A Concordance to the Poetry of
BYRON

A Concordance to the Poetry of

BYRON

Edited by
Ione Dodson Young

Volume I

Printed by
Best Printing Company, Inc.

Austin, Texas
1975

Volume I

FOREWORD

It may seem out of keeping to introduce a newly-published work upon an elegiac note, but it seems appropriate here. Ione Young's *Concordance* to the complete poems of Byron is undoubtedly the last concordance to be made without the assistance of a computer. It is then fitting to congratulate Mrs. Young on the completion of an enormous task, and to congratulate ourselves that at last we have this indispensable tool for the use of Byron readers and scholars.

Among the important poets of the Romantic Period, why a concordance to the poems of Byron has been the last to be compiled is understandable. The bulk of Byron's work is rivalled only by that of Wordsworth; thus the immensity of the undertaking has over the years put off less doughty scholars than Mrs. Young. At this point one is reminded of the somewhat ironical remark "by way of apology" of F. S. Ellis in his "Introduction" to the Shelley concordance published over seventy years ago: "The making of a concordance is but a simple matter needing only patience, industry and time." These are, as he modestly states, "humble requisites," but they are not all. A great deal of hard thought and careful judgment goes into the selection and arrangement of the material involved in such a vast project as this, where one seeks to give the user access to every significant word in the canon of a poet's work. It might be appropriate to say here that of Mr. Ellis's triad of patience, industry and time, the time Mrs. Young has devoted to this work has been taken from the busy life of a full-time teacher of English literature at Southwest Texas State College in San Marcos, Texas. Anyone who has ever taught "full time," as the popular phrase has it, knows what this implies.

There is another reason, I think, why the Byron concordance has been the last to appear. Unlike Wordsworth, or Shelley, or Keats, Byron has not been thought of as a poet who expressed himself in highly individualistic diction. There has not been thought to be—at least, it is not readily apparent—a Byronic vocabulary as there is a Shelleyan vocabulary or, to leave the period for the moment, a Yeatsian one. We do not have in Byron a particularly symbolic or mythopoeic poet whose intricate language patterns invite detailed study. But Byron's vocabulary is interesting. It reflects a mind chameleonic and retentive; it is much less slap-dash than it looks at first glance. Byron's mastery of colloquial speech—even his use of vulgarisms—is the source of a wide-ranging power which has been increasingly recognized and admired in this century. I shall not attempt to tell the reader of Byron what he should find in this area, but encourage him to take a closer look at Byron's language. The tool is here for his use, and Mrs. Young deserves our thanks in providing it for him.

Willis W. Pratt
Professor of English
The University of Texas

vii

INTRODUCTION

As Professor Pratt says in the foreword, this may be considered the last of the handmade concordances. Now that machines perform with phenomenal speed and accuracy the tedious tasks of compiling and checking data, it seems unlikely that anyone would undertake to prepare a concordance without the aid of a computer, even though much pleasure would be lost on the unfeeling machine.

The Byron concordance was begun before the era of computer concordances. In 1940-41 a grant from the Works Projects Administration to the English Department of the University of Minnesota made the first step possible—making and indexing file cards containing lines of Byron's poetry. These cards were later secured by the University of Texas Library for use by Professors Willis Pratt and Guy Steffan in preparing the variorum edition of *Don Juan.* The value to them of this material, even its raw state, pointed up the need for someone to edit and publish it. I approached the task in 1956 and worked at it sporadically for five years. Then a research grant from Southwest Texas State College enabled me to employ student assistants and work intensively for the next four years at a task that proved to be more complicated and more interesting than could have been imagined.

First, the 230 boxes of file cards had to be checked for accuracy in number and arrangement. Some sample words chosen at random were traced throughout the Cambridge text and others through a sizeable portion of it. When the number of entries for a word seemed suspiciously small, a check was made of the entire text or sections where the word would most likely occur. When incomplete lists were expanded, the two lists provided at least a partial check for each other. In only one instance were omissions discovered, and that one was relatively insignificant. Three occurrences of "thee"—a word included only when it is part of a rhyme or appears in italics or full capitals—were found in rhyming lines of the dramas, one in *Manfred* and two in *Heaven and Earth.*

When this work was done, some of the partial lists expanded, and a format planned, information on the cards was typed onto 14" by 17" pages to be reproduced by the offset method of printing. The number of times these pages needed proofreading was never determined. All were proofed twice, half of them three times, and some as many as five times. We hope that our efforts were adequate.

After expansions and discards, we were working with 236 boxes of cards, estimated to number around 285,000, including nearly 25,000 guide cards. To say that our task was an arduous one is an understatement, but the tedium was relieved by the beauty and wit of Byron's poetry.

The Byron concordance is based on the Cambridge edition of *The Complete Poetical Works of Byron,* edited by Paul Elmer More and published by Houghton Mifflin Company. Each line quoted is followed by a page reference to this text, a short title, an act or canto number when there is one, and a line number. In one instance line numbers in the concordance do not correspond to those in the text because on page 799 of the *Works* lines 1561-69 are erroneously numbered 1661-1669. These errors have been corrected; however, errors in numbering single lines have not been corrected, since corrections would tend to confuse rather than help the reader.

With minor exceptions each line in the concordance is quoted as it appears in the Cambridge text and is indexed under all significant words in the line. Punctuation and capitalization are the same except that terminal punctuation, accent marks, and italics are omitted and no words are typed in full capitals. As a rule, misspellings that are obviously printing errors have been corrected, but some that are questionable have been retained if correction would not significantly alter the indexing of the word. One example is a single occurrence of "Shakespeare's," which is probably a printing error but could be a variant of Byron's usual spelling, "Shakspeare's." Variants that are clearly Byron's have been retained, such as "et coetera" for "et cetera" and "Souvaroff" for "Suwarrow."

Homographs are listed under a single index word except when one of the words is a proper noun, as, for example, "Eve" and "eve," "Will" and "will."

Hyphenated words are indexed as such, and a cross reference to each hyphenated word is given when the second half of the word is indexed in its order. For example, under "room" are found references to "ball-room," "drawing-room," "green-room," and "spirit-room."

Like "the grosser parts" of young Juan's expurgated books, foreign language lines and some lines containing unusual foreign terms have been placed in an appendix, "which saves, in fact, the trouble of an index" for individual words in these lines.

Partial Lists and Omitted Words

Partial lists, as a rule, include occurrences of a word when it is part of a rhyme or when it appears in the text in italics or full capitals. However, in the case of "I," "I'd," "I'll," "I'm," and "I've," all entries are included except those found in the dramas. The purpose here was to include Byron's references to himself, and the surest and simplest way was to include all occurrences of these words except those in the dramas, where "I" would not be Byron. Objective and possessive forms of the first person singular were also collected but were omitted to save time and space when it became apparent that these forms so frequently appeared in context with "I" that their inclusion would be largely superfluous.

In the case of homographs, when one of the words is a significant word, all occurrences of it are included. For example, all entries of the noun "art" are listed, but those of the verb form follow the general rule explained above.

Because so many words are partially listed which would have been omitted had it not seemed important to provide in the concordance an opportunity of studying Byron's rhymes, the number of omitted words is small.

PARTIAL LISTS

a	beneath	for	indeed	nor	shall	though	what
about	between	forth	is	not	she	through	when
after	both	from	it	now	should	thus	whence
again	by		its		so	thy	where
against		had	I've	o'er	some	till	whether
all	can	has		of	still	'tis	which
along	canst	hast	less	off	such	to	while
although	could	hath	let	oft		too	who
am		have		on	that	'twas	whom
among	did	he	may	once	that's	'twere	whose
an	do	her	me	one	the	'twill	why
and	does	here	might	only	thee		will
any	done	him	mine	or	their	under	wilt
are	down	himself	more	our	theirs	until	with
around		his	most	ours	then	upon	within
art	each	how	must	over	thence	us	without
at	e'er		my	own	there		would
away	either	I	myself		therefore	very	
	ere	I'd		round	these		yes
be	even	if	ne'er		they	was	yet
been	ever	I'll	neither	said	thine	we	you
before	every	I'm	never	say	this	were	your
behind		in	no	says	those	wert	yours

OMITTED WORDS

amid	doth	he's	it's	mid	shalt	thro'
cannot	'gainst	however	itself	'mid	she's	we're
dost	hadst	into	may'st	often	than	wouldst

Also omitted are words from titles and stage directions. Thus there are no references to Alcibiades, Antony, and Socrates as they appear in *The Deformed Transformed,* for they are mentioned only in the stage directions.

Key to Abbreviated Titles

Abbreviation	Title	Page
Abydos 1	The Bride of Abydos, Canto I	323
Abydos 2	The Bride of Abydos, Canto II	329
Adams	Epitaph on John Adams, of Southwell	224
Address-A	Address Spoken at the Opening of Drury-Lane Theatre	169
Address-B	Parenthetical Address	170
Address-C	Address Intended To Be Recited at the Caledonian Meeting	182
Address-D	Condolatory Address to Sarah Countess of Jersey	183
Adieu	The Adieu	145
Ad Lesbiam	Translation from Catullus. Ad Lesbiam	87
Adrian	Adrian's Address to His Soul When Dying	87
A Fan	On Finding a Fan	148
Age	The Age of Bronze	298
Album	Lines Written in an Album, at Malta	157
Alva	Oscar of Alva	101
Anacreon-A	From Anacreon. 'I wish to tune my quivering lyre'	88
Anacreon-B	From Anacreon. ''Twas now the hour when Night had driven'	88
Anacreon-C	Translation from Anacreon	139
Answer-A	Answer to Some Elegant Verses	118
Answer-B	Answer to a Beautiful Poem, Entitled 'The Common Lot'	127
Answer-C	Answer to —'s Professions of Affection	227
Aristom	Aristomenes	205
Athos	Fragment from the 'Monk of Athos'	161
Augusta-A	Stanzas to Augusta. 'When all around grew drear and dark'	209
Augusta-B	Stanzas to Augusta. 'Though the day of my destiny's over'	210
Augusta-C	Epistle to Augusta	210
Avatar	The Irish Avatar	201
Away	'Away, Away, Ye Notes of Woe!'	165
Babylon	By the Rivers of Babylon We Sat Down and Wept	222
Ballad-A	A Very Mournful Ballad on the Siege and Conquest of Alhama	194
Ballad-B	Ballad to the Tune of 'Sally in Our Alley'	233
Ballat	Another Simple Ballat	234
Bards	English Bards and Scotch Reviewers	241
Becher-A	Lines Addressed to the Rev. J. T. Becher	128
Becher-B	Egotism. A Letter to J. T. Becher	144
Belshaz-A	To Belshazzar	185
Belshaz-B	Vision of Belshazzar	220
Beppo	Beppo	440
Blacket	Epitaph for Joseph Blacket	163
Blank Leaf	Lines Written on a Blank Leaf of the 'Pleasures of Memory'	169
Blessington	To the Countess of Blessington	205
Bloom	'Oh! Snatch'd Away in Beauty's Bloom'	218
Blues 1	The Blues, Eclogue First	277
Blues 2	The Blues, Eclogue Second	280
Bowles	Bowles and Campbell	237
Bray	The New Vicar of Bray	238
Braziers	'The Braziers, It Seems, Are Preparing To Pass'	236
Cadiz	The Girl of Cadiz	159
Cain 1	Cain, Act I	627
Cain 2	Cain, Act II	636
Cain 3	Cain, Act III	646
Calmar	The Death of Calmar and Orla	129
Caroline-A	To Caroline. 'Think'st thou I saw thy beauteous eyes'	90
Caroline-B	To Caroline. 'You say you love, and yet your eye'	90
Caroline-C	To Caroline. 'When I hear you express an affection so warm'	91
Caroline-D	To Caroline. 'Oh when shall the grave hide for ever my sorrow'	91
Castlereagh	'Here's a Happy New Year! But with Reason.' 'I send you an epitaph for Castlereagh'	235
Casuists	Queries to Casuists	145
Catullus	Translation from Catullus. 'Ye Cupids, droop each little head'	87
Cephalonia	Journal in Cephalonia	240
Chillon	The Prisoner of Chillon	402
Churchill	Churchill's Grave	190
Clare	To the Earl of Clare	137
Clay	'When Coldness Wraps This Suffering Clay'	220
Conquest	The Conquest	239
Corinth	The Siege of Corinth	384
Cornelian-A	The Cornelian	113
Cornelian-B	On a Cornelian Heart Which Was Broken	168
Corsair 1	The Corsair, Canto I	338
Corsair 2	The Corsair, Canto II	347
Corsair 3	The Corsair, Canto III	355
Critics	To a Knot of Ungenerous Critics	141
Dallas	[R. C. Dallas]	226
Damaetas	Damaetas	100
Dante Ded	The Prophecy of Dante, Dedication	455
Dante 1	The Prophecy of Dante, Canto I	456
Dante 2	The Prophecy of Dante, Canto II	458
Dante 3	The Prophecy of Dante, Canto III	460
Dante 4	The Prophecy of Dante, Canto IV	463
Darkness	Darkness	189
Dead	'And Thou Art Dead, as Young and Fair'	167
Death-A	On the Death of Mr. Fox	114
Death-B	On the Death of a Young Lady	84
Deformed 1	The Deformed Transformed, Part I	722
Deformed 2	The Deformed Transformed, Part II	735

Abbreviation	Title	Page
Deformed 3	The Deformed Transformed, Part III	742
Delawarr	To George, Earl Delawarr	136
Devil's Dr	The Devil's Drive	175
Doctor	'Dear Doctor, I Have Read Your Play'	231
Dog	Inscription on the Monument of a Newfoundland Dog	154
Dorset	To the Duke of Dorset	93
Dream	The Dream	213
Duel	The Duel	197
Dull Road	'Through Life's Dull Road, So Dim and Dirty'	236
Elegy	Elegy	237
Embargo	'Oh How I Wish That an Embargo'	225
Endorsement	Endorsement to the Deed of Separation, in the April of 1816	236
E. N. Long	To Edward Noel Long, Esq.	133
Epigrams	Epigrams	238
Epilogue	Epilogue	234
Epitaph	Epitaph on a Friend	85
Euthanasia	Euthanasia	166
Examination	Thoughts Suggested by a College Examination	111
Faliero 1	Marino Faliero, Doge of Venice, Act 1	499
Faliero 2	Marino Faliero, Doge of Venice, Act II	509
Faliero 3	Marino Faliero, Doge of Venice, Act III	518
Faliero 4	Marino Faliero, Doge of Venice, Act IV	528
Faliero 5	Marino Faliero, Doge of Venice, Act V	538
False	'Were My Bosom as False as Thou Deem'st It To Be'	221
Farce	'Brave Champions! Go on with the Farce'	237
Fare Thee	Fare Thee Well	207
Farewell-A	Farewell to the Muse	148
Farewell-B	'Farewell! If Ever Fondest Prayer'	151
First Kiss	The First Kiss of Love	92
Florence	To Florence	157
Foscari 1	The Two Foscari, Act I	595
Foscari 2	The Two Foscari, Act II	601
Foscari 3	The Two Foscari, Act III	608
Foscari 4	The Two Foscari, Act IV	615
Foscari 5	The Two Foscari, Act V	620
Fragment-A	A Fragment. 'When, to their airy hall, my fathers' voice'	85
Fragment-B	Fragment Written Shortly after the Marriage of Miss Chaworth	95
Fragment-C	A Fragment. 'Could I remount the river of my years'	191
Fragment-D	Fragment. 'I would to heaven that I were so much clay'	745
Francesca	Francesca of Rimini	476
Freedom	'When a Man Hath No Freedom To Fight for at Home'	236
French-A	From the French. 'Must thou go, my glorious Chief'	186
French-B	From the French. 'Aegle, beauty and poet, has two little crimes'	237
Friend-A	To a Youthful Friend	153
Friend-B	Epistle to a Friend	164
Gazelle	'The Wild Gazelle'	217
Giaour	The Giaour	310
Goblet	'Fill the Goblet'	155
God Maddens	'God Maddens Him Whom 'Tis His Will To Lose'	230
Gold	[Love and Gold]	179
Granta	Granta—A Medley	95
Greece	Last Words on Greece	206
Gulf	Stanzas Written in Passing the Ambracian Gulf	159
Hales-Owen	Verses Found in a Summer House at Hales-Owen	171
Happy	'Well! Thou Art Happy'	154
Harold 1	Childe Harold's Pilgrimage, Canto I	3
Harold 2	Childe Harold's Pilgrimage, Canto II	19
Harold 3	Childe Harold's Pilgrimage, Canto III	35
Harold 4	Childe Harold's Pilgrimage, Canto IV	53
Harriet	To Harriet	151
Harrow-A	On a Distant View of the Village and School of Harrow on the Hill	96
Harrow-B	Lines Written beneath an Elm in the Churchyard of Harrow	138
Harrow-C	On Revisiting Harrow	150
Haunts	'If Sometimes in the Haunts of Men'	168
Hay	'The World Is a Bundle of Hay'	237
Heaven	Heaven and Earth	655
Highlander	'When I Roved a Young Highlander'	135
High World	'If That High World'	217
Hindoo	Stanzas to a Hindoo Air	204
Hints	Hints from Horace	256
Hodgson	Lines to Mr. Hodgson	156
Hoppner	On the Birth of John William Rizzo Hoppner	233
Horace	Translation from Horace	88
Ich Dien	Ich Dien	228
Impromptu-A	Impromptu, in Reply to a Friend	174
Impromptu-B	Impromptu	239
I Read	'I Read the "Christabel"'	230
I Saw	'I Saw Thee Weep'	218
Island 1	The Island, Canto I	415
Island 2	The Island, Canto II	419
Island 3	The Island, Canto III	426
Island 4	The Island, Canto IV	430
I Would	'I Would I Were a Careless Child'	135
J.C.H.	Farewell Petition to J. C. H., Esq.	224
Jephtha	Jephtha's Daughter	218
Jerusalem	On the Day of the Destruction of Jerusalem by Titus	221
Jessy	Stanzas to Jessy	143
Jordan	'On Jordan's Banks'	217
Juan Ded	Don Juan, Dedication	745
Juan 1	Don Juan, Canto I	747
Juan 2	Don Juan, Canto II	774

Abbreviation	Title	Page
Juan 3	Don Juan, Canto III	801
Juan 4	Don Juan, Canto IV	816
Juan 5	Don Juan, Canto V	831
Juan 6	Don Juan, Canto VI	852
Juan 7	Don Juan, Canto VII	867
Juan 8	Don Juan, Canto VIII	878
Juan 9	Don Juan, Canto IX	896
Juan 10	Don Juan, Canto X	907
Juan 11	Don Juan, Canto XI	918
Juan 12	Don Juan, Canto XII	929
Juan 13	Don Juan, Canto XIII	941
Juan 14	Don Juan, Canto XIV	955
Juan 15	Don Juan, Canto XV	968
Juan 16	Don Juan, Canto XVI	980
Juan 17	Don Juan, Canto XVII	996
Julian	Julian [A Fragment]	184
Keats	'Who Kill'd John Keats?'	237
Lachin	Lachin y Gair	117
L Adieu	Love's Last Adieu	99
Lads	'As the Liberty Lads o'er the Sea'	229
Lady-A	Stanzas to a Lady	92
Lady-B	To a Lady Who Presented to the Author a Lock of Hair	101
Lady-C	To a Lady Who Presented the Author with the Velvet Band Which Bound Her Tresses	128
Lady-D	To a Lady. 'Oh! had my fate been join'd with thine'	134
Lady-E	To a Lady on Being Asked My Reason for Quitting England in the Spring	155
Lady-F	Stanzas to a Lady on Leaving England	156
Lady Byron	Lines on Hearing That Lady Byron Was Ill	212
L'Amitie	L'Amitie est L'Amour sans Ailes	131
Lara 1	Lara, Canto I	366
Lara 2	Lara, Canto II	375
Leaving NA	On Leaving Newstead Abbey	86
Love, Death	[Love and Death]	205
Lucietta	Lucietta. A Fragment	239
Lucifer	Thoughts for a Speech of Lucifer, in the Tragedy of 'Cain'	237
Maid	'Maid of Athens, Ere We Part'	160
Malta	Farewell to Malta	163
Manfred 1	Manfred, Act I	478
Manfred 2	Manfred, Act II	483
Manfred 3	Manfred, Act III	491
Marble	'In This Beloved Marble View'	229
Mariamne	Herod's Lament for Mariamne	221
Marion	To Marion	100
Marsus	Translation of the Epitaph on Virgil and Tibullus	87
Martial	Martial. Lib. I. Epig. I.	239
Masters	On a Change of Masters at a Great Public School	93
Mazeppa	Mazeppa	406
Medea	Translation from the Medea of Euripides	111
Minerva	The Curse of Minerva	268
Monody	Monody on the Death of the Right Hon. R. B. Sheridan	192

Abbreviation	Title	Page
Moore-A	Fragment of an Epistle to Thomas Moore	227
Moore-B	'As the Liberty Lads o'er the Sea': 'What are you doing now'	229
Morgante	The Morgante Maggiore	466
Mrs. Lamb	To the Hon. Mrs. George Lamb	173
Murray-A	'To Hook the Reader, You, John Murray'	230
Murray-B	'My Dear Mr. Murray'	232
Music-A	Stanzas for Music. 'I speak not, I trace not'	182
Music-B	Stanzas for Music. 'There's not a joy the world can give'	185
Music-C	Stanzas for Music. 'There be none of Beauty's daughters'	188
Music-D	Stanzas for Music: 'They say that Hope is happiness'	223
My Boat	'My Boat Is on the Shore'	230
My Son	To My Son	150
Napoleon	Napoleon's Farewell	186
New Song	New Song to the Tune of	235
Newstead-A	Elegy on Newstead Abbey	119
Newstead-B	To an Oak at Newstead	149
Newstead-C	Newstead Abbey	164
New Year	'Here's a Happy New Year! But with Reason'	235
Nihil	[E Nihilo Nihil; or an Epigram Bewitched]	232
Nisus	The Episode of Nisus and Euryalus	105
Nonsense	'You Ask for a "Volume of Nonsense" '	236
Not False	'Thou Art Not False, But Thou Art Fickle'	172
Ode-A	Ode to Napoleon Buonaparte	180
Ode-B	Ode from the French	187
Ode-C	Ode to a Lady Whose Lover Was Killed	200
Ode-D	An Ode to the Framers of the Frame Bill	225
Oh You	'Oh You, Who in All Names Can Tickle the Town'	226
Once	'Once Fairly Set Out on His Party of Pleasure'	228
On Eyes	On the Eyes of Miss A— H—	143
On Star	On the Star of 'The Legion of Honour'	188
Orchomenus	Lines Written in the Travellers' Book at Orchomenus	162
Orford	'For Orford and for Waldegrave'	238
Origin	On Being Asked What Was the 'Origin of Love'	173
Orraca	'What News, What News? Queen Orraca'	225
Ossian-A	Ossian's Address to the Sun in 'Carthon'	139
Ossian-B	A Version of Ossian's Address to the Sun	140
Paine	'Here's a Happy New Year! But with Reason'. 'In digging up your bones, Tom Paine'	235

Abbreviation	Title	Page
Pangs	'What Matter the Pangs of a Husband and Father'	238
Parisina	Parisina	396
Parker	Elegiac Stanzas on the Death of Sir Peter Parker, Bart.	183
Parting	On Parting	162
Penelope	To Penelope, January 2, 1821	236
Picture	Lines Written beneath a Picture	161
Pignus	Pignus Amoris	140
Pigot	Reply to Some Verses of J. M. B. Pigot, Esq., on the Cruelty of His Mistress	115
Pisa	Stanzas Written on the Road between Florence and Pisa	204
Pitt	'Here's a Happy New Year! But with Reason'. 'Another for Pitt'	235
Plays	'Good Plays Are Scarce'	225
Po	Stanzas to the Po	198
Portuguese-A	From the Portuguese. 'Tu mi chamas'	175
Portuguese-B	From the Portuguese. Another Version	175
Prayer	The Prayer of Nature	132
Prologue	An Occasional Prologue	113
Prometheus-A	From the Prometheus Vinctus of Aeschylus	89
Prometheus-B	Prometheus	191
Quaker	To a Beautiful Quaker	112
Quotation	On the Quotation	173
Recoll	Childish Recollections	122
Remember-A	'Remember Thee! Remember!'	171
Remember-B	'Remember Him Whom Passion's Power'	174
Remembrance	Remembrance	128
Remind	'Remind Me Not, Remind Me Not'	152
Revanche	[La Revanche]	174
Rogers	On Sam Rogers	196
Romaic-A	Translation of the Romaic Song	162
Romaic-B	Translation of a Romaic Love Song	172
Romance	To Romance	118
Rousseau	Lines Written in 'Letters to an Italian Nun and an English Gentleman: By J. J. Rousseau: Founded on Facts'	86
Roving	'So We'll Go No More a Roving'	229
Sadness	'And Dost Thou Ask the Reason of My Sadness?'	229
Sardan 1	Sardanapalus, Act I	550
Sardan 2	Sardanapalus, Act II	561
Sardan 3	Sardanapalus, Act III	571
Sardan 4	Sardanapalus, Act IV	578
Sardan 5	Sardanapalus, Act V	587
Saul-A	Song of Saul before His Last Battle	219
Saul-B	Saul	219
Sennacherib	The Destruction of Sennacherib	222
She Walks	'She Walks in Beauty'	216
Silver	'If for Silver, or for Gold'	234
Sketch	A Sketch	208
Skull	Lines Inscribed upon a Cup Formed from a Skull	153
Sleepless	'Sun of the Sleepless'	220
Snuff-Box	[Napoleon's Snuff-Box]	238
Soliloquy	Soliloquy of a Bard in the Country	142
Song	Song	150
Sonnet-A	Sonnet, To Genevra	175
Sonnet-B	Sonnet, To the Same	175
Sonnet-C	Sonnet to Lake Leman	192
Sonnet-D	Sonnet on the Nuptials of the Marquis Antonio Cavalli	199
Sonnet-E	Sonnet to the Prince Regent	199
Sonnet-F	Sonnet on Chillon	402
Sotheby	'No Infant Sotheby, Whose Dauntless Head'	231
Soul-A	'Bright Be the Place of Thy Soul'	151
Soul-B	'My Soul Is Dark'	218
Soul-C	Epigram on an Old Lady Who Had Some Curious Notions Respecting the Soul	223
Spell	'The Spell Is Broke, The Charm Is Flown'	159
Spirit	'A Spirit Pass'd before Me'	222
Stanzas-A	Stanzas. 'I heard thy fate without a tear'	186
Stanzas-B	Stanzas. 'Could Love for ever'	199
Storm	Stanzas Composed during a Thunder-Storm	158
Strahan	'Strahan, Tonson, Lintot of of the Times'	234
Strephon	To the Sighing Strephon	116
Struggle	'One Struggle More, and I Am Free'	166
Substitute	Substitute for an Epitaph	161
Suliotes	Song to the Suliotes	240
Swimming	Written after Swimming from Sestos to Abydos	160
Tasso	The Lament of Tasso	436
The Chain	'The Chain I Gave'	168
The Harp	'The Harp the Monarch Minstrel Swept'	216
The Tear	The Tear	114
Thurlow-A	'When Thurlow This Damn'd Nonsense Sent'	226
Thurlow-B	To Lord Thurlow	227
Thy Days	'Thy Days Are Done'	218
Thyrza	To Thyrza	165
Tibullus	Imitation of Tibullus	87
Time-A	'There Was a Time, I Need Not Name'	152
Time-B	To Time	171
To—A	To —. 'Oh! well I know your subtle Sex'	143
To—B	To—. 'But once I dared to lift my eyes'	205
To Anne-A	To Anne	147
To Anne-B	To the Same	147
To Author	To the Author of a Sonnet Beginning ' "Sad Is My Verse," You Say, "And Yet No Tear" '	147
To D—	To D—	85
To Dives	[To Dives (William Beckford). A Fragment]	223
To E—	To E—	85
To Eliza	To Eliza	116

xiv

Abbreviation	Title	Page
To Ellen	Imitated from Catullus. To Ellen	88
To Emma	To Emma	89
To Her	'Here's to Her Who Long'	228
To Ianthe	To Ianthe	2
To Lesbia	To Lesbia	98
To M—	To M —	97
To Mary	To Mary, on Receiving Her Picture	98
To M.S.G.-A	To M. S. G. 'Whene'er I view those lips of thine'	90
To M.S.G.-B	To M. S. G. 'When I dream that you love me, you'll surely forgive'	97
To Woman	To Woman	97
True Gate	'Would You Go to the House by the True Gate'	236
Vain Lady	To a Vain Lady	146
Valley	In the Valley of Waters'	222
Vanity	All Is Vanity, Saith the Preacher'	219
Vaults	On a Royal Visit to the Vaults	228
Venice-A	Venice	196
Venice-B	Ode on Venice	452
Vision	The Vision of Judgment	283
Vittorelli	Translation from Vittorelli	195
Waltz	The Waltz	272

Abbreviation	Title	Page
War Song	Translation of the Famous Greek War Song	161
Weep-A	'And Wilt Thou Weep When I Am Low?'	152
Weep-B	'Oh! Weep for Those'	217
Weeping	Lines to a Lady Weeping	168
Werner 1	Werner; or, The Inheritance, Act I	671
Werner 2	Werner; or, The Inheritance, Act II	683
Werner 3	Werner; or, The Inheritance, Act III	695
Werner 4	Werner; or, The Inheritance, Act IV	704
Werner 5	Werner; or, The Inheritance, Act V	713
When We	'When We Two Parted'	151
Windsor	Windsor Poetics	228
Year	On This Day I Complete My Thirty-Sixth Year	206
Youth	'Youth, Nature, and Relenting Jove'	225
Young Lady	Lines Addressed to a Young Lady	99

Acknowledgments

To all who helped me prepare the Byron concordance I gladly acknowledge my debt. Most of all, I am indebted to the University of Minnesota English Department and the Works Projects Administration for providing the original mass of material. To Professors Pratt and Steffan and the University of Texas Library I owe thanks for making this material available to me and to Houghton Mifflin Company for the use of the Cambridge edition of Byron's poetry.

I am especially grateful to Professor Pratt for his inestimable contribution as consultant for the past nine years and for writing the foreword. It was in his Byron class at the University of Texas that I became interested in Byron, and it was at his suggestion that I undertook the preparation of these volumes.

My thanks are due also to Southwest Texas State College for a research grant; to the student assistants who worked with me on this grant; and to Miss Mary Louise Hightower and Mr. George C. Miller, two of my colleagues who gave generously of their time to help proofread the typescript.

Ione Young

A

But now I fear her trip will be a	225	Embargo		5
Or if you only would but tell in a	231	Doctor		50
Except that since those times was never known a	442	Beppo		133
And no Venetian audience could endure a	444	Beppo		247
But not as yet imagined it could be a	757	Juan	1	686
Say I; by which quotation there is meant a	772	Juan	1	1691
They were relations, and for them he had a	777	Juan	2	189
I can't but say it seems to me most truly a	800	Juan	2	1659
Does these things for us, and whenever newly a	800	Juan	2	1661
And through her clear brunette complexion shone a	828	Juan	4	750
Lord H. Amundeville and Lady A.	947	Juan	13	408
Present, Lords A. B. C.'--Earls, dukes, by name	947	Juan	13	426
So animated that it might allure a	951	Juan	13	619
Is worth a tour to Rome, although no more a	960	Juan	14	315
The 'tout ensemble' of his movements wore a	960	Juan	14	317
A single shade's sufficient to entrance a	995	Juan	16	974

ABACK

| Or if I'm wrong, I'll not be ta'en aback | 938 | Juan | 12 | 566 |

ABANDON

For a time they abandon the cave and the chase	30	Harold	2	662
Abandon Ocean's children; in the fall	57	Harold	4	152
Though my heart they enthral, I'd abandon them all	115	Pigot		23
The spirits I have raised abandon me	481	Manfred	1	262

ABANDON'D

When Love has abandon'd the bowers	162	Romaic-A		14
To honour thine abandon'd Urn	168	Haunts		28
Of self-upheld abandon'd power	180	Ode-A		63
Lone, lost, abandon'd in their utmost need	302	Age		290
With slow, despairing oar, the abandon'd skiff	418	Island	1	173
Be satisfied--you are not all abandon'd	583	Sardan	4	324
Which tells me we are not abandon'd quite	656	Heaven		76
What shall become of your abandon'd garment	728	Deformed	1	422

ABANDONMENT

Abandonment of reason to resign	74	Harold	4	1136
Are bent upon this rash abandonment	624	Foscari	5	236
Abandonment), return'd my salutation	677	Werner	1	389

ABANDONS

She abandons me now--but the page of her story	186	Napoleon		3
Abandons, Heaven forgets me; in the dearth	439	Tasso		200
But Christ his servants ne'er abandons long	470	Morgante		260

ABASE

| I did abase myself as much in being | 585 | Sardan | 4 | 465 |

ABASEMENT

(See also SELF-ABASEMENT)

Or I have quaff'd me down to their abasement	558	Sardan	1	489
You spoke of your abasement. And I feel it	585	Sardan	4	488
In their abasement. I will have none such	636	Cain	2	12

ABASH'D

But if you abash'd are	232	Murray-B		16
Wondering they turn, abash'd, while each to each	340	Corsair	1	147
And then, abash'd at its own joy, withdrew	760	Juan	1	892
And all abash'd, too, at the general stare	858	Juan	6	358

ABATE

Nought that he saw his sadness could abate	17	Harold	1	832
In strength to bear what time can not abate	36	Harold	3	62
When Venice was an envy, might abate	454	Venice-B		104
As day advanced the weather seem'd to abate	777	Juan	2	233
Whose force description only would abate	843	Juan	5	771
Nor bate (abate) their hearers of an inch	953	Juan	13	780
That awful yawn which sleep can not abate	954	Juan	13	808

ABATED

The instant that the waters have abated	693	Werner	2	654
The dove did, trusting that they have abated	696	Werner	3	50
Abated? Is there hope of that? There was	696	Werner	3	51
Their speed abated or their strength grew dull	865	Juan	6	854

ABATEMENT

Abatement of your punishment, the Giunta	538	Faliero	5	23
Their quick abatement), and I'll have him safe	687	Werner	2	285
To watch for the abatement of the river	687	Werner	2	311

ABATES

| Abates. Think'st thou, that were it well for him | 690 | Werner | 2 | 490 |

ABATING

| It is abating. That is well. But how | 694 | Werner | 2 | 697 |
| The waters are abating; a few hours | 698 | Werner | 3 | 173 |

ABBEY

An abbey once, a regal fortress now	120	Newstead-A		57
Now lies in the Abbey	235	Pitt		4
In some old abbey, or a trout not stale	292	Vision		485

ABBEY

The abbey, no great way from Manopell	466	Morgante		42
An abbey which in a lone desert lay	468	Morgante		150
Of a great mountain's brow the abbey stood	468	Morgante		155
How to the abbey he had found his road	468	Morgante		168
'To the abbey I will gladly marshal you	471	Morgante		363
And onwards to the abbey went their way	472	Morgante		384
Then to the abbey they went on together	472	Morgante		433
On to the abbey, though by no means near	474	Morgante		515
And to the abbey then return'd with speed	475	Morgante		594
The abbot, abbey, and this solitude	475	Morgante		610
Before the abbey many years ago	476	Morgante		675
Upon your tomb in Westminster's old abbey	896	Juan	9	12
To Norman Abbey whirl'd the noble pair	948	Juan	13	433
The noble guests, assembled at the Abbey	951	Juan	13	625
Who after rummaging the Abbey through thick	988	Juan	16	509

ABBEY'S

| In the last moment of the abbey's foe | 476 | Morgante | | 677 |
| But then the Abbey's worth the whole collection | 921 | Juan | 11 | 200 |

ABBOT

The abbot was call'd Clermont, and by blood	468	Morgante		153
Said the abbot, 'You are welcome; what is mine	468	Morgante		169
The manna's falling now,' the abbot cried	469	Morgante		210
Dear abbot,' Roland unto him replied	469	Morgante		212
'Abbot,' he said, 'I want to find that fellow	469	Morgante		219
Said the abbot, 'Let not my advice seem shallow	469	Morgante		221
The abbot sign'd the great cross on his front	469	Morgante		233
As the abbot had directed, kept the line	469	Morgante		236
Ask the abbot pardon, as I wish you would	471	Morgante		368
Where waited them the abbot in great doubt	472	Morgante		434
The abbot, looking through upon the giant	472	Morgante		439
Said quickly, 'Abbot, be thou of good cheer	472	Morgante		442
Thence, with due thanks, the abbot God adored	473	Morgante		447
The abbot: many days they did repose	473	Morgante		474
The abbot show'd a chamber, where array'd	473	Morgante		477
So did the abbot, and set wide the gate	474	Morgante		520
The abbot, who to all did honour great	474	Morgante		533
The abbot said, 'The steeple may do well	474	Morgante		577
The abbot by the hand he took one day	475	Morgante		597
The abbot, abbey, and this solitude	475	Morgante		610
Now when the abbot Count Orlando heard	475	Morgante		617
The abbot said to him, 'Come in and see	476	Morgante		664
The abbot said to them, 'I give you all	476	Morgante		667
My lord, the abbot of St. Maurice craves	491	Manfred	3	19
Who will be mine. The abbot, if it please	711	Werner	4	447

ABBOTS

| Abbots to abbots, in a line, succeed | 120 | Newstead-A | | 38 |

ABBOT'S

| And thus our abbot's favour bought | 318 | Giaour | | 817 |

ABDALLAH

| By that same hand Abdallah--Selim bled | 336 | Abydos | 2 | 654 |

ABDALLAH'S

In war Abdallah's arm was strong	331	Abydos	2	218
Dismiss'd Abdallah's hence to heaven	331	Abydos	2	239
Abdallah's Pachalick was gain'd	331	Abydos	2	250
Abdallah's honours were obtain'd	331	Abydos	2	253
He in Abdallah's palace grew	331	Abydos	2	278
'Tis thine--Abdallah's Murderer	335	Abydos	2	576

ABDICATE

| To have the courtesy to abdicate | 615 | Foscari | 4 | 35 |
| My wish to abdicate, it was refused me | 621 | Foscari | 5 | 40 |

ABDICATED

| The Furies seize her abdicated reign | 272 | Minerva | | 280 |

ABDICATION

| Why press this abdication now? The feelings | 619 | Foscari | 4 | 265 |

ABEL

The prayers of Abel link'd to deeds of Cain	420	Island	2	72
Abel, I'm sick at heart: but it will pass	628	Cain	1	58
Weeps when he's named; and Abel lifts his eyes	631	Cain	1	250
Although my brother Abel oft implores	632	Cain	1	309
With Abel on an altar. Saidst thou not	632	Cain	1	323
He, too, looks smilingly on Abel. I	644	Cain	2	554
Two altars, which our brother Abel made	647	Cain	3	96
Thy brother Abel. Welcome, Cain! My brother	648	Cain	3	162
The peace of God be on thee! Abel, hail	648	Cain	3	163
Unfit for mortal converse: leave me, Abel	649	Cain	3	184
Abel, I pray thee, sacrifice alone	649	Cain	3	190
I have seen the elements still'd. My Abel, leave me	649	Cain	3	206
What? Where am I? alone! Where's Abel? where	651	Cain	3	322
Abel! I pray thee, mock me not! I smote	651	Cain	3	327
Abel! what's this?--who hath done this? He moves not	651	Cain	3	363
Are in my heart. My best beloved, Abel	652	Cain	3	384

ABEL
Where is thy brother Abel? Am I then — 653 Cain 3 468
O Abel! Peace be with him! But with me — 654 Cain 3 561
Thou who dost rather make me dream that Abel — 664 Heaven 669
And dream'd that aught of Abel was in her — 664 Heaven 676

ABELARD
Where Abelard, through twenty years of death — 433 Island 4 223

ABEL'S
But Abel's earnest prayer has wrought upon me — 632 Cain 1 325
In Adam's, and in Abel's, and in mine — 640 Cain 2 254
Art thou not Abel's brother? We are brethren — 644 Cain 2 588
And Abel's pious ministry, recall thee — 648 Cain 3 175
Uniting with our children Abel's offspring — 654 Cain 3 560

ABENCERRAGE
The Abencerrage, Granada's flower — 194 Ballad-A 47
Has dwelt the memory of Abencerrage — 302 Age 329

ABERDEEN
The travell'd thane, Athenian Aberdeen — 248 Bards 509
Let Aberdeen and Elgin still pursue — 256 Bards 1027

ABERNETHY
We tease mild Baillie, or soft Abernethy — 912 Juan 10 336

ABERRATIONS
Such aberrations than we men of rigour — 969 Juan 15 84

ABET
You, who abet them? I forgive this, for — 603 Foscari 2 125
Does he abet you in your accusation — 691 Werner 2 533

ABETTORS
And then she had all Seville for abettors — 750 Juan 1 220

ABEYANCE
Though circumstance may keep it in abeyance — 534 Faliero 4 407
Till then, the truth is in abeyance. Pause not — 541 Faliero 5 259
Laws reach'd this village) are all in abeyance — 703 Werner 3 562
While things were in abeyance, Ribas sent — 872 Juan 7 297
While this high post of honour's in abeyance — 913 Juan 10 385

ABHOR
Its health; but what it then detested, still abhor — 66 Harold 4 684
And as the Turks abhor long conversations — 449 Beppo 566
Which they abhor, confound not with the cause — 454 Venice-B 93
But I can act even what I most abhor — 487 Manfred 2 297
That abhor them doubly for the deeds — 520 Faliero 3 116
Must I abhor and do. Away! away — 527 Faliero 3 642
Instinct of life, which I abhor, as I — 629 Cain 1 113
Which stands before me; I cannot abhor him — 633 Cain 1 404
And who hath brought him there?--I--who abhor — 652 Cain 3 371
Who shall abhor thee though thou wert their sire — 653 Cain 3 440
I abhor death, because that thou must die — 664 Heaven 707
Abhor, condemn, abjure the mortal made — 800 Juan 2 1666
Sultans too much abhor this sort of sin — 853 Juan 6 53
By habit to what their own hearts abhor — 886 Juan 8 494

ABHOR'D
And snatch'd thy shrinking Gods to northern climes abhor'd — 21 Harold 2 135
The hills with Latian echoes; I abhor'd — 66 Harold 4 672
And once my breast abhor'd deceit — 134 Lady-D 35
Whom servile Rome obey'd, and yet abhor'd — 183 Address-D 2
Exalted o'er thy less abhor'd compeers — 209 Sketch 103
On this occasion his own work abhor'd — 285 Vision 43
Must be your souls, if you have not abhor'd — 291 Vision 382
It warm'd the heart of one abhor'd — 320 Giaour 1035
Alike all time abhor'd, all place — 322 Giaour 1196
In word and deed obey'd, in soul abhor'd — 377 Lara 1 167
As if his heart abhor'd that coming day — 381 Lara 2 473
For that, like thine, abhor'd control — 399 Parisina 297
Which he abhor'd to view below — 403 Chillon 91
Be it to the earth's end, from this abhor'd — 611 Foscari 3 238
Of life, and the abhor'd — 660 Heaven 362
Where the name of his country is abhor'd — 686 Werner 2 194
Abhor'd both mystery and blood, and yet — 720 Werner 5 481
Was neither much beloved nor yet abhor'd — 755 Juan 1 515
To prove himself the thing he most abhor'd — 764 Juan 1 1112
And of a wife by whom he was abhor'd — 863 Juan 6 716
Their country; and as traitors are abhor'd — 870 Juan 7 174
Admiring those (by dainty dames abhor'd — 903 Juan 9 427
How her great name is now throughout abhor'd — 915 Juan 10 530

ABHORRED
Parches the heart; and the abhorred grate — 436 Tasso 7
The abhorred race — 660 Heaven 341

ABHORRENCE
I read abhorrence on thy brow — 321 Giaour 1161
With God and man's abhorrence for its gains — 746 Juan Ded 112

ABHORRENT
Abhorrent policy (which holds all ties — 611 Foscari 3 194
Show even nature's self abhorrent — 736 Deformed 2 118

ABHORRETH
But Peace abhorreth artificial — 29 Harold 2 575
Though, by the Power who abhorreth human blood — 712 Werner 4 524

ABHORRING
(See also LIFE-ABHORRING)
Pollute the plains, alike abhorring both — 302 Age 323
His mind abhorring this had fix'd her throne — 371 Lara 1 349
From out their grasp, and he abhorring tyrants — 526 Faliero 3 502

ABHORS
Abhors this station of inglorious rest — 105 Nisus 22
But many a skilful judge abhors to see — 262 Hints 413
Admires the plunder but abhors the thief — 271 Minerva 198

ABIDE
But he whom Sadness sootheth may abide — 34 Harold 2 869
Through hostile legions must abide by chance — 106 Nisus 60
And here it soothes him to abide — 318 Giaour 800
I will abide by Doge Faliero's counsel — 524 Faliero 3 415
Or for the sake of decency abide — 766 Juan 1 1246

ABIDETH
He abideth night and day — 985 Juan 16 340

ABILITY
I don't know that there may be much ability — 970 Juan 15 153

ABJECT
So abject--yet alive — 180 Ode-A 4
My abject fortune, wither'd fame so low — 361 Corsair 3 359
This happens in the most contemn'd and abject — 623 Foscari 5 148

ABJURE
We repent, we abjure, we will break from our chain — 182 Music-A 7
Abjure the mummery of the German schools — 249 Bards 582
Abjure bad Macon's false and felon test — 471 Morgante 357
Abhor, condemn, abjure the mortal made — 800 Juan 2 1666

ABJURED
The monk abjured a world he ne'er could view — 120 Newstead-A 22
Now lost, abjured, for one--his friend, his all — 373 Lara 1 525
Even in that very hour and vow, they abjured — 525 Faliero 3 495

ABJURES
The Chili chief abjures his foreign lord — 302 Age 277

ABJURING
It was but abjuring my creed to efface — 221 False 3

ABLE
Or take my physic while I'm able — 163 Malta 53
Here! Have you not been able to complete — 520 Faliero 3 125
Able to work a will so good and general — 572 Sardan 3 44
'Tis time enough to ask it when he's able — 675 Werner 1 245
Able to trace the villain who hath robb'd him — 689 Werner 2 420
Who to stop his steps are able — 736 Deformed 2 82
And he who understands it would be able — 745 Juan Ded 31
That even the able seaman, deeming his — 778 Juan 2 261
And show that late hours, wine, and love are able — 809 Juan 3 527
While the right hand which wrote it still is able — 829 Juan 4 789
And, running out as fast as I was able — 835 Juan 5 262
Stretch'd in the street, and able scarce to pant — 835 Juan 5 264
Might teach them this much better than I'm able — 839 Juan 5 472
Those navigators must be able seamen — 852 Juan 6 11
Young people at his time of life should be able — 910 Juan 10 171
He was now growing up like a green tree, able — 910 Juan 10 173
An exquisite small chapel had been able — 949 Juan 13 525
For weapons; but what Muse since Homer's able — 976 Juan 15 491

ABLER
Aid which he added to your abler succour — 693 Werner 2 649

ABLUTIONS
And now he rose; and after due ablutions — 863 Juan 6 729

ABODE
Abode of gods, whose shrines no longer burn — 19 Harold 2 22
Of life and sufferance make its firm abode — 58 Harold 4 182
Without an ark for wretched man's abode — 68 Harold 4 827
A fit abode wherein appear enshrined — 78 Harold 4 1391
He drives their exiles from their blest abode — 120 Newstead-A 46
No very great way from a bishop's abode — 176 Devil's Dr 30
Here in their first abode you still may meet — 193 Monody 55
Its sound aspired to Heaven and there abode — 217 The Harp 15
Why should we call them from their dark abode — 251 Bards 709
And now no boor can seek his last abode — 252 Bards 785
And Pallas hail'd me in her own abode — 269 Minerva 74
Why wouldst thou leave calm Hartwell's green abode — 305 Age 514

ABODE

As from her fond abode she fled	388	Corinth	379
Whether in convent she abode	401	Parisina	515
The darkness of my dim abode	406	Chillon	360
And somewhat stoop'd by his marine abode	425	Island 2	489
The secret places of their new abode	432	Island 4	164
Therefore, just Lord! from out thy high abode	466	Morgante	5
And stretch'd himself at ease in this abode	470	Morgante	307
Must rather be the abode of gods than one	588	Sardan 5	55
I would not leave your ancient first abode	594	Sardan 5	426
Your treasure, your abode, your sacred relics	594	Sardan 5	430
Though in this most obscure abode of men	703	Werner 3	554
Abode of the true God, and his true saint	731	Deformed 1	606
Beside his mistress in some soft abode-	748	Juan 1	46
A taste seen in the choice of his abode	808	Juan 3	444
Of living in their insular abode	811	Juan 3	648
'We must be near some place of man's abode	837	Juan 5	353

ABODES

Nor fix on fond abodes to circumscribe thy pray'r	49	Harold 3	859
Lausanne and Ferney, ye have been the abodes	51	Harold 3	977
Of woods and cornfields, and the abodes of men	214	Dream	33
Of the abodes of men	413	Mazeppa	624
To the abodes of those who govern her	485	Manfred 2	135
That with the dwellers of the dark abodes	491	Manfred 3	36
Gods, as some say, or the abodes of gods	566	Sardan 2	260
To leave abodes like this: but when I feel	614	Foscari 3	412
His very cellars might be kings' abodes	931	Juan 12	70

ABOLISH

Abolish hell	661	Heaven	464

ABOLISH'D

Abolish'd cuckoldom with much applause	266	Hints	671
In part. I would not have his bulls abolish'd	739	Deformed 2	275
To hold some sinecures he wish'd abolish'd	990	Juan 16	623

ABOLITION

What 'twas ere Abolition; and the thing	831	Juan 4	916

ABOMINABLE

Abominable Man no more allays	450	Beppo	636
As that abominable tittle-tattle	935	Juan 12	343

ABORTION

The sole abortion! Would that I had been so	722	Deformed 1	3

ABORTIONS

Beyond the dwarfing city's pale abortions	886	Juan 8	522

ABOUND

Here dons, grandees, but chiefly dames abound	15	Harold 1	724
Rock, river, forest, mountain, all abound	26	Harold 2	428
Yet since in danger courts abound	138	Clare	79
Such as abound in Venice, would be loud	509	Faliero 2	64
Of those pedestrian Paphians who abound	922	Juan 11	236
And beauteous, even where beauties most abound	941	Juan 13	14
Of folly's fruit; for though your fools abound	953	Juan 13	757

ABOUNDED

Of his whole army, which so much abounded	881	Juan 8	222
'Tis odd, but true,--last war the News abounded	947	Juan 13	423

ABOUNDING

But Thou, exulting and abounding river	42	Harold 3	442

ABOUNDS

The feast, the song, the revel here abounds	11	Harold 1	487
A lady with apologies abounds	768	Juan 1	1405

ABOUT

And always are prating about and about it	145	Casuists	2
Yet if you could bring about	196	Rogers	23
For some resource to turn himself about	285	Vision	28
And never knew much what it was about	287	Vision	171
Would that the royal guests it girds about	304	Age	424
And, writhing half my form about	410	Mazeppa	387
'Tis time, belike, to put our helm about	426	Island 2	515
Some weeks before Shrove Tuesday comes about	440	Beppo	3
What you, she, it, or they, may be about	445	Beppo	310
My cloak is round his middle strapp'd about	445	Beppo	331
Juan the gate gain'd, turn'd the key about	770	Juan 1	1495
They knew not where nor what they were about	786	Juan 2	764
To those who like their company, about	861	Juan 6	559
So little do we know what we're about in	898	Juan 9	135
Of Titans, giants, fellows of great	901	Juan 9	302
And dig, and sweat, and turn themselves about	901	Juan 9	315
Till all the arts at length are brought about	901	Juan 9	317
I said that Lady Pinchbeck had been talk'd about	935	Juan 12	369
But now no more the ghost of Scandal stalk'd about	935	Juan 12	371
And several of her best bon-mots were hawk'd about	935	Juan 12	373
They are wrong--that's not the way to set about it	969	Juan 15	97

ABOUT

Without their seeing what he was about	978	Juan	15	656

ABOVE

But thee--and one above	6	Harold	1	149
In softness as in firmness far above	13	Harold	1	591
But when he saw the evening star above	25	Harold	2	361
Where'er we gaze, around, above, below	26	Harold	2	426
Nodding above; behold black Acheron	27	Harold	2	456
Above, strange groups adorn'd the corridor	28	Harold	2	508
Blest cares! all other feelings far above	28	Harold	2	547
Above its prostrate brethren of the cave	33	Harold	2	811
Mountains above, Earth's, Ocean's plain below	33	Harold	2	848
And Ardennes waves above them her green leaves	39	Harold	3	235
Which now beneath them, but above shall grow	39	Harold	3	240
Though high above the sun of glory glow	42	Harold	3	401
That love was pure, and, far above disguise	43	Harold	3	490
Above, the frequent feudal towers	43	Harold	3	509
But these recede. Above me are the Alps	45	Harold	3	590
Thy trees take root in Love; the snows above	50	Harold	3	925
The clouds above me to the white Alps tend	52	Harold	3	1017
Above the dogeless city's vanish'd sway	55	Harold	4	31
Christ's mighty shrine above his martyr's tomb	78	Harold	4	1371
Long'd for a deathless lover from above	79	Harold	4	1452
Darken above our bones, yet fondly deem'd	80	Harold	4	1527
Hurtling above our bones, yet fondly deem'd	88	Horace		10
Howl above thy tufted shade	95	Fragment-B		4
But now she glimmer'd from above	101	Alva		19
The distant spires above the valleys gleam	107	Nisus		118
Iulus then:--'By all the powers above	107	Nisus		139
Alone she came, all selfish fears above	107	Nisus		181
Listening he runs--above the waving trees	109	Nisus		323
Which hover faithful hearts above	111	Medea		28
How wilt thou tower above thy fellow peers	126	Recoll		298
Oh! could I soar above these feeble lays	127	Recoll		357
Still lingering pause above each checker'd leaf	127	Recoll		405
Like relics left of saints above	128	Lady-C		4
Lochlin. Join the song of bards above my	130	Calmar		85
on the rocks above. Lightly wheel the he-	130	Calmar		107
hawks scream above their prey	131	Calmar		157
Above the dear-loved peaceful seat	134	E. N. Long		99
But while these soar above me, unchanged as before	136	Highlander		43
Rose whom the Deities above	139	Anacreon-C		13
Oh! thou that roll'st above thy glorious Fire	139	Ossian-A		1
Thou far above their utmost fury borne	140	Ossian-B		19
How much thy friendship was above	146	Adieu		63
Stolen from celestial spheres above	150	Song		6
Wilt sigh above my place of rest	152	Weep-A		8
But, above all, if thou wouldst hold	164	Friend-B		13
Thy joys below, thy hopes above	164	Friend-B		17
For whirling above--underneath--and around	179	Devil's Dr		217
Who hath so glow'd above the page where fame	182	Address-C		1
And Triumph weeps above the brave	183	Parker		4
Then the few whose spirits float above the wreck of happiness	185	Music-B		5
Shine above the revel rout	196	Venice-A		4
Than the wail above the dead	207	Fare Thee		30
Save joy above the ruin thou hast wrought	209	Sketch		80
Its boughs above a monument	210	Augusta-A		28
And, above all, a lake I can behold	211	Augusta-C		63
To sounds that seem as from above	217	The Harp		19
Above or Love, Hope, Hate, or Fear	220	Clay		25
For her who soars alone above	221	Mariamne		15
Above the works and thoughts of Man	229	Marble		2
And, whatever sky's above me	230	My Boat		7
Present him raving and above all law	259	Hints		174
Above all things, Dan Poet, if you can	260	Hints		292
Below, his name--above, behold his deeds	270	Minerva		108
His wings, like thunder-clouds above some coast	288	Vision		187
Above is more august; to judge of kings	293	Vision		539
'Above the sun repeat, then, what thou hast	293	Vision		553
Varied above, but still alike below	298	Age		27
Mankind, where least above the brutes	311	Giaour		154
Darkness above, despair beneath	314	Giaour		437
Above, the mountain rears a peak	315	Giaour		553
Devotion wafts the mind above	321	Giaour		1135
They told me wild waves roll'd above	323	Giaour		1306
Pure as the prayer which Childhood wafts above	325	Abydos	1	167
The only star it hail'd above	329	Abydos	2	15
The sea-birds shriek above the prey	335	Abydos	2	603
And mourn'd above his turban stone	335	Abydos	2	619
That shine beneath, while dark above	336	Abydos	2	665
And scarce a glimpse of mercy from above	344	Corsair	1	401
If there be life below, and hope above	344	Corsair	1	451
For her in sooth my voice would mount above	354	Corsair	2	486
The life thou leav'st below, denied above	359	Corsair	3	236
Loud sung the wind above; and, doubly loud	359	Corsair	3	248
Above some object of her doubt or dread	361	Corsair	3	413
As its far shadow frown'd above the mast	362	Corsair	3	458
And here--at once behold, beneath her sex	363	Corsair	3	514
And grieve what may above thy senseless bier	375	Lara	2	13
Above them shone the crescent curling	387	Corinth		259
Painted in heavenly hues above	394	Corinth		950

ABOVE

There were the dead above, and the dead below	395	Corinth		973
Of aught around, above, beneath	396	Parisina		34
When rose thy casque above thy brow	399	Parisina		301
The sky above, and men around	400	Parisina		374
The flat and turfless earth above	404	Chillon		160
His empty chain above it leant	404	Chillon		162
And seem above both wounds and woe	407	Mazeppa		96
Dark as above us is the sky	409	Mazeppa		211
And doth a roof above me close	414	Mazeppa		798
The arctic sun rose broad above the wave	418	Island	1	169
Which lifts its peak a cloud above the main	418	Island	1	175
Above their naked bones, and feels delight	418	Island	1	191
We'll cull the flowers that grow above the dead	419	Island	2	7
And all our dreams of better life above	420	Island	2	121
Through clefts above let in a sober'd ray	431	Island	4	132
Above me, hark! the long and maniac cry	437	Tasso		65
Oh! not dismay'd--but awed, like One above	438	Tasso		135
Heart, soul, and all that seems as from above	447	Beppo		436
For these restored the Cross, that from above	454	Venice-B		114
Above the far Atlantic!--She has taught	454	Venice-B		144
And many meteors, and above thy tomb	461	Dante	3	39
Eternal honour, you will go above	471	Morgante		348
Yet pierces downward, onward, or above	482	Manfred	1	296
I hear ye momently above, beneath	482	Manfred	1	338
The order which thine own would rise above	486	Manfred	2	217
Bid him bow down to that which is above him	489	Manfred	2	416
'Tis strange--even those who do despair above	492	Manfred	3	101
The stars are forth, the moon above the tops	495	Manfred	3	261
By some well-timed concessions. But, above	504	Faliero	1	342
Within, above, around, than in this city	516	Faliero	2	506
Rather than yield to one above me in	518	Faliero	2	703
And both await without.--But, above all	545	Faliero	5	550
When we shall gather like the stars above us	551	Sardan	1	57
It seems unto the stars which are above us	560	Sardan	1	604
Of aught above it, or below it--nothing	566	Sardan	2	266
Grieve more above the blighted name and ashes	584	Sardan	4	394
By those above, till they wax'd fearful; then	597	Foscari	1	115
Upon their knees, perhaps have mourn'd above them	603	Foscari	2	121
Which floats above the place where we now stand	614	Foscari	3	376
Up to the lights above us, in the azure	631	Cain	1	277
Nor would: I would be aught above--beneath	632	Cain	1	303
Above what they have done	660	Heaven		421
Above its first and best inhabitants	665	Heaven		729
Am thus condemn'd to weep above in vain	670	Heaven		1194
A wave the less may roll above your head	676	Werner	1	303
Above his outward fortunes. There I differ	677	Werner	1	400
All to one home. Your language is above	680	Werner	1	543
Without--within--above--below--Heaven help me	683	Werner	2	12
You have guess'd, no doubt, that I was born above	700	Werner	3	311
Above our house! My father! I acquit you	702	Werner	3	489
May howl above his ashes (as they did	703	Werner	3	577
And, above all, these stiff and heavy jewels	714	Werner	5	71
The joyous crowd above, the numberless	714	Werner	5	109
A man above his station; and if not	717	Werner	5	285
Which frown above us. You remember,--or	718	Werner	5	326
Above, and many altar shrines below	731	Deformed	1	613
Pile above pile of everlasting wall	731	Deformed	1	618
So far above the cunning powers of hell	749	Juan	1	131
I mean the seraph way of those above	757	Juan	1	680
By all the vows below to powers above	760	Juan	1	867
Kept above water, with an oar for mast	781	Juan	2	482
But who is their purveyor from above	795	Juan	2	1359
With cliffs above, and a broad sandy shore	796	Juan	2	1410
Into one focus, kindled from above	797	Juan	2	1483
Above them their dessert grew on its vine	805	Juan	3	246
A like gold bar above her instep roll'd	810	Juan	3	570
Of sense and song above your graves may hiss	815	Juan	3	894
Look up to thine and to thy Son's above	815	Juan	3	916
In vain the dews of Heaven descend above	825	Juan	4	559
He was above the vulgar by his mien	832	Juan	5	70
'No--only two at present above ground	833	Juan	5	155
In which we left him several lines above	856	Juan	6	224
Above her brow, lay dreaming soft and warm	860	Juan	6	523
Kept up; and above all, the where and how	864	Juan	6	791
And above all be comb'd even to a hair	867	Juan	6	940
Flame was shower'd forth above, as well's below	883	Juan	8	356
'But heaven,' as Cassio says, 'is above all	898	Juan	9	145
Self-love--which, when some sort of thing above	905	Juan	9	539
Above, below, by turnpikes great or small	906	Juan	9	636
'Tis said (for I'll not answer above ground	907	Juan	10	3
Born in a second wedlock; and above	911	Juan	10	255
And, above all, an Englishwoman's roves	922	Juan	11	260
Above his burnt-out brain, and sapless cinders	925	Juan	11	477
Ye villains!' and above all keep a sharp eye	929	Juan	11	677
Above the ice had like a skater glided	932	Juan	12	196
Above all, I beg all men to forbear	967	Juan	14	785

ABRAHAM

Oh, holy Abraham! dost thou see the sight	307	Age	695

ABRAHAM'S

Not without Abraham's seed can Russia march	307	Age	684

ABREAST

As were some hundred youngsters all abreast	885	Juan	8	443

ABROAD

Abroad, or at home, your remembrance imparting	86	Leaving NA		23
And here one night abroad they dared to roam	124	Recoll		179
And seek abroad the love denied at home	125	Recoll		216
That outlaws were abroad	158	Storm		28
But none abroad, and few at home	160	Cadiz		55
And of unholy nature, are abroad	491	Manfred	3	30
How fares it with you? have you been abroad	511	Faliero	2	161
But still their spirit walks abroad. Though years	517	Faliero	2	610
Rather let them be borne abroad upon	594	Sardan	5	477
Foul rumours were abroad; I have also read	605	Foscari	2	223
There are more spirits abroad than have been laid	721	Werner	5	541
Abroad i' the fields. Let us but leave it there	728	Deformed	1	428
A single cry would bring them all abroad	837	Juan	5	357
They lived till some Bashaw was sent abroad	850	Juan	5	1212
Like an imperial peacock stalk abroad	876	Juan	7	589
Outward dislike, which don't look well abroad	911	Juan	10	253
Abroad, such things decide few women's fate	938	Juan	12	509
Abroad, though doubtless they do much amiss	940	Juan	12	629
Sung, or rehearsed the last dance from abroad	954	Juan	13	828
That faithful were through thick and thin, abroad	967	Juan	14	763

ABROGATE

Seeking to abrogate all law, can claim	541	Faliero	5	231

ABRUPT

Starts from the day abrupt and fearfully	361	Corsair	3	409

ABRUPTLY

Lest the ray flash abruptly on the lid	353	Corsair	2	399

ABRUPTNESS

By its abruptness--all it hath of ill	495	Manfred	3	308
The abruptness of my entrance and my bearing	542	Faliero	5	334

ABRUZZI

Erected in the Abruzzi to his glory	466	Morgante	43

ABSENCE

Absence has made me prone to roving	98	To Lesbia		26
Enjoy'd, from absence, with enraptured zest	121	Newstead-A		116
Absence, my friend, can only tell	132	L'Amitie		59
And mourns o'er thine absence with me	162	Romaic-A		36
Thy truth in absence to divine	168	The Chain		6
That absence proved his worth,--that absence fix'd	183	Address-D		9
And in absence blasts and sears you	197	Rogers		46
Of absence, shame, pride, hate, revenge, remorse	336	Abydos	2	644
Unmoved by absence, firm in every clime	342	Corsair	1	295
'In Conrad's absence wouldst thou have it glad	343	Corsair	1	366
Permit my absence--peace be with thee! Peace	348	Corsair	2	97
Except the absence of the chief it sought	376	Lara	2	106
Awaits the absence of the thing it fear'd	377	Lara	2	124
But that long absence from his native clime	377	Lara	2	170
His friends the more for his long absence prized him	452	Beppo		781
I pray, and thou, too, prince, permit my absence	552	Sardan	1	100
In absence, and attracts us to each other	557	Sardan	1	473
At such a moment now is safe in absence	586	Sardan	4	533
Are not so numerous as to spare your absence	589	Sardan	5	117
At so much price as to require your absence	605	Foscari	2	246
Years had roll'd o'er my absence. Hardly hours	647	Cain	3	59
During thine absence, whereupon to offer	647	Cain	3	97
Absence, I'm sovereign; and the baron is	682	Werner	1	687
Fare in our absence? Stralenheim knows nothing	698	Werner	3	221
To excuse your absence to the count your father	705	Werner	4	101
In a like absence? But 'tis vain to urge you	709	Werner	4	333
Abstracted, distant, given to long absence	711	Werner	4	421
Until the hours of absence should run through	764	Juan	1	1126
Has in his absence wedded some rich miser	804	Juan	3	186
Perceiving in his absence such expenses	806	Juan	3	278
More easy by the absence of all men	856	Juan	6	250
Of absence lay one's old resentments level	915	Juan	10	527
The absence of that more sublime construction	917	Juan	10	606
Who fought, and fight, in absence, too, my battles	967	Juan	14	767
Like virtue; and the absence of pretension	970	Juan	15	111
Or modesty, or absence, or inanity	978	Juan	15	622

ABSENCES

Wives in their husbands' absences grow subtler	804	Juan	3	175

ABSENT

But thinking on an absent wife	6	Harold	1	164
Long absent Harold re-appears at last	36	Harold	3	66
Joy was not always absent from his face	43	Harold	3	467
Well to that heart might his these absent greetings pour	43	Harold	3	495
Our troops and leaders mourn their absent chief	105	Nisus		30
On every side they seek his absent friend	109	Nisus		320

ABSENT

Say, will you mourn my absent name	118 Romance		53
Absent or present, still to thee	169 Blank Leaf		1
And being so--the absent are the dead	191 Fragment-C		11
The absent are the dead--for they are cold	192 Fragment-C		15
Her consort still is absent, and her crew	344 Corsair	1	414
And oft when present--absent from my thought	354 Corsair	2	520
A long, long absent gladness in his glance	362 Corsair	3	491
But one is absent from the mouldering file	366 Lara	1	41
Awake their absent echoes in his ear	373 Lara	1	523
And thus I answer for mine absent guest	376 Lara	2	56
And he must answer for the absent head	377 Lara	2	155
If some few should be tardy or absent them	524 Faliero	3	386
Be found among the absent. Say not so	530 Faliero	4	192
But found the monarch absent. And I too	564 Sardan	2	154
I needs must say but one, and he is absent	678 Werner	1	478
Absent, I took upon myself the care	702 Werner	3	484
I've known the absent wrong'd four times a day	804 Juan	3	200
She had no pulse, but death seem'd absent still	824 Juan	4	475
For some had absent lovers, all had friends	954 Juan	13	833
True, he was absent, and, 'twas rumour'd, took	961 Juan	14	355
How sweet the task to shield an absent friend	994 Juan	16	879
But seldom pay the absent, nor would look	994 Juan	16	892

ABSENTEES

There also were some Irish absentees	951 Juan	13	664

ABSOLUTE

And wives, as in life, aim at absolute sway	117 To Eliza		27
To draw conclusions absolute of aught	494 Manfred	3	207
Definitive and absolute! To the point	623 Foscari	5	165
For me, I deem an absolute autocrat	899 Juan	9	183

ABSOLUTION

With absolution such as may	400 Parisina		417
Let him have absolution. I dispense with	565 Sardan	2	239
That begg'd Pedrillo for an absolution	779 Juan	2	351

ABSOLVE

Thou wilt absolve me from the deed	320 Giaour		1038
That doom shall half absolve thy sin	391 Corinth		637
Its mercy may absolve thee yet	398 Parisina		212
And all we can absolve thee shall be pardon'd	492 Manfred	3	87

ABSOLVED

And be absolved by his upright compeers	515 Faliero	2	436
Thy husband yet may be absolved. He is	598 Foscari	1	213
Was satisfied---not that you are absolved	692 Werner	2	588

ABSOLVING

For when one near display'd the absolving cross	382 Lara	2	477

ABSORB

It has no shape; but will absorb all things	631 Cain	1	259
Upon such things would very near absorb	774 Juan	2	45

ABSORB'D

And thus I am absorb'd, and this is life	46 Harold	3	689
Though souls absorb'd like mine allow	322 Giaour		1225
Absorb'd in passion's and in nature's thirst	427 Island	3	74
Absorb'd in thine; the world was past away	439 Tasso		172
But is absorb'd in sufferance or in joy	496 Manfred	3	395
You were absorb'd in thought, and he who now	511 Faliero	2	153

ABSORBING
(See also ALL-ABSORBING, EARTH-ABSORBING)

In that absorbing sigh perchance more blest	47 Harold	3	750
Such is the absorbing hate when warring nations meet	64 Harold	4	567
But vacancy absorbing space	405 Chillon		243
We know not how, the absorbing fire	409 Mazeppa		243
The maid and boy, in one absorbing soul	423 Island	2	305
In the absorbing, sweeping, whole revenge	526 Faliero	3	541
To you in that absorbing element	594 Sardan	5	433

ABSORBS

Absorbs each wish it felt before	111 Medea		8
With a pure feeling which absorbs and awes	192 Monody		5

ABSTAIN'D

All except Juan, who throughout abstain'd	784 Juan	2	653

ABSTINENCE

By daily abstinence and nightly prayer	32 Harold	2	741
I grant his household abstinence; I grant	290 Vision		359
His mind seems nourish'd by that abstinence	339 Corsair	1	76

ABSTRACT

Nor ever had for abstract fame much passion	898 Juan	9	108
Fired with an abstract love of virtue, she	961 Juan	14	362

ABSTRACTED

Abstracted, distant, much given to long absence	711 Werner	4	421

ABSTRACTING

Can hardly be suspected of abstracting	698 Werner	3	209

ABSTRACTION

His soul, in deep abstraction sudden sunk	373 Lara	1	483
As an abstraction--for--you know not what	744 Deformed	3	132
Feel some abstraction when they gaze on her	982 Juan	16	107
Who wonder'd at the abstraction of his air	992 Juan	16	771

ABSTRUSE

Prayers are too tedious, lectures too abstruse	259 Hints		227
The sciences, and most of all the abstruse	752 Juan	1	314
I think that Dante's more abstruse ecstatics	803 Juan	3	87
For feelings causeless, or at least abstruse	819 Juan	4	176

ABSTRUSER

Of Earth, whom the abstruser powers permit	485 Manfred	2	123

ABSURD

Your passion appears most absurd	116 Strephon		34
Why bend to the proud, or applaud the absurd	129 Becher-A		23
However trifling, which may seem absurd	267 Hints		802
Contemptuous once, and now no less absurd	271 Minerva		254
Besides, our friend Scamp is to-day so absurd	278 Blues	1	42
To you 't would seem absurd as vain	409 Mazeppa		286
Which surely is exceedingly absurd	442 Beppo		176
Said he; 'don't let us make ourselves absurd	451 Beppo		717
Shed his young blood for his absurd lampoon	512 Faliero	2	241
Absurd insinuations--ignorance	693 Werner	2	637
Sweet playful phrases, which would seem absurd	818 Juan	4	111
To bring the other three here was absurd	874 Juan	7	478
Or 'God be with you!'--and 'tis not absurd	920 Juan	11	93
They wonder'd how a young man so absurd	992 Juan	16	757

ABSURDER

And now still absurder	232 Murray-B		28

ABSURDITY

Though their system's absurdity keeps it unknown	282 Blues	2	110
To mend the people's an absurdity	918 Juan	10	677

ABSURDLY

Absurdly varying, he at last engraves	257 Hints		47

ABUNDANCE

Is rank abundance, and a rotten harvest	557 Sardan	1	463

ABUSE

My counsel will get but abuse	116 Strephon		16
Train'd to invent and skilful to abuse	142 Soliloquy		40
You disparage my parts with insidious abuse	279 Blues	1	109
'Why, my dear Lucifer, would you abuse	292 Vision		497
A man some women like, and yet abuse	443 Beppo		237
Against the people to abuse their hands	526 Faliero	3	562
In my o'er-fervent youth; but for the abuse	672 Werner	1	80
As hell--mere mortals who their power abuse	894 Juan	8	983
Think not, fair creatures, that I mean to abuse you all	933 Juan	12	219
When we no more can use, or even abuse thee	953 Juan	13	800
Of coxcombry or conquest: no abuse	969 Juan	15	92

ABUSED

Abused his art, till Nature, with a blush	256 Hints		3
Nor I alone, are injured and abused	507 Faliero	1	489
Worn out, scorn'd, spurn'd, abused; what matters then	512 Faliero	2	267
To further their design was ne'er abused	522 Faliero	3	238
Enjoy'd them, loved them, and, alas! abused them	672 Werner	1	78
And, turning up her nose, with looks abused	766 Juan	1	1267
The mercy he had granted oft abused	808 Juan	3	428
He praised the present, and abused the past	811 Juan	3	625
Except Napoleon, or abused it more	897 Juan	9	66

ABUSES

Or all the figures Castlereagh abuses	849 Juan	5	1141

ABYSS

The flashing mass foams shaking the abyss	65 Harold	4	616
Thou, who didst call the Furies from the abyss	75 Harold	4	1183
Reverse of her decree than in the abyss	77 Harold	4	1355
And send us prying into the abyss	79 Harold	4	1486
Hark! forth from the abyss a voice proceeds	80 Harold	4	1495
They slept on the abyss without a surge	190 Darkness		77
And voices from the deep abyss reveal'd	216 Dream		200
His isles had floated on the abyss of time	290 Vision		335
Cares little into what abyss	321 Giaour		1158
Where the mind rots congenial with the abyss	439 Tasso		235
Forth from the abyss of time which is to be	458 Dante	2	5
Whose splendour from the black abyss is flung	463 Dante	3	188
Even in the foaming strength of its abyss	492 Manfred	3	111
Float up from the abyss of time to be	548 Faliero	5	738
Forth from the abyss, looking as he could coil	642 Cain	2	398
Holds, and the abyss, and the immensity	645 Cain	2	632
Some wandering star, which shoots through the abyss	656 Heaven		87

ABYSS

The abyss of crime (though not of such crime), I	703	Werner	3	534
Contempt, but from the bathos' vast abyss	815	Juan	3	892
And swimming long in the abyss of thought	898	Juan	9	141
Clings to its teat--sticks to me through the abyss	911	Juan	10	220
Some waltz; some draw; some fathom the abyss	936	Juan	12	413
If from great nature's or our own abyss	955	Juan	14	1

ACADEMIC

Secures its owner's academic fame	124	Recoll		154
To quit his academic occupation	778	Juan	2	294

ACADEMICIANS

As also of the first academicians	898	Juan	9	130

ACADEMIE

Hush'd 'Academie' sigh'd in silent awe	444	Beppo		250

ACARNANIA'S

To traverse Acarnania's forest wide	30	Harold	2	618

ACCELERATED

In their accelerated graves, nor will	620	Foscari	4	330

ACCENT

Still must each accent to my bosom suit	343	Corsair	1	369
Than glance could well reveal or accent breathe	367	Lara	1	78
With look collected, but with accent cold	372	Lara	1	429
Without an accent of reply	391	Corinth		664
And, starting to each accent, sprang	411	Mazeppa		458
That not a single accent seems uncouth	445	Beppo		350
The barrier which that hesitating accent	558	Sardan	1	482
With an Ionian accent, low and sweet	793	Juan	2	1199
Said Lolah, with an accent rather rough	858	Juan	6	350
Is musical--a dying accent driven	949	Juan	13	500

ACCENTS

That I in feeblest accents must adore	14	Harold	1	624
The Forum, where the immortal accents glow	72	Harold	4	1007
In faltering accents sweetly mild	88	Anacreon-B		14
His whispering accents then the youth repress'd	108	Nisus		237
And pour these accents, shrieking as he flies	110	Nisus		366
Hear'st thou the accents of despair	132	Prayer		2
The Nine, in anguish'd accents thus he spoke	142	Soliloquy		6
In accents once imagined true	152	Time-A		15
Whose busy accents whisper blame	174	Remember-B		14
Ah! then repeat those accents never	175	Portuguese-A		6
When our child's first accents flow	207	Fare Thee		34
Like cavern'd winds, the hollow accents came	219	Saul-B		12
Those accents scarcely mark'd before	322	Giaour		1233
Oh! wild as the accents of lovers' farewell	323	Abydos	1	18
As sneeringly these accents fell	325	Abydos	1	126
Thus prompt his accents and his actions still	339	Corsair	1	79
But shall we see them? will their accents bless	339	Corsair	1	112
He heard those accents never heard too oft	343	Corsair	1	344
'My fondest, faintest, latest accents hear	343	Corsair	1	359
That smooth'd his accents, soften'd in his eye	351	Corsair	2	262
And these his accents had a sound of mirth	353	Corsair	2	456
To trust their accents to Medora's ear	356	Corsair	3	92
Which spoke before her accents--'Thou must die	359	Corsair	3	279
To deem them accents of another land	369	Lara	1	232
Those strange wild accents; his the cry that	370	Lara	1	276
broke				
Till louder accents rung on Lara's ear	372	Lara	1	418
Those accents, as his native mountains dear	373	Lara	1	522
The accents his scarce-moving pale lips spoke	381	Lara	2	459
And once, as Kaled's answering accents ceased	381	Lara	2	466
He bends to hear his accents bless	400	Parisina		416
These the last accents Hugo spoke	401	Parisina		454
To the sky these accents go	401	Parisina		492
In madlier accents rose despair	401	Parisina		499
The accents tremulous and weak	409	Mazeppa		251
Enough to leave my accents free	415	Mazeppa		824
These the sole accents from his tongue that fell	418	Island	1	167
The lofty accents of whose sighing bough	419	Island	2	11
With prettier name in softer accents spoke	440	Beppo		38
These were the accents utter'd by her tongue	476	Francesca		12
The accents rattle. Give thy prayers to Heaven	497	Manfred	3	404
Suwarrow, though engaged with accents high	875	Juan	7	515

ACCEPT

Accept then my concession	138	Clare		69
Lady, accept the box a hero wore	238	Snuff-Box		1
And to your chiefs: accept me or reject me	523	Faliero	3	329
Nor would she deign to accept divided passion	554	Sardan	1	268
Accept the tardy penitence of demons	617	Foscari	4	176
Accept the homage of respect? I do	620	Foscari	5	15
Accept it as 'tis given--proceed. 'The Ten	621	Foscari	5	16
Nor would accept them if he could, you, signors	625	Foscari	5	327
Accept from out thy humble first of shepherd's	649	Cain	3	237
Aught unto thee? but yet accept it for	649	Cain	3	240
As I have said, you shall. I accept the omen	694	Werner	2	716
How to accept a better in his turn	790	Juan	2	1024
Be such as I can properly accept	840	Juan	5	574

ACCEPT

For sometimes they accept some long pursuer	934	Juan	12	289
Of friendship which you may accept or pass	937	Juan	12	451
The civil list he deigns to accept (obliging all	988	Juan	16	494

ACCEPTABLE

The gift would be acceptable to me	476	Morgante		663
His sacrifices are acceptable	644	Cain	2	558

ACCEPTANCE

Think not upon my offering's acceptance	650	Cain	3	286
In his acceptance of the victims. His	650	Cain	3	297
Had his acceptance. If thou lov'st thyself	650	Cain	3	313
Such as both may make worthy your acceptance	694	Werner	2	718

ACCEPTATION

His acceptation of their duty. Yes	500	Faliero	1	44
His subjects by his gracious acceptation	988	Juan	16	495

ACCEPTED

A propos--Is your play then accepted at last	281	Blues	2	74
Is offer'd and accepted! Could a slave	308	Age		759

ACCEPTING

Accepting you in mercy for his own	471	Morgante		370

ACCESS

And we have open'd regular access	576	Sardan	3	325
A moment's access to his dungeon. I'll	608	Foscari	4	432
Had access to the antechamber. Doubtless	683	Werner	2	18
No difficult access to any. Good sir	683	Werner	2	39
Access, save the Hungarian and yourself	684	Werner	2	59
Bars all access, and may do for some hours	694	Werner	2	696

ACCESSARIES

Those truffles too are no bad accessaries	976	Juan	15	537

ACCESSIBLE

While, placed 'midst clefts the least accessible	434	Island	4	309

ACCESSORY

An accessory, as I have cause to guess	965	Juan	14	604

ACCIDENT

Though accident, blind contact, and the strong	73	Harold	4	1118
An accident should chance to touch	410	Mazeppa		346
To-morrow for a natural accident	619	Foscari	4	269
We came up by mere accident, and just	676	Werner	1	288
Whom either accident or enterprise	716	Werner	5	234
Saw one, whom such an accident befell	835	Juan	5	275
Was favour'd by an accident or blunder	884	Juan	8	362

ACCIDENTS

And wrong are accidents, and men grow pale	69	Harold	4	835
These little accidents should ne'er transpire	277	Waltz		253
(Those happy accidents which render	408	Mazeppa		175
Birth, wealth, health, beauty, are her accidents	606	Foscari	2	341
Your works, or accidents, or whatsoe'er	637	Cain	2	112

ACCLAIM

In whose acclaim the loftiest voices vied	193	Monody		39

ACCLAMATION

And Thou by acclamation Queen	200	Ode-C		7
One acclamation rent the sky again	435	Island	4	412
There also were two wits by acclamation	952	Juan	13	729

ACCOMPANIED

Accompanied with a convulsive splash	780	Juan	2	422
And afterwards accompanied us through	876	Juan	7	571
Duly accompanied by shrieks and groans	895	Juan	8	1074

ACCOMPANIES

Is't true my wife accompanies me? Yes	612	Foscari	3	278

ACCOMPANY

A moment to accompany the Doge	526	Faliero	3	546
Accompany our guests, or charm away	551	Sardan	1	65
Well, sir, we will accompany you hence	568	Sardan	2	414
So you accompany your faithful guard	591	Sardan	2	265
Permitted to accompany my husband	606	Foscari	2	283
I have sued to accompany thee hence	610	Foscari	3	140
We will accompany, with due respect	624	Foscari	5	270
To accompany the intendant. Baron Stralenheim	681	Werner	1	645
'Will please to accompany those gentlemen	841	Juan	5	642

ACCOMPLICE

Your guiltiest accomplice: now you may	519	Faliero	3	62
Will be your most unmerciful accomplice	527	Faliero	3	637
For your accomplice? Father, do not raise	719	Werner	5	426

ACCOMPLICES

Slaves, tools, accomplices--no friends	332	Abydos	2	302
Are fully proved by your accomplices	538	Faliero	5	27

ACCOMPLICES

Say, who were your accomplices? The Senate	538	Faliero	5	54
Upon your power. Your chief accomplices	540	Faliero	5	169
The prince. Thy vile accomplices have died	546	Faliero	5	564
Up to this hall. Are you accomplices	697	Werner	3	131

ACCOMPLISH

I pledge myself to accomplish this--but would	691	Werner	2	506
Air can accomplish, with his wide wings waving	917	Juan	10	620

ACCOMPLISH'D

But there now was a 'call' and accomplish'd debaters	178	Devil's Dr		160
Exist: and what can our accomplish'd art	420	Island	2	101
A feud. But when all is accomplish'd, when	620	Foscari	4	324
Young, handsome, and accomplish'd, who was said	922	Juan	11	255
To save his fame with each accomplish'd belle	925	Juan	11	419
We have no accomplish'd blackguards, like Tom Jones	955	Juan	13	879
Serene, accomplish'd, cheerful but not loud	970	Juan	15	113

ACCOMPLISHMENT

A floating balance of accomplishment	936	Juan	12	410
As if she rated such accomplishment	986	Juan	16	378

ACCOMPLISHMENTS

His accomplishments! His!!! and thy country convince	203	Avatar		66
No wonder such accomplishments should turn	444	Beppo		273
Then for accomplishments of chivalry	751	Juan	1	301
Had left all the accomplishments she taught her	936	Juan	12	405
Whose sole accomplishments were quite a booty	972	Juan	15	270

ACCOMPTS

Of peculation; such as in accompts	684	Werner	2	43
At sixty years, and draw the accompts of evil	767	Juan	1	1335

ACCORD

This much, dear maid, accord; nor question why	3	To Ianthe		34
Have all been borne, and broken by the accord	38	Harold	3	177
Accord me such a being? Do I err	81	Harold	4	1591
The love of fame with this can ill accord	105	Nisus		23
Accord with brother, sire, or stranger guest	263	Hints		498
I grant him all the kindest can accord	290	Vision		366
With carriage) coming of his own accord	296	Vision		704
Nor aught that knighthood may accord, deny	372	Lara	1	477
If this thou dost accord, albeit	391	Corinth		635
Scarce twice the space they must accord my bier	439	Tasso		184
'And here our doctors are of one accord	472	Morgante		401
Whatever be its purport, to accord	542	Faliero	5	323
They would accord some time for your repose	602	Foscari	2	39
Accord with your will, they will make it theirs	620	Foscari	5	3
Upon reflection must accord in this	621	Foscari	5	25
Accord a pardon like a Paradise	649	Cain	3	230
Of your brave bands of their own bold accord	733	Deformed	1	802
Suffering each other's foibles by accord	755	Juan	1	517
It fell down of its own accord before	862	Juan	6	610
Poor Frederick, why did she accord perusals	934	Juan	12	270
With which the winds of heaven can claim accord	952	Juan	13	739

ACCORDANT

A feeling more accordant with his strain	59	Harold	4	278

ACCORDED
(See also SELF-ACCORDED)

Hast been of such, 'twill be accorded now	213	Lady Byron		18
Be pass'd, and thine accorded there	317	Giaour		684
By him whom Heaven accorded none	331	Abydos	2	265
Even as thou wilt: and for the grace accorded	491	Manfred	2	536
In the respect accorded by mankind	512	Faliero	2	256
Freedom of speech accorded to the dying	539	Faliero	5	113
Which yet remain of the accorded hour	546	Faliero	5	581
Will be accorded to a third request	603	Foscari	2	105
Hours are accorded you to give an answer	621	Foscari	5	35
Accorded with her Moorish origin	754	Juan	1	442

ACCORDING

According as their souls were form'd to sink or climb	58	Harold	4	198
Twined with my heart's according strings	132	L'Amitie		67
According to the doubtful story	160	Swimming		14
(According to compact) the wit in the dungeon	226	Oh You		8
That mingle there in well according bands	371	Lara	1	392
According to the proverb,--although no man	441	Beppo		67
A pagan king, according to the story	466	Morgante		45
Make our assurance doubly sure, according	518	Faliero	2	669
According to my honour and my conscience	621	Foscari	5	46
According to the curse:--must I do more	647	Cain	3	110
According to his wont, to meet with Irad	658	Heaven		244
A lodging, or a grave, according as	675	Werner	1	227
According to your order, and beneath	700	Werner	3	372
According to the Orient tale. She is	710	Werner	4	382
According to all hints I could collect	751	Juan	1	258
According to some good old woman's tale	758	Juan	1	760

ACCORDING

According to direction, then received	775	Juan	2	66
Or 'Ca ira,' according to the fashion all	812	Juan	3	676
One of the two, according to your choice	819	Juan	4	193
From crowns to kicks, according to their vices	834	Juan	5	216
With arguments according to their 'forte	837	Juan	5	383
To lodge there when a war broke out, according	850	Juan	5	1202
According to the ancient epic laws	851	Juan	5	1267
So styled according to the usual forms	854	Juan	6	98
Were they, according to the best report	857	Juan	6	317
According to the artillery's hits or misses	876	Juan	7	603
According as you take things well or ill	917	Juan	10	639
If it be chance; or if it be according	919	Juan	11	25
According as their minds or backs are bent	936	Juan	12	412
According as the skies their shadows threw	948	Juan	13	464
Is poesy, according as the mind glows	956	Juan	14	60
According to the best of dictionaries	976	Juan	15	541
The guests were placed according to their roll	977	Juan	15	587

ACCORDS

But retirement accords with the tone of my mind	128	Becher-A		3
Accords not with the freeborn soul	135	I Would		6
To you, ye children of--whom chance accords	275	Waltz		101
What the whole earth accords, beholding not	489	Manfred	2	414
The state accords her worthiest servants; nay	532	Faliero	4	320
Was such as fire accords to a wet blanket	806	Juan	3	288

ACCOST

Yet with smooth smile his tyrant can accost	32	Harold	2	787
Which sways them, I would not accost yon infant	648	Cain	3	129

ACCOUNT

Account of Ezzelin at Lara's hands	377	Lara	2	132
Destroy'd by him, or through him, the account	620	Foscari	4	318
Pursue it on their own account. Here comes	685	Werner	2	144
Of his arrival, and the time; the account, too	687	Werner	2	274
Had often turn'd the art to some account	787	Juan	2	836
She now kept house upon her own account	806	Juan	3	304
That, adding to the account his Highness' years	853	Juan	6	68
Account for everything which may look bad	882	Juan	8	244

ACCOUNTANT

A strict accountant of his beads	181	Ode-A		68

ACCOUNTS

We've not yet closed accounts, and we shall see yet	447	Beppo		493
The last, if late accounts be accurate	830	Juan	4	890
You're right on both accounts to hold your tongue	833	Juan	5	127

ACCOUTREMENTS

Completed his accoutrements, as Night	425	Island	2	498

ACCREDITED

Who must be courteous to the accredited	923	Juan	11	314

ACCRUE

The fame that could accrue to him	388	Corinth		397

ACCUMULATE

Distort the truth, accumulate the lie	193	Monody		77

ACCUMULATED

Accumulated ills. Accumulated	611	Foscari	3	230
To inherit agonies accumulated	634	Cain	1	446

ACCUMULATES

Makes greater, and accumulates my curse	464	Dante	4	114
So soon!--so late--each hour accumulates	523	Faliero	3	352

ACCUMULATING

To what thy sons' sons' sons, accumulating	642	Cain	2	430

ACCURATE

And accurate as any other vision	289	Vision		272
The last, if late accounts be accurate	830	Juan	4	890
All very accurate, you must allow	896	Juan	8	1100

ACCURATELY

Until the sum was accurately scann'd	835	Juan	5	230

ACCURSED

When Paphos fell by time--accursed Time	14	Harold	1	666
And thus--accursed be the day and year	270	Minerva		147
Alike reserved for aye to stand accursed	271	Minerva		205
The accursed Hun, more brutal than of old	307	Age		689
Lost Leila's love, accursed Giaour	316	Giaour		619
From spectre more accursed than they	318	Giaour		786
Accursed Dervise!--these thy tidings--thou	349	Corsair	2	140
Accursed was the moment when he bore	358	Corsair	3	187
The accursed breath of dungeon-dew	404	Chillon		214
Accursed was the book and he who wrote	477	Francesca		41
Accursed! what have I to do with days	480	Manfred	1	169
On the accursed tyranny which rides	531	Faliero	4	237
In their accursed bosoms. You know not	603	Foscari	2	115

ACCURSED

Accursed be the city where the laws	608	Foscari	2	419
In that accursed isle of slaves, and captives	610	Foscari	3	133
Accursed	670	Heaven		1120
By means of this accursed gold; but now	698	Werner	3	179
Keep off from me as from your foe! Accursed	699	Werner	3	274
And only took--Accursed gold! thou liest	711	Werner	4	438
Accursed be this blood that flows so fast	722	Deformed	1	33
And thee! What do I see? Accursed jackals	740	Deformed	2	309
Throbb'd in accursed dreams, which sometimes spread	791	Juan	2	1070

ACCURSING

When these are tainted by the accursing breath	503	Faliero	1	218

ACCURST

'Thou youth accurst, thy life shall pay for all	110	Nisus		360
Foredoom'd by God--by man accurst	181	Ode-A		140
'Gainst Nature's voice seduced to deeds accurst	223	To Dives		2
Had Lara from that night, to him accurst	378	Lara	2	236

ACCUSAL

Cain! clear thee from this horrible accusal	652	Cain	3	400

ACCUSALS

(Friends of the party), who begin accusals	934	Juan	12	268

ACCUSATION

The accusation and defence: if we	292	Vision		503
And long debate on Steno's accusation	499	Faliero	1	4
Alike by accusation or defence	538	Faliero	5	61
The accusation of the bribes was proved	600	Foscari	1	301
Does he abet you in your accusation	691	Werner	2	533
An accusation for a sentence	709	Werner	4	305

ACCUSE

And, madly, godlike Providence accuse	85	Death-B		18
When dames accuse 'tis bootless to deny	142	Soliloquy		34
In phrensy then their fate accuse	321	Giaour		1152
Accuse not, hate not him who wears the spoils	341	Corsair	1	190
Oh, Fate!--accuse thy folly, not thy fate	343	Corsair	1	339
To lands where, save their conscience, none accuse	418	Island	1	212
The culprit be whom I accuse of treason	539	Faliero	5	77
Who dares accuse my country? Men and angels	611	Foscari	3	240
I accuse no man. Then you acquit me, baron	691	Werner	2	544
I know not whom to accuse, or to acquit	691	Werner	2	545
As you accuse. You hint the basest injury	692	Werner	2	601
Is free, and quick with virtuous wrath to accuse	703	Werner	3	537
I accuse no man, save in my defence	717	Werner	5	299
Just as a friar may accuse his vow	849	Juan	5	1134
They accuse me--Me--the present writer of	867	Juan	7	17
Since I've grown moral, still I must accuse you all	933	Juan	12	221
Let none accuse Old England's hospitality	947	Juan	13	391
The last is apt the former to accuse	997	Juan	17	44

ACCUSED

Accused of what till now my heart disdain'd	360	Corsair	3	322
My station near the accused too, Michel Steno	500	Faliero	1	69
The apparent crimes of the accused disclose	600	Foscari	1	310
But that's a trifle. I stand here accused	691	Werner	2	540
Again! Am I accused or no? Go to	692	Werner	2	589
Some have accused me of a strange design	817	Juan	4	33
Has been accused (I doubt not by conspiracy	839	Juan	5	482
And next his savage virtue he accused	849	Juan	5	1133
Some people have accused me of misanthropy	899	Juan	9	156
The accused to think their lordships would determine	949	Juan	13	547

ACCUSER

Stands sentinel, accuser, judge, and spy	193	Monody		70
Nor thy accuser. Though the hour is past	596	Foscari	1	74
Have an accuser, let it be a man	691	Werner	2	552
You, count, have made yourself accuser--judge	717	Werner	5	300

ACCUSERS

Words wild as these, accusers like to thee	372	Lara	1	456
Unnamed accusers in the dark	385	Corinth		132
You are at once offenders and accusers	540	Faliero	5	167

ACCUSER'S

Methinks the accuser's rest is long indulged	375	Lara	2	28

ACCUSES

Unless--First, who accuses me? All things	715	Werner	5	158

ACCUSING

And feed on bitter fruits without accusing Fate	36	Harold	3	63

ACCUSTOM'D

And long accustom'd bondage uncreate	31	Harold	2	696
For I have been accustom'd to entwine	64	Harold	4	545
But the old mansion, and the accustom'd hall	215	Dream		160
Again to that accustom'd couch must creep	375	Lara	1	630

ACCUSTOM'D

From travellers accustom'd from a boy	441	Beppo		55
Or one, or all, in your accustom'd forms	480	Manfred	1	180
And may be cross'd by the accustom'd barks	590	Sardan	5	204
Who love us are accustom'd to descend	655	Heaven		2
He hath not been accustom'd to admission	679	Werner	1	526
The sights he was accustom'd to behold	808	Juan	3	429
Who were accustom'd, as a sort of god	876	Juan	7	587

ACESTES'

Nor Troy nor king Acestes' realms restrain	107	Nisus		179

ACHAIAN

Her place of birth, her own Achaian shore	253	Bards		872

ACHAIA'S

Resign Achaia's lyre, and strike your own	254	Bards		890

ACHATES

He, like Achates, faithful to the tomb	766	Juan	1	1270

ACHE

And silent ache for thee	163	Parting		20
Why must my head ache where his gentle brow lay	204	Hindoo		6
Ache with the annual tributes of a spouse	274	Waltz		94
No stiff-starch'd stays make meddling fingers ache	275	Waltz		140
Beneath the crown which makes his head ache, like	700	Werner	3	337
Which make my head and heart ache, as both throb	714	Werner	5	72
Struck not on memory, though a heavy ache	824	Juan	4	493

ACHED

And ached in sleepless silence long	218	Soul-B		14

ACHELOUS'

Till he did greet white Achelous' tide	30	Harold	2	620

ACHERON

Peace waits us on the shores of Acheron	20	Harold	2	61
Nodding above; behold black Acheron	27	Harold	2	456

ACHERUSIA'S

He pass'd bleak Pindus, Acherusia's lake	26	Harold	2	415

ACHES
(See also HEART-ACHES)

Till the sense aches with gazing to behold	33	Harold	2	832
And bloodless, with its sleepless sorrow aches	40	Harold	3	295
Aches with orchestras which he pays to hear	261	Hints		308
How my brain aches beneath thee! and my temples	504	Faliero	1	294
My heart aches bitterly. I pray you sit	625	Foscari	5	287
Expansion--at which my soul aches to think	637	Cain	2	108
(My heart or head aches with the memory yet	954	Juan	13	852

ACHIEVE

Can man achieve without the friendly steed	16	Harold	1	745
This daring soul which could achieve no less	727	Deformed	1	326

ACHIEVED

A pageant? In my life I have achieved	504	Faliero	1	300
Tasks not less difficult--achieved for them	504	Faliero	1	301
Great things were now to be achieved at table	975	Juan	15	489

ACHILLES

A boy Achilles, with the centaur's lyre	420	Island	2	85
And thine--I've seen--Achilles! do no more	422	Island	2	219
I love but thee! Even so Achilles loved	741	Deformed	2	381
Achilles ordered dinner for new comers	789	Juan	2	984
Entomb'd the bravest of the brave, Achilles	826	Juan	4	603
And though his name, than Ajax or Achilles	883	Juan	8	306
Named after thee, Achilles), and quite through 't	889	Juan	8	669

ACHILLES'

Save change: I've stood upon Achilles' tomb	829	Juan	4	807
Achilles' self was not more grim and gory	868	Juan	7	110

ACHING

But as he gazed on truth his aching eyes grew dim	8	Harold	1	323
Thou still hadst lived to bless my aching sight	85	Epitaph		9
In love can soothe the aching breast	111	Medea		12
Not to the aching frame alone confined	122	Recoll		5
To dazzle, though they please, my aching sight	122	Recoll		42
Has pillow'd oft this aching head	144	Jessy		22
That this poor aching breast now nourishes	653	Cain	3	487

ACHITOPHEL

Can sneer at him who drew 'Achitophel	815	Juan	3	896

ACIDS

As acids rouse a dormant alkali	914	Juan	10	428
Some acids with the sweets--for she was heady	975	Juan	15	484

ACKNOWLEDGE

Which Truth would acknowledge complete	178	Devil's Dr		184

ACKNOWLEDGE
I own it--I know it--acknowledge it--what	279 Blues	1	107
Whom all arts shall acknowledge as their lord	464 Dante	4	59
If you acknowledge the Redeemer blest	471 Morgante		355
Who in the very punishment acknowledge	546 Faliero	5	563
Acknowledge that more loving dust	655 Heaven		54
To be created, and to acknowledge him	666 Heaven		842
Acknowledge aught of dread of death or foe	889 Juan	8	693

ACKNOWLEDGED
Mourn'd by the few my soul acknowledged here	138 Harrow-B		32
And other minds acknowledged my dominion	816 Juan	4	20

ACKNOWLEDGMENT
For it is worse, being full of acknowledgment	503 Faliero	1	238

ACME
The acme of Sardanapalus, who	571 Sardan	3	10

ACORN
I reck not if an acorn gave it birth	963 Juan	14	468

ACQUAINTANCE
For finding one in each acquaintance	144 Becher-B		34
Our new acquaintance) Torquil. 'Aught of new	425 Island	2	501
Condemns the evil done my new acquaintance	471 Morgante		324
Our better acquaintance; relatives should be	674 Werner	1	200
More permanent acquaintance. How now, fellow	734 Deformed	1	814
Amongst her numerous acquaintance, all	753 Juan	1	433
And made him a good friend, but bad acquaintance	808 Juan	3	432
The purchaser of Juan and acquaintance	836 Juan	5	313
Her second, to cut only his--acquaintance	849 Juan	5	1106
Our old acquaintance; and at least I'll try	918 Juan	10	668
Can form a slight acquaintance with fresh air	926 Juan	11	520
And thus acquaintance grew, at noble routs	944 Juan	13	185
A large acquaintance lets not Virtue slumber	945 Juan	13	235

ACQUAINTANCES
My own acquaintances? You have to learn	691 Werner	2	522

ACQUAINTED
Though thy soul with my grief was acquainted	210 Augusta-B		5
Acquainted with all feelings save despair	421 Island	2	178
Acquainted with thy vainly echo'd name	490 Manfred	2	508
Our near, though not acquainted neighbourhood	491 Manfred	3	28
To him who first acquainted him with man	652 Cain	3	437
So let us be acquainted, as we ought	833 Juan	5	102

ACQUIESCE
Must acquiesce, while sterner hearts applaud	416 Island	1	68
Reflected upon this, but acquiesce	614 Foscari	3	383

ACQUIESCED
Because, though young, he acquiesced with suavity	944 Juan	13	171

ACQUIESCENCE
The acquiescence in all things which tend	213 Lady Byron		56

ACQUIRE
Acquire the deep and bitter power to give	830 Juan	4	852

ACQUIRED
Whate'er thou hast acquired from then till now	467 Morgante		54
Midst every natural and acquired distinction	717 Werner	5	266
But how faith is acquired, and then ensured	753 Juan	1	373
Though I acquired--but I pass over that	753 Juan	1	418
Which is acquired in Nature's good old college	791 Juan	2	1088
Might have from time acquired some slight defect	988 Juan	16	508

ACQUIT
I accuse no man. Then you acquit me, baron	691 Werner	2	544
I know not whom to accuse, or to acquit	691 Werner	2	545
Above our house! My father! I acquit you	702 Werner	3	489

ACQUITTAL
By this most rank--I will not say--acquittal	503 Faliero	1	237
For such as him a dungeon were acquittal	515 Faliero	2	438

ACQUITTANCE
Have ruffled mine, he will, for all acquittance	509 Faliero	2	54
By thy descendant, merit such acquittance	519 Faliero	3	40
The acquittance of the interest of the debt	685 Werner	2	184

ACQUITTED
This creeping, coward, rank, acquitted felon	502 Faliero	1	185
He acquitted both himself and horse: the squires	959 Juan	14	266

ACRES
And acres told upon the appointed day	306 Age		589

ACRES'
As through his palms Bob Acres' valour oozed	849 Juan	5	1129

ACROCERAUNIAN
Th' Acroceraunian mountains of old name	66 Harold	4	658

ACRO-CORINTH'S
And sit with me on Acro-Corinth's brow	385 Corinth		45

ACROPOLIS
Than yon tower-capp'd Acropolis	385 Corinth		69
To our theme.--The man who has stood on the Acropolis	919 Juan	11	49

ACROSS
His bow across his shoulders flung	89 Anacreon-B		27
Across the green in numbers fly	95 Granta		68
He stepp'd across the sea	176 Devil's Dr		28
Across her gently-budding breast	325 Abydos	1	183
Across the desert, or before the gale	333 Abydos	2	393
Stood Christian, with his arms across his chest	427 Island	3	86
There came a heaviness across my heart	528 Faliero	4	4
And swept, as 'twere, across their hearts' delight	819 Juan	4	163

ACT
Can act, is acting there against man's life	18 Harold	1	894
To act and suffer, but remount at last	46 Harold	3	693
Yours is the godlike act, be yours the praise	107 Nisus		124
Did they act like your blooming coquette	115 Pigot		24
An act like this, can simple thanks repay	126 Recoll		283
And that last act, though not thy worst	181 Ode-A		141
Had been an act of purer fame	181 Ode-A		149
There are moments which act as a plough	205 Blessington		14
Nor unregarded will the act pass by	258 Hints		131
Repeal that act! again let Humour roam	261 Hints		359
Unless they act like us and our allies	266 Hints		702
Which is to act as we are bid to do	287 Vision		176
From out the whole but such and such an act	289 Vision		269
In act to assert his right or wrong, and show	289 Vision		291
Nor midst my sins such act record	320 Giaour		1037
Not mine the act, though I the cause	320 Giaour		1061
Demons in act but Gods at least in face	341 Corsair	1	194
In act alone obeys, his air commands	374 Lara	1	561
The rattle-snake's in act to strike	412 Mazeppa		536
To act whatever duty bade them do	433 Island	4	282
When the first act is ended by a dance	445 Beppo		327
Did not my verse embalm full many an act	458 Dante	1	148
On Gan in that rash act he seem'd to take	468 Morgante		138
Kiss'd my mouth, trembling in the act all over	477 Francesca		40
But I can act even what I most abhor	487 Manfred	2	297
And why not live and act with other men	493 Manfred	3	124
I saw the president in act to seal	500 Faliero	1	27
His peers will scarce protect him; such an act	500 Faliero	1	34
His own still conscience smote him for the act	509 Faliero	2	42
To act in trust as your commander, till	518 Faliero	2	697
Than live another day to act the tyrant	523 Faliero	3	301
I blame you not, you act in your vocation	527 Faliero	3	577
You acted, and you act on your free will	527 Faliero	3	623
'My own free will and act,' and yet you err	527 Faliero	3	635
And yet I act no more on my free will	527 Faliero	3	638
The act of opening the forbidden lattice	529 Faliero	4	94
'Tis not my office to reply, but act	536 Faliero	4	567
To miss it thus!--We took him in the act	537 Faliero	4	613
Guards! let their mouths be gagg'd, even in the act	539 Faliero	5	102
Sit here, do well to act in their vocation	542 Faliero	5	317
I think the statue looks in act to speak	570 Sardan	2	535
The last drops from his helm, he stood in act	577 Sardan	3	356
And greatest to all mortals; crowning act	591 Sardan	5	229
He's right.--Let him go free.--My life's last act	592 Sardan	5	335
And act befittingly. I shall not fail	592 Sardan	5	347
'Tis done, I thank you. Thus the act confirm'd	601 Foscari	2	10
That they have power to act at their discretion	604 Foscari	2	201
Without our act or choice as birth, so that	607 Foscari	2	363
He could not now act otherwise. A show	611 Foscari	3	226
To impede the act, I must no less obey	616 Foscari	4	115
The act was passing, it might have suspended	619 Foscari	4	261
Whom we now act against not only saved	619 Foscari	4	310
To the deceased, so you would act the part	626 Foscari	5	359
Although reluctantly. My first act shall not	690 Werner	2	492
To deem he would descend to such an act	695 Werner	2	757
Return--'twas a most kind act in the count	706 Werner	4	137
Or act so carelessly, in that which is	709 Werner	4	350
Discovery in the act could make me know	719 Werner	5	412
That I should act what you could think? We have done	720 Werner	5	453
He stood in act to speak, or rather stammer	766 Juan	1	1297
Was but a moment's act.--Ah! well-a-day	769 Juan	1	1445
For they, who were most ravenous in the act	784 Juan	2	627
His brow, as if in act to butt, and then	805 Juan	3	255
Of magic ladies who, by one sole act	805 Juan	3	271
Perhaps you prophesy some sudden act	806 Juan	3	316
In arms, at least, he stood, in act to spring	821 Juan	4	311
Which was an odd one; a troop going to act	826 Juan	4	636
I think with Alexander, that the act	835 Juan	5	249

ACT

Of eating, with another act or two	835 Juan	5	250
Because a foolish or imprudent act	865 Juan	6	828
Of which, howe'er the Muse describes each act	877 Juan	7	643
Which youth would not act ill to keep in mind	907 Juan	9	669
It grows an act of patriotic charity	941 Juan	12	707
Though apt to act with fire upon occasion	943 Juan	13	109
Stood like Caractacus in act to rally	948 Juan	13	443
And only think, or act, or feel, with reference	992 Juan	16	726
Has been declared an act of inurbanity	997 Juan	17	55

ACTED

And I have acted well my part	164 Friend-B		33
And so have acted heretofore	173 Quotation		22
Unless 'twere acted by O'Neill	232 Doctor		86
Are better told than acted on the stage	260 Hints		268
Seems to have acted on them like a spell	287 Vision		164
Those grand heroics acted as a spell	297 Vision		817
Things light or lovely in their acted time	352 Corsair	2	350
Their own scant numbers acted all the few	427 Island	3	53
You acted, and you act on your free will	527 Faliero	3	623
But the sea acted as a strong emetic	776 Juan	2	168
Acted upon the living as on wire	883 Juan	8	327
If you have acted once a generous part	897 Juan	9	29
Your face--but you have acted on the whole	909 Juan	10	127
As if they acted with the heart instead	922 Juan	11	268
But whatsoe'er she wish'd, she acted right	962 Juan	14	454
So well she acted all and every part	993 Juan	16	817
Who are strongly acted on by what is nearest	993 Juan	16	824

ACTING

Can act, is acting there against man's life	18 Harold	1	894
Of late events, acting upon a frame	581 Sardan	4	169
Might end in acting as his own 'Jack Ketch	866 Juan	6	925

ACTION

No borrow'd grace of action must be seen	112 Examination		37
In all the arts of scenic action old	113 Prologue		12
His life is action	200 Stanzas-B		32
We loathe the action which exceeds belief	260 Hints		288
In saying eloquence meant 'Action, action	304 Age		501
'Twas strange--in youth all action and all life	367 Lara	1	115
How glorious in its action and itself	482 Manfred	1	299
Let each repair for action to his post	524 Faliero	3	365
Let them be dealt upon. And now to action	526 Faliero	3	507
The hour of action I have stood as calm	534 Faliero	4	446
Saint Mark and Liberty!'--Now--now to action	535 Faliero	4	473
And my superiority in action	540 Faliero	5	205
A monarch into action, to forego	560 Sardan	1	655
In the late action scarcely more appall'd	588 Sardan	5	77
Is time for union and for action, not	719 Werner	4	428
In action and endurance than thyself	724 Deformed	1	108
Placed in the rear in action--but your foes	733 Deformed	1	795
In speech as sharp in action--and that's more	733 Deformed	1	810
His brain about the action of the sky	758 Juan	1	742
So that a suit or action were made good	766 Juan	1	1277
With graceful action, science not a jot	827 Juan	4	707
As good men wear who have done a virtuous action	845 Juan	5	856
And one good action in the midst of crimes	889 Juan	8	713
May be the hoarder's principle of action	931 Juan	12	82
Whose loss in the late action we regret	948 Juan	13	431

ACTIONS

Thus prompt his accents and his actions still	339 Corsair	1	79
It doth; but actions are our epochs: mine	484 Manfred	2	52
Such actions from our hands: we'll wash away	521 Faliero	3	201
Such is our trust in all thine actions. Now	521 Faliero	3	209
And which am I to be? your actions leave	522 Faliero	3	242
When the survivors of long years and actions	525 Faliero	3	450
Through his great actions and the Senate's insults	538 Faliero	5	63
Your actions show it. Might I ask your name	686 Werner	2	189
Learn to divine and judge his actions. Young	689 Werner	2	437
He sends me here a spy upon your actions	697 Werner	3	154
Whose actions I ape	728 Deformed	1	387
But here are men who fought in gallant actions	871 Juan	7	265
To trace all actions to their secret springs	963 Juan	14	469

ACTIUM

Actium, Lepanto, fatal Trafalgar	25 Harold	2	356
But Actium, lost for Cleopatra's eyes	853 Juan	6	31

ACTIUM'S

Full beams the moon on Actium's coast	159 Gulf		2

ACTIVE

Drive o'er the sward the ball with active force	124 Recoll		131
Deprived of active force	146 Adieu		50
The active agony of grief	172 Time-B		19
To witness many an active deed	326 Abydos	1	237
A stalwart, active, soldier-looking stripling	687 Werner	2	254
Active, though not so sprightly, as a page	753 Juan	1	427
An active hermit, even in age the child	886 Juan	8	503
Who, like Don Juan, takes an active share	927 Juan	11	546

ACTIVITY

And woman in activity. Let's see	729 Deformed	1	496
Where London streets ferment in full activity	919 Juan	11	60

ACTOR

So that if any actor miss'd his part	748 Juan	1	83

ACTORS

Both are but theatres where the chief actors rot	76 Harold	4	1251
Of embryo actors, to the Drama new	113 Prologue		16
And full-grown actors are endured once more	249 Bards		565
And actors copy nature--when they can	258 Hints		152
That the taste of the actors at best is so so	281 Blues	2	77
Is it cast yet? The actors are fighting for parts	282 Blues	2	85
This makes your actors, artists, and romancers	993 Juan	16	825

ACTOR'S

So pride shall doubly nerve the actor's powers	170 Address-A		64

ACTS

Is all that desperate Valour acts in vain	12 Harold	1	555
Best prize of better acts, they bear away	15 Harold	1	736
In bloodier acts conclude those who with blood began	29 Harold	2	567
And he that acts as wise men ought	159 Spell		7
In five facetious acts comes thundering on	250 Bards		603
Or Marmion's acts of darkness, fitter food	254 Bards		939
Eke out your acts, I pray, with mortal man	260 Hints		292
His name could sadden and his acts surprise	342 Corsair	1	273
And half mistook for fate the acts of will	371 Lara	1	336
Despatches, judgments, acts, reprieves, reports	500 Faliero	1	9
Such things that acts and sees, unseen, though felt	520 Faliero	3	96
Whose acts have raised up such avengers; but	521 Faliero	3	192
From out the guilty? all their acts are one	524 Faliero	3	406
As senators for arbitrary acts	526 Faliero	3	505
And kind, and art not fit for such base acts	531 Faliero	4	245
Near sixteen lustres crowded with brave acts	543 Faliero	5	359
The worst acts of one energetic master	552 Sardan	1	119
Acts of this clay! 'Tis true I have not shed	557 Sardan	1	449
Be in the past acts you were pleased to praise	586 Sardan	4	499
A people's records, and a hero's acts	594 Sardan	5	443
Of the state's real acts as of the grave's	598 Foscari	1	185
Nor in thine eyes, nor in thine acts,--where then	603 Foscari	2	140
Dreaded to have its acts beheld by others	622 Foscari	5	131
And gentle preludes to strong acts--Go on	623 Foscari	5	167
With us acts are exempt from time, and we	635 Cain	1	532
You saved my life--and acts like these beget	693 Werner	2	677
In all his acts--but chiefly by his marriage	694 Werner	2	726
And thinks chaotically, as it acts	735 Deformed	1	886
To plays in five, and operas in three acts	771 Juan	1	1620
Like Titus' youth, and Caesar's earliest acts	814 Juan	3	827
Let radicals its other acts attack	946 Juan	13	343
But mostly sings of human things and acts	957 Juan	14	100

ACTUAL

Imprisonment and actual torture? Double	617 Foscari	4	156
(Save for the actual loss) is lucky also	687 Werner	2	289
It is an actual fact, that he, commander	873 Juan	7	409
By way of lesson against actual Turks	873 Juan	7	420
What were the actual and official duties	903 Juan	9	402

ACTUALLY

Whereas this story's actually true	771 Juan	1	1616

ACUTE

The very tendon which is most acute	889 Juan	8	667

ACUTEST

That she had puzzled all the acutest hinters	962 Juan	14	443

ADA

Ada, sole daughter of my house and heart	35 Harold	3	2

ADAH

Wilt thou frown even on me? No, Adah! no	628 Cain	1	56
Than the birds' matins; and my Adah, my	630 Cain	1	184
And sighs a prayer; and Adah looks on me	631 Cain	1	252
The offering is more his than mine--and Adah	632 Cain	1	326
And leave us? Ay. And me? Beloved Adah	632 Cain	1	344
Thou errest, Adah!--was not the tree that	633 Cain	1	349
What dreads my Adah? This is no ill spirit	633 Cain	1	411
For thee, my Adah, I choose not--it was	634 Cain	1	429
My sister Adah.--All the stars of heaven	643 Cain	2	460
Not like fair Adah and the seraphim	644 Cain	2	535
My sister Adah, leave us for awhile	648 Cain	3	172
Adah!--come hither! Death is in the world	651 Cain	3	370

ADAH'S

Like Adah's face: I turn from earth and heaven	643 Cain	2	473

ADAM

From Adam till now, has with wretchedness strove	93 First Kiss		22

ADAM

Ah! must the sons of Adam lose it twice	459 Dante	2	49
They did inhabit. Adam is the first	640 Cain	2	269
Adam, could e'er have been in Eden, as	640 Cain	2	275
Superior to your own? Had Adam not	641 Cain	2	361
Behold, my son! said Adam, how from evil	643 Cain	2	503
Even Adam and my mother both are fair	644 Cain	2	534
Where thou shalt multiply the race of Adam	645 Cain	2	620
A son of Adam! What doth the earth-born here	663 Heaven		588
Ere Eve gave Adam knowledge for her dower	670 Heaven		1133
Or Adam his first hymn of slavery sung	670 Heaven		1134
This Paradise?--(As Adam did between	694 Werner	2	722
From the red earth, like Adam	728 Deformed	1	384
He stood like Adam lingering near his garden	769 Juan	1	1437
And huge tombs worse--mankind, since Adam fell	839 Juan	5	470
That one would think the first who bore it 'Adam	870 Juan	7	200
Since Adam, with a fall or with an apple	907 Juan	10	8
That Adam, call'd 'The happiest of men	962 Juan	14	440
Adam exchanged his Paradise for ploughing	965 Juan	14	617

ADAMANT

Is more secure than walls of adamant, when	460 Dante	2	129
Doubt not our soldiers. Were the walls of ada-mant	732 Deformed	1	747
Or adamant, to find the world a spirit	918 Juan	11	7

ADAMANTINE

Man and his hopes an adamantine wall	69 Harold	4	870

ADAMITE

A war unworthy: to an Adamite	656 Heaven		69
To hear an Adamite speak riddles to me	663 Heaven		622

ADAMITES

(See also PRE-ADAMITES)

Heaven first each day before the Adamites	662 Heaven		560

ADAMS

John Adams lies here, of the parish of Southwell	224 Adams		1
Was made by Mrs. Adams, where she cries	953 Juan	13	767

ADAM'S

All the costumes since Adam's, right or wrong	293 Vision		526
In Adam's, and in Abel's, and in mine	640 Cain	2	254
With Cain's, the eldest born of Adam's, blood	664 Heaven		655
Seth, the last offspring of old Adam's dotage	664 Heaven		658
Must lift their eyes to Adam's God in vain	667 Heaven		885
To one of Adam's race	667 Heaven		929
And bear what Adam's race must bear, and can	668 Heaven		961
Renew not Adam's fall	668 Heaven		972
Heroes and chiefs, the flower of Adam's bastards	735 Deformed	1	883
Like Adam's recollection of his fall	762 Juan	1	1011
Souls to save, since Eve's slip and Adam's fall	898 Juan	9	147
Who would suppose, from Adam's simple ration	976 Juan	15	549

ADAPT

Adapt your language to your hero's state	258 Hints		128

ADAPTED

(Though in a garb adapted to its present	677 Werner	1	388
But not at all adapted to my rhymes	747 Juan	1	24
Of monitors adapted to recall	809 Juan	3	515
Look'd more adapted to be put to bed	857 Juan	6	326

ADD

Founders of sects and systems, to whom add	41 Harold	3	381
Would add to the souls of our tyrants delight	92 Caroline-D		14
Would I could add Remembrance too	128 Remembrance		7
To add one star to royal state	138 Clare		74
Ev'n now thou'rt nightly seen to add	153 Friend-A		57
But could not add a night to woe	172 Time-B		24
And, England! add their stubborn strength to thine	182 Address-C		10
To mourn the vanish'd beam and add our mite	194 Monody		99
Add Conscience, too, this bargain is your own	227 Answer-C		6
If to thy bells thou wouldst but add a cap	246 Bards		340
If you can add a little, say why not	257 Hints		83
That I may add you to my other saints	297 Vision		792
Will add to theirs a name of fear	311 Giaour		119
That seem to add but guilt to woe	321 Giaour		1154
They come--'tis but to add to slaughter	335 Abydos	2	555
Nor add a sacrifice which were in vain	433 Island	4	250
Adores thee still;--and add, that when the towers	439 Tasso		236
Fly, and one current to the ocean add	455 Venice-B		158
To add to the vain-glorious list of those	456 Dante	1	53
And, let me add, disparity of tempers	510 Faliero	2	87
And add too, that his mind is liberal	518 Faliero	2	687
That thou wouldst add a brother to our cause	521 Faliero	3	207
Many to your poor client, Bertram; add	530 Faliero	4	133
And all which circumstance can add to aid them	538 Faliero	5	28
Add the corporeal rack, you may: these limbs	542 Faliero	5	303
Not to add to each other's natural burthen	556 Sardan	1	398
Must dare to add my feeble voice to that	560 Sardan	1	640

ADD

To add it to the memory of others	586 Sardan	4	510
In deeds, and days, and sway, and, let me add	607 Foscari	2	402
And blighted like to mine, which I will add	608 Foscari	3	26
Those tears, or add my own. I could weep now	614 Foscari	3	420
But add, that if another hour would better	620 Foscari	5	2
Cold to your years and services, they add	621 Foscari	5	29
In fact but add to), shall endure and do	642 Cain	2	432
Thou shalt not:--add not impious works to impious	650 Cain	3	294
Add thy deep curse to Eve's upon his head	653 Cain	3	448
To add thy silence to the silent night	657 Heaven		161
You (as I still am rather faint) would add	686 Werner	2	242
I said I was so--and would add, with truth	695 Werner	3	16
Add further, that I have sent this slight addi-tion	706 Werner	4	111
Which is so call'd or thought, that you may add me	723 Deformed	1	85
Shall be plain Arnold still. We'll add a title	730 Deformed	1	543
To add a story to the Tower of Babel	745 Juan	Ded	32
They only add them all in an appendix	752 Juan	1	351
Besides, I've no more on this head to add	826 Juan	4	589
And stripp'd and look'd to--But why should I add	835 Juan	5	269
Thus much however I may add,--her years	843 Juan	5	777
And scorn to add a syllable untrue	861 Juan	6	555
A path, to add his own slight arm and forces	882 Juan	8	239
And when you add to this, her womanhood	905 Juan	9	561
Add what may be call'd marriage in disguise	906 Juan	9	608
You'll add to Matrimony's list of cures	937 Juan	12	480
But I shall add them in a brief appendix	964 Juan	14	543
Was apt to add a colouring from her own	970 Juan	15	130
'But add the words,' cried Henry, 'which you made	985 Juan	16	305

ADDED

His country's ruin added to the mass	62 Harold	4	407
Till the sun's rays with added flame were fill'd	71 Harold	4	980
The lute I added sweet in sound	168 The Chain		2
With the Editor added to make up the three	179 Devil's Dr		245
With added ornaments around them roll'd	275 Waltz		97
His name was added to the glorious roll	415 Island	1	21
Were added after, to the earnest prayer	417 Island	1	93
But merely added to the oath his eyes	428 Island	3	136
They parted with this added aid; afar	430 Island	4	41
Crawl'd on, and added but another link	516 Faliero	2	561
Before Bertuccio added to our cause	524 Faliero	3	392
I made no wars, I added no new imposts	556 Sardan	1	404
That I have added to her diadem	601 Foscari	2	19
In which (he added with a gracious smile	619 Foscari	4	296
Our own, but added others to her sway	619 Foscari	4	311
Aid which he added to your abler succour	693 Werner	2	649
Added to those his lady with such vigour	766 Juan	1	1286
To these was added Juan, who, before	783 Juan	2	619
Added to his connection with the sea	790 Juan	2	996
With one or two small senses added, just	801 Juan	2	1695
Especially when added to the power	828 Juan	4	752
And then he added, that he needs must say	840 Juan	5	550
She added to Juanna, their new guest	858 Juan	6	364
(She added in a soft and piteous tone	862 Juan	6	654
The imperial bride--and added, 'Let the boat	866 Juan	6	898
But when I've added that the elder Jack Smith	869 Juan	7	154
And added greatly to the missing list	870 Juan	7	216
To this we have added since, the love of money	953 Juan	13	795
They added graceful necks, white hands and arms	954 Juan	13	856
But ere he went, he added a slight hint	964 Juan	14	545
With all the added charm of form and feature	974 Juan	15	412
Added her sweet voice to the lyric sound	985 Juan	16	318
He added modestly, when rebels rail'd	990 Juan	16	622

ADDER

My voice; but as the adder, deaf and fierce	456 Dante	1	65
As he who treads on flowers is from the adder	569 Sardan	2	469
As the stripes that streak an adder	735 Deformed	2	26

ADDER-LIKE

Worm-like 'twas trampled, adder-like avenged	344 Corsair	1	399

ADDER'S

Of thine to me is as an adder's eye	206 Greece		6
Of life. The man who dies by the adder's fang	544 Faliero	5	463
To one whose foot was on an adder's path	613 Foscari	3	351

ADDING

Adding every trait that's hideous	197 Rogers		56
With adding ranks and raging boast	394 Corinth		923
From adding to the vulture's feast	414 Mazeppa		816
His friend, too, adding a new saving clause	837 Juan	5	374
Adding, that this was commonest and best	844 Juan	5	838
That, adding to the account his Highness' years	853 Juan	6	68
And adding still a little through each cross	930 Juan	12	28

ADDIO'S

The 'Lasciami's,' and quavering 'Addio's	986 Juan	16	405

ADDISON'S

Like Addison's 'faint praise,' so wont to damn	994 Juan	16	876

ADDITION
'Tis for some small addition to the temple 559 Sardan 1 593
Where it was strongest the required addition 591 Sardan 5 243
Add further, that I have sent this slight addition 706 Werner 4 111
And this addition with such gems was bound 841 Juan 5 630
That with the addition of a slight pelisse 911 Juan 10 239

ADDITIONAL
And help them with a lie or two additional 751 Juan 1 242

ADDITIONS
Not finding that the additions much encumber 802 Juan 3 24

ADDLES
But to hear a vile jargon which addles my brains 280 Blues 2 21

ADDRESS
It came to pass that when he did address 29 Harold 2 613
Who joyful in the fond address 141 Critics 15
To Him address thy trembling prayer 146 Adieu 107
An address, and present it themselves all in
  brass 237 Braziers 2
Away! address thy prayers to Heaven 398 Parisina 209
You must address the council. 'Twere in vain 505 Faliero 1 361
But wherefore not address you to the Council 516 Faliero 2 544
Address our own above!--Lead on, we are ready 539 Faliero 5 125
Then, as a prince, address thee to thy doom 543 Faliero 5 392
Let us address us then, since so it must be 611 Foscari 3 247
In your address, nor yet too arrogant 698 Werner 3 213
That morning--either in address or force 718 Werner 5 350
Himself a favourite, ventured to address 875 Juan 7 514
That calm patrician polish in the address 945 Juan 13 266
By nature soft, his whole address held off 970 Juan 15 105

ADDRESS'D
His glowing friend address'd the Dardan boy 106 Nisus 38
The elder first address'd the hoary band 106 Nisus 98
Then he address'd himself to Satan: 'Why 292 Vision 489
The playful girl's appeal address'd 326 Abydos 1 274
For ever thus, address'd with awe. I ne'er 558 Sardan 1 485
Address'd to Milan's duke, in the full knowledge 600 Foscari 1 296
And many thoughts; but afterwards address'd 610 Foscari 3 163
The vinous Greek to whom he had address'd 806 Juan 3 334
They thus address'd--and Lambro's visage fell 807 Juan 3 346
To Juan, who was nearest him, address'd 885 Juan 8 445
'Tis not addressed to you--the more's the pity 909 Juan 10 130
Then Henry turn'd to Juan, and address'd 985 Juan 16 273

ADDRESSES
But these are my addresses from the throne 814 Juan 3 861

ADDRESSING
Addressing him in tones which seem'd to thank 885 Juan 8 455
For Adeline, addressing few words to him 977 Juan 15 599

ADDS
Adds fragrance and fruit to the tree 162 Romaic-A 10
Adds an ell growth to his egregious ears 266 Hints 736
Which adds all other agony to thirst 351 Corsair 2 319
And merely adds another throb to pain 381 Lara 2 425
Repletion rather adds to what he feels 835 Juan 5 244
It adds an outward grace unto their carriage 937 Juan 12 494

ADDUCE
He will adduce such reasons as will warrant 560 Sardan 1 618

ADELINE
The Lady Adeline Amundeville 941 Juan 13 9
The Lady Adeline Amundeville 942 Juan 13 90
Sweet Adeline, amidst the gay world's hum 942 Juan 13 100
But Adeline had not the least occasion 945 Juan 13 241
There also was of course in Adeline 945 Juan 13 265
But Adeline was not indifferent: for 945 Juan 13 281
Lord Henry and the Lady Adeline 947 Juan 13 393
My Dian of the Ephesians, Lady Adeline 961 Juan 14 363
But Adeline was far from that ripe age 962 Juan 14 425
The Lady Adeline, as soon's she saw 963 Juan 14 475
The Lady Adeline resolved to take 963 Juan 14 481
Our gentle Adeline had one defect 966 Juan 14 673
My business is with Lady Adeline 966 Juan 14 719
To thus much Adeline would not advance 967 Juan 14 734
Whether Don Juan and chaste Adeline 967 Juan 14 769
It is not clear that Adeline and Juan 968 Juan 14 791
The Lady Adeline Amundeville 968 Juan 15 34
The Lady Adeline, right honourable 969 Juan 15 41
But Adeline was of the purest vintage 969 Juan 15 49
Fair Adeline, the more ingenuous 969 Juan 15 73
Adeline, no deep judge of character 970 Juan 15 129
When Adeline, in all her growing sense 971 Juan 15 217
Had Adeline read Malthus? I can't tell 972 Juan 15 297
But Adeline, who probably presumed 973 Juan 15 305
But Adeline determined Juan's wedding 973 Juan 15 313
Of Adeline, Aurora was omitted 974 Juan 15 378
When Adeline replied with some disgust 974 Juan 15 389

ADELINE
If--' But here Adeline, who seem'd to pique 974 Juan 15 397
Why Adeline had this slight prejudice 974 Juan 15 409
Since Adeline was liberal by nature 974 Juan 15 414
It was not envy--Adeline had none 974 Juan 15 425
The dashing and proud air of Adeline 975 Juan 15 441
Adeline and Don Juan rather blended 975 Juan 15 483
Aurora and the Lady Adeline 977 Juan 15 594
For Adeline, addressing few words to him 977 Juan 15 599
With her was rare: and Adeline, who as yet 978 Juan 15 642
Than Adeline (such is advice) advised 982 Juan 16 92
That something was the matter--Adeline 984 Juan 16 239
Fair Adeline enquired, 'If he were ill 984 Juan 16 251
'The last time was--' --'I pray,' said Adeline 985 Juan 16 289
'Jest!' quoth Milor; 'why, Adeline, you know 985 Juan 16 297
For Adeline is half a poetess 985 Juan 16 306
Fair Adeline, with eyes fix'd on the ground 985 Juan 16 316
Fair Adeline, though in a careless way 986 Juan 16 377
Thus Adeline would throw into the shade 986 Juan 16 393
Was Adeline well versed, as compositions 986 Juan 16 416
Of Adeline, in bringing this same lay 987 Juan 16 450
But Adeline was occupied by fame 993 Juan 16 801
On Adeline while playing her grand role 993 Juan 16 811
Some doubt how much of Adeline was real 993 Juan 16 816
While Adeline dispensed her airs and graces 993 Juan 16 841
But with the Lady Adeline the most 994 Juan 16 856
Meanwhile sweet Adeline deserved their praises 994 Juan 16 865

ADELINE'S
The Lady Adeline's serene severity 961 Juan 14 401
Heaven knows! But Adeline's malicious eyes 978 Juan 15 623

ADEN
Blooming as Aden in its earliest hour 333 Abydos 2 409

ADEPT
In lies an adept, in deceit a fiend 100 Damaetas 4
An adept next in penmanship she grows 208 Sketch 15
The adept who pursues it. All the sins 606 Foscari 2 338
Her maid Antonia, who was an adept 764 Juan 1 1116

ADHERE
Whose hue and fragrance to thy work adhere 249 Bards 534

ADHERES
Parch'd to the throat my tongue adheres 87 Ad Lesbiam 14

ADIEU
If friends he had, he bade adieu to none 5 Harold 1 86
'Adieu, adieu! my native shore 5 Harold 1 118
Tread on each other's kibes. A long adieu 14 Harold 1 679
Adieu, fair Cadiz! yea, a long adieu 18 Harold 1 873
And bade to Christian tongues a long adieu 26 Harold 2 380
Adieu to thee, fair Rhine! How long delighted 44 Harold 3 563
Adieu to thee again! a vain adieu 44 Harold 3 572
From the seat of his ancestors, bids you adieu 86 Leaving NA 22
Adieu, ye chiefs renown'd in arms 88 Anacreon-A 19
Adieu the clang of war's alarms 88 Anacreon-A 20
You bid a long adieu to peace 89 To Emma 36
Oh, God! the fondest, last adieu 89 To Emma 40
Again, thou best beloved, adieu 90 Caroline-A 21
Without a sigh which bids adieu 91 Caroline-B 26
Invoke them no more, bid adieu to the muse 92 First Kiss 11
To these again! nor let me linger o'er 94 Dorset 87
Or prunes them for ever, in love's last adieu 99 L Adieu 4
Or death disunite us in love's last adieu 99 L Adieu 8
Nor taste we the poison of love's last adieu 99 L Adieu 12
Till chill'd by the winter of love's last adieu 99 L Adieu 16
Thy reason has perish'd with love's last adieu 99 L Adieu 20
The mountains reverberate love's last adieu 99 L Adieu 24
He ponders in frenzy on love's last adieu 100 L Adieu 28
And dreads not the anguish of love's last adieu 100 L Adieu 32
The shroud of affection is love's last adieu 100 L Adieu 36
The atonement is ample in love's last adieu 100 L Adieu 40
His cypress, the garland of love's last adieu 100 L Adieu 44
Marion, adieu! oh, pr'ythee slight not 100 Marion 39
Adieu, fond race! a long adieu 118 Romance 57
To which I long have bade a last adieu 122 Recoll 32
Our first kind greetings, and our last adieu 124 Recoll 187
Or weeping Virtue sigh'd a faint adieu 127 Recoll 408
Love, Hope, and Joy, alike adieu 128 Remembrance 6
Adieu, then, ye hills where my childhood was bred 136 Highlander 45
Thou sweet flowing Dee, to thy waters adieu 136 Highlander 46
And sigh again, adieu 137 Clare 12
Adieu, thou Hill! where early joy 145 Adieu 1
Adieu, my youthful friends or foes 145 Adieu 5
Adieu, ye hoary Regal Fanes 145 Adieu 11
Adieu! while memory still is mine 145 Adieu 18
Adieu, ye mountains of the clime 145 Adieu 21
Yet why to thee adieu 145 Adieu 32
Adieu! you are not now forgot 145 Adieu 43
Your lover should bid you a lasting adieu 147 To Anne-B 14
The present--which seals our eternal Adieu 149 Farewell-A 40
And when we bid adieu to youth 153 Friend-A 25

ADIEU

Mary, adieu! I must away	155	Happy		17
And bless thee in my last adieu	156	Lady-F		62
Adieu, ye joys of La Valette	163	Malta		1
Adieu, sirocco, sun, and sweat	163	Malta		2
Adieu, thou palace rarely enter'd	163	Malta		3
Adieu, ye mansions where--I've ventured	163	Malta		4
Adieu, ye cursed streets of stairs	163	Malta		5
Adieu, ye merchants often failing	163	Malta		7
Adieu, thou mob for ever railing	163	Malta		8
Adieu, ye packets--without letters	163	Malta		9
Adieu, ye fools--who ape your betters	163	Malta		10
Adieu, thou damned'st quarantine	163	Malta		11
Adieu that stage which makes us yawn, sirs	163	Malta		13
Adieu his Excellency's dancers	163	Malta		14
Adieu to Peter--whom no fault's in	163	Malta		15
Adieu, ye females fraught with graces	163	Malta		17
Adieu, red coats, and redder faces	163	Malta		18
Adieu, the supercilious air	163	Malta		19
Farewell to these, but not adieu	163	Malta		25
'Tis past--to them and thee adieu	169	Chain		19
Sigh'd his last thanks, and wept his last adieu	170	Address-A		35
Adieu, fair thing! without upbraiding	173	Quotation		25
Adieu, dear maid! I must not speak	179	Gold		33
Maddening o'er that long adieu	186	French-A		4
My chief, my king, my friend, adieu	187	French-A		33
Retired, but not as bidding her adieu	215	Dream		100
Yet once again, adieu! ere this the sail	255	Bards		1017
One kiss--one more--another--Oh! Adieu	345	Corsair	1	465
That mute adieu to those who stem the surge	345	Corsair	1	528
Rage in his eye and threats in his adieu	358	Corsair	3	195
Farewell to life, but not adieu to thee	380	Lara		359
His sole adieu to those around	401	Parisina		476
Adieu, my worthy nephew.--Hollow bauble	504	Faliero	1	288
Adieu, my Angiolina. Let me be	515	Faliero	2	497
And that? Is yours. Hark! Now! Adieu, Assyria	595	Sardan	5	492
As you; but I curse not. Adieu, good signors	624	Foscari	5	223
Adieu. Yet hold--we had better keep together	706	Werner	4	134
Here is the garden-key--Fly--fly--Adieu	769	Juan	1	1454
And I must even survive this last adieu	771	Juan	1	1575

ADIEUS

| From this alone no fond adieus I seek | 107 | Nisus | | 185 |

ADJACENT

| I met in the adjacent hall, who, with | 677 | Werner | 1 | 385 |

ADJOINING

| Before Baal's shrine, in the adjoining hall | 594 | Sardan | 5 | 421 |
| And once or twice I heard him, from the adjoining | 620 | Foscari | 4 | 347 |

ADJOURN'D

| With which the court adjourn'd; and till it meets | 602 | Foscari | 2 | 64 |

ADJUNCTS

| Vain adjuncts, lavish'd its true bloom, and health | 528 | Faliero | 4 | 44 |

ADJURATION

| To thine adjuration bow'd | 479 | Manfred | 1 | 58 |

ADJURE

| I do adjure thee, pass not o'er thy threshold | 532 | Faliero | 4 | 312 |

ADMINISTER'D

| To judge my son? I have administer'd | 607 | Foscari | 2 | 369 |

ADMIRABLE

| It is. Oh, admirable laws of Venice | 542 | Faliero | 5 | 312 |
| And this was admirable; for so hot | 880 | Juan | 8 | 121 |

ADMIRAL

As doth the pilot of an admiral galley	534	Faliero	4	429
The admiral, his brother, say as much	605	Foscari	2	208
And Admiral Ribas (known in Russian story	871	Juan	7	275

ADMIRARI

| Great happiness of the 'Nil Admirari | 844 | Juan | 5 | 800 |
| Perhaps from Horace: his 'Nil admirari | 945 | Juan | 13 | 273 |

ADMIRATION

To those whose admiration shall succeed	3	To Ianthe		26
Save Admiration glancing harmless by	24	Harold	2	273
Their admiration thy best weapon shone	41	Harold	3	365
Howe'er we gaze with admiration	101	Marion		45
Then do not admiration smother	143	On Eyes		5
I saw you--my anger became admiration	147	To Anne-A		11
Could bid me from fond admiration refrain	147	To Anne-B		6
Of coxcombry in admiration loud	423	Island	2	337
A king's esteem--the whole world's admiration	578	Sardan	3	429
Than admiration due where nature's rich	801	Juan	2	1683
The people's awe and admiration raising	839	Juan	5	478
And mien excited general admiration	923	Juan	11	306
Secure of admiration, its impression	945	Juan	13	247

ADMIRATION

| But on the whole, to general admiration | 959 | Juan | 14 | 265 |

ADMIRATIONS

| The admirations and the speculations | 986 | Juan | 16 | 402 |

ADMIRE

Which all admire but many dread to view	26	Harold	2	382
Admire, exult--despise--laugh, weep,--for here	71	Harold	4	973
We must admire, but still despair	97	To M--		7
Some will love, and all admire	100	Marion		12
Ages on ages shall your fate admire	110	Nisus		403
Some other admire, who will melt with your fire	115	Pigot		19
The world admire thee, and thy friends adore	126	Recoll		323
Mine eyes admire, my heart adores thee still	138	Harrow-B		8
Where none but girls and striplings dare admire	142	Soliloquy		13
Whom but to see is to admire	158	Florence		19
What I loved I now merely admire	205	Blessington		11
A fund for contemplation;--to admire	211	Augusta-C		58
Genius must guide when wits admire the rhyme	252	Bards		773
What few admire--irregularity	262	Hints		414
Admire their patience through each sacrifice	307	Age		653
Admire their justice, which would fain deny	307	Age		656
Thy listless eyes so much admire	324	Abydos	1	91
In Conrad's form seems little to admire	341	Corsair	1	195
But they who pitied not could yet admire	416	Island	1	76
Yet thy true lovers more admire by far	425	Island	2	458
Because the Turks so much admire philogyny	448	Beppo		555
Admire and sigh, and then succumb and bleed	453	Venice-B		79
'Not to admire is all the art I know	844	Juan	5	801
Whose drapery hints we may admire them freely	949	Juan	13	544

ADMIRED

Ye who beheld (oh! sight admired and mourn'd	169	Address-A		5
What most admired each scrutinizing eye	183	Address-D		5
Of two fair virgins, modest, though admired	195	Vittorelli		1
No city Wordsworth, more admired than read	231	Sotheby		3
While these in turn admired the paler glow	422	Island	2	246
I might be fear'd, admired, respected, loved	727	Deformed	1	359
The same things cannot always be admired	802	Juan	3	52
The rosy flood of twilight's sky admired	815	Juan	3	902
From his translation; but had none admired	844	Juan	5	807
They all alike admired their new connection	857	Juan	6	320
Juan admired these highways of free millions	917	Juan	10	612
I don't know which was more admired or less	923	Juan	11	307
Daughters admired his dress, and pious mothers	924	Juan	11	383
Of charms that should or should not be admired	954	Juan	13	862
A full-grown Cupid, very much admired	960	Juan	14	322
Admired, adored; but also so correct	962	Juan	14	442
The supper too discuss'd, the dames admired	981	Juan	16	58

ADMIRERS

| Admirers still,--but men are so debased | 448 | Beppo | | 535 |

ADMIRES

My muse admires digression	138	Clare		72
Admires the strain she cannot comprehend	244	Bards		152
Whose plaintive strain each love-sick miss admires	246	Bards		299
Admires the plunder but abhors the thief	271	Minerva		198
Or Regent, who admires such kind of food	745	Juan	Ded	12
(None trusts the sex more, or so much admires	804	Juan	3	173
And then of course the circle much admires	986	Juan	16	373

ADMIRING

With eyes admiring, oh, believe me	87	Rousseau		11
Whilst I, admiring, too remiss	89	To Emma		21
And when the admiring circle mark	159	Storm		61
Lamented by admiring foes	184	Parker		18
Admiring Nature's universal throne	424	Island	2	383
Baba and Juan, which last stood admiring	844	Juan	5	795
Admiring this new native of the deep	859	Juan	6	480
Admiring those (by dainty dames abhorr'd	903	Juan	9	427
Admiring more Minerva than the Graces	978	Juan	15	675

ADMISSION

And sentence from the court! This full admission	542	Faliero	5	298
Requests admission to the Giunta's presence	542	Faliero	5	307
He hath not been accustom'd to admission	679	Werner	1	526

ADMIT

Admit not Love into thy breast	179	Gold		11
To woman's step admit her vow	327	Abydos	1	314
Admit him, he may be on public service	504	Faliero	1	325
Admit him, and retire; but call up quickly	530	Faliero	4	125
You do confess then, and admit the justice	541	Faliero	5	266
Which would admit the wife, in the full hope	542	Faliero	5	313
He!--but admit him. Must I then retire	604	Foscari	2	189
Of your apparent prudence should admit	677	Werner	1	411
Admit him, ne'ertheless. Ah! 'Tis, then, Werner	715	Werner	5	149
Admit, reject, contemn; and what know you	955	Juan	14	18

ADMITS

But yet this last my candid Muse admits — 142 Soliloquy 15
If he, that vain old man, whom truth admits — 183 Address-D 17
My humble tenement admits — 231 Doctor 56
Which nothing through its bars admits, save day — 437 Tasso 13
And therefore safer, and as such admits — 524 Faliero 3 394
Who is no paviour, nor admits a barge — 900 Juan 9 246

ADMITTED

Implores to be admitted. Is he a stranger — 529 Faliero 4 114
And Philip Calendaro, have admitted — 540 Faliero 5 175
Say, conscript fathers, shall she be admitted — 542 Faliero 5 308
Will not be admitted o'er the threshold. And — 599 Foscari 1 278
That your illustrious lady be admitted — 608 Foscari 3 35
You may be admitted. And what shall I say — 608 Foscari 2 434
Be thus admitted, though as novices — 616 Foscari 4 87
Admitted to our lands? Assuredly — 699 Werner 3 251
Admitted a small party as night fell — 922 Juan 11 229
Admitted as an aspirant to all — 925 Juan 11 426
Yet, if examined, it might be admitted — 997 Juan 17 23

ADMONISH

Time to admonish them again. Forbear — 615 Foscari 4 16

ADMONISHED

Would not be thus admonished — 404 Chillon 208

ADMONITION

Without a word of previous admonition — 764 Juan 1 1109

ADOPT

No longer repine, adopt this design — 116 Pigot 25
By these fell tyrants to adopt is such — 520 Faliero 3 115
They gave me to adopt all fitting means — 522 Faliero 3 237
With violence: if that thou wilt adopt it — 650 Cain 3 306

ADOPTED

A mode adopted since by modern youth — 980 Juan 16 4

ADOPTION

Besides, adoption as a son — 331 Abydos 2 264

ADORATION

This sort of adoration of the real — 801 Juan 2 1687

ADORE

That I in feeblest accents must adore — 14 Harold 1 624
How sweet it were in concert to adore — 20 Harold 2 68
Since now he vainly urged him to adore — 24 Harold 2 278
Which sages venerate and bards adore — 34 Harold 2 862
Where the bow'd waters meet him, and adore — 51 Harold 3 945
Their children's children would in vain adore — 63 Harold 4 509
His sovereign virtues--still we Trajan's name
adore — 71 Harold 4 999
Of wonder pleased, or awe which would adore — 79 Harold 4 1425
All I forget, but to adore thee — 97 To Woman 6
For me, I adore some twenty or more — 115 Pigot 21
The world admire thee, and thy friends adore — 126 Recoll 323
For then it beat but to adore thee — 134 Lady-D 36
Long to adore such brittle toys — 143 To--A 14
Be false, my sweet Anne, when I cease to adore
you — 147 To Anne-A 16
Which utters its song to adore thee — 162 Romaic-A 7
That led them to adore — 180 Ode-A 25
To listen and adore thee — 188 Music-C 14
The north and nature taught me to adore — 423 Island 2 296
Enter'd, he said that he was taught to adore — 468 Morgante 165
Christ I adore, who is the genuine Lord — 471 Morgante 335
Him, whom I now require you to adore — 472 Morgante 398
Its beauty. And why not adore? Our father — 635 Cain 1 495
Shall they adore — 661 Heaven 430
Adore and burn — 665 Heaven 779
Would he adore a sultan? he obey — 746 Juan Ded 87
A lovely statue we almost adore — 801 Juan 2 1686

ADORED

Oh thou that wert so happy, so adored — 80 Harold 4 1514
Oh! when, my adored, in the tomb will they place
me — 92 Caroline-D 21
How shall thy glorious name adored — 133 Prayer 55
Yes; my adored, yet most unkind — 152 Time-A 17
Forgive me, adored one!--forsake, if thou wilt — 182 Music-A 10
Doubly shall she be adored — 188 Ode-B 76
Thou radiant and adored deceit — 188 On Star 3
Votary and Shrine, the adoring and the adored — 201 Ode-C 76
And all that Hope adored and lost — 223 Music-D 7
'I loved her, Friar! nay, adored — 320 Giaour 1029
Adored the Alp, and loved the Apennine — 422 Island 2 285
Neuha--the fond, the faithful, the adored — 429 Island 3 187
How Salem's shrine was won, and how adored — 437 Tasso 32
And, if you please, by you may be adored — 471 Morgante 336
Thence then it beat but, the abbot God adored — 473 Morgante 447
Of the poor child of clay which so adored him — 655 Heaven 23
How would I have adored thee, but thou wouldst
not — 658 Heaven 237

ADORED

And we, who ne'er for ages have adored — 661 Heaven 431
Let us resign even what we have adored — 667 Heaven 890
Be the decree adored — 670 Heaven 1152
My Ulric! my adored! I have been full oft — 672 Werner 1 61
She loved, and was beloved--she adored — 798 Juan 2 1521
Of sentiment; and he she most adored — 903 Juan 9 429
That worse than worst of foes, the once adored — 915 Juan 10 534
Much I respect, and much I have adored — 958 Juan 14 209
Admired, adored; but also so correct — 962 Juan 14 442

ADORER

(See also BAAL-ADORER)

Thyself by thine adorer, what befell — 72 Harold 4 1059
Sate Laura by the side of her Adorer — 451 Beppo 695

ADORERS

Thy saint adorers count the rosary — 15 Harold 1 714

ADORES

And doth the Power that man adores ordain — 12 Harold 1 553
Mine eyes admire, my heart adores thee still — 138 Harrow-B 8
The heart which adores you should wish to dis-
sever — 147 To Anne-B 2
Adores thee still;--and add, that when the towers — 439 Tasso 236
Adores the Invisible only. But the symbols — 635 Cain 1 496
As he adores the Highest, death becomes — 655 Heaven 24
She's young--all beautiful--adores you--is — 710 Werner 4 371
In Catherine's reign, whom glory still adores — 863 Juan 6 735

ADORING

Too much adoring; whatsoe'er thy birth — 72 Harold 4 1034
Yet, still, this fond bosom regrets, while adoring — 91 Caroline-C 5
Votary and Shrine, the adoring and the adored — 201 Ode-C 76
Adoring him in his least works display'd — 666 Heaven 791

ADORN

And sundry signatures adorn the roll — 8 Harold 1 295
What smiles the lovers' cheeks adorn — 103 Alva 172
Soon will the day those eastern clouds adorn — 109 Nisus 283
Dull as the pictures which adorn their halls — 112 Examination 53
Still, to adorn his humble youth — 113 Cornelian-A 17
But bless the scroll which fairer words adorn — 127 Recoll 409
Not though a thousand more adorn — 128 Lady-C 21
No more yon azure vault with rays adorn — 139 Ossian-A 27
To raise the subject, or adorn the scene — 259 Hints 208
Must not adorn him to the grave — 401 Parisina 439
Round the Patrician left-legs, which adorn — 830 Juan 4 879

ADORN'D

(See also GEM-ADORN'D)

Above, strange groups adorn'd the corridor — 28 Harold 2 508
No lovelier mien adorn'd the ranks of Troy — 105 Nisus 9
Whose radiance mock'd the ruin it adorn'd — 169 Address-A 6
With more than finny tenants, and adorn'd — 205 Aristom 7
Had Cottle still adorn'd the counter's side — 247 Bards 406
Whose gilded cymbals, more adorn'd than clear — 254 Bards 895
These Cecrops placed, this Pericles adorn'd — 269 Minerva 101
Which oft in sport adorn'd her hand before — 353 Corsair 2 412
Adorn'd the triumph of Eugene — 386 Corinth 142
Had fairer form adorn'd the shore — 386 Corinth 228
That which adorn'd the brain of Donna Inez — 748 Juan 1 88
The limb which it adorn'd its only mould — 810 Juan 3 564

ADORNER

Adorner of the ruin, comforter — 74 Harold 4 1163

ADORNING

Sad thought! to lose the spouse that was adorning — 802 Juan 3 55

ADORNMENT

In fit adornment for the evening banquet — 559 Sardan 1 602

ADORNMENTS

With these adornments, o'er each slumbering head — 360 Corsair 3 309

ADORNS

Save where Tritonia's airy shrine adorns — 33 Harold 2 812
In stars adorns the vault of heaven — 97 To M-- 22
Culture again adorns the gladdening vale — 121 Newstead-A 119
Fair Ida's bower adorns the landscape round — 123 Recoll 122

ADOWN

Fresh legions pour adown the Pyrenees — 18 Harold 1 910
Till day declines adown the West — 91 Caroline-B 30
Adown in agonizing dew — 104 Alva 236

ADRIAN

That Adrian rear'd when drooping Science mourn'd — 269 Minerva 102
Was Alp, the Adrian renegade — 385 Corinth 114
To see your anger, like our Adrian waves — 502 Faliero 1 175
Though low and far, as e'er the Adrian wave — 528 Faliero 4 13
Thine Adrian sea-breeze, how it fans my face — 597 Foscari 1 125

ADRIAN
To lash up from the deep the Adrian waves   617 Foscari   4 129
Rooted where once the Adrian wave flow'd o'er 815 Juan   3 932

ADRIA'S
That e'er on Adria's waters play'd   386 Corinth   192
The song and oar of Adria's gondolier   761 Juan   1 971

ADRIATIC
The spouseless Adriatic mourns her lord   56 Harold   4   91
To curb the Adriatic main   88 Horace   7
While either Adriatic shore   163 Malta   27
And when the Adriatic bore   386 Corinth   198
Her husband sail'd upon the Adriatic   443 Beppo   193
He left this Adriatic Ariadne   443 Beppo   224
Be broad upon the Adriatic, there   528 Faliero   3 647

ADRIATIC'S
The Adriatic's free to wed another   623 Foscari   5 192

ADRIFT
Has turn'd some thousand gallant hearts adrift 676 Werner 1 334

A-DRY
And fall, for lack of moisture, quite a-dry, Bob 745 Juan Ded 24

ADULATE
It is not that I adulate the people   899 Juan   9 193

ADULATION
(See also SELF-ADULATION)
Let Adulation wait on kings   132 L'Amitie   77
To the smooth agonies of adulation   633 Cain   1 383

ADULATIONS
He varied with some skill his adulations   812 Juan   3 670

ADULTERATE
And gore-faced Treason sprung from her adulterate
  joy   12 Harold   1 512

ADULTERATION
Not quite adultery, but adulteration   937 Juan   12 504
Till old, may undergo adulteration   969 Juan   15   48

ADULTERER'S
Than the adulterer's arrow through his heel 726 Deformed 1 308

ADULTERESS
From an adulteress boastful of her guilt   548 Faliero   5 766

ADULTEROUS
Or with adulterous whisper to alloy   423 Island   2 338
Vile assignations, and adulterous beds   442 Beppo   127

ADULTERY
What men call gallantry, and gods adultery   754 Juan   1 503
Not quite adultery, but adulteration   937 Juan   12 504

ADVANCE
Awake, ye sons of Spain! awake! advance   10 Harold   1 405
And lowly bending to the lists advance   15 Harold   1 732
For 'tis his nature to advance or die   51 Harold   3 964
Thou movest--but increasing with the advance 78 Harold   4 1396
But should I fall,--and he who dares advance 106 Nisus   59
When Edward bade his conquering bands advance 111 Examination 15
I will not advance, by the rules of romance   116 Strephon   21
Her book, they say, was in advance   231 Doctor   65
First in the ranks see Joan of Arc advance   244 Bards   205
On earth, yet ventured in my face to advance 287 Vision   147
Through Calpe's strait the rolling tides advance 302 Age   282
Such have been, such shall be, such are. Advance 303 Age   376
And, issuing from the grove, advance   316 Giaour   606
And the dusk Spahi's bands advance   385 Corinth   77
And onward we advance   412 Mazeppa   592
In one vast squadron they advance   413 Mazeppa   674
Shall foreign standard to thy walls advance 460 Dante   2   99
Vincenzo.--Sir, you may advance--what would you 505 Faliero 1 357
Let them advance and strike at their own bosoms 522 Faliero 3 218
But nothing will advance; no, not a moment   621 Foscari   5   60
Advance! And thou? Fear not--without me thou 639 Cain   2 204
I know not whither; you must not advance   696 Werner   3   91
Then his next neighbour. You must not advance 696 Werner 3 101
As hath been done, mere conquest to advance 378 Juan   8   22
But those who scaled, found out that their
  advance   884 Juan   8 361
Advance beyond, while they could pass for new 962 Juan   14 420
To thus much Adeline would not advance   967 Juan   14 734

ADVANCED
When Atreus' sons advanced to war   88 Anacreon-A   5
Advanced to claim his friend with honest joy 124 Recoll   195
Are you so far advanced as to hazard this? Why 279 Blues 1   95
So well advanced the ranks before   393 Corinth   833

ADVANCED
When there advanced the nations out of Spain 467 Morgante   106
Has been, and ever shall be, far advanced   733 Deformed 1 798
Than many persons more advanced in life   776 Juan   2 116
As day advanced the weather seem'd to abate 777 Juan   2 233
And he advanced, though with but a bad grace 844 Juan   5 841
Nor work advanced, nor cover'd way was there 868 Juan   7   87
Advanced in all their azure's highest hue   924 Juan   11 396
And he arose, advanced--the shade retreated 996 Juan   16 994

ADVANCEMENT
In all fair objects of advancement, which   530 Faliero   4 136
I became Doge, or dream'd of such advancement 605 Foscari 2 204

ADVANCES
As the chief who to combat advances   162 Romaic-A   25
Advances with exasperated rap   969 Juan   15   62

ADVANCING
As with advancing age your woes increase   161 Athos   23
Strew'd beneath the advancing banner   187 Ode-B   62
Still, still advancing   200 Stanzas-B   39
The shadows of the rocks advancing   312 Giaour   169
To meet the ocean, which, advancing still   670 Heaven   1173
And still more nearly to the place advancing 805 Juan   3 225
Advancing to the nearest dinner tray   806 Juan   3 329
'Twas nine, when still advancing undismay'd 870 Juan   7 227
By the advancing Muscovite--the groan   889 Juan   8 695

ADVANTAGE
(See also 'VANTAGE)
This scroll--Fear not; they are for your
  advantage   515 Faliero   2 446
And here the advantage is my own, I ween   771 Juan   1 1611
And may become of great advantage when   785 Juan   2 740
Had all the advantage, too, of not being air 792 Juan   2 1136
Losing the advantage of a virtuous station   799 Juan   2 1604
In years he had the advantage of time's sequel 943 Juan 13 155
These forty days' advantage of her years   962 Juan   14 409

ADVANTAGES
Of Prudence, with advantages annex'd   213 Lady Byron   55
All our advantages are those of fortune   606 Foscari   2 340
Hinted the vast advantages which they   840 Juan   5 546
These were advantages: and then he thought   943 Juan   13 161

ADVENT
Then receive him as best such an advent becomes 202 Avatar   19

ADVENTURE
Preys upon high adventure, nor can tire   41 Harold   3 376
And each adventure so sublimely tells   245 Bards   252
Adventure makes it needful. Certainly   700 Werner   3 371

ADVENTURED
Now he adventured on a shore unknown   26 Harold   2 381

ADVENTURERS
To be more pensive: we adventurers   734 Deformed 1 861

ADVENTURES
I shall proceed with his adventures is   771 Juan   1 1586
Intrigues, adventures of the common school   818 Juan   4 133
Seems fertile in adventures strange and new 842 Juan   5 662
Some rumour also of some strange adventures 922 Juan   11 257
But his adventures form a sorry sight   942 Juan   13   70

ADVENTUROUS
Or, in adventurous numbers, neatly aims   257 Hints   29
Pity he loved adventurous life's variety   806 Juan   3 327
At once adventurous and contemplative   830 Juan   4 850

ADVERSARY
Than would your adversary, who dared say so 709 Werner   4 327

ADVERSE
It chanced that adverse winds once drove his bark 29 Harold 2 595
If some Rutulian arm, with adverse blow   106 Nisus   61
Fortune an adverse wayward course may run   108 Nisus   203
Gifford was born beneath an adverse star   252 Bards   778
And Afric's coast and Calpe's adverse height 255 Bards   1019
They have cause, since Sapienza's adverse day 504 Faliero 1 328

ADVERSITY
Worse than adversity the Childe befell   4 Harold   1   33
If they be in adversity, they'll learn   582 Sardan   4 280
Of man's adversity all things grow daring   585 Sardan   4 469
And sharp Adversity, will teach at last   816 Juan   4   10
Adversity is the first path to truth   936 Juan   12 397

ADVERTISE
'Tis twenty guineas, as they advertise   171 Address-B   50
Who advertise new poems by your looks   830 Juan   4 859

ADVERTISED
I've advertised, but see my books   231 Doctor   29

ADVERTISEMENT
Than an advertisement, or much the same   947 Juan   13   404

ADVICE
Advice at least's disinterested   100 Marion   32
Without thy dear advice, no great design   107 Nisus   168
Whate'er the scene, let this advice have weight   258 Hints   127
Despises all advice too much to mend   264 Hints   562
But why this vain advice? once publish'd, books   265 Hints   659
Said the abbot, 'Let not my advice seem shallow   469 Morgante   221
The advice was sound; but, let them live: we
   will not   569 Sardan   2   495
Reprove me more for my advice. And if   570 Sardan   2   512
None can say that this was not good advice   769 Juan   1 1457
And then, by the advice of some old ladies   770 Juan   1 1519
Of good advice--and two or three of credit   775 Juan   2   72
And that's one comfort for my lost advice   901 Juan   9   287
Ah, if you had but follow'd my advice   961 Juan   14   376
'That good but rarely came from good advice   963 Juan   14   528
She had a good opinion of advice   971 Juan   15   225
And after so much excellent advice   977 Juan   15   616
Than Adeline (such is advice) advised   982 Juan   16   92

ADVICES
To change them, my advices bring sure tidings   586 Sardan   4   544
Best wait for further and more sure advices   705 Werner   4   97

ADVISE
Will Wordsworth, if I might advise   235 Epilogue   16
A turn of time at which I would advise   450 Beppo   650
His daughter--had not sent before to advise   806 Juan   3   292

ADVISED
Of the last axiom, he advised his spouse   963 Juan   14   530
She seriously advised him to get married   971 Juan   15   232
Than Adeline (such is advice) advised   982 Juan   16   92

ADVISER
Their first adviser, and their last resort   123 Recoll   102
And ancient Maid's a sage adviser   151 Harriet   4

ADVOCATES
Nor spare melodious advocates of lust   245 Bards   290
Then advocates, inquisitors, and judges   750 Juan   1   223

AEGEAN
Woo'd by each Aegean wind   160 Maid   8
Beside the confines of the Aegean main   161 Athos   1
When sailing o'er the Aegean wave   166 Struggle   30
Which charm'd our days in each Aegean clime   261 Hints   345
On shore of Euxine or Aegean sea   265 Hints   617
Again the Aegean, heard no more afar   269 Minerva   49
In the Aegean, ere a squall); it near'd   292 Vision   452
As the deep billows of the Aegean roar   298 Age   17
Break o'er th' Aegean, mindful of the day   302 Age   287
Again the Aegean, heard no more afar   356 Corsair ·3   49

AEGINA
Aegina lay, Piraeus on the right   61 Harold   4   393

AEGINA'S
On old Aegina's rock and Hydra's isle   268 Minerva   7
On old Aegina's rock and Idra's isle   355 Corsair   3   7

AEGIS
Where was thine Aegis, Pallas, that appall'd   21 Harold   2   118
Her idle aegis bore no Gorgon now   269 Minerva   80

AEGLE
Aegle, beauty and poet, has two little crimes   237 French-B   1

AENEAS
And lead Aeneas from Evander's halls   105 Nisus   36
I track'd Aeneas through the walks of fate   106 Nisus   46
Then shall Aeneas in his pride return   107 Nisus   111
Aeneas and Ascanius shall combine   107 Nisus   137
When great Aeneas wears Hesperia's crown   107 Nisus   154

AENEIDS
And for their Aeneids, Iliads, and Odysseys   752 Juan   1   326

AEOLIAN
And sometimes, on Aeolian wings   145 Adieu   39
Or breathe those sweet Aeolian strains   150 Song   5
As on the Aeolian harp, his fitful wings   418 Island   1   171
But Longbow wild as an Aeolian harp   952 Juan   13   738

AEOLUS
To Aeolus a constant sacrifice   425 Island   2   444

AERIAL
Like an aerial ship it tack'd, and steer'd   292 Vision   454
In comfort, at their own aerial ease   294 Vision   588
Through an aerial universe of endless   637 Cain   2   107
Her eyebrow's shape was like th' aerial bow   754 Juan   1   483

AESOP'S
Ah! how much happier were good Aesop's frogs   303 Age   406

AETHER'S
Through trackless realms of aether's space   133 Prayer   42

AETNA
Athos, Olympus, Aetna, Atlas, made   66 Harold   4   663
Some thought it was Mount Aetna, some the high-
   lands   786 Juan   2   799

AETNA'S
That boils in Aetna's breast of flame   321 Giaour   1102

AETOLIA'S
And from his further bank Aetolia's wolds espied   30 Harold   2   621

AFAR
Flashing afar,--and at his iron feet   10 Harold   1   428
He lurks, nor casts his heavy eye afar   11 Harold   1   496
Childe Harold hail'd Leucadia's cape afar   25 Harold   2   353
Tambourgi! Tambourgi! thy 'larum afar   30 Harold   2   649
And the deep thunder peal on peal afar   39 Harold   3   221
In us such love and reverence from afar   49 Harold   3   831
Her voice their only ransom from afar   57 Harold   4   139
Fill'd with the face of heaven, which from afar   59 Harold   4   253
Ungrateful Florence! Dante sleeps afar   63 Harold   4   505
Shine from a sister valley; and afar   81 Harold   4 1559
Or Tyrian Cadmus roved afar   88 Anacreon-A   6
And gray her towers are seen afar   102 Alva   22
Am I by thee despised and left afar   106 Nisus   41
Queen of the sky, whose beams are seen afar   110 Nisus   342
To one who has roved on the mountains afar   118 Lachin   38
Which glares a meteor from afar   128 Answer-B   8
leave thy friend afar? Chief of Oithona! not   130 Calmar   63
It shines from afar like the glories of old   164 Newstead-C   3
Beat the loud alarm afar   194 Ballad-A   22
For happy are they now reposing afar   204 Avatar   113
Looking afar if yet her lover's steed   214 Dream   73
The future cheats us from afar   223 Music-D   10
Whose steps have press'd, whose eye has mark'd
   afar   253 Bards   869
Again the Aegean, heard no more afar   269 Minerva   49
Look to the Baltic--blazing from afar   271 Minerva   213
The deathshot hissing from afar   316 Giaour   639
And morning came--and still thou wert afar   343 Corsair   1   380
Whose ray of beauty reach'd him from afar   345 Corsair   1   512
The galleys feed the flames--and I afar   349 Corsair   2   139
Again the Aegean, heard no more afar   356 Corsair   3   49
He thought on her afar, his lonely bride   362 Corsair   3   462
His only follower from those climes afar   373 Lara   1   512
Bay'd from afar complainingly   396 Corinth   1070
Beheld her frailty from afar   397 Parisina   58
But yet, afar, from man to man   401 Parisina   479
No twinkling taper from afar   413 Mazeppa   617
Which fix'd my dull eyes from afar   414 Mazeppa   785
They parted with this added aid; afar   430 Island   4   41
(For beauty's sometimes best set off afar   442 Beppo   116
Fragrant as fair, and recognised afar   464 Dante   4   77
Shone through the rents of ruin; from afar   495 Manfred   3   274
And holding on its course; but there, afar   610 Foscari   3   132
Thy hour is yet afar, and matter cannot   641 Cain   2   374
Thou hast seen them from afar. And what of that   643 Cain   2   451
An Eden kept afar from sight   656 Heaven   73
Afar, a dwarf buffoon stood telling tales   805 Juan   3   265
Of time and tide rolls on, and bears afar   980 Juan   15   789

AFFAIR
Shall be one, if you leave the affair to me   295 Vision   680
The latter yours, good Michael; so the affair   295 Vision   690
I can't tell whether Julia saw the affair   755 Juan   1   537
In Marinet's affair--in fact, 'twas shabby   896 Juan   9   10
Rather than life a mere affair of breath   898 Juan   9   128
The exact affair on which he was sent o'er   922 Juan   11   252
I have seen that sad affair of the late Queen   929 Juan   11   660
That's your affair, not mine: a real spirit   941 Juan   12   695
Who, one might think, was something in the
   affair   961 Juan   14   354

AFFAIRS
In such affairs there probably are few   446 Beppo   422
'Tis in arranging all my friends' affairs   750 Juan   1   183
Few changes e'er can better their affairs   799 Juan   2 1605
Although, no doubt, her first of love affairs   802 Juan   3   29
Then having settled his marine affairs   804 Juan   3   145
He left to his vizier all state affairs   850 Juan   5 1179
'There is a tide in the affairs of men   852 Juan   6   1
There is a tide in the affairs of women   852 Juan   6   9

AFFAIRS
Thought (what in state affairs is most essential   923 Juan   11   278
Where none were dreamt of, unto love's affairs   944 Juan   13   197
When your affairs come round, one way or t'other   961 Juan   14   383
But we'll say nothing of affairs of state   991 Juan   16   716

AFFECT
Affect a candour which thou canst not feel   247 Bards   375
Who, least affecting, still affect the most   252 Bards   816
Nor write, and so they don't affect the muse   449 Beppo   570
Affect no more than lightning a conductor   916 Juan   10   568

AFFECTATION
Where Affectation holds her seat   118 Romance   35
'The tenor's voice is spoilt by affectation   827 Juan   4   689

AFFECTED
Is 'quite refreshing,' in the affected phrase   889 Juan   8   714
And yet 'tis not affected, I opine   956 Juan   14   94
Nothing affected, studied, or constructive   969 Juan   15   91

AFFECTING
All modern arts affecting to despise   112 Examination   56
Who, least affecting, still affect the most   252 Bards   816
And vice in misery affecting still   682 Werner   1   706

AFFECTION
When I hear you express an affection so warm   91 Caroline-C   1
Whom still affection taught me to defend   93 Dorset   3
With bright but mild affection shine   97 To M--   2
For in visions alone your affection can live   97 To M.S.G.-B   3
Our souls with fond affection glow not   98 To Lesbia   2
The shroud of affection is love's last adieu   100 L Adieu   36
Henceforth affection, sweetly thus begun   107 Nisus   165
Thus Nisus all his fond affection proved   110 Nisus   397
But if affection gently thrills   111 Medea   9
Cherish'd affection only bids them flow   122 Newstead-A   146
Affection is not dead   131 L'Amitie   4
Affection for a time may sleep   132 L'Amitie   53
Nor less the affection I cherish'd for you   136 Delawarr   4
No more with affection shall memory blending   136 Delawarr   13
I will not complain, and though chill'd is
  affection   137 Delawarr   21
The bond of affection no longer endures   137 Delawarr   30
A victim, nearly from affection   144 Becher-B   41
Ah, surely affection ennobles the strain   148 Farewell-A   22
Since early affection and love are o'ercast   149 Farewell-A   34
But thou wert not fated affection to share   149 Newstead-B   15
And dreams that affection can never take wing   155 Goblet   10
So shall Affection   200 Stanzas-B   61
Ascending with affection truly loyal   276 Waltz   199
Affection chain'd her to that heart   325 Abydos   1 191
From all affection and from all contempt   342 Corsair   1 272
She took his lady also in affection   755 Juan   1   531
Dante and Milton, and of both the affection   802 Juan   3   75
A lonely pure affection unopposed   808 Juan   3   453
Of their exchanging glances of affection   818 Juan   4   104
Call'd brotherly affection, could not move   914 Juan   10   422

AFFECTIONS
Whom youth and youth's affections bound to me   34 Harold   2   892
Small power the nipp'd affections have to grow   43 Harold   3   485
Peopling it with affections; but he found   51 Harold   3   969
Love from amongst her griefs?--for such the
  affections are   70 Harold   4   909
Alas! our young affections run to waste   73 Harold   4   1072
And a new spring of noble affections arise   202 Avatar   26
May the strong curse of crush'd affections light   209 Sketch   85

AFFECTION'S
Still they call forth my warm affection's tear   85 Death-B   23
If thus affection's strength prevails   104 Alva   243
To fair affection's truth unknown   111 Medea   50
But the test of affection's a Tear   114 The Tear   4
Who laugh to scorn Affection's name   141 Pignus   26
Affection's tale upon the cheek   144 Jessy   14
Affection's heart-drops, gushing o'er   165 Thyrza   23
Affection's mingling tears were ours   165 Thyrza   28
Affection's fondest pledge was worn   318 Giaour   778

AFFECTS
Nor shrinks the female eye, nor ev'n affects to
  mourn   15 Harold   1   692
Perhaps affects me; I am a thing of feelings   672 Werner   1   19
Besides the loss (which, I must own, affects me   686 Werner   2   216
Of yours are common to me, it affects me   707 Werner   4   202

AFFIANCED
With faith to him with whom I was affianced   513 Faliero   2 345

AFFIDAVIT
I do declare, upon an affidavit   965 Juan   14   633

AFFIRM
Oh! cease to affirm that man, since his birth   93 First Kiss   21
No; I affirm. I have betray'd myself   507 Faliero   1 530

AFFIRMATION
Nor affirmation truth, if nature's sense   538 Faliero   5   51

AFFIX
To affix so slight a penalty to that   501 Faliero   1 107

AFFLICTED
On that too long afflicted shore   395 Corinth   1029

AFFLICTING
Afflicting young folks with a sort of dizziness   877 Juan   7   664

AFFLICTION
The apostle of affliction, he who threw   47 Harold   3   726
Or ill-repress'd affliction, her pure thoughts   215 Dream   139

AFFLICTION'S
Affliction's semblance bends not o'er thy tomb   85 Epitaph   17
Affliction's self deplores thy youthful doom   85 Epitaph   18

AFFLUENCE
The affluence of my soul--which one day was   487 Manfred   2 235

AFFORD
And to the Lusians did her aid afford   6 Harold   1   221
Let the poor squalid splendour thy wreck can
  afford   202 Avatar   53
Afford hysterical relief   231 Doctor   6
Nor slight applause will candid pens afford   257 Hints   71
And ocean written o'er would not afford   460 Dante   3   6
Peopled with dusty atoms which afford   609 Foscari   3 102
Our flocks and wilderness afford.--Go, Japhet   657 Heaven   196
Than can afford it. 'Tis a poor sick man   678 Werner   1   473
At least to those of incomes which afford   863 Juan   6   718
The awkward squad, and could afford to squander   873 Juan   7   411
Save such as Southey can afford to give   912 Juan   10   292

AFFORDED
Afforded hope, and offer'd chance of flight   348 Corsair   2   74

AFFORDING
They're right; our days are too brief for affording 919 Juan   11   29

AFFORDS
And Beaumont's pilfer'd Caratach affords   249 Bards   572
As but to lovers a true sense affords   818 Juan   4   110

AFFRAY
A popular affray in the public square   717 Werner   5   256

AFFRIGHT
Though a smile may delight, yet a frown won't
  affright   116 Strephon   23
Fierce as a bride when first she feels affright   266 Hints   691
The Corsair vow'd protection, soothed affright   351 Corsair   2   267
Increased his fury and affright   411 Mazeppa   455
Whence her fair hair rose twining with affright   890 Juan   8   738

AFFRIGHTED
(See also HALF-AFFRIGHTED)
When Health, affrighted, spreads her rosy wing   122 Recoll   3

AFFRONT
Which was a foul affront to you, and even   501 Faliero   1 108
By the affront of Steno, and with cause   509 Faliero   2   27
By a gross affront to your attendant damsels   515 Faliero   2 432
It had been an affront on this occasion   933 Juan   12   237

AFFRONTED
I have affronted death, but in the war   486 Manfred   2 229

AFFRONTING
In politesse, and have a sound affronting in't   923 Juan   11   342

AFLOAT
And keep the ship afloat, though three feet yet   777 Juan   2   235
That still could keep afloat the struggling tars   780 Juan   2   403
Were counted in them when they got afloat   781 Juan   2   432
And drivels seas to set it well afloat   814 Juan   3   880
Frail mariners afloat without a chart   964 Juan   14   589

AFOOT
But all afoot, the light-limb'd Matadore   15 Harold   1   739

AFORESAID
So well not one of the aforesaid paints   753 Juan   1   374
(The aforesaid Baba) just then to do more   865 Juan   6   822
The animals aforesaid occupied   913 Juan   10   401

AFRAID

Anxious to please, of pleasing half afraid	125 Recoll		270
Afraid of shame, unknown to other fears	242 Bards		34
Too low a third crawls on, afraid to fly	257 Hints		45
His vassals more amazed nor less afraid	370 Lara	1	270
Not afraid to demand it? Not afraid	674 Werner	1	175
Egad! I am afraid. You look as if	674 Werner	1	176
Something of which its masters are afraid	746 Juan	Ded	107
'Tis surely Juan now--No! I'm afraid	756 Juan	1	607
Of goblins, but still more of men afraid	764 Juan	1	1123
His berth a little damp, and him afraid	777 Juan	2	200
But was used sparingly,--some were afraid	784 Juan	2	650
Which she must still pursue howe'er afraid	820 Juan	4	253
He whisper'd Juan not to be afraid	845 Juan	5	853
Occurr'd what often happens, I'm afraid	940 Juan	12	675
But then the roll-call draws them back afraid	957 Juan	14	131

AFRESH

'Tis the old aspiration breathed afresh	302 Age		268
On Shylock's shore behold them stand afresh	307 Age		702
Afresh, for they were waxing out of date	488 Manfred	2	366

AFRIC

Europe and Afric on each other gaze	22 Harold	2	191
Afric, with all its Moors. In very truth	729 Deformed	1	498
Afric is all the sun's, and as her earth	823 Juan	4	441
For Europe ploughs in Afric like 'bos piger	938 Juan	12	558

AFRICA

Some went to Africa, some stay'd in Spain	754 Juan	1	447
Thou moral Washington of Africa	965 Juan	14	652

AFRIC'S

While Afric's echoes thrill'd with Moorish matrons' wail	9 Harold	1	395
And Afric's coast and Calpe's adverse height	255 Bards		1019

AFRIT

Glared on the Moslems' eyes some Afrit sprite	349 Corsair	2	150

AFRITS

Go--and with Gouls and Afrits rave	318 Giaour		784

AFT

'Her flag?'--'I had no glass: but fore and aft	426 Island	2	512
Survey'd him fore and aft with eyes observant	469 Morgante		239
Which struck her aft, and made an awkward rift	777 Juan	2	211

AFTER

But curse my fate for ever after	101 Lady-B		44
May once by read--but never after	148 To Author		10
Which on the wind came roaring after	410 Mazeppa		382
Leaves us so doubly serious shortly after	450 Beppo		632
Sermons and soda-water the day after	796 Juan	2	1424
A pipe, too, and a drum, and shortly after	805 Juan	3	223
Honour was more before their names than after	952 Juan	13	682
But after, there are sometimes certain signs	977 Juan	15	573

AFTERNOON

The tropic afternoon of Toobonai	420 Island	2	106
And thus they walk'd out in the afternoon	796 Juan	2	1407
I canter by the spot each afternoon	829 Juan	4	817

AFTERNOONS

His afternoons he pass'd in visits, luncheons	926 Juan	11	513

AFTER-SILENCE

But in the after-silence on the shore	213 Lady Byron		11

AFTER-TIME

How in some desperate feud of after-time	432 Island	4	199

AFTER-TIMES

Such doom may be your own in after-times	894 Juan	8	996

AFTERWARD

And afterward, if he must needs destroy	881 Juan	8	189
Koutousow, he who afterward beat back	887 Juan	8	553

AFTERWARDS

And many thoughts; but afterwards address'd	610 Foscari	3	163
In Canea--afterwards the freedom of	612 Foscari	3	275
Although their porter afterwards confess'd	750 Juan	1	189
And afterwards accompanied us through	876 Juan	7	571

AFTER-WARRIORS

To after-warriors more	180 Ode-A		20

AGACERIE

Began to treat him with some small 'agacerie	960 Juan	14	328

AGAIN

(See also AGEN)

Till I come back again	6 Harold	1	153

AGAIN

But long ere I come back again	6 Harold	1	188
Alas! I cannot smile again	17 Harold	1	838
Well--I will dream that we may meet again	20 Harold	2	77
Revel and feast assumed the rule again	28 Harold	2	535
When Thebes Epaminondas rears again	32 Harold	2	793
The dregs were wormwood; but we fill'd again	36 Harold	3	74
Self-exiled Harold wanders forth again	37 Harold	3	136
Soft eyes look'd love to eyes which spake again	38 Harold	3	187
One moment of the mightiest, and again	40 Harold	3	318
And mounts in spray the skies, and thence again	65 Harold	4	622
And overpowers the page where it would bloom again	73 Harold	4	1098
What do I gaze on? Nothing: Look again	77 Harold	4	1325
That I might live for love and you again	87 Tibullus		4
To Jove's great son I raise again	88 Anacreon-A		14
Will never wish to hear again	96 Granta		76
While many an eye which ne'er again	101 Alva		13
In thee her much-loved child may live again	108 Nisus		190
And though we ne'er may meet again	112 Quaker		3
Years must elapse ere I tread you again	118 Lachin		34
'Tis past, and thus she will not sin again	123 Recoll		96
She died, but ne'er will die again	128 Answer-B		24
When Memory bids them bud again	128 Lady-C		16
But, oh, 't will wake again	132 L'Amitie		54
And hope, my God, to thee again	133 Prayer		63
I think those days may come again	133 E. N. Long		12
To trace those days and hours again	137 Clare		11
Nor canst thou glad his aged eyes again	139 Ossian-A		22
And echoes back his Patron's voice again	142 Soliloquy		20
And kindly bade me tune my Lyre again	143 Soliloquy		68
Till smiles should restore me to rapture again	147 To Anne-B		8
Tell us you'll read them o'er again	148 To Author		16
Or, if it chance to wake again	148 A Fan		17
When I scarcely can hope to behold them again	148 Farewell-A		24
Till Memory hail'd the words again	150 Harrow-C		8
The thought that ne'er shall sleep again	151 Farewell-B		12
Though thou wilt never love again	152 Time-A		18
Sweet lady! speak those words again	152 Weep-A		2,22
Will view thy mind estranged again	153 Friend-A		12
Never to think of it again	156 Lady-F		16
Perchance I view her cliffs again	158 Florence		12
I'll hie me to its haunts again	164 Friend-B		44
To bid us meet--no--ne'er again	165 Thyrza		8
I would not wish thee here again	165 Thyrza		48
I dare not trust those sounds again	165 Away		4
Then back to busy life again	166 Struggle		4
Nor thou nor I can feel again	167 Dead		63
The lonely hour presents again	168 Haunts		3
In peace we vow'd to meet again	173 Quotation		6
To him who must not love again	174 Revanche		12
For me they shall not weep again	174 Remember-B		44
But these will be furnish'd again and again	176 Devil's Dr		15
So he sat him on his box again	177 Devil's Dr		97
That rogue! how could Westminster chuse him again	178 Devil's Dr		167
And Nature must first have unmade him again	178 Devil's Dr		181
Would never have gone again	179 Devil's Dr		230
Breaks never to unite again	180 Ode-A		24
To shame the world again	181 Ode-A		97
We will part,--we will fly to--unite it again	182 Music-A		8
He knew not--but, recall'd to Life again	184 Julian		39
The shore to which their shiver'd sail shall never stretch again	185 Music-B		8
But never melt again	186 Stanzas-A		16
Though wither'd, thy tear will unfold it again	186 Napoleon		20
There he ne'er shall charge again	188 Ode-B		70
The pall of a past world; and then again	189 Darkness		30
But none retraced their steps again	196 Venice-A		20
But left long wrecks behind: and now again	198 Po		17
Could that long-wither'd spot but be verdant again	202 Avatar		25
Which thou ne'er canst know again	207 Fare Thee		8
With a convulsion--then arose again	214 Dream		84
That sound shall charm it forth again	218 Soul-B		6
Each royal vampire wakes to life again	228 Windsor		8
The royal Vampires join and rise again	228 Vaults		8
You visit him on earth again	235 Paine		3
Once laid aside, but now assumed again	242 Bards		20
Such as none heard before, or will again	246 Bards		352
Another epic! Who inflicts again	247 Bards		385
That, ere they reach the top, fall lumbering back again	247 Bards		417
And given the spirit to the world again	247 Bards		442
'My son,' she cried, 'ne'er thirst for gore again	248 Bards		498
Let Comedy assume her throne again	249 Bards		581
Why slumbers Gifford? let us ask again	253 Bards		820
No more through rolling clouds to soar again	253 Bards		842
Or Common Sense assert her rights again	254 Bards		930
Nor burn damn'd Drury if it rise again	261 Hints		372
Then at two hours past midnight we all meet again	283 Blues	2	156
'Look to the earth, I said, and say again	290 Vision		329
He had sung against all battles, and again	297 Vision		777
Have wept enough--for what?--to weep again	298 Age		8
And higher worlds than this are his again	299 Age		88

AGAIN

The conqueror's yet unbroken heart! Again	301	Age	201
Holds back the invader from her soil again	302	Age	319
But such she is not, nor shall be again	303	Age	353
He falls indeed, perhaps to rise again	308	Age	723
When shall such hero live again	310	Giaour	6
No hand shall close its clasp again	313	Giaour	327
But three shall never mount again	313	Giaour	576
I could not pass it by again	318	Giaour	795
Forbade him e'er to smile again	318	Giaour	856
But break--before it bend again	319	Giaour	936
I wish she had not loved again	320	Giaour	1055
So would I live and love again	321	Giaour	1120
I saw her; yes, she lived again	322	Giaour	1272
To-morrow sees it bloom again	336	Abydos	2	680
Yet, in the whole, who paused to look again	341	Corsair	1	199
Had left him joy, and means to give again	342	Corsair	1	260
And he deceived me--for--he came again	344	Corsair	1	449
The white sail set--she dared not look again	345	Corsair	1	502
Yet much I long to view that chief again	351	Corsair	2	270
And stanch'd the blood she saves to shed again	351	Corsair	2	281
And once unclosed--but once may close again	353	Corsair	2	401
Too harshly told him that he lived again	353	Corsair	2	432
Would that with freedom it were thine again	356	Corsair	3	65
Reply not, tell not now thy tale again	360	Corsair	3	296
''Tis mine!--my blood-red flag! again--again	362	Corsair	3	492
The chief of Lara is return'd again	366	Lara	1	11
Not unrejoiced to see him once again	367	Lara	1	95
And once beheld, would ask of him again	371	Lara	1	368
And deem'st thou me unknown too? Gaze again	372	Lara	1	439
As unfamiliar, or, if roused again	374	Lara	1	588
The word I pledged for his I pledge again	375	Lara	2	41
From that red floor he ne'er had risen again	376	Lara	2	72
By circumstance compell'd to plunge again	378	Lara	2	232
But those that waver turn to smite again	380	Lara	2	373
Meantime his followers charge, and charge again	380	Lara	2	392
For that faint throb which answers not again	382	Lara	2	497
And bear my spirit back again	384	Corinth	37
And oft, too oft, implores again	384	Corinth	41
Who perish'd there, be piled again	385	Corinth	66
Never, oh never, we meet again	390	Corinth	574
Make a pause, and turn again	393	Corinth	778
When he fell to earth again	395	Corinth	1034
Had frozen her sense to sleep again	397	Parisina	115
The hot blood ebb'd and flow'd again	398	Parisina	226
Without the power to fill again	402	Parisina	571
It ceased, and then it came again	405	Chillon	253
None lived to love me so again	405	Chillon	276
And when I did descend again	406	Chillon	359
And Moscow's walls were safe again	407	Mazeppa	8
New realms to lose them back again	408	Mazeppa	134
But on my lips they died again	409	Mazeppa	250
'I loved, and was beloved again	409	Mazeppa	282
I loved, and was beloved again	409	Mazeppa	295
Have paid their insult back again	410	Mazeppa	392
That one day I should come again	411	Mazeppa	410
Dying, to feel the same again	412	Mazeppa	564
They brought me into life again	415	Mazeppa	846
That boat and ship shall never meet again	418	Island	1	176
The savage foe escaped, to seek again	418	Island	1	195
Back to a sword, and dies and lives again	427	Island	3	58
Half whistle half a tune, and pause again	428	Island	3	114
To find it trivial, smiled and wept again	429	Island	3	192
A lion looks upon his cubs again	429	Island	3	210
But she and Torquil must not part again	429	Island	3	224
They gaze upon them--now they lose again	429	Island	3	231
They watch'd awhile to see him float again	431	Island	4	71
They had gain'd a central realm of earth	431	Island	4	119
But Christian bade them seek their shore again	433	Island	4	249
One acclamation rent the sky again	435	Island	4	412
Would I not pay them back these pangs again	438	Tasso	100
Return'd and wept alone, and dream'd again	438	Tasso	164
You once have seen, but ne'er will see again	441	Beppo	104
Where people dance, and sup, and dance again	447	Beppo	458
Keen the desire to see his home again	452	Beppo	754
And then he talks of life, and how again	453	Venice-B	45
Had not his valour driven them back again	467	Morgante	108
Stretch'd forth her arms to clasp her lord again	468	Morgante	133
Love, who to none beloved to love again	476	Francesca	7
He's Tyrant again	488	Manfred	2	321
We only give to take again	488	Manfred	2	354
Again	668	Heaven	986
Again revisit Stralenheim's chamber? and	702	Werner	3	468
Or, being mounted, e'er got down again	748	Juan	1	70
In case our lord the king should go to war again	751	Juan	1	302
This heathenish cross restored the breed again	754	Juan	1	457
And when he look'd upon his watch again	758	Juan	1	750
Mine is the victim, and would be again	770	Juan	1	1532
And there he stood to take, and take again	775	Juan	2	87
Had greater need to nerve themselves again	785	Juan	2	742
And turn'd, believing that he call'd again	791	Juan	2	1076
He woke and gazed, and would have slept again	793	Juan	2	1185
Such worthies Time will never see again	800	Juan	2	1646
Yielding to their small hands, draws back again	805	Juan	3	256
To bid men come, and go, and come again	807	Juan	3	370

AGAIN

Her nails were touch'd with henna; but again	810	Juan	3	598
A hundred thousand men might fight again	826	Juan	4	614
Drew himself up to his full height again	844	Juan	5	814
Grow deadly pale, and then blush back again	847	Juan	5	992
The moment, till too late to come again	852	Juan	6	5
Their Delhis mann'd some boats, and sail'd again	871	Juan	7	243
A moment--and all will be life again	878	Juan	7	693
Immediately in others grew again	878	Juan	8	16
Knew when and how 'to cut and come again	882	Juan	8	278
Who thus could form a line and fight again	884	Juan	8	373
Then comes 'the tug of war';--'t will come again	884	Juan	8	405
Threw them all down into the ditch again	887	Juan	8	568
The death-disgorging rampart once again	888	Juan	8	629
And the sad, second moon grows dim again	892	Juan	8	900
So Cuvier says;--and then shall come again	901	Juan	9	297
Now that the Lion's fall'n, may rise again	925	Juan	11	444
The praise of persecution; gaze again	945	Juan	13	261
Through the huge arch, which soars and sinks again	949	Juan	13	501
The hunters fought their fox-hunt o'er again	955	Juan	13	863
She had consented to create again	962	Juan	14	439
Your writers, who must either draw again	971	Juan	15	206

AGAINST
(See also 'GAINST)

Streams like the thunder-storm against the wind	69	Harold	4	875
Their prejudice against or for this noble	533	Faliero	4	367
Against the people; but to set them free	548	Faliero	5	714

AGAMEMNON

Brave men were living before Agamemnon	747	Juan	1	33

AGATE

Of porphyry, jasper, agate, and all hues	64	Harold	4	533

AGE
(See also NON-AGE, PATENT-AGE)

Have pass'd to darkness with the vanish'd age	17	Harold	1	805
Love conquers age--so Hafiz hath averr'd	29	Harold	2	561
And yet how lovely in thine age of woe	33	Harold	2	801
Age shakes Athena's tower but spares gray Marathon	33	Harold	2	836
What is the worst of woes that wait on age	35	Harold	2	918
In soul and aspect as in age: years steal	36	Harold	3	70
Itself expired, but leaving them an age	50	Harold	3	885
Such is the refuge of our youth and age	56	Harold	4	46
Of Este, which for many an age made good	60	Harold	4	311
The Roman saw these tombs in his own age	62	Harold	4	402
Rotting from sire to son, and age to age	69	Harold	4	839
To Freedom's cause, in every age and clime	69	Harold	4	867
Perchance she died in age--surviving all	70	Harold	4	919
But here youth offers to old age the food	77	Harold	4	1342
And dwell an age on every kiss	88	To Ellen	4
That age will come on, when remembrance, deploring	91	Caroline-C	7
When age chills the blood, when our pleasures are past	93	First Kiss.	25
Sixteen was then our utmost age	98	To Lesbia	9
In vain do we vow for an age to be true	99	L Adieu	6
Restore the prop of sinking age	103	Alva	130
The hope of Alva's age is o'er	103	Alva	143
Her feeble age from dangers of the main	107	Nisus	180
Do thou, my prince, her failing age sustain	108	Nisus	189
Since the refinement of this polish'd age	113	Prologue	1
Matured by age, the garb of prudence wears	123	Recoll	66
Ah, no! amidst the gloomy calm of age	127	Recoll	401
Dear are the days of youth! Age dwells	129	Calmar	1
was the arm of the king. Age withered not	130	Calmar	45
Age will not every hope destroy	133	E.N. Long	25
If frowning Age, with cold control	133	E.N. Long	33
And even in age at heart a child	133	E.N. Long	46
But thou, perhaps, like me with age must bend	139	Ossian-A	25
Age, dark unlovely Age, appears at length	139	Ossian-A	30
For age is dark, unlovely, as the light	140	Ossian-B	37
And heartless Age perhaps will smile	141	Pignus	17
From vice to save thus virtuous Age	141	Critics	51
The clouds of Age her Sun o'ercast	141	Critics	64
Ere age has wrinkled o'er my face	150	My Son	26
The age of our nectar shall gladden our own	156	Goblet	30
As with advancing age your woes increase	161	Athos	23
With the worst anarchs of the age	165	Friend-B	54
Nor age can chill, nor rival steal	167	Dead	24
The present hours, the future age	184	Parker	11
In his mind, age, face, or figure	197	Rogers	61
An age shall fleet like earthly year	220	Clay	27
And Babel's men of age	220	Belshaz-B	29
The royal vices of our age demand	242	Bards	39
Survey the precious works that please the age	243	Bards	122
To please the females of our modest age	245	Bards	272
His style in youth or age is still the same	246	Bards	313
Let all the scandals of a former age	247	Bards	373
Give, as thy last memorial to the age	249	Bards	584
Freed at that age when reason's shield is lost	251	Bards	691
So dull in youth, so drivelling in his age	251	Bards	733

AGE

The host of idiots that infest her age	255 Bards		994
And sketch the striking traits of every age	259 Hints		218
Manhood declines--age palsies every limb	260 Hints		251
In this nice age, when all aspire to taste	262 Hints		394
Which they call a disgrace to the age and the nation	277 Blues	1	31
'If I have kept my secret half an age	295 Vision		652
Attest it many a deathless age	311 Giaour		127
A life of pain, an age of crime	312 Giaour		264
But ne'er shall Hassan's Age repose	313 Giaour		316
Has been thy lot from youth to age	320 Giaour		976
Hope of thine age, thy twilight's lonely beam	336 Abydos	2	659
Had swept an age of terror, grief, and crime	362 Corsair	3	457
Of foreign aspect and of tender age	366 Lara	1	48
That speeds the specious tale from age to age	368 Lara	1	188
And make Age smile and dream itself to youth	371 Lara	1	394
And pleased not him the sports that please his age	373 Lara	1	542
Many a vanish'd year and age	385 Corinth		46
Yet Azo's age was wretched still	402 Parisina		578
Six in youth, and one in age	402 Chillon		18
Six summers, in my earlier age	408 Mazeppa		130
This change was wrought, too, long ere age	408 Mazeppa		195
And haunted to our very age	409 Mazeppa		229
In the long lapse from youth to age	409 Mazeppa		303
The godless age, where gold disturbs no dreams	418 Island	1	216
Which certain people call a 'certain age	442 Beppo		170
Which yet the most uncertain age appears	442 Beppo		171
Whate'er his youth had suffer'd, his old age	452 Beppo		785
The aid of age to turn its course apart	453 Venice-B		29
The flow and ebb of each recurring age	453 Venice-B		58
I am not of this people nor this age	458 Dante	1	143
But in a farther age shall rise along	462 Dante	3	106
The age which I anticipate, no less	464 Dante	4	71
Shall be the Age of Beauty; and while whelms	464 Dante	4	72
Thus, in its old age, did Mount Rosenberg	483 Manfred	1	360
Why, on thy brow the seal of middle age	484 Manfred	2	49
Of cheerful old age and a quiet grave	484 Manfred	2	69
Thus, without prelude:--Age and zeal, my office	491 Manfred	3	26
Old in their youth, and die ere middle age	493 Manfred	3	140
Have nothing of old age; and his bold brow	509 Faliero	2	20
To youth in woman, and old age in man	512 Faliero	2	257
I sway'd such passions; nor was this my age	513 Faliero	2	314
The blighted old age of Faliero, shall	515 Faliero	2	456
But one such day occurs within an age	515 Faliero	2	473
There might be some, whose age and qualities	521 Faliero	3	146
There Age essaying to recall the past	528 Faliero	4	35
Will yield with age to crushing iron; but	542 Faliero	5	304
Thou tremblest, Faliero! 'Tis with age, then	548 Faliero	5	704
Youth without honour, age without respect	549 Faliero	5	788
By right of blood, derived from age to age	574 Sardan	3	169
To wax more weak with age. I did not see	601 Foscari	2	7
No less than age. That's new--when spared they either	604 Foscari	2	199
Must youth support itself on age, and I	614 Foscari	3	426
'Twill break his heart. Age has no heart to break	615 Foscari	4	4
If I could have foreseen that my old age	623 Foscari	5	178
Of the realm, while his age permitted him	625 Foscari	5	313
So massy, vast, yet green in their old age	670 Heaven		1135
Of age, if 'tis a day. Which epoch makes	677 Werner	1	377
Oh, heavens! I left him in a green old age	689 Werner	2	380
But for your age and folly I would--Help	691 Werner	2	511
Whom the old man--the grandsire (as old age	694 Werner	2	736
And may your age be happy!--I will kiss	704 Werner	3	594
The nature of thine age, nor of thy blood	709 Werner	4	348
Against your age and nature! Who at twenty	710 Werner	4	364
Or Cleopatra at sixteen--an age	725 Deformed	1	200
The age discovers he is not the true one	747 Juan	1	4
But can't find any in the present age	747 Juan	1	38
Young Juan now was sixteen years of age	753 Juan	1	425
Prefer a spouse whose age is short of thirty	754 Juan	1	496
Not only of the age, and year, but moon	759 Juan	1	819
This is the age of oddities let loose	762 Juan	1	1021
At that age he would be too old for slaughter	766 Juan	1	1234
A year or two's an age when rightly spent	791 Juan	2	1085
A day of gold from out an age of iron	806 Juan	3	283
Just as old age is creeping on apace	808 Juan	3	469
This is a liberal age, and thoughts are free	817 Juan	4	54
By age in earth: her days and pleasures were	825 Juan	4	565
Was Juan,--who, an awkward thing at his age	828 Juan	4	735
Who say strange things for so correct an age	829 Juan	4	780
Until the memory of an age is fled	829 Juan	4	811
And age, and sex, were in the market ranged	832 Juan	5	50
As most at his age are, of hope and health	832 Juan	5	58
The captives, seem'd to mark their looks and age	834 Juan	5	203
Perhaps the fault of her soft sex and age	848 Juan	5	1086
Of whom all such as came of age were stow'd	850 Juan	5	1210
The Age of Gold (when gold was yet unknown	859 Juan	6	434
Extremely common in this age, whose metal	859 Juan	6	439
A lady of a 'certain age,' which means	861 Juan	6	546
Himself in at the age when all grow good	861 Juan	6	596
I mean, that every age and every year	877 Juan	7	658
Think what it is to be in your old age	880 Juan	8	106

AGE

Of his old age in wilds of deepest maze	886 Juan	8	488
An active hermit, even in age the child	886 Juan	8	503
Spared neither sex nor age in their career	893 Juan	8	946
Besides, he was of that delighted age	905 Juan	9	545
The truth; and though grief her old age might shorten	906 Juan	9	645
Of age, and looking back to youth, give one tear	910 Juan	10	216
Whose age, and what was better still, whose nation	911 Juan	10	259
Talk not of seventy years as age; in seven	928 Juan	11	641
Which is most barbarous is the middle age	929 Juan	12	2
For when they happen at a riper age	936 Juan	12	394
Sleeps from the chivalry of this bright age	946 Juan	13	350
But what we can we glean in this vile age	953 Juan	13	769
An age may come, Font of Eternity	955 Juan	14	21
But Adeline was far from that ripe age	962 Juan	14	425
A page where Time should hesitate to print age	969 Juan	15	53
Can't, like ripe age, in gormandize excel	977 Juan	15	558
Has not the natural stays of strict old age	978 Juan	15	678
An age--expectant, powerless, with his eyes	983 Juan	16	194

AGED

(See also MIDDLE-AGED)

Fresh is the green beneath those aged trees	27 Harold	2	443
Oh! where, Dodona, is thine aged grove	27 Harold	2	469
Along that aged venerable face	28 Harold	2	557
Boast of the aged! lesson of the young	34 Harold	2	861
He, who grown aged in this world of woe	36 Harold	3	37
Her aged trees rise thick as once the slain	64 Harold	4	580
This aged heart was almost broke	104 Alva		208
And, quivering, strain'd them to his aged breast	107 Nisus		128
Nor canst thou glad his aged eyes again	139 Ossian-A		22
Out then spake an aged Moor	194 Ballad-A		31
Aged or young, the living or the dead	247 Bards		432
Yet think upon, thou somewhat aged youth	304 Age		458
Deep thought was in his aged eye	324 Abydos	1	25
Aged or young, in the Christian shape	392 Corinth		695
Though aged, he was so iron of limb	393 Corinth		792
Minotti lifted his aged eye	395 Corinth		960
Shook their white aged heads o'er me, and said	438 Tasso		158
Nor the false edge of aged appetite	513 Faliero	2	311
But not such death as fits an aged man	546 Faliero	5	616
Would have but drawn upon his aged head	611 Foscari	3	228
Even aged men, be, or appear to be	619 Foscari	4	275
Certainly aged--what her years might be	861 Juan	6	547
Child, or an aged, helpless man or two	894 Juan	8	988
They err'd, as aged men will do; but by	923 Juan	11	281
For like an aged aunt, or tiresome friend	934 Juan	12	308
Less like a young wife than an aged sister	964 Juan	14	552
Since burning aged women (save a few	997 Juan	17	51

AGEN

And monks might deem their time was come agen	4 Harold	1	62

AGENCY

Now to my task.--Mysterious Agency	479 Manfred	1	28

AGENT

A supernatural agent--or a mouse	983 Juan	16	158

AGENTS

These eyes; and, though my agents still have kept	679 Werner	1	494

AGES

But worse than steel, and flame, and ages slow	19 Harold	2	6
Ages, but not oblivion, feebly brave	33 Harold	2	816
A bony heap, through ages to remain	45 Harold	3	605
Full flashes on the soul the light of ages	52 Harold	3	1023
With the remorse of ages; and the crown	63 Harold	4	510
The double night of ages, and of her	67 Harold	4	721
And famous through all ages! but beneath	67 Harold	4	762
Ages and realms are crowded in this span	71 Harold	4	976
Must yield its pomp and wait till ages are its dower	74 Harold	4	1161
Rome for the sake of ages, Glory sheds	77 Harold	4	1319
Ages on ages shall your fate admire	110 Nisus		403
Years roll on years; to ages, ages yield	120 Newstead-A		37
Thy vaults where dead of feudal ages sleep	122 Newstead-A		142
On thy leaves yet the day-beam of ages may shine	149 Newstead-B		27
Hellenes of past ages	162 War Song		15
And blend, while ages roll away	169 Blank Leaf		11
Through unborn ages, to endure this blight	190 Churchill		18
The ashes of a thousand ages spread	192 Fragment-C		25
Of ages, the first, last, the saviour, the one	202 Avatar		44
To reign! in that word see, ye ages, comprised	203 Avatar		62
Till they groan like thy people, through ages of woe	203 Avatar		82
But that was in the earlier ages	233 Nihil		12
Who rends the veil of ages long gone by	253 Bards		875
To conquer ages, and with time to cope	254 Bards		950
'So let him stand, through ages yet unborn	271 Minerva		207
Some ages hence our genealogic tree	277 Waltz		254
Of ages, since mankind have known the rule	290 Vision		348
While the dark shades of forty ages stood	300 Age		145

AGES

Through eight long ages of alternate gore	301 Age		263
On the line that it left long ages ago	388 Corinth		437
Contain'd the dead of ages gone	395 Corinth		966
The wish--which ages have not yet subdued	416 Island	1	37
In bloody chronicles of ages past	456 Dante	1	58
Within the ages which before me pass	463 Dante	4	40
And hours--all tortured into ages--hours	482 Manfred	1	334
To those which I must number: ages--ages	484 Manfred	2	46
For ages I've done, and shall still be renewing	488 Manfred	2	351
By ages of prosperity and freedom	528 Faliero	3	654
That moment would have changed the face of ages	537 Faliero	4	624
When they were freed, and flourish'd ages after	541 Faliero	5	254
I perish, but not unavenged; far ages	548 Faliero	5	737
Which shames both them and thee to coming ages	555 Sardan	1	290
A line of thirteen ages, and the lives	575 Sardan	3	234
For ages, 'That the city ne'er should yield	590 Sardan	5	196
To lesson ages, rebel nations, and	594 Sardan	5	441
Who guard the tempting tree. When thousand ages	631 Cain	1	230
By ages!--and I must be sire of such things	634 Cain	1	447
And the infinity of endless ages	645 Cain	2	640
I had borrowed more by a few drops of ages	647 Cain	3	66
The ages prophesied, upon our seed	648 Cain	3	121
His grief will be of ages, or at least	655 Heaven		26
And we, who ne'er for ages have adored	661 Heaven		431
For ages. But what have these done, their far	731 Deformed	1	658
True: but those walls have girded in great ages	733 Deformed	1	756
Who in the earlier ages raised a bustle	752 Juan	1	323
To meet the ingenuous youth of future ages	752 Juan	1	356
Of ages; to what straits old Time reduces	813 Juan	3	798
Of ages on its water-frètted halls	820 Juan	4	259
Where twenty ages gather o'er a name	829 Juan	4	796
All ears, though long; all ages, though so short	877 Juan	7	626
Which makes all female ages equal--when	905 Juan	9	546
Of all the barbarous middle ages, that	929 Juan	12	1
Whose tale belongs to 'Hallam's Middle Ages	933 Juan	12	240
Country, where a young couple of the same ages	938 Juan	12	514
Look back o'er ages, ere unto the stake fast	955 Juan	14	13
A dull and family likeness through all ages	957 Juan	14	119
Lash'd from the foam of ages; while the graves	980 Juan	15	791
Its glory, through all ages shining sunny	988 Juan	16	519
Because as Ages upon Ages push on	997 Juan	17	43
The loftiest minds outrun their tardy ages	998 Juan	17	69

AGE'S

Half an age's contempt was an error of fame	203 Avatar		67
Will right these great men, and this age's severity	282 Blues	2	100
Their luckier votaries, till old age's tedium	910 Juan	10	175

AGES'

But 'twas not all long ages' lore, nor all	423 Island	2	288

AGGRAVATE

But aggravate the crime you have not prevented	940 Juan	12	639

AGGRAVATED

Since aggravated errors on the part	603 Foscari	2	106

AGGREGATE

A daily plague, which in the aggregate	958 Juan	14	185

AGGRESSION

Even unprovok'd aggression to repel	142 Soliloquy		28
Between him and aggression! Father!--Eve	651 Cain	3	369

AGHAST

With gaping wonderment had stared aghast	30 Harold	2	634
Aghast, confused, his fears to madness rise	110 Nisus		365
Some little scandals eke: but all aghast	451 Beppo		693
The good old gentleman was quite aghast	778 Juan	2	289

AGIS

Agis and Faliero! Hast thou more	548 Faliero	5	718

AGITATED

Orlando, seeing him thus agitated	472 Morgante		441
Has been more agitated than his wont	509 Faliero	2	23
For she seem'd agitated, flush'd, and frighten'd	861 Juan	6	575
So agitated was she with her error	863 Juan	6	711

AGITATES

Or agitates his anxious breast	95 Granta		39

AGITATION

Their breath is agitation, and their life	42 Harold	3	388
With me; the hour of agitation came	534 Faliero	4	443

AGO

And cheeks all pale, which but an hour ago	38 Harold	3	210
Whose holy dust was scatter'd long ago	66 Harold	4	706
A year ago you swore, fond she	236 Endorsement		1
The man who cut his country's long ago	238 Epigrams		8
Have long ago suffered censure	239 Bray		45

AGO

Since they were both damn'd long ago and still in	293 Vision		566
Her vultures, too, were gorged not long ago	304 Age		473
On the line that it left long ages ago	388 Corinth		437
For, sonless left long years ago	393 Corinth		803
How a young chief, a thousand moons ago	432 Island	4	195
But to my story.--'Twas some years ago	442 Beppo		161
Some days ago I should have ask'd your leave	475 Morgante		605
Before the abbey many years ago	476 Morgante		675
They crown'd him long ago	479 Manfred	1	61
To me most solemnly an hour ago	505 Faliero	1	415
Not long ago the senators embarking	509 Faliero	2	4
Six hours ago, and now thy brother rebel	520 Faliero	3	80
Long years ago--so long, they are a doubt	546 Faliero	5	591
An hour ago I should have felt it. And	567 Sardan	2	370
You did not doubt me a few hours ago	586 Sardan	4	495
Ago to Carmagnuola. The attainted	619 Foscari	4	288
An hour ago I should have felt it. And	622 Foscari	5	88
There five and thirty years ago was I	624 Foscari	5	245
And that is five and thirty years ago	625 Foscari	5	284
Left it some dozen years ago. And then	675 Werner	1	267
I served; but it is many years ago	676 Werner	1	331
Some days ago that look'd the likeliest journey	678 Werner	1	425
Some hours ago, and I some days: henceforth	680 Werner	1	541
How can I hope! An hour ago methought	680 Werner	1	583
Some hours ago might teach him fellow-feeling	681 Werner	1	608
Some months ago. The devil he did! Why, yes	684 Werner	2	109
An hour ago you would have given your soul	724 Deformed	1	140
Hint that some six of seven good years ago	772 Juan	1	1692
Thus Horace wrote we all know long ago	844 Juan	5	805
Saw--'--'Well, no matter, 'twas so long ago	985 Juan	16	299

AGONIES

Whose agonies are evils of a day	66 Harold	4	701
Flowers whose wild odours breathe but agonies	73 Harold	4	1076
With all its infinite of agonies	489 Manfred	2	385
In all these agonies,--and woke and found thee	580 Sardan	4	165
To the smooth agonies of adulation	633 Cain	1	383
To inherit agonies accumulated	634 Cain	1	446
Through agonies unspeakable, and clogg'd	639 Cain	2	245
With agonies eternal, to innumerable	639 Cain	2	246
With agonies unutterable, though	643 Cain	2	509
Of life be on him! and his agonies	652 Cain	3	422
An immortality of agonies	663 Heaven		627
And saw his agonies with such sublimity	750 Juan	1	231
And natural agonies, with a slight shade	876 Juan	7	548
Are purchased by all agonies and crimes	894 Juan	8	994

AGONISE

To seal his lip, but agonise his brow	374 Lara	1	607

AGONISED

Stands on her tripod, agonised, and full	865 Juan	6	850

AGONISING

But sad his light to agonising eyes	268 Minerva		25
But sad his light to agonising eyes	355 Corsair	3	25
Of human nature's agonising voice	885 Juan	8	472

AGONIZED

When agonized hands that cease to guard	377 Lara	2	117

AGONIZING

Adown in agonizing dew	104 Alva		236

AGONY

As on a place of agony and strife	46 Harold	3	691
Of their great agony, wrung out from this	65 Harold	4	619
Consents to death, but conquers agony	76 Harold	4	1254
A father's love and mortal's agony	79 Harold	4	1434
The active agony of grief	172 Time-B		19
The pang, the agony, the doubt	172 Romaic-B		2
The agony they do not show	191 Prometheus-B		9
The Agony of Pleasure and of Pain	201 Ode-C		35
A hollow agony which will not heal	213 Lady Byron		21
Unknowing of its cause of agony	214 Dream		61
Revenge is lost in agony	221 Marianne		3
That fiery festival of agony	302 Age		339
Memorial of thine agony	318 Giaour		780
The clenched hand, the pause of agony	341 Corsair	1	236
Which downcast droop'd in tearless agony	345 Corsair	1	469
Which adds all other agony to thirst	351 Corsair	2	319
It was an agony--but now forgot	381 Lara	2	413
In outworn nature's agony	407 Mazeppa		34
My swoln limbs from their agony	411 Mazeppa		454
For I have battled with mine agony	437 Tasso		21
Oh agony! that centuries should reap	453 Venice-B		14
Or joy that ends in agony or faintness	487 Manfred	2	264
Nor agony, nor, greater than all these	492 Manfred	3	69
Groans are not words, nor agony assent	538 Faliero	5	50
Then, in the last gasp of thine agony	549 Faliero	5	792
Which our internal, restless agony	587 Sardan	5	36
And the deep agony of his pale wife	601 Foscari	1	355
The agony to which they must be heirs	667 Heaven		870

AGONY
And the birds scream their agony through air   669 Heaven   1065
Of some strong swimmer in his agony   780 Juan   2   424
Oh! dearest father, in this agony   821 Juan   4   300
Gulbeyaz proved in that brief agony   865 Juan   6   847
By the infinities of agony   879 Juan   8   99

AGRANTE
By the great Milo of Agrante fell   476 Morgante   674

AGRARIAN
The grand agrarian alchymy, high rent   306 Age   581
And prop the hill of these agrarian ants   307 Age   651
With his Agrarian laws the high estate   910 Juan   10   195

AGREE
And here I agree   239 Bray   22
The youth, the bloom, the beauty which agree   442 Beppo   109
Earth's mist with their pure pinions not agree   463 Dante   3   171
'Tis past. I cannot but agree with you   501 Faliero   1   104
Thou dost agree with me in understanding   568 Sardan   2   427
So says the proverb--and I quite agree   748 Juan   1   60
Agree to a short armistice with truth   811 Juan   3   664
And don't agree at all with the wise Roman   853 Juan   6   54
If I agree that what is, is; then this I call   919 Juan   11   35

AGREEABLE
The favour of the empress was agreeable   910 Juan   10   169
A quality agreeable to woman   960 Juan   14   285

AGREED
On one great point the council are agreed   106 Nisus   89
But all were agreed that our debts should
  increase   178 Devil's Dr   165
While all agreed that in his cheek and eye   431 Island   4   89
And said, with great respect, he had agreed   475 Morgante   598
We are agreed, then? Yes. Heaven's peace be
  with him   625 Foscari   5   318
His parents ne'er agreed except in doting   750 Juan   1   195

AGREEING
So call'd, because, the name and thing agreeing   441 Beppo   43
Until I see both sides for once agreeing   898 Juan   9   126

AGROUND
Running aground, was taken by the Turks   871 Juan   7   240

AGUE
For he was drown'd, and I've the ague   160 Swimming   20
Ague in its cold fit, they fill'd their boat   782 Juan   2   503
What they should laugh at--the mere ague still   943 Juan   13   135

AGUISH
For wit hath no great friend in aguish folks   991 Juan   16   707

AH
Ah! may'st thou ever be what now thou art   3 To Ianthe   10
Ah me! in sooth he was a shameless wight   3 Harold   1   14
Ah, happy she! to 'scape from him whose kiss   4 Harold   1   41
Ah me! what hand can pencil guide, or pen   7 Harold   1   238
Ah! such, alas, the hero's amplest fate   9 Harold   1   397
Ah, monarchs! could ye taste the mirth ye mar   11 Harold   1   501
Ah Spain! how sad will be thy reckoning-day   12 Harold   1   546
Ah! that to these were given such peaceful shades   14 Harold   1   655
Ah, Vice, how soft are thy voluptuous ways   14 Harold   1   661
Ah, grievance sore and listless dull delay   22 Harold   2   176
Ah, happy years! once more who would not be a boy   23 Harold   2   207
Ah, Greece, they love thee least who owe thee
  most   32 Harold   2   789
Ah! then and there was hurrying to and fro   38 Harold   3   208
Ah! no, far fly from me attempts so vain   85 Death-B   19
Ah, none!--a father's tears will cease to flow   85 Epitaph   25
Ah! fly not from the candid youth   87 Rousseau   15
Ah! gentle, fleeting, wav'ring sprite   87 Adrian   1
Ah, Lesbia! though 'tis death to me   87 Ad Lesbiam   9
Could I desist?--ah! never-never   88 To Ellen   12
(Ah! little did I think the dart   89 Anacreon-B   29
Ah! if thou canst, o'ercome regret   90 Caroline-A   22
Ah! did that breast with ardour glow   90 Caroline-B   5
Ah! what are words to love like mine   91 Caroline-B   21
Ah! would these joyous moments last   91 Caroline-B   37
That voice!--ah, no, 'tis but the blast   91 Caroline-B   39
But ah! my girl, you do not love   91 Caroline-B   48
Ah! though myself, by nature haughty, wild   94 Dorset   37
Ah! frown not, sweet lady, unbend your soft brow   98 To M.S.G.-B   13
Here I can trace--ah, no! that eye   98 To Mary   9
Ah! happier far, had he the morn survey'd   108 Nisus   257
Ah! must he rush his comrade's fate to share   110 Nisus   334
Ah, hapless dame! no sire bewails   111 Medea   45
Ah! there my young footsteps in infancy wander'd   117 Lachin   9
Ah! were you destined to die at Culloden   117 Lachin   27
Ah, vain defence! the hostile traitor's siege   120 Newstead-A   61
Ah happy days! too happy to endure   121 Newstead-A   129
Ah! sure some stronger impulse vibrates here   125 Recoll   213

AH
I hear again,--but ah! no brother's voice   125 Recoll   234
Ah, no! amidst the gloomy calm of age   127 Recoll   401
Ah! whilst I tread this earthly sphere   133 Prayer   47
Ah! though the present brings but pain   133 E. N. Long   11
Ah! since thy angel form is gone   134 Lady-D   17
Ah! why do dark'ning shades conceal   135 I Would   19
Ah! splendour has raised, but embitter'd, my lot   136 Highlander   29
Will Mary be there to receive me?--ah, no   136 Highlander   44
Ah, Mary! what home could be mine but with you   136 Highlander   48
And we may meet--ah! never   137 Clare   18
But, ah! without the thoughts which then were
  mine   138 Harrow-B   12
Ah what avails it thus to waste my time   142 Soliloquy   7
Ah! must he rise unpunish'd from the feast   142 Soliloquy   45
That when they part--they part?--ah no   144 Jessy   31
Ah, heedless girl! why thus disclose   146 Vain Lady   1
Ah, no! for those hours can no longer be mine   148 Farewell-A   20
Ah, droop not, my Oak! lift thy head for a while   149 Newstead-B   17
But, ah, in spite of Hope's endeavour   150 Harrow-C   14
Ah, William, were thine own the same   150 My Son   8
Ah, no--though moralists reprove   150 My Son   21
Ah, joyous season! when the mind   153 Friend-A   29
Ah! who would think that form had past   158 Florence   29
How welcome were its shade!--ah, no   158 Storm   11
Ah, tell me, my soul! must I perish   162 Romaic-A   29
Ah! wherefore art thou lowly laid   165 Thyrza   4
But where is thine?--Ah! where art thou   165 Thyrza   42
Ah! happy if each tear of thine   168 Weeping   3
Ah! Love was never yet without   172 Romaic-B   1
My light of life! ah, tell me why   172 Romaic-B   25
Ah! sure such grief is fancy's scheming   173 Not False   23
The 'Origin of Love!'--Ah! why   173 Origin   1
Ah! then repeat those accents never   175 Portuguese-A   6
Still let them pause--ah! little do they know   193 Monody   63
Ah! how much colder   199 Stanzas-B   21
Ah! whither strays the immortal mind   220 Clay   2
Ah! couldst thou--thou wouldst pardon now   221 Marianne   7
Ah, what can tombs avail!--since these disgorge   228 Windsor   9
The Quarterly--Ah, Sir, if you   231 Doctor   47
Ah! how much juster were thy muse's hap   246 Bards   339
While Kenney's World--ah! where is Kenney's wit   249 Bards   570
Such are we now. Ah! wherefore should we turn   250 Bards   608
Ah! who would take their titles with their rhymes   251 Bards   722
Shall these approach the muse? ah, no! she flies   255 Bards   963
'A groat.'--'Ah, bravo! Dick hath done the sum   264 Hints   519
Ah! let me cease; in vain my bosom burns   265 Hints   619
(Ah! too regardless of his chaplain's yawn   267 Hints   764
Yes, 'twas Minerva's self; but, ah! how changed   269 Minerva   75
And, ah! though still the brightest of the sky   269 Minerva   85
Ah, no! from Morier's pages down to Galt's   275 Waltz   131
Ah! Sir Richard, good morning; I've brought you
  some friends   280 Blues   2   26
Ah! how much happier were good Aesop's frogs   303 Age   406
Repletion? Ah! in thy dejected looks   305 Age   510
Ah! thine was not the temper or the taste   305 Age   518
For ah! 'the loaves and fishes,' once so high   306 Age   606
Ah! where shall either victim rest   314 Giaour   411
Ah! fondly youthful hearts can press   316 Giaour   645
Ah! had she but an earthly grave   321 Giaour   1124
I had'--Ah! have I now?--a friend   322 Giaour   1221
Ah! were thy beauties e'er so cold   323 Giaour   1293
Ah! deem I right? the Pacha's plan   327 Abydos   1   309
Ah! were I sever'd from thy side   327 Abydos   1   319
Ah! yonder see the Tchocadar   328 Abydos   1   449
Ah! how without can blood be spilt   330 Abydos   2   126
Ah! wherefore did he turn to look   335 Abydos   2   563
Ah, happy! but of life to lose the worst   336 Abydos   2   641
Ah, wherefore not consume it--and depart   336 Abydos   2   650
Ah! never loved he half so much as now   346 Corsair   1   582
Ah! now they fight in firmest file no more   350 Corsair   2   247
Was hush'd so deep--ah! happy if in death   352 Corsair   2   393
Ah! rather ask what will not Woman dare   353 Corsair   2   407
Ah! little reck'd that chief of womanhood   358 Corsair   3   196
Ah! since that fatal night, though brief the time   362 Corsair   3   456
This Conrad mark'd, and felt--ah! could he less   363 Corsair   3   523
Ah! happier if it ne'er with guilt had glow'd   371 Lara   1   353
Ah, pause! nor yet put out the social smile   419 Island   2   54
And, 'stead of trousers (ah! too early torn   425 Island   2   480
My Neuha! ah! and must my fate pursue   426 Island   2   526
But whatsoe'er betide, ah, Neuha! now   426 Island   2   528
But, ah, how different! 'tis the cause makes all   433 Island   4   261
Ah! to what effort would it not persuade   455 Dante   Ded   14
Italia? Ah! to me such things, foreshown   458 Dante   2   16
Ah! must the sons of Adam lose it twice   459 Dante   2   49
Ah, Manuel! thou art elderly and wise   494 Manfred   3   213
Ah! he unveils his aspect: on his brow   496 Manfred   3   336
Ah! dared I speak my feelings! Give them breath   506 Faliero   1   433
Calmer? Ay, calmer, my good lord.--Ah, why   511 Faliero   2   175
Ah, no!--As I have ever shared your kindness   512 Faliero   2   213
Ah! no; it is the certainty of all   527 Faliero   3   607
Ah! one moment sooner   537 Faliero   4   615
Ah! the plebeian Brutus, is he gone   540 Faliero   5   179
Ah! little boots it now to recollect   547 Faliero   5   640

AH

The lifted sword in air--Ah! hark! it falls	549	Faliero	5	820
Ah, Myrrha! I have been where we shall be	579	Sardan	4	47
Ah! do not name it. Well, then, mark me: when	584	Sardan	4	375
Ah! Wherefore do you start? Did I do so	585	Sardan	4	453
What voice is that?--'T is Barbarigo's! Ah	596	Foscari	1	79
And we must wait on't. Ah! a voice of wail	599	Foscari	1	228
Not signed? Ah, I perceive my eyes begin	601	Foscari	2	6
Will the gleam let me trace them? Ah	608	Foscari	3	16
Ah! they relent, then--I had ceased to hope it	608	Foscari	3	35
I will be with thee. Ah! if it were so	610	Foscari	3	110
Of late, is mercy. Ah! you never yet	611	Foscari	3	206
Ah, father! though I must and will depart	616	Foscari	4	99
Some water! Ah, he is dying! Now, I'm ready	617	Foscari	4	185
Ah! the devil come to insult the dead! Avaunt	618	Foscari	4	218
He understands me. Ah! I thought it would be so	618	Foscari	4	239
Its saviour first, then victim. Ah! that seems	619	Foscari	4	308
I am the son of Marco Memmo. Ah	623	Foscari	5	198
I am, but only to these gates.--Ah	625	Foscari	5	80
Ah! now you look as look'd my husband	625	Foscari	5	302
Ah! Thou look'st almost a god; and	629	Cain	1	128
Ah! didst thou tempt my mother	630	Cain	1	193
Ah! I thought it was a being: who could do	631	Cain	1	261
By thy own flesh. Ah me! and did they perish	640	Cain	2	279
Too fiercely, but not fatally. Ah, why	651	Cain	3	328
With stony lifelessness! Ah, cruel Cain	651	Cain	3	365
Brute of the forest? Ah! a livid light	652	Cain	3	390
Our bower. Ah, little knows he what he weeps for	654	Cain	3	520
Alone can do so. Ah! he speaks of death	663	Heaven		642
To life before it. Ah! smilest thou still in scorn	665	Heaven		722
Ah! why	667	Heaven		924
Ah, no! Why! wouldst thou have it so? I would	671	Werner	1	9
Discover'd! then I'll stab--Ah! Josephine	683	Werner	1	736
And rip the hunter's entrails. Ah! I care not	695	Werner	3	9
That corner's turn'd--so--ah! no!--right! it draws	701	Werner	3	418
Breathing around you, save my mother's? Ah	702	Werner	3	494
So cannot say. Ah! here's the lady Ida	706	Werner	4	150
Upon a journey past the frontier. Ah	708	Werner	4	282
By those he rules and those he ranks with. Ah	709	Werner	4	321
He hath no confidence! Ah! can I hope it	711	Werner	4	428
Admit him, ne'ertheless. Ah! 'Tis, then, Werner	715	Werner	5	149
Farewell! He hath clear'd the staircase. Ah! I hear	721	Werner	5	508
The noon of this same ever-scorching glory? Ah	733	Deformed	1	786
Ah! behold yon bleeding spectre	736	Deformed	2	71
Ah, now you recognise him! My brain's crush'd	739	Deformed	2	301
In the fair form I wear, to please you? Ah	743	Deformed	3	90
And so you love. Ah! could I be beloved	744	Deformed	3	134
But, ah! he died; and buried with him lay	751	Juan	1	265
Was but a moment's act.--Ah! well-a-day	769	Juan	1	1445
Which makes it fatal to be loved? Ah, why	801	Juan	3	10
Ah! what is man? what perils still environ	806	Juan	3	281
Ah! no;--the voices of the dead	812	Juan	3	732
Ah! surely nothing dies but something mourns	816	Juan	3	960
Ah! why the liver wilt thou thus attack	823	Juan	4	419
Ah! must I then the only minstrel be	830	Juan	4	863
To thee both oh! and ah! belong of right	904	Juan	9	514
Ah! if he had, how much he would have miss'd her	914	Juan	10	424
Ah, nut-brown partridges! Ah, brilliant pheasants	950	Juan	13	599
And ah, ye poachers!--'T is no sport for peasants	950	Juan	13	600
But oh, ambrosial cash! Ah! who would lose thee	953	Juan	13	799
Ah, if you had but follow'd my advice	961	Juan	14	376
Ah!--what should follow slips from my reflection	968	Juan	15	1
An 'Oh!' or 'Ah!' of joy or misery	968	Juan	15	6
Ah! who can tell? Or rather, who can not	968	Juan	15	25
I see--I see--Ah, no!--'tis not--yet 'tis	995	Juan	16	938

AHA

'Aha!' quoth he, 'what have we here	177	Devil's Dr		95

AHEAD

Though right ahead the roaring breakers lay	787	Juan	2	828

AHEM

I tried at Ilderim; Ahem	230	I Read		3

AHOLIBAMAH

Celestial natures? But, Aholibamah	655	Heaven		11
And proud Aholibamah spurns me also	657	Heaven		169
I did not speak to thee, Aholibamah	664	Heaven		662
Soft lights which were not mine? Aholibamah	664	Heaven		705
They are none. Aholibamah, own thy God	665	Heaven		724

AID

And to the Lusians did her aid afford	6	Harold	1	221
Yes, she, whose gen'rous aid her name endears	21	Harold	2	115
For foreign arms and aid they fondly sigh	31	Harold	2	717
To aid thy mind's development, to watch	53	Harold	3	1076

AID

No hollow aid; alone--man with his God must strive	60	Harold	4	297
Not now in snow, which asks the lyric Roman's aid	66	Harold	4	666
The strings their former aid refuse	89	Anacreon-B		42
It is not war their aid demands	102	Alva		93
Without thy aid no glory shall be mine	107	Nisus		167
To aid their cause implore the gods in vain	108	Nisus		218
What force, what aid, what stratagem essay	110	Nisus		335
aid of Erin	130	Calmar		34
The aid, which once improved their light	134	E. N. Long		80
Nor Hope, nor Memory yield their aid	134	Lady-D		23
Without the aid of reason	137	Clare		39
Invoke those kindred passions' aid	141	Critics		5
Thy rhymes, without the aid of magic	148	To Author		9
The aid which once improved their light	148	A Fan		6
In aid of others' let me shine	154	Skull		14
Nor ask the aid of idle song	163	Malta		44
Of aid from them--She was the Universe	190	Darkness		82
The pen! foredoom'd to aid the mental throes	242	Bards		11
If Inspiration should her aid refuse	245	Bards		259
Behold, a chosen band shall aid thy plan	248	Bards		506
But thou, with powers that mock the aid of praise	254	Bards		931
And for expression's aid, 'tis said, or sung	258	Hints		155
His book, with Longman's liberal aid, shall pass	264	Hints		547
Had built St. Paul's without the aid of Wren	266	Hints		668
Not to such deeds did Pallas lend her aid	271	Minerva		215
For a spice of your wit in an epilogue's aid	282	Blues	2	83
To aid him ere he should be quite worn out	285	Vision		30
At length with jostling, elbowing, and the aid	295	Vision		673
Disdain, defy, the tardy aid of art	299	Age		82
The aid evaded, and the cold delay	302	Age		294
Thou hast to aid thee, should his lot be thine	304	Age		460
To aid these bankrupt tyrants in their need	307	Age		679
One cry to Mahomet for aid	321	Giaour		1082
They yield such aid as Pity's haste supplies	357	Corsair	3	116
Without some aid how here could I remain	360	Corsair	3	315
Refused to aid his heavy heart's demand	364	Corsair	3	586
Rush where the sound invoked their aid to save	369	Lara	1	208
But few remain to aid his voice and hand	379	Lara	2	310
Without a hope from mercy's aid	394	Corinth		895
As not disdaining priestly aid	401	Parisina		465
For thousands fell that flight to aid	407	Mazeppa		19
A transient slumber's fitful aid	407	Mazeppa		38
They parted with this added aid; afar	430	Island	4	41
The aid of age to turn its course apart	453	Venice-B		29
Our power would thine aid would nought be found	470	Morgante		286
Ye cannot, or ye will not, aid me. Say	480	Manfred	1	165
I lean no more on super-human aid	481	Manfred	1	265
The aid of holy men, and heavenly patience	484	Manfred	2	34
But they can nothing aid me. I have sought	485	Manfred	2	136
That I can aid thee. To do this thy power	487	Manfred	2	245
And died unpardon'd--though he call'd in aid	487	Manfred	2	280
I 'gin to fear that thou art past all aid	493	Manfred	3	136
In aid to overthrow these swoln patricians	504	Faliero	1	307
I should not need the dubious aid of strangers	508	Faliero	1	589
His aid; and if reluctant, he no less	518	Faliero	2	670
And all which circumstance can add to aid them	538	Faliero	5	28
To aid our judgment in a trial arduous	541	Faliero	5	227
She has no breath, no pulse!--Guards! lend your aid	547	Faliero	5	689
With aught officious aid would bring to quell it	593	Sardan	5	361
That thought would scarcely aid me to endure it	609	Foscari	4	97
Thus hesitate? 'The Ten' have call'd in aid	616	Foscari	4	76
Let me support you--paler--ho! some aid there	617	Foscari	4	184
No aid? Call in assistance! 'Tis all over	625	Foscari	5	309
Inexorable claim without my aid	652	Cain	3	377
They cannot aid thee. But they soothe me--now	657	Heaven		163
The hour will come in which celestial aid	663	Heaven		641
I cannot, must not, aid you. 'T is decreed	669	Heaven		1070
This is one of the 'strangers to whose aid	678	Werner	1	468
The chief part of whatever aid was render'd	679	Werner	1	480
If I could aid you--journeying the same way	679	Werner	1	536
I cannot aid, and will not witness such	682	Werner	1	700
Was his chief aid in yesterday's escape	685	Werner	2	146
Though slighter, yet not slight, to aid these men	686	Werner	2	244
Aid which he added to your abler succour	693	Werner	2	649
Should aid each other. It is a damn'd world, sir	695	Werner	3	42
Through the dim Gothic glass by pious aid	697	Werner	3	114
To nothing that may tempt me! Else--Heaven aid me	701	Werner	3	413
Lady, need aid of mine. I must not now	707	Werner	4	210
To aid me. But I'll aid you now. In what	715	Werner	5	141
Have made me both at present. You shall aid me	719	Werner	5	379
My fullest, freest aid. Then fare you well	721	Werner	5	522
Would aid his likeness! If I must partake	723	Deformed	1	41
Who make men without women's aid have long	728	Deformed	1	436
Removed; the aid of--No, my gallant boy	736	Deformed	2	132
Words!--Canst thou aid her? I will try. A sprinkling	741	Deformed	2	376
If you seek aid from me--or else be silent	743	Deformed	3	107
But not a servant stirr'd to aid the fight	769	Juan	1	1467
But soon Philosophy came to my aid	800	Juan	2	1673
With some small aid from scissors, paint, and tweezers	841	Juan	5	634
By this old black enchanter's unsought aid	842	Juan	5	664

AID

Except his majesty, who, with her aid	856 Juan	6	251
Her aid to fair Juanna, whose excess	860 Juan	6	483
Without the aid of prince or plenipo	864 Juan	6	758
And then he call'd his brethren to his aid	867 Juan	6	937
Seeing arrive an aid so opportune	885 Juan	8	442
'Twere not for want of lamps to aid his dodging his	922 Juan	11	221
Without the aid of too sincere a poet	929 Juan	11	688
To aid the damsel and destroy the caitiff	942 Juan	13	74

AIDED

Had Fortune aided Nature's care	113 Cornelian-A		25
I have still aided, cherish'd, loved, and urged you	568 Sardan	2	393
And cannot I, who aided in this work	635 Cain	1	528
I would have aided you, and also have	719 Werner	5	380
The Turkish fire, and aided by their own	870 Juan	7	234
With their attendant aided our escape	876 Juan	7	570
And that which farther aided them to strive	884 Juan	8	374

AIDING

Commanding, aiding, animating all	380 Lara	2	368
With him, aiding heart and hand	394 Corinth		908
By aiding me in my dissuasion of	707 Werner	4	208

AIDS

Rise--tho' these shores few aids to Life supply	185 Julian		46
Whose ghostly whiteness aids its gloom	312 Giaour		239
That aids his envious treachery	316 Giaour		613
And all that speaks and aids the naval art	346 Corsair	1	588
Yet aids the warrior worthy of his birth	460 Dante	2	124
Besides, their resurrection aids our glories	751 Juan	1	245

AIERY

| Of her high aiery; let what we now | 544 Faliero | 5 | 432 |

AIGRETTE

| An emerald aigrette with Haidee's hair in't | 811 Juan | 3 | 614 |

AILS

'What ails thee, Dervise? eat--dost thou suppose	348 Corsair	2	117
What ails him? 'Nothing!' or a Monarch who	743 Deformed	3	97
Of charms to make good gold and cure bad ails	805 Juan	3	269

AIM

In sooth 'twere sad to thwart their noble aim	11 Harold	1	472
Yet with a nobler aim than in his youth's fond prime	37 Harold	3	99
They were gigantic minds, and their steep aim	51 Harold	3	981
My blood from out thy being were an aim	53 Harold	3	1091
To cheer thy mother's years shall be my aim	108 Nisus		201
And wives, as in life, aim at absolute sway	117 To Eliza		27
Noble his object, glorious is his aim	162 Orchomenus		3
Surely I once beheld a nobler aim	212 Augusta-C		102
Let spectre-mongering Lewis aim, at most	254 Bards		919
Cock'd, fired, and miss's his man--but gain'd his aim	273 Waltz		22
Being, end, aim, religion--rent, rent, rent	306 Age		631
Ambition, glory, love, the common aim	367 Lara	1	79
Alas, such is our nature! all but aim	417 Island	1	115
And the smoke rose between them and their aim	434 Island	4	296
(Though such was not my ambition's end or aim	456 Dante	1	52
From overfeeling good or ill; and aim	463 Dante	4	12
That stone seems with good will and aim applied	469 Morgante		214
The aim of their existence was not mine	485 Manfred	2	148
Have miss'd their chief aim--the extinction of	584 Sardan	4	377
Strike with a better aim! Ay, if we conquer	587 Sardan	4	581
In all her mystery. Hear me--they who aim	603 Foscari	2	86
At Foscari, aim no less at his father	603 Foscari	2	87
They have taken my son from me, and now aim	622 Foscari	5	84
Our swords when drawn must cross, our engines aim	676 Werner	1	348
Most likely to attain her aim--his heart	846 Juan	5	1120
Where every body has some separate aim	937 Juan	12	461
At which all modern nations vainly aim	943 Juan	13	158
In russet jacket:--lynx-like is his aim	950 Juan	13	597
Not stings, and flits through ether without aim	952 Juan	13	710
As all must blend whose part it is to aim	993 Juan	16	805

AIM'D

Aim'd with her poison'd arrows, but to miss	61 Harold	4	345
Coquettish in ambition--still he aim'd	68 Harold	4	818
Once, and but once, she aim'd a deadly blow	123 Recoll		81
The rustic's musket aim'd against my life	126 Recoll		274
Too nearly, deadly aim'd to err	335 Abydos	2	575
And still, all deadly aim'd and hot	394 Corinth		939
His last ball had been aim'd, but from his breast	434 Island	4	333
Alone is aim'd at. But discarded princes	615 Foscari	4	60

AIMS

| Or, in adventurous numbers, neatly aims | 257 Hints | | 29 |

AIR

(See also MOUNTAIN-AIR, NIGHT-AIR, OPEN-AIR)

AIR

Oh! there is sweetness in the mountain air	9 Harold	1	349
Their various arms that glitter in the air	10 Harold	1	435
And smug apprentice gulp their weekly air	15 Harold	1	696
To whom the boundless air alone were home	37 Harold	3	130
The clear air for a while (a passing guest	47 Harold	3	721
Where not a beam nor air nor leaf is lost	49 Harold	3	839
With Nature's realms of worship, earth and air	49 Harold	3	858
Thine air is the young breath of passionate thought	50 Harold	3	924
The earth to her embrace compels the powers of air	52 Harold	3	1021
Floats through the azure air, an island of the blest	59 Harold	4	243
There is a tomb in Arqua;--rear'd in air	59 Harold	4	262
The air around with beauty. We inhale	62 Harold	4	434
If through the air a zephyr more serene	65 Harold	4	605
Or the light air of Egypt's graceful queen	70 Harold	4	905
Buried in air, the deep blue sky of Rome	71 Harold	4	991
And still the eloquent air breathes--burns with Cicero	72 Harold	4	1008
Or wert,--a young Aurora of the air	72 Harold	4	1030
Not in the air shall these my words disperse	75 Harold	4	1203
And the low night-breeze waves along the air	76 Harold	4	1291
In air with Earth's chief structures, though their frame	78 Harold	4	1403
He never sought to cleave the air	87 Catullus		10
Loud rings in air the chapel bell	96 Granta		69
Change that discontented air	100 Marion		3
Shall sound his glories high in air	105 Alva		314
As some young rose, whose blossom scents the air	110 Nisus		379
But leave at once thy realms of air	118 Romance		21
High poised in air the massy weapon hung	126 Recoll		275
dwells in his hall of air: he will rejoice in	130 Calmar		73
Declaring with a coxcomb's native air	142 Soliloquy		43
Mine will not all be lost in air	151 Farewell-B		3
Where air and sea with rocks and woods conspire	161 Athos		14
Adieu, the supercilious air	163 Malta		19
With lively air, and open heart	163 Malta		41
Have thrown such speaking sadness in thine air	175 Sonnet-A		5
And a feast for the fowls of the Air	176 Devil's Dr		52
And she look'd to heaven with that frenzied air	176 Devil's Dr		70
What spread from face to face that wondering air	183 Address-D		7
It soars, and mingles in the air	187 Ode-B		7
It roll'd in air, the warrior's guide	187 Ode-B		53
And the shorn Sun grew dim in air	188 On Star		17
Swung blind and blackening in the moonless air	189 Darkness		5
The winds were wither'd in the stagnant air	190 Darkness		80
Air, so softly supercilious	196 Rogers		28
The twilight air, unharm'd by summer's heat	198 Po		24
And mellow'd Sadness in thine air	200 Ode-C		14
Perhpas a kinder clime, or purer air	211 Augusta-C		44
Till the swoln bubble bursts--and all is air	243 Bards		134
Its way back into earth, and fire, and air	286 Vision		84
'Michael!' replied the Prince of Air, 'even here	289 Vision		305
Quick in its motions, with an air of vigour	294 Vision		595
With now an air of gloom, or savage mirth	294 Vision		598
I've scarcely been ten minutes in the air	295 Vision		694
To earth, air, ocean, all that felt or feel	301 Age		228
Shall sink while there's an echo left to air	301 Age		250
No breath of air to break the wave	310 Giaour		1
How welcome is each gentle air	310 Giaour		19
And mark'd the mild angelic air	311 Giaour		74
His aspect and his air impress'd	312 Giaour		204
The air, and verdure o'er the ground	313 Giaour		304
That livid cheek, that stony air	319 Giaour		907
But yet it hath an air of gloom	329 Abydos	2	84
That melts in the liquid word	336 Abydos	2	714
Flung o'er that spot of earth the air of hell	349 Corsair	2	156
A conqueror's more than captive's air is seen	351 Corsair	2	301
'What is that form? if not a shape of air	353 Corsair	2	433
Full on his brow, as if from morning air	361 Corsair	3	397
Their freezing aspect and averted air	362 Corsair	3	465
They deem'd him better than his air express'd	367 Lara	1	114
All was so still, so soft in earth and air	368 Lara	1	167
In act alone obeys, his air commands	374 Lara	1	561
With thoughtful visage and imperious air	375 Lara	1	625
With self-confiding, coldly patient air	375 Lara	2	30
His blade is bared,--in him there is a air	380 Lara	2	609
She talk'd all idly unto shapes of air	384 Lara	2	609
Over the earth, and through the air	384 Corinth		38
Calm, clear, and azure as the air	387 Corinth		253
As rose the Muezzin's voice in air	387 Corinth		266
And see the worms of the earth, and fowls of the air	389 Corinth		491
Stirr'd by the breath of the wintry air	391 Corinth		621
Hath she sunk in the earth, or melted in air	391 Corinth		676
And gather from her air and gait	398 Parisina		154
And folded arms, and freezing air	398 Parisina		164
Save one:--what cleaves the silent air	401 Pariaina		488
To whom the goodly earth and air	402 Chillon		9
First came the loss of light, and air	405 Chillon		233
That there was something in her air	409 Mazeppa		273
But chill the air although in June	412 Mazeppa		522
The very air was mute	413 Mazeppa		661

AIR

They stop--they start--they snuff the air	413 Mazeppa		698
Of those who saw no hope, save sea and air	417 Island	1	94
Where Chimborazo, over air, earth, wave	420 Island	2	77
When every flower was bloom, and air was balm	420 Island	2	107
His bark was borne; the sport of wave and air	421 Island	2	174
The youth which makes one rainbow of the air	423 Island	2	299
In such an hour, to break the air so still	424 Island	2	418
His foremast air, and somewhat rolling gait	425 Island	2	476
Flowing o'er ocean as it stream'd in air	431 Island	4	102
Where lay her lover, saw a sail in air	435 Island	4	376
When the impatient thirst of light and air	436 Tasso		6
Song, scene, or air, when he cried 'seccatura	444 Beppo		248
The world beheld them with indulgent air	446 Beppo		429
And of the fresher air, which he would seek	453 Venice-B		47
Our strength away in wrestling with the air	453 Venice-B		62
Troubles the clotted air, of late so blue	459 Dante	2	78
Of poesy, which peoples but the air	463 Dante	4	34
If it be so.--Spirits of earth and air	479 Manfred	1	41
As e'er revolved round sun in air	480 Manfred	1	113
Earth, ocean, air, night, mountains, winds, thy star	480 Manfred	1	132
And a spirit of the air	481 Manfred	1	224
A pastoral fable) pipes in the liberal air	482 Manfred	1	311
Is goodly, his mien manly, and his air	482 Manfred	1	324
The difficult air of the iced mountain's top	485 Manfred	2	157
As in itself hath power upon the air	486 Manfred	2	181
And spirits that do compass air and earth	486 Manfred	2	182
Daughter of Air! I tell thee, since that hour	486 Manfred	2	221
Hail to our Master!--Prince of Earth and Air	488 Manfred	2	371
My power extends no further. Prince of air	490 Manfred	2	481
A whisper, or a murmur, or an air	500 Faliero	1	57
O'ersweep all bounds and foam itself to air	502 Faliero	1	176
Whether the air will calm my spirits; 'tis	528 Faliero	4	24
The very air in Venice, and makes men	531 Faliero	4	238
Thine eyes are clear with youth;--the air puts on	534 Faliero	4	458
And for a moment, poised in middle air	535 Faliero	4	485
Into the air, and cries from tens of thousands	535 Faliero	4	501
The lifted sword in air--Ah! hark! it falls	549 Faliero	5	820
The free air of the city, and we'll shorten	568 Sardan	2	441
Let's leave this place, the air grows thick and choking	569 Sardan	2	458
Air worshippers? that is, when it is angry	572 Sardan	3	50
As sweeps the air and deluges the earth	576 Sardan	3	318
Purged by the flames, and wither'd in the air	580 Sardan	4	162
Faintness of o'erwrought passion: in the air	584 Sardan	4	418
The air with clamour) build the palaces	587 Sardan	5	27
The winds of heaven, and scatter'd into air	594 Sardan	5	478
Of air, yon window which o'erlooks the waters	596 Foscari	1	88
Of foreign air he draws seems a slow poison	600 Foscari	1	292
High in the air on her return to greet	608 Foscari	3	13
In my native air that buoy'd my spirits up	610 Foscari	3	129
And the sweet freedom of the earth and air	610 Foscari	3	145
Perhaps, in the air. I doubt not. Father--wife	617 Foscari	4	190
Not even its opposite, Love, so peoples air	620 Foscari	4	336
Earth, ocean, air, and fire, and with the day	627 Cain	1	10
To right, as in the dim blue air the eye	635 Cain	1	491
I tread on air, and sink not; yet I fear	636 Cain	2	1
Borne on the air, of which I am the prince	636 Cain	2	3
Air, where ye roll along, as I have seen	637 Cain	2	103
So thickly in the upper air, that I	639 Cain	2	209
Thou rulest in the upper air	656 Heaven		83
What other? That I know not; but her air	657 Heaven		179
Shall vex our joys in middle air	661 Heaven		427
No sign yet hangs its banner in the air	662 Heaven		549
What have we here? Shapes of both earth and air	662 Heaven		576
And the birds scream their agony through air	669 Heaven		1065
Hath wound itself around the dying air	669 Heaven		1077
An air and port and eye, which would have better	677 Werner	1	386
They served to air them, at the least as long	678 Werner	1	420
His sixteen quarterings, for as much fresh air	688 Werner	2	328
As air, despite the waters; let us hence	700 Werner	3	348
In years. 'Tis nothing; but if 'twere, the air	707 Werner	4	218
Not as with air, but by some subterrane	723 Deformed	1	79
The model in air	724 Deformed	1	167
Let him fleet on. Be air, thou hemlock-drinker	725 Deformed	1	229
As thou wavest in air	728 Deformed	1	399
From their proud nostrils, burns the very air	729 Deformed	1	514
Paws the ground and snuffs the air	730 Deformed	1	548
And the air is in trouble	742 Deformed	3	40
Their odours in the air	742 Deformed	3	71
Possess'd an air and grace by no means common	754 Juan	1	487
She seem'd by the distraction of her air	760 Juan	1	876
Sooner shall this blue ocean melt to air	776 Juan	2	147
The fourth day came, but not a breath of air	782 Juan	2	553
That waved in forest-tops, and smooth'd the air	787 Juan	2	820
They nearly reach'd her heel; and in her air	789 Juan	2	926
Was coarser; and her air, though firm, less free	789 Juan	2	974
Besides, I hate all mystery, and that air	789 Juan	2	987
Had all the advantage, too, of not being air	792 Juan	2	1136
And wrapt him closer, lest the air, too raw	792 Juan	2	1142
As o'er him lay the calm and stirless air	792 Juan	2	1148
'Stop!' cried Philosophy, with air so Grecian	801 Juan	2	1679
Over his shoulder, with a Bacchant air	806 Juan	3	338

AIR

The very air seem'd lighter from her eyes	810 Juan	3	586
Of ocean?--No, of air; and then he makes	814 Juan	3	878
And not a breath crept through the rosy air	815 Juan	3	911
Earth, air, stars,--all that springs from the great Whole	815 Juan	3	927
The heavens, and earth, and air, seem'd made for them	818 Juan	4	98
Stirr'd with her dream, as rose-leaves with the air	820 Juan	4	232
Terror to earth, and tempest to the air	823 Juan	4	452
And ever-dying Gladiator's air	824 Juan	4	486
Yet has a sentimental kind of air	827 Juan	4	678
Have got a travell'd air, which speaks you one	827 Juan	4	699
And air--earth--water--fire live--and we dead	836 Juan	5	310
The lady rising up with such an air	843 Juan	5	761
But just remark'd with air sedate and wise	851 Juan	5	1237
As doth a rainbow the just clearing air	855 Juan	6	184
Beating for love, as the caged bird's for air	855 Juan	6	208
Her shape, her hair, her air, her everything	856 Juan	6	274
Then one vast fire, air, earth, and stream embraced	879 Juan	8	53
He rush'd, while earth and air were sadly shaken	882 Juan	8	263
Air 'midst the rest, who kept their valiant faces	882 Juan	8	271
When the stripp'd forest bows to the bleak air	889 Juan	8	700
The letter open with an air which posed	903 Juan	9	460
As my friend Jeffrey writes with such an air	908 Juan	10	86
From the enjoyment of the earth and air	916 Juan	10	543
But doubtless as the air, though seldom sunny	916 Juan	10	559
Air can accomplish, with his wide wings waving	917 Juan	10	620
I don't know what the reason is--the air	919 Juan	11	38
An air as sentimental as Mozart's	924 Juan	11	371
Can form a slight acquaintance with fresh air	926 Juan	11	520
Dissolving in the waltz to some soft air	927 Juan	11	550
Besides the mark'd distinction of his air	940 Juan	12	678
And I shall take a much more serious air	967 Juan	14	789
Or that he had an air of innocence	971 Juan	15	221
But still her aspect had an air so lonely	973 Juan	15	347
And with an air, to say the least, imperious	974 Juan	15	390
The dashing and proud air of Adeline	975 Juan	15	441
Once, twice, thrice pass'd, repass'd--the thing of air	983 Juan	16	177
To put the question with an air sedate	985 Juan	16	278
The air of ' 'Twas a Friar of Orders Gray	985 Juan	16	304
For he mutters his prayer in the midnight air	985 Juan	16	323
The lawyers in the study; and in air	989 Juan	16	571
Who wonder'd at the abstraction of his air	992 Juan	16	771
Her Grace, too, had a sort of air rebuked	998 Juan	17	110

AIR-BALLOONS

Of air-balloons, and of the many bars	758 Juan	1	734

AIRED
(See ARED)

AIRIEST

Too subtle for the airiest human head	918 Juan	11	4

AIRS

For such are the airs of these fanciful fairs	115 Pigot		9
'Three who have stolen their witching airs from Cupid	171 Address-B		33
One envoy's letters, six composers' airs	274 Waltz		73
Beheld her airs and triumph, and all that	448 Beppo		548
While Adeline dispensed her airs and graces	993 Juan	16	841

AIRY

Yes, this was once Ambition's airy hall	20 Harold	2	48
Save where Tritonia's airy shrine adorns	33 Harold	2	812
With airy images, and shapes which dwell	36 Harold	3	44
At airy distance, with majestic motion	55 Harold	4	12
When, to their airy hall, my fathers' voice	85 Fragment-A		1
Who lead'st along, in airy dance	118 Romance		3
And roamis romantic o'er her airy fields	122 Recoil		30
My soul shall float on airy wing	133 Prayer		54
Though now on airy visions borne	133 E. N. Long		47
Soft as the last drops round heaven's airy bow	175 Sonnet-B		8
Its airy step and glorious eye	217 Gazelle		5
Invisible his airy wings	336 Abydos	2	691
And bathed his brow with airy balm	388 Corinth		361
The airy joys of social solitudes	422 Island	2	267
Even as the arrow finds the airy king	570 Sardan	2	570
The airy child of vapour and the sun	785 Juan	2	730
And love of glory's but an airy lust	829 Juan	4	802
An airy instrument, with which he sought	830 Juan	4	893
Of things destroy'd and left in airy doubt	901 Juan	9	300
Upon their airy confine, half-seas-over	915 Juan	10	488
But a mere airy and fantastic basis	956 Juan	14	55
But, light and airy, stood on the alert	960 Juan	14	289

AISLE

Yet strength was pillar'd in each massy aisle	4 Harold	1	58
Pillar'd into many an aisle	196 Venice-A		28
Slow sweeps he through the column'd aisle	319 Giaour		884

AISLE

As in some old cathedral's glimmering aisle   431 Island   4   133
The fretted pinnacle, the aisle, the nave   432 Island   4   153
In a grand arch, which once screen'd many an
  aisle   948 Juan   13   467

AISLED

Power, Glory, Strength, and Beauty, all are
  aisled   78 Harold   4   1385

AISLES

Though slaughter streams along her aisles   395 Corinth   959
Till all thine aisles be peopled with the dead   519 Faliero   3   28

AJAR

The door of which was half ajar, I saw   718 Werner   5   331
A kind of shock that sets one's heart ajar   775 Juan   2   110

AJAX

Patroclus, Ajax, or Protesilaus   826 Juan   4   607
This simile enough for Ajax, Juan   882 Juan   8   231
And though his name, than Ajax or Achilles   883 Juan   8   306

AKIN

Yet not the joy to which it seems akin   353 Corsair   2   452
Of the Familiar's torch, which seems akin   609 Foscari   3   53
And yet the time is not akin to thought   678 Werner   1   450

ALABASTER

And Alabaster and Morgante hover   468 Morgante   158
And flung by Passamont and Alabaster   469 Morgante   200
And Alabaster he found out below   470 Morgante   290
When Alabaster heard his deep voice ring   470 Morgante   295
I left your Passamont and Alabaster   471 Morgante   328
White, waxen, and as alabaster pale   865 Juan   6   868
Like to a lighted alabaster vase   890 Juan   8   768

ALACK

'Tis not my fault--I kept good watch--Alack   763 Juan   1   1092

ALACRITY

With light alacrity and gaze of pride   363 Corsair   3   498
Such confident alacrity. Your doubts   519 Faliero   3   52
I once had great alacrity in wielding   829 Juan   4   781
Was made with all alacrity: the first   873 Juan   7   394

ALADDIN'S

Yes! ready money is Aladdin's lamp   931 Juan   12   96

ALARIC

Stern Alaric and Havoc on their way   21 Harold   2   119
Know, Alaric and Elgin did the rest   269 Minerva   104
Alaric was a gentle foeman   736 Deformed   2   64

ALARICS

But yielded to the Alarics, the Alarics   734 Deformed   1   846

ALARIC'S

In Alaric's time? No, slave! in the first
  Caesar's   734 Deformed   1   855

ALARM

No fear, no wild alarm he knew   87 Catullus   7
Beat the loud alarm afar   194 Ballad-A   22
His name shall beat the alarm, like Ziska's drum   300 Age   130
With Echo for their chorus; nor the alarm   424 Island   2   422
My own from his, not to alarm him into   679 Werner   1   496
Like Ziska's skin, to beat alarm to all   682 Werner   1   695
To scold a little at the false alarm   862 Juan   6   627

ALARM'D

My visions fled, alarm'd I rose   88 Anacreon-A   11
But yet that heart, alarm'd or weak   326 Abydos   1   261
Ere night, alarm'd, their isle is traversed o'er   365 Corsair   3   681
His host alarm'd, his murmuring squires
  distress'd   376 Lara   2   108
So much alarm'd that she is quite alarming   445 Beppo   307
Fool! hence--what else should despotism alarm'd   569 Sardan   2   450
Have been alarm'd; but as the intendant is   702 Werner   3   483
The empress was alarm'd, and her physician   912 Juan   10   306

ALARMING

And near, the beat of the alarming drum   39 Harold   3   222
So much alarm'd that she is quite alarming   445 Beppo   307
Thing quite in course, and not at all alarming   757 Juan   1   687
And makes men's miseries of alarming brevity   782 Juan   2   512

ALARMS

Who, free from Jealousy's alarms   87 Ad Lesbiam   3
Adieu the clang of war's alarms   88 Anacreon-A   20
Has fill'd that breast with fond alarms   99 Young Lady   4
Then Nisus,--'Calm thy bosom's fond alarms   106 Nisus   53
Volscens with question loud the pair alarms   109 Nisus   307
Unite in concert with increased alarms   120 Newstead-A   56

ALARUM
(See also 'LARUM)

Ring the alarum bell! let folly quake   249 Bards   579
Peal in one wide alarum!--Go not forth   530 Faliero   4   167

ALAS

And that loved one, alas! could ne'er be his   4 Harold   1   40
Ah! such, alas, the hero's amplest fate   9 Harold   1   397
And now I view thee, 'tis, alas! with shame   14 Harold   1   623
Alas! too oft condemn'd for him to bear and bleed   16 Harold   1   746
Enough, alas, in humble homes remain   16 Harold   1   798
Alas! I cannot smile again   17 Harold   1   838
Nor yet, alas, the dreadful work is done   18 Harold   1   909
Come, blue-eyed maid of heaven!--but thou, alas   19 Harold   2   1
Alas, when mingling souls forget to blend   23 Harold   2   205
(Alas, her woes will still pervade my strain   32 Harold   2   751
Lingering like me, perchance, to gaze, and sigh
  'Alas   33 Harold   2   818
Over the unreturning brave,--alas   39 Harold   3   238
Of then destruction is; and now, alas   62 Harold   4   410
Alas, the lofty city! and alas   67 Harold   4   730
Alas, for Tully's voice, and Virgil's lay   67 Harold   4   734
Alas, for Earth, for never shall we see   67 Harold   4   737
Her new-born Numa thou--with reign, alas, too
  brief   72 Harold   4   1026
Alas! our young affections run to waste   73 Harold   4   1072
Alas! developed, opens the decay   76 Harold   4   1284
Alas! I wish'd but to o'ercome the pain   87 Tibullus   3
Who sighs, alas! but sighs in vain   87 Catullus   16
'Alas!' replies the wily child   88 Anacreon-B   13
Alas! that pang will be severe   89 To Emma   5
Alas, it were unhallow'd bliss   90 To M.S.G.-A   4
Alas! you can not love like me   90 Caroline-B   16
Alas! they love not long, who love so well   94 Dorset   86
Fonder, alas! they ne'er can be, love   98 To Lesbia   36
Alas! can pangs like these be just   103 Alva   144
'Alas!' the hapless sire replied   104 Alva   205
Alas! that eyes which beam'd with love   105 Alva   295
Alas, some slumber who shall wake no more   108 Nisus   226
Alas! again no more we meet   113 Quaker   41
Drooping, alas! we fall to rise no more   114 Prologue   20
Alas! must perish altogether   118 Romance   64
To Ida now, alas! for ever lost   123 Recoll   110
The smiles of beauty (for, alas! I've known   125 Recoll   199
Except, alas! thy jealous stings   131 L'Amitie   37
My youthful nymphs, alas! are flown   133 E. N. Long   63
Attempts, alas! to find in many   134 Lady-D   20
Though near, alas! distinctly flow   137 Clare   26
Piercing like yours, like yours, alas! unseen   140 Ossian-A   52
And much, alas! I think he needs it   148 To Author   6
The last, alas! can ne'er survive   148 A Fan   15
My visions are flown, to return,--alas, never   148 Farewell-A   12
Alas! whenever folly calls   153 Friend-A   53
And when, alas! our brains are gone   154 Skull   15
But mine, alas! has stood the blow   156 Lady-F   46
And show'd, alas! in each caress   164 Friend-B   39
But lull the chords, for now, alas   165 Away   6
Alas, it gleam'd upon her grave   166 Struggle   32
'Ay, but to die, and go,' alas   167 Euthanasia   29
Alas! they could not teach thee thine   168 The Chain   8
Severe the fate of modern fools, alas   171 Hales-Owen   9
Alas! I find them poison'd too   172 Romaic-B   8
Alas! too late, I dearly know   172 Romaic-B   43
This heart, alas! perverted long   174 Remember-B   29
Alas! for them, though not for thee   184 Parker   33
Alas! the sound--he sunk into Despair   184 Julian   27
'Friends! ye have, alas! to know   194 Ballad-A   36
Alas! how many things have been   197 Duel   44
And I was, what I am, Alas   197 Duel   50
Alas! it is delusion all   223 Music-D   9
A fourth, alas! were more than we could bear   245 Bards   228
The first of poets was, alas! but man   246 Bards   370
And we and ours, alas! are due to fate   258 Hints   91
'Alas, poor Yorick!' now forever mute   261 Hints   335
Alas! I cannot 'strike at wretched kernes   265 Hints   602
Alas! woe worth the scribbler! often seen   266 Hints   725
If so, alas! 'tis nature in the man   267 Hints   751
Though fallen, alas! this vengeance yet is mine   270 Minerva   159
Alas, Sir Harry is no Hercules   271 Minerva   194
On Pallas calls,--but calls, alas! too late   271 Minerva   250
But the heat forced me out in the best part--alas   281 Blues   2   35
In this poor planet's conquest; nor, alas   290 Vision   315
Alas! why pass'd he too the Rubicon   300 Age   138
Beholds him conquer but, alas! not die   301 Age   204
Alas! why must the same Atlantic wave   301 Age   253
Alas! thou wilt not conquer, but purvey   304 Age   475
Alas, the country! how shall tongue or pen   305 Age   568
Alas! how could his cabinet thus err   308 Age   721
Alas! that name was not for thee   315 Giaour   518
Alas! though both bestow'd in vain   319 Giaour   870
And I, alas! too late to save   320 Giaour   1070
Alas! the breast that inly bleeds   321 Giaour   1155
Alas! the dreamer first must sleep   322 Giaour   1259
Alas! around a shadow prest   323 Giaour   1296

ALAS

And I, alas! am Giaffir's child	330 Abydos	2	180
To one, alas! assign'd in vain	331 Abydos	2	235
Avenge his lord? alas! too late	332 Abydos	2	282
No prize, alas!--but yet a welcome sail	339 Corsair	1	85
That met my sight--it near'd--Alas! it pass'd	343 Corsair	1	386
Alas! those eyes beheld his rocky tower	346 Corsair	1	579
A long-known voice--alas! too vainly near	359 Corsair	3	257
Alas! this love, that hatred are the first	360 Corsair	3	351
Alas, he told not! but he did awake	368 Lara	1	129
That hears him not--alas, that cannot hear	369 Lara	1	234
Alas! that heedlessness of all around	373 Lara	1	488
Alas! too like in confidence are each	373 Lara	1	506
Alas! they blaze too widely for the flight	379 Lara	2	329
Alas! we must awake before	397 Parisina		47
Alas! my own was full as chill	404 Chillon		222
A band of chiefs!--alas! how few	407 Mazeppa		45
My sight return'd, though dim, alas	412 Mazeppa		577
How slow, alas, he came	413 Mazeppa		644
Alas! his deck was trod by unwilling feet	415 Island	1	25
Awake! awake!--Alas, it is too late	416 Island	1	52
Alas, such is our nature! all but aim	417 Island	1	115
Seems far less fragile, and, alas! more free	417 Island	1	136
Alas! for them the flower of mankind bleeds	419 Island	2	37
Alas! for them our fields are rank with weeds	419 Island	2	38
The plash of hostile oars.--Alas! who made	429 Island	3	215
And if my eyes reveal'd it, they, alas	438 Tasso		126
Irreparably soon decline, alas	447 Beppo		477
Alas! how bitter is his country's curse	457 Dante	1	69
Alas! with what a weight upon my brow	457 Dante	1	130
Faints o'er the labour unapproved--Alas	463 Dante	4	38
The ashes thou shalt ne'er obtain--Alas	465 Dante	4	140
And recommended: 'Alas! unto such ill	476 Francesca		16
Alas! he's mad--but yet I must not leave him	484 Manfred	2	59
Things in my path which are no more. Alas	493 Manfred	3	135
Alas! lost mortal! what with guests like these	496 Manfred	3	333
Alas! how pale thou art--thy lips are white	496 Manfred	3	402
But yet one prayer--Alas! how fares it with thee	497 Manfred	3	410
Alas! my friend, you seek it of the twain	505 Faliero	1	359
Alas! I must not think of them, but those	508 Faliero	1	616
Pride, Angiolina! Alas! none is left me	511 Faliero	2	206
That he was linking thee to shame!--Alas	512 Faliero	2	274
Alas! why will you thus consider it	514 Faliero	2	409
To those who hear, and those who speak. Alas	538 Faliero	5	
Alas! I fain you died in peace with me	539 Faliero	5	130
Is he condemn'd? Alas! And was he guilty	543 Faliero	5	343
Not in this case with justice. Alas! signor	543 Faliero	5	363
Unto the rock: but as there are--alas	544 Faliero	5	422
Still falling--I have done with Time. Alas	546 Faliero	5	582
Still keep--Thou turn'st so pale! Alas! she faints	547 Faliero	5	688
He must be roused. Alas! there is no sound	551 Sardan	1	27
To be indulgent to my own. Alas	555 Sardan	1	325
Do more? Alas! my lord, with common men	559 Sardan	1	578
Alas! thou art pale, and on thy brow the drops	579 Sardan	4	38
And children. Alas! Hear me, sister, like	584 Sardan	4	368
I strive to keep it from my thoughts. Alas	588 Sardan	5	75
Might sadden even a victory. Alas	590 Sardan	5	178
Command us. I command!--Alas! my life	598 Foscari	1	200
They shall not balk my entrance. Alas! this	599 Foscari	1	258
Alas! how should you? she knows not herself	603 Foscari	2	85
As it, alas! has been, to ostracism	608 Foscari	2	425
His own and his beloved's name. Alas	608 Foscari	3	24
How dost thou? How are those worn limbs? Alas	609 Foscari	3	45
I may breathe many years. Alas! and this	609 Foscari	3	94
I ne'er saw aught here like a ray. Alas	609 Foscari	3	106
Alas! I little thought so lingeringly	614 Foscari	3	411
My son, you are feeble; take this hand. Alas	614 Foscari	3	455
Look back. I pray you think of me. Alas	616 Foscari	4	108
Where are your storms? In human breasts. Alas	616 Foscari	4	123
Your hand! Take it. Alas, how thine own trembles	617 Foscari	4	180
Alas! I have shed some--always thanks to you	626 Foscari	5	357
Dost thou not live? Must I not die? Alas	628 Cain	1	29
Alas! I scarcely now know what it is	632 Cain	1	295
It is not tranquil. Alas, no! and you	635 Cain	1	481
And I will weep for thee. Alas! those tears	635 Cain	1	516
Fallen, all had stood. Alas, the hopeless wretches	641 Cain	2	362
Taught thee to know thyself? Alas! I seem	645 Cain	2	625
Alas! thou sinnest now, my Cain: thy words	647 Cain	3	93
Oh, Anah! But she loves thee not. Alas	657 Heaven		168
Alas! what am I better than ye are	659 Heaven		282
Alas! what else is love but sorrow? Even	665 Heaven		727
Alas! where shall they dwell	668 Heaven		990
And have of late been sickly, as, alas	672 Werner	1	20
Enjoy'd them, loved them, and, alas! abused them	672 Werner	1	78
Even to our very hopes.--Ha! ha! Alas!	673 Werner	1	113
The river has o'erflowed. Alas! we have known	674 Werner	1	210
I have my doubts if he means well. Alas	681 Werner	1	648
Away! Alas, that I should doubt of thee	683 Werner	1	751
Alas! I have had that upon my soul	688 Werner	2	367
Think as he speaks. Alas! long years of grief	690 Werner	2	500
What have I done? Alas! what had I done	697 Werner	3	108

ALAS

Alas! what is a menial to a deathbed	707 Werner	4	190
Alas! Love never did so. Then 'tis time	710 Werner	4	388
Did he who own'd it die in his bed? Alas	712 Werner	4	503
And by the dawn there will be work. Alas	731 Deformed	1	604
But thy hearths, alas! oh, Rome	736 Deformed	2	100
Alas! that the first beat of the only heart	741 Deformed	2	389
But who, alas! can love, and then be wise	761 Juan	1	933
Alas! 'twas not in them, but in thy power	773 Juan	1	1711
Say very often to myself, 'Alas	773 Juan	1	1754
Their veil and petticoat--Alas! to dwell	774 Juan	2	44
Or rather stomach, which, alas! attends	776 Juan	2	162
Had left their bodies; and what's worse, alas	781 Juan	2	434
Alas! they were so young, so beautiful	798 Juan	2	1529
Alas! for Juan and Haidee! they were	798 Juan	2	1537
Alas! the love of women! it is known	799 Juan	2	1585
He hears--alas! no music of the spheres	805 Juan	3	219
He did not know (alas! how men will lie	806 Juan	3	297
Alas! his country show'd no path to praise	808 Juan	3	438
Alas! there is no instinct like the heart	817 Juan	4	80
'Alas!' said Juan, ''t were a tale distressing	833 Juan	5	125
Alas! man makes that great which makes him little	838 Juan	5	465
Where all the passions have, alas! but one vent	856 Juan	6	256
Newton (that proverb of the mind), alas	867 Juan	7	37
Alas! what to their memory can lack	868 Juan	7	109
Whose statues warm (I fear, alas! too true 'tis	903 Juan	9	406
Unequal matches, such as are, alas	910 Juan	10	187
Alas, that glory should be chill'd by snow	914 Juan	10	469
Alas! could she but fully, truly, know	915 Juan	10	529
Alas, how deeply painful is all payment	917 Juan	10	625
The world in which a man was born?' Alas	927 Juan	11	594
Besides (alas! his taste--forgive and pity	938 Juan	12	543
Alas! must noblest views, like an old song	942 Juan	13	77
Alas! to them of ready cash bereft	946 Juan	13	355
The days of Comedy are gone, alas	953 Juan	13	749
'Alas, poor ghost!'--What unexpected woes	953 Juan	13	775
Alas! worlds fall--and woman, since she fell'd	958 Juan	14	177
But till that point d'appui is found, alas	966 Juan	14	671
Alas! by all experience, seldom yet	967 Juan	14	753
In their resolves--alas! that I should say so	969 Juan	15	44
By death, when we are left, alas! behind	973 Juan	15	350
It was not--but 'tis easier far, alas	975 Juan	15	431
Alas! I must leave undescribed the gibier	977 Juan	15	561
But I have dined, and must forego, alas	977 Juan	15	567
Treating a topic which, alas! but brings	980 Juan	15	782
That scarlet cloak, alas! unclosed with rigour	988 Juan	16	535
There were some country wags too--and, alas	991 Juan	16	689
Alas! her star must fade like that of Dian	995 Juan	16	915
Came over Juan's ear, which throbb'd, alas	995 Juan	16	957
They reveal'd--alas! that e'er they should	996 Juan	16	1030

ALASHTAR

Because of Alashtar	232 Murray-B		17

ALBAN

And from the Alban Mount we now behold	81 Harold	4	1572

ALBANIA

Land of Albania, where Iskander rose	25 Harold	2	334
Land of Albania, let me bend mine eyes	25 Harold	2	338

ALBANIAN

The Turk, the Greek, the Albanian, and the Moor	28 Harold	2	511
The wild Albanian kirtled to his knee	28 Harold	2	514
Here the Albanian proudly treads the ground	28 Harold	2	527

ALBANIA'S

Morn dawns; and with it stern Albania's hills	25 Harold	2	370
To greet Albania's chief, whose dread command	26 Harold	2	418
Fierce are Albania's children, yet they lack	29 Harold	2	577

ALBANO'S

And near Albano's scarce divided waves	81 Harold	4	1558
Here danced Albano's boys, and here the sea shone	950 Juan	13	565

ALBEIT

And strike, albeit with untaught melody	5 Harold	1	111
Albeit unworthy of the prey-bird's maw	18 Harold	1	905
Would still, albeit in vain, the heavy heart divest	23 Harold	2	216
Love kept aloof, albeit not far remote	24 Harold	2	274
And, sunk albeit in thought as he was wont	25 Harold	2	368
Nor shrank from one albeit unworthy thee	34 Harold	2	894
Albeit my brow thou never shouldst behold	53 Harold	3	1072
Albeit too dazzling for a dotard's sight	183 Address-D		44
Albeit for such I could despise a crown	206 Greece		3
Albeit against my own perchance	325 Abydos	1	125
And must I say? albeit my heart rebel	360 Corsair	3	292
If this thou dost accord, albeit	391 Corinth		635
Albeit my birth and name be base	399 Parisina		282
He feels his spirits soaring--albeit weak	453 Venice-B		46
These mountains, albeit that they are obscure	468 Morgante		178
Pray--albeit but in thought,--but die not thus	497 Manfred	3	405
Nor doom ye guiltless; albeit better men	566 Sardan	2	291

ALBEIT

Albeit his marble face majestical	570 Sardan	2	532
Albeit thou watchest with 'the seven	655 Heaven		40
Albeit thou art not; 'tis a word I cannot	664 Heaven		667
(Albeit I never pass'd them), I'll not answer	696 Werner	3	103
And Juan and his friend, albeit they heard	837 Juan	5	394
Unconscious, albeit turn'd of quick seventeen	859 Juan	6	430
Even I--albeit I'm sure I did not know it	925 Juan	11	437
Albeit my years were less discreet than few	934 Juan	12	300
Albeit all human history attests	953 Juan	13	790
And eats her parents, albeit the digestion	955 Juan	14	10
'Twixt place and patriotism--albeit compell'd	990 Juan	16	620

ALBIN'S

Though far from Albin's craggy shore	158 Florence		9

ALBION

Of mighty strength, since Albion was allied	6 Harold	1	220
The shouts are France, Spain, Albion, Victory	10 Harold	1	444
Albion was happy in Athena's tears	21 Harold	2	110
Albion, to thee: the Ocean queen should not	57 Harold	4	151
For though I fly from Albion	156 Lady-F		17
'Fair Albion, smiling, sees her son depart	162 Orchomenus		1
Be known, perchance, when Albion is no more	254 Bards		945
And rise more worthy, Albion, of thy name	255 Bards		998
'Tis thine at once, fair Albion! to have been	255 Bards		1001
And left lost Albion hated and alone	271 Minerva		220
And Gaul shall weep ere Albion wear her chains	272 Minerva		284
Nay, frown not, Albion! for the torch was thine	272 Minerva		307
How first to Albion found thy Waltz her way	274 Waltz		58
Shall·noble Albion pass without a phrase	305 Age		528
'Twas a great banquet, such as Albion old	991 Juan	16	666

ALBION'S

Whilome in Albion's isle there dwelt a youth	3 Harold	1	10
When Albion's lessening shores could grieve or glad mine eye	35 Harold	3	9
Yet still are you dearer than Albion's plain	118 Lachin		36
For long as Albion's heedless sons submit	248 Bards		502
The floating fence of Albion's feebler crag	454 Venice-B		146
At the first sight of Albion's chalky belt	915 Juan	10	516
Don Juan now saw Albion's earliest beauties	916 Juan	10	545
Make this a sacred part of Albion's isle	921 Juan	11	192

ALBUERA

Oh, Albuera, glorious field of grief	11 Harold	1	459
Not Albuera lavish of the dead	18 Harold	1	920

ALBYN'S

The war-note of Lochiel, which Albyn's hills	39 Harold	3	227
She on high Albyn's dusky hills may raise	182 Address-C		21
To see proud Albyn's tartans as a belt	308 Age		773

ALCAEUS

Lo! sad Alcaeus wanders down the vale	247 Bards		419

ALCHEMY

The stubborn heart, its alchemy begun	73 Harold	4	1106

ALCHYMIC

Of some alchymic furnace, from whence broke	918 Juan	10	659

ALCHYMIST

A little king, a lucky alchymist	700 Werner	3	340
And prophet, pontiff, doctor, alchymist	732 Deformed	1	675

ALCHYMY

The grand agrarian alchymy, high rent	306 Age		581
The ghost of this rouleau. Here's alchymy	684 Werner	2	76
Joy of its alchymy, and to repeat	800 Juan	2	1621

ALCIBIADES

Because he had, like Alcibiades	969 Juan	15	87

ALCIDES

Alcides with the distaff now he seem'd	68 Harold	4	809
Alcides and his glorious deeds	88 Anacreon-A		15
The demi-diety, Alcides, in	514 Faliero	2	390
Before, that he were Grecian. If Alcides	575 Sardan	3	218

ALCINA

That magic palace of Alcina shows	307 Age		662

ALDABELLA

Which Aldabella thought extremely strange	468 Morgante		139

ALDABELLE

And when she saw him coming, Aldabelle	468 Morgante		132

ALDERMAN

Wild as the wife of alderman or peer	266 Hints		693
To hail their brother, Vich Ian Alderman	308 Age		770
A priest, a shark, an alderman, or pike	794 Juan	2	1256
But most, an alderman struck apoplectic	809 Juan	3	525

ALDERMAN

Who loved blood·as an alderman loves marrow	868 Juan	7	64

ALE

Vain as their honours, heavy as their ale	112 Examination		59
The chicken's toughness, and the lack of ale	224 J.C.H.		15
Twin Doric minstrels, drunk with Doric ale	266 Hints		732
But where is now the goodly audit ale	306 Age		590
But such as wafts its cloud o'er grog or ale	425 Island	2	437
Sweet is old wine in bottles, ale in barrels	762 Juan	1	1005
A mighty mug of moral double ale	989 Juan	16	580

ALEHOUSE

But daub a shipwreck like an alehouse sign	257 Hints		32

ALEPPO

He was a merchant trading to Aleppo	443 Beppo		199

ALERT

But here 'tis fit we keep on the alert in	469 Morgante		197
Suwarrow chiefly was on the alert	874 Juan	7	433
But, light and airy, stood on the alert	960 Juan	14	289

ALETHES

Moved by the speech, Alethes here exclaim'd	107 Nisus		120

ALETHES'

And old Alethes' casque defends his brows	108 Nisus		216

ALEXANDER

Than a mere Alexander, and, unstain'd	71 Harold	4	997
Rather a worm than such an Alexander	304 Age		479
I think with Alexander, that the act	835 Juan	5	249
But oh, thou grand legitimate Alexander	863 Juan	6	737
I am neither Alexander nor Hephaestion	898 Juan	9	107
Shut up the bald-coot bully Alexander	965 Juan	14	657

ALEXANDER'S

Though Alexander's urn a show be grown	298 Age		31
Since Alexander's days till now	408 Mazeppa		103

ALEXIS

From Corydon unkind Alexis turns	265 Hints		620

ALFAQUI

Out then spake old Alfaqui	194 Ballad-A		41
Moor Alfaqui! Moor Alfaqui	195 Ballad-A		71

ALFIERI'S

Angelo's, Alfieri's bones, and his	63 Harold	4	484

ALFONSO

And where Alfonso bade his poet dwell	60 Harold	4	319
Alfonso! how thy ducal pageants shrink	60 Harold	4	331
Like king Alfonso. When I thus see double	297 Vision		807
Alfonso was the name of Julia's lord	755 Juan	1	513
For Don Alfonso; and she inly swore	760 Juan	1	866
By this time Don Alfonso was arrived	763 Juan	1	1097
'In heaven's name, Don Alfonso, what d'ye mean	764 Juan	1	1130
Search, then, the room!'--Alfonso said, 'I will	764 Juan	1	1136
A husband like Alfonso at my side	764 Juan	1	1158
'Yes, Don Alfonso! husband now no more	764 Juan	1	1161
Ungrateful, perjured, barbarous Don Alfonso	764 Juan	1	1167
The Senhor Don Alfonso stood confused	766 Juan	1	1265
But Don Alfonso stood with downcast looks	766 Juan	1	1281
Alfonso saw his wife, and thought of Job's	766 Juan	1	1294
Or madam dies.'--Alfonso mutter'd, 'D--n her	767 Juan	1	1301
What's to be done? Alfonso will be back	767 Juan	1	1345
Now, Don Alfonso entering, but alone	768 Juan	1	1377
Alfonso paused a minute--then begun	768 Juan	1	1385
Alfonso ne'er to Juan had alluded	768 Juan	1	1410
Alfonso closed his speech, and begg'd her pardon	769 Juan	1	1433
Alfonso first examined well their fashion	769 Juan	1	1447
But met Alfonso in his dressing-gown	769 Juan	1	1463
Alfonso, pommell'd to his heart's desire	769 Juan	1	1468
Alfonso grappled to detain the foe	769 Juan	1	1481
Alfonso leaning, breathless, by the door	770 Juan	1	1492
And how Alfonso sued for a divorce	770 Juan	1	1503

ALFONSO'S

That Inez had, ere Don Alfonso's marriage	755 Juan	1	527
And complimented Don Alfonso's taste	755 Juan	1	534
Perhaps to open Don Alfonso's eyes	759 Juan	1	807
And then of Don Alfonso's fifty years	760 Juan	1	852
Could enter into Don Alfonso's head	764 Juan	1	1106
In Don Alfonso's facts, which just now wore	767 Juan	1	1310
Alfonso's loves with Inez were well known	768 Juan	1	1402
Like throwing Juan in Alfonso's way	768 Juan	1	1416
Haste--haste! I hear Alfonso's hurrying feet	769 Juan	1	1455
Alfonso's sword had dropp'd ere he could draw it	769 Juan	1	1473
Alfonso's days had not been in the land	769 Juan	1	1478

ALGIERS

Who took Algiers, declares I used him vilely	765 Juan	1	1184

ALHAMA
Woe is me, Alhama	194 Ballad-A		5ff
Woe is me, Alhama	195 Ballad-A		55ff
'But on my soul Alhama weighs	195 Ballad-A		86

ALHAMA'S
How Alhama's city fell	194 Ballad-A		7
Have obtain'd Alhama's hold	194 Ballad-A		39
For Alhama's loss displeased	195 Ballad-A		74

ALHAMBRA
| To the Alhambra spurring in | 194 Ballad-A | | 14 |
| When the Alhambra walls he gain'd | 194 Ballad-A | | 16 |

ALHAMBRA'S
| High Alhambra's loftiest stone | 195 Ballad-A | | 77 |
| And to the Alhambra's wall with speed | 195 Ballad-A | | 103 |

ALI
Ali reclined, a man of war and woes	28 Harold	2	554
A chief ever glorious like Ali Pashaw	31 Harold	2	684
Which defied the arms of Ali	240 Suliotes		8

ALICANT
| Guitars and castanets from Alicant | 803 Juan | 3 | 134 |

ALIENS
| And aliens from your God, Farewell | 668 Heaven | | 989 |
| (As it is call'd) are aliens to each other | 699 Werner | 3 | 258 |

ALIGHT
On Wordswords, for instance, I seldom alight	282 Blues	2	97
For angels to alight on, as the spot	659 Heaven		296
But let the consequence alight on him	716 Werner	5	201
Around us ever, rarely to alight	867 Juan	7	2

ALIGHTING
| Alighting cheerly to inspire | 385 Corinth | | 107 |
| Alighting rarely:--were she but a hornet | 952 Juan | 13 | 711 |

ALIKE
All have their fooleries; not alike are thine	15 Harold	1	711
Alike beheld beneath pale Hecate's blaze	22 Harold	2	193
Churchman and votary alike despised	26 Harold	2	391
That those who loathe alike the Frank and Turk	29 Harold	2	602
Preserves alike its bounds and boundless fame	33 Harold	2	839
Thine is a scene alike where souls united	44 Harold	3	565
His task and mine alike are nearly done	81 Harold	4	1569
Alike the Armada's pride or spoils of Trafalgar	82 Harold	4	1629
To him, alike, are always known	87 Ad Lesbiam		7
By Death's unequal hand alike controll'd	87 Marsus		3
But now tears and curses, alike unavailing	92 Caroline-D		13
Alike for courts, and camps, or senates fit	94 Dorset		70
And lull'd alike the cares of brute and man	106 Nisus		86
Alike through life esteem'd, thou godlike boy	107 Nisus		169
While friends and foes alike his talents own	114 Death-A		32
Their sneers or censures I alike despise	119 Answer-A		44
His name and precepts be alike forgot	123 Recoll		118
These shall survive alike when son and sire	124 Recoll		157
While future hope and fear alike unknown	127 Recoll		375
Festering alike in shrouds, consume	128 Answer-B		32
Love, Hope, and Joy, alike adieu	128 Remembrance		6
His beams alike to all displays	134 E. N. Long		72
To flourish alike, or to perish together	147 To Anne-B		12
Though smile and sigh alike are vain	159 Storm		69
Alike she knows not to dissemble	160 Cadiz		28
When love and life alike were new	166 Struggle		42
Alike been all employ'd in vain	168 Cornelian-B		4
Must sue alike for pardon or for praise	170 Address-A		53
To her and thee alike is given	173 Mrs. Lamb		6
And both were young--yet not alike in youth	214 Dream		43
Our bards and censors are so much alike	243 Bards		92
While Milton, Dryden, Pope, alike forgot	244 Bards		187
Renown'd alike; whose genius ne'er confines	250 Bards		600
Alike the rustic and mechanic soul	252 Bards		790
And 'scape alike the law's and muse's wrath	253 Bards		826
Our life and language must alike obey	258 Hints		104
Times dear alike to puritan or pope	262 Hints		376
Are damn'd alike by gods and men and columns	265 Hints		588
Alike reserved for aye to stand accursed	271 Minerva		205
See all alike of more or less bereft	271 Minerva		243
Who gods and men alike disdain'd to hear	271 Minerva		248
In some few qualities alike--for hock	274 Waltz		33
With vests or ribands--deck'd alike in hue	276 Waltz		175
Varied above, but still alike below	298 Age		27
Alike the better-seeing shade will smile	300 Age		119
Pollute the plains, alike abhorring both	302 Age		323
Contented subjects, all alike tax-proof	305 Age		533
I speak not of the Sovereigns--they're alike	307 Age		706
Alike must Wealth and Poverty	313 Giaour		344
His faith and race alike unknown	318 Giaour		807
Alike all time abhor'd, all place	322 Giaour		1196
Earth--sea alike--our world within our arms	333 Abydos	2	453
Lone, wild, and strange, he stood alike exempt	342 Corsair	1	271

ALIKE
Arrives, let him alike these orders mark	346 Corsair	1	566
Equipp'd for deeds alike on land or deep	347 Corsair	1	604
My thanks and praise alike are due--now hear	358 Corsair	3	176
His steel and impious prayer attract alike	359 Corsair	3	266
Well speeds alike the banquet and the ball	371 Lara	1	388
Alike in naked helplessness recline	375 Lara	1	641
Alike without their monumental stone	383 Lara	2	599
But sound and sight alike are gone	401 Parisina		497
Alike mysterious and intense	409 Mazeppa		239
Alike uplifted gloriously to God	424 Island	2	375
Perchance might suit alike with either race	425 Island	2	485
Shall find alike such sounds for every theme	458 Dante	2	26
Half dust, half deity, alike unfit	482 Manfred	1	301
Thy mind and body are alike unfit	483 Manfred	2	2
Endless, and all alike, as sands on the shore	484 Manfred	2	54
Heaven will alike forgive you and your foes	512 Faliero	2	263
Alike to them Marcello or Cornaro	533 Faliero	4	373
Alike by accusation or defence	538 Faliero	5	61
Distract within, both will alike prove fatal	552 Sardan	1	126
Alike made difficult; but I have such	596 Foscari	1	43
Sweeps after that before it, alike whelming	596 Foscari	1	58
Without a name, is alike nothing, when	607 Foscari	2	411
To me all hours are alike. Let them approach	620 Foscari	5	4
For then we are all alike; is't not so, Cain	648 Cain	3	143
Only one parent. I have lost alike	690 Werner	2	487
Likeness and fame alike rest in some panes	697 Werner	3	122
Her dowry; and her veil, in form alike	789 Juan	2	973
Were link'd alike, as for the common people he	803 Juan	3	127
I said they were alike, their features and	822 Juan	4	353
The time must come, when both alike decay'd	829 Juan	4	829
And were all clad alike; like Juan, too	844 Juan	5	787
They all alike admired their new connection	857 Juan	6	320
Alike might puzzle either wit or dunce	861 Juan	6	588
His jest alike in face of friend or foe	887 Juan	8	558
With good, and bad, and worse, alike prolific	889 Juan	8	708
Such was his tact, he could alike delight	960 Juan	14	325
At the full board, and sit alike delighted	989 Juan	16	597

ALIQUID
| 'Surgit amari aliquid'--the toll | 917 Juan | 10 | 624 |

ALIT
| And once so near me he alit | 414 Mazeppa | | 776 |

ALIVE
And our breasts, which alive with such sympathy glow	91 Caroline-C		22
'Here's to my boy! alive or dead	104 Alva		227
So abject--yet alive	180 Ode-A		4
All damn'd, though yet alive	225 Orraca		4
And sends his goods to market--all alive	247 Bards		389
Since Jonas only springs alive from whales	264 Hints		540
Dug up from dust, though buried when alive	266 Hints		722
Burst from your lead and be yourselves alive	275 Waltz		136
He saw him bound; and bleeding--but alive	357 Corsair	3	109
Yet seem'd as lately they had been alive	367 Lara	1	82
Of one that haunts him still, alive or dead	377 Lara	2	156
But felt that I was still alive	404 Chillon		224
Alive and fetterless;--but silent all	427 Island	3	81
That he's alive, he's dead, or should be so	444 Beppo		280
Well, that's the prettiest shawl--as I'm alive	451 Beppo		732
Oh, that he were alive, and I in ashes	508 Faliero	1	587
Or that he were alive ere I be ashes	508 Faliero	1	588
Not now:--being still alive, I'd have him live	512 Faliero	2	236
The dust we tread upon was once alive	579 Sardan	4	65
Alive, or dead, for prince or paladin	604 Foscari	2	161
Alive to love, are yet awake to terror	614 Foscari	3	374
You touch me not alive. Alive or dead	739 Deformed	2	298
Alive or dead, thou essence of all beauty	741 Deformed	2	380
Or be alive again--again all hoar	746 Juan	Ded	84
That lures, to flay alive, the young beginner	806 Juan	3	286
At least to all those who were left alive	884 Juan	8	372
I wonder people should be left alive	930 Juan	12	11

ALKALI
| As acids rouse a dormant alkali | 914 Juan | 10 | 428 |

ALL
Some days of joyaunce are decreed to all	32 Harold	2	743
Whose fertile bounties here extend to all	45 Harold	3	588
Is shameful to the nations,--most of all	57 Harold	4	150
Perchance she died in age--surviving all	70 Harold	4	919
On their foundations, and unalter'd all	77 Harold	4	1303
Which gathers shadow, substance, life, and all	79 Harold	4	1477
Thy beauty must enrapture all	97 To M--		19
But he, who foretold the fate of all	108 Nisus		243
'Thou youth accurst, thy life shall pay for all	110 Nisus		360
Though my heart they enthral, I'd abandon them all	115 Pigot		23
If since on Granta's failings, known to all	123 Recoll		93
Must share the common tomb of all	128 Answer-B		14
For Cora's eye will shine on all	134 E. N. Long		70
My hope, my comforter, my all	135 I Would		42

ALL

That he, who sang before all	137 Clare		45
'Tis Vanity, which rules you all	143 To-A		7
For like the Sun, it shines on All	143 On Eyes		4
Each Nymph, of course, was all perfection	144 Becher-B		28
Too soon forget they loved at all	153 Friend-A		8
Come to task all	157 Hodgson		10
Poor Joe is gone, but left his all	163 Blacket		3
Like mine, is wild and worthless all	174 Remember-B		34
Some paid rather more--but all worse dress'd than Waiters	178 Devil's Dr		162
'Aye--Aye'--quoth he--''t is the way with them all	178 Devil's Dr		197
Against it I would warn all	179 Devil's Dr		220
But thou, the weakest, worst of all	185 Belshaz-A		7
Then he fell:--so perish all	187 Ode-B		34
To them thy banks were lovely as to all	192 Sonnet-C		5
Which all embraced--and lighten'd over all	193 Monody		35
Thy Lover died, as All	201 Ode-C		59
Shivering thine imaged charms and all	201 Ode-C		73
Or, has it not bound thee the fastest of all	203 Avatar		71
Thy Grattan, thy Curran, thy Sheridan, all	204 Avatar		114
The kind--and thee the most of all	210 Augusta-A		36
Deserved to be dearest of all	210 Augusta-B		44
That he was wretched, but she saw not all	214 Dream		94
A thought unseen, but seeing all	220 Clay		10
Alas! it is delusion all	223 Music-D		9
So now they're condemn'd by no Judges at all	225 Ode-D		24
They voted me to Newgate all	235 New Song		7
Ode, epic, elegy, have at you all	242 Bards		46
Traduced by liars, and forgot by all	251 Bards		684
And 'tis some praise in peers to write at all	251 Bards		720
If your heart triumph when the hands of all	259 Hints		215
To all their income, and to--twice its tax	265 Hints		648
They storm the types, they publish, one and all	266 Hints		713
Form'd a sepulchral melodrame. Of all	286 Vision		73
A part of that vast all they held of old	291 Vision		379
Around our congress, and dispense with all	293 Vision		516
Assembled, and exclaim'd, 'My friends of all	293 Vision		530
Was really, truly, nobody at all	295 Vision		640
Times present, past, to come, heaven, hell, and all	297 Vision		806
The blest Alliance, which says three are all	303 Age		395
One half the poet's, all the gourmand's art	305 Age		523
Kings, conquerors, and markets most of all	305 Age		575
She stood superior to them all	315 Giaour		499
The youngest, most beloved of all	318 Giaour		768
To me she gave her heart, that all	320 Giaour		1068
I grant my love imperfect, all	321 Giaour		1141
My father was to Giaffir all	331 Abydos	2	197
I sought by turns, and saw them all	332 Abydos	2	357
Friendship for each, and faith to all	332 Abydos	2	371
And some--and I have studied all	332 Abydos	2	375
He was thy hope--thy joy--thy love--thine all	336 Abydos	2	636
To pay the injuries of some on all	342 Corsair	1	264
Ay--Pride can veil, and Courage brave it all	352 Corsair	2	359
'Yes, loth indeed! my soul is nerved to all	354 Corsair	2	468
He snatch'd the lamp--its light will answer all	364 Corsair	3	591
Each trace wax'd fainter of his course, till all	366 Lara	1	27
There was in him a vital scorn of all	370 Lara	1	313
The words of many, and the eyes of all	373 Lara	1	484
Now lost, abjured, for one--his friend, his all	373 Lara	1	525
And mark'd that sudden strife so mark'd of all	374 Lara	1	593
Nor gale breathe forth one sigh for thee, for all	375 Lara	2	16
And he, incensed and heedless of them all	376 Lara	2	92
By mingling with his own the cause of all	378 Lara	2	240
In this the struggle was the same with all	379 Lara	2	269
But that vain victory hath ruined all	379 Lara	2	284
Commanding, aiding, animating all	380 Lara	2	368
Sought thee in safety through foes and all	390 Corinth		566
For I had buried one and all	405 Chillon		320
And they seem'd joyous each and all	406 Chillon		352
A shock to one--a thunderbolt to all	407 Mazeppa		14
And thus it was; but yet through all	407 Mazeppa		39
And knew him in the midst of all	407 Mazeppa		73
My days and nights were nothing, all	409 Mazeppa		301
To-morrow would have given him all	414 Mazeppa		753
That I had nought to fear, that all	415 Mazeppa		835
Yet then, even then, his feelings ceased not all	417 Island	1	155
To rise, if just, a spirit o'er them all	421 Island	2	162
But 'twas not all long ages' lore, nor all	423 Island	2	288
Alive and fetterless;--but silent all	427 Island	3	81
But, ah, how different! 'tis the cause makes all	433 Island	4	261
But now the die was to be thrown, and all	433 Island	4	275
Told all she had seen, and all she hoped, and all	435 Island	4	389
None! save that One, the veriest wretch of all	438 Tasso		92
Than I have time to tell now, or at all	441 Beppo		77
Which we're obliged to hiss, and spit, and sputter all	445 Beppo		352
One hates an author that's all author, fellows	449 Beppo		593
You still may mark her cheek, out-blooming all	450 Beppo		672
Laura, who knew it would not do at all	450 Beppo		673
'Sir' (quoth the Turk), ''tis no mistake at all	451 Beppo		704
Save the few spirits, who, despite of all	453 Venice-B		80

ALL

The soul's emasculation saddens all	461 Dante	3	84
'Because his love of justice unto all	472 Morgante		393
'But they in Christ have firmest hope, and all	472 Morgante		409
The abbot said to them, 'I give you all	476 Morgante		667
She'd tell thee 'twas for all her little ones	506 Faliero	1	472
How say you? all! Whom wouldst thou spare? I spare	520 Faliero	3	143
The work is half your own. And should be all mine	596 Foscari	1	32
And must I leave them--all? You must. Not one	614 Foscari	3	386
I cannot wish them all they have inflicted	617 Foscari	4	172
All! the consummate fiends! A thousand fold	617 Foscari	4	173
All die--there is what must survive. The Other	637 Cain	2	72
Never to have been stung at all, than to	643 Cain	2	507
For then we are all alike; is't not so, Cain	648 Cain	3	143
So perish all	662 Heaven		536
No--all of heaven, they are so beautiful	662 Heaven		577
And dearer, silent friends and brethren, all	668 Heaven		966
What! wilt thou leave us all--all--all behind	669 Heaven		1094
The little rivulet which freshen'd all	670 Heaven		1182
Though pennyless all	732 Deformed	1	700
Her wit (she sometimes tried at wit) was Attic all	748 Juan	1	91
For she had not even one--the worst of all	749 Juan	1	128
Inform us truly, have they not hen-peck'd you all	749 Juan	1	176
By contrast, which is what we just were wishing all	751 Juan	1	246
And saw into herself each day before all	751 Juan	1	306
And so they were submitted first to her, all	752 Juan	1	310
Which ancient mass-books often are, and this all	752 Juan	1	363
Who saw those figures on the margin kiss all	752 Juan	1	365
Amongst her numerous acquaintance, all	753 Juan	1	433
But sweeter still than this, than these, than all	762 Juan	1	1009
Were one not punish'd, all would be outrageous	763 Juan	1	1104
Doubt upon me, confusion over all	765 Juan	1	1226
I can't say that it puzzles me at all	774 Juan	2	17
They would have eat her, olive-branch and all	786 Juan	2	760
Of nature's oracle--first love,--that all	798 Juan	2	1511
Or 'Ca ira,' according to the fashion all	812 Juan	3	676
What, silent still? and silent all	812 Juan	3	731
Vengeance on him who was the cause of all	821 Juan	4	292
And arm'd from boot to turban, one and all	822 Juan	4	374
And sung of love; the fierce name struck through all	824 Juan	4	523
With more than one profession, gains by all	827 Juan	4	666
Who came at stated moments to invite all	827 Juan	4	715
A rueful glance upon the waves (which bright all	828 Juan	4	717
Too often in its fury overcoming all	829 Juan	4	803
From out the wide destruction, which, entombing all	829 Juan	4	805
Were landed in the market, one and all	830 Juan	4	902
Those who will leave you of no sex at all	841 Juan	5	600
They spoke by signs--that is, not spoke at all	842 Juan	5	713
I'm a philosopher; confound them all	855 Juan	6	169
I might describe, as I have seen it all	858 Juan	6	404
She never thought about herself at all	859 Juan	6	432
And that so loudly, that upstarted all	861 Juan	6	561
The numbers are too great for them to flatter all	863 Juan	6	704
And some of us have felt thus 'all amort	865 Juan	6	845
To laugh at all things--for I wish to know	867 Juan	7	15
What, after all, are all things--but a show	867 Juan	7	16
'Twas much that he was understood at all	874 Juan	7	446
Or that the Russian army should repent all	876 Juan	7	598
The columns were in movement one and all	879 Juan	8	65
This chieftain--somehow would not yield at all	891 Juan	8	832
Some hundreds breathed--the rest were silent all	894 Juan	8	1016
I by and may tell you, if at all	896 Juan	8	1108
For she was homeless, houseless, helpless; all	896 Juan	8	1122
'But heaven,' as Cassio says, 'is above all	898 Juan	9	145
By night, as do that mercenary pack all	899 Juan	9	211
And scent the prey their masters would attack all	899 Juan	9	213
Since lately there have been no rents at all	900 Juan	9	252
Maintain thou art the best: for after all	903 Juan	9	442
A man' (as Giles says); for though she would widow all	904 Juan	9	503
Love, that great opener of the heart and all	906 Juan	9	634
As 'Auld Lang Syne' brings Scotland, one and all	909 Juan	10	137
There's glory again for you, gentle reader! All	916 Juan	10	581
A fool whose bells have ceased to ring at all	918 Juan	10	688
That all's ideal--all ourselves: I'll stake the	918 Juan	11	11
Admitted as an aspirant with	925 Juan	11	426
And scorn his temperate board, as none at all	930 Juan	12	22
(That make old Europe's journals squeak and gibber all	930 Juan	12	36
Or pleasure? Who make politics run glibber all	930 Juan	12	38
Commands--the intellectual lord of all	931 Juan	12	72
Think not, fair creatures, that I mean to abuse you all	933 Juan	12	219
Since I've grown moral, still I must accuse you all	933 Juan	12	221
To the lot of him who scarce pursued at all	934 Juan	12	292
Those polar summers, all sun, and some ice	939 Juan	12	576
That lady, who should be at home to all	940 Juan	12	632

ALL

The grand arcanum's not for men to see all	958	Juan	14	173
And now, that we may furnish with some matter all	979	Juan	15	743
My smiles must be sincere or not at all	980	Juan	15	762
And therefore, mortals, cavil not at all	981	Juan	16	41
Titus exclaim'd, 'I've lost a day!' Of all	981	Juan	16	85
In chisell'd stone and painted glass, and all	982	Juan	16	127
Though princes the possessor were besieging all	988	Juan	16	492
The civil list he deigns to accept (obliging all	988	Juan	16	494

ALL-IN-ALL

An all-in-all sufficient self-director	749	Juan	1	115

ALLA

By Alla! I would answer nay	315	Giaour		482
He call'd on Alla--but the word	317	Giaour		681
At solemn sound of 'Alla Hu	317	Giaour		734
One prayer to Alla all he made	321	Giaour		1083
With angels shared, by Alla given	321	Giaour		1133
For, Alla! sure thy lips are flame	328	Abydos	1	396
Such still to guilt just Alla sends	332	Abydos	2	301
This hath he sworn by Alla and his sword	347	Corsair	2	6
The Saick was bound; but Alla did not smile	348	Corsair	2	68
Alla il Alla! Vengeance swells the cry	350	Corsair	2	235
God and the Prophet--Alla Hu	392	Corinth		713

ALL-ABSORBING

Is more than ours; the all-absorbing flame	424	Island	2	378

ALLAH

The city won for Allah from the Giaour	31	Harold	2	729
Allah! forbid that e'er he ought	328	Abydos	1	442
Hark to the Allah shout! a band	393	Corinth		819
As the Turk's 'Allah!' or the Roman's more	428	Island	3	127
And only shouted, 'Allah!' and 'Bis Millah	868	Juan	7	104
Hurra! and Allah! and--one moment more	878	Juan	7	695
And one enormous shout of 'Allah!' rose	879	Juan	8	57
Resounded 'Allah!' and the clouds which close	879	Juan	8	61
All sounds it pierceth 'Allah! Allah! Hu	879	Juan	8	64
He shouted 'Allah!' and saw Paradise	893	Juan	8	915

ALLAHS

Our friends the Turks, who with loud 'Allahs' now	872	Juan	7	329

ALLAH'S

'Thou may'st forgive though Allah's self detest	362	Corsair	3	469

ALLAN

Allan had early learn'd control	102	Alva		67
At length young Allan join'd the bride	102	Alva		101
Allan, with these through Alva fly	103	Alva		114
For youthful Allan still remain'd	103	Alva		157
And Allan is my last resource	104	Alva		211
But why does Allan trembling stand	104	Alva		230
Oh, never more shall Allan rise	104	Alva		276
And Mora's eye could Allan move	105	Alva		293

ALLAN'S

But Allan's locks were bright and fair	102	Alva		63
While Allan's soul belied his form	102	Alva		73
And Allan's face was wondrous fair	103	Alva		162
To bless thy Allan's happy lot	104	Alva		202
The crimson glow of Allan's face	104	Alva		233
To pour the light on Allan's eyes	104	Alva		274
And Allan's barbed arrow lay	104	Alva		279
Ambition nerved young Allan's hand	105	Alva		285
Swift is the shaft from Allan's bow	105	Alva		289
Oh! that is Allan's nuptial bed	105	Alva		300
Shall Allan's deeds on harp-strings raise	105	Alva		306

ALL-APPROVING

The courteous host, and all-approving guest	375	Lara	1	629

ALLAY

With knowledge, nor allay my thousand fears	641	Cain	2	334
'Twas something calculated to allay	901	Juan	9	284

ALLAY'D

Known unto all,--or hope and dread allay'd	52	Harold	3	1008
Robed in the lightnings which his hand allay'd	303	Age		387
And, when the fatal waters are allay'd	667	Heaven		895
Blazed, and the cannon's roar was scarce allay'd	895	Juan	8	1060
Into a rivulet; and thus allay'd	948	Juan	13	461

ALLAYS

Abominable Man no more allays	450	Beppo		636

ALL-BLASTING

This boundless upas, this all-blasting tree	74	Harold	4	1129

ALL-CLARETLESS

Leaving all-claretless the unmoisten'd throttle	962	Juan	14	459

ALL-CLOUDLESS

Except the all-cloudless glory (which few men's is	897	Juan	9	61

ALL-CONFESS'D

And in this scene of all-confess'd inanity	868	Juan	7	45

ALL-CONSUMING

Awakes an all-consuming fire	111	Medea		20

ALLEGE

Continued Michael, 'George Rex, or allege	295	Vision		654

ALLEGIANCE

Before, even in their oath of false allegiance	525	Faliero	3	494

ALLEGORY

If Job be allegory or a fact	289	Vision		267
The allegory) a mere type, no more	793	Juan	2	1238

ALLEMANDE

Then there was God knows what 'a l'Allemande	976	Juan	15	521

ALL-ENDURING

With a sedate and all-enduring eye	41	Harold	3	349

ALLER

But 'laissez aller'--knights and dames I sing	971	Juan	15	193

ALL-ETHEREAL

Till struck,--forth flies the all-ethereal dart	438	Tasso		116

ALLEVIATION

By mild reciprocal alleviation	556	Sardan	1	400

ALL-EVIL

He loved--his own all-evil son	397	Parisina		102

ALLEY

From Grub-street to Fop's Alley	233	Ballad-B		6
Some rowing in an Alley	234	Ballad-B		54
Squeezed in 'Fop's Alley,' jostled by the beaux	261	Hints		311
Should now be butcher'd in a civic alley	836	Juan	5	296

ALLEYS

And walk in alleys rather than the street	263	Hints		470
Where the green alleys windingly allure	445	Beppo		334

ALL-FAMOUS

For they are damn'd; that once all-famous oath	872	Juan	7	354

ALL-FORGOTTEN

As all-forgotten in that watchful trance	373	Lara	1	545

ALL-FOURS

Now on all-fours, now on tip-toe	196	Rogers		33

ALL-GASPING

A drop to moisten life's all-gasping springs	418	Island	1	194

ALL-GLORIOUS

All-glorious burst from ocean? why not dart	562	Sardan	2	20

ALL-GOOD

He is all-powerful, must all-good, too, follow	628	Cain	1	77

ALL-GREAT

(Which you proclaim) of the all-great and good	635	Cain	1	484

ALL-HALLOW'D

Hence to where our all-hallow'd ark uprears	668	Heaven		1015

ALLIANCE

Humph! I can't say I know any happy alliance	278	Blues	1	71
The blest Alliance, which says three are all	303	Age		395
Yet, as the immediate cause of the alliance	526	Faliero	3	533
Could brook the alliance; and could ne'er be brought	684	Werner	2	99
I think that with this holy new alliance	772	Juan	1	1681
'La Belle Alliance' of dunces down at zero	925	Juan	11	443

ALLIANCES

We made alliances of blood and marriage	525	Faliero	3	444
At such alliances his sires would frown	754	Juan	1	452

ALLIED

Of mighty strength, since Albion was allied	6	Harold	1	220
Keen contest and destruction near allied	42	Harold	3	439
Of comrades, in friendship and mischief allied	96	Harrow-A		6
Deplored by those in early days allied	138	Harrow-B		33
The whisper'd thought of hearts allied	165	Thyrza		31
In Youth, Birth, Beauty, genially allied	199	Sonnet-D		7
When sense and wit with poesy allied	243	Bards		105
Blank verse is now, with one consent, allied	258	Hints		117
But there are human natures so allied	685	Werner	2	133

ALLIED
I think too well of blood allied to mine   695 Werner   2   756
Were sate, like ugly imps, as if allied   842 Juan   5   692
Out between friends as well as allied nations   884 Juan   8   380

ALLIES
Unless they act like us and our allies   266 Hints   702
All outlets seem'd secured. Their new allies   427 Island   3   45
As will out-sparkle our allies--your planets   562 Sardan   2   47
Europe has slaves, allies, kings, armies still   747 Juan   Ded 127
The simple olives, best allies of wine   977 Juan   15   577

ALL-INEXORABLE
And all-inexorable in their cry   509 Faliero   2   65

ALL-JARR'D
To her all-jarr'd and wandering mind   400 Parisina   379

ALL-KNOWING
Since the all-knowing cherubim love least   634 Cain   1   422

ALL-NAMELESS
Since that all-nameless hour. I have no dread   479 Manfred   1   24

ALLOT
It was the scene which passion must allot   51 Harold   3   970

ALLOTMENT
No matter where--their chief's allotment this   339 Corsair   1   59
I see it not in their allotment here   643 Cain   2   517
It seems when this allotment was made out   828 Juan   4   729

ALLOTS
He allots one poor husband to share amongst four 116 To Eliza   11
Chamber of state, her gratitude allots you   611 Foscari   3   218
Your services, the state allots the appanage   623 Foscari   5   171

ALLOTTED
Th' allotted hour of daily sport is o'er   124 Recoll   149
To where my allotted band is under arms   526 Faliero   3   549
Of toiling breathers in allotted tasks   587 Sardan   5   34
Have some allotted dwelling--as all things   644 Cain   2   574
In thine allotted ocean-tent   670 Heaven   1143

ALLOW
Here giant weeds a passage scarce allow   7 Harold   1   283
Match me those Houries, whom ye scarce allow   13 Harold   1   607
And Boileau, whose rash envy could allow   60 Harold   4   340
If you, ye chiefs, and fortune will allow   106 Nisus   107
And crowds allow to both a partial fame   126 Recoll   336
And bless'd were the scenes of our youth, I allow 136 Delawarr   10
As philosophers allow   157 Hodgson   70
For my part all men must allow   233 Nihil   17
This truth at least let satire's self allow   243 Bards   123
In modern physics, we can scarce allow   267 Hints   760
I allow our friend Scamp hath this day done his
  best   281 Blues   2   41
Though souls absorb'd like mine allow   322 Giaour   1225
If shrines that ne'er approach allow   327 Abydos   1   313
Yet would I fain, did time allow, disclose   344 Corsair   1   456
But this--time--hope--nor even thy strength allow 354 Corsair   2   463
He, fast as fetter'd limbs allow, pursued   361 Corsair   3   391
Unman me not; the hour will not allow   426 Island   2   529
As much as such a moment would allow   428 Island   3   154
And melancholy gift high powers allow   461 Dante   3   27
And hast, and may'st have, if thou wilt allow   467 Morgante   52
And honours on his head, could thus allow   541 Faliero   5   242
As to allow his voice in such high matter   596 Foscari   1   85
Your hand, too, shakes, my lord: allow me, thus 601 Foscari   2   9
Allow me to inquire who profited   716 Werner   5   192
That being about the number I'll allow   801 Juan   2   1724
'No?' quoth the other; 'yet you will allow   834 Juan   5   180
All who have loved, or love, will still allow   853 Juan   6   44
'Twas foolish, nervous, as she must allow   862 Juan   6   660
There's fortune even in fame, we must allow   871 Juan   7   262
And yet, like all men else, I must allow   877 Juan   7   637
All very accurate, you must allow   896 Juan   8   1100
Death's a reformer, all men must allow   910 Juan   10   200
But what is to be done? I can't allow   920 Juan   11   118
Mix'd Gothic, such as artists all allow   948 Juan   13   436
As clear as such a climate will allow   982 Juan   16   100

ALLOWANCE
When shipwreck's short allowance grows too scanty 784 Juan   2   663

ALLOWANCES
And all allowances besides of plunder   891 Juan   8   817

ALLOW'D
Man and his Maker--but of things allow'd   69 Harold   4   848
A melancholy halo scarce allow'd   79 Harold   4   1483
'True! he allow'd them to pray God: but as   291 Vision   385
Before the Pacha's will allow'd to speak   348 Corsair   2   64
Had the time allow'd to wound   394 Corinth   870

ALLOW'D
Her person if allow'd at large to run   810 Juan   3   580
Continued: 'Your old regiment's allow'd   875 Juan   7   499
My debt in being thus allow'd to die   875 Juan   7   517
The night was dark, and the thick mist allow'd   878 Juan   8   41
As soon as 'Crowner's quest' allow'd, pursued   920 Juan   11   139
As far as her own gentle heart allow'd   974 Juan   15   362

ALLOWS
To us bequeath--'tis all their fate allows   182 Address-C   19
Each to his humour--Comus all allows   250 Bards   650
Which Gaul allows and still Hesperia lends   260 Hints   300
The field is universal, and allows   746 Juan   Ded   53
She was all which pure ignorance allows   798 Juan   2   1517
Is all that life allows the luckiest sinner   806 Juan   3   284
At least as far as bienseance allows   964 Juan   14   532

ALLOY
When Pleasure blends no base alloy   141 Pignus   22
We are jealous!--who's not?--thou hast no such
  alloy   155 Goblet   19
That whatever he means won't alloy what he says   281 Blues   2   68
Or with adulterous whisper to alloy   423 Island   2   338
Can that low vice alloy so much ambition   682 Werner   1   678
Of being, without alloy of fop or beau   940 Juan   12   671
Who like to mix some slight alloy with fame   956 Juan   14   70

ALLOY'D
And with the ills of Eld mine earlier years
  alloy'd   35 Harold   2   926

ALL-PEOPLED
The myriad myriads--the all-peopled earth   635 Cain   1   519

ALL-PERVADING
Save to the Spirit's all-pervading eye   661 Heaven   499

ALL-PITILESS
Of an all-pitiless demon held me back   486 Manfred   2   232

ALL-POWERFUL
He is all-powerful, must all-good,too, follow   628 Cain   1   77
But here he is all-powerful; and has spread   689 Werner   2   406

ALL-PROLIFIC
And what doth Gaul, the all-prolific land   304 Age   484

ALL-RIPE
As these; and our all-ripe and gushing valleys   682 Werner   1   711

ALL'S
'Tis but envy, when all's done   197 Rogers   66
When all's gone--to the rainbow's latest ray   429 Island   3   207
They here! all's lost--yet will I make an effort 536 Faliero   4   548
Stand to your arms, and guard the door--all's
  lost   536 Faliero   4   579
All's silent, and all's lost! Now, Doge,
  denounce me   536 Faliero   4   599
He's gone; and told no more than that all's lost 575 Sardan   3   231
Again the love-fit's on him, and all's lost   577 Sardan   3   401
My sister:--all's prepared to make your safety   584 Sardan   4   369
All's silent now. Perhaps all's over; but   599 Foscari   1   248
All's to be fear'd, where all is to be gain'd   694 Werner   2   745
All's ready, my good lord! I am not sleepy   700 Werner   3   356
All's ready. Idenstein has kept his word   701 Werner   3   431
Comrades, help, ho! All's darkness   739 Deformed 2   302
The tree of knowledge has been pluck'd--all's
  known   762 Juan   1   1012
(A race of mere impostors, when all's done   789 Juan   2   942
Then dressing, nursing, praying, and all's over   799 Juan   2   1600
That all's ideal--all ourselves: I'll stake the 918 Juan   11   11

ALL-SEARCHING
True Passion must the all-searching changes prove 201 Ode-C   34

ALL-SEEING
And grow unto the spot, all-seeing but unseen   76 Harold   4   1242
And deem, because we see, we are all-seeing   898 Juan   9   124

ALL-SOFTENING
Than that all-softening, overpowering knell   837 Juan   5   391

ALL-SPREADING
The cause of this all-spreading happiness   635 Cain   1   483

ALL-STRANGLING
Her, whom the surges of the all-strangling deep   667 Heaven   941

ALL-SUFFICIENT
A something all-sufficient for the heart   964 Juan   14   585

ALL-SWAYING
With the all-swaying majesty of kings   504 Faliero   1   291

ALL-SWEEPING
Where Death sits robed in his all-sweeping
  shadow   516 Faliero 2 503

ALLUDED
Alfonso ne'er to Juan had alluded 768 Juan 1 1410

ALLURE
No splendid vices glitter'd to allure 121 Newstead-A 131
Where the green alleys windingly allure 445 Beppo 334
Who to immoral courses would allure us 800 Juan 2 1651
Possess'd, the ore, of which mere hopes allure 930 Juan 12 59
So animated that it might allure a 951 Juan 13 619
Firstly, they must allure the conversation 953 Juan 13 777

ALLURED
They might have used it better, but, allured 48 Harold 3 781
When the meteor of conquest allured me too far 186 Napoleon 6
They had not spoken; but they felt allured 798 Juan 2 1493
When he allured poor Dolon:--you had better 954 Juan 13 839

ALLURES
With notes and preface, all that most allures 297 Vision 788
Form not the true temptation which allures 814 Juan 3 869
I know its mighty empire now allures 899 Juan 9 181

ALLURING
Their passes more alluring to the view 460 Dante 2 117

ALLUSIONS
Will hint allusions never meant. Ne'er doubt 929 Juan 11 695
Reaping allusions private and inglorious 944 Juan 13 196

ALL-WHITE
The groan, the roll in dust, the all-white eye 879 Juan 8 101

ALL-WISE
God, the Eternal! Infinite! All-wise 627 Cain 1 1

ALLY
The foe, the victim, and the fond ally 10 Harold 1 445
With Athens, old ally! 162 War Song 24
Your old ally yet mourns perfidious war 271 Minerva 214
But Lusitania, kind and dear ally 271 Minerva 233
And, if you please, as friends we will ally us 471 Morgante 349
You are the sole ally we covet now 508 Faliero 1 575
This great ally who renders it more sure 524 Faliero 3 393
She keeps it for you like a true ally 939 Juan 12 592

ALMA
The studious sons of Alma Mater 95 Granta 28
Still we respect thee, 'Alma Venus Genetrix 995 Juan 16 920

ALMAIN
Iberian, Almain, Lombard, and the beast 459 Dante 2 84

ALMANACK
Its sessions form our only almanack 946 Juan 13 344

ALMANZOR
Though mad Almanzor rhymed in Dryden's days 258 Hints 119

ALMAS
Can Egypt's Almas--tantalising group 275 Waltz 127
While dance the Almas to wild minstrelsy. 347 Corsair 2 36

ALMIGHTINESS
Almightiness. And lo! his mildest and 665 Heaven 770

ALMIGHTY
And when the Almighty lifts his fiercest scourge 6 Harold 1 212
Her rushing wings--Oh, she who was Almighty
  hail'd   67 Harold 4 756
Great Jove, to whose almighty throne 89 Prometheus-A 1
From star to star to reach the almighty throne 456 Dante 1 17
Like that Jerusalem which the almighty He 456 Dante 1 61
My many wrongs, and thine almighty rod 457 Dante 1 120
The seraph voices, touch the Almighty Mind 460 Dante 3 19
Thou earliest minister of the Almighty 493 Manfred 3 182
Midst the chief relics of almighty Rome 495 Manfred 3 271
Of this almighty Death, who is, it seems 631 Cain 1 255
Pleasing or painful, little or almighty 647 Cain 3 62
That secret rests with the Almighty giver 656 Heaven 117
And, gather'd under his almighty wings 661 Heaven 463
Than their last cries shall shake the Almighty
  purpose   662 Heaven 547
Those downcast eyes beneath the Almighty dove 815 Juan 3 918

ALMIGHTY'S
Thou glorious mirror, where the Almighty's form 82 Harold 4 1639
Bow down beneath the Almighty's Throne 146 Adieu 106
And thus unjust the Almighty's self be thought 472 Morgante 408

ALMONTE'S
The victory was Almonte's else; his sight 467 Morgante 102

ALMORO
That Almoro Donato, as I said 600 Foscari 1 307

ALMOST
With pleasure drugg'd, he almost long'd for woe 4 Harold 1 53
Then turn to hate a world he had almost forgot 23 Harold 2 243
Since the fierce Carthaginian almost won thee 52 Harold 3 1024
That two, or one, are almost what they seem 53 Harold 3 1065
Almost thy very growth, to view thee catch 53 Harold 3 1078
And reap from earth, sea, joy almost as dear 81 Harold 4 1583
'Tis almost time to stop, indeed 96 Granta 96
This aged heart was almost broke 104 Alva 208
Here, then, our almost unfledged wings we try 113 Prologue 17
Who hopes, yet almost dreads, to meet your praise 114 Prologue 22
I look'd in your face, and I almost forgave you 147 To Anne-A 4
And almost deem the sentence sweet 174 Remember-B 48
While Powers of mind almost of boundless range 194 Monody 109
Almost sicken to servility 196 Rogers 30
I feel almost at times as I have felt 211 Augusta-C 49
Almost like a reality--the one 216 Dream 205
I'm almost dead, and always dizzy 232 Doctor 88
England could boast a judge almost the same 247 Bards 439
That ever glorious, almost fatal fray 248 Bards 465
And--almost crush'd beneath the glorious news 274 Waltz 71
It almost quench'd his innate thirst of evil 285 Vision 46
Of almost every body born to die 286 Vision 120
Almost as scanty, of days less remote 293 Vision 528
His very rival almost deem'd him such 298 Age 12
'Almost as quickly as he conquer'd Spain 308 Age 724
And Giaffir almost call'd me coward 327 Abydos 1 361
This tale whose close is almost nigh 331 Abydos 2 277
My almost drunkenness of heart 332 Abydos 2 344
And now almost they touch the cave 334 Abydos 2 511
And almost met the meeting wave 335 Abydos 2 546
So full--that feeling seem'd almost unfelt 345 Corsair 1 473
Yet once almost he stopp'd--and nearly gave 345 Corsair 1 515
Yet would I ask--almost my lip denies 357 Corsair 3 105
And made it almost mockery yet to weep 364 Corsair 3 608
And stupor almost lull'd it into rest 365 Corsair 3 647
They see, they recognize, yet almost deem 367 Lara 1 53
His eye was almost seal'd, but not forsook 369 Lara 1 221
From other lands, almost a stranger grown 372 Lara 1 473
With hand, whose almost careless coolness spoke 376 Lara 2 59
Almost to blackness in its demon hue 376 Lara 2 74
He almost turn'd the thirsty point on those 376 Lara 2 81
Now girt with numbers, now almost alone 380 Lara 2 376
They feel its freshness, and almost partake 380 Lara 2 410
When Cynthia's light almost gave way to morn 383 Lara 2 552
Though he heard the sound, and could almost tell 389 Corinth 450
To grasp the spoil he almost reach'd 395 Corinth 1012
That almost made the dungeon bright 404 Chillon 195
Had almost need of such a rest 406 Chillon 365
Which almost look'd like want of head 408 Mazeppa 165
And almost on the break of day 410 Mazeppa 333
At times I almost thought, indeed 411 Mazeppa 448
The dizzy race seem'd almost done 413 Mazeppa 641
That now almost ingulfs, then leaves to creep 418 Island 1 186
That rock'd her heart till almost heard to throb 429 Island 3 198
The prow now almost lay within its length 430 Island 4 48
So much as to be thought almost invincible 443 Beppo 208
She almost lost all appetite for victual 443 Beppo 227
In law he was almost as good as dead, he 444 Beppo 276
I think 'twould almost be worth while to pension 449 Beppo 613
And then come to themselves, almost or quite 451 Beppo 710
As to desert would almost be a wrong 470 Morgante 262
Almost our equal?--Can it be that thou 496 Manfred 3 367
The blood and sweat of almost eighty years 502 Faliero 1 150
Through almost sixty years, and still for Venice 506 Faliero 1 463
Nay, more, almost triumphant--listen then 522 Faliero 3 250
Is almost wronging such a night as this 529 Faliero 4 111
How goes the night? Almost upon the dawn 534 Faliero 4 415
Thou dost almost anticipate my heart 557 Sardan 1 469
And yet it almost shames me, we shall have 562 Sardan 2 81
I almost wish now, what I never wish'd 575 Sardan 3 217
Lost almost past recovery. Zames! Where 575 Sardan 3 228
So like we almost deem it permanent 587 Sardan 5 15
I grow almost a convert to your Baal 588 Sardan 5 48
For those who almost broke thee? Let him rest 596 Foscari 1 67
As long ere she resume her arms! 'Tis almost 601 Foscari 2 13
Wax very old--old almost as my years 620 Foscari 5 9
Thou look'st almost a god; and--I am none 629 Cain 1 128
And has almost recover'd from his drenching 675 Werner 1 257
Fell sick, almost to death. He should have died 677 Werner 1 407
Almost a mile off, and which only leads 683 Werner 2 24
Inadequate thanks, you almost check even them 685 Werner 2 150
A poor man almost in his grasp, a child 694 Werner 2 743
Although I almost wish you had the baron's 696 Werner 3 61
The stars are almost faded, and the grey 704 Werner 3 581
Had almost then forgot him in my son 715 Werner 5 129
Youth, strength, and beauty, almost superhuman 717 Werner 5 245
I am almost enamour'd of her, as 741 Deformed 2 413

ALMOST

Whose suicide was almost an anomaly	749	Juan	1 118
Him almost man; but she flew in a rage	753	Juan	1 429
Their looks cast down, their greetings almost dumb	755	Juan	1 555
And almost might have made a Tarquin quake	756	Juan	1 598
I'm almost sorry that I e'er begun	761	Juan	1 920
And seems to me almost a sort of blunder	764	Juan	1 1151
I favor'd none--nay, was almost uncivil	765	Juan	1 1182
But almost every other country's blue	775	Juan	2 94
Seem'd almost prying into his for breath	788	Juan	2 898
Don Juan, almost famish'd, and half drown'd	790	Juan	2 1028
A mast was almost crumbled to a crutch	790	Juan	2 1054
A lovely statue we almost adore	801	Juan	2 1686
Is good to govern--almost as a Guelf	807	Juan	3 376
But almost sanctify the sweet excess	819	Juan	4 207
And stumbled almost every step she made	820	Juan	4 251
'Our baritone I almost had forgot	827	Juan	4 705
They almost lost their way, and had to pick it	836	Juan	5 325
He look'd in almost all respects a maid	841	Juan	5 635
O'er them in almost pyramidic pride	842	Juan	5 694
An almost twelvemonth's constancy endangers	845	Juan	5 848
And rapture's self will seem almost a pain	845	Juan	5 876
And they had wasted now almost a quarter	847	Juan	5 976
Almost as far as Petersburgh and lend	863	Juan	6 740
And almost every day, in sad reality	877	Juan	7 659
I almost lately have begun to doubt	881	Juan	8 201
Grew dumb, for you might almost hear a linnet	885	Juan	8 470
Were almost as much virgins as before	894	Juan	8 1032
Almost as much as on a new despatch	904	Juan	9 487
With poets almost clergymen, or wholly	925	Juan	11 452
He almost honour'd him for his docility	944	Juan	13 170
And rated him almost a whipper-in	959	Juan	14 272
I sometimes almost think that eyes have ears	977	Juan	15 601
Almost an hair's breadth too much on one side	984	Juan	16 232
So that I almost think that the same skin	998	Juan	17 87

ALMS

The largess shall be only dealt in alms	711	Werner	4 471

ALOFT

Sustains aloft the battery's iron load	12	Harold	1 532
When placed aloft in godlike state	89	Prometheus-A	11
Oh, live then, my Oak! tow'r aloft from the weeds	149	Newstead-B	21
From aloft the signal's streaming	157	Hodgson	5
And clouds aloft and tides below	329	Abydos	2 10
And more than all, his blood-red flag aloft	345	Corsair	1 529
Or the faint dying day-hymn stole aloft	815	Juan	3 910

ALONE

But pomp and power alone are woman's care	5	Harold	1 78
And have no friend, save these alone	6	Harold	1 148
'And now I'm in the world alone	6	Harold	1 182
With human hearts--to what?--a dream alone	11	Harold	1 455
When all were changing thou alone wert true	18	Harold	1 875
Alone o'er steeps and foaming falls to lean	23	Harold	2 223
This is to be alone; this, this is solitude	23	Harold	2 234
Now Harold felt himself at length alone	26	Harold	2 379
In all save form alone, how changed! and who	31	Harold	2 711
And be alone on earth, as I am now	35	Harold	2 921
To whom the boundless air alone were home	37	Harold	3 130
And roused the vengeance blood alone could quell	38	Harold	3 206
Thou hadst been made to stand or fall alone	41	Harold	3 362
Is it not better, then, to be alone	46	Harold	3 671
In solitude where we are least alone	49	Harold	3 843
Not on those summits solely, nor alone	50	Harold	3 936
I stood and stand alone,--remember'd or forgot	52	Harold	3 1048
No hollow aid; alone--man with his God must strive	60	Harold	4 297
The wreath which Dante's brow alone had worn before	60	Harold	4 315
Standing with half its battlements alone	70	Harold	4 886
Thus much alone we know--Metella died	70	Harold	4 926
In him alone. Can Nature show so fair	73	Harold	4 1093
Standest alone, with nothing like to thee	78	Harold	4 1379
Obeys thee; thou goest forth, dread, fathomless, alone	82	Harold	4 1647
Farewell! with him alone may rest the pain	83	Harold	4 1673
A friend, whom death alone could sever	85	To D--	2
While solitary friendship sighs alone	85	Epitaph	28
My epitaph shall be my name alone	86	Fragment-A	8
Reserved for him, and him alone	87	Ad Lesbiam	8
By death alone I can avoid your hate	87	Tibullus	6
My lyre recurs to love alone	88	Anacreon-A	8
Love, Love alone, my lyre shall claim	88	Anacreon-A	25
These scenes I must retrace alone	89	To Emma	31
In sighs alone it breathed my name	90	Caroline-A	16
With me alone it joy could know	90	Caroline-B	6
Your voice alone declares your flame	90	Caroline-B	13
When these declare, 'that pomp alone should wait	93	Dorset	21
And dooms my fall, I fain would fall alone	94	Dorset	40
For in visions alone your affection can live	97	To M.S.G.-B	3
'Tis I that am alone to blame	98	To Lesbia	13
They echo to the gale alone	102	Alva	28

ALONE

'These deeds, my Nisus, shalt thou dare alone	106	Nisus	39
Alone she came, all selfish fears above	107	Nisus	181
From this alone no fond adieus I seek	107	Nisus	185
'Nor this alone, but many a gift beside	108	Nisus	200
'Me, me,--your vengeance hurl on me alone	110	Nisus	367
Unpitied, helpless, and alone	111	Medea	52
Still, not for her alone we wish respect	113	Prologue	9
For Pitt, and Pitt alone, has dared to ask	114	Death-A	36
With women alone he had peopled his heaven	116	To Eliza	8
Not to the aching frame alone confined	122	Recoll	5
Perhaps their last memorial these alone	124	Recoll	159
When names of these, like ours, alone survive	124	Recoll	182
Yet, why should I alone with such delight	125	Recoll	209
Alone, though thousand pilgrims fill the way	125	Recoll	236
To mix in friendship, or to sigh alone	125	Recoll	241
To thee alone, unrivall'd, would belong	126	Recoll	289
Ambition's slave alone would toil for more	126	Recoll	324
Justice awards it to my friend alone	126	Recoll	340
For all my humble fame, to him alone	127	Recoll	355
I think with pleasure on the past alone	127	Recoll	376
Yes, to the past alone my heart confine	127	Recoll	377
was the pride of Orla:--gentle alone to Calmar	129	Calmar	26
dark-haired Orla, 'and mine alone. What is	130	Calmar	56
alone?' said fair-haired Calmar. 'Wilt thou	130	Calmar	62
dust of Erin? Let me fall alone. My father	130	Calmar	72
from sleep; but did he rise alone? No	130	Calmar	126
'What were the chase to me alone? Who	131	Calmar	173
Worth worlds of bliss, that thought alone	131	L'Amitie	19
In one, and one alone, deceived	132	L'Amitie	61
Shall those who live for self alone	132	Prayer	33
And bids me feel for self alone	133	E. N. Long	38
And Carolina sighs alone	134	E. N. Long	65
But what it sought in thee alone	134	Lady-D	19
How cheerless feels the heart alone	135	I Would	27
One image alone on my bosom impress'd	135	Highlander	13
As the last of my race, I must wither alone	136	Highlander	27
Devoted to love and to friendship alone	137	Delawarr	28
The recollection seems alone	137	Clare	7
Where now alone I muse, who oft have trod	138	Harrow-B	3
But thou still mov'st alone, of light the Source	139	Ossian-A	9
Alone thou shinest forth--for who can rise	140	Ossian-B	9
Who loved me for myself alone	141	Pignus	8
For feeling Souls alone 'twas meant	141	Critics	66
Desire alone which makes you melt	143	To--A	8
So dearly wreathed with mine alone	143	Jessy	2
That mine alone should press it more	144	Jessy	20
A Mouth which smiles on me alone	144	Jessy	23
Let Pride alone condemn	146	Adieu	70
By nightly skies and storms alone	146	Adieu	97
Your frowns, lovely girl, are the Fates which alone	147	To Anne-B	5
Can the lips sing of Love in the desert alone	148	Farewell-A	17
But transient in thy breast alone	152	Time-A	12
And when I perish, thou alone	152	Weep-A	7
And those, and those alone, may claim	153	Friend-A	39
Who labours, fights, lives, breathes for him alone	154	Dog	10
In the goblet alone no deception is found	155	Goblet	4
And ev'n in crowds am still alone	156	Lady-F	23
Thus, when thou view'st this page alone	157	Album	3
Bow down my head alone	159	Storm	40
Think of me, sweet! when alone	161	Maid	20
In gazing when alone	163	Parting	10
If rest alone be in the tomb	165	Thyrza	47
Man was not form'd to live alone	166	Struggle	10
Whose judging voice and eye alone direct	170	Address-A	54
(This deep discovery is mine alone	171	Address-B	26
For now I bear the weight alone	171	Time-B	8
One star alone shot forth a spark	172	Time-B	27
As if a dream alone had charm'd	173	Not False	22
It seem'd as if for me alone	173	Mrs. Lamb	7
Or dread of death alone	180	Ode-A	43
Alone--how look'd he round	180	Ode-A	49
'Tis not on youth's smooth cheek the blush alone, which fades so fast	185	Music-B	3
Thee alone no doom can bow	187	French-A	12
Of all which lives, alone is life to me	191	Fragment-C	10
Since we were friends; for I alone	197	Duel	45
But let not his name be thine idol alone	203	Avatar	85
Far--far away! and alone along the billow	204	Hindoo	4
Are mine alone	206	Year	8
Methought that joy and health alone could be	213	Lady Byron	3
The Boy of whom I spake;--he was alone	214	Dream	79
That God alone was to be seen in Heaven	215	Dream	125
The Wanderer was alone as heretofore	216	Dream	185
For her who soars alone above	221	Mariamne	15
Whose leaves for me alone were blooming	221	Mariamne	20
And the tents were all silent, the banners alone	222	Sennacherib	19
Is basely purchased, not with gold alone	227	Answer-C	5
Are in danger alone	239	Bray	32
Not fann'd alone by Victory's fleeting wing	239	Conquest	5
St. Luke alone can vanquish the disease	245	Bards	280
Nor this alone; but, pausing on the road	246	Bards	357

ALONE

Forsakes the rest, and cleaves to thee alone	249 Bards	537
His scenes alone had damn'd our sinking stage	251 Bards	734
Alone impels the modern bard to sing	253 Bards	852
Yet not with thee alone his name should live	254 Bards	943
With commerce, given alone to arms and arts	263 Hints	512
In song alone Apollo's will was told	266 Hints	686
Ice in a crowd and lava when alone	266 Hints	696
Alone and friendless on the magic shore	269 Minerva	57
Though not for him alone revenge shall wait	271 Minerva	209
And left lost Albion hated and alone	271 Minerva	220
With death alone are laurels cheaply bought	272 Minerva	294
Intoxicates alone the heedless heart	274 Waltz	36
Waltz--Waltz alone--both legs and arms demands	275 Waltz	113
The natural compound left alone to fight	286 Vision	83
I hardly know too if not quite alone am I	286 Vision	101
He reign'd o'er millions to serve me alone	289 Vision	312
Freedom to worship--not alone your Lord	291 Vision	380
Thou stand'st alone unrivall'd, till the fire	300 Age	183
But not alone within the hoariest clime	302 Age	314
And not alone where, plunged in night, a crowd	302 Age	316
Nor these alone; Columbia feels no less	307 Age	680
Yes, but for these and these alone	311 Giaour	85
For this, and this alone, renown'd	311 Giaour	160
And did he fly or fall alone	313 Giaour	278
'Tis left to fly or fall alone	314 Giaour	409
Was seen, but seen alone to speed	315 Giaour	470
And now I go--but go alone	317 Giaour	688
And from its torment 'scape alone	317 Giaour	749
But broods within his cell alone	318 Giaour	806
When met alone would fain retire	318 Giaour	847
And sterner hearts alone may feel	319 Giaour	920
Even bliss- 'twere woe alone to bear	319 Giaour	942
One mate, and one alone, will take	321 Giaour	1171
By me alone be duty taught	324 Abydos 1	43
I could not; and to view alone	324 Abydos 1	59
The nameless charms unmark'd by her alone	325 Abydos 1	177
To these alone my thoughts aspire	328 Abydos 1	406
Oh! when alone along the sky	329 Abydos 2	6
God! am I left alone on earth	330 Abydos 2	166
He ever went to war alone	332 Abydos 2	329
One word alone can paint to thee	332 Abydos 2	349
Nor these alone, for each right hand	334 Abydos 2	505
Alone and dewy, coldly pure and pale	337 Abydos 2	731
''Tis he--'tis Conrad; here--as wont--alone	340 Corsair 1	133
Along the govern'd aspect, speak alone	341 Corsair 1	232
Felt--that for him earth held but her alone	345 Corsair 1	480
And wrapt a breast bestow'd on heaven alone	348 Corsair 2	60
I taste nor bread nor banquet--save alone	349 Corsair 2	130
Must he alone of all retain his breath	351 Corsair 2	292
And left proud Conrad fetter'd and alone	351 Corsair 2	325
May writhe, rebel--the weak alone repent	352 Corsair 2	335
Alone he sate, in solitude had scann'd	352 Corsair 2	372
One thought alone he could not, dared not meet	352 Corsair 2	374
And was she here? and is he now alone	355 Corsair 2	538
Which thee and thine alone of all could spare	358 Corsair 3	174
'Tis not his life alone may claim such care	358 Corsair 3	185
In words alone I am not wont to chafe	358 Corsair 3	192
Its peal wax'd fainter--ceased--he felt alone	359 Corsair 3	268
Well have I earn'd--nor here alone--the meed	359 Corsair 3	286
Amid so many, hers alone is dark	364 Corsair 3	570
Repell'd approach and show'd him still alone	367 Lara 1	108
His page approach'd, and he alone appear'd	369 Lara 1	235
In trembling pairs (alone they dared not) crawl	369 Lara 1	259
But seems as searching his, and his alone	371 Lara 1	406
Though, like Count Lara, now return'd alone	372 Lara 1	472
From deeds, and deeds alone, may he discern	373 Lara 1	508
His faith in reverence and in deeds alone	374 Lara 1	555
In act alone obeys, his air commands	374 Lara 1	561
And all within that hall seem'd left alone	374 Lara 1	615
The menials felt their usual awe alone	377 Lara 2	174
Prepared to meet, but not alone, the worst	378 Lara 2	237
In either cause, one rage alone possess'd	379 Lara 2	274
The wary foe alone hath turn'd their mood	379 Lara 2	294
And Lara's soul alone seems still unbent	379 Lara 2	309
His eye alone proclaim'd, 'We will not part	380 Lara 2	357
Now girt with numbers, now almost alone	380 Lara 2	376
To Kaled, whom their meaning reach'd alone	381 Lara 2	447
Their import those who heard could judge alone	381 Lara 2	455
And some as scatter'd and alone	384 Corinth	25
Alone, did Alp, the renegade	386 Corinth	178
He stood alone among the host	387 Corinth	296
He stood alone--a renegade	387 Corinth	306
He stood alone amidst his band	387 Corinth	308
While he alone, where thousands pass'd	388 Corinth	354
Darkly, sternly, and all alone	394 Corinth	947
My life must linger on alone	398 Parisina	202
Thou didst not give me life alone	399 Parisina	292
The heart which love of thee alone can bind	402 Sonnet-F	4
And we were three--yet, each alone	403 Chillon	49
And still we were--or seem'd--alone	413 Mazeppa	667
Methought I felt too much alone	415 Mazeppa	839
Bound, naked, bleeding, and alone	415 Mazeppa	851
Of wandering with the moon and love alone	419 Island 2	40

Not me alone, but one so sweet and true	426 Island 2	527
Back on themselves,--their sins remain'd alone	427 Island 3	42
And but for this alone the whole might seem	431 Island 4	81
Nor these alone, for all had been prepared	432 Island 4	165
And tasteless food, which I have eat alone	437 Tasso	14
Return'd and wept alone, and dream'd again	438 Tasso	164
And could not sleep with ease alone at night	443 Beppo	228
If the free Switzer yet bestrides alone	454 Venice-B	129
Love so ineffable and so alone	456 Dante 1	21
Their days in endless strife, and die alone	458 Dante 1	152
Could be so; but alone she will not war	460 Dante 2	123
For thee alone they have no arm to save	461 Dante 3	48
How servile is the task to please alone	461 Dante 3	87
Built up between us, and will die alone	465 Dante 4	148
Then forth alone from Paris went the chief	468 Morgante	127
From savage brutes alone, too fierce to tame	469 Morgante	181
As to a brother dear I speak alone	469 Morgante	222
Who, seeing him alone in this design	469 Morgante	238
A savage serpent fell on me alone	471 Morgante	339
We were alone, quite unsuspiciously	477 Francesca	33
Thou canst never be alone	481 Manfred 1	207
These were my pastimes, and to be alone	486 Manfred 2	169
Alone, but with them gentler powers than mine	486 Manfred 2	206
It rests with thee alone--command her voice	490 Manfred 2	482
I fear them not, and feel for theirs alone	490 Manfred 2	516
But I would fain confer with thee alone	491 Manfred 3	24
I leave to heaven,--'Vengeance is mine alone	492 Manfred 3	63
The lion is alone, and so am I	493 Manfred 3	123
Away! I'll die as I have lived--alone	496 Manfred 3	350
'Tis fit I were alone. Ere I depart	504 Faliero 1	281
Nor I alone, are injured and abused	507 Faliero 1	489
And leave the palace? You must come alone	508 Faliero 1	583
At midnight I will be alone and mask'd	508 Faliero 1	594
Would he were come! for I alone have power	509 Faliero 2	24
Do you still keep apart, and walk alone	511 Faliero 2	176
We will not strike for private wrongs alone	516 Faliero 2	527
Is in our power: he comes alone with me	518 Faliero 2	671
Far better than we can, to whom alone	524 Faliero 3	419
But a brief passage--I would go alone	537 Faliero 4	629
Alone can profit you on earth or heaven	538 Faliero 5	32
Where you alone could minister. I knew not	541 Faliero 5	210
I would have stood alone amidst your tombs	541 Faliero 5	263
I am devoted unto God alone	545 Faliero 5	544
Alone will be beholders of thy doom	546 Faliero 5	555
Thyself alone, but these vast realms, from all	559 Sardan 1	574
May show him how alone a king can leave	561 Sardan 1	712
Alone you dare not. Alone! foolish slave	564 Sardan 2	162
I'll on alone. Alone! Thrones hold but one	568 Sardan 2	390
Go forth, and conquer! Now, I am alone	574 Sardan 3	173
To bear alone, that we must mingle sorrows	581 Sardan 4	230
Alone with him! How many a year has pass'd	582 Sardan 4	235
Those infants, not alone from the blind love	582 Sardan 4	260
But could not I remain, alone? What! leave	584 Sardan 4	380
What, shall he die alone?--I live alone	584 Sardan 4	407
He shall not die alone; but lonely too	584 Sardan 4	408
Alone--I seek no partners but in pleasure	585 Sardan 4	482
Alone creates it, kindles, and may quench it	587 Sardan 4	572
I am alone. And is all lost? Our walls	589 Sardan 5	141
Forgot the custom; and although alone	594 Sardan 5	454
Away!--I'll walk alone. As you please, signor	598 Foscari 1	152
Not for the laws alone, for those you have strain'd	605 Foscari 2	250
Not me alone, but all who dwell here, could	605 Foscari 2	274
And I shall be alone; no men--no books	610 Foscari 3	112
Their tents were pitch'd together--I'm alone	611 Foscari 3	190
Till he himself shall brood in it alone	613 Foscari 3	339
Alone is aim'd at. But discarded princes	615 Foscari 4	60
Alone can answer; they are rarely wont	616 Foscari 4	66
Of such support! But for myself alone	617 Foscari 4	139
And not alone refused, but ye exacted	621 Foscari 5	41
Perhaps you fain would be alone? Alone	621 Foscari 5	66
Alone, come all the world around me, I	621 Foscari 5	67
I fain would be alone a little while	628 Cain 1	57
Let him crowd orb on orb: he is alone	629 Cain 1	152
Could master all things:--but I thought alone	630 Cain 1	175
Wert happy--Be thou happy, then, alone	634 Cain 1	461
Which humbles me and mine. Alone I could not	634 Cain 1	463
Alone, thou say'st, be happy? Alone! Oh, my God	634 Cain 1	469
Who could be happy and alone, or good	634 Cain 1	470
Yet thy God is alone; and is he happy	634 Cain 1	474
Will he return? Ay, woman! he alone	635 Cain 1	537
Abel, I pray thee, sacrifice alone	649 Cain 3	190
Revere him, then--but let it be alone	649 Cain 3	194
What? Where am I? alone! Where's Abel? where	651 Cain 3	322
Henceforth alone--we never must meet more	653 Cain 3	446
I alone must not weep. My office is	654 Cain 3	547
I must proceed alone. Then peace be with thee	658 Heaven	213
Rather than see his mates endure alone	660 Heaven	417
Alone can do so. Ah! he speaks of death	663 Heaven	642
Who could alone have made mine happy, she	664 Heaven	651
It would not be to live, alone exempt	664 Heaven	698
When earth must be alone	665 Heaven	777
Our doom is sorrow: not to us alone	667 Heaven	930

ALONE

And we are alone	668	Heaven	963
Yes. And from these alone. And that is something	672	Werner 1	37
Hath wasted, not alone my strength, but means	672	Werner 1	51
Far worse than solitude. Alone, I had died	672	Werner 1	66
That I would be alone; but to your business	674	Werner 1	205
Alone preserved my freedom--till I left	680	Werner 1	567
That he suspects me's certain. I'm alone	681	Werner 1	626
Hath something which I like not; and alone	687	Werner 2	296
His death alone can save you:--Thank your God	690	Werner 2	457
Father and son, and stand alone. But stay	690	Werner 2	488
Alone. I will retire with you. Not so	693	Werner 2	672
His claims alone were too contemptible	694	Werner 2	741
Alone, unknown,--a solitary grave	703	Werner 3	572
Alone, and leave all other thoughts to me	704	Werner 3	592
What? That he died alone. The general rumour	707	Werner 4	185
He could not die neglected or alone	707	Werner 4	189
It were not well that you alone of all	708	Werner 4	243
Ulric, I wish to speak with you alone	708	Werner 4	277
Jewels nor gold; his life alone was sought	716	Werner 5	196
Blood became ice. But he was all alone	718	Werner 5	318
Had found you waking, Heaven alone can tell	718	Werner 5	354
I did not enter Prague alone; and should I	719	Werner 5	390
I am not alone; nor merely the vain heir	721	Werner 5	534
Them both!--My Josephine! we are now alone	722	Werner 5	552
I am not alone a soldier, but the soldiers	733	Deformed 1	811
Let him alone; he's brave, and ever has	734	Deformed 1	819
To crack those walls alone. You may sneer, since	734	Deformed 1	866
And they themselves alone the real 'Nothings	743	Deformed 3	102
That Poesy has wreaths for you alone	745	Juan Ded	38
Since gold alone should not have been its price	745	Juan Ded	44
With virtues equall'd by her wit alone	748	Juan 1	76
Standing alone beside his desolate hearth	751	Juan 1	285
Him up to learn his catechism alone	753	Juan 1	414
Who cannot leave alone our helpless clay	754	Juan 1	499
She sate, but not alone; I know not well	759	Juan 1	833
Is first and passionate love--it stands alone	762	Juan 1	1010
Now, Don Alfonso entering, but alone	768	Juan 1	1377
It might be that her silence sprang alone	768	Juan 1	1406
They were alone, but not alone as they	798	Juan 2	1497
To them but mockeries of the past alone	799	Juan 2	1589
One man alone at first her heart can move	802	Juan 3	22
They kindly leave us, though not quite alone	808	Juan 3	471
Their place of birth alone is mute	812	Juan 3	698
And musing there an hour alone	812	Juan 3	703
Leaving my people to proceed alone	814	Juan 3	859
That trash of such sort not alone evades	815	Juan 3	891
The lady and her lover, left alone	815	Juan 3	901
They were alone once more; for them to be	817	Juan 4	73
The eagle soars alone; the gull and crow	820	Juan 4	223
She dream'd of being alone on the sea-shore	820	Juan 4	241
She died, but not alone; she held within	825	Juan 4	553
Those sufferings Dante saw in hell alone	829	Juan 4	840
A kind of death comes o'er us all alone	838	Juan 5	455
Could yet be known unto the fates alone	850	Juan 5	1220
'Besides, I hate to sleep alone,' quoth she	858	Juan 6	377
Alone, for reasons which don't matter; you	858	Juan 6	386
That the young stranger should not lie alone	862	Juan 6	644
Her neck alone was seen, but that was found	863	Juan 6	675
Would not alone have made him insecure	865	Juan 6	829
At length they found mere cannonade alone	871	Juan 7	236
In safety to the waggons, where alone	876	Juan 7	557
He found himself alone, and friends retiring	881	Juan 8	216
Alone can save the earth from hell's pollution	884	Juan 8	408
He was not all alone: around him grew	886	Juan 8	513
And felt--though done with life--he was alone	893	Juan 8	936
So much the better!--I may stand alone	929	Juan 11	711
But if Love don't, Cash does, and Cash alone	931	Juan 12	105
Nor by mustachios moved, were let alone	937	Juan 12	486
For letting that pure sanctuary alone	944	Juan 13	212
Were vanish'd to be what they call alone	947	Juan 13	387
But in a higher niche, alone, but crown'd	948	Juan 13	481
In Guido's famous fresco which alone	960	Juan 14	314
In fact, his manner was his own alone	970	Juan 15	100

ALONG

More merrily along	5	Harold 1	141
Dark Guadiana rolls his power along	9	Harold 1	379
And many a varied shore to sail along	25	Harold 2	318
As woo'd the eye and thrill'd the Bosphorus along	32	Harold 2	755
The death-bolts deadliest the thinn'd files along	39	Harold 3	259
Thus Harold inly said, and pass'd along	43	Harold 3	460
Of a dark eye in woman! Far along	49	Harold 3	863
The colouring of the scenes which fleet along	52	Harold 3	1042
And miscreator, makes and helps along	74	Harold 4	1123
I saw the sprightly wand'rers pour along	125	Recoll	205
Tell me, ye hoary few, who glide along	127	Recoll	385
From mountain to mountain I bounded along	136	Highlander	18
No more so idly pass along	153	Friend-A	75
Her hours can gaily glide along	163	Malta	43
'Thus lifted gloriously, you'll sweep along	171	Address-B	39
Thy name, our charging hosts along	219	Thy Days	13

ALONG

Immeasurable measures move along	244	Bards	149
A few brief generations fleet along	254	Bards	953
With native eloquence he soars along	257	Hints	65
Still let it bear the hearer's soul along	258	Hints	140
He speaks, but, as his subject swells along	259	Hints	203
And oft had Hassan's Youth along	313	Giaour	312
And fate, and fury, drive along	316	Giaour	635
Such were the sounds that thrill'd the rocks along	338	Corsair 1	45
Then shall my handmaids while the time along	344	Corsair 1	435
And pass'd his shaking hand along	399	Parisina	228
They saw me strangely bound along	413	Mazeppa	696
With crazy oar and shatter'd strength along	418	Island 1	187
A limb was broken, and he droop'd along	434	Island 4	327
And under the Rialto shoot along	442	Beppo	154
The echo of thy tyrant's voice along	453	Venice-B	22
But in a farther age shall rise along	462	Dante 3	106
Said, 'I will go, and while he lies along	470	Morgante	258
Love to one death conducted us along	476	Francesca	10
Of mortals whom thy lure hath led along	760	Juan 1	846
And vesper bell's that rose the boughs along	815	Juan 3	940
Still he forgot not his disguise:--along	856	Juan 6	233
At length they rose, like a white wall along	915	Juan 10	513
Blushing with Bacchant coronals along	950	Juan 13	602

ALONZO

Where, as Zanga, I trod on Alonzo o'erthrown	96	Harrow-A	18
Alonzo! best and dearest of my friends	125	Recoll	243

ALOOF

His arms a dart, he fights aloof, nor more	16	Harold 1	744
Love kept aloof, albeit not far remote	24	Harold 2	274
And fellow-countrymen have stood aloof	29	Harold 2	593
Shall Grub-street dine, while duns are kept aloof	249	Bards	547
White cliffs, that held invasion far aloof	305	Age	532
That kept at least frivolity aloof	367	Lara 1	110
Stern, and aloof a little from the rest	427	Island 3	85
The desperate trio held aloof their fate	434	Island 4	319
Too long her armed wrath hath kept aloof	457	Dante 1	85
Or if their destiny be born aloof	464	Dante 4	107
He keeps aloof from all the revels? But	563	Sardan 2	97
Aloof from desolation! My last prayer	595	Sardan 5	490
Aloof, save fear of famine! All is low	607	Foscari 2	351
He has valets now enough: has stood aloof then	678	Werner 1	437
Theirs on him, policy has held aloof	679	Werner 1	495
Takes care of us. Keep thought aloof from hosts	734	Deformed 1	864
Kept still aloof the crew, who, ere they sunk	778	Juan 2	279
And patient spirit held aloof his fate	785	Juan 2	700
Her office was to keep aloof or smother	856	Juan 6	246
Was such as rather seem'd to keep aloof	970	Juan 15	107

ALOUD

Back to the joyous Alps who call to her aloud	49	Harold 3	868
Nor coin'd my cheek to smiles, nor cried aloud	52	Harold 3	1052
Aloud, a scheme less moral than 'twas clever	297	Vision	774
Roused discipline aloud proclaims their cause	418	Island 1	203
To some she whispers, others speaks aloud	448	Beppo	515
Have voices, tongues to cry aloud for me	747	Juan Ded	126
Aloud because his feelings were too tender	863	Juan 6	707

ALP

Like climbing some great Alp, which still doth rise	78	Harold 4	1397
Was Alp, the Adrian renegade	385	Corinth	114
To Alp, who well repaid the trust	386	Corinth	155
Alone, did Alp, the renegade	386	Corinth	178
When Alp, beneath his Christian name	386	Corinth	185
The tent of Alp was on the shore	387	Corinth	284
Was Alp, despite his flight and crimes	388	Corinth	391
Still by the shore Alp mutely mused	388	Corinth	424
And Alp knew, by the turbans that roll'd on the sand	389	Corinth	466
Alp turn'd him from the sickening sight	389	Corinth	479
Alp look'd to heaven, and grew on high	391	Corinth	651
Alp at their head; his right arm is bare	392	Corinth	705
Alp is but known by the white arm bare	393	Corinth	830
As he saw Alp staggering bow	394	Corinth	859
The sharp shot dash'd Alp to the ground	394	Corinth	875
When Alp, her fierce assailant, fell	394	Corinth	913
Adored the Alp, and loved the Apennine	422	Island 2	285
In feeble colours, when the eye--from the Alp	459	Dante 2	62

ALPHA

Thus Juan learn'd his alpha beta better	794	Juan 2	1303

ALPHABET

Your alphabet. And wherefore do you not	732	Deformed 1	672
It answers better to resolve the alphabet	732	Deformed 1	673
And Greek--the alphabet--I'm nearly sure	748	Juan 1	98
Of Dido's alphabet; and this is rational	881	Juan 8	183

ALPINE

In the sun's face, like yonder Alpine snow	45	Harold 3	642

ALPINE

Of soil supports them 'gainst the Alpine shocks	58	Harold	4	175
Of glory streams along the Alpine height	59	Harold	4	237
Here are the Alpine landscapes which create	211	Augusta-C		57
On the Alpine vales below	392	Corinth		744
Of ocean's alpine azure rose and fell	427	Island	3	72
Rocking their Alpine brethren; filling up	483	Manfred	1	355
That overpowers some Alpine river's rush	792	Juan	2	1126
Flow'd like an Alpine torrent which the sun	810	Juan	3	578
Within an Alpine hollow, when the wind	820	Juan	4	234
Or the snow minaret on an Alpine steep	860	Juan	6	540

ALPS

Chimaera's alps extend from left to right	27	Harold	2	453
But these recede. Above me are the Alps	45	Harold	3	590
Back to the joyous Alps who call to her aloud	49	Harold	3	868
Hath spread himself a couch, the Alps have rear'd a throne	51	Harold	3	976
The clouds above me to the white Alps tend	52	Harold	3	1017
Down the deep Alps; nor would the hostile horde	61	Harold	4	383
The infant Alps, which--had I not before	66	Harold	4	650
Ye Alps, which view'd him in his dawning flights	300	Age		135
Besides, within the Alps, to every woman	444	Beppo		281
Oh! when the strangers pass the Alps and Po	460	Dante	2	101
Are the Alps weaker than Thermopylae	460	Dante	2	116
To make the Alps impassable; and we	460	Dante	2	144
Myself, and thee--a peasant of the Alps	484	Manfred	2	63
From the Alps to the Caucasus ride we, or fly	730	Deformed	1	567
The Alps and their snow	732	Deformed	1	692

ALP'S

And Alp's career a moment check'd	393	Corinth		848
Alp's already with the slain	394	Corinth		866
The Alp's snow summit nearer heaven is seen	463	Dante	3	186

ALREADY

My years already doubly number thine	3	To Ianthe		20
Deface the scenes, already how defaced	34	Harold	2	876
To him my tribute is already paid	123	Recoll		120
A debt already paid in pain	172	Time-B		16
He the venom has already	197	Rogers		64
As if we witness'd all already done	259	Hints		206
Have taken already, and still will continue	282	Blues	2	105
Don't call upon Scamp, who's already so harass'd	282	Blues	2	122
Already; and I merely argued his	293	Vision		509
The rest thou dost already know	322	Giaour		1200
Already at his feet hath sunk	334	Abydos	2	540
Already doubled is the cape--our bay	339	Corsair	1	89
Already shared the captives and the prize	347	Corsair	2	10
Already polish'd by the hand divine	355	Corsair	2	542
One day to him--the wretch already mine	358	Corsair	3	170
Already reddening on thy guilty cheeks	358	Corsair	3	183
Our bark is tossing--'tis already day	362	Corsair	3	433
Whose words already might my heart have wrung	376	Lara	2	46
Already they perceive its tranquil beam	379	Lara	2	322
Already they descry--is yon the bank	379	Lara	2	324
Alp's already with the slain	394	Corinth		866
And lop the already lifeless head	395	Corinth		991
But yet--they are already past	397	Parisina		46
My wounds already scarr'd with cold	411	Mazeppa		489
I wish'd the goal already won	411	Mazeppa		508
With leafy couch already made	415	Mazeppa		862
And she had waited several years already	444	Beppo		278
Their children's children's doom already brought	458	Dante	2	4
Ruin, already proud of the deeds done	459	Dante	2	73
By several pens already praised; but they	466	Morgante		29
Leonardo Aretino said already	466	Morgante		33
They are too long already.--Hence--begone	480	Manfred	1	170
Seems tottering already. Mountains have fallen	483	Manfred	1	353
It matters not--my soul was scorch'd already	484	Manfred	2	73
'Tis taught already;--many a night on the earth	489	Manfred	2	407
Content thyself with what thou know'st already	494	Manfred	3	212
This eve already. Herman! I command thee	494	Manfred	3	255
Which hath already given three dukes to Venice	502	Flaiero	1	160
Had been already where--how soon, I care not	504	Faliero	1	349
Matured and strengthen'd. We're enough already	508	Faliero	1	574
Already spent in unavailing plaints	522	Faliero	3	270
I am indeed already lost in wonder	530	Faliero	4	182
Upon your engines, gorged with pangs already	538	Faliero	5	47
A city's glory--we have laid already	540	Faliero	5	159
Already. You oppress'd the prince and people	541	Faliero	5	248
And please your enemies--a host already	542	Faliero	5	279
The torture! you have put me there already	542	Faliero	5	301
He hath already own'd to his own guilt	543	Faliero	5	354
I am already; and my blood will rise	545	Faliero	5	526
Lo, where they come! already I perceive	551	Sardan	1	37
Curse not thyself--millions do that already	552	Sardan	1	97
They say thy sceptre's turn'd to that already	556	Sardan	1	373
Already captive? can I not even breathe	560	Sardan	1	621
I have foretold already--thou wilt win it	563	Sardan	2	140
It is already, or at least they march'd	576	Sardan	3	336
Has not already shown to those who live	579	Sardan	4	55
By their two leaders, are already up	586	Sardan	4	546
(The tears of all the good are thine already	589	Sardan	5	158
What, crown'd already?--But, proceed. Beleses	592	Sardan	5	289
My lord,--the soldiers are already charged	593	Sardan	5	356
Me to the dust already. Get thee hence	593	Sardan	5	379
Our powers are such. But he has twice already	615	Foscari	4	41
Already mention'd in our former congress	623	Foscari	5	172
The fruits, or neither! One is yours already	630	Cain	1	208
No other choice. Your sire has chosen already	634	Cain	1	427
To know there are such realms. We knew already	641	Cain	2	376
To you already, in your little world	645	Cain	2	653
Be contrite? for my father's sin, already	648	Cain	3	118
Hark! hark! already we can hear the voice	661	Heaven		486
Too much already hast thou deign'd	667	Heaven		928
Already grasps each drowning hill	670	Heaven		1174
Friends. You appear to have drunk enough already	674	Werner	1	201
Already proved by greater perils than	693	Werner	2	643
Shalt thou be mine? I am, methinks, already	700	Werner	3	339
Already done as much. What do you mean	704	Werner	4	38
All--all--And you to me are so already	707	Werner	4	171
Already are at the portal. Have you sent	713	Werner	5	2
I am so already. Feel how my heart beats	713	Werner	5	29
You slew him!--Wretch! He was already slain	718	Werner	5	316
What! shrink already, being what you are	728	Deformed	1	450
And you are old in the world's ways already	729	Deformed	1	490
I swear. Spare thine already forfeit soul	740	Deformed	2	356
Would be for a disease already cured	744	Deformed	3	163
And offer poison long already mix'd	746	Juan	Ded	96
Her young philosopher was grown already	753	Juan	1	400
Who've made 'us youth' wait too--too long already	762	Juan	1	996
Who had already perish'd, suffering madly	784	Juan	2	639
But I have spoken of all this already	796	Juan	2	1365
And oh! ye gentlemen who have already	804	Juan	3	193
Suppose,--but you already have supposed	848	Juan	5	1041
Already many a once love-beaten breast	866	Juan	6	915
But on the thirteenth, when already part	872	Juan	7	305
After the hardships you've already borne	875	Juan	7	492
The troops, already disembark'd, push'd on	880	Juan	8	113
Our kill'd, already piled up to the chin	890	Juan	8	782
Already they beheld the silver showers	906	Juan	9	629
If that they were not married all already	972	Juan	15	240
Or wed already, who object to this	972	Juan	15	251
Beyond the charmers we have already cited	974	Juan	15	380
Waking already, and return'd at length	983	Juan	16	199
My trembling Lyre already several strings	998	Juan	17	101

AL-SIRAT'S

Though on Al-Sirat's arch I stood	315	Giaour		483

ALSO

Perchance to me thine also wanders	112	Quaker		28
And also for the Surry (sic	233	Ballad-B		26
Can also, when a hobbling line appears	262	Hints		435
Will you go? There's Miss Lilac will also be present	280	Blues	1	142
And he for her had also wept	398	Parisina		183
But left her vices also to their heirs	418	Island	1	220
And why not also Torquil and his bride	433	Island	4	218
It may perhaps be also to your zest	441	Beppo		93
Wrote rhymes, sang songs, could also tell a story	444	Beppo		259
I also like to dine on becaficas	445	Beppo		337
Also Ansuigi, the gay time to pass	467	Morgante		68
And also made a breakfast of his own	469	Morgante		218
Would that I could save them and Venice also	524	Faliero	3	427
And Pania also. Can aught have befallen them	576	Sardan	3	303
May also be in danger scarce less imminent	592	Sardan	5	328
Foul rumours were abroad; I have also read	605	Foscari	2	223
That were too human, also. But it was not	606	Foscari	2	279
May I not see them also? No--not here	613	Foscari	3	364
In nature being earth also--more in wisdom	630	Cain	1	222
Also the cabinet, if portable	684	Werner	2	54
Search empty pockets; also, to arrest	684	Werner	2	70
(Save for the actual loss) is lucky also	687	Werner	2	289
Your gold. I also know, that were I even	691	Werner	2	561
That's very well. You also know your place, too	699	Werner	3	300
I would have aided you, and also have	719	Werner	5	380
I'll take it for so much. Take also that	719	Werner	5	396
Also some culverins upon the walls	731	Deformed	1	614
Also a dealer in the sword and dagger	738	Deformed	2	205
And also of his mother, if you'd rather	748	Juan	1	56
'Tis also pleasant to be deem'd magnaninous	750	Juan	1	235
A thousand pities also with respect	751	Juan	1	262
As Numa's (who was also named Pompilius	751	Juan	1	279
She took his lady also in affection	755	Juan	1	531
He also found that he had lost his dinner	758	Juan	1	752
Thus parents also are at times short-sighted	759	Juan	1	793
Breathes also to the heart, and o'er it throws	761	Juan	1	911
Were there not also Russians, English, many	765	Juan	1	1189
Me also, since the time so opportune is	765	Juan	1	1198
They also lie too--under a mistake	772	Juan	1	1664
Started the stern-post, also shatter'd the	777	Juan	2	212
Was also great with which they had to cope	779	Juan	2	324
He also stuff'd his money where he could	781	Juan	2	465
And also for the biscuit-casks and butter	781	Juan	2	488
But in this case I also must remark	786	Juan	2	753

ALSO

A reef between them also now began	787 Juan	2	829
They also gave a petticoat apiece	791 Juan	2	1061
I study, also Blair, the highest reachers	795 Juan	2	1318
Are also learnt from Ceres and from Bacchus	795 Juan	2	1351
Of human frailty, folly, also crime	802 Juan	3	34
They sometimes also get a little tired	802 Juan	3	50
But now their eyes and also lips were dry	806 Juan	3	301
But Shakespeare also says, 'tis very silly	811 Juan	3	607
Also our hero's lot, howe'er unpleasant	831 Juan	4	930
She has served me also much the same as you	833 Juan	5	111
And also when my second ran away	833 Juan	5	152
Or, if it were, if also his digestion	835 Juan	5	234
Sigh'd Juan, muttering also some slight oaths	841 Juan	5	605
And also could you look a little modest	843 Juan	5	728
(Of which I have also seen some six or seven	843 Juan	5	748
As also at the race and county balls	844 Juan	5	824
And as she also risk'd her life to get out	847 Juan	5	972
I also would suggest the fitting time	847 Juan	5	977
And also, as may be presumed, she laid	847 Juan	5	1028
And half of that opinion's also mine	847 Juan	5	1032
It also gently hints to them that others	848 Juan	5	1098
Was also certain that the earth was square	850 Juan	5	1194
His empire also was without a bound	850 Juan	5	1197
Her comrades, also, thought themselves undone	851 Juan	5	1243
The heathen also, though with lesser latitude	854 Juan	6	82
Also beneath the canopy of beds	855 Juan	6	194
Katinka ask'd her also whence she came	858 Juan	6	347
'She also had compassion and a bed	858 Juan	6	376
While gentle writers also love to lift	863 Juan	6	702
Also arose about the self-same time	863 Juan	6	713
Also to have the sacking of a town	869 Juan	7	141
Was also in three columns, with a thirst	873 Juan	7	398
Also he dress'd up, for the nonce, fascines	873 Juan	7	417
Also the General Markow, Brigadier	879 Juan	8	81
His orders, also to receive his pensions	884 Juan	8	391
Another column also suffer'd much	888 Juan	8	617
To make him prisoner, was also dish'd	888 Juan	8	640
Your houris also have a natural pleasure	892 Juan	8	897
As also of the first academicians	898 Juan	9	130
Also the softer silks were heard to rustle	907 Juan	9	653
As also did Miss Protasoff then there	907 Juan	9	670
This we pass over. We will also pass	910 Juan	10	185
Their fare; and also pause besides, to fuddle	916 Juan	10	566
Republics also get involved a bit	930 Juan	12	45
And Marriage also may exist without	931 Juan	12	118
But though I also had reform'd before	934 Juan	12	301
Though several also keep their perpendicular	937 Juan	12	467
And some of them high names: I have also known	937 Juan	12	482
There's also nightly, to the uninitiated	937 Juan	12	489
And now and then it also suits my rhymes	942 Juan	13	60
Lord Henry also liked to be superior	943 Juan	13	145
Also the solace of an overcharge	946 Juan	13	360
Also a foreigner of high condition	947 Juan	13	415
'Tis also subject to the double danger	959 Juan	14	250
Admired, adored; but also so correct	962 Juan	14	442
Her beauty also seem'd to form no clog	974 Juan	15	381
Also the conference which we have seen	977 Juan	15	597
Their docile esquires also did the same	994 Juan	16	854

ALTADA

And pleasure, good Altada, to which glory	571 Sardan	3	12
Altada--Zames--forth, and arm ye! There	573 Sardan	3	119
Altada, arm yourself and return here	573 Sardan	3	125
Altada! Where's Altada? Waiting, sire	574 Sardan	3	166
Dead. And Altada? Dying. Pania? Sfero	589 Sardan	5	139

ALTAR

His altar the high places and the peak	49 Harold	3	852
An offering to thine altar from the queen	68 Harold	4	780
Who kneels to the god, on his altar of light	100 L Adieu		41
To Fiction's motley altar turn	141 Critics		14
Before an Altar--with a gentle bride	215 Dream		146
Even at the altar, o'er his brow there came	215 Dream		149
The Altar and Throne	239 Bray		31
The Altar itself	239 Bray		34
Pure is the flame which o'er her altar burns	245 Bards		291
Minotti stood o'er the altar stone	394 Corinth		948
To the high altar on they go	395 Corinth		996
And thy sad floor an altar; for 'twas trod	402 Sonnet-F		10
Stand crown'd, but bound and helpless, at the altar	541 Faliero	5	209
A priest's for the high altar, even unto	605 Foscari	2	256
Come, Foscari, take the hand the altar gave you	614 Foscari	3	433
With Abel on an altar. Saidst thou not	632 Cain	1	323
One altar may suffice; I have no offering	647 Cain	3	104
And altar without gore, may win thy favour	650 Cain	3	267
Thine altar, with its blood of lambs and kids	650 Cain	3	292
Words! let that altar stand--'tis hallow'd now	650 Cain	3	295
Brother, give back! thou shalt not touch my altar	650 Cain	3	305
Massy and bloody! snatch'd from off the altar	652 Cain	3	392
The altar, gazing on his Trojan bride	726 Deformed	1	275
Above, and many altar shrines below	731 Deformed	1	613
As though it were an altar; now his foot	737 Deformed	2	162

ALTAR

Even at the altar foot, whence I look down	740 Deformed	2	345

ALTAR-PIECE

Like cherubs round an altar-piece they cling	809 Juan	3	477

ALTAR-PIECES

There also are some altar-pieces, though	288 Vision		229

ALTAR-PLACE

The dying embers of an altar-place	189 Darkness		58

ALTARS

A thousand altars rise, for ever blazing bright	14 Harold	1	674
And bear these altars o'er the long-reluctant brine	21 Harold	2	99
But not for you will Freedom's altars flame	31 Harold	2	725
And Greece her very altars eyes in vain	32 Harold	2	750
Not for such purpose were these altars placed	34 Harold	2	877
Who worship, here are altars for their beads	77 Harold	4	1321
But thou, of temples old or altars new	78 Harold	4	1378
Thine altars with the produce of the chase	110 Nisus		346
Though there his altars are no more divine	268 Minerva		10
Though there his altars are no more divine	355 Corsair	3	10
O'er wither'd fields, and ruin'd altars	388 Corinth		383
A priest at her altars, a chief in her halls	392 Corinth		711
Like altars ranged along the broad canal	529 Faliero	4	79
Strikes his own altars. That were a dread omen	570 Sardan	2	553
With new kings rise new altars. But, proceed	592 Sardan	5	291
Two altars, which our brother Abel made	647 Cain	3	96
What shall I do? Choose one of those two altars	649 Cain	3	210
Take them! If thou must be induced with altars	650 Cain	3	252
It is too late. I will build no more altars	650 Cain	3	288
In that which it may purchase from your altars	712 Werner	4	500
Mightier founders of those altars	736 Deformed	2	115
My altars are the mountains and the oceans	815 Juan	3	926

ALTAR'S

I see thee to the altar's foot	179 Gold		31

ALTER

And canst not alter now	167 Dead		22
And 'thy true faith can alter never	173 Quotation		1
And will not alter what you can't defend	267 Hints		790
Will alter nothing which I have to say	621 Foscari	5	38
To alter his intent	668 Heaven		959
I cannot stop to alter words once written	906 Juan	9	612

ALTERATIONS

These few short years make wondrous alterations	755 Juan	1	551
In short, the list of alterations bothers	928 Juan	11	638

ALTER'D

Yet Time, who changes all, had alter'd him	36 Harold	3	69
When thou wert changed, they alter'd too	169 The Chain		17
That pouting lip and alter'd eye	172 Romaic-B		26
And the tide rising in my alter'd eye	212 Augusta-C		72
So alter'd since last year his pen is	231 Doctor		37
With some faint hope his alter'd lay	327 Abydos	1	293
'Tis Morn--and o'er his alter'd features play	355 Corsair	2	555
Faded, or alter'd into something new	820 Juan	4	274
But times are alter'd since, a rhyming lover	830 Juan	4	882

ALTERING

Than can be hid by altering his shirt; he	909 Juan	10	116

ALTERNATE

And mass and revel were alternate seen	8 Harold	1	336
Alternate converse, and their plans unfold	106 Nisus		88
The reeking weapon bears alternate stains	109 Nisus		272
By love's alternate joy and woe	161 Maid		17
Through eight long ages of alternate gore	301 Age		263
His thoughts on love and hate alternate dwell	357 Corsair	3	133
The empire of the alternate victor's breast	379 Lara	2	275

ALTERNATELY

Must myrtle and cypress alternately strew	100 L Adieu		42

ALTERNATIVE

The blest alternative of fraud or force	333 Abydos	2	435
'The last alternative befits me best	376 Lara	2	55
To the alternative of a decree	621 Foscari	5	48

ALTHOUGH

But I digress: of all appeals,--although	837 Juan	5	385
Aught of a serious, sorrowing kind, although	846 Juan	5	949
There was a way to end their strife, although	864 Juan	6	756
Long banquets and too many guests, although	992 Juan	16	730

ALTO
(See CONTRA-ALTO)

ALTOGETHER

Because not altogether of such clay	75 Harold	4	1214

ALTOGETHER

Alas! must perish altogether	118	Romance		64
Is of a fair complexion altogether	442	Beppo		138
He groan'd with joy to see them altogether	467	Morgante		80
Dependent on the public altogether	771	Juan	1	1587
He caged in one huge hamper altogether	804	Juan	3	144
Could altogether call the past to mind	826	Juan	4	595
Or got rid of the parties altogether	867	Juan	6	948
A little spoil'd, but not so altogether	936	Juan	12	387
A lady altogether to his mind	940	Juan	12	644

ALVA

Allan, with these through Alva fly	103	Alva	114

ALVA'S

Where Alva's hoary turrets rise	101	Alva	3
On Alva's casques of silver play'd	101	Alva	6
Faded is Alva's noble race	102	Alva	21
But who was last of Alva's clan	102	Alva	25
Why grows the moss on Alva's stone	102	Alva	26
On Alva's dusky hills of wind	102	Alva	54
Assembled wave in Alva's hall	102	Alva	90
The hope of Alva's age is o'er	103	Alva	143
Throng through the gate of Alva's hall	103	Alva	178
For Alva's sons knew Oscar well	105	Alva	284

ALWAY

Though alway changing, in her aspect mild	25	Harold	2	326

ALWAYS

Joy was not always absent from his face	43	Harold	3	467
And music meets not always now the ear	55	Harold	4	22
To him, alike, are always known	87	Ad Lesbiam		7
And always are prating about and about it	145	Casuists		2
Not always doom'd its heat to smother	148	A Fan		18
I'm almost dead, and always dizzy	232	Doctor		88
In him, I hope, will always fit so	233	Hoppner		2
And is always as nobly requited	236	Freedom		6
Two objects always should the poet move	264	Hints		531
Kind Nature always will perform her part	266	Hints		698
Always the ladies, and sometimes their lords	275	Waltz		102
A scholar always, now and then a wit	305	Age		524
And there are hues not always faded	318	Giaour		863
Why Giaffir always seem'd thy foe	330	Abydos	2	179
Not always knightly spurs are worn	399	Parisina		270
Besides, they always smell of bread and butter	445	Beppo		312
Are always so preposterously jealous	447	Beppo		440
Those brazen creatures always suit their taste	448	Beppo		536
And not be always thieving on the main	452	Beppo		756
I've heard the Count and he were always friends	452	Beppo		788
He in the cabinet being always ready	466	Morgante		37
'Orlando must we always then obey	467	Morgante		88
I wish for your great gallantry always	472	Morgante		382
The jealous vigilance which always led you	541	Faliero	5	214
Thus always, none would ever dare degrade thee	561	Sardan	1	677
So we should be, were justice always done	566	Sardan	2	302
As I do always. Go to, you're a child	600	Foscari	1	328
Will reach it always. See how he shrinks from me	613	Foscari	3	314
Alas! I have shed some--always thanks to you	626	Foscari	5	357
Why wilt thou always mourn for Paradise	646	Cain	3	37
Our race hath always dwelt apart from thine	664	Heaven		660
So patient always. I should like to know	697	Werner	3	138
Always the attribute of innocence	712	Werner	4	536
True; the devil's always ugly; and your beauty	729	Deformed	1	523
A cloud of your own raising. Not so always	744	Deformed	3	149
The English always use to govern d--n	749	Juan	1	112
Which always spoils the breed, if it increases	754	Juan	1	456
A real husband always is suspicious	759	Juan	1	785
So much, he always doubted I was married	765	Juan	1	1175
Prologue is always certain throes, and throbs	766	Juan	1	1292
A lady always distant from the fact	768	Juan	1	1422
Have always done so; 't is of no great use	768	Juan	1	1426
But then exceptions always prove its worth	774	Juan	2	14
(A virgin always on her maid relies	790	Juan	2	1042
And fed by spoonfuls, else they always burst	794	Juan	2	1264
Love, though good always, is not quite so good	795	Juan	2	1354
Came always back to coffee and Haidee	796	Juan	2	1368
Was that in which the heart is always full	798	Juan	2	1531
Is always so to women; one sole bond	799	Juan	2	1594
For surely if we always could perceive	801	Juan	2	1698
The same things cannot always be admired	802	Juan	3	52
And always changed as true as any needle	811	Juan	3	634
'Tis that our nature cannot always bring	816	Juan	4	27
And always envy, though we deem it frantic	818	Juan	4	144
Not always signs with him of calmest mood	821	Juan	4	307
He always is complaining of his lot	827	Juan	4	709
(Because the world won't read him, always snarling	830	Juan	4	870
Is always much more splendid than a king	831	Juan	4	918
Provided always your great goodness still	840	Juan	5	575
'Twere nothing--for her eyes flash'd always fire	848	Juan	5	1066
His majesty was always so polite	850	Juan	5	1164
Was princely, as the proofs have always shown	850	Juan	5	1222
And looking, as he always look'd, perceived	851	Juan	5	1234
But always at a most provoking height	862	Juan	6	608

ALWAYS

Oh, foolish mortals! Always taught in vain	875	Juan	7	541
In such good company as always throng	881	Juan	8	190
But always without malice: if he warr'd	881	Juan	8	193
Great men have always scorn'd great recompenses	897	Juan	9	57
Have always had a tendency to spare	899	Juan	9	166
And always used her favourites too well	904	Juan	9	500
With rhyme, but always leant less to improving	906	Juan	9	590
But always choosing with deliberation	913	Juan	10	383
Oh, ye ambrosial moments! always upper	927	Juan	11	563
Not what you seem, but always what you see	929	Juan	11	680
I have always liked you better than I state	933	Juan	12	220
Peruse! 'T is always with a moral end	934	Juan	12	306
And if my thunderbolt not always rattles	941	Juan	12	697
The fair sex should be always fair; and no man	941	Juan	13	23
Be wary, watch the time, and always serve it	943	Juan	13	140
Always a patriot, and sometimes a placeman	943	Juan	13	168
Where people always did as they were bid	944	Juan	13	179
On which the Muse has always sought to enter	946	Juan	13	302
Always premising that said son at college	946	Juan	13	335
By humouring always what they might assert	960	Juan	14	291
Is that for which the sex are always seeking	964	Juan	14	586
'Tis strange,--but true; for truth is always strange	968	Juan	14	801
Dissimulation always sets apart	968	Juan	15	22
And always have done, somehow these good looks	978	Juan	15	671
In virgins--always in a modest way	979	Juan	15	687
To keep our holy beacons always bright	979	Juan	15	716
I always knock my head against some angle	979	Juan	15	725
Is always greatest at a miracle	981	Juan	16	36
'Tis always best to take things upon trust	981	Juan	16	44
Though sometimes faintly flush'd--and always clear	993	Juan	16	799

AM

God help us all! God help me too! I am	286	Vision		113
Replies of Moslem faith I am	313	Giaour		359
When I am nothing, let that which I was	516	Faliero	2	509
I am at peace: the peace of certainty	547	Faliero	5	654
I am, but only to these gates.--Ah! Hark	625	Foscari	5	280
Then you are free from guilt. Oh, am I?--say	712	Werner	4	519
''Tis strange--the Hebrew noun which means "I am"	749	Juan	1	111
To think so: for half English as I am	920	Juan	11	94
There also was--the sinner that I am	976	Juan	15	501

AMAIN

And there we'll prick our steeds amain	316	Giaour	570

AMARI

'Surgit amari aliquid'--the toll	917	Juan	10	624

AMASS'D

Where gorgeous Tyranny hath thus amass'd	71	Harold	4	970
Of monarchs--from the bloody rolls amass'd	290	Vision		349

AMASSES

No circulating library amasses	450	Beppo	619

AMATEUR

The supplicator being an amateur	992	Juan	16	754

AMATORY

Eggs, oysters, too, are amatory food	795	Juan	2	1358
He may resume his amatory care	804	Juan	3	189
When amatory poets sing their loves	831	Juan	5	1
She could repay each amatory look you lent	904	Juan	9	493
Made up upon an amatory pattern	905	Juan	9	557
Was chosen from out an amatory score	934	Juan	12	299
Of amatory egotism the Tuism	982	Juan	16	103
Or tiptoe of an amatory Miss	995	Juan	16	942

AMAUN

Nor raised the craven cry, Amaun	316	Giaour	603

AMAZE

Fair Florence found, in sooth with some amaze	24	Harold	2	280
Of one to stone converted by amaze	45	Harold	3	621
He sobs, he dies,--the troop in wild amaze	110	Nisus		353
Search for thy form, in vain and mute amaze	183	Address-D		14
Of keen enquiry and of mute amaze	372	Lara	1	410

AMAZED

'Yet at the thing you'd never be amazed	170	Address-B		7
His vassals more amazed nor less afraid	370	Lara	1	270
Nor less amazed, that such a blot	410	Mazeppa		348
The boat's crew look'd amazed o'er sea and shore	431	Island	4	68
His wondering mates, amazed within their bark	432	Island	4	207

AMAZEMENT

Where wild Amazement shrieking--kneeling--throws	349	Corsair	2	184
While gazed the rest in dumb amazement round	381	Lara	2	449

AMAZING

The women only thought it quite amazing	448	Beppo	533
Bless me! your beard is of amazing growth	451	Beppo	726

AMAZING
A town of gardens, walls, and wealth amazing   839 Juan   5   474

AMAZON
This modern Amazon and queen of queans   864 Juan   6   764

AMAZONIAN
Waving her more than Amazonian blade   303 Age   369

AMAZONS
Yet are Spain's maids no race of Amazons   13 Harold   1   585

AMBASSADOR
The Doge will choose his own ambassador   606 Foscari   2   326

AMBASSADORS
All the ambassadors of all the powers   906 Juan   9   625
Ambassadors began as 'twere to hustle   907 Juan   9   651

AMBER
Are thrown the fragrant beads of amber   329 Abydos   2   65
When tipp'd with amber, mellow, rich, and ripe   425 Island   2   455
As beautiful and clear as the amber waves   726 Deformed   1   268
There the large olive rains its amber store   823 Juan   4   433
With amber mouths of greater price or less   838 Juan   5   422
Thoughts quite as yellow, but less clear than
    amber   981 Juan   16   84

AMBIGUOUS
(Transferr'd to those ambiguous things that ape   275 Waltz   141
Her vile, ambiguous method of flirtation   907 Juan   9   647

AMBITION
Can love, or sorrow, fame, ambition, strife   36 Harold   3   40
Ambition steel'd thee on too far to show   41 Harold   3   353
As heretofore because ambition was self-will'd   48 Harold   3   778
Coquettish in ambition--still he aim'd   68 Harold   4   818
And vile Ambition, that built up between   69 Harold   4   869
Cured all ambition? Did the conquerors heap   72 Harold   4   1004
Love, fame, ambition, avarice--'tis the same   73 Harold   4   1113
Ambition nerved young Allan's hand   105 Alva   285
Ambition might prompt me at once to go forth   129 Becher-A   6
Where stern Ambition once forsook   159 Gulf   7
With false Ambition what had I to do   212 Augusta-C   97
But Great Ambition will misrule   233 Ballad-B   45
And avarice seizes all ambition leaves   260 Hints   254
Than his ambition, though with scarce a bound   299 Age   94
Ambition tore the links apart   325 Abydos   1   192
Love shows all changes--Hate, Ambition, Guile   341 Corsair   1   229
Ambition, glory, love, the common aim   367 Lara   1   79
Ambition in his humbled hour   407 Mazeppa   21
And yet my love without ambition grew   438 Tasso   121
The thirst of their ambition was not mine   485 Manfred   2   147
Their own desire, not my ambition, made   525 Faliero   3   446
Ambition--she has seen thrones shake, and loves   583 Sardan   4   302
I leave it; though born noble, my ambition   598 Foscari   1   193
Imperfect happiness or high ambition   621 Foscari   5   79
Dust! limit thy ambition; for to see   645 Cain   2   611
Can that low vice alloy so much ambition   682 Werner   1   678
Of Anak? Why not? Glorious ambition   726 Deformed   1   295
Pride, fame, ambition, to fill up his heart   770 Juan   1   1549
Ambition was my idol, which was broken   773 Juan   1   1729
A little breath, love, wine, ambition, fame   774 Juan   2   31
Ambition, Avarice, Vengeance, Glory, glue   834 Juan   5   174
By commonest ambition, that when passion   853 Juan   6   26
For love, war, or ambition, which reward   910 Juan   10   174
Ambition rends, and gaming gains a loss   930 Juan   12   26
Had ever been his sole and whole ambition   990 Juan   16   634
To some small plan of interest or ambition   992 Juan   16   727

AMBITION'S
There shall they rot, Ambition's honour'd fools   10 Harold   1   450
Nor low Ambition's honours lost   17 Harold   1   846
Yes, this was once Ambition's airy hall   20 Harold   2   48
Ambition's life and labours all were vain   38 Harold   3   161
Ambition's slave alone would toil for more   126 Recoll   .   324
Say, can ambition's fever'd dream bestow   127 Recoll   393
One, who in stern ambition's pride   165 Friend-B   51
Ambition's less than littleness   180 Ode-A   18
Till, goaded by ambition's sting   187 Ode-B   32
Ambition's dreams expiring, love's regret   352 Corsair   2   342
Hate's working brain, and lull'd ambition's wile   375 Lara   1   635
(Though such was not my ambition's end or aim   456 Dante   1   52
These quench'd a moment her ambition's thirst   904 Juan   9   469
Blood only serves to wash Ambition's hands   904 Juan   9   472

AMBITIOUS
Ambitious hopes ne'er cross'd my dreams; and
    should   513 Faliero   2   346
What must we dread? Ambitious treachery   555 Sardan   1   332
Or hate of the ambitious Foscari   595 Foscari   1   10

AMBLE
And Pegasus hath a psalmodic amble   925 Juan   11   453

AMBO
'Arcades ambo,' id est--blackguards both   828 Juan   4   744

AMBRACIA'S
Ambracia's gulf behold, where once was lost   26 Harold   2   397

AMBROSIAL
The ambrosial aspect, which, beheld, instils   62 Harold   4   435
So up thy hill, ambrosial Richmond, heaves   247 Bards   413
Than thou, ambrosial Waltz, when first the moon   274 Waltz   91
Ambrosial and sulphureous, as they sprang   297 Vision   815
Worthy of this ambrosial sin, so shown   762 Juan   1   1014
Of these ambrosial, Pharisaic times   889 Juan   8   715
His beard, he puff'd his pipe's ambrosial gales   893 Juan   8   967
Oh, ye ambrosial moments! always upper   927 Juan   11   563
But oh, ambrosial cash! Ah! who would lose thee   953 Juan   13   799

AMBUSCADE
The feign'd retreat, the nightly ambuscade   379 Lara   2   296

AMBUSH
And anchor'd where his ambush meant to lie   347 Corsair   1   600
In ambush laid, who had perceived him loiter   919 Juan   11   82

AMBUSH'D
The lately ambush'd foes appear   316 Giaour   605

AMEN
Amen! May Heaven forgive them! And will you   512 Faliero   2   264
And Heaven have mercy on their souls! Amen   539 Faliero   5   98
Have heard you. So will God, I trust. Amen   628 Cain   1   25
He hath said it, and I say, Amen   668 Heaven   985
With the kind world's amen--'Who would have
    thought it   933 Juan   12   208

AMENABLE
Amenable, I look on them--as such   526 Faliero   3   506

AMEND
Spare, yet amend, the faults of youth   132 Prayer   12
For Virtue pardons those she would amend   208 Sketch   36
Or other civic means, to amend thy fortunes   673 Werner   1   141
They vow to amend their lives, and yet they don't   832 Juan   5   47

AMENDED
Bestow'd her customs, and amended theirs   418 Island   1   219
The law must be remodell'd or amended   540 Faliero   5   186

AMENDMENT
Without amendment, and he answers, 'Burn   267 Hints   786
Fit for amendment; but as prince, I never   607 Foscari   2   397

AMENDS
But they're lent to two friends, who make me
    amends   176 Devil's Dr   21
Waltzing shall rear, to make our name amends   277 Waltz   256
How much she'll make amends for past miscarriage   447 Beppo   494
With wealth and talking make him some amends   452 Beppo   786
Might for long lying make himself amends   811 Juan   3   662
And I know nothing which could make amends   909 Juan   10   91

AMERCE
Thy venom, and my state thou didst amerce   457 Dante   1   67

AMERCED
Amerced for doubts beyond thy little life   636 Cain   2   15
Come thou shalt be amerced for sins unknown   646 Cain   3   24

AMERICA
Thine eye along America and France   290 Vision   344
One freeman more, America, to thee   455 Venice-B   160
'Tis said the great came from America   762 Juan   1   1041
While yet America was in her non-age   971 Juan   15   216

AMIABLE
With amiable modesty, decline   297 Vision   794
These amiable descriptions from the scribes   814 Juan   3   830
Three fireships lost their amiable existence   870 Juan   7   219
She merely was deem'd amiable and witty   935 Juan   12   372

AMIABLY
'Tis thus the good will amiably err   970 Juan   15   131

AMID
Soon shall thy voice be lost amid the throng   34 Harold   2   884
And wayworn strangers shrink amid the blast   139 Ossian-A   34
'Scapes unsearch'd amid the racket   157 Hodgson   15
Do thou, amid the fair white walls   159 Storm   53
His way amid his Delis took   326 Abydos   1   236
Amid so many, hers alone is dark   364 Corsair   3   570
That I remember'd them amid the maze   547 Faliero   5   622
But, had I seen that form amid ten thousand   688 Werner   2   364

AMIDST

Of thee hereafter.--Ev'n amidst my strain	14	Harold	1	639
Slowly he falls amidst triumphant cries	16	Harold	1	786
And if amidst a scene, a shock so rude	18	Harold	1	877
Amidst the grove that crowns yon tufted hill	26	Harold	2	433
Amidst no common pomp the despot sate	28	Harold	2	500
That sound the first amidst the festival	38	Harold	3	201
Power dwelt amidst her passions; in proud state	42	Harold	3	425
A ruin amidst ruins; there to track	59	Harold	4	219
No more amidst the meaner dead find room	63	Harold	4	521
An Iris sits, amidst the infernal surge	65	Harold	4	642
Amidst this wreck, where thou hast made a shrine	74	Harold	4	1171
Or if, amidst the comrades of thy youth	93	Dorset		29
The stranger's gone,--amidst the crew	104	Alva		254
Iulus holds amidst the chiefs his place	108	Nisus		220
Volscens he seeks amidst the gathering host	110	Nisus		387
Ah, no! amidst the gloomy calm of age	127	Recoll		401
Thus if amidst the gathering storm	133	E. N. Long		5
But thou, amidst the fulness of thy joy	140	Ossian-B		15
In time forbear; amidst the throng	153	Friend-A		73
Yet here, amidst this barren isle	158	Florence		5
What bliss amidst these solitudes to share	161	Athos		24
Amidst those pictured charms, whose loveliness	183	Address-D		15
And last of all, amidst the gaping crew	271	Minerva		195
She flits amidst the phantoms of the hour	308	Age		733
With them he could seem gay amidst the gay	370	Lara	1	298
In self-defence, amidst the strife of men	378	Lara	2	233
He stood alone amidst his band	387	Corinth		308
At least to die amidst the horde	411	Mazeppa		504
Seem'd rooted in the deep amidst its calm	422	Island	2	223
Both nourish'd amidst nature's native scenes	422	Island	2	276
Might still be miss'd amidst the world of waves	427	Island	3	36
Attracts our eye amidst the rudest gale	430	Island	4	6
And if, Cassandra-like, amidst the din	458	Dante	2	10
Amidst the clash of swords and clang of helms	464	Dante	4	70
Sovereigns shall pause amidst their sport of war	464	Dante	4	79
I plunged amidst mankind--Forgetfulness	487	Manfred	2	239
And dwell the tuneless birds of night, amidst	495	Manfred	3	283
Amidst the noblest of our dames in public	515	Faliero	2	433
Those horrid bodements which, amidst the throng	529	Faliero	4	107
I would have stood alone amidst your tombs	541	Faliero	5	263
Amidst thy many murders, think of mine	549	Faliero	5	793
Along the gallery, and amidst the damsels	551	Sardan	1	41
Is my true realm, amidst bright eyes and faces	571	Sardan	3	2
A green spot amidst desert centuries	586	Sardan	4	513
And, masqued as a young gondolier, amidst	597	Foscari	1	97
Thy wrath! for she is pure amidst the failing	658	Heaven		234
They are gone! They have disappear'd amidst the roar	669	Heaven		1088
While safe amidst the elemental strife	669	Heaven		1095
Amidst its perils. Yet I will retire	681	Werner	1	638
Amidst the elements, whilst younger trees	689	Werner	2	382
And living amidst commerce-fetching burghers	694	Werner	2	727
In which you rank amidst our chiefest nobles	712	Werner	4	540
Amidst the people in the church, I dream'd not	716	Werner	5	188
Stature, and bearing; and amidst them all	717	Werner	5	265
Yet be Rome amidst thine anguish	736	Deformed	2	101
And ashes! Yes, thine own amidst the rest	739	Deformed	2	265
Amidst the skeletons of that gaunt crew	787	Juan	2	812
Amidst the barren sand and rocks so rude	799	Juan	2	1580
Amidst the savage deeds he had done and seen	808	Juan	3	452
Amidst the roar of liberated Rome	816	Juan	3	963
'My boy!' said he, 'amidst this motley crew	832	Juan	5	97
Amidst some groaning thousands dying near	879	Juan	8	83
So order'd it, amidst these sulphury revels	883	Juan	8	350
Amidst such scenes--though this was quite a new one	884	Juan	8	412
Amidst the bodies lull'd in bloody rest	889	Juan	8	728
Her hidden face was plunged amidst the dead	890	Juan	8	739
For saving her amidst the wild insanity	896	Juan	8	1118
In sight, then lost amidst the forestry	917	Juan	10	652
Or sat amidst the bricks of Nineveh	919	Juan	11	54
And found him not amidst the various progenies	922	Juan	11	219
To sit amidst the ruins of their guilt	939	Juan	12	623
Sweet Adeline, amidst the gay world's hum	942	Juan	13	100
On the most favour'd; and amidst the blaze	954	Juan	13	262
Amidst the court a Gothic fountain play'd	949	Juan	13	513
Amidst life's infinite variety	970	Juan	15	146
Amidst this tumult of fish, flesh, and fowl	977	Juan	15	585

AMISS

Nor made atonement when he did amiss	4	Harold	1	38
And Satan had taken it much amiss	179	Devil's Dr		231
Makes me regret whate'er you do amiss	292	Vision		496
And seem to think it would not be amiss	293	Vision		571
Theirs, to believe no prey nor plan amiss	339	Corsair	1	60
Let me not deem that mercy shown amiss	361	Corsair	3	367
The bard I quote from does not sing amiss	757	Juan	1	701
In deep despair, lest he had done amiss	760	Juan	1	893
That passengers would find it much amiss	778	Juan	2	259
Some people prefer wine--'tis not amiss	819	Juan	4	190
Explains the garb which Juan took amiss	846	Juan	5	912
But it suffices--little was amiss	858	Juan	6	405
That nobody can ever take amiss	859	Juan	6	467
Could not at first expound what was amiss	861	Juan	6	592

AMISS

But I'm resolved to say nought that's amiss	932	Juan	12	174
Abroad, though doubtless they do much amiss	940	Juan	12	629
Of Platonism, which leads so oft amiss	967	Juan	14	731
Thought her predictions went not much amiss	978	Juan	15	643
Now this he really rather took amiss	992	Juan	16	779

AMMON

Wines too, which might again have slain young Ammon	976	Juan	15	515

AMMON'S

Which Ammon's son ran proudly round	329	Abydos	2	47
Ammon's (ill pleased with one world and one father	835	Juan	5	248

AMONG

So noted ancient roundelays among	9	Harold	1	381
From peak to peak the rattling crags among	49	Harold	3	864
His dust; and lies it not her Great among	63	Harold	4	515
Her step, though light, less fleet among	386	Corinth		209
A dame who kept up discipline among	856	Juan	6	237
A kind of pride that he should be among	915	Juan	10	517

AMONGST

To meditate amongst decay, and stand	59	Harold	4	218
Love from amongst her griefs?--for such the affections are	70	Harold	4	909
He allots one poor husband to share amongst four	116	To Eliza		11
While now amongst thy female peers	147	Vain Lady		17
Inquire amongst your fellow-lodgers	227	Thurlow-B		14
The spheres, we shall catch cold amongst these clouds	293	Vision		531
And if my name amongst the number were	463	Dante	3	183
I could not be amongst ye: but there are	489	Manfred	2	445
A mighty thing amongst the mean, and such	493	Manfred	3	120
I would have dash'd amongst them, asking few	504	Faliero	1	306
Feel with their friends; for who is he amongst them	507	Faliero	1	495
What if I were to trust myself amongst you	508	Faliero	1	582
And pluck me down amongst them? Would they could	508	Faliero	1	614
Thinking that even amongst these wicked men	520	Faliero	3	145
Amongst you?--Israel, speak! what means this mystery	522	Faliero	3	217
Ay, and the first amongst us, as thou hast been	523	Faliero	3	337
Have made them deadly; if there be amongst them	524	Faliero	3	421
And he, the ribald, whom I see amongst you	541	Faliero	5	222
How red he glares amongst those deepening clouds	561	Sardan	2	3
My father was amongst them, too; but he	581	Sardan	4	177
To make libations amongst men. I've not	594	Sardan	5	453
Thy father sits amongst thy judges. True	596	Foscari	1	82
Amongst us), all that history has bequeath'd	607	Foscari	2	404
Cast me out from amongst them as an offering	617	Foscari	4	144
To move betimes. Methinks I see amongst you	623	Foscari	5	195
Who shall--be thou amongst the first. I never	632	Cain	1	307
Yes--death, too, is amongst the debts we owe her	646	Cain	3	44
Shall be amongst your race in different forms	661	Heaven		480
His form. And 'tis to be amongst these sovereigns	682	Werner	1	724
I am the worst-clothed and least named amongst them	695	Werner	3	24
Aught like him? How he tower'd amongst them all	713	Werner	5	42
Who feels himself the guilty one amongst us	716	Werner	5	202
Many amongst them were reported of	716	Werner	5	237
Amongst them there was said to be one man	717	Werner	5	243
Amongst the stars, which these poor cretures deem	735	Deformed	1	891
To bring one down amongst them, and set fire	735	Deformed	1	893
They tamed him down amongst them: to destroy	753	Juan	1	396
Amongst her numerous acquaintance, all	753	Juan	1	433
Particularly amongst sun-burnt nations	755	Juan	1	552
Conceal'd amongst his premises; 'tis true	768	Juan	1	1413
To be put up for auction amongst Tartars	832	Juan	5	64
It chanced amongst the other people lotted	832	Juan	5	77
Juan amongst the damsels in disguise	851	Juan	6	1235
The favourite; but what's favour amongst four	854	Juan	6	90
Amongst them all, hard blows to inflict or ward	869	Juan	7	150
Was happiest amongst mortals anywhere	886	Juan	8	485
Pick'd out amongst his followers with some skill	891	Juan	8	811
Amongst live poets and blue ladies, past	926	Juan	11	498
Amongst the higher spirits of the day	926	Juan	11	503
Amongst a people famous for reflection	927	Juan	11	559
Amongst the paths of being 'taken in	932	Juan	12	195
Amongst the sex in little things or great	933	Juan	12	218
Amongst you, about Leila's education	933	Juan	12	224
By way of sprinkling, scatter'd amongst these	951	Juan	13	663
Nem. con. amongst the women, which I grieve	978	Juan	15	666
Amongst our own most musical of nations	986	Juan	16	406
But both were thrown away amongst the fens	991	Juan	16	706

AMOR

The 'Mamma Mia's!' and the 'Amor Mio's	986	Juan	16	403

AMOROUS

Which glows yet smoother from his amorous clutch	13	Harold	1	600
With emblems well devised by amorous pride	42	Harold	3	436

AMOROUS

To soothe thy softer hours with amorous flames	107 Nisus		160
Have quitted every amorous poet	137 Clare		41
She need not fear the amorous rhyme	141 Critics		59
When schoolboys vent their amorous flames in verse	142 Soliloquy		17
These amorous nothings in revealing	147 Vain Lady		30
Be warm, but pure; be amorous, but be chaste	246 Bards		306
To soothe the mania of the amorous throng	246 Bards		344
Then he was faithful, too, as well as amorous	444 Beppo		265
I therefore do denounce all amorous writing	831 Juan	5	9
In short, the maxim for the amorous tribe is	854 Juan	6	135
And somewhat mechante in her amorous sphere	963 Juan	14	498

AMORT

And some of us have felt thus 'all amort	865 Juan	6	845

AMOS

And Amos Cottle strikes the lyre in vain	247 Bards		396
Oh, Amos Cottle!--Phoebus! what a name	247 Bards		399
Oh, Amos Cottle! for a moment think	247 Bards		401

AMOUNT

The unpaid amount of Catherine's bloody debt	300 Age		160
Yet could his corporal pangs amount to half	823 Juan	4	427
To exact of Cupid's bills the full amount	904 Juan	9	495
To gather to a somewhat large amount, he	990 Juan	16	613

AMPHIBIOUS

The amphibious desert of the dank morass	421 Island	2	158
Which struck and flash'd like an amphibious steel	431 Island	4	110
And watch if aught approach'd the amphibious lair	435 Island	4	375
But to denounce the amphibious sort of harlot	937 Juan	12	495

AMPHION

And old Amphion, such were minstrels then	266 Hints		667

AMPHITHEATRE

Nature's volcanic amphitheatre	27 Harold	2	452
Thine amphitheatre, where Romans sate	303 Age		420
Life to their amphitheatre, as well	731 Deformed	1	627
The city, or the amphitheatre	731 Deformed	1	631
Form'd like an amphitheatre, each dwelling	870 Juan	7	183

AMPLE

And Knowledge spreads them on her ample lap	67 Harold	4	725
The atonement is ample in love's last adieu	100 L Adieu		40
Magnus his ample front sublime uprears	111 Examination		2
His would have been an ample share	113 Cornelian-A		27
Secure behind her ample shield	142 Critics		87
What if thy deep and ample stream should be	198 Po		5
Which have appear'd against you; and more ample	540 Faliero	5	162
Where the sublime soars forth on wings more ample	752 Juan	1	334
But there were ample reasons for it, none	768 Juan	1	1389
Like bubbles on an ocean much less ample	898 Juan	9	102

AMPLER

And ampler canvass woos the wind from high	362 Corsair	3	485

AMPLEST

Ah! such, alas, the hero's amplest fate	9 Harold	1	397

AMPLIFIED

He amplified to every lord's content	306 Age		580

AMPLIFY

And amplify: you lose much by concision	974 Juan	15	404

AMPLY

Supplied, and amply too, by innocence	171 Hales-Owen		4

AMULET

Her mother's sainted amulet	329 Abydos	2	69

AMUNDEVILLE

The Lady Adeline Amundeville	941 Juan	13	9
The Lady Adeline Amundeville	942 Juan	13	90
Lord H. Amundeville and Lady A	947 Juan	13	408
The Lady Adeline Amundeville	968 Juan	15	34
When the Lord of the Hill, Amundeville	985 Juan	16	325
But still with the house of Amundeville	985 Juan	16	339
Amundeville is lord by day	986 Juan	16	357

AMUSE

Perhaps may amuse, yet they never can move	92 First Kiss		18
Though still our deeds amuse the youthful race	124 Recoll		165
Should I see nothing else to amuse me to-night	177 Devil's Dr		120
Though themes of innocence amuse him best	245 Bards		257
Young men should travel, if but to amuse	776 Juan	2	125
Whose chiefly harmless talent was to amuse	952 Juan	13	685

AMUSED

Men go not to be lectured, but amused	261 Hints		364
Not one, except the attorney, was amused	766 Juan	1	1269

AMUSEMENT

And yield at least amusement in the race	242 Bards		42
Some for amusement, others for old grudges	750 Juan	1	224
Which I with their amusement will connect	772 Juan	1	1667
As an amusement after the Divan	863 Juan	6	726
In his resumed amusement. 'I confess	875 Juan	7	516
Her next amusement was more fanciful	904 Juan	9	473

AMUSEMENTS

It scorns amusements which are not of price	261 Hints		306

AN

Anacreon only had the soul to tie an	995 Juan	16	917

ANACREON

Anacreon, Tom Little, Tom Moore, or Tom Brown	226 Oh You		2
Described by Mahomet, and Anacreon Moore	759 Juan	1	829
Anacreon only had the soul to tie an	995 Juan	16	917

ANACREON'S

Anacreon's morals are a still worse sample	752 Juan	1	330
It made Anacreon's song divine	812 Juan	3	751

ANACYNDARAXES

The king, and son of Anacyndaraxes	555 Sardan	1	297

ANAH

Of Earth, and love her as he once loved Anah	655 Heaven		30
Oh, Anah! But she loves thee not. Alas	657 Heaven		168
She loves another. Anah! No; her sister	657 Heaven		178
Ay, but not Anah: she but loves her God	657 Heaven		181
To perishable beings. Oh, my Anah	658 Heaven		227
Although they obscure it for an hour. My Anah	658 Heaven		236
The pleasant places where I thought of Anah	659 Heaven		284
Anah! oh, God! and with her--Japhet! Lo	663 Heaven		587
The approaching chaos. Anah! Anah! my	663 Heaven		595
Deserve her. Farewell, Anah! I have said	663 Heaven		612
Thus. Fearest thou, my Anah? Yes, for thee	663 Heaven		629
But thou, my Anah! let me call thee mine	664 Heaven		666
Part with, although I must from thee. My Anah	664 Heaven		668
Anah! and thou?--Whate'er our God decrees	664 Heaven		693
Leave not my Anah to the swallowing tides	668 Heaven		1018
Where thou, and Anah, shalt partake our lot	669 Heaven		1041
Come, Anah! quit this chaos-founded prison	669 Heaven		1078
Anah unto these eyes	669 Heaven		1092

ANAH'S

Towards Anah's tents, round which he hovers nightly	658 Heaven		246

ANAK

Of Anak? Why not? Glorious ambition	726 Deformed	1	295

ANALOGIES

Is shown through nature's whole analogies	967 Juan	14	748

ANALOGY

And said there was analogy between 'em	748 Juan	1	106

ANALYSE

Well, we won't analyse--our story must	906 Juan	9	609

ANARCHS

Imperial anarchs, doubling human woes	26 Harold	2	404
With the worst anarchs of the age	165 Friend-B		54

ANARCHY

And Anarchy assumed her attributes	72 Harold	4	1014
The clouds of anarchy from Britain's skies	121 Newstead-A		102
And all things in the anarchy of sloth	560 Sardan	1	631

ANATOMICAL

Although his anatomical construction	782 Juan	2	533

ANATOMY

In this anatomy, I've finish'd now	801 Juan	2	1722

ANCESTOR

And, like my ancestor Semiramis	554 Sardan	1	227
And was: the ancestor of heroes, too	580 Sardan	4	147

ANCESTORS

From the seat of his ancestors, bids you adieu	86 Leaving NA		22
One of our Ancestors was gored	197 Duel		6
Blush to find ancestors, who would have blush'd	612 Foscari	3	302
An atom of their ancestors from earth	619 Foscari	4	277
Erected by your ancestors, is still	711 Werner	4	454
But people's ancestors are history's game	864 Juan	6	749
I can't complain, whose ancestors are there	912 Juan	10	281

ANCESTRAL

For my ancestral faults or mine the wound	75 Harold	4	1190

ANCESTRY

Vain of our ancestry as they of theirs	170 Address-A		45

ANCESTRY
Which fits your ancestry, your rank, and virtues 542 Faliero 5 325
Of rank and ancestry? in this worn cheek 673 Werner 1 118

ANCHIALUS
There's Tarsus and Anchialus, both built 555 Sardan 1 284
In one day built Anchialus and Tarsus 555 Sardan 1 298

ANCHISES
Or to more deeply blest Anchises? or 62 Harold 4 452

ANCHOR
The anchor dropp'd; it lay along the deep 422 Island 2 234
Her anchor parts; but still her snowy sail 430 Island 4 5
At anchor under the seraglio wall 830 Juan 4 900
To slacken sail, and anchor with our rhyme 851 Juan 5 1268
He had brought his spending to a handsome anchor 911 Juan 10 244
Theirs is the best bower anchor, the chain cable 930 Juan 12 19

ANCHOR'D
Whose bark drives on and on, and anchor'd ne'er
  shall be 46 Harold 3 670
Where is Gonsalvo?' 'In the anchor'd bark 340 Corsair 1 154
Yon bark hath hardly anchor'd in the bay 344 Corsair 1 413
And anchor'd where his ambush meant to lie 347 Corsair 1 600
Where last he anchor'd rear'd its giant shape 362 Corsair 3 455
Where lay she? had she anchor'd?'--'No, but still 426 Island 2 510
Extremely tranquil, anchor'd at its station 870 Juan 7 188

ANCHORING
The sails are furl'd; and anchoring round she
  swings 339 Corsair 1 98

ANCHORITE
Might shake the saintship of an anchorite 5 Harold 1 94
The dim, though large-eyed winged anchorite 424 Island 2 426
Bronzed o'er some lean and stoic anchorite 950 Juan 13 572

ANCHORITE'S
Is more than at an anchorite's supper shown 290 Vision 365
Is as an anchorite's, were it but holy 491 Manfred 3 42

ANCHORS
Blow fair, thou breeze!--she anchors ere the dark 339 Corsair 1 88
The anchors rise, the sails unfurling fast 345 Corsair 1 526

ANCIENT
If ancient tales say true nor wrong these holy
  men 4 Harold 1 63
So noted ancient roundelays among 9 Harold 1 381
Lo, Chivalry, your ancient goddess, cries 10 Harold 1 406
Her strength, her wealth, her site of ancient days 14 Harold 1 658
Ancient of days! august Athena! where 19 Harold 2 10
The latest relic of her ancient reign 21 Harold 2 93
Well deem'd the little God his ancient sway was
  o'er 24 Harold 2 279
Beneath the shadow of that ancient mount 25 Harold 2 366
Might once again renew their ancient butcher-work 29 Harold 2 603
Here, where the ancient paid thee homage long 75 Harold 4 1182
Ancient; and these three mortal things are still 77 Harold 4 1302
When thinking on these ancient towers 89 To Emma 11
As ancient Rome, fast falling to disgrace 93 Masters 3
And poised with easy arm his ancient shield 106 Nisus 92
An ancient cup, which Tyrian Dido gave 107 Nisus 151
Though sometimes with the tales of ancient day 124 Recoll 171
Oft have we drain'd the font of ancient lore 125 Recoll 253
From ancient lineage, not unworthy sprung 126 Recoll 302
If ancient Virgins croaking censures raise 142 Soliloquy 10
A young Physician, though an ancient Man 143 Soliloquy 62
Some ancient Dames, of virtue fiery 144 Becher-B 21
An ancient Maid's a sage adviser 151 Harriet 4
The ancient world was won and lost 159 Gulf 4
That chief of ancient song 162 War Song 26
This greeting o'er, the ancient rule obey'd 170 Address-A 66
'Tis a new barouche, and an ancient peer 177 Devil's Dr 96
River, that rollest by the ancient walls 198 Po 1
There was an ancient mansion, and before 214 Dream 76
Whether on ancient tombs thou takest thy stand 245 Bards 269
Rake from each ancient dunghill ev'ry pearl 246 Bards 371
A foal well worthy of her ancient dam 255 Bards 971
Yet whether right or wrong the ancient rules 262 Hints 431
Unhappy Greece! thy sons of ancient days 263 Hints 509
Bow Irish jig and ancient rigadoon 275 Waltz 110
Each new, quite new (except some ancient tricks 276 Waltz 173
But kindly; Satan met his ancient friend 289 Vision 286
Proverbial wiles and ancient craft 311 Giaour 158
Of ancient fool and modern knave 320 Giaour 1007
Unlike the heroes of each ancient race 341 Corsair 1 193
Her ancient civic boast--'the Free 385 Corinth 130
The chief of Este's ancient sway 398 Parisina 134
To snatch some glimpses of his ancient reign 425 Island 2 473
In ancient arts by moderns mimick'd ill 441 Beppo 84
Deplores the ancient woes which both befell 466 Morgante 19
Wise Hamo, and the ancient Salamone 467 Morgante 75
'Our ancient fathers living the desert in 469 Morgante 193

ANCIENT
'Tis of an ancient vintage; many a day 484 Manfred 2 18
And ancient conqueror. Some wine, I say 553 Sardan 1 205
Their shouts come ringing through the ancient
  halls 575 Sardan 3 251
I would not leave your ancient first abode 594 Sardan 5 426
The ancient world for love. I cannot blame him 725 Deformed 1 237
I'll therefore take our ancient friend Don Juan 747 Juan 1 6
Which ancient mass-books often are, and this all 752 Juan 1 363
Of ancient days, ere tyranny grew strong 824 Juan 4 520
To so respectable an ancient rite 840 Juan 5 562
According to the ancient epic laws 851 Juan 5 1267
Those ancient good intentions, which once shaved 881 Juan 8 206
(That which some ancient Muse or modern wit 889 Juan 8 668
From our old crash, some mystic, ancient strain 901 Juan 9 299
That he was not an ancient debauchee 914 Juan 10 426
A modern Ancient Pistol--by the hilts 925 Juan 11 456
So when he saw each ancient dame a suitor 935 Juan 12 333
And the sky shows that very ancient gray 959 Juan 14 221
That ancient line, in the pale moonshine 986 Juan 16 347
He reach'd the ancient wall, then stood stone
  still 996 Juan 16 1000

ANCONA
But bred within the March of old Ancona 828 Juan 4 746

AND
'The former is the devil's scripture, and 295 Vision 689
Of Freedom, which their fathers fought for, and 454 Venice-B 136
Weeps with her sister, who remembers and 466 Morgante 18
Floating upon the azure desert, and 668 Heaven 964
That they bred in and in, as might be shown 754 Juan 1 454
But for the present, gentle reader! and 774 Juan 1 1761
His suite consisted of three servants and 777 Juan 2 193
And Zoe, when the eggs were ready, and 792 Juan 2 1161
There was no want of lofty mirrors, and 810 Juan 3 545
I said they were alike, their features and 822 Juan 4 353
And pulling out reluctant purses, and 835 Juan 5 226
Of a small iron door, 'twas open'd, and 836 Juan 5 322
All this she told with some confusion and 862 Juan 6 617
Juanna should be taken from her, and 862 Juan 6 655
If he speak truth, she is Christ's sister, and 879 Juan 8 71
As much of German as of Sanscrit, and 885 Juan 8 450
The courtiers stared, the ladies whisper'd, and 902 Juan 9 361
I have seen small poets, and great prosers, and 929 Juan 11 665
In one point only were you settled--and 933 Juan 12 225
The squires familiarly formal, and 991 Juan 16 673

ANDALUSIAN
The Andalusian courser in the van 303 Age 373
Or Andalusian girl from mass returning 939 Juan 12 594
And Juan, like a true-born Andalusian 944 Juan 13 183

ANDALUSIA'S
When her war-song was heard on Andalusia's shore 10 Harold 1 413
Tells that the foe was Andalusia's guest 12 Harold 1 517
The song of love than Andalusia's maids 14 Harold 1 653

ANDES
Where the roots of the Andes 479 Manfred 1 92

ANDES'
On Andes' and on Athos' peaks unfurl'd 302 Age 274

ANDREWS
Miles Andrews still his strength in couplets try 251 Bards 717

ANDROMACHE
She comes!--the Andromache (but not Racine's 308 Age 755

ANECDOTE
With stores of anecdote, and grains of sense 225 J. C. H. 52
And here I must an anecdote relate 903 Juan 9 399

ANENT
Spirit would name, and therefore even I won't
  anent 923 Juan 11 340

ANEW
Who but would deem their bosoms burn'd anew 31 Harold 2 713
Millions of tongues record thee, and anew 40 Harold 3 311
The cold--the changed--perchance the dead--anew 59 Harold 4 215
The dying chords are strung anew 88 Anacreon-A 11
But turn to gaze again, and find anew 183 Address-D 41
And Merry's metaphors appear anew 252 Bards 763
So many kingdoms fitted up anew 285 Vision 36
In orisons resumed anew 317 Giaour 733
That tale is old, but love anew 329 Abydos 2 18
Have need of rest before they toil anew 344 Corsair 1 415
Raise, fan, sustain--till life returns anew 357 Corsair 3 118
As if she stanch'd anew some phantom's wound 384 Lara 2 619
Since he set its edge anew 400 Parisina 404
As 'twere anew, the gaps of centuries 495 Manfred 3 295

ANGEL

Ah! since thy angel form is gone	134	Lady-D	17
For the Angel of Death spread his wings on the blast	222	Sennacherib	9
The heiress? The angel! The devil! why, man	278	Blues 1	63
I say she's an angel. Say rather an angle	278	Blues 1	67
'Saint porter,' said the angel, 'prithee rise	287	Vision	132
The angel. 'Well! he won't find kings to jostle	287	Vision	140
The angel answer'd, 'Peter! do not pout	287	Vision	169
Depends upon his deeds,' the Angel said	293	Vision	546
Poland! o'er which the avenging angel past	300	Age	161
Angel of Death! ¡'tis Hassan's cloven crest	317	Giaour	716
If ever evil angel bore	319	Giaour	912
Fresh as the Angel o'er a new inn door	447	Beppo	451
Benign and pious, bid an angel flee	466	Morgante	6
That here an angel was sent down from heaven	476	Morgante	656
Now the destroying Angel hovers o'er	535	Faliero 4	482
Come away. Seest thou not? I see an angel	632	Cain 1	337
Wert present; was it some more hostile angel	652	Cain 3	388
Angel of Light! be merciful, nor say	653	Cain 3	486
I love our God less since his angel loved me	655	Heaven	12
While all his race are slumbering? Angel! what	663	Heaven	589
To be repeated. Angel! or whate'er	663	Heaven	614
Angel! forgive this stripling's fond despair	668	Heaven	979
My better angel! such I have ever found thee	673	Werner 1	149
All had been known at once. My guardian angel	698	Werner 3	219
Her guardian angel had given up his garrison	749	Juan 1	132
And thus like to an angel o'er the dying	792	Juan 2	1145
Each was an angel, and earth paradise	800	Juan 2	1632

ANGELIC
(See also ARCH-ANGELIC)

While thus they spake, the angelic caravan	287	Vision	177
And mark'd the mild angelic air	311	Giaour	74
Pure from the fire to join the angelic race	456	Dante 1	10
Mortals the nearest to the angelic nature	512	Faliero 2	209
I am angelic: wouldst thou be as I am	637	Cain 2	78
In their true place, with the angelic choir	666	Heaven	798
Still flashes in the angelic hands	669	Heaven	1052

ANGELICAL

Of essences angelical, who wore	288	Vision	243

ANGELICALLY

His black-eyed maids of Heaven, angelically kind	13	Harold 1	611

ANGELO'S

Angelo's, Alfieri's bones, and his	63	Harold 4	484

ANGELS

And weeping angels lead her to those bowers	84	Death-B	15
Lest angels might dispute the prize	97	To M--	14
'Though women are angels, yet wedlock's the devil	116	To Eliza	16
The immortal wars which gods and angels wage	258	Hints	105
The angels all were singing out of tune	285	Vision	9
Six angels and twelve saints were named his clerks	285	Vision	32
What angels shrink from: even the very devil	285	Vision	42
And true, we learn the angels are all Tories	288	Vision	208
The make of angels and archangels, since	288	Vision	226
As angels can; next, like Italian twilight	292	Vision	482
The angels had of course enough of song	296	Vision	731
Or angels, now could stop the torrent; so	297	Vision	811
The angels stopp'd their ears and plied their pinions	297	Vision	818
I know not if the angels weep, but men	298	Age	7
With angels shared, by Alla given	321	Giaour	1133
Of the embrace of angels with a sex	493	Manfred 3	177
And thy surrounding angels; my past power	496	Manfred 3	373
Yes--the same sin that overthrew the angels	512	Faliero 2	207
Who dares accuse my country? Men and angels	611	Foscari 3	240
Whom have we here?--A shape like to the angels	628	Cain 1	80
If I shrink not from these, the fire-arm'd angels	629	Cain 1	91
The angels we have seen. Are there, then, others	632	Cain 1	340
The angels and the mortals to make happy	634	Cain 1	476
Or in his angels, who are like to thee	635	Cain 1	504
Could I stand here? His angels are within	636	Cain 1	552
Who names me demon to his angels; they	636	Cain 2	7
I may be in the rest as angels are	637	Cain 2	77
Of men nor angels, looks like something which	640	Cain 2	257
But you have seen his angels. Rarely. But	644	Cain 2	556
For angels to alight on, as the spot	659	Heaven	296
Angels shall tire their wings, but find no spot	660	Heaven	353
Have wings like angels, and like them salute	662	Heaven	559
But all good angels have forsaken earth	663	Heaven	593
That ye too know not? Angels! angels! ye	663	Heaven	618
The fellowship of angels. These are they, then	665	Heaven	736
That earth by angels must be left untrod	666	Heaven	785
When all good angels left the world, ye stay'd	666	Heaven	808
The angels, from his further snares exempt	666	Heaven	854
Listen! Yes. I have heard the angels sing	732	Deformed 1	688
Of old the angels of her earliest sex	741	Deformed 2	414
Such as the angels think so very fine	756	Juan 1	627
With prophets, houris, angels, saints, descried	893	Juan 8	919

ANGEL'S

Save the recording angel's black bureau	285	Vision	20
Cain! Cain! It soundeth like an angel's tone	653	Cain 3	467
'Tis that an angel's bride disdains to weep	667	Heaven	914

ANGELS'

From the fiends' leader to the angels' prince	288	Vision	228

ANGER

Which; though sometimes they frown, yet rarely anger dames	24	Harold 2	288
Extend not your anger to sleep	97	To M.S.G.-B	2
What though from private pique her anger grew	142	Soliloquy	29
I saw you--my anger became admiration	147	To Anne-A	11
For present anger and for future gold	213	Lady Byron	45
Nor woo that anger which he will not show	265	Hints	622
From his large eye no flashing anger broke	373	Lara 1	493
Eager with anger, their strong arms made way	433	Island 4	239
To see your anger, like our Adrian waves	502	Faliero 1	175
I am ashamed of my own anger now	503	Faliero 1	266
And not an impulse of mere anger; though	534	Faliero 4	453
May have the crawler crush'd, but feels no anger	544	Faliero 5	464
Convey'd the Host aroused my rash young anger	546	Faliero 5	597
Are judges who give way to anger? they	599	Foscari 2	275
The Eternal anger? My beloved Cain	628	Cain 1	55
The promise that his anger would stop short	673	Werner 1	95
Now they reach thee in their anger	736	Deformed 2	85
Coldness, even disdain or hate	756	Juan 1	583
Her anger pitch'd into a lower tune	848	Juan 5	1085
Her anger, and beseech'd she'd hear him through	865	Juan 6	811

ANGER'S

Of transient Anger's hasty blush	312	Giaour	237

ANGIOLIN

Angiolin of Bayonne, and Oliver	467	Morgante	71

ANGIOLINA

Pride, Angiolina? Alas! none is left me	511	Faliero 2	206
Yes, Angiolina. Do not marvel: I	515	Faliero 2	442
Sweet Angiolina! I must to my cabinet	515	Faliero 2	480
Adieu, my Angiolina. Let me be	515	Faliero 2	497
Then farewell, Angiolina!--one embrace	547	Faliero 5	671

ANGIOLINI

Let Angiolini bare her breast of snow	250	Bards	628

ANGLE

I say she's an angel. Say rather an angle	278	Blues 1	67
Nearer. Here is a darksome angle--so	701	Werner 3	419
To some odd angle for which all were straining	880	Juan 8	156
Angle, the soi-disant mathematician	952	Juan 13	691
I always knock my head against some angle	979	Juan 15	725

ANGLED

Who having angled all his life for fame	449	Beppo	578

ANGLES

Few angles were there in her form, 'tis true	857	Juan 6	333
Which Satan angles with for souls, like flies	889	Juan 8	688
The serious Angles in the eloquence	960	Juan 14	298

ANGLICE

By Souvaroff, or Anglice Suwarrow	868	Juan 7	63

ANGLING

And angling, too, that solitary vice	954	Juan 13	845

ANGRANTE

Descended from Angrante: under cover	468	Morgante	154

ANGRIEST

So that wildest of waves, in their angriest mood	388	Corinth	428

ANGRILY

But loud complaint, however angrily	507	Faliero 1	553

ANGRY

His angry tail; red rolls his eye's dilated glow	16	Harold 1	755
before his angry spear: but mild was the	129	Calmar	19
And angry clouds are pouring fast	158	Storm	3
The lightning of Love's angry glance	172	Romaic-B	20
The angry essence of her deadly will	208	Sketch	46
Where angry Townly 'lifts his voice on high	258	Hints	132
And men look angry in the proper place	258	Hints	148
Or the sad influence of the angry moon	267	Hints	806
Nought heeded they the Pacha's angry cry	349	Corsair 2	159
And Heaven must punish on its angry day	363	Corsair 3	526
And fiercer shook his angry falchion now	376	Lara 2	75
Though with fiery eyes, and angry roar	392	Corinth	725
An angry man, ye may opine	410	Mazeppa	342
Was nothing to his angry might	411	Mazeppa	451
My indignant bones, because her angry gust	457	Dante 1	81
Orlando, angry too with Carloman	468	Morgante	125

ANGRY
Robed as with angry clouds: he stands between   495 Manfred   3   325
A miscreant's angry breath may blast it all   514 Faliero   2   421
But then thou must withdraw, for angry friends   530 Faliero   4   146
Nothing. I know that there are angry spirits   531 Faliero   4   223
His fury, like an angry boy's, to master   541 Faliero   5   243
Air worshippers? that is, when it is angry   572 Sardan   3   50
His angry word once o'er, he shed no blood   807 Juan   3   382
Upon their prey, as darts an angry asp   822 Juan   4   382
You can't suppose Gulbeyaz' angry brow   848 Juan   5 1048
Like other angry ladies of her nation   867 Juan   6   949
Upon his angry sultanship, pell-mell   892 Juan   8   868
And wild dismay o'er every angry cousin   934 Juan   12   267
Were angry--as they well might, to be sure   992 Juan   16   756

ANGUISH
Yet other offspring soothe his anguish here   85 Epitaph   22
The anguish of a last embrace   89 To Emma   34
But when our cheeks with anguish glow'd   90 Caroline-A   9
Its querulous grief, when in anguish like this   92 Caroline-D   8
And dreads not the anguish of love's last adieu   100 L Adieu   32
And fret with self-created anguish   101 Lady-B   12
That anguish never can o'ertake her   113 Quaker   46
Doth through my cloud of anguish shine   152 Weep-A   10
To wean me from mine anguish here   165 Thyrza   52
Count o'er thy days from anguish free   167 Euthanasia   34
In silent anguish I sustain   172 Romaic-B   34
The lover's anguish or the friend's complaint   258 Hints   110
His anguish doubling by his own 'encore   261 Hints   310
Deep were my anguish, thus compell'd   328 Abydos   1 435
For I have anguish yet to bear--and how   437 Tasso   44
Grey-hair'd with anguish, like these blasted
    pines   482 Manfred   1 327
Sorrow and anguish   488 Manfred   2 343
To love us, cometh anguish with disgrace   667 Heaven   932
Might date for years, did Anguish make the dial   709 Werner   4 314
Yet be Rome amidst thine anguish   736 Deformed   2 101
So deep an anguish wrung Gulbeyaz' brow   865 Juan   6 836

ANGUISH'D
'Oh no!' the anguish'd sire rejoin'd   103 Alva   109
The Nine, in anguish'd accents thus he spoke   142 Soliloquy   6

ANGUS
When Angus hail'd his eldest born   102 Alva   38
And Angus hails another son   102 Alva   50
And Angus on his Oscar smiled   102 Alva   82
'Why comes not Oscar,' Angus said   102 Alva   102
And Angus said, if one year more   103 Alva   165
'With all my soul,' old Angus said   104 Alva   225
On Angus bending low the knee   104 Alva   262

ANGUS'
And Angus' cheek with wonder glows   103 Alva   195
Oblivion press'd old Angus' breast   104 Alva   271

ANIMAL
But what of that? the animal shows blood   305 Age   567
A better portion for the animal   643 Cain   2 506
Man's a strange animal, and makes strange use   762 Juan   1 1017
Who were not quite so fond of animal food   783 Juan   2 618
Who shoes the glorious animal with stilts   925 Juan   11 455

ANIMALS
All animals are glad at sight of food   474 Morgante   523
Of the forbidden tree. But animals   641 Cain   2 357
With thy sublime of humps, the animals   724 Deformed   1 105
He chose from several animals he saw   803 Juan   3 139
Will wonder where such animals could sup   901 Juan   9 307
Live animals: an old maid of threescore   913 Juan   10 398
The animals aforesaid occupied   913 Juan   10 401

ANIMATE
(See also RE-ANIMATE)
Some higher sparks should animate   181 Ode-A   105
With not a friend to animate, and tell   359 Corsair   3 228
I'll animate the ideal marble, till   726 Deformed   1 263

ANIMATED
Degraded mass of animated dust   154 Dog   18
Than we! for ours are animated logs   303 Age   407
Though multiplied to animated atoms   636 Cain   2   47
All to be animated for this only   639 Cain   2 248
So animated that it might allure a   951 Juan   13 619

ANIMATING
Commanding, aiding, animating all   380 Lara   2 368

ANIMATION
That clay, where once such animation beam'd   84 Death-B   6
Know, in a word, 'tis Animation   101 Marion   56
This earth's animation   728 Deformed   1 417
Each pulse to animation, till beneath   788 Juan   2 902
Without the animation of the wind   981 Juan   16   72

ANIMATION
At first, then kindling into animation   985 Juan   16 317

ANIMOSITY
Nor say the deeds of animosity   144 Becher-B   30
No process proved connubial animosity   850 Juan   5 1182

ANIMUS
And what the lawyers call a 'malus animus   750 Juan   1 237

ANJOU
I read a sheet of Marg'ret of Anjou; Can you   230 I Read   4

ANJOU'S
Have publish'd Anjou's Margaret   230 Murray-A   2

ANKLE
About the prettiest ankle in the world   810 Juan   3 576
Before a petticoat and peeping ankle   959 Juan   14 216

ANKLES
A canto--then their feet and ankles,--well   774 Juan   2   46
And bosoms, arms, and ankles glancing bare   861 Juan   6 572

ANLACE
And, all unsex'd, the anlace hath espoused   12 Harold   1 560

ANNAL
Space for the annal, yet it shall go forth   460 Dante   3   7

ANNALISTS
And 'gainst those few your annalists have
    thunder'd   932 Juan   12 150

ANNALS
Long shall thine annals and immortal tongue   34 Harold   2 859
And annals graved in characters of flame   61 Harold   4 374
Even in the olden time, Rome's annals say   70 Harold   4 903
How you fought, how you died, still her annals
    can tell   86 Leaving NA   16
Turn to the annals of a former day   94 Dorset   65
Fox shall in Britain's future annals shine   114 Death-A   33
And shine in fashion's annals   137 Clare   36
Dear are the days which made our annals bright   170 Address-A   42
As ever Britain's Annals knew   197 Duel   17
The cause of the curses all annals contain   203 Avatar   63
Say! will not Caledonia's annals yield   254 Bards   935
And left it; and his annals too behold   290 Vision   339
As ever the dark annals of the deep   418 Island   1 199
Of their perturbed annals could attract   458 Dante   1 146
Back to its antique lustre in our annals   508 Faliero   1 620
The annals of hereafter; but if not   519 Faliero   3   75
And never have been--read it in our annals   523 Faliero   3 303
In any annals, the Doge Faliero   540 Faliero   5 138
In memory, and yet they live in annals   546 Faliero   5 592
Our annals say not. Then I will say for them   553 Sardan   1 180
Look to the annals of thine empire's founders   559 Sardan   1 594
Which date the flight of time, but make no annals 582 Sardan   4 295
Our annals draw perchance unto their close   582 Sardan   4 296
An era of sweet peace 'midst bloody annals   586 Sardan   4 512
Which they term annals, history, what you will   610 Foscari   3 115
Something new in the annals of great sieges   731 Deformed   1 636
Up annals, revelations, poesy   923 Juan   11 294
Mock tyrants, when Rome's annals wax'd but dirty 926 Juan   11 480
Divorced or doing thereanent. Ye annals   928 Juan   11 626
The annals of full many a line undone   948 Juan   13 478

ANNE
Oh, Anne! your offences to me have been grievous 147 To Anne-A   1
Be false, my sweet Anne, when I cease to adore
    you   147 To Anne-A   16
Oh say not, sweet Anne, that the Fates have
    decreed   147 To Anne-B   1
Then say not, sweet Anne, that the Fates have
    decreed   147 To Anne-B   13

ANNE'S
Anne's Eye is liken'd to the Sun   143 On Eyes   1

ANNESLEY
Hills of Annesley! bleak and barren   95 Fragment-B   1

ANNEX
Your 'imprimatur' will ye not annex   830 Juan   4 860
An innocent predominance annex   967 Juan   14 739

ANNEX'D
Of Prudence, with advantages annex'd   213 Lady Byron   55
With any penalty annex'd they please   616 Foscari   4 104

ANNIHILATE
The things it may annihilate   191 Prometheus-B   22
Thou didst annihilate the earth to me   439 Tasso   173
That tone, that word, annihilate long years   582 Sardan   4 244

ANNIHILATED

Annihilated senates--Roman, too	67	Harold	4	745
What's this in one annihilated city	894	Juan	8	989

ANNIHILATES

Or over-cold annihilates the charm	854	Juan	6	120

ANNIHILATING

In that annihilating voice	392	Corinth		760
And when the annihilating waters roar	660	Heaven		420

ANNIHILATION

For the annihilation of all life	668	Heaven		1036

ANNOUNCE

Exulting shouts announce the finish'd race	121	Newstead-A		128
An earthquake should announce so great a fall	561	Sardan	2	10
Announce 'the Ten's' decree. That tenderness	612	Foscari	3	258
As to announce his visits a long while	850	Juan	5	1165

ANNOUNCED

While the deep war-drum's sound announced the close of day	28	Harold	2	513
Announced the fact--what then?--it lost its fame	264	Hints		568
Announced that any heard or deem'd him nigh	364	Corsair	3	584
Some streaks announced the coming sun	413	Mazeppa		643
Had not announced the heartless wrath within	543	Faliero	5	391
My father's ark of safety hath announced it	662	Heaven		539
Announced her rank; twelve rings were on her hand	810	Juan	3	571
Rush'd where the thickest fire announced most foes	882	Juan	8	256
A slender streak of blood announced how near	890	Juan	8	754
Announced with no less pomp than victory's winner	948	Juan	13	427
Each carriage was announced, and ladies rose	994	Juan	16	851

ANNOUNCING

Announcing the appointment of that lover of	872	Juan	7	311

ANNOY

His humble hope, and peace annoy	141	Critics		58
If your cool friend annoy you now and then	267	Hints		795
Will one day work me more annoy	325	Abydos	1	133
Which now is leagued young Freedom to annoy	877	Juan	7	631
With martial stoicism, nought seem'd to annoy	893	Juan	8	965

ANNOY'D

A something wherewithal to be annoy'd	965	Juan	14	627

ANNUAL

And annual marriage now no more renew'd	56	Harold	4	92
Too lucky if it prove not annual	231	Doctor		24
Whose annual strains, like armies, take the field	244	Bards		204
Beards of a week and nails of annual growth	263	Hints		468
Ache with the annual tributes of a spouse	274	Waltz		94
Luxuriant with their annual leaves	411	Mazeppa		472
No exhibition glares with annual pictures	450	Beppo		622
Till Rome awoke, and had an annual triumph	537	Faliero	4	649

ANNUITIES

'Tis said that persons living on annuities	782	Juan	2	513

ANNUL

Of counsel to nonsuit, or to annul	770	Juan	1	1508
Prompts deeds eternity can not annul	798	Juan	2	1533
Her third was feminine enough to annul	904	Juan	9	477

ANNULL'D

Has been annull'd by the death-bed confession	600	Foscari	1	303

ANNULS

How in an hour the power which gave annuls	38	Harold	3	156

ANOINT

Anoint our bodies with the fragrant oil	419	Island	2	26

ANOINTED

Crown'd and anointed from on high	185	Belshaz-A		6
The anointed high-priest--Of what god or demon	592	Sardan	5	290

ANOMALY

Whose suicide was almost an anomaly	749	Juan	1	118

ANON

Four days are sped, but with the fifth, anon	6	Harold	1	200
Swept into wrecks anon by Time's ungentle tide	7	Harold	1	287
Restless it rolls, now fix'd, and now anon	10	Harold	1	427
As page and slave anon were passing out and in	28	Harold	2	540
But ever and anon of griefs subdued	58	Harold	4	199
And pale, and pacing to and fro: anon	214	Dream		80
Nor sleeps with Sleeping Beauties, but anon	250	Bards		602
Anon my voice shall vindicate my hand	362	Corsair	3	436
For ever and anon she threw	414	Mazeppa		810
Anon the torchlight dance shall fling its sheen	419	Island	2	31
I'll answer that anon.--Away with me	483	Manfred	1	377

ANON

Was there but one who--but of her anon	485	Manfred	2	153
Thou'lt know anon--Come! Come! I have commanded	496	Manfred	3	344
But we shall see anon. How now--what tidings	500	Faliero	1	37
What mean you?--but we'll know anon. Art sure	533	Faliero	4	339
We'll embark anon. Fair nymphs, who deign	551	Sardan	1	54
And ever and anon some falling bolt	570	Sardan	2	551
All fresh and faithful; they'll be here anon	575	Sardan	3	261
Anon--what the whole earth shall ne'er forget	591	Sardan	5	285
I would know why. You will know why anon	616	Foscari		70
I'll follow you anon. If not, I will	628	Cain	1	62
He will be here anon. What ho, there! bustle	675	Werner	1	258
But we will talk of that anon. Remember	688	Werner	2	359
Anon, we shall perceive his real sway	704	Werner	4	19
Let us retire; they will be here anon	714	Werner	5	68
Fling my cloak o'er what will be dust anon	736	Deformed	2	130
We'll talk of that anon.--'Tis sweet to hear	761	Juan	1	969
For ever and anon a something shook	820	Juan	4	228
Anon--she was released, and then she stray'd	820	Juan	4	249
Anon her thin wan fingers beat the wall	824	Juan	4	521
For ever and anon comes Indigestion	918	Juan	11	17
But ever and anon, to soothe your vision	950	Juan	13	561

ANONYMOUS

I think that all the world are grown anonymous	676	Werner	1	284
For making squares and streets anonymous	944	Juan	13	202

ANOTHER

And had been glorious in another day	4	Harold	1	22
Another, hideous sight! unseam'd appears	16	Harold	1	770
Sweet Florence, could another ever share	24	Harold	2	266
On one another; pity ceased to melt	48	Harold	3	783
From thee! if in another station born	60	Harold	4	332
Wrecks of another world whose ashes still are warm	62	Harold	4	414
Is of another temper, and I roam	64	Harold	4	550
Another view, not less renown'd for wit	94	Dorset		69
Another year is quickly past	102	Alva		49
And Angus hails another son	102	Alva		50
Say, hadst thou ne'er another boy	104	Alva		203
Another to the last replies	112	Quaker		10
By another possest, may she live ever blest	115	The Tear		33
Another Henry the kind gift recalls	120	Newstead-A		43
Another chief impels the foaming steed	121	Newstead-A		135
Another crowd pursue the panting hart	121	Newstead-A		136
Whilst I, in combat with another foe	126	Recoll		277
And Mary's given to another	134	E. N. Long		66
Bestow'd by thee upon another	134	Lady-D		12
Each, murmuring, seeks another course	137	Clare		23
Its former warmth around another	148	A Fan		20
Quaff while thou canst: another race	154	Skull		17
I should not seek another zone	156	Lady-F		11
To quit another spot on earth	157	Florence		4
Another--'tis to tell	158	Storm		18
'Another Marlborough points to Blenheim's story	171	Address-B		23
For the sake of another crime more	178	Devil's Dr		212
Some charm that well rewards another view	183	Address-D		42
Hath lost, another wealth, or fame	195	Ballad-A		94
And thou wert wedded to another	197	Duel		25
And I at last another wedded	197	Duel		26
Lovedst me not: another was	197	Duel		48
Another; even now she loved another	214	Dream		71
Between them stands another sceptred thing	228	Windsor		3
Between them stands another sceptred thing	228	Vaults		3
I dare not venture on another	231	Doctor		40
He'll drivel another Phrosine	232	Murray-B		18
He mounted another as preacher	238	Bray		12
There's another, that's slyer	239	Lucietta		6
Another epic! Who inflicts again	247	Bards		385
Another soars, inflated with bombast	257	Hints		44
But coats must claim another artisan	257	Hints		54
Who (ere another Thalaba appears	265	Hints		655
Another name with his pollutes my shrine	270	Minerva		119
At sea--which drew most souls another way	285	Vision		8
Said, 'There's another star gone out, I think	287	Vision		128
And, growing bigger, took another guise	292	Vision		453
He was his father: upon which another	294	Vision		607
Another, that he was a duke, or knight	294	Vision		609
Presto! his face changed, and he was another	294	Vision		618
Another Babel soars--but Britain ends	307	Age		649
Those gibes had cost another dear	324	Abydos	1	110
To bid thee with another dwell	326	Abydos	1	197
Another! and a braver man	326	Abydos	1	198
But first--Oh! never wed another	330	Abydos	2	163
Another--and another--and another	334	Abydos	2	501
Another falls--but round him close	335	Abydos	2	543
Another came--Oh God! 'twas thine at last	343	Corsair	1	387
One kiss--one more--another--Oh! Adieu	345	Corsair	1	465
'Thou lov'st another then?--but what to me	354	Corsair	2	491
And hide from one--perhaps another there	354	Corsair	2	510
Or seek another and give mine release	355	Corsair	2	526
Perchance but snatch'd her from another grave	357	Corsair	3	114
Another word and--nay--I need no more	358	Corsair	3	186
Or else he had not seen another sun	359	Corsair	3	247

ANOTHER

Thou lov'st another--and I love in vain	360	Corsair	3	297
Yet scarcely heeded these--another light	361	Corsair	3	400
Another chequers o'er the shadow'd floor	364	Corsair	3	596
Another morn--another bids them seek	365	Corsair	3	682
Another chief consoled his destined bride	366	Lara	1	35
But lack of tidings from another clime	366	Lara	1	51
To deem them accents of another land	369	Lara	1	232
An erring spirit from another hurl'd	370	Lara	1	316
Another sex, when match'd with that smooth cheek	374	Lara	1	577
Another ere he left his mountain-shore	374	Lara	1	585
Man has another day to swell the past	375	Lara	2	3
And merely adds another throb to pain	381	Lara	2	425
And still another hurried glance would snatch	383	Lara	2	569
'Tis but another anxious night	387	Corinth		288
And Azo found another bride	401	Parisina		530
Another mistress, or new book	408	Mazeppa		142
I did not think to see another	410	Mazeppa		334
I little deem'd another day	414	Mazeppa		716
Another look on me she cast	415	Mazeppa		833
Another sign she made, to say	415	Mazeppa		834
Which, kindled by another, grows the same	424	Island	2	379
But nature's ebb. Beside him was another	428	Island	3	103
Another course had been their choice--but where	433	Island	4	235
To gather moisture for another flight	435	Island	4	372
But takes at once another, or another's	442	Beppo		144
I'll take another when I'm next at leisure	448	Beppo		504
One has false curls, another too much paint	448	Beppo		521
And self and live-stock to another bottom	452	Beppo		770
But I will make another tongue arise	458	Dante	2	23
Which make men hate themselves and one another	465	Dante	4	122
Another, to revenge his fellow farrow	473	Morgante		501
Their fountains find another channel--thus	483	Manfred	1	359
Which is another kind of ignorance	489	Manfred	2	433
Another evening; yon red cloud, which rests	494	Manfred	3	237
I learn'd the language of another world	495	Manfred	3	267
May win it from another kinder heart	501	Faliero	1	132
I had another reason. What was that	507	Faliero	1	556
Another day like that would be the best	515	Faliero	2	471
Crawl'd on, and added but another link	516	Faliero	2	561
Than live another day to act the tyrant	523	Faliero	3	301
Nobly avenged before another night	525	Faliero	3	487
Also, another thing thou knowest not	552	Sardan	1	134
And thine and mine; and in another day	555	Sardan	1	330
For he who loves another loves himself	558	Sardan	1	533
But when another speaks of Greece, it wounds me	559	Sardan	1	571
Calm thee. Thy speech seems of another world	579	Sardan	4	40
Her left, another, fill'd with--what I saw not	580	Sardan	4	112
I turn'd from one face to another, in	580	Sardan	4	118
'Twas well you enter'd by another portal	585	Sardan	4	454
The beings of another and worse world	606	Foscari	2	311
Another region with their flocks and herds	610	Foscari	3	158
What, if he will not? We'll elect another	615	Foscari	4	36
And I another; and it seems to me	616	Foscari	4	79
In presence of another he says little	620	Foscari	4	345
But add, that if another hour would better	620	Foscari	5	2
Another land, and who so bless'd and blessing	621	Foscari	5	74
The Adriatic's free to wed another	623	Foscari	5	192
Said 'tis another life? Till now he hath	639	Cain	2	241
'Tis like another world; a liquid sun	642	Cain	2	392
Can we not make another? Where? Here, or	646	Cain	3	38
But make another of thine own before	650	Cain	3	287
To try another sacrifice, 'tis thine	650	Cain	3	307
Another sacrifice! Give way, or else	650	Cain	3	308
The native of another and worse world	651	Cain	3	343
She loves another. Anah! No; her sister	657	Heaven		178
If not her words, tells me she loves another	657	Heaven		180
Another element shall be the lord	660	Heaven		361
The past seems paradise. Another day	680	Werner	1	585
Appears to have been committed. There's another	683	Werner	2	27
And wept to see another day go down	688	Werner	2	376
But there's another whom he tracks more keenly	697	Werner	3	142
You may have better luck another chase	699	Werner	3	281
But this!--another look! Gaze on it freely	700	Werner	3	327
Leave me scarce hearing for another sound	701	Werner	3	405
As e'er another prince of the empire. Why	704	Werner	4	8
At peace! and all at peace with one another	713	Werner	5	26
More general than another. I'll not hear	713	Werner	5	39
Yes: if you want another victim, strike	721	Werner	5	512
If there would be another unlike thee	722	Deformed	1	14
I' the sun. Behold another! Who is he	725	Deformed	1	209
But if I give another form, it must be	728	Deformed	1	434
Slain, another climbs the barrier	736	Deformed	2	94
And so did Bourbon, in another sense	737	Deformed	2	168
That foam is their foundation. So, another	739	Deformed	2	294
To lengthen fetters by another fix'd	746	Juan	Ded	95
Is brought up much more wisely than another	751	Juan	1	296
Kept this herself, and gave her son another	752	Juan	1	368
Which, by the Virgin's grace, let in another	756	Juan	1	604
Only another time, I trust, you'll tell us	766	Juan	1	1245
And then flew out into another passion	769	Juan	1	1448
Spurr'd her to teach another generation	775	Juan	2	80
Whisper'd another, and thus it went round	783	Juan	2	578
She snatch'd it, and refused another morsel	794	Juan	2	1271

ANOTHER

Pleasure or pain to one another living	798	Juan	2	1536
Another despot of the kind	813	Juan	3	759
Another outcry for 'a little boat	814	Juan	3	879
Thus was another Eden; they were never	817	Juan	4	74
When two pure hearts are pour'd in one another	819	Juan	4	205
And blew; another answer'd to the call	822	Juan	4	372
We'll put about, and try another tack	826	Juan	4	591
Another time he might have liked to see 'em	826	Juan	4	599
'Tis true, it gets another bright and fresh	834	Juan	5	169
Of eating, with another act or two	835	Juan	5	250
'I see you've bought another girl; 'tis pity	851	Juan	5	1239
Another part of history; for the dishes	867	Juan	6	955
Its sanguinary way good--then another	887	Juan	8	546
Another column also suffer'd much	888	Juan	8	617
May have another name for half we scan	891	Juan	8	827
On one another, and each lovely lisper	906	Juan	9	621
Our soarings with another sort of question	918	Juan	11	19
The family vault receives another lord	927	Juan	11	592
To-morrow sees another race as gay	929	Juan	11	674
And ought to go by quite another name	931	Juan	12	120
How far it profits is another matter	936	Juan	12	401
Also there bin another pious reason	944	Juan	13	201
I'll have another figure in a trice	945	Juan	13	289
To the Greek kalends of another session	946	Juan	13	354
One system eats another up, and this	955	Juan	14	5
I hardly could compose another line	956	Juan	14	90
Marvell'd at merit of another nation	959	Juan	14	267
Go to the coffee-house, and take another	961	Juan	14	384
Another gentle common-place or two	964	Juan	14	546
But there's another little thing, I own	965	Juan	14	653
Or else 'twill cost us all another million	966	Juan	14	664

ANOTHER'S

In vengeance, gloating on another's pain	16	Harold	1	795
But ne'er forget another's woe	133	E. N. Long		42
I've tried another's fetters too	156	Lady-F		55
I've seen my bride another's bride	164	Friend-B		25
Founded on another's woe	207	Fare Thee		16
Her nimble feet danced off another's head	274	Waltz		88
To gain your own or snatch another's bride	275	Waltz		106
Another's ardent look without regret	277	Waltz		241
That moulds another's weakness to its will	341	Corsair	1	184
Of fixing memory on another's heart	371	Lara	1	364
To covet there another's bride	397	Parisina		66
But takes at once another, or another's	442	Beppo		144
'Tis writ on high--your wrong must pay another's	471	Morgante		325
This cautious feeling for another's pain	484	Manfred	2	80
Have found, in searching for another's dross	689	Werner	2	423
Of one another's minds, at last have grown	745	Juan	Ded	36
Her eyes another's eye could shed a tear	846	Juan	5	952
He still preferr'd his own neck to another's	866	Juan	6	928
Mournful--but mournful of another's crime	973	Juan	15	358
His word had the same value as another's	990	Juan	16	616
Of which another's bosom is the zone	994	Juan	16	912

ANSELMO

Few dare, though now Anselmo sought his tower	365	Corsair	3	679
Anselmo, with thy company proceed	536	Faliero	4	583

ANSELMO'S

Double the guard, and when Anselmo's bark	346	Corsair	1	565
Last eve Anselmo's bark return'd, and yet	356	Corsair	3	71
Then seek Anselmo's cavern, to report	357	Corsair	3	121
Wrings with a cordial grasp Anselmo's hand	363	Corsair	3	504

ANSUIGI

Also Ansuigi, the gay time to pass	467	Morgante		68

ANSWER

What answer shall she make	6	Harold	1	169
At what? can he avouch--or answer what he claim'd	68	Harold	4	819
Might answer to the martial strain	194	Ballad-A		24
No tears, but tenderness to answer mine	211	Augusta-Q		4
Time taught him a deep answer--when she loved	214	Dream		70
But now to my letter--to yours 'tis an answer	226	Oh You		5
Who, tempted thus, can answer for the rest	276	Waltz		229
First ask him for his answer to my letter	295	Vision		656
Hears 'the lie' echo for his answer round	304	Age		489
By Alla! I would answer nay	315	Giaour		482
But, Selim, thou must answer why	328	Abydos	1	408
To such, brief answer and contemptuous eye	339	Corsair	1	81
One question answer, then in peace depart	349	Corsair	2	134
Of--"Dost thou love?" and burn to answer, "No	354	Corsair	2	506
The--quick your answer--tell me where he lies	357	Corsair	3	106
Thou need'st not answer--thy confession speaks	358	Corsair	3	182
They own the signal, answer to the hail	363	Corsair	3	494
She raised her eye, her only answer there	363	Corsair	3	542
He snatch'd the lamp--its light will answer all	364	Corsair	3	591
Doubt not my fitting answer to requite	372	Lara	1	433
Thy heart must answer, though thine ear would shun	372	Lara	1	438
He deign'd no answer, but his head he shook	372	Lara	1	446
'A word!--I charge thee stay, and answer here	372	Lara	1	449

ANSWER

And thus I answer for mine absent guest	376	Lara	2	56
And he must answer for the absent head	377	Lara	2	155
With fires that answer fast and well	385	Corinth		93
Is all the answer, with the threat of worse	416	Island	1	70
And who dare answer 'No!' to Mutiny	416	Island	1	82
They hail'd again--no answer; yet once more	434	Island	4	291
Then flew the only answer to be given	434	Island	4	299
And soul--but who shall answer where it went	434	Island	4	352
What answer Beppo made to these demands	452	Beppo		745
When he received an answer so injurious	470	Morgante		248
But, if I'm asked, this answer shall be given	476	Morgante		655
Answer, or I will teach you what I am	480	Manfred	1	158
We answer as we answer'd; our reply	480	Manfred	1	159
I'll answer that anon.--Away with me	483	Manfred	1	377
Hast thou no gentler answer?--Yet bethink thee	487	Manfred	2	255
The sternest answer can but be the Grave	487	Manfred	2	273
And that is nothing;--if they answer not	487	Manfred	2	274
An answer and his destiny--he slew	487	Manfred	2	278
With the blood of a million he'll answer my care	488	Manfred	2	322
What doth he here then? Let him answer that	489	Manfred	2	443
Of such, to answer unto what I seek	489	Manfred	2	447
And what of this? I answer with the Roman	492	Manfred	3	97
What art thou, unknown being? answer!--speak	496	Manfred	3	340
How many are ye? I'll not answer that	507	Faliero	1	528
Thus far I'll answer you--your secret's safe	508	Faliero	1	568
What would you have me answer? I would have you	508	Faliero	1	570
What was the Doge's answer? That he was	509	Faliero	2	1
I married. And the second? Needs no answer	510	Faliero	2	124
Freedom from me to choose, and urged in answer	513	Faliero	2	323
The Doge--what answer gave he? That there was	516	Faliero	2	536
Else I could answer.--Let us to the meeting	520	Faliero	3	82
If he be worm or no, may answer for me	522	Faliero	3	263
The offence grows his, and let him answer it	526	Faliero	3	532
And thou dost well to answer that it was	527	Faliero	3	634
And not before? I cannot answer this	530	Faliero	4	187
Against the senate I will answer. Well	533	Faliero	4	380
I am not warranted to answer that	537	Faliero	4	641
I'll answer for thee--'tis a certain Bertram	537	Faliero	4	642
I shall but answer that which will offend you	542	Faliero	5	278
The question--but you answer it ere spoken	542	Faliero	5	336
For mercy, and be answer'd as they answer	543	Faliero	5	388
I speak to thee in answer to yon signor	544	Faliero	5	409
That's a hard question, but I answer, Yes	555	Sardan	1	344
Will send my answer through thy babbling troop	556	Sardan	1	348
Ingratitude? I will not pause to answer	557	Sardan	1	428
They cannot answer; when the priests speak for them	559	Sardan	1	592
What doth this mean? The prince must answer that	565	Sardan	2	196
Where is the proof? I'll answer that, if once	565	Sardan	2	200
And I will answer all. Why, if I thought so	565	Sardan	2	212
Depart, and not to bear your answer. Ay	568	Sardan	2	413
A question as an answer to his question	590	Sardan	5	172
I wait the answer. Answer, slave! How long	592	Sardan	5	307
But must I bear no answer? Yes,--I ask	592	Sardan	5	342
Do so. Is that thy answer? Thou shalt see	594	Sardan	5	422
I understand thee, but I must not answer	598	Foscari	1	202
True--none dare answer here save on the rack	598	Foscari	1	203
They ought to answer; for it is well known	600	Foscari	1	306
That answer only shows you know not Venice	603	Foscari	2	84
Doge! have you aught in answer? Something from	606	Foscari	2	323
With the like answer--doubt and dreadful surmise	609	Foscari	3	76
Alone can answer; they are rarely wont	616	Foscari	4	66
Hours are accorded you to give an answer	621	Foscari	5	35
We grieve for such an answer; but it cannot	621	Foscari	5	58
And will they press their answer on the Doge	622	Foscari	5	119
And I to answer. What? My only answer	623	Foscari	5	163
Your answer, Duke! Your answer, Francis Foscari	623	Foscari	5	177
So rashly? 'twill give scandal. Answer that	623	Foscari	5	203
One answer to all questions, ''T was his will	628	Cain	1	75
I cannot answer. Were I quiet earth	631	Cain	1	287
I cannot answer this immortal thing	633	Cain	1	403
That which it really is, I cannot answer	639	Cain	2	220
Like them? Let He who made thee answer that	640	Cain	2	293
Springs good! What didst thou answer? Nothing; for	643	Cain	2	504
He will not answer to that name; for brethren	651	Cain	3	354
Japhet, I cannot answer thee; yet, yet	663	Heaven		599
To give an answer; or if not, to put	675	Werner	1	246
An answer, not an echo. You may seek	679	Werner	1	529
Both from the walls. I am not used to answer	679	Werner	1	530
And wonder that I answer not--not knowing	680	Werner	1	549
Fail, you must send on others, till the answer	680	Werner	1	592
I'll answer you. Most probably an Austrian	686	Werner	2	191
But--Show the spot, and then I'll answer you	686	Werner	2	250
If the judge ask'd me, I would answer 'No	692	Werner	2	623
To you I answer thus. With all my heart	692	Werner	2	624
(Albeit I never pass'd them), I'll not answer	696	Werner	3	103
And have look'd through him): it will answer thus	698	Werner	3	205
Answer? Are you or are you not the assassin	702	Werner	3	463
Hence! hence! I must not hear your answer--Look	704	Werner	3	580
You shall not answer--Pardon me that I	704	Werner	3	583
To me: I'll answer for the event as far	704	Werner	3	587
And answer that yourself. He's very youthful	704	Werner	4	23
Her answer, I'll give mine. But 'tis your office	710	Werner	4	397
	710	Werner	4	397
Pause ere you answer: is no other name	715	Werner	5	163
Further than justice asks. Answer at once	715	Werner	5	169
The answer--You are jealous. And of whom	744	Deformed	3	136
A ready answer, which at once enables	768	Juan	1	1394
For I have found it answer--so may you	775	Juan	2	104
The answer eloquent, where the soul shines	794	Juan	2	1293
He'll answer all for better or for worse	807	Juan	3	359
And answer, 'Let one living head	812	Juan	3	734
Where men have souls or bodies she must answer	827	Juan	4	672
To answer in a very clear oration	861	Juan	6	589
For any further answer that he found	865	Juan	6	835
He made no answer; but he took the city	874	Juan	7	424
In answer made an inclination to	885	Juan	8	451
For all the answer to his proposition	888	Juan	8	641
To answer Ribas' summons to give way	893	Juan	8	960
'Tis said (for I'll not answer above ground	907	Juan	10	3
Jury of matrons, scarce knew what to answer	924	Juan	11	404
Pray did you see her answer to his letter	934	Juan	12	280
An end to answer, or a plan to lay	937	Juan	12	462

ANSWER'D

Which answer'd not with a caress--he died	189	Darkness		54
And thus he answer'd--'Well, I do not know	190	Churchill		11
Because he answer'd, and because	195	Ballad-A		63
The angel answer'd, 'Peter! do not pout	287	Vision		169
It be?' Then Satan answer'd, 'There are many	293	Vision		519
Aught further?' Junius answer'd, 'You had better	295	Vision		655
'Tis answer'd--'Well ye speed, my gallant crew	349	Corsair	2	167
He ask'd no question--all were answer'd now	365	Corsair	3	623
He ceased; and Lara answer'd, 'I am here	375	Lara	2	43
'Demand thy life!' He answer'd not: and then	376	Lara	2	71
And echo answer'd from the hill	387	Corinth		263
Mazeppa answer'd, 'Ill betide	408	Mazeppa		107
I could have answer'd with a sigh	411	Mazeppa		441
He answer'd, and then fell	413	Mazeppa		691
Laugh'd, and the sound was answer'd by the rocks	431	Island	4	118
Orlando answer'd, 'This I'll see, be sure	469	Morgante		231
Orlando answer'd, 'Baron just and pious	471	Morgante		345
To which Morgante answer'd, 'I'm content	471	Morgante		360
Orlando answer'd, 'Like a ship's mast rather	474	Morgante		548
Orlando answer'd, 'If my counsel still	474	Morgante		565
Morgante answer'd, 'Let them pay in hell	474	Morgante		579
Orlando answer'd, 'If there should lie loose	476	Morgante		660
Is as the future, present. Art thou answer'd	480	Manfred	1	151
We answer as we answer'd; our reply	480	Manfred	1	159
And the answer'd owls are hooting	481	Manfred	1	197
And in that silence I am more than answer'd	490	Manfred	2	480
Which answer'd me--many things answer'd me	490	Manfred	2	509
Till I am answer'd. How, sir! do you menace	507	Faliero	1	529
I answer'd your first question when I said	510	Faliero	2	123
For mercy, and be answer'd as they answer	543	Faliero	5	388
It is the curse of kings to be so answer'd	551	Sardan	1	63
And ask'd of thee, and thou hast answer'd--but	562	Sardan	2	29
Between us, but he answer'd not--I fill'd it	579	Sardan	4	93
I'm answer'd! When a king asks twice, and has	590	Sardan	5	171
'The good day or good night?' his Dogeship answer'd	619	Foscari	4	294
Is manifest, then you shall all be answer'd	621	Foscari	5	57
He answer'd quickly, and must so be answer'd	622	Foscari	5	121
Must be answer'd on the instant, as the bound	699	Werner	3	285
Would I have answer'd. Sir, you wed for love	710	Werner	4	360
E'er answer'd thus till now? Did you not warn me	710	Werner	4	365
And answer'd but to nature's just demands	751	Juan	1	294
But has not answer'd like the apparatus	762	Juan	1	1035
And that the medicine answer'd very well	767	Juan	1	1342
And no great good seem'd answer'd if she staid	768	Juan	1	1382
To stay there had not answer'd her intent	775	Juan	2	59
All one an hour hence.' Juan answer'd, 'No	778	Juan	2	282
And blew; another answer'd to the call	822	Juan	4	372
When Juan answer'd--'Spanish!' he replied	833	Juan	5	105
I have answer'd all your questions without pressing	833	Juan	5	123
More easily than answer'd,--that he had tried	864	Juan	6	795
Were briskly fired and answer'd in due order	872	Juan	7	304
This dialogue; for he who answer'd knew	874	Juan	7	471
'Then up with me!'--But Juan answer'd, 'Look	890	Juan	8	785
For cousins also, answer'd the same day	911	Juan	10	236
And answer'd, like a statesman or a prophet	963	Juan	14	519
Had stirr'd him, answer'd in a way to cloud it	987	Juan	16	480

ANSWERED

To which the giant answered, 'So I will	474	Morgante		552
The buried Prophet answered to the Hag	487	Manfred	2	275

ANSWEREST

My lord, my life! why answerest thou so coldly	551	Sardan	1	62

ANSWERING

Answering each other on the Palatine	71	Harold	4	951
And once, as Kaled's answering accents ceased	381	Lara	2	466
Of boatmen answering back with verse for verse	529	Faliero	4	100

ANSWERING
Answering to Heaven for what they did on earth 540 Faliero 5 178
In answering yours. I wish I could engage him 687 Werner 2 258
Two blankets stitch'd together, answering ill 781 Juan 2 483
Recall'd his answering spirits back from death 788 Juan 2 900
Answering the Christian thunders with like voices 879 Juan 8 52
From answering she began to question; this 978 Juan 15 641

ANSWERLESS
Are questions answerless, and yet incessant 860 Juan 6 504

ANSWERS
And Jura answers, through her misty shroud 49 Harold 3 867
Which answers to all doubts so eloquently well 52 Harold 3 1003
The last smile which answers to mine 210 Augusta-B   10
Without amendment, and he answers, 'Burn 267 Hints   786
'Where is my child?' an Echo answers--'Where 336 Abydos 2 663
What answers Lara? to its centre shrunk 373 Lara 1 482
Brief were his answers, and his questions 373 Lara 1 547
And questions of his state; he answers not 381 Lara 2 440
For that faint throb which answers not again 382 Lara 2 497
Who answers? How now, brother? The queen's
  brother 551 Sardan 1 79
It answers better to resolve the alphabet 732 Deformed 1 673
How answers each bold Bacchanal 812 Juan 3 742
A few brief questions; and the answers gave 826 Juan 4 630
She liked quick answers in all conversations 864 Juan 6 803
His answers with a very graceful bow 907 Juan 9 659
'Quite well; yes,--no.'--These answers were
  mysterious 984 Juan 16 257

ANTECHAMBER
A priest is waiting in the antechamber 539 Faliero 5 106
Had access to the antechamber. Doubtless 683 Werner 2 18
He best knows; but within an antechamber 718 Werner 5 330
The antechamber--search them under, over 765 Juan 1 1218

ANTEDATE
And bid it antedate the joys of arms 272 Minerva   292

ANTELOPE
With timid fawn or antelope 325 Abydos 1 137
Bent like an antelope a Paphian pair 843 Juan 5 763

ANTELOPES
Like frighten'd antelopes. No: like the dam 577 Sardan 3 378

ANTEROS
Eros and Anteros, at Gadara 486 Manfred 2 187

ANTHEM
A dirge, an anthem o'er the dead 166 Away   12
Incense or anthem to the skies 318 Giaour   805
But when the anthem shakes the choir 319 Giaour   887
The owl his anthem, where the silenced quire 949 Juan 13 495

ANTHILL
Unto their anthill: how the pismires then 735 Deformed 1 894

ANTHONY
('Twas snow that brought St. Anthony to reason 755 Juan 1 508
If Anthony be well remember'd yet 853 Juan 6 29

ANTHONY'S
Like 'Anthony's by Caesar,' by the few 974 Juan 15 423

ANTHROPOPHAGI
What Anthropophagi are nine of ten 968 Juan 14 813

ANTIC
With frolic quaint their antic jests expose 124 Recoll   139
So call'd; the Antic long hath ceased to hear 898 Juan 9 92

ANTI-CHRIST
Younder stands Anti-Christ! How now, schismatic 738 Deformed 2 242
Destroy proud Anti-Christ. I am a Christian 738 Deformed 2 244

ANTI-CHRISTIAN
Yet left more anti-christian foes than they 302 Age   333

ANTICIPATE
If hope anticipate the words of truth 125 Recoll   248
The age which I anticipate, no less 464 Dante 4 71
To anticipate the sentence of the Forty 500 Faliero 1 24
Thou dost almost anticipate my heart 557 Sardan 1 469
Unto the timid who anticipate 579 Sardan 4 51
'Tis not for me to anticipate the pleasure 606 Foscari 2 285
To let their thoughts anticipate their purpose 616 Foscari 4 67
To anticipate my immortality 637 Cain 2 94
And none liked to anticipate the blow 778 Juan 2 286
As eager to anticipate their grave 780 Juan 2 412
Anticipate the Prophet's paradise 841 Juan 5 648
May settle; but far be't from me to anticipate 867 Juan 6 951

ANTICIPATED
The Highland seer's anticipated woes 182 Address-C   24
Anticipated freedom share 333 Abydos 2 381
Quiver with the anticipated wrenching 598 Foscari 1 160
Has been anticipated: it is known 612 Foscari 3 259
About this time, as might have been anticipated 910 Juan 10 177
They are young, but know not youth--it is
  anticipated 927 Juan 11 585

ANTICIPATES
'Done!' cried Asmodeus, 'he anticipates 296 Vision   706
Despair anticipates such things. Despair 590 Sardan 5 222

ANTICIPATING
The worthy Pania, from anticipating 569 Sardan 2 463
Anticipating aught about the matter 967 Juan 14 786

ANTI-CLIMAX
Let this not seem an anti-climax:--'Oh 914 Juan 10 465

ANTIDOTES
Applying poisons there as antidotes 625 Foscari 5 278
Dispell'd by antidotes. But as thou saidst 643 Cain 2 510

ANTIENT
Wondrous as antient war or hero 233 Nihil   21

ANTI-JACOBIN
Then grew a hearty anti-jacobin 297 Vision   775
An Eastern anti-jacobin at last 811 Juan 3 627

ANTIPATHIES
Antipathies--but to recur, ere long 74 Harold 4 1120

ANTIPATHY
Such pure antipathy to poisons as 625 Foscari 5 295
Besides the antipathy with which we met 687 Werner 2 277
There's something of antipathy, as 'twere 802 Juan 3 41

ANTIPODES
Their mothers as the antipodes of Timon 864 Juan 6 746
Simple, serene, the antipodes of shame 886 Juan 8 501
Would show mankind their souls' antipodes 968 Juan 14 808

ANTIQUARIANS
(The antiquarians who can settle time 881 Juan 8 179

ANTIQUE
Of former sovereigns, and the antique brood 60 Harold 4 310
Where, as a monument of antique art 68 Harold 4 787
Within an antique Oratory stood 214 Dream   78
That in the antique Oratory shook 215 Dream   151
In rude but antique portraiture around 368 Lara 1 138
No solemn, antique gentleman of rhyme 449 Beppo   577
Back to its antique lustre in our annals 508 Faliero 1 620
Their antique energy of mind, all that 610 Foscari 3 152
And thus they form a group that's quite antique 798 Juan 2 1551
The antique Persians taught three useful things 980 Juan 16 1
Or step ran sadly through that antique house 983 Juan 16 156

ANTIQUES
Misshapen monuments and maim'd antiques 256 Bards   1030

ANTITHESIS
A kind antithesis to Congreve's rockets 762 Juan 1 1030
Which forms, in fact, true love's antithesis 802 Juan 3 58
The sober, sad antithesis to glowing 959 Juan 14 222
The grand antithesis to great ennui 968 Juan 15 11

ANTITHETICALLY
Whose spirit antithetically mixt 40 Harold 3 317

ANTONIA
Her maid Antonia, who was an adept 764 Juan 1 1116
But Julia mistress, and Antonia maid 764 Juan 1 1121
'Oh!' sobb'd Antonia, 'I could tear their eyes
  out 765 Juan 1 1216
(Antonia! let me have a glass of water 766 Juan 1 1236
'Perhaps 'tis of Antonia you are jealous 766 Juan 1 1241
Antonia! where's my pocket-handkerchief 766 Juan 1 1256
Antonia bustled round the ransack'd room 766 Juan 1 1266
But sage Antonia cut him short before 766 Juan 1 1298
Antonia let him--not a little sore 767 Juan 1 1308
Antonia puzzled; Julia did not speak 767 Juan 1 1351
Antonia cried out 'Rape!' and Julia 'Fire 769 Juan 1 1466
Antonia in hysterics, Julia swoon'd 770 Juan 1 1491

ANTONIA'S
Following Antonia's motions here and there 766 Juan 1 1274
Antonia's skill was put upon the rack 767 Juan 1 1347
Antonia's patience now was at a stand 767 Juan 1 1357

ANTONIES
Thy charms might raise new Antonies 159 Gulf   16

ANTONIO

Antonio, take my mask and cloak, and light	528 Faliero	4	19
It seems the voice of Bertram--go, Antonio	530 Faliero	4	130
What, ho!--Antonio--Pedro--to the door	533 Faliero	4	328

ANTONY

O'er which from empire she lured Antony	298 Age		30
Titus the master, Antony the slave	800 Juan	2	1634

ANTRES

What 'antres vast and deserts idle' then	968 Juan	14	809

ANTS

And prop the hill of these agrarian ants	307 Age		651
'Go to these ants, thou sluggard, and be wise	307 Age		652

ANVIL

The anvil of his speech received the hammer	767 Juan	1	1299

ANXIETY

His own anxiety, his heart, too, bleeding	807 Juan	3	366

ANXIOUS

When you must quit your anxious lover	89 To Emma		2
Your image fills my anxious breast	91 Caroline-B		29
Or agitates his anxious breast	95 Granta		39
The year of anxious trembling past	103 Alva		171
My labouring soul, with anxious thought oppress'd	105 Nisus		21
With anxious tremors, yet unawed by fear	106 Nisus		95
What fears, what anxious hopes, attend the chase	121 Newstead-A		126
Anxious to please, of pleasing half afraid	125 Recoll		270
Why should my anxious breast repine	131 L'Amitie		1
All duly anxious to leave little work	303 Age		410
And woman's gentler anxious tone is heard	339 Corsair	1	109
To anxious eyes what hour is ever late	346 Corsair	1	590
While many an anxious glance her large dark eye	357 Corsair	3	137
Meanwhile long anxious, weary, still the same	358 Corsair	3	208
And set the anxious frame that lately shook	364 Corsair	3	600
Cold in the many, anxious in the few	366 Lara	1	32
Perceives not Lara that his anxious page	380 Lara	2	390
'Tis but another anxious night	387 Corinth		288
So very anxious, clever, fine, and jealous	449 Beppo		595
Though my breast feels too anxious; I will try	528 Faliero	4	23
The dread of more: it is an anxious hour	588 Sardan	5	74
As being anxious to resume my journey	687 Werner	2	312
With stern and anxious glance gazed back upon	718 Werner	5	333
But Inez was so anxious, and so clear	759 Juan	1	801
Which make all bodies anxious to get out	906 Juan	9	594
Because he ne'er seem'd anxious to seduce	969 Juan	15	90

ANY

My heart no more can rest with any	134 Lady-D		18
To you, or I, or any other	143 On Eyes		7
But you may choose Jack Wilkes as well as any	293 Vision		520
I like a beef-steak, too, as well as any	446 Beppo		379
'Tis said they use no better than a dog any	448 Beppo		557
Near them Giusaffa's would seem few, if any	466 Morgante		48
But had a different husband, any husband	513 Faliero	2	276
The world? In this case--yes. In any case	709 Werner	4	303
(Nuptial examples are as good as any	807 Juan	3	396
To cutting short their hopes of having any	848 Juan	5	1056
Makes us believe ourselves as good as any	905 Juan	9	544
Changes in youth, to be surprised at any	936 Juan	12	392
Of character, in those at least who have got any	957 Juan	14	128
The marriage state, the best or worst of any	967 Juan	14	758
Pious and pure, beyond what I can term any	972 Juan	15	285

ANYBODY

And more of both than any body knows	297 Vision		784
That anybody should disturb you so	858 Juan	6	371
As any body on the elected roll	911 Juan	10	275
With any body in a ride or walk	970 Juan	15	152

ANYBODY'S

In any body's business but the king's	963 Juan	14	522

ANYTHING

In short, do anything, except prescribe	143 Soliloquy		58
Be something, any-thing, but--mean	153 Friend-A		76
Speak--speak of anything but love	164 Friend-B		18
Whiche'er may please you--anything but sleep	258 Hints		142
And raise a laugh with anything--but wit	259 Hints		160
Were quaint and careless, anything but chaste	262 Hints		430
'Tis clear, are fit for anything but rhymes	264 Hints		522
What should thy sons do?--anything but weep	452 Venice-B		6
Lose anything except my own esteem	567 Sardan	2	342
The rack, the grave, all--any thing with thee	609 Foscari	3	40
To bear the brand of bloodshed? Pshaw! leave any thing	703 Werner	3	548
But if there's anything in which I shine	750 Juan	1	182
But not a page of any thing that's loose	752 Juan	1	318
His Pegasus, nor anything that's his	772 Juan	1	1642
Or think of any thing excepting thee	776 Juan	2	150
His muse made increment of any thing	812 Juan	3	677

ANYTHING

Could hardly carry anything away	843 Juan	5	741
I won't be bail for anything beyond	844 Juan	5	792
Done anything exceedingly unkind	899 Juan	9	163
Of any thing which nature would express	945 Juan	13	268
That any thing he views can greatly please	945 Juan	13	271
'Tis pleasant, if then anything is pleasant	959 Juan	14	223
In any thing, however she might flatter	966 Juan	14	698
From any thing, this epic will contain	980 Juan	16	18

ANYWHERE

Any where, where we might respire unfetter'd	607 Foscari	2	381
They might behold their parent anywhere	613 Foscari	3	365
Is it for this I scarce went anywhere	765 Juan	1	1179
A kingdom or confusion anywhere	847 Juan	5	1027
No sign that it was circular anywhere	850 Juan	5	1196
Waves at spring-tide, or women anywhere	856 Juan	6	267
Was happiest amongst mortals anywhere	886 Juan	8	485

ANYWISE

But those who sate ne'er stirr'd in anywise	838 Juan	5	428

AONIAN

Where Attic flowers Aonian odours breathe	254 Bards		884

APACE

Each spurs his jaded Pegasus apace	243 Bards		145
Night wears apace, my last of earthly rest	361 Corsair	3	369
The hogs on t'other, and he brush'd apace	473 Morgante		514
You improve apace;--two changes in an instant	729 Deformed	1	489
He studied steadily, and grew apace	753 Juan	1	389
Just as old age is creeping on apace	808 Juan	3	469
Rush back upon his heart, which fill'd apace	846 Juan	5	933
With the first draught intoxicates apace	905 Juan	9	532
His travels to the capital apace	920 Juan	11	140
When her soft, liquid words run on apace	960 Juan	14	286

APART

Apart he stalk'd in joyless reverie	4 Harold	1	50
Here woman's voice is never heard: apart	28 Harold	2	541
With blood, and each sate sullenly apart	189 Darkness		40
But that which keepeth us apart is not	198 Po		37
The deadly bullet turn'd apart	201 Ode-C		64
It is the same, together or apart	212 Augusta-C		125
Ambition tore the links apart	325 Abydos	1	192
And oft her Koran conn'd apart	330 Abydos	2	103
He seem'd, like him he served, to live apart	374 Lara	1	550
And thus together, yet apart	403 Chillon		54
But far apart--and well it were	411 Mazeppa		485
No power in death can tear our names apart	440 Tasso		244
The aid of age to turn its course apart	453 Venice-B		29
Are kept apart and nursed in the devotion	454 Venice-B		135
As by himself it chanced he sate apart	468 Morgante		118
Do you still keep apart, and walk alone	511 Faliero	2	176
If all of these even should be set apart	524 Faliero	2	410
Apart; her voice that clove through all the din	577 Sardan	3	392
We were in an existence all apart	580 Sardan	4	128
His power. I dwell apart; but I am great	632 Cain	1	305
Apart--what's this? Enter! Can I return	639 Cain	2	199
His lips, too, are apart; why then he breathes	651 Cain	3	339
Our race hath always dwelt apart from thine	664 Heaven		660
Its snow through all;--her soft lips lie apart	766 Juan	1	1263
'Man's life is of man's life a thing apart	770 Juan	1	1545
Once all in all, but now a thing apart	773 Juan	1	1715
Felt as if never more to beat apart	798 Juan	2	1528
When they from their sweet friends are torn apart	816 Juan	3	955
Would wither less than these two torn apart	817 Juan	4	79
Should an hour come to bid them breathe apart	819 Juan	4	211
And lips apart, which show'd the pearls beneath	860 Juan	6	520
Apart from one who had no sin to show	863 Juan	6	671
With all its veil of mystery drawn apart	893 Juan	8	916
If that politeness set it not apart	932 Juan	12	173
(While yet the church was Rome's) stood half apart	948 Juan	13	466
The politicians, in a nook apart	955 Juan	13	865
For reasons which I choose to keep apart	958 Juan	14	166
She call'd her husband now and then apart	963 Juan	14	515
Dissimulation always sets apart	968 Juan	15	22
Apart from the surrounding world, and strong	974 Juan	15	375

APARTMENT

When? where? This night I'll bring to your apartment	508 Faliero	1	579
To watch before the apartment of the women	575 Sardan	3	230
Apartment, mutter forth the words--'My son	620 Foscari	4	348
Here? no; but in the prince's own apartment	675 Werner	1	231
'Tis a fine building, but decay'd. The apartment	676 Werner	1	310
To his own apartment, about the same time	683 Werner	2	25
You've made the apartment in a fit condition	765 Juan	1	1211
Of the apartment--and appear'd quite new	809 Juan	3	532
Juan from the apartment: with a sign	822 Juan	4	394
With furniture an exquisite apartment	839 Juan	5	511
The apartment, on a sudden she scream'd out	861 Juan	6	560

APARTMENTS
There, in apartments small and damp   95 Granta   29
In the remote apartments: let a guard   573 Sardan   3   122
But when they reach'd their own apartments, there   856 Juan   6   265

APATHY
And never gaze on it with apathy   212 Augusta-C   86
Where cold Obstruction's apathy   311 Giaour   81
And apathy of limb, the dull beginning   453 Venice-B   39
The negligence, the apathy, the evils   552 Sardan   1   116
Itself to apathy, for we must steep   816 Juan   4   28

APATHY'S
Are wafted far distant on Apathy's wing   148 Farewell-A   8

APE
The artist and his ape, to teach and tell   63 Harold   4   470
Adieu ye fools--who ape your betters   163 Malta   10
Ape the swoln dialogue of kings and queens   261 Hints   338
('Transferr'd to those ambiguous things that ape   275 Waltz   141
From chains, would gladly be their tyrant's ape   299 Age   98
Of heaven's, as man is mimick'd by the ape   303 Age   397
And the worst despot's far less human ape   465 Dante   4   127
The Romans (and we ape then) gave a crown   620 Foscari   4   312
Whose actions I ape   728 Deformed   1   387
In Italy he'd ape the 'Trecentisti   812 Juan   3   687

APELLES
Which with Apelles and old Phidias   463 Dante   4   42

APENNINE
Once more upon the woody Apennine   66 Harold   4   649
Adored the Alp, and loved the Apennine   422 Island   2   285
Which overhangs the Apennine, my mind's eye   456 Dante   1   38
Which waft him where the Apennine looks down   458 Dante   1   169

APERTURE
Her light through thy sole aperture; to those   77 Harold   4   1320

APES
The apes of him who humbled once the proud   69 Harold   4   853
He apes the selfish prudence of his sire   260 Hints   244
Apes Treason from without. Question no further   591 Sardan   5   270
No fashion made them apes of her distortions   886 Juan   8   526

APHRODITE'S
A form like Aphrodite's in her shell   420 Island   2   132

APICIAN
Apician table, and Horatian ode   305 Age   515

APICIUS
Whereon Apicius would bestow his benison   976 Juan   15   518

APICIUS'
As temperance, if at Apicius' board   290 Vision   364

APIECE
They also gave a petticoat apiece   791 Juan   2   1061
And others of twelve consonants apiece   869 Juan   7   117

APING
Rose also, as if aping their chief shades   580 Sardan   4   138

APIS
Be for their monarch, or their ox-god Apis   595 Sardan   5   485

APISH
At apish distance; but as yet none have   68 Harold   4   798

APOCALYPSE
As told in the Apocalypse. No eyes   485 Manfred   2   102

APOLLO
Though here no more Apollo haunts his grot   14 Harold   1   634
Apollo still thy long, long summer gilds   33 Harold   2   825
If Apollo should e'er his assistance refuse   92 First Kiss   9
Apollo sink, and Shakspeare cease to reign   169 Address-A   4
To me, divine Apollo, grant--O   226 Thurlow-A   7
Restore Apollo to his vacant throne   252 Bards   807
'Tis high time for a 'Sic me servait Apollo   280 Blues   1   156
Meantime Apollo plucks me by the ear   817 Juan   4   55

APOLLO'S
'Then thus to form Apollo's crown   227 Thurlow-B   10
For this we spurn Apollo's venal son   244 Bards   183
Thy muse a sprite, Apollo's sexton thou   245 Bards   268
As Vulcan's feet to bear Apollo's frame   257 Hints   56
In song alone Apollo's will was told   266 Hints   686
Cantos would do; but at Apollo's pleading   936 Juan   12   438

APOLOGIES
And, sure, apologies are due   138 Clare   68
A lady with apologies abounds   768 Juan   1   1405

APOLOGIST
Faith cants, perplex'd apologist of sin   262 Hints   380

APOLOGUE
Apologue, fable, poesy, and parable   979 Juan   15   705

APOLOGY
Were forced to make an odd sort of apology   752 Juan   1   327
Although my opinion may require apology   803 Juan   3   83
So much less fight as might form an apology   892 Juan   8   860

APOPLECTIC
But most, an alderman struck apoplectic   809 Juan   3   525

APOSTASY'S
Apostasy's so fashionable, too   747 Juan   Ded   134

APOSTATE
Apostate from your gentle train   118 Romance   54
That mild apostate from poetic rule   245 Bards   236
Apostate from his own vile faith   316 Giaour   616

APOSTLE
The apostle of affliction, he who threw   47 Harold   3   726
'And who is George the Third?' replied the
  apostle   287 Vision   138
Like Peter the Apostle,--and he fish'd   790 Juan   2   1002

APOSTLES
'And one of our apostles, Saul once named   473 Morgante   457
Twin-named from the apostles John and Paul   508 Faliero   1   602
That all the Apostles would have done as they did   757 Juan   1   664

APOSTOLIC
Scoffing; and apostolic statues climb   71 Harold   4   989
And sweated through his apostolic skin   288 Vision   198

APOSTROPHE
To hail her with the apostrophe--'O thou   982 Juan   16   102

APOTHECARY'S
Beyond the best apothecary's art   776 Juan   2   163

APPAL
Then mightst thou more appal; or, less desired   61 Harold   4   379
These might the boldest sylph appal   97 To M--   17
To cheer--to pierce--to please--or to appal   193 Monody   36
Be driven to excesses which once could appal   238 Pangs   6
In part of your disdain, it doth appal me   502 Faliero   1   174
You would appal your slaves to further slavery   538 Faliero   5   49
'Tis easy to astonish or appal   588 Sardan   5   79
While the mere victor's may appal or stun   878 Juan   8   38
'Shadows the soul of Richard' may appal   980 Juan   15   766
When he can't tell what 'tis that doth appal   996 Juan   16   1006

APPALL'D
Appall'd, an owlet's larum chill'd with dread   12 Harold   1   563
Where was thine Aegis, Pallas, that appall'd   21 Harold   2   118
Internal fear appall'd his soul   104 Alva   247
While Hope retires appall'd, and clings to life   122 Recoll   10
Shrank back appall'd, and trembled for their home   169 Address-A   12
Appall'd by truths imparted now   334 Abydos   2   488
Nor less his change of form appall'd the sight   349 Corsair   2   143
Whom blood appall'd not,--their regards perplex   363 Corsair   3   515
Bertuccio--What! are you all appall'd to see   522 Faliero   3   215
With the same aspect, which appall'd me more   579 Sardan   4   98
In the late action scarcely more appall'd   588 Sardan   5   77
Indulge a smile at that which once appall'd   591 Sardan   5   239
Appall'd, turn their despairing eyes on me   617 Foscari   4   142
The host will be appall'd,--but vengeance!
  vengeance!   736 Deformed   2   127
But what cold Sceptic hath appall'd your faith   743 Deformed   3   112

APPALLING
Not less appalling cells, the 'leaden roofs   507 Faliero   1   533
Yet in ruin still appalling   736 Deformed   2   114

APPALS
All that expands the spirit, yet appals   45 Harold   3   596
Appals an audience with a monarch's death   260 Hints   278
Appals the gazing mourner's heart   311 Giaour   82
Whose name appals the fiercest of his crew   340 Corsair   1   175
Aught they behold or hear their thought appals   370 Lara   1   265
Perhaps there's nothing--I'll not say appals   838 Juan   5   445

APPANAGE
And sold, and be an appanage to those   548 Faliero   5   749
The homage and the appanage of sovereignty   554 Sardan   1   259
An appanage of twenty hundred golden   621 Foscari   5   30
Your services, the state allots the appanage   623 Foscari   4   171
Lord of a prince's appanage, and honour'd   709 Werner   4   320

APPARATUS
But has not answer'd like the apparatus   762 Juan   1   1035

APPAREL
(See also BED-APPAREL)
With all the apparel of the state, petitions   500 Faliero   1   8
And the apparel of the grave. Do you   626 Foscari   5   342
Without the apparel of being circumspect   962 Juan   14   444

APPARELL'D
Apparell'd as becomes the brave   324 Abydos   1   21

APPARENT
Apparent sovereign of our hundred isles   522 Faliero   3   255
The apparent crimes of the accused disclose   600 Foscari   1   310
Of your apparent prudence should admit   677 Werner   1   411
Like small stars through the milky way apparent   811 Juan   3   612
So that the heir apparent still was found   850 Juan   5   1223

APPARENTLY
Prepare to attack: they have apparently   586 Sardan   4   548

APPEAL
Their doom, nor heed the suppliant's appeal   12 Harold   1   554
Arose to Heaven in her appeal from man   193 Monody   42
But why to brain-scorch'd bigots thus appeal   262 Hints   373
Hear! hear Prometheus from his rock appeal   301 Age   227
The playful girl's appeal address'd   326 Abydos   1   274
For they appeal from tyranny to God   402 Sonnet-F   14
For Florence. I appeal from her to Thee   457 Dante   1   125
Who sent up my appeal unto the Forty   500 Faliero   1   32
Yet without remedy: you can appeal   501 Faliero   1   110
In case your fresh appeal should be rejected   502 Faliero   1   155
Appeal again! art thou my brother's son   502 Faliero   1   157
I can appeal to my past government   523 Faliero   3   304
If any person doubt it, I appeal   771 Juan   1   1617
Some talk of an appeal unto some passion   837 Juan   5   377
And 'gainst the body makes a strong appeal   910 Juan   10   157
In an appeal to the unborn, whom they   932 Juan   12   138

APPEAL'D
As sovereign, I appeal'd unto my subjects   502 Faliero   1   144
Milton appeal'd to the Avenger, Time   746 Juan   Ded   74

APPEALING
A holiness appealing to all hearts   77 Harold   4   1317

APPEALS
When Famine appeals and when Poverty groans   226 Ode-D   26
The poet meant, no doubt, and thus appeals   757 Juan   1   705
But I digress: of all appeals,--although   837 Juan   5   385

APPEAR
(See also RE-APPEAR)
Spain's realms appear whereon her shepherds tend   9 Harold   1   355
How poor their forms appear! how languid, wan,
    and weak   13 Harold   1   602
Birds, beasts of prey, and wilder men appear   26 Harold   2   377
Here men of every clime appear to make resort   28 Harold   2   504
Which utter'd, to the hearer's eye appear   33 Harold   2   844
Save darken'd Jura, whose capt heights appear   48 Harold   3   809
Heights which appear as lovers who have parted   49 Harold   3   879
A fit abode wherein appear enshrined   78 Harold   4   1391
Thy sister-lights would scarce appear   97 To M--   26
In life's last conflict 'twill appear   98 To Mary   27
That Oscar might once more appear   103 Alva   150
The faithful pair before the throne appear   106 Nisus   96
Others appear more conscious of defect   113 Prologue   10
When Truth in a glance should appear   114 The Tear   2
Thy laws in nature's works appear   132 Prayer   38
Till death's unfathom'd gulf appear   137 Clare   29
Bids every Fiend unmask'd appear   141 Critics   42
In that dread hour ere death appear   165 Thyrza   19
And, self-condemn'd, appear to smile   168 Haunts   11
And Truth itself appear a lie   179 Gold   8
And haughty lineaments, appear   200 Ode-C   3
Oh! in the lightning let thy glance appear   218 Jordan   9
And then methought it did appear   218 I Saw   3
Bid the prophet's form appear   219 Saul-B   2
'Let the men of lore appear   220 Belshaz-B   21
Twin sacred titles, which combined appear   224 J.C.H.   3
In turns appear, to make the vulgar stare   243 Bards   133
And Merry's metaphors appear anew   252 Bards   763
But now, worn down, appear in native brass   254 Bards   898
Though those shall sink, which now appear to
    thrive   258 Hints   102
But so Thalia pleases to appear   258 Hints   125
Make it appear as if it might have been   259 Hints   172
There his works will appear--Sir, they reach to
    the Ganges   281 Blues   2   62
I claim my subject: and will make appear   289 Vision   307
How vain, how worse than vain, at length appear   298 Age   33
The lately ambush'd foes appear   316 Giaour   605
To thee, old man, my deeds appear   321 Giaour   1160
And I, before its rays appear   322 Giaour   1279
Think not I am what I appear   327 Abydos   1   381
I am not, love! what I appear   328 Abydos   1   482

APPEAR
Makes even their mightiest deeds appear his own   341 Corsair   1   185
To them the very rocks appear to smile   363 Corsair   3   556
Appear--a highborn and a welcome guest   371 Corsair   1   365
That hath no business to appear   405 Chillon   298
(Let not this metaphor appear a scoff   425 Island   2   494
Which seems to him, to them too must appear   472 Morgante   410
Of darkness, making his bright realm appear   472 Morgante   430
Orlando, seeing him so soon appear   474 Morgante   517
Which gives me power upon you--Rise! appear   479 Manfred   1   36
Who is undying,--Rise! appear!--Appear   479 Manfred   1   40
I do compel ye to my will. Appear   479 Manfred   1   49
But choose a form--in that we will appear   481 Manfred   1   163
Appear!--Appear!--Appear   490 Manfred   2   466
Appear less forward in the cause than we are   517 Faliero   2   575
Some worthier should appear. If I have found
    such   518 Faliero   2   698
Even aged men, be, or appear to be   619 Foscari   4   275
Appear to join the innumerable stars   636 Cain   2   41
Forgive, my Seraph! that such thoughts appear   656 Heaven   70
Appear! Appear   656 Heaven   77
Friends. You appear to have drunk enough already   674 Werner   1   201
In haste, though even the elements appear   679 Werner   1   501
But, here! the despots of the north appear   682 Werner   1   720
And may appear so when the dog-star rages   745 Juan   Ded   30
'Tis sweet to see the evening star appear   761 Juan   1   973
They shall appear before your curious eyes   790 Juan   2   990
And as the spot where they appear he nears   805 Juan   3   217
The skin relieved appear more fairly fair   810 Juan   3   602
This way of writing will appear exotic   817 Juan   4   42
'Ay,' quoth his friend, 'I thought it would
    appear   833 Juan   5   147
Her thoughts, at least till now, appear to have
    been   859 Juan   6   428
Which makes the southern autumn's day appear   950 Juan   13   610
Appearances appear to form the joint   951 Juan   13   643
'Tis time that some new prophet should appear   979 Juan   15   717
Appear to wake, and shadows wild and quaint   982 Juan   16   141

APPEARANCE
Moved doubtless by his wife's appearance in   601 Foscari   1   378
Your bosom (for the appearance of the man   695 Werner   2   750
Would Stralenheim's appearance in Bohemia   699 Werner   3   249
May not think much of London's first appearance   919 Juan   11   55

APPEARANCES
Appearances; and views a criminal   703 Werner   3   538
Appearances appear to form the joint   951 Juan   13   643

APPEAR'D
Where demi-gods appear'd, as records tell   20 Harold   2   42
And marvel where the spoil could have appear'd   76 Harold   4   1282
When, lo! a Hercules in Fox appear'd   114 Death-A   19
As once this pledge appear'd a token   134 Lady-D   2
Appear'd in the glory of hats, boots and gaiters   178 Devil's Dr   161
What Tyre appear'd in her meridian hour   255 Bards   1000
Her form appear'd from Phidias' plastic hand   269 Minerva   78
Of half-a-crown, a little speck appear'd   292 Vision   450
And blight a form--till thine appear'd, Gulnare   354 Corsair   2   489
In silence, darkling, each appear'd to wait   356 Corsair   3   89
His doubts appear'd to wrong--nor yet she knew   358 Corsair   3   200
Within his breast appear'd no more to strive   367 Lara   1   81
With eye more curious he appear'd to scan   368 Lara   1   132
His page approach'd, and he alone appear'd   369 Lara   1   235
Appear'd less welcome now to Lara's sight   369 Lara   1   256
In him inexplicably mix'd appear'd   370 Lara   1   289
But his were silent, his appear'd to stray   373 Lara   1   486
Then, sudden silent when his form appear'd   377 Lara   2   123
Where foe appear'd to press, or friend to fall   380 Lara   2   369
Return'd no more--that night appear'd his last   383 Lara   2   549
Which, when it least appear'd to melt   402 Parisina   551
And thus when they appear'd at last   406 Chillon   375
Beside the jutting rock the few appear'd   427 Island   3   59
Led him to where the rock appear'd to jut   431 Island   3   129
The sound revived him, or appear'd to wake   434 Island   4   329
Appear'd, so that Tithonus scratch'd his brow   466 Morgante   24
For late there have appear'd three giants rough   469 Morgante   186
Courteous and kind to your great worth appear'd   475 Morgante   621
Appear'd to skirt the horizon, yet they stood   495 Manfred   3   281
On foreign shores, in all things your appear'd   514 Faliero   2   418
Which have appear'd against you; and more ample   540 Faliero   5   162
And not a leaf appear'd about to fall   670 Heaven   1187
Spared you the trouble; but had I appear'd   698 Werner   3   216
And may sound better.--He appear'd to me   717 Werner   5   269
Men such as you appear'd in height of mind   717 Werner   5   288
Appear'd like two poor harmless women, who   764 Juan   1   1122
Was used--nor sail nor shore appear'd in sight   779 Juan   2   327
Water appear'd; yet, though the people knew   779 Juan   2   331
And all within its arch appear'd to be   785 Juan   2   724
The land appear'd a high and rocky coast   786 Juan   2   793
But none of them appear'd to share his woes   788 Juan   2   869
She was, appear'd distinct, and tall, and fair   788 Juan   2   920
Of the apartment--and appear'd quite new   809 Juan   3   532
Most love, possession, unto them appear'd   818 Juan   4   127

APPEAR'D
And that brief dream appear'd a life too long   820 Juan   4   272
He saw some fellow captives, who appear'd   826 Juan   4   633
Appear'd to him but as the magic vapour   918 Juan   10   658
Next, that 'he never judged from what appear'd   963 Juan   14   523
In cowl and beads and dusky garb, appear'd   983 Juan   16   162
And yet his looks appear'd to sanction both   984 Juan   16   258
To bear on what appear'd to her the subject   987 Juan   16   451

APPEAR'DST
Appear'dst thou not to Paris in this guise   62 Harold   4   451

APPEAREST
'Think not thou art what thou appearest   327 Abydos   1   383

APPEARING
Known but to them, at least appearing such   818 Juan   4   109

APPEARS
(See also RE-APPEARS)
Another, hideous sight! unseam'd appears   16 Harold   1   770
The decorated car appears, on high   16 Harold   1   788
Plod the last sands of life,--where not a flower
    appears   35 Harold   3   27
An universal deluge, which appears   68 Harold   4   826
He in dimpling smiles appears   100 Marion   7
And what was once his bliss appears his bane   100 Damaetas   14
Dreary and dark appears the sylvan scene   109 Nisus   314
Thy form appears through night, through day   112 Quaker   30
Your passion appears most absurd   116 Strephon   34
E'en now the gulf appears in view   118 Romance   59
And what would be justice appears a disgrace   136 Delawarr   16
Age, dark unlovely Age, appears at length   139 Ossian-A   30
For though in garb of Galen he appears   143 Soliloquy   59
Thou grow'st old--who does not?--but on earth
    what appears   155 Goblet   15
'Tis strange it still appears divine   173 Mrs. Lamb   4
And though the eye may sparkle still, 'tis where
    the ice appears   185 Music-B   12
On his right hand behold a Sejanus appears   203 Avatar   86
And there is not a furrow appears   205 Blessington   15
And all, that was, at once appears   220 Clay   16
The work of each immortal bard appears   244 Bards   193
Appears the beggar which his grandsire was   250 Bards   657
Can also, when a hobbling line appears   262 Hints   435
Who (ere another Thalaba appears   265 Hints   655
The room with transient glance appears to skim   271 Minerva   187
But she appears! Verona sees her shorn   308 Age   749
His boat appears--not five oars' length   335 Abydos   2   547
Nor know I why this next appears the last   342 Corsair   1   312
Thou more than Moslem when the cup appears   344 Corsair   1   430
Far on the horizon's verge appears a speck   362 Corsair   3   482
Silent as him he served, his faith appears   373 Lara   1   516
On dun Cithaeron's ridge appears   385 Corinth   71
Appears, to his distemper'd eyes   414 Mazeppa   750
Such as appears to rise out from the deep   425 Island   2   464
Which yet the most uncertain age appears   442 Beppo   171
And lo! an eighth appears,--'I'll see no more   448 Beppo   527
And even the Lion all subdued appears   453 Venice-B   19
To him appears renewal of his breath   453 Venice-B   43
And lo! a monstrous herd of swine appears   473 Morgante   493
How lovely he appears! his little cheeks   646 Cain   3   10
Least to be tempted messenger appears   665 Heaven   771
The distant thunder's harbinger, appears   668 Heaven   1012
Appears to have been committed. There's another   683 Werner   2   27
But, great as He appears, and is to you   744 Deformed   3   141
Waved and o'ershading her wan cheek, appears   766 Juan   1   1260
(That modern phrase appears to me sad stuff   768 Juan   1   1419
Be on this sheet, 'tis not what it appears   770 Juan   1   1535
But there is something when man's eye appears   846 Juan   5   939
But by 'the bookish theoric' it appears   853 Juan   6   66
And lo! a fifth appears;--and what is she   861 Juan   6   545
He climb'd to where the parapet appears   887 Juan   8   564
To me appears a stiff yet grand erection   921 Juan   11   199
Where mingled and yet separate appears   966 Juan   14   693
For me appears a question far too nice   974 Juan   15   413
A visitant at intervals appears   981 Juan   16   52

APPEAR'ST
As thou appear'st to love her. I have said   709 Werner   4   344

APPEASE
Who can appease like her a lover's ghost   13 Harold   1   580
Volscens must soon appease his comrade's ghost   110 Nisus   388
But would not to appease him tell   191 Prometheus-B   30
Will save him living or appease him dead   357 Corsair   3   128
To appease the waves. The billow which destroys
    me   617 Foscari   4   145

APPEASED
If shades by carnage be appeased   393 Corinth   809
The stranger, much appeased by what he heard   451 Beppo   715

APPELLANTS
The major part of such appellants go   746 Juan   Ded   71

APPENDAGE
A dull and desolate appendage. Gaze   945 Juan   13   258

APPENDIX
They only add them all in an appendix   752 Juan   1   351
But I shall add them in a brief appendix   964 Juan   14   543

APPETITE
And long had fed his youthful appetite   5 Harold   1   95
The health and appetite of Rizzo   233 Hoppner   4
I've sung his health and appetite   233 Nihil   31
Such, landlords! was your appetite for war   306 Age   636
She almost lost all appetite for victual   443 Beppo   227
Nor the false edge of aged appetite   513 Faliero   2   311
Will cease, like any other appetite   644 Cain   2   531
A traveller's appetite. But are you sure   675 Werner   1   275
Feel now his appetite increased much more   784 Juan   2   621
A most prodigious appetite: the steam   793 Juan   2   1219
Such appetite in one she had deem'd dead   794 Juan   2   1260
I wonder if his appetite was good   835 Juan   5   233
With the prophetic eye of appetite   837 Juan   5   400
Of claret, sandwich, and an appetite   838 Juan   5   459
For which he own'd a present appetite   840 Juan   5   564
I wish you a good appetite.'--'Farewell   842 Juan   5   666
And that outrageous appetite for lies   889 Juan   8   687
He shows more appetite for words than war   951 Juan   13   668

APPETITES
And lusts, and appetites, and vanities   607 Foscari   2   345
Their chief, and all their kindled appetites   733 Deformed   1   751
For having used their appetites so sadly   784 Juan   2   640
And others still their appetites constrain'd   784 Juan   2   651

APPLAUD
I strike my strain, far distant, to applaud   13 Harold   1   605
Crowd to applaud the happy morn   102 Alva   40
And, if you can't applaud, at least forgive   114 Prologue   36
Why bend to the proud, or applaud the absurd   129 Becher-A   23
But as some hands applaud, a venal few   250 Bards   606
Heavens! how the vulgar stare! how crowds applaud   252 Bards   769
Nor care if courts and crowds applaud or hiss   256 Bards   1062
Applaud in thunder at the curtain's fall   259 Hints   .216
Must acquiesce, while sterner hearts applaud   416 Island   1   68
Precedence! I perceived it, and applaud   699 Werner   3   298

APPLAUDING
And other victors fill the applauding skies   254 Bards   952
And drain'd the draught with an applauding cheer   417 Island   1   104
And waving kerchiefs, and applauding hands   597 Foscari   1   103

APPLAUDS
Rather than sleep, why John applauds it too   250 Bards   607
Nor less applauds, as in politeness bound   986 Juan   16   374

APPLAUSE
(See also SELF-APPLAUSE)
In murmur'd pity or loud-roar'd applause   76 Harold   4   1244
To yield applause far, far surpassing mine   107 Nisus   138
Victory crown'd not your fall with applause   117 Lachin   28
Your strong yet just reproof extorts applause   119 Answer-A   3
Or when my first harangue received applause   127 Recoil   351
His will at least be her applause   141 Critics   12
And share with these applause, a godlike bribe   143 Soliloquy   57
Forbear to mock us with misplaced applause   170 Address-A   63
Why son and I both beg for your applause   171 Address-B   54
Than all he shall not force on our applause   183 Address-D   32
Let these, or such as these, with just applause   254 Bards   891
No just applause her honour'd name shall lose   255 Bards   995
Nor slight applause will candid pens afford   257 Hints   71
Whether they seek applause by smile or tear   259 Hints   163
Old comedies still meet with much applause   263 Hints   445
Nor do they merit. slight applause who choose   263 Hints   451
Abolish'd cuckoldom with much applause   266 Hints   671
I defy him to beat this day's wondrous applause   281 Blues   2   39
Hath lost his place and gain'd the world's
    applause   299 Age   80
The glorious meed of popular applause   811 Juan   3   655
Let this fifth canto meet with due applause   851 Juan   5   1269
With its proud brow, it merits slight applause   872 Juan   7   318
There was enthusiasm and much applause   873 Juan   7   370
His little captive gain'd him some applause   896 Juan   8   1117
And now in this new field, with some applause   959 Juan   14   257
But this I must say in my own applause   980 Juan   16   12

APPLAUSES
While, to swell my young pride, such applauses
    resounded   96 Harrow-A   19

APPLE
Presented Eve her apple   177 Devil's Dr   112
For an Apple should grieve   239 Impromptu-B   5
Like them, too, without having shared the apple   641 Cain   2   364
As was the apple in thy mother's eye   644 Cain   2   529
The son of her who snatch'd the apple spake   645 Cain   2   614

APPLE

One good gift has the fatal apple given	646	Cain	2	664
And in the midst a golden apple grew	861	Juan	6	601
But visions of an apple and a bee	862	Juan	6	634
When Newton saw an apple fall, he found	907	Juan	10	1
Since Adam, with a fall or with an apple	907	Juan	10	8

APPLES

Like to the apples on the Dead Sea's shore	40	Harold	3	303
Man fell with apples, and with apples rose	907	Juan	10	9
Since Eve ate apples, much depends on dinner	953	Juan	13	792

APPLIANCES

I have order'd fire and all appliances	675	Werner	1	238
All the appliances which purchase modes	680	Werner	1	581

APPLICATION

A further application of yon engine	539	Faliero	5	71
A former application did so; but	539	Faliero	5	73
Shrinks from the application of hot towels	776	Juan	2	180
His steady application as a dancer	924	Juan	11	406

APPLIED

Hot from the hands promiscuously applied	277	Waltz		234
That stone seems with good will and aim applied	469	Morgante		214
It is illegal, and, as now applied	536	Faliero	4	564
Perhaps 'twas in a different way applied	767	Juan	1	1343
And all lips were applied unto all ears	906	Juan	9	618
To freedom, he applied (a grief and a bore	923	Juan	11	326
Unless a marriage was applied to mend	972	Juan	15	262

APPLIES

This is a long description, but applies	428	Island	3	117

APPLY

May feel the lash that Virtue must apply	251	Bards		706
A rack. Apply it then before the dawn	533	Faliero	4	343
Or that of her to whom he might apply	972	Juan	15	238

APPLYING

Applying poisons there as antidotes	625	Foscari	5	278

APPOINTED

Of cherubim appointed to that post	295	Vision		674
And acres told upon the appointed day	306	Age		589
Sit newly on me, and you were appointed	505	Faliero	1	393
Is Zames? Posted with the guard appointed	575	Sardan	3	229
The delegates appointed to convey	620	Foscari	4	352
To-morrow is the appointed festival	708	Werner	4	235

APPOINTING

Appointing Zames chief? I did. Where's Zames	589	Sardan	5	138

APPOINTMENT

Announcing the appointment of that lover of	872	Juan	7	311

APPRECIATED

And there is much which could not be appreciated	958	Juan	14	175

APPREHEND

I apprehend less treachery than weakness	517	Faliero	2	591
His noble memory. I apprehend	678	Werner	1	467
I do not apprehend you. That may be	699	Werner	3	261

APPREHENDS

Love, which the gentle heart soon apprehends	476	Francesca		4

APPREHENSION

Begin to fail in apprehension, and	620	Foscari	5	8
Nor could aught, save the eye of apprehension	680	Werner	1	572
That is not here--confirm my apprehension	694	Werner	2	689

APPREHENSIONS

Of idle apprehensions, which like wind	883	Juan	8	316

APPREHENSIVE

But apprehensive of his spectral guest	995	Juan	16	933

APPRENTICE

And smug apprentice gulp their weekly air	15	Harold	1	696

APPRISING

Apprising me? They wish'd to spare your feelings	604	Foscari	2	198

APPRIZE

Knock, and apprize the Count of my approach	494	Manfred	3	256

APPROACH

Son of the morning, rise! approach you here	19	Harold	2	19
Let such approach this consecrated land	34	Harold	2	873
Now they approach the trench, and view the walls	109	Nisus		303
Approach and touch--Nay do not turn	141	Critics		35
Blest is the man who dares approach the bower	253	Bards		867
Shall these approach the muse? ah, no! she flies	255	Bards		963

APPROACH

Approach the lip which all, without restraint	277	Waltz		242
Approach, thou craven crouching slave	311	Giaour		108
If shrines that ne'er approach allow	327	Abydos	1	313
We dare not yet approach--thou know'st his mood	340	Corsair	1	137
Approach intrusive on that mood of fear	341	Corsair	1	238
Repell'd approach and show'd him still alone	367	Lara	1	108
Shall ne'er approach his haughty eye	401	Parisina		443
As if our faint approach to meet	413	Mazeppa		687
Approach, retire, wheel round and round	413	Mazeppa		700
Voluptuous as the first approach of sleep	420	Island	2	134
But nothing more. Approach me as ye are	480	Manfred	1	179
I will approach him nearer. To be thus	482	Manfred	1	326
I must approach him cautiously; if near	483	Manfred	1	351
As I approach the core of my heart's grief	486	Manfred	2	193
Knock, and apprize the Count of my approach	494	Manfred	3	256
I crave a second grace for this approach	495	Manfred	3	306
They came not near me, such approach gave umbrage	525	Faliero	3	471
He sues to be permitted to approach you	529	Faliero	4	119
We have the privilege to approach the presence	564	Sardan	2	153
To heed no time nor presence, but approach you	585	Sardan	4	445
Hark! You are right; some steps approach, but slowly	588	Sardan	5	87
Let me approach, I pray you, for a breath	596	Foscari	1	87
Let him approach. I must not speak with him	596	Foscari	1	89
To me all hours are alike. Let them approach	620	Foscari	5	4
Inasmuch as it shows that I approach	624	Foscari	5	265
Approach the things of earth most beautiful	643	Cain	2	454
Without approach to mine. And, to say truth	695	Werner	2	755
We approach, tell me--Why look you so? Do I	702	Werner	3	459
You were the demon, but that your approach	723	Deformed	1	94
I would approach thee, worthy her, and him	740	Deformed	2	308
The approach of home to husbands and to sires	804	Juan	3	169
Motion'd to Juan to approach, and then	844	Juan	5	810
Gaunt famine never shall approach the throne	894	Juan	8	1007
Through this, and much, and more, is the approach	921	Juan	11	177

APPROACH'D

His page approach'd, and he alone appear'd	369	Lara	1	235
But fail'd--and she approach'd, and made	415	Mazeppa		820
And watch if aught approach'd the amphibious lair	435	Island	4	375
The more approach'd, and dearest were they free	459	Dante	2	69
One has approach'd the Doge, and now they strip	549	Faliero	5	807
And some till now grew larger as we approach'd	638	Cain	2	168
And yet I have approach'd that sun, and seen	647	Cain	3	56

APPROACHES

And champion human fears.--The night approaches	487	Manfred	2	298
Mellowing the last hours as the night approaches	515	Faliero	2	460
The hour approaches, and we must prepare	571	Sardan	2	602
The hour approaches, and the wind is fair	614	Foscari	3	396
Why should I quail from him who now approaches	629	Cain	1	92
Who has seen yesterday?--But here approaches	677	Werner	1	373
Society) you can't tell how he approaches	723	Deformed	1	97

APPROACHETH

And that the hour approacheth, should indulge	658	Heaven		258

APPROACHING

Beat thy Divan's approaching hour	324	Abydos	1	74
That for itself can woo the approaching fight	338	Corsair	1	17
That when the approaching crowd his arm withheld	376	Lara	2	80
Through the approaching darkness of the wood	425	Island	2	460
Neuha, and pointing to the approaching foes	430	Island	4	58
So long approaching me?--I saw you not	511	Faliero	2	152
Beheld their fate merged in the approaching fight	534	Faliero	4	432
It is approaching. You decline to plead, then	540	Faliero	5	182
In clouds that seem approaching fast, and show	570	Sardan	2	539
We were approaching, which, begirt with light	638	Cain	2	182
By the approaching deluge! by the earth	659	Heaven		323
The approaching chaos. Anah! Anah! my	663	Heaven		595
Till, in approaching, were at length descried	872	Juan	7	343
But Juan felt, though not approaching home	917	Juan	10	645
Like a meek tradesman when, approaching palely	969	Juan	15	59

APPROBATION

(See also SELF-APPROBATION)

And if their approbation we experience	771	Juan	1	1591
The public approbation I expect	772	Juan	1	1665
'Sufficiently' (he said) 'his approbation	840	Juan	5	559
Without our knowledge or our approbation	857	Juan	6	300
'She could not too much give her approbation	911	Juan	10	257

APPROPRIATE

That's an appropriate simile, that jackal	899	Juan	9	209

APPROPRIATELY

Thus most appropriately has been shown	859	Juan	6	436

APPROVE

Since cold each kinder heart that might approve	34	Harold	2	889
How I approve my courage in the fight	474	Morgante		554
His highness to peruse and to approve	501	Faliero	1	77
So that the contemplator might approve	545	Faliero	5	510

APPROVE
Of Salemenes, to approve his zeal   560 Sardan   1   646
They speak your language, watch your nod, approve 622 Foscari   5   142
The moment cometh to approve thy strength   369 Heaven   1056
I know not that even now--but will approve   719 Werner   5   388
And, therefore, doubtless to approve the truth   963 Juan   14   529

APPROVED
Approved by thee, and thus approved by all   521 Faliero 3   208
Can only be approved by proofs. You see   686 Werner   2   233
(A thing approved as saving time and toil   939 Juan   12   606
She approved his silence; she perhaps mistook   994 Juan   16   890

APPROVER
Or an approver, or a mere spectator   927 Juan   11   543

APPROVES
'Tis an old lesson; Time approves it true   24 Harold   2   307

APPROVING
(See also ALL-APPROVING)
The approving 'Good!' (by no means GOOD in law   449 Beppo   586

APRIL
Is an eternal April to the ground   65 Harold   4   625

APROPOS
Apropos--Is your play then accepted at last   281 Blues   2   74
Oh, ye great authors!--'Apropos des bottes   901 Juan   9   281

A-PROPOS
And a-propos of monks, their piety   965 Juan   14   645
As a-propos of hope or retrospection   968 Juan   15   3

APT
Pardon my Muse, who apt to prate is   163 Malta   31
Your dialogue is apt and smart   231 Doctor   11
The unwieldy old white horse is apt at last   305 Age   564
May show, though little apt to vaunt   327 Abydos   1   365
As youth is apt in, so as not to check   514 Faliero 2   359
A kind man, I am apt to think, as some   521 Faliero 3   174
In Prague for peace restored. You are apt to
    follow   708 Werner   4   236
Are apt to carry things with a high hand   854 Juan   6   83
And apt to be transferr'd to the first buyer   854 Juan   6   126
Apt to wear out on trifling provocations   892 Juan   8   856
Is apt to tire: a calm and shallow station   898 Juan   9   142
But I am apt to grow too metaphysical   901 Juan   9   321
With which great states such things are apt to
    push on   913 Juan   10   357
Requires decorum, and is apt to double   924 Juan   11   367
Of being apt to talk at a great rate   933 Juan   12   222
People are apt to blame the Fates, forsooth   936 Juan   12   395
Although when long a little apt to weary us   941 Juan   13   6
Though apt to act with fire upon occasion   943 Juan   13   109
And apt to sow an author's wheat with tares   944 Juan   13   195
Your men of business are not apt to express   965 Juan   14   606
Are apt exceedingly to run to seed   965 Juan   14   648
Because she was not apt, like some of us   969 Juan   15   75
Was apt to add a colouring from her own   970 Juan   15   130
The last is apt the former to accuse   997 Juan   17   44
Cheerful--but, sometimes, rather apt to whimper   998 Juan   17   85

APTER
Will find me apter to requite your service   679 Werner   1   520

APTLY
My mind with many a form which aptly seems   56 Harold   4   59

AQUA-VITA
Was lost by getting at some aqua-vita   781 Juan   2   448

ARAB
He is an Arab to my sight   325 Abydos   1   144
If all our Arab tales divulge or dream   358 Corsair 3   157
On Arab sands the false mirage which offers   529 Faliero 4   66
An Arab horse, a stately stag, a barb   774 Juan   2   41
Unlike the honest Arab thieves so brave   790 Juan   2 1038
An Arab with a stranger for a guest   799 Juan   2 1564
Of wonderful replies from Arab jokers   805 Juan   3   268
The Arab lore and poet's song were done   815 Juan   3   899
So Arab deserts drink in summer's rain   904 Juan   9   470
She cannot step as does an Arab barb   939 Juan   12   593
The wilds, as doth an Arab turn'd avenger   959 Juan   14   254

ARABIA
To marshal half the horsemen of Arabia   573 Sardan   3   107
And Mocha's berry, from Arabia pure   809 Juan   3   499

ARABIA'S
Arabia's monstrous, wild, and wondrous son   244 Bards   212

ARABIC
To prove with Hebrew and with Arabic   289 Vision   266

ARABLE
By those who sow them in a land that's arable   979 Juan   15   707

ARABS
He had travell'd 'mongst the Arabs, Turks, and
    Franks   811 Juan   3   665

ARAB'S
On Jordan's banks the Arab's camels stray   217 Jordan   1
And there the Arab's camel kneels   385 Corinth   81
Placed in the Arab's clime, he would have been   421 Island   2   179
There's not a foal of Arab's breed   730 Deformed 1   549

ARAB-SPEARS
These words went through his soul like Arab-
    spears   846 Juan   5   935

ARABY
Through Araby the sandy   233 Ballad-B   34
With Chili, Hellas, or with Araby   421 Island   2   200
Of Egypt and her neighbour Araby   612 Foscari 3   294
Or your Kochlini race of Araby   729 Deformed 1   512

ARAGON
(His sire was of Castile, his dam from Aragon   751 Juan   1   300

ARAMINTA
That prodigy, Miss Araminta Smith   925 Juan   11   413

ARARAT
Through the deep clouds o'er rocky Ararat   655 Heaven   3
Which opens to the heart of Ararat   658 Heaven   249

ARARAT'S
On Ararat's late secret crest   657 Heaven   149

ARBACES
Arbaces! are you mad? Have I not render'd   564 Sardan   2   167
Who dares assail Arbaces? I! Indeed   564 Sardan   2   184
Treason--Arbaces! treachery and Beleses   565 Sardan   2   198
But no, it cannot be: the Mede Arbaces   565 Sardan   2   213
Bestow it on Arbaces. So I should   565 Sardan   2   223
A despised monarch. Look to it, Arbaces   568 Sardan   2   392
And if I win, Arbaces is my servant   568 Sardan   2   402
Soon as Arbaces and Beleses reach'd   572 Sardan   3   77
An audience. Let him speak. The King Arbaces   592 Sardan   5   288

ARBITER
Of lord of thee and arbiter of war   82 Harold   4 1626
The Arbiter of others' fate   180 Ode-A   39
Our arbiter of pleasure and of play   250 Bards   643

ARBITRARY
Time! on whose arbitrary wing   171 Time-B   1
As senators for arbitrary acts   526 Faliero 3   505

ARBITRATES
As custom arbitrates, whose shifting sway   258 Hints   103

ARBOURS
And arbours shade them from the summer heat   124 Recoll   136

ARC
First in the ranks see Joan of Arc advance   244 Bards   205

ARCADES
'Arcades ambo,' id est--blackguards both   828 Juan   4   744

ARCADIA
Arcadia displays but a region of dreams   93 First Kiss   19

ARCADIAN
Than placed in all th' Arcadian groves   101 Lady-B   39
The Arcadian Evocators to compel   487 Manfred 2   282

ARCADIANS
They and their bills, 'Arcadians both,' are left   946 Juan   13   353

ARCANUM'S
The grand arcanum's not for men to see all   958 Juan   14   173

ARCH
(See also O'ER-ARCH)
Look on its broken arch, its ruin'd wall   20 Harold   2   46
And noble arch in proud decay   43 Harold   3   512
The keystones of the arch!--though all were o'er   55 Harold   4   35
The arch of triumph! and for this the tears   68 Harold   4   824
On what were chambers, arch crush'd, column strown   71 Harold   4   957
Whose arch or pillar meets me in the face   71 Harold   4   986
Triumph, arch, pillar, all he doth displace   71 Harold   4   988
Its topmost arch and gently pauses there   76 Harold   4 1289
Arch, empire, each thing round thee, and man plods   77 Harold   4 1310
Thy yawning arch betokens slow decay   121 Newstead-A   138
arch of the rainbow; and smile through the   131 Calmar   203

ARCH
The very Fiend's arch mock .... 181 Ode-A 142
Weeps Triumph o'er each levell'd arch .... 188 Ode-B 72
Of light and darkness forms an arch sublime ...... 192 Monody 8
Many have pass'd that Arch of pain .... 196 Venice-A 19
Whose path was through one long triumphal arch ... 301 Age 222
'Tis gold, not steel, that rears the conqueror's
  arch .... 307 Age 685
Though on Al-Sirat's arch I stood .... 315 Giaour 483
Each ivied arch, and pillar lone .... 319 Giaour 881
Extends its arch before the growing gale .... 418 Island .... 1 ... 226
Howe'er 'its arch may swell, its colours move .... 423 Island .... 2 ... 344
The arch uprear'd by nature's architect .... 432 Island .... 4 ... 147
Bent its broad arch: her breath began to fail .... 435 Island .... 4 ... 378
It is not noon; the sunbow's rays still arch ..... 485 Manfred ... 2 95
And all within its arch appear'd to be .... 785 Juan ...... 2 ... 724
So much as under a triumphal arch .... 880 Juan ...... 8 ... 164
In a grand arch, which once screen'd many an
  aisle .... 948 Juan ..... 13 ... 467
In gazing on that venerable arch .... 948 Juan ..... 13 ... 472
Through the huge arch, which soars and sinks
  again .... 949 Juan ..... 13 ... 501
And when you may not be sublime, be arch .... 971 Juan ..... 15 ... 211
To these? They are rags or dust. Where is the
  arch .... 976 Juan ..... 15 ... 530

ARCHANGEL
'Twas the archangel Michael: all men know .... 288 Vision 225
The Archangel bow'd, not like a modern beau ...... 289 Vision 281
To urge against him,' said the Archangel. 'Why .. 293 Vision 554
'And who and what art thou?' the Archangel said .. 295 Vision 649
Father! and thou, archangel, thou .... 667 Heaven 945

ARCHANGELIC
That arch-angelic hierarch, the first .... 288 Vision 242
Athwart the sound of archangelic songs .... 460 Dante 3 13
From his once archangelic throne .... 667 Heaven 934

ARCHANGELS
The make of angels and archangels, since .... 288 Vision 226
The archangels. And still loftier than the
  archangels .... 634 Cain ...... 1 ... 415
Leaving the archangels at his right hand dim ..... 666 Heaven 845

ARCHANGEL'S
The Archangel's trump, not Glory's, must awake ... 40 Harold .... 3 ... 275
As if the Archangel's voice he heard .... 397 Parisina 84

ARCH'D
Black eyes, arch'd brows, and sweet expressions
  still .... 441 Beppo 82
Which arch'd the horizon like a fiery cloud ...... 879 Juan 8 43

ARCHDEACON
Until his late Life by Archdeacon Coxe .... 813 Juan ...... 3 ... 816

ARCH-ENEMY
To eat the head of his arch-enemy .... 784 Juan ...... 2 ... 659

ARCHER
Let Archer plant the horns on Sullen's brows ..... 261 Hints 361

ARCHER'S
The old archer's shafts, perhaps the early grave . 817 Juan 4 95

ARCHERY
As moon-struck bards complain, by Love's sad
  archery .... 15 Harold .... 1 ... 728

ARCHES
Arches on arches! as it were that Rome .... 74 Harold .... 4 .. 1144
Their azure arches through the long expanse ...... 268 Minerva 13
Their azure arches through the long expanse ...... 355 Corsair ... 3 13
The trees which grew along the broken arches ..... 495 Manfred ... 3 ... 272
Of other men. And those scarce mortal arches .... 731 Deformed .. 1 ... 617
Shouts, bridges, arches, pensions from a nation .. 878 Juan 8 27

ARCHIMEDES
Like Archimedes, I leave earth as 'twas .... 966 Juan ..... 14 ... 672

ARCHIPELAGO
Which stemm'd the studded archipelago .... 422 Island .... 2 ... 251

ARCHITECT
The Architect of all on which we tread .... 190 Churchill 20
The arch uprear'd by nature's architect .... 432 Island .... 4 ... 147
And the bold Architect unto whose care .... 464 Dante 4 57
Bricklayer of Babel, call'd an architect .... 988 Juan ..... 16 ... 506
From town, viz., architect and dealer, were ...... 989 Juan ..... 16 ... 573

ARCHITECTURE
Of architecture, those Titanian fabrics .... 529 Faliero ... 4 83
Who give themselves to architecture wholly .... 839 Juan ...... 5 ... 500

ARCHITRAVE
The architrave some earthquake might erect .... 432 Island .... 4 ... 148

ARCH-OPPRESSORS
The thing these arch-oppressors fain would make
  me .... 505 Faliero ... 1 ... 352

ARCHWAY
(A hollow archway by the sun unseen .... 431 Island .... 4 ... 123

ARCTIC
His arctic charge around the pole .... 88 Anacreon-B ... 4
The arctic sun rose broad above the wave .... 418 Island .... 1 ... 169

ARDENNES
And Ardennes waves above them her green leaves ... 39 Harold .... 3 ... 235

ARDENT
Hast seen my ardent flame too well .... 90 To M.S.G.-A ... 14
But who can dare thine ardent gaze .... 97 To M-- 20
Is this a bridegroom's ardent flame .... 102 Alva 98
Marking each ardent youth, ordain'd to die .... 119 Newstead-A 15
Another's ardent look without regret .... 277 Waltz 241
'Tis true he had no ardent love for peace .... 808 Juan ...... 3 ... 437

ARDENTLY
As ardently for glory as you dared .... 685 Werner .... 2 ... 161

ARDOUR
Ah! did that breast with ardour glow .... 90 Caroline-B 5
With equal ardour seems to burn .... 91 Caroline-B 34
With equal ardour fired and warlike joy .... 106 Nisus 37
'In vain you damp the ardour of my soul .... 106 Nisus 79
Plunging with ardour from the shore .... 146 Adieu 48
Half to the ardour which its birth bestows .... 193 Monody 76
In vain their stubborn ardour he would tame ...... 379 Lara ...... 2 ... 292
The hero's ardour, or the lover's sighs .... 458 Dante 2 25
The chase with such an ardour as will scarce ..... 708 Werner .... 4 ... 237
Danger and spoil with ardour much increased ...... 873 Juan ...... 7 ... 390

ARDUOUS
Our souls to compass through each arduous way .... 68 Harold .... 4 ... 772
To aid our judgment in a trial arduous .... 541 Faliero ... 5 ... 227

ARE
And claim a kindred with you; for ye are .... 49 Harold .... 3 ... 829
If my fame should be, as my fortunes are .... 56 Harold 4 80
Love from amongst her griefs?--for such the af-
  fections are .... 70 Harold .... 4 ... 909
would speak in sighs: faint and broken are .... 130 Calmar 92
Though, like all things which I have loved, they
  are .... 212 Augusta-C 79
On things that were not, and on things that are .. 213 Lady Byron 34
Nor dare we think on what we are .... 223 Music-D 12
But if you abash'd are .... 232 Murray-B 16
Who takes our laws and worship as they are .... 263 Hints 499
And sometimes these so froward are .... 408 Mazeppa 139
And even in Italy such places are .... 440 Beppo 37
Venetian women were, and so they are .... 442 Beppo 114
Before thee at thy quest their spirits are .... 480 Manfred ... 1 ... 134
We are observed, and have been. We observed ..... 520 Faliero ... 3 84
That are in danger, and that make the danger ..... 532 Faliero ... 4 ... 275
That is, where mortals are, not where they must
  be .... 583 Sardan .... 4 ... 327
Change us he may, but not o'erwhelm; we are ...... 656 Heaven 120
Save what we seem! save what we are--sick
  beggars .... 673 Werner .... 1 ... 112
My journey hence. So then you are the man .... 700 Werner .... 3 ... 316
All--all--And you to me are so already .... 707 Werner .... 4 ... 171
At mercy of the waves, whose mercies are .... 779 Juan ...... 2 ... 335
For we all know that English people are .... 794 Juan ...... 2 .. 1241
Have sung of heaven and hell, or marriage, are .. 802 Juan 3 74
Till our own weakness shows us what we are .... 816 Juan 4 8
But it was all a mystery. Here we are .... 836 Juan ...... 5 ... 305
And scarce secure, as such digressions are fair . 867 Juan ...... 6 ... 959
There have been and are heroes who begun .... 881 Juan ...... 8 ... 170
Mark how it laughs and scorns at all you are ..... 898 Juan 9 89
Tyrants and sycophants have been and are .... 899 Juan ...... 9 ... 188
Catherine was generous,--all such ladies are .... 906 Juan ...... 9 ... 633
Who is but first of slaves? The nations are .... 916 Juan ..... 10 ... 538
And insolence no doubt is what they are .... 923 Juan ..... 11 ... 321
I mean to show things really as they are .... 934 Juan ..... 12 ... 314
How little do we know that which we are .... 980 Juan ..... 15 ... 787

AREA
The lists are oped, the spacious area clear'd .... 15 Harold .... 1 ... 720

AREA'S
And oft-times through the area's echoing door .... 28 Harold .... 2 ... 509

ARED
Or e'er in new Utopias were ared   25· Harold   2   322

ARENA
The throng'd arena shakes with shouts for more   15 Harold   1   690
Within the same arena where they see   69 Harold   4   845
The arena swims around him--he is gone   76 Harold   4 1259
On the arena void--seats crush'd--walls bow'd   76 Harold   4 1277
But dragg'd again upon the arena, stood   378 Lara   2   260
In the arena (as right well they might   731 Deformed   1   624

ARETINO
Leonardo Aretino said already   466 Morgante   33

ARGIVE
Not thus my sire in Argive combats fought   106 Nisus   44
Nor left such bowls an Argive robber's prey   107 Nisus   148

ARGO
Had kept in port the good ship Argo   225 Embargo   2
Thus Argo plough'd the Euxine's virgin foam   418 Island   1   229
Like the first old Greek privateer, the Argo   782 Juan   2   528
Much passion, since the merchant-ship, the Argo   965 Juan   14   607

ARGUE
They argue the point with much furious Invective   145 Casuists   5

ARGUED
The place where Death's grand cause is argued
  o'er   289 Vision   275
Already; and I merely argued his   293 Vision   509

ARGUMENT
Or force, or forge fit argument of song   461 Dante   3   91
Shall be his sacred argument. The loss   462 Dante   3   130
But let us change the argument. My child   512 Faliero   2   270
I hate it, as I hate an argument   962 Juan   14   463
And now I will give up all argument   979 Juan   15   745
There is a common-place book argument   997 Juan   17   33

ARGUMENTS
I have prepared such arguments as will not   615 Foscari   4   50
With arguments according to their 'forte   837 Juan   5   383
And pass'd for arguments of good endurance   924 Juan   11   412

ARGUS
The martial Argus, whose not hundred eyes   308 Age   741
And that his Argus--bites him by the breeches   804 Juan   3   184

ARGYLE
Of vice and folly, Greville and Argyle   250 Bards   639

ARIADNE
He left his Adriatic Ariadne   443 Beppo   224

ARIADNE'S
When the clear sky show'd Ariadne's Isle   344 Corsair   1   444

ARID
The incessant fever of that arid thirst   418 Island   1   189
And revels o'er their vild and arid waves   493 Manfred   3   131

ARIEL
(Not the most 'dainty Ariel') and perplexes   918 Juan   11   18

ARIGHT
His eye seem'd dubious if it saw aright   353 Corsair   2   430
You are not guilty? Do I hear aright   692 Werner   2   621

ARIMANES
To the Hall of Arimanes, for to-night   488 Manfred   2   312
Glory to Arimanes! on the earth   489 Manfred   2   387
Glory to Arimanes! we who bow   489 Manfred   2   390
Glory to Arimanes! we await   489 Manfred   2   392
Refuse to Arimanes on his throne   489 Manfred   2   413
Great Arimanes, doth thy will avouch   490 Manfred   2   450

ARINO
Avolio, and Arino, and Othone   467 Morgante   73

ARION'S
Meantime some rude Arion's restless hand   22 Harold   2   185

ARIOSTO
And, like the Ariosto of the North   61 Harold   4   359
We'll turn the tale, by Ariosto told   344 Corsair   1   439
The world, not quite so great as Ariosto   814 Juan   3   864
Of Smollett, Prior, Ariosto, Fielding   829 Juan   4   779

ARIOSTO'S
The lightning rent from Ariosto's bust   61 Harold   4   361

ARISBA'S
Saved from Arisba's stately domes o'erthrown   107 Nisus   146

ARISE
In every peal she calls, 'Awake! arise   10 Harold   1   411
The cross descends, thy minarets arise   25 Harold   2   340
Arise; and, as the clouds along them break   25 Harold   2   374
All the sons of the mountains arise at the note   30 Harold   2   651
Such as Columbia saw arise when she   69 Harold   4   858
Or water but the desert; whence arise   73 Harold   4 1073
And unavenged?--Arise! ye Goths, and glut your ire   76 Harold   4 1269
Are not a spoil for him,--thou dost arise   82 Harold   4 1613
Here lies our path; lest any hand arise   108 Nisus   233
A monarch bade thee from that wild arise   120 Newstead-A   25
That will arise, though empires fall   128 Answer-B   16
war. Speak, ye chiefs! Who will arise   130 Calmar   54
To mark a friend's remains these stones arise   154 Dog   25
Sons of the Greeks, arise   161 War Song   1
And (Muse of Fitzgerald arise with a rhyme   176 Devil's Dr   47
Some new Napoleon might arise   181 Ode-A   96
Shall arise in communion   188 Ode-B   93
And a new spring of noble affections arise   202 Avatar   26
Nor less new schools of Poetry arise   243 Bards   135
Arise! let blest remembrance still inspire   252 Bards   805
Arise, my Jeffrey! or my inkless pen   265 Hints   599
Or, starting from her slumbers, deign'd arise   274 Waltz   63
And good arise; the portal past--he stood   288 Vision   235
Of Salamis!--there, there the waves arise   302 Age   288
For outworn Europe? With the sound arise   303 Age   380
Arise and make again your own   311 Giaour   115
Kneels he, nor recks he when arise   318 Giaour   804
Arise from out the earth which drank   385 Corinth   61
The visions which arise without a sleep   438 Tasso   165
And then, God knows what mischief may arise   442 Beppo   125
Of lesser torment, whence men may arise   456 Dante   1   9
But I will make another tongue arise   458 Dante   2   23
Lie like the ocean waves ere winds arise   459 Dante   2   37
Will not in vain arise to where belongs   460 Dante   3   15
The genius of my country shall arise   464 Dante   4   74
Florence, by his great bounty dost arise   467 Morgante   51
Know, that no more my wonder will arise   473 Morgante   452
You may be sure, should each desire arise   473 Morgante   469
Have made me sorrow till the tears arise   476 Francesca   21
So shall our blood more readily arise   539 Faliero   5   118
Their lineage. But arise, my pious friends   572 Sardan   3   34
Thoughts which arise within me, as if they   630 Cain   1   174
To good. Strange good, that must arise from out   643 Cain   2   493
Arise like Titan from the sea's immersion   746 Juan   Ded   70
Think'st thou, could he--the blind Old Man--arise   746 Juan   Ded   81
Aud love than either; and there would arise   754 Juan   1   477
The longings of the cannibal arise   783 Juan   2   575
But one arise--we come, we come   812 Juan   3   735
There might arise some pouting petty care   846 Juan   5   950
Arise, when we see emperors fall with oats   900 Juan   9   256
And hence arise the woes of sentiment   965 Juan   14   630

ARISEN
Till, like Babel, the new royal dome hath arisen   203 Avatar   74

ARISES
Such as arises when a nation bleeds   80 Harold   4 1497
Upon our project. At what hour arises   508 Faliero   1   598

ARISING
Arising from such rustic roofs;--the hill   214 Dream   35
Arising out of business, often brought   943 Juan   13   114

ARISTIPPUS
And Aristippus, a material crew   800 Juan   2 1650

ARISTOCRACY
The spirit of this aristocracy   521 Faliero   3   161
By the foul aristocracy: he could not   526 Faliero   3   526
Let to the Morning Post its aristocracy   814 Juan   3   838
Among the proudest of our aristocracy   938 Juan   12   526

ARISTOCRAT
And he thought, as a 'quondam aristocrat   177 Devil's Dr   137

ARISTOCRATIC
To this o'ergrown aristocratic Hydra   506 Faliero   1   450
Aristocratic as was ever seen   879 Juan   8   76
And turn on things which no aristocratic   923 Juan   11   339
But all was gentle and aristocratic   955 Juan   13   873
Of gout, which rusts aristocratic hinges   984 Juan   16   272

ARISTOTLE
Wild Nature!--Grand Shakspeare! And down
  Aristotle   282 Blues   2   115
La Harpe, thine Aristotle, beckons on   304 Age   455
Of Aristotle and the Rules, 'tis fit   761 Juan   1   959
Or, Every Poet his own Aristotle   772 Juan   1 1632
From Aristotle passim.--See Ποιητικης.   816 Juan   3   984
As those of Aristotle, though sometimes   972 Juan   15   255

ARISTOTLE'S
With strict regard to Aristotle's rules   771 Juan   1 1602

ARITHMETIC

Or turning marriage into arithmetic	973 Juan	15	304
Requires arithmetic beyond my forces	976 Juan	15	548
The poets of arithmetic are they	993 Juan	16	833

ARITHMETICIAN

I am not, like Cassio, 'an arithmetician	853 Juan	6	65

ARK

Without an ark for wretched man's abode	68 Harold	4	827
In this eternal ark of worship undefiled	78 Harold	4	1386
Since first the leaky ark reposed in mud	246 Bards		354
(What harm, if David danced before the ark	261 Hints		320
Not decent David, when before the ark	274 Waltz		83
Toss'd by the deluge in their common ark	307 Age		647
The Dove of peace and promise to mine ark	333 Abydos	2	397
His chief, commits him to his fragile ark	418 Island	1	166
And fly her as the raven fled the ark	418 Island	1	232
Yet, yet a moment!--Fly, thou light ark, fly	430 Island	3	240
Than now were wafted in that slender ark	435 Island	4	400
My father's ark of safety hath announced it	662 Heaven		539
The ark which shall receive a remnant of	664 Heaven		653
What, hath this dreamer, with his father's ark	664 Heaven		708
Save in our ark, or let me be no more	667 Heaven		949
Hence to where our all-hallow'd ark uprears	668 Heaven		1015
Thou sitt'st within thy guarded ark	669 Heaven		1096
As if a Spanish ship were Noah's ark	775 Juan	2	62
Since Noah's ark went cruising here and there	782 Juan	2	526
And had it been the dove from Noah's ark	786 Juan	2	757

ARKLESS

That without which my soul, like the arkless dove	456 Dante	1	24

ARM

Now must the pastor's arm his lambs defend	9 Harold	1	357
Arm! Arm! it is--it is--the cannon's opening roar	38 Harold	3	198
Too glorious, were this all his mighty arm had done	69 Harold	4	855
Ay, and the red right arm of Jove	88 Horace		9
Beneath whose arm the Hydra bleeds	88 Anacreon-A		16
If some Rutulian arm, with adverse blow	106 Nisus		61
Whose manly arm may snatch me back by force	106 Nisus		67
And poised with easy arm his ancient shield	106 Nisus		92
Brave Nisus here arrests his comrade's arm	109 Nisus		279
Rage nerves his arm, fate gleams in every blow	110 Nisus		390
Your arm, brave boy, arrested his career	126 Recoil		279
was the arm of the king. Age withered not	130 Calmar		45
feeble is my arm in fight. Could I see thee	130 Calmar		64
arm: he shudders in his blood. He rolls	130 Calmar		133
When persecution's arm is dead	137 Clare		53
This hand, though but feeble, would arm in thy fight	203 Avatar		107
This arm would be thy bark, or breast thy bier	206 Love, Death		8
Could no other arm be found	207 Fare Thee		18
Wave the white arm, and point the pliant toe	250 Bards		629
Pressing one radiant arm just where below	289 Vision		283
The very fetters which his arm broke through	301 Age		257
Nor Homer's),--Lo! on Pyrrhus' arm she leans	308 Age		756
Yes! the right arm, yet red from Waterloo	308 Age		757
He raised his arm, and fiercely raised	312 Giaour		241
Thou, when thine arm should bend the bow	324 Abydos	1	85
And--but his arm is little worth	325 Abydos	1	135
In war Abdallah's arm was strong	331 Abydos	2	218
It was no mortal arm that bore	337 Abydos	2	719
Last time, it more fatigued my arm than foes	340 Corsair	1	166
Sweeps his long arm--that sabre's whirling sway	349 Corsair	2	170
And scarce an arm dare rise to guard its head	349 Corsair	2	175
Its white arm raised a lamp, yet gently hid	353 Corsair	2	398
This arm redeem'd thee from a fiery tomb	354 Corsair	2	498
That when the approaching crowd his arm withheld	376 Lara	2	80
Where had his arm unwarlike caught that art	377 Lara	2	143
And Death hath stricken down yon arm of pride	380 Lara	2	383
That raised his arm to point where such had been	381 Lara	2	471
Her rounded arm show'd white and bare	390 Corinth		558
Have felt the arm they would debase	390 Corinth		592
Alp at their head; his right arm is bare	392 Corinth		705
But his veteran arm was full of might	393 Corinth		782
Their leader's nervous arm is bare	393 Corinth		821
Alp is but known by the white arm bare	393 Corinth		830
Where'er that mighty arm is seen	393 Corinth		837
Who--were his arm a moment free	398 Parisina		169
My arm of strength, my soul of flame	399 Parisina		291
And the headsman, with his bare arm ready	400 Parisina		401
But what avail'd the club and spear, and arm	427 Island	3	47
They pull'd; her arm, though delicate, was free	430 Island	4	45
For thee alone they have no arm to save	461 Dante	3	48
That Michel Steno'--Nephew, thine arm! Nay	501 Faliero	1	101
But thou wouldst arm thee, wouldst thou not, if needful	556 Sardan	1	361
And this slight arm, and die a king at least	564 Sardan	2	170
To arm himself, although but for a moment	573 Sardan	3	95
Altada--Zames--forth, and arm ye! There	573 Sardan	3	119
Altada, arm yourself and return here	573 Sardan	3	125

ARM

Think not of me--a single soldier's arm	576 Sardan	3	287
Which girds your arm? A scratch from brave Beleses	577 Sardan	3	365
Cloven with arm still lustier, breast more daring	597 Foscari	1	105
Thine arm. Take mine, sir; 'tis my duty to	597 Foscari	1	149
Lend me your arm, good signor. You turn pale	617 Foscari	4	183
Marina! art thou willing? Here's my arm	624 Foscari	5	254
So high a guest--Pray take my arm, my lord	678 Werner	1	459
Rest in this arm. We may meet by and by	693 Werner	2	644
Where is it? In the shoulder, not the sword arm	738 Deformed	2	217
My feebleness of arm that reach'd him not	739 Deformed	2	260
And half retiring from the glowing arm	761 Juan	1	914
Around his scarce-clad limbs; and the fair arm	788 Juan	2	906
They turn'd to rest; and, each clasp'd by an arm	797 Juan	2	1471
Gleam in the moonlight; and her white arm clasps	798 Juan	2	1546
Of arms (in the East all arm)--and various dyes	805 Juan	3	215
One large gold bracelet clasp'd each lovely arm	810 Juan	3	561
Juan replied, 'Not while this arm is free	821 Juan	4	314
One on the arm, the other on the head	822 Juan	4	392
On her sire's arm, which until now scarce held	823 Juan	4	463
One arm had on a bandage rather bloody	832 Juan	5	86
Else they shall feel the weight of this my arm	841 Juan	5	651
And raising up an arm as moonlight fair	843 Juan	5	765
With great blue eyes, a lovely hand and arm	857 Juan	6	323
One with her flush'd cheek laid on her white arm	860 Juan	6	521
While their beloved friends began to arm	876 Juan	7	607
By merely wielding with poetic arm	877 Juan	7	627
A path, to add his own slight arm and forces	882 Juan	8	239
Your arm, and I'll bet Moscow to a dollar	890 Juan	8	775
Raise but an arm! 'twill brush their web away	900 Juan	9	217
A single laugh demolish'd the right arm	942 Juan	13	82
Juan put forth one arm--Eternal powers	996 Juan	16	1001
His other arm forth--Wonder upon wonder	996 Juan	16	1018

ARMADAS

And triumphs o'er the armadas of mankind	417 Island	1	139

ARMADA'S

Alike the Armada's pride or spoils of Trafalgar	82 Harold	4	1629

ARMAMENT

So near a hostile armament	390 Corinth		537

ARMAMENTS

The armaments which thunderstrike the walls	82 Harold	4	1621

ARM-CHAIR

There is the sofa, there the great arm-chair	765 Juan	1	1219

ARM-CHEST

As when the arm-chest held its brighter trust	425 Island	2	497

ARM'D
(See also FIRE-ARM'D)

His breast was arm'd 'gainst fate, his wants were few	26 Harold	2	383
Sprung forth a Pallas, arm'd and undefiled	69 Harold	4	859
Nations have arm'd in madness, the strange fate	80 Harold	4	1536
Arm'd thus, to make their bosoms bleed	98 To Lesbia		33
Arm'd, thence they go, while all th' assembled train	108 Nisus		217
And arm'd with Kings to strive	180 Ode-A		2
And, arm'd in proof, the gauntlet cast at once	256 Bards		1065
Thus arm'd with beauty would she check	315 Giaour		512
Each arm'd, as best becomes a man	315 Giaour		521
'Arm'd?'--'I expect so;--sent on the look-out	426 Island	2	514
Of the arm'd boats which hurried to complete	429 Island	3	219
The boat drew nigh, well arm'd, and firm the crew	433 Island	4	281
And arm'd, excepting those of the Sixteen	516 Faliero	2	556
Shall be so sooner. Now--my spear! I'm arm'd	573 Sardan	3	144
In every forest, or a mere arm'd truce	685 Werner	2	171
Was vengeance. But though arm'd with a short poniard	718 Werner	5	347
And summon lackeys, arm'd with fire and sword	764 Juan	1	1111
And arm'd from boot to turban, one and all	822 Juan	4	374
Of the arm'd river, while with straggling light	878 Juan	7	685

ARMED

Of armed horse and many a warlike store	28 Harold	2	506
Each robber chief upheld his armed halls	42 Harold	3	426
Would not be seen the armed torrents pour'd	61 Harold	4	382
Yes, close her with your armed bosoms round	303 Age		360
Than if an armed foe were near	390 Corinth		534
A spot--a mast--a sail--an armed deck	362 Corsair	3	483
Well has each steed obey'd the armed heel	380 Lara	2	362
Too long her armed wrath hath kept aloof	457 Dante	1	85

ARMENIAN

In several oaths--Armenian, Turk, and Greek	791 Juan	2	1103

ARMIDA'S

Wrought change with all Armida's fairy art	755 Juan	1	567

ARMIES

When Athens' armies fell at Syracuse	57 Harold	4	136
armies: but the blazing oaks gleam through	130 Calmar		36
Whose annual strains, like armies, take the field	244 Bards		204
To which the march of armies trampled them	703 Werner	3	565
Europe has slaves, allies, kings, armies still	747 Juan	Ded	127
The armies of the Christian Empress Catherine	875 Juan	7	512
The hum of armies gathering rank on rank	878 Juan	7	682
Which of the armies would have cause to mourn	888 Juan	8	614

ARMISTICE

Agree to a short armistice with truth	811 Juan	3	664

ARMORIAL

A race, with old armorial lists o'erspread	94 Dorset		57

ARMOUR

And with light armour we may learn to bear	211 Augusta-C		46
Dance forth--sans armour thou shalt take the field	273 Waltz		12
Much armour was, and hung up certain bows	473 Morgante		478
'If you want armour or aught else, go in	476 Morgante		657
Some armour, ere our journey we begin	476 Morgante		661
Was cover'd with old armour like a crust	476 Morgante		666
A chief in armour is their Suzerain	533 Faliero	4	377
Perhaps. I have the goodliest armour, and	556 Sardan	1	362
And never changed their chains but for their armour	556 Sardan	1	382
My armour there. And wilt thou? Will I not	573 Sardan	3	99
Your post is near our person. King! your armour	573 Sardan	3	126
They are his weapons, not his armour, for	613 Foscari	3	317
Suspicion is a heavy armour, and	681 Werner	1	665
And helms, and twisted armour, and long swords	697 Werner	3	119
Through our friend's armour there, with greater ease	726 Deformed	1	307
Good night! Prepare our armour for the assault	735 Deformed	1	877
But his armour is rusty	742 Deformed	3	28
Generals, some all in armour, of the old	949 Juan	13	553
With massy plate for armour, knives and forks	975 Juan	15	490

ARMOUR-BEARER

Next Remus' armour-bearer, hapless, fell	108 Nisus		245

ARMOURER

This let the Armourer with speed dispose	340 Corsiar	1	165

ARMOUR'S

Hearken to the armour's clank	735 Deformed	2	22

ARMOURY

Is all in readiness in the armoury	573 Sardan	3	120
What, Sfero! I will seek the armoury	574 Sardan	3	214

ARMS

And Policy regain'd what arms had lost	8 Harold	1	302
Their various arms that glitter in the air	10 Harold	1	435
Though thus in arms they emulate her sons	13 Harold	1	587
His arms a dart, he fights aloof, nor more	16 Harold	1	744
Though man and man's avenging arms assail	16 Harold	1	767
For foreign arms and aid they fondly sigh	31 Harold	2	717
By their right minds the conquest must be wrought	31 Harold	2	722
The morn the marshalling in arms,--the day	39 Harold	3	247
Mother of Arts, as once of arms; thy hand	62 Harold	4	417
'Arms and the Man,' whose re-ascending star	81 Harold	4	1562
Adieu, ye chiefs renown'd in arms	88 Anacreon-A		19
While close your arms around me fold	91 Caroline-B		35
I fold a statue in my arms	91 Caroline-B		44
And hear the din of arms no more	101 Alva		4
Eager to gild his arms with hostile blood	105 Nisus		2
Thy heart beats fiercely to the din of arms	106 Nisus		54
Chariots and bridles, mix'd with arms, are seen	108 Nisus		227
What silver arms with various art emboss'd	109 Nisus		285
'Stand, stragglers! stand! why early thus in arms	109 Nisus		308
The mirth of feasts, the clang of burnish'd arms	120 Newstead-A		54
to the hero, and call the chief to arms	130 Calmar		51
The din of arms came to the ear of Fingal	131 Calmar		145
arms. Oscar shakes the spear. The eagle	131 Calmar		149
In arms against the foe	161 War Song		6
Which millions rush'd in arms to greet	188 On Star	4	
In one embrace let these arms again enfold him	205 Hindoo		14
For the Man is his country's--the Arms are the Prince's	228 Ich Dien		2
Which defied the arms of Ali	240 Suliotes		8
If Jeffrey died, except within her arms	248 Bards		479
Arms nor the gown, priests, lawyers, volunteers	261 Hints		334
With commerce, given alone to arms and arts	263 Hints		512
Whose arts and arms but live in poets' lore	269 Minerva		58
Since o'er the Dardan field in arms she ranged	269 Minerva		76
Arms gave the first his right, the last had none	270 Minerva		111
And bid it antedate the joys of arms	272 Minerva		292
Are now extended up from legs to arms	273 Waltz		2
Waltz--Waltz alone--both legs and arms demands	275 Waltz		113
'Arts, arms, and George, and glory, and the isles	305 Age		530
Those arms that ne'er shall lose their hold	316 Giaour		652

ARMS

Yet died he as in arms he stood	317 Giaour		737
I care not; so my arms enfold	323 Giaour		1294
Her graceful arms in meekness bending	325 Abydos	1	182
At one kind word those arms extending	325 Abydos	1	184
I've arms, and friends, and vengeance near	327 Abydos	1	382
Yet what thou means't by "arms" and "friends	328 Abydos	1	412
There arms were piled, not such as wield	330 Abydos	2	122
Those arms thou see'st my band have brought	332 Abydos	2	315
Earth--sea alike--our world within our arms	333 Abydos	2	453
So that those arms cling closer round my neck	334 Abydos	2	455
The silent slaves with folded arms that wait	335 Abydos	2	630
Select the arms--to each his blade assign	338 Corsair	1	49
Her long fair hair lay floating o'er his arms	345 Corsair	1	470
Their arms are strong, yet merciful to-day	347 Corsair	2	21
His arms were folded on his dark-green vest	347 Corsair	2	53
They search--they find--they save: with lusty arms	350 Corsair	2	215
But who is she whom Conrad's arms convey	350 Corsair	2	221
Borne in his arms through fire from yon Serai	358 Corsair	3	180
Yet on his might ever there remain	361 Corsair	3	421
Their arms scarce forbear a rough embrace	363 Corsair	3	501
Her arms are meekly folded on that breast	363 Corsair	3	518
With folded arms and long attentive eye	371 Lara	1	402
Within his arms the form that felt no more	382 Lara	2	505
The arms they taught to bear; and now	385 Corinth		119
And folded arms, and freezing air	398 Parisina		164
A match ignoble for her arms	399 Parisina		259
He ceased, and stood with folded arms	399 Parisina		318
Felt if his arms in order good	407 Mazeppa		80
His arms were all his own, our Europe's growth	425 Island	2	486
Of arms; and we have got some guns to bear	426 Island	2	522
Their arms aside to revel in its dew	427 Island	3	76
Stood Christian, with his arms across his chest	427 Island	3	86
Her arms, and flung the foam from off her locks	431 Island	4	117
Their nuptial vault, his arms outstretch'd, and press'd	433 Island	4	225
Eager with anger, their strong arms made way	433 Island	4	239
Against the arms which must be wielded here	433 Island	4	252
Prepared their arms, and with that gloomy eye	433 Island	4	255
Their arms were poised, and glitter'd in the sky	434 Island	4	290
Hath hearts, and hands, and arms, and hosts to bring	460 Dante	2	132
He, too, shall sing of arms and Christian blood	462 Dante	3	121
Stretch'd forth her arms to clasp her lord again	468 Morgante		133
The giant ran to fetch his arms, quite furious	470 Morgante		247
'But to bear arms and wield the lance; indeed	476 Morgante		649
For their great purpose; they have arms, and means	507 Faliero	1	519
Wretch! darest thou name my son? He died in arms	508 Faliero	1	585
The hoped-for fleet. Are all supplied with arms	517 Faliero	2	643
To arms!--we are betray'd--it is the Doge	522 Faliero	3	211
And all now under arms by Israel's order	524 Faliero	3	362
Within whose court will be drawn out in arms	524 Faliero	3	376
To where my allotted band is under arms	526 Faliero	3	549
The white arms and the raven hair--the braids	529 Faliero	4	54
The groans of men--the clash of arms--the sound	530 Faliero	4	165
Stand to your arms, and guard the door--all's lost	536 Faliero	4	579
Your arms! To arms! The king's in danger. Monarch	572 Sardan	3	70
Of arms--and now--and now--Ho, Sfero, ho	574 Sardan	3	197
Waved arms, more dazzling with their own born whiteness	577 Sardan	3	395
In arms again; and, serrying their ranks	586 Sardan	4	547
I am with you. Ho, my arms! again, my arms	587 Sardan	4	584
Of arms, and records, monuments, and spoils	594 Sardan	5	431
Will take me as a mother to her arms	597 Foscari	1	143
As long are she resume her arms! 'Tis almost	601 Foscari	2	13
Off with your arms!--That bell! My God! My God	625 Foscari	5	307
Look! how he laughs and stretches out his arms	648 Cain	3	149
Been clasp'd again in these long-empty arms	672 Werner	1	57
Come to my arms again! Why, thou look'st all	688 Werner	3	361
And gilded crosiers, and cross'd arms, and cowls	697 Werner	3	118
House! Leave your arms; ye have no further need	740 Deformed	2	338
Just as his feeble arms could strike no more	787 Juan	2	851
And Juan sunk to sleep within her arms	798 Juan	2	1554
Of arms (in the East all arm)--and various dyes	805 Juan	3	215
Mix'd in each other's arms, and heart in heart	819 Juan	4	209
In arms, at least, in act to spring	821 Juan	4	311
His arms were like a serpent's coil: then flew	822 Juan	4	381
And cooks in motion with their clean arms bared	837 Juan	5	398
And, wrestling both his arms into a gown	841 Juan	5	623
With gentle force her white arms he unwound	847 Juan	5	1003
There's nothing whets the beak, or arms the claw	848 Juan	5	1059
And bosoms, arms, and ankles glancing bare	861 Juan	6	572
I don't know whether they had arms or crest	869 Juan	7	147
Now under arms. Ho! Katskoff, take him to	875 Juan	7	523
Their arms, as hens their wings about their young	875 Juan	7	536
Arms to which men will never more resort	877 Juan	7	628
'Observe your lover when he leaves your arms	885 Juan	8	423
Her hundred arms and legs, and fain outrun her	909 Juan	10	94
In royalty's vast arms he sigh'd for beauty	912 Juan	10	296
Their vigour in a thousand arms is dissipated	927 Juan	11	587

ARMS

His host, with broad arms 'gainst the thunder-
  stroke   948 Juan   13 444
With her Son in her blessed arms, look'd round 948 Juan   13 483
They added graceful necks, white hands and arms 954 Juan   13 856

ARMY

Satan next took the army list in hand   178 Devil's Dr   185
With a legion of cooks, and an army of slaves   202 Avatar   20
Around a slaughter'd army lay   407 Mazeppa   3
A Turkish army had march'd o'er   411 Mazeppa   436
Our standing army, and disbanded seamen   446 Beppo   385
Who knock'd his army down with icy hammer   447 Beppo   482
The chiefless army of the dead, which late   459 Dante   2 92
And some time General of the Fleet and Army   544 Faliero   5 479
To head an army than to rule a harem   551 Sardan   1   23
Of our too needy army, that their chief   734 Deformed   1 839
Months with the Russian army here and there   833 Juan   5 118
Or that the Russian army should repent all   876 Juan   7 598
The army, like a lion from his den   878 Juan   8   11
Of his whole army, which so much abounded   881 Juan   8 222
The Russian army upon this occasion   894 Juan   8 1018
Made up by youth, fame, and an army tailor   902 Juan   9 346
Of all the standing army who stood by   906 Juan   9 624

ARMY'S

Such as an army's baffled strength delays   70 Harold   4 885
Because the army's grown more popular   747 Juan   1   29
And cared as little for his army's loss   877 Juan   7 613

ARNAUT

Stain'd with the best of Arnaut blood   315 Giaour   525
Though now array'd in Arnaut garb   316 Giaour   615

ARNO

But Arno wins us to the fair white walls   62 Harold   4 424
Along the banks where smiling Arno sweeps   62 Harold   4 430
On Arno, till he perches, it may be   458 Dante   1 170
Like Arno in the summer, to a shallow   908 Juan   10   50

ARNOLD

Shall be plain Arnold still. We'll add a title 730 Deformed   1 543
'Count Arnold:' it hath no ungracious sound   730 Deformed   1 544
More swiftly, not less surely. Arnold, your   733 Deformed   1 804
To think on? Arnold! I will lead the attack   734 Deformed   1 835
But, Philibert, we'll in to council. Arnold   734 Deformed   1 872
Hold, Arnold! I am first. Not so, my lord   736 Deformed   2 123
'Tis nothing--lend me your hand. Arnold! I
  am sped   736 Deformed   2 128
And saw no equal. Arnold, shouldst thou see   737 Deformed   2 145
To die within the wall! Hence, Arnold, hence   737 Deformed   2 148
Why, Arnold! hold thine own: thou hast in hand 738 Deformed   2 203

ARNOLD'S

But let their merriest notes be Arnold's knell 723 Deformed   1   72

ARNO'S

In Arno's dome of Art's most princely shrine   64 Harold   4 542

AROINT

And so that no explosion cry 'Aroint   951 Juan   13 645

AROMATIC

Came breathing o'er the aromatic south   425 Island   2 435

AROSE

Music arose with its voluptuous swell   38 Harold   3 186
The pilgrims of his genius. He arose   59 Harold   4 266
Sudden the stranger-chief arose   103 Alva   193
Hence, let us haste!'--their brother guards arose 106 Nisus   81
I arose with the dawn; with my dog as my guide 136 Highlander   17
And warm to the skies my devotions arose   136 Highlander   23
Here might I sleep where all my hopes arose   138 Harrow-B   25
Where free Byzantium once arose   158 Florence   34
The Waves arose and roll'd beneath the blast   184 Julian   3
Arose and o'ershadow'd the earth with her name 186 Napoleon   2
Arose to Heaven in her appeal from man   193 Monody   42
Ere Tully arose in the zenith of Rome   202 Avatar   41
With a convulsion--then arose again   214 Dream   84
How wondrous bright thy blooming morn arose   223 To Dives   6
Egypt! from whose all dateless tombs arose   300 Age   141
Arose unheeded or unheard   317 Giaour   682
Again his rage repell'd--until arose   358 Corsair   3 206
Fearfully the yell arose   394 Corinth   897
Deep-mouth'd arose, and doubly harsh   396 Corinth   1066
No hope arose of being freed   414 Mazeppa   767
Neuha arose, and Torquil: twilight's hour   424 Island   2 398
As floor'd him so that he no more arose   473 Morgante   507
Or at the least learn whence the crimes arose   545 Faliero   5 511
The waves as they arose, and prouder still   597 Foscari   1 110
Each bloodier than the former. I arose   714 Werner   5   97
Arose a clatter might awake the dead   763 Juan   1 1083
The pleasant scandal which arose next day   770 Juan   1 1501
With slow and staggering effort he arose   788 Juan   2 865

AROSE

And thus upon his elbow he arose   793 Juan   3 1193
While one new tear arose in Haidee's eye   819 Juan   4 168
Then shrieking, she arose, and shrieking fell   821 Juan   4 281
And whirl'd her brain to madness; she arose   825 Juan   4 530
Sad strife arose, for they were so cross-grain'd 828 Juan   4 741
And wafted far arose a rich perfume   842 Juan   5 678
Also arose about the self-same time   863 Juan   6 713
And he arose, advanced--the shade retreated   996 Juan   16 994

AROUND

He fell, and falling nations mourn'd around   20 Harold   2   39
But one vast realm of wonder spreads around   33 Harold   2 830
The dust thy courser's hoof, rude stranger
  spurns around   34 Harold   2 854
The Nymphs and Tritons danced around   89 Prometheus-A   15
'Oh search, ye chiefs! oh search around   103 Alva   113
The war-cry rises, thundering hoofs around   109 Nisus   325
The glittering scene, the fluttering groups
  around   125 Recoll   197
I hate the slaves that cringe around   135 I Would   12
That thy dark-waving branches would flourish
  around   149 Newstead-B   3
To breathe a sweet religious calm around   161 Athos   15
And the long shadow lingers the ruin around   164 Newstead-C   8
For whirling above--underneath--and around   179 Devil's Dr   217
Of all the herd that throng around   179 Gold   17
That with all this I still can look around   212 Augusta-C   119
While many of his tribe slumber'd around   215 Dream   122
While all his train of hovering sylphs around   254 Bards   899
Seek'st thou the cause of loathing?--look around 269 Minerva   94
The cavern'd echoes wake around   312 Giaour   183
But few that saw, so calmly gazed around   351 Corsair   2 303
Broke from within, and all was night around   364 Corsair   3 582
That darts in seeming playfulness around   367 Lara   1   75
In rude but antique portraiture around   368 Lara   1 138
Alas! that heedlessness of all around   373 Lara   1 488
In many a tale from those around   397 Parisina   121
The sky above, and men around   400 Parisina   374
With the block before and the guards around   400 Parisina   400
His sole adieu to those around   401 Parisina   476
Worshipp'd at holy distance, and around   438 Tasso   130
The fiddlers trembled as he look'd around   444 Beppo   251
His glaring disk around   668 Heaven   1006
Then rising haughtily he glanced around   847 Juan   5 1005
Many and beautiful lay those around   860 Juan   6 513
A tide of well-clad waiters, and around   922 Juan   11 234
He started; and perceiving smiles around   992 Juan   16 746
From all the 'squires and 'squiresses around   992 Juan   16 770

AROUSE

Arouse thee, Gifford! be thy promise claim'd   253 Bards   829
Should arouse the saints within   735 Deformed   2   8

AROUSED

Is it for this the Spanish maid, aroused   12 Harold   1 558
Convey'd the Host aroused my rash young anger   546 Faliero   5 597

AROYNT

Quarter, in case he bade them not 'aroynt   893 Juan   8 931

ARQUA

There is a tomb in Arqua;--rear'd in air   59 Harold   4 262
They keep his dust in Arqua where he died   59 Harold   4 271
The immortal exile; Arqua, too, her store   64 Harold   4 529

ARQUEBUSS

With arquebuss and ataghan   315 Giaour   522

ARRAGON

The knife of Arragon, Toledo's steel   303 Age   370

ARRAIGN

And shall presumptuous mortals Heaven arraign   85 Death-B   17
Though I ne'er shall presume to arraign the decree 91 Caroline-C   14
T' arraign my fate, my voice forbear   103 Alva   139
'If you have aught to arraign in him, the tomb 293 Vision   547
You do not then in aught arraign our equity   541 Faliero   5 271
Than ye or I stand ready to arraign you   566 Sardan   2 292
Whom and whose house you arraign, reviving
  viper   717 Werner   5 298

ARRAIGN'D

Arraign'd before thy beauty's throne   99 Young Lady   19
Patrician, and arraign'd upon the charge   501 Faliero   1   79

ARRANGE

Though doubts of their well doing, to arrange   867 Juan   6 954

ARRANGEMENT

The Count and Laura made their new arrangement 446 Beppo   417

ARRANGEMENTS

Which lasted, as arrangements sometimes do   446 Beppo   418

ARRANGING
'Tis in arranging all my friends' affairs 750 Juan 1 183
Arranging them like books on the same shelf 972 Juan 15 243

ARRAS
Like the figures on arras, that gloomily glare 391 Corinth 620
Arras they prick'd and curtains with their swords 764 Juan 1 1143
Most people as it plays along the arras 983 Juan 16 160

ARRAY
And church and court did mingle their array 8 Harold 1 335
And Havoc scarce for joy can number their array 10 Harold 1 440
Bursting to light in terrible array 21 Harold 2 122
Here mingled in their many-hued array 28 Harold 2 512
Battle's magnificently-stern array 39 Harold 3 248
Her name in story, and her long array 55 Harold 4 29
When they were braided, and her proud array 70 Harold 4 923
In grim array the crimson cross demand 119 Newstead-A 10
Who proudly fall in her array 189 On Star 40
Of trees, in circular array, so fix'd 214 Dream 37
In grim array though Lewis' spectres rise 249 Bards 596
To murmur loudly through their long array 296 Vision 724
Their long array of sapphire and of gold 356 Corsair 3 52
His numbers melting fast from their array 379 Lara 2 307
Even at the moment when they should array 495 Manfred 3 304
The seed of the then world may thus array 631 Cain 1 232
The decorated street, the long array 714 Werner 5 112
Of human hearts, than all the long array 761 Juan 1 925
In all the flashing of their full array 838 Juan 5 444
Array her limbs; but Juan standing mute 840 Juan 5 580
With all the damsels in their long array 855 Juan 6 202
At the given signal join'd to their array 856 Juan 6 226
To wield them in their terrible array 878 Juan 8 10
The world gave ground before her bright array 942 Juan 13 85
To draw up in array a single day-bill 976 Juan 15 493

ARRAY'D
There sits in parchment robe array'd and by 8 Harold 1 292
In costly sheen and gaudy cloak array'd 15 Harold 1 738
Array'd in many a dun and purple streak 25 Harold 2 373
She who was named Eternal, and array'd 67 Harold 4 752
The Sun in human limbs array'd, and brow 79 Harold 4 1443
Which this poetic marble hath array'd 79 Harold 4 1462
A numerous crowd, array'd in white 95 Granta 67
Her chiefs in gleaming mail array'd 101 Alva 8
With cypress crown'd, array'd in weeds 118 Romance 42
Though now array'd in Arnaut garb 316 Giaour 615
In summer garments be our limbs array'd 419 Island 2 47
Fantastically, it may be, array'd 425 Island 2 462
That sound a dread? All around them seem'd
 array'd 429 Island 3 216
Of Torquil's knife struck fire; and thus array'd 432 Island 4 144
Hath robed thee with a glory, and array'd 438 Tasso 133
The abbot show'd a chamber, where array'd 473 Morgante 477
They are array'd, and eager for the signal 533 Faliero 4 351
And now being femininely all array'd 841 Juan 5 633
A child of Nature, carelessly array'd 859 Juan 6 475
Array'd herself with mantle, gem, and veil 863 Juan 6 692
That they must instantly be well array'd 867 Juan 6 939
It was no mouse, but lo! a monk, array'd 983 Juan 16 161

ARRAYS
With humbler care her form arrays 386 Corinth 207
Mix'd with those bitter thoughts the soul arrays 429 Island 3 205
And in whatever aspect it arrays 756 Juan 1 581

ARREAR
And claims his long arrear of northern blood 271 Minerva 226
And yet was in arrear of human ills 285 Vision 24
For all the fasts are now left in arrear 474 Morgante 528

ARREARS
The troops have long arrears of pay, oft
 promised 504 Faliero 1 333
Are discontented for their long arrears 507 Faliero 1 493

ARREST
(See also MOCK-ARREST)
Who could then her wing arrest 188 Ode-B 65
Many passengers arrest one 196 Rogers 19
All, tinged with varied hues, arrest the eye 269 Minerva 47
All tinged with varied hues, arrest the eye 356 Corsair 3 47
The hands, which trembled at thy voice, arrest 416 Island 1 56
In close arrest.' Proceed. My lord, 'tis
 finish'd 501 Faliero 1 98
The Forty hath decreed a month's arrest 503 Faliero 1 241
No. A month's arrest. Is it not enough 512 Faliero 2 224
With what? a mulct or an arrest? With death 516 Faliero 2 516
See that none pass--arrest this man! Take care 533 Faliero 4 329
I arrest thee of high treason! Me 536 Faliero 4 549
To arrest two traitors. Guards! Within there!
 Satraps 564 Sardan 2 156
From Brandenburg's elector, for the arrest 680 Werner 1 564
Search empty pockets; also, to arrest 684 Werner 2 70

ARREST
He gave the word,--'Arrest or slay the Frank 822 Juan 4 376

ARRESTED
Your arm, brave boy, arrested his career 126 Recoll 279
That sprung at first to his arrested eyes 372 Lara 1 422
Whom thou suspectest?--Let them be arrested 556 Sardan 1 346

ARRESTS
Brave Nisus here arrests his comrade's arm 109 Nisus 279
Some name arrests the passer-by 157 Album 2

ARRIVAL
But found on my arrival, that, besides 541 Faliero 5 213
Of his arrival, and the time; the account, too 687 Werner 2 274
Of his arrival, so that no one stirr'd 806 Juan 3 293

ARRIVALS
And long the latest of arrivals halts 926 Juan 11 534

ARRIVE
That the time must arrive, when, no longer
 retaining 91 Caroline-C 9
While thus they speak, the hour must soon arrive 124 Recoll 181
Yet the day may arrive when the mountains once
 more 136 Highlander 41
If but to see what next can well arrive 211 Augusta-C 32
Arrive with Ofratanes. Did you not 589 Sardan 5 136
From sleep, and judge! Should that day e'er
 arrive 690 Werner 2 446
Seeing arrive an aid so opportune 885 Juan 8 442

ARRIVED
Arrived a young and noble dame 102 Alva 78
Arrived the dearly destined morn 103 Alva 170
Arrived to rob him of his prize 414 Mazeppa 751
The hour arrived, no matter where 415 Mazeppa 865
Arrived there, a prodigious noise he hears 473 Morgante 489
The hour arrived--and it became 480 Manfred 1 116
They penetrate to where they then arrived 588 Sardan 5 67
I had arrived a few hours sooner! Ay 691 Werner 2 507
Together, and together we arrived 717 Werner 5 280
By this time Don Alfonso was arrived 763 Juan 1 1097
So nobody arrived on shore but him 787 Juan 2 848
Nor yet had he arrived but for the oar 787 Juan 2 849
But Grey was not arrived, and Chatham gone 940 Juan 12 656
Arrived, retired to his; but to despond 995 Juan 16 924

ARRIVES
Arrives--to-night must break thy chain 334 Abydos 2 482
Arrives, let him alike these orders mark 346 Corsair 1 566
The foe arrives, who long had search'd the field 381 Lara 2 432
And both regardless; when the hour arrives 527 Faliero 3 611
That hour arrives, I can but offer thanks 679 Werner 1 489
Arrives from Frankfort, from the commandant 680 Werner 1 593
Is used until the truth arrives too late 802 Juan 3 44
Are spurn'd in turn, until her turn arrives 934 Juan 12 282

ARRIVING
Arriving like a rush of mighty wind 287 Vision 178
Arriving at the summit of a hill 804 Juan 3 161
He knew not why, arriving at this pass 881 Juan 8 227
The greater is the pleasure in arriving 916 Juan 10 575

ARROGANCE
The arrogance of something higher than 692 Werner 2 611

ARROGANT
By strange delay and arrogant reply 546 Faliero 5 598
In your address, nor yet too arrogant 698 Werner 3 213

ARROW
The shaft hath just been shot--the arrow bright 79 Harold 4 1445
With poison tipt, his arrow flies 89 Anacreon-B 43
And send the whistling arrow far 102 Alva 60
And Allan's barbed arrow lay 104 Alva 279
'Who shot the arrow 237 Keats 5
Of him who felt the Dardan's arrow 329 Abydos 2 45
To bear him like an arrow to that height. 364 Corsair 3 576
The erring arrow launch aside 400 Parisina 362
An arrow for his bow, and lifts his head 473 Morgante 492
Morgante at a venture shot an arrow 473 Morgante 497
Even as the arrow finds the airy king 570 Sardan 2 570
Make him a mark too royal. Every arrow 574 Sardan 3 206
An arrow pierced his brain, while, scattering 577 Sardan 3 355
Ere Paris' arrow flew. I gaze upon him 726 Deformed 1 282
Than the adulterer's arrow through his heel 726 Deformed 1 308
Ne'er with such force the swiftest arrow flew 789 Juan 2 934
An arrow for the heart like a sweet voice 970 Juan 15 104

ARROWS
Ne'er yet for one thine arrows flew so fast 34 Harold 2 906
Aim'd with her poison'd arrows, but to miss 61 Harold 4 345
Or pour his arrows through th' embattled field 105 Nisus 4
That Love had arrows, well I knew 172 Romaic-B 7

ARROWS
To me the arrows of satiric song   242 Bards   38
Those winged words like arrows sped   326 Abydos   1 224
The club, and rain our arrows o'er the field   419 Island   2 42
Shrunk to a scabbard, with his arrows at   902 Juan   9 355

ARROW'S
The arrow's flown, and dearly shalt thou rue it   229 Sadness   9
The shaft is sped, the arrow's in his breast   380 Lara   2 381

ARROWY
By the blue rushing of the arrowy Rhone   46 Harold   3 673

ARSENAL
I am the chief of the arsenal, employ'd   505 Faliero   1 379
Chief of the arsenal ere I came from Rome   505 Faliero   1 394
Ay, doubtless they have echo'd o'er the arsenal   506 Faliero   1 420
Now in the Arsenal, who holds command   511 Faliero   2 137
Of many of our cause into the arsenal   517 Faliero   2 640
Within the arsenal, and hold all ready   518 Faliero   2 660
And the quick Cassius of the Arsenal   540 Faliero   5 180

ARSENIEW
Though led by Arseniew, that great son of
  slaughter   879 Juan   8 68

ARSNIEW
Meknop, Serge Lwow, Arsniew of modern Greece   869 Juan   7 115

ART
Ah! may'st thou ever be what now thou art   3 To Ianthe   10
Or fence of art, like China's vasty wall   9 Harold   1 365
Was not unskilful in the spoiler's art   24 Harold   2 291
Art, Glory, Freedom fail, but Nature still is
  fair   33 Harold   2 827
In mockery of man's art; and these withal   45 Harold   3 586
And Otway, Radcliffe, Schiller, Shakspeare's art   58 Harold   4 158
Of all Art yields, and Nature can decree   59 Harold   4 229
Chain'd to the chariot of triumphal Art   62 Harold   4 445
Than Art in galleries: though a work divine   64 Harold   4 547
Our little life, nor Bard prescribe his art   66 Harold   4 690
Where, as a monument of antique art   68 Harold   4 787
As thine ideal breast! what'er thou art   72 Harold   4 1029
Share with immortal transports? Could thine art   73 Harold   4 1066
Oh Love! no habitant of earth thou art   73 Harold   4 1081
Of art and piety--Pantheon!--pride of Rome   77 Harold   4 1314
To art a model; and to him who treads   77 Harold   4 1318
Of art and its great masters, who could raise   79 Harold   4 1427
A grief too deep to trust the sculptor's art   85 Epitaph   14
I hate you, ye cold compositions of art   92 First Kiss   13
Though strong as mortal art could give   98 To Mary   2
Must all the painter's art defy   98 To Mary   11
Lifeless, unfeeling as thou art   98 To Mary   18
Nor time, nor place, nor art have moved it   101 Lady-B   6
What silver arms with various art emboss'd   109 Nisus   285
Though little versed in any art beside   111 Examination   10
To sigh the dupe of female art   143 To-A   18
Which made thee fickle as thou art   153 Friend-A   16
The sculptor's art exhausts the pomp of woe   154 Dog   3
To trace the birth and nursery of art   162 Orchomenus   2
And fashion's ease, without its art   163 Malta   42
Beloved dust! since dust thou art   166 Away   14
Since he who wears thee feels thou art   168 Cornelian-B   7
On Drury first your Siddons' thrilling art   169 Address-A   31
That beam hath sunk, and now thou art   172 Time-B   29
In some 'tis Nature, some 'tis Art   179 Gold   21
All Evil Spirit as thou art   181 Ode-A   77
And what he is, and what thou art   198 Duel   51
Such as my feelings were and are, thou art   198 Po   11
Wrung from the vain Romancer's art   200 Ode-C   18
What she had made the pupil of her art   208 Sketch   17
We were and are--I am, even as thou art   212 Augusta-C   123
The serpent of the field, by art   219 Vanity   17
'Tis thine to offer with corrupting art   227 Answer-C   7
Beyond the Bard's defeated aim   229 Marble   6
The play's concoction full of art   231 Doctor   12
The Art of Cookery, and mine   234 Strahan   15
Then let Ausonia, skill'd in every art   250 Bards   618
With art the charms which nature could not spare   250 Bards   665
For all the mutilated blocks of art   256 Bards   1032
Abused his art, till Nature, with a blush   256 Hints   3
Like certain tailors, limited in art   257 Hints   52
'Tis not enough, ye bards, with all your art   258 Hints   137
And truth and fiction with such art compounds   259 Hints   211
For art too rude, for nature too refined   262 Hints   390
Or if, till roofs received the vagrant art   262 Hints   439
Nor write at all, unless to teach the art   263 Hints   487
Without much grace or weight or art, will hold   263 Hints   506
If verse be studied with some show of art   266 Hints   697
Yet art and nature join'd will win the prize   266 Hints   701
That art and nature may compare their styles   270 Minerva   180
The head to hock belongs, thy subtler art   274 Waltz   35
In science and art, I'll be cursed if I know   280 Blues   2   10
Is to see Nature's triumph o'er all that is art   282 Blues   2   114

ART
Disdain, defy, the tardy aid of art   299 Age   82
One half the poet's, all the gourmand's art   305 Age   523
Thus passion's fire, and woman's art   319 Giaour   932
'Tis all too late--thou wert, thou art   322 Giaour   1190
But, shape or shade! whate'er thou art   323 Giaour   1315
By nature but enlarged by art   330 Abydos   2   101
To Love, whose deadliest bane is human Art   334 Abydos   2   459
Still sways their souls with that commanding art   340 Corsair   1   177
Long may her own be lighter than thou art   343 Corsair   1   324
And all that speaks and aids the naval art   346 Corsair   1   588
'Well, as thou wilt--ascetic as thou art   349 Corsair   2   133
He had (if .'twere not nature's boon) an art   371 Lara   363
Then all was stern collectedness and art   376 Lara   2   77
Where had his arm unwarlike caught that art   377 Lara   2   143
The stubborn wall that mocks the leaguer's art   379 Lara   2   300
With deeper skill in war's black art   385 Corinth   97
Brightest in dungeons, Liberty! thou art   402 Sonnet-F   2
Since thou hast learn'd the art so well   408 Mazeppa   110
Now let them reap the harvest of their art   419 Island   2   43
Exist: and what can our accomplish'd art   420 Island   2   101
Their art seem'd nature--such the skill to sweep   429 Island   3   181
To lift my love so lofty as thou art   437 Tasso   51
Oh that I had the art of easy writing   446 Beppo   401
For his reward the Guelf's ascendant art   457 Dante   1   90
And Art itself seem into Nature wrought   462 Dante   3   117
Art shall resume and equal even the sway   463 Dante   4   41
By the perfection of thine art   481 Manfred   1   246
My long pursued and superhuman art   487 Manfred   2   242
Whatever thou art   490 Manfred   2   455
Its false and true enchantments--art and nature   529 Faliero   4   63
Depraving nature's frailty to an art   549 Faliero   5   785
Of the destructive art of healing, to   619 Foscari   4   282
A very Ovid in the art of hating   622 Foscari   5   136
Picker and stealer, without art or genius   684 Werner   57
Or deal you in the black art? I deal plainly   697 Werner   3   132
For her Feinagle's were an useless art   748 Juan   1   85
Wrought change with all Armida's fairy art   755 Juan   1   567
On Love! how perfect is thy mystic art   760 Juan   1   843
To love too much has been the only art   770 Juan   1   1533
All other magazines of art or science   772 Juan   1   1683
The illusion's gone for ever, and thou art   773 Juan   1   1717
Beyond the best apothecary's art   776 Juan   2   163
Had often turn'd the art to some account   787 Juan   2   836
The power of art was turn'd to nothing, for   810 Juan   3   599
The world was not for them, nor the world's art   819 Juan   4   213
To feel for more is the true social art   834 Juan   5   199
Which puzzled Nature much to know what Art meant   839 Juan   5   512
'Not to admire is all the art I know   844 Juan   5   801
The cutting off his head was not the art   849 Juan   5   1119
Self-love in man, too, beats all female art   855 Juan   6   149
So beautiful that art could little mend her   863 Juan   6   709
As well as dilettanti in war's art   872 Juan   7   309
Here War forgot his own destructive art   888 Juan   8   653
Whene'er he can; for there is little art   889 Juan   8   683
War's a brain-spattering, windpipe-slitting art   896 Juan   9   27
He who has nought to gain can have small art: he   899 Juan   9   205
Seeing how Art can make her work more grand   902 Juan   9   349
Beneath his art. The dame, press'd to disclose
  them   903 Juan   9   407
Was what he call'd the 'Art of Happiness   945 Juan   13   274
An art on which the artists greatly vary   945 Juan   13   275
These last had disappear'd--a loss to art   948 Juan   13   468
The wits watch'd every loophole for their art   955 Juan   13   867
Pars parva fui,' but still art and part   958 Juan   14   162
Lord Henry heard her plans of artless art   963 Juan   14   517
And turning human nature to an art   968 Juan   15   20
The art of living in all climes with ease   969 Juan   15   88
Professors of that genial art, and patrons   972 Juan   15   291
And fruits, and ice, and all that art refines   977 Juan   15   569
He had the art of drawing people out   978 Juan   15   655
A thing of temperament and not of art   993 Juan   16   821

ARTEM
Secundem artem: but although we sneer   912 Juan   10   330

ARTERIES
The electric blood with which their arteries run   462 Dante   3   162

ARTERY
(See CAROTID-ARTERY-CUTTING)

ARTHUR
And Arthur struts in mimic majesty   261 Hints   340

ARTHUR'S
Nor hunt the bloodhounds back to Arthur's Seat   247 Bards   437
Arthur's steep summit nodded to its base   248 Bards   474
Young Arthur's eyes, can ours or nature bear   260 Hints   280

ARTICLE
To write an article thou canst not shun   265 Hints   624
I like that article of war. Come hither   693 Werner   2   665
I'm for a handsome article his creditor   772 Juan   1   1675

ARTICLE

Should let itself be snuff'd out by an article	925 Juan	11	472
Even where the article at highest rate is	971 Juan	15	228
He read an article the king attacking	983 Juan	16	207

ARTICLES

And render the believers in our "Articles" sensible	179 Devil's Dr		247
Of some of our forthcoming Articles	231 Doctor		46
To furnish articles for the Debats	308 Age		718
With other articles of ladies fair	764 Juan	1	1141
Light classic articles of female want	803 Juan	3	132
Of articles which nobody required	839 Juan	5	509
Than other articles of female dress	855 Juan	6	148
And one by one her articles of dress	860 Juan	6	481
(Whose articles are like the 'Thirty-nine	947 Juan	13	418

ARTIFICE

At such inhuman artifice of pain	600 Foscari	1	336

ARTIFICERS

As new artificers for their equipment	517 Faliero	2	641

ARTIFICIAL

But Peace abhorreth artificial joys	29 Harold	2	575
Of wit, we loathe an artificial strain	266 Hints		700
A dazzling mass of artificial light	528 Faliero	4	33
With nature manners which are artificial	971 Juan	15	199

ARTILLERY

Let off the artillery, which Milton mentions	291 Vision		415
Of far artillery which seem'd to bid	714 Werner	5	114
When just as the artillery ceased, and paused	715 Werner	5	130
They'd crack them. Hunger is a sharp artillery	732 Deformed	1	748
Of our artillery and his own: 'tis said	890 Juan	8	781
Seems Love turn'd a lieutenant of artillery	902 Juan	9	352

ARTILLERY'S

According to the artillery's hits or misses	876 Juan	7	603
Nought to be seen save the artillery's flame	878 Juan	8	42

ARTISAN

Then thy spruce citizen, wash'd artisan	15 Harold	1	695
But coats must claim another artisan	257 Hints		54
Even from this hour; the meanest artisan	501 Faliero	1	137
A famous artisan, a cunning sculptor	738 Deformed	2	204

ARTISANS

Full of reproof, because our artisans	505 Faliero	1	383
As a good jest to jolly artisans	506 Faliero	1	422

ARTIST

The artist and his ape, to teach and tell	63 Harold	4	470
Can do no more. Then let the artist share	463 Dante	4	36

ARTISTS

Poets and painters, as all artists know	257 Hints		15
Still with his hireling artists let him prate	270 Minerva		169
An art on which the artists greatly vary	945 Juan	13	275
Mix'd Gothic, such as artists all allow	948 Juan	13	436
The friend of artists, if not arts,--the owner	988 Juan	16	498
This makes your actors, artists, and romancers	993 Juan	16	825

ARTIST'S

Enormous model doom'd the artist's toils	78 Harold	4	1364

ARTLESS

For his was not that open, artless soul	4 Harold	1	69
I heard his seeming artless tale	89 Anacreon-B		21
Such is my artless song to thee	100 Marion		33
The artless Helicon I boast is youth	119 Anacreon-A		23
When every artless bosom throbs with truth	123 Recoll		58
Lord Henry heard her plans of artless art	963 Juan	14	517

ARTLESSLY

Would give up artlessly both heart and head	969 Juan	15	78

ARTS

But form'd for all the witching arts of love	13 Harold	1	586
Ere Greece and Grecian arts by barbarous hands were quell'd	19 Harold	1	953
But Harold on such arts no more relied	24 Harold	2	295
States fall, arts fade, but Nature doth not die	55 Harold	4	24
Mother of Arts, as once of arms; thy hand	62 Harold	4	417
Relic of nobler days and noblest arts	77 Harold	4	1315
'Away, away, your flattering arts	86 Rousseau		1
Dear, simple girl, those flattering arts	86 Rousseau		5
All modern arts affecting to despise	112 Examination		56
In all the arts of scenic action old	113 Prologue		12
For arts like these at bounteous tables fed	142 Soliloquy		41
'In arts and sciences our isle hath shone	171 Address-B		25
'Thee we invoke, your sister arts implore	171 Address-B		29
To guide whose hand the sister arts combine	253 Bards		861
Master of arts! as hells and clubs proclaim	260 Hints		241

ARTS

With commerce, given alone to arms and arts	263 Hints		512
Whose arts and arms but live in poets' lore	269 Minerva		58
So, instead of 'beaux arts,' we may say 'la belle passion	277 Blues	1	4
As usual in that most litigious of arts	282 Blues	2	86
'Arts, arms, and George, and glory, and the isles	305 Age		530
By arts that veil and oft preserve the proud	346 Corsair	1	540
In ancient arts by moderns mimick'd ill	441 Beppo		84
Whom all arts shall acknowledge as their lord	464 Dante	4	59
If go you will, guard well against their arts	469 Morgante		229
Nursed in effeminate arts from youth to manhood	575 Sardan	3	222
New times, new climes, new arts, new men; but still	661 Heaven		478
He learn'd the arts of riding, fencing, gunnery	751 Juan	1	303
Arts, sciences, no branch was made a mystery	752 Juan	1	311
The arts, at least all such as could be said	752 Juan	1	315
Of his own nature, and the various arts	762 Juan	1	1018
Where grew the arts of war and peace	812 Juan	3	691
The arts of which these lands were once the font	837 Juan	5	366
All arts to teach their subjects to destroy	890 Juan	8	736
Till all the arts at length are brought about	901 Juan	9	317
But Juan was a bachelor--of arts	924 Juan	11	369
Theology, fine arts, or finer stays	936 Juan	12	418
By no quite lawful marriage of the arts	949 Juan	13	530
The friend of artists, if not arts,--the owner	988 Juan	16	498
Have in their several arts or parts ascendance	990 Juan	16	652

ART'S

In Arno's dome of Art's most princely shrine	64 Harold	4	542
Art's works; nor must the delicate waters sleep	72 Harold	4	1041
And Art's mistaken gratitude shall raise	464 Dante	4	84

AS

To paint those charms which varied as they beam'd	3 To Ianthe		7
To such as see thee not my words were weak	3 To Ianthe		8
As fair in form, as warm yet pure in heart	3 To Ianthe		12
Oh! let that eye, which, wild as the Gazelle's	3 To Ianthe		28
Wins as it wanders, dazzles where it dwells	3 To Ianthe		30
And long as kinder eyes a look shall cast	3 To Ianthe		38
Of him who hail'd thee, loveliest as thou wast	3 To Ianthe		43
As if the memory of some daily feud	4 Harold	1	66
As glad to waft him from his native home	5 Harold	1	101
And frequent turn to linger as you go	7 Harold	1	253
And here and there, as up the crags you spring	7 Harold	1	261
Once form'd thy Paradise, as not aware	7 Harold	1	276
But now, as if a thing unblest by Man	7 Harold	1	281
Thy fairy dwelling is as lone as thou	7 Harold	1	282
So deem'd the Childe, as o'er the mountains he	8 Harold	1	315
But as he gazed on truth his aching eyes grew dim	8 Harold	1	323
Onward he flies, nor fix'd as yet the goal	8 Harold	1	328
Far as the eye discerns, withouten end	9 Harold	1	354
For proud each peasant as the noblest duke	9 Harold	1	375
But wields not, as of old, her thirsty lance	10 Harold	1	407
Are met--as if at home they could not die	10 Harold	1	447
As o'er thy plain the Pilgrim prick'd his steed	11 Harold	1	460
As whilome he was wont the leagues to cheer	11 Harold	1	506
No! as he speeds, he chants 'Viva el Rey	11 Harold	1	508
And, far as mortal eye can compass sight	12 Harold	1	533
In softness as in firmness far above	13 Harold	1	591
Her mind is nobler sure, her charms perchance as great	13 Harold	1	593
As Greece can still bestow, though Glory fly her glades	14 Harold	1	656
The Pleasures fled, but sought as warm a clime	14 Harold	1	668
Soon as the matin bell proclaimeth nine	15 Harold	1	713
From crimes as numerous as her beadsmen be	15 Harold	1	717
As moon-struck bards complain, by Love's sad archery	15 Harold	1	728
Four steeds that spurn the rein, as swift as shy	16 Harold	1	790
Who late so free as Spanish girls were seen	17 Harold	1	806
Love has no gift so grateful as his wings	17 Harold	1	815
Though now it moves him as it moves the wise	17 Harold	1	820
And as in Beauty's bower he pensive sate	17 Harold	1	834
To charms as fair as those that soothed his happier day	17 Harold	1	836
Where demi-gods appear'd as records tell	20 Harold	2	42
Yet if, as holiest men have deem'd, there be	20 Harold	2	64
Be as it may Futurity's behest	20 Harold	2	80
Cold as the crags upon his native coast	21 Harold	2	102
His mind as barren and his heart as hard	21 Harold	2	103
Nor feels as lovers o'er the dust they loved	21 Harold	2	128
But Harold felt not as in other times	22 Harold	2	143
When the fresh breeze is fair as breeze may be	22 Harold	2	147
Strains his shrill pipe as good or ill betides	22 Harold	2	161
Thoughtless, as if on shore they still were free to rove	22 Harold	2	189
Such as on lonely Athos may be seen	23 Harold	2	236
As breezes rise and fall and billows swell	23 Harold	2	251
Thus Harold deem'd, as on that lady's eye	24 Harold	2	271
As long as aught was worthy to pursue	24 Harold	2	294
But knew him as his worshipper no more	24 Harold	2	276
Climes, fair withal as ever mortal head	25 Harold	2	320

AS

And as the stately vessel glided slow	25	Harold	2	365
And, sunk albeit in thought as he was wont	25	Harold	2	368
Arise; and, as the clouds along them break	25	Harold	2	374
Reposes gladly on as smooth a vale	27	Harold	2	480
As ever Spring yclad in grassy dye	27	Harold	2	481
As page and slave anon were passing out and in	28	Harold	2	540
As winds come lightly whispering from the west	30	Harold	2	626
And, as the flames along their faces gleam'd	30	Harold	2	645
Wnat mark is so fair as the breast of a foe	30	Harold	2	660
Shall view us as victors, or view us no more	31	Harold	2	692
As woo'd the eye and thrill'd the Bosphorus along	32	Harold	2	755
'Twas, as if darting from her heavenly throne	32	Harold	2	762
Let sage or cynic prattle as he will	32	Harold	2	772
Not such as prate of war but skulk in peace	32	Harold	2	785
Yet are thy skies as blue, thy crags as wild	33	Harold	2	819
Thine olive ripe as when Minerva smiled	33	Harold	2	821
As on the morn to distant Glory dear	33	Harold	2	842
As Pallas and the Muse unveil their awful lore	34	Harold	2	863
And be alone on earth, as I am now	35	Harold	2	921
And then we parted,--not as now we part	35	Harold	3	4
And the waves bound beneath me as a steed	35	Harold	3	11
Though the strain'd mast should quiver as a reed	35	Harold	3	14
Still must I on; for I am as a weed	35	Harold	3	16
And bear it with me, as the rushing wind	35	Harold	3	22
I would essay as I have sung to sing	35	Harold	3	31
With form our fancy, gaining as we give	36	Harold	3	48
The life we image, even as I do now	36	Harold	3	49
Invisible but gazing, as I glow	36	Harold	3	52
In soul and aspect as in age: years steal	36	Harold	3	70
Fire from the mind as vigour from the limb	36	Harold	3	71
And he, as one, might 'midst the many stand	36	Harold	3	87
Fit speculation, such as in strange land	36	Harold	3	89
As their own beams; and earth, and earth-born jars	37	Harold	3	120
To which it mounts, as if to break the link	37	Harold	3	125
Droop'd as a wild-born falcon with clipt wing	37	Harold	3	129
As eagerly the barr'd-up bird will beat	37	Harold	3	132
Which, though 'twere wild,--as on the plunder'd wreck	37	Harold	3	141
As the ground was before, thus let it be	37	Harold	3	150
Its gifts, transferring fame as fleeting too	38	Harold	3	157
Such as Harmodius drew on Athens' tyrant lord	38	Harold	3	180
And all went merry as a marriage-bell	38	Harold	3	188
As if the clouds its echo would repeat	38	Harold	3	196
And there were sudden partings, such as press	39	Harold	3	212
Dewy with nature's tear-drops, as they pass	39	Harold	3	236
And one as all a ghastly gap did make	40	Harold	3	272
Even as a broken mirror, which the glass	40	Harold	3	289
As nothing did we die; but Life will suit	40	Harold	3	301
For daring made thy rise as fall: thou seek'st	40	Harold	3	322
Even as a flame unfed which runs to waste	42	Harold	3	394
And there they stand, as stands a lofty mind	42	Harold	3	415
Their hopes were not less warm, their souls were full as brave	42	Harold	3	432
Making thy waves a blessing as they flow	42	Harold	3	443
Thy waves would vainly roll, all sweeping as they seem	43	Harold	3	459
On such as smile upon us; the heart must	43	Harold	3	472
For this in such as him seems strange of mood	43	Harold	3	479
And there was one soft breast, as hath been said	43	Harold	3	487
But yet reject them not as such	44	Harold	3	519
For I have cherish'd them as dear	44	Harold	3	520
On such as wield her weapons; he had kept	44	Harold	3	552
Is to the mellow Earth as Autumn to the year	44	Harold	3	571
The wild rocks shaped as they had turrets been	45	Harold	3	585
A race of faces happy as the scene	45	Harold	3	587
Gather around these summits, as to show	45	Harold	3	597
And looks as with the wild-bewildered gaze	45	Harold	3	620
Which feeds it as a mother who doth make	46	Harold	3	675
Kissing its cries away as these awake	46	Harold	3	677
As on a place of agony and strife	46	Harold	3	691
Though young, yet waxing vigorous, as the blast	46	Harold	3	695
And dust is as it should be, shall I not	46	Harold	3	703
Of me and of my soul, as I of them	47	Harold	3	708
Of words, like sunbeams, dazzling as they past	47	Harold	3	732
His love was passion's essence--as a tree	47	Harold	3	734
As from the Pythian's mystic cave of yore	47	Harold	3	762
As heretofore because ambition was self-will'd	48	Harold	3	778
This quiet sail is as a noiseless wing	48	Harold	3	801
Sounds sweet as if a Sister's voice reproved	48	Harold	3	804
But breathless, as we grow when feeling most	49	Harold	3	834
And silent, as we stand in thoughts too deep	49	Harold	3	835
Yet lovely in your strength, as is the light	49	Harold	3	862
As if they did rejoice o'er a young earthquake's birth	49	Harold	3	877
Heights which appear as lovers who have parted	49	Harold	3	879
His lightnings, as if he did understand	50	Harold	3	893
That in such gaps as desolation work'd	50	Harold	3	894
But as it is, I live and die unheard	50	Harold	3	912
With a most voiceless thought, sheathing it as a sword	50	Harold	3	913
And living as if earth contain'd no tomb	50	Harold	3	917
But light leaves, young as joy, stands where it stood	51	Harold	3	948
A wit as various,--gay, grave, sage, or wild	51	Harold	3	988

AS

Breathed most in ridicule,--which, as the wind	51	Harold	3	992
And when it shall revive, as is our trust	52	Harold	3	1011
May be permitted, as my steps I bend	52	Harold	3	1019
So young as to regard men's frown or smile	52	Harold	3	1046
As loss or guerdon of a glorious lot	52	Harold	3	1047
Yet this was in my nature:--as it is	53	Harold	3	1083
Yet, though dull Hate as duty should be taught	53	Harold	3	1085
Should be shut from thee, as a spell still fraught	53	Harold	3	1087
As yet such are around thee, but thy fire	53	Harold	3	1097
As, with a sigh, I deem thou mightst have been to me	53	Harold	3	1102
As from the stroke of the enchanter's wand	55	Harold	4	4
Such as I sought for, and at moments found	56	Harold	4	60
If my fame should be, as my fortunes are	56	Harold	4	80
Thin streets, and foreign aspects, such as must	57	Harold	4	133
See! as they chant the tragic hymn, the car	57	Harold	4	140
Was as a fairy city of the heart	57	Harold	4	155
According as their souls were form'd to sink or climb	58	Harold	4	198
As Day and Night contending were, until	59	Harold	4	248
With a new colour as it gasps away	59	Harold	4	260
And venerably simple, such as raise	59	Harold	4	277
Clear as its current, glide the sauntering hours	60	Harold	4	291
In melancholy bosoms, such as were	60	Harold	4	300
There seems as 'twere a curse upon the seats	60	Harold	4	309
Patron or tyrant, as the changing mood	60	Harold	4	313
Even as the beasts that perish, save that thou	60	Harold	4	335
Great as thou art, yet parallel'd by those	61	Harold	4	352
The friend of Tully. As my bark did skim	61	Harold	4	390
In ruin, even as he had seen the desolate sight	61	Harold	4	396
Mother of Arts, as once of arms; thy hand	62	Harold	4	417
We stand as captives and would not depart	62	Harold	4	446
And gazing in thy face as toward a star	62	Harold	4	455
Shower'd on his eyelids, brow, and mouth, as from an urn	62	Harold	4	459
The gods become as mortals, and man's fate	63	Harold	4	463
Such as the great of yore, Canova is to-day	63	Harold	4	495
In death as life? Are they resolved to dust	63	Harold	4	501
Yet for this want more noted, as of yore	64	Harold	4	524
Come back before me, as his skill beguiles	64	Harold	4	554
The Earth to them was as a rolling bark	64	Harold	4	568
Her aged trees rise thick as once the slain	64	Harold	4	580
The fall of waters! rapid as the light	65	Harold	4	615
As if to sweep down all things in its track	65	Harold	4	638
Like spirits of the spot, as 'twere for fame	66	Harold	4	660
A world is at our feet as fragile as our clay	66	Harold	4	702
But Rome is as the desert where we steer	67	Harold	4	726
Where, as a monument of antique art	68	Harold	4	787
At apish distance; but as yet none have	68	Harold	4	798
And blood of earth flow on as they have flow'd	68	Harold	4	825
Such as Columbia saw arise when she	69	Harold	4	858
Firm as a fortress, with its fence of stone	69	Harold	4	884
Such as an army's baffled strength delays	70	Harold	4	885
Was she as those who love their lords, or they	70	Harold	4	901
It seems as if I had thine inmate known	70	Harold	4	929
As I now hear them, in the fading light	71	Harold	4	949
Tully was not so eloquent as thou	71	Harold	4	982
As thine ideal breast! whate'er thou art	72	Harold	4	1029
Of summer-birds sing welcome as ye pass	72	Harold	4	1048
And Love, which dies as it was born, in sighing	73	Harold	4	1065
Which spring beneath her steps as Passion flies	73	Harold	4	1078
The naked eye, thy form, as it should be	73	Harold	4	1085
The mind hath made thee, as it peopled heaven	73	Harold	4	1086
As haunts the unquench'd soul--parch'd--wearied--wrung--and riven	73	Harold	4	1089
Conceive in boyhood and pursue as men	73	Harold	4	1095
Is bitterer still. As charm by charm unwinds	73	Harold	4	1100
Some phantom lures, such as we sought at first	73	Harold	4	1111
Arches on arches! as it were that Rome	74	Harold	4	1144
As 'twere its natural torches, for divine	74	Harold	4	1148
As rots the souls of those whom I survey	75	Harold	4	1215
To the small whisper of the as paltry few	75	Harold	4	1219
As man was slaughter'd by his fellow man	76	Harold	4	1245
Dashing or winding as its torrent strays	76	Harold	4	1273
Fresh as a nursing mother, in whose vein	77	Harold	4	1330
With life, as our freed souls rejoin the universe	77	Harold	4	1359
See thy God face to face as thou dost now	78	Harold	4	1394
And as the ocean many bays will make	78	Harold	4	1407
Is but of gradual grasp: and as it is	78	Harold	4	1415
And he himself as nothing:--if he was	79	Harold	4	1473
Such as arises when a nation bleeds	80	Harold	4	1497
Whose shock was as an earthquake's, and opprest	81	Harold	4	1547
And, calm as cherish'd hate, its surface wears	81	Harold	4	1555
All coil'd into itself and round, as sleeps the snake	81	Harold	4	1557
And reap from earth, sea, joy almost as dear	81	Harold	4	1583
As if there were no man to trouble what is clear	81	Harold	4	1584
These are thy toys, and, as the snowy flake	82	Harold	4	1627
Such as creation's dawn beheld, thou rollest now	82	Harold	4	1638
For I was as it were a child of thee	82	Harold	4	1654
And laid my hand upon thy mane--as I do here	82	Harold	4	1656
The King of Terrors seized her as his prey	84	Death-B		7
Throbb'd with deep sorrow as thine own	90	Caroline-A		8
And as thy tongue essay'd to speak	90	Caroline-A		15

AS

	Page	Title	Line
Which God has proclaim'd as the fate of his creatures	91	Caroline-C	15
But as death, my beloved, soon or late shall o'ertake us	91	Caroline-C	21
And quaff the contents as our nectar below	91	Caroline-C	28
As ancient Rome, fast falling to disgrace	93	Masters	3
So you, degenerate, share as hard a fate	93	Masters	5
Such as were ne'er before enforced in schools	93	Masters	12
There sleep, unnoticed as the gloomy vaults	94	Dorset	55
As first in rank, the first in talent too	94	Dorset	62
And gild their pinions as the moments flew	94	Dorset	82
Scenes hail'd, as exiles hail their native shore	94	Dorset	88
No more, as once, in social hours rejoice	94	Dorset	105
Will leave thee glorious, as he found thee great	94	Dorset	112
I'll turn mine eye, as night grows later	95	Granta	26
As every sense is steep'd in wine	95	Granta	56
Even as a band of raw beginners	96	Granta	78
As reclining, at eve, on yon tombstone I lay	96	Harrow-A	14
Where, as Zanga, I trod on Alonzo o'erthrown	96	Harrow-A	18
Or, as Lear, I pour'd forth the deep imprecation	96	Harrow-A	21
I regarded myself as a Garrick revived	96	Harrow-A	24
For did those eyes as planets roll	97	To M--	25
Though strong as mortal art could give	98	To Mary	2
Lifeless, unfeeling as thou art	98	To Mary	18
Yet, as perchance one trembling tear	99	Young Lady	13
Love twined round their childhood his flow'rs as they grew	99	L Adieu	14
Counsel like mine is as a brother's	100	Marion	35
Then let us meet, as oft we've done	101	Lady-B	33
Keen as the lightning of the storm	102	Alva	75
The big tear starting as he spoke	104	Alva	206
But Oscar's breast is cold as clay	104	Alva	277
As yet a novice in the martial strife	105	Nisus	12
A soul heroic, as his form was fair	105	Nisus	14
As one unfit to share the toils of war	106	Nisus	42
So may I triumph, as I speak the truth	106	Nisus	57
Through wine and blood, commingling as they flow	109	Nisus	273
When, as chaste Dian, here thou deign'st to rove	110	Nisus	344
And pour these accents, shrieking as he flies	110	Nisus	366
As some young rose, whose blossom scents the air	110	Nisus	379
Now dearer as my peaceful home	111	Medea	34
As all around sit wrapt in speechless gloom	111	Examination	5
Dull as the pictures which adorn their halls	112	Examination	53
Vain as their honours, heavy as their ale	112	Examination	59
Sad as their wit, and tedious as their tale	112	Examination	60
As thus our glances oft conversed	112	Quaker	21
For as on thee my memory ponders	112	Quaker	27
And blushes modest as the giver	113	Cornelian-A	4
As fearful that I might refuse it	113	Cornelian-A	10
And sparkling as I held it near	113	Cornelian-A	14
As all his errors slumber'd in the grave	114	Death-A	16
As he bends o'er the wave which may soon be his grave	115	The Tear	15
May we meet, as we part, with a Tear	115	The Tear	40
As ye pass by the tomb where my ashes consume	115	The Tear	43
As your fair was so devilish reserved	116	Strephon	12
Such love as you plead is pure love indeed	116	Strephon	35
From this we suppose (as indeed well we may	117	To Eliza	25
And wives, as in life, aim at absolute sway	117	To Eliza	27
As daily I strode through the pine-cover'd glade	117	Lachin	12
Confess that woman's false as fair	118	Romance	23
Soon as the gloaming spreads her waning shade	120	Newstead-A	34
And Nature triumphs as the tyrant dies	121	Newstead-A	104
Earth shudders as her caves receive his bones	121	Newstead-A	107
Their joys were many, as their cares were few	121	Newstead-A	132
Hours splendid as the past may still be thine	122	Newstead-A	155
And bless thy future as thy former day	122	Newstead-A	156
As when through clouds that pour the summer storm	122	Recoll	17
And tease the grumbling rustic as he goes	124	Recoll	140
As speakers each supports an equal name	126	Recoll	335
As infant laurels round my head were twined	126	Recoll	348
While Care as yet withheld her venom'd tooth	127	Recoll	390
As those where Youth her garland twined for you	127	Recoll	400
Is not so dear to me as this	128	Lady-C	10
Deceit is a stranger as yet to my soul	129	Becher-A	33
As roll the waves of the ocean on	130	Calmar	139
men of Lochlin on the chiefs. As, breaking	131	Calmar	141
of a chief? Bright as the gold of the	131	Calmar	159
soul, Orla! yet soft to me as the dew of	131	Calmar	176
Again, as once, in converse gay	132	L'Amitie	48
Our raptured visions as before	133	E.N. Long	22
Yes, as you knew me in the days	133	E.N. Long	43
As, when the ebbing flames are low	134	E.N. Long	79
As many a boy and girl remembers	134	E.N. Long	84
As once this pledge appear'd a token	134	Lady-D	2
And rude as the rocks where my infancy grew	135	Highlander	6
As I felt, when a boy, on the crag-cover'd wild	135	Highlander	12
I arose with the dawn; with my dog as my guide	136	Highlander	17
As the last of my race, I must wither alone	136	Highlander	27
But while these soar above me, unchanged as before	136	Highlander	43
Was such as pleasure seldom showers	137	Clare	5
As when one parent spring supplies	137	Clare	19
Nor mingle as before	137	Clare	27
As void of wit and moral	137	Clare	48
Perhaps they would do quite as well	137	Clare	61
Be still as you were wont to be	138	Clare	94
Spotless as you've been known to me	138	Clare	95
Be still as you are now	138	Clare	96
Oh! as I trace again thy winding hill	138	Harrow-B	7
Where, as they once were wont, my limbs recline	138	Harrow-B	11
And seem to whisper, as they gently swell	138	Harrow-B	15
Round as the shield which graced my god-like Sire	139	Ossian-A	2
As gleams the moonbeam through the broken cloud	139	Ossian-A	31
Swift as your wings my happier days have past	140	Ossian-A	49
Keen as your storms is Sorrow's chilling blast	140	Ossian-A	50
Round as the orb of my forefathers' shield	140	Ossian-B	2
For Age is dark, unlovely, as the light	140	Ossian-B	37
Glimmering uncertain as they hurry past	140	Ossian-B	39
As by the fix'd decrees of Heaven	140	Pignus	1
When such as you revile my Name	142	Critics	91
Such, such as you will serve to show	142	Critics	95
Parsons as well as other folks must live	142	Soliloquy	22
As in the field of combat, side by side	143	Soliloquy	81
I've lived, as many other men live	144	Becher-B	5
As certain stanzas also show it	144	Becher-B	19
But not so wicked as they make me	145	Becher-B	58
For such a cursed place as This is	145	Becher-B	64
But as Love of Existence itself's the beginning	145	Casuists	3
Fresh as in Love's bewitching dream	146	Adieu	56
As the ivy and oak, in the forest entwined	147	To Anne-A	9
In one who felt as once he felt	148	A Fan	1
As when the ebbing flames are low	148	A Fan	5
As many a boy and girl remembers	148	A Fan	10
And as he, with his boys, shall revisit this spot	149	Newstead-B	33
Repentance placed them as before	150	Harrow-C	9
Bright as thy mother's in their hue	150	My Son	2
In word, as well as Deed	151	Harriet	6
As thy soul shall immortally be	151	Soul-A	6
As still my soul hath been to thee	152	Time-A	4
None, none hath sunk so deep as this	152	Time-A	9
Transient as every faithless kiss	152	Time-A	11
With every feeling soft as thine	152	Weep-A	18
As half reproach'd yet raised desire	152	Remind	15
As if in kisses to expire	152	Remind	18
And senseless as the mouldering stone	153	Remind	35
Which made thee fickle as thou art	153	Friend-A	16
As rolls the ocean's changing tide	153	Friend-A	17
As glow-worms sparkle through the night	153	Friend-A	51
As flies along the gay parterre	153	Friend-A	63
Which seems, as marshy vapours move	153	Friend-A	66
Warmly, as it was wont to do	154	Happy	4
That friends, rosy wine! are so faithful as thou	155	Goblet	12
That truth, as of yore, is confined to the bowl	155	Goblet	24
As some lone bird, without a mate	156	Lady-F	19
Yet still beats on as it begun	156	Lady-F	47
With charms perchance as fair to view	156	Lady-F	56
And I would fain have loved as well	156	Lady-F	57
Stuck together close as wax	157	Hodgson	30
As the hatchway down he rolls	157	Hodgson	54
As philosophers allow	157	Hodgson	70
Then laugh on--as I do now	157	Hodgson	72
As o'er the cold sepulchral stone	157	Album	1
Reflect on me as on the dead	157	Album	7
And who so cold as look on thee	158	Florence	25
As spot of thy nativity	158	Florence	40
And lightnings, as they play	158	Storm	6
'Twere hard if aught so fair as thou	159	Storm	47
As in those hours of revelry	159	Storm	51
Florence! whom I will love as well	159	Gulf	9
As ever yet was said or sung	159	Gulf	10
Had bards as many realms as rhymes	159	Gulf	15
And he that acts as wise men ought	159	Spell	7
But lives, as saints have died, a martyr	159	Spell	8
And as along her bosom steal	160	Cadiz	13
And swam for Love, as I for Glory	160	Swimming	16
As yet unspoil'd by sacrilegious hands	161	Athos	8
As with advancing age your woes increase	161	Athos	23
Ten thousand just as fit for him as you	161	Substitute	4
As the branch, at the bidding of Nature	162	Romaic-A	9
As the chief who to combat advances	162	Romaic-A	25
With verse immortal as his sole	163	Blacket	10
As bad--but in a different way	163	Malta	24
As here, indeed, I need not flatter	163	Malta	38
In the dome of my Sires as the clear moonbeam falls	164	Newstead-C	1
As fond and faultless as her child	164	Friend-B	30
Have kiss'd as if without design	164	Friend-B	37
Had flow'd as fast--as now they flow	165	Thyrza	24
Sweet Thyrza! waking as in sleep	166	Away	25
Is silent--ah, were mine as still	166	Struggle	46
Though cold as e'en the dead can be	166	Struggle	47
Will shrink, as shrinks the ebbing breath	167	Euthanasia	22
And thou art dead, as young and fair	167	Dead	1
As aught of mortal birth	167	Dead	2
As fervently as thou	167	Dead	20

AS

As stars that shoot along the sky	167 Dead	53
Shine brightest as they fall from high	167 Dead	54
As once I wept, if I could weep	167 Dead	55
As all can tell, who share, like me	169 Blank Leaf	3
As glared the volumed blaze, and ghastly shone	169 Address-A	13
The skies with lightnings awful as their own	169 Address-A	14
As soars this fane to emulate the last	169 Address-A	27
Names such as hallow still the dome we lost	169 Address-A	30
Vain of our ancestry as they of theirs	170 Address-A	45
To claim the sceptred shadows as they pass	170 Address-A	47
As if Sir Fretful wrote 'the slumberous' verse	170 Address-B	5
'Tis twenty guineas, as they advertise	171 Address-B	50
When vice and folly mark them as they pass	171 Hales-Owen	10
Whose love is as sincere as sweet	173 Not False	10
As if a dream alone had charm'd	173 Not False	22
Enjoy the moments as they flee	173 Quotation	30
It seem'd as if for me alone	173 Mrs. Lamb	7
Our hearts as fond, thy hand more free	174 Remember-B	22
Far may thy days, as heretofore	174 Remember-B	25
As if its guilt had made thee mine	174 Remember-B	52
Soft as the last drops round heaven's airy bow	175 Sonnet-B	8
Life is as transient as the inconstant sigh	175 Portuguese-A	11
To see my manor as much as I may	176 Devil's Dr	17
But first as he flew, I forgot to say	176 Devil's Dr	31
Nor his work done half as well	176 Devil's Dr	39
As round her fell her long fair hair	176 Devil's Dr	69
The Devil first saw, as he thought, the Mail	177 Devil's Dr	91
To redeem as he came away	177 Devil's Dr	106
And never such a treat, as--the epistle of one 'Vetus	177 Devil's Dr	125
But he heard, as he purposed to enter in there	177 Devil's Dr	135
And he thought, as a 'quondam aristocrat	177 Devil's Dr	137
As natural to him as its hole to a Mouse	178 Devil's Dr	156
And others as suited their fancies	178 Devil's Dr	164
Of hearing him talk as he ought	178 Devil's Dr	178
As he swallow'd down the bacon he wish'd himself a Jew	178 Devil's Dr	211
And as one of them wrote down the pronoun 'We	179 Devil's Dr	243
For thee, and such as thee, behold	179 Gold	25
All Evil Spirit as thou art	181 Ode-A	77
If thou hadst died as honour dies	181 Ode-A	95
Is vile as vulgar clay	181 Ode-A	101
That Earth is now as free	181 Ode-A	124
And, if a mortal, had as proudly died	181 Ode-A	144
As if that foolish robe could wring	181 Ode-A	156
And our days seem as swift, and our moments more sweet	182 Music-A	15
The blood which flow'd with Wallace flows as free	182 Address-C	11
These are not lessen'd, these are still as bright	183 Address-D	43
As he had slept not fainted in that hour	185 Julian	55
And woke from Slumber--as the Birds awake	185 Julian	56
'Tis but as ivy-leaves around the ruin'd turret wreath	186 Music-B	15
Oh could I feel as I have felt,--or be what I have been	186 Music-B	17
Or weep as I could once have wept, o'er many a vanish'd scene	186 Music-B	18
As springs in deserts found seem sweet, all brackish though they be	186 Music-B	19
As cavern'd waters wear the stone	186 Stanzas-A	11
But thy weakness decrees I should leave as I found thee	186 Napoleon	11
Dear as both have been to me	187 French-A	6
As his foes I now implore	187 French-A	36
As then shall shake the world with wonder	187 Ode-B	15
As o'er heaven shall then be bright'ning	187 Ode-B	17
Such as he of Naples wears	187 Ode-B	42
Once--as the Moon sways o'er the tide	187 Ode-B	52
And, as it onward rolling rose	187 Ode-B	58
Freedom, such as God hath given	188 Ode-B	83
When, as if its sound were causing	188 Music-C	5
As an infant's asleep	188 Music-C	12
As thou didst lighten through all space	188 On Star	16
Wore an unearthly aspect, as by fits	189 Darkness	23
Died, and their bones were tombless as their flesh	189 Darkness	45
Their eyes as it grew lighter, and beheld	190 Darkness	65
And their masts fell down piecemeal; as they dropp'd	190 Darkness	76
So soon, and so successless? As I said	190 Churchill	19
Of which we are but dreamers;--as he caught	190 Churchill	25
As 'twere the twilight of a former Sun	190 Churchill	26
Some certain coins of silver, which as 'twere	190 Churchill	34
Were not as things that gods despise	191 Prometheus-B	4
But baffled as thou wert from high	191 Prometheus-B	39
But bid it flow as now--until it glides	191 Fragment-C	5
As midnight in my solitude?--O Earth	192 Fragment-C	31
To them thy banks were lovely as to all	192 Sonnet-C	5
Sink on the heart, as dew along the flower	192 Monody	4
Even as the tenderness that hour instils	192 Monody	19
Till vanquish'd senates trembled as they praised	193 Monody	46
Complete in kind--as various in their change	194 Monody	110
As may disgust the ear of kings	195 Ballad-A	68

AS

And as these things the old Moor said	195 Ballad-A	101
'Twas carried, as the King decreed	195 Ballad-A	104
The King weeps as a woman o'er	195 Ballad-A	107
Mark that (as he masks the bilious	196 Rogers	27
To thee, as he, the Slayer, stood	197 Duel	9
For I can boast a race as true	197 Duel	15
As ever Britain's Annals knew	197 Duel	17
We must endure it as a test	198 Duel	53
Wild as thy wave, and headlong as thy speed	198 Po	8
Such as my feelings were and are, thou art	198 Po	11
And such as thou art were my passions long	198 Po	12
As various as the climates of our birth	198 Po	40
Is all meridian, as if never fann'd	198 Po	43
Live as I lived, and love as I have loved	199 Po	50
As from a dream	200 Stanzas-B	49
As through the past	200 Stanzas-B	72
Perchance might look on Love as Crime	200 Ode-C	9
And not as common Mortals love	201 Ode-C	30
Thy Lover died, as All	201 Ode-C	59
As thou within	201 Ode-C	71
Constant to thee as in its hour	201 Ode-C	81
As many a baffled Heart can tell	201 Ode-C	84
Then receive him as best such an advent becomes	202 Avatar	19
Were he God--as he is but the commonest clay	202 Avatar	30
(As the bankrupt's profusion his ruin would hide	203 Avatar	54
With what monarchs ne'er give, but as wolves yield their prey	203 Avatar	60
Deep, deep as the gore which he shed on her soil	203 Avatar	90
My vote, as a freeman's still voted thee free	203 Avatar	106
Who are gone, but I weep them no longer as once	204 Avatar	112
'Tis but as a dead-flower with May-dew besprinkled	204 Pisa	6
Were I now as I was, I had sung	205 Blessington	5
And my heart is as grey as my head	205 Blessington	12
There are moments which act as a plough	205 Blessington	14
But is deep in my soul as my brow	205 Blessington	16
And men and nature reel'd as if with wine	206 Love, Death	14
Of thine to me is as an adder's eye	206 Greece	6
Is lone as some volcanic isle	206 Year	10
As many a nameless slander deftly shows	208 Sketch	16
Eternal evil latent as she lurks	208 Sketch	52
Till the black slime betray her as she crawls	209 Sketch	48
As in a mirror of itself defined	209 Sketch	72
As loathsome to thyself as to mankind	209 Sketch	88
Black--as thy will for others would create	209 Sketch	90
Oh, may thy grave be sleepless as the bed	209 Sketch	93
Down to the dust!--and, as thou rott'st away	209 Sketch	97
That watch'd me as a seraph's eye	209 Augusta-A	14
Thou stood'st, as stands a lovely tree	210 Augusta-A	25
As the breasts I believed in with me	210 Augusta-B	14
Recalling, as it lies beyond redress	211 Augusta-C	14
I feel almost at times as I have felt	211 Augusta-C	49
Come as of yore upon me, and can melt	211 Augusta-C'	53
Such scenes as those wherein my life begun	212 Augusta-C	91
I know myself secure, as thou in mine	212 Augusta-C	122
We were and are--I am, even as thou art	212 Augusta-C	123
And is it thus?--it is as I foretold	213 Lady Byron	5
The bitter harvest in a woe as real	213 Lady Byron	24
I would not do by thee as thou hast done	213 Lady Byron	60
A portion of ourselves as of our time	213 Dream	10
As 'twere the cape of a long ridge of such	214 Dream	30
Fair as herself--but the boy gazed on her	214 Dream	41
As the sweet moon on the horizon's verge	214 Dream	44
Even as a brother--but no more; 'twas much	214 Dream	64
His bow'd head on his hands, and shook as 'twere	214 Dream	83
Into a kind of quiet: as he paused	214 Dream	88
Was traced, and then it faded, as it came	215 Dream	98
Retired, but not as bidding her adieu	215 Dream	100
As if its lid were charged with unshed tears	215 Dream	135
The Starlight of his Boyhood;--as he stood	215 Dream	148
As in that hour--a moment o'er his face	215 Dream	153
Was traced--and then it faded as it came	215 Dream	155
As by the sickness of the soul; her mind	215 Dream	169
The Wanderer was alone as heretofore	216 Dream	185
To sounds that seem as from above	217 The Harp	19
A step as fleet, an eye more bright	217 Gazelle	7
That the blood of thy child is as pure	218 Jephtha	10
As the blessing I beg ere it flow	218 Jephtha	11
And forget not I smiled as I died	218 Jephtha	20
Fond wretch! as if her step disturb'd the dead	218 Bloom	10
As clouds from yonder sun receive	218 I Saw	9
Saul saw, and fell to earth, as falls the oak	219 Saul-B	13
Its years as moments shall endure	220 Clay	28
And wrote as if on sand	220 Belshaz-B	12
Were my bosom as false as thou deem'st it to be	221 False	1
As the God who permits thee to prosper doth know	221 False	10
Had reflected the last beam of day as it blazed	221 Jerusalem	10
And scatter'd and scorn'd as thy people may be	221 Jerusalem	19
And breathed in the face of the foe as he pass'd	222 Sennacherib	10
And cold as the spray of the rock-beating surf	222 Sennacherib	16
And as my damp hair stiffen'd, thus it spake	222 Spirit	6
In our souls, as the wind that hath died on the hill	223 Valley	6

AS

As dead as her dead leaf those mute harps must be	223 Valley	10
As curst an old Lady as ever was seen	223 Soul-C	2
In Wit, in Genius, as in Wealth the first	223 To Dives	5
One song for self and Fletcher quite as well	224 J.C.H.	8
To-morrow be with me, as soon as you can, sir	226 Oh You	6
And owls sent to Athens, as wonders	227 Thorlow-B	19
Who, lovely as ever, seem'd just as delighted	228 Moore-A	24
With majesty's presence as those she invited	228 Moore-A	25
As the Liberty lads o'er the sea	229 Lads	1
Though black as his heart its hue	229 Lads	11
Though the heart be still as loving	229 Roving	3
And the moon be still as bright	229 Roving	4
(At least, it has not been as yet	230 Murray-A	4
Because as how, if you should fail	230 Murray-A	8
As I gasp'd upon the brink	230 My Boat	14
With that water, as this wine	230 My Boat	17
As I was saying, Sir, the Room	231 Doctor	52
As ready to print off	232 Murray-B	8
But as yet I have writ off	232 Murray-B	10
As you'll see in the trash he calls Tasso's	232 Murray-B	30
While others are or would seem as sick	233 Nihil	15
Wondrous as antient war or hero	233 Nihil	21
He writes as well as any Miss	233 Ballad-B	9
And barren as each valley	233 Ballad-B	38
As William Wordsworth is for once	234 Epilogue	5
As William Wordsworth is for once	235 Epilogue	7
But as few as you please of the day	235 New Year	4
As member for the Mobby O	235 New Song	16
As under Walpole Bobby O	235 New Song	20
And, as that is the case, you had best put to press	236 Nonsense	7
And is always as nobly requited	236 Freedom	6
The perusal of whom (as I told you at Mestri	237 Braziers	8
Fool! live as I live--as thy father lives	237 Lucifer	2
And if, as the opinion goes	238 Orford	9
As the saint keeps her charity back for 'the Ball	238 Pangs	8
In his doctrine, at least as a teacher	238 Bray	9
As a knave or a fool	238 Bray	11
He mounted another as preacher	238 Bray	12
From such as himself, who would render	239 Bray	33
As a sinner, you can't care what Sin does	239 Bray	42
Should be free as the former from evil	239 Impromptu-B	3
As our ploughshare is the Sabre	240 Suliotes	13
And shall we own such judgment? no--as soon	242 Bards	75
And hail their voice as truth, their word as law	243 Bards	86
Go on; my rhyme will tell you as you read	243 Bards	96
And, rear'd by taste, bloom'd fairer as they grew	243 Bards	108
And raised the people's, as the poet's fame	243 Bards	112
What varied wonders tempt us as they pass	243 Bards	131
As even in ruin bids the language live	244 Bards	198
Tells us strange tales, as other travellers do	245 Bards	223
As thou art strong in verse, in mercy, spare	245 Bards	227
As soft as evening in his favourite May	245 Bards	238
As sweet, but as immoral, in his lay	245 Bards	288
Ere miss as yet completes her infant years	246 Bards	346
Such as none heard before, or will again	246 Bards	352
Write, as if St. John's soul could still inspire	247 Bards	377
As Sisyphus against the infernal steep	247 Bards	411
His blossoms wither as the blast prevails	247 Bards	423
A coward brood, which mangle as they prey	247 Bards	430
To sentence letters, as he sentenced men	247 Bards	443
With hand less mighty, but with heart as black	247 Bards	444
With voice as willing to decree the rack	247 Bards	445
As yet hath taught him is to find a flaw	247 Bards	447
Skill'd to condemn as to traduce mankind	248 Bards	457
On such occasions, feel as much as man	248 Bards	477
Caught it, as Danae caught the golden show'r	248 Bards	495
For long as Albion's heedless sons submit	248 Bards	502
Give, as thy last memorial to the age	249 Bards	584
But as some hands applaud, a venal few	250 Bards	606
As for the smaller fry, who swarm in shoals	251 Bards	707
Whose hairs grow hoary as his rhymes grow worse	251 Bards	730
Such damning fame as Dunciads only give	252 Bards	751
Feel as they write, and write but as they feel	253 Bards	817
Let these, or such as these, with just applause	254 Bards	891
As first in freedom, dearest to the muse	255 Bards	996
Let coxcombs, printing as they come from far	255 Bards	1025
Or low Dubost--as once the world has seen	256 Hints	7
Poets and painters, as all artists know	257 Hints	15
As pertness passes with a legal gown	257 Hints	24
As Vulcan's feet to bear Apollo's frame	257 Hints	56
(As Pitt has furnish'd us a word or two	257 Hints	75
As well as William Pitt and Walter Scott	257 Hints	84
Reform in writing, as in parliament	257 Hints	88
As forests shed their foliage by degrees	257 Hints	89
Though as a monarch nods, and commerce calls	258 Hints	93
As custom arbitrates, whose shifting sway	258 Hints	103
This point, as puzzling as a Chancery suit	258 Hints	114
Make it appear as if it might have been	259 Hints	172
Soft as the gentler breathing of the lute	259 Hints	201
He speaks, but, as his subject swells along	259 Hints	203
As if we witness'd all already done	259 Hints	206
Gives, as each page improves upon the sight	259 Hints	209
Master of arts! as hells and clubs proclaim	260 Hints	241
As oft at home, with revelry and rhyme	261 Hints	346
As pious Calvin saw Servetus blaze	262 Hints	377
Poetic more, as philosophic, fame	263 Hints	456
I'll labour gratis as a grinder's wheel	263 Hints	485
'Tis just as well to think before you write	263 Hints	492
Who models his deportment as may best	263 Hints	497
Who takes our laws and worship as they are	263 Hints	499
As joint exemplar of his life and verse	263 Hints	504
Is poor as Irus or an Irish mine	264 Hints	530
As pictures, so shall poems be; some stand	264 Hints	571
Again, my Jeffrey!--as that sound inspires	265 Hints	589
Fires, such as gentle Caledonians feel	265 Hints	591
As bold in Billingsgate, though less renown'd	265 Hints	626
As if at table some discordant dish	265 Hints	627
Should shock our optics, such as frogs for fish	265 Hints	628
As oil in lieu of butter men decry	265 Hints	629
Fierce as a bride when first she feels affright	266 Hints	691
Mild as the same upon the second night	266 Hints	692
Wild as the wife of alderman or peer	266 Hints	693
Fool on, as fluent as an Orpheus' head	266 Hints	720
Till, lo! that modern Midas, as he hears	266 Hints	735
Dull as his sermons, but not half so brief	267 Hints	768
As when the dying vicar will not die	267 Hints	778
As critics kindly do, and authors ought	267 Hints	794
As the Scotch fiddle, with its touching tune	267 Hints	805
As yawning waiters fly Fitzscribble's lungs	268 Hints	808
As prelate's homily or placeman's speech	268 Hints	810
Long as the last years of a lingering lease	268 Hints	811
'A rope! help, Christians, as ye hope for grace	268 Hints	817
Prick not the poet's conscience as a curse	268 Hints	834
Not, as in northern climes, obscurely bright	268 Minerva	3
Gilds the green wave that trembles as it glows	268 Minerva	6
Who lived and died as none can live or die	268 Minerva	32
With cornice glimmering as the moonbeams play	269 Minerva	37
As thus, within the walls of Pallas' fane	269 Minerva	55
Oft as the matchless dome I turn'd to scan	269 Minerva	59
Not such as first, by her divine command	269 Minerva	77
Foul as their soil and frigid as their snows	270 Minerva	142
As dull Boeotia gave a Pindar birth	270 Minerva	150
As once of yore in some obnoxious place	270 Minerva	155
Be all the sons as senseless as the sire	270 Minerva	166
Some calm spectator, as he takes his view	271 Minerva	196
As Egypt chose an onion for a god	272 Minerva	258
His deeper deeds as yet we know by name	272 Minerva	299
Thy legs must move to conquer as they fly	273 Waltz	9
As heaven-born Pitt can testify below	274 Waltz	40
Of true despatches and as true gazettes	274 Waltz	68
Of Heyne, such as should not sink the packet	274 Waltz	78
As Love or Hymen your endeavours guide	275 Waltz	105
The lady's in return may grasp as much	276 Waltz	194
As princely paunches offer to her touch	276 Waltz	195
Asmodeus struck so bright a stroke as this	276 Waltz	223
Will wear as green a bough for him as me	277 Waltz	255
As one finds every author in one of those places	277 Blues	1	21
That it is, as the phrase goes, extremely 'refreshing	277 Blues	1	25
Pray get out of this hobble as fast as you can	278 Blues	1	64
I say she's a Blue, man, as blue as the ether	278 Blues	1	69
What? I perhaps may as well hold my tongue	278 Blues	1	75
You forget Lady lilac's as rich as a Jew	278 Blues	1	77
Her life is as good as your own, I will bet	278 Blues	1	82
Let her live, and as long as she likes; I demand	278 Blues	1	83
My talent is decent, as far as it goes	279 Blues	1	88
And so, as I can't, will you furnish a few	279 Blues	1	92
Are you so far advanced as to hazard this	279 Blues	1	96
So far as to tremble to tell her in rhyme	279 Blues	1	97
What I've told her in prose, at least, as sublime	279 Blues	1	98
As sublime!--Mr. Tracy--I've nothing to say	279 Blues	1	101
Stick to prose--as sublime!!--but I wish you good day	279 Blues	1	102
I've a card, and shall go: but at present, as soon	279 Blues	1	133
As friend Scamp shall be pleased to step down from the moon	279 Blues	1	134
Who are brought to my house as an inn, to my cost	280 Blues	2	18
Would to God I were deaf! as I'm not, I'll be dumb	280 Blues	2	25
And their gatherers, as Homer sung warriors and kings	281 Blues	2	49
He has just got a place. 'As a footman? For shame	281 Blues	2	50
To wear a new livery; the more, as 'tis not	281 Blues	2	54
And fear,' as the Greek says: for 'purging the mind	282 Blues	2	80
As is usual in that most litigious of arts	282 Blues	2	87
Of the soul; 'tis the seizing of shades as they pass	283 Blues	2	140
To the knight, as a landlord, much more than the Duke	283 Blues	2	147
And 'a pull all together,' as they say	285 Vision	7
As boats are sometimes by a wanton whale	285 Vision	16

AS

Which peopled earth no better, hell as wont	285	Vision	50
One half as mad, and t'other no less blind	286	Vision	64
What nature made him at his birth, as bare	286	Vision	86
As the mere million's base unmummied clay	286	Vision	87
God knows, as helpless as the devil can wish	286	Vision	114
As one day will be that immortal fry	286	Vision	119
Waving a goodly wing, which glow'd, as glows	287	Vision	133
If I had had my sword, as I had once	287	Vision	149
So as to make a martyr, never sped	287	Vision	159
He did as doth the puppet--by its wire	287	Vision	172
Which is to act as we are bid to do	287	Vision	176
Cleaving the fields of space, as doth the swan	287	Vision	179
As he drew near, he gazed upon the gate	288	Vision	193
As made Saint Peter wish himself within	288	Vision	196
As things were in this posture, the gate flew	288	Vision	209
In either's eye, as if 'twere less their will	289	Vision	254
As sets aside the slightest thought of trick	289	Vision	270
And accurate as any other vision	289	Vision	272
He turn'd as to an equal not too low	289	Vision	285
With more hauteur, as might an old Castilian	289	Vision	287
His duties as a king and mortal, say	289	Vision	303
That as he was my worshipper in dust	289	Vision	308
'And these but as a kind of quit-rent, to	290	Vision	321
Assert my right as lord; and even had	290	Vision	322
I such an inclination, 'twere (as you	290	Vision	323
(I have the workmen safe); but as a tool	290	Vision	346
Nations as men, home subjects, foreign foes	290	Vision	354
As temperance, if at Apicius' board	290	Vision	357
As one of Satan's most sublime inventions	291	Vision	416
As have the privilege of their damnation	291	Vision	418
They are proud of this--as very well they may	291	Vision	425
From our sun to its earth,--as we can tell	291	Vision	435
Of locusts numerous as the heavens saw these	292	Vision	460
Who damn'd away his eyes as heretofore	292	Vision	466
As the first coachman will; and 'midst the war	292	Vision	470
Bitter as clubs in cards are against spades	292	Vision	478
As angels can; next, like Italian twilight	292	Vision	482
He turn'd all colours--as a peacock's tail	292	Vision	483
As to speak first? there's choice enough	293	Vision	518
But you may choose Jack Wilkes as well as any	293	Vision	520
Almost as scanty, of days less remote	293	Vision	528
As we shall see), and jostled hands and knees	294	Vision	590
That look'd as it had been a shade on earth	294	Vision	594
But as you gazed upon its features, they	294	Vision	599
As oft as they their minds: though in full sight	294	Vision	613
'Three gentlemen at once' (as sagely says	294	Vision	626
Are fill'd as well without the latter too	295	Vision	644
For certain sure to claim them as his due	295	Vision	646
Thyself if false, as him if true? Thou wast	295	Vision	661
His way, and look'd as if his journey cost	295	Vision	676
Of Skiddaw (where as usual it still rain'd	295	Vision	685
I snatch'd him up just as you see him there	295	Vision	692
And scribbles as if head clerk to the Fates	296	Vision	708
When such an ass as this, like Balaam's, prates	296	Vision	710
Convulsed the skies, as during a debate	296	Vision	738
As at a farce; till, grown quite desperate	296	Vision	742
Was by no means so ugly as his case	296	Vision	750
But that indeed was hopeless as can be	296	Vision	751
With one still greater, as is yet the mode	296	Vision	754
Become as base a critic as e'er crawl'd	297	Vision	780
As it was once, but I would make you shine	297	Vision	798
Has more of brass in it, and is as well blown	297	Vision	800
Ambrosial and sulphureous, as they sprang	297	Vision	815
Those grand heroics acted as a spell	297	Vision	817
By their own rottenness, light as an elf	298	Vision	836
As Welborn says--'the devil turn'd precisian	298	Vision	840
As for the rest, to come to the conclusion	298	Vision	841
As the deep billows of the Aegean roar	298	Age	17
And, as thy nature urges, weep or smile	299	Age	54
Weep to perceive him mourning, as he dines	299	Age	59
As if his ashes found their latest home	300	Age	121
But be it as it is--the time may come	300	Age	129
Beheld the desert peopled, as from hell	300	Age	149
But left thee as he found thee, still a waste	300	Age	162
Thou other element! as strong and stern	300	Age	185
Before their sovereign,--sovereign as before	301	Age	206
A name eternal as the rolling year	301	Age	230
While Washington's a watchword, such as ne'er	301	Age	249
Such as repulsed the Persian from the shore	302	Age	270
Lotted by thousands, as a meet reward	302	Age	308
Demand her fields as lists to prove the sword	302	Age	321
That seed is sown and reap'd, as oft the Moor	302	Age	326
Of heaven's, as man is mimick'd by the ape	303	Age	397
Were so far like, as never to get out	304	Age	425
As eager for a plaudit as a realm	304	Age	436
And just as fit for flirting as the helm	304	Age	437
To be a kind host and as good a guest	305	Age	521
But honour them as portion of the show	307	Age	698
A common coin as ever mint could strike	307	Age	707
As his dismissal in the Moniteur	308	Age	720
'Almost as quickly as he conquer'd Spain	308	Age	724
And the ex-empress grows as ex a wife	308	Age	762
To see proud Albyn's tartans as a belt	308	Age	773

AS

As if for Gods, a dwelling-place	310	Giaour	47
But springs as to preclude his care	310	Giaour	56
It is as though the fiends prevail'd	311	Giaour	62
As if to him it could impart	311	Giaour	83
High as thine own in days of yore	311	Giaour	145
As meteor-like thou glidest by	312	Giaour	197
My gaze of wonder as he flew	312	Giaour	201
One glance he snatch'd, as if his last	312	Giaour	217
But pale as marble o'er the tomb	312	Giaour	238
As doubting to return or fly	312	Giaour	243
As Slumber starts at owlet's scream	312	Giaour	248
Swift as the hurl'd on high jerreed	312	Giaour	251
Then sped as if by death pursued	312	Giaour	260
For infinite as boundless space	313	Giaour	273
As springing high the silver dew	313	Giaour	301
Within that dome as yet Decay	313	Giaour	336
I watch'd it as it sank, methought	314	Giaour	376
As rising on its purple wing	314	Giaour	388
Then leaves him, as it soars on high	314	Giaour	394
With hue as bright, and wing as wild	314	Giaour	397
From rose to tulip as before	314	Giaour	413
In circle narrowing as its glows	314	Giaour	424
'Twas then she went as to the bath	314	Giaour	453
As large, as languishingly dark	315	Giaour	476
Bright as the jewel of Giamschid	315	Giaour	479
As midst her handmaids in the hall	315	Giaour	498
As rears her crest the ruffled Swan	315	Giaour	507
Her heart as tender to her mate	315	Giaour	516
Each arm'd, as best becomes a man	315	Giaour	521
The chief before, as deck'd for war	315	Giaour	523
The Chiaus spake, and as he said	316	Giaour	571
As rolls the river into ocean	316	Giaour	620
As the sea-tide's opposing motion	316	Giaour	622
Thus--as the stream and ocean greet	316	Giaour	632
With waves that madden as they meet	316	Giaour	633
And crimson as those clouds of morn	316	Giaour	662
As if the hour that seal'd his fate	317	Giaour	671
As dark as his that bled below	317	Giaour	674
There sleeps as true an Osmanlie	317	Giaour	729
As e'er at Mecca bent the knee	317	Giaour	730
As ever scorn'd forbidden wine	317	Giaour	731
Yet died he as in arms he stood	317	Giaour	737
But first, on earth as Vampire sent	317	Giaour	755
As cursing thee, thou cursing them	318	Giaour	765
I saw him urge as fleet a steed	318	Giaour	791
As ever served a horseman's need	318	Giaour	792
As death were stamp'd upon his brow	318	Giaour	797
And rave as to some bloody hand	318	Giaour	827
As if that eye and latter smile	318	Giaour	848
Then fix once more as if for ever	318	Giaour	854
As if his sorrow or disdain	318	Giaour	855
As if the Gorgon there had bound	319	Giaour	896
Lo!--mark ye, as the harmony	319	Giaour	905
It is as if the dead could feel	319	Giaour	945
And shudder, as the reptiles creep	319	Giaour	947
It is as if the desert-bird	319	Giaour	951
Such as thy penitents unfold	320	Giaour	979
Dark as to thee my deeds may seem	320	Giaour	999
To save or slay, as these require	320	Giaour	1020
As filed the troop to where they fell	321	Giaour	1079
Fierce as the gloomy vulture's now	321	Giaour	1159
Tell him, unheeding as I was	322	Giaour	1237
Throbb'd to the very brain as now	322	Giaour	1262
As something welcome, new, and dear	322	Giaour	1264
As through yon pale gray cloud the star	322	Giaour	1274
Which now I gaze on, as on her	322	Giaour	1275
As meet my eye, yet mock my touch	323	Giaour	1292
Where the virgins are soft as the roses they twine	323	Abydos	1	14
Can he smile on such deeds as his children have done	323	Abydos	1	17
Oh! wild as the accents of lovers' farewell	323	Abydos	1	18
Apparell'd as becomes the brave	324	Abydos	1	21
And, as thou knowest that for me	324	Abydos	1	66
As sneeringly these accents fell	325	Abydos	1	126
Sweet as the desert fountain's wave	325	Abydos	1	152
Fair as the first that fell of womankind	325	Abydos	1	158
Dazzling as that, oh! too transcendent vision	325	Abydos	1	162
Soft as the memory of buried love	325	Abydos	1	166
Pure as the prayer which Childhood wafts above	325	Abydos	1	167
And red to pale, as through her ears	326	Abydos	1	223
As if that breast were marble too	326	Abydos	1	276
As the stream late conceal'd	327	Abydos	1	332
As the bolt bursts on high	327	Abydos	1	336
Be only known to us as now	327	Abydos	1	370
As on that night of stormy water	329	Abydos	2	2
May nerve young hearts to prove as true	329	Abydos	2	19
As heaven itself to Selim dear	330	Abydos	2	90
And starting oft, as through the glade	330	Abydos	2	92
There arms were piled, not such as wield	330	Abydos	2	122
As I preserve that awful oath	331	Abydos	2	192
With venom subtle as his soul	331	Abydos	2	238
Besides, adoption as a son	331	Abydos	2	264
As if my weak unwilling hand	332	Abydos	2	327

AS

As if my spirit pierced them through	332	Abydos	2	347
Blest--as the Muezzin's strain from Mecca's wall	333	Abydos	2	402
Soft--as the melody of youthful days	333	Abydos	2	404
Dear--as his native song to Exile's ears	333	Abydos	2	406
Blooming as Aden in its earliest hour	333	Abydos	2	409
To thee be Selim's tender as thine own	333	Abydos	2	423
No--as each crest save his may feel	334	Abydos	2	538
There as his last step left the land	335	Abydos	2	561
As shaken on his restless pillow	335	Abydos	2	605
It looks as planted by Despair	336	Abydos	2	674
But soft as harp that Houri strings	336	Abydos	2	692
As if they loved in vain	336	Abydos	2	698
For there, as Helle's legends tell	337	Abydos	2	721
As weeping Beauty's cheek at Sorrow's tale	337	Abydos	2	732
Our thoughts as boundless and our souls as free	338	Corsair	1	2
Far as the breeze can bear, the billows foam	338	Corsair	1	3
And unto ears as rugged seem'd a song	338	Corsair	1	46
''T is he--'t is Conrad; here--as wont--alone	340	Corsair	1	133
But, this as if he guess'd, with head aside	340	Corsair	1	151
As if within that murkiness of mind	341	Corsair	1	211
Man as himself, the secret spirit free	341	Corsair	1	248
He cursed those virtues as the cause of ill	342	Corsair	1	257
And scorn'd the best as hypocrites who hid	342	Corsair	1	267
Oft could he sneer at others as beguiled	342	Corsair	1	283
As kindle high to-night (but blow, thou breeze	342	Corsair	1	321
Then trembles into silence as before	343	Corsair	1	350
Though vain its ray as it had never been	343	Corsair	1	354
And reach'd the chamber as the strain gave o'er	343	Corsair	1	364
As bright as this invites us not to roam	344	Corsair	1	391
At such as seem'd the fairest; thrice the hill	344	Corsair	1	425
One moment gazed--as if to gaze no more	345	Corsair	1	479
Again he hurries on--and as he hears	345	Corsair	1	521
As marks his eye the seaboy on the mast	345	Corsair	1	525
When echo'd to the heart as from his own	346	Corsair	1	549
Ah! never loved he half so much as now	346	Corsair	1	582
May watch as idly when thy power is nigh	348	Corsair	2	94
Along his cheek, and tranquillized as fast	348	Corsair	2	110
He shunn'd as if some poison mingled there	348	Corsair	2	114
'Well, as thou wilt--ascetic as thou art	349	Corsair	2	133
And blushes o'er his error, as he eyes	350	Corsair	2	233
The Pacha woo'd as if he deem'd the slave	351	Corsair	2	265
As if his homage were a woman's right	351	Corsair	2	268
That leaves the rest as once unseen, unsought	352	Corsair	2	339
That shines like snow and falls on earth as mute	353	Corsair	2	405
As if the last he could enjoy on earth	353	Corsair	2	457
Mine eye ne'er ask'd if others were as fair	354	Corsair	2	490
Whose hearts on hearts as faithful can repose	354	Corsair	2	494
That signs o'er visions--such as mine hath wrought	354	Corsair	2	496
Who share such love as I can never know	355	Corsair	2	532
And noiseless as a lovely dream is gone	355	Corsair	2	537
Not, as in northern climes, obscurely bright	355	Corsair	3	3
Gilds the green wave that trembles as it glows	355	Corsair	3	6
Who lived and died as none can live or die	356	Corsair	3	32
With cornice glimmering as the moonbeams play	356	Corsair	3	37
Though wild, as now, far different were the tale	356	Corsair	3	73
They yield such aid as Pity's haste supplies	357	Corsair	3	116
Whose deeds are daring as their hearts are true	357	Corsair	3	130
But inly views his victim as he bleeds	357	Corsair	3	140
Were offer'd rich as Stamboul's diadem	357	Corsair	3	154
Had proved unwilling as unfit to die	358	Corsair	3	217
As if some faithless friend had spurn'd his groan	359	Corsair	3	269
'T is as his heart foreboded--that fair she	359	Corsair	3	273
And beauteous still as hermit's hope can paint	359	Corsair	3	275
Though fond as mine her bosom, form more fair	360	Corsair	3	298
And gathering, as he could, the links that bound	361	Corsair	3	388
He, fast as fetter'd limbs allow, pursued	361	Corsair	3	391
Full on his brow, as if from morning air	361	Corsair	3	397
As if she late had bent her leaning head	361	Corsair	3	412
As now they froze before that purple stain	361	Corsair	3	425
Once more his limbs are free as mountain wind	362	Corsair	3	441
As if they there transferr'd that iron weight	362	Corsair	3	443
Resistance were as useless as if Seyd	362	Corsair	3	450
As its far shadow frown'd above the mast	362	Corsair	3	458
He veil'd his face and sorrow'd as he pass'd	362	Corsair	3	459
Returns their greeting as a chief may greet	363	Corsair	3	503
As he had fann'd them freshly with his wing	363	Corsair	3	554
As soon could he have linger'd there for day	364	Corsair	3	594
In that last grasp as tenderly were strain'd	364	Corsair	3	606
As if she scarcely felt, but feign'd a sleep	364	Corsair	3	607
But spares, as yet, the charm around her lips	364	Corsair	3	614
Yet, yet they seem as they forebore to smile	364	Corsair	3	615
Each feeling pure--as falls the dropping dew	365	Corsair	3	664
To those that wander as to those that stay	366	Lara	1	50
Yet seem'd as lately they had been alive	367	Lara	1	82
And--as himself would have it seem--unknown	367	Lara	1	88
As hardly worth a stranger's care to know	367	Lara	1	92
As if to startle all save him away	368	Lara	1	146
He wandering mused, and as the moonbeam shone	368	Lara	1	191
Dimm'd in the lamp, as loth to break the night	369	Lara	1	202
Cold as the marble where his length was laid	369	Lara	1	211
Pale as the beam that o'er his features play'd	369	Lara	1	212
Though mix'd with terror, senseless as he lay	369	Lara	1	217

AS

They were not such as Lara should avow	369	Lara	1	238
As heretofore he fill'd the passing hours	369	Lara	1	253
As evening saddens o'er the dark grey walls	370	Lara	1	266
When such as saw that suffering shudder yet	370	Lara	1	280
At times, a heart as not by nature hard	370	Lara	1	304
Such weakness as unworthy of its pride	370	Lara	1	306
And steel'd itself, as scorning to redeem	370	Lara	1	307
As if the worst had fall'n which could befall	370	Lara	1	314
His thoughts so forth as to offend the view	371	Lara	1	360
But seems as searching his, and his alone	371	Lara	1	406
As if distrusting that the stranger threw	372	Lara	1	412
But as thou wast and art--nay, frown not, lord	372	Lara	1	451
But as thou wast and art, on thee looks down	372	Lara	1	453
Words wild as these, accusers like to thee	372	Lara	1	456
To-morrow, here or elsewhere, as may best	372	Lara	1	469
I pledge myself for thee, as not unknown	372	Lara	1	471
And, as he pass'd him, smiling met the frown	373	Lara	1	498
Silent as him he served, his faith appears	373	Lara	1	516
Those accents, as his native mountains dear	373	Lara	1	522
Yet not such blush as mounts when health would show	373	Lara	1	532
As all-forgotten in that watchful trance	373	Lara	1	545
As if 'twas Lara's less than his desire	374	Lara	1	562
As unfamiliar, or, if roused again	374	Lara	1	588
Start to the sound, as but remember'd then	374	Lara	1	589
That rises as the busy bosom sinks	374	Lara	1	602
As if on something recognised right well	374	Lara	1	611
To bound as doubting from too black a dream	374	Lara	1	621
Such as we know is false, yet dread in sooth	375	Lara	1	622
But mighty Nature bounds as from her birth	375	Lara	2	5
As if he loathed the ineffectual strife	376	Lara	2	85
As if to search how far the wound he gave	376	Lara	2	87
Such as long power and overgorged success	377	Lara	2	149
Such as himself might fear, and foes would form	377	Lara	2	154
New havoc, such as civil discord blends	377	Lara	2	164
The million judged but of him as they found	378	Lara	2	197
They could encounter as a veteran may	379	Lara	2	303
As deep, but far too tranquil for despair	380	Lara	2	345
It trembled not in such an hour as this	380	Lara	2	355
And then, as his faint breathing waxes low	381	Lara	2	422
Scarce glances on him as on one forgot	381	Lara	2	441
And once, as Kaled's answering accents ceased	381	Lara	2	466
Whether (as then the breaking sun from high	381	Lara	2	468
As if his heart abhorr'd that coming day	381	Lara	2	473
As if such but disturb'd the expiring man	382	Lara	2	486
He gazed, as if not yet had pass'd away	382	Lara	2	500
As if even yet too much its surface show'd	383	Lara	2	571
He caught a glimpse, as of a floating breast	383	Lara	2	578
Such as the busy brain of Sorrow paints	384	Lara	2	610
As if she stanch'd anew some phantom's wound	384	Lara	2	619
As a pillow beneath the resting head	384	Corinth		13
As if their waters chafed to meet	385	Corinth		56
The stream of slaughter as it sank	385	Corinth		62
And far and wide as eye can reach	385	Corinth		79
As any chief that ever stood	385	Corinth		99
Remains as yet impregnable	385	Corinth		106
And as the fabric sank beneath	386	Corinth		167
The flame, as loud the ruin crash'd	386	Corinth		170
Calm, clear, and azure as the air	387	Corinth		253
But murmur'd meekly as the brook	387	Corinth		255
And, as they fell around them furling	387	Corinth		258
As rose the Muezzin's voice in air	387	Corinth		266
Such as when winds and harp-strings meet	387	Corinth		271
Such as a sudden passing-bell	387	Corinth		282
High and eternal, such as shone	388	Corinth		366
As from her fond abode she fled	388	Corinth		379
And through this night, as on he wander'd	388	Corinth		392
As his measured step on the stone below	389	Corinth		452
Clank'd, as he paced it to and fro	389	Corinth		453
As ye peel the fig when its fruit is fresh	389	Corinth		459
As it slipp'd through their jaws, when their edge grew dull	389	Corinth		461
As they lazily mumbled the bones of the dead	389	Corinth		462
All regarding man as their prey	389	Corinth		493
Hurriedly, as you may see	390	Corinth		515
As he heard the night-wind sigh	390	Corinth		520
But it was unrippled as glass may be	390	Corinth		524
As those thin fingers, long and white	391	Corinth		603
As he look'd on the face, and beheld its hue	391	Corinth		607
And her motionless lips lay still as death	391	Corinth		612
With aught of change, as the eyes may seem	391	Corinth		618
As they seem, through the dimness, about to come down	391	Corinth		624
As the gusts on the tapestry come and go	391	Corinth		627
As if that morn were a jocund one	391	Corinth		679
And the flap of the banners that flit as they're borne	391	Corinth		685
As the wolves, that headlong go	392	Corinth		723
Even as they fell, in files they lay	392	Corinth		735
As the spring-tides, with heavy plash	392	Corinth		739
As he saw Alp staggering bow	394	Corinth		859
Before his words, as with a blow	394	Corinth		860
To heaven, as if to waft it there	394	Corinth		957

AS

As if an earthquake pass'd 395 Corinth 1024
As twilight melts beneath the moon away 396 Corinth 14
Though her ear expects as soft a tale 396 Parisina 22
And heedless as the dead are they 396 Parisina 33
As if all else had pass'd away 396 Parisina 35
As if that parting were the last 397 Parisina 52
As if each calmly conscious star 397 Parisina 57
For such as he was wont to bless 397 Parisina 78
As if the Archangel's voice he heard 397 Parisina 84
Sounds fearful as the breaking billow 397 Parisina 94
Although as yet his voice be dumb 398 Parisina 146
As tear on tear grows gathering still 398 Parisina 282
Who would not do as I have done 398 Parisina 204
Throbb'd as if back upon his brain 398 Parisina 225
Thou tauntedst me--as little worth 399 Parisina 258
That should have won as haught a crest 399 Parisina 267
As ever waved along the line 399 Parisina 268
Such maddering moments as my past 399 Parisina 280
And, harsh as sounds thy hard decree 399 Parisina 310
As err'd the sire, so err'd the son 399 Parisina 314
And not an ear but felt as wounded 399 Parisina 320
As ice were in her curdled blood 400 Parisina 335
(As bowstrings, when relax'd by rain 400 Parisina 361
It is a lovely hour as yet 400 Parisina 407
As his last confession pouring 400 Parisina 413
With absolution such as may 400 Parisina 417
As he there did bow and listen 400 Parisina 420
Yet they shudder'd as they saw 400 Parisina 429
As if they dared not look on death 401 Parisina 448
Strike'--and as the word he said 401 Parisina 452
He died, as erring man should die 401 Parisina 462
As not disdaining priestly aid 401 Parisina 465
Still as the lips that closed in death 401 Parisina 477
As down the deadly blow descended 401 Parisina 481
That, as a mother's o'er her child 401 Parisina 490
And those who heard it, as it past 401 Parisina 500
Her name--as if she ne'er had been 401 Parisina 504
As him who wither'd in the grave 402 Parisina 533
When, struggling as they rise to start 402 Parisina 561
Worn, as if thy cold pavement were a sod 402 Sonnet-F 12
As men's have grown from sudden fears 402 Chillon 4
Finish'd as they had begun 402 Chillon 19
Dying as their father died 402 Chillon 23
As they of yore were wont to be 403 Chillon 66
To him, with eyes as blue as heaven 403 Chillon 75
For he was beautiful as day 403 Chillon 79
As to young eagles being free 403 Chillon 81
And thus he was as pure and bright 403 Chillon 86
The other was as pure of mind 403 Chillon 92
Our bread was such as captives' tears 404 Chillon 134
I begg'd them, as a boon, to lay 404 Chillon 152
Was as a mockery of the tomb 404 Chillon 191
Whose tints as gently sunk away 404 Chillon 192
As a departing rainbow's ray 404 Chillon 193
Alas! my own was full as chill 404 Chillon 222
As shrubless crags within the mist 405 Chillon 238
Close slowly round me as before 405 Chillon 262
Creeping as it before had done 405 Chillon 264
That bird was perch'd, as fond and tame 405 Chillon 266
Lone--as the corse within its shroud 405 Chillon 293
Lone--as a solitary cloud 405 Chillon 294
Avoiding only, as I trod 405 Chillon 312
As then to me he seem'd to fly 406 Chillon 355
Fell on me as a heavy load 406 Chillon 361
It was as is a new-dug grave 406 Chillon 362
And half I felt as they were come 406 Chillon 379
Faithless as their vain votaries, men 407 Mazeppa 6
As once the nations round him lay 407 Mazeppa 44
Himself as rough, and scarce less old 407 Mazeppa 55
But he was hardy as his lord 407 Mazeppa 66
As thy Bucephalus and thou 408 Mazeppa 104
Rich as a salt or silver mine 408 Mazeppa 157
As if from heaven he had been sent 408 Mazeppa 159
As few could match beneath the throne 408 Mazeppa 161
'Tis said, as passports into heaven 408 Mazeppa 178
But smooth, as all is rugged now 408 Mazeppa 189
Such as our Turkish neighbourhood 409 Mazeppa 209
Dark as above us is the sky 409 Mazeppa 211
As though it were a joy to die 409 Mazeppa 219
And such as I am love indeed 409 Mazeppa 226
As is Mazeppa to the last 409 Mazeppa 231
Conveying, as the electric wire 409 Mazeppa 242
I watch'd her as a sentinel 409 Mazeppa 262
(May ours this dark night watch as well 409 Mazeppa 263
Play'd on for hours, as if her will 409 Mazeppa 268
Even as a flash of lightning there 409 Mazeppa 272
All incoherent as they were 409 Mazeppa 276
To you 'twould seem absurd as vain 409 Mazeppa 286
Or o'er their passions, or as you 409 Mazeppa 288
As I resign'd me to my fate 410 Mazeppa 338
Who look'd as though the speed of thought 410 Mazeppa 361
Wild as the wild deer, and untaught 410 Mazeppa 363
As I was darted from my foes 410 Mazeppa 380

AS

When launch'd, as on the lightning's flash 411 Mazeppa 408
At length I play'd them one as frank 411 Mazeppa 416
But yet he swerved as from a blow 411 Mazeppa 457
As from a sudden trumpet's clang 411 Mazeppa 459
All furious as a favour'd child 412 Mazeppa 518
But headlong as a wintry stream 412 Mazeppa 526
I felt as on a plank at sea 412 Mazeppa 553
My undulating life was as 412 Mazeppa 557
And thicken'd, 'as it were, with glass 412 Mazeppa 578
As rose the moon upon my right 413 Mazeppa 613
Panting as if his heart would burst 413 Mazeppa 665
As if our faint approach to meet 413 Mazeppa 687
As if it only were a snare 414 Mazeppa 729
Not quite as men are base or good 414 Mazeppa 745
But as their nerves may be endued 414 Mazeppa 746
As doubtful that the former trance 414 Mazeppa 804
Could not as yet be o'er 414 Mazeppa 805
I must not strive as yet to break 415 Mazeppa 822
As I shall yeild when safely there 415 Mazeppa 859
Swam high, as eager of the coming ray 415 Island 1 10
Where Nature owns a nation as her child 416 Island 1 43
In hands as steel'd to do the deadly rest 416 Island 1 74
As promises the death their hands deny 416 Island 1 88
Remorse for the black deed as yet half done 417 Island 1 157
As on the Aeolian harp, his fitful wings 418 Island 1 171
Which welcomes, as a well, the clouds that burst 418 Island 1 190
To tell as true a tale of dangers past 418 Island 1 198
As ever the dark annals of the deep 418 Island 1 199
And bread itself is gather'd as a fruit 418 Island 1 214
Away with this! behold them as they were 418 Island 1 221
As stately swept the gallant vessel by 418 Island 1 224
And fly her as the raven fled the ark 418 Island 1 232
Shall sadly please us as we lean below 419 Island 2 12
In song, where fame as yet hath left no sign 420 Island 2 81
Or gathering mountain echoes as they glide 420 Island 2 90
That life knows no such rapture as the gale 420 Island 2 118
As childhood dates within our colder clime 420 Island 2 125
The infant of an infant world, as pure 420 Island 2 127
Voluptuous as the first approach of sleep 420 Island 2 134
Her smiles and tears had pass'd, as light winds pass 421 Island 2 151
And they who fall but fall as worlds will fall 421 Island 2 161
As bold a rover as the sands have seen 421 Island 2 180
And braved their thirst with as enduring lip 421 Island 2 181
As Ishmael, wafted on his desert-ship 421 Island 2 182
The fair-hair'd Torquil, free as ocean's spray 421 Island 2 210
Broad as the cloud along the horizon flings 422 Island 2 225
Light as a nereid in her ocean sledge 422 Island 2 231
Doth not the myrtle leave as sweet a shade 423 Island 2 317
These bugbears, as their terrors show too well 423 Island 2 331
With faith and feelings naked as her form 423 Island 2 340
She stood as stands a rainbow in a storm 423 Island 2 341
As in the north he mellow o'er the deep 424 Island 2 361
But fiery, full, and fierce, as if he left 424 Island 2 362
As dives a hero headlong to his grave 424 Island 2 365
Now smiling and now silent, as the scene 424 Island 2 404
Lovely as Love--the spirit!--when serene 424 Island 2 405
As, far divided from his parent deep 424 Island 2 408
The woods droop'd darkly, as inclined to rest 424 Island 2 412
Not such as would have been a lover's choice 424 Island 2 417
As ever started through a sea-bird's bill 424 Island 2 429
But such as wafts its cloud o'er grog or ale 425 Island 2 437
Opposed its vapour as the lightning flash'd 425 Island 2 442
Such as appears to rise out from the deep 425 Island 2 464
But brawny as the boar's; and hung beneath 425 Island 2 490
As when the arm-chest held its brighter trust 425 Island 2 497
Completed his accoutrements, as Night 425 Island 2 498
Which robes the cannon as he wings a tomb 426 Island 3 2
As to a mother's bosom flies the child 426 Island 3 16
As men not all unused to meditate 426 Island 3 29
And dared as what was likely to have been 426 Island 3 32
And straggling into ocean as it might 427 Island 3 64
Close on the wild, wide ocean, yet as pure 427 Island 3 67
And fresh as innocence, and more secure 427 Island 3 68
As the shy chamois' eye o'erlooks the steep 427 Island 3 70
Drank as they do who drink their last, and threw 427 Island 3 75
As wondering how so many still were found 427 Island 3 80
Each sought his fellow's eyes, as if to call 427 Island 3 82
As though their voices with their cause had died 427 Island 3 84
Along his cheek was livid now as lead 427 Island 3 88
Still as a statue, with his lips comprest 427 Island 3 91
Rough as a bear, but willing as a brother 428 Island 3 104
Then hurry as in haste--then quickly stop 428 Island 3 112
As the Turk's 'Allah!' or the Roman's more 428 Island 3 127
And as he knew not what to say, he swore 428 Island 3 132
And shrunk as fearful of his own caress 428 Island 3 150
As much as such a moment would allow 428 Island 3 154
Even as he spoke, around the promontory 428 Island 3 165
Buoyant as wings, and flitting through the spray 429 Island 3 174
As if to be assured 'twas him she grasp'd 429 Island 3 190
Then gazed upon the pair, as in his den 429 Island 3 209
As heedless of his further destinies 429 Island 3 212
She, as she caught the first glimpse o'er the bay 429 Island 3 218

AS

And towards a group of islets, such as bear	429	Island	3	227
As life is on each paddle's flight to-day	429	Island	3	236
White as a white sail on a dusky sea	430	Island	4	1
The rest was one bleak precipice, as e'er	430	Island	4	25
And firm as ever grappled with the sea	430	Island	4	46
With vigour they pull'd on, and as they came	430	Island	4	63
Steep, harsh, and slippery as a berg of ice	431	Island	4	70
White as a sepulchre above the pair	431	Island	4	77
Who left no marble (mournful as an heir	431	Island	4	78
Still as their oars receded from the crag	431	Island	4	91
Flowing o'er ocean as it stream'd in air	431	Island	4	102
Was as a native's of the element	431	Island	4	107
The way, then upward soar'd; and as she spread	431	Island	4	116
As in some old cathedral's glimmering aisle	431	Island	4	133
And she herself, as beautiful as night	432	Island	4	176
She, as he gazed with grateful wonder, press'd	432	Island	4	189
Old as eternity, but not outworn	432	Island	4	193
Then dived--it seem'd as if to rise no more	432	Island	4	206
Was love, though buried strong as in the grave	433	Island	4	222
As much unheeded as if life were o'er	433	Island	4	228
And yield as victims, or die sword in hand	433	Island	4	246
They stood, the three, as the three hundred stood	433	Island	4	259
Obdurate as a portion of the rock	433	Island	4	278
Dark as a sullen cloud before the sun	433	Island	4	280
Careless of danger, as the onward wind	434	Island	4	283
Which peal'd in vain and flatten'd as they fell	434	Island	4	298
After the first fierce peal, as they pull'd nigher	434	Island	4	301
The crag, as doth a falcon reft of young	434	Island	4	328
But, as they near'd, he rear'd his weapon high	434	Island	4	332
As his foe fell; then, like a serpent, coil'd	434	Island	4	336
Look'd desperate as himself along the deep	434	Island	4	338
As long as hand could hold, he held them fast	434	Island	4	348
The shadow lessen'd as it clear'd the bay	435	Island	4	382
To watch as for a rainbow in the skies	435	Island	4	384
And welcomed Torquil as a son restored	435	Island	4	408
As only the yet infant world displays	435	Island	4	420
To lift my love so lofty as thou art	437	Tasso		51
But let them go, or torture as they will	437	Tasso		57
As rapid rivers into ocean pour	437	Tasso		63
With needless torture, as their tyrant will	437	Tasso		72
To be forgetful as I am forgot	437	Tasso		81
Branding my thoughts as things to shun and fear	438	Tasso		99
As dwells the gather'd lightning in its cloud	438	Tasso		114
And for a moment all things as they were	438	Tasso		119
My brain against these bars, as the sun flash'd	439	Tasso		210
That such as I could love, who blush'd to hear	439	Tasso		229
As none in life could rend thee from my heart	440	Tasso		245
All people, as their fancies hit, may choose	440	Beppo		22
Such as in Monmouth-street, or in Rag Fair	440	Beppo		35
'Tis as we take a glass with friends at parting	441	Beppo		47
And you at Rome would do as Romans do	441	Beppo		66
Such as of old were copied from the Grecians	441	Beppo		83
The face recalls some face, as 'twere with pain	441	Beppo		103
As very fair, but yet suspect in fame	442	Beppo		130
He was a man as dusky as a Spaniard	443	Beppo		201
Though colour'd as it were, within a tanyard	443	Beppo		203
So much as to be thought almost invincible	443	Beppo		208
As partings often are, or ought to be	443	Beppo		218
And thought of wearing weeds, as well she might	443	Beppo		226
A Count of wealth, they said, as well as quality	443	Beppo		239
The fiddlers trembled as he look'd around	444	Beppo		251
Sold pictures, and was skilful in the dance as	444	Beppo		260
Then he was faithful, too, as well as amorous	444	Beppo		265
Who still become more constant as they cool	444	Beppo		272
In law he was almost as good as dead, he	444	Beppo		276
Close to the lady as a part of dress	445	Beppo		316
His is no sinecure, as you may guess	445	Beppo		318
Beauteous as cloudless, nor be forced to borrow	445	Beppo		342
And sounds as if it should be writ on satin	445	Beppo		347
Soft as her clime, and sunny as her skies	445	Beppo		360
I like a beef-steak, too, as well as any	446	Beppo		379
Not caring as I ought for critics' cavils	446	Beppo		414
Which lasted, as arrangements sometimes do	446	Beppo		418
As happy as unlawful love could make them	446	Beppo		426
Heart, soul, and all that seems as from above	447	Beppo		436
It was the Carnival, as I have said	447	Beppo		441
Laura, when dress'd, was (as I sang before	447	Beppo		449
A pretty woman as was ever seen	447	Beppo		450
Fresh as the Angel o'er a new inn door	447	Beppo		451
As much as saying, they're below your notice	447	Beppo		464
And as for Fortune--but I dare not d--n her	447	Beppo		486
Because, just as the stanza likes to make it	448	Beppo		499
May lurk beneath each mask; and as my sorrow	448	Beppo		510
As is supposed the case with northern nations	449	Beppo		564
And as the Turks abhor long conversations	449	Beppo		566
Unknown as bells within a Turkish steeple	449	Beppo		612
Upon the living manners, as they pass us	450	Beppo		621
And as, perhaps, they would not highly flatter	450	Beppo		627
(As to their palace stairs the rowers glide	451	Beppo		694
The lady's changing cheek, as well it might	451	Beppo		706
And cutting stays, as usual in such cases	451	Beppo		712
Well, that's the prettiest shawl--as I'm alive	451	Beppo		732

AS

Lonely he felt, at times, as Robin Crusoe	452	Beppo		757
In contrast with their fathers--as the slime	453	Venice-B		8
Church, palace, pillar, as a mourner greets	453	Venice-B		18
And as he whispers knows not that he gasps	453	Venice-B		48
Are of as high an order--they must go	453	Venice-B		65
Ye men, who pour your blood for kings as water	453	Venice-B		67
And glorying as you tread the glowing bars	453	Venice-B		75
As if his senseless sceptre were a wand	454	Venice-B		140
And moving, as a sick man in his sleep	455	Venice-B		153
Wept over, 'but thou wouldst not!' As the bird	456	Dante	1	62
My voice; but as the adder, deaf and fierce	456	Dante	1	65
As thou hast been in peril, and in pain	457	Dante	1	122
Worthless as they who wrought it. 'Tis the doom	458	Dante	1	149
As lofty and more sweet, in which express'd	458	Dante	2	24
That every word, as brilliant as thy skies	459	Dante	2	27
And wistfully implores, as 'twere, for help	459	Dante	2	66
Mountains and waters, do ye not as they	460	Dante	2	111
To thee, my country! whom before as now	461	Dante	3	25
Is not as once it shone o'er thee, forgive	461	Dante	3	29
Native to thee as summer to thy skies	461	Dante	3	45
Such as all they must breathe who are debased	461	Dante	3	60
And raise their notes as natural and high	461	Dante	3	67
And looks on prostitution as a duty	461	Dante	3	79
As guest is slave, his thoughts become a booty	461	Dante	3	81
He sings, as the Athenian spoke, with pebbles	462	Dante	3	96
And Italy shall hail him as the Chief	462	Dante	3	103
Of Freedom wreathe him with as green a leaf	462	Dante	3	105
As poor a thing as e'er was spawn'd to reign	462	Dante	3	145
Such as all flesh shall flock to kneel in: ne'er	464	Dante	4	53
As this, to which all nations shall repair	464	Dante	4	55
Whom all arts shall acknowledge as their lord	464	Dante	4	59
Such as I saw them such as all shall see	464	Dante	4	65
Fragrant as fair, and recognised afar	464	Dante	4	77
As swept off sooner; in all deadly things	465	Dante	4	121
Yearn'd, as the captive toiling at escape	465	Dante	4	129
As in the old time, till the hour be come	465	Dante	4	152
As it should still obey, the helm, my mind	466	Morgante		26
His virtues as I wish to see them: thou	466	Morgante		50
In Roncesvalles, as the villain plann'd too	467	Morgante		60
As for myself, I shall repass the mounts	467	Morgante		111
As by himself it chanced he sate apart	468	Morgante		118
As 'Welcome, my Orlando, home,' she said	468	Morgante		135
And far as pagan countries roam'd astray	468	Morgante		146
As you perceive, yet without fear or blame	469	Morgante		179
As to a brother dear I speak alone	469	Morgante		222
As knowing sure that you will lose your life	469	Morgante		224
As the abbot had directed, kept the line	469	Morgante		236
Then ask'd him, 'If he wish'd to stay as servant	469	Morgante		240
God, not to serve as footboy in your train	470	Morgante		244
As show'd a sample of his skill in slinging	470	Morgante		252
So that he swoon'd with pain as if he died	470	Morgante		255
As to desert would almost be a wrong	470	Morgante		262
Yet, harsh and haughty, as he lay he bann'd	470	Morgante		277
'I come to preach to you, as to your brothers	471	Morgante		321
And, if you please, as friends we will ally us	471	Morgante		349
And made much of his convert, as he cried	471	Morgante		362
Ask the abbot pardon, as I wish you would	471	Morgante		368
And, as I said, to be your vassal too	472	Morgante		381
Just as you tell me 'tis in heaven obey'd	472	Morgante		421
He Christ believes as Christian must be rated	473	Morgante		443
Yourself to Christ, as once you were a foe	473	Morgante		456
One day, as with Orlando they both stray'd	473	Morgante		475
As floor'd him so that he no more arose	473	Morgante		507
As though they wish'd to burst at once, they ate	474	Morgante		529
And gorged so that, as if the bones had been	474	Morgante		530
And said, 'I am as light as any feather	474	Morgante		546
To render, as the gods do, good for ill	474	Morgante		563
As you have done to him, will do to you	474	Morgante		568
As Nessus did of old beyond all cure	474	Morgante		570
With these as much is done as with this cowl	476	Morgante		650
Precisely as the war occurr'd they drew him	476	Morgante		679
And there was Milo as he overthrew him	476	Morgante		680
As I will tell in the ensuing story	476	Morgante		687
That, as thou seest, yet, yet it doth remain	476	Francesca		9
So as his dim desires to recognise	476	Francesca		24
I will do even as he who weeps and says	477	Francesca		30
I swoon'd as if by death I had been smote	477	Francesca		45
And fell down even as a dead body falls	477	Francesca		46
It will not burn so long as I must watch	478	Manfred	1	2
Have been to me as rain unto the sands	479	Manfred	1	23
As their summits to heaven	479	Manfred	1	94
It was a world as fresh and fair	480	Manfred	1	112
As e'er revolved round sun in air	480	Manfred	1	113
Is as the future, present. Art thou answer'd	480	Manfred	1	151
The lightning of my being, is as bright	480	Manfred	1	155
Pervading, and far darting as your own	480	Manfred	1	156
We answer as we answer'd; our reply	480	Manfred	1	159
If, as thou say'st, thine essence be as ours	480	Manfred	1	161
As music on the waters; and I see	480	Manfred	1	177
But nothing more. Approach me as ye are	480	Manfred	1	179
As unto him may seem most fitting--Come!	481	Manfred	1	187
Thou art wrapt as with a shroud	481	Manfred	1	208
As a thing that, though unseen	481	Manfred	1	214

As thy shadow on the spot	481	Manfred	1	219
For there it coil'd as in a brake	481	Manfred	1	237
To thy wish, but as a fear	481	Manfred	1	257
Behold the tall pines dwindled as to shrubs	482	Manfred	1	276
Proud as a freeborn peasant's, at this distance	482	Manfred	1	325
For the wind's pastime--as thus--thus they shall be	483	Manfred	1	367
And loved each other as we should not love	484	Manfred	2	27
Endless, and all alike, as sands on the shore	484	Manfred	2	54
As told in the Apocalypse. No eyes	485	Manfred	2	102
As in itself hath power upon the air	486	Manfred	2	181
Such as, before me, did the Magi, and	486	Manfred	2	185
As I do thee;--and with my knowledge grew	486	Manfred	2	188
As I approach the core of my heart's grief	486	Manfred	2	194
For madness as a blessing--'tis denied me	486	Manfred	2	228
As from a stream in winter, though the chill	487	Manfred	2	269
Save one, whom I held, as he swam, by the hair	488	Manfred	2	328
Is of no common order, as his port	489	Manfred	2	422
As far as is compatible with clay	489	Manfred	2	426
As clay hath seldom borne; his aspirations	489	Manfred	2	428
Too much, as I loved thee: we were not made	490	Manfred	2	491
The deadliest sin to love as we have loved	490	Manfred	2	493
Even as thou wilt: and for the grace accorded	491	Manfred	2	536
As I directed? All, my lord, are ready	491	Manfred	3	4
Is as an anchorite's, were it but holy	491	Manfred	3	42
But fall, even as the mountain-cataract	492	Manfred	3	109
Had they been wisely mingled; as it is	493	Manfred	3	163
Even as our outward aspects;--thou dost rise	493	Manfred	3	194
I ne'er shall see thee more. As my first glance	493	Manfred	3	196
As if they had forgotten heaven	494	Manfred	3	229
'Twas twilight, as it may be now, and such	494	Manfred	3	236
Count Manfred was, as now, within his tower	494	Manfred	3	242
As he, indeed, by blood was bound to do	494	Manfred	3	247
As 'twere anew, the gaps of centuries	495	Manfred	3	295
Robed as with angry clouds: he stands between	495	Manfred	3	325
To render up my soul to such as these	496	Manfred	3	349
Away! I'll die as I have lived--alone	496	Manfred	3	350
Have made thee--What are they to such as thee	496	Manfred	3	382
Heaven as it were beneath me. Fare thee well	497	Manfred	3	408
I have sent frequently, as you commanded	499	Faliero	1	2
He sits as rapt in duty; but whene'er	500	Faliero	1	10
Decided; but as yet his doom's unknown	500	Faliero	1	26
Ay, such as the Avogadori did	500	Faliero	1	31
As the due forms of judgment are gone through	500	Faliero	1	40
And secret as the grave to which they doom	500	Faliero	1	61
Will be as could be wish'd. Say on. 'Decreed	501	Faliero	1	86
To them, as being your subjects. But 'tis not	501	Faliero	1	109
As sovereign, I appeal'd unto my subjects	502	Faliero	1	144
And patron of her house, as if there were	503	Faliero	1	209
Did you expect as his fit punishment	503	Faliero	1	220
Was I not injured as a husband? scorn'd	503	Faliero	1	224
As man? reviled, degraded, as a prince	503	Faliero	1	225
Whether as fellow-citizen who sues	503	Faliero	1	245
For justice, or as sovereign who commands it	503	Faliero	1	246
At least, just now--a life so vile as his	503	Faliero	1	257
But be not thou too rash, as I have been	503	Faliero	1	265
The sun and you, as an ill-omen'd cloud	503	Faliero	1	276
As doth become your near and faithful kinsman	504	Faliero	1	286
Let me resume thee as I would a vizor	504	Faliero	1	293
My soul as serves the generous steed his lord	504	Faliero	1	305
In such a sort as will not leave the task	504	Faliero	1	310
Herculean, though as yet 'tis but a chaos	504	Faliero	1	311
So long as to remember Zara's siege	505	Faliero	1	389
As patron of a galley: my new office	505	Faliero	1	397
Was given as the reward of certain scars	505	Faliero	1	398
To his successor as a helpless plaintiff	505	Faliero	1	401
As a good jest to jolly artisans	506	Faliero	1	422
Who, as he sung the merry stave, exulted	506	Faliero	1	425
They'll do as much by Barbaro, no doubt	506	Faliero	1	432
However vile, to such a thing as I am	506	Faliero	1	438
As it might chance to be our country's 'vantage	506	Faliero	1	461
Being of an order of such spirits, as	508	Faliero	1	562
Noble and brave as aught of consular	508	Faliero	1	618
Such chastisement as will enforce respect	509	Faliero	2	30
May reach the soul of ribalds such as Steno	509	Faliero	2	51
Such as abound in Venice, would be loud	509	Faliero	2	64
As they would look out for an ornament	510	Faliero	2	71
And would seem honest, as they must seem fair	510	Faliero	2	74
Such have I found him as my father said	510	Faliero	2	102
Such as in years had been more meet to match	510	Faliero	2	119
As not betraying their full import, yet	511	Faliero	2	178
As you have risen, with an unalter'd brow	511	Faliero	2	203
Ah, no!--As I have ever shared your kindness	512	Faliero	2	213
Long as he can; he has ceased to merit death	512	Faliero	2	237
As a true feeling for your welfare, and	514	Faliero	2	355
As youth is apt in, so as not to check	514	Faliero	2	359
Such estimation in your eyes as these	514	Faliero	2	365
For such as him a dungeon were acquittal	515	Faliero	2	438
Mellowing the last hours as the night approaches	515	Faliero	2	460
To make my country honour'd. As her servant	515	Faliero	2	465
And pure as theirs; but this has been denied me	515	Faliero	2	468
As e'er they were by pestilence or war	516	Faliero	2	508
Such as I counsell'd you, with your own hand	516	Faliero	2	518
As 'tis, our cause looks prosperous still	516	Faliero	2	535
No punishment for such as Barbaro	516	Faliero	2	537
Had kept me in his eye, as meditating	516	Faliero	2	542
Yet as he has no mistress, and no wife	517	Faliero	2	592
And only look on death as beautiful	517	Faliero	2	603
Elapse, and others share as dark a doom	517	Faliero	2	611
As sceptre: these unmanly creeping things	517	Faliero	2	630
As with a spell. It shall be broken soon	517	Faliero	2	632
As new artificers for their equipment	517	Faliero	2	641
As far as I have seen, we are enough	518	Faliero	2	653
That if once stirr'd and baffled, as he has been	518	Faliero	2	682
Your own command as leader? Even so	518	Faliero	2	693
To act in trust as your commander, till	518	Faliero	2	697
As you yourselves shall own more worthy, think you	518	Faliero	2	699
I am with you, as I have ever been	518	Faliero	2	713
If it so please you, do as much by me	519	Faliero	3	63
'Tis in such deeds as we are now upon	520	Faliero	3	98
Deem'st thou the souls of such a race as mine	520	Faliero	3	99
With stung plebeians? It had been as well	520	Faliero	3	102
So wrong'd as I, so fall'n, so loudly call'd	520	Faliero	3	113
As when the viper hath been cut to pieces	521	Faliero	3	148
Deserve and have. Why, I should think as soon	521	Faliero	3	151
One in the jaw of the swoln serpent, as	521	Faliero	3	153
So let them die as one! Should one survive	521	Faliero	3	158
He would be dangerous as the whole; it is not	521	Faliero	3	159
A kind man, I am apt to think, as some	521	Faliero	3	174
As far among the foe as any he	521	Faliero	3	182
In brotherhood, as I have made it known	521	Faliero	3	206
To take his choice--as brother, or as victim	522	Faliero	3	241
As I described them. Speak to them. Ay, speak	522	Faliero	3	248
As one of you hath said, an old, unarm'd	522	Faliero	3	252
Although dress'd out to head a pageant, as	523	Faliero	3	283
As delegate of tyrants. Such I am not	523	Faliero	3	302
To sit in state as for a sovereign's picture	523	Faliero	3	310
My present power such as it is--not that	523	Faliero	3	321
Such as I am, I offer me to you	523	Faliero	3	328
Ay, and the first amongst us, as thou hast been	523	Faliero	3	337
And therefore safer, and as such admits	524	Faliero	3	394
As faithless leaves drop from the o'erblown flower	525	Faliero	3	430
So, as they let me wither, let them perish	525	Faliero	3	433
And seeming not all dead, as long as two	525	Faliero	3	457
Their friend and made a sovereign, as boys make	525	Faliero	3	496
As senators for arbitrary acts	526	Faliero	3	505
Amenable, I look on them--as such	526	Faliero	3	506
Yet, as the immediate cause of the alliance	526	Faliero	3	533
I would repay him as he merits; may I	526	Faliero	3	536
Without distinction, as it fell of yore	526	Faliero	3	543
Have crush'd dictators, as the popular steel	526	Faliero	3	557
Nor wore them in your heart of hearts, as I have	527	Faliero	3	586
As we went forth to take our prey arcund	527	Faliero	3	590
As if these high-born men were steers for shambles	527	Faliero	3	628
A knell was sounding as distinct and clear	528	Faliero	4	12
Though low and far, as e'er the Adrian wave	528	Faliero	4	13
Which show'd all things, but nothing as they were	528	Faliero	4	34
The sight of beauty as the parch'd pilgrim's	529	Faliero	4	65
Fair as the moonlight of which it seems part	529	Faliero	4	92
Is almost wronging such a night as this	529	Faliero	4	111
But do as I implore thee;--stir not forth	530	Faliero	4	162
As I now counsel--but if not, thou art lost	530	Faliero	4	181
As suits your station, the more humble Bertram	531	Faliero	4	212
Madden as in the last hours of the plague	531	Faliero	4	239
As vice and villany would put thee to	531	Faliero	4	246
Such as ourselves received it, or augmented	531	Faliero	4	253
As the capricious mercy of such things	532	Faliero	4	266
As thou and those who have set thee to thy task-work	532	Faliero	4	267
As noble, nay, even nobler than thine own	532	Faliero	4	271
Thy safety and thy welfare; wealth such as	532	Faliero	4	319
Sure as all gentle means can make; and if	533	Faliero	4	340
Bertram, I'll reason with thee as we go	533	Faliero	4	348
As well had there been time to have got together	533	Faliero	4	354
Methinks, my lord, 'tis better as it is	533	Faliero	4	357
As yesterday a thousand to the senate	534	Faliero	4	402
As the first wine-cup leads to the long revel	534	Faliero	4	410
As doth the pilot of an admiral galley	534	Faliero	4	429
To steel me to a purpose such as made	534	Faliero	4	437
As were the dead who lay around me: this	534	Faliero	4	447
Even as the eagle overlooks his prey	535	Faliero	4	484
And slay as if Death had but this one gate	535	Faliero	4	518
A murmur as of distant voices, and	535	Faliero	4	523
Then here must be my station, as becomes	536	Faliero	4	544
It is illegal, and, as now applied	536	Faliero	4	564
I am placed here as guard upon thy person	536	Faliero	4	568
And not as judge or to decide	536	Faliero	4	569
They die then in their duty, as will I	536	Faliero	4	589
As rebel slave of a revolted council	537	Faliero	4	600
As thou saidst even now--then do thine office	537	Faliero	4	605
As delegated from the Doge, the signal	537	Faliero	4	615
As men whose triumph is not in success	537	Faliero	4	626
Yet if they send us, as 'tis like, together	537	Faliero	4	630

AS

As we had dealt on them, but with less pomp	537	Faliero	4	637
The years of coming time, as bearing record	538	Faliero	5	8
The earth as being the Christian bulwark 'gainst	538	Faliero	5	11
Do you be brief as I am, and believe me	538	Faliero	5	39
As well as in the islands, that we hope	540	Faliero	5	149
Of such a crime, as on the old Roman tables	540	Faliero	5	188
As sons 'gainst sires, and princes 'gainst their realms	540	Faliero	5	194
As would with treason mount to tyranny	540	Faliero	5	197
You--you, who sit there, traitors as ye are	540	Faliero	5	203
Is here in virtue of his office, as	541	Faliero	5	224
And novel as the present: he was set	541	Faliero	5	228
Decreed as sentence! Base as was his crime	541	Faliero	5	238
A provocation as a young man's petulance	541	Faliero	5	245
As would have made Venetian history	541	Faliero	5	252
As you have done upon my heart while living	541	Faliero	5	265
But such blasphemers 'gainst all honour, as	542	Faliero	5	316
Guiltless as thy own bosom. Is it so	543	Faliero	5	350
Nor, as thou seest, doth he deny it now	543	Faliero	5	355
Have begg'd as famish'd mendicants for bread	543	Faliero	5	386
Have wept as they will cry unto their God	543	Faliero	5	387
For mercy, and be answer'd as they answer	543	Faliero	5	388
Then, as a prince, address thee to thy doom	543	Faliero	5	392
But since that cannot be, as Christians let us	543	Faliero	5	404
For such as he is: would that others had	544	Faliero	5	413
Despised him as I pity! I prefer	544	Faliero	5	414
To me the scorner's words were as the wind	544	Faliero	5	421
Unto the rock: but as there are--alas	544	Faliero	5	422
Light as the whirlwind on the waters; souls	544	Faliero	5	424
Their hopes is breathed on, jealous as the eagle	544	Faliero	5	431
And the great enemy of man, as subject	545	Faliero	5	493
The place wherein as Doge thou shouldst be painted	545	Faliero	5	496
As Doge, clad in the ducal robes and cap	545	Faliero	5	516
As falls the lion by the hunters, girt	546	Faliero	5	566
United to thee as thy subjects, and	546	Faliero	5	573
As such for ever, on the self-same spot	546	Faliero	5	575
And signory as podesta and captain	546	Faliero	5	594
And as he rose from earth again, he raised	546	Faliero	5	601
But not such death as fits an aged man	546	Faliero	5	616
Of life, as if they form'd a spectral voice	547	Faliero	5	623
That on my day of landing here as Doge	547	Faliero	5	629
The Riva della Paglia, as the wont is	547	Faliero	5	638
I know to be as worthless as the dust	547	Faliero	5	646
And weak as worthless, more than instruments	547	Faliero	5	647
Ay, palpable as I see thy sweet face	547	Faliero	5	666
One look!--how cold her hand!--as cold as mine	547	Faliero	5	694
I hasten, let my voice be as a spirit	548	Faliero	5	725
Ye winds, which flutter'd o'er as if you loved it	548	Faliero	5	727
And fill'd my swelling sails as they were wafted	548	Faliero	5	728
As these old veins, oft drain'd in shielding her	548	Faliero	5	747
Even in the palace where they sway'd as sovereigns	548	Faliero	5	763
As in the monstrous grasp of their conception	549	Faliero	5	774
Strike as I struck the foe! Strike as I would	549	Faliero	5	798
Have struck those tyrants! Strike deep as my curse	549	Faliero	5	799
And I must be his friend as well as subject	550	Sardan	1	4
Which he should be, as easily as the thing	551	Sardan	1	20
As femininely garb'd, and scarce less female	551	Sardan	1	42
And you will form a heaven as bright as theirs	551	Sardan	1	58
As I have said, let all dispose their hours	551	Sardan	1	81
To language such as this: yet urge me not	552	Sardan	1	107
Come, I'm indulgent, as thou knowest, patient	552	Sardan	1	143
As thou hast often proved--speak out, what moves thee	552	Sardan	1	144
As king the kingdoms thou didst leave as hero	553	Sardan	1	164
Forth as a conqueror. By all the stars	553	Sardan	1	169
Not much as man. What, ho! my cupbearer	553	Sardan	1	203
To gladden that of man, as some ornament	554	Sardan	1	223
A mortal still in name as in his grave	554	Sardan	1	226
And him as a true man, who did his utmost	554	Sardan	1	240
I married her as monarchs wed--for state	554	Sardan	1	260
And loved her as most husbands love their wives	554	Sardan	1	261
Thy sires have been revered as gods--In dust	555	Sardan	1	314
As such their hearts are something. So my dogs' are	556	Sardan	1	391
And better, as more faithful:--but, proceed	556	Sardan	1	392
The meanest vassal as the loftiest monarch	556	Sardan	1	397
I let them pass their days as best might suit them	556	Sardan	1	406
Passing my own as suited me. Thou stopp'st	556	Sardan	1	407
As powerful in thy realm. Farewell! Farewell	557	Sardan	1	432
As I am heedless; and the slaves deserve	557	Sardan	1	435
Blood as I might have done, in oceans, till	557	Sardan	1	450
I have heard thee talk of as the favourite pastime	559	Sardan	1	565
Well, then, how wouldst thou save me, as thou saidst	559	Sardan	1	572
He will adduce such reasons as will warrant	560	Sardan	1	618
And thou? I shall be king, as heretofore	561	Sardan	1	671
As fountain of all life, and symbol of	561	Sardan	2	16
As of wrath to its days? Hear me! oh, hear me	562	Sardan	2	22
I have prepared as many glittering spears	562	Sardan	2	46
As will out-sparkle our allies--your planets	562	Sardan	2	47

AS

As it would quit its place in the blue ether	562	Sardan	2	65
As firm in fight as Babylonia's captain	562	Sardan	2	77
As skilful in Chaldea's worship: now	562	Sardan	2	78
A sword which hath been drawn as oft as thine	565	Sardan	2	202
As the light breeze of midnight crisps the broad	566	Sardan	2	257
Gods, as some say, or the abodes of gods	566	Sardan	2	260
As others hold, or simply lamps of night	566	Sardan	2	261
As I have said, I will not deem ye guilty	566	Sardan	2	290
Must oft receive her right as a mere favour	566	Sardan	2	304
To use them as ye will--but from this hour	567	Sardan	2	320
As must make madness of delay. And yet	567	Sardan	2	333
Methought he look'd like Nimrod as he spoke	567	Sardan	2	352
Even as the proud imperial statue stands	567	Sardan	2	353
Had held his life but lightly--as it is	567	Sardan	2	371
I must forgive you, even as he forgave us	567	Sardan	2	372
With you. And would, perhaps, betray as well	568	Sardan	2	384
As quit me? That's a sacerdotal thought	568	Sardan	2	385
At present, let us hence as best we may	568	Sardan	2	426
This order as a sentence? Why, what other	568	Sardan	2	428
As he who treads on flowers is from the adder	569	Sardan	2	469
You may know that hereafter; as it is	569	Sardan	2	478
Hard, but as lofty as the rock, and free	570	Sardan	2	520
But as our mould is, must the produce be	570	Sardan	2	523
Frowns as the shadows of the evening dim	570	Sardan	2	533
As auguries of Jove. Jove!--ay, your Baal	570	Sardan	2	549
As on the river's brink. Not so; these walls	570	Sardan	2	562
Even as the arrow finds the airy king	570	Sardan	2	570
I thought you were exempt from this, as from	571	Sardan	2	589
Fill full! why this is as it should be: here	571	Sardan	3	1
Happy as fair! Here sorrow cannot reach	571	Sardan	3	3
They were, as all thy royal line have been	571	Sardan	3	8
As thy wish would imply. And your gods, then	572	Sardan	3	45
And pelting us even now. The Persian prays	572	Sardan	3	51
As Salemenes fear'd; the faithless satraps	572	Sardan	3	72
Soon as Arbaces and Beleses reach'd	572	Sardan	3	77
In Hades! if there be, as I believe	574	Sardan	3	158
The king, the king fights as he revels. Ho	574	Sardan	3	213
As though it were a bed of roses, deserves	575	Sardan	3	224
This realm as province. Hark! they come--they come	575	Sardan	3	267
Prove victor, as it seems even now he must	576	Sardan	3	307
As sweeps the air and deluges the earth	576	Sardan	3	318
But there's enough of that shed; as for wine	577	Sardan	3	349
As I am now. I live again--henceforth	577	Sardan	3	362
As it stream'd o'er her; her blue veins that rose	577	Sardan	3	389
As a lute's pierceth through the cymbal's clash	577	Sardan	3	393
Orders as I had given and then return	578	Sardan	3	407
Omnipotent o'er such a heart as his	578	Sardan	3	423
Or deep, deep sleep, so as to be unfathom'd	578	Sardan	4	5
For then we are happiest, as, it may be, we	578	Sardan	4	7
Shoots o'er his features, as the sudden gust	578	Sardan	4	11
And gave them to me as a realm to share	578	Sardan	4	25
Who hunted fellow-creatures as if brutes	578	Sardan	4	29
A shore where mind survives, 'twill be as mind	579	Sardan	4	57
Here--here--even where we are, guests as we were	579	Sardan	4	79
I frown'd upon him as a king should frown	579	Sardan	4	96
Till I grew stone, as they seem'd half to be	580	Sardan	4	122
Of sympathy between us, as if they	580	Sardan	4	125
At last I sate, marble as they, when rose	580	Sardan	4	131
Rose also, as if aping their chief shades	580	Sardan	4	138
Stood dull as in our temples, but she still	580	Sardan	4	155
Embraced me, while I shrunk from her, as if	580	Sardan	4	156
Such as might try the sternest. I am better	581	Sardan	4	171
I perish--as is probable: well thought	581	Sardan	4	206
I think as you do of my sister's wish	581	Sardan	4	224
And look upon me as you look'd upon me	582	Sardan	4	257
Of a fond mother, but as a fond woman	582	Sardan	4	261
Bravely--and, won, wear it wisely, not as I	582	Sardan	4	275
So little cared for as his own; and if	582	Sardan	4	288
As one, for they are nothing if I fall	583	Sardan	4	304
Nor dote even on thy beauty--as I've doted	583	Sardan	4	337
To profit by them--as the miner lights	583	Sardan	4	344
Ends as such partings end, in no departure	583	Sardan	4	364
I thought as much, and yielded against all	583	Sardan	4	365
As yet beat in these kingdoms. The time presses	584	Sardan	4	389
The homage of mankind as their born due	585	Sardan	4	435
(As you are like to lose the one you sway'd	585	Sardan	4	464
I did abase myself as much in being	585	Sardan	4	465
Your paramour, as though you were a peasant	585	Sardan	4	466
Against the falling; but as I am not	585	Sardan	4	470
And such gifts, as, if you had not been all	585	Sardan	4	478
Upon the palace towers as the swift galley	586	Sardan	4	539
To that which keeps all earth from being as fragile	588	Sardan	5	45
As I am in this form. Come, look upon it	588	Sardan	5	46
As now he reigns in heaven, so once on earth	588	Sardan	5	49
As in late midnight conflict in the very	588	Sardan	5	61
We are as much shut in even from the sound	588	Sardan	5	68
Of peril as from glory. But they reach'd	588	Sardan	5	69
In fight, as he had spared him in his peril	588	Sardan	5	85
Are not so numerous as to spare your absence	589	Sardan	5	117
As you would not permit me to expire	589	Sardan	5	120
As 'tis, I have not outlived them. You wax paler	589	Sardan	5	127

AS

Thou shalt be mourn'd for as thou wouldst be mourn'd	589	Sardan	5	152
Place it beneath my canopy, as though	589	Sardan	5	165
A question as an answer to his question	590	Sardan	5	172
Who can so feel it as I feel? but yet	590	Sardan	5	179
As time and means permit. About it straight	590	Sardan	5	212
And bring me back, as speedily as full	590	Sardan	5	213
As children at discover'd bugbears. 'Tis	591	Sardan	5	240
As was reported; I have order'd there	591	Sardan	5	241
You have done your duty faithfully, and as	591	Sardan	5	245
Along its golden frame--as bearing for	591	Sardan	5	252
Things as catch fire and blaze with one sole spark	591	Sardan	5	277
Given up as hostages. The generous victors	592	Sardan	5	306
At the same peril, if refused, as now	592	Sardan	5	322
New monarchs of an hour's growth as despotic	592	Sardan	5	324
As sovereigns swathed in purple, and enthroned	592	Sardan	5	325
Such as is that of Nimrod, to destroy	592	Sardan	5	330
Be such as will not speedily exhaust	593	Sardan	5	359
To the new comers. Frame the whole as if	593	Sardan	5	364
But not so rare, my Pania, as thou think'st it	593	Sardan	5	374
Upon the trumpet as you quit the palace	593	Sardan	5	387
And as you sail, turn back; but still keep on	593	Sardan	5	391
As ye bequeath'd it, this bright part of it	594	Sardan	5	429
Which most personifies the soul as leaving	594	Sardan	5	434
And pure as is my love to thee, shall they	594	Sardan	5	472
And better as my country than my kingdom	595	Sardan	5	494
As the torch in thy grasp. 'T is fired! I come	595	Sardan	5	498
To the ducal chambers, as he pass'd the threshold	596	Foscari	1	30
Of the first as shall make the second needless	596	Foscari	1	44
Our state as render retribution easier	596	Foscari	1	47
Thy path of desolation, as the wave	596	Foscari	1	57
Who shrieks within its riven ribs, as gush	596	Foscari	1	60
I could as blindly and remorselessly	596	Foscari	1	64
As to allow his voice in such high matter	596	Foscari	1	85
As the state's safety--And his son's. I'm faint	596	Foscari	1	86
Bounding o'er yon blue tide, as I have skimm'd	597	Foscari	1	95
And, masqued as a young gondolier, amidst	597	Foscari	1	97
My gay competitors, noble as I	597	Foscari	1	98
Plebeian as patrician, cheer'd us on	597	Foscari	1	101
The waves as they arose, and prouder still	597	Foscari	1	110
As show'd that I had search'd the deep: exulting	597	Foscari	1	117
Will take me as a mother to her arms	597	Foscari	1	143
Away!--I'll walk alone. As you please, signor	598	Foscari	1	152
But keep off from me till 'tis issued. As	598	Foscari	1	158
And the cold drops strain through my brow, as if	598	Foscari	1	161
Of yon terrific chamber are as hidden	598	Foscari	1	179
As from the people. Save the wonted rumours	598	Foscari	1	181
Nor wholly disbelieved; men know as little	598	Foscari	1	184
Of the state's real acts as of the grave's	598	Foscari	1	185
An hour since, face to face, as judge and culprit	599	Foscari	1	219
I have endured as much in giving life	599	Foscari	1	242
To those who will succeed them, as they can	599	Foscari	1	243
As they have enter'd--many never, but	599	Foscari	1	257
But as a culprit. Yes, but to his country	600	Foscari	1	299
That Almoro Donato, as I said	600	Foscari	1	307
As I do always. Go to, you're a child	600	Foscari	1	328
Infirm of feeling as of purpose, blown	600	Foscari	1	329
As was forced on him; but he did not cry	600	Foscari	1	337
His state descend to his children, as it must	601	Foscari	1	352
He's silent in his hate, as Foscari	601	Foscari	1	361
As long ere she resume her arms! 'Tis almost	601	Foscari	2	13
'The Ten;' but as the court no longer sate	602	Foscari	2	58
But they have crush'd. Nor crush'd as yet--I live	603	Foscari	2	91
For all that yet is past, as many years	603	Foscari	2	93
Nor palliate, as parent or as Duke	603	Foscari	2	98
As palsied as their hearts are hard, they counsel	603	Foscari	2	112
Cabal, and put men's lives out, as if life	603	Foscari	2	113
Do as they have done by yours, and you yourself	603	Foscari	2	124
Cloke their soul's hoarded triumph, as a fit one	604	Foscari	2	148
As far as I have borne it, what is was	604	Foscari	2	150
The admiral, his brother, say as much	605	Foscari	2	208
As I said, suddenly. Is that so strange	605	Foscari	2	214
In my mind half so natural as theirs	605	Foscari	2	217
To poison. 'Tis perhaps as true as most	605	Foscari	2	225
Your fathers were mine enemies, as bitter	605	Foscari	2	228
As their son e'er can be, and I no less	605	Foscari	2	229
At so much price as to require your absence	605	Foscari	2	246
As would have made you nothing. But in all things	605	Foscari	2	248
(I do not speak of you but as a single	605	Foscari	2	251
Were I disposed to brawl; but, as I said	605	Foscari	2	254
It galls you:--well, you are his equal, as	606	Foscari	2	290
To one as noble. What, or whose, then, is	606	Foscari	2	295
Process of my poor husband! Treat me as	606	Foscari	2	314
Than to the threshold, saving such as pass	606	Foscari	2	321
With as we may, and least in humblest stations	607	Foscari	2	347
The greatest as the meanest--nothing rests	607	Foscari	2	358
And still towards death, a thing which comes as much	607	Foscari	2	362
Without our act or choice as birth, so that	607	Foscari	2	363
Observ'st, obey'st such laws as make old Draco's	607	Foscari	2	393

AS

Fit for amendment; but as prince, I never	607	Foscari	2	397
Such rank as is permitted, or the meanest	607	Foscari	2	410
Would stifle nature's! Had I as many sons	608	Foscari	2	420
As I have years, I would have given them all	608	Foscari	2	421
As it, alas! has been, to ostracism	608	Foscari	2	425
So far with a weak woman as deny me	608	Foscari	2	431
So far take on myself, as order that	608	Foscari	2	433
For Venice but with such a yearning as	608	Foscari	3	11
Fittest for such a chronicle as this	608	Foscari	3	27
Which only can be read, as writ, by wretches	608	Foscari	3	28
As I had been without it. Couldst thou see here	609	Foscari	3	59
And the grey twilight of such glimmerings as	609	Foscari	3	62
More woful--such as this small dungeon, where	609	Foscari	3	93
Which men bequeath as portraits, and they were	610	Foscari	3	116
And here? At once--by better means, as briefer	610	Foscari	3	137
As well as home and heritage? My husband	610	Foscari	3	139
As threads which may be broken at her pleasure	611	Foscari	3	195
But--I can leave them, children as they are	611	Foscari	3	198
Which, as compared with what you have undergone	611	Foscari	3	205
Since you must love it, as it seems), and this	611	Foscari	3	217
Your exile as he bears it. Blame him not	611	Foscari	3	224
Which might have been forbidden now, as 'twas	611	Foscari	3	233
As spy upon us, or as hostage for us	612	Foscari	3	255
As how? I have inform'd him, not so gently	612	Foscari	3	260
Doubtless, as your nice feelings would prescribe	612	Foscari	3	261
Freedom as is the first imprisonment	612	Foscari	3	277
For him or such as he is. He receives them	612	Foscari	3	283
As they are offer'd. May they thrive with him	612	Foscari	3	284
This lady, of a house noble as yours	612	Foscari	3	288
Nobler! How nobler? As more generous	612	Foscari	3	289
And why not say as soon the 'generous man	612	Foscari	3	295
More than in years; and mine, which is as old	612	Foscari	3	297
As yours, is better in its product, nay	612	Foscari	3	298
A moment, as the eternal fire ere long	613	Foscari	3	313
To scatter o'er his kind as he thinks fit	613	Foscari	3	316
The hangman shrinks from, as all men from him	613	Foscari	3	331
How have you sped? We are wretched, signor, as	613	Foscari	3	332
And how feel you? As rocks. By thunder blasted	613	Foscari	3	334
As such I recommend it, as I would	613	Foscari	3	350
As worthiest, you, sir, noble Loredano	614	Foscari	3	381
Yes, light us on, as to a funeral pyre	614	Foscari	3	423
Bidding farewell? A last. As soon he shall	615	Foscari	4	13
As the first of his son's last banishment	615	Foscari	4	20
As much of ceremony as you will	615	Foscari	4	31
I have prepared such arguments as will not	615	Foscari	4	50
Of the sire as has fallen upon the son	615	Foscari	4	56
As long as he can drag them: 'tis his throne	615	Foscari	4	59
Most true. I say no more. As we hope, signor	616	Foscari	4	82
Be thus admitted, though as novices	616	Foscari	4	87
A point of time, as beacon to my heart	616	Foscari	4	103
And pleasant breezes, as I call upon you	616	Foscari	4	126
As the Phenicians did on Jonah, then	617	Foscari	4	143
Cast me out from amongst them as an offering	617	Foscari	4	144
(As I forgive you), for the gift of life	617	Foscari	4	162
Which you bestow'd upon me as my sire	617	Foscari	4	163
While he lived, he was theirs, as fits a subject	618	Foscari	4	205
As died their father. Oh, what best of blessings	618	Foscari	4	210
Eight months of such hypocrisy as is	619	Foscari	4	302
To private havoc, such as between him	620	Foscari	4	320
With phantoms, as this madness of the heart	620	Foscari	4	337
Against it at this moment. As you please	620	Foscari	4	354
Wax very old--old almost as my years	620	Foscari	5	9
Accept it as 'tis given--proceed. 'The Ten	621	Foscari	5	16
As I have laid down dearer things than life	621	Foscari	5	54
As my poor Foscari? Nothing was wanting	621	Foscari	5	75
I have seen him pass through such an ordeal as	622	Foscari	5	98
This from you. Oh, they'll hear as much one day	623	Foscari	5	145
From your imperial oath as sovereign	623	Foscari	5	169
Himself so far ungrateful, as to place	623	Foscari	5	181
As sign of our esteem. Not eight hours, signor	623	Foscari	5	189
As old as I am, and I'm very old	624	Foscari	5	215
To fall upon you! else they would, as erst	624	Foscari	5	218
In such a curse as mine, provoked by such	624	Foscari	5	222
As you; but I curse not. Adieu, good signors	624	Foscari	5	223
Inasmuch as it shows that I approach	624	Foscari	5	265
As sovereign--I go out as citizen	624	Foscari	5	274
By the same portals, but as citizen	625	Foscari	5	275
Applying poisons there as antidotes	625	Foscari	5	278
Most fit for such an hour as this. Why so	625	Foscari	5	293
Such pure antipathy to poisons as	625	Foscari	5	295
Had better now be seated, nor as yet	625	Foscari	5	301
Ah! now you look as look'd my husband	625	Foscari	5	302
Shall be such as befits his name and nation	625	Foscari	5	311
And made your power as proud as was his glory	625	Foscari	5	323
As far as touches torturing the living	625	Foscari	5	333
As Doge, but simply as a senator	626	Foscari	5	352
Of such. Well, sirs, your will be done! as one day	626	Foscari	5	360
My boy! thou speakest as I spoke, in sin	628	Cain	1	39
And do as he doth. Wilt thou not, by brother	628	Cain	1	52
Beauteous, and yet not all as beautiful	629	Cain	1	94
As he hath been, and might be: sorrow seems	629	Cain	1	95
Instinct of life, which I abhor, as I	629	Cain	1	113

AS

No more? It may be thou shalt be as we	629	Cain	1	120
As he saith--which I know not, nor believe	629	Cain	1	141
Thoughts which arise within me, as if they	630	Cain	1	174
Have stood before thee as I am: a serpent	630	Cain	1	191
Had been enough to charm ye, as before	630	Cain	1	192
And become gods as we.' Were those his words	630	Cain	1	202
They were, as I have heard from those who heard them	630	Cain	1	203
To them a shape I scorn, as I scorn all	631	Cain	1	234
Both them who sinn'd and sinn'd not, as an ill	631	Cain	1	284
But shall I know it? As I know not death	631	Cain	1	286
As yet have bow'd unto my father's God	632	Cain	1	308
Are ripe, and glowing as the light which ripens	632	Cain	1	336
But he is welcome, as they were: they deign'd	632	Cain	1	341
Not as thou lovest Cain. Oh, my God	633	Cain	1	364
Things which will love each other as we love	633	Cain	1	371
Them?--And as I love thee, my Cain! go not	633	Cain	1	372
Than was the serpent, and as false. As true	633	Cain	1	390
Dissatisfied and curious thoughts--as thou	633	Cain	1	400
Which, as I know it not, I dread not, though	634	Cain	1	466
To right, as in the dim blue air the eye	635	Cain	1	491
In seeming: as the silent sunny noon	635	Cain	1	506
With things that look as if they would be suns	635	Cain	1	511
As populous as this: at present there	635	Cain	1	540
Believe in me, as a conditional creed	636	Cain	2	21
Of Paradise. How should I? As we move	636	Cain	2	34
And as it waxes little, and then less	636	Cain	2	36
Methinks they both, as we recede from them	636	Cain	2	40
Which are around us; and, as we move on	636	Cain	2	42
As frail and few so happy--Spirit! I	637	Cain	2	60
Know nought of death, save as a dreadful thing	637	Cain	2	61
Of which I have heard my parents speak, as of	637	Cain	2	62
It be as thou hast said (and I within	637	Cain	2	66
I may be in the rest as angels are	637	Cain	2	77
I am angelic: wouldst thou be as I am	637	Cain	2	78
So humbly in their pride as to sojourn	637	Cain	2	84
Air, where ye roll along, as I have seen	637	Cain	2	103
They may be! Let me die as atoms die	637	Cain	2	113
I dare behold? As yet, thou hast shown nought	638	Cain	2	134
As I have shown thee much which cannot die	638	Cain	2	142
Had no beginning, have had one as mean	638	Cain	2	158
As thou; and mightier things have been extinct	638	Cain	2	159
And some till now grew larger as we approach'd	638	Cain	2	168
I seek it not; but as I know there are	639	Cain	2	192
But if it be as I have heard my father	639	Cain	2	221
Nor wear the form of man as I have view'd it	639	Cain	2	253
As the most beautiful and mighty which	640	Cain	2	265
As much superior unto all thy sire	640	Cain	2	274
Adam, could e'er have been in Eden, as	640	Cain	2	275
Yes, from their earth, as thou wilt fade from thine	640	Cain	2	280
But was mine theirs? It was. But not as now	640	Cain	2	281
Which struck a world to chaos, as a chaos	640	Cain	2	287
Material as thou art. And I must be	640	Cain	2	292
Inferior as thy petty feelings and	640	Cain	2	296
Of your poor attributes is such as suits	640	Cain	2	301
Knowledge was barr'd as poison. But behold	640	Cain	2	307
It cannot be: thou now beholdest as	640	Cain	2	315
As you for him. You would not have their doom	641	Cain	2	360
Forth from the abyss, looking as he could coil	642	Cain	2	398
Was not thy quest for knowledge? Yes, as being	642	Cain	2	435
My eyes with pleasant tears as I behold	643	Cain	2	465
As the day closes over Eden's walls	643	Cain	2	471
To gaze on it. 'Tis fair as frail mortality	643	Cain	2	474
Ev'n he who made us must be, as the maker	643	Cain	2	486
Dispell'd by antidotes. But as thou saidst	643	Cain	2	510
As was the apple in thy mother's eye	644	Cain	2	529
Have some allotted dwelling--as all things	644	Cain	2	574
To separate? Are ye not as brethren in	644	Cain	2	586
His creatures, as thou say'st we are, or show me	645	Cain	2	602
I battle it against him, as I battled	645	Cain	2	636
He as a conqueror will call the conquer'd	645	Cain	2	648
Of your existence, such as it must be	646	Cain	2	663
A gloomy tree, which looks as if it mourn'd	646	Cain	3	4
Lashes, dark as the cypress which waves o'er them	646	Cain	3	28
Shows more of fear than worship, as a bribe	647	Cain	3	102
Life to so much of sorrow as he must	648	Cain	3	133
Reflected in each other, as they are	648	Cain	3	145
Flutters as wing'd with joy. Talk not of pain	648	Cain	3	152
As yet he hath no words to thank thee, but	648	Cain	3	155
Singing in thunder round me, as have made me	649	Cain	3	183
If, as my elder, I revered thee not	649	Cain	3	197
My brother, as the elder, offer first	649	Cain	3	220
And I will follow--as I may. Oh God	649	Cain	3	223
His children all lost, as they might have been	649	Cain	3	227
The mercy which is thy delight as to	649	Cain	3	229
In itself nothing--as what offering can be	649	Cain	3	239
Thine attributes seem many, as thy works	650	Cain	3	250
Good to thee, inasmuch as they have not	650	Cain	3	263
Strike him, or spare him, as thou wilt! since all	650	Cain	3	273
Life cannot be so slight, as to be quench'd	651	Cain	3	351
As if he would not have asserted his	652	Cain	3	376
Speak, and assure us, wretched as we are	652	Cain	3	394

AS

All bonds I break between us, as he broke	652	Cain	3	410
In such sort as may show our God that we	652	Cain	3	417
As he did by his brother! May the swords	652	Cain	3	425
May the clear rivers turn to blood as he	652	Cain	3	432
Nothing except to leave thee, much as I	653	Cain	3	463
As yet unpeopled? Thou hast slain thy brother	653	Cain	3	484
Exemption from such deeds as thou hast done	653	Cain	3	499
Is there more? let me meet it as I may	654	Cain	3	502
As the ground thou must henceforth till; but he	654	Cain	3	504
Thou slew'st was gentle as the flocks he tended	654	Cain	3	505
As he adores the Highest, death becomes	655	Heaven		24
Of Earth, and love her as he once loved Anah	655	Heaven		30
All seraph as he is, I'd spurn him from me	655	Heaven		34
As he hath made me of the least	656	Heaven		58
For thee, immortal essence as thou art	656	Heaven		66
Of as eternal essence, and must war	656	Heaven		121
Thee in as warm a fold	656	Heaven		130
As--but descend, and prove	656	Heaven		131
As though they bore to-morrow's light	656	Heaven		138
Return'd to night, as rippling foam	657	Heaven		153
Perhaps she looks upon them as I look	657	Heaven		164
Becometh more so as it looks on beauty	657	Heaven		166
Had love been met with love: as 'tis, I leave her	657	Heaven		175
I take thy taunt as part of thy distemper	657	Heaven		188
And would not feel as thou dost for more shekels	657	Heaven		189
As if such useless and discolour'd trash	657	Heaven		193
Sigh to the stars, as wolves howl to the moon	657	Heaven		197
With gloom as sad: it is a hopeless spot	657	Heaven		205
As not being of them: turn thy steps aside	658	Heaven		211
As a star in the clouds, which cannot quench	658	Heaven		235
He said; but as I fear, to bend his steps	658	Heaven		245
For angels to alight on, as the spot	659	Heaven		296
Whose love had made me love thee more; but as	659	Heaven		317
Such as--Oh God! and canst thou--In the name	659	Heaven		320
As even to hear this wide destruction named	660	Heaven		404
Without such grief and courage, as should rather	660	Heaven		405
As of a different order in the sphere	660	Heaven		413
And scorn thy sire as the surviving one	660	Heaven		423
Beside the lamb, as though he were his brother	661	Heaven		445
Till all things shall be as they were	661	Heaven		446
Where man no more can fall as once he fell	661	Heaven		468
Shall oversweep the future, as the waves	661	Heaven		482
Still, as they were from the beginning, blind	661	Heaven		493
As on the fourth day of creation, when	662	Heaven		552
A void: without man, time, as made for man	662	Heaven		572
Which has no fountain; as his race will be	662	Heaven		574
Welcome as Eden. It may be they come	663	Heaven		584
Then ye are lost, as they are lost. So be it	663	Heaven		624
If they love as they are loved, they will not shrink	663	Heaven		625
As thine, and mine: a God of love, not sorrow	665	Heaven		726
Far less the sons of God; but as our God	665	Heaven		748
And, as the latest birth of his great word	666	Heaven		793
As they wax proud within	666	Heaven		806
Dost thou not err as we	666	Heaven		818
Made him as suns to a dependent star	666	Heaven		844
And meet the wave, as we would meet the sword	667	Heaven		891
Obey him, as we shall obey	667	Heaven		903
And as your pinions bear ye back to heaven	667	Heaven		910
The blow, though not unlook'd for, falls as new	667	Heaven		922
Live as he wills it--die, when he ordains	667	Heaven		953
But they are numerous now as are the waves	668	Heaven		974
Shorn as ye are of all celestial power	668	Heaven		988
Earth groans as if beneath a heavy load	668	Heaven		995
But be, when passion passeth, good as thou	668	Heaven		1033
Rebel! thy words are wicked, as thy deeds	669	Heaven		1049
Some clouds sweep on as vultures for their prey	669	Heaven		1071
While others, fix'd as rocks, await the word	669	Heaven		1072
As was the eagle's nestling once within	669	Heaven		1082
But as we know the worst	670	Heaven		1123
Yet, as his word	670	Heaven		1151
No; let me die, as I have lived, in faith	670	Heaven		1168
And have of late been sickly, as, alas	672	Werner	1	20
Kept his eye on me, as the snake upon	673	Werner	1	84
Entailing, as it were, my sins upon	673	Werner	1	92
We had not felt our poverty but as	673	Werner	1	136
Thou mightst have earn'd thy bread, as thousands earn it	673	Werner	1	139
In youth was such as to unmake as empire	673	Werner	1	153
Egad! I am afraid. You look as if	674	Werner	1	176
I say you have been our lodger, and as yet	674	Werner	1	184
As e'er was gilt upon a trader's board	674	Werner	1	187
And the valet, and the cattle; but as yet	675	Werner	1	218
As it is fit that men in office should be	675	Werner	1	221
A lodging, or a grave, according as	675	Werner	1	227
As fits a noble guest:--'tis damp, no doubt	675	Werner	1	232
No doubt you'll have a swingeing sum as recompense	676	Werner	1	291
Then, as we never met before, and never	676	Werner	1	321
Pray, pardon me; my health--Even as you please	676	Werner	1	326
To live as they best may; and, to say truth	676	Werner	1	335
And not unkind as to an unknown stranger	677	Werner	1	362

AS

As most good fellows are, by pain or pleasure	677	Werner	1	369
To have seen better days, as who has not	677	Werner	1	372
At least in beauty: as for majesty	677	Werner	1	396
He's poor as Job, and not so patient; but	677	Werner	1	401
That's true; but pity, as you know, does make	677	Werner	1	413
And so I thought they might as well be lodged	678	Werner	1	417
Here as at the small tavern, and I gave them	678	Werner	1	418
They served to air them, at the least as long	678	Werner	1	420
As they could pay for fire-wood. Poor souls! Ay	678	Werner	1	421
A blaze of torches from without. As sure	678	Werner	1	429
As destiny, his excellency's come	678	Werner	1	430
All roaring 'Help!' but offering none; and as	678	Werner	1	439
For duty (as you call it)--I did mine then	678	Werner	1	440
Now, as he one day will forever lie	679	Werner	1	518
As sometimes happens to the better clad	680	Werner	1	546
Still as the breathless interval between	681	Werner	1	636
I wot of: it will serve me as a den	681	Werner	1	640
I help'd to save him, as in peril; but	681	Werner	1	654
And have risk'd more than drowning for as much	682	Werner	1	669
Of yours be stretch'd as parchment on a drum	682	Werner	1	694
As these; and our all-ripe and gushing valleys	682	Werner	1	711
Rain'd, as it were, the beverage which makes glad	682	Werner	1	714
To wring his soul--as the bleak elements	682	Werner	1	723
That twenty years of usage, such as no	682	Werner	1	726
Ulric! I love my son, as thou didst me	682	Werner	1	734
The man call'd Werner's poor! Poor as a miser	683	Werner	2	19
Of peculation; such as in accompts	684	Werner	2	43
Where all men take their prey; as also in	684	Werner	2	45
We scorn it as we do board-wages. Then	684	Werner	2	50
Have been so poor a spirit as to hazard	684	Werner	2	52
And educated as his heir; but then	684	Werner	2	93
A house as Siegendorf's. The grandsire ill	684	Werner	2	98
And grandsire's qualities,--impetuous as	684	Werner	2	106
The former, and deep as the latter; but	684	Werner	2	107
An hour so critical as was the eve	684	Werner	2	111
As there was something strange and mystic in him	685	Werner	2	122
That they will seek for peril as a pleasure	685	Werner	2	135
As ardently for glory as you dared	685	Werner	2	161
In an as perilous, but opposite, element	685	Werner	2	163
Is but a petty war, as the times show us	685	Werner	2	170
My lord, not much as yet, except conjecture	686	Werner	2	215
Some rumour of it reach'd me as I pass'd	686	Werner	2	227
You (as I still am rather faint) would add	686	Werner	2	242
None; so let's march: we'll talk as we go on	686	Werner	2	249
Handsome as Hercules ere his first labour	687	Werner	2	255
For years I've track'd, as does the bloodhound, never	687	Werner	2	267
As snakes and lions shrink back from each other	687	Werner	2	278
As those who fare well everywhere, when they	687	Werner	2	300
As being anxious to resume my journey	687	Werner	2	312
The Oder to divide, as Moses did	687	Werner	2	318
His sixteen quarterings, for as much fresh air	688	Werner	2	328
As would have fill'd a bladder, while he lay	688	Werner	2	329
'Tis strange they should, when such as he may put them	688	Werner	2	334
He comes not only as a son, but saviour	688	Werner	2	344
I must be known here but as Werner. Come	688	Werner	2	360
As you say that 'tis perilous)--but i' the pomp	688	Werner	2	373
Of his broad lands as to make mine the foremost	689	Werner	2	391
As he betray'd last night; and I, perhaps	689	Werner	2	411
Is sick; a stranger; and as such not now	689	Werner	2	419
Even to your deadliest for; and he, as 'twere	690	Werner	2	455
Deem yourself safe, as young and brave; but learn	690	Werner	2	464
Think as he speaks. Alas! long years of grief	690	Werner	2	500
I'll honour you so much as save your throat	691	Werner	2	513
Such as would leave your scutcheon but a blank	692	Werner	2	565
Except such villains as ne'er had it? You	692	Werner	2	573
Can vouch your courage, and, as far as my	692	Werner	2	583
As you accuse. You hint the basest injury	692	Werner	2	601
As you have said, 'tis true I owe you something	692	Werner	2	603
You, baron, I believe; but as the effect	693	Werner	2	628
Am I concern'd? As one who did so much	694	Werner	2	698
Watch him!--as you would watch the wild boar when	694	Werner	2	703
As I have said, you shall. I accept the omen	694	Werner	2	716
Such as both may make worthy your acceptance	694	Werner	2	718
This Paradise?--(As Adam did between	694	Werner	2	722
Whom the old man--the grandsire (as old age	694	Werner	2	736
As it went chilly downward to the grave	694	Werner	2	738
Is pitiful)--he is a wretch, as likely	695	Werner	2	751
To have robb'd me as the fellow more suspected	695	Werner	2	752
A shelter?--wanting such myself as much	695	Werner	3	5
As e'er the hunted deer a covert--Or	695	Werner	3	6
As undeservedly as you. Again	695	Werner	3	17
As I? Or any other honest man	695	Werner	3	18
Because I feel it) as may leave no nightmare	695	Werner	3	38
You are no thief, nor I; and, as true men	695	Werner	3	41
So is the nearest of the two next, as	695	Werner	3	43
Therefore I'll stick by this, as being loth	696	Werner	3	45
An epitaph as larceny upon my tomb	696	Werner	3	47
To-morrow I will try the waters as	696	Werner	3	49
Rightly; for how should such a wretch as I	696	Werner	3	59
As I have said: it leads through winding walls	696	Werner	3	87
(So thick as to bear paths within their ribs	696	Werner	3	88

AS

As frail as any other life or glory	697	Werner	3	124
You have divined the man? As sure as you	697	Werner	3	128
But must break through them, as an unarm'd carle	697	Werner	3	160
The topic--You mean to pursue it, as	697	Werner	3	169
As such is now your own. With this you must	698	Werner	3	188
Of me as aught of kindred with yourself	698	Werner	3	222
Your father knew you not as I do. Scorpions	698	Werner	3	230
And I embrace it, as I did my son	699	Werner	3	246
Situate as we are now, although the first	699	Werner	3	252
Possessor might, as usual, prove the strongest	699	Werner	3	253
(As it is call'd) are aliens to each other	699	Werner	3	258
And ooze too, from the bottom, as the lead doth	699	Werner	3	267
Keep off from me as from your foe! Accursed	699	Werner	3	274
Must be answer'd on the instant, as the bound	699	Werner	3	285
I fear that men must draw their chariots, as	699	Werner	3	288
But come, I'll serve thee; thou shalt be as free	700	Werner	3	347
As air, despite the waters; let us hence	700	Werner	3	348
Sits on me as a cloud along the sky	700	Werner	3	360
All folly. Were the locks (as I desired	700	Werner	3	369
Of him who saved your master, as a litany	701	Werner	3	378
As through a crevice or a key-hole in	701	Werner	3	408
In such a den as this. Pray Heaven it lead me	701	Werner	3	412
Lands, freedom, life,--and yet he sleeps as soundly	702	Werner	3	452
Perhaps, as infancy, with gorgeous curtains	702	Werner	3	453
Such as when--Hark! what noise is that? Again	702	Werner	3	455
Insane or insolent! Reply, sir, as	702	Werner	3	461
Of Stralenheim? I never was as yet	702	Werner	3	464
Did not you this night (as the night before	702	Werner	3	466
As from mine eyes! But Stralenheim is dead	702	Werner	3	478
'Tis horrible! 'tis hideous, as 'tis hateful	702	Werner	3	479
Have been alarm'd; but as the intendant is	702	Werner	3	483
Link'd with the Hungarian's, or preferr'd as poorest	703	Werner	3	547
As heir of Siegendorf: if Idenstein	703	Werner	3	557
Here, save as such--without lands, influence	703	Werner	3	567
Obscure as his deserts, without a scutcheon	703	Werner	3	573
May howl above his ashes (as they did	703	Werner	3	577
To me: I'll answer for the event as far	704	Werner	3	587
As regards you, and that is the chief point	704	Werner	3	588
As my first duty which shall be observed	704	Werner	3	589
Though made by a new grave: but as for wassail	704	Werner	4	5
His feudal hospitality as high	704	Werner	4	7
As e'er another prince of the empire. Why	704	Werner	4	8
Fared passing well; but as for merriment	704	Werner	4	10
As yet he hath been courteous as he's bounteous	704	Werner	4	15
And we all love him. His reign is as yet	704	Werner	4	16
And strong and beautiful as a young tiger	704	Werner	4	24
Perhaps a true one. Pity, as I said	704	Werner	4	26
Already done as much. What do you mean	704	Werner	4	38
As--What? The war (you love so much) leaves living	704	Werner	4	42
Such as old Tilly loved. And who loved Tilly	705	Werner	4	45
He--might prevent it. As you say he's fond	705	Werner	4	56
You'd better ask himself. I would as soon	705	Werner	4	58
The knees of Homicide; sprinkled, as it were	705	Werner	4	71
You know it well? As well as on that night	706	Werner	4	107
To our force with you and Wolffe, as herald of	706	Werner	4	112
At this time, as my father loves to keep	706	Werner	4	114
As woman should be loved, fairly and solely	706	Werner	4	123
And do as I have said. I will. But to	706	Werner	4	136
To hail her as his daughter. Wondrous kind	706	Werner	4	140
Especially as little kindness till	706	Werner	4	141
It sounds so cold, as if you thought upon	706	Werner	4	155
Proud (as is birth's prerogative); but under	707	Werner	4	180
Had such as you been near him on his journey	707	Werner	4	182
All dreams are false. And yet I see him as	707	Werner	4	194
Because you look as if you saw a murderer	707	Werner	4	199
Infects me, to my shame: but as all feelings	707	Werner	4	201
The chase with such an ardour as will scarce	708	Werner	4	237
Then pray you be as punctual to its notes	708	Werner	4	271
As I directed: and by his best speed	708	Werner	4	279
As thou appear'st to love her. I have said	709	Werner	4	344
Obey you in espousing her? As far	710	Werner	4	369
As you feel, nothing, but all life for her	710	Werner	4	370
Such as rounds common life into a dream	710	Werner	4	373
For any woman; and as what I fix	710	Werner	4	395
The eyes of feminine, as though they were	710	Werner	4	408
Throng round him as a leader: but with me	711	Werner	4	427
Though he died not by me or mine, as much	711	Werner	4	444
As if he were my brother! I have ta'en	711	Werner	4	445
His orphan Ida--cherish'd her as one	711	Werner	4	446
For one unknown, the same as for the proudest	711	Werner	4	480
As he did me. I do not love him now	712	Werner	4	492
As I can one day God's. Nor did he die	712	Werner	4	512
As unemploy'd. Except by one day's knowledge	712	Werner	4	517
Of this man weighs on me, as if I shed it	712	Werner	4	523
For, as I said, though I be innocent	712	Werner	4	530
As if he had fallen by me or mine. Pray for me	712	Werner	4	532
Be calm as innocence. But calmness is not	712	Werner	4	535
As well as your brave son; and smooth your aspect	712	Werner	4	541
As far as the man's dress and figure could	713	Werner	5	5
Which seem'd as if they rather came from heaven	713	Werner	5	22

AS

In the world's eye, as goodly. There's, for instance	714	Werner	5	58
Which make my head and heart ache, as both throb	714	Werner	5	72
I live! and as I live, I saw him	714	Werner	5	86
With all the nobles, and as I look'd down	714	Werner	5	98
No more, then? I look'd, as a dying soldier	715	Werner	5	120
As on the loftiest and the loveliest head	715	Werner	5	125
When just as the artillery ceased, and paused	715	Werner	5	130
A crime as--Give it utterance, and then	715	Werner	5	156
Ulric, repel this calumny, as I	716	Werner	5	179
My God! you look--How? As on that dread night	716	Werner	5	184
By Stralenheim's death? Was't I--as poor as ever	716	Werner	5	193
These hints, as vague as vain, attach no less	716	Werner	5	199
And courage as unrivall'd, were proclaim'd	717	Werner	5	246
And show them as they are--even in their faces	717	Werner	5	259
'This is the man!' though he was then, as since	717	Werner	5	261
As she doth to the daring, and on whom	717	Werner	5	271
Near to this man, as if my point of fortune	717	Werner	5	274
So high, as now I find you, in my then	717	Werner	5	286
Men such as you appear'd in height of mind	717	Werner	5	288
As much as made a crevice of the fastening	718	Werner	5	313
Do thou as much! Be patient! I can not	718	Werner	5	324
As I see yours; but yours they were not, though	718	Werner	5	336
Distinct as I beheld them, though the expression	718	Werner	5	338
For him at any time, as had been proved	718	Werner	5	349
But ne'er slept guilt as Werner slept that night	718	Werner	5	356
As might have envied mine, I offer'd you	719	Werner	5	373
As Stralenheim is. Are you so dull	719	Werner	5	409
As never to have hit on this before	719	Werner	5	410
Whose life I saved from impulse, as, unknown	720	Werner	5	456
Known as our foe--but not from vengeance. He	720	Werner	5	458
As stranger I preserved him, and he owed me	720	Werner	5	462
It seems: I might have guess'd as much. Oh fool	720	Werner	5	485
(As I too) of the opposite door which leads	720	Werner	5	487
'Twas as I said--the wretch hath stript my father	721	Werner	5	515
But as thou hast--hence, hence--and do thy best	722	Deformed	1	5
More high, if not so broad as that of others	722	Deformed	1	7
So beautiful and lusty, and as free	722	Deformed	1	18
As the free chase they follow, do not spurn me	722	Deformed	1	19
Our milk has been the same. As is the hedgehog's	722	Deformed	1	20
As foolish hens at times hatch vipers, by	722	Deformed	1	26
Would rise a snake to sting them, as they have stung me	722	Deformed	1	39
Vile form--from the creation, as it hath	723	Deformed	1	65
Now, knife, stand firmly, as I fain would fall	723	Deformed	1	75
Not as with air, but by some subterrane	723	Deformed	1	79
Spirit or man? As man is both, why not	723	Deformed	1	82
As the cloud-shapen giant	724	Deformed	1	163
Come as ye were	724	Deformed	1	165
Bright as the Iris	724	Deformed	1	169
But not as a mock Caesar. Let him pass	725	Deformed	1	196
As if he knew the worthlessness of those	725	Deformed	1	235
No. As you leave me choice, I am difficult	726	Deformed	1	241
Which he wears as the sun his rays--a something	726	Deformed	1	250
As beautiful and clear as the amber waves	726	Deformed	1	268
All vow'd to Sperchius as they were--behold them	726	Deformed	1	272
And him--as he stood by Polixena	726	Deformed	1	273
He stood i' the temple! Look upon him as	726	Deformed	1	280
As if I were his soul, whose form shall soon	726	Deformed	1	283
I am impatient. As a youthful beauty	726	Deformed	1	288
Would rise against thee now, as if to hunt	726	Deformed	1	304
In Styx. Then let it be as thou deem'st best	727	Deformed	1	310
Thou shalt be beauteous as the thing thou seest	727	Deformed	1	311
And strong as what it was, and--I ask not	727	Deformed	1	312
As still are free to both, to compensate	727	Deformed	1	319
Form'd as thou art. I may dismiss the mould	727	Deformed	1	324
In feeling, on my heart as on my shoulders	727	Deformed	1	332
Had made me something--as it has made heroes	727	Deformed	1	351
Of the same mould as mine. You lately saw me	727	Deformed	1	352
And sweeter to my heart. As I am now	727	Deformed	1	358
Would be beloved. As thou showest me	727	Deformed	1	361
The poet's god, clothed in such limbs as are	727	Deformed	1	368
As the being who made him	728	Deformed	1	386
Be as fair as, when blowing	728	Deformed	1	390
As thou wavest in air	728	Deformed	1	399
But his voice as the warble	728	Deformed	1	402
Ay, as the dunghill may conceal a gem	728	Deformed	1	432
Which is now set in gold, as jewels should be	728	Deformed	1	433
I will be as you were, and you shall see	728	Deformed	1	447
Yourself for ever by you, as your shadow	728	Deformed	1	448
From seeing what you were? Do as thou wilt	728	Deformed	1	451
Tugging as usual at each other's hearts	729	Deformed	1	500
Around their manes, as common insects swarm	729	Deformed	1	516
But looks as serious though serene as night	730	Deformed	1	530
As many attributes; but as I wear	730	Deformed	1	534
Swifter as it waxes higher	730	Deformed	1	552
But be winged as a griffin	730	Deformed	1	562
A comet, and destroying as it sweeps	730	Deformed	1	594
Of joy (as once of torture unto him	731	Deformed	1	610
In the arena (as right well they might	731	Deformed	1	624
Life to their amphitheatre, as well	731	Deformed	1	627
As Dacia men to die the eternal death	731	Deformed	1	628

AS

The sun goes down as calmly, and perhaps	731	Deformed	1	638
And loved his laurels better as a wig	731	Deformed	1	645
(So history says) than as a glory. Thus	731	Deformed	1	646
I saw your Romulus (simple as I am)	731	Deformed	1	648
Be spilt till the choked Tiber be as red	731	Deformed	1	653
As e'er 'twas yellow, it will never wear	731	Deformed	1	654
And why should they not sing as well as swans	731	Deformed	1	665
As mounts each firm foot	732	Deformed	1	708
Upon the eve of conquest such as ours	732	Deformed	1	745
The beauty of our host, and brave as beauteous	733	Deformed	1	788
And generous as lovely. We shall find	733	Deformed	1	789
For you have seen that back--as general	733	Deformed	1	794
In danger's face as yours, were you the devil	733	Deformed	1	799
Slight crooked friend's as snake-like in his words	733	Deformed	1	805
As in his deeds. Your highness much mistakes me	733	Deformed	1	806
In speech as sharp in action--and that's more	733	Deformed	1	810
And worse even for their friends than foes, as being	734	Deformed	1	812
I'll lie--it is as easy: then you'll praise me	734	Deformed	1	817
To-morrow. I have heard as much, my lord	734	Deformed	1	836
That we will fight as well, and rule much better	734	Deformed	1	852
Is yours, as in the field. In both we prize it	734	Deformed	1	874
And thinks chaotically, as it acts	735	Deformed	1	886
As the tides obey the moon	735	Deformed	2	16
Regular as rolling water	735	Deformed	2	18
As the stripes that streak an adder	735	Deformed	2	26
Awful as thy brother's crime	735	Deformed	2	38
As the earthquake saps the hill	735	Deformed	2	42
Numerous as wolves, and stronger	736	Deformed	2	60
Fight as thou wast wont to vanquish	736	Deformed	2	102
Turn, as doth the lion baited	736	Deformed	2	120
Till they are conquerors--then do as you may	736	Deformed	2	136
As though it were an altar; now his foot	737	Deformed	2	162
Their hose as they have doff'd their hats, 'twould be	737	Deformed	2	178
A blessing, as a mark the less for plunder	737	Deformed	2	179
Who slays Cellini will have work'd as hard	738	Deformed	2	212
As e'er thou didst upon Carrara's blocks	738	Deformed	2	213
Beheld mankind, as mere spectators of	738	Deformed	2	227
Meantime, pursue thy sport as I do mine	738	Deformed	2	232
Why, such I fain would show me. True--as men are	738	Deformed	2	236
And thy Son's Mother, now receive me as	740	Deformed	2	307
Have as much right as he. But to the issue	740	Deformed	2	311
As you are bold within it. Mercy! mercy	740	Deformed	2	330
As red as Tiber now runs, for your baptism	740	Deformed	2	341
It is for God to judge thee as thou art	740	Deformed	2	360
But not less pure (pure as it left me then	741	Deformed	2	366
Good words, however, are as well at times	741	Deformed	2	375
I say she lives. And will she live? As much	741	Deformed	2	393
As dust can. Then she is dead! Bah! bah! You are so	741	Deformed	2	394
Such as you think so, such as you now are	741	Deformed	2	396
Softly! As softly as they bear the dead	741	Deformed	2	400
I am almost enamour'd of her, as	741	Deformed	2	413
Colonna, as I told you! Oh! I know	742	Deformed	2	427
As he yawns in the hall	742	Deformed	3	30
As towers in our time	742	Deformed	3	59
Olimpia! I thought as much--go on	743	Deformed	3	109
As an abstraction--for--you know not what	744	Deformed	3	132
Is as a shadow of the Sun. The Orb	744	Deformed	3	138
Is mighty--as you mortals deem--and to	744	Deformed	3	139
But, great as He appears, and is to you	744	Deformed	3	141
Upon a Sky which you revile as dull	744	Deformed	3	144
Now Love in you is as the Sun--a thing	744	Deformed	3	147
All wretched as I am, I would not quit	744	Deformed	3	164
To be her heart as she is mine	744	Deformed	3	168
To deem as a most logical conclusion	745	Juan	Ded	37
Scope to all such as feel the inherent glow	746	Juan	Ded	54
To worth as freedom, wisdom as to wit	747	Juan	Ded	118
My politics as yet are all to educate	747	Juan	Ded	133
Of such as these I should not care to vaunt	747	Juan	1	5
Were French, and famous people, as we know	747	Juan	1	19
So, as I said, I'll take my friend Don Juan	747	Juan	1	40
Forbids all wandering as the worst of sinning	748	Juan	1	52
Could never make a memory so fine as	748	Juan	1	87
As if she deem'd that mystery would ennoble 'em	748	Juan	1	104
Even her minutest motions went as well	749	Juan	1	133
As those of the best time-piece made by Harrison	749	Juan	1	134
Perfect she was, but as perfection is	749	Juan	1	137
The world, as usual, wickedly inclined	749	Juan	1	149
They lived respectably as man and wife	750	Juan	1	204
But as he had some lucid intermissions	750	Juan	1	211
Just as the Spartan ladies did of yore	750	Juan	1	227
I'm not to blame, as you well know--no more is	751	Juan	1	243
As Numa's (who was also named Pompilius	751	Juan	1	279
The arts, at least all such as could be said	752	Juan	1	315
Ovid's a rake, as half his verses show him	752	Juan	1	329
So much indeed as to be downright rude	752	Juan	1	342
As Saint Augustine in his fine Confessions	753	Juan	1	375
I recommend as much to every wife	753	Juan	1	384
With all the promise of as fine a face	753	Juan	1	387
As e'er to man's maturer growth was given	753	Juan	1	388

AS

To school (as God be praised that I have none	753	Juan	1	412
As well as all the Greek I since have lost	753	Juan	1	419
I think I pick'd up too, as well as most	753	Juan	1	421
Active, though not so sprightly, as a page	753	Juan	1	427
Of many charms in her as natural	753	Juan	1	437
As sweetness to the flower, or salt to ocean	753	Juan	1	438
That they bred in and in, as might be shown	754	Juan	1	454
Sprung up a branch as beautiful as fresh	754	Juan	1	460
As if her veins ran lightning; she, in sooth	754	Juan	1	486
They lived together, as most people do	755	Juan	1	516
Juan she saw, and, as a pretty child	755	Juan	1	545
But as for Juan, he had no more notion	755	Juan	1	559
As if her heart had deeper thoughts in store	755	Juan	1	571
Even by its darkness; as the blackest sky	756	Juan	1	578
As being the best judge of a lady's case	756	Juan	1	600
And then there are such things as love divine	756	Juan	1	625
Such as the angels think so very fine	756	Juan	1	627
Platonic, perfect, 'just such love as mine	756	Juan	1	629
That all the Apostles would have done as they did	757	Juan	1	664
In feelings quick as Ovid's Miss Medea	757	Juan	1	684
But not as yet imagined it could be a	757	Juan	1	686
'Oh Love! in such a wilderness as this	757	Juan	1	697
As all have found on trial, or may find	757	Juan	1	708
Or 'transport,' as we knew all that before	757	Juan	1	711
Even as the page is rustled while we look	758	Juan	1	755
As if 'twere one whereon magicians bind	758	Juan	1	758
Though watchful as the lynx, they ne'er discover	759	Juan	1	794
When Julia sate within as pretty a bower	759	Juan	1	827
As e'er held houri in that heathenish heaven	759	Juan	1	828
But then, no doubt, it equally as true is	760	Juan	1	863
As if it said, 'Detain me, if you please	760	Juan	1	883
She would have shrunk as from a toad, or asp	760	Juan	1	886
I care not for new pleasures, as the old	761	Juan	1	943
In the design, and as I have a high sense	761	Juan	1	958
'Tis sweet to listen as the night-winds creep	761	Juan	1	974
Bay deep-mouth'd welcome as we draw near home	762	Juan	1	978
No doubt in fable, as the unforgiven	762	Juan	1	1015
Are ways to benefit mankind, as true	763	Juan	1	1055
Perhaps, as shooting them at Waterloo	763	Juan	1	1056
'Twas, as the watchmen say, a cloudy night	763	Juan	1	1073
Even as a summer sky's without a cloud	763	Juan	1	1078
Poor Donna Julia, starting as from sleep	764	Juan	1	1113
As if she had just now from out them crept	764	Juan	1	1118
Of looking in the bed as well as under	764	Juan	1	1152
But, as my maid's undrest, pray turn your spies out	765	Juan	1	1215
I leave you to your conscience as before	766	Juan	1	1253
Like skies that rain and lighten; as a veil	766	Juan	1	1259
Quick, thick, and heavy--as a thunder-shower	766	Juan	1	1288
Reluctantly, still tarrying there as late as	767	Juan	1	1307
An awkward look; as he revolved the case	767	Juan	1	1311
Nothing so dear as an unfilch'd good name	767	Juan	1	1317
So much as when we call our old debts in	767	Juan	1	1334
But that can't be, as has been often shown	768	Juan	1	1404
Are such as fit with ladies' feet, but these	769	Juan	1	1442
At last, as they more faintly wrestling lay	769	Juan	1	1484
The passion which still rages as before	771	Juan	1	1558
As roll the waves before the settled wind	771	Juan	1	1564
As vibrates my fond heart to my fix'd soul	771	Juan	1	1568
And yet I may as well the task fulfil	771	Juan	1	1571
It trembled as magnetic needles do	771	Juan	1	1580
Exactly as you please, or not,--the rod	772	Juan	1	1647
And if, as I believe, thy vein be good	774	Juan	1	1771
And as the veering wind shifts, shift our sails	774	Juan	2	28
As if a Spanish ship were Noah's ark	775	Juan	2	62
(As every kind of parting has its stings	775	Juan	2	69
As I, who've cross'd it oft, know well enough	775	Juan	2	84
So Juan wept, as wept the captive Jews	776	Juan	2	121
But die, as many an exiled heart hath died	776	Juan	2	139
Of us dies with them as each fond hope ends	776	Juan	2	166
But the sea acted as a strong emetic	776	Juan	2	168
But they could not come at the leak as yet	777	Juan	2	220
As day advanced the weather seem'd to abate	777	Juan	2	233
The wind blew fresh again: as it grew late	777	Juan	2	237
To lose their lives, as well as spoil their diet	778	Juan	2	260
As upon such occasions tars will ask	778	Juan	2	263
As rum and true religion: thus it was	778	Juan	2	266
The high wind made the treble, and as bass	778	Juan	2	268
As if Death were more dreadful by his door	778	Juan	2	277
And never had as yet a quiet day	779	Juan	2	316
That made his eyelids as a woman's be	779	Juan	2	342
And others went on as they had begun	779	Juan	2	354
As now might render their long suffering less	779	Juan	2	364
As there were but two blankets for a sail	780	Juan	2	380
As eager to anticipate their grave	780	Juan	2	412
The boats, as stated, had got off before	780	Juan	2	425
It seem'd as if they had exchanged their care	781	Juan	2	443
As o'er the cutter's edge he tried to cross	781	Juan	2	452
His father's, whom he loved, as ye may think	781	Juan	2	458
As every rising wave his dread renew'd	781	Juan	2	469
So that themselves as well as hopes were damp'd	781	Juan	2	479
She had a curious crew as well as cargo	782	Juan	2	527
But as they had but one oar, and that brittle	782	Juan	2	551

AS

As a great favour one of the fore-paws	783	Juan	2	566
He died as born, a Catholic in faith	783	Juan	2	605
The surgeon, as there was no other fee	783	Juan	2	609
And such things as the entrails and the brains	783	Juan	2	614
As if not warn'd sufficiently by those	784	Juan	2	638
As fattest; but he saved himself, because	784	Juan	2	642
Which served them as a sort of spongy pitcher	784	Juan	2	675
As a full pot of porter, to their thinking	784	Juan	2	679
As the rich man's in hell, who vainly scream'd	785	Juan	2	684
As if to win a part from off the weight	785	Juan	2	702
It is as well to think so, now and then	785	Juan	2	738
Was not so safe for roosting as a church	786	Juan	2	756
As morning broke, the light wind died away	786	Juan	2	769
And seem'd as if they had no further care	786	Juan	2	780
And higher grew the mountains as they drew	786	Juan	2	794
The spray into their faces as they splash'd	787	Juan	2	808
As they drew nigh the land, which now was seen	787	Juan	2	817
As once (a feat on which ourselves we prided	787	Juan	2	839
As for the other two, they could not swim	787	Juan	2	847
Just as his feeble arms could strike no more	787	Juan	2	851
And the hard wave o'erwhelm'd him as 'twas dash'd	787	Juan	2	852
And as he gazed, his dizzy brain spun fast	788	Juan	2	873
And down he sunk; and as he sunk, the sand	788	Juan	2	874
As fair a thing as e'er was form'd of clay	788	Juan	2	880
To kindle fire, and as the new flames gave	788	Juan	2	917
As one who was a lady in the land	789	Juan	2	928
Were black as death, their lashes the same hue	789	Juan	2	930
'Tis as the snake late coil'd, who pours his length	789	Juan	2	935
For, as you know, the Spanish women banish	789	Juan	2	956
As black, but quicker, and of smaller size	789	Juan	2	976
Which are (as I must own) of female growth	789	Juan	2	979
And sometimes caught as many as he wish'd	790	Juan	2	1004
Her dowry was as nothing to her smiles	790	Juan	2	1020
As far as in her lay, 'to take him in	790	Juan	2	1031
They made a fire,--but such a fire as they	790	Juan	2	1049
Materials as were cast up round the bay	790	Juan	2	1051
Who smooth'd his pillow, as she left the den	791	Juan	2	1074
(The heart will slip, even as the tongue and pen	791	Juan	2	1078
And Zoe spent hers, as most women do	791	Juan	2	1086
Which hastens, as physicians say, one's fate	792	Juan	2	1116
Although the mortal, quite as fresh and fair	792	Juan	2	1135
And then she stopp'd, and stood as if in awe	792	Juan	2	1140
Should reach his blood, then o'er him still as death	792	Juan	2	1143
As o'er him lay the calm and stirless air	792	Juan	2	1148
That sleep which seem'd as it would ne'er awake	792	Juan	2	1168
Hush'd as the babe upon its mother's breast	793	Juan	2	1178
Droop'd as the willow when no winds can breathe	793	Juan	2	1179
Fair as the crowning rose of the whole wreath	793	Juan	2	1181
Soft as the callow cygnet in its nest	793	Juan	2	1182
As with an effort she began to speak	793	Juan	2	1196
Whence Melody descends as from a throne	793	Juan	2	1208
And Juan gazed as one who is awoke	793	Juan	2	1209
As all his latter meals had been quite raw	794	Juan	2	1252
And, as he interrupted not, went eking	794	Juan	2	1285
As he who studies fervently the skies	794	Juan	2	1301
As was the case, at least, where I have been	795	Juan	2	1308
As for the ladies, I have nought to say	795	Juan	2	1321
Some feelings, universal as the sun	795	Juan	2	1331
Were such as could not in his breast be shut	795	Juan	2	1332
He was in love,--as you would be, no doubt	795	Juan	2	1334
As o'er a bed of roses the sweet south	795	Juan	2	1344
Besides her maid's as pretty for their size	795	Juan	2	1364
To her, as 'twere, the kind of being sent	796	Juan	2	1371
Not as of yore to carry off an Io	796	Juan	2	1391
Free as a married woman, or such other	796	Juan	2	1395
Female, as where she likes may freely pass	796	Juan	2	1396
So much as to propose to take a walk	796	Juan	2	1403
Guarded by shoals and rocks as by an host	796	Juan	2	1411
Lay at this period quiet as the sky	797	Juan	2	1443
As I have said, upon an expedition	797	Juan	2	1450
Which then seems as if the whole earth it bounded	797	Juan	2	1459
Work'd by the storms, yet work'd as it were plann'd	797	Juan	2	1469
Such kisses as belong to early days	797	Juan	2	1484
As if their souls and lips each other beckon'd	798	Juan	2	1494
They were alone, but not alone as they	798	Juan	2	1497
As if there were no life beneath the sky	798	Juan	2	1503
Felt as if never more to beat apart	798	Juan	2	1528
And Haidee, being devout as well as fair	798	Juan	2	1541
As they who watch o'er what they love while sleeping	799	Juan	2	1568
And their revenge is as the tiger's spring	799	Juan	2	1590
Deadly, and quick, and crushing; yet, as real	799	Juan	2	1591
Is in its cause as its effect so sweet	800	Juan	2	1619
(Though she was masqued then as a fair Venetian	801	Juan	2	1680
Some favour'd object; and as in the niche	801	Juan	2	1685
In the same object graces quite as killing	801	Juan	2	1699
As when she rose upon us like an Eve	801	Juan	2	1700
How pleasant for the heart as well as liver	801	Juan	2	1704
And darkness and destruction as on high	801	Juan	2	1708

AS

Two hundred and odd stanzas as before	801 Juan	2	1723
As those who dote on odours pluck the flowers	801 Juan	3	13
As you may find, whene'er you like to prove her	802 Juan	3	21
There's something of antipathy, as 'twere	802 Juan	3	41
And merely practised as a sea-attorney	803 Juan	3	112
Were link'd alike, as for the common people he	803 Juan	3	127
As cavalier servente, or despise her	804 Juan	3	190
Of colour'd garbs, as bright as butterflies	805 Juan	3	216
And as the spot where they appear he nears	805 Juan	3	217
Like dervises, who turn as on a pivot, he	805 Juan	3	230
While peaceful as if still an unwean'd lamb	805 Juan	3	251
His brow, as if in act to butt, and then	805 Juan	3	255
Crimson as cleft pomegranates, their long tresses	805 Juan	3	259
Was such as fire accords to a wet blanket	806 Juan	3	288
Is good to govern--almost as a Guelf	807 Juan	3	376
(Nuptial examples are as good as any	807 Juan	3	396
With temperance in pleasure, as in food	808 Juan	3	420
Such as lit onward to the Golden Fleece	808 Juan	3	435
Just as old age is creeping on apace	808 Juan	3	469
Their bread as ministers and favourties (that's	810 Juan	3	542
As plentiful as in a court, or fair	810 Juan	3	544
With buttons form'd of pearls as large as peas	810 Juan	3	557
And, clinging as if loath to lose its hold	810 Juan	3	566
Around, as princess of her father's land	810 Juan	3	569
To offer his young pinion as her fan	810 Juan	3	584
And pure as Pysche ere she grew a wife	810 Juan	3	589
Her eyelashes, though dark as night, were tinged	810 Juan	3	593
Surmounted as its clasp--a glowing crescent	811 Juan	3	615
As the psalm says, 'inditing a good matter	811 Juan	3	624
And always changed as true as any needle	811 Juan	3	634
And, singing as he sung in his warm youth	811 Juan	3	663
To 'do at Rome as Romans do,' a piece	812 Juan	3	671
Himself from being as pliable as Pindar	812 Juan	3	680
Even as I sing, suffuse my face	812 Juan	3	722
You have the Pyrrhic dance as yet	812 Juan	3	743
Such chains as his were sure to bind	813 Juan	3	760
Such as the Doric mothers bore	813 Juan	3	764
May turn his name up, as a rare deposit	813 Juan	3	808
As most essential to their hero's story	814 Juan	3	831
The world, not quite so great as Ariosto	814 Juan	3	864
As the far bell of vesper makes him start	816 Juan	3	957
And then as an improvement 'twill be shown	816 Juan	3	982
Nothing so difficult as a beginning	816 Juan	4	1
Our sin the same, and hard as his to mend	816 Juan	4	6
Man,--and, as we would hope,--perhaps the devil	816 Juan	4	11
But as the torrent widens towards the ocean	816 Juan	4	15
As boy, I thought myself a clever fellow	816 Juan	4	17
I chose a modern subject as more meet	817 Juan	4	48
Who have imputed such designs as show	817 Juan	4	51
As but to lovers a true sense affords	818 Juan	4	110
As rarely they beheld throughout their round	818 Juan	4	123
Oh beautiful! and rare as beautiful	818 Juan	4	129
The past still welcome as the present thought	819 Juan	4	160
Even as they gazed, a sudden tremor came	819 Juan	4	162
And swept, as 'twere, across their hearts' de-light	819 Juan	4	163
As if their last day of a happy date	819 Juan	4	171
Juan gazed on her as to ask his fate	819 Juan	4	173
For beings passionate as Sappho's song	819 Juan	4	214
Unseen as sings the nightingale; they were	820 Juan	4	218
Stirr'd with her dream, as rose-leaves with the air	820 Juan	4	232
Or as the stirring of a deep clear stream	820 Juan	4	233
And ran, but it escaped her as she clasp'd	820 Juan	4	256
Which froze to marble as it fell,--she thought	820 Juan	4	264
Pale as the foam that froth'd on his dead brow	820 Juan	4	266
Dear as her father had been to Haidee	821 Juan	4	286
Deal with me as thou wilt, but spare this boy	821 Juan	4	304
Oft came and went, as there resolved to die	821 Juan	4	310
Then look'd close at the flint, as if to see	821 Juan	4	318
Stern as her sire: 'On me,' she cried, 'let death	821 Juan	4	332
She stood as one who champion'd human fears	822 Juan	4	339
She drew up to her height, as if to show	822 Juan	4	342
For she, too, was as one who could avenge	822 Juan	4	349
There was resemblance, such as true blood wears	822 Juan	4	356
And looking on her, as to look her through	822 Juan	4	363
He raised his whistle, as the word he said	822 Juan	4	371
Upon their prey, as darts an angry asp	822 Juan	4	382
And as the soil is, so the heart of man	823 Juan	4	440
Afric is all the sun's, and as her earth	823 Juan	4	441
Even as the Simoom sweeps the blasted plains	823 Juan	4	456
And her head droop'd as when the lily lies	824 Juan	4	467
The ruling passion, such as marble shows	824 Juan	4	481
But fix'd as marble's unchanged aspect throws	824 Juan	4	483
She woke at length, but not as sleepers wake	824 Juan	4	489
Then to the wall she turn'd as if to warp	824 Juan	4	517
As one who ne'er had dwelt among the sick	825 Juan	4	531
And flew at all she met, as on her foes	825 Juan	4	532
Brief, but delightful--such as had not staid	825 Juan	4	566
And as my Muse is a capricious elf	826 Juan	4	590
To be Italians, as they were in fact	826 Juan	4	634
'As for the figuranti, they are like	827 Juan	4	673

AS

'As for the men, they are a middling set	827 Juan	4	681
And as a servant some preferment get	827 Juan	4	685
Lady to lady, well as man to man	828 Juan	4	726
They placed him o'er the women as a scout	828 Juan	4	733
Bright--and as black and burning as a coal	828 Juan	4	749
And though thus chain'd, as natural her hand	828 Juan	4	756
As boys love rows, my boyhood liked a squabble	829 Juan	4	785
The grass upon my grave will grow as long	829 Juan	4	791
'Tis as a snowball which derives assistance	829 Juan	4	797
Who would as 'twere identify their dust	829 Juan	4	804
As if the peasant's coarse comtempt were vented	829 Juan	4	835
As on the beach the waves at last are broke	830 Juan	4	845
If in the course of such a life as was	830 Juan	4	849
Men, who partake all passions as they pass	830 Juan	4	851
Their images again as in a glass	830 Juan	4	853
Why then I'll swear, as poet Wordy swore	830 Juan	4	869
As some one somewhere sings about the sky	830 Juan	4	874
Blue as the garters which serenely lie	830 Juan	4	878
As well as the sublime discovery's date	830 Juan	4	892
As renegadoes; while in hapless group	831 Juan	4	925
The females stood, as one by one they pick'd 'em	831 Juan	4	927
And pair their rhymes as Venus yokes her doves	831 Juan	5	3
As Ovid's verse may give to understand	831 Juan	5	6
Except in such a way as not to attract	831 Juan	5	10
Between the Bosphorus, as they lash and lave	832 Juan	5	37
Used to it, no doubt, as eels are to be flay'd	832 Juan	5	56
As most at his age are, of hope and health	832 Juan	5	58
So let us be acquainted, as we ought	833 Juan	5	102
She has served me also much the same as you	833 Juan	5	111
Will hardly leave you (as she's not your wife	833 Juan	5	131
As if the corn-sheaf should oppose the sickle	833 Juan	5	134
'Tis not my present lot, as I have said	833 Juan	5	142
Such as I, too, would shed if in your place	833 Juan	5	150
And capabilities, as to discover	834 Juan	5	204
As is a slave by his intended bidder	834 Juan	5	209
Some by a place--as tend their years or natures	834 Juan	5	214
As though they were in a mere Christian fair	835 Juan	5	221
Just as my great coat was about me cast	835 Juan	5	259
And, running out as fast as I was able	835 Juan	5	262
(As he bled inwardly, no hideous river	835 Juan	5	278
So as I gazed on him, I thought or said	835 Juan	5	280
In awe: he said, as the centurion saith	836 Juan	5	285
But let me quit the theme; as such things claim	836 Juan	5	300
From me: I gazed (as oft I have gazed the same	836 Juan	5	302
But let us to the story as before	836 Juan	5	312
As fast as oars could pull and water float	836 Juan	5	316
As they were plodding on their winding way	836 Juan	5	329
As they were threading on their way, there came	836 Juan	5	337
And various hues, as is the Turkish wont	837 Juan	5	364
And nearer as they came, a genial savour	837 Juan	5	369
More tender, as we every day behold	837 Juan	5	390
As the black eunuch enter'd with his brace	838 Juan	5	425
Just as one views a horse to guess his price	838 Juan	5	430
As wondering what the devil a noise that is	838 Juan	5	440
But saddens more by night as well as day	838 Juan	5	446
As is a theatre lit up by gas	838 Juan	5	462
Where echo woke as if from a long slumber	839 Juan	5	506
As if the milky way their feet was under	839 Juan	5	524
But such as fit an Asiatic breech	840 Juan	5	541
But they as soon shall circumcise my head	840 Juan	5	568
Sir!--as I said, as soon as I have supt	840 Juan	5	572
Be such as I can properly accept	840 Juan	5	574
As dress yourself--' and pointed out a suit	840 Juan	5	578
As not being in a masquerading mood	840 Juan	5	581
Said Baba; 'but pray do as I desire	840 Juan	5	586
Which girt a slight chemise as white as milk	841 Juan	5	612
Which--as we say--or, as the Scotch say, whilk	841 Juan	5	614
As suited the ensemble of his toilet	841 Juan	5	631
Which is not quite so light as you may deem	841 Juan	5	652
It seem'd as though they came upon a shrine	842 Juan	5	679
Were sate, like ugly imps, as if allied	842 Juan	5	692
The hinges being as smooth as Rogers' rhymes	842 Juan	5	708
As is the custom of those Eastern climes	842 Juan	5	710
As Baba with his fingers made them fall	843 Juan	5	715
Juan a moment, as this pair so small	843 Juan	5	717
It was as if their little looks could poison	843 Juan	5	719
To Juan some slight lessons as his guide	843 Juan	5	722
'Twould be as well, and (though there's not much in't	843 Juan	5	725
As Venus rose with from the wave, on them	843 Juan	5	762
And raising up an arm as moonlight fair	843 Juan	5	765
Her presence was as lofty as her state	843 Juan	5	769
Such as was Mary's Queen of Scots; true--tears	844 Juan	5	781
As far as outward show may correspond	844 Juan	5	791
As also at the race and county balls	844 Juan	5	824
On such as these the lip too fondly lingers	845 Juan	5	844
As you will see, if she you love shall bring hers	845 Juan	5	846
As if well used to the retreating trade	845 Juan	5	851
As good men wear who have done a virtuous action	845 Juan	5	856
Blood-red as sunset summer clouds which range	845 Juan	5	861
As if she rather order'd than was granting	845 Juan	5	872
Was thrown as 'twere about the neck of you	845 Juan	5	875
As though they were quite conscious of her station	845 Juan	5	884

AS

They trod as upon necks; and to complete	845	Juan	5	885
A poniard deck'd her girdle, as the sign	845	Juan	5	887
Had been her slaves' chief pleasure, as her will	845	Juan	5	892
As we may ascertain with due precision	846	Juan	5	919
And left his cheeks as pale as snowdrops blowing	846	Juan	5	934
Like molten lead, as if you thrust a pike in	846	Juan	5	942
And as she also risk'd her life to get	847	Juan	5	972
Gulbeyaz, who look'd on him as her debtor	847	Juan	5	989
This was an awkward test, as Juan found	847	Juan	5	1001
Besides, as has been said, she was so fair	847	Juan	5	1025
As even in a much humbler lot had made	847	Juan	5	1026
And also, as may be presumed, she laid	847	Juan	5	1028
As water through an unexpected leak	848	Juan	5	1094
To be impaled, or quarter'd as a dish	849	Juan	5	1122
As through his palms Bob Acres' valour oozed	849	Juan	5	1129
Just as a friar may accuse his vow	849	Juan	5	1134
Or as a dame repents her of her oath	849	Juan	5	1135
Just as a languid smile began to flatter	849	Juan	5	1142
'Is it,' exclaim'd Gulbeyaz, 'as you say	849	Juan	5	1153
And, Christian! mingle with them as you may	849	Juan	5	1157
And as you'd have me pardon your past scorning	849	Juan	5	1158
As to announce his visits a long while	850	Juan	5	1165
He was as good a sovereign of the sort	850	Juan	5	1173
As any mention'd in the histories	850	Juan	5	1174
Were ruled as calmly as a Christian queen	850	Juan	5	1184
Of whom all such as came of age were stow'd	850	Juan	5	1210
Was princely, as the proofs have always shown	850	Juan	5	1222
As suits a matron who has play'd a prank	850	Juan	5	1228
As those whose wives have made them fit for heaven	851	Juan	5	1232
And looking, as he always look'd, perceived	851	Juan	5	1234
Spoilt, as a pipe of claret is when prick'd	851	Juan	5	1261
Meanwhile, as Homer sometimes sleeps, perhaps	851	Juan	5	1271
As are the billows when the breeze is brisk	853	Juan	6	22
Gave what I had--a heart: as the world went, I	853	Juan	6	38
As the tribunals show through many a session	853	Juan	6	78
And as four wives must have quadruple claims	854	Juan	6	87
Gulbeyaz was the fourth, and (as I said	854	Juan	6	89
Not only as a sin, but as a bore	854	Juan	6	92
They are put on as easily as a hat	854	Juan	6	108
As a rule, but truth may, if you translate it	854	Juan	6	144
Yet disappointed joys are woes as deep	855	Juan	6	156
As any man's clay mixture undergoes	855	Juan	6	157
Our least of sorrows are such as we weep	855	Juan	6	158
A favourite horse fallen lame just as he's mounted	855	Juan	6	164
As certain;--these are paltry things, and yet	855	Juan	6	167
As after reading Athanasius' curse	855	Juan	6	178
As doth a rainbow the just clearing air	855	Juan	6	184
Upon, in sheets white as what bards call 'driven	855	Juan	6	197
Perhaps as wretched if a peasant's quean	855	Juan	6	200
Beating for love, as the caged bird's for air	855	Juan	6	208
My wish is quite as wide, but not so bad	855	Juan	6	212
I know not how, but good as any other	856	Juan	6	244
Of beauties cool as an Italian convent	856	Juan	6	255
Continue. As I said, this goodly row	856	Juan	6	259
Their guards being gone, and, as it were a truce	856	Juan	6	270
So silly as to buy slaves who might share	857	Juan	6	286
They all found out as few, or fewer, specks	857	Juan	6	292
Whether there are such things as sympathies	857	Juan	6	299
Companion something newer still, as 'twere	857	Juan	6	306
(To save description), fair as fair can be	857	Juan	6	316
Lolah was dusk as India and as warm	857	Juan	6	321
As if she pitied her for being there	858	Juan	6	356
What say you, child?'--Dudu said nothing, as	858	Juan	6	391
I might describe, as I have seen it all	858	Juan	6	404
Dudu, as has been said, was a sweet creature	858	Juan	6	409
'Kiss' rhymes to 'bliss' in fact as well as verse	859	Juan	6	471
Which pass'd well off--as she could do no less	860	Juan	6	485
Oh ye! whose fate it is, as once 'twas mine	860	Juan	6	491
And shown themselves as ghosts of better taste	860	Juan	6	511
And fair brows gently drooping, as the fruit	860	Juan	6	518
And smiling through her dream, as through a cloud	860	Juan	6	524
As, slightly stirring in her snowy shroud	860	Juan	6	526
'Twas night, but there were lamps, as hath been said	860	Juan	6	530
(As night-dew, on a cypress glittering, tinges	860	Juan	6	535
A fourth as marble, stature-like and still	860	Juan	6	537
White, cold, and pure, as looks a frozen rill	860	Juan	6	539
As ere that awful period intervenes	861	Juan	6	550
And bright as any meteor ever bred	861	Juan	6	573
As fast as ever husband by his mate	861	Juan	6	579
Which, as all spoke at once and more than once	861	Juan	6	586
But, being 'no orator as Brutus is	861	Juan	6	591
That just as her young lip began to ope	862	Juan	6	613
Began, as is the consequence of fear	862	Juan	6	626
And, as the quietest of all, she might	862	Juan	6	645
At least to dream so loudly as just now	862	Juan	6	658
'Twas foolish, nervous, as she must allow	862	Juan	6	660
Where she then was, as her sound sleep disclosed	862	Juan	6	667
As thus Juanna spoke, Dudu turn'd round	863	Juan	6	673
Are true as truth has ever been of late	863	Juan	6	680
As passion rises, with its bosom worn	863	Juan	6	691

AS

Indeed on any other: as a man	863	Juan	6	722
At hand, as one may like to have a fan	863	Juan	6	724
As an amusement after the Divan	863	Juan	6	726
As greatest of all sovereigns and w----s	863	Juan	6	736
Almost as far as Petersburgh and lend	863	Juan	6	740
Their mothers as the antipodes of Timon	864	Juan	6	746
But as it was, his Highness had to hold	864	Juan	6	761
If matters had been managed as desired	864	Juan	6	789
And as his speech grew still more broken-kneed	864	Juan	6	805
Juan was given in charge, as hath been stated	865	Juan	6	814
As soon as they re-enter'd their own room	865	Juan	6	819
As if she had received a sudden blow	865	Juan	6	838
She stood a moment as a Pythoness	865	Juan	6	849
The heart asunder;--then, as more or less	865	Juan	6	853
White, waxen, and as alabaster pale	865	Juan	6	868
May serve perhaps as outlines or slight hints	865	Juan	6	872
A feeling in each footstep, as disclosed	866	Juan	6	885
Might end in acting as his own 'Jack Ketch	866	Juan	6	925
And scarce secure, as such digressions are fair	867	Juan	6	959
And such as they are, such my present tale is	867	Juan	7	9
As little as the moon stops for the baying	868	Juan	7	53
Who loved blood as an alderman loves marrow	868	Juan	7	64
So placed as to impede the fire of those	868	Juan	7	79
But the town ditch below was deep as ocean	868	Juan	7	83
And walls as thick as most skulls born as yet	868	Juan	7	90
Two batteries, cap-a-pie, as our St. George	868	Juan	7	91
But as the Danube could not well be waded	868	Juan	7	102
It seems, has got an ear as well as trumpet	869	Juan	7	120
As e'er was virgin of a nuptial chime	869	Juan	7	124
All proper men of weapons, as e'er scoff'd high	869	Juan	7	131
But such a godfather's as good a card	869	Juan	7	148
Their country; and as traitors are abhorr'd	870	Juan	7	174
But a third motive was as probably	870	Juan	7	189
Unless they are game as bull-dogs and fox-terriers	870	Juan	7	192
As they who print them think is necessary	870	Juan	7	206
While, though 'twas dawn, the Turks slept fast as ever	870	Juan	7	224
Names great as any that the roll of Fame has	871	Juan	7	256
As gallantly as ever heroes fought	871	Juan	7	266
Had been as short in youth as indigestion	871	Juan	7	284
He died beneath a tree, as much unblest on	871	Juan	7	286
As e'er was locust on the land it blasted	871	Juan	7	288
Who measured men as you would do a steeple	872	Juan	7	296
As well as dilettanti in war's art	872	Juan	7	309
But as it was mere lust of power to o'er-arch all	872	Juan	7	317
Lovely as those which ripen'd Eden's fruit	872	Juan	7	327
As roll the waters to the breathing wind	873	Juan	7	379
Or as a little dog will lead the blind	873	Juan	7	381
(This metaphor, I think, holds good as aught	873	Juan	7	387
As sometimes happens in a great extremity	873	Juan	7	404
Just as you'd break a sucking salamander	873	Juan	7	412
Is twice as strong as that where you were wounded	875	Juan	7	488
Low as the compliment deserved. Suwarrow	875	Juan	7	498
For cash and conquest, as if from a cushion	875	Juan	7	508
Their arms, as hens their wings about their young	875	Juan	7	536
As leaving a small family at large	876	Juan	7	568
Look'd on as if in doubt if they could trust	876	Juan	7	578
As they could read in all eyes. Now to them	876	Juan	7	586
Who were accustom'd, as a sort of god	876	Juan	7	587
Who calculated life as so much dross	877	Juan	7	611
And as the wind a widow'd nation's wail	877	Juan	7	612
And cared as little for his army's loss	877	Juan	7	613
As wife and friends did for the boils of Job	877	Juan	7	615
As terrible as that of Ilion	877	Juan	7	619
To vie with thee would be about as vain	877	Juan	7	638
As for a brook to cope with ocean's flood	877	Juan	7	639
When my poor Greece was once, as now, surrounded	877	Juan	7	652
As purple to the Babylonian harolt	877	Juan	7	667
Here pause we for the present--as even then	878	Juan	7	689
These are but vulgar oaths, as you may deem	878	Juan	8	2
Unriddled, and as my true Muse expounds	878	Juan	8	5
As hath been done, mere conquest to advance	878	Juan	8	22
Which rock'd as 'twere beneath the mighty noises	879	Juan	8	54
In the same moment, loud as even the roar	879	Juan	8	58
As brave as ever faced both bomb and ball	879	Juan	8	69
Just now behaved as in the Holy Land	879	Juan	8	72
Aristocratic as was ever seen	879	Juan	8	76
Had set to work as briskly as their brothers	880	Juan	8	116
Cheerful as children climb the breasts of mothers	880	Juan	8	118
Quite orderly, as if upon parade	880	Juan	8	120
Which really pour'd as if all hell were raining	880	Juan	8	158
So much as under a triumphal arch	880	Juan	8	164
A glance on the dull clouds (as thick as starch	881	Juan	8	166
Which stiffen'd heaven) as if he wish'd for day	881	Juan	8	167
With something not much better, or as bad	881	Juan	8	171
As any other notion, and not national	881	Juan	8	184
In such good company as always throng	881	Juan	8	190
Stopp'd for a minute, as perhaps he ought	881	Juan	8	228
As travellers follow over bog and brake	882	Juan	8	252
An 'ignis fatuus;' or as sailors stranded	882	Juan	8	253
Fill'd as with lightning--for his spirit shared	882	Juan	8	259
The hour, as is the case with lively brains	882	Juan	8	260

AS

And as he rush'd along, it came to pass he	882	Juan	8	265
But now reduced, as in a bulky volume	882	Juan	8	268
Who had 'retreated,' as the phrase is when	882	Juan	8	274
Which did not combat like the devil, as yet	883	Juan	8	294
Man quite as quietly as blows the monsoon	883	Juan	8	309
With many other warriors, as we said	883	Juan	8	322
Acted upon the living as on wire	883	Juan	8	327
They fell as thick as harvests beneath hail	883	Juan	8	337
Proving that trite old truth, that life's as	883	Juan	8	339
As any other boon for which men stickle	883	Juan	8	340
And swept, as gales sweep foam away, whole ranks	883	Juan	8	347
All neck or nothing, as, like pitch or rosin	883	Juan	8	355
Flame was shower'd forth above, as well's below	883	Juan	8	356
Or those who thought it brave to wait as yet	884	Juan	8	360
Out between friends as well as allied nations	884	Juan	8	380
As say that Wellington at Waterloo	884	Juan	8	383
As tigers combat with an empty craw	884	Juan	8	389
So much into the raw as quite to wrong her	884	Juan	8	398
At last it takes to weapons such as men	884	Juan	8	403
Walk'd o'er the walls of Ismail, as if nursed	884	Juan	8	411
As warm in heat as feminine in feature	884	Juan	8	416
As is the hunter's at the five-bar gate	885	Juan	8	434
He hated cruelty, as all men hate	885	Juan	8	439
As were some hundred youngsters all abreast	885	Juan	8	443
Who came as if just dropp'd down from the moon	885	Juan	8	444
(As Pistol calls it), but a young Livonian	885	Juan	8	448
As much of German as of Sanscrit, and	885	Juan	8	450
As soon as thunder, 'midst the general noise	885	Juan	8	471
Their choice than life, forgive them, as beguiled	886	Juan	8	493
He show'd himself as kind as mortal can	886	Juan	8	512
And fresh as is a torrent or a tree	886	Juan	8	520
And wander'd up and down as in a dream	887	Juan	8	572
Until they reach'd, as daybreak was expanding	887	Juan	8	573
Just as Koutousow's most 'forlorn' of 'hopes	887	Juan	8	579
But as it happens to brave men, they blunder'd	887	Juan	8	597
Fatal to bishops as to soldiers--these	888	Juan	8	602
Cossacques were all cut off as day was breaking	888	Juan	8	603
Leaving as ladders their heap'd carcasses	888	Juan	8	606
Troops as are meant to march with greatest glory on	888	Juan	8	620
Seized fast, as if 'twere by the serpent's head	888	Juan	8	659
And howl'd for help as wolves do for a meal	888	Juan	8	662
As do the subtle snakes described of old	888	Juan	8	664
The blood may gush out, as the Danube's flow	889	Juan	8	691
As the year closing whirls the scarlet leaves	889	Juan	8	699
As oaks blown down with all their thousand winters	889	Juan	8	704
For checker'd as is seen our human lot	889	Juan	8	707
I sketch your world exactly as it goes	889	Juan	8	712
And shudder;--while, as beautiful as May	889	Juan	8	725
Has feelings pure and polish'd as a gem	890	Juan	8	732
As he turn'd o'er each pale and gory cheek	890	Juan	8	750
And she was chill as they, and on her face	890	Juan	8	753
As the last link with all she had held dear	890	Juan	8	758
With infant terrors, glared as from a trance	890	Juan	8	766
On great occasions, such as an attack	890	Juan	8	771
On cities, as hath been the present case	890	Juan	8	772
Such as he thought the least given up to prey	891	Juan	8	812
As human beings, or his ways are odd	891	Juan	8	828
Or 'sultan,' as the author (to whose nod	891	Juan	8	830
Are they--now furious as the sweeping wave	891	Juan	8	845
Now moved with pity: even as sometimes nods	891	Juan	8	846
As obstinate as Swedish Charles at Bender	892	Juan	8	852
As being a virtue, like terrestrial patience	892	Juan	8	855
So much less fight as might form an apology	892	Juan	8	860
Struck at his friends, as babies beat their nurses	892	Juan	8	864
As great a scorner of the Nazarene	892	Juan	8	882
As ever Mahomet pick'd out for a martyr	892	Juan	8	883
As though there were one heaven and none besides	892	Juan	8	910
Stopp'd as if once more willing to concede	893	Juan	8	930
As he before had done. He did not heed	893	Juan	8	932
As he look'd down upon his children gone	893	Juan	8	935
As carelessly as hurls the moth her wing	893	Juan	8	939
As if he had three lives, as well as tails	893	Juan	8	968
All by which hell is peopled, or as sad	894	Juan	8	982
As hell--mere mortals who their power abuse	894	Juan	8	983
Was here (as heretofore and since) let loose	894	Juan	8	984
Are hints as good as sermons, or as rhymes	894	Juan	8	998
As when the French, that dissipated nation	894	Juan	8	1028
Were almost as much virgins as before.	894	Juan	8	1032
And as, in the great joy of your millennium	895	Juan	8	1082
As now occur, I thought that I would pen you 'em	895	Juan	8	1084
As we now gaze upon the mammoth's bones	895	Juan	8	1091
As the real purpose of a pyramid	895	Juan	8	1096
As the first Canto promised. You have now	896	Juan	8	1098
But though your years as man tend fast to	896	Juan	9	15
A prop not quite so certain as before	896	Juan	9	20
The Spanish, and the French, as well as Dutch	896	Juan	9	21
I don't mean to reflect--a man so great as	897	Juan	9	49
Though as an Irishman you love potatoes	897	Juan	9	53

AS

And as a high-soul'd minister of state is	897	Juan	9	63
As these new cantos touch on warlike feats	897	Juan	9	73
Suns as rays--worlds like atoms--years like hours	898	Juan	9	104
As also of the first academicians	898	Juan	9	130
There's no such thing as certainty, that's plain	898	Juan	9	133
As any of Mortality's conditions	898	Juan	9	134
'But heaven,' as Cassio says, 'is above all	898	Juan	9	145
As is the Christian dogma rather rough	899	Juan	9	198
As much from mobs as kings--from you as me	899	Juan	9	200
May still expatiate freely, as will I	899	Juan	9	207
By night, as do that mercenary pack all	899	Juan	9	211
(As being the brave lions' keen providers	900	Juan	9	215
As yet are strongly stinging to be free	900	Juan	9	224
Where blood was talk'd of as we would of water	900	Juan	9	227
And carcasses that lay as thick as thatch	900	Juan	9	228
Between these nations as a main of cocks	900	Juan	9	231
As if he wish'd that she should fare less ill	900	Juan	9	243
As sometimes have been greater sages' lots	901	Juan	9	283
And brilliant breeches, bright as a Cairn Gorme	902	Juan	9	341
White stocking drawn uncurdled as new milk	902	Juan	9	343
Behold him placed as if upon a pillar! He	902	Juan	9	351
His side as a small sword, but sharp as ever	902	Juan	9	356
Just then; as they are rather numerous found	902	Juan	9	364
A lover as had cost her many a tear	903	Juan	9	431
Victory; and pausing as she saw him kneel	903	Juan	9	455
As an East Indian sunrise on the main	904	Juan	9	468
In vain!--As fall the dews on quenchless sands	904	Juan	9	471
Almost as much as on a new despatch	904	Juan	9	487
When wroth--while pleased, she was as fine a figure	904	Juan	9	490
As those who like things rosy, ripe, and succulent	904	Juan	9	491
A man' (as Giles says); for though she would widow all	904	Juan	9	503
Nations, she liked man as an individual	904	Juan	9	504
Makes us believe ourselves as good as any	905	Juan	9	544
As bold as Daniel in the lion's den	905	Juan	9	548
To make a twilight in, just as Sol's heat is	905	Juan	9	551
(The last, if they have soul, are quite as good	905	Juan	9	563
Or better, as the best examples say	905	Juan	9	564
Selfish in its beginning as its end	905	Juan	9	578
As flourishing in every Christian land	906	Juan	9	606
As they beheld; the younger cast some leers	906	Juan	9	620
Smiled as she talk'd the matter o'er; but tears	906	Juan	9	622
Of rubles rain, as fast as specie can	906	Juan	9	630
Ambassadors began as 'twere to hustle	907	Juan	9	651
As if born for the ministerial trade	907	Juan	9	660
(As it will look sometimes with the first stare	907	Juan	9	668
As also did Miss Protasoff then there	907	Juan	9	670
With her then, as in humble duty bound	907	Juan	9	673
And though so much inferior, as I know	907	Juan	10	21
I wish to do as much by poesy	907	Juan	10	24
Where ships have founder'd, as doth many a boat	907	Juan	10	32
So narrow as to shame their wintry brink	908	Juan	10	51
Hectic and brief as summer's day nigh done	908	Juan	10	62
As may be won by favour of the moon	908	Juan	10	67
As my friend Jeffrey writes with such an air	908	Juan	10	86
As Caesar wore his robe you wear your gown	909	Juan	10	120
(As far as rhyme and criticism combine	909	Juan	10	123
As 'Auld Lang Syne' brings Scotland, one and all	909	Juan	10	137
And though, as you remember, in a fit	909	Juan	10	145
But his just now were spread as is a cushion	910	Juan	10	165
About this time, as might have been anticipated	910	Juan	10	177
On our fresh feelings, but--as being participated	910	Juan	10	180
Unequal matches, such as are, alas	910	Juan	10	187
But one who is not so youthful as she was	910	Juan	10	189
If I can stave off thought, which--as a whelp	911	Juan	10	219
Of this odd labyrinth; or as the kelp	911	Juan	10	221
Holds by the rock; or as a lover's kiss	911	Juan	10	222
Drains its first draught of lips:--but, as I said	911	Juan	10	223
As purple clouds befringe the sun; but most	911	Juan	10	231
As the sole sign of man's being in his senses	911	Juan	10	247
And no less to God's Son, as well as Mother	911	Juan	10	250
Loud as the virtues thou dost loudly vaunt	911	Juan	10	267
But went to heaven in as sincere a way	911	Juan	10	274
As any body on the elected roll	911	Juan	10	275
Such as the conqueror William did repay	911	Juan	10	278
Yet as they founded churches with the produce	912	Juan	10	287
Which shrink from touch, as monarchs do from rhymes	912	Juan	10	291
Save such as Southey can afford to give	912	Juan	10	292
As well as further drain the wither'd form	912	Juan	10	300
Poor little thing! She was as fair as docile	913	Juan	10	409
As rare in living beings as a fossile	913	Juan	10	411
As acids rouse a dormant alkali	914	Juan	10	428
Although ('twill happen as our planet guides	914	Juan	10	429
As patriots (now and then) may love a nation	914	Juan	10	435
Owing to him;--as also her salvation	914	Juan	10	437
But Juan, season'd, as he well might be	915	Juan	10	510
Upon the captive, freedom? He's as far	916	Juan	10	542
Who watches o'er the chain, as they who wear	916	Juan	10	544
But doubtless as the air, though seldom sunny	916	Juan	10	559
Along the road, as if they went to bury	916	Juan	10	565

AS

Leavening his blood as cayenne doth a curry	916	Juan	10	570
As going at full speed--no matter where its	916	Juan	10	571
Were pointed out as usual by the bedral	916	Juan	10	679
He breathed a thousand Cressys, as he saw	916	Juan	10	686
As the smart boys spurr'd fast in their career	917	Juan	10	611
The earth, as scarce the eagle in the broad	917	Juan	10	619
With the York mail;--but onward as we roll	917	Juan	10	623
As Machiavel shows those in purple raiment	917	Juan	10	627
Just as the day began to wane and darken	917	Juan	10	635
According as you take things well or ill	917	Juan	10	639
The sun went down, the smoke rose up, as from	917	Juan	10	641
As some have qualified that wondrous place	917	Juan	10	644
As one who, though he were not of the race	917	Juan	10	646
Dirty and dusky, but as wide as eye	917	Juan	10	650
Appear'd to him but as the magic vapour	918	Juan	10	658
The gloomy clouds, which o'er it as a yoke	918	Juan	10	661
He paused--and so will I; as doth a crew	918	Juan	10	665
To tell you truths you will not take as true	918	Juan	10	669
As several people think such hazards rude	919	Juan	11	28
Perhaps; but as I suffer from the shocks	919	Juan	11	39
Exposed to lose his life as well as breeches	919	Juan	11	88
To think so: for half English as I am	920	Juan	11	94
Who fell, as rolls an ox o'er in his pasture	920	Juan	11	101
And roar'd out, as he writhed his native mud in	920	Juan	11	102
And offering, as usual, late assistance	920	Juan	11	108
As if his veins would pour out his existence	920	Juan	11	110
Let me die where I am!' And as the fuel	920	Juan	11	124
As soon as 'Crowner's quest' allow'd, pursued	920	Juan	11	139
Through Groves, so call'd as being void of trees	921	Juan	11	161
Mount Pleasant, as containing nought to please	921	Juan	11	163
Of twilight, as the party cross'd the bridge	921	Juan	11	184
Like gold as in comparison to dross	921	Juan	11	203
As also bonfires made of country seats	922	Juan	11	211
As thunder'd knockers broke the long seal'd spell	922	Juan	11	227
Admitted a small party as night fell	922	Juan	11	229
The mob stood, and as usual several score	922	Juan	11	235
And as romantic heads are pretty painters	922	Juan	11	259
Yet as the consequences are as bright	922	Juan	11	267
As if they acted with the heart instead	922	Juan	11	268
That they as easily might do the youngster	923	Juan	11	279
As hawks may pounce upon a woodland songster	923	Juan	11	280
They err'd, as aged men will do; but by	923	Juan	11	281
Bestow'd upon him, as the public learn'd	923	Juan	11	311
More than on continents--as if the sea	923	Juan	11	335
This subject quote; as it would be schismatic	923	Juan	11	341
Juan, as an inveterate patrician	924	Juan	11	359
An air as sentimental as Mozart's	924	Juan	11	371
Such as no gentleman can quite refuse	924	Juan	11	382
Thought such an opportunity as this is	924	Juan	11	389
His steady application as a dancer	924	Juan	11	406
Into as furious English), with her best look	925	Juan	11	415
Juan knew several languages--as well	925	Juan	11	417
Admitted as an aspirant to all	925	Juan	11	426
The coteries, and, as in Banquo's glass	925	Juan	11	427
As every paltry magazine can show its	925	Juan	11	432
But I will fall at least as fell my hero	925	Juan	11	445
Nor reign at all, or as a monarch reign	925	Juan	11	446
Just as he really promised something great	925	Juan	11	466
Much as they might have been supposed to speak	925	Juan	11	469
With the same feelings as you'd coax a vampire	926	Juan	11	485
And let the Babel round run as it may	927	Juan	11	541
And look on as a mourner, or a scorner	927	Juan	11	542
Yawning a little as the night grows later	927	Juan	11	544
Our hero, as a hero, young and handsome	927	Juan	11	577
As will environ a conspicuous man. Some	927	Juan	11	581
And ugliness, disease, as toil and trouble	927	Juan	11	583
Where are the Grenvilles? Turn'd as usual Where	928	Juan	11	623
Talk not of seventy years as age; in seven	928	Juan	11	641
To-morrow sees another race as gay	929	Juan	11	674
But 'tis as well at once to understand	929	Juan	11	686
For being as much the subject of attack	929	Juan	11	708
As ever yet was any work sublime	929	Juan	11	709
And as for other love, the illusion's o'er	930	Juan	12	14
And scorn his temperate board, as none at all	930	Juan	12	22
High ground, as virgin Cynthia sways the tides	931	Juan	12	110
And as for 'Heaven being Love,' why not say honey	931	Juan	12	111
My Jeffrey held him up as an example	931	Juan	12	127
As serious as if I had for inditers	932	Juan	12	156
And then men stare, as if a new ass spake	933	Juan	12	205
To be pursued as food for inanition	933	Juan	12	214
The women much divided--as is usual	933	Juan	12	217
As beautiful as her own native land	933	Juan	12	227
As Juan was a person of condition	933	Juan	12	236
And all her points as thorough-bred to show	933	Juan	12	246
Such as--'Unless Miss (Blank) meant to have chosen	934	Juan	12	269
As I'll tell Aurea at to-morrow's rout	934	Juan	12	278
I mean to show things really as they are	934	Juan	12	314
Not as they ought to be: for I avow	934	Juan	12	315
As that abominable tittle-tattle	935	Juan	12	343
As better knowing why they should be so	935	Juan	12	362
That daughters of such mothers as may know	935	Juan	12	364

AS

As who has not, if female, young, and pretty	935	Juan	12	370
To the next comer; or--as it will tell	936	Juan	12	407
According as their minds or backs are bent	936	Juan	12	412
With music; the most moderate shine as wits	936	Juan	12	415
Although the highest: but as swords have hilts	936	Juan	12	443
'The royal game of Goose,' as I may say	937	Juan	12	460
I don't mean this as general, but particular	937	Juan	12	465
And lived, as did the broken-hearted fair	937	Juan	12	487
And all by having tact as well as taste	938	Juan	12	528
With such a chart as may be safely stuck to	938	Juan	12	557
Construction as your cures for hectic phthisics	939	Juan	12	571
As a reserve, a plunge into remorse	939	Juan	12	584
Than storms it as a foe would take a city	939	Juan	12	590
She cannot step as does an Arab barb	939	Juan	12	593
Nor wear as gracefully as Gauls her garb	939	Juan	12	595
(A thing approved as saving time and toil	939	Juan	12	606
They lose their caste at once, as do the Parias	939	Juan	12	618
Perhaps this is as it should be;--it is	939	Juan	12	625
For her return to Virtue--as they call	940	Juan	12	631
And as for chastity, you'll never bind it	940	Juan	12	637
Which flash'd as far as where the musk-bull browses	940	Juan	12	654
Of such a throne as is the proudest station	940	Juan	12	660
And full of promise, as the spring of prime	940	Juan	12	668
And Juan was received, as hath been said	940	Juan	12	673
Exposed him, as was natural, to temptation	940	Juan	12	679
And as my object is morality	940	Juan	12	683
As Philip's son proposed to do with Athos	940	Juan	12	688
And critically held as deleterious	941	Juan	13	4
As an old temple dwindled to a column	941	Juan	13	8
The kindest may be taken as a test	941	Juan	13	22
Reluctant as all placemen to resign	941	Juan	13	34
That all their glory, as a composition	942	Juan	13	87
I tell the tale as it is told, nor dare	942	Juan	13	97
As most men do, the little or the great	943	Juan	13	146
And, as he thought, in country much the same	943	Juan	13	156
Where people always did as they were bid	944	Juan	13	179
Could back a horse, as despots ride a Russian	944	Juan	13	184
As in freemasonry a higher brother	944	Juan	13	188
As many other noble scions were	944	Juan	13	219
Of counsellors,' as Solomon has said	944	Juan	13	226
But as 'there's safety' grafted in the number	945	Juan	13	233
Was faint, as of an every-day possession	945	Juan	13	248
In such a sort as cannot leave behind	945	Juan	13	252
Just as a mandarin finds nothing fine	945	Juan	13	269
As a volcano holds the lava more	945	Juan	13	283
And as the good ships sent upon that message	946	Juan	13	307
And young beginners may as well commence	946	Juan	13	313
As many doubts as any other doctrine	946	Juan	13	327
Sigh--as the postboys fasten on the traces	946	Juan	13	352
Or generous draft, conceded as a gift	946	Juan	13	357
And changed as quickly as hearts after marriage	946	Juan	13	364
As many guests, or more; before whom groan	947	Juan	13	389
As many covers, duly, daily, laid	947	Juan	13	390
And oaks as olden as their pedigree	947	Juan	13	399
As thus: 'On Thursday there was a grand dinner	947	Juan	13	425
Mix'd Gothic, such as artists all allow	948	Juan	13	436
The dappled foresters--as day awoke	948	Juan	13	446
Broad as transparent, deep, and freshly fed	948	Juan	13	450
According as the skies their shadows threw	948	Juan	13	464
When each house was a fortalice, as tell	948	Juan	13	477
As hinting more (unless our judgments warp us	949	Juan	13	551
Of martyrs awed, as Spagnoletto tainted	950	Juan	13	567
As if 'twould to a second spring resign	950	Juan	13	611
As what is lost in green is gain'd in yellow	950	Juan	13	616
But ta'en at hazard as the rhyme may run	951	Juan	13	662
Come out and glimmer'd as a six weeks' star	951	Juan	13	670
Who did not hate so much the sin as sinner	952	Juan	13	694
As beautiful and bounding as a steed	952	Juan	13	734
But Longbow wild as an Aeolian harp	952	Juan	13	738
Or solitary, as they chose to bear	954	Juan	13	820
Met the morn as they might. If fine, they rode	954	Juan	13	826
But full of cunning as Ulysses' whistle	954	Juan	13	838
As Phidian forms cut out of marble Attic	955	Juan	13	875
There now are no Squire Westerns as of old	955	Juan	13	876
But fair as then, or fairer to behold	955	Juan	13	878
But gentlemen in stays, as stiff as stones	955	Juan	13	880
Much as old Saturn ate his progeny	955	Juan	14	6
Is poesy, according as the mind glows	956	Juan	14	60
But just to play with, as an infant plays	956	Juan	14	64
The monde, exactly as they ought to paint	957	Juan	14	147
Why do their sketches fail them as inditers	958	Juan	14	157
As Captain Parry's voyage may do to Jason's	958	Juan	14	172
The world (as, since that history less polite	958	Juan	14	178
Condemn'd to child-bed, as men for their sins	958	Juan	14	183
But as to women, who can penetrate	958	Juan	14	187
To fly from, as from hungry pikes a roach	958	Juan	14	203
Are there oft dull and dreary as a dun	959	Juan	14	231
But be it as it may, a bard must meet	959	Juan	14	236
The wilds, as doth an Arab turn'd avenger	959	Juan	14	254
Some hoped things might not turn out as they fear'd	961	Juan	14	347
As they will do like leaves at the first breeze	961	Juan	14	382

AS

But mix'd with pity, pure as e'er was penn'd	962	Juan	14	406
And (as her junior by six weeks) his youth	962	Juan	14	408
If but to keep thy credit as a mower	962	Juan	14	424
As I have said in--I forget what page	962	Juan	14	429
My Muse despises reference, as you have guess'd	962	Juan	14	430
I hate it, as I hate a drove of cattle	962	Juan	14	461
Who whirl the dust as simooms whirl the sand	962	Juan	14	462
I hate it, as I hate an argument	962	Juan	14	463
The Lady Adeline, as soon's she saw	963	Juan	14	475
Such measures as she thought might best impede	963	Juan	14	482
And next a quarrel (as he seem'd to fret	963	Juan	14	495
Bewitching, torturing, as they freeze or glow	963	Juan	14	503
At least as far as bienseance allows	964	Juan	14	532
Such as are coin'd in conversation's mint	964	Juan	14	547
Retired; and, as went out, calmly kiss'd her	964	Juan	14	551
Proportion'd, as a poplar or a pole	964	Juan	14	565
Still there was something wanting, as I've said	964	Juan	14	569
An accessory, as I have cause to guess	965	Juan	14	604
Convey'd Medea as her supercargo	965	Juan	14	608
As far as I know, that the church receives	965	Juan	14	620
Much as a monk may do within his cell	965	Juan	14	644
As now with those of soi-disant sound mind	966	Juan	14	668
Like Archimedes, I leave earth as 'twas	966	Juan	14	672
As she had seen nought claiming its expansion	966	Juan	14	676
And gather'd as they run like growing water	966	Juan	14	702
Upon her mind; the more so, as her breast	966	Juan	14	703
As obstinacy, both in men and women	966	Juan	14	709
But of such friendship as man's may to man be	967	Juan	14	735
She was as capable as woman can be	967	Juan	14	736
Will there, as also in the ties of blood	967	Juan	14	738
But true--as, if expedient, I could prove	967	Juan	14	762
To leave them hovering, as the effect is fine	967	Juan	14	773
That in our youth, as dangerous a passion	968	Juan	14	794
As e'er brought man and woman to the brink	968	Juan	14	795
As few would ever dream could form the link	968	Juan	14	797
With self-love in the centre as their pole	968	Juan	14	812
As a-propos of hope or retrospection	968	Juan	15	3
As though the lurking thought had follow'd free	968	Juan	15	4
Or miniature at least, as is my notion	968	Juan	15	14
And as for love--O love!--We will proceed	968	Juan	15	33
A pretty name as one would wish to read	968	Juan	15	35
They differ as wine differs from its label	969	Juan	15	45
Bright as a new Napoleon from its mintage	969	Juan	15	51
Or glorious as a diamond richly set	969	Juan	15	52
But oft denied, as patience 'gins to fail, he	969	Juan	15	61
And take as many heroes as Heaven pleases	969	Juan	15	72
Where she was interested (as was said	969	Juan	15	74
Unto such feelings as seem'd innocent	969	Juan	15	79
As, if they told the truth, could well be shown	969	Juan	15	98
Was such as rather seem'd to keep aloof	970	Juan	15	107
So as to make them feel he knew his station	970	Juan	15	118
And eke the wise, as has been often shown	970	Juan	15	132
But speculating as I cast mine eye	970	Juan	15	148
I rattle on exactly as I'd talk	970	Juan	15	151
Just as I feel the 'Improvvisatore	970	Juan	15	160
Such as the times may furnish. 'Tis a flight	971	Juan	15	194
Or starch, as are the edicts statesmen utter	971	Juan	15	212
As women hate half measures, on the whole	971	Juan	15	223
Some difficulties, as in his own preference	972	Juan	15	237
Observed as strictly both at board and bed	972	Juan	15	254
As those of Aristotle, though sometimes	972	Juan	15	255
Strangely enough as yet without miscarriage	972	Juan	15	275
This he (as far as I can understand) meant	972	Juan	15	300
As on the whole it is an even chance	973	Juan	15	308
There was Miss Millpond, smooth as summer's sea	973	Juan	15	321
A Russ or Turk--the one's as good as t'other	973	Juan	15	336
In eyes which sadly shone, as seraphs' shine	973	Juan	15	355
Radiant and grave--as pitying man's decline	973	Juan	15	357
She look'd as if she sat by Eden's door	973	Juan	15	359
As far as her own gentle heart allow'd	974	Juan	15	362
To novel power; and as she was the last	974	Juan	15	367
As seeking not to know it; silent, lone	974	Juan	15	370
As grows a flower, thus quietly she grew	974	Juan	15	371
Her spirit seem'd as seated on a throne	974	Juan	15	374
Against her being mention'd as well fitted	974	Juan	15	382
Made Juan wonder, as no doubt he must	974	Juan	15	387
And therefore fittest, as of his persuasion	974	Juan	15	394
As usual--the same reason which she late did	974	Juan	15	400
As pure as sanctity itself from vice	974	Juan	15	411
Who look upon them as they ought to do	974	Juan	15	424
Much as she would have seen a glow-worm shine	975	Juan	15	443
More warm, as lovely, and not less sincere	975	Juan	15	461
Was such as lies between a flower and gem	975	Juan	15	464
And, as my friend Scott says, 'I sound my warison	975	Juan	15	467
Serf, lord, man, with such skill as none would share it, if	975	Juan	15	470
As congresses of late do) of the Lady	975	Juan	15	482
As white as Cleopatra's melted pearls	976	Juan	15	520
As form a science and a nomenclature	976	Juan	15	551
Taste or the gout,--pronounce it as inclines	977	Juan	15	571
But various as the various meats display'd	977	Juan	15	588
No damsel, but a dish, as hath been said	977	Juan	15	590
Was not such as to encourage him to shine	977	Juan	15	598

AS

Which piques a preux chevalier--as it ought	977	Juan	15	610
Or something which was nothing, as urbanity	977	Juan	15	618
And look'd as much as if to say, 'I said it	978	Juan	15	625
Because it sometimes, as I have seen or read it	978	Juan	15	627
As once or twice to smile, if not to listen	978	Juan	15	640
With her was rare: and Adeline, who as yet	978	Juan	15	642
As if each charming word were a decree	978	Juan	15	652
But innocently so, as Socrates	978	Juan	15	682
So much as I do any kind of wrangle	979	Juan	15	723
And also meek as a metaphysician	979	Juan	15	730
As Eldon on a lunatic commission	979	Juan	15	732
But as subservient to a moral use	979	Juan	15	740
Was dangerous;--I think she is as harmless	980	Juan	15	751
As some who labour more and yet may charm less	980	Juan	15	752
Our bubbles; as the old burst, new emerge	980	Juan	15	790
And as she treats all things, and ne'er retreats	980	Juan	16	17
Receive as gospel, and which grow more rooted	981	Juan	16	47
As all truths must, the more they are disputed	981	Juan	16	48
Thoughts quite as yellow, but less clear than amber	981	Juan	16	84
As clear as such a climate will allow	982	Juan	16	100
Then, as the night was clear though cold, he threw	982	Juan	16	129
As doubtless should be people of high birth	982	Juan	16	134
Look living in the moon; and as you turn	982	Juan	16	138
As if to ask how you can dare to keep	982	Juan	16	143
As Juan mused on mutability	983	Juan	16	153
Most people as it plays along the arras	983	Juan	16	160
With steps that trod as heavy, yet unheard	983	Juan	16	164
He moved as shadowy as the sisters weird	983	Juan	16	166
But slowly; and as he pass'd Juan by	983	Juan	16	167
As stands a statue, stood: he felt his hair	983	Juan	16	181
And would have pass'd the whole off as a dream	983	Juan	16	197
All there was as he left it: still his taper	983	Juan	16	201
Burnt, and not blue, as modest tapers use	983	Juan	16	202
He woke betimes; and, as may be supposed	984	Juan	16	217
She look'd, and saw him pale, and turn'd as pale	984	Juan	16	241
But for the rest, as he himself seem'd loth	984	Juan	16	262
'You look,' quoth he, 'as if you had had your rest	985	Juan	16	275
Graceful as Dian, when she draws her bow	985	Juan	16	301
As touch'd, and plaintively began to play	985	Juan	16	303
And 'tis held as faith, to their bed of death	985	Juan	16	343
Say nought to him as he walks the hall	986	Juan	16	361
As o'er the grass the dew	986	Juan	16	364
Nor less applauds, as in politeness bound	986	Juan	16	374
As if she rated such accomplishment	986	Juan	16	378
As the mere pastime of an idle day	986	Juan	16	379
Would now and then as 'twere without display	986	Juan	16	381
As did the Cynic on some like occasion	986	Juan	16	388
In Babylon's bravuras--as the home	986	Juan	16	409
Was Adeline well versed, as compositions	986	Juan	16	416
Upon her friends, as everybody ought	986	Juan	16	420
Thoughts, boundless, deep, but silent too as Space	987	Juan	16	432
They pass'd as such things do, for superstition	987	Juan	16	474
But as Lord Henry was a connoisseur	988	Juan	16	497
Pale as if painted so; her cheek being red	989	Juan	16	554
By nature, as in higher dames less hale	989	Juan	16	555
Both busy (as a general in his tent	989	Juan	16	574
Because, as suits their rank and situation	989	Juan	16	589
And, as the isthmus of the grand connection	989	Juan	16	599
His word had the same value as another's	990	Juan	16	616
As for his place, he could but say this of it	990	Juan	16	631
He was as independent--ay, much more	990	Juan	16	649
As common soldiers, or a common--shore	990	Juan	16	651
Thus on the mob all statesmen are as eager	990	Juan	16	655
To prove their pride, as footmen to a beggar	990	Juan	16	656
'Twas a great banquet, such as Albion old	991	Juan	16	666
Was wont to boast--as if a glutton's tray	991	Juan	16	667
As between English beef and Spartan broth	991	Juan	16	719
Bacchus and Ceres being, as we know	992	Juan	16	732
And sitting as if nail'd upon his chair	992	Juan	16	740
Though knives and forks clank'd round as in a fray	992	Juan	16	741
And hastily--as nothing can confound	992	Juan	16	748
This was no bad mistake, as it occurr'd	992	Juan	16	753
Were angry--as they well might, to be sure	992	Juan	16	756
Especially as he had been renown'd	992	Juan	16	772
As Juan should have known, had not his senses	993	Juan	16	791
Her aspect was as usual, still--not stern	993	Juan	16	795
As deep seas in a sunny atmosphere	993	Juan	16	800
As all must blend whose part it is to aim	993	Juan	16	805
(Especially as the sixth year is ending	993	Juan	16	806
Which she went through as though it were a dance	993	Juan	16	812
Five, as they might do in a modest way	993	Juan	16	835
However, the day closed, as days must close	994	Juan	16	849
And curtsying off, as curtsies country dame	994	Juan	16	852
As music chimes in with a melodrame	994	Juan	16	878
'Tis true he saw Aurora look as though	994	Juan	16	889
In making him as silent as a ghost	994	Juan	16	898
Ray fades on ray, as years on years depart	995	Juan	16	916
And full of sentiments, sublime as billows	995	Juan	16	921

AS

The night was as before: he was undrest	995 Juan	16	929
It is the sable friar as before	995 Juan	16	946
With awful footsteps regular as rhyme	995 Juan	16	947
Or (as rhymes may be in these days) much more	995 Juan	16	948
As wide as if a long speech were to come	995 Juan	16	964
His eyes were open, and (as was before	995 Juan	16	967
Dreadful as Dante's rhima, or this stanza	995 Juan	16	972
The door flew wide,--not swiftly, but, as fly	996 Juan	16	977
Don Juan shook, as erst he had been shaken	996 Juan	16	985
He shudder'd, as no doubt the bravest cowers	996 Juan	16	1005
Gleam'd forth, as through the casement's ivy shroud	996 Juan	16	1015
Which beat as if there was a warm heart under	996 Juan	16	1020
He found, as people on most trials must	996 Juan	16	1021
As ever lurk'd beneath a holy hood	996 Juan	16	1026
The next are such as are not doomed to lose	997 Juan	17	5
The next are 'only Children,' as they are styled	997 Juan	17	9
As far as words make rules--our common notion	997 Juan	17	18
Because as Ages upon Ages push on	997 Juan	17	43
Mischief in families, as some know or knew	997 Juan	17	53
Might be fill'd up, as vainly as before	997 Juan	17	66
And so for one will I--as well I may	998 Juan	17	76
Just as I make my mind up every day	998 Juan	17	78
Such as enables Man to show his strength	998 Juan	17	91
As if he had combated with more than one	998 Juan	17	107
Seem'd pale and shiver'd, as if she had kept	998 Juan	17	111

ASCANIUS

Aeneas and Ascanius shall combine	107 Nisus		137

ASCEND

Some Richmond-hill ascend, some scud to Ware	15 Harold	1	704
Whence the rapt spirit may ascend to Heaven	161 Athos		21
Nor will Melpomeme ascend her throne	262 Hints		443
But I was curious to ascend	406 Chillon		328
Whose grassy cairns ascend along the shore	422 Island	2	218
So that the sacrifice ascend to heaven	517 Faliero	2	604
Shall prayer ascend	670 Heaven		1115
Ere thou ascend it. God forgive thee, man	740 Deformed	2	347

ASCENDANCE

Have in their several arts or parts ascendance	990 Juan	16	652

ASCENDANCY

That claims and keeps ascendancy	318 Giaour		841

ASCENDANT

For his reward the Guelf's ascendant art	457 Dante	1	90

ASCENDED

(See also RE-ASCENDED)

And here ascended from the coast	318 Giaour		809
That sky whence Christ ascended from the cross	731 Deformed	1	608

ASCENDENCY

To catch that crest's ascendency	187 Ode-B		57

ASCENDING

(See also RE-ASCENDING)

How view the column of ascending flames	272 Minerva		305
Ascending with affection truly loyal	276 Waltz		199
Ascending slowly by the rock-hewn way	340 Corsair	1	123
And dashes off the ascending waves	412 Mazeppa		591

ASCENDS

He who ascends to mountain-tops, shall find	42 Harold	3	397
Undying Love's, who here ascends a throne	50 Harold	3	933
Far different incense now ascends to heaven	120 Newstead-A		79
Ascends the path familiar to his eye	364 Corsair	3	580
That horrid voice ascends to heaven	401 Parisina		495

ASCENSION

Oh! Muse prepare for thy Ascension	233 Nihil		35

ASCERTAIN

To ascertain the atmospheric state	830 Juan	4	894
As we may ascertain with due precision	846 Juan	5	919

ASCERTAIN'D

Have not exactly ascertain'd the Pole	946 Juan	13	308
Of these is not exactly ascertain'd	982 Juan	16	122

ASCETIC

'Well, as thou wilt--ascetic as thou art	349 Corsair	2	133
But certes it conducts to lives ascetic	973 Juan	15	303

ASHAM'D

And gods were not asham'd on't, why should we	266 Hints		688

ASHAMED

Make bad men better, or at least ashamed	253 Bards		830
Then beat with quicker pulse, ashamed	387 Corinth		280
And thou, Leonora! thou--who wert ashamed	439 Tasso		228

ASHAMED

Kind father, but I really was ashamed	475 Morgante		606
I am ashamed of my own anger now	503 Faliero	1	266
They are ashamed of that mad moment's impulse	522 Faliero	3	246
The slave that gave it might be well ashamed	587 Sardan	4	579
And art thou not ashamed	660 Heaven		400
She made the cleverest people quite ashamed	748 Juan	1	77
I'm very sorry, very much ashamed	761 Juan	1	951
I am ashamed of having shed these tears	766 Juan	1	1237
Men grow ashamed of being so very fond	802 Juan	3	49
Caesar himself would be ashamed of fame	968 Juan	14	816
And what was worse, was not ashamed to show it	987 Juan	16	424
Perhaps she was ashamed of seeming frail	989 Juan	16	557
And then to be ashamed of such mistaking	996 Juan	16	988

ASHES

All ashes to the taste. Did man compute	40 Harold	3	304
Beneath its base are heroes' ashes hid	44 Harold	3	539
Yet, peace be with their ashes for by them	52 Harold	3	1004
My ashes in a soil which is not mine	56 Harold	4	74
Wrecks of another world whose ashes still are warm	62 Harold	4	414
Ashes which make it holier, dust which is	63 Harold	4	479
The Scipios' tomb contains no ashes now	66 Harold	4	707
To crush the imperial urn whose ashes slept sublime	71 Harold	4	990
Though I be ashes; a far hour shall wreak	75 Harold	4	1204
His way through thorns to ashes--glorious dome	77 Harold	4	1311
His shrunken ashes, raise this dome. How smiles	78 Harold	4	1366
Thy bridal's fruit is ashes; in the dust	80 Harold	4	1523
The spot where now thy mouldering ashes lie	85 Epitaph		12
Which held his clan's great ashes stood	105 Alva		302
If in the spoiler's power my ashes lie	106 Nisus		70
As ye pass by the tomb where my ashes consume	115 The Tear		43
Till blackening ashes and the lonely wall	169 Address-A		15
The feeble ashes, and their feeble breath	190 Darkness		62
The ashes of a thousand ages spread	192 Fragment-C		25
He was your brother--bear his ashes hence	194 Monody		108
The Fruit of Fire is Ashes	201 Ode-C		31
And her ashes still float to their home o'er the tide	201 Avatar		2
I am ashes where once I was fire	205 Blessington		9
And where our fathers' ashes be	217 Gazelle		21
A virgin phoenix from her ashes risen	244 Bards		210
The urn may shine, the ashes will not glow	298 Age		28
As if his ashes found their latest home	300 Age		121
Ere yet her husband's ashes have had time	308 Age		751
(If e'er those awful ashes can grow cold	308 Age		753
Snatch from the ashes of your sires	311 Giaour		116
Contains no fabled hero's ashes	329 Abydos	2	34
The lip of ashes, and the cheek of flame	374 Lara	1	599
Down the ashes shower like rain	395 Corinth		1036
Yet when their ashes in their nook are laid	423 Island	2	316
The kindling ashes to his kindled breast	433 Island	4	226
The sparkles of our ashes. One great clime	454 Venice-B		133
Hath left its leader's ashes at the gate	459 Dante	2	94
And from thine ashes boundless spirits rise	461 Dante	3	41
Till they are ashes and repose with me	462 Dante	3	109
The ashes thou shalt ne'er obtain--Alas	465 Dante	4	140
Ashes to ashes--merry let us be	472 Morgante		422
And planets turn to ashes at his wrath	489 Manfred	2	382
And strew'd my head with ashes; I have known	489 Manfred	2	409
Oh, that he were alive, and I in ashes	508 Faliero	1	587
Or that he were alive ere I be ashes	508 Faliero	1	588
Moulder'd into a mite of ashes, hold	519 Faliero	3	19
Strew flowers o'er her deliverers' ashes, then	519 Faliero	3	72
Where the Dead Sea hath quench'd two cities' ashes	526 Faliero	3	544
But they perhaps will let our ashes mingle	537 Faliero	4	658
They had conjured up stern Nimrod from his ashes	557 Sardan	1	420
From whence I sprung are--what I see them--ashes	565 Sardan	2	242
And not gone tracking it through human ashes	571 Sardan	3	15
In ashes. Darest thou so much? I dare all things	574 Sardan	3	160
Grieve more above the blighted name and ashes	584 Sardan	4	394
Speak further of the rites due to such ashes	590 Sardan	5	167
And then a mount of ashes, but a light	594 Sardan	5	440
True, the commingling fire will mix our ashes	594 Sardan	5	471
Be ashes here than aught that lives elsewhere	597 Foscari	1	139
The exile of the disinterred ashes	616 Foscari	4	112
They have no further power upon those ashes	618 Foscari	4	204
A martyr's ashes now lie there, which make it	618 Foscari	4	220
Have roll'd o'er your dead ashes, and your seed's	631 Cain	1	231
Earth's fruits be ashes in his mouth--the leaves	652 Cain	3	428
May howl above his ashes (as they did	703 Werner	3	577
Ashes are feeble foes: it is more easy	720 Werner	5	436
And revive the heroic ashes	735 Deformed	2	9
And ashes! Yes, thine own amidst the rest	739 Deformed	2	265
And Father's house from ashes. These are nothing	743 Deformed	3	123
The ashes of our hopes, is a deep grief	807 Juan	3	407
And shiver them to ashes, but to trail	817 Juan	4	70
Her cheek turn'd ashes, ears rung, brain whirl'd round	865 Juan	6	837
Spare, or smite rarely--man's make millions ashes	879 Juan	8	48
'Ashes to ashes'--why not lead to lead	879 Juan	8	80

ASHORE

And there he went ashore without delay   804 Juan   3   153

ASHUR

And the widows of Ashur are loud in their wail 222 Sennacherib   21

ASIA

O'er prostrate Asia;--thou, who with thy frown   67 Harold   4   744
Europe and Asia, you being quite at ease   832 Juan   5   38
Asia, where Kaff looks down upon the Kurds   863 Juan   6   688

ASIAN

Did many a Roman chief and Asian king   26 Harold   2   400
The childish helplessness of Asian women   571 Sardan   2   590
The European with the Asian shore   831 Juan   5   17
The Asian pomp of Ottoman parade   838 Juan   5   408

ASIA'S

Recording Freedom's smile and Asia's tear   34 Harold   2   852
Where Asia's bounds and ours divide   393 Corinth   812

ASIATIC

And views opposed the Asiatic plain   161 Athos   3
To this our Asiatic side   332 Abydos   2   294
She had the Asiatic eye   409 Mazeppa   208
But such as fit an Asiatic breech   840 Juan   5   541
Began to clothe each Asiatic hill   863 Juan   6   683
And taciturn Asiatic disposition   933 Juan   12   210
To make his little wild Asiatic tame   935 Juan   12   334

ASIDE

I turn'd aside to pay my homage here   14 Harold   1   640
Nor from the base pursuit had turn'd aside   24 Harold   2   293
(Unless aside thy purple had been thrown   41 Harold   3   367
Aside for ever: it may be a sound   58 Harold   4   204
In pity turn'd the death aside   99 Young Lady   12
Who turns aside from real woe   118 Romance   39
Perchance not blood shall turn aside   165 Friend-B   52
But he turn'd aside and look'd from the ridge   176 Devil's Dr   53
But to the theme:--now laid aside too long   208 Sketch   37
Once laid aside, but now assumed again   242 Bards   20
See honest Hallam lay aside his fork   249 Bards   548
No matter, throw your ornaments aside   267 Hints   797
As sets aside the slightest thought of trick   289 Vision   270
His robe of pride was thrown aside   330 Abydos   2   131
But, this as if he guess'd, with head aside   340 Corsair   1   151
The sword aside--in vain--the blood o'erflows   349 Corsair   2   185
Which may not, dare not see, but turns aside   365 Corsair   3   660
But his heart was swollen, and turn'd aside   391 Corinth   653
The erring arrow launch aside   400 Parisina   362
Even that must now be thrown aside   401 Parisina   440
And all my bonds aside were cast   406 Chillon   376
They snort--they foam--neigh--swerve aside   413 Mazeppa   706
In swifter ripples stream aside the seas   418 Island   1   227
Their arms aside to revel in its dew   427 Island   3   76
Begins, and prudery flings aside her fetter   440 Beppo   12
And forests like a wolf, nor turn aside   494 Manfred   3   225
Aside the dignities which I have borne   523 Faliero   3   343
Nor turn aside to strike at such a prey   526 Faliero   3   522
To chains, but laid aside to carry weapons   526 Faliero   3   563
Are capable of turning them aside   534 Faliero   4   414
As not being of them: turn thy steps aside   658 Heaven   211
You turn aside--I did so. But--Hear me   690 Werner   2   459
Lay dying, and the stranger dash'd aside   701 Werner   3   382
Aside these nodding plumes and dragging trains 714 Werner   5   70
Aside intrigue: 'tis rarely worth the trouble   741 Deformed 2   440
These I could bear, but cannot cast aside   771 Juan   1   1557
Which makes not others smile; then turn'd aside 819 Juan   4   178
Was on the point of being set aside   837 Juan   5   404
And turns aside his scythe to vulgar things   844 Juan   5   780
He mutter'd (but the last was given aside   844 Juan   5   819
Were laid aside; but not before she offer'd   860 Juan   6   482
Some laid aside like an old Opera hat   928 Juan   11   619
Required. Aurora scarcely look'd aside   977 Juan   15   619
Aside his very mirror soon was put   984 Juan   16   228
Now this (but we will whisper it aside   986 Juan   16   385

ASK

Ask ye, Boeotian shades, the reason why   15 Harold   1   706
And dost thou ask what secret woe   17 Harold   1   841
What is that worst? Nay do not ask   18 Harold   1   869
Nor ask so dear a breast to feel one pang for mine 24 Harold 2   270
I ask not the pleasures that riches supply   30 Harold   2   669
Heart, soul could seek, tongue ask.--Away with
    words, draw near   71 Harold   4   972
That ask the eye--so here condense thy soul   78 Harold   4   1408
Ask thine own heart; 'twill bid thee, boy, forbear 93 Dorset   31
Dorset, farewell! I will not ask one part   94 Dorset   91
Yet why do I ask?--to distraction a prey   99 Adieu   19
Then grant, thou God! I ask no more   103 Alva   135
For Pitt, and Pitt alone, has dared to ask   114 Death-A   36
All I ask--all I wish--is a Tear   115 The Tear   48
I ask but this--again to rove   135 I Would   15
I ask no atonement but days like the past   137 Delawarr   36

ASK

I ask no pledge to make me blest   163 Parting   9
Nor ask the aid of idle song   163 Malta   44
And ask, for what is such a place meant   163 Malta   50
Ask if I felt no secret pain   164 Friend-B   32
I will not ask where thou liest low   167 Dead   10
That cruel question ask of me   173 Love   2
Which seem'd to ask if a God were there   176 Devil's Dr   71
All I ask is to divide   187 French-A   37
To give the tribute Glory need not ask   194 Monody   98
Ask more than patience   200 Stanzas-B   77
The world is all before me; I but ask   212 Augusta-C   81
Yet let me ponder well, before I ask   224 J.C.H.   27
Then Rogers shall ask us for laurel   227 Thurlow-B   24
And dost thou ask the reason of my sadness   229 Sadness   1
Go, ask (if he will be sincere   233 Ballad-B   19
You ask for a 'Volume of Nonsense   236 Nonsense   1
Then should you ask me, why I venture o'er   243 Bards   93
Why slumbers Gifford? let us ask again   253 Bards   820
And grant in turn the pardon which we ask   257 Hints   18
Ask not his thoughts, or follow his desire   267 Hints   788
Go, ask thy bosom who deserves them most   272 Minerva   310
He means nothing; nay, ask him. Pray, sir! did
    you mean   281 Blues   2   66
But where's the proctor who will ask his son   286 Vision   93
First ask him for his answer to my letter   295 Vision   656
Thy dying ask revenge in vain   316 Giaour   578
I do not ask him not to blame   322 Giaour   1244
I do not ask him not to mourn   322 Giaour   1247
And ask the squalid peasant how   331 Abydos   2   258
But ask no land beyond my sabre's length   333 Abydos   2   433
Is famed and fear'd--they ask and know no more 339 Corsair   1   62
'Oh! are they safe? we ask not of success   339 Corsair   1   111
More I must ask, and food the slaves shall bring 348 Corsair 2   101
Ah! rather ask what will not Woman dare   353 Corsair   2   407
Nor ask or what or who the sign may bring   353 Corsair   2   420
Yet would I ask--almost my lip denies   357 Corsair   3   105
Might be redeem'd nor ask a long remorse   367 Lara   1   64
And once beheld, would ask of him again   371 Lara   1   368
'Tis Lara!--further wouldst thou mark or ask   372 Lara   1   435
His heart's dearest wish; let him ask it, and have 392 Corinth   718
Ask the abbot pardon, as I wish you would   471 Morgante   368
Ask of us subjects, sovereignty, the power   480 Manfred   1   140
Ye offer so profusely what I ask   480 Manfred   1   146
Bethink ere thou dismiss us, ask again   480 Manfred   1   167
And ask them what it is we dread to be   487 Manfred   2   272
I know not what I ask, nor what I seek   490 Manfred   2   501
We will ask justice; if it be denied   502 Faliero   1   167
You ask redress of me! Go to the Forty   506 Faliero   1   430
Ask of the bleeding pelican why she   506 Faliero   1   470
I had but little more to ask or hope   515 Faliero   2   462
Ask me not--tempt me not with such a question   524 Faliero   3   417
Again, I tell thee, ask not; but by all   530 Faliero   4   170
Go, ask your racks what they have wrung from us 538 Faliero   5   42
What do you mean? Ask of the suffering people 538 Faliero   5   55
I ask of you, but silence for myself   542 Faliero   5   297
I would not ask so much for me still living   547 Faliero   5   674
I would thou wouldst not ask me; the next moment 556 Sardan   1   347
Glory! what's that? Ask of the gods thy fathers 559 Sardan   1   591
To count its throbs, not quicken them, and ask 570 Sardan   2   529
Questions which mortal never dared to ask me   570 Sardan   2   530
And I would ask, if this your palace were   572 Sardan   3   53
Must not be wanting now. I ask no guard   576 Sardan   3   288
Know'st thou of wounds? yet wherefore do I ask 577 Sardan   3   375
Aught--all that she can ask--but such a meeting 581 Sardan   4   218
That what they ask in aught that touches on   581 Sardan   4   221
I pray thee, brother, leave me. Since you ask it 582 Sardan 4   234
I ask no more--but let us hence together   583 Sardan   4   353
That thou shouldst come and dare to ask of me   592 Sardan   5   320
But must I bear no answer? Yes,--I ask   592 Sardan   5   342
I ask no more than a Venetian grave   597 Foscari   1   144
Why do I ask? Thy paleness--'Tis the Joy   609 Foscari   3   46
I have nought to ask. Nor aught to thank for?
    No   628 Cain   1   28
Than a mere serpent: ask the cherubim   631 Cain   1   229
Ask the Destroyer. Who? The Maker--call him   631 Cain   1   263
To be our guests--will he? Wilt thou? I ask   632 Cain   1   342
Ask Eve, your mother: bears she not the knowledge 633 Cain   1   391
Ask of your sire, the exile fresh from Eden   635 Cain   1   479
Of his first-born son: ask your own heart   635 Cain   1   480
That thirst; not ask thee to partake of fruits 636 Cain   1   556
And therefore do I ask of thee, if thou   637 Cain   2   89
And wherefore did it fall? Ask him who fells   640 Cain   2   284
Ask him who made thee greater than myself   665 Heaven   768
'Tis time enough to ask it when he's able   675 Werner   1   245
Ask not! but let us think where we shall go   683 Werner   1   742
Your actions show it. Might I ask your name   686 Werner   2   189
Why did you leave him? Can you ask that question 689 Werner 2   384
I do not ask for hints, and surmises   691 Werner   2   556
You're right: I ask for shelter at the hand   695 Werner   3   29
Ask that at Magdebourg--or for that matter   705 Werner   4   46
You'd better ask himself. I would as soon   705 Werner   4   58
Ask the lion why he laps not milk   705 Werner   4   59
No! Oh, my God! do you? Why do you ask   707 Werner   4   198

ASK

Indeed I do not:--ask of Rodolph. Truly	707 Werner	4	215
And strong as what it was, and--I ask not	727 Deformed	1	312
How mortals lie by instinct! If you ask	743 Deformed	3	92
Would I ask wherefore? Yes! and not believe	744 Deformed	3	135
And if the man should ask, 'tis but denial	756 Juan	1	623
'Twill one day ask you why you used me so	766 Juan	1	1254
As upon such occasions tars will ask	778 Juan	2	263
Must breakfast--and betimes, lest they should ask it	792 Juan	2	1151
(Such things, in fact, it don't ask much to mar	802 Juan	3	78
To ask him awkward questions on the way	804 Juan	3	155
You'd better ask our mistress who's his heir	806 Juan	3	342
Could not the blockhead ask for a balloon	814 Juan	3	888
Juan gazed on her as to ask his fate	819 Juan	4	173
And these are things which ask a tender tear	833 Juan	5	149
And conscience ask a curious sort of question	835 Juan	5	236
And, should you ask how she, a sultan's bride	846 Juan	5	914
Of one who dared to ask if 'he had loved	846 Juan	5	964
Her third, to ask him where he had been bred	849 Juan	5	1107
Could you ask such a question?--but we will	856 Juan	6	258
'From Spain.'--'But where is Spain?'--'Don't ask such stuff	858 Juan	6	348
What that is--ask the pig who sees the wind	877 Juan	7	672
But ask him what he thinks of in a year hence	919 Juan	11	56
And should you doubt, pray ask of your next neighbour	923 Juan	11	324
Ask a blind man, the best judge. You'll attack	938 Juan	12	564
I ask in turn,--Why do you play at cards	956 Juan	14	83
That--but ask any woman if she'd choose	958 Juan	14	198
And ask them how they like to be in thrall	965 Juan	14	660
As if to ask how you can dare to keep	982 Juan	16	143
To ask the reverend person what he wanted	983 Juan	16	184
I ask but this of mine, to--not defend	994 Juan	16	880

ASKALON'S

Near Askalon's towers, John of Horistan slumbers	86 Leaving NA		11

ASKANCE

The cold repulse, the look askance	172 Romaic-B		19
Till Giaffir's quail'd and shrunk askance	325 Abydos	1	130
By a look scarce perceptibly askance	993 Juan	16	814

ASK'D

Were ask'd to sing, by joy forsaken	96 Granta		87
'All thou hast ask'd, receive,' the prince replied	108 Nisus		199
Which lay unread around it. And I ask'd	190 Churchill		7
You have ask'd for a verse--the request	205 Blessington		1
'Why slumbers Gifford?' once was ask'd in vain	253 Bards		819
Then give me all I ever ask'd--a tear	343 Corsair	1	361
To send his soul--he scarcely ask'd to heaven	351 Corsair	2	291
Mine eye ne'er ask'd if others were as fair	354 Corsair	2	490
That ask'd from form so fair no more than this	363 Corsair	3	550
He ask'd no question--all were answer'd now	365 Corsair	3	623
And ask'd if greater dwelt beyond the sky	368 Lara	1	126
Vain was all question ask'd her of the past	382 Lara	2	526
I ask'd not why, and reck'd not where	406 Chillon		371
This Torquil ask'd with half-upbraiding eye	430 Island	4	53
Then ask'd him, 'If he wish'd to stay as servant	469 Morgante		240
Some days ago I should have ask'd your leave	475 Morgante		605
I ask'd no remedy but from the law	502 Faliero	1	141
Some sacrifices ask'd a single victim	503 Faliero	1	259
Would now repeat the question which I ask'd	524 Faliero	3	391
Boon which I ever ask'd Assyria's king	560 Sardan	1	658
And ask'd of thee, and thou hast answer'd--but	562 Sardan	2	29
He never ask'd it. Doubt not, he will have it	565 Sardan	2	224
Thou askest.--What of me? may soon be ask'd	609 Foscari	3	75
I ask'd for even those outlines of their kind	610 Foscari	3	114
For the only boon I would have ask'd or taken	612 Foscari	3	282
Then why is evil--he being good? I ask'd	643 Cain	2	490
I ask'd for something better than your name	674 Werner	1	177
Is ask'd in kindness. When I know it such	679 Werner	1	533
And never thought to have ask'd so much. This tone	692 Werner	2	571
You too! I merely ask'd a simple question	692 Werner	2	622
If the judge ask'd me, I would answer 'No	692 Werner	2	623
If the earth's princes ask'd no more. Be silent	734 Deformed	1	830
Yet when they ask'd her for her depositions	750 Juan	1	213
I ask'd the doctors after his disease	751 Juan	1	270
Haidee spoke not of scruples, ask'd no vows	798 Juan	2	1513
He ask'd the meaning of this holiday	806 Juan	3	333
He ask'd no further questions, and proceeded	807 Juan	3	385
Thus, usually, when he was ask'd to sing	812 Juan	3	673
Katinka ask'd her also whence she came	858 Juan	6	347
To this long catechism of questions, ask'd	864 Juan	6	794
An English lady ask'd of an Italian	903 Juan	9	401
And ask'd why such a structure had been raised	916 Juan	10	592
Late authors ask'd him for a hint or two	924 Juan	11	398
Ask'd next day, 'If men ever hunted twice	959 Juan	14	280
Then ask'd her Grace what news were of the duke of late	984 Juan	16	269

ASKED

Who, when asked for a remedy, sent them a rope	226 Ode-D		32
But, if I'm asked, this answer shall be given	476 Morgante		655

ASKEST

Thou askest.--What of me? may soon be ask'd	609 Foscari	3	75

ASKING

Asking some succour for Charity's sake	225 Ode-D		6
With many an asking smile and wondering stare	363 Corsair	3	512
And asking if indeed the day were done	424 Island	2	369
By Neuha, asking where they had been chased	435 Island	4	410
And other things which may be had for asking	440 Beppo		8
I would have dash'd amongst them, asking few	504 Faliero	1	306
Asking of his own heart what brought him here	522 Faliero	3	264
(At least to me) by asking you to share	676 Werner	1	324
Few can obtain by asking. Pardon me	677 Werner	1	367
And now I think on't, asking after you	699 Werner	3	283
And asking now and then for cast-off dresses	797 Juan	2	1456
She saw them watch her without asking why	824 Juan	4	499
Conjecturing, wondering, asking a narration	861 Juan	6	587
On which, at the third asking of the bans	992 Juan	16	745

ASKS

Not now in snow, which asks the lyric Roman's aid	66 Harold	4	666
With all that Virtue asks of Homage thine	183 Address-D		34
And even in him it asks the name of Love	342 Corsair	1	286
It is the cause, and not our will, which asks	521 Faliero	3	200
I'm answer'd! When a king asks twice, and has	590 Sardan	5	171
You owe to the unknown, who asks no more	692 Werner	2	570
Further than Justice asks. Answer at once	715 Werner	5	169

ASK'ST

Ask'st thou the difference? From fair Phyles' towers	270 Minerva		129
'Thou ask'st if I can love? be this the proof	847 Juan	5	1009

ASLEEP

As an infant's asleep	188 Music-C		12
Destroying--saving--prison'd--and asleep	352 Corsair	2	391
The king had been an hour asleep	415 Mazeppa		869
Like a huge lion in the sun asleep	422 Island	2	235
The baron was asleep in the great chair	683 Werner	2	33
How should I? I was fast asleep. And so	686 Werner	2	201
In short, I was asleep upon a chair	686 Werner	2	234
The bare knife in your hand, and earth asleep	690 Werner	2	454
And on it Stralenheim!--Asleep! And yet	718 Werner	5	315
Was not asleep--'Yes, search and search,' she cried	764 Juan	1	1154
Asleep: they shook them by the hand and head	786 Juan	2	783
He did not fall asleep just after dinner	960 Juan	14	288

ASMODEUS

Asmodeus struck so bright a stroke as this	276 Waltz		223
The devil Asmodeus to the circle made	295 Vision		675
Such trash below your wing, Asmodeus dear	296 Vision		702
'Done!' cried Asmodeus, 'he anticipates	296 Vision		706

ASP

Rivets the living links, the enormous asp	79 Harold	4	1439
She would have shrunk as from a toad, or asp	760 Juan	1	886
Upon their prey, as darts an angry asp	822 Juan	4	382

ASPECT

Though alway changing, in her aspect mild	25 Harold	2	326
In soul and aspect as in age: years steal	36 Harold	3	70
A gray and grief-worn aspect of old days	45 Harold	3	618
The stillness of their aspect in each trace	46 Harold	3	646
The ambrosial aspect, which, beheld, instils	62 Harold	4	435
And most serene of aspect, and most clear	65 Harold	4	592
Of a sublimer aspect? Majesty	78 Harold	4	1384
A deep cold settled aspect nought can shake	81 Harold	4	1556
While that icy aspect chills us	100 Marion		13
With aspect fair and honey'd tongue	132 L'Amitie		76
And o'er the changing aspect flits	174 Impromptu-A		3
With such an aspect, by his colours blent	175 Sonnet-A		9
Wore an unearthly aspect, as by fits	189 Darkness		23
And his present aspect--Beauty	196 Rogers		26
The selfsame aspect, and the quivering shock	215 Dream		150
Meet in her aspect and her eyes	216 She Walks		4
A Spirit of a different aspect waved	288 Vision		186
The aspect of a god; but this ne'er nursed	288 Vision		244
A civil aspect: though they did not kiss	289 Vision		278
To his whole aspect, which, though rather grave	296 Vision		749
Such is the aspect of this shore	311 Giaour		90
His aspect and his air impress'd	312 Giaour		204
His aspect glares within the porch	319 Giaour		890
But little from his aspect learn'd	326 Abydos	1	258
There breathe but few whose aspect might defy	341 Corsair	1	215
Along the govern'd aspect, speak alone	341 Corsair	1	232
The solemn aspect, and the high-born eye	346 Corsair	1	543
Their freezing aspect and averted air	362 Corsair	3	465
That death with gentler aspect wither'd there	364 Corsair	3	604

ASPECT

Full many a stoic eye and aspect stern	365	Corsair	3	636
Of foreign aspect and of tender age	366	Lara	1	48
His aspect all that terror gives the grave	369	Lara	1	200
That oft awake his aspect could disclose	369	Lara	1	223
Along the stranger's aspect, fix'd and stern	372	Lara	1	413
But from his aspect might be more than guess'd	374	Lara	1	583
Than Lara's aspect unto others wore	374	Lara	1	613
Along his aspect an unwonted hue	380	Lara	2	351
Save that pale aspect, where the eye, though dim	381	Lara	2	430
Their eyes were feverish, and their aspect worn	427	Island	3	61
The aspect and the form of breathing men	478	Manfred	1	8
The steady aspect of a clear large star	480	Manfred	1	178
Who is most powerful of ye, take such aspect	481	Manfred	1	186
Tinge thy celestial aspect, and make tame	485	Manfred	2	117
The aspect of a tumbling tempest's foam	487	Manfred	2	305
And the aspect thou worest	490	Manfred	2	464
Ah! he unveils his aspect: on his brow	496	Manfred	3	336
An aspect of eternity: his thoughts	509	Faliero	2	18
Drinks life, and light, and glory from her aspect	514	Faliero	2	398
Have worn this aspect yet for many a year	528	Faliero	4	50
With honest mates, and bear a cheerful aspect	531	Faliero	4	232
With the same aspect, which appall'd me more	579	Sardan	4	98
Yes, the enlarged but noble aspect of	580	Sardan	4	133
Nor look--yet he was soft of voice and aspect	582	Sardan	4	241
Now to reproof: methinks your aspect speaks	586	Sardan	4	530
Inveterate enemies. Now it bears an aspect	593	Sardan	5	366
How looks my father? With his wonted aspect	598	Foscari	1	163
The self-same aspect, to my very sire	598	Foscari	1	171
So I could see thee with a quiet aspect	610	Foscari	3	144
Yet of a sterner and a sadder aspect	628	Cain	1	81
And yet they have an aspect, which, though not	640	Cain	2	256
The fatal fruit, nor even of the same aspect	642	Cain	2	410
His aspect--I have led him here, and giv'n	652	Cain	3	374
Less goodly in their aspect, in their years	660	Heaven		395
And by her aspect she might be a prince's	677	Werner	1	392
The aspect of a secret enemy	678	Werner	1	448
Of his wife's dignified but foreign aspect	687	Werner	2	276
In aspect and demeanour. True, dear child	708	Werner	4	245
As well as your brave son; and smooth your aspect	712	Werner	4	541
Even to this hateful aspect. Let me wash	723	Deformed	1	45
And for his aspect, look upon the fountain	723	Deformed	1	98
You see his aspect--choose it, or reject	725	Deformed	1	193
His aspect may be fair, but suits me not	725	Deformed	1	197
With the wide nostrils and Silenus' aspect	725	Deformed	1	218
And manly aspect look like Hercules	725	Deformed	1	231
For I, too, love a change. Your aspect is	727	Deformed	1	370
And his aspect the brightest	728	Deformed	1	410
And blooming aspect, Huon; for he looks	730	Deformed	1	526
What clouds his royal aspect? 'Nothing,' 'Nothing	743	Deformed	3	99
And in whatever aspect it arrays	756	Juan	1	581
Of a soft cheek and aspect delicate	785	Juan	2	698
Unequal in its aspect here and there	787	Juan	2	818
His slender frame and pallid aspect lay	788	Juan	2	879
With here and there a creek, whose aspect wore	796	Juan	2	1412
More like and like to Lambro's aspect grew	820	Juan	4	276
But fix'd as marble's unchanged aspect throws	824	Juan	4	483
Which has at times an aspect of the oddest	843	Juan	5	727
A third's all pallid aspect offer'd more	860	Juan	6	531
In aspect, plainly clad, besmear'd with dust	876	Juan	7	582
Along the aspect, whether smooth or rough	902	Juan	9	382
Parisian aspect which upset old Troy	903	Juan	9	421
Glory and triumph o'er her aspect burst	904	Juan	9	467
But still her aspect had an air so lonely	973	Juan	15	347
All youth--but with an aspect beyond time	973	Juan	15	356
Her aspect was as usual, still--not stern	993	Juan	16	795

ASPECTS

Thin streets, and foreign aspects, such as must	57	Harold	4	133
Each other's aspects--saw, and shriek'd, and died	190	Darkness		66
With strange and dusky aspects; he was not	215	Dream		109
Presented well-known aspects to the view	429	Island	3	172
Even as our outward aspect;--thou dost rise	493	Manfred	3	194
The guilty; but with all this, in their aspects	500	Faliero	1	62
Of various aspects, buy of one expression	580	Sardan	4	115
Wear more magnetic aspects: I will on	701	Werner	3	424
And thus the chilliest aspects may concentre	945	Juan	13	298
Start from the frames which fence their aspects stern	982	Juan	16	142

ASPEN

And with their thin aspen faces and fix'd eyes	733	Deformed	1	767

ASPERSE

Matrons may sure their characters asperse	142	Soliloquy		18

ASPIRANT

Admitted as an aspirant to all	925	Juan	11	426
Perhaps she wish'd an aspirant profounder	962	Juan	14	453

ASPIRANTS

Attain'd by noble aspirants. To such	598	Foscari	1	192

ASPIRATION

'Tis the old aspiration breathed afresh	302	Age		268

ASPIRATIONS

That in our aspirations to be great	49	Harold	3	827
These aspirations in their scope incline	56	Harold	4	79
As clay hath seldom borne; his aspirations	489	Manfred	2	428
And noble aspirations in my youth	492	Manfred	3	105
Employ the minutes left in aspirations	547	Faliero	5	651
Longings sublime, and aspirations high	758	Juan	1	738

ASPIRE

That only Heaven to which Earth's children may aspire	25	Harold	2	351
In its own narrow being, but aspire	41	Harold	3	373
Let the young and the brilliant aspire	205	Blessington		17
Who dares aspire if thou must cease to hope	252	Bards		802
In fine, to whatsoever you aspire	257	Hints		37
If some Drawcansir you aspire to draw	259	Hints		173
In this nice age, when all aspire to taste	262	Hints		394
Ye, who aspire to 'build the lofty rhyme	267	Hints		781
To these alone my thoughts aspire	328	Abydos	1	406
And some to higher thoughts aspire	333	Abydos	2	379
Where all his hopes to see his name aspire	417	Island	1	161

ASPIRED

Its sound aspired to Heaven and there abode	217	The Harp		15
A polish'd nation's praise aspired to claim	243	Bards		111
Her virgin hand aspired to claim	386	Corinth		186
From the Tarpeian. He aspired to treason	537	Faliero	4	651
One who aspired to be what made thee, and	629	Cain	1	126

ASPIRES

Eternal captive, to her God aspires	195	Vittorelli		8
In mangled prose, nor e'en aspires to rhyme	246	Bards		322

ASPIRING

Say--shall this new, nor less aspiring pile	169	Address-A		17
Lost!--why, who is the aspiring chief who dared	558	Sardan	1	536
Knowing such things, aspiring to such things	637	Cain	2	52
And clear thought; and thou wouldst go on aspiring	645	Cain	2	608
'Tis an aspiring one, whate'er the tenement	724	Deformed	1	145

ASPRAMONT

'And even at Aspramont thou didst begin	467	Morgante		97

ASS

There's something in a stupid ass	234	Epilogue		1
The bard who soars to elegise an ass	245	Bards		262
When for the night some lately titled ass	250	Bards		656
Must mount her Pegasus, a full-grown ass	255	Bards		970
When such an ass as this, like Balaam's, prates	296	Vision		710
Do so, and take yon old ass with you. Hence	687	Werner	2	252
A--never mind; his tutor, an old ass	774	Juan	2	20
An ass was practising recitative	827	Juan	4	696
Cheapening an ox, an ass, a lamb, or kid	835	Juan	5	222
Science enough, which levels to an ass	867	Juan	7	35
For a much longer time; then, like an ass	882	Juan	8	229
Then, like an ass, he went upon his way	882	Juan	8	233
And then men stare, as if a new ass spake	933	Juan	12	205

ASSAIL

Though man and man's avenging arms assail	16	Harold	1	767
Yet let not canker'd Calumny assail	114	Death-A		27
Unyielding pangs assail the drooping mind	122	Recoil		6
If such may be the Ills which men assail	193	Monody		87
And yet, though storms and blight assail	336	Abydos	2	677
Where sallying ranks the trench assail	385	Corinth		103
Against the outworn creature they assail	439	Tasso		203
Await the moment to assail and tear	463	Dante	3	175
Which, in this scorpion nest of vice, assail	513	Faliero	2	300
Who dares assail Arbaces? I! Indeed	564	Sardan	2	184
Of one whose hate is mask'd but to assail	780	Juan	2	388
They were all summer: lightning might assail	817	Juan	4	69
He judged them proper to assail the works	873	Juan	7	422

ASSAILANT

When Alp, her fierce assailant, fell	394	Corinth		913
Their every shot told; while the assailant fell	434	Island	4	313

ASSAILANTS

Pervious to the assailants? For the present	590	Sardan	5	201

ASSAILANT'S

And fired it into one assailant's pudding	920	Juan	11	100

ASSAIL'D

A thousand battles have assail'd thy banks	43	Harold	3	451
Of Heaven, again assail'd, if Heaven the while	51	Harold	3	984
Till every lawless soldier who assail'd	72	Harold	4	1015
Even dogs assail'd their masters, all save one	189	Darkness		47
Against the seraphs they assail'd	311	Giaour		63
Their smoke assail'd his startled beak	396	Corinth		1077

ASSOCIATES
Associates of the festive hour 135 I Would 36
Not only over his associates, but 717 Werner 5 248

ASSOCIATION
This undesired association in 622 Foscari 5 140

ASSUAGE
Ere toil his thirst for travel can assuage 8 Harold 1 331
Time will assuage an infant brother's woe 85 Epitaph 26
Would my lips breathe a flame which no stream could
  assuage 92 Caroline-D 10
Too justly moved for mercy to assuage 358 Corsair 3 164
A word can kindle and a word assuage 377 Lara 2 146
He clasps the hand that pang which would assuage 381 Lara 2 426
Unless he could assuage the woe 403 Chillon 90
For ne'er can man his conscience all assuage 416 Island 1 63
So that we can our native sun assuage 905 Juan 9 549

ASSUAGES
The fount, at which the panting mind assuages 52 Harold 3 1028

ASSUAGING
But violent things will sooner bear assuaging 808 Juan 3 461

ASSUME
(See also RE-ASSUME)
Had made Despair a smilingness assume 37 Harold 3 140
Of an Italian night, where the deep skies assume 74 Harold 4 1152
And all assume a varied hue 118 Romance 14
Let Comedy assume her throne again 249 Bards 581
When Prudence would his voice assume 322 Giaour 1230
Assume the distaff--not the brand 324 Abydos 1 100
Came not again, or Lara could assume 370 Lara 1 268
That thus you dare assume a lawless function 536 Faliero 4 566
Assume to win them? Who is he should dread 558 Sardan 1 537
Are girt about by demons, who assume 633 Cain 1 398
Some one must be found to assume the shape 728 Deformed 1 441
Assume, then leave us on our freezing way 867 Juan 7 8
Days better drawn before, or else assume 971 Juan 15 207

ASSUMED
Revel and feast assumed the rule again 28 Harold 2 535
And Anarchy assumed her attributes 72 Harold 4 1014
Once laid aside, but now assumed again 242 Bards 20
Link'd with success, assumed and kept with skill 341 Corsair 1 183
Upon the spot where it was first assumed 545 Faliero 5 520
Or said her cheeks assumed the deepest dyes 848 Juan 5 1067
Strict, and his mind assumed a manlier vigour 969 Juan 15 86

ASSUMES
So honour'd but assumes a stronger, bitterer claim 40 Harold 3 279
Each youth his varied plaid assumes 102 Alva 91
Assumes the ghastly stare of death 128 Answer-B 18
Yon heaven assumes a varied glow 133 E.N.Long 7

ASSURANCE
With calm assurance to that blessed place 492 Manfred 3 81
Make our assurance doubly sure, according 518 Faliero 2 669
For the assurance of the vacant space 590 Sardan 5 211
I was thrust back, with the assurance that 602 Foscari 2 60
At Hamburgh those who would have made assurance 679 Werner 1 498
A modest confidence and calm assurance 924 Juan 11 410
Modest I am--yet with some slight assurance 998 Juan 17 82

ASSURE
(See also RE-ASSURE)
And then assure us that their rights are thine 464 Dante 4 100
Speak, and assure us, wretched as we are 652 Cain 3 394
But show me any place. I do assure you 696 Werner 3 68
I assure you I meant nothing,--a mere sport 705 Werner 4 63
You sneer, and I assure you this is true 775 Juan 2 103
Excuse my freedom, when I here assure you 866 Juan 6 919
And I assure you, that like virgin honey 933 Juan 12 247

ASSURED
As if to be assured 'twas him she grasp'd 429 Island 3 190
To trust them with the secret, till assured 520 Faliero 3 128
Refusal would offend you. Be assured 711 Werner 4 470
Tell me--and be assured, that since you stain 765 Juan 1 1231
And glides away, assured she never hurts ye 926 Juan 11 496
Perhaps 'twas hardly quite assured enough 970 Juan 15 109

ASSUREDLY
To what it may conduct. Assuredly 509 Faliero 2 38
Next to the Doge. To the Doge? Assuredly 533 Faliero 4 337
Stand good in law? Assuredly, Whoe'er 539 Faliero 5 76
Unto thy children--Most assuredly 643 Cain 2 513
Admitted to our lands? Assuredly 699 Werner 3 251

ASSURES
Assures the future that my love will last 344 Corsair 1 407

ASSYRIA
Assyria, Greece, Rome, Carthage, what are they 82 Harold 4 1631
Were all Assyria raging round the walls 560 Sardan 1 623
Sole in Assyria, or with them elsewhere 561 Sardan 1 673
To serve and save Assyria. Heaven itself 568 Sardan 2 395
One for Assyria! Rather say for Bactria 575 Sardan 3 264
Assyria is not all the earth; we'll find 583 Sardan 4 355
Which once were mightiest in Assyria--than 584 Sardan 4 395
Queen of Assyria, departed hence 585 Sardan 4 452
And that? Is yours. Hark! Now! Adieu, Assyria 595 Sardan 5 492

ASSYRIAN
The Assyrian came down like the wolf on the fold 222 Sennacherib 1
And, should I chance to slay the Assyrian wight 230 Murray-A 16
A Grecian, Syrian, or Assyrian tale 446 Beppo 406
Till now, no drop from an Assyrian vein 557 Sardan 1 455

ASSYRIANS
These our Assyrians to the solar shores 553 Sardan 1 174
The Assyrians know no pleasure but their king's 572 Sardan 3 58

ASSYRIA'S
An idol foreign to Assyria's worship 553 Sardan 1 197
Respect, the tutelage of Assyria's heirs 554 Sardan 1 258
Reluctant love even from Assyria's lord 554 Sardan 1 267
Boon which I ever ask'd Assyria's king 560 Sardan 1 658
Taking his last look of Assyria's empire 561 Sardan 2 2
Hour of Assyria's years. And yet how calm 561 Sardan 2 9
Have been more zealous for Assyria's weal 565 Sardan 2 228
Assyria's idols! Let him be released 565 Sardan 2 247
This fatal night. Farewell, Assyria's line 575 Sardan 3 253

ASTARTE
Astarte 490 Manfred 2 453
To look upon the same--Astarte!--No 490 Manfred 2 473
Astarte! my beloved! speak to me 490 Manfred 2 487
The Lady Astarte, his--Hush! who comes here 494 Manfred 3 248

ASTERISK
The Earl of--Asterisk, and Lady--Blank 276 Waltz 203

ASTLEY'S
For Astley's circus Upton writes 233 Ballad-B 25

ASTOLFO
The Dane; Astolfo there too did resort 467 Morgante 67

ASTONISH
'Tis easy to astonish or appal 588 Sardan 5 79

ASTONISH'D
The astonish'd slaves, and shun the fated hall 369 Lara 1 260
The rebels than astonish'd his true subjects 588 Sardan 5 78
In fact much more astonish'd than delighted 806 Juan 3 295

ASTONISHMENT
The giant his astonishment betray'd 470 Morgante 270

ASTOUNDED
To the astounded kingdoms all inert 41 Harold 3 332

ASTRAY
The gift,--a fate, or will, that walk'd astray 211 Augusta-C 28
Has lured in turn, and all have led astray 251 Bards 694
Are led astray by some peculiar lure 257 Hints 41
But Laura could not thus be led astray 450 Beppo 646
And far as pagan countries roam'd astray 468 Morgante 146
Of the sad consequence of going astray 935 Juan 12 350

ASTREA
Astrea declares that some penance is due 100 Adieu 38

ASTRINGENT
Is not a thing of that astringent quality 851 Juan 5 1252

ASTROLOGER
Though but a young astrologer, the stars 576 Sardan 3 276

ASTRONOMER
But lover, poet, or astronomer 982 Juan 16 105

ASTRONOMY
But my best canto, save one on astronomy 941 Juan 12 703

ASTYANAX
The young Astyanax of modern Troy 308 Age 730

ASUNDER
When 'tis full 'twill burst asunder 187 Ode-B 13
Asunder, and the flashing of its hinges 288 Vision 210
Pours the link'd band through ranks asunder riven 380 Lara 2 361
He moveth--earthquakes rend the world asunder 488 Manfred 2 378
But let her come. I go. We have lived asunder 581 Sardan 4 227
Together; but our dwellings are asunder 644 Cain 2 581

ASUNDER

Our roads must lie asunder, though they tend	680	Werner	1	542
The heart asunder;--then, as more or less	865	Juan	6	853

ASYLUM

Oh! dark asylum of a Vandal race	255	Bards		981
They found asylum oft and ne'er reproof	377	Lara	2	187
Such was the stern asylum Neuha chose	430	Island	4	29
They seem'd to promise an asylum sure	469	Morgante		180
His shelterer's asylum to the risk	702	Werner	3	508
This tower. This is the second safe asylum	719	Werner	5	386

AT

Can I say to you more? I see what you'd be at	279	Blues	1	108
Why dost thou not expire at once in hearts	584	Sardan	4	427
Never to have been stung at all, than to	643	Cain	2	507
Although 'tis true that you turn'd out a Tory at	745	Juan	Ded	3
And now, my Epic Renegade! what are ye at	745	Juan	Ded	5
Few mortals know what end they would be at	763	Juan	1	1061
Good God! I wonder what they would be at	867	Juan	7	22
Shrunk to a scabbard, with his arrows at	902	Juan	9	355
And don't know justly what we would be at	929	Juan	12	5
But thou art the most difficult to rhyme at	932	Juan	12	189
Though certainly more difficult to rhyme at	959	Juan	14	228
Mountains, and all we can be most sublime at	959	Juan	14	230
(I'll take the likeness I can first come at	997	Juan	17	29

ATAGHAN

And silver-sheathed ataghan	313	Giaour		355
With arquebuss and ataghan	315	Giaour		522
Resign'd carbine or ataghan	316	Giaour		602

ATALANTIS

For I disdain to write an Atalantis	929	Juan	11	685

ATAR-GUL'S

The Persian Atar-gul's perfume	326	Abydos	1	270

ATE

As though they wish'd to burst at once, they ate	474	Morgante		529
And stared, but neither ate nor drank, but stared	580	Sardan	4	121
They ate up all they had, and drank their wine	782	Juan	2	546
The sailors ate the rest of poor Pedrillo	783	Juan	2	616
The sailors ate him, all save three or four	783	Juan	2	617
He ate, and he was well supplied: and she	794	Juan	2	1257
Who ate, last war, more Yankees than he kill'd	952	Juan	13	700
Since Eve ate apples, much depends on dinner	953	Juan	13	792
Much as old Saturn ate his progeny	955	Juan	14	6

ATE

Be trampled on, while Death and Ate range	457	Dante	1	117

ATE'S

Let not your quench'd hearths be Ate's	736	Deformed	2	104

ATHANASIAN

Of an Athanasian Trinity	179	Devil's Dr		246

ATHANASIUS'

As after reading Athanasius' curse	855	Juan	6	178

ATHENA

Ancient of days! august Athena! where	19	Harold	2	10
Athena, no! thy plunderer was a Scot	270	Minerva		128

ATHENA'S

Well didst thou speak, Athena's wisest son	20	Harold	2	55
Aught to displace Athena's poor remains	21	Harold	2	105
Albion was happy in Athena's tears	21	Harold	2	110
Age shakes Athena's tower but spares gray Marathon	33	Harold	2	836

ATHENIAN

A Spartan firmness with Athenian wit	126	Recoll		292
The travell'd thane, Athenian Aberdeen	248	Bards		509
The Athenian wears again Harmodius' sword	302	Age		276
He sings, as the Athenian spoke, with pebbles	462	Dante	3	96

ATHENIANS

Athenians. Look upon him well. He is	725	Deformed	1	211

ATHENIAN'S

Th' Athenian's glowing style, or Tully's fire	112	Examination		30
That rolls below the Athenian's grave	310	Giaour		2

ATHENS

Where the Etrurian Athens claims and keeps	62	Harold	4	425
Maid of Athens, ere we part	160	Maid		1
Maid of Athens! I am gone	161	Maid		19
Athens holds my heart and soul	161	Maid		22
With Athens, old ally	162	War Song		24
He comes to Athens, and he writes his name	162	Orchomenus		4
And owls sent to Athens, as wonders	227	Thurlow-B		19
What Athens was in science, Rome in power	255	Bards		999
But Rome decay'd, and Athens strew'd the plain	255	Bards		1003

ATHENS

When, Athens! here thy wisest look'd his last	268	Minerva		20
When, Athens! here thy Wisest look'd his last	355	Corsair	3	20
Fair Athens! could thine evening face forget	356	Corsair	3	60
In Spain, and Lucca, Athens, every where	977	Juan	15	580

ATHENS'

When Athens' children are with hearts endued	33	Harold	2	794
Such as Harmodius drew on Athens' tyrant lord	38	Harold	3	180
When Athens' armies fell at Syracuse	57	Harold	4	136

ATHIRST

I feel athirst--will no one bring me here	625	Foscari	5	290

ATHOS

Such as on lonely Athos may be seen	23	Harold	2	236
Athos, Olympus, Aetna, Atlas, made	66	Harold	4	663
With lowering port majestic Athos stands	161	Athos		6
Athos and Ida, with a dashing sea	298	Age		15
As Philip's son proposed to do with Athos	940	Juan	12	688

ATHOS'

On Andes' and on Athos' peaks unfurl'd	302	Age		274

ATHWART

Athwart the foaming brine	6	Harold	1	191
And pass'd his hand athwart his face	389	Corinth		508
In cloud and flame athwart the heaven	395	Corinth		1026
And up and down, and then athwart	405	Chillon		308
Which fling their fragrance far athwart the deep	419	Island	2	62
Athwart the sound of archangelic songs	460	Dante	3	13
Over the gleams that flash athwart thy gloom	461	Dante	3	37
A beam of hope athwart the future years	562	Sardan	2	21
Nations athwart the deep: the golden rays	930	Juan	12	60

ATLANTIC

Through billows Atlantic to steer	115	The Tear		14
Shall crown the Atlantic like the hero's bust	299	Age		112
Alas! why must the same Atlantic wave	301	Age		253
Which freed the Atlantic! May we hope the same	303	Age		379
Above the far Atlantic!--She has taught	454	Venice-B		144
Spain--Italy--the new Atlantic world	729	Deformed	1	497
O'er far Atlantic continents or islands	986	Juan	16	412

ATLANTIC'S

Shrink vainly from the roused Atlantic's roar	302	Age		281

ATLAS

Athos, Olympus, Aetna, Atlas, made	66	Harold	4	663
He sunk, an Atlas bending 'neath the weight	114	Death-A		17
He stood like Atlas, with a world of words	844	Juan	5	825

ATMOSPHERE

Driven o'er the lowering atmosphere that nurst	193	Monody		93
A frown upon the atmosphere	405	Chillon		297
The moon? Late; but the atmosphere is thick and dusky	508	Faliero	1	599
Might strike them: this is not their atmosphere	614	Foscari	3	379
Seem'd full of life even when their atmosphere	638	Cain	2	183
And live but on the atmosphere; your feasts	707	Werner	4	220
Round her she made an atmosphere of life	810	Juan	3	585
Were nothing but the natural atmosphere	918	Juan	10	663
As deep seas in a sunny atmosphere	993	Juan	16	800

ATMOSPHERIC

To ascertain the atmospheric state	830	Juan	4	894

ATOM

Had their prophet possess'd half an atom of sense	116	To Eliza		5
An atom of their ancestors from earth	619	Foscari	4	277
Hath changed no atom of his early nature	682	Werner	1	729

ATOMS

Were all her atoms of unleaven'd ore	307	Age		664
Ye were not meant for me--Earth! take these atoms	483	Manfred	1	370
Innumerable atoms; and one desert	484	Manfred	2	55
Peopled with dusty atoms which afford	609	Foscari	3	102
Though multiplied to animated atoms	636	Cain	2	47
They may be! Let me die as atoms die	637	Cain	2	113
Yet unborn myriads of unconscious atoms	639	Cain	2	247
This hateful compound of her atoms, and	723	Deformed	1	59
If there be atoms of him left, or even	726	Deformed	1	254
There is a cause at times. Oh, yes! when atoms jostle	744	Deformed	3	150
Suns as rays--worlds like atoms--years like hours	898	Juan	9	104

ATONE

Which shall atone for years; none need despair	48	Harold	3	794
If I sin in my dream, I atone for it now	98	To M.S.G.-B		15
Say, what dire penance can atone	99	Young Lady		17
For this can wealth or title's sound atone	125	Recoll		223
Can vice atone for crimes by prayer	132	Prayer		4
Shall they by Faith for guilt atone	132	Prayer		35
Shame mounts to rage that must atone or die	350	Corsair	2	236

ATONE
Hence to thy God, who for ye did atone | 471 Morgante | | 341
To avert the fatal moment, and atone | 546 Faliero | 5 | 619
Of Milan, and his sufferings half atone for | 595 Foscari | 1 | 16
Atone for this mysterious, nameless sin | 647 Cain | 3 | 91
Like mine. Yet I have done, to atone for thee | 711 Werner | 4 | 442

ATONED
Their earthly errors, so they be atoned | 492 Manfred | 3 | 83
Remember that my faults, though not atoned for | 584 Sardan | 4 | 392
Long sufferings have atoned. My father's death | 672 Werner | 1 | 81

ATONEMENT
Nor made atonement when he did amiss | 4 Harold | 1 | 38
The least atonement I can make | 99 Young Lady | | 25
The atonement is ample in love's last adieu | 100 L Adieu | | 40
I ask no atonement but days like the past | 137 Delawarr | | 36
I thought from my wrath no atonement could save you | 147 To Anne-A | | 2
Sheds fast atonement for its first delay | 349 Corsair | 2 | 171
And the commencement of atonement is | 492 Manfred | 3 | 84
To gladden that of man, as some atonement | 554 Sardan | 1 | 223
Of thousands, tears of millions, for atonement | 589 Sardan | 5 | 157
How know we that some such atonement one day | 647 Cain | 3 | 85
The harmless for the guilty? what atonement | 647 Cain | 3 | 87
Still some atonement that I save the man | 697 Werner | 3 | 110

ATONING
With an atoning smile a more than earthly crown | 67 Harold | 4 | 747

ATREUS'
When Atreus' sons advanced to war | 88 Anacreon-A | | 5

ATROCIOUS
Austere? Atrocious! The old human fiends | 603 Foscari | 2 | 108
Was in her eyes a thing the most atrocious | 753 Juan | 1 | 432
And keeps the atrocious reader in suspense | 967 Juan | 14 | 774

ATROCITIES
To their atrocities, than could a volume | 539 Faliero | 5 | 120

ATROCITY
From that atrocity. What then? That you | 610 Foscari | 3 | 125

ATROPOS
Nor shears of Atropos before their visions | 782 Juan | 2 | 510

ATTACH
These hints, as vague as vain, attach no less | 716 Werner | 5 | 199

ATTACH'D
'Why?--Why?--Besides, Fred really was attach'd | 934 Juan | 12 | 273

ATTACHES
That opposition only more attaches | 964 Juan | 14 | 535

ATTACHING
But none unite in one attaching maze | 44 Harold | 3 | 579

ATTACHMENT
Till death their attachment to royalty seal'd | 86 Leaving NA | | 20
The attachment of years in a moment expires | 136 Delawarr | | 6

ATTACK
His first attack, wide waving to and fro | 16 Harold | 1 | 754
I can't attack, when Beauty forms the shield | 142 Soliloquy | | 36
If he has changed--why, so must we: the attack | 563 Sardan | 2 | 129
Prepare to attack: they have apparently | 586 Sardan | 4 | 548
In strength enough to venture an attack | 586 Sardan | 4 | 554
To think on? Arnold! I will lead the attack | 734 Deformed | 1 | 835
And how to parry the renew'd attack | 767 Juan | 1 | 1349
Without whom Venus will not long attack us | 795 Juan | 2 | 1352
Ah! why the liver wilt thou thus attack | 823 Juan | 4 | 419
The Russians now were ready to attack | 868 Juan | 7 | 105
To attack the Turk's flotilla, which lay nigh | 870 Juan | 7 | 187
In short, this last attack, though rich in glory | 871 Juan | 7 | 273
Presaging a most luminous attack | 873 Juan | 7 | 364
'You served at Widdin?'--'Yes.'--'You led the attack | 874 Juan | 7 | 481
Off each attack, when people are in quest | 881 Juan | 8 | 198
On great occasions, such as an attack | 890 Juan | 8 | 771
And scent the prey their masters would attack all | 899 Juan | 9 | 213
The first attack at once proved the Divinity | 919 Juan | 11 | 41
For being as much the subject of attack | 929 Juan | 11 | 708
Ask a blind man, the best judge. You'll attack | 938 Juan | 12 | 564
Let radicals its other acts attack | 946 Juan | 13 | 343

ATTACK'D
He thought that a fierce serpent had attack'd him | 471 Morgante | | 313
In their vocation) had not been attack'd | 826 Juan | 4 | 638
And with all passions in their turn attack'd | 831 Juan | 5 | 14
The third, in columns two, attack'd by water | 873 Juan | 7 | 400
But now the town is going to be attack'd | 877 Juan | 7 | 645
But of the portion which attack'd by water | 879 Juan | 8 | 66

ATTACKING
He read an article the king attacking | 983 Juan | 16 | 207

ATTACKS
Before the still renew'd attacks | 394 Corinth | | 936
Against the attacks of over-potent foes | 712 Werner | 4 | 528

ATTAIN
For fear that plenty should attain the poor | 306 Age | | 601
Save our best hunters, may attain: his garb | 482 Manfred | 1 | 323
Might probably attain both in the end | 840 Juan | 5 | 547
Most likely to attain her aim--his heart | 849 Juan | 5 | 1120
That all is dubious which man may attain | 898 Juan | 9 | 131

ATTAIN'D
Attain'd by noble aspirants. To such | 598 Foscari | 1 | 192
And have not yet attain'd to much success | 945 Juan | 13 | 276

ATTAINING
With all its stars; and with a stretch attaining | 839 Juan | 5 | 525
Of any one's attaining to his station | 903 Juan | 9 | 414

ATTAINMENT
And an attainment, all would be in vain | 53 Harold | 3 | 1092

ATTAINTED
Of their attainted gore from the high gates | 566 Sardan | 2 | 286
Ago to Carmagnuola. The attainted | 619 Foscari | 4 | 288
My attainted predecessor, stern Faliero | 624 Foscari | 5 | 232

ATTEMPT
Haste, haste, nor dare attempt reply | 103 Alva | | 116
Failing in this our first attempt to soar | 113 Prologue | | 19
With thee even clumsy cits attempt to bounce | 275 Waltz | | 157
Yet now too few--the attempt were rash | 334 Abydos | 2 | 517
The vain attempt should bring but doom to both | 354 Corsair | 2 | 467
And got clear off, although the attempt was rash | 452 Beppo | | 763
Attempt succeeds, and Venice, render'd free | 519 Faliero | 3 | 68
To march; and on my attempt to use the power | 572 Sardan | 3 | 79
Why did they not, at least, attempt the passage | 687 Werner | 2 | 316
Who died in the then great attempt to climb | 916 Juan | 10 | 589

ATTEMPTING
In any case, attempting a reply | 768 Juan | 1 | 1427

ATTEMPTS
Ah! no, far fly from me attempts so vain | 85 Death-B | | 19
Attempts, alas! to find in many | 134 Lady-D | | 20
Yet what avail their vain attempts to please | 249 Bards | | 566

ATTEND
Scatter'd the clouds away, and on that name attend | 60 Harold | 4 | 324
'Attend, nor judge from youth our humble plan | 106 Nisus | | 100
What fears, what anxious hopes, attend the chase | 121 Newstead-A | | 126
May regal smiles attend you | 138 Clare | | 75
Where few attend, 'tis useless to indite | 142 Soliloquy | | 11
And gravely tells--attend, each beauteous miss | 246 Bards | | 359
While honours, doubly merited, attend | 253 Bards | | 865
And they are ready to attend the Doge | 546 Faliero | 5 | 556
Not even a Foscari.--Sir, I attend you | 598 Foscari | 1 | 173
To attend my husband for a limited number | 602 Foscari | 2 | 52
Is rising--we are ready to attend you | 617 Foscari | 4 | 178
A moment in my chamber. I attend you | 679 Werner | 1 | 522
And self would know what duty to attend | 875 Juan | 7 | 520
In health--when ill, we call them to attend us | 912 Juan | 10 | 331

ATTENDANCE
The Ten are in attendance on your highness | 547 Faliero | 5 | 670
A melancholy one--to call the attendance | 620 Foscari | 5 | 6
Who do not give professional attendance | 990 Juan | 16 | 654

ATTENDANT
The bowl a bribed attendant bore | 331 Abydos | 2 | 244
By a gross affront to your attendant damsels | 515 Faliero | 2 | 432
The gentle girl and her attendant,--one | 788 Juan | 2 | 914
With their attendant aided our escape | 876 Juan | 7 | 570

ATTENDANTS
And then, his rarely call'd attendants said | 368 Lara | 1 | 135
Through my attendants, and so many peopled | 686 Werner | 2 | 220
Contrived to glide through all my own attendants | 686 Werner | 2 | 238
She spake some words to her attendants, who | 844 Juan | 5 | 785

ATTENDED
And I to be attended. Once more, father | 617 Foscari | 4 | 179

ATTENDING
With him the same dire fate attending Rome | 93 Masters | | 15
Attending on their chieftain's call | 102 Alva | | 92

ATTENDS
If friends, they're the first. But the luncheon attends | 280 Blues | 2 | 27

ATTENDS
She attends you. Then good morrow, my kind kins-
men   708 Werner   4   268
Or rather stomach, which, alas! attends   776 Juan   2   162

ATTENTION
In mute attention, and his care, which guess'd 374 Lara   1   556
Perhaps even more attention than is due   836 Juan   5   301
Which your sublime attention may be worth   849 Juan   5 1150
All the attention possible, and seen   876 Juan   7   556
A general object of attention, made   907 Juan   9   658
To some she show'd attention of that kind   945 Juan   13   250

ATTENTIONS
With food and raiment, and those soft attentions 789 Juan   2   978
Juan was drawn thus into some attentions   978 Juan   15   633
Its kind attentions to their proper pale   989 Juan   16   582

ATTENTIVE
With folded arms and long attentive eye   371 Lara   1   402

ATTENTIVELY
This pledge attentively I view'd   113 Cornelian-A 13

ATTEST
Ye starry spheres! thou conscious Heaven! attest 110 Nisus   369
This fact in Virtue's name let Crabbe attest   253 Bards   857
What more I owe let gratitude attest   269 Minerva   103
Attest it many a deathless age   311 Giaour   127
This bed of death--attest my truth   322 Giaour   1189
And Paswan's rebel hordes attest   331 Abydos   2   220
I gage my life, my falchion to attest   373 Lara   1   480
Who kindlest and who quenchest suns!--Attest   548 Faliero   5   735
Turn to thy seraphs: if they attest it not   665 Heaven   723

ATTESTS
This fabric's birth attests the potent spell   169 Address-A   25
Albeit all human history attests   953 Juan   13   790

ATTIC
Dims the green beauties of thine Attic plain   31 Harold   2   705
Redemption rose up in the Attic Muse   57 Harold   4   138
To scan precisely metres Attic   95 Granta   38
Scans Attic metres with a critic's ken   111 Examination   12
A turn for punning, call it Attic salt   242 Bards   68
The rival candidates for Attic fame   249 Bards   595
Where Attic flowers Aonian odours breathe   254 Bards   884
Shall I, I say, suppress my Attic salt   265 Hints   650
And envies Lais all her Attic beaux   271 Minerva   192
His wife would mount, at times, her highest attic 443 Beppo   197
Her wit (she sometimes tried at wit) was Attic
all   748 Juan   1   91
Her Attic forehead, and her Phidian nose   857 Juan   6   332
None, save the Spanish fly and Attic bee   900 Juan   9   223
And yet the British 'Damme''s rather Attic   923 Juan   11   337
As Phidian forms cut out of marble Attic   955 Juan   13   875
And really, if the sage sublime and Attic   979 Juan   15   683
For a spoil'd carpet--but the 'Attic Bee   986 Juan   16   391

ATTICA
Yet in famed Attica such lovely dales   26 Harold   2   410
And look'd down over Attica; or he   919 Juan   11   50

ATTICS
They stare not on the stars from out their attics 450 Beppo   623

ATTILA
Our fathers did not fly from Attila   517 Faliero   2   623
O'erwhelming Attila; the ocean's queen   538 Faliero   5   16
When she, who built 'gainst Attila a bulwark   548 Faliero   5   743
Unto a bastard Attila, without   548 Faliero   5   745
Or like our fathers, driven by Attila   610 Foscari   3   160

ATTITUDE
In humble attitude they sue   95 Granta   59
Declining was his attitude   390 Corinth   510
With much suspicion in his attitude   766 Juan   1 1275
And take what kings call 'an imposing attitude 854 Juan   6   84
Herself in her sublimest attitude   899 Juan   9   174

ATTITUDES
With all the attitudes of self-applause   296 Vision   760

ATTORNEY
(See also SEA-ATTORNEY)
With that sublime of rascals your attorney   765 Juan   1 1203
Not one, except the attorney, was amused   766 Juan   1 1269
The attorney last, who linger'd near the door   767 Juan   1 1306
But see the world is only one attorney   922 Juan   11   224

ATTORNEYS-GENERAL
Attorneys-general, awful to the sight   949 Juan   13   550

ATTRACT
Attract thy fairy fingers near the lyre   3 To Ianthe   42
Howe'er the flowing locks attract us   101 Marion   47
May mine attract thy pensive eye   157 Album   4
His steel and impious prayer attract alike   359 Corsair   3   266
Of their perturbed annals could attract   458 Dante   1   146
Except in such a way as not to attract   831 Juan   5   10
By which such sirens can attract our great   973 Juan   15   334
Faults which attract because they are not tame 975 Juan   15   453

ATTRACTED
At times attracted, yet perplex'd the view   341 Corsair   1   210
Again attracted every eye   399 Parisina   324

ATTRACTEST
High on the monarch's diadem, attractest   700 Werner   3   335

ATTRACTION
I would, but--There must be attraction much
higher   278 Blues   1   59
Made the attraction, and the black the wo   286 Vision   76
There is a fastening attraction which   633 Cain   1   407
Deepest attraction; for when to the view   789 Juan   2   932

ATTRACTIONS
Half her attractions--probably from pity   939 Juan   12   588
Of his attractions marr'd the fair perspective 969 Juan   15   93

ATTRACTIVE
That 'metal's attractive.' No doubt--to the
pocket   280 Blues   1   143
Great wish to please--a most attractive dower   828 Juan   4   751

ATTRACTS
Attracts the younger hero's wandering eyes   109 Nisus   288
False glare attracts, but more offends the eye 254 Bards   902
Attracts, when History's volumes are a toil   420 Island   2   95
Attracts our eye amidst the rudest gale   430 Island   4   6
In absence, and attracts us to each other   557 Sardan   1   473
For too much truth, at first sight, ne'er
attracts   957 Juan   14   102
And more attracts by all it doth conceal   958 Juan   14   212
To feel that flattery which attracts the proud 978 Juan   15   662

ATTRIBUTE
Their earliest fault in fable, and attribute   631 Cain   1   233
Always the attribute of innocence   712 Werner   4   536

ATTRIBUTED
His judges, was attributed to witchcraft   717 Werner   5   249

ATTRIBUTES
And Anarchy assumed her attributes   72 Harold   4 1014
Glanced like a spectre's attributes, and gave   369 Lara   1   199
Least like to thee in attributes divine   464 Dante   4   98
Boasting these idle attributes, because   486 Manfred   2   192
This is not all; the passions, attributes   489 Manfred   2   434
Nor of my attributes; I have shared your splen-
dour   571 Sardan   2   592
Of your poor attributes is such as suits   640 Cain   2   301
Thine attributes seem many, as thy works   650 Cain   3   250
As many attributes; but as I wear   730 Deformed 1   534

ATTRIBUTING
Their epitaph, attributing their deaths   605 Foscari   2   224

ATTUNED
Attuned to love her languid lyre   133 E. N. Long   60
Or sings to her attuned guitar   160 Cadiz   43
Attuned by voices more or less divine   954 Juan   13   851

AU
And God knows who besides in 'au' and 'ow   884 Juan   8   386

AUBURN
Their auburn, those locks must wave thin to the
breeze   91 Caroline-C   10
To lift those auburn locks on high   150 Song   12
And boasted locks of red or auburn hue   246 Bards   298
And auburn waves of gemm'd and braided hair   353 Corsair   2   403
That sparkled o'er the auburn of her hair   788 Juan   2   922
Her hair, I said, was auburn; but her eyes   789 Juan   2   929
Down her white neck long floating auburn curls 805 Juan   3   237
Her hair's long auburn waves down to her heel   810 Juan   3   577
One with her auburn tresses lightly bound   860 Juan   6   517

AUCTION
To be put up for auction amongst Tartars   832 Juan   5   64

AUCTIONEER
Dan Phoebus takes me for an auctioneer   950 Juan   13   588

AUCTIONS
At all such auctions knew how to prevail   846 Juan   5   910

AUDACIA
And then there was the Miss Audacia Shoestring 973 Juan 15 329

AUDACIOUS
Audacious brawlers? Sire, your justice. Or 564 Sardan 2 180
And laughing from my lip the audacious brine 597 Foscari 1 108
You have few to speak. What means the audacious prater 734 Deformed 1 832

AUDIBLE
With dazzling smiles, and wishes audible 597 Foscari 1 102

AUDIBLY
Scarce audibly. I must proceed. This stroke 620 Foscari 4 349

AUDIENCE
For nature then an English audience felt 243 Bards 116
The audience take their turn upon the floor 250 Bards 659
Nor drugg'd their audience with the tragic stuff 251 Bards 736
Command your audience or to smile or weep 258 Hints 141
Appals an audience with a monarch's death 260 Hints 278
Now the bard, glad to get an audience, which 296 Vision 713
And no Venetian audience could endure a 444 Beppo 247
Craves audience of your highness. I'm unwell 504 Faliero 1 317
An audience. Let him speak. The King Arbaces 591 Sardan 5 288
Requests an audience. Bid her enter. Poor 602 Foscari 2 45
The noble dame Marina craves an audience 621 Foscari 5 64
He hath an ignorant audience. Yes! her heart beats 741 Deformed 2 388

AUDIT
But where is now the goodly audit ale 306 Age 590

AUGHT
Hath aught like thee in truth or fancy seem'd 3 To Ianthe 5
Had been pollution unto aught so chaste 4 Harold 1 42
Can despots compass aught that hails their sway 11 Harold 1 456
Lest aught unseen should lurk to thwart his speed 15 Harold 1 743
If aught of young Remembrance then remain 20 Harold 2 79
Aught to displace Athena's poor remains 21 Harold 2 105
With aught beneath him, if he would preserve 22 Harold 2 168
As long as aught was worthy to pursue 24 Harold 2 294
In aught that tries the heart how few withstand the proof 29 Harold 2 594
If aught that's kindred cheer the welcome hearth 34 Harold 2 865
Grieving, if aught inanimate e'er grieves 39 Harold 3 237
Of aught but rest; a fever at the core 41 Harold 3 377
With a proud caution, love, or hate, or aught 52 Harold 3 1036
Aught that recalls the daily drug which turn'd 66 Harold 4 676
By aught than Romans Rome should thus be laid 67 Harold 4 751
Aught but a phantasy, and could be class'd 79 Harold 4 1474
Let it be aught but banishment 99 Young Lady 36
Would aught to her impede his way 103 Alva 112
Celestial pair, if aught my verse can claim 110 Nisus 401
If aught may soothe when life resigns her power 138 Harrow-B 20
In aught that reminds us of thee 151 Soul-A 12
A kindred care for aught but one 156 Lady-F 60
'Twere hard if aught so fair as thou 159 Storm 47
As aught of mortal birth 167 Dead 2
Than aught, except its living years 168 Dead 72
Shall weep that aught of thee can die 169 Blank Leaf 8
Or offer aught like thee 201 Ode-C 42
Or, if aught in my bosom can quench for an hour 204 Avatar 125
When it sparkled o'er aught that was bright in my story 204 Pisa 15
Aught with one loved save love and liberty 205 Love, Death 4
Of aught save laurel, or for such could die 206 Greece 4
Oh, Sheridan! if aught can move thy pen 249 Bards 580
Rage, love, and aught but moralize, in song 260 Hints 298
Young men with aught but elegance dispense 264 Hints 541
But what is shame, or what is aught to him 267 Hints 743
Can aught from cold Kamschatka to Cape Horn 275 Waltz 129
Of aught but tears--save those shed by collusion 286 Vision 68
Which would have made aught save a saint exclaim 287 Vision 126
'If you have aught to arraign in him, the tomb 293 Vision 547
Aught further?' Junius answer'd, 'You had better 295 Vision 655
Aught that I deem a worthy prize 320 Giaour 1017
Aught that beseems a man in thee 324 Abydos 1 84
Friends to each other, foes to aught beside 333 Abydos 2 427
If aught his lips essay'd to groan 335 Abydos 2 581
And who dare question aught that he decides 340 Corsair 1 172
Ev'n insects sting for aught they seek to save 343 Corsair 1 326
They little deem of aught in peril's shape 348 Corsair 2 90
It may seem strange--if there be aught to dread 349 Corsair 2 127
If in aught evil, for thy sake the crime 360 Corsair 3 317
Aught they behold or hear their thought appals 370 Lara 1 265
It was not love perchance, nor hate, nor aught 371 Lara 1 365
And aught that wealth or lofty lineage claims 371 Lara 1 384
If thou, Sir Ezzelin, hast aught to show 372 Lara 1 467
Nor aught that knighthood may accord deny 372 Lara 1 477
If aught he loved, 'twas Lara; but was shown 374 Lara 1 554
With aught of pity where its wrath had fix'd 377 Lara 2 148
With aught of change, as the eyes may seem 391 Corinth 618
Of aught around, above, beneath 396 Parisina 34

AUGHT
Than aught we know beyond our little day 417 Island 1 120
Aught from experience, that chill touch-stone whose 421 Island 2 147
These wither when for aught save blood they burn 423 Island 2 315
Our new acquaintance) Torquil. 'Aught of new 425 Island 2 501
And watch if aught approach'd the amphibious lair 435 Island 4 375
Aught save his eulogy, and find, and seize 461 Dante 3 90
Than aught less than the Homeric page may bear 463 Dante 4 27
'If you want armour or aught else, go in 476 Morgante 657
To draw conclusions absolute of aught 494 Manfred 3 207
Or aught that intimates a coming step 500 Faliero 1 12
Are you aware, from aught you have perceived 500 Faliero 1 52
Noble and brave as aught of consular 508 Faliero 1 618
Or aught save their past choice. 'Tis their past choice 510 Faliero 2 129
Say--is there aught that you would will within 511 Faliero 2 166
The little sway now left the Duke? or aught 511 Faliero 2 167
Of aught in Venice, and forego all claim 513 Faliero 2 308
Nor aught can turn me from my destiny 527 Faliero 3 618
I am. Nor is there aught which shall impede me 531 Faliero 4 194
Will hear you; if you have aught to confess 538 Faliero 5 24
You do not then in aught arraign our equity 541 Faliero 5 271
Nor would we aught with him, nor now, nor ever 544 Faliero 5 457
Have I aught else to undergo save death 545 Faliero 5 547
Faliero! hast thou aught further to commend 548 Faliero 5 705
To be aught save a monarch; else for me 556 Sardan 1 411
To think of aught save festivals. Thou hast not 558 Sardan 1 524
Of aught above it, or below it--nothing 566 Sardan 2 266
If aught of ill betide her, better I 576 Sardan 3 295
And Pania also. Can aught have befallen them 576 Sardan 3 303
That ornament was ever aught to me 577 Sardan 3 370
Hear those sweet lips grow eloquent in aught 578 Sardan 3 431
Aught--all that she can ask--but such a meeting 581 Sardan 4 218
That what they ask in aught that touches on 581 Sardan 4 221
Shall know from me of aught but what may honour 582 Sardan 4 277
Nor she aught but--Despise the favourite slave 585 Sardan 4 459
So fleeting, we can scarcely call it aught 587 Sardan 5 16
Their present force, or aught save treachery 589 Sardan 5 143
With aught officious aid would bring to quell it 593 Sardan 5 361
Be ashes here than aught that lives elsewhere 597 Foscari 1 139
Doge! have you aught in answer? Something from 606 Foscari 2 323
I ne'er saw aught here like a ray. Alas 609 Foscari 3 106
Aught in its favour, who would praise like thee 611 Foscari 3 246
If race be aught, it is in qualities 612 Foscari 3 296
So that the thing be done. You may, for aught 615 Foscari 4 32
Farewell! Farewell! Is there aught else? No-- nothing 617 Foscari 4 182
Avail you aught. I can submit to all things 621 Foscari 5 59
To burst, if aught of venom touches it 625 Foscari 5 296
I have nought to ask. Nor aught to thank for? No 628 Cain 1 28
So? and can aught grieve save humanity 629 Cain 1 97
Now met I aught to sympathise with me 630 Cain 1 187
Speak aught of knowledge which I would not know 631 Cain 1 244
Aught else but dust! That is a grovelling wish 631 Cain 1 289
Nor would: I would be aught above--beneath 632 Cain 1 303
Aught save a sharer or a servant of 632 Cain 1 304
Bear all--and worship aught. Then follow me 632 Cain 1 331
Nor form of mightiest brute, nor aught that is 640 Cain 2 263
Tempt thee or them to aught that's new or strange 642 Cain 2 411
Aught unto thee? but yet accept it for 649 Cain 3 240
Of aught save their delay. My sister, though 655 Heaven 7
Such pangs decreed to aught save me 655 Heaven 48
And dream'd that aught of Abel was in her 664 Heaven 676
Now near its last, can aught restore 669 Heaven 1091
Shall aught divide us. The storm of the night 671 Werner 1 18
None hold us here for aught save what we seem 673 Werner 1 111
Excuse me: have I said aught to offend you 676 Werner 1 315
Who he may be, or what, or aught of him 677 Werner 1 402
Nor could aught, save the eye of apprehension 680 Werner 1 572
If there were aught to carry off, my lord 686 Werner 2 224
Have not forgotten aught; and oft-times in 688 Werner 2 371
Well, sir! Have you aught with me? What should I 691 Werner 2 537
Aught that you know, superior; but proceed 691 Werner 2 555
True; and aught done to save or to obtain it 694 Werner 2 746
Of me as aught of kindred with yourself 698 Werner 3 222
Aught that can touch you. No one knows you here 703 Werner 3 556
And learn if he would aught with me before 705 Werner 4 92
Been aught of kindred! Would we never had 706 Werner 4 164
Could aught of his sound on it:--but come quickly 708 Werner 4 275
Count Siegendorf, command you aught? I am bound 708 Werner 4 281
Am aught connected with that city. Then 709 Werner 4 288
Of aught so beautiful. The flowers, the boughs 713 Werner 5 16
With aught more bitter. Never shall it do so 713 Werner 5 31
Aught like him? How he tower'd amongst them all 713 Werner 5 42
Of aught save him. Yet there are other men 713 Werner 5 57
See aught save heaven, to which my eyes were raised 714 Werner 5 65
Save you, in nature, can love aught like me 722 Deformed 1 11
I will. Thou canst? Perhaps. Would you aught else 724 Deformed 1 119
Thy principle of life, is aught to me 735 Deformed 1 881

AUGHT

With aught of soul would combat if he were	737 Deformed	2	195
They saw not in themselves aught to condemn	818 Juan	4	100
Lay Juan, nor could aught renew the beat	820 Juan	4	269
To try if I could wrench aught out of death	836 Juan	5	303
Than she from aught at which the eye could cavil	845 Juan	5	870
With aught which looks like despotism in view	845 Juan	5	877
Aught of a serious, sorrowing kind, although	846 Juan	5	949
In all her life with aught save prayers and praise	847 Juan	5	971
For aught we know.) Renown's all hit or miss	871 Juan	7	261
(This metaphor, I think, holds good as aught	873 Juan	7	387
Acknowledge aught of dread of death or foe	889 Juan	8	693
Houris, or aught except his florid race	893 Juan	8	923
With you, than aught (save Scott) in your proud city	909 Juan	10	132
Take lives, take wives, take aught except men's purses	917 Juan	10	626
My natural temper's really aught but stern	926 Juan	11	493
Because the sun, and stars, and aught that shines	959 Juan	14	229
Anticipating aught about the matter	967 Juan	14	786
And when aught is to befall	986 Juan	16	346

AUGMENT

They but augment the deep and sweeping thoughts	517 Faliero	2	612

AUGMENTED

His business so augmented of late years	285 Vision		25
Such as ourselves received it, or augmented	531 Faliero	4	253

AUGMENTS

Augments its ore, and is itself a mine	248 Bards		497

AUGUR

I augur right of courage and of worth	372 Lara	1	475
That happy love could augur or recall	435 Island	4	390
Which they may augur.--King, I am your subject	559 Sardan	1	543
Demanding whether he should augur him	619 Foscari	4	293
From sire to son to augur good or ill	753 Juan	1	405
If I might augur, I should rate but low	925 Juan	11	478

AUGUR'D

Their evil judgment augur'd of the worst	377 Lara	2	177
While others scoff'd his augur'd miseries	417 Island	1	130
Which augur'd of the dead, however quick	912 Juan	10	309

AUGUREST

Let me hope better than thou augurest	568 Sardan	2	425

AUGURIES

Or view, while shadowy auguries disclose	182 Address-C		23
As auguries of Jove. Jove!--ay, your Baal	570 Sardan	2	549

AUGURS

'Twas false thou know'st; but let such augurs rue	360 Corsair	3	333

AUGUR'S

His omens more than augur's skill evince	108 Nisus		242

AUGURY

Of indistinct but awful augury	519 Faliero	3	6
All augury of foes or friends; and like	576 Sardan	3	315
That's a black augury! it has been said	590 Sardan	5	195
Defying augury with that fond kiss	819 Juan	4	188

AUGUST

Ancient of days! august Athena! where	19 Harold	2	10
Above is more august; to judge of kings	293 Vision		539
To mingle with a body so august	616 Foscari	4	81
'Tis not mere splendour makes the show august	940 Juan	12	663
To recommence in August--now was done	946 Juan	13	330

AUGUSTAN

While Caesar's chambers and the Augustan halls	495 Manfred	3	289

AUGUSTINE

As Saint Augustine in his fine Confessions	753 Juan	1	375
But Saint Augustine has the great priority	981 Juan	16	37

AUGUSTUS

And Lord Augustus Fitz-Plantagenet	952 Juan	13	695
At Lord Augustus Fitz-Plantagenet	960 Juan	14	336
Poor Lord Augustus Fitz-Plantagenet	961 Juan	14	352
With Lord Augustus Fitz-Plantagenet	963 Juan	14	496

AULD

Are over: Here's a health to 'Auld Lang Syne	909 Juan	10	125
And when I use the phrase of 'Auld Lang Syne	909 Juan	10	129
As 'Auld Lang Syne' brings Scotland, one and all	909 Juan	10	137
I care not--'tis a glimpse of 'Auld Lang Syne	909 Juan	10	144

AUNT

Or the ear-trumpet of my good old aunt	911 Juan	10	269
Each aunt, each cousin, hath her speculation	933 Juan	12	257

AUNT

For like an aged aunt, or tiresome friend	934 Juan	12	308

AUNTS

Marrying their cousins--nay, their aunts, and nieces	754 Juan	1	455

AUREA

As I'll tell Aurea at to-morrow's rout	934 Juan	12	278

AURORA

Or wert,--a young Aurora of the air	72 Harold	4	1030
Aurora borealis spread its fringes	288 Vision		214
The name of this Aurora I'll not mention	450 Beppo		665
And young Aurora kiss'd her lips with dew	792 Juan	2	1132
A versified Aurora Borealis	867 Juan	7	11
Or, like a flying Hour before Aurora	960 Juan	14	313
Aurora Raby, a young star who shone	973 Juan	15	341
Of Adeline, Aurora was omitted	974 Juan	15	378
As that prim, silent, cold Aurora Raby	974 Juan	15	392
With which Aurora on those baubles look'd	974 Juan	15	418
Little Aurora deem'd she was the theme	975 Juan	15	433
Was Nature's all: Aurora could not be	975 Juan	15	462
Aurora and the Lady Adeline	977 Juan	15	594
Aurora sat with that indifference	977 Juan	15	609
Required. Aurora scarcely look'd aside	977 Juan	15	619
Aurora at the last (so history mentions	978 Juan	15	637
Aurora, who in her indifference	978 Juan	15	657
Aurora, who look'd more on books than faces	978 Juan	15	673
He thought Aurora Raby's eyes more bright	982 Juan	16	91
Aurora Raby with her large dark eyes	984 Juan	16	247
Aurora--since we are touching upon taste	987 Juan	16	425
Aurora, with her pure and placid mien	994 Juan	16	883
'Tis true he saw Aurora look as though	994 Juan	16	889
And certainly Aurora had renew'd	994 Juan	16	901

AURORA'S

And till Aurora's dawn his skill display'd	108 Nisus		258
And bids me curse Aurora's ray	113 Quaker		34
And the vine blushes like Aurora's lip	931 Juan	12	69
Aurora's spirit was not of that kind	978 Juan	15	648
Was, that he caught Aurora's eye on his	992 Juan	16	777
Smile of Aurora's there was nought to pique	992 Juan	16	782

AUSONIA

Then let Ausonia, skill'd in every art	250 Bards		618
Unite Ausonia to the mighty main	302 Age		285

AUSONIA'S

Nor in her eye Ausonia's glance is burning	939 Juan	12	596

AUSONIAN

Are ye not brave? Yes, yet the Ausonian soil	460 Dante	2	131

AUSPICES

Renew'd with no kind auspices:--to feel	52 Harold	3	1032
Born under auspices which make us more	421 Island	2	206

AUSPICIOUS

Auspicious queen of childish joys	118 Romance		2
Auspicious to these suffering isles	168 Weeping		6
Were worthier of your hopes, Auspicious Pair	199 Sonnet-D		10
By an auspicious hope, which shall look up	492 Manfred	3	80

AUSTER

By Auster on the billows spent	88 Horace		6
And waken Auster, sovereign of the tempest	617 Foscari	4	130

AUSTERE

Though on his brow were graven lines austere	43 Harold	3	464
Wild but not rude, awful yet not austere	44 Harold	3	570
Simple, erect, severe, austere, sublime	77 Harold	4	1306
That destiny austere, and yet serene	463 Dante	3	184
The austere Pantheon, into heaven shall soar	464 Dante	4	50
The proud, the fiery, the austere--austere	509 Faliero	2	36
The gentle and the austere are both against me	571 Sardan	3	579
Your most austere of counsellors, would now	577 Sardan	3	347
Indifferent, not austere.--My lord! Zarina	582 Sardan	4	242
Of your lord render them still more austere	603 Foscari	2	107
Austere? Atrocious! The old human fiends	603 Foscari	2	108
She was a Catholic, too, sincere, austere	974 Juan	15	361

AUSTEREST

The austerest form of naked majesty	68 Harold	4	776

AUSTERITIES

And wherefore blame gaunt wealth's austerities	930 Juan	12	54

AUSTERITY

Nor Virtue teach austerity--till now	208 Sketch		30
Which soften'd down the hoar austerity	495 Manfred	3	293
But Juan also shared in her austerity	962 Juan	14	405

AUSTERLITZ
Then flamed of Austerlitz the blest despatch   274 Waltz   69

AUSTRIA
Austria! which saw thy twice-ta'en capital   300 Age   153
Oh, cruel mockery! Could not Austria spare   308 Age   735

AUSTRIAN
The Suabian sued, and now the Austrian reigns   57 Harold   4   100
Gaul, Austrian and Muscovite heroes sublime   176 Devil's Dr   46
The Austrian. Well, that's over now, and peace   676 Werner   1   333
I'll answer you. Most probably an Austrian   686 Werner   2   191

AUSTRIA'S
And she, proud Austria's mournful flower   181 Ode-A   109

AUTHOR
Which stamp'd disgrace on all an author writ   113 Prologue   4
To paint a pang the author ne'er can know   119 Answer-A   22
Knew you the rumpus which the author raised   170 Address-B   8
This shall the author choose, or that reject   257 Hints   69
Whose author is perhaps the first we meet   262 Hints   401
Yet if an author, spite of foe or friend   264 Hints   561
You're an author--a poet--And think you that I   277 Blues   1   12
As one finds every author in one of those places   277 Blues   1   21
Their author, like the Niger's mouth, will bother   295 Vision   647
The world to say if there be mouth or author   295 Vision   648
(Himself an author) only for his prose   296 Vision   744
One hates an author that's all author, fellows   449 Beppo   593
A missionary author, just to preach   449 Beppo   615
Treat a dissenting author very martyrly   772 Juan   1 1688
Or 'sultan,' as the author (to whose nod   891 Juan   8   830

AUTHORITY
Would bring contempt on all authority   500 Faliero   1   35
Who claims protection from authority   507 Faliero   1   546
To that authority, can hardly be   507 Faliero   1   548
Even on the throne of his authority   512 Faliero   2   229
And, covetous of brief authority   518 Faliero   2   701
I could enforce for my authority   605 Foscari   2   253
Will wait for even the show of that authority   681 Werner   1   624
In gold, in numbers, rank, authority   681 Werner   1   628
(I have the authority to do so by   694 Werner   2   693
And soon, it may be, with authority   697 Werner   3   143
I have no authority to tell the reason   840 Juan   5   592
Some people would impose now with authority   981 Juan   16   33

AUTHORS
From authors of historic use   95 Granta   46
The unfledged MS. authors come   234 Strahan   6
Have all of your authors exhausted their store   236 Nonsense   2
To these, when authors bend in humble awe   243 Bards   85
Since authors sometimes seek the field of Mars   248 Bards   463
Dear authors! suit your topics to your strength   257 Hints   59
And yet, God knows! what may not authors do   260 Hints   289
As critics kindly do, and authors ought   267 Hints   794
No; I left a round dozen of authors and others   278 Blues   1   36
It might be of yore; but we authors now look   283 Blues   2   146
Jews, authors, generals, charlatans, combine   307 Age   710
For authors fear description might disparage   802 Juan   3   68
Oh! ye great authors luminous, voluminous   900 Juan   9   273
Oh, ye great authors!--'Apropos des bottes   901 Juan   9   281
Late authors ask'd him for a hint or two   924 Juan   11   398
He saw ten thousand living authors pass   925 Juan   11   429
Some say, that authors only snatch, by bribing   957 Juan   14   148

AUTHOR'S
The lover's solace and the author's pride   242 Bards   14
Learn, if thou canst, to yield thine author's
   sense   246 Bards   301
In him an author's luckless lot behold   247 Bards   397
And caring little for the author's ease   446 Beppo   398
Their favour in an author's cap's a feather   771 Juan   1 1589
And apt to sow an author's wheat with tares   944 Juan   13   195

AUTO
The faith's red 'auto,' fed with human fuel   302 Age   336

AUTOCRAT
How should the autocrat of bondage be   302 Age   300
The autocrat of waltzes and of war   304 Age   435
For me, I deem an absolute autocrat   899 Juan   9   183

AUTOCRATIC
The fair czarina's autocratic crest   913 Juan   10   390

AUTUMN
Is to the mellow Earth as Autumn to the year   44 Harold   3   571
Whose friends, like autumn leaves by tempests
   whirl'd   127 Recoll   387
Like the leaves of the forest when Autumn hath
   blown   222 Sennacherib   7
Sear'd by the autumn blast of grief   322 Giaour   1256
I like on Autumn evenings to ride out   445 Beppo   329

AUTUMN
While Autumn winds were at their evening song   486 Manfred   2   168
Which Autumn plants upon the perish'd leaf   490 Manfred   2   471
Ruffles the autumn leaves, that drooping cling   578 Sardan   4   14
To entertain, this autumn, a select   947 Juan   13   410
The mellow autumn came, and with it came   950 Juan   13   593
An English autumn, though it hath no vines   950 Juan   13   601

AUTUMNAL
Of her consuming cheek the autumnal leaf-like red   70 Harold   4   918
Ere strown by those autumnal eves   411 Mazeppa   473

AUTUMN'S
'Twas on a Grecian autumn's gentle eve   25 Harold   2   352
'Twas a raw day of Autumn's bleak beginning   832 Juan   5   41
Which makes the southern autumn's day appear   950 Juan   13   610

AVAIL
Again he comes; nor dart nor lance avail   16 Harold   1   765
Without thee what will they avail   89 To Emma   32
His prayer he sends; but what can prayers avail   108 Nisus   221
Yet, should our feeble efforts nought avail   114 Prologue   33
Oh! what can idle words avail   163 Parting   15
Ah, what can tombs avail!--since these disgorge   228 Windsor   9
What now can tombs avail, since these disgorge   228 Vaults   9
Yet what avail their vain attempts to please   249 Bards   566
Could now avail the promised prey   316 Giaour   592
For them no fortress can avail,--the den   460 Dante   2   127
But they avail not: I have done men good   478 Manfred   1   17
Avail him of his spells--to call thee thus   485 Manfred   2   125
Now is your time, perhaps it may avail ye   538 Faliero   5   25
Avail myself of this sole moment to   584 Sardan   4   420
What can avail such words? To let him know   612 Foscari   3   267
It could avail thee! but no less thou hast it   617 Foscari   4   159
Avail you aught. I can submit to all things   621 Foscari   5   59
Which can avail thee nothing, save to rouse   628 Cain   1   54
If that a mortal blessing may avail thee   648 Cain   3   157
And three dead, whom their strength could not
   avail   787 Juan   2   805
'Eat, drink, and love, what can the rest avail us   800 Juan   2 1655

AVAIL'D
Nor bolts nor bars against their strength avail'd   124 Recoll   176
For other's weal avail'd on high   151 Farewell-B   2
His new-born tameness nought avail'd   413 Mazeppa   632
But what avail'd the club and spear, and arm   427 Island   3   47
And Roland not avail'd him of his targe   470 Morgante   299
But this avail'd not: I have had my foes   478 Manfred   1   19
But this avail'd not:--Good, or evil, life   479 Manfred   1   21
Avail'd for either; neither change of place   825 Juan   4   542

AVAILS
Ah what avails it thus to waste my time   142 Soliloquy   7
Yet what avails the sanguine poet's hope   254 Bards   949
That which avails him nothing: he hath found it   583 Sardan   4   346

AVALANCHE
The avalanche--the thunderbolt of snow   45 Harold   3   595
The Avalanche in his hand   479 Manfred   1   65

AVALANCHES
Why sleep the idle avalanches so   460 Dante   2   103
Ye avalanches, whom a breath draws down   482 Manfred   1   336

AVALANCHE'S
Like the avalanche's snow   392 Corinth   743

AVANT
But 'en avant!' The light loves languish o'er   992 Juan   16   729

AVARICE
Love, fame, ambition, avarice--'tis the same   73 Harold   4 1113
And avarice seizes all ambition leaves   260 Hints   254
With him old avarice found its hoard secure   378 Lara   2   202
Two thalers. No more! Out upon your avarice   682 Werner   1   677
For stepdame Nature's avarice at first   727 Deformed 1   320
I think I must take up with avarice   773 Juan   1 1728
Ambition, Avarice, Vengeance, Glory, glue   834 Juan   5   174
Whose avarice all disbursements did importune   906 Juan   9   643

AVARICIOUS
From out my pocket's avaricious nook   190 Churchill   33
By the snares of this avaricious fiend   673 Werner   1   105
He's mean, deceitful, avaricious. You   690 Werner   2   463

AVAUNT
Scotch reels, avaunt! and country-dance, forego   275 Waltz   111
Tear him in pieces!--Hence! Avaunt!--he's mine   489 Manfred   2   420
Avaunt!--Pronounce--what is thy mission? Come   496 Manfred   3   339
Avaunt! ye evil ones!--Avaunt! I say   496 Manfred   3   352
Ah! the devil come to insult the dead! Avaunt   618 Foscari   4   218
Avaunt! ye exulting demons of the waste   660 Heaven   379

AVE

Ave Maria! o'er the earth and sea	815 Juan	3	903
Ave Maria! blessed be the hour	815 Juan	3	905
Ave Maria! 'tis the hour of prayer	815 Juan	3	913
Ave Maria! 'tis the hour of love	815 Juan	3	914
Ave Maria! may our spirits dare	815 Juan	3	915
Ave Maria! oh that face so fair	815 Juan	3	917

AVENGE

Who can avenge so well a leader's fall	13 Harold	1	581
'Saint!' replied Satan, 'you do well to avenge	291 Vision		397
Avenge his lord? alas! too late	332 Abydos	2	282
The first may turn, but not avenge the blow	342 Corsair	1	277
And battled to avenge or die	385 Corinth		140
Could I free Venice, and avenge my wrongs	504 Faliero	1	345
To punish and avenge--I will not say	506 Faliero	1	436
Those who would live to think on 't, and avenge me	507 Faliero	1	542
Some for escape, they live but to avenge	524 Faliero	3	404
And oftentimes avenge them; bury mine	542 Faliero	5	292
It may be, time too will avenge it. Canst thou	657 Heaven		172
I told you so. And will you not avenge me	739 Deformed	2	255
For she, too, was as one who could avenge	822 Juan	4	349

AVENGED

I am too well avenged!--but 'twas my right	213 Lady Byron		13
And be avenged, or turn them into friend	213 Lady Byron		27
When Venus half avenged Minerva's shame	270 Minerva		122
Wrongs avenged, and Moslem dying	318 Giaour		825
Worm-like 'twas trampled, adder-like avenged	344 Corsair	1	399
Wrong'd, spurn'd, reviled--and it shall be avenged	360 Corsair	3	321
Then God and man are both avenged	391 Corinth		648
That half avenged the city's fall	394 Corinth		912
I am too well avenged, for you still love me	513 Faliero	2	281
Nobly avenged before another night	525 Faliero	3	487
And in their native beauty stood avenged	810 Juan	3	597

AVENGER

Time, the avenger! unto thee I lift	74 Harold	4	1169
She hurls the spear, her love's avenger	160 Cadiz		40
To break the chain, yet--yet the Avenger stops	460 Dante	2	139
Milton appeal'd to the Avenger, Time	746 Juan	Ded	74
If Time, the Avenger, execrates his wrongs	746 Juan	Ded	75
For soon or late Love is his own avenger	825 Juan	4	584
The wilds, as doth an Arab turn'd avenger	959 Juan	14	254

AVENGERS

To warm these slow avengers of the seas	342 Corsair	1	322
Avengers o'er their bodies rose	394 Corinth		932
Than in more loud avengers. Do not doubt them	517 Faliero	2	579
Whose acts have raised up such avengers; but	521 Faliero	3	192

AVENGES

Man wrongs, and Time avenges, and my name	456 Dante	1	50
So vile he 'scaped the doom which oft avenges	811 Juan	3	637

AVENGING

Though man and man's avenging arms assail	16 Harold	1	767
His was the thunder, his the avenging rod	193 Monody		43
Poland! o'er which the avenging angel past	300 Age		161
Revives--and where? in that avenging clime	301 Age		264
Beneath avenging Monkir's scythe	317 Giaour		748
Avenging men upon their enemies	488 Manfred	2	362

AVENTICUM

Levell'd Aventicum, hath strew'd her subject lands	45 Harold	3	625

AVENUE

Entering a separate avenue, and still	524 Faliero	3	372

AVENUES

All rushing through their thousand avenues	352 Corsair	2	341

AVER

Upon my shoulders, here I must aver	946 Juan	13	340

AVERAGE

That being about their average numeral	925 Juan	11	430
May average on the whole with parturition	958 Juan	14	186

AVERAGED

And averaged each from ten to a hundred dollars	803 Juan	3	120

AVERMENTS

Deceit, averments incompatible	213 Lady Byron		51

AVERNUS

And noxious vapours from Avernus risen	461 Dante	3	59

AVERR'D

Love conquers age--so Hafiz hath averr'd	29 Harold	2	561
Averr'd, and known--and daily, hourly seen	69 Harold	4	849

AVERR'D

And none perhaps the true one. Some averr'd	685 Werner	2	114

AVERSE

And struggle not to feel averse in vain	354 Corsair	2	508
Burning for pleasure, not averse from strife	367 Lara	1	116
Because my nature was averse from life	493 Manfred	3	125
Besides being much averse from such a fate	784 Juan	2	643

AVERSION

That friendship, pity, or aversion knew	371 Lara	1	375
And left his widow to her own aversion	751 Juan	1	272
But scandal's my aversion--I protest	753 Juan	1	407
But Lambro saw all these things with aversion	806 Juan	3	277
Writ in a manner which is my aversion	814 Juan	3	848

AVERSIONS

His friendships, therefore, and no less aversions	943 Juan	13	129

AVERT

Yet Heaven avert that ever thou	17 Harold	1	839
Could sighs avert his dart's relentless force	85 Epitaph		6
Could not avert his own untimely fall	108 Nisus		244
Avert from me the death of sin	132 Prayer		8
Avert the death of sin	146 Adieu		114
And vain was the hope to avert our decline	164 Newstead-C		15
To avert the fatal moment, and atone	546 Faliero	5	619
But this the gods avert! I am content	571 Sardan	2	595
Surely a father's blessing may avert	648 Cain	3	159
True, father: and to avert those pangs from one	711 Werner	4	463
I would avert perdition. I meant not	711 Werner	4	478

AVERTED

But tears in Hope's averted eye	185 Belshaz-A		22
The averted eye of the reluctant muse	308 Age		726
Their freezing aspect and averted air	362 Corsair	3	465
With eyes averted, and with gloomy brows	542 Faliero	5	337

AVOCATION

Were once my avocation. Nothing moves you	743 Deformed	3	85

AVOGADORI

Ay, such as the Avogadori did	500 Faliero	1	31
To them once more, or to the Avogadori	501 Faliero	1	111
By the reference of the Avogadori	507 Faliero	1	558
Avogadori, order that the Doge	540 Faliero	5	143
By the Avogadori, all the proofs	540 Faliero	5	161
But these are closed: the Ten, the Avogadori	546 Faliero	5	553

AVOID

By death alone I can avoid your hate	87 Tibullus		6
All men avoid bad writers' ready tongues	268 Hints		807
Avoid it--Virtue ebbs and Wisdom errs	355 Corsair	2	547
Despise--but, it may be, avoid the life	594 Sardan	5	448
Or Doge? Why, no; not if I can avoid it	598 Foscari	1	189
If that thou wouldst avoid their doom, forget	665 Heaven		761
To spare both that I would avoid all bustle	700 Werner	3	321

AVOIDED

(And inner trembling for the avoided peril	702 Werner	3	506
Even though himself avoided the occasion	940 Juan	12	680

AVOIDING

Avoiding only, as I trod	405 Chillon		312

AVOIDS

And in the western wave avoids thy gaze	140 Ossian-B		8
The man avoids me, knows that I now know him	694 Werner	2	702

AVOLIO

Avolio, and Arino, and Othone	467 Morgante		73

AVON'S

Of Avon's bard remembering scarce the name	111 Examination		22

AVOUCH

At what? can he avouch--or answer what he claim'd	68 Harold	4	819
Great Arimanes, doth they will avouch	490 Manfred	2	450
And what are they who do avouch these things	492 Manfred	3	43
(This even rebellion must avouch); yet hear	583 Sardan	4	341
Within a dungeon, where he may avouch	687 Werner	2	286

AVOUCH'D

But what her words avouch'd, her charms had done	359 Corsair	3	246
Avouch'd his death (such people never die	806 Juan	3	299

AVOUCHES

And that was all he sought--so he avouches	600 Foscari	1	300
If he avouches not my honour. I	692 Werner	2	582

AVOW

Beauties that ev'n a cynic must avow	13 Harold	1	606
I had friends!--who has not?--but what tongue will avow	155 Goblet		11

AVOW

Did more than he was wont avow	324	Abydos	1	31
Say, why must I no more avow	328	Abydos	1	426
They were not such as Lara should avow	369	Lara	1	238
Beats the strong heart, though less the lips avow	382	Lara	2	535
Believe him not--and yet!--And you avow it	689	Werner	4	435
Will do. I avow it is a growth so monstrous	716	Werner	5	180
Not as they ought to be: for I avow	934	Juan	12	315
Connexions stronger then he chose to avow	985	Juan	16	292

AVOWAL

Avowal of your treason: on the verge	538	Faliero	5	30
What then? Will my avowal on yon rack	539	Faliero	5	75
Persisting in his first avowal; but	598	Foscari	1	177

AVOW'D

And the intent of tyranny avow'd	69	Harold	4	851
Whate'er the grief his soul avow'd	398	Parisina		187
Complains of warmth, and, this complaint avow'd	448	Beppo		517
Mortal--be thy wish avow'd	479	Manfred	1	59
But he avow'd the letter to the Duke	595	Foscari	1	15
Avow'd his crime in not denying that	605	Foscari	2	267
Which some supposed (though he had not avow'd it	987	Juan	16	479

AVOWS

Confirms his crimes, but he avows them not	600	Foscari	1	294

AWAIT

If life eternal may await the lyre	25	Harold	2	350
Not such thy sons who whilome did await	31	Harold	2	697
But if, through the course of the years which await me	97	Harrow-A		33
Doubtless await such young, exalted worth	107	Harold	2	136
Class-honours, medals, fellowships, await	112	Examination		24
Shall joy or woe my steps await	113	Quaker		38
And spoil the blisses that await him	134	Lady-D		14
Await the poet, skilful in his choice	257	Hints		64
Better still toil for masters, than await	302	Age		304
And there await the coming shock	316	Giaour		583
Might entering lead where axe and stake await	358	Corsair	3	213
What woes await on lawless love	386	Corinth		227
The elements await but for the word	459	Dante	2	44
Await the moment to assail and tear	463	Dante	3	175
Glory to Arimanes! we await	489	Manfred	2	392
O'er the few days or hours which yet await	515	Faliero	2	455
And both await without.--But, above all	545	Faliero	5	550
He comes! Shall I await him? yes, and front him	551	Sardan	1	44
I will await here your return. The place	573	Sardan	3	153
And I await to second, not disturb her	578	Sardan	4	23
Is to await the onset. I detest	586	Sardan	4	556
We but await the signal. It is long	594	Sardan	5	468
Not so: they shall await you in my chamber	614	Foscari	3	385
To await their coming here, and join them in	622	Foscari	5	117
I call thee, I await thee, and I love thee	656	Heaven		93
Bid thee await the world-dissolving wave	660	Heaven		406
While others, fix'd as rocks, await the word	669	Heaven		1072
And, seeing the case hopeless, I await	687	Werner	2	314
If such a joy await me, it must double	688	Werner	2	345
Dare you await the event of a few minutes	719	Werner	5	383
A thousand scimitars await the word	821	Juan	4	295
They parted for the present--these to await	876	Juan	7	602
To one small grass-grown patch (which must await	910	Juan	10	197
Which can await warm youth in its wild race	932	Juan	12	180
Await those who have studied their bon-mots	953	Juan	13	776

AWAITED

Awaited but the usual chances	408	Mazeppa		174

AWAITEDST

Awaitedst there the field's event	332	Abydos	2	336

AWAITING

Awaiting each his lord's behest	324	Abydos	1	22
And the Nubian awaiting the sire's award	324	Abydos	1	35

AWAITS

Or in his cave awaits the tempest's short-lived shock	27	Harold	2	468
Or kingly death, which awaits us to-day	219	Saul-A		12
Awaits the absence of the thing it fear'd	377	Lara	2	124
Hugo, the priest awaits on thee	398	Parisina		207
By the old barbarians, there awaits the new	459	Dante	2	74
Awaits us. Now the dwindling stars begin	701	Werner	3	434
Your harp, which by the way awaits you with	708	Werner	4	265
'Tis true that death awaits both you and me	778	Juan	2	283
Awaits them, treachery is all their trust	799	Juan	2	1595
Awaits at last even those who longest miss	817	Juan	4	94
Awaits it, each new meeting or election	919	Juan	11	72

AWAKE

Nor mote my shell awake the weary Nine	3	Harold	1	8
Awake, ye sons of Spain! awake! advance	10	Harold	1	405
In every peal she calls, 'Awake! arise	10	Harold	1	411
And ne'er, at least like me, awake	18	Harold	1	864

AWAKE

The Archangel's trump, not Glory's, must awake	40	Harold	3	275
Kissing its cries away as these awake	46	Harold	3	677
And quote in classic raptures, and awake	66	Harold	4	671
Dost thou not hear my heart?--Awake! thou shalt, and must	75	Harold	4	1188
But let that pass--I sleep, but thou shalt yet awake	75	Harold	4	1197
But when awake, your lips I seek	91	Caroline-B		41
Will sleep in the grave till the blast shall awake us	91	Caroline-C		23
To awake will be torture sufficient	98	To M.S.G.-B		20
No minstrel dare the theme awake	105	Alva		310
Awake, with it my fancy teems	113	Quaker		31
their locks; yet they do not awake. The	131	Calmar		156
Awake me to a world like this	135	I Would		24
Awake the pangs that pass not by	151	Farewell-B		11
Remembrance never must awake	155	Happy		34
Awake and join thy numbers	162	War Song		23
'And sleeping pangs awake--and--but away	170	Address-B		13
And woke from Slumber--as the Birds awake	185	Julian		56
And yet may thy heart leap awake to my voice	186	Napoleon		22
Awake! (not Greece--she is awake	207	Year		25
Awake, my spirit! Think through whom	207	Year		26
'Awake a louder and a lofter strain	246	Bards		351
Awake, George Colman! Cumberland, awake	249	Bards		578
'Awake a louder and a loftier strain	259	Hints		195
The sleep of him who kept the world awake	299	Age		66
From earth; why then art thou awake	323	Giaour		1305
Bares with its buried woes, till Pride awake	352	Corsair	2	356
Awake her handmaids, with the matrons leave	357	Corsair	3	119
Alas, he told not! but he did awake	368	Lara	1	129
That oft awake his aspect could disclose	369	Lara	1	223
Awake their absent echoes in his ear	373	Lara	1	523
For then, ear, eyes, and heart would all awake	374	Lara	1	591
The thirst of vengeance now awake	395	Corinth		989
Alas! we must awake before	397	Parisina		47
But those she call'd were not awake	415	Mazeppa		831
Awake, bold Bligh! the foe is at the gate	416	Island	1	51
Awake! awake!--Alas, it is too late	416	Island	1	52
But soon Orlando found himself awake	468	Morgante		140
With words, but deeds. Keep thou awake that energy	557	Sardan	1	429
I must awake him--yet not yet: who knows	578	Sardan	4	16
Seems nothing. Is the king so soon awake	581	Sardan	4	173
Alive to love, are yet awake to terror	614	Foscari	3	374
Kiss him, at least not now: he will awake soon	646	Cain	3	14
Awake!--why liest thou so on the green earth	651	Cain	3	324
I am awake at last--a dreary dream	652	Cain	3	378
Had madden'd me;--but he shall ne'er awake	652	Cain	3	379
Slept with thee, to awake with thine awakening	711	Werner	4	437
Am I awake? are these my father's halls	720	Werner	5	479
Arose a clatter might awake the dead	763	Juan	1	1083
And warm, in case by chance he should awake	791	Juan	2	1060
That sleep which seem'd as it would ne'er awake	792	Juan	2	1168
To stir her viands, made him quite awake	793	Juan	2	1223
The eye might doubt if it were well awake	811	Juan	3	605
But wide awake she was, and round her bed	861	Juan	6	569

AWAKED

That it had been relief to have awaked you	515	Faliero	2	488

AWAKEN

In vain will Italy's broad sun awaken	301	Age		197
Its hope awaken and its spirit soar	338	Corsair	1	22
By the chords you would awaken	390	Corinth		518
Sunbeams, awaken	728	Deformed	1	416
Oh ye seven hills! awaken	735	Deformed	2	11
And tried to awaken them, but found them dead	786	Juan	2	784
His own internal ghost began to awaken	996	Juan	16	989

AWAKEN'D
(See also SCARCE-AWAKEN'D)

The dead have been awaken'd--shall I sleep	240	Cephalonia		1
The Rubicon of man's awaken'd rights	300	Age		139
But 'twill not be--the spark's awaken'd--lo	301	Age		260
Of verse do more than reach the awaken'd heart	420	Island	2	102
But when the winds awaken'd, shot forth wings	422	Island	2	224
Better by me awaken'd than rebellion	554	Sardan	1	248
'Tis sweet to be awaken'd by the lark	762	Juan	1	981

AWAKENING

Awakening without wounding the touch'd heart	66	Harold	4	692
Slept with thee, to awake with thine awakening	711	Werner	4	437

AWAKES

Awakes an all-consuming fire	111	Medea		20
How heavily he sighs! he starts--awakes	353	Corsair	2	428
Melt into morn, and Light awakes the world	375	Lara	2	2
And he to that embrace awakes	397	Parisina		75
And loving him? Soft! he awakes. Sweet Enoch	648	Cain	3	139
No bugle awakes him with life-and-death call	742	Deformed	3	33
With mist, and every bird with him awakes	791	Juan	2	1110
Then dress, then dinner, then awakes the world	926	Juan	11	521

AWAKING
Of Consciousness awaking to her woes   19 Harold   1   941
But with a hope.--Awaking with a start   35 Harold   3   5

AWARD
(See also LAW-AWARDED)
And the Nubian awaiting the sire's award   324 Abydos   1   35
He now be call'd in to receive the reward   540 Faliero   5   141
His last award, will have the long grass grow   925 Juan   11   476

AWARDS
Justice awards it to my friend alone   126 Recoll   340

AWARE
Once form'd thy Paradise, as not aware   7 Harold   1   276
Then the Moors, by this aware   194 Ballad-A   26
Nor lift your load, before you're quite aware   257 Hints   61
And execute ere thought be half aware   374 Lara   1   605
Are you aware, from aught you have perceived   500 Faliero   1   52
And our more chosen comrades, is aware   520 Faliero   3   131
But they were not aware that there are things   534 Faliero   4   451
Here come our colleagues. Is the Duke aware   623 Foscari   5   151
Are you aware my father is no more   688 Werner   2   379
Dare you insinuate? What? Are you aware   696 Werner   3   62
Discoveries made, but none could be aware   755 Juan   1   539
Getting the boats out, being well aware   779 Juan   5   358
Aware of their due royal rights o'er men   847 Juan   5 1024
Aware this kind of baggage never thrives   876 Juan   7   559

AWAY
Will laugh to flee away   6 Harold   1   173
The Grave shall bear the chiefest prize away   10 Harold   1   439
The broken tools, that tyrants cast away   11 Harold   1   453
Best prize of better acts, they bear away   15 Harold   1   736
Sudden he stops; his eye is fix'd away   16 Harold   1   756
And gaze, untired, the morn, the noon, the eve
    away   27 Harold   2   450
Some high-capp'd Tartar spurr'd his steed away   28 Harold   2   510
And this is much, and all which will not pass
    away   40 Harold   3   315
But these and half their fame have pass'd away   43 Harold   3   452
But these are deeds which should not pass away   45 Harold   3   635
And Pierre can not be swept or worn away   55 Harold   4   34
With a new colour as it gasps away   59 Harold   4   260
Which shows a distant prospect far away   60 Harold   4   285
Which is not of the pangs that pass away   60 Harold   4   304
An earthquake reel'd unheededly away   64 Harold   4   563
The conqueror's sword in bearing fame away   67 Harold   4   733
We wither from our youth, we gasp away   73 Harold   4 1108
Hopes sapp'd, name blighted, Life's life lied away   75 Harold   4 1212
Were with his heart and that was far away   76 Harold   4 1262
Which streams too much on all years, man, have
    reft away   76 Harold   4 1287
For thou hast ta'en the bird away   88 Catullus   20
But now new scenes invite me far away   93 Dorset   34
Peace, that reflection never frown'd away   94 Dorset   83
In fruitless hope was pass'd away   103 Alva   166
The vision charms the hours away   113 Quaker   33
They pass the dreary winter's eve away   124 Recoll   172
The rolling seasons pass away   128 Address-B   25
Shall wing the laughing hours away   134 E. N. Long   104
And frequent mused the twilight hours away   138 Harrow-B   10
Weigh'd down with years the hills dissolve away   139 Ossian-B   12
The mountain oaks are seen to fall away   140 Ossian-B   11
From Dryden, Milbourne tears the palm away   143 Soliloquy   79
And smile to steal the heart away   150 My Son   4
Wilt shine awhile, and pass away   153 Friend-A   50
Mary, adieu! I must away   155 Happy   17
Ere call'd but for a time away   165 Thyrza   27
That all those charms have pass'd away   167 Dead   35
The leaves must drop away   167 Dead   40
Could wash a father's fault away   168 Weeping   4
And blend, while ages roll away   169 Blank Leaf   11
'And sleeping pangs awake--and--but away   170 Address-B   13
And watch that no souls shall be poach'd away   176 Devil's Dr   18
To redeem as he came away   177 Devil's Dr   106
But thou must eat thy heart away   180 Ode-A   54
Cast crowns for rosaries away   180 Ode-A   66
To all that pass away   181 Ode-A   103
Are all thy playthings snatch'd away   181 Ode-A   162
There's not a joy the world can give like that it
    takes away   185 Music-B   1
When thy bright promise fades away   189 On Star   35
In summer's twilight weeps itself away   192 Monody   2
Thy floods subside, and mine have sunk away   198 Po   16
Such servile devotion might shame him away   202 Avatar   32
Hearts can thus be torn away   207 Fare thee   24
Down to the dust!--and, as thou rott'st away   209 Sketch   97
And dash'd the darkness all away   209 Augusta-A   20
Like a wild bay of breakers, melts away   211 Augusta-C   37
Upon it till it could not pass away   214 Dream   50
His kingdom pass'd away   220 Belshaz-B   42
But I mark'd not the twilight beam melting away   221 Jerusalem   14
Were scatter'd all weeping away   222 Babylon   6

AWAY
And our hearts were so full of the land far away   223 Valley   4
Thus run our time and tongues away   232 Doctor   83
But the Pastry Cook carried away   234 Ballat   8
And roareth away   239 Bray   16
Men pardon, if his follies pass away   251 Bards   728
The spoiler swept that soaring lyre away   253 Bards   833
And now at once I tear the veil away   256 Bards   1043
Fool'd, pillaged, dunn'd, he wastes his terms
    away   260 Hints   239
On whores, spies, singers wisely shipp'd away   260 Hints   302
'Expunge that stanza, lop that line away   267 Hints   784
Droops o'er the bales no bark may bear away   272 Minerva   268
The farewell beam of Feeling past away   311 Giaour   100
Hath brush'd its brightest hues away   314 Giaour   407
Upon that eve she fled away   314 Giaour   448
Till these in horror shrink away   318 Giaour   785
Without the power to scare away   319 Giaour   949
And watch'd his spirit ebb away   321 Giaour   1086
But Heaven in wrath would turn away   322 Giaour   1242
'How strange he thus should turn away   326 Abydos   1   264
May sing these gloomy thoughts away   327 Abydos   1   294
All, one by one, have died away   329 Abydos   2   60
The evening beam that smiles the clouds away   333 Abydos   2   400
With me this hour away--away   334 Abydos   2   485
Morn slowly rolls the clouds away   335 Abydos   2   583
Cling to his couch and sicken years away   338 Corsair   1   28
This hour--it cannot be--this hour away   344 Corsair   1   412
Nor be thou lonely; though thy lord's away   344 Corsair   1   460
Again he mans himself and turns away   346 Corsair   1   584
It shines a lake of fire!--away--away   349 Corsair   2   137
Dash'd his high cap, and tore his robe away   349 Corsair   2   146
From reeking pile and combat's wreck away   350 Corsair   2   222
Farewell--morn breaks--and I must now away   355 Corsair   2   533
That dash'd her garments oft, and warn'd away   356 Corsair   3   80
To wear but till the gilding frets away   360 Corsair   3   343
All words would now be vain--away--away   362 Corsair   3   432
What she has done no tears can wash away   363 Corsair   3   525
'Tis idle all; moons roll on moons away   366 Corsair   3   687
Years had roll'd on, and fast they speed away   366 Lara   1   49
And saw them smile or sigh their hours away   367 Lara   1   100
From all communion he would start away   368 Lara   1   134
As if to startle all save him away   368 Lara   1   146
And yet they glide like happiness away   368 Lara   1   158
And half contemptuous turn'd to pass away   372 Lara   1   447
In far forgetfulness away--away   373 Lara   1   487
In haughty silence slowly strode away   376 Lara   2   94
All dread by slow degrees had worn away   377 Lara   2   173
And famine wrings, and fever sweeps away   379 Lara   2   306
'Twas Lara bleeding fast from life away   381 Lara   2   417
Scarce Kaled seem'd to know, but turn'd away   381 Lara   2   472
He gazed, as if not yet had pass'd away   382 Lara   2   500
To follow me so far away   385 Corinth   43
A hundred years have roll'd away   386 Corinth   151
The chiefs of Venice wrung away   386 Corinth   216
Nor wish'd for wings to flee away   387 Corinth   250
Tyrant and slave are swept away   388 Corinth   370
Who had stolen from the hills, but kept away   389 Corinth   475
Remnants of things that have pass'd away   389 Corinth   505
Lightly and brightly breaks away   391 Corinth   680
Unaneled he pass'd away   394 Corinth   894
Some fell on the shore, but, far away   395 Corinth   1039
Would rend those tender limbs away   395 Corinth   1047
As twilight melts beneath the moon away   396 Parisina   14
As if all else had pass'd away   396 Parisina   35
Which pants for one away   397 Parisina   74
That dream this morning pass'd away   398 Parisina   200
Wipe our mortal stains away   400 Parisina   418
With marks that will not wear away   403 Chillon   40
Was wither'd on the stalk away   404 Chillon   175
Whose tints as gently sunk away   404 Chillon   192
'Twas near his castle, far away   410 Mazeppa   331
And on he foam'd--away!--away   410 Mazeppa   378
But fast we fled, away, away   411 Mazeppa   442
How heavily it roll'd away   413 Mazeppa   647
Wide o'er the wave--away! away! away   418 Island   1   207
'And but for me!" he said, and turn'd away   429 Island   3   208
She fix'd him in her own. Away! away   429 Island   3   225
To baffle the pursuit.--Away! away   429 Island   3   235
They paused and search'd in vain, then pull'd
    away   431 Island   4   83
Yet glitter'd, but at distance--hurl'd away   434 Island   4   349
But no! it came not; fast and far away   435 Island   4   381
Successful love may sate itself away   437 Tasso   59
Absorb'd in thine; the world was past away   439 Tasso   172
Is more than I know. He was cast away   452 Beppo   746
Steals vein by vein and pulse by pulse away   453 Venice-B   41
He did; and scow'd him in some nook away   475 Morgante   593
To recreant mortality--Away   486 Manfred   2   220
Of freedom, the forbidden fruit.--Away   488 Manfred   2   369
Retire, or 'twill be dangerous--Away   495 Manfred   3   315
Once more I summon him--Away! away   496 Manfred   3   358
Of heaven and all its saints, my lord--Away   501 Faliero   1   119
In the first burst of passion, pour away   509 Faliero   2   16

AWAY

And I am tainted, and must wash away	519	Faliero	3	14
Such actions from our hands: we'll wash away	521	Faliero	3	201
Must I abhor and do. Away! away	527	Faliero	3	642
I thank thee, Night! for thou hast chased away	529	Faliero	4	106
Take it--I am unarm'd,--and then away	532	Faliero	4	264
Accompany our guests, or charm away	551	Sardan	1	65
Is now no more. Away with me--away	575	Sardan	3	255
All are the sons of circumstance: away	576	Sardan	3	320
The carcasses of Inde--away! away	578	Sardan	4	33
'Tis heal'd--I had forgotten it. Away	587	Sardan	4	577
Who slew me: and when you have borne away	593	Sardan	5	385
Or in some clammy drops, soon wiped away	601	Foscari	1	359
Of the sad mountaineer, when far away	610	Foscari	3	179
Floating on the free waves--away	611	Foscari	3	237
And I will find an hour to wipe away	614	Foscari	3	419
My eyes swim strangely--where's the door? Away	617	Foscari	4	186
But very fair. All that must pass away	644	Cain	2	536
Defies it: though this life must pass away	656	Heaven		108
Only the evil shall be put away	660	Heaven		377
With your pure equals. Hence! away! away	666	Heaven		812
Shall pass away	666	Heaven		863
It cometh! hence, away	668	Heaven		1013
Besides those of the place, and bore away	686	Werner	2	239
And fire, fire away	732	Deformed	1	726
Your ranks more than the enemy. Away	740	Deformed	2	321
Because at least the past were pass'd away	745	Fragment-D		3
His house was sold, his servants sent away	751	Juan	1	267
Thus would he while his lonely hours away	758	Juan	1	761
For want of facts would all be thrown away	761	Juan	1	964
'My dear, I was the first who came away	764	Juan	1	1128
The moment he has sent his fools away	767	Juan	1	1346
And Juan throttled him to get away	769	Juan	1	1482
In the mean time, to pass her hours away	775	Juan	2	73
Immediately the masts were cut away	778	Juan	2	249
Without their will, they carried them away	779	Juan	2	314
He watch'd it wistfully, until away	785	Juan	2	717
As morning broke, the light wind died away	786	Juan	2	769
And how this heavy faintness pass'd away	788	Juan	2	885
But that, like other things, has pass'd away	795	Juan	2	1325
Yet for all that keep not too long away	804	Juan	3	199
Her father watch'd, she turn'd her eyes away	824	Juan	4	506
Its dwellings down, its tenants pass'd away	825	Juan	4	570
And also when my second ran away	833	Juan	5	152
Could hardly carry anything away	843	Juan	5	741
In holy matrimony snores away	861	Juan	6	580
Yet for all this he did not run away	881	Juan	8	168
Raise but an arm! 'twill brush their web away	900	Juan	9	217
Certes it would have been but thrown away	901	Juan	9	286
'Tis only that they love to throw away	919	Juan	11	75
Cervantes smiled Spain's chivalry away	942	Juan	13	81
Would not be driven away	985	Juan	16	328

AWE

Long mark the battle-field with hideous awe	18	Harold	1	907
Which others hail'd with real or mimic awe	24	Harold	2	283
Thy right, and awe the robbers back, who press	61	Harold	4	377
In them suspended, reck'd not of the awe	64	Harold	4	572
With a deep awe, yet all distinct from fear	75	Harold	4	1237
Of wonder pleased, or awe which would adore	79	Harold	4	1425
Would awe his fix'd determined mind in vain	88	Horace		8
Who young obey'd their lords in silent awe	124	Recoll		167
With not the less of sorrow and of awe	190	Churchill		4
'He who holds no laws in awe	195	Ballad-A		56
More darkly sin, by satire kept in awe	242	Bards		35
To these, then authors bend in humble awe	243	Bards		85
With those who did not hold the saints in awe	291	Vision		388
The menials felt their usual awe alone	377	Lara	2	174
Even the stern stood chill'd with awe	400	Parisina		427
Some lurking remnant of their former awe	416	Island	1	77
A goddess rise--so deem'd they in their awe	432	Island	4	212
Hush'd 'Academe' sigh'd in silent awe	444	Beppo		250
For ever thus, address'd with awe. I ne'er	558	Sardan	1	485
Which means that men are kept in awe and law	559	Sardan	1	585
And then she stopp'd, and stood as if in awe	792	Juan	2	1140
In awe: he said, as the centurion saith	836	Juan	5	285
The people's awe and admiration raising	839	Juan	5	478
Had not come up in time to cast an awe	884	Juan	8	387
Even the bold Churchman's tomb excited awe	916	Juan	10	588
There was awe in the homage which she drew	974	Juan	15	373
Transgresses the great bounds of love or awe	997	Juan	17	14

AWEARY

Hold, madman!--though aweary of thy life	483	Manfred	1	371

AWED

(See also OVER-AWED)

Be wavering, which long awed and awes mankind	299	Age		86
Oh! not dismay'd--but awed, like One above	438	Tasso		135
Of martyrs awed, as Spagnoletto tainted	950	Juan	13	567

AWES

(See also O'ER-AWES)

With a pure feeling which absorbs and awes	192	Monody		5

AWES

Be wavering, which long awed and awes mankind	299	Age		86
Thy spirit less upholds them than it awes	305	Age		555
That seems to shun the sight, and awes if seen	346	Corsair	1	542
Beats quick; he awes me, and yet draws me near	633	Cain	1	409
Which awes, but yet offends not? in the field	704	Werner	4	29

AWE-STRUCK

Who to the awe-struck world unlock'd Elysium's gates	7	Harold	1	242
While awe-struck nations hail'd the magic name	244	Bards		192

AWFUL

(See also CHASTELY-AWFUL)

As Pallas and the Muse unveil their awful lore	34	Harold	2	863
Since upon night so sweet such awful morn could rise	39	Harold	3	216
Wild but not rude, awful yet not austere	44	Harold	3	570
Silence again resumes her awful sway	121	Newstead-A		95
In awful grandeur, when thou movest on high	140	Ossian-B		5
The skies with lightnings awful as their own	169	Address-A		14
Much that is awful, more that's dear	200	Ode-C		4
Untold and awful still	220	Belshaz-B		28
Gone were the terrors of her awful brow	269	Minerva		79
His voice into that awful note of woe	296	Vision		716
(If e'er those awful ashes can grow cold	308	Age		753
In awful whiteness o'er the shore	316	Giaour		630
Made manifest by awful sign	319	Giaour		911
As I preserve that awful oath	331	Abydos	2	192
Lifeless, but life-like, and awful to sight	391	Corinth		623
A stalking oracle of awful phrase	449	Beppo		585
An awful spirit. Hast thou further question	491	Manfred	2	532
His servant echoes back the awful word	492	Manfred	3	65
It is an awful chaos--light and darkness	493	Manfred	3	164
I see a dusk and awful figure rise	495	Manfred	3	322
Of indistinct but awful augury	519	Faliero	3	6
More mysteries, and awful ones! But now	532	Faliero	4	279
Of our most awful, but inexorable	542	Faliero	5	340
An awful night. Oh yes, for those who have	572	Sardan	3	39
It seems an awful shadow--if I may	634	Cain	1	467
Pass on, and gaze upon the past. 'Tis awful	640	Cain	2	290
Then, why so awful in thy speech? I said	648	Cain	3	131
Yet awful Thing of Shadows, speak to me	659	Heaven		329
So near the awful close! For these must drop	662	Heaven		563
Awful as thy brother's crime	735	Deformed	2	38
The consequence was awful in the extreme	784	Juan	2	626
(For sleep is awful), and on tiptoe crept	792	Juan	2	1141
Before the consequences grow too awful	803	Juan	3	95
Is awful to the vessel near the rock	808	Juan	3	460
It was a moment of that awful kind	821	Juan	4	287
As ere that awful period intervenes	861	Juan	6	550
That awful pause, dividing life from death	878	Juan	7	690
But still it falls in vast and awful splinters	889	Juan	8	703
It is an awful topic--but 'tis not	889	Juan	8	705
Before him summ'd the awful scroll and read it	916	Juan	10	558
Of which your lawful awful wedlock fount is	929	Juan	11	702
Attorneys-general, awful to the sight	949	Juan	13	550
That awful yawn which sleep can not abate	954	Juan	13	808
Without an awful wish to plunge within it	956	Juan	14	40
With awful footsteps regular as rhyme	995	Juan	16	947
Nigh and more nigh the awful echoes drew	995	Juan	16	965

AWFULLEST

And be this peal its awfullest and last	536	Faliero	4	535

AWHILE

Farewell awhile to him and thee	5	Harold	1	124
Though here awhile he learn'd to moralize	8	Harold	1	319
Himself awhile the victim of distress	29	Harold	2	589
They flourish awhile in the season of truth	99	Adieu		15
But leave her awhile, she shortly will smile	115	Pigot		7
To her awhile resigns her youthful train	123	Recoll		125
Dispel awhile the sense of ill	135	I Would		30
And for awhile my sorrows cease	152	Weep-A		11
Wilt shine awhile, and pass away	153	Friend-A		50
Dispel awhile the sense of ill	166	Struggle		22
Oh, pardon that in crowds awhile	168	Haunts		9
O'er taste awhile these pseudo-bards prevail	243	Bards		137
She ceased awhile, and thus I dared reply	270	Minerva		123
But driven from thence awhile, yet not for aye	302	Age		286
Glad for awhile to heave unconscious breath	375	Lara	1	642
There they yet may breathe awhile	394	Corinth		920
And throbb'd awhile, then beat no more	412	Mazeppa		543
But now the dance is o'er--yet stay awhile	419	Island	2	53
They watch'd awhile to see him float again	431	Island	4	71
Must yield awhile to this necessity	584	Sardan	4	385
My sister Adah, leave us for awhile	648	Cain	3	172

AWKWARD

Which is an awkward Jobby O	235	New Song		8
But shy and awkward at first coming out	445	Beppo		306
Is awkward from the--How now, Henrick? why	705	Werner	4	89
Poor Julia's heart was in an awkward state	756	Juan	1	593
An awkward look; as he revolved the case	767	Juan	1	1311

AWKWARD

Juan contrived to give an awkward blow	769 Juan	1	1485
An awkward spectacle their eyes before	769 Juan	1	1490
I can't but say it is an awkward sight	775 Juan	2	89
Which struck her aft, and made an awkward rift	777 Juan	2	211
To ask him awkward questions on the way	804 Juan	3	155
Was Juan,--who, an awkward thing at his age	828 Juan	4	735
His garment's novelty, and his being awkward	841 Juan	5	618
This was an awkward test, as Juan found	847 Juan	5	1001
The dagger close at hand, which made it awkward	849 Juan	5	1114
A kind of state more awkward than uncommon	853 Juan	6	50
This awkward business without harm to others	866 Juan	6	927
The awkward squad, and could afford to squander	873 Juan	7	411
To them, poor things, it is an awkward scrape	876 Juan	7	574
And he could even withstand that awkward test	885 Juan	8	421
It soothes the awkward squad of the rejected	934 Juan	12	287
An awkward inclination to go wrong	935 Juan	12	380
And fortune, has an awkward part to play	937 Juan	12	458
Epoch, that awkward corner turn'd for days	941 Juan	13	26
Some pleasant jesting at the awkward stranger	959 Juan	14	252
There is an awkward thing which much perplexes	964 Juan	14	577
He sate with feelings awkward to express	995 Juan	16	934

AWL

Employs a pen less pointed than his awl	252 Bards		766

AWOKE

Awoke the jocund birds to early song	43 Harold	3	462
Not so of yore awoke your mighty sire	259 Hints		199
That I awoke--and lo! it was no dream	308 Age		776
Before the guardian slaves awoke	324 Abydos	1	68
Morn ne'er awoke them with such brilliant beams	342 Corsair	1	320
Awoke him with a sunken heart	387 Corinth		337
Till Rome awoke, and had an annual triumph	537 Faliero	4	649
Of them and theirs, awoke and found them not	611 Foscari	3	214
The stars had not gone down when I awoke	718 Werner	5	358
If they had never been awoke before	763 Juan	1	1084
And Juan gazed as one who is awoke	793 Juan	2	1209
And starting, she awoke, and what to view	820 Juan	4	278
And so--she awoke with a great scream and start	862 Juan	6	616
The dappled foresters--as day awoke	948 Juan	13	446

AWRY

And then swung back; nor close--but stood awry	996 Juan	16	979

AXE

Chopp'd by the axe, looks rough and little worth	69 Harold	4	879
Might entering lead where axe and stake await	358 Corsair	3	213
Than e'er can stain the axe of mine	399 Parisina		240
Feels if the axe be sharp and true	400 Parisina		403
Upon the axe which near him shone	400 Parisina		424

AXIOM

Of the last axiom, he advised his spouse	963 Juan	14	530

AXIOMS

Happy the youth in Euclid's axioms tried	111 Examination		9

AXIS

Well--well, the world must turn upon its axis	774 Juan	2	25

AY

A country with--ay, or without mankind	56 Harold	4	68
Ay, and the red right arm of Jove	88 Horace		9
'Ay, but to die, and go,' alas	167 Euthanasia		29
Ay, roar in his train! let thine orators lash	202 Avatar		33
Ay! 'Build him a dwelling!' let each give his mite	203 Avatar		73
And careless Dryden--'Ay, but Pye has not	243 Bards		100
Ay, but Macheath's example--psha!--no more	261 Hints		367
Ay! there he is at it. Poor Scamp! better join	280 Blues	1	151
Ay--yours are the plays for exciting our 'pity	282 Blues	2	79
Ay, shout! inscribe! rear monuments of shame	304 Age		426
Some moments, ay, one treacherous hour	311 Giaour		86
Ay! let me like the ocean-Patriarch roam	333 Abydos	2	388
Ay--let the loud winds whistle o'er the deck	334 Abydos	2	454
'To-night, Lord Conrad?' 'Ay! a set of sun	340 Corsair	1	158
He was a villain--ay--reproaches shower	342 Corsair	1	305
Ay, let them slumber, peaceful be their dreams	342 Corsair	1	319
Ay--Pride can veil, and Courage brave it all	352 Corsair	2	358
'Ay, in my chains! my steps will gently tread	360 Corsair	3	308
'To-morrow!--ay, to-morrow!' further word	373 Lara	1	490
Ay, 'twas,--when Casimir was king	408 Mazeppa		128
'Does Christian know this?'--'Ay; he has piped all hands	426 Island	2	520
The last infirmity of evil. Ay	482 Manfred	1	290
Ay--father! I have had those earthly visions	492 Manfred	3	104
What doth he here? Why--what doth he here	496 Manfred	3	331
Ay, if a poor man: Steno's a patrician	500 Faliero	1	20
Ay, such as the Avogadori did	500 Faliero	1	31
Patient--ay, proud, it may be, of dishonour	502 Faliero	1	195
Although the cause--Ay, think upon the cause	503 Faliero	1	272
Ay, doubtless they have echo'd o'er the arsenal	506 Faliero	1	420
Wouldst thou be sovereign lord of Venice? Ay	506 Faliero	1	447
I have fought and bled; commanded, ay, and con-quer'd	506 Faliero	1	459

AY

Calmer? Ay, calmer, my good lord.--Ah, why	511 Faliero	2	175
Is he one of our order? Ay, in spirit	518 Faliero	2	674
As I described them. Speak to them. Ay, speak	522 Faliero	3	248
Ay, and the first amongst us, as thou hast been	523 Faliero	3	337
Ay, so it seems, and so it is to you	527 Faliero	3	574
Ay, there it is--you feel not, nor do I	527 Faliero	3	624
Ay, is it even so? Excuse me, Bertram	532 Faliero	4	272
Ay, send thy miserable ruffians forth	536 Faliero	4	587
Ay, ay	540 Faliero	5	142
Ay, but he must not die! Spare his few years	543 Faliero	5	356
Ay, palpable as I see thy sweet face	547 Faliero	5	666
Unheard of! ay, there's not a history	548 Faliero	5	712
Peril to thee--Ay, from dark plots and snares	558 Sardan	1	517
Business to-morrow. Ay, or death to-night	560 Sardan	1	649
They shall have temples--ay, and priests; and thou	562 Sardan	2	71
Ay, and the most devout for brave--thou hast not	562 Sardan	2	75
Soldiers, hew down the rebel! Soldiers! Ay	564 Sardan	2	161
Depart, and not to bear your answer. Ay	568 Sardan	2	413
Ay, my good lord. For my own part, I should be	570 Sardan	2	542
As auguries of Jove. Jove!--ay, your Baal	570 Sardan	2	549
The very palace. They are here, then;--ay	575 Sardan	3	250
And thine no less. Ay, Myrrha, but the woman	580 Sardan	4	148
Ay, and pursuit too; but till then, my voice	586 Sardan	4	555
Strike with a better aim! Ay, if we conquer	587 Sardan	4	581
For a king's obsequies? Ay, for a kingdom's	593 Sardan	5	368
Ay, I am used to such a summons! Ay	597 Foscari	1	147
No more. How! wouldst thou share a dungeon? Ay	609 Foscari	3	39
The fate of myriads more. Ay--we but hear	610 Foscari	3	168
Ay, there it is; 'tis like a mother's curse	611 Foscari	3	186
Ay, he may veil beneath a marble brow	613 Foscari	3	309
The stoic of the state? Here! Ay, weep on!	618 Foscari	4	214
My brethren, will we not? Ay!--Ay! You shall not	624 Foscari	5	272
Ay, they are fatherless! I thank you. We	626 Foscari	5	348
Ay, upon one condition. Name it. That	632 Cain	1	299
And leave us? Ay. And me? Beloved Adah	632 Cain	1	344
Of knowledge? Ay--to our eternal sorrow	633 Cain	1	350
Ay--but not blessed. If the blessedness	634 Cain	1	416
Will he return? Ay, woman! he alone	635 Cain	1	537
Yea, or things higher. Ay, and serpents too	638 Cain	2	171
Yon blue immensity, is boundless? Ay	645 Cain	2	595
Fitting to shadow slumber. Ay, the last	646 Cain	3	8
Of what? Of Paradise!--Ay! dream of it	646 Cain	3	31
Ay, but not Anah: she but loves her God	657 Heaven		181
Ay, day will rise; but upon what?--a chaos	662 Heaven		566
Ay, father! but when they are gone	668 Heaven		962
Thou namest--ay, the wind howls round them, and	672 Werner	1	31
As they could pay for fire-wood. Poor souls! Ay	678 Werner	1	421
So, so, it thickens! Ay, 'the commandant	681 Werner	1	616
His right must yield to ours. Ay, if at Prague	689 Werner	2	405
My mother! Ay! I thought so: you have now	690 Werner	2	486
I had arrived a few hours sooner! Ay	691 Werner	2	507
I am your equal. You! Ay, sir: and, for	691 Werner	2	554
Ay--could you see it, you would say so--but	694 Werner	2	715
Oh, do not hate me! Hate my father! Ay	698 Werner	3	228
Blood! Why does yours start from your cheeks? Ay! doth it	706 Werner	4	157
But dark deeds (ay, the darkest, if all Rumour	709 Werner	4	337
By a cut-throat! Ay!--you may look upon me	712 Werner	4	510
And could--ay, perhaps, should (if our self-safety	712 Werner	4	526
Be silenced. Ay, with half of my domains	719 Werner	5	404
Of your domains; a thousand, ay, ten thousand	721 Werner	5	535
Ay, the superior of the rest. There is	727 Deformed	1	316
Ay, as the dunghill may conceal a gem	728 Deformed	1	432
You are well enter'd now. Ay; but my path	730 Deformed	1	569
Ay, but not idle. Work yourself with words	734 Deformed	1	831
The Bourbon from the wall. Ay, did he so	738 Deformed	2	207
Ay, 'gainst an oak. A forest, when it suits me	738 Deformed	2	230
Ay, slave or master, 'tis all one: methinks	741 Deformed	2	374
'Ay,' quoth his friend, 'I thought it would appear	833 Juan	5	147
'Ay, every inch a' duke; there were twelve peers	951 Juan	13	674
He was as independent--ay, much more	990 Juan	16	649

AYE

But one sad losel soils a name for aye	4 Harold	1	23
Fondly we hope 'twill last for aye	97 To Woman		19
But bliss be aye her heart's partaker	113 Quaker		48
Friends lost to me for aye, except in dreams	122 Recoll		34
Aye, ye have Souls, and dark ones too	143 To-A		10
Remember thee! Aye, doubt it not	171 Remember-A		5
'Aye--Aye'--quoth he--'tis the way with them all	178 Devil's Dr		197
Thou overflow'st thy banks, and not for aye	198 Po		14
It lives, it reigns--'aye, every inch a king	228 Vaults		7
Alike reserved for aye to stand accursed	271 Minerva		205
But driven from thence awhile, yet not for aye	302 Age		286
Should doom him there for aye to dwell	318 Giaour		821
The Bourbon for aye	732 Deformed	1	724

A-YEAR

Their cash, to show how much they have a-year	919 Juan	11	76

AZAZIEL
I love Azaziel more than--oh, too much   655 Heaven   8
Azaziel not less, were he mortal; yet   655 Heaven   19
My own Azaziel! be but here   656 Heaven   79
They come! he comes!--Azaziel! Haste   657 Heaven   143
They have touch'd earth! Samiasa! My Azaziel   657 Heaven   159
How have Azaziel, or myself, brought on thee   663 Heaven   609
Had Samiasa and Azaziel been   666 Heaven   797
Azaziel   667 Heaven   918
And thou, Azaziel! No   667 Heaven   936

AZO
He hears--Why doth Prince Azo start   397 Parisina   83
And Azo spake:--'But yesterday   398 Parisina   198
And here stern Azo hid his face   398 Parisina   223
And Azo found another bride   401 Parisina   530

AZO'S
Bespeaks her guilt and Azo's shame   397 Parisina   92
And Azo's tortured heart and ear   397 Parisina   130
A monument of Azo's wife   400 Parisina   351
Through Azo's palace-lattice driven   401 Parisina   494
And from Prince Azo's voice, by none   401 Parisina   508
Yet Azo's age was wretched still   402 Parisina   578

AZRAEL
Even Azrael, from his deadly quiver   327 Abydos   1   323

AZURE
The tender azure of the unruffled deep   7 Harold   1   247
Floats through the azure air, an island of the
    blest   59 Harold   4   243
Of comtemplation; and the azure gloom   74 Harold   4 1151
Time writes no wrinkle on thine azure brow   82 Harold   4 1637
His glossy curls, his azure wing   89 Anacreon-B   33
'Gainst him who rules the sky and azure main   89 Prometheus-A   8
Whose azure floats in liquid fire   98 To Mary   10
How sweetly shines through azure skies   101 Alva   1
the azure eye of Mora? Why should her   130 Calmar   81
No more yon azure vault with rays adorn   139 Ossian-A   27
O Thou! who rollest in yon azure field   140 Ossian-B   1
Blest be that lip and azure eye   150 Song   17
Veiling the azure orbs below   152 Remind   21
The azure grave of many a Roman   159 Gulf   6
The languid azure eye surpasses   159 Cadiz   8
Had never pass'd the Azure rocks   225 Embargo   4
Their azure arches through the long expanse   268 Minerva   13
The azure fields of heaven, of that be sure   291 Vision   396
In azure column proudly gleaming   316 Giaour   623
Their azure arches through the long expanse   355 Corsair   3   13
Calm, clear, and azure as the air   387 Corinth   253
A lovely bird, with azure wings   405 Chillon   268
Of ocean's alpine azure rose and fell   427 Island   3   72
With the azure and vermillion   479 Manfred   1   54
And this proud city, and these azure waters   547 Faliero   5   656
Up to the lights above us, in the azure   631 Cain   1   277
Of glorious azure which floats on beyond us   642 Cain   2   384
Floating upon the azure desert, and   668 Heaven   964
No azure more shall robe the firmament   669 Heaven   1074
Red sun sinks down behind the azure hill   797 Juan   2   1458
Of azure, pink, and white was her chemise   810 Juan   3   555
But still from that sublimer azure hue   986 Juan   16   421

AZURE'S
Advanced in all their azure's highest hue   924 Juan   11   396

B
Present, Lords A. B. C.'--Earls, dukes, by name 947 Juan   13   426

BAAL
And the idols are broke in the temple of Baal   222 Sennacherib   22
Each country book-club bows the knee to Baal   243 Bards   138
Though 'twere against myself. By the god Baal 552 Sardan   1   111
Till summer heats wear down. O glorious Baal   553 Sardan   1   159
Shame me! by Baal, the cities, though well built 555 Sardan   1   291
I have, by Baal! done all I could to soothe them 556 Sardan   1   403
Where? With Baal, Nimrod, and Semiramis   561 Sardan   1   672
And dinn'd, and deafen'd with dead men and Baal 566 Sardan   2   250
Nor Baal, though an oracular deity   570 Sardan   2   531
As auguries of Jove. Jove!--ay, your Baal   570 Sardan   2   549
His father Baal, the god Sardanapalus   571 Sardan   3   28
Than his recover'd kingdom. Baal himself   576 Sardan   3   312
I grow almost a convert to your Baal   588 Sardan   5   48

BAAL-ADORER
The Baal-adorer bows on Sinai's steep   217 Jordan   3

BAAL'S
Before Baal's shrine, in the adjoining hall   594 Sardan   5   421

BABA
While he was dressing, Baba, their black friend 840 Juan   5   545
Baba eyed Juan, and said, 'Be so good   840 Juan   5   577
Said Baba; 'but pray do as I desire   840 Juan   5   586

BABA
Said Baba, 'to be curious; 'twill transpire   840 Juan   5   590
That I unsex'd my dress?' But Baba, stroking   841 Juan   5   598
The negro Baba help'd a little too   841 Juan   5   621
Was hardly long enough; but Baba found   841 Juan   5   626
While Baba made him comb his head and oil it   841 Juan   5   632
And Baba smilingly exclaim'd, 'You see, sirs   841 Juan   5   636
'You, sir,' said Baba, nodding to the one   841 Juan   5   641
'Blockhead! come on, and see,' quoth Baba; while 842 Juan   5   657
Baba led Juan onward room by room   842 Juan   5   674
As Baba with his fingers made them fall   843 Juan   5   715
Before they enter'd, Baba paused to hint   843 Juan   5   721
A lady; Baba stopp'd, and kneeling sign'd   843 Juan   5   756
What all this meant: while Baba bow'd and bended 843 Juan   5   759
She sign'd to Baba, who first kiss'd the hem   843 Juan   5   766
Who wore their uniform, by Baba chosen   844 Juan   5   788
Baba and Juan, which last stood admiring   844 Juan   5   795
Baba, when all the damsels were withdrawn   844 Juan   5   809
Baba, indignant at this ill-timed pride   844 Juan   5   817
Baba proposed that he should kiss the hand   844 Juan   5   832
Baba retire, which he obey'd in style   845 Juan   5   850
And Baba, who had ne'er been known to fail   846 Juan   5   908
The lash to Baba:--but her grand resource   849 Juan   5   1111
Further, old Baba rather briskly enter'd   849 Juan   5   1144
And here she summon'd Baba, and required   864 Juan   6   785
Baba, with some embarrassment, replied   864 Juan   6   793
When Baba saw these symptoms, which he knew   865 Juan   6   809
(The aforesaid Baba) just then to do more   865 Juan   6   822
And thrown into the sea.--Thus Baba spoke   865 Juan   6   831
Baba thought she would faint, but there he err'd 865 Juan   6   842
Baba, who knew by experience when to talk   866 Juan   6   873
Gulbeyaz stopp'd and beckon'd Baba:--'Slave   866 Juan   6   889
But one which Baba did not like to brave   866 Juan   6   891
And of this Baba willingly took note   866 Juan   6   902
My bidding!' Baba vanish'd, for to stretch   866 Juan   6   923

BABA'S
But not by Baba's fault, he said, and swore on 865 Juan   6   815
For Baba's function stopt short at the door   865 Juan   6   820

BABBLER
Produce this babbler--or redeem the pledge   376 Lara   2   51

BABBLERS
We must have no third babblers thrust between us 720 Werner   5   478

BABBLING
The clear brook babbling through the goodly plain 257 Hints   26
Must pore where babbling waters flow   324 Abydos   1   88
At the new transient flame; no babbling crowd   423 Island   2   336
Which echoes Madness in her babbling moods   438 Tasso   90
Will send my answer through thy babbling troop 556 Sardan   1   348
From its vile babbling roots, till you shall
    utter   623 Foscari   5 158

BABE
Herself more sweetly rears the babe she bears   28 Harold   2   548
She clasps a babe to whom her breast yields no
    relief   80 Harold   4 1503
The babe which ought to have been mine   164 Friend-B   38
Sweet babe of one and twenty years   235 Epilogue   12
The babe unborn thy dread intent may rue   245 Bards   233
And brother Coleridge lull the babe at nurse   254 Bards   918
Babe of a city birth! from sixpence take   264 Hints   517
Like crying babe and beaten hound   396 Corinth   1072
Hush'd as the babe upon its mother's breast   793 Juan   2   1178
Clash'd 'gainst the scimitar, and babe and mother 887 Juan   8   548
A half-starved babe, a wreck upon Life's ocean 997 Juan   17   20

BABEL
Till, like Babel, the new royal dome hath arisen 203 Avatar   74
Of Babel, and thought of the day   222 Babylon   2
Another Babel soars--but Britain ends   307 Age   649
A Carthage, and a Tyre, an Ocean Babel   547 Faliero   5 660
Now, though towering like a Babel   736 Deformed   2   81
Well done, old Babel! Ha! right nobly battled   739 Deformed   2 266
To add a story to the Tower of Babel   745 Juan   Ded   32
Methinks the story of the tower of Babel   839 Juan   5   471
Babel was Nimrod's hunting-box, and then   839 Juan   5   473
Of that same Babel, or because they won't   839 Juan   5   492
And let the Babel round run as it may   927 Juan   11   541
The Gothic Babel of a thousand years   947 Juan   13   396
Bricklayer of Babel, call'd an architect   988 Juan   16   506

BABELS
More Babels, without new dispersion, than   732 Deformed   1 677

BABEL'S
Oh! weep for those that wept by Babel's stream 217 Weep-B   1
And Babel's men of age   220 Belshaz-B   29
By Babel's waters, still remembering Sion   776 Juan   2   122

BABES
(See also FOSTER-BABES)

BABES
And frighten foolish babes, the Lord knows why   244 Bards   160
The cry of women, and the shrieks of babes   530 Faliero   4 164
Their hands in sacred vows--have danced their
    babes   603 Foscari   2 120
Like an invasion of their babes and sucklings   848 Juan   5 1060

BABIES
Struck at his friends, as babies beat their
    nurses   892 Juan   8 864

BABY
A wandering baby who can fear   89 Anacreon-B   20
Oh! I should be a baby fool   143 To--A   17
She marvell'd 'what he saw in such a baby   974 Juan   15 391

BABYLON
Unless, like he of Babylon   181 Ode-A   131
Of Babylon and Media. With our troops   568 Sardan   2 409
Him hence to meet me. Where? At Babylon   593 Sardan   5 352
Rome, Babylon, Tyre, Carthage, Nineveh   885 Juan   8 477
Of travellers to mighty Babylon   921 Juan   11 178

BABYLONIAN
But here the Babylonian whore hath built   8 Harold   1 338
On Babylonian river's border   96 Granta   88
Or Babylonian walls. Yet these are trophies   555 Sardan   1 279
As purple to the Babylonian harlot   877 Juan   7 667

BABYLONIA'S
As firm in fight as Babylonia's captain   562 Sardan   2   77

BABYLON'S
A glorious triumph still; proud Babylon's   739 Deformed   2 262
For Babylon's than Russia's royal harlot   910 Juan   10 207
In Babylon's bravuras--as the home   986 Juan   16 409

BABY'S
But felt for all the baby's woe   89 Anacreon-B   24

BACCHANAL
Wreath'd with rich grapes and Bacchanal devices   676 Werner   1 296
In Bacchanal profusion reel to earth   762 Juan   1 986
How answers each bold Bacchanal   812 Juan   3 742

BACCHANALS
And from his fellow bacchanals would flee   4 Harold   1   47

BACCHANAL'S
Let the wine flow around the old Bacchanal's
    throne   203 Avatar   83

BACCHANT
Over his shoulder, with a Bacchant air   806 Juan   3 338
Blushing with Bacchant coronals along   950 Juan   13 602

BACCHANTE
Pair'd off with a Bacchante blooming visage   828 Juan   4 736

BACCHANT'S
Command me in all service save the Bacchant's   569 Sardan   2 482

BACCHUS
Bacchus and Mars to rule the camp combine   108 Nisus   229
Within whose bosom infant Bacchus broods   422 Island   2 255
There was a certain Bacchus, was there not   553 Sardan   1 194
And skirts of these our realms lie not, this
    Bacchus   554 Sardan   1 212
Save that his jocund eye hath more of Bacchus   725 Deformed   1 232
Are also learnt from Ceres and from Bacchus   795 Juan   2 1351
While Bacchus pours out wine, or hands a jelly   795 Juan   2 1357
Bacchus and Ceres being, as we know   992 Juan   16 732

BACHELOR
When wicked wives, who love some bachelor   855 Juan   6 187
To wish him back a bachelor now and then   892 Juan   8 902
He was a bachelor, which is a matter   924 Juan   11 361
But Juan was a bachelor--of arts   924 Juan   11 369

BACK
Till I come back again   6 Harold   1 153
But long ere I come back again   6 Harold   1 188
Back to the struggle, baffled in the strife   18 Harold   1 889
Beat back keen winter's blast, and welcomed
    summer's heat   26 Harold   2 387
Where is the foe that ever saw their back   29 Harold   2 579
That gives them back their fathers' heritage   31 Harold   2 716
And timely echo'd back the measured oar   32 Harold   2 758
Recall its virtues back and vanquish Time and Fate 33 Harold   2 800
Leap kindly back to kindness, though disgust   43 Harold   3 473
Back to the joyous Alps who call to her aloud   49 Harold   3 868
Back on the heart the weight which it would fling 58 Harold   4 203
But my soul wanders; I demand it back   59 Harold   4 217
Thy right, and awe the robbers back, who press   61 Harold   4 377

BACK
Come back before me, as his skill beguiles   64 Harold   4 554
With many windings, through the vale:--Look back   65 Harold   4 636
Thou tomb! and other days come back on me   70 Harold   4 930
But yielded back his conquests: he was more   71 Harold   4 996
To whom she renders back the debt of blood   77 Harold   4 1344
Brings prudence back in proper season   100 Marion   26
Whose manly arm may snatch me back by force   106 Nisus   67
Back to redeem the Latian spoiler's prey   110 Nisus   336
Calls back the vanish'd days to rapture given   122 Recoll   13
In tracing back the years of youth   131 L'Amitie   5
Fortune! take back these cultured lands   135 I Would   9
Take back this name of splendid sound   135 I Would   10
The stars start back and hide them in the sky   140 Ossian-B   6
And echoes back his Patron's voice again   142 Soliloquy   20
Thy vaults will echo back my knell   145 Adieu   33
Those eyes threw back a glance so sweet   152 Remind   14
Lord knows when we shall come back   157 Hodgson   66
Give, oh, give me back my heart   160 Maid   2
Untainted back to thine   162 Parting   4
Then back to busy life again   166 Struggle   4
Shrank back appall'd, and trembled for their home 169 Address-A   12
And reason's voice be echo'd back by ours   170 Address-A   65
Back to my breast the wanderers shrink   175 Impromptu-A   7
And baffled back the fiery-crested Dane   182 Address-C   4
Was but the menace which flung back   191 Prometheus-B 27
Bring back with joy   200 Stanzas-B   64
Compress'd back to the heart   200 Ode-C   13
But back to our theme! Back to despots and
    slaves   202 Avatar   49
Let me not die till he comes back o'er the billow 205 Hindoo   12
Back on thy bosom with reflected blight   209 Sketch   86
And her who was his destiny, came back   215 Dream   164
Its eye shall roll through chaos back   220 Clay   18
Flash'd back on the last glance I gave to thy
    wall   221 Jerusalem   4
Or send it back to Doctor Donne   227 Thurlow-B   7
As the saint keeps her charity back for 'the
    Ball   238 Pangs   8
That, ere they reach the top, fall lumbering
    back again   247 Bards   417
Nor hunt the bloodhounds back to Arthur's Seat   247 Bards   437
Back to the sway they forfeited before   248 Bards   451
Holland, with Henry Petty at his back   249 Bards   542
But should I back return, no tempting press   255 Bards   1023
For brains may be o'erloaded, like the back   264 Hints   536
May travel back to Quito--on a trunk   265 Hints   662
Bear back my mandate to thy native shore   270 Minerva   158
Yet marks the mighty back and length of limb   271 Minerva   188
Or, back returning, sees rejected stores   272 Minerva   269
Back to my theme.--O Muse of motion say   274 Waltz   57
Brunck's heaviest tome for ballast, and, to back
    it   274 Waltz   77
Back to the ball-room speed your spectred host   275 Waltz   137
Your friends, or he'll pay you back in your own
    coin   280 Blues   1 152
Its way back into earth, and fire, and air   286 Vision   84
Is Lucifer come back with all this clatter   287 Vision   136
Back on its trunk: it may be very well   287 Vision   166
Up the back stairs, or such freemasonry   291 Vision   428
The same high spirit which beat back the Moor   301 Age   262
Holds back the invader from her soil again   302 Age   319
Back to the barbarous realm from whence they
    sprung   302 Age   331
But harden'd back whene'er the morning's raw   304 Age   441
How nobly gave he back the Poles their Diet   304 Age   446
A dubious scent would lure the bipeds back   305 Age   561
In softest incense back to heaven   310 Giaour   31
Beats back the current many a rood   316 Giaour   624
His back to earth, his face to heaven   317 Giaour   668
His hood fly back, his dark hair fall   319 Giaour   894
His back was to the dashing spray   335 Abydos   2 569
Back to your duty--for my course prepare   340 Corsair   1 156
And on himself roll back his scrutiny   341 Corsair   1 220
To give thee back to all endear'd below   355 Corsair   2 531
She stopp'd--threw back her dark far-floating
    hair   361 Corsair   3 410
Yet grieve to win him back without a blow   363 Corsair   3 507
Roll'd back the clouds) the morrow caught his eye 381 Lara   2 469
Flung back the hand which held the sacred gift   382 Lara   2 485
And bear my spirit back again   384 Corinth   37
They turn'd him on his back; his breast   394 Corinth   885
Thither bending sternly back   394 Corinth   914
Throbb'd as if back upon his brain   398 Parisina   225
Back the stain'd and heaving trunk   401 Parisina   457
A sigh shrunk back on every breast   401 Parisina   484
But flow back to the fountain head   402 Parisina   564
But then by dull degrees came back   405 Chillon   259
Had brought me back to feel and think   405 Chillon   278
My seventy years of memory back   408 Mazeppa   126
New realms to lose them back again   408 Mazeppa   134
The Ukraine back again to live   409 Mazeppa   305
Upon his back with many a thong   410 Mazeppa   371
Howl'd back my curse; but 'midst the tread   410 Mazeppa   388

BACK

Have paid their insult back again	410	Mazeppa	392
Their troop came hard upon our back	411	Mazeppa	494
'My thoughts came back; where was I? Cold	412	Mazeppa	569
Back from the solitary world	413	Mazeppa	654
His back with many a bloody thong	413	Mazeppa	697
Then plunging back with sudden bound	413	Mazeppa	701
And then subsiding back to death	414	Mazeppa	789
But those she wafted still look'd back to home	418	Island 1	230
Which spurn in columns back the baffled spray	419	Island 2	15
But lo! night comes, the Mooa woos us back	419	Island 2	29
And falls back on the foaming crowd behind	426	Island 3	23
Back on themselves,--their sins remain'd alone	427	Island 3	42
Back to a sword, and dies and lives again	427	Island 3	58
Cast one glance back, and clench'd his hand, and shook	434	Island 4	339
Would I not pay them back these pangs again	438	Tasso	100
Will back their own opinions with a wager	443	Beppo	216
Festoon'd, much like the back scene of a play	445	Beppo	325
Some six and thirty stanzas back, and so	447	Beppo	442
The sense of earth and earthly things come back	457	Dante 1	131
Back to their native mansion: soon they find	463	Dante 3	170
Its fire back to the hell from whence it sprung	463	Dante 3	192
To fly back to thee in despite of wrong	465	Dante 4	130
Had not his valour driven them back again	467	Morgante	108
Thinking that he a back of iron had	474	Morgante	539
But lend a hand to place him on my back	474	Morgante	564
'But help him on my back,' Morgante said	474	Morgante	573
I felt myself degraded back to them	486	Manfred 2	172
The gifts of our great knowledge, and shrink'st back	486	Manfred 2	219
Of an all-pitiless demon held me back	486	Manfred 2	232
Back by a single hair, which would not break	486	Manfred 2	233
But, like an ebbing wave, it dash'd me back	487	Manfred 2	237
Forbears to pant for death, and yet draws back	487	Manfred 2	268
His servant echoes back the awful word	492	Manfred 3	65
The dying Roman thrust him back, and said	492	Manfred 3	94
Spurn back, and scorn ye!--But thy many crimes	496	Manfred 3	381
And greater criminals?--Back to thy hell	496	Manfred 3	384
My own hereafter.--Back, ye baffled fiends	496	Manfred 3	400
Back to its antique lustre in our annals	508	Faliero 1	620
And I would soothe you back to what you were	512	Faliero 2	222
I have thought on 't till--but let me lead you back	514	Faliero 2	410
Which I must do to pay them back for theirs	520	Faliero 3	117
A moment back, and you were all impatience	526	Faliero 3	569
Call back your nerves to your own purpose, nor	527	Faliero 3	596
Who but give back what they have drain'd from millions	527	Faliero 3	604
Nor my own feelings--both compel me back	527	Faliero 3	639
Than torches glared back by a gaudy glass	529	Faliero 4	70
Of boatmen answering back with verse for verse	529	Faliero 4	100
Which makes me call thee back; we must not part thus	531	Faliero 4	197
When sallow burghers slunk back to their tents	533	Faliero 4	384
Himself perhaps even now draws grating back	535	Faliero 4	529
Back to my duty. But thou spakest of peril	558	Sardan 1	516
Seen me turn back from battle. No; I own thee	562	Sardan 2	76
Here, fellow, take thy weapon back. Well, sirs	565	Sardan 2	195
Monarch, take back your signet. No, retain it	565	Sardan 2	219
Their way back to the harem. If the king	576	Sardan 3	306
Let him not sink back into luxury	578	Sardan 3	416
But if I fail, then they must win it back	582	Sardan 4	274
She will recover. Pray, keep back.--I must	584	Sardan 4	419
On which the future would turn back and smile	586	Sardan 4	514
So bright, so rolling back the clouds into	587	Sardan 5	10
Beat back by valour: now at once we have	588	Sardan 5	71
Who had seen you fall, and falter'd back. Whom heard ye	589	Sardan 5	111
To call back--But I will not weep for thee	589	Sardan 5	151
And bring me back, as speedily as full	590	Sardan 5	213
And as you sail, turn back; but still keep on	593	Sardan 5	391
Flinging the billows back from my drench'd hair	597	Foscari 1	107
Back to your cheek: Heaven send you strength to bear	597	Foscari 1	131
Demurr'd: a messenger was sent back to	602	Foscari 2	57
I was thrust back, with the assurance that	602	Foscari 2	60
To back his suit. Dishonour'd!--he dishonour'd	604	Foscari 2	163
Who totters back in chains to tortures and	604	Foscari 2	169
Back to my heart, and left my cheeks like thine	609	Foscari 3	49
Look not so stern--but get you back, and pore	612	Foscari 3	299
Is one away from Venice, I look back	614	Foscari 3	414
Look back. I pray you think of me. Alas	616	Foscari 4	108
Till the sea dash me back on my own shore	617	Foscari 4	131
A shrine. Get thee back to thy place of torment	618	Foscari 4	221
Than calling it at moments back to this	619	Foscari 4	254
Whence he shall come back to thee in an hour	635	Cain 1	524
Who shall return, save One) shall come back to thee	635	Cain 1	539
Art thou not nearer? look back to thine earth	637	Cain 2	118
Or, if it irk thee, turn thee back and till	640	Cain 2	309
Now let us back to earth! And wherefore didst thou	642	Cain 2	433
But few! and some of those but bitter. Back	646	Cain 2	654

Hath given thee back to us. So Soon? 'Tis scarcely	647	Cain 3	53
It back to dust again--for what? Thou know'st	647	Cain 3	74
Brother, give back! thou shalt not touch my altar	650	Cain 3	305
Stand back till I have strew'd this turf along	651	Cain 3	314
Give thee back this.--Now for the wilderness	654	Cain 3	544
I must back to my rest. And so would I	657	Heaven	198
And scatter back the mists in floating folds	659	Heaven	291
Back to your inner caves	660	Heaven	383
Back to thy tents, insulting son of Noah	663	Heaven	602
I came to call ye back to your fit sphere	666	Heaven	820
And as your pinions bear ye back to heaven	667	Heaven	910
May have return'd back to his grandsire, and	673	Werner 1	89
As snakes and lions shrink back from each other	687	Werner 2	278
Your couriers are turn'd back--I have out-stripp'd them	687	Werner 2	309
Stand back, and let me look on thee again	688	Werner 2	337
Of your sire's feudal mansion, I look'd back	688	Werner 2	374
Where is the baron? Gone back to his chamber	699	Werner 3	282
But rather strove to trample back to hell	702	Werner 3	474
Back to my heart, which beats for you, sweet cousin	706	Werner 4	161
Which gave us back our own, in the same moment	708	Werner 4	252
Nature was never call'd back by remonstrance	709	Werner 4	334
Was over, and we march'd back in procession	714	Werner 5	107
Of tracing back my way, I saw a glimmer	718	Werner 5	308
With stern and anxious glance gazed back upon	718	Werner 5	333
That back of thine may bear its burthen; 'tis	722	Deformed 1	6
Deep in the fountain to scare back the cattle	723	Deformed 1	51
Resolve back to her elements, and take	723	Deformed 1	60
Are not far from me. Do not send me back	724	Deformed 1	131
Whence they float back before us. Hence, triumvir	726	Deformed 1	244
Back into hieroglyphics. Like your statesman	732	Deformed 1	674
We have turn'd back on no men	732	Deformed 1	697
Turn back from shadowy menaces of shadows	733	Deformed 1	763
For you have seen that back--as general	733	Deformed 1	794
To call them back into their separate cages	752	Juan 1	358
Of calling wholly back its self-control	760	Juan 1	908
With more than half the city at his back	763	Juan 1	1090
What's to be done? Alfonso will be back	767	Juan 1	1345
Call'd back the tangles of her wandering hair	767	Juan 1	1354
Thrown back a moment with the glancing hand	775	Juan 2	50
To beg the beggar, who could not rain back	785	Juan 2	685
Should suck him back to her insatiate grave	787	Juan 2	860
And tingling vein, seem'd throbbing back to life	788	Juan 2	887
And then once more his feelings back were brought	788	Juan 2	894
Recall'd his answering spirits back from death	788	Juan 2	900
Look'd back upon him, and a moment stay'd	791	Juan 2	1075
Came always back to coffee and Haidee	796	Juan 2	1368
And bring our hearts back to their starting-post	804	Juan 3	168
Yielding to their small hands, draws back again	805	Juan 3	256
Earth! render back from out thy breast	812	Juan 3	727
Brought back the sense of pain without the cause	824	Juan 4	495
Back to old thoughts, wax'd full of fearful meaning	824	Juan 4	512
With Juan, left half-kill'd some stanzas back	826	Juan 4	592
The captives back to their sad berths; each threw	827	Juan 4	716
A quantity of clothes fit for the back	840	Juan 5	531
You started back in horror to survey	842	Juan 5	698
To heaving back the portal folds: it scared	843	Juan 5	716
Rush back upon his heart, which fill'd apace	846	Juan 5	933
Call'd back the stoic to his eyes, which shone	846	Juan 5	965
Grow deadly pale, and then blush back again	847	Juan 5	992
Back to their chambers, those long galleries	855	Juan 6	205
So let us back to Lilliput, and guide	856	Juan 6	222
Count Damas drove them back into the water	871	Juan 7	247
'What follow'd?'--'A shot laid me on my back	875	Juan 7	485
Turn'd back within its socket,--that reward	879	Juan 8	102
And rally back his Romans to the field	881	Juan 8	224
And led them back into the heaviest fire	883	Juan 8	328
Now back to thy great joys, Civilisation	886	Juan 8	538
Koutousow, he who afterward beat back	887	Juan 8	553
It happen'd was himself beat back just now	887	Juan 8	556
Up Johnson came, with hundreds at his back	890	Juan 8	773
To wish him back a bachelor now and then	892	Juan 8	902
And throwing back a dim look on his brows	893	Juan 8	943
Was imaged back in blood, the sea of slaughter	894	Juan 8	976
But pray give back a little to the nation	897	Juan 9	48
First out of, and then back again to chaos	901	Juan 9	295
Of age, and looking back to youth, give one tear	910	Juan 10	216
Thus far, go forth, thou lay, which I will back	929	Juan 11	706
Could back a horse, as despots ride a Russian	944	Juan 13	184
Back to the night wind by the waterfall	949	Juan 13	503
Her way back to the world by dint of plottery	951	Juan 13	654
May the rose call back its true colour soon	955	Juan 13	886
Look back o'er ages, ere unto the stake fast	955	Juan 14	13
How clay shrinks back from more quiescent clay	955	Juan 14	27
It occupies me to turn back regards	956	Juan 14	85
But then the roll-call draws them back afraid	957	Juan 14	131
Knew that he had a rider on his back	959	Juan 14	256
Upon whose back 'tis better not to venture	964	Juan 14	584
Back to his chamber, shorn of half his strength	983	Juan 16	200

BACK
That bring Lochaber back to eyes that roam   986 Juan   16   411
And then swung back; nor close--but stood awry   996 Juan   16   979
Back fell the sable frock and dreary cowl   996 Juan   16   1029

BACKBITER
And from bishop sink into backbiter   239 Bray   54

BACKBITING
Is the numerous, humorous, backbiting crew   280 Blues   2   16

BACK'D
He back'd his steed, his homeward path he took   376 Lara   2   95
Is nothing worth, and not an instant back'd him   471 Morgante   315
And fish, and soup, by some side dishes back'd   835 Juan   5   253

BACKGAMMON
Like a backgammon board the place was dotted   832 Juan   5   73

BACKGROUND
This he discreetly kept in the background   865 Juan   6   833
Our ridicules are kept in the back-ground   953 Juan   13   753

BACKS
Are there no fools whose backs demand the scourge   253 Bards   822
With banded backs against the wall   393 Corinth   779
A band of iron rustics at our backs   533 Faliero   4   389
Who backs a horse, or bears a hawk, or wears   704 Werner   4   33
From ogling all their charms from breasts to backs   856 Juan   6   232
Sometimes a little heavy on the backs   864 Juan   6   767
They had but little baggage at their backs   872 Juan   7   340
Having been used to serve on horses' backs   887 Juan   8   589
But what he did, was to lay on their backs   890 Juan   8   743
According as their minds or backs are bent   936 Juan   12   412

BACK-SHOP
My back-shop glut, my shelves encumber   231 Doctor   32

BACKWARD
And flies unconscious o'er each backward year   23 Harold   2   211
Shall yet redeem thee, and, all backward driven   62 Harold   4   422
Then backward o'er the plain his eyes extend   109 Nisus   319
And backward to the den of his despair   301 Age   211
Thus the first were backward bent   392 Corinth   730
The waves a moment backward bent   395 Corinth   1022
And backward to the forest fly   413 Mazeppa   707
Flattering: they are beaten backward from the palace   576 Sardan   3   324
His toilet, though no doubt a little backward   841 Juan   5   620
Though he deserved it well for being so backward   849 Juan   5   1118
Backward and forward to the echoes faint   982 Juan   16   139

BACKWARDS
Instead of heaven, they stumbled backwards o'er   880 Juan   8   159

BACK-WOODSMAN
The General Boon, back-woodsman of Kentucky   886 Juan   8   484

BACON
As he swallow'd down the bacon he wish'd himself a Jew   178 Devil's Dr   211
Who hating hogs, yet wish'd to save their bacon   872 Juan   7   336
By thy humane discovery, Friar Bacon   882 Juan   8   264
You know, or don't know, that great Bacon saith   956 Juan   14   57
Was it not so, great Locke? and greater Bacon   970 Juan   15   137

BACON'S
Now, like Friar Bacon's brazen head, I've spoken   773 Juan   1   1733
Like Shakespeare's stealing deer, Lord Bacon's bribes   813 Juan   3   826

BACTRIA
Good her retreat to Bactria. And how many   553 Sardan   1   178
Have fled to Bactria, leaving to the ravens   553 Sardan   1   183
Brought Persia, Media, Bactria, to the realm   553 Sardan   1   190
One for Assyria! Rather say for Bactria   575 Sardan   3   264

BACTRIAN
The Bactrian, Samian sage, and all who taught the right   20 Harold   2   72

BACTRIANS
The Bactrians, now led on by Salemenes   572 Sardan   3   86
My faithful Bactrians, I will henceforth be   575 Sardan   3   265
Faster that I could follow with my Bactrians   576 Sardan   3   337

BAD
That saddening hour when bad men hotlier press   29 Harold   2   590
Doth lesson happier men, and shames at least the bad   29 Harold   2   612
Bad rhymes, and those who write them   137 Clare   57
As bad--but in a different way   163 Malta   24
He never had found them quite so bad   179 Devil's Dr   234
To trouble with bad hopes, or evil wish   215 Dream   138
If the bad never triumph, then God is with thee   221 False   5

BAD
Make bad men better, or at least ashamed   253 Bards   830
Democritus himself was not so bad   263 Hints   463
All men avoid bad writers' ready tongues   268 Hints   807
That may be, Mr. Tracy, but shows damn'd bad taste   279 Blues   1   106
Oh, fie! And for shame! You're too bad. Very good   281 Blues   2   64
Of constancy to a bad, ugly woman   286 Vision   96
And synagogues have made a damn'd bad purchase   286 Vision   112
Well know) superfluous; they are grown so bad   290 Vision   324
And now the bard could plead his own bad cause   296 Vision   759
All is exploded--be it good or bad   298 Age   9
Or, at the worst, a foe ignobly bad   376 Lara   2   48
Are pardon'd their bad hearts for their worse brains   435 Island   4   356
And sweating plays so middling, bad were better   449 Beppo   592
Abjure bad Macon's false and felon test   471 Morgante   357
Turn poison in bad minds. And good ones make   583 Sardan   4   320
Like Theban breathren: when a part is bad   699 Werner   3   259
'Tis no bad policy: this union with   706 Werner   4   131
Comrade. They are but bad company, your highness   734 Deformed   1   812
She next decided he was only bad   750 Juan   1   212
And the long-boat's condition was but bad   780 Juan   2   379
Of charms to make good gold and cure bad ails   805 Juan   3   269
And made him a good friend, but bad acquaintance   808 Juan   3   432
Rejoin'd the other, 'when our bad luck mends here   834 Juan   5   190
'Tis bad, and may be better--all men's lot   834 Juan   5   194
Poor fellow! for some reason, surely bad   835 Juan   5   265
Groups of bad statues, tables, chairs, and pictures   843 Juan   5   751
And he advanced, though with but a bad grace   844 Juan   5   841
And works of the same pottery, bad or good   849 Juan   5   1101
That is, we cannot pardon their bad taste   854 Juan   6   129
A bad old woman making a worse will   855 Juan   6   165
My wish is quite as wide, but not so bad   855 Juan   6   212
All bad propensities in fifteen hundred   856 Juan   6   247
With something not much better, or as bad   881 Juan   8   171
Account for every thing which may look bad   882 Juan   8   244
With good, and bad, and worse, alike prolific   889 Juan   8   708
All that the body perpetrates of bad   894 Juan   8   978
They talk'd bad French or Spanish, and upon its   924 Juan   11   397
And still pursues the right;--to curb the bad   942 Juan   13   67
Regretting much that she had chosen so bad a line   961 Juan   14   365
There's nought in this bad world like sympathy   961 Juan   14   369
They are but bad pilots when the weather's rough   961 Juan   14   379
If bad, the best way's certainly to tease on   974 Juan   15   403
Those truffles too are no bad accessaries   976 Juan   15   537
This was no bad mistake, as it occurr'd   992 Juan   16   753
But what was bad, she did not blush in turn   993 Juan   16   793

BADDISH
These books would be but baddish bail   230 Murray-A   9

BADE
If friends he had, be bade adieu to none   5 Harold   1   86
And years, that bade thy worship to expire   19 Harold   2   5
And bade to Christian tongues a long adieu   26 Harold   2   380
And where Alfonso bade his poet dwell   60 Harold   4   319
And round Orestes bade them howl and hiss   75 Harold   4   1184
Bade they obey, and gave me to command   93 Dorset   6
She bade a secret lightning lurk   97 To M--   15
Had bade serenity return   103 Alva   147
She bade his wounded pride rebel   105 Alva   294
When Edward bade his conquering bands advance   111 Examination   15
A monarch bade thee from that wild arise   120 Newstead-A   25
And bade the pious inmates rest in peace   120 Newstead-A   42
To which I long have bade a last adieu   122 Recoll   32
What though one sad dissension bade us part   126 Recoll   303
And bade them burn with fiercer glow   134 E.N.Long   81
And bade her blast a heart she never knew   142 Soliloquy   30
And kindly bade me tune my Lyre again   143 Soliloquy   68
And bade them burn with fiercer glow   148 A Fan   7
But his, whose neglect may have bade thee expire   149 Newstead-B   12
And bade him curse his future fate   155 To A Lady-E   4
And bade him have no fear   177 Devil's Dr   98
And bade thee cling to me through every shock   206 Love, Death   7
And bade no more rejoice   220 Belshaz-B   18
Because I bade the people pull   235 New Song   3
Him who bade England bow to Normandy   239 Conquest   2
Zeal for her honour bade me here engage   255 Bards   993
What lost a world and bade a hero fly   355 Corsair   2   549
But--good or ill--it bade her not depart   363 Corsair   3   546
They bade me to destruction dash   411 Mazeppa   409
And bade him 'speed and prosper.' She would take   430 Island   4   39
But Christian bade them seek their shore again   433 Island   4   249
To act whatever duty bade them do   433 Island   4   282
Feel I not wroth with those who bade me dwell   437 Tasso   82
Orlando bade him take care of Rondello   469 Morgante   217
Once more he bade him lay his burden by   475 Morgante   590
My lord, you bade me wait on you at sunset   493 Manfred   3   172
The nobleness with which you bade me speak   513 Faliero   2   304
They--Bade thee stretch me on their horrid engine   598 Foscari   1   155
Besides, I bade him 'good night' in the hall   683 Werner   2   23
Don Juan bade his valet pack his things   775 Juan   2   65

BADE
Old Lambro bade them take him to the shore	822	Juan	4	395
Who bade on till the hundreds reach'd eleven	831	Juan	4	910
The lady eyed him o'er and o'er, and bade	845	Juan	5	849
All earthly goods save tithes) and bade them push on	875	Juan	7	510
Quarter, in case he bade them not 'aroynt	893	Juan	8	931
And bade him counsel Juan. With a smile	963	Juan	14	516

BADGE
Bears in his cap the badge of crimson hue	12	Harold	1	523
Such is the badge that knighthood ever wore	383	Lara	2	591
Which his blood made a badge of glory and	731	Deformed	1	609

BADLY
Have understood Charles badly, and wrote worse	466	Morgante		32
Before, being badly seconded just then	888	Juan	8	627
To find how very badly she selected	934	Juan	12	288

BADNESS
| Knew you these lines--the badness of the best | 170 | Address-B | | 10 |

BAD'ST
| Would the hope, which thou once bad'st me cherish | 162 | Romaic-A | | 31 |
| Thou bad'st my say I was so once--Oh! now | 718 | Werner | 5 | 323 |

BAFFLE
Yet, yet, I may baffle the hosts that surround us	186	Napoleon		21
However link'd to baffle such design	379	Lara	2	337
To baffle the pursuit.--Away! away	429	Island	3	235
The spells which I have studied baffle me	481	Manfred	1	263
Even to the city, and so baffle all	556	Sardan	1	350
All we have now to think of is to baffle	699	Werner	3	244
To baffle such, than countermine a mole	720	Werner	5	437

BAFFLED
(See also OFT-BAFFLED)
Since baffled Triumph droops on Lusitania's coast	8	Harold	1	305
Back to the struggle, baffled in the strife	18	Harold	1	889
The heart, lone mourner of its baffled zeal	23	Harold	2	201
Of baffled foes was watch'd along the plain	44	Harold	3	559
Such as an army's baffled strength delays	70	Harold	4	885
Disarm'd and baffled by your conquering hand	126	Recoll		281
The baffled friends of Fiction start	141	Critics		39
And baffled back the fiery-crested Dane	182	Address-C		4
But baffled as thou wert from high	191	Prometheus-B		39
As many a baffled Heart can tell	201	Ode-C		84
Then let the ties of baffled love	210	Augusta-A		37
To baffled millions which have gone before	212	Augusta-C		104
Though baffled oft is ever won	311	Giaour		125
With baffled thirst and famine, grim	313	Giaour		296
Which nor defeated hope, nor baffled wile	342	Corsair	1	297
But chafes my pride thus baffled in the snare	343	Corsair	1	336
Fell'd--bleeding—baffled of the death he sought	351	Corsair	2	277
While baffled, weaken'd by this fatal fray	357	Corsair	3	149
Escaped the baffled wreath that strove to bind	364	Corsair	3	620
With hope still baffled still to be renew'd	367	Lara	1	104
And troubled manhood follow'd baffled youth	370	Lara	1	324
To love, long baffled by the unequal match	378	Lara	2	208
And palls the patience of his baffled heart	379	Lara	2	301
Or baffled Persia's despot fled	385	Corinth		60
When baffled feelings withering droop	387	Corinth		321
Which spurn in columns back the baffled spray	419	Island	2	15
Like vultures baffled of their previous prey	433	Island	4	240
And none have baffled, many fallen before me	478	Manfred	1	20
Have baffled me; my gains to-day will scarce	482	Manfred	1	319
And we are baffled also. Hear me, hear me	490	Manfred	2	486
My own hereafter.--Back, ye baffled fiends	496	Manfred	3	400
That if once stirr'd and baffled, as he has been	518	Faliero	2	682
They baffled me, 'twas a patrician's duty	525	Faliero	3	474
One day of baffled crime must not efface	543	Faliero	5	358
Why, like a man--a hero; baffled, but	553	Sardan	1	176
And to be baffled thus! We are not baffled	672	Werner	1	75
Baffled the long pursuit of Stralenheim	673	Werner	1	100
Had baffled the slow hounds in their pursuit	680	Werner	1	570
Brennus was a baffled foeman	736	Deformed	2	110
Like a mere log, and baffled our intent	778	Juan	2	252
Of baffled heroes, who stood shyly near	887	Juan	8	582
Their baffled rage and pain; while waxing colder	890	Juan	8	749
And baffled the assaults of all their host	893	Juan	8	956

BAFFLING
| Was light and baffling.'--'When the sun declined | 426 | Island | 2 | 509 |

BAG
Your Quarto two-pounds, or your Twopenny Post Bag	226	Oh You		4
Hived in our bosoms like the bag o' the bee	773	Juan	1	1709
Full grows his bag, and wonderful his feats	950	Ju n	13	598

BAGATELLE
| And bear Swift's motto, 'Vive la bagatelle | 261 | Hints | 34 | 344 |

BAGGAGE
| Baggage from the quay is lowering | 157 | Hodgson | | 19 |

BAGGAGE
They had but little baggage at their backs	872	Juan	7	340
To the other baggage, or to the sick tent	875	Juan	7	528
Aware this kind of baggage never thrives	876	Juan	7	559
Coach, chariot, luggage, baggage, equipage	946	Juan	13	346

BAGG'D
| Some are soon bagg'd, and some reject three dozen | 934 | Juan | 12 | 265 |
| Had bagg'd this poacher upon Nature's manor | 988 | Juan | 16 | 544 |

BAGS
| To faint, and damaged bread wet through the bags | 782 | Juan | 2 | 495 |
| Containing ingots, bags of dollars, coins | 931 | Juan | 12 | 90 |

BAH
Dreading the deep damnation or his 'bah	444	Beppo		254
As dust can. Then she is dead! Bah! bah! You are so	741	Deformed	2	394
Or a 'Ha! ha!' or 'Bah!'--a yawn, or 'Pooh	968	Juan	15	7

BAIL
| These books would be but baddish bail | 230 | Murray-A | | 9 |
| I won't be bail for anything beyond | 844 | Juan | 5 | 792 |

BAILLIE
| We tease mild Baillie, or soft Abernethy | 912 | Juan | 10 | 336 |

BAIRAM
| To-night, the Bairam feast's begun | 312 | Giaour | | 229 |
| Of Bairam through the boundless East | 314 | Giaour | | 452 |

BAIT
| But by a thread, like sharks who have gorged the bait | 434 | Island | 4 | 320 |
| To bait their tender, or their tenter, hooks | 967 | Juan | 14 | 776 |

BAITED
| Turn, as doth the lion baited | 736 | Deformed | 2 | 120 |

BAITING
| I left Don Juan with his horses baiting | 901 | Juan | 9 | 331 |

BAITS
First caresses, and then baits you	197	Rogers		48
And leaves old sinners to be young ones' baits	446	Beppo		432
Or thrown to lions, or made baits for fish	849	Juan	5	1124
May be the baits for gentlemen or lords	936	Juan	12	419

BAIZE
| Upon thy table's baize so green | 234 | Strahan | | 9 |

BAKED
When the hot sun hath baked the reeking soil	661	Heaven		454
And their baked lips, with many a bloody crack	784	Juan	2	681
Baked, fried, or burnt, turn'd inside-out, or drown'd	901	Juan	9	293

BAKES
| And bakes its unadulterated loaves | 422 | Island | 2 | 262 |

BAKING
| But will keep baking, broiling, burning on | 754 | Juan | 1 | 500 |

BALAAM
| To Balaam, and from tongue to ear o'erflows | 933 | Juan | 12 | 206 |

BALAAM"S
| When such an ass as this, like Balaam's, prates | 296 | Vision | | 710 |

BALANCE
Weigh'd in the balance, hero dust	181	Ode-A		100
Oh! early in tne balance weigh'd	185	Belshaz-A		17
He, in the balance weigh'd	220	Belshaz-B		43
How light the balance of his humbler pains	341	Corsair	1	192
To weigh kings in the balance, and to speak	488	Manfred	2	368
Were weigh'd i' the balance, 'gainst the foulest stain	502	Faliero	1	151
Our fate is trembling in the balance, and	536	Faliero	4	572
To balance such a foe, if such there be	596	Foscari	1	81
Is no more in the balance weigh'd with that	603	Foscari	2	133
Shall tremble in the balance, till the great	645	Cain	2	643
Weigh'd at its proper value in the balance	695	Werner	3	36
And find a deuced balance with the devil	767	Juan	1	1336
Who hold the balance of the world? Who reign	930	Juan	12	33
A floating balance of accomplishment	936	Juan	12	410
I've seen them balance even the scale with fighters	958	Juan	14	155

BALANCED
| And will you leave it unerased? Till balanced | 596 | Foscari | 1 | 54 |

BALANCING
| In balancing the profit and the loss | 878 | Juan | 8 | 19 |

BALCONY
They look when leaning over the balcony 441 Beppo 87
Particularly seen from a balcony 442 Beppo 115
Guards! lead them forth, and upon the balcony 539 Faliero 5 92

BALD
Like laurels on the bald first Caesar's head 76 Harold 4 1293
The phantom's bald; my quest is beauty. Could I 725 Deformed 1 190

BALD-COOT
Shut up the bald-coot bully Alexander 965 Juan 14 657

BALD-HEAD
Now. Well! the first of Caesars was a bald-head 731 Deformed 1 644

BALD-HEADS
Held in the bondage of ten bald-heads; and 611 Foscari 3 244

BALDNESS
Your bays may hide the baldness of your brows 745 Juan Ded 49

BALDOVIN
Walter of Lion's Mount, and Baldovin 467 Morgante 76

BALD-PATED
Cleave yon bald-pated shaveling to the chine 738 Deformed 2 239

BALDRIC
He saw their terror, from his baldric drew 349 Corsair 2 165
Give me the cuirass--so: my baldric; now 573 Sardan 3 127
This cuirass fits me well, the baldric better 574 Sardan 3 163

BALE
Of souls in hopeless bale; and from that place 456 Dante 1 8
A glimpse of sunshine set some hands to bale 778 Juan 2 303
And made them bale without a moment's ease 781 Juan 2 478

BALEA
Yes, Balea, thank the monarch, kiss the hem 563 Sardan 2 111

BALE-FIRES
The bale-fires flash on high; from rock to rock 10 Harold 1 419

BALEFUL
Whose baleful stings your breasts pervade 141 Critics 6
The baleful burthen of this honest song 208 Sketch 38

BALES
Droops o'er the bales no bark may bear away 272 Minerva 268
While they thrust sheets, shirts, jackets, bales
 of muslin 777 Juan 2 224

BALGOUNIE'S
The Dee, the Don, Balgounie's brig's black wall 909 Juan 10 139

BALK
Their numbers balk their own retreat 394 Corinth 925
They shall not balk my entrance. Alas! this 599 Foscari 1 258
I will not balk your humour, though untoward 680 Werner 1 558
This passion might blow o'er, nor dared to balk 866 Juan 6 875

BALK'D
But were all ramm'd and jamm'd (but to be balk'd 294 Vision 589
Balk'd of its wish; or fiercer still 412 Mazeppa 519

BALKS
That strict restraint, which, broken, ever balks 22 Harold 2 169

BALL
In motley robe to dance at masking ball 32 Harold 2 745
Yet shows of what she was, when shell and ball 44 Harold 3 556
The ball obey'd some hell-born guide 99 Young Lady 10
Drive o'er the sward the ball with active force 124 Recoll 131
Together we impell'd the flying ball 125 Recoll 257
He then popp'd his head in a royal Ball 178 Devil's Dr 193
Oh! enviously destined Ball 201 Ode-C 72
And the saint patronizes her 'Charity Ball 238 Pangs 4
As the saint keeps her charity back for 'the Ball 238 Pangs 8
Would even proscribe thee from a Paris ball 275 Waltz 152
The ball begins; the honours of the house 276 Waltz 184
Terpsichore, forgive!--at every ball 277 Waltz 250
Some erring blade or ball should glance 334 Abydos 2 532
When, at the instant, hiss'd the ball 335 Abydos 2 571
A flash is seen--the ball beyond their bow 362 Corsair 3 488
Well speeds alike the banquet and the ball 371 Lara 1 388
Which crumbles with the ponderous ball 385 Corinth 90
There flash'd no fire and there hiss'd no ball 389 Corinth 447
Whence issued late the fated ball 394 Corinth 911
His last ball had been aim'd, but from his breast 434 Island 4 333
For dance, and song, and serenade, and ball 441 Beppo 75
Its proper name, perhaps, were a masqued ball 447 Beppo 459
At the next London or Parisian ball 450 Beppo 671
Among three thousand people at a ball 450 Beppo 675
But ere it fall, that thundering ball 479 Manfred 1 66

BALL
His own shall roll before you like a ball 822 Juan 4 370
As brave as ever faced both bomb and ball 879 Juan 8 69
Count Chapeau-Bras, too, had a ball between 879 Juan 8 74
More than the cap; in fact, the ball could mean 879 Juan 8 78
Of hopes and fears which shake a single ball 927 Juan 11 568
But next to dressing for a rout or ball 981 Juan 16 81

BALLAD
In Spain, he'd make a ballad or romance on 812 Juan 3 683

BALLAD-MONGER
Behold the ballad-monger Southey rise 244 Bards 202

BALLADS
(See also HEART-BALLADS)
If still in Berkley ballads most uncivil 245 Bards 231
Forsooth, scarce fit for ballads in the street 827 Juan 4 710

BALLAD'S
For one long-cherish'd ballad's simple stave 420 Island 2 87

BALLAST
Brunck's heaviest tome for ballast, and, to back
 it 274 Waltz 77
In getting out goods, ballast, guns, and treasure 804 Juan 3 160

BALLAST-STONES
Such slings, clubs, ballast-stones, that yield
 you must 469 Morgante 226

BALLET-MASTER
Not like a ballet-master in the van 960 Juan 14 303

BALLOON
(See also AIR-BALLOONS)
Borne in the vast balloon of Busby's song 171 Address-B 40
Could not the blockhead ask for a balloon 814 Juan 3 888

BALL-PILED
The ball-piled pyramid, the ever-blazing match 12 Harold 1 539

BALL-ROOM
And every ball-room echoes with her name 275 Waltz 108
Back to the ball-room speed your spectred host 275 Waltz 137
The ball-room ere the sun begins to rise 450 Beppo 654
A ball-room bard, a foolscap, hot-press darling 830 Juan 4 866

BALLS
I saw him, last week, at two balls and a party 227 Moore-A 17
Making balls for the ladies, and bows to his foes 228 Once 4
I've seen some balls and revels in my time 450 Beppo 657
Her hair was dripping, and the very balls 820 Juan 4 261
As also at the race and county balls 844 Juan 5 824
And what with masquerades, and fetes, and balls 937 Juan 12 455
You may see such at all the balls and dinners 938 Juan 12 525

BALM
The pleasing balm of mortal ills 111 Medea 11
So sweet a balm to soothe your hours of woe 127 Recoll 394
And be that thought thy sorrow's balm 331 Abydos 2 188
And bathed his brow with airy balm 388 Corinth 361
When every flower was bloom, and air was balm 420 Island 2 107
And lying on their weariness like balm 782 Juan 2 540

BALM-BREATHING
Since the balm-breathing kiss of this magical
 miss 116 Strephon 13

BALSAMS
But the unnatural balsams merely blight 286 Vision 85

BALTIC
Look to the Baltic--blazing from afar 271 Minerva 213

BALTIC'S
Their roar even with the Baltic's--so you be 864 Juan 6 743
Something about the Baltic's navigation 913 Juan 10 358

BAMBOO
Chewing a piece of bamboo and some lead 784 Juan 2 654

BAN
Lie under the state's ban; their chief, thy
 nephew 545 Faliero 5 538
A prodigal son, beneath his father's ban 684 Werner 2 84
Who queer a flat? Who (spite of Bow-street's ban 920 Juan 11 149

BANANA
The ripe banana from the mellow hill 432 Island 4 174

BAND
(See also MOUNTAIN-BAND)
When Cava's traitor-sire first call'd the band 9 Harold 1 389

BAND

And therefore did he take a trusty band	30 Harold	2	617
Oh Love! young Love! bound in thy rosy band	32 Harold	2	771
Of a proud, brotherly, and civic band	45 Harold	3	612
Flashing and cast around. Of all the band	50 Harold	3	891
Though the harsh custom of our youthful band	93 Dorset		5
Even as a band of raw beginners	96 Granta		78
The elder first address'd the hoary band	106 Nisus		98
Just at this hour a band of Latian horse	109 Nisus		297
Their chief's retainers, an immortal band	119 Newstead-A		12
To lead the band where godlike Falkland fell	120 Newstead-A		76
Here first remember'd be the joyous band	123 Recoll		99
And none more dear than Ida's social band	125 Recoll		242
Now last, but nearest, of the social band	126 Recoll		325
This Band, which bound thy yellow hair	128 Lady-C		1
through the slumbering band. Half	130 Calmar		108
The Leader of the wrathful Band	141 Critics		47
Who to this zealous Band belong	142 Critics		78
Or joins Devotion's choral band	160 Cadiz		47
No band of friends or heirs be there	166 Euthanasia		5
To gaze on Beauty's band without its chief	183 Address-D		22
And I wept with the world o'er the patriot band	204 Avatar		111
By gibb'ring spectres hail'd, thy kindred band	245 Bards		270
Behold, a chosen band shall aid thy plan	248 Bards		506
Has crush'd, without remorse, your numerous band	251 Bards		744
Of ne plus ultra ultras and their band	304 Age		485
The foremost of the band is seen	313 Giaour		356
Nor of his little band a man	316 Giaour		601
Nor even his Pacha's turban'd band	326 Abydos	1	246
Each brother led a separate band	331 Abydos	2	231
Those arms thou see'st my band have brought	332 Abydos	2	315
Girt by my band, Zuleika at my side	333 Abydos	2	412
And since, though parted from my band	334 Abydos	2	472
But yet my band not far from shore	334 Abydos	2	515
The foremost of the prying band	334 Abydos	2	541
His band are plunging in the bay	335 Abydos	2	551
Then rose his band to duty--not from sleep	347 Corsair	1	603
Far from his band, and battling with a host	351 Corsair	2	275
Snatch'd from the flames and thy more fearful band	353 Corsair	2	438
The one of all my band that would not die	354 Corsair	2	473
But once cut off--the remnant of his band	357 Corsair	3	151
Disabled, shorn of half his might and band	358 Corsair	3	167
Seyd is mine enemy, had swept my band	361 Corsair	3	360
And these thy yet surviving band shall join	362 Corsair	3	435
He thought of all--Gonsalvo and his band	362 Corsair	3	460
Long mourn'd his band whom none could mourn beside	366 Corsair	3	691
And thousands dwindled to a scanty band	379 Lara	2	311
A moment's pause--'tis but to breathe their band	379 Lara	2	332
Thy band may perish, or thy friends may flee	380 Lara	2	358
Pours the link'd band through ranks asunder riven	380 Lara	2	361
He stood alone amidst his band	387 Corinth		308
Who cheer'd the band and waved the sword	388 Corinth		398
The foremost of these were the best of his band	389 Corinth		467
Hark to the Allah shout! a band	393 Corinth		819
The remnant of his gallant band	394 Corinth		909
The turban'd victors, the Christian band	395 Corinth		1017
A band of chiefs!--alas! how few	407 Mazeppa		45
And then he said: 'Of all our band	407 Mazeppa		97
Our dwindled band is now too few to strive	428 Island	3	160
The leader of the band he had undone	433 Island	4	272
And if I were but in a gown and band	448 Beppo		541
A band of brethren, valiant hearts and true	507 Faliero	1	512
To lead a band of--patriots: when I lay	523 Faliero	3	342
Of the brave, joyous, reckless, glorious band	525 Faliero	3	458
To join my band; let each be prompt to marshal	526 Faliero	3	515
To where my allotted band is under arms	526 Faliero	3	549
A band of iron rustics at our backs	533 Faliero	4	389
Secured a band of desperate men, supposed	716 Werner	5	231
A band of children, round a snow-white ram	805 Juan	3	249
Below her breast was fasten'd with a band	810 Juan	3	573

BANDAGE

From wounds whose only bandage might be chains	427 Island	3	78
But war on water. And that bandage, sire	577 Sardan	3	364
He should begin, and take the bandage from	710 Werner	4	389
One arm had on a bandage rather bloody	832 Juan	5	86
His bandage slipp'd down into a cravat	902 Juan	9	353

BANDAGES

Stood calling out for bandages and lint	920 Juan	11	111

BANDED

Pierced by the shaft of banded nations through	38 Harold	3	160
Who, of all the despots banded	187 Ode-B		28
With banded backs against the wall	393 Corinth		779

BANDIT

Of bandit warfare; each troop with its chief	685 Werner	2	128
A bandit of the woods, I could have borne it	692 Werner	2	618

BANDITTI

However, not to be so, but banditti	716 Werner	5	233

BANDITTI

Match'd with Bourbon's black banditti	736 Deformed	2	65

BANDS

The station'd bands, the never-vacant watch	12 Harold	1	536
To Oscar's nuptials throng the bands	102 Alva		95
When Edward bade his conquering bands advance	111 Examination		15
To mingling bands of fairy elves	118 Romance		22
In rival bands between the wickets run	124 Recoll		130
Thus join the bands, whom mutual wrong	316 Giaour		634
First of the bold Timariot bands	326 Abydos	1	203
That mingle there in well according bands	371 Lara	1	392
And the dusk Spahi's bands advance	385 Corinth		77
The bands are rank'd; the chosen van	386 Corinth		234
Had bread and bastinadoes, till some bands	452 Beppo		749
Lusatia's woods are tenanted by bands	676 Werner	1	338
He had join'd the black bands, who lay waste Lusatia	685 Werner	2	124
They say he is leagued with the 'black bands' who still	709 Werner	4	301
The black bands came over	732 Deformed	1	691
Of your brave bands of their own bold accord	733 Deformed	1	802
Where the praetorian bands take up the matter	926 Juan	11	482

BANE

And there hath been thy bane; there is a fire	41 Harold	3	371
And what was once his bliss appears his bane	100 Damaetas		14
That seat,--like seats, the bane of Freedom's realm	227 Answer-C		3
To Love, whose deadliest bane is human Art	334 Abydos	2	459
A seventh's thin muslin surely will be her bane	448 Beppo		526
A wife's dishonour was the bane of Troy	544 Faliero	5	438

BANISH

For that--would banish its repose	90 To M.S.G.-A		8
'Oh! banish care'--such ever be	164 Friend-B		1
Lull the lone heart, and 'banish care	164 Friend-B		6
It is not drain'd to banish care	168 Haunts		18
Can banish from the sky	218 I Saw		12
Howe'er our stifled tears we banish	402 Parisina		560
There are thoughts thou canst not banish	481 Manfred	1	205
They will not banish me again?--No--no	597 Foscari	1	133
Because he fears not death; and banish him	600 Foscari	1	289
For, as you know, the Spanish women banish	789 Juan	2	956
(The hypocrite!), will banish them like Marius	939 Juan	12	622
Or serious, are the topics I must banish	967 Juan	14	781
Of those sweet bitter thoughts which banish sleep	995 Juan	16	927

BANISH'D
(See also SELF-BANISH'D)

While Florence vainly begs her banish'd dead, and weeps	64 Harold	4	531
A hapless banish'd wretch to roam	111 Medea		36
Thy nights are banish'd from the realms of sleep	213 Lady Byron		19
If banish'd Romeo feign'd nor sigh nor tear	258 Hints		145
Both banish'd by the sovereign cordial 'Waltz	275 Waltz		146
Had banish'd all the beauty from her cheek	361 Corsair	3	427
In bitterness that banish'd all remorse	379 Lara	2	271
Was banish'd from each lip and ear	401 Parisina		506
Thy Tuscan Bard, the banish'd Ghibelline	459 Dante	2	34
Banish'd, and far upon their way. They live, then	570 Sardan	2	573
You banish'd from his palace and tore down	625 Foscari	5	324
The daughter of a banish'd man, who lives	694 Werner	2	733

BANISHMENT

Let it be aught but banishment	99 Young Lady		36
With the world's war and years and banishment	456 Dante	1	32
Florence dooms me but death or banishment	462 Dante	3	138
Their banishment will leave me still sound sleep	569 Sardan	2	497
James Foscari return to banishment	605 Foscari	2	269
And yet you see how, from their banishment	610 Foscari	3	150
As the first of his son's last banishment	615 Foscari	4	20
To share her beauty and her banishment	899 Juan	9	176

BANK

And from his further bank Aetolia's wolds espied	30 Harold	2	621
Buys land, and shrewdly trusts not to the Bank	260 Hints		246
(Then Phoebus first found credit in a bank	266 Hints		718
So rent may rise, bid bank and nation fall	306 Age		640
Its bank been soothed by Beauty's song	313 Giaour		313
The calm wave rippled to the bank	314 Giaour		375
His resting-place the bank that curbs the brook	374 Lara	1	549
Already they descry--is yon the bank	379 Lara	2	324
Heaved up the bank, and dash'd it from the shore	383 Lara	2	567
Up the repelling bank	412 Mazeppa		604
Upon his Turkish bank,--and never	415 Mazeppa		857
Against a bank, and spoke not, but he bled	427 Island	3	98
To root from out a bank a rock or two	470 Morgante		292
Howling and dripping on the bank, whilst I	701 Werner	3	381
To save the credit of their breaking bank	850 Juan	5	1230
Upon the Danube's left branch and left bank	868 Juan	7	66
Of Danube's bank took formidable charge	868 Juan	7	93
Along the leaguer'd wall and bristling bank	878 Juan	7	684

BANK

Which makes bank credit like a bank of vapour	930 Juan	12	32
Or paper turn'd to money by the Bank	951 Juan	13	637

BANKER

That's the Bard, the Beau, the Banker	196 Rogers		22
The banker--broker--baron--brethren, speed	307 Age		678
That in the lieu of drawing on his banker	911 Juan	10	242

BANKER'S

And Mrs. Rabbi, the rich banker's squaw	951 Juan	13	630

BANKLESS

Past my own dwelling, but that it is bankless	642 Cain	2	387

BANKRUPT

But one, repentant o'er a bankrupt state	271 Minerva		249
To aid these bankrupt tyrants in their need	307 Age		679

BANKRUPTCIES

Our trifling bankruptcies in the Gazette	446 Beppo		388

BANKRUPT'S

(As the bankrupt's profusion his ruin would hide	202 Avatar		54

BANKS
(See also FOG-BANKS)

Whilome upon his banks did legions throng	9 Harold	1	382
And woods along the banks are waving high	27 Harold	2	484
When, down the steep banks winding warily	27 Harold	4	490
When my Delhis come dashing in blood o'er the banks	31 Harold	2	687
Leap from Eurotas' banks, and call thee from the tomb	31 Harold	2	701
Till sparkling billows seem'd to light the banks they lave	32 Harold	2	764
Thus on the banks of thy majestic Rhine	42 Harold	3	409
Through banks whose beauty would endure for ever	42 Harold	3	444
A thousand battles have assail'd thy banks	43 Harold	3	451
Between the banks which bear the vine	43 Harold	3	499
But one thing want these banks of Rhine	44 Harold	3	514
Still sweeten more these banks of Rhine	44 Harold	3	535
Still springing o'er thy banks, though Empires near them fall	45 Harold	3	589
Along the banks where smiling Arno sweeps	62 Harold	4	430
Thy grassy banks whereon the milk-white steer	65 Harold	4	590
Where on Cam's sedgy banks supine they lie	112 Examination		51
narrow dwelling on the banks of Lubar	130 Calmar		69
Like a stream which burst its banks	187 Ode-B		46
Between their outworn banks of wither'd flowers	191 Fragment-C		4
To them thy banks were lovely as to all	192 Sonnet-C		5
Thou overflow'st thy banks, and not for aye	198 Po		14
Both tread thy banks, both wander on thy shore	198 Po		35
On Jordan's banks the Arab's camels stray	217 Jordan		1
On her green banks a greener wreath she wove	255 Bards		987
In vain shall Seine look up along his banks	300 Age		191
Thy predecessor on the banks of Pruth	304 Age		459
Shorn of her bishops, banks, and dividends	307 Age		648
Along the banks that bound her tide	315 Giaour		510
There's fearful news from Danube's banks	328 Abydos	1	457
Its banks are fringed with many a goodly tree	368 Lara	1	161
The banks of Po two greater still than he	462 Dante	3	107
On banks redeem'd from the rude ocean's ooze	517 Faliero	2	625
Or whiten with their bones the banks of Ganges	555 Sardan	1	276
Which fringe his banks: but whether they may be	566 Sardan	2	259
O'erfloods its banks, and hath destroy'd the bulwark	590 Sardan	5	194
To reach distinctly from its banks. Then fly	593 Sardan	5	390
Sprinkle the dusky groves and the green banks	637 Cain	2	124

BANN'D

Are bann'd, and barr'd--forbidden fare	402 Chillon		10
Yet, harsh and haughty, as he lay he bann'd	470 Morgante		277

BANNER

Yet, Freedom, yet thy banner, torn but flying	69 Harold	4	874
Strew'd beneath the advancing banner	187 Ode-B		62
The sword, the banner, and the field	206 Year		21
Radiant with glory, like a banner streaming	288 Vision		219
Beheld his banner flouting thy Madrid	300 Age		152
Where Cortes' and Pizarro's banner flew	302 Age		266
The waving banner, and the clapping door	370 Lara	1	261
'Tis Otho's banner, the pursuer's spear	379 Lara	2	327
There is not a banner in Moslem war	393 Corinth		834
Beneath the traitor Prince's banner met	459 Dante	2	93
Spread like a banner at the gate of heaven	460 Dante	3	10
Upon you! Ye blue waves, which bore my banner	548 Faliero	5	726
No sign yet hangs its banner in the air	662 Heaven		549
When first Bohemia raised her banner 'gainst	676 Werner	1	332
Where I have pitch'd my banner. Come then! raise her up	741 Deformed	2	399
Wax'd broad and waving, like a banner free	785 Juan	2	726
They found that he had fought beneath their banner	874 Juan	7	448

BANNER

Flung hovering graces o'er him like a banner	907 Juan	9	664
The constable, beneath a warrant's banner	988 Juan	16	543

BANNER'D

The banner'd pomp of war, the glittering files	272 Minerva		285
Our banner'd and escutcheon'd gallery, I	714 Werner	5	100

BANNERS

Where are those bloody banners which of yore	9 Harold	1	391
Banners on high, and battles pass'd below	42 Harold	3	420
But there no more his banners rise	102 Alva		35
And o'er his corse no banners wave	105 Alva		303
High crested banners wave thy walls within	120 Newstead-A		52
O'er Gael and Saxon mingling banners shine	182 Address-C		9
With banners glancing	200 Stanzas-B		40
That host with their banners at sunset were seen	222 Sennacherib		6
And the tents were all silent, the banners alone	222 Sennacherib		19
Hail, spirit-stirring Waltz!--beneath whose banners	273 Waltz		19
Bought also; and the torches, cloaks, and banners	286 Vision		71
Bowls on the board, and banners on the wall	366 Lara	1	6
The banners droop'd along their staves	387 Corinth		257
He look'd to the banners--each flag lay still	390 Corinth		527
And the flap of the banners that flit as they're borne	391 Corinth		685
Which fight beneath the banners of the wind	426 Island	3	24
Hallow'd her sheltering banners, which incessant	454 Venice-B		115
The red-cross banners where the first red Cross	462 Dante	3	128
Their flashing banners, folded still on high	661 Heaven		497
Our banners shall be glorious! Think of that	704 Werner	3	591
The banners, and the nobles, and the knights	713 Werner	5	17
Until I waved my banners from its height	740 Deformed	2	329
Were their reward for following Billy's banners	912 Juan	10	284

BANNIER

Your Bannier, and your Torstenson and Weimar	685 Werner	2	140

BANNOCKS

Turn beef to bannocks, cauliflowers to kail	248 Bards		525

BANQUET

There no forced banquet claims the sated guest	20 Harold	2	62
And banquet on a transient bliss	128 Lady-C		12
Then bring me wine, the banquet bring	166 Struggle		9
Belshazzar! from the banquet turn	185 Belshaz-A		1
Yet loathe the banquet which perforce	317 Giaour		761
Removed the banquet, and the last pilaff	347 Corsair	2	31
Nor show'd high relish for the banquet prest	348 Corsair	2	107
I taste nor bread nor banquet--save alone	349 Corsair	2	130
Well speeds alike the banquet and the ball	371 Lara	1	388
Than courtiers at a banquet would	407 Mazeppa		92
A banquet in the flesh it cover'd o'er	432 Island	4	172
And I can banquet like a beast of prey	437 Tasso		16
Of banquet, dance, and revel, are forgot	440 Tasso		238
The music, and the banquet, and the wine	528 Faliero	4	51
For an especial banquet; at the hour	551 Sardan	1	50
Name it. That thou this night forbear the banquet	556 Sardan	1	353
Forbear the banquet! Not for all the plotters	556 Sardan	1	355
In fit adornment for the evening banquet	559 Sardan	1	602
And you will join us at the banquet? Sire	569 Sardan	2	480
And rushes from the banquet to the battle	575 Sardan	3	223
In thy own chair--thy own place in the banquet	580 Sardan	4	102
A joyous banquet past. And this libation	594 Sardan	5	456
Expectant of the banquet. We will lay	714 Werner	5	69
Of red Bellona's banquet. 'Tis a scratch	738 Deformed	2	215
Lambro's reception at his people's banquet	806 Juan	3	287
Of this our banquet we must sometimes change	867 Juan	6	956
With evening came the banquet and the wine	954 Juan	13	849
'Twas a great banquet, such as Albion old	991 Juan	16	666

BANQUETED

At least they banqueted upon your gods	555 Sardan	1	317

BANQUETEERS

The banqueteers had dropp'd off one by one	981 Juan	16	59

BANQUETING

Thou shalt not pine where all are banqueting	348 Corsair	2	102

BANQUETS

Thy Holland's banquets shall each toil repay	248 Bards		519
Blest be the banquets spread at Holland House	249 Bards		544
For us, even banquets fond regret supply	338 Corsair	1	37
In castle halls, and social banquets, nurse not	707 Werner	4	221
Like skulls at Memphian banquets, to the mind	809 Juan	3	516
Long banquets and too many guests, although	992 Juan	16	730

BANQUET'S

Can see a smile, unless in some broad banquet's	558 Sardan	1	486

BANQUO'S

While thus Remembrance borrows Banquo's glass	170 Address-A		46

BANQUO'S
For fear, like Banquo's kings, they reach a score 448 Beppo   528
Each in their turn like Banquo's monarchs stalk   747 Juan   1   13
Like Banquo's offspring;--floating past me seems   909 Juan   10   142
The coteries, and, as in Banquo's glass   925 Juan   11   427

BANS
But love sans bans is both a sin and shame   931 Juan   12   119
On which, at the third asking of the bans   992 Juan   16   745

BAPTISM
With Nature's baptism,--'tis to him ye must   65 Harold   4   611
With blood even at their baptism. Prithee, peace 705 Werner   4   72
As red as Tiber now runs, for your baptism   740 Deformed   2   341

BAPTISMAL
Where the baptismal font baptized me God's   741 Deformed   2   364

BAPTIZE
Baptize yourself with zeal, since you repent   471 Morgante   359
Which Thetis had forgotten to baptize   726 Deformed   1   309
You shall baptize them. What! in holy water   729 Deformed   1   520
Baptize posterity, or future clay   932 Juan   12   140

BAPTIZED
(See also RE-BAPTIZED)
Baptized thine Image in its flood   201 Ode   3   78
And was baptized a Christian; and then show'd   468 Morgante   167
Hath baptized thee with a curse   481 Manfred   1   223
Where the baptismal font baptized me God's   741 Deformed   2   364
Baptized in molten gold, and swathed in dun   785 Juan   2   732
Thetis baptized her mortal son in Styx   817 Juan   4   31

BAR
(See also FIVE-BAR)
Of hasty growth and blight, and dull Oblivion bar   56 Harold   4   81
To the soft side of the heart, or wisely bar   70 Harold   4   908
Tully reposed from Rome; and where yon bar   81 Harold   4   1564
I drew the bar, and by the light   89 Anacreon-B   25
The Bar and read the 'Times   177 Devil's Dr   124
For many a bar, and many a feud   197 Duel   39
A fatal dream--for many a bar   205 To--B   9
Of the Bar, or the Gown, or the House   232 Murray-B   57
Nor roars reform for senate, church, and bar   263 Hints   500
All are not Erskines who mislead the bar   264 Hints   584
To Mecca's dome might bar my pilgrimage   349 Corsair   2   132
And flash'd the lightning by the latticed bar   359 Corsair   3   260
Since bar and bolt no more his steps preclude   361 Corsair   3   390
Stone, bar, moat, bridge, or barrier left   410 Mazeppa   396
They peep from out the blind, or o'er the bar   442 Beppo   118
I may not overleap the eternal bar   465 Dante   4   147
Ever some bar 'gainst our intents to bring   467 Morgante   82
'Tis only at the bar and in the dungeon   686 Werner   2   209
Was hapless in their nuptials, for some bar   802 Juan   3   76
A like gold bar above her instep roll'd   810 Juan   3   570
And epic, if plain truth should prove no bar   896 Juan   8   1101
It laughs not--there is now no fleshy bar   898 Juan   9   91
Have such a prescience, it should be no bar   899 Juan   9   190
No less a victim to the bolt and bar   916 Juan   10   540
When for a passport, or some other bar   923 Juan   11   325
Who bound the bar or senate in their spell   928 Juan   11   604
Yet inexperience could not be his bar   938 Juan   12   550
In senates, at the bar, in wordy feud   944 Juan   13   229
Who limits all his battles to the bar   951 Juan   13   666
Is, that whatever bar the reason rears   981 Juan   16   54

BARACAN
And the striped white gauze baracan that bound
    her   810 Juan   3   559
But a white baracan, and so transparent   811 Juan   3   610

BARB
That fiery barb so sternly rein'd   312 Giaour   258
I know him by his jet-black barb   316 Giaour   614
Is his heart more cold, or his barb less swift   317 Giaour   700
Bound where thou wilt, my barb! or glide, my prow 333 Abydos   2   394
But like a warrior bounding on his barb   349 Corsair   2   145
An Arab horse, a stately stag, a barb   774 Juan   2   41
She cannot step as does an Arab barb   939 Juan   12   593

BARBADOES
And honest men from Iceland to Barbadoes   909 Juan   10   101

BARBARIAN
Roll the barbarian tide, and sue to be forgiven   62 Harold   4   423
And up the steep barbarian monarchs ride   67 Harold   4   715
Hail'd a barbarian in her Caesar's place   93 Masters   4
Not the barbarian, with his mask of peace   302 Age   299
And the harsh sound of the barbarian drum   453 Venice-B   20
Round a barbarian Vice of Kings' Vicegerent   548 Faliero   5   762
If these barbarian Greeks of the far shores   554 Sardan   1   211
Forgive this monstrous love for a barbarian   574 Sardan   3   183
Still the world's masters! Civilised, barbarian   734 Deformed   1   848
Not a barbarian, but much worse than that   899 Juan   9   184

BARBARIANS
When less barbarians would have cheer'd him less   29 Harold   2   592
There were his young barbarians all at play   76 Harold   4   1265
But basely stole what less barbarians won   270 Minerva   112
By the old barbarians, there awaits the new   459 Dante   2   74
By fresh barbarians, on thy brow replaced   461 Dante   3   56
That he is hated of his own barbarians   561 Sardan   1   702

BARBARIAN'S
But only the barbarian's--we have both   419 Island   2   68

BARBARIC
From the dull yoke of her barbaric foes   59 Harold   4   268
Barbaric dwellings on their shatter'd site   61 Harold   4   398
The half barbaric Moscow's minarets   300 Age   169
Barbaric blood can reconcile us now   535 Faliero   4   495
Full of barbaric carving, paint, and gilding   790 Juan   2   1016

BARBARIGO'S
What voice is that?--'Tis Barbarigo's! Ah   596 Foscari   1   79

BARBARISM
Wealth, vice, corruption,--barbarism at last   71 Harold   4   967
Confess its barbarism when compared with thine   459 Dante   2   32

BARBARITY
Shows the soul from barbarity clear   115 The Tear   10
To me it seems the worst barbarity   608 Foscari   2   428

BARBARO
Barbaro. What was the cause? or the pretext   505 Faliero   1   378
This morning comes the noble Barbaro   505 Faliero   1   382
They'll do as much by Barbaro, no doubt   506 Faliero   1   432
No punishment for such as Barbaro   516 Faliero   2   537

BARBAROSSA
(Like Barbarossa to the Pope), to beg him   615 Foscari   4   34

BARBAROUS
Ere Greece and Grecian arts by barbarous hands
    were quell'd   19 Harold   1   953
Their barbarous, yet their not indecent, glee   30 Harold   2   644
In barbarous Latin doom'd to wrangle   95 Granta   44
Back to the barbarous realm from whence they
    sprung   302 Age   331
And the mournful sound of the barbarous horn   391 Corinth   684
With barbarous blows they gash the dead   395 Corinth   990
Were not each barbarous horde a nobler prey   460 Dante   2   107
For these are very barbarous and robust   469 Morgante   230
The savage Hun, and not less barbarous Frank   538 Faliero   5   13
He would tread down the barbarous crowds, and
    triumph   561 Sardan   1   707
Upon it barbarous. Sorrow preys upon   619 Foscari   4   251
Ungrateful, perjured, barbarous Don Alfonso   764 Juan   1   1167
A joint upon their barbarous spits they put on   793 Juan   2   1228
Of all the barbarous middle ages, that   929 Juan   12   1
Which is most barbarous is the middle age   929 Juan   12   2

BARBARY
A nobler breed. Match me in Barbary   729 Deformed   1   511

BARBED
And Allan's barbed arrow lay   104 Alva   279

BARBERS
No Sunday tankards foam, no barbers shave   250 Bards   635

BARBERS'
There barbers' blocks with periwigs in curl   921 Juan   11   173

BARBETTE
Case-mated one, and t'other 'a barbette   868 Juan   7   92

BARD
Than those whereof such things the bard relates   7 Harold   1   241
Historian, bard, philosopher, combined   51 Harold   3   989
And bids him thank the bard for freedom and his
    strains   57 Harold   4   144
Thy choral memory of the Bard divine   57 Harold   4   147
The Bard of Prose, creative spirit, he   63 Harold   4   498
Proscribed the bard whose name for evermore   63 Harold   4   508
Our little life, nor Bard prescribe his art   66 Harold   4   690
He was in sooth a genuine bard   92 Lady-A   13
Or had the bard at Christmas written   101 Lady-B   23
What minstrel gray, what hoary bard   105 Alva   305
Of Avon's bard remembering scarce the name   111 Examination   22
An infant bard at least may claim   118 Romance   55
Some loftier bard shall sing thy glorious name   125 Recoll   249
Fictions and dreams inspire the bard   132 L'Amitie   81
Which every bard has trod before   134 E. N. Long   92
Poor Little! sweet, melodious bard   137 Clare   43
The modest bard, like many a bard unknown   162 Orchomenus   5
Tread lightly--where the bard is laid   163 Blacket   7
That's the Bard, the Beau, the Banker   196 Rogers   22

BARD

A sweeter language and a luckier bard	199	Sonnet-D	9
And the bard in my bosom is dead	205	Blessington	10
For thee the bard up Pindus climbs	234	Strahan	3
Of prostituted muse and hireling bard	244	Bards	182
The work of each immortal bard appears	244	Bards	193
A bard may chant too often and too long	245	Bards	226
And, like his bard, confounded night with day	245	Bards	250
Conceive the bard the hero of the story	245	Bards	254
The bard who soars to elegise an ass	245	Bards	262
Oh, wonder-working Lewis! monk, or bard	245	Bards	265
Nor teach the Lusian bard to copy Moore	246	Bards	308
On dull devotion--Lo! the Sabbath bard	246	Bards	320
The bard sighs forth a gentle episode	246	Bards	358
If chance some bard, though once by dunces fear'd	246	Bards	365
Yet say! why should the bard at once resign	247	Bards	426
Have we no living bard of merit?--none	249	Bards	577
Truth! rouse some genuine bard, and guide his hand	251	Bards	687
No matter--when some bard in virtue strong	251	Bards	701
One common Lethe waits each hapless bard	252	Bards	749
Are there no sins for satire's bard to greet	253	Bards	823
Alone impels the modern bard to sing	253	Bards	852
Scotland! still proudly claim thy native bard	254	Bards	941
Thus many a bard describes in pompous strain	257	Hints	25
For you, young bard! whom luckless fate may lead	259	Hints	191
When such a word contents a British bard	262	Hints	416
And must the bard his glowing thoughts confine	262	Hints	417
To end at once:.--that bard for all is fit	264	Hints	543
(A limping leader, but a lofty bard	266	Hints	682
Should some rich bard (but such a monster now	267	Hints	759
But if (true Bard!) you scorn to condescend	267	Hints	789
For any bard to poison, hang, or drown	268	Hints	828
Thy bard forgot thy praises were his theme	277	Waltz	249
And my Lord Seventy-four, who protects our dear Bard	282	Blues 2	117
Now the bard, glad to get an audience, which	296	Vision	713
The bard Saint Peter pray'd to interpose	296	Vision	743
And now the bard could plead his own bad cause	296	Vision	759
A princess was no love-mate for a bard	438	Tasso	123
And hapless situation for a bard	446	Beppo	400
Thy Tuscan Bard, the banish'd Ghibelline	459	Dante 2	34
His spirit. Thus the Bard too near the throne	461	Dante 3	85
The Bard of Chivalry, will both consume	462	Dante 3	150
'What think'st thou?' said the bard; when I unbended	476	Francesca	15
And a Greek bard his minstrel, a Greek tomb	575	Sardan 3	226
Too much their modest bard by this omission	752	Juan 1	349
The bard I quote from does not sing amiss	757	Juan 1	701
For my part, I'm a moderate-minded bard	761	Juan 1	941
Still gentler purchaser! the bard--that's I	774	Juan 1	1762
A ball-room bard, a foolscap, hot-press darling	830	Juan 4	866
Had been call'd 'Jemmy,' after the great bard	869	Juan 7	146
For after years of travel by a bard in	917	Juan 10	603
Is heaven, and heaven is love:'--so sings the bard	931	Juan 12	98
There was the young bard Rackrhyme, who had newly	951	Juan 13	669
But be it as it may, a bard must meet	959	Juan 14	236
So much, the bard had really been prophetic	987	Juan 16	445

BARDS

(See also PSEUDO-BARDS)

Happier in this than mightiest bards have been	14	Harold 1	630
As moon-struck bard complain, by Love's sad archery	15	Harold 1	728
Which sages venerate and bards adore	34	Harold 2	862
Sophists, Bards, Statesmen, all unquiet things	41	Harold 3	382
The Bards of Hell and Chivalry: first rose	61	Harold 4	354
Let keener bards delight in satire's sting	123	Recoll	79
fall, raise the song of bards; and lay me by	130	Calmar	60
Lochlin. Join the song of bards above my	130	Calmar	85
be ours on high: the bards will mingle the	130	Calmar	95
bards raised the song	131	Calmar	188
Had bards as many realms as rhymes	159	Gulf	15
Ye Bards! to whom the Drama's Muse is dear	194	Monody	105
The Room's so full of wits and bards	231	Doctor	53
And others, neither bards nor wits	231	Doctor	55
Of all the twice ten thousand bards	233	Ballad-B	1
Our bards and censors are so much alike	243	Bards	92
When all to feebler bards resign their place	243	Bards	118
No dearth of bards can be complain'd of now	243	Bards	124
These are the bards to whom the muse must bow	244	Bards	186
Not so with us, though minor bards, content	244	Bards	199
Lords too are bards, such things at times befall	251	Bards	719
Though Crusca's bards no more our journals fill	252	Bards	759
And you, associate bards! who snatch'd to light	253	Bards	881
Shouldst leave to humbler bards ignoble lays	254	Bards	932
To crown the bards that haunt her classic grove	255	Bards	988
Oh! would thy bards but emulate thy fame	255	Bards	997
And urge thy bards to gain a name like thine	255	Bards	1010
'Tis not enough, ye bards, with all your art	258	Bards	137
Our enterprising bards pass nought untried	263	Hints	450
If all our bards, more patient of delay	263	Hints	457
Verse too was justice, and the bards of Greece	266	Hints	669

BARDS

Though this has happen'd to more bards than one	268	Hints	821
Of female wits, boy bards--in short, a fool	449	Beppo	584
Are bards; the kindled marble's bust may wear	463	Dante 4	25
And bards burn what they call their 'midnight taper	773	Juan 1	1742
Yet there will still be bards: though fame is smoke	830	Juan 4	841
Upon, in sheets white as what bards call 'driven	855	Juan 6	197
And heroes are but made for bards to sing	880	Juan 8	109
(I wish your bards would sing it rather better	896	Juan 9	24
Of bards and prosers, words are void of colour	960	Juan 14	320
Bards may sing what they please about Content	965	Juan 14	628
But speakers, bards, diplomatists, and dancers	993	Juan 16	827

BARD'S

The Sabine farm was till'd, the weary bard's delight	81	Harold 4	1566
Beyond the Bard's defeated art	229	Marble	6
To the bard's tomb, and not the warrior's column	829	Juan 4	828

BARDSHIP

And boys shall hunt your bardship up and down	263	Hints	478

BARE

From her bare bosom let me take my fill	25	Harold 2	327
And laid those proud roofs bare to Summer's rain	44	Harold 3	561
In bare and desolated bosoms: mute	58	Harold 4	183
With her unmantled neck, and bosom white and bare	77	Harold 4	1332
But his breast was bare, with the red wounds there	104	Alva	259
Houseless and homeless--bare both breast and limb	184	Julian	29
Shrunken and sinewless, and ghastly bare	219	Saul-B	10
Let Angiolini bare her breast of snow	250	Bards	628
Thy breast--if bare enough--requires no shield	273	Waltz	11
What nature made him at his birth, as bare	286	Vision	86
And left a channel bleak and bare	315	Giaour	559
To bare the sabre's edge before a slave	347	Corsair 2	19
Did Lara too his willing weapon bare	376	Lara 2	62
The rock unworn its base doth bare	388	Corinth	434
All the rest was shaven and bare	389	Corinth	470
Her rounded arm show'd white and bare	390	Corinth	553
Alp at their head; his right arm is bare	392	Corinth	705
Their leader's nervous arm is bare	393	Corinth	821
Alp is but known by the white arm bare	393	Corinth	830
But sheathed it ere the point was bare	397	Parisina	108
Kneeling on the bare cold ground	400	Parisina	399
And the headsman, with his bare arm ready	400	Parisina	401
Curl'd half down his neck so bare	400	Parisina	422
Who rears on its bare breast her callow brood	430	Island 4	17
And bare, at once, Captivity display'd	436	Tasso	11
Which shuns their reef so horrible and bare	458	Dante 1	141
Orlando had Cortana bare in hand	470	Morgante	273
On the bare ground, have I bow'd down my face	489	Manfred 2	408
The priest is robed, the scimitar is bare	545	Faliero	549
Leave bare your borough, Sir Intendant! True	686	Werner 2	223
The bare knife in your hand, and earth asleep	690	Werner 2	454
There is your sword; and when you bare it next	693	Werner 2	630
From glistening waves, and skies so hot and bare	787	Juan 2	822
But that part of the coast being shoal and bare	804	Juan 3	150
Are good manure for their more bare biography	814	Juan 3	844
That isle is now all desolate and bare	825	Juan 4	569
And bosoms, arms, and ankles glancing bare	861	Juan 6	572
Shorn of its best and loveliest, and left bare	889	Juan 8	702
Who painted their bare limbs, but not with gore	895	Juan 8	1088
Which shall lay bare her bosom to the sword	915	Juan 10	532
In lieu of a bare blade and brazen front	920	Juan 11	117

BARED

Would that breast were bared before thee	207	Fare Thee	5
Strike the bosom that's bared for thee now	218	Jephtha	4
His blade is bared,--in him there is an air	380	Lara 2	344
When, bared to meet the headsman's stroke	401	Parisina	474
No matter; I have bared my brow	412	Mazeppa	567
And cooks in motion with their clean arms bared	837	Juan 5	398

BARE-HEADED

He fights till now bare-headed, and by far	574	Sardan 3	202

BARES

Bares with its buried woes, till Pride awake	352	Corsair 2	356

BARGAIN

Add Conscience, too, this bargain is your own	227	Answer-C	6
Are idle; Israel says the bargain stands	306	Age	635
So that their bargain sounded like a battle	835	Juan 5	223
And when 'twas found straightway the bargain closed	845	Juan 5	900

BARGAINS

Bore off his bargains to a gilded boat	836	Juan 5	314

BARGAIN'S
The precious bargain's cheap--in faith, not I   247 Bards   392

BARGE
Who is no paviour, nor admits a barge   900 Juan   9   246
To be transmitted, like the Lord Mayor's barge 936 Juan   12   406

BARING
In baring to revive that lifeless breast   382 Lara   2   516
Jew Rothschild, and his fellow-Christian, Baring 930 Juan 12   40

BARITONE
'Our baritone I almost had forgot   327 Juan   4   705

BARK
(See also DOG-BARK)
'With thee, my bark, I'll swiftly go   6 Harold   1   190
It chanced that adverse winds once drove his bark 29 Harold 2   595
Whose bark drives on and on, and anchor'd ne'er
   shall be   46 Harold   3   670
The friend of Tully. As my bark did skim   61 Harold   4   390
The Earth to them was as a rolling bark   64 Harold   4   563
Built me a little bark of hope, once more   70 Harold   4   938
See still the little painted bark   89 To Emma   25
Yet Oscar's bark is seldom slow   102 Alva   108
The bark unfurls her snowy sail   156 Lady-F   2
Thy bark hath long been gone   158 Storm   38
The Bark--the Crew--the very Wreck is gone   184 Julian   11
But come--The bark that bears us hence shall find 185 Julian   50
Is it his bark which my dreary dreams discover 204 Hindoo   3
This arm would be thy bark, or breast thy bier 206 Love, Death   8
And my bark is on the sea   230 My Boat   2
Droops o'er the bales no bark may bear away   272 Minerva   268
The power to bark and bite, to toss and gore   303 Age   405
Whose bark in sheltering cove below   310 Giaour   38
My humble bark would gladly wait   313 Giaour   363
Thou, my Zuleika, share and bless my bark   333 Abydos   2   396
Time presses, floats my bark, and here   334 Abydos   2   479
Yes--she is ours--a home-returning bark   339 Corsair   1   87
The bark he views, and tell him we would greet 340 Corsair   1   135
Where is Gonsalvo?' 'In the anchor'd bark   340 Corsair   1   154
Yon bark hath hardly anchor'd in the bay   344 Corsair   1   413
He sees his bark, he notes how fair the wind   345 Corsair   1   519
Double the guard, and when Anselmo's bark   346 Corsair   1   565
Were these--my bark--my sword--my love--my God 354 Corsair   2   477
My bark is sunk or captive; but my love   354 Corsair   2   485
Last eve Anselmo's bark return'd, and yet   356 Corsair   3   71
And therefore came I, in my bark of war   361 Corsair   3   362
Our bark is tossing--'tis already day   362 Corsair   3   433
Their little bark her men of watch descry   362 Corsair   3   484
They were too busy to bark at him   389 Corinth   457
And the slight bark so laden and so frail   417 Island   1   132
No more he said; but urging to the bark   418 Island   1   165
These spurn their country with their rebel bark 418 Island   1   231
To bear the bark of others' happiness   421 Island   2   143
His bark was borne; the sport of wave and air   421 Island   2   174
Freights the frail bark and urges to the cove   429 Island   3   238
His wondering mates, amazed within their bark   432 Island   4   207
When I prepared my bark first to obey   466 Morgante   25
You think to doom to me. The bark is ready   533 Faliero   4   346
Upon the bark of some tall tree, which bears   608 Foscari   3   23
Their bark and branches--what were they? That
   which   641 Cain   2   347
'Tis sweet to hear the watch-dog's honest bark 762 Juan   1   977
Because the tackle of our shatter'd bark   786 Juan   2   755
Like Charon's bark of spectres, dull and pale   786 Juan   2   803
One bark blew up, a second near the works   871 Juan   7   239

BARKLESS
Wrecks of a single winter, barkless, branchless 482 Manfred 1   328

BARKS
That lagging barks may make their lazy way   22 Harold   2   175
Two mighty barks of the North, so pour the   131 Calmar   140
Barks of the North, so rise the chiefs of   131 Calmar   143
Winds gave our barks to Morven:--the   131 Calmar   187
The barks, like small birds through a lowering
   sky   429 Island   3   180
Gliding into the throng of barks which stud   509 Faliero   2   6
And may be cross'd by the accustom'd barks   590 Sardan   5   204
Thence launch the regal barks, once form'd for
   pleasure   591 Sardan   5   260
Barks mann'd with revellers in their best garbs 714 Werner   5   110

BARNAVE
Barnave, Brissot, Condorcet, Mirabeau   747 Juan   1   17

BARNS
Safe in their barns, these Sabine tillers sent 306 Age   618

BAROMETER
For parliament is our barometer   946 Juan   13   342

BARON
Not unavenged the raging baron yields   120 Newstead-A   65
The banker--broker--baron--brethren, speed   307 Age   678
I would dissuade you, baron, from this strife   469 Morgante   223
Orlando answer'd, 'Baron just and pious   471 Morgante   345
Oft, perfect baron! have I heard of you   472 Morgante   379
Travel for your rich count or full-blown baron 676 Werner   1   342
These old walls will be noisy soon. The baron   673 Werner   1   451
Tenfold. The baron is retired to rest   680 Werner   1   596
To accompany the intendant. Baron Stralenheim   681 Werner   1   645
And wealthy baron, and the unknown Werner   681 Werner   1   650
Absence, I'm sovereign; and the baron is   682 Werner   1   687
A baron pillaged in a prince's palace   683 Werner   2   2
The baron is determined not to lose   683 Werner   2   9
To fish the baron from the Oder. Not   683 Werner   2   29
The baron was asleep in the great chair   683 Werner   2   33
The baron would find means to silence him   684 Werner   2   88
Puzzle your baron to unravel. Why   684 Werner   2   103
The baron, and the Saxon stranger, who   685 Werner   2   145
There goes my noble, feudal, self-will'd baron 688 Werner   2   323
The baron has been robb'd, and upon me   691 Werner   2   518
In Germany. The baron shall decide   691 Werner   2   532
I accuse no man. Then you acquit me, baron   691 Werner   2   544
You, baron, I believe; but as the effect   693 Werner   2   628
Baron, I do beseech you! I must be   693 Werner   2   660
Of him who robb'd the baron. Are you sure   697 Werner   3   127
Of this same baron to make way for him   698 Werner   3   177
Where is the baron? Gone back to his chamber   699 Werner   3   282
For this fair orphan of the baron, and   706 Werner   4   139
Then grew between them. The late baron died   706 Werner   4   142
The baron lost in that last outrage neither   716 Werner   5   195
And spoke more of the baron than the monk   949 Juan   13   528

BARONESS
He is to espouse the gentle Baroness   705 Werner   4   65
The Baroness Ida lost in Countess Siegendorf   706 Werner   4   129
Without your echo? Pardon me, fair baroness   707 Werner   4   206

BARONET
From Sir George Beaumont, Baronet   235 Epilogue   18

BARONETS
Yea, baronets have ink'd the bloody hand   266 Hints   716
To muse-mad baronets or madder lords   266 Hints   730

BARONIAL
In their baronial feuds and single fields   42 Harold   3   433

BARONIES
Where baronies and orders both invite   307 Age   694

BARONS
Of the mail-cover'd Barons, who proudly to battle 86 Leaving NA   5
Steel barons, molten the next generation   949 Juan   13   537

BARON'S
Frankfort. Methinks the baron's own experience 631 Werner   1   607
The baron's chamber, that it can't be he   683 Werner   2   22
Which forms the baron's household's unimpeach'd 683 Werner   2   41
And for the baron's gold--if 'tis not found   684 Werner   2   73
Although I almost wish you had the baron's   696 Werner   3   61
The baron's coin, when he could thus convert   698 Werner   3   210
And to the baron's self hereafter--'tis   700 Werner   3   320
Ida of Stralenheim, the late baron's heiress   705 Werner   4   66
The object of the baron's hate and fears   719 Werner   5   417

BARONY
His barony or county to repel   678 Werner   1   435

BAROSSA
Bear witness, bright Barossa! thou canst tell   271 Minerva   231

BAROSSA'S
Not all the marvels of Barossa's fight   18 Harold   1   919

BAROUCHE
'Tis a new barouche, and an ancient peer   177 Devil's Dr   96
Barouche, which had the glory to display once   913 Juan   10   389

BARRACKS
All wrath in barracks, palaces, or cots   901 Juan   9   285

BARRACK'S
Or graven stone found in a barrack's station   813 Juan   3   806

BARR'D
Combined marauders, half-way, barr'd egress   29 Harold   2   615
Are bann'd, and barr'd--forbidden fare   402 Chillon   10
To my barr'd windows, and to bend   406 Chillon   329
The reason why our gate was barr'd to you   468 Morgante   175
Wisely they did to keep their portals barr'd   549 Faliero   5   823
Knowledge was barr'd as poison. But behold   640 Cain   2   307
And bounteous planter of barr'd Paradise   644 Cain   2   553
My father barr'd me from my father's house   674 Werner   1   158

BARR'D
Follow! They have barr'd the narrow passage up 739 Deformed 2 272

BARR'D-UP
As eagerly the barr'd-up bird will beat 37 Harold 3 132

BARREL
(See also GUN-BARREL)
Puns, and a prince within a barrel pent 249 Bards 562

BARRELS
(See also DOUBLE-BARRELS)
Sweet is old wine in bottles, ale in barrels 762 Juan 1 1005

BARREN
His mind as barren and his heart as hard 21 Harold 2 103
Childe Harold sail'd, and pass'd the barren spot 25 Harold 2 343
What from this barren being do we reap 69 Harold 4 829
Hills of Annesley! bleak and barren 95 Fragment-B 1
Yet here, amidst this barren isle 158 Florence 5
But who shall hear it? on that barren Sand 184 Julian 19
And barren as each valley 233 Ballad-B 38
A barren soil, where Nature's germs, confined 270 Minerva 133
Whose barren beach with frequent wrecks is paved 288 Vision 188
With clashing hosts, who strew'd the barren sand 300 Age 149
But shiver'd fragments on the barren ground 365 Corsair 3 677
Barren and cold, on which the wild waves break 484 Manfred 2 56
The barren sands which bear no shrubs to blast 493 Manfred 3 130
Left barren the great house of Foscari 599 Foscari 1 240
From fertile Italy, to barren islets 610 Foscari 3 161
A broken corse upon the barren Lido 617 Foscari 4 132
And blush at my own barren gratitude 685 Werner 2 152
An unknown barren beach for burial ground 788 Juan 2 872
Amidst the barren sand and rocks so rude 799 Juan 2 1580
They're barren, and not worth the pains to pull 953 Juan 13 758

BARRENNESS
Rooted in barrenness, where nought below 58 Harold 4 174
This barrenness of spirit, and to be 482 Manfred 1 287
And crush their blossoms into barrenness 527 Faliero 3 616
Were barrenness in Venice! Would my mother 618 Foscari 4 211

BARRIER
Ne barrier wall, ne river deep and wide 9 Harold 1 366
If the deep barrier be of earth or sea 192 Fragment-C 20
And form the barrier which Napoleon found 303 Age 361
Sleep on the surface of the barrier stream 379 Lara 2 323
Stone, bar, moat, bridge, or barrier left 410 Mazeppa 396
Thy own sweet will shall be the only barrier 551 Sardan 1 74
The barrier which that hesitating accent 558 Sardan 1 482
His dungeon barrier, like the lover's record 608 Foscari 3 22
When the great barrier of the deep is rent 660 Heaven 392
Has not God made a barrier between earth 665 Heaven 741
And gushing oceans every barrier rend 670 Heaven 1118
How he glares upon the barrier 735 Deformed 2 24
Slain, another climbs the barrier 736 Deformed 2 94

BARRIERS
From the dark barriers of that rugged clime 26 Harold 2 406

BARROW
Or Southey or Barrow 237 Keats 8
Is now a lone and nameless barrow 329 Abydos 2 49
Barrow, South, Tillotson, whom every week 795 Juan 2 1317

BARROWS
High barrows, without marble or a name 826 Juan 4 609

BARS
But Jealousy has fled: his bars, his bolts 17 Harold 1 801
The bars survive the captive they enthral 40 Harold 3 286
Nor bolts nor bars against their strength
    avail'd 124 Recoll 176
Then gaze upon it through thy dungeon bars 304 Age 431
This hour bestows, or ever bars escape 334 Abydos 2 463
Wash through the bars when winds were high 403 Chillon 120
Which nothing through its bars admits, save day 437 Tasso 13
My brain against these bars, as the sun flash'd 439 Tasso 210
And glorying as you tread the glowing bars 453 Venice-B 75
Seas, mountains, and the horizon's verge for
    bars 465 Dante 4 133
Except the occupiers of those bars 549 Faliero 5 806
Bars all access, and may do for some hours 694 Werner 2 696
Of air-balloons, and of the many bars 758 Juan 1 734

BARTER
Their game of lives, and barter breath for fame 11 Harold 1 469
What wretch with me would barter woe 172 Romaic-B 30
And pirates barter all that's left behind 272 Minerva 264
The yellow dust they try to barter with us 657 Heaven 192
For which Philosophy might barter Wisdom 710 Werner 4 376
Deformity should only barter with 726 Deformed 1 285

BARTERS
Dependence barters for her bitter bread 267 Hints 774
Lurk'd Christianity; which sometimes barters 874 Juan 7 454

BARTHOLOMEW
Of Saint Bartholomew, which makes his cowl 287 Vision 157
From Saint Bartholomew we have saved our skin 837 Juan 5 348

BASE
Her fellows flee--she checks their base career 13 Harold 1 578
See round thy giant base a brighter choir 14 Harold 1 649
The marble column's yet unshaken base 20 Harold 2 83
Nor from the base pursuit had turn'd aside 24 Harold 2 293
Beneath its base are heroes' ashes hid 44 Harold 3 539
At thy bathed base the bloody Caesar lie 68 Harold 4 778
And the base pageant last upon the scene 69 Harold 4 871
Thou nameless column with the buried base 71 Harold 4 983
Prison'd in marble; bubbling from the base 72 Harold 4 1042
Yet let us ponder boldly; 'tis a base 74 Harold 4 1135
When Pleasure blends no base alloy 141 Pignus 22
No more so base a thing be seen 153 Friend-A 74
Earth rock'd beneath thee to her base 188 On Star 15
Of failing Wisdom yields a base delight 193 Monody 60
If she ever gave birth to a being so base 203 Avatar 96
Save that there was no sea to lave its base 214 Dream 31
A mighty mixture of the great and base 244 Bards 170
Arthur's steep summit nodded to its base 248 Bards 474
Shall shake your tyrant empire to its base 271 Minerva 222
As the mere million's base unmummied clay 286 Vision 87
Which would have placed them upon the same base 291 Vision 387
Offended with such base low likenesses 291 Vision 431
Become as base a critic as e'er crawl'd 297 Vision 780
The rock unworn its base doth bare 388 Corinth 434
He sate him down at a pillar's base 389 Corinth 507
Albeit my birth and name be base 399 Parisina 282
Or statue from its base o'erthrown 400 Parisina 349
Not quite as men are base or good 414 Mazeppa 745
We'll make no running fight, for that were base 426 Island 2 517
Beneath a rock whose jutting base protrudes 426 Island 3 19
With nought but soundless waters for its base 430 Island 4 50
My spirit with her light; and to the base 456 Dante 1 12
A dome, its image, while the base expands 464 Dante 4 51
And quiver to his cavern'd base 479 Manfred 1 74
Left a base slur to pass from mouth to mouth 502 Faliero 1 189
But the base insult done your state and person 506 Faliero 1 439
Of all in seeming, but of all most base 506 Faliero 1 479
By sweet revenge on all that's base in Venice 508 Faliero 1 621
And kind, and art not fit for such base acts 531 Faliero 4 591
Than thou and thy base myrmidons,--live on 536 Faliero 4 591
Decreed as sentence! Base as was his crime 541 Faliero 5 238
Are spawn'd in courts by base intrigues, and
    baser 565 Sardan 2 207
Shall ever use that base word, with which men 604 Foscari 2 147
Touch it not, dungeon miscreants! your base
    office 618 Foscari 4 198
All these vain ceremonies are base insults 625 Foscari 5 276
With a meek brow, whose base humility 647 Cain 3 101
With a base heart so far subdued and tamed 660 Heaven 403
Except the base and blind 660 Heaven 410
Guilty of this base theft? No, no--I cannot 695 Werner 3 20
And one base sin hath done me less ill than 697 Werner 3 147
Base infamy; repentance must retrieve it 702 Werner 3 449
You! Base calumniator! I. 'Twill rest 717 Werner 5 303
Ere your very base be shaken 735 Deformed 2 12
Nor coin my self-love to so base a vice 745 Juan Ded 42
That flight was base and dastardly, and no man 756 Juan 1 611
Resting its bright base on the quivering blue 785 Juan 2 723
Like to a torrent which a mountain's base 792 Juan 2 1125
While weeds and ordure rankly round the base 829 Juan 4 824
Not reckoning him to be a 'base Bezonian 885 Juan 8 447
Power's base purveyors, who for pickings prowl 899 Juan 9 212
Which makes one drunk at once, without the base 905 Juan 9 534
Even with the very ore which makes them base 931 Juan 12 78
Yet could not speak or move; but, on its base 983 Juan 16 180

BASED
The rainbow, based on ocean, span the sky 761 Juan 1 976

BASELY
Is basely purchased, not with gold alone 227 Answer-C 5
But basely stole what less barbarians won 270 Minerva 112
And makes the many basely quail to one 349 Corsair 2 173
Of public places, where they basely brave 447 Beppo 469
I have not vilely found, or basely sought 458 Dante 1 177
Shall yield, and bloodlessly and basely yield 548 Faliero 5 744
Basely--Say, bravely. Somewhat of both, perhaps 567 Sardan 2 339

BASENESS
Which Flattery fool'd not, Baseness could not
    blind 208 Sketch 22
Time's lesson, of man's baseness or his own 424 Island 2 396
Of human baseness. Pardon is for men 544 Faliero 5 459

BASER
Worn, but unstooping to the baser crowd	42 Harold	3	416
Or raised the venal voice of baser prostitutes	72 Harold	4	1017
I sought it not by any baser lure	456 Dante	1	49
To baser passions. He bestow'd my hand	510 Faliero	2	98
And find none. To fall from him now were baser	561 Sardan	1	694
Are spawn'd in courts by base intrigues, and baser	565 Sardan	2	207
The baser sides of literature and life	909 Juan	10	106

BASEST
As you accuse. You hint the basest injury	692 Werner	2	601

BASHAW
They lived till some Bashaw was sent abroad	850 Juan	5	1212
'Tis true; the reason is, that the Bashaw	850 Juan	5	1215

BASHFULLY
All bashfully to struggle into light	860 Juan	6	528

BASHFULNESS
So sweet the blush of Bashfulness	326 Abydos	1	228

BASHKIR
To ploughshares, shave and wash thy Bashkir hordes	304 Age		467

BASIN
The musico is but a crack'd old basin	827 Juan	4	682

BASINS
Whose scatter'd streams from granite basins burst	340 Corsair	1	127
And sparkled into basins, where it spent	949 Juan	13	518

BASIS
Even upon such a basis hast thou built	213 Lady Byron		35
And form'd a basis of esteem, which ends	943 Juan	13	119
But a mere airy and fantastic basis	956 Juan	14	55

BASK
It is but in her summer's sun to bask	212 Augusta-C		83
In Plenty's sunshine Fortune's minions bask	250 Bards		654
To bask by the huge hearths of those old halls	483 Manfred	2	12
But bask beneath the clime which knows no winter	644 Cain	2	523
Had made him lately bask in his bride's beauty	863 Juan	6	728

BASK'D
I have bask'd in the beam of a dark rolling eye	155 Goblet		6
Is he not of the kind which bask'd beneath	642 Cain	2	400

BASKED
Childe Harold basked him in the noontide sun	4 Harold	1	28

BASKET
She drew out her provision from the basket	792 Juan	2	1152

BASKING
Who now are basking in their full-blown pride	971 Juan	15	179

BASQUINA
The basquina and the mantilla, they	789 Juan	2	959

BASS
The high wind made the treble, and as bass	778 Juan	2	268
And for the bass, the beast can only bellow	827 Juan	4	690

BASSO
Soprano, basso, even the contra-alto	444 Beppo		255

BASTARD
Of bastard Caesar, following him of old	68 Harold	4	803
The Bastard kept, like lions, his prey fast	239 Conquest		7
If you will breed this bastard of your brains	267 Hints		791
And well I know within that bastard land	270 Minerva		131
Believe him bastard of a brighter race	270 Minerva		168
I am no bastard in my soul	399 Parisina		296
I love the language, that soft bastard Latin	445 Beppo		345
Unto a bastard Attila, without	548 Faliero	5	745
They are childless, then? There is or was a bastard	694 Werner	2	735

BASTARDISED
And I an outcast, bastardised by practice	698 Werner	3	176

BASTARDS
Heroes and chiefs, the flower of Adam's bastards	735 Deformed	1	883

BASTARDY
Shall bear about their bastardy in triumph	548 Faliero	5	768
(It might be) bastardy on me, and on	720 Werner	5	449

BASTINADOES
Had bread and bastinadoes, till some bands	452 Beppo		749

BASTING
With Fox's lard was basting William Pitt	294 Vision		581

BASTION
Each step opposed a bastion to their wrath	434 Island	4	308
But a stone bastion, with a narrow gorge	868 Juan	7	89
Which rain'd from bastion, battery, parapet	882 Juan	8	290
Of the next bastion, fired away like devils	883 Juan	8	346
Only to draw them 'twixt two bastion corners	887 Juan	8	599
They took the bastion, which the Seraskier	888 Juan	8	631
Upon a taken bastion, where there lay	889 Juan	8	721
But the stone bastion still remains, wherein	890 Juan	8	778
But the stone bastion still kept up its fire	893 Juan	8	953
Himself or bastion, little matter'd now	893 Juan	8	970

BASTIONS
Bombs, drums, guns, bastions, batteries, bayonets, bullets	877 Juan	7	623

BASTION'S
Though he stood beneath the bastion's frown	389 Corinth		448

BAT
The Bat builds in his haram bower	313 Giaour		292
The flapping bat, the night song of the breeze	370 Lara	1	264

BATCH
What nation or what kingdom bore the batch	469 Morgante		187
Next of new knights, the fresh and glorious batch	904 Juan	9	519

BATCHES
Of 'elegant' et coetera, in fresh batches	936 Juan	12	423

BATE
Nor bate (abate) their hearers of an inch	953 Juan	13	780

BATH
A mirror and a bath for Beauty's youngest daughters	65 Harold	4	594
'Twas then she went as to the bath	314 Giaour		453
Reclined and feverish in the bath	331 Abydos	2	240
A bath, a breakfast, and the finest eyes	795 Juan	2	1362
Espoused two partners (milliners of Bath	814 Juan	3	840
Though once she was seen reading the 'Bath Guide	987 Juan	16	442

BATHED
At thy bathed base the bloody Caesar lie	68 Harold	4	773
What fruitless tears have bathed thy honour'd bier	85 Epitaph		2
And bathed his brow with airy balm	388 Corinth		361

BATHERS
Some pretty shell, is best for moderate bathers	898 Juan	9	144

BATHES
And bathes every wound with a Tear	115 The Tear		20

BATHING
Or, bathing, nursing, making love, and clothing	449 Beppo		568
And, bathing his chill temples, tried to soothe	788 Juan	2	901
Well--Juan, after bathing in the sea	796 Juan	2	1367
That bathing pass'd for nothing; Juan seem'd	796 Juan	2	1370

BATHOS
Where the Divers of Bathos lie drown'd in a heap	227 Moore-A		7

BATHOS'
Contempt, but from the bathos' vast abyss	815 Juan	3	892

BATHS
Deeming it midnight:--Temples, baths, or halls	71 Harold	4	960
Like Russians rushing from hot baths to snows	939 Juan	12	581

BATING
For, bating Covent Garden, I can hit on	440 Beppo		39

BATS
Where now the bats their wavering wings extend	120 Newstead-A		33
And bats in general insurrection, till	701 Werner	3	403

BATTALION
March'd with the brave battalion of Polouzki	888 Juan	8	608

BATTER
I sing them both, and am about to batter	868 Juan	7	60
To get at thee not batter down a wall	903 Juan	9	444
They say his system 'tis in vain to batter	918 Juan	11	3

BATTER'D
Foil'd by a woman's hand, before a batter'd wall	13 Harold	1	584
Fór behind those batter'd breaches	240 Suliotes		15
By the resistance of the chase they batter'd	883 Juan	8	296

BATTERIES
In all the planets, and hell's batteries	291 Vision		414

BATTERIES

Two batteries, cap-a-pie, as our St. George	868 Juan	7	91
The Russians, having built two batteries on	870 Juan	7	177
The Russian batteries were incomplete	870 Juan	7	201
In the new batteries erected there	870 Juan	7	214
Land batteries, work'd their guns with great precision	871 Juan	7	235
In the mean time, the batteries proceeded	872 Juan	7	302
New batteries were erected, and was held	873 Juan	7	401
Bombs, drums, guns, bastions, batteries, bayonets, bullets	877 Juan	7	623
Beyond the Russian batteries a few toises	879 Juan	8	50
The Turkish batteries thrash'd them like a flail	883 Juan	8	341
Their column, though the Turkish batteries thunder'd	887 Juan	8	593

BATTERING

To slay the Pagans who resisted, battering	875 Juan	7	511
Worn out with battering Ismail's stubborn wall	896 Juan	8	1110

BATTERS

Lie round the battery; but still it batters	890 Juan	8	783

BATTERY

Or where the battery, guarded well	385 Corinth		105
From battery to battlement	386 Corinth		162
To take a battery on the right; the others	880 Juan	8	114
Which rain'd from bastion, battery, parapet	882 Juan	8	290
Lie round the battery; but still it batters	890 Juan	8	783
He whose whole life has been assault and battery	897 Juan	9	35
Buzz round 'the Fortune' with their busy battery	933 Juan	12	255

BATTERY'S

Sustains aloft the battery's iron load	12 Harold	1	532

BATTISTA

Pedro, Battista, help me down below	776 Juan	2	156
Battista, though (a name call'd shortly Tita	781 Juan	2	447

BATTLE

Red Battle stamps his foot, and Nations feel the shock	10 Harold	1	422
The sabre is sheathed and the battle is o'er	30 Harold	2	664
Hail the bright clime of battle and of song	34 Harold	2	858
And such the storm of battle on this day	64 Harold	4	560
To battle with the ocean and the shocks	70 Harold	4	939
Of the mail-cover'd Barons, who proudly to battle	86 Leaving NA		5
But he raises the foe when in battle laid low	115 The Tear		19
Equal were their swords in battle; but fierce	129 Calmar		25
would share the spoils of battle with Calmar	131 Calmar		174
The battle, long he stood	162 War Song		34
He in the thickest battle died	201 Ode-C		43
I have won the great battle for thee	218 Jephtha		15
Some with the Watch to battle	233 Ballad-B		50
Then battle for freedom wherever you can	236 Freedom		7
Up to battle! Sons of Suli	240 Suliotes		1
But when the field is fought, the battle won	272 Minerva		297
Their brethren out to battle--why? for rent	306 Age		619
For Freedom's battle once begun	311 Giaour		123
Who falls in battle 'gainst a Giaour	317 Giaour		745
He died too in the battle broil	321 Giaour		1080
From where the battle roars, the billows chafe	339 Corsair	1	113
He had seen battle, he had brooded lone	361 Corsair	3	418
How the sounding battle goes	392 Corinth		757
All redly through the battle ride	399 Parisina		236
Because of the great battle in which fell	466 Morgante		44
You have seen blood in battle, shed it, both	527 Faliero	3	601
For if they should do battle, 'twill be more	536 Faliero	4	542
Seen me turn back from battle. No; I own thee	562 Sardan	2	76
Soldier goes not forth thus exposed to battle	573 Sardan	3	140
I follow. You! to battle? If it were so	573 Sardan	3	151
And rushes from the banquet to the battle	575 Sardan	3	223
They battle it beyond the wall, and not	588 Sardan	5	60
The fight goes. My best brother! And the battle	589 Sardan	5	132
Their boys who died in battle, is it written	602 Foscari	2	75
The universal heritage, to battle	607 Foscari	2	346
In battle: the rewards are equal. Now	620 Foscari	4	315
I battle it against him, as I battled	645 Cain	2	636
With the blood reeking from each battle plain	661 Heaven		477
Whose youth may better battle with them.--Hence	704 Werner	3	593
Upon the dawn of a world-winning battle	710 Werner	4	410
You said he died in his bed, not battle. He	712 Werner	4	507
Blood than came there in battle. It--or some	716 Werner	5	211
Be serious? On the eve of battle, no	734 Deformed	1	859
The fugitives, or battle with the desperate	737 Deformed	2	174
To make the Cretans bloodier in battle	793 Juan	2	1240
So that their bargain sounded like a battle	835 Juan	5	223
Proved death in battle equal to a pension	874 Juan	7	464
Like Roland's horn in Roncesvalles' battle	918 Juan	10	696
When man in battle or in quarrel tilts	936 Juan	12	445
A battle, wreck, or history of the heart	958 Juan	14	164

BATTLE-CHARGER

Some who on battle-charger prance	316 Giaour		607

BATTLED

Falling for France whose rights he battled to resume	44 Harold	3	544
And battled to avenge or die	385 Corinth		140
Would still have battled for that scanty crew	433 Island	4	248
Yet to the very last they battled well	434 Island	4	321
For I have battled with mine agony	437 Tasso		21
Never--till I have battled with this fiend	495 Manfred	3	330
I battle it against him, as I battled	645 Cain	2	636
Well done, old Babel! Ha! right nobly battled	739 Deformed	2	266
So long I've battled either more or less	956 Juan	14	91

BATTLE-DAY

Of these they had not deem'd: the battle-day	379 Lara	2	302

BATTLE-FIELD

Long mark the battle-field with hideous awe	18 Harold	1	907
The Battle-field, where Persia's victim horde	33 Harold	2	840
Or in an order for a battle-field	730 Deformed	1	546
Whose every battle-field is holy ground	878 Juan	8	35
To the true portrait of one battle-field	879 Juan	8	96

BATTLE-FIRE

Who would not brave the battle-fire, the wreck	339 Corsair	1	95

BATTLEMENT

And magic in the ruin'd battlement	74 Harold	4	1159
While yet may frown one battlement	319 Giaour		879
Thou, who wouldst see this battlement	324 Abydos	1	93
From battery to battlement	386 Corinth		162
Shines o'er its craggy battlement	388 Corinth		375
From Chillon's snow-white battlement	403 Chillon		111
And, save the scarce seen battlement	411 Mazeppa		432
A lofty battlement. And there! Not even	733 Deformed	1	769
From battlement to battlement. Then conquer	733 Deformed	1	780
His hand is on the battlement--he grasps it	737 Deformed	2	161

BATTLEMENTS
(See also GARDEN-BATTLEMENTS)

Stands when its wind-worn battlements are gone	40 Harold	3	285
And the bleak battlements shall bear no future blow	42 Harold	3	423
Beneath these battlements, within those walls	42 Harold	3	424
Standing with half its battlements alone	70 Harold	4	886
Through thy battlements, Newstead, the hollow winds whistle	86 Leaving NA		1
Their crackling battlements all cleft	410 Mazeppa		403
And battlements which guard his joyous hours	439 Tasso		237
A grove which springs through levell'd battlements	495 Manfred	3	284
The cherubim-defended battlements	629 Cain	1	90
Led you o'er Rome's eternal battlements	740 Deformed	2	332

BATTLE-PLAIN

The captive died upon the battle-plain	379 Lara	2	273

BATTLE-PLAINS

Of worms--on battle-plains or listed spot	76 Harold	4	1250

BATTLES

Banners on high, and battles pass'd below	42 Harold	3	420
A thousand battles have assail'd thy banks	43 Harold	3	451
In strife with the storm, when their battles were won	186 Napoleon		14
He had sung against all battles, and again	297 Vision		777
The battles of the monarchs of the wild	731 Deformed	1	621
For they remember battles, fires, and wrecks	777 Juan	2	244
The beef and battles both were owing to her	794 Juan	2	1248
Leave battles to the Turkish hordes	812 Juan	3	739
Of all our modern battles, I will bet	871 Juan	7	271
Battles to the command, Field-Marshal Souvaroff	872 Juan	7	312
Yet, in the end, except in Freedom's battles	878 Juan	8	31
To battles, sieges, and that kind of pleasure	881 Juan	8	191
The worst of tempests and the best of battles	941 Juan	12	699
Who limits all his battles to the bar	951 Juan	13	666
Who fought, and fight, in absence, too my battles	967 Juan	14	767

BATTLE'S

Enough of Battle's minions! let them play	11 Harold	1	468
Battle's magnificently-stern array	39 Harold	3	248
But fiery Nisus stems the battle's tide	110 Nisus		385
And the battle's wreck lay thickest	187 Ode-B		61
Or carried onward in the battle's van	300 Age		127
Was never seen in battle's van	326 Abydos	1	199
Knock'd at that heart unmoved by battle's yell	350 Corsair	2	201
And tempest's breath, and battle's rage	385 Corinth		47
Upon the slain when battle's o'er	411 Mazeppa		477
The death-cry drowning in the battle's roar	878 Juan	7	696
A field of battle's ghastly wilderness	892 Juan	8	894

BATTLE-WORD

Shall be the battle-word	219 Thy Days		14

115

BATTLING

Battling with nations, flying from the field	41 Harold	3	335
Far from his band, and battling with a host	351 Corsair	2	275
When battling on the parent soil	387 Corinth		305
Of sweet sensations, battling with the blood	453 Venice-B	•	31
Battling at Zara, did the hecatombs	519 Faliero	3	38
Which even the Phrygians felt when battling long	561 Sardan	1	705
And they continued battling hand to hand	769 Juan	1	1474
Warriors thereon were battling furiously	842 Juan	5	683

BAUBLE

Then throw the worthless bauble by	185 Belshaz-A		14
Adieu, my worthy nephew.--Hollow bauble	504 Faliero	1	288
That shining mockery, the ducal bauble	548 Faliero	5	702

BAUBLES

(For glittering baubles are not left to boys	127 Recoll		398
With which Aurora on those baubles look'd	974 Juan	15	418

BAWL

Still must I hear?--shall hoarse Fitzgerald bawl	241 Bards		1
And 'tis for an election that they bawl	293 Vision		534

BAWLERS

Her sale sent home some disappointed bawlers	831 Juan	4	909

BAWLING

They make a never intermitting bawling	451 Beppo		684

BAXTER

And Simeon kicks, where Baxter only 'shoves	262 Hints		382

BAY
(See also MIDNIGHT-BAY)

And winds are rude in Biscay's sleepless bay	6 Harold	1	199
Full in the centre stands the bull at bay	16 Harold	1	775
In yonder rippling bay, their naval host	26 Harold	2	399
His petty hope in some near port or bay	82 Harold	4	1619
The birds and beasts and famish'd men at bay	189 Darkness		49
Like a wild bay of breakers, melts away	211 Augusta-C		37
Cheer on the pack! the quarry stands at bay	256 Bards		1044
'Mid sullen calm, and silent bay	319 Giaour		967
The scatter'd lights that skirt the bay	329 Abydos	2	59
His band are plunging in the bay	335 Abydos	2	551
Already doubled is the cape--our bay	339 Corsair	1	89
To where their watch-tower beetles o'er the bay	340 Corsair	1	124
Yon bark hath hardly anchor'd in the bay	344 Corsair	1	413
And soon the night glass through the narrow bay	346 Corsair	1	595
In Coron's bay floats many a galley light	347 Corsair	2	1
What star--what sun is bursting on the bay	349 Corsair	2	136
The boats are darting o'er the curly bay	364 Corsair	3	559
Inured to hunters, he was found at bay	378 Lara	2	256
From Patra to Euboea's bay	386 Corinth		217
In many a winding creek and bay	388 Corinth		363
Calm or high, in main or bay	388 Corinth		432
Pick'd by the birds, on the sands of the bay	389 Corinth		478
Even unto Piraeus' bay	392 Corinth		766
And the foes, whom he singly kept at bay	393 Corinth		794
At bay, destroying many a foe	411 Mazeppa		506
Once more his eyes shall hail the welcome bay	418 Island	1	208
When summer's sun went down the coral bay	419 Island	2	2
'Belike,' said Ben, 'you might not from the bay	426 Island	2	506
She, as she caught the first glimpse o'er the bay	429 Island	3	218
They clear the breakers, dart along the bay	429 Island	3	226
In some bleak crag or deeply-hidden bay	433 Island	4	242
The shadow lessen'd as it clear'd the bay	435 Island	4	382
A thousand proas darted o'er the bay	435 Island	4	405
Of pirates landing in a neighbouring bay	452 Beppo		750
My spirit where it cannot turn at bay	672 Werner	1	63
You rather look like one would turn at bay	695 Werner	3	8
Bay deep-mouth'd welcome as we draw near home	762 Juan	1	978
A devil of a sea rolls in that bay	775 Juan	2	83
And the rest rubb'd their eyes and saw a bay	786 Juan	2	773
Materials as were cast up round the bay	790 Juan	2	1051
The silent ocean, and the starlight bay	798 Juan	2	1499
The very Botany Bay in moral geography	814 Juan	3	842

BAYARD

May serve instead: it did the same for Bayard	736 Deformed	2	139

BAY'D

Bay'd from afar complainingly	396 Corinth		1070
The watch-dog bay'd beyond the Tiber; and	495 Manfred	3	275

BAYES

To purge in spring--like Bayes--before I write	263 Hints		480

BAYETH

But the hound bayeth loudly	742 Deformed	3	34

BAYING

As little as the moon stops for the baying	868 Juan	7	53

BAY'NET

Now views the column-scattering bay'net jar	12 Harold	1	564

BAYONET

Thy limbs are bound, the bayonet at thy breast	416 Island	1	55
Close to thy throat the pointed bayonet laid	416 Island	1	72
These, with a bayonet, not so free from rust	425 Island	2	496
Was teaching his recruits to use the bayonet	873 Juan	7	408
And made them charge with bayonet these machines	873 Juan	7	419
The reeking bayonet and the flashing blade	887 Juan	8	547
Of the bright bayonet, and they all should hurry on	888 Juan	8	622
The bayonet pierces and the sabre cleaves	889 Juan	8	697

BAYONETS

Bombs, drums, guns, bastions, batteries, bayonets, bullets	877 Juan	7	623
And sixteen bayonets pierced the Seraskier	888 Juan	8	648
Of all the five, on bayonets met his lot	892 Juan	8	876
Unto the bayonets which had pierced his young	893 Juan	8	942

BAYONNE

Angiolin of Bayonne, and Oliver	467 Morgante		71

BAYS

To such resign the strife for fading bays	34 Harold	2	886
And as the ocean many bays will make	78 Harold	4	1407
To me no bays belong	132 L'Amitie		84
My own and others' bays I'm twining	227 Thurlow-A		11
Their bays are sere, their former laurels fade	244 Bards		176
Resign their hallow'd bays to Walter Scott	244 Bards		188
Then be it so; and may his withering bays	267 Hints		753
Your bays may hide the baldness of your brows	745 Juan	Ded	49

BAY'S

Nodding at midnight o'er the calm bay's breast	30 Harold	2	625

BE
(See also BE'T, CAN'T-BE, WOULD-BE)

That, sheening far, celestial seems to be	6 Harold	1	226
From crimes as numerous as her beadsmen be	15 Harold	1	717
Still, still pursues, where-e'er I be	17 Harold	1	859
Yet if, as holiest men have deem'd, there be	20 Harold	1	64
Blush, Caledonia, such thy son could be	21 Harold	2	95
When the fresh breeze is fair as breeze may be	22 Harold	2	147
What is my being? thou hast ceased to be	34 Harold	2	895
As the ground was before, thus let it be	37 Harold	3	150
What! shall reviving Thraldom again be	38 Harold	3	167
Away with these! true Wisdom's world will be	42 Harold	3	406
I know that they must wither'd be	44 Harold	3	518
Whose bark drives on and on, and anchor'd ne'er shall be	46 Harold	3	670
Nothing to loathe in nature, save to be	46 Harold	3	684
Reft of its carnal life, save what shall be	46 Harold	3	700
Kindled he was, and blasted; for to be	47 Harold	3	736
Thou wert not sent for slumber! let me be	49 Harold	3	870
To make these felt and feeling, well may be	50 Harold	3	898
Though I have found them not, that there may be	53 Harold	3	1060
Yet was I born where men are proud to be	56 Harold	4	69
Are honour'd by the nations--let it be	56 Harold	4	83
And is the loveliest, and must ever be	59 Harold	4	222
From clouds, but of all colours seems to be	59 Harold	4	239
Of a new world, than only thus to be	65 Harold	4	634
And Livy's pictured page!--but these shall be	67 Harold	4	735
With a deaf heart which never seem'd to be	68 Harold	4	815
Can tyrants but by tyrants conquer'd be	69 Harold	4	856
Even for thy tomb a garland let it be	72 Harold	4	1024
The naked eye, thy form, as it should be	73 Harold	4	1085
Whose root is earth, whose leaves and branches be	74 Harold	4	1130
Forsook his former city, what could be	78 Harold	4	1382
Peasants bring forth in safety.--Can it be	80 Harold	4	1513
And he and I must part--so let it be	81 Harold	4	1568
Of youthful sports was on thy breast to be	82 Harold	4	1649
Equal to Jove that youth must be	87 Ad Lesbiam		1
Nor then my soul should sated be	88 To Ellen		5
Mine, my beloved, thou ne'er shalt be	90 To M.S.G.-A		20
Than all the living forms could be	98 To Mary		19
When humbled in the dust, let some one be	106 Nisus		65
The hour when man must cease to be	135 I Would		20
Be still as you were wont to be	138 Clare		94
As thy soul shall immortally be	151 Soul-A		6
May its verdure like emeralds be	151 Soul-A		10
Since it will ne'er forgotten be	152 Time	1	2
Whate'er thou art or e'er shalt be	152 Time	1	23
And thou and I shall cease to be	152 Remind		6
Nor be what all in turn must be	153 Friend-A		44
And who that dear loved one may be	156 Lady-F		49
Nor be, what man should ever be	158 Florence		27
That glorious city still shall be	158 Florence		38
Though Fate forbids such things to be	159 Gulf		17
'Oh! banish care'--such ever be	164 Friend-B		1
Though cold as e'en the dead can be	166 Struggle		47
'Tis something better not to be	167 Euthanasia		36
Ill-fated Heart! and can it be	168 Cornelian-B		1

BE

And bids the Drama be where she hath been	169	Address-A		24
But live--until I cease to be	173	Origin		8
Let deep and dreary silence be	174	Revanche		7
And every drop of grief shall be	174	Revanche		15
Though long and mournful must it be	174	Remember-B		45
Whate'er my secret thoughts may be	179	Gold		34
All quell'd--Dark Spirit! what must be	180	Ode-A		35
This soul, in its bitterest blackness, shall be	182	Music-A		14
Lost to our eyes the present forms shall be	183	Address-D		29
Thy life, thy fall, thy fame shall be	184	Parker		22
Deep for the dead the grief must be	184	Parker		35
Thou gazest in mute wonder--more may be	185	Julian		48
As springs in deserts found seem sweet, all brackish though they be	186	Music-B		19
And soon, oh Goddess! may we be	189	On Star		41
The gardener of that ground, why it might be	190	Churchill		8
Since thus divided--equal must it be	192	Fragment-C		19
Though thy beard so hoary be	195	Ballad-A		72
What if thy deep and ample stream should be	198	Po		5
I had not left my clime, nor should I be	199	Po		46
To make thyself beloved? and to be	199	Sonnet-E		10
Where should the happy Lover be	201	Ode-C		40
What still a dream must be	205	To-B		8
But there thou wert--and still wouldst be	210	Augusta-A		30
She was my early friend, and now shall be	212	Augusta-C		87
I had been better than I now can be	212	Augusta-C		94
Methought that joy and health alone could be	213	Lady Byron		3
A marvel and a secret--Be it so	216	Dream		201
And where our fathers' ashes be	217	Gazelle		21
Within our veins its currents be	219	Thy Days		11
Such are mine; and such shall be	219	Saul-B		19
Its glance dilate o'er all to be	220	Clay		22
Were my bosom as false as thou deem'st it to be	221	False		1
And scatter'd and scorn'd as thy people may be	221	Jerusalem		19
Was once our only Hope to be	223	Music-D		6
As dead as her dead leaf those mute harps must be	223	Valley		10
But now I fear her trip will be a	225	Embargo		5
In short, your tragedy would be	231	Doctor		15
For who e'er would be	239	Bray		23
Not seek great Jeffrey's, yet like him will be	242	Bards		61
Be warm, but pure; be amorous, but be chaste	246	Bards		306
Then if your verse is what all verse should be	266	Hints		687
That spot where hearts were once supposed to be	276	Waltz		191
History was ever stain'd as his will be	290	Vision		357
Being clay myself. Let not those spirits be	291	Vision		430
I don't see wherefore letters should not be	295	Vision		641
At least a quarter it can hardly be	295	Vision		695
But that indeed was hopeless as can be	296	Vision		751
The little that he was and sought to be	299	Age		92
How should the autocrat of bondage be	302	Age		300
Shrine of the mighty! can it be	311	Giaour		106
Howe'er deserved her doom might be	320	Giaour		1066
Know--for the fault, if fault there be	324	Abydos	1	55
'What, sullen yet? it must not be	326	Abydos	1	277
Perchance I am, at least shall be	327	Abydos	1	368
She dream'd what Paradise might be	330	Abydos	2	105
Far better with the dead to be	330	Abydos	2	176
But harsher still my tale must be	332	Abydos	2	304
The deepest murmur of this lip shall be	334	Abydos	2	456
Such hath it been--shall be--beneath the sun	341	Corsair	1	187
Is this--'tis nothing--nothing e'er can be	354	Corsair	2	492
To meet his passion--but it would not be	354	Corsair	2	501
Art thou not he? whose deeds--' 'Whate'er I be	372	Lara	1	455
To him had Venice ceased to be	385	Corinth		129
Secure in paradise to be	387	Corinth		300
More wakeful than the humblest be	388	Corinth		351
O'er that which hath been, and o'er that which must be	389	Corinth		503
But it was unrippled as glass may be	390	Corinth		524
What Venice made me, I must be	391	Corinth		671
None of my pure race shall be	394	Corinth		863
Her son, thy rival, soon shall be	399	Parisina		247
As they of yore were wont to be	403	Chillon		66
To hoard my life, that his might be	404	Chillon		170
I sometimes deem'd that it might be	405	Chillon		287
And the whole earth would henceforth be	405	Chillon		322
Fetter'd or fetterless to be	406	Chillon		373
Or at this hour I should not be	408	Mazeppa		199
It was enough for me to be	409	Mazeppa		259
And he had reason good to be	410	Mazeppa		344
No vision it could be	410	Mazeppa		814
The silence, till my strength should be	415	Mazeppa		823
What! could you make her out? It cannot be	426	Island	2	504
For me, my lot is what I sought; to be	428	Island	3	163
But thou art dearest still, and I should be	438	Tasso		142
And then I lost my being all to be	439	Tasso		171
By grief, years, weariness--and it may be	439	Tasso		232
As partings often are, or ought to be	443	Beppo		218
Are level with the waters, there shall be	452	Venice-B		2
The everlasting to be which hath been	453	Venice-B		59
Three paces and then faltering:--better be	455	Venice-B		154
On Arno, till he perches, it may be	458	Dante	1	170
Forth from the abyss of time which is to be	458	Dante	2	5

BE

Oh! more than these illustrious far shall be	461	Dante	3	52
Storm be still scatter'd? Yes, and it must be	462	Dante	3	167
Of thinking, and without him nought could be	466	Morgante		4
And I a Christian am disposed to be	471	Morgante		344
Orlando with Morgante reason'd: 'Be	472	Morgante		386
Ashes to ashes,--merry let us be	472	Morgante		422
Orlando said, 'I really think you'll be	474	Morgante		555
That wheresoe'er you go I too shall be	475	Morgante		631
What must he be you cannot love when known	634	Cain	1	421
Thou canst not tell,--and never be	655	Heaven		47
The little shells of ocean's least things be	662	Heaven		505
But ignorance must ever be	666	Heaven		803
My pangs can be but brief; but thine would be	667	Heaven		926
Such would it be	668	Heaven		958
May now return with me. It may not be	668	Heaven		982
His blood less noble than such blood should be	754	Juan	1	451
Caress'd him often--such a thing might be	755	Juan	1	546
A moment at the door, that we may be	766	Juan	1	1247
My poem's epic, and is meant to be	771	Juan	1	1593
But that's impossible, and cannot be	776	Juan	2	146
'Give us more grog,' they cried, 'for it will be	778	Juan	2	281
That made his eyelids as a woman's be	779	Juan	2	342
If any laughter at such times could be	780	Juan	2	396
And if Pedrillo's fate should shocking be	784	Juan	2	657
And all within its arch appear'd to be	785	Juan	2	724
Her hair had silver only, bound to be	789	Juan	2	972
And that a shipwreck'd youth would hungry be	792	Juan	2	1154
By a distant organ, doubting if he be	793	Juan	2	1210
But dreams of what has been, no more to be	795	Juan	2	1328
Though foe to love; and yet they could not be	817	Juan	4	62
They were alone once more; for them to be	817	Juan	4	73
'If it should be so,--but--it cannot be	819	Juan	4	183
Strange state of being! (for 'tis still to be	820	Juan	4	239
The ocean-buried, risen from death, to be	821	Juan	4	284
Thy garment's hem with transport, can it be	821	Juan	4	302
The tumulus--of whom? Heaven knows! 't may be	826	Juan	4	606
Ah! must I then the only minstrel be	830	Juan	4	863
Where I beheld what never was to be	831	Juan	5	28
Whate'er thy power, and great it seems to be	847	Juan	5	1014
A throne, the world, the universe, to be	853	Juan	6	19
They wonder'd how Gulbeyaz, too, could be	857	Juan	6	285
(To save description), fair as fair can be	857	Juan	6	316
And then I have the worst dreams that can be	858	Juan	6	381
What are we? and whence came we? what shall be	860	Juan	6	502
Certainly aged--what her years might be	861	Juan	6	547
Their roar even with the Baltic's--so you be	864	Juan	6	743
Summers could renovate, though they should be	872	Juan	7	326
Will join your former regiment, which should be	875	Juan	7	522
The servile and the vain, such names will be	878	Juan	8	39
His cap and head, which proves the head to be	879	Juan	8	75
So Cowper says--and I begin to be	885	Juan	8	475
Said Juan: 'Whatsoever is to be	891	Juan	8	793
And thus your houri (it may be) disputes	892	Juan	8	903
And those that sate upon them, let it be	895	Juan	8	1090
You please (it causes all the things which be	903	Juan	9	451
His youth was not the chastest that might be	914	Juan	10	430
But Juan, season'd, as he well might be	915	Juan	10	510
With 'To be let' upon their doors proclaim'd	921	Juan	11	166
To turn out both, or either, it may be	925	Juan	11	460
He deems it is his proper place to be	927	Juan	11	549
Be hypocritical, be cautious, be	929	Juan	11	679
What Juan saw and underwent shall be	929	Juan	11	689
In this twelfth Canto 'tis my wish to be	932	Juan	12	155
But of such friendship as man's may to man be	967	Juan	14	735
She was as capable as woman can be	967	Juan	14	736
Whatever follows ne'ertheless may be	968	Juan	15	2
With a slight shade of blue too, it might be	973	Juan	15	325
Was Nature's all: Aurora could not be	975	Juan	15	462
A proud humility, if such there be	978	Juan	15	650
Had it not happen'd scalding hot to be	984	Juan	16	236
Who, though they prove not two and two to be	993	Juan	16	834

BEACH

Shall leave on the beach the long galley and oar	30	Harold	2	667
Whose barren beach with frequent wrecks is paved	288	Vision		188
The beach where shelving to the deep	335	Abydos	2	594
When hand grasps hand uniting on the beach	339	Corsair	1	104
The verge where ends the cliff, begins the beach	346	Corsair	1	534
The glad waves dancing on the yellow beach	362	Corsair	3	447
Strives through the surge, bestrides the beach, and high	364	Corsair	3	579
Or stretch'd on the beach, or our saddles spread	384	Corinth		12
The turban'd cohorts throng the beach	385	Corinth		80
He wander'd on, along the beach	389	Corinth		440
The beach which lay before him, high and dry	787	Juan	2	844
Roll'd on the beach, half-senseless, from the sea	787	Juan	2	856
An unknown barren beach for burial ground	788	Juan	2	872
And walking out upon the beach, below	790	Juan	2	1025
Drooping and dewy on the beach he lay	796	Juan	2	1406
And the small ripple split upon the beach	796	Juan	2	1417
They fear'd no eyes nor ears on that lone beach	798	Juan	2	1505
As on the beach the waves at last are broke	830	Juan	4	845

BEACON

Theme of the young, and beacon of the wise	25 Harold	2	335
Till then--no beacon on the cliff	329 Abydos	2	57
Still would I rise to rouse the beacon fire	343 Corsair	1	377
Sinks with its beam upon the beacon height	356 Corsair	3	67
'Tis now the beacon of thy safety--now	360 Corsair	3	354
The lights are high on beacon and from bower	364 Corsair	3	567
A beacon which had cheer'd ten thousand nights	428 Island	3	108
A beacon in the horizon for a day	594 Sardan	5	439
A point of time, as beacon to my heart	616 Foscari	4	103
No more to be the beacon of the world	659 Heaven		295

BEACON'D

| The fogs of London, through which, dimly beacon'd | 291 Vision | | 438 |

BEACONS

Where yonder beacons half-expiring beam	106 Nisus		101
Were burnt for beacons; cities were consumed	189 Darkness		13
Eternal beacons of consummate crime	253 Bards		828
The beacons blaze their wonted stations round	363 Corsair	3	558
The beacons of surrounding foes	407 Mazeppa		29
To keep our holy beacons always bright	979 Juan	15	716

BEACON-TOWER

| The Owl usurps the beacon-tower | 313 Giaour | | 294 |

BEAD

| And proffer'd to his touch the holy bead | 382 Lara | 2 | 478 |

BEADS

Who worship, here are altars for their beads	77 Harold	4	1321
Or counts her beads with fairy hand	160 Cadiz		45
A strict accountant of his beads	181 Ode-A		68
'Mid counted beads, and countless prayer	320 Giaour		972
Are thrown the fragrant beads of amber	329 Abydos	2	65
His only bends in seeming o'er his beads	357 Corsair	3	139
Some were those who counted beads	384 Corinth		19
His beads and sins are all recounted	401 Parisina		432
A Turk, with beads in hand and pipe in mouth	826 Juan	4	622
Saint from his beads to join the jocund race	951 Juan	13	620
In cowl and beads and dusky garb, appear'd	983 Juan	16	162

BEADSMEN

| From crimes as numerous as her beadsmen be | 15 Harold | 1 | 717 |

BEAK

Here roams the wolf, the eagle whets his beak	25 Harold	2	376
His breast and beak against his wiry dome	37 Harold	3	133
How did thy numbing beak and silent fang	300 Age		189
Proud Wellington, with eagle beak so curl'd	305 Age		534
Where vultures whet the thirsty beak	315 Giaour		554
Whose beak unlocks her bosom's stream	319 Giaour		952
Greets like the welcome of his tuneless beak	364 Corsair	3	562
Their smoke assail'd his startled beak	396 Corinth		1077
So cold and stark the raven's beak	411 Mazeppa		480
Whose whetted beak and far-pervading eye	423 Island	2	310
Then swoops with his unerring beak.--Thou day	535 Faliero	4	487
The eagle's beak between those eyes which ne'er	725 Deformed	1	186
There's nothing whets the beak, or arms the claw	848 Juan	5	1059

BEAKERS

| My mild and midnight beakers to the brim | 823 Juan | 4 | 423 |

BEAKS

| O'er which their hungry beaks delay | 335 Abydos | 2 | 604 |

BEAM
(See also DAY-BEAM, MOON-BEAM, NIGHT-BEAM, STAR-BEAM)

He look'd and met its beam without a thought	24 Harold	2	272
With thy unquenched beam, lost Liberty	31 Harold	2	714
Still in his beam Mendeli's marbles glare	33 Harold	2	826
Where not a beam nor air nor leaf is lost	49 Harold	3	839
That ever left the sky on the deep soul to beam	63 Harold	4	477
The beam pours in, for time and skill will couch the blind	74 Harold	4	1143
Give me the mild beam of the soul-breathing glance	92 First Kiss		3
More dear is the beam of the past to my soul	97 Harrow-A		32
Howe'er those orbs may wildly beam	97 To M--		6
A beam from under hazel brows	97 To Woman		16
But where's the beam so sweetly straying	98 To Mary		14
Where yonder beacons half-expiring beam	106 Nisus		101
With honour's soul, united beam in thee	126 Recoll		300
In Morven dwelt the chief, a beam of	129 Calmar		16
me a silver beam of night. Bear my sword	131 Calmar		178
Truth!--wherefore did thy hated beam	135 I Would		23
But thy bright beam unchanged for ever glows	139 Ossian-A		16
No more beam the eyes which my dream could inspire	148 Farewell-A		11
May wake the beam that lurks below	150 Song-A		16
For eyes that ne'er like thine could beam	152 Remind		29
I have bask'd in the beam of a dark rolling eye	155 Goblet		6
Then turn'd from earth its tender beam	166 Away		28
That beam hath sunk, and now thou art	172 Time-B		29
A night, with every star, save Dian's beam	183 Address-D		28

BEAM

Star of the brave!--whose beam hath shed	188 On Star		1
The beam of Song, the blaze of Eloquence	193 Monody		28
To mourn the vanish'd beam and add our mite	194 Monody		99
Whose tearful beam glows tremulously far	220 Sleepless		2
Had reflected the last beam of day as it blazed	221 Jerusalem		10
But I mark'd not the twilight beam melting away	221 Jerusalem		14
O'er the hush'd deep the yellow beam he throws	268 Minerva		5
On such an eve his palest beam he cast	268 Minerva		19
The farewell beam of Feeling past away	311 Giaour		100
Bestirr'd it more,--'twas but the beam	314 Giaour		378
Has shrunk before the summer beam	315 Giaour		558
That quench'd, what beam shall break my night	321 Giaour		1146
No warrior chides her peaceful beam	329 Abydos	2	42
The evening beam that smiles the clouds away	333 Abydos	2	400
Hope of thine age, thy twilight's lonely beam	336 Abydos	2	659
Nor woos the summer beam	336 Abydos	2	688
O'er the hush'd deep the yellow beam he throws	355 Corsair	3	5
On such an eve his palest beam he cast	355 Corsair	3	19
Sinks with its beam upon the beacon height	356 Corsair	3	67
The stars are studding, each with imaged beam	368 Lara	1	156
Pale as the beam that o'er his features play'd	369 Lara	1	212
Flowers in the valley, splendour in the beam	375 Lara	2	7
Already they perceive its tranquil beam	379 Lara	2	322
Which runs all redly till the morning beam	380 Lara	2	367
But brighter still the beam was thrown	400 Parisina		423
Which seem'd to melt to its own beam	409 Mazeppa		215
And went and came with wandering beam	414 Mazeppa		786
Chipp'd by the beam, a nursling of the day	430 Island	4	23
My latest look: thou wilt not beam on one	494 Manfred	3	198
A beam of hope athwart the future years	562 Sardan	2	21
Her cheek all purple with the beam of youth	754 Juan	1	484
Laid with one blast the ship on her beam ends	777 Juan	2	240
Upon his senses, and the kindling beam	793 Juan	2	1221
A spectral resident--whose pallid beam	921 Juan	11	190
While the mild emerald's beam shades down the dies	930 Juan	12	63
Which flow'd on for a moment in the beam	975 Juan	15	437

BEAM'D

To paint those charms which varied as they beam'd	3 To Ianthe		7
At Cleopatra's feet,--and now himself he beam'd	68 Harold	4	810
Like stars to shepherds' eyes:--'twas but a meteor beam'd	80 Harold	4	1530
That clay, where once such animation beam'd	84 Death-B		6
Alas! that eyes which beam'd with love	105 Alva		295
But Soul beam'd forth in every spark	315 Giaour		477

BEAMING

Still beaming through the lover's strain	128 Answer-B		22
Victory beaming from her breast	188 Ode-B		66
And from the gate thrown open issued beaming	288 Vision		217

BEAMS
(See also MOONBEAMS)

As their own beams; and earth, and earth-born jars	37 Harold	3	120
Its brilliant hues with all their beams unshorn	66 Harold	4	646
And your eye beams a ray which can never deceive	91 Caroline-C		4
Life beams not for us with one ray that can cheer	92 Caroline-D		18
Your eye for conquest beams prepared	98 To Lesbia		31
Still in truant beams they play	100 Marion		20
His dark eye shone through beams of truth	102 Alva		66
Queen of the sky, whose beams are seen afar	110 Nisus		342
Soon a new morn's restoring beams dispel	121 Newstead-A		101
Gilds with faint beams the crystal dews of rain	122 Recoll		19
No more with Hope the future beams	128 Remembrance		2
His beams alike to all displays	134 E. N. Long		72
Whence are the beams, O Sun! thy endless blaze	139 Ossian-A		3
Her sinking beams beneath the Western wave	139 Ossian-A		8
Now hateful are thy beams which wake no more	140 Ossian-A		39
Whence are thy beams? From what eternal store	140 Ossian-B		3
Bright beams the rising Sun of Fame	142 Critics		92
From it such Beams of Beauty fall	143 On Eyes		2
Full beams the moon on Actium's coast	159 Gulf		2
Thy parting glance, which fondly beams	163 Parting		5
'When in your fostering beams you bid us live	171 Address-B		55
And bright around, with quivering beams beset	269 Minerva		39
Behold where Dian's beams disdain to shine	270 Minerva		120
I know the solar beams take up more time	292 Vision		442
Her offspring chill'd; its beams are now forsaken	301 Age		198
Of all her beams--while nations gaze and mourn	308 Age		750
Where the flowers ever blossom, the beams ever shine	323 Abydos	1	6
Morn ne'er awoke them with such brilliant beams	342 Corsair	1	320
The beams, without the Hope of yesterday	355 Corsair	2	556
And, bright around with quivering beams beset	356 Corsair	3	39
Their fancy paints the friends that trim the beams	364 Corsair	3	564
But had not marr'd (though in his beams he grew	373 Lara	1	530
And his evening beams are shed	400 Parisina		411
The stars from broader beams began to creep	415 Island	1	11
Of the indulgent beams, which show, yet hide	528 Faliero	4	41
And bow'd my head beneath thy mid-day beams	562 Sardan	2	25

BEAMS

And thou of beams	656	Heaven	98
His warmth behind in memory of his beams	682	Werner 1	717
Or he himself girt with its beams, I could	701	Werner 3	416
And the young beams of the excluded sun	791	Juan 2	1092
But death is imaged in their shadowy beams	983	Juan 16	150

BEAR
(See also SHE-BEAR)

The Grave shall bear the chiefest prize away	10	Harold 1	439
Let me some remnant, some memorial bear	14	Harold 1	645
Best prize of better acts, they bear away	15	Harold 1	736
Alas! too oft condemn'd for him to bear and bleed	16	Harold 1	746
I bear, corroding joy and youth	17	Harold 1	842
And bear these altars o'er the long-reluctant brine	21	Harold 2	99
And bear it with me, as the rushing wind	35	Harold 3	22
In strength to bear what time can not abate	36	Harold 3	62
And the bleak battlements shall bear no future blow	42	Harold 3	423
Between the banks which bear the vine	43	Harold 3	499
Than join the crushing crowd, doom'd to inflict or bear	46	Harold 3	679
With their own hopes and have been vanquish'd, bear	48	Harold 3	791
Bear, know, feel and yet breathe--into one word	50	Harold 3	910
May temper it to bear,--it is but for a day	58	Harold 4	189
Uptorn must bear the hyaena bigot's wrong	63	Harold 4	520
What race of chiefs and heroes did she bear	70	Harold 4	895
It will not bear the brightness of the day	76	Harold 4	1286
With souls you'd dispense, but this last who could bear it	116	To Eliza	12
me a silver beam of night. Bear my sword	131	Calmar	178
Bear it, ye breezes, to the seat	131	L'Amitie	8
Which bear the turtle to her nest	135	I Would	54
To bear me from love and from beauty for ever	147	To Anne-B	4
He learnt to bear his load of grief	155	Lady-E	6
Bear a hand, you jolly tar, you	157	Hodgson	51
Oh, ye condemn'd the ills of life to bear	161	Athos	22
Must bear the love it cannot show	163	Parting	19
To bear, forgiving and forgiven	165	Thyrza	54
Since earthly eye but ill can bear	167	Dead	44
But not to bear a stranger's touch	168	The Chain	10
For now I bear the weight alone	171	Time-B	8
When future wanderers bear the storm	172	Time-B	35
With no one to bear it, but Thomas a Tyrwhitt	177	Devil's Dr	121
And though fond of the flesh--yet I never could bear it	179	Devil's Dr	223
Could with thy gentle image bear depart	183	Address-D	20
Bear hearts electric--charged with fire from Heaven	193	Monody	90
He was your brother--bear his ashes hence	194	Monody	108
But for the love I bore, and still must bear	209	Sketch	99
It is that they bear me from thee	210	Augusta-B	16
And with light armour we may learn to bear	211	Augusta-C	46
Yet it shall bear me on	230	My Boat	10
Well might triumphant genii bear thee hence	245	Bards	219
A fourth, alas! were more than we could bear	245	Bards	228
Bear witness Gifford, Sotheby, Macneil	253	Bards	818
As Vulcan's feet to bear Apollo's frame	257	Hints	56
What weight your shoulders will, or will not, bear	257	Hints	62
Still let it bear the hearer's soul along	258	Hints	140
Young Arthur's eyes, can ours or nature bear	260	Hints	280
And bear Swift's motto, 'Vive la bagatelle	261	Hints	344
Form'd, save in ode, to bear a serious strain	262	Hints	406
Must bear privations with unruffled face	266	Hints	704
Fear'd like a bear just bursting from his cage	268	Hints	838
Bear back my mandate to thy native shore	270	Minerva	158
Bear witness, bright Barossa! thou canst tell	271	Minerva	231
Droops o'er the bales no bark may bear away	272	Minerva	268
To you of nine years less, who only bear	275	Waltz	95
How few could feel for what he had to bear	299	Age	74
And drive the camel than purvey the bear	302	Age	313
The bear may rush into the lion's toils	304	Age	463
But what of that? the Gaul may bear the guilt	306	Age	587
Bear witness, Greece, thy living page	311	Giaour	126
'The burthen ye so gently bear	313	Giaour	360
But this empurpled pledge to bear	317	Giaour	720
But if a dagger's form it bear	319	Giaour	930
Even bliss--'twere woe alone to bear	319	Giaour	942
Save transient ills that all must bear	320	Giaour	975
Than bear a life of lingering woes	320	Giaour	1003
The weak must bear, the wretch must crave	320	Giaour	1025
And this too was I born to bear	321	Giaour	1162
But bear this ring, his own of old	322	Giaour	1251
Or farther with thee bear my soul	323	Giaour	1317
Are the hearts which they bear, and the tales which they tell	323	Abydos 1	19
Think'st thou that I could bear to part	327	Abydos 1	317
That strand of strife may bear	335	Abydos 2	587
They scarce can bear the morn to break	336	Abydos 2	701
Far as the breeze can bear, the billows foam	338	Corsair 1	3
'Where is our chief? for him we bear report	340	Corsair 1	117

BEAR

'There let him stay--to him this order bear	340	Corsair 1	155
The slaves bear round for rigid Moslems' use	347	Corsair 2	34
Those waves that would not bear me from the shore	348	Corsair 2	84
To note how much the life yet left could bear	351	Corsair 2	311
It is enough--I breathe--and I can bear	354	Corsair 2	482
But harder still the heart's recoil to bear	354	Corsair 2	509
Yet doubts how well the shrinking flesh may bear	359	Corsair 3	233
And change the sentence I deserve to bear	359	Corsair 3	285
Chance guides his steps--a freshness seems to bear	361	Corsair 3	396
She watch'd his features till she could not bear	362	Corsair 3	464
To bear him like an arrow to that height	364	Corsair 3	576
They raise him, bear him;--hush! he breathes, he speaks	369	Lara 1	225
With which that chieftain's brow would bear him down	373	Lara 1	499
To hold the stirrup, or to bear the sword	374	Lara 1	565
And bear within them to the neighbouring state	379	Lara 2	316
And bear my spirit back again	384	Corinth	37
The arms they taught to bear; and now	385	Corinth	119
But thee will I bear to a lovely spot	390	Corinth	587
Which urged to guilt, but could not bear	400	Parisina	354
My limbs; and I found strength to bear	411	Mazeppa	488
To bear the bark of others' happiness	421	Island 2	143
Eager to hope, but not less firm to bear	421	Island 2	177
Of arms; and we have got some guns to bear	426	Island 2	522
Rough as a bear, but willing as a brother	428	Island 3	104
To bear you hence to where a hope may dwell	428	Island 3	162
She was a warrior's daughter, and could bear	429	Island 3	193
And towards a group of islets, such as bear	429	Island 3	227
The wave which bore them still their foes would bear	433	Island 4	236
'Tis ours to bear, not judge the dead; and they	435	Island 4	353
Long years!--It tries the thrilling frame to bear	436	Tasso	1
For I have anguish yet to bear--and how	437	Tasso	44
In mockery through them. If I bear and bore	439	Tasso	211
Hoary and hopeless, but less hard to bear	458	Dante 1	137
Without the power that makes them bear a crown	458	Dante 1	167
Harder to bear and less deserved, for I	462	Dante 3	140
So be it: we can bear.--But thus all they	463	Dante 4	20
Than aught less than the Homeric page may bear	463	Dante 4	27
Yet some have been untouch'd who learn'd to bear	463	Dante 3	179
To bear a burthen and to serve a need	464	Dante 4	89
'Put down, nor bear him further the desert in	475	Morgante	591
'But in my heart I bear through every clime	475	Morgante	609
'But to bear arms and wield the lance; indeed	476	Morgante	649
This giant up to heaven may bear his soul	476	Morgante	652
To look within; and yet I live, and bear	478	Manfred 1	7
Do I not bear it?--Look on me--I live	484	Manfred 2	42
My lot with living being: I can bear	484	Manfred 2	76
However wretchedly, 'tis still to bear	484	Manfred 2	77
Bear what thou dorest	490	Manfred 2	462
Say that thou loath'st me not, that I do bear	490	Manfred 2	494
The barren sands which bear no shrubs to blast	493	Manfred 3	130
What I have done is done; I bear within	496	Manfred 3	387
The parchment which will bear the Forty's judgment	500	Faliero 1	28
That a Venetian prince must bear? Old Dandolo	502	Faliero 1	201
Bear witness for me thou, my injured subject	506	Faliero 1	481
To bear you from the senate. From the senate	511	Faliero 2	155
I cannot bear to leave you thus. Come then	515	Faliero 2	499
I am no brawler; but can bear myself	521	Faliero 3	181
Think on the wrongs we bear, the rights we claim	526	Faliero 3	512
Bear with me! Step by step, and blow on blow	527	Faliero 3	605
Must be, and think what I have been! Bear with me	527	Faliero 3	620
Which bear away the weaker: noble blood	531	Faliero 4	218
With honest mates, and bear a cheerful aspect	531	Faliero 4	232
Bear me a prisoner? Firstly to 'the Ten	533	Faliero 4	336
And learn (if souls so much obscured can bear	536	Faliero 4	593
For a short respite--must we bear or die	538	Faliero 5	53
Yet could not bear in silence to your graves	542	Faliero 5	284
Here was I crown'd, and here, bear witness, Heaven	548	Faliero 5	700
Shall bear about their bastardy in triumph	548	Faliero 5	768
Fill full, and bear it quickly. Is this moment	553	Sardan 1	208
Bitterer to bear than any punishment	559	Sardan 1	542
My lords, I bear an order from the king	568	Sardan 2	405
Depart, and not to bear your answer. Ay	568	Sardan 2	413
Interpretation should it bear? it is	568	Sardan 2	429
King, wilt thou bear this mad impiety	571	Sardan 3	31
What I have dreamt:--and canst thou bear to hear it	579	Sardan 4	72
I can bear all things, dreams of life or death	579	Sardan 4	73
To bear alone, that we must mingle sorrows	581	Sardan 4	230
Bear her to where her children are embark'd	584	Sardan 4	421
Quite fall'n, nor now disposed to bear reproaches	585	Sardan 4	471
Enough of heaven to enable them to bear	587	Sardan 5	30
But doubt it. Wherefore did ye bear me here	588	Sardan 5	94
To bear you to this hall. 'Twas not ill done	588	Sardan 5	97
To this which beats so bitterly. Now, bear	589	Sardan 5	163
But must I bear no answer? Yes,--I ask	592	Sardan 5	342
In which they would have revell'd, I bear with me	594	Sardan 5	432

BEAR

Back to your cheek: Heaven send you strength to bear	597 Foscari	1	131
But onward--I have borne it--I can bear it	598 Foscari	1	162
Have him bear more than mortal pain, in silence	599 Foscari	1	238
We all must bear our tortures. I have not	599 Foscari	1	239
How feeble and forlorn! I cannot bear	601 Foscari	1	380
I must bear these reproaches, though they wrong me	603 Foscari	2	138
You were the last to bear it. Would it were so	604 Foscari	2	153
Your pleasure! I bear that of 'the Ten.' They	604 Foscari	2	192
Utter'd within these walls I bear no further	606 Foscari	2	320
I know if mind may bear us up, or no	610 Foscari	3	107
On earth to bear. Have I not borne? Too much	611 Foscari	3	202
He said not which. I would that you could bear	611 Foscari	3	223
Will be more merciful than man, and bear me	617 Foscari	4	146
Dead, but still bear me to a native grave	617 Foscari	4	147
Bear hence the body. Signors, if it please you	619 Foscari	4	246
Am now and evermore. But we will bear it	621 Foscari	5	68
There is one burthen which I beg you bear	623 Foscari	5	205
We are going: do you fear that we shall bear	624 Foscari	5	213
And do not thirst to know, and bear a mind	631 Cain	1	245
That bear the form of earth-born being. Ah!	631 Cain	1	260
Bear all--and worship aught. Then follow me!	632 Cain	1	331
Bear with what we have borne, and love me--I	633 Cain	1	359
His secret, and he keeps it. We must bear	635 Cain	1	486
Shape; for I never saw such. They bear not	640 Cain	2	261
Their seed will bear fresh fruit there ere the summer	650 Cain	3	283
That I may bear to hear my own again	651 Cain	3	357
So shall our children be. I will bear Enoch	653 Cain	3	456
This punishment is more than he can bear	653 Cain	3	477
From me a being I ne'er loved to bear	654 Cain	3	515
Think'st thou my boy will bear to look on me	654 Cain	3	523
To meet them! Oh, for wings to bear	657 Heaven		144
Mine hath enabled me to bear her scorn	657 Heaven		171
And as your pinions bear ye back to heaven	667 Heaven		910
And bear what Adam's race must bear, and can	668 Heaven		961
But ours is with thee; we will bear ye far	669 Heaven		1039
For the cup's sake I'll bear the cupbearer	677 Werner	1	375
Thought. Must I bear this? Pshaw! we all must bear	692 Werner	2	610
I've seen you brave the elements, and bear	692 Werner	2	614
Must I bear to be deem'd a thief? If 'twere	692 Werner	2	617
(So thick as to bear paths within their ribs	696 Werner	3	88
Thou wouldst say: I must bear it and deserve it	703 Werner	3	512
To bear the brand of bloodshed? Pshaw! leave any thing	703 Werner	3	548
What name? You have no name, since that you bear	703 Werner	3	551
That back of thine may bear its burthen; 'tis	722 Deformed	1	6
The helmless dromedary!--and I'll bear	724 Deformed	1	117
But bear with me: indeed you'll find me useful	729 Deformed	1	491
More knows whom he must bear	730 Deformed	1	550
Of our song bear the burden	732 Deformed	1	725
Whose name you bear like other curs--And kings	734 Deformed	1	856
He speaks the truth; the heretics will bear	739 Deformed	2	287
But somewhat late i' the day. Where shall we bear her	741 Deformed	2	392
Softly! As softly as they bear the dead	741 Deformed	2	400
Now I desert not mine. Soft! bear her hence	741 Deformed	2	411
Neglect, indeed, requires a saint to bear it	749 Juan	1	155
But now I'll bear no more, nor here remain	764 Juan	1	1159
These I could bear, but cannot cast aside	771 Juan	1	1557
And bear with life, to love and pray for you	771 Juan	1	1576
Thou shalt not bear false witness like 'the Blues	772 Juan	1	1643
They live upon the love of life, and bear	782 Juan	2	522
Quick to perceive, and strong to bear, and meant	808 Juan	3	421
But violent things will sooner bear assuaging	808 Juan	3	461
A moment more will bring the sight to bear	821 Juan	4	323
Would bear such outrage, and forbear to kill	822 Juan	4	366
Through years or moons the inner weight to bear	825 Juan	4	563
Whom to the spot their school-boy feelings bear	826 Juan	4	621
To bear the compliments of many a bore	830 Juan	4	867
And never having dreamt what 'twas to bear	846 Juan	5	948
You don't sleep soundly, and I cannot bear	858 Juan	6	370
For killing nothing but a bear or buck, he	886 Juan	8	486
The bear is civilised, the wolf is mild	890 Juan	8	733
Bear it, ye Muses, on your brightest wing	894 Juan	8	1004
To bear these crosses) for each waning prude	895 Juan	8	1046
In fact, the only Christian she could bear	914 Juan	10	449
Heaven's brandy, though our brain can hardly bear it	918 Juan	11	16
Should neither court neglect, nor dread to bear it	941 Juan	12	696
Or solitary, as they chose to bear	954 Juan	13	820
That which humanity may bear, or bear not	961 Juan	14	390
To bear a son and heir--and one miscarriage	962 Juan	14	448
If once their phantasies be brought to bear	970 Juan	15	126
To bear on what appear'd to her the subject	987 Juan	16	451
This they must bear with and, perhaps, much more	998 Juan	17	70

BEARABLE

'Tis said it makes reality more bearable	979 Juan	15	709

BEARD

It is not that yon hoary lengthening beard	29 Harold	2	559
With his beard so white to see	194 Ballad-A		42
Though thy beard so hoary be	195 Ballad-A		72
Then curl'd his very beard with ire	316 Giaour		593
But if thy beard had manlier length	325 Abydos	1	122
Now let it tear thy beard in idle grief	336 Abydos	2	655
He tore his beard, and foaming fled the fight	349 Corsair	2	181
Bless me! your beard is of amazing growth	451 Beppo		726
'Beppo! that beard of yours becomes you not	451 Beppo		737
Dare beard me now, and Insolence within	591 Sardan	5	269
What's here? whose broad brow and whose curly beard	725 Deformed	1	230
And begg'd by every hair of Mahomet's beard	866 Juan	6	903
His beard, he puff'd his pipe's ambrosial gales	893 Juan	8	967
Thirdly, that 'Juan had more brain than beard	963 Juan	14	525

BEARDED
(See also WHITE-BEARDED)

The bearded Turk, that rarely deigns to speak	28 Harold	2	521
Around, the bearded chiefs he came to lead	347 Corsair	2	30
Beneath each bearded pacha's glance	385 Corinth		78
Shawl'd to the nose, and bearded to the eyes	850 Juan	5	1170

BEARDLESS

And beardless bloom yet graced the gallant boy	105 Nisus		10
And beardless faces;--I did not for this	503 Faliero	1	211
He with the beardless chin and garments torn	875 Juan	7	494
Blushing and beardless; and yet ne'ertheless	902 Juan	9	370

BEARDS

They thought shaving their beards a disaster	232 Murray-B		48
And beer undrawn, and beards unmown, display	250 Bards		636
Beards of a week and nails of annual growth	263 Hints		468
On long pearl-colour'd beards and crimson crosses	697 Werner	3	117
With beards and whiskers, and the like, the fond	903 Juan	9	420

BEARER
(See also ARMOUR-BEARER, PENNANT-BEARER)

The bearer of such boon may wait	326 Abydos	1	214
So let their bearer sleep 'neath something like one	679 Werner	1	517

BEARING
(See also THUNDER-BEARING)

The conqueror's sword in bearing fame away	67 Harold	4	733
And bearing still a breast so tried	210 Augusta-A		43
Thou who art bearing my buckler and bow	219 Saul-A		5
And nauseous words past mentioning or bearing	451 Beppo		688
Taking all shapes and bearing many names	493 Manfred	3	148
A villain, whom for his unbridled bearing	514 Faliero	4	422
'Tis a strange hour, and a suspicious bearing	529 Faliero	4	120
Thy bearing, and this strange and hurried mode	530 Faliero	4	139
The years of coming time, as bearing record	538 Faliero	5	8
The abruptness of my entrance and my bearing	542 Faliero	5	334
However harsh and hard in his own bearing	552 Sardan	4	120
This very night, and in my further bearing	586 Sardan	4	500
Along its golden frame--as bearing for	591 Sardan	5	252
Feel no remorse at bearing off the gold	593 Sardan	5	383
Her circumstances must excuse her bearing	626 Foscari	5	366
In bearing. I have also served, and can	676 Werner	1	328
May be this stranger? He too hath a bearing	677 Werner	1	399
The man, his bearing, and the mystery	687 Werner	2	273
But of his bearing. Men speak lightly of him	709 Werner	4	295
Stature, and bearing; and amidst them all	717 Werner	5	265
In all that nameless bearing of his limbs	726 Deformed	1	249
Instead of bearing up without debate	828 Juan	4	742

BEARINGS

In other bearings, I should rather lay	687 Werner	2	294
That, when I see the subject in its bearings	691 Werner	2	503
Our general situation in its bearings	698 Werner	3	172

BEARS

Bears in his cap the badge of crimson hue	12 Harold	1	523
Denotes how soft that chin which bears his touch	13 Harold	1	595
Staggering, but stemming all, his lord unharm'd he bears	16 Harold	1	773
The ocean queen, the free Britannia, bears	21 Harold	2	113
Herself more sweetly rears the babe she bears	28 Harold	2	548
Such conduct bears Philanthropy's rare stamp	29 Harold	2	610
Bears the cloud onwards: in that Tale I find	35 Harold	3	23
Fatal to him who bears, to all who ever bore	41 Harold	3	378
Watering the tree which bears his lady's name	59 Harold	4	269
The moral lesson bears, drawn from such pilgrimage	62 Harold	4	405
By the distracted waters, bears serene	66 Harold	4	645
The ocean o'er its boundary, and bears	81 Harold	4	1552
The reeking weapon bears alternate stains	109 Nisus		272
Messapus' helm his head in triumph bears	109 Nisus		294
How bears her breast the torturing hour	181 Ode-A		111
But come--The bark that bears us hence shall find	185 Julian		50
Who thy blood-bought title bears	187 Ode-B		43
The wave that bears my tears returns no more	198 Po		33

BEARS

By pugilistic pupils, and by bears	259	Hints		230
Where scarce a blackleg bears a brighter name	260	Hints		242
Bears in his belt the scimitar	315	Giaour		524
And he bears the gift at his saddle bow	317	Giaour		705
A message from the Bulbul bears	326	Abydos	1	288
Each bears a prize of unregarded charms	350	Corsair	2	216
She bears her down majestically near	362	Corsair	3	486
Despite of every yoke she bears	388	Corinth		416
Which bears at once the cup and milk and fruit	422	Island	2	259
For centuries: may he who bears it now	491	Manfred	3	32
Too long--at least so thinks the Doge. How bears he	500	Faliero	1	5
Bears but the scars of mind, the thoughts of years	509	Faliero	2	21
Which bears the name of Nimrod's chalice. Hence	553	Sardan	1	207
He's gone; and on his finger bears my signet	557	Sardan	1	433
To the star-read Chaldean, bears upon	561	Sardan	2	12
It was not this I meant, but that which bears	573	Sardan	3	130
Inveterate enemies. Now it bears an aspect	593	Sardan	5	360
'The Ten.' Who bears it? Noble Loredano	604	Foscari	2	188
Upon the bark of some tall tree, which bears	608	Foscari	3	23
The Hall not far from hence, which bears on high	610	Foscari	3	120
Your exile as he bears it. Blame him not	611	Foscari	3	224
How death itself bears witness to thy deeds	619	Foscari	4	244
May I pass on? You may. How bears the Doge	620	Foscari	4	343
Ask Eve, your mother: bears she not the know- ledge	633	Cain	1	391
Which bears them. Thou hast seen both worms and worlds	637	Cain	2	126
By what it bears of beautiful, untoiling	641	Cain	2	332
Its own exuberance, it bears double value	694	Werner	2	712
Who backs a horse, or bears a hawk, or wears	704	Werner	4	33
It bears its burthen;--but my heart! Will it	722	Deformed	1	8
Who bears the golden horn, and wears such bright	730	Deformed	1	525
Bears vegetables, in a grumbling way	782	Juan	2	534
Which bears the same relation to the real	881	Juan	8	208
Which bears the greatest likeness to Pall Mall	958	Juan	14	171
Love bears within its breast the very germ	967	Juan	14	745
Of time and tide rolls on, and bears afar	980	Juan	15	789

BEAR'S

To turn the bear's and wolf's and fox's guide	301	Age		210

BEAR-SKINS

In this gay clime of bear-skins black and furry	910	Juan	10	203

BEAR'ST

Nor care what land thou bear'st me to	6	Harold	1	192

BEAST

Like Saint John's foretold beast; but ours are born	285	Vision		55
And I can banquet like a beast of prey	437	Tasso		16
Iberian, Almain, Lombard, and the beast	459	Dante	2	84
Where nor fish, beast, bird, nor worm	729	Deformed	1	466
And for the bass, the beast can only bellow	827	Juan	4	690
Or any interesting beast of prey	848	Juan	5	1050
That sad inexplicable beast of prey	902	Juan	9	394

BEASTS

Birds, beasts of prey, and wilder men appear	26	Harold	2	377
Even as the beasts that perish, save that thou	60	Harold	4	335
The birds and beasts and famish'd men at bay	189	Darkness		49
Mightiest of all Dunedin's beasts of chase	265	Hints		597
Led all wild beasts but women by the ear	266	Hints		664
Beasts of the forest, all gathering there	389	Corinth		492
Track'd like wild beasts, like them they sought the wild	426	Island	3	15
For 'tis our nature strikes us down: the beasts	453	Venice-B		63
Against domestic beasts with watch and ward	469	Morgante		184
And left them to the savage beasts and birds	472	Morgante		432
Hark! even the forest beasts howl forth their prayer	669	Heaven		1062
Transform'd their lords to beasts (but that's a fact	805	Juan	3	272
Bills, beasts, and men, and--no! not womankind	855	Juan	6	170
A mixture of wild beasts and demigods	891	Juan	8	844
Besides fish, beasts, and birds. 'The sparrow's fall	899	Juan	9	149

BEAT

Beat back keen winter's blast, and welcomed summer's heat	26	Harold	2	387
As eagerly the barr'd-up bird will beat	37	Harold	3	132
A thousand hearts beat happily; and when	38	Harold	3	185
And near, the beat of the alarming drum	39	Harold	3	222
Until that heart shall cease to beat	85	To D--		8
Where first my heart responsive beat	131	L'Amitie		9
For then it beat but to adore thee	134	Lady-D		36
They Both must heave, or cease to beat	144	Jessy		28
Can bid Life's pulses beat	146	Adieu		74
The breast, which beat to former joy	150	My Son		35
Beat the loud alarm afar	194	Ballad-A		22

BEAT

Beat 'gainst their prison	200	Stanzas-B		83
Still must mine, though bleeding, beat	207	Fare Thee		26
He beat all three--and blew it out	225	Youth		4
I defy him to beat this day's wondrous applause	281	Blues	2	39
Besides, I beat him hollow at the last	293	Vision		557
His name shall beat the alarm, like Ziska's drum	300	Age		130
The same high spirit which beat back the Moor	301	Age		262
To thoughts with which my heart beat high	324	Abydos	1	62
Beat thy Divan's approaching hour	324	Abydos	1	74
More free her timid bosom beat	330	Abydos	2	95
Scarce beat that bosom where his image dwelt	345	Corsair	1	472
No--no--the storm may beat upon his brow	368	Lara	1	178
That ceased to beat, the look that made them start	370	Lara	1	278
His lip was silent, scarcely beat his heart	380	Lara	2	356
Then beat with quicker pulse, ashamed	387	Corinth		280
And throbb'd awhile, then beat no more	412	Mazeppa		543
Of the dusk bosoms that beat high below	419	Island	2	52
He stood; and, save a slight beat of his foot	427	Island	3	94
With fluttering fear, her heart beat thick and high	435	Island	4	379
That beat, the mind that was temptation proof	457	Dante	1	87
And fight beneath the chief who beat the Huns there	505	Faliero	1	390
Ne'er beat for any of the noble youth	510	Faliero	2	118
As yet beat in these kingdoms. The time presses	584	Sardan	4	389
Beat back by valour: now at once we have	588	Sardan	5	71
Thy foes, must be thy victims: wilt thou beat	596	Foscari	1	66
More loving, or more loyal, never beat	604	Foscari	2	157
Must I consume my own, which never beat	608	Foscari	3	10
Let me see, doth it beat? methinks--No!--no	651	Cain	3	341
Hath beat for thee, and then will beat more vainly	658	Heaven		232
Like Ziska's skin, to beat alarm to all	682	Werner	1	695
To beat the bushes, and the day looks promising	705	Werner	4	77
All hearts but one may beat in kindness for me	709	Werner	4	324
Beat Germany's drums	732	Deformed	1	730
Think'st thou I beat for hares when lions roar	738	Deformed	2	197
Alas! that the first beat of the only heart	741	Deformed	2	389
I ever wish'd to beat with mine should vibrate	741	Deformed	2	390
And hear the heart beat with the love it granted	758	Juan	1	766
I praise your vast forbearance not to beat	765	Juan	1	1197
The waters beat while he thereto was lash'd	787	Juan	2	854
Felt as if never more to beat apart	798	Juan	2	1528
Hope, care, nor love, beyond, her heart beat here	799	Juan	2	1616
And oh! that quickening of the heart, that beat	800	Juan	2	1617
Lay Juan, nor could aught renew the beat	820	Juan	4	269
Lay at her heart, whose earliest beat still true	824	Juan	4	494
Anon her thin wan fingers beat the wall	824	Juan	4	521
In thinking that their enemy is beat	872	Juan	7	332
Koutousow, he who afterward beat back	887	Juan	8	553
It happen'd was himself beat back just now	887	Juan	8	556
For those for whom it soon shall cease to beat	888	Juan	8	652
Struck at his friends, as babies beat their nurses	892	Juan	8	864
Which beat as if there was a warm heart under	996	Juan	16	1020

BEATEN
(See also BREAKER-BEATEN, LOVE-BEATEN, WEATHER-BEATEN)

And freely wander from the beaten way	259	Hints		180
Like crying babe and beaten hound	396	Corinth		1072
Be silent then, and live on, to be beaten	507	Faliero	1	505
Flattering: they are beaten backward from the palace	576	Sardan	3	324
We have beaten all foemen	732	Deformed	1	695
(Or beaten, of you insist on grammar, though	872	Juan	7	333
Was beaten--though the Prussians say so too	884	Juan	8	384
Beating or beaten she will laugh the same	896	Juan	9	5

BEATING
(See also ROCK-BEATING)

Egeria! thy all heavenly bosom beating	72	Harold	4	1055
She bids the beating heart with rapture bound	258	Hints		153
Oft his beating fingers went	390	Corinth		514
Rock'd by the beating of her mother's heart	485	Manfred	2	113
And, beating 'gainst his bosom, Haidee's heart	798	Juan	2	1527
Beating for love, as the caged bird's for air	855	Juan	6	208
Beating or beaten she will laugh the same	896	Juan	9	5

BEATRICE

Midst whom my own bright Beatrice bless'd	456	Dante	1	11
Oh Beatrice! whose sweet limbs the sod	456	Dante	1	18
My own Beatrice, I would hardly take	457	Dante	1	99
But Dante's Beatrice and Milton's Eve	803	Juan	3	79
By Beatrice, and not a mistress--I	803	Juan	3	82

BEATS

My pulse beats quick, my breath heaves short	87	Ad Lesbiam		15
Thy heart beats fiercely to the din of arms	106	Nisus		54
Yet still beats on as it begun	156	Lady-F		47
Howe'er it beats, it beats sincerely	160	Cadiz		30

BEATS

Beats back the current many a rood	316	Giaour		624
No heart that beats reply to mine	323	Giaour		1289
Each pulse beats quicker, and all bosoms seem	374	Lara	1	620
It beats no more, but Kaled will not part	382	Lara	2	495
'It beats!'--Away, thou dreamer! he is gone	382	Lara	2	498
Beats the strong heart, though less the lips avow	382	Lara	2	535
And her cheek grows pale, and her heart beats quick	396	Parisina		24
Nor fluttering throb, that beats with hopes or wishes	479	Manfred	1	26
Which sinks with sorrow, or beats quick with pain	487	Manfred	2	263
To this which beats so bitterly. Now, bear	589	Sardan	5	163
How faintly beats this heart--this pulse! The light	617	Foscari	4	188
Beats quick; he awes me, and yet draws me near	633	Cain	1	409
How my heart beats! Let us proceed upon	655	Heaven		4
Back to my heart, which beats for you, sweet cousin	706	Werner	4	161
I am so already. Feel how my heart beats	713	Werner	5	29
He hath an ignorant audience. Yes! her heart beats	741	Deformed	2	388
And louder than her breathing beats her heart	766	Juan	1	1264
The heroic bosom beats no more	812	Juan	3	716
Self-love in man, too, beats all female art	855	Juan	6	149
(Which will come over things), beats love or liquor	930	Juan	12	29
The pointer ranges, and the sportsman beats	950	Juan	13	596

BEAU

That's the Bard, the Beau, the Banker	196	Rogers		22
The Archangel bow'd, not like a modern beau	289	Vision		281
Is but a heightening of the 'beau ideal	801	Juan	2	1688
Of being, without alloy of fop or beau	940	Juan	12	671
Are grown of the beau monde a part potential	958	Juan	14	154

BEAUMONT

From Sir George Beaumont, Baronet	235	Epilogue	18

BEAUMONTS

Not that our Bens or Beaumonts show the worse	258	Hints	123

BEAUMONT'S

And Beaumont's pilfer'd Caratach affords	249	Bards	572

BEAUTEOUS

Beneath yon mountain's ever beauteous brow	7	Harold	1	280
Yet to the beauteous form he was not blind	17	Harold	1	819
Yet fresh the memory of that beauteous face	85	Death-B		22
Think'st thou I saw thy beauteous eyes	90	Caroline-A		1
When Nature stamp'd thy beauteous birth	97	To M--		9
Here I behold its beauteous hue	98	To Mary		13
And Oscar claim'd the beauteous bride	102	Alva		81
My bird of love! my beauteous mate	172	Romaic-B		27
And gravely tells--attend, each beauteous miss	246	Bards		359
And beauteous still as hermit's hope can paint	359	Corsair	3	275
Beauteous as cloudless, not be forced to borrow	445	Beppo		342
Oh! my own beauteous land! so long laid low	460	Dante	2	136
The high moon sails upon her beauteous way	529	Faliero	4	74
The summer dwelling on its beauteous border	561	Sardan	1	686
Who didst create these best and beauteous beings	627	Cain	1	15
Beauteous, and yet not all as beautiful	629	Cain	1	94
More beautiful than beauteous things remote	643	Cain	2	459
Breath will be still'd at once! All beauteous world	659	Heaven		312
Thou shalt be beauteous as the thing thou seest	727	Deformed	1	311
The beauty of our host, and brave as beauteous	733	Deformed	1	788
The strangest thing was, beauteous, she was wholly	859	Juan	6	429
Juan, I said, was a most beauteous boy	903	Juan	9	417
How beauteous are rouleaus! how charming chests	931	Juan	12	89
And beauteous, even where beauties most abound	941	Juan	13	14
A beauteous ripple of the brilliant stream	975	Juan	15	435

BEAUTIES

And safely view thy ripening beauties shine	3	To Ianthe		22
What beauties doth Lisboa first unfold	6	Harold	1	216
Beauties that ev'n a cynic must avow	13	Harold	1	606
Ev'n on a plain no humble beauties lie	27	Harold	2	482
Dims the green beauties of thine Attic plain	31	Harold	2	705
A blending of all beauties,--streams and dells	42	Harold	3	411
What daughter of her beauties was the heir	70	Harold	4	896
New beauties still are daily bright'ning	98	To Lesbia		30
How'er those beauties may distract us	101	Marion		48
Live thou--such beauties I would fain preserve	106	Nisus		63
England! thy beauties are tame and domestic	118	Lachin		37
Whose beauties I shall not rehearse	134	E. N. Long		89
But vainly now on me thy beauties blaze	140	Ossian-B		21
Yet, Mary, all thy beauties seem	146	Adieu		55
To see thy beauties fade	167	Dead		47
Nor sleeps with Sleeping Beauties, but anon	250	Bards		602
To grace the beauties of your native tongue	254	Bards		886
Where frequent beauties strike the reader's view	264	Hints		557
I mark'd the beauties of the land and main	269	Minerva		56

BEAUTIES

Say--would you make those beauties quite so cheap	276	Waltz		233
Ah! were thy beauties e'er so cold	323	Giaour		1293
Bows to your beauties, soften'd, but intense	419	Island	2	60
Thy naked beauties--Give me a cigar	425	Island	2	459
But luckily these beauties are no 'Blues	449	Beppo		574
The beauties of the sunbow which bends o'er thee	485	Manfred	2	118
While the fair populace of crowding beauties	597	Foscari	1	100
Of beauties cool as an Italian convent	856	Juan	6	255
Of any supernumerary beauties	859	Juan	6	464
Her beauties seized the unconscious hour of night	860	Juan	6	527
Which hovers oft about some married beauties	903	Juan	9	404
Don Juan now saw Albion's earliest beauties	916	Juan	10	545
And to the beauties of a foreign dame	939	Juan	12	574
And beauteous, even where beauties most abound	941	Juan	13	14
Where time through heroes and through beauties steers	947	Juan	13	398
Also some beauties of Sir Peter Lely	949	Juan	13	543
Seen beauties brought to market by the score	957	Juan	14	140
And the pale smile of beauties in the grave	982	Juan	16	145

BEAUTIFIER

To, Time! the beautifier of the dead	74	Harold	4	1162

BEAUTIFUL

Her glance how wildly beautiful! how much	13	Harold	1	598
How to make madness beautiful, and cast	47	Harold	3	730
More beautiful than our fantastic sky	56	Harold	4	52
The beautiful, the brave--the lords of earth and sea	59	Harold	4	225
Thy very weeds are beautiful, thy waste	59	Harold	4	231
Horribly beautiful! but on the verge	65	Harold	4	640
Thou wert a beautiful thought, and softly bodied forth	72	Harold	4	1035
And nostril beautiful disdain and might	79	Harold	4	1447
Since your beautiful main your flame has repaid	116	Strephon		5
For beautiful in death are they	189	On Star		39
Was beautiful which peopled every stream	205	Aristomenes		6
And both were young, and one was beautiful	214	Dream		42
So cloudless, clear, and purely beautiful	215	Dream		124
What a beautiful word! Very true; 'tis so soft	277	Blues	1	26
A beautiful and mighty Thing of Light	288	Vision		218
The young, the beautiful, the brave	329	Abydos	2	4
For he was beautiful as day	403	Chillon		79
(When day was beautiful to me	403	Chillon		80
All that was beautiful and new	414	Mazeppa		742
How beautiful are these! how happy they	419	Island	2	16
And she herself, as beautiful as night	432	Island	4	176
That thou wert beautiful, and I not blind	437	Tasso		55
Yes! thou, so beautiful, shalt feel the sword	459	Dante	2	46
Hideous or beautiful to me. Let him	481	Manfred	1	185
Why are ye beautiful? I cannot love ye	481	Manfred	1	270
With a pervading vision.--Beautiful	482	Manfred	1	297
How beautiful is all this visible world	482	Manfred	1	298
Beautiful Spirit! with thy hair of light	485	Manfred	2	107
Beautiful Spirit! in thy calm clear brow	485	Manfred	2	119
That which I love would still be beautiful	487	Manfred	2	288
More beautiful than they, which did draw down	493	Manfred	3	178
Of the snow-shining mountains.--Beautiful	495	Manfred	3	262
Leaving that beautiful which still was so	495	Manfred	3	296
So young, so beautiful, so good, so pure	513	Faliero	2	279
And only look on death as beautiful	517	Faliero	2	603
King, she is here. Away! Beautiful being	557	Sardan	1	468
Hath usher'd it! How beautiful in heaven	587	Sardan	5	2
More beautiful in that variety	587	Sardan	5	4
And lovely ones, my beautiful!--but here me	594	Sardan	5	412
Be thou still free and beautiful, and far	595	Sardan	5	489
Of manhood's strength. My beautiful, my own	597	Foscari	1	123
Her beautiful towers in the receding distance	611	Foscari	3	208
Beauteous, and yet not all as beautiful	629	Cain	1	94
Which are so beautiful: shall they, too, die	631	Cain	1	278
It is a beautiful star; I love it for	635	Cain	1	494
And brighter, yet less beautiful and powerful	635	Cain	1	505
So beautiful, unnumber'd, and endearing	635	Cain	1	512
It it not glorious? Oh, thou beautiful	637	Cain	2	98
How beautiful ye are! how beautiful	637	Cain	2	111
That they are beautiful in their own sphere	638	Cain	2	128
And that the light, which makes both beautiful	638	Cain	2	129
Haughty, and high, and beautiful, and full	640	Cain	2	259
Now breathing; mighty yet and beautiful	640	Cain	2	264
As the most beautiful and mighty which	640	Cain	2	265
Oh, what a beautiful world it was! And is	641	Cain	2	329
By what it bears of beautiful, untoiling	641	Cain	2	332
Ill cannot come: they are too beautiful	643	Cain	2	450
Approach the things of earth most beautiful	643	Cain	2	454
More beautiful than beauteous things remote	643	Cain	2	459
But if thou dost possess a beautiful	643	Cain	2	482
Thou lovest it, because 'tis beautiful	644	Cain	2	528
Cease to be beautiful! how can that be	644	Cain	2	532
The fruits of the earth, the early beautiful	647	Cain	3	105
Methinks a being that is beautiful	657	Heaven		165
No--all of heaven, they are so beautiful	662	Heaven		577
To save this beautiful--these beautiful	663	Heaven		616
Be general, not for two, though beautiful	665	Heaven		758

BEAUTIFUL

And beautiful they are, but not the less	665	Heaven	759
I loved him--beautiful he was: oh heaven	666	Heaven	846
And ye to woman's--beautiful she is	666	Heaven	856
Twelve years! he was but eight then:--beautiful	672	Werner 1	59
He was, and beautiful he must be now	672	Werner 1	60
My dream is realised--how beautiful	688	Werner 2	340
And strong and beautiful as a young tiger	704	Werner 4	24
She's young--all beautiful--adores you--is	710	Werner 4	371
Of aught so beautiful. The flowers, the boughs	713	Werner 5	16
So beautiful and lusty, and as free	722	Deformed 1	18
More lovely than the last. How beautiful	725	Deformed 1	212
As beautiful and clear as the amber waves	726	Deformed 1	268
Of all we know or dream of beautiful	727	Deformed 1	336
Beautiful shadow	728	Deformed 1	380
They are beautiful, and cannot, sure, be demons	729	Deformed 1	522
In Rome. How pale! how beautiful! how lifeless	741	Deformed 2	379
The beautiful half-clay, and nearly spirit	741	Deformed 2	412
You are beautiful and brave! the first is much	743	Deformed 3	120
Sprung up a branch as beautiful as fresh	754	Juan 1	460
How beautiful she look'd! her conscious heart	759	Juan 1	841
To keep them beautiful, or leave them neat	764	Juan 1	1142
Extracts emotions beautiful and new	773	Juan 1	1708
About this time a beautiful white bird	786	Juan 2	745
Besides, so very beautiful was she	790	Juan 2	1019
Alas! they were so young, so beautiful	798	Juan 2	1529
Beauty upon the beautiful they lighted	800	Juan 2	1627
'Tis the perception of the beautiful	801	Juan 2	1689
'Tis beautiful to see a matron bring	809	Juan 3	475
So beautiful--its very shape would charm	810	Juan 3	565
They were so soft and beautiful, and rife	810	Juan 3	587
Sink o'er the earth so beautiful and soft	815	Juan 3	908
Oh beautiful! and rare as beautiful	818	Juan 4	129
Were late he trod, her beautiful, her own	823	Juan 4	460
Glazed o'er her eyes--the beautiful, the black	825	Juan 4	551
Made her a beautiful embodied storm	848	Juan 5	1080
Young, beautiful, and daring--who would risk	853	Juan 6	18
And fresh, and 'beautiful exceedingly	857	Juan 6	283
Many and beautiful lay those around	860	Juan 6	513
So beautiful that art could little mend her	863	Juan 6	709
So beautiful, so fleeting, to the Muse	877	Juan 7	669
And shudder;--while, as beautiful as May	889	Juan 8	725
How beautiful that moment! and how odd is	906	Juan 9	597
As beautiful as her own native land	933	Juan 12	227
As beautiful and bounding as a steed	952	Juan 13	734
And then her dress--what beautiful simplicity	994	Juan 16	863

BEAUTIFULLY

Now brightly bold or beautifully shy	3	To Ianthe	29
How beautifully parted! No; you shall not	646	Cain 3	13
More beautifully, than he did on Rome	731	Deformed 1	639
Oh! 'darkly, deeply, beautifully blue	830	Juan 4	873

BEAUTY

Though Beauty long hath there been matchless deem'd	2	To Ianthe	2
Mix'd in one mighty scene, with varied beauty glow	7	Harold 1	251
To me no pleasure Beauty brings	17	Harold 1	851
All that gay Beauty from her bondsmen claims	24	Harold 2	285
Her Beauty and her Chivalry, and bright	38	Harold 3	183
Through banks whose beauty would endure for ever	42	Harold 3	444
Some fresher beauty varying round	44	Harold 3	529
But of ideal beauty, which became	47	Harold 3	740
A beauty and a mystery, and create	49	Harold 3	830
Binding all things with beauty;--'twould disarm	49	Harold 3	849
The swiftest thought of beauty, here extend	51	Harold 3	913
Those days are gone, but Beauty still is here	55	Harold 4	23
The fatal gift of beauty, which became	61	Harold 4	371
The air around with beauty. We inhale	62	Harold 4	434
Dazzled and drunk with beauty, till the heart	62	Harold 4	443
Might gather o'er her beauty, and a gloom	70	Harold 4	913
Or, it might be, a beauty of the earth	72	Harold 4	1032
Of its own beauty is the mind diseased	73	Harold 4	1090
Nor worth nor beauty dwells from out the mind's	73	Harold 4	1102
Power, Glory, Strength, and Beauty, all are aisled	78	Harold 4	1385
All that ideal beauty ever bless'd	79	Harold 4	1454
Not worth, nor beauty, have her life redeem'd	84	Death-B	8
Or beauty charm the spectre from his prey	85	Epitaph	8
Then he who tells thee of thy beauty	87	Rousseau	17
The blushing beauty by thy side	89	Prometheus-A	12
Thy beauty must enrapture all	97	To M--	19
Vex'd to behold such beauty here	99	Young Lady	6
For beauty crown'd the fair-hair'd boy	103	Alva	160
'Twas his, with beauty, valour's gifts to share	105	Nisus	13
And lingering beauty hovers round the dead	110	Nisus	384
Which beauty shows, and sheds perfume	113	Cornelian-A	22
While Youth and Beauty form the female shield	114	Prologue	31
When love was bliss, and Beauty form'd our heaven	122	Recoll	14
The smiles of beauty (for, alas! I've known	125	Recoll	199
The smiles of beauty, though those smiles were dear	125	Recoll	201
The locks that were sacred to beauty, and you	136	Highlander	40
Rose, Wine, and Beauty, all my own	139	Anacreon-C	26
Forth in thy Beauty here thou deign'st to shine	139	Ossian-A	5

BEAUTY

Whether thy locks in Orient Beauty stream	139	Ossian-A	23
Look'st forth in beauty, laughing them to scorn	140	Ossian-B	20
Like Ossian lose thy beauty and thy strength	140	Ossian-B	28
While Youth and Strength and Beauty all are thine	140	Ossian-B	36
I can't attack, when Beauty forms the shield	142	Soliloquy	36
From it such Beams of Beauty fall	143	On Eyes	2
With beauty like yours, oh, how vain the contention	147	To Anne-A	13
To bear me from love and from beauty for ever	147	To Anne-B	4
When cold is the beauty which dwelt in my soul	148	Farewell-A	15
And still may thy branches their beauty display	149	Newstead-B	24
The friend of Beauty in distress	158	Florence	28
But vain the wish--for Beauty still	167	Euthanasia	21
Thy beauty still survives unfading	173	Quotation	27
How much more, Lake of Beauty! do we feel	192	Sonnet-C	10
And his present aspect--Beauty	196	Rogers	26
In Youth, Birth, Beauty, genially allied	199	Sonnet-D	7
And Beauty, Victor even of Time	200	Ode-C	2
Here--thou so redolent of Beauty	201	Year	49
Of beauty be	207	Year	32
Nor Genius swell, nor Beauty render vain	208	Sketch	27
Daughters and sons of Beauty,--but behold	215	Dream	131
She walks in beauty, like the night	216	She Walks	1
And Beauty and Canova can	229	Marble	4
Aegle, beauty and poet, has two little crimes	237	French-B	1
There is booty--there is Beauty	240	Suliotes	5
The smile of beauty, and the flush of wine	250	Bards	648
A Calmuck beauty with a Cossack wit	304	Age	438
Have swept the lines where beauty lingers	311	Giaour	73
But beauty with that fearful bloom	311	Giaour	96
So Beauty lures the full-grown child	314	Giaour	396
Till charm, and hue, and beauty gone	314	Giaour	408
Or Beauty, blighted in an hour	314	Giaour	414
Thus arm'd with beauty would she check	315	Giaour	512
For all that Beauty sighs to grant	316	Giaour	648
In colour though varied, in beauty may vie	323	Abydos 1	12
Though many a beauty droop'd in prison'd bower	342	Corsair 1	291
And these the notes the bird of beauty sung	343	Corsair 1	346
Whose ray of beauty reach'd him from afar	345	Corsair 1	512
With all the care defenceless beauty claims	350	Corsair 2	218
Had banish'd all the beauty from her cheek	361	Corsair 3	427
A night of beauty, mock'd such breast as his	368	Lara 1	180
Of beauty, and the form of grace	390	Corinth	543
Where Beauty watch'd to imitate	398	Parisina	152
In beauty, wassail, wine, and treasure	414	Mazeppa	738
Found beauty link'd with many a dusky form	422	Island 2	245
The mutual beauty which the sternest feel	423	Island 2	302
Thy lineaments in beauty that dismay'd	438	Tasso	134
But Thou--when all that Birth and Beauty throws	440	Tasso	241
Whose tints are truth and beauty at their best	441	Beppo	89
No, nor ideal beauty, that fine name	441	Beppo	98
The youth, the bloom, the beauty which agree	442	Beppo	109
Italian beauty! didst thou not inspire	445	Beppo	362
Thou, in the pride of Beauty and of Youth	455	Dante Ded	9
And show thy beauty in its fullest light	460	Dante 2	143
Leans sculptured Beauty, which Death cannot blight	461	Dante 3	40
The harlotry of genius, which, like beauty	461	Dante 3	77
With beauty so surpassing all below	463	Dante 4	30
Shall be the Age of Beauty; and while whelms	464	Dante 4	72
All beauty upon earth, compell'd to praise	464	Dante 4	82
To look upon thy beauty--nothing further	485	Manfred 2	132
But soften'd all, and temper'd into beauty	486	Manfred 2	202
Beauty like yours? or since have you ne'er seen	510	Faliero 2	120
His object was to place your orphan beauty	513	Faliero 2	298
Which made me covetous of girlish beauty	513	Faliero 2	312
A pride not in your beauty, but your conduct	514	Faliero 2	362
In all his marble-chisell'd beauty, or	514	Faliero 2	389
And making firm the whole with grace and beauty	523	Faliero 3	294
And bridal beauty, in the unwholesome press	528	Faliero 4	45
The sight of beauty as the parch'd pilgrim's	529	Faliero 4	65
Save me, my beauty! Thou art very fair	559	Sardan 1	553
Shall blaze with beauty and with light, until	560	Sardan 1	603
Is gone--and leaves his beauty, not his knowledge	562	Sardan 2	31
I see their brilliancy and feel their beauty	566	Sardan 2	267
Nor dote even on thy beauty--as I've doted	583	Sardan 4	337
Birth, wealth, health, beauty, are her accidents	606	Foscari 2	341
Fiend! tempt me not with beauty; thou art fairer	633	Cain 1	389
Thy beauty and thy love--my love and joy	634	Cain 1	448
Its beauty. And why not adore? Our father	635	Cain 1	495
Had more of beauty. Hast thou ne'er beheld him	642	Cain 2	404
And judge their beauty near. I have done this	643	Cain 2	455
Being beyond all beauty in thine eyes	643	Cain 2	483
And when her beauty disappears, methinks	644	Cain 2	539
He who creates all beauty will lose more	644	Cain 2	540
Of strength, of bloom, of beauty, and of joy	648	Cain 3	141
Unborn, undying beauty in thine eyes	655	Heaven	51
Becometh more so as it looks on beauty	657	Heaven	166
The eternal beauty of undying things	657	Heaven	167
So varied and so terrible in beauty	658	Heaven	268
Restore the beauty of her birth	661	Heaven	466
The rest of the stern Cainites, save in beauty	664	Heaven	672
Our race; behold their stature and their beauty	664	Heaven	688

BEAUTY

Who seek earth's daughters for their beauty? Patriarch	665	Heaven	739
Save his who made, what beauty and what power	666	Heaven	847
To that you show for beauty; but I pledge you	677	Werner 1	383
Much beauty, and more majesty. And that	677	Werner 1	394
At least in beauty: as for majesty	677	Werner 1	396
Youth, strength, and beauty, almost super-human	717	Werner 5	245
Shadows of beauty	724	Deformed 1	157
Shadows of beauty	725	Deformed 1	181
The phantom's bald; my quest is beauty. Could I	725	Deformed 1	190
The earth's perfection of all mental beauty	725	Deformed 1	221
The extremest beauty, if the proverb's true	726	Deformed 1	286
I am impatient. As a youthful beauty	726	Deformed 1	288
On beauty in that sex which is the type	727	Deformed 1	335
You inhabited your present dome of beauty	728	Deformed 1	444
True; the devil's always ugly; and your beauty	729	Deformed 1	523
The beauty of our host, and brave as beauteous	733	Deformed 1	788
A form of beauty, and an	737	Deformed 2	187
Alive or dead, thou essence of all beauty	741	Deformed 2	380
'Nothing'--an outshone Beauty what has made	743	Deformed 3	94
Nor wealth, nor youth, nor power, nor rank, nor beauty	743	Deformed 3	130
Sheds beauty and deep softness o'er the whole	761	Juan 1	910
And beauty, all concentrating like rays	797	Juan 2	1482
Beauty upon the beautiful they lighted	800	Juan 2	1627
Profusion with young beauty covers o'er	801	Juan 2	1684
At wassail in their beauty and their pride	809	Juan 3	484
A beauty at the season's close grown hectic	809	Juan 3	521
And in their native beauty stood avenged	810	Juan 3	597
Beauty and love were Haidee's mother's dower	823	Juan 4	389
Mourns o'er the beauty of the Cyclades	825	Juan 4	576
Valour was his, and beauty dwelt with her	825	Juan 4	580
Of beauty, flattery, threats, a shilling,--no	837	Juan 5	387
Her beauty of that overpowering kind	843	Juan 5	770
Her blood was high, her beauty scarce of earth	845	Juan 5	893
And although sensitive to beauty, he	847	Juan 5	967
Of a young downright beauty in this case	848	Juan 5	1040
Although her beauty was enough to vex	857	Juan 6	290
Yet of a beauty that would drive you crazy	857	Juan 6	328
Had made him lately bask in his bride's beauty	863	Juan 6	728
To share her beauty and her banishment	899	Juan 9	176
Beauty springs forth, and Nature's self turns paler	902	Juan 9	348
Of youth, and vigour, beauty, and those things	908	Juan 10	39
Which set the beauty off in which he glow'd	911	Juan 10	230
In royalty's vast arms he sigh'd for beauty	912	Juan 10	296
Their love, their virtue, beauty, education	958	Juan 14	191
Whate'er thou takest, spare a while poor Beauty	969	Juan 15	65
For this an heiress, and for that a beauty	972	Juan 15	266
Her beauty also seem'd to form no clog	974	Juan 15	381
Own'd to a penchant, though discreet, for beauty	978	Juan 15	680
Some praised her beauty; others her great grace	994	Juan 16	857
Unless some Beauty with a kiss should bribe	998	Juan 17	96

BEAUTY-BREATHING

When from his beauty-breathing pencil born	175	Sonnet-A	10

BEAUTY'S

And as in Beauty's bower he pensive sate	17	Harold 1	834
The smoothness and the sheen of beauty's cheek	36	Harold 3	93
Last eve in Beauty's circle proudly gay	39	Harold 3	245
A mirror and a bath for Beauty's youngest daughters	65	Harold 4	594
The cheeks which sprung from beauty's mould	98	To Mary	7
The lips which made me beauty's slave	98	To Mary	8
Arraign'd before thy beauty's throne	99	Young Lady	19
Nor dare to call the blush from Beauty's cheek	113	Prologue	6
The lustre of a beauty's eye	128	Answer-B	17
And yet, while Beauty's praise is thine	137	Clare	49
Cease, if you prize your beauty's reign	147	Vain Lady	33
But beauty's self hath ceased to charm	152	Weep-A	19
To gaze on Beauty's band without its chief	183	Address-D	22
There be none of Beauty's daughters	188	Music-C	1
But never yet did Beauty's Zone	201	Ode-C	23
Oh! snatch'd away in beauty's bloom	218	Bloom	1
I sunn'd my heart in beauty's eyes	219	Vanity	5
Thence shall I stray through beauty's native clime	255	Bards	1021
Its bank been soothed by Beauty's song	313	Giaour	313
Of ladye-love, and beauty's chain	321	Giaour	1104
To fix one spark of Beauty's heavenly ray	325	Abydos 1	171
So bright the tear in Beauty's eye	326	Abydos 1	226
As weeping Beauty's cheek at Sorrow's tale	337	Abydos 2	732
Nor beauty's preference, and the rival's pain	367	Lara 1	106
And the gay dance of bounding Beauty's train	371	Lara 1	389
(For beauty's sometimes best set off afar	442	Beppo	116
Warranted virgin; beauty's brightest colours	830	Juan 4	907
Itself with beauty's frail inanity	905	Juan 9	581

BEAUVEAU

'Soupe a la Beauveau.' whose relief was dory	976	Juan 15	503

BEAUX

While punctual beaux reward the grateful notes	252	Bards	797
Squeezed in 'Fop's Alley,' jostled by the beaux	261	Hints	311
And envies Lais all her Attic beaux	271	Minerva	192
So, instead of 'beaux arts,' we may say 'la belle passion	277	Blues 1	4

BEAVER

Prefer my nightcap to my beaver	163	Malta	55

BECAFICAS

I also like to dine on becaficas	445	Beppo	337

BECALM'D

That the sail was becalm'd between the seas	781	Juan 2	474

BECAME

When Marathon became a magic word	33	Harold 2	843
Too long and darkly, till my brain became	36	Harold 3	56
But in Man's dwellings he became a thing	37	Harold 3	127
Who woo'd thee once, thy vassal, and became	41	Harold 3	329
Where he became a being) whose desire	47	Harold 3	722
But of ideal beauty, which became	47	Harold 3	740
The fatal gift of beauty, which became	61	Harold 4	371
I saw you--my anger became admiration	147	To Anne-A	11
Till Guilt became Sublime	201	Ode-C	22
That, seen, became a part of sight	321	Giaour	1128
To other ears that death became thee well	359	Corsair 3	229
These and the pale pure cheek became the bier	364	Corsair 3	621
A latent fierceness that far more became	374	Lara 1	580
And merely like a spur became	411	Mazeppa	452
And in my tongue the thirst became	411	Mazeppa	462
Since I became the Cossack's guest	415	Mazeppa	843
Became a slave of course, and for his pay	452	Beppo	748
He join'd the rogues and prosper'd, and became	452	Beppo	751
With dinners, where he oft became the laugh of them	452	Beppo	783
And of the faith became a trump, whose sounding	473	Morgante	463
The hour arrived--and it became	480	Manfred 1	116
Became religion, and the heart ran o'er	495	Manfred 3	298
To have you dragg'd to prison, I became	519	Faliero 3	61
Till they became my subjects; then fell from me	525	Faliero 3	429
My name became the synonyme of death	557	Sardan 1	451
I became Doge, or dream'd of such advancement	605	Foscari 2	204
Blood became ice. But he was all alone	718	Werner 5	318
The land he made not Rome's, while Rome became	725	Deformed 1	188
The hearers of her case became repeaters	750	Juan 1	222
Inez became sole guardian, which was fair	751	Juan 1	293
It was for this that I became a bride	764	Juan 1	1156
Became divested of his native modesty	774	Juan 2	8
And the ship creak'd, the town became a speck	775	Juan 2	99
And I became a prisoner to the foe	875	Juan 7	486
The earth, which he became like a fell'd tree	893	Juan 8	926
Became a kind of fashionable mystery	933	Juan 12	216
Those became one who soon were to be two	934	Juan 12	302

BECASSE

The chaste description even of a 'becasse	977	Juan 15	568

BECAUSE

And when they smiled because he deem'd it near	38	Harold 3	203
Partly because they blend me with his line	39	Harold 3	255
Because they yet may meet thine eye	44	Harold 3	521
As heretofore because ambition was selfwill'd	48	Harold 3	778
Nor claim a passing sigh, because it told for whom	63	Harold 4	522
Less than it feels, because the weapon which it wields	64	Harold 4	549
Because the deadly days which we have seen	69	Harold 4	868
Because not altogether of such clay	75	Harold 4	1214
And wherefore slaughter'd? wherefore, but because	76	Harold 4	1246
Only because the scene's a garden	101	Lady-B	16
Because my youth is fled	131	L'Amitie	2
Because that heart is not the same	148	A Fan	4
Because I cannot love but one	156	Lady-F	6
Because her bosom is not colder	160	Cadiz	52
And take my rhyme--because 'tis 'gratis	163	Malta	32
Because the Catholics would not rise	177	Devil's Dr	146
Because my homely phrase the truth would tell	191	Churchill	38
Because he answer'd, and because	195	Ballad-A	63
Because it reminds me of thine	210	Augusta-B	12
Because as how, if you should fail	230	Murray-A	8
Because of Alashtar	232	Murray-B	17
Because I bade the people pull	235	New Song	3
Because I would reform the den	235	New Song	15
Because they want to run their rigs	235	New Song	19
Because if a live dog, 'tis said	238	Orford	5
They write for food--and feed because they write	249	Bards	553
Or lose one point, because they wrote in verse	258	Hints	124
Because, in scenes exciting joy or grief	260	Hints	287
Because it costs him dear, and makes him dress	261	Hints	316
Because Parnassus, though a mount divine	264	Hints	529
New wars, because the old succeed so well	276	Waltz	169
How can you know that? there are two more. Because	281	Blues 2	38

BECAUSE

Because the last we saw here had a tussle	287	Vision		142
To thee and thine, because nor wine nor lust	289	Vision		310
Nay, not so much;--they hate thee, man, because	305	Age		554
And do not deign to smite because they may	347	Corsair	2	22
Not cankering less because the more conceal'd	352	Corsair	2	353
'Why should I seek? because--Oh! didst thou not	359	Corsair	3	288
Because, despite thy crimes, that heart is moved	360	Corsair	3	294
But not in pity, not because he ought	371	Lara	1	339
Because the worst is ever nearest truth	375	Lara	1	623
Because, forsooth, I could not claim	399	Parisina		260
Because our mother's brow was given	403	Chillon		74
Because I could have smiled to see	404	Chillon		124
Because unto himself he seem'd	410	Mazeppa		351
She fear'd no ill, because she knew it not	421	Island	2	149
Not less because I suffer it unbent	437	Tasso		54
Like steel in tempering fire? because I loved	439	Tasso		205
Because I loved what not to love, and see	439	Tasso		206
So call'd, because, the name and thing agreeing	441	Beppo		43
Because they have no sauces to their stews	441	Beppo		52
Who do such things because they know no better	442	Beppo		124
Because she had a 'cavalier servente	442	Beppo		136
Because it slips into my verse with ease	442	Beppo		168
Because I never heard, nor could engage	442	Beppo		172
Because in Christian countries 'tis a rule	443	Beppo		186
Because they know the world, and are at ease	444	Beppo		303
Because the skies are not the most secure	445	Beppo		332
Because, were I to ponder to infinity	447	Beppo		487
Because, just as the stanza likes to make it	448	Beppo		499
Because I'm rather hippish, and may borrow	448	Beppo		508
Because the Turks so much admire philogyny	448	Beppo		555
Because when once the lamps and candles fail	450	Beppo		655
My indignant bones, because her angry gust	457	Dante	1	81
Before the storm because its breath is rough	461	Dante	3	24
Because of the great battle in which fell	466	Morgante		44
Displeased he was with Gan because he said it	468	Morgante		119
'Because his love of justice unto all	472	Morgante		393
Because he was one of his family	475	Morgante		588
Boasting these idle attributes, because	486	Manfred	2	192
Because my nature was averse from life	493	Manfred	3	125
Because 'tis now degraded. 'Tis even so	502	Faliero	1	204
Because she took an old man for her lord	503	Faliero	1	207
Full of reproof, because our artisans	505	Faliero	1	383
Because my general is Doge, and will not	505	Faliero	1	408
To do yourself due right? Because the man	507	Faliero	1	545
Of which they feel the want, but not because	510	Faliero	2	72
And, secondly, because of all these men	534	Faliero	4	398
Because the Doge, who should protect the law	541	Faliero	5	230
Because he turn'd a fruit to an enchantment	554	Sardan	1	235
Because I have not shed their blood, nor led them	554	Sardan	1	274
Because he loved a Lydian queen: thou seest	556	Sardan	1	377
Because they are near; and all who are remote	557	Sardan	1	443
Because they are far. But if it should be so	557	Sardan	1	444
If then they hate me, 'tis because I hate not	557	Sardan	1	459
If they rebel, 'tis because I oppress not	557	Sardan	1	460
Because thou dost not fear, I fear for thee	560	Sardan	1	667
Because I cannot keep it with my own	565	Sardan	2	222
And chiefly thou, my priest, because I doubt thee	566	Sardan	2	276
Because for something or for nothing this	567	Sardan	2	365
Because my place is here. And when I am gone	573	Sardan	3	150
Because all passions in excess are female	577	Sardan	3	381
Because it changed not; and I turn'd for refuge	579	Sardan	4	99
Because I ever dreaded to intrude	585	Sardan	4	443
Perhaps because I merit them too often	585	Sardan	4	472
Because he fears not death; and banish him	600	Foscari	1	289
Because all earth, except his native land	600	Foscari	1	290
Pause in her full career, because a woman	600	Foscari	1	315
Because we have brief time for preparation	612	Foscari	3	286
Because we have waited long enough, and he	616	Foscari	4	63
Humanity! Because his son is dead	619	Foscari	4	259
Life--Toil! and wherefore should I toil?--because	628	Cain	1	65
And he is good.' How know I that? Because	628	Cain	1	76
Because 'ye should not eat the fruits of life	630	Cain	1	201
To that which is omnipotent, because	633	Cain	1	385
I see them, but I know them not. Because	641	Cain	2	373
Because this evil only was the path	643	Cain	2	492
And is more than myself because I love it	644	Cain	2	527
Thou lovest it, because 'tis beautiful	644	Cain	2	528
Because thou hast thought of this ere now. And if	644	Cain	2	560
For our child's canopy? Because its branches	646	Cain	3	6
And it may be with other names, because	650	Cain	3	249
I abhor death, because that thou must die	664	Heaven		707
Because it takes not life, but life's sole solace	673	Werner	1	103
That, ere you know my route? Because there is	679	Werner	1	538
It was to seek his parents; some because	685	Werner	2	115
Because they love their lives too! Yet, he's right	688	Werner	2	333
I am a fool to lose myself because	691	Werner	2	527
Are practising your power on me, because	692	Werner	2	598
All--all suspected me: and why? because	695	Werner	3	23
Because I feel it) as may leave no nightmare	695	Werner	3	38
Because an undescribable--but 'tis	700	Werner	3	368
Because 'tis dusky. And if I do so	703	Werner	3	540

BECAUSE

It only was because your presence sent it	706	Werner	4	160
Because you look as if you saw a murderer	707	Werner	4	199
Receive it, 'tis because I know too well	711	Werner	4	469
Then wherefore seek? Because I cannot rest	715	Werner	5	144
I speak to you, Count Siegendorf, because	716	Werner	5	203
As doth the bolt, because it stood between us	720	Werner	5	460
Because thou wert my first-born, and I knew not	722	Deformed	1	13
His form, why not his power? Is it because	723	Deformed	1	42
Since I have risk'd my soul because I find not	725	Deformed	1	238
In turn, because of this vile crooked clog	727	Deformed	1	340
Because you know no better than the dull	730	Deformed	1	582
Because he leapt a ditch ('twas then no wall	731	Deformed	1	650
Because no man could understand his neighbour	732	Deformed	1	680
Perhaps because they cannot feel the jolting	741	Deformed	2	401
Because at least the past were pass'd away	745	Fragment-D		3
Gasping on deck, because you soar too high, Bob	745	Juan	Ded	23
Fearless--because no feeling dwells in ice	747	Juan	Ded	119
Because the army's grown more popular	747	Juan	1	29
He died: and most unluckily, because	751	Juan	1	257
Because of filthy loves of gods and goddesses	752	Juan	1	322
Because it is a marketable vice	755	Juan	1	512
Because that number rarely much endears	760	Juan	1	854
Because, no doubt, 'twas for his dirty fee	765	Juan	1	1207
And, secondly, I pity not, because	767	Juan	1	1329
I trace this scrawl because I cannot rest	770	Juan	1	1543
Because the first is crazed beyond all hope	772	Juan	1	1635
Because they tell me 'twere in vain to try	772	Juan	1	1686
Because, till people know what's come to pass	781	Juan	2	438
Because the sea ran higher every minute	781	Juan	2	455
Because they still can hope, nor shines the knife	782	Juan	2	509
And Juan, who had still refused, because	783	Juan	2	562
As fattest; but he saved himself, because	784	Juan	2	642
Because the tackle of our shatter'd bark	786	Juan	2	755
Because it left encouragement behind	786	Juan	2	790
Because the good old man had so much 'νους.'	790	Juan	2	1037
Because her mistress would not let her break	792	Juan	2	1167
Because 'tis liquor only, and being far	794	Juan	2	1243
Him past all bounds, because she smiled to see	794	Juan	2	1259
Rather by deeds than words, because the case	794	Juan	2	1266
'Twas well, because health in the human frame	795	Juan	2	1347
Who please,--the more because they preach in vain	796	Juan	2	1422
And all because a lady fell in love	823	Juan	4	408
And then give way, subdued because surrounded	823	Juan	4	430
Because the publisher declares, in sooth	828	Juan	4	774
(Because the world won't read him, always snarling	830	Juan	4	870
(Because this Canto has become too long	831	Juan	4	931
Because if drown'd, they can't--if spared, they won't	832	Juan	5	48
Because one poet travell'd 'mongst the Turks	836	Juan	5	336
Because they can't find out the very spot	839	Juan	5	491
Of that same Babel, or because they won't	839	Juan	5	492
Because he had journey'd fifty miles, and found	850	Juan	5	1195
The women up, because, in sad reality	851	Juan	5	1250
And next she gave her (I say her, because	859	Juan	6	457
Because 'tis pleasant, so that it be pure	859	Juan	6	468
Because all gentle readers have the gift	863	Juan	6	700
Aloud because his feelings were too tender	863	Juan	6	707
Because a foolish or imprudent act	865	Juan	6	828
Because the Turks could never be persuaded	868	Juan	7	98
Because, though I am but a simple noddy	869	Juan	7	165
Because they were constructed in a hurry	870	Juan	7	202
And why? because a little--odd--old man	873	Juan	7	391
Because he runs before it like a pig	877	Juan	7	674
And why?--because it brings self-approbation	878	Juan	8	25
Because it then received no injury	879	Juan	8	77
Because their thoughts had never been the prey	886	Juan	8	523
Because it might not solace 'ears polite	890	Juan	8	742
Because deform'd, yet died all game and bottom	892	Juan	8	879
This special honour was conferr'd, because	896	Juan	8	1113
And deem, because we see, we are all-seeing	898	Juan	9	124
Why do they call me misanthrope? Because	899	Juan	9	167
Because he could no more digest his dinner	900	Juan	9	264
Because each lover look'd a sort of king	905	Juan	9	556
Because the clergy take the thing in hand	906	Juan	9	604
Because she put a favourite to death	906	Juan	9	646
Because December, with his breath so hoary	908	Juan	10	70
And why? because she's changeable and chaste	908	Juan	10	81
Because they are so;--a male Mrs. Fry	918	Juan	10	670
'Twill be because our notion is not high	923	Juan	11	283
Because the times have hardly left them one tenant	928	Juan	11	632
Because, you'll say, nought calls for such a trial	930	Juan	12	55
Because she thought him a good heart at bottom	935	Juan	12	386
Because indifference begins to lull	941	Juan	13	29
Also because the figure and the face	941	Juan	13	31
It is because I cannot well do less	942	Juan	13	59
Because it makes us smile: his hero's right	942	Juan	13	66
Because its own good pleasure hath decided	943	Juan	13	128
Because bold Britons have a tongue and free quill	943	Juan	13	157
Because, though young, he acquiesced with suavity	944	Juan	13	171
Because the monks preferr'd a hill behind	948	Juan	13	439

BECAUSE

Because--such was his magic power to please	952 Juan	13	687
Or hunt: the young, because they liked the sport	953 Juan	13	802
And hardly heaven--because it never ends	954 Juan	13	835
Down to the harp--because to music's charms	954 Juan	13	855
In youth I wrote because my mind was full	956 Juan	14	79
And now because I feel it growing dull	956 Juan	14	80
Because the sun, and stars, and aught that shines	959 Juan	14	229
It is because I do not know them yet	964 Juan	14	542
Because he mopeth idly in his shell	965 Juan	14	642
Because 'tis frailer, doubtless, than a stanch one	966 Juan	14	678
In him, because she thought he was in danger	967 Juan	14	727
Because she was not apt, like some of us	969 Juan	15	75
Because he had, like Alcibiades	969 Juan	15	87
Because he ne'er seem'd anxious to seduce	969 Juan	15	90
Because I hate even democratic royalty	971 Juan	15	184
Partly perhaps because a fresh sensation	971 Juan	15	220
A third, because there can be no objections	972 Juan	15	272
Because it breeds no more mouths than it nourishes	972 Juan	15	276
Because he either meant to sneer at harmony	972 Juan	15	281
Perhaps because 'twas fallen: her sires were proud	974 Juan	15	364
Because she did not pin her faith on feature	975 Juan	15	448
Faults which attract because they are not tame	975 Juan	15	453
Because it sometimes, as I have seen or read it	978 Juan	15	627
Because my business is to dress society	979 Juan	15	741
Because I'd rather it should be forgot	980 Juan	15	765
Because 'tis so. Who nibble, scribble, quibble, he	981 Juan	16	39
Was great, because his master brook'd no less	984 Juan	16	223
Because the present tale has oft been told	985 Juan	16	295
Because she said her temper had been tried	987 Juan	16	444
Because, as suits their rank and situation	989 Juan	16	589
Because the neighbouring Scotch Earl of Gift-gabbit	989 Juan	16	604
Because as Ages upon Ages push on	997 Juan	17	43
Heedless of pricks because it was obtuse	997 Juan	17	46
Because he fix'd it; and, to stop his talking	997 Juan	17	58

BECHER

Candour compels me, Becher! to commend	118 Answer-A		1
Dear Becher, you tell me to mix with mankind	128 Becher-A		1
But Becher! you're a reverend pastor	145 Becher-B		53
Say, Becher, I shall be forgiven	145 Becher-B		65

BECK

And Conrad following, at her beck, obey'd	362 Corsair	3	448
Are at thy beck and bidding, Child of Clay	480 Manfred	1	133

BECKET'S

Black Edward's helm, and Becket's bloody stone	916 Juan	10	578

BECKON

Then rising, start, and beckon him to fly	384 Lara	2	621
And beckon me away! So let them! Wilt thou	733 Deformed	1	762

BECKON'D

Beckon'd the natives round her to their prows	429 Island	3	221
Blazed through the clouds of death and beckon'd hence	433 Island	4	264
He beckon'd to the foremost, who drew nigh	434 Island	4	331
As if their souls and lips each other beckon'd	798 Juan	2	1494
Gulbeyaz stopp'd and beckon'd Baba:--'Slave	866 Juan	6	889

BECKONING

And all his Houris beckoning through	315 Giaour		486
But bright, and long, and beckoning years	414 Mazeppa		757

BECKONS

And Learning beckons from her temple's door	124 Recoll		150
But me she beckons from the earth	146 Adieu		85
La Harpe, thine Aristotle, beckons on	304 Age		455
Which beckons onward to his grave	318 Giaour		830
And beckons with beseeching hands	323 Giaour		1299

BECOME

Such tears become thine eye	6 Harold	1	155
In the hot throng, where we become the spoil	46 Harold	3	657
I live not in myself, but I become	46 Harold	3	680
The gods become as mortals, and man's fate	63 Harold	4	463
Lest their own judgments should become too bright	69 Harold	4	836
That we become a part of what has been	76 Harold	4	1241
Is to become no longer free	99 Young Lady		26
Frowns become not one so fair	100 Marion		4
The soul's meridian don't become her	134 E. N. Long		75
Ere thirty may become, I ween	138 Clare		65
Or say these glances don't become her	143 On Eyes		6
They do divide our being; they become	213 Dream		9
Which is not of the earth; she was become	215 Dream		172
I labour to be brief --become obscure	257 Hints		42
Sad words, no doubt, become a serious face	258 Hints		147
Become its reproach. I've no sort of objection	282 Blues	2	101

BECOME

Become as base a critic as e'er crawl'd	297 Vision		780
'Twere worse than bondage to become his bride	354 Corsair	2	524
What better name may slumber's bed become	375 Lara	1	638
He fell his soul become more light	388 Corinth		358
Who still become more constant as they cool	444 Beppo		272
But Tiber shall become a mournful river	460 Dante	2	100
As guest is slave, his thoughts become a booty	461 Dante	3	81
(Which casts up misty columns that become	492 Manfred	3	112
And be a living lie, who would become	492 Manfred	3	119
Of mortals on the earth, who do become	493 Manfred	3	139
As doth become your near and faithful kinsman	504 Faliero	1	286
Who would become a throne, or overthrow one	518 Faliero	2	676
Oh, what a villain I become for thee	532 Faliero	4	316
Become a precedent 'gainst such haught traitors	540 Faliero	5	196
Chambers: the palace has become a fortress	588 Sardan	5	62
Than should become a sovereign's retreat	621 Foscari	5	32
And become gods as we.' Were those his words	630 Cain	1	202
This is a vision, else I am become	651 Cain	3	342
Become the master of my rights, and lord	673 Werner	1	86
Pretended den of refuge, rose	718 Werner	5	345
A spur in its halt movements, to become	727 Deformed	1	317
What shall become of your abandon'd garment	728 Deformed	1	422
Any one else--they were become traditional	751 Juan	1	244
Whate'er the cause might be, they had become	755 Juan	1	553
What will become on't--I'm in such a fright	767 Juan	1	1363
And may become of great advantage when	785 Juan	2	740
Become a thing, or nothing, save to rank	813 Juan	3	803
I feel my heart become so sympathetic	823 Juan	4	413
'Twould not become myself to dwell upon	827 Juan	4	697
(Because this Canto has become too long	831 Juan	4	931
This poem will become a moral model	831 Juan	5	16
Some thought her dress did not so much become her	856 Juan	6	275
Men become wolves on any slight occasion	899 Juan	9	160
Old enemies who have become new friends	908 Juan	10	89
Old flames, new wives, become our bitterest foes	909 Juan	10	95
When nature wears the gown that doth become her	947 Juan	13	379

BECOMES

The race of life becomes a hopeless flight	46 Harold	3	666
All earth becomes their monument	183 Parker		8
Becomes extinguish'd, soon--too soon--expires	195 Vittorelli		6
Then receive him as best such an advent becomes	202 Avatar		19
The p--x becomes his passage to degrees	260 Hints		238
That best becomes an Eastern night	312 Giaour		179
Each arm'd, as best becomes a man	315 Giaour		521
Apparrell'd as becomes the brave	324 Abydos	1	21
How well such deed becomes the turban'd brave	347 Corsair	2	18
Becomes the bravest, if they feel for men	380 Lara	2	347
Or what becomes of damage and divorces	444 Beppo		296
Becomes exceeding tedious to my mind	446 Beppo		395
'Beppo! that beard of yours becomes you not	451 Beppo		737
From the quick sense of honour, which becomes	510 Faliero	2	108
Then here must be my station, as becomes	536 Faliero	4	544
And thus becomes so in diffusing joy	634 Cain	1	477
As he adores the Highest, death becomes	655 Heaven		24
No matter what becomes on't. That's ungracious	728 Deformed	1	429
Of life. The planet wheels till it becomes	730 Deformed	1	593
The ear becomes more Irish, and less nice	821 Juan	4	328
What was a paradox becomes a truth or	997 Juan	17	47

BECOMETH

Becometh more so as it looks on beauty	657 Heaven		166

BECOMING

There's nothing so becoming to the face	768 Juan	1	1424
Thought it would be becoming to die drunk	778 Juan	2	280
But in a style becoming his condition	913 Juan	10	352
'Tis so becoming to the soul and face	961 Juan	14	370
Juan replied, with all becoming deference	971 Juan	15	233

BED

(See also CHILD-BED, DEATH-BED, MARRIAGE-BED)

A little rill of scanty stream and bed	65 Harold	4	582
Worthy a king's--or more--a Roman's bed	70 Harold	4	894
Goes late to bed, yet early rises	95 Granta		32
Oh! that is Allan's nuptial bed	105 Alva		300
With clay the grave's eternal bed	133 Prayer		58
In dew-drops o'er my narrow bed	146 Adieu		96
When stretch'd on fever's sleepless bed	166 Struggle		33
Wave gently o'er my dying bed	166 Euthanasia		4
Though Earth received them in her bed	167 Dead		5
One vigil o'er thy bed	167 Dead		58
That they sent even him to his brimstone bed	178 Devil's Dr		174
Would woo thee to a loveless bed	179 Gold		30
Wake us from a widow's bed	207 Fare Thee		32
Oh, may thy grave be sleepless as the bed	209 Sketch		93
That ever breaking Bed, beyond repair	224 J.C.H.		19
But brought to bed at forty-nine	231 Doctor		70
While none but menials o'er the bed of death	251 Bards		682
But find in thine, like pagan Plato's bed	261 Hints		349
None stand by his low bed--though even the mind	299 Age		85
For the stream has shrunk from its marble bed	313 Giaour		297
Should seek and share her narrow bed	321 Giaour		1126

BED
This bed of death --attest my truth | 322 Giaour | | 1189
Thy pride of heart, thy bride for Osman's bed | 336 Abydos | 2 | 656
Ours the fresh turf and not the feverish bed | 338 Corsair | 1 | 30
What better name may slumber's bed become | 375 Lara | 1 | 638
Our sleep fell soft on the hardest bed | 384 Corinth | | 9
Than now might yield a warrior's bed | 388 Corinth | | 344
And Hugo is gone to his lonely bed | 397 Parisina | | 65
I've seen the sick and ghastly bed | 404 Chillon | | 182
My step profaned their lowly bed | 405 Chillon | | 315
And made for him a leafy bed | 407 Mazeppa | | 59
And little cared for bed and board | 407 Mazeppa | | 67
A bed nor comfortless nor new | 415 Mazeppa | | 863
Not like a 'bed of violets' on the gale | 425 Island | 2 | 436
Which smothers women in a bed of feather | 442 Beppo | | 140
The peasant's harvest from his turbid bed | 460 Dante | 2 | 106
My breast upon its rocky bosom's bed | 482 Manfred | 1 | 279
As though it were a bed of love, deserves | 575 Sardan | 3 | 224
Is he--Our bridal bed is now his bier | 622 Foscari | 5 | 110
Our little Enoch sleeps upon yon bed | 646 Cain | 3 | 2
Travel-tired, and lately risen from a bed | 678 Werner | 1 | 474
When he will take himself to bed. Before | 680 Werner | 1 | 600
And yet I must to bed; I fain would say | 700 Werner | 3 | 357
Did he who own'd it die in his bed? Alas | 712 Werner | 4 | 503
You said he died in his bed, not battle. He | 712 Werner | 4 | 507
I look'd through and beheld a purple bed | 718 Werner | 5 | 314
'Twas midnight--Donna Julia was in bed | 763 Juan | 1 | 1081
To hold a levee round his lady's bed | 764 Juan | 1 | 1110
Under the bed they search'd, and there they found | 764 Juan | 1 | 1145
Of looking in the bed as well as under | 764 Juan | 1 | 1152
Young Juan slipp'd half-smother'd, from the bed | 767 Juan | 1 | 1320
He had a bed of furs, and a pelisse | 791 Juan | 2 | 1057
Had made her mistress quit her bed to trace | 794 Juan | 2 | 1268
As o'er a bed of roses the sweet south | 795 Juan | 2 | 1344
Ocean their witness, and the cave their bed | 800 Juan | 2 | 1628
With their rough faces throng'd about the bed | 836 Juan | 5 | 290
Her fifth, to call her maids and go to bed | 849 Juan | 5 | 1109
To make the nuptial couch a 'Bed of Ware | 854 Juan | 6 | 96
A bed is not a throne, and they may sleep | 855 Juan | 6 | 154
Look'd more adapted to be put to bed | 857 Juan | 6 | 326
'She also had compassion and a bed | 858 Juan | 6 | 376
But wide awake she was, and round her bed | 861 Juan | 6 | 569
Bed for the dream she had been obliged to hear | 862 Juan | 6 | 630
Rose the sultana from a bed of splendour | 863 Juan | 6 | 705
But to sit up while others lie in bed | 924 Juan | 11 | 63
And sedges, brooding in their liquid bed | 948 Juan | 13 | 454
The Greek Eve, Helen, from the Spartan's bed | 964 Juan | 14 | 573
Observed as strictly both at board and bed | 972 Juan | 15 | 254
Undrest, and rather slowly went to bed | 984 Juan | 16 | 212
And 'tis held as faith, to their bed of death | 985 Juan | 16 | 343
'Tis white, at least when they just rise from bed | 989 Juan | 16 | 556

BED-APPAREL
Shall furnish forth the bed-apparel; for | 675 Werner | 1 | 264

BED-CLOTHES
Contrived to fling the bed-clothes in a heap | 764 Juan | 1 | 1117

BEDDED
To Strangers vow'd, with strangers bedded | 197 Duel | | 28

BEDDING
Without the expense and the suspense of bedding | 895 Juan | 8 | 1048

BEDECK
The spoil of nations shall bedeck my bride | 333 Abydos | 2 | 413

BEDECKS
Bedecks her cap with bells of every clime | 242 Bards | | 30

BEDEW
For this these tears our cheeks bedew | 89 To Emma | | 38
Though Freedom's blood thy plain bedew | 187 Ode-B | | 2
And may serve therefore to bedew these rhymes | 889 Juan | 8 | 717

BEDEW'D
Robed half in mist, bedew'd with snowy rills | 25 Harold | 2 | 372
With tears the burning cheek of each bedew'd | 107 Nisus | | 129
Methought one drop the stone bedew'd | 113 Cornelian-A | | 15
That field with blood bedew'd in vain | 329 Abydos | 2 | 23
'Twas strange--that robber, thus with gore bedew'd | 351 Corsair | 2 | 263
Bedew'd his spirit in his calmer hours | 808 Juan | 3 | 448

BED-FELLOW
Despair your bed-fellow--then rise, but not | 690 Werner | 2 | 445
Lest their too lawful bed-fellow should wake | 855 Juan | 6 | 192

BEDFORD
Though burnt by wicked Bedford for a witch | 244 Bards | | 207

BEDIMM'D
Celestial tears bedimm'd her large blue eye | 269 Minerva | | 86

BEDLAM
Than see this royal Bedlam bigot range | 291 Vision | | 395
But Bedlam still exists with its sage fetter | 921 Juan | 11 | 195
Shut up the world at large , let Bedlam out | 966 Juan | 14 | 665

BEDLAMITES
Like birds, or boys, or bedlamites broke loose | 856 Juan | 6 | 266

BEDRAL
Were pointed out as usual by the bedral | 916 Juan | 10 | 579

BEDS
Vile assignations, and adulterous beds | 442 Beppo | | 127
Also beneath the canopy of beds | 855 Juan | 6 | 194
The whole Oda from their beds at halfpast three | 862 Juan | 6 | 636
Who make the beds of those who won't take quarter | 892 Juan | 8 | 885

BEE
(See also QUEEN-BEE)
There the blithe bee his fragrant fortress builds | 33 Harold | 2 | 823
And flowers the fairest that may feast the bee | 368 Lara | 1 | 162
Good out of evil. Happier than the bee | 583 Sardan | 4 | 321
And stepping with the bee from flower to flower | 671 Werner | 1 | 6
And the honey bee is clinging | 743 Deformed | 3 | 72
Hived in our bosoms like the bag o' the bee | 773 Juan | 1 | 1709
A bee flew out and stung her to the heart | 862 Juan | 6 | 615
But visions of an apple and a bee | 862 Juan | 6 | 634
None, save the Spanish fly and Attic bee | 900 Juan | 9 | 223
For a spoil'd carpet--but the 'Attic Bee' | 986 Juan | 16 | 391

BEECHES
Plucks up pines, beeches, poplar-trees, and oaks | 469 Morgante | | 202

BEEF
Turn beef to bannocks, cauliflowers to kail | 248 Bards | | 525
A portion of their beef up from below | 780 Juan | 2 | 373
Beef, veal, and mutton, better for digestion | 782 Juan | 2 | 536
But beef is rare within these oxless isles | 793 Juan | 2 | 1225
I say that beef is rare, and can't help thinking | 793 Juan | 2 | 1233
Fed upon beef--I won't say much of beer | 794 Juan | 2 | 1242
That beef and battles both were owing to her | 794 Juan | 2 | 1248
Than could roast beef in our rough John Bull way | 977 Juan | 15 | 564
As between English beef and Spartan broth | 991 Juan | 16 | 719

BEEF-STEAK
I like a beef-steak, too, as well as any | 446 Beppo | | 379
The best of remedies is a beef-steak | 775 Juan | 2 | 101
And long for food, but chiefly a beef-steak | 793 Juan | 2 | 1224
Like Esau for my birthright a beef-steak | 837 Juan | 5 | 352

BEE-LIKE
Heard,--and that bee-like, bubbling, busy hum | 919 Juan | 11 | 63

BEEN
Happier in this than mightiest bards have been | 14 Harold | 1 | 630
And mortal foot hath ne'er or rarely been | 23 Harold | 2 | 220
That he who there at such an hour hath been | 23 Harold | 2 | 239
Thy throne had still been thine, or never been | 40 Harold | 3 | 321
The wild rocks shaped as they had turrets been | 45 Harold | 3 | 585
And thou, too, perish, Pompey? have ye been | 68 Harold | 4 | 782
And fatal have her Saturnalia been | 69 Harold | 4 | 866
Who love the lords of others?--such have been | 70 Harold | 4 | 902
That we become a part of what has been | 76 Harold | 4 | 1241
Farewell! a word that must be, and hath been | 83 Harold | 4 | 1666
Her countless hoards would his have been | 113 Cornelian A | | 31
Those fairy bowers, where all in turn have been | 122 Recoll | | 16
The joyous days which ours have been | 133 E. N. Long | | 3
To Tempests thus exposed my Fate has been | 140 Ossian | 1 | 51
Thus might the Record now have been | 150 Harrow-C | | 13
Through every turn of life hath been | 153 Friend-A | | 46
Not what he was, but what he should have been | 154 Dog | | 6
But could I be what I have been | 156 Lady-F | | 7
Of what we are, and what we've been | 156 Lady-F | | 44
'Twill soothe to be, where thou hast been | 158 Florence | | 44
And know, whatever thou hast been | 167 Euthanasia | | 35
For well I know, that such had been | 168 Haunts | | 33
And bids the Drama be where she hath been | 169 Address-A | | 24
To think that God's fair world hath been | 181 Ode-A | | 80
Oh could I feel as I have felt,--or be what I have been | 186 Music-B | | 17
Such things should be--if such have ever been | 193 Monody | | 96
Alas! how many things have been | 197 Duel | | 44
Where never Sovereign yet had been | 200 Ode-C | | 8
If my inheritance of storms hath been | 211 Augusta-C | | 17
'Tis thine at once, fair Albion! to have been | 255 Bards | | 1001
Make it appear as if it might have been | 259 Hints | | 172
And come what may, I have been blest | 321 Giaour | | 1115
Of all our golden youth had been | 322 Giaour | | 1239
To be what I have ever been | 328 Abydos | 1 | 419
Oh! yet--for there my steps have been | 329 Abydos | 2 | 28
Though vain its ray as it had never been | 343 Corsair | 1 | 354
That useless flood of grief had never been | 365 Corsair | 3 | 653
Whate'er he be, 'twas not what he had been | 367 Lara | 1 | 66
They scarce knew what, but more than should have been | 368 Lara | 1 | 142

BEEN

Burst forth, and made him all he once had been	378	Lara	2	246
Stern, unambitious, silent, he had been	378	Lara	2	258
Where but for him that strife had never been	381	Lara	2	415
That raised his arm to point where such had been	381	Lara	2	471
From lingering where her chieftain's blood had been	383	Lara	2	601
Since he, their mightiest chief, had been	387	Corinth		318
The bravest be, or late have been	393	Corinth		838
Here, throughout the siege, had been	395	Corinth		981
Her name--as if she ne'er had been	401	Parisina		505
Placed in the Arab's clime, he would have been	421	Island	2	179
And dared as what was likely to have been	426	Island	3	32
Where few but Nature's footsteps yet had been	433	Island	4	254
The maniac and his tyrant. Had I been	439	Tasso		177
The everlasting to be which hath been	453	Venice-B		59
And task most hopeless; but some such have been	463	Dante	3	182
If it had not for good Gherardo been	467	Morgante		101
And gorged so that, as if the bones had been	474	Morgante		530
Must be near thee, and hath been	481	Manfred	1	215
But what wouldst have? the empire has been founded	559	Sardan	1	596
Had Samiasa and Azaziel been	666	Heaven		797
A charlatan, a coxcomb--and have been	761	Juan	1	927
But vaccination certainly has been	762	Juan	1	1029
Ere such a monster's victim I had been	764	Juan	1	1132
As was the case, at least, where I have been	795	Juan	2	1308
About the time and place where he had been	804	Juan	3	156
On that beloved daughter; she had been	808	Juan	3	450
And children still they should have ever been	818	Juan	4	114
And worse off than we hitherto have been	837	Juan	5	350
Gulbeyaz was an empress, but had been	855	Juan	6	199
Her thoughts, at least till now, appear to have been	859	Juan	6	428
In fact they can be safe. You should have been	876	Juan	7	558
There have been and are heroes who begun	881	Juan	8	170
Which holds what might have been the noblest nation	915	Juan	10	522
But if I had been at Timbuctoo, there	938	Juan	12	559
With more of the monastic than has been	949	Juan	13	522
(Take her at thirty, that is) to have been	958	Juan	14	199
But this is not my maxim: had it been	961	Juan	14	385
But that in love such idleness has been	965	Juan	14	603
Would some believe that such a tale had been	965	Juan	14	636

BEER

His brothel, and his beer	177	Devil's Dr		100
And beer undrawn, and beards unmown, display	250	Bards		636
Have no objection to a pot of beer	446	Beppo		380
Fed upon beef--I won't say much of beer	794	Juan	2	1242
And when I think upon a pot of beer	917	Juan	10	609
Discuss'd (he hated beer yclept the 'small	989	Juan	16	579

BEES

A populous solitude of bees and birds	51	Harold	3	950
Like summer bees that hum around his mane	422	Island	2	237
Of bees, the voice of girls, the song of birds	762	Juan	1	983
Which, being join'd, like swarming bees they clung	798	Juan	2	1495
That honey of your fashionable bees	993	Juan	16	846

BEE'S

Enough to gratify a bee's slight munchings	926	Juan	11	517

BEETLES

To where his watch-tower beetles o'er the bay	340	Corsair	1	124

BEFALL

Lords too are bards, such things at times befall	251	Bards		719
As if the worst had fall'n which could befall	370	Lara	1	314
Well done; nor could it otherwise befall	472	Morgante		411
Of that which will befall them. Yes, proud city	519	Faliero	3	7
What farther hath befallen or may befall	896	Juan	8	1106
And when aught is to befall	986	Juan	16	346

BEFALLEN

And Pania also. Can aught have befallen them	576	Sardan	3	303
What farther hath befallen or may befall	896	Juan	8	1106

BEFELL

Worse than adversity the Childe befell	4	Harold	1	33
Thyself by thine adorer, what befell	72	Harold	4	1059
Of what befell in Parne's vale	315	Giaour		528
What next befell me then and there	405	Chillon		231
Deplores the ancient woes which both befell	466	Morgante		19
No matter how or why the thing befell	759	Juan	1	837
Saw one, whom such an accident befell	835	Juan	5	275
Of what befell our hero in the land	929	Juan	11	682
What then? I only know it so befell	981	Juan	16	28

BEFIT

In smiles that least befit who wear them most	365	Corsair	3	639

BEFITS

The world befits a busy brain	164	Friend-B		43
Which it befits Count Lara's ear to know	372	Lara	1	468
'The last alternative befits me best	376	Lara	2	55
Of honour which befits your rank, and wait	568	Sardan	2	416
Shall be such as befits his name and nation	625	Foscari	5	311

BEFITTINGLY

And act befittingly. I shall not fail	592	Sardan	5	347

BEFORE

The lord of lowing herds; but not before	15	Harold	1	741
But cannot hope for rest before	17	Harold	1	856
Nor now preserved the walls he loved to shield before	21	Harold	2	126
But those scarfs of blood-red shall be redder, before	30	Harold	2	663
For Europe's flowers long rooted up before	38	Harold	3	174
And nearer, clearer, deadlier than before	38	Harold	3	197
Did he not this for France, which lay before	47	Harold	3	765
The wreath which Dante's brow alone had worn before	60	Harold	4	315
The infant Alps, which--had I not before	66	Harold	4	650
That, with the freshness wearing out before	66	Harold	4	681
From all I may be or have been before	81	Harold	4	1600
Which but belong'd to thee before	99	Young Lady		24
Who braved what woman never braved before	106	Nisus		77
Absorbs each wish it felt before	111	Medea		8
My native soil! beloved before	111	Medea		33
One last long look on what we were before	124	Recoll		186
Our raptured visions as before	133	E. N. Long		22
Which every bard has trod before	134	E. N. Long		92
Through scenes my youth hath known before	135	I Would		16
And delight but in days I have witness'd before	136	Highlander		28
But while these soar above my, unchanged as before	136	Highlander		43
Nor mingle as before	137	Clare		27
Like me, the happy scenes they knew before	138	Harrow-B		6
The sense of joy which thrill'd my breast before	140	Ossian-A		40
But none had ever prest before	144	Jessy		18
Repentance placed them as before	150	Harrow-C		9
I sigh for all I knew before	155	Lady-E		12
Fill the goblet again! for I never before	155	Goblet		1
Secure of his conquest before	162	Romaic-A		26
With things that never pleased before	166	Struggle		6
The plaint she dare not speak before	168	Haunts		8
Had sold all their souls long before	178	Devil's Dr		210
And vainly preach'd before	180	Ode-A		22
Who ne'er gave cause to mourn before	184	Parker		36
Never did I droop before	187	French-A		34
The Moon, their mistress, had expired before	190	Darkness		79
In these words the king before	194	Ballad-A		32
She rules the circle which she served before	208	Sketch		40
Ere that or thou can fade these eyes before	212	Augusta-C		78
To baffled millions which have gone before	212	Augusta-C		104
There was an ancient mansion, and before	214	Dream		76
We knew before	255	Plays		4
Though of seven volumes none before	233	Nihil		27
Or any other thing that's false, before	242	Bards		79
The path which Pope and Gifford trod before	243	Bards		94
Back to the sway they forfeited before	248	Bards		451
And tell the tale of what she was before	254	Bards		946
It form'd no thieves--the thief was form'd before	261	Hints		368
The land where Phoebus never frown'd before	268	Minerva		28
With George the Third's--and ended long before	275	Waltz		134
Why so? To do justice to what goes before	282	Blues	2	91
The cherubs and the saints bow'd down before	288	Vision		241
The spirits were in neutral space, before	289	Vision		273
Before their sovereign,--sovereign as before	301	Age		206
These are the themes thus sung so oft before	305	Age		542
From rose to tulip as before	314	Giaour		413
His features I have scann'd before	318	Giaour		788
Where every hue that charm'd before	322	Giaour		1198
Those accents scarcely mark'd before	322	Giaour		1233
I'll watch him closer than before	325	Abydos	1	143
My love thou surely knew'st before	328	Abydos	1	387
Than thou hast heard or thought before	328	Abydos	1	473
But know me all I was before	330	Abydos	2	171
On promise to return before	332	Abydos	2	341
Then trembles into silence as before	343	Corsair	1	350
That juggling fiend--who never spake before	352	Corsair	2	332
Which oft in sport adorn'd her hand before	353	Corsair	2	412
The land where Phoebus never frown'd before	355	Corsair	3	28
That conflict, deadlier far than all before	358	Corsair	3	219
Not that he came, but came not long before	366	Lara	1	46
Of the things to come than the things before	389	Corinth		500
And crush the wall they have crumbled before	392	Corinth		703
Each and all had been ta'en before	393	Corinth		791
Buried he lay, where thousands before	393	Corinth		813
So well advanced the ranks before	393	Corinth		833
Alas! we must awake before	397	Parisina		47
And stand the eternal throne before	397	Parisina		88
Close slowly round me as before	405	Chillon		262

BEFORE

I never saw its like before	405	Chillon	271
No trace of man: the year before	411	Mazeppa	435
And wore my feelings out before	412	Mazeppa	527
Which lay around--behind--before	413	Mazeppa	655
And each time nearer than before	414	Mazeppa	774
The waters with their world were all before	415	Island 1	5
Till Europe taught them better than before	418	Island 1	218
Your scenes sublime, from those beloved before	423	Island 2	297
Dissolve this clog and clod of clay before	424	Island 2	390
They offer'd quarter louder than before	434	Island 4	292
Laura, when dress'd, was (as I sang before	447	Beppo	449
Into a fane surpassing all before	464	Dante 4	52
Orlando knock'd, but none would ope, before	468	Morgante	163
But you were lost and damm'd to hell before	473	Morgante	472
And hover round the mountain, where before	668	Heaven	998
At day-dawn before	732	Deformed 1	704
Or 'transport,' as we knew all that before	757	Juan 1	711
If they had never been awoke before	763	Juan 1	1084
I leave you to your conscience as before	766	Juan 1	1253
But sage Antonia cut him short before	766	Juan 1	1298
An awkward spectacle their eyes before	769	Juan 1	1490
The passion which still rages as before	771	Juan 1	1558
Me and my epic brethren gone before	771	Juan 1	1610
Can make the fool of which they made before	773	Juan 1	1723
Against sea-sickness: try it, sir, before	775	Juan 2	102
Resist his stomach, ne'er at sea before	777	Juan 2	184
Got to the spirit-room, and stood before	778	Juan 2	275
They tried the pumps again, and though before	778	Juan 2	301
The boats, as stated, had got off before	780	Juan 2	425
To these was added Juan, who, before	783	Juan 2	619
To heave into the deep with those before	787	Juan 2	806
Two hundred and odd stanzas as before	801	Juan 2	1723
They could not look more rosy than before	810	Juan 3	600
When Haidee threw herself her boy before	821	Juan 4	331
But let us to the story as before	836	Juan 5	312
It fell down of its own accord before	862	Juan 6	610
The way which they had never trod before	880	Juan 8	147
In search of glory, should look on before	882	Juan 8	247
Were almost as much virgins as before	894	Juan 8	1032
A prop not quite so certain as before	896	Juan 9	20
But though I also had reform'd before	934	Juan 12	301
But he had seen so much good love before	938	Juan 12	532
Remember, reader! you have had before	941	Juan 12	698
And Medes, would ne'er revoke what went before	943	Juan 13	132
It is the sable friar as before	995	Juan 16	946
His eyes were open, and (as was before	995	Juan 16	967
Might be fill'd up, as vainly as before	997	Juan 17	66

BEFOREHAND

(Or if set out beforehand, these may send	441	Beppo	61
With deadly cozenage, eight long months before- hand	619	Foscari 4	301

BEFRINGE

As purple clouds befringe the sun; but most	911	Juan 10	231

BEG

One boon I beg, the nearest to my heart	107	Nisus	176
Why son and I both beg for your applause	171	Address-B	54
As the blessing I beg ere it flow	218	Jephtha	11
I beg you'll permit me to say	235	New Year	2
Where rustics earn'd, and now may beg, their bread	260	Hints	304
A thing that you would purchase, beg, or steal	441	Beppo	101
When thy patricians beg their bitter bread	548	Faliero 5	757
And beg you to live on for his sake till	575	Sardan 3	246
(Like Barbarossa to the Pope), to beg him	615	Foscari 4	34
There is one burthen which I beg you bear	623	Foscari 5	205
And when I beg of any one, it shall be	677	Werner 1	365
But then, I beg it may be understood	757	Juan 1	694
But beg 'Security' will bolt the door	757	Juan 1	712
To beg his pardon when I err a bit	761	Juan 1	960
I wish to sleep, and beg you will take care	765	Juan 1	1221
And beg they'll take my word about the moral	772	Juan 1	1666
To beg the beggar, who could not rain back	785	Juan 2	685
Could he not beg the loan of Charles's Wain	814	Juan 3	883
And beg his British godship's humble pardon	964	Juan 14	596
Above all, I beg all men to forbear	967	Juan 14	785

BEGAN

(See also 'GAN)

In bloodier acts conclude those who with blood began	29	Harold 2	567
The native revels of the troop began	30	Harold 2	636
'With patience' (thus Hyrtacides began	106	Nisus	99
Without improvement since he first began	143	Soliloquy	61
And began to cram from a plate of ham	178	Devil's Dr	207
The Monarch's wrath began to rise	195	Ballad-A	62
Began to cloy	200	Stanzas-B	68
Shades of those belles whose reign began of yore	275	Waltz	133
Michael began: 'What wouldst thou with this man	289	Vision	297
Hath he wrought since his mortal race began	289	Vision	299
Began in youth's first bloom and flush to reign	290	Vision	331

BEGAN

Began to cough, and hawk, and hem, and pitch	296	Vision	715
For swords began to clash and shouts to swell	349	Corsair 2	155
Nor seem'd to know his life but then began	382	Lara 2	487
Her life began and closed in woe	401	Parisina	529
My heart began once more to thrill	412	Mazeppa	576
The stars from broader beams began to creep	415	Island 1	11
And the first breath began to stir the palm	420	Island 2	108
Bent its broad arch: her breath began to fail	435	Island 4	378
And with my years my soul began to pant	439	Tasso	166
This form of verse began, I can't well break it	448	Beppo	501
One day he openly began to say	467	Morgante	87
Was ruled, ere earth began, by me	480	Manfred 1	111
Began to glitter with the climbing moon	494	Manfred 3	241
By speaking of myself much: I began	716	Werner 5	222
'Which pye being open'd they began to sing	745	Juan Ded	9
Who call'd her Chaste, methinks, began too soon	760	Juan 1	899
Began at once to scream, and yawn, and weep	764	Juan 1	1115
And blood ('twas from the nose) began to flow	769	Juan 1	1483
At sunset they began to take in sail	777	Juan 2	206
A reef between them also now began	787	Juan 2	829
As with an effort she began to speak	793	Juan 2	1196
Their bonds whene'er some Zephyr caught began	810	Juan 3	583
O'erthrown even men, he soon began to show	832	Juan 5	92
Receipts in full, began to think of dining	835	Juan 5	232
Began to blush up to the eyes, and then	847	Juan 5	991
So he began to stammer some excuses	849	Juan 5	1137
Just as a languid smile began to flatter	849	Juan 5	1142
Began to sing, dance, chatter, smile, and play	856	Juan 6	272
That just as her young lip began to ope	862	Juan 6	613
Began, as is the consequence of fear	862	Juan 6	626
Began to clothe each Asiatic hill	863	Juan 6	683
Her cheek began to flush, her eyes to sparkle	864	Juan 6	807
At length she rose up, and began to walk	866	Juan 6	877
Began to signalise the Russ retreat	872	Juan 7	330
Glory began to dawn with due sublimity	873	Juan 7	406
But here a sort of scene began to ensue	875	Juan 7	529
While their beloved friends began to arm	876	Juan 7	607
Thicker than leaves the lives began to fall	879	Juan 8	67
Still closer sulphury clouds began to smother	887	Juan 8	550
Began to lay about with steel and lead	888	Juan 8	644
Ambassadors began as 'twere to hustle	907	Juan 9	651
Just as the day began to wane and darken	917	Juan 10	635
Began to treat him with some small 'agacerie	960	Juan 14	328
This noble personage began to look	960	Juan 14	337
Began to think the duchess' conduct free	961	Juan 14	364
More foes by this same scroll: when I began it, I	975	Juan 15	478
From answering she began to question: this	978	Juan 15	641
Began to dread she'd thaw to a coquette	978	Juan 15	644
And being present, now began to express	984	Juan 16	254
As touch'd, and plaintively began to play	985	Juan 16	303
And therefore Juan now began to rally	987	Juan 16	465
(Of weariness or scorn), began to feel	993	Juan 16	815
His own internal ghost began to awaken	996	Juan 16	989

BEGET

For glances beget ogles, ogles sighs	442	Beppo	121
You saved my life--and acts like these beget	693	Werner 2	677

BEGETS

Of blood to crowds begets the thirst of more	534	Faliero 4	409

BEGETTING

For graciously begetting George the Fourth	274	Waltz	46

BEGGAR

Appears the beggar which his grandsire was	250	Bards	657
Than the rejected beggar--he's a slave	501	Faliero 1	135
A beggar, and should know the thing thou talk'st of	672	Werner 1	35
Told you I was a beggar? You yourself	677	Werner 1	356
I am a beggar in all save his trade	677	Werner 1	364
To beg the beggar, who could not rain back	785	Juan 2	685
To prove their pride, as footmen to a beggar	990	Juan 16	656
A beggar and a queen,' or was (of late	991	Juan 16	714

BEGGAR'D

To find the beggar'd Werner in the seat	716	Werner 5	189

BEGGARS

Let thy beggars and helots their pittance unite	203	Avatar	75
Beggars for nobles, panders for a people	548	Faliero 5	753
Save what we seem! save what we are--sick beggars	673	Werner 1	112
We'll send out villains to strip beggars, and	684	Werner 2	69

BEGGAR'S

The beggar's vice, which can but overwhelm	290	Vision	342
Gives license to the humblest beggar's head	293	Vision	548
Might move compassion, like a beggar's rags	506	Faliero 1	442
Nay, more, a beggar's are his own, and these	506	Faliero 1	443

BEGG'D

I begg'd them, as a boon, to lay	404	Chillon	152
Have begg'd as famish'd mendicants for bread	543	Faliero 5	386

BEGG'D

Alfonso closed his speech, and begg'd her pardon	769 Juan	1	1433
That begg'd Pedrillo for an absolution	779 Juan	2	351
And begg'd they would excuse her; she'd get over	862 Juan	6	663
To prove reluctant, and begg'd leave to crave!	866 Juan	6	893
And begg'd by every hair of Mahomet's beard	866 Juan	6	903
Begg'd to bring up the little girl and out	933 Juan	12	243

BEGGING

Oaths, boxing, begging,--all, save rout and race	261 Hints		328
(I say young, begging to be understood	288 Vision		237
In begging him, for God's sake, just to show	892 Juan	8	859

BEGIN
(See also 'GIN)

Yet mark their mirth--ere lenten days begin	31 Harold	2	738
And found the goal when others just begin	100 Damaetas		10
When e'en thy smiles begin to pall	135 I Would		44
You could hardly begin with a less work	232 Murray-B		21
Beware--for God's sake, don't begin like Bowles	259 Hints		194
E'en now the songs of Solyma begin	262 Hints		379
Ere, pack'd up for their journey, they begin it	292 Vision		443
Where thousand thoughts begin, to end in one	365 Corsair	3	642
That waited but a signal to begin	377 Lara	2	163
'And even at Aspramont thou didst begin	467 Morgante		97
Some armour, ere our journey we begin	476 Morgante		661
The mists begin to rise from up the valley	482 Manfred	1	343
Not signed? Ah, I perceive my eyes begin	601 Foscari	2	6
Begin to fail in apprehension, and	620 Foscari	5	8
Till now I fought them off, but they begin	620 Foscari	5	10
And even to move but slowly must begin	623 Foscari	5	194
Our search for t' other. You had best begin	697 Werner	3	136
Awaits us. Now the dwindling stars begin	701 Werner	3	434
He should begin, and take the bandage from	710 Werner	4	389
My way is to begin with the beginning	748 Juan	1	50
You'd best begin with truth, and when you've lost your	762 Juan	1	1023
At least 'twas rather early to begin	767 Juan	1	1332
My teeth begin to chatter, my veins freeze	769 Juan	1	1446
In health and purse, begin your day to date	792 Juan	2	1118
So Cowper says--and I begin to be	885 Juan	8	475
'Wherefore the ravishing did not begin	895 Juan	8	1052
To end or to begin with; the next grand	906 Juan	9	602
Preach to poor rogues? And wherefore not begin	918 Juan	10	674
But I am sick of politics. Begin	932 Juan	12	193
(Friends of the party), who begin accusals	934 Juan	12	268
But now I will begin my poem. 'Tis	936 Juan	12	425
Firstly, begin with the beginning (though	950 Juan	13	581
Unless her habits should begin to mend	962 Juan	14	404
Yes, I'll begin a thorough reformation	979 Juan	15	748

BEGINNER

Of such a young beginner	137 Clare		63
You must not check a Young Beginner	144 Becher-B		16
That lures, to flay alive, the young beginner	806 Juan	3	286

BEGINNERS

Even as a band of raw beginners	96 Granta		78
But they who blunder thus are raw beginners	938 Juan	12	521
And young beginners may as well commence	946 Juan	13	313
While those who are not beginners should have sense	946 Juan	13	315

BEGINNING

But as Love of Existence itself's the beginning	145 Casuists		3
She said--'pray are the rapes beginning	177 Devil's Dr		82
And apathy of limb, the dull beginning	453 Venice-B		39
In the beginning was the Word next God	466 Morgante		1
This was in the beginning, to my mode	466 Morgante		3
Shall be like their beginning--memorable	583 Sardan	4	298
What mean you? Lo! there is the blood beginning	618 Foscari	4	240
Had no beginning, have had one as mean	638 Cain	2	158
Still, as they were from the beginning, blind	661 Heaven		493
From the beginning, and shall do so ever	664 Heaven		661
Thy heart from the beginning: but for this	673 Werner	1	135
My way is to begin with the beginning	748 Juan	1	50
Beginning with 'Formosum Pastor Corydon	752 Juan	1	336
Of the Humane Society's beginning	762 Juan	1	1036
Been stove in the beginning of the gale	780 Juan	2	378
At least in the beginning, ere one tires	803 Juan	3	102
Nothing so difficult as a beginning	816 Juan	4	1
'Twas a raw day of Autumn's bleak beginning	832 Juan	5	41
Which they hit off at once in the beginning	859 Juan	6	414
Selfish in its beginning as its end	905 Juan	9	578
Of epic Love's beginning, end, and middle	935 Juan	12	360
Firstly, begin with the beginning (though	950 Juan	13	581
In this sort, end at least with the beginning	950 Juan	13	584

BEGINNINGS

Beginnings are fair faces, ends mere fishes	939 Juan	12	578

BEGINS
(See also 'GINS)

But when the rising moon begins to climb	76 Harold	4	1288

BEGINS

The ball begins; the honours of the house	276 Waltz		184
The verge where ends the cliff, begins the beach	346 Corsair	1	534
Which thus begins so courteously and well	372 Lara	1	460
Fever begins upon the brain	412 Mazeppa		560
Begins, and prudery flings aside her fetter	440 Beppo		12
The ball-room ere the sun begins to rise	450 Beppo		654
The old man fainted. It begins to work, then	596 Foscari	1	31
The fruit of our forbidden tree begins	628 Cain	1	30
And now that it begins, let it be borne	652 Cain	3	416
Begins to grizzle the black hair of night	704 Werner	3	582
Until the chase begins; then draw thou off	706 Werner	4	135
On a lee-shore, till it begins to blow	937 Juan	12	499
Because indifference begins to lull	941 Juan	13	29

BEGIRT

She dwelt, begirt with growing Infancy	215 Dream		130
Begirt with many a gallant slave	324 Abydos	1	20
Begirt by thousands in his swarming hall	378 Lara	2	215
In vast canoes, begirt with bolts of flame	422 Island	2	221
You'd better walk about begirt with briars	440 Beppo		25
Hath begirt thee with a snare	481 Manfred	1	225
Begirt with spies for guards, with robes for power	525 Faliero	3	479
We were approaching, which, begirt with light	638 Cain	2	182
Enormous liquid plains, and some begirt	638 Cain	2	187
Sick, poor--begirt too with the flooding rivers	680 Werner	1	579
And, for the sovereign's head, my own begirt	698 Werner	3	183

BEGONE

They are too long already.---Hence--begone	480 Manfred	1	170
Let us begone, my child, the time is pressing	516 Faliero	2	513
Begone! Not I	668 Heaven		1020
In these dull pageantries. Begone! and rail	713 Werner	5	13
Let it not be more fatal still!- Begone	721 Werner	5	503
Begone!' she cried, with kindling eyes--'and do	866 Juan	6	922

BEGOT

To all his vices, without what begot	290 Vision		372
Begot in sin, to die in shame	399 Parisina		312
Begot me--thee--and all the few that are	634 Cain	1	443
Than Jose, who begot our hero, who	748 Juan	1	71
Begot--but that's to come--Well, to renew	748 Juan	1	72
To save a sire who blush'd that he begot him	892 Juan	8	880

BEGOTTEN
(See also LOVE-BEGOTTEN)

Thy not too lawfully begotten 'Waltz	273 Waltz		14
After the fall too soon was I begotten	654 Cain	3	506
Warm in our veins,--strong Cain! who was begotten	664 Heaven		656
Or swears that Ceres hath begotten Famine	873 Juan	7	360

BEGRUDGES

For Liverpool such a concession begrudges	225 Ode-D		23

BEGS

While Florence vainly begs her banish'd dead, and weep weeps	64 Harold	4	531
Who begs his bread, if 'tis refused by one	501 Faliero	1	131

BEGUILE

Which I would seize, in passing, to beguile	52 Harold	3	1043
When dreams of your presence my slumbers beguile	98 To M.S.G.-B		19
Wouldst thou wandering hearts beguile	100 Marion		15
The lips may beguile with a dimple or smile	114 The Tear		3
With tales of mystic rites beguile	132 Prayer		16
Of those who spoke but to beguile	146 Vain Lady		8
Unread (unless, since books beguile disease	260 Hints		237
The foster'd feud encouraged to beguile	302 Age		293
All--save immortal dreams that could beguile	329 Abydos	2	26
Revel and rout the evening hours beguile	347 Corsair	2	25

BEGUILED

Of brains (if brains they had) he them beguiled	8 Harold	1	299
And mirthful strains the hours beguiled	89 Prometheus-A		14
Let the Priest, who beguiled	239 Bray		25
There linger'd we, beguiled too long	324 Abydos	1	71
But once beguiled and ever more beguiling	325 Abydos	1	161
Oft could he sneer at others as beguiled	342 Corsair	1	283
Betray'd too early, and beguiled too long	365 Corsair	3	663
Their choice than life, forgive them, as beguiled	886 Juan	8	493

BEGUILES

Come back before me, as his skill beguiles	64 Harold	4	554
That playfulness of Sorrow ne'er beguiles	353 Corsair	2	448
Beguiles his charger from the combat's rage	380 Lara	2	391

BEGUILING

Now no more, the hours beguiling	95 Fragment-B		5
I do not believe it beguiling	210 Augusta-B		11
But once beguiled and ever more beguiling	325 Abydos	1	161

BEGUN

Before his weary pilgrimage begun	5 Harold	1	85

BEGUN

It deepens still, the work is scarce begun   18 Harold   1   911
Again I seize the theme, then but begun   35 Harold   3   21
My daughter! with thy name this song begun   53 Harold   3 1067
The stubborn heart, its alchemy begun   73 Harold   4 1106
Have left us nearly where we had begun   81 Harold   4 1579
Henceforth affection, sweetly thus begun   107 Nisus   165
The one long graved, the other just begun   124 Recoll   156
On the same day our studious race begun   126 Recoll   329
Yet still beats on as it begun   156 Lady-F   47
And the carnage begun, when resistance is done   176 Devil's Dr   75
Though unequall'd, preceded, the task was begun   202 Avatar   42
Such scenes as those wherein my life begun   212 Augusta-C   91
Thy days are done, thy fame begun   218 Thy Days   1
Begun in folly, ended in disgrace   251 Bards   681
Though drench'd with gore, his woes are but begun   272 Minerva   298
For Freedom's battle once begun   311 Giaour   123
To-night, the Bairam feast's begun   312 Giaour   229
Begun in folly, closed in tears   314 Giaour   399
He saw rebellion there begun   325 Abydos   1   118
These cherish'd thoughts with life begun   328 Abydos   1   425
Completes his fury what their fear begun   349 Corsair   2   172
Will sinking see impalement's pangs begun   351 Corsair   2   315
'Twas hardly midnight when that fray begun   352 Corsair   2   384
But the rampart is won, and the spoil begun   393 Corinth   769
My life begun and ends the same   399 Parisina   313
Finish'd as they had begun   402 Chillon   19
Returning where my walk begun   405 Chillon   311
When first my courser's race begun   411 Mazeppa   507
Ere his repast begun   414 Mazeppa   772
Begun the praises of a thousand years   433 Island   4   266
But stories somehow lengthen when begun   452 Beppo   792
Begun and died upon the gentle wind   495 Manfred   3   279
Commenced to-morrow; but, 'tis begun   518 Faliero   2   655
Had thus begun to sound. Are all the passes   537 Faliero   4   616
Is the day indeed begun   735 Deformed   2   4
But closed the tyrant-hater he begun   746 Juan   Ded   80
I'm almost sorry that I e'er begun   761 Juan   1   920
Alfonso paused a minute--then begun   768 Juan   1 1385
And others went on as they had begun   779 Juan   2   357
Were served out to the people, who begun   781 Juan   2   494
And more robust of figure,--then begun   788 Juan   2   916
Return we to Don Juan. He begun   795 Juan   2 1329
Small social parties just begun to dine   805 Juan   3   242
And he begun a long low island song   824 Juan   4   ...
Turn'd to the merchant, and begun to bid   834 Juan   5   218
There have been and are heroes who begun   881 Juan   8   170
I almost lately have begun to doubt   881 Juan   8   201
I've not begun what we have to go through   936 Juan   12   428
Ends. When the body of the book's begun   940 Juan   12   690
The man was well-nigh dead, ere men begun   997 Juan   17   61

BEHALF

Than hosts can do in his behalf. What, ho   573 Sardan   3   98
Has done in our behalf,--nothing. How,--nothing   673 Werner   1   133
Come you to stir yourself in his behalf   681 Werner   1   652
Your courteous courage did in my behalf   685 Werner   2   154
In the behalf of our departed friends   712 Werner   4   485
Some tongues without will wag in my behalf   719 Werner   5   392
In its behalf, let those deny who will   981 Juan   16   56

BEHAVE

Which is not fairly to behave   238 Orford   3
May teach us better to behave when masters   834 Juan   5   184

BEHAVED

And prettily behaved! He knows his station   699 Werner   3   296
Just now behaved as in the Holy Land   879 Juan   8   72
He had behaved with courage and humanity   896 Juan   8 1114
Behaved no better than a common sempstress   906 Juan   9   616

BEHAVIOUR

And put himself upon his good behaviour   837 Juan   5   373

BEHELD

Shall thus be first beheld, forgotten last   3 To Ianthe   40
When first Spain's queen beheld the black-eyed boy   12 Harold   1   511
Beheld her smile in Danger's Gorgon face   13 Harold   1   574
Still he beheld, nor mingled with the throng   17 Harold   1   828
Patience! and ye shall hear what he beheld   19 Harold   1   950
Alike beheld beneath pale Hecate's blaze   22 Harold   3   193
Last noon beheld them full of lusty life   39 Harold   3   244
The ambrosial aspect, which, beheld, instils   62 Harold   4   435
Beheld him win two realms, and, happier, yield
    his breath   67 Harold   4   765
Who hath beheld decline upon my brow   75 Harold   4 1200
I have beheld the Ephesian's miracle   78 Harold   4 1372
I have beheld Sophia's bright roofs swell   78 Harold   4 1375
Beheld her Iris.--Thou, too lonely lord   70 Harold   4 1519
Beheld it last by Calpe's rock unfold   81 Harold   4 1574
Such as creation's dawn beheld, thou rollest now   82 Harold   4 1638
Beheld by eyes that mourn yet cannot weep   94 Dorset   90
Beheld in death her fading ray   101 Alva   16
Once I beheld a splendid dream   135 I Would   21

BEHELD

'Tis long since I beheld that eye   156 Lady-F   13
In one short hour beheld the blazing fane   169 Address-A   3
Ye who beheld (oh! sight admired and mourn'd   169 Address-A   5
And had he beheld their 'Nourjahad   179 Devil's Dr   229
Their eyes as it grew lighter, and beheld   190 Darkness   65
Surely I once beheld a nobler aim   212 August-C   102
I beheld thee, oh Sion! when render'd to Rome   221 Jerusalem   2
I beheld but the death-fire that fed on thy fane   221 Jerusalem   7
While I stood on the height, and beheld the
    decline   221 Jerusalem   11
A spirit pass'd before me: I beheld   222 Spirit   1
Beheld thee twirling to a Saxon tune   274 Waltz   92
When I beheld you in your jesting way   294 Vision   578
Beheld the desert peopled, as from hell   300 Age   148
Beheld his banner flouting thy Madrid   300 Age   152
For where is he that hath beheld   316 Giaour   565
With dread beheld, with gloom beholding   319 Giaour   885
(Woe to the head whose eye beheld   324 Abydos   1   38
To wed with one I ne'er beheld   328 Abydos   1   436
Alas! those eyes beheld his rocky tower   346 Corsair   1   579
Conrad beheld the danger, he beheld   350 Corsair   2   241
The better warriors who beheld him near   351 Corsair   2   306
One hour beheld him since the tide he stemm'd   352 Corsair   2   388
Who that beheld that sun upon thee set   356 Corsair   3   59
Whose inmates first beheld whom first they sought   356 Corsair   3   86
But what he' had beheld he shunn'd to show   367 Lara   1   91
And things more timid that beheld him near   367 Lara   1   111
Whate'er his frenzy dream'd or eye beheld   369 Lara   1   247
And once beheld, would ask of him again   371 Lara   1   368
As he look'd on the face, and beheld its hue   391 Corinth   607
Beheld her frailty from afar   397 Parisina   58
And when the Cossack maid beheld   414 Mazeppa   817
Revered Parnassus, and beheld the steep   423 Island   2   286
The strener spirits who beheld that meeting   429 Island   3   201
The world beheld them with indulgent air   446 Beppo   429
Beheld her airs and triumph, and all that   448 Beppo   548
And in a recent quarrel I beheld him   517 Faliero   2   585
Beheld their fate merged in the approaching fight   534 Faliero   4   432
This, thy presumed descendant, ne'er beheld   553 Sardan   1   163
The hall of our tribunal, and beheld   601 Foscari   1   366
That they beheld them perish piecemeal, nor   602 Foscari   2   76
I would that they beheld their father in   613 Foscari   3   366
Dreaded to have its acts beheld by others   622 Foscari   5   131
He is not God--nor God's: I have beheld   633 Cain   1   412
Saith that he has beheld the God himself   635 Cain   1   500
Beheld them from the skirts of Paradise   636 Cain   2   39
But that on drawing near them I beheld   639 Cain   2   213
Had more of beauty. Hast thou ne'er beheld him   642 Cain   2   404
Within those glorious orbs which we beheld   643 Cain   2   447
And to what end have I beheld these things   645 Cain   2   622
The promised wonders which thou hast beheld   647 Cain   3   47
I had beheld the immemorial works   647 Cain   3   63
Beheld till half an hour since? Sir, I thank you   677 Werner   1   360
'Tis twenty years since I beheld him with   679 Werner   1   493
Made him what you beheld. I'm sorry for it   681 Werner   1   664
The intendant gave (for I have not beheld her   687 Werner   2   275
I look'd through and beheld a purple bed   718 Werner   5   314
Oh! God of fathers! I beheld his features   718 Werner   5   335
Distinct as I beheld them, though the expression   718 Werner   5   338
Beheld a conqueror, or look'd along   725 Deformed   1   187
Of shape;--my dam beheld my shape was hopeless   727 Deformed   1   344
Beheld mankind, as mere spectators of   738 Deformed   2   227
Beheld his native Spain receding far   775 Juan   2   106
As rarely they beheld throughout their round   818 Juan   4   123
Where I beheld what never was to be   831 Juan   5   28
Yet smelt roast-meat, beheld a huge fire shine   837 Juan   5   397
When he beheld his latest hero grace   893 Juan   8   925
The soldiers, who beheld him drop his point   893 Juan   8   929
As they beheld; the younger cast some leers   906 Juan   9   620
Already they beheld the silver showers   906 Juan   9   629
No more to be beheld but in such visions   986 Juan   16   415
Beheld between the country and the town   991 Juan   16   723

BEHELDEST

Thou who beheldest, 'mid the assassins' din   68 Harold   4   777

BEHEMOTH

At the foaming behemoth   742 Deformed   3   57

BEHEST

Be as it may Futurity's behest   20 Harold   2   80
To offer something to their high behest   106 Nisus   94
Hear then in silence Pallas' stern behest   270 Minerva   161
Awaiting each his lord's behest   324 Abydos   1   22

BEHESTS

Thy dread behests ne'er disobey   89 Prometheus-A   4

BEHIND

Oft trod, that never leaves a trace behind   23 Harold   2   245
Which, ebbing, leave a sterile track behind   35 Harold   3   25
That, if no joy, no sorrow lurk'd
    behind   36 Harold   3   86

BEHIND

Not without cause; and should I leave behind	56 Harold	4	70
The blight and blackening which it leaves behind	58 Harold	4	211
Came Megara before me, and behind	61 Harold	4	392
The loudest still the tempest leaves behind	69 Harold	4	877
Forms from the floating wreck which Ruin leaves behind	70 Harold	4	936
One spot, to leave a worthless name behind	94 Dorset		54
Will sweep my name, nor leave a trace behind	94 Dorset		94
And left their hounds in speed behind	102 Alva		56
Limping Decorum lingers far behind	119 Answer-A		12
No trace of thee remains behind	131 L'Amitie		36
And who would then remain behind	168 Haunts		27
Oh, ne'er my tyrant leave behind	181 Ode-A		89
Set with their Sun, but still have left behind	193 Monody		29
Their sunshine leaves a glow behind	218 I Saw		15
But leaves its darken'd dust behind	220 Clay		4
In deserts which he left behind	233 Ballad-B		39
But the greatest of Glory's behind	234 Ballat		33
Leave wondering comprehension far behind	252 Bards		758
I doubt if you'll leave us an equal behind	282 Blues	2	81
He died--but left his subjects still behind	286 Vision		63
And pirates barter all that's left behind	272 Minerva		264
The wrack by passion left behind	322 Giaour		1254
She told nor whence, nor why she left behind	382 Lara	2	528
Which the Soul's war doth leave behind	402 Parisina		544
And grieved for those he left behind	404 Chillon		189
All human dwellings left behind	411 Mazeppa		425
Left shrubs, and trees, and wolves behind	411 Mazeppa		492
And falls back on the foaming crowd behind	426 Island	3	23
Is of the leaves it strews, nor looks behind	434 Island	4	284
And dim the little light that's left behind	437 Tasso		71
Something shall leave it half an hour behind	448 Beppo		512
And vulture passions flying close behind	463 Dante	3	174
The hurricane I left behind	479 Manfred	1	102
What! wilt thou leave us all--all--all behind	669 Heaven		1094
And botching, patching, leaving still behind	746 Juan	Ded	106
But that's no matter, and the worst's behind	750 Juan	1	190
Withdrew itself from his, but left behind	755 Juan	1	563
But to proceed--for there is more behind	767 Juan	1	1318
Because it left encouragement behind	786 Juan	2	790
Than on the name a person leaves behind	813 Juan	3	812
And then my stoicism leaves nought behind	855 Juan	6	172
And, what was stranger, never look'd behind	882 Juan	8	234
Upon reflection, knowing that behind	883 Juan	8	314
A hospital, a church,--and leave behind	931 Juan	12	75
In such a sort as cannot leave behind	945 Juan	13	252
Of the two principles, but leaves behind	946 Juan	13	326
Because the monks preferr'd a hill behind	948 Juan	13	439
The world is all before me--or behind	956 Juan	14	65
By death, when we are left, alas! behind	973 Juan	15	350
Or like a billow left by storms behind	981 Juan	16	71

BEHMEN

Not all the reveries of Jacob Behmen	852 Juan	6	13

BEHOLD

Behold the hall where chiefs were late convened	8 Harold	1	288
Vain Sophistry! in these behold the tools	10 Harold	1	452
Shall I unmoved behold the hallow'd scene	14 Harold	1	632
Behold a train more fitting to inspire	14 Harold	1	652
Behold through each lack-lustre, eyeless hole	20 Harold	2	50
Behold each mighty shade reveal'd to sight	20 Harold	2	71
Ambracia's gulf behold, where once was lost	26 Harold	2	397
Nodding above; behold black Acheron	27 Harold	2	456
Till the sense aches with gazing to behold	33 Harold	2	832
To wear it? who can curiously behold	36 Harold	3	92
With a fit mind the might which I behold	46 Harold	3	649
Albeit my brow thou never shouldst behold	53 Harold	3	1072
We stand and in that form and face behold	62 Harold	4	438
The wealthiest Roman's wife. Behold his love or pride	70 Harold	4	927
Behold the Imperial Mount! 'tis thus the mighty falls	71 Harold	4	963
Hear me, my mother Earth! behold it, Heaven	75 Harold	4	1208
And from the Alban Mount we now behold	81 Harold	4	1572
Oh! may my shade behold no sculptured urns	85 Fragment-A		5
He would, unmoved, unawed behold	88 Horace		12
Again I behold where for hours I have ponder'd	96 Harrow-A		13
That all must love thee who behold thee	97 To Woman		2
Here I behold its beauteous hue	98 To Mary		13
Vex'd to behold such beauty here	99 Young Lady		6
There, unconfined, behold each grazing steed	109 Nisus		277
To-night no veteran Roscii you behold	113 Prologue		11
If a glimpse of redemption you wish to behold	117 To Eliza		19
There, deeply carved, behold! each tyro's name	124 Recoll		153
A heart untainted, we in thee behold	126 Recoll		310
When, haply, some light-waving locks I behold	136 Highlander		37
Behold a portly Female stand	141 Critics		48
When I scarcely can hope to behold them again	148 Farewell-A		24
Ye! who perchance behold this simple urn	154 Dog		23
In me behold the only skull	154 Skull		2

BEHOLD

When I behold that wondrous scene	158 Florence		42
Of all who venture to behold her	160 Cadiz		50
Behold the coming strife	162 War Song		14
Stranger! behold, interr'd together	163 Blacket		1
So I behold them not	167 Dead		13
For thee, and such as thee, behold	179 Gold		25
Behold! while yet before thee burn	185 Belshaz-A		3
And ne'er can be what once we did behold	192 Fragment-C		16
Where I would walk in spirit, and behold	192 Fragment-C		37
Behold the host! delighting to deprave	193 Monody		73
The current I behold will sweep beneath	198 Po		21
They might behold her	199 Stanzas-B		22
On his right hand behold a Sejanus appears	203 Avatar		86
And then expire of the joy--but to behold him	205 Hindoo		15
Look on her features! and behold her mind	209 Sketch		71
And, above all, a lake I can behold	211 Augusta-C		63
Daughters and sons of Beauty,--but behold	215 Dream		131
And the mountains behold me no more	218 Jephtha		6
King, behold the phantom seer	219 Saul-B		4
Is it thou, O King? Behold	219 Saul-B		17
A night-beam Sorrow watcheth to behold	220 Sleepless		7
Behold the Helen of the heart	229 Marble		8
Then your face we might behold	234 Silver		4
Behold the blessings of a lucky lot	237 Elegy		1
Behold! in various throngs the scribbling crew	243 Bards		143
Behold the ballad-monger Southey rise	244 Bards		202
Behold her statue placed in glory's niche	244 Bards		208
Behold!--ye tarts! one moment spare the text	246 Bards		309
In him an author's luckless lot behold	247 Bards		397
Behold, a chosen band shall aid thy plan	248 Bards		506
Behold the new Petronius of the day	250 Bards		642
Behold him Freshman! forced no more to groan	259 Hints		225
Behold a quarto!--Tarts must tell the rest	266 Hints		728
Below, his name--above, behold his deeds	270 Minerva		108
Behold where Dian's beams disdain to shine	270 Minerva		120
And left it; and his annals too behold	290 Vision		339
Behold a candidate with unturn'd coat	293 Vision		535
'He is what you behold him, and his doom	293 Vision		545
A sillier fellow you will scarce behold	296 Vision		699
Behold the grand result in yon lone isle	299 Age		53
Sigh to behold the eagle's lofty rage	299 Age		55
Behold the scales in which his fortune hangs	299 Age		63
Resplendent sight! Behold the coxcomb Czar	304 Age		434
Where Midas might again his wish behold	307 Age		660
On Shylock's shore behold them stand afresh	307 Age		702
Even robbers tremble to behold	315 Giaour		532
And tell him--what thou dost behold	322 Giaour		1252
Survey our empire and behold our home	338 Corsair	1	4
Behold his soul, the rest that soothes his lot	341 Corsair	1	244
Behold--but who hath seen, or e'er shall see	341 Corsair	1	247
Behold but bloody shore and fiery waves	349 Corsair	2	158
Behold how well or ill those pangs are borne	351 Corsair	2	317
His steps the chamber gain, his eyes behold	364 Corsair	3	597
Aught they behold or hear their thought appals	370 Lara	1	265
Immortal man! behold her glories shine	375 Lara	2	9
But he better could brook to behold the dying	389 Corinth		481
On its table still behold	395 Corinth		998
Away with this! behold them as they were	418 Island	1	221
They scarcely can behold their male relations	449 Beppo		562
Flash'd o'er the future, bidding men behold	458 Dante	2	3
When I behold your form with my own eyes	473 Morgante		454
I would behold ye face to face. I hear	480 Manfred	1	175
Behold! Oh God! if it be thus, and thou	481 Manfred	1	188
Behold the tall pines dwindled as to shrubs	482 Manfred	1	276
Behold she cometh. Say, where hast thou been	488 Manfred	2	358
Behold my blood! the first time it e'er flow'd	505 Manfred	1	387
We must behold no object save our country	517 Faliero	2	602
Had these rash men proceeded; but, behold	522 Faliero	3	245
But still I quiver to behold what I	527 Faliero	3	619
Behold my order from the assembled Ten	536 Faliero	4	552
The Doge stands to behold the chase of bulls	539 Faliero	5	94
Behold, and feel, and suffer, be a lesson	544 Faliero	5	433
Into eternity, and I behold	547 Faliero	5	665
Your swords. My lord, behold my scimitar	564 Sardan	2	157
Fools treachery--and, behold, upon the sudden	567 Sardan	2	364
Which gave me to behold your face again	582 Sardan	4	269
But let me not behold them; they unman me	584 Sardan	4	402
Behold him more! Nay, sister, I must be obey'd	584 Sardan	4	405
Sardanapalus, wilt thou thus behold me	584 Sardan	4	413
Deep fosses, or behold them sprawl on spikes	586 Sardan	4	559
Those eyes, which never may behold it more	588 Sardan	5	42
In the camp of the conquerors; behold	592 Sardan	5	295
Who rule behold us. There is one who does	596 Foscari	1	72
Stretch'd forth a hand to save them? You behold me	602 Foscari	2	77
Should I behold this sympathy? or shall	603 Foscari	2	141
I am what you behold. And that's a mystery	606 Foscari	2	331
That's sudden. Shall I not behold my father	611 Foscari	3	221
Indeed, our last of meetings? You behold	613 Foscari	3	357
They might behold their parent anywhere	613 Foscari	3	365
Behold the state's care for its sons and mothers	614 Foscari	3	395
Prepare my children to behold their father	614 Foscari	3	402
Thou cowardly murderer by law, behold	619 Foscari	4	243

BEHOLD
Behold, your work's completed! Is there then   625 Foscari   5   308
Behold thy father cheerful and resign'd   628 Cain   1   51
Worship or worship not, thou shalt behold   636 Cain   2   13
We and thy sons will try. But now, behold   637 Cain   2   97
Show me. Dar'st thou behold? How know I what   638 Cain   2   133
I dare behold? As yet, thou hast shown nought   638 Cain   2   134
Wouldst thou behold things mortal or immortal   638 Cain   2   136
That which was clay, and such thou shalt behold 638 Cain   2   165
Thou seekest to behold death and dead things   639 Cain   2   191
To such, I would behold at once what I   639 Cain   2   195
Must one day see perforce. Behold! 'Tis dark-
ness   639 Cain   2   196
And true. Behold these phantoms! they were once 640 Cain   2   291
Knowledge was barr'd as poison. But behold   640 Cain   2   307
My eyes with pleasant tears as I behold   643 Cain   2   465
Behold, my son! said Adam, how from evil   643 Cain   2   503
Thine offerings. Where are thine? Behold them
here   649 Cain   3   214
Behold them in their various bloom and ripeness 649 Cain   3   219
Woman, behold the serpent's work, behold   652 Cain   3   382
Behold, thou drivest him from the face of earth 653 Cain   3   478
Now shines! and now, behold! it hath   657 Heaven   152
Shall they drop off. Behold their last tomorrow 660 Heaven   349
Our race; behold their stature and their beauty 664 Heaven   688
To save an earth-born being; and behold   665 Heaven   734
Than to behold the universal tomb   670 Heaven   1192
Than to behold my boy and my boy's mother   674 Werner   1   161
Behold my father, or--What? An assassin   702 Werner   3   460
By mine, and you behold me! I behold   709 Werner   4   318
Behold me! I have seen the murderer   714 Werner   5   84
This prodigy, if only to behold him   717 Werner   5   254
Resembling them--behold them in Count Ulric's   718 Werner   5   337
That our eyes may behold   724 Deformed 1   166
I' the sun. Behold another! Who is he   725 Deformed 1   209
I will look further. Lo! behold again   725 Deformed 1   216
All vow'd to Sperchius as they were--behold them 726 Deformed 1   272
Is thickest, that I may behold it in   729 Deformed 1   494
Mix'd with what we now behold   735 Deformed 2   34
Than behold such hosts pollute   736 Deformed 2   69
Ah! behold yon bleeding spectre   736 Deformed 2   71
The Olympic games. When I behold a prize   738 Deformed 2   228
The cross, beneath which he is crush'd; behold
him   740 Deformed 2   313
It was such pleasure to behold him, such   796 Juan   2 1377
The sights he was accustom'd to behold   808 Juan   3   429
The sparkling gems beneath you might behold   811 Juan   3   611
Ere what we least wish to behold will sleep   816 Juan   4   30
Sigh'd to behold them of their hours bereft   817 Juan   4   61
Break with the first fall: they can ne'er behold 817 Juan   4   84
With no great voice, is pleasing to behold   827 Juan   4   661
More tender, as we every day behold   837 Juan   5   390
When they behold the brave oppress'd with odds 891 Juan   8   842
Behold the world! and curse your victories   897 Juan   9   72
Behold him placed as if upon a pillar! He   902 Juan   9   351
The lawyer and the critic but behold   909 Juan   10   105
But fair as then, or fairer to behold   955 Juan   13   878
Their union was a model to behold   966 Juan   14   687
How differently the world would men behold   968 Juan   14   804
Shepherd, or swain, whoever may behold   982 Juan   16   106
Were something very glorious to behold   991 Juan   16   668

BEHOLDER
In that queer dress, for fear that some beholder 452 Beppo   742
When the beholder knows a Doge conspired   545 Faliero   5   512
So that the philosophical beholder   805 Juan   3   263

BEHOLDERS
The fellow-feeling in the saints beholders   287 Vision   163
Alone will be beholders of thy doom   546 Faliero   5   555
And cry to all beholders, Lo! a villain   698 Werner   3   185
They put beholders in a tender taking   857 Juan   6   340
Which leads beholders on a boggy walk   873 Juan   7   366

BEHOLDEST
It cannot be: thou now beholdest as   640 Cain   2   315

BEHOLDING
With dread beheld, with gloom beholding   319 Giaour   885
Beholding with the dark eye of a seer   465 Dante   4   149
What the whole earth accords, beholding not   489 Manfred   4   414
Save in beholding thine; yet--Yet! what yet   551 Sardan   1   73
Venice without beholding him or you   611 Foscari   3   232
When he spurns high the dust, beholding his   724 Deformed 1   114
Into each other--and, beholding this   797 Juan   2 1479

BEHOLDS
Beholds the rainbow of her future years   3 To Ianthe   17
In one broad glance the soul beholds   220 Clay   15
Beholds him conquer but, alas! not die   301 Age   204
And the powerless moon beholds them flow   388 Corinth   430
And heaven beholds her face within   409 Mazeppa   223
And never meet, but each beholds the mirror   525 Faliero   3   453
And measures it by that which it beholds   647 Cain   3   61

BEHOLDS
The while the wicked world beholds delighted   759 Juan   1   795
Beholds her own shy, shadowy image pass   859 Juan   6   478

BEHOLD'ST
When thou behold'st them, drooping nigh   44 Harold   3   523

BEHOOVES
But let it be in silence, as behooves thee   537 Faliero   4   606

BEHOVED
By British hands, which it had best behoved   21 Harold   2   131

BEING
That, being, thou wouldst be again, and go   20 Harold   2   31
What is my being? thou hast ceased to be   34 Harold   2   895
A being more intense, that we endow   36 Harold   3   47
In its own narrow being, but aspire   41 Harold   3   373
Spurning the clay-cold bonds which round our being
cling   46 Harold   3   697
Where he became a being) whose desire   47 Harold   3   722
But hath a part of being, and a sense   49 Harold   3   840
A truth, which through our being then doth melt 49 Harold   3   844
My blood from out thy being were an aim   53 Harold   3 1091
My hopes of being remember'd in my line   56 Harold   4   77
What from this barren being do we reap   69 Harold   4   829
The being who upheld it through the past   79 Harold   4 1469
Accord me such a being? Do I err   81 Harold   4 1591
And being so--the absent are the dead   191 Fragment-C   11
Of breathless being?--darken'd and intense   192 Fragment-C   30
If she ever gave birth to a being so base   203 Avatar   96
That gave me being, gave me that which marr'd   211 Augusta-C   27
They do divide our being; they become   213 Dream   9
He had no breath, no being, but in hers   214 Dream   51
For, the liquor he drank being too much for one 224 Adams   5
With these and being healthy   233 Ballad-B   44
So the Doctor being found   238 Bray   7
The native genius with their being given   254 Bards   909
And find small sympathy in being sick   260 Hints   276
They may range freely--being damn'd the same   291 Vision   424
It being a sort of knighthood, or gilt key   291 Vision   426
Being clay myself. Let not those spirits be   291 Vision   430
We had the poor wretch safe (without being bored 296 Vision   703
A different web being by the Destinies   298 Vision   830
Being, end, aim, religion--rent, rent, rent   306 Age   631
Hath lost its charm by being caught   314 Giaour   405
As to young eagles being free   403 Chillon   81
The being we so much did love   404 Chillon   161
But soon his wrath being o'er, he took   408 Mazeppa   141
Who, being unpension'd, made a satire   408 Mazeppa   149
The being whom I loved the most   409 Mazeppa   261
No hope arose of being freed   414 Mazeppa   767
With each new being born or to be born   432 Island   4   194
And then I lost my being all to be   439 Tasso   171
This feast is named the Carnival, which being   441 Beppo   41
In many a nameless being we retrace   442 Beppo   110
And being natural, naturally please   444 Beppo   304
Without being forced to bid my groom be sure   445 Beppo   330
Her dearest friends for being dress'd so ill   448 Beppo   520
Which being finish'd, here the story ends   452 Beppo   790
And yet, being mortal still, have no repose   457 Dante   1   112
The being--and even yet he may be born   461 Dante   3   53
He in the cabinet being always ready   466 Morgante   37
The much-renown'd St. Dennis being the cause   467 Morgante   70
'If thou rememberest being in Gascony   467 Morgante   105
And being return'd to where Orlando stood   470 Morgante   249
Till, one day, by the Spirit being inflamed   473 Morgante   459
There being a want of water in the place   473 Morgante   481
The lightning of my being, is as bright   480 Manfred   1   155
Yet pause: being here, our will would do thee
service   480 Manfred   1   171
My lot with living being: I can bear   484 Manfred   2   76
Father or mother, mistress, friend, or being   486 Manfred   2   195
A being of the race thou dost despise   486 Manfred   2   216
Of earth and heaven, from which no power, nor
being   489 Manfred   2   435
But being met is deadly,--such hath been   493 Manfred   3   133
What art thou, unknown being? answer!--speak   496 Manfred   3   340
To them, as being your subjects. But 'tis not   501 Faliero   1   109
The justice due unto the humblest being   503 Faliero   1   214
For it is worse, being full acknowledgment   503 Faliero   1   238
Speak out; fear nothing; being stung at heart   505 Faliero   1   404
To sue for justice, being in the course   507 Faliero   1   544
Being of an order of such spirits, as   508 Faliero   1   562
Not now:--being still alive, I'd have him live 512 Faliero   2   236
Being weak and worthless? I have lived too long 512 Faliero   2   269
To what I urged.--All these things being noted 514 Faliero   2   411
The only being who was constant to me   532 Faliero   4   295
I am settled and bound up, and being so   534 Faliero   4   422
The earth as being the Christian bulwark 'gainst 538 Faliero 5   11
And being lost, take what I would have taken   541 Faliero   5   262
And there, the ducal crown being first resumed 545 Faliero   5   519
The sons are in the lowest scale of being   549 Faliero   5   770
His sloth and shame by only being that   551 Sardan   1   19

BEING

Being bought without a tear. But that is not	554	Sardan	1	244
King, she is here. Away! Beautiful being	557	Sardan	1	468
His offspring needs none. But being innocent	566	Sardan	2	299
And humbly? No, sir, proudly--being honest	567	Sardan	2	376
Death all than such a being! And the end	580	Sardan	4	130
Uncall'd for:--I retire. Yet stay--being here	585	Sardan	4	446
I did abase myself as much in being	585	Sardan	4	465
To that which keeps all earth from being as fragile	588	Sardan	5	45
'Tis part of our instruction. War being constant	588	Sardan	5	102
Our clew being well nigh wound out, let's be cheerful	591	Sardan	5	237
Of the gross stains of too material being	594	Sardan	5	425
You have no cause, being what I am; but were I	605	Foscari	2	235
Our days on seasons; our whole being on	607	Foscari	2	356
I see the man--what mean'st thou? Caution! Being	613	Foscari	3	345
No doubt, are worth it. Being worth our lives	616	Foscari	4	89
A place within the sanctuary; but being	616	Foscari	4	·92
But the decree being render'd, I obey	623	Foscari	5	186
Master of spirits. And being so, canst thou	629	Cain	1	99
Of being that which I am--and thou art	629	Cain	1	135
The other may be still. How so? By being	630	Cain	1	209
In nature being earth also--more in wisdom	630	Cain	1	222
That bear the form of earth-born being. Ah	631	Cain	1	260
I thought it was a being: who could do	631	Cain	1	261
Such evil things to beings save a being	631	Cain	1	262
Be taught the mystery of my being. Follow	632	Cain	1	319
In multiplying our being multiply	633	Cain	1	370
Yes--in his works. But in his being? No	635	Cain	1	502
Or the dull mass of life, that, being life	639	Cain	2	225
And being of all things the sole thing certain	641	Cain	2	370
Was not thy quest for knowledge? Yes, as being	642	Cain	2	435
Which being nearest to thine eyes is still	643	Cain	2	458
You think so, being not her brother. Mortal	643	Cain	2	478
Being beyond all beauty in thine eyes	643	Cain	2	483
Then why is evil--he being good? I ask'd	643	Cain	2	490
How came ye, being spirits wise and infinite	644	Cain	2	585
For being dust, and grovelling in the dust	647	Cain	3	114
Not being omnipotent, nor fit to judge	650	Cain	3	277
From me a being I ne'er loved to bear	654	Cain	3	515
Methinks a being that is beautiful	657	Heaven		165
I pity thee. Me! why? For being happy	657	Heaven		186
As not being of them: turn thy steps aside	658	Heaven		211
Thyself for being his son	660	Heaven		424
From whom we had our being? Look upon	664	Heaven		687
To save an earth-born being; and behold	665	Heaven		734
In being here	666	Heaven		819
Being gone, 'twill be less difficult to die	667	Heaven		943
Run hazard of being drown'd (although I own	676	Werner	1	299
A tatter'd splendour. What a state of being	682	Werner	1	707
But, peace being made soon after his departure	685	Werner	2	119
Your lordship, being robb'd, don't recognise	686	Werner	2	204
The rogue; how should I, not being robb'd, identify	686	Werner	2	205
Deadly, without being natural prey to either	687	Werner	2	280
As being anxious to resume my journey	687	Werner	2	312
Who taught you thus to brand an unknown being	689	Werner	2	427
With such a being and my father? Every thing	689	Werner	2	433
He being lodged far off, and in a chamber	695	Werner	2	754
If it be so, being much disposed to do	695	Werner	3	10
Therefore I'll stick by this, as being loth	696	Werner	3	45
But being taken for him might conduct	700	Werner	3	318
(The old nobles being divided from their children	715	Werner	5	140
If such be thy desire; and yet, by being	726	Deformed	1	301
As the being who made him	728	Deformed	1	386
What! shrink already, being what you are	728	Deformed	1	450
And worse even for their friends than foes, as being	734	Deformed	1	813
'Which pye being open'd they began to sing	745	Juan	Ded	9
At being disappointed in your wish	745	Juah	Ded	18
Being only injured by his own assertion	746	Juan	Ded	68
Or, being mounted, e'er got down again	748	Juan	1	70
Instead of being scatter'd through the pages	752	Juan	1	354
As being the best judge of a lady's case	756	Juan	1	600
Juan being then grown up to man's estate	757	Juan	1	674
His temper not being under great command	769	Juan	1	1476
But I being fond of true philosophy	773	Juan	1	1753
His headache being increased by every billow	777	Juan	2	198
Getting the boats out, being well aware	779	Juan	2	358
But being thirstiest at the moment, he	783	Juan	2	611
Besides being much averse from such a fate	784	Juan	2	643
Without being much more horrible than Dante	784	Juan	2	664
But being naked, she was shock'd, you know	790	Juan	2	1029
She being wiser by a year or two	791	Juan	2	1084
Had all the advantage, too, of not being air	792	Juan	2	1136
Besides, being less in love, she yawn'd a little	792	Juan	2	1155
Being no Grecian; but he had an ear	793	Juan	2	1202
Because 'tis liquor only, and being far	794	Juan	2	1243
But Zoe, being older than Haidee	794	Juan	2	1261
Next they--he being naked, save a tatter'd	794	Juan	2	1273

BEING

Is pleasant, besides being true love's essence	795	Juan	2	1348
To her, as 'twere, the kind of being sent	796	Juan	2	1371
So that, her father being at sea, she was	796	Juan	2	1394
Man, being reasonable, must get drunk	796	Juan	2	1425
And forth they wander'd, her sire being gone	797	Juan	2	1449
Which, being join'd, like swarming bees they clung	798	Juan	2	1495
Had run the risk of being damn'd for ever	798	Juan	2	1540
And Haidee, being devout as well as fair	798	Juan	2	1541
Theirs being an unnatural situation	799	Juan	2	1606
And yet last night, being at a masquerade	800	Juan	2	1670
That being about the number I'll allow	801	Juan	2	1724
Men grow ashamed of being so very fond	802	Juan	3	49
Toss'd overboard unsaleable (being old	803	Juan	3	124
But that part of the coast being shoal and bare	804	Juan	3	150
Of the true reason of his not being sad	804	Juan	3	205
The cause being past his guessing or unriddling	805	Juan	3	222
He--being a man who seldom used a word	806	Juan	3	289
Her tears, too, being return'd into their fount	806	Juan	3	303
These rascals, being new comers, knew not whom	807	Juan	3	345
Their fury being spent by its own shock	808	Juan	3	462
He being paid to satirize or flatter	811	Juan	3	623
His polar star being one which rather ranges	811	Juan	3	635
And being fluent (save indeed when fee'd ill	811	Juan	3	638
But now being lifted into high society	811	Juan	3	657
He deem'd, being in a lone isle, among friends	811	Juan	3	660
Himself from being as pliable as Pindar	812	Juan	3	680
An independent being in his day	813	Juan	3	819
Being pride, which leads the mind to soar too far	816	Juan	4	7
'Tis being too epic, and I must cut down	816	Juan	4	978
But all these, save the last, being obsolete	817	Juan	4	47
Strange state of being! (for 'tis still to be	820	Juan	4	239
She dream'd of being alone on the sea-shore	820	Juan	4	241
But after being fired at once or twice	821	Juan	4	327
She recognized no being, and no spot	824	Juan	4	507
To be so being; in a gushing stream	824	Juan	4	526
But closed its little being without light	825	Juan	4	556
But being qualified in one way yet	827	Juan	4	683
But being the prima donna's near relation	827	Juan	4	693
Her cargo, from the plague being safe and sound	830	Juan	4	901
Europe and Asia, you being quite at ease	832	Juan	5	38
They look'd like persons being led to sentence	836	Juan	5	317
There being no such profusion in the North	836	Juan	5	332
But no one dreams of ever being short	837	Juan	5	384
Was on the point of being set aside	837	Juan	5	404
As not being in a masquerading mood	840	Juan	5	581
His garment's novelty, and his being awkward	841	Juan	5	618
And now being femininely all array'd	841	Juan	5	633
The hinges being as smooth as Rogers' rhymes	842	Juan	5	708
When, being made her property at last	846	Juan	5	924
Felt most indignant still at not being free	847	Juan	5	968
That being the last thing a proud woman tries	847	Juan	5	998
Earth being only made for queens and kings	847	Juan	5	1020
Though he deserved it well for being so backward	849	Juan	5	1118
For being the last wife of the Emperour	850	Juan	5	1167
Her reason being weak, her passions strong	853	Juan	6	61
It being (not now, but only while a lad	856	Juan	6	214
The giant thought of being a Titan's bride	856	Juan	6	220
Their guards being gone, and as it were a truce	856	Juan	6	270
Being somewhat large, and languishing, and lazy	857	Juan	6	327
As if she pitied her for being there	858	Juan	6	356
But, being no orator as Brutus is	861	Juan	6	591
But ended in his being found out and sack'd	865	Juan	6	830
This being the case, may show us what Fame is	871	Juan	7	257
This fellow, being six foot high, could raise	872	Juan	7	293
And every difficulty being dispell'd	873	Juan	7	405
My debt in being this allow'd to die	875	Juan	7	517
Being much too gross to see them in detail	876	Juan	7	610
Being grenadiers, they mounted one by one	880	Juan	8	117
The lightest being the safest: at a distance	885	Juan	8	437
They knew not where, being carried by the stream	887	Juan	8	570
The city, without being farther hamper'd	887	Juan	8	596
Then being taken by the tail--a stump	888	Juan	8	601
But could not eat them, being in his turn	888	Juan	8	610
Before, being badly seconded just then	888	Juan	8	627
As being a virtue, like terrestrial patience	892	Juan	8	855
And being told the latter, sent a bey	893	Juan	8	959
Such tales being for the tea-hours of some tabby	896	Juan	9	14
May like being praised for every lucky blunder	897	Juan	9	38
You did great things; but not being great in mind	897	Juan	9	79
I should be glad to know that which is being	898	Juan	9	122
The consequence is, being of no party	899	Juan	9	201
(As being the brave lions' keen providers	900	Juan	9	215
Which, being the damn'dest part of matrimony	905	Juan	9	559
On our fresh feelings, but--as being participated	910	Juan	10	181
As the sole sign of man's being in his senses	911	Juan	10	247
And being told it was 'God's house,' she said	916	Juan	10	593
To set up vain pretence of being great	918	Juan	10	691
Being quite perspicuous and extremely fair	919	Juan	11	36
And being somewhat choleric and sudden	920	Juan	11	98
Through Groves, so call'd as being void of trees	921	Juan	11	161
In the great world,--which, being interpreted	924	Juan	11	353

BEING
That being about their average numeral   925 Juan   11   430
Sets up for being a sort of moral me   925 Juan   11   458
Being tired in time, and, neither least nor last   926 Juan   11   500
Change grows too changeable, without being new   928 Juan   11   646
For being too excursive in his homages   929 Juan   11   704
For being as much the subject of attack   929 Juan   11   708
And as for 'Heaven being Love,' why not say honey   931 Juan   12   111
Amongst the paths of being 'taken in   932 Juan   12   195
Of being apt to talk at a great rate   933 Juan   12   222
Who might not profit much by being at large   935 Juan   12   328
For being a most exemplary wife   935 Juan   12   376
Being long married, and thus set at large   936 Juan   12   404
It does nor good nor harm; being merely meant   937 Juan   12   452
Of being, without alloy of fop or beau   940 Juan   12   671
Just to console sad glory for being glorious   945 Juan   13   256
But from being farmers, we turn gleaners, glean-
  ing   953 Juan   13   761
Without the apparel of being circumspect   962 Juan   14   444
Whose virtue lies in never being detected   963 Juan   14   488
Her Grace, too, pass'd for being an intrigante   963 Juan   14   497
And being of the council call'd 'the Privy   964 Juan   14   537
And being consumptive, live on a milk diet   973 Juan   15   328
A lovely being, scarcely form'd or moulded   973 Juan   15   343
Against her mention'd as well fitted   974 Juan   15   382
Being no sibyl in the new world's ways   975 Juan   15   446
Half virtues and whole vices being combined   975 Juan   15   452
At risk of being quizz'd for superstition   984 Juan   16   220
And being present, now began to express   984 Juan   16   254
Pale as if painted so; her cheek being red   989 Juan   16   554
Bacchus and Ceres being, as we know   992 Juan   16   732
The supplicator being an amateur   992 Juan   16   754
The night before; but being sick of shaking   996 Juan   16   986
At whatsoever risk of being defeated   996 Juan   16   998
Being wan and worn, with eyes that hardly brook'd   998 Juan   17   108

BEINGS
(See also FELLOW-BEINGS)
Till he had peopled them with beings bright   37 Harold   3   119
To the mind's purified beings; 'twas the ground   51 Harold   3   971
The beings of the mind are not of clay   55 Harold   4   37
These wondrous beings of his Fancy, wrought   193 Monody   53
Beings who ne'er each other can resign   212 Augusta-C   124
With beings brighter than have been, and give   214 Dream   21
I saw two beings in the hues of youth   214 Dream   27
The beings which surrounded him were gone   216 Dream   186
Their thoughts to meaner beings; they compress'd   463 Dante   4   4
With thought and beings of our thought reflected   463 Dante   4   35
Powers, passions, all I see in other beings   479 Manfred 1   22
For if the beings, of whom I was one   486 Manfred 2   170
And sees a hundred beings, now in earth   525 Faliero 3   455
With beings of a higher order. Insects   544 Faliero 5   435
And higher beings suffer; 'tis the charter   544 Faliero 5   462
Of women, and of beings less than women   551 Sardan   1   31
Part! Have not all past human beings parted   585 Sardan   4   474
The beings of another and worse world   606 Foscari 2   311
Or shadow, madest beings to enjoy them   627 Cain   1   12
Who didst create these best and beauteous beings   627 Cain   1   15
The reach of beings innocent, and curious   630 Cain   1   198
Such evil things to beings save a being   631 Cain   1   262
Are beings past, and shadows still to come   638 Cain   2   175
What these superior beings are or were   640 Cain   2   308
Of endless beings; skirr'd extinguish'd worlds   647 Cain   3   64
Two beings here erect them unto these   650 Cain   3   254
To perishable beings. Oh, my Anah   658 Heaven   227
New beings--years--diseases--sorrow--crime   661 Heaven   456
Beings even in death so fair   662 Heaven   527
One of those beings to whom Fortune bends   717 Werner   5   270
Both beings are more swift, more strong, more
  mighty   724 Deformed 1   107
Like human beings during civil war   779 Juan   2   336
Thus the frail beings we would fondly cherish   802 Juan   3   15
But Time, which brings all beings to their level   816 Juan   4   9
But like two beings born from out a rill   818 Juan   4   117
For beings passionate as Sappho's song   819 Juan   4   214
As human beings, or his ways are odd   891 Juan   8   828
As rare in living beings as a fossile   913 Juan   10   411
Of beings, stars, and this unriddled wonder   919 Juan   11   23

BEING'S
Yet cling to Being's severing link   217 High World   12
And man, o'erlaboured with his being's strife   375 Lara   1   632
For a departing being's soul   400 Parisina   394

BELDAME
In one day--what could that blood-loving beldame   555 Sardan   1   285
If your priests lie not! And thou, ghastly   578 Sardan   4   31

BELDAMES
It is to love the lovely beldames still   276 Waltz   219

BELDAM'S
Than a scared beldam's dreaming of the dead   567 Sardan   2   350

BELEAGUER'D
The last frail reed of our beleaguer'd hopes   589 Sardan   5   135
And was beleaguer'd both by land and water   868 Juan   7   62

BELESES
The gods but in decay. Beleses, why   562 Sardan   2   36
Treason--Arbaces! treachery and Beleses   565 Sardan   2   198
Follow me. Beleses! Now, what think you   567 Sardan   2   322
Soon as Arbaces and Beleses reach'd   572 Sardan   3   77
Which girds your arm? A scratch from brave
  Beleses   577 Sardan   3   365
But he did bravely. Slew he not Beleses   588 Sardan   5   81
What, crown'd already?--But, proceed. Beleses   592 Sardan   5   289
Whate'er it be. Commend me to Beleses   592 Sardan   5   350
Is for the excellent Beleses. Why   594 Sardan   5   457

BELFRY
With all the bells I'd carry yonder belfry   474 Morgante   576

BELGIUM'S
And Belgium's capital had gather'd then   38 Harold   3   182

BELIAL
And give both Belial and his dance their due   274 Waltz   28
Where Belial, upon duty for the day   294 Vision   580

BELIE
(Unless Report does much belie them   144 Becher-B   22
And made my cheek belie my heart   164 Friend-B   34
Nor, mute, that the world might belie   210 Augusta-B   32
He will not that untainted line belie   372 Lara   1   476
What they have found me, they belie; that which   557 Sardan   1   424
He deign'd not to belie his soul in songs   746 Juan   Ded   77

BELIED
While Allan's soul belied his form   102 Alva   73
Fear'd, shunn'd, ere youth had lost her force   342 Corsair 1   261
His brow belied him if his soul was sad   371 Lara   1   398

BELIEF
We loathe the action which exceeds belief   260 Hints   288
Their belief with blood have seal'd   402 Chillon   22
Our institutions and our strong belief   492 Manfred 3   60
Within thy power, but in the firm belief   507 Faliero 1   524
To your belief in heaven--to your mild virtues   514 Faliero 2   375
Of your belief renounce it, could he see   738 Deformed 2   246
Like most in the belief in which they're bred   783 Juan   2   606
Beyond a single gentleman's belief   807 Juan   3   408
For certain reasons my belief is serious   980 Juan   15   760
'Gainst such belief, there's something stronger
  still   981 Juan   16   55

BELIES
Her eyes beseem, her heart belies, her zone   266 Hints   695

BELIEVE
Now lads on shore may sigh, and maids believe   22 Harold   2   183
But let us part fair foes; I do believe   53 Harold   3 1059
An unseen seraph, we believe in thee   73 Harold   4 1082
With eyes admiring, oh, believe me   87 Rousseau   11
Believe me, only does his duty   87 Rousseau   18
Ne'er them, my beloved, that I do not believe   91 Caroline-C   2
Believe them not;--they point the path to shame   93 Dorset   25
How prompt are striplings to believe her   97 To Woman   12
For months you may try, yet, believe me, a sigh   115 Pigot   3
In friendship I early was taught to believe   129 Becher-A   26
If thou canst venture to believe   146 Vain Lady   16
Believe me, what I am, thy friend   158 Florence   24
Tyrants shall believe and tremble   188 Ode-B   102
Thus spoke he,--'I believe the man of whom   190 Churchill   27
But by sudden wrench, believe not   207 Fare Thee   23
I do not believe it beguiling   210 Augusta-B   11
Believe a woman or an epitaph   242 Bards   78
Believe me, Moschus, like that picture   256 Hints   11
Believe not all who laud your false 'sublime   267 Hints   782
Hear and believe, for Time will tell the rest   270 Minerva   162
Believe him bastard of a brighter race   270 Minerva   168
Freed from the bit, believe themselves with wings   299 Age   46
And they who listen may believe   312 Giaour   166
And some have been who could believe   336 Abydos   2   707
Theirs, to believe no prey nor plan amiss   339 Corsair 1   60
We promise, hope, believe--there breathes despair   345 Corsair 1   490
The more I should believe in her divinity   447 Beppo   488
For stories--but I don't believe the half of them   452 Beppo   784
We give you freely, since that you believe   468 Morgante   170
They'll one day fling the mountain, I believe   469 Morgante   216
The master of a galley, I believe   504 Faliero 1   322
I do believe you; and I know you true   513 Faliero 2   348
And droop their heads; believe me, they are such   522 Faliero 3   247
Do you be brief as I am, and believe me   538 Faliero 5   39
I cannot--no--even now believe these things   543 Faliero 5   342
And if he can deny the proofs, believe him   543 Faliero 5   349
That were an union I will not believe   565 Sardan   2   199
In Hades! if there be, as I believe   574 Sardan   3   158
Believe it. Should he shrink, I cannot cease   599 Foscari 1   234

BELIEVE

That were too much: believe me, 'twas not meet	600	Foscari	1	312
Such power I do believe there might exist	624	Foscari	5	221
As he saith--which I know not, nor believe	629	Cain	1	141
Believe--and sink not! doubt--and perish! thus	636	Cain	2	5
A man shall say to a man, 'Believe in me	636	Cain	2	18
Believe in me, as a conditional creed	636	Cain	2	21
I'll not believe it--for I thirst for good	642	Cain	2	443
I must go with thee. Irad, no; believe me	658	Heaven		208
Believe him not--and yet!--And you avow it	689	Werner	2	435
You, baron, I believe; but as the effect	693	Werner	2	628
What the devil would you have? You don't believe me	695	Werner	3	19
I do believe in thee! thou art the spirit	700	Werner	3	345
The assassin, 'twill be well--if not, believe me	703	Werner	3	575
Believe me, 'twould be mark'd in any house	708	Werner	4	249
Ravage the frontier. And will you believe	709	Werner	4	302
Looks likest what the boors believe to be	723	Deformed	1	100
Would I ask wherefore? Yes! and not believe	744	Deformed	3	135
They blush, and we believe them; at least I	768	Juan	1	1425
Thou shalt believe in Milton, Dryden, Pope	772	Juan	1	1633
Not to believe my verse and their own eyes	772	Juan	1	1660
And if, as I believe, thy vein be good	774	Juan	1	1771
They hired him, though to hear him you'd believe	827	Juan	4	695
Believe the Jews, those unbelievers, who	839	Juan	5	495
Must be believed, though they believe not you	839	Juan	5	496
Are very silent when they once believe	874	Juan	7	429
He never would believe the city won	891	Juan	8	836
You hardly think such things were true	895	Juan	8	1083
Makes us believe ourselves as good as any	905	Juan	9	544
Believe that virtue thaw'd before the river	911	Juan	10	264
And yet who can believe it? I would shatter	918	Juan	11	5
On purpose to believe so much the more	919	Juan	11	48
Virtuous she was--and had been, I believe	935	Juan	12	338
Which those most swear to who believe them most	947	Juan	13	419
Would some believe that such a tale had been	965	Juan	14	636
So that I verily believe if they	971	Juan	15	178
I say I do believe a haunted spot	980	Juan	15	763
The sceptics who would not believe Columbus	981	Juan	16	32
Who bids all men believe the impossible	981	Juan	16	38
Believe:--if 'tis improbable you must	981	Juan	16	42

BELIEVED

As the breasts I believed in with me	210	Augusta-B		14
All that his heart believed not--yet foretold	364	Corsair	3	598
Where yet she scarce believed that he was not	383	Lara	2	605
Girt on, though useless, he believed, to him	473	Morgante		480
Believed itself forgotten, and was fool'd	528	Faliero	4	42
When he was failing. I believed that swoon	601	Foscari	1	346
A third believed he wish'd to serve in war	685	Werner	2	118
And ne'er believed in negatives, till these	766	Juan	1	1279
She hoped he would improve--perhaps believed	775	Juan	2	70
More than can be believed, or even thought	782	Juan	2	523
Must be believed, though they believe not you	839	Juan	5	496
Some ne'er believed one half of what they heard	961	Juan	14	349
All nations have believed that from the dead	981	Juan	16	51
For such sights, though the tale is half believed	985	Juan	16	287

BELIEVER

Which doth your true believer so much please	855	Juan	6	179

BELIEVERS

And render the believers in our "Articles" sensible	179	Devil's Dr		247
To see them true believers, but no less	840	Juan	5	554
The True Believers:--and her infant brow	917	Juan	10	598

BELIEVES

She firmly believes she will go to the Moon	223	Soul-C		4
He Christ believes as Christian must be rated	473	Morgante		443
And like the demon who believes and trembles	527	Faliero	3	641
Misrule the mortal who believes him slave	710	Werner	4	355

BELIEVING

And you will smile at their believing	86	Rousseau		3
He left believing and betray'd	321	Giaour		1179
Believing every hillock green	329	Abydos	2	33
Glares round thee, in the scarce believing eyes	416	Island	1	61
Am mortal, and believing that the race	565	Sardan	2	241
Believing that I could survive what thou	589	Sardan	5	154
And turn'd, believing that he call'd again	791	Juan	2	1076

BELIEV'ST

If thou believ'st what striplings say	146	Vain Lady		10

BELIKE

'Belike,' said Ben, 'you might not from the bay	426	Island	2	506
'T is time, belike, to put our helm about	426	Island	2	515
Belike;--I'm a civilian. Fool! are not	693	Werner	2	657

BELINGHIERI

And gentle Belinghieri too came there	467	Morgante		72

BELISARIUS

Caesar and Pompey, Mahomet, Belisarius	800	Juan	2	1643

BELL
(See also DINNER-BELL, MARRIAGE-BELL, PASSING-BELL, STORM-BELL, VESPER-BELL)

Soon as the matin bell proclaimeth nine	15	Harold	1	713
Loud rings in air the chapel bell	96	Granta		69
The school where, loud warn'd by the bell, we resorted	96	Harrow-A		11
In lingering tones resounds the distant bell	124	Recoll		148
I really wish that Peter Bell	235	Epilogue		8
Ring the alarum bell! let folly quake	249	Bards		579
Venice the bell from every city bore	441	Beppo		78
The great bell of Saint Mark's, which may not be	524	Faliero	3	367
Many and martial; while the bell tolls on	524	Faliero	3	378
Saint Mark's great bell at dawn shall find me wakeful	526	Faliero	3	510
Doubt not, Saint Mark's great bell shall wake all Venice	528	Faliero	3	645
Of rolling drum, shrill trump, and hollow bell	530	Faliero	4	166
Then it is time to strike upon the bell	534	Faliero	4	416
Where swings the sullen huge oracular bell	535	Faliero	4	531
Unless that fearful bell be silenced soon	536	Faliero	4	580
Saint Mark's great bell is soon about to toll	624	Foscari	5	227
The bell! St. Mark's, which tolls for the election	625	Foscari	5	281
The bell tolls on!--let's hence--my brain's on fire	625	Foscari	5	304
Off with your arms!--That bell! My God! My God	625	Foscari	5	307
Or in the desert heard the camel's bell	784	Juan	2	671
The 'little boatman' and his 'Peter Bell	815	Juan	3	895
While swung the deep bell in the distant tower	815	Juan	3	909
As the far bell of vesper makes him start	816	Juan	3	957
When all around rang like a tocsin bell	862	Juan	6	668
Thy waiters running mucks at every bell	916	Juan	10	548
The silvery bell rang, not for 'dinner ready	975	Juan	15	486

BELLA

(And other chief points of a 'bella donna	828	Juan	4	748

BELLE

So, instead of 'beaux arts,' we may say 'la belle passion	277	Blues	1	4
Prescribed, by way of blister, a young belle	767	Juan	1	1340
To save his fame with each accomplish'd belle	925	Juan	11	419
'La Belle Alliance' of dunces down at zero	925	Juan	11	443

BELLES

Shades of those belles whose reign began of yore	275	Waltz		133
With the pride of our belles who have made it the fashion	277	Blues	1	3

BELLI

Oh thou 'teterrima causa' of all 'belli	903	Juan	9	433

BELL-MOUTH'D

Lit match, bell-mouth'd musquetoon	735	Deformed	2	31
His bell-mouth'd goblet makes me feel quite Danish	950	Juan	13	575

BELLONA

O'er whose gay trappings stern Bellona smiles	272	Minerva		286
Bellona, what you will--they mean but wars	878	Juan	8	8

BELLONA'S

Of red Bellona's banquet. 'Tis a scratch	738	Deformed	2	215

BELLOW

Yet still they deign'd to hiccup or to bellow	811	Juan	3	654
And for the bass, the beast can only bellow	827	Juan	4	690

BELLOWING

From their down-toppling nests; and bellowing herds	64	Harold	4	575

BELLOWINGS

Dart follows dart; lance, lance; loud bellowings speak his woes	16	Harold	1	764

BELLOWS

Unless to puff them with a pair of bellows	449	Beppo		597

BELLS
(See also CHURCH-BELLS)

His quick bells wildly jingling on the way	11	Harold	1	507
Bedecks her cap with bells of every clime	242	Bards		30
What merry sounds proceed from Oxford bells	246	Bards		336
Or, still in bells delighting, finds a friend	246	Bards		337
If to thy bells thou wouldst but add a cap	246	Bards		340
The browsing camels' bells are tinkling	317	Giaour		689
The Convent bells are ringing	400	Parisina		386
The death-hymn peals and the hollow bells knoll	400	Parisina		395
Unknown as bells within a Turkish steeple	449	Beppo		612

BELLS
With all the bells I'd carry yonder belfry   474 Morgante   576
But, for the bells, you've broken them, I wot 474 Morgante   578
Mix'd with the sweet bells of the sauntering herd 482 Manfred 1 312
When the merry bells are ringing   742 Deformed   3   68
Turkey contains no bells, and yet men dine   837 Juan   5 393
A fool whose bells have ceased to ring at all 918 Juan   10 688

BELL'S
Last of the howling host which once was Bell's 252 Bards   761
And vesper bell's that rose the boughs along 815 Juan   3 940

BELL-WETHER
Or a bell-wether form the flock's connection 873 Juan   7 382

BELONG
Ill suits the passions which belong to youth   29 Harold   2 560
To thee alone, unrivall'd, would belong   126 Recoll   289
To me no bays belong   132 L'Amitie   84
Who to this zealous Band belong   142 Critics   78
My friend, what magic spells belong   169 Blank Leaf   2
For them bewail, to them belong   184 Parker   12
Such is the force of wit! but not belong   242 Bards   37
To whom such glittering ornaments belong   245 Bards   296
His strain will teach what numbers best belong 258 Hints   107
But not to them do woful things belong   442 Beppo   158
Did not belong to what I knew of life   491 Manfred   3   8
Which now belong to history, soothe the days 525 Faliero   3 451
Such kisses as belong to early days   797 Juan   2 1484
To thee both oh! and ah! belong of right   904 Juan   9 514

BELONG'D
Which but belong'd to thee before   99 Young Lady   24

BELONGS
This ribband belongs to an "order of Merit"   177 Devil's Dr   122
The head to hock belongs, thy subtler art   274 Waltz   35
Belongs to all of us, you understand   295 Vision   691
Will not in vain arise to where belongs   460 Dante   3   15
She is not of our order, but belongs   490 Manfred   2 484
Your grief is private, it belongs to me   512 Faliero   2 218
Small dungeon is all that belongs to thee   609 Foscari   3   95
More noble name belongs to common thieves   689 Werner   2 426
Belongs to empires, and has been but borne   730 Deformed   1 538
Whose tale belongs to 'Hallam's Middle Ages' 933 Juan   12 240

BELOVED
Oh, ever loving, lovely, and beloved   34 Harold   2 900
And more beloved existence. That which Fate   56 Harold   4   40
Some less majestic, less beloved head   80 Harold   4 1507
Mine, my beloved, thou ne'er shalt be   90 To M.S.G.-A   20
Again, thou best beloved, adieu   90 Caroline-A   21
Ne'er think, my beloved, that I do not believe 91 Caroline-C   2
'Tis this, my beloved, which spreads gloom o'er
  my features   91 Caroline-C   13
But as death, my beloved, soon or late shall
  o'ertake us   91 Caroline-C   21
My native soil! beloved before   111 Medea   33
Yet, Caledonia, beloved are thy mountains   117 Lachin   5
Recall one scene so much beloved to view   127 Recoll   399
Like striplings, mutually beloved   137 Clare   2
Whilst blessing your beloved name   138 Clare   100
Of those beloved, those vanish'd hours   152 Remind   2
Beloved and fair Haidee   162 Romaic-A   2
Beloved but false Haidee   162 Romaic-A   34
Divided, yet beloved in vain   165 Thyrza   6
Beloved dust! since dust thou art   166 Away   14
To make thyself beloved? and to be   199 Sonnet-E   10
Yet, though I cannot be beloved   206 Year   3
There was but one beloved face on earth   214 Dream   48
She knew she was by him beloved,--she knew   214 Dream   91
Nor given him cause to deem himself beloved   215 Dream   141
In this beloved marble view   229 Marble   2
Though spurn'd by others, yet beloved by me   242 Bards   22
The youngest, most beloved of all   318 Giaour   768
Without her, most beloved in this   330 Abydos   2 111
But first, beloved Zuleika! hear   331 Abydos   2 211
'I loved, and was beloved again   409 Mazeppa   282
I loved, and was beloved again   409 Mazeppa   295
Your scenes sublime, from those beloved before 423 Island   2 297
A foe beloved, and offspring of a foe   432 Island   4 201
Love, who to none beloved to love again   476 Francesca   7
Astarte! my beloved! speak to me   490 Manfred   2 487
To be beloved on trust for what I feel   571 Sardan   2 596
Gather like night dew. My beloved, hush   579 Sardan   4   39
'Twas time. My best beloved! My true wife   608 Foscari   3   37
So loving, so beloved; the native of   621 Foscari   5   73
To be beloved more than all save thee   627 Cain   1   16
The Eternal anger? My beloved Cain   628 Cain   1   55
Own and beloved, she, too, understands not   630 Cain   1 185
And leave us? Ay. And me? Beloved Adah   632 Cain   1 344
Of all beloved things thou lovest her   643 Cain   2 511
Are in my heart. My best beloved, Abel   652 Cain   3 384
Scarce less beloved, where I despair'd for her 659 Heaven   286

BELOVED
In vain, and long, and still to be beloved   663 Heaven   596
My Ulric!--my beloved!--can it be   688 Werner   2 338
The prosperous and beloved Siegendorf   709 Werner   4 319
For thee? Beloved, when thou lovest me not   709 Werner   4 323
Oh, my sweet mother! My beloved child   713 Werner   5   27
Would be beloved. As thou showest me   727 Deformed   1 361
I love, and I shall be beloved! Oh, life   728 Deformed   1 420
Of flowers, that flower beloved the most   742 Deformed   3   14
For these you may be stript of--but beloved   744 Deformed   3 131
And so you love. Ah! could I be beloved   744 Deformed   3 134
Was neither much beloved nor yet abhorr'd   755 Juan   1 515
Beloved and loving many; all is o'er   770 Juan   1 1554
Beloved Julia, hear me still beseeching   776 Juan   2 159
She loved, and was beloved--she adored   798 Juan   2 1521
For there it lies so tranquil, so beloved   799 Juan   2 1569
On that beloved daughter; she had been   808 Juan   3 450
A nymph and her beloved, all unseen   818 Juan   4 118
Beloved and deplored; while slowly stray'd   860 Juan   6 534
Beloved in her own way, and rather whisk   853 Juan   6   20
While their beloved friends began to arm   876 Juan   7 607

BELOVED'S
His own and his beloved's name. Alas   608 Foscari   3   24

BELOW
And e'en for change of scene would seek the
  shades below   4 Harold   1   54
Or disappointed passion lurk'd below   4 Harold   1   67
The vine on high, the willow branch below   7 Harold   1 250
Blasted below the dun hot breath of war   11 Harold   1 498
Where'er we gaze, around, above, below   26 Harold   2 426
Circled the wide extending court below   28 Harold   2 507
Mountains above, Earth's, Ocean's plain below 33 Harold   2 848
So that no wonder waits him; nor below   36 Harold   3   39
An Earthquake's spoil is sepulchred below   37 Harold   3 146
Must look down on the hate of those below   42 Harold   3 400
Banners on high, and battles pass'd below   42 Harold   3 420
How Earth may pierce to Heaven, yet leave vain man
  below   45 Harold   3 598
Imperishably pure beyond all things below   45 Harold   3 643
Of those whose eyes are only turn'd below   47 Harold   3 714
Rooted in barrenness, where nought below   58 Harold   4 174
Know, that the lightning sanctifies below   61 Harold   4 368
Into thy statue's form and look like gods below 63 Harold   4 443
Their spoils here? Yes; and in yon field below 72 Harold   4 1005
And quaff the contents as our nectar below   91 Caroline-C   28
One feeble spirit seeks the shades below   109 Nisus   274
Mild Charity's glow, to us mortals below   115 The Tear   9
O'er their last scene of happiness below   127 Recoll   384
Or the mist of the tempest that gather'd below 135 Highlander   4
On mortals here below   137 Clare   6
May wake the beam that lurks below   150 Song-A   16
Veiling the azure orbs below   152 Remind   21
And storied urns record who rests below   154 Dog   4
Should a rival bow down to our idol below   155 Goblet   18
Thy joys below, thy hopes above   164 Friend-B   17
Though every joy is fled below   166 Struggle   7
For I find we have much better manners below 178 Devil's Dr   151
Nameless, but dear to gentle hearts below   192 Monody   14
Thy welcome of tyrants had plunged thee below 203 Avatar   103
She deems that all could be like her below   208 Sketch   34
A mind at peace with all below   216 She Walks   17
And the last thought that soothes me below   218 Jephtha   12
Which roll'd on in freedom below   222 Babylon   8
But ere he sunk below Cithaeron's head   268 Minerva   29
Below, his name--above, behold his deeds   270 Minerva   108
As heaven-born Pitt can testify below   274 Waltz   40
Finding their charges past all care below   285 Vision   18
Whatever has been wisely done below   287 Vision   168
Pressing one radiant arm just where below   289 Vision   283
Trust that, whatever may occur below   292 Vision   494
Of him; I've kings enough below, God knows   293 Vision   512
Said Wilkes, 'are cherubs; and that soul below 293 Vision   542
Their place below: for me, I have forgiven   293 Vision   567
I saw a taper, far below me, wink   295 Vision   686
Such trash below your wing, Asmodeus dear   296 Vision   702
By no means often was his case below   296 Vision   714
Varied above, but still alike below   298 Age   27
That rolls below the Athenian's grave   310 Giaour   2
Whose bark in sheltering cove below   310 Giaour   38
When left to roll its folds below   315 Giaour   497
As dark as his that bled below   317 Giaour   674
My days, though few, have pass'd below   320 Giaour   982
My hope on high--my all below   322 Giaour   1183
And clouds aloft and tides below   329 Abydos   2   10
The greaves below his knee that wound   330 Abydos   2 145
If there be life below, and hope above   344 Corsair   1 451
Of flames on high and torches from below   349 Corsair   2 153
To give thee back to all endear'd below   355 Corsair   2 531
But here he sank below Cithaeron's head   356 Corsair   3   29
The life thou leav'st below, denied above   359 Corsair   3 236
My life--my love--my hatred--all below   361 Corsair   3 374
Booms harmless, hissing to the deep below   362 Corsair   3 489

BELOW

And veil'd--thought shrinks from all that lurk'd below	364 Corsair	3	610
The proud, the wayward, who have fix'd below	365 Corsair	3	632
In turn he tried--he ransack'd all below	367 Lara	1	119
Thus coldly passing all that pass'd below	371 Lara	1	351
Her isthmus idly spread below	385 Corinth		64
And the fringe of the foam may be seen below	388 Corinth		436
As his measured step on the stone below	389 Corinth		452
On the Alpine vales below	392 Corinth		744
There were dead above, and the dead below	395 Corinth		973
All that mingled there below	395 Corinth		1031
To press, not shade, the orbs below	398 Parisina		180
The song for the dead below	400 Parisina		392
But whatsoe'er its end below	401 Parisina		528
Nothing more remain'd below	402 Parisina		546
The living stream lies quick below	402 Parisina		555
Which he abhorr'd to view below	403 Chillon		91
A thousand feet in depth below	403 Chillon		108
Below the surface of the lake	403 Chillon		115
On high--their wide long lake below	406 Chillon		335
My senses climb up from below	412 Mazeppa		552
But volumes lurk'd below his fierce farewell	418 Island	1	168
Shall sadly please us as we lean below	419 Island	2	12
Of the dusk bosoms that beat high below	419 Island	2	52
Or link'd to all we know of heaven below	424 Island	2	376
While far below the vast and sullen swell	427 Island	3	71
Dash'd downward in the thundering foam below	429 Island	3	176
Diving for turtle in the depths below	432 Island	4	196
Then plunged: the rock below received like glass	434 Island	4	341
But calm and careless heaved the wave below	435 Island	4	367
With pilfering pranks and petty pains, below	439 Tasso		193
Like the lost Pleiad seen no more below	442 Beppo		112
While yet Canova can create below	446 Beppo		368
As much as saying, they're below your notice	447 Beppo		464
The demagogues of fashion of fashion: all below	447 Beppo		478
With beauty so surpassing all below	463 Beppo	4	30
In daily jeopardy the place below	468 Morgante		160
And Alabaster he found out below	470 Morgante		290
In hell below, and damn'd in great confusion	472 Morgante		406
Where he was wont to drink below the mountain	473 Morgante		488
Of aught above it, or below it--nothing	566 Sardan	2	266
A cell so far below the water's level	614 Foscari	3	377
Tremble, ye mountains, soon to shrink below	662 Heaven		502
When no good spirit longer lights below	663 Heaven		598
While from below	667 Heaven		881
Surely celestial mercy lurks below	667 Heaven		946
Is drown'd below the ford, with five post-horses	675 Werner	1	215
Without--within--above--below--Heaven help me	683 Werner	2	12
A prince's chamber, lay below my knife	690 Werner	2	468
Which shot along the glancing tide below	714 Werner	5	111
Above, and many altar shrines below	731 Deformed	1	613
A guard in sight; they wisely keep below	733 Deformed	1	770
To supersede all warblers here below	745 Juan	Ded	19
And for the fame you would engross below	745 Juan	Ded	52
By all the vows below to powers above	760 Juan	1	867
Pedro, Battista, help me down below	776 Juan	2	156
But let us die like men, not sink below	778 Juan	2	284
A portion of their beef up from below	780 Juan	2	373
And walking out upon the beach, below	790 Juan	2	1025
They gazed upon the glittering sea below	797 Juan	2	1475
Below her breast was fasten'd with a band	810 Juan	3	573
And for his theme--he seldom sung below it	811 Juan	3	622
And ships, by thousands, lay below	812 Juan	3	709
Young innate feelings all have felt below	818 Juan	4	141
Flock o'er their carrion, just like men below	820 Juan	4	224
The sharp rocks look'd below each drop they caught	820 Juan	4	263
Up in a little creek below a wall	836 Juan	5	319
Pointed to Juan who remain'd below	843 Juan	5	768
But the town ditch below was deep as ocean	868 Juan	7	83
Grass before scythes, or corn below the sickle	883 Juan	8	338
Flame was shower'd forth above, as well's below	883 Juan	8	356
Above, below, by turnpikes great or small	906 Juan	9	636
To make such puppets of us things below	909 Juan	10	124
Think of the Thunderer's falling down below	914 Juan	10	467
Such thoughts are quite below the strain they have chosen	936 Juan	12	435
She made the earth below seem holy ground	948 Juan	13	485
At eighteen, though below her feet still panted	962 Juan	14	437
Which nodded to the nation's spoils below	976 Juan	15	531
Below his window waved (of course) a willow	982 Juan	16	118
Below stairs on the score of second courses	989 Juan	16	588

BELSHAZZAR

Belshazzar! from the banquet turn	185 Belshaz-A		1
The words which shook Belshazzar in his hall	809 Juan	3	517

BELSHAZZAR'S

'Belshazzar's grave is made	220 Belshaz-B		41

BELT

Like lauwine loosen'd from the mountain's belt	57 Harold	4	106
Starts from its belt--he rends his captive's chains	57 Harold	4	143

BELT

His waist was bound with a broad belt round	104 Alva		257
The gems which stud the monarch's golden belt	109 Nisus		290
And form'd a circle like Orion's belt	288 Vision		204
To see proud Albyn's tartans as a belt	308 Age		773
Bears in his belt the scimitar	315 Giaour		524
And from his belt a sabre swung	330 Abydos	2	139
His belt and cloak were o'er his shoulders flung	346 Corsair	1	560
With swordless belt, and fetter'd hand	398 Parisina		139
And whether they had chafed his belt	407 Mazeppa		85
Link'd to his belt, a matrimonial pair	425 Island	2	493
And drawing from his belt a pistol, he	821 Juan	4	316
That stretches to the stony belt, which girds	863 Juan	6	687
At the first sight of Albion's chalky belt	915 Juan	10	516

BELTANE

For him thy Beltane yet may burn	104 Alva		220

BELTS

With luminous belts, and floating moons, which took	638 Cain	2	188

BELUS

Or why or how he hath divined it, Belus	558 Sardan	1	508
My liege--the son of Belus! he blasphemes	565 Sardan	2	236
We thank--Priest! keep your thanksgivings for Belus	566 Sardan	2	298

BELUS'

What is shall be the past of Belus' race	555 Sardan	1	331

BEN

Cam Hobhouse! but by wags Byzantian Ben	224 J.C.H.		2
Were satisfied with Chaucer and old Ben	262 Hints		428
'What cheer, Ben Bunting?' cried (when in full view	425 Island	2	500
'Ey, ey!' quoth Ben, 'not new, but news enow	426 Island	2	502
'Belike,' said Ben, 'you might not from the bay	426 Island	2	506
'Ey, ey; for that 'tis all the same to Ben	426 Island	2	519
'Right,' quoth Ben, 'that will do for the marines	426 Island	2	531
Ben Bunting, who essay'd to wash, and wipe	428 Island	3	105
Revived Ben Bunting from his pipe profound	428 Island	3	134

BENCH

He still for the Bench would be driving	238 Bray		15
The Bench too seats or suits full many a debtor	921 Juan	11	197

BENCHES

But the benches are cramm'd, like a garden in flower	277 Blues	1	2
Are puzzles to the most precautious benches	989 Juan	16	552

BEND

Pride! bend thine eye from heaven to thine estate	10 Harold	1	400
I tremble, and can only bend the knee	14 Harold	1	626
E'er deign'd to bend her chastely-awful eyes	17 Harold	1	822
Who with the weight of years would wish to bend	23 Harold	2	203
Land of Albania, let me bend mine eyes	25 Harold	2	338
And of lofty fountains, and the bend	51 Harold	3	955
May be permitted, as my steps I bend	52 Harold	3	1019
The graceful bend and the voluptuous swell	63 Harold	4	472
Yet still, though we bend with a feign'd resignation	92 Caroline-D		17
When youthful parasites, who bend the knee	93 Dorset		17
Taught by their sire to bend the bow	102 Alva		53
We'll bend our course to yonder mountain's brow	106 Nisus		108
Lest grief should bend my parent to the grave	107 Nisus		184
Now where Messapus dwelt they bend their way	109 Nisus		275
Then from the tents their cautious steps they bend	109 Nisus		295
To him, with suppliant smiles, they bend the head	112 Examination		65
What 'tis to bend before Love's mighty throne	125 Recoll		200
Why bend to the proud, or applaud the absurd	129 Becher-A		23
dost thou bend thy brow, chief of Oithona	130 Calmar		113
Unless they bend in pompous form	132 Prayer		22
Will bend before thy potent throne	139 Anacreon-C		25
But thou, perhaps, like me with age must bend	139 Ossian-A		25
Bend the canvass o'er the mast	156 Hodgson		4
I ne'er shall bend mine eyes on thee	158 Florence		16
And, though it will not bend to gold	160 Cadiz		31
Must she too bend, must she too share	181 Ode-A		113
To these, when authors bend in humble awe	243 Bards		85
Now to the Drama let us bend our eyes	261 Hints		351
But with a graceful oriental bend	289 Vision		282
But break--before it bend again	319 Giaour		936
Nay, start not--no--nor bend thy knee	320 Giaour		1036
Thou, when thine arm should bend the bow	324 Abydos	1	85
And sportive dolphins bend them through the spray	364 Corsair	3	560
He raised the humble but to bend the proud	378 Lara	2	253
But yet they reach the stream, and bend to taste	380 Lara	2	409
To my barr'd windows, and to bend	406 Chillon		329
Where these weak spirits round thee bend	480 Manfred	1	129
That bows to him who made things but to bend	631 Cain	1	235
But I will bend to neither. Ne'er the less	632 Cain	1	315

BEND

He said; but, as I fear, to bend his steps	658 Heaven		245
When the swoln clouds unto the mountains bend	670 Heaven		1116
Would Juan bend, though 'twere to Mahomet's bride	844 Juan	5	821
About his ears, and nathless would not bend	844 Juan	5	826
Heads bow, knees bend, eyes watch around a throne	847 Juan	5	1015
In prose I bend my humble verse) doth call	891 Juan	8	831

BENDED

What all this meant: while Baba bow'd and bended	843 Juan	5	759

BENDER

As obstinate as Swedish Charles at Bender	892 Juan	8	852

BENDING

And lowly bending to the lists advance	15 Harold	1	732
Thus bending o'er the vessel's laving side	23 Harold	2	208
On Angus bending low the knee	104 Alva		262
He sunk, an Atlas bending 'neath the weight	114 Death-A		17
And whistling o'er the bending mast	156 Lady-F		3
Her graceful arms .in meekness bending	325 Abydos	1	182
And senseless bending o'er his saddle-bow	380 Lara	2	389
Thither bending sternly back	394 Corinth		914
'Twas bending close o'er his, and the small mouth	788 Juan	2	897
Her hand on his, and bending on him eyes	847 Juan	5	994
Their plates--without it might be too much bending	991 Juan	16	676

BENDS

Affliction's semblance bends not o'er thy tomb	85 Epitaph		17
Or bends the languid eyelid down	100 Marion		9
Thus, sweetly drooping, bends his lovely head	110 Nisus		383
As he bends o'er the wave which may soon be his grave	115 The Tear		15
But bends not now before thy throne	118 Romance		48
Drooping, she bends o'er pensive Fancy's urn	126 Recoll		343
Then raves for...; to that Mentor bends	271 Minerva		251
Nor bends on woman's form his eyes	314 Giaour		440
And o'er him bends that foe with brow	317 Giaour		673
And now within the valley bends	317 Giaour		704
It bends and melts--though still the same	319 Giaour		925
He bends him slightly, but his lips are mute	340 Corsair	1	142
'Call Pedro here!' He comes, and Conrad bends	346 Corsair	1	561
Down to the cabin with Gonsalvo bends	346 Corsair	1	585
He slept--Who o'er his placid slumber bends	352 Corsair	2	394
His only bends in seeming o'er his beads	357 Corsair	3	139
It bends--it falls--and all is o'er	394 Corinth		945
He bends to hear his accents bless	400 Parisina		416
The beauties of the sunbow which bends o'er thee	485 Manfred	2	118
One of those beings to whom Fortune bends	717 Werner	5	270

BENEATH
(See also 'NEATH)

On sloping mounds, or in the vale beneath	7 Harold	1	270
Nor saved your brethren ere they sank beneath	10 Harold	1	417
And far beneath the earth and ocean spread	42 Harold	3	402
And famous through all ages! but beneath	67 Harold	4	762
Such pangs my nature sinks beneath	87 Ad Lesbiam		23
And on the crimson'd rocks beneath	101 Alva		9
And sunk the yawning grave beneath	128 Answer-B		20
To gaze on the torrent that thunder'd beneath	135 Highlander		3
But mocks the woe that lurks beneath	166 Struggle		19
All green and wildly fresh without, but worn and grey beneath	186 Music-B		16
The current I behold will sweep beneath	198 Po		21
Gazing--the one on all that was beneath	214 Dream		40
Disdain'd to sink beneath	219 Thy Days		10
Darkness above, despair beneath	314 Giaour		437
The name of him that was beneath	329 Abydos	2	52
The breezy freshness of the deep beneath	346 Corsair	1	536
All these seem'd his, and something more beneath	367 Lara	1	77
So much he soar'd beyond, or sunk beneath	371 Lara	1	345
Than that he loved! Oh! never yet beneath	382 Lara	2	512
And as the fabric sank beneath	386 Corinth		167
Of aught around, above, beneath	396 Parisina		34
But here, upon the earth beneath	398 Parisina		213
Could this be still the earth beneath	400 Parisina		373
One on the earth, and one beneath	404 Chillon		219
And, pointing to the helpless prow beneath	417 Island	1	153
But brawny as the boar's; and hung beneath	425 Island	2	490
When Eloisa's form was lower'd beneath	433 Island	4	224
Flung over these dim words engraved beneath	545 Faliero	4	499
Each pulse to animation, till beneath	788 Juan	2	902
And she bent o'er him, and he lay beneath	793 Juan	2	1177
The worlds to come of both, or fall beneath	802 Juan	3	69
(For that's the name they like to pray beneath	809 Juan	3	524
Which once-named myriads nameless lie beneath	829 Juan	4	815
And lips apart, which show'd the pearls beneath	860 Juan	6	520
A red lip, with two rows of pearls beneath	996 Juan	16	1014

BENEDICKS

Ye Benedicks! hear me, and listen with rapture	117 To Eliza	18

BENEDICTION

With the Lord's great reward and benediction	475 Morgante	637

BENEFACTOR

And thou art lost!--thou! my sole benefactor	532 Faliero	4	294

BENEFACTRESS

With a young benefactress,--so was she	795 Juan	2	1335

BENEFIT

To councils held to benefit mankind	303 Age		393
The public benefit; and what the state	619 Foscari	4	267
Not make them,--though he reap the benefit	728 Deformed	1	439
Are ways to benefit mankind, as true	763 Juan	1	1055
For the great benefit of those who know	898 Juan	9	115
Or do they benefit mankind? Lean miser	931 Juan	12	87

BENEFITS

Perhaps too natural; for benefits	583 Sardan	4	319

BENEVOLENCE

Of thine omnipotent benevolence	649 Cain	3	235

BENEVOLENT

And all kinds of benevolent machines	873 Juan	7	376

BENIGN

Shed o'er me your languor benign	97 To M.S.G.-B		6
Benign and pious, bid an angel flee	466 Morgante		6
Of thy benign and quiet influence	529 Faliero	4	109
Benign Ceruleans of the second sex	830 Juan	4	858

BENIGNANT

Benignant o'er those blessed isles	310 Giaour	8

BENIGNLY

Be to my verses then benignly kind	466 Morgante	15

BENINTENDE

Sage Benintende, now chief judge of Venice	544 Faliero	5	408

BENISON

'Then go you with God's benison and mine	469 Morgante	234
Whereon Apicius would bestow his benison	976 Juan	15	518

BENS

Not that our Bens or Beaumonts show the worse	258 Hints	123

BENT

His fabled golden tribute bent to pay	6 Harold	1	204
And weave their web again; some, bow'd and bent	58 Harold	4	194
Unto the things of earth, which Time hath bent	74 Harold	4	1156
Bent on your knees the Boon receive	141 Critics		19
For every thought is bent to prove	160 Cadiz		35
But never bent beneath till now	165 Thyrza		44
That still unbroke, though gently bent	210 Augusta-A		26
Bent o'er the desk, or, born to useful toils	247 Bards		407
But our good fathers never bent their brains	262 Hints		425
He merely bent his diabolic brow	289 Vision		289
He who hath bent him o'er the dead	311 Giaour		68
Though bent on earth thine evil eye	312 Giaour		196
His brow was bent, his eye was glazed	312 Giaour		240
With steel unsheathed, and carbine bent	316 Giaour		579
As e'er at Mecca bent the knee	317 Giaour		730
The tower by war or tempest bent	319 Giaour		878
Yet there we follow but the bent assign'd	333 Abydos	2	428
Bows his bent head; his hand salutes the floor	347 Corsair	2	47
As if she late had bent her leaning head	361 Corsair	3	412
But Lara's prostrate form he bent beside	369 Lara	1	241
But to a moment's thought that purpose bent	376 Lara	2	83
Who cursed the tyranny to which he bent	377 Lara	2	158
Bent was his head, and hidden was his brow	383 Lara	2	561
And o'er his brow, so downward bent	390 Corinth		513
Thus the first were backward bent	392 Corinth		730
Blazed, as he bent no more to rise	394 Corinth		880
The waves a moment backward bent	395 Corinth		1022
That bent not to the roughest breeze	411 Mazeppa		467
No nation's eyes would on their tomb be bent	433 Island	4	267
Bent its broad arch: her breath began to fail	435 Island	4	378
And Laura's brow a frown had rarely bent	443 Beppo		182
For mine is not a nature to be bent	456 Dante	1	34
Are bent upon this rash abandonment	624 Foscari	5	236
Thou ne'er hadst bent to him who made thee? Yes	632 Cain	1	324
Why should our hymn be raised, our knees be bent	670 Heaven		1124
The pleasant trees that o'er our noonday bent	670 Heaven		1180
And o'er him bent his sire, and never raised	785 Juan	2	705
Then changed like to a bow that's bent, and then	785 Juan	2	727
Bent with hush'd lips, that drank his scarce-drawn breath	792 Juan	2	1144
And she bent o'er him, and he lay beneath	793 Juan	2	1177
On him her flashing eyes a moment bent	824 Juan	4	516
Bent like an antelope a Paphian pair	843 Juan	5	763
In ordering matters after his own bent	872 Juan	7	299
Now Mars, now Momus; and when bent to storm	874 Juan	7	439

BENT
March'd forth with nerve and sinews bent to slay 878 Juan 8 12
Following the bent of body or of mind 899 Juan 9 165
Was bent with grief that Mahomet should resign 917 Juan 10 599
According as their minds or backs are bent 936 Juan 12 412
All matchless creatures, and yet bent on matches 936 Juan 12 424
Of nations, and had never bent or bow'd 974 Juan 15 366
Shall 'fool me to the top up of my bent 979 Juan 15 747

BENTLEY'S
Yet prizing Bentley's, Brunck's, or Porson's note 112 Examination 57

BENUMB
There are some feelings Time cannot benumb 58 Harold 4 170
Guilt would benumb his palsied hand 105 Alva 311
And for the present, I would not benumb 212 Augusta-C 117
Of these things, or by ridicule benumb 980 Juan 15 758

BENUMB'D
We feel benumb'd and wish to be no more 213 Lady Byron 10
Despair benumb'd her breast and eye 334 Abydos 2 522

BENVENUTO
Well said, my man of marble! Benvenuto 738 Deformed 2 210

BENVOLIO
'Tis strange Benvolio suffers such a show 261 Hints 326

BEPPO
Our Beppo:--when copied, I'll send it 232 Murray-B 12
His name Giuseppe, call'd more briefly, Beppo 443 Beppo 200
Till Beppo should return from his long cruise 443 Beppo 235
With scarce a hope that Beppo could return 444 Beppo 275
To speak, cries 'Beppo! what's your pagan name 451 Beppo 725
'Beppo! that beard of yours becomes you not 451 Beppo 737
What answer Beppo made to these demands 452 Beppo 745

BEQUEATH
To us bequeath--'tis all their fate allows 182 Address-C 19
And, dying in despondency, bequeath 462 Dante 3 152
We should bequeath to our posterity 531 Faliero 4 252
He will bequeath none; nothing but a name 550 Sardan 1 16
I will dare all things to bequeath it them 582 Sardan 4 273
Which men bequeath as portraits, and they were 610 Foscari 3 116
Bequeath that science to thy children, and 645 Cain 2 628
Endure, and, harder still, bequeath; but since 648 Cain 3 134
Might have one; or, in short, he did bequeath 711 Werner 4 482
No, not bequeath--but I bestow this sum 711 Werner 4 483

BEQUEATH'D
Here Burgundy bequeath'd his tombless host 45 Harold 3 604
Of names which unto you bequeath'd a name 51 Harold 3 978
Boccaccio to his parent earth bequeath'd 63 Harold 4 514
Bequeath'd the name of Washington 182 Ode-A 170
Of light no likeness is bequeath'd--no name 193 Monody 25
Bequeath'd by bleeding sire to son 311 Giaour 124
In what he hath bequeath'd us?--in what guise 445 Beppo 365
Bequeath'd, a heritage of heart and hand 454 Venice-B 137
As ye bequeath'd it, this bright part of it 594 Sardan 5 429
Amongst us), all that history has bequeath'd 607 Foscari 2 404
Bequeath'd to me? I leave them my inheritance 639 Cain 2 234
Our mother Eve bequeath'd us--but my heart 656 Heaven 107

BEQUEATHING
Bequeathing their hereditary rage 69 Harold 4 841

BEQUEATHS
Bequeaths of free, and History of sublime 453 Venice-B 77

BEQUEST
Nor e'er be robb'd: their spoils are a bequest 695 Werner 2 763

BEREFT
While thus of both bereft, the nymph-queen doubly
    sigh'd 24 Harold 2 261
'O God! my boy,' he cries, 'of me bereft 109 Nisus 321
Nature of verdure and flow'rs has bereft you 118 Lachin 35
Though now of Love and time bereft 161 Picture 2
See all alike of more or less bereft 271 Minerva 243
Of subsidies and Hanover bereft 274 Waltz 43
By hope unblest, of fame bereft 332 Abydos 2 332
To throb o'er those of life bereft 402 Parisina 570
The world for ever, earth of light bereft 424 Island 2 363
The weight of clay again,--too soon bereft 456 Dante 1 3
Of which young passion cannot be bereft 756 Juan 1 590
Sigh'd to behold them of their hours bereft 817 Juan 4 61
Alas! to them of ready cash bereft 946 Juan 13 355

BERENICE'S
'Tis said that Berenice's hair 97 To M-- 21

BERG
Steep, harsh, and slippery as a berg of ice 431 Island 4 70

BERGAMASK
Bertram, the Bergamask! With what vile tools 537 Faliero 4 644

BERGAMO
Bertram, of Bergamo,--would you question him 540 Faliero 5 173
And Bergamo no less are hers; her realm 602 Foscari 2 21

BERKELEY
When Bishop Berkeley said 'there was no matter 918 Juan 11 1

BERKLEY
If still in Berkley ballads most uncivil 245 Bards 231

BERLIN
Who, crush'd at Jena, crouch'd at Berlin, fell 300 Age 157
And thence through Berlin, Dresden, and the like 915 Juan 10 481

BERRY
And Mocha's berry, from Arabia pure 809 Juan 3 499

BERRY'S
Though to the rest the sober berry's juice 347 Corsair 2 33

BERTH
And shut himself at night within his berth 470 Morgante 303
His berth a little damp, and him afraid 777 Juan 2 200
Or with a famish'd boat's-crew had your berth 784 Juan 2 670

BERTHA
Shall change with Thetis' son, and I with Bertha 728 Deformed 1 377

BERTHS
Passengers their berths are clapt in 157 Hodgson 35
The captives back to their sad berths; each threw 827 Juan 4 716

BERTRAM
I do not doubt the elder; but in Bertram 517 Faliero 2 580
I have known Bertram long; there doth not breathe 517 Faliero 2 589
Who is expected momently. Where's Bertram 520 Faliero 3 124
Bertram, we must be firm! Look to it well 521 Faliero 3 166
Bertram; I have an eye upon thee. Who 521 Faliero 3 167
For sneer, nor for suspicion! Calm thee, Bertram 521 Faliero 3 198
Have they e'er shown, or felt, or feign'd it?
    Bertram 524 Faliero 3 400
It seems the voice of Bertram--go, Antonio 530 Faliero 4 130
Many to your poor client, Bertram; add 530 Faliero 4 133
Bertram, I have known thee long. From childhood,
    signor 531 Faliero 4 198
Bertram, 'tis thou who hast forgotten them 531 Faliero 4 208
As suits your station, the more humble Bertram 531 Faliero 4 212
Has proved to me, the poor plebeian Bertram 531 Faliero 4 220
Some villains have been tampering with thee,
    Bertram 531 Faliero 4 241
Was it not thus thou saidst, my gentle Bertram 531 Faliero 4 253
Ay, is it even so? Excuse me, Bertram 532 Faliero 4 272
Fie, Bertram! that was not a craft for thee 532 Faliero 4 284
And send for Marc Cornaro:--fear not, Bertram 533 Faliero 4 333
Bertram, I'll reason with thee as we go 533 Faliero 4 348
I'll answer for thee--'tis a certain Bertram 537 Faliero 4 642
Bertram, the Bergamask! With what vile tools 537 Faliero 4 644
The coward Bertram, would--Peace, Calendaro 539 Faliero 5 128
Bertram, of Bergamo,--would you question him?
    No 540 Faliero 5 173

BERTRAM'S
Bertram's and old Soranzo's, both of whom 517 Faliero 2 574

BERTUCCIO
That Israel Bertuccio has secured him 511 Faliero 2 143
The Senator Bertuccio, your kinsman 511 Faliero 2 146
Worthy Bertuccio, I have known you ever 518 Faliero 2 708
Most welcome.--Brave Bertuccio, thou art late 521 Faliero 3 203
Bertuccio--What! are you all appall'd to see 522 Faliero 3 215
Was this your trust in your true chief Bertuccio 522 Faliero 3 232
Before Bertuccio added to our cause 524 Faliero 3 392
Come hither, my Bertuccio--one embrace 535 Faliero 4 476
Noble Bertuccio, we must now remove you 537 Faliero 4 655
And two others, Israel Bertuccio 540 Faliero 5 174

BERTUCCIO'S
My nephew, brave Bertuccio's messenger 536 Faliero 4 546

BESEECH
I do beseech you, lean upon us! No! 625 Foscari 5 305
Baron, I do beseech you! I must be 693 Werner 2 660
Said--'Lady, I beseech you to suppose them 903 Juan 9 403

BESEECH'D
Her anger, and beseech'd she'd hear him through 865 Juan 6 811

BESEECHING
And beckons with beseeching hands 323 Giaour 1299
And shut out God from our beseeching eyes 670 Heaven 1141

BESEECHING

| Beseeching she no further would refuse | 769 Juan | 1 | 1439 |
| Beloved Julia, hear me still beseeching | 776 Juan | 2 | 159 |

BESEEM

The three so mingled did beseem	188 On Star		29
Her eyes beseem, her heart belies, her zone	266 Hints		695
Beseem your mutual judgment, speak the rest	372 Lara	1	470
Beseem one of thy station; I would promise	530 Faliero	4	137

BESEEM'D

| Beseem'd this palace in its brightest days | 677 Werner | 1 | 387 |
| Which well beseem'd the 'Devil's drawing-room | 917 Juan | 10 | 643 |

BESEEMING

| Beseeming all men ill but most the man | 29 Harold | 2 | 564 |

BESEEMS

| Aught that beseems a man in thee | 324 Abydos | 1 | 84 |

BESET

Tempted by love, by storms beset	113 Quaker		39
Ere quite with her snares you're beset	116 Pigot		30
With joy elate, by snares beset	132 L'Amitie		78
And bright around, with quivering beams beset	269 Minerva		39
Near these, with emerald rays beset	329 Abydos	2	67
Had Selim won, betray'd, beset	335 Abydos	2	559
Within a narrower ring compress'd, beset	350 Corsair	2	245
Endanger'd glory, life itself beset	352 Corsair	2	343
And, bright around with quivering beams beset	356 Corsair	3	39
But man and destiny beset him there	378 Lara	2	255
The tortures which beset my path	412 Mazeppa		530
Giggling with all the gallants who beset her	440 Beppo		14
Beset with all the thorns that line a crown	504 Faliero	1	289
Beset with drowsy guards and drunken courtiers	563 Sardan	2	131
In this extensive city, sore beset	882 Juan	8	292
So many troubles from her birth beset her	958 Juan	14	195

BESETS

| And of all sins most easily besets | 512 Faliero | 2 | 208 |

BESHREW

| From men and their delights. Beshrew the hour | 494 Manfred | 3 | 226 |

BESIDE

Who did for me what none beside have done	34 Harold	2	893
In him this glow'd when all beside had ceased to glow	43 Harold	3	486
Her resurrection; all beside--decay	67 Harold	4	736
With long-drawn names that grace no page beside	94 Dorset		46
'Nor this alone, but many a gift beside	108 Nisus		200
Though little versed in any art beside	111 Examination		10
One wish, nor breathed a thought beside	137 Clare		32
And unremember'd by the world beside	138 Harrow-B		34
To woo,--and--Lord knows what beside	160 Swimming		15
Beside the confines of the Aegean main	161 Athos		1
Ours too the glance none saw beside	165 Thyrza		29
Though all the world forget beside	168 Haunts		31
A stranger stood beside his shivering form	184 Julian		40
And they were enemies. They met beside	189 Darkness		57
I stood beside the grave of him who blazed	190 Churchill		1
And these, when all was lost beside	210 Augusta-A		41
Did not still walk beside thee--but at times	213 Lady Byron		49
Beside thee ceased to shine	218 I Saw		6
Obey'd by all who nought beside obey	242 Bards		28
True Briton all beside, I here am French	260 Hints		271
Whate'er their follies, and their faults beside	263 Hints		449
Write but like Wordsworth, live beside a lake	263 Hints		475
Strange--that where all is peace beside	310 Giaour		58
But wears our garb in all beside	319 Giaour		901
Whate'er beside it makes, hath made me free	331 Abydos	2	225
Friends to each other, foes to aught beside	333 Abydos	2	427
And others' gifts show'd mean beside his word	346 Corsair	1	548
She knelt beside him and his hand she press'd	362 Corsair	3	468
Long mourn'd his band whom none could mourn beside	366 Corsair	3	691
That still beside his open'd volume lay	368 Lara	1	145
But Lara's prostrate form he bent beside	369 Lara	1	241
To do what few or none would do beside	371 Lara	1	342
Whose darkness none beside should penetrate	381 Lara	2	453
Beside her eye had less of blue	390 Corinth		551
And what unto them is the world beside	396 Parisina		29
A husband's trusting heart beside	397 Parisina		68
Beside his monarch and his steed	407 Mazeppa		50
Fiercely beside thy cot the mutineer	416 Island	1	53
Beside the jutting rock the few appear'd	427 Island	3	59
But nature's ebb. Beside him was another	428 Island	3	103
The dancers and their dresses, too, beside	451 Beppo		692
Of heaven and hell and every thing beside	466 Morgante		11
Beside, wherever you are borne by fate	586 Sardan	4	501
And wish you this with me beside you? No	617 Foscari	4	135
Beside the lamb, as though he were his brother	661 Heaven		445
Beside the fire, and slumbers; and has order'd	680 Werner	1	598
Beside him. But you do not see his face	707 Werner	4	197

BESIDE

I know the assassin. Where is he? Beside you	715 Werner	5	176
Beside his mistress in some soft abode	748 Juan	1	46
Don Juan's parents lived beside the river	748 Juan	1	63
Standing alone beside his desolate hearth	751 Juan	1	285
Her throne and power, and every thing beside	857 Juan	6	288
Dudu said nothing, but sat down beside	858 Juan	6	353
George Washington had thanks and nought beside	897 Juan	9	60
The sound than sense)--beside all these pretences	906 Juan	9	591
(With more beside if Juan had not stopp'd 'em	912 Juan	10	326
Nodding beside my lady in his carriage	946 Juan	13	362
Spared by some chance when all beside was spoil'd	948 Juan	13	484
At least nine, and a ninth beside of ten	971 Juan	15	204

BESIDES

For all besides are sophists, from thy thrift	74 Harold	4	1167
And who there besides but Corinna de Stael	178 Devil's Dr		195
Besides my style is the romantic	233 Nihil		13
Besides all this, must have some genius too	265 Hints		652
To Germany, what owe we not besides	274 Waltz		49
Besides, our friend Scamp is to-day so absurd	278 Blues	1	42
Besides there were the Spaniard, Dutch, and Dane	292 Vision		473
Besides, I beat him hollow at the last	293 Vision		557
On earth besides; except some grumbling voice	296 Vision		755
Upon all topics; 'twas, besides, his bread	297 Vision		763
Besides, adoption as a son	331 Abydos	2	264
And such besides were too discreetly wise	368 Lara	1	151
Besides the wound that sent his soul to rest	383 Lara	2	541
Wer't not impossible, besides a shame	441 Beppo		102
Besides, within the Alps, to every woman	444 Beppo		281
Besides, they always smell of bread and butter	445 Beppo		312
Who think of something else besides the pen	449 Beppo		604
And less distrusted. But, besides all this	507 Faliero	1	555
Besides on all the spirits of his comrades	511 Faliero	2	139
They are--besides, it matters not; the chiefs	537 Faliero	4	618
But found on my arrival, that, besides	541 Faliero	5	213
Besides, of all the fruit of these long years	547 Faliero	5	677
Besides, he hates the effeminate thing that governs	563 Sardan	2	95
And thrice a thousand harlotry besides	563 Sardan	2	126
Besides, I know of these all clay can know	566 Sardan	2	265
I should not merit mine. Besides, you heard	571 Sardan	2	577
These white hairs! And I feel, besides, that mine	613 Foscari	3	358
To whom we owe so much besides our birth	646 Cain	3	43
One's heart commit these follies; and besides	678 Werner	1	414
And seems to like that none should sleep besides	681 Werner	1	612
And you shall have besides, in sparkling coin	682 Werner	1	676
Besides, I bade him 'good night' in the hall	683 Werner	2	23
Besides the loss (which, I must own, affects me	686 Werner	2	216
Besides those of the place, and bore away	686 Werner	2	239
Besides the antipathy with which we met	687 Werner	2	277
Have skimm'd it lightly: so that now, besides	694 Werner	2	711
Besides, he was a soldier, and a brave one	695 Werner	2	758
Besides, I never should obtain the half	700 Werner	3	323
Besides, the search--I will provide against	703 Werner	3	555
Of words, no more; besides, had it been otherwise	705 Werner	4	64
At such a time and place. Besides, the Heaven	708 Werner	4	251
Besides, he sometimes frightens me. How so	713 Werner	5	52
The fates of others oft depend; besides	717 Werner	5	272
For black--it is so honest, and besides	727 Deformed	1	373
And harquebusses, and what not; besides	731 Deformed	1	615
Fall;--and besides, his now escape may furnish	739 Deformed	2	278
Besides, the prince is all for the land-service	747 Juan	1	31
Besides her good old grandmother (who doted	750 Juan	1	221
Besides, their resurrection aids our glories	751 Juan	1	245
Leaving at last not much besides chronology	759 Juan	1	823
And while she ponder'd this, besides much more	760 Juan	1	870
Besides, it wanted but few hours of day	767 Juan	1	1350
Silence is best; besides there is a tact	768 Juan	1	1418
Besides, in Canto Twelfth, I mean to show	772 Juan	1	1655
Besides being much averse from such a fate	784 Juan	2	643
Besides, I hate all mystery, and that air	789 Juan	2	987
Besides, so very beautiful was she	790 Juan	2	1019
Besides, being less in love, she yawn'd a little	792 Juan	2	1155
Is pleasant, besides being true love's essence	795 Juan	2	1348
Besides her maid's as pretty for their size	795 Juan	2	1364
Besides, I've no more on this head to add	826 Juan	4	589
And long besides.'--'Oh! if 'tis really so	833 Juan	5	126
Besides, I'm hungry, and just now would take	837 Juan	5	351
Besides, as has been said, she was so fair	847 Juan	5	1025
'Besides, I hate to sleep alone,' quoth she	858 Juan	6	377
The holy camel's hump, besides the Koran	865 Juan	6	816
Your wars eternally, besides enjoying	880 Juan	8	111
Besides its lava, with all sorts of shot	880 Juan	8	123
Which fills a regiment (besides their pay	883 Juan	8	333
And God knows who besides in 'au' and 'ow	884 Juan	8	386
No common language; and besides, in time	885 Juan	8	458
And all allowances besides of plunder	891 Juan	8	817
As though there were one heaven and none besides	892 Juan	8	910
Their friends from foes,--besides such things from haste	895 Juan	8	1036
Besides fish, beasts, and birds. 'The sparrow's fall	899 Juan	9	149

BESIDES

Besides, the empress sometimes liked a boy	902 Juan	9	375
Besides, he was of that delighted age	905 Juan	9	545
Besides Platonic love, besides the love	906 Juan	9	585
Upon his cabinet, besides the presents	906 Juan	9	631
Besides, he had some qualities which fix	908 Juan	10	73
And still less was it sensual; for besides	914 Juan	10	425
Besides some veins of iron, lead, or copper	915 Juan	10	475
Their fare; and also pause besides, to fuddle	916 Juan	10	566
Besides the ministers and underlings	923 Juan	11	313
Cash rules the grove, and fells it too besides	931 Juan	12	106
'Why?- Why?--Besides, Fred really was attach'd	934 Juan	12	273
Besides, he had found out he was no tutor	935 Juan	12	329
Besides their knowledge of the world, and sense	935 Juan	12	349
Besides those soothing speeches of the pleaders	938 Juan	12	519
Besides (alas! his taste--forgive and pity	938 Juan	12	543
Besides, he had not seen of several hundred	940 Juan	12	643
Besides the mark'd distinction of his air	940 Juan	12	678
Besides the most sublime of--Heaven knows what else	941 Juan	12	701
Besides, the sad's a source of the sublime	941 Juan	13	5
Besides, my Muse by no means deals in fiction	957 Juan	14	97
Than these things; and besides, I wish to spare 'em	958 Juan	14	165
Besides there might be falsehood in what's stated	960 Juan	14	334
Besides, his conduct, since in England, grew more	969 Juan	15	85
The prospect and their morals: and besides	972 Juan	15	263
Great thoughts we catch from thence (besides a cold	982 Juan	16	108

BESIEGE

With suits and prosecutions they besiege us	853 Juan	6	77

BESIEGERS

Then he gazed on a town by besiegers taken	176 Devil's Dr		77
(More potent than a king) by these besiegers	591 Sardan	5	263

BESIEGER'S

It struck even the besieger's ear	387 Corinth	276

BESIEGING

Though princes the possessor were besieging all	988 Juan	16	492

BESMEAR'D

The page was so besmear'd with blood and dust	285 Vision		40
A fair-hair'd scalp, besmear'd with blood and weeds	434 Island	4	345
To him thou now see'st so besmear'd with blood	653 Cain	3	491
In aspect, plainly clad, besmear'd with dust	876 Juan	7	582

BESOM

With a soft besom will I sweep your halls	918 Juan	10	671

BESPANGLED

Bespangled with those isles of light	387 Corinth	246

BESPEAK

Nor e'en your eyes your love bespeak	90 Caroline-B		12
So femininely white it might bespeak	374 Lara	1	576
What did that sudden sound bespeak	390 Corinth		530
Thy garb and gait bespeak thee of high lineage	483 Manfred	2	7
In those who rarely smile, their smiles bespeak	992 Juan	16	780

BESPEAKS

Bespeaks the pageant of their splendid trust	57 Harold	4	130
Bespeaks her guilt and Azo's shame	397 Parisina		92

BESPOKE

One sigh Zuleika's thought bespoke	326 Abydos	1	254
Bespoke remembrance only too profound	373 Lara	1	489
There was a something which bespoke command	789 Juan	2	927
Was what her dress bespoke, a damsel fair	857 Juan	6	282

BESPRENT

There seem'd to be besprent a deal of gilding	837 Juan	5	363

BESPRINKLED

'Tis but as a dead-flower with May-dew besprinkled	204 Pisa	6

BESPRINKLING

She saw the dews of eve besprinkling	317 Giaour	691

BEST

Best prize of better acts, they bear away	15 Harold	1	736
Pursue what Chance or Fate proclaimeth best	20 Harold	2	60
By British hands, which it had best behoved	21 Harold	2	131
Brisk Confidence still best with woman copes	24 Harold	2	305
And those who know it best, deplore it most	24 Harold	2	308
And sought her more and more, and loved her best in wrath	25 Harold	2	333
Their admiration thy best weapon shone	41 Harold	3	365
Did but of Rome's best Son remind her more	64 Harold	4	526
The land which loved thee so that none could love thee best	81 Harold	4	1548

BEST

Again, thou best beloved, adieu	90 Caroline-A		21
Our deities the first best boon have given	107 Nisus		133
Who speaks the fastest's sure to speak the best	112 Examination		46
Should, after all, our best endeavours fail	114 Prologue		34
Alonzo! best and dearest of my friends	125 Recoll		243
But those who best deserve you	138 Clare		34
For silence is the best prescription	144 Becher-B		31
Thou know'st the best, I feel the most	156 Lady-F		52
Still to laugh by far the best is	157 Hodgson		71
Delirium is our best deceiver	159 Spell		4
'Twere hard to say who fared the best	160 Swimming		17
Well hast thou left in life's best bloom	165 Thyrza		45
Knew you these lines--the badness of the best	170 Address-B		10
And the best thing he saw was a broken bridge	176 Devil's Dr		55
'Tis the best sound I've heard,' quoth he, 'since my palm	177 Devil's Dr		111
But the last joke of all was by far the best	177 Devil's Dr		117
Yes--one--the first--the last--the best	182 Ode-A		167
One what best his love might claim	195 Ballad-A		93
Since things like these are best forgot	197 Duel		22
Then receive him as best such an advent becomes	202 Avatar		19
Ever glorious Grattan! the best of the good	202 Avatar		37
Her glance was the best of the rays that surround thee	204 Pisa		14
A soldier's grave, for thee the best	207 Year		38
And all that's best of dark and bright	216 She Walks		3
(Best form for letters from a distant land	224 J.C.H.		49
(Which, by the way, the old Bore's best is	231 Doctor		26
And, as that is the case, you had best put to press	236 Nonsense		7
Though themes of innocence amuse him best	245 Bards		257
All love thy strain, but children like it best	246 Bards		342
Have foil'd the best of critics, needs the worst	246 Bards		368
And, peace be with you! 'tis your best reward	252 Bards		750
'Tis sheer ill-nature--don't the world know best	252 Bards		772
Though nature's sternest painter, yet the best	253 Bards		858
Of Grub-street, and of Grosvenor-place the best	254 Bards		928
And be thy praise his first, his best reward	254 Bards		942
His strain will teach what numbers best belong	258 Hints		107
Mad wag! who pardon'd none, nor spared the best	261 Hints		331
Who models his deportment as may best	263 Hints		497
Fiction does best when taught to look like truth	264 Hints		537
With all his best endeavours, only squall	264 Hints		554
But poesy between the best and worst	265 Hints		585
Europe's worst dauber, and poor Britain's best	270 Minerva		176
Of kings the best--and last, not least in worth	274 Waltz		45
Such was the time when Waltz might best maintain	276 Waltz		178
Till you think you can turn them best to your own use	279 Blues	1	110
Indeed the best poems at first rather fail	279 Blues	1	122
But the heat forced me out in the best part--alas	281 Blues	2	35
You have lost such a lecture! The best of the ten	281 Blues	2	37
I allow our friend Scamp hath this day done his best	281 Blues	2	41
That the taste of the actors at best is so so	281 Blues	2	77
With the best doctrines till we quite o'er flow	286 Vision		109
Of clay obscures our best conceptions, saving	288 Vision		223
For at the best he will but be your neighbour	294 Vision		576
And cried,'For God's sake, stop, my friend! 'twere best	296 Vision		727
A mild Epicurean, form'd, at best	305 Age		520
Our last, our best, our only orator	305 Age		552
That best becomes an Eastern night	312 Giaour		179
Each arm'd, as best becomes a man	315 Giaour		521
Stain'd with the best of Arnaut blood	315 Giaour		525
Wet with thine own best blood shall drip	318 Giaour		781
And know'st thou not who loves thee best	327 Abydos	1	298
But life is hazard at the best; and here	333 Abydos	2	444
His heart's best blood is on the water	335 Abydos	2	556
And scorn'd the best as hypocrites who hid	342 Corsair	1	267
See, I have pluck'd the fruit that promised best	344 Corsair	1	423
And sometimes with the wisest and the best	353 Corsair	2	450
I am a slave, a favour'd slave at best	354 Corsair	2	503
To-morrow, here or elsewhere, as may best	372 Lara	1	469
'The last alternative befits me best	376 Lara	2	55
Desperate, though few, the last and best remain'd	379 Lara	2	312
Whose best success were sacrilege	388 Corinth		401
The foremost of these were the best of his band	389 Corinth		467
'I come from my rest to him I love best	390 Corinth		563
Of the Mussulman bravest and best is at hand	393 Corinth		820
I ought to do--and did my best	403 Chillon		71
Those best and earliest lyres of harmony	424 Island	2	421
Blighting my life in best of its career	438 Tasso		98
Whose tints are truth and beauty at their best	441 Beppo		89
(For beauty's sometimes best set off afar	442 Beppo		116
Laura was blooming still, had made the best	443 Beppo		177
To see what lady best stood out the season	450 Beppo		660
'Such things, perhaps, we'd best discuss within	451 Beppo		716
Of the eternal Triad,--first, last, best	456 Dante	1	13
Their inspiration, and perchance the best	463 Dante	4	2
Best speak the truth when there's a reason why	467 Morgante		109
Doing the very best that in him lay	470 Morgante		291

BEST

'Twere best to carry him into some wood	474	Morgante		559
Save our best hunters, may attain: his garb	482	Manfred	1	323
On those whom I best loved: I never quell'd	484	Manfred	2	85
The best and purest feelings of our nature	510	Faliero		97
Have urged against her right; my best friend's child	513	Faliero	2	339
Another day like that would be the best	515	Faliero	2	471
Which is your best security. There's not	520	Faliero	3	111
Oh men! what are ye, and our best designs	535	Faliero	4	516
Lord President, 'twere best proceed to judgment	539	Faliero	5	87
To mock and mar your sovereign's best intents	541	Faliero	5	215
And in thy best maturity of mind	546	Faliero	5	608
I let them pass their days as best might suit them	556	Sardan	1	406
Employ'd it for the best. Pronounce in person	565	Sardan	2	189
The trusty, rough, true soldier--the best captain	565	Sardan	2	214
At present, let us hence as best we may	568	Sardan	2	426
My brother, my best subject, better prince	569	Sardan	2	487
And with your best speed to the walls without	572	Sardan	3	69
We are nerved to look on such things. Best extract	588	Sardan	5	103
A woman, the best chamber company	589	Sardan	5	119
The fight goes. My best brother! And the battle	589	Sardan	5	132
Would fain die with you! My best! my last friends!	593	Sardan	5	400
And did not they? The grave knows best: they died	605	Foscari	2	213
You best know if I should be so. I do	605	Foscari	2	221
And this is hell: the best is, that it is not	607	Foscari	2	365
Her best and bravest from her. Tyranny	607	Foscari	2	387
Of Rome and Carthage in their best times, when	607	Foscari	2	405
'Twas time. My best beloved! My true wife	608	Foscari	3	37
My best Marina!--and our children? They	611	Foscari	3	192
Let me support him--my best love! Oh, God	617	Foscari	4	187
As died their father. Oh, what best of blessings	618	Foscari	4	210
Of twenty-five of the best born patricians	621	Foscari	5	18
My best to save his honours, and opposed	622	Foscari	5	125
You talk unwarily. 'Twere best they hear not	622	Foscari	5	144
And those of--Best retain it for your children	626	Foscari	5	347
Who didst create these best and beauteous beings	627	Cain	1	15
Could he but crush himself, 'twere the best boon	630	Cain	1	154
All foul and fulsome, and the very best	637	Cain	2	55
The tree in Eden? Eve, thy mother, best	642	Cain	2	401
Are in my heart. My best beloved, Abel	652	Cain	3	384
Above its first and best inhabitants	665	Heaven		729
But which is best, a dead eternity	667	Heaven		901
In the mean time, my best reward would be	676	Werner	1	294
To live as they best may; and, to say truth	676	Werner	1	335
An hour is past I'll do my best to serve him	680	Werner	1	601
That you know best. Or, if it were so, how	681	Werner	1	651
Soldiers and desperadoes! Heaven best knows	685	Werner	2	132
Keep the best shortly, and the last for all men	691	Werner	2	524
Have with you? You know best, if yesterday's	691	Werner	2	538
The priests say (and no doubt they should know best	696	Werner	3	44
Suspicion; but you best know--what--and why	696	Werner	3	78
Our search for t'other. You had best begin	697	Werner	3	136
The best and sweetest feeling of our hearts	699	Werner	3	276
Best wait for further and more sure advices	705	Werner	4	97
As I directed: and by his best speed	708	Werner	4	279
But--Best of all! for this is pure religion	712	Werner	4	493
You have said so, and know best. Father! I have spoken	712	Werner	4	520
Barks mann'd with revellers in their best garbs	714	Werner	5	110
Thou best dost know the innocence of him	715	Werner	5	166
He best knows; but within an antechamber	718	Werner	5	330
But as thou hast--hence, hence--and do thy best	722	Deformed	1	5
Greece look'd her last upon her best, the instant	726	Deformed	1	281
In Styx. Then let it be as thou deem'st best	727	Deformed	1	310
Have done the best which spirit may to make	727	Deformed	1	329
And drank the best dew	728	Deformed	1	407
Cabala; their best brick-work, wherewithal	732	Deformed	1	684
With your best friends? You had far best be quiet	739	Deformed	2	253
Took Jewry; but the Romans had the best then	739	Deformed	2	270
The best away. And that were shame! Go to	739	Deformed	2	288
As those of the best time-piece made by Harrison	749	Juan	1	134
And even the wisest, do the best they can	749	Juan	1	163
And so I interfered, and with the best	750	Juan	1	185
And then this best and weakest woman bore	750	Juan	1	225
To whom it may be best to have recourse	751	Juan	1	252
Juan was taught from out the best edition	752	Juan	1	345
And certainly this course was much the best	755	Juan	1	532
As being the best judge of a lady's case	756	Juan	1	600
Of its disease; he did the best he could	758	Juan	1	725
At best, no better than a go-between	761	Juan	1	928
You'd best begin with truth, and when you've lost your	762	Juan	1	1023
All propagated with the best intentions	763	Juan	1	1051
To say the best, it was extreme ill-breeding	768	Juan	1	1388
Silence is best, besides there is a tact	768	Juan	1	1418
The best is that in short-hand ta'en by Gurney	770	Juan	1	1511

BEST

The best of mothers and of educations	774	Juan	2	5
The best of remedies is a beef-steak	775	Juan	2	101
Beyond the best apothecary's art	776	Juan	2	163
But still 'tis best to struggle to the last	779	Juan	2	309
Their best clothes, as if going to a fair	779	Juan	2	354
They did their best to modify their case	782	Juan	2	499
But the best dish that e'er was cook'd since Homer's	789	Juan	2	983
Was not exactly the best way to save	790	Juan	2	1034
And therefore, with her maid, she thought it best	790	Juan	2	1041
She knew that the best feelings must have victual	792	Juan	2	1153
The best of life is but intoxication	796	Juan	2	1426
Found in one sigh the best interpreter	798	Juan	2	1510
And made thy best interpreter a sigh	801	Juan	3	12
Robb'd for his daughter by the best of fathers	803	Juan	3	136
And certainly he show'd the best of breeding	807	Juan	3	362
Squeezed through the rind, which makes it best for use	809	Juan	3	496
Was freedom's best and bravest friend	813	Juan	3	756
And no doubt of all methods 'tis best	819	Juan	4	189
All that the best can mingle and express	819	Juan	4	204
The loveliest, chastest, best, but--quite a fool	830	Juan	4	888
Of the best feelings of mankind, which grow	837	Juan	5	389
We know where things and men must end at best	839	Juan	5	501
Adding, that this was commonest and the best	844	Juan	5	838
But no doubt every thing is for the best	852	Juan	6	6
Of--but Chronology best knows the years	853	Juan	6	48
Are the best tokens (to a modest mind	854	Juan	6	117
Were they, according to the best report	857	Juan	6	317
And every couch is occupied; you had best	858	Juan	6	366
I did my very boyish best to shine	860	Juan	6	493
What pedigree the best would have to show	864	Juan	6	752
Be too minute; an outline is the best	864	Juan	6	783
His best to obey in what he had been task'd	864	Juan	6	796
But which is best, you know no more than I	867	Juan	7	32
Three of the Smiths were Peters; but the best	869	Juan	7	149
Or loved, it was with what we call 'the best	881	Juan	8	194
So that you scarce could say who best had chosen	884	Juan	8	357
Shorn of its best and loveliest, and left bare	889	Juan	8	702
You are 'the best of cut-throats:'--do not start	896	Juan	9	25
He who sleeps best may be the most content	898	Juan	9	120
Some pretty shell, is best for moderate bathers	898	Juan	9	144
At least he pays no rent, and has best right	900	Juan	9	249
Maintain thou art the best: for after all	903	Juan	9	442
Our veins, when things call'd sovereigns think it best	904	Juan	9	479
Or better, as the best examples say	905	Juan	9	564
And was not the best wife, unless we call	906	Juan	9	638
Which wafted him from Petersburgh: the best	913	Juan	10	388
Where juniper expresses its best juice	915	Juan	10	499
Don Juan, having done the best he could	920	Juan	11	137
But the old way is best for the purblind	922	Juan	11	212
Into as furious English), with her best look	925	Juan	11	415
But don't pretend to settle which was best	928	Juan	11	656
Theirs is the best bower anchor, the chain cable	930	Juan	12	19
And several of her best bon-mots were hawk'd about	935	Juan	12	373
And these vicissitudes tell best in youth	936	Juan	12	393
Ask a blind man, the best judge. You'll attack	938	Juan	12	564
Into the best society: and there	940	Juan	12	674
The worst of tempests and the best of battles	941	Juan	12	699
But my best canto, save one on astronomy	941	Juan	12	703
To show the people the best way to break	941	Juan	12	708
I'll leave them to their taste, no doubt the best	941	Juan	13	18
Or even mere fashion, which indeed's the best	944	Juan	13	222
To lose those best months in a sweaty city	947	Juan	13	380
The very best of vineyards is the cellar	950	Juan	13	608
'Tne best first speech that ever yet was made	952	Juan	13	720
While Strongbow's best things might have come from Cato	952	Juan	13	736
But seize the last word, which no doubt's the best	953	Juan	13	784
You bind yourself, and call some mode the best one	955	Juan	14	14
And shone in the best part of dialogue	960	Juan	14	290
Theirs was that best of unions, past all doubt	961	Juan	14	339
Whose ripeness is but bitter at the best	962	Juan	14	426
Such measures as she thought might best impede	963	Juan	14	482
'Tis best to pause, and think, ere you rush on	963	Juan	14	511
Herself that her intentions were the best	966	Juan	14	699
The marriage state, the best or worst of any	967	Juan	14	758
Few men dare show their thoughts of worst or best	968	Juan	15	21
We'll do our best to make the best on 't:--March	971	Juan	15	209
And morally decided, the best state is	971	Juan	15	230
Of the best class, and better than her class	973	Juan	15	340
Is wanting, and our best ties in the tomb	973	Juan	15	352
If bad, the best way's certainly to tease on	974	Juan	15	403
According to the best of dictionaries	976	Juan	15	541
The simple olives, best allies of wine	977	Juan	15	577
Make more impression than the best of books	978	Juan	15	672
Twin opposites, the second is the best	979	Juan	15	692
This was the mode of Cyrus, best of kings	980	Juan	16	3
'Tis always best to take things upon trust	981	Juan	16	44

BEST
'What friar?' said Juan; and he did his best | 985 Juan | 16 | 277
Which best it is to encounter--Ghost, or none | 998 Juan | 17 | 105

BE'ST
Oh Doubt!--if thou be'st Doubt, for which some
   take thee | 918 Juan | 11 | 13

BESTIR
It is your province.--Sirs, bestir yourselves | 623 Foscari | 5 | 204

BESTIRR'D
Bestirr'd it more,--'twas but the beam | 314 Giaour | | 378

BESTOW
As Greece can still bestow, though Glory fly her
   glades | 14 Harold | 1 | 656
That thoughts of thee and thine on polish'd
   breasts bestow | 19 Harold | 2 | 9
Can we bestow, which you may not despise | 107 Nisus | | 132
May no marble bestow the splendour of woe | 115 The Tear | | 45
Say, can ambition's fever'd dream bestow | 127 Recoll | | 393
Yet if blest to the utmost that love can bestow | 155 Goblet | | 17
And a palace bestow for a poor-house and prison | 203 Avatar | | 76
I have lost for that faith more than thou canst
   bestow | 221 False | | 9
Moravians, rise! bestow some meet reward | 246 Bards | | 319
The little left behind it to bestow | 277 Waltz | | 247
Again bestow the wreaths we gently woo | 419 Island | 2 | 57
But--thou mayst die. Will death bestow it on me | 480 Manfred | 1 | 148
From them what they could not bestow, and now | 485 Manfred | 2 | 137
And with that hand did he bestow your heart | 510 Faliero | 2 | 84
Bestow it on Arbaces. So I should | 565 Sardan | 2 | 223
No, not bequeath--but I bestow this sum | 711 Werner | 4 | 483
Nature's mistaken largess to bestow | 724 Deformed | 1 | 111
Whereon Apicius would bestow his benison | 976 Juan | 15 | 518

BESTOW'D
And the wolf dies in silence,--not bestow'd | 58 Harold | 4 | 185
If thou shouldst fall, on her shall be bestow'd | 108 Nisus | | 208
Bestow'd by thee upon another | 134 Lady-D | | 12
Hail thou! who on my birth bestow'd | 171 Time-B | | 5
Love had bestow'd a richer Mail | 201 Ode-C | | 65
Her infant friendship had bestow'd on him | 214 Dream | | 66
Reproachful term bestow'd but to upbraid | 273 Waltz | | 4
Alas! though both bestow'd in vain | 319 Giaour | | 870
Nor deem'd that gifts bestow'd on better men | 342 Corsair | 1 | 259
And wrapt a breast bestow'd on heaven alone | 348 Corsair | 2 | 60
By Conrad's mandate safely were bestow'd | 351 Corsair | 2 | 257
Bestow'd her customs, and amended theirs | 418 Island | 1 | 219
Due to my father, who bestow'd my hand | 510 Faliero | 2 | 81
He did so, or it had not been bestow'd | 510 Faliero | 2 | 85
To baser passions. He bestow'd my hand | 510 Faliero | 2 | 98
See that the women are bestow'd in safety | 573 Sardan | 3 | 121
Which you bestow'd upon me as my sire | 617 Foscari | 4 | 163
Bestow'd upon him, as the public learn'd | 923 Juan | 11 | 311

BESTOWER
And vultures to the heart of the bestower | 463 Dante | 4 | 17

BESTOWING
So oft bestowing Brunswickers and brides | 274 Waltz | | 50
Bestowing fire from heaven, and then, too late | 463 Dante | 4 | 15

BESTOWS
The charter to chastise which she bestows | 44 Harold | 3 | 551
Mnestheus to guard the elder youth bestows | 108 Nisus | | 215
Half to the ardour which its birth bestows | 193 Monody | | 76
With half the fervour Hate bestows | 316 Giaour | | 649
This hour bestows, or ever bars escape | 334 Abydos | 2 | 463
Bestows on most of mortal mould and birth | 370 Lara | 1 | 322
Him who bestows it, wherefore dost thou limit | 561 Sardan | 2 | 17
The endless soot bestows a tint far deeper | 909 Juan | 10 | 115

BESTRIDES
Strives through the surge, bestrides the beach,
   and high | 364 Corsair | 3 | 579
If the free Switzer yet bestrides alone | 454 Venice-B | | 129
Bestrides the Hartz Mountain | 724 Deformed | 1 | 164

BESTRIDING
Bestriding a proud steed, in the dim light | 520 Faliero | 3 | 88
But proudly still bestriding the high waves | 610 Foscari | 3 | 131

BESTRODE
The Giant steed, to be bestrode by Death | 485 Manfred | 2 | 101

BEST'S
(The best's at Florence--see it, if ye will | 441 Beppo | | 86

BEST-SOWN
(Though best-sown projects very often reap ill | 449 Beppo | | 614

BET
And I'll bet that your Journal | 232 Murray-B | | 34
Her life is as good as your own, I will bet | 278 Blues | 1 | 82
And there were several offer'd any bet | 443 Beppo | | 213
Still their salvation was an even bet | 777 Juan | 2 | 222
Of all our modern battles, I will bet | 871 Juan | 7 | 271
The walls were won, but 'twas an even bet | 888 Juan | 8 | 613
Your arm, and I'll bet Moscow to a dollar | 890 Juan | 8 | 775
Good at all things, but better at a bet | 952 Juan | 13 | 696
You'll never guess, I'll bet you millions,
   milliards | 968 Juan | 14 | 799

BE 'T
Be 't mine to seek for glory with my sword | 105 Nisus | | 24
Far be 't from me the 'virgin's mind' to 'taint | 119 Answer-A | | 25
Far be 't from me unkindly to upbraid | 252 Bards | | 755
May settle; but far be 't from me to anticipate | 867 Juan | 6 | 951
The sufferers--be 't in heart or intellect | 997 Juan | 17 | 15

BETA
Thus Juan learn'd his alpha beta better | 794 Juan | 2 | 1303

BETAKE
The rascals, perhaps, may betake them to robbing | 225 Ode-D | | 9
Betake thee--Giaffir I can greet | 328 Abydos | 1 | 454
Unto the nearest hut themselves betake | 882 Juan | 8 | 254

BETE
When Congreve's fool could vie with Moliere's
   bete | 953 Juan | 13 | 750

BETHINK
Then, lovely dame, bethink thee! and beware | 358 Corsair | 3 | 184
Bethink ere thou dismiss us, ask again | 480 Manfred | 1 | 167
Bethink thee, is there then no other gift | 480 Manfred | 1 | 172
Hast thou no gentler answer?--Yet bethink thee | 487 Manfred | 2 | 255
My life insures me that. How long, bethink you | 583 Sardan | 4 | 325
Or question save those--High-born dame! bethink
   thee | 598 Foscari | 1 | 204

BETHOUGHT
And bethought himself what next to do | 176 Devil's Dr | | 6
And then a slave bethought her of a harp | 824 Juan | 4 | 513

BETIDE
Whatever weal or woe betide | 133 Prayer | | 50
Lest evil unforeseen betide | 141 Critics | | 23
With honest Wonder what might next betide | 185 Julian | | 61
Reign is concluded; whatsoe'er betide | 294 Vision | | 574
Mazeppa answer'd, 'Ill betide | 408 Mazeppa | | 107
But whatsoe'er betide, ah, Neuha! now | 426 Island | 2 | 528
And may be better; but whate'er betide | 513 Faliero | 2 | 285
Nor now, nor ever; whatsoe'er betide | 531 Faliero | 4 | 209
But it has touch'd me, and, whate'er betide | 567 Sardan | 2 | 340
Love me, whate'er betide. My chiefest glory | 574 Sardan | 3 | 171
If aught of ill betide her, better I | 576 Sardan | 3 | 295
But just suppose that moment should betide | 757 Juan | 1 | 669
What may this midnight violence betide | 764 Juan | 1 | 1133

BETIDES
Whate'er betides, I've known the worst | 18 Harold | 1 | 868
Strains his shrill pipe as good or ill betides | 22 Harold | 2 | 161

BETIMES
Nurtured in blood betimes, his heart delights | 16 Harold | 1 | 794
Bred in the courts betimes, though all that law | 247 Bards | | 446
They whose young souls receive this rust betimes | 264 Hints | | 521
A Serf, that rose betimes to thread the wood | 383 Lara | 2 | 554
To move betimes. Methinks I see amongst you | 623 Foscari | 5 | 195
More words on you. Call me betimes. Good night | 701 Werner | 3 | 386
No--no--I'd send him out betimes to college | 753 Juan | 1 | 415
Is glittering youth, which I have spent betimes | 773 Juan | 1 | 1735
Must breakfast--and betimes, lest they should ask
   it | 792 Juan | 2 | 1151
The gentlemen got up betimes to shoot | 953 Juan | 13 | 801
He woke betimes; and, as may be supposed | 984 Juan | 16 | 217

BETOKEN
Betoken love--that love was mine | 321 Giaour | | 1110
Of his fierce pulse betoken a condition | 912 Juan | 10 | 308

BETOKENS
Thy yawning arch betokens slow decay | 121 Newstead A | | 138

BETOOK
He suddenly betook him to his sling | 470 Morgante | | 296

BETRAY
May now betray some simpler hearts | 86 Rousseau | | 2
The thousand thoughts I now betray to thee | 198 Po | | 7
Till the black slime betray her as she crawls | 208 Sketch | | 48
Her eye, her cheek, betray no inward strife | 308 Age | | 761
Though fortune frown, or falser friends betray | 333 Abydos | 2 | 419
Lest he to Conrad rather should betray | 341 Corsair | 1 | 221

BETRAY

Betray no further than the bitter smile	341	Corsair	1	230
Still must my song my thoughts, my soul betray	343	Corsair	1	368
May melt, but not betray to woman's grief	345	Corsair	1	518
And still too faithful to betray one fear	380	Lara	2	349
I will disclose--ensnare--betray--destroy	532	Faliero	4	315
With you. And would, perhaps, betray as well	568	Sardan	2	384
Friends fail--slaves fly--and all betray'd--and, more	586	Sardan	4	526
And if he did betray you, 'twas with truth	633	Cain	1	352
Of truth;--such truths are treason; they betray	870	Juan	7	173
But thus it is some women will betray us	964	Juan	14	576

BETRAY'D

Even through the closest searment half betray'd	32	Harold	2	776
Which betray'd not, or crush'd not, or wept not her cause	202	Avatar		8
This man the Washington of worlds betray'd	301	Age		234
If won, to equal ills betray'd	314	Giaour		400
Betray'd his rage, but no remorse	321	Giaour		1092
He left believing and betray'd	321	Giaour		1179
And all, before repress'd, betray'd	327	Abydos	1	346
With foes subdued, or friends betray'd	332	Abydos	2	285
Had Selim won, betray'd, beset	335	Abydos	2	559
And not the traitors who betray'd him still	342	Corsair	1	258
Nor cared he now if rescued or betray'd	362	Corsair	3	449
Betray'd too early, and beguiled too long	365	Corsair	3	663
Betray'd a feeling that recall'd to these	370	Lara	1	273
The sweeping fierceness which his soul betray'd	377	Lara	2	141
Against the country he betray'd	387	Corinth		307
When he betray'd Bianca's truth	397	Parisina		104
Else had his rising heart betray'd	398	Parisina		196
The giant his astonishment betray'd	470	Morgante		270
No; I affirm. I have betray'd myself	507	Faliero	1	530
To arms!--we are betray'd--it is the Doge	522	Faliero	3	211
The signory of Venice! You betray'd me	540	Faliero	5	202
He is a traitor, and betray'd the state	543	Faliero	5	370
Thee and thy race, for which we are betray'd	669	Heaven		1111
As he betray'd last night; and I, perhaps	689	Werner	2	411
Betray'd by you and him (for now I saw	718	Werner	5	343
Yet she betray'd at times a gleam of sense	825	Juan	4	537
The traits of sleeping sorrow, and betray'd	860	Juan	6	532
Which hesitation more betray'd than mask'd	864	Juan	6	798
Juan had not betray'd himself; in fact	865	Juan	6	826

BETRAYER

The slaves, who now hail their betrayer with hymns	203	Avatar		72

BETRAYING

As not betraying their full import, yet	511	Faliero	2	178
Yet ne'er betraying this in conversation	970	Juan	15	116
Betraying only now and then her soul	993	Juan	16	813

BETRAYS

Your cheek no sign of love betrays		90	Caroline-A		4
Not one poor trembler only fear betrays		114	Prologue		21
Which still the splendour of its orb betrays		193	Monody		58
Whose thistle well betrays the niggard earth		270	Minerva		135
Not oft betrays to standers by		324	Abydos	1	27
Each has some fear, and he who least betrays		352	Corsair	2	360
Nor mark of vulgar toil that hand betrays		374	Lara	1	575
More wild and high than woman's eye betrays		374	Lara	1	579
But passion most dissembles, yet betrays		756	Juan	1	577

BETROTH'D

And my betroth'd. He hath left thee no brother	652	Cain	3	407

BETS

After male loss of time, and hearts, and bets	934	Juan	12	283

BETTER

Best prize of better acts, they bear away	15	Harold	1	736
And clings to thoughts now better far removed	34	Harold	2	902
Is it not better, then, to be alone	46	Harold	3	671
Is it not better thus our lives to wear	46	Harold	3	678
They might have used it better, but, allured	48	Harold	3	781
Better be whelm'd beneath the waves, and shun	57	Harold	4	115
The strength of better thoughts, and seek their prey	60	Harold	4	299
So shall a better spring less bitter fruit bring forth	69	Harold	4	882
Hath but one page,--'tis better written here	71	Harold	4	969
Were form'd for better things than sneering	100	Marion		30
Much better, in such snowy weather	101	Lady-B		38
Better to hold the sparkling grape	154	Skull		9
In better praises than in mine	163	Malta		40
Which better bosoms would bewail	164	Friend-B		22
My Thyrza's pledge in better days	166	Struggle		41
'Tis something better not to be	167	Euthanasia		36
The better days of life were ours	167	Dead		28
Yet better I sustain thy load	171	Time-B		7
For I find we have much better manners below	178	Devil's Dr		151
But thou deserv'st a better heart	179	Gold		23

BETTER

Yet better had he neither known	181	Ode-A		71
And learn like better men to die	185	Belshaz-A		16
Better hadst thou still been leading	187	Ode-B		38
I had been better than I now can be	212	Augusta-C		94
Fame, peace, and hope--and all the better life	213	Lady Byron		39
Who did not love her better:--in her home	215	Dream		128
What better men have been in better times	224	J.C.H.		40
Oh well done Lord E----n! and better done R----r	225	Ode-D		1
Stockings fetch better prices than lives	225	Ode-D		14
There's Byron, too, who once did better	231	Doctor		33
Verse hath a better sale than prose	238	Orford		10
Better to err with Pope than shine with Pye	243	Bards		102
'What art thou better, meddling fool, than they	251	Bards		698
Make bad men better, or at least ashamed	253	Bards		830
Can make thee better, nor poor Hewson's worse	255	Bards		984
Are better told than acted on the stage	260	Hints		268
Bloodshed 'tis surely better to retrench	260	Hints		272
Plays make mankind no better, and no worse	261	Hints		370
Better let him than all the world deride	267	Hints		798
How watch'd thy better sons his farewell ray	268	Minerva		21
Ay! there he is at it. Poor Scamp! better join	280	Blues	1	151
Which peopled earth no better, hell as wont	285	Vision		50
A better farmer ne'er brush'd dew from lawn	286	Vision		61
Be saving, all the better; for not one am I	286	Vision		99
Of those who think damnation better still	286	Vision		100
Better than did this weak and wooden head	287	Vision		160
With better sense and hearts, whom history mentions	289	Vision		295
That hell has nothing better left to do	290	Vision		325
Heaven cannot make them better, nor I worse	290	Vision		328
I can have fifty better souls than this	293	Vision		507
Aught further?' Junius answer'd, 'You had better	295	Vision		655
Yet Vanity herself had better taught	301	Age		241
Better still serve the haughty Mussulman	302	Age		302
Better still toil for masters, than await	302	Age		304
Better succumb even to their own despair	302	Age		312
Better reclaim thy deserts, turn thy swords	304	Age		466
For thrones; the table sees thee better placed	305	Age		519
The phrase much better leaving out the land	306	Age		599
Better to sink beneath the shock	319	Giaour		969
Though better to have died with those	320	Giaour		1002
May better grace a brother's bier	322	Giaour		1250
Disguised things seen by better light	330	Abydos	2	117
Far better with the dead to live	330	Abydos	2	176
Nor deem'd that gifts bestow'd on better men	342	Corsair	1	259
The rest no better than the thing he seem'd	342	Corsair	1	266
Should war with nature and its better will	344	Corsair	1	397
The better warriors who beheld him near	351	Corsair	2	306
That might have better kept so true a brand	354	Corsair	2	484
How watch'd thy better sons his farewell ray	355	Corsair	3	21
Thee from the flames, which better far--but--no	358	Corsair	3	188
The love of youth, the hope of better years	365	Corsair	3	626
They deem'd him better than his air express'd	367	Lara	1	114
And wasted powers for better purpose lent	370	Lara	1	326
And left the better feelings all at strife	371	Lara	1	329
Of higher birth he seem'd, and better days	374	Lara	1	574
What better name may slumber's bed become	375	Lara	1	638
Yet sense seem'd left, though better were its loss	382	Lara	2	476
But vain her voice, till better days	388	Corinth		386
Who there in better cause had bled	388	Corinth		395
But he better could brook to behold the dying	389	Corinth		481
The brightest by the better born	399	Parisina		271
A little talk of better days	404	Chillon		198
Till Europe taught them better than before	418	Island	1	218
And all our dreams of better life above	420	Island	2	121
Thou smilest?--Smile; 'tis better thus than sigh	421	Island	2	201
Of wonder warn'd to better sympathy	422	Island	2	241
The other better self, whose joy or woe	424	Island	2	377
Their better feelings, if such were, were thrown	427	Island	3	41
In hopeless visions of our better days	429	Island	3	206
Who, born perchance for better things, had set	433	Island	4	273
But all unquench'd is still my better part	438	Tasso		112
The skies (and the more duskily the better	440	Beppo		10
You'd better walk about begirt with briars	440	Beppo		25
But something better still, so very real	441	Beppo		99
Who do such things because they know no better	442	Beppo		124
A better seaman never yet did man yard	443	Beppo		205
'Tis said they use no better than a dog any	448	Beppo		557
And sweating plays so middling, bad were better	449	Beppo		592
Scott, Rogers, Moore, and all the better brothers	449	Beppo		603
But these are better than the gloomy errors	453	Venice-B		32
Better, though each man's life-blood were a river	455	Venice-B		149
Three paces and then faltering;--better be	455	Venice-B		154
When thou art better, I will be thy guide	483	Manfred	2	4
And be of better cheer. Come, taste my wine	483	Manfred	2	17
To higher hope and better thoughts; the first	492	Manfred	3	62
Better that sixty of my fourscore years	504	Faliero	1	348
The whole must be extinguish'd;--better that	504	Faliero	1	350
Be better you should quit me; he seems rapt	510	Faliero	2	134
And may be better; but whate'er betide	513	Faliero	2	285
For better fortunes than to share in mine	515	Faliero	2	501
Better bow down before the Hun, and call	517	Faliero	2	627

BETTER

Will better have supplied my care. These orders	517 Faliero	2	636
Know your friend better; but you all shall judge	518 Faliero	2	705
Far better than we can, to whom alone	524 Faliero	3	419
Methinks, my lord, 'tis better as it is	533 Faliero	4	357
Were it not better to record the facts	545 Faliero	5	509
I cannot leave her thus, and yet 'tis better	547 Faliero	5	690
Of council; it were better I retire	551 Sardan	1	77
But the false satraps who provide no better	553 Sardan	1	155
That she had better woven within her palace	553 Sardan	1	181
And if I did, 'twere better than a trophy	554 Sardan	1	243
Better by me awaken'd than rebellion	554 Sardan	1	248
And better, as more faithful:--but, proceed	556 Sardan	1	392
The peaceful only: if they rouse me, better	557 Sardan	1	419
'Tis sometimes better to be fear'd than loved	559 Sardan	1	581
So let me fall like the pluck'd rose!--far better	560 Sardan	1	652
And that is better than the power to smile	561 Sardan	1	670
I should not love him better, but myself	561 Sardan	1	698
And be the warrior? Why not both? The better	562 Sardan	2	80
For neither, sire, say better. I will wait	566 Sardan	2	269
Nor doom ye guiltless; albeit better men	566 Sardan	2	291
No--but it had been better to have died	567 Sardan	2	361
Your servant! Why not? better than be slave	568 Sardan	2	403
Let me hope better than thou augurest	568 Sardan	2	425
My brother, my best subject, better prince	569 Sardan	2	487
Is not this better now than Nimrod's huntings	571 Sardan	3	5
Better than mortals. Friends, a thought has struck me	572 Sardan	3	48
This is of better metal, though less rich	573 Sardan	3	134
This cuirass fits me well, the baldric better	574 Sardan	3	163
If aught of ill betide her, better I	576 Sardan	3	295
Such as might try the sternest. I am better	581 Sardan	4	171
My better bodings. But it must not be	584 Sardan	4	366
You save the better part of what is left	584 Sardan	4	387
'Twere better thus, perhaps, than prolong either	587 Sardan	4	574
Strike with a better aim! Ay, if we conquer	587 Sardan	4	581
The dust of both into one urn. The better	594 Sardan	5	476
And better as my country than my kingdom	595 Sardan	5	494
So I be buried in my birth-place: better	597 Foscari	1	138
'Twere better to retire. I pray thee do so	599 Foscari	1	252
Now, you will know me better. Are you, then	604 Foscari	2	145
Better for him he never had been born	604 Foscari	2	154
Better for me.--I have seen our house dishonour'd	604 Foscari	2	155
Indeed all you have said. I better bore	604 Foscari	2	173
Died suddenly. And if they did so, better	605 Foscari	2	210
The water! There. I thank you: I am better	608 Foscari	3	31
And here? At once--by better means, as briefer	610 Foscari	3	137
Will one day thank you better. You do well	612 Foscari	3	270
As yours, is better in its product, nay	612 Foscari	3	298
Known Loredano. You may know him better	613 Foscari	3	353
And twice it was refused. The better reason	615 Foscari	4	43
Is it the light?--I am faint. He will be better	617 Foscari	4	189
But add, that if another hour would better	620 Foscari	5	2
May the next duke be better than the present	624 Foscari	5	224
Had better now be seated, nor as yet	625 Foscari	5	301
I know the former better than yourselves	626 Foscari	5	363
'Tis better I should be so. Wherefore so	628 Cain	1	27
Since better may not be without. There is	635 Cain	1	489
But had done better in not planting it	642 Cain	2	439
A better portion for the animal	643 Cain	2	506
Till ye know better its true fount; and judge	646 Cain	2	661
To myriads is within him! better 'twere	648 Cain	3	124
'Twere better that he ceased to live, than give	648 Cain	3	132
'Twere better that he never had been born	648 Cain	3	136
But thee the better: I care not for that	649 Cain	3	192
Thy burnt flesh-off'ring prospers better; see	650 Cain	3	284
Better thus than that he should weep for me	655 Heaven		32
I loved her well; I would nave loved her better	657 Heaven		174
Alas! what am I better than ye are	659 Heaven		282
May'st know me better; and thy sister know	663 Heaven		604
And better. Let me die with this, and them	665 Heaven		764
He riseth, but his better light is gone	668 Heaven		1004
I must hope better still,--at least we have yet	673 Werner	1	99
My better angel! such I have ever found thee	673 Werner	1	149
I ask'd for something better than your name	674 Werner	1	177
By the face you put on it. Better, sir	674 Werner	1	178
Better or worse, like matrimony: what	674 Werner	1	179
Our better acquaintance; relatives should be	674 Werner	1	200
Would please him better than the table after	675 Werner	1	270
To have seen better days, as who has not	677 Werner	1	372
An air and port and eye, which would have better	677 Werner	1	386
Instantly, knaves! 'Tis he! I'm better now	678 Werner	1	461
As sometimes happens to the better clad	680 Werner	1	546
Be better. I have neither, and will venture	682 Werner	1	672
For your lord's losses! He hath found a better	684 Werner	2	77
Exactly like the rest, or rather better	686 Werner	2	208
To fault; but here I have him, and that's better	687 Werner	2	269
And you, my lord? Better in rest than purse	687 Werner	2	302
Oh, God! He faints! No--I am better now	688 Werner	2	356
But I trust better, and that all is yours	689 Werner	2	393
And that the depth is rich in better things	690 Werner	2	497
That I keep better company. You shall	691 Werner	2	523
You may have better luck another chase	699 Werner	2	281
Certain. That's well; but had been better, if	703 Werner	3	510

BETTER

Whose youth may better battle with them.--Hence	704 Werner	3	593
So better times are come at last; to these	704 Werner	4	1
You'd better ask himself. I would as soon	705 Werner	4	58
Adieu. Yet hold--we had better keep together	706 Werner	4	134
Be sure I'll sound it better than your bugles	708 Werner	4	270
I thought you knew it better than to take	709 Werner	4	304
The deadliest and the stanchest. Better still	712 Werner	4	487
And may sound better.--He appear'd to me	717 Werner	5	269
The splay feet and low stature! I had better	725 Deformed	1	219
It must be peace-time, and no better fare	728 Deformed	1	427
And scarce a better to be found on earth	729 Deformed	1	502
What ho! my chargers! Never yet were better	729 Deformed	1	508
Why not? The deeper sinner, better saint	729 Deformed	1	521
Because you know no better than the dull	730 Deformed	1	582
And that is better than the bitter truth	730 Deformed	1	585
And loved his laurels better as a wig	731 Deformed	1	645
It answers better to resolve the alphabet	732 Deformed	1	673
That we will fight as well, and rule much better	734 Deformed	1	852
From better company, have kept your own	745 Juan	Ded	34
A better cavalier ne'er mounted horse	748 Juan	1	69
'Twere better to have two of five-and-twenty	754 Juan	1	492
Such thoughts, and be the better when they're over	756 Juan	1	622
At best, no better than a go-between	761 Juan	1	928
'Twere better, sure, to die so, than be shut	767 Juan	1	1327
Grieved, but, perhaps, her feelings may be better	770 Juan	1	1527
So that he had much better cause to grieve	776 Juan	2	115
Beef, veal, and mutton, better for digestion	782 Juan	2	536
Having no paper, for the want of better	783 Juan	2	591
'Twas better that he did not; for, in fact	784 Juan	2	625
Night fell: this seem'd a better omen still	786 Juan	2	752
But finding no place for their landing better	787 Juan	2	831
A better swimmer you could scarce see ever	787 Juan	2	837
How to accept a better in his turn	790 Juan	2	1024
Better than her knew what, in fact, she meant	791 Juan	2	1083
Shows stars and women in a better light	793 Juan	2	1216
Thus Juan learn'd his alpha beta better	794 Juan	2	1303
A better welcome to the tempest-tost	796 Juan	2	1413
Few changes e'er can better their affairs	799 Juan	2	1605
But all the better, for the happy pair	804 Juan	3	187
You'd better ask our mistress who's his heir	806 Juan	3	342
And that good wine ne'er wash'd down better fare	807 Juan	3	356
He'll answer all for better or for worse	807 Juan	3	359
For something better, if not wholly good	808 Juan	3	422
Perhaps no better than they have treated me	817 Juan	4	50
The least glance better understood than words	818 Juan	4	106
It were much better to have both than neither	819 Juan	4	200
May teach us better to behave when masters	834 Juan	5	184
'Tis bad, and may be better--all men's lot	834 Juan	5	194
'Tis therefore better looking before leaping	837 Juan	5	358
Might teach them this much better than I'm able	839 Juan	5	472
'Twould greatly tend to better their condition	840 Juan	5	551
'So much the better,' Juan said, 'for them	841 Juan	5	650
Juan's was good; and might have been still better	847 Juan	5	985
Morals were better, and the fish no worse	850 Juan	5	1192
That they have nothing better near, or newer	859 Juan	6	470
And shown themselves as ghosts of better taste	860 Juan	6	521
The true effect, and so we had better not	864 Juan	6	782
Conceal'd her features better than a veil	865 Juan	6	866
In war than love, he had better lead the assault	875 Juan	7	496
Which is still better; thus in verse to wage	880 Juan	8	110
With something not much better, or as bad	881 Juan	8	171
Perhaps may find it better than a new one	882 Juan	8	232
In short, howe'er our better faith derides	892 Juan	8	908
(I wish your bards would sing it rather better	896 Juan	9	24
Or better, as the best examples say	905 Juan	9	564
Behaved no better than a common sempstress	906 Juan	9	616
Such Clytemnestra, though perhaps 'tis better	906 Juan	9	639
Whose age, and what was better still, whose nation	911 Juan	10	259
Unless you make their betters better:--Fy	918 Juan	10	679
To the old text, still better:--lest it should	919 Juan	11	26
The Druids' groves are gone--so much the better	921 Juan	11	193
Which grows no better, though 'tis time it should	926 Juan	11	512
So much the better!--I may stand alone	929 Juan	11	711
I have always liked you better than I state	933 Juan	12	220
Would be much better taught beneath the eye	933 Juan	12	231
And after all poor Frederick may do better	934 Juan	12	279
As better knowing why they should be so	935 Juan	12	362
Turn out much better for the Smithfield Show	935 Juan	12	366
Good at all things, but better at a bet	952 Juan	13	696
Is better than a humdrum tete-a-tete	953 Juan	13	748
When he allured poor Dolon:--you had better	954 Juan	13	839
Trade will be all the better for these Cantos	957 Juan	14	112
All this were very well, and can't be better	958 Juan	14	193
In short, there never was a better hearer	960 Juan	14	296
'Tis better on the whole to have felt and seen	961 Juan	14	389
It were much better to be wed or dead	963 Juan	14	509
And pass, for want of better, though not new	964 Juan	14	548
Upon whose back 'tis better not to venture	964 Juan	14	584
Some truths are better kept behind a screen	965 Juan	14	638

BETTER
But all are better than the sigh supprest | 968 Juan | 15 | 17
Days better drawn before, or else assume | 971 Juan | 15 | 207
Of the best class, and better than her class | 973 Juan | 15 | 340
But draw the long bow better now than ever | 980 Juan | 16 | 8
And knew no better in her immorality | 989 Juan | 16 | 559
The love of higher things and better days | 994 Juan | 16 | 905

BETTER'D
All shall be better'd. What we have to do | 689 Werner | 2 | 387

BETTERING
In this small hope of bettering future ill | 286 Vision | | 102

BETTERS
Adieu, ye fools--who ape your betters | 163 Malta | | 10
Her wondering betters wait behind her chair | 208 Sketch | | 6
But you've others his betters | 232 Murray-B | | 31
'Tis hard to venture where our betters fail | 259 Hints | | 183
From poets, or the moralists their betters | 809 Juan | 3 | 512
It betters present times with me or you | 834 Juan | 5 | 179
That ye are dogs--your betters far--ye may | 868 Juan | 7 | 50
Unless you make their betters better:--Fy | 918 Juan | 10 | 679

BETTERS'
May live to carve your betters | 738 Deformed | 2 | 209

BETTER-SEEING
Alike the better-seeing shade will smile | 300 Age | | 119

BETTY
Thus, when he tells the tale of Betty Foy | 245 Bards | | 247

BETWEEN
(See also GO-BETWEEN, 'TWIXT)
The forest's growth, and Gothic walls between | 45 Harold | 3 | 584
It is the hush of night, and all between | 48 Harold | 3 | 806
Now, where the swift Rhone cleaves his way between | 49 Harold | 3 | 878
I speak not of men's creeds--they rest between | 69 Harold | 4 | 847
And vile Ambition, that built up between | 69 Harold | 4 | 869
And flowing flasks, and scatter'd troops between | 108 Nisus | | 228
With brakes entangled, scarce a path between | 109 Nisus | | 313
Rocks rise, and rivers roll between | 146 Adieu | | 53
Or Friendship's tears, Pride rush'd between | 150 Harrow-C | | 15
Roll'd like a river wide between | 197 Duel | | 41
Our time, nay, our eternity, between | 292 Vision | | 502
But these were few and far between | 411 Mazeppa | | 470
Colour'd, and silver paper leaved between | 447 Beppo | | 454
Robed as with angry clouds: he stands between | 495 Manfred | 3 | 325
There's only one slight difference between | 771 Juan | 1 | 1609
The distant dog-bark; and perceived between | 805 Juan | 3 | 212
Count Chapeau-Bras, too, had a ball between | 879 Juan | 8 | 74
The usual progress of intrigues between | 910 Juan | 10 | 186
By some odd chance too, he was placed between | 977 Juan | 15 | 593
But his eyes may be seen from the folds between | 986 Juan | 16 | 351
There is a difference, says the song, 'between | 991 Juan | 16 | 713

BETWIXT
Extreme in all things! hadst thou been betwixt | 40 Harold | 3 | 320
Thou pendulum betwixt a smile and tear | 71 Harold | 4 | 975
Betwixt the Hellenic and the Phrygian shore | 298 Age | | 18
Which ever rises betwixt thee and me | 551 Sardan | 1 | 75
That there are worse things betwixt earth and
heaven | 566 Sardan | 2 | 314
Choose betwixt love and knowledge--since there is | 634 Cain | 1 | 426
Morocco, betwixt Egypt and Tangier | 858 Juan | 6 | 352

BEVERAGE
His thirst with such pure beverage. No matter | 450 Beppo | | 637
A beverage for Turks and Christians both | 451 Beppo | | 722
Suggest a purpler beverage. Blood--doubtless | 577 Sardan | 3 | 348
Rain'd, as it were, the beverage which makes
glad | 682 Werner | 1 | 714
A sad, sour, sober beverage--by time | 802 Juan | 3 | 38
The beverage was various sherbets | 809 Juan | 3 | 494

BEVY
On the rack of cross questions, by all the blue
bevy | 280 Blues | 1 | 148
Each bevy with the merchant in his station | 832 Juan | 5 | 51

BEWAIL
Doom'd to bewail the blasphemy of laws | 45 Harold | 3 | 615
But now I scarcely shall bewail my fate | 87 Tibullus | | 5
Which better bosoms would bewail | 164 Friend-B | | 22
For them bewail, to them belong | 184 Parker | | 12
Bewail her now uncountry gentlemen | 305 Age | | 569
No more her sorrows I bewail | 311 Giaour | | 164
I breathe the sorrows I bewail | 323 Giaour | | 1321
When we know what all are, we must bewail us | 867 Juan | 7 | 13

BEWAILING
For poor is the soul which bewailing rehearses | 92 Caroline-D | | 7
Could they view us our sad separation bewailing | 92 Caroline-D | | 15

BEWAILING
While each bewailing | 200 Stanzas-B | | 50

BEWAILS
Ah, hapless dame! no sire bewails | 111 Medea | | 45

BEWARE
But trust not this; too easy youth, beware | 24 Harold | 2 | 263
Beware lest blundering Brougham destroy the sale | 248 Bards | | 524
Beware--for God's sake, don't begin like Bowles | 259 Hints | | 194
Let those who shape its edge, beware | 319 Giaour | | 931
Then, lovely dame, bethink thee! and beware | 358 Corsair | 3 | 184
You have it; but beware! you know not whom | 692 Werner | 2 | 599
Ida, beware! there's blood upon that hand | 721 Werner | 5 | 548
Beware! beware! of the Black Friar | 985 Juan | 16 | 321
But beware! beware! of the Black Friar | 986 Juan | 16 | 353

BEWILDER
And then, still further to bewilder 'em | 230 Murray-A | | 5

BEWILDER'D
(See also WILD-BEWILDERED)
My thoughts bewilder'd in the fond surprise | 125 Recoll | | 203
While poor John Bull, bewilder'd with the scene | 250 Bards | | 604
My brain bewilder'd--do not madden quite | 362 Corsair | 3 | 473
Bewilder'd with the dazzling blast | 412 Mazeppa | | 515
So Juan stood, bewilder'd on the deck | 775 Juan | 2 | 97

BEWILDERING
Romance, my youthful Head bewildering | 144 Becher-B | | 39
Two things for dying people quite bewildering | 779 Juan | 2 | 344

BEWITCH'D
Of rocks bewitch'd that open to the knockers | 805 Juan | 3 | 270

BEWITCHING
Fresh as in Love's bewitching dream | 146 Adieu | | 56
Bewitching, torturing, as they freeze or glow | 963 Juan | 14 | 503

BEY
Is kinsman of the Bey Oglou | 326 Abydos | 1 | 206
This kinsman Bey of Carasman | 327 Abydos | 1 | 310
To me and mine leave Osman Bey | 327 Abydos | 1 | 379
And would'st thou save that haughty Bey | 334 Abydos | 2 | 483
And being told the latter, sent a bey | 893 Juan | 8 | 959

BEYOND
And guileless beyond Hope's imagining | 3 To Ianthe | | 14
And visit scorching climes beyond the sea | 4 Harold | 1 | 52
That will not look beyond the tomb | 17 Harold | 1 | 855
A land of souls beyond that sable shore | 20 Harold | 2 | 65
Beyond the fitting medium of desire | 41 Harold | 3 | 374
Imperishably pure beyond all things below | 45 Harold | 3 | 643
But unto us she hath a spell beyond | 55 Harold | 4 | 28
Beyond where splendid shines the orb of day | 84 Death-B | | 14
Is there no cause beyond the common claim | 125 Recoll | | 211
A fame beyond the glories of the proud | 127 Recoll | | 365
Beyond the rapture of succeeding years | 127 Recoll | | 392
Some shall exist beyond the grave | 127 Answer-B | | 4
And live beyond the bounds of Time | 132 Prayer | | 36
But waft thy name beyond the sky | 151 Farewell-B | | 4
Born far beyond the mountains, but his blood | 198 Po | | 42
Recalling, as it lies beyond redress | 211 Augusta-C | | 14
If that high world, which lies beyond | 217 High World | | 1
That ever breaking Bed, beyond repair | 224 J.C.H. | | 19
Beyond Imagination's power | 229 Marble | | 5
Beyond the Bard's defeated art | 229 Marble | | 6
Could bid your lines beyond a morning live | 252 Bards | | 752
A strain far, far beyond thy humble reach | 254 Bards | | 908
And Glory knew no clime beyond her Greece | 269 Minerva | | 62
Shall vengeance follow far beyond the tomb | 271 Minerva | | 202
True; feeling is truest then, far beyond question | 283 Blues | 2 | 160
'Tis every tittle true, beyond suspicion | 289 Vision | | 271
Extended far beyond the mere controls | 291 Vision | | 419
And far beyond the Moslem's power | 314 Giaour | | 457
Are pass'd beyond the outer gate | 324 Abydos | 1 | 37
Beyond my weaker sense extends | 328 Abydos | 1 | 413
But ask no land beyond my sabre's length | 333 Abydos | 2 | 433
Without one hope on earth beyond thy love | 344 Corsair | 1 | 400
Beyond the wandering freedom which I lost | 348 Corsair | 2 | 72
All--all--before--beyond--the deadliest fall | 352 Corsair | 2 | 359
A flash is seen--the ball beyond their bow | 362 Corsair | 3 | 488
Oh! for a wing beyond the falcon's flight | 364 Corsair | 3 | 575
No train is his beyond a single page | 366 Lara | 1 | 47
And ask'd if greater dwelt beyond the sky | 368 Lara | 1 | 126
So much he soar'd beyond, or sunk beneath | 371 Lara | 1 | 345
Above his station, and beyond his years | 373 Lara | 1 | 517
No gift beyond that bitter boon--our birth | 374 Lara | 1 | 553
Which fix'd him beyond the power to start | 390 Corinth | | 598
Beyond the blow that to the block | 401 Parisina | | 486
Beyond the swift Borysthenes | 408 Mazeppa | | 116
When stirr'd beyond its calmer mood | 412 Mazeppa | | 534
To stretch beyond the sight | 412 Mazeppa | | 609
They who have revell'd beyond measure | 414 Mazeppa | | 737

BEYOND

Than aught we know beyond our little day	417	Island	1	120
Beyond the sound whose charm is half divine	420	Island	2	82
Beyond itsekf, and must retrace its way	421	Island	2	189
The isle they loved beyond their native shore	426	Island	3	12
At an external life beyond our fate	463	Dante	4	13
As Nessus did of old beyond all cure	474	Morgante		570
We have no forms, beyond the elements	430	Manfred	1	181
Have been beyond the dwellers of the earth	489	Manfred	2	429
Powers deeper still beyond--I come in quest	489	Manfred	2	446
And seek the things beyond mortality	491	Manfred	2	528
He sinks beyond the mountain. Doth he so	493	Manfred	3	173
The watch-dog bay'd beyond the Tiber; and	495	Manfred	3	275
Some cypresses beyond the time-worn breach	495	Manfred	3	280
Beyond may breed us double danger. See	516	Faliero	2	554
Beyond the compass of the human voice	548	Faliero	5	721
Beyond my easy nature. 'Tis beyond	552	Sardan	1	108
Beyond his palace walls, or if he stirs	553	Sardan	1	157
Beyond them, 'tis but to some mountain palace	553	Sardan	1	158
Beyond the palace walls to-night, but make	570	Sardan	2	555
A shore beyond the Styx: and if there be not	574	Sardan	3	159
Sent me here to conduct you hence, beyond	575	Sardan	3	243
They are safe beyond the Median's grasp, the rebels	584	Sardan	4	376
And beyond nature--'tis nor mutual	585	Sardan	4	457
Beyond a vision, 'tis so transiently	587	Sardan	5	17
They battle it beyond the wall, and not	588	Sardan	5	60
Within us lives beyond:--thou readest mine	589	Sardan	5	160
But the poor wretch has suffer'd beyond nature's	595	Foscari	1	12
Voice of the many) somewhat beyond what	605	Foscari	2	252
For us to look beyond. But still I must	616	Foscari	4	107
I have been so beyond the common lot	617	Foscari	4	166
Ends with his life, and goes not beyond murder	618	Foscari	4	199
From louder tongues than mine: they have gone beyond	623	Foscari	5	146
I thought the dead had been beyond even you	626	Foscari	5	334
The snares beyond the walls of Paradise	628	Cain	1	43
Which, knowing nought beyond their shallow senses	636	Cain	2	9
The worlds beyond thy little world, nor be	636	Cain	2	14
Amerced for doubts beyond thy little life	636	Cain	2	15
And science still beyond them, were chain'd down	637	Cain	2	53
And see thou show'st me things beyond my power	637	Cain	2	80
Beyond all power of my born faculties	637	Cain	2	81
For I was made of it. 'Tis now beyond thee	638	Cain	2	146
Couldst not have gone beyond thy world. On! on	639	Cain	2	205
That there was death. But not what was beyond it	641	Cain	2	377
A state, and many states beyond thine own	641	Cain	2	379
Of glorious azure which floats on beyond us	642	Cain	2	384
Being beyond all beauty in thine eyes	643	Cain	2	483
Beyond our wonted range. Was he of those	648	Cain	3	166
Jehovah! this is punishment beyond	652	Cain	3	385
That I must live beyond ye? Where shall be	659	Heaven		283
Nought to his eye beyond the deep, his grave	662	Heaven		513
An hour beyond his will	667	Heaven		905
Something beyond our outward sufferings (though	672	Werner	1	46
And leaves us--no! this is beyond me!--but	672	Werner	1	52
Their castle walls--beyond them 'tis but doubtful	676	Werner	1	341
Your station. Is it? Or, at least, beyond	680	Werner	1	544
My state beyond despair; and now, 'tis such	680	Werner	1	584
And with a brow of thought beyond his years	687	Werner	2	256
Beyond the two first windings; if you do	696	Werner	3	102
For that would make our ties beyond all doubt	698	Werner	3	194
The same to your pursuers. Once beyond	698	Werner	3	200
A week beyond their funeral rites their sway	703	Werner	3	569
But what beyond 'tis not ours to pronounce	705	Werner	4	48
For manly sports beyond the castle walls	710	Werner	4	403
Beyond the world they brighten, with a sigh	727	Deformed	1	337
Thou waxest insolent, beyond the privilege	734	Deformed	1	815
The resurrection is beyond me. Slave	741	Deformed	2	373
Beyond you--and your Jealousy's of Earth	744	Deformed	3	148
That is to say, a thought beyond the common	756	Juan	1	613
If people go beyond, 'tis quite a crime	756	Juan	1	639
And wonderful beyond all wondrous measure	763	Juan	1	1058
Shall supersede beyond all doubt all those	771	Juan	1	1627
Because the first is crazed beyond all hope	772	Juan	1	1635
Beyond the best apothecary's art	776	Juan	2	163
Our Juan, who, with sense beyond his years	778	Juan	2	274
Your labouring people think beyond all question	782	Juan	2	535
Hush'd into depths beyond the watcher's diving	799	Juan	2	1574
Buys them in marriage--and what rests beyond	799	Juan	2	1598
Hope, care, nor love, beyond, her heart beat here	799	Juan	2	1616
So that all hands were busy beyond measure	804	Juan	3	159
A life which made them happy beyond measure	806	Juan	3	308
Beyond a single gentleman's belief	807	Juan	3	408
While I soliloquize beyond expression	814	Juan	3	860
And tall beyond her sex, and their compeers	822	Juan	4	341
But when the offer went beyond, they knew	831	Juan	4	911
I won't be bail for anything beyond	844	Juan	5	792
When things beyond the common have occurr'd	865	Juan	6	846
A thing to wonder at beyond most wondering	874	Juan	7	436
Beyond the Russian batteries a few toises	879	Juan	8	50
Beyond the rules of posting,--and the mob	884	Juan	8	399
Beyond the dwarfing city's pale abortions	886	Juan	8	522
Although no doubt it was beyond all price	901	Juan	9	288

BEYOND

And had retain'd his boyish look beyond	903	Juan	9	418
Since, thou hast settled beyond all surmises	903	Juan	9	440
If once beyond her boudoir's precincts in ye went	904	Juan	9	501
To follow him beyond the drawing-room	908	Juan	10	37
Beyond its dimm'd eye's sphere,--but would much rather	908	Juan	10	47
Saloon, room, hall, o'erflow beyond their brink	926	Juan	11	533
And your cold people are beyond all price	946	Juan	13	303
And what not, though he rode beyond all price	959	Juan	14	279
Advance beyond, while they could pass for new	962	Juan	14	420
She was a pitch beyond a coxcomb's flight	962	Juan	14	452
This I could prove beyond a single doubt	966	Juan	14	669
Pious and pure, beyond what I can term any	972	Juan	15	285
All youth--but with an aspect beyond time	973	Juan	15	356
Beyond the charmers we have already cited	974	Juan	15	380
Her place was far beyond it, and her mind	974	Juan	15	426
Requires arithmetic beyond my forces	976	Juan	15	543
In some things, mine's beyond all contradiction	980	Juan	16	15
Beyond the rumour which such spots unfold	983	Juan	16	172
The worlds beyond this world's perplexing waste	987	Juan	16	429
Heaving between this world and worlds beyond	995	Juan	16	922

BEZONIAN

Not reckoning him to be a 'base Bezonian	885	Juan	8	447

BIANCA'S

When he betray'd Bianca's truth	397	Parisina		104

BIAS

These city slaves have all their private bias	533	Faliero	4	366
Love lay not down his cheek there): some strong bias	710	Werner	4	353
The lurking bias, be it truth or error	956	Juan	14	45

BIBLE

No less on history than the Holy Bible	295	Vision		688
And read your Bible, sir, and mind your purse	773	Juan	1	1760

BIBLIOPOLE'S

On the bibliopole's shelves, it is only two paces	277	Blues	1	20

BICKERING

The bickering sabres' shivering jar	316	Giaour		636
Or whirl around the bickering blade	385	Corinth		113

BICKERINGS

No--I'll not hear of such things. These vain bickerings	565	Sardan	2	206
No bickerings, no connubial turmoil	966	Juan	14	686

BID

But bid me with my wreath one matchless lily blend	3	To Ianthe		36
Bid man be valiant ere he merit such	13	Harold	1	597
The fault of a friend, bid an enemy live	30	Harold	2	658
You bid a long adieu to peace	89	To Emma		36
I bid thee now a last farewell	90	To M.S.G.-A		32
Invoke them no more, bid adieu to the muse	92	First Kiss		11
Ask thine own heart; 'twill bid thee, boy, forbear	93	Dorset		31
And bid him drain the dregs of pleasure's bowl	100	Damaetas		12
And bid him from the task retire	98	To Mary		12
Bid shuddering Nature shrink beneath the blow	122	Recoll		8
Can bid Life's pulses beat	146	Adieu		74
Could bid me from fond admiration refrain	147	To Anne-B		6
Your lover should bid you a lasting adieu	147	To Anne-B		14
No touch can bid its warmth return	148	A Fan		16
And bid their lids each other seek	152	Remind		20
And when we bid adieu to youth	153	Friend-A		25
Each kindred brute might bid thee blush for shame	154	Dog		22
And though I bid thee now farewell	158	Florence		41
To bid us meet--no--ne'er again	165	Thyrza		8
'When in your fostering beams you bid us live	171	Address-B		55
A charm, to bid thy lover live	172	Romaic-B		32
Who bid pretty well--but they cheated him, though	177	Devil's Dr		90
Had bid for and carried away from the Lobby	178	Devil's Dr		159
But bid it flow as now--until it glides	191	Fragment-C		5
Then part in friendship,--and bid good-night	200	Stanzas-B		60
Still bid the bursting spirit soar	217	The Harp		18
But bid the strain be wild and deep	218	Soul-B		9
Bid the prophet's form appear	219	Saul-B		2
And bid a long 'good night to Marmion	244	Bards		184
Could bid your lines beyond a morning live	252	Bards		752
Whose magic touch can bid the canvass glow	253	Bards		863
Requires no sacred theme to bid us list	255	Bards		968
If unprovoked thou once could bid me bleed	265	Hints		607
That bid the foe defiance ere they come	272	Minerva		288
And bid it antedate the joys of arms	272	Minerva		292
Which is to act as we are bid to do	287	Vision		176
To bid us blush for these old chains, or break	303	Age		389
The last to bid the cry of warfare cease	305	Age		570
And when land crumbles, bid firm paper crash	306	Age		639
So rent may rise, bid bank and nation fall	306	Age		640
And the world trembles to bid brokers break	307	Age		667

BID

Or blade to bid thy foeman bleed	319	Giaour		929
To bid the sins of others cease	320	Giaour		973
When thou canst bid my Leila live	322	Giaour		1210
To bid thee with another dwell	326	Abydos	1	197
My life, Oh! bid me be thy slave	330	Abydos	2	183
Though Glory, Nature, Reason, Freedom, bid	423	Island	2	324
And thus they bid farewell to carnal dishes	441	Beppo		49
The sea, to bid their cook, or wife, or friend	441	Beppo		59
And bid once more her faithful heart rejoice	443	Beppo		236
Without being forced to bid my groom be sure	445	Beppo		330
With dim sepulchral light, bid me forget	458	Dante	2	17
Which cheers the birds to song shall bid them glow	461	Dante	3	66
His chisel bid the Hebrew, at whose word	464	Dante	4	61
Benign and pious, bid an angel flee	466	Morgante		6
Bid him bow down to that which is above him.	489	Manfred	2	416
I cannot speak to her--but bid her speak	490	Manfred	2	474
And bid our friends prepare their companies	516	Faliero	2	549
And bid the galley be prepared. There is	551	Sardan	1	52
I'll not insult him thus, to bid him render	565	Sardan	2	216
And bid thee guard me there--where thou shouldst shield	576	Sardan	3	293
I do not bid thee not to shed them--'twere	584	Sardan	4	399
Requests an audience. Bid her enter. Poor	602	Foscari	2	45
Bid to his dukedom. When embarks the son	615	Foscari	4	11
Still fruitful? Did I bid her pluck them not	630	Cain	1	196
Bid thee await the world-dissolving wave	660	Heaven		406
And bid those clouds and waters take a shape	664	Heaven		717
And I obey; you bid me turn a chamberer	710	Werner	4	404
Of far artillery which seem'd to bid	714	Werner	5	114
I am unarm'd, count; bid your son lay down	716	Werner	5	207
Or I would bid them fall and crush me! Fly	721	Werner	5	499
He knew not wherefore, that which he was bid	767	Juan	1	1304
Ring for your valet--bid him quickly bring	797	Juan	2	1433
To bid men come, and go, and come again	807	Juan	3	370
Should an hour come to bid them breathe apart	819	Juan	4	211
Turn'd to the merchant, and begun to bid	834	Juan	5	218
But bid my women form the milky way	849	Juan	5	1155
Bid Ireland's Londonderry's Marquess show	902	Juan	9	387
Where people always did as they were bid	944	Juan	13	179
Upon my head have bid their thunders break	956	Juan	14	75

BIDDER

As is a slave by his intended bidder	834	Juan	5	209

BIDDING

That feels relief by bidding sorrow flow	4	Harold	1	70
Of rock-built cities, bidding nations quake	82	Harold	4	1622
As the branch, at the bidding of Nature	162	Romaic-A		9
Retired, but not as bidding her adieu	215	Dream		100
Flash'd o'er the future, bidding men behold	458	Dante	2	3
Mortal! to thy bidding bow'd	479	Manfred	1	50
Thy bidding to bide	479	Manfred	1	97
Are at thy beck and bidding, Child of Clay	480	Manfred	1	133
My bidding, it may help thee to thy wishes	487	Manfred	2	251
His bidding, nor did I neglect my duty	489	Manfred	2	389
Would do the bidding of their lord without	533	Faliero	4	371
Recruit his phalanx--spill your blood at bidding	555	Sardan	1	304
About my sick couch. Hence! and do my bidding	589	Sardan	5	122
Bidding farewell? A last. As soon he shall	615	Foscari	4	13
Prince! I have done your bidding. What command	620	Foscari	5	5
By my sire to Jehovah's bidding? May	659	Heaven		300
Her bidding; wearily but willingly	722	Deformed	1	29
And taking lately, by Suwarrow's bidding	833	Juan	5	119
My bidding!' Baba vanish'd, for to stretch	866	Juan	6	923
By bidding others carry while they ride	943	Juan	13	152

BIDE

Thy bidding to bide	479	Manfred	1	97

BIDS

He bids to sober joy that here sojourns	14	Harold	1	680
That bids me loathe my present state	17	Harold	1	847
'Tis night, when Meditation bids us feel	23	Harold	2	199
When Gratitude or Valour bids them bleed	29	Harold	2	584
And bids him thank the bard for freedom and his strains	57	Harold	4	144
Thou formest in his fortunes bids us think	60	Harold	4	329
From the seat of his ancestors, bids you adieu	86	Leaving NA		22
Which bids us part to meet no more	89	To Emma		6
Without a sigh which bids adieu	91	Caroline-B		26
Revives my hopes, and bids me live	98	To Mary		4
Bids her he fondly loved depart	111	Medea		51
And bids me curse Aurora's ray	113	Quaker		34
And bids devotion's hallow'd echoes cease	120	Newstead-A		44
Cherish'd affection only bids them flow	122	Newstead-A		146
When Memory bids them bud again	128	Lady-C		16
Bids me live but to hope for posterity's praise	129	Becher-A		14
And bids the war of tempests cease	133	E. N. Long		10
And bids me feel for self alone	133	E. N. Long		38
Bids every Fiend unmask'd appear	141	Critics		42
No jealousy bids me reprove	147	Vain Lady		34
Till Heaven in mercy bids your pain and sorrows cease	161	Athos		26

BIDS

And bids the Drama be where she hath been	169	Address-A		24
That bids a genuine love despair	179	Gold		4
That bids them worship at thy shrine	179	Gold		22
As even in ruin bids the language live	244	Bards		198
She bids thee 'mend thy line, and sin no more	245	Bards		294
To spurn the rod a scribbler bids me kiss	256	Bards		1061
She bids the beating heart with rapture bound	258	Hints		153
Bids not his tongue, but heart, philosophise	263	Hints		502
Gives all it can, and bids us take the rest	273	Waltz		24
No treacherous powder bids conjecture quake	275	Waltz		139
And Leipsic's treason bids the unvanquish'd yield	301	Age		208
Another morn--another bids them seek	365	Corsair	3	682
But I am he who bids it pass	479	Manfred	1	70
Heaven bids us to forgive our enemies	512	Faliero	2	260
And feel for what their duty bids them do	517	Faliero	2	583
And bids us sit and see its sharp infliction	600	Foscari	1	326
The firstlings of the flock to him who bids	630	Cain	1	181
Who bids all men believe the impossible	981	Juan	16	38

BIENSEANCE

At least as far as bienseance allows	964	Juan	14	532

BIER

And Fancy hover o'er thy bloodless bier	19	Harold	1	942
Which stretch'd his father on a bloody bier	38	Harold	3	205
What fruitless tears have bathed thy honour'd bier	85	Epitaph		2
And my corse shall recline on its bier	115	The Tear		42
This arm would be thy bark, or breast thy bier	206	Love, Death		8
Where glory decks the hero's bier	206	Year		19
Unless, perchance, from his cold bier she turns	252	Bards		811
May better grace a brother's bier	322	Giaour		1250
These and the pale pure cheek became the bier	364	Corsair	3	621
And grieve what may above thy senseless bier	375	Lara	2	13
Scarce twice the space they must accord my bier	439	Tasso		184
Thou thought'st me doubtless for the bier outlaid	470	Morgante		266
Is he--Our bridal bed is now his bier	622	Foscari	5	110

BIG

Tears, big tears, gush'd from the rough soldier's lid	44	Harold	3	542
And the big rain comes dancing to the earth	49	Harold	3	874
The big tear starting as he spoke	104	Alva		206
I saw thee weep--the big bright tear	218	I Saw		1
Of brains that labour, big with verse or prose	242	Bards		12
Big, bright, and fast, unknown to her they fell	345	Corsair	1	487
Gleam'd on the dew-drops big and damp	397	Parisina		117
The big rain pattering on the roof. No more	572	Sardan	3	65

BIGAMY

Are prosecuted for that false crime bigamy	891	Juan	8	835

BIGGER

I'll sing them in a book that's bigger	233	Nihil		34
And, growing bigger, took another guise	292	Vision		453
Now it wax'd little, then again grew bigger	294	Vision		597
Wordsworth's last quarto, by the way, is bigger	814	Juan	3	845
Her preference of a boy to men much bigger	905	Juan	9	571

BIGOT

When Self and Church demand a bigot zeal	112	Examination		62
Than see this royal Bedlam bigot range	291	Vision		395
The bigot monarch and the butcher priest	302	Age		334

BIGOTED

And yet so nursed and bigoted to strife	42	Harold	3	390

BIGOTS

Though prudes may condemn me, and bigots reprove	92	First Kiss		14
Let bigots rear a gloomy fane	132	Prayer		13
To bigots and to sects unknown	146	Adieu		105
But why to brain-scorch'd bigots thus appeal	262	Hints		373
Redeeming worlds to be by bigots shaken	970	Juan	15	141

BIGOT'S

Uptorn must bear the hyaena bigot's wrong	63	Harold	4	520
A bigot's shrine, nor despot's throne	181	Ode-A		72

BILE

From the bile, whose blackening river	197	Rogers		57
If this precaution soften't not my bile	263	Hints		481
But to his pious bile gave vent	410	Mazeppa		324
The liver is the lazaret of bile	801	Juan	2	1713
Nought's more sublime than energetic bile	848	Juan	5	1076
Indeed I've not the necessary bile	926	Juan	11	492

BILIOUS

Mark that (as he masks the bilious	196	Rogers		27
He had been ill brought up, and was born bilious	751	Juan	1	280
Would that I were less bilious--but, oh, fie on 't	998	Juan	17	77

BILL

(See also DAY-BILL, HAWK'S-BILL)

BILL
And tailors' lays be longer than their bill | 252 Bards | | 796
For the bill here, it seems, is defray'd by the
  host | 280 Blues | 2 | 19
He's buried; save the undertaker's bill | 286 Vision | | 90
Vain his complaint,--my lord presents his bill | 299 Age | | 75
In vain the Commons pass their patriot bill | 306 Age | | 597
As ever started through a sea-bird's bill | 424 Island | 2 | 429
A scolding wife, a sullen son, a bill | 855 Juan | 6 | 161
Jack Thomson and Bill Thomson; all the rest | 869 Juan | 7 | 145
Must I pass over in my bill of fare | 977 Juan | 15 | 578

BILLET-DOUX
And will look well upon a billet-doux | 730 Deformed | 1 | 545

BILLETS
To his billets? Why waltz with him? Why, I
  pray | 934 Juan | 12 | 271

BILLIARDS
Then there were billiards; cards, too, but
  no dice | 954 Juan | 13 | 841
It all sprung from a harmless game at billiards | 968 Juan | 14 | 800

BILLING
Billing or cooing now | 229 Moore-B | | 7

BILLINGSGATE
As bold in Billingsgate, though less renown'd | 265 Hints | | 626
(See Billingsgate) made even the tongue more free | 923 Juan | 11 | 336

BILLOW
His head heaves with the heaving billow | 335 Abydos | 2 | 606
Far--far away! and alone along the billow | 204 Hindoo | | 4
Let me not die till he comes back o'er the
  billow | 205 Hindoo | | 12
And hence extended by the billow | 337 Abydos | 2 | 727
Sounds fearful as the breaking billow | 397 Parisina | | 94
The cloven billow flash'd from off her prow | 415 Island | 1 | 3
Herself a billow in her energies | 421 Island | 2 | 142
Like her smooth billow, saw their moments glide | 424 Island | 2 | 355
To appease the waves. The billow which destroys
  me | 617 Foscari | 4 | 145
His headache being increased by every billow | 777 Juan | 2 | 198
Regaled two sharks, who follow'd o'er the billow | 783 Juan | 2 | 615
And dolphin's leap, and little billow crost | 797 Juan | 2 | 1446
'Neath which her breast heaved like a little
  billow | 810 Juan | 3 | 556
Stirr'd up and down her bosom like a billow | 865 Juan | 6 | 862
Or like a billow left by storms behind | 981 Juan | 16 | 71
Let in the rippling sound of the lake's billow | 982 Juan | 16 | 116

BILLOWS
(See also MOUNTAIN-BILLOWS)
In sullen billows, murmuring and vast | 9 Harold | 1 | 380
As breezes rise and fall and billows swell | 23 Harold | 2 | 251
Till sparkling billows seem'd to light the banks
  they lave | 32 Harold | 2 | 764
And trusted to thy billows far and near | 82 Harold | 4 | 1655
By Auster on the billows spent | 88 Horace | | 6
Through billows Atlantic to steer | 115 The Tear | | 14
Our pliant limbs the buoyant billows bore | 125 Recoll | | 262
And seeks the rocks where billows roll | 135 I Would | | 8
I breasted the billows of Dee's rushing tide | 136 Highlander | | 19
From out the billows pierced the sable sky | 184 Julian | | 6
His course unto the billows--late escaped | 184 Julian | | 35
If their billows excite an emotion | 210 Augusta-B | | 15
As the deep billows of the Aegean roar | 298 Age | | 17
Than ne'er to brave the billows more | 319 Giaour | | 964
In the light of its billows | 327 Abydos | 1 | 335
To where the strand and billows met | 335 Abydos | 2 | 560
The rushing billows choked the tone | 335 Abydos | 2 | 582
Far as the breeze can bear, the billows foam | 338 Corsair | 1 | 3
From where the battle roars, the billows chafe | 339 Corsair | 1 | 113
Making the very billows look less free | 422 Island | 2 | 227
Which nodded o'er the billows high and hoary | 428 Island | 3 | 166
The billows round the promontory brought | 429 Island | 3 | 214
They skim the blue tops of the billows; fast | 429 Island | 3 | 229
And billows purpler than the ocean's, making | 587 Sardan | 5 | 13
Flinging the billows back from my drench'd hair | 597 Foscari | 1 | 107
The billows and be safe. I will not say | 636 Cain | 2 | 20
Could Juan's passion, while the billows roar | 777 Juan | 2 | 183
Of billows; but at intervals there gush'd | 780 Juan | 2 | 421
As are the billows when the breeze is brisk | 853 Juan | 6 | 22
And made the very billows pay them toll | 915 Juan | 10 | 520
And full of sentiments, sublime as billows | 995 Juan | 16 | 921

BILLOW'S
And rarely ceased the haughty billow's roar | 796 Juan | 2 | 1414

BILLOWS'
Or dost thou dread the billows' rage | 5 Harold | 1 | 136
He watch'd the billows' melancholy flow | 25 Harold | 2 | 367
Save through the billows' glassy veil of green | 431 Island | 4 | 124

BILLS
The quick-eyed lizard rustles, and the bills | 72 Harold | 4 | 1047
Than the bills of the week (though they trouble
  me sore | 280 Blues | 2 | 15
I'll have him gagg'd--'twas one of his own bills | 294 Vision | | 584
The inflammation of his weekly bills | 806 Juan | 3 | 280
Bills, beasts, and men, and--no! not womankind | 855 Juan | 6 | 170
The rest were Jacks and Gills and Wills and Bills | 869 Juan | 7 | 153
Mortality! thou hast thy monthly bills | 879 Juan | 8 | 92
To exact of Cupid's bills the full amount | 904 Juan | 9 | 495
His bills in, and however we may storm | 912 Juan | 10 | 302
Thy long, long bills, whence nothing is deducted | 916 Juan | 10 | 552
Who did not limit much his bills per week | 916 Juan | 10 | 555
And tradesmen, with long bills and longer faces | 946 Juan | 13 | 351
They and their bills, 'Arcadians both,' are left | 946 Juan | 13 | 353

BILL'S
And cannot find a bill's small items costly | 922 Juan | 11 | 244

BILLY
And Chatham, so like his friend Billy | 177 Devil's Dr | | 144
Why, how now, Billy Bowles | 237 Bowles | | 5

BILLY'S
Were their reward for following Billy's banners | 912 Juan | 10 | 284

BIN
Also there bin another pious reason | 944 Juan | 13 | 201

BIND
The spectres whom no exorcism can bind | 58 Harold | 4 | 214
'Twill bind my soul in bonds to thee | 128 Lady-C | | 6
Yet shall you never bind me fast | 143 To-A | | 13
If early habits--those false links, which bind | 208 Sketch | | 43
Lo! wreaths of yew, not laurel, bind thy brow | 245 Bards | | 267
What should it be that thus their faith can bind | 341 Corsair | 1 | 181
Oh! this is all that still to earth can bind | 354 Corsair | 2 | 487
Escaped the baffled wreath that strove to bind | 364 Corsair | 3 | 620
When headsman's hands prepared to bind | 401 Parisina | | 446
And bind his wound--then calmly lit his pipe | 428 Island | 3 | 106
To bind me in existence--in a life | 490 Manfred | 2 | 498
Which bind the good more firmly. When, oppress'd | 513 Faliero | 2 | 294
Would not suffice to bind where virtue is not | 514 Faliero | 2 | 392
Ties which bind man to man, to emulate | 599 Foscari | 1 | 263
I would bind in my youth and glorious years | 706 Werner | 4 | 120
Hath but two objects, how to serve and bind | 746 Juan | Ded | 115
As if 'twere one whereon magicians bind | 758 Juan | 1 | 758
Such chains as his were sure to bind | 813 Juan | 3 | 760
Good to the soul which we no more can bind | 820 Juan | 4 | 238
But here he was!--where each tie that can bind | 885 Juan | 8 | 427
Who neither wishes to be bound nor bind | 899 Juan | 9 | 206
And as for chastity, you'll never bind it | 940 Juan | 12 | 637
You bind yourself, and call some mode the best
  one | 955 Juan | 14 | 14

BINDER
And sent them down stairs to the binder | 234 Ballat | | 7

BINDING
Binding all things with beauty;--'twould disarm | 46 Harold | 3 | 849
A league is still a compact, and more binding | 532 Faliero | 4 | 300

BINDS
Ideal shape of such; yet still it binds | 73 Harold | 4 | 1103
Which binds us in your humble train | 101 Marion | | 54
Or binds his brow | 206 Year | | 20
Yet binds them to their trysting-place | 397 Parisina | | 60
Which link the burning chain that binds | 409 Mazeppa | | 240

BIOGRAPHY
Are good manure for their more bare biography | 814 Juan | 3 | 844

BIPEDS
A dubious scent would lure the bipeds back | 305 Age | | 561

BIRD
(See also DESERT-BIRD, SEA-BIRD, WILD-BIRD)
As eagerly the barr'd-up bird will beat | 37 Harold | 3 | 132
At intervals, some bird from out the brakes | 48 Harold | 3 | 817
Dim o'er the bird of darkness' native site | 71 Harold | 4 | 950
My Lesbia's favourite bird is dead | 87 Catullus | | 3
For thou hast ta'en the bird away | 88 Catullus | | 20
As some lone bird, without a mate | 156 Lady-F | | 19
A bird of free and careless wing | 172 Romaic-B | | 13
My bird of love! my beauteous mate | 172 Romaic-B | | 27
My bird! relent: one note could give | 172 Romaic-B | | 31
To the poor bird whose pinion fluttering down | 206 Greece | | 7
And a bird in the solitude singing | 210 Augusta-B | | 47
Torn from thy parent bird to form a pen | 242 Bards | | 9
The loveliest bird of Franguestan | 315 Giaour | | 506
And like the bird whose pinions quake | 318 Giaour | | 842
'Tis true, that, like that bird of prey | 321 Giaour | | 1163
The bird that sings within the brake | 321 Giaour | | 1169

BIRD

The bird that tears that prostrate form	335 Abydos	2	613
A bird unseen--but not remote	336 Abydos	2	690
And these the notes the bird of beauty sung	343 Corsair	1	346
A wild bird and a wanderer	384 Corinth		39
To see such bird in such a nest	403 Chillon		78
It was the carol of a bird	405 Chillon		252
That bird was perch'd, as fond and tame	405 Chillon		266
A lovely bird, with azure wings	405 Chillon		268
Sweet bird! I could not wish for thine	405 Chillon		282
The tropic bird wheel'd rockward to his nest	424 Island	2	413
The startled echo of the ocean bird	430 Island	4	16
Wept over, 'but thou wouldst not!' As the bird	456 Dante	1	62
And bird, wolf, vulture, more humane than they	459 Dante	2	85
Hath ripp'd her bosom; had the bird a voice	506 Faliero	1	471
The fluttering bird, hath ere this time out-stept me	673 Werner	1	85
Deserted by the bird she thought a nightingale	710 Werner	4	381
Where nor fish, beast, bird, nor worm	729 Deformed	1	466
The first bird of the covey! he has fallen	737 Deformed	2	164
About this time a beautiful white bird	786 Juan	2	745
'Twas well this bird of promise did not perch	786 Juan	2	754
With mist, and every bird with him awakes	791 Juan	2	1110
And her voice was the warble of a bird	793 Juan	2	1203
To see her bird reposing in his nest	795 Juan	2	1340
And flew to her young mate like a young bird	798 Juan	2	1518
To the young bird the parent's brooding wings	815 Juan	3	947
(That royal bird, whose tail's a diadem	876 Juan	7	590
I think I hear a little bird, who sings	884 Juan	8	395
And where is 'Fum' the Fourth, our 'royal bird	928 Juan	11	612
To quaff a brook which murmur'd like a bird	948 Juan	13	448

BIRD-LIKE

Her right hand--her lank, bird-like right hand--stood	580 Sardan	4	110

BIRDS

(See also MOCK-BIRDS, SEA-BIRDS, SONG-BIRDS, SUMMER-BIRDS)

Birds, beasts of prey, and wilder men appear	26 Harold	2	377
With all her reckless birds upon the wing	40 Harold	3	269
Awoke the jocund birds to early song	43 Harold	3	462
A populous solitude of bees and birds	51 Harold	3	950
Which reigns when mountains tremble, and the birds	64 Harold	4	573
Clip not our pinions ere the birds can fly	113 Prologue		18
Shrieking their dirge, ill-omen'd birds resort	121 Newstead-A		99
Birds, yet in freedom, shun the net	172 Romaic-B		9
And woke from Slumber--as the Birds awake	185 Julian		56
And gnash'd their teeth and howl'd. The wild birds shriek'd	189 Darkness		32
The birds and beasts and famish'd men at bay	189 Darkness		49
Birds breed not vipers, tigers nurse not lambs	257 Hints		20
Like birds when soars the falcon; and they felt	288 Vision		202
Pick'd by the birds, on the sands of the bay	389 Corinth		478
The wild birds flew; the wild dogs fled	396 Corinth		1059
And hear the warbling birds! the damsels said	419 Island	2	4
The barks, like small birds through a lowering sky	429 Island	3	180
The haunt of birds, a desert to mankind	430 Island	4	11
The note of meaner birds, and every tongue	459 Dante	2	31
Which cheers the birds to song shall bid them glow	461 Dante	3	66
These birds of Paradise but long to flee	463 Dante	3	169
And left them to the savage beasts and birds	472 Morgante		432
For brutes of burthen, not for birds of prey	484 Manfred	2	36
Where the birds dare not build, nor insect's wing	485 Manfred	2	158
Startled the slumbering birds from the hush'd boughs	490 Manfred	2	506
And dwell the tuneless birds of night, amidst	495 Manfred	3	283
Made and far sweeter voices of the birds	662 Heaven		557
And the birds scream their agony through air	669 Heaven		1065
And sent forth evening songs from sweetest birds	670 Heaven		1181
Of flight, that if thou wert a snail, not birds	700 Werner	3	351
In vain. The birds--how joyously they sing	723 Deformed	1	70
Of birds on yon oak	728 Deformed	1	403
With birds from their nest	742 Deformed	3	41
To the buds; and birds are winging	743 Deformed	3	73
Of bees, the voice of girls, the song of birds	762 Juan	1	983
A language, too, but like to that of birds	818 Juan	4	108
Like birds, or boys, or bedlamites broke loose	856 Juan	6	266
And singing birds without were heard to warble	864 Juan	6	779
(Widows of forty were these birds long caged	895 Juan	8	1051
Besides fish, beasts, and birds. 'The sparrow's fall	899 Juan	9	149
For cats and birds more penchant ne'er display'd	913 Juan	10	399

BIRD'S

(See also PREY-BIRD'S, SEA-BIRD'S)

Nor matin bird's new voice was borne	413 Mazeppa		663
The forest shade--the green bough--the bird's voice	643 Cain	2	468
The vesper bird's which seems to sing of love	643 Cain	2	469

BIRD'S

Beating for love, as the caged bird's for air	855 Juan	6	203

BIRDS'

(See also PREY-BIRDS')

Than the birds' matins; and my Adah, my	630 Cain	1	184

BIRD'S-EYE

A bird's-eye view, too, of that wild, Society	957 Juan	14	107

BIRON

Which gave her dukes the graceless name of 'Biron	914 Juan	10	460

BIRTH

Oh, thou! in Hellas deem'd of heavenly birth	3 Harold	1	1
To give the Morrow birth	5 Harold	1	127
From birth till death enslaved; in word, in deed, unmann'd	31 Harold	2	710
Their birth, their blood, and that sublime record	32 Harold	2	790
When Grecian mothers shall give birth to men	33 Harold	2	795
(So perish monuments of mortal birth	33 Harold	2	808
And scarce regret the region of his birth	34 Harold	2	870
Mix'd with thy spirit, blended with thy birth	36 Harold	3	53
The enslavers and the enslaved, their death and birth	45 Harold	3	638
Breathed from the birth of time: the veil they rent	48 Harold	3	772
As if they did rejoice o'er a young earthquake's birth	49 Harold	3	877
Too much adoring; whatsoe'er thy birth	72 Harold	4	1034
Though from our birth the faculty divine	74 Harold	4	1139
Born with her birth. No; he shall not expire	77 Harold	4	1345
To view the huge design which sprung from such a birth	78 Harold	4	1368
Which from the birth of monarchy hath rung	80 Harold	4	1534
Since title deck'd my higher birth	85 To E--		6
Oh! cease to affirm that man, since his birth	93 First Kiss		21
On one by birth predestined to be great	93 Dorset		22
When Nature stamp'd thy beauteous birth	97 To M--		9
Fair shone the sun on Oscar's birth	102 Alva		37
Nor wealth nor birth their treasures yield	113 Cornelian-A		18
Unsullied only where it marks your birth	127 Recoll		404
'Unknown the region of his birth	127 Answer-B		5
Perchance I may strive to distinguish my birth	129 Becher-A		8
Rose by far the fairest birth	139 Anacreon-C		9
My name obscure, unmark'd my birth	146 Adieu		86
Derision sneers upon thy birth	150 My Son		15
A Father guards thy birth, my Boy	150 My Son		24
Unknown to glory, but upheld by birth	154 Dog		2
The distant shore which gave me birth	157 Florence		2
Display who gave us birth	161 War Song		4
To trace the birth and nursery of art	162 Orchomenus		2
As aught of mortal birth	167 Dead		2
This fabric's birth attests the potent spell	169 Address-A		25
Hail thou! who on my birth bestow'd	171 Time-B		5
Lament that even thou hadst birth	185 Belshaz-A		23
Wild meteor of immortal birth	188 On Star		5
With their breath, and from their birth	188 Ode-B		85
Where are the past?--and wherefore had they birth	192 Fragment-C		32
Half to the ardour which its birth bestows	193 Monody		76
As various as the climates of our birth	198 Po		40
In Youth, Birth, Beauty, genially allied	199 Sonnet-D		7
For the dungeon he quits is the place of his birth	202 Avatar		16
Till now, when the isle which should blush for his birth	203 Avatar		89
If she ever gave birth to a being so base	203 Avatar		96
It cannot quit its place of birth	217 Gazelle		17
And where the furthest heaven had birth	220 Clay		19
Some years before your birth, to Rogers	227 Thurlow-B		16
Tongues have expired with those who gave them birth	244 Bards		196
Her place of birth, her own Achaian shore	253 Bards		872
Babe of a city birth! from sixpence take	264 Hints		517
Emblem of all to whom the land gives birth	270 Minerva		136
As dull Boeotia gave a Pindar birth	270 Minerva		150
What nature made him at his birth, as bare	286 Vision		86
But nought to mark its breeding or its birth	294 Vision		596
Knows not his name, or but his death, and birth	298 Age		36
To date the birth and death of all it hid	299 Age		104
Freedom and peace to that which boasts his birth	301 Age		248
Where Freedom dates her birth with that of Time	302 Age		215
Spark of that flame, perchance of heavenly birth	311 Giaour		11
Ere from the cloud that gave it birth	315 Giaour		50
From joyaunce ne'er derived its birth	318 Giaour		858
I never loved him from his birth	325 Abydos	1	134
Who blest thy birth and bless thee now	325 Abydos	1	157
That saw my solitary birth	330 Abydos	2	168
And how my birth, disclosed to me	331 Abydos	2	224
To these should I my birth disclose	331 Abydos	2	272
The knowledge of my birth secured	332 Abydos	2	290
That white rose takes its tender birth	336 Abydos	2	716
Bestows on most of mortal mould and birth	370 Lara	1	322
And if from Lara's blood and gentle birth	372 Lara	1	474

BIRTH

No gift beyond that bitter boon--our birth	374	Lara	1	553
Of higher birth he seem'd and better days	374	Lara	1	574
But mighty Nature bounds as from her birth	375	Lara	2	5
Whom birth and nature meant not for his foes	378	Lara	2	235
His gentle sires--he drew his birth	385	Corinth		116
And with thy very crime, my birth	399	Parisina		257
Albeit my birth and name be base	399	Parisina		282
So fit a pair had never birth	408	Mazeppa		102
Our means, our birth, our nation, and our name	417	Island	1	117
Highborn (a birth at which the herald smiles	422	Island	2	214
Once renegades to that which gave them birth	426	Island	3	14
It is no marvel; from my very birth	438	Tasso		149
But Thou--when all that Birth and Beauty throws	440	Tasso		241
When Faintness, the last mortal birth of Pain	453	Venice-B		38
That which it was the moment ere our birth	453	Venice-B		55
Yet aids the warrior worthy of his birth	460	Dante	2	124
There where the farthest suns and stars have birth	460	Dante	3	9
His country's, and might die where he had birth	465	Dante	4	136
Of the form of thy birth	490	Manfred	2	458
How many years is 't? Ere Count Manfred's birth	494	Manfred	3	215
The rights of place and choice, of birth and service	502	Faliero	1	147
In evil hour was I so born; my birth	506	Faliero	1	454
From my equality with you in birth	540	Faliero	5	204
Well? 'Tis thy natal ruler--thy birth planet	562	Sardan	2	66
From birth to manhood! My life waits your breath	592	Sardan	5	326
Birth, wealth, health, beauty, are her accidents	606	Foscari	2	341
Without our act or choice as birth, so that	607	Foscari	2	363
Forgive--What? My poor mother, for my birth	617	Foscari	4	160
Before thy birth: let me not see renew'd	628	Cain	1	40
To which that birth has brought me. Why did he	628	Cain	1	69
Here let me die: for to give birth to those	637	Cain	2	68
Cursed he not me in giving me my birth	639	Cain	2	228
Cursed he not me before my birth, in daring	639	Cain	2	229
To whom we owe so much besides our birth	646	Cain	3	43
Before our birth, or need have victims to	647	Cain	3	90
Restore the beauty of her birth	661	Heaven		466
Thy death is nearer than thy recent birth	661	Heaven		501
And, as the latest birth of his great word	666	Heaven		793
Oh! my dear father's tents, my place of birth	669	Heaven		1044
And worthy by its birth to match with ours	673	Werner	1	128
But had my birth been all my claim to match	673	Werner	1	130
Thy birth, thy hopes, thy pride; nought save thy sorrows	673	Werner	1	146
My husband pants! and such his pride of birth	682	Werner	1	725
Certain. I have lived and served here since my birth	683	Werner	2	15
His birth is doubtful. How so? His sire made	684	Werner	2	94
Have rank by birth and soldiership, and friends	685	Werner	2	165
Of doubtful birth, can startle a grandee	694	Werner	2	744
Noble by birth, of one of the first houses	709	Werner	4	293
In Saxony. I talk not of his birth	709	Werner	4	294
Of wonderful endowments: birth and fortune	717	Werner	5	244
Means my good lord! That you have given birth	721	Werner	5	546
And mischief-making monkey from his birth	750	Juan	1	194
And how the deuce they ever could have birth	758	Juan	1	731
Sweet to the father is his first-born's birth	762	Juan	1	990
Their place of birth alone is mute	812	Juan	3	698
For good or evil, burning from its birth	823	Juan	4	443
Before Pelides' death, or Homer's birth	829	Juan	4	832
'To hear and to obey' had been from birth	845	Juan	5	889
Though what is soul or mind, their birth or growth	855	Juan	6	175
Her very place of birth was but a spectre	896	Juan	8	1125
But I am half a Scot by birth, and bred	909	Juan	10	135
But though I owe it little but my birth	915	Juan	10	523
In birth, in rank, in fortune likewise equal	943	Juan	13	153
So many troubles from her birth beset her	958	Juan	14	195
I reck not if an acorn gave it birth	963	Juan	14	468
Proud of his birth, and proud of every thing	964	Juan	14	554
Although her birth and wealth had given her vogue	974	Juan	15	379
As doubtless should be people of high birth	982	Juan	16	134
The company whose birth, wealth, worth, has cost	998	Juan	17	100

BIRTHDAY

Than any since the birthday of typography	814	Juan	3	846

BIRTHDAYS

On birthdays, glorious with a star and string	964	Juan	14	558

BIRTHPLACE

Clarens, sweet Clarens, birthplace of deep Love	50	Harold	3	923
Birthplace of heroes, sanctuary of saints	459	Dante	2	58
Which had its birthplace in a star condemn'd	479	Manfred	1	44
I have quitted my birthplace	479	Manfred	1	96
My fathers' and my birthplace, whose dear spires	506	Faliero	1	464
So I be buried in my birth-place: better	597	Foscari	1	138

BIRTHRIGHT

Our manors and our birthright stood	197	Duel		31
Thou sold'st thy birthright, Esau! for a mess	306	Age		632
Like Esau, for my birthright a beef-steak	837	Juan	5	352

BIRTHS

So different in their births, tongues, sexes, natures	591	Sardan	5	232
And the new births of both their stale virginities	814	Juan	3	855
And noble births, nor dread the enumeration	962	Juan	14	412

BIRTH'S

Proud (as is birth's prerogative); but under	707	Werner	4	180

BIS

And only shouted, 'Allah!' and 'Bis Millah	868	Juan	7	104

BISCAY'S

And winds are rude in Biscay's sleepless bay	6	Harold	1	199

BISCUIT

Two casks of biscuit and a keg of butter	779	Juan	2	367

BISCUIT-CASKS

And also for the biscuit-casks and butter	781	Juan	2	488

BISHOP
(See also COUNT-BISHOP)

Which made Dr. Nott not a bishop	238	Bray		6
And from bishop sink into backbiter	239	Bray		54
I smote the tardy bishop at Treviso	504	Faliero	1	339
Of festival, the sluggish bishop who	546	Faliero	5	596
When Bishop Berkeley said 'there was no matter	918	Juan	11	1
A difference ''twixt a bishop and a dean	991	Juan	16	717

BISHOPS

Shorn of her bishops, banks, and dividends	307	Age		648
'Have I not had two bishops at my feet	765	Juan	1	1193
Fatal to bishops as to soldiers--these	888	Juan	8	602
But though three bishops told her the transgression	914	Juan	10	443
Bishops, who had not left a single sermon	949	Juan	13	549
Queens, bishops, knights, rooks, pawns; the world's a game	952	Juan	13	706

BISHOP'S

No very great way from a bishop's abode	176	Devil's Dr		30

BISMILLAH

'Bismillah! now the peril's past	316	Giaour		568

BIT
(See also FROST-BIT)

Fit retribution! Gaul may champ the bit	38	Harold	3	163
The devil a bit of	232	Murray-B		11
Who's so damnably bit	232	Murray-B		61
Freed from the bit, believe themselves with wings	299	Age		46
With slacken'd bit and hoof of speed	312	Giaour		181
White is the foam of their champ on the bit	392	Corinth		700
Mouths bloodless to the bit or rein	413	Mazeppa		681
And bit her lips (for else she might have scream'd	753	Juan	1	430
To beg his pardon when I err a bit	761	Juan	1	960
Of a foe o'er him, snatch'd at it, and bit	889	Juan	8	666
Some heiresses have bit at sharpers' hooks	928	Juan	11	635
Republics also get involved a bit	930	Juan	12	45

BITCHES

Like lap-dogs, the least civil sons of b---s	923	Juan	11	328
Than witches, b--ches, or physicians brew	976	Juan	15	496
Not witches only b---ches--who create	997	Juan	17	52

BITE

The power to bark and bite, to toss and gore	303	Age		405
And pick it up, and bite it to the core	862	Juan	6	612
That madmen may not bite you on a visit	921	Juan	11	196

BITES

The foremost Tartar bites the ground	316	Giaour		573
The steed bites the bridle	742	Deformed	3	25
And that his Argus--bites him by the breeches	804	Juan	3	184

BITING

Beneath the biting wind and heavy rain	672	Werner	1	26

BITS

The country for some missing bits of coin	700	Werner	3	325
And there we go:--but where? five bits of lead	836	Juan	5	306

BITTEN

But after inky thumbs and bitten nails	262	Hints		385

BITTER

Some bitter o'er the flowers its bubbling venom flings	17	Harold	1	818
And feed on bitter fruits without accusing Fate	36	Harold	3	63
So shall a better spring less bitter fruit bring forth	69	Harold	4	382

BITTER

A dying father's bitter curse	105	Alva	315
Thou bitter pledge! thou mournful token	166	Struggle	49
The bitter moments thou hast given	172	Time-B	10
Are doubly bitter from that thought	172	Not False	4
And that too bitter moment o'er	174	Remember-B	27
The bitter harvest in a woe as real	213	Lady Byron	24
Thou canst not hear my bitter pleading	221	Marianne	6
Smug Sydney too thy bitter page shall seek	248	Bards	512
Dependence barters for her bitter bread	267	Hints	774
Bitter as clubs in cards are against spades	292	Vision	478
Too bitter--is it not so?--in thy gloom	295	Vision	662
As if that eye and bitter smile	318	Giaour	848
And shown by many a bitter sign	321	Giaour	1111
Through many a busy bitter scene	322	Giaour	1238
Betray no further than the bitter smile	341	Corsair 1	230
Too faithful, though to bitter bondage chain'd	360	Corsair 3	323
No gift beyond that bitter boon--our birth	374	Lara 1	553
The bitter print of each convulsive nail	377	Lara 2	116
In youth a bitter Nazarene	387	Corinth	319
More revenge in bitter speaking	394	Corinth	868
Oh! that parting hour was bitter	400	Parisina	426
They play'd me then a bitter prank	411	Mazeppa	413
Which felt exhaustion's deep and bitter drouth	417	Island 1	148
Mix'd with those bitter thoughts the soul arrays	429	Island 3	205
Alas! how bitter is his country's curse	457	Dante 1	69
A bitter lesson; but it leaves me free	458	Dante 1	176
To gloomy verdure and to bitter fruit	521	Faliero 3	165
When thy patricians beg their bitter bread	548	Faliero 5	757
Your fathers were mine enemies, as bitter	605	Foscari 2	228
I judge but by the fruits--and they are bitter	628	Cain 1	78
For its own bitter sake? None--nothing! 'tis	642	Cain 2	445
But few! and some of those but bitter. Back	646	Cain 2	654
That bitter laugh! Who would read in this form	673	Werner 1	114
With aught more bitter. Never shall it do so	713	Werner 5	31
And that is better than the bitter truth	730	Deformed 1	585
Welcome the bitter hunchback! and his master	733	Deformed 1	787
Thou bitter slave! to name him at this time	737	Deformed 2	140
Up Juan sprung to Haidee's bitter shriek	821	Juan 4	289
Acquire the deep and bitter power to give	830	Juan 4	852
Which (though I hate to say a thing that's bitter	910	Juan 10	204
Perhaps he long'd in bitter frosts for climes	912	Juan 10	293
Which form that bitter draught, the human species	916	Juan 10	584
Whose ripeness is but bitter at the best	962	Juan 14	426
Of those sweet bitter thoughts which banish sleep	995	Juan 16	927

BITTERER

So honour'd but assumes a stronger, bitterer claim	40	Harold 3	279
Is bitterer still. As charm by charm unwinds	73	Harold 4	1100
And then against them bitterer than ever	297	Vision	772
And is herself the cause of bitterer tears	552	Sardan 1	95
Bitterer to bear than any punishment	559	Sardan 1	542
And if there were no other nearer, bitterer	598	Foscari 1	208

BITTEREST

That peaceful still 'twixt bitterest foemen flow	9	Harold 1	374
This soul, in its bitterest blackness, shall be	182	Music-A	14
God grant you feel not then the bitterest grief	766	Juan 1	1255
Old flames, new wives, become our bitterest foes	909	Juan 10	95

BITTERLY

To this which beats so bitterly. Now, bear	589	Sardan 5	163
My heart aches bitterly. I pray you sit	625	Foscari 5	287

BITTERNESS

The child of love, though born in bitterness	53	Harold 3	1094
Scarce seen, but with fresh bitterness imbued	58	Harold 4	201
Were those hours--can their joy or their bitterness cease	182	Music-A	6
Of half its bitterness for one so dear	183	Address-A	34
Of bitterness--thy Hope--thy heart so dull	184	Julian	43
Felt without bitterness--but full and clear	192	Monody	15
Rush,--the swoln flood of bitterness I pour	196	Vittorelli	13
Till Nothing but the Bitterness remain	201	Ode-A	36
Such mirth hath less of play than bitterness	344	Corsair 1	419
And smiles in bitterness--but still it smiles	353	Corsair 2	449
In bitterness that banish'd all remorse	379	Lara 2	271
Till its unsocial bitterness is gone	437	Tasso	15
I weed all bitterness from out my breast	438	Tasso	107
Rocks, and the salt-surf weeds of bitterness	484	Manfred 2	58
Of bitterness--until this last loud insult	525	Faliero 3	490
And pangs, and bitterness; these were the fruits	641	Cain 2	356
The bitterness of tears	655	Heaven	49
The wholesome bitterness of life, know well	695	Werner 3	32

BITTERS

I have tasted the sweets and the bitters of love	129	Becher-A	25
'Tis true there be some bitters with the sweets	981	Juan 16	21

BITUMEN

And the lakes of bitumen	479	Manfred 1	90

BITUMINOUS

The dungeon vapours its bituminous smoke	609	Foscari 3	55

BIVARAMBLA

Of Bivarambla on he goes	194	Ballad-A	4

BLACK
(See also BRIGHT-BLACK, COAL-BLACK, DEATH-BLACK, JET-BLACK)

Mark'd her black eye that mocks her coal-black veil	13	Harold 1	569
Nodding above; behold black Acheron	27	Harold 2	456
Black with the miner's blast, upon her height	44	Harold 3	555
And now again 'tis black,--and now, the glee	49	Harold 3	875
All things are here of him; from the black pines	51	Harold 3	941
And thy limbs black with lightning--dost thou yet	68	Harold 4	791
Or sparkles black, or mildly throws	97	To Woman	15
Now swift or slow, now black or clear	137	Clare	23
Of the black and sulphurous fight	187	Ode-A	55
Extinguish'd with a crash--and all was black	189	Darkness	21
Black with the rude collision, inly torn	193	Monody	91
By the black wind that chills the polar flood	198	Po	44
Till the black slime betray her as she crawls	208	Sketch	48
Black--as thy will for others would create	209	Sketch	90
Though black as his heart its hue	229	Lads	11
With hand less mighty, but with heart as black	247	Bards	444
Black eyes, black ringlets, but--a bottle nose	257	Hints	58
New ornaments for black and royal guards	276	Waltz	164
Of scribblers, wits, lecturers, white, black, and blue	280	Blues 2	17
Save the recording angel's black bureau	285	Vision	20
Made the attraction, and the black the wo	286	Vision	76
Black Hassan from the Haram flies	314	Giaour	439
From the black cloud that bound it	327	Abydos 1	337
More glittering eye, and black brow's sabler gloom	349	Corsair 2	149
Though its black orb those long low lashes' fringe	373	Lara 1	538
To bound as doubting from too black a dream	374	Lara 1	621
With deeper skill in war's black art	385	Corinth	97
Wring the black drop from thy heart	390	Corinth	579
The past a blank, the future black	400	Parisina	364
I only stirr'd in this black spot	404	Chillon	212
And bounded by a forest black	411	Mazeppa	431
Headed by one black mighty steed	413	Mazeppa	702
With her black eyes so wild and free	414	Mazeppa	812
Remorse for the black deed as yet half done	417	Island 1	157
A black rock rears its bosom o'er the spray	430	Island 4	10
Black eyes, arch'd brows, and sweet expressions still	441	Beppo	82
Mankind with her black eyes for looking at her	443	Beppo	184
And large black eyes that flash on you a volley	445	Beppo	355
Of half a century bloody and black	458	Dante 1	135
Whose splendour from the black abyss is flung	463	Dante 3	188
The black blood in its blackest spring	481	Manfred 1	235
Canst thou be black with evil?--say not so	484	Manfred 2	81
The black plague flew o'er it	488	Manfred 2	336
Let it be black among your dreams; and when	503	Faliero 1	274
And freedom to the rest, or leave it black	509	Faliero 1	622
Thou must be cleansed of the black blood which makes thee	519	Faliero 3	8
To syllable black deeds into smooth names	519	Faliero 3	58
But this day, black within the calendar	535	Faliero 4	504
Black with a double treason, now will earn	537	Faliero 4	646
And for this funeral marriage, this black union	546	Faliero 5	584
Her large black eyes, that flash'd through her long hair	577	Sardan 3	388
From their black gulf to daunt the living--Myrrha	579	Sardan 4	37
That's a black augury! it has been said	590	Sardan 5	195
Those black and bloody leaves, his heart and brain	606	Foscari 2	336
And black with smoke, and red with--Speak, my son	652	Cain 3	393
And a black circle, bound	668	Heaven	1005
He had join'd the black bands, who lay waste Lusatia	685	Werner 2	124
Or deal you in the black art? I deal plainly	697	Werner 3	132
Begins to grizzle the black hair of night	704	Werner 3	582
They say he is leagued with the 'black bands' who still	709	Werner 4	301
For black--it is so honest, and besides	727	Deformed 1	373
Shall our bonny black horses skim over the ground	730	Deformed 1	566
They are black ones, to be sure. So, you are learn'd	731	Deformed 1	666
The black bands came over	732	Deformed 1	691
Cannon's black mouth, shining spear	735	Deformed 2	30
Match'd with Bourbon's black banditti	736	Deformed 2	65
Her streaming hair; the black curls strive, but fail	766	Juan 1	1261
Their throats were ovens, their swoln tongues were black	785	Juan 2	683
Just like a black eye in a recent scuffle	785	Juan 2	735
Were black as death, their lashes the same hue	789	Juan 2	930
As black, but quicker, and of smaller size	789	Juan 2	976
And when, at last, he open'd his black eyes	790	Juan 2	1044
And his black curls were dewy with the spray	792	Juan 2	1174

BLACK

Their large black eyes, and soft seraphic cheeks	805	Juan	3	258
For those large black eyes were so blackly fringed	810	Juan	3	595
Juan had on a shawl of black and gold	811	Juan	3	609
Dwarfs, dancing girls, black eunuchs, and a poet	811	Juan	3	618
I see their glorious black eyes shine	813	Juan	3	775
That large black prophet eye seem'd to dilate	819	Juan	4	169
Of her black eyes seem'd turn'd to tears, and mirk	820	Juan	4	262
That I must have recourse to black Bohea	823	Juan	4	414
Glazed o'er her eyes--the beautiful, the black	825	Juan	4	551
Bright--and as black and burning as a coal	828	Juan	4	749
Meantime (yon old black eunuch seems to eye us	834	Juan	5	191
Just now a black old neutral personage	834	Juan	5	201
Let's knock that old black fellow on the head	837	Juan	5	343
As the black eunuch enter'd with his brace	838	Juan	5	425
To thrust its black eyes through the door or lattice	838	Juan	5	439
The black, however, without hardly deigning	839	Juan	5	521
I wish to be perspicuous; and the black	840	Juan	5	529
While he was dressing, Baba, their black friend	840	Juan	5	545
By this old black enchanter's unsought aid	842	Juan	5	664
Whose colour was not black, nor white, nor grey	842	Juan	5	700
Her brow grew black, but she would not upbraid	847	Juan	5	997
And then his Highness' eunuchs, black and white	850	Juan	5	1162
His Highness cast around his great black eyes	851	Juan	5	1233
The black bough) tear-drops through her eyes' dark fringes	860	Juan	6	536
A low soft ottoman), and black despair	865	Juan	6	861
For seeing one with ribands, black and blue	885	Juan	8	453
And black silk neckcloth--and replied, 'You're right	891	Juan	8	791
White, black, or copper--the dead bones will grin	898	Juan	9	96
A scarlet coat, black facings, a long plume	902	Juan	9	338
A quintessential laudanum or 'black drop	905	Juan	9	533
Too wise to look through optics black or blue	905	Juan	9	568
The Dee, the Don, Balgounie's brig's black wall	909	Juan	10	139
In this gay clime of bear-skins black and furry	910	Juan	10	203
Black Edward's helm, and Becket's bloody stone	916	Juan	10	578
By those who love to say that white is black	929	Juan	11	710
Black letter upon foolscap, while our hair	930	Juan	12	7
Upon the black loam long manured by Vice	934	Juan	12	319
No doubt I should be told that black is fair	938	Juan	12	560
It is. I will not swear that black is white	938	Juan	12	561
But I suspect in fact that white is black	938	Juan	12	562
An eye's an eye, and whether black or blue	941	Juan	13	19
Who look'd a white lamb, yet was a black sheep	951	Juan	13	632
A little black upon this new flirtation	960	Juan	14	338
O Wilberforce! thou man of black renown	965	Juan	14	649
Broke in upon by the Black Friar of late	985	Juan	16	276
'Oh! have you never heard of the Black Friar	985	Juan	16	281
Beware! beware! of the Black Friar	985	Juan	16	321
But beware! beware! of the Black Friar	986	Juan	16	353
Then grammercy! for the Black Friar	986	Juan	16	365
Her black, bright, downcast, yet espiegle eye	989	Juan	16	561

BLACKBIRD

And be the only Blackbird in the dish	745	Juan	Ded	20

BLACKBIRDS

Like 'four and twenty Blackbirds in a pye	745	Juan	Ded	8

BLACKEN

Which strove to blacken o'er thy ray	209	Augusta-A		18
And of its cold protector, blacken round	365	Corsair	3	676

BLACKEN'D

But o'er the blacken'd memory's blighting dream	43	Harold	3	458
Now daily mutters o'er his blacken'd fame	377	Lara	2	122
All blacken'd there and reeking lay	396	Corinth		1056

BLACKENING

Blackening her lovely domes with traces rude	11	Harold	1	481
The blight and blackening which it leaves behind	58	Harold	4	211
Beneath the covert of the blackening smoke	106	Nisus		105
From the swoll'n veins the blackening torrents pour	108	Nisus		251
Nisus no more the blackening shade conceals	110	Nisus		363
Oblivion's blackening lake is seen	118	Romance		61
Till blackening ashes and the lonely wall	169	Address-A		15
Swung blind and blackening in the moonless air	189	Darkness		5
From the bile, whose blackening river	197	Rogers		57
From off the scorch'd and blackening roof	410	Mazeppa		405
From out yon tuft of blackening firs	413	Mazeppa		670
By blackening publicly his sovereign's consort	515	Faliero	2	435

BLACKENS

The veil which blackens o'er this blighted name	545	Faliero	5	503

BLACKER

Perchance the second blacker than the first	271	Minerva		206
With each convulsion, in a blacker gush	381	Lara	2	421

BLACKEST

The brightest or blackest, is fill'd with my fame	186	Napoleon		4
Who thundering comes on blackest steed	312	Giaour		180
To blackest shade, nor will endure a guide	365	Corsair	3	661
The black blood in its blackest spring	481	Manfred	1	235
To many men the blackest. It may be	697	Werner	3	133
Even by its darkness; as the blackest sky	756	Juan	1	578

BLACK-EYED

When first Spain's queen beheld the black-eyed boy	12	Harold	1	511
His black-eyed maids of Heaven, angelically kind	13	Harold	1	611
What do I see? The black-eyed Roman, with	725	Deformed	1	185
Who only saw the black-eyed girls in green	892	Juan	8	884
These black-eyed virgins make the Moslems fight	892	Juan	8	909
Who on a lark, with black-eyed Sal (his blowing	921	Juan	11	151

BLACKGUARD

And blackguard Hunt and Cobby O	235	New Song		12

BLACKGUARDS

'Arcades ambo,' id est--blackguards both	828	Juan	4	744
We have no accomplish'd blackguards, like Tom Jones	955	Juan	13	879

BLACKING

And a long eulogy of 'patent blacking	983	Juan	16	208

BLACK-IT

And if he did, 'twere shame to 'Black-it	163	Blacket		16

BLACKLEG

Where scarce a blackleg bears a brighter name	260	Hints		242
Horse by a blackleg, broadcloth by a tailor	834	Juan	5	207

BLACKLY

It glides along the water looking blackly	442	Beppo		150
For those large black eyes were so blackly fringed	810	Juan	3	595

BLACKNESS

In the same dust and blackness, and we pass	62	Harold	4	412
This soul, in its bitterest blackness, shall be	182	Music-A		14
The blackness of my bosom wore	322	Giaour		1199
Almost to blackness in its demon hue	376	Lara	2	74
I felt the blackness come and go	412	Mazeppa		550
And all is ice and blackness,--and the earth	453	Venice-B		54

BLACKS

And dwarfs and blacks, and such like things, that gain	810	Juan	3	541
All save the blacks seem'd jaded with vexation	832	Juan	5	53
With whites and blacks, in groups on show for sale	832	Juan	5	74
Four blacks were at his elbow in a trice	841	Juan	5	640
You have freed the blacks--now pray shut up the whites	965	Juan	14	656

BLACK-SMITH

And that his father was an honest black-smith	869	Juan	7	156

BLACKSTONE'S

While Blackstone's on the shelf neglected laid	111	Examination		20

BLADDER

Like wind compress'd and pent within a bladder	294	Vision		591
As would have fill'd a bladder, while he lay	688	Werner	2	329

BLADDERS

On those bouyant supporters, the bladders of rhyme	227	Moore-A		4

BLADE

The idle forge that form'd Toledo's blade	303	Age		347
Waving her more than Amazonian blade	303	Age		369
Down glanced that hand, and grasp'd his blade	312	Giaour		246
Or blade to bid thy foeman bleed	319	Giaour		929
But brands of foreign blade and hilt	330	Abydos	2	124
Upon its steel direct my blade	331	Abydos	2	190
Some erring blade or ball should glance	334	Abydos	2	532
Select the arms--to each his blade assign	338	Corsair	1	49
Till the blade glimmers in the grasp of death	350	Corsair	2	252
The skill with which he wielded his keen blade	377	Lara	2	142
His blade is bared,--in him there is an air	380	Lara	2	344
Or whirl around the bickering blade	385	Corinth		113
He look'd on the long grass--it waved not a blade	390	Corinth		525
So is the blade of his scimitar	392	Corinth		706
Nor of its fields a blade of grass	410	Mazeppa		397
Full in thine eyes is waved the glittering blade	416	Island	1	71
A few shrunk wither'd twigs, and from the blade	432	Island	4	143
Take mine. I will. But in your heart the blade	564	Sardan	2	158
The reeking bayonet and the flashing blade	887	Juan	8	547
In lieu of a bare blade and brazen front	920	Juan	11	117

BLADES
From the point of encountering blades to the hilt 392 Corinth 767
Which scarcely rose much higher than grass blades 884 Juan 8 376

BLAIR
I study, also Blair, the highest reachers 795 Juan 2 1318

BLAKE
And keep your bushy locks a year from Blake 263 Hints 476

BLAMABLE
A habit rather blamable, which is 870 Juan 7 193

BLAME
Here, where the Roman millions blame or praise 76 Harold 4 1274
'Tis I that am alone to blame 98 To Lesbia 13
And made us blush that you forbore to blame 170 Address-A 57
In sooth 'twere hard to blame thy haste 173 Quotation 10
Whose busy accents whisper blame 174 Remember-B 14
Nor can I blame thee, though it be my lot 206 Love, Death 23
Yet I blame not the world, nor despise it 210 Augusta-B 33
A schoolboy freak, unworthy praise or blame 242 Bards 49
Or, kind to dulness, do you fear to blame 250 Bards 611
Nor one facetious paragraph of blame 265 Hints 614
But then I blame the man himself much less 293 Vision 563
I do not ask him not to blame 322 Giaour 1244
Yet harsh be they that blame 336 Abydos 2 709
Not much could Conrad of his sentence blame 352 Corsair 2 370
Where history's pen its praise or blame supplies 368 Lara 1 189
But haughty still and loth himself to blame 371 Lara 1 331
Teasing with blame, excruciating with praise 449 Beppo 589
As you perceive, yet without fear or blame 469 Morgante 179
But blame our ignorance and this poor place 475 Morgante 624
I blame you not, you act in your vocation 527 Faliero 3 577
I understand you, now. And blame me? No 593 Sardan 5 369
Your exile as he bears it. Blame him not 611 Foscari 3 224
The ancient world for love. I cannot blame him 725 Deformed 1 237
But, if you rue it after, blame not me 741 Deformed 2 403
I'm not to blame, as you well know--no more is 751 Juan 1 243
The blame on me, unless you wish they were 803 Juan 3 92
But then their own Polygamy's to blame 851 Juan 5 1262
And so must tell the truth, howe'er you blame it 853 Juan 6 60
And wherefore blame gaunt wealth's austerities 930 Juan 12 54
For silly wards will bring their guardians blame 935 Juan 12 332
People are apt to blame the Fates, forsooth 936 Juan 12 395
Of passions, too, I have proved enough to blame 956 Juan 14 68
A heterogeneous mass of glorious blame 975 Juan 15 451

BLAMED
But secretly himself Orlando blamed 475 Morgante 587
The lost days of time past, which may be blamed 475 Morgante 604
His patient, and perhaps was to be blamed 889 Juan 8 678
That is, when they succeed; but greatly blamed 966 Juan 14 708

BLAMES
Who blames it but the envious fool 92 Lady-A 5
Yet rarely blames unjustly, now declare 256 Bards 1070

BLANC
Glaciers of bleak Mont Blanc both far and near 66 Harold 4 656
Mont Blanc is the monarch of mountains 479 Manfred 1 60

BLANCH
Will blanch a faithful cheek 6 Harold 1 165

BLAND
Kinder than polish'd slaves though not so bland 29 Harold 2 606
A little pressure, thrilling, and so bland 755 Juan 1 564
It may seem strange to find his manners bland 807 Juan 3 373
In liquid lines mellifluously bland 831 Juan 5 2

BLANDISHMENTS
Once passion's tumultuous blandishments knew 99 L Adieu 26
And who, though proof against all blandishments 544 Faliero 5 428

BLANK
A blank; a thing to count and curse 172 Time-B 30
And rhyme and blank maintain an equal race 243 Bards 146
Breaks into blank the Gospel of St. Luke 246 Bards 323
More books of blank upon the sons of men 247 Bards 386
With rhyme by Hoare, and epic blank by Hoyle 255 Bards 966
But which deserves the laurel, rhyme or blank 258 Hints 111
Blank verse is now, with one consent, allied 258 Hints 117
The Earl of--Asterisk, and Lady--Blank 276 Waltz 203
He had written much blank verse, and blanker
  prose 297 Vision 783
The past a blank, the future black 400 Parisina 364
For all was blank, and bleak, and grey 405 Chillon 239
With all their blank, or dismal stains, than is 610 Foscari 3 119
Such as would leave your scutcheon but a blank 692 Werner 2 565
And when his bones are dust, his grave a blank 813 Juan 3 801
The blank grey was not made to blast their hair 817 Juan 4 67
Such as--'Unless Miss (Blank) meant to have
  chosen 934 Juan 12 269

BLANK
With other Countesses of Blank--but rank 951 Juan 13 633

BLANK-BLANK
At Blank-Blank Square;--for we will break no
  squares 944 Juan 13 193
Lord Henry's mansion was in Blank-Blank Square 944 Juan 13 200
At Henry's mansion then, in Blank-Blank Square 944 Juan 13 217

BLANKER
He had written much blank verse, and blanker
  prose 297 Vision 783

BLANKET
And Melville's Mantle prove a blanket too 252 Bards 748
Was such as fire accords to a wet blanket 806 Juan 3 288

BLANKETS
As there were but two blankets for a sail 780 Juan 2 380
Two blankets stitch'd together, answering ill 781 Juan 2 483

BLANK-VERSE
Prose poets like blank-verse, I'm fond of rhyme 771 Juan 1 1605

BLASE
A little 'blase'--'tis not to be wonder'd 940 Juan 12 645

BLASPHEME
Voluptuous Waltz! and dare I thus blaspheme 277 Waltz 248
I would not so blaspheme our country's creed 554 Sardan 1 232
Blaspheme not: these are serpent's words. Why
  not 628 Cain 1 35
Blaspheme and groan 670 Heaven 1167
Went raging mad--Lord! how they did blaspheme 784 Juan 2 628

BLASPHEMED
And most devoutly Macon still blasphemed 470 Morgante 278
And Juan, too, blasphemed an octave higher 769 Juan 1 1470

BLASPHEMER
Blasphemer! darest thou murmur even now 668 Heaven 1028

BLASPHEMERS
But such blasphemers 'gainst all honour, as 542 Faliero 5 316

BLASPHEMES
My liege--the son of Belus! he blasphemes 565 Sardan 2 236

BLASPHEMIES
With blasphemies enough to break their jaws 451 Beppo 683
But while his crude, rude blasphemies he heard 470 Morgante 279
And villanous jests, and blasphemies obscene 502 Faliero 1 191
'That Scriptures out of church are blasphemies 953 Juan 13 768

BLASPHEMING
Women screeching, tars blaspheming 157 Hodgson 7
Lying at its foot blaspheming 736 Deformed 2 92

BLASPHEMOUS
'Tis blasphemous; I know one may be damn'd 286 Vision 106

BLASPHEMY
Doom'd to bewail the blasphemy of laws 45 Harold 3 615
Shrink not from blasphemy, 'twill pass for wit 242 Bards 72
And the half-inarticulate blasphemy 437 Tasso 68
This blasphemy, had never fallen upon thee 513 Faliero 2 278
Strange sounds of wailing, blasphemy, devotion 778 Juan 2 271
Platonic blasphemy, the soul of swearing 924 Juan 11 344

BLAST
(See also ALL-BLASTING)
One blast might chill him into misery 4 Harold 1 31
Beat back keen winter's blast, and welcomed
  summer's heat 26 Harold 2 387
Long shall the voyager, with th' Ionian blast 34 Harold 2 857
Black with the miner's blast, upon her height 44 Harold 3 555
Though young, yet waxing vigorous, as the blast 46 Harold 3 695
There the hot shaft should blast whatever therein
  lurk'd 50 Harold 3 895
The escutcheon and shield, which with every blast
  rattle 86 Leaving NA 7
Oh, shield me from the wintry blast 88 Anacreon-B 17
That voice!--ah, no, 'tis but the blast 91 Caroline-B 39
Will sleep in the grave till the blast shall
  awake us 91 Caroline-C 23
I blast not the fiends who have hurl'd me from
  bliss 92 Caroline-D 6
And seek to blast the honours of thy name 93 Dorset 26
He spreads his young wing, he retires with the
  blast 100 L Adieu 35
Shall dastard tongues essay to blast the name 114 Death-A 9
The man doom'd to sail with the blast of the gale 115 The Tear 13
Chill'd by misfortune's wintry blast 128 Remembrance 4
blast of the mountain 129 Calmar 15

BLAST

We heed no more the wintry blast	133	E. N. Long		57
How do thy branches, moaning to the blast	138	Harrow-B		13
And wayworn strangers shrink amid the blast	139	Ossian-A		34
Keen as your storms is Sorrow's chilling blast	140	Ossian-A		50
Loud o'er the plain is heard the northern blast	140	Ossian-B		40
She will not blast her native strain	141	Critics		10
And bade her blast a heart she never knew	142	Soliloquy		30
Untouch'd, then, my Lyre shall reply to the blast	148	Farewell-A		29
Loud sings on high the fresh'ning blast	156	Lady-F		4
Had braved the death-wing'd tempest's blast	158	Florence		31
Chill and mirk is the nightly blast	158	Storm		1
The Waves arose and roll'd beneath the blast	184	Julian		3
For the Angel of Death spread his wings on the blast	222	Sennacherib		9
On half-strung harps whine mournful to the blast	244	Bards		154
His hopes have perish'd by the northern blast	247	Bards		421
His blossoms wither as the blast prevails	247	Bards		423
When fame's loud trump hath blown its noblest blast	254	Bards		957
The fleets that sweep before the eastern blast	299	Age		107
Roused by the blast of winter, rave	316	Giaour		627
Sear'd by the autumn blast of grief	322	Giaour		1256
Oh! how the chill blast on my bosom blew	343	Corsair	1	381
His bugle--brief the blast--but shrilly blew	349	Corsair	2	166
By that tremendous blast	395	Corinth		1027
The eagle rode the rising blast	406	Chillon		353
Bewilder'd with the dazzling blast	412	Mazeppa		515
I swept upon the blast	479	Manfred	1	105
The barren sands which bear no shrubs to blast	493	Manfred	3	130
A miscreant's angry breath may blast it all	514	Faliero	2	421
Which, like the sheeted fire from heaven, must blast	526	Faliero	3	542
Beneath the mountain shadow; or the blast	578	Sardan	4	13
All safe off to your boats, blow one long blast	593	Sardan	5	386
The snow on the hills cannot blast her bower	742	Deformed	3	10
Laid with one blast the ship on her beam ends	777	Juan	2	240
The blank grey was not made to blast their hair	817	Juan	4	67
Sadder than owl-songs or the midnight blast	961	Juan	14	394

BLASTED

Blasted below the dun hot breath of war	11	Harold	1	498
Kindled he was, and blasted; for to be	47	Harold	3	736
His Holy of Holies, nor be blasted by his brow	78	Harold	4	1395
Then the Eagle, whose gaze in that moment was blasted	186	Napoleon		15
At once, and blasted by the thunder-stroke	219	Saul-B		14
The thunder came; that bolt hath blasted both	365	Corsair	3	672
Grey-hair'd with anguish, like these blasted pines	482	Manfred	1	327
And how feel you? As rocks. By thunder blasted	613	Foscari	3	334
Even as the Simoom sweeps the blasted plains	823	Juan	4	456
The bleeding flower and blasted fruit of love	825	Juan	4	560
As e'er was locust on the land it blasted	871	Juan	7	288

BLASTS

Scowling defiance on the blasts of fate	119	Newstead-A		8
Thy face, O Sun, no rolling blasts deform	139	Ossian-A		19
And in absence blasts and sears you	197	Rogers		46

BLAZE

Alike beheld beneath pale Hecate's blaze	22	Harold	2	193
When gleaming with meridian blaze	97	To M--		18
Retiring from the garish blaze of day	120	Newstead-A		20
Though sunk the radiance of his former blaze	122	Recoll		23
With him I would wish to expire in the blaze	129	Becher-A		16
blaze of oak dim-twinkles through the night	130	Calmar		99
Whence are the beams, O Sun! thy endless blaze	139	Ossian-A		3
The pale Moon sickens in thy brightening blaze	140	Ossian-B		7
But vainly now on me thy beauties blaze	140	Ossian-B		21
Consumed in Glory's blaze	146	Adieu		84
Now quenches all their blaze in night	148	A Fan		8
As glared the volumed blaze, and ghastly shone	169	Address-A		13
Eternity flash'd through thy blaze	188	On Star		8
The beams of Song, the blaze of Eloquence	193	Monody		28
No torch is kindled at its blaze	206	Year		11
I saw thee smile--the sapphire's blaze	218	I Saw		5
Nor blaze with guilty glare through future time	253	Bards		827
As pious Calvin saw Servetus blaze	262	Hints		377
But one unclouded blaze of living light	268	Minerva		4
Vesuvius shows his blaze, an usual sight	300	Age		181
Lest spies less true should let the blaze expire	343	Corsair	1	378
Their galleys blaze--why not their city too	350	Corsair	2	195
But one unclouded blaze of living light	355	Corsair	3	4
The beacons blaze their wonted stations round	363	Corsair	3	558
The unwonted faggots' hospitable blaze	366	Lara	1	8
Of skies more cloudless, moons of purer blaze	368	Lara	1	176
Alas! they blaze too widely for the flight	379	Lara	2	329
I saw its turrets in a blaze	410	Mazeppa		402
Wrapp'd in one blaze; the pure, yet funeral pile	424	Island	2	380
Humming like flies around the newest blaze	449	Beppo		587
Shall blaze with beauty and with light, until	560	Sardan	1	603
Things as catch fire and blaze with one sole spark	591	Sardan	5	277

BLAZE

A blaze of torches from without. As sure	678	Werner	1	429
Not even a sprightly blunder's spark can blaze	746	Juan	Ded	101
And the blood's lava, and the pulse a blaze	797	Juan	2	1486
A little scorch'd at present with the blaze	889	Juan	8	718
In one voluptuous blaze,--and then he died	893	Juan	8	920
Thousands blaze, love, hope, die,--how happy they	908	Juan	10	64
On him the diamond pours its brilliant blaze	930	Juan	12	62
On the most favour'd; and amidst the blaze	945	Juan	13	262
Imposed not upon her: she saw her blaze	975	Juan	15	442

BLAZED

On the smooth shore the night-fires brightly blazed	30	Harold	2	631
I stood beside the grave of him who blazed	190	Churchill		1
Which shook the nations through his lips and blazed	193	Monody		45
Had reflected the last beam of day as it blazed	221	Jerusalem		10
Blazed, as he bent no more to rise	394	Corinth		880
Then seized a torch which blazed thereby	395	Corinth		962
Blazed through the clouds of death and beckon'd hence	433	Island	4	264
Then flash'd the flint, and blazed the volleying flame	434	Island	4	295
Blazed o'er the general revel of the night	435	Island	4	416
While the whole rampart blazed like Etna, when	879	Juan	8	55
Blazed, and the cannon's roar was scarce allay'd	895	Juan	8	1060

BLAZES

It blazes there but will not burn	141	Critics		36
Exhales her odours, blazes, and expires	255	Bards		960

BLAZING

(See also EVER-BLAZING)

Now on the smoke of blazing bolts she flies	10	Harold	1	409
A thousand altars rise, for ever blazing bright	14	Harold	1	674
armies: but the blazing oaks gleam through	130	Calmar		36
by the side of the blazing oak. Strumon	130	Calmar		134
The same art ever, blazing in the sky	140	Ossian-B		16
In one short hour beheld the blazing fane	169	Address-A		3
And men were gather'd round their blazing homes	189	Darkness		14
Look to the Baltic--blazing from afar	271	Minerva		213
Would flying burghers mark the blazing town	272	Minerva		304
A conscious twilight of his blazing reign	299	Age		90
Her turret-torch was blazing high	329	Abydos	2	7
Far flash'd on high a blazing torch	334	Abydos	2	500
His blazing galleys still distract his sight	349	Corsair	2	180
And down came blazing rafters, strown	396	Corinth		1053
Of slaves and traitors. In this blazing palace	595	Sardan	5	480

BLAZON

Can blazon evil deeds or consecrate a crime	4	Harold	1	27
And Love, which lent a blazon to their shields	42	Harold	3	435
No fiction of fame shall blazon my name	115	The Tear		47
And blazon Britain's thousand glories higher	417	Island	1	162
And blazon o'er the door their names in brass	922	Juan	11	248

BLAZON'D

Where blazon'd glare names known to chivalry	8	Harold	1	294
If they require it to be blazon'd forth	509	Faliero	2	69

BLAZON-ROLL

Their pure high blood, their blazon-roll of glories	519	Faliero	3	32

BLEACH'D

Let their bleach'd bones and blood's unbleaching stain	18	Harold	1	906

BLEACHED

Shall perish, and their bleached bones shall lurk	661	Heaven		439

BLEAK

More bleak to view the hills at length recede	9	Harold	1	351
He pass'd bleak Pindus, Acherusia's lake	26	Harold	2	415
In bleak Thermopylae's sepulchral strait	31	Harold	2	699
And the bleak battlements shall bear no future blow	42	Harold	3	423
Of bleak, gray granite into life it came	58	Harold	4	179
Glaciers of bleak Mont Blanc both far and near	66	Harold	4	656
Four brothers enrich'd with their blood the bleak field	86	Leaving NA		18
Hills of Annesley! bleak and barren	95	Fragment-B		1
I loved my bleak regions, nor panted for new	135	Highlander		14
I left my bleak home, and my visions are gone	136	Highlander		25
And left a channel bleak and bare	315	Giaour		559
For all was blank, and bleak, and grey	405	Chillon		239
The rest was one bleak precipice, as e'er	430	Island	4	25
In some bleak crag or deeply-hidden bay	433	Island	4	242
To wring his soul--as the bleak elements	682	Werner	1	723
'Twas a raw day of Autumn's bleak beginning	832	Juan	5	41
When the stripp'd forest bows to the bleak air	889	Juan	8	700

BLEAKNESS
If Britain mourn her bleakness, we can tell her — 950 Juan 13 607

BLEATING
Thy suing to these men were but the bleating — 543 Faliero 5 394
And piteous bleating of its restless dam — 643 Cain 2 497
To the pain of the bleating mothers which — 650 Cain 3 300

BLED
Cities from out their sepulchres. Men bled — 68 Harold 4 795
And only healer when the heart hath bled — 74 Harold 4 1164
In the sad midnight, while thy heart still bled — 80 Harold 4 1508
What though he knows not how his fathers bled — 111 Examination 13
The humbler ranks, the lowly brave, who bled — 182 Address-C 15
Reversing the spot where you bled — 237 Farce 2
As dark as his that bled below — 317 Giaour 674
Had bled or wept to see him die — 335 Abydos 2 616
By that same hand Abdallah--Selim bled — 336 Abydos 2 654
He bled, and fell; but not with deadly wound — 376 Lara 2 69
Since first Timoleon's brother bled — 385 Corinth 59
Who there in better cause had bled — 388 Corinth 395
Had fought and bled in mutual sacrifice — 427 Island 3 46
Against a bank, and spoke not, but he bled — 427 Island 3 98
The breast which would have bled for her, the heart — 457 Dante 1 86
Hast thou not bled? and hast thou still to bleed — 458 Dante 2 15
Shed where Christ bled for man; and his high harp — 462 Dante 3 122
I have fought and bled; commanded, ay, and conquer'd — 506 Faliero 1 459
By those for whom thou hast bled. No, I will speak — 507 Faliero 1 506
Which I have bled for, and thou foreign earth — 548 Faliero 5 730
He but requested to be bled to death — 783 Juan 2 601
The surgeon had his instruments, and bled — 783 Juan 2 602
And Persian carpets, which the heart bled to stain — 810 Juan 3 539
Must we but blush?--Our fathers bled — 812 Juan 3 726
(As he bled inwardly, no hideous river — 835 Juan 5 278
Which for the last, though not the first, time bled — 836 Juan 5 292
In vain he kick'd, and swore, and writhed, and bled — 888 Juan 8 661

BLED'ST
The heart for which thou bled'st is bleeding — 221 Mariamne 2

BLEED
Happier, that while all younger hearts shall bleed — 3 To Ianthe 24
A scene where mingling foes should boast and bleed — 11 Harold 1 462
Nor bleed these patriots with their country's wounds — 11 Harold 1 489
Alas! too oft condemn'd for him to bear and bleed — 16 Harold 1 746
So may he make each curst oppressor bleed — 18 Harold 1 898
When Gratitude or Valour bids them bleed — 29 Harold 2 584
The heart's bleed longest, and but heal to wear — 48 Harold 3 789
I planted,--they have torn me--and I bleed — 56 Harold 4 89
Bleed gladiator-like, and still engage — 69 Harold 4 844
I bleed withal, and, had it been conferr'd — 75 Harold 4 1191
Arm'd thus, to make their bosoms bleed — 98 To Lesbia 33
That instant, Davus, it deserves to bleed — 126 Recoil 286
Till Fate can ordain that his bosom shall bleed — 147 To Anne-B 15
But would you make our bosoms bleed — 148 To Author 13
And smile to see them bleed — 176 Devil's Dr 14
But there are breasts that bleed with thee — 184 Parker 25
If unprovoked thou once could bid me bleed — 265 Hints 607
Nor tamely stand to bleed — 316 Giaour 584
Or blade to bid thy foeman bleed — 319 Giaour 929
Long have I led them--not to vainly bleed — 343 Corsair 1 331
Who but the love of him he dooms to bleed — 350 Corsair 2 223
That hated tyrant, Conrad--he must bleed — 360 Corsair 3 319
They bleed within that silent cell--his breast — 362 Corsair 3 479
Looks on the bleeding foe that made him bleed — 381 Lara 2 439
No more to combat and to bleed — 407 Mazeppa 4
Them on where each would foremost bleed — 409 Mazeppa 292
And therefore do I weep and inly bleed — 437 Tasso 41
Admire and sigh, and then succumb and bleed — 453 Venice-B 79
Hast thou not bled? and hast thou still to bleed — 458 Dante 2 15
Nor sect, nor faction, did I bleed or sweat — 506 Faliero 1 468
Millions of hearts which bleed to lend it lustre — 700 Werner 3 338
To share their sports or pleasures. Must I bleed too — 722 Deformed 1 37
Juan, who saw the moon's late minion bleed — 920 Juan 11 109
Or wish to make a rival's bosom bleed — 939 Juan 12 614

BLEEDING
Mix'd on the bleeding stream, by floating hosts oppress'd — 9 Harold 1 386
Foil'd, bleeding, breathless, furious to the last — 16 Harold 1 774
The last poor plunder from a bleeding land — 21 Harold 1 114
Yet still, my girl, this bleeding breast — 90 Caroline-A 7
And heals the bleeding wounds of wearied hate — 121 Newstead-A 112
Forbade my bleeding breast to own — 156 Lady-F 59
My wounded soul, my bleeding breast — 172 Romaic-B 41
The bleeding phantom of each martial form — 182 Address-C 25

BLEEDING
France o'er hosts of hirelings bleeding — 187 Ode-B 39
Still must mine, though bleeding, beat — 207 Fare Thee 26
And where shall Israel lave her bleeding feet — 217 Weep-B 5
The heart for which thou bled'st is bleeding — 221 Mariamne 2
Drank the last life-drop of his bleeding breast — 253 Bards 848
Bequeath'd by bleeding sire to son — 311 Giaour 124
With wounded wing, or bleeding breast — 314 Giaour 410
Fell'd--bleeding--baffled of the death he sought — 351 Corsair 2 277
Some bleeding--all most wretched--these the few — 356 Corsair 3 87
He saw him bound; and bleeding--but alive — 357 Corsair 3 109
They raised the bleeding Otho, and the Leech — 376 Lara 2 89
'Twas Lara bleeding fast from life away — 381 Lara 2 417
Looks on the bleeding foe that made him bleed — 381 Lara 2 439
Bound, naked, bleeding, and alone — 415 Mazeppa 851
Together, bleeding, thirsty, faint, and few — 426 Island 3 26
Rome at her feet lies bleeding; and the hue — 459 Dante 2 76
Ask of the bleeding pelican why she — 506 Faliero 1 470
Down to the earth, strew'd with their bleeding fruit — 527 Faliero 3 615
Pale, bleeding, and a man with a raised knife — 707 Werner 4 196
And bleeding like a sacrifice. My own — 718 Werner 5 317
The bleeding body--but it moved no more — 718 Werner 5 334
Ah! behold yon bleeding spectre — 736 Deformed 2 71
But sunk again upon his bleeding knee — 788 Juan 2 866
His own anxiety, his heart, too, bleeding — 807 Juan 3 366
No novels e'er had set their young hearts bleeding — 818 Juan 4 148
O'er the sharp shingles with her bleeding feet — 820 Juan 4 250
The bleeding flower and blasted fruit of love — 825 Juan 4 560

BLEEDS
Vainly his incense soars, his victim bleeds — 20 Harold 2 26
Such as arises when a nation bleeds — 80 Harold 4 1497
Beneath whose arm the Hydra bleeds — 88 Anacreon-A 16
In vain beneath unnumber'd wounds he bleeds — 110 Nisus 391
Whose breast for every bosom bleeds — 118 Romance 44
Alas! the breast that inly bleeds — 321 Giaour 1155
But inly views his victim as he bleeds — 357 Corsair 3 140
For Fame is there to say who bleeds — 389 Corinth 487
Alas! for them the flower of mankind bleeds — 419 Island 2 37
For what? My heart bleeds for you. For me, signor — 602 Foscari 2 27
The body bleeds in the presence of the assassin — 619 Foscari 4 242
And talk of weapons unto that which bleeds — 669 Heaven 1054

BLENCH
But blench not thou--thy simplest tress — 327 Abydos 1 353
And do their worst: I shall not blench for them — 556 Sardan 1 357
Which, it may be, are menaced;--yet I blench not — 558 Sardan 1 531

BLEND
But bid me with my wreath one matchless lily blend — 3 To Ianthe 36
Alas, when mingling souls forget to blend — 23 Harold 2 205
And grief with grief continuing, still to blend — 34 Harold 2 907
Partly because they blend me with his line — 39 Harold 3 255
My voice shall with thy future visions blend — 53 Harold 3 1073
The insulted mind he sought to quench, and blend — 60 Harold 4 321
Blend a celestial with a human heart — 73 Harold 4 1064
The choir did oft their mingling vespers blend — 120 Newstead-A 35
We learn at length our faults to blend — 153 Friend-A 38
And blend, while ages roll away — 169 Blank Leaf 11
When heart with heart delights to blend — 322 Giaour 1219
Blend every thought, do all--but disunite — 333 Abydos 2 425
Of murmuring Liberty's wide waves, which blend — 863 Juan 6 742
A maddening spirit which would strive to blend — 905 Juan 9 580
As all must blend whose part it is to aim — 993 Juan 16 805

BLENDED
Mix'd with thy spirit, blended with thy birth — 36 Harold 3 53
For Freedom's hand had blended them — 188 On Star 23
And ne'er shall its soft tones be blended — 222 Babylon 17
Adeline and Don Juan rather blended — 975 Juan 15 483

BLENDING
A blending of all beauties,--streams and dells — 42 Harold 3 411
With an immortal's patience blending. Vain — 79 Harold 4 1435
No more with affection shall memory blending — 136 Delawarr 13
At once such majesty with sweetness blending — 175 Sonnet-B 13
And blending every colour into one — 785 Juan 2 734
Without more preface, in her blue eyes blending — 846 Juan 5 925
And dignity with courtesy so blending — 993 Juan 16 804

BLENDS
The verse which blends the censor with the friend — 118 Answer-A 2
When Pleasure blends no base alloy — 141 Pignus 22
New havoc, such as civil discord blends — 377 Lara 2 164
And blends itself into the soul, until — 587 Sardan 5 20

BLENHEIM
Wat Tyler--Rhymes on Blenheim--Waterloo — 297 Vision 768

BLENHEIM'S
'Another Marlborough points to Blenheim's story — 171 Address-B 23

BLENT

Rider and horse,--friend, foe,--in one red burial			
blent	39 Harold	3	252
With such an aspect, by his colours blent	175 Sonnet-A		9
Though sometimes with our visions blent	656 Heaven		74
But must with thyself be blent	729 Deformed	1	469

BLESS

With none who bless us, none whom we can bless	23 Harold	2	229
Thou still hadst lived to bless my aching sight	85 Epitaph		9
A soul, if well matured, to bless mankind	93 Dorset		36
To bless thy Allan's happy lot	104 Alva		202
What poor rewards can bless your deeds on earth	107 Nisus		135
Her dying hours with pious conduct bless	108 Nisus		191
But bless the hour when Pitt resign'd his breath	114 Death-A		2
Loudly carousing, bless their lord's return	121 Newstead-A		118
And bless thy future as thy former day	122 Newstead-A		156
I bless the former, and forgive the last	123 Recoll		54
But bless the scroll which fairer words adorn	127 Recoll		409
Your coming days and years may bless	138 Clare		92
Her favour'd worshippers will bless	141 Critics		16
And bless thee in my last adieu	156 Lady-F		62
And bless the gods--I've got a fever	163 Malta		56
I bless thy purer soul even now	174 Remember-B		19
For who would lift a hand, except to bless	199 Sonnet-E		8
Think of him whose prayer shall bless thee	207 Fare Thee		39
And Memory wakes the thoughts that bless	223 Music-D		3
And bless the promise which his form displays	250 Bards		623
On Britain's sons and bless our genial isle	252 Bards		788
We bless thee still--for George the Third is left	274 Waltz		44
A good deal older--Bless me! is he blind	293 Vision		544
To bless the sacred 'bread and salt	313 Giaour		343
Shall bless thee with a father's name	318 Giaour		769
And thou wilt bless thee from the rage	320 Giaour		977
To bless his memory ere I died	322 Giaour		1241
Who blest thy birth and bless thee now	325 Abydos	1	157
But conscious shepherds bless it still	329 Abydos	2	43
Thou, my Zuleika, share and bless my bark	333 Abydos	2	396
But shall we see them? will their accents bless	339 Corsair	1	112
For such as he was wont to bless	397 Parisina		78
He bends to hear his accents bless	400 Parisina		416
Which two worlds bless for civilising both	425 Island	2	487
Bless me! your beard is of amazing growth	451 Beppo		726
To--bless me! did I ever? No, I never	451 Beppo		735
All hearts are happy, and all voices bless	571 Sardan	3	17
The pleasures of a parent! Bless him, Cain	648 Cain	3	154
His heart will, and thine own too. Bless thee,			
boy	648 Cain.	3	156
But bless him ne'er the less. Our brother comes	648 Cain	3	161
I turn'd to bless the spot	670 Heaven		1186
By the immortal wish and power to bless	819 Juan	4	208
Which made him daily bless his own neutrality	866 Juan	6	936

BLESS'D

'My father bless'd me fervently	6 Harold	1	150
All that ideal beauty ever bless'd	79 Harold	4	1454
Our children should obey her child, and bless'd	80 Harold	4	1528
No Oscar bless'd his father's sight	103 Alva		155
Since Oscar's form has bless'd my sight	104 Alva		210
But bless'd thy mother in so dear a son	108 Nisus		204
And few were my wants, for my wishes were bless'd	135 Highlander		15
And bless'd were the scenes of our youth, I allow	136 Delawarr		10
Too much invited to be bless'd	174 Remember-B		6
Think of him thy love had bless'd	207 Fare Thee		40
Though priest nor bless'd, nor marble deck'd the			
mound	382 Lara	2	523
That I may be happy, and he may be bless'd	390 Corinth		564
The silver vessels saints had bless'd	395 Corinth		995
Midst whom my own bright Beatrice bless'd	456 Dante	1	11
Unlaurell'd upon earth, but far more bless'd	463 Dante	4	6
By all thou hast of bless'd in hope or memory	530 Faliero	4	175
A world out of our own, and be more bless'd	583 Sardan	4	356
Another land, and who so bless'd and blessing	621 Foscari	5	74
For not the bless'd sherbet, sublimed with snow	797 Juan	2	1436

BLESSED

The Sabbath comes, a day of blessed rest	15 Harold	1	684
In the orbs of the blessed to shine	151 Soul-A		4
Oh lady! blessed be that tear	152 Weep-A		13
That--but I know thy blessed bosom fraught	175 Sonnet-A		6
And Mary's blessed likeness stands	196 Venice-A		36
Seems blessed harmony to Lamb and Lloyd	254 Bards		906
Benignant o'er those blessed isles	310 Giaour		8
But praying blessed Jesu, he was set	471 Morgante		316
'Then,' quoth the giant, 'blessed be Jesu	472 Morgante		377
One of the blessed, and that I shall die	490 Manfred	2	496
With calm assurance to that blessed place	492 Manfred	3	81
Ay--but not blessed. If the blessedness	634 Cain	1	416
Within our nostrils, who hath blessed us	649 Cain	3	225
Blessed are the dead	670 Heaven		1148
Still blessed be the Lord	670 Heaven		1158
Ave Maria! blessed be the hour	815 Juan	3	905
With her Son in her blessed arms, look'd round	948 Juan	13	483

BLESSEDNESS

| Ay--but not blessed. If the blessedness | 634 Cain | 1 | 416 |
| Of 'single blessedness,' and thought it good | 895 Juan | 8 | 1044 |

BLESSES

| The innocence which happy childhood blesses | 805 Juan | 3 | 261 |

BLESSETH

| Thy presence honours them, and blesseth those | 491 Manfred | 3 | 22 |

BLESSING

Making thy waves a blessing as they flow	42 Harold	3	443
Into a boundless blessing, which may vie	51 Harold	3	966
Fain would I waft such blessing upon thee	53 Harold	3	1101
Oh memory! thou choicest blessing	97 To Woman		7
For the first of my prayers was a blessing on you	136 Highlander		24
Whilst blessing your beloved name	138 Clare		100
A blessing never meant for me	168 Haunts		33
'A double blessing your rewards impart	171 Address-B		51
Blessing him they served so well	187 French-A		16
Kiss his foot with thy blessing, his blessings			
denied	202 Avatar		56
As the blessing I beg ere it flow	218 Jephtha		11
Delightful Bowles! still blessing and still blest	246 Bards		341
Whatever blessing waits a genuine Scot	249 Bards		530
A blessing cheaply purchased, the world knows	304 Age		452
Meantime we stand expectant of your blessing	475 Morgante		615
For madness as a blessing--'tis denied me	486 Manfred	2	223
I could not dissipate; and with the blessing	529 Faliero	4	103
It must be borne. Father, your blessing! Would	617 Foscari	4	153
Another land, and who so bless'd and blessing	621 Foscari	5	74
Oh, God! who loving, making, blessing all	627 Cain	1	18
If that a mortal blessing may avail thee	648 Cain	3	157
Surely a father's blessing may avert	648 Cain	3	159
A blessing, as a mark the less for plunder	737 Deformed	2	179
Thou canst not be my blessing or my curse	773 Juan	1	1716
'Have you no friends?'--'I had--but, by God's			
blessing	833 Juan	4	121
A blessing is sound sleep--Juanna lay	861 Juan	6	578
Smooth'd even the Simplon's steep, and by God's			
blessing	905 Juan	9	527
Heroes must die; and by God's blessing 'tis	921 Juan	11	154

BLESSINGS

Kiss his foot with thy blessing, his blessings			
denied	202 Avatar		56
Behold the blessings of a lucky lot	237 Elegy		1
He tasted empire's blessings and its curse	299 Age		96
And share the blessings which themselves prepared	306 Age		613
Draw blessings from the mountaineer	315 Giaour		540
Rose up, imploring Heaven to send me blessings	535 Faliero	4	502
My wife! Now blessings on thee for that word	583 Sardan	4	309
As died their father. Oh, what best of blessings	618 Foscari	4	210
And next, that we are here to share its blessings	708 Werner	4	255
I thought she had loved me. Blessings on your			
Creed	743 Deformed	3	110

BLESSINGTON'S

| Beneath Blessington's eyes | 239 Impromptu-B | | 1 |

BLEST

Who strike, blest hirelings! for their country's			
good	11 Harold	1	473
For me 'twere bliss enough to know thy spirit			
blest	20 Harold	2	81
More blest the life of godly eremite	23 Harold	2	235
Blest cares! all other feelings far above	28 Harold	2	547
In that absorbing sigh perchance more blest	47 Harold	3	750
Floats through the azure air, an island of the			
blest	59 Harold	4	243
Or to more deeply blest Anchises? or	62 Harold	4	452
From Jove to Jesus--spared and blest by time	77 Harold	4	1308
Blest into mother, in the innocent look	77 Harold	4	1336
'What stranger breaks my blest repose	88 Anacreon-B		12
From what blest inspiration your sonnets would			
flow	92 First Kiss		7
They blest her dear propitious light	101 Alva		18
Slow roll'd the moons, but blest at last	103 Alva		169
By another possest, may she live ever blest	115 The Tear		33
He drives them exiles from their blest abode	120 Newstead-A		46
Ida! blest spot, where Science holds her reign	122 Recoll		43
To love a stranger, friendship made me blest	123 Recoll		56
From learning's labour is the blest retreat	123 Recoll		114
Of those with whom I lived supremely blest	125 Recoll		252
By every son of grateful Ida blest	127 Recoll		363
Blest by the tongues that charm'd my youthful ear	138 Harrow-B		31
And Sleep my soul with gentle visions blest	140 Ossian-A		44
When Life is blest without a crime	141 Pignus		23
It vow'd to make me sweetly blest	144 Jessy		19
The spot which passion blest	146 Adieu		54
Oh! blest had my fate been, and happy my lot	149 Farewell-A		35
Blest be that lip and azure eye	150 Song-A		17
For why should we mourn for the blest	151 Soul-A		16
Thy husband's blest--and 'twill impart	154 Happy		5

BLEST

Line	Page	Work		
While thou art blest I'll not repine	155	Happy		18
Yet if blest to the utmost that love can bestow	155	Goblet		17
Which once my warmest wishes blest	156	Lady-F		10
I ask no pledge to make my blest	163	Parting		9
But if in worlds more blest than this	165	Thyrza		49
And blest with Virtue's soul and Fortune's store	199	Sonnet-D		8
Oh! blest be thine unbroken light	209	Augusta-A		13
More blest each palm that shades those plains	217	Gazelle		13
Delightful Bowles! still blessing and still blest	246	Bards		341
Blest be the banquets spread at Holland House	249	Bards		544
Oh! blest retreats of infamy and ease	250	Bards		668
With names of greater note in blest repose	252	Bards		754
Arise! let blest remembrance still inspire	252	Bards		805
Blest is the man who dares approach the bower	253	Bards		867
But doubly blest is he whose heart expands	253	Bards		873
Then, hapless Britain! be thy rulers blest	255	Bards		1011
"Blest paper credit;" who shall dare to sing	271	Minerva		245
Then flamed of Austerlitz the blest despatch	274	Waltz		69
Blest was the time Waltz chose for her debut	276	Waltz		161
For whose blest surnames--vide Morning Post	276	Waltz		205
The blest Alliance, which says three are all	303	Age		395
Thrice blest Verona! since the holy three	303	Age		412
By every breeze and season blest	310	Giaour		29
Without even savage virtue blest	311	Giaour		155
And come what may, I have been blest	321	Giaour		1115
I would not, if I might, be blest	322	Giaour		1269
Who blest thy birth and bless thee now	325	Abydos	1	157
To clasp the neck of him who blest	325	Abydos	1	185
Blest--as the Muezzin's strain from Mecca's wall	333	Abydos	2	402
The blest alternative of fraud or force	333	Abydos	2	435
No danger daunts the pair his smile hath blest	333	Abydos	2	450
At length--'twas noon--I hail'd and blest the mast	343	Corsair	1	385
To share his splendour, and seem very blest	354	Corsair	2	504
Blest are the early hearts and gentle hands	371	Lara	1	391
My words, so may I mingle with the blest	373	Lara	1	481
If you acknowledge the Redeemer blest	471	Morgante		355
With the blest tone which made me! Even so	482	Manfred	1	317
The blest are the dead	488	Manfred	3	346
Instants so high and blest? Blest! He hath been	583	Sardan	4	361
And loved by a young heart, too deeply blest	801	Juan	3	4
Than your sires' 'Islands of the Blest	812	Juan	3	700
Must we but weep o'er days more blest	812	Juan	3	725
Of tyrants, and been blest from shore to shore	897	Juan	9	68

BLEW

Line	Page	Work		
The sails were fill'd, and fair the light winds blew	5	Harold	1	100
Blew where it listed, laying all things prone	51	Harold	3	993
Full swiftly blew the swift Siroc	159	Storm		41
Blew for a little life, and made a flame	190	Darkness		63
He beat all three--and blew it out	225	Youth		4
Then Michael blew his trump, and still'd the noise	296	Vision		753
Oh! how the chill blast on my bosom blew	343	Corsair	1	381
List!--'tis the bugle--Juan shrilly blew	345	Corsair	1	464
Meantime, the steady breeze serenely blew	346	Corsair	1	591
His bugle--brief the blast--but shrilly blew	349	Corsair	2	166
Embark'd, the sail unfurl'd, the light breeze blew	362	Corsair	3	452
And o'er it blew the mountain breeze	406	Chillon		347
Ere Fiji blew the shell of war, when foes	419	Island	2	35
Before the winds blew Europe o'er these climes	419	Island	2	66
A goodly night; the cloudy wind which blew	528	Faliero	4	25
Increased at night, until it blew a gale	777	Juan	2	202
The wind blew fresh again: as it grew late	777	Juan	2	237
Again the weather threaten'd,--again blew	779	Juan	2	329
Than what it had been, for so strong it blew	780	Juan	2	428
'Twas a rough night, and blew so stiffly yet	781	Juan	2	473
So changeable had been the winds that blew	786	Juan	2	798
And blew; another answer'd to the call	822	Juan	4	372
They blew up in the middle of the river	870	Juan	7	223
One bark blew up, a second near the works	871	Juan	7	239
Towards which the impatient wind blew half a gale	915	Juan	10	507

BLIGH

Line	Page	Work		
Awake, bold Bligh! the foe is at the gate	416	Island	1	51
When Bligh in stern reproach demanded where	417	Island	1	159

BLIGHT

Line	Page	Work		
The blight of life--the demon Thought	17	Harold	1	860
When shall her Olive-Branch be free from blight	18	Harold	1	922
But Peace destroy'd what War could never blight	44	Harold	3	560
In fatal penitence, and in the blight	46	Harold	3	663
Of hasty growth and blight, and dull Oblivion bar	56	Harold	4	81
For ye are names no time nor tyranny can blight	57	Harold	4	126
The blight and blackening which it leaves behind	58	Harold	4	211
Through unborn ages, to endure this blight	190	Churchill		18
But should there be to whom the fatal blight	193	Monody		59
All passion blight	200	Stanzas-B		57
Back on thy bosom with reflected blight	209	Sketch		86
But thou and thine shall know no blight	210	Augusta-A		33
For blight and desolation, compass'd round	216	Dream		188
But the unnatural balsams merely blight	286	Vision		85
And yet, though storms and blight assail	336	Abydos	2	677
And blight a form--till thine appear'd, Gulnare	354	Corsair	2	489
Her lover lived,--nor foes nor fears could blight	429	Island	3	195
With all her seasons to repair the blight	454	Venice-B		97
Leans .sculptured Beauty, which Death cannot blight	461	Dante	3	40
In Venice save the Doge, this blight, this brand	513	Faliero	2	277
The bloom or blight of all men's happiness	709	Werner	4	351
Blossom and bough lie wither'd with one blight	825	Juan	4	558

BLIGHTED

Line	Page	Work		
Which blighted their life's bloom and then departed	50	Harold	3	884
Hopes sapp'd, name blighted, Life's life lied away	75	Harold	4	1212
And brand a nearly blighted name	174	Remember-B		16
Sear'd in heart, and lone, and blighted	208	Fare Thee		59
Or Beauty, blighted in an hour	314	Giaour		414
Yet dear to him my blighted name	322	Giaour		1227
Mark how that lone and blighted bosom sears	341	Corsair	1	245
By blighted and remorseful years	401	Parisina		517
And woo Compassion to a blighted name	439	Tasso		217
A blighted trunk upon a cursed root	482	Manfred	1	329
The blighted old age of Faliero, shall	515	Faliero	2	456
And left me a lone blighted thorny stalk	525	Faliero	3	431
The veil which blackens o'er this blighted name	545	Faliero	5	503
Grieve more above the blighted name and ashes	584	Sardan	4	394
And blighted like to mine, which I will add	608	Foscari	3	26
Wait till, like me, your hopes are blighted, till	690	Werner	2	442
Till some confounded escapade has blighted	759	Juan	1	797
To part with all till every hope was blighted	778	Juan	2	255

BLIGHTER

Line	Page	Work		
For this temporary blighter	197	Rogers		70

BLIGHTING

Line	Page	Work		
But o'er the blacken'd memory's blighting dream	43	Harold	3	458
Blighting my life in best of its career	438	Tasso		98
The blighting venom of his sweltering heart	515	Faliero	2	427

BLIND

Line	Page	Work		
Yet to the beauteous form he was not blind	17	Harold	1	819
'Gainst whom he raged with fury strange and blind	47	Harold	3	756
Oh, for one hour of blind old Dandolo	57	Harold	4	107
Though accident, blind contact, and the strong	73	Harold	4	1118
The beam pours in, for time and skill will couch the blind	74	Harold	4	1143
Against their blind omnipotence a weight	80	Harold	4	1538
For once forgetting to be blind	113	Cornelian-A		26
Is Fortune painted truly--blind	179	Gold		26
By gazing on thyself grown blind	180	Ode-A		12
Swung blind and blackening in the moonlight air	189	Darkness		5
Which Flattery fool'd not, Baseness could not blind	208	Sketch		22
Heedless and blind to Wisdom's wasted light	222	Spirit		12
Away with old Homer the blind	234	Ballat		21
Yet warm not wanton, dazzled but not blind	275	Waltz		150
One half as mad, and t'other no less blind	286	Vision		64
With an old soul, and both extremely blind	287	Vision		182
When this old, blind, mad, helpless, weak, poor worm	290	Vision		330
A good deal older--Bless me! is he blind	293	Vision		544
The blind old man of Scio's rocky isle	329	Abydos	2	27
Not blind to fate, I see, where'er I rove	333	Abydos	2	416
Why should I seek?--hath misery made thee blind	360	Corsair	3	290
On Grief's vain eye--the blindest of the blind	365	Corsair	3	659
For it was not the blind capricious rage	377	Lara	2	145
In blind confusion on the foe they press	379	Lara	2	286
Those eyes which would not brook such blind	401	Parisina		447
Blind, boundless, mute, and motionless	405	Chillon		250
And my crush'd heart fell blind and sick	405	Chillon		317
That thou wert beautiful, and I not blind	437	Tasso		55
They peep from out the blind, or o'er the bar	442	Beppo		118
But the world, blind and ignorant, don't prize	466	Morgante		49
Spinning around me--I grow blind--What art thou	483	Manfred	1	376
Those infants, not alone from the blind love	582	Sardan	4	260
Except the base and blind	660	Heaven		410
Still, as they were from the beginning, blind	661	Heaven		493
Which winds its blind but living path beneath you	720	Werner	5	438
Practise in the cool twilight. You are blind	733	Deformed	1	773
Nothing can blind a mortal like to light	744	Deformed	3	146
Think'st thou, could he--the blind Old Man--arise	746	Juan	Ded	81
Eutropius of its many masters,--blind	747	Juan	Ded	117
Unless this world, and t'other too, be blind	767	Juan	1	1316
To all, except one image, madly blind	771	Juan	1	1566
If, after all, there should be some so blind	772	Juan	1	1657
Nor inflammations redden his blind eye	776	Juan	2	176
The present century was growing blind	813	Juan	3	814
Of forms and features; it would strike you blind	843	Juan	5	774
Or as a little dog will lead the blind	873	Juan	7	381
Over the hills, a fire enough to blind	882	Juan	8	236
Oft are soon closed, all heroes are not blind	883	Juan	8	313
Ask a blind man, the best judge. You'll attack	938	Juan	12	564

BLIND
Follies trick'd out so brightly that they blind   975 Juan   15   454

BLINDED
And thine!--but I am blinded by the torch   609 Foscari   3   58

BLINDER
I'll show you a poet that's blinder   234 Ballat   22

BLINDEST
On Grief's vain eye--the blindest of the blind   365 Corsair   3   659

BLINDFOLD
Blindfold he runs groping for fame   234 Ballat   26
A blindfold bondage, where your hire is blows   453 Venice-B   70

BLINDING
Nor faster falls the blinding snow   412 Mazeppa   512

BLINDLY
The sand, nor blindly rushes on his foe   16 Harold   1   752
Short was the conflict; furious, blindly rash   376 Lara   2   67
I could as blindly and remorselessly   596 Foscari   1   64
Or pandering blindly to his own disgrace   759 Juan   1   788

BLINDNESS
And then reproach her with thine own cold blind-
ness   552 Sardan   1   92
Things whose enjoyment was to be in blindness   640 Cain   2   305
For Blindness is the first-born of Excess   666 Heaven   807
And turn him like the Cyclops mad with blindness   808 Juan   3   456

BLINDS
And such the frenzy, whose convulsion blinds   64 Harold   4   561

BLINK
Dogs blink their covey, flints withhold the spark   264 Hints   555

BLINKS
Measure in darkness distance); but it blinks   701 Werner   3   407

BLISS
Who soon had left her charms for vulgar bliss   4 Harold   1   43
For me 'twere bliss enough to know thy spirit
blest   20 Harold   2   81
Still would I steep my lips in bliss   88 To Ellen   3
In songs of bliss and sighs of flame   88 Anacreon-A   26
Since now our dream of bliss is past   89 To Emma   3
Yet I forego that bliss divine   90 To M.S.G.-A   3
Alas, it were unhallow'd bliss   90 To M.S.G.-A   4
Nor melts like mine in dewy bliss   90 Caroline-B   20
Let us pass round the cup of love's bliss in full
measure   91 Caroline-C   27
I blast not the fiends who have hurl'd me from
bliss   92 Caroline-D   6
Thus doom'd but to gaze upon bliss   98 To M.S.G.-B   16
And what was once his bliss appears his bane   100 Damaetas   14
But bliss be aye her heart's partaker   113 Quaker   48
When love was bliss, and Beauty form'd our heaven   122 Recoll   14
And banquet on a transient bliss   128 Lady-C   12
Worth worlds of bliss, that thought alone   131 L'Amitie   19
Prepare a fancied bliss or woe   132 Prayer   30
By every bliss my childhood knew   133 E. N. Long   53
A visionary scene of bliss   135 I Would   22
The bliss which wing'd those rosy hours   137 Clare   4
Partners of former bliss or woes   145 Adieu   6
And care for not Hope, who are certain of bliss   156 Goblet   28
Which gave me bliss or misery   156 Lady-F   14
What bliss amidst these solitudes to share   161 Athos   24
Impart some portion of thy bliss   165 Thyrza   51
Then to the things whose bliss or woe   174 Remember-B   33
Pronounce--if ever in your days of bliss   276 Waltz   222
Even bliss--'twere woe alone to bear   319 Giaour   942
Who falls from all he knows of bliss   321 Giaour   1157
His bower in other worlds of bliss   330 Abydos   2   110
Thus ever fade my fairy dreams of bliss   344 Corsair   1   411
And heedless, harmless wantonness of bliss   633 Cain   1   402
Who folds in clouds the fonts of bliss and woe   656 Heaven   118
Where all was peace, and innocence, and bliss   749 Juan   1   141
Here is the empire of thy perfect bliss   757 Juan   1   699
'Kiss' rhymes to 'bliss' in fact as well as verse   859 Juan   6   471

BLISSES
And spoil the blisses that await him   134 Lady-D   14
(Uncertainty is one of many blisses   876 Juan   7   605

BLISTER
Prescribed, by way of blister, a young belle   767 Juan   1   1340

BLISTER'D
Blister'd and scorch'd, and, stagnant on the sea   783 Juan   2   570

BLITHE
There the blithe bee his fragrant fortress builds   33 Harold   2   823

BLITHE
There the blithe youngster, just return'd from
Spain   250 Bards   672
Produced blithe Punch and merry Madame Joan   261 Hints   324

BLITHER
Nor find a motlier crew nor blither   384 Corinth   23

BLOAT
Though Bristol bloat him with the verdant fat   247 Bards   394

BLOATED
And life that bloated Ease can never hope to
share   9 Harold   1   350
To swell one bloated Chief's unwholesome reign   12 Harold   1   550
Your strength a name, your bloated wealth a dream   272 Minerva   262
Helping to swell our tyrant's bloated strength   516 Faliero   2   564
Of a few bloated despots needed more   534 Faliero   4   436
On life's worn confine, jaded, bloated, sated   918 Juan   10   690

BLOCK
Down to a block--immortal rebel! See   67 Harold   4   760
'You should all block your doors   239 Bray   20
With the block before and the guards around   400 Parisina   400
Upon the block he bow'd his head   401 Parisina   453
Beyond the blow that to the block   401 Parisina   486
Like him she saw upon the block   401 Parisina   523
In a great cause: the block may soak their gore   517 Faliero   2   607

BLOCKHEAD
Could not the blockhead ask for a balloon   814 Juan   3   888
'Blockhead! come on, and see,' quoth Baba, while   842 Juan   5   657

BLOCKHEADS
Had heard these blockheads sing before him   96 Granta   82

BLOCKS
Are worthy of the mountains from whose blocks   58 Harold   4   178
For all the mutilated blocks of art   256 Bards   1032
As e'er thou didst upon Carrara's blocks   738 Deformed   2   213
There barbers' blocks with periwigs in curl   921 Juan   11   173

BLONDE
She was a fine and somewhat full-blown blonde   960 Juan   14   329

BLONDO
Except Soranzo, Nicoletto Blondo   518 Faliero   2   658

BLOOD
(See also LIFE-BLOOD and COLD-BLOODED)
Pour'd forth his blood beneath the assassin's
knife   7 Harold   1   266
That men forget the blood which she hath spilt   8 Harold   1   340
To shed before his Shrine the blood he deems most
sweet   10 Harold   1   431
While boyish blood is mantling, who can 'scape   14 Harold   1   662
Nurtured in blood betimes, his heart delights   16 Harold   1   794
Some native blood was seen thy streets to dye   18 Harold   1   878
Not all the blood at Talavera shed   18 Harold   1   918
Blood follows blood, and, through their mortal
span   29 Harold   2   566
In bloodier acts conclude those who with blood
began   29 Harold   2   567
When his Delhis come dashing in blood o'er the
banks   31 Harold   2   687
May wind their path of blood along the West   31 Harold   2   735
Their birth, their blood, and that sublime   32 Harold   2   790
Till the blood tinge his plumage, so the heat   37 Harold   3   134
And roused the vengeance blood alone could quell   38 Harold   3   206
Thy tide wash'd down the blood of yesterday   43 Harold   3   455
Of our own soul turn all our blood to tears   46 Harold   3   664
My blood from out thy being were an aim   53 Harold   3   1091
And blood she bore o'er subject earth and sea   57 Harold   4   121
Making the sun like blood, the earth a tomb   60 Harold   4   305
To shed thy blood and drink the tears of thy
distress   61 Harold   4   378
Quaff blood and water; nor the stranger's sword   61 Harold   4   385
Blood, pulse, and breast confirm the Dardan
Shepherd's prize   62 Harold   4   450
A name of blood from that day's sanguine rain   65 Harold   4   583
And blood of earth flow on as they have flow'd   68 Harold   4   825
But France got drunk with blood to vomit crime   69 Harold   4   865
With household blood and wine, serenely wore   71 Harold   4   998
The field of freedom, faction, fame, and blood   72 Harold   4   1009
But now my blood shall not sink in the ground   75 Harold   4   1193
My mind may lose its force, my blood its fire   75 Harold   4   1226
All this rush'd with his blood.--Shall he expire   76 Harold   4   1268
The blood is nectar;--but what doth she there   77 Harold   4   1331
To whom she renders back the debt of blood   77 Harold   4   1344
Four brothers enrich'd with their blood the bleak
field   86 Leaving NA   18
When age chills the blood, when our pleasures are
past   93 First Kiss   25
For they were stain'd with kindred blood   105 Alva   304

BLOOD

Eager to gild his arms with hostile blood	105	Nisus	2
'Now,' cries the first, 'for deeds of blood prepare	108	Nisus	231
Through wine and blood, commingling as they flow	109	Nisus	273
Here sheathe the steel, my blood is all your own	110	Nisus	368
While my blood is thus warm I ne'er shall reform	116	Strephon	25
The blood of traitors smears the purple plain	120	Newstead-A	66
marked in blood. Lochlin's sons had fled	129	Calmar	18
dreams were of blood. They lift the spear	130	Calmar	38
moss; live to revenge me in the blood of	130	Calmar	84
dim with the gore of my father. The blood	130	Calmar	119
soar on the blood of slumber. Rise, Mathon	130	Calmar	123
arm: he shudders in his blood. He rolls	130	Calmar	133
blood. Fierce is the look of the gloomy	131	Calmar	163
hall. It is not pure from blood: but it	131	Calmar	180
Oh! more than tears of blood can tell	151	Farewell-B	6
My blood runs coldly through my breast	152	Weep-A	6
Till their hated blood shall flow	161	War Song	7
Expired in seas of blood	162	War Song	36
Perchance not blood shall turn aside	165	Friend-B	52
My curdling blood, my madd'ning brain	172	Romaic-B	33
For the field ran so red with the blood of the dead	176	Devil's Dr	40
Was slaked with blood of Rome	180	Ode-A	56
And Earth hath spilt her blood for him	181	Ode-A	82
The blood which flow'd with Wallace flows as free	182	Address-C	11
Though Freedom's blood thy plain bedew	187	Ode-B	2
Turning rivers into blood	187	Ode-B	21
Pouring nations' blood like water	188	Ode-B	89
Like lava roll'd thy stream of blood	188	On Star	13
Our tears and blood must flow for thee	189	On Star	34
With blood, and each sate sullenly apart	189	Darkness	40
(Oh had it been but other blood	197	Duel	10
For land to land, even blood to blood	197	Duel	29
And then there was the Curse of blood	197	Duel	42
Born far beyond the mountains, but his blood	198	Po	42
My blood is all meridian; were it not	199	Po	45
Thy Blood grew Ice when his was shed	201	Ode-C	57
That Heart's last throb was thine, that blood	201	Ode-C	77
Like their blood which has flow'd, and which yet has to flow	203	Avatar	84
Mark, how the channels of her yellow blood	209	Sketch	65
A touch of hers, his blood would ebb and flow	214	Dream	59
That the blood of thy child is as pure	218	Jephtha	10
When this blood of thy giving hath gush'd	218	Jephtha	17
The generous blood that flow'd from thee	219	Thy Days	9
Stretch me that moment in blood at thy feet	219	Saul-A	7
They call'd for the harp--but our blood they shall spill	223	Valley	7
The blood and dust of both--to mould a George	228	Windsor	10
The blood and dirt of both to mould a George	228	Vaults	10
Bought their freedom, and cheaply, with blood	229	Lads	?
Flesh, limbs, and blood the former make their own	270	Minerva	115
And claims his long arrear of northern blood	271	Minerva	226
Who paid for vulgar, with her royal blood	274	Waltz	51
The page was so besmear'd with blood and dust	285	Vision	40
Her youth--their blood flows faster than her wines	301	Age	194
But what of that? the animal shows blood	305	Age	567
True, blood and treasure boundlessly were spilt	306	Age	586
Blood, sweat, and tear-wrung millions--why? for rent	306	Age	621
And, gorged with blood, you grumble at a scar	306	Age	637
The blood that warm'd his heart is shed	313	Giaour	319
Stain'd with the best of Arnaut blood	315	Giaour	525
Yet dripping with the blood he spilt	316	Giaour	656
Peace to the brave! whose blood is spilt	317	Giaour	721
And unavenged, at least in blood	317	Giaour	738
And suck the blood of all thy race	317	Giaour	758
Wet with thine own best blood shall drip	318	Giaour	781
There's blood upon that dinted sword	320	Giaour	1032
'The cold in clime are cold in blood	321	Giaour	1099
No, nor the blood so near my own	325	Abydos	1	141
That blood--he hath not heard--no more	325	Abydos	1	142
We Moslem reck not much of blood	326	Abydos	1	200
That field with blood bedew'd in vain	329	Abydos	2	23
Ah! how without can blood be spilt	330	Abydos	2	126
My father's blood in every vein	331	Abydos	2	207
Nor I forgive a father's blood	331	Abydos	2	269
His heart's best blood is on the water	335	Abydos	2	556
Fast from his breast the blood is bubbling	335	Abydos	2	579
What quench'd its ray?--the blood that thou hast shed	336	Abydos	2	661
And careless eye the blood that dims its shine	338	Corsair	1	50
And calmly talk'd--and yet he talk'd of blood	347	Corsair	1	606
The sword aside--in vain--the blood o'erflows	349	Corsair	2	185
And flame for flame and blood for blood must tell	350	Corsair	2	237
And stanch'd the blood she saves to shed again	351	Corsair	2	281
'Gulnare! if for each drop of blood a gem	357	Corsair	3	153
Oh! slight but certain pledge of crime--'tis blood	361	Corsair	3	417
That spot of blood, that light but guilty streak	361	Corsair	3	426
Blood he had view'd--could view unmoved--but then	361	Corsair	3	428

BLOOD

Whom blood appall'd not,--their regards perplex	363	Corsair	3	515
For him that poniard smote, that blood was spilt	363	Corsair	3	528
His blood in temperate seeming now would flow	371	Lara	1	352
And if from Lara's blood and gentle birth	372	Lara	1	474
Nor gout of blood, nor shred of mantle torn	376	Lara	2	112
Had made a path for blood and giant sin	377	Lara	2	162
Less blood perchance hath bought a richer spoil	379	Lara	2	331
And blood is mingled with the dashing stream	380	Lara	2	366
These only told that somewhere blood was spilt	383	Lara	2	547
From lingering where her chieftain's blood had been	383	Lara	2	601
And pays in blood oppression's ills	384	Cornith	29
But could the blood before her shed	385	Corinth	58
Triumphant in the fields of blood	385	Corinth	100
Profuse of blood, untired in toil	387	Corinth	304
Deep in the tide of their warm blood lying	389	Corinth	482
Froze through his blood by their touch that night	391	Corinth	604
Sabres and swords with blood were gilt	392	Corinth	768
That splash in the blood of the slippery street	393	Corinth	774
Converted by Christ to his blood so divine	395	Corinth	1003
Not I, but thou his blood dost shed	398	Parisina	220
The hot blood ebb'd and flow'd again	398	Parisina	226
Hath shed more blood in cause of thine	399	Parisina	239
As ice were in her curdled blood	400	Parisina	335
'No--yours my forfeit blood and breath	401	Parisina	449
Their belief with blood have seal'd	402	Chillon	22
I've seen it rushing forth in blood	404	Chillon	179
Stain'd with his own and subjects' blood	407	Mazeppa	18
The fever in his blood forbade	407	Mazeppa	37
He had such wealth in blood and ore	408	Mazeppa	160
Hath mingled with our Polish blood	409	Mazeppa	210
(Sprung from a race whose rising blood	412	Mazeppa	533
My blood reflow'd though thick and chill	412	Mazeppa	574
They would not dip their souls at once in blood	416	Island	1	79
The sun-born blood suffused her neck, and threw	420	Island	2	137
These wither when for aught save blood they burn	423	Island	2	315
But still the hunter's blood was on their horn	427	Island	3	62
Yet dabbled with his lately flowing blood	428	Island	3	148
Who dyed Thermopylae with holy blood	433	Island	4	260
However boldly their warm blood was spilt	433	Island	4	269
A fair-hair'd scalp, besmear'd with blood and weeds	434	Island	4	345
Of sweet sensations, battling with the blood	453	Venice-B	31
Ye men, who pour your blood for kings as water	453	Venice-B	67
She drank no blood, nor fatten'd on the dead	454	Venice-B	112
Rights cheaply earn'd with blood.--Still, still, for ever	455	Venice-B	148
Who sleeps to dream of blood, and waking glows	457	Dante	1	114
He, too, shall sing of arms and Christian blood	462	Dante	3	121
The electric blood with which their arteries run	462	Dante	3	162
Wean'd for an hour from blood, to turn and gaze	464	Dante	4	80
Is sprung from out the noble blood of France	467	Morgante	56
The abbot was call'd Clermont, and by blood	468	Morgante	153
Him who was born of Mary's holiest blood	468	Morgante	166
Than fits me for such gentle blood to express	475	Morgante	622
The black blood in its blackest spring	481	Manfred	1	235
Stain not our pure vales with thy guilty blood	483	Manfred	1	372
Away, away! there's blood upon the brim	484	Manfred	2	21
I say 'tis blood--my blood! the pure warm stream	484	Manfred	2	24
Blood, but not hers--and yet her blood was shed	486	Manfred	2	214
With the blood of a million he'll answer my care	488	Manfred	2	322
As he, indeed, by blood was bound to do	494	Manfred	3	247
The blood and sweat of almost eighty years	502	Faliero	1	150
The nephew of a Doge? and of that blood	502	Faliero	1	159
His blood had gilt the threshold; for the carle	503	Faliero	1	230
There's blood upon thy face--how came it there	503	Faliero	1	363
Behold my blood! the first time it e'er flow'd	505	Faliero	1	387
This blood had been wash'd out in other blood	505	Faliero	1	411
With the plebeian blood, and treasure wrung	507	Faliero	1	500
They might wring blood from me, but treachery never	507	Faliero	1	536
To female virtue, and to noble blood	509	Faliero	2	31
Shed his young blood for his absurd lampoon	512	Faliero	2	241
Does not the law of Heaven say blood for blood	512	Faliero	2	244
Do not the laws of man say blood for honour	512	Faliero	2	248
Say not the laws of nations blood for treason	512	Faliero	2	250
I trusted to the blood of Loredano	514	Faliero	2	372
Of honesty in such infected blood	514	Faliero	2	386
Save the regards due to the blood and sweat	515	Faliero	2	463
No, Calendaro; these same drops of blood	516	Faliero	2	525
Turn sick at sight of blood, although a villain's	517	Faliero	2	586
Thou must be cleansed of the black blood which makes thee	519	Faliero	3	8
Where all the pregnant hearts of our bold blood	519	Faliero	3	18
Their pure high blood, their blazon-roll of glories	519	Faliero	3	32
Of blood which spouts through hoary scalps is not	521	Faliero	3	188
Which must be exorcised with blood,--and then	523	Faliero	3	288
We made alliances of blood and marriage	525	Faliero	3	444
Who? My own friends by blood and courtesy	527	Faliero	3	571
And can I see them dabbled o'er with blood	527	Faliero	3	592
You have seen blood in battle, shed it, both	527	Faliero	3	601
The roar of waters in the cry of blood	528	Faliero	3	649

BLOOD

And through my spirit chill'd my blood, until	528	Faliero	4	8
Spilt noble blood, I guarantee thy safety	530	Faliero	4	145
He who has shed patrician blood--I come	530	Faliero	4	153
To save patrician blood, and not to shed it	530	Faliero	4	154
Which bear away the weaker: noble blood	531	Faliero	4	218
Sooner than spill thy blood, I peril mine	532	Faliero	4	268
Of blood to crowds begets the thirst of more	534	Faliero	4	409
Barbaric blood can reconcile us now	535	Faliero	4	495
Are a few drops of human blood? 'tis false	535	Faliero	4	511
The blood of tyrants is not human; they	535	Faliero	4	512
Of blood, and they who use thee will reward thee	537	Faliero	4	603
Or place us there again; we have still some blood left	538	Faliero	5	43
So shall our blood more readily arise	539	Faliero	5	118
Who made you what you are, and quench in blood	540	Faliero	5	158
Have something of the blood of brighter days	541	Faliero	5	274
I am already; and my blood will rise	545	Faliero	5	526
Which drank this willing blood from many a wound	548	Faliero	5	731
Shedding so much blood in her last defence	548	Faliero	5	746
Thou den of drunkards with the blood of princes	549	Faliero	5	794
The blood of Nimrod and Semiramis	550	Sardan	1	6
Of blood and chains? The despotism of vice	552	Sardan	1	114
Won with thy blood, and toil, and time, and peril	553	Sardan	1	165
That he shed blood by oceans; and no god	554	Sardan	1	234
I pray thee, change the theme: my blood disdains	554	Sardan	1	265
Because I have not shed their blood, nor led them	554	Sardan	1	274
Recruit his phalanx--spill your blood at bidding	555	Sardan	1	304
Blood as I might have done, in oceans, till	557	Sardan	1	450
If I must shed blood, it shall be by force	557	Sardan	1	454
They are so blotted o'er with blood, I cannot	559	Sardan	1	595
The natural foes of all the blood of Greece	561	Sardan	1	703
Like the blood he predicts. If not in vain	561	Sardan	2	4
His blood dishonour'd, and himself disdain'd	563	Sardan	2	101
By right of blood, derived from age to age	574	Sardan	3	169
Rather than dip my hands in holy blood	575	Sardan	3	274
Suggest a purpler beverage. Blood--doubtless	577	Sardan	3	348
A goblet, bubbling o'er with blood; and on	580	Sardan	4	111
Shame not our blood with trembling, but remember	581	Sardan	4	232
A pluck at them, or perish in hot blood	587	Sardan	4	563
I am sped, then! With the blood that fast must follow	589	Sardan	5	105
If I redeem it, I will give thee blood	589	Sardan	5	156
Of blood from Spartans! Though these did not weep	602	Foscari	2	74
You have seen your son's blood flow, and your flesh shook not	603	Foscari	2	129
Is our own blood and kin to shrink from us	604	Foscari	2	182
In blood, in mind, in means; and that they know	605	Foscari	2	242
The sacrifice of my own blood and quiet	605	Foscari	2	257
Without expectancy, has sent the blood	609	Foscari	3	48
The blood of myriads reeking up to heaven	611	Foscari	3	241
Of his high blood. Thus much I've learnt, although	612	Foscari	3	291
To freeze their young blood in its natural current	613	Foscari	3	368
Of noble blood may), one day hope to be	616	Foscari	4	84
What mean you? Lo! there is the blood beginning	618	Foscari	4	240
And I, who would have given my blood for him	622	Foscari	5	100
Nothing but sobs through blood, for this!-- Sage signors	623	Foscari	5	159
If thou lov'st blood, the shepherd's shrine, which smokes	650	Cain	3	255
How heav'n licks up the flames when thick with blood	650	Cain	3	285
Thine altar, with its blood of lambs and kids	650	Cain	3	292
Which fed on milk, to be destroy'd in blood	650	Cain	3	293
The fumes of scorching flesh and smoking blood	650	Cain	3	299
Give way!--thy God loves blood!--then look to it	650	Cain	3	310
And yet there are no dews! 'Tis blood--my blood	651	Cain	3	345
It is not blood; for who would shed his blood	651	Cain	3	362
May the clear rivers turn to blood as he	652	Cain	3	432
The voice of thy slain brother's blood cries out	653	Cain	3	470
To drink thy brother's blood from thy rash hand	653	Cain	3	473
To him thou now see'st so besmear'd with blood	653	Cain	3	491
And I who have shed blood cannot shed tears	654	Cain	3	521
Blood darkens earth and heaven! what thou now art	654	Cain	3	530
And might have temper'd this stern blood of mine	654	Cain	3	559
Of men! that one of my blood, knowing well	658	Heaven		256
With the blood reeking from each battle plain	661	Heaven		477
With Cain's, the eldest born of Adam's, blood	664	Heaven		655
Has come down in that haughty blood which springs	664	Heaven		664
The wind to which it waves: my blood is frozen	671	Werner	1	8
Play'd round my heart: blood is not water, cousin	674	Werner	1	198
And that's enough for your right noble blood	679	Werner	1	515
I think too well of blood allied to mine	695	Werner	2	756
Thou art too late! I'll nought to do with blood	697	Werner	3	150
Especially the next in blood. Blood! 'tis	699	Werner	3	254
And so it should be, when the same in blood	699	Werner	3	257
Of gentle blood! I have important reasons	700	Werner	3	314
With blood even at their baptism. Prithee, peace	705	Werner	4	72
Our pedigree, and only weigh'd our blood	706	Werner	4	156
Blood! Why does yours start from your cheeks? Ay! doth it	706	Werner	4	157

BLOOD

The nature of thine age, nor of thy blood	709	Werner	4	348
To shed more blood? or--Oh! if it should be	711	Werner	4	431
In these dim days of heresies and blood	711	Werner	4	457
Gnashing of teeth, and tears of blood, and fire	711	Werner	4	461
'Tis yours, or theirs. Is there no blood upon it	712	Werner	4	501
No; but there's worse than blood--eternal shame	712	Werner	4	502
His death was fathomlessly deep in blood	712	Werner	4	506
Yet say I am not guilty! for the blood	712	Werner	4	522
Though, by the Power who abhorreth human blood	712	Werner	4	524
For bloodshed stopt, let blood you shed not rise	712	Werner	4	543
Blood than came there in battle. It--or some	716	Werner	5	211
Blood became ice. But he was all alone	718	Werner	5	318
Abhorr'd both mystery and blood, and yet	720	Werner	5	481
Ida, beware! there's blood upon that hand	721	Werner	5	548
Accursed be this blood that flows so fast	722	Deformed	1	33
Unto what brought me into life? Thou blood	723	Deformed	1	54
Must it be sign'd in blood? Not in your own	724	Deformed	1	147
Whose blood then? We will talk of that hereafter	724	Deformed	1	148
Now then!--A little of your blood. For what	724	Deformed	1	153
Of blood take the guise	728	Deformed	1	395
Of blood. Then wipe them, and see clearly. Why	730	Deformed	1	571
Through scenes of blood and lust, till I am here	730	Deformed	1	588
Which his blood made a badge of glory and	731	Deformed	1	609
Was brother's blood; and if its native blood	731	Deformed	1	652
Shed Rome's blood, he was your brother	736	Deformed	2	108
I see thee purple with the blood of Rome	740	Deformed	2	361
I offer him a blood less holy	741	Deformed	2	365
'Tis mix'd with blood. There is no cleaner now	741	Deformed	2	378
As I am blood, bone, marrow, passion, feeling	745	Fragment-D		2
The blood of monarchs with his prophecies	746	Juan	Ded	83
Of Moor or Hebrew blood, he traced his source	748	Juan	1	67
(Her blood was not all Spanish, by the by	754	Juan	1	443
His blood less noble than such blood should be	754	Juan	1	451
Ruin'd its blood, but much improved its flesh	754	Juan	1	458
By blood or ink; 'tis sweet to put an end	762	Juan	1	1002
When old King David's blood grew dull in motion	767	Juan	1	1341
Why, don't you know that it may end in blood	768	Juan	1	1366
His blood was up: though young, he was a Tartar	769	Juan	1	1471
And blood ('twas from the nose) began to flow	769	Juan	1	1483
Some blood, and several footsteps, but no more	770	Juan	1	1494
My blood still rushes where my spirit's set	771	Juan	1	1563
And out they spoke of lots for flesh and blood	783	Juan	2	583
For his congealing blood, and senses dim	788	Juan	2	884
Heaven knows what cash he got or blood he spilt	790	Juan	2	1013
Had dyed it with the headlong blood, whose race	792	Juan	2	1123
Should reach his blood, then o'er him still as death	792	Juan	2	1143
For love must be sustain'd like flesh and blood	795	Juan	2	1356
Pours forth at last the heart's blood turn'd to tears	801	Juan	2	1711
And turn'd her pure heart's purest blood to tears	801	Juan	3	8
His angry word once o'er, he shed no blood	807	Juan	3	382
And shed the blood of Scio's vine.	812	Juan	3	740
The Heracleidan blood might own	813	Juan	3	766
We know not this--the blood flows on too fast	816	Juan	4	14
Pure blood to stagnate, their great hearts to fail	817	Juan	4	66
Then turn'd to Juan, in whose cheek the blood	821	Juan	4	309
Replied, 'Your blood be then on your own head	821	Juan	4	317
Her father's blood before her father's face	822	Juan	4	351
There was resemblance, such as true blood wears	822	Juan	4	356
With the blood running like a little brook	822	Juan	4	390
The Moorish blood partakes the planet's hour	823	Juan	4	444
His blood was running on the very floor	823	Juan	4	459
Were dabbled with the deep blood which ran o'er	823	Juan	4	466
Weak still with loss of blood, he scarce could urge	826	Juan	4	629
With human blood that column was cemented	829	Juan	4	833
Perhaps his recent loss of blood might pull	832	Juan	5	61
Sell flesh and blood. When dinner has opprest one	835	Juan	5	238
And is this blood, then, form'd but to be shed	836	Juan	5	308
The blood of all his line's Castilian lords	844	Juan	5	827
And into her clear cheek the blood was brought	845	Juan	5	860
Her blood was high, her beauty scarce of earth	845	Juan	5	893
Felt the warm blood, which in his face was glowing	846	Juan	5	932
And then her thirst of blood was quench'd in tears	848	Juan	5	1088
It teaches them that they are flesh and blood	848	Juan	5	1097
Who loved blood as an alderman loves marrow	868	Juan	7	64
'Let there be blood!' says man, and there's a sea	872	Juan	7	322
Of blood and tears must flow the unebbing sea	875	Juan	7	544
And not much sympathy for blood, survey'd	876	Juan	7	546
But still we moderns equal you in blood	877	Juan	7	640
Oh blood and thunder! and oh blood and wounds	878	Juan	8	1
So was his blood stirr'd while he found resist- ance	885	Juan	8	433
Blood, until heated--and even then his own	885	Juan	8	439
Whose blood the puddle greatly did enrich	887	Juan	8	563
Now thaw'd into a marsh of human blood	887	Juan	8	584
The blood may gush out, as the Danube's flow	889	Juan	8	691
A slender streak of blood announced how near	890	Juan	8	754

BLOOD

Was imaged back in blood, the sea of slaughter	894 Juan	8	976
Where blood was talk'd of as we would of water	900 Juan	9	227
Of blood and water, leaden Castlereagh	903 Juan	9	398
Blood only serves to wash Ambition's hands	904 Juan	9	472
I 'scotch'd not kill'd' the Scotchman in my blood	909 Juan	10	151
Valour; much also to the blood he show'd	911 Juan	10	228
Which with the blood too readily will claim kin	912 Juan	10	318
In neither clime, time, blood, with her defender	914 Juan	10	455
Leavening his blood as cayenne doth a curry	916 Juan	10	570
His brush with all the blood of all the sainted	950 Juan	13	568
Will there, as also in the ties of blood	967 Juan	14	738
Blood is not water; and where shall we find	973 Juan	15	348
It makes my blood boil like the springs of Hecla	979 Juan	15	735
Spangled with gems--the monk made his blood curdle	995 Juan	16	952
Forth into something much like flesh and blood	996 Juan	16	1028

BLOOD-BOUGHT

Who thy blood-bought title bears	187 Ode-B		43

BLOOD-DROPS

And blood-drops, sprinkled o'er his yellow hair	428 Island	3	101

BLOOD-HORSE

Dash'd on like a spurr'd blood-horse in a race	885 Juan	8	432

BLOODHOUND

The bloodhound mob on their patrician prey	536 Faliero	4	597
For years I've track'd, as does the bloodhound, never	687 Werner	2	267
No. A rare blood-hound, when his own is heated	737 Deformed	2	159

BLOODHOUNDS

Nor hunt the bloodhounds back to Arthur's Seat	247 Bards		437
'Tis a great name for blood-hounds. There's a demon	734 Deformed	1	857
Should ever be those blood-hounds, from whose wild	829 Juan	4	838

BLOODIER

In bloodier acts conclude those who with blood began	29 Harold	2	567
I've 'scaped a bloodier hour than this	316 Giaour		596
Once bloody mortals--and now bloodier idols	578 Sardan	4	30
Each bloodier than the former. I arose	714 Werner	5	97
To make the Cretans bloodier in battle	793 Juan	2	1240

BLOODIEST

Go, read whate'er is writ of bloodiest strife	18 Harold	1	892

BLOODLESS

And Fancy hover o'er thy bloodless bier	19 Harold	1	942
And bloodless, with its sleepless sorrow aches	40 Harold	3	295
To hide her bloodless heart's soul-harden'd scheming	209 Sketch		60
Bloodless are these limbs, and cold	219 Saul-B		18
All bloodless wax'd his look	220 Belshaz-B		19
That of his valour show'd the bloodless hue	248 Bards		487
Mouths bloodless to the bit or rein	413 Mazeppa		681
For he I own is, or at least was, bloodless	568 Sardan	2	434
And how obtain'd?--that knife! 'Tis bloodless-- yet	683 Werner	1	740
If you regret your enemy's bloodless death	712 Werner	4	505
But press'd her bloodless lip to Juan's cheek	767 Juan	1	1352

BLOODLESSLY

Shall yield, and bloodlessly and basely yield	548 Faliero	5	744

BLOOD-LOVING

In one day--what could that blood-loving beldame	555 Sardan	1	285

BLOOD-RED

His blood-red tresses deep'ning in the sun	10 Harold	1	424
But those scarfs of blood-red shall be redder, before	30 Harold	2	663
See how the heroes' blood-red plumes	102 Alva		89
The blood-red signal glitters in the gale	339 Corsair	1	86
And more than all, his blood-red flag aloft	345 Corsair	1	529
''Tis mine--my blood-red flag! again--again	362 Corsair	3	492
Blood-red as sunset summer clouds which range	845 Juan	5	861

BLOOD'S

Let their bleach'd bones and blood's unbleaching stain	18 Harold	1	906
A drop of water! Blood's the only liquid	737 Deformed	2	166
Well, his blood's up; and if a little's shed	738 Deformed	2	199
And the blood's lava, and the pulse a blaze	797 Juan	2	1486

BLOODSHED

Bloodshed 'tis surely better to retrench	260 Hints		272
Well, all is remedied, and without bloodshed	569 Sardan	2	466
To bear the brand of bloodshed? Pshaw! leave any thing	703 Werner	3	548

BLOODSHED

For bloodshed stopt, let blood you shed not rise	712 Werner	4	543

BLOODSHOT

Flow'd from their bloodshot eyes, all red with strife	893 Juan	8	951

BLOODSTAIN

Bloodstain the breach through which they pass	392 Corinth		697

BLOOD-STAIN'D

Or blood-stain'd guilt repenting solace found	120 Newstead-A		23

BLOODY

Where are those bloody banners which of yore	9 Harold	1	391
In themes of bloody fray or gallant fight	25 Harold	2	359
Is lawless law; for with a bloody hand	26 Harold	2	419
Then tore with bloody talon the rent plain	38 Harold	3	159
Which stretch'd his father on a bloody bier	38 Harold	3	205
But they who fought are in a bloody shroud	42 Harold	3	421
At thy bathed base the bloody Caesar lie	68 Harold	4	778
Such were the bloody Circus' genial laws	76 Harold	4	1247
But here, where Murder breathed her bloody steam	76 Harold	4	1270
That bloody Mars recall'd them there	194 Ballad-A		27
Yea, baronets have ink'd the bloody hand	266 Hints		716
Of monarchs--from the bloody rolls amass'd	290 Vision		349
The unpaid amount of Catherine's bloody debt	300 Age		160
Oh, bloody and most bootless Waterloo	301 Age		223
With bloody spur along the shore	315 Giaour		471
And rave as to some bloody hand	318 Giaour		827
Behold but bloody shore and fiery waves	349 Corsair	2	158
And that last gasp hath burst his bloody girth	380 Lara	2	397
When on Carlowitz' bloody plain	386 Corinth		143
They leave before a bloody track	394 Corinth		915
The verdure flies the bloody sod	411 Mazeppa		438
His back with many a bloody thong	413 Mazeppa		697
In bloody chronicles of ages past	456 Dante	1	58
Of half a century bloody and black	458 Dante	1	135
The bloody chaos yet expects creation	459 Dante	2	42
The bloody scroll of our millennial wrongs	460 Dante	3	11
But the gladiators' bloody Circus stands	495 Manfred	3	287
If we should fail, employing bloody means	519 Faliero	3	76
A bold and bloody despot from his throne	562 Sardan	2	84
Once bloody mortals--and now bloodier idols	578 Sardan	4	30
An era of sweet peace 'midst bloody annals	586 Sardan	4	512
Those black and bloody leaves, his heart and brain	606 Foscari	2	336
Thy pious knife? Give way! this bloody record	650 Cain	3	303
Massy and bloody! snatch'd from off the altar	652 Cain	3	392
'Gainst whom thy breath would blow thy bloody slander	715 Werner	5	167
A man who wash'd his bloody hands, and oft	718 Werner	5	332
First flowers of the bloody meadows	735 Deformed	2	50
And their baked lips, with many a bloody crack	784 Juan	2	681
One arm had on a bandage rather bloody	832 Juan	5	86
Like hail, to make a bloody diuretic	879 Juan	8	91
Thus on they wallow'd in the bloody mire	880 Juan	8	153
Stars, medals, and a bloody sword in hand	885 Juan	8	454
Napoleon on his bold and bloody track	887 Juan	8	555
Amidst the bodies lull'd in bloody rest	889 Juan	8	728
You'll find ten thousand handsome coxcombs bloody	892 Juan	8	896
Its bloody bond, and saved perhaps some pretty	894 Juan	8	987
With bloody hands he wrote his first despatch	895 Juan	8	1061
Though bold and bloody, was the kind of thing	905 Juan	9	554
Black Edward's helm, and Becket's bloody stone	916 Juan	10	578
'Oh Jack! I'm floor'd by that 'ere bloody French- man	920 Juan	11	104
The cravat stain'd with bloody drops fell down	920 Juan	11	129

BLOODY-EYED

Instead--a grey-hair'd, wither'd, bloody-eyed	580 Sardan	4	104

BLOODY-HANDED

And bloody-handed, ghastly, ghostly thing	580 Sardan	4	105

BLOOM

For chiefs like ours in vain may laurels bloom	8 Harold	1	303
The negligently grand, the fruitful bloom	44 Harold	3	581
Which blighted their life's bloom and then de- parted	50 Harold	3	884
With breath all incense and with cheek all bloom	50 Harold	3	915
And overpowers the page where it would bloom again	73 Harold	4	1098
Your cheek's soft bloom is unimpair'd	98 To Lesbia		29
And beardless bloom yet graced the gallant boy	105 Nisus		10
In Nature's wild luxuriance bloom	113 Cornelian-A		24
But bloom in fresh, unfading spring	128 Answer-B		28
Which bloom among the fairy bowers	133 E. N. Long		30
Well hast thou left in life's best bloom	165 Thyrza		45
The flower in ripen'd bloom unmatch'd	167 Dead		37
But still for living wit the wreaths may bloom	170 Address-A		36
But the tender bloom of heart is gone, ere youth itself be past	185 Music-B		4
He comes in the promise and bloom of threescore	202 Avatar		21
Oh! snatch'd away in beauty's bloom	218 Bloom		1

BLOOM

Bloom fresh in satire, though they fade in praise	267 Hints		754
Began in youth's first bloom and flush to reign	290 Vision		331
To bloom along the fairy land	310 Giaour		55
But beauty with that fearful bloom	311 Giaour		96
Their bloom in blushes ever new	315 Giaour		495
Where bloom my native valley's bowers	322 Giaour		1220
Wax faint o'er the gardens of Gul in her bloom	323 Abydos	1	8
Bloom flowers in urns of China's mould	329 Abydos	2	79
To-morrow sees it bloom again	336 Abydos	2	680
By which the rest shall bloom and live	402 Parisina		581
With all the while a cheek whose bloom	404 Chillon		190
For these most bloom where rests the warrior's head	419 Island	2	8
When every flower was bloom, and air was balm	420 Island	2	107
The youth, the bloom, the beauty which agree	442 Beppo		109
Whose bloom could after dancing dare the dawn	450 Beppo		664
Can this be death? there's bloom upon her cheek	490 Manfred	2	468
Wealthier and wiser, in the ripest bloom	513 Faliero	2	332
Vain adjuncts, lavish'd its true bloom, and health	528 Faliero	4	44
Which generally leave some flowers to bloom	547 Faliero	5	679
In the first dawn and bloom of young creation	643 Cain	2	475
Blossom and bud, and bloom of flowers and fruits	647 Cain	3	106
Of strength, of bloom, of beauty, and of joy	648 Cain	3	141
Behold them in their various bloom and ripeness	649 Cain	3	219
The bloom or blight of all men's happiness	709 Werner	4	351
The bloom, too, had return'd to Haidee's cheeks	806 Juan	3	302
We left our hero, Juan, in the bloom	908 Juan	10	33
Meridian-born, to bloom in. This opinion	913 Juan	10	346
A fruit to bloom upon their withering bough	933 Juan	12	242

BLOOM'D

Have choked up the rose which late bloom'd in the way	86 Leaving NA		4
But bloom'd in calm domestic quiet	134 Lady-D		32
And, rear'd by taste, bloom'd fairer as they grew	243 Bards		108
Though fair they rose, and might have bloom'd at last	247 Bards		420
Bloom'd also in less transitory hues	924 Juan	11	378

BLOOMFIELD

Lo! Burns and Bloomfield, nay, a greater far	252 Bards		777
Bloomfield! why not on brother Nathan too	252 Bards		782

BLOOMING
(See also OUT-BLOOMING)

The helpless looks of blooming infancy	43 Harold	3	480
Did they act like your blooming coquette	115 Pigot		24
Still may thy blooming sons thy name revere	127 Recoll		381
When Cytherea's blooming Boy	139 Anacreon-C		15
Kiss thy soft cheeks' blooming tinge	160 Maid		10
Whose leaves for me alone were blooming	221 Marianne		20
How wondrous bright thy blooming morn arose	223 To Dives		6
Blooming as Aden in its earliest hour	333 Abydos	2	409
A blooming boy, a truant mutineer	421 Island	2	209
Laura was blooming still, had made the best	443 Beppo		177
Little deems our young blooming sleeper there	648 Cain	3	122
Or if the sweet and blooming fruits of earth	650 Cain	3	259
Blooming and bright, with golden hair, and stature	726 Deformed	1	247
And blooming aspect, Huon; for he looks	730 Deformed	1	526
Pair'd off with a Bacchante blooming visage	828 Juan	4	736
And Lady Marys blooming into girls	949 Juan	13	540
For which see Shakspeare's ever blooming garden	964 Juan	14	594
They have at hand a blooming glut of brides	972 Juan	15	264

BLOOMS

Blooms blushing to her lover's tale	310 Giaour		25
One spot exists, which ever blooms	336 Abydos	2	670
For, Tyranny, there blooms no bud for thee	454 Venice-B		100
Revived in thee, blooms forth to man restored	459 Dante	2	48

BLOSSOM

As some young rose, whose blossom scents the air	110 Nisus		379
I cannot call one single blossom mine	125 Recoll		238
Or sweep one blossom from the trees	310 Giaour		18
Where the flowers ever blossom, the beams ever shine	323 Abydos	1	6
Blossom and bud, and bloom of flowers and fruits	647 Cain	3	106
Yet quivers every leaf, and drops each blossom	668 Heaven		994
Blossom and bough lie wither'd with one blight	825 Juan	4	558

BLOSSOM'D

And hills all rich with blossom'd trees	43 Harold	3	500

BLOSSOMING

By bushy brake, and wild flowers blossoming	340 Corsair	1	125

BLOSSOMS

Thy tree hath lost its blossoms, and the rind	69 Harold	4	878
Are clothed with early blossoms, through the grass	72 Harold	4	1046
His blossoms wither as the blast prevails	247 Bards		423
The young pomegranate's blossoms strew	315 Giaour		494

BLOSSOMS

And crush their blossoms into barrenness	527 Faliero	3	616
Their summer blossoms by the surges lopp'd	670 Heaven		1137
Of these brief blossoms the immediate fruits	892 Juan	8	904

BLOT

And blot with tears the sable lines of grief	127 Recoll		406
We must not quarrel for a blot or two	264 Hints		558
And blot life's latest scene with calumny	359 Corsair	3	231
Nor less amazed, that such a blot	410 Mazeppa		348
If I do blot thy final page with tears	437 Tasso		35
To fix the blot on you. And on me only	715 Werner	5	162

BLOTTED

To view each loved one blotted from life's page	35 Harold	2	920
And blotted out the line for ever	150 Harrow-C		16
They are so blotted o'er with blood, I cannot	559 Sardan	1	595

BLOW
(See also DEATH-BLOW)

To meditate 'gainst friends the secret blow	16 Harold	1	799
Blow! swiftly blow, thou keel-compelling gale	22 Harold	2	172
Who would be free themselves must strike the blow	31 Harold	2	721
Round him are icy rocks, and loudly blow	42 Harold	3	403
And the bleak battlements shall bear no future blow	42 Harold	3	423
If some Rutulian arm, with adverse blow	106 Nisus		61
And clear thy road with many a deadly blow	108 Nisus		236
Rage nerves his arm, fate gleams in every blow	110 Nisus		390
Bid shuddering Nature shrink beneath the blow	122 Recoll		8
Once, and but once, she aim'd a deadly blow	123 Recoll		81
Fought on, unconscious of th' impending blow	126 Recoll		278
A hapless victim yielding to the blow	143 Soliloquy		76
But mine, alas! has stood the blow	156 Lady-F		46
To weep or wish the coming blow	166 Euthanasia		6
I faint, I die beneath the blow	172 Romaic-B		6
By a slave's dishonest blow	187 Ode-B		51
Of a most disastrous blow	194 Ballad-A		37
Though it smile upon the blow	207 Fare Thee		14
There cannot be pain in the blow	218 Jephtha		8
Exchanging many a midnight blow	234 Ballad-B		51
'Twas thine own genius gave the final blow	253 Bards		839
His teeth were set on edge, he could not blow	297 Vision		824
And crushing nations with a stupid blow	303 Age		409
Faithless to him, he gave the blow	320 Giaour		1064
Hath nought to dread from outward blow	321 Giaour		1156
And watch unfolding roses blow	324 Abydos	1	89
Blow fair, thou breeze!--she anchors ere the dark	339 Corsair	1	88
The first may turn, but not avenge the blow	342 Corsair	1	277
As kindle high to-night (but blow, thou breeze	342 Corsair	1	321
Unless some gay caprice suggests the blow	347 Corsair	2	23
No craven he, and yet he dreads the blow	349 Corsair	2	178
Are on this cast; Corsair! 'tis but a blow	361 Corsair	3	375
One blow shall cancel with our future fears	361 Corsair	3	379
Yet grieve to win him back without a blow	363 Corsair	3	507
Recoil before their leader's look and blow	380 Lara	2	375
These Kaled snatches: dizzy with the blow	380 Lara	2	388
Mustering his last feeble blow	393 Corinth		843
Before his words, as with a blow	394 Corinth		860
Interchanged the blow and thrust	394 Corinth		902
Dealing wounds with every blow	394 Corinth		917
That the blow may be both swift and steady	400 Parisina		402
As down the deadly blow descended	401 Parisina		481
Beyond the blow that to the block	401 Parisina		486
Done to death by sudden blow	401 Parisina		491
With every now and then a blow	408 Mazeppa		113
But yet he swerved as from a blow	411 Mazeppa		457
And that the only lesson was a blow	438 Tasso		161
When there is but required a single blow	460 Dante	2	138
My petty wrong, for what is a mere blow	506 Faliero	1	437
Had I sate down too humbly with this blow	507 Faliero	1	550
Set all in readiness to strike the blow	516 Faliero	2	550
Their blow upon the others, when they see	520 Faliero	3	139
I have disposed all for a sudden blow	523 Faliero	3	350
And vigilant, expectant of some blow	524 Faliero	3	364
To the palace to prepare all for the blow	526 Faliero	3	517
Bear with me! Step by step, and blow on blow	527 Faliero	3	605
'Tis mine to sound the knell, and strike the blow	527 Faliero	3	612
To strike the blow so suddenly. Such blows	534 Faliero	4	391
All safe off to your boats, blow one long blast	593 Sardan	5	386
And only done to daunt me:--'twas a blow	651 Cain	3	330
And but a blow. Stir--stir--nay, only stir	651 Cain	3	331
The blow, though not unlook'd for, falls as new	667 Heaven		922
'Gainst whom thy breath would blow thy bloody slander	715 Werner	5	167
Juan contrived to give an awkward blow	769 Juan	1	1485
Death shuns the wretch who fain the blow would meet	771 Juan	1	1574
I was most ready to return a blow	772 Juan	1	1694
For the sky show'd it would come on to blow	777 Juan	2	207
And none liked to anticipate the blow	778 Juan	2	286
With twilight it again came on to blow	786 Juan	2	761
With him it never was a word and blow	807 Juan	3	381
And his one blow left little work for two	807 Juan	3	384

BLOW

Pale, statue-like, and stern, she woo'd the blow	822 Juan	4	340
'On the rough deep. But this last blow--' and here	833 Juan	5	145
As if she had received a sudden blow	865 Juan	6	838
This passion might blow o'er, nor dared to balk	866 Juan	6	875
With deadlier engines and a speedier blow	877 Juan	7	635
'Twas blow for blow, disputing inch by inch	888 Juan	8	615
For the same blow which laid her mother here	890 Juan	8	756
How eager all the earth is for the blow	915 Juan	10	531
On a lee-shore, till it begins to blow	937 Juan	12	499

BLOWING

Favourable breezes blowing	156 Hodgson		3
Be as fair as, when blowing	728 Deformed	1	390
These to secure in this strong blowing weather	804 Juan	3	143
And left his cheeks as pale as snowdrops blowing	846 Juan	5	934
Who on a lark, with black-eyed Sal (his blowing	921 Juan	11	151
With a sirocco, for example, blowing	959 Juan	14	218

BLOWN

(See also FULL-BLOWN)

His eye is sparkling and his breath hath blown	50 Harold	3	938
Like the leaves of the forest when Autumn hath blown	222 Sennacherib		7
When fame's loud trump hath blown its noblest blast	254 Bards		957
On whom the stigma might perhaps be blown	295 Vision		637
Has more of brass in it, and is as well blown	297 Vision		800
Borne from a short frail pipe, which yet had blown	425 Island	2	438
To be blown down by his imperious breath	567 Sardan	3	326
Infirm of feeling as of purpose, blown	600 Foscari	1	329
I'm dark; I've blown my fingers--number'd o'er	701 Werner	3	400
As oaks blown down with all their thousand winters	889 Juan	8	704
And mine's a bubble, not blown up for praise	956 Juan	14	63

BLOWS

Our men in buckram shall have blows enough	256 Bards		1049
But first, ere came the rallying host to blows	350 Corsair	2	253
Worn out with toil and tired with changing blows	353 Corsair	2	415
With barbarous blows they gash the dead	395 Corinth		990
Where cries reply to curses, shrieks to blows	437 Tasso		86
A blindfold bondage, where your hire is blows	453 Venice-B		70
And make men's fickle breath the wind that blows	456 Dante	1	55
Next to the other. Having seen such blows	473 Morgante		509
Is it the pain of blows, or shame of blows	512 Faliero	2	246
To strike the blow so suddenly. Such blows	534 Faliero	4	391
Ne'er blows in all its blustering freedom? 'Twas so	614 Foscari	3	398
The blows upon his cutlass, and then put	822 Juan	4	387
Amongst them all, hard blows to inflict or ward	869 Juan	7	150
Man quite as quietly as blows the monsoon	883 Juan	8	309
'Fling up a straw, 'twill show the way the wind blows	956 Juan	14	58

BLOW'S

Your weakness. How? Strike! so the blow's repeated	564 Sardan	2	181

BLUCHER

And that if Blucher, Bulow, Gneisenau	884 Juan	8	385

BLUE

(See also DARK-BLUE, DEEP-BLUE)

Whose large blue eyes, fair locks, and snowy hands	5 Harold	1	93
Fades o'er the waters blue	5 Harold	1	119
Fresh feres will dry the bright blue eyes	6 Harold	1	176
Welcome, welcome, ye dark blue waves'	6 Harold	1	194
Three gaudy standards flout the pale blue skies	10 Harold	1	443
Fair Cadiz, rising o'er the dark blue sea	15 Harold	1	712
He that has sail'd upon the dark blue sea	22 Harold	2	145
Which looks o'er waves so blue, skies so serene	23 Harold	2	238
And had he doted on those eyes so blue	24 Harold	2	296
Kissing, not ruffling, the blue deep's serene	30 Harold	2	627
Yet are thy skies as blue, thy crags as wild	33 Harold	2	819
When last I saw thy young blue eyes they smiled	35 Harold	3	3
Where a blue sky, and glowing clime, extends	37 Harold	3	111
And peasant girls, with deep blue eyes	43 Harold	3	506
By the blue rushing of the arrowy Rhone	46 Harold	3	673
Of blue Friuli's mountains; Heaven is free	59 Harold	4	238
The bright blue waters with a fanning wind	61 Harold	4	391
Buried in air, the deep blue sky of Rome	71 Harold	4	991
The sweetness of the violet's deep blue eyes	72 Harold	4	1052
Upon the blue Symplegades. Long years	81 Harold	4	1576
Roll on, thou deep and dark blue Ocean, roll	81 Harold	4	1603
The eye that rolls in glossy blue	97 To Woman		14
Which gave a lustre to its blue	98 To Mary		15
On eyes of blue or lips carnation	101 Marion		46
The blue flames curdle o'er the hearth	103 Alva		184
blue waves. Erin's sons fell beneath his	130 Calmar		30
our sails rose on the blue waves. The	131 Calmar		186

BLUE

Or bounding o'er the dark blue wave	135 I Would		4
When I see the soft blue of a love-speaking eye	136 Highlander		35
Two whom I loved had eyes of Blue	144 Becher-B		25
Those flaxen locks, those eyes of blue	150 My Son		1
Although her eye be not of blue	159 Cadiz		5
Look o'er the dark blue sea	159 Storm		56
Triumphant sons of truest blue	163 Malta		26
Thine eyes' blue tenderness, thy long fair hair	175 Sonnet-A		1
Which horror froze in the blue eye clear	176 Devil's Dr		67
One, the blue depth of Seraph's eyes	188 On Star		26
Will thy yard of blue riband, poor Fingal, recall	203 Avatar		69
And they were canopied by the blue sky	215 Dream		123
Came o'er that eye of blue	218 I Saw		2
And oft by yon blue gushing stream	218 Bloom		6
When the blue wave rolls nightly on deep Galilee	222 Sennacherib		4
And wore but a starless blue coat, and in kersey	228 Moore-A		22
Hibernian Strangford! with thine eyes of blue	246 Bards		297
Spread its light wings of saffron and of blue	248 Bards		523
Whose postscripts prate of dyeing 'heroines blue	260 Hints		290
Celestial tears bedimm'd her large blue eye	269 Minerva		86
New troopers strut, new turncoats blush in blue	276 Waltz		176
A fair lady--A spinster? Miss Lilac! The Blue	278 Blues	1	62
I say she's a Blue, man, as blue as the ether	278 Blues	1	69
On the rack of cross questions, by all the blue bevy	280 Blues	1	148
Of scribblers, wits, lecturers, white, black, and blue	280 Blues	2	17
Broke out of bounds o'er the ethereal blue	285 Vision		14
Of thirty regiments in red, green, and blue	292 Vision		488
Break the blue crystal of the seas	310 Giaour		17
These waters blue that round you lave	311 Giaour		110
Far, dark, along the blue sea glancing	312 Giaour		168
Which freezes o'er its lifeless blue	318 Giaour		774
His eye look'd o'er the dark blue water	326 Abydos	1	242
'O'er the glad waters of the dark blue sea	338 Corsair	1	1
The tender blue of that large loving eye	345 Corsair	1	493
Too bright, too blue, for my captivity	348 Corsair	2	86
The blue waves sport around the stern they urge	362 Corsair	3	481
Sinks those blue orbs in that long last eclipse	364 Corsair	3	613
Blue roll the waters, blue the sky	387 Corinth		244
Beside her eye had less of blue	390 Corinth		551
And on the wave is deeper blue	396 Parisina		9
But round their orbs of deepest blue	400 Parisina		332
To him, with eyes as blue as heaven	403 Chillon		75
When skies are blue and earth is gay	405 Chillon		299
And the blue Rhone in fullest flow	406 Chillon		336
Even he too loves at times the blue lagoon	419 Island	2	19
O'er whose blue bosom rose the starry isles	422 Island	2	252
He who first met the Highlands' swelling blue	422 Island	2	280
And the blue sky spread round them like a lake	424 Island	2	414
His brow was pale, his blue eyes sunken in	427 Island	3	100
They skim the blue tops of the billows fast	429 Island	3	229
Or deem'd him mad, or prey to the blue shark	432 Island	4	208
With brighter stars, and robes with deeper blue	459 Dante	2	53
Troubles the clotted air, of late so blue	459 Dante	2	78
In the blue depth of the waters	479 Manfred	1	76
Waved dark in the blue midnight, and the stars	495 Manfred	3	273
Rising at distance o'er the blue Lagoon	506 Faliero	1	465
What ocean is to earth, spreads its blue depths	529 Faliero	4	72
That no stroke errs. And you, ye blue sea-waves	535 Faliero	4	490
Upon you! Ye blue waves, which bore my banner	548 Faliero	5	726
As it would quit its place in the blue ether	562 Sardan	2	65
I love to watch them in the deep blue vault	566 Sardan	2	253
As it stream'd o'er her; her blue veins that rose	577 Sardan	3	389
Bounding o'er yon blue tide, as I have skimm'd	597 Foscari	1	95
So does the earth, and sky, the blue of ocean	598 Foscari	1	164
To right, as in the dim blue air the eye	635 Cain	1	491
Yon small blue circle, swinging in far ether	636 Cain	2	29
Is this blue wilderness of interminable	637 Cain	2	102
Oh, how we cleave the blue! The stars fade from us	638 Cain	2	144
The very blue of the empurpled night	638 Cain	2	179
The deep blue noon of night, lit by an orb	643 Cain	2	461
Yon blue immensity, is boundless? Ay	645 Cain	2	595
Half open, from beneath them the clear blue	646 Cain	3	29
And opens wide his blue eyes upon thine	648 Cain	3	150
Of earth nought left but the unbroken blue	660 Heaven		364
A cloud comes o'er his blue eyes suddenly	713 Werner	5	53
And she lifts up her dewy eye of blue	742 Deformed	3	11
'Tis that I still retain my 'buff and blue	747 Juan	Ded	132
At midnight on the blue and moonlit deep	761 Juan	1	970
And clap a white cape on their mantles blue	763 Juan	1	1069
But almost every other country's blue	775 Juan	2	94
Sooner shall this blue ocean melt to air	776 Juan	2	147
Lull'd them like turtles sleeping on the blue	782 Juan	2	541
The sea and sky were blue, and clear, and mild	782 Juan	2	556
Resting its bright base on the quivering blue	785 Juan	2	723
Where the blue veins look'd shadowy, shrunk, and weak	792 Juan	2	1173
The sands untumbled, the blue waves untost	797 Juan	2	1444
And all the stars that crowded the blue space	799 Juan	2	1583

BLUE
Embroider'd delicately o'er with blue   809 Juan   3   510
On crimson satin, border'd with pale blue   809 Juan   3   530
Forlorn, and gazing on the deep blue surge   826 Juan   4   627
From the blue skies derived a double blue   828 Juan   4   718
Oh! 'darkly, deeply, beautifully blue   830 Juan   4   873
Blue as the garters which serenely lie   830 Juan   4   878
By measuring 'the intensity of blue   830 Juan   4   895
Broke foaming o'er the blue Symplegades   831 Juan   5   34
Without more preface, in her blue eyes blending 846 Juan   5   925
With great blue eyes, a lovely hand and arm   857 Juan   6   323
Just when the fading lamps waned dim and blue   861 Juan   6   557
And her proud brow's blue veins to swell and
   darkle   864 Juan   6   808
For seeing one with ribands, black and blue   885 Juan   8   453
In its meridian, her blue eyes or gray   905 Juan   9   562
Too wise to look through optics black or blue   905 Juan   9   568
Scotch plaids, Scotch snoods, the blue hills, and
   clear streams   909 Juan   10   138
The seventh will bring blue devils or a dun   912 Juan   10   304
The blue sea's border; and Don Juan felt   915 Juan   10   514
Now) you may cross the blue deep and white foam 924 Juan   11   347
Which now he found was blue instead of green   924 Juan   11   408
Amongst live poets and blue ladies, past   926 Juan   11   498
But it is time that I should hoist my 'blue Peter 928 Juan   11   653
Of white cliffs, white necks, blue eyes, bluer
   stockings   938 Juan   12   535
An eye's an eye, and whether black or blue   941 Juan   13   19
Its windings through the woods; now clear, now
   blue   948 Juan   13   463
Blue devils, and blue-stockings, and romances   965 Juan   14   631
Hath got blue devils for his morning mirrors   968 Juan   15   28
With a slight shade of blue too, it might be   973 Juan   15   325
Whose heart was fix'd upon a star or blue string 973 Juan   15   331
Burnt, and not blue, as modest tapers use   983 Juan   16   202
She also had a twilight tinge of 'Blue   986 Juan   16   417
Her laughing blue eyes with a glance could seize 993 Juan   16   844
But still the shade remain'd: the blue eyes
   glared   996 Juan   16   1009

BLUEBOTTLE
Sir George thinks exactly with Lady Bluebottle   282 Blues   2   116
For God's sake, my Lady Bluebottle, check not   282 Blues   2   133

BLUEBOTTLES
The bluest of bluebottles you e'er saw   449 Beppo   588

BLUEBOTTLE'S
I'm engaged to the Lady Bluebottle's collation   279 Blues   1   137
With a glass of Madeira at Lady Bluebottle's   280 Blues   1   160

BLUE-COAT
Drawn by the blue-coat misses of a coterie   830 Juan   4   872

BLUE-EYED
Come, blue-eyed maid of heaven!--but thou, alas   19 Harold   2   1
Glenalvon's blue-eyed daughter came   102 Alva   80
his boy; but the blue-eyed Mora spreads the   130 Calmar   74
to blue-eyed Mora; let it hang in my empty   131 Calmar   179
blue-eyed Mora; but not harmless was thy   131 Calmar   196
'Mortal!' the blue-eyed maid resumed, 'once more 270 Minerva   157
And who is he? the blue-eyed northern child   421 Island   2   163

BLUELY
The river from the lake, all bluely dash'd   966 Juan   14   694

BLUEMOUNT
Lady Bluemount--Miss Lilac--be pleased, pray, to
   place ye   281 Blues   2   31
Lady Bluemount! a glass of Madeira? With
   pleasure   281 Blues   2   46

BLUER
Of white cliffs, white necks, blue eyes, bluer
   stockings   938 Juan   12   535

BLUES
And for Sotheby's Blues have deserted Sam Rogers 226 Oh You   12
But consider, dear Inkel, she's one of the 'Blues 279 Blues   1   100
Blues, dandies, and dowagers, and secondhand
   scribes   280 Blues   1   158
By the rag, tag, and bobtail, of those they call
   'Blues   280 Blues   2   23
But luckily these beauties are no 'Blues   449 Beppo   574
Thou shalt not bear false witness like 'the Blues 772 Juan   1   1643
The Blues, that tender tribe who sigh o'er
   sonnets   924 Juan   11   393

BLUEST
And bluest skies that harmonise the whole   26 Harold   2   429
The bluest of bluebottles you e'er saw   449 Beppo   588

BLUE-STOCKING
Sappho the sage blue-stocking, in whose grave   800 Juan   2   1636

BLUE-STOCKINGS
Blue devils, and blue-stockings, and romances   965 Juan   14   631

BLUE-STOCKING'S
Do you think me subdued by a Blue-stocking's eye 279 Blues   1   96

BLUFF-HEAD
But from the bluff-head, where I watch'd to-day 426 Island   2   507

BLUNDER
I write in haste; excuse each blunder   231 Doctor   41
What then? the self-same blunder Pope has got   243 Bards   99
Won half by blunder, half by treachery   301 Age   225
They make some blunder, which their ladies tell
   us   759 Juan   1   784
And seems to me almost a sort of blunder   764 Juan   1   1151
I have but one simile, and that's a blunder   859 Juan   6   455
Was favour'd by an accident or blunder   884 Juan   8   362
May like being praised for every lucky blunder   897 Juan   9   38
The world, which at the worst's a glorious
   blunder   919 Juan   11   24
But they who blunder thus are raw beginners   938 Juan   12   521
That he had made at first a silly blunder   996 Juan   16   1022

BLUNDER'D
That he had somehow blunder'd into debt   443 Beppo   211
Young women, and correct them when they blunder'd 856 Juan   6   248
But as it happens to brave men, they blunder'd   887 Juan   8   597
The tenth or twentieth name would be but
   blunder'd   932 Juan   12   148

BLUNDERING
Beware lest blundering Brougham destroy the sale 248 Bards   524
A blundering novice in his new French grammar   447 Beppo   434
His haste: impatience is a blundering guide   927 Juan   11   558

BLUNDERS
Or Liverpool weeps o'er his blunders   227 Thurlow-B   21
Than some wives (who make blunders no less stupid 902 Juan   9   359
In this: whatever other blunders lie   946 Juan   13   339

BLUNDER'S
Not even a sprightly blunder's spark can blaze   746 Juan   Ded   101

BLUNT
Could blunt the sabre's edge or clear the can-
   non's smoke   12 Harold   1   530
Expel the venom and not blunt the dart   73 Harold   4   1069
My pen is blunt, my ink is low   96 Granta   95
A plain blunt show of briefly-spoken seeming   209 Sketch   59
And, blunt myself, give edge to others' steel   263 Hints   436
Shall never blunt its edge on meaner men   265 Hints   600
With sabre keen or blunt jerreed   326 Abydos   1   238
Perhaps you think by this blunt brevity   538 Faliero   5   37
I have been a soldier, and perhaps am blunt   676 Werner   1   327
A kind of blunt compassion for the sad   832 Juan   5   93

BLUNTS
Which, once partaken, blunts the sabre's edge   348 Corsair   2   120

BLUSH
(See also DAY-BLUSH)
What fruits of fragrance blush on every tree   6 Harold   1   209
And fain would blush, if blush they could, for
   shame   8 Harold   1   309
Blush, Caledonia, such thy son could be   21 Harold   2   95
Nor blush for those who conquer'd on that plain   45 Harold   3   603
But yet no blush to mine replies   90 Caroline-B   11
Nor dare to call the blush from Beauty's cheek   113 Prologue   6
What modest maid without a blush   147 Vain Lady   23
Each kindred brute might bid thee blush for shame 154 Dog   22
And made us blush that you forbore to blame   170 Address-A   57
And blush for every pang it cost   174 Remember-B   11
Its rose of whiteness with the brightest blush   175 Sonnet-B   3
To make man blush there was but one   182 Ode-A   171
'Tis not on youth's smooth cheek the blush alone,
   which fades so fast   185 Music-B   3
Till now, when the isle which should blush for his
   birth   203 Avatar   89
Abused his art, till Nature, with a blush   256 Hints   3
'Mortal!'--'twas thus she spake--'that blush of
   shame   269 Minerva   89
New troopers strut, new turncoats blush in blue 276 Waltz   176
Might once have been mistaken for a blush   276 Waltz   189
To bid us blush for these old chains, or break   303 Age   339
Of transient Anger's hasty blush   312 Giaour   237
So sweet the blush of Bashfulness   326 Abydos   1   228
And rising with the wonted blush of morn   351 Corsair   2   316
The swarthy blush recolours in his cheeks   369 Lara   1   226
The cheek where oft the unbidden blush shone
   through   373 Lara   1   531
Yet not such blush as mounts when health would
   show   373 Lara   1   532
And her blush returns, and her bosom heaves   396 Parisina   26

BLUSH

The blush would make its way, and all but speak	420	Island 2	136
All Giggle, Blush; half Pertness and half Pout	445	Beppo	308
The blush of earth embracing with her heaven	485	Manfred 2	116
How darest thou name me and not blush? Not blush	552	Sardan 1	88
And made thee weep and blush? I should do both	558	Sardan 1	514
I blush that we should owe our lives to such	567	Sardan 2	343
And I should blush far more to take the grantor's	567	Sardan 2	345
Blush to find ancestors, who would have blush'd	612	Foscari 3	302
And most enduring:--Shall I blush for him	664	Heaven	686
And blush at my own barren gratitude	685	Werner 2	152
Can neither blush with shame nor pale with fear	727	Deformed 1	374
They blush, and we believe them; at least I	768	Juan 1	1425
From heart to cheek is curb'd into a blush	792	Juan 2	1124
For Greeks a blush--for Greece a tear	812	Juan 3	724
Must we but blush?--Our fathers bled	812	Juan 3	726
Began to blush up to the eyes, and then	847	Juan 5	991
Grow deadly pale, and then blush back again	847	Juan 5	992
The new-bought virgin, made her blush and shake	851	Juan 5	1242
A slight blush, a soft tremor, a calm kind	854	Juan 6	113
Of favouritism, but not yet in the blush	908	Juan 10	34
Meaning a virgin's first blush at a rout	933	Juan 12	245
At the first blush; for a fair Briton hides	939	Juan 12	587
But what was bad, she did not blush in turn	993	Juan 16	793

BLUSH'D

Blush'd at the praise of their own loveliness	38	Harold 3	211
And Mora's tender bosom blush'd	103	Alva	196
Even passion blush'd to plead for more	165	Thyrza	36
That it blush'd like the waves of hell	176	Devil's Dr	41
Blush'd upon Sleep and Lord Castlereagh	178	Devil's Dr	170
My goblets blush'd from every vine	219	Vanity	3
That such as I could love, who blush'd to hear	439	Tasso	229
Blush to find ancestors, who would have blush'd	612	Foscari 3	302
She blush'd, and frown'd not, but she strove to speak	760	Juan 1	895
I can't tell why she blush'd, nor can expound	863	Juan 6	677
To save a sire who blush'd that he begot him	892	Juan 8	880
Fair virgins blush'd upon him; wedded dames	924	Juan 11	377

BLUSHES

Whene'er we meet my blushes rise	90	Caroline-B	9
She blushes, curt'sies, frowns--in short she	100	Marion	23
And blushes modest as the giver	113	Cornelian-A	4
There is a Face whose Blushes tell	144	Jessy	13
Their bloom in blushes ever new	315	Giaour	495
And blushes o'er his error, as he eyes	350	Corsair 2	233
His blushes make them look a little pale	450	Beppo	656
Perhaps some virtuous blushes;--let them go	745	Juan Ded	50
And burning blushes, though for no transgression	756	Juan 1	587
Blushes for those who will not:--but to sigh	923	Juan 11	300
And the vine blushes like Aurora's lip	931	Juan 12	69
To patriot sympathy a Briton's blushes	959	Juan 14	276
Than to wax white--for blushes are for quality	989	Juan 16	560

BLUSHING

Peeps blushing on the revel's laughing crew	14	Harold 1	676
When shall she breathe her from the blushing toil	18	Harold 1	923
Tell not the deed to blushing Europe's ears	21	Harold 2	112
The blushing beauty by thy side	89	Prometheus-A	12
For these this toy of blushing hue	141	Pignus	5
Again thou'lt smile, and blushing shun	159	Storm	65
The offended guests would not, with blushing, see	171	Hales-Owen	7
Lo! blushing Itch, coy nymph, enamour'd grown	249	Bards	536
Blooms blushing to her lover's tale	310	Giaour	25
At least I feel my cheek, too, blushing	328	Abydos 1	399
And redly ran his blushing waters down	894	Juan 8	1012
Blushing and beardless; and yet ne'ertheless	902	Juan 9	370
Blushing with Bacchant coronals along	950	Juan 13	602

BLUSTERING

Ne'er blows in all its blustering freedom? 'Twas so	614	Foscari 3	398

BOA

He lay coil'd like the boa in the wood	807	Juan 3	380

BOABDIL

Boabdil wept, of Donna Julia's kin	754	Juan 1	446

BOAR

So that the boar, defunct, lay tripp'd up near	473	Morgante	500
Watch him!--as you would watch the wild boar when	694	Werner 2	703
The howling hounds, the boar makes for the thicket	704	Werner 4	32
Hunts not the wretched coney, but the boar	724	Deformed 1	124

BOARD
(See also PIRATE-BOARD)

And soon on board the Lusian pilots leap	6	Harold 1	205
Prepared and spread the plenteous board within	28	Harold 2	537
Or gay assemble round the festive board	119	Newstead-A	11
Ere we sail on board the Packet	157	Hodgson	16
Ere you've been an hour on board	157	Hodgson	24

BOARD

Ev'n on board the Lisbon Packet	157	Hodgson	80
'Next to seeing a lord at the council board	177	Devil's Dr	101
From the charm'd council to the festive board	193	Monody	37
Without 'the Board of Longitude	234	Strahan	22
Whose old-establish'd board of joint controls	266	Hints	677
This was a handsome board--at least for heaven	285	Vision	33
As temperance, if at Apicius' board	290	Vision	364
A cup too on the board was set	330	Abydos 2	127
With all a hermit's board would scarce deny	339	Corsair 1	74
But come, the board is spread; our silver lamp	344	Corsair 1	433
Bowls on the board, and banners on the wall	366	Lara 1	6
But if they would--they could'--around the board	368	Lara 1	153
And little cared for bed and board	407	Mazeppa	67
Born of the fruit; for board the plantain spread	432	Island	170
First at the board in this unhappy process	595	Foscari 1	25
As e'er was gilt upon a trader's board	674	Werner 1	187
To save one half the people then on board	780	Juan 2	384
On board of one of these, and under hatches	822	Juan 4	399
We were transferr'd on board her in a hurry	827	Juan 4	653
Like a backgammon board the place was dotted	832	Juan 5	73
The eunuch made a sign to those on board	836	Juan 5	327
And scorn his temperate board, as none at all	930	Juan 12	22
Their table was a board to tempt even ghosts	953	Juan 13	787
Observed as strictly both at board and bed	972	Juan 15	254
At the full board, and sit alike delighted	989	Juan 16	597

BOARDING-BRAND

Be the edge sharpen'd of my boarding-brand	340	Corsair 1	163

BOARDS

Gods! o'er those boards shall Folly rear her head	249	Bards	586
And wounded several shutters, and some boards	764	Juan 1	1144

BOARD-WAGES

We scorn it as we do board-wages. Then	684	Werner 2	50

BOARS

Fish in the woods, and boars beneath the waves	257	Hints	48
So that the giant's join'd by all the boars	473	Morgante	496
With the dead boars and with that brimful vase	474	Morgante	518
If she hath no wild boars, she hath a tame	951	Juan 13	623

BOAR'S

But brawny as the boar's; and hung beneath	425	Island 2	490
The boar's in the wood	742	Deformed 3	35

BOARS'

Will bring you six boars' heads for trophies home	707	Werner 4	226

BOAST

A scene where mingling foes should boast and bleed	11	Harold 1	462
Still does he mark it with triumphant boast	12	Harold 1	520
Fair is proud Seville; let her country boast	14	Harold 1	657
But not the modern Pict's ignoble boast	21	Harold 2	100
Are rarely seen; nor can fair Tempe boast	26	Harold 2	411
If Greece one true-born patriot still can boast	32	Harold 2	784
Boast of the aged! lesson of the young	34	Harold 2	861
If not, o'er one fallen despot boast no more	38	Harold 3	172
Than when she was a boast, a marvel, and a show	58	Harold 4	162
And call'd, proud boast! the British drama forth	94	Dorset	68
The pride of princes, and the boast of song	94	Dorset	74
The artless Helicon I boast is youth	119	Answer-A	23
Probus, the pride of science, and the boast	123	Recoll	109
Well canst thou boast, to lead in senates fit	126	Recoll	291
Dost thou repeat, in childish boast	146	Vain Lady	13
Some hour propitious to our prayers may boast	169	Address-A	29
'But hold, you say, this self-complacent boast	171	Address-B	45
Who could boast o'er France defeated	187	Ode-B	30
For I can boast a race as true	197	Duel	15
The Muse may boast--the World must own	233	Ballad-B	7
The scourge of England and the boast of France	244	Bards	206
Boeotian Cottle, rich Bristowa's boast	247	Bards	387
England could boast a judge almost the same	247	Bards	439
Boast of thy country and Britannia's guide	248	Bards	501
May Moorland weavers boast Pindaric skill	252	Bards	795
Yet still some genuine sons 'tis hers to boast	252	Bards	815
At once the boast of learning, and disgrace	255	Bards	982
I've braved it--not for honour's boast	320	Giaour	1012
His corse may boast its urn and narrow cave	338	Corsair 1	33
Yet was I brave--mean boast where all are brave	343	Corsair 1	325
And great the gathering crews, and loud the boast	347	Corsair 2	9
Might warrant more than even the Pacha's boast	347	Corsair 2	44
I had no death to fear, nor wealth to boast	348	Corsair 2	71
Which Stamboul's sultan there can boast	385	Corinth	110
Her ancient civic boast--'the Free	385	Corinth	130
Not his the loud fanatic boast	387	Corinth	297
With adding ranks and raging boast	394	Corinth	923
But, strange to say, they rarely boast	408	Mazeppa	179
Even Greece can boast but one Thermopylae	427	Island 3	56
You have more patience than I care to boast	516	Faliero 1	530
Whom these unsettled times forbid to boast	686	Werner 2	192
Heroes of the immortal boast	735	Deformed 2	48

BOAST
For there one learns--'tis not for me to boast	753 Juan	1	417
Yet, if I name my guilt, 'tis not to boast	770 Juan	1	1541
Would she be proud, or boast herself the free	916 Juan	10	537
None than themselves could boast a longer line	947 Juan	13	397
Was wont to boast--as if a glutton's tray	991 Juan	16	667

BOASTED
(See also LONG-BOASTED)
And mix unbleeding with the boasted slain	19 Harold	1	933
Of worthless dust which from thy boasted line	60 Harold	4	327
Of all their boasted self-denial	95 Granta		64
And boasted locks of red or auburn hue	246 Bards		298
And boasted that he could not flatter	408 Mazeppa		150

BOASTER
My lord, I am no boaster of my love	571 Sardan	2	591

BOASTFUL
From an adulteress boastful of her guilt	548 Faliero	5	766

BOASTING
Partake his jest with boasting boys	321 Giaour		1174
Boasting these idle attributes, because	486 Manfred	2	192

BOASTS
Freedom and peace to that which boasts his birth	301 Age		248
Not the loud recreant wretch who boasts and flies	352 Corsair	2	362
Of the New World the Spaniard boasts about	695 Werner	3	34
The sentimental boasts to be unmoved	964 Juan	14	582

BOAT
(See also LONG-BOAT, STEAM-BOAT)
Enough for my rude boat, where should I steer	70 Harold	4	944
Stop the boat--I'm sick--oh Lord	157 Hodgson		22
My boat is on the shore	230 My Boat		1
All in my little boat, against a Galley	230 Murray-A		15
Start on the fisher's eye like boat	312 Giaour		170
His boat appears--not five oars' length	335 Abydos	2	547
A broken torch, an oarless boat	335 Abydos	2	592
Repair the boat, replace the helm or oar	338 Corsair	1	51
Her boat descending from the latticed stern	339 Corsair	1	100
'They are--nay more, embark'd; the latest boat	346 Corsair	1	557
Then to his boat with haughty gesture sprung	346 Corsair	1	570
At length a fisher's humble boat by night	348 Corsair	2	73
It came at last--a sad and shatter'd boat	356 Corsair	3	85
Hoist out the boat at once, and slacken sail	363 Corsair	3	495
With the first boat descends he for the shore	364 Corsair	3	573
On the rougher plank of our gliding boat	384 Corinth		11
'Hoist out the boat!' was now the leader's cry	416 Island	1	81
The boat is lower'd with all the haste of hate	416 Island	1	85
That boat and ship shall never meet again	418 Island	1	176
The boat drew nigh, well arm'd, and firm the crew	433 Island	4	281
'Tis a long cover'd boat that's common here	442 Beppo		147
The Count and Laura found their boat at last	451 Beppo		689
Signor! the boat is at the shore--the wind	617 Foscari	4	177
That a tight boat will live in a rough sea	779 Juan	2	359
Nine in the cutter, thirty in the boat	781 Juan	2	431
And for the boat--the crew kept crowding in it	781 Juan	2	456
Ague in its cold fit, they fill'd their boat	782 Juan	2	503
'Tis thus with people in an open boat	782 Juan	2	521
The fifth day, and their boat lay floating there	782 Juan	2	555
The men within the boat, and in this guise	786 Juan	2	750
The boat made way; yet now they were so low	786 Juan	2	763
And at the bottom of the boat three were	786 Juan	2	782
They ran the boat for shore,--and overset her	787 Juan	2	832
He still was in the boat and had but dozed	788 Juan	2	891
He wishes for 'a boat' to sail the deeps	814 Juan	3	877
Another outcry for 'a little boat'	814 Juan	3	879
They laid him in a boat, and plied the oar	822 Juan	4	397
Bore off his bargains to a gilded boat	836 Juan	5	314
The imperial bride--and added, 'Let the boat	866 Juan	6	898
But what if carrying sail capsize the boat	898 Juan	9	139
Where ships have founder'd, as doth many a boat	907 Juan	10	32

BOATMAN
The 'little boatman' and his 'Peter Bell	815 Juan	3	895

BOATMAN'S
The swain, and chase the boatman's fear	329 Abydos	2	56

BOATMEN
Now our boatmen quit their mooring	157 Hodgson		17
Of boatmen answering back with verse for verse	529 Faliero	4	100

BOATS
(See also STEAM-BOATS)
As boats are sometimes by a wanton whale	285 Vision		16
The boats are darting o'er the curly bay	364 Corsair	3	559
Of the arm'd boats which hurried to complete	429 Island	3	219
All safe off to your boats, blow one long blast	593 Sardan	5	386
Some hoisted out the boats; and there was one	779 Juan	2	350
Getting the boats out, being well aware	779 Juan	2	358
The other boats, the yawl and pinnace, had	780 Juan	2	377

BOATS
And two boats could not hold, far less be stored	780 Juan	2	383
The boats put off o'ercrowded with their crews	780 Juan	2	406
The boats, as stated, had got off before	780 Juan	2	425
'Pedlars,' and 'Boats,' and 'Waggons!' Oh! ye shades	814 Juan	3	889
To find our way to Marmora without boats	843 Juan	5	734
Their Delhis mann'd some boats, and sail'd again	871 Juan	7	243
Boats when 'twas water, skating when 'twas ice	954 Juan	13	843

BOAT'S
(See also LONG-BOAT'S, SEABOAT'S)
The boat's crew look'd amazed o'er sea and shore	431 Island	4	68

BOATS'
Within a hundred boats' length was the foe	430 Island	4	51

BOAT'S-CREW
Or with a famish'd boat's-crew had your berth	784 Juan	2	670

BOATSWAIN'S
Hark, to the Boatswain's call, the cheering cry	22 Harold	2	158

BOAZ
You may be Boaz, and I--modest Ruth	953 Juan	13	764

BOB
Fletcher! Murray! Bob! where are you	157 Hodgson		49
Johanna Southcote or Bob Southey raving	288 Vision		224
Bob Southey! You're a poet--Poet-laureate	745 Juan	Ded	1
You, Bob! are rather insolent, you know	745 Juan	Ded	17
Gasping on deck, because you soar too high, Bob	745 Juan	Ded	23
And fall, for lack of moisture, quite a-dry, Bob	745 Juan	Ded	24
An epic from Bob Southey every spring	814 Juan	3	868
As through his palms Bob Acres' valour oozed	849 Juan	5	1129

BOBBIN
So if we can hang them for breaking a bobbin	225 Ode-D		11

BOBBY
As under Walpole Bobby O	235 New Song		20

BOB-MAJOR
Like a bob-major from a village steeple	877 Juan	7	680

BOBTAIL
By the rag, tag, and bobtail, of those they call 'Blues	280 Blues	2	23

BOCCACCIO
Boccaccio to his parent earth bequeath'd	63 Harold	4	514

BOCCACCIO'S
Evergreen forest! which Boccaccio's lore	815 Juan	3	934

BODE
To bode him no great good, he deprecated	865 Juan	6	810

BODED
To thee hath never boded good	328 Abydos	1	440
I would have boded so much to myself	564 Sardan	2	142
Boded no good, whatever it express'd	806 Juan	3	332
A thing which victory by no means boded	880 Juan	8	126

BODEMENTS
Those horrid bodements which, amidst the throng	529 Faliero	4	107
Tremendous bodements; let it do its office	535 Faliero	4	534

BODES
The close and sultry summer's day, which bodes	576 Sardan	3	316
Come hither, mynheer! But so much haste bodes	686 Werner	2	247

BODICES
But never put on pantaloons or bodices	752 Juan	1	324

BODIED
Till I had bodied forth the heated mind	70 Harold	4	935
Thou wert a beautiful thought, and softly bodied forth	72 Harold	4	1035

BODIES
Not content with depriving your bodies of spirit	116 To Eliza		10
Avengers o'er their bodies rose	394 Corinth		932
Anoint our bodies with the fragrant oil	419 Island	2	26
Of minds and bodies in captivity	437 Tasso		66
Fresh souls and bodies, all foredoom'd to be	637 Cain	2	59
For killing bodies, and for saving souls	763 Juan	1	1050
Had left their bodies; and what's worse, alas	781 Juan	2	434
Where men have souls or bodies she must answer	827 Juan	4	672
But on they march'd, dead bodies trampling o'er	880 Juan	8	149
Over a heap of bodies, felt his heel	888 Juan	8	658
Amidst the bodies lull'd in bloody rest	889 Juan	8	728
Those movements, those improvements in our bodies	906 Juan	9	593
Which make all bodies anxious to get out	906 Juan	9	594

BODIES
Of physics, bodies whether short or tall 983 Juan 16 190
Such bodies could have souls, or souls such
  bodies 992 Juan 16 768

BODILESS
The bodiless thought? the Spirit of each spot 46 Harold 3 705
A bodiless enjoyment--born and dying 482 Manfred 1 316

BODING
Deep in whose darkly boding ear 321 Giaour 1077
And thus some boding flash'd through either frame 819 Juan 4 166

BODINGS
Say--that his bodings came to pass 322 Giaour 1234
Perchance, but for the bodings of his breast 363 Corsair 3 547
My better bodings. But it must not be 584 Sardan 4 366

BODY
So mix his body with the dust! It might 286 Vision 81
Of almost every body born to die 286 Vision 120
And more of both than any body knows 297 Vision 784
But of every wound his body bore 393 Corinth 790
The tempest-born in body and in mind 421 Island 2 168
His body crush'd into one gory mass 434 Island 4 342
And doom this body forfeit to the fire 457 Dante 1 68
And fell down even as a dead body falls 477 Francesca 46
Thy mind and body are alike unfit 483 Manfred 2 2
Of my full youth, while yet my body served 504 Faliero 1 304
The poisonous heads of whose envenom'd body 506 Faliero 1 451
Of one long chain; one mass, one breath, one body 521 Faliero 3 155
A single emanation from one body 524 Faliero 3 407
Of my own breath and body--so far that 564 Sardan 2 171
For mind nor body: let me have a couch 577 Sardan 3 340
The body hence. Where? To my proper chamber 589 Sardan 5 164
To mingle with a body so august 616 Foscari 4 81
Oh, Foscari! We must remove the body 618 Foscari 4 197
The body bleeds in the presence of the assassin 619 Foscari 4 242
Bear hence the body. Signors, if it please you 619 Foscari 4 246
Where? To the chamber where the body lies 622 Foscari 5 114
The body of his son. And call Marina 624 Foscari 5 208
It may turn out with the live or dead body 675 Werner 1 228
Save on his body. Part of his own household 702 Werner 3 482
The bleeding body--but it moved no more 718 Werner 5 334
Exemption from some maladies of body 737 Deformed 2 188
The body of your Credence? No one--but 743 Deformed 3 114
The very thing which every body feels 757 Juan 1 707
And then they left off eating the dead body 784 Juan 2 656
Which every body does without who can 828 Juan 4 724
May make up for a bullet in his body 869 Juan 7 163
And he whose very body was all mind 885 Juan 8 429
For one rough, weather-beaten, veteran body 892 Juan 8 895
All that the body perpetrates of bad 894 Juan 8 978
Following the bent of body or of mind 899 Juan 9 165
Not only in the body but the proem 899 Juan 9 171
And 'gainst the body makes a strong appeal 910 Juan 10 157
As any body on the elected roll 911 Juan 10 275
On that sweet ore which every body nurses 917 Juan 10 630
Decide, and every body one day will 919 Juan 11 31
His pockets first and then his body riddled 920 Juan 11 136
Where every body has some separate aim 937 Juan 12 461
Ends. When the body of the book's begun 940 Juan 12 690
The goodliest soil of body and of mind 941 Juan 13 16
Certes it was not body; he was well 964 Juan 14 564
The luck of finding every body solvent 969 Juan 15 56
With any body in a ride or walk 970 Juan 15 152
Help contradicting them, and every body 979 Juan 15 698
And every body out of their own sphere 991 Juan 16 672
Hinting that soul and body on the whole 996 Juan 16 991
It touch'd no soul, nor body, but the wall 996 Juan 16 1002

BODY-GUARD
In the prince's body-guard--if you succeed 682 Werner 1 675

BODY'S
Their body's self turn'd soul with the intense 462 Dante 3 163

BOEHM'S
To-night to Mrs. Boehm's masquerade 447 Beppo 445

BOEOTIA
Survey Boeotia;--Caledonia's ours 270 Minerva 130
As dull Boeotia gave a Pindar birth 270 Minerva 150

BOEOTIAN
Ask ye, Boeotian shades, the reason why 15 Harold 1 706
By Jeffrey's heart or Lambe's Boeotian head 242 Bards 82
Boeotian Cottle, rich Bristowa's boast 247 Bards 387
And that deep-mouth'd Boeotian 'Savage Landor 925 Juan 11 463

BOG
As travellers follow over bog and brake 882 Juan 8 252

BOGGLE
She had stood fire too long and well, to boggle 450 Beppo 647

BOGGY
Which leads beholders on a boggy walk 873 Juan 7 366

BOGLE
In mind, a sort of sentimental bogle 927 Juan 11 564

BOHEA
That I must have recourse to black Bohea 823 Juan 4 414

BOHEMIA
When first Bohemia raised her banner 'gainst 676 Werner 1 332
The mountains of Bohemia and Silesia 685 Werner 2 125
I stand well with the elector; in Bohemia 685 Werner 2 176
It is the richest of the rich Bohemia 694 Werner 2 708
The route on to Bohemia, though encumber'd 698 Werner 3 197
Would Stralenheim's appearance in Bohemia 699 Werner 3 249
Which skirt Bohemia--even into Lusatia 716 Werner 5 236

BOHEMIAN
To the Bohemian mountains many a sunset 688 Werner 2 375
An old Bohemian--an imperial gipsy 699 Werner 3 290
A gipsy or Bohemian, 'tis the same 699 Werner 3 291

BOIL
And boil in endless torture; while the sweat 65 Harold 4 618
The mists boil up around the glaciers; clouds 482 Manfred 1 346
Of cities, that boil over with their scum 919 Juan 11 64
It makes my blood boil like the springs of Hecla 979 Juan 15 735

BOIL'D
Mere roast and boil'd no epicure invites 265 Hints 633
That boil'd your bones, unless you paid them
  double 440 Beppo 32
Cloves, cinnamon, and saffron too were boil'd 809 Juan 3 503
Boil'd up, and proved her truly of his race 822 Juan 4 352
Boil'd in his veins, and rather than descend 844 Juan 5 828

BOILEAU
And Boileau, whose rash envy could allow 60 Harold 4 340

BOILING
In its own eddy boiling and o'erwrought 36 Harold 3 57
And pray, what follows from his boiling brain 259 Hints 196
Is boiling; but for thy dear sake 331 Abydos 2 208
Which flings it broad and boiling sheet on sheet 429 Island 3 177
Lie low beneath the boiling of the deep 659 Heaven 289
To show its boiling surf, and bounding spray 787 Juan 2 820

BOILINGLY
Rise boilingly higher 479 Manfred 1 91

BOILS
That boils in Aetna's breast of flame 321 Giaour 1102
I have proved them; and my spirit boils up when 681 Werner 1 658
And the loud breaker boils against the rock 763 Juan 1 1071
As wife and friends did for the boils of Job 877 Juan 7 615

BOISTEROUS
For all the boisterous joys that ever shook 587 Sardan 5 26

BOIST'ROUS
Where boist'rous joy is but a name 135 I Would 40

BOLD
Now brightly bold or beautifully shy 3 To Ianthe 29
Here the bold peasant storm'd the dragon's nest 12 Harold 1 519
He sways a nation, turbulent and bold 26 Harold 2 420
Where some bold river breaks the long expanse 27 Harold 2 483
The frailties of a heart so soft, yet bold 68 Harold 4 808
Bold in the field, and favour'd by the Nine 94 Dorset 71
While bold Pomposus bravely stay'd at home 124 Recoll 180
Prudence and sense, a spirit bold and free 126 Recoll 299
Who made that bold diversion 162 War Song 29
That the Christian, stern and bold 194 Ballad-A 38
And you miss'd your bold stroke for a mitre 239 Bray 51
He rear'd his bold and birlliant throne on high 239 Conquest 6
As bold in Billingsgate, though less renown'd 265 Hints 626
From a bold Briton in her wonted praise 305 Age 529
First of the bold Timariot bands 326 Abydos 1 203
More mildly firm than petulantly bold 372 Lara 1 430
Their wonder at the calmness of the bold 374 Lara 1 595
Or song heroically bold 403 Chillon 61
The Ukraine's hetman, calm and bold 407 Mazeppa 56
Prolong'd endurance tames the bold 412 Mazeppa 524
Awake, bold Bligh! the foe is at the gate 416 Island 1 51
Then forward stepp'd the bold and froward boy 417 Island 1 151
Which her bold bow flings off with dashing ease 418 Island 1 228
As bold a rover as the sands have seen 421 Island 2 180
And the bold Architect unto whose care 464 Dante 4 57
And do you right upon the bold delinquent 501 Faliero 1 114
Have nothing of old age; and his bold brow 509 Faliero 2 20
This man, I hear, is bold and popular 511 Faliero 2 140
Where all the pregnant hearts of our bold blood 519 Faliero 3 18
See the bold chiefs, who would reform a state 522 Faliero 3 226
'Tis bold, but feasible if I assist it 523 Faliero 3 347
A bold and bloody despot from his throne 562 Sardan 2 84
Is, at the least, a bold one, and not temper'd 565 Sardan 2 234

BOLD

And my desire. The boy, they say, 's a bold one	687	Werner	2	263
Of your brave bands of their own bold accord	733	Deformed	1	802
As you are bold within it. Mercy! mercy	740	Deformed	2	330
Against all noble maladies he's bold	776	Juan	2	173
All this, the most were patient, and some bold	779	Juan	2	332
How answers each bold Bacchanal	812	Juan	3	742
This spirit's well, but it may wax too bold	841	Juan	5	595
The Briton must be bold who really durst	884	Juan	8	381
Napoleon on his bold and bloody track	887	Juan	8	555
As bold as Daniel in the lion's den	905	Juan	9	548
Though bold and bloody, was the kind of thing	905	Juan	9	554
Even the bold Churchman's tomb excited awe	916	Juan	10	588
Bold Britons, we are now on Shooter's Hill	917	Juan	10	640
Because bold Britons have a tongue and free quill	943	Juan	13	157
But innocence is bold even at the stake	963	Juan	14	485
There were some hunters bold, and coursers keen	991	Juan	16	681

BOLDER

Or told my love, with hope grown bolder	98	To Lesbia		8
Those deeds the bolder spirit plainly did	342	Corsair	1	268

BOLDEST

The boldest steer but where their ports invite	46	Harold	3	668
These might the boldest sylph appal	97	To M--		17
E'en then the boldest start from public sneers	242	Bards		33

BOLDLY

Yet let us ponder boldly; 'tis a base	74	Harold	4	1135
Dares all things boldly but to lie	153	Friend-A		30
And boldly pilfers from the Pentateuch	246	Bards		324
But boldly clasps, and thrusts you from her gates	271	Minerva		230
They doubtless boldly did--but who are safe	339	Corsair	1	114
Beneath the gulf wherein they boldly leapt	431	Island	4	104
However boldly their warm blood was spilt	433	Island	4	269
Who live by lies, yet dare not boldly lie	923	Juan	11	285
Also a so-so matron boldly fight	951	Juan	13	653
Boldly referring to the list of peers	962	Juan	14	411

BOLERO

She mingles in the gay Bolero	160	Cadiz		42
He glanced like a personified Bolero	960	Juan	14	312

BOLERO'S

Fandango's wriggle, or Bolero's bound	275	Waltz		126

BOLIVAR

Forgets Pizarro to shout Bolivar	301	Age		252
From climes of Washington and Bolivar	303	Age		383

BOLOGNA

From an old Roman princess at Bologna	827	Juan	4	664

BOLOTOO

Like voices of the gods from Bolotoo	419	Island	2	6

BOLT

Is of the tree no bolt of thunder cleaves	61	Harold	4	365
As the bolt bursts on high	327	Abydos	1	336
Slow turns the grating bolt and sullen key	359	Corsair	3	272
Since bar and bolt no more his steps preclude	361	Corsair	3	390
The thunder came; that bolt hath blasted both	365	Corsair	3	672
And ever and anon some falling bolt	570	Sardan	2	551
But what have I to do with this? No bolt	702	Werner	3	480
As doth the bolt, because it stood between us	720	Werner	5	460
But beg 'Security' will bolt the door	757	Juan	1	712
Do pray undo the bolt a little faster	763	Juan	1	1093
No less a victim to the bolt and bar	916	Juan	10	540

BOLTED

No sooner was it bolted, than--Oh shame	767	Juan	1	1313

BOLTS

(See also DEATH-BOLTS, THUNDER-BOLTS)

Now on the smoke of blazing bolts she flies	10	Harold	1	409
But Jealousy has fled: his bars, his bolts	17	Harold	1	801
The bolts loud roll from pole to pole	104	Alva		265
Nor bolts nor bars against their strength avail'd	124	Recoll		176
In vast canoes, begirt with bolts of flame	422	Island	2	221
And guards, and bolts, and walls, and now and then	856	Juan	6	252

BOMB

Was fired before the exploding bomb	386	Corinth		166
As brave as ever faced both bomb and ball	879	Juan	8	69
At shrinking from a bullet or a bomb	883	Juan	8	302

BOMBARD

The first was to bombard it, and knock down	870	Juan	7	179

BOMBAST

Another soars, inflated with bombast	257	Hints		44

BOMBAZEEN

Miss Bombazeen, Miss Mackstay, Miss O'Tabby	951	Juan	13	629

BOMBS

Bombs, drums, guns, bastions, batteries, bayonets, bullets	877	Juan	7	623

BONAPARTE

Oh, ye great bulletins of Bonaparte	877	Juan	7	649

BOND

Friendship, the dear peculiar bond of youth	123	Recoll		57
The bond of affection no longer endures	137	Delawarr		30
Great things within you. You shall have no bond	724	Deformed	1	150
Is always so to women; one sole bond	799	Juan	2	1594
Yet 'tis 'so nominated in the bond	802	Juan	3	53
Which is but a precarious bond, in sooth	854	Juan	6	125
Its bloody bond, and saved perhaps some pretty	894	Juan	8	987

BONDAGE

And long accustom'd bondage uncreate	31	Harold	2	696
Of death, depopulation, bondage, fears	38	Harold	3	176
Of mortal bondage, by these spirits supplied	56	Harold	4	42
Disease, death, bondage--all the woes we see	74	Harold	4	1132
Shall burst the bondage of the grave	128	Answer-B		44
A bondage or a trade	201	Ode-C		48
And forgot for a moment my bondage to come	221	Jerusalem		6
How should the autocrat of bondage be	302	Age		300
The spirit to its bondage broke	311	Giaour		162
'Twere worse than bondage to become his bride	354	Corsair		524
Too faithful, though to bitter bondage chain'd	360	Corsair	3	323
A blindfold bondage, where your hire is blows	453	Venice-B		70
In the degree of bondage, we forget	574	Sardan	3	194
Held in the bondage of ten bald-heads; and	611	Foscari	3	244
Establish'd between them and bondage, they	856	Juan	6	271

BONDMEN

To the defilement of usurping bondmen	594	Sardan	5	427

BONDS

(See also VILLAIN-BONDS)

That his frail bonds to fleeting life are broke	27	Harold	2	474
Spurning the clay-cold bonds which round our being cling	46	Harold	3	697
We'll love without bonds, but we'll love you for ever	117	To Eliza		36
'Twill bind my soul in bonds to thee	128	Lady-C		6
No--from oppressive bonds relieved	132	L'Amitie		63
'Twas thine to break the bonds of loving	134	Lady-D		8
And thought of shaking off my bonds of clay	211	Augusta-C		30
Still by the church's bonds unchain'd	386	Corinth		197
To rend and gnash my bonds in twain	404	Chillon		148
And all my bonds aside were cast	406	Chillon		376
My bonds forbade to loose my hold	411	Mazeppa		490
To rend the bonds so starkly tied	413	Mazeppa		636
In common! and sweet bonds which link old friend- ships	525	Faliero	3	449
The slave hath lost all save her bonds. I love him	561	Sardan	1	690
All bonds I break between us, as he broke	652	Cain	3	410
Where shall I turn me not to view its bonds	747	Juan	Ded	121
Their bonds whene'er some Zephyr caught began	810	Juan	3	583
When freed from bonds (which are of no great use	856	Juan	6	268

BONDSMAN'S

The bondsman's peace, who sighs for all he lost	32	Harold	2	786

BONDSMEN

All that gay Beauty from her bondsmen claims	24	Harold	2	285
Hereditary bondsmen! know ye not	31	Harold	2	720
Slaves--nay, the bondsmen of a slave	311	Giaour		151

BOND-STREET

To scrawl in verse) from Bond-street or the Square	251	Bards		712

BONE

Save that wherein at last they crumble bone by bone	11	Harold	1	458
The last poor brute securely gnaws the bone	270	Minerva		116
Light was the touch, but it thrill'd to the bone	390	Corinth		596
Not a stone on their turf, nor a bone in their graves	393	Corinth		817
Save a scatter'd scalp or bone	395	Corinth		1052
Smashing the very bone; and he fell dead	473	Morgante		508
As I am blood, bone, marrow, passion, feeling	745	Fragment-D		2
Which on rough roads leaves scarcely a whole bone	900	Juan	9	235
Eleven thousand maidenheads of bone	915	Juan	10	495
Ends in a rusty casque and dubious bone	916	Juan	10	582

BONES

Let their bleach'd bones and blood's unbleaching stain	18	Harold	1	906
The bones of Laura's lover: here repair	59	Harold	4	264
Angelo's, Alfieri's bones, and his	63	Harold	4	484
Their bones, distinguish'd from our common clay	63	Harold	4	500
Of gem and marble, to encrust the bones	64	Harold	4	534
Darken above our bones, yet fondly deem'd	80	Harold	4	1527

BONES
My Oscar's whiten'd bones must lie   103 Alva   134
Earth shudders as her caves receive his bones   121 Newstead-A   107
I died: let earth my bones resign   154 Skull   6
Who strew'd our earth with hostile bones   180 Ode-A   6
In vain their bones unburied lie   183 Parker   7
Died, and their bones were tombless as their flesh   189 Darkness   45
Along my bones the creeping flesh did quake   222 Spirit   5
And breaking of frames lead to breaking of bones   226 Ode-D   28
In digging up your bones, Tom Paine   235 Paine   1
Here lie the bones of Castlereagh   235 Castlereagh   3
And printers' devils shake their weary bones   243 Bards   126
Whose table earth--whose dice were human bones   299 Age   52
Her honour, fame, and faith demand his bones   300 Age   125
Denied his bones a holier grave   337 Abydos 2   724
Or could the bones of all the slain   385 Corinth   65
As they lazily mumbled the bones of the dead   389 Corinth   462
Above their naked bones, and feels delight   418 Island 1   191
That boil'd your bones, unless you paid them double   440 Beppo   32
My indignant bones, because her angry gust   457 Dante 1   81
Thou'rt mine--my bones shall be within thy breast   458 Dante 2   20
And there are bones so many, and so many   466 Morgante   47
And gorged so that, as if the bones had been   474 Morgante   530
My bones had then been quiet in their depth   483 Manfred 1   365
From wither'd bones, and skulls, and heap'd up dust   486 Manfred 2   176
Or whiten with their bones the banks of Ganges   555 Sardan 1   276
Shall perish, and their bleached bones shall lurk   661 Heaven   439
The dull and dropping rain saps in their bones   672 Werner 1   32
Ye jackals! gnaw the bones the lion leaves   740 Deformed 2   322
One breaks your bones, one sets them in their sockets   762 Juan 1   1028
And when his bones are dust, his grave a blank   813 Juan 3   801
I pass each day where Dante's bones are laid   829 Juan 4   825
As we now gaze upon the mammoth's bones   895 Juan 8   1091
White, black, or copper--the dead bones will grin   898 Juan 9   96
In lieu of sons, of these he made no bones   955 Juan 14   8

BONFIRES
As also bonfires made of country seats   922 Juan 11   211

BON-MOT
To introduce a bon-mot head and ears   955 Juan 13   868
Imbibed the gay bon mot, or happy hoax   991 Juan 16   709

BON-MOTS
And several of her best bon-mots were hawk'd about   935 Juan 12   373
Await those who have studied their bon-mots   953 Juan 13   776

BONN
Except three days of calm when off Cape Bonn   452 Beppo   768
But Juan posted on through Manheim, Bonn   915 Juan 10   489

BONNE
If that a 'bonne fortune' be really 'bonne   963 Juan 14   512
There was a goodly 'soupe a la bonne femme   976 Juan 15   497
But though a 'bonne vivante,' I must confess   976 Juan 15   509

BONNET
My cap was the bonnet, my cloak was the plaid   117 Lachin   10
When you must doff the ducal bonnet from   540 Faliero 5   154
The ducal bonnet from his head--and now   549 Faliero 5   808
Or rather bonnet, which the fair sex wear   854 Juan 6   109

BONNETS
Line the interior of their heads or bonnets   924 Juan 11   395
And settled bonnets by the newest code   954 Juan 13   830

BONNIVARD
By Bonnivard!--May none those marks efface   402 Sonnet-F   13

BONNY
Shall our bonny black horses skim over the ground   730 Deformed 1   566

BONOS
And solace your slight lapse 'gainst 'bonos mores   961 Juan 14   399

BONY
A bony heap, through ages to remain   45 Harold 3   605
His foot, in bony whiteness, glitter'd there   219 Saul-B   9
And Famine, with her gaunt and bony growth   872 Juan 7   358

BOOBIES
At length they caught two boobies and a noddy   784 Juan 2   655

BOOBY
The spouse of Potiphar, the Lady Booby   848 Juan 5   1042

BOOK
(See also NOTE-BOOK, PRAYER-BOOK)
When S---- condemns a book he never read   142 Soliloquy   42

BOOK
Return to scribbling, or a book   163 Malta   52
For this was 'the book' which, of yore, Job, sorely smitten   179 Devil's Dr   235
To him the book of Night was open'd wide   216 Dream   199
Her book, they say, was in advance   231 Doctor   65
I'll sing them in a book that's bigger   233 Nihil   34
A book's a book, although there's nothing in't   242 Bards   52
By more or less, are sung in every book   246 Bards   355
The book which, sillier than a sick man's dreams   256 Hints   12
Then print your book, once more return to town   263 Hints   477
Let every book that suits your theme be read   263 Hints   493
His book, with Longman's liberal aid, shall pass   264 Hints   547
From the same book, in how polite a way   289 Vision   262
A bust delay'd, a book refused, can shake   299 Age   65
His walk the wood, his sport some foreign book   374 Lara 1   548
Another mistress, or new book   408 Mazeppa   142
Accursed was the book and he who wrote   477 Francesca   41
This, too, was a seal'd book to little Juan   753 Juan 1   377
Sometimes he turn'd to gaze upon the book   758 Juan 1   753
Divided in twelve books; each book containing   771 Juan 1   1594
'Go, little book, from this my solitude   774 Juan 1   1769
And read (the only book she could) the lines   794 Juan 2   1291
Turns oftener to the stars than to his book   794 Juan 2   1302
The book which treats of this erroneous pair   803 Juan 3   94
A book, friend, single lady, or a glass   838 Juan 5   458
And decorates the book of Common Prayer   855 Juan 6   183
Set down his sayings in her common-place book   925 Juan 11   416
Who, in his common-place book, had a page   953 Juan 13   773
There is a common-place book argument   997 Juan 17   33

BOOK-CLUB
Each country book-club bows the knee to Baal   243 Bards   138

BOOKISH
But by 'the bookish theoric' it appears   853 Juan 6   66

BOOKMAKING
Or, if you prefer the bookmaking of women   236 Nonsense   11

BOOKS
(See also GUIDE-BOOKS, MASS-BOOKS)
That books were only meant for drudging fools   93 Dorset   23
Ere my young mind was sacrificed to books   211 Augusta-C   52
These books would be but baddish bail   230 Murray-A   9
I've advertised, but see my books   231 Doctor   29
I bought me some books tother day   234 Ballat   6
And quit his books, for fear of growing double   245 Bards   240
More books of blank upon the sons of men   247 Bards   386
Condemn'd to make the books which once he sold   247 Bards   398
Unread (unless, since books beguile disease   260 Hints   237
(Who ne'er despises books that bring him brass   264 Hints   548
But pardon equally to books or men   264 Hints   559
But why this vain advice? once publish'd books   265 Hints   659
Those Books of Martyrs to the rage for rhyme   266 Hints   724
Them written without heads; and books, we see   295 Vision   643
It may be, still, like dull books on a shelf   298 Vision   838
There Chateaubriand forms new books of martyrs   307 Age   714
Books, for his volume heretofore was Man   368 Lara 1   131
With books and solitude, nor made the night   494 Manfred 3   222
That you have written in your books of commerce   596 Foscari 1   49
And I shall be alone; no men--no books   610 Foscari 3   112
In silent books, which, in their silence, say   662 Heaven   542
Or Mrs. Trimmer's books on education   749 Juan 1   123
And open'd certain trunks of books and letters   750 Juan 1   218
There poets find materials for their books   758 Juan 1   717
Divided in twelve books; each book containing   771 Juan 1   1594
At the first two books having too much truth   828 Juan 4   772
Oh! ye, who make the fortunes of all books   830 Juan 4   857
When the sale of new books is not so fleet   870 Juan 7   205
These first twelve books are merely flourishes   936 Juan 12   429
And tumbled books, or criticised the pictures   954 Juan 13   810
And that their books have but one style in common   957 Juan 14   151
The surest way for ladies and for books   967 Juan 14   775
Arranging them like books on the same shelf   972 Juan 15   243
Make more impression than the best of books   978 Juan 15   672
Aurora, who look'd more on books than faces   978 Juan 15   673

BOOK'S
(See also GUIDE-BOOK'S)
A book's a book, although there's nothing in't   242 Bards   52
Ends. When the body of the book's begun   940 Juan 12   690
I wish she had: his book's the eleventh commandment   972 Juan 15   298

BOOKSELLER
His bookseller - John Murray   233 Ballad-B   20

BOOKSELLER'S
That's my bookseller's business; I care not for sale   279 Blues 1   121

BOOK-SHELVES
Along thy sprucest book-shelves shine   234 Strahan   13

BOOM
No more they shriek'd their horror, boom for boom 426 Island 3 7

BOOMING
Long booming of each peal on peal, o'ercame 879 Juan 8 46

BOOMS
Booms harmless, hissing to the deep below 362 Corsair 3 489
At half-past eight o'clock, booms, hencoops,
   spars 780 Juan 2 401

BOON
Thou art? Is this a boon so kindly given 20 Harold 2 30
Sick--sick; unfound the boon--unslaked the thirst 73 Harold 4 1109
Our deities the first best boon have given 107 Nisus 133
One boon I beg, the nearest to my heart 107 Nisus 176
The sweetest boon the gods have given 111 Medea 16
The dearest boon that Life has given 140 Pignus 3
Bent on your knees the Boon receive 141 Critics 19
A boon 'tis idle then to give 166 Struggle 38
Refused thee even the boon to die 191 Prometheus-B 23
The bearer of such boon may wait 326 Abydos 1 214
He had (if 'twere not nature's boon) an art 371 Lara 1 363
No gift beyond that bitter boon--our birth 374 Lara 1 553
And for my breath, that hasty boon 399 Parisina 298
I begg'd them, as a boon, to lay 404 Chillon 152
Perchance, from this the boon of sleep 408 Mazeppa 122
Inevitable--even a boon 414 Mazeppa 726
The rulers of the invisible? A boon 485 Manfred 2 140
A boon, my noble patron; you have granted 530 Faliero 4 132
Boon which I ever ask'd Assyria's king 560 Sardan 1 658
For the only boon I would have ask'd or taken 612 Foscari 3 282
Could he but crush himself, 'twere the best
   boon 630 Cain 1 154
Strong palpitation rises, 'tis her boon 800 Juan 2 1662
As any other boon for which men stickle 883 Juan 8 340
The General Boon, back-woodsman of Kentucky 886 Juan 8 484
Cite is, that Boon lived hunting up to ninety 886 Juan 8 496

BOONS
Those boons to all that know thee known 171 Time-B 6
Of his celestial boons to you and yours 646 Cain 2 656

BOOR
And now no boor can seek his last abode 252 Bards 785

BOORS
Looks likest what the boors believe to be 723 Deformed 1 100
Of the immortal Peter's polish'd boors 899 Juan 9 179
The boors cried 'Dang it! who'd have thought
   it--?' Sires 959 Juan 14 268

BOOT
'Tis fifty years, and three to boot 197 Duel 3
He strides and stamps along with creaking boot 267 Hints 775
To sell his labours and his soul to boot 464 Dante 4 90
Reproaches, which boot nothing. Is it--is it 613 Foscari 3 356
And arm'd from boot to turban, one and all 822 Juan 4 374

BOOTED
What booted it to traverse o'er 413 Mazeppa 656

BOOTES
Bootes, only, seem'd to roll 88 Anacreon-B 3

BOOTIES
Thy packets, all whose passengers are booties 916 Juan 10 549

BOOTLESS
Oh, bloody and most bootless Waterloo 301 Age 223
When dames accuse 'tis bootless to deny 142 Soliloquy 34
Not with your gold. With bootless insolence 692 Werner 2 605

BOOTS
With scorn of man, it little boots to know 43 Harold 3 483
It boots not that, together bred 153 Friend-A 21
Appear'd in the glory of hats, boots and gaiters 178 Devil's Dr 161
His night devotes, despite of spur and boots 273 Waltz 17
The why, the where--what boots it now to tell 344 Corsair 1 454
And those sustain'd he--boots it well or ill 359 Corsair 3 242
It skills not, boots not, step by step to trace 366 Lara 1 21
What boots the oft-repeated tale of strife 379 Lara 2 264
Further interrogation, which boots nothing 541 Faliero 5 270
Ah! little boots it now to recollect 547 Faliero 5 640

BOOTY
There is booty--there is Beauty 240 Suliotes 5
The lust of booty and the thirst of hate 379 Lara 2 288
As guest is slave, his thoughts become a booty 461 Dante 3 81
A rebel's booty: forth, and do your bravest 574 Sardan 3 162
Oh for a glass of max! We've miss'd our booty 920 Juan 11 123
Gaunt Gourmand! with whole nations for your booty 969 Juan 15 69
Whose sole accomplishments were quite a booty 972 Juan 15 270

BOOZE
Booze in the ken, or at the spellken hustle 920 Juan 11 148

BORDER
On Babylonian river's border 96 Granta 88
If thus he harangues when he passes my border 178 Devil's Dr 152
The wilder slogan of a border feud 254 Bards 912
The summer dwelling on its beauteous border 561 Sardan 1 686
Whose high waves o'ersweep the border 735 Deformed 2 19
And round them ran a yellow border too 809 Juan 3 508
The upper border, richly wrought, display'd 809 Juan 3 509
And fourscore cannon on the Danube's border 872 Juan 7 303
The blue sea's border; and Don Juan felt 915 Juan 10 514

BORDER'D
On crimson satin, border'd with pale blue 809 Juan 3 530

BORDERING
Along the bordering lake 6 Harold 1 167

BORDER-NOBLES
Decoy young border-nobles through the wood 244 Bards 153

BORDER-STREAM
Who by their border-stream their march oppose 379 Lara 2 335

BORE
Where is that standard which Pelagio bore 9 Harold 1 388
The fabled Hebrew wanderer bore 17 Harold 1 854
Fatal to him who bears, to all who ever bore 41 Harold 3 378
Broken and trembling to the yoke she bore 48 Harold 3 767
And blood she bore o'er subject earth and sea 57 Harold 4 121
And fetter'd thousands bore the yoke of war 57 Harold 4 137
Which bore them to Eternity; they saw 64 Harold 4 569
That brightness in her eye she bore when Rome was
   free 67 Harold 4 738
It is enough in sooth that once we bore 80 Harold 4 1493
Our pliant limbs the buoyant billows bore 125 Recoll 262
Have seen the infant, which she bore 164 Friend-B 27
How long his senses bore its chilling chain 184 Julian 38
Wafts unto death the breast it bore so high 206 Greece 8
But for the love I bore, and still must bear 209 Sketch 99
Let not seven stanzas written by a bore 238 Snuff-Box 3
Her idle aegis bore no Gorgon now 269 Minerva 80
But for God's sake let's go, or the Bore will be
   here 280 Blues 1 154
Of pension or place;--but the subject's a bore 282 Blues 2 107
A talisman to all save him who bore 299 Age 106
Nor maid nor page behind him bore 315 Giaour 472
The pistols which his girdle bore 315 Giaour 529
A stain on every bush that bore 316 Giaour 665
If ever evil angel bore 319 Giaour 912
His brow no high-crown'd turban bore 330 Abydos 2 132
How little love they bore such guest 331 Abydos 2 221
The bowl a bribed attendant bore 331 Abydos 2 244
It was no mortal arm that bore 337 Abydos 2 719
And tottering to the couch his bride he bore 345 Corsair 1 478
Ere yet his tongue the trusted tidings bore 347 Corsair 2 48
She left his side: his signet-ring she bore 353 Corsair 2 411
Sadly she sate on high--Impatience bore 356 Corsair 3 77
Accursed was the moment when he bore 358 Corsair 3 187
'Twas worn, perhaps decay'd, yet silent bore 358 Corsair 3 218
Kaled his name, though rumour said he bore 374 Lara 1 584
Their marvel how the high-born Lara bore 374 Lara 1 596
The weak yet still untiring knee that bore 382 Lara 2 493
And when, in raising him from where he bore 382 Lara 2 504
And lifting thence the burthen which he bore 383 Lara 2 566
But if in sooth a star its bosom bore 383 Lara 2 590
Against his countrymen he bore 385 Corinth 118
And when the Adriatic bore 386 Corinth 198
Than she, the matchless stranger, bore 386 Corinth 229
So gallantly bore he the brunt of the fray 393 Corinth 783
But of every wound his body bore 393 Corinth 790
Not the matrons that them bore 395 Corinth 1048
Kinglike the monarch bore his fall 407 Mazeppa 40
They bore me to the nearest hut 415 Mazeppa 845
And what was he who bore it?--I may err 425 Island 2 446
She bore down on us, till the wind grew still 426 Island 2 511
With its broad leaf, or turtle-shell which bore 432 Island 4 171
And how, when undeceived, the pair they bore 432 Island 4 215
The wave which bore them still their foes would
   bear 433 Island 4 236
In mockery through them. If I bear and bore 439 Tasso 211
Venice the bell from every city bore 441 Beppo 78
The rest are but a vulgar set, the bore 447 Beppo 468
What nation or what kingdom bore the batch 469 Morgante 187
Had I been present when you bore this insult 516 Faliero 2 531
I had borne all--it hurt me, but I bore it 525 Faliero 3 488
Yet left the duke. All this I bore, and would 541 Faliero 5 219
His life, while earth yet bore his cruelties 544 Faliero 5 443
Upon you! Ye blue waves, which bore my banner 548 Faliero 5 726
Which bore it, shall be nothing. At the least 575 Sardan 3 238
Press'd by a nobler weight than e'er it bore 591 Sardan 5 250
Indeed all you have said. I better bore 604 Foscari 2 173

BORE

You bore this goblet, and it is not broken	625 Foscari	5	297
As though they bore to-morrow's light	656 Heaven		138
Of Hamburgh, who has got a wife who bore	674 Werner	1	189
Of Kruitzner (such the name I then bore), when	680 Werner	1	565
Besides those of the place, and bore away	686 Werner	2	239
From her who bore me would still reconcile me	723 Deformed	1	44
The brightest which the world e'er bore, and give thee	724 Deformed	1	138
And then this best and weakest woman bore	750 Juan	1	225
Of poets and romancers:--You're a bore	761 Juan	1	926
They so embellish, that 'tis quite a bore	771 Juan	1	1614
From which away so fair and fast they bore	775 Juan	2	100
But the boy bore up long, and with a mild	785 Juan	2	699
He bore these sneers against his near relations	807 Juan	3	365
Such as the Doric mothers bore	813 Juan	3	764
And then they bound him where he fell, and bore	822 Juan	4	393
O'ercharged with rain: her summon'd handmaids bore	824 Juan	4	468
And bore him with some gaiety and grace	826 Juan	4	546
To bear the compliments of many a bore	830 Juan	4	867
Bore off his bargains to a gilded boat	836 Juan	5	314
Not only as a sin, but as a bore	854 Juan	6	92
Upon the golden fruit the vision bore	862 Juan	6	614
The discipline of the whole haram bore	865 Juan	6	818
That one would think the first who bore it 'Adam	870 Juan	7	200
For six hours bore they without intermission	870 Juan	7	233
His youth and constitution bore him through	912 Juan	10	339
Was given to her favourite, and now bore his	913 Juan	10	392
Tell them Sir William Curtis is a bore	918 Juan	10	685
Private, though publicly important, bore	922 Juan	11	250
To freedom, he applied (a grief and a bore	923 Juan	11	326
But since they are, that epoch is a bore	930 Juan	12	12
And then, even then, some bore may make them lose it	955 Juan	13	872
There's little left but to be bored or bore	957 Juan	14	142
Who, in his life-time, each, was deem'd a Bore	997 Juan	17	68

BOREALIS

Aurora borealis spread its fringes	288 Vision		214
A versified Aurora Borealis	867 Juan	7	11

BORED

We had the poor wretch safe (without being bored	296 Vision		703
Form'd of two mighty tribes, the Bores and Bored	953 Juan	13	760
There's little left but to be bored or bore	957 Juan	14	142

BORES

Preserve of bores, who ought to be made game	951 Juan	13	624
Form'd of two mighty tribes, the Bores and Bored	953 Juan	13	760

BORE'S

(Which, by the way, the old Bore's best is	231 Doctor	26

BOREST

Bear what thou borest	490 Manfred	2	462

BORN

(See also BRAIN-BORN, DESERT-BORN, EARTH-BORN, FIRST-BORN, FOREST-BORN, FREE-BORN, GOD-BORN, HEAVEN-BORN, HELL-BORN, HIGH-BORN, MERIDIAN-BORN, NEW-BORN, NOBLY-BORN, OCEAN-BORN, QUICK-BORN, SCARCE-BORN, SEA-BORN, SELF-BORN, SUN-BORN, TEMPEST-BORN, TRUE-BORN, WILD-BORN, and FIRST-BORN'S, SIN-BORN'S)

Poor, paltry slaves! yet born 'midst noblest scenes	7 Harold	1	234
(Born beneath some remote inglorious star	25 Harold	2	358
The child of love, though born in bitterness	53 Harold	3	1094
Yet was I born where men are proud to be	56 Harold	4	69
From thee! if in another station born	60 Harold	4	332
Thy countrymen, before thee born to shine	61 Harold	4	353
Was modern Luxury of Commerce born	62 Harold	4	431
And love, which dies as it was born, in sighing	73 Harold	4	1065
Born with her birth. No; he shall not expire	77 Harold	4	1345
When Angus hail'd his eldest born	102 Alva		38
But, born beneath a brighter sun	160 Cadiz		21
Ere born to life and living woe	167 Euthanasia		32
When from his beauty-breathing pencil born	175 Sonnet-A		10
Jar in the music which was born their own	193 Monody		62
Born far beyond the mountains, but his blood	198 Po		42
Born in the garret, in the kitchen bred	208 Sketch		1
Bent o'er the desk, or, born to useful toils	247 Bards		407
The sixteenth story, where himself was born	248 Bards		481
Gifford was born beneath an adverse star	252 Bards		778
Scottish or Irish, born in Wilts or Wales	259 Hints		168
Like Saint John's foretold beast; but ours are born	285 Vision		55
Of almost every body born to die	286 Vision		120
Who, born no king, made monarchs draw his car	299 Age		44
Who, bred a statesman, still wast born a wit	305 Age		549
For what were all these country patriots born	305 Age		572
And this too was I born to bear	321 Giaour		1162
Born of high lineage, link'd in high command	367 Lara	1	97
The brightest by the better born	399 Parisina		271

BORN

But all men are not born to reign	409 Mazeppa		237
Twin giants, born by Freedom to her spheres	420 Island	2	76
Born in a tent, perhaps a Tamerlane	421 Island	2	185
Born under auspices which make us more	421 Island	2	206
Both born beneath a sea-presiding star	422 Island	2	275
The wave of these born playmates of the deep	429 Island	3	182
Born of the fruit; for board the plantain spread	432 Island	4	170
With each new being born or to be born	432 Island	4	194
Who, born perchance for better things, had set	433 Island	4	273
Were of the softer order--born of Love	454 Venice-B		111
Where I was born, but where I would not die	455 Dante	Ded	2
The being--and even yet he may be born	461 Dante	3	53
Or if their destiny be born aloof	464 Dante	4	107
Him who was born of Mary's holiest blood	468 Morgante		166
'The land where I was born sits by the seas	476 Francesca		1
And thou! beneath its influence born	480 Manfred	1	124
A bodiless enjoyment--born and dying	482 Manfred	1	315
Born from the knowledge of its own desert	496 Manfred	3	396
The sentence pass'd on Michel Steno, born	501 Faliero	1	78
You know the full offence of this born villain	502 Faliero	1	184
Yet, thou wast born, and still hast lived, patrician	506 Faliero	1	453
In evil hour was I so born; my birth	506 Faliero	1	454
From me and mine; and, born of those who made	514 Faliero	2	416
The eldest born of Fear, which makes you brave	522 Faliero	3	224
I was not born to shrink from idle threats	530 Faliero	4	189
If born a peasant, he had been a man	550 Sardan	1	14
To have reach'd an empire: to an empire born	550 Sardan	1	15
Although a Greek, and born a foe to monarchs	559 Sardan	1	546
We'll die where we were born--in our own halls	575 Sardan	3	258
Waved arms, more dazzling with their own born whiteness	577 Sardan	3	395
The homage of mankind as their born due	585 Sardan	4	435
To which we tend, for which we're born, and thread	591 Sardan	5	235
I leave it; though born noble, my ambition	598 Foscari	1	193
Men, who have been of women born and suckled	603 Foscari	2	110
Better for him he never had been born	604 Foscari	2	154
When he was born: those drops were ominous	604 Foscari	2	180
Of twenty-five of the best born patricians	621 Foscari	5	18
The prince of whom he was the elder born	621 Foscari	5	82
But thou, my eldest born, art silent still	628 Cain	1	26
I sought not to be born; nor love the state	628 Cain	1	68
Born on the same day, of the same womb; and	632 Cain	1	328
Born of the same sole womb, in the same hour	633 Cain	1	368
Born with me--but I love nought else. Our parents	634 Cain	1	430
We were not born then--and if we had been	634 Cain	1	433
Beyond all power of my born faculties	637 Cain	2	81
Meekly! He is the second born of flesh	644 Cain	2	547
'Twere better that he never had been born	648 Cain	3	136
Born ere this dying herd! They come like clouds	659 Heaven		339
With Cain's, the eldest born of Adam's, blood	664 Heaven		655
The eldest born of man, the strongest, bravest	664 Heaven		685
Born to be plough'd with years, and sown with cares	667 Heaven		871
Why was he born	669 Heaven		1101
Why was I born	670 Heaven		1189
True--to a peasant. Should the nobly born	672 Werner	1	38
But I was born to wealth, and rank, and power	672 Werner	1	77
To lift thee to the state we both were born for	673 Werner	1	126
Whose vassal you were born, knave? No--the prince's	682 Werner	1	685
Father born in a humble state could nerve	682 Werner	1	727
But, I born nobly also, from by father's	682 Werner	1	730
You are nobly born? I have heard my kinsmen say so	686 Werner	2	188
You have guess'd, no doubt, that I was born above	700 Werner	3	311
(But few our native fellow vassals born	704 Werner	4	40
Who were born in them, and bred up upon	705 Werner	4	70
Out, hunchback! I was born so, mother! Out	722 Deformed	1	1
To taunt me with my born deformity	723 Deformed	1	102
Been born with it! But since I may choose further	725 Deformed	1	215
No. I was not born for philosophy	725 Deformed	1	227
In Seville was he born, a pleasant city	748 Juan	1	57
Or gentlemen, who, though well born and bred	749 Juan	1	171
He had been ill brought up, and was born bilious	751 Juan	1	280
Which some are born with, but the most part learn	758 Juan	1	739
All things that have been born were born to die	773 Juan	1	1755
Were settled long ere Juan's sire was born	777 Juan	2	188
He died as born, a Catholic in faith	783 Juan	2	605
Must share it,--Happiness was born a twin	796 Juan	2	1376
Haidee was Passion's child, born where the sun	799 Juan	2	1610
Although they both are born in the same clime	802 Juan	3	36
Born to some friend, who holds his wife and riches	804 Juan	3	183
But like two beings born from out a rill	818 Juan	4	117
Love was born with them, in them, so intense	819 Juan	4	215
Legitimacy its born votaries, when	847 Juan	5	1023
Though not all born of the same sires and mothers	849 Juan	5	1102
And walls as thick as most skulls born as yet	868 Juan	7	90
Was born in Cumberland among the hills	869 Juan	7	155
As if born for the ministerial trade	907 Juan	9	660

BORN

Born in a second wedlock; and above	911 Juan	10	255
The world' in which a man was born?' Alas!	927 Juan	11	594
Both wits--one born so, and the other bred	953 Juan	13	743
Except perhaps that you were born to die	955 Juan	14	19
Born with that happy soul which seldom faints	959 Juan	14	245
Were more;--but I was born for opposition	971 Juan	15	176
When an heir is born, he's heard to mourn	986 Juan	16	345
Poor soul! for she was country born and bred	989 Juan	16	558

BORNE

(See also CAR-BORNE)

Have all been borne, and broken by the accord	38 Harold	3	177
Existence may be borne, and the deep root	58 Harold	4	181
Hear me not; but if calmly I have borne	74 Harold	4	1176
Borne, like thy bubbles, onward. From a boy	82 Harold	4	1650
To what unknown region borne	87 Adrian		3
Was borne on high by the whirlwind's wing	104 Alva		268
Though now on airy visions borne	133 E. N. Long		47
Thou far above their utmost fury borne	140 Ossian-B		19
Oft have I borne the weight of ill	165 Thyrza		43
I know not if I could have borne	167 Dead		46
Borne in the vast balloon of Busby's song	171 Address-B		40
Of men that such a yoke had borne	180 Ode-A		60
And borne o'er breakers reach'd the craggy shore	184 Julian		7
Was thine--and thou hast borne it well	191 Prometheus-B		25
By clouds surrounded, and on whirlwinds borne	193 Monody		92
Borne in our old unchanged career, we move	198 Po		18
The Spartan, borne upon his shield	206 Year		23
Borne on the breath of hyberborean gales	274 Waltz		59
With Waltz compare or after Waltz be borne	275 Waltz		130
But now is borne away by thee	318 Giaour		779
These limbs that buoyant wave hath borne	329 Abydos	2	30
Borne by my steed, or wafted by my sail	333 Abydos	2	392
Behold how well or ill those pangs are borne	351 Corsair	2	317
Borne in his arms through fire from yon Serai	358 Corsair	3	180
But none are there, and not a brake hath borne	376 Lara	2	111
And the flap of the banners that flit as they're borne	391 Corinth		685
Corinth's sons were downward borne	392 Corinth		746
Nor matin bird's new voice was borne	413 Mazeppa		663
His bark was borne; the sport of wave and air	421 Island	2	174
Borne from a short frail pipe, which yet had blown	425 Island	2	438
But must be borne. I stoop not to despair	437 Tasso		20
And all that may be borne, or can debase	439 Tasso		197
In toil, and many troubles borne in vain	457 Dante	1	124
Borne onward with a wing that cannot tire	462 Dante	3	114
It must be borne, and these wild starts are useless	484 Manfred	2	41
As clay hath seldom borne; his aspirations	489 Manfred	2	428
And this is to be borne! I say not that	502 Faliero	1	154
Aside the dignities which I have borne	523 Faliero	3	343
I had borne all--it hurt me, but I bore it	525 Faliero	3	488
Borne by thy hand before the shuddering people	532 Faliero	4	287
Have borne, until my very hearth was stain'd	541 Faliero	5	220
My boys--I could have borne it were I childless	582 Sardan	4	283
And impulse--borne away with every breath	583 Sardan	4	331
Beside, wherever you are borne by fate	586 Sardan	4	501
Who slew me: and when you have borne away	593 Sardan	5	385
Rather let them be borne abroad upon	594 Sardan	5	477
And your limbs?. Limbs! how often have they borne me	597 Foscari	1	94
But onward--I have borne it--I can bear it	598 Foscari	1	162
Had he but borne a little, little longer	603 Foscari	2	99
And feel it nothing. I have borne so much	603 Foscari	2	127
As far as I have borne it, what it was	604 Foscari	2	150
Have borne this--though I know not. Wherefore not	610 Foscari	3	166
On earth to bear. Have I not borne? Too much	611 Foscari	3	202
What is this to the things thou hast borne in silence	617 Foscari	4	155
It must be borne. Father, your blessing! Would	617 Foscari	4	158
I thought I could have borne it, when I saw him	622 Foscari	5	104
Bear with what we have borne, and love me--I	633 Cain	1	359
Borne on the air, of which I am the prince	636 Cain	2	3
And now that it begins, let it be borne	652 Cain	3	416
Have borne all this, I'll not say patiently	672 Werner	1	44
Except in thee--but we have borne it. Well	672 Werner	1	45
To me, who have borne so much with him, and for him	690 Werner	2	495
A bandit of the woods, I could have borne it	692 Werner	2	618
The first in yours. I could have borne yon noble's	693 Werner	2	636
And would you ne'er had borne the useless name	721 Werner	5	531
Which makes me lonely. Nay, I could have borne	727 Deformed	1	341
Belongs to empires, and has been but borne	730 Deformed	1	538
'Twas borne by the rude wave wherein 'twas cast	785 Juan	2	718
And all which must be borne, and never told	817 Juan	4	86
Which I deplore so much; for I have borne	833 Juan	5	143
Him borne into the house and up the stair	835 Juan	5	268
After the hardships you've already borne	875 Juan	7	492
Whate'er is to be--borne--but not resign	891 Juan	8	799
To your instructor. Juan now was borne	917 Juan	10	634
And such a straw, borne on by human breath	956 Juan	14	59

BOROUGH

The rotten borough of the human heart	227 Answer-C		8
Leave bare your borough, Sir Intendant! True	686 Werner	2	223
A borough is comprised along the height	868 Juan	7	74

BOROUGHS

For rotten boroughs, never show my wit	265 Hints		644
Burrowing for boroughs like a rat or rabbit	989 Juan	16	602

BORROW

The heart thus wither'd, seeks in vain to borrow	229 Sadness		7
I borrow my comparisons from clay	291 Vision		429
Beauteous as cloudless, nor be forced to borrow	445 Beppo		342
Because I'm rather hippish, and may borrow	448 Beppo		508
These phrases of refinement I must borrow	923 Juan	11	330

BORROW'D

No borrow'd grace of action must be seen	112 Examination		37
'Flame! fire! and flame!!' (words borrow'd from Lucretius	170 Address-B		11
Were his borrow'd glories dim	187 French	1	27
Though soft the echo, scorn a borrow'd tone	254 Bards		889
Flock o'er the deck, in Neptune's borrow'd car	425 Island	2	467
And borrow'd the Count's smallclothes for a day	452 Beppo		780
Although you borrow'd all that e'er the muses	849 Juan	5	1139
Perhaps we have borrow'd this from the Chinese	945 Juan	13	272

BORROWED

I had borrowed more by a few drops of ages	647 Cain	3	66

BORROWING

By borrowing a new one from an ox	762 Juan	1	1032

BORROWS

While thus Remembrance borrows Banquo's glass	170 Address-A		46

BORYSTHENES

Beyond the swift Borysthenes	408 Mazeppa		116
To-morrow the Borysthenes	415 Mazeppa		855

BOS

For Europe ploughs in Afric like 'bos piger	938 Juan	12	558

BOSCAN

Boscan, or Garcilasso;--by the wind	758 Juan	1	754

BOSNIAC

Remember'd yet in Bosniac song	331 Abydos	2	219

BOSOM

Repented he, but in his bosom slept	5 Harold	1	105
If I thy guileless bosom had	6 Harold	1	156
New shores descried make every bosom gay	6 Harold	1	201
Fresh lessons to the thinking bosom, how	7 Harold	1	285
Her fate, to every freeborn bosom dear	14 Harold	1	642
But now his wayward bosom was unmoved	17 Harold	1	812
Though in thy name the slaves her bosom wrung	21 Harold	2	111
And once again thy hapless bosom gored	21 Harold	2	134
And ne'er again the boy his bosom sought	24 Harold	2	277
From her bare bosom let me take my fill	25 Harold	2	327
The parted bosom clings to wonted home	34 Harold	2	864
Of his impeded soul would through his bosom eat	37 Harold	3	135
And in its tenderer hour on that his bosom dwelt	43 Harold	3	477
Or the pure bosom of its nursing lake	46 Harold	3	674
Sown deep, even in the bosom of the North	69 Harold	4	881
Egeria! thy all heavenly bosom beating	72 Harold	4	1055
With thy unmantled neck, and bosom white and bare	77 Harold	4	1332
Spurning him from thy bosom to the skies	82 Harold	4	1616
But lightly o'er her bosom moved	87 Catullus		8
Which racks my breast your fickle bosom please	87 Tibullus		2
Yet, still, this fond bosom regrets, while adoring	91 Caroline-C		5
When calling the dead, in earth's bosom laid low	91 Caroline-C		24
Which rests in the bosom, though hope is denied	96 Harrow-A		8
With jealous doubt my bosom heaves not	98 To Lesbia		18
My bosom still esteems you dearly	98 To Lesbia		24
Upon that thrilling bosom fell	99 Young Lady		14
Down a cheek which outrivals thy bosom in hue	99 L Adieu		18
And Oscar's bosom scorn'd to fear	102 Alva		71
But Oscar's bosom knew to feel	102 Alva		72
And Mora's tender bosom blush'd	103 Alva		196
Pierced the fair side, the snowy bosom gored	110 Nisus		376
Then on his bosom sought his wonted place	110 Nisus		399
May that fair bosom never know	113 Quaker		53
Then quit her, my friend! your bosom defend	116 Pigot		29
Whose breast for every bosom bleeds	118 Romance		44
Torment her bosom with unholy fires	119 Answer-A		34
But warm his bosom with impassion'd glow	122 Newstead-A		148
When every artless bosom throbs with truth	123 Recoll		58
And truth indignant all his bosom swell	123 Recoll		76
To no fond bosom link'd by kindred ties	125 Recoll		228
Oh! thus, the desire in my bosom for fame	129 Becher-A		13
bosom of Orla. Theirs is one stream of	131 Calmar		162
My bosom glows with former fire	132 L'Amitie		43

BOSOM

Oh, may my bosom never learn	133	E. N. Long	39
How cold must be my bosom now	135	I Would	43
No feeling, save one, to my bosom was dear	135	Highlander	7
One image alone on my bosom impress'd	135	Highlander	13
When pride steels the bosom, the heart is unbend-ing	136	Delawarr	15
My bosom is calm'd by the simple reflection	137	Delawarr	23
Invite the bosom to recall the past	138	Harrow-B	14
Would hide my bosom where it loved to dwell	138	Harrow-B	22
There is a Bosom all my own	144	Jessy	21
Till Fate can ordain that this bosom shall bleed	147	To Anne-B	15
This bosom, responsive to rapture no more	148	Farewell 1	5
For still in thy bosom are life's early seeds	149	Newstead-B	23
I would not give thee bosom pain	152	Weep-A	4
To keep my bosom warm	158	Storm	32
And as along her bosom steal	160	Cadiz	13
Because her bosom is not colder	160	Cadiz	52
Will nought to my bosom restore thee	162	Romaic-A	23
By all unto thy bosom dear	164	Friend-B	16
Had taught my bosom how to brook	165	Thyrza	11
Where could my vacant bosom turn	168	Haunts	26
With him unto thy bosom dearer	173	Quotation	29
What there thy bosom must endure	174	Remember-B	40
That--but I know thy blessed bosom fraught	175	Sonnet-A	6
O'er Ocean's heaving bosom sent	183	Parker	6
Thy bosom overboils, congenial river	198	Po	15
Than in that bosom once his own	201	Ode-C	25
Without that bosom kept its place	201	Ode-C	70
Or, if aught in my bosom can quench for an hour	204	Avatar	125
Oh! my lone bosom!--oh! my lonely Pillow	205	Hindoo	16
And the bard in my bosom is dead	205	Blessington	10
The fire that on my bosom preys	206	Year	9
Back on thy bosom with reflected blight	209	Sketch	86
His bosom in its solitude; and then	215	Dream	152
Strike the bosom that's bared for thee now	218	Jephtha	4
Were my bosom as false as thou deem'st it to be	221	False	1
How wakes my bosom to its wonted fires	265	Hints	590
Ah! let me cease; in vain my bosom burns	265	Hints	619
Go, ask thy bosom who deserves them most	272	Minerva	310
From where the garb just leaves the bosom free	276	Waltz	190
Pride in his heavenly bosom, in whose core	288	Vision	245
The blackness of my bosom wore	322	Giaour	1199
No word from Selim's bosom broke	326	Abydos 1	253
Unheeded o'er his bosom flew	326	Abydos 1	275
More free her timid bosom beat	330	Abydos 2	95
Mark how that lone and blighted bosom sears	341	Corsair 1	245
The only pang my bosom dare not brave	343	Corsair 1	357
Still must each accent to my bosom suit	343	Corsair 1	369
Oh! how the chill blast on my bosom blew	343	Corsair 1	381
The grapes' gay juice thy bosom never cheers	344	Corsair 1	429
Scarce beat that bosom where his image dwelt	345	Corsair 1	472
And felt that all which Freedom's bosom cheers	348	Corsair 2	87
His guilty bosom, but that breast he mann'd	352	Corsair 2	373
Though fond as mine her bosom, form more fair	360	Corsair 3	298
That nearly veil'd her face and bosom fair	361	Corsair 3	411
Though worse than frenzy could that bosom fill	363	Corsair 3	520
So springs the exulting bosom to that mirth	371	Lara 1	396
That rises as the busy bosom sinks	374	Lara 1	602
Vain Otho gave his bosom to the gash	376	Lara 2	68
The sullen calm that long his bosom kept	378	Lara 2	242
But if in sooth a star its bosom bore	383	Lara 2	590
And oft would snatch it from her bosom there	384	Lara 2	617
Within whose heated bosom throngs	385	Corinth	127
Nought conceal'd her bosom shining	390	Corinth	555
Many a bosom, sheathed in brass	392	Corinth	731
And her blush returns, and her bosom heaves	396	Parisina	26
Each gazer's bosom held his breath	401	Parisina	478
Still was his seal'd-up bosom haunted	402	Parisina	557
Her wild and warm yet faithful bosom knew	421	Island 2	145
O'er whose blue bosom rose the starry isles	422	Island 2	252
Within whose bosom infant Bacchus broods	422	Island 2	255
Wrapp'd his wean'd bosom in its dark delight	423	Island 2	307
For the broad bosom of his nursing wave	424	Island 2	411
As to a mother's bosom flies the child	426	Island 3	16
A black rock rears its bosom o'er the spray	430	Island 4	10
Forth from her bosom the young savage drew	431	Island 4	137
The buttress from some mountain's bosom hurl'd	432	Island 4	149
That nought on earth could more my bosom move	456	Dante 1	22
And in his bulky bosom made incision	470	Morgante	302
Such fervour in his bosom bred each word	475	Morgante	619
For thousand virtues which your bosom fosters	475	Morgante	630
Hath ripp'd her bosom; had the bird a voice	506	Faliero 1	471
Guiltless as thy own bosom. Is it so	543	Faliero 5	350
My very soul seem'd mouldering in my bosom	610	Foscari 3	135
Out of this bosom? was not he, their father	633	Cain 1	367
Of which thy bosom is the germ. O Cain	635	Cain 1	521
In your own bosom--where the outward fails	646	Cain 2	669
Have lain within this bosom, folded from	658	Heaven	230
The elements; this bosom, which in vain	658	Heaven	231
Are howling from the mountain's bosom	668	Heaven	992
To see him to my bosom clinging so	669	Heaven	1100
The last were in my bosom rather than	693	Werner 2	635
Is ever doting) took to warm his bosom	694	Werner 2	737

BOSOM

Your bosom (for the appearance of the man	695	Werner 2	750
A bosom whereon he his head might lay	758	Juan 1	765
Which trembled like the bosom where 'twas placed	761	Juan 1	915
Their very walk would make your bosom swell	774	Juan 2	38
A sigh from his heaved bosom--and hers, too	788	Juan 2	912
More than within the bosom of a nun	795	Juan 2	1333
And, beating 'gainst his bosom, Haidee's heart	798	Juan 2	1527
If love paternal in his bosom pleaded	807	Juan 3	389
There his worn bosom and keen eye would melt	808	Juan 3	414
The heroic bosom beats no more	812	Juan 3	716
Of those with which his Haidee's bosom bounded	823	Juan 4	423
As passion rises, with its bosom worn	863	Juan 6	691
Stirr'd up and down her bosom like a billow	865	Juan 6	862
Until each high, heroic bosom burn'd	875	Juan 7	507
Within her bosom (which was not too tough	902	Juan 9	380
My bosom underwent a glorious glow	907	Juan 10	19
His bosom,--for he never had a sister	914	Juan 10	423
Which shall lay bare her bosom to the sword	915	Juan 10	532
Or wish to make a rival's bosom bleed	939	Juan 12	614
Of which another's bosom is the zone	994	Juan 16	912

BOSOM'D

Space bosom'd not a lovelier star	480	Manfred 1	115

BOSOMS

Who but would deem their bosoms burn'd anew	31	Harold 2	713
Exchanged the look few bosoms may withstand	32	Harold 2	769
But quiet to quick bosoms is a hell	41	Harold 3	370
On self-condemning bosoms, it were here	44	Harold 3	568
In bare and desolated bosoms: mute	58	Harold 4	183
In melancholy bosoms, such as were	60	Harold 4	300
Ye rhymers, whose bosoms with phantasy glow	92	First Kiss	5
Arm'd thus, to make their bosoms bleed	98	To Lesbia	33
Shall join our bosoms and our souls in one	107	Nisus	166
And all our bosoms felt, rehearsed	112	Quaker	22
Still let some mercy in your bosoms live	114	Prologue	35
Whose bosoms heave with fancied fears	118	Romance	51
With feelings warm, with bosoms true	132	L'Amitie	66
But would you make our bosoms bleed	148	To Author	13
Which better bosoms would bewail	164	Friend-B	22
The essence of great bosoms now no more	192	Fragment-C	40
Bury your steel in the bosoms of Gath	219	Saul-A	4
And our heads on our bosoms all droopingly lay	223	Valley	3
Yes, close her with your armed bosoms round	303	Age	360
So widely spread, few bosoms well could brook	372	Lara 1	419
Each pulse beats quicker, and all bosoms seem	374	Lara 1	620
Of the dusk bosoms that beat high below	419	Island 2	52
His faults are those that dwell in the high bosoms	510	Faliero 2	103
That wedded bosoms could permit themselves	510	Faliero 2	127
Let them advance and strike at their own bosoms	522	Faliero 3	218
And bracelets; swanlike bosoms, and the necklace	529	Faliero 4	55
In their great bosoms. Who would have foreseen	540	Faliero 5	192
In their accursed bosoms. You know not	603	Foscari 2	115
Hived in our bosoms like the bag o' the bee	773	Juan 1	1709
Are laid within our bosoms but to perish	802	Juan 3	16
Their bosoms who have been induced to roam	804	Juan 3	164
With his rude scythe such gentle bosoms; he	817	Juan 4	60
Their delicate limbs; a thousand bosoms there	855	Juan 6	207
And bosoms, arms, and ankles glancing bare	861	Juan 6	572

BOSOM'S

To make thy bosom's heaven a hell	90	To M.S.G.-A	16
Had claim'd his faithless bosom's care	103	Alva	164
Then Nisus,--'Calm thy bosom's fond alarms	106	Nisus	53
The dictate of my bosom's care	113	Quaker	44
To check my bosom's fondest thought	133	E. N. Long	15
I conquer half my bosom's sadness	134	Lady-D	40
Yet thrills my bosom's chords	146	Adieu	62
This bosom's desolation dooming	221	Marianne	22
The vacant bosom's wilderness	319	Giaour	939
Whose beak unlocks her bosom's stream	319	Giaour	952
Feel--to the rising bosom's inmost core	338	Corsair 1	21
And there rose not a heave o'er her bosom's swell	391	Corinth	614
My breast upon its rocky bosom's bed	482	Manfred 1	279
Sustain'd his head upon her bosom's charms	798	Juan 2	1556

BOSPHORUS

As woo'd the eye and thrill'd the Bosphorus along	32	Harold 2	755
Between the Bosphorus, as they lash and lave	832	Juan 5	37
Each villa on the Bosphorus looks a screen	837	Juan 5	367
You know how near us the deep Bosphorus floats	843	Juan 5	732

BOSS'D

Which still, though gemm'd and boss'd with gold	315	Giaour	531

BOTANY

The very Botany Bay in moral geography	814	Juan 3	842

BOTCHING

And botching, patching, leaving still behind	746	Juan Ded	106

BOTH

The flowers which yield the most of both	113 Cornelian-A		23
Fair Venus! how I pity both	160 Swimming		8
That both had been recall'd from Heaven	173 Mrs. Lamb		8
And, gazing upon either, both required	195 Vittorelli		4
But an Insect in both	232 Murray-B		64
Thy country sends a spoiler worse than both	269 Minerva		98
Why, Jack, I'll be frank with you--something of both	278 Blues	1	79
Pollute the plains, alike abhorring both	302 Age		323
The stern or feeble sovereign, one or both	302 Age		340
Though sworn by one, hath bound us both	327 Abydos	1	350
In danger's hour to guard us both	331 Abydos	2	191
The vain attempt should bring but doom to both	354 Corsair	2	467
The thunder came; that bolt hath blasted both	365 Corsair	3	672
Not so in him; his breast had buried both	370 Lara	1	285
The Serfs contemn'd the one, and hated both	378 Lara	2	229
Surprised and seized us both	410 Mazeppa		326
But only the barbarian's--we have both	419 Island	2	68
Which two worlds bless for civilising both	425 Island	2	487
A beverage for Turks and Christians both	451 Beppo		722
Why, what are things? Both partly; but what doth	638 Cain	2	137
Enough?--why should ye differ? We both reign	645 Cain	2	597
Jehovah loves thee well. Both well, I hope	649 Cain	3	191
Such as both may make worthy your acceptance	694 Werner	2	718
Before her glass. You both see what is not	726 Deformed	1	289
Instead of quarrelling, had they been but both in	750 Juan	1	197
And these two tended him, and cheer'd him both	789 Juan	2	977
And sweet sensations should have welcomed both	822 Juan	4	359
'Arcades ambo,' id est--blackguards both	828 Juan	4	744
But in a mighty hall or gallery, both in	838 Juan	5	453
Which mostly ends in some small breach of both	849 Juan	5	1136
Is more than I know--the deuce take them both	855 Juan	6	176
Since John has lately lost the use of both	872 Juan	7	356
Nay, he had wounded, though but slightly, both	892 Juan	8	865
And yet his looks appear'd to sanction both	984 Juan	16	258
And yet great heroes have been bred by both	991 Juan	16	720

BOTHER

Their author, like the Niger's mouth, will bother	295 Vision		647

BOTHERBY

And you, Mr. Botherby--Oh, my dear lady	281 Blues	2	32
While you live, my dear Botherby, never defend	281 Blues	2	72
However, to save my friend Botherby trouble	282 Blues	2	89
Oh! my dear Mr. Botherby! sympathise!--I	282 Blues	2	129

BOTHERBYS

No bustling Botherbys have they to show 'em	449 Beppo		575

BOTHERBY'S

There were Renegade's epics, and Botherby's plays	279 Blues	1	123
Of old Botherby's spouting ex-cathedra tone	280 Blues	1	150

BOTHERS

His head for such a wife no mortal bothers	442 Beppo		143
Into a camp: I know that nought so bothers	876 Juan	7	566
In short, the list of alterations bothers	928 Juan	11	638

BOTTES

Oh, ye great authors!--'Apropos des bottes	901 Juan	9	281

BOTTLE

Black eyes, black ringlets, but--a bottle nose	257 Hints		58
I'll call the work 'Longinus o'er a Bottle	772 Juan	1	1631
What say you to a bottle of champagne	945 Juan	13	290
I hate a motive, like a lingering bottle	962 Juan	14	457
Or like a soda bottle when its spray	981 Juan	16	69
A reel within a bottle is a mystery	988 Juan	16	537

BOTTLE-CONJURER

Which to that bottle-conjurer, John Bull	872 Juan	7	347

BOTTLES

Sweet is old wine in bottles, ale in barrels	762 Juan	1	1005

BOTTOM

He first sank to the bottom--like his works	298 Vision		833
And self and live-stock to another bottom	452 Beppo		770
My pen is at the bottom of a page	452 Beppo		739
And ooze too, from the bottom, as the lead doth	699 Werner	3	267
And at the bottom of the boat three were	786 Juan	2	782
Because deform'd, yet died all game and bottom	892 Juan	8	879
There was the purest Platonism at bottom	914 Juan	10	431
Because she thought him a good heart at bottom	935 Juan	12	386
Are they, at bottom virtuous even when vicious	939 Juan	12	582

BOUDOIR

Retired into her boudoir, a sweet place	864 Juan	6	770
The scenes like Catherine's boudoir at threescore	887 Juan	8	543
A door that's in or boudoir out of the way	927 Juan	11	539

BOUDOIR'S

If once beyond her boudoir's precincts in ye went	904 Juan	9	501

BOUGH

The orange tints that gild the greenest bough	7 Harold	1	248
Keep to thy self thy wither'd bough	227 Thurlow-B		6
Will wear as green a bough for him as me	277 Waltz		255
And hew the bough that bought his children's food	383 Lara	2	555
Between me and yon chestnut's bough	408 Mazeppa		204
The lofty accents of whose sighing bough	419 Island	2	11
From the tall bough where they have perch'd so long	423 Island	2	327
The forest shade--the green bough--the bird's voice	643 Cain	2	468
The green bough from the forest. Now 'tis set	723 Deformed	1	66
Blossom and bough lie wither'd with one blight	825 Juan	4	558
The black bough) tear-drops through her eyes dark fringes	860 Juan	6	536
To its own bough, and dangled yet in sight	862 Juan	6	607
A fruit to bloom upon their withering bough	933 Juan	12	242

BOUGHS

The boughs and winding turns his steps mislead	109 Nisus		316
Thou drooping Elm! beneath whose boughs I lay	138 Harrow-B		9
For centuries still may thy boughs lightly wave	149 Newstead-B		29
Its boughs above a monument	210 Augusta-A		28
It is the hour when from the boughs	396 Parisina		1
The waving boughs with fury scathe	402 Parisina		584
The boughs gave way, and did not tear	411 Mazeppa		487
Startled the slumbering birds from the hush'd boughs	490 Manfred	2	506
Faintly and motionless to their loved boughs	578 Sardan	4	15
The sweeping tempest through its groaning boughs	658 Heaven		222
Of aught so beautiful. The flowers, the boughs	713 Werner	5	16
Let these hyacinth boughs	728 Deformed	1	396
To you I envy neither fruit nor boughs	745 Juan	Ded	51
And vesper bell's that rose the boughs along	815 Juan	3	940
And from beneath his boughs were seen to sally	948 Juan	13	445

BOUGHT

(See also BLOOD-BOUGHT, DEAR-BOUGHT, NEW-BOUGHT)

And here we earn'd the conquest dearly bought	124 Recoll		144
Her heart can ne'er be bought or sold	160 Cadiz		29
Who doom'd thee to be bought or sold	179 Gold		27
The 'moral lesson' dearly bought	188 Ode-B		78
Did glut himself again;--a meal was bought	189 Darkness		39
Since thy triumph was bought by thy vow	218 Jephtha		3
Bought their freedom, and cheaply, with blood	229 Lads		2
I bought me some books tother day	234 Ballat		6
With death alone are laurels cheaply bought	272 Minerva		294
For these things may be bought at their true worth	286 Vision		69
Bought also; and the torches, cloaks, and banners	286 Vision		71
And thus our abbot's favour bought	318 Giaour		817
I never loved--he bought me--somewhat high	360 Corsair	3	329
Less blood perchance hath bought a richer spoil	379 Lara	2	331
And hew the bough that bought his children's food	383 Lara	2	555
Dearly they have bought us, dearly still may buy	428 Island	3	157
May strike to those whose red right hands have bought	454 Venice-B		147
Shall pour in sacrifice.--She shall be bought	548 Faliero	5	748
Being bought without a tear. But that is not	554 Sardan	1	244
A good deal may be bought for fifty Louis	760 Juan	1	864
Bought up for different purposes and passions	830 Juan	4	904
How some were bought by pachas, some by Jews	831 Juan	4	922
Some bought the jet, while others chose the pale	832 Juan	5	76
Are bought up, others by a warlike leader	834 Juan	5	213
Most proper for the Christians he had bought	840 Juan	5	536
There was no end unto the things she bought	845 Juan	5	901
She order'd him directly to be bought	846 Juan	5	907
'I see you've bought another girl; 'tis pity	851 Juan	5	1239
So precious that it was not to be bought	988 Juan	16	491

BOUNCE

With thee even clumsy cits attempt to bounce	275 Waltz		157

BOUND

(See also ICE-BOUND, SOIL-BOUND, SPELL-BOUND)

Bound to the earth, he lifts his eye to heaven	20 Harold	2	28
Oh Love! young Love! bound in thy rosy band	32 Harold	2	771
Whom youth and youth's affections bound to me	34 Harold	2	892
And the waves bound beneath me as a steed	35 Harold	3	11
Which unto his was bound by stronger ties	43 Harold	3	488
The haughtiest breast its wish might bound	44 Harold	3	530
Striking the electric chain wherewith we are darkly bound	58 Harold	4	207
From rock to rock leaps with delirious bound	65 Harold	4	628
His waist was bound with a broad belt round	104 Alva		257
At length, in spells no longer bound	118 Romance		5
This Band, which bound thy yellow hair	128 Lady-C		1
the gathering chiefs bound on the plain	130 Calmar		127
yet bound on the hills of Morven	131 Calmar		170
and Calmar. When Swaran was bound	131 Calmar		185

BOUND

With dusky leaves my temples bound	139	Anacreon-C	20
Well stitch'd, and with morocco bound	163	Blacket	6
And his works shall be bound in Morocco d'Enfer	177	Devil's Dr	131
Come tell me who to thee is bound	179	Gold	19
There are links which must break in the chain that has bound us	186	Napoleon	23
Or, has it not bound thee the fastest of all	203	Avatar	71
The tie which bound the first endures the last	212	Augusta-C	128
Exulting yet may bound	217	Gazelle	2
Of bound and letter'd, red and gold	233	Ballad-B	23
She bids the beating heart with rapture bound	258	Hints	153
Bound to no clime and victors of the grave	270	Minerva	152
Fandango's wriggle, or Bolero's bound	275	Waltz	126
'Gainst Satan's couriers bound for their own clime	292	Vision	446
You know we're bound to that in every way	296	Vision	712
In two octavo volumes, nicely bound	297	Vision	787
Than his ambition, though with scarce a bound	299	Age	94
In lash for lash, and bound for bound	312	Giaour	184
Along the banks that bound her tide	315	Giaour	510
Swift from their steeds the riders bound	316	Giaour	575
As if the Gorgon there had bound	319	Giaour	896
From the black cloud that bound it	327	Abydos 1	337
Though sworn by one, hath bound us both	327	Abydos 1	350
With silvery scales were sheathed and bound	330	Abydos 2	146
Bound where thou wilt, my barb! or glide, my prow	333	Abydos 2	394
One bound he made, and gain'd the sand	334	Abydos 2	539
Ours with one pang--one bound--escapes control	338	Corsair 1	32
Will see the Pirates bound--their haven won	347	Corsair 2	13
The Saick was bound; but Alla did not smile	348	Corsair 2	68
He saw him bound; and bleeding--but alive	357	Corsair 3	109
But bound and fix'd in fetter'd solitude	358	Corsair 3	222
And gathering, as he could, the links that bound	361	Corsair 3	388
To bound as doubting from too black a dream	374	Lara 1	621
One to their cause inseparably bound	378	Lara 2	231
That bound to Lara Kaled's heart and brain	382	Lara 2	537
I burst my chain with one strong bound	404	Chillon	210
Which bound me to my failing race	404	Chillon	217
Yet bound her to the place, though not	409	Mazeppa	269
They bound me on, that menial throng	410	Mazeppa	370
Had bound my neck in lieu of rein	410	Mazeppa	386
They bound me to his foaming flank	411	Mazeppa	415
But no--my bound and slender frame	411	Mazeppa	450
Thus bound in nature's nakedness	412	Mazeppa	532
But err'd, for I was fastly bound	412	Mazeppa	541
My limbs were bound; my force had fail'd	413	Mazeppa	633
They saw me strangely bound along	413	Mazeppa	696
Then plunging back with sudden bound	413	Mazeppa	701
And there from morn till twilight bound	414	Mazeppa	718
Bound, naked, bleeding, and were	415	Mazeppa	851
Thy limbs are bound, the bayonet at thy breast	416	Island 1	55
Not over-tightly bound, nor nicely spread	425	Island 2	479
Nor bound between Distraction and Disease	438	Tasso	94
The 'prima donna's' tuneful heart would bound	444	Beppo	253
He thought himself in duty bound to do so	452	Beppo	755
Bound for Corfu: she was a fine polacca	452	Beppo	759
Quails from his inspiration, bound to please	461	Dante 3	86
Which form'd the Christian's and the pagan's bound	468	Morgante	152
And I to thee, oh Lord! am ever bound	470	Morgante	282
And the clankless chain hath bound thee	481	Manfred 1	259
As he, indeed, by blood was bound to do	494	Manfred 3	247
What is it thou and thine are bound to do	531	Faliero 4	248
I am settled and bound up, and being so	534	Faliero 4	422
Stand crown'd, but bound and helpless, at the altar	541	Faliero 5	209
Now I am cooler. You have bound it with	577	Sardan 3	368
Reply, not listen. And your wound! 'Tis bound	587	Sardan 4	576
And a black circle, bound	668	Heaven	1005
Must be answer'd on the instant, as the bound	699	Werner 3	285
A wise magician, who has bound the devil	700	Werner 3	341
Count Siegendorf, command you aught? I am bound	708	Werner 4	281
Count, you are bound to hear me. I came hither	716	Werner 5	186
Her hair had silver only, bound to be	789	Juan 2	972
Yet deem'd herself in common pity bound	790	Juan 2	1030
But three Ragusan vessels, bound for Scio	796	Juan 2	1392
And the striped white gauze baracan that bound her	810	Juan 3	559
For theirs were buoyant spirits, never bound	818	Juan 4	125
And then they bound him where he fell, and bore	822	Juan 4	393
But to the narrative:--The vessel bound	830	Juan 4	897
One person thrice in holy wedlock bound	833	Juan 5	157
And this addition with such gems was bound	841	Juan 5	630
His empire also was without a bound	850	Juan 5	1197
One with her auburn tresses lightly bound	860	Juan 6	517
Who neither wishes to be bound nor bind	899	Juan 9	206
With her then, as in humble duty bound	907	Juan 9	673
Who bound the bar or senate in their spell	928	Juan 11	604
Chaste were his steps, each kept within due bound	960	Juan 14	305
The charming of these charmers, who seem bound	985	Juan 16	314
Nor less applauds, as in politeness bound	986	Juan 16	374
Even in the country circle's narrow bound	992	Juan 16	774

BOUNDARY

The ocean o'er its boundary, and bears	81	Harold 4	1552
A boundary between the things misnamed	213	Dream	2
Against the boundary it scarcely wet	797	Juan 2	1448

BOUNDED

(See also HORIZON-BOUNDED)

From Lochlin, Swaran bounded o'er the	129	Calmar	29
From mountain to mountain I bounded along	136	Highlander	18
Who reach'd the river, bounded from his horse	383	Lara 2	565
And bounded by a forest black	411	Mazeppa	431
Which then seems as if the whole earth it bounded	797	Juan 2	1459
Their leader sang--and bounded to her song	805	Juan 3	239
Of those with which his Haidee's bosom bounded	823	Juan 4	428

BOUNDING

(See also HIGH-BOUNDING)

With braided tresses bounding o'er the green	17	Harold 1	808
And bounding hand in hand, man link'd to man	30	Harold 2	638
'Tis his to chase the bounding roe	102	Alva	106
Bounding convulsive, flies the gasping head	108	Nisus	250
Or bounding o'er the dark blue wave	135	I Would	4
Her forever bounding spirit	188	Ode-B	100
The hero bounding at his country's call	272	Minerva	289
But like a warrior bounding on his barb	349	Corsair 2	145
And why had Lara cross'd the bounding main	366	Lara 1	12
And the gay dance of bounding Beauty's train	371	Lara 1	389
Its bounding crystal frolick'd in the ray	427	Island 3	65
His bounding nereid over the broad sea	435	Island 4	392
Bounding o'er yon blue tide, as I have skimm'd	597	Foscari 1	95
To show its boiling surf and bounding spray	787	Juan 2	830
Went bounding for the island of the free	915	Juan 10	506
As beautiful and bounding as a steed	952	Juan 13	734

BOUNDLESS

Preserves alike its bounds and boundless fame	33	Harold 2	839
To whom the boundless air alone were home	37	Harold 3	130
Into a boundless blessing, which may vie	51	Harold 3	966
This boundless upas, this all-blasting tree	74	Harold 4	1129
Dark-heaving;--boundless, endless, and sublime	82	Harold 4	1643
Then hope is lost; in boundless grief	103	Alva	127
While Fancy holds her boundless reign	118	Romance	13
Earth, ocean, heaven, thy boundless throne	132	Prayer	20
Whose mantle is yon boundless sky	146	Adieu	117
The boundless power to cherish or reject	170	Address-A	55
While Powers of mind almost of boundless range	194	Monody	109
Bright is the diadem, boundless the sway	219	Saul-A	11
Eternal, boundless, undecay'd	220	Clay	9
For infinite as boundless space	313	Giaour	273
Of Bairam through the boundless East	314	Giaour	452
Our thoughts as boundless and our souls as free	338	Corsair 1	2
Blind, boundless, mute, and motionless	405	Chillon	250
We gain the top: a boundless plain	412	Mazeppa	605
And from thine ashes boundless spirits rise	461	Dante 3	41
And boundless, and of an ethereal hue	642	Cain 2	388
Yon blue immensity, is boundless? Ay	645	Cain 2	595
To perfect knowledge of the boundless skies	758	Juan 1	735
Thoughts, boundless, deep, but silent too as Space	987	Juan 16	432

BOUNDLESSLY

True, blood and treasure boundlessly were spilt	306	Age	586

BOUNDLESSNESS

Shall wonder at his boundlessness of realm	658	Heaven	242

BOUNDS

Deem ye what bounds the rival realms divide	9	Harold 1	361
But ere the mingling bounds have far been pass'd	9	Harold 1	378
Bounds with one lashing spring the mighty brute	16	Harold 1	750
Epirus' bounds recede and mountains fail	27	Harold 2	478
Preserves alike its bounds and boundless fame	33	Harold 2	839
No torrent can quench it, no bounds can repress	129	Becher-A	12
Ryno bounds in joy. Ossian stalks in his	131	Calmar	148
And live beyond the bounds of Time	132	Prayer	36
Where northward Macedonia bounds the flood	161	Athos	2
While Gayton bounds before th' enraptured looks	250	Baris	624
We know not where to fix their several bounds	259	Hints	212
Broke out of bounds o'er the ethereal blue	285	Vision	14
He bounds, he flies, until his footsteps reach	346	Corsair 1	533
But mighty Nature bounds as from her birth	375	Lara 2	5
Scarce break on the bounds of the land for a rood	388	Corinth	429
Where Asia's bounds and ours divide	393	Corinth	812
I saw no bounds on either side	411	Mazeppa	465
Our bounds, or taste the stones shower'd down for bread	469	Morgante	198
O'ersweep all bounds and foam itself to air	502	Faliero 1	176
Was there to envy in the narrow bounds	631	Cain 1	240
Him past all bounds, because she smiled to see	794	Juan 2	1259
Which bounds Ravenna's immemorial wood	815	Juan 3	931
To fix the due bounds of this dangerous quality	966	Juan 14	712
Transgresses the great bounds of love or awe	997	Juan 17	14

BOUNTEOUS
For arts like these at bounteous tables fed   142 Soliloquy   41
Has proved too bounteous to be kind   179 Gold   28
He play'd the courteous lord and bounteous host   377 Lara   2   191
And bounteous planter of barr'd Paradise   644 Cain   2   553
As yet he hath been courteous as he's bounteous   704 Werner   4   15

BOUNTIES
Whose fertile bounties here extend to all   45 Harold   3   588
Not that I mean her bounties to disparage   447 Beppo   492
(I mean in Fortune's matrimonial bounties   929 Juan   11   700

BOUNTY
For bounty cheers not his delay   313 Giaour   341
Florence, by his great bounty dost arise   467 Morgante   51
I little thought his bounty would conduct me   505 Faleiro   1   400
To some civility, to others bounty   990 Juan   16   611

BOURBON
From Brennus to the Bourbon, never, never   459 Dante   2   98
And free companion of the gallant Bourbon   730 Deformed   1   573
The Bourbon hath given orders for the assault   731 Deformed   1   603
With Bourbon, the rover   732 Deformed   1   693
Here's to the Bourbon for ever   732 Deformed   1   699
With the Bourbon we'll gather   732 Deformed   1   703
With the Bourbon we'll mount o'er   732 Deformed   1   711
Oh, the Bourbon! the Bourbon   732 Deformed   1   723
The Bourbon for aye   732 Deformed   1   724
Oh, the Bourbon! the Bourbon   732 Deformed   1   735
We'll follow the Bourbon   732 Deformed   1   737
That they will be repulsed, with Bourbon for   733 Deformed   1   750
And mine? To follow glory with the Bourbon   735 Deformed   1   876
The Bourbon! Bourbon! On, boys! Rome is ours   737 Deformed   2   156
And so did Bourbon, in another sense   737 Deformed   2   168
The Bourbon from the wall. Ay, did he so   738 Deformed   2   207

BOURBON'S
For I provoked it:--but the Bourbon's breast   733 Deformed   1   797
Match'd with Bourbon's black banditti   736 Deformed   2   65
The Bourbon's spirit shall command them still   736 Deformed   2   134

BOURN
Unto that rather somewhat misty bourn   883 Juan   8   323

BOURNE
Now having pass'd the gloomy bourne   87 Catullus   13

BOUT
Warm bout are broken into their new tricks   881 Juan   8   175

BOUTS
Were sonnets to herself, or 'bouts rimes   987 Juan   16   448

BOUWAH
Bouwah! Bouwah! Suliotes   240 Suliotes   4ff

BOW
(See also SADDLE-BOW)
And bow the knee to Pomp that loves to varnish
   guilt   8 Harold   1   341
The glorious main expanding o'er the bow   22 Harold   2   150
Thy fanes, thy temples to thy surface bow   33 Harold   2   805
The flying Mede, his shaftless broken bow   33 Harold   2   846
Before the Chastener humbly let me bow   35 Harold   2   922
Or view the Lord of the unerring bow   79 Harold   4   1441
His bow across his shoulders flung   89 Anacreon-B   27
Than swift he seized his slender bow   89 Anacreon-B   38
'My bow can still impel the shaft   89 Anacreon-B   46
Taught by their sire to bend the bow   102 Alva   53
Swift is the shaft from Allan's bow   105 Alva   289
But when the hostile chiefs at length bow down   107 Nisus   153
But never from thy golden bow   111 Medea   17
She's now most divine, and I bow at the shrine   116 Strephon   7
The courtier's supple bow and sneering smile   126 Recoll   317
I hail the sky's celestial bow   133 E. N. Long   8
Bow down beneath the Almighty's Throne   146 Adieu   106
Should a rival bow down to our idol below   155 Goblet   18
Bow down my head alone   159 Storm   40
Soft as the last drops round heaven's airy bow   175 Sonnet-B   8
Thee alone no doom can bow   187 French-A   12
Chasten'd bow, and mock humility   196 Hints   29
Pride, which not a world could bow   208 Fare Thee   50
Nor Fortune change, Pride raise, nor Passion bow   208 Sketch   29
The cedars bow, the mountains nod   217 The Harp   14
Thou who art bearing my buckler and bow   219 Saul-A   5
Pierced by shafts of many a bow   219 Saul-B   26
Him who bade England bow to Normandy   239 Conquest   2
These are the bards to whom the muse must bow   244 Bards   186
May shoot a little with a lengthen'd bow   257 Hints   16
Bow Irish jig and ancient rigadoon   275 Waltz   110
And he bares the gift at his saddle bow   317 Giaour   705
Thou, when thine arm should bend the bow   324 Abydos   1   85
Thou see'st yon bow--it hath a string   324 Abydos   1   104
A flash is seen--the ball beyond their bow   362 Corsair   3   488

BOW
Could bow to Lara, not descend to them   374 Lara   1   573
The reed in storms may bow and quiver   391 Corinth   669
As he saw Alp staggering bow   394 Corinth   859
As he there did bow and listen   400 Parisina   420
Which her bold bow flings off with dashing ease   418 Island   1   228
For what were simple bow and savage spear   433 Island   4   251
Whom you may bow to without looking grave   447 Beppo   467
Whose sons must bow them at a monarch's motion   454 Venice-B   139
And tyrants threat, and meeker victims bow   460 Dante   3   23
Tread on the universal necks that bow   464 Dante   4   99
An arrow for his bow, and lifts his head   473 Morgante   492
Could make the mountain bow   479 Manfred   1   73
Glory to Arimanes! we who bow   489 Manfred   2   390
The necks of men, bow down before his throne   489 Manfred   2   391
Bow down and worship! I do know the man   489 Manfred   2   400
Bow down and worship, slave! What, know'st thou
   not   489 Manfred   2   402
Bid him bow down to that which is above him   489 Manfred   2   416
Better bow down before the Hun, and call   517 Faliero   2   627
Nor bow the knee before a civic senate   533 Faliero   4   376
A sword of such a temper; and a bow   556 Sardan   1   363
These men would bow me down with. Never, never   586 Sardan   4   508
And bow me to the Duke. Are you content   606 Foscari   2   330
Why should I bow to thee? Hast thou ne'er bow'd   632 Cain   1   311
A mild and many-colour'd bow   657 Heaven   150
Now do yours. Hence, and bow and cringe him here   678 Werner   1   441
I bow beneath them. You shall say so when   685 Werner   2   186
Her zone to Venus, or his bow to Cupid   753 Juan   1   439
Her eyebrow's shape was like th' aerial bow   754 Juan   1   483
To pay them with; and some look'd o'er the bow   779 Juan   2   349
Then changed like to a bow that's bent, and then   785 Juan   2   727
And, laying down my pen, I make my bow   801 Juan   2   1726
And now and then, with tough strings of the bow   842 Juan   5   709
Heads bow, knees bend, eyes watch around a throne   847 Juan   5   1015
Katinka, too; and with a gentle bow   858 Juan   6   395
Ismail's no more! The crescent's silver bow   893 Juan   8   972
For I have drawn much less with a long bow   896 Juan   8   1102
His bow converted into a cock'd hat   902 Juan   9   357
His answers with a very graceful bow   907 Juan   9   659
Differ, except in robbing with a bow   920 Juan   11   116
Is idle; let us like most others bow   923 Juan   11   301
With fascination in his very bow   940 Juan   12   667
To draw the bow, to ride, and speak the truth   980 Juan   16   2
But draw the long bow better now than ever   980 Juan   16   8
Graceful as Dian, when she draws her bow   985 Juan   16   301

BOW'D
First bow'd beneath the brunt of Hellas' sword   33 Harold   2   841
Bow'd to the inborn tyranny of years   47 Harold   3   766
Where the bow'd waters meet him, and adore   51 Harold   3   965
I have not flatter'd its rank breath, nor bow'd   52 Harold   3   1050
And weave their web again; some, bow'd and bent   58 Harold   4   194
The yoke that is upon us doubly bow'd   69 Harold   4   850
Perchance she died in youth: it may be, bow'd   70 Harold   4   910
On the arena void--seats crush'd--walls bow'd   76 Harold   4   1277
When Friendship bow'd before the shrine of truth   127 Recoll   411
Bow'd to the dust the Drama's tower of pride   169 Address-A   2
Who bow'd so low the knee   180 Ode-A   11
And Monarchs bow'd the trembling limb   181 Ode-A   84
His bow'd head on his hands, and shook as 'twere   214 Dream   83
The cherubs and the saints bow'd down before   288 Vision   241
The Archangel bow'd, not like a modern beau   289 Vision   281
Satan bow'd, and was silent. 'Well, if you   297 Vision   793
In silence bow'd the virgin's head   326 Abydos   1   219
And bow'd her head, and turn'd her to depart   355 Corsair   2   536
Whose brow was bow'd beneath the glance he gave   363 Corsair   3   532
He seized his cloak, his head he slightly bow'd   373 Lara   1   496
And therefore bow'd he for a space   398 Parisina   227
Upon the block he bow'd his head   401 Parisina   453
Meekly had he bow'd and pray'd   401 Parisina   464
My limbs are bow'd, though not with toil   402 Chillon   5
And passing bow'd and mingled with her chat   448 Beppo   550
'Twas not for them, their necks were too much
   bow'd   454 Venice-B   90
I bow'd my visage, and so kept it till   476 Francesca   14
Mortal! to thy bidding bow'd   479 Manfred   1   50
To thine adjuration bow'd   479 Manfred   1   58
On the bare ground, have I bow'd down my face   489 Manfred   2   408
And bow'd my head beneath thy mid-day beams   562 Sardan   2   25
Bow'd down by such oppression; yes, I thought   622 Foscari   5   105
As yet have bow'd unto my father's God   632 Cain   1   303
Why should I bow to thee? Hast thou ne'er bow'd   632 Cain   1   311
He who bows not to him has bow'd to me   632 Cain   1   314
What all this meant: while Baba bow'd and bended   843 Juan   5   759
They bow'd obeisance and withdrew, retiring   844 Juan   5   793
Had bow'd themselves before th' imperial eyes   855 Juan   6   203
And bow'd her throbbing head o'er trembling knees   865 Juan   6   856
'He shall if that he dare.' Here Juan bow'd   875 Juan   7   497
Are bow'd, and put the sun out like a taper   918 Juan   10   662
Of nations, and had never bent or bow'd   974 Juan   15   366

BOWELS
Bowels (but they were forgotten   196 Rogers   9

BOWELS
Purges the eyes and moves the bowels | 231 Doctor | | 3
And tears his bowels, rather than survive | 733 Deformed | 1 | 777
About the lower region of the bowels | 776 Juan | 2 | 178

BOWER
(See also GARDEN-BOWER)
And none did love him; though to hall and bower | 4 Harold | 1 | 73
Heard her light, lively tones in Lady's bower | 13 Harold | 1 | 570
And as in Beauty's bower he pensive sate | 17 Harold | 1 | 834
Nor quit my silent humble bower | 111 Medea | | 39
In the shade of her bower I remember the hour | 115 The Tear | | 31
Fair Ida's bower adorns the landscape round | 123 Recoll | | 122
Smile in thy bower, but quit thee with a tear | 127 Recoll | | 382
Ye tenants of the classic bower | 145 Adieu | | 16
Of rapture in the secret bower | 201 Ode-C | | 82
Blest is the man who dares approach the bower | 253 Bards | | 867
The Bat builds in his haram bower | 313 Giaour | | 292
Find joy within her broken bower | 314 Giaour | | 415
The faithless slave that broke her bower | 315 Giaour | | 535
Is worthiest an immortal bower | 317 Giaour | | 746
That none can pierce that secret bower | 324 Abydos | 1 | 79
Than thee, companion of her bower | 328 Abydos | 1 | 423
His bower in other worlds of bliss | 330 Abydos | 2 | 110
For thee in those bright isles is built a bower | 333 Abydos | 2 | 408
And buds unshelter'd by a bower | 336 Abydos | 2 | 686
Though many a beauty droop'd in prison'd bower | 342 Corsair | 1 | 291
The lights are high on beacon and from bower | 364 Corsair | 3 | 567
And if she sits in Este's bower | 396 Parisina | | 19
No more in palace, hall, or bower | 401 Parisina | | 503
Which led me to that lady's rocky bower | 409 Mazeppa | | 299
Came sad and softly to their rocky bower | 424 Island | 2 | 399
With all could cheer or deck their sparry bower | 432 Island | 4 | 186
Were easy in the isolated bower | 563 Sardan | 2 | 130
Our bower. Ah, little knows he what he weeps for | 654 Cain | 3 | 520
The snow on the hills cannot blast her bower | 742 Deformed | 3 | 10
When Julia sate within as pretty a bower | 759 Juan | 1 | 827
She and her wave worn love had made their bower | 799 Juan | 2 | 1581
But after all it is the only 'bower | 926 Juan | 11 | 518
Theirs is the best bower anchor, the chain cable | 930 Juan | 12 | 19
But in the country ladies seek their bower | 955 Juan | 13 | 883

BOWERS
(See also VINTAGE-BOWERS)
And weeping angels lead her to those bowers | 84 Death-B | | 15
No more we meet in yonder bowers | 98 To Lesbia | | 25
Those fairy bowers, where all in turn have been | 122 Recoll | | 16
Which bloom among the fairy bowers | 133 E. N. Long | | 30
Lyaeus! in thy bowers of pleasure | 139 Anacreon-C | | 21
When Man, expell'd from Eden's bowers | 155 Lady-E | | 1
When Love has abandon'd the bowers | 162 Romaic-A | | 14
Where bloom my native valley's bowers | 322 Giaour | | 1220
Then feast like spirits in their promised bowers | 419 Island | 2 | 22
Till they were exiled from their earlier bowers | 749 Juan | 1 | 140
He thought of wood-nymphs and immortal bowers | 758 Juan | 1 | 747
With cypress branches hast thou wreathed thy
  bowers | 801 Juan | 3 | 11
Through orange bowers, and jasmine, and so forth | 836 Juan | 5 | 330

BOWING
The face of thy high heaven, bowing his own | 649 Cain | 3 | 242
Stands sleek and slavish, bowing at his door | 464 Dante | 4 | 94

BOWL
But seeks not now the harlot and the bowl | 8 Harold | 1 | 327
And fill'd the bowl, and trimm'd the cheerful
  lamp | 29 Harold | 2 | 608
And bid him drain the dregs of pleasure's bowl | 100 Damaetas | | 12
'Fill high the bowl the table round | 104 Alva | | 221
Roused by the sneer, he raised the bowl | 104 Alva | | 245
Though gay companions o'er the bowl | 135 I Would | | 29
Mingle with the genial bowl | 139 Anacreon-C | | 1
When drain'd is the nectar which gladdens the
  bowl | 148 Farewell-A | | 13
That truth, as of yore, is confined to the bowl | 155 Goblet | | 24
Will deeply embitter the bowl | 162 Romaic-A | | 18
Though gay companions o'er the bowl | 166 Struggle | | 21
I'd dash to earth the sweetest bowl | 168 Haunts | | 23
The bowl a Moslem must not drain | 315 Giaour | | 548
What need of words? the deadly bowl | 331 Abydos | 2 | 236
The bowl a bribed attendant bore | 331 Abydos | 2 | 244
Or if she fell by bowl or steel | 401 Parisina | | 519
And raise it in his followers--'Ho! the bowl | 417 Island | 1 | 99
Strike up the dance! the cava bowl fill high | 419 Island | 2 | 45
Fill high the bowl with Samian wine | 812 Juan | 3 | 749
Fill high the bowl with Samian wine | 813 Juan | 3 | 761ff

BOWLES
Way, how now, Billy Bowles | 237 Bowles | | 5
And art thou not their prince, harmonious Bowles | 246 Bards | | 331
Delightful Bowles! still blessing and still blest | 246 Bards | | 341
She quits poor Bowles for Little's purer strain | 246 Bards | | 348
Bowles! in thy memory let this precept dwell | 246 Bards | | 361
From silly Hafiz up to simple Bowles | 251 Bards | | 708

BOWLES
Let sonneteering Bowles his strains refine | 254 Bards | | 925
Beware--for God's sake, don't begin like Bowles | 259 Hints | | 194

BOWLS
Nor left such bowls an Argive robber's prey | 107 Nisus | | 148
What bowls and mantles in confusion toss'd | 109 Nisus | | 286
Bowls on the board, and banners on the wall | 366 Lara | 1 | 6

BOWS
Rome--Rome imperial, bows her to the storm | 62 Harold | 4 | 411
So the spirit bows before thee | 188 Music-C | | 13
Bows to thee--by thee forsaken | 208 Fare Thee | | 51
The Baal-adorer bows on Sinai's steep | 217 Jordan | | 3
Making balls for the ladies, and bows to his foes | 228 Once | | 4
Each country book-club bows the knee to Baal | 243 Bards | | 138
Bows his bent head; his hand salutes the floor | 347 Corsair | 2 | 47
Bows to your beauties, soften'd, but intense | 419 Island | 2 | 60
Much armour was, and hung up certain bows | 473 Morgante | | 473
The worship of the land, which bows the knee | 565 Sardan | 2 | 237
That bows to him who made things but to bend | 631 Cain | 1 | 235
He who bows not to him has bow'd to me | 632 Cain | 1 | 314
Whose every drop bows them down nearer earth | 672 Werner | 1 | 27
When the stripp'd forest bows to the bleak air | 889 Juan | 8 | 700
High dash'd the spray, the bows dipp'd in the sea | 915 Juan | 10 | 508
Bows have they, generally with two strings | 980 Juan | 16 | 5
Retired: with most unfashionable bows | 994 Juan | 16 | 853

BOWSHOT
Within a bowshot. Where the Caesars dwelt | 495 Manfred | 3 | 282
A bow-shot of the 'Riva di Schiavoni | 614 Foscari | 3 | 400

BOWSPRIT
Foremast and bowsprit were cut down, and they | 778 Juan | 2 | 253

BOW-STREET
Grenadiers, Volunteers, Bow-street Police | 225 Ode-D | | 18
And Bow-street myrmidons stood laughing by | 248 Bards | | 467
At home, our Bow-street gemmen keep the laws | 451 Beppo | | 685

BOW-STREET'S
Who queer a flat? Who (spite of Bow-street's ban | 920 Juan | 11 | 149

BOWSTRING
About a bow-string--quite in vain; not yet | 844 Juan | 5 | 820
Of years to fill a bowstring or the throne | 850 Juan | 5 | 1218

BOWSTRINGS
(As bowstrings, when relax'd by rain | 400 Parisina | | 361

BOWSTRUNG
His lately bowstrung brother caused his rise | 850 Juan | 5 | 1172

BOX
(See also HUNTING-BOX)
When the box of Pandora was open'd on earth | 156 Goblet | | 25
So he sat him on his box again | 177 Devil's Dr | | 97
Lady, accept the box a hero wore | 238 Snuff-Box | | 1
Must go to Jackson ere they dare to box | 265 Hints | | 638
(For sometimes we must box without the muffle | 785 Juan | 2 | 736

BOXER
Or a good boxer, into a sad pickle | 883 Juan | 8 | 342
For, like a racer, or a boxer training | 943 Juan | 13 | 143

BOXES
'Sustains her part' in all the 'upper' boxes | 171 Address-B | | 38
O'erwhelm with sound the boxes, gallery, pit | 259 Hints | | 159
Nor much to climb; through little boxes framed | 921 Juan | 11 | 164

BOXING
Oaths, boxing, begging,--all, save rout and race | 261 Hints | | 328
Lounging and boxing; and the twilight hour | 926 Juan | 11 | 514

BOY
(See also HERO-BOY, SCHOOL-BOY)
When first Spain's queen beheld the black-eyed
  boy | 12 Harold | 1 | 511
Away, thou heedless boy! prepare the spear | 16 Harold | 1 | 757
Ah, happy years! once more who would not be a boy | 23 Harold | 2 | 207
Here, too, his boy essay'd the dreadful leap | 24 Harold | 2 | 259
And ne'er again the boy his bosom sought | 24 Harold | 2 | 277
The mother of a moment, o'er thy boy | 80 Harold | 4 | 1509
Borne, like thy bubbles, onward. From a boy | 82 Harold | 4 | 1650
At this lone hour the Paphian boy | 88 Anacreon-B | | 7
Ask thine own heart; 'twill bid thee, boy,
  forbear | 93 Dorset | | 31
In law an infant and in years a boy | 100 Damaetas | | 1
'Nor chase nor wave my boy delay | 103 Alva | | 110
For beauty crown'd the fair-hair'd boy | 103 Alva | | 160
Say, hadst thou ne'er another boy | 104 Alva | | 203
'Here's to my boy! alive or dead | 104 Alva | | 227
And beardless bloom yet graced the gallant boy | 105 Nisus | | 10
His glowing friend address'd the Dardan boy | 106 Nisus | | 38

BOY

Her only boy, reclined in endless sleep	106	Nisus	74
Still dwells the Dardan spirit in the boy	107	Nisus	122
Alike through life esteem'd, thou godlike boy	107	Nisus	169
More than a boy, in wisdom and in grace	108	Nisus	219
Th' exulting boy the studded girdle wears	109	Nisus	293
'O God! my boy,' he cries, 'of me bereft	109	Nisus	321
The hapless boy a ruffian train surround	109	Nisus	329
And, raging, on the boy defenceless flew	110	Nisus	362
The light effusions of a heedless boy	119	Answer-A	40
When now the boy is ripen'd into man	123	Recoll	67
My eyes, my heart, proclaim'd me still a boy	125	Recoll	196
Nor yet are you forgot, my jocund boy	125	Recoll	265
Your arm, brave boy, arrested his career	126	Recoll	279
his boy; but the blue-eyed Mora spreads the	130	Calmar	74
In mind again a boy	132	L'Amitie	44
As many a boy and girl remembers	134	E. N. Long	84
As I felt, when a boy, on the crag-cover'd wild	135	Highlander	12
When Cytherea's blooming Boy	139	Anacreon-C	15
Thus to disturb a harmless Boy	141	Critics	57
And crush, oh! noble conquest! crush a Boy	143	Soliloquy	66
Where Science seeks each loitering boy	145	Adieu	3
Will not the laughing boy despise	147	Vain Lady	25
As many a boy and girl remembers	148	A Fan	10
And touch thy father's heart, my Boy	150	My Son	6
And pardon all the past, my Boy	150	My Son	12
A Father's heart is thine, my Boy	150	My Son	18
A Father's heart is thine, my Boy	150	My Son	24
In justice done to thee, my Boy	150	My Son	30
Will ne'er desert its pledge, my Boy	150	My Son	36
Thou, too, hast ceased to be a boy	153	Friend-A	24
The heart of a mistress some boy may estrange	155	Goblet	13
The winged boy, Love	200	Stanzas-B	86
Fair as herself--but the boy gazed on her	214	Dream	41
The boy had fewer summers, but his heart	214	Dream	46
The Boy of whom I spake;--he was alone	214	Dream	79
The Boy was sprung to manhood: in the wilds	215	Dream	106
Well, I will tell it thee, unfeeling boy	229	Sadness	2
My boy Hobbie O	235	New Song	2ff
The idiot mother of 'an idiot boy	245	Bards	248
Whom you speak to? Right well, boy, and so does 'the Row	277	Blues	1	11
Of that fair boy his sire shall ne'er embrace	299	Age	84
The mother of the hero's hope, the boy	308	Age	729
'Come hither, boy--what, no reply	325	Abydos	1	119
'Much I misdoubt this wayward boy	325	Abydos	1	132
I would not have thee wed a boy	326	Abydos	1	208
His only boy had met his fate	393	Corinth	806
Then forward stepp'd the bold and froward boy	417	Island	1	151
A boy Achilles, with the centaur's lyre	420	Island	2	85
Where sat the songstress with the stranger boy	420	Island	2	111
A blooming boy, a truant mutineer	421	Island	2	209
The infant rapture still survived the boy	423	Island	2	290
The maid and boy, in one absorbing soul	423	Island	2	305
Torquil, my boy! what cheer? Ho! brother, ho	425	Island	2	431
'And is it thus?' he cried, 'unhappy boy	428	Island	3	145
Even Christian gazed upon the maid and boy	429	Island	3	203
Down plunged she through the cave to rouse her boy	435	Island	4	388
And such a truant boy would end in woe	438	Tasso	160
From travellers accustom'd from a boy	441	Beppo	55
Of female wits, boy bards--in short, a fool	449	Beppo	584
By such a boy to be no longer guided	467	Morgante	96
Why, yes!--boy, you perceive it then at last	503	Faliero	1	244
Continue what thou pleasest. Boy, retire	554	Sardan	246
Open--How feel you? Like a boy--Oh Venice	597	Foscari	1	93
My track like a sea-bird---I was a boy then	597	Foscari	1	121
And happier than his father. The rash boy	603	Foscari	2	94
The last!--my boy!--the last time I shall see	608	Foscari	2	438
Have heard thee name my name--our name! My boy	613	Foscari	3	342
Even on these dull damp walls, and--Boy! no tears	614	Foscari	3	415
Now he is mine--my broken-hearted boy	618	Foscari	4	206
You tremble. 'Tis the knell of my poor boy	625	Foscari	5	286
A sovereign should die standing. My poor boy	625	Foscari	5	306
My boy! thou speakest as I spoke, in sin	628	Cain	1	39
A watching shepherd boy, who offers up	630	Cain	1	180
I wrestled with the lion, when a boy	631	Cain	1	257
My disinherited boy! 'Tis but a dream	646	Cain	3	32
Have I not thee, our boy, our sire, and brother	646	Cain	3	41
His heart will, and thine own too. Bless thee, boy	648	Cain	3	156
A murderer in my boy, and of his father	653	Cain	3	488
Think'st thou my boy will bear to look on me	654	Cain	3	523
Silence, vain boy! each word of thine's a crime	668	Heaven	978
My boy	669	Heaven	1107
Further. Take comfort,--we shall find our boy	672	Werner	1	72
Upon my boy his father's faults and follies	673	Werner	1	98
Than to behold my boy and my boy's mother	674	Werner	1	161
And my desire. The boy, they say, 's a bold one	687	Werner	2	263
Ulric! My father, Siegendorf! Hush! boy	688	Werner	2	357
Who taught you, long-sought and ill-found boy! that	689	Werner	2	430
The frontier, and you're safe. My noble boy	698	Werner	3	201
The least we'll meet again once more. My boy	698	Werner	3	226

BOY

If nature--Oh, my boy! what unknown woes	702	Werner	3	487
The fugitive? Boy! since I fell into	703	Werner	3	533
The chamber. Then, my boy! thou art guiltless still	718	Werner	5	322
From Macedon's boy	725	Deformed	1	178
The unshorn boy of Peleus, with his locks	726	Deformed	1	267
Of Thetis's boy	728	Deformed	1	381
Like to the lovely boy lost in the forest	730	Deformed	1	527
Removed; the aid of--No, my gallant boy	736	Deformed	2	132
At twelve he was a fine, but quiet boy	753	Juan	1	394
But the boy bore up long, and with a mild	785	Juan	2	699
The boy expired--the father held the clay	785	Juan	2	713
All tranquilly the shipwreck'd boy was lying	792	Juan	2	1147
Paid daily visits to her boy, and took	796	Juan	2	1386
As boy, I thought myself a clever fellow	816	Juan	4	17
And Juan was a boy of saintly breeding	818	Juan	4	150
Deal with me as thou wilt, but spare this boy	821	Juan	4	304
When Haidee threw herself her boy before	821	Juan	4	331
'My boy!' said he, 'amidst this motley crew	832	Juan	5	97
There was not now a luggage boy but sought	873	Juan	7	389
He's a fine boy. The women may be sent	875	Juan	7	527
But Juan was quite 'a broth of a boy	881	Juan	8	185
Exclaiming;--'Juan! Juan! On, boy! brace	890	Juan	8	774
Besides, the empress sometimes liked a boy	902	Juan	9	375
Juan, I said, was a most beauteous boy	903	Juan	9	417
Her preference of a boy to men much bigger	905	Juan	9	571
All my boy feelings, all my gentler dreams	909	Juan	10	140
Though on the whole, no doubt, the Dardan boy	964	Juan	14	574

BOY-GOD

Her, and the boy-God on her knee	394	Corinth	955

BOYHOOD

I loved her from my boyhood; she to me	57	Harold	4	154
Conceive in boyhood and pursue as men	73	Harold	4	1095
Ye dreams of my boyhood, how much I regret you	96	Harrow-A	25
The Starlight of his Boyhood;--as he stood	215	Dream	148
Had Lara's daring boyhood govern'd men	366	Lara	1	20
From boyhood, ever ready to assist thee	530	Faliero	4	135
As boys love rows, my boyhood liked a squabble	829	Juan	4	785

BOYHOOD'S

And even in simple boyhood's opening dawn	93	Dorset	19

BOYISH

While boyish blood is mantling, who can 'scape	14	Harold	1	662
Doth lean his boyish form along the rock	27	Harold	2	467
Each early boyish friend, or youthful foe	123	Recoll	52
Who join'd with me in every boyish sport	123	Recoll	101
Yet greets the triumph of my boyish mind	126	Recoll	347
Has cured my boyish soul of Dreaming	144	Becher-B	44
Had quench'd at length my boyish flame	155	Happy	22
In fondness brotherly and boyish, I	654	Cain	3	537
Against your own example? Boyish sophist	710	Werner	4	366
He buoy'd his boyish limbs, and strove to ply	787	Juan	2	842
I did my very boyish best to shine	860	Juan	6	493
You love this boyish, new, seraglio guest	866	Juan	6	917
And had retain'd his boyish look beyond	903	Juan	9	418

BOYS
(See also SEA-BOYS)

'My spouse and boys dwell near thy hall	6	Harold	1	166
The boys in childhood chased the roe	102	Alva	55
Then in his warm embrace the boys he press'd	107	Nisus	127
Thy votive train of girls and boys	118	Romance	4
(For glittering baubles are not left to boys	127	Recoll	398
And as he, with his boys, shall revisit this spot	149	Newstead-B	33
Is but for boys	200	Stanzas-B	87
So we, boys, we	229	Lads	3
Up my boys and do your duty	240	Suliotes	6
And boys shall hunt your bardship up and down	263	Hints	478
Our boys (save those whom public schools compel	264	Hints	513
Partake his jest with boasting boys	321	Giaour	1174
That there were few, or boys or men	408	Mazeppa	183
Where yet my boys are, and that fatal she	458	Dante	1	172
Their friend and made a sovereign, as boys make	525	Faliero	3	496
Unman my heart, and the poor boys will weep	581	Sardan	4	211
My boys--I could have borne it were I childless	582	Sardan	4	283
Certain, and of the boys too, our last hopes	584	Sardan	4	370
Their boys who died in battle, is it written	602	Foscari	2	75
Bustle, my boys! we are at fault. In what	697	Werner	3	145
Now, boys! On! on! And off! Eternal powers	736	Deformed	2	126
The Bourbon! Bourbon! On, boys! Rome is ours	737	Deformed	2	156
As boys love rows, my boyhood liked a squabble	829	Juan	4	785
Like birds, or boys, or bedlamites broke loose	856	Juan	6	266
An uniform to boys is like a fan	877	Juan	7	668
His five brave boys no less the foe defied	892	Juan	8	853
No more it doth, its ploughs but change their boys	908	Juan	10	55
As the smart boys spurr'd fast in their career	917	Juan	10	611
To herd with boys, or hoard with good threescore	930	Juan	12	110
Here danced Albano's boys, and here the sea shone	950	Juan	13	565
The first thing boys like after play and fruit	953	Juan	13	803

BOY'S
His fury, like an angry boy's, to master 541 Faliero 5 243
Than to behold my boy and my boy's mother 674 Werner 1 161
And 'tis no boy's play. Now he strikes them down 737 Deformed 2 160
And the boy's eyes, which the dull film half glazed 785 Juan 2 709
'Twas the boy's 'mite,' and, like the 'widow's,' may 853 Juan 6 41

BRACE
As the black eunuch enter'd with his brace 838 Juan 5 425
And for one kiss would fain imprint a brace 845 Juan 5 845
Exclaiming;--'Juan! Juan! On, boy! brace 890 Juan 8 774

BRACED
Where pistols unadorn'd were braced 330 Abydos 2 138
Around his waist are forests braced 479 Manfred 1 64

BRACELET
One large gold bracelet clasp'd each lovely arm 810 Juan 3 561

BRACELETS
And bracelets; swanlike bosoms, and the necklace 529 Faliero 4 55

BRACKISH
As springs in deserts found seem sweet, all brackish though they be 186 Music-B 19

BRAEMAR
You rest with your clan in the caves of Braemar 117 Lachin 30

BRAG
For hang me if I know of which you may most brag 226 Oh You 3

BRAGANZA
On Braganza 157 Hodgson 58

BRAHMINS
Of highest caste--the Brahmins of the ton 951 Juan 13 660

BRAIDED
(See also SERPENT-BRAID)
With braided tresses bounding o'er the green 17 Harold 1 808
When they were braided, and her proud array 70 Harold 4 923
With braided hair, and bright-black eye 323 Giaour 1300
And auburn waves of gemm'd and braided hair 353 Corsair 2 403

BRAIDS
The white arms and the raven hair--the braids 529 Faliero 4 54
In braids behind; and though her stature were 788 Juan 2 924

BRAIN
When busy Memory flashes on my brain 20 Harold 2 76
Too long and darkly, till my brain became 36 Harold 3 56
But to that gentle touch, through brain and breast 47 Harold 3 748
Have I not had my brain sear'd, my heart riven 75 Harold 4 1211
Two insulated phantoms of the brain 77 Harold 4 1327
Of narrow brain, yet of a narrower soul 93 Masters 7
pierced his eye. His brain gushes through 130 Calmar 137
But in my breast and in my brain 151 Farewell-B 10
The world befits a busy brain 164 Friend-B 43
My curdling blood, my madd'ning brain 172 Romaic-B 33
And the Heart's Spectre flitting through the brain 201 Ode-C 37
'Twill flow, and cease to burn my brain 218 Soul-B 8
'Twas ill report that urged my brain to madness 229 Sadness 3
All hail, M. P.! from whose infernal brain 245 Bards 273
Prompt thy crude brain, and claim thee for a scribe 246 Bards 364
If Commerce fills the purse, she clogs the brain 247 Bards 395
The petrifactions of a plodding brain 247 Bards 416
And pray, what follows from his boiling brain 259 Hints 196
Dilutes with drivel every drizzly brain 270 Minerva 140
But smile--though all the pangs of brain and heart 299 Age 81
And darts into her desperate brain 314 Giaour 432
If bursting heart, and madd'ning brain 321 Giaour 1107
Throbb'd to the very brain as now 322 Giaour 1262
My brain bewilder'd--do not madden quite 362 Corsair 3 473
It was the very weakness of his brain 365 Corsair 3 650
Hate's working brain, and lull'd ambition's wile 375 Lara 1 635
That bound to Lara Kaled's heart and brain 382 Lara 2 537
Such as the busy brain of Sorrow paints 384 Lara 2 610
That crash'd through the brain of the infidel 394 Corinth 877
Throbb'd as if back upon his brain 398 Parisina 225
And each frail fibre of her brain 400 Parisina 360
But then within my brain it wrought 404 Chillon 155
A light broke in upon my brain 405 Chillon 251
Then through my brain the thought did pass 409 Mazeppa 271
My heart turn'd sick, my brain grew sore 412 Mazeppa 542
Fever begins upon the brain 412 Mazeppa 560
My heart, and sparks that cross'd my brain 414 Mazeppa 793
Works through the throbbing eyeball to the brain 436 Tasso 9

BRAIN
My brain against these bars, as the sun flash'd 439 Tasso 210
Should rise up in high treason to his brain 461 Dante 3 95
Orlando, in whose brain all was not well 468 Morgante 134
O'er thy heart and brain together 481 Manfred 1 260
And my brain reels--and yet my foot is firm 482 Manfred 1 283
How my brain aches beneath thee! and my temples 504 Faliero 1 294
An arrow pierced his brain, while, scattering 577 Sardan 3 355
If that this moment is not gain'd. My brain turns 584 Sardan 4 415
Those black and bloody leaves, his heart and brain 606 Foscari 2 336
That which adorn'd the brain of Donna Inez 748 Juan 1 88
That you might 'brain them with their lady's fan 749 Juan 1 165
Her brain, though in a dream! (and then she sigh'd 757 Juan 1 667
His brain about the action of the sky 758 Juan 1 742
And as he gazed, his dizzy brain spun fast 788 Juan 2 873
Or if, too classic for his vulgar brain 814 Juan 3 885
The tears rush'd forth from her o'erclouded brain 824 Juan 4 527
And whirl'd her brain to madness; she arose 825 Juan 4 530
Her cheek turn'd ashes, ears rung, brain whirl'd round 865 Juan 6 837
So lofty that I feel my brain turn round 907 Juan 9 677
Which is a signal to my nerves and brain 907 Juan 9 679
Heaven's brandy, though our brain can hardly bear it 918 Juan 11 16
Above his burnt-out brain, and sapless cinders 925 Juan 11 477
Thirdly, that 'Juan had more brain than beard 963 Juan 14 525

BRAIN-BORN
With brain-born dreams of evil all their own 20 Harold 2 59

BRAINS
Of brains (if brains they had) he them beguiled 8 Harold 1 299
Instead of Brains, a fine Ingredient 144 Becher-B 38
And when, alas! our brains are gone 154 Skull 15
Of brains that labour, big with verse or prose 242 Bards 12
Who rack their brains for lucre, not for fame 244 Bards 178
Uncheck'd by megrims of patrician brains 261 Hints 357
But our good fathers never bent their brains 262 Hints 425
For brains may be o'erloaded, like the back 264 Hints 536
If you will breed this bastard of your brains 267 Hints 791
But to hear a vile jargon which addles my brains 280 Blues 2 21
Are pardon'd their bad hearts for their worse brains 435 Island 4 356
They knock the brains out first--which makes them heirs 695 Werner 2 761
And such things as the entrails and the brains 783 Juan 2 614
The hour, as is the case with lively brains 882 Juan 8 260
The ocean's tides and mortals' brains she sways 982 Juan 16 111

BRAIN'S
The bell tolls on!--let's hence--my brain's on fire 625 Foscari 5 304
Ah, now you recognise him! My brain's crush'd 739 Deformed 2 301
From his own brain's oppression while it reels 835 Juan 5 246

BRAIN-SCORCH'D
But why to brain-scorch'd bigots thus appeal 262 Hints 373

BRAIN-SPATTERING
War's a brain-spattering, windpipe-slitting art 896 Juan 9 27

BRAKE
O'er brake and craggy brow 158 Storm 34
Recall'd at morning from the branched brake 185 Julian 57
The bird that sings within the brake 321 Giaour 1169
But here young Selim silence brake 324 Abydos 1 47
By bushy brake, and wild flowers blossoming 340 Corsair 1 125
But none are there, and not a brake hath borne 376 Lara 2 111
For there it coil'd as in a brake 481 Manfred 1 237
As travellers follow over bog and brake 882 Juan 8 252
Around: the wildfowl nestled in the brake 948 Juan 13 453

BRAKES
At intervals, some bird from out the brakes 48 Harold 3 817
With brakes entangled, scarce a path between 109 Nisus 313

BRAMINS
Where gentle hearts, like Bramins, sit and smile 424 Island 2 381

BRANCH
(See also OLIVE-BRANCH)
The vine on high, the willow branch below 7 Harold 1 250
As the branch, at the bidding of Nature 162 Romaic-A 9
'I lay my branch of laurel down 227 Thurlow-B 1
Thou 'lay thy branch of laurel down 227 Thurlow-B 2
The olive branch, which still she deign'd to clasp 269 Minerva 83
And withers not though branch and leaf 336 Abydos 2 667
The last bud of the rival branch at once 706 Werner 4 132
For every branch of every science known 748 Juan 1 74
Arts, sciences, no branch was made a mystery 752 Juan 1 311

BRANCH
Sprung up a branch as beautiful as fresh   754 Juan   1   460
Where the wild branch of the cork forest grew   757 Juan   1   716
Upon the Danube's left branch and left bank   868 Juan   7   66
For war cuts up not only branch, but root   872 Juan   7   328
So that the branch a goodly-verdure flings   963 Juan   14   467

BRANCHED
Recall'd at morning from the branched brake   185 Julian   57

BRANCHES
Which feeds these deadly branches: for it were   40 Harold   3   300
Of stirring branches, and the bud which brings   51 Harold   3   956
Whose root is earth, whose leaves and branches be   74 Harold   4   1130
High, through those elms, with hoary branches
  crown'd   123 Recoll   121
Their branches on the gale   131 L'Amitie   22
Spot of my youth! whose hoary branches sigh   138 Harrow-B   1
How do thy branches, moaning to the blast   138 Harrow-B   13
That thy dark-waving branches would flourish
  around   149 Newstead-B   3
And still may thy branches their beauty display   149 Newstead-B   24
While the branches thus gratefully shelter his
  grave   149 Newstead-B   31
The tainted branches of the tree   402 Parisina   579
Is it the wind those branches stirs   413 Mazeppa   671
Lovely in all its branches to all eyes   464 Dante   4   76
Composed of branches, logs of wood, and earth   470 Morgante   306
Their bark and branches--what were they? That
  which   641 Cain   2   347
For our child's canopy? Because its branches   646 Cain   3   6
The branches shake, and some loose stones have
  fallen   702 Werner   3   456
With cypress branches hast thou wreathed thy
  bowers   801 Juan   3   11
Through the waved branches o'er the greensward
  glancing   805 Juan   3   227
Know not, since knowledge saw her branches stript 903 Juan   9   438

BRANCHING
The branching stag swept down with all his herd   948 Juan   13   447

BRANCHLESS
Wrecks of a single winter, barkless, branchless   482 Manfred   1   328
Without their sap, how branchless were the trunk   797 Juan   2   1429

BRAND
(See also BOARDING-BRAND)
Shake the red cloak, and poise the ready brand   16 Harold   1   779
And wasted far and near with glaive and brand   30 Harold   2   616
While Envy waved her burning brand   105 Alva   287
And brand a nearly blighted name   174 Remember-B   16
But having buy my keys, and not my brand   287 Vision   151
Who leads them on with foreign brand   316 Giaour   608
Which quivers round that faithless brand   316 Giaour   658
Assume the distaff--not the brand   324 Abydos   1   100
Refused the bridle or the brand   332 Abydos   2   328
Is ready with a sheathless brand   334 Abydos   2   506
And fragments of each shiver'd brand   335 Abydos   2   588
They game--carouse--converse--or whet the brand   338 Corsair   1   48
In pensive posture leaning on the brand   340 Corsair   1   131
That might have better kept so true a brand   354 Corsair   2   484
But since the dagger suits thee less than brand   361 Corsair   3   380
It was too late to check the wasting brand   379 Lara   2   278
And that not once a useless brand   399 Parisina   237
And waved along the vault her kindled brand   432 Island   4   162
Which snared me here, and with the brand of
  shame   439 Tasso   215
And wear a deeper brand and gaudier chain   464 Dante   4   106
Cortana clave the skull like a true brand   470 Morgante   275
Stamp'd the same brand upon a peasant's stool   503 Faliero   1   229
In Venice save the Doge, this blight, this brand   513 Faliero   2   277
Breaks through, as from a thunder-cloud! yon
  brand   652 Cain   3   391
Who taught you thus to brand an unknown being   689 Werner   2   427
To bear the brand of bloodshed? Pshaw! leave any
  thing   703 Werner   3   548
Himself--a felon's brand? The man who is   720 Werner   5   450

BRANDED
By dire reviewers should be branded   137 Clare   47

BRANDENBURG
To rise. I speak of Brandenburg, wherein   685 Werner   2   175
An order of the house of Brandenburg   694 Werner   2   694

BRANDENBURG'S
From Brandenburg's elector, for the arrest   680 Werner   1   564

BRANDING
In many a branding page and burning line   271 Minerva   204
Branding my thoughts as things to shun and fear   438 Tasso   99

BRANDISH
The reply was the brandish of sabre and spear   392 Corinth   720

BRANDS
Wide o'er the realm they wave their kindling
  brands   272 Minerva   281
Ungrateful fool! since but for brands   320 Giaour   1042
But brands of foreign blade and hilt   330 Abydos   2   124
And snatch'd in startled haste unbelted brands   369 Lara   1   210
Where Hymen's torch but brands one strumpet more 818 Juan   4   135

BRANDY
'Brandy for heroes!' Burke could once exclaim   417 Island   1   101
Meantime I drink to your return in brandy   450 Beppo   640
Heaven's brandy, though our brain can hardly bear
  it   918 Juan   11   16

BRANDY'S
(In love or brandy's fervent fermentation   923 Juan   11   310

BRARA
And on towards Brara prick'd him o'er the plain   468 Morgante   131

BRASS
Before St. Mark still glow his steeds of brass   57 Harold   4   109
With fronts of brass and feet of clay   180 Ode-A   27
If the idol of brass find his feet are of clay   203 Avatar   58
An address, and present it themselves all in
  brass   237 Braziers   2
But now, worn down, appear in native brass   254 Bards   898
(Who ne'er despises books that bring him brass   264 Hints   548
Of native brass or law-awarded gold   275 Waltz   98
Of velvet, gilding, brass, and no great dearth   286 Vision   67
The brass of both his epitaph and tomb   295 Vision   658
Has more of brass in it, and is as well blown   297 Vision   800
Many a bosom, sheathed in brass   392 Corinth   731
The mirror, sire? Yes, sir, of polish'd brass   573 Sardan   3   146
I think it may be of 'Corinthian Brass'   859 Juan   6   441
And blazon o'er the door their names in brass   922 Juan   11   248

BRAST
Mid wounds, and clinging darts, and lances brast   16 Harold   1   776

BRATS
And goblin brats, of Gilpin Horner's brood   244 Bards   157
Of feeding brats the moment his wife weans   932 Juan   12   168

BRATTLING
Jarr'd but not drown'd by the loud brattling; her   577 Sardan   3   394

BRAVE
And must they fall? the young, the proud, the
  brave   12 Harold   1   549
Oh! who is more brave than a dark Suliote   30 Harold   2   653
Ages, but not oblivion, feebly brave   33 Harold   2   816
The lamps shone o'er fair women and brave men   38 Harold   3   184
Over the unreturning brave,--alas   39 Harold   3   238
Such scorn of man had help'd to brave the shock   41 Harold   3   363
Their hopes were not less warm, their souls were
  full as brave   42 Harold   3   432
Brief, brave, and glorious was his young career   44 Harold   3   545
The beautiful, the brave--the lords of earth and
  sea   59 Harold   4   225
Yes! yield those lips, for which I'd brave   90 To M.S.G.-A   29
It shakes the shield of Oscar brave   102 Alva   34
Both, both were brave: the Saxon spear   102 Alva   69
Unknown the secret enterprise I brave   107 Nisus   183
Brave Nisus here arrests his comrade's arm   109 Nisus   279
'Ill-starr'd, though brave, did no visions
  foreboding   117 Lachin   25
Though oft repulsed, by guile o'ercomes the brave 120 Newstead-A   62
Your arm, brave boy, arrested his career   126 Recoll   279
The fair, the brave, the good must die   128 Answer-B   19
What censure, what danger, what woe would I brave 129 Becher-A   18
Brave shades of chiefs and sages   162 War Song   13
Thy choice is most ignobly brave   180 Ode-A   45
The humbler ranks, the lowly brave, who bled   182 Address-C   15
The Coronach's wild requiem to the brave   182 Address-C   30
That left a likeness of the brave or just   183 Address-D   4
And Triumph weeps above the brave   183 Parker   4
Every peril he must brave   187 French-A   38
Contains the 'bravest of the brave'   187 Ode-B   10
Star of the brave!--whose beam hath shed   188 On Star   1
Star of the brave! thy ray is pale   189 On Star   31
And teach it what to brave or brook   209 Augusta-A   22
Brave Champions! go on with the farce   237 Farce   1
So may her few, the letter'd and the brave   270 Minerva   151
Clime of the unforgotten brave   311 Giaour   103
Peace to the brave! whose blood is spilt   317 Giaour   721
And welcome with a kiss the brave   317 Giaour   744
Too meek to meet, or brave despair   319 Giaour   919
Than ne'er to brave the billows more   319 Giaour   964
Death is but what the haughty brave   320 Giaour   1024
Apparell'd as becomes the brave   324 Abydos   1   21
Now I have motive to be brave   327 Abydos   1   362
The young, the beautiful, the brave   329 Abydos   2   4
How had the brave who fell exulted now   338 Corsair   1   42
Who would not brave the battle-fire, the wreck   339 Corsair   1   95

BRAVE

Yet was I brave--mean boast where all are brave	343 Corsair	1	325
The only pang my bosom dare not brave	343 Corsair	1	357
How well such deed becomes the turban'd brave	347 Corsair	2	18
Ay--Pride can veil, and Courage brave it all	352 Corsair	2	358
They heard and rose, and, tremulously brave	369 Lara	1	207
O'er which the following brave may rise	387 Corinth		240
They follow'd him, for he was brave	387 Corinth		310
But none so lovely and so brave	402 Parisina		532
And wear the wreaths that sprung from out the brave	419 Island	2	28
Is hurl'd down headlong, like the foremost brave	426 Island	3	22
No less of human bravery than the brave	427 Island	3	52
More brave than firm, and more disposed to dare	428 Island	3	123
Of public places, where they basely brave	447 Beppo		469
Are ye not brave? Yes, yet the Ausonian soil	460 Dante	2	131
The gay, the learn'd, the generous, and the brave	461 Dante	3	44
Conflict, and final triumph of the brave	462 Dante	3	125
Noble and brave as aught of consular	508 Faliero	1	618
Brave, generous; rich in all the qualities	510 Faliero	2	100
The brave, the chivalrous, how little deem'd	512 Faliero	2	272
The signal. These brave words have breathed new life	516 Faliero	2	558
The truly brave are soft of heart and eyes	517 Faliero	2	587
Trusty and brave, with head and heart to plan	518 Faliero	2	709
And chiefly thou, Ordelafo the brave	519 Faliero	3	36
Of you have found me; and if brave or no	521 Faliero	3	175
Most welcome.--Brave Bertuccio, thou art late	521 Faliero	3	203
The eldest born of Fear, which makes you brave	522 Faliero	3	224
Of the brave, joyous, reckless, glorious band	525 Faliero	3	458
My nephew, brave Bertuccio's messenger	536 Faliero	4	546
To brave your judges to postpone the sentence	538 Faliero	5	38
Even let them have their way, brave Calendaro	539 Faliero	5	115
Near sixteen lustres crowded with brave acts	543 Faliero	5	359
The truly brave are generous to the fallen	543 Faliero	5	379
I' the heel o'erthrew the bravest of the brave	544 Faliero	5	437
Quaff'd by the line of Nimrod. 'Twas a brave one	562 Sardan	2	53
Ay, and the most devout for brave--thou hast not	562 Sardan	2	75
The hilt quits not this hand. How! dost thou brave me	564 Sardan	2	159
Which girds your arm? A scratch from brave Beleses	577 Sardan	3	365
I over-ruled him. Well, the fault's a brave one	589 Sardan	5	147
Learnt but in eighty years. Brave Carmagnuola	619 Foscari	4	303
Even when the waters wax'd too fierce to brave	668 Heaven		1000
Brave, I know, by my living now to say so	685 Werner	2	158
Epitome of what brave chivalry	687 Werner	2	324
Deem yourself safe, as young and brave; but learn	690 Werner	2	464
I've seen you brave the elements, and bear	692 Werner	2	614
Between me and a brave inheritance	694 Werner	2	706
Besides, he was a soldier, and a brave one	695 Werner	2	758
Dim with brave knights and holy hermits, whose	697 Werner	3	121
Then his brave son, Count Ulric--there's a knight	704 Werner	4	21
Nonsense! they are all brave iron-visaged fellows	705 Werner	4	44
He you; for the brave ever love each other	707 Werner	4	178
As well as your brave son; and smooth your aspect	712 Werner	4	541
The beauty of our host, and brave as beauteous	733 Deformed	1	788
Of your brave bands of their own bold accord	733 Deformed	1	802
You are brave, and that's enough for me; and quick	733 Deformed	1	809
Let him alone; he's brave, and ever has	734 Deformed	1	819
Worthy a brave man's liking. Were ye such	740 Deformed	2	316
You are beautiful and brave! the first is much	743 Deformed	3	120
Brave men were living before Agamemnon	747 Juan	1	33
Brave Inez now set up a Sunday school	775 Juan	2	74
Then shriek'd the timid, and stood still the brave	780 Juan	2	410
Unlike the honest Arab thieves so brave	790 Juan	2	1038
Entomb'd the bravest of the brave, Achilles	826 Juan	4	603
But one which Baba did not like to brave	866 Juan	6	891
O'er the promoted couple of brave men	875 Juan	7	537
As brave as ever faced both bomb and ball	879 Juan	8	69
Or those who thought it brave to wait as yet	884 Juan	8	360
But as it happens to brave men, they blunder'd	887 Juan	8	597
March'd with the brave battalion of Polouzki	888 Juan	8	608
But to our subject: a brave Tartar khan	891 Juan	8	829
But flank'd by five brave sons(such is polygamy	891 Juan	8	833
To take him was the point. The truly brave	891 Juan	8	841
When they behold the brave oppress'd with odds	891 Juan	8	842
His five brave boys no less the foe defied	892 Juan	8	853
Who still have shown themselves more brave than witty	899 Juan	9	180
(As being the brave lions' keen providers	900 Juan	9	215

BRAVED

Who braved what woman never braved before	106 Nisus		77
Had braved the death-wing'd tempest's blast	158 Florence		31
I've braved it--not for honour's boast	320 Giaour		1012
And braved their thirst with as enduring lip	421 Island	2	181
When thou and thine have braved	660 Heaven		390

BRAVELY

The dullest sailer wearing bravely now	22 Harold	2	152
'Bravely, old man, this health has sped	104 Alva		229
While bold Pomposus bravely stay'd at home	124 Recoll		180
Whose were the sons that bravely fought and fell	271 Minerva		232
Rest from your task--so--bravely done	314 Giaour		370
So smoothly, bravely, brilliantly she went	431 Island	4	108
Hath wash'd since winter.--Come, 'tis bravely done	483 Manfred	1	385
Basely--Say, bravely. Somewhat of both, perhaps	567 Sardan	2	339
Bravely--and, won, wear it wisely, not as I	582 Sardan	4	275
But he did bravely. Slew he not Beleses	588 Sardan	5	81
But bravely rush'd on his first heavenly night	892 Juan	8	907

BRAVER

Another! and a braver man	326 Abydos	1	198

BRAVERY

No less of human bravery than the brave	427 Island	3	52

BRAVES

The soldier braves death for a fanciful wreath	115 The Tear		17
My courser's broad breast proudly braves	412 Mazeppa		590
An Indian widow braves for custom? Then	594 Sardan	5	467

BRAVEST

And his was of the bravest, and when shower'd	39 Harold	3	258
Contains the 'bravest of the brave	187 Ode-B		10
And Britain's bravest victor was the last	239 Conquest		8
Becomes the bravest, if they feel for men	380 Lara	2	347
Of the Mussulman bravest and best is at hand	393 Corinth		820
The bravest be, or late have been	393 Corinth		838
I' the heel o'erthrew the bravest of the brave	544 Faliero	5	437
And own the bravest for the most devout	562 Sardan	2	74
A rebel's booty: forth, and do your bravest	574 Sardan	3	162
Her best and bravest from her. Tyranny	607 Foscari	2	387
The eldest born of man, the strongest, bravest	664 Heaven		685
He was the fairest and the bravest of	725 Deformed	1	210
Was freedom's best and bravest friend	813 Juan	3	756
Entomb'd the bravest of the brave, Achilles	826 Juan	4	603
Putting the very bravest, who were knock'd	883 Juan	8	343
He shudder'd, as no doubt the bravest cowers	996 Juan	16	1005

BRAVO

'A groat.'--'Ah, bravo! Dick hath done the sum	264 Hints		519
(The Lord forgive him!), 'Bravo! grand! divine	267 Hints		772
His 'bravo' was decisive, for that sound	444 Beppo		249

BRAVO'S

But loathed the bravo's trade and laugh'd at marshal wight	25 Harold	2	360

BRAVURAS

le those bravuras (which I still am learning	939 Juan	12	598
In Babylon's bravuras--as the home	986 Juan	16	409

BRAWL

The mangled victim of a drunken brawl	251 Bards		685
Be interrupted by a private brawl	521 Faliero	3	180
And desperate libertines who brawl in taverns	531 Faliero	4	228
Were I disposed to brawl; but, as I said	605 Foscari	2	254

BRAWLER

I am no brawler; but can bear myself	521 Faliero	3	181

BRAWLERS

Audacious brawlers? Sire, your justice. Or	564 Sardan	2	180

BRAWLING

And shining in the brawling brook, where-by	60 Harold	4	290
By tyrannous faction and the brawling crowd	456 Dante	1	35

BRAWLS

Brawls must end here. They shall. You have wrong'd me, Ulric	693 Werner	2	633

BRAWNY

Edina's brawny sons and brimstone page	256 Bards		1048
While brawny brutes in stupid wonder stare	271 Minerva		181
But brawny as the boar's; and hung beneath	425 Island	2	490

BRAY

A new Vicar of Bray	239 Bray		17
Except that his bray lost his living	239 Bray		18

BRAYING

The braying trumpet and the hoarser drum	120 Newstead-A		55

BRAYS

He brays, the laureat of the long-ear'd kind	245 Bards		264

BRAZEN

The brazen Steeds are glittering o'er	196 Venice-A		5
The brazen trump, the spirit-stirring drum	272 Minerva		287

BRAZEN

That brazen lamp but dimly threw	330 Abydos	2	118
Those brazen creatures always suit their taste	448 Beppo		536
Now, like Friar Bacon's brazen head, I've spoken	773 Juan	1	1733
The brazen uppermost). Kind reader! pass	859 Juan	6	443
In lieu of a bare blade and brazen front	920 Juan	11	117
Then roll the brazen thunders of the door	926 Juan	11	526

BRAZEN-COLOUR'D

Save where their brazen-colour'd edges streak	668 Heaven	1009

BRAZEN-IMAGED

She-wolf, whose brazen-imaged dugs impart	68 Harold	4	785

BRAZIERS

The braziers, it seems, are preparing to pass	237 Braziers	1

BRAZILS

Presented by the Prince of the Brazils	897 Juan	9	42

BREACH

Famed for contemptuous breach of sacred ties	228 Windsor		1
Probes to the quick where'er he makes his breach	268 Hints		843
His skill to pierce the promised breach	386 Corinth		180
Bloodstain the breach through which they pass	392 Corinth		697
'There the breach lies for passage, the ladder to scale	392 Corinth		715
Some cypresses beyond the time-worn breach	495 Manfred	3	280
To watch the breach occasion'd by the waters	591 Sardan	5	244
Charge me with such a breach of faith. No; thou	607 Foscari	2	392
Which mostly ends in some small breach of both	849 Juan	5	1136
I doubt few readers e'er would mount the breach	871 Juan	7	280
You were the first i' the breach?'--'I was not slack	875 Juan	7	483

BREACHES

For behind those batter'd breaches	240 Suliotes	15

BREAD
(See also DATE-BREAD)

He does not speak for Virtue, but for bread	142 Soliloquy		24
Who daily scribble for your daily bread	251 Bards		742
Where rustics earn'd, and now may beg, their bread	260 Hints		304
Dependence barters for her bitter bread	267 Hints		774
New laws to hang the rogues that roar'd for bread	276 Waltz		165
Upon all topics; 'twas, besides, his bread	297 Vision		763
But bread was high, the farmer paid his way	306 Age		588
To bless the sacred 'bread and salt	313 Giaour		343
Nor tastes the sacred bread and wine	318 Giaour		815
Not all who break his bread are true	331 Abydos	2	271
Earth's coarsest bread, the garden's homeliest roots	339 Corsair	1	71
To break or mingle bread with friends or foes	349 Corsair	2	126
I taste nor bread nor banquet--save alone	349 Corsair	2	130
Our bread was such as captives' tears	404 Chillon		134
And just enough of water and of bread	416 Island	1	89
And bread itself is gather'd as a fruit	418 Island	1	214
For food the cocoa-nut, the yam, the bread	432 Island	4	169
Besides, they always smell of bread and butter	445 Beppo		312
Had bread and bastinadoes, till some bands	452 Beppo		749
Our bounds, or taste the stones shower'd down for bread	469 Morgante		198
Who begs his bread, if 'tis refused by one	501 Faliero	1	131
You never broke their bread, nor shared their salt	527 Faliero	3	580
To lead a temperate life, and break thy bread	531 Faliero	4	231
Have begg'd as famish'd mendicants for bread	543 Faliero	5	386
When thy patricians beg their bitter bread	548 Faliero	5	757
The bread we eat? For what must I be grateful	647 Cain	3	113
Thou mightst have earn'd thy bread, as thousands earn it	673 Werner	1	139
In the same thicket where he hew'd for bread	697 Werner	3	162
Bread has been made (indifferent) from potatoes	762 Juan	1	1033
Some pounds of bread, though injured by the wet	779 Juan	2	370
To faint, and damaged bread wet through the bags	782 Juan	2	495
For breakfast, of eggs, coffee, bread, and fish	791 Juan	2	1064
But there were eggs, fruit, coffee, bread, fish, honey	792 Juan	2	1159
Their bread as ministers and favourites (that's	810 Juan	3	542
Let this one toil for bread--that rack for rent	898 Juan	9	119
On them and bread 'twas oft my luck to dine	977 Juan	15	581

BREADTH

The breadth of pavement, and yon shrine where fame is	921 Juan	11	189
Almost an hair's breadth too much on one side	984 Juan	16	232

BREAD-TREE

The bread-tree, which, without the ploughshare, yields	422 Island	2	260

BREAK
(See also DAY-BREAK, HEART-BREAK)

BREAK

Such partings break the heart they fondly hope to heal	5 Harold	1	90
Arise; and, as the clouds along them break	25 Harold	2	374
To which it mounts, as if to break the link	37 Harold	3	125
And thus the heart will break, yet brokenly live on	40 Harold	3	288
Heaves like a long-swept wave about to break	66 Harold	4	668
And if my voice break forth, 'tis not that now	75 Harold	4	1198
Thou seest not all; but piecemeal thou must break	78 Harold	4	1405
The spell should break of this protracted dream	82 Harold	4	1659
His harp in shuddering chords would break	105 Alva		312
And break through her slight-woven net	116 Pigot		26
I break the fetters of my youth	118 Romance		6
And till those vital chords shall break	132 L'Amitie		68
'Twas thine to break the bonds of loving	134 Lady-D		8
To break the rudely sounding shell	137 Clare		62
To break 'such flies upon the wheel	142 Critics		82
I thought my jealous heart would break	154 Happy		10
My foolish heart be still, or break	155 Happy		36
And the wild waves that break with murmuring sound	161 Athos		17
Or break the heart to which thou'rt press'd	166 Struggle		52
But the Devil remain'd till the Break of Day	178 Devil's Dr		169
We repent, we abjure, we will break from our chain	182 Music-A		7
And man shall not break it--whatever thou mayst	182 Music-A		12
There are links which must break in the chain that has bound us	186 Napoleon		23
Be broken--thine will never break	210 Augusta-A		38
And break at once--or yield to song	218 Soul-B		16
And break him on the wheel he meant for me	256 Bards		1060
Or break the compact which herself had made	271 Minerva		216
Out of 'Elegant Extracts.' Well, now we break up	283 Blues	2	154
Break o'er th' Aegean, mindful of the day	302 Age		287
To bid us blush for these old chains, or break	303 Age		389
And the world trembles to bid brokers break	307 Age		667
No breath of air to break the wave	310 Giaour		1
Break the blue crystal of the seas	310 Giaour		17
But break--before it bend again	319 Giaour		936
That quench'd, what beam shall break my night	321 Giaour		1146
He comes not, for he cannot break	323 Giaour		1304
I'd joy to see thee break a lance	325 Abydos	1	124
That gnaws and yet may break his chain	331 Abydos	2	206
Not all who break his bread are true	331 Abydos	2	271
Arrives--to-night must break thy chain	334 Abydos	2	482
They scarce can bear the morn to break	336 Abydos	2	701
Must break my chain before it dried my tears	348 Corsair	2	88
To break or mingle bread with friends or foes	349 Corsair	2	126
'One effort--one--to break the circling host	350 Corsair	2	243
To snatch the mirror from the soul--and break	352 Corsair	2	357
And this will break a heart so more than kind	354 Corsair	2	488
Remember, captive, 'tis to break thy chain	355 Corsair	2	529
To curse the wither'd heart that would not break	368 Lara	1	130
Dimm'd in the lamp, as loth to break the night	369 Lara	1	202
Some few, perchance, may break and pass the line	379 Lara	2	336
Scarce break on the bounds of the land for a rood	388 Corinth		429
Which his worshippers drank at the break of day	395 Corinth		1004
For so it seem'd on her to break	400 Parisina		384
And almost on the break of day	410 Mazeppa		333
'Twas scarcely yet the break of day	410 Mazeppa		377
I must not strive as yet to break	415 Mazeppa		822
But ere he break--a deed is to be done	415 Island	1	16
In such an hour, to break the air so still	424 Island	2	418
But with all Heaven t' himself; that day will break as	445 Beppo		341
Their chains so slight, 'twas not worth while to break them	446 Beppo		428
This form of verse began, I can't well break it	448 Beppo		501
With blasphemies enough to break their jaws	451 Beppo		683
To break the chain, yet--yet the Avenger stops	460 Dante	2	139
My heart shall be pour'd over thee and break	461 Dante	3	34
Break no commandment, for high heaven is there	463 Dante	4	32
Barren and cold, on which the wild waves break	484 Manfred	2	56
Back by a single hair, which would not break	486 Manfred	2	233
To lead a temperate life, and break thy bread	531 Faliero	4	231
The tempest may break out which overwhelms thee	555 Sardan	1	329
My heart will break. Now you know all--decide	584 Sardan	4	383
Have those without will break their way through hosts	590 Sardan	5	181
That's strange. I pray thee break that loyal silence	590 Sardan	5	186
And so the Council must break up, and Justice	600 Foscari	1	314
'Twill break his heart. Age has no heart to break	615 Foscari	4	4
I cannot break my oath. Reduce us not	621 Foscari	5	47
All bonds I break between us, as he broke	652 Cain	3	410
No more to have the morning sun break forth	659 Heaven		290
The wave shall break upon your cliffs; and shells	662 Heaven		504
And they will sing! and day will break! Both near	662 Heaven		562
A second host from heaven, to break heaven's law	666 Heaven		859
The verge where brighter morns were wont to break	668 Heaven		1010
Then canst thou wish for that which must break mine	671 Werner	1	13

BREAK

But must break through them, as an unarm'd carle	697 Werner	3	160
Like the poor fly, but break it not. Take heed	709 Werner	4	309
Break her heart for a man who has none to break	710 Werner	4	379
Or break or climb o'er	732 Deformed	1	706
I could breathe on and break it	743 Deformed	3	78
And break the--Which commandment is't they break	758 Juan	1	780
And break a promise after having made it her	772 Juan	1	1677
Because her mistress would not let her break	792 Juan	2	1167
She had no need of this, day ne'er will break	810 Juan	3	603
He counted them at break of day	812 Juan	3	711
Would break your shield, however broad	813 Juan	3	772
Break with the first fall: they can ne'er behold	817 Juan	4	84
To break the lifeless splendour of the whole	838 Juan	5	448
I yield thus far; but soon will break the charm	841 Juan	5	653
Just as you'd break a sucking salamander	873 Juan	7	413
To break the rules by bringing one's own bride	876 Juan	7	565
Is perpetrated ere a word can break	885 Juan	8	461
But now I choose to break off in the middle	896 Juan	8	1109
With his despatch, forgot to break the seal	903 Juan	9	456
To show the people the best way to break	941 Juan	12	708
At Blank-Blank Square;--for we will break no squares	944 Juan	13	193
Upon my head have bid their thunders break	956 Juan	14	75
They break their ranks and gladly leave the drill	957 Juan	14	130
Wherewith we break our bubbles on the ocean	968 Juan	15	12
To see men let these scoundrel sovereigns break law	979 Juan	15	736

BREAKER

And the loud breaker boils against the rock	763 Juan	1	1071

BREAKER-BEATEN

It was a wild and breaker-beaten coast	796 Juan	2	1409

BREAKERS

The Night-winds sigh, the breakers roar	5 Harold	1	120
Of the loud breakers, and the ceaseless roar	70 Harold	4	940
I wanton'd with thy breakers--they to me	82 Harold	4	1651
And borne o'er breakers reach'd the craggy shore	184 Julian		7
I watch'd thee on the breakers, when the rock	206 Love, Death		5
Like a wild bay of breakers, melts away	211 Augusta-C		37
His feet the foremost breakers lave	335 Abydos	2	550
Their sport, the dashing breakers and the chase	416 Island	1	47
They clear the breakers, dart along the bay	429 Island	3	226
We skim its rugged breakers, which put on	487 Manfred	2	304
Deeming themselves the breakers of the ocean	739 Deformed	2	292
Unless with breakers close beneath her lee	779 Juan	2	360
Some swore that they heard breakers, others guns	786 Juan	2	767
Though right ahead the roaring breakers lay	787 Juan	2	828
Turns up more dangerous breakers than the Euxine	832 Juan	5	40
Of breakers has not daunted my slight, trim	907 Juan	10	30

BREAKER'S

The desert, forest, cavern, breaker's foam	37 Harold	3	113
Swift-gliding o'er the breaker's whitening edge	422 Island	2	230

BREAKFAST

Now his breakfast, now his verses	157 Hodgson		55
And also made a breakfast of his own	469 Morgante		218
For breakfast, of eggs, coffee, bread, and fish	791 Juan	2	1064
Must breakfast--and betimes, lest they should ask it	792 Juan	2	1151
And so, she cook'd their breakfast to a tittle	792 Juan	2	1157
And, the first breakfast spoilt, prepared a new one	792 Juan	2	1166
A bath, a breakfast, and the finest eyes	795 Juan	2	1362
For love or breakfast; private, pleasing, lone	864 Juan	6	771
But System doth reverse the Titan's breakfast	955 Juan	14	9
The morning came--and breakfast, tea and toast	998 Juan	17	98

BREAKING

There have been tears and breaking hearts for thee	39 Harold	3	262
For breaking slumbers of delight	113 Quaker		35
men of Lochlin in the chiefs. As, breaking	131 Calmar		141
At the sound of my trumpet, breaking	162 War Song		17
One pang, exults--while mine is breaking	172 Romaic-B		36
Send me kind dreams to keep my heart from breaking	205 Hindoo		10
That ever breaking Bed, beyond repair	224 J.C.H.		19
So if we can hang them for breaking a bobbin	225 Ode-D		11
And breaking of frames lead to breaking of bones	226 Ode-D		28
While eddying whirl and breaking wave	316 Giaour		626
This breaking heart and throbbing head	321 Giaour		1125
Though rising gale and breaking foam	329 Abydos	2	8
Whether (as then the breaking sun from high	381 Lara	2	468
Sounds fearful as the breaking billow	397 Parisina		94
I've seen it on the breaking ocean	404 Chillon		180
The morning now was on the point of breaking	450 Beppo		649
And thou fresh breaking Day, and you, ye Mountains	481 Manfred	1	269
On the swift whirl of the new breaking wave	486 Manfred	2	161
For breaking in upon your meditation	511 Faliero	2	145

BREAKING

Like a small bubble breaking with the wave	575 Sardan	3	237
But grief is lonely, and the breaking in	619 Foscari	4	250
Breaking only rank by rank	735 Deformed	2	21
Still breaking, but with stamina so steady	762 Juan	1	998
To save the credit of their breaking bank	850 Juan	5	1230
Stole on your spirit like a May-day breaking	857 Juan	6	338
Cossacques were all cut off as day was breaking	888 Juan	8	603
Into the excursive, breaking the indentures	922 Juan	11	261
They run before the wind through high seas breaking	964 Juan	14	590
But what with keeping some, and breaking others	990 Juan	16	615

BREAK-NECK

Repay my break-neck travail.--What is here	482 Manfred	1	320

BREAKS

Where some bold river breaks the long expanse	27 Harold	2	483
But hark!--that heavy sound breaks in once more	38 Harold	3	195
The same, and still the more, the more it breaks	40 Harold	3	292
The midland ocean breaks on him and me	81 Harold	4	1571
'What stranger breaks my blest repose	88 Anacreon-B		12
But, pall'd with vice, he breaks his former chain	100 Damaetas		13
It breaks the stillness of the night	103 Alva		121
'Tis this which breaks the heart thou grievest	173 Not False		5
Breaks never to unite again	180 Ode-A		24
While sun is quench'd or system breaks	220 Clay		23
If our weight breaks them down and we sink in the flood	227 Moore-A		5
Breaks into blank the Gospel of St. Luke	246 Bards		323
The starved mechanic breaks his rusting loom	272 Minerva		271
Smile--for the fetter'd eagle breaks his chain	299 Age		87
'Tis late to think--but soft, his slumber breaks	353 Corsair	2	427
Farewell--morn breaks--and I must now away	355 Corsair	2	533
Breaks, yet unsated with the dance	386 Corinth		211
Lightly and brightly breaks away	391 Corinth		680
When he breaks from the town, and none escape	392 Corinth		694
Whose every wave breaks on a living shore	483 Manfred	1	349
Methinks the day breaks--is it not so? look	534 Faliero	4	457
Has ceased, and the moon breaks forth in her brightness	573 Sardan	3	142
Of the immortal sovereigns. Now he breaks	588 Sardan	5	56
Breaks in on our deliberations? No	600 Foscari	1	316
Will be--But wherefore breaks it not? Why live I	617 Foscari	4	151
Breaks through, as from a thunder-cloud! yon brand	652 Cain	3	391
One breaks your bones, one sets them in their sockets	762 Juan	1	1028
Or breaks their hopes, or hearts, or heads, or necks	778 Juan	2	246
And 'tis, no doubt, a sight to see when breaks	791 Juan	2	1108
The moon breaks, half unveil'd each further charm	860 Juan	6	525

BREAST

That smile for which my breast might vainly sigh	3 To Ianthe		32
Yet deem not thence his breast a breast of steel	5 Harold	1	87
Or he shall calm his breast, or learn experience sage	8 Harold	1	332
By all forgotten, save the lonely breast	19 Harold	1	932
And woo the vision to my vacant breast	20 Harold	1	78
A flashing pang! of which the weary breast	23 Harold	2	215
Nor ask so dear a breast to feel one pang for mine	24 Harold	2	270
Not much he kens, I ween, of woman's breast	24 Harold	2	298
That breast imbued with such immortal fire	25 Harold	2	348
His breast was arm'd 'gainst fate, his wants were few	26 Harold	2	383
Here winds of gentlest wing will fan his breast	27 Harold	2	444
Who never quits the breast no meaner passion shares	28 Harold	2	549
Nodding at midnight o'er the calm bay's breast	30 Harold	2	625
What mark is so fair as the breast of a foe	30 Harold	2	660
He of the breast which fain no more would feel	36 Harold	3	67
His breast and beak against his wiry dome	37 Harold	3	133
They reach'd no nobler breast than thine, young, gallant Howard	39 Harold	3	261
Are theirs! One breast laid open were a school	41 Harold	3	386
In one fond breast to which his own would melt	43 Harold	3	476
And there was one soft breast, as hath been said	43 Harold	3	487
Whose breast of waters broadly swells	43 Harold	3	498
The haughtiest breast its wish might bound	44 Harold	3	530
But to that gentle touch, through brain and breast	47 Harold	3	748
Deep into Nature's breast the spirit of her hues	48 Harold	3	823
Are ye like those within the human breast	50 Harold	3	903
My breast, or that of others, for a while	52 Harold	3	1044
Blood, pulse, and breast confirm the Dardan Shepherd's prize	62 Harold	4	450
Did they not to her breast their filial earth intrust	63 Harold	4	504
Such seeds within her breast, or Europe no such shore	69 Harold	4	864
As thine ideal breast! whate'er thou art	72 Harold	4	1029
And didst thou not, thy breast to his replying	73 Harold	4	1063

BREAST

Shaped by some solitary nymph, whose breast	79 Harold	4	1451
She clasps a babe to whom her breast yields no relief	80 Harold	4	1503
From thy Sire's to his humblest subject's breast	81 Harold	4	1545
Of youthful sports was on thy breast to be	82 Harold	4	1649
Detach'd thee from my breast for ever	85 To D--		4
True, she has forced thee from my breast	85 To D--		5
On thy dear breast I'll lay my head	85 To D--		11
Raise a flame in the breast for the war-laurell'd wreath	86 Leaving NA		10
Which racks my breast your fickle bosom please	87 Tibullus		2
My breast was never pity's foe	89 Anacreon-B		23
His little fingers chill my breast	89 Anacreon-B		32
Reposing on my breast you lay	89 To Emma		20
Whene'er I dream of that pure breast	90 To M.S.G.-A		5
Yes! yield that breast, to seek despair	90 To M.S.G.-A		33
Yet still, my girl, this bleeding breast	90 Caroline-B		7
Ah! did that breast with ardour glow	90 Caroline-B		5
Your image fills my anxious breast	91 Caroline-B		29
'Tis then your breast, no longer cold	91 Caroline-B		33
Or agitates his anxious breast	95 Granta		39
Unfaded your memory dwells in my breast	96 Harrow-A		26
Since your sweet breast is still the same	98 To Lesbia		15
Has fill'd that breast with fond alarms	99 Young Lady		4
Still Hope, breathing peace through the grief-swollen breast	99 L Adieu		9
Love's a stranger to thy breast	100 Marion		6
But his breast was bare, with the red wounds there	104 Alva		259
Oblivion press'd old Angus' breast	104 Alva		271
But Oscar's breast is cold as clay	104 Alva		277
Thou know'st my deeds, my breast devoid of fear	106 Nisus		47
And, quivering, strain'd them to his aged breast	107 Nisus		128
And pierced proud Rhamnes through his panting breast	108 Nisus		238
His coward breast behind a jar he hides	109 Nisus		269
And sanguine torrents mantle o'er his breast	110 Nisus		378
The breast where love is wont to glow	111 Medea		2
Can rouse the tortured breast no more	111 Medea		6
In love can soothe the aching breast	111 Medea		12
In vain, to drive thee from my breast	112 Quaker		7
His form had fix'd her fickle breast	113 Cornelian-A		30
This hope to my breast is most near	115 The Tear		38
Whose image must fill my whole breast	116 Strephon		30
Whose breast for every bosom bleeds	118 Romance		44
The maid whose virgin breast is void of guile	119 Answer-A		27
Hours of my youth! when, nurtured in my breast	123 Recoll		55
Yet with a breast of such materials made	125 Recoll		269
Oh no! whene'er my breast forgets the deed	126 Recoll		285
Would make that breast with indignation burn	126 Recoll		319
While hope of dawning honours fill'd my breast	127 Recoll		354
It finds an echo in each youthful breast	127 Recoll		364
Whose yellow locks wave o'er the breast	131 Calmar		158
Why should my anxious breast repine	131 L'Amitie		1
For none but these my breast shall wake	132 L'Amitie		69
And once my breast abhorr'd deceit	134 Lady-D		35
My breast requires the sullen glen	135 I Would		51
When fate shall chill at length this fever'd breast	138 Harrow-B		17
My breast by no tumultuous Passion torn	139 Ossian-A		38
The sense of joy which thrill'd my breast before	140 Ossian-A		40
Such soften'd feelings in my breast	144 Jessy		10
Still nearest to my breast	146 Adieu		52
Still near my breast thy gift I wear	146 Adieu		65
And thou hast known a stranger's breast	150 My Son		14
The breast, which beat to former joy	150 My Son		35
But in my breast and in my brain	151 Farewell-B		10
But transient in thy breast alone	152 Time-A		12
My blood runs coldly through my breast	152 Weep-A		6
With eyes so languid, breast so fair	152 Remind		11
When thus reclining on my breast	152 Remind		13
And who would in a breast confide	153 Friend-A		19
My breast would thrill before thy look	155 Happy		26
Could I repose upon the breast	156 Lady-F		9
Forbade my bleeding breast to own	156 Lady-F		59
Or, since that has left my breast	160 Maid		3
Nor one memorial for a breast	163 Parting		11
Though painful, welcome to my breast	166 Struggle		50
Thine image from my breast may fade	168 Haunts		2
My wounded soul, my bleeding breast	172 Romaic-B		41
That yielding breast, that melting eye	174 Remember-B		5
Back to my breast the wanderers shrink	175 Impromptu-A		7
Ere his breast or his face, or his tongue, or his pen	178 Devil's Dr		182
Admit not Love into thy breast	179 Gold		11
How bears her breast the torturing hour	181 Ode-A		111
Remembrance from thy breast	181 Ode-A		157
Houseless and homeless--bare both breast and limb	184 Julian		29
Though wit may flash from fluent lips, and mirth distract the breast	185 Music-B		13
Victory beaming from her breast	188 Ode-B		66
Whose breast is gently heaving	188 Music-C		11
Still warming its folds in the breast of a king	203 Avatar		100

BREAST

But my Hippocrene was but my breast	205 Blessington		3
This arm would be thy bark, or breast thy bier	206 Love, Death		8
Wafts unto death the breast it bore so high	206 Greece		8
Would that breast were bared before thee	207 Fare Thee		5
Would that breast, by thee glanced over	207 Fare Thee		9
With longing breast and undeluded ear	208 Sketch		20
And bearing still a breast so tried	210 Augusta-A		43
And with a breast unknowing its own crimes	213 Lady Byron		50
Tribes of the wandering foot and weary breast	217 Weep-B		9
And the soul wears out the breast	230 Roving		6
Let Angiolini bare her breast of snow	250 Bards		628
Drank the last life-drop of his bleeding breast	253 Bards		848
Lulls his chafed breast from elemental war	269 Minerva		50
Thy breast--if bare enough--requires no shield	273 Waltz		11
Hail, moving Muse! to whom the fair one's breast	273 Waltz		23
The breast thus publicly resign'd to man	276 Waltz		214
For prurient nature still will storm the breast	276 Waltz		223
One common cause makes myriads of one breast	302 Age		272
Without one free or valiant breast	311 Giaour		156
There's none within his rider's breast	312 Giaour		188
A troubled memory on my breast	312 Giaour		205
By all that most distracts the breast	312 Giaour		268
And oft upon his mother's breast	313 Giaour		310
With wounded wing, or bleeding breast	314 Giaour		410
His breast with wounds unnumber'd riven	317 Giaour		667
Should rend her rash devoted breast	319 Giaour		955
Within thy pure and pitying breast	320 Giaour		981
Yet, lurks a wish within my breast	320 Giaour		994
That boils in Aetna's breast of flame	321 Giaour		1102
Alas! the breast that inly bleeds	321 Giaour		1155
They shrink upon my lonely breast	323 Giaour		1297
Across her gently-budding breast	325 Abydos	1	183
As if that breast were marble too	326 Abydos	1	275
Come, lay thy head upon my breast	327 Abydos	1	301
To guard from winds of heaven the breast	330 Abydos	2	89
Clung like a cuirass to his breast	330 Abydos	2	144
My breast is offer'd--take thy fill	330 Abydos	2	175
Yet well my toils shall that fond breast repay	333 Abydos	2	418
Despair benumb'd her breast and eye	334 Abydos	2	522
Fast from his breast the blood is bubbling	335 Abydos	2	579
My breast before the time when it must feel	344 Corsair	1	417
Fire in his glance, and wildness in his breast	346 Corsair	1	531
And wrapt a breast bestow'd on heaven alone	348 Corsair	2	60
Shone his mail'd breast, and flash'd his sabre's ray	349 Corsair	2	147
His guilty bosom, but that breast he mann'd	352 Corsair	2	373
Oh! that this dotage of his breast would cease	355 Corsair	2	525
Lulls his chafed breast from elemental war	356 Corsair	3	50
Now fare thee well--more peace be with thy breast	361 Corsair	3	368
They bleed within that silent cell--his breast	362 Corsair	3	479
Her arms are meekly folded on that breast	363 Corsair	3	518
Perchance, but for the bodings of his breast	363 Corsair	3	547
The indistinctness of the suffering breast	365 Corsair	3	641
That fearful empire which the human breast	366 Lara	1	15
Within his breast appear'd no more to strive	367 Lara	1	81
A night of beauty, mock'd such breast as his	368 Lara	1	180
A breast that needed not ideal woe	369 Lara	1	246
Not so in him; his breast had buried both	370 Lara	1	285
In self-inflicted penance of a breast	370 Lara	1	309
His presence haunted still; and from the breast	371 Lara	1	379
True, in his words it broke not from his breast	374 Lara	1	582
The empire of the alternate victor's breast	379 Lara	2	275
The truth, and not the terror of his breast	380 Lara	2	353
The shaft is sped, the arrow's in his breast	380 Lara	2	381
He saw the head his breast would still sustain	382 Lara	2	506
The breast of man such trusty love may breathe	382 Lara	2	513
In baring to revive that lifeless breast	382 Lara	2	516
They laid him in the earth, and on his breast	383 Lara	2	540
He caught a glimpse, as of a floating breast	383 Lara	2	578
The mail weigh'd lead-like on his breast	387 Corinth		339
His head was drooping on his breast	390 Corinth		511
This first false passion of his breast	391 Corinth		655
They turn'd him on his back; his breast	394 Corinth		885
With sudden wing and ruffled breast	396 Corinth		1073
And clasps her Lord unto the breast	397 Parisina		73
Go! woman of the wanton breast	398 Parisina		219
I had a sword--and have a breast	399 Parisina		266
A sigh shrunk back on every breast	401 Parisina		484
That even in death his freeborn breast	404 Chillon		156
My courser's broad breast proudly braves	412 Mazeppa		590
Thy limbs are bound, the bayonet at thy breast	416 Island	1	55
The levell'd muskets circle round thy breast	416 Island	1	73
Which shadows o'er the vineyard in her breast	422 Island	2	257
And flings off famine from its fertile breast	422 Island	2	264
To stifle even the breath within his breast	427 Island	3	92
Who rears on its bare breast her callow brood	430 Island	4	17
Her shelter'd love to her impassion'd breast	432 Island	4	190
The kindling ashes to his kindled breast	433 Island	4	226
His last ball had been aim'd, but from his breast	434 Island	4	333
I weed all bitterness from out my breast	438 Tasso		107
And look to thee with undivided breast	438 Tasso		147
Against the breast that cherish'd thee was stirr'd	457 Dante	1	66
The breast which would have bled for her, the heart	457 Dante	1	86

BREAST

And Carthage ruins, my lone breast may burn	457 Dante	1	105
Thou'rt mine--my bones shall be within thy breast	458 Dante	2	20
While the scorch'd mountain, from whose burning breast	463 Dante	4	189
'The Lord descended to the virgin breast	471 Morgante		353
By thy cold breast and serpent smile	481 Manfred	1	242
My breast upon its rocky bosom's bed	482 Manfred	1	279
And thy breast heaves--and in thy gasping throat	496 Manfred	3	403
Ne'er from that moment could this breast have known	512 Faliero	2	242
Re-man your breast; I feel no such remorse	527 Faliero	3	621
Though my breast feels too anxious; I will try	528 Faliero	4	23
Within the breast which trusted to his truth	532 Faliero	4	304
Of human life must spring from woman's breast	559 Sardan	1	557
Cloven with arm still lustier, breast more daring	597 Foscari	1	105
Within a human breast. I would not change	604 Foscari	2	158
Crowd in my breast to burning, when I hear	631 Cain	1	254
That this poor aching breast now nourishes	653 Cain	3	487
The same breast, clasp'd thee often to my own	654 Cain	3	536
To Samiasa's breast	657 Heaven		146
Buried in its immeasurable breast	668 Heaven		967
For I provoked it;--but the Bourbon's breast	733 Deformed	1	797
Is yet within her breast, and may revive	741 Deformed	2	405
Nothing but what was good, her breast was peaceable	757 Juan	1	661
'My breast has been all weakness, is so yet	771 Juan	1	1561
Hush'd as the babe upon its mother's breast	793 Juan	2	1178
Were such as could not in his breast be shut	795 Juan	2	1332
And then on the pale cheek her breast now warms	799 Juan	2	1558
A child the moment when it drains the breast	799 Juan	2	1562
Of such quicksilver clay that in his breast	800 Juan	2	1667
Pillow'd upon a fair and happy breast	801 Juan	3	2
And place them on their breast--but place to die	801 Juan	3	14
'Neath which her breast heaved like a little billow	810 Juan	3	556
Below her breast was fasten'd with a band	810 Juan	3	573
Earth! render back from out thy breast	812 Juan	3	727
Thou bring'st the child, too, to the mother's breast	815 Juan	3	952
And breast maternal wean'd at once for ever	817 Juan	4	78
And call'd from Juan's breast a faint low sigh	819 Juan	4	167
And then dismiss'd the omen from her breast	819 Juan	4	187
Herself upon his breast, and there she grew	847 Juan	5	1000
A sincere woman's breast,--for over-warm	854 Juan	6	119
Through the heaved breast the dream of some far shore	860 Juan	6	533
And hid her face within Juanna's breast	863 Juan	6	674
Which fable places in her breast of wail	863 Juan	6	694
Already many a once love-beaten breast	866 Juan	6	915
May win perhaps a riband at the breast	880 Juan	8	104
And here he was--who upon woman's breast	884 Juan	8	417
And hide her little palpitating breast	889 Juan	8	727
Upon the Russian steel his breast he flung	893 Juan	8	938
Though hoary now, and with a withering breast	908 Juan	10	45
Upon her mind; the more so, as her breast	966 Juan	14	703
Love bears within its breast the very germ	967 Juan	14	745
Except itself;--such is the human breast	981 Juan	16	75

BREASTED

I breasted the billows of Dee's rushing tide	136 Highlander	19

BREASTPLATE

A breastplate for thine hour of need	319 Giaour	928

BREASTS

That thoughts of thee and thine on polish'd breasts bestow	19 Harold	2	9
In their shut breasts their petty misery	66 Harold	4	697
And our breasts, which alive with such sympathy glow	91 Caroline-C		22
Whose baleful stings your breasts pervade	141 Critics		6
But there are breasts that bleed with thee	184 Parker		25
Breasts to whom all the strength of feeling given	193 Monody		89
As the breasts I believed in with me	210 Augusta-B		14
So much for human ties in royal breasts	308 Age		763
Whate'er his fate--the breasts he form'd and led	357 Corsair	3	127
Where are your storms? In human breasts. Alas	616 Foscari	4	123
Although, were Momus' lattice in your breasts	695 Werner	3	25
To think such breasts must suckle slaves	813 Juan	3	778
From ogling all their charms from breasts to backs	856 Juan	6	232
Cheerful as children climb the breasts of mothers	880 Juan	8	118

BREATH

Their game of lives, and barter breath for fame	11 Harold	1	469
Blasted below the dun hot breath of war	11 Harold	1	498
Where'er the surge may sweep, the tempest's breath prevail	35 Harold	3	18
Savage and shrill! But with the breath which fills	39 Harold	3	230
Their breath is agitation, and their life	42 Harold	3	388
The breath which made him wretched; yet he knew	47 Harold	3	729
Fix'd Passion holds his breath, until the hour	48 Harold	3	793

BREATH

With breath all incense and with cheek all bloom	50 Harold	3	915
Thine air is the young breath of passionate thought	50 Harold	3	924
His eye is sparkling and his breath hath blown	50 Harold	3	938
His soft and summer breath, whose tender power	50 Harold	3	939
I have not flatter'd its rank breath, nor bow'd	52 Harold	3	1050
I would not their vile breath should crisp the stream	63 Harold	4	474
Beheld him win two realms, and, happier, yield his breath	67 Harold	4	765
Kiss'd by the breath of heaven, seems colour'd by its skies	72 Harold	4	1053
The fickle reek of popular breath, the tongue	80 Harold	4	1532
What sighs re-echo'd to thy parting breath	85 Epitaph		3
My pulse beats quick, my breath heaves short	87 Ad Lesbiam		15
The titled child whose future breath may raise	93 Dorset		14
To fate how I long to resign my frail breath	97 To M.S.G.-B		11
Fame, fame is cheaply earn'd by fleeting breath	106 Nisus		51
May I resign this fleeting breath	111 Medea		33
But bless the hour when Pitt resign'd his breath	114 Death-A		2
Rise on the night-rolling breath of the gale	117 Lachin		18
Whirlwinds, responsive, greet his labouring breath	121 Newstead-A		106
Their lives did not end when they yielded their breath	129 Becher-A		19
Uninjured by time or the rude winter's breath	149 Newstead-B		28
Chill is thy Breath thou breeze of night	150 Song		13
Will shrink, as shrinks the ebbing breath	167 Euthanasia		22
To thee the breath of life	180 Ode-A		31
With their breath, and from their birth	188 Ode-B		85
The feeble ashes, and their feeble breath	190 Darkness		62
Is proud, and makes the breath of glory real	192 Sonnet-C		14
And when convulsive throes denied my breath	206 Love, Death		17
Away thy breath	207 Year		36
And dreams in their development have breath	213 Dream		5
A breath to forms which can outlive all flesh	214 Dream		22
He had no breath, no being, but in hers	214 Dream		51
Tny spirit on our breath	219 Thy Days		12
But through it there roll'd not the breath of his pride	222 Sennacherib		14
Wash thy red wounds, or watch thy wavering breath	251 Bards		683
He'll risk no living for a little breath	267 Hints		770
Borne on the breath of hyberborean gales	274 Waltz		59
No breath of air to break the wave	310 Giaour		1
That parts not quite with parting breath	311 Giaour		95
Beneath whose widely-wasting breath	313 Giaour		284
But not the breath of human life	322 Giaour		1193
Heave his thick breath and shake his palsied head	338 Corsair	1	29
And deem'd the breath that faintly fann'd thy sail	343 Corsair	1	373
His breath choked gasping with the volumed smoke	350 Corsair	2	213
His last faint quittance rendering with his breath	350 Corsair	2	251
Must he alone of all retain his breath	351 Corsair	2	292
He slept in calmest seeming, for his breath	352 Corsair	2	392
To lips where Love had lavish'd all his breath	363 Corsair	3	552
Glad for awhile to heave unconscious breath	375 Lara	1	642
In the next tone of Lara's gathering breath	380 Lara	2	342
That panting thirst which scorches in the breath	380 Lara	2	402
More than Lara's his voice and breath	381 Lara	2	457
But gasping heaved the breath that Lara drew	382 Lara	2	490
And tempest's breath, and battle's rage	385 Corinth		47
The trench is dug, the cannon's breath	385 Corinth		87
The shattering shell's volcanic breath	386 Corinth		168
And he felt not a breath come over his cheek	390 Corinth		529
And her words came forth without her breath	* 391 Corinth		613
Stirr'd by the breath of the wintry air	391 Corinth		621
Sigh, nor word, nor struggling breath	394 Corinth		891
Thou gav'st, and may'st resume my breath	399 Parisina		241
And for my breath, that hasty boon	399 Parisina		298
'No--yours my forfeit blood and breath	401 Parisina		449
Each gazer's bosom held his breath	401 Parisina		478
The accursed breath of dungeon-dew	404 Chillon		214
But silence, and a stirless breath	405 Chillon		247
My breath came gaspingly and thick	405 Chillon		316
Of gentle breath and hue	406 Chillon		350
'Away!--away!--My breath was gone	410 Mazeppa		375
If this were human breath I drew	412 Mazeppa		600
And then again a little breath	414 Mazeppa		790
Thou call'st the loyal with thy menaced breath	416 Island	1	66
And the first breath began to stir the palm	420 Island	2	108
To stifle even the breath within his breast	427 Island	3	92
Bent its broad arch: her breath began to fail	435 Island	4	378
To him appears renewal of his breath	453 Venice-B		43
And made men's fickle breath the wind that blows	456 Dante	1	55
Me breath, but in her sudden fury thrust	457 Dante	1	79
Before the storm because its breath is rough	461 Dante	3	24
Which the breath of twilight builds	479 Manfred	1	52
A stir, a motion, even a breath, would bring	482 Manfred	1	278
The breath of degradation and of pride	482 Manfred	1	304
Ye avalanches, whom a breath draws down	482 Manfred	1	336
But words are breath--look on me in my sleep	486 Manfred	2	222
Nor breath from the worm upwards is exempt	489 Manfred	2	436

BREATH

The red-hot breath of the most lone Simoom	493	Manfred	3 128
Nor will I hence, while I have earthly breath	496	Manfred	3 361
When these are tainted by the accursing breath	503	Faliero	1 218
Ah! dared I speak my feelings! Give them breath	506	Faliero	1 433
It were indeed no more, if human breath	509	Faliero	2 60
A miscreant's angry breath may blast it all	514	Faliero	2 421
Of one long chain; one mass, one breath, one body	521	Faliero	3 155
I stake my fame (and I had fame), my breath	523	Faliero	3 325
A breath to sigh for them, a tongue to speak	525	Faliero	3 460
I would not hold my breath on such a tenure	532	Faliero	4 265
She has no breath, no pulse!--Guards! lend your aid	547	Faliero	5 689
For all the popular breath that e'er divided	556	Sardan	1 386
The breath of heaven? Tell prince Salemenes	560	Sardan	1 622
Of my own breath and body--so far that	564	Sardan	2 171
Although upon this breath of mine depends	566	Sardan	2 281
To be blown down by his imperious breath	567	Sardan	2 326
You are wounded--give some wine. Take breath, good Pania	572	Sardan	3 73
And impulse--borne away with every breath	583	Sardan	4 331
I took the rabble's shouts for love, the breath	586	Sardan	4 519
Like mine or any other subject's breath	587	Sardan	4 570
From birth to manhood! My life waits your breath	592	Sardan	5 326
Let me approach, I pray you, for a breath	596	Foscari	1 87
The long-suspended breath, again I spurn'd	597	Foscari	1 119
My only Venice--this is breath! Thy breeze	597	Foscari	1 124
To him is one wide prison, and each breath	600	Foscari	1 291
About by every breath, shook by a sigh	600	Foscari	1 330
Our fame is in men's breath, our lives upon	607	Foscari	2 354
Less than their breath; our durance upon days	607	Foscari	2 355
Long ceased to breathe our breath, have theirs, thou say'st	644	Cain	2 578
Who made us, and who breathed the breath of life	649	Cain	3 224
Breath will be still'd at once! All beauteous world	659	Heaven	312
And no breath	660	Heaven	351
And not enquired their Maker's breath of me	666	Heaven	802
There's not a breath of wind upon the hill	668	Heaven	993
And roll the waters o'er his placid breath	669	Heaven	1108
The breath which is his own	670	Heaven	1154
And shall I, for a little gasp of breath	670	Heaven	1166
Before the breath of menials, and their master	692	Werner	2 575
'Gainst whom thy breath would blow thy bloody slander	715	Werner	5 167
And when at length they're out of breath, they sigh	769	Juan	1 1429
A little breath, love, wine, ambition, fame	774	Juan	2 31
The fourth day came, but not a breath of air	782	Juan	2 553
Pedrillo, and so gently ebb'd his breath	783	Juan	2 603
Seem'd almost prying into his for breath	788	Juan	2 898
Bent with hush'd lips, that drank his scarce-drawn breath	792	Juan	2 1144
Till pausing at the last her breath to take	794	Juan	2 1287
Are things that really take away the breath	809	Juan	3 526
And not a breath crept through the rosy air	815	Juan	3 911
Except mere breath; and since the silent shore	817	Juan	4 93
Until she sobb'd for breath, and soon they were	820	Juan	4 246
Had stopp'd this Canto, and Don Juan's breath	821	Juan	4 330
No sign, save breath, of having left the grave	824	Juan	4 504
'But yesterday and who had mightier breath	835	Juan	5 283
Nods from the tree, was slumbering with soft breath	860	Juan	6 519
Thousands of whom were drawing their last breath	878	Juan	7 692
Her steady breath (which some months the same still is	883	Juan	8 310
Retire a little, merely to take breath	883	Juan	8 320
The breath of morn and man, where foot by foot	887	Juan	8 551
Mark how its lipless mouth grins without breath	898	Juan	9 88
Rather than life a mere affair of breath	898	Juan	9 128
Because December, with his breath so hoary	908	Juan	10 70
Should not veer round with every breath, nor seize	909	Juan	10 103
His breath,--he from his swelling throat untied	920	Juan	11 127
Lets out impatiently his rushing breath	955	Juan	14 31
And such a straw, borne on by human breath	956	Juan	14 59
The ghost had a remarkably sweet breath	996	Juan	16 1012

BREATHE

But now the wild flowers round them only breathe	7	Harold	1 272
Each volley tells that thousands cease to breathe	10	Harold	1 420
When shall she breathe her from the blushing toil	18	Harold	1 923
A life within itself, to breathe without mankind	37	Harold	3 108
Bear, know, feel and yet breathe--into one word	50	Harold	3 910
Flowers whose wild odours breathe but agonies	73	Harold	4 1076
Torture and Time, and breathe when I expire	75	Harold	4 1229
Would my lips breathe a flame which no stream could assuage	92	Caroline-D	10
Henceforth I breathe but for thy sake	99	Young Lady	27
Then let me breathe this parting prayer	113	Quaker	43
To Thee I breathe my humble strain	133	Prayer	61
Or breathe those sweet Aeolian strains	150	Song	5
To breathe a sweet religious calm around	161	Athos	15
Yes, Thyrza! yes, they breathe of thee	166	Away	13

BREATHE

In vain my lyre would lightly breathe	166	Struggle	17
I speak not, I trace not, I breathe not thy name	182	Music-A	1
That race is gone--but still their children breathe	182	Address-C	7
Millions with him he but to inherit	188	Ode-B	99
The envious who but breathe in others' pain	193	Monody	72
Her eyes will look on thee, when she shall breathe	198	Po	23
And the heart must pause to breathe	230	Roving	7
Where Attic flowers Aonian odours breathe	254	Bards	884
I breathe the sorrows I bewail	323	Giaour	1321
Without--can only strangers breathe	329	Abydos	2 51
There breathe but few whose aspect might defy	341	Corsair	1 215
There checks his speed, but pauses, less to breathe	346	Corsair	1 535
It is enough--I breathe--and I can bear	354	Corsair	2 482
What--speak not, breathe not--for I know it well	357	Corsair	3 104
Than glance could well reveal or accent breathe	367	Lara	1 78
The men with whom he felt condemn'd to breathe	371	Lara	1 346
Nor gale breathe forth one sigh for thee, for all	375	Lara	2 16
A moment's pause--'tis but to breathe their band	379	Lara	2 332
The breast of man such trusty love may breathe	382	Lara	2 513
There they yet may breathe awhile	394	Corinth	920
They only for each other breathe	396	Parisina	36
A name she dare not breathe by day	397	Parisina	72
Howe'er unworthy now to breathe	397	Parisina	109
Together, for an hour, could breathe	398	Parisina	215
She had forgotten:--did she breathe	400	Parisina	372
My brothers--both had ceased to breathe	404	Chillon	220
With syllables which breathe of the sweet South	445	Beppo	348
Me forth to breathe elsewhere, so reassume	457	Dante	1 80
Such as all they must breathe who are debased	461	Dante	3 60
A heritage enriching all who breathe	462	Dante	3 154
A conflict of its elements, and breathe	482	Manfred	1 303
My joy was in the Wilderness, to breathe	485	Manfred	2 156
To breathe my scorn upon ye--earthly strength	496	Manfred	3 362
I have known Bertram long; there doth not breathe	517	Faliero	2 589
Rather than breathe in slavery! If there are so	543	Faliero	5 377
I do not dare to breathe my own desire	551	Sardan	1 69
Already captive? can I not even breathe	560	Sardan	1 621
I breathe more freely. This great hour has proved	577	Sardan	3 342
Where their fond votaries repose and breathe	587	Sardan	5 28
I may breathe many years. Alas! and this	609	Foscari	3 94
May breathe it without prejudice. I have not	614	Foscari	3 382
We breathe not by a mortal measurement	635	Cain	1 535
Breathe save the erect ones? How the lights recede	638	Cain	2 173
My spirit buoys thee up to breathe in regions	641	Cain	2 321
Long ceased to breathe our breath, have theirs, thou say'st	644	Cain	2 578
Why, so--that's well--thou breath'st! breathe upon me	651	Cain	3 332
A brighter world than this, where thou shalt breathe	669	Heaven	1085
Who play'st with thine own guilt! Of all that breathe	715	Werner	5 165
In spirit. Cover up my dust, and breathe not	737	Deformed	2 151
That I have ceased to breathe. Away! and be	737	Deformed	2 152
I could breathe on and break it	743	Deformed	3 78
Droop'd as the willow when no winds can breathe	793	Juan	2 1179
Should an hour come to bid them breathe apart	819	Juan	4 211
In lovers' parts his passion more to breathe	827	Juan	4 711
To breathe destruction on its winding way	878	Juan	8 14

BREATHED

And soft voluptuous couches breathed repose	28	Harold	2 553
This breathed itself to life in Julie, this	47	Harold	3 743
Breathed from the birth of time: the veil they rent	48	Harold	3 772
Breathed most in ridicule,--which as the wind	51	Harold	3 992
With many a sweet and solemn requiem breathed	63	Harold	4 516
But here, where Murder breathed her bloody steam	76	Harold	4 1270
In sighs alone it breathed my name	90	Caroline-A	16
Oh! if these wishes are not breathed in vain	94	Dorset	110
Full foes enough to-night have breathed their last	109	Nisus	282
One wish, nor breathed a thought beside	137	Clare	32
And breathed in the face of the foe as he pass'd	222	Sennacherib	10
'Tis the old aspiration breathed afresh	302	Age	268
A moment breathed him from his speed	312	Giaour	219
'And she was lost--and yet I breathed	322	Giaour	1192
The childish thought was hardly breathed	326	Abydos	1 283
He lived--he breathed--he moved--he felt	327	Abydos	1 327
Breathed Conrad's spirit, and forbade despair	357	Corsair	3 126
And breathed new vigour in his shaken frame	369	Lara	1 250
When Lara's lip breathed forth the words of home	373	Lara	1 521
I told it not, I breathed it not, it was	438	Tasso	124
Have breathed a pestilence upon us all	506	Faliero	1 452
The signal. These brave words have breathed new life	516	Faliero	2 558
Their hopes is breathed on, jealous as the eagle	544	Faliero	5 431
Too often breathed out in a woman's hearing	559	Sardan	1 560

BREATHED

Who made us, and who breathed the breath of life	649 Cain	3	224
Who breathed to destroy	725 Deformed	1	180
Beneath the lie this State-thing breathed o'er thee	747 Juan	Ded	124
Some hundreds breathed--the rest were silent all	894 Juan	8	1016
He breathed a thousand Cressys, as he saw	916 Juan	10	586

BREATHER

My spirit; I'm a forester and breather	707 Werner	4	222

BREATHERS

Of toiling breathers in allotted tasks	587 Sardan	5	34

BREATHES

There breathes a living fragrance from the shore	48 Harold	3	811
And still the eloquent air breathes--burns with Cicero	72 Harold	4	1008
A tinge of years, but breathes the flame with which 'twas wrought	79 Harold	4	1467
And though so sweet it breathes my name	90 Caroline-B		14
Nor breathes a murmur 'gainst the will of fate	122 Newstead-A		152
Orla. He breathes not; but his eye is still	131 Calmar		164
Breathes our thoughts from Earth to Heaven	139 Anacreon-C		12
Who labours, fights, lives, breathes for him alone	154 Dog		10
Breathes o'er the page her purity of soul	249 Bards		558
It breathes the same dark spirit now	318 Giaour		796
We promise, hope, believe--there breathes despair	345 Corsair	1	490
They raise him, bear him;--hush! he breathes, he speaks	369 Lara	1	225
Well,--let that pass,--there breathes not one	398 Parisina		203
Than breathes his mimic murmurer in the shell	424 Island	2	407
You have cause, sire; for on the earth there breathes not	578 Sardan	3	426
His lips, too, are apart; why then he breathes	651 Cain	3	339
He breathes not; and his hands drop down from mine	651 Cain	3	364
She breathes! But no, 'twas nothing, or the last	741 Deformed	2	384
Faint flutter life disputes with death. She breathes	741 Defromed	2	385
Breathes also to the heart, and o'er it throws	761 Juan	1	911
Love, who heroically breathes a vein	776 Juan	2	179
Which breathes of nations saved, not worlds undone	878 Juan	8	36
Compassion breathes along the savage mind	891 Juan	8	848

BREATHETH

He breatheth--and a tempest shakes the sea	488 Manfred	2	375

BREATHING

(See also BALM-BREATHING, BEAUTY-BREATHING, SOUL-
BREATHING)

And chiefless castles breathing stern farewells	42 Harold	3	413
Still Hope, breathing peace through the grief-swollen breast	99 L Adieu		9
And lips, though silent, breathing love	152 Remind		12
Her breathing moment on the bridge where Time	192 Monody		7
Soft as the gentler breathing of the lute	259 Hints		201
That form was nought but breathing clay	315 Giaour		481
No breathing form within my grasp	323 Giaour		1288
The mind, the Music breathing from her face	325 Abydos	1	179
And freshness breathing from each silver spring	340 Corsair	1	126
But gather'd breathing from the happier dead	351 Corsair	2	274
He stood a stranger in this breathing world	370 Lara	1	315
A breathing but devoted warrior lay	381 Lara	2	416
And then, as his faint breathing waxes low	381 Lara	2	422
Scarce breathing more than that he loved so well	382 Lara	2	511
Had his free breathing been denied	404 Chillon		142
Came breathing o'er the aromatic south	425 Island	2	435
And paradise was breathing in the sigh	429 Island	3	199
The aspect and the form of breathing men	478 Manfred	1	8
A living voice, a breathing harmony	482 Manfred	1	315
I had no sympathy with breathing flesh	485 Manfred	2	151
We have breathing time: yet once more charge, my friends	575 Sardan	3	263
Yet breathing stone, for I felt life in them	580 Sardan	4	123
Now breathing; mighty yet and beautiful	640 Cain	2	264
All temporary breathing creatures their	644 Cain	2	576
Breathing around you, save my mother's? Ah	702 Werner	3	494
Let each breathing heart dilated	736 Deformed	2	119
And louder than her breathing beats her heart	766 Juan	1	1264
Breathing all gently o'er his cheek and mouth	795 Juan	2	1343
In a new face 'the ugliest creature breathing	857 Juan	6	296
As roll the waters to the breathing wind	873 Juan	7	379

BREATHINGS

He is no more--these breathings are his last	79 Harold	4	1471
Soften'd with the first breathings of the spring	529 Faliero	4	73

BREATHING-TIME

Brief breathing-time! the turban'd host	394 Corinth		922

BREATHLESS

Foil'd, bleeding, breathless, furious to the last	16 Harold	1	774
But breathless, as we grow when feeling most	49 Harold	3	834
Of breathless being?--darken'd and intense	192 Fragment-C		30
Crownless, breathless, headless fall	219 Saul-B		29
To their superior, all in breathless rout	472 Morgante		436
Where all is breathless save thyself. Gaze on	641 Cain	2	322
Still as the breathless interval between	681 Werner	1	636
I'm breathless! You must also furnish me	699 Werner	3	307
Alfonso leaning, breathless, by the door	770 Juan	1	1492
There, breathless, with his digging nails he clung	787 Juan	2	857
Lay in a breathless, hush'd, and stony sleep	860 Juan	6	538

BREATH'ST

Why, so--that's well--thou breath'st! breathe upon me	651 Cain	3	332

BRED

(See also ILL-BRED, THOROUGH-BRED, WELL-BRED)

And bred in darkness, lest the truth should shine	74 Harold	4	1141
Adieu, then, ye hills where my childhood was bred	136 Highlander		45
Born in the garret, in the kitchen bred	208 Sketch		1
Bred in the courts betimes, though all that law	247 Bards		446
It boots not that, together bred	153 Friend-A		21
Who, bred a statesman, still wast born a wit	305 Age		549
The hearts within thy valleys bred	311 Giaour		147
'From unbelieving mother bred	324 Abydos	1	82
Was he not bred in Egripo	327 Abydos	1	375
Bred to a throne, perhaps unfit to reign	421 Island	2	186
A thousand wrongs unto the monks they bred	472 Morgante		389
Such fervour in his bosom bred each word	475 Morgante		619
No tyrant, though bred up to tyranny	518 Faliero	2	678
Was bred a soldier, not a senator	538 Faliero	5	36
A young heir, bred to wealth and luxury	685 Werner	2	130
Who were born in them, and bred up upon	705 Werner	4	70
Or gentleman, who, though well born and bred	749 Juan	1	171
That they bred in and in, as might be shown	754 Juan	1	454
Like most in the belief in which they're bred	783 Juan	2	606
All hope; to look upon her sweet face bred	824 Juan	4	478
But bred within the March of old Ancona	828 Juan	4	746
Her third, to ask him where he had been bred	849 Juan	5	1107
And bright as any meteor ever bred	861 Juan	6	573
The ladies,--who by no means had been bred	875 Juan	7	530
But I am half a Scot by birth, and bred	909 Juan	10	135
His holy temples in the lands which bred	917 Juan	10	597
And about twice two thousand people bred	924 Juan	11	355
Than those bred up by prudes without a heart	935 Juan	12	368
Both wits--one born so, and the other bred	953 Juan	13	743
To like too readily, or too high bred	969 Juan	15	76
The island girl, bred up by the lone sea	975 Juan	15	460
My Muse hath bred, and still perhaps may breed	975 Juan	15	477
For I was bred a moderate Presbyterian	979 Juan	15	728
Poor soul! for she was country born and bred	989 Juan	16	558
And yet great heroes have been bred by both	991 Juan	16	720
Though too well bred to quiz men to their faces	993 Juan	16	843

BREECH

But such as fit an Asiatic breech	840 Juan	5	541

BREECHES

Must put on my breeches, and wait on the Heathcote	226 Oh You		14
-mere breeches whisk'd round, in a waltz with the Jersey	228 Moore-A		23
With a clean shirt, and very spacious breeches	794 Juan	2	1280
And that his Argus--bites him by the breeches	804 Juan	3	184
And brilliant breeches, bright as a Cairn Gorme	902 Juan	9	341
Exposed to lose his life as well as breeches	919 Juan	11	88

BREECHES'

But keep your hands out of his breeches' pocket	917 Juan	10	632

BREED

Birds breed not vipers, tigers nurse not lambs	257 Hints		20
If you will breed this bastard of your brains	267 Hints		791
A Tartar of the Ukraine breed	410 Mazeppa		360
Vain doubt! his swift and savage breed	412 Mazeppa		510
Who seem'd the patriarch of his breed	413 Mazeppa		703
Beyond may breed us double danger. See	516 Faliero	2	554
They eat, and drink, and live, and breed together	521 Faliero	3	156
A nobler breed. Match me in Barbary	729 Deformed	1	511
There's not a foal of Arab's breed	730 Deformed	1	549
And eat your thoughts--till they breed snakes within you	743 Deformed	3	108
Which always spoils the breed, if it increases	754 Juan	1	456
This heathenish cross restored the breed again	754 Juan	1	457
Where waves might wash, and seals might breed and lurk	820 Juan	4	260
Huger than twelve of our degenerate breed	950 Juan	13	556
But Strongbow's wit was of more polish'd breed	952 Juan	13	732
But form good housekeepers, to breed a nation	958 Juan	14	192

BREED
My Muse hath bred, and still perhaps may breed 975 Juan 15 477

BREEDING
(See also ILL-BREEDING)
But nought to mark its breeding or its birth 294 Vision 596
My lord, excuse this poor man's want of breeding 679 Werner 1 525
Though this looks like it: this is the true
  breeding 700 Werner 3 313
Was, that his breeding should be strictly moral 752 Juan 1 308
That Pasiphae promoted breeding cattle 793 Juan 2 1239
With such true breeding of a gentleman 806 Juan 3 323
And certainly he show'd the best of breeding 807 Juan 3 362
And Juan was a boy of saintly breeding 818 Juan 4 150
To him whose breeding matches with his quality 944 Juan 13 192

BREEDS
That fellow even in hell breeds farther ills 294 Vision 583
And your departure breeds such sorrow here 475 Morgante 645
Because it breeds no more mouths than it
  nourishes 972 Juan 15 276

BREEZE
(See also NIGHT-BREEZE, SEA-BREEZE)
When the fresh breeze is fair as breeze may be 22 Harold 2 147
To waste on sluggish hulks the sweetest breeze 22 Harold 2 177
From heaven itself he may inhale the breeze 27 Harold 2 445
Swelling the breeze that sigh'd along the
  lengthening glen 27 Harold 2 495
And when a transient breeze swept o'er the wave 32 Harold 2 761
Dance in the soft breeze in a fairy mass 72 Harold 4 1051
Calm or convulsed--in breeze, or gale, or storm 82 Harold 4 1641
Their auburn, those locks must wave thin to the
  breeze 91 Caroline-C 10
Tumultuous voices swell the passing breeze 109 Nisus 324
The hunters' cry hangs lengthening on the breeze 121 Newstead-A 124
they lie on Erin. The breeze of ocean lifts 131 Calmar 155
Swept by the breeze that fans thy cloudless sky 138 Harrow-B 2
Breeze of the night in gentler sighs 150 Song 1
But Breeze of night again forbear 150 Song 9
Chill is thy Breath thou breeze of night 150 Song 13
Each breeze from foggy mount and marshy plain 270 Minerva 139
And if at times a transient breeze 310 Giaour 16
By every breeze and season blest 310 Giaour 29
Far as the breeze can bear, the billows foam 338 Corsair 1 3
Blow fair, thou breeze!--she anchors ere the dark 339 Corsair 1 88
The breeze will freshen when the day is done 340 Corsair 1 159
As kindle high to-night (but blow, thou breeze 342 Corsair 1 321
In three days (serve the breeze) the sun shall
  shine 346 Corsair 1 567
Meantime, the steady breeze serenely blew 346 Corsair 1 591
Embark'd, the sail unfurl'd, the light breeze
  blew 362 Corsair 3 452
Still onward, fair the breeze, nor rough the
  surge 362 Corsair 3 480
The flapping bat, the night song of the breeze 370 Lara 1 264
And o'er it blew the mountain breeze 406 Chillon 347
And a low breeze crept moaning by 411 Mazeppa 440
That bent not to the roughest breeze 411 Mazeppa 467
The breeze now sank, now whisper'd from his cave 418 Island 1 170
The breeze springs up; the lately flapping sail 418 Island 1 225
Of his true sons, who riot in the breeze 425 Island 2 470
A cooling breeze which crisps the broad clear
  river 551 Sardan 1 53
As the light breeze of midnight crisps the broad 566 Sardan 2 257
My only Venice--this is breath! Thy breeze 597 Foscari 1 124
They dared not take it in for all the breeze 781 Juan 2 476
Save in the breeze that came not; savagely 783 Juan 2 572
As are the billows when the breeze is brisk 853 Juan 6 22
As they will do like leaves at the first breeze 961 Juan 14 382

BREEZES
As breezes rise and fall and billows swell 23 Harold 2 251
Bear it, ye breezes, to the seat 131 L'Amitie 8
Favourable breezes blowing 156 Hodgson 3
Breezes foul and tempests murky 157 Hodgson 67
And pleasant breezes, as I call upon you 616 Foscari 4 126

BREEZY
The breezy freshness of the deep beneath 346 Corsair 1 536

BRENNUS
From Brennus to the Bourbon, never, never 459 Dante 2 98
Brennus was a baffled foeman 736 Deformed 2 110

BRENTA
The deep-dyed Brenta, where their hues instil 59 Harold 4 250
(Long ere I dreamt of dating from the Brenta 772 Juan 1 1693

BRENTFORD
To Hampstead, Brentford, Harrow make repair 15 Harold 1 699

BRENT'S
Where Brent's cool waves in limpid currents stray 124 Recoll 134

BRESCIA
The gems of Brescia and Ravenna; Crema 601 Foscari 2 20

BRETHREN
(See also ESAU-BRETHREN)
Nor saved your brethren ere they sank beneath 10 Harold 1 417
Above its prostrate brethren of the cave 33 Harold 2 811
Their brethren out to battle--why? for rent 306 Age 619
The banker--broker--baron--brethren, speed 307 Age 678
And hated hosts seem brethren to the sight 348 Corsair 2 122
How much I grieve about my brethren dead 472 Morgante 419
Rocking their Alpine brethren; filling up 483 Manfred 1 355
My pious brethren, the scared peasantry 492 Manfred 3 44
Then I must summon up my brethren.---Rise 496 Manfred 3 351
Whose brethren, parents, children, wives, or
  sisters 507 Faliero 1 496
A band of brethren, valiant hearts and true 507 Faliero 1 512
Inflicted on our brethren or ourselves 516 Faliero 2 563
Hence, brethren, to our posts, and may this be 526 Faliero 3 508
The rage of the worst war--the war of brethren 559 Sardan 1 575
Is dead; so is young Foscari and his brethren 619 Foscari 4 304
My brethren, will we not? Ay!--Ay! You shall
  not 624 Foscari 5 272
To do himself and them full justice. Brethren 625 Foscari 5 314
To separate? Are ye not as brethren in 644 Cain 2 586
Art thou not Abel's brother? We are brethren 644 Cain 2 588
He will not answer to that name; for brethren 651 Cain 3 354
Brethren, rejoice 661 Heaven 484
Brethren, rejoice 662 Heaven 514
Fly, brethren, fly 662 Heaven 532
I glory in my brethren and our fathers 664 Heaven 691
And dearer, silent friends and brethren, all 668 Heaven 966
My brethren and my brethren's herds 670 Heaven 1179
The spark which lights the matchlock, we are
  brethren 677 Werner 1 352
Like Theban brethren: when a part is bad 699 Werner 3 259
Call not thy brothers brethren! Call me not 722 Deformed 1 24
In giving to his brethren their full meed 746 Juan Ded 62
Me and my epic brethren gone before 771 Juan 1 1610
And then he call'd his brethren to his aid 867 Juan 6 937

BRETHREN'S
He cut his brethren's hands off at these words 472 Morgante 431
My brethren and my brethren's herds 670 Heaven 1179

BREVIARIES
They lay their breviaries to sleep, and work 474 Morgante 524

BREVITY
Perhaps you think by this blunt brevity 538 Faliero 5 37
And makes men's miseries of alarming brevity 782 Juan 2 512

BREW
With which I could not brew a pastoral 959 Juan 14 235
Than witches, b--ches, or physicians brew 976 Juan 15 496

BREW'D
That e'er were brew'd from elements or gore 941 Juan 12 700

BREWING
Damnation for others brewing 179 Devil's Dr 240
Where every kind of mischief's daily brewing 932 Juan 12 179

BRIAREAN
Could I not shatter the Briarean sceptre 504 Faliero 1 297

BRIAREUS
Oh, enviable Briareus! with thy hands 856 Juan 6 217

BRIARS
You'd better walk about begirt with briars 440 Beppo 25

BRIBE
And share with these applause, a godlike bribe 143 Soliloquy 57
But if some new-born whim, or larger bribe 246 Bards 363
Shows more of fear than worship, as a bribe 647 Cain 3 102
Bribe the intendant for his old caleche 698 Werner 3 189
Must be recited, and--without a bribe 897 Juan 9 78
Unless some Beauty with a kiss should bribe 998 Juan 17 96

BRIBED
The bowl a bribed attendant bore 331 Abydos 2 244
I used no poison, bribed no subtle master 619 Foscari 4 281
I've bribed my grandmother's review--the British 772 Juan 1 1672

BRIBES
A person yet by prayers, or bribes, or tears 442 Beppo 173
The accusation of the bribes was proved 600 Foscari 1 301
Females with portions, brides and bribes for
  nobles 614 Foscari 3 394
Like Shakespeare's stealing deer, Lord Bacon's
  bribes 813 Juan 3 826
Whether you're paid by government in bribes 900 Juan 9 276

BRIBING
Some say, that authors only snatch, by bribing 957 Juan 14 148

BRICK
Hath piled in her brick mountains, o'er dead
kings 595 Sardan 5 483
A mighty mass of brick, and smoke, and shipping 917 Juan 10 649

BRICKLAYER
Bricklayer of Babel, call'd an architect 988 Juan 16 506

BRICKS
(Though Claudius Rich, Esquire, some bricks has
got 839 Juan 5 493
Or sat amidst the bricks of Nineveh 919 Juan 11 54
Of bricks, to let the dust in at your ease 921 Juan 11 165

BRICK-WORK
Cabala; their best brick-work, wherewithal 732 Deformed 1 684

BRIDAL
'And where should our bridal couch be spread 390 Corinth 581
And bridal beauty, in the unwholesome press 528 Faliero 4 15
Is he--Our bridal bed is now his bier 622 Foscari 5 110
And the first year of sovereigns is bridal 704 Werner 4 18
Just at the close of the first bridal year 881 Juan 8 212
Before the bridal hours have danced their measure 892 Juan 8 899
He flits on the bridal eve 985 Juan 16 342

BRIDAL'S
Thy bridal's fruit is ashes; in the dust 80 Harold 4 1523

BRIDE
For him who dared prefer a mortal bride 24 Harold 2 258
Shall win the young bride with her long flowing
hair 30 Harold 2 671
But now a bride and mother--and now there 80 Harold 4 1543
Since first Hesione thy bride 89 Prometheus-A 10
And Oscar claim'd the beauteous bride 102 Alva 81
At length young Allan join'd the bride 102 Alva 101
If with high-bounding pride he return to his
bride 115 The Tear 21
I've seen my bride another's bride 164 Friend-B 25
Thy still imperial bride 181 Ode-A 110
Lovely and young, herself a happy bride 199 Sonnet-D 2
And Thou his widow--not his bride 201 Ode-C 45
To the long-cherish'd isle which he loved like
his--bride 201 Avatar 4
Before an Altar--with a gentle bride 215 Dream 146
Fierce as a bride when first she feels affright 266 Hints 691
To gain your own or snatch another's bride 275 Waltz 106
Till woo'd by danger, his yet weeping bride 301 Age 220
The imperial daughter, the imperial bride 308 Age 727
'Tis said he goes to woo a bride 315 Giaour 533
'Lady, a fearful bride thy Son hath wed 317 Giaour 718
I must not see thee Osman's bride 330 Abydos 2 156
The spoil of nations shall bedeck my bride 333 Abydos 2 413
Thy pride of heart, thy bride for Osman's bed 336 Abydos 2 656
And tottering to the couch his bride he bore 345 Corsair 1 478
'Twere worse than bondage to become his bride 354 Corsair 2 524
He thought on her afar, his lonely bride 362 Corsair 3 462
And fair the monument they gave his bride 366 Corsair 3 692
Another chief consoled his destined bride 366 Lara 1 35
The maid who might have been his bride 390 Corinth 545
There thou yet shalt be my bride 390 Corinth 589
'Francesca!--Oh, my promised bride 393 Corinth 853
To covet there another's bride 397 Parisina 66
In him who made her not his bride 397 Parisina 106
The minion of his father's bride 398 Parisina 171
But wrong for wrong: this deem'd thy bride 399 Parisina 253
And made thy own my destined bride 399 Parisina 308
And Azo found another bride 401 Parisina 530
The husband of the bride of Toobonai 421 Island 2 211
Against them, save the bride of Toobonai 429 Island 3 217
Was all that told of Torquil and his bride 431 Island 4 80
Proud and exulting in his mermaid bride 432 Island 4 214
And why not also Torquil and his bride 433 Island 4 218
And thou, oh Virgin! daughter, mother, bride 466 Morgante 9
I should have sought none though a peasant's
bride 510 Faliero 2 79
And a young bride: for in my fieriest youth 513 Faliero 2 313
The Sons of Heaven by many a mortal bride 660 Heaven 398
'Tis that an angel's bride disdains to weep 667 Heaven 914
My Werner, when you deign'd to choose for bride 673 Werner 1 122
The altar, gazing on his Trojan bride 726 Deformed 1 275
Tobias' future bride (and after all 741 Deformed 2 418
The bride and her lover 742 Deformed 3 3
The bride and her lover 742 Deformed 3 64
It was for this that I became a bride 764 Juan 1 1156
Haidee was Nature's bride, and knew not this 799 Juan 2 1609
Would Juan bend, though 'twere to Mahomet's bride 844 Juan 5 821
She was a sultan's bride (thank Heaven, not mine 845 Juan 5 888
And, should you ask how she, a sultan's bride 846 Juan 5 914
'Bride of the Sun! and Sister of the Moon 849 Juan 5 1145

BRIDE
The giant thought of being a Titan's bride 856 Juan 6 220
(If that his Highness wearied of his bride 857 Juan 6 287
The imperial bride--and added, 'Let the boat 866 Juan 6 898
To break the rules by bringing one's own bride 876 Juan 7 565
Or hawk, or bride, most mortals after one 881 Juan 8 174
Of import both to virgin and to bride 924 Juan 11 362
Upon an heiress or his neighbour's bride 927 Juan 11 554
But in old England, when a young bride errs 938 Juan 12 511
Of what she had gone through with--since a bride 987 Juan 16 446

BRIDEGROOM
Why sends not the Bridegroom his promised gift 317 Giaour 699

BRIDEGROOMS
That future bridegrooms swore, and sigh'd, and
paid it 924 Juan 11 392
That bridegrooms, after they are fairly groom'd 973 Juan 15 309

BRIDEGROOM'S
Is this a bridegroom's ardent flame 102 Alva 98
The bridegroom's health is deeply quaff'd 103 Alva 190

BRIDES
So oft bestowing Brunswickers and brides 274 Waltz 50
His hours, and rivals opium and his brides 425 Island 2 451
Females with portions, brides and brides for
nobles 614 Foscari 3 394
For rich men and their brides to lay their heads 855 Juan 6 196
Thought not upon the charms of four young brides 892 Juan 8 906
Without cash, Malthus tells you--'take no brides 931 Juan 12 108
They have at hand a blooming glut of brides 972 Juan 15 264

BRIDE'S
(See also SISTER-BRIDE'S)
Had made him lately bask in his bride's beauty 863 Juan 6 728

BRIDGE
I stood in Venice on the Bridge of Sighs 55 Harold 4 1
And the best thing he saw was a broken bridge 176 Devil's Dr 55
Her breathing moment on the bridge where Time 192 Monody 7
Divided by the 'Bridge of Sighs 196 Venice-A 14
Stone, bar, moat, bridge, or barrier left 410 Mazeppa 396
And I would pass the fearful 'Bridge of Sighs 507 Faliero 1 537
'The Ten.'--When we had reach'd 'the Bridge of
Sighs 602 Foscari 2 54
Your 'Bridge of Sighs,' your strangling chamber,
and 606 Foscari 2 309
The Bridge which few repass. I am silent. Why 616 Foscari 4 75
Continue. When we reach'd the Muldau's bridge 714 Werner 5 108
I tell thee, be not rash; a golden bridge 737 Deformed 2 185
Of twilight, as the party cross'd the bridge 921 Juan 11 184

BRIDGES
Shouts, bridges, arches, pensions from a nation 878 Juan 8 27

BRIDLED
But the thoughts we cannot bridle 208 Fare Thee 55
Refused the bridle or the brand 332 Abydos 2 328
With spur and bridle undefiled 410 Mazeppa 364
And his spouse took his bridle on this change 468 Morgante 141
The steed bites the bridle 742 Deformed 3 25

BRIDLED
Are they not bridled?--Venice, lost and won 57 Harold 4 112
The steeds are all bridled, and snort to the rein 392 Corinth 698
The Misses bridled, and the matrons frown'd 961 Juan 14 346

BRIDLES
Chariots and bridles, mix'd with arms, are seen 108 Nisus 227

BRIEF
Who could foresee thee, in a space so brief 11 Harold 1 461
Brief, brave, and glorious was his young career 44 Harold 3 545
Her new-born Numa thou--with reign, alas, too
brief 72 Harold 4 1026
The hour draws nigh, a few brief days will close 94 Dorset 77
A month's brief lapse, perhaps a day's 153 Friend-A 11
A few, brief, rolling seasons o'er 158 Florence 11
Too brief for our passion, too long for our peace 182 Music-A 5
There, where death's brief pang was quickest 187 Ode-B 60
True, the great of her bright and brief era are
gone 201 Avatar 5
Is a brief feeling of a trivial date 211 Augusta-C 59
A few brief generations fleet along 254 Bards 953
I labour to be brief--become obscure 257 Hints 42
Whate'er you teach, be brief, if you design 264 Hints 533
Dull as his sermons, but not half so brief 267 Hints 768
Brief thought to distant friendship's claim 322 Giaour 1226
And the brief epitaph in danger's day 338 Corsair 1 39
To such brief answer and contemptuous eye 339 Corsair 1 81
Yet thus sincere--'tis cheering, though so brief 340 Corsair 1 119
His bugle--brief the blast--but shrilly blew 349 Corsair 2 166
Brief time had Conrad now to greet Gulnare 350 Corsair 2 225

BRIEF

Ah! since that fatal night, though brief the time	362 Corsair	3	456
If greeted once; however brief the date	371 Lara	1	374
Brief were his answers, and his questions	373 Lara	1	547
Brief breathing-time! the turban'd host	394 Corinth		922
Or thought how brief such moments last	397 Parisina		45
And for a brief delay demands	399 Parisina		231
A few brief hours or days that must	399 Parisina		278
Wondering that summer show'd so brief a sun	424 Island	2	368
The sound. 'Here's one,' was all the brief reply	425 Island	2	433
But brief their time for good or evil thought	429 Island	3	213
Till its dried wing relapsed from its brief height	435 Island	4	371
Orlando one day heard this speech in brief	468 Morgante		117
For this brief moment to descend	480 Manfred	1	128
And his brief term of mock-arrest will pass	515 Faliero	2	439
And, covetous of brief authority	518 Faliero	2	701
But a brief passage--I would go alone	537 Faliero	4	629
Your object? Freedom! You are brief, sir	538 Faliero	5	34
Do you be brief as I am, and believe me	538 Faliero	5	39
Let it be brief, and we ourselves will be	546 Faliero	5	571
But nothing 'gainst the truth of that brief record	555 Sardan	1	294
Than either the brief life or the wide realm	558 Sardan	1	530
Be brief. I am charged by Salemenes to	560 Sardan	1	614
Briefly; but in that brief cool calm inhale	587 Sardan	5	29
A few brief minutes for his tortured limbs	595 Foscari	1	6
In this brief parley, and must now redeem it	597 Foscari	1	91
The dates of their despair, the brief words of	608 Foscari	3	18
Because we have brief time for preparation	612 Foscari	3	286
A few brief words of truth shame the devil's servants	613 Foscari	3	311
Intercheck'd with an instant of brief pleasure	634 Cain	1	453
While a brief truce	661 Heaven		448
After the bright course of a few brief morrows	662 Heaven		565
My pangs can be but brief; but thine would be	667 Heaven		926
Own brief connection led me, honour. Then	692 Werner	2	584
So brief and burning, with a lady's zone	706 Werner	4	121
With such brief greeting. You have heard our bugle	708 Werner	4	233
And yet I had horrid dreams! and such brief sleep	718 Werner	5	357
Be brief in your decision! I will be so	719 Werner	5	393
And that brief dream appear'd a life too long	820 Juan	4	272
Brief, but delightful--such as had not staid	825 Juan	4	566
A few brief questions; and the answers gave	826 Juan	4	630
Gulbeyaz proved in that brief agony	865 Juan	6	847
Of these brief blossoms the immediate fruits	892 Juan	8	904
Hectic and brief as summer's day nigh done	908 Juan	10	62
The lawyer's brief is like the surgeon's knife	909 Juan	10	110
They're right; our days are too brief for affording	919 Juan	11	29
And then she drops a brief and modern curtsy	926 Juan	11	495
In brief, the little orphan of the East	935 Juan	12	383
But I shall add them in a brief appendix	964 Juan	14	543

BRIEFER

And here? At once--by better means, as briefer	610 Foscari	3	137

BRIEFLY

His name Giuseppe, call'd more briefly, Beppo	443 Beppo		200
Briefly; but in that brief cool calm inhale	587 Sardan	5	29
'What are ye?'--'What you see us.' Briefly pass'd	874 Juan	7	470

BRIEFLY-SPOKEN

A plain blunt show of briefly-spoken seeming	209 Sketch		59

BRIERS

The doubts that rise like briers in our path	697 Werner	3	159

BRIG

Hail'd a strange brig--Corpo di Caio Mario	826 Juan	4	652
Say, that he scuds before it like a brig	877 Juan	7	676

BRIGADIER

Also the General Markow, Brigadier	879 Juan	8	81

BRIGADIERS

But wishing to be one day brigadiers	869 Juan	7	140

BRIGAND

A brigand than the robber-chief. I cannot	607 Foscari	2	391

BRIGANDS

Lure on the broken brigands to their fate	379 Lara	2	289

BRIGANTINE

Or brigantine, or pink, of no great tonnage	971 Juan	15	215

BRIGHT

Fresh feres will dry the bright blue eyes	6 Harold	1	176
A thousand altars rise, for ever blazing bright	14 Harold	1	674
Hail the bright clime of battle and of song	34 Harold	2	858
Till he had peopled them with beings bright	37 Harold	3	119

BRIGHT

Her Beauty and her Chivalry, and bright	38 Harold	3	183
And partly that bright names will hallow song	39 Harold	3	257
Could man but leave thy bright creation so	42 Harold	3	445
Pray for his gallant spirit's bright repose	44 Harold	3	548
If in your bright leaves we would read the fate	49 Harold	3	825
Of a bright sun can make sufficient holiday	60 Harold	4	288
The bright blue waters with a fanning wind	61 Harold	4	391
Lest their own judgments should become too bright	69 Harold	4	836
With their large eyes all glistening gray and bright	71 Harold	4	952
I have beheld Sophia's bright roofs swell	78 Harold	4	1375
The shaft hath just been shot--the arrow bright	79 Harold	4	1445
Bright are the deeds thine earlier sires display	94 Dorset		66
With bright but mild affection shine	97 To M--		2
They lightly wheel the bright claymore	102 Alva		59
But Allan's locks were bright and fair	102 Alva		63
A bright example of maternal love	107 Nisus		182
Sheds forth a silver radiance, glancing bright	109 Nisus		306
The green sparkles bright with a Tear	115 The Tear		16
Gave place to the rays of the bright polar star	117 Lachin		14
Bright in idea gleams thy lofty spire	122 Recoll		45
A bright renown shall be enjoy'd	128 Answer-B		39
of a chief? Bright as the gold of the	131 Calmar		159
Now bright in rays divine	131 L'Amitie		14
But thy bright beam unchanged for ever glows	139 Ossian-A		16
To thy bright canopy the mourner flies	140 Ossian-A		42
Once bright, thy Silence lull'd my frame to rest	140 Ossian-A		43
Bright through the world enlivening radiance pour	140 Ossian-B		32
Bright beams the rising Sun of Fame	142 Critics		92
Bright as thy mother's in their hue	150 My Son		2
Bright be the place of thy soul	151 Soul-A		1
Let the Sunbeam be bright for the younger of days	164 Newstead-C		5
Dear are the days which made our annals bright	170 Address-A		42
Whose bright claymore and hardihood of hand	182 Address-C		5
Bright though they be, thine own had render'd less	183 Address-D		16
These are not lessen'd, these are still as bright	183 Address-D		43
Her bright chain o'er the deep	188 Music-C		10
Of three bright colours, each divine	188 On Star	21	
When thy bright promise fades away	189 On Star		35
The bright sun was extinguish'd, and the stars	189 Darkness		2
A holy concord--and a bright regret	192 Monody		11
The flash of Wit, the bright Intelligence	193 Monody		27
Bright with the hues of his Promethean heat	193 Monody		56
Her bright eyes will be imaged in thy stream	198 Po		29
True, the great of her bright and brief era are gone	201 Avatar		5
Than to see the bright eyes of the dear one discover	204 Pisa		11
When it sparkled o'er aught that was bright in my story	204 Pisa		15
And all that's best of dark and bright	216 She Walks		3
A step as fleet, an eye more bright	217 Gazelle		7
I saw thee weep--the big bright tear	218 I Saw		1
Bright is the diadem, boundless the sway	219 Saul-A		11
A thousand bright lamps shone	220 Belshaz-B		3
The lamps around were bright	220 Belshaz-B		37
How wondrous bright thy blooming morn arose	223 To Dives		6
And the moon be still as bright	229 Roving		4
Not, as in northern climes, obscurely bright	268 Minerva		3
And bright around, with quivering beams beset	269 Minerva		39
Bear witness, bright Barossa! thou canst tell	271 Minerva		231
Asmodeus struck so bright a stroke as this	276 Waltz		223
But bringing up the rear of this bright host	288 Vision		185
With all the myriads of bright worlds which pass	290 Vision		317
And not a star but shines too bright	312 Giaour		214
'Twas sweet, when cloudless stars were bright	313 Giaour		305
With hue as bright, and wing as wild	314 Giaour		397
Bright as the jewel of Giamschid	315 Giaour		479
On him shall glance for ever bright	317 Giaour		742
So bright the tear in Beauty's eye	326 Abydos	1	226
And many a bright emblazon'd rhyme	329 Abydos	2	74
For thee in those bright isles is built a bower	333 Abydos	2	408
As bright as this invites us not to roam	344 Corsair	1	391
Big, bright, and fast, unknown to her they fell	345 Corsair	1	487
Through Coron's lattices the lamps are bright	347 Corsair	2	2
Too bright, too blue, for my captivity	348 Corsair	2	86
That starts at once--bright--pure--from Pity's mine	355 Corsair	2	541
Not, as in northern climes, obscurely bright	355 Corsair	3	3
And, bright around with quivering beams beset	356 Corsair	3	39
There be bright faces in the busy hall	366 Lara	1	5
In windings bright and mazy like the snake	368 Lara	1	166
So wildly, spiritually bright	387 Corinth		247
There sate a lady, youthful and bright	390 Corinth		532
Lurk'd beneath his corslet bright	393 Corinth		789
His bright brown locks must now be clipp'd	401 Parisina		435
And thus he was as pure and bright	403 Chillon		86
That almost made the dungeon bright	404 Chillon		195
The bright broad river's gushing tide	412 Mazeppa		583
But bright, and long, and beckoning years	414 Mazeppa		757
And is it mortal, yon bright eye	414 Mazeppa		801
The memory bright with many a festival	419 Island	2	34

BRIGHT

Changing its hues with bright variety	423 Island	2	342
Midst whom my own bright Beatrice bless'd	456 Dante	1	11
Loved ere I knew the name of love, and bright	456 Dante	1	30
By the transparency of his bright dream	462 Dante	3	118
Conduct? shall their bright plumage on the rough	462 Dante	3	166
Of darkness, making his bright realm appear	472 Morgante		430
A bright deformity on high	480 Manfred	1	122
The lightning of my being, is as bright	480 Manfred	1	155
And thou, the bright eye of the universe	482 Manfred	1	271
Of this most bright intelligence, until	486 Manfred	2	190
The moon is rising broad, and round, and bright	487 Manfred	2	299
Shall be succeeded by a bright millennium	535 Faliero	4	505
And all which makes them eminent and bright	547 Faliero	5	657
And see the bright gems of the glittering girls	551 Sardan	1	39
And you will form a heaven as bright as theirs	551 Sardan	1	58
Is my true realm, amidst bright eyes and faces	571 Sardan	3	2
So bright, so rolling back the clouds into	587 Sardan	5	10
As ye bequeath'd it, this bright part of it	594 Sardan	5	429
Of what is visible; and yon bright star	635 Cain	1	498
Each bright and sparkling--what dost think of them	638 Cain	2	127
Had deem'd them rather the bright populace	639 Cain	2	210
Before thy bright wings worlds be driven	655 Heaven		42
More bright than those of day	656 Heaven		99
Their bright way through the parted night	656 Heaven		136
After the bright course of a few brief morrows	662 Heaven		565
Thou bright eye of the Mine! thou loadstar of	700 Werner	3	331
Bright as the Iris	724 Deformed	1	169
Blooming and bright, with golden hair, and stature	726 Deformed	1	247
Who bears the golden horn, and wears such bright	730 Deformed	1	525
This precious thing of dust--this bright Olimpia	744 Deformed	3	153
(Who does not often claim the bright reversion	746 Juan	Ded	66
Bright with intelligence, and fair, and smooth	754 Juan	1	482
Bright and immaculate, unmix'd and pure	756 Juan	1	626
By gusts, and many a sparkling hearth was bright	763 Juan	1	1075
Resting its bright base on the quivering blue	785 Juan	2	723
Bright hues when out of doors, and yet, while wave	789 Juan	2	957
Bright Phoebus, while the mountains still are wet	791 Juan	2	1109
Spread like a rosy ocean, vast and bright	797 Juan	2	1474
Of colour'd garbs, as bright as butterflies	805 Juan	3	216
Those their bright rise had lighted to such joys	818 Juan	4	122
With his broad bright, and dropping orb were gone	819 Juan	4	172
A rueful glance upon the waves (which bright all	828 Juan	4	717
Bright--and as black and burning as a coal	828 Juan	4	749
Casts off its bright skin yearly like the snake	834 Juan	5	168
''Tis true, it gets another bright and fresh	834 Juan	5	169
But every fool describes in these bright days	838 Juan	5	410
The giant door was broad, and bright, and high	842 Juan	5	681
Object on object flash'd so bright and fast	843 Juan	5	742
But o'er her bright brow flash'd a tumult strange	845 Juan	5	859
Bright with the very weakness he reproved	846 Juan	5	966
And bright as any meteor ever bred	861 Juan	6	573
Of wolves, will the bright muse withdraw one ray	868 Juan	7	54
More evil in an hour, than thirty bright	872 Juan	7	325
To their two selves, one whole bright bulletin	880 Juan	8	152
Of the bright bayonet, and they all should hurry on	888 Juan	8	622
And bright eternity without disguise	893 Juan	8	917
And brilliant breeches, bright as a Cairn Gorme	902 Juan	9	341
Yet as the consequences are as bright	922 Juan	11	267
Those bright moths fluttering round a dying flame	939 Juan	12	572
The world gave ground before her bright array	942 Juan	13	85
Sleeps from the chivalry of this bright age	946 Juan	13	350
Bright as a new Napoleon from its mintage	969 Juan	15	51
To keep our holy beacons always bright	979 Juan	15	716
He thought Aurora Raby's eyes more bright	982 Juan	16	91
Glanced, without pausing, on him a bright eye	983 Juan	16	168
Her black, bright, downcast, yet espiegle eye	989 Juan	16	561
For he had two, both tolerably bright	996 Juan	16	982

BRIGHT-BLACK

With braided hair, and bright-black eye	323 Giaour		1300

BRIGHTEN

Beyond the world they brighten, with a sigh	727 Deformed	1	337

BRIGHTEN'D

And the broad moon has brighten'd. What a stillness	528 Faliero	4	27
Brighten'd, and for a moment seem'd to roam	785 Juan	2	710

BRIGHTENING

Thy youth, in thee, thus hourly brightening	3 To Ianthe		16
The pale Moon sickens in thy brightening blaze	140 Ossian-B		7

BRIGHTER

See round thy giant base a brighter choir	14 Harold	1	649
A brighter glance her form reflected gave	32 Harold	2	763
And multiply in us a brighter ray	55 Harold	4	39
But, born beneath a brighter sun	160 Cadiz		21
To me they speak of brighter days	165 Away		5

BRIGHTER

A brighter name to lure mankind	181 Ode-A		90
Lights which ought to burn the brighter	197 Rogers		69
For him could Time unfold a brighter doom	201 Ode-C		41
With beings brighter than have been, and give	214 Dream		21
The Czar's look, I own, was much brighter and brisker	228 Moore-A		20
Where scarce a blackleg bears a brighter name	260 Hints		242
Believe him bastard of a brighter race	270 Minerva		168
But brighter traits with evil mix'd	318 Giaour		862
Where the soul glows beneath a brighter star	373 Lara	1	513
But brighter still the beam was thrown	400 Parisina		423
So shall their brighter hues contrast the glow	419 Island	2	51
As when the arm-chest held its brighter trust	425 Island	2	497
With brighter stars, and robes with deeper blue	459 Dante	2	53
No hero would in history look brighter	466 Morgante		36
Have something of the blood of brighter days	541 Faliero	5	274
Who knew no brighter gems than summer wreaths	560 Sardan	1	603
And brighter, yet less beautiful and powerful	635 Cain	1	505
In the dim twilight, brighter than yon world	637 Cain	2	125
To brighter destinies, if so she deems them	657 Heaven		176
The verge where brighter morns were wont to break	668 Heaven		1010
A brighter world than this, where thou shalt breathe	669 Heaven		1085
You have open'd brighter prospects to my eyes	727 Deformed	1	357
Our coming, and look brighter when we come	762 Juan	1	980
Or fresher, brighter; but the year gone through	834 Juan	5	170
Which still elsewhere may rouse a brighter spring	897 Juan	9	84
They can transfigure brighter than a Raphael	970 Juan	15	128
And nothing brighter gleam'd through the saloon	981 Juan	16	63

BRIGHTEST

The brightest through these parted hills hath fork'd	50 Harold	3	892
Has moments like their brightest; but the weight	63 Harold	4	464
Shine brightest as they fall from high	167 Dead		54
Its rose of whiteness with the brightest blush	175 Sonnet-B		3
The brightest or blackest, is fill'd with my fame	186 Napoleon		4
And, ah! though still the brightest of the sky	269 Minerva		85
Hath brush'd its brightest hues away	314 Giaour		407
The brightest by the better born	399 Parisina		271
Brightest in dungeons, Liberty! thou art	402 Sonnet-F		2
Yon earliest, and the brightest, which so quivers	562 Sardan	2	64
The brightest and most glorious of your life	577 Sardan	3	343
The brightest future, without the sweet past	664 Heaven		701
Beseem'd this palace in its brightest days	677 Werner	1	387
The brightest which the world e'er bore, and give thee	724 Deformed	1	138
And his aspect the brightest	728 Deformed	1	410
In whom our brightest days we would retrace	808 Juan	3	467
Warranted virgin; beauty's brightest colours	830 Juan	4	907
Who with the brightest Georgians might compare	857 Juan	6	284
Bear it, ye Muses, on your brightest wing	894 Juan	8	1004

BRIGHTLY

Now brightly bold or beautifully shy	3 To Ianthe		29
On the smooth shore the night-fires brightly blazed	30 Harold	2	631
Yon sunny sea heaves brightly, and remains	59 Harold	4	246
Too brightly on the unprepared mind	74 Harold	4	1142
Through thousand summers brightly gone	388 Corinth		367
Lightly and brightly breaks away	391 Corinth		680
Brightly it sparkles to plunderers' eyes	395 Corinth		1001
Follies trick'd out so brightly that they blind	975 Juan	15	454

BRIGHTNESS

That brightness in her eye she bore when Rome was free	67 Harold	4	738
It will not bear the brightness of the day	76 Harold	4	1286
The brightness of old to illumine our Hall	164 Newstead-C		14
Not smoke from brightness, but from darkness-- light	259 Hints		210
Henceforth in all the bronze of brightness shine	273 Waltz		5
Yet still between his Darkness and his Brightness	289 Vision		279
Around the waves' phosphoric brightness broke	346 Corsair	1	572
A moment's brightness pass'd along his brow	428 Island	3	153
And marshall'd me the way in all their brightness	567 Sardan	2	348
Has ceased, and the moon breaks forth in her brightness	573 Sardan	3	142
The brightness of our city, and her domes	598 Foscari	1	165
With the brightness of a bubble	743 Deformed	3	76
And knew such brightness was but the reflection	818 Juan	4	103

BRIGHT'NING

Was my eye, 'stead of tears, with red fury flakes bright'ning	92 Caroline-D		9
New beauties still are daily bright'ning	98 To Lesbia		30
As o'er heaven shall then be bright'ning	187 Ode-B		17

BRIG'S

The Dee, the Don, Balgounie's brig's black wall	909 Juan	10	139

BRILLIANCY

I see their brilliancy and feel their beauty	566 Sardan	2	267

BRILLIANT
The brilliant, fair, and soft,--the glories of old days	44 Harold	3	580
Its brilliant hues with all their beams unshorn	66 Harold	4	646
Seem'd stealing o'er thy brilliant cheek	152 Remind		23
Let the young and the brilliant aspire	205 Blessington		17
He rear'd his bold and brilliant throne on high	239 Conquest		6
Morn ne'er awoke them with such brilliant beams	342 Corsair	1	320
With dark but brilliant skin, and dewy eye	429 Island	3	185
That every word, as brilliant as thy skies	459 Dante	2	27
And make it broader; the same brilliant sky	461 Dante	3	65
Than the huge brilliant luminous orbs which swung	639 Cain	2	208
And brilliant breeches, bright as a Cairn Gorme	902 Juan	9	341
So brilliant, where the list of routs and dances is	928 Juan	11	627
On him the diamond pours its brilliant blaze	930 Juan	12	62
Ah, nut-brown partridges! Ah, brilliant pheasants	950 Juan	13	599
Doubtless it is a brilliant masquerade	957 Juan	14	133
With the new Venus of their brilliant ocean	962 Juan	14	436
A beauteous ripple of the brilliant stream	975 Juan	15	435
Exulting in their brilliant lucubrations	989 Juan	16	576
A brilliant diner out, though but a curate	991 Juan	16	698

BRILLIANTLY
So smoothly, bravely, brilliantly she went	431 Island	4	108

BRIM
And life's enchanted cup but sparkles near the brim	36 Harold	3	72
And fill'd his goblet to the brim	104 Alva		226
The wild-dog howls o'er the fountain's brim	313 Giaour		295
Away, away! there's blood upon the brim	484 Manfred	2	21
When o'er the brim the sparkling bumpers reach	796 Juan	2	1419
My mild and midnight beakers to the brim	823 Juan	4	423

BRIMFUL
With the dead boars and with that brimful vase	474 Morgante		518

BRIMM'D
His goblets brimm'd with every costly wine	5 Harold	1	96

BRIMSTONE
That they sent even him to his brimstone bed	178 Devil's Dr		174
Edina's brawny sons and brimstone page	256 Bards		1048
And smooth'd the brimstone of that street of hell	881 Juan	8	207

BRINE
Without a sigh he left, to cross the brine	5 Harold	1	98
Athwart the foaming brine	6 Harold	1	191
And bear these altars o'er the long-reluctant brine	21 Harold	2	99
But treasures all to hermits of the brine	416 Island	1	92
Wiped with her hair the brine from Torquil's eyes	431 Island	3	127
And laughing from my lip the audacious brine	597 Foscari	1	108

BRING
To doubtful conflict, certain slaughter bring	26 Harold	2	401
Let her bring from the chamber her many-toned lyre	30 Harold	2	675
I turn'd from all she brought to those she could not bring	40 Harold	3	270
Which is itself, no changes bring surprise	56 Harold	4	66
And slight withal may be the things which bring	58 Harold	4	202
So shall a better spring less bitter fruit bring forth	69 Harold	4	882
Peasants bring forth in safety.--Can it be	80 Harold	4	1513
Love and hope upon earth bring no more consolation	92 Caroline-D		19
Which bring together the imprudent	95 Granta		52
Bring me hemlock--since mine is ungrateful	162 Romaic-A		15
His name would bring more credit than his verse	162 Orchomenus		8
Then bring me wine, the banquet bring	166 Struggle		9
When Time, or soon or late, shall bring	166 Euthanasia		1
The glowing portraits, fresh from life, that bring	193 Monody		51
Yet if you could bring about	196 Rogers		23
Bring back with joy	200 Stanzas-B		64
'Let every other bring his own	227 Thurlow-B		17
Will bring it safe in his portmanteau	232 Murray-B		6
Or Greeks to bring upon their stages	233 Nihil		11
And what should she bring me for paper	234 Ballat		13
And Sermons to thy mill bring grist	234 Strahan		18
(Who ne'er despises books that bring him brass	264 Hints		548
Than is to bring to land a late-hook'd fish	286 Vision		116
He will return; but now, the moments bring	344 Corsair	1	452
More I must ask, and food the slaves shall bring	348 Corsair	2	101
Nor ask or what or who the sign may bring	353 Corsair	2	420
Is link'd a mirth--it doth not bring relief	353 Corsair	2	447
The vain attempt should bring but doom to both	354 Corsair	2	467
I fear that henceforth 'twill but bring disgust	354 Corsair	2	522
'"Bring forth the horse!"--the horse was brought	410 Mazeppa		358
In a soil where the mothers bring forth men	460 Dante	2	125
Hath hearts, and hands, and arms, and hosts to bring	460 Dante	2	132
Ever some bar 'gainst our intents to bring	467 Morgante		82

BRING
A stir, a motion, even a breath, would bring	482 Manfred	1	278
Would bring contempt on all authority	500 Faliero	1	35
But bring me to the knowledge of your chiefs	508 Faliero	1	576
When? where? This night I'll bring to your apartment	508 Faliero	1	579
He hath no harm; bring me my sword and cloak	533 Faliero	4	330
Bring me the golden goblet thick with gems	553 Sardan	1	206
But now I know thee. Bring down my spear too	573 Sardan	3	109
Sfero--I had forgotten--bring the mirror	573 Sardan	3	145
And bring him a new spear and his own helmet	574 Sardan	3	201
Bring me some water. 'Tis the first time in	577 Sardan	3	345
To change them, my advices bring sure tidings	586 Sardan	4	544
And bring me back, as speedily as full	590 Sardan	5	213
Bring cedar, too, and precious drugs, and spices	591 Sardan	5	278
Bring frankincense and myrrh, too, for it is	591 Sardan	5	280
With aught officious aid would bring to quell it	593 Sardan	5	361
Bring in the prisoner! Signor, you hear the order	597 Foscari	1	146
But did not; for my hope was to bring forth	599 Foscari	1	246
I bring you food. I pray you set it down	608 Foscari	3	29
To bring them up to serve the state, and die	618 Foscari	4	209
I thank you. If the tidings which you bring	618 Foscari	4	233
I feel athirst--will no one bring me here	625 Foscari	5	290
Shall they not love and bring forth things that love	633 Cain	1	365
Marry, and bring forth dust! I should have loved	655 Heaven		18
Than all our father's herds would bring if weigh'd	657 Heaven		190
Can bring no pang like this. Fly! fly	667 Heaven		942
Which could bring compensation for past sorrow	672 Werner	1	74
What brings you here? Why, what should bring me here	674 Werner	1	206
March, vassals! I'm your leader, and will bring	693 Werner	2	662
Will bring his summon'd myrmidons from Frankfort	698 Werner	3	174
Into the deep, and bring up slime and mud	699 Werner	3	266
Will bring you six boars' heads for trophies home	707 Werner	4	226
And gather wood! I will: but when I bring it	722 Deformed	1	16
But you reject him? If his form could bring me	725 Deformed	1	223
To bring one down amongst them, and set fire	735 Deformed	1	893
Ring for your valet--bid him quickly bring	797 Juan	2	1433
And if 'tis lost, life hath no more to bring	799 Juan	2	1588
And bring our hearts back to their starting-post	804 Juan	3	168
'Tis beautiful to see a matron bring	809 Juan	3	475
The reader; but 'twould not be hard to bring	814 Juan	3	870
'Tis that our nature cannot always bring	816 Juan	4	27
Years could but bring them cruel things or wrong	819 Juan	4	212
On the first foe whom Lambro's call might bring	821 Juan	4	312
A moment more will bring the sight to bear	821 Juan	4	323
And like the soil beneath it will bring forth	823 Juan	4	445
Which the West Indian market scarce would bring	831 Juan	4	914
A single cry would bring them all abroad	837 Juan	5	357
As you will see, if she you love shall bring hers	845 Juan	5	846
I should but bring disgrace upon the dyer	848 Juan	5	1068
Bring down the fruit, which still perversely clung	862 Juan	6	606
Bring the two slaves!' she said in a low tone	866 Juan	6	890
To bring the other three here was absurd	874 Juan	7	478
Will bring the other, ere the lake-like brow	908 Juan	10	59
The seventh will bring blue devils or a dun	912 Juan	10	304
Wars, revels, loves--do these bring men more ease	931 Juan	12	85
Begg'd to bring up the little girl and 'out	933 Juan	12	243
For silly wards will bring their guardians blame	935 Juan	12	332
To bring what was a jest to a serious end	978 Juan	15	630
That bring Lochaber back to eyes that roam	986 Juan	16	411

BRINGEST
Oh, Hesperus! thou bringest all good things	815 Juan	3	945

BRINGING
But bringing up the rear of this bright host	288 Vision		185
Bringing warm water, wreathing her long tresses	797 Juan	2	1455
By bringing women here? They shall be shown	876 Juan	7	555
To break the rules by bringing one's own bride	876 Juan	7	565
Of Adeline, in bringing this same lay	987 Juan	16	450

BRINGS
To me no pleasure Beauty brings	17 Harold	1	851
Of stirring branches, and the bud which brings	51 Harold	3	956
Each year brings forth its millions; but how long	61 Harold	4	347
But brings, with new torture, the curse of to-day	91 Caroline-D		4
Brings prudence back in proper season	100 Marion		26
Celestial consolation brings	131 L'Amitie		7
Ah! though the present brings but pain	133 E. N. Long		11
That brings a Lethe for despair	168 Haunts		20
And brings life near in utter nakedness	216 Dream		182
Hail, Sympathy! thy soft idea brings	246 Bards		327
Her lover brings the lemonade, she sips	448 Beppo		518
The cup which brings oblivion of a chain	454 Venice-B		87
For what he brings the nations, 'tis the furthest	561 Sardan	2	8
With the burnt offerings, which he daily brings	647 Cain	3	100
A voice of woe from Zillah brings me here	652 Cain	3	380
Where could he rest them, while the whole space brings	662 Heaven		512
What brings you here? Why, what should bring me here	674 Werner	1	206

194

BRINGS
Or any other thing that brings regret 778 Juan 2 245
But Time, which brings all beings to their level 816 Juan 4 9
She hardly knew, to such perfection brings 847 Juan 5 1022
Your slave brings tidings--he hopes not too soon 849 Juan 5 1149
And why?--because it brings self-approbation 878 Juan 8 25
As 'Auld Lang Syne' brings Scotland, one and all 909 Juan 10 137
Care, like a housekeeper, brings every week 912 Juan 10 301
And this reflection brings me to plain physics 939 Juan 12 573
Treating a topic which, alas! but brings 980 Juan 15 782
Or like an opiate, which brings troubled rest 981 Juan 16 73

BRING'ST
Thou bring'st the child, too, to the mother's
  breast 815 Juan 3 952

BRINK
That keeps us from yon heaven which woos us to
  its brink 37 Harold 3 126
Walks by thy brink, and there perchance recalls 198 Po 3
That we so tremble on the brink 217 High World 10
As I gasp'd upon the brink 230 My Boat 14
The dullest, fattest weeds on Lethe's brink 267 Hints 756
But to the point; while hovering o'er the brink 295 Vision 684
Along the brink at Twilight's close 313 Giaour 317
There he might rest--but on Destruction's brink 345 Corsair 1 514
Between me and the eternal brink 404 Chillon 216
And cheering from my dungeon's brink 405 Chillon 277
And to the fountain's brink precisely pours 473 Morgante 495
I stand, and on the torrent's brink beneath 482 Manfred 1 275
Of him who made you, stand not on that brink 483 Manfred 1 363
Stands plotting on the brink of their pure graves 520 Faliero 3 101
As on the river's brink. Not so; these walls 570 Sardan 2 562
The wall which skirted near the river's brink 590 Sardan 5 189
The river's brink is too remote, its stream 593 Sardan 5 388
The brink, thou feel'st an inward shrinking from 594 Sardan 5 414
With tenderness--stood howling on the brink 781 Juan 2 460
So narrow as to shame their wintry brink 908 Juan 10 51
And yet 'tis very puzzling on the brink 910 Juan 10 158
Had kept him from the brink of Hippocrene 924 Juan 11 407
Saloon, room, hall, o'erflow beyond their brink 926 Juan 11 533
The woods sloped downwards to its brink, and
  stood 948 Juan 13 455
As e'er brought man and woman to the brink 968 Juan 14 795

BRINSLEY
Ere Garrick fled, or Brinsley ceased to write 170 Address-A 43

BRISK
Wakes the brisk harmony that sailors love 22 Harold 2 186
Brisk Confidence still best with woman copes 24 Harold 2 305
When some brisk youth, the tenant of a stall 252 Bards 765
And brisk Thalia takes a serious tone 258 Hints 130
As are the billows when the breeze is brisk 853 Juan 6 22

BRISKER
The Czar's look, I own, was much brighter and
  brisker 228 Moore-A 20

BRISKLY
Further, old Baba rather briskly enter'd 849 Juan 5 1144
Were briskly fired and answer'd in due order 872 Juan 7 304
Had set to work as briskly as their brothers 880 Juan 8 116

BRISSOT
Barnave, Brissot, Condorcet, Mirabeau 747 Juan 1 17

BRISTLING
The bristling palisade, the fosse o'erflow'd 12 Harold 1 535
His bristling locks of sable, brow of gloom 369 Lara 1 197
Upon the courser's bristling mane 411 Mazeppa 445
No sullen ship lay bristling o'er the foam 435 Island 4 403
That peep'd up bristling through his serpent hair 579 Sardan 4 91
Look upon the bristling wall 735 Deformed 2 27
Rose over the town's right side, in bristling
  tier 868 Juan 7 95
Along the leaguer'd wall and bristling bank 878 Juan 7 684
When up the bristling Moslem rose at last 879 Juan 8 51

BRISTOL
Though Bristol bloat him with the verdant fat 247 Bards 394
Without high heels, white plume, and Bristol
  stone 262 Hints 444

BRISTOWA'S
Boeotian Cottle, rich Bristowa's boast 247 Bards 387

BRITAIN
And laid the scene of love in Britain 101 Lady-B 24
Thou cutt'st thy throat that Britain may be saved 238 Epigrams 4
While grateful Britain yields the praise she owes 248 Bards 520
And Britain fall, the bulwark of the world 255 Bards 1006
Then, hapless Britain! be thy rulers blest 255 Bards 1011
And happy Britain, wealth, and Freedom's smiles 305 Age 531

BRITAIN
Another Babel soars--but Britain ends 307 Age 649
More wealth than Britain ever had to lose 307 Age 663
How rich is Britain! not indeed in mines 307 Age 668
No place that's call'd 'Piazza' in Great Britain 440 Beppo 40
Though Britain owes (and pays you too) so much 896 Juan 9 17
Renown'd for ruining Great Britain gratis 897 Juan 9 64
Great Britain, which the Muse may penetrate 932 Juan 12 190
In Britain--which of course true patriots find 941 Juan 13 15
If Britain mourn her bleakness, we can tell her 950 Juan 13 607

BRITAIN'S
He, too, is fall'n, who Britain's loss supplied 114 Death-A 21
Fox shall in Britain's future annals shine 114 Death-A 33
The clouds of anarchy from Britain's skies 121 Newstead-A 102
When Britain's 'May is in the sere 164 Friend-B 46
As ever Britain's Annals knew 197 Duel 17
And Britain's bravest victor was the last 239 Conquest 8
On Britain's sons and bless our genial isle 252 Bards 788
'Daughter of Jove! in Britain's injured name 270 Minerva 125
Europe's worst dauber, and poor Britain's best 270 Minerva 176
Late majesty of Britain's case with you 293 Vision 510
And blazon Britain's thousand glories higher 417 Island 1 162
Briton no more, had once been Britain's still 434 Island 4 288
I recollect Great Britain's coast looks white 775 Juan 2 93
Of Britain's youth depends upon their weight 885 Juan 8 436
Of Britain's present wealth and happiness 944 Juan 13 232

BRITANNIA
Britannia sickens, Cintra! at thy name 8 Harold 1 307
The ocean queen, the free Britannia, bears 21 Harold 2 113
Britannia must prosper with councils like yours 225 Ode-D 2

BRITANNIA'S
Boast of thy country and Britannia's guide 248 Bards 501
To do what oft Britannia's self had done 271 Minerva 212
Nelson was once Britannia's god of war 747 Juan 1 25

BRITISH
Oh, dome displeasing unto British eye 8 Harold 1 289
What! shall it e'er be said by British tongue 21 Harold 2 109
By British hands, which it had best behoved 21 Harold 2 131
And call'd, proud boast! the British drama forth 94 Dorset 68
Of northern climes and British ladies 159 Cadiz 2
'O British poesy, whose powers inspire 171 Address-B 27
While British critics suffer scenes like these 249 Bards 567
When such a word contents a British bard 262 Hints 416
Our British Commons sometimes deign to 'hear 304 Age 490
I've bribed my grandmother's review--the British 772 Juan 1 1672
A wanderer from the British world of fashion 795 Juan 2 1322
Our British friend, 'these are the wives of
  others 876 Juan 7 562
Between the British cabinet and Russian 913 Juan 10 355
And yet the British 'Damme''s rather Attic 923 Juan 11 337
And beg his British godship's humble pardon 964 Juan 14 596

BRITON
True Briton all beside, I here am French 260 Hints 271
Proclaims thee Briton, once a noble name 269 Minerva 90
A true-born Briton may the deed disclaim 270 Minerva 126
From a bold Briton in her wonted praise 305 Age 529
Briton no more, had once been Britain's still 434 Island 4 288
The Briton must be bold who really durst 884 Juan 8 381
At the first blush; for a fair Briton hides 939 Juan 12 587

BRITONS
Conquest and Fame: but Britons rarely swerve 22 Harold 2 170
Britons our judges, Nature for our guide 170 Address-A 72
Degenerate Britons! are ye dead to shame 250 Bards 610
And modern Britons glory in their sires 255 Bards 990
Which Britons deem their 'uti possidetis 913 Juan 10 360
Bold Britons, we are now on Shooter's Hill 917 Juan 10 640
Because bold Britons have a tongue and free quill 943 Juan 13 157

BRITON'S
A terrier, too, which once had been a Briton's 803 Juan 3 140
To patriot sympathy a Briton's blushes 959 Juan 14 276

BRITTLE
Long to adore such brittle toys 143 To--A 14
Is Fame like his so brittle 225 Plays 3
She deem'd the window-frames and shutters brittle 443 Beppo 229
But as they had but one oar, and that brittle 782 Juan 2 551
Could stir his pulse, or make his faith feel
  brittle 828 Juan 4 759
What speaks of Heaven should by no means be
  brittle 839 Juan 5 467

BROAD
Till the broad sun withdraws his lessening ray 22 Harold 2 173
To the broad column which rolls on, and shows 65 Harold 4 631
The Tiber winds, and the broad ocean laves 81 Harold 4 1560
His waist was bound with a broad belt round 104 Alva 257
Wafted on Time's broad pinion, yours is fame 110 Nisus 402

BROAD

Yes, I will hope that Time's broad wing	133	E. N. Long	27
To cross thy stream, broad Hellespont	160	Swimming	4
In dreams that day's broad light can not remove	217	The Harp	20
In one broad glance the soul beholds	220	Clay	15
In broad St. Gile's or in Tottenham-road	251	Bards	710
In vain will Italy's broad sun awaken	301	Age	197
Thine own 'broad Hellespont' still dashes	329	Abydos 2	36
Of Otho's lands and Lara's broad domain	383	Lara 2	557
And o'er that fair broad brow were wrought	402	Parisina	539
The bright broad river's gushing tide	412	Mazeppa	583
My courser's broad breast proudly braves	412	Mazeppa	590
The arctic sun rose broad above the wave	418	Island 1	169
Broad as the cloud along the horizon flings	422	Island 2	225
The broad sun set, but not with lingering sweep	424	Island 2	360
For the broad bosom of his nursing wave	424	Island 2	411
The musket swung behind his shoulders broad	425	Island 2	488
Which flings it broad and boiling sheet on sheet	429	Island 3	177
With its broad leaf, or turtle-shell which bore	432	Island 4	171
Bent its broad arch: her breath began to fail	435	Island 4	378
His bounding nereid over the broad sea	435	Island 4	392
The moon is rising broad, and round, and bright	487	Manfred 2	299
Be broad upon the Adriatic, there	528	Faliero 3	647
And the broad moon has brighten'd. What a stillness	528	Faliero 4	27
Like altars ranged along the broad canal	529	Faliero 4	79
A cooling breeze which crisps the broad clear river	551	Sardan 1	53
Can see a smile, unless in some broad banquet's	558	Sardan 1	486
As the light breeze of midnight crisps the broad	566	Sardan 2	257
And the foe too; and in the moon's broad light	574	Sardan 3	204
And the broad fillet which crowns both. Ye gods	574	Sardan 3	208
The river's broad and swoln, and umcommanded	591	Sardan 5	262
Broad eminence I was invested duke	624	Foscari 5	242
Of the broad sun which ripen'd them, may seem	650	Cain 3	262
Day's broad orb drop behind its head at even	659	Heaven	293
While man shall long in vain for his broad wings	662	Heaven	510
Of his broad lands as to make mine the foremost	689	Werner 2	391
More high, if not so broad as that of others	722	Deformed 1	7
What's here? whose broad brow and whose curly beard	725	Deformed 1	230
They pass'd the broad Po	732	Deformed 1	694
Wax'd broad and waving, like a banner free	785	Juan 2	726
With cliffs above, and a broad sandy shore	796	Juan 2	1410
Whence the broad moon rose circling into sight	797	Juan 2	1476
Would break your shield, however broad	813	Juan 3	772
With his broad, bright, and dropping orb were gone	819	Juan 4	172
The giant door was broad, and bright, and high	842	Juan 5	681
If rather broad, made stocks rise and their holders	903	Juan 9	416
The earth, as scarce the eagle in the broad	917	Juan 10	619
His host, with broad arms 'gainst the thunder-stroke	948	Juan 13	444
Broad as transparent, deep, and freshly fed	948	Juan 13	450

BROADCLOTH

Horse by a blackleg, broadcloth by a tailor	834	Juan 5	207

BROADENING

Broadening to grins, he colour'd more than once	992	Juan 16	747

BROADER

Scarce broader than my dungeon floor	406	Chillon	345
The stars from broader beams began to creep	415	Island 1	11
And make it broader; the same brilliant sky	461	Dante 3	65
Speed, for the day grows broader. Send me soon	535	Faliero 4	477

BROADLY

Whose breast of waters broadly swells	43	Harold 3	498
Of ours, although they propagate more broadly	972	Juan 15	286

BROADSIDE

Before they give their broadside. By and by	918	Juan 10	666

BROGUED

There Paddy brogued 'By Jasus!'--'What's your wull	292	Vision	467

BROIL

He died too in the battle broil	321	Giaour	1080
Long war without and frequent broil within	377	Lara 2	161
What has occurred, some rash and sudden broil	530	Faliero 4	142
A foreign foe invade, or civil broil	552	Sardan 1	125

BROILING

And when--To be sure it was broiling; but then	281	Blues 2	36
His gains repay his broiling brow	331	Abydos 2	259
So that her female friends, with envy broiling	448	Beppo	547
But will keep baking, broiling, burning on	754	Juan	500

BROKE

That his frail bonds to fleeting life are broke	27	Harold 2	474
Broke by the share of every rustic plough	33	Harold 2	807

BROKE

Nearest to Heaven's, broke o'er a father's grave	45	Harold 3	629
His hand, but broke his scythe, there is a power	74	Harold 4	1158
Old in the world, though scarcely broke from school	100	Damaetas	8
This aged heart was almost broke	104	Alva	208
What though we never silence broke	112	Quaker	13
When lightning broke the gloom	158	Storm	10
The spell is broke, the charm is flown	159	Spell	1
And all her chains are broke	162	War Song	12
The chain is broke, the music mute	169	The Chain	13
Chain'd by the trunk he vainly broke	180	Ode-A	48
And thy light broke on human eyes	188	On Star	11
And broke the die--in moulding Sheridan	194	Monody	118
Broke it no more	201	Ode-C	54
Of the Ionian waters broke a dread	205	Aristomenes	3
And the idols are broke in the temple of Baal	222	Sennacherib	22
Broke out of bounds o'er the ethereal blue	285	Vision	14
And realised the phrase of 'hell broke loose	292	Vision	464
The very fetters which his arm broke through	301	Age	257
The spirit to its bondage broke	311	Giaour	162
The faithless slave that broke her bower	315	Giaour	535
I on Zuleika's slumber broke	324	Abydos 1	65
No word from Selim's bosom broke	326	Abydos 1	253
My thraldom for a season broke	332	Abydos 2	340
And day broke dreary on my troubled view	343	Corsair 1	382
Why--thou wert worse than he who broke his vow	344	Corsair 1	441
Around the waves' phosphoric brightness broke	346	Corsair 1	572
But still from room to room his way he broke	350	Corsair 2	214
That ne'er till now so broke upon his sleep	359	Corsair 3	251
Broke from within, and all was night around	364	Corsair 3	582
Those strange wild accents; his the cry that broke	370	Lara 1	276
From his large eye no flashing anger broke	373	Lara 1	493
True, in his words it broke not from his breast	374	Lara 1	582
And from his eye the gladiator broke	378	Lara 2	263
So sad, so deep, and hesitating broke	381	Lara 2	458
He heard a tramp--a horse and horseman broke	383	Lara 2	558
And ere that faithless truce was broke	386	Corinth	222
The camels from their keepers broke	396	Corinth	1061
Save the few which from him broke	401	Parisina	473
A light broke in upon my brain	405	Chillon	251
Or broke its cage to perch on mine	405	Chillon	280
And on the thought my words broke forth	409	Mazeppa	275
The waters broke my hollow trance	412	Mazeppa	587
In masses broke into the light	413	Mazeppa	612
His feverish lips thus broke their gloomy spell	418	Island 1	163
Broke the luxurious silence of the skies	420	Island 2	104
A human figure broke the solitude	425	Island 2	461
You with his monks so oft have broke the peace	470	Morgante	245
Not with my hand, but heart--which broke her heart	486	Manfred 2	212
I broke through his slumbers	488	Manfred 2	318
You never broke their bread, nor shared their salt	527	Faliero 3	580
The realms he wasted, and the hearts he broke	554	Sardan 1	219
For those who almost broke thee? Let him rest	596	Foscari 1	67
The foam which broke around me, and pursued	597	Foscari 1	120
Broke forth in a slight shuddering, though rarely	601	Foscari 1	358
When his distracted wife broke through into	601	Foscari 1	365
The hearts which broke in silence of that parting	610	Foscari 3	171
All bonds I break between us, as he broke	652	Cain 3	410
God said unto him, 'Shine!' and he broke forth	662	Heaven	553
Until at length the smother'd fire broke out	750	Juan 1	207
When you broke in upon us with your fellows	766	Juan 1	1243
Day has not broke--there's no one in the street	769	Juan 1	1456
Burglariously broke his coffin's lid	773	Juan 1	1750
New broke, a cameleopard, a gazelle	774	Juan 2	42
A squall came on, and while some guns broke loose	777	Juan 2	238
Day broke, and the wind lull'd: the masts were gone	778	Juan 2	298
As morning broke, the light wind died away	786	Juan 2	769
The morn broke, and found Juan slumbering still	791	Juan 2	1089
Not yet a dreamer, till the spell is broke	793	Juan 2	1211
Each hour to drown her, yet she could not die	820	Juan 4	248
As on the beach the waves at last are broke	830	Juan 4	845
Broke foaming o'er the blue Symplegades	831	Juan 5	34
And then her sex's shame broke in at last	848	Juan 5	1091
To lodge there when a war broke out, according	850	Juan 5	1202
Like birds, or boys, or bedlamites broke loose	856	Juan 6	266
Not all the clamour broke her happy state	861	Juan 6	581
That broke for nothing on their sleeping ear	862	Juan 6	628
Within these walls to be broke in upon	862	Juan 6	642
Was shown, and some more noble heart broke through	894	Juan 8	986
Of some alchymic furnace, from whence broke	918	Juan 10	659
As thunder'd knockers broke the long seal'd spell	922	Juan 11	227
What time he chose for dress, and broke his fast	954	Juan 13	823
He broke, 'tis true, some statutes of the laws	959	Juan 14	261
Then broke his packet, to see what was in't	964	Juan 14	549
To indicate a Cupidon broke loose	969	Juan 15	94
Broke in upon me by the Black Friar of late	985	Juan 16	276
True, she said little--'twas the rest that broke	994	Juan 16	873

BROKEN

The broken tools, that tyrants cast away	11 Harold	1	453
The mountain-howitzer, the broken road	12 Harold	1	534
Look on its broken arch, its ruin'd wall	20 Harold	2	46
That strict restraint, which, broken, ever balks	22 Harold	2	169
The flying Mede, his shaftless broken bow	33 Harold	2	846
He wears the shatter'd links of the world's broken chain	38 Harold	3	162
Have all been borne, and broken by the accord	38 Harold	3	177
Even as a broken mirror, which the glass	40 Harold	3	289
Broken and trembling to the yoke she bore	48 Harold	3	767
With desolation, and a broken claim	53 Harold	3	1088
Their sceptre broken, and their sword in rust	57 Harold	4	131
O'er steps of broken thrones and temples, Ye	66 Harold	4	700
Tay trumpet voice, though broken now and dying	69 Harold	4	876
A faith whose martyrs are the broken heart	73 Harold	4	1083
would speak in sighs: faint and broken are	130 Calmar		92
For then my peace had not been broken	134 Lady-D		4
As gleams the moonbeam through the broken cloud	139 Ossian-A		31
Thy vows are all broken	151 When We		13
While wand'ring through each broken path	158 Storm		33
And thou recall'st the broken vow	174 Revanche		11
And the best thing he saw was a broken bridge	176 Devil's Dr		55
While the broken line enlarging	188 Ode-B		67
Be broken--thine will never break	210 Augusta-A		38
Weep for the harp of Judah's broken shell	217 Weep-B		3
That the frames of the fools may be first to be broken	226 Ode-D		31
Of Glass to be broken	239 Bray		40
With broken lyre and cheek serenely pale	247 Bards		418
Her helm was dinted, and the broken lance	269 Minerva		81
What shall return?--the conqueror's broken car	301 Age		200
Find joy within her broken bower	314 Giaour		415
Small broken crags of granite gray	315 Giaour		562
This broken tale was all we knew	323 Giaour		1333
A broken torch, an oarless boat	335 Abydos	2	592
Peace to thy broken heart and virgin grave	336 Abydos	2	640
To lips whose broken sighs such fragrance fling	363 Corsair	3	553
They find on shore a seaboat's broken chain	365 Corsair	3	685
Lure on the broken brigands to their fate	379 Lara	2	289
And fain would wake, in souls too broken	388 Corinth		384
So well had they broken a lingering fast	389 Corinth		464
Strew'd the earth like broken glass	392 Corinth		732
With broken swords and helms o'erthrown	395 Corinth		972
And listen'd to each broken word	397 Parisina		82
Those ties are broken--not by me	398 Parisina		205
Her broken heart, my sever'd head	399 Parisina		248
Was broken in this fatal place	404 Chillon		218
But so it was:--my broken chain	405 Chillon		304
O'er channell'd rock and broken bush	406 Chillon		338
Restrain'd them longer than their broken law	416 Island	1	78
And injured navies urge their broken laws	418 Island	1	204
Till now, when she has forged her broken chain	427 Island	3	57
Love's broken murmur and more broken sigh	433 Island	4	230
A limb was broken, and he droop'd along	434 Island	4	327
With this last bruise upon a broken reed	437 Tasso		42
Elopements, broken vows and hearts and heads	442 Beppo		128
(A broken Dandy lately on my travels	446 Beppo		410
But, for the bells, you've broken them, I wot	474 Morgante		578
By the power which hath broken	490 Manfred	2	476
And some of wither'd or of broken hearts	493 Manfred	3	145
The trees which grew along the broken arches	495 Manfred	3	272
As with a spell. It shall be broken soon	517 Faliero	2	632
Playthings, to do their pleasure--and be broken	525 Faliero	3	497
The day at last has broken. What a night	587 Sardan	5	1
Your hand; this broken weapon but prolongs	589 Sardan	5	128
As threads which may be broken at her pleasure	611 Foscari	3	195
He has seen his son's half broken, and, except	615 Foscari	4	5
A broken corse upon the barren Lido	617 Foscari	4	132
You bore this goblet, and it is not broken	625 Foscari	5	297
The untrodden forest, only broken by	658 Heaven		221
The fountains of the great deep shall be broken	661 Heaven		490
Of the old man's death, whose heart was broken by it	684 Werner	2	112
Ambition was my idol, which was broken	773 Juan	1	1729
Some broken planks, and oars, that to the touch	790 Juan	2	1052
Was broken words, they thought a language there	798 Juan	2	1508
He hers, until they end in broken gasps	798 Juan	2	1550
The heart--which may be broken: happy they	817 Juan	4	81
A broken pillar, not uncouthly hewn	829 Juan	4	821
To teach him greater, had his own leg broken	879 Juan	8	88
Warm bout are broken into their new tricks	881 Juan	8	175
Broken in carriages, and all the phantasies	928 Juan	11	629
When once you have broken their confounded ice	946 Juan	13	304
Nor broken my own head, nor that of Priscian	971 Juan	15	190

BROKEN-HEARTED

That they can meet no more, though broken-hearted	49 Harold	3	881
Half broken-hearted	151 When We		3
Feel broken-hearted	199 Stanzas-B		17
Now he is mine--my broken-hearted boy	618 Foscari	4	206
And lived, as did the broken-hearted fair	937 Juan	12	487

BROKEN-KNEED

And as his speech grew still more broken-kneed	864 Juan	6	806

BROKENLY

And thus the heart will break, yet brokenly live on	40 Harold	3	288

BROKENNESS

In helpless, hopeless, brokenness of heart	365 Corsair	3	655
In quicken'd brokenness that came	401 Parisina		525

BROKER

The banker--broker--baron--brethren, speed	307 Age		678

BROKERS

And the world trembles to bid brokers break	307 Age		667

BRONZE

Henceforth in all the bronze of brightness shine	273 Waltz		5
From the rich peasant cheek of ruddy bronze	445 Beppo		354
Venetian (who see few steeds save of bronze	612 Foscari	3	292
Of gilded bronze, and carved in curious guise	842 Juan	5	682

BRONZED

Bronzed o'er some lean and stoic anchorite	950 Juan	13	572

BROOD

Where Desolation plants her famish'd brood	11 Harold	1	483
Of Wahab's rebel brood, who dared divest	31 Harold	2	733
Of former sovereigns, and the antique brood	60 Harold	4	310
And brood in secret o'er those hours of joy	127 Recoll		373
Than nurse the earth-worm's slimy brood	154 Skull		10
Like the great Father of the giant brood	161 Athos		5
And goblin brats, of Gilpin Horner's brood	244 Bards		157
A coward brood, which mangle as they prey	247 Bards		430
No! though contempt hath mark'd the spurious brood	252 Bards		813
If one with wit the parent brood disgrace	270 Minerva		167
''Tis true, they are a lawless brood	332 Abydos	2	363
And shown their rashness to that erring brood	379 Lara	2	295
Who rears on its bare breast her callow brood	430 Island	4	17
One Passamont was foremost of the brood	468 Morgante		157
Her callow brood. What letters are these which	608 Foscari	3	14
Till he himself shall brood in it alone	613 Foscari	3	339

BROODED

He had seen battle, he had brooded lone	361 Corsair	3	418
His mind the more o'er this its mystery brooded	768 Juan	1	1414

BROODING

While brooding in thy prison'd rage	181 Ode-A		129
Of darkly brooding thoughts. My fancy is	504 Faliero	1	312
Brooding with him in mutual hate and fear	526 Faliero	3	500
To the young bird the parent's brooding wings	815 Juan	3	947
And sedges, brooding in their liquid bed	948 Juan	13	454

BROODS

The Mind, that broods o'er guilty woes	314 Giaour		422
But broods within his cell alone	318 Giaour		806
Within whose bosom infant Bacchus broods	422 Island	2	255
How lonely every freeborn creature broods	820 Juan	4	221
Just at the very time when he least broods	823 Juan	4	405

BROOK

And scarce a name distinguisheth the brook	9 Harold	1	370
And shining in the brawling brook, where-by	60 Harold	4	290
Lay where their roots are; but a brook hath ta'en	65 Harold	4	581
Or even the piping cry of lips that brook	77 Harold	4	1337
Had taught my bosom how to brook	165 Thyrza		11
There is an eye which could not brook	167 Dead		8
And teach it what to brave or brook	209 Augusta-A		22
The harp I yet can brook to hear	218 Soul-B		2
The clear purple babbling through the goodly plain	257 Hints		26
Should brook such stranger's further stay	318 Giaour		819
Nor 'scape the glance they scarce can brook	318 Giaour		845
So widely spread, few bosoms well could brook	372 Lara	1	419
His resting-place the bank that curbs the brook	374 Lara	1	549
But murmur'd meekly as the brook	387 Corinth		255
But he better could brook to behold the dying	389 Corinth		481
Those eyes which would not brook such blind	401 Parisina		447
In life when others could not brook to dream	484 Manfred	2	78
Could brook the alliance; and could ne'er be brought	684 Werner	2	99
I will not brook a human voice--scarce dare	690 Werner	2	460
However--but in friendship. I will brook	693 Werner	2	645
My soul might brook to open it more widely	695 Werner	3	26
Of such a follower, but will brook no leader	736 Deformed	2	125
And would not brook at all this sort of thing	772 Juan	1	1695
And Haidee's sweet lips murmur'd like a brook	820 Juan	4	230
With the blood running like a little brook	822 Juan	4	390
To brook a ruffled rose-leaf by his side	863 Juan	6	708
As for a brook to cope with ocean's flood	877 Juan	7	639
Kill a man's family, and he may brook it	917 Juan	10	631
To quaff a brook which murmur'd like a bird	948 Juan	13	448
But such small licences must lovers brook	960 Juan	14	339
Or what his consort did: if he could brook	961 Juan	14	357

BROOK'D

And Passion's host, that never brook'd control	20 Harold	2	52
Yet well thy soul hath brook'd the turning tide	41 Harold	3	343
Ill brook'd high Lara scrutiny like this	371 Lara	1	404
A spirit deep that brook'd not to be chid;	374 Lara	1	559
But that wild tale she brook'd not to unfold	382 Lara	2	538
He was not one who brook'd delay	398 Parisina		132
And though her dignity brook'd no complaining	913 Juan	10	374
He neither brook'd nor claim'd superiority	970 Juan	15	120
For there are few things by mankind less brook'd	974 Juan	15	420
Was great, because his master brook'd no less	984 Juan	16	223
Being wan and worn, with eyes that hardly brook'd	998 Juan	17	108

BROOKS

Love brooks not a degraded throne	200 Stanzas-B		45
In happy childhood; trees, and flowers, and brooks	211 Augusta-C		50
What brooks it now to ponder upon this	539 Faliero	5	129
Young Juan wander'd by the glassy brooks	757 Juan	1	713

BROOK'S

Nor pause at the brook's side to drink	730 Deformed	1	556

BROOM'S

A legal broom's a moral chimney-sweeper	909 Juan	10	113

BROOMSTICKS

New white-sticks, gold-sticks, broomsticks, all new sticks	276 Waltz		174

BROTH
(See also VIPER-BROTH)

They made a most superior mess of broth	789 Juan	2	981
But Juan was quite 'a broth of a boy	881 Juan	8	185
As between English beef and Spartan broth	991 Juan	16	719

BROTHEL

His brothel, and his beer	177 Devil's Dr		100

BROTHER
(See also FOSTER-BROTHER)

(For one who hath no friend, no brother there	10 Harold	1	433
Nor Oscar nor his brother came	102 Alva		100
'And is it thus a brother hails	104 Alva		241
Hence, let us haste!'--their brother guards arose	106 Nisus		81
What brother springs a brother's love to seek	125 Recoll		225
Yet doom his brother to expire	132 Prayer		26
The love which you felt was the love of a brother	136 Delawarr		3
At once a brother and a son	150 My Son		28
He was your brother--bear his ashes hence	194 Monody		108
Even as a brother--but no more; 'twas much	214 Dream		64
And take for pet a brother fowl	226 Dallas		5
And every brother rake will smile to see	251 Bards		699
Bloomfield! why not on brother Nathan too	252 Bards		782
And brother Coleridge lull the babe at nurse	254 Bards		918
Accord with brother, sire, or stranger guest	263 Hints		498
Was sure he was his mother's cousin's brother	294 Vision		608
To hail their brother, Vich Ian Alderman	308 Age		770
Zuleika! I am not thy brother	330 Abydos	2	164
'Oh! not my brother!--yet unsay	330 Abydos	2	165
That brother wrought a brother's fall	331 Abydos	2	199
Each brother led a separate band	331 Abydos	2	231
'Oh! fly--no more--yet now my more than brother	334 Abydos	2	502
This said, his brother Pirate's hand he wrung	346 Corsair	1	569
Since first Timoleon's brother fell	385 Corinth		59
When my last brother droop'd and died	403 Chillon		46
I said my nearer brother pined	404 Chillon		126
Torquil, my boy! what cheer! Ho! brother, ho	425 Island	2	431
Rough as a bear, but willing as a brother	428 Island	3	104
Thy brother hates--but I can not detest	438 Tasso		109
Go! tell thy brother, that my heart, untamed	439 Tasso		231
The faction Chief is but the Sultan's brother	465 Dante	4	126
As to a brother dear I speak alone	469 Morgante		222
Saying, 'My brother, so devout and good	471 Morgante		367
Orlando, like a worthy brother, said	473 Morgante		482
Six hours ago, and now thy brother rebel	520 Faliero	3	80
That thou wouldst add a brother to our cause	521 Faliero	3	207
To take his choice--as brother, or as victim	522 Faliero	3	241
He hath wrong'd my sister, still he is my brother	550 Sardan	1	2
Who answers? How now, brother? The queen's brother	551 Sardan	1	79
Which said thou wouldst not leave me. Sire! your brother	552 Sardan	1	86
His consort's brother, minion of Ionia	552 Sardan	1	87
Thou wilt lose both, and both for ever! Brother	552 Sardan	1	105
Humanise thee: my surly, chiding brother	554 Sardan	1	230
The queen is silent. And why not her brother	554 Sardan	1	270
Even in the chase. Hast ever seen them, brother	556 Sardan	1	367
Against his foes. And now against his brother	565 Sardan	2	203
You must have been deceived, my brother. First	565 Sardan	2	209
Give him his sword. My lord, and king, and brother	565 Sardan	2	248

BROTHER

My brother, my best subject, better prince	569 Sardan	2	487
And, prithee, think more gently of thy brother	570 Sardan	2	517
Is the chief victor? where's the king? Here, brother	576 Sardan	3	329
Know'st thou, my brother, where I lighted on	577 Sardan	3	376
With my stern brother? I shall soon be jealous	578 Sardan	3	425
Look like thy brother, Death,--so still--so stirless	578 Sardan	4	6
Yes, brother, and I would I had not slept	581 Sardan	4	174
I pray thee, brother, leave me. Since you ask it	582 Sardan	4	234
Nor hands; but I gave both. Your brother said	582 Sardan	4	251
A brother I have injured--children whom	583 Sardan	4	305
Inhuman brother! wilt thou thus weigh out	583 Sardan	4	360
Here when I had remann'd myself. My brother	584 Sardan	4	403
Man may despoil his brother man of all	586 Sardan	4	524
The fight goes. My best brother! And the battle	589 Sardan	5	132
Receive a token from your dying brother	589 Sardan	5	137
But fatal. Oh, my brother! I would give	589 Sardan	5	148
The admiral, his brother, say as much	605 Foscari	2	208
And do as he doth. Wilt thou not, my brother	628 Cain	1	52
Precede me, brother--I will follow shortly	628 Cain	1	59
Be on your spirit, brother! And this is	628 Cain	1	64
Of an eternal curse; my brother is	630 Cain	1	179
Although my brother Abel oft implores	632 Cain	1	309
I will. My brother, I have come for thee	632 Cain	1	332
Must not my daughter love her brother Enoch	633 Cain	1	363
When I think how soon I shall see my brother	634 Cain	1	472
His brother, and our children, and our parents	634 Cain	1	473
Spirit, I have said it. Cain! my brother! Cain	636 Cain	1	559
But for thy sons and brother? Let them share it	639 Cain	2	232
With me, their sire and brother! What else is	639 Cain	2	233
You think so, being not her brother. Mortal	643 Cain	2	473
And I thee who lov'st nothing. And thy brother	644 Cain	2	543
Sufficiently to see they love your brother	644 Cain	2	557
Art thou not Abel's brother? We are brethren	644 Cain	2	588
Have I not thee, our boy, our sire, and brother	646 Cain	3	41
Two altars, which our brother Abel made	647 Cain	3	96
But bless him ne'er the less. Our brother comes	648 Cain	3	161
Thy brother Abel. Welcome, Cain! My brother	648 Cain	3	162
Term him! your words are strange to-day, my brother	648 Cain	3	171
At least, without me. Brother, I should ill	649 Cain	3	195
My brother, as the elder, offer first	649 Cain	3	220
Oh, brother, pray! Jehovah's wroth with thee	650 Cain	3	280
Brother, give back! thou shalt not touch my altar	650 Cain	3	305
Since he loves lives. What hast thou done, my brother	651 Cain	3	317
Brother! Oh, God! receive thy servant, and	651 Cain	3	318
Cain? Can it be that I am he? My brother	651 Cain	3	323
Comfort poor Zillah:--she has but one brother	651 Cain	3	335
What shall I say to him?--My brother! No	651 Cain	3	353
Dost thou there, brother? Doth he sleep? Oh, heav'n	651 Cain	3	360
My brother to his cold and still embrace	652 Cain	3	375
Curse him not, mother, for he is my brother	652 Cain	3	406
And my betroth'd. He hath left thee no brother	652 Cain	3	407
As he did by his brother! May the swords	652 Cain	3	425
Where is thy brother Abel? Am I then	653 Cain	3	468
As yet unpeopled? Thou hast slain thy brother	653 Cain	3	484
A dreary, and an early doom, my brother	654 Cain	3	545
Where is his brother Japhet? He went forth	658 Heaven		243
Beside the lamb, as though he were his brother	661 Heaven		445
Our brother Satan fell; his burning will	666 Heaven		832
As if he were my brother? I have ta'en	711 Werner	4	445
Trembled in his who slew her brother. So	726 Deformed	1	279
Who warr'd with his brother	732 Deformed	1	734
Of a people without brother	735 Deformed	2	52
Priam's offspring loved their brother	736 Deformed	2	73
Shed Rome's blood, he was your brother	736 Deformed	2	108
To all the brother tars who may have need hence	777 Juan	2	229
Without even the incumbrance of a brother	796 Juan	2	1397
And mother, brother, guardian, she had none	797 Juan	2	1451
Which mix'd all feelings, friend, child, lover, brother	819 Juan	4	203
His lately bowstrung brother caused his rise	850 Juan	5	1172
Who wish'd they had a brother just like her	857 Juan	6	310
Inform'd him that he had a little brother	911 Juan	10	254
Nor brother, father, sister, daughter love	914 Juan	10	418
Perhaps you'll have a visit from the brother	937 Juan	12	475
As in freemasonry a higher brother	944 Juan	13	188
She took up with some foreign younger brother	973 Juan	15	335

BROTHERHOOD

To know no brotherhood, and take from earth	374 Lara	1	552
And by thy brotherhood of Cain	481 Manfred	1	249
In brotherhood, as I have made it known	521 Faliero	3	206
For nonsense. Nay, it is their brotherhood	732 Deformed	1	682

BROTHERHOOD'S

My brotherhood's with those who have no children	643 Cain	2	479

BROTHERLESS

For brotherless she was, save in the name	214	Dream		65
Now. And I none!--Who makes me brotherless	651	Cain	3	336
Shrink from the deed which leaves thee brotherless	653	Cain	3	464

BROTHERLY

Of a proud, brotherly, and civic band	45	Harold	3	612
In fondness brotherly and boyish, I	654	Cain	3	537
Call'd brotherly affection, could not move	914	Juan	10	422

BROTHERS

Four brothers enrich'd with their blood the bleak field	86	Leaving NA		18
All, all that brothers should be, but the name	125	Recoll		264
My brothers--both had ceased to breathe	404	Chillon		220
Scott, Rogers, Moore, and all the better brothers	449	Beppo		603
'I come to preach to you, as to your brothers	471	Morgante		321
The brothers sicken'd shortly: he is sovereign	596	Foscari	1	38
Of your three goodly brothers, now in earth	616	Foscari	4	113
Speak to me kindly. Though my brothers are	722	Deformed	1	17
Call not thy brothers brethren! Call me not	722	Deformed	1	24
But then they only seem so many brothers	756	Juan	1	616
That urns and pipkins are but fragile brothers	849	Juan	5	1100
By service with my military brothers	876	Juan	7	564
Had set to work as briskly as their brothers	880	Juan	8	116
Inquired his income, and if he had brothers	924	Juan	11	384
Have taken up at length with younger brothers	928	Juan	11	634
And daughters, brothers, sisters, kith or kin	972	Juan	15	242

BROTHER'S

Time will assuage an infant brother's woe	85	Epitaph		26
Counsel like mine is as a brother's	100	Marion		35
A brother's fond remembrance	104	Alva		242
A brother's death-groan echoes there	105	Alva		316
What brother springs a brother's love to seek	125	Recoll		225
I hear again,--but ah! no brother's voice	125	Recoll		234
(Very sorry, no doubt, since the cause is a brother's	278	Blues	1	37
May better grace a brother's bier	322	Giaour		1250
'This rose to calm my brother's cares	326	Abydos	1	287
That brother wrought a brother's fall	331	Abydos	2	199
But little deem'd a brother's wrath	331	Abydos	2	242
By him a brother's murder stain'd	331	Abydos	2	254
My brother's soul was of that mould	404	Chillon		140
My brother's soul come down to me	405	Chillon		288
Appeal again! art thou my brother's son	502	Faliero	1	157
Of half a century on his brother's brow	525	Faliero	3	454
My brother's and my own, and shed by me	651	Cain	3	346
My brother's keeper? Cain! what hast thou done	653	Cain	3	469
The voice of thy slain brother's blood cries out	653	Cain	3	470
To drink thy brother's blood from thy rash hand	653	Cain	3	473
From him who shed the first, and that a brother's	664	Heaven		665
Was brother's blood; and if its native blood	731	Deformed	1	652
Awful as thy brother's crime	735	Deformed	2	38

BROTHERS'

My brothers' graves without a sod	405	Chillon		313

BROUGHAM

Beware lest blundering Brougham destroy the sale	248	Bards		524

BROUGHT

The midnight brought the signal-sound of strife	39	Harold	3	246
I turn'd from all she brought to those she could not bring	40	Harold	3	270
Morn came and went--and came, and brought no day	189	Darkness		6
Of gods brought forth the high heroic race	205	Aristom		10
Brought on when ills habitually recur	211	Augusta-C		43
But brought to bed at forty-nine	231	Doctor		70
Who are brought to my house as an inn, to my cost	280	Blues	2	18
Ah! Sir Richard, good morning; I've brought you some friends	280	Blues	2	26
Now dead, and brought before the Lord? What ill	289	Vision		298
And brought him off for sentence out of hand	295	Vision		693
Great largess to these walls he brought	318	Giaour		816
Those arms thou see'st my band have brought	332	Abydos	2	315
Had brought me back to feel and think	405	Chillon		278
'"Bring forth the horse!"--the horse was brought	410	Mazeppa		358
They brought me into life again	415	Mazeppa		846
The billows round the promontory brought	429	Island	3	214
Which said--'Has Neuha brought me here to die	430	Island	4	54
I can't tell who first brought the custom in	444	Beppo		284
Their mother, the cold partner who hath brought	458	Dante		173
Their children's children's doom already brought	458	Dante	2	4
Ye mock me--but the power which brought ye here	480	Manfred	1	152
Is't nothing to have brought into contempt	512	Faliero	2	254
They might be certain that whoe'er was brought	522	Faliero	3	239
Asking of his own heart what brought him here	522	Faliero	3	264
Without doubt, he will be brought up to trial	539	Faliero	5	78
Be brought before the council. And the rest	540	Faliero	5	144
When shall they be brought up? When all the chiefs	540	Faliero	5	145

BROUGHT

An injured husband brought the Gauls to Clusium	544	Faliero	5	440
Ere we were summon'd here--we would have brought	549	Faliero	5	825
Brought Persia, Media, Bactria, to the realm	553	Sardan	1	190
He but be brought to think so: this I doubt of	563	Sardan	2	103
Brought from the spoils of India--but be speedy	573	Sardan	3	147
Now brought upon thee. Had I never loved	584	Sardan	4	430
This herald has been brought before me, craving	591	Sardan	5	287
To which that birth has brought me. Why did he	628	Cain	1	69
Which my sire brought us--Death; thou hast shown me much	644	Cain	2	570
And who hath brought him there?--I--who abhor	652	Cain	3	371
Of death, whom I have brought upon the earth	652	Cain	3	420
How have Azaziel, or myself, brought on thee	663	Heaven		609
I brought him forth in woe	669	Heaven		1098
Could brook the alliance; and could ne'er be brought	684	Werner	2	99
Which brought me here was chiefly that, but I	689	Werner	2	422
Mother; for if I brought thee forth, it was	722	Deformed	1	25
Unto what brought me into life? Thou blood	723	Deformed	1	54
Of the then untamed desert, brought to joust	731	Deformed	1	623
For all the glory your conversion brought	745	Juan	Ded	43
(The jury brought their verdict in 'Insanity	749	Juan	1	120
He had been ill brought up, and was born bilious	751	Juan	1	280
Is brought up much more wisely than another	751	Juan	1	296
('Twas snow that brought St. Anthony to reason	755	Juan	1	508
But no device could be brought into play	767	Juan	1	1343
The nine days' wonder which was brought to light	770	Juan	1	1502
The Queen of Denmark, for Ophelia brought	776	Juan	2	133
Brought forth in purple, cradled in vermilion	785	Juan	2	731
And then once more his feelings back were brought	788	Juan	2	894
Charm'd with each other, all things charm'd that brought	819	Juan	4	159
Brought back the sense of pain without the cause	824	Juan	4	495
Thus to their extreme verge the passions brought	830	Juan	4	846
Twelve negresses from Nubia brought a price	831	Juan	4	913
What brought you here?'--'Oh! nothing very rare	833	Juan	5	114
Those honourable scars which brought him fame	836	Juan	5	298
Wondering what next, till the caique was brought	836	Juan	5	318
And there, you see, this turn has brought us through	837	Juan	5	359
And into her clear cheek the blood was brought	845	Juan	5	860
Whate'er she saw and coveted was brought	845	Juan	5	897
And brought before the empress, who had made	867	Juan	6	941
They brought him and his comrades to head-quarters	874	Juan	7	450
A yard or two of ground, which brought them nigher	880	Juan	8	155
To be produced when brought up to the test	881	Juan	8	196
Till all the arts at length are brought about	901	Juan	9	317
And thirdly he who brought you the despatch	904	Juan	9	520
He had brought his spending to a handsome anchor	911	Juan	10	244
He might--and brought them up with skill, in time	925	Juan	11	418
Of vestals brought into the marriage mart	935	Juan	12	367
Arising out of business, often brought	943	Juan	13	114
'Tis the whole spirit brought to a quintessence	945	Juan	13	297
I have brought this world about my ears, and eke	956	Juan	14	73
Seen beauties brought to market by the score	957	Juan	14	140
But since beneath it upon earth we are brought	958	Juan	14	204
But here a messenger brought in despatches	964	Juan	14	536
As e'er brought man and woman to the brink	968	Juan	14	795
If once their phantasies be brought to bear	970	Juan	15	126
There was a picture-dealer who had brought	988	Juan	16	489
Had brought the capo d'opera, not for sale	988	Juan	16	503
Brought to survey these grey walls, which though so thick	988	Juan	16	507

BROW

(See also LAUREL-BROW'D)

Strange pangs would flash along Childe Harold's brow	4	Harold	1	65
Beneath yon mountain's ever beauteous brow	7	Harold	1	280
Wrote on his faded brow curst Cain's unresting doom	17	Harold	1	827
Nay, smile not at my sullen brow	17	Harold	1	837
Monastic Zitza, from thy shady brow	26	Harold	2	424
Spirit of freedom! when on Phyle's brow	31	Harold	2	702
What stamps the wrinkle deeper on the brow	35	Harold	2	919
To wear it ever on thy lip and brow	41	Harold	3	356
Though on his brow were graven lines austere	43	Harold	3	464
Albeit my brow thou never shouldst behold	53	Harold	3	1072
The wreath which Dante's brow alone had worn before	60	Harold	4	315
He! with a glory round his furrow'd brow	60	Harold	4	337
And the false semblance but disgraced his brow	61	Harold	4	366
On thy sweet brow is sorrow plough'd by shame	61	Harold	4	373
Shower'd on his eyelids, brow, and mouth, as from an urn	62	Harold	4	459
Which Petrarch's laureate brow supremely wore	63	Harold	4	511
Win to the brow, 'tis his; and if ye trace	65	Harold	4	606
What are the laurels of the Caesar's brow	71	Harold	4	984
Who hath beheld decline upon my brow	75	Harold	4	1200
He leans upon his hand--his manly brow	76	Harold	4	1253
His Holy of Holies, nor be blasted by his brow	78	Harold	4	1395

BROW

The Sun in human limbs array'd, and brow	79	Harold	4	1443
Time writes no wrinkle on thine azure brow	82	Harold	4	1637
No threat'ning tyrant's darkling brow	88	Horace		3
Or round the steep brow of the churchyard I wander'd	96	Harrow-A		15
Ah! frown not, sweet lady, unbend your soft brow	98	To M.S.G.-B		13
Your polish'd brow no cares have crost	98	To Lesbia		5
Marion, why that pensive brow	100	Marion		1
But who is he, whose darken'd brow	103	Alva		181
We'll bend our course to yonder mountain's brow	106	Nisus		108
War's dread machines o'erhang thy threatening brow	120	Newstead-A		59
The polish'd brow where once you shone	128	Lady-C		22
of the dark brow." Why should tears dim	130	Calmar		80
dost thou bend thy brow, chief of Oithona	130	Calmar		113
the gloomy brow. 'Mathon of Lochlin	130	Calmar		117
And virtues crown your brow	138	Clare		93
A Mask each canker'd brow shall hide	141	Critics		24
Spread roses o'er my brow	145	Adieu		2
Sunk chill on my brow	151	When We		10
O'er brake and craggy brow	158	Storm		34
And clouds the brow,' or fills the eye	174	Impromptu-A		4
Transferr'd his by-word to thy brow	181	Ode-A		126
The eye that gladdens, and the brow serene	183	Address-D		36
Go! dash the roses from thy brow	185	Belshaz-A		9
Unknowing who he was upon whose brow	190	Darkness		68
With scarce fewer wrinkles than sins on his brow	202	Avatar		31
What are garlands and crowns to the brow that is wrinkled	204	Pisa		5
Why must my head ache where his gentle brow lay	204	Hindoo		6
But is deep in my soul as my brow	205	Blessington		16
Or binds his brow	206	Year		20
And he did calm himself, and fix his brow	214	Dream		87
Even at the altar, o'er his brow there came	215	Dream		149
And on that cheek, and o'er that brow	216	She Walks		13
With the dew on his brow and the rust on his mail	222	Sennacherib		18
Lo! wreaths of yew, not laurel, bind thy brow	245	Bards		267
Gone were the terrors of her awful brow	269	Minerva		79
His brow was like the deep when tempest-toss'd	288	Vision		189
He merely bent his diabolic brow	289	Vision		289
And but for that chill, changeless brow	311	Giaour		80
Of foreign garb and fearful brow	312	Giaour		231
His brow was bent, his eye was glazed	312	Giaour		240
I know him by his pallid brow	316	Giaour		611
And o'er him bends that foe with brow	317	Giaour		673
Has gain'd our nearest mountain's brow	317	Giaour		702
As death were stamp'd upon his brow	318	Giaour		797
That pale brow wildly wreathing round	319	Giaour		895
I have not quail'd to danger's brow	320	Giaour		1027
But look--'tis written on my brow	320	Giaour		1057
I read abhorrence on thy brow	321	Giaour		1161
But could not, for my burning brow	322	Giaour		1261
This brow that then will burn no more	323	Giaour		1313
His pensive cheek and pondering brow	324	Abydos	1	30
His brow no high-crown'd turban bore	330	Abydos	2	132
His gains repay his broiling brow	331	Abydos	2	259
And cry, Remembrance saddening o'er each brow	338	Corsair	1	41
Flush in the cheek, or damp upon the brow	341	Corsair	1	242
A laughing wildness half unbent his brow	353	Corsair	2	455
Surveys his brow--would soothe his gloom of mind	357	Corsair	3	136
Full on his brow, as if from morning air	361	Corsair	3	397
They meet--upon her brow, unknown, forgot	361	Corsair	3	414
Whose brow was bow'd beneath the glance he gave	363	Corsair	3	532
By the first glance on that still, marble brow	365	Corsair	3	624
There grew one flower beneath its rugged brow	365	Corsair	3	670
That brow in furrow'd lines had fix'd at last	367	Lara	1	67
His brow fell darker, and his words more few	367	Lara	1	94
No--no--the storm may beat upon his brow	368	Lara	1	178
His bristling locks of sable, brow of gloom	369	Lara	1	197
And still defiance knit his gather'd brow	369	Lara	1	216
And, by the changes of his cheek and brow	369	Lara	1	237
It is a sight the careful brow might smooth	371	Lara	1	393
His brow belied him if his soul was sad	371	Lara	1	398
Upon his brow no outward passion spoke	373	Lara	1	492
With which that chieftain's brow would bear him down	373	Lara	1	499
That brow whereon his native sun had sate	373	Lara	1	529
And o'er his brow the dampening heart-drops threw	374	Lara	1	600
To seal his lip, but agonise his brow	374	Lara	1	607
For Lara's brow upon the moment grew	376	Lara	2	73
Than when his foe's was levell'd at his brow	376	Lara	2	76
Save that damp brow which rests upon his knees	381	Lara	2	429
To look on Lara's brow--where all grew night	381	Lara	2	475
With brow repulsive, and with gesture swift	382	Lara	2	484
Bent was his head, and hidden was his brow	383	Lara	2	561
And sit with me on Acro-Corinth's brow	385	Corinth		45
The turban girt his shaven brow	385	Corinth		120
The turban on his hot brow press'd	387	Corinth		338
And bathed his brow with airy balm	388	Corinth		361
Lepanto's gulf; and, on the brow	388	Corinth		364
And o'er his brow, so downward bent	390	Corinth		513
The feverish glow of his brow was gone	391	Corinth		605
From off thy faithless brow, and swear	391	Corinth		631

BROW

And brow were stain'd with gore and dust	394	Corinth		886
And o'er his brow the burning lamp	397	Parisina		116
With downcast eyes and knitting brow	398	Parisina		163
Stern and erect his brow was raised	398	Parisina		186
One look upon that deathlike brow	398	Parisina		195
For on his brow the swelling vein	398	Parisina		224
When rose thy casque above thy brow	399	Parisina		301
And never smile his brow unbended	402	Parisina		538
And o'er that fair broad brow were wrought	402	Parisina		539
Because our mother's brow was given	403	Chillon		74
My very soul from out my brow	408	Mazeppa		191
A brow like a midsummer lake	409	Mazeppa		220
No matter; I have bared my brow	412	Mazeppa		567
Now rose like startled vipers o'er his brow	427	Island	3	90
His brow was pale, his blue eyes sunken in	427	Island	3	100
A moment's brightness pass'd along his brow	428	Island	3	153
And Laura's brow a frown had rarely bent	443	Beppo		182
To the high dama's brow, more melancholy	445	Beppo		357
'Sir,' said the Count, with brow exceeding grave	451	Beppo		697
My brow with hopes of triumph,--let them go	457	Dante	1	109
Alas! with what a weight upon my brow	457	Dante	1	130
By fresh barbarians, on thy brow replaced	461	Dante	3	56
More poesy upon its speaking brow	463	Dante	4	26
Appear'd, so that Tithonus scratch'd his brow	466	Morgante		24
Of a great mountain's brow the abbey stood	468	Morgante		155
Why, on thy brow the seal of middle age	484	Manfred	2	49
Beautiful Spirit! in thy calm clear brow	485	Manfred	2	119
Ah! he unveils his aspect: on his brow	496	Manfred	3	336
Without investing the insulted brow	504	Faliero	1	290
A moody brow and mutter'd threats had made me	507	Faliero	1	551
Have nothing of old age; and his bold brow	509	Faliero	2	20
And let such strong emotions stamp your brow	511	Faliero	2	177
As you have risen, with an unalter'd brow	511	Faliero	2	203
Of half a century on his brother's brow	525	Faliero	3	454
A damp like death rose o'er my brow. I strove	528	Faliero	4	9
To risk your sacred brow beneath--and trust me	573	Sardan	3	133
Along her most transparent brow; her nostril	577	Sardan	3	390
Alas! thou art pale, and on thy brow the drops	579	Sardan	4	38
Female in garb, and crown'd upon the brow	580	Sardan	4	106
And the cold drops strain through my brow, as if	598	Foscari	1	161
And princely brow of his old father, which	601	Foscari	1	357
Couldst thou but read--'Tis not upon thy brow	603	Foscari	2	139
Ay, he may veil beneath a marble brow	613	Foscari	3	309
With such an earnest brow, upon thy tablets	626	Foscari	5	368
Why wilt thou wear this gloom upon thy brow	628	Cain	1	53
With a meek brow, whose base humility	647	Cain	3	101
Wouldst thou with me? To mark upon thy brow	653	Cain	3	498
My brow, but nought to that which is within it	654	Cain	3	501
From its tremendous brow? no more to have	659	Heaven		292
Why is thy brow severe	666	Heaven		795
That pure severe serenity of brow	667	Heaven		947
Patriarch, be still a father! smooth thy brow	668	Heaven		1029
And famine-hollow'd brow, the lord of halls	673	Werner	1	119
And with a brow of thought beyond his years	687	Werner	2	256
Even to your brow again. And if it fled	706	Werner	4	159
Beneath their glitter o'er my brow and zone	714	Werner	5	73
His brow was girt with laurels more than hairs	725	Deformed	1	192
What's here? whose broad brow and whose curly beard	725	Deformed	1	230
Her smooth brow crisp--'Oh, nothing!'--a young heir	743	Deformed	3	95
Each eye a sermon, and her brow a homily	749	Juan	1	114
Her glossy hair was cluster'd o'er a brow	754	Juan	1	481
Young, yet her elder, and of brow less grave	788	Juan	2	915
Her brow was overhung with coins of gold	788	Juan	2	921
Her brow was white and low, her cheek's pure dye	789	Juan	2	937
His brow, as if in act to butt, and then	805	Juan	3	255
A king sate on the rocky brow	812	Juan	3	707
Pale as the foam that froth'd on his dead brow	820	Juan	4	266
An open brow a little mark'd with care	832	Juan	5	85
But o'er her bright brow flash'd a tumult strange	845	Juan	5	859
To cross her brow, she wonder'd how so near	846	Juan	5	951
Her brow grew black, but she would not upbraid	847	Juan	5	997
You can't suppose Gulbeyaz' angry brow	848	Juan	5	1048
And Love's a god, or was before the brow	853	Juan	6	46
But she rose up, and kiss'd the matron's brow	858	Juan	6	393
Above her brow, lay dreaming soft and warm	860	Juan	6	523
So deep an anguish wrung Gulbeyaz' brow	865	Juan	6	836
And her brow clear'd, but not her troubled eye	866	Juan	6	879
With its proud brow, it merits slight applause	872	Juan	7	318
Upon them his slow brow and piercing eye	874	Juan	7	467
On her unwrinkled brow, nor could you view	886	Juan	8	517
Had scarr'd her brow, and left its crimson trace	890	Juan	8	757
Though modest, on his unembarrass'd brow	907	Juan	9	661
Will bring the other, ere the lake-like brow	908	Juan	10	59
The True Believers:--and her infant brow	917	Juan	10	598
She rings the world's 'Te Deum,' and her brow	923	Juan	11	299
Though royalty was written on his brow	940	Juan	12	669
What are the fillets on the victor's brow	976	Juan	15	529
(Who watch'd the changes of Don Juan's brow	985	Juan	16	290

BROWN

(See also LIGHT-BROWN, NUT-BROWN)

BROWN
Disclosing rock and slope and forest brown   22 Harold   2   195
How brown the foliage of the green hill's grove   30 Harold   2   624
'Tis Orla, the brown chief of Oithona   131 Calmar   192
Anacreon, Tom Little, Tom Moore, or Tom Brown   226 Oh You   2
'Tis midnight: on the mountains brown   387 Corinth   242
His bright brown locks must now be clipp'd   401 Parisina   435
Good teeth, with curling rather dark brown hair   832 Juan   5   83

BROWNER
And on the leaf a browner hue   396 Parisina   10

BROWS
A beam from under hazel brows   97 To Woman   16
And old Alethes' casque defends his brows   108 Nisus   216
With Roses crown our jovial brows   139 Anacreon-C   5
The brows of men by the despairing light   189 Darkness   22
Let Archer plant the horns on Sullen's brows   261 Hints   361
To you, ye husbands of ten years! whose brows   274 Waltz   93
Black eyes, arch'd brows, and sweet expressions
  still   441 Beppo   82
With eyes averted, and with gloomy brows   542 Faliero   5 337
His brows to changed expression, till at times   570 Sardan   2 534
To place it on his brows. Slain! unrewarded   577 Sardan   3 357
And wave o'er his brows   728 Deformed   1 398
Your bays may hide the baldness of your brows   745 Juan   Ded 49
And jestest with the brows of mightiest men   800 Juan   2 1642
Who clear'd her sparkling eyes and smooth'd her
  brows   850 Juan   5 1227
And fair brows gently drooping, as the fruit   860 Juan   6 518
Were there, with brows that did not much invite   949 Juan   13 546
'Gainst rhyme I never should have knock'd my brows 971 Juan   15 189

BROW'S
More glittering eye, and black brow's sabler   349 Corsair   2 149
And murmurs rise, and Otho's brow's o'ercast   375 Lara   2   32
And her proud brow's blue veins to swell and
  darkle   864 Juan   6 808

BROWSE
To browse beneath the midnight dews   407 Mazeppa   65

BROWSES
Which flash'd as far as where the musk-bull
  browses   940 Juan   12 654

BROWSETH
Browseth; and, pensive o'er his scatter'd flock   27 Harold   2 465

BROWSING
The browsing camels' bells are tinkling   317 Giaour   689

BRUISE
With this last bruise upon a broken reed   437 Tasso   42

BRUISERS
Be all the bruisers cull'd from all St. Giles   270 Minerva   179

BRUITED
Was ne'er more bruited in men's minds than now   40 Harold   3 327

BRUMMEL
Where's Brummel? Dish'd. Where's Long Pole
  Wellesley? Diddled   928 Juan   11 609

BRUNCK'S
Yet prizing Bentley's, Brunck's, or Porson's note 112 Examination   57
Brunck's heaviest tome for ballast, and, to back
  it   274 Waltz   77

BRUNETTE
And through her clear brunette complexion shone a 828 Juan   4 750

BRUNSWICK
Ere the daughter of Brunswick is cold in her grave 201 Avatar   1

BRUNSWICKERS
So oft bestowing Brunswickers and brides   274 Waltz   50

BRUNSWICK'S
Sate Brunswick's fated chieftain; he did hear   38 Harold   3 200

BRUNT
First bow'd beneath the brunt of Hellas' sword   33 Harold   2 841
Is scathed by fiery passion's brunt   312 Giaour   195
So gallantly bore he the brunt of the fray   393 Corinth   783

BRUSA'S
To Brusa's walls for safety sent   332 Abydos   2 335

BRUSH
Saw cits grow centaurs underneath his brush   256 Hints   4
Raise but an arm! 'twill brush their web away   900 Juan   9 217
And brush a web or two from off the walls   918 Juan   10 672
His brush with all the blood of all the sainted   950 Juan   13 568

BRUSH'D
A better farmer ne'er brush'd dew from lawn   286 Vision   61
Hath brush'd its brightest hues away   314 Giaour   407
The hogs on t'other, and he brush'd apace   473 Morgante   514

BRUSHES
Of stockings, slippers, brushes, combs, complete   764 Juan   1 1140
But leaps, and bursts, and sometimes foxes'
  brushes   959 Juan   14 274

BRUSSELS
And robes sweet friendship in a Brussels lace   961 Juan   14 372

BRUTAL
And foes disabled in the brutal fray   16 Harold   1 777
Of this brutal Lisbon Packet   157 Hodgson   64
The accursed Hun, more brutal than of old   307 Age   689
And drove them with their brutal yells to seek   890 Juan   8 746

BRUTE
Bounds with one lashing spring the mighty brute   16 Harold   1 750
And lull'd alike the cares of brute and man   106 Nisus   86
Each kindred brute might bid thee blush for shame 154 Dog   22
Nor e'en the pawing of the wilder Brute   184 Julian   22
With the skill of an Orpheus to soften the brute   202 Avatar   45
Each brute hath its nature, a king's is to reign   203 Avatar   61
The last poor brute securely gnaws the bone   270 Minerva   116
For danger levels man and brute   407 Mazeppa   51
Plain, forest, river? Man nor brute   413 Mazeppa   657
The weary brute still stagger'd on   413 Mazeppa   666
The man of genius as the meanest brute   464 Dante   4   88
And treats me like a brute, the brute may turn   505 Faliero   1 376
Nor form of mightiest brute, nor aught that is   640 Cain   2 263
Brute of the forest? Ah! a livid light   652 Cain   3 390
Worn for a husband,--or some other brute   791 Juan   2 1112
The rudest brute that roams Siberia's wild   890 Juan   8 731

BRUTE-LIKE
And trample, brute-like, o'er each flower   310 Giaour   52

BRUTES
And flap their useless wings; the wildest brutes   189 Darkness   34
While brawny brutes in stupid wonder stare   271 Minerva   181
A sight unmatch'd since Orpheus and his brutes   273 Waltz   18
Mankind, where least above the brutes   311 Giaour   154
This common courage which with brutes we share   343 Corsair   1 327
Like brutes within an iron den   404 Chillon   137
From savage brutes alone, too fierce to tame   469 Morgante   181
For brutes of burthen, and for birds of prey   484 Manfred   2   36
To one wide desert chase of brutes, who were   557 Sardan   1 422
Old hunter of the earliest brutes! and ye   578 Sardan   4   28
Who hunted fellow-creatures as if brutes   578 Sardan   4   29
Where even the brutes, in their despair   661 Heaven   442
Like brutes;--and thus his dangerous post kept he 778 Juan   2 285

BRUTI
And we shall be like the two Bruti in   519 Faliero   3   74

BRUTUS
When Brutus made the dagger's edge surpass   67 Harold   4 732
The thought of Brutus--for his was not there   183 Address-D   8
Roused millions do what single Brutus did   423 Island   2 325
If Brutus had not lived? He died in giving   517 Faliero   2 615
Ah! the plebian Brutus, is he gone   540 Faliero   5 179
But, being 'no orator as Brutus is   861 Juan   6 591
Of Brutus at the pageant of Tiberius   974 Juan   15 386

BRUTUS'
The Caesar's pageant, shorn of Brutus' bust   64 Harold   4 525
Than Cato's sister, or than Brutus' mother   725 Deformed   1 199

BRYANT
They say so (Bryant says the contrary   826 Juan   4 604

BUBBLE
Till the swoln bubble bursts--and all is air   243 Bards   134
And fairy fables bubble none but youth   264 Hints   538
Nor say one mass to cool the caldron's bubble   440 Beppo   31
Like a small bubble breaking with the wave   575 Sardan   3 237
With the brightness of a bubble   743 Deformed   3   76
And mine's a bubble, not blown up for praise   956 Juan   14   63
'Bubble and squeak' would spoil my liquid lay   977 Juan   15 566

BUBBLES
Borne, like thy bubbles, onward. From a boy   82 Harold   4 1650
But bubbles on thy surface; and the key   192 Fragment-C   34
While they are but its bubbles, ignorant   739 Deformed   2 293
Like bubbles on an ocean much less ample   898 Juan   9 102
Its little torrent in a thousand bubbles   949 Juan   13 519
Wherewith we break our bubbles on the ocean   968 Juan   15   12
Our bubbles; as the old burst, new emerge   980 Juan   15 790

BUBBLING
Some bitter o'er the flowers its bubbling venom
  flings   17 Harold   1 818

BUBBLING
Whose bubbling did a genial freshness fling	28 Harold	2	552
Down where the shallower wave still tells its bubbling tales	65 Harold	4	603
Prison'd in marble; bubbling from the base	72 Harold	4	1042
He sinks into thy depths with bubbling groan	82 Harold	4	1610
Fast from his breast the blood is bubbling	335 Abydos	2	579
Or from the bubbling streamlet's grassy side	420 Island	2	89
A goblet, bubbling o'er with blood; and on	580 Sardan	4	111
A solitary shriek, the bubbling cry	780 Juan	2	423
He heard his rivulet's light bubbling run	805 Juan	3	211
Heard,--and that bee-like, bubbling, busy hum	919 Juan	11	63

BUCENTAUR
The Bucentaur lies rotting unrestored	56 Harold	4	93
The Bucentaur, like the columnar cloud	547 Faliero	5	632

BUCEPHALUS
As thy Bucephalus and thou	408 Mazeppa		104

BUCK
For killing nothing but a bear or buck, he	886 Juan	8	486

BUCKET
Morgante on his neck the bucket took	473 Morgante		511

BUCKLER
The casque, the buckler, and the fiery steed	107 Nisus		155
Thou who art bearing my buckler and bow	219 Saul-A		5
Ho, there!--But seek not for the buckler: 'tis	573 Sardan	3	100

BUCKLERS
Upon their bucklers for a winding sheet	64 Harold	4	566

BUCKRAM
Our men in buckram shall have blows enough	256 Bards		1049

BUD
Of stirring branches, and the bud which brings	51 Harold	3	956
From the first hour of empire in the bud	72 Harold	4	1011
She sees her little bud put forth its leaves	77 Harold	4	1340
When Memory bids them bud again	128 Lady-F		16
Nipp'd in the bud by Caledonian gales	247 Bards		422
The first, the freshest bud of Feeling's soil	420 Island	2	96
For, Tyranny, there blooms no bud for thee	454 Venice-B		100
Blossom and bud, and bloom of flowers and fruits	647 Cain	3	106
The last bud of the rival branch at once	706 Werner	4	132
And far away, the last bud of her race	933 Juan	12	228

BUDA'S
By Buda's wall and Danube's side	386 Corinth		215

BUDDING
(See also GENTLY-BUDDING)
Thy budding years a lengthen'd term deserve	106 Nisus		64
The budding sprouts of those that you shall wear	275 Waltz		96
'Tis true, your budding Miss is very charming	445 Beppo		305
Luxuriant, budding; cheerful without mirth	859 Juan	6	419
The colour of a budding rose's crest	863 Juan	6	676
Their tender parents in their budding days	997 Juan	17	6

BUDGELL
Budgell, a rogue and rhymester, for no good	268 Hints		823

BUDGELL'S
I'll tell you Budgell's story,--and have done	268 Hints		822

BUDS
And buds unshelter'd by a bower	336 Abydos	2	686
To the buds; and birds are winging	743 Deformed	3	73

BUFF
'Tis that I still retain my 'buff and blue	747 Juan	Ded	132

BUFFALO
On the stately buffalo	392 Corinth		724
Were I to taunt a buffalo with this	732 Deformed	1	103

BUFFALO'S
Give me the strength then of the buffalo's foot	724 Deformed	1	113

BUFFO
By one of these, the buffo of the party	826 Juan	4	641

BUFFOON
A would-be satirist, a hired buffoon	255 Bards		975
Of a buffoon. You mean I speak the truth	734 Deformed	1	816
Afar, a dwarf buffoon stood telling tales	805 Juan	3	265
Hero, buffoon, half-demon, and half-dirt	874 Juan	7	437

BUFFOONERY
Were all kinds of buffoonery and dress	442 Beppo		164

BUFFOON'RY'S
On those shall Farce display Buffoon'ry's mask	249 Bards		588

BUFFOONS
Well may they smile on Italy's buffoons	250 Bards		614
Intoxicating glare, when the buffoons	558 Sardan	1	487
Or any such like sovereign buffoons	816 Juan	3	970

BUGBEAR
The bugbear he hath built to scare the world	664 Heaven		709

BUGBEARS
These bugbears, as their terrors show too well	423 Island	2	331
As children at discover'd bugbears. 'Tis	591 Sardan	5	240

BUGLE
Sling on thy bugle--see that free from rust	340 Corsair	1	161
List!--'tis the bugle--Juan shrilly blew	345 Corsair	1	464
His bugle--brief the blast--but shrilly blew	349 Corsair	2	166
Invited Conrad's bugle, and the din	349 Corsair	2	187
Full fifteen summers. Hark, my lord, the bugle	707 Werner	4	204
With such brief greeting. You have heard our bugle	708 Werner	4	233
No bugle awakes him with life-and-death call	742 Deformed	3	33
The trump and bugle till he spake were dumb	836 Juan	5	287

BUGLES
Be sure I'll sound it better than your bugles	708 Werner	4	270

BUILD
Where are its golden roofs? where those who dared to build	71 Harold	4	981
Would build up all her triumphs in one dome	74 Harold	4	1146
To build for giants, and for his vain earth	78 Harold	4	1365
To build his own upon thy deathless fame	125 Recoll		250
Ay! 'Build him a dwelling!' let each give his mite	203 Avatar		73
Ye, who aspire to 'build the lofty rhyme	267 Hints		781
While eagles scarce build higher than the crest	422 Island	2	256
In spots where eagles might have chosen to build	434 Island	4	312
I dare to build the imitative rhyme	455 Dante	Ded	4
Where the birds dare not build, nor insect's wing	485 Manfred	2	158
Nor sweated them to build up pyramids	555 Sardan	1	278
The air with clamour) build the palaces	587 Sardan	5	27
For a great sacrifice I build the pyre	591 Sardan	5	281
It is too late. I will build no more altars	650 Cain	3	288
And build thy city o'er the drown'd earth's grave	660 Heaven		408
They build more--Oh, thou everlasting sneerer	732 Deformed	1	685
Shows that we build when we should but entomb us	839 Juan	5	504
Oh! ye who build up monuments, defiled	900 Juan	9	259
To build a college, or to found a race	931 Juan	12	74
To build up common things with common places	956 Juan	14	56

BUILDING
'Tis a fine building, but decay'd. The apartment	676 Werner	1	310
But this I know, it was a spacious building	790 Juan	2	1015
It was indeed a wide extensive building	837 Juan	5	361

BUILDINGS
Near ruin'd buildings--never have been proved	598 Foscari	1	183
More modern buildings and those built of yore	838 Juan	5	454
With buildings in the Oriental taste	868 Juan	7	67
The public buildings and the private too	870 Juan	7	180
New buildings of correctest conformation	988 Juan	16	511

BUILDING'S
The holy building's massy door	196 Venice	1	6

BUILDS
There the blithe bee his fragrant fortress builds	33 Harold	2	823
The Bat builds in his haram bower	313 Giaour		292
Thou, in whose pleasant places Summer builds	459 Dante	2	54
Which the breath of twilight builds	479 Manfred	1	52
He there builds up a formidable dyke	814 Juan	3	849

BUILT
(See also ROCK-BUILT)
But here the Babylonian whore hath built	8 Harold	1	338
Poor child of Doubt and Death, whose hope is built on reeds	20 Harold	2	27
And vile Ambition, that built up between	69 Harold	4	869
Built me a little bark of hope, once more	70 Harold	4	938
Even upon such a basis hast thou built	213 Lady Byron		35
Had built St. Paul's without the aid of Wren	266 Hints		668
For thee in those bright isles is built a bower	333 Abydos	2	408
Against the Tartars built of old	411 Mazeppa		434
Sought out their cottage built beneath the palm	424 Island	2	403
And built herself a chapel of the seas	432 Island	4	160
Carved at the prow, built lightly, but compactly	442 Beppo		148
Or fanes be built of grandeur yet unknown	464 Dante	4	66
Built up between us, and will die alone	465 Dante	4	148
When she, who built 'gainst Attila a bulwark	548 Faliero	5	743
Who built up this vast empire, and wert made	553 Sardan	1	160
There's Tarsus and Anchialus, both built	555 Sardan	1	284
Built for a whim, recorded with a verse	555 Sardan	1	289
Shame me! by Baal, the cities, though well built	555 Sardan	1	291

BUILT

In one day built Anchialus and Tarsus — 555 Sardan 1 298
The bugbear he hath built to scare the world — 664 Heaven 709
When man built less against the elements — 696 Werner 3 100
Philosopher, and what not, they have built — 732 Deformed 1 676
He was a Greek, and on his isle had built — 790 Juan 2 1009
More modern buildings and those built of yore — 838 Juan 5 454
The Russians, having built two batteries on — 870 Juan 7 177
When they built up unto his darling trees — 886 Juan 8 506
Have built and laid out ground at such a rate — 950 Juan 13 587

BULBUL

A message from the Bulbul bears — 326 Abydos 1 288
It were the Bulbul; but his throat — 336 Abydos 2 694

BULK

Hurl the dark bulk along, scarce seen in dashing
by — 16 Harold 1 791
Which heaved from wave to wave its trampling bulk — 422 Island 2 233
In full, voluptuous, but not o'ergrown bulk — 996 Juan 16 1031

BULKY

And in his bulky bosom made incision — 470 Morgante 302
But now reduced, as is a bulky volume — 882 Juan 8 268

BULL
(See also MUSK-BULL)

On foams the bull, but not unscathed he goes — 16 Harold 1 761
Full in the centre stands the bull at bay — 16 Harold 1 775
And the greatest of all is John Bull — 237 Hay 4
While poor John Bull, bewilder'd with the scene — 250 Bards 604
A wandering Peregrine, or plain John Bull — 259 Hints 166
Here crash'd a sturdy oath of stout John Bull — 292 Vision 465
The bull of Phalaris renews his roar — 303 Age 357
Of the young bull, until the milkmaid finds — 722 Deformed 1 22
This is no bull, although it sounds so; for — 860 Juan 6 529
'I've heard of stories of a cock and bull — 862 Juan 6 633
How Peace should make John Bull the Frenchman's
foe — 870 Juan 7 176
Which to that bottle-conjurer, John Bull — 872 Juan 7 347
Exchanged for 'thin potations' by John Bull — 929 Juan 11 671
Than could roast beef in our rough John Bull way — 977 Juan 15 564
Bull something of the lower world's condition — 979 Juan 15 734

BULL-DOG

A bull-dog, and a bullfinch, and an ermine — 913 Juan 10 393

BULL-DOGS

Unless they are game as bull-dogs and fox-
terriers — 870 Juan 7 192

BULLET

The deadly bullet turn'd apart — 201 Ode-C 64
A bullet whistled o'er his head — 316 Giaour 572
Whose bullet through the night-air sang — 335 Abydos 2 574
Stray bullet of our lansquenets, who might — 733 Deformed 1 772
May make up for a bullet in his body — 869 Juan 7 163
At shrinking from a bullet or a bomb — 883 Juan 8 302

BULLETIN

He fell, immortal in a bulletin — 869 Juan 7 160
Praise) if a man's name in a bulletin — 869 Juan 7 162
To their two selves, one whole bright bulletin — 880 Juan 8 152

BULLETINS

Oh, ye great bulletins of Bonaparte — 877 Juan 7 649

BULLETS

'Though far and near the bullets hiss — 316 Giaour 595
Kill'd by five bullets from an old gun-barrel — 835 Juan 5 272
Bombs, drums, guns, bastions, batteries, bayonets,
bullets — 877 Juan 7 623

BULLET'S

Impell'd the bullet's viewless course — 99 Young Lady 7

BULLETS'

While the rock rattled with the bullets' knell — 434 Island 4 297

BULL-FIGHTS

Except to bull-fights, mass, play, rout, and
revel — 765 Juan 1 1180

BULLFINCH

A bull-dog, and a bullfinch, and an ermine — 913 Juan 10 393

BULL-FROG'S

The bull-frog's note, from out the marsh — 396 Corinth 1065

BULLIED

Who butcher'd half the earth, and bullied t'other — 917 Juan 10 648

BULLIES

Unless these bullies of eternal pains — 435 Island 4 355

BULLS

The Doge stands to behold the chase of bulls — 539 Faliero 5 94
In part. I would not have his bulls abolish'd — 739 Deformed 2 275

BULL'S

Or roams the herd beneath the bull's protection — 873 Juan 7 380
Put to trial John Bull's partial patience — 884 Juan 8 382

BULLY

There was Parolles, too, the legal bully — 951 Juan 13 665
Shut up the bald-coot bully Alexander — 965 Juan 14 657

BULOW

And that if Blucher, Bulow, Gneisenau — 884 Juan 8 385

BULWARK

And Europe's bulwark 'gainst the Ottomite — 57 Harold 4 123
In war my bulwark, and in peace my joy — 107 Nisus 170
And Britain fall, the bulwark of the world — 255 Bards 1006
Dashing against the outward Lido's bulwark — 528 Faliero 4 15
The earth as being the Christian bulwark 'gainst — 538 Faliero 5 11
When she, who built 'gainst Attila a bulwark — 548 Faliero 5 743
Sole bulwark of all right. Away, I say — 569 Sardan 2 457
There is no bulwark. No, nor in the palace — 570 Sardan 2 566
O'erfloods its banks, and hath destroy'd the
bulwark — 590 Sardan 5 194

BULWARKS

Whose bulwarks were not then in vain — 388 Corinth 405

BUMPER

And think, for every bumper I shall quaff — 676 Werner 1 302
The foam which made its virgin bumper gay — 981 Juan 16 67

BUMPERS

When o'er the brim the sparkling bumpers reach — 796 Juan 2 1419
Expedient of full bumpers; for the eye — 905 Juan 9 535

BUNDLE

The world is a bundle of hay — 237 Hay 1

BUNGLER

A bungler even in its disgusting trade — 746 Juan Ded 105

BUNTING

'What cheer, Ben Bunting?' cried (when in full
view — 425 Island 2 500
Ben Bunting, who essay'd to wash, and wipe — 428 Island 3 105
Revived Ben Bunting from his pipe profound — 428 Island 3 134

BUON

Strange too in my 'buon camerado' Scott — 931 Juan 12 125

BUONAPARTE

France, too, had Buonaparte and Dumourier — 747 Juan 1 15
She fell with Buonaparte--What strange thoughts — 900 Juan 9 255
Had Buonaparte won at Waterloo — 966 Juan 14 713

BUONAPARTE'S

Though now transferr'd to Buonaparte's 'fiat — 274 Waltz 56
Why would you trouble Buonaparte's reign — 306 Age 577
Than Buonaparte's cancer: could I dash on — 898 Juan 9 110
The shade of Buonaparte's noble daring — 930 Juan 12 39

BUOYANT

Our pliant limbs the buoyant billows bore — 125 Recoll 262
On those buoyant supporters, the bladders of
rhyme — 227 Moore-A 4
I feel so elastic--'so buoyant--so buoyant — 282 Blues 2 131
These limbs that buoyant wave hath borne — 329 Abydos 2 30
But ere he well could mark the buoyant trunk — 383 Lara 2 580
Buoyant as wings, and flitting through the spray — 429 Island 3 174
For theirs were buoyant spirits, never bound — 818 Juan 4 125

BUOY'D
(See also RE-BUOY'D)

The pair, buoy'd up on Hope's exulting wing — 106 Nisus 83
For all corrupted things are buoy'd like corks — 298 Vision 835
In my native air that buoy'd my spirits up — 610 Foscari 3 129
He buoy'd his boyish limbs, and strove to ply — 787 Juan 2 842

BUOYS

My spirit buoys thee up to breathe in regions — 641 Cain 2 321

BURDEN

Some trouble. When his burden down he laid — 295 Vision 677
Once more he bade him lay his burden by — 475 Morgante 590
Now, Cain! I will divide thy burden with thee — 654 Cain 3 551
A burden to the earth, myself, and shame — 723 Deformed 1 53
Of our song bear the burden — 732 Deformed 1 725
Set to some thousands ('tis the usual burden — 988 Juan 16 514

BURDENS

How some to burdens were obliged to stoop — 831 Juan 4 923

BURDETT

There's I and Burdett--Gentlemen | 235 New Song | | 11

BUREAU

Save the recording angel's black bureau | 285 Vision | | 20

BURGAGE

Also a lawsuit upon tenures burgage | 988 Juan | 16 | 523

BURGH

This burgh and Frankfort; so far's in our favour | 698 Werner | 3 | 196

BURGHER

And been an Hanseatic burgher? Excellent | 673 Werner | 1 | 142

BURGHERS

Would flying burghers mark the blazing town | 272 Minerva | | 304
When sallow burghers slunk back to their tents | 533 Faliero | 4 | 384
Still further on these obscure petty burghers | 681 Werner | 1 | 632
And living amidst commerce-fetching burghers | 694 Werner | 2 | 727
To petty burghers, who leave once a year | 724 Deformed | 1 | 126

BURGLARIOUS

When this burglarious, larcenous felony | 683 Werner | 2 | 26

BURGLARIOUSLY

Burglariously broke his coffin's lid | 773 Juan | 1 | 1750

BURGOYNE

Prince Ferdinand, Granby, Burgoyne, Keppel, Howe | 747 Juan | 1 | 10

BURGUNDY

Here Burgundy bequeath'd his tombless host | 45 Harold | 3 | 604
Nor Burgundy in all its sunset glow | 797 Juan | 2 | 1438

BURIAL

Rider and horse,--friend, for,--in one red burial blent | 39 Harold | 3 | 252
His burial made some pomp; there was profusion | 286 Vision | | 66
An unknown barren beach for burial ground | 788 Juan | 2 | 872
Men are but maggots of some huge Earth's burial | 901 Juan | 9 | 312

BURIED
(See also DEEP-BURIED, OCEAN-BURIED)

Had buried long his hopes, no more to rise | 17 Harold | 1 | 825
Fall'n states and buried greatness, o'er a land | 59 Harold | 4 | 220
And buried Learning rose, redeem'd to a new morn | 62 Harold | 4 | 432
Like Scipio, buried by the upbraiding shore | 63 Harold | 4 | 506
Thou nameless column with the buried base | 71 Harold | 4 | 983
Buried in air, the deep blue sky of Rome | 71 Harold | 4 | 991
Raked from repose in search for buried gold | 121 Newstead-A | | 88
And think my heart is buried here | 157 Album | | 8
And more thy buried love endears | 168 Dead | | 71
'Samuel, raise thy buried head | 219 Saul-B | | 3
Expires unwept--is buried--let him rot | 260 Hints | | 262
Dug up from dust, though buried when alive | 266 Hints | | 722
He's buried; save the undertaker's bill | 286 Vision | | 90
I saw him buried where he fell | 323 Giaour | | 1303
Soft as the memory of buried love | 325 Abydos | 1 | 166
For all the treasures buried far | 327 Abydos | 1 | 357
Bares with its buried woes, till Pride awake | 352 Corsair | 2 | 356
Not so in him; his breast had buried both | 370 Lara | 1 | 285
Buried he lay, where thousands before | 393 Corinth | | 813
For I had buried one and all | 405 Chillon | | 320
Was love, though buried strong as in the grave | 433 Island | 4 | 222
The buried Prophet answered to the Hag | 487 Manfred | 2 | 275
Lay buried in torpor | 498 Manfred | 2 | 316
Buried, and raised again--consumed by worms | 580 Sardan | 4 | 161
So I be buried in my birth-place: better | 597 Foscari | 1 | 138
Buried in its immeasurable breast | 668 Heaven | | 967
But, ah! he died; and buried with him lay | 751 Juan | 1 | 265
Half buried in the tresses which it grasps | 798 Juan | 2 | 1548
And, buried, sinks beneath its offspring's doom | 829 Juan | 4 | 812
But buried in the heap of such transactions | 871 Juan | 7 | 267
And had just buried the fair-faced Lanskoi | 902 Juan | 9 | 376
Glimmer on high; their buried locks still wave | 982 Juan | 16 | 147

BURKE

Now Burke, now Tooke, he grew to people's fancies | 294 Vision | | 631
'Brandy for heroes!' Burke could once exclaim | 417 Island | 1 | 101

BURLESQUE

Turns what was once romantic to burlesque | 816 Juan | 4 | 24

BURLETTA

The curtain dropp'd, the gay burletta o'er | 250 Bards | | 658

BURN

Abode of gods, whose shrines no longer burn | 19 Harold | 2 | 22
Nor ceased to burn till kingdoms were no more | 47 Harold | 3 | 764
With lava kisses melting while they burn | 62 Harold | 4 | 458
With equal ardour seems to burn | 91 Caroline-B | | 34
For him thy Beltane yet may burn | 104 Alva | | 220

BURN

These burn with one pure flame of generous love | 105 Nisus | | 15
Would make that breast burn with indignation burn | 126 Recoll | | 319
And bade them burn with fiercer glow | 134 E. N. Long | | 81
It blazes there but will not burn | 141 Critics | | 36
And bade them burn with fiercer glow | 148 A Fan | | 7
Some careful hand may teach to burn | 148 A Fan | | 14
Your hearts shall burn, your hopes expire | 172 Romaic-B | | 12
I burn, and feebly flutter there | 172 Romaic-B | | 16
Behold! while yet before thee burn | 185 Belshaz-A | | 3
Lights which ought to burn the brighter | 197 Rogers | | 69
'Twill flow, and cease to burn my brain | 218 Soul-B | | 8
Nor burn damn'd Drury if it rise again | 261 Hints | | 372
Burn all your last three works--and half the next | 265 Hints | | 658
Without amendment, and he answers, 'Burn | 267 Hints | | 786
Must burn before its surface shine | 319 Giaour | | 923
This brow that then will burn no more | 323 Giaour | | 1313
With thoughts that burn--in rays that melt | 327 Abydos | 1 | 331
Of--"Dost thou love?" and burn to answer, "No | 354 Corsair | 2 | 506
They did not know how hate can burn | 387 Corinth | | 322
These wither when for aught save blood they burn | 423 Island | 2 | 315
What! do not yet the red-hot ploughshares burn | 453 Venice-B | | 71
And Carthage ruins, my lone breast may burn | 457 Dante | 1 | 105
It will not burn so long as I must watch | 478 Manfred | 1 | 2
Adore and burn | 665 Heaven | | 779
Which may protect me at a pinch. Burn still | 701 Werner | 3 | 426
My eyeballs burn and throb, but have no tears | 770 Juan | 1 | 1536
And bards burn what they call their 'midnight taper | 773 Juan | 1 | 1742
To burn a town which never did them harm | 876 Juan | 7 | 608
Without resistance, see their city burn | 888 Juan | 8 | 612
Must burn more mildly ere it can enlighten | 922 Juan | 11 | 216

BURN'D

Who but would deem their bosoms burn'd anew | 31 Harold | 2 | 713
Than if for other hearts I burn'd | 152 Remind | | 28
And burn'd poor Moscow like a tub of 'tar | 170 Address-B | | 20
His constant pipe, which never yet burn'd dim | 425 Island | 2 | 475
And distant from each other burn'd the lights | 860 Juan | 6 | 506
Until each high, heroic bosom burn'd | 875 Juan | 7 | 507
A lamp burn'd high, while he leant from a niche | 982 Juan | 16 | 125
Which still in Juan's candlesticks burn'd high | 996 Juan | 16 | 981

BURNING
(See also EVER-BURNING, HEART-BURNING)

And burning with high hope, shall moulder cold and low | 39 Harold | 3 | 243
Along his burning page, distemper'd though it seems | 47 Harold | 3 | 742
Thou couldst not feel my burning cheek | 90 Caroline-A | | 13
While Envy waved her burning brand | 105 Alva | | 287
With tears the burning cheek of each bedew'd | 107 Nisus | | 129
Burning with wrath, he view'd his soldiers fall | 110 Nisus | | 359
While thousands, throng'd around the burning dome | 169 Address-A | | 11
Till Lethe quench life's burning stream | 171 Remember-A | | 2
The Roman, when his burning heart | 180 Ode-A | | 55
Of the eagle's burning crest | 187 Ode-B | | 63
In many a branding page and burning line | 271 Minerva | | 204
The Inquisition, with her burning feast | 302 Age | | 335
But could not, for my burning brow | 322 Giaour | | 1261
Vain voice! the spirit burning but unbent | 352 Corsair | 2 | 334
'Tis more than nature's; like the burning might | 357 Corsair | 3 | 101
Burning for pleasure, not averse from strife | 367 Lara | 1 | 116
That for a burning moment fever'd there | 373 Lara | 1 | 535
In vain impels the burning mouth to crave | 380 Lara | 2 | 404
Nor his, what burning patriots feel | 387 Corinth | | 302
And o'er his brow the burning lamp | 397 Parisina | | 116
Those furrows which the burning share | 402 Parisina | | 541
Which link the burning chain that binds | 409 Mazeppa | | 240
O'er those who, burning in the new-born fire | 420 Island | 2 | 115
While the scorch'd mountain, from whose burning breast | 463 Dante | 3 | 189
The burning wreck of a demolish'd world | 479 Manfred | 1 | 45
His vitals with her burning hands, till he | 518 Faliero | 2 | 685
The burning oracle of all that live | 561 Sardan | 2 | 15
Crowd in my breast to burning, when I hear | 631 Cain | 1 | 254
Our brother Satan fell; his burning will | 666 Heaven | | 832
So brief and burning, with a lady's zone | 706 Werner | 4 | 121
Burning in a quenchless lot | 729 Deformed | 1 | 464
Ye who weep o'er Carthage burning | 735 Deformed | 2 | 55
But will keep baking, broiling, burning on | 754 Juan | 1 | 500
For that compression in its burning core | 755 Juan | 1 | 573
And burning blushes, though for no transgression | 756 Juan | 1 | 587
The seventh day, and no wind--the burning sun | 783 Juan | 2 | 569
And all the burning tongues the passions teach | 798 Juan | 2 | 1509
And when those deep and burning moments pass'd | 798 Juan | 2 | 1553
The hand from burning underneath them placed | 809 Juan | 3 | 502
Where burning Sappho loved and sung | 812 Juan | 3 | 705
My own the burning tear-drop laves | 813 Juan | 3 | 777
For good or evil, burning from its birth | 823 Juan | 4 | 443
Bright--and as black and burning as a coal | 828 Juan | 4 | 749
Of burning streets, like moonlight on the water | 894 Juan | 8 | 975
Far flash'd her burning towers o'er Danube's stream | 894 Juan | 8 | 1011

BURNING

Could rhyme, like Nero, o'er a burning city 895 Juan 8 1072
Nor in her eye Ausonia's glance is burning 939 Juan 12 596
Since burning aged women (save a few 997 Juan 17 51

BURNISH'D

The mirth of feasts, the clang of burnish'd arms 120 Newstead-A 54

BURNS

Of true devotion monkish incense burns 14 Harold 1 682
And still the eloquent air breathes--burns with Cicero 72 Harold 4 1008
It burns with no responsive glow 90 Caroline-B 19
Here is a soul with hope immortal burns 106 Nisus 49
But the tear which now burns on my cheek may impart 182 Music-A 3
Pure is the flame which o'er her altar burns 245 Bards 291
Lo! Burns and Bloomfield, nay, a greater far 252 Bards 777
To deck the turf that wraps her minstrel, Burns 252 Bards 812
Ah! let me cease; in vain my bosom burns 265 Hints 619
Burns the slow flame, eternal--but unseen 343 Corsair 1 352
Before them burns the lamp, and spreads the chart 346 Corsair 1 587
The ever-burning lamp that burns without 594 Sardan 5 420
No, let me die! It must not be. It burns 654 Cain 3 500
From their proud nostrils, burns the very air 729 Deformed 1 514
Like Burns (whom Doctor Currie well describes 814 Juan 3 828

BURNT

(See also SUN-BURNT)

Were burnt for beacons; cities were consumed 189 Darkness 13
Though burnt by wicked Bedford for a witch 244 Bards 207
And burnt my lips up with her noisome kisses 580 Sardan 4 150
With the burnt offerings, which he daily brings 647 Cain 3 100
Thy burnt flesh-off'ring prospers better; see 650 Cain 3 284
Christians have burnt each other, quite persuaded 757 Juan 663
Baked, fried, or burnt, turn'd inside-out, or drown'd 901 Juan 9 293
Burnt, and not blue, as modest tapers use 983 Juan 16 202

BURNT-OUT

Above his burnt-out brain, and sapless cinders 925 Juan 11 477

BURROWING

Burrowing for boroughs like a rat or rabbit 989 Juan 16 602

BURST

Or burst the vanish'd Hero's lofty mound 20 Harold 2 37
A cry of horror burst from every tongue 126 Recoll 276
Shall burst the bondage of the grave 128 Answer-B 44
E'er burst from its mortal control 151 Soul-A 3
Clouds burst, skies flash, oh, dreadful hour! 158 Storm 29
When 'tis full 'twill burst asunder 187 Ode-B 13
Like a stream which burst its banks 187 Ode-B 46
Thoughts which have turn'd to thunder--scorch-- and burst 193 Monody 94
Within her walls, burst into tears 195 Ballad-A 109
Or else this heavy heart will burst 218 Soul-B 12
And the thunderbolt burst on the conqueror's head 221 Jerusalem 16
Wrath's vial on thy lofty head hath burst 223 To Dives 4
Her fetters burst, and just released from prison 244 Bards 209
Till, burst at length, their watery head o'erflows 270 Minerva 141
Now should they burst on thy devoted coast 272 Minerva 309
Burst from your lead and be yourselves alive 275 Waltz 136
But no,--their embers soon will burst the mould 308 Age 754
She burst into a laughter so extreme 308 Age 775
That sound had burst his waking dream 312 Giaour 247
That heart hath burst--that eye was closed 335 Abydos 2 619
Burst forth in one wild cry--and all was still 336 Abydos 2 639
Whose scatter'd streams from granite basins burst 349 Corsair 1 127
Up rose the Dervise with that burst of light 349 Corsair 2 142
And burst within--and it were death to wait 349 Corsair 2 183
'Oh! burst the Haram--wrong not on your lives 350 Corsair 2 202
That frantic echo burst the sleeping ear 369 Lara 1 206
Burst forth, and made him all he once had been 378 Lara 2 246
And that last gasp hath burst his bloody girth 380 Lara 2 397
And charged to crush him--let it burst 391 Corinth 662
And burst his girth, and tore his rein 396 Corinth 1064
Then burst her voice in one long shriek 400 Parisina 347
I burst my chain with one strong bound 404 Chillon 210
Panting as if his heart would burst 413 Mazeppa 665
Which welcomes, as a well, the clouds that burst 418 Island 1 190
Match'd with that burst of nature, even in thought 420 Island 2 120
And burst and madden'd with disdain and grief 468 Morgante 128
As though they wish'd to burst at once, they ate 474 Morgante 529
And burst, while cold on earth lay head and hoof 474 Morgante 542
And he has burst;--to this what say you, count 474 Morgante 547
But he will make you burst, you may be sure 474 Morgante 572
In the first burst of passion, pour away 509 Faliero 2 16
And relatives, in the first burst of vengeance 530 Faliero 4 147
Over my mood, when its first burst was spent 534 Faliero 4 450
Though my heart burst, it shall be silent.--Speak 544 Faliero 5 475
All-glorious burst from ocean? why not dart 562 Sardan 2 20

BURST

Will burst all cerement, even a living grave's 609 Foscari 3 81
To burst, if aught of venom touches it 625 Foscari 5 296
And burst 670 Heaven 1117
Enough of the Order to have burst two peasants 675 Werner 1 223
And then of these some part burst into tears 786 Juan 2 777
And fed by spoonfuls, else they always burst 794 Juan 2 1264
The fire burst forth from her Numidian veins 823 Juan 4 455
A vein had burst, and her sweet lips' pure dyes 823 Juan 4 465
So that he spoke not, but burst into tears 840 Juan 5 540
And waited but the signal's voice to burst 846 Juan 5 936
Will oftentimes make deadly quarrels burst 873 Juan 7 396
Glory and triumph o'er her aspect burst 884 Juan 8 379
And was not likely all at once to burst 904 Juan 9 467
Our bubbles; as the old burst, new emerge 963 Juan 14 491
                                              980 Juan 15 790

BURSTING

Bursting to light in terrible array 21 Harold 2 122
And deeply swells the bursting storm 104 Alva 252
Still bid the bursting spirit soar 217 The Harp 18
Fear'd like a bear just bursting from his cage 268 Hints 838
If bursting heart, and madd'ning brain 321 Giaour 1107
What star--what sun is bursting on the bay 349 Corsair 2 136
Curst Gan, with envy bursting, had such need 467 Morgante 85
Than mounted there, the bursting organ's peal 713 Werner 5 23
Now overhead a rainbow, bursting through 785 Juan 2 721
Taught to conceal, their bursting hearts despond 799 Juan 2 1596
A pretty lad, but bursting with conceit 827 Juan 4 706

BURSTS

Once more through all he bursts his thundering way 16 Harold 1 780
Bursts from my heart and mingles with the strain 19 Harold 1 928
Which bursts when Nature's feelings newly flow 183 Address-C 32
Till the swoln bubble bursts--and all is air 243 Bards 134
Who bursts the chains of millions to renew 301 Age 256
As the bolt bursts on high 327 Abydos 1 336
But when the day-blush bursts from high 336 Abydos 2 705
He climbs the crackling stair, he bursts the door 350 Corsair 2 211
Keep a firm rein upon these bursts of passion 528 Faliero 3 651
A twilight tempest, bursts forth in such thunder 576 Sardan 3 317
But leaps, and bursts, and sometimes foxes' brushes 959 Juan 14 274

BURTHEN

The baleful burthen of this honest song 208 Sketch 38
'The burthen ye so gently bear 313 Giaour 360
Their burthen round Sigaeum's steep 335 Abydos 2 601
Wrapt round some burthen at his saddle-bow 383 Lara 2 560
And lifting thence the burthen which he bore 383 Lara 2 566
To bear a burthen and to serve a need 464 Dante 4 89
For brutes of burthen, not for birds of prey 484 Manfred 2 36
Until he reel'd beneath his heavy burthen 546 Faliero 5 600
Not to add to each other's natural burthen 556 Sardan 1 398
There is one burthen which I beg you bear 623 Foscari 5 205
That back of thine may bear its burthen; 'tis 722 Deformed 1 6
It bears its burthen;--but my heart! Will it 722 Deformed 1 8
Death left no doubt, and the dead burthen lay 785 Juan 2 715

BURTHENS

Kick off their burthens, meaning the high classes 929 Juan 11 664

BURTHENSOME

Less burthensome to his immense existence 629 Cain 1 150

BURY

Bury your steel in the bosoms of Gath 219 Saul-A 4
And flings them, our community to bury 469 Morgante 203
And oftentimes avenge them; bury mine 542 Faliero 5 292
To me to bury and to mourn; but if 614 Foscari 3 391
Along the road, as if they went to bury 916 Juan 10 565

BUSBY

And Master G--- recites what Doctor Busby sings 170 Address-B 16
Oh! for the flow of Busby or of Fitz 274 Waltz 25

BUSBY'S

Borne in the vast balloon of Busby's song 171 Address-B 40

BUSEY

The Ladies Scilly, Busey;--Miss Eclat 951 Juan 13 628

BUSH

A stain on every bush that bore 316 Giaour 665
O'er channell'd rock and broken bush 406 Chillon 338

BUSHES

To beat the bushes, and the day looks promising 705 Werner 4 77
Who, after a long chase o'er hills, dales, bushes 959 Juan 14 278

BUSHY

And keep your bushy locks a year from Blake 263 Hints 476
By bushy brake, and wild flowers blossoming 340 Corsair 1 125

BUSIER
And found in busier scenes relief   155 Lady-E   8

BUSINESS
But still to business he held fast   163 Blacket   11
What business had they there at such a time   215 Dream   166
Damn'd business for my Miss Medea, etc., etc.   225 Embargo   6
That's my bookseller's business; I care not for
    sale   279 Blues   1   121
Terrestrial business fill'd nought in the sky   285 Vision   19
His business so augmented of late years   285 Vision   25
My business and your own is not to enquire   287 Vision   174
Or business carries them in search of game   291 Vision   423
So lets 's to business: why this general call   293 Vision   532
The very business you are now upon   296 Vision   707
That hath no business to appear   405 Chillon   298
It hath no business where thou art a guest   438 Tasso   108
Let him refer his business to the council   504 Faliero   1   319
My lord, a man without, on urgent business   529 Faliero   4   113
Business to-morrow. Ay, or death to-night   560 Sardan   1   649
Our business is with night--'tis come. But not   562 Sardan   2   40
And now, sir, to your business. 'Tis decreed   605 Foscari   2   260
We have higher business for our own. This day   615 Foscari   4   18
I will be legislator in this business   615 Foscari   4   39
About the business you provided for him   618 Foscari   4   225
You would deprive this old man of all business   619 Foscari   4   256
And has done miracles i' the way of business   674 Werner   1   192
That I would be alone; but to your business   674 Werner   1   205
I know no further. It is a strange business   686 Werner   2   229
I have pledged myself to do so; and the business   689 Werner   2   421
Be you the man or no, 'tis not my business   700 Werner   3   322
Save mine, stain'd in this business? Trifling
    villain   715 Werner   5   164
When I grow weary of it, I have business   735 Deformed   1   890
Come, count, to business. True. I'll weep
    hereafter   737 Deformed   2   155
And put the business past all kind of doubt   750 Juan   1   208
Sees half the business in a wicked way   760 Juan   1   902
Under pretence of business indispensable   765 Juan   1   1202
He had no business to commit a sin   767 Juan   1   1330
From this my subject, has no business here   794 Juan   2   1244
Which put off business to the ensuing session   814 Juan   3   862
Would reconcile him to the business quite   840 Juan   5   566
This awkward business without harm to others   866 Juan   6   927
Turns out to be a butcher in great business   877 Juan   7   663
His morns he pass'd in business--which, dissected   926 Juan   11   505
Was like all business a laborious nothing   926 Juan   11   506
And now to business.--O my gentle Juan   932 Juan   12   177
Arising out of business, often brought   943 Juan   13   114
In any body's business but the king's   963 Juan   14   522
Your men of business are not apt to express   965 Juan   14   606
My business is with Lady Adeline   966 Juan   14   719
Because my business is to dress society   979 Juan   15   741

BUSKIN
And knew all niceties of the sock and buskin   444 Beppo   246

BUST
Is the spot mark'd with no colossal bust   37 Harold   3   147
Their tomb was simple, and without a bust   45 Harold   3   633
The lightning rent from Ariosto's bust   61 Harold   4   361
Could not her quarries furnish forth one bust   63 Harold   4   503
The Caesar's pageant, shorn of Brutus' bust   64 Harold   4   525
Gave to the vulgar gaze each glorious bust   183 Address-D   3
A bust delay'd, a book refused, can shake   299 Age   65
Shall crown the Atlantic like the hero's bust   299 Age   112
Are bards; the kindled marble's bust may wear   463 Dante   4   25
On his vast bust, whence a huge quiver rose   579 Sardan   4   89
A name, a wretched picture, and worse bust   773 Juan   1   1744
There was an Irish lady, to whose bust   789 Juan   2   947
But only give a bust of marriages   802 Juan   3   60
And this omission, like that of the bust   974 Juan   15   385
It press'd upon a hard but glowing bust   996 Juan   16   1019

BUSTLE
Now all was bustle, and the menial train   28 Harold   2   536
A general bustle spread throughout the throng   296 Vision   729
The busy sounds, the bustle of the shore   345 Corsair   1   523
He will be here anon. What ho, there! bustle   675 Werner   1   258
Bustle, my boys! we are at fault. In what   697 Werner   3   145
To spare both that I would avoid all bustle   700 Werner   3   321
Who in the earlier ages raised a bustle   752 Juan   1   323
And could be very busy without bustle   883 Juan   8   312
But when the levee rose, and all was bustle   907 Juan   9   649
Who in his time had made heroic bustle   920 Juan   11   146
There was much bustle too, and preparation   989 Juan   16   587

BUSTLED
Antonia bustled round the ransack'd room   766 Juan   1   1266

BUSTLING
No bustling Botherbys have they to show 'em   449 Beppo   575
I thought our bustling host without had said   676 Werner   1   318

BUSTS
Their eyes on honour'd forms whose busts around
    them close   77 Harold   4   1323

BUSY
When busy Memory flashes on my brain   20 Harold   2   76
The hoarse command, the busy humming din   22 Harold   2   156
He heard the busy hum of warrior-men   27 Harold   2   494
While busy preparation shook the court   28 Harold   2   501
But spare its relics--let no busy hand   34 Harold   2   875
Of busy cities, now in vain display'd   60 Harold   4   286
Are swept for ever from this busy world   127 Recoll   388
This busy scene of splendid woe   135 I Would   46
The world befits a busy brain   164 Friend-B   43
Then back to busy life again   166 Struggle   4
Whose busy accents whisper blame   174 Remember-B   14
My hands are full, my head so busy   232 Doctor   87
And rising ports along the busy shore   258 Hints   97
With even the busy Northern Isle unknown   298 Age   41
Through many a busy bitter scene   322 Giaour   1238
For the wild-bird, the busy springes set   338 Corsair   1   53
The busy sounds, the bustle of the shore   345 Corsair   1   523
Shrieks the shrill whistle--ply the busy hands   346 Corsair   1   574
Well, since we met, hath sped my busy time   360 Corsair   3   316
There are bright faces in the busy hall   366 Lara   1   5
That rises as the busy bosom sinks   374 Lara   1   602
Such as the busy brain of Sorrow paints   384 Lara   2   610
They were too busy to bark at him   389 Corinth   457
Of gondolas--and to the busy hum   453 Venice-B   25
Chamber swims round and round--and shadows busy   453 Venice-B   51
And busy with thy name; a noble name   491 Manfred   3   31
A roused mechanic in your busy plot   520 Faliero   3   112
Thou camest hither I was busy writing   609 Foscari   3   67
Pass on. We sought the Doge. He's busy, look   618 Foscari   4   224
The busy have no time for tears. And therefore   619 Foscari   4   255
Thou busy devil, rising in my heart   697 Werner   3   149
So that all hands were busy beyond measure   804 Juan   3   159
A busy character in the dull scene   818 Juan   4   116
'Right! I was busy, and forgot. Why, you   875 Juan   7   521
For he was dizzy, busy, and his veins   882 Juan   8   258
And could be very busy without bustle   883 Juan   8   312
Heard,--and that bee-like, bubbling, busy hum   919 Juan   11   63
Buzz round 'the Fortune' with their busy battery   933 Juan   12   255
He also had been busy seeing sights   940 Juan   12   649
There were two lawyers busy on a mortgage   988 Juan   16   521
Both busy (as a general in his tent   989 Juan   16   574

BUT
The worst can be but mine   167 Dead   29
Since earthly eye but ill can bear   167 Dead   44
'And sleeping pangs awake--and--but away   170 Address-B   13
That--but I know thy blessed bosom fraught   175 Sonnet-A   6
If his eyes were good, he but saw by night   177 Devil's Dr   85
'Tis done--but yesterday a King   180 Ode-A   1
Which man seem'd made but to obey   180 Ode-A   33
To oppose them, but--In Venice 'but' 's a traitor   616 Foscari   4   73
Ay, but not Anah: she but loves her God   657 Heaven   181
He gave me life--he taketh but   670 Heaven   1153
Suspects, 'tis but suspicion, and he is   703 Werner   3   558
For my part I say nothing--nothing--but   753 Juan   1   409
At last they did get at it really, but   777 Juan   2   221
To hear new words, and to repeat them; but   795 Juan   2   1330
Haidee and Juan were not married, but   803 Juan   3   89
The second had his cheek laid open; but   822 Juan   4   385
She was not violently lively, but   857 Juan   6   337
Which was a mixture of all metals, but   859 Juan   6   442
Bellona, what you will--they mean but wars   878 Juan   8   8
I should be loth to march without you, but   891 Juan   8   807
And, after all, what is a lie? 'Tis but   923 Juan   11   289
To take some trouble with his toilet, but   984 Juan   16   226

BUTCHER
Or to the butcher to purvey the lamb   286 Vision   117
The bigot monarch and the butcher priest   302 Age   334
At last of one patrician! Butcher me   522 Faliero   3   228
Of the lamb to the butcher, or the cry   543 Faliero   5   395
Vernon, the butcher Cumberland, Wolfe, Hawke   747 Juan   1   9
Turns out to be a butcher in great business   877 Juan   7   663
Before they butcher. Little Leila gazed   916 Juan   10   591

BUTCHER'D
Butcher'd to make a Roman holiday   76 Harold   4   1267
Should now be butcher'd in a civic alley   836 Juan   5   296
Who butcher'd half the earth, and bullied t'other   917 Juan   10   648

BUTCHER'S
When demagogues would with a butcher's knife   990 Juan   16   637

BUTCHER-WORK
Might once again renew their ancient butcher-work   29 Harold   2   603
You feel not--you go to this butcher-work   527 Faliero   3   627

BUTCHERY
Is butchery, sometimes a single sorrow   876 Juan   7   551

BUTE
Than Bute and Grafton, and shall be unwilling   293 Vision   564

BUTLER
And daughters sometimes run off with the butler   804 Juan   3   176

BUTS
But me no 'buts,' unless you would pass o'er   616 Foscari   4   74

BUTT
With maudlin Clarence in his Malmsey butt   767 Juan   1   1328
His brow, as if in act to butt, and then   805 Juan   3   255

BUTTER
As oil in lieu of butter men decry   265 Hints   629
Besides, they always smell of bread and butter   445 Beppo   312
Two casks of biscuit and a keg of butter   779 Juan   2   367
And also for the biscuit-casks and butter   781 Juan   2   488

BUTTER'D
Of which he butter'd both sides; 'twould delay   297 Vision   764
Lord Henry said his muffin was ill butter'd   984 Juan   16   244

BUTTERFLIES
Of colour'd garbs, as bright as butterflies   805 Juan   3   216
Who think that novelties are butterflies   933 Juan   12   213

BUTTERFLY
Pleasure shall, like a butterfly new caught   462 Dante   3   115
Spare him--he's none: a mere court butterfly   588 Sardan   5   90
My Muse, the butterfly hath but her wings   952 Juan   13   709

BUTTERY
Weights, measures, larder, cellar, buttery   684 Werner   2   44

BUTTON
He tore the topmost button from his vest   434 Island   4   334

BUTTONS
With buttons form'd of pearls as large as peas   810 Juan   3   557

BUTTRESS
The buttress from some mountain's bosom hurl'd   432 Island   4   149

BUTTRESSES
Some fifty buttresses--and roused the rats   701 Werner   3   402

BUXOM
Some voices of the buxom middle-aged   895 Juan   8   1049

BUY
My sabre shall win what the feeble must buy   30 Harold   2   670
What gold could never buy   228 To Her   4
Fresh fish from Hippocrene! who'll buy? who'll
   buy   247 Bards   391
Weighs well and wisely what to sell or buy   260 Hints   257
Cannot find the new volume I wanted to buy   277 Blues   1   19
Whatever you publish, am ready to buy   279 Blues   1   120
I shall think of him oft when I buy a new hat   281 Blues   2   61
Since with me came a heart he could not buy   360 Corsair   3   330
Dearly they have bought us, dearly still may buy   428 Island   3   157
And buy repentance, ere they grow devout   440 Beppo   5
Walk or ride to the Strand, and buy in gross   441 Beppo   60
A third--where did she buy that frightful turban   448 Beppo   522
Or buy in selfish marriage some young victim   513 Faliero   2   319
Next Juan stood, till some might choose to buy   832 Juan   5   80
I wish to G--d that somebody would buy us   834 Juan   5   192
So silly as to buy slaves who might share   857 Juan   6   286

BUYER
And apt to be transferr'd to the first buyer   854 Juan   6   126

BUYING
And buying other's grief at any price   213 Lady Byron   46

BUYS
Buys land, and shrewdly trusts not to the Bank   260 Hints   246
Buys them in marriage--and what rests beyond   799 Juan   2   1598
They have a king who buys and sells   813 Juan   3   768

BUZZ
And here the buzz of eager nations ran   76 Harold   4   1243
Buzz round 'the Fortune' with their busy battery   933 Juan   12   255

BUZZING
And here, where buzzing nations choked the ways   76 Harold   4   1271

BY
(See also PASSER-BY, WHERE-BY)
But long ere scarce a third of his pass'd by   4 Harold   1   32
There sits in parchment robe array'd, and by   8 Harold   1   292

BY
The humblest of thy pilgrims passing by   13 Harold   1   618
Hurl the dark bulk along, scarce seen in dashing
   by   16 Harold   1   791
Unmoved the Moslem sits, the light Greek carols by   21 Harold   2   90
Or schoolboy Midshipman that, standing by   22 Harold   2   160
Save Admiration glancing harmless by   24 Harold   2   273
Nor niggard of his cheer; the passer by   27 Harold   2   439
And Laos wide and fierce came roaring by   27 Harold   2   488
Whither I know not; but the hour's gone by   35 Harold   3   8
When the whole host of hatred stood hard by   41 Harold   3   347
With its own flickering, or a sword laid by   42 Harold   3   395
And food for meditation, nor pass by   50 Harold   3   921
And majesty flash their full lightnings by   79 Harold   4   1448
We hence may meet, and pass each other by   94 Dorset   99
fall, raise the song of bards; and lay me by   130 Calmar   60
Through many a weary day gone by   141 Pignus   13
Awake the pangs that pass not by   151 Farewell-B   11
Endear'd by days gone by   159 Storm   58
While day and night roll darkling by   172 Romaic-B   4
In envious dimness pass'd thy portrait by   183 Address-D   48
Then throw the worthless bauble by   185 Belshaz-A   14
The church of St. Mark--which stands hard by   196 Venice-A   31
Before its fourth in time had pass'd me by   212 Augusta-C   112
May glance in tameless transport by   217 Gazelle   6
And Bow-street myrmidons stood laughing by   248 Bards   467
Who rends the veil of ages long gone by   253 Bards   875
Nor unregarded will the act pass by   258 Hints   131
And dull were his that pass'd them heedless by   269 Minerva   48
Or distant lightning on the horizon by night   292 Vision   486
As meteor-like thou glidest by   312 Giaour   197
He winds around; he hurries by   312 Giaour   210
Pass heedless and unheeded by   313 Giaour   345
The nearest oar that's scatter'd by   314 Giaour   367
No: gayer insects fluttering by   314 Giaour   416
Reveals too much of times gone by   318 Giaour   835
Will scarce delay the passer by   319 Giaour   877
Not oft betrays to standers by   324 Abydos   1   27
Or stand with smiles unmurmuring by   328 Abydos   1   402
He shunn'd, nor sought, but coldly pass'd them by   342 Corsair   1   290
Secure, unnoted, Conrad's prow pass'd by   347 Corsair   1   599
And dull were his that pass'd them heedless by   356 Corsair   3   48
She drops her veil, and stands in silence by   363 Corsair   3   517
That smile might reach his lip but pass'd not by   370 Lara   1   301
It were too much for Lara to pass by   372 Lara   1   427
Their growth but glanced unheeded by   402 Parisina   535
And a low breeze crept moaning by   411 Mazeppa   440
As stately swept the gallant vessel by   418 Island   1   224
It glanced on Torquil, who lean'd faintly by   428 Island   3   144
But did not merit to expire by her   457 Dante   1   71
Once more he bade him lay his burden by   475 Morgante   590
Though thou seest me not pass by   481 Manfred   1   212
Not by me, but by the ungrateful nobles   519 Faliero   3   34
Of his departure had been sent him by   777 Juan   2   191
Of good example; pity that so few by   848 Juan   5   1044
To educate--ye youth of Europe--you by   848 Juan   5   1046
The second object was to profit by   870 Juan   7   185
Of all the standing army who stood by   906 Juan   9   624
They err'd, as aged men will do; but by   923 Juan   11   281
But slowly; and as he pass'd Juan by   983 Juan   16   167

BY AND BY
Rest in this arm. We may meet by and by   693 Werner   2   644
Ulric, you'll come and hear me? By and by   708 Werner   4   269
'Perhaps we shall be one day, by and by   834 Juan   5   189
The same, Katinka, until by and by   858 Juan   6   387
The people by and by will be the stronger   884 Juan   8   396
I by and by may tell you, if at all   896 Juan   8   1108
Just now,--but by and by the Truth will show 'em   899 Juan   9   173
Before they give their broadside. By and by   918 Juan   10   666
Just now enough; but by and by I'll prattle   918 Juan   10   695
But this won't do, save by and by; and he   927 Juan   11   545
Tells an odd story, of which by and by   985 Juan   16   284

BY THE BY
(Her blood was not all Spanish, by the by   754 Juan   1   443
(Who, by the by, when clever, are more handy   933 Juan   12   252

BYE
Now, Strephon, good bye; I cannot deny   116 Strephon   33

BYRON
There's Byron, too, who once did better   231 Doctor   33

BY-WORD
Her very by-word sprung from victory   57 Harold   4   119
Transferr'd his by-word to thy brow   181 Ode-A   126
It is a word--nay, worse--a worthless by-word   501 Faliero   1   129
Into a by-word; and the doubly felon   515 Faliero   2   430

BYZANTIAN
Cam Hobhouse! but by wags Byzantian Ben   224 J.C.H.   2

BYZANTINE
From the Byzantine maid's unsleeping spirit   487 Manfred   2   277

BYZANTIUM
Where free Byzantium once arose   158 Florence   34

BYZANTIUM'S
Th' octogenarian chief, Byzantium's conquering
  foe   57 Harold   4 108

C
E--- is a wife, and C--- a mother   133 E. N. Long   64
S---, W---, C---, L---d, and L---e   225 Orraca   3
Present, Lords A.B.C.'--Earls, dukes, by name   947 Juan   13 426

CA
Or 'Ca ira,' according to the fashion all   812 Juan   3 676

CABAL
Or some unknown cabal, caprice   331 Abydos   2 266
Cabal, and put men's lives out, as if life   603 Foscari   2 113
Cabal in commonwealth, nor secret means   605 Foscari   2 232

CABALA
Cabala; their best brick-work, wherewithal   732 Deformed   1 684

CABIN
'Hey day! call you that a cabin   157 Hodgson   37
Down to the cabin with Gonsalvo bends   346 Corsair   1 585
The gallant chief within his cabin slept   415 Island   1   17
Sorrow and shame are handmaids of your cabin   690 Werner   2 443
From his dull cabin, found himself a slave   826 Juan   4 626

CABIN'D
Is chain'd and tortured--cabin'd, cribb'd,
  confined   74 Harold   4 1140
Wounded and fetter'd, 'cabin'd, cribb'd, confined   826 Juan   4 593

CABINET
Alas! how could his cabinet thus err   308 Age   721
He in the cabinet being always ready   466 Morgante   37
Sweet Angiolina! I must to my cabinet   515 Faliero   2 480
A cabinet with letters, papers, and   683 Werner   2   36
Also the cabinet, if portable   684 Werner   2   54
My cabinet before me with some gold   686 Werner   2 235
Upon his cabinet, besides the presents   906 Juan   9 631
Between the British cabinet and Russian   913 Juan   10 355
Lord Henry walk'd into his cabinet   964 Juan   14 538

CABLE
Hoarse o'er her side the rustling cable rings   339 Corsair   1   97
Theirs is the best bower anchor, the chain cable   930 Juan   12   19

CABLE'S
Within a cable's length their vessels lay   870 Juan   7 228

CACIQUE
Cacique in Mexico, and prince in Wales   245 Bards   222
Young Freedom plumes the crest of each cacique   302 Age   279
Fix'd upon Chili's shore, a proud cacique   421 Island   2 183

CADENCE
Whilst to the gale in mournful cadence wave   124 Recoll   161
Soften'd by distance to a hymn-like cadence   732 Deformed   1 687

CADES
Floats scumlike uppermost, and these Jack Cades   815 Juan   3 893

CADIZ
But Cadiz, rising on the distant coast   14 Harold   1 659
Fair Cadiz, rising o'er the dark blue sea   15 Harold   1 712
Adieu, fair Cadiz! yea, a long adieu   18 Harold   1 873
If Cadiz yet be free   159 Storm   54
Like me, the lovely girl of Cadiz   159 Cadiz   4
Enchants you like the Girl of Cadiz   160 Cadiz   24
May match the dark-eyed Girl of Cadiz   160 Cadiz   56
Cadiz perhaps--but that you soon may see   748 Juan   1   62
She sent her son to be shipp'd off from Cadiz   770 Juan   1 1520
I said that Juan had been sent to Cadiz   774 Juan   2   33
Her son to Cadiz only to embark   775 Juan   2   58
Was a small present made to him at Cadiz   784 Juan   2 647

CADMUS
Or Tyrian Cadmus roved afar   88 Anacreon-A   6
You have the letters Cadmus gave   812 Juan   3 747

CAESAR
At thy bathed base the bloody Caesar lie   68 Harold   4 778
Of bastard Caesar, following him of old   68 Harold   4 803
From Caesar the dreaded to George the despised   203 Avatar   64
His country's Caesar, Europe's Hannibal   301 Age   239
Had Caesar known but Cleopatra's kiss   423 Island   2 318
But try the Caesar, or the Catiline   509 Faliero   1 625
But not as a mock Caesar. Let him pass   725 Deformed   1 196
I trust. Then call me Caesar. Why, that name   730 Deformed   1 537
Caesar thou shalt be. For myself, my name   730 Deformed   1 542
And a worse name. I'm Caesar and a hunch-back   731 Deformed   1 643

CAESAR
And the first Caesar with his triumphs flits   733 Deformed   1 779
Oh, Love! of whom great Caesar was the suitor   800 Juan   2 1633
Caesar and Pompey, Mahomet, Belisarius   800 Juan   2 1643
Caesar himself, who, in the very sight   881 Juan   8 221
No Caesar, but a fine young lad, who fought   881 Juan   8 226
As Caesar wore his robe you wear your gown   909 Juan   10 120
Caesar himself would be ashamed of fame   968 Juan   14 816
Like 'Anthony's by Caesar,' by the few   974 Juan   15 423

CAESAREAN
To where the last Caesarean fortress stood   815 Juan   3 933

CAESARS
Had fix'd him with the Caesars in his fate   68 Harold   4 822
Within a bowshot. Where the Caesars dwelt   495 Manfred   3 282
Refused the diadem of all the Caesars   502 Faliero   1 202
Caesars have fallen, and even patrician hands   526 Faliero   3 556
Now. Well! the first of Caesars was a bald-head   731 Deformed   1 644
Retain'd her sway o'er nations, and the Caesars   734 Deformed   1 845

CAESAR'S
Look where the second Caesar's trophies rose   26 Harold   2 402
The Caesar's pageant, shorn of Brutus' bust   64 Harold   4 525
What are the laurels of the Caesar's brow   71 Harold   4 984
Like laurels on the bald first Caesar's head   76 Harold   4 1293
Hail'd a barbarian in her Caesar's place   93 Masters   4
Of sin and slaughter--from the Caesar's school   290 Vision   350
Thou Rome, who saw'st thy Caesar's deeds outdone   300 Age   137
And what have Caesar's deeds and Caesar's fame   423 Island   2 320
More near from out the Caesars' palace came   495 Manfred   3 276
While Caesar's chambers and the Augustan halls   495 Manfred   3 289
Said, 'Caesar's wife must not even be suspected   502 Faliero   1 198
In Alaric's time? No, slave! in the first
  Caesar's   734 Deformed   1 855
Like Titus' youth, and Caesar's earliest acts   814 Juan   3 827
Outbalances all Caesar's victories   853 Juan   6   32
Oh, Caesar's Commentaries! now impart, ye   877 Juan   7 653

CAFTAN
His calpac rent--his caftan red   317 Giaour   717

CAGE
Tamed to her cage, nor feels a wish to rove   28 Harold   2 544
Thou Timour! in his captive's cage   181 Ode-A   127
Fear'd like a bear just bursting from his cage   268 Hints   838
Reduced to nibble at his narrow cage   299 Age   56
When cities cage us in a social home   333 Abydos   2 437
Or broke its cage to perch on mine   405 Chillon   280
If they were fitted for the purposed cage   834 Juan   5 205

CAGED
He caged in one huge hamper altogether   804 Juan   3 144
Beating for love, as the caged bird's for air   855 Juan   6 208
In cities caged. The present case in point I   886 Juan   8 495
(Widows of forty were these birds long caged   895 Juan   8 1051

CAGES
To call them back into their separate cages   752 Juan   1 358

CAIN
What may the fruit be yet?--I know not, Cain was
  Eve's   77 Harold   4 1341
There read of Cain the curse and crime   320 Giaour   1058
But like the nephew of a Cain   331 Abydos   2 204
The prayers of Abel link'd to deeds of Cain   420 Island   2   72
And by thy brotherhood of Cain   481 Manfred   1 249
And the mere instinct of the first-born Cain   534 Faliero   4 405
Son Cain, my first-born, wherefore art thou
  silent   627 Cain   1   22
Her fruits with little labour. Cain, my son   628 Cain   1   50
The Eternal anger? My beloved Cain   628 Cain   1   55
Which cometh not. Cain! walk not with this
  spirit   633 Cain   1 358
Not as thou lovest Cain. Oh, my God   633 Cain   1 364
Them?--And as I love thee, my Cain! go not   633 Cain   1 372
Nearer, and nearer:--Cain--Cain--save me from him   633 Cain   1 410
His worship is but fear. Oh, Cain! choose love   634 Cain   1 428
Should we not love them and our children, Cain   634 Cain   1 434
I am not wretched, Cain, and if thou   634 Cain   1 460
Of which thy bosom is the germ. O Cain   635 Cain   1 521
But that's a mystery. Cain, come on with me   635 Cain   1 536
Spoke with our mother first. Cain! thou hast
  heard   636 Cain   1 554
Spirit, I have said it. Cain! my brother! Cain   636 Cain   1 559
Hush! tread softly, Cain. I will; but wherefore   646 Cain   3   1
Dear Cain! Nay, do not whisper o'er our son   646 Cain   3   35
Cain! that proud spirit who withdrew thee hence   646 Cain   3   45
Alas! thou sinnest now, my Cain: thy words   647 Cain   3   93
Touch not the child--my child! thy child! Oh,
  Cain   648 Cain   3 127
Oh Cain! look on him; see how full of life   648 Cain   3 140
For then we are all alike; is't not so, Cain   648 Cain   3 143
When thou art gentle. Love us, then, my Cain   648 Cain   3 147

CAIN

The pleasures of a parent! Bless him, Cain	648	Cain	3	154
Thy brother Abel. Welcome, Cain! My brother	648	Cain	3	162
We mean to sacrifice. Farewell, my Cain	648	Cain	3	173
Nor suffer any. Cain! what meanest thou	650	Cain	3	289
He did--Cain, give me--give me thy hand; and tell	651	Cain	3	320
Cain? Can it be that I am he? My brother	651	Cain	3	323
Thy murderer. Then may God forgive him! Cain	651	Cain	3	334
'Tis Cain; and watching by my husband. What	651	Cain	3	359
With stony lifelessness! Ah, cruel Cain	651	Cain	3	365
Or what hath done this deed?--speak, Cain, since thou	652	Cain	3	387
Speak, Cain! and say it was not thou! It was	652	Cain	3	396
Cain! clear thee from this horrible accusal	652	Cain	3	400
Hence, fratricide! henceforth that word is Cain	652	Cain	3	438
Cain! get thee forth: we dwell no more together	653	Cain	3	444
Cain! thou hast heard, we must go forth. I am ready	653	Cain	3	455
And the great God. Cain! Cain! Hear'st thou that voice	653	Cain	3	466
Cain! Cain! It soundeth like an angel's tone	653	Cain	3	467
My brother's keeper? Cain! what hast thou done	653	Cain	3	469
On Cain, so that he may go forth in safety	653	Cain	3	495
Who slayeth Cain, a sevenfold vengeance shall	653	Cain	3	496
Now, Cain! I will divide thy burden with thee	654	Cain	3	551
Against the metal of the sons of Cain	657	Heaven		191
But of the sons of Cain	662	Heaven		520
Children of Cain? From what? And is it so	663	Heaven		617
Warm in our veins,--strong Cain! who was begotten	664	Heaven		656
Offspring of Cain, thy father did so! But	664	Heaven		678
The God of Seth as Cain, I must obey	664	Heaven		694
From out the race of Cain; the sons of heaven	665	Heaven		738
It seems; and, of that few, the race of Cain	667	Heaven		884
Were graves permitted to the seed of Cain	668	Heaven		977
My Leipsic, and my Mount Saint Jean seems Cain	925	Juan	11	442

CAINA

But Caina waits for him our life who ended	476	Francesca		11

CAINITES

The rest of the stern Cainites, save in beauty	664	Heaven		672

CAIN'S

Wrote on his faded brow curst Cain's unresting doom	17	Harold	1	827
The last and loveliest of Cain's race, could share	664	Heaven		652
With Cain's, the eldest born of Adam's, blood	664	Heaven		655
A righteous death, unlike the seed of Cain's	667	Heaven		954

CAIO

Hail'd a strange brig--Corpo di Caio Mario	826	Juan	4	652

CAIQUE

Glanced many a light caique along the foam	32	Harold	2	765
And fearful for his light caique	312	Giaour		172
Wondering what next, till the caique was brought	836	Juan	5	318

CAIRN

And brilliant breeches, bright as a Cairn Gorme	902	Juan	9	341

CAIRNS

Whose grassy cairns ascend along the shore	422	Island	2	218

CAITIFF

To aid the damsel and destroy the caitiff	942	Juan	13	74

CAJOLES

Cajoles; there Wellington forgets to fight	307	Age		713

CALAIS

I said at Calais and have not forgot it	446	Beppo		370

CALAMITIES

Yet still, to increase your calamities more	116	To Eliza		9

CALAMITY

Calamity the nations with distress	464	Dante	4	73
Thy lore unto calamity? Why not	561	Sardan	2	18
This last calamity? With desperate firmness	620	Foscari	4	344
You scoff even at your own calamity	743	Deformed	3	86
And such calamity! how wert thou fallen	743	Deformed	3	87

CALCINED

Till thy hard heart be calcined into dust	209	Sketch		91

CALCULATE

Unless a man can calculate his means	932	Juan	12	167

CALCULATED

He gazed; Morgante's height he calculated	473	Morgante		449
And then--they calculated on his ransom	832	Juan	5	72
Who calculated life as so much dross	877	Juan	7	611
'Twas something calculated to allay	901	Juan	9	284

CALCULATING

Of this cool, calculating fiend, who walks	681	Werner	1	618
Not calculating how much they condensed	990	Juan	16	614

CALCULATION

In short, she was a walking calculation	749	Juan	1	121
For any sage's creed or calculation	907	Juan	10	4
Or revel in the joys of calculation	931	Juan	12	80
And hers were those which can face calculation	962	Juan	14	410

CALCULATORS

To calculators when they count on woman	960	Juan	14	344

CALDERON

All Calderon and greater part of Lope	748	Juan	1	82

CALDRON

Where reeking London's smoky caldron simmers	445	Beppo		344

CALDRONS

Their walls, to fill their household caldrons with	724	Deformed	1	127

CALDRON'S

Nor say one mass to cool the caldron's bubble	440	Beppo		31

CALECHE

In a most miserable old caleche	677	Werner	1	405
Bribe the intendant for his old caleche	698	Werner	3	189

CALEDON

Whether in Caledon or Italy	909	Juan	10	102

CALEDONIA

Blush, Caledonia, such thy son could be	21	Harold	2	95
Yet, Caledonia, beloved are thy mountains	117	Lachin		5
Yet Caledonia claims some native worth	270	Minerva		149

CALEDONIAN

Nipp'd in the bud by Caledonian gales	247	Bards		422

CALEDONIANS

Fires, such as gentle Caledonians feel	265	Hints		591

CALEDONIA'S

But Caledonia's goddess hover'd o'er	248	Bards		490
Say! will not Caledonia's annals yield	254	Bards		935
Survey Boeotia;--Caledonia's ours	270	Minerva		130

CALEDON'S

Hath fix'd high Caledon's unconquer'd name	182	Address-C		2

CALENDAR

But this day, black within the calendar	535	Faliero	4	504

CALENDARO

There is a certain Philip Calendaro	511	Faliero	2	136
No, Calendaro; these same drops of blood	516	Faliero	2	524
All leading qualities? No, Calendaro	518	Faliero	2	704
You, Calendaro, can pronounce, who have seen me	521	Faliero	3	176
Save Israel and Philip Calendaro	534	Faliero	4	399
And you, too, Philip Calendaro, what	539	Faliero	5	67
Even let them have their way, brave Calendaro	539	Faliero	5	115
The coward Bertram, would--Peace, Calendaro	539	Faliero	5	128
And Philip Calendaro, have admitted	540	Faliero	5	175

CALENDARS

When thou art noted in our calendars	545	Faliero	5	491

CALENTURES

The calentures of music which o'ercome	986	Juan	16	413

CALF

Some leaden calf--but whom it matters not	243	Bards		141
And case his volumes in congenial calf	251	Bards		738
Refused to kill the fatted calf; and, therefore	684	Werner	2	86

CALF-SKIN

And hang a calf-skin on those recreant lines	251	Bards		740

CALIDA

'Non ego hoc ferrem calida juventa	772	Juan	1	1689

CALIGULA

An obscene gesture cost Caligula	544	Faliero	5	442

CALL
(See also ROLL-CALL)

Mine dares not call thee from thy sacred hill	3	Harold	1	4
And when they on their father call	6	Harold	1	168
Or call with truth one span of earth their own	11	Harold	1	457
Hark, to the Boatswain's call, the cheering cry	22	Harold	2	158
The Muezzin's call doth shake the minaret	28	Harold	2	530
Leap from Eurotas' banks, and call thee from the tomb	31	Harold	2	701

CALL

But History's purchased page to call them great	42	Harold	3	430
Back to the joyous Alps who call to her aloud	49	Harold	3	868
Thoughts which should call down thunder and the flame	51	Harold	3	983
Thou, who didst call the Furies from the abyss	75	Harold	4	1183
Thy former realm, I call thee from the dust	75	Harold	4	1187
In Saxon times, which we are wont to call	77	Harold	4	1301
Still here forth my warm affection's tear	85	Death-B		23
Shall call my spirit, joyful in their choice	85	Fragment-A		2
Obedient to her call he flew	87	Catullus		6
Attending on their chieftain's call	102	Alva		92
Would call, thy Oscar might return	104	Alva		218
Roused by their call, nor court again repose	106	Nisus		82
Nor dare to call the blush from Beauty's cheek	113	Prologue		6
And call thy sylvan female choir	118	Romance		45
I cannot call one single blossom mine	125	Recoil		238
to the hero, and call the chief to arms	130	Calmar		51
Father of Light, on thee I call	132	Prayer		5
To Thee, my God, to thee I call	133	Prayer		49
Who dare not call their words their own	142	Critics		84
Who dare not call their very thoughts their own	143	Soliloquy		56
Father of Light! to Thee I call	146	Adieu		111
'Hey day! call you that a cabin	157	Hodgson		37
You call me still your life.---Oh! change the word	175	Portuguese-B		1
I shall hint to friend Moloch to call him to order	178	Devil's Dr		153
But there now was a 'call' and accomplish'd debaters	178	Devil's Dr		160
Then turn thee and call on the Chief of thy choice	186	Napoleon		24
'Wherefore call on us, O King	194	Ballad-A		33
Which some call fine, and some call frantic	233	Nihil		14
What did the House upon this call	235	New Song		5
A turn for punning, call it Attic salt	242	Bards		68
Why should we call them from their dark abode	251	Bards		709
Shall hoary Granta call her sable sons	255	Bards		961
Nor call a ghost, unless some cursed scrape	260	Hints		293
It will not do to call our fathers fools	262	Hints		432
And wayward voices, at their owner's call	264	Hints		553
The hero bounding at his country's call	272	Minerva		289
Which they call a disgrace to the age and the nation	277	Blues	1	31
To call you to this hotbed. I own it--'tis true	278	Blues	1	61
Is there one which I dare call my own any more	280	Blues	2	7
By the rag, tag, and bobtail, of those they call 'Blues	280	Blues	2	23
Don't call upon Scamp, who's already so harass'd	282	Blues	2	122
I'll trouble you to call your witnesses	291	Vision		408
My call for witnesses? I did not mean	292	Vision		498
By multo-scribbling Southey.--'Then we'll call	293	Vision		514
So lets's to business: why this general call	293	Vision		532
'Call Junius!' From the crowd a shadow stalk'd	294	Vision		585
'Tis, that what Junius we are wont to call	295	Vision		639
To call George Washington, and John Horne Tooke	295	Vision		670
Who now assemble at the holy call	303	Age		394
And call his vassals to submit	316	Giaour		598
'Now call me the chief of the Haram guard	324	Abydos	1	263
Call Haroun--he can tell it out	331	Abydos	2	247
But chiefly to my council call	333	Abydos	2	377
To pilgrims pure and prostrate at his call	333	Abydos	2	403
No--though again he call me coward	334	Abydos	2	536
And thought the voice of wrath a sacred call	342	Corsair	1	263
'Call Pedro here!' He comes, and Conrad bends	346	Corsair	1	561
A sound--a voice--a shriek--a fearful call	369	Lara	1	204
The gather'd chieftains come to Otho's call	375	Lara	2	20
They form no longer to their leader's call	379	Lara	2	285
In midnight call to wonted prayer	387	Corinth		267
Obey'd his voice, and came to call	407	Mazeppa		72
Were near at my command or call	415	Mazeppa		836
The freedom which can call each grot a home	416	Island	1	41
With no distracting world to call her off	423	Island	2	334
Each sought his fellow's eyes, as if to call	427	Island	3	82
While all can hear, none heed his neighbour's call	438	Tasso		91
And so we'll call her Laura, if you please	442	Beppo		167
Which certain people call a 'certain age	442	Beppo		170
And we may call this (not to say the worst	444	Beppo		287
The Spaniards call the person a 'Cortejo	444	Beppo		291
Coach, servants, gondola, he goes to call	445	Beppo		319
They only call a little on their saints	451	Beppo		709
And call captivity a kindness meant	462	Dante	3	134
Nor without justice holy could we call	472	Morgante		397
I call upon ye by the written charm	479	Manfred	1	35
Mortals call death hath nought to do with us	480	Manfred	1	163
I call upon thee! and compel	481	Manfred	1	250
May call thee lord? I only know their portals	483	Manfred	2	10
The homage of these waters.--I will call her	485	Manfred	2	106
Avail him of his spells--to call thee thus	485	Manfred	2	125
Still in my science--I can call the dead	487	Manfred	2	271
Within few hours I shall not call in vain	487	Manfred	2	292
Call up the dead--my question is for them	489	Manfred	2	449
Uncharnel? One without a tomb--call up	490	Manfred	2	452
Better bow down before the Hun, and call	517	Faliero	2	627

CALL

I call them up, and them and thee to witness	519	Faliero	3	30
In this--I cannot call it commonwealth	523	Faliero	3	276
Call back your nerves to your own purpose, nor	527	Faliero	3	596
Admit him, and retire; but call up quickly	530	Faliero	4	125
Which makes me call thee back; we must not part thus	531	Faliero	4	197
Until the council call ye to your trial	537	Faliero	4	634
I shall be with the Eternal.--Call her women	547	Faliero	5	693
More frequently, and he did well to call me	558	Sardan	1	515
I have no call for either. Salemenes	567	Sardan	2	321
Thou wouldst digest what some call treason, and	567	Sardan	2	363
I know not what to call it; but it reckons	570	Sardan	2	526
Now call upon thy planets, will they shoot	576	Sardan	3	280
Whom you call glorious. So I term you also	581	Sardan	4	181
So fleeting, we can scarcely call it aught	587	Sardan	5	16
To call back--But I will not weep for thee	589	Sardan	5	151
Even by my presence: when the last call sounds	596	Foscari	1	77
And were the first to call out for assistance	601	Foscari	1	345
Dost thou see this? Child--child--Call me not 'child	602	Foscari	2	70
In circumstances which would call forth tears	602	Foscari	2	73
And dies. You call this weakness! It is strength	611	Foscari	3	182
And pleasant breezes, as I call upon you	616	Foscari	4	126
This edict. Let him call up into life	619	Foscari	4	273
We must be speedy: let us call together	620	Foscari	4	351
A melancholy one--to call the attendance	620	Foscari	5	6
The body of his son. And call Marina	624	Foscari	5	208
No aid? Call in assistance! 'Tis all over	625	Foscari	5	309
Who didst divide the wave from wave, and call	627	Cain	1	7
God! who didst call the elements into	627	Cain	1	9
The gates of what they call their Paradise	630	Cain	1	169
Ask the Destroyer. Who? The Maker--call him	631	Cain	1	263
Can call them living. Yet they lived. Where? Where	640	Cain	2	267
He as a conqueror will call the conquer'd	645	Cain	2	648
But if he gives you good--so call him: if	646	Cain	2	659
I call thee, I await thee, and I love thee	656	Heaven		93
And call his nestlings up with fruitless yell	662	Heaven		508
But thou, my Anah! let me call thee mine	664	Heaven		666
I came to call ye back to your fit sphere	666	Heaven		820
For duty (as you call it)--I did mine then	678	Werner	1	440
Call such your mother. You have seen the woman	694	Werner	2	730
Which I call helpless; if you now deny it	695	Werner	3	30
Werner, or what else? Call me Werner still	700	Werner	3	343
Who saved your life. I think they call him 'Ulric	700	Werner	3	374
More words on you. Call me betimes. Good night	701	Werner	3	386
Your long-lost, late-found son.---Let's call my mother	704	Werner	3	585
Shall I call forth your excellency's suite	705	Werner	4	78
Why do you call me 'cousin'? Are we not so	706	Werner	4	153
'Cousin' again. Nay, then I'll call you sister	706	Werner	4	162
But I can wait! Dear Ida! Call me Ida	707	Werner	4	172
Why wilt thou call me prosperous, while I fear	709	Werner	4	322
For son I dare not call thee--What say'st thou	719	Werner	5	400
Call me by that worst name of parent. What	721	Werner	5	545
Call not thy brothers brethren! Call me not	722	Deformed	1	24
Is never diabolical. I'll call him	729	Deformed	1	524
I trust. Then call me Caesar. Why, that name	730	Deformed	1	537
Unless you call me pope instead. Well, then	730	Deformed	1	541
Of what these creatures call eternity	739	Deformed	2	291
How stanch a friend is what you call a fiend	741	Deformed	2	409
No bugle awakes him with life-and-death call	742	Deformed	3	33
No! no! you would be loved--what you call loved	743	Deformed	3	128
In short, in all things she was fairly what I call	748	Juan	1	93
And what the lawyers call a 'malus animus	750	Juan	1	237
To call them back into their separate cages	752	Juan	1	358
There was the Donna Julia, whom to call	753	Juan	1	435
What men call gallantry, and gods adultery	754	Juan	1	503
Fond of a little love (which I call leisure	761	Juan	1	942
Call me the only virtuous wife in Spain	765	Juan	1	1188
Who is the man you search for? how d'ye call	765	Juan	1	1228
So much as when we call our old debts in	767	Juan	1	1334
Of rhetoric, which the learn'd call 'rigmarole	768	Juan	1	1392
I'll call the work 'Longinus o'er a Bottle	772	Juan	1	1631
And bards burn what they call their 'midnight taper	773	Juan	1	1742
For, after all, we cannot call thee devil	800	Juan	2	1640
Men call inconstancy is nothing more	801	Juan	2	1682
Hark! rising to the ignoble call	812	Juan	3	741
I know that what our neighbours call 'longueurs	814	Juan	3	865
Inherent--what we mortals call romantic	818	Juan	4	143
I have seen such--but must not call to mind	821	Juan	4	288
Smiled scornfully, and said, 'Within my call	821	Juan	4	294
On the first foe whom Lambro's call might bring	821	Juan	4	312
And blew; another answer'd to the call	822	Juan	4	372
Of what she was, and is, if ye could call	824	Juan	4	525
Could altogether call the past to mind	826	Juan	4	595
The things down, said, 'Incense me, and I call	841	Juan	5	599
Her fifth, to call her maids and go to bed	849	Juan	5	1109
And take what kings call 'an imposing attitude	854	Juan	6	84

CALL

Which it can either pain or evil call	855 Juan	6	173
Upon, in sheets white as what bards call 'driven	855 Juan	6	197
Which some call 'the sublime:' I wish they'd try it	859 Juan	6	422
Matron and maids, and those whom you may call	861 Juan	6	563
To call men love-begotten or proclaim	864 Juan	6	745
What sages call Chance, Providence, or Fate	876 Juan	7	604
When I call 'fading' martial immortality	877 Juan	7	657
So be they her inspirers! Call them Mars	878 Juan	8	7
Or loved, it was with what we call 'the best	881 Juan	8	194
Unto his call, unlike 'the spirits from	883 Juan	8	298
At least nine tenths of what we call so;--God	891 Juan	8	826
In prose I bend my humble verse) doth call	891 Juan	8	831
Of what it had been; there the Muezzin's call	896 Juan	8	1126
Why do they call me misanthrope? Because	899 Juan	9	167
To be the first of what we used to call	900 Juan	9	250
I ne'er decide what I shall say, and this I call	901 Juan	9	325
Some call thee 'the worst cause of war,' but I	903 Juan	9	441
And was not the best wife, unless we call	906 Juan	9	638
In health--when ill, we call them to attend us	912 Juan	10	331
If I agree that what is, is; then this I call	919 Juan	11	35
O Gold! Why call we misers miserable	930 Juan	12	7
Why call the miser miserable? as	930 Juan	12	49
While he, despising every sensual call	931 Juan	12	71
The fool will call such mania a disease	931 Juan	12	83
I call such things transmission; for there is	936 Juan	12	409
For her return to Virtue--as they call	940 Juan	12	563
Were vanish'd to be what they call alone	947 Juan	13	387
May the rose call back its true colour soon	955 Juan	13	886
You bind yourself, and call some mode the best one	955 Juan	14	14
Which pretty women--the sweet souls!--call soul	964 Juan	14	563
Before you learn to call this superstition	980 Juan	15	784

CALL'D

When Cava's traitor-sire first call'd the band	9 Harold	1	389
The southern Scott, the minstrel who call'd forth	61 Harold	4	357
And call'd, proud boast! the British drama forth	94 Dorset		68
Ere call'd but for a time away	165 Thyrza		27
The Fourth of the fools and oppressors call'd 'George!'	203 Avatar		80
They call'd for the harp--but our blood they shall spill	223 Valley		7
And call'd to the Maid to remind her	234 Ballat		12
Mute, though he votes, unless when call'd to cheer	260 Hints		249
Call'd county meetings, and enforced the laws	266 Hints		672
Be call'd to labour when he thinks to dine	266 Hints		705
Of ocean call'd him king: through many a storm	290 Vision		334
Thus spoke the Demon (late call'd 'multifaced	293 Vision		513
In their high praise and glory; he had call'd	297 Vision		778
He call'd the Prophet, but his power	317 Giaour		679
He call'd on Alla--but the word	317 Giaour		681
Thrice clapp'd his hands, and call'd his steed	326 Abydos	1	232
And Giaffir almost call'd me coward	327 Abydos	1	361
And then, his rarely call'd attendants said	368 Lara	1	135
He call'd on Nature's self to share the shame	371 Lara	1	332
And Lara call'd his page, and went his way	373 Lara	1	510
I call'd, for I was wild with fear	404 Chillon		206
I call'd, and thought I heard a sound	404 Chillon		209
My life but to have call'd her mine	410 Mazeppa		314
And call'd the radiance from their cars	413 Mazeppa		650
Which scarcely could be call'd a voice	414 Mazeppa		781
But those she call'd were not awake	415 Mazeppa		831
Nor cause for such: they call'd me and mad--and why	437 Tasso		48
No place that's call'd 'Piazza' in Great Britain	440 Beppo		40
So call'd, because, the name and thing agreeing	441 Beppo		43
Row'd by two rowers, each call'd 'Gondolier	442 Beppo		149
His name Giuseppe, call'd more briefly, Beppo	443 Beppo		200
Of well-bred persons, call'd 'the World;' but I	447 Beppo		471
They enter'd and for coffee call'd--it came	451 Beppo		721
And call'd the 'kingdom' of a conquering foe	454 Venice-B		122
The abbot was call'd Clermont, and by blood	468 Morgante		153
And Mahomet he call'd; but Mahomet	471 Morgante		314
I then have call'd ye from your realms in vain	480 Manfred	1	164
And died unpardon'd--though he call'd in aid	487 Manfred	2	280
Or those who have call'd thee	490 Manfred	2	479
For I have call'd on thee in the still night	490 Manfred	2	505
Was call'd in, that no moment might be lost	500 Faliero	1	48
I call'd no judges but those named by law	502 Faliero	1	143
Why so is he who smote you. He is call'd so	505 Faliero	1	373
For those who are call'd to the high destinies	517 Faliero	1	598
So wrong'd as I, so fall'n, so loudly call'd	520 Faliero	3	113
He now be call'd in to receive the award	540 Faliero	5	141
Of virtue, looking not to what is call'd	544 Faliero	5	419
Which I was delegated with, they call'd	572 Sardan	3	80
You here! Who call'd you? No one--but I heard	585 Sardan	4	437
The labyrinth of mystery call'd life	591 Sardan	5	236
Who.are all earth, and I, who am call'd upon	607 Foscari	2	368
Thus hesitate? 'The Ten' have call'd in aid	616 Foscari	4	76
My country call'd me here to exercise	621 Foscari	5	45
Many of the same kind (at least so call'd	642 Cain	2	405

CALL'D

And in the worship of our God call'd not	649 Cain	3	198
Hungarian. Which is call'd? It matters little	675 Werner	1	283
Since no one cares to tell me what he's call'd	676 Werner	1	285
The man call'd Werner's poor! Poor as a miser	683 Werner	2	19
(As it is call'd) are aliens to each other	699 Werner	3	258
Nature was never call'd back by remonstrance	709 Werner	4	334
Of senators and princes; but you have call'd me	716 Werner	5	190
Which is so call'd or thought, that you may add me	723 Deformed	1	85
A noble stream, and call'd the Guadalquivir	748 Juan	1	64
For Inez call'd some druggists and physicians	750 Juan	1	209
He died of the slow fever call'd the tertian	751 Juan	1	271
Who call'd her chaste, methinks, begun too soon	760 Juan	1	899
Call'd back the tangles of her wandering hair	767 Juan	1	1354
The ship, call'd the most holy 'Trinidada	777 Juan	2	185
Battista, though (a name call'd shortly Tita	781 Juan	2	447
He had an only daughter, call'd Haidee	790 Juan	2	1017
And turn'd, believing that he call'd again	791 Juan	2	1076
And call'd her father's old slaves up, who swore	791 Juan	2	1102
Like earthquakes from the hidden fire call'd 'central	801 Juan	2	1720
A drowsy frowzy poem, call'd the 'Excursion	814 Juan	3	847
And call'd from Juan's breast a faint low sigh	819 Juan	4	167
Call'd social, haunts of Hate, and Vice, and Care	820 Juan	4	220
Till what is call'd in Ossian the fifth Duan	831 Juan	4	936
Which might have call'd Diana's chorus 'cousin	844 Juan	5	790
Call'd back the stoic to his eyes, which shone	846 Juan	5	965
Or whether they were 'maids' who call'd her mother	856 Juan	6	242
And then he call'd his brethren to his aid	867 Juan	6	937
The fortress is call'd Ismail, and is placed	868 Juan	7	65
Sixteen call'd Thomson, and nineteen named Smith	869 Juan	7	144
Had been call'd 'Jemmy,' after the great bard	869 Juan	7	146
Not that his manhood could be call'd in question	871 Juan	7	282
(Here he call'd up a Polish orderly	875 Juan	7	524
And these he call'd on; and, what's strange, they came	883 Juan	8	297
Open'd the gate call'd 'Kilia', to the groups	887 Juan	8	581
Call'd 'Saviour of the Nations'--not yet saved	897 Juan	9	39
So call'd; the Antic long hath ceased to hear	898 Juan	9	92
Our veins, when things call'd sovereigns think it best	904 Juan	9	479
Add what may be call'd marriage in disguise	906 Juan	9	608
Of what is call'd eternity, to stare	910 Juan	10	159
Call'd brotherly affection, could not move	914 Juan	10	422
Through Groves, as call'd as being void of trees	921 Juan	11	161
Through 'Rows' most modestly call'd 'Paradise	921 Juan	11	167
Is call'd on to support his claim, or show it	925 Juan	11	435
Call'd 'Parks' where there is neither fruit nor flower	926 Juan	11	516
About what's call'd success, or not succeeding	936 Jaun	12	434
A jest at Vice by Virtue's call'd a crime	941 Juan	13	3
Peace, war, the taxes, and what's call'd the 'Nation	941 Juan	13	42
Was what he call'd the 'Art of Happiness	945 Juan	13	274
Death, so call'd, is a thing which makes men weep	955 Juan	14	23
And were her object only what's call'd glory.	957 Juan	14	103
That Adam, call'd 'The happiest of men	962 Juan	14	440
She call'd her husband now and then apart	963 Juan	14	515
And being of the council call'd 'the Privy	964 Juan	14	537
There is a flower call'd 'Love in Idleness	964 Juan	14	593
Whether their talk was of the kind call'd 'small	967 Juan	14	780
Were things but only call'd by their right name	968 Juan	14	815
Why call'd he 'Harmony' a state sans wedlock	972 Juan	15	279
But for that hour, call'd half-hour, given to dress	975 Juan	15	487
That cookery could have call'd forth such resources	976 Juan	15	550
Bricklayer of Babel, call'd an architect	988 Juan	16	506
And throw down old--which he call'd restoration	988 Juan	16	512
To be call'd up for her examination	989 Juan	16	568
Though not exactly what's call'd 'open house	989 Juan	16	592
They err--'tis merely what is call'd mobility	993 Juan	16	820
Of what is call'd the world, and the world's ways	994 Juan	16	907

CALLED

spears were in their hands. Fingal called his	130 Calmar		42
My services have called me up those steps	624 Foscari	5	243
For what is sometimes called poetic diction	889 Juan	8	686
Called 'Cavalier servente?'--a Pygmalion	903 Juan	9	405
In a most natural whirl, called 'gravitation	907 Juan	10	6
He felt like other plants called sensitive	912 Juan	10	290

CALLEST

Thou livest. When? On what thou callest earth	640 Cain	2	268

CALLING

When calling the dead, in earth's bosom laid low	91 Caroline-C		24
And here a sentry stands within your calling	451 Beppo		686
From me and from my calling; yet so young	493 Manfred	3	137
Than calling it at moments back to this	619 Foscari	4	254

CALLING

For calling you a hero. Philibert	734	Deformed	1	818
Of calling wholly back its self-control	760	Juan	1	908
Stood calling out for bandages and lint	920	Juan	11	111

CALLOUS

But now, so callous grown, so changed since youth	256	Bards		1057
And callous, save to crime	311	Giaour		152
My scars are callous, or I should have dash'd	439	Tasso		209
Indifferent from the first or callous grown	755	Juan	1	542

CALLOW

Who rears on its bare breast her callow brood	430	Island	4	17
Her callow brood. What letters are these which	608	Foscari	3	14
Soft as the callow cygnet in its nest	793	Juan	2	1182

CALLS

In every peal she calls, 'Awake! arise	10	Harold	1	411
Calls forth a sweeter though ignoble praise	14	Harold	1	660
Where Revel calls, and Laughter, vainly loud	35	Harold	2	911
When least we deem of such, calls up to view	58	Harold	4	213
Calls for my spirit's homage, yet it yields	64	Harold	4	548
Calls back the vanish'd days to rapture given	122	Recoll		13
rise! The son of Connal calls; thy	130	Calmar		124
Heedless when Morning calls thee to the skies	140	Ossian-B		34
In vain he calls each Muse in order down	142	Soliloquy		3
Alas! whenever folly calls	153	Friend-A		53
My way-worn countryman, who calls	158	Storm		15
And this the world calls frenzy; but the wise	216	Dream		177
Who is he that calls the dead	219	Saul-B		16
As you'll see in the trash he calls Tasso's	232	Murray-B		30
Cuts the light pack, or calls the rattling main	250	Bards		673
Though as a monarch nods, and commerce calls	258	Hints		93
On Pallas calls,--but calls, alas! too late	271	Minerva		250
He makes a solitude, and calls it--peace	333	Abydos	2	431
These Juan calls--they come--to their salute	340	Corsair	1	141
Which calls up green and native fields to view	610	Foscari	3	173
He calls his wife. Is she not so? No more	694	Werner	2	731
Who calls? I--Siegendorf! Take these, and fly	720	Werner	5	491
And still it half calls up the realms of fairy	831	Juan	5	27
Sometimes calls 'murder,' and at others 'glory	870	Juan	7	208
Debt he calls wealth, and taxes Paradise	872	Juan	7	357
He was what Erin calls, in her sublime	881	Juan	8	177
(As Pistol calls it), but a young Livonian	885	Juan	8	448
Calls Ilion's the first damages on record	903	Juan	9	424
Because, you'll say, nought calls for such a trial	930	Juan	12	55
In making men what courtesy calls friends	943	Juan	13	120

CALL'ST

| Thou call'st the loyal with thy menaced breath | 416 | Island | 1 | 66 |

CALM

Nor calm domestic peace had ever deign'd to taste	4	Harold	1	45
Or he shall calm his breast, or learn experience sage	8	Harold	1	332
Pass we the calm, the gale, the change, the tack	23	Harold	2	246
Nodding at midnight o'er the calm bay's breast	30	Harold	2	625
Melt to calm twilight, they feel overcast	42	Harold	3	392
With a calm languor, which, though to the eye	60	Harold	4	292
And, calm as cherish'd hate, its surface wears	81	Harold	4	1555
Calm or convulsed--in breeze, or gale, or storm	82	Harold	4	1641
Be calm, my soul! he yet may live	103	Alva		138
Then Nisus,--'Calm thy bosom's fond alarms	106	Nisus		53
The hold calm of sacred love	111	Medea		26
An, no! amidst the gloomy calm of age	127	Recoll		401
But bloom'd in calm domestic quiet	134	Lady-D		32
To make that calm contentment mine	135	I Would		47
And calm its cares and passions into rest	138	Harrow-B		18
Yet was I calm: I knew the time	155	Happy		25
To breathe a sweet religious calm around	161	Athos		15
Who hath not shared that calm so still and deep	192	Monody		9
And he did calm himself, and fix his brow	214	Dream		87
And he stood calm and quiet, and he spoke	215	Dream		156
So soft, so calm, yet eloquent	216	She Walks		14
Walk'd out of his depth and was lost in a calm sea	227	Moore-A		10
From calm reflection, comfort or relief	229	Sadness		8
The calm possession of their native field	247	Bards		435
The other half pursued its calm career	248	Bards		473
And, sad and sombre mid the holy calm	269	Minerva		45
Some calm spectator, as he takes his view	271	Minerva		196
And when the tumult dwindled to a calm	298	Vision		847
Which hushes all! a calm, unstormy wave	298	Age		22
Why wouldst thou leave calm Hartwell's green abode	305	Age		514
So fair, so calm, so softly seal'd	311	Giaour		88
The calm wave rippled to the bank	314	Giaour		375
'Mid sullen calm, and silent bay	319	Giaour		967
And calm the lonely lioness	322	Giaour		1216
'This rose to calm my brother's cares	326	Abydos	1	287
But, gentle love, this transport calm	331	Abydos	2	185

CALM

Though smooth his voice and calm his general mien	341	Corsair	1	207
Calm their loud fears, sustain their sinking frames	350	Corsair	2	217
And, dun and sombre 'mid the holy calm	356	Corsair	3	45
So calm, the waters scarcely seem to stray	368	Lara	1	157
With eye, though calm, determined not to spare	376	Lara	2	61
The sullen calm that long his bosom kept	378	Lara	2	242
Henceforth a calm spectator of life's scene	378	Lara	2	259
And he regards them with a calm disdain	381	Lara	2	435
And calm, till murmuring death gasp'd hoarsely near	381	Lara	2	461
Calm, clear, and azure as the air	387	Corinth		253
Cool was the silent sky, though calm	388	Corinth		360
Calm or high, in main or bay	388	Corinth		432
The ocean's calm within their view	390	Corinth		550
He faded, and so calm and meek	404	Chillon		186
The Ukraine's hetman, calm and bold	407	Mazeppa		56
Die calm, or calmer oft than he	414	Mazeppa		739
Seem'd rooted in the deep amidst its calm	422	Island	2	223
Slowly the pair, partaking nature's calm	424	Island	2	402
But calm and careless heaved the wave below	435	Island	4	367
The struggle to be calm, and cold distress	438	Tasso		102
Except three days of calm when off Cape Bonn	452	Beppo		768
O'er my calm Hall of Coral	479	Manfred	1	84
Beautiful Spirit! in thy calm clear brow	485	Manfred	2	119
Thou may'st retire. There is a calm upon me	491	Manfred	3	6
With calm assurance to that blessed place	492	Manfred	3	81
Calm, but not overcast, he stood resign'd	500	Faliero	1	71
Cheer up, be calm; this transport is uncall'd for	501	Faliero	1	102
The means, and calm yourself. Hold, nephew: this	503	Faliero	1	233
The day is overcast, but the calm wave	511	Faliero	2	162
For sneer, nor for suspicion! Calm thee, Bertram	521	Faliero	3	198
Whether the air will calm my spirits; 'tis	528	Faliero	4	24
How sweet and soothing is this hour of calm	529	Faliero	4	105
The hour of action I have stood as calm	534	Faliero	4	446
Of thy far father-land. Nay, weep not--calm thee	559	Sardan	1	566
Hour of Assyria's years. And yet how calm	561	Sardan	2	9
The steel will reach the earthly. But be calm	570	Sardan	2	571
Crisps the reluctant lake that lay so calm	578	Sardan	4	12
Calm thee. Thy speech seems of another world	579	Sardan	4	40
Briefly; but in that brief cool calm inhale	587	Sardan	5	29
Be calm! I am; but oh, thou eternal God	598	Foscari	1	211
Their sting is honester. I pray you, calm you	612	Foscari	3	266
But I have seen him sometimes in a calm	615	Foscari	4	8
Will nothing calm you? Never yet did mariner	616	Foscari	4	124
The little I have shown thee into calm	645	Cain	2	607
Would have composed thy mind into the calm	647	Cain	3	49
Some strong delusion; it will calm thee. No	649	Cain	3	203
Nothing can calm me more. Calm! say I? Never	649	Cain	3	204
Knew I what calm was in the soul, although	649	Cain	3	205
When sporting on the face of the calm deep	657	Heaven		156
Have come upon me. Peace! what peace? the calm	658	Heaven		219
My love, be calmer! I am calm. To me	671	Werner	1	1
I'll say so. I am calm--live on! That's more	691	Werner	2	530
Be calm as innocence. But calmness is not	712	Werner	4	535
Which look'd so calm, and the celestial hymns	713	Werner	5	21
I could not deem it earth-born: but be calm	716	Werner	5	181
Could I be calm? Think you that I have heard	719	Werner	5	430
No, she is calm, and meek, and silent with me	743	Deformed	3	117
For on the third day there came on a calm	782	Juan	2	538
As o'er him lay the calm and stirless air	792	Juan	2	1148
On one side, and the deep sea calm and chill	797	Juan	2	1462
Then calm, concentrated, and still, and slow	807	Juan	3	379
Calm in his voice, and calm within his eye	821	Juan	4	306
So calm; though pierced through stomach, heart, and lung	835	Juan	5	276
A slight blush, a soft tremor, a calm kind	854	Juan	6	113
Where all was harmony, and calm, and quiet	859	Juan	6	418
The calm Dudu so turbulently wake	861	Juan	6	568
Is apt to tire: a calm and shallow station	898	Juan	9	142
While every thing around was calm and still	919	Juan	11	61
A modest confidence and calm assurance	924	Juan	11	410
The kinder veteran with calm words will court you	935	Juan	12	357
That calm patrician polish in the address	945	Juan	13	266
Survey'd him with a kind of calm surprise	984	Juan	16	248

CALMAR

hall of clouds! Such is Calmar. The gray	129	Calmar		11
eye of Calmar; soft was the flow of his yellow locks	129	Calmar		20
was the pride of Orla:--gentle alone to Calmar	129	Calmar		26
Orla. Calmar stood by his side. Their	130	Calmar		41
alone!' said fair-haired Calmar. 'Wilt thou	130	Calmar		62
'Calmar,' said the chief of Oithona, 'why	130	Calmar		70
thinks it is the tread of Calmar. Let her	130	Calmar		77
not say, "Calmar has fallen by the steel of	130	Calmar		78
voice curse Orla, the destroyer of Calmar	130	Calmar		82
Live, Calmar! Live to raise my stone of	130	Calmar		83
Orla, from the voice of Calmar. My ghost	130	Calmar		87
names of Orla and Calmar	130	Calmar		96
said fair-haired Calmar: 'we are in the	130	Calmar		114
'Fly! Calmar, fly!' said dark-haired Orla	130	Calmar		128
the wound, and foams on the spear of Calmar	130	Calmar		138

CALMAR
his friend. 'Tis Calmar: he lies on the 131 Calmar 161
hand is grasped in Calmar's; but Calmar 131 Calmar 166
heal the wounds of heroes. Calmar may 131 Calmar 169
'Never more shall Calmar chase the 131 Calmar 171
would share the spoils of battle with Calmar 131 Calmar 174
and Calmar. When Swaran was bound 131 Calmar 185
thine, Calmar! Lovely wast thou, son of 131 Calmar 195
thy praise, Calmar! It dwells on the voice 131 Calmar 199

CALMAR'S
hand is grasped in Calmar's; but Calmar 131 Calmar 166

CALM'D
My bosom is calm'd by the simple reflection 137 Delawarr 23

CALMER
The chief companion of a calmer lot 211 Augusta-C 48
'Tis calmer than thy heart, young Giaour 312 Giaour 190
In earlier days, and calmer hours 322 Giaour 1218
Thou com'st to claim a calmer grave 323 Giaour 1311
When stirr'd beyond its calmer mood 412 Mazeppa 534
Die calm, or calmer oft than he 414 Mazeppa 739
Except to see you oftener and calmer 511 Faliero 2 174
Calmer? Ay, calmer, my good lord.--Ah, why 511 Faliero 2 175
Thyself, and canst not injure them--be calmer 547 Faliero 5 663
No, he seems calmer. Oh, thou God of Quiet 578 Sardan 4 3
My love, be calmer! I am calm. To me 671 Werner 1 1
Bedew'd his spirit in his calmer hours 808 Juan 3 448
In currents through the calmer water spread 948 Juan 13 452

CALMEST
He slept in calmest seeming, for his breath 352 Corsair 2 392
Not always signs with him of calmest mood 821 Juan 4 307

CALMING
Calming the lightning which he thence hath riven 301 Age 246

CALMLY
Hear me not; but if calmly I have borne 74 Harold 4 1176
In gentle stream so calmly run 144 Jessy 30
That with such change can calmly cope 180 Ode-A 42
All thou calmly dost resign 187 French-A 30
While sate the catholic Moloch, calmly cruel 302 Age 337
And calmly talk'd--and yet he talk'd of blood 347 Corsair 1 606
He calmly met the curious eyes that scann'd 348 Corsair 2 62
But few that saw, so calmly gazed around 351 Corsair 2 303
She gazed in wonder: 'Can he calmly sleep 353 Corsair 2 421
Its pulse nor check'd--nor quicken'd--calmly cold 354 Corsair 2 512
As if each calmly conscious star 397 Parisina 57
And bind his wound--then calmly lit his pipe 428 Island 3 106
She pointed calmly to the craggy isle 430 Island 4 38
How they had gladly lived and calmly died 433 Island 4 217
The mode and means: if you had calmly heard me 503 Faliero 1 252
And calmly wash those hands incarnadine 527 Faliero 3 630
Let me die calmly; you may grant me this 542 Faliero 5 295
You muse right calmly: and can you so watch 587 Sardan 5 39
You, who can talk thus calmly of a son 602 Foscari 2 72
So calmly with its gold and crimson glory 611 Foscari 3 212
The sun goes down as calmly, and perhaps 731 Deformed 1 638
Calmly she heard each calumny that rose 750 Juan 1 230
Were ruled as calmly as a Christian queen 850 Juan 5 1184
Smoking his pipe quite calmly 'midst the din 890 Juan 8 780
Where the chief pacha calmly held his post 893 Juan 8 954
And rather calmly into the heart glides 939 Juan 12 589
Retired; and, as went out, calmly kiss'd her 964 Juan 14 551
Had she known this, she would have calmly smiled 975 Juan 15 439

CALMNESS
Thy current's calmness; oft from out it leaps 65 Harold 4 599
The sullen calmness of despair 155 Happy 32
Which still would meet with joy, with calmness
 part 342 Corsair 1 301
Resumed the calmness which before forsook 348 Corsair 2 112
Could this mean peace? the calmness of the good 373 Lara 1 504
Their wonder at the calmness of the bold 374 Lara 1 595
We'll take it; but may do all this in calmness 502 Faliero 1 168
And cool them into calmness! How unlike 597 Foscari 1 127
Be calm as innocence. But calmness is not 712 Werner 4 535

CALMS
There's nought, no doubt, so much the spirit
 calms 778 Juan 2 265

CALM'ST
Who calm'st the elemental war 133 Prayer 43
Who calm'st the elemental war 146 Adieu 116

CALMUCK
A Calmuck beauty with a Cossack wit 304 Age 438
He said,--and in the kindest Calmuck tone 876 Juan 7 553

CALMUCKS
Before a company of Calmucks, drilling 874 Juan 7 458

CALOYER
Here dwells the caloyer, nor rude is he 27 Harold 2 438
'How name ye yon lone Caloyer 318 Giaour 787

CALPAC
His calpac rent--his caftan red 317 Giaour 717

CALPE'S
Through Calpe's straits survey the steepy shore 22 Harold 2 190
Beheld it last by Calpe's rock unfold 81 Harold 4 1574
And Afric's coast and Calpe's adverse height 255 Bards 1019
Through Calpe's strait the rolling tides advance 302 Age 282

CALUMNIATED
And the calumniated queen Semiramis 839 Juan 5 480

CALUMNIATOR
You! Base calumniator! I. 'Twill rest 717 Werner 5 303

CALUMNIES
To all the growing calumnies of time 509 Faliero 1 623

CALUMNY
From the loud roar of foaming calumny 75 Harold 4 1218
Yet let not canker'd Calumny assail 114 Death-A 27
And pile the Pyramid of Calumny 193 Monody 78
And blot life's latest scene with calumny 359 Corsair 3 231
Long years of outrage, calumny, and wrong 436 Tasso 3
Of calumny and scorn. And what redress 503 Faliero 1 219
Upon his coward calumny. 'Twere fit 509 Faliero 2 44
Each calumny they can to sink their sovereigns 556 Sardan 1 379
Ulric, repel this calumny, as I 716 Werner 5 179
Calmly she heard each calumny that rose 750 Juan 1 230

CALVIN
As pious Calvin saw Servetus blaze 262 Hints 377

CALYPSO
And thou may'st find a new Calypso there 24 Harold 2 265

CALYPSO'S
But not in silence pass Calypso's isles 23 Harold 2 253
Then think upon Calypso's isles 159 Storm 57

CAM
Cam Hobhouse! but by wags Byzantian Ben 224 J.C.H. 2
Whose Helicon is duller than her Cam 255 Bards 972

CAMA'S
On Cama's verdant margin placed 145 Adieu 17

CAMBRIAN
Imports old stories from the Cambrian coast 247 Bards 388

CAMBRIDGE
But when we at Cambridge were 235 New Song 21

CAMBYSES
A new Cambyses thundering in their ear 300 Age 144

CAMBYSES'
Over Cambyses' host the desert spread 460 Dante 2 108

CAME
And Laos wide and fierce came roaring by 27 Harold 2 488
But from the chambers came the mingling din 28 Harold 2 539
It came to pass that when he did address 29 Harold 2 613
Then came his fit again, which to o'ercome 37 Harold 3 131
For then he was inspired, and from him came 47 Harold 3 761
It came, it cometh, and will come,--the power 48 Harold 3 795
They came like truth, and disappear'd like dreams 56 Harold 4 56
Of bleak, gray granite into life it came 58 Harold 4 179
Return to whence they came--with like intent 58 Harold 4 193
Came Megara before me, and behind 61 Harold 4 392
And came--and saw--and conquer'd! But the man 68 Harold 4 811
Glenalvon's blue-eyed daughter came 102 Alva 80
Nor Oscar nor his brother came 102 Alva 100
And whence the dreadful stranger came 105 Alva 281
Alone she came, all selfish fears above 107 Nisus 181
Nor less the other's deadly vengeance came 109 Nisus 265
Here Probus came, the rising fray to quell 124 Recoll 177
The din of arms came to the ear of Fingal 131 Calmar 145
To redeem as he came away 177 Devil's Dr 106
The Night came on the Waters--all was rest 184 Julian 1
Morn came and went--and came, and brought no day 189 Darkness 6
Came tame and tremulous; and vipers crawl'd 189 Darkness 35
Thus came the Heritage to thee 197 Duel 12
Came through a line of yore renown'd 197 Duel 14
The earthquake came, and rock'd the quivering wall 206 Love, Death 13
While that placid sleep came o'er thee 207 Fare Thee 7
And when the cloud upon us came 209 Augusta-A 17
And yet they came unsought, and with me grew 212 Augusta-C 99
A change came o'er the spirit of my dream 214 Dream 75

CAME

Was traced, and then it faded, as it came 215 Dream 98
A change came o'er the spirit of my dream 215 Dream 105
Even at the altar, o'er his brow there came 215 Dream 149
Was traced--and then it faded as it came 215 Dream 155
And her who was his destiny, came back 215 Dream 164
A change came o'er the spirit of my dream 216 Dream 184
Came o'er that eye of blue 218 I Saw 2
Like cavern'd winds, the hollow accents came 219 Saul-B 12
Came forth against the wall 220 Belshaz-B 11
The Assyrian came down like the wolf on the fold 222 Sennacherib 1
Deep sleep came down on every eye save mine 222 Spirit 3
How came you in Hob's pound to cool 235 New Song 1
That all may learn from whence the plunderer came 269 Minerva 105
She came--Waltz came, and with her certain sets 274 Waltz 67
To one and all the lovely stranger came 275 Waltz 107
And nodded o'er his keys; when, lo! there came 286 Vision 122
That all the saints came out and took him in 287 Vision 154
'He came to his sceptre young; he leaves it old 290 Vision 337
The shadow came--a tall, thin, gray-hair'd figure 294 Vision 593
Woe to that hour he came or went 313 Giaour 279
He came, he went, like the Simoom 313 Giaour 282
Since first among our freres he came 318 Giaour 799
Say--that his bodings came to pass 322 Giaour 1234
Zuleika came; and Giaffir felt 325 Abydos 1 187
And morning came--and still thou wert afar 343 Corsair 1 380
Another came--Oh God! 'twas thine at last 343 Corsair 1 387
And he deceived me--for--he came again 344 Corsair 1 449
Around, the bearded chiefs he came to lead 347 Corsair 2 30
But first, ere came the rallying host to blows 350 Corsair 2 253
Through guards and dunnest night how came it there 353 Corsair 2 406
It came at last--a sad and shatter'd boat 356 Corsair 3 85
The second--third--and still she came not there 359 Corsair 3 245
Came storm and darkness in their mingling might 359 Corsair 3 249
A light step came--it paused--it moved once more 359 Corsair 3 271
Yet changed since last within that cell she came 359 Corsair 3 276
Since with me came a heart he could not buy 360 Corsair 3 330
And therefore came I, in my bark of war 361 Corsair 3 362
The thunder came; that bolt hath blasted both 365 Corsair 3 672
Nor sent, nor came he, till conjecture grew 366 Corsair 3 31
And Conrad comes not, came not since that day 366 Corsair 3 688
Not that he came, but came not long before 366 Lara 1 46
Rests at his heart; the custom'd morning came 369 Lara 1 249
Came not again, or Lara could assume 370 Lara 1 268
To Otho's hall came Lara with the rest 371 Lara 1 386
''Tis he!--how came he thence?--what doth he here 372 Lara 1 426
The colour of young Kaled went and came 374 Lara 1 598
Where was this Ezzelin, who came and went 376 Lara 2 99
Came fast enquiry, which unfolded nought 376 Lara 2 105
The moment came, the hour when Otho thought 378 Lara 2 212
With him his gentle daughter came 386 Corinth 224
And her words came forth without her breath 391 Corinth 613
Inward and onward the Mussulman came 395 Corinth 964
The foe came on, and few remain 395 Corinth 986
So near they came, the nearest stretch'd 395 Corinth 1011
And down came blazing rafters, strown 396 Corinth 1053
So came upon his soul the shock 397 Parisina 98
From thee in all their vigour came 399 Parisina 290
In quicken'd brokenness that came 401 Parisina 525
First came the loss of light, and air 405 Chillon 233
It ceased, and then it came again 405 Chillon 253
But then by dull degrees came back 405 Chillon 259
But through the crevice where it came 405 Chillon 265
A kind of change came in my fate 405 Chillon 300
My breath came gaspingly and thick 405 Chillon 316
And then new tears came in my eye 406 Chillon 356
At last men came to set me free 406 Chillon 370
Obey'd his voice, and came to call 407 Mazeppa 72
Which on the wind came roaring after 410 Mazeppa 382
Their troop came hard upon our back 411 Mazeppa 494
'My thoughts came back; where was I? Cold 412 Mazeppa 569
How slow, alas, he came 413 Mazeppa 644
Came thickly thundering on 413 Mazeppa 686
On came the troop--they saw him stoop 413 Mazeppa 695
And went and came with wandering beam 414 Mazeppa 786
'She came with mother and with sire 415 Mazeppa 840
Who came and conquer'd; such, wherever rise 420 Island 2 99
She, when the thunder-bearing strangers came 422 Island 2 220
Came sad and softly to their rocky bower 424 Island 2 399
Came breathing o'er the aromatic south 425 Island 2 435
A little stream came tumbling from the height 427 Island 3 63
Show'd that his faintness came not from despair 428 Island 3 102
Onward it came--and, lo! a second follow'd 428 Island 3 169
With vigour they pull'd on, and as they came 430 Island 4 63
But no! it came not; fast and far away 435 Island 4 381
The chiefs came down, around the people pour'd 435 Island 4 407
Which ever playing round me came and smiled 437 Tasso 38
They enter'd and for coffee call'd--it came 451 Beppo 721
And how came you to keep away so long 451 Beppo 727
When words were things that came to pass, and thought 458 Dante 2 2
And gentle Belinghieri too came there 467 Morgante 72
The son of Pepin:--when his knights came hither 467 Morgante 79

CAME

'When hither to inhabit first we came 468 Morgante 177
Which nearly crush'd Rondell, came tumbling over 469 Morgante 207
The giant from his sleep; and he came forth 471 Morgante 310
And to the gate he came with great regret 471 Morgante 318
Came the sound of thy spells 479 Manfred 1 83
My injuries came down on those who loved me 484 Manfred 2 84
The course of my existence; but there came 493 Manfred 3 134
More near from out the Caesars' palace came 495 Manfred 3 276
My lord, I came away upon the moment 500 Faliero 1 66
There's blood upon thy face--how came it there 505 Faliero 1 363
Chief of the arsenal ere I came from Rome 505 Faliero 1 394
Then wherefore came you here? I come for justice 505 Faliero 1 407
They came not near me, such approach gave umbrage 525 Faliero 3 471
There came a heaviness across my heart 528 Faliero 4 5
With me; the hour of agitation came 534 Faliero 4 443
The marvel is, it came not until now 546 Faliero 5 589
Have written otherwise. Though they came down 567 Sardan 2 347
Strange to thy heart--how came it on thy lips 603 Foscari 2 137
Came you here to insult us, or remain 612 Foscari 3 254
You came here to enjoy a heartless triumph 613 Foscari 3 325
Of cold looks upon manifold griefs! You came 613 Foscari 3 326
When I came here. The galley floats within 614 Foscari 3 399
And their desponding shades came flitting round 616 Foscari 4 114
What 'twas which shook us all--but nothing came 631 Cain 1 274
Thou didst before I came upon thee. How 637 Cain 2 95
Ere we came down into this phantom realm 643 Cain 2 449
How came ye, being spirits wise and infinite 644 Cain 2 585
From earth they came, to earth let them return 650 Cain 3 282
I came to call ye back to your fit sphere 666 Heaven 820
That which I came to do: till now we trod 666 Heaven 323
(Where I doff'd mine for these, and came on hither 675 Werner 1 256
We came up by mere accident, and just 676 Werner 1 288
To-night), I know not. But how came he here 677 Werner 1 404
I came upon the frontier; the free city 680 Werner 1 566
Fit to decide. But I came here to seek you 687 Werner 2 308
He hath been plunder'd too, since he came hither 689 Werner 2 418
Came the thought ne'er into your mind last night 697 Werner 3 166
Shall I forget him! Here I came most poor 701 Werner 3 437
Which seem'd as if they rather came from heaven 713 Werner 5 22
Count, you are bound to hear me. I came hither 716 Werner 5 186
Blood than came there in battle. It--or some 716 Werner 5 211
The black bands came over 732 Deformed 1 691
And how the goddesses came down to men 758 Juan 1 748
'Tis said the great came from America 762 Juan 1 1041
'My dear, I was the first who came away 764 Juan 1 1128
The only mischief was, it came too late 769 Juan 1 1458
Lights came at length, and men, and maids, who found 769 Juan 1 1489
A squall came on, and while some guns broke loose 777 Juan 2 238
But now there came a flash of hope once more 778 Juan 2 297
Then came the carpenter, at last, with tears 779 Juan 2 337
For on the third day there came on a calm 782 Juan 2 538
The fourth day came, but not a breath of air 782 Juan 2 553
Save in the breeze that came not; savagely 783 Juan 2 572
But ere they came to this, they that day shared 783 Juan 2 585
It came and went, and flutter'd round them till 786 Juan 2 751
With twilight it again came on to blow 786 Juan 2 761
And down the cliff the island virgin came 792 Juan 2 1129
She came into the cave, but it was merely 795 Juan 2 1339
And every morn his colour freshlier came 795 Juan 2 1345
Came always back to coffee and Haidee 796 Juan 2 1368
Then came her freedom, for she had no mother 796 Juan 2 1393
But soon Philosophy came to my aid 800 Juan 2 1673
Thus she came often, not a moment losing 803 Juan 3 103
He is, nor whence he came--and little care 807 Juan 3 354
In small fine China cups, came in at last 809 Juan 3 500
Even as they gazed, a sudden tremor came 819 Juan 4 162
Oft came and went, as there resolved to die 821 Juan 4 310
Some twenty of his train came, rank on rank 822 Juan 4 375
Corruption came not in each mind to kill 824 Juan 4 477
The harper came, and tuned his instrument 824 Juan 4 514
Short solace, vain relief!--thought came too quick 825 Juan 4 529
Who came at stated moments to invite all 827 Juan 4 715
For night was closing ere they came to land 836 Juan 5 326
As they were threading on their way, there came 836 Juan 5 337
And nearer as they came, a genial savour 837 Juan 5 369
It seem'd as though they came upon a shrine 842 Juan 5 679
But not by the same door through which came in 844 Juan 5 794
First came her damsels, a decorous file 850 Juan 5 1161
Before he came, especially at night 850 Juan 5 1166
But then they never came to 'the Seven Towers 850 Juan 5 1200
Of whom all such as came of age were stow'd 850 Juan 5 1210
Katinka ask'd her also whence she came 858 Juan 6 347
By which its nomenclature came to pass 859 Juan 6 435
What are we? and whence came we? what shall be 860 Juan 6 502
Neither, came crowding like the waves of ocean 861 Juan 6 564
Then out it came at length, that to Dudu 865 Juan 6 813
For some time, till they came in nearer view 872 Juan 7 339
And as he rush'd along, it came to pass he 882 Juan 8 265
Just at this crisis up came Johnson too 882 Juan 8 273
And these he call'd on; and, what's strange, they came 883 Juan 8 297

CAME

Came mounting quickly up, for it was now	883 Juan	8	354
Who came as if just dropp'd down from the moon	885 Juan	8	444
Crime came not near him--she is not the child	886 Juan	8	489
Up came John Johnson (I will not say 'Jack	890 Juan	8	769
Up Johnson came, with hundreds at his back	890 Juan	8	773
And swearing if the infant came to ill	891 Juan	8	813
Haustus' (And here the surgeon came and cupp'd him	912 Juan	10	
From Poland they came on through Prussia Proper	915 Juan	10	473
Came up, all marvelling at such a deed	920 Juan	11	107
The mellow autumn came, and with it came	950 Juan	13	593
That when a culprit came for condemnation	952 Juan	13	703
'His country's pride,' he came down to the country	952 Juan	13	728
With evening came the banquet and the wine	954 Juan	13	849
At sixteen she came out; presented, vaunted	962 Juan	14	433
'That good but rarely came from good advice	963 Juan	14	528
Though God knows whence it came from; there was, too	976 Juan	15	498
Though he came in his might, with King Henry's right	985 Juan	16	329
And lo! upon that day it came to pass	991 Juan	16	693
The evening also waned--and coffee came	994 Juan	16	850
Came over Juan's ear, which throbb'd, alas	995 Juan	16	957
The morning came--and breakfast, tea and toast	998 Juan	17	98

CAMEL

The camel labours with the heaviest load	58 Harold	4	184
And drive the camel than purvey the bear	302 Age		313
And there the Arab's camel kneels	385 Corinth		81
Through needles' eyes it easier for the camel is	828 Juan	4	775

CAMELEOPARD

New broke, a cameleopard, a gazelle	774 Juan	2	42

CAMELS

Stood camels grazing, and some goodly steeds	215 Dream		119
On Jordan's banks the Arab's camels stray	217 Jordan		1
The camels from their keepers broke	396 Corinth		1061

CAMEL'S

He rode upon a Camel's hump	233 Ballad-B		33
Or in the desert heard the camel's bell	784 Juan	2	671
And long, long deserts scorch the camel's foot	823 Juan	4	438
The holy camel's hump, besides the Koran	865 Juan	6	816

CAMELS'

The browsing camels' bells are tinkling	317 Giaour		689

CAMERADO

Strange too in my 'buon camerado' Scott	931 Juan	12	125

CAMERON'S

And wild and high the 'Cameron's gathering' rose	39 Harold	3	226

CAMESE

In his snowy camese and his shaggy capote	30 Harold	2	654

CAMEST

Thou camest hither I was busy writing	609 Foscari	3	67
Nor part from thee; thou camest in such a guise	711 Werner	4	440

CAMILLA

Like swift Camilla, he scarce skimm'd the ground	960 Juan	14	307

CAMOENS

To him let Camoens, Milton, Tasso yield	244 Bards		203
By dressing Camoens in a suit of lace	246 Bards		304
And swear that Camoens sang such notes of yore	254 Bards		922

CAMP

Here was the camp, the watch-flame, and the host	12 Harold	1	518
The camp, the host, the fight, the conqueror's career	33 Harold	2	845
Seest thou yon camp, with torches twinkling dim	105 Nisus		25
Bacchus and Mars to rule the camp combine	108 Nisus		229
To Turnus' camp pursue their destined course	109 Nisus		298
Did the senate or camp my exertions require	129 Becher-A		5
Behind, the camp; before him lay	388 Corinth		362
In the camp of the conquerors; behold	592 Sardan	5	295
Marauders from the hostile camp. They proved	716 Werner	5	232
And for his tongue, the camp is full of licence	734 Deformed	1	822
The court, camp, church, the vessel, and the mart	770 Juan	1	1547
But to the tale:--great joy unto the camp	873 Juan	7	361
The fleet and camp saluted with great grace	873 Juan	7	371
The whole camp rung with joy; you would have thought	873 Juan	7	385
Of the assault, and all the camp was in	874 Juan	7	426
Into a camp: I know that nought so bothers	876 Juan	7	566
'Love rules the camp, the court, the grove,'-- 'for love	931 Juan	12	97
Now if the 'court,' and 'camp,' and 'grove,' be not	931 Juan	12	121

CAMPAIGN

Than in thy Greek gazette of that campaign	877 Juan	7	636
''Twas only the fatigue of last campaign	912 Juan	10	320

CAMPBELL

Remarks on Mr. Campbell	237 Bowles		4
Come forth, oh Campbell! give thy talents scope	252 Bards		801
Scott, Rogers, Campbell, Moore, and Crabbe will try	746 Juan	Ded	55
Sir Walter reign'd before me; Moore and Campbell	925 Juan	11	449

CAMPBELLS

Crabbes, Campbells, Crokers, Freres, and Wards	231 Doctor		54

CAMPBELL'S

And Campbell's Hippocrene is somewhat drouthy	772 Juan	1	1633

CAMPS

Alike for courts, and camps, or senates fit	94 Dorset		70
Our church and state, our courts and camps, concede	264 Hints		581
If 'courts' and 'camps' be quite so sentimental	931 Juan	12	104
Without cash, camps were thin, and courts were none	931 Juan	12	107
In camps, in ships, in cottages, or courts	959 Juan	14	244

CAMP'S

No doubt, the camp's the school of civic rights	734 Deformed	1	853

CAM'S

Where on Cam's sedgy banks supine they lie	112 Examination		51
King's Coll., Cam's stream, stain'd windows and old walls	257 Hints		28

CAM'ST

Why cam'st thou not in time to save him from	651 Cain	3	366

CAN

And Beauty and Canova can	229 Marble		4
I read a sheet of Marg'ret of Anjou; Can you	230 I Read		4
The Tolbooth felt--for marble sometimes can	248 Bards		476
And actors copy nature--when they can	258 Hints		152
Above all things, Dan Poet, if you can	260 Hints		291
May Heaven forgive you, for he never can	267 Hints		752
In private may resist him--if it can	276 Waltz		215
Pray get out of this hobble as fast as you can	278 Blues	1	64
From out his havresack and can	407 Mazeppa		87
Of such defence the Powers of Evil can	439 Tasso		201
I pray thee take heed of me, till I can	470 Morgante		287
But will not, can not be so now. I doubt it	568 Sardan	2	435
But--I can leave them, children as they are	611 Foscari	3	198
To make way for much meaner than we can	638 Cain	2	160
Who can redeems thee. And why him and can	665 Heaven		766
And bear what Adam's race must bear, and can	668 Heaven		961
And even the wisest, do the best they can	749 Juan	1	163
No courtier could, and scarcely woman can	806 Juan	3	325
Which every body does without who can	828 Juan	4	724
He show'd himself as kind as mortal can	886 Juan	8	512
Of rubles rain, as fast as specie can	906 Juan	9	630
Yet undiscover'd treasure. What I can	922 Juan	11	222
And seem to say, 'Resist us if you can	969 Juan	15	95
For how could it go on? Explain who can	990 Juan	16	647

CANAAN

No land of Canaan, full of milk and honey	307 Age		670

CANAL

Damm'd like the dull canal with locks and chains	455 Venice-B		152
Like altars ranged along the broad canal	529 Faliero	4	79
The landing-place of the canal. No. I	624 Foscari	5	239

CANALS

Impetuous rivers stagnate in canals	258 Hints		94
And up and down the long canals they go	442 Beppo		153
On her canals, where God takes sea and land	900 Juan	9	247
And cut through such canals of contradiction	979 Juan	15	703

CANCEL

Repentance will cancel the vow you have made	136 Delawarr		20
One blow shall cancel with our future fears	361 Corsair	3	379
Oh! never canst thou cancel half her debt	372 Lara	1	441
Now choose more wisely, could they cancel it	510 Faliero	2	131
Could cancel the inexorable past	543 Faliero	5	403
Your feelings cannot cancel a sole pang	586 Sardan	4	543

CANCELL'D
(See also HALF-CANCELL'D)

That kindness cancell'd fear in those who heard	346 Corsair	1	547
Perhaps his guilt, has cancell'd all the little	693 Werner	2	647

CANCER

He's the cancer of his species	197 Rogers		71
Than Buonaparte's cancer: could I dash on	898 Juan	9	110

CANDELIGHT
That sort of farthing candelight which glimmers   445 Beppo   343

CANDIA
Witness Troy's rival, Candia! Vouch it, ye   57 Harold   4   124
Return to Candia. Then my last hope's gone   610 Foscari   3   126
Your sentence, then? Return to Candia? True   612 Foscari   3   272
Of Candia, Cyprus, Rhodes, or other islands   786 Juan   2   800

CANDID
Ah! fly not from the candid youth   87 Rousseau   19
Candid and liberal, with a heart of steel   126 Recoll   271
But yet this last my candid Muse admits   142 Soliloquy   15
And showers their odours on thy candid sheets   249 Bards   533
Nor slight applause will candid pens afford   257 Hints   71

CANDIDATE
The candidate for college prizes   95 Granta   30
Behold a candidate with unturn'd coat   293 Vision   535
Of the official candidate. I'll touch   990 Juan   16   662

CANDIDATES
Lo! candidates and voters lie   95 Granta   13
The rival candidates for Attic fame   249 Bards   595
Of candidates requesting to be placed   913 Juan   10   379

CANDIDE
Voltaire says 'No:' he tells you that Candide   835 Juan   5   241

CANDIOTE
That decks the wandering Candiote   330 Abydos   2   142
Which howl'd about my Candiote dungeon and   597 Foscari   1   129
His candiote exile, I had hopes--he has quench'd
   them   603 Foscari   2   100
A Candiote cloak, which to the knee might reach   840 Juan   5   539

CANDLE
She snuff'd the candle, curtsied, and withdrew   768 Juan   1   1384
Their moon, their sun, their gas, their farthing
   candle   936 Juan   12   448

CANDLE-LIGHT
Their last dramatic work by candle-light   267 Hints   766

CANDLES
Because when once the lamps and candles fail   450 Beppo   655
To Virgin Mary several pounds of candles   770 Juan   1   1518
Of candles to their saints--but there were none   779 Juan   2   348

CANDLESTICKS
Which still in Juan's candlesticks burn'd high   996 Juan   16   981

CANDOUR
Candour compels me, Becher! to commend   118 Answer-A   1
Though Cleon's candour would the palm divide   126 Recoll   338
A thread of candour with a web of wiles   209 Sketch   58
Affect a candour which thou canst not feel   247 Bards   375
This of his candour seem'd the sable dew   248 Bards   486

CANDOUR'S
Which Envy, wearing Candour's sacred mask   114 Death-A   35
Instructs his son from candour's path to shrink   123 Recoll   69
Yet candour's self compels me now to own   126 Recoll   339

CANDY
(See also SUGAR-CANDY)
Than their he relatives), like flies o'er candy   933 Juan   12   254

CANEA
In Canea--afterwards the freedom of   612 Foscari   3   275

CAN GRANDE
'Can Grande' (which I venture to translate   303 Age   417

CANKER
The worm, the canker, and the grief   206 Year   7
And the mind's canker in its savage mood   436 Tasso   5
Or worse; for it has been a canker in   673 Werner   1   134

CANKER'D
Yet let not canker'd Calumny assail   114 Death-A   27
A Mask each canker'd brow shall hide   141 Critics   24

CANKERING
Hath slowly work'd her cankering way   313 Giaour   337
Not cankering less because the more conceal'd   352 Corsair   2   353
That iron is a cankering thing   403 Chillon   38

CANKERS
Let us have done with that which cankers life   720 Werner   5   468

CANKER-WORM
My heart!--a never-dying canker-worm   701 Werner   3   440
For causes young or old: the canker-worm   912 Juan   10   298

CANNAE'S
While Waterloo with Cannae's carnage vies   45 Harold   3   608

CANNIBAL
The longings of the cannibal arise   783 Juan   2   575

CANNING
There was Canning for War, and Whitbread for
   peace   178 Devil's Dr   163
From Canning, the tall wit   232 Murray-B   58
Even this thy genius, Canning! may permit   305 Age   548

CANNING'S
While Canning's colleagues hate him for his wit   255 Bards   1015

CANNON
By Christian cannon piecemeal rent   324 Abydos   1   94
The cannon are pointed, and ready to roar   392 Corinth   702
Which robes the cannon as he wings a tomb   426 Island   3   2
While two and twenty cannon duly set   868 Juan   7   94
And fourscore cannon on the Danube's border   872 Juan   7   303
Three hundred cannon threw up their emetic   879 Juan   8   89
And the loud cannon peal'd his hoarsest strains   882 Juan   8   262
The very cannon, deafen'd by the din   885 Juan   8   469

CANNONADE
Off Ismail, and commenced a cannonade   870 Juan   7   229
At length they found mere cannonade alone   871 Juan   7   236
In preparations for a cannonade   877 Juan   7   618

CANNON'S
Could blunt the sabre's edge or clear the
   cannon's smoke   12 Harold   1   530
Arm! Arm! it is--it is--the cannon's opening roar   38 Harold   3   198
The trench is dug, the cannon's breath   385 Corinth   87
Than the late cannon's volume, this word--'Werner 715 Werner   5   134
Cannon's black mouth, shining spear   735 Deformed   2   30
Blazed, and the cannon's roar was scarce allay'd   895 Juan   8   1060

CANNON-SHOT
Within a cannon-shot length of the place   873 Juan   7   373

CANOE
Their unexploring navy, the canoe   416 Island   1   46
The sea-born sailor of his shell canoe   417 Island   1   134
The sea-spread net, the lightly-launch'd canoe   422 Island   2   250
Oh, for a sole canoe! though but a shell   428 Island   3   161
And now what refuge but their frail canoe   430 Island   4   52
Each dawn had wafted there her light canoe   432 Island   4   183
Hid the canoe that Neuha there had left   435 Island   4   394
Just like a coffin clapt in a canoe   442 Beppo   151

CANOES
For the first time were wafted in canoes   419 Island   2   36
In vast canoes, begirt with bolts of flame   422 Island   2   221
Embark'd their guests and launch'd their light
   canoes   429 Island   3   222
And now the two canoes in chase divide   429 Island   3   233
Ere the canoes divided, near the spot   430 Island   4   33

CANONGATE
Flow'd all the Canongate with inky streams   248 Bards   485

CANONICAL
Is that which may be christen'd love canonical   906 Juan   9   603

CANONICALLY
(To talk canonically) wax a son   726 Deformed   1   294

CANONIZATION
Canonization for the self-same cause   930 Juan   12   53

CANOPIED
(See also O'ER-CANOPIED)
And they were canopied by the blue sky   215 Dream   123

CANOPY
But gaze beneath thy cloudy canopy   14 Harold   1   628
The well-reeved guns, the netted canopy   22 Harold   2   155
With her most starry canopy; and seating   72 Harold   4   1058
To thy bright canopy the mourner flies   140 Ossian-A   42
O'er the corse of thy lord in thy canopy laid   149 Newstead-B   30
His canopy the stone   220 Belshaz-B   46
Without or couch or canopy   388 Corinth   342
With starless skies my canopy   408 Mazeppa   201
And show'd a self-born Gothic canopy   432 Island   4   146
Place it beneath my canopy, as though   589 Sardan   165
From his snow canopy of cliffs and clouds   610 Foscari   3   180
For our child's canopy? Because its branches   646 Cain   3   6
Spread for his canopy, o'er silken pillows   702 Werner   3   454
Under a canopy, and there reclined   843 Juan   5   754
These are beneath the canopy of heaven   855 Juan   6   193
Also beneath the canopy of beds   855 Juan   6   194
With thick'ning canopy the conflict o'er   879 Juan   8   62

CANOPY
On tiptoe through their sea-coal canopy   917 Juan   10   654

CANOVA
Such as the great of yore, Canova is today   63 Harold   4   495
And Beauty and Canova can   229 Marble   4
While yet Canova can create below   446 Beppo   368

CANST
I will. Thou canst? Perhaps. Would you aught else   724 Deformed   1   119

CANT
Till, after cloying the gazettes with cant   747 Juan   1   3
And recollect the time when all this cant   829 Juan   4   783

CAN'T
The premium can't exceed the price they pay   112 Examination   72
And, if you can't applaud, at least forgive   114 Prologue   36
Still I can't contradict, what so oft has been said   116 To Eliza   15
Precepts of prudence curb, but can't control   119 Answer-A   9
Shall these, by creeds they can't expound   132 Prayer   29
I can't attack, when Beauty forms the shield   142 Soliloquy   36
For, Faith, I can't withstand Temptation   145 Becher-B   68
Why we should weep I can't find out   147 To Author   3
Why? I really can't discover   197 Rogers   60
But in this last I can't determine   233 Nihil   6
As a sinner, you can't care what Sin does   239 Bray   42
And smile at folly, if we can't at wit   261 Hints   342
And will not alter what you can't defend   267 Hints   790
And cockneys practise what they can't pronounce   275 Waltz   158
Humph! I can't say I know any happy alliance   278 Blues   1   71
And so, as I can't, will you furnish a few   279 Blues   1   92
I really can't say that they much evince   288 Vision   230
I can't tell who first brought the custom in   444 Beppo   284
And when I can't find that, I put a worse on   446 Beppo   413
Excepting that it can't be spoilt by rain   447 Beppo   462
This form of verse began, I can't well break it   448 Beppo   501
And may be pardon'd, since they can't be punish'd   590 Sardan   5   218
The baron's chamber, that it can't be he   683 Werner   2   22
My present seeming. I can't say I did   700 Werner   3   312
You can't deny his train of followers   704 Werner   4   39
To me than to my son. I can't help that   716 Werner   5   200
Society) you can't tell how he approaches   723 Deformed   1   97
But can't find any in the present age   747 Juan   1   38
But this I heard her say, and can't be wrong   748 Juan   1   109
I can't say much for friend or yet relation   751 Juan   1   253
I can't help thinking Juvenal was wrong   752 Juan   1   339
I can't but say that his mamma was right   753 Juan   1   378
I can't tell whether Julia saw the affair   755 Juan   1   537
I can't help thinking puberty assisted   758 Juan   1   744
And then--God knows what next--I can't go on   761 Juan   1   919
I can't tell how, or why, or what suspicion   764 Juan   1   1105
I can't tell why she should take all this trouble   764 Juan   1   1119
But that can't be, as has been often shown   768 Juan   1   1404
I can't help putting in my claim to praise   774 Juan   1   1774
I can't say that it puzzles me at all   774 Juan   2   17
I can't describe it, though so much it strike   774 Juan   2   39
I can't but say it is an awkward sight   775 Juan   2   89
I can't say that she gave them any tea   792 Juan   2   1158
I say that beef is rare, and can't help thinking   793 Juan   2   1233
I can't but say it seems to me most truly a   800 Juan   2   1659
And sigh, 'I can't get out,' like Yorick's starling   830 Juan   4   868
Because if drown'd, they can't--if spared, they won't   832 Juan   5   48
Because they can't find out the very spot   839 Juan   5   491
Where I can't say or gold or diamond flings   843 Juan   5   749
You can't suppose Gulbeyaz' angry brow   848 Juan   5   1048
I can't tell why she blush'd, nor can expound   863 Juan   6   677
You can't repeat nine names from each Gazette   871 Juan   7   272
Quite disappear'd--the gods know how! (I can't   882 Juan   8   243
And 'farmers' can't raise Ceres from her fall   900 Juan   9   254
I can't complain, whose ancestors are there   912 Juan   10   281
And though I can't help thinking 'twas scarce fair   912 Juan   10   285
But what is to be done? I can't allow   920 Juan   11   118
In thunder, holds the way it can't well miss   921 Juan   11   158
Or can't do otherwise than lie, but do it   923 Juan   11   287
Such is your cold coquette, who can't say 'No   937 Juan   12   497
Can't form a friendship, but the world o'er-awes it   938 Juan   12   515
I can't oblige you, reader, to read on   941 Juan   12   694
I can't exactly trace their rule of right   951 Juan   13   649
The gulf of rock yawns,--you can't gaze a minute   956 Juan   14   39
And yet I can't help scribbling once a week   956 Juan   14   77
But this can't well be true, just now; for writers   958 Juan   14   153
All this were very well, and can't be better   958 Juan   14   193
Which never meets, and therefore can't fall out   961 Juan   14   360
That like to make a quarrel, when they can't   963 Juan   14   501
But now I can't tell where it may not run   971 Juan   15   172
Had Adeline read Malthus? I can't tell   972 Juan   15   297

CAN'T
With things I can't withstand or understand   976 Juan   15   523
Can't, like ripe age, in gormandize excel   977 Juan   15   558
Of which I can't tell whence their knowledge springs   977 Juan   15   604
Yet mix'd so slightly, that you can't complain   981 Juan   16   22
I can't tell why, to this dissimulation   985 Juan   16   315
One can't tell how it e'er got in or out   988 Juan   16   538
When he can't tell what 'tis that doth appal   996 Juan   16   1006

CANTABS
Of verse (the name with which we Cantabs please   816 Juan   3   975

CAN'T-BE
The would-be wits and can't-be gentlemen   449 Beppo   606

CANTEMIR
Of Cantemir, or Knolles, where few shine   850 Juan   5   1175
So Cantemir can tell you, or De Tott   856 Juan   6   245

CANTER
I canter by the spot each afternoon   829 Juan   4   817
I think to canter gently through a hundred   936 Juan   12   440

CANTERBURY
On with the horses! Off to Canterbury   916 Juan   10   561
They saw at Canterbury the cathedral   916 Juan   10   577

CANTICLES
The land of Song--and Canticles you know   743 Deformed   3   84

CANTO
Hermilda's first and second canto   226 Thurlow-A   8
To set up this ultimate Canto   232 Murray-B   3
That ever penn'd a canto   233 Ballad-B   2
Here ends this canto.--Need I sing, or say   770 Juan   1   1497
Besides, in Canto Twelfth, I mean to show   772 Juan   1   1655
A canto--then their feet and ankles,--well   774 Juan   2   46
Perhaps it may be lined with this my canto   776 Juan   2   128
Each canto of the twelve, or twenty-four   801 Juan   2   1725
Oh!--the third canto--and the pretty pair   811 Juan   3   646
In England a six canto quarto tale   812 Juan   3   682
(In copying) this long canto into two   816 Juan   3   979
Had stopp'd this Canto, and Don Juan's breath   821 Juan   4   330
(Because this Canto has become too long   831 Juan   4   931
Let this fifth canto meet with due applause   851 Juan   5   1269
This Canto, ere my Muse perceives fatigue   877 Juan   7   678
As the first Canto promised. You have now   896 Juan   8   1098
In this twelfth Canto 'tis my wish to be   932 Juan   12   155
Here the twelfth Canto of our introduction   940 Juan   12   689
But my best canto, save one on astronomy   941 Juan   12   703
To the next Canto; where perhaps I shall   967 Juan   14   782
Our Hero was, in Canto the Sixteenth   998 Juan   17   89

CANTOS
Lines forty thousand, cantos twenty-five   247 Bards   390
Ere your first score of cantos time unrolls   259 Hints   193
To pass, than those two cantos into families   828 Juan   4   776
As these new cantos touch on warlike feats   897 Juan   9   73
But how shall I relate in other cantos   929 Juan   11   681
That from the first of Cantos up to this   936 Juan   12   427
Cantos would do; but at Apollo's pleading   936 Juan   12   438
Trade will be all the better for these Cantos   957 Juan   14   112

CANTS
Faith cants, perplex'd apologist of sin   262 Hints   380

CANVAS
(See also CANVASS)
Nor rag of canvas, what could they expect   778 Juan   2   308

CANVASS
And the rent canvass fluttering strew the gale   35 Harold   3   15
Who canvass there with all their might   95 Granta   11
Bend the canvass o'er the mast   156 Hodgson   4
You hate the house--why canvass, then   235 New Song   13
Whose magic touch can bid the canvass glow   253 Bards   863
His costly canvass with each flatter'd face   256 Hints   2
And ampler canvass woos the wind from high   362 Corsair   3   485
Some cordage, canvass, sails, and lines, and twine   416 Island   1   91
And from the outspread canvass gladly wrings   418 Island   1   193
I've seen no rag of canvass on the sea   426 Island   2   505
Or deify the canvass till it shine   463 Dante   4   29
On canvass or on stone; and they who mar   464 Dante   4   81
Nimrods, whose canvass scarce contain'd the steed   950 Juan   13   558
They fill the canvass up--and 'verbum sat'   970 Juan   15   125
Nor canvass what so 'eminent a hand' meant   973 Juan   15   302
Along the canvass; their eyes glance like dreams   982 Juan   16   148

CAP
Bears in his cap the badge of crimson hue   12 Harold   1   523
The Delhi with his cap of terror on   28 Harold   2   518
My cap was the bonnet, my cloak was the plaid   117 Lachin   10

CAP
Bedecks her cap with bells of every clime   242 Bards   30
If to thy bells thou wouldst but add a cap   246 Bards   340
Conspicuous by his yellow cap   315 Giaour   550
And these his lofty cap rose proudly o'er   348 Corsair   2   58
Dash'd his high cap, and tore his robe away   349 Corsair   2 146
And wore the ducal cap I trample on   502 Faliero   1 203
This cap is not the monarch's crown; these robes   506 Faliero   1 441
As Doge, clad in the ducal robes and cap   545 Faliero   5 516
This ducal cap the diadem of earth   603 Foscari   2   80
His cap and head, which proves the head to be   879 Juan   8   75
More than the cap; in fact, the ball could mean   879 Juan   8   78
I have seen crowns worn instead of a fool's cap   929 Juan   11 661
There was a country girl in a close cap   988 Juan   16 531

CAPABILITIES
And capabilities, as to discover   834 Juan   5 204

CAPABLE
A slumbering thought, is capable of years   214 Dream   25
Grows capable of all things for revenge   518 Faliero   2 686
Are capable of turning them aside   534 Faliero   4 414
She was as capable as woman can be   967 Juan   14 736

CAPACITY
With more capacity for love than earth   370 Lara   1 321
The mind then hath capacity of time   647 Cain   3   60
If such can e'er be drawn by man's capacity   966 Juan   14 718

CAP-A-PIE
All cap-a-pie from head to heel   410 Mazeppa   329
Two batteries, cap-a-pie, as our St. George   868 Juan   7   91

CAPARISON'D
Richly caparison'd, a ready row   28 Harold   2 505
Its walls there was a steed caparison'd   214 Dream   77
He shall be straight caparison'd. How many   705 Werner   4   85

CAPE
Childe Harold hail'd Leucadia's cape afar   25 Harold   2 353
As 'twere the cape of a long ridge of such   214 Dream   30
Can aught from cold Kamschatka to Cape Horn   275 Waltz   129
Already doubled is the cape--our bay   339 Corsair   1   89
Screen'd from espial by the jutting cape   347 Corsair   1 601
Sunk he in Contemplation, till the Cape   362 Corsair   3 454
You like by way of doublet, cape, or cloak   440 Beppo   34
Except three days of calm when off Cape Bonn   452 Beppo   768
And clap a white cape on their mantles blue   763 Juan   1 1069
Some he disposed of off Cape Matapan   803 Juan   3 121
But now was not much pleased with Cape Sigaeum   826 Juan   4 600

CAPEL
And Capel Lofft declares 'tis quite sublime   252 Bards   774
The cobbler-laureats sing to Capel Lofft   266 Hints   734

CAPER
And my internal spirit cut a caper   907 Juan   10   20

CAPERERS
Columbia's caperers to the warlike whoop   275 Waltz   128

CAPET
With Capet or Napoleon   188 Ode-B   80

CAPITAL
And Belgium's capital had gather'd then   38 Harold   3 182
Our giant capital, whose squares are spread   260 Hints   303
Austria! which saw thy twice-ta'en capital   300 Age   153
Numbered by hordes, a human capital   302 Age   306
My journey to the capital, curtail'd   541 Faliero   5 217
In lieu of capital, with slaves for senates   548 Faliero   5 752
Great capital perchance is ours to-morrow   734 Deformed   1 843
With slaves to sell off in the capital   830 Juan   4 898
That pleasant capital of painted snows   901 Juan   9 336
And Konigsberg the capital, whose vaunt   915 Juan   10 474
His travels to the capital apace   920 Juan   11 140

CAPITALS
Girt with the silent crimes of Capitals   11 Harold   1 493
And monarchs tremble in their capitals   82 Harold   4 1623

CAPITOL
Where the car climb'd the capitol; far and wide   67 Harold   4 716
While stands the Capitol, immortal dome   110 Nisus   405
With the geese in the Capitol, which gabbled   537 Faliero   4 648

CAPITULATION
To frighten them into capitulation   870 Juan   7 190

CAPO
Had brought the capo d'opera, not for sale   988 Juan   16 503

CAPON'S
But this I know, that this roast capon's fat   807 Juan   3 355

CAPOTE
The little shepherd in his white capote   27 Harold   2 466
In his snowy camese and his shaggy capote   30 Harold   2 654
The cloak of white; the thin capote   330 Abydos   2 141
There lies a white capote   335 Abydos   2 595
Waits but my chief--' 'My sword, and my capote   346 Corsair   1 558
Whether we couch'd in our rough capote   384 Corinth   10

CAPP'D
(See HIGH-CAPP'D, TOWER-CAPPED)

CAPRICE
And each well known caprice of wave and wind   23 Harold   2 247
Caprice must be my only reason   98 To Lesbia   16
In whom Caprice had seem'd a duty   201 Ode-C   50
From infant's play, and man's caprice   314 Giaour   403
Or some unknown cabal, caprice   331 Abydos   2 266
Unless some gay caprice suggests the blow   347 Corsair   2   23
'Twas not a foolish dotard's vile caprice   513 Faliero   2 310
And no great mischief's done by their caprice   771 Juan   1 1590
In what way feminine caprice may dissipate   867 Juan   6 952
Nine times in ten 'tis but caprice or fashion   939 Juan   12 611

CAPRICES
Judge then, if her caprices e'er stood still   845 Juan   5 894
A lover with caprices soft and dear   963 Juan   14 500
But nature's nature, and has more caprices   974 Juan   15 415
And morals of the country from caprices   989 Juan   16 547

CAPRICIOUS
For it was not the blind capricious rage   377 Lara   2 145
As the capricious mercy of such things   532 Faliero   4 266
Love's a capricious power: I've known it hold   776 Juan   2 169
And as my Muse is a capricious elf   826 Juan   4 590
Into gazettes; but Fame (capricious strumpet   869 Juan   7 119

CAPS
I, at whose name the million's caps were flung   535 Faliero   4 500
Some leathern caps, and what remain'd of shoes   783 Juan   2 586
Some who once set their caps at cautious dukes   928 Juan   11 633

CAP'S
Their favour in an author's cap's a feather   771 Juan   1 1589

CAPSIZE
But what if carrying sail capsize the boat   898 Juan   9 139

CAPT
Save darken'd Jura, whose capt heights appear   48 Harold   3 809

CAPTAIN
Now we've reach'd her, lo! the captain   157 Hodgson   33
From Captain Noah down to Captain Cook   246 Bards   356
By Captain Parry's crew, in 'Melville's Sound   288 Vision   216
Down with them both! our traitorous captain, and   522 Faliero   3 212
And signory as podesta and captain   546 Faliero   5 594
As firm in fight as Babylonia's captain   562 Sardan   2   77
The trusty, rough, true soldier--the best captain   565 Sardan   2 214
In his rough eyes, and told the captain he   779 Juan   2 338
As Captain Parry's voyage may do to Jason's   958 Juan   14 172

CAPTAINS
A list of ships, and captains, and kings reigning   771 Juan   1 1596
Should captains the remark, or critics, make   772 Juan   1 1663

CAPTAIN'S
And view'd their captain's fate with piteous eyes   417 Island   1 129

CAPTIOUS
To fly from the captious coquette   116 Pigot   28

CAPTIVATE
Which would so captivate, I ween   226 Dallas   2

CAPTIVE
And track to his covert the captive on shore   30 Harold   2 668
The bars survive the captive they enthral   40 Harold   3 286
Conqueror and captive of the earth art thou   40 Harold   3 325
Or wealth redeem from foes my captive corse   106 Nisus   68
Nay more, twelve slaves, and twice six captive
  dames   107 Nisus   159
Struggling in vain, a captive to the crew   109 Nisus   332
The last single Captive to millions in war   186 Napoleon   8
Eternal captive, to her God aspires   195 Vittorelli   8
A captive in the land   220 Belshaz-B   33
The Zegri, and the captive victors, flung   302 Age   330
The flames around their captive close   314 Giaour   425
From which the captive gladly steals   332 Abydos   2 299
His captive, though with dread resigning   332 Abydos   2 339
'A captive Dervise, from the pirate's nest   347 Corsair   2   49
Contain'd this captive and his court   352 Corsair   2 369
My bark is sunk or captive; but my love   354 Corsair   2 485
Remember, captive, 'tis to break thy chain   355 Corsair   2 529
The captive died upon the battle-plain   379 Lara   2 273

CAPTIVE

The fugitive, the captive, or the slain	435 Island	4	358
A captive, sees his half of manhood gone	461 Dante	3	83
Yearn'd, as the captive toiling at escape	465 Dante	4	129
The Captive Usurper	488 Manfred	2	314
And learn thou to be captive.--It hath ceased	536 Faliero	4	595
Already captive? can I not even breathe	560 Sardan	1	621
To worse than captive rebels. Let us trace them	576 Sardan	3	309
Pania yet lives; but Sfero's fled, or captive	589 Sardan	5	140
So Juan wept, as wept the captive Jews	776 Juan	2	121
Those captive soothers of a captive's hours	864 Juan	6	776
Don Juan raised his little captive from	890 Juan	8	751
His little captive gain'd him some applause	896 Juan	8	1117
Upon the captive, freedom? He's as far	916 Juan	10	542

CAPTIVES

We stand as captives and would not depart	62 Harold	4	446
Enchains the captives of their hate	196 Venice-A		16
Though fairest captives daily met his eye	342 Corsair	1	289
Already shared the captives and the prize	347 Corsair	2	10
She was a slave--from such may captives claim	358 Corsair	3	202
Of whom our captives often sing, related	556 Sardan	1	375
In that accursed isle of slaves, and captives	610 Foscari	3	133
He saw some fellow captives, who appear'd	826 Juan	4	633
The captives back to their sad berths; each threw	827 Juan	4	716
The captives, seem'd to mark their looks and age	834 Juan	5	203
With his two captives, by so queer a road	837 Juan	5	355
One or two stared the captives in the face	838 Juan	5	429
There captives led in triumph droop the eye	842 Juan	5	685
Captives just now escaped,' was the reply	874 Juan	7	469

CAPTIVE'S

Starts from its belt--he rends his captive's chains	57 Harold	4	143
Thou Timour! in his captive's cage	181 Ode-A		127
'Pacha! the fetter'd captive's mourning eye	348 Corsair	2	81
A conqueror's more than captive's air is seen	351 Corsair	2	301
Stern Seyd, still pondering o'er his Captive's fate	357 Corsair	3	132
Saved by his tribe but for a captive's woe	432 Island	4	202
And the poor captive's tale is graven on	608 Foscari	3	21
Those captive soothers of a captive's hours	864 Juan	6	776

CAPTIVES'

Our bread was such as captives' tears	404 Chillon		134

CAPTIVITY

Too bright, too blue, for my captivity	348 Corsair	2	86
But ne'er from strife, captivity, remorse	361 Corsair	3	422
But knowing well captivity	405 Chillon		281
And bare, at once, Captivity display'd	436 Tasso		11
Of minds and bodies in captivity	437 Tasso		66
And call captivity a kindness meant	462 Dante	3	134
But he has been condemn'd into captivity	515 Faliero	2	437
Than his prolong'd captivity;--I am punish'd	622 Foscari	5	107

CAPTURE

A fugitive--' 'Thy capture where and when	348 Corsair	2	66
His capture could but wait thy first command	358 Corsair	3	168
'His capture could!--and shall I then resign	358 Corsair	3	169
First Ismail's capture caught your fancy quite	904 Juan	9	518

CAPTURED

We have captured a king	732 Deformed	1	696

CAPTURES

By winds and waves, and some important captures	803 Juan	3	114

CAPULETS

The vaunted tomb of 'all the Capulets	303 Age		415

CAR

The decorated car appears, on high	16 Harold	1	788
Or the car rattling o'er the stony street	38 Harold	3	191
The mustering squadron, and the clattering car	39 Harold	3	218
See! as they chant the tragic hymn, the car	57 Harold	4	140
Where the car climb'd the capitol; far and wide	67 Harold	4	716
Her car half round yon sable heaven	88 Anacreon-B		2
Winter presides in his cold icy car	117 Lachin		22
Night quits her car, the twinkling stars decline	139 Ossian-A		6
Dramatic 'spirit drives a conquering car	170 Address-B		19
Who, born no king, made monarchs draw his car	299 Age		44
What shall return?--the conqueror's broken car	301 Age		200
Flock o'er the deck, in Neptune's borrow'd car	425 Island	2	467
Why, Nature's self detains the victor's car	460 Dante	2	121
His car (but temper'd by his sire's command	466 Morgante		22

CARACTACUS

Stood like Caractacus in act to rally	948 Juan	13	443

CARASMAN

But yet the line of Carasman	326 Abydos	1	201
This kinsman Bey of Carasman	327 Abydos	1	310

CARATACH

And Beaumont's pilfer'd Caratach affords	249 Bards		572

CARATS

Carats may it weigh?--Come, Werner, I will wing thee	700 Werner	3	355

CARAVAGGIO'S

Or gloomy Caravaggio's gloomier stain	950 Juan	13	571

CARAVAN

While thus they spake, the angelic caravan	287 Vision		177
Than swell the Cossaque's prowling caravan	302 Age		303
Or heaving whelm the helpless caravan	823 Juan	4	439
Of the long caravan, which in the chill	863 Juan	6	685

CARBINE

With steel unsheathed, and carbine bent	316 Giaour		573
Resign'd carbine or ataghan	316 Giaour		602
Whose voice is heard? whose carbine rang	335 Abydos	2	573

CARBINE-LOCK

My carbine-lock springs worthy of my trust	340 Corsair	1	162

CARBINE'S

Till within the range of a carbine's reach	389 Corinth		441

CARBONADOED

Have Carbonaro cooks not carbonadoed	305 Age		508

CARBONARO

Have Carbonaro cooks not carbonadoed	305 Age		508

CAR-BORNE

dream. I will seek car-borne Cuthullin. If I	130 Calmar		59

CARCASS

Carcass pick'd out from some mummy	196 Rogers		8
For there his carcass he might freely fling	268 Hints		819
Gorging and growling o'er carcass and limb	389 Corinth		456
The rebels' lines, his carcass down the river	592 Sardan	5	313
Worth naming so, would dwell in such a carcass	724 Deformed	1	144

CARCASSES

But nothing rests, save carcasses and wrecks	484 Manfred	2	57
The carcasses of Inde--away! away	578 Sardan	4	33
Has been o'er carcasses: mine eyes are full	730 Deformed	1	570
They lay like carcasses; and hope was none	783 Juan	2	571
Leaving as ladders their heap'd carcasses	888 Juan	8	606
And carcasses that lay as thick as thatch	900 Juan	9	228

CARD

I've a card, and shall go: but at present, as soon	279 Blues	1	133
But such a godfather's as good a card	869 Juan	7	148
Intentions,' which form all mankind's trump card	881 Juan	8	195
Received instructions how to play his card	913 Juan	10	366

CARDINAL

What have we here? A cardinal or two	737 Deformed	2	175

CARDS

Bitter as clubs in cards are against spades	292 Vision		478
Then there were billiards; cards, too, but no dice	954 Juan	13	841
I ask in turn,--Why do you play at cards	956 Juan	14	83
May drop in without cards, and take their station	989 Juan	16	596

CARE

But pomp and power alone are woman's care	5 Harold	1	78
Nor care what land thou bear'st me to	6 Harold	1	192
Doth care for cleanness of surtout or shirt	7 Harold	1	232
A fair but froward infant her own care	46 Harold	3	676
But chirup'd oft, and, free from care	87 Catullus		11
With care I tend my weary guest	89 Anacreon-B		31
Had claim'd his faithless bosom's care	103 Alva		164
Thy pious care may raise a simple tomb	106 Nisus		71
Struck with a filial care so deeply felt	108 Nisus		195
The dictate of my bosom's care	113 Quaker		44
Had Fortune aided Nature's care	113 Cornelian-A		25
The tender guidance of a father's care	125 Recoll		220
While Care as yet withheld her venom'd tooth	127 Recoll		390
It claims my warmest, dearest care	128 Lady-C		3
From any claim a kindred care	138 Clare		83
With pious care from wreck I'll save it	141 Pignus		30
Who claims a fostering Mother's care	141 Critics		54
Although his meanest care	146 Adieu		110
Oh! hardy thou wert--even now little care	149 Newstead-B		13
My care for thee shall purchase peace	150 My Son		10
I care not when I quit the scene	153 Friend-A		48
Will deign to own a kindred care	153 Friend-A		70
And care not for Hope, who are certain of bliss	156 Goblet		28
A kindred care for aught but one	156 Lady-F		60

CARE

'Have a care! that case holds liquor	157	Hodgson	21
A quiet refuge from each earthly care	161	Athos	20
Dear object of defeated care	161	Picture	1
'Oh! banish care'--such ever be	164	Friend-B	1
Lull the lone heart, and 'banish care	164	Friend-B	6
It is not drain'd to banish care	168	Haunts	18
Thy gentle care for him, who now	168	Haunts	34
Have years of care for thine and thee	168	Cornelian-B	3
I should have deem'd thee doom'd to earthly care	175	Sonnet-A	8
In taking care of Number One	176	Devil's Dr	62
May lighten well her heart's maternal care	183	Address-C	37
They sink, and turn to care	186	Stanzas-A	10
Even in this low world of care	188	Ode-B	97
That humbler Harmonist of care on Earth	194	Monody	112
What care I for the wreaths that can only give glory	204	Pisa	8
The hope, the fear, the jealous care	206	Year	13
Though his care she must forego	207	Fare thee	36
From me demand but little of my care	212	Augusta-C	106
As a sinner, you can't care what Sin does	239	Bray	42
Care not for feeling--pass your proper jest	242	Bards	73
Indeed!--'tis granted, faith!--but what care I	243	Bards	101
This cord receive, for thee reserved with care	248	Bards	458
Nor care if courts and crowds applaud or hiss	256	Bards	1062
So you indeed, with care (but be content	257	Hints	77
In sooth I do not know, or greatly care	262	Hints	437
That's my bookseller's business; I care not for sale	279	Blues	1	121
Finding their charges past all care below	285	Vision	18
Small care hath he of what his tomb consists	300	Age	117
But springs as to preclude his care	310	Giaour	56
Seems one that claims your utmost care	313	Giaour	361
Thyself without a crime or care	320	Giaour	974
I care not; so my arms enfold	323	Giaour	1294
To Haroun's care with women left	332	Abydos	2	331
My lot hath long had little of my care	343	Corsair	1	335
'Receive these tablets and peruse with care	346	Corsair	1	563
With all the care defenceless beauty claims	350	Corsair	2	218
'Tis not his life alone may claim such care	358	Corsair	3	185
As hardly worth a stranger's care to know	367	Lara	1	92
The common pleasure or the general care	367	Lara	1	102
But 'twas a hectic tint of secret care	373	Lara	1	534
In mute attention, and his care, which guess'd	374	Lara	1	556
Light care had he for life, and less for fame	378	Lara	2	248
And slung them with a more than common care	383	Lara	2	575
With humbler care her form arrays	386	Corinth	207
Thy youthful love, paternal care	399	Parisina	251
If lopp'd with care, a strength may give	402	Parisina	580
And for the like had little care	404	Chillon	131
My latest care, for whom I sought	404	Chillon	169
For time, and care, and war, have plough'd	408	Mazeppa	190
Yet shunn'd and dreaded with such care	414	Mazeppa	728
Was now his grateful sense of former care	417	Island	1	160
Who could resist themselves even, hardest care	463	Dante	3	181
And the bold Architect unto whose care	464	Dante	4	57
Orlando bade them take care of Rondello	469	Morgante	217
'Take care he don't revenge himself, though dead	474	Morgante	569
Why stood I not beneath it? Friend! have a care	483	Manfred	1	361
With the blood of a million he'll answer my care	488	Manfred	2	322
And he was a subject well worthy my care	488	Manfred	2	329
Our power, increasing thine, demands our care	489	Manfred	2	396
Had been already where--how soon, I care not	504	Faliero	1	349
You have more patience than I care to boast	516	Faliero	2	530
Let us but deal upon them, and I care not	516	Faliero	2	565
Will better have supplied my care. These orders	517	Faliero	2	636
You can; I care not. Israel, are these men	522	Faliero	3	229
See that none pass--arrest this man! Take care	533	Faliero	4	329
When men have shrunk from the ignoble care	559	Sardan	1	561
Worlds, or the lights of worlds, I know nor care not	566	Sardan	2	262
And I--I know not what, and care not; but	569	Sardan	2	489
A peasant's stool, I care not what: so--now	577	Sardan	3	341
Were past the sense of fear. Hate on; I care not	605	Foscari	2	237
I care not for his frowns! We can but die	613	Foscari	3	319
Behold the state's care for its sons and mothers	614	Foscari	3	395
I care, depute the Council on their knees	615	Foscari	4	33
With care, although 'tis past all farther harm	624	Foscari	5	206
But thee the better: I care not for that	649	Cain	3	192
Until 'tis spilt or check'd--how soon, I care not	671	Werner	1	11
This way, your excellency:--have a care	678	Werner	1	456
All places here. O Ulric! have a care	693	Werner	2	674
And rip the hunter's entrails. Ah! I care not	695	Werner	3	9
Greatly to care. But hark! they come! Who come	696	Werner	3	64
Absent, I took upon myself the care	702	Werner	3	484
And wherefore? Were you seen? The officious care	715	Werner	5	136
Takes care of us. Keep thought aloof from hosts	734	Deformed	1	864
Of such as these I should not care to vaunt	747	Juan	1	5
For native Spanish she had no great care	748	Juan	1	101
Which, with a long minority and care	751	Juan	1	291
Perhaps she did not know, or did not care	755	Juan	1	541
I care not for new pleasures, as the old	761	Juan	1	943
I wish to sleep, and beg you will take care	765	Juan	1	1221

CARE

CARE

For reputations he had little care	766	Juan	1	1276
It seem'd as if they had exchanged their care	781	Juan	2	443
And seem'd as if they had no further care	786	Juan	2	780
Its gentle touch and trembling care, a sigh	788	Juan	2	903
And lifting him with care into the cave	788	Juan	2	913
Hope, care, nor love, beyond, her heart beat here	799	Juan	2	1616
He may resume his amatory care	804	Juan	3	189
He is, nor whence he came--and little care	807	Juan	3	354
The 'Vates irritabilis' takes care	811	Juan	3	642
What was it made them thus exempt from care	818	Juan	4	140
Call'd social, haunts of Hate, and Vice, and Care	820	Juan	4	220
An open brow a little mark'd with care	832	Juan	5	85
The eunuch, having eyed them o'er with care	834	Juan	5	217
More circumstances? vain was every care	835	Juan	5	270
'What you may be, I neither know nor care	840	Juan	5	585
There might arise some pouting petty care	846	Juan	5	950
And I of your young charge will take due care	858	Juan	6	374
With cost, and care, and warmth induced to shoot	860	Juan	6	516
By the North Pole,--they sought her cause of care	861	Juan	6	574
Inquiries after them with kindest care	867	Juan	6	942
Their haste, or waste, I neither know nor care	870	Juan	7	210
Nor care a pinch of snuff about his corps	882	Juan	8	248
Of care or gain: the green woods were their portions	886	Juan	8	524
We don't much care with whom we may engage	905	Juan	9	547
Our young lieutenant to the genial care	907	Juan	9	666
I care not--'tis a glimpse of 'Auld Lang Syne	909	Juan	10	144
Care, like a housekeeper, brings every week	912	Juan	10	301
Must steer with care through all that glittering sea	927	Juan	11	547
Let him take care that that which he pursues	927	Juan	11	555
My Muses do not care a pinch of rosin	936	Juan	12	433
And care but for discoveries and not deeds	940	Juan	12	636
Take care what you reply to such a letter	954	Juan	13	840
Some heart-aches had been spared me: yet I care not	961	Juan	14	386
With no great care for what is nicknamed glory	970	Juan	15	147
Child to the care of guardians good and kind	973	Juan	15	346
I write the world, nor care if the world read	975	Juan	15	475

CARED

But this none knew, nor haply cared to know	4	Harold	1	68
A spot he long'd to see, nor cared to leave	25	Harold	2	354
Nor cared he who were winning	176	Devil's Dr	78
Who cared about the corpse? The funeral	286	Vision	75
Cared little, so that they were duly fed	303	Age	403
He cared not what he soften'd, but subdued	346	Corsair	1	552
Nor cared he now if rescued or betray'd	362	Corsair	3	449
What cared he for the freedom of the crowd	378	Lara	2	252
And little cared for bed and board	407	Mazeppa	67
Talking, she knew not why and cared not what	448	Beppo	546
Between the state and me. They shall be cared for	548	Faliero	5	710
Their safety shall be cared for. Get thee hence, then	570	Sardan	2	516
So little cared for as his own; and if	582	Sardan	4	288
Our children will be cared for by the Doge	611	Foscari	3	219
Cared for--what would he more? Die in his robes	622	Foscari	5	123
So there were quarrels, cared not for the cause	766	Juan	1	1271
Little cared they for Mahomet or Mufti	869	Juan	7	133
And cared as little for his army's loss	877	Juan	7	613
He knew not where he was, nor greatly cared	882	Juan	8	257
Juan, who cared not a tobacco-stopper	915	Juan	10	477
Cared most about; it need not now be pleaded	932	Juan	12	133
Profit he cared not for, let others reap it	990	Juan	16	644

CAREEN

With orders to the people to careen	804	Juan	3	158

CAREER

Her fellows flee--she checks their base career	13	Harold	1	578
The skill that yet may check his mad career	16	Harold	1	759
The camp, the host, the fight, the conqueror's career	33	Harold	2	845
Brief, brave, and glorious was his young career	44	Harold	3	545
A glorious and a long career pursue	94	Dorset	61
Diverted from its first career	99	Young Lady	8
In Glory's romantic career	115	The Tear	18
Your arm, brave boy, arrested his career	126	Recoil	179
Thus side by side we pass'd our first career	126	Recoil	331
Borne in our old unchanged career, we move	198	Po	18
The other half pursued its calm career	248	Bards	473
Thus far I've held my undisturb'd career	256	Bards	1037
Moscow! thou limit of his long career	300	Age	171
Thus held his thoughts their dark career	325	Abydos	1	112
Why did I doubt their quickness of career	349	Corsair	2	168
So steel'd by pondering o'er his far career	352	Corsair	2	364
And Alp's career a moment check'd	393	Corinth	848
He flew upon his far career	411	Mazeppa	447
His first and last career is done	413	Mazeppa	694
Blighting my life in best of its career	438	Tasso	98
Against the giant rush'd in fierce career	473	Morgante	502
By which we could pursue a fit career	475	Morgante	643

CAREER
Pause in her full career, because a woman   600 Foscari   1   315
Warrior from warrior in their grim career   881 Juan   8   210
Spared neither sex nor age in their career   893 Juan   8   946
As the smart boys spurr'd fast in their career   917 Juan   10   611
'Tis true, that thy career is not a new one   932 Juan   12   181
God help us! Since we have need on our career   979 Juan   15   715

CAREERING
Careering cleave the folded felt   326 Abydos   1   248

CAREFUL
His careful sire chalks forth some wary plan   123 Recoll   68
Some careful hand may teach to burn   148 A Fan   14
The careful pilot of my proper woe   211 Augusta-C   24
It is a sight the careful brow might smooth   371 Lara   1   393
Yet, be not rash--be careful of your life   583 Sardan   4   299
The watchful mothers, and the careful sisters   933 Juan   12   251
From these they will be careful to select   972 Juan   15   265

CARELESS
I would I were a careless child   135 I Would   1
A bird of free and careless wing   172 Romaic-B   13
And careless Dryden--'Ay, but Pye has not   243 Bards   100
Were quaint and careless, anything but chaste   262 Hints   430
All that a careless eye could see   330 Abydos   2   149
And careless eye the blood that dims its shine   338 Corsair   1   50
The careless guard that did not see me fly   348 Corsair   2   93
With hand, whose almost careless coolness spoke   376 Lara   2   59
A careless thing, who placed his choice in chance   421 Island   2   175
Careless of danger, as the onward wind   434 Island   4   283
But calm and careless heaved the wave below   435 Island   4   367
Glut the more careless swords of those leagued
  with us   535 Faliero   4   470
There is a careless courage which corruption   550 Sardan   1   10
Without the knowledge of the careless sovereign   574 Sardan   3   212
Resumed its careless life, and rose to drain   643 Cain   2   500
And careless voices, knowing not the cause   687 Werner   2   271
He was a mortal of the careless kind   749 Juan   1   145
On its own strength, with careless nerves and
  thews   882 Juan   8   286
Juan, though careless, young, and magnifique   916 Juan   10   553
Or careless; but the effort was not valid   985 Juan   16   279
Fair Adeline, though in a careless way   986 Juan   16   377

CARELESSLY
Or act so carelessly, in that which is   709 Werner   4   350
One hand on Juan's carelessly was thrown   760 Juan   1   871
A child of Nature, carelessly array'd   859 Juan   6   475
As carelessly as hurls the moth her wing   893 Juan   8   939
Than my forerunners. Carelessly I sing   896 Juan   8   1103

CARELESSNESS
In carelessness or mirth   167 Dead   7
Coldness of mien, and carelessness of praise   367 Lara   1   70
With something between carelessness and trouble   428 Island   3   116
In my sight, but with carelessness; mysterious   710 Werner   4   420

CARES
And joyful in a mother's gentlest cares   28 Harold   2   546
Blest cares! all other feelings far above   28 Harold   2   547
Your polish'd brow no cares have crost   98 To Lesbia   5
And lull'd alike the cares of brute and man   106 Nisus   86
Of cares o'erwhelming our conflicting state   114 Death-A   18
Their joys were many, as their cares were few   121 Newstead-A   132
And calm its cares and passions into rest   138 Harrow-B   18
Who the devil cares for more   157 Hodgson   78
Who cares if mimic heroes lived or not   259 Hints   170
(Unlucky Tavell! doom'd to daily cares   259 Hints   229
Cares little into what abyss   321 Giaour   1158
'This rose to calm my brother's cares   326 Abydos   1   287
Are well resign'd for cares--for joys like these   333 Abydos   2   415
Not that he had no cares to vex   408 Mazeppa   137
And no one notices, nor cares a pin   444 Beppo   286
On an old man oft moved with many cares   511 Faliero   2   171
You know what daily cares oppress all those   511 Faliero   2   182
Which might not yield to any cares of mine   571 Sardan   2   598
Have I not cares enow, and pangs enow   581 Sardan   4   229
Kind to relieve him from the cares of state   615 Foscari   4   3
Of the republic, and the o'erwhelming cares   621 Foscari   5   20
Born to be plough'd with years, and sown with
  cares   667 Heaven   871
Her surface. And that's not the worst: who cares   672 Werner   1   29
Since no one cares to tell me what he's call'd   676 Werner   1   285
Which late you wore, or were? Who cares? Let
  wolves   728 Deformed   1   424
Not having of my own domestic cares   750 Juan   1   184
Some run away, and but exchange their cares   799 Juan   2   1603
For no one cares for matrimonial cooings   802 Juan   3   61
Continued still her hospitable cares   804 Juan   3   149
Were once her cares, how idle seem'd they now   820 Juan   4   268
I know not if he had domestic cares   850 Juan   5   1181
The soul out (like the stone) with petty cares   855 Juan   6   160
While the poor rich wretch, object of these cares   934 Juan   12   263

CARE'S
Unless your care's exact, your judgment nice   257 Hints   49

CARESS
And show'd, alas! in each caress   164 Friend-B   39
Which answer'd not with a caress--he died   189 Darkness   54
To find in Hope but the renew'd caress   193 Monody   85
To seize and share the dear caress   316 Giaour   646
That dreaming sigh and warm caress   397 Parisina   77
Like other charmers, wooing the caress   425 Island   2   456
And shrunk as fearful of his own caress   428 Island   3   150
Not mine to tell the rapturous caress   433 Island   4   219

CARESS'D
And lovely forms caress'd me   219 Vanity   4
And stand a critic, hated yet caress'd   242 Bards   74
But more caressing seems when most caress'd   275 Waltz   144
Which mutely clasp'd, imploringly caress'd   345 Corsair   1   477
Caress'd him often--such a thing might be   755 Juan   1   546
To see it--the king hiss'd, and then caress'd   928 Juan   11   655

CARESSES
Her caresses shall lull me, her music shall
  soothe   30 Harold   2   674
And curl'd to give her neck caresses   160 Cadiz   16
First caresses, and then baits you   197 Rogers   48
Or give, like her, caresses to a score   277 Waltz   245
And suited to her soft caresses, told   432 Island   4   191
Of heads, than their caresses of the heart   854 Juan   6   112

CARESSING
But more caressing seems when most caress'd   275 Waltz   144
His child caressing and carest   325 Abydos   1   186

CAREST
His child caressing and carest   325 Abydos   1   186

CARETH
What careth she for hearts when once possess'd   24 Harold   2   300

CARGO
Fraught with this cargo--and her fairest freight   274 Waltz   79
Her only cargo such a scant supply   416 Island   1   87
To get up part of the cargo, and what not   777 Juan   2   219
She had a curious crew as well as cargo   782 Juan   2   527
Her cargo, from the plague being safe and sound   830 Juan   4   901
The filling up their whole connubial cargo   863 Juan   6   719

CARGOES
The cargoes he confiscated, and gain   790 Juan   2   1005

CARING
And caring little for the author's ease   446 Beppo   398
Not caring as I ought for critics' cavils   446 Beppo   414

CARLE
But every carle can lord it o'er thy land   31 Harold   2   707
His blood had gilt the threshold; for the carle   503 Faliero   1   230
That's right. A gallant carle, and fit to be   682 Werner   1   673
But must break through them, as an unarm'd carle   697 Werner   3   160

CARLISLE
The paralytic puling of Carlisle   251 Bards   726
Let Stott, Carlisle, Matilda, and the rest   254 Bards   927

CARLO
There rose a Carlo Dolce or a Titian   950 Juan   13   563

CARLOMAN
Orlando, angry too with Carloman   468 Morgante   125
At least return once more to Carloman   470 Morgante   288

CARLOWITZ'
When on Carlowitz' bloody plain   386 Corinth   143

CARLTON
'I have a state-coach at Carlton House   176 Devil's Dr   19
With Carlton, or with other houses? Try   918 Juan   10   675
Wheels whirl from Carlton palace to Soho   946 Juan   13   347

CARMAGNUOLA
Ago to Carmagnuola. The attainted   619 Foscari   4   288
Of Carmagnuola, eight months ere he died   619 Foscari   4   299
Learnt but in eighty years. Brave Carmagnuola   619 Foscari   4   303
I never smiled on them. Was Carmagnuola   619 Foscari   4   305

CARMEN
This first, you'll have, perhaps, a second
  'Carmen   308 Age   778

CARNAGE
While Waterloo with Cannae's carnage vies   45 Harold   3   608
To all save carnage, that, beneath the fray   64 Harold   4   562
And three unhappy slaves the carnage swell   108 Nisus   246

CARNAGE

With **murder** glutted, and in carnage rolls	109	Nisus	262
Too flush'd with carnage, and with conquest warm	109	Nisus	280
And the carnage begun, when resistance is done	176	Devil's Dr	75
We hate the carnage while we see the trick	260	Hints	275
Till at the crowning carnage, Waterloo	285	Vision	38
Mark! where his carnage and his conquests cease	333	Abydos	2	430
And him she saw, where thickest carnage spread	351	Corsair	2	273
And Carnage smiled upon her daily dead	379	Lara	2	281
And all but the after carnage done	393	Corinth	770
If shades by carnage be appeased	393	Corinth	809
And thus for wider carnage taught to pant	746	Juan	Ded	91
Records Ravenna's carnage on its face	829	Juan	4	823
'Carnage' (so Wordsworth tells you) 'is God's daughter	879	Juan	8	70
Of carnage, like the Nile's sun-sodden slime	888	Juan	8	655
Of carnage, when this old man was pierced through	893	Juan	8	947
Of carnage--and I think he was more glad in her	896	Juan	8	1119

CARNAL

Save concubines and carnal companie	4	Harold	1	17
Reft of its carnal life, save what shall be	46	Harold	3	700
They would all turn perfectly carnal	179	Devil's Dr	222
And thus they bid farewell to carnal dishes	441	Beppo	49

CARNATION

On eyes of blue or lips carnation	101	Marion	46
And Juan grew carnation with vexation	993	Juan	16	787

CARNATION'D

(Carnation'd like a sleeping infant's cheek	485	Manfred	2	112

CARNIVAL

And join the mimic train of merry Carnival	32	Harold	2	746
He glitter'd through the Carnival	386	Corinth	190
Hold o'er the dead their carnival	389	Corinth	455
This feast is named the Carnival, which being	441	Beppo	41
Of all the places where the Carnival	441	Beppo	73
The carnival was at its height, and so	442	Beppo	163
It was the Carnival, as I have said	447	Beppo	441
Guilty on the last night of Carnival	501	Faliero	1	89
Last carnival she made a deal of strife	827	Juan	4	662
She, too, was fortunate last carnival	827	Juan	4	668

CARNIVAL'S

But the Carnival's coming	229	Moore-B	9
The Carnival's coming	229	Moore-B	11

CARNIVOROUS

But man is a carnivorous production	782	Juan	2	529

CARO.

I read Glenarvon, too, by Caro. Lamb--God damn	230	I Read	7

CAROL

Or chirps the grasshopper one good-night carol more	48	Harold	3	814
It was the carol of a bird	405	Chillon	252

CAROLINA

And Carolina sighs alone	134	E. N. Long	65

CAROLINE

(See CARO.)

CAROLINES

Where are the Lady Carolines and Franceses	928	Juan	11	625

CAROLS

How carols now the lusty muleteer	11	Harold	1	504
Unmoved the Moslem sits, the light Greek carols by	21	Harold	2	90

CAROTID-ARTERY-CUTTING

Carotid-artery-cutting Castlereagh	914	Juan	10	468

CAROUSAL

The long carousal shakes the illumined hall	371	Lara	1	387

CAROUSALS

Join'd the carousals of the great and gay	367	Lara	1	99

CAROUSE

Where Scotchmen feed, and critics may carouse	249	Bards	545
They game--carouse--converse--or whet the brand	338	Corsair	1	48
Have 'public days,' when all men may carouse	989	Juan	16	591

CAROUSING

Loudly carousing, bless their lord's return	121	Newstead-A	118
Carousing with the vassals; but the paths	483	Manfred	2	13

CARP

With which I still can harp, and carp, and fiddle	896	Juan	8	1105
At Longbow's phrases you might sometimes carp	953	Juan	13	742

CARPE

But 'carpe diem,' Juan, 'carpe, carpe	929	Juan	11	673

CARPENTER

Then came the carpenter, at last, with tears	779	Juan	2	337

CARPET

Tobacco on a little carpet;--Troy	893	Juan	8	963
For a spoil'd carpet--but the 'Attic Bee	986	Juan	16	391

CARPETED

Haidee and Juan carpeted their feet	809	Juan	3	529

CARPETS

And Persian carpets, which the heart bled to stain	810	Juan	3	539
So costly were they; carpets every stich	839	Juan	5	518

CARR

Snatch his own wreath of ridicule from Carr	255	Bards	1026

CARRARA'S

As e'er thou didst upon Carrara's blocks	738	Deformed	2	213

CARRIAGE

For itself, or what follows--But here comes your carriage	283	Blues	2	164
With carriage) coming of his own accord	296	Vision	704
In time to drag him through his carriage window	676	Werner	1	289
To help him from his carriage, and present	678	Werner	1	432
From out that carriage when he would have given	678	Werner	1	434
Forgot with him her very prudent carriage	755	Juan	1	528
Upon the whole his carriage was serene	832	Juan	5	66
(A cursed sort of carriage without springs	900	Juan	9	234
Walk'd on behind his carriage, o'er the summit	919	Juan	11	66
Behind his carriage; and, like handy lads	919	Juan	11	83
But Juan now is stepping from his carriage	922	Juan	11	240
It adds an outward grace unto their carriage	937	Juan	12	494
Nodding beside my lady in his carriage	946	Juan	13	362
Each carriage was announced, and ladies rose	994	Juan	16	851

CARRIAGES

Behind their carriages their new portmanteau	776	Juan	2	127
Through crowds and carriages, but waxing thinner	922	Juan	11	226
Broken in carriages, and all the phantasies	928	Juan	11	629

CARRIED

Had bid for and carried away from the Lobby	178	Devil's Dr	159
'Twas carried, as the King decreed	195	Ballad-A	104
A Carrier who carried his can to his mouth well	224	Adams	2
He carried so much, and he carried so fast	224	Adams	3
He could carry no more--so was carried at last	224	Adams	4
When coals to Newcastle are carried	227	Thurlow-B	18
But the Pastry Cook carried away	234	Ballat	8
Or carried onward in the battle's van	300	Age	127
All Tartar-like he carried him	407	Mazeppa	71
Which must be carried one by one before	588	Sardan	5	66
Had carried from their usual haunt--the forests	716	Werner	5	235
Without their will, they carried them away	779	Juan	2	314
That carried off his neighbour by the thigh	787	Juan	2	846
They knew not where, being carried by the stream	887	Juan	8	570
When matters must be carried by the touch	888	Juan	8	621
For morals, marriage; and this question carried	971	Juan	15	231
And then he had good looks;--that point was carried	978	Juan	15	665

CARRIER

A Carrier who carried his can to his mouth well	224	Adams	2

CARRIES

Or business carries them in search of game	291	Vision	423
And carries fan and tippet, gloves and shawl	445	Beppo	320

CARRION

Flock o'er their carrion, just like men below	820	Juan	4	224

CARRI-ON

He could not carry off,--so he's now carri-on	224	Adams	6

CARRY

He could carry no more--so was carried at last	224	Adams	4
He could not carry off,--so he's now carri-on	224	Adams	6
They'll find where they're going much more than they carry	237	Braziers	4
And carry prose or rhyme, and this my lay	466	Morgante	27
And carry them unto the holy monks	472	Morgante	424
'Twere best to carry him into some wood	474	Morgante	559
The giant said, 'Then carry him I will	474	Morgante	561
Since that to carry me he was so slack	474	Morgante	562
To lift or carry this dead courser, who	474	Morgante	567
With all the bells I'd carry yonder belfry	474	Morgante	576
Morgante said, 'I'll carry him for certain	475	Morgante	592
To chains, but laid aside to carry weapons	526	Faliero	3	563
Be thine! Now let us carry forth our children	654	Cain	3	555

CARRY
If there were aught to carry off, my lord   686 Werner   2   224
And carry precept to the highest pitch   772 Juan   1   1630
And carry away, perhaps, a mast or so   777 Juan   2   208
And carry them to shore; these hopes were fine   782 Juan   2   550
Not as of yore to carry off an Io   796 Juan   2   1391
'Nay,' quoth the maid, 'the Sultan's self shan't
  carry me   842 Juan   5   671
Could hardly carry anything away   843 Juan   5   741
Are apt to carry things with a high hand   854 Juan   6   83
By bidding others carry while they ride   943 Juan   13   152

CARRYING
By carrying off Count Cesare Cicogna   827 Juan   4   663
But what if carrying sail capsize the boat   898 Juan   9   139

CARRYINGS
To whom your midnight carryings off and drownings 606 Foscari   2   305

CARS
So many conquerors' cars were daily driven   285 Vision   35
And call'd the radiance from their cars   413 Mazeppa   650
Beneath his cars of Ceres groan the roads   931 Juan   12   68

CART
Our Muse, like that of Thespis, kept a cart   262 Hints   440

CARTE
Resolved to thrust the mystery carte and tierce   996 Juan   16   997

CARTHAGE
Assyria, Greece, Rome, Carthage, what are they   82 Harold   4   1631
And Carthage ruins, my lone breast may burn   457 Dante   1   105
A Carthage, and a Tyre, an Ocean Babel   547 Faliero   5   660
Of Rome and Carthage in their best times, when   607 Foscari   2   405
Ye who weep o'er Carthage burning   735 Deformed   2   55
Rome, Babylon, Tyre, Carthage, Nineveh   885 Juan   8   477
For Fame's a Carthage not so soon rebuilt   939 Juan   12   624

CARTHAGINIAN
Since the fierce Carthaginian almost won thee   52 Harold   3   1024

CARTHAGINIAN'S
For there the Carthaginian's warlike wiles   64 Harold   4   553

CARTRIDGES
You should but give few cartridges to such   888 Juan   8   619
But oh! ye modern heroes with your cartridges   976 Juan   15   535

CARVE
I'll carve our passage through the heedless foe   108 Nisus   235
To such let others carve their way   320 Giaour   1014
May live to carve your betters'   738 Deformed   2   209

CARVED
(See also RUDE-CARVED)
There, deeply carved, behold! each tyro's name   124 Recoll   153
A turban carved in coarsest stone   317 Giaour   723
The carved crests, and curious hues   395 Corinth   969
Carved at the prow, built lightly, but compactly   442 Beppo   148
Then he hath carved his monument. I yet   738 Deformed   2   208
Of gilded bronze, and carved in curious guise   842 Juan   5   682
With a carved lady on a monument   861 Juan   6   544

CARVING
Full of barbaric carving, paint, and gilding   790 Juan   2   1016

CARVINGS
Symmetrical, but deck'd with carvings quaint   949 Juan   13   514

CASCADE
Around the verge of that cascade   313 Giaour   309
Its outlet dash'd into a deep cascade   948 Juan   13   457
And he stood gazing out on the cascade   982 Juan   16   119

CASE
'Have a care! that case holds liquor   157 Hodgson   21
With--still to keep him in good case   233 Hoppner   3
In case you should not know 'em   233 Ballad-B   12
And, as that is the case, you had best put to
  press   236 Nonsense   7
But, in love, oft the case is   239 Lucietta   4
And case his volumes in congenial calf   251 Bards   738
(Unless his case be much misunderstood)   268 Hints   824
Make out a case to be exempt from woe   289 Vision   293
Late majesty of Britain's case with you   293 Vision   510
By no means often was his case below   296 Vision   714
Was by no means so ugly as his case   296 Vision   750
This is the case in England; at least was   447 Beppo   473
As is supposed the case with northern nations   449 Beppo   564
'Morgante, I could wish you in this case   473 Morgante   483
I know I have done too little in this case   475 Morgante   623
In case your fresh appeal should be rejected   502 Faliero   1   155
The wavering of the weak, in case of conflict   536 Faliero   4   541

CASE
Not in this case with justice. Alas! signor   543 Faliero   5   363
Their just pretensions to the crown in case   581 Sardan   4   205
In case he should survive. Poor gentleman   675 Werner   1   240
For which I promise you, in case you e'er   676 Werner   1   298
In that case, I much wonder that a person   677 Werner   1   410
And, seeing the case hopeless, I await   687 Werner   2   314
Think if it were your own case! Oh, just God   696 Werner   3   70
Is roused: such is not here the case; he died   703 Werner   3   571
The world? In this case--yes. In any case   709 Werner   4   303
Last,--yours has lately been a common case   745 Juan   Ded   4
The hearers of her case became repeaters   750 Juan   1   222
In case our lord the king should go to war again   751 Juan   1   302
And pitying sore his mutilated case   752 Juan   1   350
As being the best judge of a lady's case   756 Juan   1   600
Of his own case, and never hit the true one   757 Juan   1   683
The last indeed's infallibly the case   759 Juan   1   790
In case he thought his wife too great a prize   759 Juan   1   803
People should hold their tongues in any case   759 Juan   1   836
An awkward look; as he revolved the case   767 Juan   1   1311
In any case, attempting a reply   768 Juan   1   1427
In Juan's case were but employ'd in vain   774 Juan   2   6
Of eyes were crying for their owner's case   781 Juan   2   446
They did their best to modify their case   782 Juan   2   499
But in this case I also must remark   786 Juan   2   753
But with our damsel this was not the case   789 Juan   2   961
And warm, in case by chance he should awake   791 Juan   2   1060
Rather by deeds than words, because the case   794 Juan   2   1266
As was the case, at least, where I have been   795 Juan   2   1308
It is a hard although a common case   808 Juan   3   465
Juan was told about their curious case   826 Juan   4   642
That there had been a lady in the case   833 Juan   5   148
I wish the case could come before a jury here   839 Juan   5   488
To gentlemen in any such like case   847 Juan   5   978
Of a young downright beauty in this case   848 Juan   5   1040
In case of any premature disclosure   866 Juan   6   912
This being the case, may show us what Fame is   871 Juan   7   257
The hour, as is the case with lively brains   882 Juan   8   260
In cities caged. The present case in point I   886 Juan   8   495
On cities, as hath been the present case   890 Juan   8   772
Quarter, in case he bade them not 'aroynt   893 Juan   8   931
In all the circumstances of the case   920 Juan   11   138
And between pity for her case and yours   937 Juan   12   479
Poor thing! Eve's was a trifling case to hers   938 Juan   12   512
Or separate maintenance, in case 'twas doom'd   973 Juan   15   307
Both in the case of lover and of friend   978 Juan   15   628
A case which to the juries we may leave   978 Juan   15   668
To state the case, it might be ta'en for granted   984 Juan   16   263

CASED
Cased like the centipede in saffron mail   209 Sketch   67

CASE-MATED
Case-mated one, and t'other 'a barbette   868 Juan   7   92

CASEMENT
But only stare from out my casement   163 Malta   49
And cautious opening of the casement, showing   529 Faliero   4   90
Rampart, wall, casement, house,--for there was
  not   882 Juan   8   291

CASEMENTS
Casements, through which the sunset streams like
  sunrise   697 Werner   3   116

CASEMENT'S
Where from this Gothic casement's height   89 To Emma   13
Gleam'd forth, as through the casement's ivy
  shroud   996 Juan   16   1015

CASES
Cases cracking   157 Hodgson   13
The only difference known between the cases   447 Beppo   447
And cutting stays, as usual in such cases   451 Beppo   712
A hint, in tender cases, is enough   768 Juan   1   1417
Common in many cases, was in this   870 Juan   7   195

CASH
Civil to sharpers, prodigal of cash   260 Hints   234
Cash cannot quell them; Pollio play'd this prank   266 Hints   717
Is it miss or the cash of mamma you pursue   278 Blues   1   78
What! would they spread their earthquake even
  o'er cash   306 Age   638
Himself, and much (heaven knows how gotten!) cash 452 Beppo   761
For an estate, or cash, or country seat   762 Juan   1   997
In my young days they lent me cash that way   782 Juan   2   519
Heaven knows what cash he got or blood he spilt   790 Juan   2   1013
Let not his mode of raising cash seem strange   803 Juan   3   105
The most by ready cash--but all have prices   834 Juan   5   215
Which leaves you minus of the cash you counted   855 Juan   6   166
For cash and conquest, as if from a cushion   875 Juan   7   508
And rich in rubles, diamonds, cash, and credit   916 Juan   10   554
Their cash, to show how much they have a-year   919 Juan   11   76
Their cash comes from, their wealth goes to a Jew 927 Juan   11   588

CASH
But if Love don't, Cash does, and Cash alone | 931 Juan | 12 | 105
Cash rules the grove, and fells it too besides | 931 Juan | 12 | 106
Without cash, camps were thin, and courts were none | 931 Juan | 12 | 107
Without cash, Malthus tells you--'take no brides | 931 Juan | 12 | 108
So Cash rules Love the ruler, on his own | 931 Juan | 12 | 109
Alas! to them of ready cash bereft | 946 Juan | 13 | 355
But oh, ambrosial cash! Ah! who would lose thee | 953 Juan | 13 | 799

CASHMIRE
A shawl, whose folds in Cashmire had been nurst | 840 Juan | 5 | 542

CASIMERE
Of yellow casimere we may presume | 902 Juan | 9 | 342

CASIMIR
Ay, 'twas,--when Casimir was king | 408 Mazeppa | | 128
John Casimir,--I was his page | 408 Mazeppa | | 129

CASK
And Hook conceal his heroes in a cask | 249 Bards | | 589
For grog, and sometimes drink rum from the cask | 778 Juan | 2 | 264
Water, a twenty-gallon cask or so | 780 Juan | 2 | 371

CASKET
Here is the key and casket. It is well | 491 Manfred | 3 | 5

CASKS
(See also BISCUIT-CASKS)
Two casks of biscuit and a keg of butter | 779 Juan | 2 | 367

CASQUE
The casque, the buckler, and the fiery steed | 107 Nisus | | 155
And old Alethes' casque defends his brows | 108 Nisus | | 216
Round the rent casque her owlet circled slow | 269 Minerva | | 87
His close but glittering casque, and sable plume | 349 Corsair | 2 | 148
When rose thy casque above thy brow | 399 Parisina | | 301
Ends in a rusty casque and dubious bone | 916 Juan | 10 | 582
That casque, which never stoop'd except to Time | 916 Juan | 10 | 587

CASQUES
On Alva's casques of silver play'd | 101 Alva | | 6

CASQUE'S
The casque's on the wall | 742 Deformed | 3 | 26

CASSANDRA
Than whom Cassandra was not more prophetic | 823 Juan | 4 | 411

CASSANDRA-LIKE
And if, Cassandra-like, amidst the din | 458 Dante | 2 | 10

CASSANDRA'S
But let me cease, and dread Cassandra's fate | 255 Bards | | 1007

CASSIO
I am not, like Cassio, 'an arithmetician | 853 Juan | 6 | 65
'But heaven,' as Cassio says, 'is above all | 898 Juan | 9 | 145

CASSIUS
And the quick Cassius of the Arsenal | 540 Faliero | 5 | 180

CAST
(See also O'ER-CAST)
And long as kinder eyes a look shall cast | 3 To Ianthe | | 38
The broken tools, that tyrants cast away | 11 Harold | 1 | 453
To cast a worthless offering at thy shrine | 24 Harold | 2 | 269
Each Palikar his sabre from his cast | 30 Harold | 2 | 637
Where, for some sin, to sorrow I was cast | 46 Harold | 3 | 692
How to make madness beautiful, and cast | 47 Harold | 3 | 730
Flashing and cast around. Of all the band | 50 Harold | 3 | 891
Wherein were cast the heroic and the free | 59 Harold | 4 | 224
O'er the dim fragments cast a lunar light | 67 Harold | 4 | 719
Are thine; no envious lot shall then be cast | 107 Nisus | | 157
On Luna's orb he cast his frenzied eye | 110 Nisus | | 340
Howe'er my future doom be cast | 131 L'Amitie | | 15
Cast crowns for rosaries away | 180 Ode-A | | 66
With curses cast them down upon the dust | 189 Darkness | | 31
Yet to such times our lingering looks are cast | 243 Bards | | 119
And, arm'd in proof, the gauntlet cast at once | 256 Bards | | 1065
On such an eve his palest beam he cast | 268 Minerva | | 19
Is it cast yet? The actors are fighting for parts | 282 Blues | 2 | 85
And cast on Lemnos' shore | 335 Abydos | 2 | 602
Hope, power, and life upon a single cast | 343 Corsair | 1 | 338
On such an eve his palest beam he cast | 355 Corsair | 3 | 19
On him she cast her dark and hurried eye | 359 Corsair | 3 | 278
Are on this cast; Corsair! 'tis but a blow | 361 Corsair | 3 | 375
He gazed on Ezzelin till Lara cast | 374 Lara | 1 | 608
Nor cast on Otho's towers a single look | 376 Lara | 2 | 96
Upon that page his eye was kindly cast | 381 Lara | 2 | 465
From the purest metal cast | 395 Corinth | | 1009
Three were in a dungeon cast | 403 Chillon | | 25

CAST
And all my bonds aside were cast | 406 Chillon | | 376
I cast my last looks up the sky | 414 Mazeppa | | 768
Another look on me she cast | 415 Mazeppa | | 833
Then cast his eyes on his companions--then | 428 Island | 3 | 113
His life upon a cast which linger'd yet | 433 Island | 4 | 274
Cast one glance back, and clench'd his hand, and shook | 434 Island | 4 | 339
Is more than I know. He was cast away | 452 Beppo | | 746
All this, and cast a wide and tender light | 495 Manfred | 3 | 292
The die is cast. Where is the place of meeting | 508 Faliero | 1 | 593
Of life upon this cast: the die was thrown | 519 Faliero | 3 | 55
My heart, my hope, my soul, upon this cast | 523 Faliero | 3 | 327
And thus, I cast all further feelings from me | 525 Faliero | 3 | 492
Who have cast lots for the first death, and they | 537 Faliero | 4 | 639
While Manlius, who hurl'd down the Gauls, was cast | 537 Faliero | 4 | 650
Pity my husband, or I cast it from me | 603 Foscari | 2 | 135
Had I been cast out like the Jews from Zion | 610 Foscari | 3 | 159
Cast me out from amongst them as an offering | 617 Foscari | 4 | 144
Would make him cast upon the spiritual nature | 630 Cain | 1 | 219
To cast down yon vile flatt'rer of the clouds | 650 Cain | 3 | 290
Of those cast out from Eden's gate | 656 Heaven | | 59
Things which had made this silkworm cast his skin | 692 Werner | 2 | 615
Spirit, till I took up with your cast shape | 731 Deformed | 1 | 642
Lie there, more like a worm than man; she cast it | 740 Deformed | 2 | 314
Where juries cast up what a wife is worth | 755 Juan | 1 | 509
Their looks cast down, their greetings almost dumb | 755 Juan | 1 | 555
He cast a rueful look or two, and did | 767 Juan | 1 | 1303
And cast their languid eyes down, and let loose | 769 Juan | 1 | 1430
These I could bear, but cannot cast aside | 771 Juan | 1 | 1557
I cast thee on the waters--go thy ways | 774 Juan | 1 | 1770
And all things, for a chance, had been cast loose | 780 Juan | 2 | 402
'Twas borne by the rude wave wherein 'twas cast | 785 Juan | 2 | 718
Materials as were cast up round the bay | 790 Juan | 2 | 1051
He was her own, her ocean-treasure, cast | 796 Juan | 2 | 1383
And now and then her eye to heaven is cast | 799 Juan | 2 | 1557
The very instant, till the change that cast | 825 Juan | 4 | 549
With whom it is our luck to cast our lot | 833 Juan | 5 | 100
Just as my great coat was about me cast | 835 Juan | 5 | 259
In such sort, that the eye along it cast | 843 Juan | 5 | 740
Passion and power, a glance on him she cast | 846 Juan | 5 | 926
His Highness cast around his great black eyes | 851 Juan | 5 | 1233
A slight example, just to cast a shade | 856 Juan | 6 | 253
Of Cossacques and their prey, turn'd round and cast | 874 Juan | 7 | 466
Had not come up in time to cast an awe | 884 Juan | 8 | 387
Of his opinion, when I see cast down | 885 Juan | 8 | 476
Paused for a moment, from the fight, and cast | 893 Juan | 8 | 927
For a new flame; a thought to cast of gloom enough | 902 Juan | 9 | 381
As they beheld; the younger cast some leers | 906 Juan | 9 | 620
Than the more glowing dames whose lot is cast | 938 Juan | 12 | 547
And what I write I cast upon the stream | 956 Juan | 14 | 87
But speculating as I cast mine eye | 970 Juan | 15 | 148
And she withdrew, but cast not down, her eye | 993 Juan | 16 | 796
And usual--Juan, when he cast a glance | 993 Juan | 16 | 810

CASTALIAN
Proscribed from tasting your Castalian tea | 830 Juan | 4 | 864

CASTALIE'S
And highland linns with Castalie's clear fount | 423 Island | 2 | 293

CASTANET
Fandango twirls his jocund castanet | 11 Harold | 1 | 500

CASTANETS
Guitars and castanets from Alicant | 803 Juan | 3 | 134

CASTE
They lose their caste at once, as do the Parias | 939 Juan | 12 | 618
Of highest caste--the Brahmins of the ton | 951 Juan | 13 | 660

CASTELLATED
Until he reach'd the castellated Rhine | 915 Juan | 10 | 482

CASTER'S
The jovial caster's set, and seven's the nick | 251 Bards | | 674

CASTIGATION
Than in the mockery of castigation | 541 Faliero | 5 | 236

CASTILE
The new Numantine soul of old Castile | 303 Age | | 355
The famous lance of chivalrous Castile | 303 Age | | 371
(His sire was of Castile, his dam from Aragon | 751 Juan | 1 | 300

CASTILIAN
With more hauteur, as might an old Castilian | 289 Vision | | 287
The blood of all his line's Castilian lords | 844 Juan | 5 | 827
And which was softest, Russian or Castilian | 924 Juan | 11 | 399

CASTING
And if I had to give a casting voice   819 Juan   4   197

CASTLE
The castle still stands, and the senate's no more 202 Avatar   10
First to the Castle of that man of woes   224 J.C.H.   9
Dunedin's castle felt a secret shock   248 Bards   469
The fish swam by the castle wall   406 Chillon   351
'Twas near his castle, far away   410 Mazeppa   331
They led me to the castle gate   410 Mazeppa   339
There is not of that castle gate   410 Mazeppa   394
And couldst say much; thou hast dwelt within the
  castle   494 Manfred   3   214
Be strung to city gates and castle walls   517 Faliero   2   609
Their castle walls--beyond them 'tis but doubtful 676 Werner   1   341
Is dead near Prague, in his castle, and my lord   684 Werner   2   80
In Castle Siegendorf! Display no gold   698 Werner   3   203
We'll meet in Castle Siegendorf--once more   704 Werner   3   590
Full numbers of retainers round the castle   706 Werner   4   115
In castle halls, and social banquets, nurse not   707 Werner   4   221
For manly sports beyond the castle walls   710 Werner   4   403
It seems, of my own castle--of my own   720 Werner   5   497

CASTLED
The castled crag of Drachenfels   43 Harold   3   496
One of the many chiefs, whose castled crags   483 Manfred   2   8

CASTLE-GATE
But turn'd in silence to his castle-gate   368 Lara   1   173

CASTLEREAGH
Blush'd upon Sleep and Lord Castlereagh   178 Devil's Dr   170
Thine own Castlereagh! let him still be thine own 203 Avatar   87
Here lie the bones of Castlereagh   235 Castlereagh   3
Oh, Castlereagh! thou art a patriot now   238 Epigrams   1
So Castlereagh has cut his throat!--The worst   238 Epigrams   5
When Castlereagh has been up long enough   296 Vision   739
And ne'er (enough) lamented Castlereagh   305 Age   538
The intellectual eunuch Castlereagh   746 Juan   Ded   88
So good--I wonder Castlereagh don't tax 'em   800 Juan   2   1624
Or all the figures Castlereagh abuses   849 Juan   5   1141
Meantime the Taxes, Castlereagh, and Debt   894 Juan   8   997
Of blood and water, leaden Castlereagh   903 Juan   9   398
Carotid-artery-cutting Castlereagh   914 Juan   10   468
Where little Castlereagh? The devil can tell   927 Juan   11   602

CASTLEREAGH'S
When Castlereagh's wife has an heir   227 Thurlow-B   23

CASTLES
And chiefless castles breathing stern farewells 42 Harold   3   413
Except our fathers' sovereignty and castles   703 Werner   3   549

CAST-OFF
And asking now and then for cast-off dresses   797 Juan   2   1456

CASTS
He lurks, nor casts his heavy eye afar   11 Harold   1   496
On giant statues casts the curious eye   271 Minerva   186
(Which casts up misty columns that become   492 Manfred   3   112
To heaven, and Zillah casts hers to the earth   631 Cain   1   251
Casts off its bright skin yearly like the snake   834 Juan   5   168

CASUALLY
And having casually glanced it through   964 Juan   14   550

CASUIST
But Juan was no casuist, nor had ponder'd   940 Juan   12   641
And 'twill perplex the casuist in morality   966 Juan   14   711

CASUISTS
Some kinder casuists are pleased to say   815 Juan   3   921

CAT
In water, sorely grieved the dog and cat   474 Morgante   531
But like conveying to the cat the mouse   790 Juan   2   1035
Two parrots, with a Persian cat and kittens   803 Juan   3   138
Ye powers! it is the--the--the--Pooh! the cat   995 Juan   16   939

CATALAN
The unerring rifle of the Catalan   303 Age   372

CATALANI'S
And worship Catalani's pantaloons   250 Bards   615

CATALOGUE
By Homer's 'Catalogue of ships' is clear   950 Juan   13   590
Now it so happen'd, in the catalogue   974 Juan   15   377

CATARACT
(See also MOUNTAIN-CATARACT)
Tells where the volumed cataract doth roll   26 Harold   2   431
Charming the eye with dread--a matchless cataract 65 Harold   4   639

CATARACTS
Of cataracts, where nursing Nature smiled   69 Harold   4   862
Though cataracts foam 'stead of smoothflowing
  fountains   117 Lachin   7

CATASTROPHE
Which your catastrophe convulses   231 Doctor   8

CATCH
Almost thy very growth, to view thee catch   53 Harold   3   1078
To catch the last gleam of the sun's setting ray 96 Harrow-A   16
To catch that crest's ascendency   187 Ode-B   57
The spheres, we shall catch cold amongst these
  clouds   293 Vision   531
Swam smoothly forth to catch the rising ray   435 Island   4   374
The stars and their development; or catch   486 Manfred   2   165
Which a shrewd gleaner and quick eye would catch
  at   500 Faliero   1   56
Hush! we perhaps may catch the sound. 'Tis vain 549 Faliero   5   815
Things as catch fire and blaze with one sole
  spark   591 Sardan   5   277
In twilight's hour, to catch a glimpse of those 628 Cain   1   86
So scarcely will catch cold in't, if he be   675 Werner   1   235
Which painters cannot catch like faces sinning   859 Juan   6   412
Those who catch cold in 'shadows of Death's
  valley   882 Juan   8   288
Which pass'd, or catch the first glimpse of the
  cliffs   915 Juan   10   512
And caught them;--what do they not catch
  methinks   942 Juan   13   95
To catch a glimpse even of a pretty peasant   959 Juan   14   224
Great thoughts we catch from thence (besides a
  cold   982 Juan   16   108

CATCHES
At which he vainly catches, flit and gleam   453 Venice-B   52
And several who sung fewer psalms than catches 991 Juan   16   688

CATECHISM
I know my catechism; I know we are cramm'd   286 Vision   108
Him up to learn his catechism alone   753 Juan   1   414
To this long catechism of questions, ask'd   864 Juan   6   794

CATERING
Than human insects, catering for spiders   900 Juan   9   216

CATHAY
From Ceylon, Inde, or far Cathay, unloads   930 Juan   12   66

CATHEDRA
(See EX-CATHEDRA)

CATHEDRAL
They saw at Canterbury the cathedral   916 Juan   10   577

CATHEDRAL'S
As in some old cathedral's glimmering aisle   431 Island   4   133

CATHERINE
Many an old woman, but no Catherine   304 Age   461
Had Catherine and the sultan understood   864 Juan   6   753
The armies of the Christian Empress Catherine   875 Juan   7   512
And Catherine, who loved all things (save her
  lord   903 Juan   9   425
Catherine, who was the grand epitome   903 Juan   9   449
Catherine, I say, was very glad to see   903 Juan   9   453
Oh Catherine! (for of all interjections   904 Juan   9   513
And Catherine (we must say thus much for
  Catherine   905 Juan   9   553
Catherine was generous,--all such ladies are   906 Juan   9   633
Love had made Catherine make each lover's fortune 906 Juan   9   641
Made the chaste Catherine look a little grim   913 Juan   10   347
So Catherine, who had a handsome way   913 Juan   10   361
Made Catherine taste next night a quiet slumber 913 Juan   10   380
Which Catherine in a moment of 'ivresse'   923 Juan   11   309

CATHERINE'S
The unpaid amount of Catherine's bloody debt   300 Age   160
In Catherine's reign, whom glory still adores   863 Juan   6   735
The scenes like Catherine's boudoir at threescore 887 Juan   8   543
Fair Catherine's pastime--who look'd on the match 900 Juan   9   230

CATHOLIC
True, the chains of the Catholic clank o'er his
  rags   202 Avatar   9
The fetters from millions of Catholic limbs   203 Avatar   70
The foe to Catholic participation   291 Vision   383
While sate the catholic Moloch, calmly cruel   302 Age   337
All countries of the Catholic persuasion   440 Beppo   2
He died as born, a Catholic in faith   783 Juan   2   605
In Catholic eyes; but told him, too, to smother 911 Juan   10   252
Those vegetables of the Catholic creed   965 Juan   14   647
She was a Catholic, too, sincere, austere   974 Juan   15   361
Juan rejoin'd--'She was a Catholic   974 Juan   15   393

CATHOLICS
Because the Catholics would not rise   177 Devil's Dr   146
And you, too, catholics! Would ye return   739 Deformed   2   283
When over Catholics the ocean rolls   781 Juan   2   435

CATILINE
But try the Ceasar, or the Catiline   509 Faliero   1   625
By Sallust in his Catiline, who chased   866 Juan   6   886

CATO
Cato died for his country, so didst thou   238 Epigrams   2
'To die like Cato,' leapt into the Thames   268 Hints   826
With all their heroes,--the last Cato stands   733 Deformed   1   776
Heroic, stoic Cato, the sententious   853 Juan   6   55
For my part, I pretend not to be Cato   867 Juan   7   30
While Strongbow's best things might have come
    from Cato   952 Juan   13   736

CATOS
Two weeds which pose our economic Catos   972 Juan   15   296

CATO'S
Than Cato's sister, or than Brutus' mother   725 Deformed   1   199

CATS
Over the floors were spread; gazelles and cats   810 Juan   3   540
For cats and birds more penchant ne'er display'd   913 Juan   10   399

CATTLE
And the valet, and the cattle; but as yet   675 Werner   1   218
Deep in the fountain to scare back the cattle   723 Deformed   1   51
That Pasiphae promoted breeding cattle   793 Juan   2   1239
For this superior yoke of human cattle   835 Juan   5   224
Makes men, like cattle, follow him who leads   883 Juan   8   304
Which is the cud eschew'd by human cattle   935 Juan   12   344
I hate it, as I hate a drove of cattle   962 Juan   14   461

CATULLUS
And you'll be Catullus, the Regent Mamurra   226 Oh You   16
'Tis Little! young Catullus of his day   245 Bards   287
Catullus, whose old laurels yield to new   303 Age   419
Catullus scarcely has a decent poem   752 Juan   1   331
Horace, Catullus, scholars, Ovid tutor   800 Juan   2   1635

CAUCASUS
Like to the dying day on Caucasus   552 Sardan   1   90
And share a cottage on the Caucasus   558 Sardan   1   499
Of cloud-fenced Caucasus, where the eagle sits   570 Sardan   2   568
At least, wear this. Wear Caucasus! why, 'tis   573 Sardan   3   138
No; to the cavern of the Caucasus   658 Heaven   265
From the Alps to the Caucasus ride we, or fly   730 Deformed   1   567
By thought of frosty Caucasus;' but few   828 Juan   4   766

CAUGHT
Maidens, like moths, are ever caught by glare   5   Harold   1   80
Who knew its votary often lost and caught   24 Harold   2   275
And caught its tone with Death's prophetic ear   38 Harold   3   202
The very Glaciers have his colours caught   50 Harold   3   926
From thee, fair Venice, have their colours caught   58 Harold   4   169
One ringlet in the dust; nor hath it caught   79 Harold   4   1466
For thrice he caught the stranger's eye   104 Alva   239
But caught within the subtle snare   172 Romaic-B   15
And the wan lustre of thy features--caught   175 Sonnet-A   2
Of which we are but dreamers;--as he caught   190 Churchill   25
Caught it, as Danae caught the golden show'r   248 Bards   495
And stooping, caught this fellow at a libel   295 Vision   687
She caught Sir William Curtis in a kilt   308 Age   768
Caught by the laughing tides that lave   310 Giaour   14
Some motion from the current caught   314 Giaour   377
Hath lost its charm by being caught   314 Giaour   405
It fell, and caught one stain of earth   315 Giaour   503
A feeling from the Godhead caught   321 Giaour   1137
My own have nearly caught the same   328 Abydos   1   398
Till--Oh, how far!--it caught a glimpse of him   345 Corsair   1   495
At length he caught it--'tis a face unknown   371 Lara   1   405
And the wild sparkle of his eye seem'd caught   373 Lara   1   536
Where had his arm unwarlike caught that art   377 Lara   2   143
Some factious phrase by cunning caught and
    spread   378 Lara   2   224
Roll'd back the clouds) the morrow caught his eye   381 Lara   2   469
He caught a glimpse, as of a floating breast   383 Lara   2   578
'Twas but a day he had been caught   410 Mazeppa   365
The sparkle of her eye I caught   414 Mazeppa   808
The courteous manners but from nature caught   417 Island   1   109
Which still reverts to what first caught the eye   422 Island   2   279
She, as she caught the first glimpse o'er the bay   429 Island   3   218
Were never caught in epigram of witticism   449 Beppo   571
Pleasure shall, like a butterfly new caught   462 Dante   3   115
Lies negligently by to be caught up   551 Sardan   1   35
Than the steel her hand held, which she caught up   577 Sardan   3   396
And a strange firefly, which was quickly caught   609 Foscari   3   104
I am to deem the plunderer is caught   686 Werner   2   197
Nets are for thrushes, eagles are not caught so   697 Werner   3   163
How fare you in your purpose? Have you caught   699 Werner   3   279

CAUGHT
And Juan caught him up, and ere he stepp'd   781 Juan   2   463
At length they caught two boobies and a noddy   784 Juan   2   655
And by good fortune, gliding softly, caught her   786 Juan   2   787
And sometimes caught as many as he wish'd   790 Juan   2   1004
Their bonds whene'er some Zephyr caught began   810 Juan   3   583
The sharp rocks look'd below each drop they
    caught   820 Juan   4   263
And caught her falling, and from off the wall   821 Juan   4   290
Juan, the latest of her whims, had caught   846 Juan   5   905
When Juan caught a glimpse of this sad sight   890 Juan   8   740
First Ismail's capture caught your fancy quite   904 Juan   9   513
And caught them;--what do they not catch
    methinks   942 Juan   13   95
Into close contact. Though reserved, nor caught   943 Juan   13   116
That few or none more than himself had caught   943 Juan   13   163
Was not exactly pleased to be so caught   977 Juan   15   614
There were two poachers caught in a steel trap   988 Juan   16   529
Was, that he caught Aurora's eye on his   992 Juan   16   777
And that in his confusion he had caught   996 Juan   16   1023

CAULDRON
Let him keep the cauldron steady   197 Rogers   63

CAULIFLOWERS
Turn beef to bannocks, cauliflowers to kail   248 Bards   525

CAULKING
To think his skull had not some need of caulking   997 Juan   17   62

CAUSA
Oh thou 'teterrima causa' of all 'belli   903 Juan   9   433

CAUSE
For some slight cause of wrath, whence life's
    warm stream must flow   16 Harold   1   800
Would he had ne'er return'd to find fresh cause
    to roam   34 Harold   2   899
All unbought champions in no princely
    cause   45 Harold   3   613
Since cause might be which skill could never
    find   47 Harold   3   758
Nor without cause; and should I leave
    behind   56 Harold   4   70
To Freedom's cause, in every age and clime   69 Harold   4   867
Thou art the cause of all her woe   88 Catullus   23
Mistake not, sweet sceptic, the cause of emotion   91 Caroline-C   17
Which I, th' unconscious cause of fear   99 Young Lady   15
To aid their cause implore the gods in vain   108 Nisus   218
Tell you that fate had forsaken your cause   117 Lachin   26
From me, the heedless and imprudent cause   119 Answer-A   4
The cause unknown, yet still to me the same   123 Recoll   84
Is there no cause beyond the common claim   125 Recoll   211
His sage instruction the primeval cause   127 Recoll   352
She will assist her votary's cause   141 Critics   11
Nor with the effect forget the cause   165 Friend-B   56
'Our twofold feeling owns its twofold cause   171 Address-B   53
Who ne'er gave cause to mourn before   184 Parker   36
Hearts and hands in one great cause   188 Ode-B   82
Which betray'd not, or crushed not, or wept not
    her cause   202 Avatar   8
The cause of the curses all annals contain   203 Avatar   63
Unknowing of its cause of agony   214 Dream   61
Nor given him cause to deem himself beloved   215 Dream   141
And dishonour the Cause of devotion   239 Bray   30
Seek'st thou the cause of loathing?--look around   269 Minerva   94
(Very sorry, no doubt, since the cause is a
    brother's   278 Blues   1   37
And is that any cause for not coming together   278 Blues   1   70
To place where Death's grand cause is argued o'er   289 Vision   275
Cause why King George by no means could or should 289 Vision   292
And now the bard could plead his own bad cause   296 Vision   759
And the stiff surgeon, who maintain'd his cause   299 Age   79
One common cause makes myriads of one breast   302 Age   272
Who heard it first had cause to grieve   312 Giaour   167
Not mine the act, though I the cause   320 Giaour   1061
Then plead my cause in that high place   322 Giaour   1212
The cause I cannot dream nor tell   328 Abydos   1   410
If thou hast cause for vengeance, see   330 Abydos   2   174
He cursed those virtues as the cause of ill   342 Corsair   1   257
Yes, smile!--but he had little cause to sneer   360 Corsair   3   324
The heart to show the effect but not the cause   370 Lara   1   284
The cause and conqueror in this sudden fray   376 Lara   2   93
Who else than Lara could have cause to fear   377 Lara   2   133
One to their cause inseparably bound   378 Lara   2   231
By mingling with his own the cause of all   378 Lara   2   240
In either cause, one rage alone possess'd   379 Lara   2   274
Who there in better cause had bled   388 Corinth   395
Hath shed more blood in cause of thine   399 Parisina   239
I will not plead the cause of crime   399 Parisina   276
The living cause of Hugo's ill   399 Parisina   327
In vain thou dost demand the cause; a curse   416 Island   1   69
Roused discipline aloud proclaims their cause   418 Island   1   203
As though their voices with their cause had died   427 Island   3   84

CAUSE

And they, the cause and sharers of the shock	433 Island	4	231
But, ah, how different! 'tis the cause makes all	433 Island	4	261
Nor cause for such: they call'd me mad--and why	437 Tasso		48
And that's the cause I rhyme upon it so	441 Beppo		94
Good cause had he to doubt the chance of war	447 Beppo		485
In this they're like our coachmen, and the cause	451 Beppo		681
Which they abhor, confound not with the cause	454 Venice-B		93
Thou art the cause; and howsoever I	455 Dante	Ded	6
The much-renown'd St. Dennis being the cause	467 Morgante		70
The Christian cause had suffer'd shamefully	467 Morgante		107
The cause of our delay to let you in	468 Morgante		173
Searching its cause in its effect; and drew	486 Manfred	2	175
Thou hast no cause; he shall not harm thee, but	495 Manfred	3	327
Will now take up the cause they once declined	501 Faliero	1	113
Although the cause--Ay, think upon the cause	503 Faliero	1	272
They have cause, since Sapienza's adverse day	504 Faliero	1	328
When Genoa conquer'd; they have further cause	504 Faliero	1	329
Barbaro. What was the cause? or the pretext	505 Faliero	1	378
At least, in such a cause. Are you much hurt	505 Faliero	1	402
That injuries like ours, sprung from one cause	507 Faliero	1	525
By the affront of Steno, and with cause	509 Faliero	2	27
I would not be a judge in my own cause	509 Faliero	2	49
As 'tis, our cause looks prosperous still. You saw	516 Faliero	2	535
Appear less forward in the cause than we are	517 Faliero	2	575
In a great cause: the block may soak their gore	517 Faliero	2	607
Of many of our cause into the arsenal	517 Faliero	2	640
My object is to make your cause end well	518 Faliero	2	694
Spirits! smile down upon me; for my cause	519 Faliero	3	41
I had been glad; and see no cause in this	521 Faliero	3	197
It is the cause, and not our will, which asks	521 Faliero	3	200
That thou wouldst add a brother to our cause	521 Faliero	3	207
Some cause to doubt the freedom of the choice	522 Faliero	3	243
Is not this man a host in such a cause	523 Faliero	3	334
Before Bertuccio added to our cause	524 Faliero	3	392
Injustice to thy comrades and thy cause	524 Faliero	3	402
Yet, as the immediate cause of the alliance	526 Faliero	3	533
The cause of which I know not: at the hour	530 Faliero	4	190
Unless thou dost detail the cause, and show	532 Faliero	4	291
Let him be told the cause--it is your history	545 Faliero	5	513
And I have been the cause, the unconscious cause	546 Faliero	5	583
And who were they who fell in such a cause	548 Faliero	5	716
And is herself the cause of bitterer tears	552 Sardan	1	95
Who should rebel? or why? what cause? pretext	554 Sardan	1	249
To plead thy sovereign's cause before his people	566 Sardan	2	307
I trust there is no cause. No cause, perhaps	566 Sardan	2	308
What cause? What cause? true,--fill the goblet up	571 Sardan	3	22
You have cause, sire; for on the earth there breathes not	578 Sardan	3	426
His wound, though slight, may cause all this, and shake	578 Sardan	4	20
On lesser charms, for no cause save that such	583 Sardan	4	338
I am content: and, trusting in my cause	586 Sardan	4	502
That's not the cause; you saw the prisoner's state	600 Foscari	1	317
I have no repose; that is, none which shall cause	602 Foscari	2	40
You have no cause, being what I am; but were I	605 Foscari	2	235
The cause of this all-spreading happiness	635 Cain	1	483
Is that a cause for thee and me to part	656 Heaven		109
What destinies? I have some cause to think	657 Heaven		177
Was there no cause assign'd? Plenty, no doubt	685 Werner	2	113
Was I, and that's the cause I know no more	686 Werner	2	202
And careless voices, knowing not the cause	687 Werner	2	271
Be he who is the stifling cause which smothers	699 Werner	3	275
The very wretch who was the cause he needed	703 Werner	3	520
Seeing my faintness, ignorant of the cause	715 Werner	5	138
There is a cause at times. Oh, yes! when atoms jostle	744 Deformed	3	150
His death contrived to spoil a charming cause	751 Juan	1	261
Whate'er the cause might be, they had become	755 Juan	1	553
But whatsoe'er the cause is, one may say	759 Juan	1	813
Forward, and there is no great cause to quake	761 Juan	1	955
And never once he has had cause to scold	765 Juan	1	1173
So there were quarrels, cared not for the cause	766 Juan	1	1271
The depositions, and the cause at full	770 Juan	1	1506
So that he had much better cause to grieve	776 Juan	2	115
But the same cause, conducive to his loss	781 Juan	2	450
The frequent fog-banks gave them cause to doubt	786 Juan	2	766
One should not rail without a decent cause	789 Juan	2	946
Is in its cause as its effect so sweet	800 Juan	2	1619
But knew the cause no more than a philosopher	804 Juan	3	208
The cause being past his guessing or unriddling	805 Juan	3	222
Of which the first ne'er knows the second cause	811 Juan	3	656
He felt a grief, but knowing cause for none	819 Juan	4	174
Vengeance on him who was the cause of all	821 Juan	4	292
If cause should be--a lioness, though tame	822 Juan	4	350
Brought back the sense of pain without the cause	824 Juan	4	495
Of gore divulged the cause) that he was dead	835 Juan	5	279
The cause of this odd travesty?'--'Forbear	840 Juan	5	589
A woman's, true; but then there is a cause	841 Juan	5	602
Your patience) shows the cause must still be stronger	848 Juan	5	1064
By the North Pole,--they sought her cause of care	861 Juan	6	574

CAUSE

The cause of killing Tchitchitzkoff and Smith	870 Juan	7	196
Thus the same cause which makes a verse want feet	870 Juan	7	203
But shortly he had cause to be content	872 Juan	7	301
Was worthy of a Spartan, had the cause	872 Juan	7	314
And all presaged good fortune to their cause	873 Juan	7	372
Which of the armies would have cause to mourn	888 Juan	8	614
And that's the cause no doubt why, if we scan	892 Juan	8	893
Unless her cause by right be sanctified	896 Juan	9	28
Increases, till you shall make common cause	900 Juan	9	222
Some call thee 'the worst cause of war,' but I	903 Juan	9	441
Of that great cause of war, or peace, or what	903 Juan	9	450
(Let deeper sages the true cause determine	913 Juan	10	395
Whate'er the cause, the church made little of it	914 Juan	10	447
I've no great cause to love that spot of earth	915 Juan	10	521
For the less cause there is for all this flurry	916 Juan	10	574
Canonization for the self-same cause	930 Juan	12	53
Has cause to wish her sire had had male heirs	934 Juan	12	264
A verdict--grievous foe to those who cause it	938 Juan	12	517
Which is the only cause that we can guess	944 Juan	13	231
The cause I know not, nor can solve; but such	949 Juan	13	511
His cause by leaning much from might to right	949 Juan	13	548
And that's one cause she meets with contradiction	957 Juan	14	101
An accessory, as I have cause to guess	965 Juan	14	604
The cause of this effect, or this defect	980 Juan	16	9
'For this effect defective comes by cause	980 Juan	16	10
Was long, and thus far there was no great cause	983 Juan	16	187
The cause, but Juan said, 'He was quite well	984 Juan	16	256
The country would have far more cause to weep it	990 Juan	16	646
Should cause more fear than a whole host's identity	996 Juan	16	1008
Whate'er the cause, are orphans in effect	997 Juan	17	16

CAUSED

The giants caused us, that the way was lost	475 Morgante		642
Who caused the giant in this place to die	476 Morgante		684
I caused to be conducted forth, and taught	514 Faliero	2	424
I've noted most; and caused the other chiefs	518 Faliero	2	651
Cursed be he who caused those tears to flow	552 Sardan	1	96
Here's no great harm done. What hath caused all this	693 Werner	2	627
Out through a fever caused by its own heat	776 Juan	2	170
Nor to the trouble which her fancies caused	845 Juan	5	902
His lately bowstrung brother caused his rise	850 Juan	5	1172
Then slacken'd it, which is the march most caused	866 Juan	6	883
With all the mystery by midnight caused	982 Juan	16	117

CAUSELESS

Is't wise or fitting, causeless to explore	764 Juan	1	1165
For feelings causeless, or at least abstruse	819 Juan	4	176

CAUSERS

But many causers:--if ye meet with such	566 Sardan	2	309

CAUSES

I well could count their causes o'er	412 Mazeppa		528
A thing which causes many 'poohs' and 'pishes	441 Beppo		53
Upon effects, not causes. Stralenheim	720 Werner	5	455
Take towns by storm: no causes can I guess	894 Juan	8	1029
You please (it causes all the things which be	903 Juan	9	451
For causes young or old: the cankerworm	912 Juan	10	298

CAUSING

When, as if its sound were causing	188 Music-C		5
A lad of sixteen causing a divorce	774 Juan	2	15

CAUTION

With a proud caution, love, or hate, or aught	52 Harold	3	1036
Yet mark one caution ere thy next Review	248 Bards		522
To use like caution in their companies	518 Faliero	2	652
In Venice, 'twill be wise to use some caution	530 Faliero	4	124
I see the man--what mean'st thou? Caution! Being	613 Foscari	3	345

CAUTIONS

Spurn'd his sage cautions? What?--and dost thou fear	558 Sardan	1	525

CAUTIOUS

The ground with cautious tread is traversed o'er	15 Harold	1	742
Then from the tents their cautious steps they bend	109 Nisus		295
Precise in style, and cautious to select	257 Hints		70
With cautious steps the thicket threading	330 Abydos	2	91
The wisdom of the cautious Frank	333 Abydos	2	378
With cautious reverence from the outer gate	347 Corsair	2	45
This cautious feeling for another's pain	484 Manfred	2	80
And wise, and just, and cautious, this I grant	500 Faliero	1	60
And cautious opening of the casement, showing	529 Faliero	4	90
With cautious hand and slow, having first undone	718 Werner	5	312
More than Pelides' heel; why then, be cautious	737 Deformed	2	193
Some who once set their caps at cautious dukes	928 Juan	11	633
Be hypocritical, be cautious, be	929 Juan	11	679
And thus Lord Henry, who was cautious as	943 Juan	13	121
(I state this, for I am cautious to a pitch	982 Juan	16	123

CAUTIOUS

Courteous and cautious therefore in his county	990 Juan	16	609

CAUTIOUSLY

Smoothly to speak, and cautiously to think	123 Recoll		70
More cautiously to write	151 Harriet		12
I must approach him cautiously; if near	483 Manfred	1	351
I'll follow him--out cautiously, though surely	493 Manfred	3	171

CAVA

Strike up the dance! the cava bowl fill high	419 Island	2	45
The cava feast, the yam, the cocoa's root	422 Island	2	258

CAVALIER

'Cavalier, and man of worth	195 Ballad-A		81
Because she had a 'cavalier servente'	442 Beppo		136
But 'Cavalier Serventes' are quite common	444 Beppo		285
But 'Cavalier Servente' is the phrase	445 Beppo		313
And that you may not, cavalier, conceive	468 Morgante		172
'For God-sake, cavalier, come in with speed	469 Morgante		209
Morgante said, 'Oh gentle cavalier	471 Morgante		329
And, 'Cavalier,' he said, 'if I have less	475 Morgante		620
A better cavalier ne'er mounted horse	748 Juan	1	69
But for a cavalier of his condition	764 Juan	1	1107
'Had it but been for a stout cavalier	768 Juan	1	1369
As cavalier servente, or despise her	804 Juan	3	190
Forty feet high, upon a cavalier	868 Juan	7	96
After the taking of the 'Cavalier	887 Juan	8	578
Called 'Cavalier servente?'--a Pygmalion	903 Juan	9	405

CAVALIERO

In short, he was a perfect cavaliero	444 Beppo		263

CAVALIERS

Four cavaliers prepare for venturous deeds	15 Harold	1	731
The gallant cavaliers, who fought in vain	948 Juan	13	479

CAVA'S

When Cava's traitor-sire first call'd the band	9 Harold	1	389

CAVE

(See also FOREST-CAVE, MOUNTAIN-CAVE, OCEAN-CAVE)

Deep in yon cave Honorius long did dwell	7 Harold	1	259
Sighs in the gale, keeps silence in the cave	14 Harold	1	637
Or in his cave awaits the tempest's short-lived shock	27 Harold	2	468
For a time they abandon the cave and the chase	30 Harold	2	662
Above its prostrate brethren of the cave	33 Harold	2	811
As from the Pythian's mystic cave of yore	47 Harold	3	762
In the still cave and forest; o'er the flower	50 Harold	3	937
What was this tower of strength? within its cave	70 Harold	4	890
This cave was surely shaped out for the greeting	72 Harold	4	1060
For Oscar search'd each mountain cave	103 Alva		126
From Ida torn, he left his sylvan cave	105 Nisus		5
Together they dwelt in the cave of	129 Calmar		27
ours has been the cave of Oithona; ours be the	130 Calmar		68
sword. It hangs in thy cave. The ghosts	131 Calmar		197
Still dwelling in my Highland cave	135 I Would		2
Pallid and cold the Moon descends to cave	139 Ossian-A		7
Why did I quit my Highland cave	145 Adieu		28
The ebon portal of thy peopled cave	192 Fragment-C		36
The wild-dove hath her nest, the fox his cave	217 Weep-B		11
And now almost they touch the cave	334 Abydos	2	511
That fearful moment when he left the cave	335 Abydos	2	634
His corse may boast its urn and narrow cave	338 Corsair	1	33
From crag to cliff they mount.--Near yonder cave	340 Corsair	1	129
Whether we lay in the cave or the shed	384 Corinth		8
Even from the cold earth of our cave	404 Chillon		151
And, half uncivilised, preferr'd the cave	416 Island	1	31
The breeze now sank, now whisper'd from his cave	418 Island	1	170
All gently to refresh the thirsty cave	420 Island	2	110
Which draws the diver to the crimson cave	420 Island	2	140
Until the earthquake tear the naiad's cave	421 Island	2	155
Around she pointed to a spacious cave	431 Island	4	121
Were there, all scoop'd by Darkness from her cave	432 Island	4	154
Into the cave which round and o'er them lay	432 Island	4	198
This tale; enough that all within that cave	433 Island	4	221
Down plunged she through the cave to rouse her boy	435 Island	4	388
Their sanctuary the name of 'Neuha's Cave	435 Island	4	414
Sullen and lonely, couching in the cave	437 Tasso		17
From the Levant hath crept into its cave	528 Faliero	4	26
My father's house shall never be a cave	590 Sardan	5	208
Ye wilds, that look eternal; and thou cave	658 Heaven		266
Before the mass of waters; and yon cave	659 Heaven		275
Nor leaves an unsearch'd cave	670 Heaven		1175
The wounded lion his cool cave. Methinks	695 Werner	3	7
Before the entrance of a cilff-worn cave	787 Juan	2	862
And lifting him with care into the cave	788 Juan	2	913
And such was she, the lady of the cave	789 Juan	2	953
To place him in the cave for present rest	790 Juan	2	1043
Fast in his cave, and nothing clash'd upon	791 Juan	2	1090
And near the cave her quick light footsteps drew	792 Juan	2	1130
She came into the cave, but it was merely	795 Juan	2	1339

CAVE

Ocean their witness, and the cave their bed	800 Juan	2	1628
The dream changed:--in a cave she stood, its walls	820 Juan	4	257
On ours, or spars within some dusky cave	983 Juan	16	149

CAVED

Who in oppression's darkness caved had dwelt	48 Harold	3	785

CAVE-GUARDED

Of thy cave-guarded spring, with years unwrinkled	72 Harold	4	1033

CAVERN

The desert, forest, cavern, breaker's foam	37 Harold	3	113
The fire in the cavern of Etna conceal'd	129 Becher-A		9
Though I shall lie low in the cavern of death	149 Newstead-B		26
On the rude cavern of the rocky isle	300 Age		120
And oft around the cavern fire	333 Abydos	2	382
Forth to the cavern mouth he stept	334 Abydos	2	519
Then seek Anselmo's cavern, to report	357 Corsair	3	121
Mount, grotto, cavern, valley search'd in vain	365 Corsair	3	684
Or cavern sparkling with its native spars	420 Island	2	130
And sleeps unwieldy in his cavern dun	430 Island	4	13
No, Irad; I will to the cavern, whose	657 Heaven		200
Or else he walks the wild up to the cavern	658 Heaven		248
No; to the cavern of the Caucasus	658 Heaven		265
Palace, or garden, paradise, or cavern	748 Juan	1	47
The secret cavern of this lurking treasure	765 Juan	1	1223
And when into the cavern Haidee stepp'd	792 Juan	2	1137
Corroding in the cavern of the heart	968 Juan	15	18

CAVERN'D

As cavern'd waters wear the stone	186 Stanzas-A		11
Like cavern'd winds, the hollow accents came	219 Saul-B		12
The cavern'd echoes wake around	312 Giaour		183
The wolves yell'd on the cavern'd hill	396 Corinth		1067
And quiver to his cavern'd base	479 Manfred	1	74
Sickness sits cavern'd in his hollow eye	694 Werner	2	685

CAVERNS

Deep in the caverns of the deadly tide	866 Juan	6	916

CAVES

Welcome, ye deserts, and ye caves	6 Harold	1	196
Why thought seeks refuge in lone caves, yet rife	36 Harold	3	43
From cities to caves of the forest he flew	99 Adieu		22
You rest with your clan in the caves of Braemar	117 Lachin		30
Earth shudders as her caves receive his bones	121 Newstead-A		107
And caves their sullen roar enclose	133 E. N. Long		56
Which, trembling in their coral caves	314 Giaour		386
Within the caves of Istakar	327 Abydos	1	358
But War had enter'd their dark caves	395 Corinth		977
Without a spirit? Are the dropping caves	424 Island	2	387
Or trusted that, if sought, their distant caves	427 Island	3	35
For ever? or, received in coral caves	431 Island	4	97
And earth's and ocean's caves familiar things	479 Manfred	1	34
In my lone wanderings, to the caves of death	486 Manfred	2	174
And woke the mountain wolves, and made the caves	490 Manfred	2	507
Back to your inner caves	660 Heaven		383
In caves, in dens, in clefts of mountains, where	661 Heaven		440
The very demons shriek it from their caves	662 Heaven		540
The voiceless sands and dropping caves, that lay	798 Juan	2	1501

CAVIL

'Oh! were I prone to cavil--or were I not the Devil	178 Devil's Dr		189
Cavil about their lives--so let them mend them	569 Sardan	2	496
I would not cavil about climes or regions	610 Foscari	3	146
Than she from aught at which the eye could cavil	845 Juan	5	870
Unless it teaches one to quote and cavil	947 Juan	13	376
And therefore, mortals, cavil not at all	981 Juan	16	41

CAVILS

Not caring as I ought for critics' cavils	446 Beppo		414

CAW

'Caw me, caw thee'--for six months hath been hatching	928 Juan	11	615

CAYENNE

Leavening his blood as cayenne doth a curry	916 Juan	10	570

CAZZANI

'Did not the Italian Musico Cazzani	765 Juan	1	1185

CEASE

Each volley tells that thousands cease to breathe	10 Harold	1	420
And Virtue vanquish all, and Murder cease to thrive	11 Harold	1	485
Cease, fool, the fate of gods may well be thine	27 Harold	2	475
Which living waves where thou didst cease to live	39 Harold	3	265
And could the ceaseless vultures cease to prey	44 Harold	3	567
And Freedom's heart, grown heavy, cease to hoard	80 Harold	4	1516
Until that heart shall cease to beat	85 To D--		8

CEASE

Ah, none!--a father's tears will cease to flow	85	Epitaph	25
Oh! cease to affirm that man, since his birth	93	First Kiss	21
If these,--but let me cease the lengthen'd strain	94	Dorset	109
Nor yet the sounds of pleasure cease	102	Alva	96
And made the tear-drop cease to flow	103	Alva	148
And bids devotion's hallow'd echoes cease	120	Newstead-A	44
And matrons, once lamenting, cease to mourn	121	Newstead-A	120
Soon must her early song for ever cease	123	Recoll	97
And bids the war of tempests cease	133	E. N. Long	10
Nor cease till Luna's waning horn	134	E. N. Long	107
The hour when man must cease to be	135	I Would	20
Now let me cease--Physician, Parson, Dame	143	Soliloquy	63
They Both must heave, or cease to beat	144	Jessy	28
And, since I soon must cease to live	146	Adieu	119
Cease, if you prize your beauty's reign	147	Vain Lady	33
Be false, my sweet Anne, when I cease to adore you	147	To Anne-A	16
No self-reproach--but, let me cease	150	My Son	9
And our sorrow may cease to repine	151	Soul-A	7
And for awhile my sorrows cease	152	Weep-A	11
And thou and I shall cease to be	152	Remind	6
Can I cease to love thee? No	161	Maid	23
Till Heaven in mercy bids your pain and sorrows cease	161	Athos	26
Apollo sink, and Shakspeare cease to reign	169	Address-A	4
But live--until I cease to be	173	Origin	8
Were those hours--can their joy or their bitterness cease	182	Music-A	6
When cease to hear thy cherish'd name	184	Parker	30
'Twill flow, and cease to burn my brain	218	Soul-B	8
And Longman smirk and critics cease to rail	224	J.C.H.	32
Here let me cease, for why should I prolong	224	J.C.H.	41
When Tories and Whigs cease to quarrel	227	Thurlow-B	22
Oh, Southey! Southey! cease thy varied song	245	Bards	225
Cease to deceive; thy pilfer'd harp restore	246	Bards	307
Who dares aspire if thou must cease to hope	252	Bards	802
But let me cease, and dread Cassandra's fate	255	Bards	1007
Ye, who seek finish'd models, never cease	262	Hints	423
Ah! let me cease; in vain my bosom burns	265	Hints	619
The past return'd, the present seem'd to cease	269	Minerva	61
E'en factions cease to charm a factious land	272	Minerva	276
The last to bid the cry of warfare cease	305	Age	570
To bid the sins of others cease	320	Giaour	973
Mark! where his carnage and his conquests cease	333	Abydos	2	430
I cease to love thee when I love mankind	344	Corsair	1	405
If at my word the helpless cease to live	350	Corsair	2	208
Oh! that this dotage of his breast would cease	355	Corsair	2	525
When agonized hands that cease to guard	377	Lara	2	117
Coumourgi, can his glory cease	386	Corinth	147
Upon that sound is doom'd to cease	397	Parisina	90
And flows--and cannot cease to flow	402	Parisina	556
The day may come when she will cease to err	457	Dante	1	73
Passion shall tear thee when all passions cease	546	Faliero	5	610
Believe it. Should he shrink, I cannot cease	599	Foscari	1	234
Existence--it will cease, and thou wilt be	629	Cain	1	118
Will cease, like any other appetite	644	Cain	2	531
Cease to be beautiful! how can that be	644	Cain	2	532
Conflict shall cease, if ever it shall cease	645	Cain	2	644
Shall cease to prey on man and on each other	661	Heaven	443
That they exist: they soon shall cease to be	665	Heaven	762
Cease, or be sorrowful in silence: cease	667	Heaven	955
So that they find the goal or cease to feel	672	Werner	1	71
Gallop o'er the west drawbridge. See they cease not	714	Werner	5	81
Whether my verse's fame be doom'd to cease	829	Juan	4	788
For those for whom it soon shall cease to hope	888	Juan	8	652
And then before sighs cease; for oft the one	908	Juan	10	58
To pain, the moment when you cease to please	909	Juan	10	104
In which the Neva's ice would cease to live	912	Juan	10	294
With rust, should surely cease to hack and hew	962	Juan	14	422

CEASED

Here ceased the swift their race, here sunk the strong	9	Harold	1	384
Though the fair goddess long hath ceased to weep	23	Harold	2	256
Oft Music changed but never ceased her tone	32	Harold	2	757
What is my being? thou hast ceased to be	34	Harold	2	895
In him this glow'd when all beside had ceased to glow	43	Harold	3	486
Nor ceased to burn till kingdoms were no more	47	Harold	3	764
On one another; pity ceased to melt	48	Harold	3	783
Ere ceased the inhuman shout which hail'd the wretch who won	76	Harold	4	1260
My task is done--my song hath ceased--my theme	82	Harold	4	1657
Forgot to smile, or ceased to weep	88	Anacreon-B	6
Cold was the feast, the revel ceased	104	Alva	269
For her his wings have ceased to spread	141	Critics	61
But beauty's self hath ceased to charm	152	Weep-A	19
Thou, too, hast ceased to be a boy	153	Friend-A	24
My life, when Thyrza ceased to live	166	Struggle	40
For thousands Death hath ceased to lower	167	Euthanasia	27
Ere Garrick fled, or Brinsley ceased to write	170	Address-A	43
Since others it hath ceased to move	206	Year	2

CEASED

Which colour'd all his objects:--he had ceased	214	Dream	55
Beside thee ceased to shine	218	I Saw	6
She ceased awhile, and thus I dared reply	270	Minerva	123
He ceased, and drew forth an MS.; and no	297	Vision	809
Or has it ceased to 'kick against the pricks	307	Age	701
E'en for thy presence ceased to pine	332	Abydos	2	351
Its peal wax'd fainter--ceased--he felt alone	359	Corsair	3	263
Had nearly ceased his memory to recall	366	Lara	1	28
That ceased to beat, the look that made them start	370	Lara	1	278
He ceased; and Lara answer'd, 'I am here	375	Lara	2	43
Inspiring hope himself had ceased to feel	380	Lara	2	371
And once, as Kaled's answering accents ceased	381	Lara	2	466
To him had Venice ceased to be	385	Corinth	129
Which conquer'd hearts they ceased to prize	386	Corinth	205
Hath ceased her shaded orb to veil	391	Corinth	646
He ceased, and stood with folded arms	399	Parisina	318
It ceased--again she thought to speak	400	Parisina	346
My brothers--both had ceased to breathe	404	Chillon	220
It ceased, and then it came again	405	Chillon	253
Yet then, even then, his feelings ceased not all	417	Island	1	155
Had ceased; and sulphury vapours upward driven	426	Island	3	3
Following the nereid? Had they ceased to weep	431	Island	4	96
Vow'd to their God, have shrieking fled, and ceased	459	Dante	2	82
My own soul's sepulchre, for I have ceased	482	Manfred	1	288
Long as he can; he has ceased to merit death	512	Faliero	2	237
Which I have never for one moment ceased	514	Faliero	2	378
And learn thou to be captive.--It hath ceased	536	Faliero	4	595
Has ceased, and the moon breaks forth in her brightness	573	Sardan	3	142
Who have ceased to mingle love? My sister! Courage	581	Sardan	4	231
That words have ceased to shake me. Oh, no doubt	603	Foscari	2	128
Ah! they relent, then--I had ceased to hope it	608	Foscari	3	36
Long ceased to breathe our breath, have theirs, thou say'st	644	Cain	2	578
'Twere better that he ceased to live, than give	648	Cain	3	132
When just as the artillery ceased, and paused	715	Werner	5	130
That I have ceased to breathe. Away! and be	737	Deformed	2	152
She ceased, and turn'd upon her pillow; pale	766	Juan	1	1257
And rarely ceased the haughty billow's roar	796	Juan	2	1414
To those who have ceased to hear such, or ne'er heard	818	Juan	4	112
Her struggles ceased with one convulsive groan	823	Juan	4	462
The Duke of Wellington had ceased to show	884	Juan	8	390
But here it seem'd his jokes had ceased to take	887	Juan	8	560
The good old khan, who long had ceased to see	893	Juan	8	922
So call'd; the Antic long hath ceased to hear	898	Juan	9	92
A fool whose bells have ceased to ring at all	918	Juan	10	688
Be gilt, who sate hath ceased to be the same	983	Juan	16	152
The lady's voice ceased, and the thrilling wires	986	Juan	16	369
But should the day come when place ceased to exist	990	Juan	16	645

CEASELESS

It is that settled, ceaseless gloom	17	Harold	1	853
This made the ceaseless toil of travel sweet	26	Harold	2	386
And could the ceaseless vultures cease to prey	44	Harold	3	567
Of the loud breakers, and the ceaseless roar	70	Harold	4	940
The ceaseless echo of the rhyming throng	119	Answer-A	20
Which rends my heart with ceaseless sigh	172	Romaic-B	3
Of ceaseless vigils; for I had the share	212	Augusta-C	110
But who forgives the senior's ceaseless verse	251	Bards	729
The searching throes of ceaseless pain	320	Giaour	1005
Against them pour'd the ceaseless shot	386	Corinth	160
Huge fragments, sapp'd by the ceaseless flow	392	Corinth	741
Thirty-four years of nearly ceaseless warfare	601	Foscari	2	14
From that Ixion grindstone's ceaseless toil	746	Juan	Ded	102
Making their summer lives one ceaseless song	815	Juan	3	938
On his soul, like a ceaseless sunrise, dart	893	Juan	8	918

CEASES

The pause in which he ceases to destroy	423	Island	2	301
And when it ceases to be so, thy love	644	Cain	2	530

CEASING

(See also NEVER-CEASING)

He frets, he fumes, and ceasing to invoke	142	Soliloquy	5
Yet not quite ceasing	200	Stanzas-B	55
Would scamper o'er the scalding soil, and ceasing	735	Deformed	1	895

CECROPS

These Cecrops placed, this Pericles adorn'd	269	Minerva	101

CEDAR

Know ye the land of the cedar and vine	323	Abydos	1	5
A cedar towering o'er the Wilderness	464	Dante	4	75
Bring cedar, too, and precious drugs, and spices	591	Sardan	5	278
Head ten times higher than the haughtiest cedar	642	Cain	2	397
Cedar and pine shall lift their tops in vain	660	Heaven	368
Her writhing, fell she like a cedar fell'd	823	Juan	4	464

CEDARS
The cedars bow, the mountains nod   217 The Harp   14
The cedars wave on Lebanon   217 Gazelle   11
Who grew like cedars round him gloriously   893 Juan   8   924

CEILING
So that I seem to stand upon the ceiling   745 Fragment-D   6

CELEBRATE
The muse may celebrate with perfect praise   263 Hints   510

CELEBRATED
And then he said, 'Oh giant celebrated   473 Morgante   451
Noble, rich, celebrated, and a stranger   927 Juan   11   578
So celebrated for his morals, when   931 Juan   12   126
Desirable, distinguish'd, celebrated   960 Juan   14   330

CELEBRITY
The diners of celebrity dined well   977 Juan   15   554

CELESTIAL
That, sheening far, celestial seems to be   6 Harold   1   226
Blend a celestial with a human heart   73 Harold   4   1064
For some celestial fruit forbidden to our wants   73 Harold   4   1080
The organ's soft celestial swell   96 Granta   71
Within those once celestial eyes   97 To M--   16
What rapture celestial is mine   97 To M.S.G.-B   8
Celestial pair, if aught my verse can claim   110 Nisus   401
Your nature so much of celestial partakes   117 To Eliza   39
Celestial consolation brings   131 L'Amitie   7
I hail the sky's celestial bow   133 E. N. Long   8
Stolen from celestial spheres above   150 Song   6
The song, celestial from thy voice   165 Thyrza   39
And fit for that celestial sign   188 On Star   22
To themes celestial told in epic song   258 Hints   108
Celestial tears bedimm'd her large blue eye   269 Minerva   86
Saint Peter sat by the celestial gate   285 Vision   1
And claim the help of his celestial peers   285 Vision   29
Saint Peter sat by the celestial gate   286 Vision   121
Away he melted in celestial smoke   295 Vision   668
A ray of no celestial hue   330 Abydos   2   119
And waters with celestial tears   336 Abydos   2   682
To embalm with his celestial flattery   462 Dante   3   144
Than ninety-nine of the celestial list   473 Morgante   468
Tinge thy celestial aspect, and make tame   485 Manfred   2   117
Of his celestial boons to you and yours   646 Cain   2   656
Celestial natures? But, Aholibamah   655 Heaven   11
The hour will come in which celestial aid   663 Heaven   641
Surely celestial mercy lurks below   667 Heaven   946
Shorn as ye are of all celestial power   668 Heaven   988
Which look'd so calm, and the celestial hymns   713 Werner   5   21
On whom her reveries celestial ran   756 Juan   1   632
Quite a celestial kaleidoscope   785 Juan   2   744
Is sharpen'd from its high celestial flavour   802 Juan   3   39

CELL
Which seem'd to him more lone than Eremite's
  sad cell   4 Harold   1   36
Why ev'n the worm at last disdains her shatter'd
  cell   20 Harold   2   45
Still unimpair'd, though old, in the soul's
  haunted cell   36 Harold   3   45
Hark to his strain and then survey his cell   60 Harold   4   317
Of an enamour'd Goddess, and the cell   73 Harold   4   1061
To which Diana's marvel was a cell   78 Harold   4   1370
Within this narrow cell reclines her clay   84 Death-B   5
Extracted from its glistening cell   99 Young Lady   16
To know some humbler grave, some narrow cell   138 Harrow-B   21
Soon must I share the gloomy cell   145 Adieu   8
And droop within their silent cell   175 Impromptu-A   8
An empire for a cell   180 Ode-A   67
Each in his incommunicative cell   192 Fragment-C   28
While high-born ladies in their magic cell   244 Bards   161
Yes, friend! for thee I'll quit my cynic cell   261 Hints   343
But broods within his cell alone   318 Giaour   806
Or pent within our penance cell   318 Giaour   820
Unto thy cell will Selim come   328 Abydos   1   464
She, of this Peri cell the sprite   329 Abydos   2   85
But in a nook within the cell   330 Abydos   2   120
Now with Gulnare, and now in Conrad's cell   357 Corsair   3   134
Shook o'er his turret cell the thunder-cloud   359 Corsair   3   259
Yet changed since last within that cell she came   359 Corsair   3   276
They bleed within that silent cell--his breast   362 Corsair   3   479
Along my cell from side to side   405 Chillon   307
Fit for this cell which wrongs me--but for thee   438 Tasso   143
Perchance in such a cell we suffer more   439 Tasso   181
A future temple of my present cell   439 Tasso   220
Ferrara him a pittance and a cell   462 Dante   3   139
The gloom of this eternal cell, which never   609 Foscari   3   51
The sole fit habitant of such a cell   613 Foscari   3   337
A cell so far below the water's level   614 Foscari   3   377
That every step I take, even from this cell   614 Foscari   3   413
Much as a monk may do within his cell   965 Juan   14   644

CELLAR
Improves our cellar, thou our living stock   274 Waltz   34
Keep up the stove--I will myself to the cellar   675 Werner   1   262
Weights, measures, larder, cellar, buttery   684 Werner   2   44
The very best of vineyards is the cellar   950 Juan   13   603

CELLARS
His very cellars might be kings' abodes   931 Juan   12   70

CELLINI
Who slays Cellini will have work'd as hard   738 Deformed 2   212

CELLS
Yes! in thy gloomy cells and shades profound   120 Newstead-A   21
The gloomy tenants, Newstead! of thy cells   121 Newstead-A   113
Then he found sixty scribblers in separate cells   179 Devil's Dr   237
Nor leave their cells for water or for wood   468 Morgante   162
Not less appalling cells, the 'leaden roofs'   507 Faliero   1   533
And hollow cells, and obscure niches, to   696 Werner   3   90
In hollow halls, with sparry roofs and cells   797 Juan   2   1470
More to secure them in their naval cells   828 Juan   4   725
The cells, too, and refectory, I ween   949 Juan   13   524

CELT
Gird the gross sirloin of a city Celt   308 Age   774

CELTIC
Mix'd Celtic memories with the Phyrgian mount   423 Island   2   292

CEMENT
A monument, whose cement hath been guilt   213 Lady Byron   36
Whate'er it now be); and Rome's earliest cement   731 Deformed 1   651

CEMENTED
Still undivided, and cemented more   43 Harold   3   492
With human blood that column was cemented   829 Juan   4   833

CEMETERIES
Will make the cemeteries populous   516 Faliero   2   507

CEMETERY
While thus they parley in the cemetery   469 Morgante   205

CENEDA
From Laurence the Count-bishop of Ceneda   545 Faliero   5   533

CENSOR
The sternest censor to the fair must yield   114 Prologue   32
The verse which blends the censor with the friend   118 Answer-A   2
Still, still despise the censor stern   133 E. N. Long   41

CENSORIOUS
The rest of the censorious throng   142 Critics   77
Although some kind, censorious friend will say   251 Bards   697
By naming streets: since men are so censorious   944 Juan   13   194

CENSORS
While these are censors, 'twould be sin to spare   243 Bards   87
Our bards and censors are so much alike   243 Bards   92

CENSURE
What censure, what danger, what woe would I brave   129 Becher-A   18
Yours is the Censure, mine the Praise   142 Critics   100
Why should his harmless censure seem offence   143 Soliloquy   53
And censure, wisely loud, be justly mute   170 Address-A   61
Have long ago suffered censure   239 Bray   45
Save censure--critics all are ready made   242 Bards   64
Lest censure hover o'er some faulty line   262 Hints   418
Lest we provoke them. True, they love not
  censure   572 Sardan   3   47

CENSURES
Their censures on the hapless victim shower   119 Answer-A   18
Their sneers or censures I alike despise   119 Answer-A   44
If ancient Virgins croaking censures raise   142 Soliloquy   10

CENT
Counts cent per cent, and smiles, or vainly frets   260 Hints   255
Year after year they voted cent. per cent   306 Age   620

CENTAUR
Into that moral centaur, man and wife   851 Juan   5   1264
And Centaur Nessus garb of mortal clothing   926 Juan   11   508
But both together form a kind of centaur   964 Juan   14   583

CENTAURS
Saw cits grow centaurs underneath his brush   256 Hints   4

CENTAUR'S
A boy Achilles, with the centaur's lyre   420 Island   2   85

CENTINEL
His wither'd centinel, Duenna sage   17 Harold   1   802

CENTIPEDE
Cased like the centipede in saffron mail   209 Sketch   67

CENTRAL
And traverse Paynim shores and pass Earth's
   central line   5 Harold   1   99
They had gain'd a central realm of earth again 431 Island 4   119
Like earthquakes from the hidden fire call'd
   'central   801 Juan   2 1720

CENTRE
Stands in the centre, eager to invade   15 Harold   1   740
Full in the centre stands the bull at bay   16 Harold   1   775
Ev'n to the centre of Illyria's vales   26 Harold   2   407
Of living water from the centre rose   28 Harold   2   551
Earth yawn'd; he stood the centre of a cloud 219 Saul-B   5
Had gain'd the centre of her softest sky   269 Minerva   64
'There, in its centre, a sepulchral lamp   343 Corsair   1   351
What answers Lara? to its centre shrunk   373 Lara   1   482
Centre of many stars! which mak'st our earth 493 Manfred   3   188
To be the centre of re-union to   536 Faliero   4   538
To centre all their force and save the king 572 Sardan   3   92
The very centre, girded by vast courts   588 Sardan   5   64
The fairest in the centre? They have but   628 Cain   1   74
And centre of surrounding things--'tis made 630 Cain   1   212
Were scarlet, from whose glowing centre grew 809 Juan   3   534
Yet in the very centre, past all price   945 Juan   13   293
A mighty window, hollow in the centre   948 Juan   13   489
With self-love in the centre as their pole 968 Juan   14   812

CENTRED
Need I say, my sweet Mary, 'twas centred in you 135 Highlander   8
His soul, his existence, are centred in you 147 To Anne-B   16
Until it centred in an only son   754 Juan   1   467

CENTRES
Which centres in a single ray of his   588 Sardan   5   52

CENTURIED
Yet through this centuried eclipse of woe   461 Dante   3   62

CENTURIES
Redeemer of dark centuries of shame   72 Harold   4 1020
For centuries still may thy boughs lightly wave 149 Newstead-B   29
For the few little years, out of centuries won 202 Avatar   7
An epic scarce ten centuries could claim   244 Bards   191
In these sad centuries of sin and slaughter 450 Beppo   635
Oh agony! that centuries should reap   453 Venice-B   14
Madden'd with centuries of drought, are loud 454 Venice-B   85
Woe! woe! the veil of coming centuries   459 Dante   2   35
For centuries: may he who bears it now   491 Manfred   3   32
As 'twere anew, the gaps of centuries   495 Manfred   3   295
Through the long centuries of thy renown   553 Sardan   1   162
A green spot amidst desert centuries   586 Sardan   4   513
If we had not for many centuries   608 Foscari   2   416
That had for centuries been known in Spain 770 Juan   1 1515
Or of some centuries to take a lease   829 Juan   4   790

CENTURION
In awe: he said, as the centurion saith   836 Juan   5   285

CENTURY
Through the thick deaths of half a century 190 Churchill   10
Of life which might have fill'd a century   212 Augusta-C   111
Of half a century bloody and black   458 Dante   1   135
Of half a century on his brother's brow   525 Faliero   3   454
With three parts of a century of years   541 Faliero   5   241
The present century was growing blind   813 Juan   3   814
Are things which in this century don't strike 814 Juan   3   853
Than might suffice a moderate century through 928 Juan   11   644
And Mitford in the nineteenth century   932 Juan   12   151
Had made more progress than for the last century 990 Juan 16   628

CEPHISUS
Where meek Cephisus sheds his scanty tide   269 Minerva   42
Where meek Cephisus pours his scanty tide   356 Corsair   3   42

CERBERUS
'Sooner will I with Cerberus exchange   291 Vision   393
I'll try to coax our Cerberus up to heaven 291 Vision   400
For sometimes he like Cerberus would seem   294 Vision   625

CEREMENT
Will burst all cerement, even a living grave's 609 Foscari 3   81

CEREMONIE
I pray ye be seated, 'sans ceremonie   280 Blues   2   28

CEREMONIES
All these vain ceremonies are base insults 625 Foscari   5   276
This master of the ceremonies is   676 Werner   1   308
With all the ceremonies of his rank   850 Juan   5 1226

CEREMONY
As much of ceremony as you will   615 Foscari   4   31
His head, until the ceremony ended   843 Juan   5   760

CERES
Are also learnt from Ceres and from Bacchus 795 Juan   2 1351
Ceres presents a plate of vermicelli   795 Juan   2 1355
Or swears that Ceres hath begotten Famine   873 Juan   7   360
And 'farmers' can't raise Ceres from her fall 900 Juan   9   254
Beneath his cars of Ceres groan the roads   931 Juan   12   68
Bacchus and Ceres being, as we know   992 Juan   16   732

CERINTHUS
Cruel Cerinthus! does the fell disease   87 Tibullus   1

CERTAIN
To doubtful conflict, certain slaughter bring 26 Harold   2   401
With joy I court a certain doom   90 To M.S.G.-A   23
A certain space to yonder Moon is given   139 Ossian-A   13
As certain stanzas also show it   144 Becher-B   19
To certain very precious scheming   144 Becher-B   42
Would certain Damsels also teach   151 Harriet   11
And care not for Hope, who are certain of bliss 156 Goblet   23
A certain Chief Justice say something like
   swearing   178 Devil's Dr   149
Some certain coins of silver, which as 'twere 190 Churchill   34
Some folks for certain have thought it was
   shocking   226 Ode-D   25
I went where one's certain to find her   234 Ballat   17
Like certain tailors, limited in art   257 Hints   52
But this is certain, since our Shakspeare's days 262 Hints   441
Nor is it certain that some sorts of verse 268 Hints   833
She came--Waltz came, and with her certain sets 274 Waltz   67
Well, one thing is certain, that some must be
   fools   282 Blues   2   124
In certain terms I shan't translate in full 292 Vision   469
For certain sure to claim them as his due   295 Vision   646
Of war so certain--yet not quite so sure   308 Age   719
Oh! slight but certain pledge of crime--'tis
   blood   361 Corsair   3   417
There was a certain Palatine   408 Mazeppa   155
A certain lady went to see the show   442 Beppo   165
Which certain people call a 'certain age   442 Beppo   170
But certain savage giants look'd him over   468 Morgante   156
Second and third, with certain slings, and throw 468 Morgante   159
Think not they lived on locusts sole, 'tis
   certain   469 Morgante   195
'So that all persons may be sure and certain 472 Morgante   425
Much armour was, and hung up certain bows   473 Morgante   478
Morgante said, 'I'll carry him for certain 475 Morgante   592
And in a certain closet, where the wall   476 Morgante   665
And certain letters, weeping, then he read 476 Morgante   685
From senates once his slaves, a certain soldier 492 Manfred   3   91
At present in repairing certain galleys   505 Faliero   1   380
Was given as the reward of certain scars   505 Faliero   1   398
A duty to a certain sign, a vice   510 Faliero   2   109
There is a certain Philip Calendaro   511 Faliero   2   136
Of that be certain: he is one who may   518 Faliero   2   668
Yet for all this, so full of certain passions 518 Faliero   2   681
They might be certain that whoe'er was brought 522 Faliero 3   239
I'll answer for thee--'tis a certain Bertram 537 Faliero   4   642
There was a certain Bacchus, was there not 553 Sardan   1   194
Certain, and of the boys too, our last hopes 584 Sardan   4   370
And all will prosper. Could I but be certain 615 Faliero   4   54
And being of all things the sole thing certain 641 Cain   2   370
But what is certain is, that he has swallow'd 675 Werner   1   222
That he suspects me's certain. I'm alone   681 Werner   1   626
Certain. I have lived and served here since my
   birth   683 Werner   2   15
And has much influence with a certain court 684 Werner   2   90
Till certain of the hearer's patience. That 686 Werner   2   232
Certain. That's well; but had been better, if 702 Werner   2   510
Is not the certain path to future praise   746 Juan   Ded   64
And open'd certain trunks of books and letters 750 Juan   1   218
I'm very certain mine would not have done so 760 Juan   1   880
Prologue is always certain throes, and throbs 766 Juan   1 1292
A certain portion of uncertain paper   773 Juan   1 1738
'Tis very certain the desire of life   782 Juan   2   505
For certain merchantmen upon the look   796 Juan   2 1390
Except some certain portions of the prey   803 Juan   3   131
Of certain stews, and roast-meats, and pilaus 837 Juan   5   370
A certain press or cupboard niched in yonder 839 Juan   5   526
Was also certain that the earth was square 850 Juan   5 1194
As certain;--these are paltry things, and yet 855 Juan   6   167
But certain 'tis they all felt for their new 857 Juan   6   305
A lady of a 'certain age,' which means   861 Juan   6   546
'Twas certain that his conduct had been pure 865 Juan   6   827
Juan and Johnson join'd a certain corps   880 Juan   8   145
A prop not quite so certain as before   896 Juan   9   20
Others talk'd learnedly of certain tumours 912 Juan   10   315
Which, though 'tis certain to perplex and
   frighten   922 Juan   11   215
That is, up to a certain point; which point 951 Juan   13   641

CERTAIN

I think that were I certain of success	956 Juan	14	89
Without the coxcombry of certain she men	959 Juan	14	248
Whose verdict for such sin a certain cure is	963 Juan	14	480
Indeed a certain fair and fairy one	973 Juan	15	339
But after, there are sometimes certain signs	977 Juan	15	573
For certain reasons my belief is serious	980 Juan	15	760

CERTAINLY

The Lord Westmoreland certainly silly	177 Devil's Dr		142
'Tis said she certainly was married	231 Doctor		67
I certainly follow, not set an example	278 Blues	1	55
If you and she marry, you'll certainly wrangle	278 Blues	1	68
Adventure makes it needful. Certainly	700 Werner	3	371
Revenge in person's certainly no virtue	750 Juan	1	239
And certainly this course was much the best	755 Juan	1	532
But vaccination certainly has been	762 Juan	1	1029
And certainly he show'd the best of breeding	807 Juan	3	362
But certainly to one deem'd dead, returning	807 Juan	3	391
And though he certainly ran many risks	856 Juan	6	227
Certainly aged--what her years might be	861 Juan	6	547
Though certainly more difficult to rhyme at	959 Juan	14	228
If bad, the best way's certainly to tease on	974 Juan	15	403
And certainly Aurora had renew'd	994 Juan	16	901

CERTAINTIES

Your doubts are certainties to all around you	692 Werner	2	596

CERTAINTY

Till grew such certainty from that suspense	356 Corsair	3	83
In hopeless certainty of mind	414 Mazeppa		722
Ah! no; it is the certainty of all	527 Faliero	3	607
I am at peace: the peace of certainty	547 Faliero	5	654
Thy safety; and the certainty that nought	560 Sardan	1	663
Suspicion into such a certainty	567 Sardan	2	332
There's no such thing as certainty, that's plain	898 Juan	9	133
Of thought we could but snatch a certainty	955 Juan	14	2

CERTES

Certes, I should have more than those	238 Orford		11
A vulgar scribbler, certes, stands disgraced	262 Hints		393
And certes often like Sir Philip Francis	294 Vision		632
Certes, far more than yet is said or thought	466 Morgante		40
And certes courteous, to leave that to the lady	710 Werner	4	393
I see, too? In my grammar, certes. I	731 Deformed	1	667
All these are, certes, entertaining facts	813 Juan	3	825
Though certes by no means so grand a sight	838 Juan	5	461
But certes matters took a different face	873 Juan	7	369
Certes it would have been but thrown away	901 Juan	9	286
Indifference certes don't produce distress	945 Juan	13	278
Certes it was not body; he was well	964 Juan	14	564
Certes, but a preventative, and therefore	972 Juan	15	247
But certes it conducts to lives ascetic	973 Juan	15	303

CERULEANS

Benign Ceruleans of the second sex	830 Juan	4	858

CERUSE

The painting and the painted; youth, ceruse	924 Juan	11	380

CERVANTES

Verse, and by Solomon and by Cervantes	867 Juan	7	24
Had not Cervantes, in that too true tale	942 Juan	13	63
Cervantes smiled Spain's chivalry away	942 Juan	13	81

CESARE

By carrying off Count Cesare Cicogna	827 Juan	4	663

CETERA
(See COETERA and ET CETERA)

CEYLON

From Ceylon, Inde, or far Cathay, unloads	930 Juan	12	66

CHAFE

At thee his rage will only chafe	334 Abydos	2	530
From where the battle roars, the billows chafe	339 Corsair	1	113
In words alone I am not wont to chafe	358 Corsair	3	192
Its mother's.--Let the coming chaos chafe	669 Heaven		1083
She was not one to weep, and rave, and chafe	823 Juan	4	429

CHAFED

Lulls his chafed breast from elemental war	269 Minerva		50
Lulls his chafed breast from elemental war	356 Corsair	3	50
As if their waters chafed to meet	385 Corinth		56
And whether they had chafed his belt	407 Mazeppa		85
And chafed at poor Dudu, who only sigh'd	862 Juan	6	631

CHAFES

But chafes my pride thus baffled in the snare	343 Corsair	1	336

CHAFF

Hope constancy in wind, or corn in chaff	242 Bards		77
Of chaff, although our gleanings be not grist	953 Juan	13	770

CHAFING

And chafing him, the soft warm hand of youth	788 Juan	2	899

CHAIN
(See also DRAG-CHAIN)

None hugg'd a conqueror's chain, save fallen Chivalry	18 Harold	1	831
Not thirty tyrants now enforce the chain	31 Harold	2	706
Still round him clung invisibly a chain	36 Harold	3	77
He wears the shatter'd links of the world's broken chain	38 Harold	3	162
A link reluctant in a fleshly chain	46 Harold	3	685
Striking the electric chain wherewith we are darkly bound	58 Harold	4	207
The old man's clench; the long envenom'd chain	79 Harold	4	1438
Is link'd the electric chain of that despair	81 Harold	4	1546
But, pall'd with vice, he breaks his former chain	100 Damaetas		13
But wouldst thou see the secret chain	101 Marion		53
Dissemble your pain, and lengthen your chain	115 Pigot		13
The chain I gave was fair to view	168 The Chain		1
That chain was firm in every link	168 The Chain		9
The chain which shiver'd in his grasp	169 The Chain		14
The chain is broke, the music mute	169 The Chain		18
False heart, frail chain, and silent lute	169 The Chain		20
By Love's or Plutus' heavier chain	179 Gold		20
We repent, we abjure, we will break from our chain	182 Music-A		7
The mountain-land which spurn'd the Roman chain	182 Address-C		3
How long his senses bore its chilling chain	184 Julian		38
There are links which must break in the chain that has bound us	186 Napoleon		23
Her bright chain o'er the deep	188 Music-C		10
The rock, the vulture, and the chain	191 Prometheus-B		7
We'd hug the chain	199 Stanzas-B		8
The holiest chain of human ties	201 Ode-C		52
Tears fall on his chain, though it drops from his hands	202 Avatar		15
Then might freedom forgive thee this dance in thy chain	202 Avatar		27
When a week's saturnalia hath loosen'd her chain	202 Avatar		52
But wear the chain	206 Year		16
Smile--for the fetter'd eagle breaks his chain	299 Age		87
Why did you chain him on yon isle so lone	306 Age		584
Of ladye-love, and beauty's chain	321 Giaour		1104
That gnaws and yet may break his chain	331 Abydos	2	206
Arrives--to-night must break thy chain	334 Abydos	2	482
Hath doom'd his death, or fix'd his chain	335 Abydos	2	566
Must break my chain before it dried my tears	348 Corsair	2	88
He found enough to load with heaviest chain	351 Corsair	2	312
And strain'd with rage the chain on which he gazed	352 Corsair	2	377
He moved his hand--the grating of his chain	353 Corsair	2	431
Remember, captive, 'tis to break thy chain	355 Corsair	2	529
What gem hath dropp'd and sparkles o'er his chain	355 Corsair	2	539
Close to the glimmering grate he dragg'd his chain	359 Corsair	3	262
A single word of mine removes that chain	360 Corsair	3	314
He had been tempted, chasten'd, and the chain	361 Corsair	3	420
They find on shore a seaboat's broken chain	365 Corsair	3	685
And Slavery half forgets her feudal chain	366 Lara	1	2
Links grace and harmony in happiest chain	371 Lara	1	390
They were not common links, that form'd the chain	382 Lara	2	536
And in each ring there is a chain	403 Chillon		37
He died--and they unlock'd his chain	404 Chillon		149
His empty chain above it leant	404 Chillon		162
I burst my chain with one strong bound	404 Chillon		210
But so it was:--my broken chain	405 Chillon		304
I had not left my recent chain	406 Chillon		358
Which link the burning chain that binds	409 Mazeppa		240
While round it swarm'd the proas' flitting chain	422 Island	2	236
Till now, when she has forged her broken chain	427 Island	3	57
The very love which lock'd me to my chain	438 Tasso		144
And freedom the mere numbness of his chain	453 Venice-B		44
The cup which brings oblivion of a chain	454 Venice-B		87
To break the chain, yet--yet the Avenger stops	460 Dante	2	139
And the first day which sees the chain enthral	461 Dante	3	82
And wear a deeper brand and gaudier chain	464 Dante	4	106
And the clankless chain hath bound thee	481 Manfred	1	259
With whom I wore the chain of human ties	486 Manfred	2	196
I shiver'd his chain	488 Manfred	2	319
Of one long chain; one mass, one breath, one body	521 Faliero	3	155
And that's the heaviest link of the long chain	561 Sardan	1	691
None else shall chain them. You hear him, and me	564 Sardan	2	172
All that look'd like a chain for me or others	583 Sardan	4	340
Meantime still struggle in the mortal chain	661 Heaven		473
Deeming the chain it wears even men may fit	746 Juan	Ded	116
Thy clanking chain, and Erin's yet green wounds	747 Juan	Ded	125
Whether the word was death, or but the chain	807 Juan	3	372
A chain o'er all she did; that is, a chain	845 Juan	5	874
And now would chain them, to the very mind	915 Juan	10	536
Who watches o'er the chain, as they who wear	916 Juan	10	544
Theirs is the best bower anchor, the chain cable	930 Juan	12	19

CHAIN'D
Chain'd to the chariot of triumphal Art   62 Harold 4 445
Is chain'd and tortured--cabin'd, cribb'd, confined   74 Harold 4 1140
Chain'd by the trunk he vainly broke   180 Ode-A 48
Chain'd to the signature of O. P. Q.   252 Bards 764
For which poor Prometheus was chain'd to his mountain   283 Blues 2 137
Some of his works about his neck were chain'd   295 Vision 683
Chain'd to the chariot of the chieftain's state   299 Age 48
Affection chain'd her to that heart   325 Abydos 1 191
Too faithful though to bitter bondage chain'd   360 Corsair 3 323
Chain'd to excess, the slave of each extreme   368 Lara 1 127
These hands are chain'd--but let me die   401 Parisina 450
They chain'd us each to a column stone   403 Chillon 48
Chain'd to the chill and stiffening steed   414 Mazeppa 764
Chain'd on the deck, where once, a gallant crew   435 Island 4 359
Lies chain'd to his lone rock by the seashore   463 Dante 4 19
And science still beyond them, were chain'd down   637 Cain 2 53
By swamping one of the prizes; he had chain'd   803 Juan 3 117
Chain'd to a rock; she knew not how, but stir   820 Juan 4 242
Wounded and chain'd, so that he cannot move   823 Juan 4 407
Were to be chain'd and lotted out per couple   828 Juan 4 727
With Raucocanti lucklessly was chain'd   828 Juan 4 737
And though thus chain'd, as natural her hand   828 Juan 4 756
Chill, and chain'd to cold earth, we lift on high 867 Juan 7 5

CHAINED
While Hugo raised his chained hands   399 Parisina 230

CHAINING
What is't but chaining   200 Stanzas-B 81

CHAIN-KISSING
Nor the steps of enslavers and chain-kissing slaves   204 Avatar 119

CHAINLESS
Eternal Spirit of the chainless Mind   402 Sonnet-F 1
His chainless mountains, 'tis but for a time   454 Venice-B 130
Is chainless. Have you all the musters ready   516 Faliero 2 569

CHAIN-PUMP
Kept two hand and one chain-pump still in use   777 Juan 2 236

CHAINS
And never knew, till then, the weight of Despots' chains   21 Harold 2 108
Kingdoms are shrunk to provinces, and chains   57 Harold 4 102
Starts from its belt--he rends his captive's chains   57 Harold 4 143
War for their chains, and rather than be free   69 Harold 4 843
Now hate rules a heart which in love's easy chains   99 L Adieu 25
In firmer chains our hearts confine   101 Lady-B 2
Our chains once dissolved and our hearts unconfined   117 To Eliza 35
The young, the old, have worn the chains of love   119 Answer-A 15
And all her chains are broke   162 War Song 12
All their chains were light to me   187 French-A 23
True, the chains of the Catholic clank o'er his rags   202 Avatar 9
And Gaul shall weep ere Albion wear her chains   272 Minerva 284
From chains, would gladly be their tyrant's ape   299 Age 98
Who bursts the chains of millions to renew   301 Age 256
To bid us blush for these old chains, or break   303 Age 389
A tyrant's secrets are but chains   332 Abydos 2 298
Oh! if he knew the weight of splendid chains   348 Corsair 1 191
The Rovers won: our limbs have worn their chains   348 Corsair 2 70
'Ay, in my chains! my steps will gently tread   360 Corsair 3 308
Silent but quick they stoop, his chains unbind   362 Corsair 3 440
When those dull chains in meeting clank'd   399 Parisina 322
I suffer'd chains and courted death   402 Chillon 12
With joy:--but not in chains to pine   403 Chillon 97
My very chains and I grew friends   406 Chillon 389
The rust which tyrants cherish on our chains   423 Island 2 323
From wounds whose only bandage might be chains   427 Island 3 78
Chains in his eye, and menace in his ear   430 Island 4 62
To cheer resistance against death or chains   433 Island 4 258
Their chains so slight, 'twas not worth while to break them   446 Beppo 428
The city it has clothed in chains, which clank   454 Venice-B 118
Damn'd like the dull canal with locks and chains   455 Venice-B 152
To chains, but laid aside to carry weapons   526 Faliero 3 563
Are all in chains, and some even now on trial   537 Faliero 4 619
Of blood and chains? The despotism of vice   552 Sardan 1 114
And never changed their chains but for their armour   556 Sardan 1 382
Degraded by that passion then by chains   559 Sardan 1 549
Are chains. Again that shout! and now the clash   574 Sardan 3 196
Who totters back in chains to tortures and   604 Foscari 2 169
Exile, or chains, or whatsoever worse   608 Foscari 2 426
The groans of slaves in chains, and men in dungeons   611 Foscari 3 242

CHAINS
With death, and chains, and exile in his hand   613 Foscari 3 315
Exchange of chains for heavier chains I owe him   614 Foscari 3 408
Denounced--dragg'd, it may be, in chains; and all   721 Werner 5 525
A tinkering slave-maker, who mends old chains   746 Juan Ded 111
Until the chains and leathers were worn through   779 Juan 2 333
Such chains as his were sure to bind   813 Juan 3 760

CHAIR
(See also ARM-CHAIR)
And marvel men should quit their easy chair   9 Harold 1 347
Thy couch of hackney, whiskey, one-horse chair   15 Harold 1 697
Placed on his chair of state, he seems a god   111 Examination 3
Pomposus fills his magisterial chair   123 Recoll 115
Her wondering betters wait behind her chair   208 Sketch 6
Mr. Scamp, you're fatigued; take your chair there, next me   280 Blues 2 29
Nor e'er before confession chair   318 Giaour 803
And he will start up from his chair, then pause   500 Faliero 1 14
Place a chair instantly. A moment's faintness   542 Faliero 5 327
In thy own chair--thy own place in the banquet   580 Sardan 4 102
He sinks!--support him!--quick--a chair--support him   625 Foscari 5 303
I'll rest me here a moment. Ho! a chair   678 Werner 1 460
He hath thrown himself into an easy chair   680 Werner 1 597
The baron was asleep in the great chair   683 Werner 2 33
The velvet chair--in his embroider'd nightgown   683 Werner 2 34
In short, I was asleep upon a chair   686 Werner 2 234
Sweeping the marble underneath her chair   865 Juan 6 859
And sitting as if nail'd upon his chair   992 Juan 16 740

CHAIRS
Groups of bad statues, tables, chairs, and pictures   843 Juan 5 751

CHAISE
(See also POST-CHAISES)
Whether they come by horse, or chaise, or coach   921 Juan 11 179

CHALDEA
By the tricks taught thee in Chaldea. Hear him   565 Sardan 2 235

CHALDEAN
Like the Chaldean he could watch the stars   37 Harold 3 118
Of the Chaldean shepherds, till they pour'd   493 Manfred 3 184
Like a Chaldean peasant to his mate   554 Sardan 1 263
To the star-read Chaldean, bears upon   561 Sardan 2 12
I would not change for your Chaldean lore   566 Sardan 2 264

CHALDEANS
Which the Chaldeans read--the restless slaves   553 Sardan 1 170

CHALDEA'S
Chaldea's seers are good   220 Belshaz-B 25
As skilful in Chaldea's worship: now   562 Sardan 2 78
And all Chaldea's starry mysteries   566 Sardan 2 251

CHALDEES
That the rebellious Medes and Chaldees, marshall'd   586 Sardan 4 545

CHALDEE'S
The Chaldee's god, which, when I gaze upon   588 Sardan 5 47

CHALET
The Chalet will be gain'd within an hour   483 Manfred 1 382

CHALICE
The poison, when pour'd from the chalice   162 Romaic-A 17
Which bears the name of Nimrod's chalice. Hence   553 Sardan 1 207

CHALK
Chalk mimics painting; then festoons are twirl'd   926 Juan 11 525

CHALKS
His careful sire chalks forth some wary plan   123 Recoll 68

CHALKY
Pleased round the chalky floor how well they trip   276 Waltz 196
At the first sight of Albion's chalky belt   915 Juan 10 516

CHALLENGE
Come on!'--That challenge is in vain   394 Corinth 865

CHAMAS'S
With 'Tu mi chamas's' from Portingale   986 Juan 16 407

CHAMBER
Let her bring from the chamber her many-toned lyre   30 Harold 2 675
'Let the chamber be clear'd.'--The train disappear'd   324 Abydos 1 32
Yes! there is light in that lone chamber   329 Abydos 2 63
And reach'd the chamber as the strain gave o'er   343 Corsair 1 364
The cloven turbans o'er the chamber spread   349 Corsair 2 174

CHAMBER

In the high chamber of his highest tower	352	Corsair	2	366
Within the Haram's secret chamber sate	357	Corsair	3	131
But in one chamber, where our path must lead	360	Corsair	3	356
From a lone chamber struck upon his sight	361	Corsair	3	401
His steps the chamber gain, his eyes behold	364	Corsair	3	597
A chamber tenantless, a steed at rest	376	Lara	2	107
Gloom o'er his chamber, cheerful was his gate	377	Lara	2	181
Within the chamber of his state	398	Parisina		133
Is this a chamber where I lie	414	Mazeppa		800
Chamber swims round and round--and shadows busy	453	Venice-B		51
The abbot show'd a chamber, where array'd	473	Morgante		477
One chamber where none enter: I would give	494	Manfred	3	209
Is here to crave your patience. Leave the chamber	505	Faliero	1	356
The lamp within my chamber. Yes, my lord	528	Faliero	4	20
To the council chamber. Duke! it may not be	536	Faliero	4	557
Into an inner chamber. Farewell, uncle	537	Faliero	4	656
Before you in your chamber at full length	540	Faliero	5	160
Guards! form the Doge's escort to his chamber	546	Faliero	5	576
A woman, the best chamber company	589	Sardan	5	119
The body hence. Where? To my proper chamber	589	Sardan	5	164
It opens to a secret chamber, placed	591	Sardan	5	248
Behind the couch in my own chamber. (Now	591	Sardan	5	249
Since it is so, farewell. Search well my chamber	593	Sardan	5	382
Within the Council Chamber. There, sir, 'tis	597	Foscari	1	92
Of yon terrific chamber are as hidden	598	Foscari	1	179
Your 'Bridge of Sighs,' your strangling chamber, and	606	Foscari	2	309
Chamber of state, her gratitude allots you	611	Foscari	3	218
You will. Where? Here, or in the ducal chamber	611	Foscari	3	222
Not so: they shall await you in my chamber	614	Foscari	3	385
Where? To the chamber where the body lies	622	Foscari	5	114
And no one walks a chamber like to ours	671	Werner	1	3
Which hath no chamber for them save beneath	672	Werner	1	28
All is in order in the damask chamber	675	Werner	1	261
The prince's chamber is prepared, with all	679	Werner	1	511
A moment in my chamber. I attend you	679	Werner	1	522
Not long since in his chamber. But these rooms	681	Werner	1	643
Away--we must to our chamber. But whence comest thou	683	Werner	1	741
But let us to our chamber. Yet one question	683	Werner	1	748
Is there no other entrance to the chamber	683	Werner	2	13
The baron's chamber, that it can't be he	683	Werner	2	22
Familiar to the chamber. Friend, how fare you	687	Werner	2	299
A prince's chamber, lay below my knife	690	Werner	2	468
Or chamber:--is the charge your own or his	691	Werner	2	543
He being lodged far off, and in a chamber	695	Werner	2	754
Lead even into the chamber of your foe	696	Werner	3	97
Where is the baron? Gone back to his chamber	699	Werner	3	282
Changed, to-day, of this chamber? for last night's	700	Werner	3	370
Again revisit Stralenheim's chamber? and	702	Werner	3	468
Of mustering the police. His chamber has	702	Werner	3	485
The countess in her chamber.--She complains	708	Werner	4	266
Portal--which open'd to the chamber, where	718	Werner	5	311
The chamber. Then, my boy! thou art guiltless still	718	Werner	5	322
And thence the chamber where you slept. If I	718	Werner	5	353
Of night which robe the chamber, or where popping	838	Juan	5	437
It was a spacious chamber (Oda is	858	Juan	6	401
There was deep silence in the chamber: dim	860	Juan	6	505
Of the 'Star Chamber' than of 'Habeas Corpus	949	Juan	13	552
The Gothic chamber, where he was enclosed	982	Juan	16	115
His chamber door wide open--and went forth	982	Juan	16	130
Back to his chamber, shorn of half his strength	983	Juan	16	200

CHAMBERER

And I obey; you bid me turn a chamberer	710	Werner	4	404

CHAMBERLAIN

Flank'd by her formidable chamberlain	308	Age		740
Than the gilt chamberlain, who, clothed and fee'd	464	Dante	4	93
The very model of a chamberlain	964	Juan	14	559

CHAMBERLAINS

And damning dulness of lord chamberlains	261	Hints		358

CHAMBERLAIN'S

Is not fenced from his chamberlain's slander, or	709	Werner	4	297

CHAMBERS

Its chambers desolate, and portals foul	20	Harold	2	47
But from the chambers came the mingling din	28	Harold	2	539
On what were chambers, arch crush'd, column strown	71	Harold	4	957
And the remember'd chambers, and the place	215	Dream		161
Of mercenaries? and her noisy chambers	304	Age		486
While Caesar's chambers and the Augustan halls	495	Manfred	3	289
How to demean himself in ducal chambers	514	Faliero	2	425
Are to keep guard on both in separate chambers	537	Faliero	4	633
Chambers: the palace has become a fortress	588	Sardan	5	62
To the ducal chambers, as he pass'd the threshold	596	Foscari	1	30

CHAMBERS

Even here, into these chambers of the unknown	598	Foscari	1	168
Ingress is given to none within those chambers	599	Foscari	1	254
For chambers? rest is all. The wretches whom	672	Werner	1	30
And lighted chambers, on my rest, and snatch	686	Werner	2	221
The outer chambers of the palace, but	686	Werner	2	228
Who shut in chambers think it loneliness	798	Juan	2	1498
A range or suite of further chambers, which	839	Juan	5	514
In kingly chambers or imperial halls	844	Juan	5	823
Back to their chambers, those long galleries	855	Juan	6	205
Huge halls, long galleries, spacious chambers, join'd	949	Juan	13	529

CHAMBER'S

For many a gilded chamber's there	313	Giaour		334

CHAMBRE

Undressing is a woe; our robe de chambre	981	Juan	16	82

CHAMELEON

Would soon restore me. I'm the true chameleon	707	Werner	4	219
It changed, of course; a heavenly chameleon	785	Juan	2	729

CHAMELEONS

Took like chameleons some slight tinge of fear	887	Juan	8	580

CHAMOIS

This way the chamois leapt: her nimble feet	482	Manfred	1	318

CHAMOIS'

As the shy chamois' eye o'erlooks the steep	427	Island	3	70

CHAMP

Fit retribution! Gaul may champ the bit	38	Harold	3	163
Their date of war, and their 'champ clos' the spheres	289	Vision		256
White is the foam of their champ on the bit	392	Corinth		700

CHAMPAGNE

For the sciences, sandwiches, hock, and champagne	283	Blues	2	157
A lobster salad, and champagne, and chat	763	Juan	1	1080
Scarcely o'erpass'd the cream of your champagne	796	Juan	2	1418
What say you to a bottle of champagne	945	Juan	13	290
And then there was champagne with foaming whirls	976	Juan	15	519
Is like the last glass of champagne, without	981	Juan	16	66
To these the invention of champagne and truffles	992	Juan	16	735

CHAMPAIGN

Champaign, dice, music, or your neighbour's spouse	250	Bards		651

CHAMPION

For he was Freedom's champion, one of those	44	Harold	3	549
And Freedom find no champion and no child	69	Harold	4	857
The forum's champion, and the people's chief	72	Harold	4	1025
Yes! where is he, the champion and the child	299	Age		49
And champion human fears.--The night approaches	487	Manfred	2	298
Champion his claims. That's well. The father whom	687	Werner	2	266
Like to the champion in the fisty ring	925	Juan	11	434
And champion him to the utmost'--he would keep it	990	Juan	16	642

CHAMPION'D

She stood as one who champion'd human fears	822	Juan	4	339

CHAMPIONS

To view these champions cheated of their fame	8	Harold	1	312
All unbought champions in no princely cause	45	Harold	3	613
Brave Champions! go on with the farce	237	Farce		1

CHANCE

Pursue what Chance or Fate proclaimeth best	20	Harold	2	60
While, chance, some scatter'd water-lily sails	65	Harold	4	602
Since chance has thrown us in the self-same sphere	94	Dorset		96
The chance of an hour may command us to part	99	L Adieu		7
Through hostile legions must abide by chance	106	Nisus		60
Vain wish! if chance some well-remember'd face	124	Recoll		193
Whom rank or chance, whom wealth or power	135	I Would		34
The chance which has lost may in future redeem you	136	Delawarr		19
Or, if it chance to wake again	148	A Fan		17
This chance is theirs, to be of use	154	Skull		24
'So now for the earth to take my chance	176	Devil's Dr		25
And, should I chance to slay the Assyrian wight	230	Murray-A		16
If chance some bard, though once by dunces fear'd	246	Bards		365
Who knows, if chance his patrons should restore	248	Bards		450
If chance some wicked wag should pass his jest	252	Bards		771
Parnassian pilgrims! ye whom chance or choice	264	Hints		577
If by some chance he walks into a well	268	Hints		815
To you, ye children of--whom chance accords	275	Waltz		101
His fate to chance, his projects to the wave	345	Corsair	1	516
Afforded hope, and offer'd chance of flight	348	Corsair	2	74
Else vainly had I pray'd or sought the chance	348	Corsair	2	91

CHANCE

Theirs is the chance--and let them use their right	353	Corsair	2	443
Chance guides his steps--a freshness seems to bear	361	Corsair	3	396
By choice the perils he by chance escaped	370	Lara	1	318
Or that 'twas chance, or some remember'd scene	381	Lara	2	470
By some strange chance, which I forget	409	Mazeppa		257
An accident should chance to touch	410	Mazeppa		346
A careless thing, who placed his choice in chance	421	Island	2	175
No further chance or choice remain'd; and right	433	Island	4	243
Good cause had he to doubt the chance of war	447	Beppo		485
I'll warn him to descend, or he may chance	482	Manfred	1	344
As it might chance to be our country's 'vantage	506	Faliero	1	461
Both honour'd by the choice or chance which leads us	616	Foscari	4	80
You were a chance and passing guest, the counterpart	676	Werner	1	319
Chance your conductor; midnight for your mantle	690	Werner	2	453
Remember, I discover'd it by chance	696	Werner	3	84
My chance at several places of resort	716	Werner	5	226
And did you so? You'll hear. Chance favour'd me	717	Werner	5	255
I turn'd, and fled--i' the dark: chance rather than	718	Werner	5	351
Chance led me here after so many moons	718	Werner	5	362
Thyself? The chance is even; we will throw	738	Deformed	2	223
And even if by chance--and who can tell	756	Juan	1	617
And swimmers, who may chance to be survivors	778	Juan	2	248
And all things, for a chance, had been cast loose	780	Juan	2	402
There was slight chance of reaching any shore	780	Juan	2	429
They thought that in such perils, more than chance	786	Juan	2	791
And warm, in case by chance he should awake	791	Juan	2	1060
Even till an iceberg it may chance to grow	829	Juan	4	799
And you and I may chance, ere morning rise	843	Juan	5	733
If fond of a chance ogle at her glass	859	Juan	6	476
What sages call Chance, Providence, or Fate	876	Juan	7	604
Juan, by some strange chance, which oft divides	881	Juan	8	209
Her life to chance; but point me out some nook	890	Juan	8	787
My chance so happen--deeds), with all who war	899	Juan	9	186
If it be chance; or if it be according	919	Juan	11	25
(A chance still), 'tis a voyage or vessel lost	946	Juan	13	312
Spared by some chance when all beside was spoil'd	948	Juan	13	484
As on the whole it is an even chance	973	Juan	15	308
By some odd chance too, he was placed between	977	Juan	15	593

CHANCED

It chanced that adverse winds once drove his bark	29	Harold	2	595
As by himself it chanced he sate apart	468	Morgante		118
If at that moment he had chanced to claw it	769	Juan	1	1477
Which in their way that moment chanced to fall	786	Juan	2	759
There chanced to be an odd male, and odd female	828	Juan	4	730
It chanced amongst the other people lotted	832	Juan	5	77
It chanced some diplomatical relations	943	Juan	13	113

CHANCELLOR

| They know the Chancellor has got | 95 | Granta | | 21 |

CHANCELLORS

| Though all Exchequer chancellors endeavour | 993 | Juan | 16 | 830 |

CHANCERY

This point, as puzzling as a Chancery suit	258	Hints		114
To a chancery suit, and messuages, and lands	751	Juan	1	290
That suit in Chancery,--which some persons plead	932	Juan	12	137
A child of Chancery, that Star-Chamber ward	997	Juan	17	28

CHANCES

Awaited but the usual chances	408	Mazeppa		174
The chances were in favour of his fall	433	Island	4	276
Their chances; they're too numerous, like the thirty	926	Juan	11	479

CHANDELIER

| Methinks the glare of yonder chandelier | 275 | Waltz | | 117 |

CHANGE

And e'en for change of scene would seek the shades below	4	Harold	1	54
Pass we the calm, the gale, the change, the tack	23	Harold	2	246
Greece, change thy lords, thy state is still the same	31	Harold	2	727
And long to change the robe of revel for the shroud	32	Harold	2	782
To change like this, a mind so far imbued	43	Harold	3	482
The sky is changed!--and such a change! Oh night	49	Harold	3	860
And now they change; a paler shadow strews	59	Harold	4	257
Change that discontented air	100	Marion		3
Yet there's pleasure, at least, in a change	116	Strephon		20

CHANGE

Newstead! what saddening change of scene is thine	121	Newstead-A		137
And change whene'er my fancy cloys	143	To--A		16
And such the change the heart displays	153	Friend-A		9
Friendship shifts with the sunbeam--thou never canst change	155	Goblet		14
Can weep no change in me	163	Parting		8
Who didst not change through all the past	167	Dead		21
Or wrong, or change, or fault in me	167	Dead		27
To trace the change to foul from fair	167	Dead		45
When she can change who loved so truly	173	Not False		11
And all thy change can be but dreaming	173	Not False		24
And if each week you change a lover	173	Quotation		21
Or change 'my life!' into 'my soul'	175	Portuguese-A		7
You call me still your life.--Oh! change the word	175	Portuguese-B		1
That with such change can calmly cope	180	Ode-A		42
Complete in kind--as various in their change	194	Monody		110
Nor Fortune change, Pride raise, nor Passion bow	208	Sketch		29
(For even to this may change of soul refer	211	Augusta-C		45
And his cheek change tempestuously--his heart	214	Dream		60
A change came o'er the spirit of my dream	214	Dream		75
A change came o'er the spirit of my dream	215	Dream		105ff
A change came o'er the spirit of my dream	216	Dream		184
My dream was past; it had no further change	216	Dream		202
Is new;' yet still from change to change we run	243	Bards		130
To change Earl Osmond's negro to a snake	260	Hints		286
And when that change was hardly well put on	294	Vision		619
Repentant of the change he made	318	Giaour		813
Which Grief could change, and Guilt could stain	319	Giaour		871
And sneer on all who cannot change	321	Giaour		1173
What change is wrought to make me shun	328	Abydos	1	427
Some change seem'd wrought within the grot	330	Abydos	2	115
Must change; but, my Zuleika, know	331	Abydos	2	194
From toil to rest, and joy in every change	338	Corsair	1	8
Nor less his change of form appall'd the sight	349	Corsair	2	143
The change to hatred were at least to feel	354	Corsair	2	518
And change the sentence I deserve to bear	359	Corsair	3	285
To hate he offer'd, with the coming change	378	Lara	2	206
Through many a change had Corinth pass'd	385	Corinth		121
With aught of change, as the eyes may seem	391	Corinth		618
With all its change of time and tide	396	Parisina		30
No check, no change, no good, no crime	405	Chillon		246
A kind of change came in my fate	405	Chillon		300
This change was wrought, too, long ere age	408	Mazeppa		195
And must their fate be hers? The eternal change	421	Island	2	159
Through every change of all the varying skies	425	Island	2	445
Those jealous whiffs, which never any change meant	446	Beppo		421
With the oft-baffled, slakeless thirst of change	457	Dante	1	115
And his spouse took his bridle on this change	468	Morgante		141
I know not what to do, till matters change	469	Morgante		192
Must change their chieftain first. Oh! I have seen	494	Manfred	3	230
Till you can change it haply for a crown	504	Faliero	1	283
And murmur deeply--any hope of change	504	Faliero	1	334
Deep at my heart--But let us change the theme	512	Faliero	2	212
But let us change the argument. My child	512	Faliero	2	270
You had been won, but thought the change your choice	514	Faliero	2	361
Vice cannot fix, and virtue cannot change	514	Faliero	2	394
And change a life of hope for one of exile	516	Faliero	2	521
In operating this great change, I claim	523	Faliero	3	297
I understand it not: why should you change	527	Faliero	3	622
Through every change. Yet, make me not a traitor	532	Faliero	4	296
May change your tone. Most true, it will do so	539	Faliero	5	72
It will not change my words, or, if it did	539	Faliero	5	74
I could not change, and would not fear.--Nay more	547	Faliero	5	627
To change the irksome theme, then, hear of vice	552	Sardan	1	140
I pray thee, change the theme: my blood disdains	554	Sardan	1	265
I like not this same sudden change of place	563	Sardan	2	117
There is some mystery: wherefore should he change it	563	Sardan	2	118
Doth he not change a thousand times a day	563	Sardan	2	119
I would not change for your Chaldean lore	566	Sardan	2	264
Changed to me only--would the change were mutual	582	Sardan	4	239
To change them, my advices bring sure tidings	586	Sardan	4	544
So that we would not change their sweet rebukes	587	Sardan	5	25
Within a human breast. I would not change	604	Foscari	2	158
Would change, for the sake of my house, the charter	607	Foscari	2	398
He knows this, or he had not sought to change them	614	Foscari	3	409
The wind may change. And if it do, it will not	616	Foscari	4	120
Change their hearts, or your lot: the galley's oars	616	Foscari	4	121
Why, what should change me? That which changes me	620	Foscari	4	322
May every element shun or change to him	652	Cain	3	434
Change us we may, but not o'erwhelm; we are	656	Heaven		120
A change at hand, and an o'erwhelming doom	658	Heaven		226
Our unexpected journey, and this change	673	Werner	1	109
What no state high or low can ever change	673	Werner	1	144
He paused to change his garments in a cottage	675	Werner	1	255

CHANGE

Small change will subdivide into a treasure	682	Werner	1	680
And hunted through each change of time, name, fortune	690	Werner	2	477
More understand each other. But to change	697	Werner	3	168
Prithee, sweet child, change--Child, indeed! I have	707	Werner	4	203
You have changed more than e'er I saw you change	707	Werner	4	217
Let's change the theme. I wish you to consider	709	Werner	4	335
The ripple of a spring change my resolve	723	Deformed	1	77
Good service. What wilt thou do for me? Change	724	Deformed	1	133
The possibility of change, I would	727	Deformed	1	328
For I, too, love a change. Your aspect is	727	Deformed	1	370
Shall change with Thetis' son, and I with Bertha	728	Deformed	1	377
Of this immortal change. In a few moments	728	Deformed	1	446
Through every change the seven-hill'd city hath	734	Deformed	1	844
Which makes me wish you'd change your lakes for ocean	745	Juan	Ded	40
Wrought change with all Armida's fairy art	755	Juan	1	567
Change horses, making history change its tune	759	Juan	1	821
The same things change their names at such a rate	802	Juan	3	46
For into a prime minister but change	803	Juan	3	107
Serenely savage, with a little change	822	Juan	4	347
Avail'd for either; neither change of place	825	Juan	4	542
The very instant, till the change that cast	825	Juan	4	549
But let me change this theme which grows too sad	825	Juan	4	585
Save change: I've stood upon Achilles' tomb	829	Juan	4	807
And then the merchant giving change, and signing	835	Juan	5	231
When he was gone, there was a sudden change	845	Juan	5	857
By way of change from their sepulchral sites	860	Juan	6	510
Of this our banquet we must sometimes change	867	Juan	6	956
Or widow, maid or mother, she can change her	904	Juan	9	509
No more it doth, its ploughs but change their boys	908	Juan	10	55
Through such a scene of change, and dread, and slaughter	914	Juan	10	442
A silent change dissolves the glittering mass	927	Juan	11	598
Change grows too changeable, without being new	928	Juan	11	646
But would not change my free thoughts for a throne	929	Juan	11	712
The obsequious landlord hath the change restored	947	Juan	13	365
Of Strongbow's talk you would not change a word	953	Juan	13	741
Of change; and how should this be otherwise	967	Juan	14	746
How oft would vice and virtue places change	968	Juan	14	805

'CHANGE

And found on 'Change a Fundling Hospital	306	Age		641
On 'Change; and even thy silver soil, Peru	930	Juan	12	47

CHANGEABLE

So changeable had been the winds that blew	786	Juan	2	798
And why? because she's changeable and chaste	908	Juan	10	81
Change grows too changeable, without being new	928	Juan	11	646
Changeable too--yet somehow 'Idem semper	998	Juan	17	83

CHANGED

In all save form alone, how changed! and who	31	Harold	2	711
Oft Music changed but never ceased her tone	32	Harold	2	757
Yet am I changed; though still enough the same	36	Harold	3	61
The sky is changed!--and such a change! Oh night	49	Harold	3	860
The cold--the changed--perchance the dead--anew	59	Harold	4	215
Is changed and solemn, like the cloudy groan	70	Harold	4	932
Thy shores are empires, changed in all save thee	82	Harold	4	1630
You say 'tis I, not you, have changed	98	To Lesbia		3
Had changed the place of declaration	101	Lady-B		26
When all I loved is changed or gone	164	Friend-B		9
When thou wert changed, they alter'd too	169	The Chain		17
And art thou changed, and canst thou hate	172	Romaic-B		28
And they are changed, and cheerless,--or if yet	192	Fragment-C		17
When fortune changed--and love fled far	209	Augusta-A		9
The Lady of his love;--Oh! she was changed	215	Dream		168
Light changed its hue, retiring from his shroud	219	Saul-B		6
But now, so callous grown, so changed since youth	256	Bards		1057
Yes, 'twas Minerva's self; but, ah! how changed	269	Minerva		75
Changed every instant--to what, none could say	294	Vision		600
Mysterious changed his countenance at least	294	Vision		612
Presto! his face changed, and he was another	294	Vision		618
And art thou, dearest, changed so much	323	Giaour		1291
And changed her cheek from pale to red	326	Abydos	1	222
My Selim, thou art sadly changed	327	Abydos	1	384
Should all be changed, to find thee faithful still	333	Abydos	2	421
His soul was changed, before his deeds had driven	342	Corsair	1	251
'Yea, strange indeed--that heart hath long been changed	344	Corsair	1	398
Yet changed since last within that cell she came	359	Corsair	3	276
I see thee shudder, but my soul is changed	360	Corsair	3	320
Who now seem'd changed and humbled:--faint and meek	363	Corsair	3	533
And they indeed were changed--'tis quickly seen	367	Lara	1	65
But Lara stirr'd not, changed not, the surprise	372	Lara	1	421
And is again; he only changed the scene	378	Lara	2	247
In hearts once changed from soft to stern	387	Corinth		323

CHANGED

So deeply changed from what he knew	391	Corinth		608
Thy heart within thee is not changed	391	Corinth		647
How changed since last her speaking eye	398	Parisina		149
Was changed for water from the moat	404	Chillon		133
They were not changed like me in frame	406	Chillon		333
Had found no native home, or found it changed	416	Island	1	30
And see thy diadem, so changed and worn	461	Dante	3	55
Look on me! the grave hath not changed thee more	490	Manfred	2	439
Than I am changed for thee. Thou lovedst me	490	Manfred	2	490
Unfix'd your quiet, you are greatly changed	512	Faliero	2	221
Has changed his slow scythe for the two-edged sword	530	Faliero	4	157
So changed from what I knew it, there glares forth	532	Faliero	4	262
That moment would have changed the face of ages	537	Faliero	4	624
And never changed their chains but for their armour	556	Sardan	1	382
If he has changed--why, so must we: the attack	563	Sardan	2	129
The night the same we destined. He hath changed	567	Sardan	2	330
A moment's pang now changed for years of crime	569	Sardan	2	500
His brows to changed expression, till at times	570	Sardan	2	534
Because it changed not; and I turn'd for refuge	579	Sardan	4	99
He loved me not: yet he seems little changed	582	Sardan	4	238
Changed to me only--would the change were mutual	582	Sardan	4	239
Once--But they have not changed. Nor ever will	582	Sardan	4	258
So changed by its convulsion, they would not	641	Cain	2	326
Perhaps even hours, ye will be changed, rent, hurl'd	659	Heaven		274
Be watch'd. If it is he, he is so changed	679	Werner	1	504
Hath changed no atom of his early nature	682	Werner	1	729
Changed, to-day, of this chamber? for last night's	700	Werner	3	370
You have changed more than e'er I saw you change	707	Werner	4	217
If not, your son does,--that the locks were changed	718	Werner	5	327
Hath changed her scarlet raiment for sackcloth	739	Deformed	2	264
Changed; for the dame grew distant, the youth shy	755	Juan	1	554
Then changed like to a bow that's bent, and then	785	Juan	2	727
It changed, of course, a heavenly chameleon	785	Juan	2	729
And always changed as true as any needle	811	Juan	3	634
The dream changed:--in a cave she stood, its walls	820	Juan	4	257
They changed from room to room--but all forgot	824	Juan	4	509
In time to his old tune; he changed the theme	824	Juan	4	522
All feelings changed, but this was last to vary	831	Juan	5	29
Poor creatures! their good looks were sadly changed	832	Juan	5	52
And changed as quickly as hearts after marriage	946	Juan	13	364

CHANGELESS

And but for that chill, changeless brow	311	Giaour		80
Which changeless rolls eternally	388	Corinth		427
Moons changing had roll'd on, and changeless found	818	Juan	4	121

CHANGELING

I am no changeling--'tis too late	391	Corinth		668

CHANGES

Yet Time, who changes all, had alter'd him	36	Harold	3	69
Which is itself, no changes bring surprise	56	Harold	4	66
When, lo! she changes in a day	97	To Woman		20
True Passion must the all-searching changes prove	201	Ode-C		34
Love swallows all changes--Hate, Ambition, Guile	341	Corsair	1	229
And, by the changes of his cheek and brow	369	Lara	1	237
One who has done great deeds, and seen great changes	518	Faliero	2	677
Why, what should change me? That which changes me	620	Foscari	4	322
But changes make not death, except to clay	638	Cain	2	163
You improve apace;--two changes in an instant	729	Deformed	1	489
Few changes e'er can better their affairs	799	Juan	2	1605
But changes night and day, too, like the sky	801	Juan	2	1706
He was a man who had seen many changes	811	Juan	3	633
The unusual quickness of these common changes	928	Juan	11	640
I have seen more changes, down from monarchs to	928	Juan	11	642
Changes in youth, to be surprised at any	936	Juan	12	392
(Who watch'd the changes of Don Juan's brow	985	Juan	16	290

CHANGING

And o'er him many changing scenes must roll	8	Harold	1	330
When all were changing thou alone wert true	18	Harold	1	875
Though alway changing, in her aspect mild	25	Harold	2	326
Patron or tyrant, as the changing mood	60	Harold	4	313
Of changing sentinels the distant hum	120	Newstead-A		53
And flies with every changing gale of spring	122	Recoil		4
As rolls the ocean's changing tide	153	Friend-A		17
And o'er the changing aspect flits	174	Impromptu-A		3
If changing cheek, and scorching vein	321	Giaour		1105
His changing cheek, his sinking heart confess	325	Abydos	1	174
To probe his heart and watch his changing cheek	341	Corsair	1	218
Worn out with toil and tired with changing blows	353	Corsair	2	415

CHANGING

To pine, the prey of every changing mood	358 Corsair	3	223
Changing its hues with bright variety	423 Island	2	342
The lady's changing cheek, as well it might	451 Beppo		706
Under its emperors, and--changing sex	730 Deformed	1	576
Moons changing had roll'd on, and changeless found	818 Juan	4	121

CHANNEL

Smiles form the channel of a future tear	35 Harold	2	916
And cross St. George's Channel and the Tweed	264 Hints		550
And left a channel bleak and bare	315 Giaour		559
These deck the shore; the waves their channel make	368 Lara	1	165
Their fountains find another channel--thus	483 Manfred	1	359
Lurk in the narrow channel which glides by	508 Faliero	1	604
But when he shrinks into his wonted channel	590 Sardan	5	203

CHANNELL'D

The channell'd waters dark and deep	314 Giaour		369
O'er channell'd rock and broken bush	406 Chillon		338

CHANNELS

Now flow in different channels	137 Clare		33
Mark, how the channels of her yellow blood	209 Sketch		65
Through thousand lazy channels in our veins	455 Venice-B		151
Of fashion,--say what streams now fill those channels	928 Juan	11	630

CHANSON

In France, for instance, he would write a chanson	812 Juan	3	681

CHANT

See! as they chant the tragic hymn, the car	57 Harold	4	140
A bard may chant too often and too long	245 Bards		226
And godly Grahame chant a stupid stave	254 Bards		924
Oh for a forty-parson power to chant	911 Juan	10	265

CHANTED

It rose, that chanted mournful strain	387 Corinth		268

CHANTERS

(See KORAN-CHANTERS)

CHANTREY

Crabbe, Malcolm, Hamilton, and Chantrey	231 Doctor		61

CHANTS

No! as he speeds, he chants 'Viva el Rey	11 Harold	1	508
While sad, she chants the solitary song	182 Address-C		27

CHAOS

Which have relapsed to chaos: here repose	63 Harold	4	483
Chaos of ruins! who shall trace the void	67 Harold	4	718
Again in crashing chaos roll'd	88 Horace		14
A mingled chaos this of war and wine	108 Nisus		230
A lump of death--a chaos of hard clay	190 Darkness		72
Its eye shall roll through chaos back	220 Clay		18
There is a war, a chaos of the mind	352 Corsair	2	328
A chaos of wild hopes and fears	400 Parisina		380
The chaos of events, where lie half-wrought	458 Dante	2	6
The bloody chaos yet expects creation	459 Dante	2	42
Whether into the marble chaos driven	464 Dante	4	60
Themselves to chaos at his high command	488 Manfred	2	374
It is an awful chaos--light and darkness	493 Manfred	3	164
Herculean, though as yet 'tis but a chaos	504 Faliero	1	311
Then--then--a chaos of all loathsome things	580 Sardan	4	159
By human passions to a human chaos	587 Sardan	5	7
Which struck a world to chaos, as a chaos	640 Cain	2	287
Of all in chaos; until they	661 Heaven		437
Ay, day will rise; but upon what?--a chaos	662 Heaven		566
The approaching chaos. Anah! Anah! my	663 Heaven		595
Its mother's.--Let the coming chaos chafe	669 Heaven		1083
First out of, and then back again to chaos	901 Juan	9	295

CHAOS-FOUNDED

Come, Anah! quit this chaos-founded prison	669 Heaven		1078

CHAOTICALLY

And thinks chaotically, as it acts	735 Deformed	1	886

CHAPEAU-BRAS

Count Chapeau-Bras, too, had a ball between	879 Juan	8	74

CHAPEL

Loud rings in air the chapel bell	96 Granta		69
That rung from a Methodist Chapel	177 Devil's Dr		110
Who lied in the Chapel	235 Pitt		3
And built herself a chapel of the seas	432 Island	4	160
An exquisite small chapel had been able	949 Juan	13	525

CHAPLAIN'S

(Ah! too regardless of his chaplain's yawn	267 Hints		764

CHAPLET

Thy chaplet must be foolscap still	227 Thurlow-B		12
Such in her chaplet infant Dian wove	368 Lara	1	163

CHAPTER

Of St. Matt. read the second and twentieth chapter	117 To Eliza		20

CHAPTERS

His prisoners, dividing them like chapters	803 Juan	3	118

CHARACTER

For character--he did not lack it	163 Blacket		15
In character--but it would not be fair	753 Juan	1	404
A busy character in the dull scene	818 Juan	4	116
And with that gentle, serious character	913 Juan	10	410
Of character, in those at least who have got any	957 Juan	14	128
Adeline, no deep judge of character	970 Juan	15	129
Juan knew nought of such a character	975 Juan	15	457

CHARACTERS

And annals graved in characters of flame	61 Harold	4	374
Matrons may sure their characters asperse	142 Soliloquy		18
The characters were still so plain	150 Harrow-C		6
True to your characters, till all be pass'd	259 Hints		181
In characters unworn by time	320 Giaour		1059
Or trace strange characters along the sand	384 Lara	2	625
New characters; the episodes are three	771 Juan	1	1597
By whose degrees all characters are class'd	987 Juan	16	427

CHARACTER'S

Of your character's panes	239 Bray		47

CHARGE

Guard thine immortal cubs, nor thy fond charge forget	68 Harold	4	792
His arctic charge around the pole	88 Anacreon-B		4
There he ne'er shall charge again	188 Ode-B		70
Up and charge, my Stratiotes	240 Suliotes		11
Around their poor old charge; who scarce knew whither	288 Vision		205
Who did not watch their charge too well	315 Giaour		466
To him this pledge I charge thee send	322 Giaour		1222
The day when Giaffir's charge was o'er	332 Abydos	2	342
They form, unite, charge, waver--all is lost	350 Corsair	2	244
'A word!--I charge thee stay, and answer here	372 Lara	1	449
When Ezzelin his charge may here unfold	375 Lara	2	23
If not the man on whom his menaced charge	377 Lara	2	135
It matters little; if they charge the foes	379 Lara	2	334
'The charge be ours! to wait for their assault	379 Lara	2	338
Meantime his followers charge, and charge again	380 Lara	2	392
A charge against him uneffaced	385 Corinth		134
Charge of the Moslem multitude	392 Corinth		748
Therefore take heed, ye Freethinkers! I charge ye	440 Beppo		24
The daring charge to raise it shall be given	464 Dante	4	58
Orlando set himself in turn to charge	470 Morgante		301
And once again, I charge thee, follow not	485 Manfred	2	94
And I do charge ye in the name--Old man	496 Manfred	3	354
Patrician, and arraign'd upon the charge	501 Faliero	1	79
Toil, charge, or duty for the state, I did not	506 Faliero	1	477
His separate charge: the Doge will now return	526 Faliero	3	516
I charge thee, give me way, or marshal me	536 Faliero	4	556
Then I may charge on horseback. Sfero, ho	573 Sardan	3	104
Be set before them, with strict charge to quit	573 Sardan	3	123
Who sent me privily upon this charge	574 Sardan	3	211
We have breathing time: yet once more charge, my friends	575 Sardan	3	263
Set on, we have them in the toil. Charge! charge	575 Sardan	3	268
My charge upon the rebels. Where's the soldier	577 Sardan	3	353
And charge once more the rebel crew who still	581 Sardan	4	184
Let me then charge! You talk like a young soldier	587 Sardan	4	564
Not clearly, and the charge of homicide	600 Foscari	1	302
Obey. I had in charge, too, from the Council	602 Foscari	2	35
Charge me with such a breach of faith. No; thou	607 Foscari	2	392
What hast thou done? Nothing. I cannot charge	617 Foscari	4	164
Or chamber:--is the charge your own or his	691 Werner	2	543
And without quibbling, to my charge. 'Tis false	715 Werner	5	170
Hold, sir, I charge you! Follow! I am proud	736 Deformed	2	124
But I must after my young charge. He is	737 Deformed	2	170
By this time i' the forum. Charge! charge	737 Deformed	2	171
The foremost in the charge or in the sally	836 Juan	5	295
And I of your young charge will take due care	858 Juan	6	374
But now I must transfer her to the charge	862 Juan	6	647
Juan was given in charge, as hath been stated	865 Juan	6	814
Of Danube's bank took formidable charge	868 Juan	7	93
And made them charge with bayonet these machines	873 Juan	7	419
The hearts of the heroic on a charge	876 Juan	7	567
The march! the charge! the shouts of either faith	878 Juan	7	694
He turn'd his eyes upon his little charge	900 Juan	9	242
This secret charge on Juan, to display	913 Juan	10	363
A goodly guardian for his infant charge	935 Juan	12	327
Our hero gladly saw his little charge	936 Juan	12	402

CHARGED
Bear hearts electric--charged with fire from Heaven	193	Monody		90
As if its lid were charged with unshed tears	215	Dream		135
And charged all faults upon the fleshly form	371	Lara	1	333
And charged to crush him--let it burst	391	Corinth		662
I am charged to tell his highness that the court	500	Faliero	1	38
Charged me to follow and inquire your pleasure	511	Faliero	2	147
Be brief. I am charged by Salemenes to	560	Sardan	1	614
I am charged to--'Tis no time for hesitation	572	Sardan	3	93
He lives--And charged me to secure your life	575	Sardan	3	245
My lord,--the soldiers are already charged	593	Sardan	5	356
I have sought you, and have found you: you are charged	715	Werner	5	154
When I first charged him with the crime--so lately	718	Werner	5	340
Till slowly charged with thunder they display	823	Juan	4	451

CHARGER
(See also BATTLE-CHARGER)
Here loud his raven charger neigh'd	312	Giaour		245
Beguiles his charger from the combat's rage	380	Lara	2	391
So that his horse, or charger, hunter, hack	959	Juan	14	255

CHARGERS
Rich are their scarfs, their chargers featly prance	15	Harold	1	733
What ho! my chargers! Never yet were better	729	Deformed	1	508

CHARGES
Finding their charges past all care below	285	Vision		18
'My charges upon record will outlast	295	Vision		657

CHARGING
There be sure was Murat charging	188	Ode-B		69
Thy name, our charging hosts along	219	Thy Days		13
When charging to the cheering cry	399	Parisina		274

CHARING
The line of lights too up to Charing Cross	921	Juan	11	201

CHARIOT
Chain'd to the chariot of triumphal Art	62	Harold	4	445
Oh thou, whose chariot roll'd on Fortune's wheel	67	Harold	4	739
A chariot in Seymour Place	176	Devil's Dr		20
Chain'd to the chariot of the chieftain's state	299	Age		48
Slave! In the victor's Chariot, when Rome triumph'd	744	Deformed	3	157
That Juan's chariot, rolling like a drum	921	Juan	11	157
Coach, chariot, luggage, baggage, equipage	946	Juan	13	346

CHARIOTEER
The charioteer along his courser's sides	108	Nisus		247

CHARIOTS
Chariots and bridles, mix'd with arms, are seen	108	Nisus		227
I fear that men must draw their chariots, as	699	Werner	3	288
Through street and square fast flashing chariots hurl'd	926	Juan	11	523

CHARIOTS'
Where the triumphal chariots' haughty march	976	Juan	15	532

CHARITABLE
So gentle, charming, charitable, chaste	938	Juan	12	527

CHARITABLY
A fourth set charitably have surmised	685	Werner	2	121

CHARITIES
With her once natural charities. But they	48	Harold	3	784

CHARITY
And the saint patronizes her 'Charity Ball	238	Pangs		4
As the saint keeps her charity back for 'the Ball	238	Pangs		8
And charity upon the hope would dwell	383	Lara	2	596
Their charity increased about their guest	790	Juan	2	1045
The virtues, even the most exalted, Charity	831	Juan	4	919
Then she was given to charity and pity	935	Juan	12	374
It grows an act of patriotic charity	941	Juan	12	707
Its motive for that charity we owe	994	Juan	16	891

CHARITY'S
Mild Charity's glow, to us mortals below	115	The Tear		9
Asking some succour for Charity's sake	225	Ode-D		6

CHARLATAN
A charlatan, a coxcomb--and have been	761	Juan	1	927

CHARLATANS
Jews, authors, generals, charlatans, combine	307	Age		710

CHARLEMAGNE
A sway surpassing that of Charlemagne	308	Age		744

CHARLEMAGNE'S
Like Charlemagne's--and all such peers in look	951	Juan	13	675

CHARLES
The royal wittol Charles, and curse the day	12	Harold	1	510
By headless Charles see heartless Henry lies	228	Windsor		2
Charles to his people, Henry to his wife	228	Windsor		5
See heartless Henry lies by headless Charles	228	Vaults		2
Charles to his people, Henry to his wife	228	Vaults		5
For which rude Charles had wept his frozen tear	300	Age		172
The wounded Charles was taught to fly	407	Mazeppa		16
And Charles of this his slender share	407	Mazeppa		93
Quoth Charles, 'Old Hetman, wherefore so	408	Mazeppa		109
And if ye marvel Charles forgot	415	Mazeppa		867
Of Charles the Emperor, whom you will find	466	Morgante		28
Have understood Charles badly, and wrote worse	466	Morgante		32
That if, like Pepin, Charles had had a writer	466	Morgante		34
And felon people whom Charles sent to hell	466	Morgante		46
Twelve paladins had Charles in court, of whom	467	Morgante		57
To him a happy seat with Charles in heaven	467	Morgante		64
Charles held; the chief, I say, Orlando was	467	Morgante		66
While Charles reposed him thus, in word and deed	467	Morgante		83
Orlando ruled court, Charles, and every thing	467	Morgante		84
To vent his spite, that thus with Charles the king	467	Morgante		86
In fact and fairness are his earning, Charles	467	Morgante		104
But much more still that Charles should give him credit	468	Morgante		120
As obstinate as Swedish Charles at Bender	892	Juan	8	852
But in the war which struck Charles from his throne	948	Juan	13	476

CHARLES'
But Charles' protecting genius hither flew	120	Newstead-A		71

CHARLES'S
Could he not beg the loan of Charles's Wain	814	Juan	3	883

CHARLEY
Much faster than ever Whig Charley went	236	True Gate		2

CHARM
Thine eyes have scarce a charm for me	17	Harold	1	852
A charm they know not; loved Parnassus fails	26	Harold	2	412
The charm of this enchanted ground	44	Harold	3	527
Eternal harmony, and sheds a charm	49	Harold	3	847
With an immaculate charm which cannot be defaced	59	Harold	4	234
A sunset charm around her, and illume	70	Harold	4	916
Is bitterer still. As charm by charm unwinds	73	Harold	4	1100
Or beauty charm the spectre from his prey	85	Epitaph		8
Could hardly charm me, when that friend was near	125	Recoll		202
To charm her ear while some remains	150	Song		7
But beauty's self hath ceased to charm	152	Weep-A		19
The spell is broke, the charm is flown	159	Spell		1
A charm, to bid thy lover live	172	Romaic-B		32
And what might make the charm still stronger	173	Quotation		15
'Tis Heaven--not man--must charm away the woe	183	Address-C		31
Some charm that well rewards another view	183	Address-D		42
And those must wait till ev'ry charm is gone	183	Address-D		45
The gay creations of his spirit charm	193	Monody		48
That sound shall charm it forth again	218	Soul-B		6
Not that a title's sounding charm can save	242	Bards		53
Sought the rapt soul to charm, nor sought in vain	243	Bards		110
Strain her fair neck, and charm the listening throng	250	Bards		631
E'en factions cease to charm a factious land	272	Minerva		276
And every charm and grace hath mix'd	310	Giaour		48
Hath lost its charm by being caught	314	Giaour		405
Till charm, and hue, and beauty gone	314	Giaour		408
Her eye's dark charm 'twere vain to tell	315	Giaour		473
But spares, as yet, the charm around her lips	364	Corsair	3	614
Beyond the sound whose charm is half divine	420	Island	2	82
Of the loud war-whoop to dispel the charm	424	Island	2	423
Of Hercules, against the sulphury charm	427	Island	3	48
I call upon ye by the written charm	479	Manfred	1	35
From thy own lip I drew the charm	481	Manfred	1	238
Nor charm in prayer, nor purifying form	492	Manfred	3	67
Accompany our guests, or charm away	551	Sardan	1	65
Had been enough to charm ye, as before	630	Cain	1	192
And make the charm effective. Take it all	724	Deformed	1	155
But then the situation had its charm	761	Juan	1	918
Yielded to the deep twilight's purple charm	797	Juan	2	1472
Have such a charm for us poor human creatures	800	Juan	2	1664
So beautiful--its very shape would charm	810	Juan	3	565
Before one charm or hope had taken wing	817	Juan	4	64
I yield thus far; but soon will break the charm	841	Juan	5	653
Or over-cold annihilates the charm	854	Juan	6	120
It would not spoil some separate charm to pare	857	Juan	6	336
The moon breaks, half unveil'd each further charm	860	Juan	6	525
Oh, thou eternal Homer! who couldst charm	877	Juan	7	625
Has Spain had heroes. While Romance could charm	942	Juan	13	84
To this grey ruin, with a voice to charm	949	Juan	13	509
With all the added charm of form and feature	974	Juan	15	412

CHARM

Which charm most people in their earlier day	974	Juan	15	419
As some who labour more and yet may charm less	980	Juan	15	752

CHARM'D

Blest by the tongues that charm'd my youthful ear	138	Harrow-B		31
These gifts were charm'd by secret spell	168	The Chain		5
As if a dream alone had charm'd	173	Not False		22
Seems Sorrow's softness charm'd from its despair	175	Sonnet-A		4
From the charm'd council to the festive board	193	Monody		37
Which charm'd our days in each Aegean clime	261	Hints		345
Where every hue that charm'd before	322	Giaour		1198
Charm'd with each other, all things charm'd that brought	819	Juan	4	159
Which charm'd the charming Mary Montagu	831	Juan	5	24
The dice seem'd charm'd, too, with his repartees	952	Juan	13	688

CHARMED

The charmed ocean's pausing	188	Music-C		6

CHARMER

Charms from the charmer, yet some never grow	844	Juan	5	783

CHARMERS

Like other charmers, wooing the caress	425	Island	2	456
Beyond the charmers we have already cited	974	Juan	15	380
The charming of these charmers, who seem bound	985	Juan	16	314

CHARMING

Charming the eye with dread--a matchless cataract	65	Harold	4	639
Oh! who hath power of charming	219	Vanity		20
Where I just had been skimming a charming critique	277	Blues	1	22
'Tis true, your budding Miss is very charming	445	Beppo		305
'That charming passage in the last new poem	449	Beppo		576
A charming woman whom we like to see	450	Beppo		668
His death contrived to spoil a charming cause	751	Juan	1	261
At six a charming child, and at eleven	753	Juan	1	386
At six, I said, he was a charming child	753	Juan	1	393
Was married, charming, chaste, and twenty-three	754	Juan	1	472
Which, with a little patience, might grow charming	757	Juan	1	688
The charming creatures lie with such a grace	768	Juan	1	1423
Which charm'd the charming Mary Montagu	831	Juan	5	24
How beauteous are rouleaus! how charming chests	931	Juan	12	89
Her charming figure and romantic history	933	Juan	12	215
So gentle, charming, charitable, chaste	938	Juan	12	527
As if each charming word were a decree	978	Juan	15	652
The charming of these charmers, who seem bound	985	Juan	16	314

CHARMS

To paint those charms which varied as they beam'd	3	To Ianthe		7
Who soon had left her charms for vulgar bliss	4	Harold	1	43
Her mind is nobler sure, her charms perchance as great	13	Harold	1	593
To charms as fair as those that soothed his happier day	17	Harold	1	836
Hard is his heart whom charms may not enslave	22	Harold	2	142
Converse with Nature's charms and view her stores unroll'd	23	Harold	2	225
What rainbow tints, what magic charms are found	26	Harold	2	427
For thy destructive charms; then, still untired	61	Harold	4	381
Charms, kindred, children--with the silver gray	70	Harold	4	920
Where are the charms and virtues which we dare	73	Harold	4	1094
Securely views thy matchless charms	87	Ad Lesbiam		4
And clasp enraptured all your charms	91	Caroline-B		42
But, placed in all thy charms before me	97	To Woman		5
This faint resemblance of thy charms	98	To Mary		1
Wafting destruction o'er thy charms	99	Young Lady		2
Unworthy with such charms to dwell	102	Alva		74
The vision charms the hours away	113	Quaker		33
And I must view thy charms no more	155	Lady-E		10
With charms perchance as fair to view	156	Lady-F		56
All charms which heedless hearts can move	158	Florence		18
Thy charms might raise new Antonies	159	Gulf		16
And if their charms be fair to view	160	Cadiz		19
In each her charms the heart must move	160	Cadiz		49
Is hush'd, and all their charms are fled	165	Away		10
And form so soft, and charms so rare	167	Dead		3
That all those charms have pass'd away	167	Dead		35
Thy youth, thy charms, thy tenderness	174	Remember-B		37
Amidst those pictured charms, whose loveliness	183	Address-D		15
Shivering thine imaged charms and all	201	Ode-C		73
Those Charms would win	201	Ode-C		74
The Tolbooth felt defrauded of his charms	248	Bards		478
With art the charms which nature could not spare	250	Bards		665
Swell the young heart with visionary charms	272	Minerva		291
Muse of the many-twinkling feet! whose charms	273	Waltz		1
Who wisely wish the charms you view to reap	276	Waltz		232
Shrunk from the charms it meant to praise	315	Giaour		514
The nameless charms unmark'd by her alone	325	Abydos	1	177
With thee all toils are sweet, each clime hath charms	333	Abydos	2	452

CHARMS

In all the wildness of dishevell'd charms	345	Corsair	1	471
Each bears a prize of unregarded charms	350	Corsair	2	216
But what her words avouch'd, her charms had done	359	Corsair	3	246
When wearier of these fleeting charms and me	360	Corsair	3	340
The well-worn charms success was sure to snatch	378	Lara	2	209
Thou saw'st, and covetedst her charms	399	Parisina		256
Till Parisina's fatal charms	399	Parisina		324
Could these have charms for rudest sea-boys, driven	417	Island	1	111
Such sounds are utter'd, and such charms display'd	455	Dante	Ded	12
Her charms to pontiffs proud, who but employ	464	Dante	4	87
The charms of earth's least mortal daughters grow	485	Manfred	2	109
On lesser charms, for no cause save that such	583	Sardan	4	338
Of many charms in her as natural	753	Juan	1	437
The charms of maid, wife, and still less of widow	773	Juan	1	1722
Sustain'd his head upon her bosom's charms	798	Juan	2	1556
And all its charms, like death without its terrors	799	Juan	2	1576
Of charms to make good gold and cure bad ails	805	Juan	3	269
Charms from the charmer, yet some never grow	844	Juan	5	783
Some stress on charms, which seldom are, if e'er	847	Juan	5	1029
His Highness gazed upon Gulbeyaz' charms	854	Juan	6	102
From ogling all their charms from breasts to backs	856	Juan	6	232
With the most regulated charms of feature	859	Juan	6	411
But Juan never left them, while they had charms	885	Juan	8	424
Thought not upon the charms of four young brides	892	Juan	8	906
Whose charms made all men speak, and women dumb	942	Juan	13	102
Down to the harp--because to music's charms	954	Juan	13	855
Of charms that should or should not be admired	954	Juan	13	862
The charms of other days, in starlight gleams	982	Juan	16	146

CHARNEL

In their proud charnel of Thermopylae	455	Venice-B		156

CHARON'S

Of Charon's ferry; you forget that his	294	Vision		573
Like Charon's bark of spectres, dull and pale	786	Juan	2	803

CHART

The ocean hath his chart, the stars their map	67	Harold	4	724
Before them burns the lamp, and spreads the chart	346	Corsair	1	587
I dare them to the proof, the chart of what	607	Foscari	2	371
With such a chart as may be safely stuck to	938	Juan	12	557
Such are--but I have lost the London Chart	944	Juan	13	216
Frail mariners afloat without a chart	964	Juan	14	589

CHARTA

Though marvelling at the name of Magna Charta	111	Examination		17

CHARTER

The charter to chastise which she bestows	44	Harold	3	551
Religion's charter their protecting shield	120	Newstead-A		39
Recalls the woes of Nature's charter	159	Spell		6
And higher beings suffer; 'tis the charter	544	Faliero	5	462
Would change, for the sake of my house, the charter	607	Foscari	2	398

CHARTERS

There Montmorenci, the sworn foe to charters	307	Age		716
Rise! for yours are holier charters	736	Deformed	2	112

CHARTS

Whose charts lay down its current to a hair	852	Juan	6	12

CHASE

Though sluggards deem it but a foolish chase	9	Harold	1	346
All join the chase, but few the triumph share	10	Harold	1	438
Thin the closed ranks, and lead in Glory's fearful chase	13	Harold	1	575
For a time they abandon the cave and the chase	30	Harold	2	662
To chase the glowing Hours with flying feet	38	Harold	3	194
No more her heroes urge the chase	102	Alva		23
'Tis his to chase the bounding roe	102	Alva		106
'Nor chase nor wave my boy delay	103	Alva		110
The drops of death each other chase	104	Alva		235
Thine altars with the produce of the chase	110	Nisus		346
Outstrip and vanquish'd in the mental chase	119	Answer-A		14
What fears, what anxious hopes, attend the chase	121	Newstead-A		126
Or chase with nimble feet its rapid course	124	Recoil		132
And chase the phantom of what once was mine	127	Recoil		378
has been the chase of the roebuck, and the	130	Calmar		66
'Never more shall Calmar chase the	131	Calmar		171
'What were the chase to me alone? Who	131	Calmar		173
Nor through the groves of Ida chase	133	E. N. Long		21
Like Israel's pillar, chase the night from heaven	169	Address-A		8
Still there are follies, e'en for me to chase	242	Bards		41
Mightiest of all Dunedin's beasts of chase	265	Hints		597
And chase the sultriness of day	313	Giaour		300
A weary chase and wasted hour	314	Giaour		393

CHASE

A chase of idle hopes and fears	314 Giaour		398
The unwonted chase each hour employs	314 Giaour		441
And scarcely in the chase could cope	325 Abydos	1	136
The swain, and chase the boatman's fear	329 Abydos	2	56
With thought of years in phantom chase misspent	370 Lara	1	325
Their sport, the dashing breakers and the chase	416 Island	1	47
The chase, the race, the liberty to roam	422 Island	2	248
'About?--Whate'er may have us now in chase	426 Island	2	516
And now the two canoes in chase divide	429 Island	3	233
The depths where divers hold the pearl in chase	431 Island	4	112
Who, disappointed of their former chase	433 Island	4	237
The Doge stands to behold the chase of bulls	539 Faliero	5	94
Health like the chase, nor glory like the war	551 Sardan	1	26
Even in the chase. Hast ever seen them, brother	556 Sardan	1	367
To one wide desert chase of brutes, who were	557 Sardan	1	422
Or my wild grandam's chase in search of kingdoms	571 Sardan	3	6
The chase of Fortune; now she hath o'ertaken	672 Werner	1	62
You may have better luck another chase	699 Werner	3	281
All ready for the chase? The dogs are order'd	705 Werner	4	75
The toils of Monday: 'twas a noble chase	705 Werner	4	81
Engaged in the chase, draw off the eighty men	705 Werner	4	105
Until the chase begins; then draw thou off	706 Werner	4	135
Count Ulric from the chase to-day. You will not	707 Werner	4	209
Sweet Ida, wish me a fair chase, and I	707 Werner	4	225
The chase with such an ardour as will scarce	708 Werner	4	237
Chase this man from my mind, although my senses	714 Werner	5	118
As the free chase they follow, do not spurn me	722 Deformed	1	19
But the chase hath no story	742 Deformed	3	44
Of empire and chase	742 Deformed	3	47
His hell-dogs, and their chase, and the fair throng	815 Juan	3	942
With us there is more law given to the chase	847 Juan	5	980
By the resistance of the chase they batter'd	883 Juan	8	296
A sylvan tribe of children of the chase	886 Juan	8	514
Thou art no novice in the headlong chase	932 Juan	12	182
Rife with more horns than hounds--she hath the chase	951 Juan	13	618
Who, after a long chase o'er hills, dales, bushes	959 Juan	14	278
To early risers after a long chase	960 Juan	14	282

CHASED

The boys in childhood chased the roe	102 Alva		55
Where love chased each fast-fleeting year	115 The Tear		26
And chased away the gloom profound	134 E. N. Long		96
They flew, and fast their fierce pursuers chased	429 Island	3	230
That eve the strangers chased them from the shore	435 Island	4	396
By Neuha, asking where they had been chased	435 Island	4	410
I thank thee, Night! for thou hast chased away	529 Faliero	4	106
Which chased the first-born out of Paradise	669 Heaven		1051
By Sallust in his Catiline, who, chased	866 Juan	6	886

CHASING

On with the giddy circle, chasing Time	37 Harold	3	98
Chasing the shades of envious night	142 Critics		93

CHASMS

With his fierce footsteps, yield in chasms a fearful vent	65 Harold	4	630

CHASSEURS

He found a number of Chasseurs, all scatter'd	883 Juan	8	295

CHASTE
(See also HALF-CHASTE)

Had been pollution into aught so chaste	4 Harold	1	42
Tomb'd in a palace? Was she chaste and fair	70 Harold	4	893
You may be prudent, fair, and chaste	91 Caroline-B		47
Her impulse chaste must needs refuse	100 Marion		22
When, as chaste Dian, here thou deign'st to rove	110 Nisus		344
But here I'll close my chaste Description	144 Becher-B		29
Or tracest chaste descriptions on thy page	245 Bards		271
Be warm, but pure; be amorous, but be chaste	246 Bards		306
Were quaint and careless, anything but chaste	262 Hints		430
What glory to the chaste Venetian dames	542 Faliero	5	315
My martial grandam, chaste Semiramis	555 Sardan	1	286
Was married, charming, chaste, and twenty-three	754 Juan	1	472
Which time hath lately render'd much more chaste	755 Juan	1	530
Who call'd her Chaste, methinks, began too soon	760 Juan	1	899
Here my chaste Muse a liberty must take	761 Juan	1	953
Chaste Muse!--well, if you must, you must)--the veil	775 Juan	2	49
Pressure of hands, perhaps even a chaste kiss	795 Juan	2	1311
Thou mak'st the chaste connubial state precarious	800 Juan	2	1641
Chaste reader, then, in any way to put	803 Juan	3	91
Some chaste liaison of the kind--I mean	804 Juan	3	194
True knights, chaste dames, huge giants, kings despotic	817 Juan	4	46
Here I might enter on a chaste description	828 Juan	4	769
She rose, and pausing one chaste moment, threw	847 Juan	5	999
With all their chaste integrity of laws	859 Juan	6	461
And then she gave Juanna a chaste kiss	859 Juan	6	465
Had made them chaste;--they ravish'd very little	894 Juan	8	1024
Of light to save the venerably chaste	895 Juan	8	1038

CHASTE

Is when chaste matrons to their other ties	906 Juan	9	607
And why? because she's changeable and chaste	908 Juan	10	81
Made the chaste Catherine look a little grim	913 Juan	10	347
'Here are chaste wives, pure lives; here people pay	919 Juan	11	73
So gentle, charming, charitable, chaste	938 Juan	12	527
Chaste was she, to detraction's desperation	942 Juan	13	105
In my young days, that chaste and goodly veil	958 Juan	14	210
Chaste were his steps, each kept within due bound	960 Juan	14	305
The chaste, and those who are not so much inspired	960 Juan	14	326
This sort of chaste liaison for a friend	963 Juan	14	508
Whether Don Juan and chaste Adeline	967 Juan	14	769
Was there chaste dame who had not in her head	972 Juan	15	252
The chaste description even of a 'becasse	977 Juan	15	568
It happen'd luckily, the chaste orb shone	982 Juan	16	99
Of knights and dames heroic and chaste too	982 Juan	16	133
And dreading the chaste echoes of her shoe	995 Juan	16	944

CHASTELY

Sad rakes to sadder husbands chastely taming	957 Juan	14	141

CHASTELY-AWFUL

E'er deign'd to bend her chastely-awful eyes	17 Harold	1	822

CHASTEN

Who chasten, with unsparing spirit	137 Clare		56
(Who chasten and who purify our hearts	587 Sardan	5	24
Prolongs my days to prove and chasten me	621 Foscari	5	50

CHASTEN'D

And meditation chasten'd down, enough	58 Harold	4	165
Chasten'd bow, and mock humility	196 Rogers		29
He had been tempted, chasten'd, and the chain	361 Corsair	3	420
Chasten'd and visited, I needs must think	617 Foscari	4	167
Chasten'd, subdued, out-worn, and taught to know	674 Werner	1	155
Which struggled through and chasten'd down the whole	754 Juan	1	480
In the more chasten'd domes of Western kings	843 Juan	5	747

CHASTENER

Before the Chastener humbly let me bow	35 Harold	2	922

CHASTENING

Gifford perchance, shall raise the chastening song	251 Bards		702

CHASTENS

While the Lord's servant chastens whom he loves	262 Hints		381

CHASTER

Start not! still chaster reader--she'll be nice hence	761 Juan	1	954
That--but my chaster ear will not receive	935 Juan	12	340

CHASTEST

The loveliest, chastest, best, but--quite a fool	830 Juan	4	888
Like chastest wives from constant husbands' sides	881 Juan	8	211
His youth was not the chastest that might be	914 Juan	10	430
Unless I knew the very chastest squares	944 Juan	13	208

CHASTISE

The charter to chastise which she bestows	44 Harold	3	551
And wink at faults they tremble to chastise	93 Dorset		16

CHASTISED

Good is rewarded, and chastised the ill	472 Morgante		391

CHASTISEMENT

On thee a double chastisement	195 Ballad-A		52
Such chastisement as will enforce respect	509 Faliero	2	30

CHASTITY

Ye, who have kept your chastity when young	847 Juan	5	1034
Their chastity in these unhappy climes	851 Juan	5	1251
And as for chastity, you'll never bind it	940 Juan	12	637

CHAT

And passing bow'd and mingled with her chat	448 Beppo		550
A lobster salad, and champagne, and chat	763 Juan	1	1080
Relieved her thoughts; dull silence and quick chat	824 Juan	4	502
To meet. However, 'tis no time to chat	924 Juan	11	350

CHATEAUBRIAND

There Chateaubriand forms new books of martyrs	307 Age		714

CHATELAINS

Their maintenance: the Chatelains must keep	676 Werner	1	340

CHATHAM

For the life of a Fox, of a Chatham the death	129 Becher-A		17
And Chatham, so like his friend Billy	177 Devil's Dr		144

CHATHAM
But Grey was not arrived, and Chatham gone | 940 Juan | 12 | 656

CHATTED
Others in monosyllable talk chatted | 838 Juan | 5 | 419

CHATTER
A smatter and chatter, gleaned out of reviews | 280 Blues | 2 | 22
My teeth begin to chatter, my veins freeze | 769 Juan | 1 | 1446
Have sung, or even a Dandy's dandiest chatter | 849 Juan | 5 | 1140
Began to sing, dance, chatter, smile, and play | 856 Juan | 6 | 272
And will not toss and chatter the night through | 858 Juan | 6 | 390

CHAUCER
What Chaucer, Spenser did, we scarce refuse | 257 Hints | | 81
Were satisfied with Chaucer and old Ben | 262 Hints | | 428

CHAUNT
To chaunt the sweet and hallow'd vesper | 160 Cadiz | | 48

CHE
Voi che entrate!' The hinge seem'd to speak | 995 Juan | 16 | 971

CHEAP
And think her ransom cheap that day | 195 Ballad-A | | 99
The precious bargain's cheap--in faith, not I | 247 Bards | | 392
Say--would you make those beauties quite so cheap | 276 Waltz | | 233

CHEAPEN'D
The king himself had cheapen'd it, but thought | 988 Juan | 16 | 493

CHEAPENING
Cheapening an ox, an ass, a lamb, or kid | 835 Juan | 5 | 222

CHEAPLY
Fame, fame is cheaply earn'd by fleeting breath | 106 Nisus | | 51
Bought their freedom, and cheaply, with blood | 229 Lads | | 2
With death alone are laurels cheaply bought | 272 Minerva | | 294
A blessing cheaply purchased, the world knows | 304 Age | | 452
Rights cheaply earn'd with blood.--Still, still, for ever | 455 Venice-B | | 148
To sell my life--not cheaply. Now, Count Ulric | 719 Werner | 5 | 399

CHEAT
Thy love is lust, thy friendship all a cheat | 154 Dog | | 19
That very cheat had cheer'd me then | 413 Mazeppa | | 621
A most enervating and filthy cheat | 637 Cain | 2 | 57

CHEATED
To view these champions cheated of their fame | 8 Harold | 1 | 312
That cheated us in slumber only | 173 Not False | | 17
Who bid pretty well--but they cheated him, though | 177 Devil's Dr | | 90
Till the eye, cheated, opens thick with tears | 791 Juan | 2 | 1072

CHEATING
Saving his soul by cheating in the ware | 870 Juan | 7 | 212

CHEATS
The future cheats us from afar | 223 Music-D | | 10

CHECK
The skill that yet may check his mad career | 16 Harold | 1 | 759
Did you inspire a cheer which he forbore to check | 37 Harold | 3 | 144
In vain I check the rising sighs | 112 Quaker | | 9
And check each impulse with prudential rein | 123 Recoll | | 60
To check my bosom's fondest thought | 133 E. N. Long | | 15
You must not check a Young Beginner | 144 Becher-B | | 16
Could nobly check its useless sighs | 167 Euthanasia | | 14
For God's sake, my Lady Bluebottle, check not | 282 Blues | 2 | 133
Thus arm'd with beauty would she check | 315 Giaour | | 512
Scarce had they time to check the rein | 316 Giaour | | 574
There lie the only rocks our course can check | 334 Abydos | 2 | 460
And check the very hands with gore imbrued | 350 Corsair | 2 | 220
Command nor duty could their transport check | 363 Corsair | 3 | 497
With none to check and few to point in time | 366 Lara | 1 | 17
It was too late to check the wasting brand | 379 Lara | 2 | 278
To check the headlong fury of that crew | 379 Lara | 2 | 291
We check those waters of the heart | 402 Parisina | | 562
No check, no change, no good, no crime | 405 Chillon | | 246
As youth is apt in, so as not to check | 514 Faliero | 2 | 359
States, stung humanity will rise to check it | 623 Foscari | 5 | 149
Inadequate thanks, you almost check even them | 685 Werner | 2 | 150
I mount. Rodolph, our friends have had a check | 705 Werner | 4 | 93
Which rushes to some shore whose shingles check | 865 Juan | 6 | 863
Men's wrongs, and rather check than punish crimes | 942 Juan | 13 | 62

CHECK'D
(See also INTERCHECK'D)
But, check'd by every tie, I may not dare | 24 Harold | 2 | 268
Check'd by thy columns, fell more sadly fair | 269 Minerva | | 68
A moment check'd his wheeling steed | 312 Giaour | | 218
He saw their terror, check'd the first despair | 349 Corsair | 2 | 161
Its pulse nor check'd--nor quicken'd--calmly cold | 354 Corsair | 2 | 512

CHECK'D
And Alp's career a moment check'd | 393 Corinth | | 848
Since it must be so, and this churl has check'd | 552 Sardan | 1 | 101
Until 'tis spilt or check'd--how soon, I care not | 671 Werner | 1 | 11
Your messengers were all check'd like myself | 687 Werner | 2 | 313
For ne'er till now she knew a check'd desire | 848 Juan | 5 | 1070
Even ye who know what a check'd woman is | 848 Juan | 5 | 1071

CHECKER'D
Still lingering pause above each checker'd leaf | 127 Recoll | | 405
That checker'd o'er the living stream | 314 Giaour | | 379
For checker'd as is seen our human lot | 889 Juan | 8 | 707

CHECKERING
Far checkering o'er the pictured window, plays | 366 Lara | 1 | 7
Some dusky shadow checkering the Rialto | 529 Faliero | 4 | 101

CHECKS
And checks his song to execrate Godoy | 12 Harold | 1 | 509
Her fellows flee--she checks their base career | 13 Harold | 1 | 578
Or checks the sympathetic sigh | 133 E. N. Long | | 36
There checks his speed, but pauses, less to breathe | 346 Corsair | 1 | 535
That checks low mirth but lacks not courtesy | 346 Corsair | 1 | 544
Checks to a lake, whose waves in circles spread | 792 Juan | 2 | 1127
If free from passion, which all friendship checks | 967 Juan | 14 | 741

CHEEK
Will blanch a faithful cheek | 6 Harold | 1 | 165
Hath Phoebus woo'd in vain to spoil her cheek | 13 Harold | 1 | 599
False to the heart, distorts the hollow cheek | 35 Harold | 2 | 912
The smoothness and the sheen of beauty's cheek | 36 Harold | 3 | 93
With breath all incense and with cheek all bloom | 50 Harold | 3 | 915
Nor coin'd my cheek to smiles, nor cried aloud | 52 Harold | 3 | 1052
And print on thy soft cheek a parent's kiss | 53 Harold | 3 | 1081
Feeding on thy sweet cheek; while thy lips are | 62 Harold | 4 | 457
Of her consuming cheek the autumnal leaf-like red | 70 Harold | 4 | 918
That cheek, which ever dimpling glows | 87 Ad Lesbiam | | 5
Thou couldst not feel my burning cheek | 90 Caroline-A | | 13
Your cheek no sign of love betrays | 90 Caroline-B | | 4
And mantle through my purpled cheek | 90 Caroline-B | | 10
So chill's the pressure of your cheek | 91 Caroline-B | | 43
Down a cheek which outrivals thy bosom in hue | 99 L Adieu | | 18
And pensive seem'd his cheek, and pale | 102 Alva | | 64
And Angus' cheek with wonder glows | 103 Alva | | 195
With tears the burning cheek of each bedew'd | 107 Nisus | | 129
No fainting mother's lips have press'd my cheek | 108 Nisus | | 186
Nor dare to call the blush from Beauty's cheek | 113 Prologue | | 6
What sister's gentle kiss has prest my cheek | 125 Recoll | | 226
This cheek now pale from early riot | 134 Lady-D | | 30
While every cheek with Laughter glows | 139 Anacreon-C | | 6
Affection's tale upon the cheek | 144 Jessy | | 14
Pale grew thy cheek and cold | 151 When We | | 5
Seem'd stealing o'er thy brilliant cheek | 152 Remind | | 23
And made my cheek belie my heart | 164 Friend-B | | 34
Thy cheek is pale with thought, but not from woe | 175 Sonnet-B | | 1
With its hollow cheek, and eyes half shut | 176 Devil's Dr | | 73
But the tear which now burns on my cheek may impart | 182 Music-A | | 3
'Tis not on youth's smooth cheek the blush alone, which fades so fast | 185 Music-B | | 3
A cheek of parchment, and an eye of stone | 209 Sketch | | 64
And his cheek change tempestuously--his heart | 214 Dream | | 60
And on that cheek, and o'er that brow | 216 She Walks | | 13
With sparkling eyes, and cheek by passion flush'd | 245 Bards | | 285
With broken lyre and cheek serenely pale | 247 Bards | | 418
And tinge with red the female reader's cheek | 249 Bards | | 556
Flush in the cheek and languish in the eyes | 276 Waltz | | 225
And there he sits by St. Paul, cheek by jowl | 287 Vision | | 155
Her eye, her cheek, betray no inward strife | 308 Age | | 761
There, mildly dimpling, Ocean's cheek | 310 Giaour | | 12
The languor of the placid cheek | 311 Giaour | | 77
That livid cheek, that stony air | 319 Giaour | | 907
If changing cheek, and scorching vein | 321 Giaour | | 1105
His pensive cheek and pondering brow | 324 Abydos | 1 | 30
His changing cheek, his sinking heart confess | 325 Abydos | 1 | 174
And changed her cheek from pale to red | 326 Abydos | 1 | 222
Thy cheek, thine eyes, thy lips to kiss | 328 Abydos | 1 | 394
At least I feel my cheek, too, blushing | 328 Abydos | 1 | 399
Would make thy waning cheek more pale | 332 Abydos | 2 | 314
And woman's eye is wet, man's cheek is pale | 335 Abydos | 2 | 622
As weeping Beauty's cheek at Sorrow's tale | 337 Abydos | 2 | 732
And tints each swarthy cheek with sallower hue | 340 Corsair | 1 | 176
Sunburnt his cheek, his forehead high and pale | 341 Corsair | 1 | 203
To probe his heart and watch his changing cheek | 341 Corsair | 1 | 218
Flush in the cheek, or damp upon the brow | 341 Corsair | 1 | 242
And pale his cheek with penance, not from fears | 347 Corsair | 2 | 56
Along his cheek, and tranquillized as fast | 348 Corsair | 2 | 110
That form, with eye so dark and cheek so fair | 353 Corsair | 2 | 402
Dash o'er her deathlike cheek the ocean dew | 357 Corsair | 3 | 117
More pale her cheek, more tremulous her frame | 359 Corsair | 3 | 277
Had banish'd all the beauty from her cheek | 361 Corsair | 3 | 427
But varying oft the colour of her cheek | 363 Corsair | 3 | 534
These and the pale pure cheek became the bier | 364 Corsair | 3 | 621

CHEEK

And, by the changes of his cheek and brow	369	Lara	1	237
The cheek where oft the unbidden blush shone through	373	Lara	1	531
Another sex, when match'd with that smooth cheek	374	Lara	1	577
The lip of ashes, and the cheek of flame	374	Lara	1	599
With cheek unchanging from its sallow gloom	376	Lara	2	57
And he felt not a breath come over his cheek	390	Corinth		529
The rose was yet upon her cheek	390	Corinth		546
And her cheek grows pale, and her heart beats quick	396	Parisina		24
And red her cheek with troubled dreams	397	Parisina		70
But never tear his cheek descended	402	Parisina		537
With all the while a cheek whose bloom	404	Chillon		190
A cheek and lip--but why proceed	409	Mazeppa		224
May peck unpierced each frozen cheek	411	Mazeppa		481
Yet full of life--for through her tropic cheek	420	Island	2	135
Along his cheek was livid now as lead	427	Island	3	88
While all agreed that in his cheek and eye	431	Island	4	89
From the rich peasant cheek of ruddy bronze	445	Beppo		354
You still may mark her cheek, out-blooming all	450	Beppo		672
The lady's changing cheek, as well it might	451	Beppo		706
(Carnation'd like a sleeping infant's cheek	485	Manfred	2	112
Can this be death? there's bloom upon her cheek	490	Manfred	2	468
And hueless cheek, and thine unquiet motions	531	Faliero	4	234
To look upon her, and her kindled cheek	577	Sardan	3	387
Back to your cheek: Heaven send you strength to bear	597	Foscari	1	131
Thy cheek is flush'd with an unnatural hue	649	Cain	3	186
Of rank and ancestry? in this worn cheek	673	Werner	1	118
Love lay not down his cheek there): some strong bias	710	Werner	4	353
Till the rose in his cheek	728	Deformed	1	389
Her cheek all purple with the beam of youth	754	Juan	1	484
Glow'd in her cheek, and yet she felt no wrong	759	Juan	1	842
Waved and o'ershading her wan cheek, appears	766	Juan	1	1260
But press'd her bloodless lip to Juan's cheek	767	Juan	1	1352
Of a soft cheek and aspect delicate	785	Juan	2	698
And her transparent cheek, all pure and warm	788	Juan	2	908
From heart to cheek is curb'd into a blush	792	Juan	2	1124
For still he lay, and on his thin worn cheek	792	Juan	2	1169
And look'd upon the lady, in whose cheek	793	Juan	2	1194
Breathing all gently o'er his cheek and mouth	795	Juan	2	1343
And then on the pale cheek her breast now warms	799	Juan	2	1558
Now pillow'd cheek to cheek, in loving sleep	820	Juan	4	225
Then turn'd to Juan, in whose cheek the blood	821	Juan	4	309
The old man's cheek grew pale, but not with dread	821	Juan	4	315
The second had his cheek laid open; but	822	Juan	4	385
And into her clear cheek the blood was brought	845	Juan	5	860
One with her flush'd cheek laid on her white arm	860	Juan	6	521
Her cheek began to flush, her eyes to sparkle	864	Juan	6	807
Her cheek turn'd ashes, ears rung, brain whirl'd round	865	Juan	6	837
As he turn'd o'er each pale and gory cheek	890	Juan	8	750
O'erspreads the cheek which seems too pure for clay	908	Juan	10	63
Will feed upon the fairest, freshest cheek	912	Juan	10	299
Along his wasted cheek, and seem'd to gravel	912	Juan	10	343
Pale as if painted so; her cheek being red	989	Juan	16	554
And something like a smile upon her cheek	992	Juan	16	778

CHEEKS

In vain fair cheeks were furrow'd with hot tears	38	Harold	3	173
And cheeks all pale, which but an hour ago	38	Harold	3	210
Her swollen cheeks with weeping glow	88	Catullus		22
For this these tears our cheeks bedew	89	To Emma		38
But when our cheeks with anguish glow'd	90	Caroline-A		9
The cheeks which sprung from beauty's mould	98	To Mary		7
What smiles the lovers' cheeks adorn	103	Alva		172
Already reddening on thy guilty cheeks	358	Corsair	3	183
The swarthy blush recolours in his cheeks	369	Lara	1	226
But oft our eyes met, and our cheeks in hue	477	Francesca		34
On sallow cheeks and sunken eyes, which should not	528	Faliero	4	49
Back to my heart, and left my cheeks like thine	609	Foscari	3	49
How lovely he appears! his little cheeks	646	Cain	3	10
His cheeks are reddening into deeper smiles	646	Cain	3	26
Blood! Why does yours start from your cheeks? Ay! doth it	706	Werner	4	157
Their large black eyes, and soft seraphic cheeks	805	Juan	3	258
The bloom, too, had return'd to Haidee's cheeks	806	Juan	3	302
And left his cheeks as pale as snowdrops blowing	846	Juan	5	934
Or said her cheeks assumed the deepest dyes	848	Juan	5	1067
Between the eyes, and Lolah on both cheeks	858	Juan	6	394
Good hours of fair cheeks are the fairest tinters	955	Juan	13	887

CHEEK'S

Your cheek's soft bloom is unimpair'd	98	To Lesbia		29
On her fair cheek's unfading hue	315	Giaour		493
Her cheek's last tinge, her eye's last spark	318	Giaour		772
Her brow was white and low, and her cheek's pure dye	789	Juan	2	937
Who gazed upon her cheek's transcendent hue	857	Juan	6	331

CHEEKS'

| Kiss thy soft cheeks' blooming tinge | 160 | Maid | | 10 |

CHEER

The heartless parasites of present cheer	5	Harold	1	76
As whilome he was wont the leagues to cheer	11	Harold	1	506
Nor niggard of his cheer; the passer by	27	Harold	2	439
If aught that's kindred cheer the welcome hearth	34	Harold	2	855
Still o'er the features, which perforce they cheer	35	Harold	2	914
Did yet inspire a cheer which he forbore to check	37	Harold	3	144
Though none, like thee, his dying hour will cheer	85	Epitaph		21
Life beams not for us with one ray that can cheer	92	Caroline-D		18
Through hours, through years, through time, 'twill cheer	98	To Mary		25
To gladden more their highland cheer	102	Alva		43
To cheer thy mother's years shall be my aim	108	Nisus		201
To cheer my last declining days	138	Clare		98
To cheer--to pierce--to please--or to appal	193	Monody		36
Then Congreve's scenes could cheer, or Otway's melt	243	Bards		115
No muse will cheer, with renovating smile	251	Bards		725
Cheer on the pack! the quarry stands at bay	256	Bards		1044
Mute, though he votes, unless when call'd to cheer	260	Hints		249
Late, late to-night will Dian cheer	329	Abydos	2	55
For Moslem mouths produce their choicest cheer	347	Corsair	2	27
Youth present cheer and promised recompense	378	Lara	2	204
And to uphold and cheer the rest	403	Chillon		70
But yet I forced it on to cheer	403	Chillon		101
To force of cheer a greater show	407	Mazeppa		95
And drain'd the draught with an applauding cheer	417	Island	1	104
Torquil, my boy! what cheer? Ho! brother, ho	425	Island	2	431
'What cheer, Ben Bunting?' cried (when in full view	425	Island	2	500
With all could cheer or deck their sparry bower	432	Island	4	186
To cheer resistance against death or chains	433	Island	4	253
Said quickly, 'Abbot, be thou of good cheer	472	Morgante		442
And be of better cheer. Come, taste my wine	483	Manfred	2	17
Cheer up, be calm; this transport is uncall'd for	501	Faliero	1	102
And thou art lord of this. Be of good cheer	579	Sardan	4	41
Who will do honour to your good cheer with	675	Werner	1	274
I thought to cheer up this old dungeon here	676	Werner	1	323
The cheer but scantily, our sizings were	704	Werner	4	12
Home to the weary, to the hungry cheer	815	Juan	3	946
Great plenty, much formality, small cheer	991	Juan	16	671

CHEER'D

When less barbarians would have cheer'd him less	29	Harold	2	592
For fancy was cheer'd by traditional story	117	Lachin		15
Though it unmann'd me, still had cheer'd	332	Abydos	2	334
Who cheer'd the band and waved the sword	388	Corinth		398
That very cheat had cheer'd me then	413	Mazeppa		621
A beacon which had cheer'd ten thousand nights	428	Island	3	108
And yet, I know not why, it cheer'd me not	528	Faliero	4	3
Plebeian as patrician, cheer'd us on	597	Foscari	1	101
And these two tended him, and cheer'd him both	789	Juan	2	977

CHEERFUL

And fill'd the bowl, and trimm'd the cheerful lamp	29	Harold	2	608
Gloom o'er his chamber, cheerful was his gate	377	Lara	2	181
Of cheerful creatures, whose most sinful deeds	453	Venice-B		26
Of cheerful old age and a quiet grave	484	Manfred	2	69
With honest mates, and bear a cheerful aspect	531	Faliero	4	232
Our clew being well nigh wound out, let's be cheerful	591	Sardan	5	237
Behold thy father cheerful and resign'd	628	Cain	1	51
Made poverty more cheerful, where each herb	682	Werner	1	712
You are not cheerful? Why should I be so	732	Deformed	1	744
Must be more cheerful. Wherefore should we think	734	Deformed	1	862
There's something cheerful in that sort of light	763	Juan	1	1077
Luxuriant, budding; cheerful without mirth	859	Juan	6	419
Cheerful as children climb the breasts of mothers	880	Juan	8	118
Or cheerful, without any 'flaws or starts	924	Juan	11	373
Serene, accomplish'd, cheerful but not loud	970	Juan	15	113
Cheerful--but, sometimes, rather apt to whimper	998	Juan	17	85

CHEERFULLY

| Millions of myriads feel it, cheerfully | 673 | Werner | 1 | 137 |

CHEERFULNESS

| And cheerfulness the handmaid of their toil | 886 | Juan | 8 | 530 |

CHEERILY

| But those hardy days flew cheerily | 384 | Corinth | | 34 |

CHEERING

Hark, to the Boatswain's call, the cheering cry	22	Harold	2	158
My eyes refuse the cheering light	87	Ad Lesbiam		21
I hail'd with smiles the cheering rays of Morn	139	Ossian-A		37
For only Morning's cheering light	150	Song		15
Yet thus sincere--'tis cheering, though so brief	340	Corsair	1	119
The haven hums with many a cheering sound	363	Corsair	3	557

CHEERING
When charging to the cheering cry — 399 Parisina 274
And cheering from my dungeon's brink — 405 Chillon 277
Thine are the hours and days when both are cheering — 646 Cain 3 21

CHEERLESS
But pallid, cheerless, and forlorn — 87 Adrian 6
Thus, while the future dark and cheerless gleams — 122 Recoll 21
How cheerless feels the heart alone — 135 I Would 27
Vain is the feeble cheerless toil — 142 Critics 97
All, all is dark and cheerless now — 146 Adieu 71
And they are changed, and cheerless,--or if yet — 192 Fragment-C 17

CHEERLY
While cheerly following where the mighty led — 182 Address-C 16
Alighting cheerly to inspire — 385 Corinth 107

CHEERS
The Spanish maid, and cheers the Spanish swain — 16 Harold 1 793
Hope cheers with wonted smiles the peaceful realm — 121 Newstead-A 111
The sun that cheers, the storm that lowers — 167 Dead 30
For bounty cheers not his delay — 313 Giaour 341
The grapes' gay juice thy bosom never cheers — 344 Corsair 1 429
And felt that all which Freedom's bosom cheers — 348 Corsair 2 87
Cheers Lara's voice, and waves or strikes his steel — 380 Lara 2 370
Cheers the tar's labour or the Turkman's rest — 425 Island 2 449
Which cheers the birds to song shall bid them glow — 461 Dante 3 66
Which cheers the sad, revives the old, inspires — 554 Sardan 1 236

CHEERY
On what I've seen or ponder'd, sad or cheery — 956 Juan 14 86

CHEESE
Yet still she rules the pastoral realm of cheese — 308 Age 746

CHEESE-PARING
Know not what visions spring from each cheese-paring — 930 Juan 12 24

CHEMISE
Of azure, pink, and white was her chemise — 810 Juan 3 555
Which girt a slight chemise as white as milk — 841 Juan 5 612

CHEMISTRY
No chemistry for them unfolds her gases — 449 Beppo 617

CHEOPS
Cheops erected the first pyramid — 773 Juan 1 1746
Since not a pinch of dust remains of Cheops — 773 Juan 1 1752

CHEQUER'D
Through few, but deeply chequer'd years — 131 L'Amitie 11
Is chequer'd with the northern light — 411 Mazeppa 428
The umbrage of the walls of Eden, chequer'd — 631 Cain 1 270
The history of divorces, which, though chequer'd — 903 Juan 9 423
Chequer'd with all the tracery of the hall — 996 Juan 16 1004

CHEQUERS
Another chequers o'er the shadow'd floor — 364 Corsair 3 596

CHERISH
That fame, and that memory, still will he cherish — 86 Leaving NA 29
Would the hope, which thou once bad'st me cherish — 162 Romaic-A 31
The boundless power to cherish or reject — 170 Address-A 55
Let Otho cherish here his polish'd guest — 372 Lara 1 461
The rust which tyrants cherish on our chains — 423 Island 2 323
The sick they should cherish — 488 Manfred 2 340
I fain would have them dutiful. I cherish — 582 Sardan 4 259
Such manure thy fields will cherish — 736 Deformed 2 98
Thus the frail beings we would fondly cherish — 802 Juan 3 15

CHERISHED
(See also LONG-CHERISHED)
For I have cherish'd them as dear — 44 Harold 3 520
Their cherish'd gaze upon thee, lovely Rhine — 44 Harold 3 576
Thoughts hid, but not less cherish'd than of old — 46 Harold 3 651
And, calm as cherish'd hate, its surface wears — 81 Harold 4 1555
Cherish'd affection only bids them flow — 122 Newstead-A 146
Nor less the affection I cherish'd for you — 136 Delawarr 4
(For cherish'd first in royal halls — 153 Friend-A 55
When cease to hear thy cherish'd name — 184 Parker 30
It hath taught me that what I most cherish'd — 210 Augusta-B 43
If there the cherish'd heart be fond — 217 High World 3
Which gleams, but warms no more its cherish'd earth — 311 Giaour 102
The cherish'd madness of my heart — 322 Giaour 1191
These cherish'd thoughts with life begun — 328 Abydos 1 425
And cherish'd most where least reveal'd — 402 Parisina 568
Most cherish'd since his natal hour — 404 Chillon 165
His chief had cherish'd only to destroy — 417 Island 1 152
Against the breast that cherish'd thee was stirr'd — 457 Dante 1 66

CHERISH'D
I have still aided, cherish'd, loved, and urged you — 568 Sardan 2 393
His orphan Ida--cherish'd her as one — 711 Werner 4 446
She must not own, but cherish'd more the while — 755 Juan 1 572
However dear or cherish'd in their day — 824 Juan 4 508
His third was sabred; and the fourth, most cherish'd — 892 Juan 8 875

CHERRY
From Cherry, Skeffington, and Mother Goose — 249 Bards 591

CHERSONESE
The tyrant of the Chersonese — 813 Juan 3 755

CHERUB
Fair cherubs, pledge of youth and joy — 150 My Son 23
A cherub flapp'd his right wing o'er his eyes — 287 Vision 130
'No,' quoth the cherub; 'George the Third is dead — 287 Vision 137
And this should be a cherub--since he loves not — 634 Cain 1 419
When he put on the cherub to perplex — 845 Juan 5 867

CHERUB-GUARDED
The cherub-guarded walls of Eden, with — 641 Cain 2 344

CHERUB-HYDRA
A Cherub-hydra round us dost thou gape — 14 Harold 1 664

CHERUBIM
Of cherubim appointed to that post — 295 Vision 674
Both cherubim and seraphim were heard — 296 Vision 723
Guarded by fiery-sworded cherubim — 630 Cain 1 170
Than a mere serpent: ask the cherubim — 631 Cain 1 229
The seraphs love most--cherubim know most — 634 Cain 1 418
Since the all-knowing cherubim love least — 634 Cain 1 422
And mingles with the song of cherubim — 643 Cain 2 470
And wings of fiery cherubim pursue him — 652 Cain 3 426
Or joining with the inferior cherubims — 656 Heaven 90
Who midst the cherubim — 666 Heaven 843
Not practise! Oh for trumps of cherubim — 911 Juan 10 268

CHERUBIM-DEFENDED
The cherubim-defended battlements — 629 Cain 1 90

CHERUBS
(Just like those cherubs, earthly ministers — 285 Vision 27
The very cherubs huddled all together — 288 Vision 201
Before him the young cherubs and saints hoary — 288 Vision 236
The cherubs and the saints bow'd down before — 288 Vision 241
Said Wilkes, 'are cherubs; and that soul below — 293 Vision 542
The cherubs and the seraphs; he looks not — 633 Cain 1 413
The childless cherubs well might envy thee — 648 Cain 3 153
Like cherubs round an altar-piece they cling — 809 Juan 3 477

CHERUBS'
By the far-flashing of the cherubs' swords — 631 Cain 1 271

CHESS
Upon their hams, were occupied at chess — 838 Juan 5 418

CHESS-BOARD
Good company's a chess-board--there are kings — 952 Juan 13 705

CHESSMAN
From our next neighbours' land, where, like a chessman — 923 Juan 11 331

CHEST
(See also ARM-CHEST)
His gory chest unveils life's panting source — 16 Harold 1 771
Stood Christian, with his arms across his chest — 427 Island 3 86
Closet and clothes' press, chest and window-seat — 764 Juan 1 1138
A miser filling his most hoarded chest — 799 Juan 2 1566

CHESTERFIELD
Yet Chesterfield, whose polish'd pen inveighs — 261 Hints 355
He thought at heart like courtly Chesterfield — 959 Juan 14 277

CHESTNUT
And the rings of chestnut hair — 400 Parisina 421
And here and there a chestnut stood — 411 Mazeppa 483

CHESTNUT'S
Between me and yon chestnut's bough — 408 Mazeppa 204

CHESTS
How beauteous are rouleaus! how charming chests — 931 Juan 12 89

CHEVALIER
There was the preux Chevalier de la Ruse — 952 Juan 13 683
Which piques a preux chevalier--as it ought — 977 Juan 15 610

CHEVALIERS
The preux chevaliers of the good old times — 683 Werner 2 325

CHEVALIERS'
For out of these three 'preux Chevaliers,' how — 871 Juan 7 258

CHEW
If living he must chew the husks still. But — 684 Werner 2 87

CHEW'D
And their dead palates chew'd the cud of pain — 454 Venice-B 91

CHEWING
Chewing a piece of bamboo and some lead — 784 Juan 2 654

CHIAN
And flasks of Samian and of Chian wine — 805 Juan 3 244

CHIAUS
The Chiaus spake, and as he said — 316 Giaour 571

CHIBOUQUE
Resign'd his gem-adorn'd chibouque — 326 Abydos 1 233

CHIBOUQUE'S
The long chibouque's dissolving cloud supply — 347 Corsair 2 35

CHICANE
That law's chicane or envious kinsmen might — 513 Faliero 2 338

CHICKEN'S
The chicken's toughness, and the lack of ale — 224 J.C.H. 15

CHICKS
The former know what's what; while new-fledged chicks — 908 Juan 10 75

CHID
A spirit deep that brook'd not to be chid — 374 Lara 1 559
Though I was chid for wandering; and the Wise — 438 Tasso 157
Just now you chid me for demanding names — 675 Werner 1 248

CHIDE
Father! for fear that thou shouldst chide — 324 Abydos 1 53
How teach her tender lips to chide — 330 Abydos 2 99
Think not I mean to chide, for I rejoice — 344 Corsair 1 431
But once perceived, his spirit seem'd to chide — 370 Lara 1 305

CHIDES
No warrior chides her peaceful beam — 329 Abydos 2 42

CHIDING
Humanise thee: my surly, chiding brother — 554 Sardan 1 230
(Although they too were chiding), which reproved me — 585 Sardan 4 442

CHIEF
(See also ROBBER-CHIEF, STRANGER-CHIEF)
Her chief is slain—she fills his fatal post — 13 Harold 1 577
What! could not Pluto spare the chief once more — 21 Harold 2 123
Did many a Roman chief and Asian king — 26 Harold 2 400
To greet Albania's chief, whose dread command — 26 Harold 2 418
Survey'd the dwelling of this chief of power — 28 Harold 2 498
Unshaken rushing on where'er their chief may lead — 29 Harold 2 585
A chief ever glorious like Ali Pashaw — 31 Harold 2 684
Each robber chief upheld his armed halls — 42 Harold 3 426
Th' octogenarian chief, Byzantium's conquering foe — 57 Harold 4 108
The forum's champion, and the people's chief — 72 Harold 4 1025
Collecting the chief trophies of her line — 74 Harold 4 1145
Both are but theatres where the chief actors rot — 76 Harold 4 1251
In air with Earth's chief structures, though their frame — 78 Harold 4 1403
The gulf is thick with phantoms, but the chief — 80 Harold 4 1500
Three days, three sleepless nights, the Chief — 103 Alva 125
Perchance the chief has only roved — 104 Alva 219
And thrice he frown'd on a chief on the ground — 104 Alva 263
The song is glory's chief reward — 105 Alva 307
Our troops and leaders mourn their absent chief — 105 Nisus 30
But not from thee, dark pile! departs the chief — 119 Newstead-A 17
Another chief impels the foaming steed — 121 Newstead-A 135
Who hail'd me chief, obedient to command — 123 Recoll 100
In Morven dwelt the chief, a beam of — 129 Calmar 16
to the hero, and call the chief to arms — 130 Calmar 51
leave thy friend afar? Chief of Oithona! not — 130 Calmar 63
'Calmar,' said the chief of Oithona, 'why — 130 Calmar 70
Lochlin: he died with gloomy Orla, the chief — 130 Calmar 79
dost thou bend thy brow, chief of Oithona — 130 Calmar 113
of a chief? Bright as the gold of the — 131 Calmar 159
'Tis Orla, the brown chief of Oithona — 131 Calmar 192
The chief who survives may recline in thy shade — 149 Newstead-B 32
That chief of ancient song — 162 War Song 26
As the chief who to combat advances — 162 Romaic-A 25
A certain Chief Justice say something like swearing — 178 Devil's Dr 149
To gaze on Beauty's band without its chief — 183 Address-D 22
Then turn thee and call on the Chief of thy choice — 186 Napoleon 24

CHIEF
Must thou go, my glorious Chief — 186 French-A 1
My chief, my king, my friend, adieu — 187 French-A 33
The Chief has fallen, but not by you — 187 Ode-B 22
With thy youthful chief competed — 187 Ode-B 29
The chief companion of a calmer lot — 211 Augusta-C 48
Earth's chief dictatress, ocean's lovely queen — 255 Bards 1002
Chief of thy foes shall Pallas still be found — 269 Minerva 93
The Chili chief abjures his foreign lord — 302 Age 277
The chief before, as deck'd for war — 315 Giaour 523
'Now call me the chief of the Haram guard — 324 Abydos 1 33
Was she, the daughter of that rude old Chief — 325 Abydos 1 168
Woe to thee, rash and unrelenting chief — 336 Abydos 2 651
But who that Chief? his name on every shore — 339 Corsair 1 61
'Where is our chief? for him we bear report — 340 Corsair 1 117
But, Juan! instant guide us to our chief — 340 Corsair 1 120
'These letters, Chief, are from the Greek—the spy — 340 Corsair 1 143
Or even that traitor chief—I've seen thee smile — 344 Corsair 1 443
But no—it must not be—a worthy chief — 345 Corsair 1 517
Waits but my chief—' 'My sword, and my capote — 346 Corsair 1 558
Yet much I long to view that chief again — 351 Corsair 2 270
A chief on land—an outlaw on the deep — 352 Corsair 2 390
Ah! little reck'd that chief of womanhood — 358 Corsair 3 196
Returns their greeting as a chief may greet — 363 Corsair 3 503
The chief of Lara is return'd again — 366 Lara 1 11
Another chief consoled his destined bride — 366 Lara 1 35
And from his chief withdrawn, he wander'd lone — 373 Lara 1 546
Except the absence of the chief it sought — 376 Lara 2 105
In vain he doth whate'er a chief may do — 379 Lara 2 290
Less loud, outlasts a people's for their chief — 382 Lara 2 525
As any chief that ever stood — 385 Corinth 99
Since he, their mightiest chief, had been — 387 Corinth 318
A priest at her altars, a chief in her halls — 392 Corinth 711
The chief, and his retreating train — 394 Corinth 918
The chief of Este's ancient sway — 398 Parisina 134
His chief would follow like a fawn — 407 Mazeppa 77
A chief of thousands, and could lead — 409 Mazeppa 291
The gallant chief within his cabin slept — 415 Island 1 17
Of those who fear the chief they sacrifice — 416 Island 1 62
And now the self-elected chief finds time — 417 Island 1 97
Who wait their chief, a melancholy crew — 417 Island 1 126
His chief had cherish'd only to destroy — 417 Island 1 152
His chief, commits him to his fragile ark — 418 Island 1 166
A patriot hero or despotic chief — 421 Island 2 204
How a young chief, a thousand moons ago — 432 Island 4 195
For then the chief and only satisfaction — 451 Beppo 719
And Italy shall hail him as the Chief — 462 Dante 3 103
The faction Chief is but the Sultan's brother — 465 Dante 4 126
Charles held; the chief, I say, Orlando was — 467 Morgante 66
Then forth alone from Paris went the chief — 468 Morgante 127
Who chose thee for his shadow? Thou chief star — 493 Manfred 3 187
Midst the chief relics of almighty Rome — 495 Manfred 3 271
Not only to the Chief of the Republic — 500 Faliero 1 50
Chief magistrate of Venice, and requests — 501 Faliero 1 76
Dishonour'd in its chief—that chief the prince — 501 Faliero 1 94
I love our house, I honour you, its chief — 502 Faliero 1 171
The leader, and the statesman, and the chief — 503 Faliero 1 268
They may be won, at least their chief at Rome — 504 Faliero 1 341
I am the chief of the arsenal, employ'd — 505 Faliero 1 379
And fight beneath the chief who beat the Huns there — 505 Faliero 1 390
Chief of the arsenal ere I came from Rome — 505 Faliero 1 394
Be our chief now—our sovereign hereafter — 507 Faliero 1 527
Wife to a prince, the chief of the Republic — 510 Faliero 2 78
Has lavish'd all its chief employs upon him — 510 Faliero 2 114
Her servant, though her chief—I would have gone — 515 Faliero 2 466
It may be, that of chief. What! and resign — 518 Faliero 2 692
For my own part, I seek no other chief — 518 Faliero 2 711
Can rest, when he, their last descendant chief — 520 Faliero 3 100
To be of your chief comrades? but no less — 521 Faliero 3 184
Was this your trust in your true chief Bertuccio — 522 Faliero 3 232
Of Venice—be our general and chief — 523 Faliero 3 338
Chief!—general!—I was general at Zara — 523 Faliero 3 339
And chief in Rhodes and Cyprus, prince in Venice — 523 Faliero 3 340
Is he not chief of the state? Perhaps at sunrise — 533 Faliero 4 338
A chief in armour is their Suzerain — 533 Faliero 4 377
Upon your power. Your chief accomplices — 540 Faliero 5 169
Sage Benintende, now chief judge of Venice — 544 Faliero 5 408
Lie under the state's ban; their chief, thy nephew — 545 Faliero 5 538
The Giunta, and the chief men of the Forty — 546 Faliero 5 554
The heads of thy chief foes before thy feet — 555 Sardan 336
The same of their chief hero, Hercules — 556 Sardan 1 376
Lost!—why, who is the aspiring chief who dared — 558 Sardan 1 536
Unto our enemies. Chief, keep your weapon — 565 Sardan 2 218
Is the chief victor? where's the king? Here, brother — 576 Sardan 3 329
Rose also, as if aping their chief shades — 580 Sardan 4 138
Have miss'd their chief aim—the extinction of — 584 Sardan 4 377
Appointing Zames chief? I did. Where's Zames — 584 Sardan 5 138
Proceed. And the chief judge, the Doge? No—he — 595 Foscari 1 23
Chief of 'the Ten.' Then why not clear him? That — 600 Foscari 1 305
Was prejudicial to the state, the chief — 623 Foscari 5 179

CHIEF

You, by your garb, Chief of the Forty! Signor	623 Foscari	5	197
The chief part of whatever aid was render'd	679 Werner	1	480
Of bandit warfare; each troop with its chief	685 Werner	2	128
Was his chief aid in yesterday's escape	685 Werner	2	146
A man pursued by my chief foe; disgraced	703 Werner	3	517
As regards you, and that is the chief point	704 Werner	3	588
To save a father is a child's chief honour	704 Werner	3	597
Beneath his chief inspection on the morn	718 Werner	5	328
Their chief, and all their kindled appetites	733 Deformed	1	751
Of our too needy army, that their chief	734 Deformed	1	839
(And other chief points of a 'bella donna	828 Juan	4	748
Had been her slaves' chief pleasure, as her will	845 Juan	5	892
The chief dame of the Oda, upon whom	865 Juan	6	817
In chief, in proper person deign'd to drill	873 Juan	7	410
Is neither man nor woman.' The chief threw on	874 Juan	7	475
Who were thus honour'd by the greatest chief	875 Juan	7	538
Where the chief pacha calmly held his post	893 Juan	8	954
Was left upon his way to the chief city	899 Juan	9	178
Her chief resource was in her own high spirit	945 Juan	13	244
Experience is the chief philosopher	970 Juan	15	133

CHIEFEST

The Grave shall bear the chiefest prize away	10 Harold	1	439
The Christians' chiefest magazine	395 Corinth		982
Which gave all these their chiefest harm	481 Manfred	1	239
I pray thee say not so: my chiefest joy	551 Sardan	1	67
Love me, whate'er betide. My chiefest glory	574 Sardan	3	171
In which you rank amidst our chiefest nobles	712 Werner	4	540

CHIEFLESS

And chiefless castles breathing stern farewells	42 Harold	3	413
The chiefless army of the dead, which late	459 Dante	2	92

CHIEFLY

Here dons, grandees, but chiefly dames abound	15 Harold	1	724
There chiefly I sought thee, there only I found thee	204 Pisa		13
But chiefly, Pallas! thine; when Hecate's glare	269 Minerva		67
But chiefly to my council call	333 Abydos	2	377
With a vice-husband, chiefly to protect her	443 Beppo		232
And chiefly thou, Ordelafo the brave	519 Faliero	3	36
And chiefly thou, my priest, because I doubt thee	566 Sardan	2	276
Given chiefly at my own expense: 'tis true	642 Cain	2	418
Which brought me here was chiefly that, but I	689 Werner	2	422
In all its acts--but chiefly by his marriage	694 Werner	2	726
But that which chiefly may, and must surprise	758 Juan	1	772
And that which chiefly proved his saving clause ·	784 Juan	2	646
But chiefly by a species of self-slaughter	787 Juan	2	815
And long for food, but chiefly a beef-steak	793 Juan	2	1224
Learning that language chiefly from its preachers	795 Juan	2	1316
Suwarrow chiefly was on the alert	874 Juan	7	433
Whose chiefly harmless talent was to amuse	952 Juan	13	685

CHIEFS

Behold the hall where chiefs were late convened	8 Harold	1	288
For chiefs like ours in vain may laurels bloom	8 Harold	1	303
And all that kings or chiefs e'er gain their toils repay	15 Harold	1	737
To the last halo of the chiefs and sages	52 Harold	3	1025
What race of chiefs and heroes did she bear	70 Harold	4	895
Scion of chiefs and monarchs, where art thou	80 Harold	4	1504
Adieu, ye chiefs renown'd in arms	88 Anacreon-A		19
Her chiefs in gleaming mail array'd	101 Alva		8
'Oh search ye chiefs! oh search around	103 Alva		113
If you, ye chiefs, and fortune will allow	106 Nisus		107
But when the hostile chiefs at length bow down	107 Nisus		153
Iulus holds amidst the chiefs his place	108 Nisus		220
Spare, spare, ye chiefs! from him your rage remove	110 Nisus		373
might. Fingal roused his chiefs to combat	130 Calmar		31
chiefs: they stood around. The king was in	130 Calmar		43
war. Speak, ye chiefs! Who will arise	130 Calmar		54
They quit the circle of the chiefs. Their	130 Calmar		97
the gathering chiefs bound on the plain	130 Calmar		127
men of Lochlin on the chiefs. As, breaking	131 Calmar		141
barks of the North, so rise the chiefs of	131 Calmar		143
Brave shades of chiefs and sages	162 War Song		13
And fallen chiefs, and fleets no more	163 Malta		28
Like Chiefs of Faction	200 Stanzas-B		31
Who, for years, were the chiefs in the eloquent war	204 Avatar		115
Warriors and chiefs! should the shaft or the sword	219 Saul-A		1
While throng'd the chiefs of every Highland clan	308 Age		769
Around, the bearded chiefs he came to lead	347 Corsair	2	30
The rising morn will view the chiefs embark	347 Corsair	2	37
From him by sterner chiefs to exile driven	378 Lara	2	198
Throughout that clime the feudal chiefs had gain'd	378 Lara	2	226
The chiefs of Venice wrung away	386 Corinth		216
The chiefs whose dust around him slumber'd	388 Corinth		403
Before proud chiefs of princely rank	399 Parisina		273
Of all the chiefs that there were rank'd	399 Parisina		321

CHIEFS

A band of chiefs!--alas! how few	407 Mazeppa		45
And dames, and chiefs, of princely port	408 Mazeppa		146
The chiefs came down, around the people pour'd	435 Island	4	407
The ducal chiefs within thee, shalt fall down	439 Tasso		223
One of the many chiefs, whose castled crags	483 Manfred	2	8
But bring me to the knowledge of your chiefs	508 Faliero	1	576
I've noted most; and caused the other chiefs	518 Faliero	2	651
With a long race of other lineal chiefs	519 Faliero	3	25
The example of their chiefs, and I for one	520 Faliero	3	140
See the bold chiefs, who would reform a state	522 Faliero	3	226
And to your chiefs: accept me or reject me	523 Faliero	3	329
They are--besides, it matters not; the chiefs	537 Faliero	4	618
When shall they be brought up? When all the chiefs	540 Faliero	5	145
By strong suspicion of the Median chiefs	572 Sardan	3	88
The general with his chiefs and men of trust	732 Deformed	1	742
Heroes and chiefs, the flower of Adam's bastards	735 Deformed	1	883
Mighty chiefs! eternal shadows	735 Deformed	2	49
Their chiefs to order,--were all cut to pieces	887 Juan	8	532
Statesmen, chiefs, orators, queens, patriots, kings	927 Juan	11	599

CHIEF'S

To swell one bloated Chief's unwholesome reign	12 Harold	1	550
Selictar, unsheathe then our chief's scimitar	31 Harold	2	639
Their chief's retainers, an immortal band	119 Newstead-A		12
Obedience to their chief's command	332 Abydos	2	368
No matter where--their chief's allotment this	339 Corsair	1	59
Some secret thought, than drag that chief's to-day	341 Corsair	1	222

CHIEFTAIN

For the lone chieftain, who majestic stalks	22 Harold	2	166
Sate Brunswick's fated chieftain; he did hear	38 Harold	3	200
Watch thou, while many a dreaming chieftain dies	108 Nisus		234
And own thee chieftain of the critic clan	248 Bards		507
The long self-exiled chieftain, is restored	366 Lara	1	4
Watch'd his late chieftain with exploring eye	417 Island	1	145
Must change their chieftain first. Oh! I have seen	494 Manfred	3	230
This chieftain--somehow would not yield at all	891 Juan	8	832

CHIEFTAINS

Till others fall where other chieftains lead	11 Harold	1	465
Her vassals combat when their chieftains flee	18 Harold	1	885
The tapers wink, the chieftains shrink	104 Alva		253
Once by a line of former chieftains worn	109 Nisus		292
On chieftains long perish'd my memory ponder'd	117 Lachin		11
The gather'd chieftains come to Otho's call	375 Lara	2	20
In vain the circling chieftains round them closed	376 Lara	2	63

CHIEFTAIN'S

Childe Harold saw them in their chieftain's tower	29 Harold	2	586
The vassals round their chieftain's hearth	102 Alva		39
Attending on their chieftain's call	102 Alva		92
Chain'd to the chariot of the chieftain's state	299 Age		48
Than those around their chieftain's state he eyes	369 Lara	1	240
With which that chieftain's brow would bear him down	373 Lara	1	499
From lingering where her chieftain's blood had been	383 Lara	2	601
The chieftain's trophy, and the poet's volume	829 Juan	4	830

CHIEFTAINSHIP

In kin and Chieftainship to me	197 Duel	11

CHILD
(See also RIVER-CHILD)

Poor child of Doubt and Death, whose hope is built on reeds	20 Harold	2	27
England, I joy no child he was of thine	21 Harold	2	96
He never-wean'd, though not her favour'd child	25 Harold	2	328
Is thy face like thy mother's, my fair child	35 Harold	3	1
When Fortune fled her spoil'd and favourite child	41 Harold	3	350
The one was fire and fickleness, a child	51 Harold	3	986
The child of love, though born in bitterness	53 Harold	3	1094
And Freedom find no champion and no child	69 Harold	4	857
Our children should obey her child, and bless'd	80 Harold	4	1528
For I was as it were a child of thee	82 Harold	4	1654
'Alas!' replies the wily child	88 Anacreon-B		13
The titled child whose future breath may raise	93 Dorset		14
Whom Indiscretion hail'd her favourite child	94 Dorset		38
Versed in hypocrisy while yet a child	100 Damaetas		5
Should play before the hero's child	102 Alva		47
Thus to obtain Glenalvon's child	102 Alva		84
In thee her much-loved child may live again	108 Nisus		190
And even in age at heart a child	133 E. N. Long		46
I would I were a careless child	135 I Would		1
What passion can dwell in the heart of a child	135 Highlander		10
What child has she of promise fair	141 Critics		53
I own myself the child of Folly	145 Becher-B		57
Will not reject a child of dust	146 Adieu		109
I hail thee, dearest child of love	150 My Son		22

CHILD

When late I saw thy favourite child	154 Happy		9
As fond and faultless as her child	164 Friend-B		30
A child of Famine dying	176 Devil's Dr		74
Vain froward child of empire! say	181 Ode-A		161
She taught the child to read, and taught so well	208 Sketch		13
That the blood of thy child is as pure	218 Jephtha		10
His own Sovereign's child	239 Bray		26
Nor woman, man, nor child will stir a pace	268 Hints		818
Or got a child on consecrated ground	268 Hints		836
Yes! where is he, the champion and the child	299 Age		49
So Beauty lures the full-grown child	314 Giaour		396
My child Zuleika's face unveil'd	324 Abydos	1	39
His child caressing and carest	325 Abydos	1	186
'Zuleika! child of gentleness	326 Abydos	1	193
And I, alas! am Giaffir's child	330 Abydos	2	180
'Where is my child?' an Echo answers--'Where	336 Abydos	2	663
By passions worthy of a fool or child	342 Corsair	1	284
On the sweet sleep of her child	395 Corinth		1045
'Tis Hugo's--he, the child of one	397 Parisina		101
That, as a mother's o'er her child	401 Parisina		490
No child, no sire, no kin had I	405 Chillon		324
All furious as a favour'd child	412 Mazeppa		518
Where Nature owns a nation as her child	416 Island	1	43
In growth a woman, though in years a child	420 Island	2	124
And who is he? the blue-eyed northern child	421 Island	2	163
As to a mother's bosom flies the child	426 Island	3	16
Of nature's child in nature's ecstasy	429 Island	3	200
And eagle-spirit of a Child of Song	436 Tasso		2
But thou, my young creation! my soul's child	437 Tasso		37
What wouldst thou, Child of Clay, with me	480 Manfred	1	131
Are at thy beck and bidding, Child of Clay	480 Manfred	1	133
Child of the Earth! or dread the worst. I know it	489 Manfred	2	405
My dearest child, forgive me--why delay	511 Faliero	2	151
At ease. 'Tis nothing, child.--But in the state	511 Faliero	2	181
But let us change the argument. My child	512 Faliero	2	270
My injured wife, the child of Loredano	512 Faliero	2	271
Come hither, child; I would a word with you	513 Faliero	2	291
Have urged against her right; my best friend's child	513 Faliero	2	339
My gentle child, forgive me; thou wert made	515 Faliero	2	500
Let us begone, my child, the time is pressing	516 Faliero	2	513
A woman or a child had made him less	517 Faliero	2	596
Although a child of greatness; he is one	518 Faliero	2	675
A child; if you are not in second childhood	527 Faliero	3	595
Why, child, I loathe all war, and warriors	559 Sardan	1	576
To shield thee from them. Child, if there be peril	570 Sardan	2	560
As I do always. Go to, you're a child	600 Foscari	1	328
Your privacy. I have none from you, my child	602 Foscari	2	47
Dost thou see this? Child--child--Call me not 'child	602 Foscari	2	70
To teach you to be less a child. From this	611 Foscari	3	199
My child! this is a phantasy of grief	619 Foscari	4	245
Touch not the child--my child! thy child! Oh, Cain	648 Cain	3	127
Of the poor child of clay which so adored him	655 Heaven		23
Peace, child of passion, peace	667 Heaven		950
Oh let this child embark	669 Heaven		1097
A poor man almost in his grasp, a child	694 Werner	2	743
My friend! my only child, sole preserver	698 Werner	3	227
Prithee, sweet child, change--Child, indeed! I have	707 Werner	4	203
In aspect and demeanour. True, dear child	708 Werner	4	245
To see my child again, and now I have found him	710 Werner	4	418
Even to my child? Or is the Hungarian near	711 Werner	4	430
Oh, my sweet mother! My beloved child	713 Werner	5	27
Poor child! Do you pity me? No; I but envy	713 Werner	5	36
The first-born child of the early sun	742 Deformed	3	8
At six a charming child, and at eleven	753 Juan	1	386
At six, I said, he was a charming child	753 Juan	1	393
Juan she saw, and, as a pretty child	755 Juan	1	545
But for a child, what piece of work is here	768 Juan	1	1371
And Ocean slumber'd like an unwean'd child	782 Juan	2	554
The other father had a weaklier child	785 Juan	2	697
The airy child of vapour and the sun	785 Juan	2	730
A child the moment when it drains the breast	799 Juan	2	1562
Haidee was Passion's child, born where the sun	799 Juan	2	1610
He loved his child, and would have wept the loss of her	804 Juan	3	207
Over the innocence of that sweet child	808 Juan	3	415
Thou bring'st the child, too, to the mother's breast	815 Juan	3	952
Damm'd from its fountain--the child from the knee	817 Juan	4	77
Which mix'd all feelings, friend, child, lover, brother	819 Juan	4	203
Have dawn'd a fair and sinless child of sin	825 Juan	4	555
At a per-centage; a child cross, dog ill	855 Juan	6	163
What say you, child?'--Dudu said nothing, as	858 Juan	6	391
A child of Nature, carelessly array'd	859 Juan	6	475
You surely are unwell, child! we must see	862 Juan	6	638
The fiat of this spoil'd child of the Night	872 Juan	7	323
Are nothing but a child of Murder's rattles	878 Juan	8	32

CHILD

A thing of impulse and a child of song	881 Juan	8	186
Even from a child, felt like a child; howe'er	884 Juan	8	418
Crime came not near him--she is not the child	886 Juan	8	489
An active hermit, even in age the child	886 Juan	8	503
A female child of ten years tried to stoop	889 Juan	8	726
Two villanous Cossacques pursued the child	890 Juan	8	729
Upon this child--I saved her--must not leave	890 Juan	8	786
This child, who is parentless, and therefore mine	891 Juan	8	800
The child's a pretty child--a very pretty	891 Juan	8	802
Child, or an aged, helpless man or two	894 Juan	8	988
But Juan turn'd his eyes on the sweet child	900 Juan	9	257
You had reason; 'twas that a young child of grace	933 Juan	12	226
The pride of a mere child with a new sash on	939 Juan	12	613
The Virgin Mother of the God-born Child	948 Juan	13	482
Child to the care of guardians good and kind	973 Juan	15	346
She had so much, or little, of the child	975 Juan	15	440
Pronounces that an 'only's' a spoilt child	997 Juan	17	11
A child of Chancery, that Star-Chamber ward	997 Juan	17	28

CHILD-BED

Condemn'd to child-bed, as men for their sins	958 Juan	14	183

CHILDE

Worse than adversity the Childe befell	4 Harold	1	33
The Childe departed from his father's hall	4 Harold	1	55
Yet marvel not, Sir Childe, that I	5 Harold	1	144
Sir Childe, I'm not so weak	6 Harold	1	163
So deem'd the Childe, as o'er the mountain he	8 Harold	1	315

CHILDE HAROLD

Childe Harold was he hight:--but whence his name	4 Harold	1	19
Childe Harold basked him in the noontide sun	4 Harold	1	28
And now Childe Harold was sore sick at heart	4 Harold	1	46
Childe Harold had a mother, not forgot	5 Harold	1	82
Childe Harold wends through many a pleasant place	9 Harold	1	345
Childe Harold sail'd, and pass'd the barren spot	25 Harold	2	343
Childe Harold hail'd Leucadia's cape afar	25 Harold	2	353
Childe Harold pass'd o'er many a mount sublime	26 Harold	2	408
Childe Harold saw, like meteors in the sky	27 Harold	2	491
Childe Harold saw them in their chieftain's tower	29 Harold	2	586
Childe Harold at a little distance stood	30 Harold	2	640

CHILDE HAROLD'S

Strange pangs would flash along Childe Harold's brow	4 Harold	1	65

CHILDHOOD

Of flowers yet fresh with childhood; on the ear	48 Harold	3	812
Friendship, whose truth let childhood only tell	94 Dorset		85
Where my thoughtless childhood stray'd	95 Fragment-B		2
Ye scenes of my childhood, whose loved recollection	96 Harrow-A		1
Love twined round their childhood his flow'rs as they grew	99 L Adieu		14
The boys in childhood chased the roe	102 Alva		55
What scenes of childhood still unsung remain	127 Recoll		370
I turn'd to those my childhood knew	132 L'Amitie		65
By every bliss my childhood knew	133 E. N. Long		53
And then with those our childhood knew	134 E. N. Long		101
Adieu, then, ye hills where my childhood was bred	136 Highlander		45
The friendships of childhood, though fleeting, are true	136 Delawarr		2
The wonted delights of our childhood retrace	136 Delawarr		14
Press'd by the turf where once my childhood play'd	138 Harrow-B		28
Why did my childhood wander forth	145 Adieu		25
The feelings of childhood, which taught thee to soar	148 Farewell-A		7
In happy childhood; trees, and flowers, and brooks	211 Augusta-C		50
And oft had Hassan's Childhood play'd	313 Giaour		308
Pure as the prayer which Childhood wafts above	325 Abydos	1	167
As childhood dates within our colder clime	420 Island	2	125
I know from childhood--which of these is thine	483 Manfred	2	15
A child; if you are not in second childhood	527 Faliero	3	595
Bertram, I have known thee long. From childhood, signor	531 Faliero	4	198
The innocence which happy childhood blesses	805 Juan	3	261
My childhood in this childishness of mine	909 Juan	10	143

CHILDHOOD'S

Endear'd to all in childhood's very name	125 Recoll		212
And childhood's gay sincerity	153 Friend-A		3
Observe his simple childhood's dawning days	259 Hints		221
From simple childhood's earliest hour	328 Abydos	1	421
Between us and our childhood's sympathy	422 Island	2	278

CHILDISH

And spend the hours in childish play	89 To Emma		18
Half the long night in childish games was pass'd	108 Nisus		255
Auspicious queen of childish joys	118 Romance		2
Will spare the childish verse, and not destroy	119 Answer-A		39
Or, dear to youth, portrays each childish scene	122 Recoll		15

CHILDISH

Our tricks of mischief, every childish game	122	Recoll	47
Davus, the harbinger of childish joy	125	Recoll	266
Till the dull knell of childish play	131	L'Amitie	26
Dost thou repeat, in childish boast	146	Vain Lady	13
Our childish days were days of joy	153	Friend-A	22
Whose verse, of all but childish prattle void	254	Bards	905
Let simple Wordsworth chime his childish verse	254	Bards	917
The childish thought was hardly breathed	326	Abydos 1	283
The childish helplessness of Asian women	571	Sardan 2	590
The gondola along in childish race	597	Foscari 1	96

CHILDISHNESS

Ida, this is mere childishness; your weakness	707	Werner 4	200
My childhood in this childishness of mine	909	Juan 10	143

CHILDLESS

Childless and crownless, in her voiceless woe	66	Harold 4	704
His wrath made many a childless foe	393	Corinth	804
My boys--I could have borne it were I childless	582	Sardan 4	283
The childless cherubs well might envy thee	648	Cain 3	153
And he who lieth there was childless. I	654	Cain 3	556
They are childless, then? There is or was a bastard	694	Werner 2	735

CHILDREN

That only Heaven to which Earth's children may aspire	25	Harold 2	351
Fierce are Albania's children, yet they lack	29	Harold 2	577
Who now shall lead thy scatter'd children forth	31	Harold 2	695
When Athens' children are with hearts endued	33	Harold 2	794
Abandon Ocean's children; in the fall	57	Harold 4	152
Their children's children would in vain adore	63	Harold 4	509
Charms, kindred, children--with the silver gray	70	Harold 4	920
Our children should obey her child, and bless'd	80	Harold 4	1528
Which the children of vanity rear	115	The Tear	46
At School I thought like other Children	144	Becher-B	37
Wherewith the children of Despair	164	Friend-B	5
In darkness my children take most delight	176	Devil's Dr	9
That race is gone--but still their children breathe	182	Address-C	7
'Sires have lost their children, wives	195	Ballad-A	91
By your children in the islands	240	Suliotes	10
I printed--older children do the same	242	Bards	50
All love thy strain, but children like it best	246	Bards	342
Dunedin! view thy children with delight	249	Bards	552
Whose generous children narrow'd not their hearts	263	Hints	511
Despatch her scheming children far and wide	270	Minerva	144
And shine like children of a happier strand	270	Minerva	154
To you, ye children of--whom chance accords	275	Waltz	101
Can he smile on such deeds as his children have done	323	Abydos 1	17
Their union grew: the children of the storm	422	Island 2	244
Both children of the isles, though distant far	422	Island 2	274
But for the children of the 'mighty mother's	449	Beppo	605
What have they given your children in return	453	Venice-B	68
Whose brethren, parents, children, wives, or sisters	507	Faliero 1	496
And makes her children with their little hands	519	Faliero 3	71
A pastime for their children. You are met	523	Faliero 3	285
Much that we let their children live; I doubt	524	Faliero 3	409
That, ere the dawn, she sets forth with her children	581	Sardan 4	201
From Nineveh with--Our children: it is true	582	Sardan 4	253
A brother I have injured--children whom	583	Sardan 4	305
And children. Alas! Hear me, sister, like	584	Sardan 4	368
Your children, with two parents and yet orphans	584	Sardan 4	381
Bear her to where her children are embark'd	584	Sardan 4	421
Upon her sleeping children, were still fix'd	586	Sardan 4	538
As children at discover'd bugbears. 'Tis	591	Sardan 5	240
His state descend to his children, as it must	601	Foscari 1	352
You soon will have no children--you deserve none	602	Foscari 2	71
When I received it. But for the poor children	604	Foscari 2	151
The ruin of their children? Under such laws, Venice	607	Foscari 2	400
My last of children! Tell him I will come	608	Foscari 2	439
My best Marina!--and our children? They	611	Foscari 3	192
But--I can leave them, children as they are	611	Foscari 3	198
Our children will be cared for by the Doge	611	Foscari 3	219
Look to my children--to your last child's children	613	Foscari 3	361
Prepare my children to behold their father	614	Foscari 3	402
Live long to be a mother to those children	617	Foscari 4	137
And I must live! Your children live, Marina	618	Foscari 4	207
My children! true--they live, and I must live	618	Foscari 4	208
Had been so! My unhappy children! What	618	Foscari 4	212
To me my husband and my children were	622	Foscari 5	96
And those of--Best retain it for your children	626	Foscari 5	347
It one day will be in your children. What	633	Cain 1	362
But we, thy children, ignorant of Eden	633	Cain 1	397
Should we not love them and our children, Cain	634	Cain 1	434
All we love in our children and each other	634	Cain 1	450
His brother, and our children, and our parents	634	Cain 1	473
Although inferior, and thy children shall	642	Cain 2	390

CHILDREN

My brotherhood's with those who have no children	643	Cain 2	479
Unto thy children--Most assuredly	643	Cain 2	513
Bequeath that science to thy children, and	645	Cain 2	628
His children all lost, as they might have been	649	Cain 3	227
From Eden, till his children do by him	652	Cain 3	424
So shall our children be. I will bear Enoch	653	Cain 3	456
Go to our children; I will follow thee	654	Cain 3	526
Be thine! Now let us carry forth our children	654	Cain 3	555
Uniting with our children Abel's offspring	654	Cain 3	560
For earth and all her children. Ha! ha! ha	659	Heaven	331
Children of dust be quench'd; and of each hue	660	Heaven	363
Children of Cain? From what? And is it so	663	Heaven	617
Righteous enough to save his children. Would	664	Heaven	648
In Paradise,--would mingle with Seth's children	664	Heaven	657
Dost thou here with these children of the wicked	665	Heaven	731
Nor perish like heaven's children with man's daughters	668	Heaven	1034
Like other parents, she spoils her worst children	704	Werner 4	43
Protected by their children. Yes, good father	711	Werner 4	455
(The old nobles being divided from their children	715	Werner 5	140
No, no; I have no children: never more	721	Werner 5	544
Ilion's children find no Hector	736	Deformed 2	72
The lisp of children, and their earliest words	762	Juan 1	984
(So children cutting teeth receive a coral	772	Juan 1	1668
For naughty children, who would rather play	775	Juan 2	75
But he, poor fellow, had a wife and children	779	Juan 2	343
A band of children, round a snow-white ram	805	Juan 3	249
To find our children running restive--they	808	Juan 3	466
Her children up (if nursing them don't thin her	809	Juan 3	476
All these were theirs, for they were children still	818	Juan 4	113
And children still they should have ever been	818	Juan 4	114
Cheerful as children climb the breasts of mothers	880	Juan 8	118
A sylvan tribe of children of the chase	886	Juan 8	514
Who fought with his five children in the van	891	Juan 8	840
As he look'd down upon his children gone	893	Juan 8	935
And lay before them with his children near	893	Juan 8	948
But ye--our children's children! think how we	895	Juan 8	1079
The next are 'only Children,' as they are styled	997	Juan 17	9
Who grow up Children only, since th' old saw	997	Juan 17	10

CHILDREN'S

Their children's lips shall echo them, and say	40	Harold 3	312
Their children's children would in vain adore	63	Harold 4	509
Who hides all verses from his children's sight	264	Hints	524
And hew the bough that bought his children's food	383	Lara 2	555
Their children's children's doom already brought	458	Dante 2	4
So long the grave of thy own children's hopes	460	Dante 2	137
Your children's sake! My gentle, wrong'd Zarina	583	Sardan 4	329
Nor in my sister-bride's, nor in my children's	640	Cain 2	255
How mothers love their children's squalls and chucklings	848	Juan 5	1062
But ye--our children's children! think how we	895	Juan 8	1079

CHILD'S

When our child's first accents flow	207	Fare Thee	34
Look to my children--to your last child's children	613	Foscari 3	361
For our child's canopy? Because its branches	646	Cain 3	6
To save a father is a child's chief honour	704	Werner 3	597
Into his dying child's mouth--but in vain	785	Juan 2	712
'And poor Juanna, too--the child's first night	862	Juan 6	641
The child's a pretty child--a very pretty	891	Juan 8	802
Perplexing for most virgins--a child's father	989	Juan 16	584

CHILI

The Chili chief abjures his foreign lord	302	Age	277
With Chili, Hellas, or with Araby	421	Island 2	200

CHILI'S

Fix'd upon Chili's shore, a proud cacique	421	Island 2	183

CHILI-VINEGAR

Ketchup, Soy, Chili-vinegar, and Harvey	441	Beppo	63

CHILL

One blast might chill him into misery	4	Harold 1	31
His little fingers chill my breast	89	Anacreon-B	32
When fate shall chill at length this fever'd breast	138	Harrow-B	17
Chill is thy Breath thou breeze of night	150	Song-A	13
Sunk chill on my brow	151	When We	10
Chill and mirk is the nightly blast	158	Storm	1
It feels, it sickens with the chill	166	Struggle	48
Nor age can chill, nor rival steal	167	Dead	24
That heavy chill has frozen o'er the fountain of our tears	185	Music-B	11
And the eyes of the sleepers wax'd deadly and chill	222	Sennacherib	11
O'er the chill marble, where the startling tread	269	Minerva	69
To chill in their inhospitable clime	308	Age	752
And but for that chill, changeless brow	311	Giaour	80
Thy heart grew chill	335	Abydos 2	635

CHILL
Oh! how the chill blast on my bosom blew   343 Corsair   1   381
And chill and nodding at the turret door   353 Corsair   2   417
Chill--wet--and misty round each stiffen'd limb   355 Corsair   2   561
Nor deem'd it cold--her chill was at her heart   356 Corsair   3   82
And its glance, though clear, was chill   390 Corinth   553
With all the deep and shuddering chill   397 Parisina   63
Lay on her soul, so deep and chill   400 Parisina   369
Alas! my own was full as chill   404 Chillon   222
The heavy hour was chill and dark   407 Mazeppa   36
But chill the air although in June   412 Mazeppa   522
My blood reflow'd though thick and chill   412 Mazeppa   574
Chain'd to the chill and stiffening steed   414 Mazeppa   764
Aught from experience, that chill touchstone
  whose   421 Island   2   147
As from a stream in winter, though the chill   487 Manfred   2   269
The lips which have been press'd to mine, a chill   558 Sardan   1   494
But here! 'Tis chill; the tapestry lets through   671 Werner   1   7
And, bathing his chill temples, tried to soothe   788 Juan   2   901
On one side, and the deep sea calm and chill   797 Juan   2 1462
Days lay she in that state unchanged, though
  chill   824 Juan   4   473
Of the long caravan, which in the chill   863 Juan   6   685
Chill, and chain'd to cold earth, we lift on high   867 Juan   7   5
In the chill dark, when courage does not glow   880 Juan   8   163
And she was chill as they, and on her face   890 Juan   8   753
Perhaps the season's chill, and their long
  station   894 Juan   8 1022
Of men's regard, the fever or the chill   943 Juan   13   136

CHILL'D
Appall'd, an owlet's larum chill'd with dread   12 Harold   1   563
Till chill'd by the winter of love's last adieu   99 L Adieu   16
Chill'd by misfortune's wintry blast   128 Remembrance   4
I will not complain, and though chill'd is
  affection   137 Delawarr   21
Were chill'd into a selfish prayer for light   189 Darkness   9
To snowy Gottenburg, was chill'd to sleep   274 Waltz   62
Her offspring chill'd; its beams are now forsaken   301 Age   198
And chill'd remembrance shudders o'er the rest   354 Corsair   2   516
But sunk, and chill'd, and petrified at last   365 Corsair   3   667
Even the stern stood chill'd with awe   400 Parisina   427
And through my spirit chill'd my blood, until   528 Faliero   4   8
By night chill'd, by day scorch'd, thus one by
  one   787 Juan   2   813
And felt her veins chill'd by the neighbouring
  sea   792 Juan   2 1156
Alas, that glory should be chill'd by snow   914 Juan   10   469

CHILLER
And waxing chiller in her courtesy   961 Juan   14   366

CHILLIEST
And thus the chilliest aspects may concentre   945 Juan   13   298

CHILLING
Whose labour'd lines in chilling numbers flow   119 Answer-A   21
Keen as your storms is Sorrow's chilling blast   140 Ossian-A   50
How long his senses bore its chilling chain   184 Julian   38
With all that chilling mystery of mien   371 Lara   1   361
He felt that chilling heaviness of heart   776 Juan   2   161

CHILLNESS
And shot a chillness to his heart   390 Corinth   597

CHILLON
Chillon! thy prison is a holy place   402 Sonnet-F   9

CHILLON'S
In Chillon's dungeons deep and old   403 Chillon   28
Lake Leman lies by Chillon's walls   403 Chillon   107
From Chillon's snow-white battlement   403 Chillon   111

CHILLS
When age chills the blood, when our pleasures are
  past   93 First Kiss   25
While that icy aspect chills us   100 Marion   13
Chills the warm tide which flows along the veins   122 Recoll   2
By the black wind that chills the polar flood   198 Po   44
That dazzles, leads, yet chills the vulgar heart   340 Corsair   1   178

CHILL'S
So chill's the pressure of your cheek   91 Caroline-B   43

CHILLY
Think on our chilly situation   101 Lady-B   31
Our cloudy climate, and our chilly women   446 Beppo   389
As it went chilly downward to the grave   694 Werner   2   738
At a sad discount: while your over chilly   854 Juan   6   127
And the heart's dew of pain sprang fast and
  chilly   865 Juan   6   839
I feel some chilly midnight shudderings   980 Juan   15   780

CHIMAERA'S
Chimaera's alps extend from left to right   27 Harold   2   453

CHIMARI
Shall the sons of Chimari, who never forgive   30 Harold   2   657
And in Chimari heard the thunder-hills of fear   66 Harold   4   657

CHIMARIOT
Chimariot, Illyrian, and dark Suliote   30 Harold   2   652

CHIMBORAZO
Where Chimborazo, over air, earth, wave   420 Island   2   77

CHIME
In every chime that jingled from Ostend   246 Bards   338
But not in flimsy Darwin's pompous chime   254 Bards   893
Let simple Wordsworth chime his childish verse   254 Bards   917
Yet something may remain perchance to chime   305 Age   546
Unbroken by the clock's funereal chime   423 Island   2   349
Must chime in to the echo of his revel   551 Sardan   1   32
And was thrust in to close the octave's chime   854 Juan   6   142
As e'er was virgin of a nuptial chime   869 Juan   7   124
Upon the ear, and sounds of horror chime   885 Juan   8   462
In mine irregularity of chime   970 Juan   15   158

CHIMERA
Their post; but theirs is merely a chimera   941 Juan   13   35

CHIMES
As music chimes in with a melodrame   994 Juan   16   878

CHIMNEY
The chimney--which would really hold a lover   765 Juan   1 1220

CHIMNEY-SMOKE
On seeing his own chimney-smoke, felt glad   804 Juan   3   203

CHIMNEY-SWEEPER
A legal broom's a moral chimney-sweeper   909 Juan   10   113

CHIN
Denotes how soft that chin which bears his touch   13 Harold   1   595
Nose and chin would shame a knocker   196 Rogers   1
He with the beardless chin and garments torn   875 Juan   7   494
Our kill'd, already piled up to the chin   890 Juan   8   782
A dimpled chin, a neck of ivory, stole   996 Juan   16 1027

CHINA
In small fine China cups, came in at last   809 Juan   3   500
Society, that china without flaw   939 Juan   12   621

CHINA'S
Or fence of art, like China's vasty wall   9 Harold   1   365
Bloom flowers in urns of China's mould   329 Abydos   2   79
In small-eyed China's crockery-ware metropolis   919 Juan   11   53

CHINE
Cleave yon bald-pated shaveling to the chine   738 Deformed   2   239

CHINESE
Moved by the Chinese nymph of tears, green tea   823 Juan   4   410
Perhaps we have borrow'd this from the Chinese   945 Juan   13   272

CHINS
Their chins upon their clenched hands, and smiled 189 Darkness   26
Have shaving too entail'd upon their chins   958 Juan   14   184

CHIOZZA
Have been disposed of. Some have fled to Chiozza 540 Faliero   5   146

CHIP
That saw'st the unfledged eaglet chip his shell   300 Age   134

CHIPP'D
Chipp'd by the beam, a nursling of the day   430 Island   4   23

CHIRPS
Or chirps the grasshopper one good-night carol
  more   48 Harold   3   814

CHIRUP'D
But chirup'd oft, and, free from care   87 Catullus   11

CHIRURGEONS
If there might be chirurgeons who could solder   890 Juan   8   747

CHISEL
His chisel bid the Hebrew, at whose word   464 Dante   4   61
Ne'er compass'd, nor less mortal chisel wrought   789 Juan   2   952

CHISELL'D
(See also MARBLE-CHISELL'D)
When exquisitely chisell'd, still lay there   824 Juan   4   482
In chisell'd stone and painted glass, and all   982 Juan   16   127

CHIVALRIC
I would not warrant thy chivalric heart   737 Deformed 2 192

CHIVALROUS
Shrunk from his deeds of chivalrous emprize   25 Harold 2 337
To do good to mankind is the chivalrous plan   236 Freedom 5
Mount, chivalrous Hidalgo! not in vain   303 Age 358
The famous lance of chivalrous Castile   303 Age 371
And chivalrous. Upon the clay   407 Mazeppa 48
The brave, the chivalrous, how little deem'd   512 Faliero 2 272

CHIVALRY
Where blazon'd glare names known to chivalry   8 Harold 1 294
Lo, Chivalry, your ancient goddess, cries   10 Harold 1 406
None hugg'd a conqueror's chain, save fallen
   Chivalry   18 Harold 1 881
Her Beauty and her Chivalry, and bright   38 Harold 3 183
The Bards of Hell and Chivalry: first rose   61 Harold 4 354
Of Cordova the Chivalry   194 Ballad-A 49
The naked knights of savage chivalry   422 Island 2 217
And fill the earth with feats of chivalry   462 Dante 3 111
The Bard of Chivalry, will both consume   462 Dante 3 150
Epitome of what brave chivalry   688 Werner 2 324
Then for accomplishments of chivalry   751 Juan 1 301
Who sang when chivalry was more Quixotic   817 Juan 4 44
Pondering on glory, chivalry, and kings   900 Juan 9 236
Cervantes smiled Spain's chivalry away   942 Juan 13 81
Sleeps from the chivalry of this bright age   946 Juan 13 350

CHOCOLATE
Lord Henry, who had now discuss'd his chocolate   984 Juan 16 265

CHOICE
Of Wealth and Wantonness, the choice retreat   29 Harold 2 572
Shall call my spirit, joyful in their choice   85 Fragment-A 2
Kind Reader! take your choice to cry or laugh   161 Substitute 1
Thy choice is most ignobly brave   180 Ode-A 45
Then turn thee and call on the Chief of thy
   choice   186 Napoleon 24
And gives the choice of death or phrenzy--choose   230 God Maddens 2
Await the poet, skilful in his choice   257 Hints 64
Parnassian pilgrims! ye whom chance or choice   264 Hints 577
A muse and heart by choice so wholly thine   265 Hints 604
But take your choice); and then it grew a cloud   292 Vision 457
As to speak first? there's choice enough--who
   shall   293 Vision 518
She is the offspring of my choice   325 Abydos 1 148
What others deem a penance is thy choice   344 Corsair 1 432
By choice the perils he by chance escaped   370 Lara 1 318
A careless thing, who placed his choice in chance   421 Island 2 175
Not such as would have been a lover's choice   424 Island 2 417
But though the choice seems native to die free   427 Island 3 55
Another course had been their choice--but where   433 Island 4 235
No further chance or choice remain'd; and right   433 Island 4 243
If only you will but oppose their choice   443 Beppo 234
I have no choice; there is no form on earth   481 Manfred 1 117
The choice of such remains--and for the last   492 Manfred 3 59
The rights of place and choice, of birth and
   service   502 Faliero 1 147
Or aught save their past choice. 'Tis their
   past choice   510 Faliero 2 129
Your father's choice. I did so; I would do so   513 Faliero 2 324
You had been won, but thought the change your
   choice   514 Faliero 2 361
Some skill, and your own choice, had mark'd me
   out   518 Faliero 2 696
To take his choice--as brother, or as victim   522 Faliero 3 241
Some cause to doubt the freedom of the choice   522 Faliero 3 243
The moments from me? The king's choice is mine   551 Sardan 1 66
But would no more, by their own choice, be human   557 Sardan 1 423
Nay, there's no other choice, but--hence, I say   569 Sardan 2 465
Of choice to single out a residence   592 Sardan 5 301
Have chosen well their envoy. 'Tis their choice   604 Foscari 2 193
Without our act or choice as birth, so that   607 Foscari 2 363
Both honour'd by the choice or chance which leads
   us   616 Foscari 4 80
No other choice. Your sire has chosen already   634 Cain 1 427
With him, or with his God, is in your choice   666 Heaven 852
My heart's first choice; which chose thee,
   knowing neither   673 Werner 1 145
Thy choice. On what condition? There's a
   question   724 Deformed 1 139
No. As you leave me choice, I am difficult   726 Deformed 1 241
Your choice. The godlike son of the sea-goddess   726 Deformed 1 266
A choice of forms, I take the one I view   727 Deformed 1 362
There is small choice: the whole race are just
   now   729 Deformed 1 499
I have heard great things of Rome. A goodly
   choice   729 Deformed 1 501
No choice was left his feelings or his pride   751 Juan 1 287
Had his first choice of morsels for his pains   783 Juan 2 610
A taste seen in the choice of his abode   808 Juan 3 444
One of the two, according to your choice   819 Juan 4 193
Would leave his proposition to their choice   840 Juan 5 555

CHOICE
Their choice than life, forgive them, as beguiled   886 Juan 8 493
So you may take your choice of this or that   903 Juan 9 452
That the young lady made a monstrous choice   934 Juan 12 304
Suppression,' Lady Pinchbeck was his choice   935 Juan 12 336
Or should it shake, the choice will more perplex   945 Juan 13 236
Hath yet a purchased choice of choicest wines   950 Juan 13 605
The devil hath not in all his quiver's choice   970 Juan 15 103

CHOICEST
Oh memory! thou choicest blessing   97 To Woman 7
For Moslem mouths produce their choicest cheer   347 Corsair 2 27
Youth of the choicest, my heart would have chosen   688 Werner 2 365
Hath yet a purchased choice of choicest wines   950 Juan 13 605

CHOIR
See round thy giant base a brighter choir   14 Harold 1 649
Our choir would scarcely be excused   96 Granta 77
And call thy sylvan female choir   118 Romance 45
The choir did oft their mingling vespers blend   120 Newstead-A 35
I would not hear a Seraph Choir   144 Jessy 11
Who in soft guise, surrounded by a choir   245 Bards 283
There the hired eunuch, the Hesperian choir   250 Bards 644
But when the anthem shakes the choir   319 Giaour 887
Such is the observance of the eternal choir   472 Morgante 416
And the responsive voices of the choir   529 Faliero 4 99
In their true place, with the angelic choir   666 Heaven 798
Composed a choir of girls, ten or a dozen   844 Juan 5 786

CHOIRS
From choirs, in one great cry of 'God be praised   714 Werner 5 95

CHOKE
They choke the feeble words that would unfold   370 Lara 1 288
Reeling with grapes red wagons choke the way   445 Beppo 335

CHOKED
In fragments, choked up vaults, and frescos
   steep'd   71 Harold 4 958
And here, where buzzing nations choked the ways   76 Harold 4 1271
Have choked up the rose which late bloom'd in the
   way   86 Leaving NA 4
The like (since Tom Sternhold was choked) never
   man saw   227 Moore-A 12
The rushing billows choked the tone   335 Abydos 2 582
His breath choked gasping with the volumed smoke   350 Corsair 2 213
Was choked within her swelling throat   400 Parisina 343
Be spilt till the choked Tiber be as red   731 Deformed 1 653
Through coaches, drays, choked turnpikes, and a
   whirl   921 Juan 11 169

CHOKENOFF
And Tschitsshakoff, and Roguenoff, and Chokenoff   869 Juan 7 116

CHOKES
Till the last rattle chokes the strangled scream   453 Venice-B 53

CHOKING
The life from out young hearts, and choking sighs   39 Harold 3 213
Let's leave this place, the air grows thick and
   choking   569 Sardan 2 458
From the Ravenstone by choking you myself   691 Werner 2 514

CHOLER
Thus, snorting with his choler, said   195 Ballad-A 68

CHOLERIC
And being somewhat choleric and sudden   920 Juan 11 98

CHOOSE
(See also CHUSE)
So hath it proved to thee and all such lot who
   choose   41 Harold 3 360
Unbodied choose a sanctuary. I twine   56 Harold 4 76
If free to choose, I cannot now restore   66 Harold 4 683
I cannot choose but look on thee   87 Ad Lesbiam 10
Choose then, relentless! and I swear   99 Young Lady 33
But now without a theme to choose   133 E. N. Long 61
They cannot choose but weep the more   184 Parker 34
Then look around, and choose thy ground   207 Year 39
Nor did Heaven choose so near an instrument   213 Lady Byron 16
And gives the choice of death or phrenzy--choose   230 God Maddens 2
Just skill'd to know the right and choose the
   wrong   251 Bards 690
This shall the author choose, or that reject   257 Hints 69
A hackney'd plot, than choose a new, and err   259 Hints 186
Nor do they merit slight applause who choose   263 Hints 451
The glory of that death they freely choose   268 Hints 832
But you may choose Jack Wilkes as well as any   293 Vision 520
For fear, for I can choose my own reviewers   297 Vision 790
All people, as their fancies hit, may choose   440 Beppo 22
She chose (and what is there they will not choose   443 Beppo 233
Look o'er the wardrobe, and take what you choose   476 Morgante 658
But choose a form--in that we will appear   481 Manfred 1 183

249

CHOOSE

Heaven and myself; I shall not choose a mortal	492 Manfred	3	54
To ponder upon what they now might choose	510 Faliero	2	128
Now choose more wisely, could they cancel it	510 Faliero	2	131
Freedom from me to choose, and urged in answer	513 Faliero	2	323
His worthy daughter, free to choose again	513 Faliero	2	331
Would choose more fitly in respect of years	513 Faliero	2	340
Them choose me for their prince, and then farewell	525 Faliero	3	447
And thou, my own Ionian Myrrha, choose	551 Sardan	1	60
The Doge will choose his own ambassador	606 Foscari	2	326
Choose betwixt love and knowledge--since there is	634 Cain	1	426
His worship is but fear. Oh, Cain! choose love	634 Cain	1	428
For thee, my Adah, I choose not--it was	634 Cain	1	429
O'er what it shadows; wherefore didst thou choose it	646 Cain	3	5
What shall I do? Choose one of those two altars	649 Cain	3	210
Choose for me: they to me are so much turf	649 Cain	3	211
And stone. Choose thou! I have chosen. 'Tis the highest	649 Cain	3	212
My Werner, when you deign'd to choose for bride	673 Werner	1	122
That we are both unarm'd; I would not choose	716 Werner	5	209
You see his aspect--choose it, or reject	725 Deformed	1	193
Been born with it! But since I may choose further	725 Deformed	1	215
Who can command all forms will choose the highest	727 Deformed	1	364
Though no man would choose thee	728 Deformed	1	453
Would not your highness choose to kiss the cross	736 Deformed	2	137
I don't choose to say much upon this head	749 Juan	1	173
'Tis a sad thing, I cannot choose but say	754 Juan	1	497
Gasps, and whatever else the owners choose	766 Juan	1	1293
Thou shalt not write, in short, but what I choose	772 Juan	1	1645
And none to be the sacrifice would choose	783 Juan	2	588
May choose between the headache and the heartache	819 Juan	4	192
But which to choose, I really hardly know	819 Juan	4	196
Hoping no very old vizier might choose	831 Juan	4	926
Next Juan stood, till some might choose to buy	832 Juan	5	80
So pick and choose--perhaps you'll be content	861 Juan	6	543
I never saw such eyes--but hark! now choose	891 Juan	8	803
But now I choose to break off in the middle	896 Juan	8	1109
May choose to tax me with; which is not fair	908 Juan	10	84
I could say more, but do not choose to encroach	921 Juan	11	181
For reasons which I choose to keep apart	958 Juan	14	166
That--but ask any woman if she'd choose	958 Juan	14	198
To jest, you'll choose some other theme just now	985 Juan	16	294

CHOOSES

Marries for money, chooses friends for rank	260 Hints		245
I wish your fate may yield ye, when she chooses	746 Juan	Ded	59

CHOOSING

You knew it, choosing me, and chose: I trusted	514 Faliero	2	368
But always choosing with deliberation	913 Juan	10	383
In play, there are two pleasures for your choosing	957 Juan	14	95

CHOPP'D

Chopp'd by the axe, looks rough and little worth	69 Harold	4	879

CHORAL

Thy choral memory of the Bard divine	57 Harold	4	147
And still the choral peal prolong	102 Alva		88
And still the choral peal prolong	103 Alva		176
Or joins Devotion's choral band	160 Cadiz		47
Thy fall, the theme of choral song	219 Thy Days		15
With choral step and voice, the virgin throng	805 Juan	3	240
And harmonised by the old choral wall	949 Juan	13	504

CHORD

Man, thou hast struck upon the chord which jars	528 Faliero	3	661

CHORDS

The dying chords are strung anew	88 Anacreon-A		11
His harp in shuddering chords would break	105 Alva		312
And till those vital chords shall break	132 L'Amitie		68
Yet thrills my bosom's chords	146 Adieu		62
But lull the chords, for now, alas	165 Away		6
No more he strikes the quivering chords with fire	121 Newstead-A		91
Restring the chords, renew the clasp	169 The Chain		16
Redoubled be her tears, its chords are riven	216 The Harp		5
Then leave, ye wise, the lyre's precarious chords	266 Hints		729
By the chords you would awaken	390 Corinth		518
In vain--in vain: strike other chords	812 Juan	3	737

CHORUS

With Echo for their chorus; nor the alarm	424 Island	2	422
Or making chorus to the creaking oar	506 Faliero	1	423
At once his chorus and his council, flash	551 Sardan	1	40
The very chorus of the tragic song	559 Sardan	1	564
Yes, if they keep to their chorus. But here comes	732 Deformed	1	741
Clamour'd in chorus to the roaring ocean	778 Juan	2	272
Which might have call'd Diana's chorus 'cousin	844 Juan	5	790
Your heart joins chorus, Fame is but a din	900 Juan	9	272

CHOSE

Had grown Suspicion's sanctuary, and chose	47 Harold	3	754
'Twas not for fiction chose Rousseau this spot	51 Harold	3	968
Which a Corporal chose to shiver	176 Devil's Dr		56
Who would not die the death they chose	184 Parker		20
And chose a topic all sublime	233 Nihil		20
As Egypt chose an onion for a god	272 Minerva		258
Blest was the time Waltz chose for her debut	276 Waltz		161
For the rough virtues chose them for their clime	290 Vision		336
Millions who found him what oppression chose	290 Vision		368
He chose the last, and when elate	332 Abydos	2	284
Yes, they who chose might smile, but some had seen	368 Lara	1	141
They knew, or chose to know: with dubious look	372 Lara	1	445
Such was the stern asylum Neuha chose	430 Island	4	29
She chose (and what is there they will not choose	443 Beppo		233
And saunter'd here and there, where'er they chose	473 Morgante		476
Who chose thee for his shadow! Thou chief star	493 Manfred	3	187
You knew it, choosing me, and chose: I trusted	514 Faliero	2	368
My heart's first choice; which chose thee, knowing neither	673 Werner	1	145
Dusky, but not uncomely. If I chose	727 Deformed	1	371
Who chose to go where'er he had a mind	749 Juan	1	147
Though several thousand people chose to try	750 Juan	1	179
Who saw their spouses kill'd, and nobly chose	750 Juan	1	228
Her great-great-grandmamma chose to remain	754 Juan	1	448
He chose from several animals he saw	803 Juan	3	139
I chose a modern subject as more meet	817 Juan	4	48
Some bought the jet, while others chose the pale	832 Juan	5	76
He chose himself to point out what he thought	840 Juan	5	535
Or solitary, as they chose to bear	954 Juan	13	820
What time he chose for dress, and broke his fast	954 Juan	13	823
When, where, and how he chose for that repast	954 Juan	13	824
Connexions stronger then he chose to avow	985 Juan	16	292
(By doing easily, whene'er she chose	986 Juan	16	394

CHOSEN

Or doom the lover you have chosen	101 Lady-B		13
For me, I fain would please the chosen few	119 Answer-A		37
The triumphs of her chosen Son	218 Thy Days		3
Behold, a chosen band shall aid thy plan	248 Bards		506
Two Jews, a chosen people, can command	307 Age		686
The bands are rank'd; the chosen van	386 Corinth		234
And he, the chosen one, whose lance	398 Parisina		167
In spots where eagles might have chosen to build	434 Island	4	312
And our more chosen comrades, is aware	520 Faliero	3	131
The end I would have chosen, had I saved	589 Sardan	5	125
Have chosen well their envoy. 'Tis their choice	604 Foscari	2	193
Chosen delegates, a school of wisdom, to	616 Foscari	4	86
Chosen, however reluctantly so chosen	616 Foscari	4	93
No other choice. Your sire has chosen already	634 Cain	1	427
And stone. Choose thou! I have chosen. 'Tis the highest	649 Cain	3	212
We have chosen, and will endure	668 Heaven		983
Youth of the choicest, my heart would have chosen	688 Werner	2	365
Thou art a conqueror; the chosen knight	730 Deformed	1	572
That I have chosen a confessor so old	765 Juan	1	1171
I yet have chosen from out the youth of Seville	765 Juan	1	1178
Who was her choice: what was said or done	799 Juan	2	1614
Who wore their uniform, by Baba chosen	844 Juan	5	788
So that you scarce could say who best had chosen	884 Juan	8	357
'And here,' he cried, 'is Freedom's chosen station	919 Juan	11	69
Such as--'Unless Miss (Blank) meant to have chosen	934 Juan	12	269
Was chosen from out an amatory score	934 Juan	12	299
Such thoughts are quite below the strain they have chosen	936 Juan	12	435
'Tis true, I might have chosen Piccadilly	944 Juan	13	209
Regretting much that she had chosen so bad a line	961 Juan	14	365

CHREMATOFF

Scherematoff and Chrematoff, Koklophti	869 Juan	7	129

CHRIST

(See also ANTI-CHRIST)

Oh, Christ! it is a goodly sight to see	6 Harold	1	207
To none, save them whose faith in Christ is sure	382 Lara	2	489
Converted by Christ to his blood so divine	395 Corinth		1003
Oh, Christ! that thus a son should stand	398 Parisina		140
Shed where Christ bled for man; and his high harp	462 Dante	3	122
But Christ his servants ne'er abandons long	470 Morgante		260
Christ I adore, who is the genuine Lord	471 Morgante		335
'But they in Christ have firmest hope, and all	472 Morgante		409
He Christ believes as Christian must be rated	473 Morgante		443
Yourself to Christ, as once you were a foe	473 Morgante		456
Long Persecuted sore the faith of Christ	473 Morgante		458
"Why dost thou persecute me thus?" said Christ	473 Morgante		460
And went for ever after preaching Christ	473 Morgante		462
That sky whence Christ ascended from the cross	731 Deformed	1	608
What wouldst thou? In the holy name of Christ	738 Deformed	2	243

CHRISTABEL

I read the Christabel; Very well	230 I Read		1

CHRISTEN'D
Is that which may be christen'd love canonical 906 Juan 9 603

CHRISTIAN
(See also ANTI-CHRISTIAN, FELLOW-CHRISTIAN)
The Paynim turban and the Christian crest 9 Harold 1 385
What hallows it upon this Christian shore 15 Harold 1 685
And bade to Christian tongues a long adieu 26 Harold 2 380
The Goth, the Christian, Time, War, Flood, and
    Fire 67 Harold 4 712
Of Christian knight or Moorish hero 160 Cadiz 44
In all the license of a Christian nation 291 Vision 384
Was ever Christian land so rich in Jews 307 Age 673
His Christian crest and haughty mien 312 Giaour 256
But only Christian in his face 318 Giaour 811
By Christian cannon piecemeal rent 324 Abydos 1 94
Pierced keener than a Christian sword 324 Abydos 1 108
Or Christian crouching in the fight 325 Abydos 1 145
Till Christian hands to Greece restore 386 Corinth 149
When Alp, beneath his Christian name 386 Corinth 185
But still his Christian origin 387 Corinth 314
The sons and the shrines of the Christian name 390 Corinth 584
Aged or young, in the Christian shape 392 Corinth 695
The turban'd victors, the Christian band 395 Corinth 1017
Christian or Moslem, which be they 395 Corinth 1041
'Does Christian know this?'--'Ay; he has piped
    all hands 426 Island 2 520
Stood Christian, with his arms across his chest 427 Island 3 86
But Christian, of a higher order, stood 428 Island 3 139
Even Christian gazed upon the maid and boy 429 Island 3 203
In one placed Christian and his comrades twain 429 Island 3 223
The skiff which wafted Christian from the shore 430 Island 4 36
In search of Christian now renew'd their race 433 Island 4 238
But Christian bade them seek their shore again 433 Island 4 249
They heard the voice of Christian shout, 'Now
    fire 434 Island 4 302
Christian died last--twice wounded; and once more 434 Island 4 323
Because in Christian countries 'tis a rule 443 Beppo 186
Our Christian usage of the parts of speech 449 Beppo 616
Less in the Mussulman than Christian way 450 Beppo 642
His wife, religion, house, and Christian name 452 Beppo 776
He, too, shall sing of arms and Christian blood 462 Dante 3 121
Who for the church and Christian faith had
    wrought 466 Morgante 39
The Christian cause had suffer'd shamefully 467 Morgante 107
And was baptized a Christian; and then show'd 468 Morgante 167
And if a Christian, speak for courtesy 471 Morgante 332
And I a Christian am disposed to be 471 Morgante 344
He Christ believes as Christian must be rated 473 Morgante 443
The earth as being the Christian bulwark 'gainst 538 Faliero 5 11
True and Christian,--strike the assaulters 736 Deformed 2 116
What, when a Christian dies? Shall I not offer 737 Deformed 2 142
A Christian 'Vade in pace'? Silence! Oh! 737 Deformed 2 143
Destroy proud Anti-Christ. I am a Christian 738 Deformed 2 244
What a good Christian you were found to be 743 Deformed 3 111
In every Christian language ever named 748 Juan 1 75
I speak of Christian lands in this comparison 796 Juan 2 1399
As though they were in a mere Christian fair 835 Juan 5 221
No Christian knoll to table, saw no line 837 Juan 5 395
Gave it a slight kick with his Christian foot 840 Juan 5 582
To supper; but, worthy Christian nun 841 Juan 5 643
Had she but been a Christian, I've a notion 845 Juan 5 895
And merely saying, 'Christian, canst thou love 846 Juan 5 927
And, Christian! mingle with them as you may 849 Juan 5 1157
Were ruled as calmly as a Christian queen 850 Juan 5 1184
That a mere Christian should be half so pretty 851 Juan 5 1240
Now, if this holds good in a Christian land 854 Juan 6 81
When they survey, with Christian eyes or Heathen 857 Juan 6 295
The armies of the Christian Empress Catherine 875 Juan 7 512
Answering the Christian thunders with like voices 879 Juan 8 52
By Christian soldiery, a single spot 883 Juan 8 293
From whence they sallied on those Christian
    scorners 887 Juan 8 600
The fifth, who, by a Christian mother nourish'd 892 Juan 8 877
As is the Christian dogma rather rough 899 Juan 9 198
As flourishing in every Christian land 906 Juan 9 606
In fact, the only Christian she could bear 914 Juan 10 449
Scott, who can paint your Christian knight or
    Saracen 975 Juan 15 469

CHRISTIANITY
By their examples of true Christianity 867 Juan 7 43
Lurk'd Christianity; which sometimes barters 874 Juan 7 454

CHRISTIANS
That the Christians, stern and bold 194 Ballad-A 38
'A rope! help, Christians, as ye hope for grace 268 Hints 817
By Christians, unto whom they gave their creed 302 Age 291
Where still the Christians yielded not 394 Corinth 927
And faint the weary Christians wax 394 Corinth 935
A beverage for Turks and Christians both 451 Beppo 722
But since that cannot be, as Christians let us 543 Faliero 5 404
Christians war against Christ's shrine 735 Deformed 2 39
Christians have burnt each other, quite persuaded 757 Juan 1 663

CHRISTIANS
Some Christians have a comfortable creed 785 Juan 2 688
Most proper for the Christians he had bought 840 Juan 5 536
By mowing Christians down on every side 892 Juan 8 851

CHRISTIAN'S
This feast a Christian's? or my friends thy foes 348 Corsair 2 118
But cursed the Christian's victory 386 Corinth 146
Which Christian's eye was train'd to mark full
    well 434 Island 4 310
Which form'd the Christian's and the pagan's
    bound 468 Morgante 152
The only true God is the Christian's God 471 Morgante 352

CHRISTIANS'
Did traitors lurk in the Christians' hold 389 Corinth 444
The Christians' chiefest magazine 395 Corinth 982

CHRISTMAS
Or had the bard at Christmas written 101 Lady-B 23
And Christmas stories tortured into rhyme 245 Bards 245
In Christmas revels, simple country folks 261 Hints 321

CHRISTMAS-DAY
'Twas Christmas-day; in Paris all his court 467 Morgante 65

CHRIST'S
Christ's mighty shrine above his martyr's tomb 78 Harold 4 1371
To be Christ's Laureate--they reward him well 462 Dante 3 137
Christians war against Christ's shrine 735 Deformed 2 39
If he speak truth, she is Christ's sister, and 879 Juan 8 71

CHRONICLE
Fittest for such a chronicle as this 608 Foscari 3 27
'Tis written in the Hebrew Chronicle 767 Juan 1 1338
Thus far our chronicle; and now we pause 851 Juan 5 1265
The third sort to be noted in our chronicle 906 Juan 9 605
Turpin's or Monmouth Geoffry's Chronicle 981 Juan 16 34

CHRONICLERS
That injured Queen by chroniclers so coarse 839 Juan 5 481

CHRONICLES
In bloody chronicles of ages past 456 Dante 1 58
Which are your chronicles, I pray you note 566 Sardan 2 313

CHRONOLOGICAL
In chronological commemoration 813 Juan 3 804

CHRONOLOGY
Leaving at last not much besides chronology 759 Juan 1 823
Of--but Chronology best knows the years 853 Juan 6 48
The strictest in chronology and virtue 962 Juan 14 419

CHRONONHOTONTHOLOGOS
When 'Chrononhotonthologos must die 261 Hints 339

CHRYSOSTOM
To Jerome and to Chrysostom inured 752 Juan 1 371

CHUCKLINGS
How mothers love their children's squalls and
    chucklings 848 Juan 5 1062

CHURCH
And church and court did mingle their array 8 Harold 1 335
Than the church links withal; and, though unwed 43 Harold 3 489
When Self and Church demand a bigot zeal 112 Examination 62
The church of St. Mark--which stands hard by 196 Venice-A 31
Nor church nor state escaped his public sneers 261 Hints 333
Nor roars reform for senate, church, and bar 263 Hints 500
Our church and state, our courts and camps,
    concede 264 Hints 581
And served the church--without demanding tithes 266 Hints 674
I know that all save England's church have
    shamm'd 286 Vision 110
Lo! Mother Church, while all religion writhes 306 Age 642
Church, state, and faction wrestle in the dark 307 Age 646
Some of mosque, and some of church 384 Corinth 20
Of a long defended church 394 Corinth 872
Still the church is tenable 394 Corinth 910
And so God save the Regent, Church, and King 446 Beppo 383
(He made the church a present, by the way 452 Beppo 778
Church, palace, pillar, as a mourner greets 453 Venice-B 18
Who for the church and Christian faith had
    wrought 466 Morgante 39
With the true church, and through the church to
    heaven 492 Manfred 3 51
And all our church can teach thee shall be taught 492 Manfred 3 86
Near to the church where sleep my sires, the same 508 Faliero 1 601
At midnight, by the church Saints John and Paul 508 Faliero 1 608
Who, though of our most faultless holy church 711 Werner 4 464
Listen!--The church was throng'd; the hymn was
    raised 714 Werner 5 93

CHURCH
Amidst the people in the church, I dream'd not	716 Werner	5	188
The church, or one, or all? for you confound	731 Deformed	1	632
For half his days were pass'd at church, the other	753 Juan	1	391
The court, camp, church, the vessel, and the mart	770 Juan	1	1547
Was not so safe for roosting as a church	786 Juan	2	756
I grant you in a church 'tis very well	838 Juan	5	466
Whate'er the cause, the church made little of it	914 Juan	10	447
A hospital, a church,--and leave behind	931 Juan	12	75
Is when, without regard to 'church or state	937 Juan	12	507
(While yet the church was Rome's) stood half apart	948 Juan	13	466
'That Scriptures out of church are blasphemies	953 Juan	13	768
As far as I know, that the church receives	965 Juan	14	620
Made Norman Church his prey	985 Juan	16	326
To turn church lands to lay	985 Juan	16	330
For he's seen in the porch, and he's seen in the church	985 Juan	16	335
There were some massy members of the church	991 Juan	16	686

CHURCH-BELLS
In like church-bells, with sigh, howl, groan, yell, prayer	885 Juan	8	463

CHURCHES
And that the other twice two hundred churches	286 Vision		111
Yet as they founded churches with the produce	912 Juan	10	287
'Untying' squires 'to fight against the churches	988 Juan	16	526

CHURCHMAN
Churchman and votary alike despised	26 Harold	2	391

CHURCHMAN'S
Even the bold Churchman's tomb excited awe	916 Juan	10	588

CHURCH'S
Still by the church's bonds unchain'd	386 Corinth		197
Through his means and the church's might be paved	914 Juan	10	438
For he is yet the church's heir	986 Juan	16	355

CHURCHYARD
Or round the steep brow of the churchyard I wander'd	96 Harrow-A		15
Who fain wouldst make Parnassus a churchyard	245 Bards		266

CHURL
Provoking envious gibe from each pedestrian churl	15 Harold	1	701
Since it must be so, and this churl has check'd	552 Sardan	1	101

CHURLISH
Think me not churlish; I would spare thyself	493 Manfred	3	157

CHUSE
That rogue! how could Westminster chuse him again	178 Devil's Dr		167

CHYMIC
'Time is, Time was, Time's past:'--a chymic treasure	773 Juan	1	1734

CHYMIST
She's a poet, a chymist, a mathematician	278 Blues	1	66

CICALAS
The shrill cicalas, people of the pine	815 Juan	3	937

CICERO
And still the eloquent air breathes--burns with Cicero	72 Harold	4	1008

CICERONIAN
He revell'd in his Ciceronian glory	952 Juan	13	724

CICISBEO
The word was formerly a 'Cicisbeo'	444 Beppo		289

CICOGNA
By carrying off Count Cesare Cicogna	827 Juan	4	663

CID
Spain! which, a moment mindless of the Cid	300 Age		151
And in each heart the spirit of the Cid	303 Age		375

CI-DEVANT
Witness those 'ci-devant jeunes hommes' who stem	957 Juan	14	143

CIGAR
Thy naked beauties--Give me a cigar	425 Island	2	459

CINCINNATI
See these inglorious Cincinnati swarm	306 Age		614

CINCINNATUS
The Cincinnatus of the West	182 Ode-A		168

CINCINNATUS
The high Roman fashion, too, of Cincinnatus	897 Juan	9	51

CINDER
Like a cinder strew'd the plain	395 Corinth		1035

CINDERS
Above his burnt-out brain, and sapless cinders	925 Juan	11	477

CINNAMON
Cloves, cinnamon, and saffron too were boil'd	809 Juan	3	503

CINTRA
Britannia sickens, Cintra! at thy name	8 Harold	1	307

CINTRA'S
And Cintra's mountain greets them on their way	6 Harold	1	202
Lo! Cintra's glorious Eden intervenes	7 Harold	1	236

CIPHER
Than shine a lonely, though a gilded cipher	598 Foscari	1	196

CIRCASSIA
Whom, if they were at home in sweet Circassia	857 Juan	6	311

CIRCASSIAN
For one Circassian, a sweet girl, were given	830 Juan	4	906

CIRCASSIANS
And there with Georgians, Russians, and Circassians	830 Juan	4	903
And therefore of Circassians had good store	863 Juan	6	725

CIRCASSIA'S
So moved on earth Circassia's daughter	315 Giaour		505

CIRCLE
Thy name shall circle round the gaping throng	11 Harold	1	466
A circle there of merry listeners stand	22 Harold	2	187
On with the giddy circle, chasing Time	37 Harold	3	98
Last eve in Beauty's circle proudly gay	39 Harold	3	245
Then in this magic circle raise the dead	76 Harold	4	1295
Despoil'd, yet perfect, with thy circle spreads	77 Harold	4	1316
They quit the circle of the chiefs. Their	130 Calmar		97
And circle in the goblet's shape	154 Skull		11
And when the admiring circle mark	159 Storm		61
She rules the circle which she served before	208 Sketch		40
Wide and more wide thy witching circle spreads	275 Waltz		155
And form'd a circle like Orion's belt	288 Vision		204
The devil Asmodeus to the circle made	295 Vision		675
In circle narrowing as its glows	314 Giaour		424
A swarming circle of his foes	335 Abydos	2	544
Around him some mysterious circle thrown	367 Lara	1	107
While the crowd in a speechless circle gather	400 Parisina		405
The levell'd muskets circle round thy breast	416 Island	3	73
Now--now--he kneels--and now they form a circle	549 Faliero	5	818
I sought thy sweet face in the circle, but	580 Sardan	4	103
Yon small blue circle, swinging in far ether	636 Cain	2	29
And a black circle, bound	668 Heaven		1005
To a sedate grey circle of old smokers	805 Juan	3	266
In the dissolving circle, all the nations'	907 Juan	9	650
The circle smiled, then whisper'd, and then sneer'd	961 Juan	14	345
And then of course the circle much admires	986 Juan	16	373

CIRCLED
Circled the wide extending court below	28 Harold	2	507
Or, circled by his fatal fire	172 Romaic-B		11
Round the rent casque her owlet circled slow	269 Minerva		87
The eye like what it circled; the thin robes	529 Faliero	4	57

CIRCLE'S
Gapes round the silent circle's peopled walls	16 Harold	1	749
Even in the country circle's narrow bound	992 Juan	16	774

CIRCLES
In viewless circles wheel'd, his falchion flies	110 Nisus		393
Through splendid circles, fashion's gaudy world	124 Recoll		189
Used in politest circles to express	445 Beppo		314
And wider, and make widening circles round us	639 Cain	2	203
Checks to a lake, whose waves in circles spread	792 Juan	2	1127
High in high circles, gentle in her own	935 Juan	12	377

CIRCLET
With an inferior circlet near it still	636 Cain	2	30

CIRCLING
Where lone Utraikey forms its circling cove	30 Harold	2	622
The feast was done, the red wine circling fast	30 Harold	2	632
These sparkling segments of that circling soul	193 Monody		34
Now round the room the circling dow'gers sweep	250 Bards		660
A Glory circling round the soul	321 Giaour		1140
'One effort--one--to break the circling host	350 Corsair	2	243
In vain the circling chieftains round them closed	376 Lara	2	63

CIRCLING
With a thousand circling wrinkles — 395 Corinth — 1038
On which the circling fetters sounded — 399 Parisina — 319
The circling white dilated grew — 400 Parisina — 333
Circling all nature, hush'd, and dim, and still — 797 Juan — 2 — 1460
Whence the broad moon rose circling into sight — 797 Juan — 2 — 1476

CIRCUIT
Retrace the circuit of my former flight — 125 Recoll — 210

CIRCULAR
Of trees, in circular array, so fix'd — 214 Dream — 37
No sign that it was circular anywhere — 850 Juan — 5 — 1196

CIRCULATING
No circulating library amasses — 450 Beppo — 619
Of one of the most circulating scandals — 770 Juan — 1 — 1514
Make some prefer the circulating medium — 910 Juan — 10 — 176

CIRCULATION
With clownish heel, your popular circulation — 901 Juan — 9 — 279

CIRCUMAMBIENT
And soon were lost in circumambient foam — 5 Harold — 1 — 103

CIRCUMCISE
But they as soon shall circumcise my head — 840 Juan — 5 — 568

CIRCUMCISED
Though sadly scoff'd at by the circumcised — 26 Harold — 2 — 389

CIRCUMCISION
If they would condescend to circumcision — 840 Juan — 5 — 552

CIRCUMFUSED
Glowing and circumfused in speechless love — 62 Harold — 4 — 460

CIRCUMSCRIBE
Nor fix on fond abodes to circumscribe thy pray'r — 49 Harold — 3 — 859

CIRCUMSCRIBETH
Though not to one dome circumscribeth she — 14 Harold — 1 — 672

CIRCUMSCRIBING
By circumscribing, with some slight restriction — 286 Vision — 103

CIRCUMSPECT
(Although their talk's obscure and circumspect — 751 Juan — 1 — 260
Without the apparel of being circumspect — 962 Juan — 14 — 444
In which you cannot be too circumspect — 987 Juan — 16 — 461

CIRCUMSPECTION
Harriet! To see such Circumspection — 151 Harriet — 1
Hut, whence wise travellers drive with circumspection — 910 Juan — 10 — 214
Who like to play the fool with circumspection — 927 Juan — 11 — 560

CIRCUMSTANCE
And Circumstance, that unspiritual god — 74 Harold — 4 — 1122
By circumstance compell'd to plunge again — 378 Lara — 2 — 232
All circumstance which may compel — 397 Parisina — 128
When struggling with the tides of circumstance — 531 Faliero — 4 — 217
Though circumstance may keep it in abeyance — 534 Faliero — 4 — 407
And all which circumstance can add to aid them — 538 Faliero — 5 — 28
Repress'd by circumstance but not destroy'd — 550 Sardan — 1 — 12
All are the sons of circumstance: away — 576 Sardan — 3 — 320
I am the very slave of circumstance — 583 Sardan — 4 — 330
Consuming but not killing. Circumstance — 600 Foscari — 1 — 293
Sin in itself? Can circumstance make sin — 633 Cain — 1 — 378
It must be he! All circumstance proclaims it — 687 Werner — 2 — 270
And circumstance, and proofs; I know enough — 691 Werner — 2 — 557
You wax too insolent. If circumstance — 692 Werner — 2 — 590
Except that circumstance is less against him — 695 Werner — 2 — 753
And every speck of circumstance unite — 715 Werner — 5 — 161
To hear related a strange circumstance — 716 Werner — 5 — 228
This circumstance may serve to give a notion — 868 Juan — 7 — 81
About; a circumstance which has confounded — 881 Juan — 8 — 220
Flung here by fate or circumstance, which tame — 885 Juan — 8 — 430
And in each circumstance of love or war — 964 Juan — 14 — 567

CIRCUMSTANCES
In circumstances which would call forth
  tears — 602 Foscari — 2 — 73
Her circumstances must excuse her bearing — 626 Foscari — 5 — 366
And long-engender'd circumstances (not — 693 Werner — 2 — 679
Have in such circumstances thrust him forth — 703 Werner — 3 — 522
Men are the sport of circumstances, when — 833 Juan — 5 — 135
The circumstances seem the sport of men — 833 Juan — 5 — 136
More circumstances? vain was every care — 835 Juan — 5 — 270
In all the circumstances of the case — 920 Juan — 11 — 138
To his own circumstances, there might lie — 972 Juan — 15 — 236
If in the circumstances which ensued — 994 Juan — 16 — 899

CIRCUS
Then to the crowded circus forth they fare — 15 Harold — 1 — 718

CIRCUS
For Astley's circus Upton writes — 233 Ballad-B — 25
The narrow circus of my dungeon wall — 437 Tasso — 23
But the gladiators' bloody Circus stands — 495 Manfred — 3 — 287
Have been the circus of an empire. Well — 734 Deformed — 1 — 850

CIRCUS'
Such were the bloody Circus' genial laws — 76 Harold — 4 — 1247

CIRQUE
Some likeness, which the glittering cirque
  confines — 931 Juan — 12 — 94

CITADEL
Coop'd in their winged sea-girt citadel — 23 Harold — 2 — 249

CITE
To name his works--he would but cite a few — 297 Vision — 767
Cite is, that Boon lived hunting up to ninety — 886 Juan — 8 — 496

CITED
Beyond the charmers we have already cited — 974 Juan — 15 — 380

CITHAERON'S
But ere he sunk below Cithaeron's head — 268 Minerva — 29
But here he sank below Cithaeron's head — 356 Corsair — 3 — 29
On dun Cithaeron's ridge appears — 385 Corinth — 71
So did the leaves on Cithaeron's hill — 390 Corinth — 528

CITIES
(See also HALF-CITIES)
And scatter'd cities crowning these — 43 Harold — 3 — 502
Of human cities torture: I can see — 46 Harold — 3 — 683
Clank over sceptred cities; nations melt — 57 Harold — 4 — 103
Of busy cities, now in vain display'd — 60 Harold — 4 — 286
These sepulchres of cities which excite — 62 Harold — 4 — 403
Cities from out their sepulchres. Men bled — 68 Harold — 4 — 795
Of rock-built cities, bidding nations quake — 82 Harold — 4 — 1622
From cities to caves of the forest he flew — 99 L Adieu — 22
Were burnt for beacons; cities were consumed — 189 Darkness — 13
The silent cities of the dead — 189 On Star — 38
Or do they in their silent cities dwell — 192 Fragment-C — 27
In cities lodged too near his lord — 315 Giaour — 543
Are more than cities and Serais to me — 333 Abydos — 2 — 391
When cities cage us in a social home — 333 Abydos — 2 — 437
By cities levell'd with the dust — 386 Corinth — 156
Which makes the distant cities wonder — 392 Corinth — 756
And sway'd the waves, like cities of the sea — 422 Island — 2 — 226
Cities and generations--fair, when free — 454 Venice-B — 99
In turbulent cities, and the tented field — 457 Dante — 1 — 123
Of Venice, first of cities? To the sentence — 501 Faliero — 1 — 95
In many lands and cities; they can tell you — 523 Faliero — 3 — 305
In distant lands--on flood, in field, in cities — 541 Faliero — 5 — 207
Or for my trophies I have founded cities — 555 Sardan — 1 — 283
I own thy merit in those founded cities — 555 Sardan — 1 — 288
Shame me! by Baal, the cities, though well built — 555 Sardan — 1 — 291
The penalty of saving cities. He — 619 Foscari — 4 — 309
If we should measure forth the cities taken — 620 Foscari — 4 — 316
Taker of cities. Yet one shadow more — 726 Deformed — 1 — 259
In cities caged. The present case in point I — 886 Juan — 8 — 475
On cities, as hath been the present case — 890 Juan — 8 — 772
O'er silenced cities, merely served to flatter — 900 Juan — 9 — 229
Of cities, that boil over with their scum — 919 Juan — 11 — 64
Whose cities Night by no means deigns to gloss — 921 Juan — 11 — 205

CITIES'
Where the Dead Sea hath quench'd two cities'
  ashes — 526 Faliero — 3 — 544

CITIZEN
(See also FELLOW-CITIZEN)
Then thy spruce citizen, wash'd artisan — 15 Harold — 1 — 695
When the soldier citizen — 187 Ode-B — 24
Of a true citizen fulfill'd, and saw — 457 Dante — 1 — 89
All that a citizen could be I was — 465 Dante — 4 — 144
(For here the sovereign is a citizen — 503 Faliero — 1 — 248
And not less loyal citizen and subject — 504 Faliero — 1 — 287
Of soldier, citizen, and friend; in all — 510 Faliero — 2 — 101
That which scarce one more favour'd citizen — 515 Faliero — 2 — 476
A Prince who fain would be a citizen — 523 Faliero — 3 — 330
It means, I am more citizen than either — 608 Foscari — 2 — 415
A crown to him who saved a citizen — 620 Foscari — 4 — 314
As sovereign--I go out as citizen — 624 Foscari — 5 — 274
By the same portals, but as citizen — 625 Foscari — 5 — 275

CITIZENS
(See also FELLOW-CITIZENS)
While throng'd the citizens with terror dumb — 39 Harold — 3 — 224
Free citizens have struck at kings ere now — 526 Faliero — 3 — 555
These citizens all lions, like their standard — 533 Faliero — 4 — 387
Your tributaries, your dumb citizens — 606 Foscari — 2 — 302
Had thousands of such citizens, and shall — 608 Foscari — 2 — 417
By the Doge Foscari, with citizens — 620 Foscari — 4 — 317
Our nobles were but citizens and merchants — 682 Werner — 1 — 709

CITRON

Where the citron and olive are fairest of fruit	323 Abydos	1	9

CITS

Saw cits grow centaurs underneath his brush	256 Hints	4
With thee even clumsy cits attempt to bounce	275 Waltz	157

CITY

And left the primal city of the land	26 Harold	2	416
The city won for Allah from the Giaour	31 Harold	2	729
Was as a fairy city of the heart	57 Harold	4	155
Oh Rome, my country! city of the soul	66 Harold	4	694
Alas, the lofty city! and alas	67 Harold	4	730
Forsook his former city, what could be	78 Harold	4	1382
That glorious city still shall be	158 Florence		38
And the seven-hill'd city seeking	162 War Song		19
In one dread night our city saw, and sigh'd	169 Address-A		1
Of an enormous city did survive	189 Darkness		56
How Alhama's city fell	194 Ballad-A		7
No city Wordsworth, more admired than read	231 Sotheby		3
But even too nasty for a city knight	262 Hints		398
Babe of a city birth! from sixpence take	264 Hints		517
Your city saddens; loud though Revel howls	271 Minerva		241
Gird the gross sirloin of a city Celt	308 Age		774
Strange rumours in our city say	314 Giaour		447
Their galleys blaze--why not their city too	350 Corsair	2	195
The city lies behind--they speed, they reach	362 Corsair	3	446
From city or from succour near	410 Mazeppa		332
Venice the bell from every city bore	441 Beppo		78
That sea-born city was in all her glory	441 Beppo		80
The city it has clothed in chains, which clank	454 Venice-B		118
The city lies sleeping	488 Manfred	2	332
The city worse than nothing--mere machines	504 Faliero	1	331
Within, above, around, that in this city	516 Faliero	2	506
Be strung to city gates and castle walls	517 Faliero	2	609
Of that which will befall them. Yes, proud city	519 Faliero	3	7
Let me but prosper, and I make this city	519 Faliero	3	45
Decreed to him by the twice rescued city	520 Faliero	3	91
To this unshackled city. A true tyrant	528 Faliero	3	655
The ocean-born and earth-commanding city	529 Faliero	4	104
These city slaves have all their private bias	533 Faliero	4	366
I, who was named Preserver of the City	535 Faliero	4	499
A city which has open'd India's wealth	538 Faliero	5	14
The throne of such a city, these lost men	538 Faliero	5	18
To portion them (leaving my city spoil	545 Faliero	5	535
And this proud city, and these azure waters	547 Faliero	5	656
Of this proud city, and I leave my curse	548 Faliero	5	740
To the unrivall'd city! What dost dread	555 Sardan	1	327
Even to the city, and so baffle all	556 Sardan	1	350
The free air of the city, and we'll shorten	568 Sardan	2	441
Within the palace or the city walls	568 Sardan	2	445
Their stations in the city, they refused	572 Sardan	3	78
We've clear'd the palace--And I trust the city	576 Sardan	3	331
For ages, 'That the city ne'er should yield	590 Sardan	5	196
The brightness of our city; and her domes	598 Foscari	1	165
I trust, have still such, Venice were no city	608 Foscari	2	418
Accursed be the city where the laws	608 Foscari	2	419
Of our departure from this much-loved city	611 Foscari	3	216
Ye tutelar saints of my own city! which	616 Foscari	4	127
Your friend? He was the safeguard of the city	619 Foscari	4	306
To him who took a city; and they gave	620 Foscari	4	313
And build thy city o'er the drown'd earth's grave	660 Heaven		408
I came upon the frontier; the free city	680 Werner	1	566
The strongest city, Prague, that fire and sword	694 Werner	2	710
Am aught connected with that city. Then	709 Werner	4	288
With the nobles of the city. I felt sure	717 Werner	5	262
To leave the city privately: we left it	717 Werner	5	279
Lord of the city which hath been earth's lord	730 Deformed	1	575
And shall the city yield? I see the giant	731 Deformed	1	605
The city, or the amphitheatre	731 Deformed	1	631
Through every change the seven-hill'd city hath	734 Deformed	1	844
O'er the city high and holy	735 Deformed	2	6
On they sweep. Oh, glorious city	736 Deformed	2	61
Rouse thee, thou eternal city	736 Deformed	2	66
In Seville was he born, a pleasant city	748 Juan	1	57
With more than half the city at his back	763 Juan	1	1090
Commands the city, and upon its site	868 Juan	7	76
He made no answer; but he took the city	874 Juan	7	424
Hurling defiance: city, stream, and shore	879 Juan	8	60
In this extensive city, sore beset	882 Juan	8	292
His thanks, and hopes to take the city soon	885 Juan	8	446
The madden'd Turks their city still dispute	887 Juan	8	552
The city, without being farther hamper'd	887 Juan	8	596
Without resistance, see their city burn	888 Juan	8	612
Rolls by the city wall; but deed nor word	889 Juan	8	692
And groans; and thus the peopled city grieves	889 Juan	8	701
Will serve when there is plunder in a city	891 Juan	8	806
He never would believe the city won	891 Juan	8	836
What's this in one annihilated city	894 Juan	8	989
Could rhyme, like Nero, o'er a burning city	895 Juan	8	1072
Was left upon his way to the chief city	899 Juan	9	178
Was a ta'en city, thirty thousand slain	904 Juan	9	466
With you, than aught (save Scott) in your proud city	909 Juan	10	132

CITY

A city which presents to the inspector	915 Juan	10	494
Toward the great city.--Ye who have a spark in	917 Juan	10	637
Meaneth the west or worst end of a city	924 Juan	11	354
Than storms it as a foe would take a city	939 Juan	12	590
To lose those best months in a sweaty city	947 Juan	13	380
A most important outwork of the city	993 Juan	16	790

CITY'S
(See also OCEAN-CITY'S)

Through many a cypress grove within each city's ken	25 Harold	2	342
Ne city's towers pollute the lovely view	27 Harold	2	460
Of sated Grandeur from the city's noise	29 Harold	2	573
Of coming ripeness, the white city's sheen	44 Harold	3	582
Above the dogeless city's vanish'd sway	55 Harold	4	31
Have dealt upon the seven-hill'd city's pride	67 Harold	4	713
That half avenged the city's fall	394 Corinth		912
And form'd the Eternal City's ornaments	459 Dante	2	56
Rose o'er the city's murmur in the night	528 Faliero	4	14
A city's glory--we have laid already	540 Faliero	5	159
The honour of our city's gone for ever	683 Werner	2	7
They flit along the eternal city's rampart	733 Deformed	1	760
Of such: the city's render'd. And mark well	740 Deformed	2	339
The city's shape suggested this, 'tis true	870 Juan	7	182
Beyond the dwarfing city's pale abortions	886 Juan	8	522
The city's taken--only part by part	888 Juan	8	649
The city's taken, but not render'd!--No	889 Juan	8	689
If yet the city's rest were won or lost	893 Juan	8	958
Of this enormous city's spreading span	922 Juan	11	220

CIVIC

Of a proud, brotherly, and civic band	45 Harold	3	612
Her ancient civic boast--'the Free	385 Corinth		130
The native mariners and civic troops	507 Faliero	1	494
Nor bow the knee before a civic senate	533 Faliero	4	376
But friend or foe will roll in civic slaughter	535 Faliero	4	497
I interfered not with their civic lives	556 Sardan	1	405
I speak of civic popular love, self-love	559 Sardan	1	584
Our quick departure proves our civic zeal	569 Sardan	2	461
No doubt, the camp's the school of civic rights	734 Deformed	1	853
From civic revelry to rural mirth	762 Juan	1	988
Should now be butcher'd in a civic alley	836 Juan	5	296

CIVIL

Thy factions, in their worse than civil war	63 Harold	4	507
When civil discord piled the fields with dead	111 Examination		14
Famed for their civil and domestic quarrels	228 Vaults		1
Civil to sharpers, prodigal of cash	260 Hints		234
A civil aspect: though they did not kiss	289 Vision		278
Saint Peter, you were wont to be more civil	291 Vision		403
New havoc, such as civil discord blends	377 Lara	2	164
On such occasions should be civil	410 Mazeppa		320
An eye to gaze upon their civil rage	458 Dante	1	147
Were civil fury raging in Saint Mark's	511 Faliero	2	201
A foreign foe invade, or civil broil	552 Sardan	1	125
And placed beneath the civil jurisdiction	717 Werner	5	240
Like human beings during civil war	779 Juan	2	336
Like lap-dogs, the least civil sons of b--s	923 Juan	11	328
You should be civil in a modest way	969 Juan	15	70
The civil list he deigns to accept (obliging all	988 Juan	16	494
Sooner 'come place into the civil list	990 Juan	16	641

CIVILIAN

Poor noble meet a mushroom rich civilian	289 Vision		288
Belike;--I'm a civilian. Fool! are not	693 Werner	2	657

CIVILISATION

The sordor of civilisation, mix'd	419 Island	2	69
So that civilisation they may learn	762 Juan	1	1046
The inconvenience of civilisation	886 Juan	8	509
Now back to thy great joys, Civilisation	886 Juan	8	538

CIVILISATION'S

And civilised Civilisation's son	422 Island	2	271

CIVILISE

Lands which no foes destroy or civilise	420 Island	2	100

CIVILISED

And civilised Civilisation's son	422 Island	2	271
Still the world's masters! Civilised, barbarian	734 Deformed	1	848
The bear is civilised, the wolf is mild	890 Juan	8	733

CIVILISING

Which two worlds bless for civilising both	425 Island	2	487

CIVILITY

To some civility, to others bounty	990 Juan	16	611

CLAD
(See also MAIL-CLAD, PLUME-CLAD, SCARCE-CLAD,
SNOW-CLAD, THIN-CLAD, WELL-CLAD)

CLAMOROUS
Although they're now and then a little clamorous 444 Beppo 267
With unimpair'd but not a clamorous grief 547 Faliero 5 687
Woman, this clamorous grief of thine, I tell thee 603 Foscari 2 132
So desolate, that the most clamorous grief 615 Foscari 4 9

CLAMOUR
Retire; the clamour of the fight is o'er 121 Newstead-A 94
Their noisome clamour? You have said they are men 556 Sardan 1 390
The air with clamour) build the palaces 587 Sardan 5 27
Not all the clamour broke her happy state 861 Juan 6 581
With such a clamour! I had thought it right 862 Juan 6 643

CLAMOUR'D
Clamour'd in chorus to the roaring ocean 778 Juan 2 272

CLAMOURS
No factious clamours can control 88 Horace 2

CLAN
(See also ROBBER-CLAN)
Yelling their uncouth dirge, long daunced the kirtled clan 30 Harold 2 639
But who was last of Alva's clan 102 Alva 25
Again the clan, in festive crowd 103 Alva 177
You rest with your clan in the caves of Braemar 117 Lachin 30
And own the chieftain of the critic clan 248 Bards 507
Than the vile foray of a plundering clan 254 Bards 937
While throng'd the chiefs of every Highland clan 308 Age 769
His island clan to where the waters spread 432 Island 4 204
Into a scene, and swell the clients' clan 963 Juan 14 492

CLANG
Sounds not the clang of conflict on the heath 10 Harold 1 415
Adieu the clang of war's alarms 88 Anacreon-A 20
The mirth of feasts, the clang of burnish'd arms 120 Newstead-A 54
is the clang of death! many are the widows 131 Calmar 151
The clang of tumult vibrate on his ears 345 Corsair 1 522
As from a sudden trumpet's clang 411 Mazeppa 459
Amidst the clash of swords and clang of helms 464 Dante 4 70
With every clang. 'Tis a perpetual knell 701 Werner 3 393
Shall clang with our tread 732 Deformed 1 722

CLANGOUR
Fire and smoke and hellish clangour 736 Deformed 2 86

CLANK
Clank over sceptred cities; nations melt 57 Harold 4 103
True, the chains of the Catholic clank o'er his rags 202 Avatar 9
His spirit wither'd with their clank 403 Chillon 98
The city it has clothed in chains, which clank 454 Venice-B 118
Hearken to the armour's clank 735 Deformed 2 22

CLANK'D
And heavy though it clank'd not; worn with pain 36 Harold 3 79
Clank'd, as he paced it to and fro 389 Corinth 453
When those dull chains in meeting clank'd 399 Parisina 322
Of feet on which the iron clank'd, the groan 608 Foscari 3 4
Though knives and forks clank'd round as in a fray 992 Juan 16 741

CLANKING
Then, only then, his clanking hands he raised 352 Corsair 2 376
Thy clanking chain, and Erin's yet green wounds 747 Juan Ded 125

CLANKLESS
And the clankless chain hath bound thee 481 Manfred 1 259

CLAN'S
Which held his clan's great ashes stood 105 Alva 302

CLANSMAN'S
And Evan's, Donald's fame rings in each clansman's ears 39 Harold 3 234

CLAP
Stumbling o'er recollections; now we clap 67 Harold 4 727
Clap thy permitted palms, kind Italy 304 Age 432
And clap a white cape on their mantles blue 763 Juan 1 1069

CLAPP'D
Thrice clapp'd his hands, and call'd his steed 326 Abydos 1 232
She clapp'd her hands, and through the gallery pour 362 Corsair 3 438
And clapp'd her hands with joy at his surprise 431 Island 3 128

CLAPPING
The waving banner, and the clapping door 370 Lara 1 261
That is--the Lady:' clapping his hands twice 841 Juan 5 639

CLAPT
Passengers their berths are clapt in 157 Hodgson 35

CLAPT
Just like a coffin clapt in a canoe 442 Beppo 151

CLAP-TRAP
Of clap-trap which your recent poets prize 789 Juan 2 988

CLARE
Now, Clare, I must return to you 138 Clare 67
In truth, dear Clare, in fancy's flight 138 Clare 70

CLARENCE
With maudlin Clarence in his Malmsey butt 767 Juan 1 1328

CLARENS
Clarens, sweet Clarens, birthplace of deep Love 50 Harold 3 923
Clarens! by heavenly feet thy paths are trod 50 Harold 3 932

CLARET
(See also ALL-CLARETLESS)
The copious use of claret is forbid too 773 Juan 1 1726
Of claret, sandwich, and an appetite 838 Juan 5 459
Spoilt, as a pipe of claret is when prick'd 851 Juan 5 1261
But then they have their claret and Madeira 941 Juan 13 37
The claret light, and the Madeira strong 950 Juan 13 606

CLARION
Nor here War's clarion, but Love's rebeck sounds 11 Harold 1 490
Thrice sounds the clarion; lo! the signal falls 16 Harold 1 747
With the silver clarion round 194 Ballad-A 19

CLARKE
There Clarke, still striving piteously 'to please 255 Bards 973

CLASH
Through sparkling spray, in thundering clash 316 Giaour 628
For swords began to clash and shouts to swell 349 Corsair 2 155
And the clash, and the shout, 'They come! they come 391 Corinth 687
For my part, I say nothing, lest we clash 452 Beppo 765
Amidst the clash of swords and clang of helms 464 Dante 4 70
The groans of men--the clash of arms--the sound 530 Faliero 4 165
Lest it should clash with thine; for thou art still 551 Sardan 1 70
It sounded like the clash of--hark again 572 Sardan 3 64
Are chains. Again that shout! and now the clash 574 Sardan 3 196
As a lute's pierceth through the cymbal's clash 577 Sardan 3 393

CLASH'D
Fast in his cave, and nothing clash'd upon 791 Juan 2 1090
Clash'd 'gainst the scimitar, and babe and mother 887 Juan 8 548
Though much in temper; but they never clash'd 966 Juan 14 690

CLASHES
Now the meeting steel first clashes 736 Deformed 2 89

CLASHING
While helmets cleft, and sabres clashing 187 Ode-B 47
With clashing hosts, who strew'd the barren sand 300 Age 149
Of sabres clashing, foemen flying 318 Giaour 824
Clashing swords, and spears transfixing 394 Corinth 901
And grappled with him, clashing steel with steel 562 Sardan 2 85
The clashing music, and the thundering 714 Werner 5 113

CLASP
Thy gentle hand to clasp in mine 44 Harold 3 515
In thee, I fondly hoped to clasp 85 To D-- 1
And clasp enraptured all your charms 91 Caroline-B 42
And clasp again the comrade of my youth 106 Nisus 58
Restring the chords, renew the clasp 169 The Chain 16
The olive branch, which still she deign'd to clasp 269 Minerva 83
Where were the rapture then to clasp the form 277 Waltz 236
No hand shall close its clasp again 313 Giaour 327
And clasp her to my desperate heart 323 Giaour 1286
I clasp--what is it that I clasp 323 Giaour 1287
To clasp the neck of him who blest 325 Abydos 1 185
But never did clasp of one so dear 391 Corinth 601
And clasp the mountain in his mind's embrace 422 Island 2 283
No, no;--they woo and clasp us to their spheres 424 Island 2 389
Stretch'd forth her arms to clasp her lord again 468 Morgante 133
I yet might be most happy. I will clasp thee 481 Manfred 1 190
'Tis flesh; grasp--clasp--yet closer, till I feel 579 Sardan 4 43
And dost me justice now. Let me once clasp 589 Sardan 5 161
Methinks, a Sylla's menace; but they clasp 733 Deformed 1 765
Yet there's no doubt she only meant to clasp 760 Juan 1 884
Surmounted as its clasp--a glowing crescent 811 Juan 3 615
His daughter; while compress'd within his clasp 822 Juan 4 378

CLASP'D
Which mutely clasp'd, imploringly caress'd 345 Corsair 1 477
He clasp'd that hand--it trembled--and his own 363 Corsair 3 539
He clasp'd her sleeping to his heart 397 Parisina 81
And smiled, and wept, and near and nearer clasp'd 429 Island 3 189

CLASP'D
The same breast, clasp'd thee often to my own 654 Cain 3 536
Been clasp'd again in these long-empty arms 672 Werner 1 57
They turn'd to rest; and, each clasp'd by an arm 797 Juan 2 1471
One large gold bracelet clasp'd each lovely arm 810 Juan 3 561
And ran, but it escaped her as she clasp'd 820 Juan 4 256

CLASPS
She clasps a babe to whom her breast yields no relief 80 Harold 4 1503
'Look on your Spain!--she clasps the hand she hates 271 Minerva 229
But boldly clasps, and thrusts you from her gates 271 Minerva 230
He clasps the hand that pang which would assuage 381 Lara 2 426
And clasps her Lord unto the breast 397 Parisina 73
That his thin finger feels not what it clasps 453 Venice-B 49
Gleam in the moonlight; and her white arm clasps 798 Juan 2 1546

CLASS
Flowers fresh in hue, and many in their class 72 Harold 4 1049
Perchance succeeded by some other class 447 Beppo 475
Her talents were of the more silent class 858 Juan 6 392
It sooner for the soul of me, and class 859 Juan 6 445
Parental feelings, and the other class 914 Juan 10 421
To keep the wheels going of the higher class 937 Juan 12 453
Yet think, a specimen of every class 953 Juan 13 747
Of the best class, and better than her class 973 Juan 15 340

CLASS'D
Class'd among creatures, when the soul can flee 46 Harold 3 686
Aught but a phantasy, and could be class'd 79 Harold 4 1474
Must what terror or policy wring forth be class'd 203 Avatar 59
With these and with their victims am I class'd 437 Tasso 74
Their sail, and deem it glory to be class'd 456 Dante 1 56
And henceforth found himself more gaily class'd 926 Juan 11 502
By whose degrees all characters are class'd 987 Juan 16 427

CLASSES
Kick off their burthens, meaning the high classes 929 Juan 11 664

CLASS-HONOURS
Class-honours, medals, fellowships, await 112 Examination 24

CLASSIC
Though classic ground and consecrated most 26 Harold 2 413
And quote in classic raptures, and awake 66 Harold 4 671
With him, for years, we search'd the classic page 123 Recoll 111
We neither conquer'd in the classic strife 126 Recoll 334
Ye tenants of the classic bower 145 Adieu 16
Of repetitions nicknamed Classic 233 Nihil 16
Whatever I was, I'm classic now 233 Nihil 18
O'er his lost works let classic Sheffield weep 247 Bards 424
And classic Hallam, much renown'd for Greek 248 Bards 513
One classic drama, and reform the stage 249 Bards 585
With hallow'd feelings for those classic lands 253 Bards 874
To crown the bards that haunt her classic grove 255 Bards 988
Good classic Louis! is it, canst thou say 305 Age 512
His classic studies made a little puzzle 752 Juan 1 321
In cloisters of the classic Salamanca 778 Juan 2 295
Light classic articles of female want 803 Juan 3 132
Or if, too classic for his vulgar brain 814 Juan 3 885
And drill'd away in the most classic Russian 875 Juan 7 506
Such classic pas--sans flaws--set off our hero 960 Juan 14 311

CLASSICAL
Their classical profiles, and glittering dresses 805 Juan 3 257
With motives the most classical and pure 988 Juan 16 499

CLATTER
Is Lucifer come back with all this clatter 287 Vision 136
Arose a clatter might awake the dead 763 Juan 1 1083
Which sets the teeth on edge; and a slight clatter 995 Juan 16 954

CLATTERING
The mustering squadron, and the clattering car 39 Harold 3 218
Beneath the clattering iron's sound 312 Giaour 182
Shakes with the clattering tramp no more 312 Giaour 254

CLAUDIUS
(Though Claudius Rich, Esquire, some bricks has got 839 Juan 5 493

CLAUSE
Making kings' rights divine, by some Draconic clause 45 Harold 3 616
All your own private fortune. That last clause 623 Foscari 5 175
And that which chiefly proved his saving clause 784 Juan 2 646
His friend, too, adding a new saving clause 837 Juan 5 374
In outward show, which is a saving clause 859 Juan 6 459
That clause is hard); and secondly, proceed 950 Juan 13 582

CLAVE
Cortana clave the skull like a true brand 470 Morgante 275

CLAW
If at that moment he had chanced to claw it 769 Juan 1 1477
There's nothing whets the beak, or arms the claw 848 Juan 5 1059

CLAWS
And without that, their poison and their claws 900 Juan 9 218

CLAY
(See also HALF-CLAY)
Nor all that heralds rake from coffin'd clay 4 Harold 1 25
Yes, Honour decks the turf that wraps their clay 10 Harold 1 451
Fame that will scarce re-animate their clay 11 Harold 1 470
He had been happy; but this clay will sink 37 Harold 3 123
The earth is cover'd thick with other clay 39 Harold 3 250
Which her own clay shall cover, heap'd and pent 39 Harold 3 251
The beings of the mind are not of clay 55 Harold 4 37
Endure and shrink not, we of nobler clay 58 Harold 4 188
Their bones, distinguish'd from our common clay 63 Harold 4 500
A world is at our feet as fragile as our clay 66 Harold 4 702
And laid him with the earth's preceding clay 68 Harold 4 769
Because not altogether of such clay 75 Harold 4 1214
Their clay creator the vain title take 82 Harold 4 1625
Within this narrow cell reclines her clay 84 Death-B 5
That clay, where once such animation beam'd 84 Death-B 6
If that with honour fail to crown my clay 86 Fragment-A 9
Friend and associate of this clay 87 Adrian 2
Oh when shall my soul wing her flight from this clay 91 Caroline-D 2
But Oscar's breast is cold as clay 104 Alva 277
Transfix'd his heart, and stretch'd him on the clay 110 Nisus 352
The humid pall of life-extinguish'd clay 120 Newstead-A 30
With clay the grave's eternal bed 133 Prayer 58
Unheeded in the clay 146 Adieu 92
Redeem'd from worms and wasting clay 154 Skull 23
With fronts of brass and feet of clay 180 Ode-A 27
Is vile as vulgar clay 181 Ode-A 101
Our life is but a load of clay 189 On Star 36
A lump of death--a chaos of hard clay 190 Darkness 72
To extricate remembrance from the clay 190 Churchill 22
I borrow my comparisons from clay 291 Vision 429
But mingled millions decomposed to clay 192 Fragment-C 24
Were he God--as he is but the commonest clay 202 Avatar 30
If the idol of brass find his feet are of clay 203 Avatar 58
Be stamp'd in the turf o'er their fetterless clay 204 Avatar 120
Even worms shall perish on thy poisonous clay 209 Sketch 98
And thought of shaking off my bonds of clay 211 Augusta-C 30
Then we mix our mouldering clay 219 Saul-B 24
When coldness wraps this suffering clay 220 Clay 1
Is light and worthless clay 220 Belshaz-B 44
Creatures of clay--vain dwellers in the dust 222 Spirit 9
As the mere million's base unmummied clay 286 Vision 87
Of clay obscures our best conceptions, saving 288 Vision 223
And that 'the sons of God,' like those of clay 289 Vision 260
Being clay myself. Let not those spirits be 291 Vision 430
That form was nought but breathing clay 315 Giaour 481
The cold consumers of their clay 319 Giaour 950
And fit thy clay to fertilise the soil 375 Lara 2 18
The haughty spirit of that humble clay 382 Lara 2 501
Claim'd kindred with their sacred clay 388 Corinth 411
Fragments of stone, rear'd by creatures of clay 389 Corinth 506
Deeply dinted in the clay 396 Corinth 1055
Theirs was unconsecrated clay 401 Parisina 511
And chivalrous. Upon the clay 407 Mazeppa 48
I thought to mingle there our clay 414 Mazeppa 765
Are far more potent o'er our yielding clay 417 Island 1 119
Dissolve this clog and clod of clay before 424 Island 1 390
Yet so relieving the o'er-tortured clay 453 Venice-B 42
The weight of clay again,--too soon bereft 456 Dante 1 3
Which still recoils from its encumbering clay 463 Dante 4 22
What wouldst thou, Child of Clay, with me 480 Manfred 1 131
Are at thy beck and bidding, Child of Clay 480 Manfred 1 133
And shall not yield to yours, though coop'd in clay 480 Manfred 1 157
Nor midst the creatures of clay that girded me 485 Manfred 2 152
And was all clay again. And then I dived 486 Manfred 2 173
Prostrate thyself, and thy condemned clay 489 Manfred 2 404
As far as is compatible with clay 489 Manfred 2 426
As clay hath seldom borne; his aspirations 489 Manfred 2 428
Of the mould of thy clay 490 Manfred 2 459
Less hardy clay--Time has but little power 509 Faliero 2 13
And do what our frail clay, thus clogg'd, hath fail'd in 537 Faliero 4 660
Acts of this clay! 'Tis true I have not shed 557 Sardan 1 449
Besides, I know of these all clay can know 566 Sardan 2 265
Am softer clay, impregnated with flowers 570 Sardan 2 522
A shadow of this cumbrous clog of clay 579 Sardan 4 59
And false, and hollow--clay from first to last 607 Foscari 2 352
How should I be so? Look on me! Poor clay 629 Cain 1 123
Poor clay! what should I tempt them for, or how 630 Cain 1 214
With worms in clay? And what art thou who dwellest 637 Cain 2 85
But changes make not death, except to clay 638 Cain 2 163
But thou art clay, and canst but comprehend 638 Cain 2 164

CLAY

That which was clay, and such thou shalt behold	638 Cain	2	165
Clay, spirit! what thou wilt, I can survey	638 Cain	2	166
Clay has its earth, and other worlds their tenants	644 Cain	2	575
Come, Zillah! Yet one kiss on yon pale clay	653 Cain	3	453
Unto some son of clay, and toil and spin	655 Heaven		16
Of the poor child of clay which so adored him	655 Heaven		23
Share the dim destiny of clay in this	656 Heaven		89
Though I be form'd of clay	656 Heaven		97
The creatures proud of their poor clay	661 Heaven		438
For perishable clay	666 Heaven		865
I would not keep this life of mine in clay	667 Heaven		904
Farewell, thou earth! ye wretched sons of clay	669 Heaven		1069
Thou clay, be all glowing	728 Deformed	1	388
Which clay can compound	728 Deformed	1	409
Clay! not dead, but soul-less	728 Deformed	1	452
Clay thou art; and unto spirit	729 Deformed	1	456
All clay is of equal merit	729 Deformed	1	457
Keep them yet ignorant that I am but clay	736 Deformed	2	135
I would to heaven that I were so much clay	745 Fragment-D		1
Who cannot leave alone our helpless clay	754 Juan	1	499
The boy expired--the father held the clay	785 Juan	2	713
As fair a thing as e'er was form'd of clay	788 Juan	2	880
Of such quicksilver clay that in his breast	800 Juan	2	1667
Our little selves re-form'd in finer clay	808 Juan	3	468
Was not for them--they had too little clay	817 Juan	4	72
The precious porcelain of human clay	817 Juan	4	83
Her human clay is kindled; full of power	823 Juan	4	442
And nothing outward tells of human clay	825 Juan	4	572
To gaze once more on the commanding clay	836 Juan	5	291
Although of clay, are yet not quite of mud	849 Juan	5	1099
As any man's clay mixture undergoes	855 Juan	6	157
For deeming human clay but common dirt	874 Juan	7	461
Their clay for the last time their souls encumber	880 Juan	8	141
From the manure of human clay, though deck'd	900 Juan	9	269
The whole thing is of clothing souls in clay	906 Juan	9	600
O'erspreads the cheek which seems too pure for clay	908 Juan	10	63
My guard! my old guard!' exclaim'd that god of clay	914 Juan	10	466
Baptize posterity, or future clay	932 Juan	12	140
How clay shrinks back from more quiescent clay	955 Juan	14	27
And he did not seem form'd of clay	985 Juan	16	334

CLAY-COLD

Spurning the clay-cold bonds which round our being cling	46 Harold	3	697

CLAYMORE

They lightly wheel the bright claymore	102 Alva		59
Whose bright claymore and hardihood of hand	182 Address-C		5
While all the Common Council cry 'Claymore	308 Age		772

CLEAN

Of weary life a moment lave it clean	65 Harold	4	610
'Tis even superfluous, since two honest, clean	292 Vision		500
Perceiving that they all were pick'd too clean	474 Morgante		532
You keep your hands clean, or I'll find out a stream	740 Deformed	2	340
With a clean shirt, and very spacious breeches	794 Juan	2	1280
And cooks in motion with their clean arms bared	837 Juan	5	398
Stript to his waistcoat, and that not too clean	876 Juan	7	583

CLEANER

'Tis mix'd with blood. There is no cleaner now	741 Deformed	2	378

CLEANNESS

Doth care for cleanness of surtout or shirt	7 Harold	1	232

CLEANSE

Resolve to cleanse this commonwealth with fire	534 Faliero	4	424
But the four rivers would not cleanse my soul	654 Cain	3	522

CLEANSED

Thou must be cleansed of the black blood which makes thee	519 Faliero	3	8

CLEAR

Could blunt the sabre's edge or clear the cannon's smoke	12 Harold	1	530
Streams from his flank the crimson torrent clear	16 Harold	1	762
And all was stainless, and on thy clear stream	43 Harold	3	456
Its clear depth yields of their far height and hue	46 Harold	3	647
The clear air for a while (a passing guest	47 Harold	3	721
Clear, placid Leman! thy contrasted lake	48 Harold	3	797
Thy margin and the mountains, dusk, yet clear	48 Harold	3	807
Clear as its current, glide the sauntering hours	60 Harold	4	291
And most serene of aspect, and most clear	65 Harold	4	592
Our hands, and cry 'Eureka!' it is clear	67 Harold	4	728
Derives from thee a sense so deep and clear	76 Harold	4	1240
No drop of that clear stream its way shall miss	77 Harold	4	1357
As if there were no man to trouble what is clear	81 Harold	4	1584
And clear thy road with many a deadly blow	108 Nisus		236

CLEAR

A manner clear or warm is useless, since	112 Examination		31
Shows the soul from barbarity clear	115 The Tear		10
Now swift or slow, now black or clear	137 Clare		28
Marr's dusky heath, and Dee's clear wave	145 Adieu		29
In the dome of my Sires as the clear moonbeam falls	164 Newstead-C		1
Which horror froze in the blue eye clear	176 Devil's Dr		67
Felt without bitterness--but full and clear	192 Monody		15
So cloudless, clear, and purely beautiful	215 Dream		124
Distinct, but distant--clear--but, oh how cold	220 Sleepless		8
Whose gilded cymbals, more adorn'd than clear	254 Bards		895
The clear brook babbling through the goodly plain	257 Hints		26
'Tis clear, are fit for anything but rhymes	264 Hints		522
All fair; 'tis but lecture for lecture. That's clear	280 Blues	1	153
Whose welcome waters, cool and clear	315 Giaour		539
When the clear sky show'd Ariadne's Isle	344 Corsair	1	444
And hoard their curses, till the coast is clear	347 Corsair	2	28
Less clear, perchance, its earthly trials pass'd	365 Corsair	3	666
But fleet his step, and clear his tones would come	373 Lara	1	520
But Lara's voice, though low, at first was clear	381 Lara	2	460
More mountain-like, through those clear skies	385 Corinth		68
Calm, clear, and azure as the air	387 Corinth		253
And its glance, though clear, was chill	390 Corinth		553
Full on his eye the clear moon shone	391 Corinth		666
And in the heaven that clear obscure	396 Parisina		11
With a clear and ghastly glitter	400 Parisina		425
While all the rest of heaven is clear	405 Chillon		296
And clear them of their dreary mote	406 Chillon		369
When all was now prepared, the vessel clear	417 Island	1	141
O'er her clear nut-brown skin a lucid hue	420 Island	2	138
And Highland linns with Castalie's clear fount	423 Island	2	293
They clear the breakers, dart along the bay	429 Island	3	226
But clear, and with a wild and liquid glance	445 Beppo		358
And got clear off, although the attempt was rash	452 Beppo		763
And that they may perceive my spirit clear	472 Morgante		428
A proof of both the giants' fate quite clear	473 Morgante		446
The steady aspect of a clear large star	480 Manfred	1	178
Beautiful Spirit! in thy calm clear brow	485 Manfred	2	119
I'll clear them on your person! You are welcome	521 Faliero	3	178
A knell was sounding as distinct and clear	528 Faliero	4	12
Thine eyes are clear with youth;--the air puts on	534 Faliero	4	458
A cooling breeze which crisps the broad clear river	551 Sardan	1	53
Chief of 'the Ten.' Then why not clear him? That	600 Foscari	1	305
Will quickly clear the harbour. O ye elements	616 Foscari	4	122
And clear thought; and thou wouldst go on aspiring	645 Cain	2	608
Half open, from beneath them the clear blue	646 Cain	3	29
In the clear waters, when they are gentle, and	648 Cain	3	146
Cain! clear thee from this horrible accusal	652 Cain	3	400
May the clear rivers turn to blood as he	652 Cain	3	432
As beautiful and clear as the amber waves	726 Deformed	1	268
But Inez was so anxious, and so clear	759 Juan	1	801
The sea and sky were blue, and clear, and mild	782 Juan	2	556
So soft, so sweet, so delicately clear	793 Juan	2	1204
Or as the stirring of a deep clear stream	820 Juan	4	233
Which she essay'd in vain to clear (how sweet	820 Juan	4	267
And through her clear brunette complexion shone a	828 Juan	4	750
And through her clear cheek the blood was brought	845 Juan	5	860
To answer in a very clear oration	861 Juan	6	589
Scotch plaids, Scotch snoods, the blue hills, and clear streams	909 Juan	10	138
Extremely wholesome, though but rarely clear	918 Juan	10	664
Traps for the traveller; every highway's clear	919 Juan	11	78
Its windings through the woods; now clear, now blue	948 Juan	13	463
By Homer's 'Catalogue of ships' is clear	950 Juan	13	590
It is not clear that Adeline and Juan	968 Juan	14	791
Truth's fountains may be clear--her streams are muddy	979 Juan	15	702
Some millions must be wrong, that's pretty clear	979 Juan	15	713
Thoughts quite as yellow, but less clear than amber	981 Juan	16	84
As clear as such a climate will allow	982 Juan	16	100
Then, as the night was clear though cold, he threw	982 Juan	16	129
Though sometimes faintly flush'd--and always clear	993 Juan	16	799

CLEAR'D

The lists are oped, the spacious area clear'd	15 Harold	1	720
Hath it indeed been plunder'd, or but clear'd	76 Harold	4	1283
'Let the chamber be clear'd.'--The train disappear'd	324 Abydos	1	32
The shadow lessen'd as it clear'd the bay	435 Island	4	382
We've clear'd the palace--And I trust the city	576 Sardan	3	331
Farewell! He hath clear'd the staircase. Ah! I hear	721 Werner	5	508
Who clear'd her sparkling eyes and smooth'd her brows	850 Juan	5	1227

CLEAR'D
And her brow clear'd, but not her troubled eye 866 Juan 6 879
He clear'd hedge, ditch, and double post, and
rail 959 Juan 14 258

CLEARER
A mutual language, clearer than the tome 37 Harold 3 115
And nearer, clearer, deadlier than before 38 Harold 3 197
With name no clearer than the names unknown 190 Churchill 6
Seem clearer to thine immortality 642 Cain 2 382
Clearer than that without, and its wide hue 785 Juan 2 725
He ne'er presumed to make an error clearer 960 Juan 14 295

CLEARING
Gleam'd the last star of night, the clearing sky 361 Corsair 3 399
As doth a rainbow the just clearing air 855 Juan 6 184

CLEARLY
But had the goddess clearly seen 113 Cornelian-A 29
Clearly and full--I love not mystery 348 Corsair 2 104
Not clearly, and the charge of homicide 600 Foscari 1 302
More clearly, then, these claims of Stralenheim 690 Werner 2 502
I see the subject now more clearly, and 698 Werner 3 171
Of blood. Then wipe them, and see clearly. Why 730 Deformed 1 571
Know very clearly--or at least lie still 919 Juan 11 32

CLEAVE
He never sought to cleave the air 87 Catullus 10
Then would I cleave the vault of heaven 135 I Would 55
Careering cleave the folded felt 326 Abydos 1 248
Some villain spy--seize--cleave him--slay him now 349 Corsari 2 141
Oh, how we cleave the blue! The stars fade from
us 638 Cain 2 144
Cleave yon bald-pated shaveling to the chine 738 Deformed 2 239

CLEAVES
Now, where the swift Rhone cleaves his way
between 49 Harold 3 878
Is of the tree no bolt of thunder cleaves 61 Harold 4 365
Velino cleaves the wave-worn precipice 65 Harold 4 614
Forsakes the rest, and cleaves to thee alone 249 Bards 537
Yet tempests wear, and lightning cleaves the rock 365 Harold 3 668
Save one:--what cleaves the silent air 401 Parisina 488
The bayonet pierces and the sabre cleaves 889 Juan 8 697

CLEAVING
(See also CLOUD-CLEAVING)
Cleaving the fields of space, as doth the swan 287 Vision 179
What hinders me from cleaving you in twain 564 Sardan 2 179

CLEFT
Now, where the quick Rhone thus hath cleft his
way 50 Harold 3 887
Of the cleft statue, with a gentle leap 72 Harold 4 1043
Mathon is cleft; his shield falls from his 130 Calmar 132
While helmets cleft, and sabres clashing 187 Ode-B 47
Since his turban was cleft by the infidel's sabre 313 Giaour 351
And cleft in twain its firmest fold 316 Giaour 660
From right to left his path he cleft 335 Abydos 2 545
Hemm'd in--cut off--cleft down--and trampled o'er 350 Corsair 2 248
And through the crevice and the cleft 403 Chillon 32
Their crackling battlements all cleft 410 Mazeppa 403
Swam round the rock, to where a shallow cleft 435 Island 4 393
With a cleft heart look on thee day by day 659 Heaven 314
Crimson as cleft pomegranates, their long tresses 805 Juan 3 259
Even Time the pitiless in sorrow cleft 817 Juan 4 59

CLEFTS
Through clefts above let in a sober'd ray 431 Island 4 132
While, placed 'midst clefts the least accessible 434 Island 4 309
Nested in pathless clefts, if treachery be 570 Sardan 2 569
In caves, in dens, in clefts of mountains, where 661 Heaven 440

CLEMENCY
Once honest. Ye are free, sirs. Sire, this
clemency 566 Sardan 2 296

CLENCH
The old man's clench; the long envenom'd chain 79 Harold 4 1438

CLENCH'D
Cast one glance back, and clench'd his hand, and
shook 434 Island 4 339

CLENCHED
Their chins upon their clenched hands, and smiled 189 Darkness 26
The clenched hand, the pause of agony 341 Corsair 1 236

CLEOFAS
No more, like Cleofas, I fly 96 Granta 98

CLEON
See honest, open, generous Cleon stand 126 Recoll 326

CLEON'S
Though Cleon's candour would the palm divide 126 Recoll 338

CLEOPATRA
Not Cleopatra on her galley's deck 274 Waltz 89
Or Cleopatra at sixteen--an age 725 Deformed 1 200

CLEOPATRA'S
At Cleopatra's feet,--and now himself he beam'd 68 Harold 4 810
Though Cleopatra's mummy cross the sea 298 Age 29
The timid tear in Cleopatra's eye 355 Corsair 2 550
Had Caesar known but Cleopatra's kiss 423 Island 2 318
Thy Cleopatra's waiting. Who is this 726 Deformed 1 245
But Actium, lost for Cleopatra's eyes 853 Juan 6 31
As white as Cleopatra's melted pearls 976 Juan 15 520

CLERGY
But no one in these parts may quiz the clergy 440 Beppo 23
Because the clergy take the thing in hand 906 Juan 9 604
The other; that's to say, the clergy, who 956 Juan 14 74

CLERGYMAN
I tell him, if a clergyman, he lies 772 Juan 1 1662

CLERGYMEN
With poets almost clergymen, or wholly 925 Juan 11 452

CLERICAL
A clerical work of our jesuits at home 279 Blues 1 127

CLERK
Ere scenes were play'd by many a reverend clerk 261 Hints 319
And scribbles as if head clerk to the Fates 296 Vision 708
(For we've no printer); and set by my clerk 684 Werner 2 67

CLERKS
Six angels and twelve saints were named his
clerks 285 Vision 32
The very clerks,--those somewhat dirty springs 923 Juan 11 317

CLERMONT
The abbot was call'd Clermont, and by blood 468 Morgante 153

CLEVER
The Devil he thought it clever 176 Devil's Dr 58
All clever men, who make their way 231 Doctor 60
Aloud, a scheme less moral than 'twas clever 297 Vision 774
So very anxious, clever, fine, and jealous 449 Beppo 595
Or, like all very clever people, could not 758 Juan 1 776
As boy, I thought myself a clever fellow 816 Juan 4 17
But Johnson was a clever fellow, who 882 Juan 8 277
But still so like, that Psyche were more clever 902 Juan 9 358
(Who, by the by, when clever, are more handy 933 Juan 12 252
By many a windings to their clever clinch 953 Juan 13 778
At speaking truth perhaps they are less clever 980 Juan 16 7
Little that's great, but much of what is clever 993 Juan 16 828

CLEVEREST
She made the cleverest people quite ashamed 748 Juan 1 77

CLEW
Our clew being well nigh wound out, let's be
cheerful 591 Sardan 5 237

CLIENT
Many to your poor client, Bertram; add 530 Faliero 4 133
My father was your father's client, I 531 Faliero 4 204

CLIENTS
My nephew and the clients of our house 524 Faliero 3 377
And for the dispositions of our clients 533 Faliero 4 379
Have not essay'd to multiply their clients 772 Juan 1 1685

CLIENTS'
Into a scene, and swell the clients' clan 963 Juan 14 492

CLIFF
(See also MOUNTAIN-CLIFF)
The torrents that from cliff to valley leap 7 Harold 1 249
Colonna's cliff, and gleams along the wave 33 Harold 2 813
That tomb which, gleaming o'er the cliff 310 Giaour 3
On cliff he hath been known to stand 318 Giaour 826
Till then--no beacon on the cliff 329 Abydos 2 57
From crag to cliff they mount.--Near yonder cave 340 Corsair 1 129
The verge where ends the cliff, begins the beach 346 Corsair 1 534
Behind his Delphian cliff he sinks to sleep 355 Corsair 3 18
Ploughs its drear progress to the scarce-seen
cliff 418 Island 1 174
And gush'd from cliff to crag with saltless spray 427 Island 3 66
When to the mountain cliff I climb'd this morn 670 Heaven 1185
The cliff, towards sunset, on that day she found 790 Juan 2 1026
And down the cliff the island virgin came 792 Juan 2 1129

CLIFFS
And points to yonder cliffs which oft were won and lost	12 Harold	1	521
And o'er her cliffs a fruitless watch to keep	24 Harold	2	257
Crushing the cliffs, which, downward worn and rent	65 Harold	4	629
Perchance I view her cliffs again	158 Florence		12
But the Devil has reach'd our cliffs so white	177 Devil's Dr		83
White cliffs, that held invasion far aloof	305 Age		532
Which I have pointed from these cliffs the while	344 Corsair	1	445
From the cliffs invading dash	392 Corinth		740
From his snow canopy of cliffs and clouds	610 Foscari	3	180
The wave shall break upon your cliffs; and shells	662 Heaven		504
With cliffs above, and a broad sandy shore	796 Juan	2	1410
Which pass'd, or catch the first glimpse of the cliffs	915 Juan	10	512
Thy cliffs, dear Dover! harbour, and hotel	916 Juan	10	546
Of white cliffs, white necks, blue eyes, bluer stockings	938 Juan	12	535

CLIFF-WORN
Before the entrance of a cliff-worn cave	787 Juan	2	862

CLIMACTERIC
Her climacteric teased her like her teens	913 Juan	10	373

CLIMATE
But here our climate is so rigid	101 Lady-B		29
His fiery climate than his tender frame	374 Lara	1	581
Our cloudy climate, and our chilly women	446 Beppo		389
Which make the English climate of our years	801 Juan	2	1712
And climate, stopp'd all scandal (now and then	911 Juan	10	260
The climate was too cold, they said, for him	913 Juan	10	345
What with a small diversity of climate	932 Juan	12	185
In that fair clime which don't depend on climate	959 Juan	14	226
As clear as such a climate will allow	982 Juan	16	100

CLIMATES
As various as the climates of our birth	198 Po		40

CLIMATE'S
Is much more common where the climate's sultry	754 Juan	1	504

CLIMAX
(See also ANTI-CLIMAX)
The climax of all scorn should hang on high	209 Sketch		102
Dreading that climax of all human ills	806 Juan	3	279
Forms a sad climax to romantic homages	938 Juan	12	518

CLIMB
Then slowly climb the many-winding way	7 Harold	1	252
To climb the trackless mountain all unseen	23 Harold	2	221
The star which rises o'er her steep, nor climb	36 Harold	3	96
According as their souls were form'd to sink or climb	58 Harold	4	198
Scoffing; and apostolic statues climb	71 Harold	4	989
But when the rising moon begins to climb	76 Harold	4	1288
Nor these will rash intruder climb	328 Abydos	1	468
My senses climb up from below	412 Mazeppa		552
Or climb the steep, and view the surf in vain	419 Island	2	13
Or break or climb o'er	732 Deformed	1	706
Cheerful as children climb the breasts of mothers	880 Juan	8	118
Was made at length with those who dared to climb	888 Juan	8	628
For a lieutenant to climb up; but skill	905 Juan	9	526
Who died in the then great attempt to climb	916 Juan	10	589
Nor much to climb; through little boxes framed	921 Juan	11	164
'Midst royal dukes and dames condemn'd to climb	926 Juan	11	535

CLIMB'D
(See also CLOMB)
Where the car climb'd the capitol; far and wide	67 Harold	4	716
And climb'd thy steep summit, oh Morven of snow	135 Highlander		2
And climb'd up to the pinnacle of power	511 Faliero	2	196
When to the mountain cliff I climb'd this morn	670 Heaven		1185
He climb'd to where the parapet appears	887 Juan	8	564

CLIMBING
Like climbing some great Alp, which still doth rise	78 Harold	4	1397
Began to glitter with the climbing moon	494 Manfred	3	241
Some liken it to climbing up a hill	773 Juan	1	1739

CLIMBS
For thee the bard up Pindus climbs	234 Strahan		3
While Franklin's quiet memory climbs to heaven	301 Age		245
He climbs the crackling stair, he bursts the door	350 Corsair	2	211
Though every wave she climbs divides us more	430 Island	4	7
Slain, another climbs the barrier	736 Deformed	2	94

CLIME
The Pleasures fled, but sought as warm a clime	14 Harold	1	668
Through many a clime 'tis mine to go	18 Harold	1	865
While o'er the parent clime prowls Murder unrestrain'd	18 Harold	1	917
From the dark barriers of that rugged clime	26 Harold	2	406

CLIME
Here men of every clime appear to make resort	28 Harold	2	504
Hail the bright clime of battle and of song	34 Harold	2	858
Where a blue sky, and glowing clime, extends	37 Harold	3	111
To Freedom's cause, in every age and clime	69 Harold	4	867
Icing the pole, or in the torrid clime	82 Harold	4	1642
A votive pilgrim in Judea's clime	119 Newstead-A		16
Adieu, ye mountains of the clime	145 Adieu		21
Through scorching clime and varied sea	158 Florence		14
Through many a clime 'tis mine to roam	160 Cadiz		53
Long he look'd down on the hosts of each clime	176 Devil's Dr		44
I had not left my clime, nor should I be	199 Po		46
And he the Sun and Thou the Clime	201 Ode-C		26
Perhaps a kinder clime, or purer air	211 Augusta-C		44
Bedecks her cap with bells of every clime	242 Bards		30
The clime that nursed the sons of song and war	253 Bards		870
Thence shall I stray through beauty's native clime	255 Bards		1021
Which charm'd our days in each Aegean clime	261 Hints		345
And Glory knew no clime beyond her Greece	269 Minerva		62
Bound to no clime and victors of the grave	270 Minerva		152
Ye quartos publish'd upon every clime	275 Waltz		124
For the rough virtues chose them for their clime	290 Vision		336
'Gainst Satan's couriers bound for their own clime	292 Vision		446
Vain was his sickness, never was a clime	299 Age		77
Revives--and where? in that avenging clime	301 Age		264
But not alone within the hoariest clime	302 Age		314
To infest the clime whose skies and laws are pure	304 Age		470
To chill in their inhospitable clime	308 Age		752
Fair clime! where every season smiles	310 Giaour		7
Clime of the unforgotten brave	311 Giaour		103
When man was worthy of thy clime	311 Giaour		146
'The cold in clime are cold in blood	321 Giaour		1099
Are emblems of deeds that are done in their clime	323 Abydos	1	2
'Tis the clime of the East; 'tis the land of the Sun	323 Abydos	1	16
With thee all toils are sweet, each clime hath charms	333 Abydos	2	452
Unmoved by absence, firm in every clime	342 Corsair	1	295
But lack of tidings from another clime	366 Lara	1	51
But that long absence from his native clime	377 Lara	2	170
Throughout that clime the feudal chiefs had gain'd	378 Lara	2	226
Along the gulf, the mount, the clime	388 Corinth		368
As childhood dates within our colder clime	420 Island	2	125
Placed in the Arab's clime, he would have been	421 Island	2	179
He shelter'd there a daughter of the clime	432 Island	4	200
Soft as her clime, and sunny as her skies	445 Beppo		360
The sparkle of our ashes. One great clime	454 Venice-B		133
Still one great clime, in full and free defiance	454 Venice-B		142
Lady! if for the cold and cloudy clime	455 Dante Ded		
'But in my heart I bear through every clime	475 Morgante		609
But bask beneath the clime which knows no winter	644 Cain	2	523
To imitate the ice-wind of their clime	682 Werner	1	721
Although they both are born in the same clime	802 Juan	3	36
Still o'er his mind the influence of the clime	808 Juan	3	441
The time, the clime, the spot, where I so oft	815 Juan	3	906
To the kind reader of our sober clime	817 Juan	4	41
That is to say in a meridian clime	847 Juan	5	979
And clime and time, and country and complexion	857 Juan	6	319
Like flowers of different hue, and clime, and root	860 Juan	6	514
A thing of much less import in that clime	863 Juan	6	717
Which flashes o'er a waste and icy clime	867 Juan	7	12
Swear that Pat's language sprung from the same clime	881 Juan	8	181
In this gay clime of bear-skins black and furry	910 Juan	10	203
In neither clime, time, blood, with her defender	914 Juan	10	455
He had then the grace, too, rare in every clime	940 Juan	12	670
In that fair clime which don't depend on climate	959 Juan	14	226

CLIMES
Not in those climes where I have late been straying	2 To Ianthe		1
And visit scorching climes beyond the sea	4 Harold	1	52
Match me, ye climes which poets love to laud	13 Harold	1	603
And snatch'd thy shrinking Gods to northern climes abhorr'd	21 Harold	2	135
Ere the cold stranger pass'd to other climes	21 Harold	2	141
Climes, fair withal as ever mortal head	25 Harold	2	320
Through distant climes condemn'd to fly	111 Medea		43
But, wandering on through distant climes	155 Lady-E		5
Of northern climes and British ladies	159 Cadiz		2
Of fiery climes he made himself a home	215 Dream		107
Of cloudless climes and starry skies	216 She Walks		2
Not, as in northern climes, obscurely bright	268 Minerva		3
Of all climes and professions, years and trades	292 Vision		476
From climes of Washington and Bolivar	303 Age		383
Not, as in northern climes, obscurely bright	355 Corsair	3	3
His only follower from those climes afar	373 Lara	1	512
Before the winds blew Europe o'er these climes	419 Island	2	66
Which seem'd so white in climes that knew no snow	422 Island	2	247
The many felt, for from all days and climes	454 Venice-B		109
And pilgrims come from climes where they have known	458 Dante	1	154

CLIMES

Sire of the seasons! Monarch of the climes	493 Manfred	3	191
To do so; having served her in all climes	507 Faliero	1	515
Hues, features, climes, times, feelings, in-tellects	591 Sardan	5	233
I would not cavil about climes or regions	610 Foscari	3	146
New times, new climes, new arts, new men; but still	661 Heaven		478
And through all climes, the snowy and the sunny	760 Juan	1	855
All European climes, by land or sea	770 Juan	1	1522
But like the climes that know nor snow nor hail	817 Juan	4	68
As is the custom of those Eastern climes	842 Juan	5	710
Their chastity in these unhappy climes	851 Juan	5	1251
Madrid's and Moscow's climes were of a piece	911 Juan	10	240
Perhaps he long'd in bitter frosts for climes	912 Juan	10	293
The art of living in all climes with ease	969 Juan	15	88

CLIMES'

More rich than other climes' fertility	59 Harold	4	232

CLINCH

By many windings to their clever clinch	953 Juan	13	778

CLING

Yet, though a dreary strain, to this I cling	35 Harold	3	32
Spurning the clay-cold bonds which round our being cling	46 Harold	3	697
Still would I kiss and cling to thee	88 To Ellen		6
Thus must I cling to some endearing hand	125 Recoll		241
Remorse and Shame shall cling to thee	171 Remember-A		3
And bade thee cling to me through every shock	206 Love, Death		7
Yet cling to Being's severing link	217 High World		12
So that those arms cling closer round my neck	334 Abydos	2	455
Cling to his couch and sicken years away	338 Corsair	1	28
The lip that there would cling for ever	397 Parisina		54
Place your foot here--here, take this staff, and cling	483 Manfred	1	379
To which frail twig they cling like drowning men	492 Manfred	3	103
Or cling to any creed of destiny	547 Faliero	5	644
When all the ills of conquer'd states shall cling thee	549 Faliero	5	780
Ruffles the autumn leaves, that drooping cling	578 Sardan	4	14
Cling to a son of Noah for our lives	664 Heaven		712
Like cherubs round an altar-piece they cling	809 Juan	3	477
Strip your green fields, and to your harvests cling	894 Juan	8	1006

CLINGING

Mid wounds, and clinging darts, and lances brast	16 Harold	1	776
To make death hateful, save an innate clinging	629 Cain	1	111
To see him to my bosom clinging so	669 Heaven		1100
And the honey bee is clinging	743 Deformed	3	72
And, clinging as if loath to lose its hold	810 Juan	3	566

CLINGS

Still to the last kind Vice clings to the tott'ring walls	11 Harold	1	494
The parted bosom clings to wonted home	34 Harold	2	864
And clings to thoughts now better far removed	34 Harold	2	902
While Hope retires appall'd, and clings to life	122 Recoll		10
To one idea fondly clings	131 L'Amitie		17
Still clings she to thy side	181 Ode-A		112
Is it madness or meanness which clings to thee now	202 Avatar		29
Fast to the doom'd offender's form it clings	342 Corsair	1	279
Yet there is one--to whom my memory clings	354 Corsair	2	474
Whate'er of peace about our hearthstone clings	815 Juan	3	949
Clings to its teat--sticks to me through the abyss	911 Juan	10	220

CLINIAS

Such was the curled son of Clinias;--wouldst thou	725 Deformed	1	213

CLINK

Keeping due time with every hammer's clink	506 Faliero	1	421

CLIP

Clip not our pinions ere the birds can fly	113 Prologue		18
Know'st thou that I can clip thy wanton wing	358 Corsair	3	191
Which for an instant clip enjoyment's wings	908 Juan	10	40

CLIPP'D

His bright brown locks must now be clipp'd	401 Parisina		435

CLIPPING

Clipping, like a pair of snuffers	197 Rogers		68

CLIPT

Droop'd as a wild-born falcon with clipt wing	37 Harold	3	129
And drooping like an eagle's with clipt pinion	913 Juan	10	350

CLITUMNUS

But thou, Clitumnus, in thy sweetest wave	65 Harold	4	586

CLOAK

In costly sheen and gaudy cloak array'd	15 Harold	1	738
Shake the red cloak, and poise the ready brand	16 Harold	1	779
Whose shade securely our design will cloak	106 Nisus		106
My cap was the bonnet, my cloak was the plaid	117 Lachin		10
The cloak of white; the thin capote	330 Abydos	2	141
My corslet--cloak--one hour--and we are gone	340 Corsair	1	160
His belt and cloak were o'er his shoulders flung	346 Corsair	1	560
He seized his cloak, his head he slightly bow'd	373 Lara	1	496
From out the wood--before him was a cloak	383 Lara	2	559
His mantling cloak before was stripp'd	401 Parisina		434
This done, Mazeppa spread his cloak	407 Mazeppa		78
You like by way of doublet, cape, or cloak	440 Beppo		34
My cloak is round his middle strapp'd about	445 Beppo		331
Antonio, take my mask and cloak, and light	528 Faliero	4	19
His face is muffled in his cloak, but both	529 Faliero	4	115
He hath no harm; bring me my sword and cloak	533 Faliero	4	330
Cloak their own treason under such an order	536 Faliero	4	551
Fling my cloak o'er what will be dust anon	736 Deformed	2	130
A Candiote cloak, which to the knee might reach	840 Juan	5	539
Of Hell shall pall them in a deeper cloak	878 Juan	7	688
And scarlet cloak (I hate the sight to see, since	988 Juan	16	532
That scarlet cloak, alas! unclosed with rigour	988 Juan	16	535

CLOAKS

Bought also; and the torches, cloaks, and banners	286 Vision		71

CLOCK

Their clock the sun, in his unbounded tow'r	424 Island	2	356
Of outposts on the never-merry clock	701 Werner	3	390

CLOCK'S

Unbroken by the clock's funereal chime	423 Island	2	349

CLOD

Thus hail'd your rulers their patrician clod	272 Minerva		257
Dissolve this clog and clod of clay before	424 Island	2	390
Been a clod of the valley,--happier nothing	727 Deformed	1	347

CLODIUS

To live like Clodius and like Falkland fall	251 Bards		686

CLOG

That clog thy young growth and assist thy decay	149 Newstead-B		22
She gave to clog the soul and feast the worm	371 Lara	1	334
Dissolve this clog and clod of clay before	424 Island	2	390
A shadow of this cumbrous clog of clay	579 Sardan	4	59
And clog the last sad sands of life with tears	593 Sardan	5	404
In turn, because of this vile crooked clog	727 Deformed	1	340
Yon hump, and lump, and clog of ugliness	728 Deformed	1	423
Her beauty also seem'd to form no clog	974 Juan	15	381

CLOGG'D

And do what our frail clay, thus clogg'd, hath fail'd in	537 Faliero	4	660
Through agonies unspeakable, and clogg'd	639 Cain	2	245
And it is clogg'd with dead even to the door	739 Deformed	2	273

CLOGS

If Commerce fills the purse, she clogs the brain	247 Bards		395
It clogs like lead Corruption's weary wing	271 Minerva		246
Which clogs the ethereal essence, have been such	489 Manfred	2	427

CLOISTER

And take my refuge in the cloister. Come	545 Faliero	5	545

CLOISTER'D

Of warriors, monks, and dames the cloister'd tomb	119 Newstead-A		3

CLOISTERS

Thy cloisters, pervious to the wintry showers	122 Newstead-A		143
In verity much rather than the cloisters	475 Morgante		628
In cloisters of the classic Salamanca	778 Juan	2	295
Elsewhere preserved: the cloisters still were stable	949 Juan	13	523

CLOKE

If subtle poniards, wrapt beneath the cloke	12 Harold	1	529
Cloke their soul's hoarded triumph, as a fit one	604 Foscari	2	148

CLOMB
(See also CLIMB'D)

We forded the river, and clomb the high hill	384 Corinth		6

CLOOTZ

Petion, Clootz, Danton, Marat, La Fayette	747 Juan	1	18

CLOS

Their date of war, and their 'champ clos' the spheres	289 Vision		256

CLOSE

Close shamed Elysium's gates, my shade shall seek for none	27 Harold	2	459

CLOSE

While the deep war-drum's sound announced the close of day	28 Harold	2	513
The thunder-clouds close o'er it, which when rent	39 Harold	3	249
Their eyes on honour'd forms whose busts around them close	77 Harold	4	1323
This is of love the final close	89 To Emma		39
While close your arms around me fold	91 Caroline-B		35
The hour draws nigh, a few brief days will close	94 Dorset		77
But here I'll close my chaste Description	144 Becher-B		29
And then those pensive eyes would close	152 Remind		19
Stuck together close as wax	157 Hodgson		30
And drove off at the close of day	177 Devil's Dr		108
Of Crime unnamed, and thy sad noon must close	224 To Dives		8
So close on each pathetic part he dwells	245 Bards		251
But now at once your fleeting labours close	252 Bards		753
Revive the cry--'Iago! and close Spain	303 Age		359
Yes, close her with your armed bosoms round	303 Age		360
Along the brink at Twilight's close	313 Giaour		317
No hand shall close its clasp again	313 Giaour		327
The flames around their captive close	314 Giaour		425
The close observer can espy	319 Giaour		868
Do all but close thy dying eye	328 Abydos	1	404
This tale whose close is almost nigh	331 Abydos	2	277
Few words remain of mine my tale to close	334 Abydos	2	464
Another falls--but round him close	335 Abydos	2	543
Behind, but close, his comrades lay	335 Abydos	2	570
Too close inquiry his stern glance would quell	341 Corsair	1	214
His close but glittering casque, and sable plume	349 Corsair	2	148
And once unclosed--but once may close again	353 Corsair	2	401
Close to the glimmering grate he dragg'd his chain	359 Corsair	3	262
But close by the shore, on the edge of the gulf	389 Corinth		473
Like the mower's grass at the close of day	392 Corinth		736
They die; but ere their eyes could close	394 Corinth		931
Nor once did those sweet eyelids close	399 Parisina		330
Can only o'er the surface close	402 Parisina		554
Close slowly round me as before	405 Chillon		262
Yet still a dark and hideous close	414 Mazeppa		733
And doth a roof above me close	414 Mazeppa		798
Close to thy throat the pointed bayonet laid	416 Island	1	72
But close in one eternal gush of love	420 Island	2	122
Close on the wild, wide ocean, yet as pure	427 Island	3	67
Disdain'd all further efforts, save to close	434 Island	4	306
With, though a hostile hand, to close his eye	434 Island	4	326
'Mid sights and sounds like these my life may close	437 Tasso		76
Close to the lady as a part of dress	445 Beppo		316
And vulture passions flying close behind	463 Dante	3	174
Perceiving that the pig was on him close	473 Morgante		505
There is a vigil, and these eyes but close	478 Manfred	1	6
In close arrest.' Proceed. My lord, 'tis finish'd	501 Faliero	1	98
Now darkling in their close toward the deep vale	516 Faliero	2	502
And show these eyes, before they close, the doom	548 Faliero	5	739
The close and sultry summer's day, which bodes	576 Sardan	3	316
Our annals draw perchance unto their close	582 Sardan	4	296
Draw near a close. I pray you take this key	591 Sardan	5	247
So near the awful close! For these must drop	662 Heaven		563
I don't much like this fellow--close and dry	676 Werner	1	304
She kept her counsel in so close a way	755 Juan	1	544
Unless with breakers close beneath her lee	779 Juan	2	360
They could not rescue him although so close	781 Juan	2	454
'Twas bending close o'er his, and the small mouth	788 Juan	2	897
Those eyes to close, though weariness and pain	793 Juan	2	1187
A beauty at the season's close grown hectic	809 Juan	3	521
Then look'd close at the flint, as if to see	821 Juan	4	318
Although her paroxysm drew towards its close	825 Juan	4	534
They follow'd close behind their sable guide	837 Juan	5	402
This massy portal stood at the wide close	842 Juan	5	689
The dagger close at hand, which made it awkward	849 Juan	5	1114
And was thrust in to close the octave's chime	854 Juan	6	142
Resounded 'Allah!' and the clouds which close	879 Juan	8	61
At other times, repulsed by the close fire	880 Juan	8	157
Just at the close of the first bridal year	881 Juan	8	212
Into close contact. Though reserved, nor caught	943 Juan	13	116
There was a country girl in a close cap	988 Juan	16	531
However, the day closed, as days must close	994 Juan	16	849
And then swung back; nor close--but stood awry	996 Juan	16	979

CLOSED

(See also SCARCE-CLOSED)

Thin the closed ranks, and lead in Glory's fearful chase	13 Harold	1	575
What deep wounds ever closed without a scar	48 Harold	3	788
Though the grave closed between us,--'twere the same	53 Harold	3	1089
Debauch, and not fatigue, his eyes had closed	108 Nisus		240
Nor closed the progress of my youthful dream	127 Recoll		368
That closed their murder'd sage's latest day	268 Minerva		22
Are gone--their oven closed, their ocean dry	306 Age		607
Begun in folly, closed in tears	314 Giaour		399
The night hath closed on Helle's stream	329 Abydos	2	39
That heart hath burst--that eye was closed	335 Abydos	2	619

CLOSED

Yea--closed before his own	335 Abydos	2	620
Of that closed eye, which opens but to pain	353 Corsair	2	400
That closed their murder'd sage's latest day	355 Corsair	3	22
By his closed eye unheeded and unfelt	355 Corsair	2	559
In vain the circling chieftains round them closed	376 Lara	2	63
Still as the lips that closed in death	401 Parisina		477
Her life began and closed in woe	401 Parisina		529
I closed my own again once more	414 Mazeppa		803
We've not yet closed accounts, and we shall see yet	447 Beppo		493
But these are closed: the Ten, the Avogadori	546 Faliero	5	553
'Twill be full soon, and may be closed for ever	620 Foscari	4	342
'Tis closed. You have said well; I will contain	646 Cain	3	17
Of a discovery. You are sure you closed it	702 Werner	3	509
But closed the tyrant-hater he begun	746 Juan	Ded	80
Closed the oration of the trusty maid	768 Juan	1	1378
Alfonso closed his speech, and begg'd her pardon	769 Juan	1	1433
And fruits, and date-bread loaves closed the repast	809 Juan	3	498
But closed its little being without light	825 Juan	4	556
And when 'twas found straightway the bargain closed	845 Juan	5	900
Oft are soon closed, all heroes are not blind	883 Juan	8	318
However, the day closed, as days must close	994 Juan	16	849

CLOSELY

In unison so closely sweet	144 Jessy		26
Yet copy not too closely, but record	259 Hints		187
No damsel faints when rather closely press'd	275 Waltz		143
So closely mingling here, that disentwined	344 Corsair	1	404
'Tis done--all closely are they shorn	401 Parisina		436
Closely, and scarcely less expert to trace	431 Island	4	111

CLOSER

I'll watch him closer than before	325 Abydos	1	143
So that those arms cling closer round my neck	334 Abydos	2	455
'Tis flesh; grasp--clasp--yet closer, till I feel	579 Sardan	4	43
And wrapt him closer, lest the air, too raw	792 Juan	2	1142
Still closer sulphury clouds began to smother	887 Juan	8	550
Closer, that all the deadlier they might wring	893 Juan	8	941

CLOSES

And the spell closes with its silent seal	36 Harold	3	65
Ere the night closes o'er the inhibited walls	629 Cain	1	88
As the day closes over Eden's walls	643 Cain	2	471

CLOSEST

Even through the closest searment half betray'd	32 Harold	2	776

CLOSET

And in a certain closet, where the wall	476 Morgante		665
Closet and clothes' press, chest and window-seat	764 Juan	1	1138
'There is the closet, there the toilet, there	765 Juan	1	1217
This pretty gentleman within the closet	767 Juan	1	1360
And Julia instant to the closet flew	769 Juan	1	1450
In digging the foundation of a closet	813 Juan	3	807

CLOSETS

On stalls must moulder, or in closets rot	249 Bards		593

CLOSING

And gathering storms around convulse the closing year	26 Harold	2	378
But thine, within the closing grate retired	195 Vittorelli		7
Towards it he moved; a scarcely closing door	361 Corsair	3	402
Coumourgi, he whose closing scene	386 Corinth		141
Closing o'er one we sought to save	406 Chillon		363
For night was closing ere they came to land	836 Juan	5	326
Of closing 'gainst the light their orbs of vision	863 Juan	6	701
As the year closing whirls the scarlet leaves	889 Juan	8	699
He saw, however, at the closing session	940 Juan	12	657

CLOTH

(See also SACK-CLOTH, TABLE-CLOTH)

Nor are you form'd to wear our sober cloth	475 Morgante		648

CLOTHE

The cork-trees hoar that clothe the shaggy steep	7 Harold	1	244
Clothe envy in the garb of honest zeal	247 Bards		376
Began to clothe each Asiatic hill	863 Juan	6	683

CLOTHED

(See also ILL-CLOTHED, WORST-CLOTHED)

Are clothed with early blossoms, through the grass	72 Harold	4	1046
Clothed in odds and ends of humour	197 Rogers		39
The city it has clothed in chains, which clank	454 Venice-B		118
Than the gilt chamberlain, who, clothed and fee'd	464 Dante	4	93
The poet's god, clothed in such limbs as are	727 Deformed	1	368
Of what I then dreamt, clothed in their own pall	909 Juan	10	141
In short, he hardly could be clothed with less	995 Juan	16	932

CLOTHES
(See also BED-CLOTHES)

Their best clothes, as if going to a fair	779	Juan	2	354
And most of them had little clothes but rags	782	Juan	2	496
A quantity of clothes fit for the back	840	Juan	5	531
'I offer you a handsome suit of clothes	841	Juan	5	601
His clothes were not curb'd to their usual cut	984	Juan	16	230

CLOTHES'

Closet and clothes' press, chest and window-seat	764	Juan	1	1138

CLOTHING

Wear his Sheep's clothing still	239	Bray		28
Or bathing, nursing, making love, and clothing	449	Beppo		568
The whole thing is of clothing souls in clay	906	Juan	9	600
Too often all the clothing, meat, or fuel	915	Juan	10	503
And Centaur Nessus garb of mortal clothing	926	Juan	11	508

CLOTTED

Troubles the clotted air, of late so blue	459	Dante	2	78

CLOTTING

Stain'd is the couch and earth with clotting gore	108	Nisus		252

CLOUD
(See also THUNDER-CLOUD)

Bears the cloud onwards: in that Tale I find	35	Harold	3	23
Or holding dark communion with the cloud	42	Harold	3	418
Leaps the live thunder! Not from one lone cloud	49	Harold	3	865
Have flung a desolate cloud o'er Venice' lovely walls	57	Harold	4	135
Home to its cloud this lightning of the mind	58	Harold	4	209
With its unemptied cloud of gentle rain	65	Harold	4	624
That weigh'd upon her gentle dust, a cloud	70	Harold	4	912
Through which all things grow phantoms, and the cloud	79	Harold	4	1480
By dreams of ill to cloud some future day	94	Dorset		84
With scarce one speck to cloud the pleasing scene	126	Recoll		327
hear the song together. One cloud shall	130	Calmar		94
As gleams the moonbeam through the broken cloud	139	Ossian-A		31
Doth through my cloud of anguish shine	152	Weep-A		10
Thy day without a cloud hath pass'd	167	Dead		50
Thy cloud could overcast the light	172	Time-B		23
Dim in the cloud, or darkling in the storm	182	Address-C		26
A crimson cloud it spreads and glows	187	Ode-B		11
And when the cloud upon us came	209	Augusta-A		17
Earth yawn'd; he stood the centre of a cloud	219	Saul-B		5
Seated their fellow-traveller on a cloud	287	Vision		184
But take your choice); and then it grew a cloud	292	Vision		457
And so it was--a cloud of witnesses	292	Vision		458
But such a cloud! No land e'er saw a crowd	292	Vision		459
Of Incas darken to a dubious cloud	302	Age		317
Ere from the cloud that gave it birth	315	Giaour		502
A sky without a cloud or sun	319	Giaour		962
As through yon pale gray cloud the star	322	Giaour		1274
From the black cloud that bound it	327	Abydos	1	337
The long chibouque's dissolving cloud supply	347	Corsair	2	35
If errs my feeble hand, the morning cloud	361	Corsair	3	384
There is no darkness like the cloud of mind	365	Corsair	3	658
Nor cloud shall gather more, nor leaf shall fall	375	Lara	2	15
In form a peak, in height a cloud	388	Corinth		376
There is a light cloud by the moon	391	Corinth		643
No--though that cloud were thunder's worst	391	Corinth		661
In cloud and flame athwart the heaven	395	Corinth		1026
Lone--as a solitary cloud	405	Chillon		294
A single cloud on a sunny day	405	Chillon		295
Which lifts its peak a cloud above the main	418	Island	1	175
Broad as the cloud along the horizon flings	422	Island	2	225
But such as wafts its cloud o'er grog or ale	425	Island	2	437
Dark as a sullen cloud before the sun	433	Island	4	280
As dwells the gather'd lightning in its cloud	438	Tasso		114
In vain, and never more (save when the cloud	456	Dante	1	37
From my mansion in the cloud	479	Manfred	1	51
Thou art gather'd in a cloud	481	Manfred	1	209
Another evening; yon red cloud, which rests	494	Manfred	3	237
The sun and you, as an ill-omen'd cloud	503	Faliero	1	276
The Bucentaur, like the columnar cloud	547	Faliero	5	632
A cloud of Parthians, hitherto reserved	576	Sardan	3	333
Not of a mere pillar form'd of cloud and flame	594	Sardan	5	438
Which cloud whate'er we gaze on, even thine eyes	609	Foscari	3	56
Under the cloud of night.--Nay, speak to me	653	Cain	3	459
Sits on me as a cloud along the sky	700	Werner	3	360
A cloud upon your thoughts. This were to be	712	Werner	4	544
A cloud comes o'er his blue eyes suddenly	713	Werner	5	53
The smallest cloud--the slightest vapour of	744	Deformed	3	142
A cloud of your own raising. Not so always	744	Deformed	3	149
Even as a summer sky's without a cloud	763	Juan	1	1078
And smiling through her dream, as through a cloud	860	Juan	6	524
And throws a cloud o'er Longman and John Murray	870	Juan	7	204
Which arch'd the horizon like a fiery cloud	879	Juan	8	43
What can ye recognise?--a gilded cloud	945	Juan	13	264
Had stirr'd him, answer'd in a way to cloud it	987	Juan	16	480
The moon peep'd, just escaped from a grey cloud	996	Juan	16	1016

CLOUD-CLEAVING

Thou winged and cloud-cleaving minister	482	Manfred	1	291

CLOUD-COMPELLING

The cloud-compelling harbinger of love	423	Island	2	345

CLOUDED

Of passion reeking from his clouded face	428	Island	3	142
When half the horizon's clouded and half free	430	Island	4	2
Although 'tis clouded by my dungeon roof	439	Tasso		188
(But rarely clouded, and when clouded, leaving	682	Werner	1	716
Whither shrinks the clouded sun	735	Deformed	2	3
Of rivalship rose in each clouded eye	906	Juan	9	623

CLOUD-FENCED

Of cloud-fenced Caucasus, where the eagle sits	570	Sardan	2	568

CLOUDLESS
(See also ALL-CLOUDLESS)

Like rays which gild a cloudless morn	128	Lady-C		23
Swept by the breeze that fans thy cloudless sky	138	Harrow-B		2
Through cloudless skies, in silvery sheen	159	Gulf		1
So cloudless, clear, and purely beautiful	215	Dream		124
Of cloudless climes and starry skies	216	She Walks		2
'Twas sweet, when cloudless stars were bright	313	Giaour		305
Of skies more cloudless, moons of purer blaze	368	Lara	1	176
Beauteous as cloudless, nor be forced to borrow	445	Beppo		342
Though your eyes dare not gaze on it when cloudless	744	Deformed	3	145

CLOUDS
(See also THUNDER-CLOUDS)

Arise; and, as the clouds along them break	25	Harold	2	374
Who can contemplate Fame through clouds unfold	36	Harold	3	95
As if the clouds its echo would repeat	38	Harold	3	196
The loftiest peaks most wrapt in clouds and snow	42	Harold	3	398
Have pinnacled in clouds their snowy scalps	45	Harold	3	592
With night, and clouds, and thunder, and a soul	50	Harold	3	897
Laughing the clouds away with playful scorn	50	Harold	3	916
The clouds above me to the white Alps tend	52	Harold	3	1017
From clouds, but of all colours seems to be	59	Harold	4	239
Scatter'd the clouds away, and on that name attend	60	Harold	4	324
Plunge in the clouds for refuge and withdraw	64	Harold	4	574
Sits on the firm-set ground--and this the clouds must claim	78	Harold	4	1404
Soon will the day those eastern clouds adorn	109	Nisus		283
Clouds there encircle the forms of my fathers	117	Lachin		23
And from thy hall of clouds descend	118	Romance		18
The clouds of anarchy from Britain's skies	121	Newstead-A		102
As when through clouds that pour the summer storm	122	Recoll		17
hall of clouds! Such is Calmar. The gray	129	Calmar		11
Night rose in clouds. Darkness veils the	130	Calmar		35
'What form rises on the roar of clouds	131	Calmar		189
Now half obscured by clouds of tears	131	L'Amitie		13
While clouds the darken'd noon deform	133	E. N. Long		6
And clouds obscure the watery moon	134	E. N. Long		88
Thou look'st from clouds and laughest at the Storm	139	Ossian-A		20
Lull'd in the clouds, nor hear the voice of Morn	139	Ossian-A		28
On eastern clouds thy yellow tresses play	140	Ossian-B		24
But sleep within thy clouds, and fail to rise	140	Ossian-B		33
Shed by the Moon when clouds deform the night	140	Ossian-B		38
The clouds of Age her Sun o'ercast	141	Critics		64
And angry clouds are pouring fast	158	Storm		3
Clouds burst, skies flash, oh, dreadful hour	158	Storm		29
Through clouds of fire the massy fragments riven	169	Address-A		7
And clouds the brow, or fills the eye	174	Impromptu-A		4
Despite some passing clouds of crime	181	Ode-A		153
And the clouds perish'd; Darkness had no need	190	Darkness		81
By clouds surrounded, and on whirlwinds borne	193	Monody		92
As clouds from yonder sun receive	218	I Saw		9
And kings of fire, of water, and of clouds	245	Bards		276
No more through rolling clouds to soar again	253	Bards		842
Clouds farther off than we can understand	291	Vision		411
The spheres, we shall catch cold amongst these clouds	293	Vision		531
And crimson as those clouds of morn	316	Giaour		662
This morning clouds upon me lower'd	327	Abydos	1	359
And clouds aloft and tides below	329	Abydos	2	10
The evening beam that smiles the clouds away	333	Abydos	2	400
Morn slowly rolls the clouds away	335	Abydos	2	583
Roll'd back the clouds) the morrow caught his eye	381	Lara	2	469
Which seems the very clouds to kiss	385	Corinth		70
Whose clouds that day grew doubly dun	386	Corinth		173
The clouds beneath him seem'd so dun	396	Corinth		1076
Nor further mercy clouds rebellion's dawn	417	Island	1	150
Which welcomes, as a well, the clouds that burst	418	Island	1	190
Blazed through the clouds of death and beckon'd hence	433	Island	4	264
The storms yet sleep, the clouds still keep their station	459	Dante	2	40
Thy moral morn, too long with clouds defaced	461	Dante	3	58
On a throne of rocks, in a robe of clouds	479	Manfred	1	62
The mists boil up around the glaciers; clouds	482	Manfred	1	346

CLOUDS

Leaving a gap in the clouds, and with the shock	483	Manfred	1	354
The clouds grow thicker--there--now lean on me	483	Manfred	1	378
Colouring the clouds, that shut me out from heaven	484	Manfred	2	29
The fretwork of some earthquake--where the clouds	487	Manfred	2	308
We have outstay'd the hour--mount we our clouds	488	Manfred	2	370
Who walks the clouds and waters--in his hand	488	Manfred	2	372
He speaketh--and the clouds reply in thunder	488	Manfred	2	376
Clouds raining from the re-ascended skies	492	Manfred	3	113
Robed as with angry clouds: he stands between	495	Manfred	3	325
Floating like light clouds 'twixt our gaze and heaven	529	Faliero	4	58
How red he glares amongst those deepening clouds	561	Sardan	2	3
In clouds that seem approaching fast, and show	570	Sardan	2	539
Art thou of those who dread the roar of clouds	570	Sardan	2	547
So bright, so rolling back the clouds into	587	Sardan	5	10
Through all the clouds, and fills my eyes with light	588	Sardan	5	57
From his snow canopy of cliffs and clouds	610	Foscari	3	180
Like an ethereal night, where long white clouds	635	Cain	1	508
Through thee and thine. The clouds still open wide	639	Cain	2	202
Along that western paradise of clouds	643	Cain	2	467
To cast down yon vile flatt'rer of the clouds	650	Cain	3	290
Through the deep clouds o'er rocky Ararat	655	Heaven		3
Who folds in clouds the fonts of bliss and woe	656	Heaven		118
The clouds from off their pinions flinging	656	Heaven		137
As a star in the clouds, which cannot quench	658	Heaven		235
The heaven which will convert her clouds to seas	659	Heaven		326
Born ere this dying world? They come like clouds	659	Heaven		339
Until the clouds look gory	661	Heaven		476
The clouds have nearly fill'd their springs	661	Heaven		489
The clouds are few, and of their wonted texture	662	Heaven		550
And bid those clouds and waters take a shape	664	Heaven		717
In clouds they overspread the lurid sky	668	Heaven		997
The clouds return into the hues of night	668	Heaven		1008
Some clouds sweep on as vultures for their prey	669	Heaven		1071
These darken'd clouds are not the only skies	669	Heaven		1087
When the swoln clouds unto the mountains bend	670	Heaven		1116
Of dark fatality, like clouds, are gathering	702	Werner	3	488
What clouds his royal aspect? 'Nothing,' 'Nothing	743	Deformed	3	99
The scattering clouds, shone, spanning the dark sea	785	Juan	2	722
Now o'er it clouds and thunder must be driven	801	Juan	2	1707
And clouds come o'er the sunset of our day	808	Juan	3	470
Like fleecy clouds about the moon, flow'd round her	810	Juan	3	560
Like summer clouds all silvery, smooth, and fair	823	Juan	4	450
Blood-red as sunset summer clouds which range	845	Juan	5	861
Resounded 'Allah!' and the clouds which close	879	Juan	8	61
A glance on the dull clouds (as thick as starch	881	Juan	8	166
Still closer sulphury clouds began to smother	887	Juan	8	550
As purple clouds befringe the sun; but most	911	Juan	10	231
The gloomy clouds, which o'er it as a yoke	918	Juan	10	661
All purged and pious from their native clouds	951	Juan	13	636
Like fleecy clouds into the sky retired	981	Juan	16	62

CLOUD-SHAPEN

As the cloud-shapen giant	724	Deformed	1	163

CLOUDY

But gaze beneath thy cloudy canopy	14	Harold	1	628
A thousand years their cloudy wings expand	55	Harold	4	5
Is changed and solemn, like the cloudy groan	70	Harold	4	932
Welcome thou cloudy veil of nightly skies	140	Ossian-A		41
To smoky towns and cloudy sky	163	Malta		22
Our cloudy climate, and our chilly women	446	Beppo		389
Lady! if for the cold and cloudy clime	455	Dante	Ded	1
A goodly night; the cloudy wind which blew	528	Faliero	4	25
'Twas, as the watchmen say, a cloudy night	763	Juan	1	1073

CLOVE

Apart; her voice that clove through all the din	577	Sardan	3	392

CLOVEN

Angel of Death! 'tis Hassan's cloven crest	317	Giaour		716
The cloven turbans o'er the chamber spread	349	Corsair	2	174
The cloven cuirass, and the helmless head	380	Lara	2	395
The cloven billow flash'd from off her prow	415	Island	1	3
Cloven with arm still lustier, breast more daring	597	Foscari	1	105
Cloven foot of thine, or the swift dromedary	723	Deformed	1	104

CLOVEN-FOOTED

Their cloven-footed terror. Do you--dare you	723	Deformed	1	101

CLOVES

Cloves, cinnamon, and saffron too were boil'd	809	Juan	3	503

CLOWNISH

With clownish heel, your popular circulation	901	Juan	9	279

CLOWNS

And harlequins and clowns, with feats gymnastical	440	Beppo		19

CLOY

Which fill'd the imperial isles so full it seem'd to cloy	80	Harold	4	1512
Began to cloy	200	Stanzas-B		68
Time can but cloy love	200	Stanzas-B		84

CLOY'D

Contented, when translated, means but cloy'd	965	Juan	14	629

CLOYING

Till, after cloying the gazettes with cant	747	Juan	1	3

CLOYS

And root from out the soul the deadly weed which cloys	73	Harold	4	1071
And change whene'er my fancy cloys	143	To--A		16
Repose but cloys him	200	Stanzas-B		43
And these were not of the vain kind which cloys	818	Juan	4	124

CLUB
(See also BOOK-CLUB)

But be true to his club and staunch to his rein	177	Devil's Dr		99
The club, and rain our arrows o'er the field	419	Island	2	42
But what avail'd the club and spear, and arm	427	Island	3	47
Leaning dejected on his club of conquest	725	Deformed	1	234

CLUBBY

You founded a Whig Clubby O	235	New Song		24

CLUBS

Master of arts! as hells and clubs proclaim	260	Hints		241
Bitter as clubs in cards are against spades	292	Vision		478
Such slings, clubs, ballast-stones, that yield you must	469	Morgante		226
But the clubs found it rather serious laughter	952	Juan	13	686
Save in the clubs no man of honour plays	954	Juan	13	842

CLUE

That labyrinth, whose clue is of the same	939	Juan	12	570
But what's reality? Who has its clue	979	Juan	15	710

CLUMSY

With thee even clumsy cits attempt to bounce	275	Waltz		157

CLUNG

Still round him clung invisibly a chain	36	Harold	3	77
To which thy weakness clung	181	Ode-A		76
Till hunger clung them, or the dropping dead	189	Darkness		50
Clung like a cuirass to his breast	330	Abydos	2	144
She rose, she sprung, she clung to his embrace	345	Corsair	1	466
The first success to Lara's numbers clung	379	Lara	2	283
To which some strange remembrance wildly clung	381	Lara	2	445
Each form'd a hideous river. Still she clung	580	Sardan	4	153
Within his grasp; he clung to it, and sore	787	Juan	2	853
There, breathless, with his digging nails he clung	787	Juan	2	857
Their lips drew near, and clung into a kiss	797	Juan	2	1480
Which, being join'd, like swarming bees they clung	798	Juan	2	1495
And Haidee clung around him; 'Juan, 'tis	821	Juan	4	297
Bring down the fruit, which still perversely clung	862	Juan	6	606
To the live leg still clung the sever'd head	889	Juan	8	672
While courage clung but to a single twig.--Am I	891	Juan	8	837
Against the light wherein she dies: he clung	893	Juan	8	940

CLUSIUM

An injured husband brought the Gauls to Clusium	544	Faliero	5	440

CLUSTER'D

Her glossy hair was cluster'd o'er a brow	754	Juan	1	481

CLUSTERING

You'd swear each clustering lock could feel	160	Cadiz		15
The glossy darkness of that clustering hair	183	Address-D		37
Pass'd the high headlands of each clustering isle	346	Corsair	1	593
Spell-bound within the clustering Cyclades	356	Corsair	3	62
Her clustering hair, whose longer locks were roll'd	788	Juan	2	923

CLUSTERS

So hang them in clusters round each Manufactory	225	Ode-D		7
That clusters round thy forehead fair	327	Abydos	1	356

CLUTCH

Which glows yet smoother from his amorous clutch	13	Harold	1	600

CLYTEMNESTRA

(The moral Clytemnestra of thy lord	213	Lady Byron		37
Such Clytemnestra, though perhaps 'tis better	906	Juan	9	639

CO.
There's Vamp, Scamp, and Mouthy, and Wordswords
  and Co.   277 Blues   1   9

COACH
(See also STAGE-COACH, STATE-COACH)
Thy coach of hackney, whiskey, one-horse chair   15 Harold   1 697
Per coach for Mrs. Pigot frank it down   224 J.C.H.   30
Coach, servants, gondola, he goes to call   445 Beppo   319
Whether they come by horse, or chaise, or coach 921 Juan   11 179
Coach, chariot, luggage, baggage, equipage   946 Juan   13 346
By various joltings of life's hackney coach   958 Juan   14 205

COACHES
The Coaches through the street so thunder   231 Doctor   42
Like mourning coaches when the funeral's done   442 Beppo   160
Through coaches, drays, choked turnpikes, and a
  whirl   921 Juan   11 169

COACHMAN
Its coachman and his coat   177 Devil's Dr   92
Of his Majesty's suite, up from coachman to
  Hetman   227 Moore-A   15
As the first coachman will; and 'midst the war   292 Vision   470

COACHMEN
In this they're like our coachmen, and the cause 451 Beppo   681

COAL
(See also SEA-COAL)
Bright--and as black and burning as a coal   828 Juan   4 749

COAL-BLACK
Mark'd her black eye that mocks her coal-black veil 13 Harold   1 569
To horse! to horse! my coal-black steed   730 Deformed   1 547

COALS
When coals to Newcastle are carried   227 Thurlow-B   18
They'd haul you o'er the coals, and stir the fires 440 Beppo   29
Sir Humphry Davy's lantern, by which coals   763 Juan   1 1052
Takes off one peck of purgatorial coals   781 Juan   2 437

COARSE
Were pleased with morrice-mumm'ry and coarse
  jokes   261 Hints   322
'Twixt too much polish and too coarse a wit   262 Hints   392
It was not that 'twas coarse and rude   404 Chillon   129
Dine and be d--d! I don't mean to be coarse   441 Beppo   71
Of loose mechanics, with all coarse foul comments 502 Faliero   1 190
But in its stead, coarse lusts of habitude   549 Faliero   5 783
As if the peasant's coarse contempt were vented 829 Juan   4 835
That injured Queen by chroniclers so coarse   839 Juan   5 481
Or to coarse efforts very loud and long   991 Juan   16 711

COARSER
Was coarser; and her air, though firm, less free 789 Juan   2 974

COARSEST
A turban carved in coarsest stone   317 Giaour   723
Earth's coarsest bread, the garden's homeliest
  roots   339 Corsair   1   71

COAST
(See also MOUNTAIN-COAST)
Since baffled Triumph droops on Lusitania's coast 8 Harold   1 305
But Cadiz, rising on the distant coast   14 Harold   1 659
Cold as the crags upon his native coast   21 Harold   2 102
From mountain-cliff to coast descending sombre
  down   23 Harold   2 198
To match some spots that lurk within this
  lowering coast   26 Harold   2 414
Full on the coast of Suli's shaggy shore   29 Harold   2 596
Themselves their monument;--the Stygian coast   45 Harold   3 606
The Latian coast where sprung the Epic war   81 Harold   4 1561
Full beams the moon on Actium's coast   159 Gulf   2
Imports old stories from the Cambrian coast   247 Bards   388
And Afric's coast and Calpe's adverse height   255 Bards   1019
Now should they burst on thy devoted coast   272 Minerva   309
His wings, like thunder-clouds above some coast 288 Vision   187
And here ascended from the coast   318 Giaour   809
His summon'd prows collect along the coast   347 Corsair   2   8
And hoard their curses, till the coast is clear 347 Corsair   2   28
Rustled like leaves from coast to coast   387 Corinth   265
I recollect Great Britain's coast looks white   775 Juan   2   93
The land appear'd a high and rocky coast   786 Juan   2 793
It was a wild and breaker-beaten coast   796 Juan   2 1409
The coast--I think it was the coast that I   797 Juan   2 1441
Was just describing--Yes, it was the coast   797 Juan   2 1442
Who dying on the coast of Ithaca   803 Juan   3 141
But that part of the coast being shoal and bare 804 Juan   3 150
Have you explored the limits of the coast   981 Juan   16   29

COASTS
From those Venetians who have skirr'd the coasts 612 Foscari   3 293

COAT
(See also BLUE-COAT)
Its coachman and his coat   177 Devil's Dr   92
The hat too old, the coat too cold to wear   224 J.C.H.   20
And wore but a starless blue coat, and in kersey 228 Moore-A   22
The first time he has turn'd both his creed and
  nis coat   281 Blues   2   55
Behold a candidate with unturn'd coat   293 Vision   535
Had turn'd his coat--and would have turn'd his
  skin   297 Vision   776
Instead of coat and smallclothes, than put on   440 Beppo   26
With nothing but the sky for a great coat   782 Juan   2 504
Just as my great coat was about me cast   835 Juan   5 259
A scarlet coat, black facings, a long plume   902 Juan   9 338

COATS
Adieu, red coats, and redder faces   163 Malta   18
For skirtless coats and skeletons of plays   249 Bards   599
And pay for poems--when they pay for coats   252 Bards   798
But coats must claim another artisan   257 Hints   54
If but thy coats are reasonably high   273 Waltz   10

COAX
I'll try to coax our Cerberus up to heaven   291 Vision   400
With the same feelings as you'd coax a vampire   926 Juan   11 485

COBBETT
Will. Cobbett has done well   235 Paine   2

COBBLER-LAUREATS
The cobbler-laureats sing to Capel Lofft   266 Hints   734

COBBLERS
Ye tuneful cobblers! still your notes prolong   252 Bards   791

COBBLES
St. Crispin quits, and cobbles for the muse   252 Bards   768

COBBLING
Cobbling at manacles for all mankind   746 Juan   Ded 110

COBBY
And blackguard Hunt and Cobby O   235 New Song   12

COBLENTZ
By Coblentz, on a rise of gentle ground   44 Harold   3 536

COCHINEAL
If from a shell-fish or from cochineal   981 Juan   16   79

COCK
And next proceeded quietly to cock   821 Juan   4 320
'I've heard of stories of a cock and bull   862 Juan   6 633
Good morrow--for the cock had crown, and light   863 Juan   6 682
Who wake in winter ere the cock can summon   960 Juan   14 283

COCK-CROW
With the first cock-crow. Which, if it end with 731 Deformed   1 634

COCK'D
So instead of a pistol he cock'd his tail   177 Devil's Dr   93
Cock'd, fired, and miss'd his man--but gain'd
  his aim   273 Waltz   22
Oh, valiant man! with sword drawn and cock'd
  trigger   765 Juan   1 1199
Upon the head, before their guns were cock'd   883 Juan   8 344
Over a cock'd hat in a crowded room   902 Juan   9 340
His bow converted into a cock'd hat   902 Juan   9 357

COCKER
Wrinkles that would puzzle Cocker   196 Rogers   2

COCKER'S
Of late years, to dispense with Cocker's rigours 993 Juan   16 831

COCK-EYED
A merry, cock-eyed, curious-looking sprite   293 Vision   521

COCKING
That cocking of a pistol, when you know   821 Juan   4 322

COCKNEY
Your veins of Cockney spirit, smile or mourn   917 Juan   10 638

COCKNEYS
And cockneys practise what they can't pronounce 275 Waltz   158
Cockneys of London! Muscadins of Paris   894 Juan   8 991

COCKS
Between these nations as a main of cocks   900 Juan   9 231

COCOA-NUT
For food the cocoa-nut, the yam, the bread   432 Island   4 169

COCOA'S
The cava feast, the yam, the cocoa's root   422 Island   2   258

CODE
A code of mercy by comparison   607 Foscari   2   394
And settled bonnets by the newest code   954 Juan   13 830

CODES
Defy all codes to image or to name them   549 Faliero   5   775
You may do your own deeming--you have codes   567 Sardan   2   379

CODGERS
I suppose that to-night you're engaged with some
  codgers   226 Oh You   11

CODICIL
A neat Codicil   238 Bray   4

COELEBS
Or 'Coelebs' Wife' set out in quest of lovers   749 Juan   1   124

COERCED
Poor thing of usages! coerced, compell'd   958 Juan   14 181

COETERA
Coetera desunt   239 Lucietta   12

COEVAL
When the coeval pride of human hands   45 Harold   3   624
The forest's trees (coeval with the hour   670 Heaven   1131

CO-EXIST
They cannot co-exist with Venice' freedom   525 Faliero   3   434

COFFEE
They enter'd and for coffee call'd--it came   451 Beppo   721
For breakfast, of eggs, coffee, bread, and fish   791 Juan   2   1064
But there were eggs, fruit, coffee, bread, fish,
  honey   792 Juan   2   1159
The coffee made, would fain have waken'd Juan   792 Juan   2   1162
Came always back to coffee and Haidee   796 Juan   2   1368
Up with the coffee, which (I think) they spoil'd   809 Juan   3   504
For tea and coffee leave us much more serious   823 Juan   4   416
He drank six cups of coffee at the least   863 Juan   6   732
And scarce to the Mogul a cup of coffee   900 Juan   9   262
The evening also waned--and coffee came   994 Juan   16 850

COFFEEHOUSE
And Lord Mount Coffeehouse, the Irish peer   765 Juan   1   1191
Go to the coffee-house, and take another   961 Juan   14 384

COFFER
Or that this crooked coffer, which contain'd   735 Deformed   1   880

COFFIN
And when the gorgeous coffin was laid low   286 Vision   78
Like dust beneath the coffin lid   401 Parisina   514
Just like a coffin clapt in a canoe   442 Beppo   151
And sends new Werters yearly to their coffin   937 Juan   12 502

COFFIN'D
Nor all that heralds rake from coffin'd clay   4 Harold   1   25
Lay cold in many a coffin'd row   395 Corinth   974
From daybreak, and when coffin'd at fourscore   792 Juan   2   1119

COFFIN'S
Scarce deem'd the coffin's lead could keep him
  fast   299 Age   102
Burglariously broke his coffin's lid   773 Juan   1   1750

COGNIAC
Unless when qualified with thee, Cogniac   823 Juan   4   417

CO-HEIRESSES
And the two fair co-heiresses Giltbedding   973 Juan   15 317

COHORN'S
The Greek or Turkish Cohorn's ignorance   884 Juan   8   363

COHORTS
And his cohorts were gleaming in purple and gold   222 Sennacherib   2
The turban'd cohorts throng the beach   385 Corinth   80

COIL
We may deplore and struggle with the coil   46 Harold   3   659
Forth from the abyss, looking as he could coil   642 Cain   2   398
And thou thyself wert like the serpent, coil   656 Heaven   127
His arms were like a serpent's coil: then flew   822 Juan   4   381

COIL'D
All coil'd into itself and round, as sleeps the
  snake   81 Harold   4   1557
As his foe fell; then, like a serpent, coil'd   434 Island   4   336
For there it coil'd as in a brake   481 Manfred   1   237

COIL'D
Should you see then the serpent, who hath coil'd   690 Werner   2   447
'Tis as the snake late coil'd, who pours his
  length   789 Juan   2   935
He lay coil'd like the boa in the wood   807 Juan   3   380

COILING
The struggle; vain, against the coiling strain   79 Harold   4   1436

COILS
But that which coils around the heart   219 Vanity   19

COIN
Your friends, or he'll pay you back in your own
  coin   280 Blues   1   152
A common coin as ever mint could strike   307 Age   707
Hath flow'd for me, nor hath the smallest coin   557 Sardan   1   456
And you shall have besides, in sparkling coin   682 Werner   1   676
The baron's coin, when he could thus convert   698 Werner   3   210
The country for some missing bits of coin   700 Werner   3   325
He pays me in the coin he owes me not   710 Werner   4   413
Nor coin my self-love to so base a vice   745 Juan   Ded 42

COINCIDENCE
A 'strange coincidence,' to use a phrase   862 Juan   6   623

COIN'D
Nor coin'd my cheek to smiles, nor cried aloud   52 Harold   3   1052
Such as are coin'd in conversation's mint   964 Juan   14 547
Coin'd from surviving superstition's mint   983 Juan   16 173

COINS
Some certain coins of silver, which as 'twere   190 Churchill   34
New coins (most new) to follow those that fled   276 Waltz   166
Her brow was overhung with coins of gold   788 Juan   2   921
Containing ingots, bags of dollars, coins   931 Juan   12 90

COKE
Also observe, that, like the great Lord Coke   979 Juan   15 689

COLBLEEN
I think of the rocks that o'ershadow Colbleen   136 Highlander   34

COLCHIAN
This cunning Colchian poison, which my father   574 Sardan   3   187
His predecessors in the Colchian days   808 Juan   3   436

COLD
(See also CLAY-COLD, OVER-COLD)
None through their cold disdain are doom'd to die   15 Harold   1   727
Cold as the crags upon his native coast   21 Harold   2   102
Cold is the heart, fair Greece, that looks on thee 21 Harold   2   127
Ere thy cold stranger pass'd to other climes   21 Harold   2   141
Since cold each kinder heart that might approve   34 Harold   2   889
And burning with high hope, shall moulder cold and
  low   39 Harold   3   243
Living in shatter'd guise, and still, and cold   40 Harold   3   294
Of cold sublimity, where forms and falls   45 Harold   3   594
And reach into thy heart,--when mine is cold   53 Harold   3   1074
Nor Torture shake, or mine would now be cold and
  dumb   58 Harold   4   171
The cold--the changed--perchance the dead--anew   59 Harold   4   215
With passions fiercer, yet a judgment cold   68 Harold   4   806
A deep cold settled aspect nought can shake   81 Harold   4   1556
Cold dews my pallid face o'erspread   87 Ad Lesbiam   17
'Tis then your breast, no longer cold   91 Caroline-B   33
I hate you, ye cold compositions of art   92 First Kiss   13
Except the dull cold stone that hides thy head   94 Dorset   50
With faint regard, or cold and distant eye   94 Dorset   100
But shuns the cold forbidding frown   100 Marion   10
Cold was the feast, the revel ceased   104 Alva   269
But Oscar's breast is cold as clay   104 Alva   277
Winter presides in his cold icy car   117 Lachin   22
If frowning Age, with cold control   133 E. N. Long   33
How cold must be my bosom now   135 I Would   43
Though cold is my heart, still it lingers with
  you   136 Highlander   32
Pallid and cold the Moon descends to cave   139 Ossian-A   7
When cold is the beauty which dwelt in my soul   148 Farewell-A   15
Pale grew thy cheek and cold   151 When We   5
As o'er the cold sepulchral stone   157 Album   1
And who so cold as look on thee   158 Florence   25
It gilds, but it warms not--'tis dazzling, but
  cold   164 Newstead-C   4
Place in a heart that ne'er was cold   164 Friend-B   14
Have seen her eyes, in cold disdain   164 Friend-B   31
Though cold as e'en the dead can be   166 Struggle   47
The cold repulse, the look askance   172 Romaic-B   19
That dull, cold sensualist, whose sickly eye   183 Address-D   47
Would that I were cold with those   187 French-A   17
And shivering scraped with their cold skeleton
  hands   190 Darkness   61
The absent are the dead--for they are cold   192 Fragment-C   15
Leave no cold traces   200 Stanzas-B   70

COLD

Ere the daughter of Brunswick is cold in her grave	201	Avatar	1
Yes, happy are they in their cold English graves	204	Avatar	117
The weak despair--the cold depart	209	Augusta-A	8
Within me,--or perhaps a cold despair	211	Augusta-C	42
Upon itself, and the wreck'd heart lies cold	213	Lady Byron	7
Which, but for this cold treason of thy heart	213	Lady Byron	40
Trafficking with them in a purpose cold	213	Lady Byron	44
He rose, and with a cold and gentle grasp	214	Dream	95
No ear so dull, no soul so cold	216	The Harp	8
Making the cold reality too real	216	Dream	183
Bloodless are these limbs, and cold	219	Saul-B	18
Distinct, but distant--clear--but, oh how cold	220	Sleepless	8
But thou art cold, my murder'd love	221	Mariamne	13
And cold as the spray of the rock-beating surf	222	Sennacherib	16
The hat too old, the coat too cold to wear	224	J.C.H.	20
And I, though with cold I have nearly my death got	226	Oh You	13
Beneath this cold slab, he	235	Pitt	2
Unless, perchance, from his cold bier she turns	252	Bards	811
Can aught from cold Kamschatka to Cape Horn	275	Waltz	129
Of his lecture, to treat him with cold tongue and praise	279	Blues	1	140
Michael, but you, and you, Saint Peter! Cold	291	Vision	381
The spheres, we shall catch cold amongst these clouds	293	Vision	531
Winds its cold folds, the tomb preserves its form	298	Age	26
The aid evaded, and the cold delay	302	Age	294
(If e'er those awful ashes can grow cold	308	Age	753
Where cold Obstruction's apathy	311	Giaour	81
Is his heart more cold, or his barb less swift	317	Giaour	700
The cold consumers of their clay	319	Giaour	950
'The cold in clime are cold in blood	321	Giaour	1099
Such cold request might sound like scorn	322	Giaour	1248
Ah! were thy beauties e'er so cold	323	Giaour	1293
Be long my lot! and cold were he	329	Abydos	2	37
Kiss'd her cold forehead--turn'd--is Conrad gone	345	Corsair	1	481
Its pulse nor check'd--nor quicken'd--calmly cold	354	Corsair	2	512
Nor deem'd it cold--her chill was at her heart	356	Corsair	3	82
And the cold flowers her colder hand contain'd	364	Corsair	3	605
And of its cold protector, blacken round	365	Corsair	3	676
Cold in the many, anxious in the few	366	Lara	1	32
Cold as the marble where his length was laid	369	Lara	1	211
With look collected, but with accent cold	372	Lara	1	429
The sickening iciness of that cold dew	374	Lara	1	601
Cold to the great, contemptuous to the high	377	Lara	2	184
With the cold grasp, but feels, and feels in vain	382	Lara	2	496
The cold, round moon shines deeply down	387	Corinth	243
Were their hands grown stiff, or their hearts wax'd cold	389	Corinth	445
But like that cold wave it stood still	390	Corinth	552
Though slight was that grasp so mortal cold	390	Corinth	599
Lay cold in many a coffin'd row	395	Corinth	974
Kneeling on the bare cold ground	400	Parisina	399
A cold electric shiver ran	401	Parisina	480
Worn, as if thy cold pavement were a sod	402	Sonnet-F	12
Or if they were--on his cold eye	402	Parisina	534
But even these at length grew cold	403	Chillon	62
Which in a palace had grown cold	404	Chillon	141
Even from the cold earth of our cave	404	Chillon	151
And my cold sweat-drops fell like rain	411	Mazeppa	444
So cold and stark the raven's beak	411	Mazeppa	480
My wounds already scarr'd with cold	411	Mazeppa	489
Or it might be my veins ran cold	412	Mazeppa	523
Cold, hunger, sorrow, shame, distress	412	Mazeppa	531
'My thoughts came back; where was I? Cold	412	Mazeppa	569
And of the cold, dull, swimming, dense	414	Mazeppa	787
In the cold drenching of the stormy night	418	Island	1	192
Cold lay they where they fell, and weltering	435	Island	4	363
The struggle to be calm, and cold distress	438	Tasso	102
Of the cold staggering race which Death is winning	453	Venice-B	40
Lady! if for the cold and cloudy clime	455	Dante	Ded	1
So long hath press'd and the cold marble stone	456	Dante	1	19
Their mother, the cold partner who hath brought	458	Dante	1	173
And burst, while cold on earth lay head and hoof	474	Morgante	542
The Glacier's cold and restless mass	479	Manfred	1	68
By thy cold breast and serpent smile	481	Manfred	1	242
Barren and cold, on which the wild waves break	484	Manfred	2	56
And fatal things pass'd harmless--the cold hand	486	Manfred	2	231
And feel a strange cold thaw upon my heart	487	Manfred	2	296
Give me thy hand. Cold--cold--even to the heart	497	Manfred	3	409
Who are not restless, cold: but there exists	517	Faliero	2	577
Its cold prerogative, we play'd together	531	Faliero	4	202
And if the cruelty in their cold eyes	543	Faliero	5	390
One look!--how cold her hand!--as cold as mine	547	Faliero	5	694
Prurient yet passionless, cold studied lewdness	549	Faliero	5	784
And then reproach her with thine own cold blindness	552	Sardan	1	92
Comes o'er my heart, a cold sense of the false-hood	558	Sardan	1	495
For seeming slain in that cold dizzy trance	588	Sardan	5	98
And the cold drops strain through my brow, as if	598	Foscari	1	161

COLD

For such a son--thou cold inveterate hater	612	Foscari	3	303
I have pierced him to the core of his cold heart	613	Foscari	3	318
Of cold looks upon manifold griefs! You came	613	Foscari	3	326
Cold to your years and services, they add	621	Foscari	5	29
My brother to his cold and still embrace	652	Cain	3	375
This cold and creeping kinsman, who so long	673	Werner	1	83
So scarcely will catch cold in't, if he be	675	Werner	1	235
Still liable to cold--and if not, why	675	Werner	1	236
To triple Time in the son's ear. I'm cold	701	Werner	3	399
It sounds so cold, as if you thought upon	706	Werner	4	155
His manner was a little cold, his spirit	707	Werner	4	179
But if my son is cold!--Who dare say that	709	Werner	4	325
Stiff and cold	729	Deformed	1	476
But what cold Sceptic hath appall'd your faith	743	Deformed	3	112
An Idol, but a cold one to your heat	744	Deformed	3	155
But be much puzzled by a cough and cold	776	Juan	2	171
Ague in its cold fit, they fill'd their boat	782	Juan	2	503
Famine, despair, cold, thirst, and heat, had done	787	Juan	2	809
And wet, and cold, and lifeless at her feet	820	Juan	4	265
And subject, when the house is thin, to cold	827	Juan	4	659
But, after all, 'tis nothing but cold snow	829	Juan	4	800
But I grow sad--and let a tale grow cold	831	Juan	5	31
White, cold, and pure, as looks a frozen rill	860	Juan	6	539
Chill, and chain'd to cold earth, we lift on high	867	Juan	7	5
Hark! through the silence of the cold, dull night	878	Juan	7	681
Those who catch cold in 'shadows of Death's valley	882	Juan	8	288
For that were vulgar, cold, and commonplace	890	Juan	8	770
Except cold weather and commiseration	894	Juan	8	1030
The climate was too cold, they said, for him	913	Juan	10	345
Of hot or cold, mercurial or sedate	932	Juan	12	186
Such is your cold coquette, who can't say 'No	937	Juan	12	497
A hidden nectar under a cold presence	945	Juan	13	299
And your cold people are beyond all price	946	Juan	13	303
When, ere the ink be dry, the sound grows cold	947	Juan	13	405
In this our party; polish'd, smooth, and cold	955	Juan	13	874
He was a cold, good, honourable man	964	Juan	14	553
Serene and noble,--conjugal, but cold	966	Juan	14	688
Now this at all events must render cold	971	Juan	15	205
As that prim, silent, cold Aurora Raby	974	Juan	15	392
Great thoughts we catch from thence (besides a cold	982	Juan	16	108
Then, as the night was clear though cold, he threw	982	Juan	16	129
But seeing him all cold and silent still	984	Juan	16	249
Quite full, right dull, guests hot, and dishes cold	991	Juan	16	670
Follow'd, his veins no longer cold, but heated	996	Juan	16	996

COLD-BLOODED

See the cold-blooded serpent, with venom full flush'd	203	Avatar	99
Cold-blooded, smooth-faced, placid miscreant	746	Juan	Ded	89

COLDER

Colder thy kiss	151	When We	6
Because her bosom is not colder	160	Cadiz	52
Ah! how much colder	199	Stanzas-B	21
And the cold flowers her colder hand contain'd	364	Corsair	3	605
As childhood dates within our colder clime	420	Island	2	125
Pray don't you think the weather here is colder	451	Beppo	740
Know then, that colder now than a pilaster	471	Morgante	327
Which colder hearts endure till they are laid	825	Juan	4	564
Their baffled rage and pain; while waxing colder	890	Juan	8	749

COLDEST

The coldest effusion which springs from my heart	148	Farewell-A	4
The coldest dames so very tender	408	Mazeppa	176

COLDLY

It is in vain that we would coldly gaze	43	Harold	3	471
My blood runs coldly through my breast	152	Weep-A	6
Which, coldly fix'd, regard the past	186	Stanzas-A	15
So coldly sweet, so deadly fair	311	Giaour	92
Alone and dewy, coldly pure and pale	337	Abydos	2	731
He shunn'd, nor sought, but coldly pass'd them by	342	Corsair	1	290
Thus coldly passing all that pass'd below	371	Lara	1	351
With self-confiding, coldly patient air	375	Lara	2	30
They coldly laugh'd--and laid him there	404	Chillon	159
My lord, my life! why answerest thou so coldly	551	Sardan	1	62
We met so rarely and so coldly in	680	Werner	1	574
And coldly dutiful, and proudly patient	743	Deformed	3	118
And looking coldly in her face, he cried	847	Juan	5	1006

COLDNESS

Secure in guarded coldness, he had mix'd	36	Harold	3	82
Which, be it wisdom, coldness, or deep pride	41	Harold	3	345
Then the mortal coldness of the soul like death itself comes down	185	Music-B	9
When coldness wraps this suffering clay	220	Clay	1
Coldness of mien, and carelessness of praise	367	Lara	1	70
From his high place with such relentless coldness	625	Foscari	5	325
But how!--obedient, but with coldness; duteous	710	Werner	4	419

COLDNESS
Yet Julia's very coldness still was kind   755 Juan   1   561
Coldness or anger, even disdain or hate   756 Juan   1   583
And whether coldness, pride, or virtue dignify   962 Juan   14   455
Such was her coldness or her self-possession   975 Juan   15   456

COLERIDGE
No drunken Coleridge with a new Lay Sermon   231 Sotheby   4
Shall gentle Coleridge pass unnoticed here   245 Bards   255
And brother Coleridge lull the babe at nurse   254 Bards   918
And Coleridge, too, has lately taken wing   745 Juan Ded 13
Like Coleridge, into a metaphysician   758 Juan   1   728
Thou shalt not set up Wordsworth, Coleridge,
   Southey   772 Juan   1 1634
Or Coleridge, long before his flighty pen   814 Juan   3   837
Some persons think that Coleridge hath the sway   925 Juan   11   461

COLIC
Or like a human colic, which is sadder   294 Vision   592

COLISEUM
Her Coliseum stands; the moonbeams shine   74 Harold   4 1147
'While stands the Coliseum, Rome shall stand   76 Harold   4 1297
When falls the Coliseum, Rome shall fall   76 Harold   4 1298

COLISEUM'S
I stood within the Coliseum's wall   495 Manfred   3   270

COLL.
King's Coll., Cam's stream, stain'd windows, and
   old walls   257 Hints   28

COLLAR
That you and I will win St. George's collar   890 Juan   8   776

COLLARS
Their gilded collars glittering in the sun   57 Harold   4   110
Glittering with their collars of gold   196 Venice-A   7
In number'd lots; they all had cuffs and collars 803 Juan   3   119

COLLATION
I'm engaged to the Lady Bluebottle's collation   279 Blues   1   137

COLLEAGUES
While Canning's colleagues hate him for his wit   255 Bards   1015
Rejoin our colleagues in the council, and   595 Foscari 1   4
Yet pause--the number of our colleagues is not   595 Foscari 1   21
The indulgence of your colleagues: but he knew it 612 Foscari 3   262
Here come our colleagues. Is the Duke aware   623 Foscari 5   151

COLLECT
His summon'd prows collect along the coast   347 Corsair 2   8
According to all hints I could collect   751 Juan   1   258
But still I think I can collect my mind   771 Juan   1 1562

COLLECTED
(See also SELF-COLLECTED)
Fraternal smiles collected round me seem   125 Recoll   230
Collected in the silent tomb   128 Answer-B   30
With look collected, but with accent cold   372 Lara   1   429

COLLECTEDNESS
Then all was stern collectedness and art   376 Lara   2   77

COLLECTING
Collecting the chief trophies of her line   74 Harold   4 1145

COLLECTION
But then the Abbey's worth the whole collection   921 Juan   11   200

COLLECTIVE
Where'er collective wisdom can parade   944 Juan   13   230

COLLECTOR
He is made a collector. Collector! How? What   281 Blues   2   60

COLLECTS
While heaviness collects the shatter'd spoils   213 Lady Byron   8
Collects such pasture for the longing sorrow   610 Foscari 3   178

COLLEGE
(See also COLL.)
The candidate for college prizes   95 Granta   30
With all the honours of his college   95 Granta   34
Who share the converse of a college hall   123 Recoll   94
No--no--I'd send him out betimes to college   753 Juan   1   415
Which is acquired in Nature's good old college   791 Juan   2 1088
Was whipt at college--a harsh sire--odd spouse   813 Juan   3   823
To build a college, or to found a race   931 Juan   12   74
Always premising that said son at college   946 Juan   13   335

COLLIER'S
And, spite of puritans and Collier's curse   261 Hints   369

COLLINI
Collini trill her love-inspiring song   250 Bards   630

COLLISION
Black with the rude collision, inly torn   193 Monody   91
And thus at the collision of thy name   438 Tasso   117

COLLOQUY
All further colloquy; and so--farewell   493 Manfred 3   159
Johnson, who knew by this long colloquy   875 Juan   7   513

COLLUSION
Of aught but tears--save those shed by collusion 286 Vision   68

COLMAN
Awake, George Colman! Cumberland, awake   249 Bards   578

COLOGNE
From thence he was drawn onwards to Cologne   915 Juan   10   493

COLONEL
(See also LIEUTENANT-COLONEL)
But could not teach a colonel waltzing   163 Malta   16

COLONIAL
'Tis there the mart of the colonial trade is   774 Juan   2   35

COLONNA
In the Colonna palace. In my father's   740 Deformed 2   337
Convey her unto the Colonna palace   741 Deformed 2   398
Colonna, as I told you! Oh! I know   742 Deformed 2   427

COLONNADE
It is a princely colonnade   196 Venice-A   21

COLONNA'S
Colonna's cliff, and gleams along the wave   33 Harold   2   813
Which, seen from far Colonna's height   310 Giaour   9

COLOR
(See COLOUR)

COLOSSAL
Is the spot mark'd with no colossal bust   37 Harold   3   147
When the colossal fabric's form is near'd   76 Harold   4 1285
Colossal copyist of deformity   78 Harold   4 1362
Has grown colossal, and can only find   78 Harold   4 1390

COLOSSUS
Than all a gold Colossus could secure   183 Address-D   12
Thou hast struck one immense Colossus down   965 Juan   14   651

COLOUR
And colour things to come with hues of Night   46 Harold   3   665
With a new colour as it gasps away   59 Harold   4   260
In colour though varied, in beauty may vie   323 Abydos   1   12
But varying oft the colour of her cheek   363 Corsair 3   534
The colour of young Kaled went and came   374 Lara   1   598
He was a Turk, the colour of mahogany   448 Beppo   553
No colour from the fleeting things without   496 Manfred 3   394
Lent a fair colour to the introduction   517 Faliero 2   639
Made my heart sick. I see the colour comes   597 Foscari 1   130
And blending every colour into one   785 Juan   2   734
And every morn his colour freshlier came   795 Juan   2 1345
Whose colour was not black, nor white, nor grey   842 Juan   5   700
Her eye dilated and her colour heighten'd   861 Juan   6   576
The colour of a budding rose's crest   863 Juan   6   666
To colour up his rays from your despatches   877 Juan   7   648
Lend to that colour a transcendent ray   905 Juan   9   566
May the rose call back its true colour soon   955 Juan   13   886
Of bards and prosers, words are void of colour   960 Juan   14   320
I know not; but her colour ne'er was high   993 Juan   16   798

COLOUR'D
(See also BRAZEN-COLOUR'D, FLESH-COLOUR'D, MANY-
   COLOUR'D, PEARL-COLOUR'D)
The mind is colour'd by thy every hue   44 Harold   3   574
Kiss'd by the breath of heaven, seems colour'd by
   its skies   72 Harold   4 1053
Which colour'd all his objects:--he had ceased   214 Dream   55
Though colour'd, as it were, within a tan-yard   443 Beppo   203
Colour'd, and silver paper leaved between   447 Beppo   454
Of colour'd garbs, as bright as butterflies   805 Juan   3   216
So that the streets of colour'd lamps are full   872 Juan   7   349
Broadening to grins, he colour'd more than once   992 Juan   16   747

COLOURING
The colouring of the scenes which fleet along   52 Harold   3 1042
Colouring the clouds, that shut me out from
   heaven   484 Manfred 2   29
Was apt to add a colouring from her own   970 Juan   15   130
The difficulty lies in colouring   971 Juan   15   197

COLOURINGS
Shorn of its glass of thousand colourings   948 Juan   13   490

COLOURS
The very Glaciers have his colours caught   50 Harold   3   926
From thee, fair Venice, have their colours caught   58 Harold   4   169
From clouds, but of all colours seems to be   59 Harold   4   239
With such an aspect, by his colours blent   175 Sonnet-A   9
Of three bright colours, each divine   188 On Star   21
Congenial colours in that soul or face   209 Sketch   70
He turn'd all colours--as a peacock's tail   292 Vision   483
Howe'er its arch may swell, its colours move   423 Island   2   344
In feeble colours, when the eye--from the Alp   459 Dante   2   62
Simpler, and yet of colours not so grave   789 Juan   2   955
And take all colours--like the hands of dyers   813 Juan   3   792
And in such colours that they seem to live   830 Juan   4   854
Warranted virgin; beauty's brightest colours   830 Juan   4   907
Oh that my words were colours! but their tints   865 Juan   6   871
A thousand and a thousand colours they   867 Juan   7   7

COLT
Or wild colt of a comet, which too soon   285 Vision   13

COLUMBIA
Such as Columbia saw arise when she   69 Harold   4   858
Nor these alone; Columbia feels no less   307 Age   680
Now new no more, save where Columbia rears   420 Island   2   75

COLUMBIA'S
Strange retribution! now Columbia's ease   18 Harold   1   915
Beneath Columbia's fervid zone   128 Lady-C   24
Columbia's caperers to the warlike whoop   275 Waltz   128
Columbia's stock hath holders not unknown   930 Juan   12   46

COLUMBUS
If some Columbus of the moral seas   968 Juan   14   807
Columbus found a new world in a cutter   971 Juan   15   214
The sceptics who would not believe Columbus   981 Juan   16   32

COLUMN
Save where some solitary column mourns   33 Harold   2   810
Nor column trophied for triumphal show   37 Harold   3   148
By a lone wall a lonelier column rears   45 Harold   3   617
To the broad column which rolls on, and shows   65 Harold   4   631
On what were chambers, arch crush'd, column strown   71 Harold   4   957
Thou nameless column with the buried base   71 Harold   4   983
Saw the long column of revolving flames   169 Address-A   9
Frowns from the height of his hoary column   196 Venice-A   10
There the white column greets her grateful ray   269 Minerva   38
How view the column of ascending flames   272 Minerva   305
When Victory's Gallic column shall but rise   299 Age   109
Hath swept the column from their tomb   311 Giaour   131
In azure column proudly gleaming   316 Giaour   623
There the white column greets her grateful ray   356 Corsair   3   38
And half a column of the pompous page   368 Lara   1   187
Nothing is there but the column stone   391 Corinth   675
Through the massy column to turn and fly   394 Corinth   929
They chain'd us each to a column stone   403 Chillon   48
And roll the sheeted silver's waving column   485 Manfred   2   97
'Tis rumour'd that the column sent against them   705 Werner   4   95
To the bard's tomb, and not the warrior's column   829 Juan   4   828
With human blood that column was cemented   829 Juan   4   833
With human filth that column is defiled   829 Juan   4   834
The column order'd on the assault scarce pass'd   879 Juan   8   195
Fell in with what was late the second column   882 Juan   8   266
The town was enter'd: first one column made   887 Juan   8   545
Where three parts of his column yet remain   887 Juan   8   576
Their column, though the Turkish batteries
    thunder'd   887 Juan   8   593
Another column also suffer'd much   888 Juan   8   617
As an old temple dwindled to a column   941 Juan   13   8
Column; date, 'Falmouth. There has lately been
    here   948 Juan   13   429

COLUMNAR
The Bucentaur, like the columnar cloud   547 Faliero   5   632

COLUMN'D
Slow sweeps he through the column'd aisle   319 Giaour   884

COLUMNS
(See also WATER-COLUMNS)
Columns and idol-dwellings, Goth or Greek   49 Harold   3   857
Its columns strew the wilderness, and dwell   78 Harold   4   1373
Couch'd among fallen columns, in the shade   215 Dream   116
The list concludes John Murray's columns   232 Nihil   2
Some stragglers skirmish round the columns still   252 Bards   760
Are damn'd alike by gods and men and columns   265 Hints   588
Check'd by thy columns, fell more sadly fair   269 Minerva   68
In red and wreathing columns flash'd   386 Corinth   169
Two or three columns, many have a stone   389 Corinth   497
There are seven columns, massy and grey   403 Chillon   29
Which spurn in columns back the baffled spray   419 Island   2   15
Than all the columns Conquest's minions rear   420 Island   2   92

COLUMNS
(Which casts up misty columns that become   492 Manfred   3   112
Proportion'd like the columns to the temple   523 Faliero   3   292
In separate columns at the self-same moment   535 Faliero   4   466
Of the red columns, where, on festal Thursday   539 Faliero   5   93
Not so:--of all his conquests a few columns   554 Sardan   1   215
Detachment of three columns took its station   873 Juan   7   395
Was also in three columns, with a thirst   873 Juan   7   398
The third, in columns two, attack'd by water   873 Juan   7   400
The columns were in movement one and all   879 Juan   8   65

COLUMN'S
The marble column's yet unshaken base   20 Harold   2   83

COLUMN-SCATTERING
Now views the column-scattering bay'net jar   12 Harold   1   564

COMB
Did Neuha with the mermaids comb her hair   431 Island   4   101
While Baba made him comb his head and oil it   841 Juan   5   632

COMBAT
Her vassals combat when their chieftains flee   18 Harold   1   885
Did nations combat to make One submit   38 Harold   3   165
And thus they dealt the combat side by side   124 Recoll   174
Whilst I, in combat with another foe   126 Recoll   277
might. Fingal roused his chiefs to combat   130 Calmar   31
life is his; rise to combat.' Mathon starts   130 Calmar   125
As in the field of combat, side by side   143 Soliloquy   81
As the chief who to combat advances   162 Romaic-A   25
Have next to combat with the female knight   230 Murray-A   17
Let him combat for that of his neighbours   236 Freedom   2
Combat than listen, were it to their father   304 Age   495
Feast there who can, nor combat till they must   347 Corsair   2   41
It flow'd in combat, or was shed by men   361 Corsair   3   429
But form'd to combat with his kind   403 Chillon   93
No more to combat and to bleed   407 Mazeppa   4
I do not combat against death, but thee   496 Manfred   3   372
They dared not. They were kept to toil and
    combat   556 Sardan   1   381
In the combat he'll not faint   730 Deformed   1   558
With aught of soul would combat if he were   737 Deformed   2   195
I combat with a mass, or not at all   738 Deformed   2   231
That of despising those we combat with   870 Juan   7   194
Which did not combat like the devil, as yet   883 Juan   8   294
As tigers combat with an empty craw   884 Juan   8   389

COMBATED
Still he combated unwounded   393 Corinth   786
As if he had combated with more than one   998 Juan   17   107

COMBATS
Not thus my sire in Argive combats fought   106 Nisus   44
For nobler combats, here, reserved his life   120 Newstead-A   75

COMBAT'S
From reeking pile and combat's wreck away   350 Corsair   2   222
Beguiles his charger from the combat's rage   380 Lara   2   391

COMB'D
And above all be comb'd even to a hair   867 Juan   6   940

COMBINATION
By the mere combination of a coterie   951 Juan   13   652

COMBINATIONS
Were combinations of disjointed things   216 Dream   174

COMBINE
Three hosts combine to offer sacrifice   10 Harold   1   441
When vice and infamy combine   95 Granta   54
And all combine to hail the draught   103 Alva   192
Aeneas and Ascanius shall combine   107 Nisus   137
Bacchus and Mars to rule the camp combine   108 Nisus   229
With him the Graces then combine   139 Anacreon-C   17
How many must combine to form one Incomprehensible   179 Devil's Dr   248
Who rack'd his little spirit to combine   183 Address-D   49
Though Murray with his Miller may combine   244 Bards   173
For fops, fools, gamesters, knaves, and lords
    combine   250 Bards   649
To guide whose hand the sister arts combine   253 Bards   861
Let judgment teach him wisely to combine   257 Hints   67
Jews, authors, generals, charlatans, combine   307 Age   710
That love and marriage rarely can combine   802 Juan   3   35
(As far as rhyme and criticism combine   909 Juan   10   123

COMBINED
Combined marauders, half-way, barr'd egress   29 Harold   2   615
Historian, bard, philosopher, combined   51 Harold   3   989
And not the whole combined and countless throng   61 Harold   4   349
To love, than rank with vice combined   85 To E--   4
And now combined they hold their nightly guard   105 Nisus   18
Twin sacred titles, which combined appear   224 J.C.H.   3
When knaves and fools combined o'er all prevail   242 Bards   31

COMBINED

Combined usurpers on the throne of taste	243 Bards		84
And all with justice deem'd the two combined	248 Bards		488
Whose mingling taste combined to cull the wreath	254 Bards		883
When all its elements convulsed, combined	352 Corsair	2	329
And the old ducal dotard, who combined	600 Foscari	1	322
Might shock a connoisseur; but when combined	949 Juan	13	531
Half virtues and whole vices being combined	975 Juan	15	452

COMBINING

Suspected of combining to destroy it	507 Faliero	1	549

COMBOLOIO

And by her comboloio lies	329 Abydos	2	72

COMBS

Of stockings, slippers, brushes, combs, complete	764 Juan	1	1140

COME

And monks might deem their time was come agen	4 Harold	1	62
The silent thought, nor from his lips did come	5 Harold	1	106
'Come hither, hither, my little page	5 Harold	1	134
Till I come back again	6 Harold	1	153
'Come hither, hither, my staunch yeoman	6 Harold	1	158
But long ere I come back again	6 Harold	1	188
Portend the deeds to come:--but he whose nod	12 Harold	1	540
Come, blue-eyed maid of heaven!--but thou, alas	19 Harold	2	1
Come--but molest not yon defenceless urn	19 Harold	2	20
As winds come lightly whispering from the west	30 Harold	2	626
When his Delhis come dashing in blood o'er the banks	31 Harold	2	687
Would they had never been, or were to come	34 Harold	2	898
Or whispering, with white lips--'The foe! They come! they come	39 Harold	3	225
Come forth her work of gladness to contrive	40 Harold	3	268
And colour things to come with hues of Night	46 Harold	3	665
It came, it cometh, and will come,--the power	48 Harold	3	795
Uprear'd of human hands. Come, and compare	49 Harold	3	856
The hour must come when such things shall be made	52 Harold	3	1007
But is not Doria's menace come to pass	57 Harold	4	111
Come back before me, or were to come	64 Harold	4	554
What are our woes and sufferance? Come and see	66 Harold	4	698
Thou tomb! and other days come back on me	70 Harold	4	930
Since now the hour is come at last	89 To Emma		1
That age will come on, when remembrance, deploring	91 Caroline-C		7
Come then, some other mode elect	99 Young Lady		31
Come, drink remembrance of the dead	104 Alva		231
throng on the green hills. They come to the	130 Calmar		33
Come rolling fresh on Fancy's eye	133 E. N. Long		4
I think those days may come again	133 E. N. Long		12
Come to task all	157 Hodgson		10
Lord knows when we shall come back	157 Hodgson		66
And when the dreaded hour shall come	169 Blank Leaf		5
His turn is come to follow me	173 Quotation		20
And the Devil has all the pleasure to come	178 Devil's Dr		177
Come tell me who to thee is bound	179 Gold		19
But come--The bark that bears us hence shall find	185 Julian		50
Past or to come, a new-born people's cry	206 Greece		2
The time shall come, nor long remote, when thou	209 Sketch		81
Come as of yore upon me, and can melt	211 Augusta-C		53
And for the remnant which may be to come	212 Augusta-C		113
We are entwined--let death come slow or fast	212 Augusta-C		127
And forgot for a moment my bondage to come	221 Jerusalem		6
Come, say, how many have been sold	233 Ballad-B		21
The unfledged MS. authors come	234 Strahan		6
Next see tremendous Thalaba come on	244 Bards		211
Come forth, oh Campbell! give thy talents scope	252 Bards		801
Let coxcombs, printing as they come from far	255 Bards		1025
That bid the foe defiance ere they come	272 Minerva		288
Come near enough--if not to touch--to taint	277 Waltz		243
That--come--do not make me speak ill of one's neighbour	278 Blues	1	51
To a man of--but come--let us shake hands. You knew	279 Blues	1	118
Have you never yet seen it? That pleasure's to come	279 Blues	1	128
Very true; let us go, then, before they can come	280 Blues	1	146
Come, come: nay, I'm off. You are right, and I'll follow	280 Blues	1	155
A rabble who know not--But soft, here they come	280 Blues	2	24
If he does, his fatigue is to come. Mr. Tracy	280 Blues	2	30
Come, a truce with all tartness:--the joy of my heart	282 Blues	2	113
Is Lucifer come back with all this clatter	287 Vision		136
'But had it come up here upon its shoulders	287 Vision		161
Of worlds past, present, or to come; no station	291 Vision		420
Pye come again? No more--no more of that	296 Vision		736
Times present, past, to come, heaven, hell, and all	297 Vision		806
As for the rest, to come to the conclusion	298 Vision		841
But be it as it is--the time may come	300 Age		129
To come, in which all empires shall expire	300 Age		184
And sketch the group--the picture's yet to come	308 Age		766
They come--their kerchiefs green they wave	317 Giaour		743

COME

And come what may, I have been blest	321 Giaour		1115
'Come hither, boy--what, no reply	325 Abydos	1	119
Come, lay thy head upon my breast	327 Abydos	1	301
Unto thy cell will Selim come	328 Abydos	1	464
Ours be the last; in time deceit may come	333 Abydos	2	436
Dauntless he stood!--''Tis come--soon past	334 Abydos	2	513
They come--'tis but to add to slaughter	335 Abydos	2	555
Thy destined lord is come too late	335 Abydos	2	624
Come when it will--we snatch the life of life	338 Corsair	1	25
These Juan calls--they come--to their salute	340 Corsair	1	141
Be silent, Conrad!--dearest! come and share	344 Corsair	1	420
But come, the board is spread; our silver lamp	344 Corsair	1	433
A feast for promised triumph yet to come	347 Corsair	2	4
'And now come torture when it will--or may	352 Corsair	2	380
I come through darkness--and I scarce know why	353 Corsair	2	439
Or when reflection comes--and come it must	354 Corsair	2	521
Medora's heart; the third day's come and gone	356 Corsair	3	68
They come with half-lit tapers in their hands	369 Lara	1	209
But fleet his step, and clear his tones would come	373 Lara	1	520
The gather'd chieftains come to Otho's call	375 Lara	2	20
Heedless if she come or go	388 Corinth		431
Of the things to come than the things before	389 Corinth		500
And he felt not a breath come over his cheek	390 Corinth		529
'I come from my rest to him I love best	390 Corinth		563
I come--and if I come in vain	390 Corinth		573
As they seem, through the dimness, about to come down	391 Corinth		624
As the gusts on the tapestry come and go	391 Corinth		627
And the clash, and the shout, 'They come! they come	391 Corinth		687
Shriller shrieks now mingling come	393 Corinth		771
Come on!'--That challenge is in vain	394 Corinth		865
But it must come, and they must part	397 Parisina		61
And it was come to love me when	405 Chillon		275
My brother's soul come down to me	405 Chillon		288
And half I felt as they were come	406 Chillon		379
That one day I should come again	411 Mazeppa		410
I felt the blackness come and go	412 Mazeppa		550
A trampling troop; I see them come	413 Mazeppa		673
The morning watch was come; the vessel lay	415 Island	1	1
They come not; they are few, and, over-awed	416 Island	1	67
Come, let us to the islet's softest shade	419 Island	2	3
Or that he would, or that he would not come	443 Beppo		214
I'll keep them for my life (to come) in prose	450 Beppo		628
And then come to themselves, almost or quite	451 Beppo		710
And so he hired a vessel come from Spain	452 Beppo		758
The day may come when she will cease to err	457 Dante	1	73
The day may come she would be proud to have	457 Dante	1	74
The sense of earth and earthly things come back	457 Dante	1	131
And pilgrims come from climes where they have known	458 Dante	1	154
Are yet to come; and on the imperial hill	459 Dante	2	72
As in the old time, till the hour be come	465 Dante	4	152
'For God-sake, cavalier, come in with speed	469 Morgante		209
I come to kill you, if it shall so please	470 Morgante		243
'I come to preach to you, as to your brothers	471 Morgante		321
The abbot said to him, 'Come in and see	476 Morgante		664
They come not yet.--Now by the voice of him	479 Manfred	1	37
As unto him may seem most fitting--Come	481 Manfred	1	187
In mountainous o'erwhelming, come and crush me	482 Manfred	1	337
Come on, we'll quickly find a surer footing	483 Manfred	1	383
Hath wash'd since winter.--Come, 'tis bravely done	483 Manfred	1	385
And be of better cheer. Come, taste my wine	483 Manfred	2	17
Let it do thus for thine. Come, pledge me fairly	484 Manfred	2	20
Or watch my watchings--Come and sit by me	486 Manfred	2	223
Is our great festival--'tis strange they come not	488 Manfred	2	313
Powers deeper still beyond--I come in quest	489 Manfred	2	446
Take it. I come to save, and not destroy	492 Manfred	3	47
The fee of what I have to come these three years	494 Manfred	3	210
Some strange things in them, Herman. Come, be friendly	494 Manfred	3	231
Avaunt!--Pronounce--what is thy mission? Come	496 Manfred	3	339
The genius of this mortal.--'tis time	496 Manfred	3	341
Thou'lt know anon--Come! Come! I have commanded	496 Manfred	3	344
Mortal! thine hour is come--Away! I say	496 Manfred	3	347
I knew, and know my hour is come, but not	496 Manfred	3	348
Then wherefore came you here? I come for justice	505 Faliero	1	407
You come to me for justice--unto me	505 Faliero	1	412
If such your power and purpose, why come here	507 Faliero	1	543
And leave the palace? You must come alone	508 Faliero	1	583
Would he were come! for I alone have power	509 Faliero	2	24
Come hither, child; I would a word with you	513 Faliero	2	291
The hour you speak of come, it will be seen so	513 Faliero	2	347
I cannot bear to leave you thus	515 Faliero	2	499
And I come here to strengthen even the strong	522 Faliero	3	272
Would that the hour were come! we will not scotch	524 Faliero	3	389
I am resolved--come on. With all my soul	528 Faliero	3	650
He who has shed patrician blood--I come	530 Faliero	4	153
What hath come to thee? in thy hollow eye	531 Faliero	4	233
I come for your last orders. It had been	533 Faliero	4	353
The Genoese are come--ho! to the rescue	535 Faliero	4	472

COME

Come hither, my Bertuccio--one embrace	535	Faliero	4	476
But this is idle. Come, sirs, do your work	537	Faliero	4	654
Must be consider'd, till the hour shall come	540	Faliero	5	153
And see be sooth, have reach'd me, and I come	542	Faliero	5	332
Nothing of good can come from such a source	544	Faliero	5	456
And take my refuge in the cloister. Come	545	Faliero	5	545
He turn'd to me, and said, 'The hour will come	546	Faliero	5	604
Thus saying, he pass'd on.--That hour is come	546	Faliero	5	617
That a sure hour will come, when their sons' sons	547	Faliero	5	655
Lo, where they come! already I perceive	551	Sardan	1	37
Speaking of him and his. They come, the slaves	551	Sardan	1	46
Come, I'm indulgent, as thou knowest, patient	552	Sardan	1	143
That ever shook a kingdom! Let them come	556	Sardan	1	356
Not one! the time may come thou may'st. It will	558	Sardan	1	506
But he is honest. Come, we'll think no more on't	558	Sardan	1	522
Come, Myrrha, let us go on to the Euphrates	559	Sardan	1	599
Why let it come then unexpectedly	560	Sardan	1	650
If the worst come, I shall be where none weep	561	Sardan	1	669
Our business is with night--'tis come. But not	562	Sardan	2	40
Grief cannot come where perfect love exists	571	Sardan	2	599
I come. There's victory in the very word	573	Sardan	3	118
Their shouts come ringing through the ancient halls	575	Sardan	3	251
This realm as province. Hark! they come--they come	575	Sardan	3	267
Thine hour is come. No, thine.--I've lately read	575	Sardan	3	275
Come down to hail us hers. This is too much	577	Sardan	3	400
Had lost a part of death to come to me	580	Sardan	4	126
I come to speak with you. How! of the queen	581	Sardan	4	199
But let her come. I go. We have lived asunder	581	Sardan	4	227
As I am in this form. Come, look upon it	588	Sardan	5	46
All that can come, and how to meet it, our	590	Sardan	5	224
That thou shouldst come and dare to ask of me	592	Sardan	5	320
As the torch in thy grasp. 'Tis fired! I come	595	Sardan	5	498
The time will come they will renew that order	598	Foscari	1	157
But here come two of 'the Ten;' let us retire	600	Foscari	1	311
The hall, and his own sufferings.--Lo! they come	601	Foscari	1	379
My last of children! Tell him I will come	608	Foscari	2	439
I come to tell thee the result of their	610	Foscari	3	122
If you come for our thanks, take them, and hence	612	Foscari	3	263
They feel not, but no less are shiver'd. Come	613	Foscari	3	335
Come, Foscari, take the hand the altar gave you	614	Foscari	3	433
Come, they are met by this time; let us join them	615	Foscari	4	48
Ah! the devil come to insult the dead! Avaunt	618	Foscari	4	218
Alone, come all the world around me, I	621	Foscari	5	67
I must look on him once more. Come with me	622	Foscari	5	109
And he is in his shroud! Come, come, old man	622	Foscari	5	111
Here come our colleagues. Is the Duke aware	623	Foscari	5	151
We come once more to urge our past request	623	Foscari	5	162
But come; my son and I will go together	624	Foscari	5	250
I will. My brother, I have come for thee	632	Cain	1	332
Come away. Seest thou not? I see an angel	632	Cain	1	337
Whence he shall come back to thee in an hour	635	Cain	1	524
But that's a mystery. Cain, come on with me	635	Cain	1	536
Who shall return, save One) shall come back to thee	635	Cain	1	539
With torture of my dooming. There will come	636	Cain	2	16
Are beings past, and shadows still to come	638	Cain	2	175
Is come. And these, too; can they ne'er repass	641	Cain	2	324
Ill cannot come: they are too beautiful	643	Cain	2	450
Both; but the time will come thou shalt see one	645	Cain	2	604
Come thou shalt be amerced for sins unknown	646	Cain	3	24
Adah!--come hither! Death is in the world	651	Cain	3	370
Come, Zillah! I must watch my husband's corse	653	Cain	3	450
Come, Zillah! Yet one kiss on yon pale clay	653	Cain	3	453
'Twill come to pass, that whoso findeth him	653	Cain	3	481
Be taken on his head. Come hither! What	653	Cain	3	497
They come! he comes!--Azaziel! Haste	657	Heaven		143
Have come upon me. Peace! what peace? the calm	658	Heaven		219
Born ere this dying world? They come like clouds	659	Heaven		339
Welcome as Eden. It may be they come	663	Heaven		584
For which I have so often pray'd.--They come	663	Heaven		586
We know thee not. The hour may come when thou	663	Heaven		603
The hour will come in which celestial aid	663	Heaven		641
Has come down in that haughty blood which springs	664	Heaven		664
Come, Anah! quit this chaos-founded prison	669	Heaven		1078
To make a world for torture.--Lo! they come	670	Heaven		1128
Save those who come to make it poorer still	674	Werner	1	168
As destiny, his excellency's come	678	Werner	1	430
Than did the elements, is come. This way	678	Werner	1	455
Come you to stir yourself in his behalf	681	Werner	1	652
Come hither, mynheer! But so much haste bodes	686	Werner	2	247
Come on, old oracle, expound thy riddle	687	Werner	2	253
I must be known here but as Werner. Come	688	Werner	2	360
Come to my arms again! Why, thou look'st all	688	Werner	2	361
I like that article of war. Come hither	693	Werner	2	665
Greatly to care. But hark! they come! Who come	696	Werner	3	64
They come! to seek elsewhere what is before them	697	Werner	3	112
Why need you come so far, then? In the search	697	Werner	3	126
Both paramount to his and mine. But come	697	Werner	3	144
Diamond, by all that's glorious! Come, I'll trust you	700	Werner	3	310
Without the forfeit of his soul. But come	700	Werner	3	342

COME

But come, I'll serve thee; thou shalt be as free	700	Werner	3	347
Carats may it weigh?--Come, Werner, I will wing thee	700	Werner	3	355
So better times are come at last; to these	704	Werner	4	1
No true knight.--Come, dear Ulric! yield to me	707	Werner	4	212
Come! I will sing to you. Ida, you scarcely	708	Werner	4	228
Ulric, you'll come and hear me? By and by	708	Werner	4	269
Could aught of his sound on it:--but come quickly	708	Werner	4	275
Of heaven, although I look'd on Ulric. Come	714	Werner	5	67
But come: you wish to kill yourself;--pursue	723	Deformed	1	87
Come as ye were	724	Deformed	1	165
Of mortals, that extremes meet. Come! Be quick	726	Deformed	1	287
Upon your pilgrimage. But come, pronounce	729	Deformed	1	492
Come, count, to business. True. I'll weep hereafter	737	Deformed	2	155
To come at. And my thirst increases--but	738	Deformed	2	221
His hour is not yet come. That shall be seen	739	Deformed	2	254
And others come: so flows the wave on wave	739	Deformed	2	290
Come on! I'm glad on 't! I will show you, slaves	740	Deformed	2	326
And do not know it. She will come to life	741	Deformed	2	395
Where I have pitch'd my banner. Come then! raise her up	741	Deformed	2	399
The spring is come	742	Deformed	3	2
The spring is come; the violet's gone	742	Deformed	3	7
The spring is come	742	Deformed	3	63
Begot--but that's to come--Well, to renew	748	Juan	1	72
To teach him manners for the time to come	750	Juan	1	200
Our coming, and look brighter when we come	762	Juan	1	980
'Come, come, 'tis no time now for fooling there	767	Juan	1	1358
Of twenty-five or thirty (come, make haste	768	Juan	1	1370
(Come, sir, get in)--my master must be near	768	Juan	1	1373
Or else the thing had hardly come to pass	774	Juan	2	22
(And so, my sober Muse--come, let's be steady	775	Juan	2	48
For the sky show'd it would come on to blow	777	Juan	2	207
But they could not come at the leak as yet	777	Juan	2	220
Because, till people know what's come to pass	781	Juan	2	438
And when the wish'd-for shower at length was come	785	Juan	2	708
The worlds to come of both, or fall beneath	802	Juan	3	69
To bid men come, and go, and come again	807	Juan	3	370
And clouds come o'er the sunset of our day	808	Juan	3	470
(Provided they don't come in after dinner	808	Juan	3	474
But one arise,--we come, we come	812	Juan	3	735
Of Pope and Dryden, are we come to this	814	Juan	3	890
Should an hour come to bid them breathe apart	819	Juan	4	211
The time may come when you may hear me too	827	Juan	4	702
Of poets who come down to us through distance	829	Juan	4	793
The time must come, when both alike decay'd	829	Juan	4	829
"Go," and he goeth; "come," and forth he stepp'd	836	Juan	5	286
I wish the case could come before a jury here	839	Juan	5	488
And now, then, you must come along with me, sirs	841	Juan	5	638
'Blockhead! come on, and see,' quoth Baba; while	842	Juan	5	657
The moment, till too late to come again	852	Juan	6	5
Stript to his shirt, was come to lead the van	873	Juan	7	392
'Whence come ye?'--'From Constantinople last	874	Juan	7	468
Who, when we come to sum up the totality	877	Juan	7	661
Past, present, and to come;--but all may yield	879	Juan	8	95
Knew when and how 'to cut and come again	882	Juan	8	278
Which made some think, and others know, a hell come	883	Juan	8	336
Had not come up in time to cast an awe	884	Juan	8	387
Then comes 'the tug of war;'--'twill come again	884	Juan	8	405
So Cuvier says;--and then shall come again	901	Juan	9	297
I never know the word which will come next	901	Juan	9	328
From thee we come, to thee we go, and why	903	Juan	9	443
But coughs will come when sighs depart--and now	908	Juan	10	57
Must come? Much rather should he court the ray	908	Juan	10	71
To come off handsomely in that regard	910	Juan	10	172
But time, the comforter, will come at last	913	Juan	10	377
Whether they come by horse, or chaise, or coach	921	Juan	11	179
You leave behind, the next of much you come	924	Juan	11	349
(Which will come over things), beats love or liquor	930	Juan	12	29
The time will come she'll wish that she had snatch'd	934	Juan	12	275
Come out and glimmer'd as a six weeks' star	951	Juan	13	670
While Strongbow's best things might have come from Cato	952	Juan	13	736
An age may come, Font of Eternity	955	Juan	14	21
When your affairs come round, one way or t'other	961	Juan	14	383
To come between mine epic and its index	964	Juan	14	544
And hate those who won't let them come to pass	978	Juan	15	632
For you have got that pleasure still to come	980	Juan	15	756
Might come or go; but Juan could not state	983	Juan	16	191
But, come, I'll set your story to a tune	985	Juan	16	300
Sooner 'come place into the civil list	990	Juan	16	641
But should the day come when place ceased to exist	990	Juan	16	645
As wide as if a long speech were to come	995	Juan	16	964
Or how is't matter trembles to come near it	995	Juan	16	976
(I'll take the likeness I can first come at	997	Juan	17	29

COMEDIES
Old comedies still meet with much applause   263 Hints   445
All comedies are ended by a marriage   802 Juan   3   66

COMEDY
The Tuscan father's comedy divine   61 Harold   4   355
Let Comedy assume her throne again   249 Bards   581
Whilst modest Comedy her verse foregoes   258 Hints   121
Farce follow'd Comedy, and reach'd her prime   261 Hints   329
The comedy is not upon the stage   304 Age   429
And Dante in his comedy has given   467 Morgante   63
The days of Comedy are gone, alas   953 Juan   13   749

COMER
Their talk, of course, ran most on the new comer   856 Juan   6   273
To the next comer; or--as it will tell   936 Juan   12   407

COMERS
To the new comers. Frame the whole as if   593 Sardan   5   364
Achilles ordered dinner for new comers   789 Juan   2   984
These rascals, being new comers, knew not whom   807 Juan   3   345
Kept for all comers at all hours to dine   810 Juan   3   552

COMES
The Sabbath comes, a day of blessed rest   15 Harold   1   684
Again he comes; nor dart nor lance avail   16 Harold   1   765
And the big rain comes dancing to the earth   49 Harold   3   874
There comes a token like a scorpion's sting   58 Harold   4   200
Comes down upon the waters; all its hues   59 Harold   4   254
Lo, where it comes like an eternity   65 Harold   4   637
'Why comes not Oscar,' Angus said   102 Alva   102
But Oscar comes not o'er the plain   103 Alva   124
A shudder comes o'er me   151 When We   19
He comes to Athens, and he writes his name   162 Orchomenus   4
None comes to stretch the hospitable hand   184 Julian   20
Then the mortal coldness of the soul like death
  itself comes down   185 Music-B   9
But he comes! the Messiah of royalty comes   202 Avatar   17
He comes in the promise and bloom of threescore   202 Avatar   21
Let me not die till he comes back o'er the billow   205 Hindoo   12
For quickly comes such knowledge, that his heart   214 Dream   92
Next comes the dull disciple of thy school   245 Bards   235
In five facetious acts comes thundering on   250 Bards   603
It is only time past which comes under my
  strictures   282 Blues   2   112
For itself, or what follows--But here comes your
  carriage   283 Blues   2   164
The king who comes has head and all entire   287 Vision   170
She comes!--the Andromache (but not Racine's   308 Age   755
Who thundering comes on blackest steed   312 Giaour   180
'Why comes he not? his steeds are fleet   317 Giaour   697
He comes not, for he cannot break   323 Giaour   1304
Enough that he who comes to woo   326 Abydos   1   205
'Call Pedro here!' He comes, and Conrad bends   346 Corsair   1   561
Or when reflection comes--and come it must   354 Corsair   2   521
With it he comes not, sends not--faithless one   356 Corsair   3   69
He comes at last in sudden loneliness   366 Lara   1   43
And Conrad comes not, came not since that day   366 Corsair   3   688
A morrow comes when they are not for thee   375 Lara   2   12
Why comes he not? Such truths to be divulged   375 Lara   2   27
Why comes not Ezzelin? The hour is past   375 Lara   2   31
And Otho comes, and leaping from his steed   381 Lara   2   438
And looks o'er the surf, but it comes not there   388 Corinth   435
From every crevice comes the shot   394 Corinth   940
We know such vision comes no more   397 Parisina   48
But lo! night comes, the Mooa woos us back   419 Island   2   29
Some weeks before Shrove Tuesday comes about   440 Beppo   3
And so the film comes o'er him--and the dizzy   453 Venice-B   50
The Lady Astarte, his--Hush! who comes here   494 Manfred   3   248
And here it comes.--What news, Vincenzo? 'Tis   500 Faliero   1   25
It comes, for the perusal of his highness   501 Faliero   1   73
This morning comes the noble Barbaro   505 Faliero   1   382
Here comes the Doge--shall I retire? It may   510 Faliero   2   133
Is in our power: he comes alone with me   518 Faliero   2   671
The master-mover.--Hark! he comes--he comes   536 Faliero   4   545
He comes! Shall I await him? yes, and front him   551 Sardan   1   44
That is, it would be happy; but--There comes   558 Sardan   1   479
Comes o'er my heart, a cold sense of the false-
  hood   558 Sardan   1   495
Than what was counted on? When the hour comes   563 Sardan   2   136
And here comes Joy's true herald. King! the sky   570 Sardan   2   537
And that reproof comes heavier on my heart   582 Sardan   4   249
Lo, where he comes! Be still, my heart! they are   596 Foscari   1   65
Made my heart sick. I see the colour comes   597 Foscari   1   130
And still towards death, a thing which comes as
  much   607 Foscari   2   362
To our departure. Who comes here? Retire   611 Foscari   3   248
See you not, he comes here to glut his hate   612 Foscari   3   305
See, the Duke comes! I have obey'd your summons   623 Foscari   5   161
Thy precept comes too late: there is no more   642 Cain   2   413
But bless him ne'er the less. Our brother comes   648 Cain   3   161
They come! he comes!--Azaziel! Haste   657 Heaven   143
But then he comes from a much damper place   675 Werner   1   234
Pursue it on their own account. Here comes   685 Werner   2   144

COMES
The order comes from Frankfort, if these waters   687 Werner   2   283
He comes not only as a son, but saviour   688 Werner   2   344
But here he comes! My noble lord, I'm here   691 Werner   2   536
Here comes the intendant: sound him with the gem   699 Werner   3   264
And here he comes! The devil! you'll hold your
  tongue   705 Werner   4   60
Go to! my lady countess comes. I'd rather   713 Werner   5   10
A cloud comes o'er his blue eyes suddenly   713 Werner   5   53
Our varied host comes   732 Deformed   1   728
Yes, if they keep to their chorus. But here
  comes   732 Deformed   1   741
Is of the self-same purple hue. He comes   737 Deformed   2   182
And when the spring comes with her host   742 Deformed   3   13
'If he comes here to take a deposition   765 Juan   1   1209
A kind of death comes o'er us all alone   838 Juan   5   455
Then comes 'the tug of war';--'twill come again   884 Juan   8   405
For ever and anon comes Indigestion   918 Juan   11   17
Their cash comes from, their wealth goes to a Jew   927 Juan   11   588
'For this effect defective comes by cause   980 Juan   16   10
He comes--but not to grieve   985 Juan   16   344
He was 'free to confess' (whence comes this
  phrase   990 Juan   16   625

COMEST
If thus thou comest in disguise   111 Medea   13
Why comes thou to tell me at this hour   530 Faliero   4   186
It throbb'd for thee, and here thou comest: let
  me   557 Sardan   1   470
Away--we must to our chamber. But whence comest
  thou   683 Werner   1   741

COMET
The Comet rolls its Influence here   141 Critics   32
The comet of a season, and I saw   190 Churchill   2
Or wild colt of a comet, which too soon   285 Vision   13
A pathless comet, and a curse   480 Manfred   1   118
A comet, and destroying as it sweeps   730 Deformed   1   594
Hence, my old comet! give the stars due warning   849 Juan   5   1156

COMETH
It came, it cometh, and will come,--the power   48 Harold   3   795
Methinks he cometh late and tarries long   79 Harold   4   1470
And the night cometh, ne'er to pass from him   365 Corsair   3   657
And the night cometh; I am old in days   456 Dante   1   44
Behold she cometh. Say, where hast thou been   488 Manfred   2   358
He cometh. Mortal! Spirit, who art thou   629 Cain   1   98
Which cometh not. Cain! walk not with this
  spirit   633 Cain   1   358
For the expected ebb which cometh not   660 Heaven   358
When the Redeemer cometh; first in pain   661 Heaven   471
To love us, cometh anguish with disgrace   667 Heaven   932
It cometh! hence, away   668 Heaven   1013
The tempest cometh; heaven and earth unite   668 Heaven   1035
The moment cometh to approve thy strength   669 Heaven   1056
It cometh like the night, and quickly)--Wait   689 Werner   2   441

COMETS
The comets herald through the crackling skies   489 Manfred   2   381
It shall out-dazzle comets. Let us think   562 Sardan   2   68

COMFORT
''Tis comfort still,' I faintly said   166 Struggle   35
Yet comfort still one selfish thought imparts   183 Address-D   23
From calm reflection, comfort or relief   229 Sadness   8
In comfort, at their own aerial ease   294 Vision   588
And this thy comfort, that, when next we meet   344 Corsair   1   462
'Twould be some comfort still, could you survive   428 Island   3   159
Thy dread and sufferance be, there's comfort yet   484 Manfred   2   33
Such things. And yet I find a comfort in   547 Faliero   5   641
And what can I reply to comfort them   581 Sardan   4   212
These men were honest: it is comfort still   593 Sardan   5   410
Lady of Lombardy: it is a comfort   601 Foscari   2   18
That they can comfort me. I would they could   618 Foscari   4   237
I cannot comfort thee. He might have lived   621 Foscari   5   71
A dreary comfort in my desolation   626 Foscari   5   340
Comfort poor Zillah:--she has but one brother   651 Cain   3   335
Comfort! We have struggled long; and they who
  strive   672 Werner   1   69
Further. Take comfort,--we shall find our boy   672 Werner   1   72
While they last, let me comfort or divide them   673 Werner   1   147
My comfort is that, wander where I may   676 Werner   1   343
Too sensitive. Take comfort, and forget   712 Werner   4   545
Suggested some slight comfort in his way   876 Juan   7   595
And that's one comfort for my lost advice   901 Juan   9   287
(If but for comfort) that all things are kind   946 Juan   13   324

COMFORTABLE
Some Christians have a comfortable creed   785 Juan   2   688
A mistress, and such comfortable quarters   832 Juan   5   63
Into a comfortable tete-a-tete   847 Juan   5   974

COMFORTED
For their decease, I pray you, comforted   472 Morgante   387

COMFORTED
Be comforted! You are innocent, and should   712 Werner   4   534

COMFORTER
Adorner of the ruin, comforter   74 Harold   4   1163
My hope, my comforter, my all   135 I Would   42
And each turn comforter to each   403 Chillon   59
But time, the comforter, will come at last   913 Juan   10   377

COMFORTLESS
On the grim smile of comfortless despair   271 Minerva   240
A bed nor comfortless nor new   415 Mazeppa   863
That comfortless we all are to our cost   475 Morgante   646

COMFORTS
Of in-door comforts still she hath a mine   950 Juan   13   613

COMIC
Seen a more comic pantomime since Titus   739 Deformed   2   269

COMING
Where Scorn her finger points through many a
    coming year   8 Harold   1   314
But all unconscious of the coming doom   11 Harold   1   486
Of coming ripeness, the white city's sheen   44 Harold   3   582
Our coming evils with a crutch-like rod   74 Harold   4   1124
The present is hell, and the coming to-morrow   91 Caroline-D   3
The coming morrow from thy youthful mind   94 Dorset   93
our coming. Who will speed through Lochlin   130 Calmar   50
Thou shalt not haunt my coming hour   132 L'Amitie   39
Your coming days and years may bless   138 Clare   92
'Zounds! my liver's coming up   157 Hodgson   62
Behold the coming strife   162 War Song   14
To weep or wish the coming blow   166 Euthanasia   6
Which scarce the shade of coming eve   218 I Saw   11
Ere the coming day is done   219 Saul-B   21
But the Carnival's coming   229 Moore-B   9
The Carnival's coming   229 Moore-B   11
Or--done!--a thousand on the coming trick   251 Bards   675
But fits thy country for her coming fate   271 Minerva   210
And desperate mans him 'gainst the coming doom   272 Minerva   272
And is that any cause for not coming together   278 Blues   1   70
Well, sir, the time's coming. Scamp! don't you
    feel sore   282 Blues   2   108
With carriage) coming of his own accord   296 Vision   704
I hear the sound of coming feet   313 Giaour   352
And there await the coming shock   316 Giaour   583
And doubt that joy, which hails our coming, short   340 Corsair   1   118
To keep in practice for the coming foe   347 Corsair   2   24
And question of his coming fain would seek   348 Corsair   2   63
Irrevocable faults and coming fate   358 Corsair   3   225
Than these were wont; and if the coming night   369 Lara   1   255
But there he was not, and with coming day   376 Lara   2   104
To hate he offer'd, with the coming change   378 Lara   2   206
As if his heart abhorr'd that coming day   381 Lara   2   473
Some streaks announced the coming sun   413 Mazeppa   643
Nor more unkind for coming soon   414 Mazeppa   727
Swam high, as eager of the coming ray   415 Island   1   10
The purpling ocean owns the coming sun   415 Island   1   15
But shy and awkward at first coming out   445 Beppo   306
Woe! woe! the veil of coming centuries   459 Dante   2   35
And when she saw him coming, Aldabelle   468 Morgante   132
Coming on this point to the same conclusion   472 Morgante   402
Or aught that intimates a coming step   500 Faliero   1   12
To wait your coming, and conduct you where   508 Faliero   1   596
The years of coming time, as bearing record   538 Faliero   5   8
I pray you pass to judgment. It is coming   539 Faliero   5   66
Which shames both them and thee to coming ages   555 Sardan   1   290
The hour is coming when he'll need all love   561 Sardan   1   693
To await their coming here, and join them in   622 Foscari   5   117
I watch'd for what I thought his coming; for   631 Cain   1   272
The hues of twilight--the sun's gorgeous coming   643 Cain   2   463
Through all the coming myriads of mankind   652 Cain   3   439
Upon thy coming doom without a feeling   659 Heaven   319
The coming desolation of an orb   659 Heaven   333
Yet a few hours their coming is delay'd   661 Heaven   496
Dread'st thou not to partake their coming doom   665 Heaven   732
Its mother's.--Let the coming chaos chafe   669 Heaven   1083
Which all the coming splendour of the lands   701 Werner   3   441
Be long in coming, he is of that kind   704 Werner   4   36
My coming, though I could but spare them ill   706 Werner   4   113
And yet my coming saves you. I said not   723 Deformed 1   93
The toil of coming here. Why so? One half   733 Deformed 1   801
Our coming, and look brighter when we come   762 Juan   1   980
Nought but the heavy sea, and coming night   779 Juan   2   328
Leaves nothing till 'the coming of the just   829 Juan   4   806
To hint that he is coming up this way   849 Juan   5   1152
Sound, and then by a cry, 'The Sultan's coming   849 Juan   5   1160
'Your coming has been unexpected here   858 Juan   6   365
But coming young from lands and scenes romantic   938 Juan   12   537
Until preferment, coming at a sure rate   991 Juan   16   700

COMITATUS
With him retired his 'posse comitatus   767 Juan   1   1305

COMMAND
'Gainst those who most transgress his high command   6 Harold   1   213
The hoarse command, the busy humming din   22 Harold   2   156
To greet Albania's chief, whose dread command   26 Harold   2   418
An empire thou couldst crush, command, rebuild   41 Harold   3   338
Which was the mightiest in its old command   59 Harold   4   221
Bade thee obey, and gave me to command   93 Dorset   6
The chance of an hour may command us to part   99 Adieu   7
Iulus greets them; at his kind command   106 Nisus   97
Who hail'd me chief, obedient to command   123 Recoll   100
By thy command I rise or fall   133 Prayer   51
But woman is made to command and deceive us   147 To Anne-A   3
And when he saw this high command   178 Devil's Dr   187
Too late thou leav'st the high command   181 Ode-A   75
No foe could tame--no tyrant could command   182 Address-C   6
He heard the king's command   220 Belshaz-B   35
At whose command 'grim women' throng in crowds   245 Bards   275
Command your audience or to smile or weep   258 Hints   141
Provincial maidens, men of high command   266 Hints   715
Not such as first, by her divine command   269 Minerva   77
Hath Wisdom's goddess never held command   270 Minerva   132
Vain is each voice where tones could once command   272 Minerva   275
Two Jews, a chosen people, can command   307 Age   686
A mightier monument command   311 Giaour   132
Without thy free consent, command   327 Abydos   1   315
But were it not that high command   330 Abydos   2   147
Nor last nor least in high command   331 Abydos   2   230
Obedience to their chief's command   332 Abydos   2   368
Wait--wave--behold--destroy--at thy command   333 Abydos   2   411
With these he mingles not but to command   339 Corsair   1   63
All these he wielded to command assent   346 Corsair   1   545
I do command thee--sit--dost hear?--obey   348 Corsair   2   100
His capture could but wait thy first command   358 Corsair   3   168
Command nor duty could their transport check   363 Corsair   3   497
And feels he yet can conquer and command   363 Corsair   3   505
Born of high lineage, link'd in high command   367 Lara   1   97
In such from him he rarely heard command   373 Lara   1   519
Left beneath his high command   394 Corinth   907
Can she command or these obey   398 Parisina   161
Were near at my command or call   415 Mazeppa   836
Dragg'd o'er the deck, no more at thy command   416 Island   1   57
By her command removed, to strengthen more   430 Island   4   35
His car (but temper'd by his sire's command   466 Morgante   22
Then will I every thing at your command do   471 Morgante   375
Must pause for my command   479 Manfred   1   67
Whose presence I command, and be the slave   487 Manfred   2   253
Themselves to chaos at his high command   488 Manfred   2   374
It rests with thee alone--command her voice   490 Manfred   2   482
This eve already. Herman! I command thee   494 Manfred   3   255
The late Doge; keeping still my old command   505 Faliero   1   396
Now in the Arsenal, who holds command   511 Faliero   2   137
I thought the Duke had held command in Venice   511 Faliero   2   159
Could I require, or you command? 'Tis well   513 Faliero   2   284
Command our swords, and rule us with a word   517 Faliero   2   631
Your own command as leader? Even so   518 Faliero   2   693
Command you no refreshment? Nought, save sleep   528 Faliero   4   21
They have command from you through me in person   534 Faliero   4   419
I can at least command myself, who listen   552 Sardan   1   106
And therefore need a soldier to command them   563 Sardan   2   93
Command me in all service save the Bacchant's   569 Sardan   2   482
The post but with their lives--command it, Zames   573 Sardan   3   124
The king's command was not to quit thee. Me   576 Sardan   3   286
You fell and fainted: 'twas his strict command   588 Sardan   5   96
Named next to the command? I did not hear   589 Sardan   5   112
'Tis my command, my last command. Wilt thou   591 Sardan   5   271
Command us. I command!--Alas! my life   598 Foscari   1   200
Command my time, when not commanded by   602 Foscari   2   48
Prince! I have done your bidding. What command   620 Foscari   5   5
Who, who, our tears, our shrieks, shall then
    command   668 Heaven   968
You are the latest stranger, and command   693 Werner   2   673
Count Siegendorf, command you aught? I am bound   708 Werner   4   281
Dare you command me? Let the man go on   716 Werner   5   206
Stop! I command--entreat--implore! Oh, Ulric   721 Werner   5   523
Such my command   725 Deformed 1   172
Who can command all forms will choose the highest   727 Deformed 1   364
The Bourbon's spirit shall command them still   736 Deformed 2   134
You are a Conqueror--command your Slave   744 Deformed 3   159
Even then their love they could not all command   767 Juan   1   1355
His temper not being under great command   769 Juan   1   1476
There was a something which bespoke command   789 Juan   2   927
Now in a person used to much command   807 Juan   3   369
Though doubtless he who can command himself   807 Juan   3   375
Fretted with gold or silver:--by command   810 Juan   3   549
For sorrow o'er each sense held stern command   828 Juan   4   754
And others rose to the command of crews   831 Juan   4   924
Of half voluptuousness and half command   845 Juan   5   864
She deem'd her least command must yield delight   847 Juan   5   1019
Battles to the command, Field-Marshal Souvaroff   872 Juan   7   312
The general who held him in command   885 Juan   8   452
That great enchanter, at whose rod's command   902 Juan   9   347
Who took by turns that difficult command   902 Juan   9   365
Howe'er our friend Don Juan might command   933 Juan   12   229

COMMAND
'Tis not in mortals to command success 943 Juan 13 137

COMMANDANT
Arrives from Frankfort, from the commandant 680 Werner 1 593
Here is a packet for the commandant 681 Werner 1 613
So, so, it thickens! Ay, 'the commandant 681 Werner 1 616
I found the military commandant 835 Juan 5 263
Perceiving then no more the commandant 882 Juan 8 241

COMMANDED
Whose nod commanded and whose voice was law 124 Recoll 168
Till lone Tyranny commanded 187 Ode-B 31
Surrounded and commanded, though not nigh 434 Island 4 317
Thou'lt know anon--Come! Come! I have commanded 496 Manfred 3 344
I have sent frequently, as you commanded 499 Faliero 1 2
I have fought and bled; commanded, ay, and
  conquer'd 506 Faliero 1 459
Of men who have commanded: too much pride 510 Faliero 2 104
Which will not be commanded. Let me hope it 528 Faliero 4 22
Command my time, when not commanded by 602 Foscari 2 48
I am commanded to inform you that 608 Foscari 3 32
The Imperial? I commanded--no--I mean 676 Werner 1 330
How you should be commanded, and who led you 740 Deformed 2 327
Perceiving nor commander nor commanded 882 Juan 8 249

COMMANDER
To act in trust as your commander, till 518 Faliero 2 697
It is an actual fact, that he, commander 873 Juan 7 409
Perceiving nor commander nor commanded 882 Juan 8 249

COMMANDETH
And mine commandeth me to set his seal 653 Cain 3 494

COMMANDING
(See also EARTH-COMMANDING)
Still sways their souls with that commanding art 340 Corsair 1 177
Commanding, aiding, animating all 380 Lara 2 368
In forked flashes a commanding tempest 570 Sardan 2 540
To gaze once more on the commanding clay 836 Juan 5 291

COMMANDMENT
Then, when he most required commandment, then 366 Lara 1 19
Break no commandment, for high heaven is there 463 Dante 4 32
And break the--Which commandment is't they break 758 Juan 1 780
I wish she had: his book's the eleventh com-
  mandment 972 Juan 15 298

COMMANDMENTS
I'll write poetical commandments, which 771 Juan 1 1626

COMMANDS
Gallant Kidd, commands the crew 157 Hodgson 34
Commands a verse, and will not be denied 199 Sonnet-D 3
In act alone obeys, his air commands 374 Lara 1 561
In all commands,' was the reply, 'straightways 473 Morgante 485
And we are vigilant.--Thy late commands 489 Manfred 2 397
For justice, or as sovereign who commands it 503 Faliero 1 246
Satraps! The king commands your presence at 563 Sardan 2 105
How vain to war with what thy God commands 669 Heaven 1058
Loiter you here? For your commands, my lord 705 Werner 4 90
The king commands us, and the doctor quacks us 774 Juan 2 29
For through the South the custom still commands 844 Juan 5 839
Commands the city, and upon its site 868 Juan 7 76
Commands--the intellectual lord of all 931 Juan 12 72

COMMEMORATE
Placed to commemorate a more than mortal lot 70 Harold 4 900

COMMEMORATION
In chronological commemoration 813 Juan 3 804
Yet there were several worth commemoration 869 Juan 7 123
And therefore worthy of commemoration 894 Juan 8 1020

COMMENCE
Then go, once more the joyous work commence 225 J.C.H. 51
On which they might repose, or even commence 779 Juan 2 317
Commence with feelings warm, and prospects high 834 Juan 5 165
And young beginners may as well commence 946 Juan 13 313
Thirdly, commence not with the end--or, sinning 950 Juan 13 583
Commenced (from such slight things will great
  commence 978 Juan 15 661

COMMENCED
And Misery's triumph commenced over Mirth 156 Goblet 26
Commenced to-morrow; but, till 'tis begun 518 Faliero 2 655
Than urge them when they have commenced, but till 534 Faliero 4 412
And now commenced a strict investigation 861 Juan 6 585
Off Ismail, and commenced a cannonade 870 Juan 7 229
Commenced (from such slight things will great
  commence 978 Juan 15 661
And promises to all--which last commenced 990 Juan 16 612

COMMENCEMENT
From life's commencement to its slow decline 212 Augusta-C 126
And the commencement of atonement is 492 Manfred 3 84

COMMEND
To one so young my strain I would commend 3 To Ianthe 35
Candour compels me, Becher! to commend 118 Answer-A 1
Though all the social tie commend 141 Pignus 10
Though the world for this commend thee 207 Fare Thee 13
No doubt you do right to commend it 232 Murray-B 9
Done in the field, commend me to my peasants 533 Faliero 4 382
Faliero! hast thou aught further to commend 548 Faliero 5 705
I would commend my nephew to their mercy 548 Faliero 5 707
Whate'er it be. Commend me to Beleses 592 Sardan 5 350
Content! I will fix here. I must commend 726 Deformed 1 265

COMMENDING
Commending every time, save times like these 260 Hints 260

COMMENDS
Thy name ennobles him who thus commends 125 Recoll 244

COMMENT
A comment on the Gospel's 'Sin no more 939 Juan 12 626

COMMENTARIES
Oh, Caesar's Commentaries! now impart, ye 877 Juan 7 653

COMMENTATOR'S
Deem this a commentator's fantasy 803 Juan 3 84

COMMENTS
Of loose mechanics, with all coarse foul comments 502 Faliero 1 190
Have fill'd their papers with their comments
  various 939 Juan 12 620

COMMERCE
Was modern Luxury of Commerce born 62 Harold 4 431
Shewing how Commerce on Liberty thrives 225 Ode-D 16
If Commerce fills the purse, she clogs the brain 247 Bards 395
Though as a monarch nods, and commerce calls 258 Hints 93
With commerce, given alone to arms and arts 263 Hints 512
That you have written in your books of commerce 596 Foscari 1 49
Or, if that seem too humble, tried by commerce 673 Werner 1 140

COMMERCE-FETCHING
And living amidst commerce-fetching burghers 694 Werner 2 727

COMMERCIAL
Seem'd to him half commercial, half pedantic 938 Juan 12 541

COMMINGLING
Commingling slowly with heroic earth 33 Harold 2 806
Through wine and blood, commingling as they flow 109 Nisus 273
True, the commingling fire will mix our ashes 594 Sardan 5 471

COMMISERATION
He surely, in commiseration 101 Lady-B 25
Gulbeyaz show'd them both commiseration 867 Juan 6 947
Except cold weather and commiseration 894 Juan 8 1030

COMMISSION
In your commission? What, my lord? This prattle 602 Foscari 2 32
Away he went then upon his commission 866 Juan 6 929
Juan, whose was a delicate commission 922 Juan 11 249
As Eldon on a lunatic commission 979 Juan 15 732

COMMIT
Though I be wrought on to commit them. When 519 Faliero 3 59
Wouldst thou have God commit a sin for thee 668 Heaven 957
One's heart commit these follies; and besides 678 Werner 1 414
In gangs of fifty, thieves commit their crimes 760 Juan 1 861
He had no business to commit a sin 767 Juan 1 1330
Commit--flirtation with the muse of Moore 772 Juan 1 1640

COMMITS
His chief, commits him to his fragile ark 418 Island 1 166

COMMITTED
For crimes committed, and the victor's threat 351 Corsair 2 296
Appears to have been committed. There's another 683 Werner 2 27

COMMITTEE
Sir, the green-room's in rapture, and so's the
  committee 282 Blues 2 78

COMMITTING
His crime? Perhaps without committing any 595 Foscari 1 14

COMMIX'D
O'er mingling man, and horse commix'd with horse 121 Newstead-A 83

COMMODIOUS
Commodious but immoral, they are found 922 Juan 11 238

COMMODITIES

For both commodities dwell by the Thames	924 Juan	11	379

COMMON

He felt, or deem'd he felt, no common glow	25 Harold	2	364
Amidst no common pomp the despot sate	28 Harold	2	500
All felt the common joy they now must feign	32 Harold	2	753
Little in common;--untaught to submit	37 Harold	3	102
Their bones, distinguish'd from our common clay	63 Harold	4	500
Who found a more than common votary there	72 Harold	4	1033
That gallant spirits scorn the common rules	93 Dorset		24
Then share with titled crowds the common lot	94 Dorset		47
But lo! no common orator can hope	112 Examination		27
Beneath one common stroke of fate expire	124 Recoll		158
Is there no cause beyond the common claim	125 Recoll		211
Montgomery! true, the common lot	127 Answer-B		1
Must share the common tomb of all	128 Answer-B		14
Then do not say the common lot	128 Answer-B		41
Which tells the common tale	131 L'Amitie		24
And of no common pang complain	148 To Author		14
Such is the common lot of man	153 Friend-A		41
Like common earth can rot	167 Dead		16
And not as common Mortals love	201 Ode-C		30
To common sense his thoughts could raise	226 Thurlow-A		5
Then let us soar to-day; no common theme	242 Bards		23
Illustrious conqueror of common sense	245 Bards		220
And common-place and common sense confounds	249 Bards		569
One common Lethe waits each hapless bard	252 Bards		749
No common is enclosed without an ode	252 Bards		786
And sure no common muse inspired thy pen	253 Bards		879
Or Common Sense assert her rights again	254 Bards		930
When common prose will serve for common things	258 Hints		134
(At least in theatres) with common sense	258 Hints		158
Whence spring their scenes, from common life or court	259 Hints		162
Or follow common fame, or forge a plot	259 Hints		169
In these plain common sense will travel far	264 Hints		583
Sir, your taste is too common; but time and posterity	282 Blues	2	99
And palace fuel to one common fire	300 Age		174
One common cause makes myriads of one breast	302 Age		272
Toss'd by the deluge in their common ark	307 Age		647
A common coin as ever mint could strike	307 Age		707
While all the Common Council cry 'Claymore	308 Age		772
The common crowd but see the gloom	318 Giaour		866
No giant frame sets forth his common height	341 Corsair	1	198
This common courage which with brutes we share	343 Corsair	1	327
Ambition, glory, love, the common aim	367 Lara	1	79
The common pleasure or the general care	367 Lara	1	102
Nor common gazers could discern the growth	370 Lara	1	286
Too high for common selfishness, he could	371 Lara	1	337
They were not common links, that form'd the chain	382 Lara	2	536
And slung them with a more than common care	383 Lara	2	575
But not a coward or a common spoil	428 Island	3	156
'Tis a long cover'd boat that's common here	442 Beppo		147
But 'Cavalier Serventes' are quite common	444 Beppo		285
Yet she but shares with them a common woe	454 Venice-B		121
A common sight to every common eye	458 Dante	1	162
The limits of man's common malice, for	465 Dante	4	143
Of common mortal trod, we nightly tread	487 Manfred	2	301
Is of no common order, as his port	489 Manfred	2	422
With common ruffians leagued to ruin states	508 Faliero	1	611
In common! and sweet bonds which link old friend-ships	525 Faliero	3	449
Do more? Alas! my lord, with common men	559 Sardan	1	578
From all the taints of common earth--while I	570 Sardan	2	521
The rest of common, heavy, human hours	587 Sardan	5	31
The only thing common to all mankind	591 Sardan	5	231
My doom is common, many are in dungeons	609 Foscari	3	98
I have been so beyond the common lot	617 Foscari	4	166
His equal? No;--I have nought in common with him	632 Cain	1	302
What ye in common have with what they had	640 Cain	2	299
Who can have nought in common with him. Sir	680 Werner	1	557
What can there be in common with the proud	681 Werner	1	649
More noble name belongs to common thieves	689 Werner	2	426
I named a villain. What is there in common	689 Werner	2	432
Of yours are common to me, it affects me	707 Werner	4	202
Such as rounds common life into a dream	710 Werner	4	373
Than common stabber! What deed of my life	719 Werner	5	424
Around their manes, as common insects swarm	729 Deformed	1	516
Round common steeds towards sunset. Mount, my lord	729 Deformed	1	517
Last,--yours has lately been a common case	745 Juan	Ded	4
To be the most remote from common use	752 Juan	1	316
Possess'd an air and grace by no means common	754 Juan	1	487
Is much more common where the climate's sultry	754 Juan	1	504
That is to say, a thought beyond the common	756 Juan	1	613
Never could she survive that common loss	757 Juan	1	668
This may seem strange, but yet 'tis very common	758 Juan	1	777
The common privileges of my sex	765 Juan	1	1170
Yet deem'd herself in common pity bound	790 Juan	2	1030
Were link'd alike, as for the common people he	803 Juan	3	127
It is a hard although a common case	808 Juan	3	465
Quite common in those countries, are a kind	809 Juan	3	514

COMMON

Intrigues, adventures of the common school	818 Juan	4	133
To match a common fury with her rage	848 Juan	5	1082
And decorates the book of Common Prayer	855 Juan	6	183
Extremely common in this age, whose metal	859 Juan	6	439
When things beyond the common have occurr'd	865 Juan	6	846
Which with your conquerors is a common prank	868 Juan	7	70
Common in many cases, was in this	870 Juan	7	195
Many of common readers give a guess	871 Juan	7	259
For deeming human clay but common dirt	874 Juan	7	461
All common fellows, who might writhe and wince	879 Juan	8	84
No common language; and besides, in time	885 Juan	8	458
Increases, till you shall make common cause	900 Juan	9	222
Behaved no better than a common sempstress	906 Juan	9	616
But at least I have shunn'd the common shore	907 Juan	10	27
While common men grow ignorantly old	909 Juan	10	109
Only the common run, who must pursue	927 Juan	11	570
The unusual quickness of these common changes	928 Juan	11	640
Which 'tis the common cry and lie to vaunt as	929 Juan	11	683
Of common likings, which make some deplore	943 Juan	13	134
To build up common things with common places	956 Juan	14	56
And that their books have but one style in common	957 Juan	14	151
Extremely disagreeable, but common	960 Juan	14	343
She merely felt a common sympathy	967 Juan	14	725
She deem'd his merits something more than common	973 Juan	15	318
Confounded him in common with the crowd	978 Juan	15	658
As common soldiers, or a common--shore	990 Juan	16	651
The poor priest was reduced to common sense	991 Juan	16	710
As far as words make rules--our common notion	997 Juan	17	18

COMMONERS

For commoners had ever them mistook	951 Juan	13	677

COMMONEST

Were he God--as he is but the commonest clay	202 Avatar		30
Adding, that this was commonest and best	844 Juan	5	838
By commonest ambition, that when passion	853 Juan	6	26
From out the commonest demands of nature	976 Juan	15	552

COMMON-PLACE

From common-place Gally	236 Nonsense		10
And common-place and common sense confounds	249 Bards		569
For that were vulgar, cold, and common-place	890 Juan	8	770
Set down his sayings in her common-place book	925 Juan	11	416
(Now for a common-place!) beneath the snow	945 Juan	13	282
Who, in his common-place book, had a page	953 Juan	13	773
A kind of common-place, even in their crimes	957 Juan	14	124
Another gentle common-place or two	964 Juan	14	546
The present, with their common-place costume	971 Juan	15	208
There is a common-place book argument	997 Juan	17	33

COMMONS

And he turn'd to 'the room' of the Commons	177 Devil's Dr		134
Search Doctors' Commons six months from my date	276 Waltz		207
With all his Lords and Commons: in the sky	293 Vision		558
Our British Commons sometimes deign to 'hear	304 Age		490
In vain the Commons pass their patriot bill	306 Age		597
He was a kind man to the commons ever	549 Faliero	5	822
Save death or Doctors' Commons--so he died	751 Juan	1	288
And founded Doctors' Commons--I have conn'd	903 Juan	9	422
The House of Commons turn'd to a tax-trap	929 Juan	11	659
Of Doctors' Commons: but she dreaded first	963 Juan	14	493
Have tied together commons, lords, and kings	990 Juan	16	640

COMMONWEALTH

The commonwealth of kings, the men of Rome	59 Harold	4	226
The name of Commonwealth is past and gone	454 Venice-B		125
Who govern this precarious commonwealth	511 Faliero	2	183
In this--I cannot call it commonwealth	523 Faliero	3	276
Condensing in a fair free commonwealth	523 Faliero	3	290
Resolve to cleanse this commonwealth with fire	534 Faliero	4	424
Cabal in commonwealth, nor secret means	605 Foscari	2	232

COMMONWEALTHS

Of commonwealths, and sovereign of himself	503 Faliero	1	269
Which purify corrupted commonwealths	517 Faliero	2	599

COMMOTION

In life commotion is the extremest point	730 Deformed	1	592
The Oda, in a general commotion	861 Juan	6	562
She put all coronets into commotion	962 Juan	14	434

COMMUNE

At times to commune with them--if that he	485 Manfred	2	124
No. Why then commune with him? he may be	648 Cain	3	168
Has deign'd to commune with me, and reveal	665 Heaven		749

COMMUNEST

Thou communest. I know that with mankind	491 Manfred	3	39

COMMUNICATES

Communicates between us, though unseen	557 Sardan	1	472
I'll to the secret passage, which communicates	681 Werner	1	634

275

COMMUNICATION

The path still open, and communication 573 Sardan 3 112
By which there's no communication with 683 Werner 2 21

COMMUNION

(See also SELF-COMMUNION)
Or holding dark communion with the cloud 42 Harold 3 418
Shall arise in communion 188 Ode-B 93
Thus with himself communion held he, till 343 Corsair 1 341
From all communion he would start away 368 Lara 1 134
So much a long communion tends 406 Chillon 390
From all communion with existence, save 439 Tasso 176
That make communion sweet, and soften pain 458 Dante 1 165
I held but slight communion; but instead 485 Manfred 2 155
In high communion with a spirit, far 648 Cain 3 165
Thou hast said it. Woe, woe, woe to such
   communion 665 Heaven 740
Masters of their own time--or in communion 954 Juan 13 819

COMMUNITY

And flings them, our community to bury 469 Morgante 203
The prayers of our community. Our convent 711 Werner 4 453

COMPACT

(According to compact) the wit in the dungeon 226 Oh You 8
A compact without more delay 232 Murray-B 51
Or break the compact which herself had made 271 Minerva 216
Was purchased by no compact with thy crew 496 Manfred 3 374
A league is still a compact, and more binding 532 Faliero 4 300
Leagues of this nature, and to keep compact 536 Faliero 4 540
In which it is mislodged. But name your compact 724 Deformed 1 146
But it will serve to keep my verse compact 768 Juan 1 1420

COMPACTLY

Carved at the prow, built lightly, but compactly 442 Beppo 148
Which ne'er had suited others so compactly 476 Morgante 672

COMPANIE

Save concubines and carnal companie 4 Harold 1 17

COMPANIES

And bid our friends prepare their companies 516 Faliero 2 549
And are the sixteen companies completed 516 Faliero 2 570
To use like caution in their companies 518 Faliero 2 652
Our companies are ready, sixty each 524 Faliero 3 361
The Sixteen and their companies will move 535 Faliero 4 465

COMPANION

Some old companion of my early race 124 Recoll 194
Companion of thy splendour in the skies 140 Ossian-B 10
The chief companion of a calmer lot 211 Augusta-C 48
Ward's creeping Companion and Louse 232 Murray-B 60
Than thee, companion of her bower 328 Abydos 1 423
And their companions, glorious by her side 432 Island 4 213
One only, to be my companion, who 466 Morgante 7
The sole companion of his wanderings 494 Manfred 3 244
An instant--yet an instant your companion 515 Faliero 2 498
Is the dim and remote companion, in 644 Cain 2 567
Must thou be my companion? Wherefore not 729 Deformed 1 485
And free companion of the gallant Bourbon 730 Deformed 1 573
At length one whisper'd his companion, who 783 Juan 2 577
Juan's companion was a Romagnole 828 Juan 4 745
Whisper'd to his companion:--'twas the same 836 Juan 5 339
In the fair form of their companion new 857 Juan 6 293
Companion something newer still, as 'twere 857 Juan 6 306

COMPANIONS

Though gay companions o'er the bowl 135 I Would 29
Though gay companions o'er the bowl 166 Struggle 21
Then cast his eyes on his companions--then 428 Island 3 113
And your companions; there's enough to load ye 591 Sardan 5 256
Of me and my companions. Very true 676 Werner 1 320
The fare of my companions and myself 676 Werner 1 325
One of those strange companions whom I fain 709 Werner 4 291

COMPANION'S

Which might be turn'd to my companion's use 476 Morgante 662

COMPANIONSHIP

Were unto him companionship; they spake 37 Harold 3 114
For such companionship, I would not now 630 Cain 1 190
With all companionship of hate and toil 661 Heaven 457

COMPANY

(See also CO.)
Must keep him company; and we might show 289 Vision 261
We were a gallant company 384 Corinth 3
The company is 'mix'd' (the phrase I quote is 447 Beppo 463
For a 'mix'd company' implies that, save 447 Beppo 465
The number wanting in your company 520 Faliero 3 126
Nor held a revel in their company 527 Faliero 3 583
Anselmo, with thy company proceed 536 Faliero 4 583
A woman, the best chamber company 589 Sardan 5 119
That there were two. There were, in company 678 Werner 1 476

COMPANY

In the meantime I crave your company 679 Werner 1 521
That I keep better company. You shall 691 Werner 2 523
Your company. We found you in the Oder 692 Werner 2 577
Wolves prowl in company. He hath the key 720 Werner 5 486
Was like one. Unless you keep company 723 Deformed 1 95
Your betters keep worse company. My betters 729 Deformed 1 486
Comrade. They are but bad company, your highness 734 Deformed 1 812
From better company, have kept your own 745 Juan Ded 34
Drest to receive so much good company 766 Juan 1 1248
To find so much good company invited 806 Juan 3 296
But in good company--the gout or stone 808 Juan 3 472
In company a very pleasant fellow 811 Juan 3 650
To those who like their company, about 861 Juan 6 559
Before a company of Calmucks, drilling 874 Juan 7 458
Suwarrow, when he saw this company 874 Juan 7 465
In such good company as always throng 881 Juan 8 190
Of the good company, can win a corner 926 Juan 11 538
Unless good company be kept too long 965 Juan 14 614
Show off--to please their company or mother 986 Juan 16 400
The company prepared to separate 987 Juan 16 482
With the substantial company engross'd 992 Juan 16 764
The company whose birth, wealth, worth, has cost 998 Juan 17 100

COMPANY'S

Good company's a chess-board--there are kings 952 Juan 13 705

COMPARATIVE

Had suffer'd more--his hardships were comparative 791 Juan 2 1095
Scott, the superlative of my comparative 975 Juan 15 468

COMPARE

Uprear'd of human hands. Come, and compare 49 Harold 3 856
'If mighty things with small we may compare 170 Address-B 17
That art and nature may compare their styles 270 Minerva 180
With Waltz or after Waltz be borne 275 Waltz 130
Compare my day and yesterday 408 Mazeppa 194
And to compare them with my Myrrha's eyes 566 Sardan 2 254
With its strange whirls and eddies can compare 852 Juan 6 14
Who with the brightest Georgians might compare 857 Juan 6 284
Few specimens yet left us can compare 948 Juan 13 437

COMPARED

All objects, if compared with these? and stem 47 Harold 3 711
Compared with other recreations 95 Granta 51
Embitters the present, compared with the past 96 Harrow-A 2
Compared with his, the Corsair's roving crew 350 Corsair 2 232
Confess its barbarism when compared with thine 459 Dante 2 32
'Twas purity compared with your protection 541 Faliero 5 239
Which, as compared with what you have undergone 611 Foscari 3 205
In all its innocence compared to what 642 Cain 2 427
Compared with our great crimes:--Sole Lord of
   light 649 Cain 3 231
They seem so niggardly, compared with what 685 Werner 2 153
Compared with what Haidee did with his treasure 806 Juan 3 310
Compared with those of our pure pearls of price 939 Juan 12 575
But rarely seen, like gold compared with paper 983 Juan 16 175
Are Tutors, Guardians, and so forth, compared 997 Juan 17 26

COMPARISON

A code of mercy by comparison 607 Foscari 2 394
Of any modern female saint's comparison 749 Juan 1 130
I speak of Christian lands in this comparison 796 Juan 2 1399
Like gold as in comparison to dross 921 Juan 11 203
Or like the old comparison of snows 934 Juan 12 323
Having wound up with this sublime comparison 975 Juan 15 465

COMPARISONS

Draws sly comparisons of these with those 271 Minerva 191
My poor comparisons must needs be teeming 288 Vision 221
I borrow my comparisons from clay 291 Vision 429
Thou smilest;--these comparisons seem high 421 Island 2 196

COMPASS

Can despots compass aught that hails their sway 11 Harold 1 456
And, far as mortal eye can compass sight 12 Harold 1 533
Our souls to compass through each arduous way 68 Harold 4 772
For ere they compass their escape 141 Critics 45
Short compass what--but, to resume 231 Doctor 51
The feeling compass--Navigation's soul 417 Island 1 96
Ye, who do compass earth about, and dwell 479 Manfred 1 31
And spirits that do compass air and earth 486 Manfred 2 182
Beyond the compass of the human voice 548 Faliero 5 721
Have nought to give but tears! But could I
   compass 622 Foscari 5 101
I cannot compass: 'tis denounced against us 631 Cain 1 283
No doubt, in little compass, round or square 767 Juan 1 1324
A voice of no great compass, and not sweet 827 Juan 4 708
Could risk or compass such strange phantasies 846 Juan 5 915

COMPASS'D

For Spain is compass'd by unyielding foes 9 Harold 1 358
For blight and desolation, compass'd round 216 Dream 188
Cut off from hope, and compass'd in the toil 379 Lara 2 330

COMPASS'D
Ne'er compass'd, nor less mortal chisel wrought 789 Juan 2 952

COMPASSION
Compassion will melt where this virtue is felt 115 The Tear 11
Compassion for him--his tame virtues; drones 290 Vision 373
For in that pause compassion snatch'd from war 350 Corsair 2 227
How deep the root from whence compassion grew 358 Corsair 3 201
For them, at least, his soul compassion knew 377 Lara 2 183
And woo Compassion to a blighted name 439 Tasso 217
By your compassion: now in peace proceed 476 Morgante 653
Might move compassion, like a beggar's rags 506 Faliero 1 442
This false compassion is a folly, and 524 Faliero 3 401
I crave, not pardon, but compassion from you 543 Faliero 5 406
By those who feel a proud compassion for thee 546 Faliero 5 567
Lest I forget in this compassion for 601 Foscari 1 369
Of feeling or compassion on his part 611 Foscari 3 227
An evangelical compassion--with 712 Werner 4 495
And their compassion grew to such a size 790 Juan 2 1046
A kind of blunt compassion for the sad 832 Juan 5 93
'She also had compassion and a bed 858 Juan 6 376
Compassion breathes along the savage mind 891 Juan 8 848

COMPASSIONATE
My keepers grew compassionate 405 Chillon 301
By the compassionate trance, poor nature's last 600 Foscari 1 285

COMPATIBLE
As far as is compatible with clay 489 Manfred 2 426
Compatible with justice, to the senate 548 Faliero 5 706
That they are not compatible, the doom 634 Cain 1 424

COMPEER
Yet it will be so; he and his compeer 462 Dante 3 149

COMPEERS
Till by the voice of him and his compeers 48 Harold 3 768
Exalted o'er thy less abhorr'd compeers 209 Sketch 103
And be absolved by his upright compeers 515 Faliero 2 436
And tall beyond her sex, and their compeers 822 Juan 4 341
Departed like the rest of their compeers 947 Juan 13 394

COMPEL
(See also CLOUD-COMPELLING, KEEL-COMPELLING)
Our boys (save those whom public schools compel 264 Hints 513
In vigilance of grief that would compel 370 Lara 1 311
All circumstance which may compel 397 Parisina 128
I do compel ye to my will. Appear 479 Manfred 1 49
I call upon thee! and compel 481 Manfred 1 250
The Arcadian Evocators to compel 487 Manfred 2 282
Nor my own feelings--both compel me back 527 Faliero 3 639
Why would the general vote compel me hither 622 Foscari 5 127

COMPELL'D
Ere yet unlucky Fame, compell'd to creep 274 Waltz 61
You compell'd me, by speaking the truth--To speak ill 278 Blues 1 53
Deep were my anguish, thus compell'd 328 Abydos 1 435
By circumstance compell'd to plunge again 378 Lara 2 232
All beauty upon earth, compell'd to praise 464 Dante 4 82
Some sucking hero is compell'd to rear 877 Juan 7 660
Unless compell'd by fate, or wave, or wind 885 Juan 8 425
Poor thing of usages! coerced, compell'd 958 Juan 14 181
'Twixt place and patriotism--albeit compell'd 990 Juan 16 620

COMPELS
The earth to her embrace compels the powers of air 52 Harold 3 1021
Candour compels me, Becher! to commend 118 Answer-A 1
Yet candour's self compels me now to own 126 Recoll 339

COMPENSATE
To compensate for many a dull hour, wasted 511 Faliero 2 170
And think if tempting man can compensate 666 Heaven 837
As still are free to both, to compensate 727 Deformed 1 319

COMPENSATION
Which could bring compensation for past sorrow 672 Werner 1 74
All compensation, gentle stranger, save 685 Werner 2 149

COMPETE
Without doors, too, she may compete in mellow 950 Juan 13 615

COMPETED
With that youthful chief competed 187 Ode-B 29

COMPETENT
Were proved by competent false witnesses 766 Juan 1 1280

COMPETITION
And then there was a general competition 933 Juan 12 234

COMPETITORS
My gay competitors, noble as I 597 Foscari 1 98

COMPLACENCY
To show with what complacency he creeps 814 Juan 3 875

COMPLACENT
(See also SELF-COMPLACENT)
And gaze complacent on congenial earth 34 Harold 2 867

COMPLAIN
Yet did not much complain 6 Harold 1 151
As moon-struck bards complain, by Love's sad archery 15 Harold 1 728
Pride might forbid e'en Friendship to complain 19 Harold 1 930
Why, Pigot, complain of this damsel's disdain 115 Pigot 1
I will not complain, and though chill'd is affection 137 Delawarr 21
And of no common pang complain 148 To Author 14
My soul nor deigns nor dares complain 151 Farewell-B 13
Will this unteach us to complain 218 Bloom 13
Lips taught to writhe, but not complain 321 Giaour 1106
So that no sort of female could complain 444 Beppo 266
Know then, oh emperor! that all complain 467 Morgante 110
I can't complain, whose ancestors are there 912 Juan 10 281
She had nothing to complain of, or reprove 966 Juan 14 685
Yet mix'd so slightly, that you can't complain 981 Juan 16 22

COMPLAINANT
But the complainant, both in one united 500 Faliero 1 51

COMPLAIN'D
No dearth of bards can be complain'd of now 243 Bards 124
I have not complain'd, sir. My good lord, forgive me 602 Foscari 2 26
Also the muffin whereof he complain'd 984 Juan 16 266

COMPLAINING
He always is complaining of his lot 827 Juan 4 709
And though her dignity brook'd no complaining 913 Juan 10 374

COMPLAININGLY
Bay'd from afar complainingly 396 Corinth 1070

COMPLAINS
Complains of warmth, and, this complaint avow'd 448 Beppo 517
The countess in her chamber.--She complains 708 Werner 4 266

COMPLAINT
There, raving, he howls his complaint to the wind 99 L Adieu 23
The lover's anguish or the friend's complaint 258 Hints 110
Vain his complaint,--my lord presents his bill 299 Age 75
Complains of warmth, and, this complaint avow'd 448 Beppo 517
But loud complaint, however angrily 507 Faliero 1 553
How sped you, Israel, in your late complaint 516 Faliero 2 514
Complaint, and Salemenes' sister seeks not 554 Sardan 1 266
Of merit, and complaint of present days 746 Juan Ded 63
'Tis said--indeed a general complaint 957 Juan 14 145

COMPLAINTS
And woos to listen to her fond complaints 384 Lara 2 611
And lived contentedly, without complaints 959 Juan 14 243

COMPLETE
Which Truth would acknowledge complete 178 Devil's Dr 184
Complete in kind--as various in their change 194 Monody 110
Thy Sovereignty would grow but more complete 199 Sonnet-E 12
When the web that we weave is complete 229 Lads 6
Our task complete like Hamet's, shall be free 242 Bards 21
And Dibdin's nonsense yield complete content 249 Bards 563
A tragedy complete in all but words 249 Bards 573
None are complete, all wanting in some part 257 Hints 51
Complete in all life's lessons--but to die 260 Hints 258
To tell thee, when the tale's complete 332 Abydos 2 362
Thus rendering the imperfect phrase complete 428 Island 3 137
Of the arm'd boats which hurried to complete 429 Island 3 219
Here! Have you not been able to complete 520 Faliero 3 125
Yet we would hear from your own lips complete 538 Faliero 5 29
The proofs and process are complete; the time 540 Faliero 5 139
Signor! complete that which you deem your duty 544 Faliero 5 467
Complete yet; two are wanting ere we can 595 Foscari 1 22
And how? You see the number is complete 596 Foscari 1 55
Or gentleman of seventy years complete 762 Juan 1 995
Of stockings, slippers, brushes, combs, complete 764 Juan 1 1140
My misery can scarce be more complete 771 Juan 1 1572
Of all our pumps:--a wreck complete she roll'd 779 Juan 2 334
And when they deem'd its moisture was complete 784 Juan 2 676
Their sofa occupied three parts complete 809 Juan 3 531
Which made their new establishment complete 811 Juan 3 619
In that complete perfection which ensures 814 Juan 3 867
They trod as upon necks; and to complete 845 Juan 5 885
The two first feelings ran their course complete 904 Juan 9 481
Of freedom shall complete their education 940 Juan 12 662
To spoil his undertaking or complete 959 Juan 14 238

COMPLETED
Completed: he leaves heirs on many thrones 290 Vision 371

COMPLETED
Completed his accoutrements, as Night	425	Island	2	498
And are the sixteen companies completed	516	Faliero	2	570
Behold, your work's completed! Is there then	625	Foscari	5	308
Our orisons completed, let us hence	628	Cain	1	47

COMPLETELY
But that which more completely faith exacts	771	Juan	1	1622
That soon his head was most completely crown'd	841	Juan	5	628
In his grave office so completely skill'd	952	Juan	13	702
Completely 'sans culotte,' and without vest	995	Juan	16	931

COMPLETES
Ere miss as yet completes her infant years	246	Bards		346
Completes his fury what their fear begun	349	Corsair	2	172

COMPLEXION
Is one of that complexion which seems made	60	Harold	4	281
Or, with a fair complexion, to expose	257	Hints		57
Is of a fair complexion altogether	442	Beppo		138
And through her clear brunette complexion shone a	828	Juan	4	750
In make, of a complexion white and ruddy	832	Juan	5	82
And clime and time, and country and complexion	857	Juan	6	319

COMPLIANCE
A free compliance with all honest wishes	514	Faliero	2	356
Unto the state, to justify compliance	542	Faliero	5	310
Instead of your compliance. Providence	621	Foscari	5	49

COMPLIANT
Too greatly fear'd, at first, to be compliant	472	Morgante		440
Which thou, compliant with my father's wish	546	Faliero	5	585

COMPLICATED
To this most foul and complicated treason	538	Faliero	5	9

COMPLICATION
Was not offence like his a complication	503	Faliero	1	226

COMPLIMENT
The flow of compliment, the slippery wile	126	Recoll		318
Of time, and time return'd the compliment	443	Beppo		178
All compliment, I hope so for your sake	451	Beppo		702
Would revel in the compliment. And yet	724	Deformed	1	106
This compliment, which drew all eyes upon	851	Juan	5	1241
Low as the compliment deserved. Suwarrow	875	Juan	7	498
Rather by deference than compliment	978	Juan	15	663

COMPLIMENTED
And complimented Don Alfonso's taste	755	Juan	1	534

COMPLIMENTS
Of soothing compliments divested	100	Marion		31
To bear the compliments of many a bore	830	Juan	4	867

COMPLY
Of Nature that with which she will comply	212	Augusta-C		82
Cannot comply with your request. His relics	626	Foscari	5	349

COMPOSE
Compose a mind like thine? Though all in one	61	Harold	4	350
Compose at once a slipper and a song	252	Bards		792
I own it: but, prithee, compose me the song	279	Blues	1	104
But who compose this senate of the few	303	Age		390
For me--compose thy limbs into their grave	654	Cain	3	540
I hardly could compose another line	956	Juan	14	90
Could write rhymes, and compose more than she wrote	986	Juan	16	418

COMPOSED
Had seen those scatter'd limbs composed	335	Abydos	2	617
Composed of branches, logs of wood, and earth	470	Morgante		306
Would have composed thy mind into the calm	647	Cain	3	49
Composed a choir of girls, ten or a dozen	844	Juan	5	786
Forgetting quite the woman (which composed	903	Juan	9	458

COMPOSERS'
One envoy's letters, six composers' airs	274	Waltz		73

COMPOSITION
And that's the moral of this composition	863	Juan	6	697
That all their glory, as a composition	942	Juan	13	87

COMPOSITIONS
I hate you, ye cold compositions of art	92	First Kiss		13
Was Adeline well versed, as compositions	986	Juan	16	416

COMPOUND
The natural compound left alone to fight	286	Vision		83
Learn'd to compound on Euxine shores, and taught me	574	Sardan	3	188
This hateful compound of her atoms, and	723	Deformed	1	59
Which clay can compound	728	Deformed	1	409

COMPOUNDS
And truth and fiction with such art compounds	259	Hints		211

COMPREHEND
To comprehend, but never love thy verse	66	Harold	4	688
Admires the strain she cannot comprehend	244	Bards		152
Which in itself can comprehend	313	Giaour		275
To comprehend the universe: nor these	486	Manfred	2	205
Would have required no words to comprehend	502	Faliero	1	178
But thou art clay, and canst but comprehend	638	Cain	2	164
But canst not comprehend the shadow of	641	Cain	2	336
Comprehend spirit wholly--but 'tis something	641	Cain	2	375
But not a word could Juan comprehend	794	Juan	2	1282
We whose minds comprehend all things? No more	836	Juan	5	311
I comprehend, for without transformation	899	Juan	9	159

COMPREHENDS
Conduct like this by no means comprehends	750	Juan	1	238

COMPREHENSION
Leave wondering comprehension far behind	252	Bards		758
His maxims, which to martial comprehension	874	Juan	7	463

COMPREHENSIONS
To females of perspicuous comprehensions	978	Juan	15	635

COMPRESS'D
Compress'd back to the heart	200	Ode-C		13
Like wind compress'd and pent within a bladder	294	Vision		591
Within a narrower ring compress'd, beset	350	Corsair	2	245
And, with a hushing sound compress'd	401	Parisina		483
Their thoughts to meaner beings; they compress'd	463	Dante	4	4
His daughter; while compress'd within his clasp	822	Juan	4	378

COMPRESSION
For that compression in its burning core	755	Juan	1	573

COMPREST
Still as a statue, with his lips comprest	427	Island	3	91

COMPRISE
Even if it should comprise a pack of fables	768	Juan	1	1398

COMPRISED
To reign! in that word see, ye ages, comprised	203	Avatar		62
A borough is comprised along the height	868	Juan	7	74
Contrived to get itself comprised within it	885	Juan	8	468

COMPROMISE
I must not compromise my soul. What soul	724	Deformed	1	143
Here was an honourable compromise	844	Juan	5	833

COMPROMISED
If not, strike home,--my life is compromised	523	Faliero	3	299
Felt restless, and perplex'd, and compromised	982	Juan	16	90

COMPUNCTION
A dying person in compunction	231	Doctor		75
Have felt the strange compunction which hath wrung you	528	Faliero	3	657
Rage, fear, hate, jealousy, revenge, compunction	801	Juan	2	1718

COMPUTE
All ashes to the taste. Did man compute	40	Harold	3	304

COMRADE
And clasp again the comrade of my youth	106	Nisus		58
The giant comrade of his pensive moods	421	Island	2	171
So much. My comrade may speak for himself	679	Werner	1	491
Hadst thou but done so! I have sought you, comrade	691	Werner	2	508
Comrade. They are but bad company, your highness	734	Deformed	1	812
She hath kill'd our comrade. Welcome such a death	740	Deformed	2	304
Count, she hath slain our comrade. With what weapon	740	Deformed	2	312
Don Juan, turning to his comrade, who	842	Juan	5	658
A wounded comrade, sprawling in his gore	880	Juan	8	160

COMRADES
Fit comrades in Elysian regions move	87	Marsus		4
Or if, amidst the comrades of thy youth	93	Dorset		29
Of comrades, in friendship and mischief allied	96	Harrow-A		6
Ye comrades of the jovial hour	145	Adieu		15
Where happier comrades in their triumph trod	182	Address-C		18
His comrades strain with desperate strength	335	Abydos	2	548
Behind, but close, his comrades lay	335	Abydos	2	570
Comrades, good night!'--The Hetman threw	415	Mazeppa		860
To leave my comrades helpless on the shoal	426	Island	2	525
In one placed Christian and his comrades twain	429	Island	3	223
How! are we comrades?--the state's ducal robes	505	Faliero	1	392
Besides on all the spirits of his comrades	511	Faliero	2	139
And our more chosen comrades, is aware	520	Faliero	3	131
To be of your chief comrades? but no less	521	Faliero	3	184

COMRADES
Our comrades are even now prepared to greet him   521 Faliero   3   205
Long live Faliero! Comrades! did I well   523 Faliero   3   333
Injustice to thy comrades and thy cause   524 Faliero   3   402
Or should be comrades, even though enemies   676 Werner   1   347
Down with them, comrades! seize upon those lamps   738 Deformed 2   238
Comrades, help, ho! All's darkness   739 Deformed 2   302
Her comrades, also, thought themselves undone   851 Juan   5   1243
They brought him and his comrades to head-
   quarters   874 Juan   7   450
In fair proportion with their comrades;--then   891 Juan   8   818

COMRADE'S
Thy comrade's honour and thy friend's delight   85 Epitaph   10
Brave Nisus here arrests his comrade's arm   109 Nisus   279
Ah! must he rush his comrade's fate to share   110 Nisus   334
Volscens must soon appease his comrade's ghost   110 Nisus   388
And when his comrade's thought each sufferer knew 783 Juan   2   581
'Your names?'--'Mine's Johnson, and my comrade's
   Juan   874 Juan   7   473

COM'ST
Thou com'st to claim a calmer grave   323 Giaour   1311
'Whence com'st thou, Dervise?' 'From the outlaw's
   den   348 Corsair   2   65

COMUS
Each to his humour--Comus all allows   250 Bards   650

CON.
Nem. con. amongst the women, which I grieve   978 Juan   15 666
To say leads oft to crim. con. with the married   978 Juan   15 667

CONCATENATION
All felt a soft kind of concatenation   857 Juan   6   302

CONCEAL
To feign the pleasure or conceal the pique   35 Harold   2   915
The heart against itself; and to conceal   52 Harold   3   1035
What I can ne'er express, yet can not all conceal   81 Harold   4   1602
Yet I conceal my love--and why   90 To M.S.G.-A   11
Ah! why do dark'ning shades conceal   135 I Would   19
A lip of lies; a face form'd to conceal   209 Sketch   61
My feelings farther.--Nor shall I conceal   212 Augusta-C   118
And Hook conceal his heroes in a cask   249 Bards   589
Why wilt thou urge me to conceal   328 Abydos   1   438
Shall be what thou must conceal   481 Manfred   1   221
Ay, as the dunghill may conceal a gem   728 Deformed 1   432
Conceal my fall--all will go well--conceal it   736 Deformed 2   129
Taught to conceal, their bursting hearts despond   799 Juan   2   1596
Dyes with his morning light,--and would conceal   810 Juan   3   579
And more attracts by all it doth conceal   958 Juan   14 212

CONCEAL'D
The fire in the cavern of Etna conceal'd   129 Becher-A   9
As the stream late conceal'd   327 Abydos   1   332
Not cankering less because the more conceal'd   352 Corsair   2   353
But not his pride, and hate no more conceal'd   377 Lara   2   128
The secret long and yet but half conceal'd   382 Lara   2   515
Nought conceal'd her bosom shining   390 Corinth   555
Conceal'd and fatal gallery. There I'll find him 702 Werner   3   497
In the poor town where Werner was conceal'd   717 Werner   5   281
That I had robb'd him. I conceal'd you--I   717 Werner   5   297
With me at last to be so. You conceal'd me   717 Werner   5   304
Conceal'd amongst his premises; 'tis true   768 Juan   1   1413
Conceal'd her features better than a veil   865 Juan   6   866

CONCEALING
While vanity prevents concealing   147 Vain Lady   32
Is worth--God knows what. 'Tis at least worth
   concealing   283 Blues   2   163

CONCEALMENT
My heart concealment weighs like sin   328 Abydos   1   444
Concealment is no more; they speak   397 Parisina   127
Concealment or escape? You may be sure   695 Werner   2   767
Imploring a few hours' concealment from   703 Werner   3   519

CONCEALS
Nisus no more the blackening shade conceals   110 Nisus   363
The haughtier thought it curbs, but scarce
   conceals   341 Corsair   1   206

CONCEDE
Our church and state, our courts and camps,
   concede   264 Hints   581
Stopp'd as if once more willing to concede   893 Juan   8   930

CONCEDED
Or generous draft, conceded as a gift   946 Juan   13 357

CONCEIT
Her who relates each fond conceit   147 Vain Lady   26
And think's thou, Scott! by vain conceit per-
   chance   244 Bards   171

CONCEIT
A pretty lad, but bursting with conceit   827 Juan   4   706

CONCEITED
Or more conceited in his petty sphere   296 Vision   700

CONCEITS
A wilderness of the most rare conceits   980 Juan   16 19

CONCEIVE
Thus only may our sons conceive the scenes we saw   18 Harold   1   908
Conceive in boyhood and pursue as men   73 Harold   4   1095
Who can conceive, who has not proved   89 To Emma   33
Yet I conceive thou'lt partly guess   112 Quaker   26
Conceive the bard the hero of the story   245 Bards   254
And that you may not, cavalier, conceive   468 Morgante   172
Cannot conceive my love for her the less   644 Cain   2   538
I was the fool of passion to conceive   693 Werner   2   641
Were not drawn from their spouses, you conceive   803 Juan   3   80
A stern repose; which you would scarce conceive   874 Juan   7   427

CONCEIVED
Is he whose head conceived, whose hand prepared   21 Harold   2   104
Conceived--utter'd--look'd--or wrote down letters
   ten   178 Devil's Dr   183
Conceived the globe he panted not to spare   298 Age   40
Conceived deliberately such a thought   702 Werner   3   473
Now you must do so. I conceived myself   718 Werner   5   342
She now conceived all difficulties past   846 Juan   5   922
Conceived that phrase was quite enough to move   846 Juan   5   928

CONCENTER'D
Its own concenter'd recompense   191 Prometheus-B 57

CONCENTRATED
Then calm, concentrated, and still, and slow   807 Juan   3   379

CONCENTRATES
Concentrates into all that's merciless   377 Lara   2   150

CONCENTRATING
And beauty, all concentrating like rays   797 Juan   2   1482

CONCENTRE
And thus the chilliest aspects may concentre   945 Juan   13 298

CONCENTRED
All is concentred in a life intense   49 Harold   3   838
Oft in concentred spirits not less daring   517 Faliero   2   578

CONCEPTION
When each conception was a heavenly guest   79 Harold   4   1456
Groan with the strong conception of their wrongs   507 Faliero   1   491
As in the monstrous grasp of their conception   549 Faliero   5   774

CONCEPTIONS
Its golden sands, and learn what great conceptions
   can   79 Harold   4   1431
Of clay obscures our best conceptions, saving   288 Vision   223
And my conceptions. What are they which dwell   637 Cain   2   83
Conceptions, 'twas that I had rarely seen   717 Werner   5   287

CONCERN
Nor sent, nor wrote, nor show'd the least concern 444 Beppo   277
'Twas surely no concern of theirs nor mine   750 Juan   1   180
'Twas strange that one so young should thus
   concern   758 Juan   1   741
There is a sort of unexprest concern   775 Juan   2   109
But here I leave the general concern   880 Juan   8   129
To Jack howe'er this gave but slight concern   883 Juan   8   325
With such small gear to give myself concern   926 Juan   11 491
But small concern about the when, or where   961 Juan   14 356
But this is not at present my concern   963 Juan   14 471
Yet grew a little pale--with what? concern   993 Juan   16 797

CONCERN'D
Am I concern'd? As one who did so much   694 Werner   2   698
At which the naval people are concern'd   747 Juan   1   30
And never dream'd his lady was concern'd   749 Juan   1   148

CONCERNING
Concerning woman's soft dominion   101 Marion   44
Concerning what they read   151 Harriet   3
She's so learned in all things, and fond of
   concerning   278 Blues   1   73

CONCERNS
Concerns your husband, and if not--Well, signor   604 Foscari   2   191

CONCERT
How sweet it were in concert to adore   20 Harold   2   68
While thus in concert they this lay half sang,
   half scream'd   30 Harold   2   648
Unite in concert with increased alarms   120 Newstead-A   56

CONCERT
'Tis mann'd; the oars keep concert to the strand 339 Corsair 1 101
Revel, and lie, oppress, and kill in concert 521 Faliero 3 157
We served and fought; we smiled and wept in
  concert 525 Faliero 3 442
And, suffering in concert, make our pangs 630 Cain 1 158
Where heart, and soul, and sense, in concert move 797 Juan 2 1485

CONCESSION
Accept then my concession 138 Clare 69
For Liverpool such a concession begrudges 225 Ode-D 23

CONCESSIONS
By some well-timed concessions. But, above 504 Faliero 1 342

CONCHS
With sounding conchs and joyous shouts to shore 432 Island 4 216

CONCISION
Of tyranny of all kinds, my concision 971 Juan 15 175
And amplify: you lose much by concision 974 Juan 15 404

CONCLUDE
In bloodier acts conclude those who with blood
  began 29 Harold 2 567
At once to conclude such a fruitless dissension 147 To Anne-A 15
With whom you'd conclude 232 Murray-B 50
And Heaven forbid I should conclude 234 Strahan 21

CONCLUDED
At last, concluded our scholastic life 126 Recoll 333
Reign is concluded; whatso'er betide 294 Vision 574
Had been the happy lover, he concluded 768 Juan 1 1412

CONCLUDES
The list concludes John Murray's columns 232 Nihil 2

CONCLUSION
As for the rest, to come to the conclusion 298 Vision 841
Coming on this point to the same conclusion 472 Morgante 402
To deem as a most logical conclusion 745 Juan Ded 37

CONCLUSIONS
Conclusions most forbidden. Then I pass'd 486 Manfred 2 177
To draw conclusions absolute of aught 494 Manfred 3 207
I'd try conclusions with those Janizaries 926 Juan 11 487

CONCOCTION
The play's concoction full of art 231 Doctor 12
Some said 'twas a concoction of the humours 912 Juan 10 317
The plan at present's simply in concoction 941 Juan 12 693

CONCORD
A holy concord--and a bright regret 192 Monody 11
And tune the concord to a finer mood 967 Juan 14 740

CONCUBINE
Years, and a fifteen-hundredth concubine 853 Juan 6 64
In his monastic concubine of snow 854 Juan 6 134

CONCUBINES
Save concubines and carnal companie 4 Harold 1 17
Four wives by law, and concubines 'ad libitum 449 Beppo 560
Than songs, and lutes, and feasts, and concubines 555 Sardan 1 281
Your king of concubines? why stir me up 562 Sardan 2 59

CONCUR
Extremely pure, which made them all concur 857 Juan 6 308

CONCUSSION
Few youthful minds can stand the strong
  concussion 910 Juan 10 163

CONDE
Fowls 'a la Conde,' slices eke of salmon 976 Juan 15 513

CONDEMN
(See also SELF-CONDEMNING)
It is not ours to judge, far less condemn 52 Harold 3 1006
Though prudes may condemn me, and bigots reprove 92 First Kiss 14
Whose souls disdain not to condemn the wrong 93 Dorset 28
Shall man condemn his race to hell 132 Prayer 21
Those who condemn, should surely deign to read 142 Soliloquy 48
Let Pride alone condemn 146 Adieu 70
Pause--ere their feebler offspring you condemn 170 Address-A 50
Grieved to condemn, the muse must still be just 245 Bards 289
Skill'd as to condemn as to traduce mankind 248 Bards 457
Condemn the unlucky curate to recite 267 Hints 765
Still, ere thou dost condemn me, pause 320 Giaour 1060
Yet the same feeling which thou dost condemn 344 Corsair 1 402
Mankind, the rather to condemn than praise 377 Lara 2 152
Forgive me or condemn me. She is silent 490 Manfred 2 475
You who condemn me, you who fear and slay me 542 Faliero 5 283
The thing which you condemn, a disposition 555 Sardan 1 322

CONDEMN
Will he condemn him? I trust not. But if 599 Foscari 1 220
I marvel they condemn him not at once 600 Foscari 1 287
And seek to save what all things now condemn 668 Heaven 1024
Condemn him not from his own mouth, but trust 690 Werner 2 494
Yet hear me still!--if you condemn me, yet 720 Werner 5 439
And so have been forgotten:--I condemn none 747 Juan 1 37
Condemn the royal lady's taste who wore 793 Juan 2 1236
Abhor, condemn, abjure the mortal made 800 Juan 2 1666
They saw not in themselves aught to condemn 818 Juan 4 100
I own it, I deplore it, I condemn it 853 Juan 6 58
And whom for this at last must we condemn 890 Juan 8 734

CONDEMNATION
Since my defence must be your condemnation 540 Faliero 5 166
That when a culprit came for condemnation 952 Juan 13 703

CONDEMN'D
(See also SELF-CONDEMN'D)
Monastic dome! condemn'd to uses vile 4 Harold 1 59
Alas! too oft condemn'd for him to bear and bleed 16 Harold 1 746
Through distant climes condemn'd to fly 111 Medea 43
Condemn'd a heart she never knew 142 Critics 72
Oh, ye condemn'd the ills of life to bear 161 Athos 22
So now they're condemn'd by no Judges at all 225 Ode-D 24
Condemn'd at length to be forgotten quite 242 Bards 17
Condemn'd to make the books which once he sold 247 Bards 398
Condemn'd to drudge, the meanest of the mean 255 Bards 977
Condemn'd to meditate and gaze 320 Giaour 993
For one so long condemn'd to toil and fast 348 Corsair 2 115
Disguised--discover'd--conquering--ta'en--
  condemn'd 352 Corsair 2 389
The men with whom he felt condemn'd to breathe 371 Lara 1 346
Thus trammell'd, thus condemn'd to Flattery's
  trebles 461 Dante 3 92
Which had its birthplace in a star condemn'd 479 Manfred 1 44
How says your highness? Steno is condemn'd 505 Faliero 1 416
What! is the sentence pass'd? is he condemn'd? 509 Faliero 2 46
But he has been condemn'd into captivity 515 Faliero 2 437
Is he condemn'd? Alas! And was he guilty 543 Faliero 5 343
Condemn'd without a crime. The triumph is 576 Sardan 3 323
And cannot pardon till I have condemn'd 583 Sardan 4 308
Has he not been condemn'd? Is none but guilt so 604 Foscari 2 176
Which is comdemn'd; nay, even the evil fly 663 Heaven 594
What he who made you glorious hath condemn'd 665 Heaven 756
Condemn'd. Oh, father! say it not. Son! son 665 Heaven 760
Am thus condemn'd to weep above in vain 670 Heaven 1194
Senates and sages have condemn'd its use 915 Juan 10 501
'Midst royal dukes and dames condemn'd to climb 926 Juan 11 535
Condemn'd to child-bed, as men for their sins 958 Juan 14 183

CONDEMNED
Prostrate thyself, and thy condemned clay 489 Manfred 2 404

CONDEMNS
When S-- condemns a book he never read 142 Soliloquy 42
She then surveys, condemns, but pities still 448 Beppo 519
Condemns the evil done my new acquaintance 471 Morgante 324

CONDENSE
That ask the eye--so here condense thy soul 78 Harold 4 1408

CONDENSED
Condensed their scatter'd rays, they would not
  form a sun 61 Harold 4 351
Its quantity is but condensed to quality 947 Juan 13 392
Not calculating how much they condensed 990 Juan 16 614

CONDENSING
Condensing in a fair free commonwealth 523 Faliero 3 290

CONDESCEND
If e'er the sinking stage could condescend 170 Address-A 58
Though printers condescend the press to soil 255 Bards 965
But if (true bard!) you scorn to condescend 267 Hints 789
Nor foes--all nations--condescend to smile 746 Juan Ded 100
If ever I should condescend to prose 771 Juan 1 1625
If they would condescend to circumcision 840 Juan 5 552
How power could condescend to do without 876 Juan 7 592

CONDESCENDED
At length he condescended to inquire 893 Juan 8 957

CONDESCENDING
And deem'd herself extremely condescending 846 Juan 5 923
My lords and ladies proudly condescending 991 Juan 16 674
This day; and watching, witching, condescending 993 Juan 16 802

CONDESCENDS
Remember Ugolino condescends 784 Juan 2 658

CONDESCENSION
And condescension to the vulgar's level 291 Vision 405
Her plumpness, her imperial condescension 905 Juan 9 570

CONDITION
And Macon would not pity my condition   471 Morgante   340
Condition that the three young princes are   592 Sardan 5 305
Ay, upon one condition. Name it. That   632 Cain 1 299
A jewel! 'Tis your own on one condition   699 Werner 3 303
Thy choice. On what condition? There's a
    question   724 Deformed 1 139
Would fully suit a widow of condition   757 Juan 1 675
And turn'd, without perceiving his condition   758 Juan 1 727
But for a cavalier of his condition   764 Juan 1 1107
You've made the apartment in a fit condition   765 Juan 1 1211
The worst of all was, that in their condition   779 Juan 2 361
And the long-boat's condition was but bad   780 Juan 2 379
''Twould greatly tend to better their condition   840 Juan 5 551
For this first fault, and that on no condition   862 Juan 6 653
Against all women of whate'er condition   866 Juan 6 931
Of the imperial favourite's condition   903 Juan 9 411
Of his fierce pulse betoken a condition   912 Juan 10 308
But in a style becoming his condition   913 Juan 10 352
Was well received by persons of condition   924 Juan 11 360
To the surprise of people of condition   933 Juan 12 212
As Juan was a person of condition   933 Juan 12 236
Also a foreigner of high condition   947 Juan 13 415
The real sufferings of their she condition   958 Juan 14 188
If I had never proved the soft condition   971 Juan 15 186
Bull something of the lower world's condition   979 Juan 15 734
Shadows;--but you must be in my condition   980 Juan 15 783
Both which are limited to no condition   992 Juan 16 728

CONDITIONAL
Believe in me, as a conditional creed   636 Cain 2 21

CONDITIONS
And laid conditions he thought very hard on   769 Juan 1 1435
Survive through very desperate conditions   782 Juan 2 508
As any of Mortality's conditions   898 Juan 9 134

CONDOLE
Nor sought he friend to counsel or condole   4 Harold 1 71
In the first place, the Council doth condole   620 Foscari 5 12

CONDOLENCE
A few words of condolence on his state   985 Juan 16 274

CONDORCET
Barnave, Brissot, Condorcet, Mirabeau   747 Juan 1 17

CONDOTTIERO
A kind of general condottiero system   685 Werner 2 127

CONDUCE
Yes; all things which conduce to other men's   621 Foscari 5 78

CONDUCIVE
But the same cause, conducive to his loss   781 Juan 2 450

CONDUCT
Such conduct bears Philanthropy's rare stamp   29 Harold 2 610
Her dying hours with pious conduct bless   108 Nisus   191
His conduct was but natural in a prince   293 Vision   560
In words too wise, in conduct there a fool   342 Corsair 1 254
Conduct? shall their bright plumage on the rough   462 Dante 3 166
I little thought his bounty would conduct me   505 Faliero 1 400
To wait your coming, and conduct you where   508 Faliero 1 596
To what it may conduct. Assuredly   509 Faliero 2 38
A pride not in your beauty, but your conduct   514 Faliero 2 362
Upon the motive, and my conduct proved   514 Faliero 2 413
To what does this conduct? To thus much, that   514 Faliero 2 420
Which overpower all others, and conduct   517 Faliero 2 613
Sent me here to conduct you hence, beyond   575 Sardan 3 243
But being taken for him might conduct   700 Werner 3 318
Their conduct was exceedingly well-bred   750 Juan 1 205
Required this conduct--which seem'd very odd   750 Juan 1 216
Conduct like this by no means comprehends   750 Juan 1 238
Immoral conduct by the fancied sway   761 Juan 1 923
Of conduct was which he observed in Greece   812 Juan 3 672
'Twas certain that his conduct had been pure   865 Juan 6 827
Steam-engines will conduct him to the moon   907 Juan 10 16
Began to think the duchess' conduct free   961 Juan 14 364
Her conduct had been perfectly correct   966 Juan 14 675
Besides, his conduct, since in England, grew more   969 Juan 15 85
Safe conduct through the rocks of re-elections   993 Juan 16 808

CONDUCTED
Him traitor Gan conducted to the tomb   467 Morgante   59
Love to one death conducted us along   476 Francesca   10
I caused to be conducted forth, and taught   514 Faliero 2 424
But what conducted, if the question's fair   833 Juan 5 116

CONDUCTOR
Chance your conductor; midnight for your mantle   690 Werner 2 453
Here their conductor tapping at the wicket   836 Juan 5 321
Affect no more than lightning a conductor   916 Juan 10 568

CONDUCTS
Conducts her generations to our tombs   519 Faliero 3 70
By the private staircase, which conducts you
    towards   624 Foscari 5 238
But certes it conducts to lives ascetic   973 Juan 15 303

CONDUCT'S
Deserves the worst, his conduct's less defensible   765 Juan 1 1206

CONEY
Hunts not the wretched coney, but the boar   724 Deformed 1 124

CONFEDERATION
Ere cursed confederation made thee France's   274 Waltz   41

CONFER
And we might then and there confer   409 Mazeppa   247
But I would fain confer with thee alone   491 Manfred 3 24
Than empires can confer, in quiet honour   540 Faliero 5 156

CONFERENCE
That moment summon'd to a conference   509 Faliero 2 2
You have held conference with him? I am weary   538 Faliero 5 64
The conference or congress (for it ended   975 Juan 15 481
Also the conference which we have seen   977 Juan 15 597

CONFERR'D
I bleed withal, and, had it been conferr'd   75 Harold 4 1191
Conferr'd on his Highness of Cumberland   178 Devil's Dr   188
This special honour was conferr'd, because   896 Juan 8 1113
Of fitting out her favourites, conferr'd   913 Juan 10 362

CONFESS
Confess that woman's false as fair   118 Romance   23
And you, Scamp!--I needs must confess I'm
    embarrass'd   282 Blues 2 121
His changing cheek, his sinking heart confess   325 Abydos 1 174
Confess and envy, yet oppose in vain   341 Corsair 1 180
They gaze and marvel how--and still confess   341 Corsair 1 201
That would confess me at so fair a shrine   353 Corsair 2 445
Confess its barbarism when compared with thine   459 Dante 2 32
Confess--confide in me--thou know'st my nature   531 Faliero 4 247
Will hear you; if you have aught to confess   538 Faliero 5 24
You do confess then, and admit the justice   541 Faliero 5 266
Of our tribunal? I confess to have fail'd   541 Faliero 5 267
You have nought to do, except confess and die   545 Faliero 5 548
Let them wring on; I am strong yet. Confess   597 Foscari 1 134
I am a judge; but must confess that part   600 Foscari 1 324
All things, my father says; but I confess   643 Cain 2 516
In his resumed amusement. 'I confess   875 Juan 7 516
Perhaps she had nothing to confess:--no matter   914 Juan 10 446
To taste:--the truth is, if men would confess   938 Juan 12 551
But though a 'bonne vivante,' I must confess   976 Juan 15 509
He was 'free to confess' (whence comes this
    phrase   990 Juan 16 625

CONFESS'D
(See also ALL-CONFESS'D)
Confess'd a love which equall'd mine   152 Time-A   6
Her heart confess'd a gentler flame   326 Abydos 1 260
Which thus confess'd without relieving pain   365 Corsair 3 651
And they the wiser, friendlier few confess'd   367 Lara 1 113
Its grief seem'd ended, but the sex confess'd   382 Lara 2 517
Having confess'd, there is no hope for you   540 Faliero 5 170
And the rack will be spared you. I confess'd   597 Foscari 1 135
Although their porter afterwards confess'd   750 Juan 1 189
Who fain would have a mutual flame confess'd   854 Juan 6 131

CONFESSION
(See also SELF-CONFESSION)
For though I will not make confession   144 Becher-B   10
Their lips are slow at Love's confession   160 Cadiz   20
Nor e'er before confession chair   318 Giaour   803
Thou need'st not answer--thy confession speaks   358 Corsair 3 182
As his last confession pouring   400 Parisina   413
That Michel Steno, by his own confession   501 Faliero 1 88
So your confession be detail'd and full   539 Faliero 5 80
And by thine own confession, of the guilt   545 Faliero 5 484
Has been annull'd by the death-bed confession   600 Foscari 1 303
Confession, and the prisoner partly having   605 Foscari 2 266
She also had no passion for confession   914 Juan 10 445

CONFESSIONAL
More constant at confessional   386 Corinth   202

CONFESSIONS
As Saint Augustine in his fine Confessions   753 Juan 1 375

CONFESSOR
Confessor! to thy secret ear   323 Giaour   1320
Nor leave a last word with our confessor   539 Faliero 5 105
I am neither confessor nor notary   706 Werner 4 149
Between his tutors, confessor, and mother   753 Juan 1 392
That I have chosen a confessor so old   765 Juan 1 1171

CONFEST
He could not--durst not--lo! the guile confest   110 Nisus   370
At least, we moderns, wisely 'tis confest   263 Hints   447
The man in all the rest might be confest   885 Juan   8   419
The only truth that yet has been confest   942 Juan   13 51

CONFIDANTE
The genial confidante, and general spy   208 Sketch   10

CONFIDE
In thy protection I confide   133 Prayer   52
And who would in a breast confide   153 Friend-A   19
Consult Lord Fanny, and confide in Curll   246 Bards   372
The maid whose folly could confide   397 Parisina   105
Confess--confide in me--thou know'st my nature   531 Faliero   4   247

CONFIDENCE
Brisk Confidence still best with woman copes   24 Harold   2   305
Where confidence and ease the watch disdain   105 Nisus   27
Alas! too like in confidence are each   373 Lara   1   506
To win no confidence, and wake no love   377 Lara   2   140
Showing his confidence and his submission   507 Faliero   1   547
It lull'd suspicion, showing confidence   516 Faliero   2   540
On a rash confidence in one we know not   518 Faliero   2   666
And have you confidence in such a project   615 Foscari   4   1
Unbounded confidence. Say on. Mysterious   693 Minerva   2   678
He hath no confidence! Ah! can I hope it   711 Werner   4   428
For the old negro's confidence in creeping   837 Juan   5   354
A modest confidence and calm assurance   924 Juan   11 410

CONFIDENT
Defying earth and confident of heaven   378 Lara   2   217
Such confident alacrity. Your doubts   519 Faliero   3   52

CONFIDENTIAL
Quite in a confidential queenly way   843 Juan   5   755

CONFIDES
And vainly in the weak defence confides   109 Nisus   270

CONFIDING
(See also SELF-CONFIDING)
Confiding have I found you, that I doubted   719 Werner   5   422

CONFINE
In firmer chains our hearts confine   101 Lady-B   2
Yes, to the past alone my heart confine   127 Recoll   377
Shall man confine his Maker's sway   132 Prayer   17
Life will not long confine   181 Ode-A   133
Now to soft themes thou scornest to confine   246 Bards   349
To themes less lofty still my lay confine   255 Bards   1009
And must the bard his glowing thoughts confine   262 Hints   417
Upon their airy confine, half-seas-over   915 Juan   10 488
On life's worn confine, jaded, bloated, sated   918 Juan   10 690
On general topics: poems must confine   924 Juan   11 351

CONFINED
Whose fate to distant homes confined their lot   14 Harold   1   631
Is chain'd and tortured--cabin'd, cribb'd,
   confined   74 Harold   4   1140
Let those they ne'er confined my lay reprove   119 Answer-A   16
Not to the aching frame alone confined   122 Recoll   5
These last should be confined to one   134 E. N. Long   74
That truth, as of yore, is confined to the bowl   155 Goblet   24
A barren soil, where Nature's germs, confined   270 Minerva   133
Guarded and watch'd, but not confined in person   592 Sardan   5   303
States to be curb'd and thoughts to be confined   746 Juan   Ded 108
Wounded and fetter'd, 'cabin'd, cribb'd, confined 826 Juan   4   593
Was not confined to feeling for her friend   961 Juan   14 402

CONFINEMENT
Confinement, too, must make them look quite
   palely   449 Beppo   565
To a month's confinement. What! the same who
   dared   505 Faliero   1   417

CONFINEMENT'S
Yet, when confinement's lingering hour was done   125 Recoll   255

CONFINES
Confines the current of the soul   133 E. N. Long   34
Beside the confines of the Aegean main   161 Athos   1
Renown'd alike; whose genius ne'er confines   250 Bards   600
Round all the confines of the yielded waist   276 Waltz   192
Some likeness, which the glittering cirque
   confines   931 Juan   12 94

CONFIRM
Blood, pulse, and breast confirm the Dardan
   Shepherd's prize   62 Harold   4   450
Thine. The king's! Yes! and let the king
   confirm it   564 Sardan   2   186
Of my inquiries, still confirm it.--Yes   687 Werner   2   272
All--all--confirm it to my mind. However   687 Werner   2   281

CONFIRM
That is not here--confirm my apprehension   694 Werner   2   689
All these confirm my statement a good deal   771 Juan   1   1621
Which should confirm, or shake, or make a faith   836 Juan   5   304
Perhaps she might wish to confirm him in it   987 Juan   16 455

CONFIRM'D
'Tis done, I thank you. Thus the act confirm'd   601 Foscari   2   10
Gently, but palpably confirm'd its grasp   760 Juan   1   882
Though oft well founded, which confirm'd but more 943 Juan   13 130

CONFIRMS
Confirms his crimes, but he avows them not   600 Foscari   1   294

CONFISCATE
Thy goods are confiscate unto the state   545 Faliero   5   487

CONFISCATED
Are all my lands confiscated? They are   545 Faliero   5   528
Under the penalty to see confiscated   623 Foscari   5   174
The cargoes he confiscated, and gain   790 Juan   2   1005

CONFITURES
But even sans 'confitures,' it no less true is   976 Juan   15 543

CONFLICT
Sounds not the clang of conflict on the heath   10 Harold   1   415
To doubtful conflict, certain slaughter bring   26 Harold   2   401
With the sharp scythe of conflict,--then to see   43 Harold   3   447
In life's last conflict 'twill appear   98 To Mary   27
Not in the conflict Havoc seeks delight   272 Minerva   295
That conflict, deadlier far than all before   358 Corsair   3   219
Short was the conflict; furious, blindly rash   376 Lara   2   67
Then again in conflict mixing   394 Corinth   900
Proclaim'd the desperate conflict o'er   395 Corinth   1028
And though the long, long conflict hath been
   spent   456 Dante   1   36
Of conflict none will hear, or hearing heed   458 Dante   2   11
Conflict, and final triumph of the brave   462 Dante   3   125
A conflict of its elements, and breathe   482 Manfred   1   303
Crash with a frequent conflict; but ye pass   482 Manfred   1   339
In dark suspicious conflict with the Doge   525 Faliero   3   499
The wavering of the weak, in case of conflict   536 Faliero   4   541
From the outward wall the fiercest conflict
   rages   573 Sardan   3   103
Goes on the conflict? Dubiously and fiercely   574 Sardan   3   199
As in late midnight conflict in the very   588 Sardan   5   61
We in our conflict! Goodness would not make   629 Cain   1   146
Conflict shall cease, if ever it shall cease   645 Cain   2   644
And, after thirty years of conflict, peace   685 Werner   2   169
With thick'ning canopy the conflict o'er   879 Juan   8   62

CONFLICTING
Even still conflicting passions shake his soul   100 Damaetas   11
When fierce conflicting passions urge   111 Medea   1
Of cares o'erwhelming our conflicting state   114 Death-A   18

CONFLICTS
Though pale with conflicts between love and
   pride   863 Juan   6   710

CONFORM
When elements to elements conform   46 Harold   3   702

CONFORMATION
New buildings of correctest conformation   988 Juan   16 511

CONFOUND
While lengthening shades his weary way confound   109 Nisus   330
(Confound me if I know what next to say   170 Address-B   14
'Confound the renegado! I have sprain'd   295 Vision   681
Which they abhor, confound not with the cause   454 Venice-B   93
The church, or one, or all? for you confound   731 Deformed 1   632
I'm a philosopher; confound them all   855 Juan   6   169
And hastily--as nothing can confound   992 Juan   16 748

CONFOUNDED
And, like his bard, confounded night with day   245 Bards   250
Till he at last confounded good and ill   371 Lara   1   335
Till some confounded escapade has blighted   759 Juan   1   797
With your confounded fantasies, to more   761 Juan   1   922
Shadows of glory! (lest I be confounded   877 Juan   7   654
About; a circumstance which has confounded   881 Juan   8   220
When once you have broken their confounded ice   946 Juan   13 304
Confounded him in common with the crowd   978 Juan   15 658

CONFOUNDING
The past confounding with the present day   122 Recoll   26

CONFOUNDS
And common-place and common sense confounds   249 Bards   569
But whether 'twas that one's own guilt con-
   founds   768 Juan   1   1403

CONFRONT
Confront a traitor. What have you to say   540 Faliero   5   164

CONFRONTED
Confronted with whole realms far and near   694 Werner   2   713

CONFUSE
Whose minglings might confuse a Newton's thought   190 Churchill   23
Shrinks from the crowd that may confuse   742 Deformed   3   15

CONFUSED
Aghast, confused, his fears to madness rise   110 Nisus   365
All was confused and undefined   400 Parisina   378
The Senhor Don Alfonso stood confused   766 Juan   1   1265
Confused, in the confusion, and distrait   992 Juan   16   739
But what confused him more than smile or stare   992 Juan   16   769

CONFUSION
All is confusion--through the vale   103 Alva   117
What bowls and mantles in confusion toss'd   109 Nisus   286
With wives who eternal confusion are spreading   117 To Eliza   22
Yet meet with no confusion there   155 Happy   30
All I saw farther, in the last confusion   298 Vision   845
The wild confusion, and the swarthy glow   349 Corsair   2   152
So much Confusion magnifies his foe   349 Corsair   2   179
In blind confusion on the foe they press   379 Lara   2   286
Until by some confusion led   408 Mazeppa   164
But a confusion worse than such   412 Mazeppa   562
In hell below, and damn'd in great confusion   472 Morgante   406
Now, knaves, what ransom for your lives?
     Confusion   536 Faliero   4   578
Doubt upon me, confusion over all   765 Juan   1   1226
Who told him to be damn'd--in his confusion   779 Juan   2   352
A rich confusion form'd a disarray   843 Juan   5   739
A kingdom or confusion anywhere   847 Juan   5   1027
All this she told with some confusion and   862 Juan   6   617
Without confusion of the sorts and sexes   918 Juan   11   22
Of wheels, and roar of voices, and confusion   921 Juan   11   170
To the performer's diffident confusion   986 Juan   16   376
Confused, in the confusion, and distrait   992 Juan   16   739
And that in his confusion he had caught   996 Juan   16   1023

CONFUTE
Though perhaps 'twere no difficult task to
     confute it   145 Casuists   6

CONGEAL
That is, till deeper griefs congeal our tears   776 Juan   2   120

CONGEAL'D
But Pride congeal'd the drop within his ee   4 Harold   1   49

CONGEALING
For his congealing blood, and senses dim   788 Juan   2   884

CONGEALS
Congeals the tear of Pity's eye   133 E. N. Long   35

CONGENIAL
And gaze complacent on congenial earth   34 Harold   2   867
Our souls at least congenial meet   85 To E--   9
To me congenial sounds your wintry Dirge   140 Ossian-A   48
There's not a kind congenial heart   156 Lady-E   39
Thy bosom overboils, congenial river   198 Po   15
Congenial colours in that soul or face   209 Sketch   70
Oh! hadst thou lived in that congenial time   247 Bards   379
And case his volumes in congenial calf   251 Bards   738
Devotes to scandal his congenial mind   255 Bards   979
Nor swore in vain; the long congenial sound   428 Island   3   133
Where the mind rots congenial with the abyss   439 Tasso   235
Stirs rudely; but, congenial with the night   529 Faliero   4   86
You seem congenial, will you wear his features   725 Deformed   1   240

CONGRATULATIONS
Round the young man with their congratulations   907 Juan   9   652

CONGRESS
Around our congress, and dispense with all   293 Vision   516
But lo! a Congress! What! that hallow'd name   303 Age   378
A congress forms their 'New Jerusalem   307 Age   693
Strange sight, this Congress! destined to unite   307 Age   704
Already mention'd in our former congress   623 Foscari   5   172
Conspiracy or Congress to be made   746 Juan   Ded   109
I have seen a Congress doing all that's mean   929 Juan   11   662
O'er congress, whether royalist or liberal   930 Juan   12   34
The conference or congress (for it ended   975 Juan   15   481

CONGRESSES
As congresses of late do) of the Lady   975 Juan   15   482

CONGREVE'S
Then Congreve's scenes could cheer, or Otway's
     melt   243 Bards   115
A kind antithesis to Congreve's rockets   762 Juan   1   1030

CONGREVE'S
When Congreve's fool could vie with Moliere's
     bete   953 Juan   13   750

CONJECTURE
By Rome.--But whither would Conjecture stray   70 Harold   4   925
No treacherous powder bids conjecture quake   275 Waltz   139
Conjecture whispers in his muttering speech   340 Corsair   1   148
Nor sent, nor came he, till conjecture grew   366 Lara   1   31
And dye conjecture with a darker hue   377 Lara   2   126
My lord, not much as yet, except conjecture   686 Werner   2   215

CONJECTURES
In various conjectures, for none knew   786 Juan   2   796

CONJECTURING
Conjecturing, wondering, asking a narration   861 Juan   6   587

CONJUGAL
All Heaven would ring with the conjugal uproar   117 To Eliza   28
Serene and noble,--conjugal, but cold   966 Juan   14   688

CONJURED
They had conjured up stern Nimrod from his ashes   557 Sardan   1   420

CONJURER
(See BOTTLE-CONJURER)

CONNAL
rise! The son of Connal calls; thy   130 Calmar   124

CONN'D
And oft her Koran conn'd apart   330 Abydos   2   103
And founded Doctors' Commons:--I have conn'd   903 Juan   9   422

CONNECT
And so she thought it prudent to connect her   443 Beppo   231
Which I with their amusement will connect   772 Juan   1   1667

CONNECTED
Herself in all matters connected with learning   278 Blues   1   74
Despair and Genius are too oft connected   463 Dante   4   39
Am aught connected with that city. Then   709 Werner   4   288
A guardian green in years, a ward connected   914 Juan   10   454

CONNECTION
With the Scripture in connection   196 Rogers   15
The dear connection   200 Stanzas ·B   63
Own brief connection led me, honour. Then   692 Werner   2   584
And that still keeping up the old connection   755 Juan   1   529
Added to his connection with the sea   790 Juan   2   996
Of fault or temper ruin'd the connection   802 Juan   3   77
Tears shed into the grave of the connection   807 Juan   3   399
They all alike admired their new connection   857 Juan   6   320
Or a bell-wether form the flock's connection   873 Juan   7   382
With modern history has but small connection   897 Juan   9   52
And, as the isthmus of the grand connection   989 Juan   16   599

CONNECTIONS
To last--of all connections the most steady   804 Juan   3   197
In love and war) how odd are the connections   904 Juan   9   515
A second for her excellent connections   972 Juan   15   271

CONNECTION'S
At their lord's, son's, or similar connection's   993 Juan   16   807

CONNECTS
The sensual for a short time but connects us   964 Juan   14   581

CONNEXION
My intimate connexion;--'Cousin Idenstein   682 Werner   1   688

CONNEXIONS
Connexions stronger then he chose to avow   985 Juan   16   292

CONNIVANCE
(See also LONG-CONNIVING)
Escape? He's gone. With your connivance? With   721 Werner   5   521

CONNOISSEUR
Might shock a connoisseur; but when combined   949 Juan   13   531
But as Lord Henry was a connoisseur   988 Juan   16   497

CONNOISSEURS
But let the connoisseurs explain their merits   288 Vision   232

CONNOISSEUR'S
Nor dreads the connoisseur's fastidious view   264 Hints   575

CONNOISSEURSHIP
How well his connoisseurship understands   63 Harold   4   471

CONNUBIAL
Of faith connubial: where it is not--where   514 Faliero   2   381

CONNUBIAL
Thou mak'st the chaste connubial state precarious   800 Juan   2   1641
There's nothing wrong in a connubial kiss   802 Juan   3   62
No process proved connubial animosity   850 Juan   5   1182
And for their rights connubial make a stand   854 Juan   6   85
The filling up their whole connubial cargo   863 Juan   6   719
No bickerings, no connubial turmoil   966 Juan   14   686

CONQUER
Too much, to conquer for the poet's sake   66 Harold   4   673
Her warriors but to conquer--she who veil'd   67 Harold   4   753
To that when further worlds to conquer fail'd   72 Harold   4   1012
I conquer half my bosom's sadness   134 Lady-D   40
Fight, conquer, till we're free   162 War Song   20
To conquer ages, and with time to cope   254 Bards   950
Thy legs must move to conquer as they fly   273 Waltz   9
On shores he wept to conquer, though unknown   298 Age   32
He wept for worlds to conquer--half the earth   298 Age   35
He 'wept for worlds to conquer!' he who ne'er   298 Age   39
Beholds him conquer, but, alas! not die   301 Age   204
Alas! thou wilt not conquer, but purvey   304 Age   475
And he may crush--not conquer--still it stings   342 Corsair   1   280
And feels he yet can conquer and command   363 Corsair   3   505
That some can conquer, and that all would claim   367 Lara   1   80
The first thy subjects have no heart to conquer   552 Sardan   1   127
Thy planets and their portents. When we conquer   562 Sardan   2   70
Go forth, and conquer! Now, I am alone   574 Sardan   3   173
No--here I stand or fall. If that you conquer   585 Sardan   4   492
Strike with a better aim! Ay, if we conquer   587 Sardan   4   581
From battlement to battlement. Then conquer   733 Deformed   1   780
You lose time--they will conquer Rome without
    thee   737 Deformed   2   149
Might conquer for himself then. Mutineer   740 Deformed   2   324
France could not even conquer your great name   896 Juan   9   3
I know not who may conquer: if I could   899 Juan   9   189

CONQUER'D
Woe to the conqu'ring, not the conquer'd host   8 Harold   1   304
The shrieks of the conquer'd, the conquerors'
    yell   30 Harold   2   678
Nor blush for those who conquer'd on that plain   45 Harold   3   603
And fought and conquer'd, and the same course
    steer'd   68 Harold   4   797
And came--and saw--and conquer'd! But the man   68 Harold   4   811
Can tyrants but by tyrants conquer'd be   69 Harold   4   856
We neither conquer'd in the classic strife   126 Recoll   334
But weakness conquer'd--swam his dizzy glance   184 Julian   36
And the last Conquer'd own'd the line   197 Duel   19
'Almost as quickly as he conquer'd Spain   308 Age   724
Which conquer'd hearts they ceased to prize   386 Corinth   205
Who came and conquer'd; such, wherever rise   420 Island   2   99
When Genoa conquer'd; they have further cause   504 Faliero   1   329
I have fought and bled; commanded, ay, and
    conquer'd   506 Faliero   1   459
Who perish'd in the field, where I since
    conquer'd   519 Faliero   3   37
Victors of him who oft had conquer'd for them   547 Faliero   5   650
When all the ills of conquer'd states shall
    cling thee   549 Faliero   5   780
Who conquer'd this same golden realm of Ind   553 Sardan   1   198
Conquer'd the whole of India, did he not   554 Sardan   1   213
She could not keep when conquer'd? Mighty though   571 Sardan   3   7
And that is--but they have not conquer'd yet   603 Foscari   2   90
Save what I am. He conquer'd; let him reign   629 Cain   1   130
He as a conqueror will call the conquer'd   645 Cain   2   648
The walls for which he conquer'd and be greater   733 Deformed   1   781

CONQUEREST
A father. If thou conquerest, they shall reign   582 Sardan   4   286

CONQUERING
Th' octogenarian chief, Byzantium's conquering foe   57 Harold   4   108
And my frame perish even in conquering pain   75 Harold   4 1227
When Edward bade his conquering bands advance   111 Examination   15
Disarm'd and baffled by your conquering hand   126 Recoll   281
Dramatic 'spirit drives a conquering car   170 Address-B   19
Disguised--discover'd--conquering--ta'en--
    condemn'd   352 Corsair   2   389
And call'd the 'kingdom' of a conquering foe   454 Venice-B   122
Of fellow-soldiers conquering without thee   576 Sardan   3   285

CONQUEROR
Conqueror and captive of the earth art thou   40 Harold   3   325
On whom we tread. For this the conqueror rears   68 Harold   4   823
For the first Conqueror gave us Ground   197 Duel   18
And left the name of conqueror more than king   239 Conquest   3
Illustrious conqueror of common sense   245 Bards   220
The cause conqueror in this sudden fray   376 Lara   2   93
That latest conqueror of Greece   386 Corinth   148
Forth as a conqueror. By all the stars   553 Sardan   1   169
And ancient conqueror. Some wine, I say   553 Sardan   1   205
Degrades the very conqueror. To have pluck'd   562 Sardan   2   83
The conqueror has left thee. Follow me   636 Cain   1   558
He as a conqueror will call the conquer'd   645 Cain   2   648

CONQUEROR
Beheld a conqueror, or look'd along   725 Deformed   1   187
Thou art a conqueror; the chosen knight   730 Deformed   1   572
You are a Conqueror--command your Slave   744 Deformed   3   159
For this great conqueror play'd the corporal   874 Juan   7   442
Suwarrow now was conqueror--a match   895 Juan   8 1057
Such as the conqueror William did repay   911 Juan   10   278
The conqueror at least; who, ere Time renders   925 Juan   11   475

CONQUERORS
By their contagion,--Conquerors and Kings   41 Harold   3   380
What want these outlaws conquerors should have   42 Harold   3   429
Cured all ambition? Did the conquerors heap   72 Harold   4 1004
Of these, the Conquerors of the earth   181 Ode-A   108
To teach a lesson conquerors will not learn   300 Age   186
Ten thousand conquerors for a single sage   301 Age   244
Kings, conquerors, and markets most of all   305 Age   575
With conquerors and virtue's other foes   456 Dante   1   57
Sons of the conquerors who overthrew   460 Dante   2   113
Conquerors on foreign shores and the far wave   461 Dante   3   46
Conquerors of high renown but full of scars   463 Dante   4   9
I leave such things to conquerors; enough   555 Sardan   1   309
In the camp of the conquerors; behold   592 Sardan   5   295
Till they are conquerors--then do as you may   736 Deformed   2   136
They all were heroes, conquerors, and cuckolds   800 Juan   2 1648
Which with your conquerors is a common prank   868 Juan   7   70

CONQUEROR'S
None hugg'd a conqueror's chain, save fallen
    Chivalry   18 Harold   1   881
The camp, the host, the fight, the conqueror's
    career   33 Harold   2   845
The conqueror's sword in bearing fame away   67 Harold   4   733
And the thunderbolt burst on the conqueror's head   221 Jerusalem   16
What shall return?--the conqueror's broken car   301 Age   200
The conqueror's yet unbroken heart! Again   301 Age   201
'Tis gold, not steel, that rears the conqueror's
    arch   307 Age   685
A conqueror's more than captive's air is seen   351 Corsair   2   301

CONQUERORS'
The shrieks of the conquer'd, the conquerors'
    yell   30 Harold   2   678
So many conquerors' cars were daily driven   285 Vision   35

CONQUERS
The Queen who conquers all must yield to thee   14 Harold   1   667
Love conquers age--so Hafiz hath averr'd   29 Harold   2   561
Consents to death, since he but conquers agony   76 Harold   4 1254
Who conquers me shall find a stubborn foe   256 Bards   1052
Their country conquers with their martyrdom   402 Sonnet-F   7

CONQUEST
Conquest and Fame: but Britons rarely swerve   22 Harold   2   170
By their right arms the conquest must be wrought   31 Harold   2   722
The milk of conquest yet within the dome   68 Harold   4   786
Your eye for conquest beams prepared   98 To Lesbia   31
Our slumbering foes of future conquest dream   106 Nisus   102
With me the conquest and the labour share   108 Nisus   232
Too flush'd with carnage, and with conquest warm   109 Nisus   280
And here we earn'd the conquest dearly bought   124 Recoll   144
And crush, oh! noble conquest! crush a Boy   143 Soliloquy   66
Secure of his conquest before   162 Romaic-A   26
When the meteor of conquest allured me too far   186 Napoleon   6
In this poor planet's conquest; nor, alas   290 Vision   315
And less to conquest than to Korans trust   347 Corsair   2   42
And those who fought for conquest strike for life   350 Corsair   2   240
To me war is no glory--conquest no   586 Sardan   4   505
Leaning dejected on his club of conquest   725 Deformed   1   234
Upon the eve of conquest such as ours   732 Deformed   1   745
A moment's error in the heat of conquest   740 Deformed   2   334
The conquest which you led to. Get you hence   740 Deformed   2   335
For cash and conquest, as if from a cushion   875 Juan   7   508
As hath been done, mere conquest to advance   878 Juan   8   22
Of conquest and its consequences, which   889 Juan   8   719
Of conquest, and his guard of grenadiers   914 Juan   10   464
Of coxcombry or conquest: no abuse   969 Juan   15   92

CONQUESTS
But yielded back his conquests: he was more   71 Harold   4   996
Mark! where his carnage and his conquests cease   333 Abydos   2   430
But gladden'd where her harmless conquests spread   454 Venice-B   113
Not so:--of all his conquests a few columns   554 Sardan   1   215
'Tis not his conquests keep his name in fashion   853 Juan   6   30

CONQUEST'S
Soon, soon shall Conquest's fiery foot intrude   11 Harold   1   480
Than all the columns Conquest's minions rear   420 Island   2   92

CONQU'RING
Woe to the conqu'ring, not the conquer'd host   8 Harold   1   304

CONRAD
''Tis he--'tis Conrad; here--as wont--alone   340 Corsair   1   133

CONRAD

'To-night, Lord Conrad?' 'Ay! at set of sun   340 Corsair 1 158
Yet they repine not--so that Conrad guides   340 Corsair 1 171
Lest he to Conrad rather should betray   341 Corsair 1 221
Yet was not Conrad thus by Nature sent   342 Corsair 1 249
My Conrad! learn the joys of peace to share   343 Corsair 1 389
Be silent, Conrad!--dearest! come and share   344 Corsair 1 420
Thus Conrad, too, will quit me for the main   344 Corsair 1 448
Kiss'd her cold forehead--turn'd--is Conrad gone 345 Corsair 1 481
Stern Conrad down, nor once he turn'd his head   345 Corsair 1 506
For well had Conrad learn'd to curb the crowd   346 Corsair 1 539
'Call Pedro here!' He comes, and Conrad bends   346 Corsair 1 561
So well could Conrad tame their fiercest mood   350 Corsair 2 219
Brief time had Conrad now to greet Gulnare   350 Corsair 2 225
Conrad beheld the danger, he beheld   350 Corsair 2 241
And left proud Conrad fetter'd and alone   351 Corsair 2 325
Sate Conrad, fetter'd in the Pacha's power   352 Corsair 2 367
Not much could Conrad of his sentence blame   352 Corsair 2 370
Their eyes had envied Conrad his repose   353 Corsair 2 416
Whate'er it was that flash'd on Conrad, now   353 Corsair 2 454
Had Conrad waited for that single sail   356 Corsair 3   74
Sits Triumph--Conrad taken, fall'n the rest   357 Corsair 3 142
What last proclaim'd they--Conrad still the same 359 Corsair 3 283
That hated tyrant, Conrad--he must bleed   360 Corsair 3 319
And Conrad following, at her beck, obey'd   362 Corsair 3 448
Up rose keen Conrad from his silent trance   362 Corsair 3 490
''Tis Conrad! Conrad!' shouting from the deck   363 Corsair 3 496
Than haughty Conrad how they win their way   363 Corsair 3 511
To Conrad turns her faint imploring eye   363 Corsair 3 516
Which--Conrad safe--to fate resign'd the rest   363 Corsair 3 519
This Conrad mark'd, and felt--ah! could he less 363 Corsair 3 523
And 'midst them Conrad seeks Medora's tower   364 Corsair 3 568
And Conrad comes not, came not since that day   366 Corsair 3 688
Without there, Herman, Weilburg, Peter Conrad   675 Werner   1 259

CONRAD'S

In Conrad's form seems little to admire   341 Corsair 1 195
'In Conrad's absence wouldst thou have it glad   343 Corsair 1 366
Secure, unnoted, Conrad's prow pass'd by   347 Corsair 1 599
Invited Conrad's bugle, and the din   349 Corsair 2 187
A stern delight was fix'd in Conrad's eye   350 Corsair 2 198
But who is she whom Conrad's arms convey   350 Corsair 2 221
By Conrad's mandate safely were bestow'd   351 Corsair 2 257
For Conrad's plans matured, at once were done   352 Corsair 2 385
His fellow's mournful guess at Conrad's fate   356 Corsair 3   90
Breathed Conrad's spirit, and forbade despair   357 Corsair 3 126
Now with Gulnare, and now in Conrad's cell   357 Corsair 3 134
How much had Conrad's memory to review   362 Corsair 3 453
On Conrad's stricken soul exhaustion prest   365 Corsair 3 646
The sun goes forth, but Conrad's day is dim   365 Corsair 3 656

CONSCIENCE

Nor livelier Satirist the conscience pierce   66 Harold 4 691
Whose conscience won't disturb their slumber   95 Granta   16
In thee the wounded conscience courts relief   120 Newstead-A 19
But saved thee all that conscience fears   174 Remember-B 10
Add Conscience, too, this bargain is your own   227 Answer-C   6
Prick not the poet's conscience as a curse   268 Hints   834
The thought that Conscience must embrace   313 Giaour   274
But conscience wrung away the power   390 Corinth   541
For ne'er can man his conscience all assuage   416 Island 1   63
Man's conscience is the oracle of God   417 Island 1 124
To lands where, save their conscience, none
  accuse   418 Island 1 212
His own still conscience smote him for the act   509 Faliero 2   42
Sorrow and shame and conscience seem at war   531 Faliero 4 235
According to my honour and my conscience   621 Foscari 5   46
A quiet conscience makes one so serene   757 Juan   1 662
I leave you to your conscience as before   766 Juan   1 1253
But at sixteen the conscience rarely gnaws   767 Juan   1 1333
Fine truths; even Conscience, too, has a tough
  job   800 Juan   2 1622
And conscience ask a curious sort of question   835 Juan   5 236
And for your conscience, only learn to nerve it 943 Juan   13 142
But leave them to the conscience of the nations 970 Juan   15 144

CONSCIENTIOUS

And, undisturb'd by conscientious qualms   246 Bards   325

CONSCIOUS

And conscious Reason whisper'd to despise   8 Harold 1 321
Ye starry spheres! thou conscious Heaven! attest 110 Nisus   369
Others appear more conscious of defect   113 Prologue   10
She whom a conscious grace shall thus refine   119 Answer-A   31
And if, when conscious on the morrow   173 Not False   15
A conscious twilight of his blazing reign   299 Age   90
But conscious shepherds bless it still   329 Abydos 2   43
As if each calmly conscious star   397 Parisina   57
But she must lay her conscious head   397 Parisina   67
And was, scarce conscious what I wist   405 Chillon   237
To which you only and the Night are conscious   527 Faliero 3 610
Be conscious to a single present spot   641 Cain   2 327
How beautiful she look'd! her conscious heart   759 Juan   1 841
As though they were quite conscious of her   845 Juan   5 884
  station

CONSCIOUSNESS

Of Consciousness awaking to her woes   19 Harold 1 941
None that, with kindred consciousness endued   23 Harold 2 231
Yet still with consciousness; and there it stands 45 Harold 3 622
Till consciousness will vainly wake   166 Away   23
With all the consciousness that he   402 Parisina   575
Space and eternity--and consciousness   484 Manfred 2   47

CONSCRIPT

Say, conscript fathers, shall she be admitted   542 Faliero 5 308

CONSECRATE

Can blazon evil deeds or consecrate a crime   4 Harold 1   27
And consecrate the oath with draught, and dance
  till morn   15 Harold 1 710

CONSECRATED

Though classic ground and consecrated most   26 Harold 2 413
Once consecrated to the sepulchre   27 Harold 2 457
Let such approach this consecrated land   34 Harold 2 873
Who glorify thy consecrated pages   52 Harold 3 1026
This consecrated name, till now assign'd   303 Age   392
The cup of consecrated gold   395 Corinth   999
This--this shall be a consecrated spot   440 Tasso   240
Have consecrated my last moments to her   623 Foscari 5 185
Which shall be consecrated to his rites   626 Foscari 5 346

CONSECRATES

On the same spot still consecrates the scene   169 Address-A   23
The glorious death that consecrates his fall   272 Minerva   290
Which consecrates our undertaking more   526 Faliero 3 534

CONSENT

For gardens seem, by one consent   101 Lady-B   17
Blank verse is now, with one consent, allied   258 Hints   117
Without thy free consent, command   327 Abydos 1 315
His hope would win without consent   386 Corinth   182
Seem'd to consent, and all events were friendly 568 Sardan 2 396
I'll not consent. You have consented to   619 Foscari 4 263
My sire and uncle--I consent. Men may   619 Foscari 4 274
He hath ta'en a jump i' the dark. But you
  consent   710 Werner 4 391
And whispering 'I will ne'er consent'--consented 761 Juan   1 936

CONSENTED

His father gods consented. Menaced, rather   571 Sardan 3   30
I'll not consent. You have consented to   619 Foscari 4 263
And whispering 'I will ne'er consent'--consented 761 Juan   1 936
Juan consented to march on through thunder   891 Juan   8 819
She had consented to create again   962 Juan   14 439

CONSENTING

No more beneath soft Eve's consenting star   11 Harold 1 499
The Queen of tides on high consenting shone   32 Harold 2 760
It is resolved, they march--consenting Night   379 Lara   2 320

CONSENTS

Consents to death, but conquers agony   76 Harold 4 1254

CONSEQUENCE

A consequence of prayer, refused the law   291 Vision   386
Have pierced his heart; and in their consequence 489 Manfred 2 437
The consequence will sanctify the deed   519 Faliero 3   73
The consequence of all which led thee here   532 Faliero 4 292
But to prevent the consequence of great ones   703 Werner 3 515
But let the consequence alight on him   716 Werner 5 201
This is the consequence of giving matter   735 Deformed 1 884
The consequence was easily foreseen   782 Juan   2 545
The consequence was awful in the extreme   784 Juan   2 626
Dismay, the usual consequence of dreams   862 Juan   6 618
Began, as is the consequence of fear   862 Juan   6 626
Sultana, think upon the consequence   866 Juan   6 906
And the sweet consequence of large society   886 Juan   8 539
The consequence is, being of no party   899 Juan   9 201
Of the sad consequence of going astray   935 Juan   12 350

CONSEQUENCES

I'll meet the consequences. You shall do so   715 Werner 5 157
Before the consequences grow too awful   803 Juan   3   95
(Although the consequences of such frisks   856 Juan   6 229
Of conquest and its consequences, which   889 Juan   8 719
Yet as the consequences are as bright   922 Juan   11 267

CONSEQUENTIAL

Of what they deem themselves most consequential 958 Juan   14 158

CONSIDER

But consider, dear Inkel, she's one of the 'Blues 279 Blues 1 100
Nay, stay, my dear fellow--consider--I'm wrong   279 Blues   1 103
Let me consider--of efficient troops   505 Faliero 1 353
Alas! why will you thus consider it   514 Faliero 2 409
'Tis not the moment to consider thus   520 Faliero 3   81
An hour's truce to consider. But an hour's   592 Sardan 5 343

CONSIDER
Let's change the theme. I wish you to consider   709 Werner   4   335
And all are to be sold, if you consider   834 Juan   5   211

CONSIDERABLE
Was reckon'd a considerable time   925 Juan   11   439
Considerable talent in my way   967 Juan   14   784

CONSIDERATION
Now take it in consideration   145 Becher-B   54
And his disguise with due consideration   864 Juan   6   790

CONSIDER'D
Must be consider'd, till the hour shall come   540 Faliero   5   153
If all things be consider'd: first, there was   774 Juan   2   18

CONSIGN
Consign their souls to man's eternal foe   355 Corsair   2   553

CONSIGN'D
And when thy sons to fetters are consign'd   402 Sonnet-F   5
Though (some, no doubt,) consign'd to powers
   which may   626 Foscari   5   335
Of every monarch, till they are consign'd   854 Juan   6   99
An order from her majesty consign'd   907 Juan   9   665

CONSIST
The party might consist of thirty-three   951 Juan   13   659

CONSISTED
His suite consisted of three servants and   777 Juan   2   193
Consisted of--we give the sex the pas'   951 Juan   13   626

CONSISTENCY
Preserve consistency from first to last   259 Hints   182
It is consistency which forms and proves it   514 Faliero   2   393

CONSISTENT
But if a writer should be quite consistent   979 Juan   15   695

CONSISTORY
And merely state, though not for the consistory   988 Juan   16   541

CONSISTS
For it only consists in the word   116 Strephon   36
Small care hath he of what his tomb consists   300 Age   117
Consists in slavery--no. I have heard it said   634 Cain   1   417

CONSOLATION
To all, save one, is consolation known   85 Epitaph   27
Love and hope upon earth bring no more
   consolation   92 Caroline-D   19
Celestial consolation brings   131 L'Amitie   7
Of this last consolation, though so scant   300 Age   124
If I could yield you any consolation   833 Juan   5   103
And, strange to say, they found some consolation   876 Juan   7   599
Drew quiet consolation through its hint   911 Juan   10   271
He had his judge's joke for consolation   952 Juan   13   704
No doubt a consolation to his dust   997 Juan   17   64

CONSOLE
Just to console sad glory for being glorious   945 Juan   13   256

CONSOLED
Another chief consoled his destined bride   366 Lara   1   35
And she would have consoled, but knew not how   846 Juan   5   945
Was much consoled by his own repartee   986 Juan   16   392

CONSOLING
Consoling us with--'Would you had thought twice   961 Juan   14   375

CONSOMME
The salmi, the consomme, the puree   977 Juan   15   562

CONSONANTS
And others of twelve consonants apiece   869 Juan   7   117

CONSORT
And desolate consort--vainly wert thou wed   80 Harold   4   1520
'I know he was a constant consort; own   290 Vision   361
Her consort still is absent, and her crew   344 Corsair   1   414
From Ermellina, consort of the Dane   468 Morgante   129
By blackening publicly his sovereign's consort   515 Faliero   2   435
Between my consort and my kinsmen. These   545 Faliero   5   537
My consort to their justice; for methinks   548 Faliero   5   708
'Tis well--I rather would consort with spirits   630 Cain   1   188
And Madame Idenstein (my consort, stranger   675 Werner   1   263
Not easy to persuade my consort of   681 Werner   1   661
For when his pious consort gave him stones   955 Juan   14   7
Or what his consort did: if he could brook   961 Juan   14   357

CONSORTEST
   Reports be true), with whom thou consortest   709 Werner   4   338

CONSORTS
And kings and consorts oft are mystified   846 Juan   5   918

CONSORT'S
His consort's brother, minion of Ionia   552 Sardan   1   87

CONSPICUOUS
Are mix'd conspicuous: some recline in groups   28 Harold   2   523
Conspicuous by his yellow cap   315 Giaour   550
That too conspicuous from the precious stones   573 Sardan   3   132
Until to some conspicuous square they pass   922 Juan   11   247
As will environ a conspicuous man. Some   927 Juan   11   581

CONSPICUOUSLY
So honour'd--and conspicuously there   70 Harold   4   898

CONSPIRACY
Conspiracy or Congress to be made   746 Juan   Ded   109
Has been accused (I doubt not by conspiracy   839 Juan   5   482

CONSPIRATORS
But shows a thousand crown'd conspirators   548 Faliero   5   713

CONSPIRE
On thee, in whom at once conspire   158 Florence   17
Where air and sea with rocks and woods conspire   161 Athos   14
For hitherto all hateful things conspire   490 Manfred   2   497
For ever, and for ever, they conspire   526 Faliero   3   561

CONSPIRED
When the beholder knows a Doge conspired   545 Faliero   5   512

CONSTABLE
Late constable of France: and now to be   730 Deformed   1   574
Good night, lord constable! thou wert a man   737 Deformed   2   157
The constable, beneath a warrant's banner   988 Juan   16   543

CONSTABLES
Did more than constables to keep the peace   266 Hints   670

CONSTANCE
Constance, King Richard, Hamlet, and the Devil   259 Hints   178

CONSTANCY
Too much for human constancy   173 Quotation   18
Hope constancy in wind, or corn in chaff   242 Bards   77
Of constancy to a bad, ugly woman   286 Vision   96
Shining with love, and hope, and constancy   429 Island   3   186
Had not one word to say of constancy   798 Juan   2   1520
An almost twelvemonth's constancy endangers   845 Juan   5   848

CONSTANT
And Venus, constant to her native sea   14 Harold   1   669
To nought else constant, hither deign'd to flee   14 Harold   1   670
My constant heart of fear disarms   98 To Mary   3
More constant they may prove, indeed   98 To Lesbia   35
Make for him a constant revel   197 Rogers   44
Constant to thee as in its hour   201 Ode-C   81
Constant to nought--save hazard and a whore   260 Hints   235
'I know he was a constant consort; own   290 Vision   361
Even Constant, their sole master of debate   304 Age   492
The only constant mourner o'er the dead   313 Giaour   287
More constant at confessional   386 Corinth   202
Their constant peril, and their scant relief   418 Island   1   178
To Aeolus a constant sacrifice   425 Island   2   444
His constant pipe, which never yet burn'd dim   425 Island   2   475
Who still become more constant as they cool   444 Beppo   272
Have traversed land and sea in constant duty   506 Faliero   1   462
The only being who was constant to me   532 Faliero   4   295
Thou speakest of them. True--true: constant
   thought   559 Sardan   1   569
Not from the council--there he is ever constant   563 Sardan   2   98
'Tis part of our instruction. War being constant   588 Sardan   5   102
Of daily toil and constant thought: I look   630 Cain   1   172
Love, constant love, has been my constant guest   800 Juan   2   1669
Like chastest wives from constant husbands' sides   881 Juan   8   211
Recruited all with constant married men   931 Juan   12   122

CONSTANTINE
Of Rome transplanted fell with Constantine   842 Juan   5   688

CONSTANTINOPLE
For the slave market of Constantinople   828 Juan   4   728
'Whence come ye?'--'From Constantinople last   874 Juan   7   468
Who has sail'd where picturesque Constantinople
   is   919 Juan   11   51
Constantinople, and such distant places   944 Juan   13   178

CONSTANTLY
In sight, but constantly in scent, had put me   687 Werner   2   268
And constantly? I think so; for I love   706 Werner   4   124

CONSTELLATION
A constellation of a sweeter ray   77 Harold   4   1353

CONSTELLATIONS
And the strange constellations which the Muse   56 Harold   4   53

CONSTERNATION
The moment of the general consternation   870 Juan   7   186

CONSTITUTE
To constitute a reader; there must go   950 Juan   13   579

CONSTITUTED
(See SELF-CONSTITUTED)

CONSTITUTION
His youth and constitution bore him through   912 Juan   10   339

CONSTITUTIONAL
A king in constitutional possession   940 Juan   12   659

CONSTITUTIONS
On constitutions and steam-boats of vapour   932 Juan   12   165

CONSTRAIN'D
And others still their appetites constrain'd   784 Juan   2   651

CONSTRUCTED
Because they were constructed in a hurry   870 Juan   7   202
They drew, constructed ladders, repair'd flaws   873 Juan   7   374

CONSTRUCTION
Although his anatomical construction   782 Juan   2   533
A kind construction upon them and me   859 Juan   6   447
The absence of that more sublime construction   917 Juan   10   606
Construction as your cures for hectic phthisics   939 Juan   12   571
You'll find it of a different construction   941 Juan   12   691

CONSTRUCTIVE
Nothing affected, studied, or constructive   969 Juan   15   91

CONSULAR
Noble and brave as aught of consular   508 Faliero   1   618

CONSULE
Consule Planco,' Horace said, and so   772 Juan   1 1690

CONSULT
Truth's Records you consult in vain   141 Critics   9
Consult Lord Fanny, and confide in Curll   246 Bards   372
'For that you may consult my title-page   295 Vision   650
Unravel. They look up to him, consult him   711 Werner   4   426

CONSULTING
Consulting 'the Society for Vice   935 Juan   12   335

CONSUME
Strange modes of merriment the hours consume   11 Harold   1   488
And all we deem delightful and consume   68 Harold   4   771
Then let the secret fire consume   90 To M.S.G.-A   21
Let it consume, thou shalt not know   90 To M.S.G.-A   22
As ye pass by the tomb where my ashes consume   115 The Tear   43
Festering alike in shrouds, consume   128 Answer-B   32
Ah, wherefore not consume it--and depart   336 Abydos   2   650
In life, to wear their hearts out, and consume   458 Dante   1   151
The Bard of Chivalry, will both consume   462 Dante   3   150
So quick and restless that it would consume   509 Faliero   2   12
To sway his nations than consume his life   551 Sardan   1   22
Must I consume my life--this little life   557 Sardan   1   438
Must I consume my own, which never beat   608 Foscari   3   10

CONSUMED
Of passion had consumed themselves to dust   43 Harold   3   470
Consumed in Glory's blaze   146 Adieu   84
Were burnt for beacons; cities were consumed   189 Darkness   13
So let him be consumed. From out the past   290 Vision   347
To view with fire their scorpion nest consumed   348 Corsair   2   80
Buried, and raised again--consumed by worms   580 Sardan   4   161
Though his possessions have been all consumed   626 Foscari   5   344

CONSUMERS
The cold consumers of their clay   319 Giaour   950
To the consumers of fish, fowl, and game   993 Juan   16   803

CONSUMING
(See also ALL-CONSUMING)
Of her consuming cheek the autumnal leaf-like red   70 Harold   4   918
Which unconsumed are still consuming   221 Mariamne   24
Consuming but not killing. Circumstance   600 Foscari   1   293
To prove the public debt is not consuming us   901 Juan   9   277

CONSUMMATE
Eternal beacons of consummate crime   253 Bards   828
the consummate fiends! A thousand fold   617 Foscari   4   173

CONSUMMATION
Fit consummation of an earthly race   251 Bards   680

CONSUMMATION
Which led to such a consummation. Lo   594 Sardan   5   449

CONSUMPTIVE
And being consumptive, live on a milk diet   973 Juan   15   328

CONTACT
Though accident, blind contact, and the strong   73 Harold   4 1118
The genial contact gently undergo   276 Waltz   209
From this lewd grasp and lawless contact warm   277 Waltz   237
In contact; and sometimes even a fair stranger's   845 Juan   5   847
Into close contact. Though reserved, nor caught   943 Juan   13   116

CONTAGION
By their contagion,--Conquerors and Kings   41 Harold   3   380
Deceit infect not, near Contagion soil   208 Sketch   23

CONTAGIOUS
Examples of this kind are so contagious   763 Juan   1 1103

CONTAIN
Lands that contain the monuments of Eld   19 Harold   1   952
The cause of the curses all annals contain   203 Avatar   63
Contain the essence of the true sublime   245 Bards   246
For sometimes they contain a deal of fun   442 Beppo   159
Our hands contain the hearts of men   488 Manfred   2   352
Why, those few lines contain the history   555 Sardan   1   295
'Tis closed. You have said well; I will contain   646 Cain   3   17
Whatever star contain thy glory   655 Heaven   38
For an immortal. If the skies contain   656 Heaven   133
Contain no longer. Softly! mighty well   701 Werner   3   417
From any thing, this epic will contain   980 Juan   16   18

CONTAIN'D
And living as if earth contain'd no tomb   50 Harold   3   917
And looking to the stars. They had contain'd   71 Harold   4   992
Which once contain'd our youth's retreat   134 E. N. Long   100
A fearful hope was all the world contain'd   189 Darkness   18
Contain'd at once his captive and his court   352 Corsair   2   369
And the cold flowers her colder hand contain'd   364 Corsair   3   605
Contain'd the dead of ages gone   395 Corinth   966
Contain'd, together with its penalty   501 Faliero   1   80
Or that this crooked coffer, which contain'd   735 Deformed   2   880
Nimrods, whose canvass scarce contain'd the steed   950 Juan   13   558
Superbly, and contain'd a world of zest   977 Juan   15   592

CONTAINING
Divided in twelve books; each book containing   771 Juan   1 1594
Mount Pleasant, as containing nought to please   921 Juan   11   163
Containing ingots, bags of dollars, coins   931 Juan   12   90

CONTAINS
The Scipios' tomb contains no ashes now   66 Harold   4   707
Contains the 'bravest of the brave   187 Ode-B   10
Contains no fabled hero's ashes   329 Abydos   2   34
A word against a world which still contains   713 Werner   5   40
Turkey contains no bells, and yet men dine   837 Juan   5   393

CONTAMINATE
Methinks thou wouldst contaminate all hands   711 Werner   4   441

CONTEMN
That just habitual scorn, which could contemn   41 Harold   3   354
With a pure passion? should I not contemn   47 Harold   3   710
Let those whose souls contemn the pleasing power   119 Answer-A   17
Which, worn by thee, ev'n slaves contemn   185 Belshaz-A   15
They may crush, but they shall not contemn   210 Augusta-B   22
Admit, reject, contemn; and what know you   955 Juan   14   18

CONTEMN'D
For whom thou wert contemn'd, reviled   330 Abydos   2   181
The Serfs contemn'd the one, and hated both   378 Lara   2   229
Contemn'd and trampled on; but the whole people   507 Faliero   5   490
This happens in the most contemn'd and abject   623 Foscari   5   148

CONTEMNED
And lavish'd treasures, and contemned virtues   555 Sardan   1   282

CONTEMNER
Dear, d--d contemner of my schoolboy songs   265 Hints   605

CONTEMPLATE
Who can contemplate Fame through clouds unfold   36 Harold   3   95
Our spirits to the size of that they contemplate   78 Harold   4 1422
Such scene his soul no more could contemplate   368 Lara   1   174

CONTEMPLATED
And more than once contemplated his size   473 Morgante   450

CONTEMPLATES
Contemplates the scenes of her youth with a tear   91 Caroline-C   8

CONTEMPLATION
Or lonely Contemplation thus might stray   44 Harold   3   566

CONTEMPLATION
Those who find contemplation in the urn .... 47 Harold 3 718
Of contemplation; and the azure gloom .... 74 Harold 4 1151
To separate contemplation the great whole .... 78 Harold 4 1406
Mid scenes where Heavenly Contemplation loves ..... 161 Athos 12
From contemplation--where serenely wrought .... 175 Sonnet-A 3
A fund for contemplation;--to admire .... 211 Augusta-C 58
Sunk he in Comtemplation, till the Cape .... 362 Corsair 3 454
And deeds, and contemplation, and have met .... 456 Dante 1 45
In that slight startle from his contemplation ..... 907 Juan 10 2
I say, Don Juan, wrapt in contemplation .... 919 Juan 11 65
The mind is lost in mighty contemplation .... 976 Juan 15 545
For contemplation rather than his pillow .... 982 Juan 16 114
'Twas a mere quiet smile of contemplation .... 992 Juan 16 785

CONTEMPLATIVE
At once adventurous and contemplative .... 830 Juan 4 850

CONTEMPLATOR
So that the contemplator might approve .... 545 Faliero 5 510

CONTEMPT
Contempt, in silence, be the pedant's lot .... 123 Recoll 117
With fervent contempt evermore to disdain you ..... 147 To Anne-A 10
Nor deem'd Contempt could thus make mirth .... 181 Ode-A 107
Half an age's contempt was an error of fame .... 203 Avatar 67
My contempt for a nation so servile, though sore .. 204 Avatar 126
No! though contempt hath mark'd the spurious
  brood .... 252 Bards 813
From all affection and from all contempt .... 342 Corsair 1 272
The Joy untasted, the contempt or hate .... 352 Corsair 2 344
With him contempt forbore to mock the poor .... 378 Lara 2 203
Would bring contempt on all authority .... 500 Faliero 1 35
Is't nothing to have brought into contempt .... 512 Faliero 2 254
Contempt, but from the bathos' vast abyss .... 815 Juan 3 892
As if the peasant's coarse contempt were vented ... 829 Juan 4 835

CONTEMPTIBLE
His claims alone were too contemptible .... 694 Werner 2 741

CONTEMPTUOUS
Famed for contemptuous breach of sacred ties ...... 228 Windsor 1
Contemptuous once, and now no less absurd .... 271 Minerva 254
To such, brief answer and contemptuous eye .... 339 Corsair 1 81
And half contemptuous turn'd to pass away .... 372 Lara 1 447
Cold to the great, contemptuous to the high .... 377 Lara 2 184
The grossest insult, most contemptuous crime ...... 502 Faliero 1 152

CONTEND
That rise--convulse--contend--that freeze or glow . 341 Corsair 1 241
Contend not with you on the winged steed .... 746 Juan Ded 58
And to contend with thoughts she could not
  smother .... 760 Juan 1 875

CONTENDED
The pale contended with the purple rose .... 793 Juan 2 1195
Others contended they were but in spring .... 856 Juan 6 278

CONTENDING
Contending tempests on his naked head .... 42 Harold 3 404
As Day and Night contending were, until .... 59 Harold 4 248
On Marston, with Rupert, 'gainst traitors
  contending .... 86 Leaving NA 17
Who, still contending in the studious race .... 122 Recoll 39
Makes even contending tribes in peace unite .... 348 Corsair 2 121
Contending with low wants and lofty will .... 482 Manfred 1 305
Mix'd, and contending without end or order .... 493 Manfred 3 166

CONTENDS
Where man contends for fame and life .... 325 Abydos 1 139

CONTENT
Next night I'll be content to freeze .... 101 Lady-B 42
Not content with depriving your bodies of spirit .. 116 To Eliza 10
But she must be content to shine .... 163 Malta 39
I am content; and for the past I feel .... 212 Augusta-C 114
And surely he should be content .... 233 Ballad-B 43
Content you with the praise you get .... 235 Epilogue 17
Not so with us, though minor bards, content .... 244 Bards 199
And Dibdin's nonsense yield complete content ...... 249 Bards 563
And, quite content, no more shall interpose .... 256 Bards 1035
So you indeed, with care (but be content .... 257 Hints 77
To heathen Greek, content with native strains ..... 262 Hints 426
Sir! Pray be content with your portion of praise .. 281 Blues 2 69
He amplified to every lord's content .... 306 Age 580
Excepting to grow moderate and content .... 306 Age 609
To which Morgante answer'd, 'I'm content .... 471 Morgante 360
So much I see you with our stay content .... 475 Morgante 608
Content thyself with what thou know'st already .... 494 Manfred 3 212
I trust, for torture--I'm content. What--him ...... 564 Sardan 2 183
Not ill content to vary the smooth scene .... 570 Sardan 2 543
But this the gods avert! I am content .... 571 Sardan 2 595
I am content: and, trusting in my cause .... 586 Sardan 4 502
For him and me; but mine would be content .... 601 Foscari 1 372

CONTENT
And bow me to the Duke. Are you content .... 606 Foscari 2 330
Are ye content? We will not interrupt .... 618 Foscari 4 226
Content thee with what is. Had we been so .... 628 Cain 1 45
And sin--and not content with their own sorrow .... 634 Cain 1 442
Seems dim and shadowy. Be content; it will .... 642 Cain 2 381
If then, like me, content with petty plunder ...... 690 Werner 2 458
Are you content? I take thee at thy word .... 724 Deformed 1 152
Content! I will fix here. I must commend .... 726 Deformed 1 265
Themselves a poetry. Less will content me .... 727 Deformed 1 369
But found would it content you? would you owe ..... 743 Deformed 3 126
Moderate in all his habits, and content .... 808 Juan 3 419
So pick and choose--perhaps you'll be content ..... 861 Juan 6 543
But shortly he had cause to be content .... 872 Juan 7 301
Why should not Life be equally content .... 898 Juan 9 99
He who sleeps best may be the most content .... 898 Juan 9 120
And till she doth, I fain must be content .... 899 Juan 9 175
Of metaphysics; others are content .... 936 Juan 12 414
A laureate's ode, or servile peer's content .... 962 Juan 14 464
Bards may sing what they please about Content ..... 965 Juan 14 628
Pursued an instant for her own content .... 986 Juan 16 380

CONTENTED
Contented subjects, all alike tax-proof .... 305 Age 533
Saying, 'Thou hast contented me, oh Lord .... 473 Morgante 448
Not even contented with a sceptre, still .... 540 Faliero 5 198
Thou now hadst been contented.--Oh, my son .... 628 Cain 1 46
Of a contented knowledge; but I see .... 647 Cain 3 50
Contented, when translated, means but cloy'd ...... 965 Juan 14 629

CONTENTEDLY
I by my faith disclose contentedly .... 471 Morgante 334
And lived contentedly, without complaints .... 959 Juan 14 243

CONTENTION
With beauty like yours, oh, how vain the
  contention .... 147 To Anne-A 13
With Hatred and Contention; Pain was mix'd .... 216 Dream 189

CONTENTIOUS
Midst a contentious world, striving where none
  are strong .... 46 Harold 3 661

CONTENTMENT
To make that calm contentment mine .... 135 I Would 47
With how much more contentment I resign .... 548 Faliero 5 701

CONTENTS
And quaff the contents as our nectar below .... 91 Caroline-C 28
When such a word contents a British bard .... 262 Hints 416
He read the first three lines of the contents ..... 297 Vision 812
Or its contents, it were impossible .... 494 Manfred 3 206
Jehovah said not that. No; he contents him .... 647 Cain 3 70
And if their full contents I do not give ye .... 964 Juan 14 541

CONTEST
Ill may such contest now the spirit move .... 34 Harold 2 887
Keen contest and destruction near allied .... 42 Harold 3 439
My whole life was a contest, since the day .... 211 Augusta-C 26
Where none contest the fields, the woods, the
  streams .... 418 Island 1 215

CONTESTED
Contested for a time, while the smooth gloss ...... 462 Dante 3 132

CONTESTS
But county contests cost him rather dearer .... 989 Juan 16 603

CONTEXT
And from its context thought she could divine ..... 985 Juan 16 291

CONTINENCE
But on the whole their continence was great .... 895 Juan 8 1041

CONTINENT
Some die, some fly, some languish on the
  Continent .... 928 Juan 11 631

CONTINENTAL
Your continental oaths are but incontinent .... 923 Juan 11 338

CONTINENTS
More than on continents--as if the sea .... 923 Juan 11 335
O'er far Atlantic continents or islands .... 986 Juan 16 412

CONTINENT'S
Match'd with the Continent's illumination .... 921 Juan 11 204

CONTINUAL
When teased with creditors' continual claims ...... 268 Hints 825
His waking a continual dread of death .... 652 Cain 3 431

CONTINUANCE
But a continuance of enduring thought .... 478 Manfred 1 4
The Question, or continuance of the trial .... 605 Foscari 2 262

CONTINUANCE
Of the continuance of the gale: to run   781 Juan   2   490

CONTINUATION
Or hints continuation of the species   752 Juan   1   319

CONTINUE
Have taken already, and still will continue   282 Blues   2   105
Continue what thou pleasest. Boy, retire   554 Sardan   1   246
Canst thou continue so, with such a world   598 Foscari   1   212
Hereafter; but we must continue now   697 Werner   3   135
For wishing to continue privily   700 Werner   3   315
Continue daily orisons for us   711 Werner   4   456
Continue. When we reach'd the Muldau's bridge   714 Werner   5   108
Let him continue. I will not detain you   716 Werner   5   221
But more or less continue still to tease on   837 Juan   5   382
Continue. As I said, this goodly row   856 Juan   6   259
'You, Lolah, must continue still to lie   858 Juan   6   385
But to continue:--I say not the first   884 Juan   8   409
Should so continue--'tis a point of honour   908 Juan   10   90
But to continue: though her years were waning   913 Juan   10   372

CONTINUED
Continued Michael, 'George Rex, or allege   295 Vision   654
Thus reasoning, they continued much to say   472 Morgante   383
And still continued pricking with the spur   474 Morgante   544
The honours they continued to receive   475 Morgante   601
At Keswick, and, through still continued fusion   745 Juan   Ded   35
And they continued battling hand to hand   769 Juan   1   1474
Continued still her hospitable cares   804 Juan   3   149
Continued: 'Your old regiment's allow'd   875 Juan   7   499

CONTINUES
No matter, George continues still to write   242 Bards   57

CONTINUING
And grief with grief continuing still to blend   34 Harold   2   907

CONTRA-ALTO
Soprano, basso, even the contra-alto   444 Beppo   255

CONTRACT
But your own will, no contract save your deeds   724 Deformed   1   151

CONTRACTED
Has not contracted much more debt than knowledge   946 Juan   13   336

CONTRACTIONS
Thus even good fame may suffer sad contractions   871 Juan   7   269

CONTRACTOR'S
Or some contractor's personal cupidity   870 Juan   7   211

CONTRADICT
Still I can't contradict, what so oft has been
said   116 To Eliza   15
If people contradict themselves, can I   979 Juan   15   697

CONTRADICTED
Or contradicted but with proud humility   944 Juan   13   172

CONTRADICTING
Help contradicting them, and every body   979 Juan   15   698

CONTRADICTION
'This may involve a seeming contradiction   475 Morgante   633
And that's one cause she meets with contradiction   957 Juan   14   101
Is that which passes with least contradiction   968 Juan   15   24
And cut through such canals of contradiction   979 Juan   15   703
In some things, mine's beyond all contradiction   980 Juan   16   15

CONTRARY
The foul, the fair, the contrary, the kind   23 Harold   2   250
Not at all; on the contrary, those of the lake   282 Blues   2   104
They say so (Bryant says the contrary   826 Juan   4   604
Has quite the contrary effect on vice   851 Juan   5   1256
The contrary; but then 'tis in the head   922 Juan   11   266
Nor seem embarrass'd--quite the contrary   993 Juan   16   794

CONTRAST
So shall their brighter hues contrast the glow   419 Island   2   51
In contrast with their fathers--as the slime   453 Venice-B   8
And what a contrast with the scene I left   528 Faliero   4   28
By contrast, which is what we just were wishing
all   751 Juan   1   246
And horrid was the contrast to the view   836 Juan   5   299

CONTRASTED
Clear, placid Leman! thy contrasted lake   48 Harold   3   797

CONTRIBUTE
Is to contribute to thine every wish   551 Sardan   1   68
'Obey the king--contribute to his treasure   555 Sardan   1   303
They do not much contribute to his glory   814 Juan   3   832

CONTRITE
Given with a gentle and a contrite spirit   647 Cain   3   108
Be contrite? for my father's sin, already   648 Cain   3   118

CONTRITION
Say farewell, and in peace: with full contrition   543 Faliero   5   405

CONTRIVANCES
And rich with all contrivances which grace   864 Juan   6   772

CONTRIVE
Come forth her work of gladness to contrive   40 Harold   3   268
Souls to contrive those smiling lures   143 To--A   11
And how so many years did you contrive   451 Beppo   734
Upon the moment could contrive with such   790 Juan   2   1050
'If you could just contrive,' he said, 'to stint   843 Juan   5   723
Paces were left, whereon you could contrive   884 Juan   8   370
But, if you can contrive, get next at supper   927 Juan   11   561

CONTRIVED
Contrived to glide through all my own attendants   686 Werner   2   238
So strangely were contrived these galleries   696 Werner   3   98
His death contrived to spoil a charming cause   751 Juan   1   261
Of any wicked woman, who contrived   763 Juan   1   1101
Contrived to fling the bed-clothes in a heap   764 Juan   1   1117
Juan contrived to give an awkward blow   769 Juan   1   1485
But in the long-boat they contrived to stow   779 Juan   2   369
Six flasks of wine; and they contrived to get   780 Juan   2   372
Contrived to help Pedrillo to a place   781 Juan   2   442
Along the rest, contrived to keep this den   856 Juan   6   254
Contrived to get itself comprised within it   885 Juan   8   468
Contrived to talk about the gods of late   925 Juan   11   468

CONTRIVES
Yet she somehow contrives that all things shall
be done   280 Blues   2   12

CONTROL
(See also SELF-CONTROL)
Whate'er this grief mote be which he could not
control   4 Harold   1   72
And Passion's host, that never brook'd control   20 Harold   2   52
Lone mother of dead empires, and control   66 Harold   4   696
To more immediate objects, and control   78 Harold   4   1409
Man marks the earth with ruin, his control   82 Harold   4   1605
No factious clamours can control   88 Horace   2
To shun fair science, or evade control   93 Dorset   12
Pomposus holds you in his harsh control   93 Masters   8
E'en suns, which systems now control   97 To M--   27
Held every sense in fast control   98 To Mary   24
Allan had early learn'd control   102 Alva   67
Replied Euryalus; 'it scorns control   106 Nisus   80
Precepts of prudence curb, but can't control   119 Answer-A   9
Then why should I live in a hateful control   129 Becher-A   35
If frowning Age, with cold control   133 E. N. Long   33
E'er burst from its mortal control   151 Soul-A   3
Slaves to the specious world's control   153 Friend-A   26
Many could a world control   187 French-A   11
A truce with remark, and let nothing control   282 Blues   2   127
All states, all things, all sovereigns they
control   307 Age   676
Holds not a Musselim's control   327 Abydos   1   374
Ours with one pang--one bound--escapes control   338 Corsair   1   32
For that, like thine, abhorr'd control   399 Parisina   297
The like control.--But to resume   409 Mazeppa   294
Which shall control the elements, whereof   480 Manfred   1   142
With any kind of troublesome control   757 Juan   1   654
With things not very subject to control   758 Juan   1   726
Of those who hold the kingdoms in control   968 Juan   14   814

CONTROLL'D
By Death's unequal hand alike controll'd   87 Marsus   3

CONTROLS
Whose old-establish'd board of joint controls   266 Hints   677
Extended far beyond the mere controls   291 Vision   419

CONTROUL
Now wakeful Grief disdains her mild controul   140 Ossian-A   45
While these impose a harsh controul   141 Pignus   27

CONTROULLESS
Your system feigns o'er the controulless core   761 Juan   1   924

CONUNDRUM
To serve in this conundrum of a dish   971 Juan   15   168

CONVALESCENCE
And every day help'd on his convalescence   795 Juan   2   1346
Ready for gaol, their place of convalescence   988 Juan   16   530

CONVENED
Behold the hall where chiefs were late convened   8 Harold   1   288

CONVENIENCE
To march; a great convenience to our men 884 Juan 8 371

CONVENIENT
She was a married woman; 'tis convenient 443 Beppo 185
''Twould be convenient; for these mutes have eyes 843 Juan 5 729
With her the latter, though at times convenient 904 Juan 9 497

CONVENT
The horrid crags by toppling convent crown'd 7 Harold 1 243
Full many a convent rears its glittering spire 161 Athos 11
For he declines the convent oath 319 Giaour 899
The Convent bells are ringing 400 Parisina 386
Whether in convent she abode 401 Parisina 515
The monks could pass the convent gate no more 468 Morgante 161
But sitting in the convent of Saint Saviour's 536 Faliero 4 559
The prayers of our community. Our convent 711 Werner 4 453
Julia was sent into a convent: she 770 Juan 1 1526
Of beauties cool as an Italian convent 856 Juan 6 255
Less on a convent than a coronet 951 Juan 13 680

CONVENTION
Convention is the dwarfish demon styled 8 Harold 1 297

CONVENTIONS
Fines, tutors, tasks, conventions threat in vain 260 Hints 231

CONVENT'S
The convent's white walls glisten fair on high 27 Harold 2 437

CONVERSATION
To partake of a luncheon and learn'd conversation 279 Blues 1 138
In tete-a-tete or general conversation 444 Beppo 300
At least her conversation was obscure 748 Juan 1 102
Grow tired of scientific conversation 749 Juan 1 172
Until too late for useful conversation 761 Juan 1 930
But no one troubled him with conversation 838 Juan 5 432

CONVERSATIONAL
But there's a conversational facility 970 Juan 15 155

CONVERSATIONIST
Kit-Cat, the famous Conversationist 953 Juan 13 772

CONVERSATIONS
And as the Turks abhor long conversations 449 Beppo 566
She liked quick answers in all conversations 864 Juan 6 803

CONVERSATION'S
Such as are coin'd in conversation's mint 964 Juan 14 547

CONVERSAZIONE
The conversazione; the duet 954 Juan 13 850

CONVERSE
Converse with Nature's charms and view her stores unroll'd 23 Harold 2 225
Though with them to converse can rarely be our lot 81 Harold 4 1593
Alternate converse, and their plans unfold 106 Nisus 88
Who share the converse of a college hall 123 Recoll 94
Again, as once, in converse gay 132 L'Amitie 48
In turn thy converse and thy song 169 Blank Leaf 4
They game--carouse--converse--or whet the brand 338 Corsair 1 48
'Tis said thou holdest converse with the things 491 Manfred 3 34
Unfit for mortal converse: leave me, Abel 649 Cain 3 184
For none likes more to hear himself converse 807 Juan 3 360
Suppose the converse of this precedent 997 Juan 17 37

CONVERSED
As thus our glances oft conversed 112 Quaker 21

CONVERSION
Mem--whenever a sudden conversion I want 178 Devil's Dr 201
Assist in their conversion. They are gone 739 Deformed 2 289
For all the glory your conversion brought 745 Juan Ded 43

CONVERT
The convert of revenge can feel 387 Corinth 325
And made much of his convert, as he cried 471 Morgante 362
They can convert it to a two-edged sword 540 Faliero 5 199
That's true, my Myrrha; and could I convert 572 Sardan 3 41
I grow almost a convert to your Baal 588 Sardan 5 48
The heaven which will convert her clouds to seas 659 Heaven 326
The baron's coin, when he could thus convert 698 Werner 3 210

CONVERTED
Of one to stone converted by amaze 45 Harold 3 621
Converted by Christ to his blood so divine 395 Corinth 1003
His bow converted into a cock'd hat 902 Juan 9 357
Converted foes should scorn to join with those 909 Juan 10 96
The little Turk refused to be converted 914 Juan 10 440

CONVERTS
Which young and fiery converts feel 385 Corinth 126

CONVEY
Convey reproof, nor further deign reply 339 Corsair 1 82
But who is she whom Conrad's arms convey 350 Corsair 2 221
The delegates appointed to convey 620 Foscari 4 352
And now I will convey thee to thy world 645 Cain 2 619
He writes for a detachment to convey me 681 Werner 1 620
Convey her unto the Colonna palace 741 Deformed 2 398

CONVEYANCE
Thought them worth purchase and conveyance, are 554 Sardan 1 217
Of his o'erset and water-logg'd conveyance 688 Werner 2 331
You'll mount with our young hero the conveyance 913 Juan 10 387

CONVEY'D
(See also RE-CONVEY'D)
Convey'd me from this idle shore 332 Abydos 2 354
How was that gentle sound convey'd 390 Corinth 526
Convey'd the Host aroused my rash young anger 546 Faliero 5 597
Convey'd me from the spot where I was stricken 589 Sardan 5 108
And sail in the same galley which convey'd him 605 Foscari 2 270
Which flatters, but is flattery convey'd 945 Juan 13 251
Convey'd Medea as her supercargo 965 Juan 14 608

CONVEYING
Conveying, as the electric wire 409 Mazeppa 242
But like conveying to the cat the mouse 790 Juan 2 1035

CONVEYS
No symptom of that love conveys 90 Caroline-B 2
Which to the dead a lingering fame conveys 420 Island 2 80

CONVICT
Convict by many witnesses and proofs 545 Faliero 5 483
Such names at present cut a convict figure 814 Juan 3 841

CONVICTED
And stand convicted of more truth than treason 759 Juan 1 814

CONVICTION
And understand my speech with full conviction 475 Morgante 635
There seems to me enough in the conviction 512 Faliero 2 230
There now rests, after such conviction of 538 Faliero 5 1

CONVINCE
We do not try by speaking to convince 112 Examination 32
His accomplishments! His!!! and thy country convince 203 Avatar 66
Whom nothing can convince save a full meal 734 Deformed 1 827

CONVINCED
Your smile soon convinced me suspicion was wrong 147 To Anne-A 8
She, for the future of her strength convinced 757 Juan 1 651

CONVINCES
Convinces all men, even a politician 974 Juan 15 406

CONVINCING
Convincing all, by demonstration plain 245 Bards 243
Oh! too convincing, dangerously dear 355 Corsair 2 543

CONVIVIAL
A few days after this convivial scene 474 Morgante 534

CONVOY
The convoy spread like wild swans in their flight 22 Harold 2 151

CONVULSE
And gathering storms around convulse the closing year 26 Harold 2 378
Which Earth and Heaven could not convulse 191 Prometheus-B 43
Yet jarring sects convulse a sister isle 272 Minerva 277
That rise--convulse--contend--that freeze or glow 341 Corsair 1 241
The quick successive throbs convulse 387 Corinth 333
Which for a moment would convulse 412 Mazeppa 573
Or sensual throbs convulse it, well I know 514 Faliero 2 384

CONVULSED
Calm or convulsed--in breeze, or gale, or storm 82 Harold 4 1641
Convulsed by gales you cannot weather 118 Romance 62
Convulsed the skies, as during a debate 296 Vision 738
Convulsed and quick, then gently raised to heaven 345 Corsair 1 500
Even Seyd, convulsed, o'erwhelm'd, with rage, surprise 349 Corsair 2 176
When all its elements convulsed, combined 352 Corsair 2 329
Convulsed and quick, then fix for ever 401 Parisina 461
He is convulsed--This is to be a mortal 491 Manfred 2 527

CONVULSES
Which your catastrophe convulses 231 Doctor 8

CONVULSES
Which thus convulses slumber: shall I wake him · 578 Sardan · 4 · 2

CONVULSION
And nurtured in convulsion,--of thy sire · 53 Harold · 3 · 1095
And such the frenzy, whose convulsion blinds · 64 Harold · 4 · 561
Or seen my mind's convulsion leave it weak · 75 Harold · 4 · 1201
With a convulsion--then arose again · 214 Dream · 84
With each convulsion, in a blacker gush · 381 Lara · 2 · 421
This is convulsion, and no healthful life · 484 Manfred · 2 · 43
And the repress'd convulsion of the high · 601 Foscari · 1 · 356
So changed by its convulsion, they would not · 641 Cain · 2 · 326
It was but a convulsion, which though short · 865 Juan · 6 · 843

CONVULSIONS
And foam and roll, with strange convulsions
    rack'd · 784 Juan · 2 · 629

CONVULSIVE
Bounding convulsive, flies the gasping head · 108 Nisus · 250
And when convulsive throes denied my breath · 206 Love, Death · 17
But one convulsive struggle still remains · 272 Minerva · 283
Starts not to more convulsive life · 327 Abydos · 1 · 344
The bitter print of each convulsive nail · 377 Lara · 2 · 116
With feeble and convulsive effort swept · 380 Lara · 2 · 406
She strove with that convulsive dream · 400 Parisina · 383
Strive with a swoln convulsive motion · 404 Chillon · 181
Accompanied with a convulsive splash · 780 Juan · 2 · 422
Her struggles ceased with one convulsive groan · 823 Juan · 4 · 462

CONYNGE
Vain rage! the mantle quits the conynge hand · 16 Harold · 1 · 781

COO
The wood-dove from the forest depth shall coo · 419 Island · 2 · 5

COOING
Billing or cooing now · 229 Moore-B · 7

COOINGS
For no one cares for matrimonial cooings · 802 Juan · 3 · 61

COOK
But the Pastry Cook carried away · 234 Ballat · 8
From Captain Noah down to Captain Cook · 246 Bards · 356
The sea, to bid their cook, or wife, or friend · 441 Beppo · 59

COOK'D
But the best dish that e'er was cook'd since
    Homer's · 789 Juan · 2 · 983
And so, she cook'd their breakfast to a tittle · 792 Juan · 2 · 1157

COOKE
No Cooke, no Kemble, can salute you here · 113 Prologue · 13

COOKERY
The Art of Cookery, and mine · 234 Strahan · 15
Of Zoe's cookery no doubt was stealing · 793 Juan · 2 · 1220
Of which perhaps the cookery rather varies · 976 Juan · 15 · 539
That cookery could have call'd forth such
    resources · 976 Juan · 15 · 550

COOKS
(See also PASTRY-COOKS, PASTRY-COOK'S)
With a legion of cooks, and an army of slaves · 202 Avatar · 20
Have Carbonaro cooks not carbonadoed · 305 Age · 508
I read all France's treason in her cooks · 305 Age · 511
What! must I go to the oblivious cooks · 830 Juan · 4 · 861
And cooks in motion with their clean arms bared · 837 Juan · 5 · 398

COOL
Nought but cool indifference thrills us · 100 Marion · 14
Where Brent's cool waves in limpid currents stray · 124 Recoll · 134
How came you in Hob's pound to cool · 235 New Song · 1
If your cool friend annoy you now and then · 267 Hints · 795
Whose welcome waters, cool and clear · 315 Giaour · 539
One drop--the last--to cool it for the grave · 380 Lara · 2 · 405
Cool was the silent sky, though calm · 388 Corinth · 360
Nor say one mass to cool the caldron's bubble · 440 Beppo · 31
A well-timed wedding makes the scandal cool · 443 Beppo · 190
Who still become more constant as they cool · 444 Beppo · 272
But not for a deliberate, false, cool villain · 512 Faliero · 2 · 227
And headed by the cool, stern Salemenes · 563 Sardan · 2 · 91
Briefly; but in that brief cool calm inhale · 587 Sardan · 5 · 29
And cool them into calmness! How unlike · 597 Foscari · 1 · 127
Of this cool, calculating fiend, who walks · 681 Werner · 1 · 618
The wounded lion his cool cave. Methinks · 695 Werner · 3 · 7
Practise in the cool twilight. You are blind · 733 Deformed · 1 · 773
His daily task had kept his fancy cool · 774 Juan · 2 · 11
The umbrage of the wood so cool and dun · 805 Juan · 3 · 213
The third, a wary, cool old sworder, took · 822 Juan · 4 · 386
Of beauties cool as an Italian convent · 856 Juan · 6 · 255
Cool, and quite English, imperturbable · 942 Juan · 13 · 108

COOL'D
To lips just cool'd in time to save · 325 Abydos · 1 · 153
Cool'd their scorch'd throats, and wash'd the
    gory stains · 427 Island · 3 · 77

COOLER
Now I am cooler. You have bound it with · 577 Sardan · 3 · 368

COOLEST
My steps have wound to try the coolest rill · 344 Corsair · 1 · 426

COOLING
And so cooling--they use it a little too oft · 277 Blues · 1 · 27
A cooling breeze which crisps the broad clear
    river · 551 Sardan · 1 · 53
It was the cooling hour, just when the rounded · 797 Juan · 2 · 1457
And sherbet cooling in the porous vase · 805 Juan · 3 · 245

COOLLY
They were only coolly reviewing · 179 Devil's Dr · 242
Nor of thy temperament, to talk so coolly · 709 Werner · 4 · 349
'You take things coolly, sir,' said Juan. 'Why · 834 Juan · 5 · 161

COOLNESS
Sprinkle its coolness, and from the dry dust · 65 Harold · 4 · 609
And flung luxurious coolness round · 313 Giaour · 303
With hand, whose almost careless coolness spoke · 376 Lara · 2 · 59

COOP'D
Coop'd in their winged sea-girt citadel · 23 Harold · 2 · 249
And shall not yield to yours, though coop'd in
    clay · 480 Manfred · 1 · 157
Of his presumption. What! am I then coop'd · 560 Sardan · 1 · 620
Though coop'd within these walls, they are strong,
    and we · 590 Sardan · 5 · 180

COOT
(See BALD-COOT)

COPE
Which it would cope with, on delighted wing · 46 Harold · 3 · 696
'Tis said with Sorrow Time can cope · 161 Picture · 5
That with such change can calmly cope · 180 Ode-A · 42
To conquer ages, and with time to cope · 254 Bards · 950
No more with sorrow meekly cope · 321 Giaour · 1151
And scarcely in the chase could cope · 325 Abydos · 1 · 136
To teach my few with numbers still to cope · 343 Corsair · 1 · 330
Of flight from foes with whom I could not cope · 354 Corsair · 2 · 471
Few of our youth could cope with him · 393 Corinth · 793
That I could cope with you, whom I had seen · 693 Werner · 2 · 642
With Crabbe it may be difficult to cope · 772 Juan · 1 · 1637
Was also great with which they had to cope · 779 Juan · 2 · 324
As for a brook to cope with ocean's flood · 877 Juan · 7 · 639

COPED
I have coped with the nations which dread me thus
    lonely · 186 Napoleon · 7

COPES
Brisk Confidence still best with woman copes · 24 Harold · 2 · 305
And join their strength to that which with thee
    copes · 460 Dante · 2 · 141

COPIED
Our Beppo:--when copied, I'll send it · 232 Murray-B · 12
Such as of old were copied from the Grecians · 441 Beppo · 83
In vineyards copied from the south of France · 445 Beppo · 328

COPIOUS
The copious use of claret is forbid too · 773 Juan · 1 · 1726

COPPER
And Estifania gull her 'Copper' spouse · 261 Hints · 362
White, black, or copper--the dead bones will grin · 898 Juan · 9 · 96
Besides some veins of iron, lead, or copper · 915 Juan · 10 · 475

COPPET
Pray--was not she interr'd at Coppet · 232 Doctor · 82

COPY
Sweet copy! far more dear to me · 98 To Mary · 17
Nor teach the Lusian bard to copy Moore · 246 Bards · 308
And actors copy nature--when they can · 258 Hints · 152
Yet copy not too closely, but record · 259 Hints · 187
In your name? In my name. I will copy them out · 279 Blues · 1 · 93
Harsh Runic copy of the South's sublime · 455 Dante · Ded · 5
Of perserverance which I would not copy · 571 Sardan · 2 · 588
She could have served him for the prompter's copy · 748 Juan · 1 · 84
Shown in the following copy of her Letter · 770 Juan · 1 · 1528

COPYING
(In copying) this long canto into two · 816 Juan · 3 · 979

COPYIST
Colossal copyist of deformity 78 Harold 4 1362

COQUETRY
Coquetry, or a wish to take the lead 939 Juan 12 612
And for coquetry, she disdain'd to wear it 945 Juan 13 246

COQUETTE
Will never obtain a coquette 115 Pigot 4
And then you may kiss your coquette 115 Pigot 8
And humbles the proudest coquette 115 Pigot 12
That yours is the rosy coquette 115 Pigot 16
And laugh at the little coquette 115 Pigot 20
Did they act like your blooming coquette 115 Pigot 24
To fly from the captious coquette 116 Pigot 28
Should lead you to curse the coquette 116 Pigot 32
Of this quickly reformed coquette 116 Strephon 8
The Spanish maid is no coquette 160 Cadiz 25
Such is your cold coquette, who can't say 'No 937 Juan 12 497
Began to dread she'd thaw to a coquette 978 Juan 15 644

COQUETTISH
Coquettish in ambition--still he aim'd 68 Harold 4 818

CORAL
Which, trembling in their coral caves 314 Giaour 386
When summer's sun went down the coral bay 419 Island 2 2
Like coral reddening through the darken'd wave 420 Island 2 139
For ever? or, received in coral caves 431 Island 4 97
O'er my calm Hall of Coral 479 Manfred 1 84
(So children cutting teeth receive a coral 772 Juan 1 1668
Mother of pearl and coral the less costly 809 Juan 3 488

CORA'S
And Cora's eye which roll'd on me 134 E. N. Long 67
For Cora's eye will snine on all 134 E. N. Long 70

CORD
This cord receive, for thee reserved with care 248 Bards 458
And snapp'd the cord, which to the mane 410 Mazeppa 385
The cord, he hurl'd a stone with strength so rude 470 Morgante 251

CORDAGE
Some cordage, canvass, sails, and lines, and
  twine 416 Island 1 91
The wind sung, cordage strain'd, and sailors
  swore 775 Juan 2 98

CORDIAL
Both banish'd by the sovereign cordial 'Waltz 275 Waltz 146
Wrings with a cordial grasp Anselmo's hand 363 Corsair 3 504
Then was the cordial pour'd, and mantle flung 788 Juan 2 905
To no men are such cordial greetings given 851 Juan 5 1231
But to deny the mob a cordial, which is 915 Juan 10 502

CORDIALS
Of herbs and cordials they produced their store 824 Juan 4 470

CORDOVA
Of Cordova the Chivalry 194 Ballad-A 49

CORDS
Meantime my cords were wet with gore 411 Mazeppa 460

CORE
Of aught but rest; a fever at the core 41 Harold 3 377
Rank at the core, though tempting to the eyes 73 Harold 4 1075
Felt the glow which now gladdens my heart to its
  core 155 Goblet 2
Hast pierced through my heart to its core 162 Romaic-A 28
Of mighty minds doth hallow in the core 192 Sonnet-C 7
Thy heart was wither'd to its Core 201 Ode-C 55
There was something so warm and sublime in the
  core 204 Avatar 123
Pride in his heavenly bosom, in whose core 288 Vision 245
Feel--to the rising bosom's inmost core 338 Corsair 1 21
As I approach the core of my heart's grief 486 Manfred 2 193
Let the throne form the core of it; I would not 593 Sardan 5 362
I have pierced him to the core of his cold heart 613 Foscari 3 318
For that compression in its burning core 755 Juan 1 573
Your system feigns o'er the controulless core 761 Juan 1 924
My shame and sorrow deep in my heart's core 770 Juan 1 1556
And pick it up, and bite it to the core 862 Juan 6 612

CORFU
Bound for Corfu: she was a fine polacca 452 Beppo 759

CORINNA
And who there besides but Corinna de Stael 178 Devil's Dr 195

CORINTH
And Corinth on the left; I lay reclined 61 Harold 4 394
Have swept o'er Corinth; yet she stands 385 Corinth 48
Through many a change had Corinth pass'd 385 Corinth 121

CORINTH
Leave not in Corinth a living one 392 Corinth 710
Lost Corinth may resist no more 394 Corinth 946
Thus was Corinth lost and won 396 Corinth 1079

CORINTHIAN
I think it may be of 'Corinthian Brass 859 Juan 6 441

CORINTH'S
(See also ACRO-CORINTH'S)
That Corinth's pedagogue hath now 181 Ode-A 125
Minotti held in Corinth's towers 386 Corinth 218
Corinth's sons were downward borne 392 Corinth 746

CORK
Where the wild branch of the cork forest grew 757 Juan 1 716

CORKS
For all corrupted things are buoy'd like corks 298 Vision 835

CORK-TREES
The cork-trees hoar that clothe the shaggy steep 7 Harold 1 244

CORN
And fields which promise corn and wine 43 Harold 3 501
Her corn and wine and oil, and Plenty leaps 62 Harold 4 428
Hope constancy in wind, or corn in chaff 242 Bards 77
To hunt, and vote, and raise the price of corn 305 Age 573
But corn, like every mortal thing, must fall 305 Age 574
Or peace or plenty, corn or oil, or wines 307 Age 669
Grass before scythes, or corn below the sickle 883 Juan 8 338
Only to keep its corn at the old price 934 Juan 12 320
The corn is cut, the manor full of game 950 Juan 13 595

CORNARO
Fought by my side, and Marc Cornaro shared 524 Faliero 3 424
And send for Marc Cornaro:--fear not, Bertram 533 Faliero 4 333
Alike to them Marcello or Cornaro 533 Faliero 4 373

CORNELIAN
The motto cut upon a white cornelian 771 Juan 1 1583

CORNELIA'S
Was she a matron of Cornelia's mien 70 Harold 4 904

CORNER
Not a corner for a mouse 157 Hodgson 14
With a scorpion in each corner 196 Rogers 4
Of the good company, can win a corner 926 Juan 11 538
Epoch, that awkward corner turn'd for days 941 Juan 13 26
A corner for herself; and therefore fiction 968 Juan 15 23
Had gather'd a large tear into its corner 989 Juan 16 562

CORNERS
Only to draw them 'twixt two bastion corners 887 Juan 8 599

CORNER'S
That corner's turn'd--so--ah! no!--right! it
  draws 701 Werner 3 418

CORNER-STONE
Who flung at my good horse yon corner-stone 469 Morgante 220
And rock their marbles to the corner-stone 518 Faliero 3 4

CORNFIELD
Fruit, foliage, crag, wood, cornfield, mountain,
  vine 42 Harold 3 412

CORNFIELDS
Of woods and cornfields, and the abodes of men 214 Dream 33

CORNIANI
Did not his countryman, Count Corniani 765 Juan 1 1187

CORNICE
With cornice glimmering as the moonbeams play 269 Minerva 37
With cornice glimmering as the moonbeams play 356 Corsair 3 37

CORNISH
Those Cornish plunderers of Parnassian wrecks 830 Juan 4 862

CORN-SHEAF
As if the corn-sheaf should oppose the sickle 833 Juan 5 134

COROLLARIES
And mysteries, and corollaries of 567 Sardan 2 380

CORONACH'S
The Coronach's wild requiem to the brave 182 Address-C 30

CORONAL
Thick wreaths shall form our coronal, like
  spring's 419 Island 2 49

CORONALS
Blushing with Bacchant coronals along 950 Juan 13 602

CORONET
Less on a convent than a coronet 951 Juan 13 680

CORONETS
Smart uniforms and sparkling coronets 934 Juan 12 281
She put all coronets into commotion 962 Juan 14 434

CORON'S
In Coron's bay floats many a galley light 347 Corsair 2 1
Through Coron's lattices the lamps are bright 347 Corsair 2 2

CORPO
Hail'd a strange brig--Corpo di Caio Mario 826 Juan 4 652

CORPORAL
Which a Corporal chose to shiver 176 Devil's Dr 56
Yet could his corporal pangs amount to half 823 Juan 4 427
For this great conqueror play'd the corporal 874 Juan 7 442
Within him, and to quell his corporal quaking 996 Juan 16 990

CORPORAL'S
His time, a corporal's duty to fulfil 873 Juan 7 412

CORPORATION
Mere freedoms of the female corporation 960 Juan 14 340

CORPOREAL
Add the corporeal rack, you may: these limbs 542 Faliero 5 303

CORPS
We'll form a very pretty corps 173 Quotation 24
Be not so quick; the honour of the corps 683 Werner 2 40
'Twas none of our corps; but some petty, trivial 684 Werner 2 56
Juan and Johnson join'd a certain corps 880 Juan 8 145
To corps, the greater part of which were corses 882 Juan 8 240
Of his own corps, nor even the corps, which had 882 Juan 8 242
Nor care a pinch of snuff about his corps 882 Juan 8 248
And so, when all his corps were dead or dying 882 Juan 8 281

CORPSE
(See also CORSE)
Is't a corpse stuck up for show 196 Rogers 13
Who cared about the corpse? The funeral 286 Vision 75
Save one, a corpse, from out the famish'd three 788 Juan 2 870

CORPSE-LIGHT
But vanish'd like a corpse-light from a grave 431 Island 4 86

CORPSES
The corpses of the world of thy young days 670 Heaven 1145
And galvanism has set some corpses grinning 762 Juan 1 1034
And handsome corpses strew'd upon the shore 791 Juan 2 1100
And though I have seen many corpses, never 835 Juan 5 274

CORPUS
And vote his "habeas corpus" into heaven 293 Vision 568
I like the Habeas Corpus (when we've got it 446 Beppo 374
Of the 'Star Chamber' than of 'Habeas Corpus 949 Juan 13 552

CORRECT
To gain the paltry suffrage of 'correct 262 Hints 420
Who say strange things for so correct an age 829 Juan 4 780
Young women, and correct them when they blunder'd 856 Juan 6 248
Midst whom we have heard, from sources quite
    correct 947 Juan 13 412
Admired, adored; but also so correct 962 Juan 14 442
Her conduct had been perfectly correct 966 Juan 14 675

CORRECTED
'Tis of our safety. Right; I stand corrected 697 Werner 3 170

CORRECTEST
New buildings of correctest conformation 988 Juan 16 511

CORRECTLY
The slow, sad stanza will correctly paint 258 Hints 109

CORRECTOR
Time! the corrector where our judgments err 74 Harold 4 1165
The Law's expounder, and the State's corrector 749 Juan 1 117

CORRESPOND
As far as outward show may correspond 844 Juan 5 791

CORRESPONDENT
To make each correspondent a new debtor 954 Juan 13 832

CORRESPONDENTS
To his Tunis correspondents, save one man 803 Juan 3 123

CORRIDOR
Above, strange groups adorn'd the corridor 28 Harold 2 508

CORRIDORE
He pass'd the portal, cross'd the corridore 343 Corsair 1 363
But, glimmering through the dusky corridore 364 Corsair 3 595

CORROBORATED
Morgante with the hands corroborated 473 Morgante 445

CORRODING
I bear, corroding joy and youth 17 Harold 1 842
With me no corroding resentment shall live 137 Delawarr 22
In that corroding secrecy which gnaws 370 Lara 1 283
Corroding in the cavern of the heart 968 Juan 15 18

CORROSIVE
Corrosive passions, feelings dull and low 457 Dante 1 132

CORRUPT
I own myself corrupt and weak 133 Prayer 39
Debased by slavery, or corrupt by power 154 Dog 16
To soften manners, but corrupt the heart 250 Bards 619
Corrupt no less than they oppress, and sap 552 Sardan 1 122

CORRUPTED
If that corrupted thing could ever such be taught 25 Harold 2 324
If his corrupted eye and wither'd heart 183 Address-D 19
Since his veins are corrupted to mud 229 Lads 12
For all corrupted things are buoy'd like corks 298 Vision 835
My mind like theirs corrupted to its grave 439 Tasso 179
Which purify corrupted commonwealths 517 Faliero 2 599

CORRUPTING
'Tis thine to offer with corrupting art 227 Answer-C 7

CORRUPTION
Of vice-entail'd Corruption; they no land 45 Harold 3 614
Wealth, vice, corruption,--barbarism at last 71 Harold 4 967
And Corruption shrunk scorch'd from the glance of
    his mind 202 Avatar 48
Corruption foil'd her, for she fear'd her glance 261 Hints 353
Corruption shakes which peril could not part 333 Abydos 2 439
The general corruption generated 526 Faliero 3 525
There is a careless courage which corruption 550 Sardan 1 10
Corruption came not in each mind to kill 824 Juan 4 477
Though they may make Corruption gape or stare 878 Juan 8 30
Corruption could not make their hearts her soil 886 Juan 8 532
Corruption for its crop) with the poor devils 910 Juan 10 198
By foul corruption into streams,--even they 923 Juan 11 319

CORRUPTION'S
Corruption's heap, the savage spoilers trod 121 Newstead-A 84
It clogs like lead Corruption's weary wing 271 Minerva 246

CORRUPTS
That world corrupts the noblest soul 153 Friend-A 28
A second marriage which corrupts the first 444 Beppo 288

CORSAIR
The Corsair vow'd protection, soothed affright 351 Corsair 2 267
'Corsair, thy doom is named! but I have power 354 Corsair 2 460
'Misdoubting Corsair! I have gain'd the guard 360 Corsair 3 312
Are on this cast; Corsair! 'tis but a blow 361 Corsair 3 375
Corsair! we meet in safety or no more 361 Corsair 3 383
Corsair! he perish'd--thou art dearly won 362 Corsair 3 431

CORSAIRS
The Corsairs, pouring, haste to where within 349 Corsair 2 186

CORSAIR'S
Compared with his, the Corsair's roving crew 350 Corsair 2 232
His Corsair's isle was once thine own domain 356 Corsair 3 64
He left a Corsair's name to other times 366 Corsair 3 695

CORSE
One gallant steed is stretch'd a mangled corse 16 Harold 1 769
The corse is piled--sweet sight for vulgar eyes 16 Harold 1 789
Then to the vulture let each corse remain 18 Harold 1 904
And o'er his corse no banners wave 105 Alva 303
Or wealth redeem from foes my captive corse 106 Nisus 68
This from the pallid corse was quickly torn 109 Nisus 291
Fox! o'er whose corse a mourning world must weep 114 Death-A 29
And my corse shall recline on its bier 115 The Tear 42
There many a pale and ruthless robber's corse 121 Newstead-A 81
O'er the corse of thy lord in thy canopy laid 149 Newstead-B 30
And he was faithful to a corse, and kept 189 Darkness 48
Heed not the corse, though a king's, in your path 219 Saul-A 3
Thy corse shall from its tomb be rent 317 Giaour 756
Must feed thy livid living corse 317 Giaour 762
Each feature of that sullen corse 321 Giaour 1091
What recks it, though that corse shall lie 335 Abydos 2 611
His corse may boast its urn and narrow cave 338 Corsair 1 33
Or pave the path with many a corse 386 Corinth 239

CORSE

His corse in dust whereon the day	404 Chillon		153
Lone--as the corse within its shroud	405 Chillon		293
A broken corse upon the barren Lido	617 Foscari	4	132
That I would rather look upon his corse	622 Foscari	5	106
A corse--a corse, it might be, fighting for them	624 Foscari	5	248
Come, Zillah! I must watch my husband's corse	653 Cain	3	450

CORSES

| To corps, the greater part of which were corses | 882 Juan | 8 | 240 |

CORSLET

| My corslet--cloak--one hour--and we are gone | 340 Corsair | 1 | 160 |
| Lurk'd beneath his corslet bright | 393 Corinth | | 789 |

CORTANA

He took Cortana, and then took Rondell	468 Morgante		130
Orlando had Cortana bare in hand	470 Morgante		273
Cortana clave the skull like a true brand	470 Morgante		275

CORTEJO

| The Spaniards call the person a 'Cortejo | 444 Beppo | | 291 |
| 'Was it for this that no Cortejo e'er | 765 Juan | 1 | 1177 |

CORTES'

| Where Cortes' and Pizarro's banner flew | 302 Age | | 266 |

CORUSCATION

| Pall Mall, and so forth, have a coruscation | 921 Juan | 11 | 202 |
| Have waned into a crescent's coruscation | 924 Juan | 11 | 388 |

CORYDON

| From Corydon unkind Alexis turns | 265 Hints | | 620 |
| Beginning with 'Formosum Pastor Corydon | 752 Juan | 1 | 336 |

COSI

| Can paint,--'Cosi viaggino i Ricchi | 947 Juan | 13 | 373 |

COSMO

| Like Cosmo. We had evils, but not such | 682 Werner | 1 | 710 |

COSMOGONY

| Oh, world! which was and is, what is cosmogony | 899 Juan | 9 | 155 |

COSSACK

A Calmuck beauty with a Cossack wit	304 Age		438
The Cossack prince rubb'd down his horse	407 Mazeppa		58
And when the Cossack maid beheld	414 Mazeppa		817

COSSACK'S

| Since I became the Cossack's guest | 415 Mazeppa | | 843 |

COSSACQUE

How shall I spell the name of each Cossacque	868 Juan	7	107
To Russian, Tartar, English, French, Cossacque	873 Juan	7	362
He made 'gainst Cossacque sabres, in the wide	913 Juan	10	405

COSSACQUES
(See also KOZACKS)

In sight two horsemen, who were deem'd Cossacques	872 Juan	7	338
Some Cossacques, hovering like hawks round a hill	874 Juan	7	443
Of Cossacques and their prey, turn'd round and cast	874 Juan	7	466
The Kozacks, or, if so you please, Cossacques	887 Juan	8	585
Cossacques were all cut off as day was breaking	888 Juan	8	603
Two villanous Cossacques pursued the child	890 Juan	8	729
The readiest way of reasoning with Cossacques	890 Juan	8	744

COSSAQUE'S

| Than swell the Cossaque's prowling caravan | 302 Age | | 303 |

COST

The paltry prize is hardly worth the cost	24 Harold	2	310
And blush for every pang it cost	174 Remember-B		11
And if dearly that error hath cost me	210 Augusta-B		37
Who are brought to my house as an inn, to my cost	280 Blues	2	18
His way, and look'd as if his journey cost	295 Vision		676
Those gibes had cost another dear	324 Abydos	1	110
'Twill cost me dear--but dread no death to-day	355 Corsair	2	534
That sad fatality hath cost me dear	438 Tasso		141
And mine at least hath cost me dear: to die	458 Dante	1	158
That comfortless we all are to our cost	475 Morgante		646
The very effort which it cost me to	534 Faliero	4	423
An obscene gesture cost Caligula	544 Faliero	5	442
On objects which could cost her sons a tear	557 Sardan	1	458
Mine inn is like to cost me dear. I heard	687 Werner	2	303
(Although it cost me half an hour in spinning	748 Juan	1	54
And must have cost his majesty a treasure	761 Juan	1	940
And yet can not regret what it hath cost	770 Juan	1	1539
Denying the receipt of what it cost	772 Juan	1	1678
Had cost his enemies a long repentance	808 Juan	3	431
Monsters, who cost a no less monstrous sum	842 Juan	5	704
Her toilet, which cost little, for she was	859 Juan	6	474
With cost, and care, and warmth induced to shoot	860 Juan	6	516

COST

A lover as had cost her many a tear	903 Juan	9	431
A moment's good thing may have cost them years	955 Juan	13	870
And since that time it need not cost much showing	965 Juan	14	621
Or else 'twill cost us all another million	966 Juan	14	664
Cost her an effort, which is a sad toil	966 Juan	14	682
The cost would be a trifle--an 'old song	988 Juan	16	513
But county contests cost him rather dearer	989 Juan	16	603
Might cost both man and master too--their places	991 Juan	16	680
Had fallen last market, cost his host three votes	992 Juan	16	760
The company whose birth, wealth, worth, has cost	998 Juan	17	100

COSTIVE

| His rhymes are of the costive kind | 233 Ballad-B | | 37 |
| With gore, like Nadir Shah, that costive sophy | 900 Juan | 9 | 260 |

COSTLY

His goblets brimm'd with every costly wine	5 Harold	1	96
In costly sheen and gaudy cloak array'd	15 Harold	1	738
His costly canvass with each flatter'd face	256 Hints		2
Such costly triumph to repay	328 Abydos	1	461
Whose porphyry pillars, and whose costly fronts	529 Faliero	4	77
Mother of pearl and coral the less costly	809 Juan	3	488
So costly were they; carpets every stitch	839 Juan	5	518
Vied with each other on this costly spot	864 Juan	6	778
And cannot find a bill's small items costly	922 Juan	11	244

COSTS

What crimes it costs to be a moment free	67 Harold	4	761
Because it costs him dear, and makes him dress	261 Hints		316
But this costs little to true Franks, who had rather	304 Age		494
It costs three francs for every mass that's said	781 Juan	2	440
How much it costs us! yet each rising throb	800 Juan	2	1618

COSTUME

| The present, with their common-place costume | 971 Juan | 15 | 208 |

COSTUMES

| All the costumes since Adam's, right or wrong | 293 Vision | | 526 |

COT

Scanty the hamlet, rare the lonely cot	27 Harold	2	463
Fields, which surround yon rustic cot	145 Adieu		41
Is yon a cot I saw, though low	158 Storm		9
The roofless cot, decay'd and rent	319 Giaour		876
By him no peasant mourn'd his rifled cot	378 Lara	2	200
Fiercely beside thy cot the mutineer	416 Island	1	53

COTERIE

Smug coterie, and literary lady	449 Beppo		608
Drawn by the blue-coat misses of a coterie	830 Juan	4	872
By the mere combination of a coterie	951 Juan	13	652

COTERIES

| The coteries, and, as in Banquo's glass | 925 Juan | 11 | 427 |

COTS

| All wrath in barracks, palaces, or cots | 901 Juan | 9 | 285 |

COTTA

| For Paphlagonia, where our kinsman Cotta | 581 Sardan | 4 | 202 |

COTTAGE

To this the peasant gave his cottage thatch	300 Age		176
The omen of a cottage gate	413 Mazeppa		616
Sate watching by the cottage wall	414 Mazeppa		807
The soil where every cottage show'd a home	422 Island	2	249
Sought out their cottage built beneath the palm	424 Island	2	403
And share a cottage on the Caucasus	558 Sardan	1	499
He paused to change his garments in a cottage	675 Werner	1	255
My lord, he tarried in the cottage where	679 Werner	1	486
But did not leave the cottage by the Oder	685 Werner	2	147

COTTAGES

| In camps, in ships, in cottages, or courts | 959 Juan | 14 | 244 |

COTTA'S

| Is safe with my three sons in Cotta's court | 593 Sardan | 5 | 394 |

COTTED
(See VILLAGE-COTTED)

COTTLE

Boeotian Cottle, rich Bristowa's boast	247 Bards		387
And Amos Cottle strikes the lyre in vain	247 Bards		396
Oh, Amos Cottle!--Phoebus! what a name	247 Bards		399
Oh, Amos Cottle! for a moment think	247 Bards		401
Had Cottle still adorn'd the counter's side	247 Bards		406

COUCH

| But Silence spreads the couch of ever welcome rest | 20 Harold | 2 | 63 |
| Hath spread himself a couch, the Alps have rear'd a throne | 51 Harold | 3 | 976 |

COUCH

The beam pours in, for time and skill will couch the blind	74	Harold	4	1143
No marble marks thy couch of lowly sleep	85	Epitaph		15
Stain'd is the couch and earth with clotting gore	108	Nisus		252
At eve, on my heath-cover'd couch of repose	136	Highlander		21
Scene of my youth and couch of my repose	138	Harrow-B		26
Yielding my couch and stretch'd me on the ground	206	Love, Death		10
The widow'd couch of fire, that thou hast spread	209	Sketch		94
I slumber not; the thorn is in my Couch	240	Cephalonia		4
And rushing from my couch, I dart	323	Giaour		1285
Cling to his couch and sicken years away	338	Corsair	1	28
Oh! many a night on this lone couch reclined	343	Corsair	1	371
And tottering to the couch his bride he bore	345	Corsair	1	478
On silken couch than o'er the rugged deep	347	Corsair	2	40
Again to that accustom'd couch must creep	375	Lara	1	630
Without or couch or canopy	388	Corinth		342
'And where should our bridal couch be spread	390	Corinth		581
Do these limbs on a couch repose	414	Mazeppa		799
With leafy couch already made	415	Mazeppa		862
The waves without sang round their couch, their roar	433	Island	4	227
Now will I to my couch, although to rest	529	Faliero	4	110
For mind nor body: let me have a couch	577	Sardan	3	340
About my sick couch. Hence! and do my bidding	589	Sardan	5	122
Behind the couch in my own chamber. (Now	591	Sardan	5	249
Stalk frowning round my couch, and, pointing towards	620	Foscari	4	332
Which might have graced his recent marriage couch	654	Cain	3	558
His couch; and, that he might be more at ease	791	Juan	2	1059
Their lady to her couch with gushing eyes	824	Juan	4	469
To make the nuptial couch a 'Bed of Ware	854	Juan	6	96
And every couch is occupied; you had best	858	Juan	6	366
Of Lolah--though her couch is not so large	862	Juan	6	648
Waved o'er his couch; he meditated, fond	995	Juan	16	926

COUCH'D

Couch'd among fallen columns, in the shade	215	Dream		116
Whether we couch'd in our rough capote	384	Corinth		10
Had yet been couch'd before her glance	398	Parisina		168
And Steno's lie, couch'd in two worthless lines	544	Faliero	5	445
Housed in a prince's palace, couch'd within	690	Werner	4	467
Are couch'd at their mother	732	Deformed	1	732
By his despatches couch'd in pithy phrase	872	Juan	7	310
There, couch'd all snugly on his pillow's nook	984	Juan	16	213

COUCHES

And soft voluptuous couches breathed repose	28	Harold	2	553
Were couches, toilets--and much more than this	858	Juan	6	403

COUCHING

Sullen and lonely, couching in the cave	437	Tasso		17

COUGH

Began to cough, and hawk, and hem, and pitch	296	Vision		715
The tumult grew; an universal cough	296	Vision		737
But be much puzzled by a cough and cold	776	Juan	2	171
Sigh like his son, than cough like his grandfather	908	Juan	10	48

COUGHS

But coughs will come when sighs depart--and now	908	Juan	10	57

COULD

Of thoughts which were not their thoughts, and still could	52	Harold	3	1056
What Nature could, but would not, do	229	Marble		3
'His capture could!--and shall I then resign	358	Corsair	3	169
Too high for common selfishness, he could	371	Lara	1	337
And yet they wrung me till I could have shriek'd	599	Foscari	1	245
And could--ay, perhaps, should (if our self-safety	712	Werner	4	526
Of its disease; he did the best he could	758	Juan	1	725
He also stuff'd his money where he could	781	Juan	2	465
Refusing his own spaniel, hardly could	783	Juan	2	620
And all her fools whom I could lay the lash on	795	Juan	2	1326
I know not who may conquer: if I could	899	Juan	9	189
Space to dispute what no one ever could	919	Juan	11	30
Don Juan, having done the best he could	920	Juan	11	137
To show she could, if it were worth her while	986	Juan	16	384

COULEUR

'Couleur de rose,' who's neither white nor scarlet	937	Juan	12	496

COUMOURGI

Coumourgi, he whose closing scene	386	Corinth		141
Coumourgi, can his glory cease	386	Corinth		147
Thus utter'd Coumourgi, the dauntless vizier	392	Corinth		719

COUNCIL

On one great point the council are agreed	106	Nisus		89

COUNCIL

'Next to seeing a lord at the council board	177	Devil's Dr		101
From the charm'd council to the festive board	193	Monody		37
While all the Common Council cry 'Claymore	308	Age		772
But chiefly to my council call	333	Abydos	2	377
In that wild council words wax'd warm and strange	357	Corsair	3	123
But still the Signory is deep in council	499	Faliero	1	3
In council, without one dissenting voice	501	Faliero	1	87
Give me the paper--''Tis decreed in council	501	Faliero	1	100
Let him refer his business to the council	504	Faliero	1	319
You must address the council. 'Twere in vain	505	Faliero	1	361
To what? to hold a council in the dark	508	Faliero	1	610
But wherefore not address you to the Council	516	Faliero	2	544
In recent council to redouble now	517	Faliero	2	637
Valiant in war, and sage in council; noble	518	Faliero	2	679
By me into this council had been led	522	Faliero	3	240
The Council and 'the Ten?' the spies, the eyes	524	Faliero	3	355
All the patricians flocking to the Council	524	Faliero	3	381
With pomp for freedom, gaolers for a council	525	Faliero	3	480
The elders of the council: I remember	527	Faliero	3	588
Of council, be it soon or late, I shall not	530	Faliero	4	191
Such council can be lawful, till the prince	536	Faliero	4	554
To the council chamber. Duke! it may not be	536	Faliero	4	557
Nor are they in the wonted Hall of Council	536	Faliero	4	558
As rebel slave of a revolted council	537	Faliero	4	600
Until the council call ye to your trial	537	Faliero	4	634
Be brought before the council. And the rest	540	Faliero	5	144
The mighty in the field, the sage in council	543	Faliero	5	352
In peril of his own life; but the council	545	Faliero	5	539
At once his chorus and his council, flash	551	Sardan	1	40
Of council; it were better I retire	551	Sardan	1	77
Not from the council--there he is ever constant	563	Sardan	2	98
But an hour only. Let us then hold council	581	Sardan	4	191
Rejoin our colleagues in the council, and	595	Foscari	1	4
Extinct, you may say this.--Let's in to council	595	Foscari	1	20
Within the Council Chamber. There, sir, 'tis	597	Foscari	1	92
I dared not disobey the Council when	598	Foscari	1	154
And so the Council must break up and Justice	600	Foscari	1	314
In council were against you. Thanks to you, sir	600	Foscari	1	321
The instance of the elders of the Council	601	Foscari	1	377
Obey. I had in charge, too, from the Council	602	Foscari	2	35
We have decided. We? 'The Ten' in council	604	Foscari	2	196
That council when you were a young patrician	605	Foscari	2	206
I never work'd by plot in council, nor	605	Foscari	2	231
Last council on thy doom. I know it--look	610	Foscari	3	123
By our united influence in the Council	615	Foscari	4	28
I care, depute the Council on their knees	615	Foscari	4	33
Lived longer than enough. Hence! in to council	616	Foscari	4	64
But pass'd here merely on our path from council	618	Foscari	4	223
In the first place, the Council doth condone	620	Foscari	5	12
But, Philibert, we'll in to council. Arnold	734	Deformed	1	872
His daily council upon ways and means	864	Juan	6	762
A general council, in which unanimity	873	Juan	7	402
And being of the council call'd 'the Privy	964	Juan	14	537

COUNCIL-FAWNER

The sanction of 'the Ten,' a council-fawner	523	Faliero	3	314

COUNCILS

Ye Orators! whom yet our councils yield	194	Monody		101
Britannia must prosper with councils like yours	225	Ode-D		2
Far from such councils, from the faithless field	271	Minerva		217
To councils held to benefit mankind	303	Age		393
And hesitating councils: day on day	516	Faliero	2	560
In earnest councils--we will not be least so	616	Foscari	4	98
That stranger to most councils, here prevail'd	873	Juan	7	403
A man known in the councils of the nation	942	Juan	13	107

COUNCIL'S

The council's resolution. I protest	620	Foscari	4	353

COUNSEL

Nor sought he friend to counsel or condole	4	Harold	1	71
And Counsel sage, and patriotic Zeal	12	Harold	1	556
Of hollow counsel, the false oracle	80	Harold	4	1533
Counsel like mine is as a brother's	100	Marion		35
My counsel will get but abuse	116	Strephon		16
Receive this counsel, and be timely wise	264	Hints		579
I have a counsel for thy gentler ear	358	Corsair	3	177
Orlando answer'd, 'If my counsel still	474	Morgante		565
I will abide by Doge Faliero's counsel	524	Faliero	3	415
As I now counsel--but if not, thou art lost	530	Faliero	4	181
If ye would fain survive me. Take this counsel	542	Faliero	5	293
By all that's good and glorious, take this counsel	560	Sardan	1	648
Let us not leave them time for further counsel	569	Sardan	2	460
If I have spared these men against thy counsel	569	Sardan	2	493
As palsied as their hearts are hard, they counsel	603	Foscari	2	112
My counsel is a kind one; for 'tis even	642	Cain	2	417
Less for my life than for your counsel. These	693	Werner	2	632
From counsel learned in those kinds of laws	751	Juan	1	259
She kept her counsel in so close a way	755	Juan	1	544
Our counsel--(Juan, mind, you must not sleep	768	Juan	1	1376
Of counsel to nonsuit, or to annul	770	Juan	1	1508

COUNSEL
Fee by a counsel, felon by a jailor   834 Juan   5   208
And bade him counsel Juan. With a smile   963 Juan   14   516

COUNSELL'D
Such as I counsell'd you, with your own hand   516 Faliero   2   518

COUNSELLORS
Your most austere of counsellors, would now   577 Sardan   3   347
Of counsellors,' as Solomon has said   944 Juan   13   226
'Of counsellors' for men, thus for the sex   945 Juan   13   234

COUNSELS
To turn my counsels far from lands like thine   270 Minerva   160
Show me the man whose counsels may have weight   272 Minerva   274
Like him a fury counsels, his revenge   468 Morgante   137

COUNSEL'S
This counsel's safe--but is it honourable   704 Werner   3   596

COUNT
Thy saint adorers count the rosary   15 Harold   1   714
Existence by enjoyment, and count o'er   40 Harold   3   305
Count o'er the joys thine hours have seen   167 Euthanasia   33
Count o'er thy days from anguish free   167 Euthanasia   34
A blank; a thing to count and curse   172 Time-B   30
Saint Peter, may I count upon your vote   293 Vision   536
Count they each said, and mark how there supine   346 Corsair   1   597
To count the hours that struggle to thine end   358 Corsair   3   227
Which it befits Count Lara's ear to know   372 Lara   1   468
Though, like Count Lara, now return'd alone   372 Lara   1   472
Ere his years could count a score   393 Corinth   800
For years--I cannot count them o'er   403 Chillon   44
I kept no count, I took no note   406 Chillon   367
A count of far and high descent   408 Mazeppa   156
To deck her Count with titles given   408 Mazeppa   177
The Count was something more than wroth   410 Mazeppa   327
Was he, the proud Count Palatine   410 Mazeppa   343
The Count for his uncourteous ride   411 Mazeppa   412
I well could count their causes o'er   412 Mazeppa   528
A Count of wealth, they said, as well as quality   443 Beppo   239
And then he was a Count, and then he knew   444 Beppo   241
The Count and Laura made their new arrangement   446 Beppo   417
The Count was at her elbow with her shawl   450 Beppo   677
The Count and Laura found their boat at last   451 Beppo   689
'Sir,' said the Count, with brow exceeding grave   451 Beppo   697
But the Count courteously invited in   451 Beppo   714
I've heard the Count and he were always friends   452 Beppo   788
It roll'd on Count Orlando's helmet good   470 Morgante   253
And he has burst;--to this what say you, count   474 Morgante   547
Now when the abbot Count Orlando heard   475 Morgante   617
Seeing this history, Count Orlando said   476 Morgante   681
To greet your presence. Peace be with Count
    Manfred   491 Manfred   3   20
Who dwell within them. Would it were so, Count   491 Manfred   3   23
How many years is't? Ere Count Manfred's birth   494 Manfred   3   215
Count Sigismund was proud, but gay and free   494 Manfred   3   220
Count Manfred was, as now, within his tower   494 Manfred   3   242
Knock, and apprize the Count of my approach   494 Manfred   3   256
The Count Val di Marino, now our Doge   510 Faliero   2   83
Count of Val di Marino, Senator   544 Faliero   5   478
To count its throbs, not quicken them, and ask   570 Sardan   2   529
Shall count me with his spoils. Away with me   575 Sardan   3   240
How turn? I did not count them   676 Werner   1   287
Travel for your rich count or full-blown baron   676 Werner   1   342
Or count (or whatsoe'er this half-drown'd noble   678 Werner   1   452
The late Count Siegendorf, his distant kinsman   684 Werner   2   79
Whom the late count reclaim'd from his son's
    hands   684 Werner   2   92
I never heard his name till now. The count   689 Werner   2   400
Methinks the old Count Siegendorf maintain'd   704 Werner   4   6
Even of the narrowest. The old count loved not   704 Werner   4   13
Then his brave son, Count Ulric--there's a knight   704 Werner   4   21
Count Ulric for a well-supported pride   704 Werner   4   28
Than the most open warfare. But Count Ulric   705 Werner   4   54
On all that I have said! Good morrow, count   705 Werner   4   73
To excuse your absence to the count your father   705 Werner   4   101
Return--'twas a most kind act in the count   706 Werner   4   137
Count Ulric from the chase to-day. You will not   707 Werner   4   209
The nobles in our marshall'd ranks. You, count   708 Werner   4   240
Count Siegendorf, command you aught? I am bound   708 Werner   4   281
His further inquisition. Count, to Hamburgh   708 Werner   4   286
God speed you! Fare ye well, Count Siegendorf   709 Werner   4   289
To woo. Count, 'tis a marriage of your making   710 Werner   4   398
In masses for his spirit. Count, if I   711 Werner   4   468
Be quick! the count will soon return: the ladies   713 Werner   5   1
The count, and Ulric, and your daughter Ida   713 Werner   5   35
The young Count Waldorf, who scarce once withdrew   714 Werner   5   59
It seems. Count, I have heard that you, or yours   715 Werner   5   152
Look at him, count, and then hear me. I hear
    thee   716 Werner   5   183
Count, you are bound to hear me. I came hither   716 Werner   5   186
I speak to you, Count Siegendorf, because   716 Werner   5   203
I am unarm'd, count; bid your son lay down   716 Werner   5   207

COUNT
You, count, have made yourself accuser--judge   717 Werner   5   300
Resembling them--behold them in Count Ulric's   718 Werner   5   337
And show'd me Werner in Count Siegendorf   718 Werner   5   363
To sell my life--not cheaply. Now, Count Ulric   719 Werner   5   399
Farewell, then! Recollect, however, Count   721 Werner   5   501
Despatch!--he's there! The count, my lord! You
    here, sir   721 Werner   5   511
A wretch to profit by our ruin! No, count   721 Werner   5   529
'Count Arnold:' it hath no ungracious sound   730 Deformed   1   544
And who then shall count o'er   732 Deformed   1   713
Come, count, to business. True. I'll weep here-
    after   737 Deformed   2   155
Holla! hold, count! Away! they must not rally   737 Deformed   2   184
Count, she hath slain our comrade. With what
    weapon   740 Deformed   2   312
Count! count! I am your servant in all things   741 Deformed   2   406
Is it for this that General Count O'Reilly   765 Juan   1 1183
Did not his countryman, Count Corniani   765 Juan   1 1187
The Count Strongstroganoff I put in pain   765 Juan   1 1190
By carrying off Count Cesare Cicogna   827 Juan   4   663
Count Damas drove them back into the water   871 Juan   7   247
Count Chapeau-Bras, too, had a ball between   879 Juan   8   74
To calculators when they count on woman   960 Juan   14   344

COUNT-BISHOP
From Laurence the Count-bishop of Ceneda   545 Faliero   5   533

COUNTED
'Mid counted beads, and countless prayer   320 Giaour   972
Some were those who counted beads   384 Corinth   19
Than what was counted on? When the hour comes   563 Sardan   2   136
Five--six hours have I counted, like the guard   701 Werner   3   389
Were counted in them when they got afloat   781 Juan   2   432
They counted thirty, crowded in a space   782 Juan   2   497
He counted them at break of day   812 Juan   3   711
Which leaves you minus of the cash you counted   855 Juan   6   166

COUNTENANCE
Mysterious changed his countenance at least   294 Vision   612
Swerved. In his countenance, I grant you, never   615 Foscari   4   7
Making the countenance a masque of rest   968 Juan   15   19

COUNTER
They leap the counter, and they leave the stall   266 Hints   714
The gamester's counter, or the statesman's dross   930 Juan   12   30

COUNTERBALANCE
A thing to counterbalance human woes   907 Juan   10   13

COUNTERMINE
To baffle such, than countermine a mole   720 Werner   5   437

COUNTERPART
Had form'd his glorious namesake's counterpart   421 Island   2   193
You were a chance and passing guest, the
    counterpart   676 Werner   1   319

COUNTER'S
Had Cottle still adorn'd the counter's side   247 Bards   406

COUNTESS
Shall you be at the Countess of Fiddlecome's rout   279 Blues   1   132
The Baroness Ida lost in Countess Siegendorf   706 Werner   4   129
The countess in her chamber.--She complains   708 Werner   4   266
Go to! my lady countess comes. I'd rather   713 Werner   5   10
Offspring of some sage husband-hunting countess   929 Juan   11   698
The Duchess of Fitz-Fulke; the Countess Crabby   951 Juan   13   627

COUNTESSES
The fashion hails--from countesses to queens   275 Waltz   153
And countesses mature in robes and pearls   949 Juan   13   542
With other Countesses of Blank--but rank   951 Juan   13   633

COUNTIES
Those who in counties have great land resources   989 Juan   16   590

COUNTING
I know not, never counting past their teens   861 Juan   6   548

COUNTLESS
And not the whole combined and countless throng   61 Harold   4   349
Victors of countless kings, or puppets of a scene   68 Harold   4   783
The yellow harvest's countless seed   88 To Ellen   10
Her countless hoards would his have been   113 Cornelian-A   31
To fight my course through passion's countless
    host   251 Bards   692
'Mid counted beads, and countless prayer   320 Giaour   972
Or into countless meteors driven   386 Corinth   171

COUNTREE
(See also COUNTRY)
And some are in a far countree   384 Corinth   30

COUNTRIES

All countries of the Catholic persuasion	440 Beppo		2
Because in Christian countries 'tis a rule	443 Beppo		186
And far as pagan countries roam'd astray	468 Morgante		146
Especially in countries near the sun	754 Juan	1	493
Quite common in those countries, are a kind	809 Juan	3	514
Of ladies of all countries at the will	856 Juan	6	260
Countries of greater heat, but lesser suction	917 Juan	10	604
All countries have their 'Lions,' but in thee	932 Juan	12	191

COUNTRY
(See also COUNTREE)

Fair is proud Seville; let her country boast	14 Harold	1	657
A country with--ay, or without mankind	56 Harold	4	68
Oh Rome, my country! city of the soul	66 Harold	4	694
My fathers! the tears of your country redress ye	86 Leaving NA		15
For the rights of a monarch their country defending	86 Leaving NA		19
By those Penates who my country love	107 Nisus		140
And Critics rise in every country Squire	142 Soliloquy		14
Let your country see you rising	162 War Song		11
To keep his country free	162 War Song		32
His accomplishments! His!!! and thy country convince	203 Avatar		66
Mankind their country--Israel but the grave	217 Weep-B		12
Since our Country, our God--Oh, my Sire	218 Jephtha		1
And my Father and Country are free	218 Jephtha		16
Cato died for his country, so didst thou	238 Epigrams		2
Each country book-club bent the knee to Baal	243 Bards		138
Boast of thy country and Britannia's guide	248 Bards		501
And save her glory, though his country fall	254 Bards		948
My country, what her sons should know too well	255 Bards		992
In Christmas revels, simple country folks	261 Hints		321
To friends and country, and to pardon foes	263 Hints		496
Or country Crispins, now grown somewhat stale	266 Hints		731
Thy country sends a spoiler worse than both	269 Minerva		98
But fits thy country for her coming fate	271 Minerva		210
'I loved my country, and I hated him	295 Vision		664
Thy wall, nor knew the country held him in	303 Age		423
Alas, the country! how shall tongue or pen	305 Age		568
For what were all these country patriots born	305 Age		572
Their love of country, millions all misspent	306 Age		626
Against the country he betray'd	387 Corinth		307
Their country conquers with their martyrdom	402 Sonnet-F		7
Men without country, who, too long estranged	416 Island	1	29
Such was the country which these strangers yearn'd	416 Island	1	49
These spurn their country with their rebel bark	418 Island	1	231
Proscribed even in their second country, they	427 Island	3	43
No grateful country, smiling through her tears	433 Island	4	265
To him who for that country would expire	457 Dante	1	70
We can have but one country, and even yet	458 Dante	2	19
To thee, my country! whom before as now	461 Dante	3	25
And to their country a redoubled wreath	462 Dante	3	156
The genius of my country shall arise	464 Dante	4	74
To make my country honour'd. As her servant	515 Faliero	2	465
We must behold no object save our country	517 Faliero	2	602
By thee, I now must do it by my country	532 Faliero	4	326
Our lives and country from thy wickedness	545 Faliero	5	495
Love none but heroes. But I have no country	561 Sardan	1	689
Than see my country languish, I will be	568 Sardan	2	399
In my own country we respect their voices	570 Sardan	2	548
Who in thy country threw--Look to the portals	572 Sardan	3	68
And better as my country than my kingdom	595 Sardan	5	494
But as a culprit. Yes, but to his country	600 Foscari	1	299
Did you but love your country like this victim	604 Foscari	2	168
My country faithfully--victoriously	607 Foscari	2	370
The country is the traitress, which thrusts forth	607 Foscari	2	386
I would have given some tears to my late country	610 Foscari	3	162
He who loves not his country can love nothing	611 Foscari	3	184
Who dares accuse my country? Men and angels	611 Foscari	3	240
Your years, so long devoted to your country	621 Foscari	5	22
My country call'd me here to exercise	621 Foscari	5	45
The country and the people whom he loved	621 Foscari	5	81
Against his country, had he a thousand lives	622 Foscari	5	93
Country and home. I loved him--how I loved him	622 Foscari	5	97
His own high dignity before his country	623 Foscari	5	182
Not useless to that country, I would fain	623 Foscari	5	184
Of the late troops, who levy on the country	676 Werner	1	339
Where the name of his country is abhorr'd	686 Werner	2	194
The country for some missing bits of coin	700 Werner	3	325
The country (nominally now at peace	705 Werner	4	50
On us for thanksgiving: first, for our country	708 Werner	4	254
Sans country or home	732 Deformed	1	736
For an estate, or cash. or country seat	762 Juan	1	997
Alas! his country show'd no path to praise	808 Juan	3	438
My country? On thy voiceless shore	812 Juan	3	714
And clime and time, and country and complexion	857 Juan	6	319
Not fighting for their country or its crown	869 Juan	7	139
Was he, since so renown'd 'in country quarters	869 Juan	7	151
Their country; and as traitors are abhorr'd	870 Juan	7	174
Defence of freedom, country, or of laws	872 Juan	7	316
'God made the country and man made the town	885 Juan	8	474
Which loves so well its country and its king	894 Juan	8	1002

COUNTRY

To free his country: Pitt too had his pride	897 Juan	9	62
A country in all senses the most dear	917 Juan	10	613
As also bonfires made of country seats	922 Juan	11	211
I have seen the country gentlemen turn squeakers	929 Juan	11	668
A moral country? But I hold my hand	929 Juan	11	684
Country, where a young couple of the same ages	938 Juan	12	514
Into a country where 'tis half a fashion	938 Juan	12	540
Of his own country;--seldom since that day	942 Juan	13	83
And, as he thought, in country much the same	943 Juan	13	156
The London winter and the country summer	947 Juan	13	377
Ere patriots their true country can remember	947 Juan	13	383
'Departure, for his country seat, to-day	947 Juan	13	407
'His country's pride,' he came down to the country	952 Juan	13	728
To be assembled at a country seat	953 Juan	13	746
But in the country ladies seek their bower	955 Juan	13	883
And once o'er several country gentlemen	959 Juan	14	264
There was a country girl in a close cap	988 Juan	16	531
And morals of the country from caprices	989 Juan	16	547
Poor soul! for she was country born and bred	989 Juan	16	558
All country gentlemen, esquired or knighted	989 Juan	16	595
Which threaten'd the whole country with perdition	990 Juan	16	636
The country would have far more cause to weep it	990 Juan	16	646
There were some country wags too--and, alas	991 Juan	16	689
Beheld between the country and the town	991 Juan	16	723
Even in the country circle's narrow bound	992 Juan	16	774
And curtsying off, as curtsies country dame	994 Juan	16	852

COUNTRY-DANCE

Scotch reels, avaunt! and country-dance, forego	275 Waltz		111

COUNTRYMAN

My way-worn countryman, who calls	158 Storm		15
Did not his countryman, Count Corniani	765 Juan	1	1187

COUNTRYMEN
(See also FELLOW-COUNTRYMEN)

Our countrymen were warring on that day	40 Harold	3	314
Thy countrymen, before thee born to shine	61 Harold	4	353
'What gift, my countrymen, what martial prize	107 Nisus		131
Against his countrymen he bore	385 Corinth		118
For Torquil's safety from his countrymen	432 Island	4	182
My friends, my family, my countrymen	516 Faliero	2	523
Were still, at least, our countrymen	813 Juan	3	754
My gentle countrymen, we will renew	918 Juan	10	667

COUNTRY'S

Who strike, blest hirelings! for their country's good	11 Harold	1	473
Nor bleed these patriots with their country's wounds	11 Harold	1	489
So may our country's name be undisgraced	34 Harold	2	879
No strain which shamed his country's creaking lyre	61 Harold	4	341
His country's ruin added to the mass	62 Harold	4	407
And have their country's marbles nought to say	63 Harold	4	502
Thy country's foes ere thou wouldst pause to feel	67 Harold	4	741
Thy country's strains record	218 Thy Days		2
For the Man is his country's--the Arms are the Prince's	228 Ich Dien		2
The man who cut his country's long ago	238 Epigrams		8
Assert thy country's honour and thine own	252 Bards		808
Thy country's voice, the voice of all the nine	254 Bards		933
The hero bounding at his country's call	272 Minerva		289
His country's Caesar, Europe's Hannibal	301 Age		239
And from his country's justice now demands	377 Lara	2	131
Thine injured country's sons to spare	391 Corinth		632
And felt, the vengeance of their country's law	427 Island	3	38
Alas! how bitter is his country's curse	457 Dante	1	69
His country's, and might die where he had birth	465 Dante	4	136
But craved his country's justice on his head	503 Faliero	1	213
As it might chance to be our country's 'vantage	506 Faliero	1	461
I would not so blaspheme our country's creed	554 Sardan	1	232
Why do I love this man? My country's daughters	561 Sardan	1	688
Would have been noble in my country's creed	561 Sardan	1	696
And the cup! 'Tis my country's custom to	594 Sardan	5	451
And merits all our country's gratitude	602 Foscari	2	24
Go and obey our country's will: 'tis not	616 Foscari	4	106
Of days, since every hour has been the country's	621 Foscari	5	52
But almost every other country's blue	775 Juan	2	94
His country's wrongs and his despair to save her	808 Juan	3	423
(It is the country's custom), but in vain	810 Juan	3	594
He died, deserving well his country's tears	888 Juan	8	637
Go! hear it in your famish'd country's cries	897 Juan	9	71
Who fatten on their country's gore, and debts	897 Juan	9	77
When a man's country's going to the devil	915 Juan	10	528
'Perhaps,' thought he, 'it is the country's wont	920 Juan	11	113
All kinds of toil, save for our country's good	926 Juan	11	511
'His country's pride,' he came down to the country	952 Juan	13	728

COUNTS

Or counts her beads with fairy hand	160 Cadiz		45

COUNTS

Retards, but never counts the hour | 172 Time-B | | 20
Counts cent per cent, and smiles, or vainly frets | 260 Hints | | 255
Here are we, counts, kings, dukes, to own thy sway | 467 Morgante | | 91
O'er which I cross'd with two and sixty counts | 467 Morgante | | 112

COUNT'S

And borrow'd the Count's smallclothes for a day | 452 Beppo | | 780

COUNTSHIP

A precious somerset! Is your countship injured | 737 Deformed | 2 | 158

COUNTY

In Nottingham county there lives at Swan Green | 223 Soul-C | | 1
Call'd county meetings, and enforced the laws | 266 Hints | | 672
Serfs of my county of Val di Marino | 533 Faliero | 4 | 370
His barony or county to repel | 678 Werner | 1 | 435
As also at the race and county balls | 844 Juan | 5 | 824
And county meetings, and the parliament | 941 Juan | 13 | 39
But county contests cost him rather dearer | 989 Juan | 16 | 603
Courteous and cautious therefore in his county | 990 Juan | 16 | 609

COUPLE

Which serves the happy couple for a tavern | 748 Juan | 1 | 48
Were to be chain'd and lotted out per couple | 828 Juan | 4 | 727
We leave this royal couple to repose | 855 Juan | 6 | 153
O'er the promoted couple of brave men | 875 Juan | 7 | 537
Country, where a young couple of the same ages | 938 Juan | 12 | 514

COUPLED

Or like a system coupled with a doubt | 981 Juan | 16 | 68

COUPLET

Help!'--'A couplet?'--'No, a cup | 157 Hodgson | | 59
Who from our couplet lopp'd two final feet | 262 Hints | | 402
A couplet, or an elegy to claim | 880 Juan | 8 | 134
Into a Russian couplet rather dull | 904 Juan | 9 | 475

COUPLETS

His creaking couplets in a tavern hall | 241 Bards | | 2
Whether he spin poor couplets into plays | 246 Bards | | 311
Miles Andrews still his strength in couplets try | 251 Bards | | 717
Tag twenty thousand couplets when they please | 265 Hints | | 642

COURAGE

Where Courage falls in her despairing files | 64 Harold | 4 | 556
New courage, he'll think upon glory and you | 86 Leaving NA | | 24
This common courage which with brutes we share | 343 Corsair | 1 | 327
Ay--Pride can veil, and Courage brave it all | 352 Corsair | 2 | 358
If thou hast courage still, and wouldst be free | 360 Corsair | 3 | 306
I augur right of courage and of worth | 372 Lara | 1 | 475
My strength, my courage, or my mind | 408 Mazeppa | | 198
Their manly courage even when deem'd in vain | 418 Island | 1 | 180
Degrades or hallows courage in its fall | 433 Island | 4 | 262
With knightly courage, treasure, or the lance | 467 Morgante | | 55
How I approve my courage in the fight | 474 Morgante | | 554
And hearts, and hopes, and faith, and patient courage | 507 Faliero | 1 | 520
I should not now be here.--Oh! noble Courage | 522 Faliero | 3 | 223
I know not well the courage or the faith | 534 Faliero | 4 | 400
There is a careless courage which corruption | 550 Sardan | 1 | 10
A desperate courage crept through every limb | 580 Sardan | 4 | 140
Who have ceased to mingle love? My sister! Courage | 581 Sardan | 4 | 231
Your courage never--nor your love till now | 586 Sardan | 4 | 496
Courage and vigilance to guard us. May they | 588 Sardan | 5 | 72
Without such grief and courage, as should rather | 660 Heaven | | 405
Their courage, strength, and length of days-- They are number'd | 664 Heaven | | 689
Your courteous courage did in my behalf | 685 Werner | 2 | 154
Can vouch your courage, and, as far as my | 692 Werner | 2 | 583
And courage as unrivall'd, were proclaim'd | 717 Werner | 5 | 246
Ugliest, and meanest of mankind, what courage | 727 Deformed | 1 | 349
Its very courage stagnates to a vice | 747 Juan | Ded | 120
Which courage gives, while poor Pedrillo's pair | 781 Juan | 2 | 445
The only hope of courage dwells | 813 Juan | 3 | 770
In the chill dark, when courage does not glow | 880 Juan | 8 | 163
In courage, was obliged to snatch a shield | 881 Juan | 8 | 223
While courage clung but to a single twig.--Am I | 891 Juan | 8 | 837
He had behaved with courage and humanity | 896 Juan | 8 | 1114
And there's a courage which grows out of fear | 955 Juan | 14 | 34

COURIER

Despatch a courier to a wizard's grave | 244 Bards | | 163
Recorded in the Moniteur and Courier | 747 Juan | 1 | 16
In writing 'Courser' by mistake for 'Courier' | 839 Juan | 5 | 487
A courier to the prince, and he succeeded | 872 Juan | 7 | 298
A courier on the spur inspired new heart | 872 Juan | 7 | 307

COURIERS

'Gainst Satan's couriers bound for their own clime | 292 Vision | | 446
Your couriers are turn'd back--I have outstripp'd them | 687 Werner | 2 | 309

COURLAND

Through Courland also, which that famous farce saw | 914 Juan | 10 | 459

COURSE

Pass we the long, unvarying course, the track | 23 Harold | 2 | 244
The third of the same moon whose former course | 67 Harold | 4 | 766
And fought and conquer'd, and the same course steer'd | 68 Harold | 4 | 797
Could tears retard the tyrant in his course | 85 Epitaph | | 5
Quick to my gate directs his course | 88 Anacreon-B | | 9
But if, through the course of the years which await me | 97 Harrow-A | | 33
Impell'd the bullet's viewless course | 99 Young Lady | | 7
'Thrice has the earth revolved her course | 104 Alva | | 209
We'll bend our course to yonder mountain's brow | 106 Nisus | | 108
Fortune an adverse wayward course may run | 108 Nisus | | 203
To Turnus' camp pursue their destined course | 109 Nisus | | 298
Distraction and discord would follow in course | 117 To Eliza | | 29
Some who yet urge the same scholastic course | 122 Recoll | | 37
Or chase with nimble feet its rapid course | 124 Recoll | | 132
Each, murmuring, seeks another course | 137 Clare | | 23
Who can o'ertake thee in thy fiery course | 139 Ossian-A | | 10
Each Nymph, of course, was all perfection | 144 Becher-B | | 28
At noontide heat their pliant course | 146 Adieu | | 47
His course unto the billows--late escaped | 184 Julian | | 35
The magnet of their course is gone, or only points in vain | 185 Music-B | | 7
And through the street directs his course | 194 Ballad-A | | 12
To fight my course through passion's countless host | 251 Bards | | 692
Mark his gay course and own the hues of heaven | 268 Minerva | | 16
Of course his perspiration was but ichor | 288 Vision | | 199
The angels had of course enough of song | 296 Vision | | 731
Each course enough? or doctors dire dissuaded | 305 Age | | 509
Our course has been right swiftly run | 314 Giaour | | 371
Disdains to light, and keeps his course | 316 Giaour | | 588
May shape the course of struggling skiff | 329 Abydos | 2 | 58
There lie the only rocks our course can check | 334 Abydos | 2 | 460
How gloriously her gallant course she goes | 339 Corsair | 1 | 91
Back to your duty--for my course prepare | 340 Corsair | 1 | 156
Upon our course--the Moslem merchant's gains | 348 Corsair | 2 | 69
Mark his gay course and own the hues of heaven | 355 Corsair | 3 | 16
Short was the course his restlessness had run | 366 Lara | 1 | 23
Each trace wax'd fainter of his course, till all | 366 Lara | 1 | 27
And such, if not yet harden'd in their course | 367 Lara | 1 | 63
Himself unheeded watch'd the stranger's course | 383 Lara | 2 | 564
On their course she hath no sway | 388 Corinth | | 433
But first, outspent with this long course | 407 Mazeppa | | 57
Her course, and gently made her liquid way | 415 Island | 1 | 2
Another course had been their choice--but where | 433 Island | 4 | 235
While yet a doubt sprung where its course might lie | 435 Island | 4 | 380
Whose course and home we knew not, nor shall know | 442 Beppo | | 111
Became a slave of course, and for his pay | 452 Beppo | | 748
The aid of age to turn its course apart | 453 Venice-B | | 29
Its course was free and regular | 480 Manfred | 1 | 114
Without a sphere, without a course | 480 Manfred | 1 | 121
The course of my existence; but there came | 493 Manfred | 3 | 134
To sue for justice, being in the course | 507 Faliero | 1 | 544
And holding on its course; but there, afar | 610 Foscari | 3 | 132
Is your course measured for ye? Or do ye | 637 Cain | 2 | 105
And the immortal star in its great course | 638 Cain | 2 | 131
After the bright course of a few brief morrows | 662 Heaven | | 565
Himself, no tidings have reveal'd his course | 673 Werner | 1 | 93
Of course. But to the point: What's to be done | 684 Werner | 2 | 62
Is Saxon, and of course my service due | 685 Werner | 2 | 179
His father's name was Jose--Don, of course | 748 Juan | 1 | 65
And certainly this course was much the best | 755 Juan | 1 | 532
Thing quite in course, and not at all alarming | 757 Juan | 1 | 687
Were in the English newspapers, of course | 770 Juan | 1 | 1504
Puzzled his tutors very much, of course | 774 Juan | 2 | 16
It changed, of course; a heavenly chameleon | 785 Juan | 2 | 729
Upon its course), pass'd oft before their eyes | 786 Juan | 2 | 748
Or thought they saw, and shaped their course for shore | 786 Juan | 2 | 774
Were mad for land, and thus their course they ran | 787 Juan | 2 | 827
(But that, of course, is rare), and then despond | 802 Juan | 3 | 51
He shaped his course to where his daughter fair | 804 Juan | 3 | 148
If in the course of such a life as was | 830 Juan | 4 | 849
Than any other scrape, a thing of course | 832 Juan | 5 | 96
Was to sit down again, and cry of course | 849 Juan | 5 | 1112
She was of course the favorite of the four | 850 Juan | 5 | 1168
Their talk, of course, ran most on the new comer | 856 Juan | 6 | 273
Its farther course, but must receive its wreck | 865 Juan | 6 | 864
The two first feelings ran their course complete | 904 Juan | 9 | 481
The effect on Juan was of course sublime | 916 Juan | 10 | 585
Like other slaves of course must pay his ransom | 927 Juan | 11 | 579
My topic, with of course the due restriction | 929 Juan | 11 | 690
They warm into a scrape, but keep of course | 939 Juan | 12 | 583
In Britain--which of course true patriots find | 941 Juan | 13 | 15
There also was of course in Adeline | 945 Juan | 13 | 265
Pursued its course, now gleaming, and now hiding | 948 Juan | 13 | 462

COURSE
Of course with some reserve and slight re-
  striction   957 Juan   14   99
But never yet (except of course a miss   972 Juan   15 249
That in the course of some six thousand years   981 Juan   16   50
Below his window waved (of course) a willow   982 Juan   16 118
Of course the others could not but express   985 Juan   16 308
And then of course the circle much admires   986 Juan   16 373
Of course these groups were scatter'd here and
  there   989 Juan   16 569

COURSER
The Andalusian courser in the van   303 Age   373
How could I deem his courser slow   317 Giaour   706
Denied the courser and the spear   332 Abydos   2   324
His wearied courser might refuse   407 Mazeppa   64
The drooping courser, faint and low   413 Mazeppa   627
Methought I heard a courser neigh   413 Mazeppa   669
To lift or carry this dead courser, who   474 Morgante   567
What courser will you please to mount? The dun   705 Werner   4   79
In writing 'Courser' by mistake for 'Courier   839 Juan   5 487

COURSERS
With well-timed croupe the nimble coursers veer   16 Harold   1 760
The gilded harness Rhamnes' coursers felt   109 Nisus   289
And o'er the dead our coursers driven   399 Parisina   303
May see our coursers graze at ease   415 Mazeppa   856
The coursers, and the incense, and the sun   713 Werner   5   19
Shall we proceed? Like gallants, on good coursers 729 Deformed 1 507
Of coursers also spake they: Henry rid   944 Juan   13 181
There were some hunters bold, and coursers keen 991 Juan   16 681

COURSER'S
The dust thy courser's hoof, rude stranger,
  spurns around   34 Harold   2 854
The charioteer along his courser's sides   108 Nisus   247
The foam that streaks the courser's side   312 Giaour   185
Rung his dark courser's hoofs of fear   312 Giaour   207
The spur hath lanced his courser's sides   312 Giaour   249
Some o'er their courser's harness leant   316 Giaour   580
But these might be from his courser's side   317 Giaour   714
And mine have lanced my courser's flank   399 Parisina   272
The thunder of my courser's speed   410 Mazeppa   389
Upon the courser's bristling mane   411 Mazeppa   445
When first my courser's race begun   411 Mazeppa   507
My courser's broad breast proudly braves   412 Mazeppa   590
The sight re-nerved my courser's feet   413 Mazeppa   688
And to and fro, like the pale courser's tail   485 Manfred   2 100

COURSERS'
Beneath their coursers' hoofs the valleys shake 121 Newstead-A   125

COURSES
And follow different courses o'er the tide   429 Island   3 234
But Heaven preserve Old England from such courses 444 Beppo   295
Who to immoral courses would allure us   800 Juan   2 1651
Of intellect expanded on two courses   976 Juan   15 546
Below stairs on the score of second courses   989 Juan   16 588

COURT
And church and court did mingle their array   8 Harold   1 335
While busy preparation shook the court   28 Harold   2 501
Circled the wide extending court below   28 Harold   2 507
With joy I court a certain doom   90 To M.S.G.-A   23
I court the effusions that spring from the heart 92 First Kiss   15
Roused by their call, nor court again repose   106 Juan   82
With eager haste they court the lord of power   112 Examination   63
Far from thy motley court I fly   118 Romance   34
Here Desolation holds her dreary court   121 Newstead-A   97
To join the vain, and court the proud   153 Friend-A   60
There must have been for thee a Court   200 Ode-C   6
Whence spring their scenes, from common life or
  court   259 Hints   162
Should some pretending scribbler of the court   267 Hints   761
The court, the Regent, like herself were new   276 Waltz   162
To note the trappings of her mimic court   308 Age   748
Contain'd at once his captive and his court   352 Corsair   2 369
Her knights and dames, her court--is there   398 Parisina   166
To gaze upon his splendid court   408 Mazeppa   145
It was a court of jousts and mimes   408 Mazeppa   151
Twelve paladins had Charles in court, of whom   467 Morgante   57
'Twas Christmas-day; in Paris all his court   467 Morgante   65
Orlando ruled court, Charles, and every thing   467 Morgante   84
For the whole court is more or less in grief   468 Morgante   115
I am charged to tell his highness that the court 500 Faliero   1   38
Within whose court will be drawn out in arms   524 Faliero   3 376
The first now stands before you in the court   540 Faliero   5 172
Then let it sleep in mine, unless you court   542 Faliero   5 287
And sentence from the court! This full admission 542 Faliero   5 298
Spare him--he's none: a mere court butterfly   588 Sardan   5   90
Is safe with my three sons in Cotta's court   593 Sardan   5 394
'The Ten;' but as the court no longer sate   602 Foscari   2   58
With which the court adjourn'd; and till it meets 602 Foscari   2   64
And has much influence with a certain court   684 Werner   2   90

COURT
Your hall's my court, your heart is my tribunal 717 Werner   5 301
The court, camp, church, the vessel, and the mart 770 Juan   1 1547
As plentiful as in a court, or fair   810 Juan   3 544
His wondrous journey to some foreign court   838 Juan   5 411
Snatch'd from a prison to preside at court   850 Juan   5 1171
Of worlds to lose, yet still, to pay my court, I 853 Juan   6   37
And so he says no more--but pays his court   871 Juan   7 253
Much less than is the hope of every court   877 Juan   7 630
The court, that watch'd each look her visage wore 904 Juan   9 461
The whole court look'd immediately most sweet   904 Juan   9 483
The whole court melted into one wide whisper   906 Juan   9 617
Must come? Much rather should he court the ray   908 Juan   10   71
At which the whole court was extremely troubled 912 Juan   10 311
'Love rules the camp, the court, the grove,'--
  'for love   931 Juan   12   97
Now if the 'court,' and 'camp,' and 'grove,' be
  not   931 Juan   12 121
I've known them court an heiress for their lover 933 Juan   12 260
The kinder veteran with calm words will court you 935 Juan   12 357
Should neither court neglect, nor dread to bear
  it   941 Juan   12 696
Court mysteries, having been himself a minister 943 Juan   13 164
Amidst the court a Gothic fountain play'd   949 Juan   13 513
No doubt, if I had wish'd to pay my court   971 Juan   15 173

COURTED
I suffer'd chains and courted death   402 Chillon   12
Juan, instead of courting courts, was courted   911 Juan   10 225

COURTEOUS
Say, courteous host, canst thou not feel it   89 Anacreon-B   48
The courteous host, and all-approving guest   375 Lara   1 629
He play'd the courteous lord and bounteous host 377 Lara   2 191
The courteous manners but from nature caught   417 Island   1 109
Courteous and kind to your great worth appear'd 475 Morgante   621
Which made me look like them--a courteous wittol 502 Faliero   1 194
Your courteous courage did in my behalf   685 Werner   2 154
As yet he hath been courteous as he's bounteous 704 Werner   4   15
And certes courteous, to leave that to the lady 710 Werner   4 393
Who must be courteous to the accredited   923 Juan   11 314
Courteous and cautious therefore in his county   990 Juan   16 609

COURTEOUSLY
Which thus begins so courteously and well   372 Lara   1 460
But the Count courteously invited in   451 Beppo   714
Pass'd, but he strove quite courteously to quell 807 Juan   3 348
Proud with the proud, yet courteously proud   970 Juan   15 117

COURTESAN
Let the poor wretch, like to the courtesan   544 Faliero   5 450

COURTESIES
All proper customs and true courtesies   467 Morgante   53
Made him my debtor for some courtesies   513 Faliero   2 293
To use all fit and proper courtesies   844 Juan   5 837

COURTESY
For Courtesy and Pity died   313 Giaour   346
That checks low mirth but lacks not courtesy   346 Corsair   1 544
With all the courtesy he deign'd his friends   346 Corsair   1 562
Much did she marvel o'er the courtesy   351 Corsair   2 261
But still I thank your courtesy or thine   353 Corsair   2 444
The unlook'd for courtesy of such a knight   372 Lara   1 434
And if a Christian, speak for courtesy   471 Morgante   332
Who? My own friends by blood and courtesy   527 Faliero   3 571
And no less to their courtesy.--Proceed   604 Foscari   2 195
To have the courtesy to abdicate   615 Foscari   4   35
You might reply with courtesy to what   679 Werner   1 532
Pray have the courtesy to make it known   765 Juan   1 1227
And you an equal courtesy should show   833 Juan   5 124
Which is required by proper courtesy   929 Juan   11 691
In making men what courtesy calls friends   943 Juan   13 120
A gentle, genial courtesy of mind   945 Juan   13 254
And waxing chiller in her courtesy   961 Juan   14 366
In courtesy their wish to see display'd   985 Juan   16 309
And dignity with courtesy so blending   993 Juan   16 804

COURTIER
One, though a courtier, lived a man of worth   94 Dorset   67
You turn'd to half a courtier ere you died   293 Vision   570
For the first courtier in the Czar's regard   302 Age   309
Where every courtier tried at rhymes   408 Mazeppa   152
But prince--Hence, I say! Here's a courtier and 589 Sardan   5 118
The sneer of the last courtier whom he has made 709 Werner   4 298
A disappointed courtier--What's the matter   743 Deformed   3   93
No courtier could, and scarcely woman can   806 Juan   3 325

COURTIERS
Than courtiers at a banquet would   407 Mazeppa   92
Beset with drowsy guards and drunken courtiers   563 Sardan   2 131
The courtiers stared, the ladies whisper'd, and 902 Juan   9 361

COURTIER'S
The courtier's supple bow and sneering smile   126 Recoll   317
Or, roughly treading on the 'courtier's kibes   901 Juan   9   278

COURTING
Juan, instead of courting courts, was courted   911 Juan   10   225

COURTLY
He thought at heart like courtly Chesterfield   959 Juan   14   277
Tall, stately, form'd to lead the courtly van   964 Juan   14   557

COURTS
Alike for courts, and camps, or senates fit   94 Dorset   70
In thee the wounded conscience courts relief   120 Newstead-A   19
Haply, in polish'd courts might be thy seat   126 Recoll   315
'Tis yours to mix in polish'd courts   137 Clare   35
Yet since in danger courts abound   138 Clare   79
Bred in the courts betimes, though all that law 247 Bards   446
Nor care if courts and crowds applaud or hiss   256 Bards   1062
Our church and state, our courts and camps,
    concede   264 Hints   581
Or raise the neck that courts the yoke   311 Giaour   163
Of courts would slide o'er his forgotten name   462 Dante   3   133
The secret custom of the courts in Venice   500 Faliero   1   54
Are spawn'd in courts by base intrigues, and
    baser   565 Sardan   2   207
Even in our courts and by the outer gate   573 Sardan   3   106
The very centre, girded by vast courts   588 Sardan   5   64
Juan, instead of courting courts, was courted   911 Juan   10   225
If 'courts' and 'camps' be quite so sentimental 931 Juan   12   104
Without cash, camps were thin, and courts were
    none   931 Juan   12   107
In camps, in ships, in cottages, or courts   959 Juan   14   244

COURTSHIP
His form, in courtship of repose   387 Corinth   335

COUSIN
I have a cousin in the lazaretto   674 Werner   1   188
Play'd round my heart: blood is not water, cousin 674 Werner   1   198
My intimate connexion;--'Cousin Idenstein   682 Werner   1   688
You are early, my sweet cousin! Not too early   706 Werner   4   151
Why do you call me 'cousin'? Are we not so   706 Werner   4   153
Back to my heart, which beats for you, sweet
    cousin   706 Werner   4   161
'Cousin' again. Nay, then I'll call you sister 706 Werner   4   162
Sister, or cousin, what you will, so that   707 Werner   4   169
Which might have call'd Diana's chorus 'cousin 844 Juan   5   790
Each aunt, each cousin, hath her speculation   933 Juan   12   257
And wild dismay o'er every angry cousin   934 Juan   12   267

COUSINS
Marrying their cousins--nay, their aunts, and
    nieces   754 Juan   1   455
For cousins also, answer'd the same day   911 Juan   10   236

COUSIN'S
Was sure he was his mother's cousin's brother   294 Vision   608

COVE
Where lone Utraikey forms its circling cove   30 Harold   2   622
Whose bark in sheltering cove below   310 Giaour   38
Freights the frail bark and urges to the cove   429 Island   3   238

COVENT
For, bating Covent Garden, I can hit on   440 Beppo   39

COVER
Which her own clay shall cover, heap'd and pent 39 Harold   3   251
Here didst thou dwell, in this enchanted cover   72 Harold   4 1054
Their ships cover the ocean. Their hosts   130 Calmar   32
Descended from Angrante: under cover   468 Morgante   154
So that he took a long leap under cover   469 Morgante   208
And cover with it o'er this giant's skin   476 Morgante   659
In high Silesia will permit and cover   705 Werner   4   103
In spirit. Cover up my dust, and breathe not   737 Deformed 2   151
For sometimes such a world of virtues cover   830 Juan   4   886

COVER'D
(See also CRAG-COVER'D, HEATH-COVER'D, MAIL-
COVER'D, PINE-COVER'D)
The earth is cover'd thick with other clay   39 Harold   3   250
A banquet in the flesh it cover'd o'er   432 Island   4   172
'Tis a long cover'd boat that's common here   442 Beppo   147
Was cover'd with old armour like a crust   476 Morgante   666
Placed at the ducal table, cover'd o'er   500 Faliero   1   7
Nor work advanced, nor cover'd way was there   868 Juan   7   87

COVERING
Yes! doff that covering, where morocco shines   251 Bards   739

COVERS
The moment night with dusky mantle covers   440 Beppo   9
And covers his ferocious eye with hands   652 Cain   3   398

COVERS
Miss Edgeworth's novels stepping from their
    covers   749 Juan   1   122
Profusion with young beauty covers o'er   801 Juan   2 1684
As many covers, duly, daily, laid   947 Juan   13   390

COVERT
And track to his covert the captive on shore   30 Harold   2   668
The covert of old trees with trunks all hoar   51 Harold   3   947
Beneath the covert of the blackening smoke   106 Nisus   105
Trusting the covert of the night, they fly   109 Nisus   310
And now the foe their covert quit   316 Giaour   597
The secret covert to which this will lead you   591 Sardan   5   254
As e'er the hunted deer a covert--Or   695 Werner   3   6
And I have none; I merely seek a covert   696 Werner   3   58

COVET
To covet there another's bride   397 Parisina   66
You are the sole ally we covet now   508 Faliero   1   575
To peace--the only victory I covet   586 Sardan   4   504
Thou shalt not covet Mr. Sotheby's Muse   772 Juan   1 1641
Of toil, is what we covet most; and yet   955 Juan   14   26

COVETED
Their only portion of the coveted kingdom   566 Sardan   2   288
Whate'er she saw and coveted was brought   845 Juan   5   897
Who never coveted their neighbour's lot   931 Juan   12   123

COVETEDST
Thou saw'st, and covetedst her charms   399 Parisina   256

COVETOUS
Which made me covetous of girlish beauty   513 Faliero   2   312
And, covetous of brief authority   518 Faliero   2   701

COVETS
Although 'twere wed to him it covets most   514 Faliero   2   387
And who and what doth not? Who covets evil   642 Cain   2   444

COVEY
Dogs blink their covey, flints withhold the spark 264 Hints   555
The first bird of the covey! he has fallen   737 Deformed 2   164

COV'RING
The earth, which is thine outward cov'ring, is 629 Cain   1   117

COWARD
His coward breast behind a jar he hides   109 Nisus   269
When the doubts of coward foes   187 French-A   19
A coward brood, which mangle as they prey   247 Bards   430
And Giaffir almost call'd me coward   327 Abydos   1   361
No--though again he call me coward   334 Abydos   2   536
Wrung from the coward crouching of despair   354 Corsair   2   481
But not a coward or a common spoil   428 Island   3   156
This creeping, coward, rank, acquitted felon   502 Faliero   1   185
Upon his coward calumny. 'Twere fit   509 Faliero   2   44
The coward Bertram, would--Peace, Calendaro   539 Faliero   5   128

COWARDICE
In discord, cowardice, cruelty, all that springs 465 Dante   4   123
Despised by cowards for greater cowardice   549 Faliero   5   772

COWARDLY
Thou cowardly murderer by law, behold   619 Foscari   4   243

COWARDS
Despised by cowards for greater cowardice   549 Faliero   5   772

COWARD'S
Were fate well worthy of a coward's halt   379 Lara   2   339

COWER'D
And cower'd to hear their own victorious trumpet 533 Faliero 4   385

COWERS
Destruction cowers to mark what deeds are done   10 Harold   1   429
The patriarch of the flock all gently cowers   805 Juan   3   252
He shudder'd, as no doubt the bravest cowers   996 Juan   16 1005

COWL
Sought shelter in the priest's protecting cowl 120 Newstead-A   28
Of Saint Bartholomew, which makes his cowl   287 Vision   157
That glares beneath his dusky cowl   318 Giaour   833
With these as much is done as with this cowl   476 Morgante   650
In cowl and beads and dusky garb, appear'd   983 Juan   16   162
'Tis shadow'd by his cowl   986 Juan   16   350
Back fell the sable frock and dreary cowl   996 Juan   16 1029

COWLS
And gilded crosiers, and cross'd arms, and cowls 697 Werner   3   118

COWPER
Where her last hopes with pious Cowper sleep   252 Bards   810
So Cowper says--and I begin to be   885 Juan   8   475

COW-POX
The cow-pox, tractors, galvanism, and gas   243 Bards   132

COW'S
A cow's shape for a mask--was only (sinking   793 Juan   2   1237

COXCOMB
For food and raiment thus the coxcomb rails   142 Soliloquy   51
And twenty scatter'd quires, the coxcomb fails   262 Hints   386
Resplendent sight! Behold the coxcomb Czar   304 Age   434
A coxcomb was he by the public voice   443 Beppo   238
A charlatan, a coxcomb--and have been   761 Juan   1   927
The quaint, old, cruel coxcomb, in his gullet   954 Juan   13   847
Now Juan, though no coxcomb in pretence   977 Juan   15   613

COXCOMBRY
Of coxcombry in admiration loud   423 Island   2   337
Without the coxcombry of certain she men   959 Juan   14   248
Of coxcombry or conquest: no abuse   969 Juan   15   92

COXCOMBRY'S
Of coxcombry's worst coxcombs e'en the pink   449 Beppo   598

COXCOMBS
Let coxcombs, printing as they come from far   255 Bards   1025
Round the throng'd gate shall sauntering coxcombs
  creep   271 Minerva   183
Of coxcombry's worst coxcombs e'en the pink   449 Beppo   598
You'll find ten thousand handsome coxcombs bloody 892 Juan   8   896
Self-love, there's safety in a crowd of coxcombs 945 Juan   13   240

COXCOMB'S
Declaring with a coxcomb's native air   142 Soliloquy   43
Recounts a flattering coxcomb's praise   147 Vain Lady   24
Some coxcomb's raillery   159 Storm   66
She was a pitch beyond a coxcomb's flight   962 Juan   14   452

COXE
Until his late Life by Archdeacon Coxe   813 Juan   3   816

COY
The woods and waters with coy nymphs that scorn'd 205 Aristom   8
Lo! blushing Itch, coy nymph, enamour'd grown   249 Bards   536

COZEN
That is to say, unskill'd to cozen   100 Marion   37

COZENAGE
With deadly cozenage, eight long months before-
  hand   619 Foscari   4   301
My lord, my lord, this is mere cozenage   692 Werner   2   594

CRABBE
Crabbe, Malcolm, Hamilton, and Chantrey   231 Doctor   61
This fact in Virtue's name let Crabbe attest   253 Bards   857
Scott, Rogers, Campbell, Moore, and Crabbe will
  try   746 Juan   Ded   55
With Crabbe it may be difficult to cope   772 Juan   1   1637

CRABBES
Crabbes, Campbells, Crokers, Freres, and Wards   231 Doctor   54

CRABBY
The Duchess of Fitz-Fulke; the Countess Crabby   951 Juan   13   627

CRAB-LIKE
Crouching and crab-like, through their sapping
  streets   453 Venice-B   13

CRACK
May unship us in a crack   157 Hodgson   68
They'd crack them. Hunger is a sharp artillery 732 Deformed   1   748
To crack those walls alone. You may sneer, since 734 Deformed 1   866
They're on the stair just now, and in a crack   763 Juan   1   1094
And their baked lips, with many a bloody crack   784 Juan   2   681
He was a jolly fellow, and could crack   887 Juan   8   557

CRACK'D
The musico is but a crack'd old basin   827 Juan   4   682
Who little thought that his own crack'd existence 837 Juan   5   403
Crack'd, shiver'd, vanish'd, scarcely gazed on,
  ere   927 Juan   11   597

CRACKING
Cases cracking   157 Hodgson   13

CRACKLING
They fell and faded--and the crackling trunks   189 Darkness   20
He climbs the crackling stair, he bursts the door 350 Corsair   2   211
And here and there some crackling dome   386 Corinth   165
Their crackling battlements all cleft   410 Mazeppa   403
When with its crackling sound the night   411 Mazeppa   427
The comets herald through the crackling skies   489 Manfred   2   381

CRACKS
For which their mouths gaped, like the cracks of
  earth   784 Juan   2   666

CRADLE
Dash o'er the old Spaniard's cradle, and would
  fain   302 Age   284
Now crawl from cradle to the grave   311 Giaour   150
Rock'd in his cradle by the roaring wind   421 Island   2   167
Her palace, in whose cradle Empire grew   459 Dante   2   55

CRADLED
Sweet be thy cradled slumbers! O'er the sea   53 Harold   3   1099
Man knows not, when from out its cradled nook   77 Harold   4   1339
When in cradled rest they lay   395 Corinth   1043
Brought forth in purple, cradled in vermilion   785 Juan   2   731

CRAFT
(See also EPISTLE-CRAFT)
Reviewing 'the ungentle craft,' and then   297 Vision   779
Proverbial wiles and ancient craft   311 Giaour   158
Is this my skill? my craft? to set at last   343 Corsair   1   337
Egad! she seem'd a wicked-looking craft   426 Island   2   513
Fie, Bertram! that was not a craft for thee   532 Faliero   4   284

CRAFTY
Each day some tempter's crafty suit   179 Gold   29

CRAG
Fruit, foliage, crag, wood, cornfield, mountain,
  vine   42 Harold   3   412
The castled crag of Drachenfels   43 Harold   3   496
For there--the Rose o'er crag or vale   310 Giaour   21
The crag is won, no more is seen   312 Giaour   255
From crag to cliff they mount.--Near yonder cave 340 Corsair   1   129
From crag to crag descending, swiftly sped   345 Corsair   1   505
Hail in each crag a friend's familiar face   422 Island   2   282
When scaling his enormous crag the wave   426 Island   3   21
And gush'd from cliff to crag with saltless spray 427 Island   3   66
Still as their oars receded from the crag   431 Island   4   91
In some bleak crag or deeply-hidden bay   433 Island   4   242
But steep the crag, and all without a path   434 Island   4   307
The crag, as doth a falcon reft of young   434 Island   4   328
The floating fence of Albion's feebler crag   454 Venice-B   146

CRAG-COVER'D
As I felt, when a boy, on the crag-cover'd wild 135 Highlander   12

CRAGGY
Or dark Sierras rise in craggy pride   9 Harold   1   364
Which loves the mountain's craggy side   135 I Would   7
Though far from Albin's craggy shore   158 Florence   9
O'er brake and craggy brow   158 Storm   34
And borne o'er breakers reach'd the craggy shore 184 Julian   7
Who dare not quit their craggy screen   316 Giaour   586
Shines o'er its craggy battlement   388 Corinth   375
The sharer of his craggy solitudes   421 Island   2   172
She pointed calmly to the craggy isle   430 Island   4   38
Remain'd unknown within his craggy nook   796 Juan   2   1388

CRAGS
The horrid crags by toppling convent crown'd   7 Harold   1   243
And here and there, as up the crags you spring   7 Harold   1   261
Ne horrid crags, nor mountains dark and tall   9 Harold   1   367
With crags, whereon those Moorish turrets rest   12 Harold   1   514
Cold as the crags upon his native coast   21 Harold   2   102
Yet are thy skies as blue, thy crags as wild   · 33 Harold   2   819
From peak to peak the rattling crags among   49 Harold   3   864
The permanent crags, tell here of Love, who sought 50 Harold   3   929
Oh for the crags that are wild and majestic   118 Lachin   39
And the famine which dwelt on her freedomless crags 202 Avatar   11
Small broken crags of granite gray   315 Giaour   562
As shrubless crags within the mist   405 Chillon   238
And you, ye crags, upon whose extreme edge   482 Manfred   1   274
Which I outlive!--Ye toppling crags of ice   482 Manfred   1   335
One of the many chiefs, whose castled crags   483 Manfred   2   8

CRAG'S
Of the crag's steep, inexorable face   430 Island   4   49
O'er the crag's headlong perpendicular   485 Manfred   2   98

CRAM
And began to cram from a plate of ham   178 Devil's Dr   207
While Southey's epics cram the creaking shelves 243 Bards   127
A turbot for relief of those who cram   976 Juan   15   499

CRAMM'D
But now this sheet is nearly cramm'd   238 Orford   13
But the benches are cramm'd, like a garden in
  flower   277 Blues   1   2
Why, the place is so cramm'd, there's not room
  for a spectre   278 Blues   1   4
I know my catechism; I know we are cramm'd   286 Vision   108
Or cramm'd twelve sheets into one little letter 954 Juan   13   831

CRANED

| And never craned, and made but few 'faux pas | 959 Juan | 14 | 259 |

CRANNIES

| Through distant crannies, of a twinkling light | 718 Werner | 5 | 309 |

CRANNYING

| All tenantless, save to the crannying wind | 42 Harold | 3 | 417 |

CRASH

Extinguish'd with a crash--and all was black	189 Darkness		21
And when land crumbles, bid firm paper crash	306 Age		639
Crash with a frequent conflict; but ye pass	482 Manfred	1	339
Louder than the loud ocean, like a crash	780 Juan	2	418
From our old crash, some mystic, ancient strain	901 Juan	9	299
Its inner crash is like an earthquake's ruin	966 Juan	14	680

CRASHAW

| With truth like Southey, and with verse like Crashaw | 811 Juan | 3 | 632 |

CRASH'D

Here crash'd a sturdy oath of stout John Bull	292 Vision		465
The flame, as loud the ruin crash'd	386 Corinth		170
That crash'd through the brain of the infidel	394 Corinth		877
When the Poles crash'd, and water was the world	432 Island	4	150

CRASHES

| That sound that crashes in the tyrant's ear | 300 Age | | 166 |
| Downward then the ladder crashes | 736 Deformed | 2 | 90 |

CRASHING

| Crashing the lance, he snuffs the spouting gore | 15 Harold | 1 | 688 |
| Again in crashing chaos roll'd | 88 Horace | | 14 |

CRAVAT

To give some rebel Pacha a cravat	842 Juan	5	711
His bandage slipp'd down into a cravat	902 Juan	9	353
The cravat stain'd with bloody drops fell down	920 Juan	11	129

CRAVE

Justice is sworn 'gainst tears, and hers would crave	45 Harold	3	630
My hands and eyes and heart, and crave of thee a gift	74 Harold	4	1170
Whose jaws eternal victims crave	88 Catullus		18
For him, whose distant relics vainly crave	182 Address-C		29
The veil of Immortality, and crave	190 Churchill		16
The weak must bear, the wretch must crave	320 Giaour		1025
In vain impels the burning mouth to crave	380 Lara	2	404
He who first downs with the red cross may crave	392 Corinth		717
It necessary for myself to crave	451 Beppo		699
I crave a second grace for this approach	495 Manfred	3	306
Is here to crave your patience. Leave the chamber	505 Faliero	1	356
I crave, not pardon, but compassion from you	543 Faliero	5	406
The Ionian Myrrha we would crave her presence	557 Sardan	1	467
Am upon duty. May we crave its purport	564 Sardan	2	155
Of--True--true--true: I crave your pardon. I	620 Foscari	5	7
The whirling river, have sent on to crave	675 Werner	1	226
If I intrude, I crave--Oh, no intrusion	675 Werner	1	250
In the meantime I crave your company	679 Werner	1	521
It is but a night's lodging which I crave	696 Werner	3	48
To prove reluctant, and begg'd leave to crave	866 Juan	6	893

CRAVED

But craved my country's justice on his head	503 Faliero	1	213
I craved his name, but this he seem'd reluctant	529 Faliero	4	117
One of the Forty; 'the Ten' having craved	541 Faliero	5	225

CRAVEN

Approach, thou craven crouching slave	311 Giaour		108
Nor raised the craven cry, Amaun	316 Giaour		603
No craven he, and yet he dreads the blow	349 Corsair	2	178
There the craven cries for quarter	393 Corinth		839
Disarm me: why such craven did I fight	470 Morgante		259

CRAVENS

| That seeks what cravens shun with more than zeal | 338 Corsair | 1 | 19 |

CRAVES

Pacha!--my limbs are faint--and nature craves	348 Corsair	2	95
My lord, the abbot of St. Maurice craves	491 Manfred	3	19
Craves audience of your highness. I'm unwell	504 Faliero	1	317
The noble dame Marina craves an audience	621 Foscari	5	64

CRAVING

And this dark heart is vainly craving	221 Mariamne		14
This herald has been brought before me, craving	591 Sardan	5	287
Had told his son to satisfy his craving	917 Juan	10	622

CRAW

| As tigers combat with an empty craw | 884 Juan | 8 | 389 |

CRAWL

The filth they leave still points out where they crawl	171 Hales-Owen		12
Now crawl from cradle to the grave	311 Giaour		150
In trembling pairs (alone they dared not) crawl	369 Lara	1	259

CRAWL'D

Came tame and tremulous; and vipers crawl'd	189 Darkness		35
Seems proud of the reptile which crawl'd from her earth	203 Avatar		91
The meanest thing that crawl'd beneath my eyes	256 Bards		1056
Become as base a critic as e'er crawl'd	297 Vision		780
And spurn the dust o'er which they crawl'd of late	299 Age		47
Crawl'd on, and added but another link	516 Faliero	2	561

CRAWLER

| May have the crawler crush'd, but feels no anger | 544 Faliero | 5 | 464 |

CRAWLING

| Here the young turtle, crawling from his shell | 430 Island | 4 | 21 |

CRAWLS

Till the black slime betray her as she crawls	208 Sketch		48
That he crawls on the surface like Vermin	232 Murray-B		63
Too low a third crawls on, afraid to fly	257 Hints		45
I'd rather be the thing that crawls	320 Giaour		990
Let him who crawls enamour'd of decay	338 Corsair	1	27
The dragon crawls from out his den	669 Heaven		1063
The quiet sheep feeds, and the tortoise crawls	826 Juan	4	616

CRAZED

| Crazed, querulous, forsaken, half forgot | 260 Hints | | 261 |
| Because the first is crazed beyond all hope | 772 Juan | 1 | 1635 |

CRAZY

With crazy oar and shatter'd strength along	418 Island	1	187
The door to open, like a crazy thing	471 Morgante		311
Yet of a beauty that would drive you crazy	857 Juan	6	328

CREAK

The iron yields, the hinges creak	394 Corinth		944
Except the creak of wheels, which on their pivot he	919 Juan	11	62
It open'd with a most infernal creak	995 Juan	16	969

CREAK'D

| And the ship creak'd, the town became a speck | 775 Juan | 2 | 99 |

CREAKING

No strain which shamed his country's creaking lyre	61 Harold	4	341
His creaking couplets in a tavern hall	241 Bards		2
While Southey's epics cram the creaking shelves	243 Bards		127
He strides and stamps along with creaking boot	267 Hints		775
Now, creaking in the ears of those who owe	454 Venice-B		119
Or making chorus to the creaking oar	506 Faliero	1	423

CREAKS

| The wreck that creaks to the wild winds, and wretch | 596 Foscari | 1 | 59 |

CREAM

My lady skims the cream of each critique	249 Bards		557
Scarcely o'erpass'd the cream of your champagne	796 Juan	2	1418
Who seem'd the cream of equanimity	973 Juan	15	323

CREATE
(See also RE-CREATE)

'Tis to create, and in creating live	36 Harold	3	46
A beauty and a mystery, and create	49 Harold	3	830
Essentially immortal, they create	55 Harold	4	38
We can recall such visions, and create	63 Harold	4	466
Which for its pleasure doth create	191 Prometheus-B		21
Black--as thy will for others would create	209 Sketch		90
Here are the Alpine landscapes which create	211 Augusta-C		57
While yet Canova can create below	446 Beppo		368
For what is poesy but to create	463 Dante	4	11
Further than to create a moment's pity	544 Faliero	5	412
Myself, with those about me, to create	610 Foscari	3	164
Who didst create these best and beauteous beings	627 Cain	1	15
Create, and re-create	630 Cain	1	163
Society itself, which should create	834 Juan	5	197
She had consented to create again	962 Juan	14	439
Not witches only b---ches--who create	997 Juan	17	52

CREATED
(See also SELF-CREATED, SMOKE-CREATED)

A wretch created to repine	152 Weep-A		20
Created by degrees an ocean-Rome	610 Foscari	3	154
Unto Jehovah, who created both	662 Heaven		570
His love unto created love? I am	665 Heaven		746
To be created, and to acknowledge him	666 Heaven		842

CREATES
A spark creates the flame--'tis the last drop   541 Faliero 5 246
Alone creates it, kindles, and may quench it   587 Sardan   4 572
He who creates all beauty will lose more   644 Cain   2 540

CREATING
'Tis to create, and in creating live   36 Harold   3   46
Creating worlds, to make eternity   629 Cain   1 149

CREATION
Within its own creation, or in thine   42 Harold   3 407
Could man but leave thy bright creation so   42 Harold   3 445
A new creation with his magic line   61 Harold   4 358
Might furnish forth creation. Italy   63 Harold   4 488
Egeria, sweet creation of some heart   72 Harold   4 1027
And fevers into false creation:--where   73 Harold   4 1091
Mere phantoms of thine own creation   87 Rousseau   8
To hail you queens of all creation   101 Marion   55
Before Creation peopled earth   220 Clay   17
Yon weak creation of such paltry things   290 Vision   319
But thou, my young creation! my soul's child   437 Tasso   37
To the fair single part of the Creation   444 Beppo   298
The bloody chaos yet expects creation   459 Dante   2   42
A Croesus in creation--I plunged deep   487 Manfred 2 236
Thy fellows in creation, thou dost rarely   491 Manfred 3   40
In the first dawn and bloom of young creation   643 Cain   2 475
Shall not stand in the sun, to shame creation   650 Cain   3 304
The little remnant of the past creation   661 Heaven   450
As on the fourth day of creation, when   662 Heaven   552
Vile form--from the creation, as it hath   723 Deformed 1   65
His stand in creation   728 Deformed 1 419
Unto the new creation, rising out   901 Juan   9 298
And every new creation hath decreased   901 Juan   9 310
Gleams only through the dawn of its creation   930 Juan   12   16

CREATIONS
The gay creations of his spirit charm   193 Monody   48
Creations of the mind?--The mind can make   214 Dream   19
The form which their creations may essay   463 Dante   4   24
But think not of these things--the mere creations 580 Sardan 4 168

CREATION'S
Such as creation's dawn beheld, thou rollest now 82 Harold   4 1638
Fire! Creation's first-born daughter   729 Deformed 1 471

CREATIVE
The Bard of Prose, creative spirit, he   63 Harold   4 498
Be for mere fancy's sport a theme creative   942 Juan   13   78

CREATOR
Of that which is of all Creator and defence   49 Harold   3 841
Their clay creator the vain title take   82 Harold   4 1625
To the Creator? Surely, 'tis well done   647 Cain   3 103

CREATOR'S
Their great Creator's purpose know   132 Prayer   32

CREATURE
Oh earth! of which he was a noble creature   300 Age   132
Against the outworn creature they assail   439 Tasso   203
This should have been a noble creature: he   493 Manfred 3 160
The innocent creature thus most vilely slander'd 502 Faliero 1 206
We operate to slay or save! This creature   537 Faliero 4 645
Dear is the helpless creature we defend   762 Juan   1 1006
The creature was his father's dog that died   783 Juan   2 563
A something to be loved, a creature meant   796 Juan   2 1373
I saw the prettiest creature, fresh from Milan   800 Juan   2 1671
How lonely every freeborn creature broods   820 Juan   4 221
In a new face 'the ugliest creature breathing   857 Juan   6 296
Dudu, as has been said, was a sweet creature   858 Juan   6 409
Pervaded him--although a generous creature   884 Juan   8 415
And when at last the pretty creature gets   934 Juan   12 285
For prejudice it was--against a creature   974 Juan   15 410

CREATURES
(See also FELLOW-CREATURES)
Class'd among creatures, when the soul can flee   46 Harold   3 686
Which God has proclaim'd as the fate of his
  creatures   91 Caroline-C   15
Of these two creatures should be thus traced out 216 Dream   204
Creatures of clay--vain dwellers in the dust   222 Spirit   9
Degrade God's creatures in his graphic spleen   256 Hints   8
Fragments of stone, rear'd by creatures of clay 389 Corinth   506
Those brazen creatures always suit their taste   448 Beppo   536
Of cheerful creatures, whose most sinful deeds   453 Venice-B   26
Nor midst the creatures of clay that girded me   485 Manfred 2 152
Sustain such creatures. True, it was more
  glorious   640 Cain   2 283
That which it was. And those enormous creatures 641 Cain   2 337
And those inordinate creatures sporting o'er   642 Cain   2 393
All temporary breathing creatures their   644 Cain   2 576
Ye are his creatures, and not mine. Then leave
  us   645 Cain   2 601
His creatures, as thou say'st we are, or show me 645 Cain   2 602

CREATURES
The creatures proud of their poor clay   661 Heaven   438
Poor creatures! are you sure? Yes, of the monkey 675 Werner 1 217
No kind--not made like other creatures, or   722 Deformed 1   36
Amongst the stars, which these poor creatures
  deem   735 Deformed 1 891
Of what these creatures call eternity   739 Deformed 2 291
The charming creatures lie with such a grace   768 Juan   1 1423
Have such a charm for us poor human creatures   800 Juan   2 1664
Yet some of you are most seraphic creatures   830 Juan   4 881
Poor creatures! their good looks were sadly
  changed   832 Juan   5   52
You never thought about those little creatures   842 Juan   5 696
Those houris, like all other pretty creatures   892 Juan   8 887
With some of those fair creatures who have prided 933 Juan   12 198
Think not, fair creatures, that I mean to abuse
  you all   933 Juan   12 219
All matchless creatures, and yet bent on matches 936 Juan   12 424

CREDENCE
Full credence to the tale they tell   397 Parisina   129
The body of your Credence? No one--but   743 Deformed 3 114

CREDENTIAL
To proper placemen, every Russ credential   922 Juan   11 274

CREDIT
How quick we credit every oath   97 To Woman   17
Must credit all we say or write   147 Vain Lady   31
His name would bring more credit than his verse 162 Orchomenus   8
New words find credit in these latter days   257 Hints   79
Expect no credit for too wondrous tales   264 Hints   539
(Then Phoebus first found credit in a bank   266 Hints   718
"Blest paper credit;" who shall dare to sing   271 Minerva   245
But he has too much credit near the throne   467 Morgante   94
But much more still that Charles should give him
  credit   468 Morgante   120
From the sky to preserve their seer and credit   576 Sardan   3 281
For my own part, I credit neither; 'tis   625 Foscari 5 299
Of good advice--and two or three of credit   775 Juan   2   72
To save the credit of their breaking bank   850 Juan   5 1230
And rich in rubles, diamonds, cash, and credit   916 Juan   10 554
Not to be overlook'd--and gave such credit   924 Juan   11 391
Which makes bank credit like a bank of vapour   930 Juan   12   32
If but to keep thy credit as a mower   962 Juan   14 424
Will pique a gentleman, for his own credit   978 Juan   15 629

CREDITED
The theme, half credited the strange tradition   987 Juan   16 476

CREDITOR
I'm for a handsome article his creditor   772 Juan   1 1675
Sole creditor whose process doth involve in't   969 Juan   15   55

CREDITORS
Of any creditors the worst a Jew it is   782 Juan   2 517
Of paying debts, which creditors regret   955 Juan   14   30

CREDITORS'
When teased with creditors' continual claims   268 Hints   825

CREDULOUS
The credulous hope of mutual minds is o'er   773 Juan   1 1725

CREECH
(So take it in the very words of Creech   844 Juan   5 804

CREED
Sapping a solemn creed with solemn sneer   52 Harold   3 999
It was but abjuring my creed to efface   221 False   3
The first time he has turn'd both his creed and
  his coat   281 Blues   2   55
By Christians, unto whom they gave their creed   302 Age   291
And keep that portion of his creed   315 Giaour   488
For he was hostile to thy creed   320 Giaour   1039
Thou, Greek in soul if not in creed   324 Abydos   1   87
Our law, our creed, our God denies   328 Abydos   1 430
And every creed and every race   332 Abydos   2 365
Safe in the dome of one who held their creed   350 Corsair 2 256
In falling away from thy father's creed   390 Corinth   576
Whatever creed be taught or land be trod   417 Island   1 123
Or cling to any creed of destiny   547 Faliero 5 644
I would not so blaspheme our country's creed   554 Sardan   1 232
Would have been noble in my country's creed   561 Sardan   1 696
Believe in me, as a conditional creed   636 Cain   2   21
I thought she had loved me. Blessings on your
  Creed   743 Deformed 3 110
So was her creed in her own innocence   760 Juan   1 848
Some Christians have a comfortable creed   785 Juan   2 688
Against the creed and morals of the land   817 Juan   4   34
And such their creed was, till they were invaded 868 Juan   7 100
For any sage's creed or calculation   907 Juan   10   4
In the faith of their procreative creed   932 Juan   12 139
Which, like a creed, ne'er says all it intends   954 Juan   13 837

CREED

Than true, hath been a creed so strictly held	958 Juan	14	179
Those vegetables of the Catholic creed	965 Juan	14	647
And thy pure creed made sanction of all ill	970 Juan	15	140

CREEDS

'Twas Jove's, 'tis Mahomet's, and other creeds	19 Harold	2	24
I speak not of men's creeds--they rest between	69 Harold	4	847
Shall these, by creeds they can't expound	132 Prayer		29
A subtle disputant on creeds	181 Ode-A		69
We were of all tongues and creeds	384 Corinth		18
And that odd impulse, which in wars or creeds	883 Juan	8	303

CREED'S

To keep one creed's a task grown quite Herculean	747 Juan	Ded	135

CREEK

He shuns the near but doubtful creek	312 Giaour		173
In many a winding creek and bay	388 Corinth		363
With here and there a creek, whose aspect wore	796 Juan	2	1412
Up in a little creek below a wall	836 Juan	5	319

CREEP

The rill runs o'er, and round, fern, flowers, and ivy creep	72 Harold	4	1044
Round the throng'd gate shall sauntering coxcombs creep	271 Minerva		183
Ere yet unlucky Fame, compell'd to creep	274 Waltz		61
And shudder, as the reptiles creep	319 Giaour		947
Then softly from the Haram creep	328 Abydos	1	465
Again to that accustom'd couch must creep	375 Lara	1	630
The stars from broader beams began to creep	415 Island	1	11
That now almost ingulfs, then leaves to creep	418 Island	1	186
Are they to those that were; and thus they creep	453 Venice-B		12
That it should flow and overflow, than creep	455 Venice-B		150
Yet didst permit the Serpent to creep in	627 Cain	1	19
So dexterous a spoiler, who could creep	686 Werner	2	219
'Tis sweet to listen as the night-winds creep	761 Juan	1	974
That all the rest creep in and form a junction	801 Juan	2	1716
Juan, and shuddering o'er his frame would creep	820 Juan	4	229

CREEPER

Retains the sable stains of the dark creeper	909 Juan	10	117

CREEPING

Whose creeping venom, sure and slow	111 Medea		19
That which creeping is to walking	196 Rogers		32
Along my bones the creeping flesh did quake	222 Spirit		5
Ward's creeping Companion and Louse	232 Murray-B		60
So thrill'd, so shudder'd every creeping vein	361 Corsair	3	424
But creeping things shall revel in their spoil	375 Lara	2	17
Creeping o'er the floor so damp	403 Chillon		34
Creeping as it before had done	405 Chillon		264
This creeping, coward, rank, acquitted felon	502 Faliero	1	185
As sceptre: these unmanly creeping things	517 Faliero	2	630
Fond parents listen'd to a creeping thing	631 Cain	1	238
And the predestined creeping things reserved	659 Heaven		299
The creeping marrow. I have been a soldier	672 Werner	1	33
This cold and creeping kinsman, who so long	673 Werner	1	83
To feel the poison through her spirit creeping	801 Juan	3	5
Just as old age is creeping on apace	808 Juan	3	469
For the old negro's confidence in creeping	837 Juan	5	354

CREEPS

To show with what complacency he creeps	814 Juan	3	875

CREMA

The gems of Brescia and Ravenna; Crema	601 Foscari	2	20

CREPT

This said, with languor to his mat he crept	352 Corsair	2	382
So feeble now--his mother's softness crept	365 Corsair	3	648
Their limbs along the crimson'd turf have crept	380 Lara	2	407
Meantime the Serf had crept to where unseen	383 Lara	2	576
And a low breeze crept moaning by	411 Mazeppa		440
From the Levant hath crept into its cave	528 Faliero	4	26
A desperate courage crept through every limb	580 Sardan	4	140
As if she had just now from out them crept	764 Juan	1	1118
(For sleep is awful), and on tiptoe crept	792 Juan	2	1141
And not a breath crept through the rosy air	815 Juan	3	911
And though it was no opiate, slumber crept	984 Juan	16	215

CRESCENT
(See also MOUNTAIN-CRESCENT)

Red gleam'd the cross, and waned the crescent pale	9 Harold	1	394
And the pale crescent sparkles in the glen	25 Harold	2	341
Idol, saint, virgin, prophet, crescent, cross	26 Harold	2	393
Since the days of our prophet the Crescent ne'er saw	31 Harold	2	683
The crescent glimmers on the hill	312 Giaour		222
The tent is pitch'd, the crescent shines	385 Corinth		75
'Gainst which he rear'd the Crescent high	385 Corinth		139
Above them shone the crescent curling	387 Corinth		259

CRESCENT

To plant the crescent o'er the cross	387 Corinth		298
Flew between earth and the unholy Crescent	454 Venice-B		116
Surmounted as its clasp--a glowing crescent	811 Juan	3	615
And the mosque crescent struggled into sight	863 Juan	6	684

CRESCENTS

Glittering like crescents o'er a Turk's pavilion	785 Juan	2	733

CRESCENT'S

Ismail's no more! The crescent's silver bow	893 Juan	8	972
Have waned into a crescent's coruscation	924 Juan	11	388

CRESSY

Paul and Hubert, too, sleep in the valley of Cressy	86 Leaving NA		13

CRESSYS

He breathed a thousand Cressys, as he saw	916 Juan	10	586

CREST

The Paynim turban and the Christian crest	9 Harold	1	385
With milk-white crest, gold spur, and light poised lance	15 Harold	1	730
While Glory crowns so many a meaner crest	19 Harold	1	934
While, on the other hand, meek Dian's crest	59 Harold	4	242
Dark Oscar's sable crest is low	105 Alva		291
Lowly to earth inclines his plume-clad crest	110 Nisus		377
Or Henry trampled on the crest of France	111 Examination		16
When I see some dark hill point its crest to the sky	136 Highlander		33
The star--the string--the crest	181 Ode-A		160
Of the eagle's burning crest	187 Ode-B		63
Young Freedom plumes the crest of each cacique	302 Age		279
His Christian crest and haughty mien	312 Giaour		256
As rears her crest the ruffled Swan	315 Giaour		507
Angel of Death! 'tis Hassan's cloven crest	317 Giaour		716
No--as each crest save his may feel	334 Abydos	2	538
'Pacha! the day is thine; and on thy crest	357 Corsair	3	141
And shook--Why sudden droops that plumed crest	380 Lara	2	380
That should have won as haught a crest	399 Parisina		267
While eagles scarce build higher than the crest	422 Island	2	256
Yet rears her crest, unconquer'd and sublime	454 Venice-B		143
Than the volcano's fierce eruptive crest	463 Dante	3	187
On Ararat's late secret crest	657 Heaven		149
Upon your dancing crest; the loftiest	715 Werner	5	124
She sits like a crest	742 Deformed	3	39
The colour of a budding rose's crest	863 Juan	6	676
I don't know whether they had arms or crest	869 Juan	7	147
The fair czarina's autocratic crest	913 Juan	10	390
And some who had but talent for their crest	944 Juan	13	220
Time sheds a moment o'er each sparkling crest	975 Juan	15	438

CRESTED
(See also FIERY-CRESTED, GOLDEN-CRESTED)

High crested banners wave thy walls within	120 Newstead-A		52

CRESTS

Morven on the scattered crests of Lochlin	131 Calmar		144
The carved crests, and curious hues	395 Corinth		969
(Not of old victors, all whose heads and crests	931 Juan	12	91

CREST'S

To catch that crest's ascendency	187 Ode-B		57

CRETANS

To make the Cretans bloodier in battle	793 Juan	2	1240
So were the Cretans--from which I infer	794 Juan	2	1247

CREUSA'S

Creusa's style but wanting to the dame	108 Nisus		202

CREVICE

From every crevice comes the shot	394 Corinth		940
And through the crevice and the cleft	403 Chillon		32
But through the crevice where it came	405 Chillon		265
Sending its pestilence through every crevice	614 Foscari	3	378
As through a crevice or a key-hole in	701 Werner	3	408
As much as made a crevice of the fastening	718 Werner	5	313

CREVICES

Glide through the crevices made by the winds	609 Foscari	3	63

CREW
(See also BOAT'S-CREW)

Peeps blushing on the revel's laughing crew	14 Harold	1	676
And well the docile crew that skilful urchin guides	22 Harold	2	162
Yet never would he join the lovers' whining crew	24 Harold	2	297
And subtler venom of the reptile crew	75 Harold	4	1220
Not so the methodistic crew	95 Granta		57
The stranger's gone,--amidst the crew	104 Alva		254
Struggling in vain, a captive to the crew	109 Nisus		332
Others, again, a pert and lively crew	124 Recoll		137

CREW

	Page	Work		Line
We'll mingle in the festive crew	134	E. N. Long		102
And I will fly the midnight crew	135	I Would		39
Rail on, Rail on, ye heartless Crew	141	Critics		1
Rail on, Rail on, ye heartless Crew	142	Critics		85
Gallant Kidd, commands the crew	157	Hodgson		34
The Bark--the Crew--the very Wreck is gone	184	Julian		11
Behold! in various throngs the scribbling crew	243	Bards		143
Let monodies on Fox regale your crew	252	Bards		747
And last of all, amidst the gaping crew	271	Minerva		195
And yet we shall have the whole crew on our kibes	280	Blues	1	157
Is the numerous, humorous, backbiting crew	280	Blues	2	16
By Captain Parry's crew, in 'Melville's Sound	288	Vision		216
But when and where I join'd the crew	332	Abydos	2	358
And for his fare--the rudest of his crew	339	Corsair	1	69
Whose name appals the fiercest of his crew	340	Corsair	1	175
Her consort still is absent, and her crew	344	Corsair	1	414
How gallant all her crew, and deigns to praise	346	Corsair	1	576
'Tis answer'd--Well ye speed, my gallant crew	349	Corsair	2	167
Compared with his, the Corsair's roving crew	350	Corsair	2	232
No sympathy with that familiar crew	374	Lara	1	571
To check the headlong fury of that crew	379	Lara	2	291
Nor find a motlier crew nor blither	384	Corinth		23
Who wait their chief, a melancholy crew	417	Island	1	126
And near, and nearer, till their dusky crew	429	Island	3	171
The boat's crew look'd amazed o'er sea and shore	431	Island	4	68
Would still have battled for that scanty crew	433	Island	4	248
The boat drew nigh, well arm'd, and firm the crew	433	Island	4	281
Chain'd on the deck, where once, a gallant crew	435	Island	4	359
Was purchased by no compact with thy crew	496	Manfred	3	374
And charge once more the rebel crew who still	581	Sardan	4	184
Gather like a locusts' crew	735	Deformed	2	36
Kept still aloof the crew, who, ere they sunk	778	Juan	2	279
And in them crowded several of the crew	780	Juan	2	426
And for the boat--the crew kept crowding in it	781	Juan	2	456
She had a curious crew as well as cargo	782	Juan	2	527
And thus it was with this our hapless crew	782	Juan	2	537
There were two fathers in this ghastly crew	785	Juan	2	689
Amidst the skeletons of that gaunt crew	787	Juan	2	812
And Aristippus, a material crew	800	Juan	2	1650
'Twixt her and Juan interposed the crew	822	Juan	4	379
Was interrupted by the pirate crew	827	Juan	4	714
'My boy!' said he, 'amidst this motley crew	832	Juan	5	97
They form'd a very nymph-like looking crew	844	Juan	5	789
But what was strangest in this virgin crew	857	Juan	6	289
He paused--and so will I; as doth a crew	918	Juan	10	665
Between the tyrant's and the tribunes' crew	927	Juan	11	590

CREWS

	Page	Work		Line
And great the gathering crews, and loud the boast	347	Corsair	2	9
The boats put off o'ercrowded with their crews	780	Juan	2	406
And others rose to the command of crews	831	Juan	4	924

CRIBB'D

	Page	Work		Line
Is chain'd and tortured--cabin'd, cribb'd, confined	74	Harold	4	1140
Wounded and fetter'd, 'cabin'd, cribb'd, confined	826	Juan	4	593

CRICKETS

	Page	Work		Line
I'm fond of fire, and crickets, and all that	763	Juan	1	1079

CRICKET'S

	Page	Work		Line
Together join'd in cricket's manly toil	125	Recoll		259

CRIED

	Page	Work		Line
Nor coin'd my cheek to smiles, nor cried aloud	52	Harold	3	1052
He cried, 'if this its strength has lost	89	Anacreon-B		40
'Old man!' he cried, 'this pledge is done	104	Alva		197
'My son,' she cried, 'ne'er thirst for gore again	248	Bards		498
But managers for once cried, 'Hold, enough	251	Bards		735
And cried, 'You may the prisoner withdraw	291	Vision		390
Of passion?'--'Passion!' cried the phantom dim	295	Vision		663
'What's this?' cried Michael; 'why, 'tis not a ghost	295	Vision		678
'Done!' cried Asmodeus, 'he anticipates	296	Vision		706
And cried, 'For God's sake, stop, my friend! 'twere best	296	Vision		727
I mean--the slaves hear now); some cried 'Off, off	296	Vision		741
For pantisocracy he once had cried	297	Vision		773
'Tis he!' the stranger cried, and those that heard	372	Lara	1	415
'Who hails?' cried Torquil, following with his eye	425	Island	2	432
'What cheer, Ben Bunting?' cried (when in full view	425	Island	2	500
'And is it thus?' he cried, 'unhappy boy	428	Island	3	145
Cried, 'Torquil, follow me, and fearless follow	430	Island	4	59
Song, scene, or air, when he cried 'seccatura	444	Beppo		248
The manna's falling now,' the abbot cried	469	Morgante		210
And made much of his convert, as he cried	471	Morgante		362
That have cried shame to every ear in Venice	506	Faliero	1	419
No tears. He cried out twice. A saint had done so	600	Foscari	1	334

CRIED

	Page	Work		Line
Now Julia found at length a voice, and cried	764	Juan	1	1129
Was not asleep--'Yes, search and search,' she cried	764	Juan	1	1154
Antonia cried out 'Rape!' and Julia 'Fire	769	Juan	1	1466
'Farewell, my Spain! a long farewell!' he cried	776	Juan	2	137
'Give us more grog,' they cried, 'for it will be	778	Juan	2	281
'Stop!' cried Philosophy, with air so Grecian	801	Juan	2	1679
Stern as her sire: 'On me,' she cried, 'let death	821	Juan	4	332
I cried upon my first wife's dying day	833	Juan	5	151
And looking coldly in her face, he cried	847	Juan	5	1006
And said that she was sorry she had cried	862	Juan	6	632
Softer than the soft Sybarite's, who cried	863	Juan	6	706
Begone!' she cried, with kindling eyes--'and do	866	Juan	6	922
'And here,' he cried, 'is Freedom's chosen station	919	Juan	11	69
The dying man cried, 'Hold! I've got my gruel	920	Juan	11	122
The boors cried 'Dang it! who'd have thought it?'--Sires	959	Juan	14	268
'But add the words,' cried Henry, 'which you made	985	Juan	16	305

CRIES
(See also OUT-CRIES)

	Page	Work		Line
Lo, Chivalry, your ancient goddess, cries	10	Harold	1	406
Slowly he falls amidst triumphant cries	16	Harold	1	786
Kissing its cries away as these awake	46	Harold	3	677
Now, cries the first, for deeds of blood prepare	108	Nisus		231
'O God! my boy,' he cries, 'of me bereft	109	Nisus		321
But when a pert Physician loudly cries	142	Soliloquy		37
Nor rather deem from nightly cries	158	Storm		27
Your hero raves, your heroine cries	231	Doctor		13
Then spouts and foams, and cries at every line	267	Hints		771
And varied cries were like those of wild geese	292	Vision		462
Of groaning victims and wild cries for life	349	Corsair	2	188
But cries 'I warn'd thee!' when the deed is o'er	352	Corsair	2	333
There the craven cries for quarter	393	Corinth		839
The sea-born infant cries, and will not sleep	424	Island	2	409
Where cries reply to curses, shrieks to blows	437	Tasso		86
To speak, cries 'Beppo! what's your pagan name	451	Beppo		725
Where late my ears rung with the damned cries	456	Dante	1	7
Into the air, and cries from tens of thousands	535	Faliero	4	501
The voice of thy slain brother's blood cries out	653	Cain	3	470
Than their last cries shall shake the Almighty purpose	662	Heaven		547
And then the mother cries, the father swears	759	Juan		799
Go! hear it in your famish'd country's cries	897	Juan	9	71
'Where is the world?' cries Young, at eighty-- 'Where	927	Juan	11	593
Was made by Mrs. Adams, where she cries	953	Juan	13	767

CRIM.

	Page	Work		Line
To say leads oft to crim. con. with the married	978	Juan	15	667

CRIME

	Page	Work		Line
Can blazon evil deeds or consecrate a crime	4	Harold	1	27
Some seek devotion, toil, war, good or crime	58	Harold	4	197
But France got drunk with blood to vomit crime	69	Harold	4	865
His fault was friendship, all his crime was love	110	Nisus		374
Whose years float on in daily crime	132	Prayer		34
When Life is blest without a crime	141	Pignus		23
But now to tremble were a crime	155	Happy		27
When thou hadst loved without a crime	174	Remember-B		23
Had he found save in downright crime	177	Devil's Dr		126
For the sake of another crime more	178	Devil's Dr		212
Despite some passing clouds of crime	181	Ode-A		153
Thy Godlike crime was to be kind	191	Prometheus-B		35
Perchance might look on Love as Crime	200	Ode-C		10
The curse which, thou say'st, is the crime of my race	221	False		4
Of Crime unnamed, and thy sad noon must close	224	To Dives		8
When Folly, frequent harbinger of crime	242	Bards		29
Eternal beacons of consummate crime	253	Bards		828
If all such mixtures then be half a crime	265	Hints		631
Reviews record this epidemic crime	266	Hints		723
So free from homicide--to doubt's a crime	299	Age		78
Where Spain was once synonymous with crime	301	Age		265
And callous, save to crime	311	Giaour		152
A life of pain, an age of crime	312	Giaour		264
But one that for thy crime must fall	318	Giaour		767
Thyself without a crime or care	320	Giaour		974
There read of Cain the curse and crime	320	Giaour		1058
Now melt into sorrow, now madden to crime	323	Abydos	1	4
If then such secrecy be crime	328	Abydos	1	445
Our souls to lighten at least a crime	350	Corsair	2	210
But now to stern Reflection each a crime	352	Corsair	2	351
She scarce had left an uncommitted crime	352	Corsair	2	387
If in aught evil, for thy sake the crime	360	Corsair	3	317
The crime--'tis none to punish those of Seyd	360	Corsair	3	318
Oh! slight but certain pledge of crime--'tis blood	361	Corsair	3	417
Had swept an age of terror, grief, and crime	362	Corsair	3	457
The thousand paths that slope the way to crime	366	Lara	1	18
Mislead his spirit equally to crime	371	Lara	1	344
Had left him stainless of oppression's crime	377	Lara	2	171

CRIME

And some foreboding that it might be crime	383 Lara	2	563
While unimpeach'd for traitorous crime	386 Corinth		188
And with thy very crime, my birth	399 Parisina		257
I will not plead the cause of crime	399 Parisina		276
My crime seems worst to human view	399 Parisina		316
Dark the crime and just the law	400 Parisina		428
No check, no change, no good, no crime	405 Chillon		246
To stun the first sensation of his crime	417 Island	1	98
Where nought is ripen'd rapidly save crime	420 Island	2	126
And then I look'd (I hope it was no crime	450 Beppo		659
Thy gentle heart will pardon me the crime	455 Dante	Ded	8
The grossest insult, most comtemptuous crime	502 Faliero	1	152
And he is pure, for now his crime is theirs	512 Faliero	2	239
That we must work by crime to punish crime	535 Faliero	4	517
Whom your patrician crimes have driven to crime	538 Faliero	5	56
The nature of your crime--our law--and peril	539 Faliero	5	90
And crime require a quick procedure; shall	540 Faliero	5	140
Of such a crime, as on the old Roman tables	540 Faliero	5	188
That nature could be filed to such a crime	540 Faliero	5	193
Decreed as sentence! Base as was his crime	541 Faliero	5	238
One day of baffled crime must not efface	543 Faliero	5	358
Even notwithstanding thine unheard-of crime	548 Faliero	5	711
Than the king recks of. Whose then is the crime	553 Sardan	1	154
A moment's pang now changed for years of crime	569 Sardan	2	500
Condemn'd without a crime. The triumph is	576 Sardan	3	323
His crime? Perhaps without committing any	595 Foscari	1	14
A high crime, which I neither can deny	603 Foscari	2	97
Avow'd his crime in not denying that	605 Foscari	2	267
Not so? For crime, I know not; but for pain	642 Cain	2	423
New beings--years--diseases--sorrow--crime	661 Heaven		456
Silence, vain boy! each word of thine's a crime	668 Heaven		978
For my own crime; a victim to my safety	703 Werner	3	518
The abyss of crime (though not of such crime), I	703 Werner	3	534
A crime as--Give it utterance, and then	715 Werner	5	156
When I first charged him with the crime--so lately	718 Werner	5	340
Awful as thy brother's crime	735 Deformed	2	38
Nor turn his very talent to a crime	746 Juan	Ded	78
If people go beyond, 'tis quite a crime	756 Juan	1	639
Of human frailty, folly, also crime	802 Juan	3	34
But here a small delay forms a great crime	847 Juan	5	981
Little was heard of criminal or crime	850 Juan	5	1186
And if one lady's slip could leave a crime on	864 Juan	6	750
But ne'ertheless I hope it is no crime	867 Juan	7	14
Rings o'er the dialogue, and many a crime	885 Juan	8	460
Crime came not near him--she is not the child	886 Juan	8	489
Engender'd monstrous shapes of every crime	888 Juan	8	656
Are prosecuted for that false crime bigamy	891 Juan	8	835
But aggravate the crime you have not prevented	940 Juan	12	639
A jest at Vice by Virtue's call'd a crime	941 Juan	13	3
Mournful--but mournful of another's crime	973 Juan	15	358

CRIMES

From crimes as numerous as her beadsmen be	15 Harold	1	717
And left without a sigh the land of war and crimes	22 Harold	2	144
But crimes that scorn the tender voice of Ruth	29 Harold	2	563
What crimes it costs to be a moment free	67 Harold	4	761
And their free thoughts be crimes, and earth have too much light	69 Harold	4	837
And Superstition's crimes, of various dyes	120 Newstead-A		27
Can vice atone for crimes by prayer	132 Prayer		4
My thoughts, my words, my crimes forgive	146 Adieu		118
Thou hear'st of one, whose deepening crimes	164 Friend-B		47
And with a breast unknowing its own crimes	213 Lady Byron		50
Aegle, beauty and poet, has two little crimes	237 French-B		1
Yet still the gods are just, and crimes are cross'd	270 Minerva		117
Even by the crimes through which it waded	318 Giaour		865
The very crimes that mar my youth	322 Giaour		1188
For crimes committed, and the victor's threat	351 Corsair	2	296
Because, despite thy crimes, that heart is moved	360 Corsair	3	294
The worst of crimes had left her woman still	363 Corsair	3	522
Link'd with one virtue and a thousand crimes	366 Corsair	3	696
'Twas all they left of virtues or of crimes	368 Lara	1	184
Was Alp, despite his flight and crimes	388 Corinth		391
And worse than all, the sudden crimes engender'd	453 Venice-B		81
She was the voyager's worship;--even her crimes	454 Venice-B		110
Spurn back, and scorn ye!--But thy many crimes	496 Manfred	3	381
Must crimes be punish'd but by other crimes	496 Manfred	3	383
We stand to hear, and not to speak. Your crimes	538 Faliero	5	26
Whom your patrician crimes have driven to crime	538 Faliero	5	56
Decapitated for his crimes.' 'His crimes	545 Faliero	5	501
'Decapitated for his crimes!'--What crimes	545 Faliero	5	508
Or at the least learn whence the crimes arose	545 Faliero	5	511
Confirms his crimes, but he avows them not	600 Foscari	1	294
The apparent crimes of the accused disclose	600 Foscari	1	310
Compared with our great crimes:--Sole Lord of light	649 Cain	3	231
The same old tears, old crimes, and oldest ill	661 Heaven		479
More patient! Ulric!--Ulric!--there are crimes	690 Werner	2	483
This is no hour to think of petty crimes	703 Werner	3	514
That there were crimes made venial by the occasion	720 Werner	5	442

CRIMES

To be the father of fresh crimes, no less	720 Werner	5	489
In gangs of fifty, thieves commit their crimes	760 Juan	1	861
Which in the North prevents precocious crimes	851 Juan	5	1253
And one good action in the midst of crimes	889 Juan	8	713
Are purchased by all agonies and crimes	894 Juan	8	994
Men's wrongs, and rather check than punish crimes	942 Juan	13	62
A kind of common-place, even in their crimes	957 Juan	14	124

CRIME'S

And then--thy crime's reward	398 Parisina		208

CRIMINAL

His summons found the destined criminal	378 Lara	2	214
Whether he be found criminal or no	686 Werner	2	212
Appearances; and views a criminal	703 Werner	3	538
Than of the criminal! Ho! Gabor! Gabor	720 Werner	5	490
Little was heard of criminal or crime	850 Juan	5	1186

CRIMINALS

And greater criminals?--Back to thy hell	496 Manfred	3	384
Now that these criminals have been disposed of	540 Faliero	5	135
Its criminals, instead of touching at	547 Faliero	5	637

CRIMSON

Nor shakes her crimson plumage in the skies	10 Harold	1	408
Bears in his cap the badge of crimson hue	12 Harold	1	523
Streams from his flank the crimson torrent clear	16 Harold	1	762
Or roll the crimson tide of war	102 Alva		24
The crimson glow of Allan's face	104 Alva		233
Or crimson poppy, sinking with the shower	110 Nisus		381
In grim array the crimson cross demand	119 Newstead-A		10
A crimson cloud it spreads and glows	187 Ode-B		11
Crimson tears will follow yet	188 Ode-B		104
And crimson as those clouds of morn	316 Giaour		662
Crimson and green were the shawls of their wear	389 Corinth		468
Rose crimson, and deposed the stars	413 Mazeppa		649
Which draws the diver to the crimson cave	420 Island	2	140
Now thou must wear an unmix'd crimson; no	535 Faliero	4	494
Thou hast no more eyes than heart to make her crimson	552 Sardan	1	89
So calmly with its gold and crimson glory	611 Foscari	3	212
On long pearl-colour'd beards and crimson crosses	697 Werner	3	117
Engraved in crimson in men's memories	703 Werner	3	553
But let them fly; the crimson kennels now	737 Deformed	2	180
Crimson as cleft pomegranates, their long tresses	805 Juan	3	259
On crimson satin, border'd with pale blue	809 Juan	3	530
All gold and crimson shone her jelick's fellow	810 Juan	3	558
To women; there is scarce a crimson varlet	877 Juan	7	669
Had scarr'd her brow, and left its crimson trace	890 Juan	8	757
Sunk, and the crimson cross glared o'er the field	894 Juan	8	973

CRIMSON'D
(See also GORE-CRIMSON'D)

And on the crimson'd rocks beneath	101 Alva		9
Their limbs along the crimson'd turf have crept	380 Lara	2	407
Was crimson'd from his veins who died to save	462 Dante	3	129

CRIMSON-SCARFED

The crimson-scarfed men of Macedon	28 Harold	2	517

CRINGE

Why crouch to her leaders, or cringe to her rules	129 Becher-A		22
I hate the slaves that cringe around	135 I Would		12
Now do yours. Hence, and bow and cringe him here	678 Werner	1	441
I cringe!--but I shall lose the opportunity	678 Werner	1	442

CRISIS

In fond suspense this crisis of their fate	114 Prologue		24
Just in the very crisis she should not	798 Juan	2	1544
Just at this crisis up came Johnson too	882 Juan	8	273

CRISP

I would not their vile breath should crisp the stream	63 Harold	4	474
Her smooth brow crisp--'Oh, nothing!'--a young heir	743 Deformed	3	95

CRISP'D

Thrown topsy-turvy, twisted, crisp'd, and curl'd	901 Juan	9	292

CRISPER

The elder ladies' wrinkles curl'd much crisper	906 Juan	9	619

CRISPIN

St. Crispin quits, and cobbles for the muse	252 Bards		768

CRISPINS

Or country Crispins, now grown somewhat stale	266 Hints		731

CRISPS

A cooling breeze which crisps the broad clear river	551 Sardan	1	53
As the light breeze of midnight crisps the broad	566 Sardan	2	257

CRISPS
Crisps the reluctant lake that lay so calm   578 Sardan   4   12

CRITIC
Is this too much? stern Critic, say not so   19 Harold   1   949
More than the verse on which the critic wrote   112 Examination   58
By critic sarcasm to be vext   137 Clare   59
Outshining every critic Light   142 Critics   94
And whenever I need a critic who can gloss over   178 Devil's Dr   203
And stand a critic, hated yet caress'd   242 Bards   74
And own thee chieftain of the critic clan   248 Bards   507
What harm? In spite of every critic elf   251 Bards   715
Remove whate'er a critic may suspect   262 Hints   419
The critic eye, and please when near at hand   264 Hints   572
When Southrons writhe upon their critic wheel   265 Hints   592
Become as base a critic as e'er crawl'd   297 Vision   780
He was a critic upon operas, too   444 Beppo   245
I'll prove that such the opinion of the critic is   816 Juan   3   983
The lawyer and the critic but behold   909 Juan   10   105

CRITICAL
Lords of the quill, whose critical assaults   263 Hints   459
An hour so critical as was the eve   684 Werner   2   111

CRITICALLY
And critically held as deleterious   941 Juan   13   4

CRITICISE
We may presume to criticise or praise   941 Juan   13   28

CRITICISED
And tumbled books, or criticised the pictures   954 Juan   13 810

CRITICISM
They cannot read, and so don't lisp in criticism   449 Beppo   569
This is true criticism, and you may kiss   772 Juan   1 1646
(As far as rhyme and criticism combine   909 Juan   10   123

CRITICS
For sense and reason (critics know it   137 Clare   40
And critics are forgot   137 Clare   54
And Critics rise in every country Squire   142 Soliloquy   14
And Longman smirk and critics cease to rail   224 J.C.H.   32
Your Orators--Critics--and Wits   232 Murray-B   33
Though grinning Critics worry   233 Ballad-B   28
Yet Critics have been very kind   234 Ballat-A   31
Though nymphs forsake, and critics may deride   242 Bards   13
Save censure--critics all are ready made   242 Bards   64
You trust in critics, who themselves are sore   242 Bards   80
While such critics, why should I forbear   243 Bards   88
Have foil'd the best of critics, needs the worst   246 Bards   368
Where Scotchmen feed, and critics may carouse   249 Bards   545
While British critics suffer scenes like these   249 Bards   567
Let squabbling critics by themselves dispute   258 Hints   113
As critics kindly do, and authors ought   267 Hints   794
And furnish food for critics, or their quills   267 Hints   804
Should captains the remark, or critics, make   772 Juan   1 1663
To critics, or to hail the setting sun   971 Juan   15   174

CRITIC'S
Scans Attic metres with a critic's ken   111 Examination   12
Learn'd to deride the critic's starch decree   256 Bards   1059
Which might defy a crotchet critic's rigour   960 Juan   14   310

CRITICS'
Not caring as I ought for critics' cavils   446 Beppo   414

CRITIQUE
A smart Critique upon St. Helena   231 Doctor   49
My lady skims the cream of each critique   249 Bards   557
Where I just had been skimming a charming
   critique   277 Blues   1   22
John Keats, who was kill'd off by one critique   925 Juan   11 465

CROAKING
To such a set of croaking sinners   96 Granta   80
If ancient Virgins croaking censures raise   142 Soliloquy   10

CROCE
And Santa Croce wants their mighty dust   64 Harold   4 523

CROCE'S
In Santa Croce's holy precincts lie   63 Harold   4 478

CROCKERY
A difference between crockery ware and plate   991 Juan   16 718

CROCKERY-WARE
In small-eyed China's crockery-ware metropolis   919 Juan   11   53

CROCODILES
And mammoths, and your winged crocodiles   901 Juan   9 304

CROESUS
A Croesus in creation--I plunged deep   487 Manfred   2 236

CROKERS
Crabbes, Campbells, Crokers, Freres, and Wards   231 Doctor   54

CROMWELL
The sagest of usurpers, Cromwell; he   67 Harold   4 758

CROMWELL'S
Like Cromwell's pranks;--but although truth
   exacts   814 Juan   3 829

CRONE
The hunter and the crone; and smiling on me   580 Sardan   4 132

CROOK
Here leans the idle shepherd on his crook   9 Harold   1 372
With 'a crook in his lot   238 Bray   2

CROOK'D
Except a little longer and less crook'd   725 Deformed   1 208

CROOKED
And crooked glaive; the lively, supple Greek   28 Harold   2 519
And thus once enter'd into crooked ways   213 Lady Byron   47
In turn, because of this vile crooked clog   727 Deformed   1 340
Slight crooked friend's as snake-like in his
   words   733 Deformed   1 805
Or that this crooked coffer, which contain'd   735 Deformed   1 880

CROP
Has generally no great crop to spare it, he   746 Juan   Ded   67
Corruption for its crop) with the poor devils   910 Juan   10 198
If the weeds o'erlive not the first crop   944 Juan   13 175

CROPS
Till time crops the leaves with unmerciful knife   99 L Adieu   3

CROSIERS
And gilded crosiers, and cross'd arms, and cowls   697 Werner   3 118

CROSS
(See also RED-CROSS)
Without a sigh he left, to cross the brine   5 Harold   1   98
Some hand erects a cross of mouldering lath   7 Harold   1 267
Red gleam'd the cross, and waned the crescent pale   9 Harold   1 394
The cross descends, thy minarets arise   25 Harold   2 340
Here the red cross (for still the cross is here   26 Harold   2 388
Idol, saint, virgin, prophet, crescent, cross   26 Harold   2 393
In grim array the crimson cross demand   119 Newstead-A   10
And I will cross the whitening foam   156 Lady-F   25
To cross thy stream, broad Hellespont   160 Swimming   4
By hellish instinct, all that cross their way   247 Bards   431
And cross St. George's Channel and the Tweed   264 Hints   550
And cross whole pages with his plaguy pen   267 Hints   796
On the rack of cross questions, by all the blue
   bevy   280 Blues   1 148
Though Cleopatra's mummy cross the sea   298 Age   29
And, save the cross above my head   323 Giaour   1325
For whom one near display'd the absolving cross   382 Lara   2 477
In him who triumph'd o'er the Cross   385 Corinth   138
To plant the crescent o'er the cross   387 Corinth   298
The cross he deem'd no more divine   390 Corinth   539
The sign of the cross, and for ever be mine   390 Corinth   578
He who first downs with the red cross may crave   392 Corinth   717
And made the sign of a cross with a sigh   395 Corinth   961
Whose threshold he shall cross no more   412 Mazeppa   514
'The curious in fish-sauce,' before they cross   441 Beppo   58
For these restored the Cross, that from above   454 Venice-B   114
The red-cross banners where the first red Cross   462 Dante   3 128
The abbot sign'd the great cross on his front   469 Morgante   233
Upon the cross, preferr'd I my petition   471 Morgante   342
With cross and garland over its green turf   484 Manfred   2   70
That a great personage, who fain would cross   674 Werner   1 213
Our swords when drawn must cross, our engines aim   676 Werner   1 348
Saint Peter, rear its dome and cross into   731 Deformed   1 607
That sky whence Christ ascended from the cross   731 Deformed   1 608
Would not your highness choose to kiss the cross   736 Deformed   2 137
The cross, beneath which he is crush'd; behold
   him   740 Deformed   2 313
This heathenish cross restored the breed again   754 Juan   1 457
But Heaven forbid that such a thought should
   cross   757 Juan   1 666
As o'er the cutter's edge he tried to cross   781 Juan   2 452
To cross her brow, she wonder'd how so near   846 Juan   5 951
At a per-centage; a child cross, dog ill   855 Juan   6 163
Was not like Jacob's) or to cross a ditch   873 Juan   7 416
Sunk, and the crimson cross glared o'er the field   894 Juan   8 973
The line of lights too up to Charing Cross   921 Juan   11 201
Now) you may cross the blue deep and white foam   924 Juan   11 347
And adding still a little through each cross   930 Juan   12   28

CROSS'D
(See also CROST)

But since he cross'd the rapid tide	160	Swimming		13
Some folly cross'd, some jest, or some debate	267	Hints		746
Yet still the gods are just, and crimes are cross'd	270	Minerva		117
He knew and cross'd me in the fray	321	Giaour		1084
He pass'd the portal, cross'd the corridore	343	Corsair	1	363
And why had Lara cross'd the bounding main	366	Lara	1	12
A Serf that cross'd the intervening vale	383	Lara	2	551
My heart, and sparks that cross'd my brain	414	Mazeppa		793
O'er which I cross'd with two and sixty counts	467	Morgante		112
Hating to be so,--cross'd me in my path	486	Manfred	2	171
Ambitious hopes ne'er cross'd my dreams; and should	513	Faliero	2	346
And may be cross'd by the accustom'd barks	590	Sardan	5	204
And gilded crosiers, and cross'd arms, and cowls	697	Werner	3	118
As I, who've cross'd it oft, know well enough	775	Juan	2	84
And some such visions cross'd her majesty	905	Juan	9	523
Of twilight, as the party cross'd the bridge	921	Juan	11	184
'An oyster may be cross'd in love,'--and why	965	Juan	14	641

CROSSES

Mark many rude-carved crosses near the path	7	Harold	1	262
On long pearl-colour'd beards and crimson crosses	697	Werner	3	117
To bear these crosses) for each waning prude	895	Juan	8	1046

CROSS-GRAIN'D

Sad strife arose, for they were so cross-grain'd	828	Juan	4	741

CROSS-LEGG'D

And here, assembled cross-legg'd round their trays	805	Juan	3	241
In the mean time, cross-legg'd, with great sang-froid	893	Juan	8	961

CROSS-QUESTION'D

But Juan, when cross-question'd on the vision	987	Juan	16	478

CROST
(See also CROSS'D)

If, kindly cruel, early Hope is crost	24	Harold	2	313
Your polish'd brow no cares have crost	98	To Lesbia		5
And why that early love was crost	156	Lady-F		51
But show where rocks our paths have crost	158	Storm		7
The sea from Paynim land he crost	318	Giaour		808
And dolphin's leap, and little billow crost	797	Juan	2	1446

CROTCHET

Which might defy a crotchet critic's rigour	960	Juan	14	310

CROUCH

Why crouch to her leaders, or cringe to her rules	129	Becher-A		22
The World's at war with tyrants--shall I crouch	240	Cephalonia		2
Yet pause and crouch beneath her feet	385	Corinth		57
The terror of his Glory?--Crouch! I say	489	Manfred	2	415

CROUCH'D

Who, crush'd at Jena, crouch'd at Berlin, fell	300	Age		157
The hearts that loathed him, crouch'd and dreaded too	342	Corsair	1	270
They crouch'd to him, for he had skill	387	Corinth		312

CROUCHES

And quench'd existence crouches in a grave	375	Lara	1	637

CROUCHING

Approach, thou craven crouching slave	311	Giaour		108
Or Christian crouching in the fight	325	Abydos	1	145
Wrung from the coward crouching of despair	354	Corsair	2	481
Crouching and crab-like, through their sapping streets	453	Venice-B		13

CROUPE

With well-timed croupe the nimble coursers veer	16	Harold	1	760

CROW
(See also COCK-CROW, OVER-CROW'D)

To feed the crow, on Talavera's plain	10	Harold	1	448
The eagle soars alone; the gull and crow	820	Juan	4	223

CROWD

Yells the mad crowd o'er entrails freshly torn	15	Harold	1	691
But 'midst the crowd, the hum, the shock of men	23	Harold	2	226
To such the gladness of the gamesome crowd	32	Harold	2	779
Then must I plunge again into the crowd	35	Harold	2	909
Unheeded, searching through the crowd to find	36	Harold	3	88
Worn, but unstooping to the baser crowd	42	Harold	3	416
Than join the crushing crowd, doom'd to inflict or bear	46	Harold	3	679
In worship of an echo; in the crowd	52	Harold	3	1053
Was death or life, the playthings of a crowd	76	Harold	4	1275
A numerous crowd, array'd in white	95	Granta		67
Crowd to applaud the happy morn	102	Alva		40

CROWD

Again the clan, in festive crowd	103	Alva		177
And all the clamorous crowd are hush'd	103	Alva		194
Speed, speed my dart to pierce yon vaunting crowd	110	Nisus		347
We speak to please ourselves, not move the crowd	112	Examination		34
I seek not glory from the senseless crowd	119	Answer-A		41
Another crowd pursue the panting hart	121	Newstead-A		136
Scenes of my youth, developed, crowd to view	122	Recoll		31
Or all the plaudits of the venal crowd	127	Recoll		366
Lost in the dull, ignoble crowd	146	Adieu		88
One insect to the fluttering crowd	153	Friend-A		58
And o'er the spot the crowd may tread	167	Dead		6
The crowd was famish'd by degrees; but two	189	Darkness		55
Had I but sooner learnt the crowd to shun	212	Augusta-C		93
Sonnets on sonnets crowd, and ode on ode	244	Bards		147
Displays a crowd of figures incomplete	256	Hints		13
Ice in a crowd and lava when alone	266	Hints		696
Crowd to the ranks of mercenary war	272	Minerva		266
And the crowd of to-day shows that one fool makes many	278	Blues	1	57
But such a cloud! No land e'er saw a crowd	292	Vision		459
'Call Junius!' From the crowd a shadow stalk'd	294	Vision		585
And not alone where, plunged in night, a crowd	302	Age		316
Crowd to the theatre with loyal rage	304	Age		428
The common crowd but see the gloom	318	Giaour		866
'Haroun--when all the crowd that wait	324	Abydos	1	36
Nor mark'd the javelin-darting crowd	326	Abydos	1	250
The tidings spread, and gathering grows the crowd	339	Corsair	1	107
Saw more than marks the crowd of vulgar men	341	Corsair	1	200
The waving kerchiefs of the crowd that urge	345	Corsair	1	527
For well had Conrad learn'd to curb the crowd	346	Corsair	1	539
Though the far shouting of the distant crowd	351	Corsair	2	304
And passing Ezzelin, he left the crowd	373	Lara	1	497
And when the crowd around and near him told	374	Lara	1	594
The crowd are gone, the revellers at rest	375	Lara	1	628
That when the approaching crowd his arm withheld	376	Lara	2	80
The mystery dearest to the curious crowd	377	Lara	2	138
What cared he for the freedom of the crowd	378	Lara	2	252
He would not shrink before the crowd	398	Parisina		188
While the crowd in a speechless circle gather	400	Parisina		405
At the new transient flame; no babbling crowd	423	Island	2	336
And falls back on the foaming crowd behind	426	Island	3	23
Now Laura moves along the joyous crowd	448	Beppo		513
Is much the same--the crowd, and pulling, hauling	451	Beppo		682
Gushing from Freedom's fountains--when the crowd	454	Venice-B		84
By tyrannous faction and the brawling crowd	456	Dante	1	35
Then future thousands crowd around their tomb	458	Dante	1	153
This crowd of palaces and prisons is not	610	Foscari	3	147
Let him crowd orb on orb: he is alone	629	Cain	1	152
Crowd in my breast to burning, when I hear	631	Cain	1	254
Can crowd eternity into an hour	635	Cain	1	533
The thief among so many? In the crowd	686	Werner	2	206
The joyous crowd above, the numberless	714	Werner	5	109
The music, and the crowd embraced in lieu	715	Werner	5	131
With the heroic crowd that now pursue	737	Deformed	2	173
Shrinks from the crowd that may confuse	742	Deformed	3	15
With the piled wood, round which the family crowd	763	Juan	1	1076
A crowd of shivering slaves of every nation	832	Juan	5	49
And raven ringlets gather'd in dark crowd	860	Juan	6	522
Self-love, there's safety in a crowd of coxcombs	945	Juan	13	240
Observant of the foibles of the crowd	970	Juan	15	115
But I must crowd all into one grand mess	976	Juan	15	505
Confounded him in common with the crowd	978	Juan	15	658

CROWDED

Then to the crowded circus forth they fare	15	Harold	1	718
Ages and realms are crowded in this span	71	Harold	4	976
Not thankless,--for within the crowded sum	212	Augusta-C		115
Crowded like waves upon me, but he was	215	Dream		113
And yet the numbers crowded in his host	347	Corsair	2	43
The launch is crowded with the faithful few	417	Island	1	125
For we are crowded in our solitudes	437	Tasso		88
Of flush'd and crowded wassailers, and wasted	528	Faliero	4	46
Near sixteen lustres crowded with brave acts	543	Faliero	5	359
And in them crowded several of the crew	780	Juan	2	426
They counted thirty, crowded in a space	782	Juan	2	497
And all the stars that crowded the blue space	799	Juan	2	1583
Over a cock'd hat in a crowded room	902	Juan	9	340
Than others crowded in the Forest's maze	997	Juan	17	4

CROWDING

While the fair populace of crowding beauties	597	Foscari	1	100
And for the boat--the crew kept crowding in it	781	Juan	2	456
Neither, came crowding like the waves of ocean	861	Juan	6	564

CROWDS

And thou shalt view thy sons in crowds to Hades hurl'd	12	Harold	1	548
Then share with titled crowds the common lot	94	Dorset		47
Or hear, unless in crowds, thy well-known voice	94	Dorset		106
Whom shivering crowds with horror see	104	Alva		264
But falls on feeble crowds without a name	109	Nisus		266
Steel, flashing, pours on steel, foe crowds on foe	110	Nisus		389

CROWDS

A hermit, 'midst of crowds, I fain must stay	125	Recoll	235
And crowds allow to both a partial fame	126	Recoll	336
Lochlin crowds around. Fly through the	130	Calmar	130
And ev'n in crowds am still alone	156	Lady-F	23
Oh, pardon that in crowds awhile	168	Haunts	9
A theme to crowds that knew them not	184	Parker	17
At whose command 'grim women' throng in crowds	245	Bards	275
Heavens! how the vulgar stare! how crowds applaud	252	Bards	769
Nor care if courts and crowds applaud or hiss	256	Bards	1062
The spirit look'd around upon the crowds	293	Vision	529
In crowds a slave, in deserts free	315	Giaour	546
That crowds on my prophetic eye: the earth	460	Dante	3	5
Whate'er be stirring; though the roar of crowds	530	Faliero	4	163
Of blood to crowds begets the thirst of more	534	Faliero	4	409
He would tread down the barbarous crowds, and triumph	561	Sardan	1	707
Too soon the scorn of crowds for crownless princes	582	Sardan	4	281
Drew crowds together. It was one of those	717	Werner	5	257
In deserts, forests, crowds, or by the shore	838	Juan	5	450
Through crowds and carriages, but waxing thinner	922	Juan	11	226
At once the 'lie' and the 'elite' of crowds	951	Juan	13	634

CROWD'S

The crowd's loud shout and ladies' lovely glance | 15 Harold 1 735

CROWN
(See also HALF-A-CROWN)

The iron crown of laurel's mimic'd leaves	61	Harold	4	362
With the remorse of ages; and the crown	63	Harold	4	510
With an atoning smile a more than earthly crown	67	Harold	4	747
Crown me with ivy from his dwelling-place	71	Harold	4	985
If that with honour fail to crown my clay	86	Fragment-A	9
When great Aeneas wears Hesperia's crown	107	Nisus	154
And virtues crown your brow	138	Clare	93
With Roses crown our jovial brows	139	Anacreon-C	5
Or crown with fancied wreaths my head	146	Adieu	77
Till manhood shall crown me, not mine is the power	149	Newstead-B	11
His wavering crown to follow woman	159	Gulf	8
Heir of his father's crown and of his wits	183	Address-D	18
Thee and thine, thy crown and realm	195	Ballad-A	53
Albeit for such I could despise a crown	206	Greece	3
'Then thus to form Apollo's crown	227	Thurlow-B	10
A crown! why, twist it how you will	227	Thurlow-B	11
They'll tell you Phoebus gave his crown	227	Thurlow-B	15
So let us Crown the Mobby O	235	New Song	32
To crown with honour thee and Walter Scott	245	Bards	278
To crown the bards that haunt her classic grove	255	Bards	988
Cut down crown influence with reforming scythes	266	Hints	673
That head of his, which could not keep a crown	287	Vision	146
Shall crown the Atlantic like the hero's bust	299	Age	112
Jove's Ida and Olympus crown the deep	423	Island	2	287
A poet's wreath shall be thine only crown	439	Tasso	225
Without the power that makes them bear a crown	458	Dante	1	167
Till you can change it haply for a crown	504	Faliero	1	283
Beset with all the thorns that line a crown	504	Faliero	1	289
This cap is not the monarch's crown; these robes	506	Faliero	1	441
To vanquish empires, and refuse their crown	535	Faliero	4	507
I will resign a crown, and make the state	535	Faliero	4	508
That head, which could not wear a crown more noble	540	Faliero	5	155
And there, the ducal crown being first resumed	545	Faliero	5	519
That ducal crown and head shall be united	546	Faliero	5	560
Shall crown to leave thee headless; honours shall	546	Faliero	5	613
Nor crown me with a single rose the less	556	Sardan	1	359
Replace the crown now tottering on your temples	569	Sardan	2	472
Their just pretensions to the crown in case	581	Sardan	4	205
And by that heedless pity risk'd a crown	588	Sardan	5	86
Even with the crown of glory in his eye	600	Foscari	1	335
The Romans (and we ape them) gave a crown	620	Foscari	4	312
A crown to him who saved a citizen	620	Foscari	4	314
Leaving it with a crown of many hues	659	Heaven	294
Beneath the crown which makes his head ache, like	700	Werner	3	337
Good morrow--for the cock had crown, and light	863	Juan	6	682
Not fighting for their country or its crown	869	Juan	7	139
A huge, dun cupola, like a foolscap crown	917	Juan	10	655

CROWN'D
(See also HIGH-CROWN'D, TOWER-CROWN'D)

The horrid crags by toppling convent crown'd	7	Harold	1	243
On yon long, level plain, at distance crown'd	12	Harold	1	513
Had all but crown'd him, on the self-same day	67	Harold	4	767
For beauty crown'd the fair-hair'd boy	103	Alva	160
With wine let every cup be crown'd	104	Alva	223
Victory crown'd not your fall with applause	117	Lachin	28
With cypress crown'd, array'd in weeds	118	Romance	42
High, through those elms, with hoary branches crown'd	123	Recoll	121
Then will I sing divinely crown'd	139	Anacreon-C	19
Crown'd with the verdure of eternal wood	161	Athos	7
Crown'd and anointed from on high	185	Belshaz-A	6
Farewell to thee, France! when thy diadem crown'd me	186	Napoleon	9

CROWN'D

To Monarchs crown'd, and some discrown'd	197	Duel	16
Was crown'd with a peculiar diadem	214	Dream	36
A meet reward had crown'd thy glorious gains	247	Bards	383
Where Kaff is clad in rocks and crown'd with snows sublime	255	Bards	1022
By nations raised, by monarchs crown'd	329	Abydos	2	48
They crown'd him long ago	479	Manfred	1	61
Stand crown'd, but bound and helpless, at the altar	541	Faliero	5	209
Here was I crown'd, and here, bear witness, Heaven	548	Faliero	5	700
But shows a thousand crown'd conspirators	548	Faliero	5	713
Lolls crown'd with roses, and his diadem	551	Serdan	1	34
Crown'd with fresh flowers like--Victims. No, like sovereigns	560	Sardan	1	606
They would be crown'd to reign o'er--let that pass	566	Sardan	2	289
Female in garb, and crown'd upon the brow	580	Sardan	4	106
Both rose, and the crown'd figures on each hand	580	Sardan	4	137
What, crown'd already?--But, proceed. Beleses	592	Sardan	5	289
Crown'd with eternal glory! Heaven, forgive	739	Deformed	2	259
That soon his head was most completely crown'd	841	Juan	5	628
No less deserving to be hang'd than crown'd	850	Juan	5	1224
Life's half-way house, where dames with virtue crown'd	861	Juan	6	597
Since first her majesty was singly crown'd	902	Juan	9	366
Crown'd by high woodlands, where the Druid oak	948	Juan	13	442
But in a higher niche, alone, but crown'd	948	Juan	13	481

CROWNED

The palaces of crowned kings--the huts | 189 Darkness 11
The table sate a range of crowned wretches | 580 Sardan 4 114

CROWNER'S

As soon as 'Crowner's quest' allow'd, pursued | 920 Juan 11 139

CROWNING

And scatter'd cities crowning these	43	Harold	3	502
Crowning the summit of the verdant mound	44	Harold	3	538
Till at the crowning carnage, Waterloo	285	Vision	38
And greatest to all mortals; crowning act	591	Sardan	5	229
Fair as the crowning rose of the whole wreath	793	Juan	2	1181

CROWNLESS

Childless and crownless, in her voiceless woe	66	Harold	4	704
Crownless, breathless, headless fall	219	Saul-B	29
Discrown'd a prince, cut off his crownless head	544	Faliero	5	448
Too soon the scorn of crowds for crownless princes	582	Sardan	4	281

CROWNS

While Glory crowns so many a meaner crest	19	Harold	1	934
Pique her and soothe in turn, soon Passion crowns thy hopes	24	Harold	2	306
Amidst the grove that crowns yon tufted hill	26	Harold	2	433
Cast crowns for rosaries away	180	Ode-A	66
And glory crowns them with redoubled wreath	182	Address-C	8
What are garlands and crowns to the brow that is wrinkled	204	Pisa	5
Taking towns at his liking and crowns at his leisure	228	Once	2
In the red cup that crowns our memory	338	Corsair	1	38
With thee, and wear no crowns but those of flowers	558	Sardan	1	500
And the broad fillet which crowns both. Ye gods	574	Sardan	3	208
From crowns to kicks, according to their vices	834	Juan	5	216
I have seen crowns worn instead of a fool's cap	929	Juan	11	661

CROW-QUILL

With a neat little crow-quill, slight and new | 771 Juan 1 1578

CRUCIFIX

The eye upon its seeming crucifix	432	Island	4	158
'Tis there, and shall be. What? The crucifix	731	Deformed	1	612
And first a little crucifix he kiss'd	783	Juan	2	607

CRUDE

Prompt thy crude brain, and claim thee for a scribe | 246 Bards 364
But while his crude, rude blasphemies he heard | 470 Morgante 279

CRUEL

If, kindly cruel, early Hope is crost	24	Harold	2	313
For its own cruel sacrifice, the kind	47	Harold	3	755
Cruel Cerinthus! does the fell disease	87	Tibullus	1
Too cruel! in vain I implore thee	162	Romaic-A	21
That cruel question ask of me	173	Origin	2
While sate the catholic Moloch, calmly cruel	302	Age	337
Oh, cruel mockery! Could not Austria spare	308	Age	735
And yet not cruel; for I would not make	493	Manfred	3	126
He who is only just is cruel; who	543	Faliero	5	364
With stony lifelessness! Ah, cruel Cain	651	Cain	3	365
Along the wave, the cruel heaven upbraid	662	Heaven	525

CRUEL
Years could but bring them cruel things or wrong 819 Juan 4 212
Good government has left them, seems but cruel 915 Juan 10 504
The cruel Nazarenes, who had laid low 916 Juan 10 596
The quaint, old, cruel coxcomb, in his gullet 954 Juan 13 847

CRUELTIES
His life, while earth yet bore his cruelties 544 Faliero 5 443

CRUELTY
In discord, cowardice, cruelty, all that springs 464 Dante 4 123
And if the cruelty in their cold eyes 543 Faliero 5 390
Whose delegated cruelty surpasses 552 Sardan 1 118
He hated cruelty, as all men hate 885 Juan 8 438

CRUISE
Till Beppo should return from his long cruise 443 Beppo 235

CRUISED
The wild seas, and wild men with whom he cruised 808 Juan 3 430

CRUISING
Since Noah's ark went cruising here and there 782 Juan 2 526
Whilst her piratical papa was cruising 803 Juan 3 104
With quiet cruising o'er the ocean woman 946 Juan 13 314

CRUMBLE
Save that wherein at last they crumble bone by
    bone 11 Harold 1 458
Which shake the world, yet crumble in the wind 417 Island 1 140

CRUMBLED
The smoking ruin, and the crumbled wall 379 Lara 2 268
And crush the wall they have crumbled before 392 Corinth 703
A mast was almost crumbled to a crutch 790 Juan 2 1054

CRUMBLES
And when land crumbles, bid firm paper crash 306 Age 639
Which crumbles with the ponderous ball 385 Corinth 90

CRUMBLING
Her palaces are crumbling to the shore 55 Harold 4 21
And crumbling piecemeal view thy heartless halls 439 Tasso 224

CRUMBS
Will take the crumbs he deigns to scatter from 563 Sardan 2 113
And transubstantiated to crumbs again 743 Deformed 3 113

CRUNCH'D
And their white tusks crunch'd o'er the whiter
    skull 389 Corinth 460

CRUPPER
Which sits for ever upon memory's crupper 927 Juan 11 565

CRUSCAN
In face of all his foes, the Cruscan quire 60 Harold 4 339

CRUSCA'S
Though Crusca's bards no more our journals fill 252 Bards 759

CRUSH
An empire thou couldst crush, command, rebuild 41 Harold 3 338
To crush the imperial urn whose ashes slept
    sublime 71 Harold 4 990
I crush the fiend with malice fraught 133 E. N. Long 17
Crush, if you can, the hopes of youth 141 Critics 7
And crush, oh! noble conquest! crush a Boy 143 Augusta-B 66
They may crush, but they shall not contemn 210 Augusta-B 22
And he may crush--not conquer--still it stings 342 Corsair 1 280
And charged to crush him--let it burst 391 Corinth 662
And crush the wall they have crumbled before 392 Corinth 703
And crush the living waters to a mass 421 Island 2 157
Crush them, ye rocks! floods whelm them, and for
    ever 460 Dante 2 102
In mountainous o'erwhelming, come and crush me 482 Manfred 1 337
And we will kneel together. Crush the worm 489 Manfred 2 419
And crush their blossoms into barrenness 527 Faliero 3 616
The offspring of their sovereign, and so crush 584 Sardan 4 374
Could he but crush himself, 'twere the best boon 630 Cain 1 154
Or I would bid them fall and crush me! Fly 721 Werner 5 499

CRUSH'D
Defies the power which crush'd thy temples gone 33 Harold 2 835
And feeling still with thee in my crush'd feelings'
    dearth 36 Harold 3 54
And the crush'd relics of their vanish'd might 62 Harold 4 401
On what were chambers, arch crush'd, column strown 71 Harold 4 957
On the arena void--seats crush'd--walls bow'd 76 Harold 4 1277
Which betray'd not, or crush'd not, or wept not
    her cause 202 Avatar 8
May the strong curse of crush'd affections light 209 Sketch 85
Has crush'd, without remorse, your numerous band 251 Bards 744
And--almost crush'd beneath the glorious news 274 Waltz 71

CRUSH'D
Who, crush'd at Jena, crouch'd at Berlin, fell 300 Age 157
And crush'd the rights of Europe and his own 301 Age 258
And my crush'd heart fell blind and sick 405 Chillon 317
The mutineers were crush'd, dispersed, or ta'en 426 Island 3 9
His body crush'd into one gory mass 434 Island 4 342
Crush'd was Napoleon by the northern Thor 447 Beppo 481
Venice is crush'd, and Holland deigns to own 454 Venice-B 127
Which nearly crush'd Rondell, came tumbling over 469 Morgante 207
And we again will be--My heart is crush'd 481 Manfred 1 191
Which crush'd the waters into mist and made 483 Manfred 1 358
Leaving one scorpion crush'd, and thousands
    stinging 516 Faliero 2 522
The feelings which they crush'd for me, long,
    long 525 Faliero 3 493
Have crush'd dictators, as the popular steel 526 Faliero 3 557
May have the crawler crush'd, but feels no anger 544 Faliero 5 464
That thou wilt now be crush'd. But not by thee 576 Sardan 3 279
But they have crush'd. Nor crush'd as yet--I
    live 603 Foscari 2 91
Oppress'd but not disgraced, crush'd, overwhelm'd 604 Foscari 2 160
Slime of a mighty universe, crush'd into 640 Cain 2 303
Or crush'd, or rising slowly from the dust 703 Werner 3 564
Till the rocks are crush'd to powder 735 Deformed 2 46
Rome be crush'd to one wide tomb 736 Deformed 2 121
Ah, now you recognise him! My brain's crush'd 739 Deformed 2 301
The cross, beneath which he is crush'd; behold
    him 740 Deformed 2 313

CRUSHES
Within the opposing scale which crushes soon or
    late 80 Harold 4 1539
And the Omnipotent who makes and crushes 659 Heaven 327

CRUSHING
Than join the crushing crowd, doom'd to inflict
    or bear 46 Harold 3 679
Crushing the cliffs, which, downward worn and rent 65 Harold 4 629
And crushing nations with a stupid blow 303 Age 409
The new Symplegades--the crushing Stocks 307 Age 659
Will yield with age to crushing iron; but 542 Faliero 5 304
But how? By a most crushing and inexorable 640 Cain 2 285
Deadly, and quick, and crushing; yet, as real 799 Juan 2 1591

CRUSIERS
Despatching single crusiers here and there 804 Juan 3 146

CRUSOE
Lonely he felt, at times, as Robin Crusoe 452 Beppo 757

CRUST
And thy soul welter in its hideous crust 209 Sketch 92
Was cover'd with old armour like a crust 476 Morgante 666

CRUSTY
And the veteran grows crusty 742 Deformed 3 29

CRUTCH
A mast was almost crumbled to a crutch 790 Juan 2 1054
You have repair'd Legitimacy's crutch 896 Juan 9 19

CRUTCH-LIKE
Our coming evils with a crutch-like rod 74 Harold 4 1124

CRY
(See also DEATH-CRY, WAR-CRY)
War, war is still the cry, 'War even to the knife 18 Harold 1 890
Hark, to the Boatswain's call, the cheering cry 22 Harold 2 158
Our hands, and cry 'Eureka!' it is clear 67 Harold 4 728
The sound shall temper with the owlets' cry 71 Harold 4 948
Or even the piping cry of lips that brook 77 Harold 4 1337
The hunters' cry hangs lengthening on the breeze 121 Newstead-A 124
A cry of horror burst from every tongue 126 Recoil 276
Kind Reader! take your choice to cry or laugh 161 Substitute 1
'My life!' with tenderest tone, you cry 175 Portuguese-A 2
And so soft to his ear was the cry of despair 176 Devil's Dr 35
But nations swell the funeral cry 183 Parker 3
In that dark Hour a long loud gather'd cry 184 Julian 5
The Sea roars on--that Cry is heard no more 184 Julian 8
And a quick desolate cry, licking the hand 189 Darkness 53
When the loud cry of trampled Hindostan 193 Monody 41
Past or to come, a new-born people's cry 206 Greece 2
The cry is up, and scribblers are my game 242 Bards 44
A cry for room, though not a phantom stirr'd 295 Vision 672
Revive the cry--'Iago! and close Spain 303 Age 359
But not for love mistake their yelling cry 305 Age 558
The last to bid the cry of warfare cease 305 Age 570
While all the Common Council cry 'Claymore 308 Age 772
Nor raised the craven cry, Amaun 316 Giaour 603
One cry to Mahomet for aid 321 Giaour 1082
Burst forth in one wild cry--and all was still 336 Abydos 2 639
And cry, Remembrance saddening o'er each brow 338 Corsair 1 41
Nought heeded they the Pacha's angry cry 349 Corsair 2 159
But sudden sunk; for on his ear the cry 350 Corsair 2 199

CRY
Alla il Alla! Vengeance swells the cry   350 Corsair   2   235
But deeply feels a single cry would shame   359 Corsair   3   234
Those strange wild accents; his the cry that
  broke   370 Lara   1   276
And cry, exulting inly, 'They are thine   375 Lara   2   10
Such is their cry--some watchword for the fight   378 Lara   2   220
None sued, for Mercy knew her cry was vain   379 Lara   2   272
A cry prophetic of their fall   387 Corinth   275
Stroke, and thrust, and flash, and cry   392 Corinth   753
The jackal's troop, in gather'd cry   396 Corinth   1069
When charging to the cheering cry   399 Parisina   274
I strove to cry--my lips were dumb   413 Mazeppa   675
'Hoist out the boat!' was now the leader's cry   416 Island   1   81
'Huzza! for Otaheite!' was the cry   417 Island   1   105
'Huzza! for Otaheite!' was the cry   418 Island   1   223
Above me, hark! the long and maniac cry   437 Tasso   65
A cry of nations o'er thy sunken halls   452 Venice-B   3
The owl's long cry, and, interruptedly   495 Manfred   3   277
And all-inexorable in their cry   509 Faliero   2   65
Upon the way let your cry be of war   524 Faliero   3   373
The roar of waters in the cry of blood   528 Faliero   3   649
The cry of women, and the shrieks of babes   530 Faliero   4   164
Remember that the cry is still 'Saint Mark   535 Faliero   4   471
Have wept as they will cry unto their God   543 Faliero   5   387
Of the lamb to the butcher, or the cry   543 Faliero   5   395
'Tis lost, all earth will cry out, thank your
  father   582 Sardan   4   289
Hark! 'Twas a cry of--No, no; not my husband's   599 Foscari   1   229
As was forced on him; but he did not cry   600 Foscari   1   337
And when we cry out against Fate, 'twere well   607 Foscari   2   342
Or with a cry which rather shamed my judges   609 Foscari   3   91
I hear our little Enoch cry within   654 Cain   3   519
And to the universal human cry   662 Heaven   530
Hark, hark! the sea-birds cry   668 Heaven   996
And cry to all beholders, Lo! a villain   698 Werner   3   185
From choirs, in one great cry of 'God be praised   714 Werner   5   95
Then summon'd, would the cry for the police   719 Werner   5   414
Have voices, tongues to cry aloud for me   747 Juan   Ded   126
That they will not cry out before they're hurt   772 Juan   1   1651
And cry that they 'the moral cannot find   772 Juan   1   1661
A solitary shriek, the bubbling cry   780 Juan   2   423
And all was stillness, save the sea-bird's cry   797 Juan   2   1445
A single cry would bring them all abroad   837 Juan   5   357
Was to sit down again, and cry of course   849 Juan   5   1112
Sound, and then by a cry, 'The Sultan's coming   849 Juan   5   1160
Nor give my voice to slavery's jackal cry   899 Juan   9   208
Which 'tis the common cry and lie to vaunt as   929 Juan   11   683
And so that no explosion cry 'Aroint   951 Juan   13   645
Or Swiss Rousseau, cry 'Voila la Pervenche   965 Juan   14   600

CRYING
Like crying babe and beaten hound   396 Corinth   1072
Of eyes were crying for their owner's case   781 Juan   2   446
Dissolved like snow before a woman crying   849 Juan   5   1128
A kerchief, crying, 'Give Sal that!'--and died   920 Juan   11   128

CRYSTAL
Lake Leman woos me with its crystal face   46 Harold   3   644
Of the most living crystal that was e'er   65 Harold   4   587
Gilds with faint beams the crystal dews of rain   122 Recoll   19
In sweetly gliding o'er thy crystal sea   192 Sonnet-C   11
Break the blue crystal of the seas   310 Giaour   17
Its bounding crystal frolick'd in the ray   427 Island   3   65
'Tis said that our Venetian crystal has   625 Foscari   3   294
Of crystal which each rattling wind proclaims   697 Werner   3   123
Soften'd by intervening crystal, and   726 Deformed   1   270
Past him in crystal, and a joy in flowers   808 Juan   3   447
These were ranged round, each in its crystal ewer   809 Juan   3   497
Crystal and marble, plate and porcelain   809 Juan   3   537

CRYSTAL-GIRDED
Thou wert to me a crystal-girded shrine   438 Tasso   129

CUB
The hunter may reserve some single cub   524 Faliero   3   411
Against the hunter flying with her cub   577 Sardan   3   382

CUBITS
His stature is twelve cubits; would you so far   726 Deformed   1   292

CUBLESS
The cubless tigress in her jungle raging   808 Juan   3   457

CUBS
Guard thine immortal cubs, nor thy fond charge
  forget   68 Harold   4   792
A lion looks upon his cubs again   429 Island   3   210
The she-bear licks her cubs into a sort   727 Deformed   1   343
From tigresses and cubs to ducks and ducklings   848 Juan   5   1058

CUCKOLDOM
Abolish'd cuckoldom with much applause   266 Hints   671

CUCKOLDS
They all were heroes, conquerors, and cuckolds   800 Juan   2   1648

CUD
And their dead palates chew'd the cud of pain   454 Venice-B   91
Which is the cud eschew'd by human cattle   935 Juan   12   344

CUDGEL
Whate'er the weapon, cudgel, fist, or foil   265 Hints   639

CUE
Into such matters, but to mind our cue   287 Vision   175
My cue for any time to be terrific   889 Juan   8   706
I'll not gainsay them; it is not my cue   941 Juan   13   17

CUFFS
In number'd lots; they all had cuffs and collars   803 Juan   3   119

CUIRASS
No Cuirass o'er that glowing heart   201 Ode-C   63
Clung like a cuirass to his breast   330 Abydos   2   144
The cloven cuirass, and the helmless head   380 Lara   2   395
The whole, which, save one cuirass, was too small   476 Morgante   669
Too heavy:--a light cuirass and my sword   573 Sardan   3   101
Give me the cuirass--so: my baldric; now   573 Sardan   3   127
This cuirass fits me well, the baldric better   574 Sardan   3   163

CULL
Which Spring and Nature cull from Earth   139 Anacreon-C   10
Whose mingling taste combined to cull the wreath   254 Bards   883
Light toil! to cull and dress thy frugal fare   344 Corsair   1   422
We'll cull the flowers that grow above the dead   419 Island   2   7
To cull some first-fruits. Why? To offer up   632 Cain   1   322
Professional; and there is nought to cull   953 Juan   13   756

CULL'D
Be all the bruisers cull'd from all St. Giles'   270 Minerva   179

CULLODEN
Ah! were you destined to die at Culloden   117 Lachin   27

CULLS
For thee Edina culls her evening sweets   249 Bards   532

CULOTTE
Completely 'sans culotte,' and without vest   995 Juan   16   931

CULPRIT
The culprit be whom I accuse of treason   539 Faliero   5   77
An hour since, face to face, as judge and culprit   599 Foscari   1   219
But as a culprit. Yes, but to his country   600 Foscari   1   299
Prisoners we'll have at least, if not the culprit   684 Werner   2   72
Who seems the culprit, and--Who seems? Who else   703 Werner   3   530
That when a culprit came for condemnation   952 Juan   13   703
The present culprit was extremely pale   989 Juan   16   553

CULTIVATE
And cultivate, or sigh when it could not   586 Sardan   4   515

CULTIVATED
Well cultivated, it will render double   939 Juan   12   608

CULTURE
Culture again adorns the gladdening vale   121 Newstead-A   119
Nor claims the culture of his hand   310 Giaour   54

CULTURED
Fortune! take back these cultured lands   135 I Would   9

CULVERIN
Rose from each heated culverin   386 Corinth   164

CULVERINS
Their culverins, and so forth, would find way   726 Deformed   1   306
Also some culverins upon the walls   731 Deformed   1   614

CULVERIN'S
When the culverin's signal is fired, then on   392 Corinth   709

CUMBER'D
More drench'd with gore, more cumber'd with the
  slain   290 Vision   352
And cumber'd with his scaly spoil   312 Giaour   175

CUMBERLAND
Conferr'd on his Highness of Cumberland   178 Devil's Dr   188
Awake, George Colman! Cumberland, awake   249 Bards   578
Vernon, the butcher Cumberland, Wolfe, Hawke   747 Juan   1   9
Was born in Cumberland among the hills   869 Juan   7   155

CUMBROUS
The cumbrous pomp of Saxon pride   135 I Would   5
A shadow of this cumbrous clog of clay   579 Sardan   4   59

CUNNING
(See also CONYNGE)

I have been cunning in mine overthrow	211 Augusta-C		23
Some factious phrase by cunning caught and spread	378 Lara	2	224
For tyranny of late is cunning grown	454 Venice-B		131
This cunning Colchian poison, which my father	574 Sardan	3	187
A famous artisan, a cunning sculptor	738 Deformed	2	204
So far above the cunning powers of hell	749 Juan	1	131
Was nothing but a valorous kind of cunning	882 Juan	8	280
But full of cunning as Ulysses' whistle	954 Juan	13	838
And smiling but in secret--cunning rogue	960 Juan	14	294

CUNNING'S

He had the skill, when Cunning's gaze would seek	341 Corsair	1	217
There lie love's feverish hope, and cunning's guile	375 Lara	1	634

CUP
(See also WINE-CUP)

And life's enchanted cup but sparkles near the brim	36 Harold	3	72
Let us pass round the cup of love's bliss in full measure	91 Caroline-C		27
With wine let every cup be crown'd	104 Alva		223
And raise thy cup with firmer hand	104 Alva		232
He said, and dash'd the cup to earth	104 Alva		248
An ancient cup, which Tyrian Dido gave	107 Nisus		151
The envied silver cup within his scope	112 Examination		28
The man who hopes t'obtain the promised cup	112 Examination		41
Help!--'A couplet?'--'No, a cup	157 Hodgson		59
The cup of woe for me to drain	165 Thyrza		46
The cup must hold a deadlier draught	168 Haunts		19
He raised young Julian. 'Is thy Cup so full	184 Julian		42
The cup of woe was quaff'd--the spirit fled	268 Minerva		30
A cup too on the board was set	330 Abydos	2	127
To quench his thirst had such a cup	331 Abydos	2	243
This cup too for the rugged knaves	332 Abydos	2	317
In the red cup that crowns our memory	338 Corsair	1	38
Ne'er for his lip the purpling cup they fill	339 Corsair	1	67
Thou more than Moslem when the cup appears	344 Corsair	1	430
The cup of woe was quaff'd--the spirit fled	356 Corsair	3	30
The cup of consecrated gold	395 Corinth		999
Which bears at once the cup and milk and fruit	422 Island	2	259
The cup which brings oblivion of a chain	454 Venice-B		87
Till this last running over of the cup	525 Faliero	3	489
A cup too much, a scuffle, and a stab	530 Faliero	4	143
Which makes the cup run o'er, and mine was full	541 Faliero	5	247
The first cup which he drains will be the last	562 Sardan	2	52
I invited him to fill the cup which stood	579 Sardan	4	92
And the cup? 'Tis my country's custom to	594 Sardan	5	451
A cup of water? I--And I--And I	625 Foscari	5	291
For the mere cup and trencher, we no doubt	704 Werner	4	9
Presented the o'erflowing cup, and said	806 Juan	3	339
Fill high the cup with Samian wine	812 Juan	3	738
Dash down yon cup of Samian wine	813 Juan	3	784
And scarce to the Mogul a cup of coffee	900 Juan	9	262
His grace, his God-knows-what: for Cupid's cup	905 Juan	9	531

CUPBEARER

Not much as man. What, ho! my cupbearer	553 Sardan	1	203
And the most tiresome. Where's my cupbearer	577 Sardan	3	344
For the cup's sake I'll bear the cupbearer	677 Werner	1	375

CUPBOARD

A certain press or cupboard niched in yonder	839 Juan	5	526

CUPID

'Three who have stolen their witching airs from Cupid	171 Address-B		33
Her zone to Venus, or his bow to Cupid	753 Juan	1	439
If she had not mistaken him for Cupid	902 Juan	9	360
A full-grown Cupid, very much admired	960 Juan	14	322

CUPIDITY

Or some contractor's personal cupidity	870 Juan	7	211

CUPIDON

To indicate a Cupidon broke loose	969 Juan	15	94

CUPIDS

Ye Cupids, droop each little head	87 Catullus		1

CUPID'S

To exact of Cupid's bills the full amount	904 Juan	9	495
His grace, his God-knows-what: for Cupid's cup	905 Juan	9	531

CUPOLA

And Cupola and minaret	196 Venice-A		33
A little cupola, more neat than solemn	829 Juan	4	826
Sophia's cupola with golden gleam	831 Juan	5	20
A huge, dun cupola, like a foolscap crown	917 Juan	10	655

CUPP'D

Haustus' (And here the surgeon came and cupp'd him	912 Juan	10	324

CUPS

A thousand cups of gold	220 Belshaz-B		5
In small fine China cups, came in at last	809 Juan	3	500
Gold cups of filigree made to secure	809 Juan	3	501
He drank six cups of coffee at the least	863 Juan	6	732

CUP'S

For the cup's sake I'll bear the cupbearer	677 Werner	1	375

CUR

Morgante said, 'Get up, thou sulky cur	474 Morgante		543

CURATE

Condemn the unlucky curate to recite	267 Hints		765
A brilliant diner out, though but a curate	991 Juan	16	698

CURB

Look through thine own, nor curb the lust of war	41 Harold	3	341
To curb the Adriatic main	88 Horace		7
And curb this rage for imitation	101 Lady-B		32
Precepts of prudence curb, but can't control	119 Answer-A		9
Or curb a runaway young star or two	285 Vision		12
And hurl the dart, and curb the steed	324 Abydos	1	86
He cannot curb his haughty mood	331 Abydos	2	268
For well had Conrad learn'd to curb the crowd	346 Corsair	1	539
His form, to curl their length and curb their sound	361 Corsair	3	389
Remember that of man, and curb this passion	501 Faliero	1	127
'Twill serve to curb his fever. Yield thee, slave	738 Deformed	2	200
The silken fillet's curb, and sought to shun	810 Juan	3	582
And still pursues the right;--to curb the bad	942 Juan	13	67
And with such hurry, that ere he could curb it	992 Juan	16	751

CURB'D

Are curb'd too much by long-recurring rhyme	262 Hints		412
'Twas the Roman curb'd the Roman	736 Deformed	2	109
States to be curb'd and thoughts to be confined	746 Juan	Ded	108
From heart to cheek is curb'd into a blush	792 Juan	2	1124
His clothes were not curb'd to their usual cut	984 Juan	16	230

CURBS

That curbs his reign	200 Stanzas-B		34
The haughtier thought it curbs, but scarce conceals	341 Corsair	1	206
That curbs to scorn the wrath it cannot hide	373 Lara	1	501
His resting-place the bank that curbs the brook	374 Lara	1	549

CURDLE

The blue flames curdle o'er the hearth	103 Alva		184
Till all thy self-thoughts curdle into hate	209 Sketch		89
At times would curdle o'er some heavy groan	885 Juan	8	440
Spangled with gems--the monk made his blood curdle	995 Juan	16	952

CURDLED

As ice were in her curdled blood	400 Parisina		335
Sate:--my veins curdled. Is this all? Upon	580 Sardan	4	109

CURDLES

And curdles a long life into one hour	214 Dream		26

CURDLING

My curdling blood, my madd'ning brain	172 Romaic-B		33
An icy sickness curdling o'er	414 Mazeppa		792
I look upon thy hands my curdling limbs	598 Foscari	1	159

CURE

Who loves, raves--'tis youth's frenzy; but the cure	73 Harold	4	1099
Included kingdoms in the cure of souls	266 Hints		678
'Of restiveness he'd cure him had he need	469 Morgante		213
As Nessus did of old beyond all cure	474 Morgante		570
Shorten the path to the eternal cure	619 Foscari	4	283
Of charms to make good gold and cure bad ails	805 Juan	3	269
That killing him is not the way to cure you	866 Juan	6	920
The regimental surgeon could not cure	889 Juan	8	677
Cure them of tours, hussar and highland dresses	918 Juan	10	682
A cure for grief--for what can ever rankle	959 Juan	14	215
Whose verdict for such sin a certain cure is	963 Juan	14	480

CURED

Not to be cured when Love itself forgets to please	24 Harold	2	315
Cured all ambition? Did the conquerors heap	72 Harold	4	1004
Has cured my boyish soul of Dreaming	144 Becher-B		44
Would be for a disease already cured	744 Deformed	3	163
The hoarse harsh waves kept time; fright cured the qualms	778 Juan	2	269
He would have hospitably cured the stranger	790 Juan	2	1039

CURELESS

Though cureless pangs may prey on me	90 To M.S.G.-A		39
To inflict a cureless wound	207 Fare Thee		20

CURES

Whose remedy only must kill ere it cures	225 Ode-D		4
Gives but one pang, and cures all pain	314 Giaour		431
You'll add to Matrimony's list of cures	937 Juan	12	480
Construction as your cures for hectic phthisics	939 Juan	12	571
Doctors less famous for their cures than fees	961 Juan	14	380

CURIOSITY

To physic idle curiosity	144 Becher-B		32
I shall not sleep to-night for curiosity	676 Werner	1	307
Nevertheless, from curiosity	701 Werner	3	410
Will not excite her too great curiosity	720 Werner	5	475
I loathe that low vice--curiosity	750 Juan	1	181
Or neither--out of curiosity	800 Juan	2	1678
And show'd but little royal curiosity	850 Juan	5	1180

CURIOUS

On giant statues casts the curious eye	271 Minerva		186
She saw in curious order set	326 Abydos	1	279
He calmly met the curious eyes that scann'd	348 Corsair	2	62
With eye more curious he appear'd to scan	368 Lara	1	132
The mystery dearest to the curious crowd	377 Lara	2	138
Why did she love him? Curious fool!--be still	382 Lara	2	530
The carved crests, and curious hues	395 Corinth		969
But I was curious to ascend	406 Chillon		328
A curious sort of somewhat scanty mat	425 Island	2	482
'The curious in fish-sauce,' before they cross	441 Beppo		58
Few questions, and I'm not of curious nature	557 Sardan	1	415
The reach of beings innocent, and curious	630 Cain	1	198
Dissatisfied and curious thoughts--as thou	633 Cain	1	400
She had a curious crew as well as cargo	782 Juan	2	527
They shall appear before your curious eyes	790 Juan	2	990
This revel seem'd a curious mode of mourning	807 Juan	3	392
Juan was told about their curious case	826 Juan	4	642
And conscience ask a curious sort of question	835 Juan	5	236
Said Baba, 'to be curious; 'twill transpire	840 Juan	5	590
Of gilded bronze, and carved in curious guise	842 Juan	5	682
Which curl in curious wreaths:--how soon the smoke	878 Juan	7	687
Of our sensations! What a curious way	906 Juan	9	599
And thus they form'd a rather curious pair	914 Juan	10	453
Had seen the world--which is a curious sight	924 Juan	11	375
Of this same mystic friar's curious doings	987 Juan	16	471
Draperied her form with curious felicity	994 Juan	16	864
And Juan, puzzled, but still curious, thrust	996 Juan	16	1017

CURIOUS-LOOKING

A merry, cock-eyed, curious-looking sprite	293 Vision		521

CURIOUSLY

To wear it? who can curiously behold	36 Harold	3	92
Some female head most curiously presumes	838 Juan	5	438

CURL

So gaily curl the waves before each dashing prow	22 Harold	2	153
And on the curl hangs pausing. Not in vain	66 Harold	4	669
Thus Pope by Curl and Dennis was destroy'd	143 Soliloquy		77
How that pale lip will curl and quiver	318 Giaour		853
The lip's least curl, the lightest paleness thrown	341 Corsair	1	231
His form, to curl their length and curb their sound	361 Corsair	3	389
Now perching on the wave's high curl, and now	429 Island	3	175
With hissing snakes, which curl around my temples	698 Werner	3	184
Which curl in curious wreaths:--how soon the smoke	878 Juan	7	687
There barbers' blocks with periwigs in curl	921 Juan	11	173
A straggling curl show'd he had been fair-hair'd	996 Juan	16	1013

CURL'D

In gently waving ringlet curl'd	128 Lady-C		18
Yet, by thine eyes and ringlets curl'd	159 Gulf		18
And curl'd to give her neck caresses	160 Cadiz		16
Proud Wellington, with eagle beak so curl'd	305 Age		534
Then curl'd his very beard with ire	316 Giaour		593
Night wanes, the vapours round the mountains curl'd	375 Lara	2	1
Curl'd half down his neck so bare	400 Parisina		422
'Up rose the sun; the mists were curl'd	413 Mazeppa		653
Was still, yet lighted; his long locks curl'd down	579 Sardan	4	88
Which curl'd about my senses, and again	714 Werner	5	105
Each sea curl'd o'er the stern, and kept them wet	781 Juan	2	477
Her locks curl'd negligently round her face	789 Juan	2	963
Thrown topsy-turvy, twisted, crisp'd, and curl'd	901 Juan	9	292
The elder ladies' wrinkles curl'd much crisper	906 Juan	9	619

CURLED

Such was the curled son of Clinias;--wouldst thou	725 Deformed	1	213

CURLING

In curling foam and mingling flood	316 Giaour		625
Above them shone the crescent curling	387 Corinth		259

CURLING

Rise curling fast beneath me, white and sulphury	482 Manfred	1	347
Good teeth, with curling rather dark brown hair	832 Juan	5	83

CURLL

Consult Lord Fanny, and confide in Curll	246 Bards		372

CURLS

Their Phlegethon, curls round the rocks of jet	65 Harold	4	620
His glossy curls, his azure wing	89 Anacreon-B		33
The sable curls in wild profusion veil	341 Corsair	1	204
One has false curls, another too much paint	448 Beppo		521
Her streaming hair; the black curls strive, but fail	766 Juan	1	1261
His dewy curls, long drench'd by every storm	788 Juan	2	910
And his black curls were dewy with the spray	792 Juan	2	1174
Down her white neck long floating auburn curls	805 Juan	3	237
His curls fell negligently o'er his front	984 Juan	16	229

CURLY

The boats are darting o'er the curly bay	364 Corsair	3	559
What's here? whose broad brow and whose curly beard	725 Deformed	1	230
And she would softly stir his locks so curly	795 Juan	2	1341
Of wrath and rhyme, when juvenile and curly	909 Juan	10	146

CURLY-HEADED

A little curly-headed, good-for-nothing	750 Juan	1	193

CURRAN

Thy Grattan, thy Curran, thy Sheridan, all	204 Avatar		114
Where Grattan, Curran, Sheridan, all those	928 Juan	11	603

CURRENCY

Which passes ghosts in currency like gold	983 Juan	16	174

CURRENT

Clear as its current, glide the sauntering hours	60 Harold	4	291
Confines the current of the soul	133 E. N. Long		34
And thus of old thy current pour'd	160 Swimming		7
The current I behold will sweep beneath	198 Po		21
Some motion from the current caught	314 Giaour		377
Beats back the current many a rood	316 Giaour		624
Fly, and one current to the ocean add	455 Venice-B		158
For their once healthful current? is it nothing	512 Faliero	2	252
The rank polluted current from the veins	534 Faliero	4	435
To freeze their young blood in its natural current	613 Foscari	3	368
Have it a healthful current. Let it flow	671 Werner	1	10
Set by a current, toward it: they were lost	786 Juan	2	795
Meantime the current, with a rising gale	786 Juan	2	801
Had soil'd the current of her sinless years	801 Juan	3	7
Whose charts lay down its current to a hair	852 Juan	6	12

CURRENTS

Where Brent's cool waves in limpid currents stray	124 Recoll		134
Within our veins its currents be	219 Thy Days		11
In currents through the calmer water spread	948 Juan	13	452

CURRENT'S

Thy current's calmness; oft from out it leaps	65 Harold	4	599
The current's pleasure. Would the dogs were in it	687 Werner	2	315

CURRIE

Like Burns (whom Doctor Currie well describes	814 Juan	3	828

CURRISH

To fly my vengeance--currish renegade	470 Morgante		268

CURRY

Leavening his blood as cayenne doth a curry	916 Juan	10	570

CURS

Against the curs of Nazareth	324 Abydos	1	98
Whose name you bear like other curs--And kings	734 Deformed	1	856

CURSE

The royal wittol Charles, and curse the day	12 Harold	1	510
There seems as 'twere a curse upon the seats	60 Harold	4	309
Not for thy faults, but mine; it is a curse	66 Harold	4	686
And pile on human heads the mountain of my curse	75 Harold	4	1206
That curse shall be Forgiveness. Have I not	75 Harold	4	1207
But brings, with new torture, the curse of to-day	91 Caroline-D		4
But curse my fate for ever after	101 Lady-B		44
A dying father's bitter curse	105 Alva		315
And bids me curse Aurora's ray	113 Quaker		34
Should lead you to curse the coquette	116 Pigot		32
voice curse Orla, the destroyer of Calmar	130 Calmar		82
Pronounced an unrelenting Curse	142 Critics		70
And bade him curse his future fate	155 Lady-E		4
A blank; a thing to count and curse	172 Time-B		30
I've lived to curse my natal day	172 Romaic-B		39

CURSE
We do not curse thee, Waterloo | 187 Ode-B | 1
And then there was the Curse of blood | 197 Duel | 42
May the strong curse of crush'd affections light | 209 Sketch | 85
For thou art pillow'd on a curse too deep | 213 Lady Byron | 22
The curse which, thou say'st, is the crime of my race | 221 False | 4
And, spite of puritans and Collier's curse | 261 Hints | 369
Prick not the poet's conscience as a curse | 268 Hints | 834
My curse shall light,--on him and all his seed | 270 Minerva | 164
And evil by their own internal curse | 290 Vision | 327
He tasted empire's blessings and its curse | 299 Age | 96
The curse for Hassan's sin was sent | 313 Giaour | 280
There read of Cain the curse and crime | 320 Giaour | 1058
To mourn--I dare not curse--the day | 330 Abydos | 2 | 167
To curse the wither'd heart that would not break | 368 Lara | 1 | 130
The curse of Him thou didst forsake | 391 Corinth | 640
Howl'd back my curse; but 'midst the tread | 410 Mazeppa | 388
In vain thou dost demand the cause; a curse | 416 Island | 1 | 69
Alas! how bitter is his country's curse | 457 Dante | 1 | 69
Makes greater, and accumulates my curse | 464 Dante | 4 | 114
And feel the curse to have no natural fear | 479 Manfred | 1 | 25
By the strong curse which is upon my soul | 479 Manfred | 1 | 47
A pathless comet, and a curse | 480 Manfred | 1 | 118
Hath baptized thee with a curse | 481 Manfred | 1 | 223
Shall be a desolation and a curse | 547 Faliero | 5 | 658
Of this proud city, and I leave my curse | 548 Faliero | 5 | 740
Have struck those tyrants! Strike deep as my curse | 549 Faliero | 5 | 799
'Twas but a murmur--Curse upon the distance | 549 Faliero | 5 | 811
It is the curse of kings to be so answer'd | 551 Sardan | 1 | 63
Curse not thyself--millions do that already | 552 Sardan | 1 | 97
Deserve that I should curse them with their wishes | 553 Sardan | 1 | 171
And they will swell the echo with a curse | 582 Sardan | 4 | 290
Ay, there it is; 'tis like a mother's curse | 611 Foscari | 3 | 186
Unjust, and--Curse it not. If I am silent | 611 Foscari | 3 | 239
In such a curse as mine, provoked by such | 624 Foscari | 5 | 222
As you; but I curse not. Adieu, good signors | 624 Foscari | 5 | 223
May shame you; but they dare not groan nor curse you | 624 Foscari | 5 | 260
Of an eternal curse; my brother is | 630 Cain | 1 | 179
Even for the innocent! Dost thou curse thy father | 639 Cain | 2 | 227
The curse is mutual 'twixt thy sire and thee | 639 Cain | 2 | 231
With them would render the curse on it useless | 641 Cain | 2 | 351
According to the curse:--must I do more | 647 Cain | 3 | 110
To save thee from the serpent's curse! It shall | 648 Cain | 3 | 158
May the eternal serpent's curse be on him | 652 Cain | 3 | 402
Curse him not, mother, for he is thy son | 652 Cain | 3 | 405
Curse him not, mother, for he is my brother | 652 Cain | 3 | 406
I curse him from my sight for evermore | 652 Cain | 3 | 409
Add thy deep curse to Eve's upon his head | 653 Cain | 3 | 448
I curse him not: his spirit be his curse | 653 Cain | 3 | 449
And curse thee not; but hold | 656 Heaven | 129
At such an hour too! Yes, curse--it will ease you | 699 Werner | 3 | 277
After--what! doth my father's curse descend | 711 Werner | 4 | 429
Oh! my dead father's curse! 'tis working now | 719 Werner | 5 | 434
Thy curse hath dug it deeper for thy sin | 722 Werner | 5 | 555
Thou canst not be my blessing or my curse | 773 Juan | 1 | 1716
No scandals made the daily press a curse | 850 Juan | 5 | 1191
With one good hearty curse I vent my gall | 855 Juan | 6 | 171
As after reading Athanasius' curse | 855 Juan | 6 | 178
Behold the world! and curse your victories | 897 Juan | 9 | 72

CURSED
But how much cursed by every lover | 97 To Woman | 9
For such a cursed place as This is | 145 Becher-B | 64
Adieu, ye cursed streets of stairs | 163 Malta | 5
Nor call a ghost, unless some cursed scrape | 260 Hints | 293
Ere cursed confederation made thee France's | 274 Waltz | 41
In science and art, I'll be cursed if I know | 280 Blues | 2 | 10
He cursed those virtues as the cause of ill | 342 Corsair | 1 | 257
It told 'twas sunset--and he cursed that sun | 345 Corsair | 1 | 475
Who cursed the tyranny to which he bent | 377 Lara | 2 | 158
But cursed the Christian's victory | 386 Corinth | 146
But cursed them in my heart, and to my haunt | 438 Tasso | 163
When lo! those cursed gondoliers had got | 450 Beppo | 679
A blighted trunk upon a cursed root | 482 Manfred | 1 | 329
Then cursed myself till sunset;--I have pray'd | 486 Manfred | 2 | 227
Cursed be he who caused those tears to flow | 552 Sardan | 1 | 96
Oh God! I dare not think on't! Cursed be | 639 Cain | 2 | 223
Cursed he not me in giving me my birth | 639 Cain | 2 | 228
Cursed he not me before my birth, in daring | 639 Cain | 2 | 229
Cursed from the earth, which open'd late her mouth | 653 Cain | 3 | 472
Or cursed be--with him who made | 669 Heaven | 1110
For a fit escort--but this cursed flood | 694 Werner | 2 | 695
Their cursed pattering feet and whirling wings | 701 Werner | 3 | 404
A new-found mammoth; and their cursed engines | 726 Deformed | 1 | 305
Some cursed the day on which they saw the sun | 779 Juan | 2 | 355
Or by one's early valet's cursed knock | 793 Juan | 2 | 1213
Pricking her fingers with those cursed pins | 860 Juan | 6 | 487

CURSED
(A cursed sort of carriage without springs | 900 Juan | 9 | 234
Love (though she had a cursed taste for war | 906 Juan | 9 | 637

CURSES
From my eye flows no tear, from my lips flow no curses | 92 Caroline-D | 5
But now tears and curses, alike unavailing | 92 Caroline-D | 13
Hobhouse muttering fearful curses | 157 Hodgson | 53
With curses cast them down upon the dust | 189 Darkness | 31
The cause of the curses all annals contain | 203 Avatar | 63
A wretch never named but with curses and jeers | 203 Avatar | 88
And hoard their curses, till the coast is clear | 347 Corsair | 2 | 28
Where cries reply to curses, shrieks to blows | 437 Tasso | 86
Muffled to whisper curses to the night | 531 Faliero | 4 | 226
To strew it with the dead. May all the curses | 652 Cain | 3 | 421
Peace! 'tis no hour for curses, but for prayer | 670 Heaven | 1112
We deem our curses vain; we must expire | 670 Heaven | 1122
For double curses will be my meed now | 722 Deformed | 1 | 34
When they dispute with sceptics; and with curses | 892 Juan | 8 | 863
Such is the shortest way to general curses | 917 Juan | 10 | 628

CURSETH
This spirit curseth us. Let him say on | 635 Cain | 1 | 522

CURSING
Yet cursing both--for both have made him sore | 260 Hints | 236
As cursing thee, thou cursing them | 318 Giaour | 765

CURST
Wrote on his faded brow curst Cain's unresting doom | 17 Harold | 1 | 827
With many a retrospection curst | 18 Harold | 1 | 866
So may he make each curst oppressor bleed | 18 Harold | 1 | 898
Curst be the hour when from their isle they roved | 21 Harold | 2 | 133
But all too late,--so are we doubly curst | 73 Harold | 4 | 1112
Oh! curst be thou, devouring grave | 88 Catullus | 17
Cut off from all but Memory he curst | 184 Julian | 30
As curst an old Lady as ever was seen | 223 Soul-C | 2
So curst the tyrants that destroy | 311 Giaour | 67
Of days no more deplored or curst | 414 Mazeppa | 756
Curst Gan, with envy bursting, had such need | 467 Morgante | 85
Was ever heard of such a curst disaster | 763 Juan | 1 | 1091
Oh, Julia! (this curst vessel pitches so | 776 Juan | 2 | 158

CURTAIL
Curtail or silence the lascivious jest | 263 Hints | 448

CURTAIL'D
O'er curtail'd dishes and o'er stinted wines | 299 Age | 60
My journey to the capital, curtail'd | 541 Faliero | 5 | 217

CURTAIN
The curtain rises--may our stage unfold | 170 Address-A | 70
The curtain dropp'd, the gay burletta o'er | 250 Bards | 658
Till the dropp'd curtain gives a glad release | 261 Hints | 314
By the Lord's grace, who hath withdrawn the curtain | 472 Morgante | 429

CURTAIN'D
Four-posted and silk curtain'd, which are given | 855 Juan | 6 | 195

CURTAINS
Perhaps, as infancy, with gorgeous curtains | 702 Werner | 3 | 453
Arras they prick'd and curtains with their swords | 764 Juan | 1 | 1143

CURTAIN'S
Applaud in thunder at the curtain's fall | 259 Hints | 216

CURTIS
She caught Sir William Curtis in a kilt | 308 Age | 768
Tell them Sir William Curtis is a bore | 918 Juan | 10 | 685

CURTSIED
She snuff'd the candle, curtsied, and withdrew | 768 Juan | 1 | 1384

CURTSIES
To some she curtsies, and to some she dips | 448 Beppo | 516
And curtsying off, as curtsies country dame | 994 Juan | 16 | 852

CURT'SIES
She blushes, curt'sies, frowns--in short she | 100 Marion | 23
(Curt'sies are neither used by Turks nor Greeks | 858 Juan | 6 | 396

CURTSY
To make her curtsy thought it right and fitting | 450 Beppo | 676
And then she drops a brief and modern curtsy | 926 Juan | 11 | 495
With the three-thousandth curtsy; there the waltz | 926 Juan | 11 | 530

CURTSYING
And curtsying off, as curtsies country dame | 994 Juan | 16 | 852

CURVED
Curved is each neck, and flowing each mane | 392 Corinth | 699

CUSHION
(See also PIN-CUSHION)
For cash and conquest, as if from a cushion ... 875 Juan 7 508
But his just now were spread as is a cushion ... 910 Juan 10 165

CUSHIONS
The velvet cushions (for a throne more meet ... 809 Juan 3 533

CUSTOM
Though the harsh custom of our youthful band ... 93 Dorset 5
As custom arbitrates, whose shifting sway ... 258 Hints 103
And seems the custom here to overthrow ... 287 Vision 167
I can't tell who first brought the custom in ... 444 Beppo 284
The secret custom of the courts in Venice ... 500 Faliero 1 54
The custom of the state to put to death ... 547 Faliero 5 636
Thou know'st the man--it is his usual custom ... 558 Sardan 1 521
And the cup? 'Tis my country's custom to ... 594 Sardan 5 451
Forgot the custom; and although alone ... 594 Sardan 5 454
An Indian widow braves for custom? Then ... 594 Sardan 5 467
'Twas an old custom of the Greek and Roman ... 785 Juan 2 739
(It is the country's custom), but in vain ... 810 Juan 3 594
Reversing the good custom of old days ... 811 Juan 3 626
As is the custom of those Eastern climes ... 842 Juan 5 710
For through the South the custom still commands ... 844 Juan 5 839
Her state (it is the custom of her nation ... 845 Juan 5 886
Than is the custom of the gentle sex ... 857 Juan 6 294

CUSTOM'D
Rests at his heart; the custom'd morning came ... 369 Lara 1 249
Of thee and Zames, and our custom'd meeting ... 579 Sardan 4 83

CUSTOM-HOUSE
Prying from the custom-house ... 157 Hodgson 11
Having no custom-house nor quarantine ... 804 Juan 3 154
Thy custom-house, with all its delicate duties ... 916 Juan 10 547

CUSTOMS
Bestow'd her customs, and amended theirs ... 418 Island 1 219
All proper customs and true courtesies ... 467 Morgante 53
Of all the customs of this polish'd nation ... 840 Juan 5 560
An outline of the customs of the East ... 859 Juan 6 460
Exacted by the customs of the East ... 863 Juan 6 730

CUSTOM'S
And all things weigh'd in custom's falsest scale ... 69 Harold 4 832

CUT
Cut to his heart again with the keen knife ... 36 Harold 3 41
Thy love of Tasso, should have cut the knot ... 57 Harold 4 148
Deeply she cut--but not erased ... 150 Harrow-C 5
Cut off from all but Memory he curst ... 184 Julian 30
So Castlereagh has cut his throat!--The worst ... 238 Epigrams 5
So He has cut his throat at last!--He! Who ... 238 Epigrams 7
The man who cut his country's long ago ... 238 Epigrams 8
Cut down crown influence with reforming scythes ... 266 Hints 673
So they've cut up our friend then? Not left him
  a tatter ... 277 Blues 1 29
When I cut ears off, I had cut him down ... 287 Vision 150
To cut from nations' hearts their 'pound of flesh ... 307 Age 703
Which cut her lord's half-shatter'd sceptre
  through ... 308 Age 758
Hemm'd in--cut off--cleft down--and trampled o'er ... 350 Corsair 2 248
But once cut off--the remnant of his band ... 357 Corsair 3 151
Cut off by some mysterious fate from those ... 378 Lara 2 234
Cut off from hope, and compass'd in the toil ... 379 Lara 2 330
I will cut off the hands from both their trunks ... 472 Morgante 423
He cut his brethren's hands off at these words ... 472 Morgante 431
As when the viper hath been cut to pieces ... 521 Faliero 3 148
No privacy of life--all were cut off ... 525 Faliero 3 470
Nor claim to ties they have cut off from others ... 526 Faliero 3 504
Which grief and shame will soon cut down to days ... 543 Faliero 5 357
Discrown'd a prince, cut off his crownless head ... 544 Faliero 5 448
The serpent's, not the lion's. Cut him down ... 564 Sardan 2 166
Enjoyment! We have cut the way short to it ... 571 Sardan 3 14
Was a rock in our way which I cut through ... 720 Werner 5 459
Now, tell me, don't you cut a pretty figure ... 765 Juan 1 1200
But sage Antonia cut him short before ... 766 Juan 1 1298
The motto cut upon a white cornelian ... 771 Juan 1 1583
Immediately the masts were cut away ... 778 Juan 2 249
Foremast and bowsprit were cut down, and they ... 778 Juan 2 253
That ever scuttled ship or cut a throat ... 806 Juan 3 322
Such names at present cut a convict figure ... 814 Juan 3 841
'Tis being too epic, and I must cut down ... 816 Juan 3 978
Cut from its forest root of years--the river ... 817 Juan 4 76
Had fallen, with his right shoulder half cut
  through ... 822 Juan 4 384
And he himself o'ermaster'd and cut down ... 823 Juan 4 458
The Parcae then cut short the further spinning ... 832 Juan 5 43
'Cut off a thousand heads, before--'--'Now, pray ... 840 Juan 5 569
Her first thought was to cut off Juan's head ... 849 Juan 5 1105
Her second, to cut only his--acquaintance ... 849 Juan 5 1106
She look'd (this simile's quite new) just cut ... 857 Juan 6 341
Whose heads were heroes, which cut off in vain ... 878 Juan 8 15
Knew when and how 'to cut and come again ... 882 Juan 8 278
Their chiefs to order,--were all cut to pieces ... 887 Juan 8 592

CUT
Cossacques were all cut off as day was breaking ... 888 Juan 8 603
Which was cut off, and scarce even then let go ... 889 Juan 8 680
By God! we'll be too late for the first cut ... 891 Juan 8 808
Just now yours were cut out in different sections ... 904 Juan 9 517
And my internal spirit cut a caper ... 907 Juan 10 20
Had such been cut in Phaeton's time, the god ... 917 Juan 10 621
He from the world had cut off a great man ... 920 Juan 11 145
The corn is cut, the manor full of game ... 950 Juan 13 595
As Phidian forms cut out of marble Attic ... 955 Juan 13 875
And cut through such canals of contradiction ... 979 Juan 15 703
His clothes were not curb'd to their usual cut ... 984 Juan 16 230
Cut through and through (oh! damnable incision ... 990 Juan 16 638
And not a joke he cut but earn'd its praise ... 991 Juan 16 699

CUTHULLIN
where is Cuthullin, the shield of Erin? He ... 130 Calmar 48
dream. I will seek car-borne Cuthullin. If I ... 130 Calmar 59

CUTLASS
His cutlass droop'd, unconscious of a sheath ... 425 Island 2 491
The blows upon his cutlass, and then put ... 822 Juan 4 387

CUTS
Cuts the light pack, or calls the rattling main ... 250 Bards 673
Much that'--'Peace, peace!' he cuts their prating
  short ... 340 Corsair 1 146
For war cuts up not only branch, but root ... 872 Juan 7 328

CUTTER
Were all that could be thrown into the cutter ... 779 Juan 2 368
Nine in the cutter, thirty in the boat ... 781 Juan 2 431
And the poor little cutter quickly swamp'd ... 781 Juan 2 480
They grieved for those who perish'd with the
  cutter ... 781 Juan 2 487
Columbus found a new world in a cutter ... 971 Juan 15 214

CUTTER'S
As o'er the cutter's edge he tried to cross ... 781 Juan 2 452

CUT-THROAT
By a cut-throat! Ay!--you may look upon me ... 712 Werner 4 510

CUT-THROATS
Of his infallibility. Well, cut-throats ... 739 Deformed 2 280
You are 'the best of cut-throats:'--do not start ... 896 Juan 9 25

CUTTING
(See also CAROTID-ARTERY-CUTTING)
And cutting stays, as usual in such cases ... 451 Beppo 712
(So children cutting teeth receive a coral ... 772 Juan 1 1668
To cutting short their hopes of having any ... 848 Juan 5 1056
The cutting off his head was not the art ... 849 Juan 5 1119

CUTT'ST
Thou cutt'st thy throat that Britain may be saved ... 238 Epigrams 4

CUVIER
So Cuvier says;--and then shall come again ... 901 Juan 9 297
Man, 'midst thy mouldy mammoths, 'grand Cuvier ... 913 Juan 10 412

CYBELE
She looks a sea Cybele, fresh from ocean ... 55 Harold 4 10

CYCLADES
Spell-bound within the clustering Cyclades ... 356 Corsair 3 62
Undreamt of in his native Cyclades ... 425 Island 2 471
The hot gales of the horrid Cyclades ... 597 Foscari 1 128
(One of the wild and smaller Cyclades ... 790 Juan 2 1010
Mourns o'er the beauty of the Cyclades ... 825 Juan 4 576

CYCLOPS
And turn him like the Cyclops mad with blindness ... 808 Juan 3 456

CYGNET
The cygnet nobly walks the water ... 315 Giaour 504
Soft as the callow cygnet in its nest ... 793 Juan 2 1182

CYMBALS
Whose gilded cymbals, more adorn'd than clear ... 254 Bards 895

CYMBAL'S
As a lute's pierceth through the cymbal's clash ... 577 Sardan 3 393

CYMON'S
Did modern swains, possess'd of Cymon's powers ... 171 Hales-Owen 5
In Cymon's manner waste their leisure hours ... 171 Hales-Owen 6

CYNIC
Beauties that ev'n a cynic must avow ... 13 Harold 1 606
Let sage or cynic prattle as he will ... 32 Harold 2 772
Yes, friend! for thee I'll quit my cynic cell ... 261 Hints 343
Be slaves who will, the cynic shall be free ... 304 Age 480
Which in a saint or cynic ever was ... 930 Juan 12 51
As did the Cynic on some like occasion ... 986 Juan 16 388

CYNICS
For sceptred cynics earth were far too wide a den 41 Harold 3 369

CYNTHIA
High ground, as virgin Cynthia sways the tides 931 Juan 12 110

CYNTHIA'S
And oft I thought at Cynthia's noon 166 Struggle 29
When Cynthia's light almost gave way to morn 383 Lara 2 552

CYPRESS
Through many a cypress grove within each city's ken 25 Harold 2 342
The cypress, hear the owl, and plod your way 66 Harold 4 699
Cypress and ivy, weed and wallflower grown 71 Harold 4 955
Must myrtle and cypress alternately strew 100 L Adieu 42
His cypress, the garland of love's last adieu 100 L Adieu 44
With cypress crown'd, array'd in weeds 118 Romance 42
But nor cypress nor yew let us see 151 Soul-A 15
And the wild cypress wave in tender gloom 218 Bloom 5
The cypress saddening by the sacred mosque 269 Minerva 43
The very cypress droops to death 313 Giaour 285
Know ye the land where the cypress and myrtle 323 Abydos 1 1
We to the cypress groves had flown 324 Abydos 1 69
The sad but living cypress glooms 336 Abydos 2 666
'Tis from her cypress summit heard 336 Abydos 2 713
The cypress saddening by the sacred mosque 356 Corsair 3 43
Of leaves, beneath the cypress. Cypress! 'tis 646 Cain 3 3
Lashes, dark as the cypress which waves o'er them 646 Cain 3 28
With cypress branches hast thou wreathed thy bowers 801 Juan 3 11
The cypress groves; Olympus high and hoar 831 Juan 5 21
(As night-dew, on a cypress glittering, tinges 860 Juan 6 535

CYPRESSES
Some cypresses beyond the time-worn breach 495 Manfred 3 280
O'ertopp'd with cypresses, dark-green and tall 836 Juan 5 320

CYPRUS
And chief in Rhodes and Cyprus, prince in Venice 523 Faliero 3 340
Then, when of Cyprus, now thy subject kingdom 549 Faliero 5 776
Of Candia, Cyprus, Rhodes, or other islands 786 Juan 2 800

CYRUS
This was the mode of Cyrus, best of kings 980 Juan 16 3

CYTHEREA'S
Like to the fabled Cytherea's zone 49 Harold 3 848
When Cytherea's blooming Boy 139 Anacreon-C 15
More Muse-like--like to Cytherea's shell 936 Juan 12 408

CZAR
Gasps for the gore of serfs and of their czar 300 Age 168
Resplendent sight! Behold the coxcomb Czar 304 Age 434
Had pass'd to the triumphant Czar 407 Mazeppa 7

CZARINA'S
The fair czarina's autocratic crest 913 Juan 10 390

CZAR'S
The Czar's look, I own, was much brighter and brisker 228 Moore-A 20
For the first courtier in the Czar's regard 302 Age 309

DABBLE
Who dabble in the pettiness of fame 456 Dante 1 54
There's nothing women love to dabble in 972 Juan 15 244

DABBLED
Yet dabbled with his lately flowing blood 428 Island 3 148
And can I see them dabbled o'er with blood 527 Faliero 3 592
Were dabbled with the deep blood which ran o'er 823 Juan 4 466

DABBLING
Nor dabbling fingers left to tell the tale 377 Lara 2 115
My dabbling in vile drugs. And art thou sure 619 Foscari 4 285
And dabbling merchants, in a mart of Jews 694 Werner 2 728
By dabbling with a jewel in your favour 698 Werner 3 218
Dabbling its sleek young hands in Erin's gore 746 Juan Ded 90

DACIA
As Dacia men to die the eternal death 731 Deformed 1 628

DACIAN
There was their Dacian mother--he, their sire 76 Harold 4 1266

DACTYLS
But ere the spavin'd dactyls could be spurr'd 296 Vision 721

DAD
(See GRAND-DAD'S)

DAGGER
Threw down the dagger--dared depart 180 Ode-A 57
That dagger, on whose hilt the gem 330 Abydos 2 135

DAGGER
But since the dagger suits thee less than brand 361 Corsair 3 380
And be it where it may--I have my dagger 701 Werner 3 425
Also a dealer in the sword and dagger 738 Deformed 2 205
Slippers of saffron, dagger rich and handy 840 Juan 5 543
The dagger close at hand, which made it awkward 849 Juan 5 1114

DAGGER'S
When Brutus made the dagger's edge surpass 67 Harold 4 732
But if a dagger's form it bear 319 Giaour 930

DAGON'S
The pillars of stone Dagon's temple on 624 Foscari 5 219

DAILY
As if the memory of some daily feud 4 Harold 1 66
By daily abstinence and nightly prayer 32 Harold 2 741
Aught that recalls the daily drug which turn'd 66 Harold 4 676
Averr'd, and known--and daily, hourly seen 69 Harold 4 849
New beauties still are daily bright'ning 98 To Lesbia 30
As daily I strode through the pine-cover'd glade 117 Lachin 12
Th' allotted hour of daily sport is o'er 124 Recoll 149
Whose years float on in daily crime 132 Prayer 34
A walking register of daily news 142 Soliloquy 39
And nightly smiles, and daily dinners 163 Malta 29
What wits! what poets dost thou daily raise 242 Bards 15
Lo! with what pomp the daily prints proclaim 249 Bards 594
Who daily scribble for your daily bread 251 Bards 742
(Unlucky Tavell! doom'd to daily cares 259 Hints 229
So many conquerors' cars were daily driven 285 Vision 35
Written without hands, since we daily view 295 Vision 612
Now daily squabbling o'er disputed rations 299 Age 58
Though fairest captives daily met his eye 342 Corsair 1 289
Now daily mutters o'er his blacken'd fame 377 Lara 2 122
And Carnage smiled upon her daily dead 379 Lara 2 281
The daily harass, and the fight delay'd 379 Lara 2 297
Grew daily tired of his dominion 408 Mazeppa 169
Which deals the daily pittance of our span 423 Island 3 350
They lock them up, and veil, and guard them daily 449 Beppo 561
I leave them to their daily 'tea is ready 449 Beppo 607
With dull and daily dissonance, repeats 453 Venice-B 21
Of many thousand years--the daily scene 453 Venice-B 57
In daily jeopardy the place below 468 Morgante 160
From off yon mountain daily raining faster 469 Morgante 199
To him War offers daily sacrifice 489 Manfred 2 383
You know what daily cares oppress all those 511 Faliero 2 182
Daily since I was Doge; but if you will 542 Faliero 5 302
Whom I see daily wave their fiery swords 628 Cain 1 84
Of daily toil and constant thought: I look 630 Cain 1 172
With the burnt offerings, which he daily brings 647 Cain 3 100
Which daily feast a thousand vassals? You 673 Werner 1 120
Do not five hundred thousand heroes daily 682 Werner 1 681
Whose daily repetition marks your duty 701 Werner 3 379
Continue daily orisons for us 711 Werner 4 456
Daily, or monthly, or three monthly; I 772 Juan 1 1684
His daily task had kept his fancy cool 774 Juan 2 11
Paid daily visits to her boy, and took 796 Juan 2 1386
Thought daily service was her only mission 797 Juan 2 1454
No scandals made the daily press a curse 850 Juan 5 1191
'Tis the vile daily drop on drop which wears 855 Juan 6 159
His daily council upon ways and means 864 Juan 6 762
Which made him daily bless his own neutrality 866 Juan 6 936
That daily shilling which makes warriors tough 883 Juan 8 334
Upon the nothings which are daily spent 898 Juan 9 101
Ye twice ten hundred thousand daily scribes 900 Juan 9 274
Employ'd for, since it is their daily labour 923 Juan 11 322
Where every kind of mischief's daily brewing 932 Juan 12 179
Indeed we see the daily proof display'd 944 Juan 13 228
As many covers, duly, daily, laid 947 Juan 13 390
A daily plague, which in the aggregate 958 Juan 14 185
O Death! thou dunnest of all duns! thou daily 969 Juan 15 57
The fourth we hear, and see, and say too, daily 970 Juan 15 166

DAINTIES
And, grateful for the dainties on his plate 249 Bards 550
'Salt seasons dainties, and my food is still 349 Corsair 2 123

DAINTY
'A dainty dish to set before the King 745 Juan Ded 11
Admiring those (by dainty dames abhorr'd 903 Juan 9 427
(Not the most 'dainty Ariel') and perplexes 918 Juan 11 18

DALE
Each hill and dale, each deepening glen and wold 33 Harold 2 834

DALES
Yet in famed Attica such lovely dales 26 Harold 2 410
Who, after a long chase o'er hills, dales, bushes 959 Juan 14 278

DALLAS
Sagacious R. C. Dallas 226 Dallas 6

DALLIANCE
Within these palace walls in silken dalliance 560 Sardan 1 627

DALMATIAN
Your merchants, your Dalmatian and Greek slaves   606 Foscari   2   301

DAM
A foal well worthy of her ancient dam   255 Bards   971
Would seek to save the spotted sire or dam   524 Faliero   3   413
Like frighten'd antelopes. No: like the dam   577 Sardan   3   378
And piteous bleating of its restless dam   643 Cain   2   497
Which sucks at midnight from the wholesome dam   722 Deformed   1   21
Of shape;--my dam beheld my shape was hopeless   727 Deformed   1   344
(His sire was of Castile, his dam from Aragon   751 Juan   1   300

DAMAETAS
Damaetas ran through all the maze of sin   100 Damaetas   9

DAMAGE
Or what becomes of damage and divorces   444 Beppo   296
To do not much less damage than the table   809 Juan   3   528

DAMAGED
Been somewhat damaged in my name to save   719 Werner   5   381
Their stock was damaged by the weather's stress   779 Juan   2   366
To faint, and damaged bread wet through the bags   782 Juan   2   495

DAMAGES
Are worse than the worst damages men pay   856 Juan   6   230
Calls Ilion's the first damages on record   903 Juan   9   424
Or whether he was taken in for damages   929 Juan   11   703
Then there's the vulgar trick of those d--d
damages   938 Juan   12   516

DAMAS
Count Damas drove them back into the water   871 Juan   7   247
The Prince de Ligne, and Langeron, and Damas   871 Juan   7   255

DAMA'S
To the high dama's brow, more melancholy   445 Beppo   357

DAMASK
All is in order in the damask chamber   675 Werner   1   261
And thick with damask flowers of silk inlaid   809 Juan   3   507

DAMASQUE
A golden scabbard on a Damasque sword   958 Juan   14   213

DAME
But his was not the love of living dame   47 Harold   3   738
Arrived a young and noble dame   102 Alva   78
Creusa's style but wanting to the dame   108 Nisus   202
Ah, hapless dame! no sire bewails   111 Medea   45
Nor find a sylph in every dame   118 Romance   19
Now let me cease--Physician, Parson, Dame   143 Soliloquy   63
To flit along from dame to dame   153 Friend-A   67
And old dame Portland fills the place of Pitt   255 Bards   1016
Macbeth's fierce dame is ready to your hand   259 Hints   176
The slaughter'd peasant and the ravish'd dame   272 Minerva   300
Leads forth the ready dame, whose rising flush   276 Waltz   188
For worlds I dare not view the dame   322 Giaour   1186
Then, lovely dame, bethink thee! and beware   358 Corsair   3   184
What hath such gentle dame to do with home   360 Corsair   3   303
Nor there, since Menelaus' dame   386 Corinth   225
Could make or mar it. Yet full many a dame   509 Faliero   2   61
You have strange thoughts for a patrician dame   510 Faliero   2   75
Or question save those--High-born dame! bethink
thee   598 Foscari   1   204
That he is known. Let the fair dame preserve   612 Foscari   3   268
The noble dame Marina craves an audience   621 Foscari   5   64
Is not your husband visible, fair dame   693 Werner   2   669
Changed; for the dame grew distant, the youth shy   755 Juan   1   554
Or as a dame repents her of her oath   849 Juan   5   1135
A dame who kept up discipline among   856 Juan   6   237
The dame replied, 'Between your dreams and you   858 Juan   6   383
The chief dame of the Oda, upon whom   865 Juan   6   817
Beneath his art. The dame, press'd to disclose
them   903 Juan   9   407
So when he saw each ancient dame a suitor   935 Juan   12   333
And to the beauties of a foreign dame   939 Juan   12   574
Was there chaste dame who had not in her head   972 Juan   15   252
And curtsying off, as curtsies country dame   994 Juan   16   852
Is like--a duckling by Dame Partlett rear'd   997 Juan   17   30

DAMES
The laughing dames in whom he did delight   5 Harold   1   92
Who round the North for paler dames would seek   13 Harold   1   601
Here dons, grandees, but chiefly dames abound   15 Harold   1   724
Which, though sometimes they frown, yet rarely
anger dames   24 Harold   2   288
Nay more, twelve slaves, and twice six captive
dames   107 Nisus   159
Of warriors, monks, and dames the cloister'd tomb   119 Newstead-A   3
When dames accuse 'tis bootless to deny   142 Soliloquy   34
Some ancient Dames, of virtue fiery   144 Becher-B   21
That dames may listen to the sound at nights   244 Bards   156
Strikes his wild lyre, whilst listening dames are
hush'd   245 Bards   286

DAMES
There is a festival, where knights and dames   371 Lara   1   383
Her knights and dames, her court--is there   398 Parisina   166
And dames, and chiefs, of princely port   408 Mazeppa   146
The coldest dames so very tender   408 Mazeppa   176
Worthy to be our first of native dames   514 Faliero   2   419
Amidst the noblest of our dames in public   515 Faliero   2   433
What glory to the chaste Venetian dames   542 Faliero   5   315
True knights, chaste dames, huge giants, kings
despotic   817 Juan   4   46
Life's half-way house, where dames with virtue
crown'd   861 Juan   6   597
Admiring those (by dainty dames abhorr'd   903 Juan   9   427
Of gentle dames, among whose recreations   907 Juan   9   654
Fair virgins blush'd upon him; wedded dames   924 Juan   11   377
'Midst royal dukes and dames condemn'd to climb   926 Juan   11   535
Nay, married dames will now and then discover   933 Juan   12   258
Than the more glowing dames whose lot is cast   938 Juan   12   547
Nor use those palisades by dames erected   963 Juan   14   487
But 'laissez aller'--knights and dames I sing   971 Juan   15   193
The supper too discuss'd, the dames admired   981 Juan   16   58
Of knights and dames heroic and chaste too   982 Juan   16   133
By nature, as in higher dames less hale   989 Juan   16   555

DAMM'D
Damm'd like the dull canal with locks and chains   455 Venice-B   152
Damm'd from its fountain--the child from the knee   817 Juan   4   77

DAMME
'Sick, ma'am, damme, you'll be sicker   157 Hodgson   23

DAMMES
While Reynolds vents his 'dammes!' 'poohs!' and
'zounds   249 Bards   568

DAMME'S
Though hardly heard through multifarious 'damme's   921 Juan   11   187
And yet the British 'Damme''s rather Attic   923 Juan   11   337
But 'Damme''s quite ethereal, though too daring   924 Juan   11   343

DAMMING
Damming the rivers with a sudden dash   483 Manfred   1   357

DAMN
And damn the verse you cannot feel   141 Critics   4
I read Glenarvon, too, by Caro. Lamb--God damn   230 I Read   7
God save the people--damn all Kings   235 New Song   31
How can you, damn your souls   237 Bowles   7
Now (damn you) get knock'd on the head   237 Farce   4
Or damn the dead with purgatorial praise   246 Bards   312
Damn'd like the devil, devil-like will damn   248 Bards   517
And double-barrels (damn them!) miss their mark   264 Hints   556
And not a whit more difficult to damn   286 Vision   115
Exclaim'd, 'G--d damn!'--those syllables intense   428 Island   3   125
And as for Fortune--but I dare not d--n her   447 Beppo   486
The English always use to govern d--n   749 Juan   1   112
Or madam dies.'--Alfonso mutter'd, 'D--n her   767 Juan   1   1301
'Tis strange that he should farther 'damn his
eyes   872 Juan   7   353
With,--'Damn your eyes! your money or your life   919 Juan   11   80
Of English, save their shibboleth, 'God damn   920 Juan   11   90
Like Addison's 'faint praise,' so wont to damn   994 Juan   16   876

DAMNABLE
With their damnable--Hold, my good friend, do
you know   277 Blues   1   10
Cut through and through (oh! damnable incision   990 Juan   16   638

DAMNABLY
Who's so damnably bit   232 Murray-B   61
Were damnably mistaken; few are slow   872 Juan   7   331

DAMNATION
Unless it ensures most infallible Damnation   179 Devil's Dr   214
Damnation for others brewing   179 Devil's Dr   240
Of those who think damnation better still   286 Vision   100
I think few worth damnation save their kings   290 Vision   320
As have the privilege of their damnation   291 Vision   418
Dreading the deep damnation of his 'bah   444 Beppo   254

DAMN'D
(See also DOUBLE-DAMN'D)
And damn'd, ere yet the whole was read   141 Critics   68
Damn'd business for my Miss Medea, etc., etc.   225 Embargo   6
All damn'd, though yet alive   225 Orraca   4
When Thurlow this damn'd nonsense sent   226 Thurlow-A   1
And Sotheby, with his damn'd Orestes   231 Doctor   25
You're in a damn'd hurry   232 Murray-B   2
Yet even then 'twould be damn'd ugly   234 Silver   6
I heard or saw so damn'd a fool   234 Friend-A   4
My play is damn'd, and Lady Noel not   237 Elegy   2
And if you won't,--you may be damn'd   238 Orford   15
Damn'd like the devil, devil-like will damn   248 Bards   517
His scenes alone had damn'd our sinking stage   251 Bards   734
Poor Virgin! damn'd some twenty times a year   258 Hints   126
We saved Irene, but half damn'd the play   260 Hints   282

DAMN'D

Nor burn damn'd Drury if it rise again	261	Hints	372
Are damn'd alike by gods and men and columns	265	Hints	588
Dear, d--d contemner of my schoolboy songs	265	Hints	605
Damn'd all their days, they posthumously thrive	266	Hints	721
And only left us thy d----d debts and dances	274	Waltz	42
That may be, Mr. Tracy, but shows damn'd bad taste	279	Blues 1	106
I wish all these people were d----d with my marriage	283	Blues 2	165
'Tis blasphemous; I know one may be damn'd	286	Vision	106
And synagogues have made a damn'd bad purchase	286	Vision	112
While I am guard, may I be damn'd myself	291	Vision	392
This was a signal unto such damn'd souls	291	Vision	417
They may range freely--being damn'd the same	291	Vision	424
Who damn'd away his eyes as heretofore	292	Vision	466
Try if kings may n't be damn'd like me or you	292	Vision	480
Since they were both damn'd long ago, and still in	293	Vision	566
Dine and be d--d! I don't mean to be coarse	441	Beppo	71
Over the damn'd before the Judgment-throne	464	Dante 4	64
In hell below, and damn'd in great confusion	472	Morgante	406
But you were lost and damn'd to hell before	473	Morgante	472
Heap'd with the damn'd like pebbles.--I am giddy	483	Manfred 1	350
The guilty saved hath damn'd his hundred judges	512	Faliero 2	238
Should aid each other. It is a damn'd world, sir	695	Werner 3	42
Although one must be damn'd for you, no doubt	761	Juan 1	946
Who told him to be damn'd--in his confusion	779	Juan 2	352
Had run the risk of being damn'd for ever	798	Juan 2	1540
So now all things are d--n'd one feels at ease	855	Juan 6	177
For they are damn'd; that once all-famous oath	872	Juan 7	354
And wrinkles, the d--d democrats, won't flatter	910	Juan 10	192
Then there's the vulgar trick of those d--d damages	938	Juan 12	516

DAMN'DEST

Which, being the damn'dest part of matrimony	905	Juan 9	559

DAMNED

Where late my ears rung with the damned cries	456	Dante 1	7

DAMNED'ST

Adieu, thou damned'st quarantine	163	Malta	11

DAMNING

Devil, whose sole delight is damning	197	Rogers	74
Such damning fame as Dunciads only give	252	Bards	751
And damning dulness of lord chamberlains	261	Hints	358
No doubt this patience, when the world is damning us	750	Juan 1	233

DAMNS

Vomits forth--and damns our souls	157	Hodgson	56

D'AMOUR

Follow'd by 'petits puits d'amour'--a dish	976	Juan 15	538

DAMP

And piled the hearth, and wrung their garments damp	29	Harold 2	607
There, in apartments small and damp	95	Granta	29
'In vain you damp the ardour of my soul	106	Nisus	79
Yet lingers 'mid thy damp and mossy tombs	122	Newstead-A	151
Youth will not damp parental fire	150	My Son	32
And as my damp hair stiffen'd, thus it spake	222	Spirit	6
Flush in the cheek, or damp upon the brow	341	Corsair 1	242
Which not the darkness of despair can damp	343	Corsair 1	353
Is trimm'd and heeds not the sirocco's damp	344	Corsair 1	434
Save that damp brow which rests upon his knees	381	Lara 2	429
Gleam'd on the dew-drops big and damp	397	Parisina	117
To fetters, and the damp vault's dayless gloom	402	Sonnet-F	6
Creeping o'er the floor so damp	403	Chillon	34
A damp like death rose o'er my brow. I strove	528	Faliero 4	9
Even on these dull damp walls, and--Boy! no tears	614	Foscari 3	415
Your hands! There's death in that damp clammy grasp	618	Foscari 4	191
In its dull damp degeneracy, to	640	Cain 2	277
As fits a noble guest:--'tis damp, no doubt	675	Werner 1	232
And devilish damp, but fine enough by torchlight	679	Werner 1	514
His berth a little damp, and him afraid	777	Juan 2	200
How long in his damp trance young Juan lay	788	Juan 2	881
Which weigh'd upon them yet, all damp and salt	793	Juan 2	1175
Or like a wisp along the marsh so damp	873	Juan 7	365

DAMP'D

So that themselves as well as hopes were damp'd	781	Juan 2	479
Although a squall or two had damp'd his raptures	803	Juan 3	116

DAMPENING

And o'er his brow the dampening heartdrops threw	374	Lara 1	600

DAMPER

But then he comes from a much damper place	675	Werner 1	234

DAMPS

In subterranean damps where the owl peep'd	71	Harold 4	959
And these vile damps, too, and yon thick green wave	614	Foscari 3	375

DAMS

But make not monsters spring from gentle dams	257	Hints	19

DAMSEL

'I lost a damsel in that hour	195	Ballad-A	96
No damsel faints when rather closely press'd	275	Waltz	143
To that lost damsel, shouldst thou leave me now	344	Corsair 1	442
Thy sovereign. Yet stay, damsel!--She's gone	576	Sardan 3	294
Though somewhat frankly said for a fair damsel	708	Werner 4	246
But with our damsel this was not the case	789	Juan 2	961
Was what her dress bespoke, a damsel fair	857	Juan 6	282
To aid the damsel and destroy the caitiff	942	Juan 13	74
No damsel, but a dish, as hath been said	977	Juan 15	590

DAMSELS

I've loved, and many damsels know it	144	Becher-B	17
Would certain Damsels also teach	151	Harriet	11
With thee our nursery damsels shed their tears	246	Bards	345
The long-conniving damsels seek	397	Parisina	124
And hear the warbling birds! the damsels said	419	Island 2	4
By a gross affront to your attendant damsels	515	Faliero 2	432
Along the gallery, and amidst the damsels	551	Sardan 1	41
Why went you not forth with the other damsels	573	Sardan 3	149
Baba, when all the damsels were withdrawn	844	Juan 5	809
First came her damsels, a decorous file	850	Juan 5	1161
Juan amongst the damsels in disguise	851	Juan 5	1235
With all the damsels in their long array	855	Juan 6	202
The damsels', who had thoughts of some great harm	862	Juan 6	525
But six old damsels, each of seventy years	895	Juan 8	1039
Damsels, and dances, revels, ready money	910	Juan 10	167

DAMSEL'S

Why, Pigot, complain of this damsel's disdain	115	Pigot	1
Lolah demanded the new damsel's name	858	Juan 6	345

DAN

Above all things, Dan Poet, if you can	260	Hints	291
Dan Phoebus takes me for an auctioneer	950	Juan 13	588

DANAE

Caught it, as Danae caught the golden show'r	248	Bards	495

DANCE

(See also COUNTRY-DANCE)

And consecrate the oath with draught, and dance till morn	15	Harold 1	710
While on the gay dance shone Night's lover-loving Queen	17	Harold 1	809
Fain would he now have join'd the dance, the song	17	Harold 1	830
Whose shadows in the glassy waters dance	27	Harold 2	485
In motley robe to dance at masking ball	32	Harold 2	745
On with the dance! let joy be unconfined	38	Harold 3	192
Dance in the soft breeze in a fairy mass	72	Harold 4	1051
Who lead'st along, in airy dance	118	Romance	3
Who move in joy, and dance along the plain	123	Recoll	126
Flies lightly through the dance of Joy	139	Anacreon-C	16
Then might freedom forgive thee this dance in thy chain	202	Avatar	27
The midnight orgy, and the mazy dance	250	Bards	647
Decorum left her for an opera dance	261	Hints	354
Dance forth--sans armour thou shalt take the field	273	Waltz	12
And give both Belial and his dance their due	274	Waltz	28
And join with me the dance, or wake the song	344	Corsair 1	436
While dance the Almas to wild minstrelsy	347	Corsair 2	36
And the gay dance of bounding Beauty's train	371	Lara 1	389
Breaks, yet unsated with the dance	386	Corinth	211
Anon the torchlight dance shall fling its sheen	419	Island 2	31
Strike up the dance! the cava bowl fill high	419	Island 2	45
But now the dance is o'er--yet stay awhile	419	Island 2	53
Of banquet, dance, and revel, are forgot	440	Tasso	238
For dance, and song, and serenade, and ball	441	Beppo	75
Sold pictures, and was skilful in the dance as	444	Beppo	260
When the first act is ended by a dance	445	Beppo	327
Where people dance, and sup, and dance again	447	Beppo	458
Which, in the lightest movement of the dance	528	Faliero 4	5
Perceived it was the Pyrrhic dance so martial	805	Juan 3	231
Song, dance, wine, music, stories from the Persian	806	Juan 3	275
You have the Pyrrhic dance as yet	812	Juan 3	743
Our virgins dance beneath the shade	813	Juan 3	774
Which might go far, but she don't dance with vigour	827	Juan 4	679
Whose smile makes all the planets dance with mirth	849	Juan 5	1148
Began to sing, dance, chatter, smile, and play	856	Juan 6	272
The only dance which teaches girls to think	926	Juan 11	531
Or, if he dance not, but hath higher views	927	Juan 11	553
Sung, or rehearsed the last dance from abroad	954	Juan 13	828

DANCE

Sometimes a dance (though rarely on field days	954	Juan 13	857
May retrograde a little in the dance	973	Juan 15	310
Like Holbein's 'Dance of Death'--but 'tis the same	973	Juan 15	312
The song was silent, and the dance expired	981	Juan 16	60
Which she went through as though it were a dance	993	Juan 16	812

DANCED

Danced on the shore the daughters of the land	32	Harold 2	766
The Nymphs and Tritons danced around	89	Prometheus-A	15
The woods of Ida danced before my eyes	125	Recoll	204
(What harm, if David danced before the ark	261	Hints	320
Her nimble feet danced off another's head	274	Waltz	88
And danced in triumph o'er the waters wide	338	Corsair 1	14
Their hands in sacred vows--have danced their babes	603	Foscari 2	120
Before the bridal hours have danced their measure	892	Juan 8	899
And parts, and hearts: he danced and sung, and had	924	Juan 11	370
Here danced Albano's boys, and here the sea shone	950	Juan 13	565
And then he danced,--all foreigners excel	960	Juan 14	297
Of pantomime;--he danced, I say, right well	960	Juan 14	299
He danced without theatrical pretence	960	Juan 14	302

DANCER

And then there's the Grotesca--such a dancer	827	Juan 4	671
Ourselves, a singer, dancer, much in fashion	905	Juan 9	540
His steady application as a dancer	924	Juan 11	406

DANCERS

Adieu his Excellency's dancers	163	Malta	14
The dancers and their dresses, too, beside	451	Beppo	692
'And then there are the dancers; there's the Nini	827	Juan 4	665
But speakers, bards, diplomatists, and dancers	993	Juan 16	827

DANCES

And only left us thy d----d debts and dances	274	Waltz	42
At Warsaw's youth, some songs, and dances	408	Mazeppa	173
Discussing all the dances gone and past	451	Beppo	691
Damsels, and dances, revels, ready money	910	Juan 10	167
So brilliant, where the list of routs and dances is	928	Juan 11	627
Reduced to practice, and perform'd like dances	965	Juan 14	632

DANCING

Long streams of light o'er dancing waves expand	22	Harold 2	182
Glass'd with its dancing light the sunny ray	43	Harold 3	874
And the big rain comes dancing to the earth	49	Harold 3	874
What with driving and visiting, dancing and dining	280	Blues 2	8
The glad waves dancing on the yellow beach	362	Corsair 3	447
She, with her paddling oar and dancing prow	422	Island 2	228
With fiddling, feasting, dancing, drinking, masquing	440	Beppo	7
Music, and dancing, fiddling, French and Tuscan	444	Beppo	242
Ladies who have been dancing, or partaking	450	Beppo	651
Whose bloom could after dancing dare the dawn	450	Beppo	664
Upon your dancing crest; the loftiest	715	Werner 5	124
And sparks of flame, like dancing fire-flies, wheel	729	Deformed 1	515
Seeing a troop of his domestics dancing	805	Juan 3	229
Link'd hand in hand, and dancing; each too having	805	Juan 3	236
Hence all this rice, meat, dancing, wine, and fiddling	806	Juan 3	305
Dwarfs, dancing girls, black eunuchs, and a poet	811	Juan 3	618
The dwarfs and dancing girls had all retired	815	Juan 3	898
Dancing all free and happy in the sun	828	Juan 4	719
He flitted to and fro a dancing light	873	Juan 7	367

DANDIES

Blues, dandies, and dowagers, and second-hand scribes	280	Blues 1	158
During the dynasty of Dandies, now	447	Beppo	474
And dandies, all are gone on the wind's wings	927	Juan 11	600
With dandies dined; heard senators declaiming	957	Juan 14	139

DANDIEST

Have sung, or even a Dandy's dandiest chatter	849	Juan 5	1140

DANDOLO

Oh, for one hour of blind old Dandolo	57	Harold 4	107
That a Venetian prince must bear? Old Dandolo	502	Faliero 1	201
Doge Dandolo survived to ninety summers	535	Faliero 4	506

DANDY

Of this poetic dandy	233	Ballad-B	36
How well the imperial dandy prates of peace	304	Age	444
(A broken Dandy lately on my travels	446	Beppo	410
In short, all things which form a Turkish Dandy	840	Juan 5	544
Each out-at-elbow peer, or desperate dandy	933	Juan 12	250
Which makes a dandy while it spoils a man	969	Juan 15	96

DANDY'S

Have sung, or even a Dandy's dandiest chatter	849	Juan 5	1140

DANE

And baffled back the fiery-crested Dane	182	Address-C	4
Besides there were the Spaniard, Dutch, and Dane	292	Vision	473
The Dane; Astolfo there too did resort	467	Morgante	67
From Ermellina, consort of the Dane	468	Morgante	129

DANG

The boors cried 'Dang it! who'd have thought it?'--Sires	959	Juan 14	268

DANGER

(The deed, the danger, and the fame be mine	105	Nisus	32
What censure, what danger, what woe would I brave	129	Becher-A	18
but little is the danger. The sons of Lochlin	130	Calmar	58
feast of shells; ours be the path of danger	130	Calmar	67
If danger demanded, were wholly your own	137	Delawarr	26
Yet since in danger courts abound	138	Clare	79
Prepared the danger to defy	141	Critics	26
She dares the deed and shares the danger	160	Cadiz	38
Are in danger alone	239	Bray	32
Till woo'd by danger, his yet weeping bride	301	Age	220
The last of danger and distress	311	Giaour	71
Had danger woo'd me on to move	320	Giaour	1010
No danger daunts the pair his smile hath blest	333	Abydos 2	450
And turn what some deem danger to delight	338	Corsair 1	18
Conrad beheld the danger, he beheld	350	Corsair 2	241
He, half forgetting danger and defeat	363	Corsair 3	502
For danger levels man and brute	407	Mazeppa	51
Their days of danger, and their nights of pain	418	Island 1	179
Careless of danger, as the onward wind	434	Island 4	283
By danger dignified, yet guiltless; hopes	484	Manfred 2	68
Beyond may breed us double danger. See	516	Faliero 2	554
That are in danger, and that make the danger	532	Faliero 4	275
A danger which would double that you escape	542	Faliero 5	288
And fear her danger; opens a new world	554	Sardan 1	238
To feel a master. What may be the danger	557	Sardan 1	436
Thus much from thee, but some impending danger	560	Sardan 1	665
What danger can they work upon the frontier	569	Sardan 2	474
Your arms! To arms! The king's in danger. Monarch	572	Sardan 3	70
May also be in danger scarce less imminent	592	Sardan 5	328
Into some greater danger than that which	701	Werner 3	421
Around him in his danger on the Oder	703	Werner 3	578
Between young persons without any danger	756	Juan 1	634
And half forgot their danger and despair	767	Juan 1	1356
The greatest danger here was from a shark	787	Juan 2	845
And sold him instantly when out of danger	790	Juan 2	1040
That, without any danger of a riot, he	811	Juan 3	661
In some shape; let none think to fly the danger	825	Juan 4	583
Danger and spoil with ardour much increased	873	Juan 7	390
From ignorance of danger, which indues	882	Juan 8	284
And what a whirlpool full of depth and danger	904	Juan 9	507
Before he can escape from so much danger	927	Juan 11	580
'Tis also subject to the double danger	959	Juan 14	250
In him, because she thought he was in danger	967	Juan 14	727

DANGEROUS

If in the dangerous game they shine to-day	15	Harold 1	734
A mortal sovereign holds her dangerous throne	24	Harold 2	264
Led them o'er rocks and past the dangerous swamp	29	Harold 2	605
Mortals, who sought and found, by dangerous roads	51	Harold 3	979
'Hence let us haste, the dangerous path is pass'd	109	Nisus	281
Remember thou that dangerous hour	174	Remember-B	3
Again she ventured on the dangerous path	358	Corsair 3	205
To pore upon its mysteries. 'Twere dangerous	494	Manfred 3	211
Retire, or 'twill be dangerous--Away	495	Manfred 3	315
He would be dangerous as the whole; it is not	521	Faliero 3	159
Should deem thee dangerous, and keep the house	531	Faliero 4	255
Of the most dangerous orders of mankind	565	Sardan 2	231
And I am hopeless. But 'tis dangerous	657	Heaven	206
His lineage on these wild and dangerous frontiers	686	Werner 2	193
I sought you, father. Is't not dangerous	697	Werner 3	151
Summer's indeed a very dangerous season·	759	Juan 1	810
A feeling dangerous to a prudent spouse	760	Juan 1	888
There is a dangerous silence in that hour	760	Juan 1	905
And purgatives are dangerous to his reign	777	Juan 2	181
Like brutes;'--and thus his dangerous post kept he	778	Juan 2	285
'Tis dangerous to read of loves unlawful	803	Juan 3	96
The dangerous life in which he had grown old	808	Juan 3	427
Turns up more dangerous breakers than the Euxine	832	Juan 5	40
Seduced by youth and dangerous examples	910	Juan 10	178
Intense intentions are a dangerous matter	966	Juan 14	700
To fix the due bounds of this dangerous quality	966	Juan 14	712
That in our youth, as dangerous a passion	968	Juan 14	794
Was dangerous;--I think she is as harmless	980	Juan 15	751

DANGEROUSLY

Oh! too convincing, dangerously dear	355	Corsair 2	543
And felt that you were dangerously insulted	508	Faliero 1	561

DANGERS

Her feeble age from dangers of the main	107	Nisus	180
Of toils rewarded, and of dangers o'er	415	Island 1	20
To tell as true a tale of dangers past	418	Island 2	198
The dangers past that make even man enjoy	423	Island 2	300
The toils and dangers of a life of war	534	Faliero 4	439

DANGER'S

Beheld her smile in Danger's Gorgon face	13	Harold 1	574
In danger's path, though not untaught to feel	126	Recoll	272
Through Danger's most destructive path	158	Florence	30
I have not quail'd to danger's brow	320	Giaour	1027
In danger's hour to guard us both	331	Abydos 2	191
And the brief epitaph in danger's day	338	Corsair 1	39
In danger's face as yours, were you the devil	733	Deformed 1	799

DANGLED

To its own bough, and dangled yet in sight	862	Juan 6	607

DANIEL

And raise this Daniel to the judgment-seat	248	Bards	453
And Daniel tamed the lions in their den	839	Juan 5	477
What Daniel read was short-hand of the Lord's	895	Juan 8	1069
As bold as Daniel in the lion's den	905	Juan 9	548

DANISH

His bell-mouth'd goblet makes me feel quite Danish	950	Juan 13	575

DANK

The amphibious desert of the dank morass	421	Island 2	158
Reeking and dank from out the slime, whose ooze	659	Heaven	306
The stars peep through the vapours dim and dank	878	Juan 7	686

DANTE

Dante, and Petrarch, and, scarce less than they	63	Harold 4	497
Ungrateful Florence! Dante sleeps afar	63	Harold 4	505
And Dante in his comedy has given	467	Morgante	63
Without being much more horrible than Dante	784	Juan 2	664
Dante and Milton, and of both the affection	802	Juan 3	75
Some persons say that Dante meant theology	803	Juan 3	81
Those sufferings Dante saw in hell alone	829	Juan 4	840
A 'wood obscure,' like that where Dante found	861	Juan 6	595

DANTE'S

The wreath which Dante's brow alone had worn before	60	Harold 4	315
And Dante's exile shelter'd by thy gate	303	Age	421
But Dante's Beatrice and Milton's Eve	803	Juan 3	79
I think that Dante's more abstruse ecstatics	803	Juan 3	87
I pass each day where Dante's bones are laid	829	Juan 4	825
I say no more than hath been said in Dante's	867	Juan 7	23
But getting nigh grim Dante's 'obscure wood'	910	Juan 10	211
Dreadful as Dante's rhima, or this stanza	995	Juan 16	972

DANTON

Petion, Clootz, Danton, Marat, La Fayette	747	Juan 1	18

DANUBE

Dark Muchtar his son to the Danube is sped	31	Harold 2	685
But where his rude hut by the Danube lay	76	Harold 4	1264
But as the Danube could not well be waded	868	Juan 7	102

DANUBE'S

There's fearful news from Danube's banks	328	Abydos 1	457
Far from our seats by Danube's tide	332	Abydos 2	295
By Buda's wall and Danube's side	386	Corinth	215
Upon the Danube's left branch and left bank	868	Juan 7	66
Of Danube's bank took formidable charge	868	Juan 7	93
And fourscore cannon on the Danube's border	872	Juan 7	303
And in the Danube's waters shone the same	879	Juan 8	44
The blood may gush out, as the Danube's flow	889	Juan 8	691
Far flash'd her burning towers o'er Danube's stream	894	Juan 8	1011

DAPHNE

Oh, Lady Daphne! let me measure you	830	Juan 4	896

DAPHNE'S

Yield me one leaf of Daphne's deathless plant	14	Harold 1	646

DAPPLE

Would never dapple into day	413	Mazeppa	646

DAPPLED

The dappled foresters--as day awoke	948	Juan 13	446

DAPPLING

The quiet night, now dappling, 'gan to wane	415	Island 1	7
The morn is dappling in the sky. Away then	534	Faliero 4	461

DARDAN

Blood, pulse, and breast confirm the Dardan Shepherd's prize	62	Harold 4	450

DARDAN

His glowing friend address'd the Dardan boy	106	Nisus	38
Save where the Dardan leaders nightly hold	106	Nisus	87
Still dwells the Dardan spirit in the boy	107	Nisus	122
Of Dardan tours let dilettanti tell	256	Bards	1033
Since o'er the Dardan field in arms she ranged	269	Minerva	76
Though on the whole, no doubt, the Dardan boy	964	Juan 14	574

DARDANELLES

Between the winding Dardanelles	326	Abydos 1	244
They heard next day--that in the Dardanelles	828	Juan 4	721

DARDAN'S

Of him who felt the Dardan's arrow	329	Abydos 2	45

DARE

By myriads, when they dare to pave their way	11	Harold 1	454
And in the horrid phalanx dare to move	13	Harold 1	588
Nor raise my voice, nor vainly dare to soar	14	Harold 1	627
But, check'd by every tie, I may not dare	24	Harold 2	268
Nor solely dare encounter hostile rage	31	Harold 2	718
But ere these matchless heights I dare to scan	45	Harold 3	599
Gazing upon the ground, with thoughts which dare not glow	47	Harold 3	715
Where meaner relics must not dare to rot	70	Harold 4	899
Where are the charms and virtues which we dare	73	Harold 4	1094
More than I here shall dare to tell	90	To M.S.G.-A	30
Which to obtain my soul would dare	90	To M.S.G.-A	35
None dare to raise the sterner voice of truth	93	Dorset	30
But who can dare thine ardent gaze	97	To M--	20
Haste, haste, nor dare attempt reply	103	Alva	116
No minstrel dare the theme awake	105	Alva	310
'These deeds, my Nisus, shalt thou dare alone	106	Nisus	39
What can his friend 'gainst thronging numbers dare	110	Nisus	333
Nor dare to call the blush from Beauty's cheek	113	Prologue	6
Simple and young, I dare not feign	132	L'Amitie	88
Who dare not call their words their own	142	Critics	84
Where none but girls and striplings dare admire	142	Soliloquy	13
Who dare not call their very thoughts their own	143	Soliloquy	56
Than dare again the specious Snare	144	Becher-B	47
Let not a Zephyr's pinion dare	150	Song	11
But dare not stand the test of day	153	Friend-A	52
Oh! who in such a night will dare	158	Storm	21
I dare not trust those sounds again	165	Away	4
The plaint she dare not speak before	168	Haunts	8
To soothe the sickly taste it dare not mend	170	Address-A	59
I dare not talk of Love to thee	179	Gold	36
It cannot feel for others' woes, it dare not dream its own	185	Music-B	10
Scarce dare trust a man with thee	187	French-A	20
If to have woo'd thee I could dare	197	Duel	33
And is she dead?--and did they dare	221	Mariamne	9
Nor dare we think on what we are	223	Music-D	12
I dare not venture on another	231	Doctor	40
Nor any dare to take thy name in vain	248	Bards	505
Or (since some men of fashion nobly dare	251	Bards	711
Let them--but hold, my muse, nor dare to teach	254	Bards	907
But if a new design you dare essay	259	Hints	179
And leave to minds which never dare invent	263	Hints	453
Must go to Jackson ere they dare to box	265	Hints	638
"Blest paper credit;" who shall dare to sing	271	Minerva	245
Voluptuous Waltz! and dare I thus blaspheme	277	Waltz	248
Is there one which I dare call my own any more	280	Blues 2	7
I dare say that his wife is still at tea	295	Vision	696
They dare not whisper to the waves	314	Giaour	387
Who dare not quit their craggy screen	316	Giaour	586
She died--I dare not tell thee how	320	Giaour	1056
For worlds I dare not view the dame	322	Giaour	1186
Ere dare to sit before his sire	324	Abydos 1	52
That stifled feeling dare not shed	326	Abydos 1	221
I dare not to my hope deny	328	Abydos 1	393
To mourn--I dare not curse--the day	330	Abydos 2	167
And seems to dare the elements to strife	339	Corsair 1	94
We dare not yet approach--thou know'st his mood	340	Corsair 1	137
And who dare question aught that he decides	340	Corsair 1	172
The only pang my bosom dare not brave	343	Corsair 1	357
And scarce an arm dare rise to guard its head	349	Corsair 2	175
Ah! rather ask what will not Woman dare	353	Corsair 2	407
When soft could feel, and when incensed could dare	358	Corsair 3	199
Before thee tortures, which the soul can dare	359	Corsair 3	232
I rush through peril which she would not dare	360	Corsair 3	299
And know, but dare not own, we gaze in vain	364	Corsair 3	602
Which may not, dare not see, but turns aside	365	Corsair 3	660
Few dare, though now Anselmo sought his tower	365	Corsair 3	679
His spirit seem'd to dare you to forget	371	Lara 1	382
Yes--there be things which we must dream and dare	374	Lara 1	604
A name she dare not breathe by day	397	Parisina	72
When waves no murmur dare to make	409	Mazeppa	222
And who dare answer 'No!' to Mutiny	416	Island 1	82
Against the many oft will dare and do	427	Island 3	54
More brave than firm, and more disposed to dare	428	Island 3	123
And as for Fortune--but I dare not d--n her	447	Beppo	486
Whose bloom could after dancing dare the dawn	450	Beppo	664

DARE

I dare to build the imitative rhyme	455 Dante	Ded	4
And you, ye men! Romans, who dare not die	460 Dante	2	112
Where the birds dare not build, nor insect's wing	485 Manfred	2	158
A thing I dare not think upon--or nothing	487 Manfred	2	291
Yet in this hour I dread the thing I dare	487 Manfred	2	293
To my own desolation. Dost thou dare	489 Manfred	2	412
Is to dare all things for a righteous end	493 Manfred	3	170
We dare not. Then it seems I must be herald	494 Manfred	3	257
That which I dare not name, and yet will do	505 Faliero	1	406
(Which they dare not refuse, at the dread signal	524 Faliero	3	382
Thy prince, of treason?--Who are they that dare	536 Faliero	4	550
You dare to disobey me, then? I serve	536 Faliero	4	560
That thus you dare assume a lawless function	536 Faliero	4	566
But this ye dare not do; for if we die there	538 Faliero	5	45
I do not dare to breathe my own desire	551 Sardan	1	69
Must dare to add my feeble voice to that	560 Sardan	1	640
Thus always, none would ever dare degrade thee	561 Sardan	1	677
Alone you dare not. Alone! foolish slave	564 Sardan	2	162
Who dare to day so!--'Tis impossible	571 Sardan	3	21
In ashes. Darest thou so much? I dare all things	574 Sardan	3	160
All that the dead dare gloomily raise up	579 Sardan	4	36
I will dare all things to bequeath it them	582 Sardan	4	273
Which sparkles at his feet; nor dare he lift	583 Sardan	4	349
Thy face seems ominous. Speak! I dare not. Dare not	590 Sardan	5	184
While millions dare revolt with sword in hand	590 Sardan	5	185
Dare beard me now, and Insolence within	591 Sardan	5	269
That thou shouldst come and dare to ask of me	592 Sardan	5	320
A problem few dare imitate, and none	594 Sardan	5	447
A Greek girl dare not do for love that which	594 Sardan	5	466
True--none dare answer here save on the rack	598 Foscari	1	203
Striven all they dare to weigh me down: be sure	605 Foscari	2	244
I dare them to the proof, the chart of what	607 Foscari	2	371
Else you dare not deal thus by them or me	624 Foscari	5	258
May shame you; but they dare not groan nor curse you	624 Foscari	5	260
Souls who dare use their immortality	629 Cain	1	137
Souls who dare look the Omnipotent tyrant in	629 Cain	1	138
I dare behold? As yet, thou shown nought	638 Cain	2	134
I dare not gaze on further. On, then, with me	638 Cain	2	135
Oh God! I dare not think on't! Cursed be	639 Cain	2	223
I must not, dare not touch what I have made thee	654 Cain	3	534
Can never meet thee more, nor even dare	654 Cain	3	538
Or warring with the spirits who may dare	656 Heaven		84
When God destroys whom you dare not destroy	660 Heaven		381
More to be mortal, than I would to dare	663 Heaven		626
But could I dare to pray in his dread hour	664 Heaven		696
I dare not think thee guilty of dishonour	683 Werner	1	744
Ulric, before you dare despise your father	689 Werner	2	436
I will not brook a human voice--scarce dare	690 Werner	2	460
May be of innocence. 'Sdeath! who dare doubt it	692 Werner	2	572
Dare you insinuate? What? Are you aware	696 Werner	3	62
I dare not use it, show it, scarce look on it	698 Werner	3	180
I'll face it. Who shall dare suspect me? Yet	702 Werner	3	492
But if my son is cold!--Who dare say that	709 Werner	4	325
Like poison in my hands; I dare not use thee	711 Werner	4	439
I dare be sworn that they grow still, nor e'er	713 Werner	5	46
I dare not say so much to him--I fear him	713 Werner	5	49
Once on a time. If you mean me, I dare	715 Werner	5	174
But ere I can proceed--dare you protect me	716 Werner	5	205
Dare you command me? Let the man go on	716 Werner	5	206
The verge--dare you hear further? I must do so	717 Werner	5	283
He, whom you dare not name, nor even I	718 Werner	5	320
Scarce dare to recollect, was not then in	718 Werner	5	321
Dare you await the event of a few minutes?	719 Werner	5	383
For son I dare not call thee--What say'st thou	719 Werner	5	400
He longs to do, but dare not. Is it strange	720 Werner	5	452
(Although you know them not) dare venture all things	720 Werner	5	473
To a demon! Who shall dare say this of Ulric	721 Werner	5	547
Again, and scarce dare think on't. Hideous wretch	723 Deformed	1	48
Their cloven-footed terror. Do you--dare you	723 Deformed	1	101
Though your eyes dare not gaze on it when cloudless	744 Deformed	3	145
That even its grossest flatterers dare not praise	746 Juan	Ded	99
And will not dare to trust itself with truth	755 Juan	1	575
Dare you suspect me, whom the thought would kill	764 Juan	1	1135
How dare you think your lady would go on so	764 Juan	1	1168
And dare not set my seal upon this sheet	771 Juan	1	1570
Ave Maria! may our spirits dare	815 Juan	3	915
'He shall if that he dare.' Here Juan bow'd	875 Juan	7	497
Glory like yours should any dare gainsay	896 Juan	9	7
Who live by lies, yet dare not boldly lie	923 Juan	11	285
I tell the tale as it is told, nor dare	942 Juan	13	97
Perhaps of all most desperate, which will dare	956 Juan	14	35
Few men dare show their thoughts of worst or best	968 Juan	15	21
As if to ask how you can dare to keep	982 Juan	16	143
When any dare a new light to present	997 Juan	17	35

DARED

Sung the loud song, and dared the deed of war	12 Harold	1	561

DARED

For him who dared prefer a mortal bride	24 Harold	2	258
Or Wahab's rebel brood, who dared divest	31 Harold	2	733
Where are its golden roofs? where those who dared to build	71 Harold	4	981
It dared to give your slumbering eyes	89 To Emma		24
Who, for thy sake, the tempest's fury dared	106 Nisus		75
For Pitt, and Pitt alone, has dared to ask	114 Death-A		36
And here one night abroad they dared to roam	124 Recoll		179
Threw down the dagger--dared depart	180 Ode-A		57
He dared depart in utter scorn	180 Ode-A		59
Whom envy dared not hate	182 Ode-A		169
By thy side for years I dared	187 French-A		13
But this I never dared--even yet	197 Duel		34
But once I dared to lift my eyes	205 To--B		1
Mine be the doom which they dared not to meet	219 Saul-A		8
For me, who, thus unask'd, have dared to tell	255 Bards		991
Thus much I've dared; if my incondite lay	256 Bards		1067
Perhaps at some pert speech you've dared to frown	267 Hints		749
She ceased awhile, and thus I dared reply	270 Minerva		123
But they that fear'd him dared not to despise	342 Corsair	1	274
He dared not raise to his that deep-blue eye	345 Corsair	1	468
The white sail set--she dared not look again	345 Corsair	1	502
Forbidden draughts, 'tis said, he dared to quaff	347 Corsair	2	32
One thought alone he could not, dared not meet	352 Corsair	2	374
She saw not, felt not this, nor dared depart	356 Corsair	3	81
In trembling pairs (alone they dared not) crawl	369 Lara	1	259
Who thus for mercy dared to interpose	376 Lara	2	82
But yet he dared not look on her	398 Parisina		189
And hers,--oh, hers!--he dared not throw	398 Parisina		194
As if they dared not look on death	401 Parisina		448
For that dark love she dared to feel	401 Parisina		520
And dared as what was likely to have been	426 Island	3	32
And mortals dared to ponder for themselves	488 Manfred	2	367
To execute the state's decree: I dared	505 Faliero	1	385
To a month's confinement. What! the same who dared	505 Faliero	1	417
Ah! dared I speak my feelings! Give them breath	506 Faliero	1	433
Why Steno dared not: when he scrawl'd his lie	509 Faliero	2	40
And have you dared to peril your friends' lives	518 Faliero	2	665
I had mark'd out some: but I have not dared	520 Faliero	3	127
He dared not--in more honourable days	526 Faliero	3	527
They dared not. They were kept to toil and combat	556 Sardan	1	381
Thou whom he spurn'd so harshly, and now dared	558 Sardan	1	512
Lost!--why, who is the aspiring chief who dared	558 Sardan	1	536
When my eye dared not meet thee. I have watch'd	562 Sardan	2	26
That is not possible: he dared not; no	565 Sardan	2	205
An hour ago, who dared to term me such	567 Sardan	2	370
Questions which mortal never dared to ask me	570 Sardan	2	530
I dared not disobey the Council when	598 Foscari	1	154
Rather than longer worship dared endure	666 Heaven		833
Never a white wing, wetted by the wave, Yet dared to soar	668 Heaven		999
As ardently for glory as you dared	685 Werner	2	161
Than would your adversary, who dared say so	709 Werner	4	327
Heard him! he dared to utter even my name	714 Werner	5	87
They dared not take it in for all the breeze	781 Juan	2	476
Of one who dared to ask if 'he had loved	846 Juan	5	964
This passion might blow o'er, nor dared to balk	866 Juan	6	875
Was made at length with those who dared to climb	888 Juan	8	628

DARES

Mine dares not call thee from thy sacred hill	3 Harold	1	4
Where nothing polish'd dares pollute her path	25 Harold	2	330
But should I fall,--and he who dares advance	106 Nisus		59
My soul nor deigns nor dares complain	151 Farewell-B		13
Dares all things boldly but to lie	153 Friend-A		30
She dares the deed and shares the danger	160 Cadiz		38
Triumphant where it dares defy	191 Prometheus-B		58
Who dares aspire if thou must cease to hope	252 Bards		802
Blest is the man who dares approach the bower	253 Bards		867
And if it dares enough, 'twere hard	320 Giaour		1050
Taught by the thing he dares to spurn	321 Giaour		1168
I know the wretch who dares demand	327 Abydos	1	371
Still Minotti dares dispute	394 Corinth		905
By the first manly hand which dares to snatch it	551 Sardan	1	36
Who dares assail Arbaces? I! Indeed	564 Sardan	2	184
A fable. Who dares say so? I!--'Tis true	605 Foscari	2	227
Who dares accuse my country? Men and angels	611 Foscari	3	240

DAREST

Thou darest them to their worst, exclaiming-- 'Fire	416 Island	1	75
Wretch! darest thou name my son? He died in arms	508 Faliero	1	585
How darest thou name me and not blush? Not blush	552 Sardan	1	88
In ashes. Darest thou so much? I dare all things	574 Sardan	3	160
Darest thou to look on Death? He has not yet	631 Cain	1	247
How darest thou look on that prophetic sky	668 Heaven		1023
Blasphemer! darest thou murmur even now	668 Heaven		1028

DARING

Yet here and there some daring mountain-band	26 Harold	2	421

DARING

With the fierce native daring which instils	39	Harold 3	232
For daring made thy rise as fall: thou seek'st	40	Harold 3	322
Was, Titan-like, on daring doubts to pile	51	Harold 3	982
Yet is the daring wish repress'd	90	To M.S.G.-A	7
Whose daring revels shock the sight	95	Granta	53
Watch every fault that Genius owes	193	Monody	75
Or prune the spirit of each daring phrase	262	Hints	421
Hast thou no weapon for my daring deed	265	Hints	608
And daring deed, and vengeful steel	321	Giaour	1108
Whose deeds are daring as their hearts are true	357	Corsair 3	130
Had Lara's daring boyhood govern'd men	366	Lara 1	20
Despair to daring, and a front to foes	380	Lara 2	365
By ever daring to be first	387	Corinth	327
And Honour's eye on daring deeds	389	Corinth	488
Of that false son and daring lover	400	Parisina	431
More dazzlingly when daring in full dress	425	Island 2	457
Against a daring housebreaker or sprite	443	Beppo	230
The daring charge to raise it shall be given	464	Dante 4	58
But by superior science, penance, daring	496	Manfred 3	375
Sudden and daring, and yet secret; 'twould	511	Faliero 2	141
Oft in concentred spirits not less daring	517	Faliero 2	578
His daring, and perhaps obtain the pardon	560	Sardan 1	619
Of man's adversity all things grow daring	585	Sardan 4	469
Cloven with arm still lustier, breast more daring	597	Foscari 1	105
Of thy fond parents, for their daring, proves	634	Cain 1	425
Cursed he not me before my birth, in daring	639	Cain 2	229
There's something daring in it;--but to steal	692	Werner 2	619
As she doth to the daring, and on whom	717	Werner 5	271
For valour, since deformity is daring	727	Deformed 1	313
This daring soul which could achieve no less	727	Deformed 1	326
'Tis necessary for the further daring	734	Deformed 1	838
Young, beautiful, and daring--who would risk	853	Juan 6	18
But 'Damme''s quite ethereal, though too daring	924	Juan 11	343
The shade of Bounaparte's noble daring	930	Juan 12	39
With those who, Pope says, 'greatly daring dine	947	Juan 13	422
For Gothic daring shown in English money	988	Juan 16	520

DARK

Welcome, welcome, ye dark blue waves	6	Harold 1	194
Or dark Sierras rise in craggy pride	9	Harold 1	364
Ne horrid crags, nor mountains dark and tall	9	Harold 1	367
Dark Guadiana rolls his power along	9	Harold 1	379
Fair Cadiz, rising o'er the dark blue sea	15	Harold 1	712
Hurl the dark bulk along, scarce seen in dashing by	16	Harold 1	791
He that has sail'd upon the dark blue sea	22	Harold 2	145
Dark Sappho, could not verse immortal save	25	Harold 2	347
Dark Suli's rocks, and Pindus' inland peak	25	Harold 2	371
From the dark barriers of that rugged clime	26	Harold 2	406
When all around was desolate and dark	29	Harold 2	597
Their gestures nimble, dark eyes flashing free	30	Harold 2	646
Chimariot, Illyrian, and dark Suliote	30	Harold 2	652
Oh! who is more brave than a dark Suliote	30	Harold 2	653
Dark Muchtar his son to the Danube is sped	31	Harold 2	685
The wandering outlaw of his own dark mind	35	Harold 3	20
Or holding dark communion with the cloud	42	Harold 3	418
Of a dark eye in woman! Far along	49	Harold 3	863
In her dark eye, prophetic of the doom	70	Harold 4	914
Redeemer of dark centuries of shame	72	Harold 4	1020
But weeds of dark luxuriance, tares of haste	73	Harold 4	1074
Those waves, we follow'd on till the dark Euxine roll'd	81	Harold 4	1575
Roll on, thou deep and dark blue Ocean, roll	81	Harold 4	1603
Or, dark in mist, descend the mountain's side	85	Fragment-A	4
One trace of dark deceit it leaves not	98	To Lesbia	20
Despair now inflames the dark tide of his veins	100	L Adieu	27
To hide their orbs in dark restraint	100	Marion	18
Dark was the flow of Oscar's hair	102	Alva	61
His dark eye shone through beams of truth	102	Alva	66
Dark is the robe which wraps his form	103	Alva	185
With him in dark Glentanar's vale	104	Alva	280
Dark Oscar's sable crest is low	105	Alva	291
Dreary and dark appears the sylvan scene	109	Nisus	314
Wake the dark echoes of the trembling ground	109	Nisus	326
He pray'd in vain; the dark assassin's sword	110	Nisus	375
I sigh for the valley of dark Loch na Garr	117	Lachin	8
Disclosed by the natives of dark Loch na Garr	117	Lachin	16
They dwell in the tempests of dark Loch na Garr	117	Lachin	24
Your deeds on the echoes of dark Loch na Garr	118	Lachin	32
The steep frowning glories of dark Loch na Garr	118	Lachin	40
But not from thee, dark pile! departs the chief	119	Newstead-A	17
Loathing the offering of so dark a death	121	Newstead-A	108
Thus, while the future dark and cheerless gleams	122	Recoll	21
From dark oblivion meant to guard	128	Answer-B	38
of the dark brow." Why should tears dim	130	Calmar	80
stranger, they mingle with the dark hair of	131	Calmar	160
friend. Raise the song when I am dark	131	Calmar	182
Whose dark ghost gleams on the red streams	131	Calmar	190
Thou seest my soul is dark within	132	Prayer	6
Or bounding o'er the dark blue wave	135	I Would	4
When I roved a young Highlander o'er the dark heath	135	Highlander	1
When I see some dark hill point its crest to the sky	136	Highlander	33

DARK

Life's evening dream is dark and dull	137	Clare	17
Age, dark unlovely Age, appears at length	139	Ossian-A	30
Dark is the night, but darker is my Soul	140	Ossian-A	46
For Age is dark, unlovely, as the light	140	Ossian-B	37
Aye, ye have Souls, and dark ones too	143	To--A	10
All, all is dark and cheerless now	146	Adieu	71
With tears the dark sepulchral deep	146	Adieu	99
My soul is dark within	146	Adieu	112
No; for myself, so dark my fate	153	Friend-A	45
I have bask'd in the beam of a dark rolling eye	155	Goblet	6
My own dark thoughts I cannot shun	156	Lady-F	29
Look o'er the dark blue sea	159	Storm	56
If, in the month of dark December	160	Swimming	1
Through dark and dread Eternity	168	Dead	69
For then, however drear and dark	172	Time-B	25
For, through thy long dark lashes low depending	175	Sonnet-B	9
All quell'd--Dark Spirit! what must be	180	Ode-A	35
In that dark Hour a long loud gather'd cry	184	Julian	5
In the dark union of insensate dust	192	Fragment-C	22
'Tis midnight--but it is not dark	196	Venice-A	1
Are not thy waters sweeping, dark, and strong	198	Po	10
When all around grew drear and dark	209	Augusta-A	1
And all that's best of dark and bright	216	She Walks	3
My soul is dark--Oh! quickly string	218	Soul-B	1
And this dark heart is vainly craving	221	Marianne	14
Dark roll'd the sympathetic waves of Forth	248	Bards	470
Why should we call them from their dark abode	251	Bards	709
Oh! dark asylum of a Vandal race	255	Bards	981
And dark the mountain's once delightful dyes	268	Minerva	26
The groves of olive scatter'd dark and wide	269	Minerva	41
'My slippery steps are safest in the dark	275	Waltz	120
And I'll take a turn with you there till 'tis dark	283	Blues 2	151
While the dark shades of forty ages stood	300	Age	145
Church, state, and faction wrestle in the dark	307	Age	646
The first dark day of nothingness	311	Giaour	70
Far, dark, along the blue sea glancing	312	Giaour	168
Rung his dark courser's hoofs of fear	312	Giaour	207
Dark tree, still sad when others' grief is fled	313	Giaour	286
The channell'd waters dark and deep	314	Giaour	369
So do the dark in soul expire	314	Giaour	433
Her eye's dark charm 'twere vain to tell	315	Giaour	473
As large, as languishingly dark	315	Giaour	476
As dark as his that bled below	317	Giaour	674
And the dark Heaven of Houris' eyes	317	Giaour	741
It breathes the same dark spirit now	318	Giaour	796
For some dark deed he will not name	318	Giaour	801
Dark and unearthly is the scowl	318	Giaour	832
His hood fly back, his dark hair fall	319	Giaour	894
Dark as to thee my deeds may seem	320	Giaour	999
To-morrow's night shall be more dark	322	Giaour	1278
Thus held his thoughts their dark career	325	Abydos 1	112
His eye look'd o'er the dark blue water	326	Abydos 1	242
That shine beneath, while dark above	336	Abydos 2	665
'O'er the glad waters of the dark blue sea	338	Corsair 1	1
Blow fair, thou breeze!--she anchors ere the dark	339	Corsair 1	88
Though his dark eyebrow shades a glance of fire	341	Corsair 1	196
Through those long, dark, and glistening lashes dew'd	345	Corsair 1	497
But waves are somewhat treacherous in the dark	347	Corsair 2	38
Lie dark and jarring with perturbed force	352	Corsair 2	330
That form, with eye so dark and cheek so fair	353	Corsair 2	402
And dark the mountain's once delightful dyes	355	Corsair 3	26
The groves of olive, scatter'd dark and wide	356	Corsair 3	41
Her own dark soul these words at once subdued	357	Corsair 3	112
While an anxious glance her large dark eye	357	Corsair 3	137
On him she cast her dark and hurried eye	359	Corsair 3	278
'Twas dark and winding, and he knew not where	361	Corsair 3	392
She stopp'd--threw back her dark far-floating hair	361	Corsair 3	410
But speechless all, deep, dark, and unexprest	362	Corsair 3	478
Amid so many, hers alone is dark	364	Corsair 3	570
The long dark lashes fringed her lids of snow	364	Corsair 3	609
Though dark the shade, it shelter'd, saved till now	365	Corsair 3	671
O'er the dark gallery, where his fathers frown'd	368	Lara 1	137
As evening saddens o'er the dark grey walls	370	Lara 1	266
A thing of dark imaginings, that shaped	370	Lara 1	317
Prying and dark, a stranger's by his mien	371	Lara 1	407
That when his long dark shadow through the porch	374	Lara 1	618
And sadly smiles his thanks to that dark page	381	Lara 2	427
So unrepentant, dark, and passionless	381	Lara 2	463
Unnamed accusers in the dark	385	Corinth	132
Dark will thy doom be, darker still	391	Corinth	649
But War had enter'd their dark caves	395	Corinth	977
So softly dark and darkly pure	396	Parisina	12
From the long dark fringe of that fair lid	400	Parisina	338
Dark the crime and just the law	400	Parisina	428
For that dark love she dared to feel	401	Parisina	520
The dark vault lies wherein we lay	403	Chillon	116
Until a day more dark and drear	407	Mazeppa	9
The heavy hour was chill and dark	407	Mazeppa	36
Dark as above us is the sky	409	Mazeppa	211

DARK

Large, dark, and swimming in the stream	409	Mazeppa		214
(May ours this dark night watch as well	409	Mazeppa		263
For all behind was dark and drear	412	Mazeppa		595
Yet still a dark and hideous close	414	Mazeppa		733
As ever the dark annals of the deep	418	Island	1	199
Wrapp'd his wean'd bosom in its dark delight	423	Island	2	307
A dark speck dotted ocean: on it flew	428	Island	3	167
With dark but brilliant skin, and dewy eye	429	Island	3	185
Dark as a sullen cloud before the sun	433	Island	4	280
Encompass'd with its dark and rolling shroud	438	Tasso		115
Heaving in dark and sullen undulation	459	Dante	2	38
Beholding with the dark eye of a seer	465	Dante	4	149
That with the dwellers of the dark abodes	491	Manfred	3	36
Waved dark in the blue midnight, and the stars	495	Manfred	3	273
To what? to hold a council in the dark	508	Faliero	1	610
Elapse, and others share as dark a doom	517	Faliero	2	611
In dark suspicious conflict with the Doge	525	Faliero	3	499
Glorious to save than slay, and slay i' the dark too	532	Faliero	4	283
I would not smite i' the dark, but rather see	535	Faliero	4	489
Peril to thee--Ay, from dark plots and snares	558	Sardan	1	517
And waking in the dark.--Go to--go to	567	Sardan	2	351
Was ranged on my left hand a haughty, dark	579	Sardan	4	84
But it grows dark and dark--the stars are gone	638	Cain	2	176
All here seems dark and dreadful. But distinct	639	Cain	2	190
Lashes, dark as the cypress which waves o'er them	646	Cain	3	28
I'm dark; I've blown my fingers--number'd o'er	701	Werner	3	400
Of dark fatality, like clouds, are gathering	702	Werner	3	488
But dark deeds (ay, the darkest, if all Rumour	709	Werner	4	337
He hath ta'en a jump i' the dark. But you consent	710	Werner	4	391
Died, I scarce know--but--he was stabb'd i' the dark	712	Werner	4	508
Especially in these dark troublous times	713	Werner	5	55
Weary with watching in the dark, and dubious	718	Werner	5	307
I turn'd, and fled--i' the dark: chance rather than	718	Werner	5	351
'Tis the morn, but dim and dark	735	Deformed	2	1
Was large and dark, suppressing half its fire	754	Juan	1	474
She lay, her dark eyes flashing through their tears	766	Juan	1	1258
But why?--we leave the reader in the dark	775	Juan	2	60
The scattering clouds, shone, spanning the dark sea	785	Juan	2	722
With the quick wave, and gain, ere it was dark	787	Juan	2	843
And saw each other's dark eyes darting light	797	Juan	2	1478
Her eyelashes, though dark as night, were tinged	810	Juan	3	593
Joy sparkling in their dark eyes like a gem	818	Juan	4	102
Oh! Powers of Heaven! what dark eye meets she there	821	Juan	4	279
In the large dark eye's mutual-darted flame	822	Juan	4	348
But her large dark eye show'd deep Passion's force	823	Juan	4	447
With resolution in his dark grey eye	832	Juan	5	79
Good teeth, with curling rather dark brown hair	832	Juan	5	83
He paused, and his dark eye grew full of gloom	833	Juan	5	139
That she was fair, or dark, or short, or tall	859	Juan	6	431
And raven ringlets gather'd in dark crowd	860	Juan	6	522
The black bough) tear-drops through her eyes' dark fringes	860	Juan	6	536
The night was dark, and the thick mist allow'd	878	Juan	8	41
In the chill dark, when courage does not glow	880	Juan	8	163
Some odd mistakes, too, happen'd in the dark	894	Juan	8	1033
Retains the sable stains of the dark creeper	909	Juan	10	117
He hath no morn nor night, but all is dark	939	Juan	12	567
Aurora Raby with her large dark eyes	984	Juan	16	247

DARK-BLUE

Receding slowly through the dark-blue deep	94	Dorset		89
Divided by the dark-blue main	158	Florence		10
I by thy source, she by the dark-blue deep	198	Po		36

DARKEN

Darken above our bones, yet fondly deem'd	80	Harold	4	1527
Of Incas darken to a dubious cloud	302	Age		317
To darken o'er the fair domain	310	Giaour		61
Just as the day began to wane and darken	917	Juan	10	635

DARKEN'D

And, scathed by fire, the greensward's darken'd vest	12	Harold	1	516
Save darken'd Jura, whose capt heights appear	48	Harold	3	809
But who is he, whose darken'd brow	103	Alva		181
While clouds the darken'd noon deform	133	E. N. Long		6
Whose gloom may suit a darken'd mind	135	I Would		52
When Earth is darken'd with tempestuous skies	139	Ossian-A		17
While their long lashes' darken'd gloss	152	Remind		22
Of breathless being?--darken'd and intense	192	Fragment-C		30
Was darken'd with her shadow, and she saw	214	Dream		93
But leaves its darken'd dust behind	220	Clay		4
Like coral reddening through the darken'd wave	420	Island	2	139
These darken'd clouds are not the only skies	669	Heaven		1087
Her serious sayings darken'd to sublimity	748	Juan	1	92
That flash'd and after darken'd in the shade	982	Juan	16	120

DARKENED

should thy yellow locks be darkened in the	130	Calmar		71

DARKENING

Distinct, though darkening with her waning phase	22	Harold	2	196
And in the door-way, darkening darkness, stood	996	Juan	16	983

DARKENS

His portrait darkens in its fading frame	366	Lara	1	34
Blood darkens earth and heaven! what thou now art	654	Cain	3	530

DARKER

Dark is the night, but darker is my Soul	140	Ossian-A		46
The Rest had eyes of darker Hue	144	Becher-B		27
And darker fate hast found	180	Ode-A		52
Or darker greenness of the scorpion's scale	209	Sketch		68
The darker secret of my own	330	Abydos	2	160
The sun hath sunk, and, darker than the night	356	Corsair	3	66
His brow fell darker, and his words more few	367	Lara	1	94
And dye conjecture with a darker hue	377	Lara	2	126
Dark will thy doom be, darker still	391	Corinth		649
And darker, and more thoughtful, who smiles not	730	Deformed	1	529

DARKEST

In darkest glances seems to roll	160	Cadiz		11
Wrapt in the darkest sable vest	329	Abydos	2	87
How dear the dream in darkest hours of ill	333	Abydos	2	420
But dark deeds (ay, the darkest, if all Rumour	709	Werner	4	337

DARK-EYED

Lands of the dark-eyed Maid and dusky Moor	22	Harold	2	192
May match the dark-eyed Girl of Cadiz	160	Cadiz		56
And when that dark-eyed lady, young Gulnare	351	Corsair	2	259
And now he turn'd him to that dark-eyed slave	363	Corsair	3	531
With an Italian exile's dark-eyed daughter	684	Werner	2	96
Our dark-eyed pages--what may be their names	729	Deformed	1	519

DARK-GLANCING

With Spain's dark-glancing daughters--deign to know	13	Harold	1	609

DARK-GREEN

His arms were folded on his dark-green vest	347	Corsair	2	53
O'ertopp'd with cypresses, dark-green and tall	836	Juan	5	320

DARK-HAIRED

--to dark-haired Orla, destroyer of heroes	129	Calmar		24
dark-haired Orla, 'and mine alone. What is	130	Calmar		56
'Fly! Calmar, fly!' said dark-haired Orla	130	Calmar		128

DARK-HEAVING

Dark-heaving;--boundless, endless, and sublime	82	Harold	4	1643

DARKLE

And her proud brow's blue veins to swell and darkle	864	Juan	6	808

DARKLED

And grimly darkled o'er the faces pale	780	Juan	2	390

DARKLING

No threat'ning tyrant's darkling brow	88	Horace		3
While day and night roll darkling by	172	Romaic-B		4
Dim in the cloud, or darkling in the storm	182	Address-C		26
Did wander darkling in the eternal space	189	Darkness		3
In silence, darkling, each appear'd to wait	356	Corsair	3	89
And in the depth of forests darkling	407	Mazeppa		27
Now darkling in their close toward the deep vale	516	Faliero	2	502
Walk darkling to their doom; which, though so nigh	662	Heaven		545

DARKLY

Too long and darkly, till my brain became	36	Harold	3	56
Striking the electric chain wherewith we are darkly bound	58	Harold	4	207
Loud shrieks a darkly gleaming form	104	Alva		250
So darkly of departed years	220	Clay		14
More darkly sin, by satire kept in awe	242	Bards		35
Till, darkly shaded from the land and deep	268	Minerva		17
Deep in whose darkly boding ear	321	Giaour		1077
Rolls darkly heaving to the main	329	Abydos	2	21
And where his frown of hatred darkly fell	341	Corsair	1	225
He deeply, darkly felt; but evil pride	351	Corsair	2	298
Till, darkly shaded from the land and deep	355	Corsair	3	17
Light was his form, and darkly delicate	373	Lara	1	528
Floating darkly downward there	390	Corinth		557
Darkly, sternly, and all alone	394	Corinth		947
So softly dark and darkly pure	396	Parisina		12
The woods droop'd darkly, as inclined to rest	424	Island	2	412
I've heard thee darkly speak of an event	494	Manfred	3	233
Of darkly brooding thoughts. My fancy is	504	Faliero	1	312
Oh! 'darkly, deeply, beautifully blue	830	Juan	4	873

DARKNESS

Have pass'd to darkness with the vanish'd age	17	Harold	1	805

DARKNESS

To those that walk in darkness: on the sea	46	Harold	3	667
Who in oppression's darkness caved had dwelt	48	Harold	3	785
And storm, and darkness, ye are wondrous strong	49	Harold	3	861
And loved to dwell in darkness and dismay	60	Harold	4	302
Mantles the earth with darkness, until right	69	Harold	4	834
And bred in darkness, lest the truth should shine	74	Harold	4	1141
To hover on the verge of darkness;--rays	79	Harold	4	1484
Through storm and darkness yawns the rending ground	80	Harold	4	1499
Since darkness o'ershadows the prospect before me	97	Harrow-A		31
Night rose in clouds. Darkness veils the	130	Calmar		35
In darkness and in dread	159	Storm		50
In darkness my children take most delight	176	Devil's Dr		9
The glossy darkness of that clustering hair	183	Address-D		37
In his native darkness share	187	French-A		28
And darkness must again prevail	189	On Star		32
And the clouds perish'd; Darkness had no need	190	Darkness		81
Of light and darkness forms an arch sublime	192	Monody		8
Hath pass'd from day to darkness--to whose hour	192	Monody		24
And dash'd the darkness all away	209	Augusta-A		20
That show'st the darkness thou canst not dispel	220	Sleepless		3
Of northern wolves, that still in darkness prowl	247	Bards		429
Or Marmion's acts of darkness, fitter food	254	Bards		939
Not smoke from brightness, but from darkness--light	259	Hints		210
Yet still between his Darkness and his Brightness	289	Vision		279
While kings, in dusty darkness hid	311	Giaour		128
Darkness above, despair beneath	314	Giaour		437
With thoughts that long in darkness dwelt	327	Abydos	1	330
That dreads the darkness and yet loathes the light	336	Abydos	2	648
Which not the darkness of despair can damp	343	Corsair	1	353
I come through darkness--and I scarce know why	353	Corsair	2	439
Came storm and darkness in their mingling might	359	Corsair	3	249
But for that deed of darkness what wert thou	362	Corsair	3	470
There is no darkness like the cloud of mind	365	Corsair	3	658
In darkness, yet so well the path was worn	376	Lara	1	102
Whose darkness none beside should penetrate	381	Lara	2	453
And then eternal darkness sunk	394	Corinth		881
In darkness found a dwelling-place	402	Chillon		16
And then of darkness too	405	Chillon		234
The darkness of my dim abode	406	Chillon		360
Dividing darkness from the dawning main	415	Island	1	8
Through the approaching darkness of the wood	425	Island	2	460
For all was darkness for a space, till day	431	Island	3	131
Were there, all scoop'd by Darkness from her cave	432	Island	4	154
'Let there be darkness!' and thou grow'st a tomb	459	Dante	2	45
Of darkness, making his bright realm appear	472	Morgante		430
Whom I have sought in darkness and in light	479	Manfred	1	30
The future, till the past be gulf'd in darkness	481	Manfred	1	267
My teeth in darkness till returning morn	486	Manfred	2	226
It is an awful chaos--light and darkness	493	Manfred	3	164
Of darkness: use them for your further rest	581	Sardan	4	187
To darkness more than light, by lending to	609	Foscari	3	54
Familiarity with what was darkness	609	Foscari	3	61
Who out of darkness on the deep didst make	627	Cain	1	2
Must one day see perforce. Behold! 'Tis darkness	639	Cain	2	196
Vacant in heaven to dwell in darkness here	660	Heaven		416
How should I make my way in darkness through	696	Werner	3	93
Measure in darkness distance); but it blinks	701	Werner	3	407
Comrades, help, ho! All's darkness	739	Deformed	2	302
The darkness of her Oriental eye	754	Juan	1	441
Even by its darkness; as the blackest sky	756	Juan	1	578
And darkness and destruction as on high	801	Juan	2	1708
In darkness--I can only hope they did	895	Juan	8	1056
There Rembrandt made his darkness equal light	950	Juan	13	570
The starry darkness round her like a girdle	995	Juan	16	951
And in the door-way, darkening darkness, stood	996	Juan	16	983

DARKNESS'.

Dim o'er the bird of darkness' native site	71	Harold	4	950

DARK'NING

Ah! why do dark'ning shades conceal	135	I Would		19

DARK-RED

'Tis rent in twain--one dark-red stain	335	Abydos	2	596

DARKSOME

Nearer. Here is a darksome angle--so	701	Werner	3	419

DARK-WAVING

That thy dark-waving branches would flourish around	149	Newstead-B		3

DARLING

A ball-room bard, a foolscap, hot-press darling	830	Juan	4	866
When they built up unto his darling trees	886	Juan	8	506

DARNLEY

Than Darnley, Ivan, or Kehama	231	Doctor		36

DAR'ST

But there be deeds thou dar'st not do	325	Abydos	1	121
'Gainst which thou wilt not strive, and dar'st not murmur	549	Faliero	5	790
What thou dar'st not deny,--the history	636	Cain	2	24
Show me. Dar'st thou behold? How know I what	638	Cain	2	133

DART

His arms a dart, he fights aloof, nor more	16	Harold	1	744
Dart follows dart; lance, lance; loud bellowings speak his woes	16	Harold	1	764
Again he comes; nor dart nor lance avail	16	Harold	1	765
Scorch'd by the Roman Jove's ethereal dart	68	Harold	4	790
Expel the venom and not blunt the dart	73	Harold	4	1069
The glory which at once upon thee did not dart	78	Harold	4	1413
(Ah! little did I think the dart	89	Anacreon-B		29
Exulting demons wing'd his dart	105	Alva		286
The dart has drunk his vital tide	105	Alva		292
Speed, speed my dart to pierce yon vaunting crowd	110	Nisus		347
Thus having said, the hissing dart he flung	110	Nisus		349
And dart destruction in sulphureous showers	120	Newstead-A		60
Time steals along, and Death uprears his dart	121	Newstead-A		134
Pointless must fall the Spectre's dart	146	Adieu		83
Prepared a light and pangless dart	165	Thyrza		14
View'd his own feather on the fatal dart	253	Bards		843
And rushing from my couch, I dart	323	Giaour		1285
And hurl the dart, and curb the steed	324	Abydos	1	86
They clear the breakers, dart along the bay	429	Island	3	226
Till struck,--forth flies the all-ethereal dart	438	Tasso		116
All-glorious burst from ocean? why not dart	562	Sardan	2	20
On his soul, like a ceaseless sunrise, dart	893	Juan	8	918
Unwithering myrtle round the unblunted dart	995	Juan	16	918

DARTED

(See also MUTUAL-DARTED)				
That darted from beneath the lid	315	Giaour		478
As I was darted from my foes	410	Mazeppa		380
The proa darted like a shooting star	430	Island	4	42
A thousand proas darted o'er the bay	435	Island	4	405

DARTER

The finny darter with the glittering scales	65	Harold	4	600

DARTING

(See also JAVELIN-DARTING)				
'Twas, as if darting from her heavenly throne	32	Harold	2	762
Darting on the opportunity	197	Rogers		49
The boats are darting o'er the curly bay	364	Corsair	3	559
Pervading, and far darting as your own	480	Manfred	1	156
And saw each other's dark eyes darting light	797	Juan	2	1478

DARTS

Mid wounds, and clinging darts, and lances brast	16	Harold	1	776
And darts into her desperate brain	314	Giaour		432
That darts in seeming playfulness around	367	Lara	1	75
Darts for a victim over all the sky	423	Island	2	311
'That Passamont has in his hand three darts	469	Morgante		225
And darts in one quick glance a long reply	794	Juan	2	1294
Upon their prey, as darts an angry asp	822	Juan	4	382

DART'S

Could sighs avert his dart's relentless force	85	Epitaph		6

DARWIN'S

But not in flimsy Darwin's pompous chime	254	Bards		893

DASH

But dash the tear-drop from thine eye	5	Harold	1	138
I'd dash to earth the sweetest bowl	168	Haunts		23
That thou shouldst from Thee dash the Draught of Life	185	Julian		44
Go! dash the roses from thy brow	185	Belshaz-A		9
Dash o'er the old Spaniard's cradle, and would fain	302	Age		284
Dash o'er her deathlike cheek the ocean dew	357	Corsair	3	117
He did not dash himself thereby, nor tear	382	Lara	2	508
But dash that turban to earth, and sign	390	Corinth		577
From the cliffs invading dash	392	Corinth		740
Away!--away!--and on we dash	410	Mazeppa		373
They bade me to destruction dash	411	Mazeppa		409
When all the waves that dash o'er thee	412	Mazeppa		554
Methought the dash of waves was nigh	412	Mazeppa		579
Damming the rivers with a sudden dash	483	Manfred	1	357
Thrill like his lyre-strings at the sight;--the dash	529	Faliero	4	96
Till the sea dash me back on my own shore	617	Foscari	4	131
Save the wild wind and the remorseless dash	780	Juan	2	420
Again to be o'ercome, again to dash on	798	Juan	2	1526
Dash down yon cup of Samian wine	813	Juan	3	784
Dash into poetry, which is but passion	830	Juan	4	847
Yet men resolved to dash through thick and thin	874	Juan	7	428
Than Buonaparte's cancer: could I dash on	898	Juan	9	110
Entreating you to pause before you dash on	935	Juan	12	358

DASH

There was the Duke of Dash, who was a--duke	951 Juan	13	673

DASH'D

Here Folly dash'd to earth the victor's plume	8 Harold	1	301
He said, and dash'd the cup to earth	104 Alva		248
In him there still is Life, the Wave that dash'd	184 Julian		13
And dash'd the darkness all away	209 Augusta-A		20
Steps stamp'd; and dash'd into the sand	335 Abydos	2	589
Dash'd his high cap, and tore his robe away	349 Corsair	2	146
That dash'd her garments oft, and warn'd away	356 Corsair	3	80
Heaved up the bank, and dash'd it from the shore	383 Lara	2	567
The sharp shot dash'd Alp to the ground	394 Corinth		875
Dash'd downward in the thundering foam below	429 Island	3	176
Dash'd on the shingles like the limpet shell	434 Island	4	314
Down the tube dash'd it, levell'd, fired, and smiled	434 Island	4	335
My scars are callous, or I should have dash'd	439 Tasso		209
But, like an ebbing wave, it dash'd me back	487 Manfred	2	237
I would have dash'd amongst them, asking few	504 Faliero	1	306
I snatch'd him in his sleep, and dash'd him 'gainst	648 Cain	3	125
Subsides soon after he again hath dash'd	657 Heaven		157
Lay dying, and the stranger dash'd aside	701 Werner	3	382
Upon destruction, shall my head be dash'd	740 Deformed	2	346
Though the two sharks still follow'd them, and dash'd	787 Juan	2	807
And the hard wave o'erwhelm'd him as 'twas dash'd	787 Juan	2	852
Dash'd on like a spurr'd blood-horse in a race	885 Juan	8	432
High dash'd the spray, the bows dipp'd in the sea	915 Juan	10	508
Its outlet dash'd into a deep cascade	948 Juan	13	457
The river from the lake, all bluely dash'd	966 Juan	14	694

DASHES

The Ocean's tempest dashes	201 Ode-C		32
Thine own 'broad Hellespont' still dashes	329 Abydos	2	36
And dashes on the pointed rock	397 Parisina		96
And dashes off the ascending waves	412 Mazeppa		591
Round which yellow Tiber dashes	735 Deformed	2	10
And the sea dashes round the promontory	763 Juan	1	1070

DASHEST

And dashest him again to earth:--there let him lay	82 Harold	4	1620

DASHING

(See also FAR-DASHING)

And Tagus dashing onward to the deep	6 Harold	1	203
Hurl the dark bulk along, scarce seen in dashing by	16 Harold	1	791
So gaily curl the waves before each dashing prow	22 Harold	2	153
When his Delhis come dashing in blood o'er the banks	31 Harold	3	687
Dashing or winding as its torrent strays	76 Harold	4	1273
Little didst thou deem, when dashing	187 Ode-B		44
Produced a play too dashing for a dunce	264 Hints		566
Athos and Ida, with a dashing sea	298 Age		15
For the gay thousands of his dashing ranks	300 Age		192
Since, dashing by the lonely shore	318 Giaour		790
His back was to the dashing spray	335 Abydos	2	569
The shout, the signal, and the dashing oar	345 Corsair	1	524
And now its dashing echo on his ear	359 Corsair	3	256
And blood is mingled with the dashing stream	380 Lara	2	366
Their sport, the dashing breakers and the chase	416 Island	1	47
Which her bold bow flings off with dashing ease	418 Island	1	228
To rust beneath the dew and dashing spray	434 Island	4	350
Is with the dashing of the spring-tide foam	453 Venice-B		10
Dashing against the outward Lido's bulwark	528 Faliero	4	15
And, standing upon deck, the dashing spray	775 Juan	2	85
Not very dashing, but extremely winning	858 Juan	6	410
Others, in that off-hand and dashing style	939 Juan	12	602
A dashing demoiselle of good estate	973 Juan	15	330
The dashing and proud air of Adeline	975 Juan	15	441

DASTARD

Shall dastard tongues essay to blast the name	114 Death-A		9

DASTARDLY

That flight was base and dastardly, and no man	756 Juan	1	611

DATE

A peasant's plaint prolongs his dubious date	10 Harold	1	399
Than mightier heroes of a longer date	42 Harold	3	428
Is a brief feeling of a trivial date	211 Augusta-C		59
And works and words but dwindle to a date	258 Hints		92
Search Doctors' Commons six months from my date	276 Waltz		207
Their date of war, and their 'champ clos' the spheres	289 Vision		256
To date the birth and death of all it hid	299 Age		104
Oh, who its dreary length shall date	313 Giaour		270
If greeted once; however brief the date	371 Lara	1	374
And demagogues yield to them but in date	465 Dante	4	120
Afresh, for they were waxing out of date	488 Manfred	2	366
Which date the flight of time, but make no annals	582 Sardan	4	295

DATE

Might date for years, did Anguish make the dial	709 Werner	4	314
In health and purse, begin your day to date	792 Juan	2	1118
As if their last day of a happy date	819 Juan	4	171
As well as the sublime discovery's date	830 Juan	4	892
I rather think the moon should date the dears	908 Juan	10	80
At a long date--till they can get a fresh one	946 Juan	13	358
Column; date, 'Falmouth. There has lately been here	948 Juan	13	429
That poets were so from their earliest date	950 Juan	13	589

DATE-BREAD

And fruits, and date-bread loaves closed the repast	809 Juan	3	498

DATED

My life is not dated by years	205 Blessington		13
And prophecy--except it should be dated	923 Juan	11	295

DATELESS

Egypt! from whose all dateless tombs arose	300 Age		141

DATES

Where Freedom dates her birth with that of Time	302 Age		315
As childhood dates within our colder clime	420 Island	2	125
The dates of their despair, the brief words of	608 Foscari	3	18
If dungeon dates say true. And what of him	609 Foscari	3	70
Hundreds of doges, and their deeds and dates	610 Foscari	3	121
I like to be particular in dates	759 Juan	1	818
In female dates, strikes Time all of a heap	962 Juan	14	416

DATING

(Long ere I dreamt of dating from the Brenta	772 Juan	1	1693

DAUB

But daub a shipwreck like an alehouse sign	257 Hints		32

DAUBER

Europe's worst dauber, and poor Britain's best	270 Minerva		176

DAUGHTER

Ada, sole daughter of my house and heart	35 Harold	3	2
Julia, the daughter, the devoted, gave	45 Harold	3	627
My daughter! with thy name this song begun	53 Harold	3	1067
My daughter! with thy name thus much shall end	53 Harold	3	1068
Night's daughter, Ignorance, hath wrapt and wrap	67 Harold	4	722
What daughter of her beauties was the heir	70 Harold	4	896
The fair-hair'd Daughter of the Isles is laid	80 Harold	4	1524
Glenalvon's blue-eyed daughter came	102 Alva		80
Weep, daughter of a royal line	168 Weeping		1
I to the marble, where my daughter lies	196 Vittorelli		12
Ere the daughter of Brunswick is cold in her grave	201 Avatar		1
Devotion and her daughter Love	217 The Harp		17
Demand that thy daughter expire	218 Jephtha		2
'Daughter of Jove! in Britain's injured name	270 Minerva		125
First duly done by daughter or by spouse	276 Waltz		185
Nothing more than the heart of her daughter and hand	278 Blues	1	84
The imperial daughter, the imperial bride	308 Age		727
A daughter? What did France's widow there	308 Age		736
So moved on earth Circassia's daughter	315 Giaour		505
There from thy daughter, sister, wife	317 Giaour		759
Hence, lead my daughter from her tower	324 Abydos	1	40
But, Haroun!--to my daughter speed	324 Abydos	1	101
Was she, the daughter of that rude old Chief	325 Abydos	1	168
He thought but of old Giaffir's daughter	326 Abydos	1	252
The lonely hope of Sestos' daughter	329 Abydos	2	5
With him his gentle daughter came	386 Corinth		224
Such was this daughter of the southern seas	421 Island	2	141
She was a warrior's daughter, and could bear	429 Island	3	193
The happiest daughter of the loving isles	432 Island	4	188
He shelter'd there a daughter of the clime	432 Island	4	200
And still more helpless nor less holy daughter	459 Dante	2	81
And thou, oh Virgin! daughter, mother, bride	466 Morgante		9
Daughter of Air! I tell thee, since that hour	486 Manfred	2	221
Deep Vengeance is the daughter of deep Silence	502 Faliero	1	169
Might now pretend to Loredano's daughter	510 Faliero	2	122
And then the daughter of my earliest friend	513 Faliero	2	330
His worthy daughter, free to choose again	513 Faliero	2	331
Ne'er weigh'd in mind with Loredano's daughter	544 Faliero	5	411
Your husband? And your son. Proceed, my daughter	602 Foscari	2	50
That is not a Venetian thought, my daughter	605 Foscari	2	276
To use for the decrees of--Daughter, know you	606 Foscari	2	287
Daughter, it is superfluous; I have long	613 Foscari	3	352
Thus leave me. Daughter! Hold thy peace, old man	618 Foscari	4	195
I am no daughter now--thou hast no son	618 Foscari	4	196
My daughter! Get thee ready; we must mourn	624 Foscari	5	209
Must not my daughter love her brother Enoch	633 Cain	1	363
That he will single forth some other daughter	655 Heaven		29
Still loves this daughter of a fated race	658 Heaven		253
Had left a daughter, whose pure pious race	664 Heaven		670

DAUGHTER
The foreign daughter of a wandering exile   673 Werner   1   123
An exile's daughter with an outcast son   673 Werner   1   124
With an Italian exile's dark-eyed daughter   684 Werner   2   96
The daughter of a banish'd man, who lives   694 Werner   2   733
To hail her as his daughter. Wondrous kind   706 Werner   4   140
The daughter of dead Stralenheim, your foe   710 Werner   4   383
The count, and Ulric, and your daughter Ida   713 Werner   5   35
Fire! Creation's first-born daughter   729 Deformed 1   471
Who left an only daughter; my narration   754 Juan   1   468
They are unworthy of my father's daughter   766 Juan   1   1238
Mistress and maid; the first was only daughter   790 Juan   2   991
He had an only daughter, call'd Haidee   790 Juan   2   1017
Robb'd for his daughter by the best of fathers   803 Juan   3   136
He shaped his course to where his daughter fair   804 Juan   3   148
His daughter--had not sent before to advise   806 Juan   3   292
On that beloved daughter; she had been   808 Juan   3   450
His daughter; while compress'd within his clasp   822 Juan   4   378
Her daughter, temper'd with a milder ray   823 Juan   4   449
'Carnage' (so Wordsworth tells you) 'is God's
  daughter   879 Juan   8   70
Nor brother, father, sister, daughter love   914 Juan   10   418
And where the Daughter, whom the Isles loved well   928 Juan   11   606
Safe with a lady, whose last grown-up daughter   936 Juan   12   403
That usual paragon, an only daughter   973 Juan   15   322
And frights--especially if 'tis a daughter   997 Juan   17   31

DAUGHTERS
With Spain's dark-glancing daughters--deign to
  know   13 Harold   1   609
Danced on the shore the daughters of the land   32 Harold   2   766
And such she was;--her daughters had their dowers   55 Harold   4   14
A mirror and a bath for Beauty's youngest
  daughters   65 Harold   4   594
By my daughters of kingdom and reason deprived   96 Harrow-A   22
Frail daughters of the wanton Eve   143 To--A   2
But Daughters say, 'although he's naughty   144 Becher-A   15
There be none of Beauty's daughters   188 Music-C   1
If daughters dread her for the mothers' sake   208 Sketch   42
Daughters and sons of Beauty,--but behold   215 Dream   131
And ye, oh her desolate daughters   222 Babylon   5
Now in loose waltz the thin-clad daughters leap   250 Bards   661
And round her flock'd the daughters of the land   274 Waltz   82
Though in your daughters' daughters yet you
  thrive   275 Waltz   135
My wife now waltzes, and my daughters shall   277 Waltz   251
Neuha, the sun-flower of the island daughters   421 Island   2   213
The charms of earth's least mortal daughters grow   485 Manfred   2   109
Entail'd on thy less virtuous daughters, grown   549 Faliero   5   778
Why do I love this man? My country's daughters   561 Sardan   1   688
To snatch the loveliest of earth's daughters from   659 Heaven   302
And all his goodly daughters   662 Heaven   522
Who seek earth's daughters for their beauty?
  Patriarch   665 Heaven   739
Nor perish like heaven's children with man's
  daughters   668 Heaven   1034
And heartless daughters--worn--and pale--and poor   746 Juan   Ded   86
The sons no more were short, the daughters plain   754 Juan   1   461
Which Eve has left her daughters since her fall   798 Juan   2   1512
Of his gazelle-eyed daughters; she was one   799 Juan   2   1612
And daughters sometimes run off with the butler   804 Juan   3   176
A lady with her daughters or her nieces   809 Juan   3   479
He had fifty daughters and four dozen sons   850 Juan   5   1209
Daughters admired his dress, and pious mothers   924 Juan   11   383
That daughters of such mothers as may know   935 Juan   12   364
And daughters, brothers, sisters, kith or kin   972 Juan   15   242

DAUGHTER'S
To mar a son's, or make a daughter's, match   275 Waltz   100
Thy Daughter's dead   336 Abydos   2   658
For thine own, thy daughter's sake   393 Corinth   850
Your nature's firmness--know your daughter's too   821 Juan   4   336
To say her daughter's feelings are trepann'd   937 Juan   12   474

DAUGHTERS'
Though in your daughters' daughters yet you
  thrive   275 Waltz   135
And kinder still their daughters' gentler fires   422 Island   2   243

DAUNCED
Yelling their uncouth dirge, long daunced the
  kirtled clan   30 Harold   2   639

DAUNIAN
To watch the movements of the Daunian host   105 Nisus   7

DAUNT
A heart his words nor deeds can daunt   327 Abydos   1   366
From their black gulf to daunt the living--Myrrha   579 Sardan   4   37
And only done to daunt me:--'twas a blow   651 Cain   3   330

DAUNTED
Of breakers has not daunted my slight, trim   907 Juan   10   30

DAUNTLESS
Still dauntless 'midst the wreck of earth he'd
  smile   88 Horace   17
Where one so dear, so dauntless, fell   184 Parker   28
No infant Sotheby, whose dauntless head   231 Sotheby   1
Dauntless he stood!--''Tis come--soon past   334 Abydos   2   513
Thus utter'd Coumourgi, the dauntless vizier   392 Corinth   719
The ruddy, reckless, dauntless hue once spread   427 Island   3   87

DAUNTS
Demands and daunts the stranger's eye   319 Giaour   880
No danger daunts the pair his smile hath blest   333 Abydos   2   450

DAVID
If David, when his toils were ended   96 Granta   81
(What harm, if David danced before the ark   261 Hints   320
Not decent David, when before the ark   274 Waltz   83
His own Goliath down to a slight David   726 Deformed 1   298
For David lived, but Juan nearly died   767 Juan   1   1344
Like David, flings smooth pebbles 'gainst a giant   884 Juan   8   402

DAVID'S
Till David's lyre grew mightier than his throne   216 The Harp   10
When old King David's blood grew dull in motion   767 Juan   1   1341

DAVUS
Davus, the harbinger of childish joy   125 Recoll   266
That instant, Davus, it deserves to bleed   126 Recoll   286
To venture a solution: 'Davus sum   942 Juan   13   98

DAVY'S
Sir Humphry Davy's lantern, by which coals   763 Juan   1   1052

DAWN
(See also DAY-DAWN)
What leagues are lost before the dawn of day   22 Harold   2   178
Thy dawn of little joys, to sit and see   53 Harold   3   1077
Such as creation's dawn beheld, thou rollest now   82 Harold   4   1638
And even in simple boyhood's opening dawn   93 Dorset   19
And till Aurora's dawn his skill display'd   108 Nisus   258
My dawn of life is overcast   128 Remembrance   5
I arose with the dawn; with my dog as my guide   136 Highlander   17
In the first year of freedom's second dawn   285 Vision   57
The dawn revives: renown'd, romantic Spain   302 Age   318
But much must yet be done ere dawn of day   346 Corsair   1   583
And shun, though day but dawn on ills increased   375 Lara   1   644
And, with to-morrow's earliest dawn   386 Corinth   231
Dawn in those yet remember'd rays   388 Corinth   387
That steed from sunset until dawn   407 Mazeppa   76
And must it dawn upon his grave   414 Mazeppa   762
Nor further mercy clouds rebellion's dawn   417 Island   1   150
Each dawn had wafted there her light canoe   432 Island   4   183
'Twas morn; and Neuha, who by dawn of day   435 Island   4   373
Whose bloom could after dancing dare the dawn   450 Beppo   664
May dawn on it weeping   488 Manfred   2   334
And of the Genoese fleet, by the first dawn   524 Faliero   3   374
Some dawn of mercy to a portion of   524 Faliero   3   395
Saint Mark's great bell at dawn shall find me
  wakeful   526 Faliero   3   510
Farewell, then,--until dawn! Success go with
  you   526 Faliero   3   550
A rack. Apply it then before the dawn   533 Faliero   4   343
How goes the night? Almost upon the dawn   534 Faliero   4   415
That, ere the dawn, she sets forth with her
  children   581 Sardan   4   201
In the first dawn and bloom of young creation   643 Cain   2   475
Into the dawn, which lighted not the yet   662 Heaven   554
Set out ere dawn. I will remain here to   703 Werner   3   525
Upon the dawn of a world-winning battle   710 Werner   4   410
And by the dawn there will be work. Alas   731 Deformed 1   604
The dawn of an eternal day, than death   733 Deformed 1   784
Of dewy dawn wound slowly round each height   863 Juan   6   686
While, though 'twas dawn, the Turks slept fast as
  ever   870 Juan   7   224
Glory began to dawn with due sublimity   873 Juan   7   406
Swore they should see him by the dawn of day   876 Juan   7   597
Gleams only through the dawn of its creation   930 Juan   12   16

DAWN'D
Where science first dawn'd on the powers of
  reflection   96 Harrow-A   3
Have dawn'd a fair and sinless child of sin   825 Juan   4   555

DAWNING
While hope of dawning honours fill'd my breast   127 Recoll   354
There is no vestige, in the Dawning light   184 Julian   9
Observe his simple childhood's dawning days   259 Hints   221
Ye Alps, which view'd him in his dawning flights   300 Age   135
Who, in my dawning time of day   408 Mazeppa   184
Methought that mist of dawning gray   413 Mazeppa   645
Dividing darkness from the dawning main   415 Island   1   8
In the first dawning of the drunken hour   416 Island   1   83

DAWNS
Morn dawns; and with it stern Albania's hills   25 Harold   2   370

DAY
(See also BATTLE-DAY, CHRISTMAS-DAY, MAY-DAY, MID-
DAY, RECKONING-DAY, SABBATH-DAY, SUMMER-DAY, WELL-
A-DAY)

And had been glorious in another day	4 Harold	1	22
Nor deém'd before his little day was done	4 Harold	1	30
The royal wittol Charles, and curse the day	12 Harold	1	510
The Sabbath comes, a day of blessed rest	15 Harold	1	684
The seventh day this, the jubilee of man	15 Harold	1	693
London, right well thou know'st the day of prayer	15 Harold	1	694
To charms as fair as those that soothed his happier day	17 Harold	1	836
How many a doubtful day shall sink in night	18 Harold	1	924
His shade from Hades upon that dread day	21 Harold	2	121
What leagues are lost before the dawn of day	22 Harold	2	178
To me by day or night she ever smiled	25 Harold	2	331
While the deep war-drum's sound announced the close of day	28 Harold	2	513
Through the long day its penance did maintain	28 Harold	2	533
Thy glorious day is o'er, but not thine years of shame	31 Harold	2	728
The morn the marshalling in arms,--the day	39 Harold	3	247
The day drags through though storms keep out the sun	40 Harold	3	287
Our countrymen were warring on that day	40 Harold	3	314
There was a day when they were young and proud	42 Harold	3	419
They were not eagles, nourish'd with the day	48 Harold	3	786
And glowing into day. We may resume	50 Harold	3	918
Perchance even dearer in her day of woe	58 Harold	4	161
May temper it to bear,--it is but for a day	58 Harold	4	189
Where the Day joins the past Eternity	59 Harold	4	241
As Day and Night contending were, until	59 Harold	4	248
Its mantle o'er the mountains; parting day	59 Harold	4	258
Of moody texture from their earliest day	60 Harold	4	301
And such the storm of battle on this day	64 Harold	4	560
Whose agonies are evils of a day	66 Harold	4	701
The trebly hundred triumphs! and the day	67 Harold	4	731
To what would one day dwindle that which made	67 Harold	4	749
His day of double victory and death	67 Harold	4	764
Had all but crown'd him, on the selfsame day	67 Harold	4	767
It may be, still a something of the day	70 Harold	4	922
It will not bear the brightness of the day	76 Harold	4	1286
Shalt one day, if found worthy, so defined	78 Harold	4	1393
Beyond where splendid shines the orb of day	84 Death-B		14
Till day declines adown the West	91 Caroline-B		30
In the death which one day will deprive you of me	91 Caroline-C		16
Yes! I have mark'd thee many a passing day	93 Dorset		33
Turn to the annals of a former day	94 Dorset		65
By dreams of ill to cloud some future day	94 Dorset		84
May one day claim our suffrage for the state	94 Dorset		98
Against the next elective day	95 Granta		12
When, lo! she changes in a day	97 To Woman		20
Could mark the rising orb of day	101 Alva		14
Hoped that one day the pibroch's strain	102 Alva		46
His natal day is like the last	102 Alva		51
'Perchance forgetful of the day	102 Alva		105
And he would name their nuptial day	103 Alva		168
My sire secured them on that fatal day	107 Nisus		147
To him Euryalus:--'No day shall shame	107 Nisus		171
Soon will the day those eastern clouds adorn	109 Nisus		283
By night heaven owns thy sway, by day the grove	110 Nisus		343
No future day shall see your names expire	110 Nisus		404
This very day, this very hour	111 Medea		37
Thy form appears through night, through day	112 Quaker		30
Retiring from the garish blaze of day	120 Newstead-A		20
And bless thy future as thy former day	122 Newstead-A		156
The orb of day unveils his distant form	122 Recoll		18
The past confounding with the present day	122 Recoll		26
Tradition treasures for a future day	124 Recoll		142
Though sometimes with the tales of ancient day	124 Recoll		171
On the same day our studious race begun	126 Recoll		329
On the same day our studious race was run	126 Recoll		330
The mouldering marble lasts its day	128 Answer-B		33
Thy temple is the face of day	132 Prayer		19
While many a tale of former day	134 E. N. Long		103
Yet the day may arrive when the mountains once more	136 Highlander		41
Through many a weary day gone by	141 Pignus		13
By day, that Form their joy supplies	144 Jessy		7
Unconscious of the day	145 Adieu		10
Are lost in the hours of Eternity's day	150 Newstead-B		40
But dare not stand the test of day	153 Friend-A		52
Why not? since through life's little day	154 Skull		21
'Hey day! call you that a cabin	157 Hodgson		37
By day or night, in weal or woe	163 Parting		17
Shall they not flow, when many a day	165 Thyrza		25
Thy day without a cloud hath pass'd	167 Dead		50
Hiss'd from the theatre the 'other day	170 Address-B		4
While day and night roll darkling by	172 Romaic-B		4
I've lived to curse my natal day	172 Romaic-B		39
What we see every day	177 Devil's Dr		86
And drove off at the close of day	177 Devil's Dr		108
He had been there many a day	178 Devil's Dr		157
But the Devil remain'd till the Break of Day	178 Devil's Dr		169
Each day some tempter's crafty suit	179 Gold		29

DAY

There was a day--there was an hour	181 Ode-A		145
Morn came and went--and came, and brought no day	189 Darkness		6
He died before my day of Sextonship	190 Churchill		13
Was a most famous writer in his day	190 Churchill		29
It may be both--but, one day end it must	192 Fragment-C		21
When the last sunshine of expiring day	192 Monody		1
When Summer's day declines along the hills	192 Monody		20
Hath pass'd from day to darkness--to whose hour	192 Monody		24
And think her ransom cheap that day	195 Ballad-A		99
And, since that day, beneath the skies	205 To--B		3
The night grows day to me	205 To--B		6
Though the day of my destiny's over	210 Augusta-B		1
My whole life was a contest, since the day	211 Augusta-C		26
Kingdoms and empires in my little day	211 Augusta-C		33
I have outlived myself by many a day	212 Augusta-C		107
The day, the hour, the sunshine, and the shade	215 Dream		162
Which heaven to gaudy day denies	216 She Walks		6
Ere the coming day is done	219 Saul-B		21
Fare thee well, but for a day	219 Saul-B		23
There rose no day, there roll'd no hour	219 Vanity		13
Had reflected the last beam of day as it blazed	221 Jerusalem		10
And now on that mountain I stood on that day	221 Jerusalem		13
Of Babel, and thought of the day	222 Babylon		2
Things of a day! you wither ere the night	222 Spirit		11
In the valley of waters we wept o'er the day	223 Valley		1
And the day returns too soon	230 Roving		10
I bought me some books tother day	234 Ballat		6
But as few as you please of the day	235 New Year		4
This day, of all our days, has done	236 Penelope		1
Each day a trumpet soundeth in mine ear	240 Cephalonia		5
And, like his bard, confounded night with day	245 Bards		250
'Tis Little! young Catullus of his day	245 Bards		287
Can none remember that eventful day	248 Bards		464
Oh, day disastrous! On her firm-set rock	248 Bards		468
Behold the new Petronius of the day	250 Bards		642
By day and night to read the works of Greece	262 Hints		424
That closed their murder'd sage's latest day	268 Minerva		22
And thus--accursed be the day and year	270 Minerva		147
To sell, and made--may Shame record the day	270 Minerva		173
His day of mercy is the day of fight	272 Minerva		296
Stick to prose--As sublime!!--but I wish you good day	279 Blues	1	102
That it threaten'd to give up the ghost t'other day	279 Blues	1	130
I allow our friend Scamp hath this day done his best	281 Blues	2	41
Each day too slew its thousands six or seven	285 Vision		37
'Twill one day finish: meantime they increase	285 Vision		53
As one day will be that immortal fry	286 Vision		119
To reach its goal--the devil not half a day	292 Vision		448
Where Belial, upon duty for the day	294 Vision		580
And take up rather more time than a day	297 Vision		766
Break o'er th' Aegean, mindful of the day	302 Age		287
Must fight next day his speech to vindicate	304 Age	.	493
Whose penknife slit a goose-quill t'other day	305 Age		539
And acres told upon the appointed day	306 Age		589
Ere the first day of death is fled	311 Giaour		69
The first dark day of nothingness	311 Giaour		70
And chase the sultriness of day	313 Giaour		300
The day shall have a stormy end	316 Giaour		664
But were I Prior, not a day	318 Giaour		818
Who shrived him on his dying day	323 Abydos	1	1332
Will one day work me more annoy	325 Abydos	1	133
How dear this very day must tell	326 Abydos	1	194
I've partisans for peril's day	327 Abydos	1	380
Save that we meet not but by day	328 Abydos	1	391
To mourn--I dare not curse--the day	330 Abydos	2	167
The day when Giaffir's charge was o'er	332 Abydos	2	342
Thought of the gloomy day and ghastly night	336 Abydos	2	647
And the brief epitaph in danger's day	338 Corsair	1	39
The breeze will freshen when the day is done	340 Corsair	1	159
And day broke dreary on my troubled view	343 Corsair	1	382
But much must yet be done ere dawn of day	346 Corsair	1	583
How many?--Ha! it cannot sure be day	349 Corsair	2	135
That by day death still forbears to slake	351 Corsair	2	320
More need of rest to nerve me for the day	352 Corsair	2	381
The sentence that remits thee scarce a day	354 Corsair	2	465
That closed their murder'd sage's latest day	355 Corsair	3	22
The night-breeze freshens; she that day had pass'd	356 Corsair	3	75
'Pacha! the day is thine; and on thy crest	357 Corsair	3	141
One day to him--the wretch already mine	358 Corsair	3	170
Roll'd day and night: his soul, could terror tame	358 Corsair	3	209
The first day pass'd; he saw not her, Gulnare	359 Corsair	3	244
The fourth day roll'd along, and with the night	359 Corsair	3	248
Starts from the day abrupt and fearfully	361 Corsair	3	409
Our bark is tossing--'tis already day	362 Corsair	3	433
And Heaven must punish on its angry day	363 Corsair	3	526
As soon could he have linger'd there for day	364 Corsair	3	594
The sun goes forth, but Conrad's day is dim	365 Corsair	3	656
And Conrad comes not, came not since that day	366 Corsair	3	688
And oft, in sudden mood, for many a day	368 Lara	1	133
And shun, though day but dawn on ills increased	375 Lara	1	644
Man has another day to swell the past	375 Lara	2	3

DAY

But there he was not, and with coming day	376 Lara	2	104
And they who watch'd might mark that, day by day	377 Lara	2	188
Day glimmers on the dying and the dead	380 Lara	2	394
As if his heart abhorr'd that coming day	381 Lara	2	473
Never our steeds for a day stood still	384 Corinth		7
Whose clouds that day grew doubly dun	386 Corinth		173
Within his tent to wait for day	388 Corinth		347
Like sparkling waves on a sunny day	391 Corinth		611
And the Noon will look on a sultry day	391 Corinth		682
Like the mower's grass at the close of day	392 Corinth		736
You might have heard it, on that day	392 Corinth		763
The dead before him, on that day	393 Corinth		784
Who fell that day beneath his ire	393 Corinth		802
And since the day, when in the strait	393 Corinth		805
Which his worshippers drank at the break of day	395 Corinth		1004
Little deem'd she such a day	395 Corinth		1046
Which follows the decline of day	396 Parisina		13
A name she dare not breathe by day	397 Parisina		72
Ere day declines, I shall have none	398 Parisina		201
Which rose upon that heavy day	400 Parisina		409
At least the knight's who died that day	401 Parisina		512
Till I have done with this new day	403 Chillon		41
For he was beautiful as day	403 Chillon		79
(When day was beautiful to me	403 Chillon		80
A polar day, which will not see	403 Chillon		82
We heard it ripple night and day	403 Chillon		117
His corse in dust whereon the day	404 Chillon		153
Less wretched now, and one day free	404 Chillon		171
He, too, was struck, and day by day	404 Chillon		174
It was not night--it was not day	405 Chillon		240
A single cloud on a sunny day	405 Chillon		295
'Twas after dread Pultowa's day	407 Mazeppa		1
Until a day more dark and drear	407 Mazeppa		9
By day and night through field and flood	407 Mazeppa		17
Since but the fleeting of a day	407 Mazeppa		46
Who, in my dawning time of day	408 Mazeppa		184
Compare my day and yesterday	408 Mazeppa		194
Wherewith we while away the day	409 Mazeppa		254
And almost on the break of day	410 Mazeppa		333
'Twas but a day he had been caught	410 Mazeppa		365
'Twas scarcely yet the break of day	410 Mazeppa		377
They little thought that day of pain	411 Mazeppa		407
That one day I should come again	411 Mazeppa		410
How many hours of night or day	412 Mazeppa		597
Would never dapple into day	413 Mazeppa		646
I little deem'd another day	414 Mazeppa		716
Me--one day o'er their realm to reign	415 Mazeppa		847
The dolphins, not unconscious of the day	415 Island	1	9
Than aught we know beyond our little day	417 Island	1	120
The sweet siesta of a summer day	420 Island	2	105
They reckon'd not, whose day was but an hour	424 Island	2	357
And asking if indeed the day were done	424 Island	2	369
Chipp'd by the beam, a nursling of the day	430 Island	4	23
For all was darkness for a space, till day	431 Island	4	131
'Twas morn; and Neuha, who by dawn of day	435 Island	4	373
Which nothing through its bars admits, save day	437 Tasso		13
But undefined and wandering, till the day	439 Tasso		169
And to this day from Venice to Verona	442 Beppo		131
By night and day, all paces, swift or slow	442 Beppo		155
Who love to see the Sun shine every day	445 Beppo		323
But with all Heaven t' himself; that day will break as	445 Beppo		341
It shall be shaved before you're a day older	451 Beppo		738
And borrow'd the Count's smallclothes for a day	452 Beppo		780
The day may come when she will cease to err	457 Dante	1	73
The day may come she would be proud to have	457 Dante	1	74
Long day, and dreary night; the retrospect	457 Dante	1	134
And the first day which sees the chain enthral	461 Dante	3	82
She held in Hellas' unforgotten day	463 Dante	4	43
The day thy Gabriel said 'All hail!' to thee	466 Morgante		12
One day he openly began to say	467 Morgante		87
And by the fount did much the day to win	467 Morgante		99
But I know who that day had won the fight	467 Morgante		100
Orlando one day heard this speech in brief	468 Morgante		117
They'll one day fling the mountain, I believe	469 Morgante		216
Saying, 'What grace to me thou'st this day given	470 Morgante		281
Till, one day, by the Spirit being inflamed	473 Morgante		459
One day, as with Orlando they both stray'd	473 Morgante		475
The abbot by the hand he took one day	475 Morgante		597
We read one day for pastime, seated nigh	477 Francesca		31
That day no further leaf we did uncover	477 Francesca		42
Moves onward day by day	479 Manfred	1	69
And the day shall have a sun	481 Manfred	1	230
And thou fresh breaking Day, and you, ye Mountains	481 Manfred	1	269
'Tis of an ancient vintage; many a day	484 Manfred	2	18
The affluence of my soul--which one day was	487 Manfred	2	235
Re-appear to the day	490 Manfred	2	461
Merrier than day; he did not walk the rocks	494 Manfred	3	224
Oh for one year! Oh! but for even a day	504 Faliero	1	303
They have cause, since Sapienza's adverse day	504 Faliero	1	328
The day is overcast, but the calm wave	511 Faliero	2	162
To lighten or divide it. Since the day	512 Faliero	2	219

DAY

The state; then live to save her still. A day	515 Faliero	2	470
Another day like that would be the best	515 Faliero	2	471
But one such day occurs within an age	515 Faliero	2	473
Thus speak I? Venice has forgot that day	515 Faliero	2	478
And hesitating councils: day on day	516 Faliero	2	560
Than live another day to act the tyrant	523 Faliero	3	301
Will one day learn. Meantime, I do devote	523 Faliero	3	319
This day and night shall be the last of peril	526 Faliero	3	513
Mere things of every day: so that thou hast not	530 Faliero	4	144
Methinks the day breaks--is it not so? look	534 Faliero	4	457
Speed, for the day grows broader. Send me soon	535 Faliero	4	477
Then swoops with his unerring beak.--Thou day	535 Faliero	4	487
And fame, and length of days--to see this day	535 Faliero	4	503
But this day, black within the calendar	535 Faliero	4	504
One day of baffled crime must not efface	543 Faliero	5	358
Upon a public day of thanksgiving	545 Faliero	5	489
Of the town of Treviso, on a day	546 Faliero	5	595
That on my day of landing here as Doge	547 Faliero	5	629
Are silently engendering of the day	548 Faliero	5	742
Like to the dying day on Caucasus	552 Sardan	1	90
In one day--what could that blood-loving beldame	555 Sardan	1	285
In one day built Anchialus and Tarsus	555 Sardan	1	298
And thine and mine; and in another day	555 Sardan	1	330
That for this day, at least, he will not quit	560 Sardan	1	616
How many a day and moon thou hast reclined	560 Sardan	1	626
And wilt thou not now tarry for a day	560 Sardan	1	633
A day which may redeem thee? Wilt thou not	560 Sardan	1	634
Into some realm of undiscover'd day	562 Sardan	2	39
Doth he not change a thousand times a day	563 Sardan	2	119
In his sire's day for mighty vice-royalties	568 Sardan	2	437
The close and sultry summer's day, which bodes	576 Sardan	3	316
And must not all the present one day part	585 Sardan	4	475
The day at last has broken. What a night	587 Sardan	5	1
A beacon in the horizon for a day	594 Sardan	5	439
Forward to be one day of the decemvirs	598 Foscari	1	188
The fiends who will one day requite them in	599 Foscari	1	264
Our only day; for, save the gaoler's torch	609 Foscari	3	103
Saw day go down upon your native spires	611 Foscari	3	211
Will one day thank you better. You do well	612 Foscari	3	270
Of destinies: each day secures him more	613 Foscari	3	321
I know his fate may one day be their heritage	614 Foscari	3	371
We have higher business for our own. This day	615 Foscari	4	18
Of noble blood may), one day hope to be	616 Foscari	4	84
'The good day or good night?' his Dogeship answer'd	619 Foscari	4	294
This from you. Oh, they'll hear as much one day	623 Foscari	5	145
Of such. Well, sirs, your will be done! as one day	626 Foscari	5	360
God! who didst name the day, and separate	627 Cain	1	5
Earth, ocean, air, and fire, and with the day	627 Cain	1	10
Born on the same day, of the same womb; and	632 Cain	1	328
It one day will be in your children. What	633 Cain	1	362
Must one day see perforce. Behold! 'Tis darkness	639 Cain	2	196
It speaks of a day past. It is the realm	639 Cain	2	218
He one day will unfold that further secret	639 Cain	2	243
Happy the day! Yes; happy! when unfolded	639 Cain	2	244
I must one day return here from the earth	640 Cain	2	312
As the day closes over Eden's walls	643 Cain	2	471
How know we that some such atonement one day	647 Cain	3	85
By night and--snakes spring up in his path	652 Cain	3	427
Be from this day, and vagabond on earth	653 Cain	3	476
Will one day hover o'er the sepulchre	655 Heaven		22
More bright than those of day	656 Heaven		99
With a cleft heart look on thee day by day	659 Heaven		314
From day	660 Heaven		378
The sun will rise upon the earth's last day	662 Heaven		551
As on the fourth day of creation, when	662 Heaven		552
Heaven first each day before the Adamites	662 Heaven		560
And they will sing! and day will break! Both near	662 Heaven		562
Their outworn pinions on the deep; and day	662 Heaven		564
Ay, day will rise; but upon what?--a chaos	662 Heaven		566
Which was ere day, and which, renew'd makes time	662 Heaven		567
Shall long outlast the sun which gave them day	666 Heaven		867
Of age, if 'tis a day. Which epoch makes	677 Werner	1	377
Now, as he one day will forever lie	679 Werner	1	518
The past seems paradise. Another day	680 Werner	1	585
Oh! that I e'er should live to see this day	683 Werner	2	6
And wept to see another day go down	688 Werner	2	376
From sleep, and judge! Should that day e'er arrive	690 Werner	2	446
I will but wait a day or two with him	698 Werner	3	223
One day. You shall be safe: let that suffice	699 Werner	3	248
To beat the bushes, and the day looks promising	705 Werner	4	77
In this, for this one day: the day looks heavy	707 Werner	4	213
I did, and do. Then fix the day. 'Tis usual	710 Werner	4	392
As I can one day God's. Nor did he die	712 Werner	4	512
In open day, by his disgrace which stamp'd	720 Werner	5	448
The nipple next day sore and udder dry	722 Deformed	1	23
My labour for the day is over now	722 Deformed	1	32
On the fair day, which sees no foul thing like	723 Deformed	1	68
It hath sustain'd your soul full many a day	728 Deformed	1	431

DAY

Whose statue turns a harper once a day	730	Deformed	1	532
On the day Remus leapt her wall. I saw him	731	Deformed	1	640
The dawn of an eternal day, than death	733	Deformed	1	784
Is the day indeed begun	735	Deformed	2	4
But somewhat late i' the day. Where shall we bear her	741	Deformed	2	392
Each day--each hour--each minute shows me more	743	Deformed	3	115
And saw into herself each day before all	751	Juan	1	306
And next day paid a visit to his mother	756	Juan	1	602
It was upon a day, a summer's day	759	Juan	1	809
'Twas on a summer's day--the sixth of June	759	Juan	1	817
Their nomenclature; there is not a day	760	Juan	1	900
Suppose from June the sixth (the fatal day	761	Juan	1	962
About the day--the era's more obscure	761	Juan	1	968
'Twill one day ask you why you used me so	766	Juan	1	1254
Besides, it wanted but few hours of day	767	Juan	1	1350
Day has not broke--there's no one in the street	769	Juan	1	1456
The pleasant scandal which arose next day	770	Juan	1	1501
I thought of a peruke the other day	773	Juan	1	1699
Infants of three years old were taught that day	775	Juan	2	77
As day advanced the weather seem'd to abate	777	Juan	2	233
Day broke, and the wind lull'd: the masts were gone	778	Juan	2	298
And never had as yet a quiet day	779	Juan	2	316
Some cursed the day on which they saw the sun	779	Juan	2	355
'Twas twilight, and the sunless day went down	780	Juan	2	385
And must have meals, at least one meal a day	782	Juan	2	530
For on the third day there came on a calm	782	Juan	2	538
On what, in fact, next day were they to dine	782	Juan	2	548
The fourth day came, but not a breath of air	782	Juan	2	553
The fifth day, and their boat lay floating there	782	Juan	2	555
On the sixth day they fed upon his hide	783	Juan	2	561
The seventh day, and no wind--the burning sun	783	Juan	2	569
But ere they came to this, they that day shared	783	Juan	2	585
The day before, fast sleeping on the water	786	Juan	2	785
By night chill'd, by day scorch'd, thus one by one	787	Juan	2	813
And Time had nothing more of night nor day	788	Juan	2	883
The cliff, towards sunset, on that day she found	790	Juan	2	1026
In health and purse, begin your day to date	791	Juan	2	1118
A purple hectic play'd like dying day	792	Juan	2	1170
Where I, like other 'dogs, have had my day	795	Juan	2	1323
And every day by daybreak--rather early	795	Juan	2	1337
And every day help'd on his convalescence	795	Juan	2	1346
For little had he wander'd since the day	796	Juan	2	1404
Sermons and soda-water the day after	796	Juan	2	1424
But changes night and day, too, like the sky	801	Juan	2	1706
He left his ship to be hove down next day	804	Juan	3	157
I've known the absent wrong'd four times a day	804	Juan	3	200
A day of gold from out an age of iron	806	Juan	3	283
So little they expected him that day	807	Juan	3	388
And clouds come o'er the sunset of our day	808	Juan	3	470
She had no need of this, day ne'er will break	810	Juan	3	603
He counted them at break of day	812	Juan	3	711
An independent being in his day	813	Juan	3	819
Of those who sail the seas, on the first day	816	Juan	3	954
The long year link'd with heavy day on day	817	Juan	4	85
As if their last day of a happy dome	819	Juan	4	171
However dear or cherish'd in their day	824	Juan	4	508
They heard next day--that in the Dardanelles	828	Juan	4	721
I pass each day where Dante's bones are laid	829	Juan	4	825
'Twas a raw day of Autumn's bleak beginning	832	Juan	5	41
I cried upon my first wife's dying day	833	Juan	5	151
'Perhaps we shall be one day, by and by	834	Juan	5	189
And such an end! that he who many a day	836	Juan	5	293
More tender, as we every day behold	837	Juan	5	390
But saddens more by night as well as day	838	Juan	5	446
Reign'd, till one summer's day he took to grazing	839	Juan	5	476
But wishing to be one day brigadiers	869	Juan	7	140
Their Gallic names upon a glorious day	870	Juan	7	171
All that the Russians did upon this day	871	Juan	7	250
(For Day ne'er saw his merits) could decree	872	Juan	7	324
The day before the assault, while upon drill	874	Juan	7	441
Swore they should see him by the dawn of day	876	Juan	7	597
And almost every day, in sad reality	877	Juan	7	659
Which stiffen'd heaven) as if he wish'd for day	881	Juan	8	167
But seeing, flashing forward, like the day	882	Juan	8	235
Cossacques were all cut off as day was breaking	888	Juan	8	603
That they should all be shot on the next day	891	Juan	8	814
A thing which happens everywhere each day	891	Juan	8	823
The web of these tarantulas each day	900	Juan	9	221
But let it go:--it will one day be found	901	Juan	9	289
Did not his deeds unriddle them each day	902	Juan	9	396
Fair weather for the day. Though rather spacious	904	Juan	9	463
Hectic and brief as summer's day nigh done	908	Juan	10	62
To hoard up warmth against a wintry day	908	Juan	10	72
For cousins also, answer'd the same day	911	Juan	10	236
Which portions out upon the judgment day	911	Juan	10	276
His services. He kiss'd hands the next day	913	Juan	10	365
Just as the day began to wane and darken	917	Juan	10	635
Decide, and every body one day will	919	Juan	11	31
He'll find it rather difficult some day	925	Juan	11	459
Amongst the higher spirits of the day	926	Juan	11	503

DAY

Whenever--which means every day--they'd shown	935	Juan	12	379
Of his own country;--seldom since that day	942	Juan	13	83
The dappled foresters--as day awoke	948	Juan	13	446
Which makes the southern autumn's day appear	950	Juan	13	610
And rank'd with what is every day display'd	952	Juan	13	719
The middle-aged to make the day more short	954	Juan	13	804
A sleep without dreams, after a rough day	955	Juan	14	25
And when upon a silent, sullen day	959	Juan	14	217
Ask'd next day, 'If men ever hunted twice	959	Juan	14	280
December's drowsy day to his dull race	960	Juan	14	284
Find one, each day of the delightful year	963	Juan	14	502
Which you should perpetrate some summer's day	965	Juan	14	654
Were shaken down, and 'dogs had had their day	971	Juan	15	180
Which charm most people in their earlier day	974	Juan	15	419
The evaporation of a joyous day	981	Juan	16	65
Titus exclaim'd, 'I've lost a day!' Of all	981	Juan	16	85
Though he is not seen by day	985	Juan	16	336
He abideth night and day	985	Juan	16	340
Amundeville is lord by day	986	Juan	16	357
As the mere pastime of an idle day	986	Juan	16	379
Of Juan's nervous feelings on that day	987	Juan	16	452
But should the day come when place ceased to exist	990	Juan	16	645
But 'twas a public feast and public day	991	Juan	16	669
And lo! upon that day it came to pass	991	Juan	16	693
Dully past o'er the dinner of the day	992	Juan	16	737
This day; and watching, witching, condescending	993	Juan	16	802
However, the day closed, as days must close	994	Juan	16	849
Just as I make my mind up every day.	998	Juan	17	78

DAY-BEAM

On thy leaves yet the day-beam of ages may shine	149	Newstead-B		27

DAY-BILL

To draw up in array a single day-bill	976	Juan	15	493

DAY-BLUSH

But when the day-blush bursts from high	336	Abydos	2	705

DAYBREAK

At day-break winding through the wood	411	Mazeppa		500
By day-break I propose that we set forth	581	Sardan	4	183
Met the great Duke at daybreak with a jest	619	Foscari	4	292
Good night! I trust to meet with him at daybreak	681	Werner	1	667
In my return. You!--Why? I went at daybreak	687	Werner	2	310
An hour ere daybreak with all means to quit	700	Werner	3	308
And yours will be a post of trust at daybreak	734	Deformed	1	875
She and her maid--and promised by daybreak	791	Juan	2	1062
From daybreak, and when coffin'd at four-score	792	Juan	2	1119
And every day by daybreak--rather early	795	Juan	2	1337
Until they reach'd, as daybreak was expanding	887	Juan	8	573

DAY-DAWN

At day-dawn it is yours. Oh, thou sweet sparkler	700	Werner	3	328
At day-dawn before	732	Deformed	1	704
For like a day-dawn she was young and pure	934	Juan	12	322

DAY-HYMN

Or the faint dying day-hymn stole aloft	815	Juan	3	910

DAYLESS

To fetters, and the damp vault's dayless gloom	402	Sonnet-F		6

DAYLIGHT

To meet the daylight after seven hours sitting	450	Beppo		674

DAYLIGHT'S

The pledge of daylight's lengthen'd hours	742	Deformed	3	20
In decent London when the daylight's o'er	922	Juan	11	237

DAYS
(See also DOG-DAYS, NOW-A-DAYS)

My days once number'd, should this homage past	3	To Ianthe		41
But spent his days in riot most uncouth	3	Harold	1	12
Four days are sped, but with the fifth, anon	6	Harold	1	200
Her strength, her wealth, her site of ancient days	14	Harold	1	658
Though to my hopeless days forever lost	19	Harold	1	938
Ancient of days! august Athena! where	19	Harold	2	10
Since the days of our prophet the Crescent ne'er saw	31	Harold	2	683
Yet mark their mirth--ere lenten days begin	31	Harold	2	738
Some days of joyaunce are decreed to all	32	Harold	2	743
Of louder minstrels in these later days	34	Harold	2	885
Roll on, vain days! full reckless may ye flow	35	Harold	2	924
Since my young days of passion--joy, or pain	35	Harold	3	28
The patch'd-up idol of enlighten'd days	38	Harold	3	168
That should their days, surviving perils past	42	Harold	3	391
Nor was all love shut from him, though his days	43	Harold	3	469
The brilliant, fair, and soft,--the glories of old days	44	Harold	3	580
A gray and grief-worn aspect of old days	45	Harold	3	618
Those days are gone, but Beauty still is here	55	Harold	4	23
The mountain-village where his latter days	59	Harold	4	272

DAYS

Because the deadly days which we have seen	69 Harold	4	868
There is a stern round tower of other days	69 Harold	4	883
Thou tomb! and other days come back on me	70 Harold	4	930
Relic of nobler days and noblest arts	77 Harold	4	1315
The hour draws nigh, a few brief days will close	94 Dorset		77
'Oh, such were the days which my infancy knew	97 Harrow-A		36
Three days, three sleepless nights, the Chief	103 Alva		125
Days roll'd along, the orb of light	103 Alva		153
And days of glory yet for him remain	120 Newstead-A		68
Ah happy days! too happy to endure	121 Newstead-A		129
Calls back the vanish'd days to rapture given	122 Recoll		13
The dear preceptor of my early days	123 Recoll		108
These young effusions of my early days	127 Recoll		358
Say, if remembrance days like these endears	127 Recoll		391
Peruse the record of your days on earth	127 Recoll		403
My days of happiness are few	128 Remembrance		3
Why waste upon folly the days of my youth	129 Becher-A		36
Dear are the days of youth! Age dwells	129 Calmar		1
Days of delight may still be mine	131 L'Amitie		3
The joyous days which ours have been	133 E. N. Long		3
I think those days may come again	133 E. N. Long		12
Yes, as you knew me in the days	133 E. N. Long		43
And delight but in days I have witness'd before	136 Highlander		28
I ask no atonement but days like the past	137 Delawarr		36
To trace those days and hours again	137 Clare		11
Your coming days and years may bless	138 Clare		92
To cheer my last declining days	138 Clare		98
Deplored by those in early days allied	138 Harrow-B		33
Thy season o'er, thy days will find their end	139 Ossian-A		26
Swift as your wings my happier days have past	140 Ossian-A		49
For could I through my days again live	144 Becher-B		7
Thou Power! who hast ruled me through infancy's days	148 Farewell-B		1
I hoped that thy days would be longer than mine	149 Newstead-B		2
Remembrance of the days that were	152 Time-A		16
Our childish days were days of joy	153 Friend-A		22
In the days of my youth, when the heart's in its spring	155 Goblet		9
Endear'd by days gone by	159 Storm		58
Let the Sunbeam be bright for the younger of days	164 Newstead-C		5
To me they speak of brighter days	165 Away		5
It was not thus in days more dear	166 Struggle		13
My Thyrza's pledge in better days	166 Struggle		41
Count o'er thy days from anguish free	167 Euthanasia		34
The better days of life were ours	167 Dead		28
Dear are the days which made our annals bright	170 Address-A		42
Scenes not unworthy Drury's days of old	170 Address-A		71
Seven days and nights of single sorrow	173 Quotation		17
Far may thy days, as heretofore	174 Remember-B		25
And our days seem as swift, and our moments more sweet	182 Music-A		15
A halo of the light of other days	193 Monody		57
The goodly work of the days of old	196 Venice-A		8
His offspring, who expired in other days	199 Sonnet-E		3
The days of our youth are the days of our glory	204 Pisa		2
My days are in the yellow leaf	206 Year		5
Like to the Pontic monarch of old days	216 Dream		191
But tell of days in goodness spent	216 She Walks		16
Thy days are done, thy fame begun	218 Thy Days		1
I strive to number o'er what days	219 Vanity		9
So gleams the past, the light of other days	220 Sleepless		5
This day, of all our days, has done	236 Penelope		1
Time was, ere yet in these degenerate days	243 Bards		103
There be they say, in these enlighten'd days	253 Bards		849
New words find credit in these latter days	257 Hints		79
Though mad Almanzor rhymed in Dryden's days	258 Hints		119
Observe his simple childhood's dawning days	259 Hints		221
Which charm'd our days in each Aegean clime	261 Hints		345
But this is certain, since our Shakspeare's days	262 Hints		441
Unhappy Greece! thy sons of ancient days	263 Hints		509
Damn'd all their days, they posthumously thrive	266 Hints		721
And tell-tale powder--all have had their days	276 Waltz		183
Pronounce--if ever in your days of bliss	276 Waltz		222
'Tis a sort of re-union for Scamp, on the days	279 Blues	1	139
My days, which once pass'd in so gentle a void	280 Blues	2	4
Almost as scanty, of days less remote	293 Vision		528
Hid him from sight--like fogs on London days	294 Vision		630
High as thine own in days of yore	311 Giaour		145
'Father! thy days have pass'd in peace	320 Giaour		971
My days, though few, have pass'd below	320 Giaour		982
Than pass my dull, unvarying days	320 Giaour		992
'In earlier days, and calmer hours	322 Giaour		1218
His days, his very hours were few	331 Abydos	2	273
Soft--as the melody of youthful days	333 Abydos	2	404
Would that those days were over! wilt thou ne'er	343 Corsair	1	388
In three days (serve the breeze) the sun shall shine	346 Corsair	1	567
The pride, but not the fire, of early days	367 Lara	1	69
Such scene reminded him of other days	368 Lara	1	175
Of higher birth he seem'd, and better days	374 Lara	1	574
Days roll along, and Otho's wounds are heal'd	377 Lara	2	127
But those hardy days flew cheerily	384 Corinth		34
But vain her voice, till better days	388 Corinth		386

DAYS

While in his thought her days are number'd	397 Parisina		119
A few brief hours or days that must	399 Parisina		278
But sleepless nights and heavy days	402 Parisina		547
A little talk of better days	404 Chillon		198
It might be months, or years, or days	406 Chillon		366
Since Alexander's days till now	408 Mazeppa		103
My days and nights were nothing, all	409 Mazeppa		301
I paid it well in after days	410 Mazeppa		393
Of days no more deplored or curst	414 Mazeppa		756
To keep, some days, the dying from the dead	416 Island	1	90
Their days of danger, and their nights of pain	418 Island	1	179
Such was this ditty of Tradition's days	420 Island	2	79
Around him days and worlds are heedless driven	424 Island	2	372
In hopeless visions of our better days	429 Island	3	206
A night succeeded by such happy days	435 Island	4	419
To live for forty days on ill-dress'd fishes	441 Beppo		51
Was most facetious in the days of yore	441 Beppo		74
Their days are either pass'd in doing nothing	449 Beppo		567
Ye happy mixtures of more happy days	450 Beppo		634
Except three days of calm when off Cape Bonn	452 Beppo		768
The many felt, for from all days and climes	454 Venice-B		109
And the night cometh; I am old in days	456 Dante	1	44
Their days in endless strife, and die alone	458 Dante	1	152
The Spirit of the fervent days of Old	458 Dante	2	1
Must pass their days in penury or pain	464 Dante	4	104
The evil days to gifted souls foreshown	465 Dante	4	150
And then reposed himself some days with her	468 Morgante		144
Through all the different periods of my days	472 Morgante		380
The abbot: many days they did repose	473 Morgante		474
A few days after this convivial scene	474 Morgante		534
The lost days of time past, which may be blamed	475 Morgante		604
Some days ago I should have ask'd your leave	475 Morgante		605
Is to remind us of our happy days	476 Francesca		26
Kingdom, and sway, and strength, and length of days	480 Manfred	1	168
Accursed! what have I to do with days	480 Manfred	1	169
(For here the patriarchal days are not	482 Manfred	1	310
Have made my days and nights imperishable	484 Manfred	2	53
Thy days of health, and nights of sleep; thy toils	484 Manfred	2	67
We are the fools of time and terror: Days	487 Manfred	2	258
In all the days of this detested yoke	487 Manfred	2	261
In all the days of past and future, for	487 Manfred	2	265
My days are number'd, and my deeds recorded	495 Manfred	3	314
And put her from him. True--but in those days	502 Faliero	1	199
Till in these late days did I see you thus	511 Faliero	2	188
I knew my days could not disturb you long	513 Faliero	2	329
No lure for me, in my most passionate days	514 Faliero	2	352
Be honour'd still by me: but may your days	515 Faliero	2	449
O'er the few days or hours which yet await	515 Faliero	2	455
Yet a few days and dream-perturbed nights	515 Faliero	2	495
Whate'er the good, may last days of life	523 Faliero	3	320
Which now belong to history, soothe the days	525 Faliero	3	451
Flit round them whispering of the days gone by	525 Faliero	3	456
He dared not--in more honourable days	526 Faliero	3	527
And many deeds and days--the senators	527 Faliero	3	572
You have been my protector, in the days	531 Faliero	4	199
A moment to the feelings of old days	534 Faliero	4	395
And fame, and length of days--to see this day	535 Faliero	4	503
That it should fall to me! and that my days	538 Faliero	5	6
Have something of the blood of brighter days	541 Faliero	5	274
Which grief and shame will soon cut down to days	543 Faliero	5	357
For the last time--the days which I denounce	547 Faliero	5	667
I let them pass their days as best might suit them	556 Sardan	1	406
Unfold the rise of days more worthy thine	561 Sardan	2	19
As of wrath to its days? Hear me! oh, hear me	562 Sardan	2	22
Than many monarchs in a length of days	582 Sardan	4	294
Where thou shalt pass thy days in peace; but on	592 Sardan	5	304
No doubt; yet most men like to live their days out	605 Foscari	2	212
Less than their breath; our durance upon days	607 Foscari	2	355
Our days on seasons; our whole being on	607 Foscari	2	356
In deeds, and days, and sway, and, let me add	607 Foscari	2	402
Prolongs my days to prove and chasten me	621 Foscari	5	50
Of days, since every hour has been the country's	621 Foscari	5	52
Three days are left you to remove from hence	623 Foscari	5	173
If you would have the three days named extended	623 Foscari	5	187
But in that hour see things of many days	635 Cain	1	525
Out of old worlds this new one in few days	635 Cain	1	527
Thine are the hours and days when both are cheering	646 Cain	3	21
May all his days be desolate! May--Hold	652 Cain	3	404
Go forth! fulfil thy days! and be thy deeds	654 Cain	3	517
A weakness of the spirit, listless days	658 Heaven		217
The destiny and evil of these days	658 Heaven		257
Ye look eternal! Yet, in a few days	659 Heaven		273
And night by night, thy number'd days and nights	659 Heaven		315
Their courage, strength, and length of days-- They are number'd	664 Heaven		689
Even had their days been left to toil their path	667 Heaven		873
Proclaims earth's last of summer days hath shone	668 Heaven		1007
The corpses of the world of thy young days	670 Heaven		1145

DAYS

That to our sorrow for these five days; since	674 Werner	1	211
To have seen better days, as who has not	677 Werner	1	372
Beseem'd this palace in its brightest days	677 Werner	1	387
Some days ago that look'd the likeliest journey	678 Werner	1	425
Some hours ago, and I some days: henceforth	680 Werner	1	541
By our Teutonic fathers in old days	696 Werner	3	99
In these dim days of heresies and blood	711 Werner	4	457
Of merit, and complaint of present days	746 Juan	Ded	63
If, fallen in evil days on evil tongues	746 Juan	Ded	73
Have moments, hours, and days, so unprepared	749 Juan	1	164
For half his days were pass'd at church, the other	753 Juan	1	391
'Twas in November, when fine days are few	763 Juan	1	1067
Alfonso's days had not been in the land	769 Juan	1	1478
My days of love are over; me no more	773 Juan	1	1721
The world will find thee after many days	774 Juan	1	1772
Days nearly o'er, might be disposed to riot	778 Juan	2	262
Having been several days in great distress	779 Juan	2	362
And the dim desolate deep: twelve days had Fear	780 Juan	2	391
In my young days they lent me cash that way	782 Juan	2	519
Who died two days before, and now had found	788 Juan	2	871
Save on the dead long summer days, which make	796 Juan	2	1415
Such kisses as belong to early days	797 Juan	2	1484
Our days, and put one's servants into mourning	802 Juan	3	56
There his few peaceful days Time had swept o'er	808 Juan	3	413
His predecessors in the Colchian days	808 Juan	3	436
In whom our brightest days we would retrace	808 Juan	3	467
Reversing the good custom of old days	811 Juan	3	626
Must we but weep o'er days more blest	812 Juan	3	725
They took it up when my days grew more mellow	816 Juan	4	19
Days lay she in that state unchanged, though chill	824 Juan	4	473
Of ancient days, ere tyranny grew strong	824 Juan	4	520
Twelve days and nights she wither'd thus; at last	825 Juan	4	545
By age in earth: her days and pleasures were	825 Juan	4	565
Some days and nights elapsed before that he	826 Juan	4	594
When nights are equal, but not so the days	832 Juan	5	42
For any length of days in such a pickle	833 Juan	5	132
The glittering lime-twigs of our latter days	834 Juan	5	175
But every fool describes in these bright days	838 Juan	5	410
Be in these days?) some infidels, who don't	839 Juan	5	490
Gulbeyaz, for the first time in her days	847 Juan	5	969
Their never knowing their own mind two days	866 Juan	6	934
This was Potemkin--a great thing in days	871 Juan	7	289
Enjoy'd the lonely, vigorous, harmless days	886 Juan	8	487
Motion was in their days, rest in their slumbers	886 Juan	8	529
They must be days: though six days smoothly run	912 Juan	10	303
For one or two days, reader, we request	913 Juan	10	386
They're right; our days are too brief for affording	919 Juan	11	29
(For in those days we had not got to gas	921 Juan	11	176
With regular descent, in these our days	936 Juan	12	420
Epoch, that awkward corner turn'd for days	941 Juan	13	26
The days of Comedy are gone, alas	953 Juan	13	749
Youth fades, and leaves our days no longer sunny	953 Juan	13	797
And the hard frost destroy'd the scenting days	954 Juan	13	844
Sometimes a dance (though rarely on field days	954 Juan	13	857
In my young days, that chaste and goodly veil	958 Juan	14	210
The difference is, that in the days of old	971 Juan	15	201
Days better drawn before, or else assume	971 Juan	15	207
Of deeds and days when they had fill'd the ear	974 Juan	15	365
The nights and days most people can remember	981 Juan	16	86
The charms of other days, in starlight gleams	982 Juan	16	146
And his mass of the days that are gone	985 Juan	16	324
Have 'public days,' when all men may carouse	989 Juan	16	591
I knew him in his livelier London days	991 Juan	16	697
However, the day closed, as days must close	994 Juan	16	849
The love of higher things and better days	994 Juan	16	905
Or (as rhymes may be in these days) much more	995 Juan	16	948
Their tender parents in their budding days	997 Juan	17	6

DAY'S

A name of blood from that day's sanguine rain	65 Harold	4	583
I sought not my home till the day's dying glory	117 Lachin		13
Her day's Meridian now is past	141 Critics		63
Yet thought that a day's separation was long	147 To Anne-A		6
A month's brief lapse, perhaps a day's	153 Friend-A		11
When the day's promise heralds early Spring	185 Julian		58
In dreams that day's broad light can not remove	217 The Harp		20
I defy him to beat this day's wondrous applause	281 Blues	2	39
Medora's heart; the third day's come and gone	356 Corsair	3	68
The long day's march had well withstood	407 Mazeppa		81
Sung sweetly to the rose the day's farewell	424 Island	2	359
Day's broad orb drop behind its head at even	659 Heaven		293
As unemploy'd. Except by one day's knowledge	712 Werner	4	517
Ride a day's hunting on an outworn jade	713 Werner	5	11
For one day's peace, after thrice ten dread years	714 Werner	5	96
Which yielded a day's life, and to their mind	786 Juan	2	788
Seeming to weep the dying day's decay	816 Juan	3	958

DAYS'

(A forty days' precaution 'gainst disease	443 Beppo		196
The nine days' wonder which was brought to light	770 Juan	1	1502

DAYS'

These forty days' advantage of her years	962 Juan	14	409

DAZZLE
(See also OUT-DAZZLE)

To dazzle, though they please, my aching sight	122 Recoll		42
And dazzle not thy deep-blue eyes--but, oh	175 Sonnet-B		5
To dazzle and dismay	181 Ode-A		106

DAZZLED

Dazzled and drunk with beauty, till the heart	62 Harold	4	443
Yet warm not wanton, dazzled but not blind	275 Waltz		150
He raised his head, and dazzled with the light	353 Corsair	2	429
To those who scan all things with dazzled eye	421 Island	2	197
If I e'er felt it, 'tis so dazzled from	688 Werner	2	351
I am not dazzled by this splendid roof	847 Juan	5	1013
Yet she was nothing dazzled by the meteor	975 Juan	15	447

DAZZLES

Wins as it wanders, dazzles where it dwells	3 To Ianthe		30
Which emanated then, and dazzles now	60 Harold	4	338
That dazzles, leads, yet chills the vulgar heart	340 Corsair	1	178
Sure 'tis no father's fondness dazzles me	688 Werner	2	363

DAZZLING

Through views more dazzling unto mortal ken	7 Harold	1	240
Feel all I see, less dazzling, but more warm	46 Harold	3	704
Of words, like sunbeams, dazzling as they past	47 Harold	3	732
These dazzling Meteors but dcccivc	141 Critics		34
It gilds, but it warms not--'tis dazzling, but cold	164 Newstead-C		4
Albeit too dazzling for a dotard's sight	183 Address-D		44
Dazzling as that, oh! too transcendent vision	325 Abydos	1	162
Bewilder'd with the dazzling blast	412 Mazeppa		515
Seen dazzling through the mist of tears	414 Mazeppa		758
Were prouder than more dazzling fame unbless'd	463 Dante	3	185
And dazzling eyes of glory, in whose form	485 Manfred	2	108
The dazzling lightnings till my eyes grew dim	486 Manfred	2	166
Which, having leapt from its more dazzling height	492 Manfred	3	110
A dazzling mass of artificial light	528 Faliero	4	33
An India in itself; yet dazzling not	529 Faliero	4	56
Waved arms, more dazzling with their own born whiteness	577 Sardan	3	395
With dazzling smiles, and wishes audible	597 Foscari	1	102
Not dazzling, and yet drawing us to them	635 Cain	1	513
Distant, and dazzling, and innumerable	643 Cain	2	448
A dazzling mass of gems, and gold, and glitter	843 Juan	5	743
But when she saw his dazzling eye wax dim	913 Juan	10	349

DAZZLINGLY

More dazzlingly when daring in full dress	425 Island	2	457

DE

And who there besides but Corinna de Stael	178 Devil's Dr		195

DEAD

The falchion flash, and o'er the yet warm dead	12 Harold	1	565
Flows there a tear of pity for the dead	18 Harold	1	900
Not Albuera lavish of the dead	18 Harold	1	920
Twined with my heart, and can I deem thee dead	20 Harold	2	75
Like to the apples on the Dead Sea's shore	40 Harold	3	303
Nor of the dead who rise upon our dreams	47 Harold	3	739
My name from out the temple where the dead	56 Harold	4	82
Of her dead Doges are declined to dust	57 Harold	4	128
The cold--the changed--perchance the dead--anew	59 Harold	4	215
No more amidst the meaner dead find room	63 Harold	4	521
While Florence vainly begs her banish'd dead, and weeps	64 Harold	4	531
Freshness in the green turf that wraps the dead	64 Harold	4	537
And Sanguinetto tells ye where the dead	65 Harold	4	584
Lone mother of dead empires, and control	66 Harold	4	696
Thou dost; but all thy foster-babes are dead	68 Harold	4	793
But who was she, the lady of the dead	70 Harold	4	892
With hectic light, the Hesperus of the dead	70 Harold	4	917
Oh, Time! the beautifier of the dead	74 Harold	4	1162
Thy haunts are ever where the dead walls rear	75 Harold	4	1238
Then in this magic circle raise the dead	76 Harold	4	1295
Fond hope of many nations, art thou dead	80 Harold	4	1505
The husband of a year! the father of the dead	80 Harold	4	1521
And, when the grave restores her dead	85 To D--		9
My Lesbia's favourite bird is dead	87 Catullus		3
When calling the dead, in earth's bosom laid low	91 Caroline-C		24
Perhaps they will leave unmolested the dead	92 Caroline-D		24
While naught divides thee from the vulgar dead	94 Dorset		49
'Here's to my boy! alive or dead	104 Alva		227
Come, drink remembrance of the dead	104 Alva		231
Which rises o'er a warrior dead	105 Alva		298
And Latian spoils and purpled heaps of dead	107 Nisus		113
And, last, his lord is number'd with the dead	108 Nisus		249
'Mid the sad flock at dead of night he prowls	109 Nisus		261
And lingering beauty hovers round the dead	110 Nisus		384
When civil discord piled the fields with dead	111 Examination		14
To friendship dead, though not untaught to feel	112 Examination		61
Would mangle still the dead, perverting truth	114 Death-A		6

DEAD

For noble spirits 'war not with the dead	114	Death-A	14
'Shades of the dead! have I not heard your voices	117	Lachin	17
From ruffian fangs escape not e'en the dead	121	Newstead-A	87
Thy vaults where dead of feudal ages sleep	122	Newstead-A	142
Affection is not dead	131	L'Amitie	4
Though doom'd no more to quit the dead	133	Prayer	60
When all its former hopes are dead	135	I Would	28
When persecution's arm is dead	137	Clare	53
And mingle with the dead	146	Adieu	80
Remembrance still hallows the dust of the dead	149	Newstead-B	36
And rhyme and revel with the dead	154	Skull	20
Reflect on me as on the dead	157	Album	7
A dirge, an anthem o'er the dead	166	Away	12
Though cold as e'en the dead can be	166	Struggle	47
To that which cannot quit the dead	166	Struggle	56
The dreamless sleep that lulls the dead	166	Euthanasia	2
And thou art dead, as young and fair	167	Dead	1
Nor hoard your honours idly for the dead	170	Address-A	41
For the field ran so red with the blood of the dead	176	Devil's Dr	40
Deep for the dead the grief must be	184	Parker	35
Such glory o'er the quick and dead	188	On Star	2
The silent cities of the dead	189	On Star	38
Till hunger clung them, or the dropping dead	189	Darkness	50
The waves were dead; the tides were in their grave	190	Darkness	78
And being so--the absent are the dead	191	Fragment-C	11
The absent are the dead--for they are cold	192	Fragment-C	15
The dead are thy inheritors--and we	192	Fragment-C	33
The Moorish King, and doom'd him dead	195	Ballad-A	69
Wrecks and the dead upon the rocky shore	201	Ode-C	33
And Thou the Vestal of the Dead	201	Ode-C	58
Of an Irishman's heart, that I envy--thy dead	204	Avatar	124
And the bard in my bosom is dead	205	Blessington	10
Voice which proclaim'd 'the Mighty Pan is dead	205	Aristom	4
Than the wail above the dead	207	Fare Thee	30
Fond wretch! as if her step disturb'd the dead	218	Bloom	10
Thou whose spell can raise the dead	219	Saul-B	1
Who is he that calls the dead	219	Saul-B	16
And is she dead?--and did they dare	221	Mariamne	9
As dead as her dead leaf those mute harps must be	223	Valley	10
I'm almost dead, and always dizzy	232	Doctor	88
A live lord must be worth two dead	238	Orford	7
The dead have been awaken'd--shall I sleep	240	Cephalonia	1
Or damn the dead with purgatorial praise	246	Bards	312
Not raised thy hoof against the lion dead	247	Bards	382
Aged or young, the living or the dead	247	Bards	432
Degenerate Britons! are ye dead to shame	250	Bards	610
Some merry manuscript of mimes, when dead	261	Hints	350
Not all the living only, but the dead	266	Hints	719
Thrills the lone heart like echoes from the dead	269	Minerva	70
And glares the Nemesis of native dead	271	Minerva	224
He's dead--and upper earth with him has done	286	Vision	89
'No,' quoth the cherub; 'George the Third is dead	287	Vision	137
Now dead, and brought before the Lord? What ill	289	Vision	298
He who hath bent him o'er the dead	311	Giaour	68
The only constant mourner o'er the dead	313	Giaour	287
The Koran verse that mourns the dead	317	Giaour	726
It is as if the dead could feel	319	Giaour	945
Of joys long dead; my hope, their doom	320	Giaour	1001
But he is dead! within the dell	323	Giaour	1302
Then lay me with the humblest dead	323	Giaour	1324
Far better with the dead to be	330	Abydos	2	176
Thy Daughter's dead	336	Abydos	2	658
When Ocean shrouds and sepulchres our dead	338	Corsair	1	36
Grief for the dead not Virtue can reprove	343	Corsair	1	360
But gather'd breathing from the happier dead	351	Corsair	2	274
But here is one denies that he is dead	357	Corsair	3	108
Will save him living or appease him dead	357	Corsair	3	128
When every hour might doom him worse than dead	358	Corsair	3	211
That fearful spot which stain'd it from the dead	363	Corsair	3	536
Which hands profane had gather'd from the dead	368	Lara	1	144
Of one that haunts him still, alive or dead	377	Lara	2	156
And Carnage smiled upon her daily dead	379	Lara	2	281
Day glimmers on the dying and the dead	380	Lara	2	394
His face was mask'd--the features of the dead	383	Lara	2	588
If dead it were, escaped the observer's dread	383	Lara	2	589
But some are dead, and some are gone	384	Corinth	24
And thought upon the glorious dead	388	Corinth	394
Hold o'er the dead their carnival	389	Corinth	455
As they lazily mumbled the bones of the dead	389	Corinth	462
Than the perishing dead who are past all pain	389	Corinth	484
O'er the weltering field of the tombless dead	389	Corinth	490
In the midst of the dying and the dead	390	Corinth	582
The dead before him, on that day	393	Corinth	784
Contain'd the dead of ages gone	395	Corinth	966
There were dead above, and the dead below	395	Corinth	973
In masses by the fleshless dead	395	Corinth	980
With barbarous blows they gash the dead	395	Corinth	990
All that of living or dead remain	395	Corinth	1018
And heedless as the dead are they	396	Corinth	33
And howling left the unburied dead	396	Corinth	1060
Shall witness for thee from the dead	399	Parisina	249

DEAD

And o'er the dead our coursers driven	399	Parisina	303
The song for the dead below	400	Parisina	392
A mind all dead to scorn or praise	402	Parisina	548
Nor reach his dying hand--nor dead	404	Chillon	146
That nip the forest's foliage dead	411	Mazeppa	474
Link'd to the dead and stiffening wretch	413	Mazeppa	710
The dying on the dead	413	Mazeppa	715
To keep, some days, the dying from the dead	416	Island	1	90
We'll cull the flowers that grow above the dead	419	Island	2	7
Which to the dead a lingering fame conveys	420	Island	2	80
There was a dead hue of eternity	431	Island	4	90
'Tis ours to bear, not judge the dead; and they	435	Island	4	353
In law he was almost as good as dead, he	444	Beppo	276
That he's alive, he's dead, or should be so	444	Beppo	280
A drunken man's dead eye in maudlin sorrow	445	Beppo	340
And their dead palates chew'd the cud of pain	454	Venice-B	91
She drank no blood, nor fatten'd on the dead	454	Venice-B	112
Of Tiber, thick with dead. The helpless priest	459	Dante	2	80
The chiefless army of the dead, which late	459	Dante	2	92
The dead whose tomb Oblivion never knew	460	Dante	2	115
But more than dead, he seem'd so stupefied	470	Morgante	256
And by the way about the giants dead	472	Morgante	385
How much I grieve about my brethren dead	472	Morgante	419
That they are dead, and have no further fear	472	Morgante	426
Smashing the very bone; and he fell dead	473	Morgante	508
With the dead boars and with that brimful vase	474	Morgante	518
But the horse, sinking with the pain, fell dead	474	Morgante	541
To lift or carry this dead courser, who	474	Morgante	567
'Take care he don't revenge himself, though dead	474	Morgante	569
The penalty who lie dead in yon grot	474	Morgante	580
And fell down even as a dead body falls	477	Francesca	46
Must wake the dead, or lay me low with them	487	Manfred	2	246
Still in my science--I can call the dead	487	Manfred	2	271
Frozen in a moment--a dead whirlpool's image	487	Manfred	2	306
The blest are the dead	488	Manfred	2	346
Call up the dead--my question is for them	489	Manfred	2	449
The dead, but sceptred sovereigns, who still rule	495	Manfred	3	300
The floor which doth divide us from the dead	519	Faliero	3	17
Till thine aisles be peopled with the dead	519	Faliero	3	28
And, if there be a spell to stir the dead	520	Faliero	3	97
And seeming not all dead, as long as two	525	Faliero	3	457
Where the Dead Sea hath quench'd two cities' ashes	526	Faliero	3	544
As were the dead who lay around me: this	534	Faliero	4	447
Weapons, and forced them! Are you sure he's dead	549	Faliero	5	826
Which sleeps at times, but is not dead within thee	557	Sardan	1	430
The worship of dead men; feeling that I	565	Sardan	2	240
And dinn'd, and deafen'd with dead men and Baal	566	Sardan	2	250
Than a scared beldam's dreaming of the dead	567	Sardan	2	350
From a dead soldier's grasp;--all these things made	577	Sardan	3	397
All that the dead dare gloomily raise up	579	Sardan	4	36
A legion of the dead. And so have I	579	Sardan	4	64
Throng'd thick and shapeless: I was dead, yet feeling	580	Sardan	4	160
She's dead--and you have slain her. 'Tis the mere	584	Sardan	4	417
Dead. And Altada? Dying. Pania? Sfero	589	Sardan	5	139
Hath piled in her brick mountains, o'er dead kings	595	Sardan	5	483
Alive, or dead, for prince or paladin	604	Foscari	2	161
Were never piled on high save o'er the dead	609	Foscari	3	73
Dead, but still bear me to a native grave	617	Foscari	4	147
He's gone! He's free! No--no, he is not dead	618	Foscari	4	193
Ah! the devil come to insult the dead! Avaunt	618	Foscari	4	218
To flow through the dead lips of Foscari	618	Foscari	4	241
Humanity! Because his son is dead	619	Foscari	4	259
His sons--and he had four--are dead, without	619	Foscari	4	284
Is dead; so is young Foscari and his brethren	619	Foscari	4	304
And my dead father. Are you then thus fix'd	620	Foscari	4	321
His sons all dead, his family depress'd	620	Foscari	4	326
Envy the dead. My lord, if you indeed	624	Foscari	5	235
I thought the dead had been beyond even you	626	Foscari	5	334
Grief is fantastical, and loves the dead	626	Foscari	5	341
Have roll'd o'er your dead ashes, and your seed's	631	Cain	1	231
Thou seekest to behold death and dead things	639	Cain	2	191
I know not. Nor what thou hast seen? The dead	648	Cain	3	177
Still yearn for their dead offspring? or the pangs	650	Cain	3	301
His eyes are open! then he is not dead	651	Cain	3	337
But he cannot be dead!--Is silence death	651	Cain	3	349
To strew it with the dead. May all the curses	652	Cain	3	421
Depart and leave the dead to me--I am	653	Cain	3	445
I will not leave thee lonely with the dead	654	Cain	3	527
Let us depart together. Oh, thou dead	654	Cain	3	528
But which is best, a dead eternity	667	Heaven	901
Blessed are the dead	670	Heaven	1148
We know not if his excellency's dead	675	Werner	1	219
It may turn out with the live or dead body	675	Werner	1	228
Is dead near Prague, in his castle, and my lord	684	Werner	2	80
Not thieves. The dead, who feel nought, can lose nothing	695	Werner	2	762

DEAD

As from mine eyes! But Stralenheim is dead	702	Werner	3	478
The daughter of dead Stralenheim, your foe	710	Werner	4	383
Thou villainous gold, and thy dead master's doom	711	Werner	4	443
And every mass no less sung for the dead	711	Werner	4	472
For whom shall mass be said? For--for--the dead	711	Werner	4	476
Of our dead enemies is worthy those	712	Werner	4	489
You said, and to none else. At dead of night	717	Werner	5	306
Oh! my dead father's curse! 'tis working now	719	Werner	5	434
Clay! not dead, but soul-less	728	Deformed	1	452
And it is clogg'd with dead even to the door	739	Deformed	2	273
You touch me not alive. Alive or dead	739	Deformed	2	298
Alive or dead, thou essence of all beauty	739	Deformed	2	380
As dust can. Then she is dead! Bah! bah! You are so	741	Deformed	2	394
Softly! As softly as they bear the dead	741	Deformed	2	400
Wishing each other, not divorced, but dead	750	Juan	1	203
Dead scandals form good subjects for dissection	751	Juan	1	248
The languages, especially the dead	752	Juan	1	313
Arose a clatter might awake the dead	763	Juan	1	1083
They won't lay out their money on the dead	781	Juan	2	439
You hardly could perceive when he was dead	783	Juan	2	604
And then they left off eating the dead body	784	Juan	2	656
Death left no doubt, and the dead burthen lay	785	Juan	2	715
And tried to awaken them, but found them dead	786	Juan	2	784
And three dead, whom their strength could not avail	787	Juan	2	805
Insensible,--not dead, but nearly so	790	Juan	2	1027
Juan slept like a top, like the dead	791	Juan	2	1066
Such appetite in one she had deem'd dead	794	Juan	2	1260
Save on the dead long summer days, which make	796	Juan	2	1415
A second hiccup'd, 'Our old master's dead	806	Juan	3	341
But certainly to one deem'd dead, returning	807	Juan	3	391
If all the dead could now return to life	807	Juan	3	393
A remnant of our Spartan dead	812	Juan	3	728
Ah! no;--the voices of the dead	812	Juan	3	732
Haidee and Juan thought not of the dead	818	Juan	4	97
Pale as the foam that froth'd on his dead brow	820	Juan	4	266
And gazing on the dead, she thought his face	820	Juan	4	273
No hideous sign proclaim'd her surely dead	824	Juan	4	476
Rather the dead, for life seem'd something new	824	Juan	4	490
The very generations of the dead	829	Juan	4	809
Of gore divulged the cause) that he was dead	835	Juan	5	279
And air--earth--water--fire live--and we dead	836	Juan	5	310
'Will it?' said Juan, sharply: 'Strike me dead	840	Juan	5	567
But on they march'd, dead bodies trampling o'er	880	Juan	8	149
Of dead and dying thousands,--sometimes gaining	880	Juan	8	154
And so, when all his corps were dead or dying	882	Juan	8	281
His soul (like galvanism upon the dead	883	Juan	8	326
Was from a pistol-shot that laid him dead	888	Juan	8	642
Her hidden heart was plunged amidst the dead	890	Juan	8	739
The old Pacha sits among some hundreds dead	890	Juan	8	779
White, black, or copper--the dead bones will grin	898	Juan	9	96
Which augur'd of the dead, however quick	912	Juan	10	309
The list grows long of live and dead pretenders	925	Juan	11	473
Her late performance had been a dead set	960	Juan	14	335
It were much better to be wed or dead	963	Juan	14	509
Now here I've got the preacher at a dead lock	972	Juan	15	280
All nations have believed that from the dead	981	Juan	16	51
But by dim lights the portraits of the dead	982	Juan	16	135
The man was well-nigh dead, ere men begun	997	Juan	17	61

DEAD-FLOWER

'Tis but as a dead-flower with May-dew besprinkled	204	Pisa		6

DEADLIER

And nearer, clearer, deadlier than before	38	Harold	3	197
The cup must hold a deadlier draught	168	Haunts		19
That conflict, deadlier far than all before	358	Corsair	3	219
Are things in Venice deadlier than the laws	530	Faliero	4	148
Your own; and, deadlier for ye, on my fears	566	Sardan	2	282
With deadlier engines and a speedier blow	877	Juan	7	635
Closer, that all the deadlier they might wring	893	Juan	8	941

DEADLIEST

The death-bolt's deadliest the thinn'd files along	39	Harold	3	259
Although to death or deadliest ill	321	Giaour		1148
Although thy Sire's my deadliest foe	331	Abydos	2	196
To Love, whose deadliest bane is human Art	334	Abydos	2	459
That owes its deadliest efforts to despair	343	Corsair	1	328
All--all--before--beyond--the deadliest fall	352	Corsair	3	359
The deadliest sin to love as we have loved	490	Manfred	2	493
Even to your deadliest foe; and he, as 'twere	690	Werner	2	455
I am his deadliest foe. You? After such	696	Werner	3	79
The deadliest and the stanchest. Better still	712	Werner	4	487

DEADLY

Sheathed in his form the deadly weapon lies	16	Harold	1	784
Their wrath how deadly! but their friendship sure	29	Harold	2	583
The grave of France, the deadly Waterloo	37	Harold	3	155
Which feeds these deadly branches: for it were	40	Harold	3	300
Because the deadly days which we have seen	69	Harold	4	868

DEADLY

And root from out the soul the deadly weed which cloys	73	Harold	4	1071
With deadly languor droops my head	87	Ad Lesbiam		18
On foes his deadly vengeance fell	102	Alva		76
On his with deadly fury placed	104	Alva		240
Who, for thy sake, war's deadly peril shared	106	Nisus		76
And clear thy road with many a deadly blow	108	Nisus		236
Nor less the other's deadly vengeance came	109	Nisus		265
Once, and but once, she aim'd a deadly blow	123	Recoil		81
The deadly bullet turn'd apart	201	Ode-C		64
The angry essence of her deadly will	208	Sketch		46
And the eyes of the sleepers wax'd deadly and chill	222	Sennacherib		11
So coldly sweet, so deadly fair	311	Giaour		92
Even Azrael, from his deadly quiver	327	Abydos	1	323
What need of words? the deadly bowl	331	Abydos	2	236
Too nearly, deadly aim'd to err	335	Abydos	2	575
Ev'n in that deadly grove	336	Abydos	2	671
Of women struck, and like a deadly knell	350	Corsair	2	200
He bled, and fell; but not with deadly wound	376	Lara	2	69
And still, all deadly aim'd and hot	394	Corinth		939
That deadly earth-shock disappear'd	396	Corinth		1058
As down the deadly blow descended	401	Parisina		481
In hands as steel'd to do the deadly rest	416	Island	1	74
As swept off sooner; in all deadly things	465	Dante	4	121
But being met is deadly,--such hath been	493	Manfred	3	133
But for the effect, the deadly deep impression	509	Faliero	2	34
That make such deadly to the sense of man	512	Faliero	2	247
Have made them deadly; if there be amongst them	524	Faliero	3	421
And deadly face--I could not recognise it	579	Sardan	4	85
With deadly cozenage, eight long months before-hand	619	Foscari	4	301
By some strange destiny, to him proved deadly	621	Foscari	5	80
The life-tree? He was hinder'd. Deadly error	631	Cain	1	292
The tree was true, though deadly. These dim realms	641	Cain	2	372
Its deadly opposite. I lately saw	643	Cain	2	494
Deadly, without being natural prey to either	687	Werner	2	280
Have ne'er return'd: that fever was most deadly	707	Werner	4	187
Its way with all deformity's dull, deadly	727	Deformed	1	330
With the deep deadly thought that they must part	785	Juan	2	704
Deadly, and quick, and crushing; yet, as real	799	Juan	2	1591
Love's the first net which spreads its deadly mesh	834	Juan	5	173
Grow deadly pale, and then blush back again	847	Juan	5	992
Deep in the caverns of the deadly tide	866	Juan	6	916
Will oftentimes make deadly quarrels burst	884	Juan	8	379
My Juan, whom I left in deadly peril	926	Juan	11	497
Some deadly shots too, Septembrizers, seen	991	Juan	16	683
Inflicted on the dish a deadly wound	992	Juan	16	750

DEAF

With a deaf heart which never seem'd to be	68	Harold	4	815
Now so deaf to duty's prayer	187	French-A		26
And the deaf tyranny of Fate	191	Prometheus-B		19
Would to God I were deaf! as I'm not, I'll be dumb	280	Blues	2	25
My voice; but as the adder, deaf and fierce	456	Dante	1	65
Upon your lives, I say. What, deaf or drunken	564	Sardan	2	176
Or deaf obedient ocean which fulfils it	662	Heaven		548
And deaf, that any other it would vex	765	Juan	1	1172
They were mis-shapen pignies, deaf and dumb	842	Juan	5	703
And shriek for water into a deaf ear	879	Juan	8	85

DEAFEN'D

The devils ran howling, deafen'd, down to hell	297	Vision		819
And dinn'd, and deafen'd with dead men and Baal	566	Sardan	2	250
The very cannon, deafen'd by the din	885	Juan	8	469
The loudest wit I e'er was deafen'd with	991	Juan	16	696

DEAL

Deal round to happy fools its speechless obloquy	75	Harold	4	1224
A devilish deal more sad than witty	147	To Author		2
Translates, misunderstood, a deal of German	231	Sotheby		2
Sorry, Sir, but I cannot deal	232	Doctor		85
I thought you had publish'd a good deal not long since	236	Nonsense		3
A good deal older--Bless me! is he blind	293	Vision		544
A good deal like a vulture in the face	296	Vision		746
Its grasp well-used to deal the sabre-stroke	376	Lara	2	60
For sometimes they contain a deal of fun	442	Beppo		159
Nor deal (thank God for that!) in mathematics	450	Beppo		624
But for all that, there is a deal of swearing	451	Beppo		687
Can deal that justice on the self-condemn'd	492	Manfred	3	77
Let us but deal upon them, and I care not	516	Faliero	2	565
Even to the last? but let them deal upon us	537	Faliero	4	636
Of those who fain must deal perforce with vice	613	Foscari	3	349
Else you dare not deal thus by them or me	624	Foscari	5	258
Deal out in his long homilies, 'tis a thing	639	Cain	2	222
Nothing--but there's a good deal to be said	684	Werner	2	63
Or deal you in the black art? I deal plainly	697	Werner	3	132
With whom you have to deal. I know too well	721	Werner	5	506
A good deal like him too, though quite the same none	747	Juan	1	35

DEAL
A good deal may be bought for fifty Louis   760 Juan   1   864
All these confirm my statement a good deal   771 Juan   1 1621
And in thy stead I've got a deal of judgment   773 Juan   1 1719
By which, no doubt, a good deal may be made   790 Juan   2 1008
Deal with me as thou wilt, but spare this boy   821 Juan   4   304
Last carnival she made a deal of strife   827 Juan   4   662
(Of which I might have a good deal to say   836 Juan   5   331
There seem'd to be besprent a deal of gilding   837 Juan   5   363
A good deal practised here upon occasion   843 Juan   5   736
She was a good deal shock'd; not shock'd at tears 846 Juan   5   937
And yawn'd a good deal with discreet surprise   861 Juan   6   584
When, after a good deal of heavy firing   881 Juan   8   215
Of present life a good deal more than we   891 Juan   8   795
Though there's a shorter a good deal than this   932 Juan   12   172
I therefore deal in generalities   965 Juan   14   640

DEALER
(See also PICTURE-DEALER)
Also a dealer in the sword and dagger   738 Deformed 2   205
From town, viz., architect and dealer, were   989 Juan   16   573

DEALING
That the sinner should suffer is only fair
  dealing   238 Pangs   7
Dealing wounds with every blow   394 Corinth   917
Robed in official purple, dealing out   522 Faliero 3   256
Ye treated him:--you did so, in so dealing   606 Foscari 2   315

DEALINGS
Are all thy dealings, but in this they pass   465 Dante   4   142

DEALS
The tongue in flattering falsehood deals   112 Quaker   15
Which deals the daily pittance of our span   423 Island   2   350
He deals on his own soul. All this is well   492 Manfred 3   78
Besides, my Muse by no means deals in fiction   957 Juan   14   97

DEALT
By their new vigour, sternly have they dealt   48 Harold   3   782
Have dealt upon the seven-hill'd city's pride   67 Harold   4   713
And thus they dealt the combat side by side   124 Recoll   174
His guards had led him, though they gently dealt 288 Vision   206
With sabre stroke right sharply dealt   326 Abydos   1   249
And the last death-blow dealt his hand   335 Abydos   2   562
Let them be dealt upon. And now to action   526 Faliero 3   507
Remember what these men have dealt to thee   528 Faliero 3   652
A service, till our foes are dealt upon   533 Faliero 4   363
As we had dealt on them, but with less pomp   537 Faliero 4   637
'Justice hath dealt upon the mighty Traitor   549 Faliero 5   828
He dealt in such? Most sure. And yet he seems   619 Foscari 4   286
The largess shall be only dealt in alms   711 Werner   4   471
Famine long hath dealt their rations   736 Deformed 2   58
To the Gazette--which doubtless fairly dealt   880 Juan   8   138
Those haughty shopkeepers, who sternly dealt   915 Juan   10   518
The most sincere that ever dealt in fiction   980 Juan   16   16

DEAN
The slightest motion would displease the Dean   112 Examination   38
You doubt--see Dryden, Pope, St. Patrick's dean   258 Hints   116
A difference ''twixt a bishop and a dean   991 Juan   16   717

DEAR
This much, dear maid, accord; nor question why   3 To Ianthe   34
Yea! none did love him--not his lemans dear   5 Harold   1   77
A few dear objects, will in sadness feel   5 Harold   1   89
Her fate, to every freeborn bosom dear   14 Harold   1   642
And mould to every taste thy dear delusive shape   14 Harold   1   665
Dear to a heart where nought was left so dear   19 Harold   1   937
None so desolate but something dear   23 Harold   2   212
Nor ask so dear a breast to feel one pang for mine 24 Harold   2   270
Dear Nature is the kindest mother still   25 Harold   2   325
Forgets that pride to pamper'd priesthood dear   26 Harold   2   390
As on the morn to distant Glory dear   33 Harold   2   842
In glens which might have made even exile dear   43 Harold   3   463
For I have cherish'd them as dear   44 Harold   3   520
To nature and to me so dear   44 Harold   3   533
Could thy dear eyes in following mine   44 Harold   3   534
Nor yet forget how Venice once was dear   55 Harold   4   25
Where all lies founder'd that was ever dear   70 Harold   4   942
And reap from earth, sea, joy almost as dear   81 Harold   4 1583
Yet is remembrance of those virtues dear   85 Death-B   21
On thy dear breast I'll lay my head   85 To D--   11
Oh, Friend, for ever loved, for ever dear   85 Epitaph   1
Dear, simple girl, those flattering arts   86 Rousseau   5
Far from my dear maternal home   88 Anacreon-B   16
Which tears me far from one so dear   89 To Emma   7
Perhaps, dear girl! for me thou'lt prize   92 Lady-A   2
Then read, dear girl! with feeling read   92 Lady-A   9
More dear is the beam of the past to my soul   97 Harrow-A   32
Sweet copy! far more dear to me   98 To Mary   17
They blest her dear propitious light   101 Alva   18
More dear thy worth and valour than my own   106 Nisus   55
Without thy dear advice, no great design   107 Nisus   168

DEAR
So dear a hope must all my soul inflame   108 Nisus   193
But bless'd thy mother in so dear a son   108 Nisus   204
To Turnus dear, a prophet and a prince   108 Nisus   241
Whose dear remains in honour'd marble sleep   114 Death-A   30
My Mary to Love once so dear   115 The Tear   30
And think that eye to truth was dear   118 Romance   30
Or, dear to youth, portrays each childish scene   122 Recoll   15
Friendship, the dear peculiar bond of youth   123 Recoll   57
The dear preceptor of my early days   123 Recoll   108
Dear honest race! though now we meet no more   124 Recoll   185
The smiles of beauty, though those smiles were
  dear   125 Recoll   201
Which whispers friendship will be doubly dear   125 Recoll   214
Those hearts, dear Ida, have I found in thee   125 Recoll   217
And none more dear than Ida's social band   125 Recoll   242
Oh! friends regretted, scenes for ever dear   126 Recoll   341
Is not so dear to me as this   128 Lady-C   10
By the dear head on which you grow   128 Lady-C   19
Dear Becher, you tell me to mix with mankind   128 Becher-A   1
Dear are the days of youth! Age dwells   129 Calmar
Each dear associate seems to say   132 L'Amitie   49
Dear Long, in this sequester'd scene   133 E. N. Long   1
In truth, dear Long, 'twas time to flee   134 E. N. Long   69
But now, dear Long, 'tis midnight's noon   134 E. N. Long   87
For thy dear sake I cannot hate him   134 Lady-D   16
No feeling, save one, to my bosom was dear   135 Highlander   7
More dear were the scenes which my infancy knew   136 Highlander   30
Oh yes, I will own we were dear to each other   136 Delawarr   1
However, dear George, for I still must esteem you 136 Delawarr   17
In truth, dear Clare, in fancy's flight   138 Clare   70
To me were doubly dear   138 Clare   99
And this will form a dear employ   141 Pignus   31
For dear I was to him who gave it   141 Pignus   32
To retrospection dear   145 Adieu   44
In that dear moment quite forgot   146 Adieu   69
And, wert thou still less dear to me   150 My Son   33
Why wert thou so dear   151 When We   20
Such precious drops are doubly dear   152 Weep-A   15
And who that dear loved one may be   156 Lady-F   49
Dear object of defeated care   161 Picture   1
The kiss, dear maid! thy lip has left   162 Parting   1
By all unto thy bosom dear   164 Friend-B   16
It was not thus in days more dear   166 Struggle   13
Nor deem that memory less dear   168 Haunts   13
That last dear duty to fulfil   168 Haunts   30
Dear are the days which made our annals bright   170 Address-A   42
I heard, before, from one so dear   173 Mrs. Lamb   3
Why did I hold thy love so dear   174 Revanche   5
My frenzy drew from eyes so dear   174 Remember-B   43
Dear words! on which my heart had doted   175 Portuguese-A   3
Adieu, dear maid! I must not speak   179 Gold   33
Fair Freedom! we may hold thee dear   181 Ode-A   86
Of half its bitterness for one so dear   183 Address-C   34
Where one so dear, so dauntless, fell   184 Parker   28
And yet thou wert surpassing dear   186 Stanzas-A   3
Dear as both have been to me   187 French-A   6
Nameless, but dear to gentle hearts below   192 Monody   14
Ye Bards! to whom the Drama's Muse is dear   194 Monody   105
The dear connection   200 Stanzas-B   63
Much that is awful, more that's dear   200 Ode-C   4
For him, the dear One in thine eyes   201 Ode-C   53
Than to see the bright eyes of the dear one
  discover   204 Pisa   11
I did remind thee of our own dear Lake   212 Moore-A   73
How pure, how dear their dwelling-place   216 She Walks   12
If in this heart a hope be dear   218 Soul-B   5
But dear to those presiding at the helm   227 Answer-C   4
I'm your man 'of all measures,' dear Tom,--so
  here goes   227 Moore-A   2
Dear Doctor, I have read your play   231 Doctor   1
Dear Doctor, I am yours   232 Doctor   90
My dear Mr. Murray   232 Murray-B   1
His songs at sixpence would be dear   233 Ballad-B   15
By your own dear native Highlands   240 Suliotes   9
To turgid ode and tumid stanza dear   245 Bards   256
Dear authors! suit your topics to your strength   257 Hints   59
Because it costs him dear, and makes him dress   261 Hints   316
Times dear alike to puritan or pope   262 Hints   376
Dear, d--d contemner of my schoolboy songs   265 Hints   605
But Lusitania, kind and dear ally   271 Minerva   233
To what purpose? You know, my dear friend, that
  in prose   279 Blues   1   87
But consider, dear Inkel, she's one of the 'Blues 279 Blues   1   100
Nay, stay, my dear fellow--consider--I'm wrong   279 Blues   1   103
And you know, my dear fellow, how heartily I   279 Blues   1   119
And you, Mr. Botherby--Oh, my dear lady   281 Blues   2   32
Never mind our friend Inkel; we all know, my dear 281 Blues   2   57
While you live, my dear Botherby, never defend   281 Blues   2   72
And my Lord Seventy-four, who protects our dear
  Bard   282 Blues   2   117
Oh! my dear Mr. Botherby! sympathise!--I   282 Blues   2   129
So shall he be in spirit, although dear   289 Vision   309
'Why, my dear Lucifer, would you abuse   292 Vision   497

DEAR

Such trash below your wing, Asmodeus dear	296 Vision		702
To seize and share the dear caress	316 Giaour		646
Yet dear to him my blighted name	322 Giaour		1227
As something welcome, new, and dear	322 Giaour		1264
Those gibes had cost another dear	324 Abydos	1	110
Oh! more than ev'n her mother dear	325 Abydos	1	149
How dear this very day must tell	326 Abydos	1	194
Oh, Selim dear! oh, more than dearest	327 Abydos	1	299
As heaven itself to Selim dear	330 Abydos	2	90
Oh! who so dear with him could dwell	330 Abydos	2	112
Is boiling; but for thy dear sake	331 Abydos	2	208
Dear--as his native song to Exile's ears	333 Abydos	2	406
How dear the dream in darkest hours of ill	333 Abydos	2	420
Friends', husbands', lovers' names in each dear word	339 Corsair	1	110
What sudden spell hath made this man so dear	353 Corsair	2	424
'Twill cost me dear--but dread no death to-day	355 Corsair	2	534
Oh! too convincing, dangerously dear	355 Corsair	2	543
If that thy heart to hers were truly dear	360 Corsair	3	300
I was not treacherous then, nor thou too dear	360 Corsair	3	325
'Gulnare!'--but she replied not--'dear Gulnare	363 Corsair	3	541
Those accents, as his native mountains dear	373 Lara	1	522
But never did clasp of one so dear	391 Corinth		601
Those relics of a home so dear	403 Chillon		102
Like his dear vessel, spoke his former state	425 Island	2	477
That sad fatality hath cost me dear	438 Tasso		141
To less than monarchs that thou couldst be dear	439 Tasso		230
I like a seacoal fire, when not too dear	446 Beppo		378
The poor dear Mussulwomen whom I mention	449 Beppo		609
And mine at least hath cost me dear: to die	458 Dante	1	158
Shall live, outliving all thou holdest dear	464 Dante	4	115
Dear abbot,' Roland unto him replied	469 Morgante		212
As to a brother dear I speak alone	469 Morgante		222
I cannot fix them. Patience, my dear uncle	501 Faliero	1	84
Who hath a home whose hearth is dear to him	503 Faliero	1	216
My fathers' and my birthplace, whose dear spires	506 Faliero	1	464
To human ties, and all that's good and dear	525 Faliero	3	438
Thou holdest dear on earth or heaven--by all	530 Faliero	4	171
Save this. Thou must not die! and think how dear	532 Faliero	4	307
Dear Cain! Nay, do not whisper o'er our son	646 Cain	3	35
Oh! think of her who holds thee dear	655 Heaven		44
Yet, Seraph dear	656 Heaven		60
Dear, dearest in themselves, and scarce less dear	666 Heaven		822
The depth beneath us hides our own dear land	668 Heaven		965
Oh! my dear father's tents, my place of birth	669 Heaven		1044
Sick, poor, and lonely. Lonely! my dear husband	672 Werner	1	64
That which will send you hence. Patience, dear Werner	674 Werner	1	208
In Tuscany, my own dear sunny land	682 Werner	1	708
Mine inn is like to cost me dear. I heard	687 Werner	2	303
Himself around all that is dear and noble	690 Werner	2	448
Dear Ulric, if I do not interrupt you	706 Werner	4	152
But I can wait! Dear Ida! Call me Ida	707 Werner	4	172
You have mine--you have me. Dear Ulric, how I wish	707 Werner	4	175
No true knight.--Come, dear Ulric! yield to me	707 Werner	4	212
In aspect and demeanour. True, dear child	708 Werner	4	245
Dear mother, I am with you. Is he not found	714 Werner	5	74
Thank Heav'n, I see you safe! Safe! Yes, dear father	721 Werner	5	543
By harbouring some dear friend extremely vicious	759 Juan	1	789
Dear is the helpless creature we defend	762 Juan	1	1006
Against the world; and dear the schoolboy spot	762 Juan	1	1007
'My dear, I was the first who came away	764 Juan	1	1128
Nothing so dear as an unfilch'd good name	767 Juan	1	1317
To whom she knew his mother's fame was dear	768 Juan	1	1408
So dear is still the memory of that dream	770 Juan	1	1540
A pleasure--like all pleasures--rather dear	794 Juan	2	1675
'I will, my dear Philosophy!' I said	800 Juan	2	1675
With his dear 'Waggoners,' around his lakes	814 Juan	3	876
Whate'er our household gods protect of dear	815 Juan	3	950
Dear unto all, but dearest to their eyes	818 Juan	4	154
Dear as her father had been to Haidee	821 Juan	4	286
However dear or cherish'd in their day	824 Juan	4	508
(Plain truth, dear Murray, needs few flowers of speech	844 Juan	5	802
I'm puzzled what to do with you, my dear	858 Juan	6	363
Out of their hides, if parchment had grown dear	869 Juan	7	135
Of deeds to human happiness most dear	877 Juan	7	662
Defended at a price extremely dear	888 Juan	8	632
As the last link with all she had held dear	890 Juan	8	758
Is rather dear!--I'm sure I mean no harm	897 Juan	9	56
He strips from man that mantle (far more dear	898 Juan	9	94
Dear Jeffrey, once my most redoubted foe	909 Juan	10	122
Thy cliffs, dear Dover! harbour, and hotel	916 Juan	10	546
A country in all senses the most dear	917 Juan	10	613
But what they please; and if that things be dear	919 Juan	11	74
In the dear offices of peace or war	923 Juan	11	323
A lover with caprices soft and dear	963 Juan	14	500
And deem'd that fallen worship far more dear	974 Juan	15	363

DEAR-BOUGHT

No dear-bought knowledge purchased by deceit	123 Recoll		64
Like them, too, without the so dear-bought knowledge	641 Cain	2	365

DEARER

Dearer than self, possesses or possess'd	23 Harold	2	213
Perchance even dearer in her day of woe	58 Harold	4	161
Whom dearer than her eyes she loved	87 Catullus		4
Now dearer as my peaceful home	111 Medea		34
Yet still are you dearer than Albion's plain	118 Lachin		36
Dearer than all the joys I've known	137 Clare		8
With time the gift is dearer grown	141 Pignus		14
On me 'twill hold a dearer claim	158 Florence		39
And every fragment dearer grown	168 Cornelian-B		6
With him unto thy bosom dearer	173 Quotation		29
Dearer and purer were, it should be thine	211 Augusta-C		2
Lovelier, not dearer, than our own of old	211 Augusta-C		64
The sweet remembrance of a dearer shore	212 Augusta-C		76
Then not for mine, but that far dearer life	344 Corsair	1	394
Nearer and nearer yet, and dearer still	459 Dante	2	68
Far dearer than his kingdom, yet he fights	576 Sardan	3	297
The heart, is dearer to their feelings or	581 Sardan	4	222
As I have laid down dearer things than life	621 Foscari	5	54
And dearer, silent friends and brethren, all	668 Heaven		966
His lands (if he hath any), and, still dearer	688 Werner	2	327
But county contests cost him rather dearer	989 Juan	16	603

DEAREST

The dearest remembrance will still be the last	93 First Kiss		27
Therefore, to guard her dearest work	97 To M--		13
To be by dearest ties related	113 Quaker		50
Alonzo! best and dearest of my friends	125 Recoll		243
This parting song, the dearest and the last	127 Recoll		372
Its claims my warmest, dearest care	128 Lady-C		3
The dearest boon that Life has given	140 Pignus		3
Had the first strain of love been the dearest, the last	149 Farewell-A		36
I hail thee, dearest child of love	150 My Son		22
Since the dearest of prizes to me's a deserter	178 Devil's Dr		200
Deserved to be dearest of all	210 Augusta-B		44
As first in freedom, dearest to the muse	255 Bards		996
And art thou, dearest, changed so much	323 Giaour		1291
Oh, Selim dear! oh, more than dearest	327 Abydos	1	299
This morn I saw thee gentlest, dearest	328 Abydos	1	385
Be silent, Conrad!--dearest! come and share	344 Corsair	1	420
To valour's praise thy last and dearest claim	359 Corsair	3	235
The mystery dearest to the curious crowd	377 Lara	2	138
His heart's dearest wish; let him ask it, and have	392 Corinth		718
His martyr'd father's dearest thought	404 Chillon		168
The last--the sole--the dearest link	404 Chillon		215
But thou art dearest still, and I should be	438 Tasso		142
Her dearest friends for being dress'd so ill	448 Beppo		520
The more approach'd, and dearest were they free	459 Dante	2	69
The nearest, dearest part of all men's honour	502 Faliero	1	188
My dearest child, forgive me--why delay	511 Faliero	2	151
You ever were my dearest offspring, when	616 Foscari	4	109
Dear, dearest in themselves, and scarce less dear	666 Heaven		822
After twelve years? My dearest mother! Yes	688 Werner	2	339
Oh heavens! and can you wish that? Dearest Ida	706 Werner	4	165
Yet died without its last and dearest offices	711 Werner	4	465
Farewell, too, dearest Julia!--(Here he drew	776 Juan	2	143
Dear unto all, but dearest to their eyes	818 Juan	4	154
Oh! dearest father, in this agony	821 Juan	4	300

DEAR-LOVED

Above the dear-loved peaceful seat	134 E. N. Long		99

DEARLY

And see how dearly earn'd Torquato's fame	60 Harold	4	318
My bosom still esteems you dearly	98 To Lesbia		24
Arrived the dearly destined morn	103 Alva		170
And love them most dearly; but yet	115 Pigot		22
And here we earn'd the conquest dearly bought	124 Recoll		144
From Jove to Hebe, dearly love	139 Anacreon-C		14
So dearly wreathed with mine alone	143 Jessy		2
Thou hast been dearly, solely mine	152 Time-A		24
'Twill love you long and love you dearly	160 Cadiz		32
Alas! too late, I dearly know	172 Romaic-B		43
The 'moral lesson' dearly bought	188 Ode-B		78
And if dearly that error hath cost me	210 Augusta-B		37
The arrow's flown, and dearly shalt thou rue it	229 Sadness		9
That deem right dearly won the field he lost	351 Corsair	2	276
Corsair! he perish'd--thou art dearly won	362 Corsair	3	431
Her tale untold, her truth too dearly proved	384 Lara	2	627
To see again, a sight they dearly earn'd	416 Island	1	50
Dearly they have bought us, dearly still may buy	428 Island	3	157
I must pay dearly for the desolation	584 Sardan	4	429
Some went off dearly; fifteen hundred dollars	830 Juan	4	905
Was dearly purchased by his land's perdition	942 Juan	13	88

DEARS

For, were the Sultan just to all his dears	853 Juan	6	70

DEARS

I rather think the moon should date the dears	908 Juan	10	80
There were the six Miss Rawbolds--pretty dears	951 Juan	13	678
Are somehow echoed to the pretty dears	977 Juan	15	603

DEARTH

And feeling still with thee in my crush'd feelings' dearth	36 Harold	3	54
And be (with prose supply my dearth of rhymes	224 J.C.H.		39
No dearth of bards can be complain'd of now	243 Bards		124
Of velvet, gilding, brass, and no great dearth	286 Vision		67
'Twas still some solace, in the dearth	403 Chillon		56
Abandons, Heaven forgets me; in the dearth	439 Tasso		200
'Tis something, in the dearth of fame	812 Juan	3	719
And yet, though I have said there was no dearth	840 Juan	5	534

DEARY

Lucietta, my deary	239 Lucietta		1

DEATH

(See also LIFE-AND-DEATH, 'SDEATH)

Tyrants and Tyrants' slaves?--the fires of Death	10 Harold	1	418
Death rides upon the sulphury Siroc	10 Harold	1	421
Poor child of Doubt and Death, whose hope is built on reeds	20 Harold	2	27
Death hath but little left him to destroy	23 Harold	2	206
From birth till death enslaved; in word, in deed, unmann'd	31 Harold	2	710
Death in the front, Destruction in the rear	33 Harold	2	849
All thou couldst have of mine, stern Death, thou hast	34 Harold	2	904
Of death, depopulation, bondage, fears	38 Harold	3	176
The enslavers and the enslaved, their death and birth	45 Harold	3	638
The spectre Death, had he substantial power to harm	49 Harold	3	850
In life and death to be the mark where Wrong	61 Harold	4	344
In death as life? Are they resolved to dust	63 Harold	4	501
His day of double victory and death	67 Harold	4	764
Heaven gives its favourites--early death; yet shed	70 Harold	4	915
And Death the sable smoke where vanishes the flame	73 Harold	4	1116
Disease, death, bondage--all the woes we see	74 Harold	4	1132
Consents to death, but conquers agony	76 Harold	4	1254
Was death or life, the playthings of a crowd	76 Harold	4	1275
Death hush'd that pang for ever; with thee fled	80 Harold	4	1510
A friend, whom death alone could sever	85 To D--		2
Whilst thou wast struggling in the pangs of death	85 Epitaph		4
Unnerved is the hand of his minstrel by death	86 Leaving NA		12
Till death their attachment to royalty seal'd	86 Leaving NA		20
Ah, Lesbia! though 'tis death to me	87 Ad Lesbiam		9
And feels a temporary death	87 Ad Lesbiam		24
By death alone I can avoid your hate	87 Tibullus		6
His death and Lesbia's grief I mourn	87 Catullus		15
In the death which one day will deprive you of me	91 Caroline-C		16
But as death, my beloved, soon or late shall o'ertake us	91 Caroline-C		21
If again in the mansion of death I embrace thee	92 Caroline-D		23
They tell us that slumber, the sister of death	97 To M.S.G.-B		9
In pity turn'd the death aside	99 Young Lady		12
Let it be death, or what thou wilt	99 Young Lady		32
Or death disunite us in love's last adieu	99 L Adieu		8
Pale in the scatter'd ranks of death	101 Alva		11
Beheld in death her fading ray	101 Alva		16
Since martial Oscar's death or flight	104 Alva		212
The drops of death each other chase	104 Alva		235
The price of honour is the sleep of death	106 Nisus		52
Unconscious whence the death, with horror gaze	110 Nisus		354
Languid in death, expires beneath the share	110 Nisus		380
Nor wounds, nor death, distracted Nisus heeds	110 Nisus		392
And death was heavenly in his friend's embrace	110 Nisus		400
A doom to me far worse than death	111 Medea		40
'Our nation's foes lament on Fox's death	114 Death-A		1
The soldier braves death for a fanciful wreath	115 The Tear		17
That should Saints after death with their spouses put up more	117 To Eliza		26
The minstrel's palsied hand reclines in death	121 Newstead-A		90
Loathing the offering of so dark a death	121 Newstead-A		108
Time steals along, and Death uprears his dart	121 Newstead-A		134
Denied in death a monumental stone	124 Recoll		160
Stern Death forbade my orphan youth to share	125 Recoll		219
Assumes the ghastly stare of death	128 Answer-B		18
For the life of a Fox, of a Chatham the death	129 Becher-A		17
death to me? I love the sleep of the mighty	130 Calmar		57
grave. Sweet will be the song of death to	130 Calmar		86
song of death to my friend? Could I give	130 Calmar		90
is the clang of death! many are the widows	131 Calmar		151
a flame. It glares in death unclosed. His	131 Calmar		165
Avert from me the death of sin	132 Prayer		8
If fate should seal my Death to-morrow	144 Becher-B		1
To Death, the parent of decay	146 Adieu		59
Avert the death of sin	146 Adieu		114

DEATH

Though I shall lie low in the cavern of death	149 Newstead-B		26
And didst thou not, since Death for thee	165 Thyrza		13
In that dread hour ere death appear	165 Thyrza		19
Deceive in life, unman in death	167 Euthanasia		24
For thousands Death hath ceased to lower	167 Euthanasia		27
The love where Death has set his seal	167 Dead		23
To death even hours like these must roll	175 Portuguese-A		5
Or dread of death alone	180 Ode-A		43
Who would not die the death they chose	184 Parker		20
Then the mortal coldness of the soul like death itself comes down	185 Music-B		9
Death; and envied those who fell	187 French-A		14
Than sold thyself to death and shame	187 Ode-B		40
For beautiful in death are they	189 On Star		39
All earth was but one thought--and that was death	189 Darkness		42
A lump of death--a chaos of hard clay	190 Darkness		72
And making Death a Victory	191 Prometheus-B		59
What is this Death?--a quiet of the heart	191 Fragment-C		7
Where Death is Pride	201 Ode-C		44
O'erflow'd with Passion even in Death	201 Ode-C		80
To thee--to thee--e'en in the gasp of death	206 Love, Death		19
Wafts unto death the breast it bore so high	206 Greece		8
The land of honourable death	207 Year		34
We are entwined--let death come slow or fast	212 Augusta-C		127
Death and existence: Sleep hath its own world	213 Dream		3
Through that which had been death to many men	216 Dream		194
That death nor heeds nor hears distress	218 Bloom		12
Thou shalt not taste of death	219 Thy Days		8
Or kingly the death, which awaits us to-day	219 Saul-A		12
Death stood all glassy in his fixed eye	219 Saul-B		7
For the Angel of Death spread his wings on the blast	222 Sennacherib		9
And I, though with cold I have nearly my death got	226 Oh You		13
Justice and death have mix'd their dust in vain	228 Windsor		7
Justice and Death have mix'd their dust in vain	228 Vaults		7
And prick'd to death expire upon her needle	230 Murray-A		18
And gives the choice of death or phrenzy--choose	230 God Maddens		2
With death doom'd to grapple	235 Pitt		1
Were Death an evil, would I let thee live	237 Lucifer		1
While none but menials o'er the bed of death	251 Bards		682
She sow'd the seeds, but death has reap'd the fruit	253 Bards		838
Scrawl on, till death release us from the strain	254 Bards		929
Appals an audience with a monarch's death	260 Hints		278
Yet, since 'tis promised at the rector's death	267 Hints		769
The glory of that death they freely choose	268 Hints		832
The glorious death that consecrates his fall	272 Minerva		290
With death alone are laurels cheaply bought	272 Minerva		294
He died!--his death made no great stir on earth	286 Vision		65
Knows not his name, or but his death and birth	298 Age		36
To date the birth and death of all it hid	299 Age		104
Ere the first day of death is fled	311 Giaour		69
The first, last look by death reveal'd	311 Giaour		89
Hers is the loveliness in death	311 Giaour		94
Then sped as if by death pursued	312 Giaour		260
The very cypress droops to death	313 Giaour		285
Around it flame, within it death	314 Giaour		438
It shall not save him from the death	316 Giaour		617
True foes, once met, are join'd till death	316 Giaour		654
Angel of Death! 'tis Hassan's cloven crest	317 Giaour		716
As death were stamp'd upon his brow	318 Giaour		797
Yet death I have not fear'd to meet	320 Giaour		1008
Death is but what the haughty brave	320 Giaour		1024
His death sits lightly; but her fate	320 Giaour		1073
Although to death or deadliest ill	321 Giaour		1148
This bed of death--attest my truth	322 Giaour		1189
Nor strike one stroke for life and death	324 Abydos	1	97
His death is all I need relate	331 Abydos	2	222
And woman, more than man, when death or woe	333 Abydos	2	440
'His head and faith from doubt and death	334 Abydos	2	468
Hath doom'd his death, or fix'd his chain	335 Abydos	2	566
No dread of death--if with us die our foes	338 Corsair	1	23
'Tis rash to meet, but surer death to wait	342 Corsair	1	315
I had no death to fear, nor wealth to boast	348 Corsair	2	71
And burst within--and it were death to wait	349 Corsair	2	183
Till the blade glimmers in the grasp of death	350 Corsair	2	252
Fell'd--bleeding--baffled of the death he sought	351 Corsair	2	277
Who more than all had striven and struck for death	351 Corsair	2	293
That day by day death still forbears to slake	351 Corsair	2	320
But he who looks on death--and silent dies	352 Corsair	2	363
Was hush'd so deep--Ah! happy if in death	352 Corsair	2	393
'Twill cost me dear--but dread no death to-day	355 Corsair	2	534
To other ears that death became thee well	359 Corsair	3	229
That death with gentler aspect wither'd there	364 Corsair	3	604
Oh! o'er the eye Death most exerts his might	364 Corsair	3	611
His death yet dubious, deeds too widely known	366 Corsair	3	694

DEATH

Yet wake to wrestle with the dread of death	375 Lara	1	643
The life or death of Lara's future fame	375 Lara	2	22
And present death, to hourly suffering life	379 Lara	2	305
How many shall but hear the voice of death	380 Lara	2	343
And Death hath stricken down yon arm of pride	380 Lara	2	383
Of those that die the soldier's fiery death	380 Lara	2	403
And that escape to death from living hate	381 Lara	2	437
From this, you might have deem'd young Kaled's death	381 Lara	2	456
And calm, till murmuring death gasp'd hoarsely near	381 Lara	2	461
Wings the far hissing globe of death	385 Corinth		88
And proved, by many a deed of death	386 Corinth		157
Who hold the thought of death in scorn	386 Corinth		237
Whate'er be the shape in which death may lower	389 Corinth		486
And her motionless lips lay still as death	391 Corinth		612
Nothing there, save death, was mute	392 Corinth		752
Heralded his way to death	394 Corinth		892
'It is not that I dread the death	399 Parisina		234
As if they dared not look on death	401 Parisina		448
Still as the lips that closed in death	401 Parisina		477
Done to death by sudden blow	401 Parisina		491
I suffer'd chains and courted death	402 Chillon		12
The death that would have set me free	404 Chillon		125
That even in death his freeborn breast	404 Chillon		156
And that forbade a selfish death	405 Chillon		230
Which neither was of life nor death	405 Chillon		248
And Death, whom he should deem his friend	414 Mazeppa		749
And my dim eyes of death had need	414 Mazeppa		766
And then subsiding back to death	414 Mazeppa		789
In vain, not silenced by the eye of death	416 Island	1	65
As promises the death their hands deny	416 Island	1	88
Exclaim'd, 'Depart at once! delay is death	417 Island	1	154
In life or death, the fearless and the free	428 Island	3	164
Where Abelard, through twenty years of death	433 Island	4	223
To cheer resistance against death or chains	433 Island	4	258
Blazed through the clouds of death and beckon'd hence	433 Island	4	264
No power in death can tear our names apart	440 Tasso		244
The sick man's lightning half an hour ere death	453 Venice-B		37
Of the cold staggering race which Death is winning	453 Venice-B		40
Be trampled on, while Death and Ate range	457 Dante	1	117
Leans sculptured Beauty, which Death cannot blight	461 Dante	3	40
Florence dooms me but death or banishment	462 Dante	3	138
From Death the Sin-born's incest with his mother	465 Dante	4	124
Love to one death conducted us along	476 Francesca		10
I swoon'd as if by death I had been smote	477 Francesca		45
But--thou mayst die. Will death bestow it on me	480 Manfred	1	148
Mortals call death hath nought to do with us	480 Manfred	1	163
Though thy death shall still seem near	481 Manfred	1	256
With the fierce thirst of death--and still unslaked	484 Manfred	2	48
The Giant steed, to be bestrode by Death	485 Manfred	2	101
In my lone wanderings, to the caves of death	486 Manfred	2	174
I have affronted death, but in the war	486 Manfred	2	229
Forbears to pant for death, and yet draws back	487 Manfred	2	268
To him Death pays his tribute; Life is his	489 Manfred	2	384
Can this be death? there's bloom upon her cheek	490 Manfred	2	468
Which walk the valley of the shade of death	491 Manfred	3	38
To shun the torments of a public death	492 Manfred	3	90
Without the violence of warlike death	493 Manfred	3	141
I do not combat against death, but thee	496 Manfred	3	372
The hand of death is on me--but not yours	496 Manfred	3	401
Death! Was I not the sovereign of the state	503 Faliero	1	221
Perhaps I pass the sentence of my death	507 Faliero	1	503
And suffering what thou hast done--fear'st thou death	507 Faliero	1	504
Long as he can; he has ceased to merit death	512 Faliero	2	237
Where Death sits robed in his all-sweeping shadow	516 Faliero	2	503
With what? a mulct or an arrest? With death	516 Faliero	2	516
For the result, which must be death or freedom	516 Faliero	2	566
We will be free in life or death! the grave	516 Faliero	2	568
And only look on death as beautiful	517 Faliero	2	603
No eyes in marble. But there are in Death	520 Faliero	3	94
To me a thing of triumph, nor the death	521 Faliero	3	189
Strike!--If I dreaded death, a death more fearful	522 Faliero	3	221
On yoke, and slavery and death may whet	526 Faliero	3	565
A damp like death rose o'er my brow. I strove	528 Faliero	4	9
And you shall perish piecemeal, by the death	533 Faliero	4	345
And slay as if Death had but this one gate	535 Faliero	4	518
Which never knells but for a princely death	535 Faliero	4	532
Who have cast lots for the first death, and they	537 Faliero	4	639
So let them die the death. We are prepared	538 Faliero	5	20
Unhappy men! prepare for instant death	539 Faliero	5	89
Where he now sits, to glut him with my death	541 Faliero	5	235
Is present infamy and death--the future	541 Faliero	5	257
And my own violent death, and thy vile life	542 Faliero	5	320
There to pronounce the death of your deliverer	543 Faliero	5	373
More terrible than death, here and hereafter	544 Faliero	5	426
Until this trial--the decree is death	545 Faliero	5	486
Have I aught else to undergo save death	545 Faliero	5	547

DEATH

The dog's death, and the wolf's; but thou shalt fall	546 Faliero	5	565
And mourn even the inevitable death	546 Faliero	5	568
Didst promise at his death, thou hast seal'd thine own	546 Faliero	5	586
And hoary hairs of shame, and both of death	546 Faliero	5	615
But not such death as fits an aged man	546 Faliero	5	616
The custom of the state to put to death	547 Faliero	5	636
When she shakes off this temporary death	547 Faliero	5	692
My death, and such a death, might settle all	548 Faliero	5	709
And death, where they are neither gods nor men	555 Sardan	1	315
Before my hour, to live in dread of death	557 Sardan	1	441
My name became the synonyme of death	557 Sardan	1	451
Fear!--I'm a Greek, and how should I fear death	558 Sardan	1	526
Business to-morrow. Ay, or death to-night	560 Sardan	1	649
Death, so it be but glorious? 'Tis a sunset	562 Sardan	2	34
Which their death had not left me. Thus you run	569 Sardan	2	498
Look like thy brother, Death,--so still--so stirless	578 Sardan	4	6
Sleep shows such things, what may not death disclose	579 Sardan	4	53
I know no evil death can show, which life	579 Sardan	4	54
Whate'er it have to fear, will not fear death	579 Sardan	4	62
I can bear all things, dreams of life or death	579 Sardan	4	73
Had lost a part of death to come to me	580 Sardan	4	126
Death all than such a being! And the end	580 Sardan	4	130
Mere mimics death in death--but I sate still	580 Sardan	4	139
His death who made their lives a jubilee	583 Sardan	4	316
And I not death. Where was the king when you	589 Sardan	5	107
The death of Salemenes, and the shouts	590 Sardan	5	174
His death. Too many far have heralded	593 Sardan	5	378
It may be, purified by death from some	594 Sardan	5	424
The death of Peter Loredano, both	596 Foscari	1	37
The wretch too happy to escape to death	600 Foscari	1	284
Because he fears not death; and banish him	600 Foscari	1	289
His and his father's death your nearest wish	601 Foscari	1	348
In pain, in peril, or in death--who are	603 Foscari	2	122
So far from strange, that never was there death	605 Foscari	2	216
And still towards death, a thing which comes as much	607 Foscari	2	362
Of death, the imprecation of despair	608 Foscari	3	5
Hath nerved me to endure the risk of death	609 Foscari	3	88
And torture positive, far worse than death	609 Foscari	3	89
(If death be a deep sleep), without a groan	609 Foscari	3	90
With death, and chains, and exile in his hand	613 Foscari	3	315
Your hands! There's death in that damp clammy grasp	618 Foscari	4	191
How death itself bears witness to thy deeds	619 Foscari	4	244
'Twas true; the question was the death resolved	619 Foscari	4	298
Was pluck'd too soon; and all the fruit is death	629 Cain	1	108
To make death hateful, save an innate clinging	629 Cain	1	111
Darest thou to look on Death? He has not yet	631 Cain	1	247
Of this almighty Death, who is, it seems	631 Cain	1	255
Of death; although I know not what it is	631 Cain	1	266
They are so lovely. What is death? I fear	631 Cain	1	281
But shall I know it? As I know not death	631 Cain	1	286
The knowledge, he was ignorant of death	631 Cain	1	294
To Death--the unknown! Methinks the tree of knowledge	634 Cain	1	454
Of knowledge--and the mystery of death	634 Cain	1	457
I think I could be so, despite of death	634 Cain	1	465
Divided with me; life and death--and time	636 Cain	1	545
All living, and all doom'd to death, and wretched	636 Cain	2	48
Know nought of death, save as a dreadful thing	637 Cain	2	61
Methinks is merely propagating death	637 Cain	2	70
He shut him forth from Paradise, with death	637 Cain	2	74
Nor ever shall--the mysteries of death	638 Cain	2	140
But changes make not death, except to clay	638 Cain	2	163
Thou seekest to behold death and dead things	639 Cain	2	191
Return! be sure: how else should death be peopled	639 Cain	2	200
Of death.--Wouldst have it present? Till I know	639 Cain	2	219
He who invented life that leads to death	639 Cain	2	224
Then what is death? What? Hath not he who made ye	639 Cain	2	240
Is life, and what ye shall have--death: the rest	640 Cain	2	300
The gates of death--By what gate have we enter'd	640 Cain	2	319
Of death and life. What thy world is, thou seest	641 Cain	2	335
And death to all things, and disease to most things	641 Cain	2	355
Of death--but knowledge still: but what knows man	641 Cain	2	368
It may be death leads to the highest knowledge	641 Cain	2	369
That there was death. But not what was beyond it	641 Cain	2	377
Which my sire brought us--Death; thou hast shown me much	644 Cain	2	570
That sight is for the other state. Of death	645 Cain	2	616
Yes--death, too, is amongst the debts we owe her	646 Cain	3	44
Might never taste of death nor human sorrow	647 Cain	3	83
Death is like sleep, and sleep shuts down our lids	651 Cain	3	338
But he cannot be dead!--Is silence death	651 Cain	3	349
Adah!--come hither! Death is in the world	651 Cain	3	370
The name of Death so deeply, that the thought	652 Cain	3	372
That of his nature, in yon--Oh death! death	652 Cain	3	411

DEATH

Of death, whom I have brought upon the earth   652 Cain   3   420
His waking a continual dread of death   652 Cain   3   431
And death itself wax womething worse than death 652 Cain   3   436
With my own death redeem him from the dust   654 Cain   3   511
As he adores the Highest, death becomes   655 Heaven   24
Her whose heart death could not keep from
  overflowing   656 Heaven   65
It may be hidden long: death and decay   656 Heaven   106
Sleep too upon the very eve of death   659 Heaven   336
Which look like death in life, and speak like
  things   659 Heaven   338
Of death   660 Heaven   346
Is made with Death, who shall forbear   661 Heaven   449
Thy death is nearer than thy recent birth   661 Heaven   501
Exempt for future sorrow's sake from death   662 Heaven   519
Beings even in death so fair   662 Heaven   527
Alone can do so. Ah! he speaks of death   663 Heaven   642
Of death to us! and those who are with us   663 Heaven   643
I abhor death, because that thou must die   664 Heaven   707
And reap'd by Death, lord of the human soil   667 Heaven   872
A righteous death, unlike the seed of Cain's   667 Heaven   954
It cannot slay us: threaten dust with death   669 Heaven   1053
Nor spangled stars be glorious: Death hath risen 669 Heaven   1075
What is there in this milk of mine, that death 669 Heaven   1105
Time--space--eternity--life--death   670 Heaven   1163
Long sufferings have atoned. My father's death 672 Werner   1   81
Fell sick, almost to death. He should have died 677 Werner   1   407
Of the old man's death, whose heart was broken
  by it   684 Werner   2   112
An obscure death to save an unknown stranger   685 Werner   2   162
Inviting death, by looking like it, while   690 Werner   2   456
His death alone can save you:--Thank your God   690 Werner   2   457
Pursue me to the death, except through shame   692 Werner   2   564
About his death--and even the place of it   706 Werner   4   145
Unlatch'd the door of death for thee? 'Twas not 711 Werner   4   434
If you regret your enemy's bloodless death   712 Werner   4   505
His death was fathomlessly deep in blood   712 Werner   4   506
By Stralenheim's death? Was't I--as poor as ever 716 Werner   5   193
His death? Or had the prince's household been   719 Werner   5   413
Living upon the death of other things   731 Deformed   1   596
The men who are to kindle them to death   731 Deformed   1   616
As Dacia men to die the eternal death   731 Deformed   1   628
And death only be mute   732 Deformed   1   710
The dawn of an eternal day, than death   733 Deformed   1   784
Death is in thy walls and under   736 Deformed   2   88
Death is upon me. But what is one life   736 Deformed   2   133
She hath kill'd our comrade. Welcome such a
  death   740 Deformed   2   304
Death hath a thousand gates; and on the marble 740 Deformed   2   344
Faint flutter life disputes with death. She
  breathes   741 Deformed   2   385
His death contrived to spoil a charming cause   751 Juan   1   261
Save death or Doctors' Commons'--so he died   751 Juan   1   288
The unexpected death of some old lady   762 Juan   1   994
Who threaten'd death--so Juan knock'd him down 769 Juan   1   1464
Death shuns the wretch who fain the blow would
  meet   771 Juan   1   1574
And flesh (which Death mows down to hay) is grass 773 Juan   1   1756
Or death of those we dote on, when a part   776 Juan   2   165
Sea-sickness death: his love was perfect, how
  else   777 Juan   2   182
As if Death were more dreadful by his door   778 Juan   2   277
'Tis true that death awaits both you and me   778 Juan   2   283
Been their familiar, and now Death was here   780 Juan   2   392
He but requested to be bled to death   783 Juan   2   601
Death left no doubt, and the dead burthen lay   785 Juan   2   715
For Death, though vanquish'd, still retired with
  strife   788 Juan   2   888
And wish'd it death in which he had reposed   788 Juan   2   893
Recall'd his answering spirits back from death 788 Juan   2   900
Were black as death, their lashes the same hue 789 Juan   2   930
Should reach his blood, then o'er him still as
  death   792 Juan   2   1143
And all its charms, like death without its
  terrors   799 Juan   2   1576
All tragedies are finish'd by a death   802 Juan   3   65
They say no more of Death or of the Lady   802 Juan   3   72
Avouch'd his death (such people never die   806 Juan   3   299
Whether the word was death, or but the chain   807 Juan   3   372
A genius who has drunk himself to death   809 Juan   3   522
The death of friends, and that which slays even
  more   817 Juan   4   91
The death of friendship, love, youth, all that is 817 Juan   4   92
The ocean-buried, risen from death, to be   821 Juan   4   284
Perchance the death of one she loved too well   821 Juan   4   285
Stern as her sire: 'On me,' she cried, 'let death 821 Juan   4   332
Like one life could not hold, nor death destroy 824 Juan   4   472
She had no pulse, but death seem'd absent still 824 Juan   4   475
And lose their own in universal death   829 Juan   4   816
Before Pelides' death, or Homer's birth   829 Juan   4   832
'Can this be death? then what is life or death 835 Juan   5   281
To try if I could wrench aught out of death   836 Juan   5   303
Death to his publisher, to him 'tis sport   838 Juan   5   413

DEATH

A kind of death comes o'er us all alone   838 Juan   5   455
Proved death in battle equal to a pension   874 Juan   7   464
That awful pause, dividing life from death   878 Juan   7   690
But when they light upon immediate death   883 Juan   8   319
Who passes for in life and death most lucky   886 Juan   8   482
Where if men seek her not, and death be more   886 Juan   8   492
Though life, and death, and victory were at stake 887 Juan   8   559
And death is drunk with gore: there's not a
  street   888 Juan   8   650
Acknowledge aught of dread of death or foe   889 Juan   8   693
Death laughs--Go ponder o'er the skeleton   897 Juan   9   81
Death laughs at all you weep for:--look upon   897 Juan   9   85
And thus Death laughs,--it is sad merriment   898 Juan   9   97
For me, I sometimes think that life is death   898 Juan   9   127
Thou gate of life and death--thou nondescript   903 Juan   9   434
Because she put a favourite to death   906 Juan   9   646
And Death, the sovereign's sovereign, though the
  great   910 Juan   10   193
He lived (not Death, but Juan) in a hurry   910 Juan   10   201
Quit; and though death had threaten'd an ejection 912 Juan   10   338
Death, so call'd, is a thing which makes men weep 955 Juan   14   23
Less from disgust of life than dread of death   955 Juan   14   32
A paper kite which flies 'twixt life and death 956 Juan   14   61
O Death! thou dunnest of all duns! thou daily   969 Juan   15   57
Like Holbein's 'Dance of Death'--but 'tis the
  same   973 Juan   15   312
By death, when we are left, alas! behind   973 Juan   15   350
A vigil there, where all but death should sleep 982 Juan   16   144
But death is imaged in their shadowy beams   983 Juan   16   150
And 'tis held as faith, to their bed of death   985 Juan   16   343
And rather variably for stony death   996 Juan   16   1010

DEATH-BED
Like Hope upon a death-bed, and, unworn   65 Harold   4   643
Which soothed his death-bed. I have not
  forgotten   513 Faliero   2   303
Has been annull'd by the death-bed confession   600 Foscari   1   303
Alas! what is a menial to a death-bed   707 Werner   4   190

DEATH-BLACK
To be left vacant, with a death-black veil   545 Faliero   5   498

DEATH-BLOW
For by the death-blow of my Hope   161 Picture   7
And the last death-blow dealt his hand   335 Abydos   2   562
Whose demon death-blow left no hope for fight   349 Corsair   2   151

DEATH-BOLTS
The death-bolts deadliest the thinn'd files along 39 Harold   3   259

DEATH-CRY
The death-cry drowning in the battle's roar   878 Juan   7   696

DEATH-DISGORGING
The death-disgorging rampart once again   888 Juan   8   629

DEATH-FIRE
I beheld but the death-fire that fed on thy fane 221 Jerusalem   7

DEATH-FIRMAN
Will laugh to scorn the death-firman   326 Abydos   1   211

DEATH-GROAN
A brother's death-groan echoes there   105 Alva   316

DEATH-HYMN
The death-hymn peals and the hollow bells knoll 400 Parisina   395

DEATHLESS
Yield me one leaf of Daphne's deathless plant   14 Harold   1   646
Long'd for a deathless lover from above   79 Harold   4   1452
Of Grecian dramas vaunts the deathless fame   111 Examination   21
To build his own upon thy deathless fame   125 Recoll   250
The record of his deathless name   128 Answer-B   12
A deathless part of him who died too soon   193 Monody   32
The matchless dialogue, the deathless wit   193 Monody   49
And soul in soul grow deathless theirs   217 High World   16
Attest it many a deathless age   311 Giaour   127
Rome liberty, but left a deathless lesson   517 Faliero   2   616
Of thine imaginary deathless tree   875 Juan   7   543

DEATHLIKE
Dash o'er her deathlike cheek the ocean dew   357 Corsair   3   117
One look upon that deathlike brow   398 Parisina   195
Recover'd from that death-like swoon   400 Parisina   357
And raise, and wring their dim and death-like
  hands   733 Deformed   1   766
Pillow'd his death-like forehead; then she wrung 788 Juan   2   909

DEATHS
Through the thick deaths of half a century   190 Churchill   10
'Doge Foscari, my debtor for the deaths   596 Foscari   1   51
The deaths of the two sons Heaven took from me 604 Foscari   2   174

DEATHS

Their epitaph, attributing their deaths 605 Foscari 2 224
His sons expire by natural deaths, and I 619 Foscari 4 279
It seems, of all deaths, the least likely for you 676 Werner 1 300
Of many deaths, it may be of their own 731 Deformed 1 664
And many deaths do they escape by this 817 Juan 4 90
('Mongst other deaths the General Ribaupierre's 887 Juan 8 566
About the present family's deaths and wooings 987 Juan 16 472

DEATH'S

And caught its tone with Death's prophetic ear 38 Harold 3 202
By Death's unequal hand alike controll'd 87 Marsus 3
Still were you happy in death's earthy slumber 117 Lachin 29
Till death's unfathom'd gulf appear 137 Clare 29
There, where death's brief pang was quickest 187 Ode-B 60
The place where Death's grand cause is argued o'er 289 Vision 275
Full in Death's face--before--and now 412 Mazeppa 568
Those who catch cold in 'shadows of Death's valley 882 Juan 8 288
Death's a reformer, all men must allow 910 Juan 10 200

DEATH-SHOT

With death-shot glowing in his fiery hands 10 Harold 1 425
The deathshot hissing from afar 316 Giaour 639
The deathshot peal'd of murder near 321 Giaour 1078

DEATH-STRUCK

Though death-struck, still his feeble frame he rears 16 Harold 1 772

DEATH-THIRST

Scorch'd with the death-thirst, and writhing in vain 389 Corinth 483

DEATH-WATCH

Like the death-watch, within our ears the ills 879 Juan 8 94

DEATH-WING'D

Had braved the death-wing'd tempest's blast 158 Florence 31

DEATH-WOUND

The drops fell from his death-wound, and he drew ill 920 Juan 11 126

DEBARR'D

Great Galileo was debarr'd the Sun 997 Juan 17 57

DEBARRING

Debarring me the usage of my own 438 Tasso 97

DEBASE

Who will debase his manly mind 153 Friend-A 71
Have felt the arm they would debase 390 Corinth 592
And all that may be borne, or can debase 439 Tasso 197

DEBASED

Debased by slavery, or corrupt by power 154 Dog 16
The long degenerate noble; the debased 302 Age 342
Who have debased me in the minds of men 438 Tasso 96
Admirers still,--but men are so debased 448 Beppo 535
Such as all they must breathe who are debased 461 Dante 3 60
Stung with strange passions, and debased 666 Heaven 809

DEBATE

Since then the same senate, nay, the same debate 94 Dorset 97
Some folly cross'd, some jest, or some debate 267 Hints 746
Convulsed the skies, as during a debate 296 Vision 738
Even Constant, their sole master of debate 304 Age 492
On visionary schemes debate 333 Abydos 2 383
They to the midnight watch protract debate 346 Corsair 1 589
I like a parliamentary debate 446 Beppo 375
And long debate on Steno's accusation 499 Faliero 1 4
Except to turn a trial to debate 542 Faliero 5 277
Instead of bearing up without debate 828 Juan 4 742
Which made a long debate; but I must halt 871 Juan 7 278
Upon debate: the papers echoed yet 952 Juan 13 717

DEBATER

And the Lord Henry was a great debater 943 Juan 13 159

DEBATERS

But there now was a 'call' and accomplish'd debaters 178 Devil's Dr 160

DEBATES

And (save debates in Warsaw's diet 408 Mazeppa 135
To hear debates whose thunder roused (not rouses 940 Juan 12 652
Listening debates not very wise or witty 947 Juan 13 382

DEBATING

Debating despots, hemm'd on either shore 302 Age 280

DEBATS

To furnish articles for the Debats 308 Age 718

DEBAUCH

Debauch; and not fatigue, his eyes had closed 108 Nisus 240

DEBAUCHEE

That he was not an ancient debauchee 914 Juan 10 426

DEBONNAIRE

However disciplined and debonnaire 940 Juan 12 676

DEBT

To whom she renders back the debt of blood 77 Harold 4 1344
They think all our homage a debt 115 Pigot 10
A debt already paid in pain 172 Time-B 16
So mind you don't get into debt 230 Murray-A 7
The unpaid amount of Catherine's bloody debt 300 Age 160
Groans beneath indigestion's heavy debt 305 Age 503
A syllable of imposts or of debt 305 Age 537
The debt of nations:--pray who made it high 307 Age 657
Of lingering tortures to repay the debt 351 Corsair 2 297
Oh! never canst thou cancel half her debt 372 Lara 1 441
That he had somehow blunder'd into debt 443 Beppo 211
Poor's rate, Reform, my own, the nation's debt 446 Beppo 386
That he has paid me! What debt did he owe you 626 Foscari 5 369
A long and just one; Nature's debt and mine 626 Foscari 5 370
The acquittance of the interest of the debt 685 Werner 2 184
A part of the long debt of duty, not 688 Werner 2 347
Doth my refusal make a debt to you 717 Werner 5 292
His life: when due, I but resumed the debt 720 Werner 5 463
Debt he calls wealth, and taxes Paradise 872 Juan 7 357
My debt in being thus allow'd to die 875 Juan 7 517
Meantime the Taxes, Castlereagh, and Debt 894 Juan 8 997
To prove the public debt is not consuming us 901 Juan 9 277
And debt, and what not, for their solace sent 941 Juan 13 40
Has not contracted much more debt than knowledge 946 Juan 13 336
The very Suicide that pays his debt 955 Juan 14 28
To tell how he reduced the nation's debt 964 Juan 14 540
And for which Nature might forego her debt 969 Juan 15 54
The debt unsunk, yet sinks all it receives 993 Juan 16 840

DEBTOR

I now depart a debtor. Fare ye well 491 Manfred 2 537
Made him my debtor for some courtesies 513 Faliero 2 293
'Doge Foscari, my debtor for the deaths 596 Foscari 1 51
And thus far I am also the state's debtor 611 Foscari 3 235
Gulbeyaz, who look'd on him as her debtor 847 Juan 5 989
And Waterloo has made the world your debtor 896 Juan 9 23
The Bench too seats or suits full many a debtor 921 Juan 11 197
To make each correspondent a new debtor 954 Juan 13 832
Some splendid debtor he would take by sap 969 Juan 15 60

DEBTS

But all were agreed that our debts should increase 178 Devil's Dr 165
O'er hoards diminish'd by young Hopeful's debts 260 Hints 256
And only left us thy d--d debts and dances 274 Waltz 42
Yes--death, too, is amongst the debts we owe her 646 Cain 3 44
So much as when we call our old debts in 767 Juan 1 1334
Who fatten on their country's gore, and debts 897 Juan 9 77
Of paying debts, which creditors regret 955 Juan 14 30

DEBT-SINKERS

Meantime, read all the national debt-sinkers 941 Juan 12 711

DEBUT

To-night you throng to witness the debut 113 Prologue 15
Blest was the time Waltz chose for her debut 276 Waltz 161
With his debut, which made a strong impression 952 Juan 13 718

DECANTED

When once decanted;--I presume to guess so 969 Juan 15 46

DECAPITATED

Decapitated for his crimes.' 'His crimes 545 Faliero 5 501
'Decapitated for his crimes!'--What crimes 545 Faliero 5 508

DECAY

And noble arch in proud decay 43 Harold 3 512
Forgets her empires with a just decay 45 Harold 3 637
Ours is a trophy which will not decay 55 Harold 4 32
To meditate amongst decay, and stand 59 Harold 4 218
Spirits which soar from ruin:--thy decay 63 Harold 4 492
Her resurrection; all beside--decay 67 Harold 4 736
Though to the last, in verge of our decay 73 Harold 4 1110
Alas! developed, opens the decay 76 Harold 4 1284
The stranger, slave, or savage; their decay 82 Harold 4 1634
Thou, the hall of my fathers, art gone to decay 86 Leaving NA 2
Receptacle of life's decay 88 Catullus 24
Prove nature a prey to decay and disease 91 Caroline-C 12
Thy yawning arch betokens slow decay 121 Newstead-A 138
Whilst honour's laurels ne'er decay 128 Answer-B 27
Oaks of the mountains fall, the rocks decay 139 Ossian-A 11
Mountains themselves by length of years decay 140 Ossian-B 12
To Death, the parent of decay 146 Adieu 59
Thy decay not the weeds that surround thee can hide 149 Newstead-B 8

DECAY

That clog thy young growth and assist thy decay	149	Newstead-B	22
It tells not of Time's or the tempest's decay	164	Newstead-C	23
I might have watch'd through long decay	167	Dead	36
A Sire's disgrace, a realm's decay	168	Weeping	2
When the glow of early thought declines in feeling's dull decay	185	Music-B	2
Love may sink by slow decay	207	Fare Thee	22
True, some decay, yet not a few revive	258	Hints	101
Yet all his spices but prolong decay	286	Vision	88
A gilded halo hovering round decay	311	Giaour	99
Within that dome as yet Decay	313	Giaour	336
Unseen to drop by dull decay	319	Giaour	968
Let him who crawls enamour'd of decay	338	Corsair	1	27
All rejoicing in his decay	389	Corinth	494
So deep, that did it not decay	397	Parisina	38
To have all feeling save the one decay	437	Tasso	61
But with a sense of its decay:--I see	439	Tasso	190
The weeds of nations in their last decay	453	Venice-B	33
The Grecian forms at least from their decay	464	Dante	4	45
Which but supplies a feeling to decay	482	Manfred	1	330
Grovel on earth in indistinct decay	495	Manfred	3	290
The gods but in decay. Beleses, why	562	Sardan	2	36
It may be hidden long: death and decay	656	Heaven	106
Seeming to weep the dying day's decay	816	Juan	3	958
A long and snake-like life of dull decay	817	Juan	4	71
Shaped by decay perchance, hath given the power	949	Juan	13	506

DECAY'D

Which, thus much we are sure, must lie decay'd	52	Harold	3	1010
And sought a refuge from their hopes decay'd	60	Harold	4	283
When decay'd, may he mingle his dust with your own	86	Leaving NA	32
But these are now decay'd	131	L'Amitie	34
Extinguish'd, not decay'd	167	Dead	52
Whose soul expired ere youth decay'd	185	Belshaz-A	19
Decay'd in thy glory, and sunk in thy worth	186	Napoleon	12
But Rome decay'd, and Athens strew'd the plain	255	Bards	1003
The roofless cot, decay'd and rent	319	Giaour	876
'Twas worn, perhaps decay'd, yet silent bore	358	Corsair	3	218
Your father's house was noble, though decay'd	673	Werner	1	127
'Tis a fine building, but decay'd. The apartment	676	Werner	1	310
Somewhat decay'd: but if we had expected	678	Werner	1	458
The time must come, when both alike decay'd	829	Juan	4	829

DECAYING

For its decaying fame and former worth	915	Juan	10	525

DECAYS

Making a marvel that it not decays	45	Harold	3	623
He stands not still, but or decays or grows	51	Harold	3	965
Youth flies, life decays, even hope is o'ercast	100	L Adieu	33
'Tis the light that should shine on a race that decays	164	Newstead-C	6

DECAY'S

(Before Decay's effacing fingers	311	Giaour	72

DECEASE

For their decease, I pray you, comforted	472	Morgante	387

DECEASED

To the deceased, so you would act the part	626	Foscari	5	359
By the deceased, who lie in famous slumber	880	Juan	8	139

DECEIT

One trace of dark deceit it leaves not	98	To Lesbia	20
With this dream of deceit half our sorrow's represt	99	L Adieu	11
In lies an adept, in deceit a fiend	100	Damaetas	4
Deceit the guilty lips impart	112	Quaker	17
And forgive her deceit with a Tear	115	The Tear	36
Romance! disgusted with deceit	118	Romance	33
No dear-bought knowledge purchased by deceit	123	Recoll	64
But that thy tongue could never forge deceit	126	Recoll	316
Deceit is a stranger as yet to my soul	129	Becher-A	33
From smooth deceit and terror sprung	132	L'Amitie	75
And once my breast abhorr'd deceit	134	Lady-D	35
No smile of Love's deceit	146	Adieu	72
Yet cannot see the slight deceit	147	Vain Lady	28
Thy smiles hypocrisy, thy words deceit	154	Dog	20
And spurns deceiver and deceit	173	Not False	8
His veracity were but deceit	178	Devil's Dr	180
Thou radiant and adored deceit	188	On Star	3
Deceit infect not, near Contagion soil	208	Sketch	23
Deceit, averments incompatible	213	Lady Byron	51
And lull'd me with a vain deceit	331	Abydos	2	201
Ours be the last; in time deceit may come	333	Abydos	2	436
Gird more deceit within a petticoat	806	Juan	3	326

DECEITFUL

(See also SELF-DECEITFUL)			
Then fare thee well, deceitful maid	134	Lady-D	21
Now 'tis thy lord that warns--deceitful thing	358	Corsair	3	190

DECEITFUL

He's mean, deceitful, avaricious. You	690	Werner	2	463

DECEIVE

Words which are things, hopes which will not deceive	53	Harold	3	1061
He never wishes to deceive thee	87	Rousseau	12
And your eye beams a ray which can never deceive	91	Caroline-C	4
I have found that a friend may profess, yet deceive	129	Becher-A	28
This will assist you to deceive	141	Critics	20
These dazzling Meteors but deceive	141	Critics	34
The words man utters to deceive	146	Vain Lady	14
But woman is made to command and deceive us	147	To Anne-A	3
Thy spirit deceive	151	When We	28
Deceive in life, unman in death	167	Euthanasia	24
And undeceived may long deceive	173	Quotation	28
Yet, oh yet, thyself deceive not	207	Fare Thee	21
Though human, thou didst not deceive me	210	Augusta-B	25
Cease to deceive; thy pilfer'd harp restore	246	Bards	307
(So fondly youthful dreams deceive	336	Abydos	2	708
It may deceive all hearts, save that within	353	Corsair	2	453
The holy father said, 'I don't deceive	469	Morgante	215
Sweeps o'er thee to the last; thou dost deceive	547	Faliero	5	662
I'll trust them. Do! They will deceive you sweetly	730	Deformed	1	584
Now though we know of old that looks deceive	978	Juan	15	670

DECEIVED

Deceived by its gigantic elegance	78	Harold	4	1398
In one, and one alone, deceived	132	L'Amitie	61
By some deceived, by others plunder'd	144	Becher-B	35
And he deceived me--for--he came again	344	Corsair	1	449
You must have been deceived, my brother. First	565	Sardan	2	209
They have deceived thee; thou shalt live. I live	629	Cain	1	109

DECEIVER

Woman, that fair and fond deceiver	97	To Woman	11
Delirium is our best deceiver	159	Spell	4
And spurns deceiver and deceit	173	Not False	8

DECEIVING

And they shall weep at your deceiving	86	Rousseau	4

DECEMBER

If, in the month of dark December	160	Swimming	1
Seek roses in December, ice in June	242	Bards	76
Their herald out of dim December	742	Deformed	3	18
Because December, with his breath so hoary	908	Juan	10	70

DECEMBER'S

December's drowsy day to his dull race	960	Juan	14	284

DECEMVIR

Decemvir, it is surely for the senate's	616	Foscari	4	85

DECEMVIRS

Forward to be one day of the decemvirs	598	Foscari	1	188

DECENCIES

Teach them the decencies of good threescore	918	Juan	10	681

DECENCY

Or for the sake of decency abide	766	Juan	1	1246

DECENT

I fain would take a decent leave	173	Quotation	26
And thus to furnish decent lining	227	Thurlow-A	10
Not decent David, when before the ark	274	Waltz	83
Werter, to decent vice though much inclined	275	Waltz	149
My talent is decent, as far as it goes	279	Blues	1	88
He was a decent sire, and middling lord	290	Vision	362
Without their decent dignity of fall	301	Age	240
Catullus scarcely has a decent poem	752	Juan	1	331
Like garden gods--and not so decent either	752	Juan	1	360
One should not rail without a decent cause	789	Juan	2	946
Pair of scarce decent trowsers--went to work	794	Juan	2	1274
After a decent time must be gallanted	802	Juan	3	28
In decent London when the daylight's o'er	922	Juan	11	237
I think I should have made a decent spouse	971	Juan	15	185

DECEPTION

I've seen too much of man's deception	144	Becher-B	11
In the goblet alone no deception is found	155	Goblet	4

DECIDE

Can such a verdict then decide	142	Critics	73
What the rest will decide I know not, but	518	Faliero	2	712
Let him decide if any should be saved	524	Faliero	3	416
Decide yourselves. You know their private virtues	524	Faliero	3	418
And not as judge to hear or to decide	536	Faliero	4	569
My heart will break. Now you know all--decide	584	Sardan	4	383
Fit to decide. But I came here to seek you	687	Werner	2	308
In Germany. The baron shall decide	691	Werner	2	532

DECIDE

Whatever dreads to die. Decide between	727	Deformed	1	355
And then decide, without great wrong to either	819	Juan	4	199
This I must leave sultanas to decide	846	Juan	5	916
The world, not the world's masters, will decide	897	Juan	9	30
'To be, or not to be?'--Ere I decide	898	Juan	9	121
I ne'er decide what I shall say, and this I call	901	Juan	9	325
Decide, and every body one day will	919	Juan	11	31
Abroad, such things decide few women's fate	938	Juan	12	509
Must the event decide between the two	966	Juan	14	715

DECIDED

(For 'tis not yet decided where they dwell	297	Vision		821
Which we won't suffer, but are quite decided	467	Morgante		95
Decided: but as yet his doom's unknown	500	Faliero	1	26
And is it then decided! must they die	526	Faliero	3	570
You were decided. It was ever thus	534	Faliero	4	442
Have slaves decided on the doom of kings	592	Sardan	5	308
We have decided. We? 'The Ten' in council	604	Foscari	2	196
(Join'd with the Doge) decided his destruction	619	Foscari	4	291
She next decided he was only bad	750	Juan	1	212
'They tell me 'tis decided; you depart	770	Juan	1	1529
Decided thus, and show'd good reason why	803	Juan	3	86
Because its own good pleasure hath decided	943	Juan	13	128
And morally decided, the best state is	971	Juan	15	230

DECIDES

Or Scottish taste decides on English wit	248	Bards		503
And who dare question aught that he decides	340	Corsair	1	172
Decides to-day must not give way before	619	Foscari	4	268

DECIMATE

For which men vainly decimate the throng	886	Juan	8	498

DECIMATED

Hath decimated Venice, put in peril	544	Faliero	5	446
Nor decimated them with savage laws	555	Sardan	1	277

DECISION

Judge with my judgment, and by my decision	297	Vision		803
To leave his reverence; but for this decision	475	Morgante		599
Of their decision? No, my lord; you know	500	Faliero	1	53
Be brief in your decision! I will be so	719	Werner	5	393

DECISIVE

His 'bravo' was decisive, for that sound	444	Beppo		249
'Tis royal. And should therefore be decisive	569	Sardan	2	503

DECK

Though thousands fall to deck some single name	11	Harold	1	471
White is the glassy deck, without a stain	22	Harold	2	163
With draughts intemperate on the sinking deck	37	Harold	3	143
Stretch'd along the deck like logs	157	Hodgson		50
With garlands deck your own Menander's head	170	Address-A		40
Promoted thence to deck her mistress' head	208	Sketch		2
No future laurels deck a noble head	251	Bards		724
What heterogeneous honours deck the peer	251	Bards		731
To deck the turf that wraps her minstrel, Burns	252	Bards		812
Not Cleopatra on her galley's deck	274	Waltz		89
Ay--let the loud winds whistle o'er the deck	334	Abydos	2	454
To move the monarch of her peopled deck	339	Corsair	1	96
They gain the vessel, on the deck he stands	346	Corsair	2	573
A spot--a mast--a sail--an armed deck	362	Corsair	3	483
''Tis Conrad!' shouting from the deck	363	Corsair	3	496
A hundred scutcheons deck with gloomy grace	366	Lara	1	39
These deck the shore; the waves their channel make	368	Lara	1	165
Disdain'd to deck a thing like me	399	Parisina		284
To deck her Count with titles given	408	Mazeppa		177
Alas! his deck was trod by unwilling feet	415	Island	1	25
Dragg'd o'er the deck, no more at thy command	416	Island	1	57
But some remain'd reluctant on the deck	417	Island	1	127
Flock o'er the deck, in Neptune's borrow'd car	425	Island	2	467
A spot to make the saved regret the deck	430	Island	4	27
With all could cheer or deck their sparry bower	432	Island	4	186
Chain'd on the deck, where once, a gallant crew	435	Island	4	359
On the horizon verged the distant deck	435	Island	4	385
There is not a plank of the hull or the deck	488	Manfred	2	326
And vainer fears. Within there!--Ye slaves, deck	561	Sardan	1	681
Gasping on deck, because you soar too high, Bob	745	Juan	Ded	23
And, standing upon deck, the dashing spray	775	Juan	2	85
So Juan stood, bewilder'd on the deck	775	Juan	2	97

DECK'D

Since title deck'd my higher birth	85	To E--		6
Of all that deck'd that passing pageantry	183	Address-D		6
And not a trapping deck'd my power	219	Vanity		15
With vests or ribands--deck'd alike in hue	276	Waltz		175
The chief before, as deck'd for war	315	Giaour		523
Though priest nor bless'd, nor marble deck'd the mound	382	Lara	2	523
And the pavilion, deck'd for our return	559	Sardan	1	601
Had deck'd her out in all the hues of heaven	830	Juan	4	908
A poniard deck'd her girdle, as the sign	845	Juan	5	887

DECK'D

From the manure of human clay, though deck'd	900	Juan	9	269
With many more by rank and fashion deck'd	947	Juan	13	414
Deck'd by the rays reflected from his host	947	Juan	13	421
Symmetrical, but deck'd with carvings quaint	949	Juan	13	514
(There's fame) young partridge fillets, deck'd with truffles	976	Juan	15	528

DECKING

Where the Mermaid is decking	479	Manfred	1	80

DECKS

Yes, Honour decks the turf that wraps their clay	10	Harold	1	451
Where glory decks the hero's bier	206	Year		19
And what dignity decks the flat face of the great man	227	Moore-A		16
That decks the wandering Candiote	330	Abydos	2	142
And majesty, which decks all other heads	546	Faliero	5	612
The water left the hold, and wash'd the decks	777	Juan	2	242

DECLAIMING

With dandies dined; heard senators declaiming	957	Juan	14	139

DECLAMATION

Or even, perhaps, the declamation prize	112	Examination		25

DECLARATION

Had changed the place of declaration	101	Lady-B		26
Is just two minutes for your declaration	847	Juan	5	983

DECLARE

When these declare, 'that pomp alone should wait	93	Dorset		21
What satellites declare her dismal reign	121	Newstead-A		98
When late I heard thy lips declare	152	Time-A		14
I have loved!--who has not?--but what heart can declare	155	Goblet		7
Declare his landlord can at least translate	249	Bards		551
Yet rarely blames unjustly, now declare	256	Bards		1070
Nor trace, nor tidings of his doom declare	366	Corsair	3	689
His sire was dust, his vassals could declare	366	Lara	1	29
Was to declare how sage, and still, and steady	753	Juan	1	399
That therefore do I previously declare	944	Juan	13	199
I do declare, upon an affidavit	965	Juan	14	633

DECLARED

Since Juliet first declared her passion	101	Lady-B		19
But had not thine own lips declared	330	Abydos	2	157
Hear, Myrrha; Salemenes has declared	558	Sardan	1	507
But Salemenes hath declared my throne	558	Sardan	1	510
By poison. When the Doge declared that he	596	Foscari	1	35
Declared, with all his grand discoveries recent	867	Juan	7	38
Has been declared an act of inurbanity	997	Juan	17	55

DECLARES

Your voice alone declares your flame	90	Caroline-B		13
Astrea declares that some penance is due	100	L Adieu		38
And Capel Lofft declares 'tis quite sublime	252	Bards		774
Who took Algiers, declares I used him vilely	765	Juan	1	1184
Because the publisher declares, in sooth	828	Juan	4	774

DECLARING

Declaring with a coxcomb's native air	142	Soliloquy		43

DECLINE

Happy, I ne'er shall see them in decline	3	To Ianthe		23
He stops, he starts, disdaining to decline	16	Harold	1	785
Of perish'd states he mourn'd in their decline	62	Harold	4	408
Who hath beheld decline upon my brow	75	Harold	4	1200
Night quits her car, the twinkling stars decline	139	Ossian-A		6
And vain was the hope to avert our decline	164	Newstead-C		15
Now hope, and he who hoped, decline	172	Romaic-B		22
And gilded thy decline	181	Ode-A		151
From life's commencement to its slow decline	212	Augusta-C		126
While I stood on the height, and beheld the decline	221	Jerusalem		11
If I decline on this occasion	231	Doctor		18
With amiable modesty, decline	297	Vision		794
Yea, foes--to me will Giaffir's hate decline	334	Abydos	2	466
Which follows the decline of day	396	Parisina		13
I saw it silently decline	403	Chillon		99
Yet do I feel at times my mind decline	439	Tasso		189
Irreparably soon decline, alas	447	Beppo		477
At these late years, decline what was the highest	506	Faliero	1	478
It is approaching. You decline to plead, then	540	Faliero	5	182
To my own sovereign. If I must decline	685	Werner	2	180
Decline all question of your guilt or innocence	692	Werner	2	593
To irrigate the dryness of decline	941	Juan	13	38
Then, if she hath not that serene decline	950	Juan	13	609
Radiant and grave--as pitying man's decline	973	Juan	15	357

DECLINED

Of her dead Doges are declined to dust	57	Harold	4	128
And the star of my fate hath declined	210	Augusta-B		2
Which lexicographers declined to do	257	Hints		76
I said his mighty heart declined	404	Chillon		127

DECLINED
With years, ye know, have not declined | 408 Mazeppa | 197
Was light·and baffling.'--'When the sun declined | 426 Island | 2 | 509
Will now take up the cause they once declined | 501 Faliero | 1 | 113
Of modesty declined the assistance proffer'd | 860 Juan | 6 | 484
Her face declined and was unseen; her hair | 865 Juan | 6 | 857
Must be declined, while life's thin thread's
   spun out | 946 Juan | 13 | 319

DECLINES
Till day declines adown the West | 91 Caroline-B | 30
When the glow of early thought declines in feel-
   ing's dull decay | 185 Music-B | 2
When Summer's day declines along the hills | 192 Monody | 20
Manhood declines--age palsies every limb | 260 Hints | 251
For he declines the convent oath | 319 Giaour | 899
Ere day declines, I shall have none | 398 Parisina | 201
And you his sister. Ere the sun declines | 653 Cain | 3 | 457

DECLINING
Declining gently, falls a fading flower | 110 Nisus | 382
Or, plunging from the green declining shore | 125 Recoll | 261
To cheer my last declining days | 138 Clare | 98
Declining was his attitude | 390 Corinth | 510

DECLIVITY
Upon a mild declivity of hill | 65 Harold | 4 | 597
Green and of mild declivity, the last | 214 Dream | 29
Descending rather quickly the declivity | 805 Juan | 3 | 226
Sunset the time, the place the same declivity | 919 Juan | 11 | 58

DECOMPOSE
The devil may decompose, but never settle | 859 Juan | 6 | 440

DECOMPOSED
But mingled millions decomposed to clay | 192 Fragment-C | 24

DECORATE
And decorate the verse herself inspires | 253 Bards | 856
Would rob poor Faith to decorate 'good works | 265 Hints | 594
Trimm'd either heads or hearts to decorate | 854 Juan | 6 | 110
Still unimpair'd, to decorate the scene | 949 Juan | 13 | 526

DECORATED
The decorated car appears, on high | 16 Harold | 1 | 788
A decorated victim led | 179 Gold | 32
The decorated street, the long array | 714 Werner | 5 | 112
And divers smoked superb pipes decorated | 838 Juan | 5 | 421

DECORATES
And decorates the book of Common Prayer | 855 Juan | 6 | 183

DECOROUS
To feel, or feign, decorous woe | 166 Euthanasia | 8
Upon decorous silence, few will twice | 296 Vision | 757
First came her damsels, a decorous file | 850 Juan | 5 | 1161
Flirtation--but decorous; the mere praise | 954 Juan | 13 | 861

DECORUM
Limping Decorum lingers far behind | 119 Answer-A | 12
To sanction Vice, and hunt Decorum down | 250 Bards | 621
Decorum left her for an opera dance | 261 Hints | 354
But here the Muse with due decorum halts | 275 Waltz | 121
Requires decorum, and is apt to double | 924 Juan | 11 | 367

DECOY
May no delights decoy | 138 Clare | 87
Decoy young border-nobles through the wood | 244 Bards | 158

DECREASED
And every new creation hath decreased | 901 Juan | 9 | 310

DECREASING
While first decreasing | 200 Stanzas-B | 54

DECREE
Of all Art yields, and Nature can decree | 59 Harold | 4 | 229
The harmony of things,--this hard decree | 74 Harold | 4 | 1127
Reverse of her decree than in the abyss | 77 Harold | 4 | 1355
United by the priest's decree | 90 To M.S.G.-A | 18
Though I ne'er shall presume to arraign the decree | 91 Caroline-C | 14
What punishment wilt thou decree | 99 Young Lady | 20
Nought shall thy dread decree prevent | 99 Young Lady | 34
Yet I deserve the stern decree | 174 Remember-B | 47
With voice as willing to decree the rack | 247 Bards | 445
Learn'd to deride the critic's starch decree | 256 Bards | 1059
No! happier made by that decree | 328 Abydos | 1 | 433
By Osman's power, and Giaffir's stern decree | 333 Abydos | 2 | 447
I form the plan, decree the spoil | 334 Abydos | 2 | 476
And, harsh as sounds thy hard decree | 399 Parisina | 310
Had only pass'd a just decree | 402 Parisina | 576
To the decree, whate'er it were;--but lo | 501 Faliero | 1 | 72
To execute the state's decree: I dared | 505 Faliero | 1 | 385
Of time or penalty--'tis a decree | 543 Faliero | 5 | 361

DECREE
Until this trial--the decree is death | 545 Faliero | 5 | 486
She might decree. And this is patriotism | 608 Foscari | 2 | 427
Announce 'the Ten's' decree. That tenderness | 612 Foscari | 3 | 258
To the alternative of a decree | 621 Foscari | 5 | 48
What you decree--decree. With this, then,
   must we | 621 Foscari | 5 | 61
You have heard it. Hear you then the last decree | 623 Foscari | 5 | 164
But the decree being render'd, I obey | 623 Foscari | 5 | 186
Jehovah's late decree | 666 Heaven | 801
In the decree | 666 Heaven | 816
Be the decree adored | 670 Heaven | 1152
(For Day ne'er saw his merits) could decree | 872 Juan | 7 | 324
As if each charming word were a decree | 978 Juan | 15 | 652

DECREED
But mix'd with pangs to Love's even loveliest
   hours decreed | 3 To Ianthe | 27
Some days of joyaunce are decreed to all | 32 Harold | 2 | 743
Were this decreed, beneath yon rising mound | 105 Nisus | 33
An instant message to their prince decreed | 106 Nisus | 90
Till royal sacrilege their doom decreed | 120 Newstead-A | 40
Oh say not, sweet Anne, that the Fates have
   decreed | 147 To Anne-B | 1
Then say not, sweet Anne, that the Fates have
   decreed | 147 To Anne-B | 13
And more decreed his glory to endure | 183 Address-D | 11
'Twas carried, as the King decreed | 195 Ballad-A | 104
Yet lived to view the doom his ire decreed | 362 Corsair | 3 | 451
Will be as could be wish'd. Say on. 'Decreed | 501 Faliero | 1 | 86
Give me the paper. ''Tis decreed in council | 501 Faliero | 1 | 100
The Forty hath decreed a month's arrest | 503 Faliero | 1 | 241
Decreed to him by the twice rescued city | 520 Faliero | 3 | 91
Decreed as sentence! Base as was his crime | 541 Faliero | 5 | 238
And now, sir, to your business. 'Tis decreed | 605 Foscari | 2 | 260
The thing's decreed. The Giunta and 'the Ten | 619 Foscari | 4 | 257
Such pangs decreed to aught save me | 655 Heaven | 48
It is decreed | 662 Heaven | 528
I cannot, must not, aid you. 'Tis decreed | 669 Heaven | 1070

DECREES
Or Heaven reverse the dread decrees of fate | 84 Death-B | 10
As by the fix'd decrees of Heaven | 140 Pignus | 1
But thy weakness decrees I should leave as I
   found thee | 186 Napoleon | 11
By whose decrees, our sinful souls to save | 250 Bards | 634
Safety, and all save honour, the decrees | 605 Foscari | 2 | 258
To use for the decrees of--Daughter, know you | 606 Foscari | 2 | 287
Anah! and thou?--Whate'er our God decrees | 664 Heaven | 693

DECREPITUDE
Not their decrepitude: and he of late | 509 Faliero | 2 | 22

DECRY
As oil in lieu of butter men decry | 265 Hints | 629
Can stand tamely in silence to hear you decry | 277 Blues | 1 | 13

DEDICATE
Meantime, Sir Laureate, I proceed to dedicate | 747 Juan | Ded | 129

DEDUCE
From whom I now deduce these moral lessons | 946 Juan | 13 | 301

DEDUCTED
Thy long, long bills, whence nothing is deducted | 916 Juan | 10 | 552

DEDUCTION
Is that your deduction? When speaking of Scamp
   ill | 278 Blues | 1 | 54

DEE
Thou sweet flowing Dee, to thy waters adieu | 136 Highlander | 46
The Dee, the Don, Balgounie's brig's black wall | 909 Juan | 10 | 139

DEED
How will posterity the deed proclaim | 8 Harold | 1 | 310
Sung the loud song, and dared the deed of war | 12 Harold | 1 | 561
So may such foes deserve the most remorseless deed | 18 Harold | 1 | 899
Tell not the deed to blushing Europe's ears | 21 Harold | 2 | 112
From birth till death enslaved; in word, in deed,
   unmann'd | 31 Harold | 2 | 710
The wrecks are all thy deed, nor doth remain | 82 Harold | 4 | 1607
(The deed, the danger, and the fame be mine | 105 Nisus | 32
Oh no! whene'er my breast forgets the deed | 126 Recoll | 285
'Son of Trenmor! mine be the deed,' said | 130 Calmar | 55
In word, as well as Deed | 151 Harriet | 6
She dares the deed and shares the danger | 160 Cadiz | 38
An equal deed hast done at length | 180 Ode-A | 51
Hast thou no weapon for my daring deed | 265 Hints | 608
A true-born Briton may the deed disclaim | 270 Minerva | 126
'First on the head of him who did this deed | 270 Minerva | 163
My wrath is wreak'd, the deed is done | 317 Giaour | 687
For some dark deed he will not name | 318 Giaour | 801
I proved it more in deed than word | 320 Giaour | 1031

DEED

Thou wilt absolve me from the deed	320 Giaour		1038
And daring deed, and vengeful steel	321 Giaour		1108
The deed that's done canst thou undo	322 Giaour		1205
To witness many an active deed	326 Abydos	1	237
How Giaffir wrought this deed of fear	331 Abydos	2	212
'The deed once done, and Paswan's feud	331 Abydos	2	248
A hand to point them to the deed	331 Abydos	2	275
No deed they've done, nor deed shall do	334 Abydos	2	474
How well such deed becomes the turban'd brave	347 Corsair	2	18
But cries 'I warn'd thee!' when the deed is o'er	352 Corsair	2	333
Of Seyd's revenge, by many a lawless deed	359 Corsair	3	287
But for that deed of darkness what wert thou	362 Corsair	3	470
A woman's hand secured that deed her own	363 Corsair	3	509
Hate of that deed but grief for her distress	363 Corsair	3	524
In word and deed obey'd, in soul abhorr'd	377 Lara	2	167
And the next word shall scarce outstrip the deed	380 Lara	2	341
From post to post, and deed to deed	385 Corinth		101
And proved, by many a deed of death	386 Corinth		157
Of rest, to nerve for many a deed	387 Corinth		293
When man would do a deed of worth	388 Corinth		419
Thou hast done a fearful deed	390 Corinth		575
But ere he break--a deed is to be done	415 Island	1	16
Remorse for the black deed as yet half done	417 Island	1	157
The deed was over! All were gone or ta'en	435 Island	4	357
Her sons, may do this with one deed--Unite	460 Dante	2	145
While Charles reposed him thus, in word and deed	467 Morgante		83
This wreck of a realm--this deed of my doing	488 Manfred	2	350
The consequence will santcify the deed	519 Faliero	3	73
Oime! Oime!--and must I do this deed	525 Faliero	3	462
Seem each a trophy of some mighty deed	529 Faliero	4	80
Thou hast done a worthy deed, and earn'd the price	537 Faliero	4	602
With them and all things. Save one deed--the last	591 Sardan	5	228
Shall spare this deed of mine, and hold it up	594 Sardan	5	446
A dotage which may justify this deed	624 Foscari	5	266
Done, that we must be victims for a deed	647 Cain	3	89
Or what hath done this deed?--speak, Cain, since thou	652 Cain	3	387
Shrink from the deed which leaves thee brotherless	653 Cain	3	464
I had not named his deed, but that thyself	664 Heaven		682
For pious purposes. A proper deed	712 Werner	4	484
Than common stabber! What deed of my life	719 Werner	5	424
Nor much disposed to wait in word or deed	864 Juan	6	802
Rolls by the city wall; but deed nor word	889 Juan	8	692
Came up, all marvelling at such a deed	920 Juan	11	107

DEEDS

Can blazon evil deeds or consecrate a crime	4 Harold	1	27
When wanton Wealth her mightiest deeds hath done	7 Harold	1	277
Destruction cowers to mark what deeds are done	10 Harold	1	429
Portend the deeds to come:--but he whose nod	12 Harold	1	540
Four cavaliers prepare for venturous deeds	15 Harold	1	731
Shrunk from his deeds of chivalrous emprize	25 Harold	2	337
The deeds that lurk beneath and stain him with disgrace	28 Harold	2	558
In deeds, not years, piercing the depths of life	36 Harold	3	38
What deeds of prowess unrecorded died	42 Harold	3	434
But these are deeds which should not pass away	45 Harold	3	635
O'er erring deeds and thoughts a heavenly hue	47 Harold	3	731
Were all thy proud historic deeds forgot	57 Harold	4	146
Where endless pleasures virtue's deeds repay	84 Death-B		16
Oh may no other fame my deeds repay	86 Fragment-A		10
To deeds of fame and notes of fire	88 Anacreon-A		2
Alcides and his glorious deeds	88 Anacreon-A		15
To other deeds my soul is strung	88 Anacreon-A		21
Bright are the deeds thine earlier sires display	94 Dorset		66
Should urge the soul to deeds of hell	105 Alva		296
Shall Allan's deeds on harp-strings raise	105 Alva		306
'These deeds, my Nisus, shalt thou dare alone	106 Nisus		39
Thou know'st my deeds, my breast devoid of fear	106 Nisus		47
What poor rewards can bless your deeds on earth	107 Nisus		135
'Now,' cries the first, 'for deeds of blood prepare	108 Nisus		231
Your deeds on the echoes of dark Loch na Garr	118 Lachin		32
Though still our deeds amuse the youthful race	124 Recoll		165
Nor say the deeds of animosity	144 Becher-B		30
Can I sing of the deeds which my Fathers have done	148 Farewell-A		25
Thine evil deeds are writ in gore	181 Ode-A		91
Save in deeds that led them on	187 Ode-B		26
The deeds he did, the fields he won	218 Thy Days		5
'Gainst Nature's voice seduced to deeds accurst	223 To Dives		2
Whose proudest deeds disgrace the name of man	254 Bards		938
Yet many deeds preserved in history's page	260 Hints		267
Below, his name--above, behold his deeds	270 Minerva		108
Hers were the deeds that taught her lawless son	271 Minerva		211
Not to such deeds did Pallas lend her aid	271 Minerva		215
His deeper deeds as yet ye know by name	272 Minerva		299
Depends upon his deeds.' the Angel said	293 Vision		546
Thou Rome, who saw'st thy Caesar's deeds outdone	300 Age		137
Thy sons to deeds sublime	311 Giaour		149
Of wayward deeds, and fitting doom	318 Giaour		867

DEEDS

Dark as to thee my deeds may seem	320 Giaour		999
In madness do those fearful deeds	321 Giaour		1153
To thee, old man, my deeds appear	321 Giaour		1160
Are emblems of deeds that are done in their clime	323 Abydos	1	2
Can he smile on such deeds as his children have done	323 Abydos	1	17
But there be deeds thou dar'st not do	325 Abydos	1	121
A heart his words nor deeds can daunt	327 Abydos	1	366
Makes even their mightiest deeds appear his own	341 Corsair	1	186
His soul was changed, before his deeds had driven	342 Corsair	1	251
Those deeds the bolder spirit plainly did	342 Corsair	1	268
Equipp'd for deeds alike on land or deep	347 Corsair	1	604
Deeds, thoughts, and words, perhaps remember'd not	352 Corsair	2	348
Grateful for deeds thou hast too rarely done	353 Corsair	2	436
Whose deeds are daring as their hearts are true	357 Corsair	3	130
His death yet dubious, deeds too widely known	366 Corsair	3	694
Art thou not he? whose deeds--' 'Whate'er I be	372 Lara	1	455
From deeds, and deeds alone, may he discern	373 Lara	1	508
His faith in reverence and in deeds alone	374 Lara	1	555
Enquiry into deeds at distance done	378 Lara	2	239
And Honour's eye on daring deeds	389 Corinth		488
Which follows fast the deeds of ill	397 Parisina		64
The prayers of Abel link'd to deeds of Cain	420 Island	2	72
And what have Caesar's deeds and Caesar's fame	423 Island	2	320
Yet reek'd, the remnant of himself and deeds	434 Island	4	346
Of cheerful creatures, whose most sinful deeds	453 Venice-B		26
Yes! the few spirits--who, despite of deeds	454 Venice-B		92
And deeds, and contemplation, and have met	456 Dante	1	45
Ruin, already proud of the deeds done	459 Dante	2	73
For your just pious deeds may you be graced	475 Morgante		636
To justify my deeds unto myself	482 Manfred	1	289
And deeds of good and ill, extreme in both	485 Manfred	2	129
My days are number'd, and my deeds recorded	495 Manfred	3	314
One who has done great deeds, and seen great changes	518 Faliero	2	677
To syllable black deeds into smooth names	519 Faliero	3	58
'Tis in such deeds as we are now upon	520 Faliero	3	98
That I abhor them doubly for the deeds	520 Faliero	3	116
And urge them on to deeds, and not to war	522 Faliero	3	273
Of deeds that else were silent, save on marble	525 Faliero	3	461
And many deeds and days--the senators	527 Faliero	3	572
By all the good deeds thou hast done to me	530 Faliero	4	177
And justify their deeds unto themselves	534 Faliero	4	456
With words, but deeds. Keep thou awake that energy	557 Sardan	1	429
In deeds, and days, and sway, and, let me add	607 Foscari	2	402
Hundreds of doges, and their deeds and dates	610 Foscari	3	121
Due to his years, his station, and his deeds	615 Foscari	4	30
How death itself bears witness to thy deeds	619 Foscari	4	244
Shown in the exemption of thy deeds from evil	649 Cain	3	247
Exemption from such deeds as thou hast done	653 Cain	3	499
Go forth! fulfil thy days! and be thy deeds	654 Cain	3	517
With other deeds between his God and him	664 Heaven		680
Rebel! thy words are wicked, as thy deeds	669 Heaven		1049
Taught me to name a ruffian from his deeds	689 Werner	2	429
But dark deeds (ay, the darkest, if all Rumour	709 Werner	4	337
At once both warm and weak invites to deeds	720 Werner	4	451
But your own will, no contract save your deeds	724 Deformed	1	151
They woo with fearless deeds the smiles of fortune	727 Deformed	1	321
As in his deeds. Your highness much mistakes me	733 Deformed	1	806
And for my deeds, I only sting when stung	733 Deformed	1	808
My word is known. So shall be my deeds	738 Deformed	2	202
Rather by deeds than words, because the case	794 Juan	2	1266
Prompts deeds eternity can not annul	798 Juan	2	1533
Amidst the savage deeds he had done and seen	808 Juan	3	452
Great deeds are doing--how shall I relate 'em	877 Juan	7	646
Of deeds to human happiness most dear	877 Juan	7	662
My chance so happen--deeds), with all who war	899 Juan	9	186
Did not his deeds unriddle them each day	902 Juan	9	396
And care but for discoveries and not deeds	940 Juan	12	636
Of deeds and days when they had fill'd the ear	974 Juan	15	365

DEEM

And monks might deem their time was come agen	4 Harold	1	62
Yet deem not thence his breast a breast of steel	5 Harold	1	87
Yet deem not these devotion's offering	7 Harold	1	263
Though sluggards deem it but foolish chase	9 Harold	1	346
Deem ye what bounds the rival realms divide	9 Harold	1	361
Scarce would you deem that Saragoza's tower	13 Harold	1	573
And lately had he learn'd with truth to deem	17 Harold	1	814
Twined with my heart, and can I deem thee dead	20 Harold	2	75
Who but would deem their bosoms burn'd anew	31 Harold	2	713
We are not what we have been, and to deem	52 Harold	3	1033
They could not deem me one of such: I stood	52 Harold	3	1054
Snares for the failing: I would also deem	53 Harold	3	1063
As, with a sigh, I deem thou mightst have been to me	53 Harold	3	1102
When least we deem of such, calls up to view	58 Harold	4	213
And all we deem delightful and consume	68 Harold	4	771
Something unearthly which they deem not of	75 Harold	4	1230
Nor deem me too happy in this	98 To M.S.G.-B		14

DEEM

Start not--nor deem my spirit fled	154	Skull		1
Nor rather deem from nightly cries	158	Storm		27
Nor deem that memory less dear	168	Haunts		13
And almost deem the sentence sweet	174	Remember-B		48
Little didst thou deem, when dashing	187	Ode-B		44
Look on the picture! deem it not o'ercharged	209	Sketch		73
Nor given him cause to deem himself beloved	215	Dream		141
Against that ridicule they deem so hard	263	Hints		466
My good old friend, for such I deem you; though	292	Vision		490
Good Mrs. Malaprop); then you might deem	294	Vision		627
Right well I view and deem thee one	312	Giaour		198
How could I deem his courser slow	317	Giaour		706
Aught that I deem a worthy prize	320	Giaour		1017
Then deem it evil, what thou wilt	321	Giaour		1143
But deem such feeble, heartless man	321	Giaour		1176
Ah! deem I right? the Pacha's plan	327	Abydos	1	309
For well may maids of Helle deem	336	Abydos	2	683
And turn what some deem danger to delight	338	Corsair	1	18
What others deem a penance is thy choice	344	Corsair	1	432
They little deem of aught in peril's shape	348	Corsair	2	90
And deem design had left me single here	349	Corsair	2	169
That deem right dearly won the field he lost	351	Corsair	2	276
Look to thyself, nor deem thy falsehood safe	358	Corsair	3	193
Let me not deem that mercy shown amiss	361	Corsair	3	367
They see, they recognize, yet almost deem	367	Lara	1	53
To deem them accents of another land	369	Lara	1	232
Of guilt, of peril, do they deem	397	Parisina		41
I own that I should deem it much	412	Mazeppa		563
And Death, whom he should deem his friend	414	Mazeppa		749
But deem him sailor or philosopher	425	Island	2	447
Or lived to deem the happiest were the slain	426	Island	3	10
And deem this proof of loyalty the real	453	Venice-B		73
Their sail, and deem it glory to be class'd	456	Dante	1	56
From out the schoolman's jargon, I should deem	491	Manfred	3	12
Thine order, and revere thine years; I deem	493	Manfred	3	155
And deem you this enough for such foul scorn	509	Faliero	2	48
That far too often makes them deem they would	510	Faliero	2	130
Your fiery nature makes you deem all those	517	Faliero	2	576
Should deem thee dangerous, and keep the house	531	Faliero	4	255
Signor! complete that which you deem your duty	544	Faliero	5	467
Rather than deem these mortals, most of whom	547	Faliero	5	645
Deem that some unknown influence, some sweet oracle	557	Sardan	1	471
We deem our happiness: let me remove	558	Sardan	1	481
Or if they think so, deem it necessary	559	Sardan	1	587
And hear him whine, it may be--Do not deem it	563	Sardan	2	88
King! do not deem so: they are with the stars	565	Sardan	2	243
As I have said, I will not deem ye guilty	566	Sardan	2	290
And kings are--But I did not deem it so	579	Sardan	4	49
They are now the only tie between us. Deem not	582	Sardan	4	262
So like we almost deem it permanent	587	Sardan	5	15
Surely he is a god! So we Greeks deem too	588	Sardan	5	53
They are to deem that I reject their terms	592	Sardan	5	346
Should never deem himself a sovereign till	596	Foscari	1	36
He judges. Then deem not the laws too harsh	596	Foscari	1	83
I will not deem it: he hath nerved himself	599	Foscari	1	249
Is far the worst of treasons. Dost thou deem	607	Foscari	2	388
I did not deem this poor place could have drawn	612	Foscari	3	250
Could I but deem them happy, I would half	634	Cain	1	436
Worship the word which strikes their ear, and deem	636	Cain	2	10
Yet deem not that thou canst escape it; thou	638	Cain	2	148
Which looks like water, and which I should deem	642	Cain	2	385
He would but deem it was the moon	656	Heaven		140
We deem our curses vain; we must expire	670	Heaven		1122
Were it a garden, I should deem thee happy	671	Werner	1	5
I am to deem the plunderer is caught	686	Werner	2	197
Should he prove other than I deem. This robbery	687	Werner	2	288
Deem yourself safe, as young and brave; but learn	690	Werner	2	464
Fools deem me knave: it is their homage. How	691	Werner	2	528
But if he be the man I deem (and that	694	Werner	2	687
To deem he would descend to such an act	695	Werner	2	757
I could not deem it earth-born: but be calm	716	Werner	5	181
I know you innocent, and deem you just	716	Werner	5	204
Or thought of mine, could make you deem me fit	719	Werner	5	425
You deem, a single moment would have made you	723	Deformed	1	91
The devil in disguise--since so you deem me	730	Deformed	1	540
Amongst the stars, which these poor creatures deem	735	Deformed	1	891
Is mighty--as you mortals deem--and to	744	Deformed	3	139
To deem as a most logical conclusion	745	Juan	Ded	37
None can deem harshlier of me than I deem	770	Juan	1	1542
And deem not, what I deem'd, my soul invincible	773	Juan	1	1704
And deem that it was saved, perhaps in vain	787	Juan	2	864
Deem this a commentator's fantasy	803	Juan	3	84
I could not deem myself a slave	812	Juan	3	706
And always envy, though we deem it frantic	818	Juan	4	144
Which for himself he seem'd to deem no worse	832	Juan	5	95
Which is not quite so light as you may deem	841	Juan	5	652
These are but vulgar oaths, as you may deem	878	Juan	8	2
To deem the woods shall be our home at last	885	Juan	8	480
And deem, because we see, we are all-seeing	898	Juan	9	124
For me, I deem an absolute autocrat	899	Juan	9	183
If this be true; for we must deem the mode	907	Juan	10	10
You'll deem, no doubt, they put it to a good use	912	Juan	10	288
Which Britons deem their 'uti possidetis	913	Juan	10	360
Weakness, for what most people deem mere vermin	913	Juan	10	397
How all the nations deem her their worst foe	915	Juan	10	533
Some deem it but the distant echo given	949	Juan	13	502
Of what they deem themselves most consequential	958	Juan	14	158
Some would not deem such women could be found	961	Juan	14	348
Than when some squeamish people deem her frail	976	Juan	15	508
Was weak enough to deem Pope a great poet	987	Juan	16	423
Are so divine, that I must deem them real	994	Juan	16	904

DEEM'D

Though Beauty long hath there been matchless deem'd	2	To Ianthe		2
Oh, thou! in Hellas deem'd of heavenly birth	3	Harold	1	1
Nor deem'd before his little day was done	4	Harold	1	30
When deem'd he no strange ear was listening	5	Harold	1	112
So deem'd the Childe, as o'er the mountains he	8	Harold	1	315
Nor let thy votary's hope be deem'd an idle vaunt	14	Harold	1	647
Which the stern dotard deem'd he could encage	17	Harold	1	804
Yet if, as holiest men have deem'd, there be	20	Harold	2	64
Thus Harold deem'd, as on that lady's eye	24	Harold	2	271
Well deem'd the little God his ancient sway was o'er	24	Harold	2	279
He felt, or deem'd he felt, no common glow	25	Harold	2	364
Might well itself be deem'd of dignity	27	Harold	2	436
And deem'd its spring perpetual--but in vain	36	Harold	3	76
And deem'd his spirit now so firmly fix'd	36	Harold	3	84
And when they smiled because he deem'd it near	38	Harold	3	203
Who deem'd thee for a time whate'er thou didst assert	41	Harold	3	333
Monarchs partook, and deem'd their dignity increased	55	Harold	4	18
Darken above our bones, yet fondly deem'd	80	Harold	4	1527
I deem'd that time, I deem'd that pride	155	Happy		21
For then I deem'd the heavenly light	166	Struggle		27
By Friendship ever deem'd too nigh	169	Blank Leaf		6
In flattering dreams I deem'd thee mine	172	Romaic-B		21
I should have deem'd thee doom'd to earthly care	175	Sonnet-A		8
Nor deem'd Contempt could thus make mirth	181	Ode-A		107
When, dreading to be deem'd too kind	209	Augusta-A		7
In Judah deem'd divine	220	Belshaz-B		6
And all with justice deem'd the two combined	248	Bards		488
At first none deem'd it his; but when his name	264	Hints		567
His very rival almost deem'd him such	298	Age		12
Scarce deem'd the coffin's lead could keep him fast	299	Age		102
Somewhat of this had Hassan deem'd	314	Giaour		459
Nor deem'd she, could he long endure	330	Abydos	2	109
That Selim late was deem'd to thee	331	Abydos	2	198
But little deem'd a brother's wrath	331	Abydos	2	242
Nor deem'd that gifts bestow'd on better men	342	Corsair	1	259
He knew himself a villain, but he deem'd	342	Corsair	1	265
And deem'd the breath that faintly fann'd thy sail	343	Corsair	1	373
The Pacha woo'd as if he deem'd the slave	351	Corsair	2	265
Nor deem'd it cold--her chill was at her heart	356	Corsair	3	82
That deem'd not till they found their energy	357	Corsair	3	96
And little deem'd he what thy heart, Gulnare	358	Corsair	3	198
Announced that any heard or deem'd him nigh	364	Corsair	3	584
They deem'd him better than his air express'd	367	Lara	1	114
All was not well, they deem'd--but where the wrong	368	Lara	1	149
So Lara deem'd, nor longer there he stood	368	Lara	1	172
But that I deem'd him scarcely less than mad	376	Lara	2	47
They deem'd him now unhappy, though at first	377	Lara	2	176
He deem'd himself mark'd out for others' hate	378	Lara	2	250
Deem'd few were slain, while more remain'd to slay	379	Lara	2	277
Of these they had not deem'd: the battle-day	379	Lara	2	302
From this, you might have deem'd young Kaled's death	381	Lara	2	456
And many deem'd her heart was won	386	Corinth		194
The cross he deem'd no more divine	390	Corinth		539
Little deem'd she such a day	395	Corinth		1046
In sooth he had not deem'd of this	397	Parisina		100
But wrong for wrong: this deem'd thy bride	399	Parisina		253
I sometimes deem'd that it might be	405	Chillon		287
The first of men, nor less he deem'd	410	Mazeppa		352
I little deem'd another day	414	Mazeppa		716
Their manly courage even when deem'd in vain	418	Island	1	180
Had from that moment deem'd the deep his home	421	Island	2	170
What deem'd they of the future or the past	423	Island	2	352
Yet still the lingering hope, which deem'd their lot	426	Island	3	33
The wound was slighter than he deem'd or fear'd	428	Island	3	152
Or deem'd him mad, or prey to the blue shark	432	Island	4	208
A goddess rise--so deem'd they in their awe	432	Island	4	212
Was deem'd a woman of the strictest principle	443	Beppo		207
She deem'd the window-frames and shutters brittle	443	Beppo		229
The brave, the chivalrous, how little deem'd	512	Faliero	2	272
All who were deem'd trustworthy; there are some	517	Faliero	2	644
Who would have deem'd it?--Ah! one moment sooner	537	Faliero	4	623
Upon their open thoughts; but still I deem'd	539	Faliero	5	111

DEEM'D

That he is deem'd a god for what he did — 553 Sardan 1 201
He did, and thence was deem'd a deity — 554 Sardan 1 214
A diadem around it. Sire, I deem'd — 573 Sardan 3 131
You deem'd! Are you too turn'd a rebel? Fellow — 573 Sardan 3 135
Myself a host that deem'd himself but guest — 579 Sardan 4 80
Had deem'd them rather the bright populace — 639 Cain 2 210
Were I the victor, his works would be deem'd — 645 Cain 2 650
With him who deem'd it hard — 666 Heaven 841
With thee, I should have deem'd it what it is — 673 Werner 1 131
I deem'd this humble garb, and route obscure — 680 Werner 1 569
The villain I am deem'd, the service render'd — 691 Werner 2 562
Must I bear to be deem'd a thief? If 'twere — 692 Werner 2 617
I therefore deem'd him wealthy. But my soul — 717 Werner 5 252
The devil speaks truth much oftener than he's deem'd — 741 Deformed 2 387
As if she deem'd that mystery would ennoble 'em — 748 Juan 1 104
'Tis also pleasant to be deem'd magnanimous — 750 Juan 1 235
And everybody but his mother deem'd — 753 Juan 1 428
Her plan she deem'd both innocent and feasible — 757 Juan 1 657
And deem not, what I deem'd, my soul invincible — 773 Juan 1 1704
And when they deem'd its moisture was complete — 784 Juan 2 676
Yet deem'd herself in common pity bound — 790 Juan 2 1030
Such appetite in one she had deem'd dead — 794 Juan 2 1260
To be her happiness, and whom she deem'd — 796 Juan 2 1374
But certainly to one deem'd dead, returning — 807 Juan 3 391
He deem'd, being in a lone isle, among friends — 811 Juan 3 660
Him whom she deem'd a habitant where dwell — 821 Juan 4 283
If the soprano might be deem'd to be male — 828 Juan 4 732
And deem'd herself extremely condescending — 846 Juan 5 923
She deem'd her least command must yield delight — 847 Juan 5 1019
In sight two horsemen, who were deem'd Cossacques — 872 Juan 7 338
She merely was deem'd amiable and witty — 935 Juan 12 372
Hath won the experience which is deem'd so weighty — 936 Juan 12 400
Since laughter now-a-days is deem'd too serious — 941 Juan 13 2
She deem'd his merits something more than common — 973 Juan 15 318
And deem'd that fallen worship far more dear — 974 Juan 15 363
Little Aurora deem'd she was the theme — 975 Juan 15 433
Of flatterers, though she deem'd he had more sense — 978 Juan 15 659
And 'Hayley's Triumphs,' which she deem'd pathetic — 987 Juan 16 443
So much he deem'd his patronage an honour — 988 Juan 16 502
Who, in his life-time, each, was deem'd a Bore — 997 Juan 17 68

DEEMEST

The works thou deemest most divine — 234 Strahan 14

DEEMING

Deeming themselves predestined to a doom — 60 Harold 4 303
Deeming it midnight:--Temples, baths, or halls — 71 Harold 4 960
In deeming such inhabit many a spot — 81 Harold 4 1592
You may do your own deeming--you have codes — 567 Sardan 2 379
Deeming me wholly his. I cannot think it — 697 Werner 3 155
Deeming themselves the breakers of the ocean — 739 Deformed 2 292
Deeming the chain it wears even men may fit — 746 Juan Ded 116
That even the able seaman, deeming his — 778 Juan 2 261
And deeming there were remedies for any ill — 781 Juan 2 471
For deeming human clay but common dirt — 874 Juan 7 461
By deeming that my Mise's conversation — 979 Juan 15 750
Deeming the sage would be much mortified — 986 Juan 16 389

DEEMS

To shed before his Shrine the blood he deems most sweet — 10 Harold 1 431
Let these too go, for waking Reason deems — 56 Harold 4 61
She deems that all could be like her below — 208 Sketch 34
Than he who deems even Seraphs insecure — 222 Spirit 8
And deems himself of Shakespeare's peers — 235 Epilogue 14
Little deems our young blooming sleeper there — 648 Cain 3 122
To brighter destinies, if so she deems them — 657 Heaven 176
With which he deems him rich. It would be well — 734 Deformed 1 829
Prophetically, or that which one deems — 862 Juan 6 622
But deems himself the first in Glory's van — 877 Juan 7 670
He deems it is his proper place to be — 927 Juan 11 549

DEEM'ST

'Deem'st thou I tremble for my life — 6 Harold 1 162
Were my bosom as false as thou deem'st it to be — 221 False 1
And deem'st thou me unknown too? Gaze again — 372 Lara 1 439
Perhaps thou deem'st this lad a Mars in heart — 468 Morgante 116
Deem'st thou the souls of such a race as mine — 520 Faliero 3 99
In Styx. Then let it be as thou deem'st best — 727 Deformed 1 310

DEEP
(See also KNEE-DEEP)

And Tagus dashing onward to the deep — 6 Harold 1 203
The tender azure of the unruffled deep — 7 Harold 1 247
Deep in yon cave Honorius long did dwell — 7 Harold 1 259
Ne barrier wall, ne river deep and wide — 9 Harold 1 366
The sister tenants of the middle deep — 23 Harold 2 254
While the deep war-drum's sound announced the close of day — 28 Harold 2 513

But hush! hark! a deep sound strikes like a rising knell — 38 Harold 3 189
And the deep thunder peal on peal afar — 39 Harold 3 221
Which, be it wisdom, coldness, or deep pride — 41 Harold 3 345
And peasant girls, with deep blue eyes — 43 Harold 3 506
Deep in its fountain, lest it overboil — 46 Harold 3 656
Is not the love of these deep in my heart — 47 Harold 3 709
What deep wounds ever closed without a scar — 48 Harold 3 788
Deep into Nature's breast the spirit of her hues — 48 Harold 3 823
And silent, as we stand in thoughts too deep — 49 Harold 3 835
Clarens, sweet Clarens, birthplace of deep Love — 50 Harold 3 923
And wonderful, and deep, and hath a sound — 51 Harold 3 974
The other, deep and slow, exhausting thought — 51 Harold 3 995
Existence may be borne, and the deep root — 58 Harold 4 181
In the deep umbrage of a green hill's shade — 60 Harold 4 284
Down the deep Alps; nor would the hostile horde — 61 Harold 4 383
That ever left the sky on the deep soul to beam — 63 Harold 4 477
Life short, and truth a gem which loves the deep — 69 Harold 4 831
Deep in the unpruned forest, 'midst the roar — 69 Harold 4 861
Sown deep, even in the bosom of the North — 69 Harold 4 881
Buried in air, the deep blue sky of Rome — 71 Harold 4 991
The sweetness of the violet's deep blue eyes — 72 Harold 4 1052
Of an Italian night, where the deep skies assume — 74 Harold 4 1152
The deep prophetic fulness of this verse — 75 Harold 4 1205
With a deep awe, yet all distinct from fear — 75 Harold 4 1237
Derives from thee a sense so deep and clear — 76 Harold 4 1240
Full swells the deep pure fountain of young life — 77 Harold 4 1333
Great Nature's Nile, whose deep stream rises higher — 77 Harold 4 1348
With some deep and immedicable wound — 80 Harold 4 1498
A deep cold settled aspect nought can shake — 81 Harold 4 1556
By the deep Sea, and music in its roar — 81 Harold 4 1597
Roll on, thou deep and dark blue Ocean, roll — 81 Harold 4 1603
The monsters of the deep are made; each zone — 82 Harold 4 1646
A grief too deep to trust the sculptor's art — 85 Epitaph 14
Deep in my tortured heart it lies — 89 Anacreon-B 44
Throbb'd with deep sorrow as thine own — 90 Caroline-A 8
Receding slowly through the dark-blue deep — 94 Dorset 89
Or puzzles o'er the deep triangle — 95 Granta 42
Or, as Lear, I pour'd forth the deep imprecation — 96 Harrow-A 21
Then hear my thought:--In deep and sullen grief — 105 Nisus 29
Deep in his throat its end the weapon found — 110 Nisus 395
To roam a dreary world in deep despair — 120 Newstead-A 47
Of all lies deep in Lethe's wave — 128 Answer-A 42
Gloaming a deep phosphoric fire — 141 Critics 29
With tears the dark sepulchral deep — 146 Adieu 99
Oh, from the deep temptation fly — 146 Vain Lady 11
Young Oak! when I planted thee deep in the ground — 149 Newstead-B 1
None, none hath sunk so deep as this — 152 Time-A 9
For him that wanders o'er the deep — 156 Lady-F 64
And deep embosom'd in his shady groves — 161 Athos 10
A star that trembled o'er the deep — 166 Away 27
(This deep discovery is mine alone — 171 Address-B 26
Let deep and dreary silence be — 174 Revanche 7
The deep thoughts that dwell in that silence of heart — 182 Music-A 4
While deep Remembrance pours to Worth — 184 Parker 15
Deep for the dead the grief must be — 184 Parker 35
Yes--deep and heavy, one by one — 186 Stanzas-A 9
Her bright chain o'er the deep — 188 Music-C 10
With a deep thought, and with a soften'd eye — 191 Churchill 40
And a firm will, and a deep sense — 191 Prometheus-B 55
If the deep barrier be of earth or sea — 192 Fragment-C 20
Who hath not shared that calm so still and deep — 192 Monody 9
Gaunt Poverty should league with deep Disease — 193 Monody 80
Their loss, so heavy and so deep — 195 Ballad-A 107
What if thy deep and ample stream should be — 198 Po 5
I by thy source, she by the dark-blue deep — 198 Po 36
Deep, deep as the gore which he shed on her soil — 203 Avatar 90
The depth of thy deep in a deeper gulf still — 203 Avatar 104
But is deep in my soul as my brow — 205 Blessington 16
In that deep midnight of the mind — 209 Augusta-A 5
For thou art pillow'd on a curse too deep — 213 Lady Byron 22
Time taught him a deep answer--when she loved — 214 Dream 70
And voices from the deep abyss reveal'd — 216 Dream 200
And feed deep thought with many a dream — 218 Bloom 8
But bid the strain be wild and deep — 218 Soul-B 9
A deep and mellow dye — 218 I Saw 10
Are wise and deep in lore — 220 Belshaz-B 30
When the blue wave rolls nightly on deep Galilee — 222 Sennacherib 4
Deep sleep came down on every eye save mine — 222 Spirit 3
My wounds are far too deep for simple grief — 229 Sadness 6
And dye it deep in the gore he has pour'd — 229 Lads 10
O'er the hush'd deep the yellow beam he throws — 268 Minerva 5
Till, darkly shaded from the land and deep — 268 Minerva 17
Till Indus rolls a deep purpureal flood — 271 Minerva 225
His brow was like the deep when tempest-toss'd — 288 Vision 189
As the deep billows of the Aegean roar — 298 Age 17
That, jutting, shadows o'er the deep — 312 Giaour 209
The channell'd waters dark and deep — 314 Giaour 369
Known but to Genii of the deep — 314 Giaour 385
Deep in whose darkly boding ear — 321 Giaour 1077
Deep thought was in his aged eye — 324 Abydos 1 25

DEEP

	Page	Work		Line
The fairest scenes of land and deep	324	Abydos	1	60
Till I, who heard the deep tambour	324	Abydos	1	73
Deep were my anguish, thus compell'd	328	Abydos	1	435
Where we may wander by the deep	328	Abydos	1	466
The beach where shelving to the deep	335	Abydos	2	594
That grief--though deep--though fatal--was thy first	336	Abydos	2	642
'Deep in my soul that tender secret dwells	343	Corsair	1	347
That hail'd him first when homeward from the deep	345	Corsair	1	510
The breezy freshness of the deep beneath	346	Corsair	1	536
His deep yet tender melody of tone	346	Corsair	1	550
Equipp'd for deeds alike on land or deep	347	Corsair	1	604
On silken couch than o'er the rugged deep	347	Corsair	2	40
A chief on land--an outlaw on the deep	352	Corsair	2	390
Was hush'd so deep--Ah! happy if in death	352	Corsair	2	393
O'er the hush'd deep the yellow beam he throws	355	Corsair	3	5
Till, darkly shaded from the land and deep	355	Corsair	3	17
How deep the root from whence compassion grew	358	Corsair	3	201
Oh! how he listen'd to the rushing deep	359	Corsair	3	250
But speechless all, deep, dark, and unexprest	362	Corsair	3	478
Booms harmless, hissing to the deep below	362	Corsair	3	489
And some deep feeling it were vain to trace	367	Lara	1	83
Too deep for words, indelible, unmix'd	370	Lara	1	282
His soul, in deep abstraction sudden sunk	373	Lara	1	483
A spirit deep that brook'd not to be chid	374	Lara	1	559
But the deep working of a soul unmix'd	377	Lara	2	147
The deep reversion of delay'd revenge	378	Lara	2	207
As deep, but far too tranquil for despair	380	Lara	2	345
Of mournful paleness, whose deep tint express'd	380	Lara	2	352
So sad, so deep, and hesitating broke	381	Lara	2	458
But where he died his grave was dug as deep	382	Lara	2	521
And that deep silence was unbroke	387	Corinth		260
Deep in the tide of their warm blood lying	389	Corinth		482
By deep interminable pride	391	Corinth		654
Which pierces the deep hills through and through	392	Corinth		761
From its deep veins lately loosed	394	Corinth		888
Massy and deep, a glittering prize	395	Corinth		1000
So deep, that did it not decay	397	Parisina		38
With all the deep and shuddering chill	397	Parisina		63
Lay on her soul, so deep and chill	400	Parisina		369
With a deep sound, to and fro	400	Parisina		389
In deep disdain were half renew'd	401	Parisina		445
In the dust, which each deep vein	401	Parisina		458
In Chillon's dungeons deep and old	403	Chillon		28
The hound's deep hate and hunter's fire	411	Mazeppa		496
Our shut eyes in deep midnight, when	412	Mazeppa		559
And fill'd the earth, from his deep throne	413	Mazeppa		651
And lift their shining eyelids from the deep	415	Island	1	12
The surge, is safe {his port is in the deep	417	Island	1	138
Which felt exhaustion's deep and bitter drouth	417	Island	1	148
The varying frowns and favours of the deep	418	Island	1	185
As ever the dark annals of the deep	418	Island	1	199
Which fling their fragrance far athwart the deep	419	Island	2	133
With all her loves around her on the deep	420	Island	2	133
Had from that moment deem'd the deep his home	421	Island	2	170
Seem'd rooted in the deep amidst its calm	422	Island	2	223
The anchor dropp'd; it lay along the deep	422	Island	2	234
Jove's Ida and Olympus crown the deep	423	Island	2	287
As in the north he mellows o'er the deep	424	Island	2	361
As, far divided from his parent deep	424	Island	2	408
Such as appears to rise out from the deep	425	Island	2	464
Its silver torrent glitter'd o'er the deep	427	Island	3	69
The wave of these born playmates of the deep	429	Island	3	182
Steals to the deep wherein his parents dwell	430	Island	4	95
And where was he, the pilgrim of the deep	431	Island	4	95
Young Neuha plunged into the deep, and he	431	Island	4	105
Deep--deeper for an instant Neuha led	431	Island	4	115
Its latent sparkle from the sapping deep	431	Island	4	140
When, fresh and springing from the deep, they saw	432	Island	4	211
Look'd desperate as himself along the deep	434	Island	4	338
Dwelling deep in my shut and silent heart	438	Tasso		113
Stamp Madness deep into my memory	439	Tasso		216
Dreading the deep damnation of his 'bah	444	Beppo		254
The dull green ooze of the receding deep	453	Venice-B		9
Than stagnate in our marsh,--or o'er the deep	455	Venice-B		157
Lift me from that deep gulf without repeal	456	Dante	1	6
The wound, too deep the wrong, and the distress	457	Dante	1	94
The inner war of passions deep and fierce	464	Dante	4	110
When Alabaster heard his deep voice ring	470	Morgante		295
The deep echo roll'd	479	Manfred	1	85
Strike deep in the earth	479	Manfred	1	93
Though thy slumber may be deep	481	Manfred	1	202
Like foam from the roused ocean of deep Hell	483	Manfred	1	348
A Croesus in creation--I plunged deep	487	Manfred	2	236
The innate tortures of that deep despair	492	Manfred	3	70
But still the Signory is deep in council	499	Faliero	1	3
Harp on the deep dishonour of our house	501	Faliero	1	93
Deep Vengeance is the daughter of deep Silence	502	Faliero	1	169
No pride, no passion, no deep sense of honour	502	Faliero	1	181
But for the effect, the deadly deep impression	509	Faliero	2	34
And the deep passions fiercely foster'd by	510	Faliero	2	105
Deep at my heart--But let us change the theme	512	Faliero	2	212
Now darkling in their close toward the deep vale	516	Faliero	2	502
A silent, solitary, deep revenge	516	Faliero	2	543
They but augment the deep and sweeping thoughts	517	Faliero	2	612
Stake our deep interest on my single thoughts	518	Faliero	2	702
I owe him such deep gratitude, that fain	526	Faliero	3	535
Were deep offence. But question even the Doge	543	Faliero	5	348
Have struck those tyrants! Strike deep as my curse	549	Faliero	5	799
Steep'd, but not drown'd, in deep voluptuousness	550	Sardan	1	13
From the deep urgency with which the prince	560	Sardan	1	638
I love to watch them in the deep blue vault	566	Sardan	2	253
Or deep, deep sleep, so as to be unfathom'd	578	Sardan	4	5
Deep fosses, or behold them sprawl on spikes	586	Sardan	4	559
As show'd that I had search'd the deep: exulting	597	Foscari	1	117
With a far-dashing stroke, and drawing deep	597	Foscari	1	118
And the deep agony of his pale wife	601	Foscari	1	355
(If death be a deep sleep), without a groan	609	Foscari	3	90
From the rough deep, with such identity	610	Foscari	3	174
Seem'd ploughing deep into your heart; you never	611	Foscari	3	210
The dungeon gloom is deep enough without you	612	Foscari	3	264
And that is vengeance. In my mind, too deep	615	Foscari	4	21
To lash up from the deep the Adrian waves	617	Foscari	4	129
Just now, though Venice totter'd o'er the deep	618	Foscari	4	231
Who out of darkness on the deep didst make	627	Cain	1	2
Streak the deep purple, and unnumber'd stars	635	Cain	1	509
Unequal, of deep valleys and vast mountains	638	Cain	2	185
Of the deep woods of earth, the hugest which	641	Cain	2	341
The deep blue noon of night, lit by an orb	643	Cain	2	461
Add thy deep curse to Eve's upon his head	653	Cain	3	448
Through the deep clouds o'er rocky Ararat	655	Heaven		3
Like the eternal thunders of the deep	656	Heaven		113
When sporting on the face of the calm deep	657	Heaven		156
The fountains of the deep, how mightest thou	658	Heaven		229
Lie low beneath the boiling of the deep	659	Heaven		289
The deep which will lay open all her fountains	659	Heaven		325
When the great barrier of the deep is rent	660	Heaven		392
The deep shall follow to their latest lair	661	Heaven		441
The fountains of the great deep shall be broken	661	Heaven		490
Nought to his eye beyond the deep, his grave	662	Heaven		513
Their outworn pinions on the deep; and day	662	Heaven		564
Dies with man, and is swallow'd in that deep	662	Heaven		573
The deep shall rise to meet heaven's overflow	667	Heaven		882
Farewell! Now rise, inexorable deep	667	Heaven		915
Her, whom the surges of the all-strangling deep	667	Heaven		941
Hark, hark! Deep sounds, and deeper still	668	Heaven		991
The former, and deep as the latter; but	684	Werner	2	107
Into the deep, and bring up slime and mud	699	Werner	3	266
His death was fathomlessly deep in blood	712	Werner	4	506
Of shouting, I heard in a deep, low voice	715	Werner	5	132
Deep in the fountain to scare back the cattle	723	Deformed	1	51
And Priam weeping, mingled with deep passion	726	Deformed	1	277
The deep hue of the ocean and the earth	731	Deformed	1	655
His, like all deep grief, plunged in solitude	757	Juan	1	692
In deep despair, lest he had done amiss	760	Juan	1	893
Sheds beauty and deep softness o'er the whole	761	Juan	1	910
At midnight on the blue and moonlit deep	761	Juan	1	970
My shame and sorrow deep in my heart's core	770	Juan	1	1556
And the dim desolate deep: twelve days had Fear	780	Juan	2	391
Into the deep without a tear or groan	785	Juan	2	696
With the deep deadly thought that they must part	785	Juan	2	704
To heave into the deep with those before	787	Juan	2	806
Away the vast, salt, dread, eternal deep	787	Juan	2	824
On one side, and the deep sea calm and chill	797	Juan	2	1462
Yielded to the deep twilight's purple charm	797	Juan	2	1472
And when those deep and burning moments pass'd	798	Juan	2	1553
The ashes of our hopes, is a deep grief	807	Juan	3	407
Than the stern, single, deep, and wordless ire	808	Juan	3	463
While swung the deep bell in the distant tower	815	Juan	3	909
They should have lived together deep in woods	820	Juan	4	217
A gentle slumber, but it was not deep	820	Juan	4	227
Or as the stirring of a deep clear stream	820	Juan	4	233
From two smart sabre gashes, deep and red	822	Juan	4	391
But her large dark eye show'd deep Passion's force	823	Juan	4	447
Were dabbled with the deep blood which ran o'er	823	Juan	4	466
Forlorn, and gazing on the deep blue surge	826	Juan	4	627
Acquire the deep and bitter power to give	830	Juan	4	852
In all, who o'er the great deep take their ways	832	Juan	5	46
'On the rough deep. But this last blow--' and here	833	Juan	5	145
You know how near us the deep Bosphorus floats	843	Juan	5	732
Of her deep purple robe, and speaking low	843	Juan	5	767
And the deep passions flashing through her form	848	Juan	5	1079
Yet disappointed joys are woes as deep	855	Juan	6	156
Admiring this new native of the deep	859	Juan	6	480
There was deep silence in the chamber: dim	860	Juan	6	505
The nightingale that sings with the deep thorn	863	Juan	6	693
So deep an anguish wrung Gulbeyaz' brow	865	Juan	6	836
By deep emotion:--you may sometimes trace	866	Juan	6	884
Deep in the caverns of the deadly tide	866	Juan	6	916
But the town ditch below was deep as ocean	868	Juan	7	83
The vasty deep,' to whom you may exclaim	883	Juan	8	299
Had feathers, when a traveller on deep ways is	900	Juan	9	240
Which threatens inundations deep and yellow	908	Juan	10	52

DEEP

Now) you may cross the blue deep and white foam	924	Juan	11	347
Nations athwart the deep: the golden rays	930	Juan	12	60
Broad as transparent, deep, and freshly fed	948	Juan	13	450
Its outlet dash'd into a deep cascade	948	Juan	13	457
Through the serene and placid glassy deep	966	Juan	14	695
Adeline, no deep judge of character	970	Juan	15	129
Deep secrets to her rolling light are told	982	Juan	16	110
Thoughts, boundless, deep, but silent too as Space	987	Juan	16	432
As deep seas in a sunny atmosphere	993	Juan	16	800
When deep sleep fell on men, and the world wore	995	Juan	16	950

DEEP-BLUE

And dazzle not thy deep-blue eyes--but, oh	175	Sonnet-B		5
He dared not raise to his that deep-blue eye	345	Corsair	1	468

DEEP-BURIED

Of Love deep-buried without resurrection	701	Werner	3	396

DEEP-DYED

The deep-dyed Brenta, where their hues instil	59	Harold	4	250

DEEPEN

Or deepen every stain	181	Ode-A		94
Skill'd by a touch to deepen scandal's tints	208	Sketch		55

DEEPEN'D

Which deepen'd now and then the sandy dint	427	Island	3	95
Through which the deepen'd glories once could enter	948	Juan	13	491

DEEPENING

Each hill and dale, each deepening glen and wold	33	Harold	2	834
And gripe and deepening of the dragon's grasp	79	Harold	4	1437
Thou hear'st of one, whose deepening crimes	164	Friend-B		47
His features' deepening lines and varying hue	341	Corsair	1	209
How red he glares amongst those deepening clouds	561	Sardan	2	3

DEEPENS

It deepens still, the work is scarce begun	18	Harold	1	911
And deepens into red the saffron water	459	Dante	2	79

DEEPER

What stamps the wrinkle deeper on the brow	35	Harold	2	919
Although no deeper Moralist rehearse	66	Harold	4	689
Had worn a deeper shade	167	Dead		49
The depth of thy deep in a deeper gulf still	203	Avatar		104
These are words of deeper sorrow	207	Fare Thee		29
Have a far deeper madness, and the glance	216	Dream		178
And in thy skull discern a deeper hell	245	Bards		282
His deeper deeds as yet ye know by name	272	Minerva		299
Of deeper passions; and, to judge their mien	341	Corsair	1	233
To deeper shades of paleness, all its red	363	Corsair	3	535
Have deeper thoughts than your dull eyes discern	382	Lara	2	533
With deeper skill in war's black art	385	Corinth		97
And on the wave is deeper blue	396	Parisina		9
And well he may--a deeper doom	397	Parisina		85
A greater wreck, a deeper fall	407	Mazeppa		13
Deep--deeper for an instant Neuha led	431	Island	4	115
With brighter stars, and robes with deeper blue	459	Dante	2	53
And wear a deeper brand and gaudier chain	464	Dante	4	106
Deeper than all yet urged, a tyrant-spell	479	Manfred	1	43
Powers deeper still beyond--I come in quest	489	Manfred	2	446
But if his insults sink no deeper in	509	Faliero	2	52
A leech's lancet would have scratch'd me deeper	587	Sardan	4	578
And I would mitigate his deeper hatred	601	Foscari	1	374
His cheeks are reddening into deeper smiles	646	Cain	3	26
Hath sadden'd thine still deeper. I had hoped	647	Cain	3	46
Hark, hark! Deep sounds, and deeper still	668	Heaven		991
Thy curse hath dug it deeper for thy son	722	Werner	5	555
Why not? The deeper sinner, better saint	729	Deformed	1	521
As if her heart had deeper thoughts in store	755	Juan	1	571
Then there were sighs, the deeper for suppression	756	Juan	1	585
That is, till deeper griefs congeal our tears	776	Juan	2	120
Of Hell shall pall them in a deeper cloak	878	Juan	7	688
The endless soot bestows a tint far deeper	909	Juan	10	115
(Let deeper sages the true cause determine	913	Juan	10	395

DEEPEST

This is the deepest of our woes	89	To Emma		37
Though first in glory, deepest in reverse	299	Age		95
And the purple of Ocean is deepest in dye	323	Abydos	1	13
The deepest murmur of this lip shall be	334	Abydos	2	456
By those that deepest feel is ill exprest	365	Corsair	3	640
But round their orbs of deepest blue	400	Parisina		332
The deepest ice which ever froze	402	Parisina		553
Must mourn the deepest o'er the fatal truth	478	Manfred	1	11
Am plunged into the deepest hell of both	720	Werner	5	482
Deepest attraction; for when to the view	789	Juan	2	932
Deepest in those who long the most to die	817	Juan	4	88
Or said her cheeks assumed the deepest dyes	848	Juan	5	1067
Of his old age in wilds of deepest maze	886	Juan	8	488

DEEP-FIX'D

That deep-fix'd pillar to the shore	337	Abydos	2	720

DEEP-GREEN

Their deep-green shadow o'er the rocky door	432	Island	4	205

DEEPLY

However deeply in men's spirits skill'd	41	Harold	3	340
Or to more deeply blest Anchises? or	62	Harold	4	452
Rolls deeply on the list'ning ear	96	Granta		72
The bridegroom's health is deeply quaff'd	103	Alva		190
And deeply swells the bursting storm	104	Alva		252
Struck with a filial care so deeply felt	108	Nisus		195
There, deeply carved, behold! each tyro's name	124	Recoll		153
Though drinking deeply, thirsting still the more	125	Recoll		254
Through few, but deeply chequer'd years	131	L'Amitie		11
Deeply she cut--but not erased	150	Harrow-C		5
Too deeply to tell	151	When We		24
Will deeply embitter the bowl	162	Romaic-A		18
Severely, deeply, vainly proved	174	Remember-B		2
Have given her power too deeply to instil	208	Sketch		45
More deeply purpled meet his mellowing glance	268	Minerva		14
He deeply felt--what mortal hearts must feel	351	Corsair	2	294
He deeply, darkly felt; but evil pride	351	Corsair	2	298
More deeply purpled meet his mellowing glance	355	Corsair	3	14
But deeply feels a single cry would shame	359	Corsair	3	234
Had sate too deeply were he left at large	377	Lara	2	136
Then deeply disappear'd. The horseman gazed	383	Lara	2	584
The cold, round moon shines deeply down	387	Corinth		243
So deeply changed from what he knew	391	Corinth		608
Deeply dinted in the clay	396	Corinth		1055
Too deeply rooted thence to vanish	402	Parisina		559
For I have been too long and deeply wreck'd	458	Dante	1	138
And murmur deeply--any hope of change	504	Faliero	1	334
My peril be the proof. You have deeply ventured	508	Faliero	1	566
What is't you feel so deeply, then, even now	514	Faliero	2	406
You have been deeply wrong'd, and now shall be	525	Faliero	3	486
I have seen you dyed ere now, and deeply too	535	Faliero	4	491
Deeply--more deeply than all things but love	585	Sardan	4	489
Not to feel deeply for your son. Was this	602	Foscari	2	31
The name of Death so deeply, that the thought	652	Cain	3	372
In all these he was much and deeply read	752	Juan	1	317
And loved by a young heart, too deeply blest	801	Juan	3	4
The henna should be deeply dyed to make	810	Juan	3	601
We ponder deeply on each past emotion	816	Juan	4	16
Oh! 'darkly, deeply, beautifully blue	830	Juan	4	873
Alas, how deeply painful is all payment	917	Juan	10	625

DEEPLY-HIDDEN

In some bleak crag or deeply-hidden bay	433	Island	4	242

DEEP-MOUTH'D

Deep-mouth'd arose, and doubly harsh	396	Corinth		1066
Bay deep-mouth'd welcome as we draw near home	762	Juan	1	978
And that deep-mouth'd Boeotian 'Savage Landor	925	Juan	11	463

DEEP'NING

His blood-red tresses deep'ning in the sun	10	Harold	1	424

DEEPS

Who dwells and revels in thy glassy deeps	65	Harold	4	601
He wishes for 'a boat' to sail the deeps	814	Juan	3	877

DEEP'S

Kissing, not ruffling, the blue deep's serene	30	Harold	2	627
We, we shall view the deep's salt sources pour'd	661	Heaven		435

DEEP-WOUNDED

Lest your deep-wounded heart, when incensed by the smart	116	Pigot		31

DEER

(See also RED-DEER'S)

They feast upon the mountain deer	102	Alva		41
deer of Morven with Orla,' said the hero	131	Calmar		172
Had follow'd there the deer and wolf	403	Chillon		104
Wild as the wild deer, and untaught	410	Mazeppa		363
As e'er the hunted deer a covert--Or	695	Werner	3	6
Like Shakspeare's stealing deer, Lord Bacon's bribes	813	Juan	3	826

DEE'S

I breasted the billows of Dee's rushing tide	136	Highlander		19
Marr's dusky heath, and Dee's clear wave	145	Adieu		29

DEFACE

Restore what Time hath labour'd to deface	21	Harold	2	88
Deface the scenes, already how defaced	34	Harold	2	876
The grosser parts; but, fearful to deface	752	Juan	1	348

DEFACED

Thy walls defaced, thy mouldering shrines removed	21	Harold	2	130
Deface the scenes, already how defaced	34	Harold	2	876
With an immaculate charm which cannot be defaced	59	Harold	4	234

DEFACED

Resentment's hand the line defaced	150 Harrow-C		4
Though my many faults defaced me	207 Fare Thee		17
Nor fall nor struggle hath defaced the grass	376 Lara	2	113
Thy moral morn, too long with clouds defaced	461 Dante	3	58
Or was at least, unless 'tis since defaced	868 Juan	7	69

DEFAME

Still urge your task, and if you can, defame	143 Soliloquy	64
Though watchful, 'twas not to defame me	210 Augusta-B	31

DEFAULT

Detect with fingers, in default of ears	262 Hints	436

DEFEAT

Retrieved three long olympiads of defeat	271 Minerva	238
He, half forgetting danger and defeat	363 Corsair	3 502
That no defeat can drive me from the Nine	956 Juan	14 92

DEFEATED

Dear object of defeated care	161 Picture		1
Who could boast o'er France defeated	187 Ode-B		30
Beyond the Bard's defeated art	229 Marble		6
Which nor defeated hope, nor baffled wile	342 Corsair	1	297
At whatsoever risk of being defeated	996 Juan	16	998

DEFECT

Others appear more conscious of defect	113 Prologue		10
Could they see thee, Eliza, they'd own their defect	116 To Eliza		3
Could remedy this lubberly defect	870 Juan	7	222
From off the marble, which had no defect	962 Juan	14	446
Our gentle Adeline had one defect	966 Juan	14	673
For one a songstress who hath no defect	972 Juan	15	267
The cause of this effect, or this defect	980 Juan	16	9
Might have from time acquired some slight defect	988 Juan	16	508

DEFECTIVE

But if Venus and Hymen should once prove defective	145 Casuists		7
'For this effect defective comes by cause	980 Juan	16	10

DEFECTS

Inherit but his fame with his defects	725 Deformed	1 191

DEFENCE
(See also SELF-DEFENCE)

Of that which is of all Creator and defence	49 Harold	3	841
Be thy sad weapon of defence, and so	61 Harold	4	386
And vainly in the weak defence confides	109 Nisus		270
Ah, vain defence! the hostile traitor's siege	120 Newstead-A		61
Extend to me thy wide defence	133 Prayer		48
Whose Innocence requires defence	141 Critics		55
'Twas in your defence. If you please, with submission	281 Blues	2	70
The accusation and defence: if we	292 Vision		503
For sudden siege and long defence prepared	344 Corsair	1	459
Of such defence the Powers of Evil can	439 Tasso		201
An enemy, save in my just defence	484 Manfred	2	86
Alike by accusation or defence	538 Faliero	5	61
In your defence? What shall I say to ye	540 Faliero	5	165
Since my defence must be your condemnation	540 Faliero	5	166
Such my defence would be, had I full scope	542 Faliero	5	289
Shedding so much blood in her last defence	548 Faliero	5	746
Than hurt in his defence. Well, sir, the rebels	572 Sardan	3	76
I accuse no man, save in my defence	717 Werner	5	299
Defence of freedom, country, or of laws	872 Juan	7	316

DEFENCELESS

Come--but molest not yon defenceless urn	19 Harold	2	20
And, raging, on the boy defenceless flew	110 Nisus		362
With all the care defenceless beauty claims	350 Corsair	2	218
Defenceless man; and yesterday you saw me	522 Faliero	3	253
And that's defenceless.--True, we have no proofs	687 Werner	2	291

DEFENCES

While the giant goes to put off his defences	470 Morgante		263
Be e'er excusable in such defences	712 Werner	4	527
By last night's ghost been driven from their defences	993 Juan	16	792

DEFEND

Now must the pastor's arm his lambs defend	9 Harold	1	357
Whom still affection taught me to defend	93 Dorset		3
Then quit her, my friend! your bosom defend	116 Pigot		29
Pray who would there be to defend or dispute it	145 Casuists		8
The first to welcome, foremost to defend	154 Dog		8
For 'gainst the rest myself I could defend	213 Lady Byron		26
And will not alter what you can't defend	267 Hints		790
While you live, my dear Botherby, never defend	281 Blues	2	72
'Twill serve thee to defend or kill	319 Giaour		927
Wait--wave--defend--destroy--at thy command	333 Abydos	2	411
I deny nothing--defend nothing--nothing	542 Faliero	5	296
Dear is the helpless creature we defend	762 Juan	1	1006
I ask but this of mine, to--not defend	994 Juan	16	880

DEFENDED
(See also CHERUBIM-DEFENDED)

Of a long defended church	394 Corinth		872
Defended at a price extremely dear	888 Juan	8	632

DEFENDER

And pray God to pay his defender	239 Bray		36
In neither clime, time, blood, with her defender	914 Juan	10	455

DEFENDING

For the rights of a monarch their country defending	86 Leaving NA	19

DEFENDS

And old Alethes' casque defends his brows	108 Nisus	216
Not all that forced politeness, which defends	256 Hints	9

DEFENSIBLE

Deserves the worst, his conduct's less defensible	765 Juan	1 1206

DEFENSIVE

My errors with defensive paradox	211 Augusta-C	22

DEFER

Which never loses though it doth defer	74 Harold	4	1168
Most willingly. You see--Defer your tale	686 Werner	2	231

DEFERENCE

To whom he show'd nor deference nor disdain	374 Lara	1	569
However, I still think, with all due deference	444 Beppo		297
The deference due even to the lightest word	606 Foscari	2	298
It must be done with all the deference	615 Foscari	4	29
Of Dudu, though they held their tongues from deference	858 Juan	6	400
Juan replied, with all becoming deference	971 Juan	15	233
Which show'd such deference to what females say	978 Juan	15	651
Rather by deference than compliment	978 Juan	15	663

DEFIANCE

Hurl their defiance far, nor yield, unless to gold	26 Harold	2	423
Perhaps the workings of defiance stir	211 Augusta-C		41
Scowling defiance on the blasts of fate	119 Newstead-A		8
To hurl defiance on a secret foe	123 Recoll		82
That bid the foe defiance ere they come	272 Minerva		288
Of mix'd defiance and despair	319 Giaour		908
And still defiance knit his gather'd brow	369 Lara	1	216
Still one great clime, in full and free defiance	454 Venice-B		142
Upon their troops, who rose in fierce defiance	572 Sardan	3	81
Hurling defiance: city, stream, and shore	879 Juan	8	60

DEFICIENT

Oh, think not my penance deficient	98 To M.S.G.-B	18
But then he is sadly deficient in whisker	228 Moore-A	21

DEFIED

Than in the world's defied rebuke	209 Augusta-A		24
By all that Hero suffered, or defied	224 J.C.H.		14
Which defied the arms of Ali	240 Suliotes		8
Who have defied the law in their excesses	520 Faliero	3	135
Ye might have then defied him. Oh! my son	628 Cain	1	34
But she defied all means they could employ	824 Juan	4	471
His five brave boys no less the foe defied	892 Juan	8	853

DEFIES

Defies the power which crush'd thy temples gone	33 Harold	2	835
Defies at first our Nature's littleness	78 Harold	4	1420
Defies the scythe of time, the torch of flame	169 Address-A		22
Retreats before him, though he still defies	349 Corsair	2	177
His silken son to save it: he defies	576 Sardan	3	314
And now defies them. How now, friend, what seek you	599 Foscari	1	250
Despair defies even despotism: there is	599 Foscari	1	267
Defies it: though this life must pass away	656 Heaven		108
All that defies the worst which pen expresses	894 Juan	8	981

DEFILE

Wind slowly through the long defile	315 Giaour	552

DEFILED

Or tear their name defiled from Slavery's mournful page	31 Harold	2	719
With human filth that column is defiled	829 Juan	4	834
Oh! ye who build up monuments, defiled	900 Juan	9	259

DEFILEMENT

To the defilement of usurping bondmen	594 Sardan	5 427

DEFILES

By Thrasimene's lake, in the defiles	64 Harold	4	551
Noisome and ghast, defiles thy sacred sod	121 Newstead-A		82
Spain, too, hath rocks, and rivers, and defiles	304 Age		462

DEFINE

To name, define by speech, or write on page	442 Beppo	174

DEFINED
Shalt one day, if found worthy, so defined   78 Harold 4 1393
As in a mirror of itself defined   209 Sketch   72

DEFINES
We hear and see, but none defines   409 Mazeppa   235

DEFINITE
Now that I know it leads to something definite   645 Cain 2 618

DEFINITIVE
Definitive and absolute! To the point   623 Foscari 5 165

DEFLENDUS
While that 'hiatus maxime deflendus   912 Juan 10 333

DEFLOWER'D
Were all deflower'd by different grenadiers   895 Juan 8 1040

DEFORM
While clouds the darken'd noon deform   133 E. N. Long   6
Thy face, O Sun, no rolling blasts deform   139 Ossian-A   19
Shed by the Moon when clouds deform the night   140 Ossian-B   38
One scene even thou canst not deform   172 Time-B   33

DEFORM'D
Because deform'd, yet died all game and bottom   892 Juan 8 879

DEFORMITY
Colossal copyist of deformity   78 Harold 4 1362
A bright deformity on high   480 Manfred 1 122
To taunt me with my born deformity   723 Deformed 1 102
Deformity should only barter with   726 Deformed 1 285
For valour, since deformity is daring   727 Deformed 1 313

DEFORMITY'S
Its way with all deformity's dull, deadly   727 Deformed 1 330

DEFRAUDED
The Tolbooth felt defrauded of his charms   248 Bards   478
They have defrauded me of both my rights   503 Faliero 1 247

DEFRAY'D
For the bill here, it seems, is defray'd by the
  host   280 Blues 2 19

DEFTLY
As many a nameless slander deftly shows   208 Sketch   16

DEFUNCT
So that the boar, defunct, lay tripp'd up near   473 Morgante   500

DEFY
Must all the painter's art defy   98 To Mary   11
Prepared the danger to defy   141 Critics   26
Triumphant where it dares defy   191 Prometheus-B   58
I defy him to beat this day's wondrous applause   281 Blues 2 39
Disdain, defy, the tardy aid of art   299 Age   82
There breathe but few whose aspect might defy   341 Corsair 1 215
I do defy ye,--though I feel my soul   496 Manfred 3 359
Is ebbing from me, yet I do defy ye   496 Manfred 3 360
Upon my strength--I do defy-deny   496 Manfred 3 380
Defy all codes to image or to name them   549 Faliero 5 775
They yet may find me--shall defy their wish   557 Sardan 1 425
I may ensure the public, and defy   772 Juan 1 1682
The truth in masquerade; and I defy   923 Juan 11 290
Which might defy a crotchet critic's rigour   960 Juan 14 310

DEFYING
Defying earth and confident of heaven   378 Lara 2 217
Defying augury with that fond kiss   819 Juan 4 188

DEGENERACY
In its dull damp degeneracy, to   640 Cain 2 277

DEGENERATE
So you, degenerate, share as hard a fate   93 Masters   5
For me, degenerate modern wretch   160 Swimming   9
Time was, ere yet in these degenerate days   243 Bards   103
Degenerate Britons! are ye dead to shame   250 Bards   610
The long degenerate noble; the debased   302 Age   342
Degenerate into hands like mine   812 Juan 3 718
Huger than twelve of our degenerate breed   950 Juan 13 556

DEGENERATED
Of hero sires who shame thy now degenerated horde   32 Harold 2 791

DEGRADATION
The degradation of our vaunted stage   249 Bards   575
The breath of degradation and of pride   482 Manfred 1 304
Of thine enjoyments a sweet degradation   637 Cain 2 56
He waged, in vengeance of her degradation   808 Juan 3 440
To say, by degradation) mingled there   810 Juan 3 543

DEGRADE
No more his mention shall my verse degrade   123 Recoll   119
Yet must I spare--nor thus my pen degrade   142 Soliloquy   49
Degrade God's creatures in his graphic spleen   256 Hints   8
Thus always, none would ever dare degrade thee   561 Sardan 1 677

DEGRADED
Youth wasted, minds degraded, honour lost   24 Harold 2 311
From what it hates in this degraded form   46 Harold 3 699
Degraded mass of animated dust   154 Dog   18
Love brooks not a degraded throne   200 Stanzas-B   45
To kindle souls within degraded flesh   302 Age   269
But more degraded; the unpeopled realm   302 Age   344
Which speak a mind not all degraded   318 Giaour   864
The Old World more degraded than the New   420 Island 2 74
And die or are degraded: for the mind   463 Dante 3 172
Than those who are degraded by the jars   463 Dante 4 7
I felt myself degraded back to them   486 Manfred 2 172
Because 'tis now degraded. 'Tis even so   502 Faliero 1 204
As man? reviled, degraded, as a prince   503 Faliero 1 225
Thou idle, gilded, and degraded toy   504 Faliero 1 292
Before he was degraded to a Doge   523 Faliero 3 323
Degraded by that passion than by chains   559 Sardan 1 549
I will not live degraded. Hadst thou felt   561 Sardan 1 676
The old man is deposed, his name degraded   620 Foscari 4 325

DEGRADES
No vice degrades that purest soul serene   126 Recoll   328
Degrades or hallows courage in its fall   433 Island 4 262
Degrades the very conqueror. To have pluck'd   562 Sardan 2 83

DEGREE
And flaunting wassailers of high and low degree   4 Harold 1 18
Ne personage of high or mean degree   7 Harold 1 231
The slain, stood in a like degree   197 Duel   8
And each did well in his degree   403 Chillon   72
Of vassal or of knight's degree   408 Mazeppa   185
In the degree of bondage, we forget   574 Sardan 3 194
And what they were thou feelest, in degree   640 Cain 2 295
In that point so precise in each degree   754 Juan 1 453
Though differing in stature and degree   857 Juan 6 318
Good people all, of every degree   932 Juan 12 153
I have named a few, not foremost in degree   951 Juan 13 661

DEGREES
The crowd was famish'd by degrees; but two   189 Darkness   55
Forgetting doggerel leads not to degrees   255 Bards   974
As forests shed their foliage by degrees   257 Hints   89
The p--x becomes his passage to degrees   260 Hints   238
Their dogs and oxen knew their own degrees   303 Age   401
All dread by slow degrees had worn away   377 Lara 2 173
But then by dull degrees came back   405 Chillon   259
Which, kindling by degrees its dewy spars   424 Island 2 400
Digression is a sin, that by degrees   446 Beppo   394
Created by degrees an ocean-Rome   610 Foscari 3 154
The wound: and by degrees the helpless wretch   643 Cain 2 499
The hand which still held Juan's, by degrees   760 Juan 1 881
But by degrees their senses were restored   798 Juan 2 1525
To dub the last of honours in degrees   816 Juan 3 976
She sunk down on her seat by slow degrees   865 Juan 6 855
But by degrees, that they were fairer far   938 Juan 12 546
Then by degrees recall'd his energies   983 Juan 16 196
Upon him by degrees, and so he slept   984 Juan 16 216
By whose degrees all characters are class'd   987 Juan 16 427

DEIFIED
Here's that which deified him--let it now   554 Sardan 1 229

DEIFY
Or deify the canvass till it shine   463 Dante 4 29

DEIGN
With Spain's dark-glancing daughters--deign to
  know   13 Harold 1 609
On man and man's research could deign do more than
  smile   51 Harold 3 985
Those who condemn, should surely deign to read   142 Soliloquy   48
No mortal eye will deign to steep   146 Adieu   98
Will deign to own a kindred care   153 Friend-A   70
If you would please the public, deign to hear   259 Hints   213
Our British Commons sometimes deign to 'hear   304 Age   490
Convey reproof, nor further deign reply   339 Corsair 1 82
And do not deign to smite because they may   347 Corsair 2 22
Will look on earth and heaven, and who will deign   462 Dante 3 143
We will embark anon. Fair nymphs, who deign   551 Sardan 1 54
Nor would she deign to accept divided passion   554 Sardan 1 268
Shall deign to expound this dream   661 Heaven   460
For them and theirs with all who deign to read   801 Juan 2 1728

DEIGN'D
Nor calm domestic peace had ever deign'd to taste   4 Harold 1 45
To nought else constant, hither deign'd to flee   14 Harold 1 670
E'er deign'd to bend her chastely-awful eyes   17 Harold 1 822
Have deign'd to praise the firstlings of my Muse   143 Soliloquy   71

DEIGN'D

The olive branch, which still she deign'd to clasp	269	Minerva	83
Or, starting from her slumbers, deign'd arise	274	Waltz	63
With all the courtesy he deign'd his friends	346	Corsair 1	562
He deign'd no answer, but his head he shook	372	Lara 1	446
But he is welcome, as they were: they deign'd	632	Cain 1	341
Has deign'd to commune with me, and reveal	665	Heaven	749
Too much already hast thou deign'd	667	Heaven	928
My Werner, when you deign'd to choose for bride	673	Werner 1	122
This worthy personage has deign'd to fix	691	Werner 2	519
He deign'd not to belie his soul in songs	746	Juan Ded	77
Yet still they deign'd to hiccup or to bellow	811	Juan 3	654
In chief, in proper person deign'd to drill	873	Juan 7	410
Frederic the Great from Molwitz deign'd to run	881	Juan 8	172
Whom France and Fortune lately deign'd to waft here	952	Juan 13	684
Whose hounds ne'er err'd, nor greyhounds deign'd to lurch	991	Juan 16	682

DEIGNEST

Thou deignest to partake their hymn	656	Heaven	91

DEIGNETH

A little moment deigneth to delay	12	Harold 1	543

DEIGNING

Thou hast forgot thy dignity in deigning	546	Faliero 5	561
The black, however, without hardly deigning	839	Juan 5	521

DEIGNS

The bearded Turk, that rarely deigns to speak	28	Harold 2	521
My soul nor deigns nor dares complain	151	Farewell-B	13
Oh! since increased refinement deigns to smile	252	Bards	787
Though all deplore when Milton deigns to doze	264	Hints	569
That frown, where gentler ocean deigns to smile	269	Minerva	54
And philanthropic Israel deigns to drain	307	Age	682
How gallant all her crew, and deigns to praise	346	Corsair 1	576
Venice is crush'd, and Holland deigns to own	454	Venice-B	127
Will take the crumbs he deigns to scatter from	563	Sardan 2	113
Deigns not to refuse thee	729	Deformed 1	455
To you the unflattering Muse deigns to inscribe	897	Juan 9	74
Or duchess, princess, empress, 'deigns to prove	905	Juan 9	541
Whose cities Night by no means deigns to gloss	921	Juan 11	205
The civil list he deigns to accept (obliging all	988	Juan 16	494

DEIGN'ST

When, as chaste Dian, here thou deign'st to rove	110	Nisus	344
Forth in thy Beauty here thou deign'st to shine	139	Ossian 1	5

DEITIES

Our deities the first best boon have given	107	Nisus	133
Rose whom the Deities above	139	Anacreon-C	13
Pursuing Deities, or in the embrace	205	Aristomenes	9
In the hands of the deities, if such	593	Sardan 5	408

DEITY

Developing in that one glance the Deity	79	Harold 4	1449
I save the Deity some worlds of trouble	297	Vision	808
Half dust, half deity, alike unfit	482	Manfred 1	301
He did, and thence was deem'd a deity	554	Sardan 1	214
Nor Baal, though an oracular deity	570	Sardan 2	531
Our tutelar deity, in a leader's shape	734	Deformed 1	863

DEJECTED

Repletion? Ah! in thy dejected looks	305	Age	510
The palm, he shares the peril, and dejected	463	Dante 4	37
Leaning dejected on his club of conquest	725	Deformed 1	234
And on our sofas makes us lie dejected	926	Juan 11	509

DEJECTION

A sweet dejection--a transparent tear	192	Monody	16
Just to relieve her spirits from dejection	976	Juan 15	512

DELATOR

Should turn delator, be the shame on him	507	Faliero 1	508

DELAY

Yet Mafra shall one moment claim delay	8	Harold 1	333
A little moment deigneth to delay	12	Harold 1	543
Ah, grievance sore and listless dull delay	22	Harold 2	176
Could youth and virtue claim a short delay	85	Epitaph	7
'Nor chase nor wave my boy delay	103	Alva	110
While the slow foot their tardy march delay	109	Nisus	299
midst of foes. Is this a time for delay	130	Calmar	115
A compact without more delay	232	Murray-B	51
If all our bards, more patient of delay	263	Hints	457
Of which he butter'd both sides; 'twould delay	297	Vision	764
The aid evaded, and the cold delay	302	Age	294
For bounty cheers not his delay	313	Giaour	341
Will scarce delay the passer by	319	Giaour	877
Did word like this--' 'Delay not thou	328	Abydos 1	477
O'er which their hungry beaks delay	335	Abydos 2	604
Sheds fast atonement for its first delay	349	Corsair 2	171

DELAY

But all I can, I will: at least delay	354	Corsair 2	464
In guerdon for their long delay	387	Corinth	291
He was not one who brook'd delay	398	Parisina	132
And for a brief delay demands	399	Parisina	231
But why delay the truth?--he died	404	Chillon	144
And she would not delay	415	Mazeppa	837
Exclaim'd, 'Depart at once! delay is death	417	Island 1	154
And Hope is nothing but a false delay	453	Venice-B	36
The cause of our delay to let you in	468	Morgante	173
Or with its ice delay	479	Manfred 1	71
My dearest child, forgive me--why delay	511	Faliero 2	151
It may be, of to-morrow's sun: delay	516	Faliero 2	553
See that they strike without delay, and with	534	Faliero 4	462
By strange delay and arrogant reply	546	Faliero 5	598
As must make madness of delay. And yet	567	Sardan 2	333
Myrrha, without delay; we must not lose	575	Sardan 3	241
Of aught save their delay. My sister, though	655	Heaven	7
And lose eternity by that delay	666	Heaven	814
This long delay was not my fault. I know it	688	Werner 2	349
And prosper; but delay not, or you are lost	720	Werner 5	494
And there he went ashore without delay	804	Juan 3	153
And now delay the progress of Don Juan	831	Juan 4	935
But here a small delay forms a great crime	847	Juan 5	981
I write what's uppermost, without delay	956	Juan 14	53

DELAY'D

A bust delay'd, a book refused, can shake	299	Age	65
Impatient of his flight delay'd	312	Giaour	244
And fail'd to frame the question they delay'd	364	Corsair 3	590
The deep reversion of delay'd revenge	378	Lara 2	207
E'en if he fail'd, he still delay'd his fall	378	Lara 2	241
The daily harass, and the fight delay'd	379	Lara 2	297
But not for vengeance, long delay'd	386	Corinth	177
So hoped for, yet delay'd, of Ofratanes	589	Sardan 5	115
Yet a few hours their coming is delay'd	661	Heaven	496

DELAYS

Such as an army's baffled strength delays	70	Harold 4	885
O'er which Remembrance yet delays	133	E. N. Long	44

DELEGATE

As delegate of tyrants. Such I am not	523	Faliero 3	302

DELEGATED

The wrath, the delegated voice of God	193	Monody	44
The Doge's delegated powers	386	Corinth	219
As delegated from the Doge, the signal	537	Faliero 4	615
Your delegated slaves--the people's tyrants	545	Faliero 5	507
Whose delegated cruelty surpasses	552	Sardan 1	118
Which I was delegated with, they call'd	572	Sardan 3	80

DELEGATES

Chosen delegates, a school of wisdom, to	616	Foscari 4	86
The delegates appointed to convey	620	Foscari 4	352

DELETERIOUS

'Tis pity wine should be so deleterious	823	Juan 4	415
And critically held as deleterious	941	Juan 13	4

DELHI

The Delhi with his cap of terror on	28	Harold 2	518

DELHIS

When his Delhis come dashing in blood o'er the banks	31	Harold 2	687
Will lure the Delhis half so far	393	Corinth	835
Their Delhis mann'd some boats, and sail'd again	871	Juan 7	243

DELIBERATE

But not for a deliberate, false, cool villain	512	Faliero 2	227

DELIBERATED

Having deliberated on the state	621	Foscari 5	19

DELIBERATELY

Conceived deliberately such a thought	702	Werner 3	473

DELIBERATION

Of their deliberation five and twenty	616	Foscari 4	77
Deliberation? If I should do so	719	Werner 5	384
But always choosing with deliberation	913	Juan 10	383

DELIBERATIONS

Breaks in on our deliberations? No	600	Foscari 1	316

DELICACIES

And when the delicacies of the law	939	Juan 12	619

DELICACY

Of early delicacy render more	672	Werner 1	40
From delicacy to Don Juan's ear	768	Juan 1	1407
Even to the delicacy of their hand	822	Juan 4	355

DELICATE
Of small and delicate proportion, keeps   65 Harold   4   596
Art's works; nor must the delicate waters sleep   72 Harold   4 1041
But in his delicate form--a dream of Love   79 Harold   4 1450
Light was his form, and darkly delicate   373 Lara   1   528
They pull'd; her arm, though delicate, was free   430 Island   4   45
For you seem delicate in health. Sir! Pray   676 Werner   1   314
Of a soft cheek and aspect delicate   785 Juan   2   698
And have ten thousand delicate inventions   789 Juan   2   980
Their delicate limbs; a thousand bosoms there   855 Juan   6   207
But still his state was delicate: the hue   912 Juan   10   341
Thy custom-house, with all its delicate duties   916 Juan   10   547
Juan, whose was a delicate commission   922 Juan   11   249
And wins even by a delicate dissent   978 Juan   15   664

DELICATELY
Reforming saints! too delicately nice   250 Bards   633
And patriotism, so delicately nice   306 Age   604
So delicately white, it trembles in   529 Faliero   4   93
So soft, so sweet, so delicately clear   793 Juan   2 1204
Embroider'd delicately o'er with blue   809 Juan   3   510

DELICIOUS
What Heaven hath done for this delicious land   6 Harold   1   208
Full from the fount of Joy's delicious springs   17 Harold   1   817

DELIGHT
Who ne in virtue's ways did take delight   3 Harold   1   11
The laughing dames in whom he did delight   5 Harold   1   92
Mark them unmoved, for he would not delight   25 Harold   2   357
From hence, if he delight kind Nature's sheen to
  see   27 Harold   2   441
A sharer in thy fierce and far delight   49 Harold   3   871
The Sabine farm was till'd, the weary bard's
  delight   81 Harold   4 1566
Were a delight; and if the freshening sea   82 Harold   4 1652
Thy comrade's honour and thy friend's delight   85 Epitaph   10
Would add to the souls of our tyrants delight   92 Caroline-D   14
Which throbs with delight to the first kiss of
  love   92 First Kiss   16
His myrtle, an emblem of purest delight   100 L Adieu   43
This warning, though it may delight not   101 Marion   40
And all my sorrows yield to one delight   107 Nisus   144
For breaking slumbers of delight   113 Quaker   35
Though a smile may delight, yet a frown won't
  affright   116 Strephon   23
Seats of delight, inspiring youthful themes   122 Recoll   33
Let keener bards delight in satire's sting   123 Recoll   79
Yet, why should I alone with such delight   125 Recoll   209
Why search for delight in the friendship of fools   129 Becher-A   24
Days of delight may still be mine   131 L'Amitie   3
And delight but in days I have witness'd before   136 Highlander   28
To wing our moments with Delight   139 Anacreon-C   8
Have fondly gazed with such delight   144 Jessy   6
For she who takes a soft delight   147 Vain Lady   29
How vain is the effort delight to prolong   148 Farewell-A   14
Or dwell with delight on the hours that are flown   148 Farewell-A   19
In moments to delight devoted   175 Portuguese-A   1
In darkness my children take most delight   176 Devil's Dr   9
And he gazed with delight from its growing height   176 Devil's Dr   37
Of failing Wisdom yields a base delight   193 Monody   60
Of praise in payment of a long delight   194 Monody   100
Devil, whose sole delight is damning   197 Rogers   74
Oh Fame!--if I e'er took delight in thy praises   204 Pisa   9
And o'er her scenes of lost delight   217 Gazelle   9
Poetic souls delight in prose insane   245 Bards   244
Dunedin! view thy children with delight   249 Bards   552
Not in the conflict Havoc seeks delight   272 Minerva   295
And lend to loneliness delight   310 Giaour   11
Faints into dimness with its own delight   325 Abydos   1   173
All that can eye or sense delight   329 Abydos   2   82
To soothe each sorrow, share in each delight   333 Abydos   2   424
And turn what some deem danger to delight   338 Corsair   1   18
A stern delight was fix'd in Conrad's eye   350 Corsair   2   198
That would not here in that gay hope delight   353 Corsair   2   442
But who in patience parts with all delight   365 Corsair   3   635
Secure that nought of evil could delight   368 Lara   1   169
Above their naked bones, and feels delight   418 Island   1   191
Or less than we delight to ponder o'er   421 Island   2   207
Wrapp'd his wean'd bosom in its dark delight   423 Island   2   307
That full-blown moment in its all delight   429 Island   3   196
Thou too art gone--and so is my delight   437 Tasso   40
To give thee honour and the earth delight   461 Dante   3   42
By thy delight in others' pain   481 Manfred   1   248
Art a delight--thou shin'st not on my heart   482 Manfred   1   273
The mercy which is thy delight as to   649 Cain   3   229
Delight   656 Heaven   72
And swept, as 'twere, across their hearts'
  delight   819 Juan   4   163
She deem'd her least command must yield delight   847 Juan   5 1019
Of gentle feminine delight, and shown   854 Juan   6   114
A topic scandal doth delight to rouse   944 Juan   13   206
Such was his tact, he could alike delight   960 Juan   14   325
Which ministers unto the soul's delight   968 Juan   15   15

DELIGHTED
Through life to dwell delighted here   44 Harold   3   531
Adieu to thee, fair Rhine! How long delighted   44 Harold   3   563
Which it would cope with, on delighted wing   46 Harold   3   696
Though not delighted, yet I must forgive   142 Soliloquy   21
Who, lovely as ever, seem'd just as delighted   228 Moore-A   24
The eye delighted, but fatigued the ear   254 Bards   896
The partial muse delighted loves to lave   255 Bards   986
And kiss the doubt from these delighted eyes   339 Corsair   1   116
The feast these hands delighted to prepare   344 Corsair   1   421
Must seem delighted with the heart he gave   351 Corsair   2   266
All the heart's hue in that delighted glow   373 Lara   1   533
To the delighted west, which revels in   562 Sardan   2   32
His frequent mission with delighted pinions   666 Heaven   790
The while the wicked world beholds delighted   759 Juan   1   795
In fact much more astonish'd than delighted   806 Juan   3   295
No less delighted to employ his leisure   881 Juan   8   192
And I shall be delighted to learn who   897 Juan   9   31
Besides, he was of that delighted age   905 Juan   9   545
Don Juan was delighted to secure   935 Juan   12   326
At the full board, and sit alike delighted   989 Juan   16   597
Delighted with their dinner and their host   994 Juan   16   855

DELIGHTFUL
And all we deem delightful and consume   68 Harold   4   771
'While Poesy,' with these delightful doxies   171 Address-B   37
Delightful Bowles! still blessing and still blest   246 Bards   341
And dark the mountain's once delightful dyes   268 Minerva   26
Delightful Waltz on tiptoe for a mate   274 Waltz   80
And dark the mountain's once delightful dyes   355 Corsair   3   26
Brief, but delightful--such as had not staid   825 Juan   4   566
What a delightful thing's a turnpike road   917 Juan   10   617
Find one, each day of the delightful year   963 Juan   14   502

DELIGHTING
Behold the host! delighting to deprave   193 Monody   73
Or, still in bells delighting, finds a friend   246 Bards   337
How quickly would I print (the world delighting   446 Beppo   405
Form'd rather for instructing than delighting   831 Juan   5   13

DELIGHTS
Nurtured in blood betimes, his heart delights   16 Harold   1   794
That I with stern delights should e'er have been
  so moved   48 Harold   3   805
All treasures, all delights, that eye or ear   71 Harold   4   971
Thy every path delights me still   132 L'Amitie   46
Where smiling Youth delights to dwell   133 E. N. Long   31
The wonted delights of our childhood retrace   136 Delawarr   14
May no delights decoy   138 Clare   87
Renew those riotous delights   164 Friend-B   4
Torments and delights me   239 Lucietta   11
Thus poetry disgusts, or else delights   265 Hints   634
When heart with heart delights to blend   322 Giaour   1219
Still the old god delights, from out the main   425 Island   2   472
From men and their delights. Beshrew the hour   494 Manfred   3   226
But theirs was love in which the mind delights   818 Juan   4   130
Temperance delights her, but long fasting ruffles   992 Juan   16   736

DELINQUENT
And do you right upon the bold delinquent   501 Faliero   1   114
Well, but now to discover the delinquent   683 Werner   2   8

DELIRIOUS
From rock to rock leaps with delirious bound   65 Harold   4   628
Of Sin delirious with its dread   404 Chillon   183
I was indeed delirious in my heart   437 Tasso   50
However they might savour of delirious   984 Juan   16   259

DELIRIOUSLY
Which sweeps the soul deliriously from life   531 Faliero   4   240

DELIRIUM
When Love's delirium haunts the glowing mind   119 Answer-A   11
Delirium is our best deceiver   159 Spell   4
Delirium gathers from the fever's height   357 Corsair   3   102

DELIS
His way amid his Delis took   326 Abydos   1   236
The turban'd Delis in the field   330 Abydos   2   123

DELIVER
Made me--And how look'd he? deliver that   500 Faliero   1   70
My lord, I will deliver your reply   504 Faliero   1   320
Let him deliver up his weapon, and   565 Sardan   2   210

DELIVERANCE
For this our most miraculous deliverance   545 Faliero   5   490
Had sent them this for their deliverance   786 Juan   2   792

DELIVER'D
Though I feel that my soul is deliver'd   210 Augusta-B   19
But if she were deliver'd safe and sound   891 Juan   8   815
Who had deliver'd well a very set   952 Juan   13   715

DELIVERER
There to pronounce the death of your deliverer   543 Faliero   5   373

DELIVERERS'
Strew flowers o'er her deliverers' ashes, then   519 Faliero   3   72

DELL
We view'd the lake, the park, the dell   89 To Emma   14
A victim in that lonely dell   317 Giaour   728
But he is dead! within the dell   323 Giaour   1302

DELLS
A blending of all beauties,--streams and dells   42 Harold   3   411

DELOS
Where Delos rose, and Phoebus sprung   812 Juan   3   692

DELPHI
Nor e'er did Delphi, when her priestess sung   14 Harold   1   650
And Delphi now, however rich of old   264 Hints   527

DELPHIAN
Behind his Delphian rock he sinks to sleep   268 Minerva   18
Behind his Delphian cliff he sinks to sleep   355 Corsair   3   18

DELPHI'S
Yes! sigh'd o'er Delphi's long-deserted shrine   3 Harold   1   6
When wandering slow by Delphi's sacred side   34 Harold   2   871
When next you visit Delphi's town   227 Thurlow-B   13
Of Delphi's hill, unshaken snow   388 Corinth   365

DELUGE
An universal deluge, which appears   68 Harold   4   826
Toss'd by the deluge in their common ark   307 Age   647
By the approaching deluge! by the earth   659 Heaven   323
Of the subsiding deluge, from its slime   661 Heaven   453
Than the eternal deluge, which devours   898 Juan   9   103

DELUGES
As sweeps the air and deluges the earth   576 Sardan   3   318

DELUSION
Alas! it is delusion all   223 Music-D   9
Which kept my optics free from all delusion   298 Vision   843
All the delusion of the dizzy scene   529 Faliero   4   62
Then there must be delusion.--What is that   643 Cain   2   457
Can make its offspring; still it is delusion   643 Cain   2   477
Some strong delusion; it will calm thee. No   649 Cain   3   203
There mails fast flying off like a delusion   921 Juan   11   172

DELUSION'S
Vain Hope! the gay delusion's past   91 Caroline-B   38

DELUSIVE
And mould to every taste thy dear delusive shape   14 Harold   1   665
Away, away! delusive power   132 L'Amitie   38

DELVED
Plough'd, delved, or plied the oar with lusty
  limb   247 Bards   409

DEMAGOGUE
Excepting the Demagogue Francis   178 Devil's Dr   166

DEMAGOGUES
The demagogues of fashion: all below   447 Beppo   478
And demagogues yield to them but in date   465 Dante   4   120
Without me, there are demagogues enough   899 Juan   9   194
When demagogues would with a butcher's knife   990 Juan   16   637

DEMAND
But my soul wanders; I demand it back   59 Harold   4   217
When Self and Church demand a bigot zeal   112 Examination   62
In grim array the crimson cross demand   119 Newstead-A   10
To demand the same free question   196 Rogers   20
From me demand but little of my care   212 Augusta-C   106
Demand that thy daughter expire   218 Jephtha   2
This duty done, let me in turn demand   224 J.C.H.   25
That I despair of all demand   231 Doctor   28
The royal vices of our age demand   242 Bards   39
Are now no fools whose backs demand the scourge   253 Bards   822
Demand a hallow'd harp--that harp is thine   254 Bards   934
Let her live, and as long as she likes; I demand   278 Blues   1   83
By the increased demand for his remarks   285 Vision   31
Her honour, fame, and faith demand his bones   300 Age   125
Demand her fields as lists to prove the sword   302 Age   321
I know the wretch who dares demand   327 Abydos   1   371
Refused to aid his heavy heart's demand   364 Corsair   3   586
To lend at thy demand a listening ear   375 Lara   2   44
'Demand thy life!' He answer'd not: and then   376 Lara   2   71
In vain thou dost demand the cause; a curse   416 Island   1   69
Now swarm forth in rebellion, and demand   583 Sardan   4   315
Now you are last; but did the state demand   616 Foscari   4   111
Not afraid to demand it? Not afraid   674 Werner   1   175

DEMAND
But this is nothing: I demand of you   692 Werner   2   566
Demand some in return;--no, no, he must not   739 Deformed   2   277
All strut, and stays, and whiskers, to demand   937 Juan   12   476

DEMANDED
If danger demanded, were wholly your own   137 Delawarr   26
They demanded the song; but, oh never   222 Babylon   9
The song they demanded in vain--it lay still   223 Valley   5
When Bligh in stern reproach demanded where   417 Island   1   159
Twice I demanded it, but was refused   604 Foscari   2   186
Lull'd even the savage hunger which demanded   783 Juan   2   595
Lolah demanded the new damsel's name   858 Juan   6   345

DEMANDING
And served the church--without demanding tithes   266 Hints   674
Demanding whether he should augur him   619 Foscari   4   293
Just now you chid me for demanding names   675 Werner   1   248

DEMANDS
Which from our sex demands such praises   87 Rousseau   15
It is not war their aid demands   102 Alva   93
This seeks the shade, but that demands the light   264 Hints   574
Waltz--Waltz alone--both legs and arms demands   275 Waltz   113
Now thou hast swill'd thy pottage, thy demands   306 Age   634
Demands and daunts the stranger's eye   319 Giaour   880
And from his country's justice now demands   377 Lara   2   131
And for a brief delay demands   399 Parisina   231
What answer Beppo made to these demands   452 Beppo   745
Our power, increasing thine, demands our care   489 Manfred   2   396
The king demands your fellow-traitor's sword   565 Sardan   2   201
And answer'd but to nature's just demands   751 Juan   1   294
And spawns his quarto, and demands your praise   838 Juan   5   412
From out the commonest demands of nature   976 Juan   15   552

DEMEAN
How to demean himself in ducal chambers   514 Faliero   2   425

DEMEANOUR
For a prince, his demeanour was rather too hearty   228 Moore-A   18
A high demeanour, and a glance that took   367 Lara   1   71
How vainly! It is said the king's demeanour   588 Sardan   5   76
In aspect and demeanour. True, dear child   708 Werner   4   245
Of mild demeanour though of savage mood   808 Juan   3   418
Showing a much more reconciled demeanour   826 Juan   4   647

DEMETRIUS
Demetrius the Macedonian, and   726 Deformed   1   258

DEMI-DIETY
The demi-diety, Alcides, in   514 Faliero   2   390

DEMIGOD
Of Fame the Moloch or the demigod   301 Age   238
Who truly looketh like a demigod   726 Deformed   1   246

DEMIGODS
Where demi-gods appear'd, as records tell   20 Harold   2   42
A mixture of wild beasts and demigods   891 Juan   8   844

DEMISE
The hour of her demise may rue   232 Doctor   80

DEMOCRACY
Season'd his pedlar poems with democracy   814 Juan   3   836

DEMOCRATIC
Because I hate even democratic royalty   971 Juan   15   184

DEMOCRATS
And wrinkles, the d--d democrats, won't flatter   910 Juan   10   192

DEMOCRITUS
Democritus himself was not so bad   263 Hints   463

DEMOISELLE
A dashing demoiselle of good estate   973 Juan   15   330

DEMOLISH'D
The burning wreck of a demolish'd world   479 Manfred   1   45
A single laugh demolish'd the right arm   942 Juan   13   82
But that with them all law would be demolish'd   990 Juan   16   624

DEMON
(See also HALF-DEMON)
Convention is the dwarfish demon styled   8 Harold   1   297
The blight of life--the demon Thought   17 Harold   1   860
Thus spoke the Demon (late call'd 'multifaced   293 Vision   513
Though like a demon of the night   312 Giaour   202
Shall know the demon for their sire   318 Giaour   764
Whose demon death-blow left no hope for fight   349 Corsair   2   151
Almost to blackness in its demon hue   376 Lara   2   74
And a strange demon, who is vexing me   439 Tasso   192
Of an all-pitiless demon held me back   486 Manfred   2   232

DEMON

And like the demon who believes and trembles	527	Faliero	3	641
The anointed high-priest--Of what god or demon	592	Sardan	5	290
In thunder. Then who was the demon? He	630	Cain	1	204
But the thing had a demon? He but woke one	631	Cain	1	226
Who names me demon to his angels; they	636	Cain	2	7
Oh, god, or demon, or whate'er thou art	636	Cain	2	26
To a demon! Who shall dare say this of Ulric	721	Werner	5	547
My horrid shadow--like a demon placed	723	Deformed	1	50
You were the demon, but that your approach	723	Deformed	1	94
Oh! then you are indeed the demon, for	724	Deformed	1	136
'Tis a great name for blood-hounds. There's a demon	734	Deformed	1	857
But when it was, she had that lurking demon	966	Juan	14	705

DEMONS

Or, it may be, with demons, who impair	60	Harold	4	298
Exulting demons wing'd his dart	105	Alva		286
But where have Demons hid thy Heart	143	To--A		20
Demons in act but Gods at least in face	341	Corsair	1	194
That these are demons: could it be else that	603	Foscari	2	117
Accept the tardy penitence of demons	617	Foscari	4	176
Are girt about by demons, who assume	633	Cain	1	398
Avaunt! ye exulting demons of the waste	660	Heaven		379
And even the very demons shall do well	661	Heaven		469
The very demons shriek it from their caves	662	Heaven		540
Demons heroic	725	Deformed	1	173
Demons who wore	725	Deformed	1	174
They are beautiful, and cannot, sure, be demons	729	Deformed	1	522
And demons howl. And man too. Let us listen	732	Deformed	1	689
By all the demons of all passions, show'd	866	Juan	6	887

DEMON'S

Yet once he struggled 'gainst the demon's sway	17	Harold	1	833
Oh! could Le Sage's demon's gift	95	Granta		1
Surely some envious demon's force	99	Young Lady		5

DEMONSTRATION

Convincing all, by demonstration plain	245	Bards		243

DEMOSTHENES

With all which Demosthenes wanted endued	202	Avatar		39
Henry, the forest-born Demosthenes	303	Age		384
Demosthenes has sanction'd the transaction	304	Age		500

DEMUR

Lord H---, indeed, may not demur	95	Granta		17
Or every thing which pass'd without demur	468	Morgante		143

DEMURR'D

Demurr'd: a messenger was sent back to	602	Foscari	2	57
Juan demurr'd at this first notice to	912	Juan	10	337

DEN

Where Superstition once had made her den	4	Harold	1	60
The den expands, and Expectation mute	16	Harold	1	748
For sceptred cynics earth were far too wide a den	41	Harold	3	369
The World, the same wide den--of thieves, or what ye will	77	Harold	4	1305
Because I would reform the den	235	New Song		15
Up to his den Sir Scribbler hies, and soon	267	Hints		747
In his own den, to scrawl some 'Life' or 'Vision	298	Vision		839
And backward to the den of his despair	301	Age		211
Is Desolation's hungry den	313	Giaour		349
'Whence com'st thou, Dervise?' 'From the outlaw's den	348	Corsair	2	65
Like brutes within an iron den	404	Chillon		137
But vainly wolves and lions seek their den	426	Island	3	17
Then gazed upon the pair, as in his den	429	Island	3	209
And form'd a refuge of the rocky den	432	Island	4	181
From long infection of a den like this	439	Tasso		234
A wanderer, while even wolves can find a den	458	Dante	1	163
For them no fortress can avail,--the den	460	Dante	2	127
Thou den of drunkards with the blood of princes	549	Faliero	5	794
And dolphins gambol in the lion's den	659	Heaven		278
The dragon crawls from out his den	669	Heaven		1063
I wot of: it will serve me as a den	681	Werner	1	640
In such a den as this. Pray Heaven it lead me	701	Werner	3	412
You ne'er had turn'd it to a den for--Thieves	703	Werner	3	511
Pretended den of refuge, to become	718	Werner	5	345
A den of thieves! No injury!--this temple	740	Deformed	2	352
Who smooth'd his pillow, as she left the den	791	Juan	2	1074
To-morrow'd see us in some other den	837	Juan	5	349
And Daniel tamed the lions in their den	839	Juan	5	477
What fear you? think you this a lion's den	841	Juan	5	646
Along the rest, contrived to keep this den	856	Juan	6	254
The army, like a lion from his den	878	Juan	8	11
The restless Titan hiccups in his den	879	Juan	8	56
Destruction's jaws into the devil's den	882	Juan	8	276
As bold as Daniel in the lion's den	905	Juan	9	548
(The den of many a diplomatic lost lie	922	Juan	11	246

DENIAL
(See also SELF-DENIAL)

Ne'er taunts you with a mock denial	160	Cadiz		34
And if the man should ask, 'tis but denial	756	Juan	1	623

DENIED

And hath denied, to every other sky	63	Harold	4	491
Which rests in the bosom, though hope is denied	96	Harrow-A		8

DENIED

Though souls are denied you by fools and by rakes	117	To Eliza		37
Denied in death a monumental stone	124	Recoll		160
And seek abroad the love denied at home	125	Recoll		216
And this can be denied by none	143	On Eyes		3
Denied in heaven the soul he held on earth	154	Dog		12
Commands a verse, and will not be denied	199	Sonnet-D		3
His soul o'er the freedom implored and denied	202	Avatar		36
Kiss his foot with thy blessing, his blessings denied	202	Avatar		56
And when convulsive throes denied my breath	206	Love, Death		17
Denied the courser and the spear	332	Abydos	2	324
Or, since that hope denied in worlds of strife	333	Abydos	2	398
Denied his bones a holier grave	337	Abydos	2	724
The life thou leav'st below, denied above	359	Corsair	3	236
For the God their foes denied	402	Chillon		24
Had his free breathing been denied	404	Chillon		142
On him for language which his lips denied	427	Island	3	83
To seek from Heaven the shelter men denied	433	Island	4	234
Of him, whom she denied a home, the grave	457	Dante	1	76
No, she denied me what was mine--my roof	457	Dante	1	83
Since to thy servants pity's ne'er denied	466	Morgante		13
For madness as a blessing--'tis denied me	486	Manfred	2	228
But he, who is denied his right by those	501	Faliero	1	133
We will ask justice; if it be denied	502	Faliero	1	167
I cannot even obtain it--'twas denied	505	Faliero	1	414
And pure as theirs; but this has been denied me	515	Faliero	2	468
Would not now be denied to us; but since	539	Faliero	5	114
A throne, or, if that be denied--You have heard	582	Sardan	4	266
This prayer of yours was twice denied before	603	Foscari	2	103
With some remorse received (though first denied	783	Juan	2	565
But oft denied, as patience 'gins to fail, he	969	Juan	15	61
A great resource to all, and ne'er denied	982	Juan	16	95

DENIES

Repose denies her requiem to his name	193	Monody		67
Which heaven to gaudy day denies	216	She Walks		6
Do more than niggard envy still denies	300	Age		114
Our law, our creed, our God denies	328	Abydos	1	430
'Oh! water--water!'--smiling Hate denies	351	Corsair	2	322
Yet would I ask--almost my lip denies	357	Corsair	3	105
But here is one denies that he is dead	357	Corsair	3	108
For Truth denies all eloquence to Woe	365	Corsair	3	645
Which he himself denies and violates	541	Faliero	5	233

DENIZEN

And roam along, the world's tired denizen	23	Harold	2	228

DENIZENS

The dingy denizens are rear'd in dirt	7	Harold	1	230

DENMARK

The Queen of Denmark, for Ophelia brought	776	Juan	2	133

DENNIS

Thus Pope by Curl and Dennis was destroy'd	143	Soliloquy		77
To rave with Dennis, and with Ralph to rhyme	247	Bards		380
I loathe an opera worse than Dennis did	260	Hints		296
The much-renown'd St. Dennis being the cause	467	Morgante		70

DENOTE

And presence here denote. His sufferings	489	Manfred	2	423

DENOTES

Denotes how soft that chin which bears his touch	13	Harold	1	595

DENOUNCE

Should dub me scribbler and denounce my muse	241	Bards		4
All's silent, and all's lost! Now, Doge, denounce me	537	Faliero	4	599
The traitor I denounce upon that rack	539	Faliero	5	85
For the last time--the days which I denounce	547	Faliero	5	667
I therefore do denounce all amorous writing	831	Juan	5	9
But to denounce the amphibious sort of harlot	937	Juan	12	495

DENOUNCED

Denounced of retribution from all time	615	Foscari	4	23
I cannot compass: 'tis denounced against us	631	Cain	1	283
When the dread hour denounced shall open wide	658	Heaven		228
Denounced--dragg'd, it may be, in chains; and all	721	Werner	5	525

DENOUNCING

Denouncing dire reproach to luckless fools	111	Examination		7

DENS

In caves, in dens, in clefts of mountains, where	661	Heaven		440

DENSE

And of the cold, dull, swimming, dense	414	Mazeppa		787
Your miserly intendant, and dense noble	695	Werner	3	22

DENSITY

Unwonted density went on before	547	Faliero	5	631

DENT

From Mr. Hammond to Dog Dent	231	Doctor		58

DENUNCIATION

Of thy denunciation, I go forth	532	Faliero	4	290
You have forgotten the denunciation	641	Cain	2	353

DENY

Glance o'er this page, nor to my verse deny	3	To Ianthe		31

DENY

In dreams deny me not to see thee here	19	Harold	1	939
Of thine imperial garment, shall deny	63	Harold	4	490
Our hearts deny it: and so young, so fair	80	Harold	4	1541
My limbs deny their slight support	87	Ad Lesbiam		16
Or, if my destiny these last deny	106	Nisus		69
If again you shall sigh, she no more will deny	115	Pigot		15
Now, Strephon, good bye; I cannot deny	116	Strephon		33
Who to woman deny the soul's future existence	116	To Eliza		2
Nor Matthew nor Mark nor St. Paul can deny it	117	To Eliza		30
Still to assent, and never to deny	123	Recoll		71
I cannot deny such a precept is wise	128	Becher-A		2
When dames accuse 'tis bootless to deny	142	Soliloquy		34
And much it grieves me to deny them	144	Becher-B		24
But every drop its lids deny	186	Stanzas-A		7
In a rhymer, 'twere strange to deny	205	Blessington		2
Admire their justice, which would fain deny	307	Age		656
I dare not to my hope deny	328	Abydos	1	393
With all a hermit's board would scarce deny	339	Corsair	1	74
Nor aught that knighthood may accord, deny	372	Lara	1	477
As promises the death their hands deny	416	Island	1	88
To the true God, who will not then deny us	471	Morgante		347
And to thee shall Night deny	481	Manfred	1	228
I am prepared for all things; but deny	496	Manfred	3	342
Upon my strength--I do defy--deny	496	Manfred	3	380
I deny nothing--defend nothing--nothing	542	Faliero	5	296
And if he can deny the proofs, believe him	543	Faliero	5	349
Nor, as thou seest, doth he deny it now	543	Faliero	5	355
Which I deny to them. We all are men	555	Sardan	1	313
A high crime, which I neither can deny	603	Foscari	2	97
Thus much they cannot well deny. And if	607	Foscari	2	377
So far with a weak woman as deny me	608	Foscari	2	431
What! would they even deny me my sire's sepulchre	610	Foscari	3	138
Did not the Doge deny this strongly? Doubtless	615	Foscari	4	25
What thou dar'st not deny,--the history	636	Cain	2	24
Deny thee shelter! earth a home! the dust	653	Cain	3	442
Which I call helpless; if you now deny it	695	Werner	3	30
You can't deny his train of followers	704	Werner	4	39
Or waste a world? since no one can deny	903	Juan	9	445
But to deny the mob a cordial, which is	915	Juan	10	502
For me, I know nought; nothing I deny	955	Juan	14	17
He who doubts all things nothing can deny	979	Juan	15	701
In its behalf, let those deny who will	981	Juan	16	56

DENYING

Who there could gaze denying thee	329	Abydos	2	38
Avow'd his crime in not denying that	605	Foscari	2	267
Denying several little things he wanted	769	Juan	1	1436
Denying the receipt of what it cost	772	Juan	1	1678
And wear my head, denying that I wear it	918	Juan	11	8

DEPART

The winds lift up their voices: I depart	35	Harold	3	7
We stand as captives and would not depart	62	Harold	4	446
Yet, ere from hence our eager steps depart	107	Nisus		175
Bids her he fondly loved depart	111	Medea		51
Ye friends of my heart, ere from you I depart	115	The Tear		37
The wise sometimes from Wisdom's ways depart	119	Answer-A		7
From me again 'twill ne'er depart	128	Lady-C		7
Too late desiring to depart	141	Critics		40
'Fair Albion, smiling, sees her son depart	162	Orchomenus		1
Threw down the dagger--dared depart	180	Ode-A		57
He dared depart in utter scorn	180	Ode-A		59
Could with thy gentle image bear depart	183	Address-D		20
The weak despair--the cold depart	209	Augusta-A		8
In mercy ne'er again depart	323	Giaour		1316
Ah, wherefore not consume it--and depart	336	Abydos	2	650
With feelings loosed to strengthen--not depart	341	Corsair	1	240
One softer feeling would not yet depart	342	Corsair	1	282
One question answer, then in peace depart	349	Corsair	2	134
And bow'd her head, and turn'd her to depart	355	Corsair	2	536
She saw not, felt not this, nor dared depart	356	Corsair	3	81
But--good or ill--it bade her not depart	363	Corsair	3	546
Nor long they flow'd--he dried them to depart	365	Corsair	3	654
Exclaim'd, 'Depart at once! delay is death	417	Island	1	154
But feast to-night! to-morrow we depart	419	Island	2	44
To-morrow for the Mooa we depart	419	Island	2	55
What do I say?--to-morrow we depart	419	Island	2	64
But can endure thy pity. I depart	485	Manfred	2	90
I now depart a debtor. Fare ye well	491	Manfred	2	537
'Tis fit I were alone. Ere I depart	504	Faliero	1	281
The glory shall depart from out thy house	546	Faliero	5	606
I humble me before you, and depart	563	Sardan	2	116
Say, we depart. My order is to see you	568	Sardan	2	412
Depart, and not to bear your answer. Ay	568	Sardan	2	413
Too oft. Am I permitted to depart	569	Sardan	2	485
Look to thine own. Permit me to depart	570	Sardan	2	515
Depart, will you not see--My sons! It may	581	Sardan	4	210
At least from thence he will depart to meet me	593	Sardan	5	353
Ere he depart? It may be the last time	608	Foscari	2	437
I shall depart, then, without meeting them	614	Foscari	3	384
Ah, father! though I must and will depart	616	Foscari	4	99
Signors, you may depart: what would you more	624	Foscari	5	212

DEPART

Farewell, sirs! You shall not depart without	624	Foscari	5	268
Depart. Ah! now you look as look'd my husband	625	Foscari	5	302
Depart and leave the dead to me--I am	653	Cain	3	445
Let us depart, nor walk the wilderness	653	Cain	3	458
Let us depart together. Oh, thou dead	654	Cain	3	528
But yet depart	667	Heaven		923
'They tell me 'tis decided; you depart	770	Juan	1	1529
But coughs will come when sighs depart--and now	908	Juan	10	57
Ray fades on ray, as years on years depart	995	Juan	16	916

DEPARTED

The Childe departed from his father's hall	4	Harold	1	55
Fair Greece, sad relic of departed worth	31	Harold	2	693
Which blighted their life's bloom and then departed	50	Harold	3	884
Pledge me departed Oscar's health	104	Alva		224
Yet even these themes are departed for ever	148	Farewell-A		10
So darkly of departed years	220	Clay		14
Of the departed, and then go their way	459	Dante	2	87
Then full of wrath departed from the place	468	Morgante		145
The glory hath departed from our house	537	Faliero	4	622
Queen of Assyria, departed hence	585	Sardan	4	452
Two hours since ye departed: two long hours	647	Cain	3	54
Ulric, this man, who has just departed, is	709	Werner	4	290
In the behalf of our departed friends	712	Werner	4	485
Departed like the rest of their compeers	947	Juan	13	394
Skirmish of wits o'er the departed; one	994	Juan	16	882

DEPARTING

Of your departing voices, is the knoll	50	Harold	3	900
Shades of heroes, farewell! your descendant, departing	86	Leaving NA		21
Departing for a distant shore	89	To Emma		8
Scrapes wealth, o'er each departing penny grieves	260	Hints		253
For a departing being's soul	400	Parisina		394
As a departing rainbow's ray	404	Chillon		193
Remaining here, you may lose all; departing	584	Sardan	4	386

DEPARTS

But not from thee, dark pile! departs the chief	119	Newstead-A		17

DEPARTURE

And your departure breeds such sorrow here	475	Morgante		645
Our quick departure proves our civic zeal	569	Sardan	2	461
Our quick departure hinders our good escort	569	Sardan	2	462
Ends as such partings end, in no departure	583	Sardan	4	364
Or after their departure; of that malady	610	Foscari	3	172
Of our departure from this much-loved city	611	Foscari	3	216
To our departure. Who comes here? Retire	611	Foscari	3	248
But, peace being made soon after his departure	685	Werner	2	119
Of his departure had been sent him by	777	Juan	2	191
Of their departure: such is modern fame	947	Juan	13	402
'Departure, for his country seat, to-day	947	Juan	13	407

DEPEND

Think'st thou existence doth depend on time	484	Manfred	2	51
Or if it must depend upon men's words	509	Faliero	2	58
Depend their own, their fortunes, and their hopes	522	Faliero	3	220
I may depend upon you? 'Twere too late	694	Werner	2	748
The fates of others oft depend; besides	717	Werner	5	272
On which the passion's self seems to depend	905	Juan	9	582
In that fair clime which don't depend on climate	959	Juan	14	226

DEPENDENCE

Dependence barters for her bitter bread	267	Hints		774

DEPENDENT

All but one poor dependent priest withdrawn	267	Hints		763
Made him as suns to a dependent star	666	Heaven		844
Dependent on the public altogether	771	Juan	1	1587

DEPENDING

For, through thy long dark lashes low depending	175	Sonnet-B		9
Depending more upon the historian's style	813	Juan	3	811

DEPENDS

Depends upon his deeds,' the Angel said	293	Vision		546
Although upon this breath of mine depends	566	Sardan	2	281
Depends upon a straw than on a storm	607	Foscari	2	360
Depends upon what depends on a rash word	693	Werner	2	675
Remember what depends on a rash word	693	Werner	2	675
Depends so much upon the gastric juice	835	Juan	5	256
Of Britain's youth depends upon their weight	885	Juan	8	436
Since Eve ate apples, much depends on dinner	953	Juan	13	792

DEPLORE

And those who know it best, deplore it most	24	Harold	2	308
We may deplore and struggle with the coil	46	Harold	3	659
In vain our fate in sighs deplore	90	Caroline-A		18
The sentence I should scarce deplore	99	Young Lady		22
With those who, scatter'd far, perchance deplore	138	Harrow-B		5
Though all deplore when Milton deigns to doze	264	Hints		569
The morn, to deplore it	488	Manfred	2	333
Which I deplore so much; for I have borne	833	Juan	5	143

DEPLORE
I own it, I deplore it, I condemn it	853 Juan	6	58
Of common likings, which make some deplore	943 Juan	13	134

DEPLORED
Deplored by those in early days allied	138 Harrow-B		33
Thou shalt not be deplored	219 Thy Days		18
Of days no more deplored or curst	414 Mazeppa		756
Beloved and deplored; while slowly stray'd	860 Juan	6	534

DEPLORES
Affliction's self deplores thy youthful doom	85 Epitaph		18
No friend thy wretched fate deplores	111 Medea		46
Deplores the ancient woes which both befell	466 Morgante		19

DEPLORING
That age will come on, when remembrance, deploring	91 Caroline-C		7
To the monk, his doom deploring	400 Parisina		414

DEPOPULATED
Would have depopulated empires, nor	528 Faliero	3	656

DEPOPULATION
Of death, depopulation, bondage, fears	38 Harold	3	176

DEPORTMENT
Who models his deportment as may best	263 Hints		497

DEPOSE
The indignant shadow to depose her wrath	487 Manfred	2	283

DEPOSED
Deposed him gently from his throne of force	68 Harold	4	768
Rose crimson, and deposed the stars	413 Mazeppa		649
The old man is deposed, his name degraded	620 Foscari	4	325
Elected, and so will I be deposed	624 Foscari	5	253
Deposed where now the eagle's offspring dwells	662 Heaven		506

DEPOSING
Even now deposing to the secret giunta	537 Faliero	4	643

DEPOSIT
She whisper'd, in great wrath--'I must deposit	767 Juan	1	1359
May turn his name up, as a rare deposit	813 Juan	3	808

DEPOSITED
Where all sighs are deposited; and now	982 Juan	16	98

DEPOSITION
But if this deposition should take place	615 Foscari	4	27
'If he comes here to take a deposition	765 Juan	1	1209

DEPOSITIONS
Yet when they ask'd her for her depositions	750 Juan	1	213
The depositions, and the cause at full	770 Juan	1	1506

DEPOTISM
Of every depotism in every nation	899 Juan	9	192

DEPRAVE
Behold the host! delighting to deprave	193 Monody		73

DEPRAVING
Depraving nature's frailty to an art	549 Faliero	5	785

DEPRAVITY
He knew the world, and would not see depravity	944 Juan	13	173

DEPRECATED
To bode him no great good, he deprecated	865 Juan	6	810

DEPRECIATED
But not the less for this to be depreciated	937 Juan	12	491

DEPRESS
Can raise with hope, depress with fear	90 To M.S.G.-A		10
To good, depress thee thus? Had I gone forth	610 Foscari	3	156

DEPRESS'D
His sons all dead, his family depress'd	620 Foscari	4	326

DEPREST
His step was feeble, and his look deprest	347 Corsair	2	54

DEPRIVE
In the death which one day will deprive you of me	91 Caroline-C		16
It could not deprive me of thee	210 Augusta-B		40
You would deprive this old man of all business	619 Foscari	4	256
Which shall deprive thee of a single good	636 Cain	1	557

DEPRIVED
Deprived of many a wholesome meal	95 Granta		43
By my daughters of kingdom and reason deprived	96 Harrow-A		22

DEPRIVED
Friendship, the power deprived of wings	132 L'Amitie		70
Deprived of active force	146 Adieu		50
Deprived of that which makes my misery	657 Heaven		187
By his nerves only? Who deprived me of	720 Werner	5	446

DEPRIVES
Thy fond fidelity for a time deprives	617 Foscari	4	138

DEPRIVING
Not content with depriving your bodies of spirit	116 To Eliza		10

DEPTH
Its clear depth yields of their far height and hue	46 Harold	3	647
Even in destruction's depth, her foreign foes	57 Harold	4	116
Its depth, and thence may draw the mind of man	79 Harold	4	1430
The thicket's depth with hurried pace they tread	109 Nisus		311
The violet still grows in the depth of thy valleys	186 Napoleon		19
One, the blue depth of Seraph's eyes	188 On Star		26
Distance, nor depth of wave, nor space of earth	198 Po		38
The depth of thy deep in a deeper gulf still	203 Avatar		104
Walk'd out of his depth and was lost in a calm sea	227 Moore-A		10
For ever in its depth endure	402 Parisina		566
A thousand feet in depth below	403 Chillon		108
And in the depth of forests darkling	407 Mazeppa		27
The wood-dove from the forest depth shall coo	419 Island	2	5
In the blue depth of the waters	479 Manfred	1	76
My bones had then been quiet in their depth	483 Manfred	1	365
Along the depth beneath, and ne'er feel dizzy	511 Faliero	2	199
We leave him to himself, that lowest depth	544 Faliero	5	458
The depth beneath us hides our own dear land	668 Heaven		965
And that the depth is rich in better things	690 Werner	2	497
From the depth of this fountain	724 Deformed	1	162
Lull'd like the depth of ocean when at rest	793 Juan	2	1180
In winter's depth, or want of rest and victual	894 Juan	8	1023
And what a whirlpool full of depth and danger	904 Juan	9	507
There was a depth of feeling to embrace	987 Juan	16	431

DEPTHS
In deeds, not years, piercing the depths of life	36 Harold	3	38
In hate, whose mining depths so intervene	49 Harold	3	880
He sinks into thy depths with bubbling groan	82 Harold	4	1610
And nothing stirr'd within their silent depths	190 Darkness		74
Whose depths unsearch'd, and fountains from the hill	421 Island	2	153
The depths where divers hold the pearl in chase	431 Island	4	112
Diving for turtle in the depths below	432 Island	4	196
What ocean is to earth, spreads its blue depths	529 Faliero	4	72
In the eternal depths of heaven	655 Heaven		39
Shall have its depths search'd by the sweeping wave	659 Heaven		277
Hush'd into depths beyond the watcher's diving	799 Juan	2	1574
Our hearts first in the depths of Lethe's spring	816 Juan	4	29

DEPUTATION
My lord, the deputation is in waiting	620 Foscari	5	1

DEPUTE
I care, depute the Council on their knees	615 Foscari	4	33

DERANGE
And these so much our orisons derange	469 Morgante		191

DERIDE
If still, from false pride, your pangs she deride	115 Pigot		17
But lo!--the papers print what you deride	171 Address-B		48
Though nymphs forsake, and critics may deride	242 Bards		13
Learn'd to deride the critic's starch decree	256 Bards		1059
Better let him than all the world deride	267 Hints		798
Though at the first I might perchance deride	971 Juan	15	181

DERIDES
In short, howe'er our better faith derides	892 Juan	8	908

DERISION
(See also SELF-DERISION)
Derision sneers upon thy birth	150 My Son		15

DERIVED
From joyance ne'er derived its birth	318 Giaour		858
By right of blood, derived from age to age	574 Sardan	3	169
The honey, nor enquire whence 'tis derived	583 Sardan	4	323
From the blue skies derived a double blue	828 Juan	4	718

DERIVES
Derives from thee a sense so deep and clear	76 Harold	4	1240
When stripp'd of this mortality, derives	496 Manfred	3	393
'Tis as a snowball which derives assistance	829 Juan	4	797

DERVISE
Nor there will wandering Dervise stay	313 Giaour		340

DERVISE

'A captive Dervise, from the pirate's nest   347 Corsair   2   49
'Whence com'st thou, Dervise?' 'From the
outlaw's den   348 Corsair   2   65
'Stay, Dervise! I have more to question--stay   348 Corsair   2   99
'What ails thee, Dervise? eat--dost thou suppose   348 Corsair   2   117
Accursed Dervise!--these thy tidings--thou   349 Corsair   2   140
Up rose the Dervise with that burst of light   349 Corsair   2   142
Up rose that Dervise--not in saintly garb   349 Corsair   2   144
They seize that Dervise!--seize on Zatanai   349 Corsair   2   160

DERVISES

Like dervises, who turn as on a pivot, he   805 Juan   3   230

DESAIX

Joubert, Hoche, Marceau, Lannes, Desaix, Moreau   747 Juan   1   21

DESCEND

But thus unlaurel'd to descend in vain   19 Harold   1   931
Ye mountains, that see us descend to the shore   31 Harold   2   691
Or, dark in mist, descend the mountain's side   85 Fragment-A   4
And from thy hall of clouds descend   118 Romance   18
I will not descend to a world I despise   128 Becher-A   4
The mountain-peasants to descend   158 Storm   19
No! when the sons of song descend to trade   244 Bards   175
Could bow to Lara, not descend to them   374 Lara   1   573
And when I did descend again   406 Chillon   359
For this brief moment to descend   480 Manfred   1   128
I'll warn him to descend, or he may chance   482 Manfred   1   344
His state descend to his children, as it must   601 Foscari   1   352
Will now descend the stairs by which I mounted   624 Foscari   5   240
Who love us are accustom'd to descend   655 Heaven   2
Descend and share my lot   656 Heaven   96
As--but descend, and prove   656 Heaven   131
To deem he would descend to such an act   695 Werner   2   757
Descend in rain and end, but spreads itself   700 Werner   3   362
After--what! doth my father's curse descend   711 Werner   4   429
Descend--the fault is mine; this fatal shore   821 Juan   4   333
In vain the dews of Heaven descend above   825 Juan   4   559
Boil'd in his veins, and rather than descend   844 Juan   5   828

DESCENDANT

Shades of heroes, farewell! your descendant,
departing   86 Leaving NA   21
By thy descendant, merit such acquittance   519 Faliero   3   40
Can rest, when he, their last descendant chief   520 Faliero   3   100
This, thy presumed descendant, ne'er beheld   553 Sardan   1   163
In lieu of her remote descendant, I   580 Sardan   4   157

DESCENDANTS

Descendants worthy both of them and thee   530 Faliero   4   174
Remote descendants, who have lived in peace   731 Deformed   1   659

DESCENDED

To us his psalms had ne'er descended   96 Granta   83
As down the deadly blow descended   401 Parisina   481
But never tear his cheek descended   402 Parisina   537
Descended from Angrante: under cover   468 Morgante   154
'The Lord descended to the virgin breast   471 Morgante   353
I am the lawful king, descended from   554 Sardan   1   250

DESCENDETH

Not oft to smile descendeth he   318 Giaour   850

DESCENDING

From mountain-cliff to coast descending sombre
down   23 Harold   2   198
Descending from the realms of joy   88 Anacreon-B   8
From these descending, sons to sires succeed   121 Newstead-A   133
Gleams like a seraph from the sky descending   175 Sonnet-B   11
Descending fast, the mountain-shadows kiss   268 Minerva   11
And Night's descending shadows hide   329 Abydos   2   22
Her boat descending from the latticed stern   339 Corsair   1   100
From crag to crag descending, swiftly sped   345 Corsair   1   505
Descending fast, the mountain shadows kiss   355 Corsair   3   11
Descending rather quickly the declivity   805 Juan   3   226

DESCENDS

The cross descends, thy minarets arise   25 Harold   2   340
And descends to the plain like the stream from
the rock   30 Harold   2   656
Pallid and cold the Moon descends to cave   139 Ossian-A   7
And warily the steep descends   317 Giaour   703
But Heaven itself descends in love   321 Giaour   1136
With the first boat descends he for the shore   364 Corsair   3   573
Upon that shore to which the Po descends   476 Francesca   2
Whence Melody descends as from a throne   793 Juan   2 1208

DESCENT

No wit for nobles, dunces by descent   265 Hints   612
A count of far and high descent   408 Mazeppa   156
His judgments, I reply, that the descent   665 Heaven   750
With regular descent, in these our days   936 Juan   12   420

DESCRIBE

Let these describe the undescribable   63 Harold   4   473
You should not, I'll describe it you exactly   442 Beppo   146
Would words describe thy past and present glow   446 Beppo   367
Made deserts. You describe it faithfully   694 Werner   2   714
How, nor can I indeed describe the where   767 Juan   1 1322
I can't describe it, though so much it strike   774 Juan   2   39
Far less describe, present the very view   831 Juan   5   23
I won't describe; description is my forte   838 Juan   5   409
I might describe, as I have seen it all   858 Juan   6   404
And this same state we won't describe: we would   910 Juan   10   209
I won't describe,--that is, if I can help   911 Juan   10   217
'Tis that, in fact, there's little to describe   958 Juan   14   160
Is more than I shall venture to describe   998 Juan   17   95

DESCRIBED

Described in every stripling's verse   134 E. N. Long   90
Shakspeare described the sex in Desdemona   442 Beppo   129
As I described them. Speak to them. Ay, speak   522 Faliero   3   248
Their quest of him I have described. Oh, Ulric   714 Werner   5   82
Described by Mahomet, and Anacreon Moore   759 Juan   1   829
Described--what's strange--in words extremely few 859 Juan   6   454
Can never be described; we all have heard   865 Juan   6   844
As do the subtle snakes described of old   888 Juan   8   664
And ne'er to be described; for to the dolour   960 Juan   14   319

DESCRIBES

Thus many a bard describes in pompous strain   257 Hints   25
Like Burns (whom Doctor Currie well describes   814 Juan   3   828
But every fool describes in these bright days   838 Juan   5   410
Of which, howe'er the Muse describes each act   877 Juan   7   643

DESCRIBING

Was just describing--Yes, it was the coast   797 Juan   2 1442
I don't much like describing people mad   825 Juan   4   587
Describing Priam's, Peleus', or Jove's son   891 Juan   8   838
That no one has succeeded in describing   957 Juan   14   146

DESCRIED

New shores descried make every bosom gay   6 Harold   1   201
Till, in approaching, were at length descried   872 Juan   7   343
With prophets, houris, angels, saints, descried   893 Juan   8   919
Is not at once too palpably descried   927 Juan   11   556

DESCRIPTION

But here I'll close my chaste Description   144 Becher-B   29
This is a long description, but applies   428 Island   3   117
By your description track him. The devil take   713 Werner   5   6
For authors fear description might disparage   802 Juan   3   68
Here I might enter on a chaste description   828 Juan   4   769
I won't describe; description is my forte   838 Juan   5   409
Whose force description only would abate   843 Juan   5   771
(To save description), fair as fair can be   857 Juan   6   316
Description; and I won't reflect,--that is   911 Juan   10   218
Is one of which there's no description recent   957 Juan   14   115
I will not make his great description less   964 Juan   14   595
The chaste description even of a 'becasse   977 Juan   15   568

DESCRIPTIONS

Or tracest chaste descriptions on thy page   245 Bards   271
These amiable descriptions from the scribes   814 Juan   3   830
Varied each ray;--but all descriptions garble   864 Juan   6   781

DESCRIPTION'S

Description's power of words   146 Adieu   64

DESCRIPTIVE

A gust--which all descriptive power transcends   777 Juan   2   239

DESCRY

Thou'lt there descry that elegance   87 Rousseau   14
Which even in torture can descry   191 Prometheus-B   56
Their little bark her men of watch descry   362 Corsair   3   484
Already they descry--is yon the bank   379 Lara   2   324

DESDEMONA

Shakspeare described the sex in Desdemona   442 Beppo   129

DESERT

The desert, forest, cavern, breaker's foam   37 Harold   3   113
I look upon the peopled desert past   46 Harold   3   690
Even in thy desert, what is like to thee   59 Harold   4   230
But Rome is as the desert where we steer   67 Harold   4   726
Or water but the desert; whence arise   73 Harold   4 1073
Oh that the Desert were my dwelling-place   81 Harold   4 1585
'Yes, on some desert rocky shore   103 Alva   133
Can the lips sing of Love in the desert alone   148 Farewell-A   17
Will ne'er desert its pledge, my Boy   150 My Son   36
Earth is no desert--ev'n to me   210 Augusta-A   44
In the desert a fountain is springing   210 Augusta-B   45
Though a desert should surround me   230 My Boat   11
Beheld the desert peopled, as from hell   300 Age   148
The exterminating war, the desert plain   303 Age   362
On desert sands 'twere joy to scan   313 Giaour   328

DESERT

The leafless desert of the mind	319	Giaour		959
Sweet as the desert fountain's wave	325	Abydos	1	152
The desert of old Priam's pride	329	Abydos	2	24
Across the desert, or before the gale	333	Abydos	2	393
Like lightning on the desert path	400	Parisina		366
The desert gap which made his pain	402	Parisina		572
And hurl thee towards a desert realm	412	Mazeppa		556
To pass the desert to a throne	415	Mazeppa		852
The amphibious desert of the dank morass	421	Island	2	158
The haunt of birds, a desert to mankind	430	Island	4	11
Than the wreck'd sailor on his desert shore	439	Tasso		182
Over Cambyses' host the desert spread	460	Dante	2	108
An abbey which in a lone desert lay	468	Morgante		150
'Our ancient fathers living the desert in	469	Morgante		193
As to desert would almost be a wrong	470	Morgante		262
To wander solitary this desert in	472	Morgante		427
'Put down, nor bear him further the desert in	475	Morgante		591
Innumerable atoms; and one desert	484	Manfred	2	55
Which dwells but in the desert and sweeps o'er	493	Manfred	3	129
Born from the knowledge of its own desert	496	Manfred	3	396
By the true touchstone of desert--success	509	Faliero		626
To one wide desert chase of brutes, who were	557	Sardan	1	422
Making a desert of fertility	557	Sardan	1	465
A green spot amidst desert centuries	586	Sardan	4	513
Floating upon the azure desert, and	668	Heaven		964
The very desert saves man from mankind	674	Werner	1	172
Of the then untamed desert, brought to joust	731	Deformed	1	623
Now I desert not mine. Soft! bear her hence	741	Deformed	2	411
Or in the desert heard the camel's bell	784	Juan	2	671

DESERT-BIRD

It is as if the desert-bird	319	Giaour		951

DESERT-BORN

To me the desert-born was led	410	Mazeppa		369

DESERTED
(See also LONG-DESERTED)

Deserted is my own good hall	5	Harold	1	130
To halls deserted, portals gaping wide	7	Harold	1	284
Though sad and deserted, I ne'er can forget you	96	Harrow-A		27
Deserted now, he scans thy gray worn towers	122	Newstead-A		141
In these, to me, deserted towers	165	Thyrza		26
And for Sotheby's Blues have deserted Sam Rogers	226	Oh You		12
What! must deserted Poesy still weep	252	Bards		809
I am not all deserted on the main	362	Corsair	3	493
The fourth and last of this deserted group	428	Island	3	109
Deserted by the bird she thought a nightingale	710	Werner	4	381
His home deserted for the lonely wood	757	Juan	1	690

DESERTER

Since the dearest of prizes to me 's a deserter	178	Devil's Dr		200

DESERTION

This were the worst desertion:--renegadoes	909	Juan	10	97

DESERT-LOVING

Of desert-loving pine, whose emerald scalp	459	Dante	2	64

DESERTS

Welcome, ye deserts, and ye caves	6	Harold	1	196
Has dried up realms to deserts:--not so thou	82	Harold	4	1635
As springs in deserts found seem sweet, all brackish though they be	186	Music-B		19
In deserts which he left behind	233	Ballad-B		39
Better reclaim thy deserts, turn thy swords	304	Age		466
In crowds a slave, in deserts free	315	Giaour		546
Nor told of wondrous wilds and deserts vast	367	Lara	1	86
Have made thee last and worst of peopled deserts	549	Faliero	5	791
I am safe, not for my own deserts, but those	663	Heaven		646
Until the very deserts know no thirst	670	Heaven		1119
Made deserts. You describe it faithfully	694	Werner	2	714
Obscure as his deserts, without a scutcheon	703	Werner	3	573
So shall he have his full deserts. The world's	734	Deformed	3	842
And long, long deserts scorch the camel's foot	823	Juan	4	438
In deserts, forests, crowds, or by the shore	838	Juan	5	450
So Arab deserts drink in summer's rain	904	Juan	9	470
What 'antres vast and deserts idle' then	968	Juan	14	809

DESERT'S

Like Pompey's pillar, in a desert's skies	299	Age		110
To dry into the desert's dust by myriads	555	Sardan	1	275

DESERT-SHIP

As Ishmael, wafted on his desert-ship	421	Island	2	182
And patient swiftness of the desert-ship	724	Deformed	1	116

DESERT-SPRING

Nor the first sparkle of the desert-spring	797	Juan	2	1437

DESERVE

So may such foes deserve the most remorseless deed	18	Harold	1	899

DESERVE

Thy budding years a lengthen'd term deserve	106	Nisus		64
But those who best deserve you	138	Clare		84
Yet I deserve the stern decree	174	Remember-B		47
Deserve those plaudits--study nature's page	259	Hints		217
Their love can scarce deserve the name	321	Giaour		1100
And change the sentence I deserve to bear	359	Corsair	3	285
Deserve the fate their fretting lips foretell	360	Corsair	3	328
Deserve and have. Why, I should think as soon	521	Faliero	3	151
Deserve that I should curse them with their wishes	553	Sardan	1	171
As I am heedless; and the slaves deserve	557	Sardan	1	435
You soon will have no children--you deserve none	602	Foscari	2	71
Deserve the name of our great father's son	649	Cain	3	196
Deserve her. Farewell, Anah! I have said	663	Heaven		612
And then--I seek no more, and scarce deserve	679	Werner	1	490
Thou wouldst say: I must bear it and deserve it	703	Werner	3	512
And giving so much happiness, deserve	710	Werner	4	377
But I deserve it. Villain, hold your peace	737	Deformed	2	141
There is no doubt that you deserve your ration	897	Juan	9	47
But do you more, Sempronius--don't deserve it	943	Juan	13	138

DESERVED

From your verses, what else she deserved	116	Strephon		10
And ill deserved the fate it found	168	The Chain		4
Good King! this thou hast deserved	194	Ballad-A		44
Deserved to be dearest of all	210	Augusta-B		44
Whose treachery deserved a grave	314	Giaour		462
Howe'er deserved her doom might be	320	Giaour		1066
Was reft at once--and he deserved his fate	365	Corsair	3	629
Of these, who have deserved them most	408	Mazeppa		180
Harder to bear and less deserved, for I	462	Dante	3	140
In love--with love, too, which perhaps deserved it	658	Heaven		215
My faults deserved--exclusion; although then	674	Werner	1	163
If ever you indeed deserved the name	764	Juan	1	1162
Though he deserved it well for being so backward	849	Juan	5	1118
Low as the compliment deserved. Suwarrow	875	Juan	7	498
No one could envy her deserved prosperity	994	Juan	16	862
Meanwhile sweet Adeline deserved their praises	994	Juan	16	865

DESERVEDLY

Faith! he hath shamed us, and deservedly	522	Faliero	3	231

DESERVES

He surely well deserves to gain them	95	Granta		33
That instant, Davus, it deserves to bleed	126	Recoll		286
How many a friend deserves the grateful strain	127	Recoll		369
But which deserves the laurel, rhyme or blank	258	Hints		111
Go, ask thy bosom who deserves them most	272	Minerva		310
(Here Satan's sole good work deserves insertion	285	Vision		47
One who deserves to be repeal'd, pronounce	524	Faliero	3	422
As though it were a bed of love, deserves	575	Sardan	3	224
That slave deserves her freedom. Freedom only	581	Sardan	4	196
That slave deserves to share a throne. Your patience	581	Sardan	4	197
Deserves the worst, his conduct's less defensible	765	Juan	1	1206

DESERVING

Some say deserving Reprehension	144	Becher-B		20
The only hypocrite deserving praise	352	Corsair	2	361
No less deserving to be hang'd than crown'd	850	Juan	5	1224
Though all deserving equally to turn	880	Juan	8	133
He died, deserving well his country's tears	888	Juan	8	637

DESERV'ST

But thou deserv'st a better heart	179	Gold		23

DESHAYES

Let wedded strumpets languish o'er Deshayes	250	Bards		622

DESIDERATUM

A long desideratum. Yes, for masters	704	Werner	4	3
And fact is truth, the grand desideratum	877	Juan	7	642

DESIGN

To view the huge design which sprung from such a birth	78	Harold	4	1368
Whose shade securely our design will cloak	106	Nisus		106
Without thy dear advice, no great design	107	Nisus		168
No longer repine, adopt this design	116	Pigot		25
Your Leader's grand design pursue	142	Critics		86
Have kiss'd, as if without design	164	Friend-B		37
But if a new design you dare essay	259	Hints		179
Whate'er you teach, be brief, if you design	264	Hints		533
While Europe wonders at the vast design	307	Age		711
When all that we design to do	332	Abydos	2	360
And deem design had left me single here	349	Corsair	2	169
However link'd to baffle such design	379	Lara	2	337
Presumptuous thus to love without design	438	Tasso		140
Who, seeing him alone in this design	469	Morgante		238
To further their design was ne'er abused	522	Faliero	3	238
The regularity of my design	748	Juan	1	51
In the design, and as I have a high sense	761	Juan	1	958

DESIGN
Some have accused me of a strange design   817 Juan   4   33
With this same legend)--'if you but design   985 Juan   16   293

DESIGN'D
The world was ne'er design'd for me   135 I Would   18
My love and my life were by nature design'd   147 To Anne-B 11
Design'd for him you rescued will be found   676 Werner   1   311

DESIGNS
Her flight to garnish Greenwood's gay designs   250 Bards   601
Oh men! what are ye, and our best designs   535 Faliero   4   516
Who have imputed such designs as snow   817 Juan   4   51
Of their designs, by saying they meant well   881 Juan   8   199

DESIRABLE
Desirable to be the Desire   305 Age   513
Desirable, distinguish'd, celebrated   960 Juan   14   330

DESIRE
Such is the most my memory may desire   3 To Ianthe   44
Nurst in the glowing lap of soft desire   14 Harold   1   654
When all is won that all desire to woo   24 Harold   2   309
Beyond the fitting medium of desire   41 Harold   3   374
Where he became a being) whose desire   47 Harold   3   722
A million scarce would quench desire   88 To Ellen   2
Wakes silver notes of soft desire   88 Anacreon-A   18
Be realized at my desire   95 Granta   2
Though they might kindle less desire   97 To M--   3
Or, in itself a god, what great desire   105 Nisus   20
The wild desire, the guilty flame   111 Medea   7
Oh! thus, the desire in my bosom for fame   129 Becher-A   13
(Whilst Truth my sole desire is nigh   141 Critics   25
Desire alone which makes you melt   143 To--A   8
As half reproach'd yet raised desire   152 Remind   15
Weaning the thoughts from every low desire   161 Athos   16
For much I view which I could most desire   211 Augusta-C   62
Ask not his thoughts, or follow his desire   267 Hints   788
Desirable to be the Desire   305 Age   513
To lift from earth our low desire   321 Giaour   1134
As if 'twas Lara's less than his desire   374 Lara   1   562
These, link'd with that desire which ever sways   377 Lara   2   151
To earn mild virtue's vain desire, repose   417 Island   1   114
With all we know of Heaven, or can desire   445 Beppo   364
Keen the desire to see his home again   452 Beppo   754
You may be sure, should each desire arise   473 Morgante   469
I have nothing to desire, or to request   511 Faliero   2   173
Their own desire, not my ambition, made   525 Faliero   3   446
I do not dare to breathe my own desire   551 Sardan   1   69
Desire, were to escape from such a land   605 Foscari   2   275
Your plots could make, and vengeance could desire
    us   613 Foscari   3   333
And my desire. The boy, they say, 's a bold one   687 Werner   2   263
Such his desire is   725 Deformed 1   171
If such be thy desire; and yet, by being   726 Deformed 1   301
What I desire to know! and will not waste   743 Deformed 3   105
To thankfulness what you desire from Passion   743 Deformed 3   127
A something in them which was not desire   754 Juan   1   478
Alfonso, pommel'd to his heart's desire   769 Juan   1 1468
'Tis very certain the desire of life   782 Juan   2   505
And firmer faith no ladye-love desire   828 Juan   4   763
Said Baba; 'but pray do as I desire   840 Juan   5   586
For ne'er till now she knew a check'd desire   848 Juan   5 1070
Would like (I think) to trust all to desire   854 Juan   6   124
But here the effect fell short of their desire   871 Juan   7   246
Are touch'd with a desire to shield and save   891 Juan   8   843

DESIRED
Then mightst thou more appal; or, less desired   61 Harold   4   379
No matter how, to the desired end   213 Lady Byron   57
Was man who more desired to rule in peace   557 Sardan   1   418
Be lawfully desired, and lawfully   598 Foscari   1   191
For heaven desired too late   666 Heaven   838
Look down on us and our so long desired   682 Werner   1   733
All folly. Were the locks (as I desired   700 Werner   3   369
But that which Donna Inez most desired   751 Juan   1   305
Though full of all things which could be desired   839 Juan   5   507
A second time desired him to kneel down   844 Juan   5   811
If matters had been managed as desired   864 Juan   6   789

DESIRES
But for the nymph whose premature desires   119 Answer-A   33
Heaven for a nobler doom their worth desires   195 Vittorelli   3
So as his dim desires to recognise   476 Francesca   24
Although inferior still to my desires   637 Cain   2   82
Indulgence of their innocent desires   803 Juan   3   98

DESIREST
What mean'st thou?--'tis thy secret; thou
    desirest   557 Sardan   1   414

DESIRING
Even with its own desiring phantasy   73 Harold   4 1087
Too late desiring to depart   141 Critics   40

DESIRING
If thus, fair Jersey, our desiring gaze   183 Address-D   13

DESIST
Could I desist?--ah! never--never   88 To Ellen   12

DESK
Bent o'er the desk, or, born to useful toils   247 Bards   407
And the sad truth which hovers o'er my desk   816 Juan   4   23
That forms this desk, of what they mean;
    lykanthropy   899 Juan   9   158

DESK'S
Shall drag my journal from the desk's recess   255 Bards   1024

DESOLATE
Its hearth is desolate   5 Harold   1   131
Lest he should view his vineyard desolate   11 Harold   1   497
Its chambers desolate, and portals foul   20 Harold   2   47
None are so desolate but something dear   23 Harold   2   212
When all around was desolate and dark   29 Harold   2   597
Passes the strength of storms in their most
    desolate hour   50 Harold   3   940
Have flung a desolate cloud o'er Venice' lovely
    walls   57 Harold   4   135
In ruin, even as he had seen the desolate sight   61 Harold   4   396
And temple more divinely desolate   74 Harold   4 1172
And desolate consort--vainly wert thou wed   80 Harold-F 4 1520
My weary heart is desolate   156 Lady-F   20
Through Silence and Shade o'er its desolate walls   164 Newstead-C   2
The Desolator desolate   180 Ode-A   37
And a quick desolate cry, licking the hand   189 Darkness   53
Is extending its steps to her desolate shore   202 Avatar   12
To her desolate shore--where the emigrant stands   202 Avatar   13
Here to be lonely is not desolate   211 Augusta-C   61
Whose shrines are desolate, whose land a dream   217 Weep-B   2
And ye, oh her desolate daughters   222 Babylon   5
Where the weeds and the desolate dust are spread   313 Giaour   298
The heart once left thus desolate   319 Giaour   943
'It is no dream--and I am desolate   345 Corsair   1   504
But was not half so desolate   405 Chillon   274
On the lone rock of desolate Despair   458 Dante   1   139
Unroof'd and desolate, how many flatterers   572 Sardan   3   54
So desolate, that the most clamorous grief   615 Foscari   4   9
From fishers' hands upon the desolate strand   617 Foscari   4   148
In the vast desolate night in search of him   631 Cain   1   268
May all his days be desolate! May--Hold   652 Cain   3   404
'Tis the most desolate, and suits my steps   654 Cain   3   553
Seized me upon this desolate frontier, and   672 Werner   1   50
May be), for whom this desolate village and   678 Werner   1   453
Standing alone beside his desolate hearth   751 Juan   1   285
And the dim desolate deep: twelve days had Fear   780 Juan   2   391
That isle is now all desolate and bare   825 Juan   4   569
A dull and desolate appendage. Gaze   945 Juan   13   258
Now yawns all desolate: now loud, now fainter   949 Juan   13   493
Have something ghastly, desolate, and dread   982 Juan   16   136

DESOLATED
In bare and desolated bosoms: mute   58 Harold   4   183
The desolated lands, the ravaged isle   302 Age   292

DESOLATING
To hear whose desolating tale   332 Abydos   2   313
Who taught her passion's desolating joy   420 Island   2   112
Must lie beneath the desolating waters   662 Heaven   523
Praying, instructing, desolating, plundering   874 Juan   7   438

DESOLATION
Where Desolation plants her famish'd brood   11 Harold   1   483
Proud though in desolation; which could find   37 Harold   3   107
That in such gaps as desolation work'd   50 Harold   3   894
With desolation, and a broken claim   53 Harold   3 1088
And I in desolation. All that was   62 Harold   4   409
Since Zion's desolation, when that He   78 Harold   4 1381
Here Desolation holds her dreary court   121 Newstead-A   97
Of this their desolation; and all hearts   189 Darkness   8
For blight and desolation, compass'd round   216 Dream   188
This bosom's desolation dooming   221 Marianne   22
And desolation; while his native Greece   298 Age   37
Hath all of desolation, save its peace   298 Age   38
In hurried desolation o'er his path   370 Lara   1   328
And Desolation reap'd the famish'd land   379 Lara   2   279
Of their own desolation   488 Manfred   2   348
To my own desolation. Dost thou dare   489 Manfred   2   412
But find a desolation. Like the wind   493 Manfred   3   127
Of rugged desolation, and fill'd up   495 Manfred   3   294
Shall be a desolation and a curse   547 Faliero   5   658
I must pay dearly for the desolation   584 Sardan   4   429
Aloof from desolation! My last prayer   595 Sardan   5   490
Thy path of desolation, as the wave   596 Foscari   1   57
A dreary comfort in my desolation   626 Foscari   5   340
Of desolation, and the stillness   658 Heaven   220
The coming desolation of an orb   659 Heaven   333
In this lone spot of wintry desolation   674 Werner   1   171

358

DESOLATION
Leave us no less desolation, nay, even more	705	Werner	4	53
Not I have made this desolation: few	822	Juan	4	365
War, pestilence, the despot's desolation	886	Juan	8	540
Howe'er the mighty locust, Desolation	894	Juan	8	1005

DESOLATION'S
| Is Desolation's hungry den | 313 | Giaour | | 349 |
| Can we in desolation's peace have rest | 668 | Heaven | | 969 |

DESOLATOR
| The Desolator desolate | 180 | Ode-A | | 37 |

DESPAIR
And Mammon wins his way where Seraphs might despair	5	Harold	1	81
Had made Despair a smilingness assume	37	Harold	3	140
There is a very life in our despair	40	Harold	3	298
Which shall atone for years; none need despair	48	Harold	3	794
The nympholepsy of some fond despair	72	Harold	4	1031
The unreach'd Paradise of our despair	73	Harold	4	1096
Is link'd the electric chain of that despair	81	Harold	4	1546
Yes! yield that breast, to seek despair	90	To M.S.G.-A		33
We must admire, but still despair	97	To M--		7
Despair now inflames the dark tide of his veins	100	L Adieu		27
'Yet he may live,--away, despair	103	Alva		137
Revenge his leader, and despair his guide	110	Nisus		386
Why thus in despair do you fret	115	Pigot		2
Away with despair, no longer forbear	116	Pigot		27
Or drive me to dreadful despair	116	Strephon		24
To roam a dreary world in deep despair	120	Newstead-A		47
Hear'st thou the accents of despair	132	Prayer		2
The sullen calmness of despair	155	Happy		32
To reconcile me with despair	161	Picture		3
Wherewith the children of Despair	164	Friend-B		5
That brings a Lethe for despair	168	Haunts		20
Seems Sorrow's softness charm'd from its despair	175	Sonnet-A		4
And so soft to his ear was the cry of despair	176	Devil's Dr		35
That bids a genuine love despair	179	Gold		4
Thy late repentance, long despair	181	Ode-A		114
Alas! the sound--he sunk into Despair	184	Julian		27
The weak despair--the cold depart	209	Augusta-A		8
Look on thine earthly victims--and despair	209	Sketch		96
Within me,--or perhaps a cold despair	211	Augusta-C		42
My wrath but doom'd my own despair	221	Marianne		11
That I despair of all demand	231	Doctor		28
On the grim smile of comfortless despair	271	Minerva		240
And backward to the den of his despair	301	Age		211
Better succumb even to their own despair	302	Age		312
Darkness above, despair beneath	314	Giaour		437
Of mix'd defiance and despair	319	Giaour		908
Too meek to meet, or brave despair	319	Giaour		919
Despair upon his dying face	321	Giaour		1094
Despair is stronger than my will	322	Giaour		1266
Waste not thine orison, despair	322	Giaour		1267
Despair benumb'd her breast and eye	334	Abydos	2	522
Hark! to the hurried question of Despair	336	Abydos	2	662
It looks as planted by Despair	336	Abydos	2	674
That owes its deadliest efforts to despair	343	Corsair	1	328
Which not the darkness of despair can damp	343	Corsair	1	353
We promise, hope, believe--there breathes despair	345	Corsair	1	490
He saw their terror, check'd the first despair	349	Corsair	2	161
Recall'd those thoughts late wandering in despair	351	Corsair	2	260
Wrung from the coward crouching of despair	354	Corsair	2	481
Breathed Conrad's spirit, and forbade despair	357	Corsair	3	126
New torments for thy life, and my despair	360	Corsair	3	337
Where lives thy grief, or perish'd his despair	366	Corsair	3	690
As deep, but far too tranquil for despair	380	Lara	2	345
Despair to daring, and a front to foes	380	Lara	2	365
Less for her own despair than him	398	Parisina		174
That guilt's detection and despair	400	Parisina		355
No more reproach--no more despair	401	Parisina		471
In madlier accents rose despair	401	Parisina		499
I learn'd to love despair	406	Chillon		374
Which would not doom me to despair	409	Mazeppa		274
They left me there to my despair	413	Mazeppa		709
Let none despond, let none despair	415	Mazeppa		854
Acquainted with all feelings save despair	421	Island	2	178
Show'd that his faintness came not from despair	428	Island	3	102
And die at once than wrestle with despair	428	Island	3	124
Such sights, and feel, and mourn, but not despair	429	Island	3	194
Gave mariners a shelter and despair	430	Island	4	26
But must be borne. I stoop not to despair	437	Tasso		20
Look on a love which knows not to despair	438	Tasso		111
On the lone rock of desolate Despair	458	Dante	1	139
Succumbs to long infection and despair	463	Dante	3	173
Despair and Genius are too oft connected	463	Dante	4	39
Is mortal here; I dwell in my despair	487	Manfred	2	243
With a nation's destruction--his flight and despair	488	Manfred	2	323
I sunk before my vain despair, and knelt	489	Manfred	2	411
The innate tortures of that deep despair	492	Manfred	3	70
'Tis strange--even those who do despair above	492	Manfred	3	101
Despair can do; and step by step disputes	575	Sardan	3	249

DESPAIR
Despair anticipates such things. Despair	590	Sardan	5	222
No; not despair precisely. When we know	590	Sardan	5	223
Despair defies even despotism: there is	599	Foscari	1	267
Of death, the imprecation of despair	608	Foscari	3	5
The dates of their despair, the brief words of	608	Foscari	3	18
Or show the place where strong Despair hath died	660	Heaven		356
Where even the brutes, in their despair	661	Heaven		442
Angel! forgive this stripling's fond despair	668	Heaven		979
Of wrath, and pity thine own world's despair	669	Heaven		1067
My state beyond despair; and now, 'tis such	680	Werner	1	584
Despair your bed-fellow--then rise, but not	690	Werner	2	445
Not of love, but despair; nor sought to win	727	Deformed	1	338
In deep despair, lest he had done amiss	760	Juan	1	893
And half forgot their danger and despair	767	Juan	1	1356
Despair of all recovery spoils longevity	782	Juan	2	511
Famine, despair, cold, thirst, and heat, had done	787	Juan	2	809
And felt again with his despair o'erwrought	788	Juan	2	892
Yet what can people do, except despair	802	Juan	3	45
His country's wrongs and his despair to save her	808	Juan	3	423
But overwrought with passion and despair	823	Juan	4	454
A low soft ottoman), and black despair	865	Juan	6	861
Snatch when despair makes human hearts less pliant	884	Juan	8	404

DESPAIR'D
| Scarce less beloved, where I despair'd for her | 659 | Heaven | | 286 |
| And then they look'd around them and despair'd | 783 | Juan | 2 | 587 |

DESPAIRING
Where Courage falls in her despairing files	64	Harold	4	556
The brows of men by the despairing light	189	Darkness		22
Some imprecation of despairing pride	369	Lara	1	220
From Lara's face his fix'd despairing view	382	Lara	2	483
And sign'd my odes "Despairing Thyrsis	408	Mazeppa		154
With slow, despairing oar, the abandon'd skiff	418	Island	1	173
Appall'd, turn their despairing eyes on me	617	Foscari	4	142
And, with hyaena-laughter, died despairing	784	Juan	2	632

DESPATCH
Despatch a courier to a wizard's grave	244	Bards		163
Despatch her scheming children far and wide	270	Minerva		144
Then flamed of Austerlitz the blest despatch	274	Waltz		69
Their lives, despatch them o'er the river towards	681	Werner	1	606
Despatch!--he's there! The count, my lord! You here, sir	721	Werner	5	511
Vassals, despatch in search of him! You see	721	Werner	5	514
You have yours--I mine. Despatch! despatch! Even so	728	Deformed	1	379
Three lines of the despatch in taking 'Schmacksmith	869	Juan	7	158
In the despatch: I knew a man whose loss	880	Juan	8	143
With bloody hands he wrote his first despatch	895	Juan	8	1061
While Juan is sent off with the despatch	896	Juan	8	1111
Was left upon his way with the despatch	900	Juan	9	226
With his despatch, forgot to break the seal	903	Juan	9	456
Almost as much as on a new despatch	904	Juan	9	487
And thirdly he who brought you the despatch	904	Juan	9	520

DESPATCH'D
And souls despatch'd to that world or to this	289	Vision		276
Despatch'd me to your sacred presence, I	560	Sardan	1	639
Serry your ranks--stand firm. I have despatch'd	575	Sardan	3	259

DESPATCHES
Of true despatches and as true gazettes	274	Waltz		68
Despatches, judgments, acts, reprieves, reports	500	Faliero	1	9
Their lies, yclep'd despatches, without risk or	850	Juan	5	1207
By his despatches couch'd in pithy phrase	872	Juan	7	310
To colour up his rays from your despatches	877	Juan	7	648
But here a messenger brought in despatches	964	Juan	14	536
Writing despatches) in their several stations	989	Juan	16	575

DESPATCHING
| Despatching single crusiers here and there | 804 | Juan | 3 | 146 |

DESPERADOES
| Soldiers and desperadoes! Heaven best knows | 685 | Werner | 2 | 132 |

DESPERATE
Is all that desperate Valour acts in vain	12	Harold	1	555
And desperate mans him 'gainst the coming doom	272	Minerva		272
As at a farce; till, grown quite desperate	296	Vision		742
For their incessant prey; the desperate wall	303	Age		366
And darts into her desperate brain	314	Giaour		432
And clasp her to my desperate heart	323	Giaour		1286
His comrades strain with desperate strength	335	Abydos	2	548
Or guilt grown old in desperate hardihood	373	Lara	1	505
But not less fitted for the desperate game	378	Lara	2	249
Desperate, though few, the last and best remain'd	379	Lara	2	312
Desperate groups, of twelve or ten	393	Corinth		777
Where the last and desperate few	394	Corinth		873
Proclaim'd the desperate conflict o'er	395	Corinth		1028
Nor desperate of all hope on high	401	Parisina		466

DESPERATE

Its desperate escape from duty's path	416	Island	1	60
How in some desperate feud of after-time	432	Island	4	199
The desperate trio held aloof their fate	434	Island	4	319
Look'd desperate as himself along the deep	434	Island	4	338
And desperate libertines who brawl in taverns	531	Faliero	4	228
A feeble female, 'midst their desperate strife	576	Sardan	3	292
A desperate courage crept through every limb	580	Sardan	4	140
This last calamity? With desperate firmness	620	Foscari	4	344
Secured a band of desperate men, supposed	716	Werner	5	231
The fugitives, or battle with the desperate	737	Deformed	2	174
Their desperate efforts seem'd all useless grown	778	Juan	2	302
Survive through very desperate conditions	782	Juan	2	508
An ominous, and wild, and desperate sound	783	Juan	2	580
While some more desperate dowager has been waging	848	Juan	5	1035
Where fights not to the last some desperate heart	888	Juan	8	651
For them in saving such a desperate foe	892	Juan	8	861
Each out-at-elbow peer, or desperate dandy	933	Juan	12	250
By rendering desperate those who had else repented	940	Juan	12	640
Perhaps of all most desperate, which will dare	956	Juan	14	35
Which after all at such a desperate rate runs	972	Juan	15	293

DESPERATION

And only not to desperation driven	75	Harold	4	1213
Poor lady! 'Tis mere desperation: she	599	Foscari	1	277
None are secure from desperation, few	690	Werner	2	465
Chaste was she, to detraction's desperation	942	Juan	13	105

DESPERATIONS

What desperations	200	Stanzas-B	78

DESPICABLE

Nor despicable state	181	Ode-A	166

DESPISE

And conscious Reason whisper'd to despise	8	Harold	1	321
But not too humbly or she will despise	24	Harold	2	302
Admire, exult--despise--laugh, weep,--for here	71	Harold	4	973
For earth's destruction thou dost all despise	82	Harold	4	1615
A theme we never can despise	92	Lady-A		4
Can we bestow, which you may not despise	107	Nisus		132
What heart unfeeling would despise	111	Medea		15
All modern arts affecting to despise	112	Examination		56
Their sneers or censures I alike despise	119	Answer-A		44
I will not descend to a world I despise	128	Becher-A		4
Still, still despise the censor stern	133	E. N. Long		41
Will not the laughing boy despise	147	Vain Lady		25
Were not as things that gods despise	191	Prometheus-B		4
Thou, who couldst trample and despise	201	Ode-C		51
Albeit for such I could despise a crown	206	Greece		3
Yet I blame not the world, nor despise it	210	Augusta-B		33
Nor fools nor follies tempt me to despise	256	Bards		1055
But they that fear'd him dared not to despise	342	Corsair	1	274
Though far the distant foe they thus despise	347	Corsair	2	11
A being of the race thou dost despise	486	Manfred	2	216
Who shall despise her!--She shall stoop to be	548	Faliero	5	750
Nor she aught but--Despise the favourite slave	585	Sardan	4	459
Despise--but, it may be, avoid the life	594	Sardan	5	448
Despise myself, yet cannot overcome	629	Cain	1	114
Ulric, before you dare despise your father	689	Werner	2	436
Further--that you despise me. Wherefore should I	698	Werner	3	237
Thank him--and despise you. 'You think'! and scarce	701	Werner	3	384
To their own good this warning to despise	772	Juan	1	1658
As cavalier servente, or despise her	804	Juan	3	190

DESPISED

Churchman and votary alike despised	26	Harold	2	391
Thou! form'd to eat, and be despised, and die	60	Harold	4	334
Am I by thee despised and left afar	106	Nisus		41
From Caesar the dreaded to George the despised	203	Avatar		64
The most despised, wrong'd, outraged, helpless wretch	501	Faliero	1	130
They smote you, and oppress'd you, and despised you	527	Faliero	3	578
Despised him as I pity! I prefer	544	Faliero	5	414
Despised by cowards for greater cowardice	549	Faliero	5	772
I told you that you had too much despised him	567	Sardan	2	356
A despised monarch. Look to it, Arbaces	568	Sardan	2	392

DESPISES

The wholly false the heart despises	173	Not False		7
(Who ne'er despises books that bring him brass	264	Hints		548
Despises all advice too much to mend	264	Hints		562
My Muse despises reference, as you have guess'd	962	Juan	14	430

DESPISING

Then manfully despising	161	War Song		9
That of despising those we combat with	870	Juan	7	194
While he, despising every sensual call	931	Juan	12	71

DESPITE

And is, despite of war and wasting fire	19	Harold	2	4

DESPITE

Of Venice think of thine, despite thy watery wall	57	Harold	4	153
Despite some passing clouds of crime	181	Ode-A		153
Despite--of all--it still may be his Grave	184	Julian		33
Her Haven, soon, despite the warning Wind	185	Julian		51
Then away despite of thunder	240	Suliotes		18
Lo! here, despite of war and wasting fire	269	Minerva		95
His night devotes, despite of spur and boots	273	Waltz		17
I am his slave--but, in despite of pride	354	Corsair	2	523
Because, despite thy crimes, that heart is moved	360	Corsair	3	294
He gazed--how long we gaze despite of pain	364	Corsair	3	601
Despite your wonder, to your own he wound	371	Lara	1	378
Was Alp, despite his flight and crimes	388	Corinth		391
Despite of every yoke she bears	388	Corinth		416
Save the few spirits, who, despite of all	453	Venice-B		80
Yes! the few spirits--who, despite of deeds	454	Venice-B		92
To fly back to thee in despite of wrong	465	Dante	4	130
Wilt thou go forth despite of this true warning	530	Faliero	4	188
I think I could be so, despite of death	634	Cain	1	465
Immortal in despite of me. I knew not	637	Cain	2	91
And spared, despite our father's sin, to make	649	Cain	3	226
Thy son, despite his folly, shall not sink	668	Heaven		1030
As air, despite the waters; let us hence	700	Werner	3	348
Despite of all their efforts and expedients	777	Juan	2	227
Despite her injured love and fiery pride	866	Juan	6	901
Before May-day: perhaps, despite his duty	912	Juan	10	295
Despite the snake Society's loud rattles	967	Juan	14	768

DESPOIL

Man may despoil his brother man of all	586	Sardan	4	524

DESPOIL'D

Despoil'd, yet perfect, with thy circle spreads	77	Harold	4	1316
It hardly could, unless the rats despoil'd	683	Werner	2	4

DESPOILERS

True, they may lay your proud despoilers low	31	Harold	2	724

DESPOND

Of mighty shadows, whose dim forms despond	55	Harold	4	30
Let none despond, let none despair	415	Mazeppa		854
Despond not: wherefore wilt thou wander thus	657	Heaven		160
Taught to conceal, their bursting hearts despond	799	Juan	2	1596
(But that, of course, is rare), and then despond	802	Juan	3	51
Arrived, retired to his; but to despond	995	Juan	16	924

DESPONDENCY

And, dying in despondency, bequeath	462	Dante	3	152

DESPONDING

And lower wheat to such desponding quarters	306	Age		583
And their desponding shades came flitting round	616	Foscari	4	114

DESPONDS

Thy late reviving Roman soul desponds	747	Juan	Ded	123

DESPOT

Amidst no common pomp the despot sate	28	Harold	2	500
If not, o'er one fallen despot boast no more	38	Harold	3	172
The miserable despot could not quell	60	Harold	4	320
Many a despot men miscall	185	Belshaz-A		5
A despot thou, and yet thy people free	199	Sonnet-E		13
Despot no more, he	200	Stanzas-B		36
Till the gluttonous despot be stuff'd to the gorge	203	Avatar		78
O'er the despot at our feet	229	Lads		9
To villain-bonds and despot sway	311	Giaour		141
No more must slave to despot say	324	Abydos	1	45
In full Divan the despot scoff'd	332	Abydos	2	326
That soil full many a wringing despot saw	377	Lara	2	159
Or baffled Persia's despot fled	385	Corinth		60
A bold and bloody despot from his throne	562	Sardan	2	84
Another despot of the kind	813	Juan	3	759

DESPOTIC

A patriot hero or despotic chief	421	Island	2	204
New monarchs of an hour's growth as despotic	592	Sardan	5	324
True knights, chaste dames, hugh giants, kings despotic	817	Juan	4	46

DESPOTISM

Of blood and chains? The despotism of vice	552	Sardan	1	114
Fool! hence--what else should despotism alarm'd	569	Sardan	2	450
Despair defies even despotism: there is	599	Foscari	1	267
With aught which looks like despotism in view	845	Juan	5	877

DESPOTS

Can despots compass aught that hails their sway	11	Harold	1	456
Has tumbled feebler despots from their sway	12	Harold	1	541
Who, of all the despots banded	187	Ode-B		28
But back to our theme! Back to despots and slaves	202	Avatar		49
Who sleep, or despots who have now forgot	290	Vision		374
Dresden surveys three despots fly once more	301	Age		205

DESPOTS

Debating despots, hemm'd on either shore	302	Age		280
To own a thousand despots in his place	517	Faliero	2	626
Of a few bloated despots needed more	534	Faliero	4	436
But, here! the despots of the north appear	682	Werner	1	720
To see despots and slaves	743	Deformed	3	81
Though despots know it not--till the progression	940	Juan	12	661
Could back a horse, as despots ride a Russian	944	Juan	13	184

DESPOT'S

A bigot's shrine, nor despot's throne	181	Ode-A		72
Sweep these mere mock-birds of the despot's song	423	Island	2	326
And the worst despot's far less human ape	465	Dante	4	127
War, pestilence, the despot's desolation	886	Juan	8	540

DESPOTS'

And never knew, till then, the weight of Despots' chains	21	Harold	2	108

DESSERT

Above them their dessert grew on its vine	805	Juan	3	246

DESTINATION

And our true destination--but not idly	720	Werner	5	461

DESTINED

In records destined never to be read	94	Dorset		58
Again had run his destined race	103	Alva		154
Arrived the dearly destined morn	103	Alva		170
To Turnus' camp pursue their destined course	109	Nisus		298
Ah! were you destined to die at Culloden	117	Lachin		27
Oh! enviously destined Ball	201	Ode-C		72
Strange sight, this Congress! destined to unite	307	Age		704
Thy destined lord is come too late	335	Abydos	2	624
Another chief consoled his destined bride	366	Lara	1	35
His summons found the destined criminal	378	Lara	2	214
Thou know'st for me was destined long	399	Parisina		255
And made thy own my destined bride	399	Parisina		308
The night the same we destined. He hath changed	567	Sardan	2	330
For although destined to the Turkish mart, he	826	Juan	4	643

DESTINIES

Our destinies o'erleap their mortal state	49	Harold	3	828
A different web being by the Destinies	298	Vision		830
As heedless of his further destinies	429	Island	3	212
And said, 'Francesca, thy sad destinies	476	Francesca		20
For those who are call'd to the high destinies	517	Faliero	2	598
Of destinies: each day secures him more	613	Foscari	3	321
To brighter destinies, if so she deems them	657	Heaven		176
What destinies? I have some cause to think	657	Heaven		177
My destinies were woven in that name	714	Werner	5	90

DESTINY

His fate the moral lurks of destiny	67	Harold	4	763
These might have been her destiny; but no	80	Harold	4	1540
Or, if my destiny these last deny	106	Nisus		69
His own funereal destiny	191	Prometheus-B		50
There yet are two things in my destiny	211	Augusta-C		7
And her who was his destiny, came back	215	Dream		164
Than destiny to make the eternal years	289	Vision		255
But man and destiny beset him there	378	Lara	2	255
Of such men's destiny beneath the sun	462	Dante	3	160
That destiny austere, and yet serene	463	Dante	3	184
Or if their destiny be born aloof	464	Dante	4	107
The star which rules thy destiny	480	Manfred	1	110
Shall be in thy destiny	481	Manfred	1	255
An answer and his destiny--he slew	487	Manfred	2	278
Nor aught can turn me from my destiny	527	Faliero	3	618
Or cling to any creed of destiny	547	Faliero	5	644
By some strange destiny, to him proved deadly	621	Foscari	5	80
Share the dim destiny of clay in this	656	Heaven		89
The destiny and evil of these days	658	Heaven		257
God hath proclaim'd the destiny of earth	662	Heaven		538
As destiny, his excellency's come	678	Werner	1	430
A maze hath my dim destiny involved me	697	Werner	3	146
My Destiny has so involved about me	709	Werner	4	307
Long with her destiny; but she sleeps well	825	Juan	4	567
From them, at least, their destiny he heard	826	Juan	4	635
But for the destiny of this young troop	831	Juan	4	921
But Destiny and Passion spread the net	942	Juan	13	93

DESTINY'S

That Destiny's relentless knife	143	Jessy		3
Though the day of my destiny's over	210	Augusta-B		1

DESTROY

Death hath but little left him to destroy	23	Harold	2	206
All suffering doth destroy, or is destroy'd	58	Harold	4	190
May no distracting thoughts destroy	111	Medea		25
Will spare the childish verse, and not destroy	119	Answer-A		63
Age will not every hope destroy	133	E. N. Long		25
Perhaps his peace I could destroy	134	Lady-D		13
The humble offerings of my Muse destroy	143	Soliloquy		65
Why thus destroy thine own repose	146	Vain Lady		3
Yet shall not these one hope destroy	150	My Son		17

DESTROY

Itself destroy'd might there destroy	174	Remember-B		30
And use destroy love	200	Stanzas-B		85
Beware lest blundering Brougham destroy the sale	248	Bards		524
Such scenes, such men, destroy the public weal	251	Bards		696
So curst the tyrants that destroy	311	Giaour		67
Wait--wave--defend--destroy--at thy command	333	Abydos	2	411
That happy madness would destroy	397	Parisina		39
His chief had cherish'd only to destroy	417	Island	1	152
Lands which no foes destroy or civilise	420	Island	2	100
O'er lakes to ruffle, not destroy, their glass	421	Island	2	152
The pause in which he ceases to destroy	423	Island	2	301
And thee, too, thee--my madness must destroy	428	Island	3	146
Shall feel the power of that which they destroy	464	Dante	4	83
Take it. I come to save, and not destroy	492	Manfred	3	47
Suspected of combining to destroy it	507	Faliero	1	549
I will disclose--ensnare--betray--destroy	532	Faliero	4	315
To save or to destroy; and you, who sit	543	Faliero	5	372
Do more, except destroy them? 'Tis most true	555	Sardan	1	287
Such as is that of Nimrod, to destroy	592	Sardan	5	330
Which name thou wilt: he makes but to destroy	631	Cain	1	264
But thee and me he never can destroy	656	Heaven		119
When God destroys whom you dare not destroy	660	Heaven		381
Should stir all heaven and earth up to destroy	669	Heaven		1106
Who breathed to destroy	725	Deformed	1	180
Destroy proud Anti-Christ. I am a Christian	738	Deformed	2	244
They tamed him down amongst them: to destroy	753	Juan	1	396
They will destroy a face which mortal thought	789	Juan	2	951
Like one life could not hold, nor death destroy	824	Juan	4	472
But which neglect is hastening to destroy	829	Juan	4	822
And love destroy; and sapping sorrow wrings	844	Juan	5	782
And afterward, if he must needs destroy	881	Juan	8	189
All arts to teach their subjects to destroy	890	Juan	8	736
The usual hirsute seasons which destroy	903	Juan	9	419
To aid the damsel and destroy the caitiff	942	Juan	13	74

DESTROY'D

O'er hearts divided and o'er hopes destroy'd	35	Harold	2	923
But Peace destroy'd what War could never blight	44	Harold	3	560
All suffering doth destroy, or is destroy'd	58	Harold	4	190
What, though the sculpture be destroy'd	128	Answer-B		37
Thus Pope by Curl and Dennis was destroy'd	143	Soliloquy		77
Itself destroy'd might there destroy	174	Remember-B		30
When Science' self destroy'd her favourite son	253	Bards		836
My life is reversed and my quiet destroy'd	280	Blues	2	3
Destroy'd but realms, and still maintain'd your prices	306	Age		579
The magic of the thunder, which destroy'd	427	Island	3	49
I loved her, and destroy'd her! With thy hand	486	Manfred	2	211
Repress'd by circumstance but not destroy'd	550	Sardan	1	12
O'erfloods its banks, and hath destroy'd the bulwark	590	Sardan	5	194
Judged and destroy'd in silence,--all things wear	598	Foscari	1	170
Destroy'd by him, or through him, the account	620	Foscari	4	318
Which e'en in Paradise destroy'd his parents	628	Cain	1	44
Or hath destroy'd in few? Lead on. Will he	635	Cain	1	530
'Twould be destroy'd so early. But why war	641	Cain	2	352
Which fed on milk, to be destroy'd in blood	650	Cain	3	293
Destroy'd!	660	Heaven		360
Cannot this earth be made, or be destroy'd	666	Heaven		828
Which ever the destroyer yet destroy'd	816	Juan	3	962
Of things destroy'd and left in airy doubt	901	Juan	9	300
And the hard frost destroy'd the scenting days	954	Juan	13	844

DESTROYER

--to dark-haired Orla, destroyer of heroes	129	Calmar		24
voice curse Orla, the destroyer of Calmar	130	Calmar		82
Domdaniel's dread destroyer, who o'erthrew	244	Bards		213
But was my own destroyer, and will be	496	Manfred	3	399
Ask the Destroyer. Who? The Maker--call him	631	Cain	1	263
Which ever the destroyer yet destroy'd	816	Juan	3	962

DESTROYING

Destroying--saving--prison'd--and asleep	352	Corsair	2	391
At bay, destroying many a foe	411	Mazeppa		506
Now the destroying Angel hovers o'er	535	Faliero	4	482
A comet, and destroying as it sweeps	730	Deformed	1	594
Half-pay for life, make mankind worth destroying	880	Juan	8	112
In more destroying Nature; and the heat	888	Juan	8	654

DESTROYS

And Pleasure, leagued with Pomp, the zest of both destroys	29	Harold	2	576
The dull satiety which all destroys	73	Harold	4	1070
The sound elates, the sight his hope destroys	109	Nisus		328
Retreat destroys him	200	Stanzas-B		44
To appease the waves. The billow which destroys me	617	Foscari	4	145
When God destroys whom you dare not destroy	660	Heaven		381
Unites the future and destroys the past	706	Werner	4	133
By the mere senses; and that which destroys	818	Juan	4	126
Kindness, destroys what little we had got	834	Juan	5	198

DESTRUCTION

Destruction cowers to mark what deeds are done	10	Harold	1	429

DESTRUCTION
Death in the front, Destruction in the rear | 33 Harold | 2 | 849
Keen contest and destruction near allied | 42 Harold | 3 | 439
Of then destruction is; and now, alas | 62 Harold | 4 | 410
For earth's destruction thou dost all despise | 82 Harold | 4 | 1615
Wafting destruction o'er thy charms | 99 Young Lady | | 2
And dart destruction in sulphureous showers | 120 Newstead-A | | 60
They bade me to destruction dash | 411 Mazeppa | | 409
Destruction face to face in all his ways | 456 Dante | 1 | 46
Pass his destruction even into a law | 457 Dante | 1 | 91
Destruction for a dowry,--this to see | 458 Dante | 1 | 174
With a nation's destruction--his flight and
despair | 488 Manfred | 2 | 323
But prove to thee the heralds of destruction | 546 Faliero | 5 | 614
The sire's destruction would not save the son | 603 Foscari | 2 | 88
(Join'd with the Doge) decided his destruction | 619 Foscari | 4 | 291
Destruction and disorder of the elements | 640 Cain | 2 | 286
Of things unhappy! To produce destruction | 643 Cain | 2 | 487
So young, so mark'd out for destruction, I | 659 Heaven | | 313
As even to hear this wide destruction named | 660 Heaven | | 404
And wherefore speak'st thou of destruction near | 666 Heaven | | 796
Destruction, till I reach my own domain | 681 Werner | 1 | 630
And yet I spared thee when my own destruction | 711 Werner | 4 | 436
Upon destruction, shall my head be dash'd | 740 Deformed | 2 | 346
And darkness and destruction as on high | 801 Juan | 2 | 1708
From out the wide destruction, which, entombing
all | 829 Juan | 4 | 805
I do not mean destruction and exposure | 866 Juan | 6 | 911
To breathe destruction on its winding way | 878 Juan | 8 | 14

DESTRUCTION'S
Even in destruction's depth, her foreign foes | 57 Harold | 4 | 116
His shadow fades away into Destruction's mass | 79 Harold | 4 | 1476
There he might rest--but on Destruction's brink | 345 Corsair | 1 | 514
The ripe green valleys with destruction's
splinters | 483 Manfred | 1 | 356
And Destruction's threaten'd son | 729 Deformed | 1 | 472
Destruction's jaws into the devil's den | 882 Juan | 8 | 276

DESTRUCTIVE
For thy destructive charms; then, still untired | 61 Harold | 4 | 381
Through Danger's most destructive path | 158 Florence | | 30
All dormant or destructive. He will perish | 493 Manfred | 3 | 167
Of the destructive art of healing, to | 619 Foscari | 4 | 282
Here War forgot his own destructive are | 888 Juan | 8 | 653

DESULTORY
Shown in this sort of desultory rhyme | 970 Juan | 15 | 154

DESUNT
Coetera desunt | 239 Lucietta | | 12

DETACH'D
Detach'd thee from my breast for ever | 85 To D-- | | 4

DETACHMENT
He writes for a detachment to convey me | 681 Werner | 1 | 620
Detachment of three columns took its station | 873 Juan | 7 | 395

DETAIL
Unless thou dost detail the cause, and show | 532 Faliero | 4 | 291
Could I do justice to the full detail | 843 Juan | 5 | 775
All that a poet drags into detail | 865 Juan | 6 | 870
Being much too gross to see them in detail | 876 Juan | 7 | 610
But could we know them in detail, perchance | 878 Juan | 8 | 18
Or mass; for should I stretch into detail | 976 Juan | 15 | 506

DETAIL'D
So your confession be detail'd and full | 539 Faliero | 5 | 80
But wish'd for a still more detail'd narration | 987 Juan | 16 | 470

DETAIN
Let him continue. I will not detain you | 716 Werner | 5 | 221
As if it said, 'Detain me, if you please | 760 Juan | 1 | 883
Alfonso grappled to detain the foe | 769 Juan | 1 | 1481

DETAIN'D
Detain'd, till all too late to part from thence | 378 Lara | 2 | 205
I was detain'd repairing shatter'd thrones | 488 Manfred | 2 | 360
'That Michel Steno be detain'd a month | 501 Faliero | 1 | 97
The intendant said, you had been detain'd by
sickness | 679 Werner | 1 | 535
The good old gentleman had been detain'd | 803 Juan | 3 | 113

DETAINS
Why, Nature's self detains the victor's car | 460 Dante | 2 | 121

DETECT
Detect with fingers, in default of ears | 262 Hints | | 436
Who soon detect, and mark where'er we fail | 263 Hints | | 461
I have seen John half detect himself a fool | 929 Juan | 11 | 672

DETECTED
Although detected, welcome still | 413 Mazeppa | | 622

DETECTED
For fear of some false note's detected flaw | 444 Beppo | | 252
I know not that, but he has been detected | 509 Faliero | 2 | 47
When foolish Steno's ribaldry detected | 512 Faliero | 2 | 220
Hath ruin'd all by that detected letter | 603 Foscari | 2 | 96
And I'm detected,--on the very eve | 680 Werner | 1 | 586
Is forced; no violence can be detected | 702 Werner | 3 | 481
Whose virtue lies in never being detected | 963 Juan | 14 | 488

DETECTION
That guilt's detection and despair | 400 Parisina | | 355

DETERMINATION
Was Julia's innocent determination | 756 Juan | 1 | 642

DETERMINE
Of what size you may quickly determine | 232 Murray-B | | 66
But in this last I can't determine | 233 Nihil | | 6
(Let deeper sages the true cause determine | 913 Juan | 10 | 395
The accused to think their lordships would
determine | 949 Juan | 13 | 547
The reason why is easy to determine | 957 Juan | 14 | 116

DETERMINED
Would awe his fix'd determined mind in vain | 88 Horace | | 8
When we met, I determined again to suspect you | 147 To Anne-A | | 7
Which show'd resolve, determined, though unknown | 373 Lara | 1 | 495
With eye, though calm, determined not to spare | 376 Lara | 2 | 61
And, till 'twas done, determined not to stir | 448 Beppo | | 532
Once more, art thou determined to go forth | 530 Faliero | 4 | 193
The baron is determined not to lose | 683 Werner | 2 | 9
She now determined that a virtuous woman | 756 Juan | 1 | 609
While Souvaroff, determined to obtain it | 873 Juan | 7 | 407
They honour'd such determined scorn of life | 893 Juan | 8 | 952
Determined, right or wrong, on friend or foe | 943 Juan | 13 | 124
But Adeline determined Juan's wedding | 973 Juan | 15 | 313

DETERR'D
Had thought one man might be deterr'd by two | 764 Juan | 1 | 1124

DETEST
Which pleased in Swift of yore, we now detest | 262 Hints | | 396
'Thou may'st forgive though Allah's self detest | 362 Corsair | 3 | 469
Thy brother hates--but I can not detest | 438 Tasso | | 109
Is to await the onset. I detest | 586 Sardan | 4 | 556
I hate inconstancy--I loathe, detest | 800 Juan | 2 | 1665
But I detest all fiction even in song | 853 Juan | 6 | 59
Men love in haste, but they detest at leisure | 942 Juan | 13 | 48

DETESTATION
To mask detestation or fear | 114 The Tear | | 6
Which seem'd to hold all verse in detestation | 296 Vision | | 730
To this my plain, sworn, downright detestation | 899 Juan | 9 | 191

DETESTED
Itself to Sorrow's most detested fruit | 40 Harold | 3 | 302
Its health; but what it then detested, still
abhor | 66 Harold | 4 | 684
He knew himself detested, but he knew | 342 Corsair | 1 | 269
In all the days of this detested yoke | 487 Manfred | 2 | 261
Farewell! at least to this detested dungeon | 614 Foscari | 3 | 404
Will rescue us from this detested dungeon | 683 Werner | 1 | 739

DETRACT
Is fix'd for ever to detract or praise | 193 Monody | | 66

DETRACTION'S
My fancy soars not on Detraction's wing | 123 Recoll | | 80
Chaste was she, to detraction's desperation | 942 Juan | 13 | 105

DETRACTS
Detracts most largely from the merit | 95 Granta | | 63

DEUCE
The deuce a soul will stay to read | 96 Granta | | 94
Who the deuce can harbour there | 157 Hodgson | | 40
And how the deuce they ever could have birth | 758 Juan | 1 | 731
Is more than I know--the deuce take them both | 855 Juan | 6 | 176
Which sometimes plays the deuce with womankind | 975 Juan | 15 | 450

DEUCED
And find a deuced balance with the devil | 767 Juan | 1 | 1336

DEVELOPED
Alas! developed, opens the decay | 76 Harold | 4 | 1284
Scenes of my youth, developed, crowd to view | 122 Recoll | | 31

DEVELOPING
Developing the mountains, leaves, and flowers | 60 Harold | 4 | 289
Developing in that one glance the Deity | 79 Harold | 4 | 1449

DEVELOPMENT
To aid thy mind's development, to watch | 53 Harold | 3 | 1076
And dreams in their development have breath | 213 Dream | | 5

DEVELOPMENT

The stars and their development; or catch	486 Manfred	2	165

DEVIATE

And deviate into matters rather dry	901 Juan	9	324

DEVIATION

A single deviation from the track	585 Sardan	4	433
For any deviation from the graces	991 Juan	16	679

DEVICE

But no device could be brought into play	767 Juan	1	1348

DEVICES

Devices quaint and frolics ever new	14 Harold	1	678
Wreath'd with rich grapes and Bacchanal devices	676 Werner	1	296

DEVIL

The devil a soul had stay'd to hear	96 Granta		92
'Though women are angels, yet wedlock's the devil	116 To Eliza		16
Who the devil cares for more	157 Hodgson		78
And wish thee rudely at the Devil	163 Malta		48
The Devil return'd to hell by two	176 Devil's Dr		1
The Devil he thought it clever	176 Devil's Dr		58
But the Devil has reach'd our cliffs so white	177 Devil's Dr		83
The Devil first saw, as he thought, the Mail	177 Devil's Dr		91
The Devil gat next to Westminster	177 Devil's Dr		133
And the Devil was shock'd--and quoth he, 'I must go	178 Devil's Dr		150
Then the Devil went down to the humbler House	178 Devil's Dr		154
But the Devil remain'd till the Break of Day	178 Devil's Dr		169
And the Devil has all the pleasure to come	178 Devil's Dr		177
'Oh! were I prone to cavil--or were I not the Devil	178 Devil's Dr		189
Were from God knows whom--and the Devil knows what	178 Devil's Dr		192
The Devil wax'd faint at the sight of this Saint	178 Devil's Dr		205
The Devil (but 'twas over) had been vastly glad	179 Devil's Dr		225
Form the devil would frighten God in	196 Rogers		12
Devil, whose sole delight is damning	197 Rogers		74
The devil a bit of	232 Murray-B		11
What mortal would not play the Devil	239 Impromptu-B		6
Thou wilt devote old women to the devil	245 Bards		232
Damn'd like the devil, devil-like will damn	248 Bards		517
Stares, wondering what the devil it can mean	250 Bards		605
Constance, King Richard, Hamlet, and the Devil	259 Hints		178
The heiress? The angel! The devil! why, man	278 Blues	1	63
What angels shrink from: even the very devil	285 Vision		42
God knows, as helpless as the devil can wish	286 Vision		114
Here Michael interposed: 'Good saint! and devil	291 Vision		401
To reach its goal--the devil not half a day	292 Vision		448
A poor unlucky devil without a shilling	293 Vision		562
'Wilkes,' said the Devil, 'I understand all this	293 Vision		569
The Devil himself seem'd puzzled even to guess	294 Vision		603
The devil Asmodeus to the circle made	295 Vision		675
As Welborn says--'the devil turn'd precisian	298 Vision		840
There was a laughing devil in his sneer	341 Corsair	1	223
And such there were on us; the devil	410 Mazeppa		319
The devil!--I'm loth to do him wrong	410 Mazeppa		321
Not like that sooty devil of Othello's	442 Beppo		139
The pious only wish'd 'the devil take them	446 Beppo		430
To turn,--and to return;--the devil take it	447 Beppo		497
Ah! the devil come to insult the dead! Avaunt	618 Foscari	4	218
Remember! The devil take these great men! they	681 Werner	1	602
Some months ago. The devil he did! Why, yes	684 Werner	1	109
The devil and his)--He doth. Hath he no right	694 Werner	2	723
What the devil would you have? You don't believe me	695 Werner	3	19
Thou busy devil, rising in my heart	697 Werner	3	149
A wise magician, who has bound the devil	700 Werner	3	341
And here he comes! The devil! you'll hold your tongue	705 Werner	4	60
By your description track him. The devil take	713 Werner	5	6
The devil you cannot lay between us. This	719 Werner	5	427
Or that the devil, to whom they liken me	722 Deformed	1	40
You may be devil. So many men are that	723 Deformed	1	84
Be interrupted? If I be the devil	723 Deformed	1	90
Your interlopers. The devil may take men	728 Deformed	1	438
The devil in disguise--since so you deem me	730 Deformed	1	540
Dog! Man! Devil! Your obedient humble servant	730 Deformed	1	586
In danger's face as yours, were you the devil	733 Deformed	1	799
I say he is the devil. Hush! keep that secret	738 Deformed	1	248
The devil, or the devil's vicar upon earth	739 Deformed	2	251
The devil speaks truth much oftener than he's deem'd	741 Deformed	2	387
Sent to the devil somewhat ere his time	747 Juan	1	8
But then she had a devil of a spirit	749 Juan	1	157
And wonders why the devil he got heirs	759 Juan	1	800
And find a deuced balance with the devil	767 Juan	1	1336
Saw Juan's last elopement with the devil	771 Juan	1	1624
(Like truant rogues) the devil, or the fool	775 Juan	2	76
A devil of a sea rolls in that bay	775 Juan	2	83
Some play the devil, and then write a novel	799 Juan	2	1608
For, after all, we cannot call thee devil	800 Juan	2	1640

DEVIL

If only from the devil they would insure us	800 Juan	2	1653
Else how the devil is it that fresh features	800 Juan	2	1663
Man,--and, as we would hope,--perhaps the devil	816 Juan	4	11
Are what I found there--but the devil a Phrygian	826 Juan	4	624
How get out? how the devil got we in	837 Juan	5	346
As wondering what the devil a noise that is	838 Juan	5	440
'What the devil shall I do with all this gauze	841 Juan	5	606
Her features all the sweetness of the devil	845 Juan	5	866
Though such a she's a devil (if that there be one	853 Juan	6	23
The devil may decompose, but never settle	859 Juan	6	440
Is to the devil now no farther prize	872 Juan	7	355
'Why, Johnson, what the devil do you mean	876 Juan	7	554
Which did not combat like the devil, as yet	883 Juan	8	294
All that the devil would do if run stark mad	894 Juan	8	980
When a man's country's going to the devil	915 Juan	10	528
(But that I never doubted, nor the Devil	919 Juan	11	42
Stone-Henge is not--but what the devil is it	921 Juan	11	194
Where little Castlereagh? The devil can tell	927 Juan	11	602
And where--oh, where the devil are the rents	928 Juan	11	608
Which takes so much--to give the devil his due	939 Juan	12	603
The devil hath not in all his quiver's choice	970 Juan	15	103
The devil was in the girl! Could it be pride	978 Juan	15	621
Gave him, to lay the devil who looks o'er Lincoln	991 Juan	16	703
The devil may take that stealthy pace of his	995 Juan	16	940

DEVILISH

As your fair was so devilish reserved	116 Strephon		12
A devilish deal more sad than witty	147 To Author		2
O'er Virgil's devilish verses and--his own	259 Hints		226
And devilish damp, but fine enough by torchlight	679 Werner	1	514
Some devilish escapade or stir, which shows	933 Juan	12	202
And that same devilish doctrine of the Persian	946 Juan	13	325

DEVILISM

Like magnetism, or devilism, or what	857 Juan	6	303

DEVIL-LIKE

Damn'd like the devil, devil-like will damn	248 Bards		517

DEVILS

Should I introduce these revels among my younger devils	179 Devil's Dr		221
And printers' devils shake their weary bones	243 Bards		126
The devils had ta'en a longer, stronger pull	285 Vision		6
Persuasion on the part of devils, or saints	297 Vision		810
The devils ran howling, deafen'd, down to hell	297 Vision		819
Of the next bastion, fired away like devils	883 Juan	8	346
Corruption for its crop) with the poor devils	910 Juan	10	198
The seventh will bring blue devils or a dun	912 Juan	10	304
Blue devils, and blue-stockings, and romances	965 Juan	14	631
Hath got blue devils for his morning mirrors	968 Juan	15	28

DEVIL'S

Or be named in the Devil's indentures	239 Bray		21
'The former is the devil's scripture, and	295 Vision		689
A few brief words of truth shame the devil's servants	613 Foscari	3	311
True; the devil's always ugly; and your beauty	729 Deformed	1	523
The devil, or the devil's vicar upon earth	739 Deformed	2	251
The devil's so very sly--she should discover	756 Juan	1	618
The devil's in the moon for mischief; they	760 Juan	1	898
The devil's in the urchin, and no good	767 Juan	1	1364
Destruction's jaws into the devil's den	882 Juan	8	276
Which well beseem'd the 'Devil's drawing-room	917 Juan	10	643

DEVIOUS

Where yonder torrent's devious waters stray	107 Nisus		116

DEVISE

That we more surely might devise together	503 Faliero	1	255

DEVISED

With emblems well devised by amorous pride	42 Harold	3	436

DEVOID

Thou know'st my deeds, my breast devoid of fear	106 Nisus		47
You seem devoid of this--wilt share it? Who	677 Werner	1	355

DEVOTE

To thee I do devote it--thou shalt take	75 Harold	4	1194
Thou wilt devote old women to the devil	245 Bards		232
I loved and love, devote the mournful lyre	461 Dante	3	26
Which doth devote thee to this trial	481 Manfred	1	253
Will one day learn. Meantime, I do devote	523 Faliero	3	319
Thus I devote thee to the infernal gods	549 Faliero	5	796

DEVOTED

Her worship, but, devoted to her rite	14 Harold	1	673
Julia, the daughter, the devoted, gave	45 Harold	3	627
Devoted to love and to friendship alone	137 Delawarr		28
In moments to delight devoted	175 Portuguese-A		1
Devoted in the stormiest hour	210 Augusta-A		31
When thus devoted to poetic dreams	247 Bards		403

DEVOTED
Now should they burst on thy devoted coast   272 Minerva   309
Should rend her rash devoted breast   319 Giaour   955
A breathing but devoted warrior lay   381 Lara   2   416
They fell devoted, but undying   388 Corinth   406
Her sons, devoted to the grave   391 Corinth   660
To be thus kiss'd by such devoted lover   477 Francesca,   38
We sprung, and you, devoted to the state   531 Faliero   4   211
I am devoted unto God alone   545 Faliero   5   544
Your years, so long devoted to your country   621 Foscari   5   22

DEVOTEE
And let not this seem strange: the devotee   424 Island   2   370
A devotee when soars the Host in sight   799 Juan   2   1563

DEVOTES
Devotes to scandal his congenial mind   255 Bards   979
His night devotes, despite of spur and boots   273 Waltz   17

DEVOTION
Of love, romance, devotion is his lay   11 Harold   1   505
Of true devotion monkish incense burns   14 Harold   1   682
There some grave Moslem to devotion stoops   28 Harold   2   525
Some seek devotion, toil, war, good or crime   58 Harold   4   197
He worships each look with such faithful devotion   91 Caroline-C   19
No more with love's former devotion we sue   100 L Adieu   34
Such servile devotion might shame him away   202 Avatar   32
Devotion and her daughter Love   217 The Harp   17
And dishonour the Cause of devotion   239 Bray   30
On dull devotion--Lo! the Sabbath bard   246 Bards   320
Devotion wafts the mind above   321 Giaour   1135
With such devotion to their ecstasy   420 Island   2   117
Are kept apart and nursed in the devotion   454 Venice-B   135
Hoard your devotion for the thunderer there   572 Sardan   3   35
Devotion was a duty, and I hated   583 Sardan   4   339
His rank and his devotion to the duties   625 Foscari   5   312
The very Lutherans have more true devotion   739 Deformed 2   285
Selected for discretion and devotion   753 Juan   1   434
Fighting, devotion, dust,--perhaps a name   774 Juan   2   32
Strange sounds of wailing, blasphemy, devotion   778 Juan   2   271
In nameless print--that I have no devotion   815 Juan   3   922
And what is that? Devotion, doubtless--how   856 Juan   6   257
To shelter their devotion from the wind   948 Juan   13   440
A hecatomb of suitors with devotion   962 Juan   14   438

DEVOTIONS
And warm to the skies my devotions arose   136 Highlander   23
So rapt in thy devotions? Dost thou stand   562 Sardan   2   37

DEVOTION'S
Yet deem not these devotion's offering   7 Harold   1   263
And bids devotion's hallow'd echoes cease   120 Newstead-A   44
Or joins Devotion's choral band   160 Cadiz   47

DEVOUR
Is such, he wills his judgment should devour   472 Morgante   394

DEVOUR'D
The meagre by the meagre were devour'd   189 Darkness   46
Devour'd by that which drowns his infant world   662 Heaven   575
Devour'd it, longing for the other too   783 Juan   2   568
And transient, and devour'd by the same harpy   929 Juan   11   675

DEVOURING
(See also LOVE-DEVOURING)
Oh! curst be thou, devouring grave   88 Catullus   17

DEVOURS
Than the eternal deluge, which devours   898 Juan   9   103

DEVOUT
And buy repentance, ere they grow devout   440 Beppo   5
Saying, 'My brother, so devout and good   471 Morgante   367
And own the bravest for the most devout   562 Sardan   2   74
Ay, and the most devout for brave--thou hast not   562 Sardan   2   75
Devout, too! Well, sir, I obey at once   708 Werner   4   256
And Haidee, being devout as well as fair   798 Juan   2   1541

DEVOUTLY
And most devoutly Macon still blasphemed   470 Morgante   278
That I devoutly wish'd the three were four   919 Juan   11   47

DEW
(See also DUNGEON-DEW, MAY-DEW, NIGHT-DEW, SPRING-DEW)
The skies which rain their plagues on men like dew 74 Harold   4   1131
Though nurtured 'mid weeds dropping pestilent dew   99 L Adieu   2
Adown in agonizing dew   104 Alva   236
And its dew is diffused in a Tear   115 The Tear   12
To steep in dew thy gaudy shrine   118 Romance   40
Where now the grass exhales a murky dew   120 Newstead-A   29
The dew I gather from thy lip   128 Lady-C   9
soul, Orla! yet soft to me as the dew of   131 Calmar   176
The dew of the morning   151 When We   9
Sink on the heart, as dew along the flower   192 Monody   4

DEW
A violet dropping dew   218 I Saw   4
With the dew on his brow and the rust on his mail   222 Sennacherib   18
Yet this is the dew   229 Lads   13
This of his candour seem'd the sable dew   248 Bards   486
A better farmer ne'er brush'd dew from lawn   286 Vision   61
As springing high the silver dew   313 Giaour   301
Dash o'er her deathlike cheek the ocean dew   357 Corsair   3   117
Each feeling pure--as falls the dropping dew   365 Corsair   3   664
The sickening iciness of that cold dew   374 Lara   1   601
Their arms aside to revel in its dew   427 Island   3   76
And sandal oil to fence against the dew   432 Island   4   168
To rust beneath the dew and dashing spray   434 Island   4   350
Gather like night dew. My beloved, hush   579 Sardan   4   39
And drank the best dew   728 Deformed 1   407
The freshness of the heart can fall like dew   773 Juan   1   1706
A drop of dew, when every drop had seem'd   785 Juan   2   686
And young Aurora kiss'd her lips with dew   792 Juan   2   1132
Falling like dew, upon a thought, produces   813 Juan   3   794
And the heart's dew of pain sprang fast and
  chilly   865 Juan   6   839
As o'er the grass the dew   986 Juan   16   364

DEW'D
Through those long, dark, and glistening lashes
  dew'd   345 Corsair   1   497

DEW-DROPS
In dew-drops o'er my narrow bed   146 Adieu   96
Gleam'd on the dew-drops big and damp   397 Parisina   117

DEWS
But that is fancy, for the starlight dews   48 Harold   3   820
Of merchant-dukes? The momentary dews   64 Harold   4   535
Cold dews my pallid face o'erspread   87 Ad Lesbiam   17
I fear, relax'd with midnight dews   89 Anacreon-B   41
Gilds with faint beams the crystal dews of rain   122 Recoll   19
Will shed around some dews of spring   133 E. N. Long   28
When the Stars are on high and the dews on the
  ground   164 Newstead-C   7
She saw the dews of eve besprinkling   317 Giaour   691
While sets that Sun and Dews of evening melt   355 Corsair   2   560
Each flower the dews have lightly wet   396 Parisina   7
To browse beneath the midnight dews   407 Mazeppa   65
And yet there are no dews! 'Tis blood--my blood   651 Cain   3   345
In vain the dews of Heaven descend above   825 Juan   4   559
In vain!--As fall the dews on quenchless sands   904 Juan   9   471

DEWY
Dewy with nature's tear-drops, as they pass   39 Harold   3   236
The morn is up again, the dewy morn   50 Harold   3   914
Nor melts like mine in dewy bliss   90 Caroline-B   20
Pity her dewy wings before him spread   114 Death-A   13
Oh! pass thy dewy fingers o'er   323 Giaour   1312
Alone and dewy, coldly pure and pale   337 Abydos   2   731
Which, kindling by degrees its dewy spars   424 Island   2   400
With dark but brilliant skin, and dewy eye   429 Island   3   185
While o'er them flapp'd the sea-bird's dewy wing   435 Island   4   364
And she lifts up her dewy eye of blue   742 Deformed 3   11
His dewy curls, long drench'd by every storm   788 Juan   2   910
And his black curls were dewy with the spray   792 Juan   2   1174
Drooping and dewy on the beach he lay   796 Juan   2   1406
Of dewy dawn wound slowly round each height   863 Juan   6   686

DEXTEROUS
So dexterous a spoiler, who could creep   686 Werner   2   219

DEXTROUS
Stretch'd by a dextrous sleight along the ground   376 Lara   2   70

DEXT'ROUS
Their passions, and are dext'rous; some by
  features   834 Juan   5   212

DEY
Had a large order from the Dey of Tripoli   803 Juan   3   128

DI
Non Di, non homines--you know the rest   296 Vision   728

DIABOLIC
He merely bent his diabolic brow   289 Vision   289

DIABOLICAL
Is never diabolical. I'll call him   729 Deformed 1   524

DIADEM
With diadem hight foolscap, lo! a fiend   8 Harold   1   290
'Tis worth thy vanish'd diadem   181 Ode-A   117
More than thy very diadem   185 Belshaz-A   12
Farewell to thee, France! when thy diadem crown'd
  me   186 Napoleon   9
Was crown'd with a peculiar diadem   214 Dream   36
Bright is the diadem, boundless the sway   219 Saul-A   11

DIADEM
She's gone, who shared my diadem   221 Mariamne   17
Were worthy of a diadem   330 Abydos   2   136
Old Ocean's purple diadem   332 Abydos   2   356
Were offer'd rich as Stamboul's diadem   357 Corsair   3   154
And see thy diadem, so changed and worn   461 Dante   3   55
With a diadem of snow   479 Manfred   1   63
Refused the diadem of all the Caesars   502 Faliero   1   202
Could I not turn thee to a diadem   504 Faliero   1   296
Lolls crown'd with roses, and his diadem   551 Sardan   1   34
A diadem around it. Sire, I deem'd   573 Sardan   3   131
The fillet of my diadem the first time   577 Sardan   3   369
That I have added to her diadem   601 Foscari   2   19
This ducal cap the diadem of earth   603 Foscari   2   80
At my too long worn diadem and ring   622 Foscari   5   85
And there the ducal diadem. And so   623 Foscari   5   191
High on the monarch's diadem, attractest   700 Werner   3   335
(That royal bird, whose tail's a diadem   876 Juan   7   590

DIAL
For a fit time--that hour is on the dial   516 Faliero   2   552
Might date for years, did Anguish make the dial   709 Werner   4   314

DIALOGUE
The matchless dialogue, the deathless wit   193 Monody   49
Your dialogue is apt and smart   231 Doctor   11
Ape the swoln dialogue of kings and queens   261 Hints   338
The dialogue is held between the Powers   289 Vision   263
This dialogue; for he who answer'd knew   874 Juan   7   471
Rings o'er the dialogue, and many a crime   885 Juan   8   460
And shone in the best part of dialogue   960 Juan   14   290

DIALOGUES
He held his dialogues; and they did teach   216 Dream   197
Long dialogues--which pass'd without a word   977 Juan   15   608
Which Plato in his dialogues dramatic   979 Juan   15   685

DIAMOND
Diamond, by all that's glorious! Come, I'll
  trust you   700 Werner   3   310
Where I can't say or gold or diamond flings   843 Juan   5   749
One monstrous diamond drew much observation   923 Juan   11   308
On him the diamond pours its brilliant blaze   930 Juan   12   62
Or glorious as a diamond richly set   969 Juan   15   52

DIAMONDS
And rich in rubles, diamonds, cash, and credit   916 Juan   10   554

DIAN
When, as chaste Dian, here thou deign'st to rove   110 Nisus   344
Late, late to-night will Dian cheer   329 Abydos   2   55
Such in her chaplet infant Dian wove   368 Lara   1   163
My Dian of the Ephesians, Lady Adeline   961 Juan   14   363
Graceful as Dian, when she draws her bow   985 Juan   16   301
Alas! her star must fade like that of Dian   995 Juan   16   915

DIANA'S
To which Diana's marvel was a cell   78 Harold   4   1370
Which might have call'd Diana's chorus 'cousin   844 Juan   5   790

DIAN'S
To gaze on Dian's wave-reflected sphere   23 Harold   2   209
While, on the other hand, meek Dian's crest   59 Harold   4   242
A night, with every star, save Dian's beam   183 Address-D   28
Hours roll'd along, and Dian's orb on high   269 Minerva   63
Behold where Dian's beams disdain to shine   270 Minerva   120

DIAPASONS
My music has some mystic diapasons   958 Juan   14   174

DIBDIN'S
And Dibdin's nonsense yield complete content   249 Bards   563

DICE
When drunkenness and dice invite   95 Granta   55
Champaign, dice, music, or your neighbour's
  spouse   250 Bards   651
Whose table earth--whose dice were human bones   299 Age   52
Have won with false dice.--Who hath been our
  Judas   537 Faliero   4   640
The dice thereon. But I lose time in prating   738 Deformed 2   224
The dice seem'd charm'd, too, with his repartees   952 Juan   13   688
Then there were billiards; cards, too, but no
  dice   954 Juan   13   841

DICEDRABBIT
His son, the Honourable Dick Dicedrabbit   989 Juan   16   606

DICK
'A groat.'--'Ah, bravo! Dick hath done the sum   264 Hints   519
Dick Dunder. That is, if he lives. And why not   281 Blues   2   44
There was Dick Dubious, the metaphysician   952 Juan   13   689
His son, the Honourable Dick Dicedrabbit   989 Juan   16   606

DICKEY
'Tis granted; and the valet mounts the dickey   947 Juan   13   369

DICTATE
The dictate of my bosom's care   113 Quaker   44

DICTATES
Can youth then hush the dictates of the heart   119 Answer-A   8

DICTATORIAL
The dictatorial wreath,--couldst thou divine   67 Harold   4   748

DICTATORS
Farmers of war, dictators of the farm   306 Age   615
Have crush'd dictators, as the popular steel   526 Faliero   3   557

DICTATRESS
Earth's chief dictatress, ocean's lovely queen   255 Bards   1002

DICTION
For what is sometimes called poetic diction   889 Juan   8   686
Though every scribe, in some slight turn of
  diction   929 Juan   11   694

DICTIONARIES
According to the best of dictionaries   976 Juan   15   541

DID
I loathe an opera worse than Dennis did   260 Hints   296
Those deeds the bolder spirit plainly did   342 Corsair   1   268
Still there was haughtiness in all he did   374 Lara   1   558
Roused millions do what single Brutus did   423 Island   2   325
How you could tear and fling the trees you late
  did   473 Morgante   453
Alas! Love never did so. Then 'tis time   710 Werner   4   388
In their own way by all the things that she did   748 Juan   1   80
That all the Apostles would have done as they did   757 Juan   1   664
If you think 'twas philosophy that this did   758 Juan   1   743
He cast a rueful look or two, and did   767 Juan   1   1303
Leander, Mr. Ekenhead, and I did   787 Juan   2   840
They haggled, wrangled, swore, too--so they did   835 Juan   5   220
But what he did, was to lay on their backs   890 Juan   8   743
In darkness--I can only hope they did   895 Juan   8   1056
You did great things; but not being great in mind   897 Juan   9   79
Permits whate'er they please, or did not long
  since   927 Juan   11   576
As usual--the same reason which she late did   974 Juan   15   400

DIDACTIC
For our remembrance your didactic line   264 Hints   534

DIDDLE
But remember Miss Diddle invites us to sup   283 Blues   2   155

DIDDLED
Full flash, all fancy, until fairly diddled   920 Juan   11   135
Where's Brummel? Dish'd. Where's Long Pole
  Wellesley? Diddled   928 Juan   11   609

DIDO
An ancient cup, which Tyrian Dido gave   107 Nisus   151

DIDO'S
Of Dido's alphabet; and this is rational   881 Juan   8   183

DID'S
The quantity of good she did's unknown   935 Juan   12   381

DIDST
Here didst thou dwell, here schemes of pleasure
  plan   7 Harold   1   279
But ne'er didst thou, fair Mount, when Greece was
  young   14 Harold   1   648
Didst never yet one mortal song inspire   19 Harold   2   2
Well didst thou speak, Athena's wisest son   20 Harold   2   55
Which living waves where thou didst cease to live   39 Harold   3   265
Thou, who didst grudge him even that fleeting span   40 Harold   3   309
Who deem'd thee for a time whate'er thou didst
  assert   41 Harold   3   333
Triumphant Sylla! thou, who didst subdue   67 Harold   4   740
With all thy vices, for thou didst lay down   67 Harold   4   746
Here didst thou dwell, in this enchanted cover   72 Harold   4   1054
And didst thou not, thy breast to his replying   73 Harold   4   1063
Thou, who didst call the Furies from the abyss   75 Harold   4   1183
Fair didst thou shine upon my earlier hours   139 Ossian-A   36
And didst thou not, since Death for thee   165 Thyrza   13
Who didst not change through all the past   167 Dead   21
Little didst thou deem, when dashing   187 Ode-B   44
As thou didst lighten through all space   188 On Star   16
The fate thou didst so well foresee   191 Prometheus-B   29
Though human, thou didst not deceive me   210 Augusta-B   25
Though woman, thou didst not forsake   210 Augusta-B   26
Though trusted, thou didst not disclaim me   210 Augusta-B   29
But of thy virtues didst thou make a vice   213 Lady Byron   43

DIDST

Cato died for his country, so didst thou	238	Epigrams	2
Thou didst not view thy Selim fall	335	Abydos 2	633
'Why should I seek? because--Oh! didst thou not	359	Corsair 3	288
The curse of Him thou didst forsake	391	Corinth	640
Thou didst not give me life alone	399	Parisina	292
Thou didst annihilate the earth to me	439	Tasso	173
Didst ever see a Gondola? For fear	442	Beppo	145
Italian beauty! didst thou not inspire	445	Beppo	362
Thy venom, and my state thou didst amerce	457	Dante 1	67
This shalt thou owe to him thou didst so wrong	459	Dante 2	33
'And even at Aspramont thou didst begin	467	Morgante	97
And thou didst shine, thou rolling moon, upon	495	Manfred 3	291
Thou didst not tempt me, and thou couldst not tempt me	496	Manfred 3	397
Thou didst not; but from out thy wolfish eye	532	Faliero 4	261
Didst promise at his death, thou hast seal'd thine own	546	Faliero 5	586
Thou didst not say so. But thou lookedst it	551	Sardan 1	84
As king the kingdoms thou didst leave as hero	553	Sardan 1	164
Who out of darkness on the deep didst make	627	Cain 1	2
God! who didst name the day, and separate	627	Cain 1	5
Who didst divide the wave from wave, and call	627	Cain 1	7
God! who didst call the elements into	627	Cain 1	·9
Who didst create these best and beauteous beings	627	Cain 1	15
Yet didst permit the Serpent to creep in	627	Cain 1	19
Oh, God! why didst thou plant the tree of knowledge	628	Cain 1	32
Ah! didst thou tempt my mother? I tempt none	630	Cain 1	193
To sway. But didst thou tempt my parents? I	630	Cain 1	213
Thou didst before I came upon thee. How	637	Cain 2	95
Now let us back to earth! And wherefore didst thou	642	Cain 2	433
Springs good! What didst thou answer? Nothing; for	643	Cain 2	504
Which thou hast shown me? Didst thou not require	645	Cain 2	623
O'er what it shadows; wherefore didst thou choose it	646	Cain 3	5
Why didst thou not take me, who first incurr'd thee	652	Cain 3	412
Didst seem to glory in him, nor to shrink	664	Heaven	683
Thou didst not mar my fortunes: my own nature	673	Werner 1	152
Ulric! I love my son, as thou didst me	682	Werner 1	734
Why didst thou spare me? I dreamt of my father	718	Werner 5	359
As e'er thou didst upon Carrara's blocks	738	Deformed 2	213

DIE

Are met--as if at home they could not die	10	Harold 1	447
And die, that living might have proved her shame	11	Harold 1	474
None through their cold disdain are doom'd to die	15	Harold 1	727
As nothing did we die; but Life will suit	40	Harold 3	301
With sorrow and supineness, and so die	42	Harold 3	393
But as it is, I live and die unheard	50	Harold 3	912
For 'tis his nature to advance or die	51	Harold 3	964
States fall, arts fade, but Nature doth not die	55	Harold 4	24
'Tis solitude should teach us how to die	60	Harold 4	295
Thou! form'd to eat, and be despised, and die	60	Harold 4	334
Of gods and men, great Nemesis! did he die	68	Harold 4	781
Proud of their trampled nature, and so die	69	Harold 4	840
I needs must gaze, but, gazing, die	87	Ad Lesbiam	12
With him his frantic sire may die	103	Alva	136
Perhaps the hero did not die	104	Alva	216
Or die with him for whom he wish'd to live	110	Nisus	338
With me to live, with me to die	111	Medea	32
Unknown, unhonour'd live, unwept for die	112	Examination	52
Ah! were you destined to die at Culloden	117	Lachin	27
Marking each ardent youth, ordain'd to die	119	Newstead-A	15
The fair, the brave, the good must die	128	Answer-B	19
She died, but ne'er will die again	128	Answer-B	24
die, and not lift the spear? No, Orla! ours	130	Calmar	65
'Mathon is mine. I shall die in joy: but	130	Calmar	129
With this fond dream, methinks, 'twere sweet to die	138	Harrow-B	23
I soon must die of melancholy	145	Becher-B	59
Instruct me how to die	146	Adieu	120
We must die--who shall not?--May our sins be forgiven	156	Goblet	31
'Ay, but to die, and go,' alas	167	Euthanasia	29
The all of thine that cannot die	168	Dead	68
Shall weep that aught of thee can die	169	Blank Leaf	8
But drag or drive us on to die	171	Time-B	4
I faint, I die beneath the blow	172	Romaic-B	6
If youth could neither fade nor die	175	Portuguese-A	4
For, like the soul, my love can never die	175	Portuguese-B	4
To die a prince--or live a slave	180	Ode-A	44
There is a tear for all that die	183	Parker	1
Who would not die the death they chose	184	Parker	20
Look upon me, and know thou shalt not die	185	Julian	47
Is it not written, thou must die	185	Belshaz-A	8
And learn like better men to die	185	Belshaz-A	16
Unfit to govern, live, or die	185	Belshaz-A	24
Too loved of all to die	186	Stanzas-A	4
Man may die--the soul's renew'd	188	Ode-B	96

DIE

Refused thee even the boon to die	191	Prometheus-B	23
And broke the die--in moulding Sheridan	194	Monody	118
Expect to die	199	Stanzas-B	19
Who truly love should die	201	Ode-C	60
Let me not die till he comes back o'er the billow	205	Hindoo	12
Of aught save laurel, or for such could die	206	Greece	4
More than this I scarce can die	208	Fare Thee	60
Where all beneath her influence droop or die	209	Sketch	78
How sweet this very hour to die	217	High World	6
In other lands to die	217	Gazelle	20
It cannot die, it cannot stay	220	Clay	3
Forgetting faith it was to die	220	Clay	32
Live on in thy faith, but in mine I will die	221	False	8
And when she does die, which I hope will be soon	223	Soul-C	3
Will die fighting, or live free	229	Lads	4
And live in prologues, though his dramas die	251	Bards	718
Him let them shun, with him let tinsel die	254	Bards	901
Complete in all life's lessons--but to die	260	Hints	258
When 'Chrononhotonthologos must die	261	Hints	339
As when the dying vicar will not die	267	Hints	778
'To die like Cato,' leapt into the Thames	268	Hints	826
Who lived and died as none can live or die	268	Minerva	32
Of almost every body born to die	286	Vision	120
Beholds him conquer, but, alas! not die	301	Age	204
To die for England--why then live?--for rent	306	Age	623
They too will rather die than shame	311	Giaour	122
The graves of those that cannot die	311	Giaour	135
Ne'er droop the wing o'er those that die	314	Giaour	417
I knew but to obtain or die	321	Giaour	1113
I die--but first I have possess'd	321	Giaour	1114
To die--and know no second love	321	Giaour	1166
I knew 'twas false--she could not die	323	Giaour	1301
With thee to live, with thee to die	328	Abydos 1	392
Which holds he here--he saw him die	331	Abydos 2	280
Their oars, 'tis but to see me die	334	Abydos 2	524
Had bled or wept to see him die	335	Abydos 2	616
No dread of death--if with us die our foes	338	Corsair 1	23
So let it be--it irks not me to die	343	Corsair 1	333
''Tis well--but Seyd escapes--and he must die	349	Corsair 2	193
Shame mounts to rage that must atone or die	350	Corsair 2	236
Would doom him ever dying--ne'er to die	351	Corsair 2	283
Yet not to hurt--I would not see thee die	353	Corsair 2	440
The one of all my band that would not die	354	Corsair 2	473
Who lived and died as none can live or die	356	Corsair 3	32
Had proved unwilling as unfit to die	358	Corsair 3	217
Which spoke before her accents--'Thou must die	359	Corsair 3	279
Yes, thou must die; there is but one resource	359	Corsair 3	280
Whose waters mock the lip of those that die	380	Lara 2	401
Of those that die the soldier's fiery death	380	Lara 2	403
And battled to avenge or die	385	Corinth	140
He sank, regretting not to die	386	Corinth	145
The foremost who rush on his strength but to die	392	Corinth	728
They perforce must do or die	394	Corinth	930
They die; but ere their eyes could close	394	Corinth	931
Farewell! I will not see thee die	398	Parisina	216
Begot in sin, to die in shame	399	Parisina	312
Would she thus hear him doom'd to die	399	Parisina	325
That some one was to die--but who	400	Parisina	371
These hands are chain'd--but let me die	401	Parisina	450
He died, as erring man should die	401	Parisina	462
He claim'd to die with eyes unbound	401	Parisina	475
I could not die	404	Chillon	228
Such was the hazard of the die	407	Mazeppa	15
As though it were a joy to die	409	Mazeppa	219
At least to die amidst the horde	411	Mazeppa	504
Can die no more than then I died	412	Mazeppa	548
Die calm, or calmer oft than he	414	Mazeppa	739
Who scarce would wait till both should die	414	Mazeppa	771
Drain every drop!--to-morrow we may die	419	Island 2	46
That life knows no such rapture as to die	420	Island 2	118
And die they do; for earthly life has nought	420	Island 2	119
We will die at our quarters, like true men	426	Island 2	518
But though the choice seems native to die free	427	Island 3	55
And die at once than wrestle with despair	428	Island 3	124
Which said--'Has Neuha brought me here to die	430	Island 4	54
And yield as victims, or die sword in hand	433	Island 4	246
But now the die was to be thrown, and all	433	Island 4	275
Enough for seizure, near enough to die	434	Island 4	318
Too late for life, but not too late to die	434	Island 4	325
Have pardon'd princes' insults and would die	438	Tasso	105
Which hath no words, 'tis that I would not die	439	Tasso	213
Where I was born, but where I would not die	455	Dante Ded	2
Of me) can I return, though but to die	456	Dante 1	40
Their days in endless strife, and die alone	458	Dante 1	152
And mine at least hath cost me dear: to die	458	Dante 1	158
And you, ye men! Romans, who dare not die	460	Dante 2	112
And die or are degraded: for the mind	463	Dante 3	172
His country's, and might die where he had birth	465	Dante 4	136
Built up between us, and will die alone	465	Dante 4	148
Who caused the giant in this place to die	476	Morgante	684
But--thou mayst die. Will death bestow it on me	480	Manfred 1	148
Nor to slumber, nor to die	481	Manfred 1	254
Loathing our life, and dreading still to die	487	Manfred 2	260

DIE

The touch that they die from	488	Manfred 2	342
One of the blessed, and that I shall die	490	Manfred 2	496
Old in their youth, and die ere middle age	493	Manfred 3	140
Away! I'll die as I have lived--alone	496	Manfred 3	350
Pray--albeit but in thought,--but die not thus	497	Manfred 3	405
Old man! 'tis not so difficult to die	497	Manfred 3	411
The die is cast. Where is the place of meeting	508	Faliero 1	593
You would not have him die for this offence	512	Faliero 2	235
But if we fail--They never fail who die	517	Faliero 2	606
Of life upon this cast: the die was thrown	519	Faliero 3	55
So let them die as one! Should one survive	521	Faliero 3	158
And is it then decided? must they die	526	Faliero 3	526
Save this. Thou must not die! and think how dear	532	Faliero 4	307
The die is thrown; but for a warlike service	533	Faliero 4	381
They die then in their duty, as will I	536	Faliero 4	589
There now is nothing left me save to die	537	Faliero 4	610
So let them die the death. We are prepared	538	Faliero 5	20
Your racks have done that for us. Let us die	538	Faliero 5	21
But this ye dare not do; for if we die there	538	Faliero 5	45
For a short respite--must we bear or die	538	Faliero 5	53
What matter a few syllables? let's die	539	Faliero 5	116
I die and pardon thee! I die and scorn thee	540	Faliero 5	134
Let me die calmly; you may grant me this	542	Faliero 5	295
Ay, but he must not die! Spare his few years	543	Faliero 5	356
No, lady, there are others who would die	543	Faliero 5	376
Then die, Faliero! since it must be so	543	Faliero 5	381
I have lived too long not to know how to die	543	Faliero 5	393
You have nought to do, except confess and die	545	Faliero 5	548
The Doge! Yes, Doge, thou hast lived and thou shalt die	546	Faliero 5	557
It is not worth so much! It were to die	557	Sardan 1	440
To die is no less natural than those	557	Sardan 1	448
But here is more upon the die--a kingdom	563	Sardan 2	139
And this slight arm, and die a king at least	564	Sardan 2	170
They mean us to die privately, but not	568	Sardan 2	444
No! I'll die here!--Away, and tell your king	575	Sardan 3	256
We'll die where we were born--in our own halls	575	Sardan 3	258
What, shall he die alone?--I live alone	584	Sardan 4	407
He shall not die alone; but lonely you	584	Sardan 4	408
Part to die for his sovereign, and why not	593	Sardan 5	372
Would fain die with you! My best! my last friends	593	Sardan 5	400
And may die under it if now repeated	595	Foscari 1	8
Live on, so the good die not, till the hour	599	Foscari 1	226
Not his--not his--he'll die in silence. What	599	Foscari 1	232
If he die unattainted? War with them too	601	Foscari 1	353
So die than live on lingeringly in pain	605	Foscari 2	211
I care not for his frowns! We can but die	613	Foscari 3	319
Be left to me to tend them; should they die	614	Foscari 3	390
To bring them up to serve the state, and die	618	Foscari 4	209
Renew this instance. I have sworn to die	621	Foscari 5	43
Cared for--what would he more? Die in his robes	622	Foscari 5	123
A sovereign should die standing. My poor boy	625	Foscari 5	306
The misery to die a subject where	625	Foscari 5	316
Dost thou not live? Must I not die? Alas	628	Cain 1	29
But live to die: and, living, see no thing	629	Cain 1	110
Think'st thou I'd take the shape of things that die	630	Cain 1	225
Which are so beautiful: shall they, too, die	631	Cain 1	278
I'm glad of that: I would not have them die	631	Cain 1	280
Here let me die: for to give birth to those	637	Cain 2	68
Who can but suffer many years, and die	637	Cain 2	69
All die--there is what must survive. The Other	637	Cain 2	72
They may be! Let me die as atoms die	637	Cain 2	113
(If that they die), or know ye in your might	637	Cain 2	114
As I have shown thee much which cannot die	638	Cain 2	142
Said nothing, save that all shall die. Perhaps	639	Cain 2	242
Did they, too, eat of it, that they must die	641	Cain 2	358
Eat, drink, toil, tremble, laugh, weep, sleep, and die	645	Cain 2	621
To us! they sinn'd, then let them die	647	Cain 3	76
Would I could die for them, so they might live	647	Cain 3	79
May he live in the pangs which others die with	652	Cain 3	435
No, let me die! It must not be. It burns	654	Cain 3	500
For thou hast loved me, and I would not die	656	Heaven	62
Until I know what I must die in knowing	656	Heaven	63
Man, earth, and fire, shall die	660	Heaven	370
And the striped tiger shall lie down to die	661	Heaven	444
All die	662	Heaven	516
All die	662	Heaven	529
Upon the earth to toil and die; and they	663	Heaven	638
I abhor death, because that thou must die	664	Heaven	707
And better. Let me die with this, and them	665	Heaven	764
Let us still walk the stars. True, earth must die	666	Heaven	825
Ye cannot die	666	Heaven	861
I hear the voice which says that all must die	667	Heaven	877
Our portion is to die	667	Heaven	899
And must we die	667	Heaven	916
Being gone, 'twill be less difficult to die	667	Heaven	943
Live as he wills it--die, when he ordains	667	Heaven	953
Then die	668	Heaven	1021
Whether they live, or die with all earth's life	669	Heaven	1090

DIE

Who die in the Lord	670	Heaven	1149
No; let me die, as I have lived, in faith	670	Heaven	1168
To die! in youth to die	670	Heaven	1190
He could not die neglected or alone	707	Werner 4	189
Did he who own'd it die in his bed? Alas	712	Werner 4	503
As I can one day God's. Nor did he die	712	Werner 4	512
Whatever dreads to die. Decide between	727	Deformed 1	355
But still, like them, must live and die, the subject	731	Deformed 1	597
Of something which has made it live and die	731	Deformed 1	598
As Dacia men to die the eternal death	731	Deformed 1	628
In such an enterprise to die is rather	733	Deformed 1	783
To die within the wall! Hence, Arnold, hence	737	Deformed 2	148
The goal is gain'd, we die, you know--and then	763	Juan 1	1064
'Twere better,. sure, to die so, than be shut	767	Juan 1	1327
All things that have been born were born to die	773	Juan 1	1755
And live and die, make love and pay our taxes	774	Juan 2	27
And such light griefs are not a thing to die on	776	Juan 2	124
But die, as many an exiled heart nath died	776	Juan 2	139
Thought it would be becoming to die drunk	778	Juan 2	280
But let us die like men, not sink below	778	Juan 2	284
And though 'tis true that man can only die once	779	Juan 2	311
And strives to strangle him before he die	780	Juan 2	416
That some, I really think, do never die	782	Juan 2	516
And who should die to be his fellow's food	783	Juan 2	584
Who die in righteousness, she lean'd; and there	792	Juan 2	1146
Unless he wish'd to die upon the place	794	Juan 2	1270
Save theirs, and that their life could never die	798	Juan 2	1504
If souls could die, had perish'd in that passion	798	Juan 2	1524
For all of theirs upon that die is thrown	799	Juan 2	1587
And place them on their breast--but place to die	801	Juan 3	14
Avouch'd his death (such people never die	806	Juan 3	299
There, swan-like, let me sing and die	813	Juan 3	782
Meant to grow old, but die in happy spring	817	Juan 4	63
Deepest in those who long the most to die	817	Juan 4	83
'Whom the gods love die young,' was said of yore	817	Juan 4	89
Why did they not then die?--they had lived too long	819	Juan 4	210
Each broke to drown her, yet she could not die	820	Juan 4	248
Oft came and went, as there resolved to die	821	Juan 4	310
I love him--I will die with him if I knew	821	Juan 4	335
Nor even Diogenes.--We live and die	867	Juan 7	31
My debt in being thus allow'd to die	875	Juan 7	517
But at the least you may die gloriously	891	Juan 8	797
That one should die, than two drag on the fetter	906	Juan 9	640
Thousands blaze, love, hope, die,--how happy they	908	Juan 10	64
But Juan was not meant to die so soon	908	Juan 10	65
Let me die where I am!' And as the fuel	920	Juan 11	124
Heroes must die; and by God's blessing 'tis	921	Juan 11	154
Some die, some fly, some languish on the Continent	928	Juan 11	631
Except perhaps that you were born to die	955	Juan 14	19

DIED

Or gazing o'er the plains where Greek and Persian died	34	Harold 2	872
What deeds of prowess unrecorded died	42	Harold 3	434
And then she died on him she could not save	45	Harold 3	632
Watering tne heart whose early flowers have died	56	Harold 4	44
They keep his dust in Arqua where he died	59	Harold 4	271
How lived, how loved, how died she? Was she not	70	Harold 4	897
Perchance she died in youth: it may be, bow'd	70	Harold 4	910
Perchance she died in age--surviving all	70	Harold 4	919
Thus much alone we know--Metella died	70	Harold 4	926
Has died into an echo; it is fit	82	Harold 4	1658
How you fought, how you died, still her annals can tell	86	Leaving NA	16
'When Oscar left my hall, or died	104	Alva	207
With him our fast-reviving hopes have died	114	Death-A	22
She died, but ne'er will die again	128	Answer-B	24
Lochlin: he died with gloomy Orla, the chief	130	Calmar	79
A Fabius and some noble Roman died	143	Soliloquy	82
I died: let earth my bones resign	154	Skull	6
But lives, as saints have died, a martyr	159	Spell	8
If thou hadst died as honour dies	181	Ode-A	95
And, if a mortal, had as proudly died	181	Ode-A	144
Died, and their bones were tombless as their flesh	189	Darkness	45
Which answer'd not with a caress--he died	189	Darkness	54
Each other's aspects--saw, and shriek'd, and died	190	Darkness	66
Even of their mutual hideousness they died	190	Darkness	67
He died before my day of Sextonship	190	Churchill	13
A deathless part of him who died too soon	193	Monody	32
He in the thickest battle died	201	Ode-C	43
Thy Lover died, as All	201	Ode-C	59
How much died with him! false or true--the dream	205	Aristomenes	5
And forget not I smiled as I died	218	Jephtha	20
In our souls, as the wind that hath died on the hill	223	Valley	6
Some say she died a Papist; Some	231	Doctor	71
Cato died for his country, so didst thou	238	Epigrams	2
If Jeffrey died, except within her arms	248	Bards	479
Who lived and died as none can live or die	268	Minerva	32

DIED

Died George the Third; although no tyrant, one	285	Vision	58
He died--but left his subjects still behind	286	Vision	63
He died!--his death made no great stir on earth	286	Vision	65
You turn'd to half a courtier ere you died	293	Vision	570
For Courtesy and Pity died	313	Giaour	346
Yet died he by a stranger's hand	317	Giaour	735
Yet died he as in arms he stood	317	Giaour	737
Though better to have died with those	320	Giaour	1002
'Twas shed for her who died for me	320	Giaour	1034
She died--I dare not tell thee how	320	Giaour	1056
He died too in the battle broil	321	Giaour	1080
For him who dies, but her who died	321	Giaour	1122
To bless his memory ere I died	322	Giaour	1241
All, one by one, have died away	329	Abydos	2	60
Who lived and died as none can live or die	356	Corsair	3	32
All lost--that softness died not, but it slept	357	Corsair	3	98
It was enough--she died--what reck'd it how	365	Corsair	3	625
The young forgot him, and the old had died	366	Lara	1	36
Some half-form'd threat in utterance there had died	369	Lara	1	219
The captive died upon the battle-plain	379	Lara	2	273
But where he died his grave was dug as deep	382	Lara	2	521
In the year since Jesus died for men	384	Corinth	1
Than his, Minotti's son, who died	393	Corinth	811
'Oh God! when died she?'--'Yesternight	394	Corinth	861
Had died or gain'd her liberty	398	Parisina	170
Yet would I that I then had died	399	Parisina	306
He died, as erring man should die	401	Parisina	462
At least the knight's who died that day	401	Parisina	512
She died by tortures less remote	401	Parisina	522
Dying as their father died	402	Chillon	23
When my last brother droop'd and died	403	Chillon	46
But why delay the truth?--he died	404	Chillon	144
He died--and they unlock'd his chain	404	Chillon	149
His own--and died the Russians' slave	407	Mazeppa	24
But on my lips they died again	409	Mazeppa	250
Can die no more than then I died	412	Mazeppa	548
As though their voices with their cause had died	427	Island	3	84
How they had gladly lived and calmly died	433	Island	4	217
And ere the word upon the echo died	434	Island	4	303
Christian died last--twice wounded; and once more	434	Island	4	323
Raphael, who died in thy embrace, and vies	445	Beppo	363
Was crimson'd from his veins who died to save	462	Dante	3	129
They felt, and loved, and died, but would not lend	463	Dante	4	3
So that he swoon'd with pain as if he died	470	Morgante	255
And pagan Passamont died unredeem'd	470	Morgante	276
And died unpardon'd--though he call'd in aid	487	Manfred	2	280
Begun and died upon the gentle wind	495	Manfred	3	279
Wretch! darest thou name my son? He died in arms	508	Faliero	1	585
Would I had died at Zara! There you saved	515	Faliero	2	469
If Brutus had not lived? He died in giving	517	Faliero	2	615
Vault where two Doges rest--my sires! who died	519	Faliero	3	23
Farewell the past! I died to all that had been	525	Faliero	3	468
Alas! I fain you died in peace with me	539	Faliero	5	130
The prince. Thy vile accomplices have died	546	Faliero	5	564
One sovereign only died, and one is dying	548	Faliero	5	715
And died for lack of farther nutriment	555	Sardan	1	318
No--but it had been better to have died	567	Sardan	2	361
Hast died for--our long royalty of race	589	Sardan	5	155
Poor Salemenes! thou hast died in time	592	Sardan	5	297
I have read their epitaph, which says they died	596	Foscari	1	34
Their boys who died in battle, is it written	602	Foscari	2	75
Died suddenly. And if they did so, better	605	Foscari	2	210
And did not they? The grave knows best: they died	605	Foscari	2	213
As died their father. Oh, what best of blessings	618	Foscari	4	210
Of Carmagnuola, eight months ere he died	619	Foscari	4	299
What, if I show to thee things which have died	638	Cain	2	141
Or show the place where strong Despair hath died	660	Heaven	356
Sooner than our white-bearded patriarchs died	667	Heaven	878
Far worse than solitude. Alone, I had died	672	Werner	1	66
Fell sick, almost to death. He should have died	677	Werner	1	407
Proceed. Died he not by your hand? Great God	702	Werner	3	469
Is roused: such is not here the case; he died	703	Werner	3	571
Then grew between them. The late baron died	706	Werner	4	142
He had not died without a friend to soothe	707	Werner	4	183
What? That he died alone. The general rumour	707	Werner	4	185
It loves?--They say he died of a fever. Say	707	Werner	4	192
Though he had not by me or mine, as much	711	Werner	4	444
Yet died without its last and dearest offices	711	Werner	4	465
You said he died in his bed, not battle. He	712	Werner	4	507
Died, I scarce know--but--he was stabb'd i' the dark	712	Werner	4	508
Nearer than Tiber. I have died for Rome	737	Deformed	2	167
Before, unluckily, Don Jose died	751	Juan	1	256
He died: and most unluckily, because	751	Juan	1	257
But, ah! he died; and buried with him lay	751	Juan	1	265
He died of the slow fever call'd the tertian	751	Juan	1	271
Save death or Doctors' Commons--so he died	751	Juan	1	288
And if in the mean time her husband died	757	Juan	1	665
Has madness seized you? would that I had died	764	Juan	1	1131
For David lived, but Juan nearly died	767	Juan	1	1344

DIED

But die, as many an exiled heart hath died	776	Juan	2	139
The creature was his father's dog that died	783	Juan	2	563
He died as born, a Catholic in faith	783	Juan	2	605
And, with hyaena-laughter, died despairing	784	Juan	2	632
But he died early; and when he was gone	785	Juan	2	692
As morning broke, the light wind died away	786	Juan	2	769
Who died two days before, and now had found	788	Juan	2	871
She died, but not alone; she held within	825	Juan	4	553
Thus lived--thus died she; never more on her	825	Juan	4	561
Who lived too long for men, but died too soon	829	Juan	4	819
He died at fifty for a queen of forty	853	Juan	6	33
He died beneath a tree, as much unblest on	871	Juan	7	286
He died, deserving well his country's tears	888	Juan	8	637
Because deform'd, yet died all game and bottom	892	Juan	8	879
In one voluptuous blaze,--and then he died	893	Juan	8	920
Epaminondas saved his Thebes, and died	897	Juan	9	58
Who died in the then great attempt to climb	916	Juan	10	589
A kerchief, crying, 'Give Sal that!'--and died	920	Juan	11	128
Died from the touch that kindled them to sound	986	Juan	16	370

DIEM

But 'carpe diem,' Juan, 'carpe, carpe	929	Juan	11	673

DIES

Without a groan, without a struggle dies	16	Harold	1	787
And the wolf dies in silence,--not bestow'd	58	Harold	4	185
Dies like the dolphin, whom each pang imbues	59	Harold	4	259
And Love, which dies as it was born, in sighing	73	Harold	4	1065
Watch thou, while many a dreaming chieftain dies	108	Nisus	234
He sobs, he dies,--the troop in wild amaze	110	Nisus	353
Nor quits the hero's grasp till Volscens dies	110	Nisus	394
And Nature triumphs as the tyrant dies	121	Newstead-A	104
In her who lives and him who dies	167	Euthanasia	16
If thou hadst died as honour dies	181	Ode-A	95
When all of Genius which can perish dies	192	Monody	22
All stab, and everybody dies	231	Doctor	14
For him who dies, but her who died	321	Giaour	1122
The worm that will not sleep--and never dies	336	Abydos	2	646
The victim's prayer, for if he drinks he dies	351	Corsair	2	323
But he who looks on death--and silent dies	352	Corsair	2	363
His doom is fix'd--he dies: and well his fate	357	Corsair	3	143
Their stepping-stone--the last who dies	387	Corinth	241
Which saw no farther: he who dies	412	Mazeppa	547
Back to a sword, and dies and lives again	427	Island	3	58
Who moves a step against them dies. Hold! hear	522	Faliero	3	214
Of life. The man who dies by the adder's fang	544	Faliero	5	463
If he dies innocent, that is to say	601	Foscari	1	349
And dies. You call this weakness! It is strength	611	Foscari	3	182
Dies with man, and is swallow'd in that deep	662	Heaven	573
What, when a Christian dies? Shall I not offer	737	Deformed	2	142
Or madam dies.'--Alfonso mutter'd, 'D--n her	767	Juan	1	1301
Of us dies with them as each fond hope ends	776	Juan	2	166
Ah! surely nothing dies but something mourns	816	Juan	3	960
Against the light wherein she dies: he clung	893	Juan	8	940
While the mild emerald's beam shades down the dies	930	Juan	12	63

DIET

But peace to her, her emperor and diet	274	Waltz	55
How nobly gave he the Poles their Diet	304	Age	446
And (save debates in Warsaw's diet	408	Mazeppa	135
To lose their lives, as well as spoil their diet	778	Juan	2	260
And being consumptive, live on a milk diet	973	Juan	15	328

DIETH

May the worm which ne'er dieth feed upon them	617	Foscari	4	174
Eternal, and the worm which dieth not	711	Werner	4	462
Save the worm which dieth not	729	Deformed	1	467

DIETY

See DEMI-DIETY

DIFFER

But wherein do they differ? I speak not	494	Manfred	3	218
Enough?--why should ye differ? We both reign	645	Cain	2	597
Above his outward fortunes. There I differ	677	Werner	4	400
Differ, except in robbing with a bow	920	Juan	11	116
That manners hardly differ more than dress	953	Juan	13	752
They differ as wine differs from its label	969	Juan	15	45

DIFFERENCE

Well doth the Spanish hind the difference know	9	Harold	1	376
Ask'st thou the difference? From fair Phyles' towers	270	Minerva	129
Mourns o'er the difference of now and then	271	Minerva	189
To be sure makes a difference. I know what is what	279	Blues	1	112
Our difference is political, and I	292	Vision	493
The only difference known between the cases	447	Beppo	447
I think so. For the difference in our years	514	Faliero	2	367
Oh God! the difference 'twixt those hours and this	531	Faliero	4	207

DIFFERENCE

There's only one slight difference between   771 Juan   1 1609
Such difference doth a few months make. You'd
  think   908 Juan   10   53
By turns the difference of the several sexes   964 Juan   14   579
The difference is, that in the days of old   971 Juan   15   201
Nor would be thus:--the difference in them   975 Juan   15   463
There is a difference, says the song, 'between   991 Juan   16   713
A difference ''twixt a bishop and a dean   991 Juan   16   717
A difference between crockery ware and plate   991 Juan   16   718
Upon the whole is greater than the difference   991 Juan   16   722

DIFFERENCES

They had their little differences, too   446 Beppo   420

DIFFERENT

Were they but so in man's, how different were
  his doom   68 Harold   4   774
For all are meteors with a different name   73 Harold   4 1115
How different now thy joyless fate   89 Prometheus-A   9
How different is my love from thine   91 Caroline-B   27
Far different incense now ascends to heaven   120 Newstead-A   79
Whose soul a different hope supplies   132 Prayer   27
Now flow in different channels   137 Clare   33
As bad--but in a different way   163 Malta   24
How different now thou meet'st my gaze   166 Struggle   43
You know, we are used to quite different graces   228 Moore-A   19
Each tugs it a different way   237 Hay   3
Yet his and Phillips' faults, of different kind   262 Hints   389
There would have been a different tale to tell   287 Vision   162
A Spirit of a different aspect waved   288 Vision   186
The world and he both wore a different form   290 Vision   332
Our different parties make us fight so shy   292 Vision   491
A different web being by the Destinies   298 Vision   830
Though wild, as now, far different were the tale   356 Corsair   3   73
Or else a different lot were mine   411 Mazeppa   486
And follow different courses o'er the tide   429 Island   3   234
But, ah, how different! 'tis the cause makes all   433 Island   4   261
Spring from a different theme!--Ye see and read   453 Venice-B   78
Through all the different periods of my days   472 Morgante   380
Your feelings now are of a different kind   511 Faliero   2   204
But had a different husband, any husband   513 Faliero   2   276
Each at their different place of rendezvous   524 Faliero   3   363
March on Saint Mark's! And there?--By different
  routes   524 Faliero   3   370
Your lot be different, I'll not weep, but share
  it   586 Sardan   4   494
So different in their births, tongues, sexes,
  natures   591 Sardan   5   232
They work by different means to the same end   603 Foscari   2   89
'Twas fit that some one of such different
  thoughts   622 Foscari   5   128
As of a different order in the sphere   660 Heaven   413
Shall be amongst your race in different forms   661 Heaven   480
Kindness was taught a different lesson. Father   682 Werner   1   731
And out of them, it is a different thing   699 Werner   3   256
Where different talents find their different
  marts   762 Juan   1 1022
Perhaps 'twas in a different way applied   767 Juan   1 1343
For sailors are, in fact, a different kind   777 Juan   2   205
Her dress was very different from the Spanish   789 Juan   2   954
Pieced out for different marts in the Levant   803 Juan   3   130
Of velvet panels, each of different hue   809 Juan   3   506
And knew the self-loves of the different nations   811 Juan   3   666
He gave the different nations something national   812 Juan   3   674
That each pull'd different ways with many an oath   828 Juan   4   743
Bought up for different purposes and passions   830 Juan   4   904
Like flowers of different hue, and clime, and
  root   860 Juan   6   514
But certes matters took a different face   873 Juan   7   369
Were all deflower'd by different grenadiers   895 Juan   8 1040
Just now yours were cut out in different sections   904 Juan   9   517
You'll find it of a different construction   941 Juan   12   691
With more ease too she'd tell a different story   957 Juan   14   104
In England ranks quite on a different list   963 Juan   14   478
But though the flower is different, with the
  French   965 Juan   14   599
The same self-interest, with a different leaning   990 Juan   16   608

DIFFERENTLY

And judge of it far differently from those   522 Faliero   3   266
How differently the world would men behold   968 Juan   14   804

DIFFERETH

Think how your essence differeth from theirs   667 Heaven   868

DIFFERING

A fellow-feeling, differing but in name   358 Corsair   3   203
Their stature, differing but in sex and years   822 Juan   4   354
All ragamuffins differing but in hue   833 Juan   5   99
Though differing in stature and degree   857 Juan   6   318

DIFFERS

Though modern practice sometimes differs quite   263 Hints   491

DIFFERS

They differ as wine differs from its label   969 Juan   15   45

DIFFICULT

Though perhaps 'twere no difficult task to
  confute it   145 Casuists   6
And not a whit more difficult to damn   286 Vision   115
The difficult air of the iced mountain's top   485 Manfred   2   157
Old man! 'tis not so difficult to die   497 Manfred   3   411
Tasks not less difficult--achieved for them   504 Faliero   1   301
But never difficult. And do you love him   510 Faliero   2   92
Alike made difficult; but I have such   596 Foscari   1   43
Let him partake it! That were difficult   613 Foscari   3   307
Being gone, 'twill be less difficult to die   667 Heaven   943
No difficult access to any. Good sir   683 Werner   2   39
To all my plans. It will be difficult   705 Werner   4   100
Then you are far more difficult to please   725 Deformed   1   198
No. As you leave me choice, I am difficult   726 Deformed   1   241
Of gaining, or--what is more difficult   741 Deformed   2   421
But very difficult, to shut their eyes   759 Juan   1   840
With Crabbe it may be difficult to cope   772 Juan   1 1637
'Twas difficult to get out such provision   779 Juan   2   363
Nothing so difficult as a beginning   816 Juan   4   1
It difficult to shun some strange mistakes   874 Juan   7   456
Who took by turns that difficult command   902 Juan   9   365
He'll find it rather difficult some day   925 Juan   11   459
Which it were rather difficult to prove   931 Juan   12   99
But thou art the most difficult to rhyme at   932 Juan   12   189
For then they are very difficult to stop   944 Juan   13   176
Forms the most difficult in punctuation   951 Juan   13   642
Is difficult. Pray tell me, can you make fast   955 Juan   14   11
But even this is difficult, Heaven knows   958 Juan   14   194
Though certainly more difficult to rhyme at   959 Juan   14   228
With sloth hath found it difficult to dwell   965 Juan   14   646
The third is still more difficult to stand to   970 Juan   15   165
A situation difficult, I ween   977 Juan   15   595
So very difficult, they say, it is   978 Juan   15   645
'Twere difficult to say what was the object   987 Juan   16   449
Perhaps these are most difficult to tame   989 Juan   16   550
'Twere difficult to say; but Juan look'd   998 Juan   17   106

DIFFICULTIES

A few hours' start, the difficulties will be   698 Werner   3   199
The present difficulties of our house   698 Werner   3   242
She now conceived all difficulties past   846 Juan   5   922
All difficulties, whether great or small   959 Juan   14   237
Some difficulties, as in his own preference   972 Juan   15   237

DIFFICULTY

One difficulty still remain'd--his hair   841 Juan   5   625
And every difficulty being dispell'd   873 Juan   7   405
The difficulty lies in colouring   971 Juan   15   197

DIFFIDENT

To the performer's diffident confusion   986 Juan   16   376

DIFFUSE

O'er her wild universe is skilful to diffuse   56 Harold   4   54
Their magical variety diffuse   59 Harold   4   256
The varied marble's veins diffuse   395 Corinth   970
Who to diffuse his glory were inclined   466 Morgante   30

DIFFUSED

And its dew is diffused in a Tear   115 The Tear   12
And woo'd the freshness Night diffused   388 Corinth   425

DIFFUSING

And thus becomes so in diffusing Joy   634 Cain   1   477

DIG

And dig the source of future tears   146 Vain Lady   4
Who dig no land for tyrants but their graves   378 Lara   2   219
Graves! If I thought so, this good sword should
  dig   568 Sardan   2   423
Placed him to dig, but not divide the wealth   583 Sardan   4   348
And dig, and sweat, and turn themselves about   901 Juan   9   315

DIGEST

Thou wouldst digest what some call treason, and   567 Sardan   2   363
Because he could no more digest his dinner   900 Juan   9   264

DIGESTION

I wish to the gods 'twas the same with digestion   283 Blues   2   161
And gentle when digestion may permit   305 Age   525
Beef, veal, and mutton, better for digestion   782 Juan   2   536
Or, if it were, if also his digestion   835 Juan   5   234
But would much rather have a sound digestion   898 Juan   9   109
And with it all the process of digestion   909 Juan   10   112
And eats her parents, albeit the digestion   955 Juan   14   10

DIGGING

And I had not the digging of this grave   190 Churchill   14
In digging up your bones, Tom Paine   235 Paine   1
Or digging in the Hunnish mines in fetters   543 Faliero   5   375

DIGGING

There, breathless, with his digging nails he clung	787 Juan	2	857
In digging the foundation of a closet	813 Juan	3	807

DIGNIFIED

By danger dignified, yet guiltless; hopes	484 Manfred	2	68
Of his wife's dignified but foreign aspect	687 Werner	2	276

DIGNIFY

And whether coldness, pride, or virtue dignify	962 Juan	14	455

DIGNIFYING

Laocoon's torture dignifying pain	79 Harold	4	1433

DIGNITIES

Aside the dignities which I have borne	523 Faliero	3	343

DIGNITY

Might well itself be deem'd of dignity	27 Harold	2	436
Monarchs partook, and deem'd their dignity increased	55 Harold	4	18
These hills seem things of lesser dignity	66 Harold	4	664
Folding his robe in dying dignity	68 Harold	4	779
And what dignity decks the flat face of the great man	227 Moore-A		16
Without their decent dignity of fall	301 Age		240
Your office, and its dignity and duty	501 Faliero	1	126
To virtue in your sex, and dignity	512 Faliero	2	258
Thou hast forgot thy dignity in deigning	546 Faliero	5	561
But for my dignity--I hold it of	621 Foscari	5	55
His dignity is look'd to, his estate	622 Foscari	5	122
His own high dignity before his country	623 Foscari	5	182
And though her dignity brook'd no complaining	913 Juan	10	374
And dignity with courtesy so blending	993 Juan	16	804

DIGRESS

But from the Drama let me not digress	260 Hints		263
But I digress: of all appeals,--although	837 Juan	5	385

DIGRESSING

But I'm digressing; what on earth has Nero	816 Juan	3	969

DIGRESSION

My muse admires digression	138 Clare		72
Digression is a sin, that by degrees	446 Beppo		394
If I have any fault, it is digression	814 Juan	3	858
Oh, pardon my digression--or at least	934 Juan	12	305
I'm 'at my old lunes'--digression, and forget	942 Juan	13	89

DIGRESSIONS

And scarce secure, as such digressions are fair	867 Juan	6	959
Since with digressions we too long have tarried	978 Juan	15	669

DIGS

And Vice, that digs her own voluptuous tomb	17 Harold	1	824

DILATE

Till, growing with its growth, we thus dilate	78 Harold	4	1421
Its glance dilate o'er all to be	220 Clay		22
And every passion into one dilate	437 Tasso		62
That large black prophet eye seem'd to dilate	819 Juan	4	169

DILATED

His angry tail; red rolls his eye's dilated glow	16 Harold	1	755
The circling white dilated grew	400 Parisina		333
Dilated from its symmetry; her lips	577 Sardan	3	391
Let each breathing heart dilated	736 Deformed	2	119
Her eye dilated and her colour heighten'd	861 Juan	6	576
Upon each other, with dilated glance	890 Juan	8	762

DILATES

To follow half on which the eye dilates	7 Harold	1	239
Nods to the storm--dilates and dotes o'er thee	459 Dante	2	65

DILATING

The flash of that dilating eye	318 Giaour		834

DILETTANTI

Of Dardan tours let dilettanti tell	256 Bards		1033
As well as dilettanti in war's art	872 Juan	7	309
And no great dilettanti in topography	887 Juan	8	590
What dilettanti do with vast parade	986 Juan	16	395

DILIGENCE

It might be seen, with diligence was sought	845 Juan	5	899

DILIGENTLY

Of genius quick, and diligently steady	466 Morgante		35

DILUTES

Dilutes with drivel every drizzly brain	270 Minerva		140

DIM

And tuned his farewell in the dim twilight	5 Harold	1	114
But as he gazed on truth his aching eyes grew dim	8 Harold	1	323
Dim with the mist of years, gray flits the shade of power	19 Harold	2	18
Of mighty shadows, whose dim forms despond	55 Harold	4	30
O'er the dim fragments cast a lunar light	67 Harold	4	719
Dim o'er the bird of darkness' native site	71 Harold	4	950
There is a dungeon, in whose dim drear light	77 Harold	4	1324
And spreads the dim and universal pall	79 Harold	4	1479
Though a tear dim his eye at this sad separation	86 Leaving NA		25
Seest thou yon camp, with torches twinkling dim	105 Nisus		25
And hostile life-drops dim my gory spear	106 Nisus		48
of the dark brow." Why should tears dim	130 Calmar		80
dim with the gore of my father. The blood	130 Calmar		119
Dim in the cloud, or darkling in the storm	182 Address-C		26
Were his borrow'd glories dim	187 French-A		27
And the shorn Sun grew dim in air	188 On Star		17
Through life's dull road, so dim and dirty	236 Dull Road		1
Of passion?'--'Passion!' cried the phantom dim	295 Vision		663
And she--the dim and melancholy star	345 Corsair	1	511
The sun goes forth, but Conrad's day is dim	365 Corsair	3	656
Through the dim lattice o'er the floor of stone	368 Lara	1	192
His lip resumes its red; his eye, though dim	369 Lara	1	227
The long dim shadows of surrounding trees	370 Lara	1	263
Guides with her star their dim and torchless flight	379 Lara	2	321
Perchance 'twas but the moon's dim twilight threw	380 Lara	2	350
Save that pale aspect, where the eye, though dim	381 Lara	2	430
And dull the film along his dim eye grew	382 Lara	2	491
He felt how faint and feebly dim	388 Corinth		396
Dim with a dull imprison'd ray	403 Chillon		30
The darkness of my dim abode	406 Chillon		360
The sky was dull, and dim, and gray	411 Mazeppa		439
My sight return'd, though dim, alas	412 Mazeppa		577
In the dim waste would indicate	413 Mazeppa		615
And my dim eyes of death had need	414 Mazeppa		766
Echoed their dim light to the mustering stars	424 Island	2	401
The dim, though large-eyed winged anchorite	424 Island	2	426
His constant pipe, which never yet burn'd dim	425 Island	2	475
And dim the little light that's left behind	437 Tasso		71
Still in these dim old eyes, now overwrought	456 Dante	1	31
With dim sepulchral light, bid me forget	458 Dante	2	17
So as his dim desires to recognise	476 Francesca		24
The dazzling lightnings till my eyes grew dim	486 Manfred	2	166
Of dim and solitary loveliness	495 Manfred	3	266
Where sleep my fathers, whose dim statues shadow	519 Faliero	3	16
Bestriding a proud steed, in the dim light	520 Faliero	3	88
Flung over these dim words engraved beneath	545 Faliero	5	499
Frowns as the shadows of the evening dim	570 Sardan	2	533
With one foot in the grave, with dim eyes, strange	603 Foscari	2	109
To right, as in the dim blue air the eye	635 Cain	1	491
In the dim twilight, brighter than yon world	637 Cain	2	125
How silent and how vast are these dim worlds	639 Cain	2	206
The tree was true, though deadly. These dim realms	641 Cain	2	372
Seems dim and shadowy. Be content; it will	642 Cain	2	381
Is the dim and remote companion, in	644 Cain	2	567
Share the dim destiny of clay in this	656 Heaven		89
Shakes them no more in their dim disbelief	662 Heaven		546
Making my dim existence radiant with	664 Heaven		704
Leaving the archangels at his right hand dim	666 Heaven		845
Through the dim Gothic glass by pious aid	697 Werner	3	114
Dim with brave knights and holy hermits, whose	697 Werner	3	121
A maze hath my dim destiny involved me	697 Werner	3	146
When the dim eye rolls vainly round for what	707 Werner	4	191
In these dim days of heresies and blood	711 Werner	4	457
Have seen else on this side of the dim shore	726 Deformed	1	243
And raise, and wring their dim and death-like hands	733 Deformed	1	766
'Tis the morn, but dim and dark	735 Deformed	2	1
Their herald out of dim December	742 Deformed	3	18
Dim image of war	742 Deformed	3	43
And, lighted at too pure a shrine to dim its	757 Juan	1	645
And the dim desolate deep: twelve days had Fear	780 Juan	2	391
Forsook the dim eyes of these shipwreck'd men	785 Juan	2	728
For his congealing blood, and senses dim	788 Juan	2	884
Circling all nature, hush'd, and dim, and still	797 Juan	2	1460
Her eye might flash on his, but found it dim	828 Juan	4	755
There was deep silence in the chamber: dim	860 Juan	6	505
Just when the fading lamps waned dim and blue	861 Juan	6	557
The stars peep through the vapours dim and dank	878 Juan	7	686
And the sad, second moon grows dim again	892 Juan	8	900
And throwing back a dim look on his sons	893 Juan	8	943
The stars, I own my telescope is dim	907 Juan	10	26
Who, though her spectacles at last grew dim	911 Juan	10	270
But when she saw his dazzling eye wax dim	913 Juan	10	349
When even the sea looks dim with all its spray	959 Juan	14	219
And now and then a nightingale) is dim	980 Juan	15	770
But by dim lights the portraits of the dead	982 Juan	16	135

DIMINISH

Distance can but diminish glory--they	643 Cain	2	452

DIMINISH'D
If once diminish'd   200 Stanzas-B   58
O'er hoards diminish'd by young Hopeful's debts   260 Hints   256
Diminish'd, dwindled to a very speck   435 Island   4   386

DIMITY
A prodigy--her morning dress was dimity   748 Juan   1   94
No matter whether russet, silk, or dimity   958 Juan   14   208

DIMLY
Would twinkle dimly through their sphere   97 To M--   28
And dimly twinkles o'er the watery plain   122 Recoll   20
The fogs of London, through which, dimly beacon'd 291 Vision   438
Dimly I view its trembling spark   322 Giaour   1277
That brazen lamp but dimly threw   330 Abydos   2   118

DIMLY-LATTICED
Those vast and dimly-latticed galleries   528 Faliero   4   32

DIMM'D
Is dimm'd for a time with a Tear   114 The Tear   8
Dimm'd in the lamp, as loth to break the night   369 Lara   1   202
Speak it, 'twill lighten thy dimm'd mind.
  Methought   579 Sardan   4   67
Beyond its dimm'd eye's sphere,--but would much
  rather   908 Juan   10   47

DIMMEST
The dimmest in the district's map, exist   682 Werner   1   702

DIMNESS
In envious dimness pass'd thy portrait by   183 Address-D   48
Faints into dimness with its own delight   325 Abydos   1   173
As they seem, through the dimness, about to come
  down   391 Corinth   624

DIMPLE
The lips may beguile with a dimple or smile   114 The Tear   3
Whose wishes dimple in a modest smile   119 Answer-A   28

DIMPLED
A dimpled chin, a neck of ivory, stole   996 Juan   16   1027

DIMPLES
Those rosy lips, whose dimples play   150 My Son   3
Into half a dozen dimples   234 Silver   3

DIMPLING
The seal Love's dimpling finger hath impress'd   13 Harold   1   594
That cheek, which ever dimpling glows   87 Ad Lesbiam   5
He in dimpling smiles appears   100 Marion   7
There, mildly dimpling, Ocean's cheek   310 Giaour   12

DIMS
Dims the green beauties of thine Attic plain   31 Harold   2   705
And careless eye the blood that dims its shine   338 Corsair   1   50

DIM-TWINKLES
blaze of oak dim-twinkles through the night   130 Calmar   99

DIN
Hush'd is the din of tongues; on gallant steeds   15 Harold   1   729
The hoarse command, the busy humming din   22 Harold   2   156
But from the chambers came the mingling din   28 Harold   2   539
Thou who beheldest, 'mid the assassins' din   68 Harold   4   777
And hear the din of arms no more   101 Alva   4
Thy heart beats fiercely to the din of arms   106 Nisus   54
Shakes with the martial music's novel din   120 Newstead-A   50
The din of arms came to the ear of Fingal   131 Calmar   145
Unscared by all the din of Melbourne house   256 Bards   1045
Invited Conrad's bugle, and the din   349 Corsair   2   187
And thunder-like the pealing din   386 Corinth   163
Heard through Cain's silence, and o'er Glory's
  din   417 Island   1   122
In public by a scene, nor raise a din   451 Beppo   718
And if, Cassandra-like, amidst the din   458 Dante   2   10
Apart; her voice that clove through all the din   577 Sardan   3   392
With all its elements! Heed not their din   669 Heaven   1084
But without there is a din   735 Deformed   2   7
That all is settled:--there was little din   874 Juan   7   430
The very cannon, deafen'd by the din   885 Juan   8   469
Smoking his pipe quite calmly 'midst the din   890 Juan   8   780
Were also heard to wonder in the din   895 Juan   8   1050
Your heart joins chorus, Fame is but a din   900 Juan   9   272
A jargon, a mere philanthropic din   918 Juan   10   678

DINDON
Relieved with 'dindon a la Parigeux   976 Juan   15   500

DINE
Shall Grub-street dine, while duns are kept aloof 249 Bards   547
Be call'd to labour when he thinks to dine   266 Hints   705
I thank you; not any more, sir, till I dine   283 Blues   2   143
A propos--Do you dine with Sir Humphry to-day   283 Blues   2   144

DINE
Would rather dine in sin on a ragout   441 Beppo   70
Dine and be d--d! I don't mean to be coarse   441 Beppo   71
I also like to dine on becaficas   445 Beppo   337
On what, in fact, next day were they to dine   782 Juan   2   548
Dine with them on his pastor and his master   784 Juan   2   624
'Tis surely fair to dine upon our friends   784 Juan   2   662
Small social parties just begun to dine   805 Juan   3   242
Kept for all comers at all hours to dine   810 Juan   3   552
Turkey contains no bells, and yet men dine   837 Juan   5   393
I've done. Now go and dine from off the plate   897 Juan   9   41
With those who, Pope says, 'greatly daring dine   947 Juan   13   422
Your stomach! Ere you dine, the French will do   977 Juan   15   572
On them and bread 'twas oft my luck to dine   977 Juan   15   581
For man therein, with eyes and heart, to dine   977 Juan   15   596

DINED
When he dined on some homicides done in ragout   176 Devil's Dr   3
But where's the monarch? hath he dined? or yet   305 Age   502
They roar'd, they dined, they drank, they swore
  they meant   306 Age   622
Who on the very loftiest kings have dined   854 Juan   6   101
And having voted, dined, drunk, gamed, and whored 927 Juan   11   591
With dandies dined; heard senators declaiming   957 Juan   14   139
The diners of celebrity dined well   977 Juan   15   554
But I have dined, and must forego, alas   977 Juan   15   567

DINER
A brilliant diner out, though but a curate   991 Juan   16   698

DINERS
The diners of celebrity dined well   977 Juan   15   554

DINES
She dines from off the plate she lately wash'd   208 Sketch   8
A party dines with me to-day   231 Doctor   59
And (except with his publisher) dines where he
  pleases   283 Blues   2   149
Weep to perceive him mourning, as he dines   299 Age   59

DINGY
The dingy denizens are rear'd in dirt   7 Harold   1   230

DINING
What with driving and visiting, dancing and
  dining   280 Blues   2   8
Receipts in full, began to think of dining   835 Juan   5   232

DINN'D
And dinn'd, and deafen'd with dead men and Baal   566 Sardan   2   250

DINNER
While seated after dinner at his ease   748 Juan   1   45
He also found that he had lost his dinner   758 Juan   1   752
Achilles ordered dinner for new comers   789 Juan   2   984
The happiest mortals even after dinner   806 Juan   3   282
Advancing to the nearest dinner tray   806 Juan   3   329
(Provided they don't come in after dinner   808 Juan   3   474
The dinner made about a hundred dishes   809 Juan   3   489
Sell flesh and blood. When dinner has opprest
  one   835 Juan   5   238
Because he could no more digest his dinner   900 Juan   9   264
Of doors 'gainst duns, and to an early dinner   922 Juan   11   228
Then dress, then dinner, then awakes the world   926 Juan   11   521
As thus: 'On Thursday there was a grand dinner   947 Juan   13   425
Who loved philosophy and a good dinner   952 Juan   13   690
Since Eve ate apples, much depends on dinner   953 Juan   13   792
He did not fall asleep just after dinner   960 Juan   14   288
The silvery bell rang, not for 'dinner ready   975 Juan   15   486
The dinner and the soiree too were done   981 Juan   16   57
Dully past o'er the dinner of the day   992 Juan   16   737
Delighted with their dinner and their host   994 Juan   16   855

DINNER-BELL
The tocsin of the soul--the dinner-bell   837 Juan   5   392
No more on this--the dinner-bell hath rung   990 Juan   16   663

DINNERS
And nightly smiles, and daily dinners   163 Malta   29
With dinners, where he oft became the laugh of
  them   452 Beppo   783
Hot suppers, dinners (fitting other places   475 Morgante   627
You may see such at all the balls and dinners   938 Juan   12   525
And diplomatic dinners, or at other   944 Juan   13   186
More with these dinners than the kill'd or
  wounded   947 Juan   13   424
Of modern dinners? where more mystery lurks   976 Juan   15   494
Gone to where victories must like dinners go   976 Juan   15   533

DINNER'S
Was rung by dinner's knell; till then all were   954 Juan   13   818

DINT
Wide-scatter'd hoof-marks dint the wounded ground 12 Harold   1   515

DINT

Nor dint of hoof, nor print of foot	413 Mazeppa		658
Which deepen'd now and then the sandy dint	427 Island	3	95
You--Gentlemen! by dint of long seclusion	745 Juan	Ded	33
And now, by dint of fingers and of eyes	794 Juan	2	1297
Do just whate'er they please, by dint of features	892 Juan	8	888
To those who, by the dint of glass and vapour	907 Juan	10	22
Her way back to the world by dint of plottery	951 Juan	13	654

DINTED

Her helm was dinted, and the broken lance	269 Minerva		81
There's blood upon that dinted sword	320 Giaour		1032
Deeply dinted in the clay	396 Corinth		1055

DINTS

They found the scatter'd dints of many a scar	383 Lara	2	542

DIOGENES

Like stern Diogenes to mock at men	41 Harold	3	368
I am Diogenes, though Russ and Hun	304 Age		476
But were I not Diogenes, I'd wander	304 Age		478
Nor even Diogenes.--We live and die	867 Juan	7	31
But London's so well lit, that if Diogenes	922 Juan	11	217
On Sunium or Hymettus, like Diogenes	977 Juan	15	583

DIP

They would not dip their souls at once in blood	416 Island	1	79
Rather than dip my hands in holy blood	575 Sardan	3	274

DIPLOMATIC

A half-way house of diplomatic rest	844 Juan	5	834
Their dirty diplomatic hands, to vent	850 Juan	5	1205
The import of this diplomatic phrase	902 Juan	9	386
Don Juan, our young diplomatic sinner	922 Juan	11	230
(The den of many a diplomatic lost lie	922 Juan	11	246
And diplomatic dinners, or at other	944 Juan	13	186

DIPLOMATICAL

It chanced some diplomatical relations	943 Juan	13	113

DIPLOMATIST

Turns a diplomatist of great eclat	308 Age		717
Both to the duchess and diplomatist	963 Juan	14	474

DIPLOMATISTS

Diplomatists of rather wavering kings	923 Juan	11	315
But speakers, bards, diplomatists, and dancers	993 Juan	16	827

DIPP'D

Sons that were unborn, when dipp'd	393 Corinth		798
That I had dipp'd the pen without effect	601 Foscari	2	8
High dash'd the spray, the bows dipp'd in the sea	915 Juan	10	508

DIPS

To some she curtsies, and to some she dips	448 Beppo		516

DIPT

Flash'd the dipt oars, and, sparkling with the stroke	346 Corsair	1	571
I dipt thee not in Styx; and 'gainst a foe	737 Deformed	2	191
May pause in pondering how all souls are dipt	903 Juan	9	436

DIRE

Is the dread sceptre and dominion dire	19 Harold	2	7
With him the same dire fate attending Rome	93 Masters		15
Say, what dire penance can atone	99 Young Lady		17
Denouncing dire reproach to luckless fools	111 Examination		7
By dire reviewers should be branded	137 Clare		47
And dooms them to a dire disgrace	141 Critics		44
Each course enough? or doctors dire dissuaded	305 Age		509
Dire was the scuffle, and out went the light	769 Juan	1	1465

DIRECT

But these with slower steps direct their way	124 Recoll		133
There must thou soon direct thy flight	146 Adieu		103
Whose judging voice and eye alone direct	170 Address-A		54
Two Jews--but not Samaritans--direct	307 Age		690
Upon its steel direct my blade	331 Abydos	2	190
Where'er your highness pleases to direct me	508 Faliero	1	595
Who pride themselves upon it; but direct me	587 Sardan	4	567
Direct your questions to my neighbour there	807 Juan	3	358

DIRECTED
(See also ILL-DIRECTED)

As the abbot had directed, kept the line	469 Morgante		236
By whom you were directed to this waste	475 Morgante		638
As I directed? All, my lord, are ready	491 Manfred	3	4
Let your march be directed, every sixty	524 Faliero	3	371
As I directed: and by his best speed	708 Werner	4	279

DIRECTION

Right and wrong which I lack for my direction	568 Sardan	2	381
In all things your direction. I would have	698 Werner	3	215
The inhibited direction: I must on	701 Werner	3	409
According to direction, then received	775 Juan	2	66

DIRECTION

Makes that of multitudes take one direction	873 Juan	7	378
You need not take them under your direction	897 Juan	9	54
And sent the doctors in a new direction	912 Juan	10	340
Direction be, so 'tis but in a hurry	916 Juan	10	572

DIRECTIONS

I have, in all directions, over Prague	713 Werner	5	4

DIRECTLY

She order'd him directly to be bought	846 Juan	5	907

DIRECTOR
(See SELF-DIRECTOR)

DIRECTS

Quick to my gate directs his course	88 Anacreon-B		9
The guardian seraph who directs thy fate	94 Dorset		111
And through the street directs his course	194 Ballad-A		12
A wisdom in the spirit, which directs	635 Cain	1	490

DIRGE

Yelling their uncouth dirge, long daunced the kirtled clan	30 Harold	2	639
Shrieking their dirge, ill-omen'd birds resort	121 Newstead-A		99
To me congenial sounds your wintry Dirge	140 Ossian-A		48
A dirge, an anthem o'er the dead	166 Away		12
Though soft, it seem'd the low prophetic dirge	343 Corsair	1	375
And screaming high their harsh and hungry dirge	435 Island	4	366
What was; no dirge, except the hollow sea's	825 Juan	4	575

DIRGES

Of his quench'd heart; and the sea dirges low	820 Juan	4	270

DIRK

Omitting turban, slippers, pistols, dirk	794 Juan	2	1278

DIRKS

Like men with turbans, scimitars, and dirks	873 Juan	7	418

DIRT
(See also HALF-DIRT)

The dingy denizens are rear'd in dirt	7 Harold	1	230
The blood and dirt of both to mould a George	228 Vaults		10
For deeming human clay but common dirt	874 Juan	7	461

DIRTY

Through life's dull road, so dim and dirty	236 Dull Road		1
To his own dirty views of promotion	239 Bray		27
The dirty language and the noisome jest	262 Hints		395
Because, no doubt, 'twas for his dirty fee	765 Juan	1	1207
From the dull palace to the dirty hovel	799 Juan	2	1607
Their dirty diplomatic hands, to vent	850 Juan	5	1205
And that's the reason he himself's so dirty	909 Juan	10	114
Dirty and dusky, but as wide as eye	917 Juan	10	650
The very clerks,--those somewhat dirty springs	923 Juan	11	317
Mock tyrants, when Rome's annals wax'd but dirty	926 Juan	11	480
O Time! why dost not pause? Thy scythe, so dirty	962 Juan	14	421

DISABLED

And foes disabled in the brutal fray	16 Harold	1	777
Disabled, shorn of half his might and band	358 Corsair	3	167

DISAFFECTION

Some wretch has made thee drunk with disaffection	531 Faliero	4	243

DISAGREEABLE

Wet, still more disagreeable and striking	846 Juan	5	940
Extremely disagreeable, but common	960 Juan	14	343

DISAPPEAR

To shine with splendour, then to disappear	140 Ossian-B		30
Flash forth, then faintly disappear	325 Abydos	1	114
Who menaced but to disappear with light	376 Lara	2	98
His presence? who had made him disappear	377 Lara	2	134
By night, and disappear with sunrise; but	705 Werner	4	52

DISAPPEARANCE

Since his strange disappearance from my father's	673 Werner	1	91
And disappearance of his servants, who	707 Werner	4	186

DISAPPEAR'D

They came like truth, and disappear'd like dreams	56 Harold	4	56
'Let the chamber be clear'd.'--The train disappear'd	324 Abydos	1	32
Then deeply disappear'd. The horseman gazed	383 Lara	2	584
That deadly earth-shock disappear'd	396 Corinth		1058
They are gone! They have disappear'd amidst the roar	669 Heaven		1088
Has disappear'd;--the door unbolted, with	683 Werner	2	38
No heir? Oh, yes; but he has disappear'd	684 Werner	2	82
The strangest is, that he too disappear'd	684 Werner	2	108
The Hungarian! He is gone! he disappear'd	702 Werner	3	495
Quite disappear'd--the gods know how! (I can't	882 Juan	8	243
These last had disappear'd--a loss to art	948 Juan	13	468

DISAPPEARING
Gazing to trace thy disappearing god   562 Sardan   2   38
And follow far the disappearing sun   819 Juan   4   170

DISAPPEARS
Before whose heavenly hues all sorrow disappears   3 To Ianthe   18
And when her beauty disappears, methinks   644 Cain   2   539

DISAPPOINT
A throne too easily--does it disappoint thee   563 Sardan   2   134

DISAPPOINTED
Or disappointed passion lurk'd below   4 Harold   1   67
The old and disappointed maid   92 Lady-A   6
Which springs from disappointed pride   142 Critics   74
Who, disappointed of their former chase   433 Island   4   237
A disappointed courtier--What's the matter   743 Deformed   3   93
At being disappointed in your wish   745 Juan   Ded   18
Was for some rum a disappointed suitor   778 Juan   2   288
Her sale sent home some disappointed bawlers   831 Juan   4   909
Yet disappointed joys are woes as deep   855 Juan   6   156
Till duly disappointed or dismiss'd   990 Juan   16   643

DISAPPOINTMENT
So that some disappointment there ensued   895 Juan   8   1042

DISAPPOINTMENT'S
Warp'd by the world in Disappointment's school   342 Corsair   1   253

DISARM
Binding all things with beauty;--'twould disarm   49 Harold   3   849
For your lip would the soul of suspicion disarm   91 Caroline-C   3
Disarm me: why such craven did I fight   470 Morgante   259
'Let him disarm; or, by my father's head   822 Juan   4   369

DISARM'D
Disarm'd and baffled by your conquering hand   126 Recoll   281
'Tis he indeed, disarm'd but undeprest   351 Corsair   2   286
Once when disarm'd and at my mercy. True   716 Werner   5   213

DISARMS
My constant heart of fear disarms   98 To Mary   3

DISARRAY
A rich confusion form'd a disarray   843 Juan   5   739

DISARRAY'D
The once impervious phalanx disarray'd   303 Age   346

DISASTER
They thought shaving their beards a disaster   232 Murray-B   48
For the poet of pedlers 'twere, sure, no disaster   281 Blues   2   53
Was ever heard of such a curst disaster   763 Juan   1   1091
Even in extremity of their disaster   784 Juan   2   623

DISASTERS
We know what slavery is, and our disasters   834 Juan   5   183

DISASTROUS
Of a most disastrous blow   194 Ballad-A   37
Oh, day disastrous! On her firm-set rock   248 Bards   468

DISAVOW
Nor falsehood disavow   167 Dead   25

DISAVOWAL
From your own lips a disavowal of   692 Werner   2   568

DISAVOW'D
My page, though nameless, never disavow'd   256 Bards   1042
And thus I should be disavow'd   408 Mazeppa   192

DISBANDED
Our standing army, and disbanded seamen   446 Beppo   385
Disbanded soldiers, discontented ruffians   531 Faliero   4   227
To risk his life and honours with disbanded   685 Werner   2   131

DISBELIEF
Shakes them no more in their dim disbelief   662 Heaven   546

DISBELIEVED
Nor wholly disbelieved: men know as little   598 Foscari   1   184

DISBURSEMENTS
Whose avarice all disbursements did importune   906 Juan   9   643

DISCARD
That she'd discard her fav'rite owl   226 Dallas   4

DISCARDED
Alone is aim'd at. But discarded princes   615 Foscari   4   60

DISCERN
And in thy skull discern a deeper hell   245 Bards   282

DISCERN
And gathering loiterers on the land discern   339 Corsair   1   99
Nor common gazers could discern the growth   370 Lara   1   286
From deeds, and deeds alone, may he discern   373 Lara   1   508
Have deeper thoughts than your dull eyes discern   382 Lara   2   533
Could discern their offspring more   395 Corinth   1049
For thence she could discern the ship with ease   443 Beppo   198
I have gain'd the gate, and can discern the Ten   549 Faliero   5   801
I could discern, methought, the assassin's eye   717 Werner   5   267
In thoughts like these true wisdom may discern   758 Juan   1   737

DISCERN'D
Discern'd before the port; form round the palace   524 Faliero   3   375

DISCERNMENT
His just discernment and your own. That's well   699 Werner   3   299
Which show'd what great discernment was the
    donor's   913 Juan   10   368
'Twill teach discernment to the sensitive   961 Juan   14   391

DISCERNS
Far as the eye discerns, withouten end   9 Harold   1   354
Till thee or thine mine evil eye discerns   265 Hints   601

DISCHARGE
More than the mere discharge of public duties   511 Faliero   2   190

DISCIPLE
Next comes the dull disciple of thy school   245 Bards   235
Yea, a disciple that would make the founder   738 Deformed   2   245

DISCIPLES
Were his fairest Disciples Waltzing   179 Devil's Dr   218

DISCIPLINE
To mourn the discipline they late disdain'd   379 Lara   2   313
Roused discipline aloud proclaims their cause   418 Island   1   203
A humbler state and discipline of heart   421 Island   1   192
Did more than Europe's discipline had done   422 Island   2   270
Him, whom the laws of discipline and Venice   505 Faliero   1   369
The secret discipline we need for such   533 Faliero   4   362
Of all who discipline our nations--No   565 Sardan   2   215
A dame who kept up discipline among   856 Juan   6   237
The discipline of the whole haram bore   865 Juan   6   818

DISCIPLINED
However disciplined and debonnaire   940 Juan   12   676

DISCLAIM
Though trusted, thou didst not disclaim me   210 Augusta-B   29
A true-born Briton may the deed disclaim   270 Minerva   126

DISCLOSE
Disclose the dwelling of the mountaineer   25 Harold   2   375
And all its thousand turns disclose   44 Harold   3   528
When all we feel, our honest souls disclose   123 Recoll   61
Ah, heedless girl! why thus disclose   146 Vain Lady   1
Or view, while shadowy auguries disclose   182 Address-C   23
What can his vaulted gallery now disclose   183 Address-D   25
Where it injures to disclose it   197 Rogers   54
To those who watch thee will disclose   200 Ode-C   16
To these should I my birth disclose   331 Abydos   2   272
Yet would I fain, did time allow, disclose   344 Corsair   1   456
That oft awake his aspect could disclose   369 Lara   1   223
I by my faith disclose contentedly   471 Morgante   334
Disclose too much? Disclose too much!--of what   511 Faliero   2   179
What is there to disclose? A heart so ill   511 Faliero   2   180
I will disclose--ensnare--betray--destroy   532 Faliero   4   315
Sleep shows such things, what may not death
    disclose   579 Sardan   4   53
The apparent crimes of the accused disclose   600 Foscari   1   310
Which, if withdrawn, would but disclose the frown   780 Juan   2   387
Beneath his art. The dame, press'd to disclose
    them   903 Juan   9   407
In which Sir Isaac Newton could disclose   907 Juan   10   11

DISCLOSED
Disclosed by the natives of dark Loch na Garr   117 Lachin   16
And how my birth, disclosed to me   331 Abydos   2   224
For him earth now disclosed no other guide   373 Lara   1   526
Disclosed for man to dread or woman weep   418 Island   1   200
Phaedra, and all which story has disclosed   848 Juan   5   1043
Where she then was, as her sound sleep disclosed   862 Juan   6   667
A feeling in each footstep, as disclosed   866 Juan   6   885
Until a royal smile at length disclosed   904 Juan   9   462
And whether it ought not to be disclosed   984 Juan   16   219

DISCLOSES
A summer's sun discloses it. Yon disk   561 Sardan   2   11

DISCLOSING
Disclosing rock and slope and forest brown   22 Harold   2   195

DISCLOSURE
In case of any premature disclosure   866 Juan   6   912

DISCOLOUR'D
Saw the discolour'd Rhine beneath its ruin run   42 Harold   3   441
Discolour'd with a lifeless red   411 Mazeppa   475
All o'er discolour'd by that reading were   477 Francesca   35
As if such useless and discolour'd trash   657 Heaven   193

DISCONSOLATE
Disconsolate will wander up and down   7 Harold   1   227

DISCONTENT
Nor is it discontent to keep the mind   46 Harold   3   655
Their good, ill, health, wealth, joy, or
   discontent   306 Age   630
On her one murmur of his discontent   342 Corsair   1   300
Intemperate triumph fades to discontent   379 Lara   2   308

DISCONTENTED
Change that discontented air   100 Marion   3
Have discontented movements stirr'd the troops   305 Age   506
I know the people to be discontented   504 Faliero   1   327
Are discontented for their long arrears   507 Faliero   1   493
Disbanded soldiers, discontented ruffians   531 Faliero   4   227
From Medes--and discontented troops and nations   558 Sardan   1   518

DISCONTENTS
Of discontents infecting the fair soil   557 Sardan   1   464

DISCORD
When civil discord piled the fields with dead   111 Examination   14
Distraction and discord would follow in course   117 To Eliza   29
Is worse than discord to my heart   166 Away   16
New havoc, such as civil discord blends   377 Lara   2   164
And Doubt and Discord step 'twixt thine and thee   460 Dante   2   140
In discord, cowardice, cruelty, all that springs   465 Dante   4   123
Since there is discord after both at least   873 Juan   7   388

DISCORDANT
But ever twangs the same discordant string   264 Hints   563
As if at table some discordant dish   265 Hints   627
Even the hoarse sea-bird's shrill, discordant
   shriek   364 Corsair   3   561
The oft discordant elements which form   536 Faliero   4   539
Rattles around me her discordant hymn   980 Juan   15   772

DISCORDS
And cannot tune those discords of narration   869 Juan   7   121

DISCORD'S
And one on tithes, which sure are Discord's
   torches   988 Juan   16   524

DISCOUNT
At a sad discount: while your over chilly   854 Juan   6   127
At sight, nor would permit you to discount   904 Juan   9   496
Hawk'd about at a discount, small or large   946 Juan   13   359

DISCOUNTED
To pay, unpaid, protested, or discounted   855 Juan   6   162
Must get itself discounted by a Jew   930 Juan   12   48

DISCOURAGED
Folks are discouraged; and most surely no men   785 Juan   2   741

DISCOURAGING
Discouraging weight upon me, like a mountain   727 Deformed   1   331

DISCOURSE
And, sobbing, thus his first discourse renew'd   107 Nisus   130

DISCOVER
For her each hour new joys discover   113 Quaker   51
Repeat old pastimes and discover new   124 Recoll   128
Why? I really can't discover   197 Rogers   60
Than to see the bright eyes of the dear one
   discover   204 Pisa   11
Is it his bark which my dreary dreams discover   204 Hindoo   3
Then thou wouldst at last discover   207 Fare Thee   11
Thy soft heart refused to discover   210 Augusta-B   3
Remembrance can discover   219 Vanity   10
Except they manage never to discover it   443 Beppo   192
Nor will you napping there discover me   474 Morgante   557
Let me discover--and this steel--Put up   520 Faliero   3   85
Well, but now to discover the delinquent   683 Werner   2   8
Is all he'll have, or wants. If I discover   703 Werner   3   574
The devil's so very sly--she should discover   756 Juan   1   618
Though watchful as the lynx, they ne'er discover   759 Juan   1   794
And make no further noise, till you discover   765 Juan   1   1222
And capabilities, as to discover   834 Juan   5   204
And if they should discover your disguise   843 Juan   5   731
With strict inquiry I could ne'er discover   861 Juan   6   554
Discover stars and sail in the wind's eye   907 Juan   10   23

DISCOVER
Nay, married dames will now and then discover   933 Juan   12   258

DISCOVER'D
Disguised--discover'd--conquering--ta'en--
   condemn'd   352 Corsair   2   389
Discover'd that my love is worth esteem   583 Sardan   4   352
As children at discover'd bugbears   591 Sardan   5   240
Discover'd! then I'll stab--Ah! Josephine   683 Werner   1   736
Remember, I discover'd it by chance   696 Werner   3   84
Would be discover'd in the human soul   968 Juan   14   810
Which he perhaps had not discover'd soon   984 Juan   16   235

DISCOVERERS
Discoverers of new worlds which take their name   461 Dante   3   47

DISCOVERIES
Where all Discoveries jumbled from the flood   246 Bards   353
Discoveries made, but none could be aware   755 Juan   1   539
What opposite discoveries we have seen   762 Juan   1   1025
Declared, with all his grand discoveries recent   867 Juan   7   38
And care but for discoveries and not deeds   940 Juan   12   636

DISCOVERING
Upon a vein of virgin ore, discovering   583 Sardan   4   345
Tiring old readers, nor discovering new   956 Juan   14   78

DISCOVERS
Discovers little silver and less gold   264 Hints   528
Discovers where the Pacha's galleys lay   346 Corsair   1   596
The age discovers he is not the true one   747 Juan   1   4
In which not Envy's self a flaw discovers   749 Juan   1   126
No friend like to a woman earth discovers   967 Juan   14   743

DISCOVERY
(This deep discovery is mine alone   171 Address-B   26
Of me, leaves all discovery far behind   673 Werner   1   110
My soul in part; but how without discovery   701 Werner   3   445
Of a discovery. You are sure you closed it   702 Werner   3   509
Discovery in the act could make me know   719 Werner   5   412
By thy humane discovery, Friar Bacon   882 Juan   8   264
What a sublime discovery 'twas to make the   918 Juan   11   9

DISCOVERY'S
As well as the sublime discovery's date   830 Juan   4   892

DISCREET
To Jeffrey go, be silent and discreet   242 Bards   69
And yawn'd a good deal with discreet surprise   861 Juan   6   584
Albeit my years were less discreet than few   934 Juan   12   300
Own'd to a penchant, though discreet, for beauty   978 Juan   15   680

DISCREETLY
And such besides were too discreetly wise   368 Lara   1   151
Must be postponed discreetly for the present   831 Juan   4   932
This he discreetly kept in the background   865 Juan   6   833

DISCREPANCIES
But of all nature's discrepancies, none   991 Juan   16   721

DISCRETION
Pray, not so fast; you both outrun discretion   291 Vision   402
That they have power to act at their discretion   604 Foscari   2   201
Discretion, and were not so peaceable   751 Juan   1   278
Selected for discretion and devotion   753 Juan   1   434
That Sage (said John) surrenders at discretion   872 Juan   7   350

DISCROWN'D
Seems royal still, though with her head
   discrown'd   80 Harold   4   1501
To Monarchs crown'd, and some discrown'd   197 Duel   16
Discrown'd a prince, cut off his crownless head   544 Faliero   5   448

DISCUSS
Why naughty women--but I won't discuss   448 Beppo   538
'Such things, perhaps, we'd best discuss within   451 Beppo   716
Young men who--though they hated to discuss   937 Juan   12   483
To show it (points we need not now discuss   969 Juan   15   77

DISCUSS'D
Discuss'd the fashion which might next prevail   954 Juan   13   829
Discuss'd the world, and settled all the spheres   955 Juan   13   866
Will be discuss'd hereafter, I opine   967 Juan   14   771
The supper too discuss'd, the dames admired   981 Juan   16   58
Lord Henry, who had now discuss'd his chocolate   984 Juan   16   265
Discuss'd (he hated beer yclept the 'small   989 Juan   16   579

DISCUSSING
Discussing all the dances gone and past   451 Beppo   691

DISCUSSION
They're at this moment in discussion   231 Doctor   63
Who (after some discussion and some doubt   828 Juan   4   731
There was just then a kind of a discussion   913 Juan   10   353

DISCUSSION
Discussion, which is neither here nor there	919 Juan	11	34
Of such discussion. She was there a guest	975 Juan	15	434
Therefore I would solicit free discussion	997 Juan	17	41

DISDAIN
None through their cold disdain are doom'd to die	15 Harold	1	727
Disdain his power, and from their rocky hold	26 Harold	2	422
Is source of wayward thought and stern disdain	32 Harold	2	780
And nostril beautiful disdain and might	79 Harold	4	1447
Whose souls disdain not to condemn the wrong	93 Dorset		28
Where confidence and ease the watch disdain	105 Nisus		27
Why, Pigot, complain of this damsel's disdain	115 Pigot		40
With fervent contempt evermore to disdain you	147 To Anne-A		10
Have seen her eyes, in cold disdain	164 Friend-B		31
Quits with disdain	200 Stanzas-B		38
Behold where Dian's beams disdain to shine	270 Minerva		120
Disdain, defy, the tardy aid of art	299 Age		82
As if his sorrow or disdain	318 Giaour		855
To whom he show'd nor deference nor disdain	374 Lara	1	569
And he regards them with a calm disdain	381 Lara	2	435
And smiled--Heaven pardon! if 'twere with disdain	382 Lara	2	481
In deep disdain were half renew'd	401 Parisina		445
And burst and madden'd with disdain and grief	468 Morgante		128
In part of your disdain, it doth appal me	502 Faliero	1	174
At peril of my life, if you disdain not	506 Faliero	1	487
Sheathe them, and hear him. I disdain to speak	522 Faliero	3	234
Jehovah's footsteps not disdain her sod	666 Heaven		787
Coldness or anger, even disdain or hate	756 Juan	1	583
Yet if perchance remember'd, still disdain you 'em	895 Juan	8	1086
For I disdain to write an Atalantis	929 Juan	11	685

DISDAIN'D
Disdain'd to sink beneath	219 Thy Days		10
The shrine where Jehovah disdain'd not to reign	221 Jerusalem		18
This thing of rhyme I ne'er disdain'd to own	256 Bards		1039
Who gods and men alike disdain'd to hear	271 Minerva		248
Her Prophet had disdain'd to show	330 Abydos	2	107
The storm roll'd onward, and disdain'd to strike	359 Corsair	3	267
Accused of what till now my heart disdain'd	360 Corsair	3	322
Nor had Sir Ezzelin his host disdain'd	375 Lara	2	38
To mourn the discipline they late disdain'd	379 Lara	2	313
Disdain'd to deck a thing like me	399 Parisina		284
Disdain'd all further efforts, save to close	434 Island	4	306
The mass are; I disdain'd to mingle with	493 Manfred	3	121
His blood dishonour'd, and himself disdain'd	563 Sardan	2	101
But to the spirits who have not disdain'd	667 Heaven		931
'Is it for this I have disdain'd to hold	765 Juan	1	1169
Hers was a phrensy which disdain'd to rave	825 Juan	4	535
And for coquetry, she disdain'd to wear it	945 Juan	13	246
(I have had of both, some not to be disdain'd	982 Juan	16	87

DISDAINING
He stops, he starts, disdaining to decline	16 Harold	1	785
Disdaining humbler rural sports	137 Clare		34
As not disdaining priestly aid	401 Parisina		465
And loves or hates, disdaining to be guided	943 Juan	13	127

DISDAINS
Why ev'n the worm at last disdains her shatter'd cell	20 Harold	2	45
And follow all that Peace disdains to seek	35 Harold	2	910
Whose downcast eye disdains the wanton leer	119 Answer-A		29
Now wakeful Grief disdains her mild controul	140 Ossian-A		45
Disdains to light, and keeps his course	316 Giaour		588
I pray thee, change the theme: my blood disdains	554 Sardan	3	265
'Tis that an angel's bride disdains to weep	667 Heaven		914

DISEASE
Still to the last it rankles, a disease	24 Harold	2	314
Here pierceth not, impregnate with disease	27 Harold	2	448
But he was phrensied by disease or woe	47 Harold	3	759
Disease, death, bondage--all the woes we see	74 Harold	4	1132
Cruel Cerinthus! does the fell disease	87 Tibullus		1
Prove nature a prey to decay and disease	91 Caroline-C		12
When slow Disease, with all her host of pains	122 Recoll		1
Till slow disease resigns his prey	146 Adieu		58
Gaunt Poverty should league with deep Disease	193 Monody		80
St. Luke alone can vanquish the disease	245 Bards		280
Unread (unless, since books beguile disease	260 Hints		237
When lost--what recks it by disease or strife	338 Corsair	1	26
That fever'd moment of his mind's disease	370 Lara	1	274
Nor bound between Distraction and Disease	438 Tasso		94
(A forty days' precaution 'gainst disease	443 Beppo		196
Some of disease, and some insanity	493 Manfred	3	144
And death to all things, and disease to most things	641 Cain	2	355
By its rich harvests, new disease, and gold	730 Deformed	1	580
Would be for a disease already cured	744 Deformed	3	163
I ask'd the doctors after his disease	751 Juan	1	270
Of its disease; he did the best he could	758 Juan	1	725
And ugliness, disease, as toil and trouble	927 Juan	11	583
The fool will call such mania a disease	931 Juan	12	83

DISEASED
Of its own beauty is the mind diseased	73 Harold	4	1030
Not inspiration, but a mind diseased	252 Bards		784
A mind diseased no remedy can physic	776 Juan	2	151

DISEASES
New beings--years--diseases--sorrow--crime	661 Heaven		456
Suppress, then, some slight feminine diseases	969 Juan	15	71

DISEMBARK'D
The pilot was misled, and disembark'd us	547 Faliero	5	634
The troops, already disembark'd, push'd on	880 Juan	8	113

DISEMBODIED
Were odds against a disembodied soul	996 Juan	16	992

DISENTWINED
So closely mingling here, that disentwined	344 Corsair	1	404

DISFIGURE
That live gazette, had scatter'd to disfigure	969 Juan	15	82

DISFIGURES
That which disfigures it; and they who war	48 Harold	3	790

DISGORGE
(See also DEATH-DISGORGING)
Ah, what can tombs avail!--since these disgorge	228 Windsor		9
What now can tombs avail, since these disgorge	228 Vaults		9

DISGORGED
Pump'd up with such effort, disgorg'd with such labour	278 Blues	1	50

DISGRACE
The deeds that lurk beneath and stain him with disgrace	28 Harold	2	558
Nor can thy lot my rank disgrace	85 To E--		10
He vows that he ne'er will disgrace your renown	86 Leaving NA		30
All, all reproach--but thy disgrace	90 To M.S.G.-A		36
As ancient Rome, fast falling to disgrace	93 Masters		3
But should a storm o'erwhelm him with disgrace	112 Examination		67
Which stamp'd disgrace on all an author writ	113 Prologue		4
And what would be justice appears a disgrace	136 Delawarr		16
And dooms them to a dire disgrace	141 Critics		44
A Sire's disgrace, a realm's decay	168 Weeping		2
Meet sordid Rage--and wrestle with Disgrace	193 Monody		84
Begun in folly, ended in disgrace	251 Bards		681
Whose proudest deeds disgrace the name of man	254 Bards		938
At once the boast of learning, and disgrace	255 Bards		982
If one with wit the parent brood disgrace	270 Minerva		167
Which they call a disgrace to the age and the nation	277 Blues	1	31
Each step from splendour to disgrace	311 Giaour		137
Or even Disgrace would lay her lover low	333 Abydos	2	441
The tale of his disgrace	398 Parisina		144
Before me can be gods, I'll not disgrace	571 Sardan	3	33
Than Jacopo's disgrace. That word again	604 Foscari	2	175
To love us, cometh anguish with disgrace	667 Heaven		932
In open day, by his disgrace which stamp'd	720 Werner	5	448
Or pandering blindly to his own disgrace	759 Juan	1	788
She never would disgrace the ring she wore	760 Juan	1	868
I should but bring disgrace upon the dyer	848 Juan	5	1068
And stinginess, disgrace her sex and station	907 Juan	9	648

DISGRACED
And the false semblance but disgraced his brow	61 Harold	4	366
These fair green walks disgraced by infamy	171 Hales-Owen		8
A vulgar scribbler, certes, stands disgraced	262 Hints		393
Hidalgo, and the peasant less disgraced	302 Age		343
My youth disgraced--the long, long wasted years	361 Corsair	3	378
Proud of some name they have disgraced, or sprung	548 Faliero	5	765
Oppress'd but not disgraced, crush'd, overwhelm'd	604 Foscari	2	160
Who for these twenty years disgraced his lineage	694 Werner	2	725
Disgraced--Who told you that I was disgraced?	695 Werner	3	13
A man pursued by my chief foe; disgraced	703 Werner	3	517

DISGRACES
Disgraces, too! 'inseparable train	171 Address-B		32

DISGUISE
Disguise ev'n tenderness if thou art wise	24 Harold	2	304
That love was pure, and, far above disguise	43 Harold	3	490
If thus thou comest in disguise	111 Medea		13
Spurn such restraint and scorn disguise	112 Quaker		20
The devil in disguise--since so you deem me	730 Deformed	1	540
Until she spoke, then through its soft disguise	754 Juan	1	475
Lest they should seem princesses in disguise	789 Juan	2	986
That this disguise may lead to no mistake	842 Juan	5	656
And if they should discover your disguise	843 Juan	5	731
His youth and features favour'd the disguise	846 Juan	5	913
Juan amongst the damsels in disguise	851 Juan	5	1235
Don Juan in his feminine disguise	855 Juan	6	201
Still he forgot not his disguise:--along	856 Juan	6	233

DISGUISE
Although they could not see through his disguise 857 Juan 6 301
And his disguise with due consideration 864 Juan 6 790
And bright eternity without disguise 893 Juan 8 917
Add what may be call'd marriage in disguise 906 Juan 9 608

DISGUISED
Foul Superstition! howsoe'er disguised 26 Harold 2 392
Disguised things seen by better light 330 Abydos 2 117
Disguised--discover'd--conquering--ta'en--condemn'd 352 Corsair 2 389
He then threw off the garments which disguised him 452 Beppo 779

DISGUISES
But she who not a thought disguises 173 Not False 9

DISGUST
Leap kindly back to kindness, though disgust 43 Harold 3 473
Pay orisons for this suspension of disgust 65 Harold 4 612
What disgust to life hast thou 100 Marion 2
Who knows thee well must quit thee with disgust 154 Dog 17
As may disgust the ear of kings 195 Ballad-A 67
From grosser incense with disgust she turns 245 Bards 292
They threw their pens down in divine disgust 285 Vision 39
I fear that henceforth 'twill but bring disgust 354 Corsair 2 522
Less from disgust of life than dread of death 955 Juan 14 32
When Adeline replied with some disgust 974 Juan 15 389

DISGUSTED
Romance! disgusted with deceit 118 Romance 33

DISGUSTING
A bungler even in its disgusting trade 746 Juan Ded 105

DISGUSTS
In tragic scene disgusts, though but in show 260 Hints 274
Thus poetry disgusts, or else delights 265 Hints 634

DISH
Who seven years since tried to dish up 238 Bray 3
As if at table some discordant dish 265 Hints 627
Not that I'm fit for such a noble dish 286 Vision 118
'A dainty dish to set before the King 745 Juan Ded 11
And be the only Blackbird in the dish 745 Juan Ded 20
But the best dish that e'er was cook'd since Homer's 789 Juan 2 983
To pay him a fresh visit, with a dish 791 Juan 2 1063
To be impaled, or quarter'd as a dish 849 Juan 5 1122
To serve in this conundrum of a dish 971 Juan 15 168
Follow'd by 'petits puits d'amour'--a dish 976 Juan 15 538
No damsel, but a dish, as hath been said 977 Juan 15 590
He sate him pensive o'er a dish of tea 984 Juan 16 234
Inflicted on the dish a deadly wound 992 Juan 16 750

DISH'D
He sought in the slave-market too, and dish'd 790 Juan 2 1006
To make him prisoner, was also dish'd 888 Juan 8 640
Where's Brummel? Dish'd. Where's Long Pole Wellesley? Diddled 928 Juan 11 609

DISHEARTEN'D
It is a portent. What! they are dishearten'd 590 Sardan 5 173

DISHES
O'er curtail'd dishes and o'er stinted wines 299 Age 60
And thus they bid farewell to carnal dishes 441 Beppo 49
The dinner made about a hundred dishes 809 Juan 3 489
And fish, and soup, by some side dishes back'd 835 Juan 5 253
Another part of history; for the dishes 867 Juan 6 955
Quite full, right dull, guests hot, and dishes cold 991 Juan 16 670

DISHEVELL'D
No maiden, with dishevell'd hair 166 Euthanasia 7
In all the wildness of dishevell'd charms 345 Corsair 1 471
Of those dishevell'd locks, I would have thinn'd 740 Deformed 2 320

DISHONEST
By a slave's dishonest blow 187 Ode-B 51
Throb feverish under thy dishonest weight 504 Faliero 1 295

DISHONOUR
And dishonour the Cause of devotion 239 Bray 30
Harp on the deep dishonour of our house 501 Faliero 1 93
Patient--ay, proud, it may be, of dishonour 502 Faliero 1 195
A wife's dishonour was the bane of Troy 544 Faliero 5 438
A wife's dishonour unking'd Rome for ever 544 Faliero 5 439
He must be there. 'Tis no dishonour--no 574 Sardan 3 215
'Tis no dishonour to have loved this man 575 Sardan 3 216
I dare not think thee guilty of dishonour 683 Werner 1 744
Dishonour! I have said it. Let us hence 683 Werner 1 745
The madness and dishonour of an instant 709 Werner 4 316

DISHONOURABLY
Dishonourably. Have you long time served 505 Faliero 1 388

DISHONOUR'D
Dishonour'd in its chief--that chief the prince 501 Faliero 1 94
Their mighty name dishonour'd all in me 519 Faliero 3 33
His blood dishonour'd, and himself disdain'd 563 Sardan 2 101
Better for me.--I have seen our house dishonour'd 604 Foscari 2 155
To back his suit. Dishonour'd!--he dishonour'd 604 Foscari 2 163
I tell thee, Doge, 'tis Venice is dishonour'd 604 Foscari 2 164
But not dishonour'd: and I leave them with 701 Werner 3 438

DISHONOUR'S
To whom dishonour's shadow is a substance 544 Faliero 5 425

DISINHERITED
My disinherited boy! 'Tis but a dream 646 Cain 3 32
Right! none. A disinherited prodigal 694 Werner 2 724

DISINTERESTED
Advice at least's disinterested 100 Marion 32

DISINTERESTEDNESS
Such pure disinterestedness of passion 933 Juan 12 259

DISINTERRED
The exile of the disinterred ashes 616 Foscari 4 112

DISJOIN'D
But though husband and wife shall at length be disjoin'd 117 To Eliza 33

DISJOINTED
Were combinations of disjointed things 216 Dream 174
O'er the disjointed mass shall vault 386 Corinth 232

DISK
A summer's sun discloses it. Yon disk 561 Sardan 2 11
His glaring disk around 668 Heaven 1006

DISLIKE
Men, even when dying, dislike inanition 779 Juan 2 365
Or show the same dislike to suitors' kisses 804 Juan 3 180
Still I have no dislike to learned natures 830 Juan 4 885
Those who dislike to look upon a fray 882 Juan 8 237
Outward dislike, which don't look well abroad 911 Juan 10 253
She show'd a great dislike to holy water 914 Juan 10 444

DISLIKES
For jealousy dislikes the world to know it 755 Juan 1 520

DISMISS
Dismiss thy guard, and trust thee to such traits 199 Sonnet-E 7
Bethink ere thou dismiss us, ask again 480 Manfred 1 167
I have no time to lose, nor thou--dismiss 530 Faliero 4 128
But I dismiss them from my mind.--Yet pause 594 Sardan 5 463
Ludwig, dismiss the train without! And so 708 Werner 4 257
Form'd as thou art. I may dismiss the mould 727 Deformed 1 324
She to dismiss her guards and he his haram 864 Juan 6 759

DISMISSAL
As his dismissal in the Moniteur 308 Age 720

DISMISS'D
Dismiss'd Abdallah's hence to heaven 331 Abydos 2 239
Dismiss'd the natives and their shallop, who 433 Island 4 247
Only dismiss'd them from our presence, who 570 Sardan 2 508
And then dismiss'd the omen from her breast 819 Juan 4 187
Till duly disappointed or dismiss'd 990 Juan 16 643

DISMAL
Couldst thou forbode the dismal hour which now 31 Harold 2 704
What satellites declare her dismal reign 121 Newstead-A 98
With all their blank, or dismal stains, than is 610 Foscari 3 119

DISMAY
And loved to dwell in darkness and dismay 60 Harold 4 302
To dazzle and dismay 181 Ode-A 106
Into recitative, in great dismay 296 Vision 722
Dismay, the usual consequence of dreams 862 Juan 6 618
John Johnson, seeing their extreme dismay 876 Juan 7 593
And wild dismay o'er every angry cousin 934 Juan 12 267
To laugh him out of his supposed dismay 987 Juan 16 454

DISMAY'D
He sue for mercy! He dismay'd 391 Corinth 657
Thy lineaments in beauty that dismay'd 438 Tasso 134
Oh! not dismay'd--but awed, like One above 438 Tasso 135

DISMOUNT
But finally he thought fit to dismount 474 Morgante 545

DISMOUNTED
And he dismounted from his horse, and spake 468 Morgante 142

DISOBEDIENCE
'Of man's first disobedience and the fruit   259 Hints   202
In disobedience to the monarch. Myrrha   576 Sardan   3   301
Be one of disobedience. Oh, he is good   690 Werner   2   493
Would sanction disobedience against all   708 Werner   4   261

DISOBEDIENT
To Sense had made me disobedient   144 Becher-B   40

DISOBEY
Thy dread behests ne'er disobey   89 Prometheus-A   4
You dare to disobey me, then? I serve   536 Faliero   4   560
I dared not disobey the Council when   598 Foscari   1   154

DISOBEY'D
I ever disobey'd; but now--So all men   591 Sardan   5   268

DISORDER
Destruction and disorder of the elements   640 Cain   2   286
No, you don't look a leech for that disorder   696 Werner   3   56

DISORDERLY
And rushing in disorderly, though led   822 Juan   4   373

DISORDERS
Exhaustion, or disorders of the same kin   912 Juan   10   316

DISOWN
Ne'er may my soul thy power disown   89 Prometheus-A   3
Must I fond Nature's claim disown   150 My Son   20
With a vile mask the Gorgon would disown   209 Sketch   63

DISPARAGE
You disparage my parts with insidious abuse   279 Blues   1   109
Not that I mean her bounties to disparage   447 Beppo   492
For authors fear description might disparage   802 Juan   3   68
It is--I meant and mean not to disparage   937 Juan   12   492
The postboys have no reason to disparage   947 Juan   13   366
Without those sad expenses which disparage   972 Juan   15   277

DISPARITY
And, let me add, disparity of tempers   510 Faliero   2   87
There was no great disparity of years   966 Juan   14   689

DISPATCH
Dispatch the letter which I must enclose   224 J.C.H.   10

DISPEL
Soon a new morn's restoring beams dispel   121 Newstead-A   101
Dispel awhile the sense of ill   135 I Would   30
By pangs which a smile would dispel   162 Romaic-A   30
Dispel awhile the sense of ill   166 Struggle   22
That show'st the darkness thou canst not dispel   220 Sleepless   3
For every ray that travels to dispel   291 Vision   437
When but a word of freedom would dispel   423 Island   2   330
Of the loud war-whoop to dispel the charm   424 Island   2   423

DISPELL'D
Since our last meeting, then, are all dispell'd   519 Faliero   3   53
Dispell'd by antidotes. But as thou saidst   643 Cain   2   510
And every difficulty being dispell'd   873 Juan   7   405

DISPENSE
With souls you'd dispense, but this last who
   could bear it   116 To Eliza   12
Still hear thy motley orators dispense   255 Bards   1013
Who, worn with use, of late would fain dispense   258 Hints   157
Young men with aught but elegance dispense   264 Hints   541
Has found out the way to dispense with Parnassus   282 Blues   2   120
Around our congress, and dispense with all   293 Vision   516
''Tis fit thy grandeur should dispense relief   467 Morgante   113
Let him have absolution. I dispense with   565 Sardan   2   239
Dispense with me--I am no wassailer   569 Sardan   2   481
The state would not dispense me from those duties   604 Foscari   2   185
For they were forced with steering to dispense   779 Juan   2   315
Of late years, to dispense with Cocker's rigours   993 Juan   16   831

DISPENSED
Exceeding sagely from that hour dispensed   757 Juan   1   653
He was all things to all men, and dispensed   990 Juan   16   610
While Adeline dispensed her airs and graces   993 Juan   16   841

DISPENSING
('The Ten,' dispensing with the stricter law   605 Foscari   2   264

DISPERSE
Not in the air shall these my words disperse   75 Harold   4   1203
Though all, who can, disperse on shore and seek   347 Corsair   2   16
Disperse then to your posts: be firm and vigilant   526 Faliero   3   511

DISPERSED
The mutineers were crush'd, dispersed, or ta'en   426 Island   3   9
Their followers are dispersed, and many taken   537 Faliero   4   620

DISPERSION
More Babels, without new dispersion, than   732 Deformed   1   677

DISPIRITED
With voice and gesture the dispirited troops   589 Sardan   5   110

DISPLACE
Aught to displace, Athena's poor remains   21 Harold   2   105
Triumph, arch, pillar, all he doth displace   71 Harold   4   988

DISPLAY
Now is thy time, to perish, or display   16 Harold   1   758
Bright are the deeds thine earlier sires display   94 Dorset   66
Pedantic inmates full display   95 Granta   6
His hbnour'd name requires no vain display   127 Recoll   362
And still may thy branches their beauty display   149 Newstead-B   24
Display who gave us birth   161 War Song   4
On those shall Farce display Buffoon'ry's mask   249 Bards   588
And beer undrawn, and beards unmown, display   250 Bards   636
The last display the free unfetter'd limb   250 Bards   663
Without display, without parade   401 Parisina   463
In Castle Siegendorf! Display no gold   698 Werner   3   203
Till slowly charged with thunder they display   823 Juan   4   451
This secret charge on Juan, to display   913 Juan   10   363
Barouche, which had the glory to display once   913 Juan   10   389
Say something to the purpose, and display   967 Juan   14   783
Would now and then as 'twere without display   986 Juan   16   381
Yet with display in fact, at times relent   986 Juan   16   382

DISPLAY'D
Of busy cities, now in vain display'd   60 Harold   4   286
All, save the lone Soracte's height, display'd   66 Harold   4   665
Earth with her haughty shadow, and display'd   67 Harold   4   754
And till Aurora's dawn his skill display'd   108 Nisus   258
To me in smiles display'd   146 Adieu   57
When that vast edifice display'd   196 Venice-A   23
All, all in earth, or skies display'd   220 Clay   11
Display'd so much of leg, or more of neck   274 Waltz   90
Than he, who heard that vow, display'd   327 Abydos   1   345
So may the Koran verse display'd   331 Abydos   2   189
For when one near display'd the absolving cross   382 Lara   2   477
Around our waists the tappa's white display'd   419 Island   2   48
And bare, at once, Captivity display'd   436 Tasso   11
Such sounds are utter'd, and such charms
   display'd   455 Dante   Ded   12
Adoring him in his least works display'd   666 Heaven   791
The upper border, richly wrought, display'd   809 Juan   3   509
His strain display'd some feeling--right or wrong   813 Juan   3   789
The negroes more philosophy display'd   832 Juan   5   55
And a magnificent large hall display'd   838 Juan   5   407
A perfect transformation here display'd   841 Juan   5   637
'Twas like the fawn, which, in the lake display'd   859 Juan   6   477
For cats and birds more penchant ne'er display'd   913 Juan   10   399
The talent and good humour he display'd   940 Juan   12   677
Indeed we see the daily proof display'd   944 Juan   13   228
And rank'd with what is every day display'd   952 Juan   13   719
Display'd some sylph-like figures in its maze   954 Juan   13   859
But various as the various meats display'd   977 Juan   15   588
In courtesy their wish to see display'd   985 Juan   16   309
To something like this when too oft display'd   986 Juan   16   397

DISPLAYING
Not in those visions to the heart displaying   2 To Ianthe   3
And some emitting sparks, and some displaying   638 Cain   2   186

DISPLAYS
The fountain of sublimity displays   79 Harold   4   1429
Till Glory's self is twilight, and displays   79 Harold   4   1482
Arcadia displays but a region of dreams   93 First Kiss   19
For these, each Hero all his power displays   114 Prologue   27
His beams alike to all displays   134 E. N. Long   72
Whose sun displays a general summer   134 E. N. Long   76
Her Sun displays perpetual Summer   143 On Eyes   8
And such the change the heart displays   153 Friend-A   9
Which all that life or earth displays   219 Vanity   11
And bless the promise which his form displays   250 Bards   623
Displays a crowd of figures incomplete   256 Hints   13
As only the yet infant world displays   435 Island   4   420
Foretells the heaviest tempest, it displays   756 Juan   1   579
His parts of speech; and in the strange displays   902 Juan   9   388
And sparkling on from heap to heap, displays   930 Juan   12   58

DISPLEASE
The slightest motion would displease the Dean   112 Examination   38
And, therefore, may the reader too displease   446 Beppo   396
Or, if that simple sentence should displease   877 Juan   7   675
Has shown, I know not why they should displease   979 Juan   15   686

DISPLEASED
And view'd, but not displeased, the revelrie   30 Harold   2   641
Though an Emperor's taste was displeased with his
   haste   176 Devil's Dr   57
For Alhama's loss displeased   195 Ballad-A   74
Displeased he was with Gan because he said it   468 Morgante   119

DISPLEASING
Oh, dome displeasing unto British eye | 8 Harold | 1 | 289
And, lest my precepts be displeasing | 101 Marion | | 41
On pain of much displeasing the gynocracy | 987 Juan | 16 | 464

DISPORTING
Disporting there like any other fly | 4 Harold | 1 | 29

DISPOSAL
Some pretty livings in disposal | 95 Granta | | 22

DISPOSE
He whom our plays dispose to good or ill | 261 Hints | | 365
Upon a point of form: you may dispose | 293 Vision | | 511
This let the Armourer with speed dispose | 340 Corsair | 1 | 165
Except two thousand ducats--these dispose of | 545 Faliero | 5 | 530
As I have said, let all dispose their hours | 551 Sardan | 1 | 81
But first of little Leila we'll dispose | 934 Juan | 12 | 321

DISPOSED
Or the Nine be disposed from your service to
  rove | 92 First Kiss | | 10
At least I feel disposed to stray, love | 98 To Lesbia | | 12
More brave than firm, and more disposed to dare | 428 Island | 3 | 123
And I a Christian am disposed to be | 471 Morgante | | 344
Are all things so disposed of in the tower | 491 Manfred | 3 | 3
I have disposed all for a sudden blow | 523 Faliero | 3 | 350
Now that these criminals have been disposed of | 540 Faliero | 5 | 135
Have been disposed of. Some have fled to
  Chiozza | 540 Faliero | 5 | 146
Quite fall'n, nor now disposed to bear reproaches | 585 Sardan | 4 | 471
Were I disposed to brawl; but, as I said | 605 Foscari | 2 | 254
Your father has disposed in such a sort | 689 Werner | 2 | 390
For which you seem disposed to pay yourself | 692 Werner | 2 | 604
If it be so, being much disposed to do | 695 Werner | 3 | 10
And not at all disposed to prove a martyr | 769 Juan | 1 | 1472
Days nearly o'er, might be disposed to riot | 778 Juan | 2 | 262
Some he disposed of off Cape Matapan | 803 Juan | 3 | 121
She did not find herself the least disposed | 863 Juan | 6 | 669
Nor much disposed to wait in word or deed | 864 Juan | 6 | 802
To be disposed of in a way so new | 875 Juan | 7 | 531
Juan felt somewhat pensive, and disposed | 982 Juan | 16 | 113
Though for the public weal disposed to venture
  high | 990 Juan | 16 | 630

DISPOSING
But all things are disposing for thy doom | 459 Dante | 2 | 43

DISPOSITION
The thing which you condemn, a disposition | 555 Sardan | 1 | 322
Itself, and show'd a feverish disposition | 912 Juan | 10 | 310
And taciturn Asiatic disposition | 933 Juan | 12 | 210

DISPOSITIONS
And for the dispositions of our clients | 533 Faliero | 4 | 379

DISPRAISE
Though passive tutors, fearful to dispraise | 93 Dorset | | 13

DISPROPORTION
Yet this strange disproportion in your years | 510 Faliero | 2 | 86

DISPROVE
If false, 'tis easy to disprove the word | 372 Lara | 1 | 452
Who says so? I. And how disprove it? By | 715 Werner | 5 | 171

DISPUTANT
A subtle disputant on creeds | 181 Ode-A | | 69

DISPUTE
Lest angels might dispute the prize | 97 To M-- | | 14
Pray who would there be to defend or dispute it | 145 Casuists | | 8
Let squabbling critics by themselves dispute | 258 Hints | | 113
Still Minotti dares dispute | 394 Corinth | | 905
Where all partake the earth without dispute | 418 Island | 1 | 213
All, all, will I dispute! And world by world | 645 Cain | 2 | 641
Dispute with him | 656 Heaven | | 85
Dispute your claim, and weave a web that may | 684 Werner | 2 | 102
The madden'd Turks their city still dispute | 887 Juan | 8 | 552
When they dispute with sceptics; and with curses | 892 Juan | 8 | 863
Space to dispute what no one ever could | 919 Juan | 11 | 30
'Tis nonsense to dispute about a hue | 941 Juan | 13 | 21

DISPUTED
Now daily squabbling o'er disputed rations | 299 Age | | 58
Disputed foot by foot, till treason, still | 301 Age | | 215
As all truths must, the more they are disputed | 981 Juan | 16 | 48

DISPUTES
Despair can do; and step by step disputes | 575 Sardan | 3 | 249
For family disputes. While you were tortured | 719 Werner | 5 | 429
Faint flutter life disputes with death. She
  breathes | 741 Deformed | 2 | 385
And thus your houri (it may be) disputes | 892 Juan | 8 | 903

DISPUTING
'Twas blow for blow, disputing inch by inch | 888 Juan | 8 | 615

DISQUIET
Disquiet your great thoughts with restless hate | 514 Faliero | 2 | 402
And you perceive your presence doth disquiet | 612 Foscari | 3 | 287

DISQUIETED
'Why is my sleep disquieted | 219 Saul-B | | 15
He has been much disquieted of late | 509 Faliero | 2 | 8

DISQUIETUDE
With mad disquietude on the dull sky | 189 Darkness | | 29

DISQUIETUDES
In pondering o'er your late disquietudes | 513 Faliero | 2 | 327

DISSATISFIED
Dissatisfied and curious thoughts--as thou | 633 Cain | 1 | 400
Dissatisfied, nor knowing what he wanted | 758 Juan | 1 | 762

DISSECTED
His morns he pass'd in business--which, dissected | 926 Juan | 11 | 505

DISSECTING
Dissecting the whole inside of a question | 909 Juan | 10 | 111

DISSECTION
Dead scandals form good subjects for dissection | 751 Juan | 1 | 248
But others ponder'd on a new dissection | 784 Juan | 2 | 637

DISSEMBLE
Dissemble your pain, and lengthen your chain | 115 Pigot | | 13
Alike she knows not to dissemble | 160 Cadiz | | 28

DISSEMBLED
(See also ILL-DISSEMBLED)
And evil dread so ill dissembled | 191 Prometheus-B | | 33

DISSEMBLERS
But all dissemblers overact their part | 267 Hints | | 780

DISSEMBLES
But passion most dissembles, yet betrays | 756 Juan | 1 | 577

DISSEMBLING
For trifling or dissembling. I have said | 719 Werner | 5 | 407

DISSENSION
What though one sad dissension bade us part | 126 Recoll | | 303
To forget our dissension we both should endeavour | 137 Delawarr | | 35
At once to conclude such a fruitless dissension | 147 To Anne-A | | 15

DISSENT
And wins even by a delicate dissent | 978 Juan | 15 | 664

DISSENTING
In council, without one dissenting voice | 501 Faliero | 1 | 87
Treat a dissenting author very martyrly | 772 Juan | 1 | 1688

DISSERT
That I dissert, like grace before a feast | 934 Juan | 12 | 307

DISSEVER
Nought should my kiss from thine dissever | 88 To Ellen | | 7
Yet woman and man ne'er were meant to dissever | 117 To Eliza | | 34
The heart which adores you should wish to
  dissever | 147 To Anne-B | | 2

DISSIMULATION
Dissimulation always sets apart | 968 Juan | 15 | 22
I can't tell why, to this dissimulation | 985 Juan | 16 | 315

DISSIMULATION'S
Who hath not seen Dissimulation's reign | 420 Island | 2 | 71

DISSIPATE
I could not dissipate; and with the blessing | 529 Faliero | 4 | 108
In what way feminine caprice may dissipate | 867 Juan | 6 | 952

DISSIPATED
And haggard with a dissipated life | 827 Juan | 4 | 658
As when the French, that dissipated nation | 894 Juan | 8 | 1028
Don Juan grew, I fear, a little dissipated | 910 Juan | 10 | 179
Their vigour in a thousand arms is dissipated | 927 Juan | 11 | 587

DISSIPATION
Some mind their household, others dissipation | 799 Juan | 2 | 1602

DISSOLUTE
To punish some more dissolute young nobles | 520 Faliero | 3 | 134

DISSOLUTION
On poor De Stael's late dissolution | 231 Doctor | | 64

DISSOLVE
Weigh'd down with years the hills dissolve away   139 Ossian-A   12
Dissolve this clog and clod of clay before   424 Island   2   390

DISSOLVED
Our chains once dissolved and our hearts
  unconfined   117 To Eliza   35
Our feuds dissolved, but not my friendship past   123 Recoll   53
Envy dissolved our ties, and not our will   126 Recoll   307
Like mountain mists at length dissolved in rain   824 Juan   4   528
Dissolved like snow before a woman crying   849 Juan   5 1128

DISSOLVES
A silent change dissolves the glittering mass   927 Juan   11   598

DISSOLVING
(See also WORLD-DISSOLVING)
Now half dissolving to a liberal thaw   304 Age   440
The long chibouque's dissolving cloud supply   347 Corsair   2   35
In the dissolving circle, all the nations'   907 Juan   9   650
Dissolving in the waltz to some soft air   927 Juan   11   550

DISSONANCE
With dull and daily dissonance, repeats   453 Venice-B   21

DISSUADE
A smile can enchant, or a tear can dissuade   91 Caroline-C   20
I would dissuade you, baron, from this strife   469 Morgante   223

DISSUADED
Each course enough? or doctors dire dissuaded   305 Age   509

DISSUASION
By aiding me in my dissuasion of   707 Werner   4   208

DISTAFF
Alcides with the distaff now he seem'd   68 Harold   4   809
Assume the distaff--not the brand   324 Abydos   1   100
Till they shall wish it turn'd into a distaff   556 Sardan   1   372
She-garb, and wielding her vile distaff, surely   575 Sardan   3   220
In this vile garb, the distaff, web, and woof   847 Juan   5 1011

DISTAFFS
A king of distaffs! But no less we owe them   567 Sardan   2   344

DISTANCE
On yon long, level plain, at distance crown'd   12 Harold   1   513
Childe Harold at a little distance stood   30 Harold   2   640
At airy distance, with majestic motion   55 Harold   4   12
At apish distance; but as yet none have   68 Harold   4   798
Where Pallas' walls at distance meet the sight   107 Nisus   109
Unchanged by time or distance, seem the same   122 Recoll   48
Their swords gleam at distance in heaps   130 Calmar   104
And heard at a distance the Highlander's song   136 Highlander   20
You knew me unalter'd by years or by distance   137 Delawarr   27
Distance, nor depth of wave, nor space of earth   198 Po   38
Which strips the distance of its fantasies   216 Dream   181
But others at a distance strike the sight   264 Hints   573
About ten million times the distance reckon'd   291 Vision   434
Not he, whose heart nor time nor distance frees   356 Corsair   3   61
Enquiry into deeds at distance done   378 Lara   2   239
The watch-fires in the distance sparkling   407 Mazeppa   28
And still reluctant distance kept   409 Mazeppa   245
Yet glitter'd, but at distance--hurl'd away   434 Island   4   349
Worshipp'd at holy distance, and around   438 Tasso   130
In dizziness of distance; when a leap   482 Manfred   1   277
Proud as a freeborn peasant's, at this distance   482 Manfred   1   325
Rising at distance o'er the blue Lagoon   506 Faliero   1   465
'Twas but a murmur--Curse upon the distance   549 Faliero   5   811
Her beautiful towers in the receding distance   611 Foscari   3   208
Distance can but diminish glory--they   643 Cain   2   452
A light! It is at distance (if I can   701 Werner   3   406
Measure in darkness distance); but it blinks   701 Werner   3   418
Soften'd by distance to a hymn-like cadence   732 Deformed   1   687
By distance mellow'd, o'er the waters sweep   761 Juan   1   972
When gazing on them, mystified by distance   775 Juan   2   95
A gentlemanly distance, not too near   821 Juan   4   325
And Ida in the distance, still the same   826 Juan   4   611
Of poets who come down to us through distance   829 Juan   4   793
He motion'd them to stop at some small distance   838 Juan   5   405
Haughty and huge, along the distance lowers   842 Juan   5   677
In this imperial hall, at distance lay   843 Juan   5   753
At some small distance, all he saw within   844 Juan   5   796
A sad miscalculation about distance   870 Juan   7   217
The lightest being the safest: at a distance   885 Juan   8   437
Keep merely firing at a foolish distance   888 Juan   8   624
And Juan's suite, late scatter'd at a distance   920 Juan   11   106

DISTANT
I strike my strain, far distant, to applaud   13 Harold   1   605
Whose fate to distant homes confined their lot   14 Harold   1   631
But Cadiz, rising on the distant coast   14 Harold   1   659
Nor mortal eye the distant end foresees   18 Harold   1   912
Beneath, the distant torrent's rushing sound   26 Harold   2   430

DISTANT
As on the morn to distant Glory dear   33 Harold   2   842
Which shows a distant prospect far away   60 Harold   4   285
Of dying thunder on the distant wind   70 Harold   4   933
Where sparkle distant worlds. Oh, holiest nurse   77 Harold   4 1356
A long low distant murmur of dread sound   80 Harold   4 1496
Far distant he goes, with the same emulation   86 Leaving NA   27
Wilt thou now wing thy distant flight   87 Adrian   4
Departing for a distant shore   89 To Emma   8
With faint regard, or cold and distant eye   94 Dorset   100
From high Southannon's distant tower   102 Alva   77
Far, distant far, the noble grave   105 Alva   301
And sought a foreign home, a distant grave   105 Nisus   6
The distant spires above the valleys gleam   107 Nisus   118
From me be ever distant far   111 Medea   24
Through distant climes condemn'd to fly   111 Medea   43
While distant mitres to their eyes are spread   112 Examination   66
Of changing sentinels the distant hum   120 Newstead-A   53
The orb of day unveils his distant form   122 Recoll   18
To scenes far distant points his paler rays   122 Recoll   24
In lingering tones resounds the distant bell   124 Recoll   148
Seat of my youth! thy distant spire   132 L'Amitie   41
When distant far from you   137 Clare   9
Are wafted far distant on Apathy's wing   148 Farewell-A   8
But, wandering on through distant climes   155 Lady-E   5
The distant shore which gave me birth   157 Florence   2
On distant England's name   158 Storm   16
And throws his mighty shade o'er seas and distant
  lands   161 Athos   9
For him, whose distant relics vainly crave   182 Address-C   29
Distinct, but distant--clear--but, oh how cold   220 Sleepless   8
(Best form for letters from a distant land   224 J.C.H.   49
Mix'd with the shades of many a distant isle   269 Minerva   53
Say with what eye along the distant down   272 Minerva   303
Or distant lightning on the horizon by night   292 Vision   486
Brief thought to distant friendship's claim   322 Giaour   1226
The loud Wul-wulleh warn his distant ear   335 Abydos   2   627
Gaze where some distant sail a speck supplies   339 Corsair   1   55
His was the lofty port, the distant mien   346 Corsair   1   541
Though far the distant foe they thus despise   347 Corsair   2   11
Though the far shouting of the distant crowd   351 Corsair   2   304
Mix'd with the shades of many a distant isle   356 Corsair   3   53
Which makes the distant cities wonder   392 Corinth   756
The distant steer forsook the yoke   396 Corinth   1062
I saw the white-wall'd distant town   406 Chillon   339
On distant heights of some strong hold   411 Mazeppa   433
Whom distant vengeance had not taught to fear   418 Island   1   206
Both children of the isles, though distant far   422 Island   2   274
Or trusted that, if sought, their distant caves   427 Island   3   35
Not distant from the isle of Toobonai   430 Island   4   9
On the horizon verged the distant deck   435 Island   4   385
'Midst glens obscure and distant lands, he found   468 Morgante   151
Of distant sentinels the fitful song   495 Manfred   3   278
He hears the jarring of a distant door   500 Faliero   1   11
A murmur as of distant voices, and   535 Faliero   4   523
And such examples will find heirs, though distant   537 Faliero   4   663
In distant lands--on flood, in field, in cities   541 Faliero   5   207
A distant voyage and an eternal sleep   568 Sardan   2   432
Of distant portals shaken by the wind   572 Sardan   3   63
In a strange land--so young, so distant? No   584 Sardan   4   382
The dove has for her distant nest, when wheeling   608 Foscari   3   12
Distant, and dazzling, and innumerable   643 Cain   2   448
Whose glittering top is like a distant star   659 Heaven   288
The distant thunder's harbinger, appears   668 Heaven   1012
The late Count Siegendorf, his distant kinsman   684 Werner   2   79
Our distant kinsman, and our nearest foe   689 Werner   2   399
A distant lamp-light is an incident   701 Werner   3   411
Abstracted, distant, much given to long absence   711 Werner   4   421
Through distant crannies, of a twinkling light   718 Werner   5   309
Changed; for the dame grew distant, the youth shy   755 Juan   1   554
A lady always distant from the fact   768 Juan   1 1422
On the snow-tops of distant hills; the streak   792 Juan   2 1171
By a distant organ, doubting if he be   793 Juan   2 1210
The distant dog-bark; and perceived between   805 Juan   3   212
Sound like a distant torrent's fall   812 Juan   3   733
While swung the deep bell in the distant tower   815 Juan   3   909
And distant from each other burn'd the lights   860 Juan   6   506
Rather too high and distant; that she threw   862 Juan   6   603
With distant shrieks were heard Heaven to upbraid   887 Juan   8   549
Constantinople, and such distant places   944 Juan   13   178
Some deem it but the distant echo given   949 Juan   13   502

DISTANTLY
To yours? Oh, yes; we are, but distantly   674 Werner   1   194

DISTEMPER
I take thy taunt as part of thy distemper   657 Heaven   188

DISTEMPERATURE
Fancy's distemperature! There is no passion   620 Foscari   4   334

DISTEMPER'D
Along his burning page, distemper'd though it
  seems   47 Harold   3   742

DISTEMPER'D
No eastern vision, no distemper'd dream   242 Bards   24
Save that distemper'd passions lent their force   379 Lara   2   270
Appears, to his distemper'd eyes   414 Mazeppa   750
Would be but a distemper'd dream. What is it   484 Manfred   2   61

DISTIL
From thy false tears I did distil   481 Manfred   1   232

DISTILL'D
Slowly distill'd into the glimmering glass   921 Juan   11   175

DISTINCT
Distinct, though darkening with her waning phase   22 Harold   2   196
With a deep awe, yet all distinct from fear   75 Harold   4   1237
Distinct, but distant--clear--but, oh how cold   220 Sleepless   8
Distinct but strange--enough they understand   369 Lara   1   231
A knell was sounding as distinct and clear   528 Faliero   4   12
All here seems dark and dreadful. But distinct   639 Cain   190
Distinct from that which we and all our sires   664 Heaven   718
Distinct and keener far upon my ear   715 Werner   5   133
Distinct as I beheld them, though the expression   718 Werner   5   338
Distinct, and high, and palpable to view   786 Juan   2   776
She was, appear'd distinct, and tall, and fair   788 Juan   2   920

DISTINCTION
And proud distinction from each other land   454 Venice-B   138
Without distinction, as it fell of yore   526 Faliero   3   543
Midst every natural and acquired distinction   717 Werner   5   266
Fast by the head; and, all distinction gone   779 Juan   2   346
Besides the mark'd distinction of his air   940 Juan   12   678
O'er Juan he could no distinction claim   943 Juan   13   154
Such small distinction between friends and foes   958 Juan   14   196

DISTINCTLY
Mellow'd and mingling, yet distinctly seen   48 Harold   3   808
Though near, alas! distinctly flow   137 Clare   26
They understood not, if distinctly heard   381 Lara   2   443
But nought distinctly seen   413 Mazeppa   614
To reach distinctly from its banks. Then fly   593 Sardan   5   390

DISTINGUISH
Perchance I may strive to distinguish my birth   129 Becher-A   8
Could they distinguish whose the features were   294 Vision   602
The fallen? and how distinguish now the innocent   524 Faliero   3   405
Now here we should distinguish; for howe'er   854 Juan   6   105

DISTINGUISH'D
Their bones, distinguish'd from our common clay   63 Harold   4   500
Far, far distinguish'd from the glittering throng   94 Dorset   73
Distinguish'd from the vulgar rank   332 Abydos   2   376
To some distinguish'd strangers in that fray   871 Juan   7   254
Upon the shades of those distinguish'd men   945 Juan   13   259
Desirable, distinguish'd, celebrated   960 Juan   14   330

DISTINGUISHETH
And scarce a name distinguisheth the brook   9 Harold   1   370

DISTINGUISHING
Distinguishing for love or hate his foes   533 Faliero   4   372

DISTORT
Distort the truth, accumulate the lie   193 Monody   77

DISTORTED
And there lay the rider distorted and pale   222 Sennacherib   17

DISTORTION
Watch each distortion of a Naldi's face   250 Bards   613
And truculent distortion of their tresses   994 Juan   16   872

DISTORTIONS
No fashion made them apes of her distortions   886 Juan   8   526

DISTORTS
False to the heart, distorts the hollow cheek   35 Harold   2   912

DISTRACT
Sadder than saddest night, for they distract the
   gaze   79 Harold   4   1485
Howe'er those beauties may distract us   101 Marion   48
Though wit may flash from fluent lips, and mirth
   distract the breast   185 Music-B   13
His blazing galleys still distract his sight   349 Corsair   2   180
Distract within, both will alike prove fatal   552 Sardan   1   126

DISTRACTED
He flies, he wheels, distracted with his throes   16 Harold   1   763
By the distracted waters, bears serene   66 Harold   4   645
Nor wounds, nor death, distracted Nisus heeds   110 Nisus   392
Distracted, to and fro, the flying slaves   349 Corsair   2   157
To stir up the distracted multitude   539 Faliero   5   101
When his distracted wife broke through into   601 Foscari   1   365

DISTRACTING
May no distracting thoughts destroy   111 Medea   25
With no distracting world to call her off   423 Island   2   334

DISTRACTION
To waft me from distraction; once I loved   48 Harold   3   802
Yet why do I ask?--to distraction a prey   99 L Adieu   19
Distraction and discord would follow in course   117 To Eliza   29
But the distraction of a various lot   198 Po   39
Nor bound between Distraction and Disease   438 Tasso   94
Lady! the natural distraction of   543 Faliero   5   344
She seem'd by the distraction of her air   760 Juan   1   876

DISTRACTS
By all that most distracts the breast   312 Giaour   268
I have sons, who shall be men. Your grief
   distracts you   622 Foscari   5   103

DISTRAIT
So much distrait he was, that all could see   984 Juan   16   238
Confused, in the confusion, and distrait   992 Juan   16   739

DISTRESS
Minions of splendour shrinking from distress   23 Harold   2   230
Himself awhile the victim of distress   29 Harold   2   589
And gathering tears, and tremblings of distress   38 Harold   3   209
To shed thy blood and drink the tears of thy
   distress   61 Harold   4   378
Rise, with thy yellow waves, and mantle her
   distress   67 Harold   4   711
Assist her wants, relieve her fond distress   108 Nisus   192
The friend of Beauty in distress   158 Florence   28
Our signal of distress   158 Storm   24
Above all pain, yet pitying all distress   175 Sonnet-B   12
That death nor heeds nor hears distress   218 Bloom   12
There man, enamour'd of distress   310 Giaour   50
The last of danger and distress   311 Giaour   71
His swarthy visage spake distress   317 Giaour   711
But soothe not--mock not my distress   322 Giaour   1217
When I forget my own distress   326 Abydos   1   195
Stood like that statue of distress   334 Abydos   2   492
Tried in temptation, strengthen'd by distress   342 Corsair   1   294
But trifle now no more with my distress   344 Corsair   1   418
Hate of that deed but grief for her distress   363 Corsair   3   524
Cold, hunger, sorrow, shame, distress   412 Mazeppa   531
The struggle to be calm, and cold distress   438 Tasso   102
The wound, too deep the wrong, and the distress   457 Dante   1   94
Calamity the nations with distress   464 Dante   4   73
From your distress: were it of public import   512 Faliero   2   215
To weather out much longer; the distress   779 Juan   2   323
Having been several days in great distress   779 Juan   2   362
Are similes at hand for the distress   848 Juan   5   1051
Of inspiration gather'd from distress   865 Juan   6   851
So much did Juan's setting off distress her   913 Juan   10   375
Indifference certes don't produce distress   945 Juan   13   278
If in my extremity of rhyme's distress   964 Juan   14   597

DISTRESS'D
His host alarm'd, his murmuring squires
   distress'd   376 Lara   2   108
And truly might it be distress'd   403 Chillon   77

DISTRESSES
But the thing of all things which distresses me
   more   280 Blues   2   14
All that we read, hear, dream, of man's
   distresses   894 Juan   8   979
That hired huzzas redeem no land's distresses   918 Juan   10   684

DISTRESSING
'Alas!' said Juan, ''twere a tale distressing   833 Juan   5   125

DISTRIBUTION
In silent horror, and their distribution   783 Juan   2   594

DISTRICT
The vassals of that district are too rude   533 Faliero   4   360

DISTRICT'S
The dimmest in the district's map, exist   682 Werner   1   702

DISTRUSTED
And less distrusted. But, besides all this   507 Faliero   1   555

DISTRUSTFULLY
Distrustfully. I will; and so provide   719 Werner   5   398

DISTRUSTING
As if distrusting that the stranger threw   372 Lara   1   412

DISTRUSTS
Distrusts thy smiles, but shakes not at thy frown 372 Lara   1   454
Distrusts me? Not I; for if I did so   521 Faliero   3   168

DISTURB
Whose conscience won't disturb their slumber 95 Granta 16
Thus to disturb a harmless Boy 141 Critics 57
May no rude hand disturb their early sleep 247 Bards 425
And thoughtless, will disturb repose 331 Abydos 2 217
They don't disturb themselves for him or her 472 Morgante 414
I knew my days could not disturb you long 513 Faliero 2 329
And I await to second, not disturb her 578 Sardan 4 23
But it were pity to disturb him till 646 Cain 3 16
To recognise. I seek not to disturb 678 Werner 1 466
Is harmless, let it not disturb you.--Gabor 693 Werner 2 629
Disturb your right, or mine, if once we were 699 Werner 3 250
And therefore paused not to disturb the slumber 763 Juan 1 1100
That anybody should disturb you so 858 Juan 6 371

DISTURBANCE
To prevent universal disturbance and riot 117 To Eliza 32

DISTURB'D
Fond wretch! as if her step disturb'd the dead 218 Bloom 10
Nor rush, disturb'd by haste, to vulgar view 346 Corsair 1 538
As if such but disturb'd the expiring man 382 Lara 2 486
Disturb'd him like the eagle in her nest 423 Island 2 309
He may not be disturb'd until eleven 680 Werner 1 599
That no one likes to be disturb'd at meals 757 Juan 1 709

DISTURBED
And after dreaming a disturbed vision 611 Foscari 3 213

DISTURBING
Without disturbing her yet slumbering guest 795 Juan 2 1342

DISTURBS
'Tis not love disturbs thy rest 100 Marion 5
The goldless age, where gold disturbs no dreams 418 Island 1 216

DISUNITE
Or death disunite us in love's last adieu 99 L Adieu 8
Blend every thought, do all--but disunite 333 Abydos 2 425

DISUNITED
Fare thee well!--thus disunited 208 Fare Thee 57

DITCH
O'er hedge and ditch, through unfrequented ways 268 Hints 814
Because he leapt a ditch ('twas then no wall 731 Deformed 1 650
But the town ditch below was deep as ocean 868 Juan 7 83
Was not like Jacob's) or to cross a ditch 873 Juan 7 416
For having thrown himself into a ditch 887 Juan 8 561
Threw them all down into the ditch again 887 Juan 8 568
He clear'd hedge, ditch, and double post, and rail 959 Juan 14 258

DITCHER
They wrung it out, and though a thirsty ditcher 784 Juan 2 677

DITCHES
Thicker grows the strife: thy ditches 736 Deformed 2 95
In ditches, fields, or wheresoe'er they felt 880 Juan 8 140
That water-land of Dutchmen and of ditches 915 Juan 10 498

DITTY
Teems not each ditty with the glorious tale 9 Harold 1 396
Such was this ditty of Tradition's days 420 Island 2 79

DIURETIC
Like hail, to make a bloody diuretic 879 Juan 8 91

DIURNAL
(Pray is it diurnal 232 Murray-B 35

DIVAN
Old Giaffir sate in his Divan 324 Abydos 1 24
Thou know'st not what in our Divan 331 Abydos 2 251
In full Divan the despot scoff'd 332 Abydos 2 326
Who look'd not lovingly on that Divan 348 Corsair 2 106
As an amusement after the Divan 863 Juan 6 726
A goodly spirit for a state divan 964 Juan 14 555

DIVAN'S
Beat thy Divan's approaching hour 324 Abydos 1 74

DIVED
But now, or where? He dived, and rose no more 431 Island 4 67
Then dived--it seem'd as if to rise no more 432 Island 4 206
And was all clay again. And then I dived 486 Manfred 2 173

DIVER
Which draws the diver to the crimson cave 420 Island 2 140

DIVERGED
Together. You diverged from that dread path 679 Werner 1 540

DIVERGING
How soon, diverging from their source 137 Clare 22

DIVERS
Where the Divers of Bathos lie drown'd in a heap 227 Moore-A 7
The depths where divers hold the pearl in chase 431 Island 4 112
Thus drownings are much talk'd of by the divers 778 Juan 2 247
And divers smoked superb pipes decorated 838 Juan 5 421

DIVERSION
Young, old, high, low, at once the same diversion share 15 Harold 1 719
Who made that bold diversion 162 War Song 29
Here was no lack of innocent diversion 806 Juan 3 273
But heaven must be diverted; its diversion 946 Juan 13 321

DIVERSIONS
Of Incest and such like diversions 233 Nihil 9

DIVERSITY
What with a small diversity of climate 932 Juan 12 185

DIVERT
Just to divert my thoughts a little space 448 Beppo 507
But Donna Inez, to divert the train 770 Juan 1 1513

DIVERTED
Diverted from its first career 99 Young Lady 8
And now, diverted by his milder sway 377 Lara 2 172
And now they were diverted by their suite 811 Juan 3 617
But heaven must be diverted; its diversion 946 Juan 13 321

DIVERTS
Its solitude, and nothing more diverts it 619 Foscari 4 252

DIVES
Unhappy Dives! in an evil hour 223 To Dives 1
As dives a hero headlong to his grave 424 Island 2 365

DIVEST
Would still, albeit in vain, the heavy heart divest 23 Harold 2 216
Or Wahab's rebel brood, who dared divest 31 Harold 2 733

DIVESTED
Of soothing compliments divested 100 Marion 31
Became divested of his native modesty 774 Juan 2 8

DIVIDE
Deem ye what bounds the rival realms divide 9 Harold 1 361
Though Cleon's candour would the palm divide 126 Recoll 338
All I ask is to divide 187 French-A 37
Were safety hopeless--rather than divide 205 Love, Death 3
Mountains and seas divide us, but I claim 211 Augusta-C 3
They do divide our being; they become 213 Dream 9
Still Skeffington and Goose divide the prize 249 Bards 597
Of sullen earth divide each winding sheet 298 Age 20
'Ye waves, divide not lovers long 329 Abydos 2 17
When those who win at length divide the prey 338 Corsair 1 40
Where Asia's bounds and ours divide 393 Corinth 812
And now the two canoes in chase divide 429 Island 3 233
And with the Spirit of the place divide 485 Manfred 2 105
To lighten or divide it. Since the day 512 Faliero 2 219
The floor which doth divide us from the dead 519 Faliero 3 17
I will divide with you; think not I waver 527 Faliero 3 606
Placed him to dig, but not divide the wealth 583 Sardan 4 348
The dungeon walls must still divide us. True 602 Foscari 2 62
I will divide this with you. Let us think 611 Foscari 3 215
Who didst divide the wave from wave, and call 627 Cain 1 7
These are my realms! So that I do divide 636 Cain 1 549
Now, Cain! I will divide thy burden with thee 654 Cain 3 551
Shall aught divide us. The storm of the night 671 Werner 1 18
While they last, let me comfort or divide them 673 Werner 1 147
The Oder to divide, as Moses did 687 Werner 2 318
With the free foresters divide no spoil 886 Juan 8 534
Which mortals generously would divide 943 Juan 13 151

DIVIDED
O'er hearts divided and o'er hopes destroy'd 35 Harold 2 923
And near Albano's scarce divided waves 81 Harold 4 1558
Divided by the dark-blue main 158 Florence 10
Divided, yet beloved in vain 165 Thyrza 6
Since thus divided--equal must it be 192 Fragment-C 19
Divided by the 'Bridge of Sighs 196 Venice-A 14
Resign'd for ever, or divided far 212 Augusta-C 80
That tie is widen'd, not divided 331 Abydos 2 195
As, far divided from his parent deep 424 Island 2 408
Ere the canoes divided, near the spot 430 Island 4 33
Many, but each divided by the wall 438 Tasso 89
He who from me can be divided ne'er 477 Francesca 39
Divided like a house against itself 532 Faliero 4 277
Nor would she deign to accept divided passion 554 Sardan 1 268
For all the popular breath that e'er divided 556 Sardan 1 386
I wish'd to thank you that you have not divided 582 Sardan 4 254

DIVIDED
Morning from night, till then divided never   627   Cain   1   6
Divided with me; life and death--and time   636   Cain   1   545
(The old nobles being divided from their children   715   Werner   5   140
Divided in twelve books; each book containing   771   Juan   1   1594
Which he divided with Pedrillo, who   783   Juan   2   567
Part was divided, part thrown in the sea   783   Juan   2   613
And now to see them, thus divided, stand   822   Juan   4   357
The women much divided--as is usual   933   Juan   12   217

DIVIDENDS
Shorn of her bishops, banks, and dividends   307   Age   648

DIVIDES
Sunset divides the sky with her, a sea   59   Harold   4   236
While naught divides thee from the vulgar dead   94   Dorset   49
Expires, the steel his sever'd neck divides   108   Nisus   248
Divides thy fate from mine   205   To--B   10
Pass'd by the river that divides the plain   383   Lara   2   556
Which on the Moslem's ottoman divides   425   Island   2   450
Though every wave she climbs divides us more   430   Island   4   7
Juan, by some strange chance, which oft divides   881   Juan   8   209

DIVIDING
Dividing darkness from the dawning main   415   Island   1   8
Whose vigorous offspring by dividing ocean   454   Venice-B   134
His prisoners, dividing them like chapters   803   Juan   3   118
That awful pause, dividing life from death   878   Juan   7   690

DIVINE
Prophetic fount, and oracle divine   27   Harold   2   470
There Harold gazes on a work divine   42   Harold   3   410
Making kings' rights divine, by some Draconic
   clause   45   Harold   3   616
Thy choral memory of the Bard divine   57   Harold   4   147
The Tuscan father's comedy divine   61   Harold   4   355
Than Art in galleries: though a work divine   64   Harold   4   547
The dictatorial wreath,--couldst thou divine   67   Harold   4   748
Though from our birth the faculty divine   74   Harold   4   1139
As 'twere its natural torches, for divine   74   Harold   4   1148
Yet I forego that bliss divine   90   To M.S.G.-A   3
By any ties but those divine   90   To M.S.G.-A   19
She fear'd that, too divine for earth   97   To--M--   11
In this life of probation for rapture divine   100   L Adieu   37
Like thine ennobled, hardly less divine   107   Nisus   178
She's now most divine, and I bow at the shrine   116   Strephon   7
Now bright in rays divine   131   L'Amitie   14
On earth thou wert all but divine   151   Soul-A   5
Thy truth in absence to divine   168   The Chain   6
Now to produce in a 'divine sestetto   171   Address-B   36
'Tis strange it still appears divine   173   Mrs. Lamb   4
Of three bright colours, each divine   188   On Star   21
Like thee, Man is in part divine   191   Prometheus-B   47
But which their doom may none divine   196   Venice-A   18
In Judah deem'd divine   220   Belshaz-B   6
And there it stood,--all formless--but divine   222   Spirit   4
To me, divine Apollo, grant--O   226   Thurlow-A   7
The works thou deemest most divine   234   Strahan   14
Because Parnassus, though a mount divine   264   Hints   529
(The Lord forgive him!), 'Bravo! grand! divine   267   Hints   772
Though there his altars are no more divine   268   Minerva   10
Not such as first, by her divine command   269   Minerva   77
And making them substance; 'tis something divine   283   Blues   2   141
They threw their pens down in divine disgust   285   Vision   39
Whose memoirs could be render'd more divine   297   Vision   796
Else may we dread the wrath divine   319   Giaour   910
And all, save the spirit of man, is divine   323   Abydos   1   15
Though there his altars are no more divine   355   Corsair   3   10
Already polish'd by the hand divine   355   Corsair   2   542
The cross he deem'd no more divine   390   Corinth   539
To fix our thoughts on things divine   394   Corinth   953
Converted by Christ to his blood so divine   395   Corinth   1003
And he was proud, ye may divine   408   Mazeppa   158
Beyond the sound whose charm is half divine   420   Island   2   82
Divine in hookas, glorious in a pipe   425   Island   2   454
And revell'd among men and things divine   437   Tasso   25
That they who kneel to idols so divine   463   Dante   4   31
Least like to thee in attributes divine   464   Dante   4   98
With us in Mary Mother's Son divine   468   Morgante   171
For Providence divine, in you and others   471   Morgante   323
Of Mary Mother, sinless and divine   471   Morgante   354
Divine the frankness of the Hungarian, who   680   Werner   1   576
Learn to divine and judge his actions. Young   689   Werner   2   437
Not any of the many could divine   750   Juan   1   178
And then there are such things as love divine   756   Juan   1   625
And here thou art a god indeed divine   757   Juan   1   700
You never could divine his real thought   806   Juan   3   324
His question, much too merry to divine   806   Juan   3   335
And must thy lyre, so long divine   812   Juan   3   717
It made Anacreon's song divine   812   Juan   3   751
A little heavy, but no less divine   813   Juan   3   818
About the right divine how far we should   835   Juan   5   237
For all was vast, still, fragrant, and divine   842   Juan   5   680
She thought hers gave a double 'right divine   847   Juan   5   1031

DIVINE
Which none divine, and every one obeys   902   Juan   9   390
Of any worship wake some thoughts divine   948   Juan   13   488
Attuned by voices more or less divine   954   Juan   13   851
Juan was something she could not divine   975   Juan   15   445
The first--but what she could not well divine   984   Juan   16   240
And from its context thought she could divine   985   Juan   16   291
Are so divine, that I must deem them real   994   Juan   16   904

DIVINED
Or why or how he hath divined it, Belus   558   Sardan   1   508
You have divined the man? As sure as you   697   Werner   3   128

DIVINELY
And temple more divinely desolate   74   Harold   4   1172
Then will I sing divinely crown'd   139   Anacreon-C   19

DIVINER
Great Socrates? And thou, Diviner still   970   Juan   15   138

DIVINEST
Who knows not, knows not man's divinest lore   13   Harold   1   622

DIVING
Diving for turtle in the depths below   432   Island   4   196
Hush'd into depths beyond the watcher's diving   799   Juan   2   1574

DIVINITIES
Have proved but dropsies, taken for divinities   814   Juan   3   856

DIVINITY
Their full divinity inadequate   62   Harold   4   461
Is still impregnate with divinity   63   Harold   4   493
His full Divinity was felt   200   Ode-C   20
The more I should believe in her divinity   447   Beppo   488
Proves his divinity,--and yet sometimes   570   Sardan   2   552
The first attack at once proved the Divinity   919   Juan   11   41

DIVISION
Power sways but by division, her resource   333   Abydos   2   434
While still Division sows the seeds of woe   460   Dante   2   134

DIVORCE
The only expedient is general divorce   117   To Eliza   31
The lawyers did their utmost for divorce   751   Juan   1   254
And how Alfonso sued for a divorce   770   Juan   1   1503
A lad of sixteen causing a divorce   774   Juan   2   15

DIVORCED
I never thought to be divorced except   624   Foscari   5   247
Wishing each other, not divorced, but dead   750   Juan   1   203
Divorced or doing thereanent. Ye annals   928   Juan   11   626

DIVORCEMENT
After twelve years divorcement from my parents   709   Werner   4   331

DIVORCES
From divorces down to dresses   197   Rogers   41
Or what becomes of damage and divorces   444   Beppo   296
The history of divorces, which, though chequer'd   903   Juan   9   423

DIVORCING
Or marriage, by divorcing them thus oddly   972   Juan   15   282

DIVULGE
If all our Arab tales divulge or dream   358   Corsair   3   157
If we divulge them, doubtless they are worth   616   Foscari   4   90

DIVULGED
Why comes he not? Such truths to be divulged   375   Lara   2   27
Of gore divulged the cause) that he was dead   835   Juan   5   279

DIZEN'D
A thing of robes and trinkets, dizen'd out   523   Faliero   3   309

DIZZINESS
In dizziness of distance; when a leap   482   Manfred   1   277
For all was doubt and dizziness; he thought   788   Juan   2   890
Afflicting young folks with a sort of dizziness   877   Juan   7   664

DIZZY
But weakness conquer'd--swam his dizzy glance   184   Julian   36
I'm almost dead, and always dizzy   232   Doctor   88
These Kaled snatches: dizzy with the blow   380   Lara   2   388
The dizzy race seem'd almost done   413   Mazeppa   641
And so the film comes o'er him--and the dizzy   453   Venice-B   50
Along the depth beneath, and ne'er feel dizzy   511   Faliero   2   199
All the delusion of the dizzy scene   529   Faliero   4   62
For seeming slain in that cold dizzy trance   588   Sardan   5   98
And as he gazed, his dizzy brain spun fast   788   Juan   2   873
For he was dizzy, busy, and his veins   882   Juan   8   258

DO
Have I not seen what human things could do   75   Harold   4   1217

DO

But ah! my girl, you do not love	91	Caroline-B		48
Warmly, as it was wont to do	154	Happy		4
All which women or which men do	197	Rogers		37
With false Ambition what had I to do	212	Augusta-C		97
What Nature could, but would not, do	229	Marble		3
Tells us strange tales, as other travellers do	245	Bards		223
Which lexicographers declined to do	257	Hints		76
And yet, God knows! what may not authors do	260	Hints		289
And hoarse with having little else to do	285	Vision		10
And yet they had even then enough to do	285	Vision		34
Which is to act as we are bid to do	287	Vision		176
That hell has nothing better left to do	290	Vision		325
Are of a former life, and what we do	293	Vision		538
But there be deeds thou dar'st not do	325	Abydos	1	121
But what could single slavery do	332	Abydos	2	281
When all that we design to do	332	Abydos	2	360
No deed they've done, nor deed shall do	334	Abydos	2	474
Much hath been done, but more remains to do	350	Corsair	2	194
In vain he doth whate'er a chief may do	379	Lara	2	290
Whate'er was to be done, would do	407	Mazeppa		69
What 'gainst their numbers could I do	410	Mazeppa		330
Against the many oft will dare and do	427	Island	3	54
To act whatever duty bade them do	433	Island	4	282
And you at Rome would do as Romans do	441	Beppo		66
Where none can make out what you say or do	442	Beppo		152
Which lasted, as arrangements sometimes do	446	Beppo		418
Of their sad rout, though he did all knight can do	467	Morgante		62
Thus those who in suspicion live must do	468	Morgante		176
Then will I every thing at your command do	471	Morgante		375
But for domestic quarrels one will do	749	Juan	1	152
Tney lived together, as most people do	755	Juan	1	516
They mean to scold, and very often do	760	Juan	1	858
But what he did, is much what you would do	760	Juan	1	890
(At least this is the thing most people do	770	Juan	1	1525
It trembled as magnetic needles do	771	Juan	1	1580
In short, I must not lead the life I did do	773	Juan	1	1724
Not knowing what himself to say, or do	781	Juan	2	468
That some, I really think, do never die	782	Juan	2	516
And Zoe spent hers, as most women do	791	Juan	2	1086
I feel this tediousness will never do	816	Juan	3	977
But next, when I'm engaged to sing there--do go	827	Juan	4	704
Replied the other, 'what can a man do	834	Juan	5	162
To ope this door, which they could really do	842	Juan	5	707
Begone!' she cried, with kindling eyes--'and do	866	Juan	6	922
And this young fellow--say what can he do	875	Juan	7	493
Or done, is light to what she'll say or do	904	Juan	9	511
That they as easily might do the youngster	923	Juan	11	279
For there's no saying what they will or may do	939	Juan	12	616
But do you more, Sempronius--don't deserve it	943	Juan	13	138
Who, 'stead of saying what you now should do	961	Juan	14	397
The first is rather more than mortal can do	970	Juan	15	163
Who look upon them as they ought to do	974	Juan	15	424
Your stomach! Ere you dine, the French will do	977	Juan	15	572
'Tis wonderful what fable will not do	979	Juan	15	708

DOCILE

And well the docile crew that skilful urchin guides	22	Harold	2	162
But spirited and docile too	407	Mazeppa		68
Poor little thing! She was as fair as docile	913	Juan	10	409
Their docile esquires also did the same	994	Juan	16	854

DOCILITY

He almost honour'd him for his docility	944	Juan	13	170

DOCKS

Who, still unlaunch'd from Grecian docks	225	Embargo		3

DOCTOR

And Master G-- recites what Doctor Busby sings	170	Address-B		16
Or send it back to Doctor Donne	227	Thurlow-B		7
Dear Doctor, I have read your play	231	Doctor		1
Dear Doctor, I am yours	232	Doctor		90
So the Doctor being found	238	Bray		7
But, Doctor, one word	239	Bray		37
And prophet, pontiff, doctor, alchymist	732	Deformed	1	675
With which the Doctor paid off an old pox	762	Juan	1	1031
The king commands us, and the doctor quacks us	774	Juan	2	29
Like Burns (whom Doctor Currie well describes	814	Juan	3	828

DOCTORS

Each course enough? or doctors dire dissuaded	305	Age		509
'And here our doctors are of one accord	472	Morgante		401
I ask'd the doctors after his disease	751	Juan	1	270
He hew'd away, like doctors of theology	892	Juan	8	862
And sent the doctors in a new direction	912	Juan	10	340
Doctors less famous for their cures than fees	961	Juan	14	380

DOCTORS'

Search Doctors' Commons six months from my date	276	Waltz		207
Save death or Doctors' Commons--so he died	751	Juan	1	288
And founded Doctors' Commons:--I have conn'd	903	Juan	9	422

DOCTORS'

Of Doctors' Commons: but she dreaded first	963	Juan	14	493

DOCTRINE

To shame the doctrine of the Sadducee	20	Harold	2	66
And this doctrine would meet with a general resistance	116	To Eliza		4
In his doctrine, at least as a teacher	238	Bray		9
And that same devilish doctrine of the Persian	946	Juan	13	325
As many doubts as any other doctrine	946	Juan	13	327

DOCTRINES

Or doctrines less severe inspire	132	Prayer		28
With the best doctrines till we quite o'erflow	286	Vision		109
Doubtless to that of doctrines the most true	875	Juan	7	533

DOCUMENTS

So let me have the proper documents	297	Vision		791

DODGING

'Twere not for want of lamps to aid his dodging his	922	Juan	11	221

DODONA

Oh! where, Dodona, is thine aged grove	27	Harold	2	469

DOE

I look'd at Wordsworth's milk-white Rylstone Doe; Hillo	230	I Read		6

DOES

As a sinner, you can't care what Sin does	239	Bray		42
That's true; but pity, as you know, does make	677	Werner	1	413

DOFF

Yes! doff that covering, where morocco shines	251	Bards		739
When you must doff the ducal bonnet from	540	Faliero	5	154
How the old red-shanks scamper! Could they doff	737	Deformed	2	177

DOFF'D

(Where I doff'd mine for these, and came on hither	675	Werner	1	256
Their hose as they have doff'd their hats, 'twould be	737	Deformed	2	178

DOG

(See also BULL-DOG, WATCH-DOG, WILD-DOG)

My dog howls at the gate	5	Harold	1	133
Perchance my dog will whine in vain	6	Harold	1	186
I arose with the dawn; with my dog as my guide	136	Highlander		17
But the poor dog, in life the firmest friend	154	Dog		7
From Mr. Hammond to Dog Dent	231	Doctor		58
Because if a live dog, 'tis said	238	Orford		5
His son's so sharp--he'll see the dog a peer	260	Hints		250
Of a dog when gone rabid, than listen two hours	278	Blues	1	48
Tny Scaligers--for what was 'Dog the Great	303	Age		416
'Tis said they use no better than a dog any	448	Beppo		557
Vile dog! 'tis past his patience to sustain	470	Morgante		246
In water, sorely grieved the dog and cat	474	Morgante		531
Dog! Man! Devil! Your obedient humble servant	730	Deformed	1	586
The creature was his father's dog that died	783	Juan	2	563
At a per-centage; a child cross, dog ill	855	Juan	6	163
Or as a little dog will lead the blind	873	Juan	7	381

DOG-BARK

The distant dog-bark; and perceived between	805	Juan	3	212

DOG-DAYS

Love with you, and been in the dog-days stung	848	Juan	5	1036

DOGE

The ocean-city's dreaded Doge	196	Venice-A		12
Too long--at least so thinks the Doge. How bears he	500	Faliero	1	5
Unto the Doge, and hasten to inform him	500	Faliero	1	29
The sentence will be sent up to the Doge	500	Faliero	1	41
Health and respect to the Doge Faliero	501	Faliero	1	75
The nephew of a Doge? and of that blood	502	Faliero	1	159
Redress. Of whom? Of God and of the Doge	505	Faliero	1	358
Sometime my general, now the Doge Faliero	505	Faliero	1	391
The late Doge; keeping still my old command	505	Faliero	1	396
Because my general is Doge, and will not	505	Faliero	1	408
The Doge of Venice, and I cannot give it	505	Faliero	1	413
He was not a shamed dotard like the Doge	506	Faliero	1	426
Hath made me Doge to be insulted: but	506	Faliero	1	455
At every hazard; and if Venice' Doge	507	Faliero	1	507
Some rumours that the Doge was greatly moved	507	Faliero	1	557
The Doge cannot suspect you? Suspect me	509	Faliero	2	39
The Count Val di Marino, now our Doge	510	Faliero	2	83
Here comes the Doge--shall I retire? It may	510	Faliero	2	133
In Venice save the Doge, this blight, this brand	513	Faliero	2	277
The Doge--what answer gave he? That there was	516	Faliero	2	536
The Doge is a mere puppet, who can scarce	516	Faliero	2	545
To arms!--we are betray'd--it is the Doge	522	Faliero	3	211

DOGE
Of Doge, but of a man who has been great   523 Faliero   3   322
Before he was degraded to a Doge   523 Faliero   3   323
Struck without special order of the Doge   524 Faliero   3   368
I will abide by Doge Faliero's counsel   524 Faliero   3   415
From the hour they made me Doge, the Doge they
  made me   525 Faliero   3   467
In dark suspicious conflict with the Doge   525 Faliero   3   499
His separate charge: the Doge will now return   526 Faliero   3   516
Doge, when I greet you next, my homage to you   526 Faliero   3   519
A moment to accompany the Doge   526 Faliero   3   546
Doge! Doge! this vacillation is unworthy   527 Faliero   3   594
Next to the Doge. To the Doge? Assuredly   533 Faliero   4   337
Doge Dandolo survived to ninety summers   535 Faliero   4   506
All's silent, and all's lost! Now, Doge,
  denounce me   537 Faliero   4   599
As delegated from the Doge, the signal   537 Faliero   4   615
You know the Doge? I served with him at Zara   538 Faliero   5   57
And, for the rest, all Venice knows her Doge   538 Faliero   5   62
The Doge stands to behold the chase of bulls   539 Faliero   5   94
In any annals, the Doge Faliero   540 Faliero   5   138
Avogadori, order that the Doge   540 Faliero   5   143
Doge--for such still you are, and by the law   540 Faliero   5   152
Their fellowship in treason with the Doge   540 Faliero   5   176
Was not the place of Doge sufficient for ye   540 Faliero   5   200
Because the Doge, who should protect the law   541 Faliero   5   230
And can it be, that the great Doge of Venice   541 Faliero   5   240
Daily since I was Doge; but if you will   542 Faliero   5   302
Were deep offence. But question even the Doge   543 Faliero   5   348
I sought to free the groaning nations! Doge   543 Faliero   5   399
Marino Faliero, Doge of Venice   544 Faliero   5   477
The place wherein as Doge thou shouldst be
  painted   545 Faliero   5   496
When the beholder knows a Doge conspired   545 Faliero   5   512
As Doge, clad in the ducal robes and cap   545 Faliero   5   516
And they are ready to attend the Doge   546 Faliero   5   556
The Doge! Yes, Doge, thou hast lived and thou
  shalt die   546 Faliero   5   557
That on my day of landing here as Doge   547 Faliero   5   629
And they who are indwellers. Doge of Venice   547 Faliero   5   669
So now the Doge is nothing, and at last   548 Faliero   5   697
The King of Sparta, and the Doge of Venice   548 Faliero   5   717
Robed in their gowns of state, ranged round the
  Doge   549 Faliero   5   802
One has approach'd the Doge, and now they strip   549 Faliero   5   807
Proceed. And the chief judge, the Doge? No--he   595 Foscari   1   23
By poison. When the Doge declared that he   596 Foscari   1   35
Orphans? But did the Doge make you so? Yes   596 Foscari   1   40
'Doge Foscari, my debtor for the deaths   596 Foscari   1   51
Or Doge? Why, no; not if I can avoid it   598 Foscari   1   189
So is the Doge; he has a son at stake   598 Foscari   1   216
Though they sweep both the Doge and son from
  life   599 Foscari   1   241
I tell thee, Doge, 'tis Venice is dishonour'd   604 Foscari   2   164
With or without the presence of the Doge   604 Foscari   2   202
I became Doge, or dream'd of such advancement   605 Foscari   2   204
Doge! have you aught in answer? Something from   606 Foscari   2   323
The Doge; it may be also from a parent   606 Foscari   2   324
My mission here is to the Doge. Then say   606 Foscari   2   325
The Doge will choose his own ambassador   606 Foscari   2   326
This means that you are more Doge than father   608 Foscari   2   414
Our children will be cared for by the Doge   611 Foscari   3   219
I feel too much thou hast not. Doge, look there   613 Foscari   3   344
Let us proceed. Doge, lead the way. The torch,
  there   614 Foscari   3   422
Did not the Doge deny this strongly? Doubtless   615 Foscari   4   25
Inform the signory from me, the Doge   618 Foscari   4   203
Pass on. We sought the Doge. He's busy, look   618 Foscari   4   224
(Join'd with the Doge) decided his destruction   619 Foscari   4   291
And the old Doge, who knew him doom'd, smiled
  on him   619 Foscari   4   300
By the Doge Foscari, with citizens   620 Foscari   4   317
May I pass on? You may. How bears the Doge   620 Foscari   4   343
With the Doge on his late and private grief   620 Foscari   5   13
Where is the Doge? This instant retired hence   622 Foscari   5   112
And will they press their answer on the Doge   622 Foscari   5   119
You are no longer Doge; you are released   623 Foscari   5   168
Live to hear this!--the first doge who e'er heard   624 Foscari   5   230
The Doge unto his private palace. Say   624 Foscari   5   271
Unto their home by the new Doge, not clad   626 Foscari   5   351
As Doge, but simply as a senator   626 Foscari   5   352

DOGELESS
Above the dogeless city's vanish'd sway   55 Harold   4   31

DOGES
Of her dead Doges are declined to dust   57 Harold   4   128
Where lie two doges who preceded me   508 Faliero   1   613
Vault where two Doges rest--my sires! who died   519 Faliero   3   23
Hundreds of doges, and their deeds and dates   610 Foscari   3   121

DOGE'S
The Doge's delegated powers   386 Corinth   219
Had he instead of on the Doge's throne   503 Faliero   1   228

DOGE'S
What was the Doge's answer? That he was   509 Faliero   2   1
Guards! form the Doge's escort to his chamber   546 Faliero   5   576
This is the Doge's palace; I am wife   599 Foscari   1   271
In Venice had to dread a Doge's frown   605 Foscari   2   239
Shall be the last of the old Doge's reign   615 Foscari   4   19

DOGESHIP
'The good day or good night?' his Dogeship
  answer'd   619 Foscari   4   294

DOGGEREL
Forgetting doggerel leads not to degrees   255 Bards   974

DOGGING
Yon score of vassals dogging at your heels   693 Werner   2   658
Dogging him yester-even. You reclosed   702 Werner   3   504

DOGMA
As is the Christian dogma rather rough   899 Juan   9   198

DOGS
(See also BULL-DOGS, HELL-DOGS, LAP-DOGS)
Then to the dogs resign the unburied slain   18 Harold   1   903
Here's a rope's end for the dogs   157 Hodgson   52
Even dogs assail'd their masters, all save one   189 Darkness   47
The dogs to be sure have got nothing to eat   225 Ode-D   10
Dogs blink their covey, flints withhold the spark   264 Hints   555
Their dogs and oxen knew their own degrees   303 Age   401
Before the dogs of Moscow fall   324 Abydos   1   96
And he saw the lean dogs beneath the wall   389 Corinth   454
Scared by the dogs, from the human prey   389 Corinth   476
The wild birds flew; the wild dogs fled   396 Corinth   1059
The current's pleasure. Would the dogs were in
  it   687 Werner   2   315
All ready for the chase? The dogs are order'd   705 Werner   4   75
Forbear! Ha! ha! here's equity! The dogs   740 Deformed   310
Knowing (dogs have such intellectual noses   781 Juan   2   461
Where I, like other 'dogs, have had my day   795 Juan   2 1323
Those servile dogs are not so proudly eyed   833 Juan   5   107
For dogs, or to be slain with pangs refined   849 Juan   5 1123
Dogs, or men!--for I flatter you in saying   868 Juan   7   49
That ye are dogs--your betters far--ye may   868 Juan   7   50
With 'schnapps'--sad dogs! whom 'Hundsfot,' or
  'Verflucter   916 Juan 10   567
Were shaken down, and 'dogs had had their day   971 Juan 15   180
For the Lord Henry, link'd with dogs and horses   989 Juan 16   586

DOG'S
(See also WATCH-DOG'S)
The scalps were in the wild dog's maw   389 Corinth   471
The dog's death, and the wolf's; but thou shalt
  fall   546 Faliero   5   565
I would have saved a peasant's or a dog's, I slew   720 Werner   5   457

DOGS'
As such their hearts are something. So my dogs'
  are   556 Sardan   1   391

DOG'S-EAR
And if a single dog's-ear of this packet   682 Werner   1   691

DOG-STAR
This female dog-star of her little sky   209 Sketch   77
And may appear so when the dog-star rages   745 Juan   Ded   30

DOING
(See also WELL-DOING)
Doing his evil will, nor less elate   42 Harold   3   427
And marvell'd what they were doing   179 Devil's Dr   238
What are you doing now   229 Moore-B   1ff
Of doing people harm about the throne   295 Vision   635
Is wound up to the lust of doing ill   437 Tasso   73
Their days are either pass'd in doing nothing   449 Beppo   567
Doing the very best that in him lay   470 Morgante   291
This wreck of a realm--this deed of my doing   488 Manfred   2   350
For doing all its duties, and replying   513 Faliero   2   344
The last night of mere words: I'd fain be doing   526 Faliero   3   509
Though doubts of their well doing, to arrange   867 Juan   6   954
Great deeds are doing--how shall I relate 'em   877 Juan   7   646
Divorced or doing thereanent. Ye annals   928 Juan 11   626
I have seen a Congress doing all that's mean   929 Juan 11   662
(By doing easily, whene'er she chose   986 Juan 16   394

DOINGS
With all its sinful doings, I must say   445 Beppo   321
Fine doings! goodly doings! honest doings   683 Werner   2   1
A long and loud farewell to its great doings   714 Werner   5   115
For my part, to such doings I'm a stranger   756 Juan   1   636
There's doubtless something in domestic doings   802 Juan   3   57
Of this same mystic friar's curious doings   987 Juan 16   471

DOLCE
There rose a Carlo Dolce or a Titian   950 Juan 13   563

DOLDRUMS

I saw her in the doldrums; for the wind	426	Island	2	508

DOLED

His food and wine were doled out duly still	299	Age		76

DOLFINO'S

Dolfino's father was my friend, and Lando	524	Faliero	3	423

DOLLAR

Your arm, and I'll bet Moscow to a dollar	890	Juan	8	775

DOLLARS

And averaged each from ten to a hundred dollars	803	Juan	3	120
Some went off dearly; fifteen hundred dollars	830	Juan	4	905
Containing ingots, bags of dollars, coins	931	Juan	12	90

DOLON

When he allured poor Dolon:--you had better	954	Juan	13	839

DOLOUR

And ne'er to be described; for to the dolour	960	Juan	14	319

DOLPHIN

Dies like the dolphin, whom each pang imbues	59	Harold	4	259

DOLPHINS

And sportive dolphins bend them through the spray	364	Corsair	3	560
The dolphins, not unconscious of the day	415	Island	1	9
Far o'er its face the dolphins sported on	435	Island	4	369
And dolphins gambol in the lion's den	659	Heaven		278

DOLPHIN'S

And dolphin's leap, and little billow crost	797	Juan	2	1446

DOLT

Than does your excellency. Dolt! Why, if	686	Werner	2	203

DOMAIN

To darken o'er the fair domain	310	Giaour		61
His Corsair's isle was once thine own domain	356	Corsair	3	64
The Serfs are glad through Lara's wide domain	366	Lara	1	1
Of Otho's lands and Lara's broad domain	383	Lara	2	557
Dominion and domain. Who knows? our son	673	Werner	1	88
Destruction, till I reach my own domain	681	Werner	1	630
On the domain) are such a sort of knaves	704	Werner	4	41
Yes, but the unsettled state of our domain	705	Werner	4	102

DOMAINS

And you will live in peace on your domains	708	Werner	4	231
Be silenced. Ay, with half of my domains	719	Werner	5	404
Of your domains; a thousand, ay, ten thousand	721	Werner	5	535

DOMDANIEL'S

Domdaniel's dread destroyer, who o'erthrew	244	Bards		213

DOME

Monastic dome! condemn'd to uses vile	4	Harold	1	59
Oh, dome displeasing unto British eye	8	Harold	1	289
That foil'd the knights in Marialva's dome	8	Harold	1	298
A dome, where flaunts she in such glorious sheen	8	Harold	1	339
Though not to one dome circumscribeth she	14	Harold	1	672
The dome of Thought, the palace of the Soul	20	Harold	2	49
His breast and beak against his wiry dome	37	Harold	3	133
In Arno's dome of Art's most princely shrine	64	Harold	4	542
The milk of conquest yet within the dome	68	Harold	4	786
Would build up all her triumphs in one dome	74	Harold	4	1146
His way through thorns to ashes--glorious dome	77	Harold	4	1311
His shrunken ashes, raise this dome. How smiles	78	Harold	4	1366
But lo, the dome, the vast and wondrous dome	78	Harold	4	1369
The lamps of gold, and haughty dome which vies	78	Harold	4	1402
While stands the Capitol, immortal dome	110	Nisus		405
His voice in thunder shakes the sounding dome	111	Examination		6
Newstead! fast-falling, once-resplendent dome	119	Newstead-A		1
In the dome of my Sires as the clear moonbeam falls	164	Newstead-C		1
While thousands, throng'd around the burning dome	169	Address-A		11
Names such as hallow still the dome we lost	169	Address-A		30
Till, like Babel, the new royal dome hath arisen	203	Avatar		74
From the last hill that looks on thy once holy dome	221	Jerusalem		1
Oft as the matchless dome I turn'd to scan	269	Minerva		59
Link'd with the fool that fired the Ephesian dome	271	Minerva		201
In Rome's Pantheon or Gaul's mimic dome	300	Age		122
When Tully fulmined o'er each vocal dome	304	Age		499
Within that dome as yet Decay	313	Giaour		336
To Mecca's dome might bar my pilgrimage	349	Corsair	2	132
And fire the dome from minaret to porch	350	Corsair	2	197
Safe in the dome of one who held their creed	350	Corsair	2	256
He left the dome of Otho, long ere morn	376	Lara	2	101
And here and there some crackling dome	386	Corinth		165
From within the plunder'd dome	393	Corinth		772
A dome, its image, while the base expands	464	Dante	4	51
You inhabited your present dome of beauty	728	Deformed	1	444

DOME

Saint Peter, rear its dome and cross into	731	Deformed	1	607
The spoils of each dome	732	Deformed	1	714
Stalking o'er thy highest dome	736	Deformed	2	83
Some dome surmounted by his meagre face	931	Juan	12	76

DOMES

Are domes where whilome kings did make repair	7	Harold	1	271
Blackening her lovely domes with traces rude	11	Harold	1	481
Saved from Arisba's stately domes o'erthrown	107	Nisus		146
Yet he prefers thee to the gilded domes	122	Newstead-A		149
To Gothic domes of mouldering stone	132	Prayer		18
The brightness of our city, and her domes	598	Foscari	1	165
In the more chasten'd domes of Western kings	843	Juan	5	747

DOMESTIC

Nor calm domestic peace had ever deign'd to taste	4	Harold	1	45
Perish'd, perchance, in some domestic feud	11	Harold	1	475
England! thy beauties are tame and domestic	118	Lachin		37
Domestic happiness will stamp thy fate	126	Recoll		321
But bloom'd in calm domestic quiet	134	Lady-D		32
And reign the Hecate of domestic hells	208	Sketch		54
Famed for their civil and domestic quarrels	228	Vaults		1
Against domestic beasts with watch and ward	469	Morgante		184
He whose domestic treason plants the poniard	532	Faliero	4	303
But for domestic quarrels one will do	749	Juan	1	152
Not having of my own domestic cares	750	Juan	1	184
Victorious virtue, and domestic truth	760	Juan	1	851
There's doubtless something in domestic doings	802	Juan	3	57
I know not if he had domestic cares	850	Juan	5	1181
With some slight heart-quake of domestic treason	944	Juan	13	205

DOMESTICS

Seeing a troop of his domestics dancing	805	Juan	3	229

DOMINATORS

We are the dominators,--each and all	480	Manfred	1	143

DOMINION

Is the dread sceptre and dominion dire	19	Harold	2	7
Where things that own not man's dominion dwell	23	Harold	2	219
He would not yield dominion of his mind	37	Harold	3	105
The fool of false dominion--and a kind	68	Harold	4	802
Concerning woman's soft dominion	101	Marion		44
And Manhood claims his stern dominion	133	E. N. Long		24
But Friendship can vary her gentle dominion	136	Delawarr		5
Grew daily tired of his dominion	408	Mazeppa		169
Dominion and domain. Who knows? our son	673	Werner	1	88
And other minds acknowledged my dominion	816	Juan	4	20

DOMINIONS

The ghosts fled, gibbering, for their own dominions	297	Vision		820
Watching this youngest star of his dominions	666	Heaven		792

DON

And don the purple vest	181	Ode-A		155
I'll therefore take our ancient friend Don Juan	747	Juan	1	6
So, as I said, I'll take my friend Don Juan	747	Juan	1	40
Narrating somewhat of Don Juan's father	748	Juan	1	55
Don Juan's parents lived beside the river	748	Juan	1	63
His father's name was Jose--Don, of course	748	Juan	1	65
Don Jose, like a lineal son of Eve	749	Juan	1	143
Don Jose and his lady quarrell'd--why	750	Juan	1	177
Don Jose and the Donna Inez led	750	Juan	1	201
Before, unluckily, Don Jose died	751	Juan	1	256
Is more than I know--But Don Juan's mother	752	Juan	1	367
Produced her Don more heirs at love than law	754	Juan	1	464
That Inez had, ere Don Alfonso's marriage	755	Juan	1	527
And complimented Don Alfonso's taste	755	Juan	1	534
In young Don Juan's favour, and to him its	756	Juan	1	643
Perhaps to open Don Alfonso's eyes	759	Juan	1	807
And then of Don Alfonso's fifty years	760	Juan	1	852
For Don Alfonso; and she inly swore	760	Juan	1	866
But keeping Julia and Don Juan still	761	Juan	1	965
By this time Don Alfonso was arrived	763	Juan	1	1097
Could enter into Don Alfonso's head	764	Juan	1	1106
'In heaven's name, Don Alfonso, what d'ye mean	764	Juan	1	1130
'Yes, Don Alfonso! husband now no more	764	Juan	1	1161
Ungrateful, perjured, barbarous Don Alfonso	764	Juan	1	1167
The Duke of Ichar, and Don Fernan Nunez	765	Juan	1	1194
The Senhor Don Alfonso stood confused	766	Juan	1	1265
But Don Alfonso stood with downcast looks	766	Juan	1	1281
In Don Alfonso's facts, which just now wore	767	Juan	1	1310
Now, Don Alfonso entering, but alone	768	Juan	1	1377
From delicacy to Don Juan's ear	768	Juan	1	1407
This was Don Juan's earliest scrape; but whether	771	Juan	1	1585
Don Juan bade his valet pack his things	775	Juan	2	65
Don Juan stood, and, gazing from the stern	775	Juan	2	105
A small old spaniel,--which had been Don Jose's	781	Juan	2	457
Don Juan, almost famish'd, and half drown'd	790	Juan	2	1028
Return we to Don Juan. He begun	795	Juan	2	1329
Leaving Don Juan and Haidee to plead	801	Juan	2	1727
Had stopp'd this Canto, and Don Juan's breath	821	Juan	4	330

DON

I leave Don Juan for the present, safe	823 Juan	4	425
Don Juan, here permitted to emerge	826 Juan	4	625
Therefore I'll make Don Juan leave the ship soon	828 Juan	4	773
And now delay the progress of Don Juan	831 Juan	4	935
Into Don Juan's head a thought, which he	836 Juan	5	338
Don Juan, turning to his comrade, who	842 Juan	5	658
Don Juan in his feminine disguise	855 Juan	6	201
Don Juan at his hands, and information	864 Juan	6	786
Don Juan, who was much more sentimental	876 Juan	7	596
Though 'twas Don Juan's first of fields, and though	880 Juan	8	161
Except Don Juan, a mere novice, whose	882 Juan	8	282
But of the first, our little friend Don Juan	884 Juan	8	410
Don Juan raised his little captive from	890 Juan	8	751
Don Juan, who had shone in the late slaughter	900 Juan	9	225
I left Don Juan with his horses baiting	901 Juan	9	331
The Dee, the Don, Balgounie's brig's black wall	909 Juan	10	139
Don Juan, who was real, or ideal	910 Juan	10	153
Don Juan grew a very polish'd Russian	910 Juan	10	161
Don Juan grew, I fear, a little dissipated	910 Juan	10	179
All private favourites of Don Juan;--for	913 Juan	10	394
Don Juan loved her, and she loved him, as	914 Juan	10	417
The blue sea's border; and Don Juan felt	915 Juan	10	514
Don Juan now saw Albion's earliest beauties	916 Juan	10	545
Don Juan had got out on Shooter's Hill	919 Juan	11	57
I say, Don Juan, wrapt in contemplation	919 Juan	11	65
Before Don Juan's feet: he could not tell	920 Juan	11	130
Don Juan, having done the best he could	920 Juan	11	137
Don Juan, our young diplomatic sinner	922 Juan	11	230
Don Juan was presented, and his dress	923 Juan	11	305
Who, like Don Juan, takes an active share	927 Juan	11	546
Howe'er our friend Don Juan might command	933 Juan	12	229
Don Juan was delighted to secure	935 Juan	12	326
Don Juan saw that microcosm on stilts	936 Juan	12	441
To wean Don Juan from the siren's wile	963 Juan	14	518
Whether Don Juan and chaste Adeline	967 Juan	14	769
To read Don Quixote in the original	967 Juan	14	778
But, right or wrong, Don Juan was without it	970 Juan	15	99
Adeline and Don Juan rather blended	975 Juan	15	483
Don Juan sat next an 'a l'Espagnole	977 Juan	15	589
(Who watch'd the changes of Don Juan's brow	985 Juan	16	290
Don Juan, when the midnight hour of pillows	995 Juan	16	923
Don Juan shook, as erst he had been shaken	996 Juan	16	985

DONALD'S

And Evan's, Donald's fame rings in each clansman's ears	39 Harold	3	234

DONATION

I have to offer humbly this donation	711 Werner	4	467

DONATIONS

Our house needs no donations, thanks to yours	711 Werner	4	473

DONATO

That Almoro Donato, as I said	600 Foscari	1	307

DONE

Nor deem'd before his little day was done	4 Harold	1	30
When wanton Wealth her mightiest deeds hath done	7 Harold	1	277
Destruction cowers to mark what deeds are done	10 Harold	1	429
Nor yet, alas, the dreadful work is done	18 Harold	1	909
Who did for me what none beside have done	34 Harold	2	893
Her thirteen hundred years of freedom done	57 Harold	4	113
Too glorious, were this all his mighty arm had done	69 Harold	4	855
His task and mine alike are nearly done	81 Harold	4	1569
Long, though not very many--since have done	81 Harold	4	1577
O'er shades where, when our race was done	89 To Emma		19
Then let us meet, as oft we've done	101 Lady-B		33
Nor soon the jocund feast was done	102 Alva		52
'Old man! he cried, 'this pledge is done	104 Alva		197
Yet, when confinement's lingering hour was done	125 Recoll		255
Can I sing of the deeds which my Fathers have done	148 Farewell-A		25
When Infancy's years of probation are done	149 Newstead-B		20
And the carnage begun, when resistance is done	176 Devil's Dr		75
'Tis but envy, when all's done	197 Rogers		66
I would not do by thee as thou hast done	213 Lady Byron		60
Ere the coming day is done	219 Saul-B		21
This day, of all our days, has done	236 Penelope		1
As if we witness'd all already done	259 Hints		206
I'll tell you Budgell's story,--and have done	268 Hints		822
To do what oft Britannia's self had done	271 Minerva		212
The Gaul retires for once, and all is done	271 Minerva		236
Yet she somehow contrives that all things shall be done	280 Blues	2	12
He's dead--and upper earth with him has done	286 Vision		89
'But since he's here, let's see what he has done	296 Vision		705
Rest from your task--so--bravely done	314 Giaour		370
My wrath is wreak'd, the deed is done	317 Giaour		687
There will he pause till all is done	319 Giaour		891
Who would but do--what he hath done	320 Giaour		1023

DONE

Yet did he but what I had done	320 Giaour		1062
Can he smile on such deeds as his children have done	323 Abydos	1	17
He read how much his wrath had done	325 Abydos	1	117
Yes, fondly, wisely hast thou done	327 Abydos	1	351
'Steer to that shore!'--they sail. 'Do this!'-- 'tis done	339 Corsair	1	77
The breeze will freshen when the day is done	340 Corsair	1	159
For Conrad's plans matured, at once were done	352 Corsair	2	385
Grateful for deeds thou hast too rarely done	353 Corsair	2	436
But what her words avouch'd, her charms had done	359 Corsair	3	246
''Tis done--he nearly waked--but it is done	362 Corsair	3	430
Enquiry into deeds at distance done	378 Lara	2	239
And all but the after carnage done	393 Corinth		770
Who would not do as I have done	398 Parisina		204
See what thy guilty love hath done	399 Parisina		294
Creeping as it before had done	405 Chillon		264
Can less have said or more have done	407 Mazeppa		100
The dizzy race seem'd almost done	413 Mazeppa		641
His first and last career is done	413 Mazeppa		694
But ere he break--a deed is to be done	415 Island	1	16
Remorse for the black deed as yet half done	417 Island	1	157
Did more than Europe's discipline had done	422 Island	2	270
And asking if indeed the day were done	424 Island	2	369
But this is o'er, my pleasant task is done	437 Tasso		33
Like mourning coaches when the funeral's done	442 Beppo		160
'Tis to be wish'd it had been sooner done	452 Beppo		791
Ruin, already proud of the deeds done	459 Dante	2	73
And for this thou hast warr'd with me.--'Tis done	465 Dante	4	146
Which shall make thee wish it done	481 Manfred	1	231
Above what they have done	660 Heaven		421
What hath he done	669 Heaven		1102
What hast thou done? Left one thing undone which	683 Werner	1	749
When heaven with the world hath done	729 Deformed	4	473
He would not justify what he had done	768 Juan	1	1387
Was all that for the present could be done	781 Juan	2	492
They glared upon each other--all was done	783 Juan	2	573
One glance at him, and said, 'Heaven's will be done	785 Juan	2	694
Famine, despair, cold, thirst, and heat, had done	787 Juan	2	809
(A race of mere impostors, when all's done	789 Juan	2	942
Who was her chosen: what was said or done	799 Juan	2	1614
The Arab lore and poet's song were done	815 Juan	3	899
I say a thing, it must at once be done	841 Juan	5	645
Who landed lower down, their landing done	880 Juan	8	115
And orders, and on all that he had done	900 Juan	9	237
Hectic and brief as summer's day nigh done	908 Juan	10	62
From what some people say 'twill be when done	941 Juan	12	692
To recommence in August--now was done	946 Juan	13	330
The dinner and the soiree too were done	981 Juan	16	57

DONNA

That which adorn'd the brain of Donna Inez	748 Juan	1	88
Now Donna Inez had, with all her merit	749 Juan	1	153
Don Jose and the Donna Inez led	750 Juan	1	201
But that which Donna Inez most desired	751 Juan	1	305
For Donna Inez dreaded the Mythology	752 Juan	1	328
'Tis not with Donna Inez I would shut	753 Juan	1	413
There was the Donna Julia, whom to call	753 Juan	1	435
Boabdil wept, of Donna Julia's kin	754 Juan	1	446
'Tis said that Donna Julia's grandmamma	754 Juan	1	463
With Donna Inez quite a favourite friend	755 Juan	1	522
That Donna Julia knew the reason why	755 Juan	1	558
And then he thought of Donna Julia's eyes	758 Juan	1	736
Is, that the Donna Inez did not tease	758 Giaour		773
'Twas midnight--Donna Julia was in bed	763 Juan	1	1081
Poor Donna Julia, starting as from sleep	764 Juan	1	1113
But Donna Inez, to divert the train	770 Juan	1	1513
But to our tale: the Donna Inez sent	775 Juan	2	57
Than did the prima donna and the tenor	826 Juan	4	648
'The prima donna, though a little old	827 Juan	4	657
(And other chief points of a 'bella donna	828 Juan	4	748
His mother, Donna Inez, finding, too	911 Juan	10	241

DONNA'S

The 'prima donna's' tuneful heart would bound	444 Beppo		253
But being the prima donna's near relation	827 Juan	4	693

DONNE

Or send it back to Doctor Donne	227 Thurlow-B		7

DONOR

So that he would have been the very donor	988 Juan	16	500

DONOR'S

Which show'd what great discernment was the donor's	913 Juan	10	368

DONS

Here dons, grandees, but chiefly dames abound	15 Harold	1	724

DON'T

The soul's meridian don't become her	134 E. N. Long		75

DON'T

Or say these glances don't become her	143	On Eyes	6
But whom I don't intend to mention	144	Becher-B	18
If you don't warrant my salvation	145	Becher-B	66
But Harriet, I don't wish to flatter	151	Harriet	7
So mind you don't get into debt	230	Murray-A	7
I don't know that--the fellow, Schlegel	231	Doctor	73
But (if they don't rob us	232	Murray-B	4
Who don't speak Italian	232	Murray-B	23
And don't stand shilly-shally	233	Ballad-B	22
She don't seem to take to the name	234	Ballat	28
If my memory don't err	235	New Song	23
'Tis sheer ill-nature--don't the world know best	252	Bards	772
Beware--for God's sake, don't begin like Bowles	259	Hints	194
And hark ye, Southey! pray--but don't be vex'd	265	Hints	657
Who owe us millions--don't we owe the queen	274	Waltz	48
You don't happen to have the Review in your pocket	278	Blues 1	35
Well, sir, the time's coming. Scamp! don't you feel sore	282	Blues 2	108
Don't call upon Scamp, who's already so harass'd	282	Blues 2	122
Said Wilkes, 'don't wait to see them laid in lead	293	Vision	550
I don't like ripping up old stories, since	293	Vision	559
It varied, till I don't think his own mother	294	Vision	620
I don't see wherefore letters should not be	295	Vision	641
Then Satan said to Michael, 'Don't forget	295	Vision	669
Dine and be d--d! I don't mean to be coarse	441	Beppo	71
I don't know how they ever can get over it	443	Beppo	191
One of few things experience don't improve	447	Beppo	438
Although I know them, really don't know why	447	Beppo	472
I only don't see why it should be thus	448	Beppo	540
They cannot read, and so don't lisp in criticism	449	Beppo	569
Nor write, and so they don't affect the muse	449	Beppo	570
One don't know what to say to them, or think	449	Beppo	596
Italian females don't do so outright	451	Beppo	708
Said he; 'don't let us make ourselves absurd	451	Beppo	717
Pray don't you think the weather here is colder	451	Beppo	740
For stories--but I don't believe the half of them	452	Beppo	784
But the world, blind and ignorant, don't prize	466	Morgante	49
The holy father said, 'I don't deceive	469	Morgante	215
They don't disturb themselves for him or her	472	Morgante	414
'Take care he don't revenge himself, though dead	474	Morgante	569
I don't know if the fact you've heard or read	474	Morgante	571
You don't know what has happen'd, then? How should we	674	Werner 1	209
It keeps us here. But what you don't know is	674	Werner 1	212
I don't much like this fellow--close and dry	676	Werner 1	304
Be spared--but never mind! I don't. But who	677	Werner 1	398
Friend! Sir! Sir! Lord--oh Lord! Why don't you say	679	Werner 1	523
You don't mean me? No, sir; I honour more	684	Werner 2	60
Who may he be? Why, don't you know, my lord	686	Werner 2	200
Your lordship, being robb'd, don't recognise	686	Werner 2	204
What the devil would you have? You don't believe me	695	Werner 3	19
No, you don't look a leech for that disorder	696	Werner 3	56
And yet I don't know that I know your place	699	Werner 3	301
I don't choose to say much upon this head	749	Juan 1	173
I don't think Sappho's Ode a good example	752	Juan 1	332
I really don't know what, nor Julia either	757	Juan 1	648
Now, tell me, don't you cut a pretty figure	765	Juan 1	1200
He had been hid--I don't pretend to say	767	Juan 1	1321
Why, don't you know that it may end in blood	768	Juan 1	1366
But if you don't, I'll lay it on, by G--d	772	Juan 1	1648
But vulgar illnesses don't like to meet	776	Juan 2	174
So good--I wonder Castlereagh don't tax 'em	800	Juan 3	1624
(Such things, in fact, it don't ask much to mar	802	Juan 3	78
(Provided they don't come in after dinner	808	Juan 3	474
Her children up (if nursing them don't thin her	809	Juan 3	476
Are things which in this century don't strike	814	Juan 3	853
I don't pretend that I quite understand	817	Juan 4	36
I don't much like describing people mad	825	Juan 4	587
Which might go far, but she don't dance with vigour	827	Juan 4	679
They vow to amend their lives, and yet they don't	832	Juan 5	47
Said Juan; 'but I really don't see how	834	Juan 5	178
Be in these days?) some infidels, who don't	839	Juan 5	490
Or if you don't the fault is not in me	840	Juan 5	528
These don't express one half what I should say	848	Juan 5	1054
Why don't they knead two virtuous souls for life	851	Juan 5	1263
And don't agree at all with the wise Roman	853	Juan 5	54
'From Spain.'--'But where is Spain?'--'Don't ask such stuff	858	Juan 6	348
You don't sleep soundly, and I cannot bear	858	Juan 6	370
Than you would make the half of;--don't say no	858	Juan 6	373
Alone, for reasons which don't matter; you	858	Juan 6	386
But that you won't--then don't--I am not less free	859	Juan 6	448
I don't know whether they had arms or crest	869	Juan 7	147
I don't know how the thing occurr'd--it might	881	Juan 8	217
For if he don't, I doubt if men will longer	884	Juan 8	394
(I don't much pique myself upon orthography	887	Juan 8	586
Or if these do not move you, don't forget	894	Juan 8	995
I don't think that you used Kinnaird quite well	896	Juan 9	9
I don't mean to reflect--a man so great as	897	Juan 9	49
Your wise men don't know much of navigation	898	Juan 9	140
(When she don't pin men's limbs in like a gaoler	902	Juan 9	350
We don't much care with whom we may engage	905	Juan 9	547
Outward dislike, which don't look well abroad	911	Juan 10	253
I don't know how it was, but he grew sick	912	Juan 10	305
Her note, she don't forget the infant girl	913	Juan 10	407
I don't know what the reason is--the air	919	Juan 11	38
I recollect some innkeepers who don't	920	Juan 11	115
I don't mean that they are passionless, but quite	922	Juan 11	265
And by we'll talk of that; and if we don't	923	Juan 11	282
I don't know which was more admired or less	923	Juan 11	307
But don't pretend to settle which was best	928	Juan 11	656
This--when I speak, I don't hint, but speak out	929	Juan 11	696
And don't know justly what we would be at	929	Juan 12	5
But if Love don't, Cash does, and Cash alone	931	Juan 12	105
Well, if I don't succeed, I have succeeded	931	Juan 12	129
I don't mean this as general, but particular	937	Juan 12	465
(Whatever people say), I don't know whether	940	Juan 12	684
But do you more, Sempronius--don't deserve it	943	Juan 13	138
Indifference certes don't produce distress	945	Juan 13	278
Sometimes a little later. I don't err	946	Juan 13	338
'Tis true, you don't--but, pale and struck with terror	956	Juan 14	41
You know, or don't know, that great Bacon saith	956	Juan 14	57
In that fair clime which don't depend on climate	959	Juan 14	226
(For foreigners don't know that a faux pas	963	Juan 14	477
I don't know what, and therefore cannot tell	964	Juan 14	562
I don't know that there may be much ability	970	Juan 15	153
And don't regret the time you may have lost	980	Juan 15	755

DOOM

Mine shall escape the doom thine eyes assign	3	To Ianthe	25
But all unconscious of the coming doom	11	Harold 1	486
Their doom, nor heed the suppliant's appeal	12	Harold 1	554
Wrote on his faded brow curst Cain's unresting doom	17	Harold 1	827
Their hope, their doom, their punishment, their law	24	Harold 2	284
The hopeless warriors of a willing doom	31	Harold 2	698
When mariners would madly meet their doom	37	Harold 3	142
Lamenting and yet envying such a doom	44	Harold 3	543
Deeming themselves predestined to a doom	60	Harold 4	303
Were they but so in man's, how different were his doom	68	Harold 4	774
In her dark eye, prophetic of the doom	70	Harold 4	914
Affliction's self deplores thy youthful doom	85	Epitaph	18
Nor yet thy doom was fix'd, nor Jove relentless frown'd	89	Prometheus	16
With joy I court a certain doom	90	To M.S.G.-A	23
Ill-fated Ida! soon must stamp your doom	93	Masters	16
Or doom the lover you have chosen	101	Lady-B	13
To mark thy love, and signalize my doom	106	Nisus	72
A doom to me far worse than death	111	Medea	40
Till royal sacrilege their doom decreed	120	Newstead-A	40
Howe'er my future doom be cast	131	L'Amitie	15
Yet doom his brother to expire	132	Prayer	26
Yet left him such a doom	180	Ode-A	61
Thee alone no doom can bow	187	French-A	12
Heaven for a nobler doom their worth desires	195	Vittorelli	3
But which their doom may none divine	196	Venice-A	18
For him could Time unfold a brighter doom	201	Ode-C	41
A strange doom is thy father's son's, and past	211	Augusta-C	13
It was of a strange order, that the doom	216	Dream	203
Mine be the doom which they dared not to meet	219	Saul-A	8
And desperate mans him 'gainst the coming doom	272	Minerva	272
'He is what you behold him, and his doom	293	Vision	545
Exaggeration? something which may doom	295	Vision	660
The doom he dreads, yet dwells upon	311	Giaour	84
Thy heroes, though the general doom	311	Giaour	130
Should doom him there for aye to dwell	318	Giaour	821
Of wayward deeds, and fitting doom	318	Giaour	867
Of joys long dead; my hope, their doom	320	Giaour	1001
Howe'er deserved her doom might be	320	Giaour	1066
His doom was seal'd--he knew it well	321	Giaour	1075
Shall I the doom I sought upbraid	321	Giaour	1116
'Tis strange--he prophesied my doom	322	Giaour	1228
That parts all else, shall doom for ever	327	Abydos 1	325
'Tis Nature's doom--but let the wretch who toils	341	Corsair 1	189
Would doom him ever dying--ne'er to die	351	Corsair 2	283
This was his doom;--the Leech, the guard, were gone	351	Corsair 2	324
'Corsair, thy doom is named! but I have power	354	Corsair 2	460
The vain attempt should bring but doom to both	354	Corsair 2	467
His doom is fix'd--he dies: and well his fate	357	Corsair 3	143
When every hour might doom him worse than dead	358	Corsair 3	211
Yet lived to view the doom his ire decreed	362	Corsair 3	451
Nor trace, nor tidings of his doom declare	366	Corsair 3	689
A heavy doom 'tis thine to meet	391	Corinth	636
That doom shall half absolve thy sin	391	Corinth	637
Dark will thy doom be, darker still	391	Corinth	649
His parent's iron hand did doom	393	Corinth	807
And well he may--a deeper doom	397	Parisina	85

DOOM

The guilt, the shame, the doom, to her	397	Parisina		126
Did Parisina wait her doom	398	Parisina		148
To see the Son fall by the doom of the Father	400	Parisina		406
To the monk, his doom deploring	400	Parisina		414
That they had wrought their doom of ill	402	Parisina		577
Which would not doom me to despair	409	Mazeppa		274
In sooth, it is a happy doom	409	Mazeppa		296
Theresa's doom I never knew	410	Mazeppa		340
What mortal his own doom may guess	415	Mazeppa		853
Link'd with the unknown name of one whose doom	421	Island	2	198
The strife was done, the vanquish'd had their doom	426	Island	3	8
Who doom to hell, themselves are on the way	435	Island	4	354
And doom this body forfeit to the fire	457	Dante	1	68
Forsooth is over and repeal'd her doom	457	Dante	1	82
Worthless as they who wrought it. 'Tis the doom	458	Dante	1	149
Their children's children's doom already brought	458	Dante	2	4
But all things are disposing for thy doom	459	Dante	2	43
What will he do to merit such a doom	462	Dante	3	146
While the horn rang so loud and knell'd the doom	467	Morgante		61
And secret as the grave to which they doom	500	Faliero	1	61
Elapse, and others share as dark a doom	517	Faliero	2	612
And such may be my doom; for here I swear	532	Faliero	4	288
You think to doom to me. The bark is ready	533	Faliero	4	346
How did they meet their doom? Think of your own	540	Faliero	5	181
His doom must be fulfill'd without remission	543	Faliero	5	360
Then, as a prince, address thee to thy doom	543	Faliero	5	392
Alone will be beholders of thy doom	546	Faliero	5	555
And show these eyes, before they close, the doom	548	Faliero	5	739
The doom of Nineveh is seal'd.--Woe--woe	555	Sardan	1	326
Nor doom ye guiltless; albeit better men	566	Sardan	2	291
I would reserve thee for a fitter doom	575	Sardan	3	273
Have slaves decided on the doom of kings	592	Sardan	5	308
But think so, to my mind the happiest doom	605	Foscari	2	273
My doom is common, many are in dungeons	609	Foscari	3	98
Last council on thy doom. I know it--look	610	Foscari	3	123
That they are not compatible, the doom	634	Cain	1	424
As you for him. You would not have their doom	641	Cain	2	360
A heavy doom was long forespoken to us	652	Cain	3	415
A dreary, and an early doom, my brother	654	Cain	3	545
A change at hand, and an o'erwhelming doom	658	Heaven		226
A doom which even some serpent, with his mate	659	Heaven		303
Upon thy coming doom without a feeling	659	Heaven		319
Walk darkling to their doom; which, though so nigh	662	Heaven		545
Dread'st thou not to partake their coming doom	665	Heaven		732
If that thou wouldst avoid their doom, forget	665	Heaven		761
Our doom is sorrow: not to us alone	667	Heaven		930
And happier in that doom	670	Heaven		1191
Thou villainous gold, and thy dead master's doom	711	Werner	4	443
So vile he 'scaped the doom which oft avenges	811	Juan	3	637
When Nero perish'd by the justest doom	816	Juan	3	961
And, buried, sinks beneath its offspring's doom	829	Juan	4	812
At present weigh'd down by a doom which had	832	Juan	5	91
Six Tartars and a drag-chain.' 'To this doom	833	Juan	5	115
''Tis not,' said Juan, 'for my present doom	833	Juan	5	137
Such doom may be your own in aftertimes	894	Juan	8	996
If such doom waits each intellectual Giant	998	Juan	17	73

DOOM'D

None through their cold disdain are doom'd to die	15	Harold	1	727
In other lands, where he was doom'd to go	19	Harold	1	951
Doom'd to bewail the blasphemy of laws	45	Harold	3	615
Than join the crushing crowd, doom'd to inflict or bear	46	Harold	3	679
And doom'd him to the zealot's ready Hell	52	Harold	3	1002
Enormous model doom'd the artist's toils	78	Harold	4	1364
In single sorrow doom'd to fade	92	Lady-A		8
In barbarous Latin doom'd to wrangle	95	Granta		35
Thus doom'd but to gaze upon bliss	98	To M.S.G.-B		16
The man doom'd to sail with the blast of the gale	115	The Tear		13
Though doom'd no more to quit the dead	133	Prayer		60
Not always doom'd its heat to smother	148	A Fan		18
Is doom'd to all who love or live	173	Not False		14
I should have deem'd thee doom'd to earthly care	175	Sonnet-A		8
Who doom'd thee to be bought or sold	179	Gold		27
The Moorish King, and doom'd him dead	195	Ballad-A		69
And now 'tis doom'd to know the worst	218	Soul-B		15
My wrath but doom'd my own despair	221	Mariamne		11
With death doom'd to grapple	235	Pitt		1
Well wert thou doom'd the last of all thy race	244	Bards		218
Most wisely doom'd to shun the public sight	251	Bards		714
(Unlucky Tavell! doom'd to daily cares	259	Hints		229
Who would be doom'd to gaze upon	319	Giaour		961
Ere I have heard and doom'd it too	334	Abydos	2	475
Hath doom'd his death, or fix'd his chain	335	Abydos	2	566
Doom'd by his very virtues for a dupe	342	Corsair	1	256
Fast to the doom'd offender's form it clings	342	Corsair	1	258
Dream they of this our preparation, doom'd	348	Corsair	2	79
Upon that sound is doom'd to cease	397	Parisina		90
Would she thus hear him doom'd to die	399	Parisina		325
The ghastly spectres which were doom'd at last	418	Island	1	197
Is doom'd to expiate his rash insult with	509	Faliero	2	29

DOOM'D

Have you to say why you should not be doom'd	539	Faliero	5	68
And miss his own Ionian, we are doóm'd	576	Sardan	3	308
And the old Doge, who knew him doom'd, smiled on him	619	Foscari	4	300
All living, and all doom'd to death, and wretched	636	Cain	2	48
Whether my verse's fame be doom'd to cease	829	Juan	4	788
Or separate maintenance, in case 'twas doom'd	973	Juan	15	307

DOOMED

The next are such as are not doomed to lose	997	Juan	17	5

DOOMING

This bosom's desolation dooming	221	Mariamne		22
With torture of my dooming. There will come	636	Cain	2	16

DOOMS

Which nips life's tree, and dooms man's worst--his second fall	69	Harold	4	873
And dooms my fall, I fain would fall alone	94	Dorset		40
And dooms them to a dire disgrace	141	Critics		44
Who but the love of him he dooms to bleed	350	Corsair	2	223
The dust she dooms to scatter, and transfer	457	Dante	1	75
Florence dooms me but death or banishment	462	Dante	3	138
And unknown dooms, and sudden executions	605	Foscari	2	308

DOOM'S

Let that too pass;--the doom's prepared	398	Parisina		206
Decided; but as yet his doom's unknown	500	Faliero	1	26

DOOMSDAY

Heaven's freeholds, in a sort of doomsday scroll	911	Juan	10	277

DOOR
(See also ROOM-DOOR)

And oft-times through the area's echoing door	28	Harold	2	509
And sable Horror guards the massy door	121	Newstead-A		96
And Learning beckons from her temple's door	124	Recoll		150
And stoop to strive with Misery at the door	193	Monody		82
But thou at least from out the jealous door	195	Vittorelli		9
The holy building's massy door	196	Venice-A		6
The Hunger, which repulsed from Sally's door	224	J.C.H.		21
(Next door to the pastry-cook's; so that when I	277	Blues	1	18
He climbs the crackling stair, he bursts the door	350	Corsair	2	211
And chill and nodding at the turret door	353	Corsair	2	417
The midnight pass'd, and to the massy door	359	Corsair	3	270
Towards it he moved; a scarcely closing door	361	Corsair	3	402
No words are utter'd; at her sign, a door	362	Corsair	3	444
He reach'd his turret door; he paused--no sound	364	Corsair	3	581
The waving banner, and the clapping door	370	Lara	1	261
Which whelms the peasant near the door	412	Mazeppa		513
And gently oped the door, and spake	415	Mazeppa		828
Their deep-green shadow o'er the rocky door	432	Island	4	205
Fresh as the Angel o'er a new inn door	447	Beppo		451
Such sight hath been unfolded by a door	464	Dante	4	54
Stands sleek and slavish, bowing at his door	464	Dante	4	94
The door to open, like a crazy thing	471	Morgante		311
He hears the jarring of a distant door	500	Faliero	1	11
What, ho!--Antonio--Pedro--to the door	533	Faliero	4	328
Stand to your arms, and guard the door--all's lost	536	Faliero	4	579
My eyes swim strangely--where's the door? Away	617	Foscari	4	186
Will to the door. It cannot be of import	674	Werner	1	170
Your humble duty at the door? I dragg'd him	678	Werner	1	433
Has disappear'd;--the door unbolted, with	683	Werner	2	38
Unlatch'd the door of death for thee? 'Twas not	711	Werner	4	434
I follow'd it, and reach'd a door--a secret	718	Werner	5	310
The door of which was half ajar, I saw	718	Werner	5	331
Skill made me gain the secret door of the hall	718	Werner	5	352
(As I too) of the opposite door which leads	720	Werner	5	487
The door sound loud behind him! He is safe	721	Werner	5	509
And it is clogg'd with dead even to the door	739	Deformed	2	273
And look'd extremely at the opening door	756	Juan	1	603
But beg 'Security' will bolt the door	757	Juan	1	712
Sleeping, most probably,--when at her door	763	Juan	1	1082
The door was fasten'd, but with voice and fist	763	Juan	1	1087
A moment at the door, that we may be	766	Juan	1	1247
The attorney last, who linger'd near the door	767	Juan	1	1306
The door was fasten'd in his legal face	767	Juan	1	1312
The door is open--you may yet slip through	769	Juan	1	1452
Alfonso leaning, breathless, by the door	770	Juan	1	1492
As if Death were more dreadful by his door	778	Juan	2	277
The solitude of passing his own door	808	Juan	3	411
Of a small iron door, 'twas open'd, and	836	Juan	5	322
To thrust its black eyes through the door or lattice	838	Juan	5	439
The giant door was broad, and bright, and high	842	Juan	5	681
To ope this door, which they could really do	842	Juan	5	707
But not by the same door through which came in	844	Juan	5	794
For Baba's function stopt short at the door	865	Juan	6	820
They reach'd the hotel: forth stream'd from the front door	922	Juan	11	233
And blazon o'er the door their names in brass	922	Juan	11	248
Then roll the brazen thunders of the door	926	Juan	11	526

388

DOOR

A door that's in or boudoir out of the way	927 Juan	11	539
An erring woman finds an opener door	940 Juan	12	630
And out of door hath showers, and mists, and sleet	959 Juan	14	234
She look'd as if she sat by Eden's door	973 Juan	15	359
His chamber door wide open--and went forth	982 Juan	16	130
He shut his door, and after having read	983 Juan	16	210
Stated) his mouth. What open'd next?--the door	995 Juan	16	968
The door flew wide,--not swiftly, but, as fly	996 Juan	16	977

DOORS
(See also TRAP-DOORS)

Thy steps within a stranger's doors	111 Medea		48
'You should all block your doors	239 Bray		20
Watch well the Haram's massy doors	326 Abydos	1	240
Which step from out our mountains to their doors	483 Manfred	2	14
Not till I pass the threshold of these doors	624 Foscari	5	226
Open, and the doors which lead from that hall	702 Werner	3	500
Bright hues when out of doors, and yet, while wave	789 Juan	2	957
And thus they parted, each by separate doors	842 Juan	5	673
With 'To be let' upon their doors proclaim'd	921 Juan	11	166
Of doors 'gainst duns, and to an early dinner	922 Juan	11	228
Tithes, taxes, duns, and doors with double knock-ings	938 Juan	12	536
Without doors, too, she may compete in mellow	950 Juan	13	615
Knockest at doors, at first with modest tap	969 Juan	15	58
Doors there were many, through which, by the laws	983 Juan	16	189

DOOR-WAY

And in the door-way, darkening darkness, stood	996 Juan	16	983

DORIA'S

But is not Doria's menace come to pass	57 Harold	4	111

DORIC

Twin Doric minstrels, drunk with Doric ale	266 Hints		732
Such as the Doric mothers bore	813 Juan	3	764

DORMANT

All dormant or destructive. He will perish	493 Manfred	3	167
As acids rouse a dormant alkali	914 Juan	10	428

DORSET

Dorset! whose early steps with mine have stray'd	93 Dorset		1
Yet, Dorset, let not this seduce thy soul	93 Dorset		11
Dorset, farewell! I will not ask one part	94 Dorset		91

DORY

'Soupe a la Beauveau,' whose relief was dory	976 Juan	15	503

DOSED

Dosed with vile drams on Sunday he was found	268 Hints		835

DOTAGE

His dotage trifled well	181 Ode-A		70
Oh! that this dotage of his breast would cease	355 Corsair	2	525
Mine too he threatens; but his dotage still	360 Corsair	3	338
His summer dotage. And he loved his queen	563 Sardan	2	125
To tears save drops of dotage, with long white	603 Foscari	2	110
A dotage which may justify this deed	624 Foscari	5	266
Seth, the last offspring of old Adam's dotage	664 Heaven		658

DOTARD

Which the stern dotard deem'd he could encage	17 Harold	1	804
Vainly the dotard mends her prudish pace	119 Answer-A		13
Meantime, the flattering, feeble dotard, West	270 Minerva		175
He was not a shamed dotard like the Doge	506 Faliero	1	426
And the old ducal dotard, who combined	600 Foscari	1	322

DOTARD'S

Albeit too dazzling for a dotard's sight	183 Address-D		44
What, am I then a toy for dotard's play	360 Corsair	3	342
'Twas not a foolish dotard's vile caprice	513 Faliero	2	310

DOTE

Ye, who have known what 'tis to dote upon	5 Harold	1	88
Nor dote even on thy beauty--as I've doted	583 Sardan	4	337
Or death of those we dote on, when a part	776 Juan	2	165
As those who dote on odours pluck the flowers	801 Juan	3	13

DOTED

And had he doted on those eyes so blue	24 Harold	2	296
Dear words! on which my heart had doted	175 Portuguese-A		3
Nor dote even on thy beauty--as I've doted	583 Sardan	4	337
(But that could scarce be, for he doted on him	685 Werner	2	117
Besides her good old grandmother (who doted	750 Juan	1	221

DOTES

Nods to the storm--dilates and dotes o'er thee	459 Dante	2	65

DOTING

Why should thy doting wretched mother weep	106 Nisus		73

DOTING

Peevish and spiteful, doting, hard to please	260 Hints		259
And not a doting homage--friendship, faith	514 Faliero	2	364
Is ever doting) took to warm his bosom	694 Werner	2	737
His parents ne'er agreed except in doting	750 Juan	1	195
The mouth of some one in his plays so doting	869 Juan	7	167

DOTTED

A dark speck dotted ocean: on it flew	428 Island	3	167
Like a backgammon board the place was dotted	832 Juan	5	73

DOUBLE
(See also REDOUBLE)

With double joy wert thou with me	43 Harold	3	505
The double night of ages, and of her	67 Harold	4	721
His day of double victory and death	67 Harold	4	764
Each flower a double fragrance flings	132 L'Amitie		47
'A double blessing your rewards impart	171 Address-B		51
On thee a double chastisement	195 Ballad-A		52
In him the double tyrant starts to life	228 Windsor		6
In him the double tyrant starts to life	228 Vaults		6
Here's a double health to thee	230 My Boat		4
And quit his books, for fear of growing double	245 Bards		240
In double portion swells thy glorious lot	249 Bards		531
At double meanings folks seem wondrous sly	258 Hints		149
I'll do what I can, though my pains must be double	282 Blues	2	90
Like king Alfonso. When I thus see double	297 Vision		807
Double the guard, and when Anselmo's bark	346 Corsair	1	565
The landmark to the double tide	385 Corinth		54
A double dungeon wall and wave	403 Chillon		113
That boil'd your bones, unless you paid them double	440 Beppo		32
And gave me thus a double right to be so	502 Faliero	1	146
Beyond may breed us double danger. See	516 Faliero	2	554
Black with a double treason, now will earn	537 Faliero	4	646
A danger which would double that you escape	542 Faliero	5	288
A double guard, withdrawing from the wall	591 Sardan	5	242
Imprisonment and actual torture? Double	617 Foscari	4	156
To the great double Mysteries! the two Principles	645 Cain	2	609
For now their torrents rush, with double roar	670 Heaven		1172
If such a joy await me, it must double	688 Werner	2	345
Its own exuberance, it bears double value	694 Werner	2	712
A double purpose. Stralenheim lost gold	698 Werner	3	206
It spread its peace o'er all, hath double claims	708 Werner	4	253
For double curses will be my meed now	722 Deformed	1	34
To prove her mistress had been sleeping double	764 Juan	1	1120
To double even the sweetness of a flower	773 Juan	1	1712
From the blue skies derived a double blue	828 Juan	4	718
She thought hers gave a double 'right divine	847 Juan	5	1031
Or double post and rail, where the existence	885 Juan	8	435
By those who scour those double vales of strife	909 Juan	10	108
Of politicians and their double front	923 Juan	11	284
Requires decorum, and is apt to double	924 Juan	11	367
The single ladies wishing to be double	937 Juan	12	463
Tithes, taxes, duns, and doors with double knockings	938 Juan	12	536
Well cultivated, it will render double	939 Juan	12	608
'Tis also subject to the double danger	959 Juan	14	250
He clear'd hedge, ditch, and double post, and rail	959 Juan	14	258
Of double nature, and thus doubly named	966 Juan	14	706
Of single gentlemen who would be double	974 Juan	15	384
Presents the problem of a double figure	988 Juan	16	536
A mighty mug of moral double ale	989 Juan	16	580

DOUBLE-BARRELS

And double-barrels (damn them!) miss their mark	264 Hints		556

DOUBLED

The rock is doubled, and the shore	312 Giaour		253
Already doubled is the cape--our bay	339 Corsair	1	89
The last may then be doubled, and the former	508 Faliero	1	573
She was and is: my reign has doubled realms	607 Foscari	2	372
The sovereign shock'd, and all his medicines doubled	912 Juan	10	312

DOUBLE-DAMN'D

Next owner for their double-damn'd post-obits	762 Juan	1	1000

DOUBLES

Which doubles what they think of the transgression	853 Juan	6	76

DOUBLET

You like by way of doublet, cape, or cloak	440 Beppo		34

DOUBLING

Imperial anarchs, doubling human woes	26 Harold	2	404
His anguish doubling by his own 'encore	261 Hints		310
The doubling rental? What an evil's peace	306 Age		595

DOUBLOONS

Doubloons a hundred I would pay	195 Ballad-A		98

DOUBLY

My years already doubly number thine	3 To Ianthe		20
While thus of both bereft, the nymph-queen doubly sigh'd	24 Harold	2	261
To leave the flagging spirit doubly weak	35 Harold	2	913
Whate'er it strikes;--yon head is doubly sacred now	61 Harold	4	369
And say, 'here was, or is,' where all is doubly night	67 Harold	4	720
The yoke that is upon us doubly bow'd	69 Harold	4	850
But all too late,--so are we doubly curst	73 Harold	4	1112
Which whispers friendship will be doubly dear	125 Recoll		214
To me were doubly dear	138 Clare		99
How doubly sweet will be the draught	139 Anacreon-C		4
To me 'tis doubly sweet to find	152 Time-A		19
Such precious drops are doubly dear	152 Weep-A		15
My pen were doubly weak	163 Parting		14
So pride shall doubly nerve the actor's powers	170 Address-A		64
Are doubly bitter from that thought	172 Not False		4
Doubly shall she be adored	188 Ode-B		76
In stream less smooth, indeed, yet doubly strong	243 Bards		114
While honours, doubly merited, attend	253 Bards		865
But doubly blest is he whose heart expands	253 Bards		873
Loud sung the wind above; and, doubly loud	359 Corsair	3	258
Such insult from a stranger, doubly sore	374 Lara	1	597
Whose clouds that day grew doubly dun	386 Corinth		173
Deep-mouth'd arose, and doubly harsh	396 Corinth		1066
And left me twice so doubly lone	405 Chillon		292
We met in secret--doubly sweet	410 Mazeppa		311
Leaves us so doubly serious shortly after	450 Beppo		632
Into a by-word; and the doubly felon	515 Faliero	2	430
Make our assurance doubly sure, according	518 Faliero	2	669
That I abhor them doubly for the deeds	520 Faliero	3	116
I thank you doubly for my life, and this	592 Sardan	5	340
Which, at this moment, doubly must oppress	621 Foscari	5	21
And how ye may be doubly widows--wives	769 Juan	1	1480
A sad tale saddens doubly, when 'tis long	833 Juan	5	128
These must seem doubly mindful of their vows	850 Juan	5	1229
Of double nature, and thus doubly named	966 Juan	14	706

DOUBT

Poor child of Doubt and Death, whose hope is built on reeds	20 Harold	2	27
No doubt can the mind of your lover invade	91 Caroline-C		18
With jealous doubt my bosom heaves not	98 To Lesbia		18
Should you own it yourselves, I would even then doubt you	117 To Eliza		38
Thy verse is 'sad' enough, no doubt	147 To Author		1
Remember thee! Aye, doubt it not	171 Remember-A		5
The pang, the agony, the doubt	172 Romaic-B		2
'Though I doubt if this drivelling encomiast of War	177 Devil's Dr		127
If ever Doubt a place possest	179 Gold		9
Doubt others' love, nor trust in mine	179 Gold		12
The miscreant who well might plunge Erin in doubt	203 Avatar		95
The papers have told you, no doubt, of the fusses	227 Moore-A		13
No doubt you do right to commend it	232 Murray-B		9
No doubt he's a rare man	232 Murray-B		25
You doubt--see Dryden, Pope, St. Patrick's dean	258 Hints		116
Sad words, no doubt, become a serious cause	258 Hints		147
Nor let a doubt obscure one verse you've made	267 Hints		800
(Very sorry, no doubt, since the cause is a brother's	278 Blues	1	37
No doubt; you by this time should know what is due	279 Blues	1	117
Well, that is a sign of some spirit. No doubt	279 Blues	1	131
That 'metal's attractive.' No doubt--to the pocket	280 Blues	1	143
I doubt if you'll leave us an equal behind	282 Blues	2	81
That he was forced, against his will no doubt	285 Vision		26
And will be judged like all the rest, no doubt	287 Vision		173
'Foolish, no doubt, and wicked, to oppress	293 Vision		561
His name a doubt to all the winds of heaven	301 Age		236
He still might doubt the tyrant's power	311 Giaour		87
Nor need'st thou doubt this speech from one	320 Giaour		1022
If thou my tale, Zuleika, doubt	331 Abydos	2	246
Yes, fear!--the doubt, the dread of losing thee	333 Abydos	2	446
'His head and faith from doubt and death	334 Abydos	2	468
And kiss the doubt from these delighted eyes	339 Corsair	1	116
And doubt that joy, which hails our coming, short	340 Corsair	1	118
Perchance from some emotion, doubt, or pride	340 Corsair	1	152
Lest Time should raise that doubt to more than dread	344 Corsair	1	447
'Tis but to sail--no doubt to-morrow's Sun	347 Corsair	2	12
Why did they doubt their quickness of career	349 Corsair	2	168
No doubt regardless if the prize were fair	358 Corsair	3	175
This fearful interval of doubt and dread	358 Corsair	3	210
Above some object of her doubt or dread	361 Corsair	3	413
One doubt from others' half withheld esteem	370 Lara	1	308
Doubt not my fitting answer to requite	372 Lara	1	433
The wondrous tale no doubt thy tongue can tell	372 Lara	1	459
Vain doubt! his swift and savage breed	412 Mazeppa		510
No doubt a liquid path to epic fame	417 Island	1	102
While yet a doubt sprung where its course might lie	435 Island	4	380

DOUBT

Good cause had he to doubt the chance of war	447 Beppo		485
I have my reasons, you no doubt suppose	450 Beppo		626
And Doubt and Discord step 'twixt thine and thee	460 Dante	2	140
Where waited them the abbot in great doubt	472 Morgante		434
Why do you tremble thus?--nay, doubt not, all	501 Faliero	1	85
Had stabb'd him on the instant. Do not doubt it	503 Faliero	1	231
With plunder. But the priests--I doubt the priesthood	504 Faliero	1	336
They'll do as much by Barbaro, no doubt	506 Faliero	1	432
Might make the world doubt whether such an union	510 Faliero	2	88
Why should you doubt it? has it ever fail'd	513 Faliero	2	290
Than in more loud avengers. Do not doubt them	517 Faliero	2	579
I do not doubt the elder; but in Bertram	517 Faliero	2	580
Yet doubt me not; it is this very feeling	520 Faliero	3	109
Some courage to doubt the freedom of the choice	522 Faliero	3	243
Outraged and trodden on, until he doubt	522 Faliero	3	262
Much that we let their children live; I doubt	524 Faliero	3	409
For I will do this! Doubt not--fear not; I	527 Faliero	3	636
Doubt not, Saint Mark's great bell shall wake all Venice	528 Faliero	3	645
Without doubt, he will be brought up to trial	539 Faliero	5	78
Merit forgiveness; else a doubt like this	543 Faliero	5	346
Long years ago--so long, they are a doubt	546 Faliero	5	591
Would it were over! Does the prophet doubt	562 Sardan	2	42
I do not doubt of victory--but the victor	562 Sardan	2	44
He but be brought to think so: this I doubt of	563 Sardan	2	103
He never ask'd it. Doubt not, he will have it	565 Sardan	2	224
And chiefly thou, my priest, because I doubt thee	566 Sardan	2	276
More than the soldier; and would doubt thee all	566 Sardan	2	277
But will not, can not be so now. I doubt it	568 Sardan	2	435
That is, their lives--it is not that I doubt	569 Sardan	2	494
You did not doubt me a few hours ago	586 Sardan	4	495
And none could make me doubt it save yourself	586 Sardan	4	497
But doubt it. Wherefore did ye bear me here	588 Sardan	5	94
The state had need of some repose. No doubt	601 Foscari	2	16
That words have ceased to shake me. Oh, no doubt	603 Foscari	2	128
No doubt; yet most men like to live their days out	605 Foscari	2	212
With the like answer--doubt and dreadful surmise	609 Foscari	3	76
I do not doubt my memory, but my life	609 Foscari	3	82
Liberation. He speaks truth. No doubt! but 'tis	614 Foscari	3	407
No doubt, are worth it. Being worth our lives	616 Foscari	4	89
Perhaps, in the air. I doubt not. Father--wife	618 Foscari	4	190
Though (some, no doubt,) consign'd to powers which may	626 Foscari	5	335
Believe--and sink not! doubt--and perish! thus	636 Cain	2	5
This seems too terrible. No doubt the other	642 Cain	2	403
A reptile's subtlety. Of that I doubt	648 Cain	3	160
As fits a noble guest:--'tis damp, no doubt	675 Werner	1	232
No doubt you'll have a swingeing sum as recompense	676 Werner	1	291
No doubt is a mere tool and spy of Stralenheim's	680 Werner	1	577
Between me and my father's house. No doubt	681 Werner	1	619
I doubt not. But our wives and families	682 Werner	1	670
Away! Alas, that I should doubt of thee	683 Werner	1	751
Was there no cause assign'd? Plenty, no doubt	685 Werner	2	113
But cannot think of sorrow now, and doubt	688 Werner	2	350
May be of innocence. 'Sdeath! who dare doubt it	692 Werner	2	572
To doubt it. Let no foolish pity shake	694 Werner	2	749
The priests say (and no doubt they should know best	696 Werner	3	44
For that would make our ties beyond all doubt	698 Werner	3	194
You have guess'd, no doubt, that I was born above	700 Werner	3	311
Past doubt, been enter'd secretly. Excuse me	702 Werner	3	486
You, my son!--doubted--And do you doubt of him	703 Werner	3	532
May produce even of the guilty's guilt. Your heart	703 Werner	3	536
For the mere cup and trencher, we no doubt	704 Werner	4	9
And she, no doubt, will soften whatsoever	705 Werner	4	67
My son, I know my own innocence, and doubt not	716 Werner	5	219
Doubt not our soldiers. Were the walls of adamant	732 Deformed	1	747
No doubt, the camp's the school of civic rights	734 Deformed	1	853
Like stars, no doubt; for that's a metaphor	741 Deformed	2	425
No doubt! for if you did, the remedy	744 Deformed	3	162
And put the business past all kind of doubt	750 Juan	1	208
No doubt this patience, when the world is damning us	750 Juan	1	233
Although no doubt his real intent was good	752 Juan	1	340
Some people whisper (but no doubt they lie	755 Juan	1	525
There surely will be little doubt with some	755 Juan	1	557
'Twas but a doubt; but ne'er magician's wand	755 Juan	1	566
The poet meant, no doubt, and thus appeals	757 Juan	1	705
The sun, no doubt, is the prevailing reason	759 Juan	1	812
But then, no doubt, it equally as true is	760 Juan	1	863
Yet there's no doubt she only meant to clasp	760 Juan	1	884
Although one must be damn'd for you, no doubt	761 Juan	1	946
No doubt in fable, as the unforgiven	762 Juan	1	1015
Because, no doubt, 'twas for his dirty fee	765 Juan	1	1207
Doubt upon me, confusion over all	765 Juan	1	1226
No doubt, in little compass, round or square	767 Juan	1	1324
I doubt, all likeness ends between the pair	769 Juan	1	1488
If any person doubt it, I appeal	771 Juan	1	1617
Shall supersede beyond all doubt all those	771 Juan	1	1627

DOUBT

No doubt we weep for those the heart endears	776 Juan	2	119
No doubt he would have been much more pathetic	776 Juan	2	167
There's nought, no doubt, so much the spirit calms	778 Juan	2	265
No doubt, the vessel was about to sink	781 Juan	2	462
Death left no doubt, and the dead burthen lay	785 Juan	2	715
The frequent fog-banks gave them cause to doubt	786 Juan	2	766
For all was doubt and dizziness; he thought	788 Juan	2	890
By which, no doubt, a good deal may be made	790 Juan	2	1008
And 'tis, no doubt, a sight to see when breaks	791 Juan	2	1108
Since, after all, no doubt the youthful pair	792 Juan	2	1150
Of Zoe's cookery no doubt was stealing	793 Juan	2	1220
Goat's flesh there is, no doubt, and kid, and mutton	793 Juan	2	1226
No doubt, less of her language than her look	794 Juan	2	1300
He was in love,--as you would be, no doubt	795 Juan	2	1334
Heaven knows how long--no doubt they never reckon'd	798 Juan	2	1490
Perplexing question; but, no doubt, the moon	800 Juan	2	1660
Although, no doubt, her first of love affairs	802 Juan	3	29
Most naturally some small doubt inspires	804 Juan	3	171
A melody which made him doubt his ears	805 Juan	3	221
No doubt whate'er might be their former strife	807 Juan	3	397
The eye might doubt if it were well awake	811 Juan	3	605
There was no doubt he earn'd his laureate pension	811 Juan	3	640
And no doubt of all methods 'tis the best	819 Juan	4	189
That doubt should mingle with my filial joy	821 Juan	4	303
Who (after some discussion and some doubt	828 Juan	4	731
And heard Troy doubted; time will doubt of Rome	829 Juan	4	808
Used to it, no doubt, as eels are to be flay'd	832 Juan	5	56
Unless he's drunk, and then no doubt he's freed	835 Juan	5	245
Has been accused (I doubt not by conspiracy	839 Juan	5	482
No doubt, in proper place, and time, and season	840 Juan	5	591
His toilet, though no doubt a little backward	841 Juan	5	620
But no doubt every thing is for the best	852 Juan	6	6
I doubt if any now could make it worse	855 Juan	6	180
A goodly sinecure, no doubt! but made	856 Juan	6	249
I doubt few readers e'er would mount the breach	871 Juan	7	280
Look'd on as if in doubt if they could trust	876 Juan	7	578
With all the pomp of power, it was a doubt	876 Juan	7	591
I almost lately have begun to doubt	881 Juan	8	201
For if he don't, I doubt if men will longer	884 Juan	8	394
I rather doubt; and I would fain say 'fie on't	884 Juan	8	406
And that's the cause no doubt why, if we scan	892 Juan	8	893
There is no doubt that you deserve your ration	897 Juan	9	47
This world, I doubt if doubt itself be doubting	898 Juan	9	136
Although no doubt it was beyond all price	901 Juan	9	288
Of things destroy'd and left in airy doubt	901 Juan	9	300
That Sphinx, whose words would ever be a doubt	902 Juan	9	395
No doubt gave pain, where each new pair of shoulders	903 Juan	9	415
For such all women are at first no doubt	906 Juan	9	596
You'll deem, no doubt, they put it to a good use	912 Juan	10	288
Oh Doubt!--if thou be'st Doubt, for which some take thee	918 Juan	11	13
But which I doubt extremely--thou sole prism	918 Juan	11	14
And insolence no doubt is what they are	923 Juan	11	321
And should you doubt, pray ask of your next neighbour	923 Juan	11	324
Will hint allusions never meant. Ne'er doubt	929 Juan	11	695
To doubt (no less than landlords of their rental	931 Juan	12	103
Excepting marriage? which is love, no doubt	931 Juan	12	114
So good an opportunity, no doubt	934 Juan	12	276
No doubt I should be told that black is fair	938 Juan	12	560
But once there (if you doubt this, prithee try	939 Juan	12	591
No doubt his sensibilities were less	940 Juan	12	648
I'll leave them to their taste, no doubt the best	941 Juan	13	18
Theirs was that best of unions, past all doubt	961 Juan	14	359
Though on the whole, no doubt, the Dardan boy	964 Juan	14	574
This I could prove beyond a single doubt	966 Juan	14	669
No doubt the secret influence of the sex	967 Juan	14	737
Sincere he was--at least you could not doubt it	970 Juan	15	101
No doubt, if I had wish'd to pay my court	971 Juan	15	173
That is, no doubt, the only reason wherefore	972 Juan	15	248
Made Juan wonder, as no doubt he must	974 Juan	15	387
Or like a system coupled with a doubt	981 Juan	16	68
I leave to those who are fond of solving doubt	988 Juan	16	540
Some doubt how much of Adeline was real	993 Juan	16	816
He shudder'd, as no doubt the bravest cowers	996 Juan	16	1005
No doubt a consolation to his dust	997 Juan	17	64

DOUBTED

Philosophers have never doubted	145 Becher-B		61
But now I doubted strength and speed	412 Mazeppa		509
'Tis the first time that honour has been doubted	502 Faliero	1	182
Which makes thee to be doubted. You should know	521 Faliero	3	171
How I do love thee! I ne'er doubted it	573 Sardan	3	108
Can be so? Not I, though just now you doubted	703 Werner	3	531
You, my son!--doubted--And do you doubt of him	703 Werner	3	532
Confiding have I found you, that I doubted	719 Werner	5	422
So much, he always doubted I was married	765 Juan	1	1175
And heard Troy doubted; time will doubt of Rome	829 Juan	4	808
He doubted not a few hours of reflection	840 Juan	5	565

DOUBTED

But no one doubted on the whole, that she	857 Juan	6	281
(But that I never doubted, nor the Devil	919 Juan	11	42
Whose fame she rather doubted with posterity	962 Juan	14	403

DOUBTERS

'Tis time to strike such puny doubters dumb as	981 Juan	16	31

DOUBTEST

Not one of all those strangers whom thou doubtest	508 Faliero	1	590

DOUBTFUL

How many a doubtful day shall sink in night	18 Harold	1	924
To doubtful conflict, certain slaughter bring	26 Harold	2	401
Than they in doubtful time of troublous need	29 Harold	2	582
According to the doubtful story	160 Swimming		14
'Tis doubtful whom to seek, or whom to shun	243 Bards		90
Or was steer'd (I am doubtful of the grammar	292 Vision		455
He shuns the near but doubtful creek	312 Giaour		173
It even were doubtful if their victim knew	352 Corsair	2	327
And more than doubtful paradise, thy heaven	359 Corsair	3	238
As doubtful that the former trance	414 Mazeppa		804
Were they once masters--but that's doubtful. Satraps	567 Sardan	2	318
Their castle walls--beyond them 'tis but doubtful	676 Werner	1	341
His birth is doubtful. How so? His sire made	684 Werner	2	94
Of doubtful birth, can startle a grandee	694 Werner	2	744

DOUBTING

At length they ventured forth, though doubting sore	29 Harold	2	601
Yet oft my doubting soul 'twill shake	166 Away		21
As doubting to return or fly	312 Giaour		243
To bound as doubting from too black a dream	374 Lara	1	621
But these were not; and doubting hope is left	377 Lara	2	120
What, doubting still? He spared our lives, nay, more	567 Sardan	2	334
Doubting if you were false or feeble: I	719 Werner	5	420
By a distant organ, doubting if he be	793 Juan	2	1210
This world, I doubt if doubt itself be doubting	898 Juan	9	136

DOUBTLESS

Doubtless, sweet girl! the hissing lead	99 Young Lady		1
Doubtless await such young, exalted worth	107 Nisus		136
Looking, doubtless, much more smugly	234 Silver		5
And doubtless the Squadron are ready with more	236 Nonsense		4
And, doubtless, holds some precious freight	313 Giaour		362
They doubtless boldly did--but who are safe	339 Corsair	1	114
Thou thought'st me doubtless for the bier outlaid	470 Morgante		266
'Tis said he is much moved,--and doubtless 'twas	500 Faliero	1	18
Ay, doubtless they have echo'd o'er the arsenal	506 Faliero	1	420
But the offender doubtless even now	509 Faliero	2	28
Oh, thou wouldst have me doubtless set up edicts	555 Sardan	1	302
Now then obey! Doubtless. Yes, to the gates	568 Sardan	2	418
Suggest a purpler beverage. Blood--doubtless	577 Sardan	3	348
Moved doubtless by his wife's appearance in	601 Foscari	1	378
Doubtless, as your nice feelings would prescribe	612 Foscari	3	261
Did not the Doge deny this strongly? Doubtless	615 Foscari	4	25
If we divulge them, doubtless they are worth	616 Foscari	4	90
His excellency will sup, doubtless? Faith	675 Werner	1	268
Had access to the antechamber. Doubtless	683 Werner	2	18
The tale is doubtless worthy the relater	716 Werner	5	217
Well spoken! And thou doubtless wilt remain	727 Deformed	1	323
(But, doubtless, nobody will be so pert	772 Juan	1	1653
Meantime, they'll doubtless please to recollect	772 Juan	1	1669
Had, doubtless, heard about the Stygian river	798 Juan	2	1542
There's doubtless something in domestic doings	802 Juan	3	57
Though doubtless he who can command himself	807 Juan	3	375
And what is that? Devotion, doubtless--how	856 Juan	6	257
The stricter doubtless grow the vestal duties	859 Juan	6	463
And doubtless would be foremost on the foe	875 Juan	7	491
Doubtless to that of doctrines the most true	875 Juan	7	533
To the Gazette--which doubtless fairly dealt	880 Juan	8	138
But doubtless they prefer a fine young man	892 Juan	8	891
Yet Europe doubtless owes you greatly more	896 Juan	9	18
But doubtless as the air, though seldom sunny	916 Juan	10	559
Abroad, though doubtless they do much amiss	940 Juan	12	629
Doubtless it is a brilliant masquerade	957 Juan	14	133
And, therefore, doubtless to approve the truth	963 Juan	14	529
Because 'tis frailer, doubtless, than a stanch one	966 Juan	14	678
As doubtless should be people of high birth	982 Juan	16	134

DOUBTLESSLY

And doubtlessly, with such a form and heart	685 Werner	2	159

DOUBTS

Was, Titan-like, on daring doubts to pile	51 Harold	3	982
Which answers to all doubts so eloquently well	52 Harold	3	1003
But no one doubts the form of flame	105 Alva		283
Ye racking doubts! ye jealous fears	111 Medea		21
When the doubts of coward foes	187 French-A		19
Perhaps they have doubts that they ever will take	282 Blues	2	103
His doubts appear'd to wrong--nor yet she knew	358 Corsair	3	200

DOUBTS
Yet doubts how well the shrinking flesh may bear   359 Corsair   3   233
Such confident alacrity. Your doubts   519 Faliero   3   52
Put to the proof; or, if you should have doubts   521 Faliero   3   177
Amerced for doubts beyond thy little life   636 Cain   2   15
I have my doubts if he means well. Alas   681 Werner   1   648
Your doubts are certainties to all around you   692 Werner   2   596
The doubts that rise like briers in our path   697 Werner   3   159
To lull all doubts, and then rejoin my father   698 Werner   3   224
I had my doubts, perhaps I have them still   753 Juan   1   401
With fluttering doubts if all be well or ill   804 Juan   3   165
Though doubts of their well doing, to arrange   867 Juan   6   954
Upon his talent Henry had no doubts   944 Juan   13   189
As many doubts as any other doctrine   946 Juan   13   327
And thus we see--who doubts the Morning Post   947 Juan   13   417
He who doubts all things nothing can deny   979 Juan   15   701

DOUBT'S
So free from homicide--to doubt's a crime   299 Age   78
I wonder (although Mars no doubt's a god I   869 Juan   7   161
But seize the last word, which no doubt's the
    best   953 Juan   13   784

DOVE
(See also WILD-DOVE, WOOD-DOVE)
'Tis but the tender fierceness of the dove   13 Harold   1   589
For years fleet away with the wings of the dove   93 First Kiss   26
But this was taught me by the dove   321 Giaour   1165
The Dove of peace and promise to mine ark   333 Abydos   2   397
And yet they seek to nestle with the dove   418 Island   1   233
That without which my soul, like the arkless dove   456 Dante   1   24
To envy every dove his nest and wings   458 Dante   1   168
The dove has for her distant nest, when wheeling   608 Foscari   3   12
Like a dove round and round its pillaged nest   658 Heaven   247
The dove did, trusting that they have abated   696 Werner   3   50
And send him like a dove of promise forth   775 Juan   2   64
Webfooted, not unlike a dove in size   786 Juan   2   746
And had it been the dove from Noah's ark   786 Juan   2   757
Those downcast eyes beneath the Almighty dove   815 Juan   3   918
Of faithful pairs (I needs must rhyme with dove   906 Juan   9   587

DOVE-EYED
By driving dove-eyed peace from thine   90 To M.S.G.-A   26

DOVER
Thy cliffs, dear Dover! harbour, and hotel   916 Juan   10   546
Even in the hopeful Isle, whose outlet's 'Dover   934 Juan   12   262

DOVES
More than for those of nightingales or doves   818 Juan   4   152
And pair their rhymes as Venus yokes her doves   831 Juan   5   3

DOVE'S
'Oh!' saith the Psalmist, 'that I had a dove's   908 Juan   10   42

DOWAGER
While some more desperate dowager has been waging   848 Juan   5   1035

DOWAGERS
Blues, dandies, and dowagers, and second-hand
    scribes   280 Blues   1   158
But sixteen dowagers, ten unwed she sages   933 Juan   12   239

DOWDYISH
A fifth's look's vulgar, dowdyish, and suburban   448 Beppo   524

DOWER
When Venice was a queen with an unequall'd dower   56 Harold   4   99
A funeral dower of present woes and past   61 Harold   4   372
Must yield its pomp and wait till ages are its
    dower   74 Harold   4   1161
With Kenneth's lands to form her dower   102 Alva   79
With Immortality her dower   229 Marble   7
And thou shalt have a noble dower   326 Abydos   1   209
Was fiery Expectation's dower   409 Mazeppa   300
Ere Eve gave Adam knowledge for her dower   670 Heaven   1133
When happiness had been their only dower   819 Juan   4   157
Beauty and love were Haidee's mother's dower   823 Juan   4   446
Great wish to please--a most attractive dower   828 Juan   4   751

DOWERS
And such she was;--her daughters had their dowers   55 Harold   4   14

DOW'GERS
Now round the room the circling dow'gers sweep   250 Bards   660

DOWN
Disconsolate will wander up and down   7 Harold   1   227
From mountain-cliff to coast descending sombre
    down   23 Harold   2   198
With all thy vices, for thou didst lay down   67 Harold   4   746
Or bends the languid eyelid down   100 Marion   9
But when the hostile chiefs at length bow down   107 Nisus   153
In vain he calls each Muse in order down   142 Soliloquy   3

DOWN
Then the mortal coldness of the soul like death
    itself comes down   185 Music-B   9
The flashes fell upon them; some lay down   189 Darkness   24
The Moorish King rides up and down   194 Ballad-A   1
To the poor bird whose pinion fluttering down   206 Greece   7
Tread reviving passions down   207 Year   29
Nor master'd Science tempt her to look down   208 Sketch   25
Per coach for Mrs. Pigot frank it down   224 J.C.H.   30
'I lay my branch of laurel down   227 Thurlow-B   1
Thou 'lay thy branch of laurel down   227 Thurlow-B   2
To sanction Vice, and hunt Decorum down   250 Bards   621
I too can hunt a poetaster down   256 Bards   1064
And nonsense in a lofty note goes down   257 Hints   23
And boys shall hunt your bardship up and down   263 Hints   478
Say with what eye along the distant down   272 Minerva   303
When I cut ears off, I had cut him down   287 Vision   150
And at the fifth line knock'd the poet down   298 Vision   827
But as thou wast and art, on thee looks down   372 Lara   1   453
With which that chieftain's brow would bear him
    down   373 Lara   1   499
The cold, round moon shines deeply down   387 Corinth   243
As they seem, through the dimness, about to come
    down   391 Corinth   624
The shatter'd town--the walls thrown down   395 Corinth   1021
And whiter sails go skimming down   406 Chillon   340
The ducal chiefs within thee, shalt fall down   439 Tasso   223
And in its own good season tramples down   454 Venice-B   132
Which waft him where the Apennine looks down   458 Dante   1   169
With an Hidalgo, who transmitted down   754 Juan   1   450
Who threaten'd death--so Juan knock'd him down   769 Juan   1   1464
Would have been vain, and they must have gone
    down   777 Juan   2   226
'Twas twilight, and the sunless day went down   780 Juan   2   385
'Tis being too epic, I must cut down   816 Juan   3   978
And he himself o'ermaster'd and cut down   823 Juan   4   458
He paused, and took a survey up and down   841 Juan   5   624
A second time desired him to kneel down   844 Juan   5   811
The first was to bombard it, and knock down   870 Juan   7   179
Of his opinion, when I see cast down   885 Juan   8   476
And redly ran his blushing waters down   894 Juan   8   1012
The cravat stain'd with bloody drops fell down   920 Juan   11   129
Thou hast struck one immense Colossus down   965 Juan   14   651

DOWNCAST
He offer'd it with downcast look   113 Cornelian-A   9
Whose downcast eye disdains the wanton leer   119 Answer-A   29
And downcast look'd, and gently spake   324 Abydos   1   49
Which downcast droop'd in tearless agony   345 Corsair   1   469
Or seen at such, with downcast eyes   386 Corinth   204
With downcast eyes and knitting brow   398 Parisina   163
For the sweet downcast virgin whose young hand   726 Deformed   1   278
But Don Alfonso stood with downcast looks   766 Juan   1   1281
Of downcast length, in whose silk shadow lies   789 Juan   2   931
Those downcast eyes beneath the Almighty dove   815 Juan   3   918
Her black, bright, downcast, yet espiegle eye   989 Juan   16   561

DOWN'D
Since by the giant I was fairly down'd   470 Morgante   284

DOWNRIGHT
Had he found save in downright crime   177 Devil's Dr   126
But for your petty, picking, downright thievery   684 Werner   2   49
So much indeed as to be downright rude   752 Juan   1   342
Of a young downright beauty in this case   848 Juan   5   1040
And yet a headlong, headstrong, downright she   853 Juan   6   17
To this my plain, sworn, downright detestation   899 Juan   9   191
In islands is, it seems, downright and thorough   923 Juan   11   334
For downright rudeness, ye may stay at home   924 Juan   11   345

DOWNS
He who first downs with the red cross may crave   392 Corinth   717

DOWN-THUNDERING
By the down-thundering of the prison-wall   454 Venice-B   82

DOWN-TOPPLING
From their down-toppling nests; and bellowing
    herds   64 Harold   4   575

DOWNWARD
Which slope his green path downward to the shore   51 Harold   3   944
The sunshine for a while, and downward go   57 Harold   4   105
Crushing the cliffs, which, downward worn and rent   65 Harold   4   629
Pass'd the first winding downward to the glen   342 Corsair   1   310
And downward to the Isthmian plain   385 Corinth   73
And o'er his brow, so downward bent   390 Corinth   513
Floating darkly downward there   390 Corinth   557
Corinth's sons were downward borne   392 Corinth   746
Dash'd downward in the thundering foam below   429 Island   3   176
Yet pierces downward, onward, or above   482 Manfred   1   296
As it went chilly downward to the grave   694 Werner   2   738
Downward then the ladder crashes   736 Deformed   2   90
And tumble downward like the flying fish   745 Juan   Ded   22

DOWNWARD
And further downward, tall and towering still, is 826 Juan 4 605
But these are trifles. Downward flies my lord 946 Juan 13 361

DOWNWARDS
The woods sloped downwards to its brink, and
   stood 948 Juan 13 455

DOWRY
Destruction for a dowry,--this to see 458 Dante 1 174
To make my dowry equal to the rank 513 Faliero 2 307
A queen, shall make your dowry worth a kingdom 585 Sardan 4 479
In the state's service, I have still my dowry 626 Foscari 5 345
Girl, you but grasp your dowry. Oh, great God 739 Deformed 2 300
Her dowry; and her veil, in form alike 789 Juan 2 973
Her dowry was as nothing to her smiles 790 Juan 2 1020

DOXIES
'While Poesy,' with these delightful doxies 171 Address-B 37

DOZE
Though all deplore when Milton deigns to doze 264 Hints 569
To toss, to tumble, doze, revive, and quake 855 Juan 6 191

DOZED
Or if he dozed, a sound, a start 387 Corinth 336
He still was in the boat and had but dozed 788 Juan 2 891

DOZEN
It shares itself among a dozen 100 Marion 38
Into half a dozen dimples 234 Silver 3
A dozen dukes, some kings, a queen--and Waltz 274 Waltz 54
No; I left a round dozen of authors and others 278 Blues 1 36
For half a dozen years without estrangement 446 Beppo 419
Left it some dozen years ago. And then 675 Werner 1 267
Rouse up some half a dozen shivering vassals 681 Werner 1 604
(Quoth he) you'll order out a dozen villains 682 Werner 1 689
And now he storms at half a dozen wretches 688 Werner 2 332
Enough to seize a dozen such? Hence! after him 693 Werner 2 659
Composed a choir of girls, ten or a dozen 844 Juan 5 786
He had fifty daughters and four dozen sons 850 Juan 6 1209
First one or two, then five, six, and a dozen 883 Juan 8 353
Some are soon bagg'd, and some reject three dozen 934 Juan 12 265
I thought, at setting off, about two dozen 936 Juan 12 437
I've known a dozen weddings made even thus 937 Juan 12 481

DOZING
Your noble guest right quickly. Yes--he's dozing 681 Werner 1 611

DR.
Do you know Dr. Nott 238 Bray 1
Which made Dr. Nott not a bishop 238 Bray 6

DRACHENFELS
The castled crag of Drachenfels 43 Harold 3 496
Which Drachenfels frowns over like a spectre 915 Juan 10 490

DRACONIC
Making kings' rights divine, by some Draconic
   clause 45 Harold 3 616

DRACO'S
Observ'st, obey'st such laws as make old Draco's 607 Foscari 2 393

DRAFT
Or generous draft, conceded as a gift 946 Juan 13 357
On ready money, or 'a draft on Ransom 969 Juan 15 64

DRAG
But drag or drive us on to die 171 Time-B 4
Shall drag my journal from the desk's recess 255 Bards 1024
Some secret thought, than drag that chief's
   to-day 341 Corsair 1 222
When he shall drag the fetter'd Rovers home 347 Corsair 2 5
They ne'er had been, than drag me on to be 504 Faliero 1 351
Rose up, methought, to drag me down to them 581 Sardan 4 176
Thank God! At least they will not drag him more 605 Foscari 2 271
As long as he can drag them: 'tis his throne 615 Foscari 4 59
In time to drag him through his carriage window 676 Werner 1 289
That one should die, than two drag on the fetter 906 Juan 9 640

DRAG-CHAIN
Six Tartars and a drag-chain.' 'To this doom 833 Juan 5 115

DRAGG'D
I have dragg'd to three-and-thirty 236 Dull Road 2
Close' to the glimmering grate he dragg'd his
   chain 359 Corsair 3 262
But dragg'd again upon the arena, stood 378 Lara 2 260
Dragg'd o'er the deck, no more at thy command 416 Island 1 57
To have you dragg'd to prison, I became 519 Faliero 3 61
Your humble duty at the door! I dragg'd him 678 Werner 1 433
Of those around me dragg'd me from the spot 715 Werner 5 137
Denounced--dragg'd; it may be, in chains; and all 721 Werner 5 525

DRAGGING
Aside these nodding plumes and dragging trains 714 Werner 5 70

DRAGON
The dragon crawls from out his den 669 Heaven 1063
Or pray Medea for a single dragon 814 Juan 3 884

DRAGON'S
Here the bold peasant storm'd the dragon's nest 12 Harold 1 519
And gripe and deepening of the dragon's grasp 79 Harold 4 1437

DRAGS
The day drags through though storms keep out the
   sun 40 Harold 3 287
All that a poet drags into detail 865 Juan 6 870

DRAIN
I know that thou wilt love me; though to drain 53 Harold 3 1090
Oh! then let us drain, while we may, draughts of
   pleasure 91 Caroline-C 25
And bid him drain the dregs of pleasure's bowl 100 Damaetas 12
The cup of woe for me to drain 165 Thyrza 46
And philanthropic Israel deigns to drain 307 Age 682
The bowl a Moslem must not drain 315 Giaour 548
At midnight drain the stream of life 317 Giaour 760
Unless he drain the wine of passion--rage 416 Island 1 64
Drain every drop!--to-morrow we may die 419 Island 2 46
Will drain one draught in memory of many 594 Sardan 5 455
Resumed its careless life, and rose to drain 643 Cain 2 500
As well as further drain the wither'd form 912 Juan 10 300

DRAIN'D
Oft have we drain'd the font of ancient lore 125 Recoll 253
When drain'd is the nectar which gladdens the
   bowl 148 Farewell-A 13
It is not drain'd to banish care 168 Haunts 18
Though swamps subdued, and marshes drain'd,
   sustain 258 Hints 95
'Tis true, the purchase nearly drain'd 331 Abydos 2 255
And drain'd the draught with an applauding cheer 417 Island 1 104
Who but give back what they have drain'd from
   millions 527 Faliero 3 604
As these old veins, oft drain'd in shielding her 548 Faliero 5 747
I, who sprung from the same womb with thee,
   drain'd 654 Cain 3 535

DRAINER
The drainer of oblivion, even the sot 968 Juan 15 27

DRAINS
The first cup which he drains will be the last 562 Sardan 2 52
A child the moment when it drains the breast 799 Juan 2 1562
Drains its first draught of lips:--but, as I said 911 Juan 10 223

DRAMA
(See also MELO-DRAMES)
And call'd, proud boast! the British drama forth 94 Dorset 68
Of embryo actors, to the Drama new 113 Prologue 16
And bids the Drama be where she hath been 169 Address-A 24
A sort of--it's no more a drama 231 Doctor 35
Now to the Drama turn--Oh! motley sight 249 Bards 560
One classic drama, and reform the stage 249 Bards 585
Since their own drama yields no fairer trace 250 Bards 616
But from the Drama let me not digress 260 Hints 263
Now to the Drama let us bend our eyes 261 Hints 351
Some drama of the marriage unities 972 Juan 15 253

DRAMAS
Of Grecian dramas vaunts the deathless fame 111 Examination 21
And live in prologues, though his dramas die 251 Bards 718

DRAMA'S
Bow'd to the dust the Drama's tower of pride 169 Address-A 2
Oh! since your fiat stamps the Drama's laws 170 Address-A 62
The Drama's homage by her herald paid 170 Address-A 67
Ye Bards! to whom the Drama's Muse is dear 194 Monody 105

DRAMATIC
Dramatic 'spirit drives a conquering car 170 Address-B 19
Though too licentious for dramatic laws 263 Hints 446
Their last dramatic work by candle-light 267 Hints 766
Which Plato in his dialogues dramatic 979 Juan 15 685

DRAMATIS
But all our dramatis personae wait 114 Prologue 23

DRAMATISE
And George and I will dramatise it for ye 171 Address-B 24

DRAMS
Dosed with vile drams on Sunday he was found 268 Hints 835
Some take a lover, some take drams or prayers 799 Juan 2 1601

DRANK

And his Soul drank their sunbeams: he was girt	215	Dream	108
For, the liquor he drank being too much for one	224	Adams	5
Drank the last life-drop of his bleeding breast	253	Bards	848
They roar'd, they dined, they drank, they swore they meant	306	Age	622
He drank one draught nor needed more	331	Abydos 2	245
Arise from out the earth which drank	385	Corinth	61
Which his worshippers drank at the break of day	395	Corinth	1004
Drank as they do who drink their last, and threw	427	Island 3	75
She drank no blood, nor fatten'd on the dead	454	Venice-B	112
Which swam before my giddy eyes, that drank	529	Faliero 4	64
Which drank this willing blood from many a wound	548	Faliero 5	731
Thrice have I drank of it, and thrice renew'd	577	Sardan 3	351
And stared, but neither ate nor drank, but stared	580	Sardan 4	121
And drank the best dew	728	Deformed 1	407
Some plunder'd, some drank spirits, some sung psalms	778	Juan 2	267
They ate up all they had, and drank their wine	782	Juan 2	546
Bent with hush'd lips, that drank his scarce-drawn breath	792	Juan 2	1144
He drank six cups of coffee at the least	863	Juan 6	732

DRAPERIED

Draperied her form with curious felicity	994	Juan 16	864

DRAPERIES

With floating draperies and with flying hair	861	Juan 6	570

DRAPERY

Some half-torn drapery scatter'd on the ground	770	Juan 1	1493
The milliners who furnish 'drapery Misses	924	Juan 11	385
Whose drapery hints we may admire them freely	949	Juan 13	544

DRAUGHT

And consecrate the oath with draught, and dance till morn	15	Harold 1	710
And all combine to hail the draught	103	Alva	192
How doubly sweet will be the draught	139	Anacreon-C	4
The draught shall be sweet to my soul	162	Romaic-A	20
The cup must hold a deadlier draught	168	Haunts	19
That thou shouldst from Thee dash the Draught of Life	185	Julian	44
He drank one draught nor needed more	331	Abydos 2	245
And drain'd the draught with an applauding cheer	417	Island 1	104
Yes; and for one sole draught of hate, forego	516	Faliero 2	519
The pleasure of that draught; for I was parch'd	577	Sardan 3	361
Will drain one draught in memory of many	594	Sardan 5	455
Looks at a draught of water, for this man	715	Werner 5	121
Preferr'd a draught from the fast-flowing veins	783	Juan 2	612
Might not have thought the scanty draught so sweet	784	Juan 2	678
Vie with that draught of hock and soda-water	797	Juan 2	1440
With the first draught intoxicates apace	905	Juan 9	532
Drains its first draught of lips:--but, as I said	911	Juan 10	223
Which form that bitter draught, the human species	916	Juan 10	584
Of the Truth's rays, spoil not my draught of spirit	918	Juan 11	15

DRAUGHTS

With draughts intemperate on the sinking deck	37	Harold 3	143
Oh! then let us drain, while we may, draughts of pleasure	91	Caroline-C	25
Forbidden draughts, 'tis said, he dared to quaff	347	Corsair 2	32

DRAW

Heart, soul could seek, tongue ask.--Away with words, draw near	71	Harold 4	972
Its depth, and thence may draw the mind of man	79	Harold 4	1430
No Siddons draw the sympathetic tear	113	Prologue	14
Oh! might we draw our omens from the past	169	Address-A	28
To draw a Lying Valet, or a Lear	259	Hints	164
If some Drawcansir you aspire to draw	259	Hints	173
Who, born no king, made monarchs draw his car	299	Age	44
And now, ye kings! they kindly draw your own	307	Age	675
Draw blessings from the mountaineer	315	Giaour	540
More beautiful than they, which did draw down	493	Manfred 3	178
To draw conclusions absolute of aught	494	Manfred 3	207
Will draw them forward: they shall pay themselves	504	Faliero 1	335
And draw down freedom on her evermore	517	Faliero 2	605
Shall draw more gazers than the thousand portraits	545	Faliero 5	505
Our annals draw perchance unto their close	582	Sardan 4	296
To make me useful: I would draw it forth	589	Sardan 5	130
Draw near a close. I pray you take this key	591	Sardan 5	247
Their matins now draw nigh--the east is kindling	662	Heaven	561
The snake but vanquish'd dust; but she will draw	666	Heaven	858
I fear that men must draw their chariots, as	699	Werner 3	288
Engaged in the chase, draw off the eighty men	705	Werner 4	105
Until the chase begins; then draw thou off	706	Werner 4	135
Bay deep-mouth'd welcome as we draw near home	762	Juan 1	978
At sixty years, and draw the accompts of evil	767	Juan 1	1335
Alfonso's sword had dropp'd ere he could draw it	769	Juan 1	1473
Only to draw them 'twixt two bastion corners	887	Juan 8	599

DRAW

To draw a high prize: now, howe'er he got her, I	934	Juan 12	295
Some waltz; some draw; some fathom the abyss	936	Juan 12	413
And draw them nightly when a ticket's sent	937	Juan 12	454
To draw the line between the false and true	966	Juan 14	717
Your writers, who must either draw again	971	Juan 15	206
To draw up in array a single day-bill	976	Juan 15	493
To draw the bow, to ride, and speak the truth	980	Juan 16	2
But draw the long bow better now than ever	980	Juan 16	8

DRAWBRIDGE

Its drawbridge and portcullis' weight	410	Mazeppa	395
Gallop o'er the west drawbridge. See they cease not	714	Werner 5	81

DRAWCANSIR

If some Drawcansir you aspire to draw	259	Hints	173
And not in literature a great Drawcansir	924	Juan 11	402

DRAWING

Whose walls o'erlook the stream; and drawing nigh	27	Harold 2	493
Precipitously steep; and drawing near	48	Harold 3	810
Or drawing from the no less kindled earth	301	Age	247
And drawing nigh, exclaim'd, with haughty sneer	372	Lara 1	425
With a far-dashing stroke, and drawing deep	597	Foscari 1	118
Not dazzling, and yet drawing us to them	635	Cain 1	513
But that on drawing near them I beheld	639	Cain 2	213
And drawing from his belt a pistol, he	821	Juan 4	316
Thousands of whom were drawing their last breath	878	Juan 7	692
That in the lieu of drawing on his banker	911	Juan 10	242
He had the art of drawing people out	978	Juan 15	655

DRAWING-ROOM

To follow him beyond the drawing-room	908	Juan 10	37
Which well beseem'd the 'Devil's drawing-room	917	Juan 10	643

DRAWLING

Of Londonderry drawling against time	869	Juan 7	126

DRAWN

(See also HALF-DRAWN, LONG-DRAWN, SCARCE-DRAWN)

The moral lesson bears, drawn from such pilgrimage	62	Harold 4	405
(For drawn from reptiles only may we trace	209	Sketch	69
Drawn from the stem of each Teutonic stud	274	Waltz	52
That sound hath drawn my foes more nigh	334	Abydos 2	525
The milk drawn from the mountain goat	404	Chillon	132
More slowly drawn, grew less and less	404	Chillon	204
But once drawn up, and their new swords well-flesh'd	520	Faliero 3	136
Within whose court will be drawn out in arms	524	Faliero 3	376
There is no more to be drawn from these men	539	Faliero 5	88
A sword which hath been drawn as oft as thine	565	Sardan 2	202
Would have but drawn upon his aged head	611	Foscari 3	228
I did not deem this poor place could have drawn	612	Foscari 3	250
Out of their love? have they not drawn their milk	633	Cain 1	366
Our swords when drawn must cross, our engines aim	676	Werner 1	348
Oh, valiant man! with sword drawn and cock'd trigger	765	Juan 1	1199
Drawn from the stars, and filter'd through the skies	801	Juan 2	1692
Were not drawn from their spouses, you conceive	803	Juan 3	80
Drawn by the blue-coat misses of a coterie	830	Juan 4	872
With all its veil of mystery drawn apart	893	Juan 8	916
For I have drawn much less with a long bow	896	Juan 8	1102
White stocking drawn uncurdled as new milk	902	Juan 9	343
From thence he was drawn onwards to Cologne	915	Juan 10	493
If such can e'er be drawn by man's capacity	966	Juan 14	718
Days better drawn before, or else assume	971	Juan 15	207
Juan was drawn thus into some attentions	978	Juan 15	633
A noise like to wet fingers drawn on glass	995	Juan 16	953

DRAWS

The fatal spell, and still it draws us on	73	Harold 4	1104
The hour draws nigh, a few brief days will close	94	Dorset	77
Draws sly comparisons of these with those	271	Minerva	191
Which draws the diver to the crimson cave	420	Island 2	140
Ye avalanches, whom a breath draws down	482	Manfred 1	336
Forbears to pant for death, and yet draws back	487	Manfred 2	268
Himself perhaps even now draws grating back	535	Faliero 4	529
Of foreign air he draws seems a slow poison	600	Foscari 1	292
Beats quick; he awes me, and yet draws me near	633	Cain 1	409
That corner's turn'd--so--ah! no!--right! it draws	701	Werner 3	418
Yielding to their small hands, draws back again	805	Juan 3	256
But then the roll-call draws them back afraid	957	Juan 14	131
Graceful as Dian, when she draws her bow	985	Juan 16	301

DRAY

In England 'twould be dung, dust, or a dray	445	Beppo	336

DRAYS

Through coaches, drays, choked turnpikes, and a whirl	921	Juan 11	169

DREAD

Or dost thou dread the billows' rage	5	Harold 1	136
Or dost thou dread a French foeman	6	Harold 1	160
Appall'd, an owlet's larum chill'd with dread	12	Harold 1	563
In whose dread name both men and maids are sworn	15	Harold 1	709
Is the dread sceptre and dominion dire	19	Harold 2	7
His shade from Hades upon that dread day	21	Harold 2	121
Which all admire but many dread to view	26	Harold 2	382
To greet Albania's chief, whose dread command	26	Harold 2	418
Let the yellow-hair'd Giaours view his horse-tail with dread	31	Harold 2	686
Known unto all,--or hope and dread allay'd	52	Harold 3	1008
Stumble o'er heaving plains, and man's dread hath no words	64	Harold 4	576
Charming the eye with dread--a matchless cataract	65	Harold 4	639
And thou, dread statue, yet existent in	68	Harold 4	775
The seal is set.--Now welcome, thou dread power	75	Harold 4	1234
A long low distant murmur of dread sound	80	Harold 4	1496
Obeys thee; thou goest forth, dread, fathomless, alone	82	Harold 4	1647
Or Heaven reverse the dread decrees of fate	84	Death-B	10
Thy dread behests ne'er disobey	89	Prometheus-A	4
Nought shall thy dread decree prevent	99	Young Lady	34
The hope of praise, the dread of shame	111	Medea	5
Seduction's dread is here no slight restraint	119	Answer-A	26
War's dread machines o'erhang thy threatening brow	120	Newstead-A	59
Thy dread omnipotence I own	132	Prayer	11
From rage he rails not, rather say from dread	142	Soliloquy	23
I view my parting hour with dread	158	Florence	8
In darkness and in dread	159	Storm	50
In that dread hour ere death appear	165	Thyrza	19
Through dark and dread Eternity	168	Dead	69
In one dread night our city saw, and sigh'd	169	Address-A	1
'Dread metaphors, which open wounds' like issues	170	Address-B	12
Or dread of death alone	180	Ode-A	43
I have coped with the nations which dread me thus lonely	186	Napoleon	7
And men forgot their passions in the dread	189	Darkness	7
And evil dread so ill dissembled	191	Prometheus-B	33
Of the Ionian waters broke a dread	205	Aristom	3
If daughters dread her for the mothers' sake	208	Sketch	42
Hadst nought to dread--in thy own weakness shielded	213	Lady Byron	29
The dread of vanish'd shadows--Are they so	214	Dream	17
Domdaniel's dread destroyer, who o'erthrew	244	Bards	213
The babe unborn thy dread intent may rue	245	Bards	233
Even Satan's self with thee might dread to dwell	245	Bards	281
But let me cease, and dread Cassandra's fate	255	Bards	1007
Too long the assembly (he was pleased to dread	297	Vision	765
He stood--some dread was on his face	312	Giaour	234
And still with little less than dread	319	Giaour	874
With dread beheld, with gloom beholding	319	Giaour	885
Else may we dread the wrath divine	319	Giaour	910
Hath nought to dread from outward blow	321	Giaour	1156
When on that dread yet lovely serpent smiling	325	Abydos 1	159
His captive, though with dread resigning	332	Abydos 2	339
Yes, fear!--the doubt, the dread of losing thee	333	Abydos 2	446
That dread shall vanish with the favouring gale	333	Abydos 2	448
'Tis sorrow so unmix'd with dread	336	Abydos 2	700
No dread of death--if with us die our foes	338	Corsair 1	23
Yet dread not this; the proof of all the past	344	Corsair 1	406
Lest Time should raise that doubt to more than dread	344	Corsair 1	447
It may seem strange--if there be aught to dread	349	Corsair 2	127
In silence eyed him with a secret dread	351	Corsair 2	309
'Twill cost me dear--but dread no death to-day	355	Corsair 2	534
'With nothing left to love, there's nought to dread	357	Corsair 3	100
This fearful interval of doubt and dread	358	Corsair 3	210
Above some object of her doubt or dread	361	Corsair 3	413
Such as we know is false, yet dread in sooth	375	Lara 1	622
Yet wake to wrestle with the dread of death	375	Lara 1	643
In dread to meet the marks of prowlers' wrath	376	Lara 2	110
All dread by slow degrees had worn away	377	Lara 2	173
Perchance his strife with Otho made him dread	378	Lara 2	192
If dead it were, escaped the observer's dread	383	Lara 2	589
With an echo dread and new	392	Corinth	762
'It is not that I dread the death	399	Parisina	234
Of Sin delirious with its dread	404	Chillon	183
I knew 'twas hopeless, but my dread	404	Chillon	207
'Twas after dread Pultowa's day	407	Mazeppa	1
When truth had nought to dread from power	407	Mazeppa	22
For until now he had the dread	407	Mazeppa	63
In the full foam of wrath and dread	410	Mazeppa	368
Disclosed for man to dread or woman weep	418	Island 1	200
That sound a dread? All around them seem'd array'd	429	Island 3	216
Since that all-nameless hour. I have no dread	479	Manfred 1	24
And when in that secret dread	481	Manfred 1	216
Thy dread and sufferance be, there's comfort yet	484	Manfred 2	33
And ask them what it is we dread to be	487	Manfred 2	272
Yet in this hour I dread the thing I dare	487	Manfred 2	293
And evil and dread	488	Manfred 2	344

DREAD

Child of the Earth! or dread the worst. I know it	489	Manfred 2	405
It is the same! Oh, God! that I should dread	490	Manfred 2	472
Whither? I dread to think; but he is gone	497	Manfred 3	413
And shake down senates, mad with wrath and dread	522	Faliero 3	227
(Which they dare not refuse, at the dread signal	524	Faliero 3	382
Surely thou ravest! what have I to dread	530	Faliero 4	183
And trembled at the thought of this dread duty	534	Faliero 4	426
Of that dread gulf which none repass, the truth	538	Faliero 5	31
They tremble at our voices--nay, they dread	539	Faliero 5	122
To the unrivall'd city! What dost dread	555	Sardan 1	327
What must we dread? Ambitious treachery	555	Sardan 1	332
That I should prize their noisy praise, or dread	556	Sardan 1	389
Before my hour, to live in dread of death	557	Sardan 1	441
A slave, and wherefore should I dread my freedom	558	Sardan 1	527
Assume to win them? Who is he should dread	558	Sardan 1	537
And if I do not dread it, why shouldst thou	560	Sardan 1	666
Of open force? We dread thy treason, not	564	Sardan 2	164
Art thou of those who dread the roar of clouds	570	Sardan 2	547
Strikes his own altars. That were a dread omen	570	Sardan 2	553
Are ended. Yet, I dread thy nature will	584	Sardan 4	393
The dread of more: it is an anxious hour	588	Sardan 5	74
What more may be imposed!--I dread to think on't	597	Foscari 1	132
In Venice had to dread a Doge's frown	605	Foscari 2	239
And dread, and toil, and sweat, and heaviness	633	Cain 1	356
Which, as I know it not, I dread not, though	634	Cain 1	466
That is the prelude. Then I dread it less	645	Cain 2	617
His waking a continual dread of death	652	Cain 3	431
Who hath provided for us this dread office	653	Cain 3	452
When the dread hour denounced shall open wide	658	Heaven	228
But could I dare to pray in his dread hour	664	Heaven	696
Together. You diverged from that dread path	679	Werner 1	540
For one day's peace, after thrice ten dread years	714	Werner 5	96
My God! you look--How? As on that dread night	716	Werner 5	184
They make you dread that they'll recite them too	760	Juan 1	860
As every rising wave his dread renew'd	781	Juan 2	469
Away the vast, salt, dread, eternal deep	787	Juan 2	824
The old man's cheek grew pale, but not with dread	821	Juan 4	315
Polygamy may well be held in dread	854	Juan 6	91
Not to be rashly touch'd. But still more dread	860	Juan 6	490
Which Hamlet tells us is a pass of dread	883	Juan 8	324
Acknowledge aught of dread of death or foe	889	Juan 8	693
With joy to save, and dread of some mischance	890	Juan 8	764
This hourly dread of all! whose threaten'd sting	897	Juan 9	86
Or, on, might dread her majesty had not room enough	902	Juan 9	379
Through such a scene of change, and dread, and slaughter	914	Juan 10	442
Should neither court neglect, nor dread to bear it	941	Juan 12	696
Less from disgust of life than dread of death	955	Juan 14	32
And noble births, nor dread the enumeration	962	Juan 14	412
No wonder then a purer soul should dread	963	Juan 14	507
But I may have, and you too, reader, dread it	977	Juan 15	576
Began to dread she'd thaw to a coquette	978	Juan 15	644
Have something ghastly, desolate, and dread	982	Juan 16	136
With some, while others, who had more in dread	987	Juan 16	475
And then his dread grew wrath, and his wrath fierce	996	Juan 16	993

DREADED

By peril, dreaded most in female eyes	43	Harold 3	493
From dreaded pangs that feeble foe to save	123	Recoll	87
And when the dreaded hour shall come	169	Blank Leaf	5
The ocean-city's dreaded Doge	196	Venice-A	12
From Caesar the dreaded to George the despised	203	Avatar	64
Are dreaded more than hostile sword	*316	Giaour	600
The hearts that loathed him, crouch'd and dreaded too	342	Corsair 1	270
Yet shunn'd and dreaded with such care	414	Mazeppa	728
Strike!--If I dreaded death, a death more fearful	522	Faliero 3	221
Because I ever dreaded to intrude	585	Sardan 4	443
Who dreaded to elect me, and have since	605	Foscari 2	243
Dreaded to have its acts beheld by others	622	Foscari 5	131
Of that existence with the dreaded name	644	Cain 2	569
For Donna Inez dreaded the Mythology	752	Juan 1	328
Of Doctors' Commons: but she dreaded first	963	Juan 14	493

DREADFUL

Hark! heard you not those hoofs of dreadful note	10	Harold 1	414
Nor yet, alas, the dreadful work is done	18	Harold 1	909
Here, too, his boy essay'd the dreadful leap	24	Harold 2	259
And whence the dreadful stranger came	105	Alva	281
Or drive me to dreadful despair	116	Strephon	24
wing of Fillan floats on the wind. Dreadful	131	Calmar	150
Clouds burst, skies flash, oh, dreadful hour	158	Storm	29
Could have effected. 'Twas a dreadful sight	601	Foscari 1	364
With the like answer--doubt and dreadful surmise	609	Foscari 3	76
Says he is something dreadful, my mother	631	Cain 1	249
I feel, it is a dreadful thing; but what	631	Cain 1	282
Know nought of death, save as a dreadful thing	637	Cain 2	61
All here seems dark and dreadful. But distinct	639	Cain 2	190
As if Death were more dreadful by his door	778	Juan 2	277
Then some leap'd overboard with dreadful yell	780	Juan 2	411

DREADFUL

Is dreadful to the shepherd and the flock	808 Juan	3	458
A dreadful impulse to each loud meander	863 Juan	6	741
A 'dreadful trade,' like his who 'gathers samphire	926 Juan	11	483
Dreadful as Dante's rhima, or this stanza	995 Juan	16	972

DREADING

Dreading each should set thee free	187 French-A		21
When, dreading to be deem'd too kind	209 Augusta-A		7
Dreading the deep damnation of his 'bah	444 Beppo		254
Loathing our life, and dreading still to die	487 Manfred	2	260
They dreading he should snatch the tyranny	526 Faliero	3	501
Dreading that climax of all human ills	806 Juan	3	279
And dreading the chaste echoes of her shoe	995 Juan	16	944

DREADS

And dreads not the anguish of love's last adieu	100 L Adieu		32
Dreads lest the subject should transport me	100 Marion		24
Who hopes, yet almost dreads, to meet your praise	114 Prologue		22
Nor dreads the connoisseur's fastidious view	264 Hints		575
The doom he dreads, yet dwells upon	311 Giaour		84
That dreads the darkness and yet loathes the light	336 Abydos	2	648
No craven he, and yet he dreads the blow	349 Corsair	2	178
What dreads my Adah? This is no ill spirit	633 Cain	1	411
Whatever dreads to die. Decide between	727 Deformed	1	355

DREAD'ST

Dread'st thou not to partake their coming doom	665 Heaven		732

DREAM

With human hearts--to what?--a dream alone	11 Harold	1	455
Or dream'd he loved, since Rapture is a dream	17 Harold	1	811
Oh, may they still of transport dream	18 Harold	1	863
Gone--glimmering through the dream of things that were	19 Harold	2	12
Still wilt thou dream on future joy and woe	20 Harold	2	34
Well--I will dream that we may meet again	20 Harold	2	77
Though friendless now, will dream it had a friend	23 Harold	2	202
And many dream withal the hour is nigh	31 Harold	2	715
So that it wean me from the weary dream	35 Harold	3	33
But o'er the blacken'd memory's blighting dream	43 Harold	3	458
That goodness is no name and happiness no dream	53 Harold	3	1066
The unruffled mirror of the loveliest dream	63 Harold	4	476
But in his delicate form--a dream of Love	79 Harold	4	1450
Its wretched essence; and to dream of fame	80 Harold	4	1489
The spell should break of this protracted dream	82 Harold	4	1659
Since now our dream of bliss is past	89 To Emma		3
Whene'er I dream of that pure breast	90 To M.S.G-A		5
It sings of Love's enchanting dream	92 Lady-A		3
Fellows who dream on lawn or stalls	95 Granta		7
When I dream that you love me, you'll surely forgive	97 To M.S.G-B		1
Should the dream of to-night but resemble the last	97 To M.S.G.-B		7
If I sin in my dream, I atone for it now	98 To M.S.G.-B		15
And--though our dream at last is ended	98 To Lesbia		23
With this dream of deceit half our sorrow's represt	99 L Adieu		11
Our slumbering foes of future conquest dream	106 Nisus		102
Oft in the progress of some fleeting dream	125 Recoll		229
Nor closed the progress of my youthful dream	127 Recoll		368
Say, can ambition's fever'd dream bestow	127 Recoll		393
dream. I will seek car-borne Cuthullin. If I	130 Calmar		59
And interrupt the golden dream	133 E. N. Long		16
Once I beheld a splendid dream	135 I Would		21
Life's evening dream is dark and dull	137 Clare		17
With this fond dream, methinks, 'twere sweet to die	138 Harrow-B		23
Fresh as in Love's bewitching dream	146 Adieu		56
My life a short and vulgar dream	146 Adieu		87
No more beam the eyes which my dream could inspire	148 Farewell-A		11
And, sooth to say, that very dream	152 Remind		26
Can still a pleasing dream restore	152 Remind		33
Away! away! my early dream	155 Happy		33
To listen, though the dream be flown	166 Away		24
Thou art but now a lovely dream	166 Away		26
Thou wert too like a dream of Heaven	168 Haunts		39
And haunt thee like a feverish dream	171 Remember-A		4
To dream of joy and wake to sorrow	173 Not False		13
As if a dream alone had charm'd	173 Not False		22
I scarcely can regret my dream	173 Mrs. Lamb		11
That turn from tracing them to dream of thee	183 Address-D		30
It cannot feel for others' woes, it dare not dream its own	185 Music-B		10
The texture of a heavenly dream	188 On Star		30
I had a dream, which was not all a dream	189 Darkness		1
Thy waters could I dream of, name, or see	198 Po		27
Mine cannot witness, even in a dream	198 Po		31
As from a dream	200 Stanzas-B		49
What still a dream must be	205 To--B		8
A fatal dream--for many a bar	205 To--B		9

DREAM

How much died with him! false or true--the dream	205 Aristom		4
A change came o'er the spirit of my dream	214 Dream		75
A change came o'er the spirit of my dream	215 Dream		105ff
A change came o'er the spirit of my dream	216 Dream		184
My dream was past; it had no further change	216 Dream		202
Whose shrines are desolate, whose land a dream	217 Weep-B		2
And feed deep thought with many a dream	218 Bloom		8
No eastern vision, no distemper'd dream	242 Bards		24
Your strength is name, your bloated wealth a dream	272 Minerva		262
They varied like a dream--now here, now there	294 Vision		604
Of this true dream, the telescope is gone	298 Vision		842
That I awoke--and lo! it was no dream	308 Age		776
That sound had burst his waking dream	312 Giaour		247
And I shall sleep without the dream	320 Giaour		997
No, father, no, 'twas not a dream	322 Giaour		1258
The cause I cannot dream nor tell	328 Abydos	1	410
How dear the dream in darkest hours of ill	333 Abydos	2	420
'It is no dream--and I am desolate	345 Corsair	1	504
Dream they of this our preparation, doom'd	348 Corsair	2	79
And noiseless as a lovely dream is gone	355 Corsair	2	537
If all our Arab tales divulge or dream	358 Corsair	3	157
The present dubious, or the past a dream	367 Lara	1	54
How woke he from the wildness of that dream	368 Lara	1	128
To soothe away the horrors of his dream	369 Lara	1	244
If dream it were, that thus could overthrow	369 Lara	1	245
Was it a dream? was his the voice that spoke	370 Lara	1	275
And make Age smile and dream itself to youth	371 Lara	1	394
Yes--there be things which we must dream and dare	374 Lara	1	604
To bound as doubting from too black a dream	374 Lara	1	621
And yet they fearless dream of spoil	388 Corinth		353
Of the restless who walk in a troubled dream	391 Corinth		619
In that tumultuous tender dream	397 Parisina		42
That dream this morning pass'd away	398 Parisina		200
She strove with that convulsive dream	400 Parisina		383
A restless dream or two, some glances	408 Mazeppa		172
Nor dream that e'er that fortress was	410 Mazeppa		401
Studded with stars;--it is no dream	412 Mazeppa		581
I know no more--my latest dream	414 Mazeppa		783
For sages' labours or the student's dream	420 Island	2	94
The vanish'd phantom of a seaman's dream	431 Island	4	82
Writhe in a dream before me and o'er-arch	457 Dante	1	108
Who sleeps to dream of blood, and waking glows	457 Dante	1	114
Shall realise a poet's proudest dream	459 Dante	2	28
By the transparency of his bright dream	462 Dante	3	118
For a rough dream had shook him slumbering	471 Morgante		312
Would be but a distemper'd dream. What is it	484 Manfred	2	61
In life what others could not brook to dream	484 Manfred	2	78
How, say you?--finish'd! Do I dream?--'tis false	501 Faliero	1	99
'Twere hopeless for humanity to dream	514 Faliero	2	385
Waking the sleepers from some hideous dream	519 Faliero	3	5
Which shook me in a supernatural dream	547 Faliero	5	624
I would but have recall'd thee from thy dream	554 Sardan	1	247
Dream; though I know it now to be a dream	579 Sardan	4	71
And dream them through in placid sufferance	587 Sardan	5	32
Laughs out, although in slumber. He must dream	646 Cain	3	30
Of what? Of Paradise!--Ay! dream of it	646 Cain	3	31
My disinherited boy! 'Tis but a dream	646 Cain	3	32
I am awake at last--a dreary dream	652 Cain	3	378
Shall deign to expound this dream	661 Heaven		460
Thou who dost rather make me dream that Abel	664 Heaven		669
My dream is realised--how beautiful	688 Werner	2	340
It was so. I sometimes dream otherwise	707 Werner	4	193
Such as rounds common life into a dream	710 Werner	4	373
You dream. I live! and as I live, I saw him	714 Werner	5	86
And now my dream is out! 'Tis not my fault	718 Werner	5	360
But dream it is what must be. Must I wait	726 Deformed	1	290
Of all we know or dream of beautiful	727 Deformed	1	336
Her brain, though in a dream! (and then she sigh'd	757 Juan	1	667
So dear is still the memory of that dream	770 Juan	1	1540
And Juan, too, was help'd out from his dream	793 Juan	2	1217
An opium dream of too much youth and reading	818 Juan	4	146
Stirr'd with her dream, as rose-leaves with the air	820 Juan	4	232
Walks o'er it, was she shaken by the dream	820 Juan	4	235
The dream changed:--in a cave she stood, its walls	820 Juan	4	257
And that brief dream appear'd a life too long	820 Juan	4	272
Her recollection; on her flash'd the dream	824 Juan	4	524
The twelve isles, and the more than I could dream	831 Juan	5	22
And smiling through her dream, as through a cloud	860 Juan	6	524
Through the heaved breast the dream of some far shore	860 Juan	6	533
She dream'd a dream, of walking in a wood	861 Juan	6	594
Bed for the dream she had been obliged to hear	862 Juan	6	630
She promised never more to have a dream	862 Juan	6	657
At least to dream so loudly as just now	862 Juan	6	658
Of all save Dudu's dream, which was no joke	865 Juan	6	832
And so they are; yet thus is Glory's dream	878 Juan	8	4
And wander'd up and down as in a dream	887 Juan	8	572
All that we read, hear, dream, of man's distresses	894 Juan	8	979
To swim or sink--I have had at least my dream	956 Juan	14	88

DREAM

As few would ever dream could form the link	968	Juan	14	797
And would have pass'd the whole off as a dream	983	Juan	16	197

DREAM'D

Forms which it sighs but to have only dream'd	2	To Ianthe		4
Oft have I dream'd of Thee, whose glorious name	13	Harold	1	621
Or dream'd he loved, since Rapture is a dream	17	Harold	1	811
I saw or dream'd of such,--but let them go	56	Harold	4	55
Dream'd not of the rebound	180	Ode-A		47
I would recall a vision which I dream'd	214	Dream		23
She dream'd what Paradise might be	330	Abydos	2	105
I have a tale thou hast not dream'd	330	Abydos	2	153
But soon he found, or feign'd, or dream'd relief	352	Corsair	2	378
Whate'er his frenzy dream'd or eye beheld	369	Lara	1	247
Of waving trees, and dream'd uncounted hours	438	Tasso		156
Return'd and wept alone, and dream'd again	438	Tasso		164
I sought not, wish'd not, dream'd not the election	541	Faliero	5	211
Say on. I saw, that is, I dream'd myself	579	Sardan	4	78
I became Doge, or dream'd of such advancement	605	Foscari	2	204
And dream'd that aught of Abel was in her	664	Heaven		676
From whence he never dream'd to rise. Methought	678	Werner	1	475
Of whom I long have dream'd in a low garb	700	Werner	3	346
Amidst the people in the church, I dream'd not	716	Werner	5	188
And never dream'd his lady was concern'd	749	Juan	1	148
My mother dream'd not in my natal hour	766	Juan	1	1239
Dream'd of a thousand wrecks, o'er which she stumbled	791	Juan	2	1099
Of whom these two years she had nightly dream'd	796	Juan	2	1372
I dream'd that Greece might still be free	812	Juan	3	704
She dream'd of being alone on the sea-shore	820	Juan	4	241
But all this time how slept, or dream'd, Dudu	861	Juan	6	553
She dream'd a dream, of walking in a wood	861	Juan	6	594
Pretensions which they never dream'd to have shown	937	Juan	12	484

DREAMER

Alas! the dreamer first must sleep	322	Giaour		1259
'It beats!'--Away, thou dreamer! he is gone	382	Lara	2	498
What, hath this dreamer, with his father's ark	664	Heaven		708
Not yet a dreamer, till the spell is broke	793	Juan	2	1211

DREAMERS

Of which we are but dreamers;--as he caught	190	Churchill		25

DREAMER'S

Not in the phrensy of a dreamer's eye	13	Harold	1	613

DREAMING

Watch thou, while many a dreaming chieftain dies	108	Nisus		234
Has cured my boyish soul of Dreaming	144	Becher-B		44
And all thy change can be but dreaming	173	Not False		24
And the lull'd winds seem dreaming	188	Music-C		8
His sleep, sans dreaming of Siberia's wastes	302	Age		311
My dreaming fear with storms hath wing'd the wind	343	Corsair	1	372
Nor only wake to war, but dreaming kill	347	Corsair	2	15
That dreaming sigh and warm caress	397	Parisina		77
Its hours of rest in dreaming this was pleasure	528	Faliero	4	47
Than a scared beldam's dreaming of the dead	567	Sardan	2	350
And after dreaming a disturbed vision	611	Foscari	3	213
Above her brow, lay dreaming soft and warm	860	Juan	6	523
Save that of dreaming once 'mal-a-propos	863	Juan	6	672

DREAMLESS

The dreamless sleep that lulls the dead	166	Euthanasia		2
The silence of that dreamless sleep	167	Dead		32
A joyous hour, or dreamless slumber more	512	Faliero	2	243
Young Juan slept all dreamless:--but the maid	791	Juan	2	1073

DREAM-PERTURBED

Yet a few days and dream-perturbed nights	515	Faliero	2	495

DREAMS

In dreams deny me not to see thee here	19	Harold	1	939
With brain-born dreams of evil all their own	20	Harold	2	59
The scenes our earliest dreams have dwelt upon	33	Harold	2	833
Nor of the dead who rise upon our dreams	47	Harold	3	739
They came like truth, and disappear'd like dreams	56	Harold	4	56
In dreams your fancied form I view	91	Caroline-B		32
Arcadia displays but a region of dreams	93	First Kiss		19
By dreams of ill to cloud some future day	94	Dorset		84
Ye dreams of my boyhood, how much I regret you	96	Harrow-A		25
When dreams of your presence my slumbers beguile	98	To M.S.G.-B		19
The soul by purer dreams possest	111	Medea		10
In sleep, it smiles in fleeting dreams	113	Quaker		32
Parent of golden dreams, Romance	118	Romance		1
And yet 'tis hard to quit the dreams	118	Romance		9
The sun of memory, glowing through my dreams	122	Recoll		22
Friends lost to me for aye, except in dreams	122	Recoll		34
'Tis done!--I saw it in my dreams	128	Remembrance		1
dreams were of blood. They lift the spear	130	Calmar		38
My hopes, my dreams, my heart was thine	131	L'Amitie		33
Fictions and dreams inspire the bard	132	L'Amitie		81

DREAMS

No dreams, save of Mary, were spread to my view	136	Highlander		22
And Dreams restore it, through the night	144	Jessy		8
And soothe her soul to dreams of love	150	Song		8
And dreams that affection can never take wing	155	Goblet		10
In flattering dreams I deem'd thee mine	172	Romaic-B		21
Is it his bark which my dreary dreams discover	204	Hindoo		3
Send me kind dreams to keep my heart from breaking	205	Hindoo		10
And dreams in their development have breath	213	Dream		5
In dreams that day's broad light can not remove	217	The Harp		20
When thus devoted to poetic dreams	247	Bards		403
The book which, sillier than a sick man's dreams	256	Hints		12
When heart meets heart again in dreams Elysian	325	Abydos	1	164
All--save immortal dreams that could beguile	329	Abydos	2	26
(So fondly youthful dreams deceive	336	Abydos	2	708
Ay, let them slumber, peaceful be their dreams	342	Corsair	1	319
Thus ever fade my fairy dreams of bliss	344	Corsair	1	411
Ambition's dreams expiring, love's regret	352	Corsair	2	342
In muttering dreams yet saw his pirate-guest	353	Corsair	2	410
His early dreams of good outstripp'd the truth	370	Lara	1	323
That sleep, the loveliest, since it dreams the least	375	Lara	1	645
And red her cheek with troubled dreams	397	Parisina		70
Like precipices in our dreams	412	Mazeppa		608
His dreams were of Old England's welcome shore	415	Island	1	19
The goldless age, where gold disturbs no dreams	418	Island	1	216
And all our dreams of better life above	420	Island	2	121
Let it be black among your dreams; and when	503	Faliero	1	274
Ambitious hopes ne'er cross'd my dreams; and should	513	Faliero	2	346
Whose reign is o'er seal'd eyelids and soft dreams	578	Sardan	4	4
I can bear all things, dreams of life or death	579	Sardan	4	73
To think of these past dreams. Let's not reproach	582	Sardan	4	246
With scorpions! May his dreams be of his victim	652	Cain	3	430
Rather than thus--But the enthusiast dreams	664	Heaven		713
The worst of dreams, the fantasies engender'd	664	Heaven		714
All dreams are false. And yet I see him as	707	Werner	4	194
And yet I had horrid dreams! and such brief sleep	718	Werner	5	357
Throbb'd in accursed dreams, which sometimes spread	791	Juan	2	1070
But dreams of what has been, no more to be	795	Juan	2	1328
But no one dreams of ever being short	837	Juan	5	384
Whate'er their dreams be, if of joys or woes	855	Juan	6	155
And then I have the worst dreams that can be	858	Juan	6	381
The dame replied, 'Between your dreams and you	858	Juan	6	383
I fear Juanna's dreams would be but few	858	Juan	6	384
Dismay, the usual consequence of dreams	862	Juan	6	618
Her future dreams should all be kept in hand	862	Juan	6	656
Is of all dreams the first hallucination	872	Juan	7	348
All my boy feelings, all my gentler dreams	909	Juan	10	140
A sleep without dreams, after a rough day	955	Juan	14	25
Along the canvass; their eyes glance like dreams	982	Juan	16	148
All mountaineers with dreams that they are nigh lands	986	Juan	16	414

DREAMT

I dreamt last night our love return'd	152	Remind		25
What I have dreamt:--and canst thou bear to hear it	579	Sardan	4	72
How can you say so! never have I dreamt	713	Werner	5	15
Why didst thou spare me? I dreamt of my father	718	Werner	5	359
(Long ere I dreamt of dating from the Brenta	772	Juan	1	1693
And, never having dreamt of falsehood, she	798	Juan	2	1519
And never having dreamt what 'twas to bear	846	Juan	5	948
More virgin valour never dreamt of flying	882	Juan	8	283
In rhymes, or dreamt (for fancy will play tricks	908	Juan	10	77
Of what I then dreamt, clothed in their own pall	909	Juan	10	141
Where none were dreamt of, unto love's affairs	944	Juan	13	197
A vigil, or dreamt rather more than slept	998	Juan	17	112

DREAR

There is a dungeon, in whose dim drear light	77	Harold	4	1324
For then, however drear and dark	172	Time-B		25
When all around grew drear and dark	209	Augusta-A		1
With something ominous and drear	387	Corinth		277
Until a day more dark and drear	407	Mazeppa		9
For all behind was dark and drear	412	Mazeppa		595
Ploughs its drear progress to the scarce-seen cliff	418	Island	1	174
The season, rather than to winter drear	950	Juan	13	612
You look down o'er the precipice, and drear	956	Juan	14	38

DREARILY

And when they now fall drearily	384	Corinth		35

DREARY

Yet, though a dreary strain, to this I cling	35	Harold	3	32
Dreary and dark appears the sylvan scene	109	Nisus		314
To roam a dreary world in deep despair	120	Newstead-A		47
Here Desolation holds her dreary court	121	Newstead-A		97
They pass the dreary winter's eve away	124	Recoll		172

DREARY

And empty the goblet, and dreary the hearth	164	Newstead-C	12
But he who through life's dreary way	166	Away	29
Let deep and dreary silence be	174	Revanche	7
Falls dreary on my heart	186	Stanzas-A	8
A dreary shroud around us, and invest	191	Fragment-C	13
The dreary dwelling where the State	196	Venice-A	15
Is it his bark which my dreary dreams discover	204	Hindoo	3
Oh, who its dreary length shall date	313	Giaour	270
Are rapture to the dreary void	319	Giaour	958
And day broke dreary on my troubled view	343	Corsair	1	382
Like one in dreary musing mood	390	Corinth	509
With glimpses of a dreary track	400	Parisina	365
And won to heaven her dreary road	401	Parisina	516
Our voices took a dreary tone	403	Chillon	63
And clear them of their dreary mote	406	Chillon	369
Who peals his dreary paean o'er the night	424	Island	2	427
Long day, and dreary night; the retrospect	457	Dante	1	134
A dreary comfort in my desolation	626	Foscari	5	340
Fades to a dreary twilight, yet I see	638	Cain	2	180
I am awake at last--a dreary dream	652	Cain	3	378
A dreary, and an early doom, my brother	654	Cain	3	545
Or dull repentance hath had dreary leisure	892	Juan	8	901
Life's sad post-horses o'er the dreary frontier	910	Juan	10	215
The dreary 'Fuimus' of all things human	946	Juan	13	318
Why drink? Why read?--To make some hour less dreary	956	Juan	14	84
Are there oft dull and dreary as a dun	959	Juan	14	231
And hence high life is oft a dreary void	965	Juan	14	625
Back fell the sable frock and dreary cowl	996	Juan	16	1029

DREGS

The dregs were wormwood; but he fill'd again	36	Harold	3	74
And bid him drain the dregs of pleasure's bowl	100	Damaetas	12
The dregs of pleasure for their vanish'd joys	513	Faliero	2	318
His dregs of life, which you have kindly shorten'd	626	Foscari	5	338

DRENCH'D

Though drench'd with gore, his woes are but begun	272	Minerva	298
More drench'd with gore, more cumber'd with the slain	290	Vision	352
Flinging the billows back from my drench'd hair	597	Foscari	1	107
Hid dewy curls, long drench'd by every storm	788	Juan	2	910

DRENCHES

And drenches handkerchiefs like towels	231	Doctor	4

DRENCHING

In the cold drenching of the stormy night	418	Island	1	192
And has almost recover'd from his drenching	675	Werner	1	257

DRESDEN

Dresden surveys three despots fly once more	301	Age	205
And thence through Berlin, Dresden, and the like	915	Juan	10	481

DRESS

All persons in the dress of gent	231	Doctor	57
Because it costs him dear, and makes him dress	261	Hints	316
Light toil! to cull and dress thy frugal fare	344	Corsair	1	422
More dazzlingly when daring in full dress	425	Island	2	457
The mat for rest; for dress the fresh gnatoo	432	Island	4	167
All kinds of dress, except the ecclesiastical	440	Beppo	21
Were all kinds of buffoonery and dress	442	Beppo	164
Close to the lady as a part of dress	445	Beppo	316
Should soil with parts of speech the parts of dress	447	Beppo	456
In that queer dress, for fear that some beholder	452	Beppo	742
As far as the man's dress and figure could	713	Werner	5	5
A prodigy--her morning dress was dimity	748	Juan	1	94
A dress through which the eyes give such a volley	775	Juan	2	55
Her dress was very different from the Spanish	789	Juan	2	954
Her dress was many-colour'd, finely spun	789	Juan	2	962
The other female's dress was not unlike	789	Juan	2	969
Their loves, and feasts, and house, and dress, and mode	811	Juan	3	647
His figure, and the splendour of his dress	832	Juan	5	67
And some seem'd much in love with their own dress	838	Juan	5	420
As dress yourself--' and pointed out a suit	840	Juan	5	578
That I unsex'd my dress?' But Baba, stroking	841	Juan	5	598
Than other articles of female dress	855	Juan	6	148
Some thought her dress did not so much become her	856	Juan	6	275
Was what her dress bespoke, a damsel fair	857	Juan	6	282
And one by one her articles of dress	860	Juan	6	481
Their dress was Moslem, but you might have guess'd	874	Juan	7	451
There lurk'd a man beneath the spirit's dress	902	Juan	9	374
Like a race-horse; much to each dress he sported	911	Juan	10	229
Don Juan was presented, and his dress	923	Juan	11	305
Daughters admired his dress, and pious mothers	924	Juan	11	383
Then dress, then dinner, then awakes the world	926	Juan	11	521
That manners hardly differ more than dress	953	Juan	13	752
What time he chose for dress, and broke his fast	954	Juan	13	823
But for that hour, call'd half-hour, given to dress	975	Juan	15	487

DRESS

So every one may dress it to his wish	976	Juan	15	540
Because my business is to dress society	979	Juan	15	741
Knock'd to inform him it was time to dress	984	Juan	16	224
And then her dress--what beautiful simplicity	994	Juan	16	863

DRESS'D
(See also ILL-DRESS'D)

Some paid rather more--but all worse dress'd than Waiters	178	Devil's Dr	162
All ready and dress'd for proceeding to spunge on	226	Oh You	7
Dress'd in a fashion now forgotten quite	293	Vision	523
And treated her genteelly, so that, dress'd	443	Beppo	179
Laura, when dress'd, was (as I sang before	447	Beppo	449
Her dearest friends for being dress'd so ill	448	Beppo	520
And well dress'd males still kept before her filing	448	Beppo	549
Although dress'd out to head a pageant, as	523	Faliero	3	283
And dress'd him, for the present, like a Turk	794	Juan	2	1276
Also he dress'd up, for the nonce, fascines	873	Juan	7	417
He dress'd; and like young people he was wont	984	Juan	16	225

DRESSES

From divorces down to dresses	197	Rogers	41
And there are dresses splendid, but fantastical	440	Beppo	17
The dancers and their dresses, too, beside	451	Beppo	692
And asking now and then for cast-off dresses	797	Juan	2	1456
Their classical profiles, and glittering dresses	805	Juan	3	257
Of all the dresses I select Haidee's	810	Juan	3	553
Cure them of tours, hussar and highland dresses	918	Juan	10	682
And you may get the wedding dresses ready	937	Juan	12	472
Their hideous wives, their horrid selves and dresses	994	Juan	16	871

DRESSETH

Look on it! and for him who dresseth it	650	Cain	3	268

DRESSING

By dressing Camoens in a suit of lace	246	Bards	304
Then dressing, nursing, praying, and all's over	799	Juan	2	1600
While he was dressing, Baba, their black friend	840	Juan	5	545
But next to dressing for a rout or ball	981	Juan	16	81

DRESSING-GOWN

But met Alfonso in his dressing-gown	769	Juan	1	1463

DREST

Of Moor and Knight, in mailed splendour drest	9	Harold	1	383
Or else at eve, in radiant glory drest	140	Ossian-B	25
Drest to receive so much good company	766	Juan	1	1248
Drest to a Sybarite's most pamper'd wishes	809	Juan	3	493
Recommendation; and to be well drest	944	Juan	13	223
Drest, voted, shone, and, may be, something more	957	Juan	14	138
But so far like a lady, that 'twas drest	977	Juan	15	591

DREW

Such as Harmodius drew on Athens' tyrant lord	38	Harold	3	180
'Here, where the sword united nations drew	40	Harold	3	313
But still their flame was fierceness, and drew on	42	Harold	3	438
Wrung overwhelming eloquence, first drew	47	Harold	3	728
I drew the bar, and by the light	89	Anacreon-B	25
A gleaming falchion from the sheath he drew	108	Nisus	210
Quick from the sheath his flaming glaive he drew	110	Nisus	361
Or, if my muse a pedant's portrait drew	123	Recoll	89
Drew tears from eyes unused to weep with you	124	Recoll	188
Here your last tears retiring Roscius drew	169	Address-A	34
My frenzy drew from eyes so dear	174	Remember-B	43
From the same fount their inspiration drew	243	Bards	107
At sea--which drew most souls another way	285	Vision	8
As he drew near, he gazed upon the gate	288	Vision	193
He ceased, and drew forth an MS.; and no	297	Vision	809
On--on he hasten'd, and he drew	312	Giaour	200
He drew the token from his vest	317	Giaour	715
He saw their terror, from his baldric drew	349	Corsair	2	165
And rarely wander'd in his speech, or drew	371	Lara	1	359
But gasping heaved the breath that Lara drew	382	Lara	2	490
His gentle sires--he drew his birth	385	Corinth	116
I only lived--I only drew	404	Chillon	213
If this were human breath I drew	412	Mazeppa	600
No joy like what it gave; her hopes ne'er drew	421	Island	2	146
But now at rest, a little remnant drew	426	Island	3	25
He drew it from his mouth, and look'd full wise	428	Island	3	135
But floating still through surf and swell, drew nigh	429	Island	3	179
The vault drew half her shadow from the scene	431	Island	4	136
Forth from her bosom the young savage drew	431	Island	4	137
Drew to their isle, that force or flight might fail	432	Island	4	180
The boat drew nigh, well arm'd, and firm the crew	433	Island	4	281
He beckon'd to the foremost, who drew nigh	434	Island	4	331
Precisely as the war occurr'd they drew him	476	Morgante	679
From thy own lip I drew the charm	481	Manfred	1	238
Searching its cause in its effect; and drew	486	Manfred	2	175
Of Endor; and the Spartan Monarch drew	487	Manfred	2	276

DREW

You drew me from my honourable toils	541 Faliero	5	206
Drew crowds together. It was one of those	717 Werner	5	257
An indescribable sensation drew me	717 Werner	5	273
Farewell, too, dearest Julia!--(Here he drew	776 Juan	2	143
And higher grew the mountains as they drew	786 Juan	2	794
As they drew nigh the land, which now was seen	787 Juan	2	817
And watch'd with eagerness each throb that drew	788 Juan	2	911
And near the cave her quick light footsteps drew	792 Juan	2	1130
She drew out her provision from the basket	792 Juan	2	1152
And without word, a sign her finger drew on	792 Juan	2	1164
Their lips drew near, and clung into a kiss	797 Juan	2	1480
Can sneer at him who drew 'Achitophel'	815 Juan	3	896
She drew up to her height, as if to show	822 Juan	4	342
Although her paroxysm drew towards its close	825 Juan	4	534
Drew all eyes on him, giving them to guess	832 Juan	5	69
Drew himself up to his full height again	844 Juan	5	814
This compliment, which drew all eyes upon	851 Juan	5	1241
But here the Mother of the Maids drew near	858 Juan	6	361
For, on the sixteenth, at full gallop, drew	872 Juan	7	337
They drew, constructed ladders, repair'd flaws	873 Juan	7	374
Drew quiet consolation through its hint	911 Juan	10	271
Drew forth a pocket pistol from his vesture	920 Juan	11	99
The drops fell from his death-wound, and he drew ill	920 Juan	11	126
One monstrous diamond drew much observation	923 Juan	11	308
To Homer's Iliad, since it drew to Troy	964 Juan	14	572
There was awe in the homage which she drew	974 Juan	15	373
Nigh and more nigh the awful echoes drew	995 Juan	16	965

DRIED

Has dried up realms to deserts:--not so thou	82 Harold	4	1635
Must break my chain before it dried my tears	348 Corsair	2	88
And dried those tears for life and fame that flow'd	351 Corsair	2	258
Nor long they flow'd--he dried them to depart	365 Corsair	3	654
They are not dried--those tears unshed	402 Parisina		563
Till its dried wing relapsed from its brief height	435 Island	4	371
Have dried the fountain of a gentle race	654 Cain	3	557
When dried to summer dust; till taught by pain	784 Juan	2	667

DRIED-UP

The furrows of long thought, and dried-up tears	35 Harold	3	24

DRIFT

If people would but see its real drift	863 Juan	6	698

DRIFTING

Drifting along the tide, without an oar	435 Island	4	395

DRILL

In chief, in proper person deign'd to drill	873 Juan	7	410
The day before the assault, while upon drill	874 Juan	7	441
They break their ranks and gladly leave the drill	957 Juan	14	130

DRILL'D

The drill'd dull lesson, forced down word by word	66 Harold	4	674
And drill'd away in the most classic Russian	875 Juan	7	506
Of his drill'd nymphs, but like a gentleman	960 Juan	14	304

DRILLING

Surveying, drilling, ordering, jesting, pondering	874 Juan	7	434
Before a company of Calmucks, drilling	874 Juan	7	458

DRINK

But mine now drink this sight of loveliness	485 Manfred	2	103
They eat, and drink, and live, and breed together	521 Faliero	3	156
Eat, drink, and love; the rest's not worth a fillip	555 Sardan	1	299
Down on your knees, and drink a measure to	571 Sardan	3	25
Eat, drink, toil, tremble, laugh, weep, sleep, and die	645 Cain	2	621
To drink thy brother's blood from thy rash hand	653 Cain	3	473
And eat, and drink, and wive	660 Heaven		402
He knows not what he says, yet shall not drink	668 Heaven		1031
And so let's have some wine, and drink unto	674 Werner	1	199
Nor pause at the brook's side to drink	730 Deformed	1	556
For grog, and sometimes drink rum from the cask	778 Juan	2	264
'Eat, drink, and love, what can the rest avail us	800 Juan	2	1655
So Arab deserts drink in summer's rain	904 Juan	9	470
Why drink? Why read?--To make some hour less dreary	956 Juan	14	84

DRINKER

(See also HEMLOCK-DRINKER)

And Sir John Pottledeep, the mighty drinker	951 Juan	13	672

DRINKING

Though drinking deeply, thirsting still the more	125 Recoll		254
With fiddling, feasting, dancing, drinking, masquing	440 Beppo		7
From drinking therein. And shall I live on	723 Deformed	1	52
He drinks--but what's drinking	742 Deformed	3	31

DRINKING

Drinking salt-water like a mountain-stream	784 Juan	2	630
They ne'er till now had known the joys of drinking	784 Juan	2	680

DRINKS

The victim's prayer, for if he drinks he dies	351 Corsair	2	323
Drinks life, and light, and glory from her aspect	514 Faliero	2	398
He drinks--but what's drinking	742 Deformed	3	31
She sits upon his knee, and drinks his sighs	798 Juan	2	1549
That drinks and still is dry. At last they perish'd	892 Juan	8	873
In love drinks all life's fountains (save tears) dry	905 Juan	9	536

DRIP

Drops the light drip of the suspended oar	48 Harold	3	813
Wet with thine own best blood shall drip	318 Giaour		781

DRIPPING

My dripping limbs I faintly stretch	160 Swimming		11
Yet dripping with the blood he spilt	316 Giaour		656
Or spread beneath the sun the dripping net	338 Corsair	1	54
'With glossy skin, and dripping mane	412 Mazeppa		601
Your heads would now be dripping the last drops	566 Sardan	2	285
Dripping with dusky gore, and trampling on	578 Sardan	4	32
Serpent, which rears his dripping mane and vasty	642 Cain	2	396
Shaking their dripping ears upon the shore	678 Werner	1	438
Howling and dripping on the bank, whilst I	701 Werner	3	381
Droop'd dripping on the oar (their jurymast	788 Juan	2	877
Her hair was dripping, and the very balls	820 Juan	4	261

DRIVE

In vain, to drive thee from my breast	112 Quaker		7
Or drive me to dreadful despair	116 Strephon		24
Drive o'er the sward the ball with active force	124 Recoll		131
To think would drive my soul to madness	134 Lady-D		38
But drag or drive us on to die	171 Time-B		4
'And,' quoth he, 'I'll take a drive	176 Devil's Dr		7
To drive this pestilence from out the land	251 Bards		688
And drive the camel than purvey the bear	302 Age		313
And fate, and fury, drive along	316 Giaour		635
Drive from our presence with his savage jeers	558 Sardan	1	513
The malice of my foes will drive me down them	624 Foscari	5	244
And drive my father forth from Paradise	627 Cain	1	20
Drive him forth o'er the wilderness, like us	652 Cain	3	423
And drive your sullen race	660 Heaven		386
Yet of a beauty that would drive you crazy	857 Juan	6	328
Hut, whence wise travellers drive with circumspection	910 Juan	10	214
But I won't weep!--and so drive on, postilions	917 Juan	10	610
That no defeat can drive me from the Nine	956 Juan	14	92

DRIVEL

He'll drivel another Phrosine	232 Murray-B		18
Dilutes with drivel every drizzly brain	270 Minerva		140

DRIVELLING

'Though I doubt if this drivelling encomiast of War	177 Devil's Dr		127
So dull in youth, so drivelling in his age	251 Bards		733

DRIVELS

And drivels seas to set it well afloat	814 Juan	3	880

DRIVEN

And the world's waste have driven him far from those	51 Harold	3	963
Shall yet redeem thee, and, all backward driven	62 Harold	4	422
And only not to desperation driven	75 Harold	4	1213
'Twas now the hour when Night had driven	88 Anacreon-B		1
A second shaft with equal force is driven	110 Nisus		356
He ne'er would have women from paradise driven	116 To Eliza		6
Are driven o'er the shoals of guilt, or ocean of excess	185 Music-B		6
Driven o'er the lowering atmosphere that nurst	193 Monody		93
Be driven to excesses which once could appal	238 Pangs		6
And tenderest tints, along their summits driven	268 Minerva		15
So many conquerors' cars were daily driven	285 Vision		35
But driven from thence awhile, yet not for aye	302 Age		286
His soul was changed, before his deeds had driven	342 Corsair	1	251
'He's gone!'--against her heart that hand is driven	345 Corsair	1	499
The hopeless past, the hasting future driven	352 Corsair	2	346
And tenderest tints, along their summits driven	355 Corsair	3	15
If he had driven her from that resting-place	363 Corsair	3	544
From him by sterner chiefs to exile driven	378 Lara	2	198
The word hath pass'd his lips, and onward driven	380 Lara	2	360
Or into countless meteors driven	386 Corinth		171
From whence thy traitor soul is driven	393 Corinth		856
The thousand shapeless things all driven	395 Corinth		1025
And o'er the dead our coursers driven	399 Parisina		303
Through Azo's palace-lattice driven	401 Parisina		494
Could these have charms for rudest seaboys, driven	417 Island	1	111

DRIVEN

Around him days and worlds are heedless driven	424 Island	2	372
Had ceased; and sulphury vapours upward driven	426 Island	3	3
Waves, and the echo of our groans is driven	460 Dante	3	12
Whether into the marble chaos driven	464 Dante	4	60
Had not his valour driven them back again	467 Morgante		108
Whom your patrician crimes have driven to crime	538 Faliero	5	56
Or like our fathers, driven by Attila	610 Foscari	3	160
That which hath driven us all from Paradise	634 Cain	1	432
Before thy bright wings worlds be driven	655 Heaven		42
Yet much is ours, whence we cannot be driven	669 Heaven		1048
Now o'er it clouds and thunder must be driven	801 Juan	2	1707
Upon, in sheets white as what bards call 'driven	855 Juan	6	197
Is musical--a dying accent driven	949 Juan	13	500
Would not be driven away	985 Juan	16	328
Some exiles from the town, who had been driven	991 Juan	16	690
By last night's ghost been driven from their defences	993 Juan	16	792

DRIVER

Even where their driver goads them, though to slaughter	453 Venice-B		66

DRIVES

The hull drives on, though mast and sail be torn	40 Harold	3	282
Whose bark drives on and on, and anchor'd ne'er shall be	46 Harold	3	670
He drives them exiles from their blest abode	120 Newstead-A		46
Dramatic 'spirit drives a conquering car	170 Address-B		19
That drives the sailor shipless to his home	453 Venice-B		11
Some gentleman, who fights, or writes, or drives	934 Juan	12	286

DRIVEST

Behold, thou drivest him from the face of earth	653 Cain	3	478

DRIVING

By driving dove-eyed peace from thine	90 To M.S.G.-A		26
By driving my favourite pace	176 Devil's Dr		22
He still for the Bench would be driving	238 Bray		15
What with driving and visiting, dancing and dining	280 Blues	2	8
At the great end of travel--which is driving	916 Juan	10	576

DRIZZLY

Dilutes with drivel every drizzly brain	270 Minerva		140

DROMEDARY

Cloven foot of thine, or the swift dromedary	723 Deformed	1	104
The helmless dromedary!--and I'll bear	724 Deformed	1	117

DRONE

Hark! Zounds, they'll be on us; I know by the drone	280 Blues	1	149
Since that rash hour, when, madden'd with the drone	504 Faliero	1	338

DRONES

Compassion for him--his tame virtues; drones	290 Vision		373

DROOP

Ye Cupids, droop each little head	87 Catullus		1
Which droop with nightly showers, I wring	89 Anacreon-B		34
Too late you may droop o'er the fond recollection	137 Delawarr		31
Ah, droop not, my Oak! lift thy head for a while	149 Newstead-B		17
And droop within their silent cell	175 Impromptu-A		8
Never did I droop before	187 French-A		34
Where all beneath her influence droop or die	209 Sketch		78
Ne'er droop the wing o'er those that die	314 Giaour		417
When baffled feelings withering droop	387 Corinth		321
Some whom no power could ever force to droop	463 Dante	3	180
And droop their heads; believe me, they are such	522 Faliero	3	247
Equal to every fortune. Droop not, 'tis	537 Faliero	4	628
Have made them--Rage--not droop--it should have been	590 Sardan	5	176
'But droop not: Fortune at your time of life	833 Juan	5	129
There captives led in triumph droop the eye	842 Juan	5	685
To this vain refuge, made the good heart droop	889 Juan	8	724

DROOP'D

Droop'd as a wild-born falcon with clipt wing	37 Harold	3	129
And his droop'd head sinks gradually low	76 Harold	4	1255
His hope now droop'd and now revived	103 Alva		151
Though many a beauty droop'd in prison'd bower	342 Corsair	1	291
Which downcast droop'd in tearless agony	345 Corsair	1	469
His limbs stretch'd fluttering, and his head droop'd o'er	382 Lara	2	492
The banners droop'd along their staves	387 Corinth		257
When my last brother droop'd and died	403 Chillon		46
The woods droop'd darkly, as inclined to rest	424 Island	2	412
His cutlass droop'd, unconscious of a sheath	425 Island	2	491
A limb was broken, and he droop'd along	434 Island	4	327
Droop'd dripping on the oar (their jurymast	788 Juan	2	877
Droop'd as the willow when no winds can breathe	793 Juan	2	1179
And her head droop'd as when the lily lies	824 Juan	4	467

DROOPING

When thou behold'st them, drooping nigh	44 Harold	3	523
Thus, sweetly drooping, bends his lovely head	110 Nisus		383
Drooping, alas! we fall to rise no more	114 Prologue		20
Unyielding pangs assail the drooping mind	122 Recoll		6
Drooping, she bends o'er pensive Fancy's urn	126 Recoll		343
Thou drooping Elm! beneath whose boughs I lay	138 Harrow-B		9
Uphold thy drooping head	167 Dead		61
And an unquiet drooping of the eye	215 Dream		134
Shall Sorrow lean her drooping head	218 Bloom		7
That Adrian rear'd when drooping Science mourn'd	269 Minerva		102
Where lay his drooping head upon her knee	384 Lara	2	613
His head was drooping on his breast	390 Corinth		511
The drooping courser, faint and low	413 Mazeppa		627
Ruffles the autumn leaves, that drooping cling	578 Sardan	4	14
Drooping and dewy on the beach he lay	796 Juan	2	1406
And seated her all drooping by his side	847 Juan	5	1004
And fair brows gently drooping, as the fruit	860 Juan	6	518
And one hand o'er the ottoman lay drooping	865 Juan	6	867
And drooping like an eagle's with clipt pinion	913 Juan	10	350

DROOPINGLY

And our heads on our bosoms all droopingly lay	223 Valley		3
That hand, so raised, how droopingly it hung	380 Lara	2	385

DROOPS

Since baffled Triumph droops on Lusitania's coast	8 Harold	1	305
With deadly languor droops my head	87 Ad Lesbiam		18
Where panting Nature droops the head	158 Florence		6
And my head droops over thee like the willow	204 Hindoo		8
Droops o'er the bales no bark may bear away	272 Minerva		268
The very cypress droops to death	313 Giaour		285
Nor droops, though spring refuse her shower	336 Abydos	2	687
And shook--Why sudden droops that plumed crest	380 Lara	2	380
Leaf,' and Imagination droops her pinion	816 Juan	4	22

DROP

(See also LIFE-DROP, TEAR-DROP)

But Pride congeal'd the drop within his ee	4 Harold	1	49
No drop of that clear stream its way shall miss	77 Harold	4	1357
When, for a moment, like a drop of rain	82 Harold	4	1609
Methought one drop the stone bedew'd	113 Cornelian-A		15
My praise was worth this drop of ink	163 Malta		36
The leaves must drop away	167 Dead		40
And be each drop in future years	168 Weeping		7
And every drop of grief shall be	174 Revanche		15
But every drop its lids deny	186 Stanzas-A		7
Were't the last drop in the well	230 My Boat		13
To their favours is such--but the subject to drop	277 Blues	1	16
And gather in that drop of time	312 Giaour		263
Unseen to drop by dull decay	319 Giaour		968
But drop for drop, for Seyd's unglutted eye	351 Corsair	2	282
'Gulnare! if for each drop of blood a gem	357 Corsair	3	153
One drop--the last--to cool it for the grave	380 Lara	2	405
Wring the black drop from thy heart	390 Corinth		579
A drop to moisten life's all-gasping springs	418 Island	1	194
Drain every drop!--to-morrow we may die	419 Island	2	46
To pick a pebble up--then let it drop	428 Island	3	111
Nor spilt one drop of water in his race	474 Morgante		516
As faithless leaves drop from the o'erblown flower	525 Faliero	3	430
A spark creates the flame--'tis the last drop	541 Faliero	5	246
Till now, no drop from an Assyrian vein	557 Sardan	1	455
To drop down the Euphrates; but ere they	581 Sardan	4	209
He breathes not; and his hands drop down from mine	651 Cain	3	364
Day's broad orb drop behind its head at even	659 Heaven		293
Shall they drop off. Behold their last tomorrow	660 Heaven		349
So near the awful close! For these must drop	662 Heaven		563
Whose every drop bows them down nearer earth	672 Werner	1	27
Like them? Oh that each drop which falls to earth	722 Deformed	1	38
Howling for a drop of water	729 Deformed	1	463
A drop of water! Blood's the only liquid	737 Deformed	2	166
A drop of dew, when every drop had seem'd	785 Juan	2	686
But words are things, and a small drop of ink	813 Juan	3	793
The sharp rocks look'd below each drop they caught	820 Juan	4	263
'Tis the vile daily drop on drop which wears	855 Juan	6	159
The soldiers, who beheld him drop his point	893 Juan	8	929
A quintessential laudanum or 'black drop	905 Juan	9	533
May drop in without cards, and take their station	989 Juan	16	596

DROPP'D

And their masts fell down piecemeal; as they dropp'd	190 Darkness		76
He dropp'd the hand he held, and with slow steps	215 Dream		99
The curtain dropp'd, the gay burletta o'er	250 Bards		658
Till the dropp'd curtain gives a glad release	261 Hints		314
What gem hath dropp'd and sparkles o'er his chain	355 Corsair	2	539
Dropp'd it should seem in more than nature's fear	369 Lara	1	214
The anchor dropp'd; it lay along the deep	422 Island	2	234
Alfonso'd sword had dropp'd ere he could draw it	769 Juan	1	1473

DROPP'D
While his salt tears dropp'd into the salt sea   776 Juan   2   130
Dropp'd in their laps, scarce pluck'd, their
  mellow store   805 Juan   3   248
A moment, and then dropp'd; 'but to resume   833 Juan   5   141
Who came as if just dropp'd down from the moon   885 Juan   8   444
The banqueteers had dropp'd off one by one   981 Juan   16   59
The guests dropp'd in--the last but one, Her
  Grace   998 Juan   17   103

DROPPING
Though nurtured 'mid weeds dropping pestilent dew   99 L Adieu   2
Yet, dropping, harden there   186 Stanzas-A   12
Till hunger clung them, or the dropping dead   189 Darkness   50
A violet dropping dew   218 I Saw   4
Each feeling pure--as falls the dropping dew   365 Corsair   3   664
Without a spirit? Are the dropping caves   424 Island   2   387
The dull and dropping rain saps in their bones   672 Werner   1   32
The voiceless sands and dropping caves, that lay   798 Juan   2 1501
With his broad, bright, and dropping orb were
  gone   819 Juan   4   172
Splendid but silent, save in one, where, dropping   838 Juan   5   435

DROPS
(See also BLOOD-DROPS, DEW-DROPS, HEART-DROPS,
LIFE-DROPS, SWEAT-DROPS, TEAR-DROPS, WATER-DROPS,)
Drops the light drip of the suspended oar   48 Harold   3   813
And through his side the last drops, ebbing slow   76 Harold   4 1256
The drops of death each other chase   104 Alva   235
Such precious drops are doubly dear   152 Weep-A   15
Soft as the last drops round heaven's airy bow   175 Sonnet-B   8
Tears fall on his chain, though it drops from his
  hands   202 Avatar   15
The drops, that through his glittering vest   326 Abydos   1   273
With drops of sadness oft to be renew'd   345 Corsair   1   498
And when resign'd, it drops a lifeless weight   354 Corsair   2   513
She drops her veil, and stands in silence by   363 Corsair   3   517
Still a few drops within it lay   395 Corinth   1006
Such drops could fall from human eyes   400 Parisina   341
No, Calendaro; these same drops of blood   516 Faliero   2   524
From a few drops from veins of hoary vampires   527 Faliero   3   603
Are a few drops of human blood? 'tis false   535 Faliero   4   511
Your heads would now be dripping the last drops   566 Sardan   2   285
The last drops from his helm, he stood in act   577 Sardan   3   356
Alas! thou art pale, and on thy brow the drops   579 Sardan   4   38
And the cold drops strain through my brow, as if   598 Foscari   1   161
Or in some clammy drops, soon wiped away   601 Foscari   1   359
To tears save drops of dotage, with long white   603 Foscari   2   110
When he was born: those drops were ominous   604 Foscari   2   180
I had borrowed more by a few drops of ages   647 Cain   3   66
Whose drops shall be less thick than would their
  graves   668 Heaven   976
Yet quivers every leaf, and drops each blossom   668 Heaven   994
When a few drops of gold might save me still   680 Werner   1   588
Not now. A few drops will suffice for this   724 Deformed   1   156
He squeezed from out a rag some drops of rain   785 Juan   2   711
But poor Dudu, with large drops in her own   862 Juan   6   650
The drops fell from his death-wound, and he drew
  ill   920 Juan   11   126
The cravat stain'd with bloody drops fell down   920 Juan   11   129
And then she drops a brief and modern curtsy   926 Juan   11   495
Which leaves few drops of that immortal rain   945 Juan   13   292

DROPSIES
Have proved but dropsies, taken for divinities   814 Juan   3   856

DROSS
Who from true worship's gold can separate thy
  dross   26 Harold   2   396
And, though the thickening dross will scarce
  refine   248 Bards   496
Purged from the dross of earth and earthly pass
  passion   594 Sardan   5   473
Have found, in searching for another's dross   689 Werner   2   423
Who calculated life as so much dross   877 Juan   7   611
To waste so much gold for a little dross   878 Juan   8   21
Like gold as in comparison to dross   921 Juan   11   203
The gamester's counter, or the statesman's dross   930 Juan   12   30

DROUGHT
Then, when their drought was quench'd, look'd
  sadly round   427 Island   3   79
Madden'd with centuries of drought, are loud   454 Venice-B   85

DROUTH
Which felt exhaustion's deep and bitter drouth   417 Island   1   148
Like flowers well water'd after a long drouth   904 Juan   9   484

DROUTHY
And Campbell's Hippocrene is somewhat drouthy   772 Juan   1 1638

DROVE
And drove at last the poilers to their shore   9 Harold   1   393
It chanced that adverse winds once drove his bark   29 Harold   2   595

DROVE
And drove off at the close of day   177 Devil's Dr   108
Which drove your race from Eden--war with all
  things   641 Cain   2   354
Count Damas drove them back into the water   871 Juan   7   247
And drove them with their brutal yells to seek   890 Juan   8   746
Pursued his path, and drove past some hotels   922 Juan   11   231
I hate it, as I hate a drove of cattle   962 Juan   14   461

DROWN
I plunged to drown in noise my fond regret   124 Recoll   191
For any bard to poison, hang, or drown   268 Hints   828
Into his lake, for there he did not drown   298 Vision   829
Shall be a voice of weeping, which shall drown   528 Faliero   3   648
Or no; your noblemen are hard to drown   675 Werner   1   220
Each broke to drown her, yet she could not die   820 Juan   4   248

DROWN'D
(See also HALF-DROWN'D)
For he was drown'd, and I've the ague   160 Swimming   20
That drown'd a single thought of thee   168 Hints   24
Get drown'd with a great many   176 Devil's Dr   63
Where the Divers of Bathos lie drown'd in a heap   227 Moore-A   7
Steep'd, but not drown'd, in deep voluptuousness   550 Sardan   1   13
Jarr'd but not drown'd by the loud brattling; her   577 Sardan   3   394
And build thy city o'er the drown'd earth's grave   660 Heaven   408
Is drown'd below the ford, with five post-horses   675 Werner   1   215
Run hazard of being drown'd (although I own   676 Werner   1   299
But if I'm drown'd? Why, you will be well paid
  for 't   681 Werner   1   668
Don Juan, almost famish'd, and half drown'd   790 Juan   2 1028
Because if drown'd, they can't--if spared, they
  won't   832 Juan   5   48
Baked, fried, or burnt, turn'd inside-out, or
  drown'd   901 Juan   9   293

DROWNING
To which frail twig they cling like drowning men   492 Manfred   3   103
Already grasps each drowning hill   670 Heaven   1174
And have risk'd more than drowning for as much   682 Werner   1   669
Ere I go hang for snatching him from drowning   691 Werner   2   535
The death-cry drowning in the battle's roar   878 Juan   7   696

DROWNINGS
To whom your midnight carryings off and drownings   606 Foscari   2   305
Thus drownings are much talk'd of by the divers   778 Juan   2   247

DROWNS
Devour'd by that which drowns his infant world   662 Heaven   575

DROWSY
And vex'd with mirth the drowsy ear of Night   3 Harold   1   13
And drowsy Silence holds her sable reign   105 Nisus   28
With the drowsy to snore--or the hungry to sup   178 Devil's Dr   172
Through drowsy guards that must that sign obey   353 Corsair   2   414
Beset with drowsy guards and drunken courtiers   563 Sardan   2   131
A drowsy frowzy poem, call'd the 'Excursion   814 Juan   3   847
December's drowsy day to his dull race   960 Juan   14   284

DRUDGE
Condemn'd to drudge, the meanest of the mean   255 Bards   977

DRUDGING
That books were only meant for drudging fools   93 Dorset   23

DRUG
Aught that recalls the daily drug which turn'd   66 Harold   4   676
Of practice against life by steel or drug   605 Foscari   2   233

DRUGG'D
With pleasure drugg'd, he almost long'd for woe   4 Harold   1   53
Nor drugg'd their audience with the tragic stuff   251 Bards   736
By Giaffir's orders drugg'd and given   331 Abydos   2   237

DRUGGISTS
For Inez call'd some druggists and physicians   750 Juan   1   209

DRUGS
Are drugs--mere drugs, Sir--now-a-days   231 Doctor   22
Bring cedar, too, and precious drugs, and spices   591 Sardan   5   278
My dabbling in vile drugs. And art thou sure   619 Foscari   4   285

DRUID
There lives one druid, who prepares in time   267 Hints   737
Crown'd by high woodlands, where the Druid oak   948 Juan   13   442

DRUIDS
With you, ye Druids! rich in native lead   251 Bards   741

DRUID'S
And 'Memory' o'er her Druid's tomb   169 Blank Leaf   7

DRUIDS'
The Druids' groves are gone--so much the better   921 Juan   11   193

DRUM

The hoarse dull drum would sleep, and Man be happy yet	11	Harold	1	503
And near, the beat of the alarming drum	39	Harold	3	222
The braying trumpet and the hoarser drum	120	Newstead-A		55
The brazen trump, the spirit-stirring drum	272	Minerva		287
His name shall beat the alarm, like Ziska's drum	300	Age		130
But, mark me, when the twilight drum	328	Abydos	1	462
Hark to the trump, and the drum	391	Corinth		683
And the harsh sound of the barbarian drum	453	Venice-B		20
Of rolling drum, shrill trump, and hollow bell	530	Faliero	4	166
Of yours be stretch'd as parchment on a drum	682	Werner	1	694
A pipe, too, and a drum, and shortly after	805	Juan	3	223
And now nought left him but the muffled drum	836	Juan	5	288
That Juan's chariot, rolling like a drum	921	Juan	11	157

DRUMMING

Fifing and drumming	229	Moore-B		14

DRUMS
(See also KETTLE-DRUMS, WAR-DRUM'S)

And when the hollow drums of war	194	Ballad-A		21
Beat Germany's drums	732	Deformed	1	730
Bombs, drums, guns, bastions, batteries, bayonets, bullets	877	Juan	7	623

DRUNK

For not yet had he drunk of Lethe's stream	17	Harold	1	813
Dazzled and drunk with beauty, till the heart	62	Harold	4	443
But France got drunk with blood to vomit crime	69	Harold	4	865
Thou saw'st 'twas duly drunk by me	104	Alva		198
The dart has drunk his vital tide	105	Alva		292
But when drunk to escape from thy malice	162	Romaic-A		19
That 'Felo de se' who, half drunk with his malmsey	227	Moore-A		9
Twin Doric minstrels, drunk with Doric ale	266	Hints		732
My soul was drunk with love, which did pervade	438	Tasso		150
The Greeks of yore made drunk their slaves to form	523	Faliero	3	284
Some wretch has made thee drunk with disaffection	531	Faliero	4	243
Friends. You appear to have drunk enough already	674	Werner	1	201
Having got drunk exceedingly to-day	745	Fragment-D		5
The second drunk, the third so quaint and mouthy	772	Juan	1	1636
Thought it would be becoming to die drunk	778	Juan	2	280
Left him so drunk, he jump'd into the wave	781	Juan	2	451
Man, being reasonable, must get drunk	796	Juan	2	1425
But to return,--Get very drunk; and when	797	Juan	2	1431
The servants all were getting drunk or idling	806	Juan	3	307
A genius who has drunk himself to death	809	Juan	3	522
Unless he's drunk, and then no doubt he's freed	835	Juan	5	245
And death is drunk with gore: there's not a street	888	Juan	8	650
Which makes one drunk at once, without the base	905	Juan	9	534
And having voted, dined, drunk, gamed, and whored	927	Juan	11	591

DRUNKARDS

And the roar of his drunkards proclaim him at last	203	Avatar		79
I saw the trees like drunkards reel	412	Mazeppa		545
Thou den of drunkards with the blood of princes	549	Faliero	5	794
The railing drunkards! why, what would they have	553	Sardan	1	151

DRUNKEN

Where drunken slumbers wrap each lazy limb	105	Nisus		26
No drunken Coleridge with a new Lay Sermon	231	Sotheby		4
The mangled victim of a drunken brawl	251	Bards		685
In the first dawning of the drunken hour	416	Island	1	83
A drunken man's dead eye in maudlin sorrow	445	Beppo		340
Enough!--yes, for a drunken galley-slave	512	Faliero	2	225
Beset with drowsy guards and drunken courtiers	563	Sardan	2	131
Upon your lives, I say. What, deaf or drunken	564	Sardan	2	176
Will he so spare? till the first drunken minute	567	Sardan	2	336

DRUNKENNESS

When drunkenness and dice invite	95	Granta		55
My almost drunkenness of heart	332	Abydos	2	344
A sudden fit of drunkenness or spleen	764	Juan	1	1134

DRURY

On Drury first your Siddons' thrilling art	169	Address-A		31
On Drury, Garrick's latest laurels grew	169	Address-A		33
Such Drury claim'd and claims--nor you refuse	170	Address-A		38
To furnish melo-drames for Drury Lane	171	Address-B		22
'Old Drury never, never soar'd so high	171	Address-B		43
To see the new Drury Lane	179	Devil's Dr		226
Nor burn damn'd Drury if it rise again	261	Hints		372

DRURY'S

Scenes not unworthy Drury's days of old	170	Address-A		71

DRY
(See also A-DRY)

Mine own would not be dry	6	Harold	1	157
Fresh feres will dry the bright blue eyes	6	Harold	1	176

DRY

Sprinkle its coolness, and from the dry dust	65	Harold	4	609
These lips are mute, these eyes are dry	151	Farewell-B		9
And my feelings (its fountain) are dry	205	Blessington		4
His hand was wither'd, and his veins were dry	219	Saul-B		8
Are gone--their oven closed, their ocean dry	306	Age		607
Love half regrets to kiss it dry	326	Abydos	1	227
Fell quench'd in tears, too late to shed or dry	362	Corsair	3	467
This mantle kept it dry; then from a nook	432	Island	4	141
So that he could not keep his visage dry	476	Morgante		686
To dry into the desert's dust by myriads	555	Sardan	1	275
Of this our palace, into the dry dust	566	Sardan	2	287
Henceforth to dry up tears, and not to shed them	654	Cain	3	548
Who shall dry up my tears? Thy spirit-lord	669	Heaven		1046
I don't much like this fellow--close and dry	676	Werner	1	304
The nipple next day sore and udder dry	722	Deformed	1	23
The beach which lay before him, high and dry	787	Juan	2	844
Much less experience of dry land than ocean	804	Juan	3	202
But now their eyes and also lips were dry	806	Juan	3	301
'Talking's dry work, I have no time to spare	806	Juan	3	340
That drinks and still is dry. At last they perish'd	892	Juan	8	873
And deviate into matters rather dry	901	Juan	9	324
Are, or would be, thou sea of life's dry land	903	Juan	9	448
In love drinks all life's fountains (save tears) dry	905	Juan	9	536
Of peeresses whose follies had run dry	933	Juan	12	232
I'll leave a single reader's eyelid dry	940	Juan	12	685
When, ere the ink be dry, the sound grows cold	947	Juan	13	405
Which the poor thing at times essay'd to dry	989	Juan	16	563

DRYAD

The palm, the loftiest dryad of the woods	422	Island	2	254

DRYDEN

From Dryden, Milbourne tears the palm away	143	Soliloquy		79
And careless Dryden--'Ay, but Pye has not	243	Bards		100
Like him great Dryden pour'd the tide of song	243	Bards		113
While Milton, Dryden, Pope, alike forgot	244	Bards		187
You doubt--see Dryden, Pope, St. Patrick's dean	258	Hints		116
Thou shalt believe in Milton, Dryden, Pope	772	Juan	1	1633
Of Pope and Dryden, are we come to this	814	Juan	3	890

DRYDEN'S

When Dryden's fool, 'unknowing what he sought	171	Hales-Owen		1
To Dryden's or to Pope's maturer muse	257	Hints		82
Though mad Almanzor rhymed in Dryden's days	258	Hints		119
And Dryden's lay made haunted ground to me	815	Juan	3	935

DRYING

The drying up a single tear has more	878	Juan	8	23

DRYNESS

To irrigate the dryness of decline	941	Juan	13	38

DUAN

Till what is call'd in Ossian the fifth Duan	831	Juan	4	936

DUB

Should dub me scribbler and denounce my muse	241	Bards		4
To dub the last of honours in degrees	816	Juan	3	976

DUBB'D

Dubb'd for thy sins a stark Miscellanist	224	J.C.H.		44

DUBIOUS

A peasant's plaint prolongs his dubious date	10	Harold	1	399
And sophists, madly vain of dubious lore	20	Harold	2	67
Dubious to trust where treachery might lurk	29	Harold	2	600
To try the dubious road	158	Storm		26
The transient mention of a dubious name	254	Bards		956
Of Incas darken to a dubious cloud	302	Age		317
A dubious scent would lure the bipeds back	305	Age		561
His eye seem'd dubious if it saw aright	353	Corsair	2	430
His death yet dubious, deeds too widely known	366	Corsair	3	694
The present dubious, or the past a dream	367	Lara	1	54
They knew, or chose to know: with dubious look	372	Lara	1	445
In words of dubious import, but fulfill'd	487	Manfred	2	285
I should not need the dubious aid of strangers	508	Faliero	1	589
Of the patricians dubious of their slaves	524	Faliero	3	356
And now more dubious of the prince they have made one	524	Faliero	3	357
'Tis dubious. Till it meets! and when it meets	602	Foscari	2	65
Weary with watching in the dark, and dubious	718	Werner	5	307
And dubious notice of your eyes and ears	730	Deformed	1	583
A thousand perils in this dubious shape	876	Juan	7	572
Lo! dusky masses steal in dubious sight	878	Juan	7	683
Which Rousseau points out to the dubious fair	885	Juan	8	422
That all is dubious which man may attain	898	Juan	9	131
Ends in a rusty casque and dubious bone	916	Juan	10	582
To me seems but a dubious kind of reed	932	Juan	12	141
Within; and what seest thou? A dubious spark	939	Juan	12	568
There was Dick Dubious, the metaphysician	952	Juan	13	689

DUBIOUSLY
Goes on the conflict? Dubiously and fiercely   574 Sardan   3   199

DUBLIN
Where are the Dublin shouts--and London hisses   928 Juan   11   622

DUBOST
Or low Dubost--as once the world has seen   256 Hints   7

DUCAL
Alfonso! how thy ducal pageants shrink   60 Harold   4   331
View ducal errors with indulgent eyes   93 Dorset   15
The ducal chiefs within thee, shalt fall down   439 Tasso   223
Placed at the ducal table, cover'd o'er   500 Faliero   1   7
Of having graven on the ducal throne   501 Faliero   1   90
And wore the ducal cap I trample on   502 Faliero   1   203
How! are we comrades?--the state's ducal robes   505 Faliero   1   392
Save Faliero, fill'd the ducal throne   505 Faliero   1   410
To stain the ducal throne with those foul words   506 Faliero   1   418
How to demean himself in ducal chambers   514 Faliero   2   425
Presiding in the hall of ducal state   522 Faliero   3   254
When you must doff the ducal bonnet from   540 Faliero   5   154
As Doge, clad in the ducal robes and cap   545 Faliero   5   516
And there, the ducal crown being first resumed   545 Faliero   5   519
That ducal crown and head shall be united   546 Faliero   5   560
That shining mockery, the ducal bauble   548 Faliero   5   702
The ducal bonnet from his head--and now   549 Faliero   5   808
To the ducal chambers, as he pass'd the threshold   596 Foscari   1   30
And the old ducal dotard, who combined   600 Foscari   1   322
This ducal cap the diadem of earth   603 Foscari   2   80
This ducal ring with which I wed the waves   603 Foscari   2   81
You will. Where? Here, or in the ducal chamber   611 Foscari   3   222
The ducal palace, marshal me to vengeance   620 Foscari   4   333
Where go you, sirrah? By the ducal order   620 Foscari   4   338
The resignation of the ducal ring   621 Foscari   5   26
Your ducal robes must be put off; but for   623 Foscari   5   170
Nor even eight minutes--There's the ducal ring   623 Foscari   5   190
And there the ducal diadem. And so   623 Foscari   5   191

DUCATS
Except two thousand ducats--these dispose of   545 Faliero   5   530
Ducats, to make retirement not less splendid   621 Foscari   5   31
A hundred golden ducats, which to find   686 Werner   2   240

DUCHESS
Noble Venetians! Duchess Faliero   542 Faliero   5   306
Or duchess, princess, empress, 'deigns to prove   905 Juan   9   541
The Duchess of Fitz-Fulke; the Countess Crabby   951 Juan   13   627
The Duchess of Fitz-Fulke, who loved 'tracasserie   960 Juan   14   327
Both to the duchess and diplomatist   963 Juan   14   474
The Duchess of Fitz-Fulke play'd with her veil   984 Juan   16   245

DUCHESS'
Began to think the duchess' conduct free   961 Juan   14   364

DUCK
Still swam--though not exactly like a duck   779 Juan   2   320

DUCKLING
Is like--a duckling by Dame Partlett rear'd   997 Juan   17   30

DUCKLINGS
From tigresses and cubs to ducks and ducklings   848 Juan   5 1058

DUCKS
From tigresses and cubs to ducks and ducklings   848 Juan   5 1058

DUDGEON
Lie down in dudgeon to sigh for the light   855 Juan   6   188

DUDU
Lolah, Katinka, and Dudu; in short   857 Juan   6   315
A kind of sleepy Venus seem'd Dudu   857 Juan   6   329
Dudu said nothing, but sat down beside   858 Juan   6   353
And I shall place Juanna with Dudu   858 Juan   6   388
What say you, child?'--Dudu said nothing, as   858 Juan   6   391
Of Dudu, though they held their tongues from
  deference   858 Juan   6   400
Dudu, as has been said, was a sweet creature   858 Juan   6   409
And thus my narrative proceeds:--Dudu   859 Juan   6   450
Dudu was fond of kissing--which I'm sure   859 Juan   6   466
But all this time how slept, or dream'd, Dudu   861 Juan   6   553
The calm Dudu so turbulently wake   861 Juan   6   568
Dudu had never pass'd for wanting sense   861 Juan   6   590
And chafed at poor Dudu, who only sigh'd   862 Juan   6   631
With you, Dudu, a good night's rest have known   862 Juan   6   646
But poor Dudu, with large drops in her own   862 Juan   6   650
As thus Juanna spoke, Dudu turn'd round   863 Juan   6   673
Then out it came at length, that to Dudu   865 Juan   6   813
At which Dudu look'd strange, and Juan silly   867 Juan   6   943

DUDU'S
But rather skim the earth; while Dudu's form   857 Juan   6   325
Of all save Dudu's dream, which was no joke   865 Juan   6   832

DUE
The wrath of thy own wrongs, or reap the due   67 Harold   4   742
To war, to war, my harp is due   88 Anacreon-A   12
Astrea declares that some penance is due   100 L Adieu   38
We give the palm where Justice points its due   114 Death-A   4
To give the palm where Justice points its due   114 Death-A   26
The praise is due, who made that fame my own   127 Recoll   356
And, sure, apologies are due   138 Clare   68
Nay more, my warmest thanks are due   142 Critics   90
To the famed throng now paid the tribute due   252 Bards   799
And we and ours, alas! are due to fate   258 Hints   91
And give both Belial and his dance their due   274 Waltz   28
But here the Muse with due decorum halts   275 Waltz   121
No doubt; you by this time should know what is
  due   279 Blues   1   117
Of elegy there was the due infusion   286 Vision   70
For certain sure to claim them as his due   295 Vision   646
My thanks and praise alike are due--now hear   358 Corsair   3   176
Her due return:--while she was gone   415 Mazeppa   838
However, I still think, with all due deference   444 Beppo   297
Thence, with due thanks, the abbot God adored   473 Morgante   447
To his high mercy is our freedom due   475 Morgante   639
No words--it is thy due. Follow me not   485 Manfred   2   92
As the due forms of judgment are gone through   500 Faliero   1   40
In forwarding the intimation due   500 Faliero   1   49
The justice due unto the humblest being   503 Faliero   1   214
Keeping due time with every hammer's clink   506 Faliero   1   421
To do yourself due right? Because the man   507 Faliero   1   545
Some sacrifice is due to slander'd virtue   509 Faliero   2   56
Due to my father, who bestow'd my hand   510 Faliero   2   81
Save the regards due to the blood and sweat   515 Faliero   2   463
Due to your rank: in this I shall obey you   537 Faliero   4   609
A patient hearing with the due respect   542 Faliero   5   324
From just infliction of due punishment   570 Sardan   2   575
The homage of mankind as their born due   585 Sardan   4   435
Without the reverence and the rapture due   588 Sardan   5   44
Speak further of the rites due to such ashes   590 Sardan   5   167
The deference due even to the lightest word   606 Foscari   2   298
Due to his years, his station, and his deeds   615 Foscari   4   30
With all due reverence we retire. My lord   621 Foscari   5   63
We will accompany, with due respect   624 Foscari   5   270
Is Saxon, and of course my service due   685 Werner   2   179
You see, sir: how he gave to each his due   699 Werner   3   297
His life: when due, I but resumed the debt   720 Werner   5   463
Instead of hoarding it with due precision   782 Juan   2   544
Save Zoe, who, although with due precision   797 Juan   2 1452
Than admiration due where nature's rich   801 Juan   2 1683
His verses rarely wanted their due feet   811 Juan   3   621
Even Petrarch's self, if judged with due severity   831 Juan   5   7
Perhaps even more attention than is due   836 Juan   5   301
As we may ascertain with due precision   846 Juan   5   919
Aware of their due royal rights o'er men   847 Juan   5 1024
Hence, my old comet! give the stars due warning   849 Juan   5 1156
Let this fifth canto meet with due applause   851 Juan   5 1269
And I of your young charge will take due care   858 Juan   6   374
And now he rose; and after due ablutions   863 Juan   6   729
And his disguise with due consideration   864 Juan   6   790
Were briskly fired and answer'd in due order   872 Juan   7   304
Glory began to dawn with due sublimity   873 Juan   7   406
Maintain'd with all the due prevarication   913 Juan   10   356
No title to point out with due precision   922 Juan   11   251
And was received with all the due grimace   922 Juan   11   275
My topic, with of course the due restriction   929 Juan   11   690
Who have a due respect for their own wishes   939 Juan   12   580
Which takes so much--to give the devil his due   939 Juan   12   603
Which judged mankind at their due estimation   945 Juan   13   245
After due search, your faith to any question   955 Juan   14   12
Chaste were his steps, each kept within due bound   960 Juan   14   305
To fix the due bounds of this dangerous quality   966 Juan   14   712
(Keeping the due proportions still in sight   971 Juan   15   198

DUENNA
His wither'd centinel, Duenna sage   17 Harold   1   802

DUET
The conversazione; the duet   954 Juan   13   850

DUETS
Oh! the long evenings of duets and trios   986 Juan   16   401

DUG
(See also NEW-DUG)
Dug up from dust, though buried when alive   266 Hints   722
But where he died his grave was dug as deep   382 Lara   2   521
The trench is dug, the cannon's breath   385 Corinth   87
Dug, like a spreading pestilence, the grave   427 Island   3   51
The first grave yet dug for mortality   654 Cain   3   541
But who hath dug that grave? Oh, earth! Oh,
  earth   654 Cain   3   542
Thy curse hath dug it deeper for thy son   722 Werner   5   555
Think if then George the Fourth should be dug up   901 Juan   9   305

DUGS
She-wolf, whose brazen-imaged dugs impart   68 Harold   4   785

DUKE

For proud each peasant as the noblest duke	9	Harold	1 375
I should think with Duke Humphry was more in your way	283	Blues	2 145
To the knight, as a landlord, much more than the Duke	283	Blues	2 147
Another, that he was a duke, or knight	294	Vision	609
In Venice' Duke to say so. Venice' Duke	501	Faliero	1 123
Who now is Duke in Venice? let me see him	501	Faliero	1 124
The Duke of Venice--There is no such thing	501	Faliero	1 128
And yet they made thee duke. They made me so	506	Faliero	1 473
I thought the Duke had held command in Venice	511	Faliero	2 159
The little sway now left the Duke? or aught	511	Faliero	2 167
To the council chamber. Duke! it may not be	536	Faliero	4 557
Yet left the duke. All this I bore, and would	541	Faliero	5 219
But he avow'd the letter to the Duke	595	Foscari	1 15
Address'd to Milan's duke, in the full knowledge	600	Foscari	1 296
Nor palliate, as parent or as Duke	603	Foscari	2 98
Am, or at least was, more than a mere duke	605	Foscari	2 241
The letter to the Duke of Milan's his	605	Foscari	2 268
Between the Duke and me on the state's service	606	Foscari	2 322
And bow me to the Duke. Are you content	606	Foscari	2 330
Met the great Duke at daybreak with a jest	619	Foscari	4 292
No more--no more of that. Will not the Duke	620	Foscari	5 14
Here come our colleagues. Is the Duke aware	623	Foscari	5 151
The Duke is with his son. If it be so	623	Foscari	5 153
See, the Duke comes! I have obey'd your summons	623	Foscari	5 161
Your answer, Duke! Your answer, Francis Foscari	623	Foscari	5 177
May the next duke be better than the present	624	Foscari	5 224
The present duke is Paschal Malipiero	624	Foscari	5 225
Broad eminence I was invested duke	624	Foscari	5 242
The Duke of Ichar, and Don Fernan Nunez	765	Juan	1 1194
The Duke of Wellington had ceased to show	884	Juan	8 390
You, my lord duke! is far above reflection	897	Juan	9 50
Shrink to a Saturn. I have seen a Duke	928	Juan	11 650
The Duke of D-- the shooting season spends	947	Juan	13 413
There was the Duke of Dash, who was a--duke	951	Juan	13 673
'Ay, every inch a' duke; there were twelve peers	951	Juan	13 674
But what is odd, none ever named the duke	961	Juan	14 353
Then ask'd her Grace what news were of the duke of late	984	Juan	16 269

DUKEDOM

From which on his return the dukedom met him	510	Faliero	2 116
Bid to his dukedom. When embarks the son	615	Foscari	4 14

DUKES

(See also MERCHANT-DUKES)

Of hoary marquises and stripling dukes	250	Bards	625
A dozen dukes, some kings, a queen--and Waltz	274	Waltz	54
Here are we, counts, kings, dukes, to own thy sway	467	Morgante	91
Which hath already given three dukes to Venice	502	Faliero	1 160
Which gave her dukes the graceless name of 'Biron	914	Juan	10 460
'Midst royal dukes and dames condemn'd to climb	926	Juan	11 535
Some who once set their caps at cautious dukes	928	Juan	11 633
Present, Lords A.B.C.'--Earls, dukes, by name	947	Juan	13 426
But whether English dukes grew rare of late	973	Juan	15 332

DUKE'S

My husband's father's palace. The Duke's palace	598	Foscari	1 206
Of the Duke's son, the innocent Duke's son	599	Foscari	1 272

DULL

The hoarse dull drum would sleep, and Man be happy yet	11	Harold	1 503
The last, the worst, dull spoiler, who was he	21	Harold	2 94
Dull is the eye that will not weep to see	21	Harold	2 129
Ah, grievance sore and listless dull delay	22	Harold	2 176
Yet, though dull Hate as duty should be taught	53	Harold	3 1085
Prohibits to dull life in this our state	56	Harold	4 41
Of hasty growth and blight, and dull Oblivion bar	56	Harold	4 81
From the dull yoke of her barbaric foes	59	Harold	4 268
The drill'd dull lesson, forced down word by word	66	Harold	4 674
The dull satiety which all destroys	73	Harold	4 1070
Except the dull cold stone that hides thy head	94	Dorset	50
Dull as the pictures which adorn their halls	112	Examination	53
For me how dull the vacant moments rise	125	Recoil	227
Till the dull knell of childish play	131	L'Amitie	26
How dull! to hear the voice of those	135	I Would	33
Life's evening dream is dark and dull	137	Clare	17
Lost in the dull, ignoble crowd	146	Adieu	88
Although by far too dull for laughter	148	To Author	12
Whatever flows is never dull	154	Skull	4
Through each dull tedious trifling part	172	Time-B	31
That dull, cold sensualist, whose sickly eye	183	Address-D	47
Of bitterness--thy Hope--thy heart so dull	184	Julian	43
When the glow of early thought declines in feeling's dull decay	185	Music-B	2
With mad disquietude on the dull sky	189	Darkness	29
No ear so dull, no soul so cold	216	The Harp	8
Through life's dull road, so dim and dirty	236	Dull Road	1
Where dull pretenders grapple for the prize	243	Bards	136
Next comes the dull disciple of thy school	245	Bards	235

DULL

On dull devotion--Lo! the Sabbath bard	246	Bards	320
Dull Maurice all his granite weight of leaves	247	Bards	414
So dull in youth, so drivelling in his age	251	Bards	733
Racks his dull memory and his duller muse	267	Hints	739
Dull as his sermons, but not half so brief	267	Hints	768
And dull were his that pass'd them heedless by	269	Minerva	48
As dull Boeotia gave a Pindar birth	270	Minerva	150
Oh say, shall dull Romaika's heavy round	275	Waltz	125
Fool's Paradise is dull to that you lost	275	Waltz	138
His keys were rusty and the lock was dull	285	Vision	2
It may be, still, like dull books on a shelf	298	Vision	838
Oh, dull Saint Helen! with thy gaoler nigh	301	Age	226
And never, even in that dull House, couldst tame	305	Age	550
Unseen to drop by dull decay	319	Giaour	968
Than pass my dull, unvarying days	320	Giaour	992
And dull were his that pass'd them heedless by	356	Corsair	3 48
And dull the film along his dim eye grew	382	Lara	2 491
Have deeper thoughts than your dull eyes discern	382	Lara	2 533
As it slipp'd through their jaws, when their edge grew dull	389	Corinth	461
When those dull chains in meeting clank'd	399	Parisina	322
Dim with a dull imprison'd ray	403	Chillon	30
But then by dull degrees came back	405	Chillon	259
The sky was dull, and dim, and gray	411	Mazeppa	439
Which fix'd my dull eyes from afar	414	Mazeppa	785
And of the cold, dull, swimming, dense	414	Mazeppa	787
And sanction with self-slaughter the dull lie	439	Tasso	214
Or left untended in a dull repose	440	Tasso	239
The dull green ooze of the receding deep	453	Venice-B	9
With dull and daily dissonance, repeats	453	Venice-B	21
The dull beginning	453	Venice-B	39
Damm'd like the dull canal with locks and chains	455	Venice-B	152
Corrosive passions, feelings dull and low	457	Dante	1 132
Goading the wise to madness; from the dull	488	Manfred	2 364
'Tis over--my dull eyes can fix thee not	497	Manfred	3 406
To compensate for many a dull hour, wasted	511	Faliero	2 170
Of the dull moon. That warrior was the sire	520	Faliero	3 89
Wish that I could lay down the dull tiara	558	Sardan	1 498
Stood dull as in our temples, but she still	580	Sardan	4 155
Even on these dull damp walls, and--Boy! no tears	614	Foscari	3 415
In number than the dust of thy dull earth	636	Cain	2 46
Or the dull mass of life, that, being life	639	Cain	2 225
In its dull damp degeneracy, to	640	Cain	2 277
The smoky harbinger of thy dull pray'rs	650	Cain	3 291
The dull and dropping rain saps in their bones	672	Werner	1 32
Cannot you humour the dull gossip till	674	Werner	1 195
Even here, in this remote, unnamed, dull spot	682	Werner	1 701
And dull suspicion are a part of his	693	Werner	2 638
Too dull for wakefulness, too quick for slumber	700	Werner	3 359
At his dull heedlessness, in leaving thus	702	Werner	3 507
In these dull pageantries. Begone! and rail	713	Werner	5 13
How so? As Stralenheim is. Are you so dull	719	Werner	5 409
Its way with all deformity's dull, deadly	727	Deformed	1 330
Because you know no better than the dull	730	Deformed	1 582
The stammering young ones of the flood's dull ooze	732	Deformed	1 678
The gross, dull, heavy, gloomy execration	734	Deformed	1 825
Upon a Sky which you revile as dull	744	Deformed	3 144
When old King David's blood grew dull in motion	767	Juan	1 1341
Are various, but they none of them are dull	770	Juan	1 1510
And the boy's eyes, which the dull film half glazed	785	Juan	2 709
Like Charon's bark of spectres, dull and pale	786	Juan	2 803
From the dull palace to the dirty hovel	799	Juan	2 1607
Without which life would be extremely dull	801	Juan	2 1693
Some dull MS. oblivion long has sank	813	Juan	3 805
A long and snake-like life of dull decay	817	Juan	4 71
A busy character in the dull scene	818	Juan	4 116
To lose itself when the old world grows dull	818	Juan	4 131
Relieved her thoughts; dull silence and quick chat	824	Juan	4 502
Her sweet face into shadow, dull and slow	825	Juan	4 550
From his dull cabin, found himself a slave	826	Juan	4 626
Yet I must own he looked a little dull	832	Juan	5 59
Their speed abated or their strength grew dull	865	Juan	6 854
Hark! through the silence of the cold, dull night	878	Juan	7 681
A glance on the dull clouds (as thick as starch	881	Juan	8 166
Or dull repentance hath had dreary leisure	892	Juan	8 901
Into a Russian couplet rather dull	904	Juan	9 475
Too dull even for the dullest of excesses	918	Juan	10 686
And after that serene and somewhat dull	941	Juan	13 25
A dull and desolate appendage. Gaze	945	Juan	13 258
Ridiculous enough, but also dull	953	Juan	13 754
And now because I feel it growing dull	956	Juan	14 80
A dull and family likeness through all ages	957	Juan	14 119
Are there oft dull and dreary as a dun	959	Juan	14 231
December's drowsy day to his dull race	960	Juan	14 284
Now grave, now gay, but never dull or pert	960	Juan	14 293
Quite full, right dull, guests hot, and dishes cold	991	Juan	16 670

DULLER

Whose Helicon is duller than her Cam	255	Bards	972

DULLER
Racks his dull memory and his duller muse   267 Hints   739
Save that it seems even duller than repose   338 Corsair   1 24

DULLEST
The dullest sailer wearing bravely now   22 Harold   2 152
The dullest, fattest weeds on Lethe's brink   267 Hints   756
Too dull even for the dullest of excesses   918 Juan   10 686

DULLS
He sweats in palling pleasures, dulls his soul   551 Sardan   1 24

DULLY
But) of fine unclipt gold, where dully rests   931 Juan   12 93
Dully past o'er the dinner of the day   992 Juan   16 737

DULNESS
To strange mysterious dulness still the friend   244 Bards   151
Or, kind to dulness, do you fear to blame   250 Bards   611
And damning dulness of lord chamberlains   261 Hints   358

DULY
Thou saw'st 'twas duly drunk by me   104 Alva   198
Up, and do your duty duly   240 Suliotes   2
First duly done by daughter or by spouse   276 Waltz   185
His food and wine were doled out duly still   299 Age   76
Cared little, so that they were duly fed   303 Age   403
All duly anxious to leave little work   303 Age   410
Mark that the signal-gun is duly fired   340 Corsair   1 167
For just and holy works were duly fed   469 Morgante   194
Sire, I shall ever duly serve my sovereign   570 Sardan   2 518
If duly taught; but, in one word, if I   691 Werner   2 551
All hearts point duly north, like trembling
  needles   700 Werner   3 333
And duly seated on the immortal hill   745 Juan   Ded 48
Who thank'd me duly by return of post   772 Juan   1 1674
Was steering duly for the port Leghorn   777 Juan   2 186
In Sicily (all singers, duly rear'd   826 Juan   4 637
While two and twenty cannon duly set   868 Juan   7 94
Duly accompanied by shrieks and groans   895 Juan   8 1074
As many covers, duly, daily, laid   947 Juan   13 390
Till duly disappointed or dismiss'd   990 Juan   16 643

DUMB
While throng'd the citizens with terror dumb   39 Harold   3 224
Nor Torture shake, or mine would now be cold
  and dumb   58 Harold   4 171
He had seen George Rose--but George was grown
  dumb   178 Devil's Dr   175
To thee, with hope and terror dumb   234 Strahan   5
Let Pastoral be dumb; for who can hope   262 Hints   387
Would to God I were deaf! as I'm not, I'll be
  dumb   280 Blues   2 25
While gazed the rest in dumb amazement round   381 Lara   2 449
Although as yet his voice be dumb   398 Parisina   146
I strove to cry--my lips were dumb   413 Mazeppa   675
Your tributaries, your dumb citizens   606 Foscari   2 302
And with their roar make wholesome nature dumb   670 Heaven   1130
I am dumb. Have you been long here? Long?
  I sought   679 Werner   1 528
Their looks cast down, their greetings almost
  dumb   755 Juan   1 555
Then he himself sunk down all dumb and shivering   785 Juan   2 719
The peasants gave the poor dumb thing a pittance   803 Juan   3 142
And that his sorrow may not be a dumb one   804 Juan   3 191
'Tis but the living who are dumb   812 Juan   3 736
The trump and bugle till he spake were dumb   836 Juan   5 287
They were mis-shapen pigmies, deaf and dumb   842 Juan   5 703
Grew dumb, for you might almost hear a linnet   885 Juan   8 470
Whose charms made all men speak, and women dumb   902 Juan   13 102
No; but you have heard--I understand--be dumb   980 Juan   15 754
'Tis time to strike such puny doubters dumb as   981 Juan   16 31
Surprise has this effect--to make one dumb   995 Juan   16 962

DUMBER
And wait until the nightingale grows dumber   947 Juan   13 381

DUMOURIER
France, too, had Buonaparte and Dumourier   747 Juan   1 15

DUMPY
Her stature tall--I hate a dumpy woman   754 Juan   1 488

DUN
Blasted below the dun hot breath of war   11 Harold   1 498
Array'd in many a dun and purple streak   25 Harold   2 373
And, dun and sombre 'mid the holy calm   356 Corsair   3 45
On dun Cithaeron's ridge appears   385 Corinth   71
Whose clouds that day grew doubly dun   386 Corinth   173
The clouds beneath him seem'd so dun   396 Corinth   1076
Fluttering between the dun wave and the sky   430 Island   4 3
And sleeps unwieldy in his cavern dun   430 Island   4 13
What courser will you please to mount? The dun   705 Werner   4 79
Baptized in molten gold, and swathed in dun   785 Juan   2 732

DUN
The umbrage of the wood so cool and dun   805 Juan   3 213
The seventh will bring blue devils or a dun   912 Juan   10 304
A huge, dun cupola, like a foolscap crown   917 Juan   10 655
Are there oft dull and dreary as a dun   959 Juan   14 231

DUNCAN
Forgetting Duncan, Nelson, Howe, and Jervis   747 Juan   1 32

DUNCE
And something in a heavy dunce   234 Epilogue   2
To Scotch marauder and to southern dunce   256 Bards   1066
Whom nature guides so writes that every dunce   262 Hints   383
Produced a play too dashing for a dunce   264 Hints   566
Alike might puzzle either wit or dunce   861 Juan   6 588
And so may every one except a dunce   935 Juan   12 347
Could hardly be united by a dunce   985 Juan   16 312
A wise man more than laughter from a dunce   992 Juan   16 749

DUNCES
If chance some bard, though once by dunces fear'd 246 Bards   365
No wit for nobles, dunces by descent   265 Hints   612
But fifty dunces can, with perfect ease   265 Hints   641
Dunces were whipt, or set upon a stool   775 Juan   2 78
'La Belle Alliance' of dunces down at zero   925 Juan   11 443

DUNCIAD
And link'd thee to the Dunciad for thy pains   247 Bards   384

DUNCIADS
Such damning fame as Dunciads only give   252 Bards   751

DUNDER
Dick Dunder. That is, if he lives. And why not   281 Blues   2 44

DUNEDIN
Dunedin! view thy children with delight   249 Bards   552

DUNEDIN'S
Dunedin's castle felt a sceret shock   248 Bards   469
Mightiest of all Dunedin's beasts of chase   265 Hints   597

DUNG
In England 'twould be dung, dust, or a dray   445 Beppo   336

DUNGEON
There is a dungeon, in whose dim drear light   77 Harold   4 1324
My thoughts their dungeon know too well   175 Impromptu-A   6
For the dungeon he quits is the place of his
  birth   202 Avatar   16
(According to compact) the wit in the dungeon   226 Oh You   8
Plunged in a dungeon, he had still been great   299 Age   71
To flit between a dungeon and a throne   301 Age   259
Then gaze upon it through thy dungeon bars   304 Age   431
Three were in a dungeon cast   403 Chillon   25
An echo of the dungeon stone   403 Chillon   64
To him this dungeon was a gulf   403 Chillon   105
A double dungeon wall and wave   403 Chillon   113
In such a dungeon could not rest   404 Chillon   157
That almost made the dungeon bright   404 Chillon   195
I saw the dungeon walls and floor   405 Chillon   261
Scarce broader than my dungeon floor   406 Chillon   345
A floating dungeon:--all was hope and home   435 Island   4 404
The narrow circus of my dungeon wall   437 Tasso   23
Although 'tis clouded by my dungeon roof   439 Tasso   188
A poet's dungeon thy most far renown   439 Tasso   226
Who has the whole world for a dungeon strong   465 Dante   4 132
For such as him a dungeon were acquittal   515 Faliero   2 438
Which howl'd about my Candiote dungeon and   597 Foscari   1 129
A dungeon, what they will, so it be here   597 Foscari   1 145
The dungeon walls must still divide us. True   602 Foscari   2 62
A moment's access to his dungeon. I'll   608 Foscari   2 432
His dungeon barrier, like the lover's record   608 Foscari   3 22
No more. How! wouldst thou share a dungeon? Ay   609 Foscari   3 39
The dungeon vapours its bituminous smoke   609 Foscari   3 55
If dungeon dates say true. And what of him   609 Foscari   3 70
More woful--such as this small dungeon, where   609 Foscari   3 93
Small dungeon! is all that belongs to thee   609 Foscari   3 95
I could endure my dungeon, for 'twas Venice   610 Foscari   3 127
The dungeon gloom is deep enough without you   612 Foscari   3 264
Farewell! at least to this detested dungeon   614 Foscari   3 404
A start of feeling in his dungeon, never   615 Foscari   4 6
Touch it not, dungeon miscreants! your base
  office   618 Foscari   4 198
I thought to cheer up this old dungeon here   676 Werner   1 323
Will rescue us from this detested dungeon   683 Werner   1 739
'Tis only at the bar and in the dungeon   686 Werner   2 209
Within a dungeon, where he may avouch   687 Werner   2 286
To plunge you, with your parents, in a dungeon   690 Werner   2 475
The whip, the rack, or dungeon at the least   806 Juan   3 317

DUNGEON-DEW
The accursed breath of dungeon-dew   404 Chillon   214

DUNGEON-LIGHT
It was not even the dungeon-light | 405 Chillon | 241

DUNGEONS
Dungeons and thrones, which the same hour
  re-fill'd | 48 Harold | 3 | 777
Oh! although in dungeons pent | 187 French-A | 22
Brightest in dungeons, Liberty! thou art | 402 Sonnet-F | 2
In Chillon's dungeons deep and old | 403 Chillon | 28
And that Saint Mark's has dungeons, and the
  dungeons | 533 Faliero | 4 | 342
Yawns dungeons at each step for thee and me | 568 Sardan | 2 | 422
Your dungeons next the palace roofs, or under | 606 Foscari | 2 | 306
My doom is common, many are in dungeons | 609 Foscari | 3 | 98
The groans of slaves in chains, and men in
  dungeons | 611 Foscari | 3 | 242

DUNGEON'S
Most noxious o'er a dungeon's walls | 320 Giaour | 991
For they have been a dungeon's spoil | 402 Chillon | 7
And cheering from my dungeon's brink | 405 Chillon | 277

DUNGHILL
Rake from each ancient dunghill ev'ry pearl | 246 Bards | 371
Ay, as the dunghill may conceal a gem | 728 Deformed | 1 | 432

DUNGHILL'S
Life knots of vipers on a dunghill's soil | 801 Juan | 2 | 1717

DUNN'D
Fool'd, pillaged, dunn'd, he wastes his terms
  away | 260 Hints | 239

DUNNEST
Through guards and dunnest night how came it
  there | 353 Corsair | 2 | 406
O Death! thou dunnest of all duns! thou daily | 969 Juan | 15 | 57

DUNS
Shall Grub-street dine, while duns are kept aloof | 249 Bards | 547
Of doors 'gainst duns, and to an early dinner | 922 Juan | 11 | 228
Tithes, taxes, duns, and doors with double
  knockings | 938 Juan | 12 | 536
O Death! thou dunnest of all duns! thou daily | 969 Juan | 15 | 57

DUODECIMO
Thy patrons wave a duodecimo | 224 J.C.H. | 48

DUOMO
(His Maggior Duomo, a smart, subtle Greek | 916 Juan | 10 | 557

DUPE
Woman his dupe, his heedless friend a tool | 100 Damaetas | 7
To sigh the dupe of female art | 143 To--A | 18
Doom'd by his very virtues for a dupe | 342 Corsair | 1 | 256
I have not been thy dupe nor am thy prey | 496 Manfred | 3 | 398

DUPLICITY
Duplicity in vain would veil | 147 Vain Lady | 20

DURA
'O dura ilia messorum!'--'Oh | 898 Juan | 9 | 113
Even Nimrod's self might leave the plains of Dura | 951 Juan | 13 | 621

DURANCE
The magazine in rocky durance stow'd | 12 Harold | 1 | 537
And the grim guards that to his durance led | 351 Corsair | 2 | 308
Less than their breath; our durance upon days | 607 Foscari | 2 | 355

DURATION
By length I mean duration; theirs endured | 798 Juan | 2 | 1489

DURING
Convulsed the skies, as during a debate | 296 Vision | 738
During the dynasty of Dandies, now | 447 Beppo | 474
During thine absence, whereupon to offer | 647 Cain | 3 | 97
In saying you were a soldier during peacetime | 677 Werner | 1 | 357
She did this during even her husband's life | 753 Juan | 1 | 383
During this inquisition, Julia's tongue | 764 Juan | 1 | 1153
Like human beings during civil war | 779 Juan | 2 | 336

DURLINDAN
And from his hand extracted Durlindan | 468 Morgante | 123

DURST
He could not--durst not--lo! the guile confest | 110 Nisus | 370
No thought, save for his Maker's service, durst | 288 Vision | 246
And why--he felt, but durst not tell | 325 Abydos | 1 | 131
The Briton must be bold who really durst | 884 Juan | 8 | 381

DUSK
Thy margin and the mountains, dusk, yet clear | 48 Harold | 3 | 807
And the dusk Spahi's bands advance | 385 Corinth | 77
Of the dusk bosoms that beat high below | 419 Island | 2 | 52

DUSK
The New World stretch'd its dusk hand to the Old | 422 Island | 2 | 239
They wait in their dusk livery of woe | 442 Beppo | 157
I see a dusk and awful figure rise | 495 Manfred | 3 | 322
Lolah was dusk as India and as warm | 857 Juan | 6 | 321

DUSKILY
The skies (and the more duskily the better | 440 Beppo | 10

DUSKY
At every turn Morena's dusky height | 12 Harold | 1 | 531
Lands of the dark-eyed Maid and dusky Moor | 22 Harold | 2 | 192
Dusky and huge, enlarging on the sight | 27 Harold | 2 | 451
On Alva's dusky hills of wind | 102 Alva | 54
Till night expands her dusky wings | 103 Alva | 120
But ruder records fill the dusky wall | 124 Recoll | 152
Or roaming through the dusky wild | 135 I Would | 3
With dusky leaves my temples bound | 139 Anacreon-C | 20
Marr's dusky heath, and Dee's clear wave | 145 Adieu | 29
Her dusky shadow mounts too high | 174 Impromptu-A | 2
She on high Albyn's dusky hills may raise | 182 Address-C | 21
With strange and dusky aspects; he was not | 215 Dream | 109
Sighs to remember on his dusky shore | 302 Age | 327
That, streak'd with dusky red, portend | 316 Giaour | 663
That glares beneath his dusky cowl | 318 Giaour | 833
He sees a dusky glimmering--shall he seek | 361 Corsair | 3 | 394
But, glimmering through the dusky corridore | 364 Corsair | 3 | 595
Their spirits wrapp'd the dusky mountain | 388 Corinth | 412
Or scatter'd spot of dusky green | 413 Mazeppa | 611
Dusky like night, but night with all her stars | 420 Island | 2 | 129
Found beauty link'd with many a dusky form | 422 Island | 2 | 245
And near, and nearer, till their dusky crew | 429 Island | 3 | 171
White as a white sail on a dusky sea | 430 Island | 4 | 1
The moment night with dusky mantle covers | 440 Beppo | 9
He was a man as dusky as a Spaniard | 443 Beppo | 201
The moon? Late; but the atmosphere is thick and
  dusky | 508 Faliero | 1 | 599
Some dusky shadow checkering the Rialto | 529 Faliero | 4 | 101
Dripping with dusky gore, and trampling on | 578 Sardan | 4 | 32
Sprinkle the dusky groves and the green banks | 637 Cain | 2 | 124
Huge dusky masses: but unlike the worlds | 638 Cain | 2 | 181
Because 'tis dusky. And if I do so | 703 Werner | 3 | 540
Dusky, but not uncomely. If I chose | 727 Deformed | 1 | 371
Its twinkle through the lattice dusky quite | 855 Juan | 6 | 190
Lo! dusky masses steal in dubious sight | 878 Juan | 7 | 683
Dirty and dusky, but as wide as eye | 917 Juan | 10 | 650
On ours, or spars within some dusky cave | 983 Juan | 16 | 149
In cowl and beads and dusky garb, appear'd | 983 Juan | 16 | 162
He sweeps along in his dusky pall | 986 Juan | 16 | 363

DUST
Regard and weigh yon dust before it flies | 20 Harold | 2 | 35
Nor feels as lovers o'er the dust they loved | 21 Harold | 2 | 128
An hour may lay it in the dust; and when | 33 Harold | 2 | 798
The dust thy courser's hoof, rude stranger,
  spurns around | 34 Harold | 2 | 854
Stop!--for thy tread is on an Empire's dust | 37 Harold | 3 | 145
And those which waved are shredless dust ere now | 42 Harold | 3 | 422
Of passion had consumed themselves to dust | 43 Harold | 3 | 470
And held within their urn one mind, one heart,
  one dust | 45 Harold | 3 | 634
And dust is as it should be, shall I not | 46 Harold | 3 | 703
To look on One whose dust was once all fire | 47 Harold | 3 | 719
By slumber, on one pillow,--in the dust | 52 Harold | 3 | 1009
Of her dead Doges are declined to dust | 57 Harold | 4 | 128
They keep his dust in Arqua where he died | 59 Harold | 4 | 271
Of worthless dust which from thy boasted line | 60 Harold | 4 | 327
In the same dust and blackness, and we pass | 62 Harold | 4 | 412
Ashes which make it holier, dust which is | 63 Harold | 4 | 479
In death as life? Are they resolved to dust | 63 Harold | 4 | 501
His dust; and lies it not her Great among | 63 Harold | 4 | 515
And Santa Croce wants their mighty dust | 64 Harold | 4 | 523
Sprinkle its coolness, and from the dry dust | 65 Harold | 4 | 609
Whose holy dust was scatter'd long ago | 66 Harold | 4 | 706
That weigh'd upon her gentle dust, a cloud | 70 Harold | 4 | 912
Whose touch turns Hope to dust,--the dust we all
  have trod | 74 Harold | 4 | 1125
Thy former realm, I call thee from the dust | 75 Harold | 4 | 1187
Heroes have trod this spot--'tis on their dust
  ye tread | 76 Harold | 4 | 1296
One ringlet in the dust; nor hath it caught | 79 Harold | 4 | 1466
And wipe the dust from off the idle name | 80 Harold | 4 | 1490
Thy bridal's fruit is ashes; in the dust | 80 Harold | 4 | 1523
And scatter flowers on the dust I love | 84 Death-B | 4
When life again to dust is given | 85 To D-- | 10
When decay'd, may he mingle his dust with your own | 86 Leaving NA | 32
That veil their dust, their follies, and their
  faults | 94 Dorset | 56
I sink forgotten in the dust | 103 Alva | 142
When humbled in the dust, let some one be | 106 Nisus | 65
Oh! moisten their dust with a Tear | 115 The Tear | 44
dust of Erin! Let me fall alone. My father | 130 Calmar | 72
If, when this dust to dust's restored | 133 Prayer | 53
To humble in the dust my face | 146 Adieu | 79

DUST

Will not reject a child of dust	146	Adieu	109
Remembrance still hallows the dust of the dead	149	Newstead-B	36
Degraded mass of animated dust	154	Dog	18
Beloved dust! since dust thou art	166	Away	14
Bow'd to the dust the Drama's tower of pride	169	Address-A	2
Weigh'd in the balance, hero dust	181	Ode-A	100
With curses cast them down upon the dust	189	Darkness	31
In the dark union of insensate dust	192	Fragment-C	22
To dust if I return, from dust I sprung	199	Po	51
Till thy hard heart be calcined into dust	209	Sketch	91
Down to the dust!--and, as thou rott'st away	209	Sketch	97
But leaves its darken'd dust behind	220	Clay	4
Creatures of clay--vain dwellers in the dust	222	Spirit	9
Justice and death have mix'd their dust in vain	228	Windsor	7
The blood and dust of both--to mould a George	228	Windsor	10
Justice and Death have mix'd their dust in vain	228	Vaults	7
Now, prone in dust, can only be revered	246	Bards	366
Dug up from dust, though buried when alive	266	Hints	722
Shake off the sordid dust of such a land	270	Minerva	153
Oh, loathed in life nor pardon'd in the dust	271	Minerva	199
The page was so besmear'd with blood and dust	285	Vision	40
So mix his body with the dust! It might	286	Vision	81
That as he was my worshipper in dust	289	Vision	308
Of 'dust to dust,' but half its tale untold	298	Age	24
And spurn the dust o'er which they crawl'd of late	299	Age	47
The rocky isle that holds or held his dust	299	Age	111
Touch the freed spirit or the fetter'd dust	300	Age	116
To form, like Guesclin's dust, her talisman	300	Age	128
Where the weeds and the desolate dust are spread	313	Giaour	298
Which saith that woman is but dust	315	Giaour	489
Our hearts to undivided dust	327	Abydos	1	326
Dust long outlasts the storied stone	329	Abydos	2	53
But Thou--thy very dust is gone	329	Abydos	2	54
Vainly thou heap'st the dust upon thy head	336	Abydos	2	652
His sire was dust, his vassals could declare	366	Lara	1	29
That hid their dust, their foibles, and their faults	368	Lara	1	186
By cities levell'd with the dust	386	Corinth	156
The chiefs whose dust around him slumber'd	388	Corinth	403
And brow were stain'd with gore and dust	394	Corinth	886
Hurling warriors in the dust	394	Corinth	903
At length roll o'er my reckless dust	399	Parisina	279
In the dust, which each deep vein	401	Parisina	458
Like dust beneath the coffin lid	401	Parisina	514
His corse in dust whereon the day	404	Chillon	153
Feel far more ere we turn to dust	412	Mazeppa	566
His soul is gone before his dust to heaven	424	Island	2	373
In England 'twould be dung, dust, or a dray	445	Beppo	336
Of wealth and glory turn'd to dust and tears	453	Venice-B	16
The dust she dooms to scatter, and transfer	457	Dante	1	75
But this shall not be granted; let my dust	457	Dante	1	77
Earth's dust by immortality refined	460	Dante	3	21
Morgante rummaged piecemeal from the dust	476	Morgante	668
Half dust, half deity, alike unfit	482	Manfred	1	301
Preach it to mortals of a dust like thine	484	Manfred	2	37
From wither'd bones, and skulls, and heap'd up dust	486	Manfred	2	176
And mind and dust, and passions and pure thoughts	493	Manfred	3	165
The dust from sepulchres to fill his hour-glass	530	Faliero	4	159
I know to be as worthless as the dust	547	Faliero	5	646
To dry into the desert's dust by myriads	555	Sardan	1	275
Thy sires have been revered as gods--In dust	555	Sardan	1	314
Flattering dust with eternity. Well, Pania	560	Sardan	1	613
Of this our palace, into the dry dust	566	Sardan	2	287
Would lick the dust in which the king lay low	572	Sardan	3	55
The dust we tread upon was once alive	579	Sardan	4	65
Me to the dust already. Get thee hence	593	Sardan	5	379
The dust of both into one urn. The better	594	Sardan	5	476
Leave them, and walk with dust? I know the thoughts	629	Cain	1	100
Of dust, and feel for it, and with you. How	629	Cain	1	101
Aught else but dust! That is a grovelling wish	631	Cain	1	289
The dust which form'd your father? Can it be	636	Cain	2	28
In number than the dust of thy dull earth	636	Cain	2	46
Unworthy what I see, though my dust is	637	Cain	2	116
Shalt soon return to earth and all its dust	638	Cain	2	149
That dust has shown me--let me dwell in shadows	640	Cain	2	314
In generations like to dust (which they	642	Cain	2	431
Dust! limit thy ambition; for to see	645	Cain	2	611
And after flattering dust with glimpses of	647	Cain	3	72
It back to dust again--for what? Thou know'st	647	Cain	3	74
For being dust, and grovelling in the dust	647	Cain	3	114
Till I return to dust? If I am nothing	648	Cain	3	115
Even to the dust, of which he is, in honour	649	Cain	3	243
Deny thee shelter! earth a home! the dust	653	Cain	3	442
With my own death redeem him from the dust	654	Cain	3	511
Marry, and bring forth dust! I should have loved	655	Heaven	18
Acknowledge that more loving dust	655	Heaven	54
The yellow dust they try to barter with us	657	Heaven	192
A portion of thy dust, I come	659	Heaven	318
Children of dust be quench'd; and of each hue	660	Heaven	363
No more to dust than is eternity	662	Heaven	569

DUST

Say'st well, though she be dust, I did not, could not	663	Heaven	611
The snake but vanquish'd dust; but she will draw	666	Heaven	858
Through time to dust, unshorten'd by God's wrath	667	Heaven	874
It cannot slay us: threaten dust with death	669	Heaven	1053
Thy hell is not hereafter! Am I dust still	696	Werner	3	71
Or crush'd, or rising slowly from the dust	703	Werner	3	564
When he spurns high the dust, beholding his	724	Deformed	1	114
Fling my cloak o'er what will be dust anon	736	Deformed	2	130
In spirit. Cover up my dust, and breathe not	737	Deformed	2	151
As dust can. Then she is dead! Bah! bah! You are so	741	Deformed	2	394
This precious thing of dust--this bright Olimpia	744	Deformed	3	153
To have, when the original is dust	773	Juan	1	1743
Since not a pinch of dust remains of Cheops	773	Juan	1	1752
Fighting, devotion, dust,--perhaps a name	774	Juan	2	32
When dried to summer dust; till taught by pain	784	Juan	2	667
To hint that flesh is form'd of fiery dust	801	Juan	2	1696
And when his bones are dust, his grave a blank	813	Juan	3	801
Who would as 'twere identify their dust	829	Juan	4	804
Protects his dust, but reverence here is paid	829	Juan	4	827
In aspect, plainly clad, besmear'd with dust	876	Juan	7	582
The groan, the roll in dust, the all-white eye	879	Juan	8	101
And the two are so mix'd with human dust	906	Juan	9	613
Of bricks, to let the dust in at your ease	921	Juan	11	165
The turnpikes glow with dust; and Rotten Row	946	Juan	13	349
Who whirl the dust as simooms whirl the sand	962	Juan	14	462
To these? They are rags or dust. Where is the arch	976	Juan	15	530
No doubt a consolation to his dust	997	Juan	17	64

DUST'S

If, when this dust to dust's restored	133	Prayer	53
And still is hallow'd by thy dust's return	457	Dante	1	101

DUSTY

While kings, in dusty darkness hid	311	Giaour	128
O'er dusty plain and smoky skies	385	Corinth	92
The dusty monuments from light recoil	431	Island	4	134
Peopled with dusty atoms which afford	609	Foscari	3	102

DUTCH

Besides there were the Spaniard, Dutch, and Dane	292	Vision	473
A monkey, a Dutch mastiff, a mackaw	803	Juan	3	137
The Spanish, and the French, as well as Dutch	896	Juan	9	21
Or Dutch with thirst--What, ho! a flask of Rhenish	950	Juan	13	576

DUTCHMEN

That water-land of Dutchmen and of ditches	915	Juan	10	498

DUTEOUS

What though his gaoler, duteous to the last	299	Age	101
And where he leads the duteous pack will follow	305	Age	557
But how!--obedient, but with coldness; duteous	710	Werner	4	419

DUTIES

His duties as a king and mortal, say	289	Vision	303
Has still been in my duties, which are many	510	Faliero	2	91
More than the mere discharge of public duties	511	Faliero	2	190
For doing all its duties, and replying	513	Faliero	2	344
Short of the duties of a king; and therefore	556	Sardan	1	408
Of human duties leads even those who claim	585	Sardan	4	434
And thought--It forms no portion of your duties	585	Sardan	4	439
I have too many duties towards you	602	Foscari	2	29
But I have other duties than a father's	604	Foscari	2	184
The state would not dispense me from those duties	604	Foscari	2	185
By duties paramount; and 'tis our first	611	Foscari	3	201
Your Giunta's duties. How!--my Giunta! Yours	622	Foscari	5	141
His rank and his devotion to the duties	625	Foscari	5	312
It is my last of duties, and may prove	626	Foscari	5	339
Fulfil a parent's duties by his side	710	Werner	4	415
The stricter doubtless grow the vestal duties	859	Juan	6	463
Where thousand loves, and ties, and duties grew	894	Juan	8	990
What were the actual and official duties	903	Juan	9	402
Thy custom-house, with all its delicate duties	916	Juan	10	547
His duties warlike, loving or official	924	Juan	11	405

DUTIFUL

And scribbling Songs grow dutiful and live	225	J.C.H.	54
They are wond'rous dutiful, and ever humble	500	Faliero	1	45
I fain would have them dutiful. I cherish	582	Sardan	4	259
And coldly dutiful, and proudly patient	743	Deformed	3	118

DUTY

Yet, though dull Hate as duty should be taught	53	Harold	3	1085
Believe me, only does his duty	87	Rousseau	18
That last dear duty to fulfil	168	Haunts	30
And they have done their duty well	168	The Chain	7
In whom Caprice had seem'd a duty	201	Ode-C	50
And found a nobler duty than to part	213	Lady Byron	42
This duty done, let me in turn demand	224	J.C.H.	25
Up, and do your duty duly	240	Suliotes	2

DUTY

Up my boys and do your duty	240	Suliotes		6
He who has learn'd the duty which he owes	263	Hints		495
Long be thine import from all duty free	274	Waltz		31
Where Belial, upon duty for the day	294	Vision		580
By me alone be duty taught	324	Abydos	1	43
To thee, and to my duty true	324	Abydos	1	75
Back to your duty--for my course prepare	340	Corsair	1	156
Then rose his band to duty--not from sleep	347	Corsair	1	603
Command nor duty could their transport check	363	Corsair	3	497
In duty patient, and sedate though young	373	Lara	1	515
Her duty, and her glory, and her joy	423	Island	2	339
To act whatever duty bade them do	433	Island	4	282
He thought himself in duty bound to do so	452	Beppo		755
And looks on prostitution as a duty	461	Dante	3	79
His bidding, nor did I neglect my duty	489	Manfred	2	389
For such are worth redemption; and my duty	493	Manfred	3	169
He sits as rapt in duty; but whene'er	500	Faliero	1	10
His acceptation of their duty. Yes	500	Faliero	1	44
Your office, and its dignity and duty	501	Faliero	1	126
Who have forgot their duty to the sovereign	503	Faliero	1	243
In all things to rely upon my duty	504	Faliero	1	285
Have traversed land and sea in constant duty	506	Faliero	1	462
Toil, charge, or duty for the state, I did not	506	Faliero	1	477
A duty to a certain sign, a vice	510	Faliero	2	109
I would not interrupt him in his duty	511	Faliero	2	156
And theirs. The senate's duty! you mistake	511	Faliero	2	157
And feel for what their duty bids them do	517	Faliero	2	588
On duty, and our leader Israel	520	Faliero	3	123
They baffled me, 'twas a patrician's duty	525	Faliero	3	474
Not least though last; but having done my duty	532	Faliero	4	325
And trembled at the thought of this dread duty	534	Faliero	4	426
They die then in their duty, as will I	536	Faliero	4	589
Have I not done my duty? Peace, thou thing	537	Faliero	4	601
Duty to heaven and man! Yet speak; I cannot	542	Faliero	5	341
Signor! complete that which you deem your duty	544	Faliero	5	467
Before we can proceed upon that duty	544	Faliero	5	468
Back to my duty. But thou spakest of peril	558	Sardan	1	516
On duty. On what duty? On the state's	564	Sardan	2	152
Am upon duty. May we crave its purport	564	Sardan	2	155
Proclaim himself your subject by that duty	565	Sardan	2	211
Devotion was a duty, and I hated	583	Sardan	4	339
You have done your duty faithfully, and as	591	Sardan	5	245
My king, in going forth upon my duty	591	Sardan	5	286
Further than thus: I have transgress'd my duty	596	Foscari	1	90
Thine arm. Take mine, sir; 'tis my duty to	597	Foscari	1	149
Whose duty 'tis to do so. 'Tis their duty	599	Foscari	1	261
Of our stern duty, which prescribes the Question	600	Foscari	1	325
A duty, paramount to every duty	616	Foscari	4	116
Is thus a seraph's duty to be shown	665	Heaven		775
Your humble duty at the door? I dragg'd him	678	Werner	1	433
For duty (as you call it)--I did mine then	678	Werner	1	440
A part of the long debt of duty, not	688	Werner	2	347
To you for remedy--teach them their duty	691	Werner	2	549
Whose daily repetition marks your duty	701	Werner	3	379
As my first duty which shall be observed	704	Werner	3	589
Go to my father, and present my duty	705	Werner	4	91
I will now pay my duty to my mother	710	Werner	4	400
Too much of duty, and too little love	710	Werner	4	412
Rise to your duty	724	Deformed	1	159
Up to your duty	725	Deformed	1	183
Save that her duty both to man and God	750	Juan	1	215
But I must do my duty--how thou hast	822	Juan	4	367
Their duty was--for they were strong, and though	842	Juan	5	705
Though an unusual fit of love, or duty	863	Juan	6	727
His time, a corporal's duty to fulfil	873	Juan	7	412
And self would know what duty to attend	875	Juan	7	520
With her then, as in humble duty bound	907	Juan	9	673
And though the duty wax'd a little hard	910	Juan	10	170
Before May-day: perhaps, despite his duty	912	Juan	10	295
But ere they could perform this pious duty	920	Juan	11	121
What though she now and then may slip from duty	969	Juan	15	67
For t'other one who promises much duty	972	Juan	15	268
And Socrates, that model of all duty	978	Juan	15	679
In politics my duty is to show John	979	Juan	15	733

DUTY'S

Now so deaf to duty's prayer	187	French-A		26
Its desperate escape from duty's path	416	Island	1	60
Preside there, and that duty's mine: on thine	536	Faliero	4	555
That duty's mine. A woman's! 'Tis the soldier's	593	Sardan	5	371

DWARF

Afar, a dwarf buffoon stood telling tales	805	Juan	3	265

DWARFING

Beyond the dwarfing city's pale abortions	886	Juan	8	522

DWARFISH

Convention is the dwarfish demon styled	8	Harold	1	297

DWARFS

I love thee most in dwarfs! A mortal of	726	Deformed	1	296
And dwarfs and blacks, and such like things, that gain	810	Juan	3	541

DWARFS

Dwarfs, dancing girls, black eunuchs, and a poet	811	Juan	3	618
The dwarfs and dancing girls had all retired	815	Juan	3	898
Two little dwarfs, the least you could suppose	842	Juan	5	691

DWELL

Then loathed he in his native land to dwell	4	Harold	1	35
'My spouse and boys dwell near thy hall	6	Harold	1	166
Deep in yon cave Honorius long did dwell	7	Harold	1	259
Here didst thou dwell here schemes of pleasure plan	7	Harold	1	279
Is that a temple where a God may dwell	20	Harold	2	44
Where things that own not man's dominion dwell	23	Harold	2	219
Then the pirates of Parga that dwell by the waves	30	Harold	2	665
With airy images, and shapes which dwell	36	Harold	3	44
And motion of the soul which will not dwell	41	Harold	3	372
Through life to dwell delighted here	44	Harold	3	531
And loved to dwell in darkness and dismay	60	Harold	4	302
And where Alfonso bade his poet dwell	60	Harold	4	319
Wherein that image shall for ever dwell	63	Harold	4	475
Here didst thou dwell, in this enchanted cover	72	Harold	4	1054
Its columns strew the wilderness, and dwell	78	Harold	4	1373
Which is his last, if in your memories dwell	83	Harold	4	1669
And dwell an age on every kiss	88	To Ellen		4
How could I dwell upon its snows	90	To M.S.G.-A		6
Unworthy with such charms to dwell	102	Alva		74
They dwell in the tempests of dark Loch na Garr	117	Lachin		24
Yet with the retrospection loves to dwell	126	Recoll		345
Where smiling Youth delights to dwell	133	E. N. Long		31
What passion can dwell in the heart of a child	135	Highlander		10
Would hide my bosom where it loved to dwell	138	Harrow-B		22
Whose ever-slumbering inmates dwell	145	Adieu		9
Or dwell with delight on the hours that are flown	148	Farewell-A		19
But few that dwell beneath the sun	156	Lady-F		53
Since where thou art I may not dwell	158	Florence		43
And lead us where they dwell	158	Storm		20
The deep thoughts that dwell in that silence of heart	182	Music-A		4
The habitations of all things which dwell	189	Darkness		12
You are the fools, not I--for I did dwell	191	Churchill		39
Or do they in their silent cities dwell	192	Fragment-C		27
Still may thy spirit dwell on mine	209	Augusta-A		21
Equivocations, and the thoughts which dwell	213	Lady Byron		52
Mourn--where their God hath dwelt, the godless dwell	217	Weep-B		4
Even Satan's self with thee might dread to dwell	245	Bards		281
Bowles! in thy memory let this precept dwell	246	Bards		351
Can heavenly mercy dwell with earthly zeal	262	Hints		374
(For 'tis not yet decided where they dwell	297	Vision		821
First, and but rose to follow! Ye who dwell	300	Age		158
And, fix'd on heavenly thrones, should dwell	311	Giaour		64
Doth Leila there no longer dwell	314	Giaour		445
Around, within, thy heart shall dwell	317	Giaour		752
Should doom him there for aye to dwell	318	Giaour		821
To bid thee with another dwell	326	Abydos	1	197
Oh! who so dear with him could dwell	330	Abydos	2	112
Nor dwell upon thy name, whate'er the tale	356	Corsair	3	57
His thoughts on love and hate alternate dwell	357	Corsair	3	133
And on the words, however light, would dwell	371	Lara	1	370
And charity upon the hope would dwell	383	Lara	2	596
And there seem'd not a pulse in her veins to dwell	391	Corinth		615
In quiet we had learn'd to dwell	406	Chillon		388
To bear you hence to where a hope may dwell	428	Island	3	162
Steals to the deep wherein his parents dwell	430	Island	4	22
Did they with ocean's hidden sovereigns dwell	431	Island	4	99
Feel I not wroth with those who bade me dwell	437	Tasso		82
While thou, Ferrara! when no longer dwell	439	Tasso		222
Ye, who do compass earth about, and dwell	479	Manfred	1	31
And for ever shalt thou dwell	481	Manfred	1	210
Is mortal here; I dwell in my despair	487	Manfred	2	243
Who dwell within them. Would it were so, Count	491	Manfred	3	23
And those who dwell in them! for near or far	493	Manfred	3	192
And dwell the tuneless birds of night, amidst	495	Manfred	3	283
His faults are those that dwell in the high bosoms	510	Faliero	2	103
Not he alone, but all who dwell here, could	605	Foscari	2	274
His power. I dwell apart; but I am great	632	Cain	1	305
Throughout all space. Where should I dwell? Where are	635	Cain	1	543
And my conceptions. What are they which dwell	637	Cain	2	83
Of matter, which seem'd made for life to dwell on	639	Cain	2	215
That dust has shown me--let me dwell in shadows	640	Cain	2	314
But do not think to dwell here till thine hour	641	Cain	2	323
Dwell near it--'tis the phantasm of an ocean	642	Cain	2	391
Ye do not dwell together? No, we reign	644	Cain	2	580
Cain! get thee forth: we dwell no more together	653	Cain	3	444
To dwell with one who hath done this? I fear	653	Cain	3	462
Vacant in heaven to dwell in darkness here	660	Heaven		416
Alas! where shall they dwell	668	Heaven		990
Worth naming so, would dwell in such a carcass	724	Deformed	1	144
Their veil and petticoat--Alas! to dwell	774	Juan	2	46
Him whom she deem'd a habitant where dwell	821	Juan	4	283
By the sea-shore, whereon she loved to dwell	825	Juan	4	568

DWELL

'Twould not become myself to dwell upon	827 Juan	4	697
To quit her gentle partner, and to dwell	863 Juan	6	670
Upon the rest 'tis not worth while to dwell	896 Juan	9	13
To those who upon land or water dwell	916 Juan	10	550
For both commodities dwell by the Thames	924 Juan	11	379
I will not dwell upon ragouts or roasts	953 Juan	13	789
With sloth hath found it difficult to dwell	965 Juan	14	646
'Tis not my purpose on his views to dwell	973 Juan	15	301
Where all the dwellers of the earth must dwell	981 Juan	16	30

DWELLERS

Of their heroic dwellers;--dost thou flow	67 Harold	4	709
Creatures of clay--vain dwellers in the dust	222 Spirit		9
Have been beyond the dwellers of the earth	489 Manfred	2	429
That with the dwellers of the dark abodes	491 Manfred	3	36
Where all the dwellers of the earth must dwell	981 Juan	16	30

DWELLEST

Are few inhabitants. Where dwellest thou	635 Cain	1	542
With worms in clay? And what art thou who dwellest	637 Cain	2	85

DWELLING

Thy fairy dwelling is as lone as thou	7 Harold	1	282
Disclose the dwelling of the mountaineer	25 Harold	2	375
Survey'd the dwelling of this chief of power	28 Harold	2	498
narrow dwelling on the banks of Lubar	130 Calmar		69
Four gray stones mark the dwelling of Orla	131 Calmar		184
Still dwelling in my Highland cave	135 I Would		2
Without the wish of dwelling there	155 Lady-E		16
And set while thou wert dwelling there	188 On Star		18
The dreary dwelling where the State	196 Venice-A		15
Ay! 'Build him a dwelling!' let each give his mite	203 Avatar		73
Had wander'd from its dwelling, and her eyes	215 Dream		170
His lone but lovely dwelling on the steep	345 Corsair	1	509
Infest his dwelling, but forbear to slay	347 Corsair	2	20
He could not miss it: near his dwelling lay	376 Lara	2	103
Dwelling deep in my shut and silent heart	438 Tasso		113
'Twas fit our quiet dwelling to secure	469 Morgante		182
My dwelling is the shadow of the night	480 Manfred	1	108
The summer dwelling on its beauteous border	561 Sardan	1	686
To make their sovereign's dwelling what it was	590 Sardan	5	182
To make thyself fit for this dwelling, thou	640 Cain	2	317
Past my own dwelling, but that it is bankless	642 Cain	2	387
Have some allotted dwelling--as all things	644 Cain	2	574
Thy dwelling, or his dwelling. I could show thee	645 Cain	2	603
Your worst dwelling with their foot	736 Deformed	2	70
Form'd like an amphitheatre, each dwelling	870 Juan	7	183

DWELLING-PLACE

The latent grandeur of thy dwelling-place	21 Harold	2	86
Crown me with ivy from his dwelling-place	71 Harold	4	985
Oh that the Desert were my dwelling-place	81 Harold	4	1585
How pure, how dear their dwelling-place	216 She Walks		12
As if for Gods, a dwelling-place	310 Giaour		47
Within--thy dwelling-place how narrow	329 Abydos	2	50
The Laras' last and longest dwelling-place	366 Lara	1	40
In darkness found a dwelling-place	402 Chillon		16

DWELLINGS
(See also IDOL-DWELLINGS)

But in Man's dwellings he became a thing	37 Harold	3	127
Barbaric dwellings on their shatter'd site	61 Harold	4	398
All human dwellings left behind	411 Mazeppa		425
He who from out their fountain dwellings raised	486 Manfred	2	186
Together; but our dwellings are asunder	644 Cain	2	581
Its dwellings down, its tenants pass'd away	825 Juan	4	570

DWELLS

Wins as it wanders, dazzles where it dwells	3 To Ianthe		30
Here dwells the caloyer, nor rude is he	27 Harold	2	438
From gray but leafy walls, where Ruin greenly dwells	42 Harold	3	414
Who dwells and revels in thy glassy deeps	65 Harold	4	601
Nor worth nor beauty dwells from out the mind's	73 Harold	4	1102
Or the rapture which dwells on the first kiss of love	92 First Kiss		4
Unfaded your memory dwells in my breast	96 Harrow-A		26
Still dwells the Dardan spirit in the boy	107 Nisus		122
Again the master on his tenure dwells	121 Newstead-A		115
Dear are the days of youth! Age dwells	129 Calmar		1
dwells in his hall of air: he will rejoice in	130 Calmar		73
thy praise, Calmar! It dwells on the voice	131 Calmar		199
If laurell'd Fame but dwells with lies	132 L'Amitie		85
Where dwells the lady of my love, when she	198 Po		2
And never wilt! Love dwells not in our will	206 Love, Death		22
To make a Pandemonium where she dwells	208 Sketch		53
So close on each pathetic part he dwells	245 Bards		251
The doom he dreads, yet dwells upon	311 Giaour		84
'Deep in my soul that tender secret dwells	343 Corsair	1	347
I felt--I feel--love dwells with--with the free	354 Corsair	2	502
As dwells the gather'd lightning in its cloud	438 Tasso		114

DWELLS

The hell which in its entrails ever dwells	463 Dante	3	193
Which dwells but in the desert and sweeps o'er	493 Manfred	3	129
And without love where dwells security	559 Sardan	1	555
It dwells upon the soul, and soothes the soul	587 Sardan	5	19
Dwells tily mind rather upon that man's name	594 Sardan	5	458
But not all: show me where Jehovah dwells	644 Cain	2	571
Deposed where now the eagle's offspring dwells	662 Heaven		506
Fearless--because no feeling dwells in ice	747 Juan	Ded	119
The only hope of courage dwells	813 Juan	3	770
There many an envoy either dwelt or dwells	922 Juan	11	245

DWELT

Whilome in Albion's isle there dwelt a youth	3 Harold	1	10
Where dwelt of yore the Lusians' luckless queen	8 Harold	1	334
The scenes our earliest dreams have dwelt upon	33 Harold	2	833
Power dwelt amidst her passions; in proud state	42 Harold	3	425
And in its tenderer hour on that his bosom dwelt	43 Harold	3	477
Who in oppression's darkness caved had dwelt	48 Harold	3	785
With the wild world I dwelt in, is a thing	48 Harold	3	798
In meditation dwelt, with learning wrought	51 Harold	3	997
But where they dwelt, the vast and sumptuous pile	57 Harold	4	129
And the soft quiet hamlet where he dwelt	60 Harold	4	280
Which in my spirit dwelt is fluttering, faint, and low	83 Harold	4	1665
Now where Messapus dwelt they bend their way	109 Nisus		275
In Morven dwelt the chief, a beam of	129 Calmar		16
Together they dwelt in the cave of	129 Calmar		27
When cold is the beauty which dwelt in my soul	148 Farewell-A		15
A stranger has dwelt in the hall of my sire	149 Newstead-B		10
Strange power of healing dwelt within the touch	185 Julian		53
Happy were those who dwelt within the eye	189 Darkness		16
Where dwelt the wise and wondrous; but by thee	192 Sonnet-C		9
With thee how proudly Love hath dwelt	200 Ode-C		19
And the famine which dwelt on her freedomless crags	202 Avatar		11
Which do remember me of where I dwelt	211 Augusta-C		51
She dwelt, begirt with growing Infancy	215 Dream		130
Mourn--where their God hath dwelt, the godless dwell	217 Weep-B		4
Where dwelt the muses at their natal hour	253 Bards		868
Where Kosciusko dwelt, remembering yet	300 Age		159
Has dwelt the memory of Abencerrage	302 Age		329
When Leila dwelt in his Serai	314 Giaour		444
With thoughts that long in darkness dwelt	327 Abydos	1	330
Scarce beat that bosom where his image dwelt	345 Corsair	1	472
And ask'd if greater dwelt beyond the sky	368 Lara	1	126
And couldst say much; thou hast dwelt within the castle	494 Manfred	3	214
A warrior and a reveller; he dwelt not	494 Manfred	3	221
Within a bowshot. Where the Caesars dwelt	495 Manfred	3	282
That such things must be dwelt upon. Your patience	525 Faliero	3	464
Our race hath always dwelt apart from thine	664 Heaven		660
Without a welcome; there he long had dwelt	808 Juan	3	412
As one who ne'er had dwelt among the sick	825 Juan	4	531
Valour was his, and beauty dwelt with her	825 Juan	4	580
There many an envoy either dwelt or dwells	922 Juan	11	245

DWINDLE

To what would one day dwindle that which made	67 Harold	4	749
And works and words but dwindle to a date	258 Hints		92
Nor dwindle to the thing I now must be	520 Faliero	3	107
The dying embers dwindle in the grate	980 Juan	15	775

DWINDLED

And when the tumult dwindled to a calm	298 Vision		847
And thousands dwindled to a scanty band	379 Lara	2	311
Our dwindled band is now too few to strive	428 Island	3	160
Diminish'd, dwindled to a very speck	435 Island	4	386
Which, if it waned and dwindled, Earth may thank	454 Venice-B		117
Behold the tall pines dwindled as to shrubs	482 Manfred	1	276
Since the last years of war had dwindled into	685 Werner		126
As an old temple dwindled to a column	941 Juan	13	8

DWINDLES

You plan a vase--it dwindles to a pot	257 Hints		33

DWINDLING

Awaits us. Now the dwindling stars begin	701 Werner	3	434

DYE

Some native blood was seen thy streets to dye	18 Harold	1	878
As ever Spring yclad in grassy dye	27 Harold	2	481
A deep and mellow dye	218 I Saw		10
And dye it deep in the gore he has pour'd	229 Lads		10
And the purple of Ocean is deepest in dye	323 Abydos	1	13
And dye conjecture with a darker hue	377 Lara	2	126
Her brow was white and low, her cheek's pure dye	789 Juan	2	937
So much the present dye, she was remote	986 Juan	16	422

D'YE

'In heaven's name, Don Alfonso, what d'ye mean	764 Juan	1	1130
Who is the man you search for? how d'ye call	765 Juan	1	1228

DYED
(See also DEEP-DYED)

That dyed thy mountain streams with gothic gore	9 Harold	1	390
His garb with sanguine spots was dyed	317 Giaour		713
Who dyed Thermopylae with holy blood	433 Island	4	260
I have seen you dyed ere now, and deeply too	535 Faliero	4	491
Had dyed it with the headlong blood, whose race	792 Juan	2	1123
The henna should be deeply dyed to make	810 Juan	3	601
Dyed purple, none at present can tell how	981 Juan	16	78

DYEING

Whose postscripts prate of dyeing 'heroines blue	260 Hints		290

DYER

I should but bring disgrace upon the dyer	848 Juan	5	1068

DYERS

And take all colours--like the hands of dyers	813 Juan	3	792

DYES

Its steady dyes while all around is torn	66 Harold	4	644
Implore the pausing step, and with their dyes	72 Harold	4	1050
And Superstition's crimes, of various dyes	120 Newstead-A		27
One tint was of the sunbeam's dyes	188 On Star		25
And dark the mountain's once delightful dyes	268 Minerva		26
An earthly peacock's tail, with heavenly dyes	287 Vision		134
A Koran of illumined dyes	329 Abydos	2	73
And dark the mountain's once delightful dyes	355 Corsair	3	26
Of arms (in the East all arm)--and various dyes	805 Juan	3	215
Dyes with his morning light,--and would conceal	810 Juan	3	579
A vein had burst, and her sweet lips' pure dyes	823 Juan	4	465
Or said her cheeks assumed the deepest dyes	848 Juan	5	1067

DYING
(See also EVER-DYING, NEVER-DYING)

Around me, and a dying Glory smiles	55 Harold	4	6
Folding his robe in dying dignity	68 Harold	4	779
Thy trumpet voice, though broken now and dying	69 Harold	4	876
Of dying thunder on the distant wind	70 Harold	4	933
Though none, like thee, his dying hour will cheer	85 Epitaph		21
The dying chords are strung anew	88 Anacreon-A		11
A dying father's bitter curse	105 Alva		315
Her dying hours with pious conduct bless	108 Nisus		191
Dying, revenged the fate of him he loved	110 Nisus		398
Though ill success obscured his dying hour	114 Death-A		12
I sought not my home till the day's dying glory	117 Lachin		13
While dying groans their painful requiem sound	120 Newstead-A		78
The dying stag seeks refuge in the Lake	121 Newstead-A		127
steps are to the host of Lochlin. The dying	130 Calmar		98
Extinguish'd with the dying embers	134 E. N. Long		86
Oft have I thought, 'twould soothe my dying hour	138 Harrow-B		19
In dying strains may float	145 Adieu		40
Extinguish'd with the dying embers	148 A Fan		12
Wave gently o'er my dying bed	166 Euthanasia		4
A child of Famine dying	176 Devil's Dr		74
When their dying shout was heard	187 French-A		15
The dying embers of an altar-place	189 Darkness		58
Ends not in dying	199 Stanzas-B		10
And hope but shed a dying spark	209 Augusta-A		3
A dying person in compunction	231 Doctor		75
As when the dying vicar will not die	267 Hints		778
The dying ask revenge in vain	316 Giaour		578
Wrongs avenged, and Moslem dying	318 Giaour		825
Despair upon his dying face	321 Giaour		1094
Who shrived him on his dying day	323 Giaour		1332
Do all but close thy dying eye	328 Abydos	1	404
Would doom him ever dying--ne'er to die	351 Corsair	2	283
Day glimmers on the dying and the dead	380 Lara	2	394
His dying tones are in that other tongue	381 Lara	2	444
His words, his looks, his dying grasp recall	384 Lara	2	615
And saw the Spartan smile in dying	388 Corinth		389
But he better could brook to behold the dying	389 Corinth		481
In the midst of the dying and the dead	390 Corinth		582
So seen by the dying lamp's fitful light	391 Corinth		622
Scorns to yield a groan in dying	393 Corinth		842
Nor on his lips one dying sob	394 Corinth		890
Dying as their father died	402 Chillon		23
Nor reach his dying hand--nor dead	404 Chillon		146
Dying, to feel the same again	412 Mazeppa		564
The dying on the dead	413 Mazeppa		715
To keep, some days, the dying from the dead	416 Island	1	90
No dying night-breeze, harping o'er the hill	424 Island	2	419
Took their last farewell of the dying sound	434 Island	4	294
And with a dying glance upbraid the sky	439 Tasso		186
And, dying in despondency, bequeath	462 Dante	3	152
A bodiless enjoyment--born and dying	482 Manfred	1	316
The dying Roman thrust him back, and said	492 Manfred	3	94
The dying Roman said, ''twas but a name	509 Faliero	2	59
Freedom of speech accorded to the dying	539 Faliero	5	113
Spoken or written of our dying words	539 Faliero	5	121
And dying men's are things which long outlive	542 Faliero	5	291
One sovereign only died, and one is dying	548 Faliero	5	715
Like to the dying day on Caucasus	552 Sardan	1	90
Its hues of dying glory. Yet what is	562 Sardan	2	33

DYING

The name of him, who, dying like a king	582 Sardan	4	292
Receive a token from your dying brother	589 Sardan	5	137
Dead. And Altada? Dying. Pania? Sfero?	589 Sardan	5	139
Some water! Ah, he is dying! Now, I'm ready	617 Foscari	4	185
Whose tenants dying, while their world is falling	656 Heaven		88
Born ere this dying world? They come like clouds	659 Heaven		339
Hath wound itself around the dying air	669 Heaven		1077
Lay dying, and the stranger dash'd aside	701 Werner	3	382
No more, then? I look'd, as a dying soldier	715 Werner	5	120
Dying intestate, Juan was sole heir	751 Juan	1	289
Two things for dying people quite bewildering	779 Juan	2	344
Men, even when dying, dislike inanition	779 Juan	2	365
Into his dying child's mouth--but in vain	785 Juan	2	712
A stranger' dying, with so white a skin	790 Juan	2	1032
And thus like to an angel o'er the dying	792 Juan	2	1145
A purple hectic play'd like dying day	792 Juan	2	1170
Who dying on the coast of Ithaca	803 Juan	3	141
Perhaps, than even the mental pangs of dying	807 Juan	3	404
Or the faint dying day-hymn stole aloft	815 Juan	3	910
Seeming to weep the dying day's decay	816 Juan	3	958
I cried upon my first wife's dying day	833 Juan	5	151
But all his great preparatives for dying	849 Juan	5	1127
Amidst some groaning thousands dying near	879 Juan	8	83
Of dead and dying thousands,--sometimes gaining	880 Juan	8	154
And so, when all his corps were dead or dying	882 Juan	8	281
A dying Moslem, who had felt the foot	889 Juan	8	665
The dying man cried, 'Hold! I've got my gruel	920 Juan	11	122
Those bright moths fluttering round a dying flame	939 Juan	12	572
Is musical--a dying accent driven	949 Juan	13	500
The dying embers dwindle in the grate	980 Juan	15	775
Than dying tapers--and the peeping moon	981 Juan	16	64

DYKE

He there builds up a formidable dyke	814 Juan	3	849

DYNASTIES

Marrying fools, restoring dynasties	488 Manfred	2	361

DYNASTY

To his unconquerable dynasty	239 Conquest		4
During the dynasty of Dandies, now	447 Beppo		474

E

E--- is a wife, and C--- a mother	133 E. N. Long		64

EACH

I turn'd to thee, to thousands, of whom each	40 Harold	3	271
Yet on he mouths--ten minutes--tedious each	268 Hints		809
Wondering they turn, abash'd, while each to each	340 Corsair	1	147
Alas! too like in confidence are each	373 Lara	1	506
And each turn comforter to each	403 Chillon		59
The suit he thought most suitable to each	840 Juan	5	537

EAGER

Stands in the centre, eager to invade	15 Harold	1	740
And here the buzz of eager nations ran	76 Harold	4	1243
Eager to gild his arms with hostile blood	105 Nisus		2
Yet, ere from hence our eager steps depart	107 Nisus		175
With eager haste they court the lord of power	112 Examination		63
Still simpering on with eager haste	153 Friend-A		62
For notice eager, pass in long review	243 Bards		144
These after husbands wing their eager flight	250 Bards		666
As eager for a plaudit as a realm	304 Age		436
But his glance follow'd far with eager eye	361 Corsair	3	387
Swam high, as eager of the coming ray	415 Island	1	10
Eager to hope, but not less firm to bear	421 Island	2	177
Eager with anger, their strong arms made way	433 Island	4	239
They are array'd, and eager for the signal	533 Faliero	4	351
Eager to keep it worthy of our Lord	666 Heaven		794
Than paid myself, had I been eager of	691 Werner	2	560
Your mother will be eager to receive you	708 Werner	4	276
As eager to anticipate their grave	780 Juan	2	412
With eager eyes, and light but hurried tread	861 Juan	6	571
How eager all the earth is for the blow	915 Juan	10	531
Full many an eager gentleman oft rues	927 Juan	11	557
Thus on the mob all statesmen are as eager	990 Juan	16	655
But Juan, eager now the truth to pierce	996 Juan	16	995

EAGERLY

As eagerly the barr'd-up bird will beat	37 Harold	3	132
I saw you eye it eagerly, and him	719 Werner	5	397
And yet the rest rush'd eagerly--no wonder	891 Juan	8	821

EAGERNESS

And watch'd with eagerness each throb that drew	788 Juan	2	911

EAGLE

Here roams the wolf, the eagle whets his beak	25 Harold	2	376
In 'pride of place' here last the eagle flew	38 Harold	3	158
arms. Oscar shakes the spear. The eagle	131 Calmar		149
Then the Eagle, whose gaze in that moment was blasted	186 Napoleon		15

EAGLE

With eagle pinion soaring to the skies	244	Bards	201
So the struck eagle, stretch'd upon the plain	253	Bards	841
Smile--for the fetter'd eagle breaks his chain	299	Age	87
Proud Wellington, with eagle beak so curl'd	305	Age	534
The eagle left his rocky nest	396	Corinth	1074
The eagle rode the rising blast	406	Chillon	353
Disturb'd him like the eagle in her nest	423	Island	2	309
Even as the eagle overlooks his prey	535	Faliero	4	484
Fool! the high eagle flies at nobler game	536	Faliero	4	590
Their hopes is breathed on, jealous as the eagle	544	Faliero	5	431
Of cloud-fenced Caucasus, where the eagle sits	570	Sardan	2	568
The eagle loves. Except his prey, I hope	707	Werner	4	224
The eagle soars alone; the gull and crow	820	Juan	4	223
'The prison'd eagle will not pair, nor I	847	Juan	5	1007
The earth, as scarce the eagle in the broad	917	Juan	10	619

EAGLES

They were not eagles, nourish'd with the day	48	Harold	3	786
Or do ye find at length, like eagles, some high nest	50	Harold	3	904
And on Parnassus seen the eagles fly	66	Harold	4	659
Of hoarded vengeance till thine eagles flew	67	Harold	4	743
Who would have tamed his eagles down to flee	68	Harold	4	812
As to young eagles being free	403	Chillon	81
While eagles scarce build higher than the crest	422	Island	2	256
In spots where eagles might have chosen to build	434	Island	4	312
Nets are for thrushes, eagles are not caught so	697	Werner	3	163

EAGLE'S

Of the eagle's burning crest	187	Ode-B	63
Sigh to behold the eagle's lofty rage	299	Age	55
But few shall soar upon that eagle's wing	461	Dante	3	70
And look in the sun's face with eagle's gaze	461	Dante	3	71
With shaft-heads feather'd from the eagle's wing	579	Sardan	4	90
Deposed where now the eagle's offspring dwells	662	Heaven	506
As was the eagle's nestling once within	669	Heaven	1082
The eagle's beak between those eyes which ne'er	725	Deformed	1	186
And drooping like an eagle's with clipt pinion	913	Juan	10	350

EAGLE-SPIRIT

And eagle-spirit of a Child of Song	436	Tasso	2

EAGLET

That saw'st the unfledged eaglet chip his shell	300	Age	134

EAGLETS

Thy prey, and gorge thine eaglets; thou art gone	482	Manfred	1	294

EAR

(See also DOG'S-EAR, LONG-EAR'D)

And vex'd with mirth the drowsy ear of Night	3	Harold	1	13
When deem'd he no strange ear was listening	5	Harold	1	112
'Mid many things most new to ear and eye	29	Harold	2	568
And caught its tone with Death's prophetic ear	38	Harold	3	202
Of flowers yet fresh with childhood; on the ear	48	Harold	3	812
And music meets not always now the ear	55	Harold	4	22
All treasures, all delights, that eye or ear	71	Harold	4	971
Tuned to her ear his grateful strain	87	Catullus	12
Rolls deeply on the list'ning ear	96	Granta	72
The din of arms came to the ear of Fingal	131	Calmar	145
Blest by the tongues that charm'd my youthful ear	138	Harrow-B	31
To charm her ear while some remains	150	Song	7
A knell to mine ear	151	When We	18
'Tis silent all!--but on my ear	166	Away	17
The sacred song that on mine ear	173	Mrs. Lamb	1
And so soft to his ear was the cry of despair	176	Devil's Dr	35
But the softest note that soothed his ear	176	Devil's Dr	64
Which even his ear found faults in	179	Devil's Dr	216
As may disgust the ear of kings	195	Ballad-A	67
With longing breast and undeluded ear	208	Sketch	20
No ear so dull, no soul so cold	216	The Harp	8
Its melting murmurs o'er mine ear	218	Soul-B	4
Each day a trumpet soundeth in mine ear	240	Cephalonia	5
The eye delighted, but fatigued the ear	254	Bards	896
To stun the public ear--at least with prose	256	Bards	1036
(Give ear, my friend, for thou hast been a scribe	257	Hints	40
What soothes the many-headed monster's ear	259	Hints	214
The ear sustains what shocks the timid eye	260	Hints	269
Hence the pert shopkeeper, whose throbbing ear	261	Hints	307
Led all wild beasts but women by the ear	266	Hints	664
Yet Pallas pluck'd each premier by the ear	271	Minerva	247
It is--my gentle public, lend thine ear	295	Vision	638
A new Cambyses thundering in their ear	300	Age	144
That sound that crashes in the tyrant's ear	300	Age	166
A Gallic senate hath more tongue than ear	304	Age	491
And must ye fall with every ear of grain	306	Age	576
And long upon my startled ear	312	Giaour	206
But not a voice mine ear to greet	313	Giaour	353
Its echoes on the throbbing ear	316	Giaour	638
Nor ear can hear nor tongue can tell	317	Giaour	753
Deep in whose darkly boding ear	321	Giaour	1077
Confessor! to thy secret ear	323	Giaour	1320
At least that met old Giaffir's ear	324	Abydos	1	106
Like Houris' hymn it meets mine ear	325	Abydos	1	147

EAR

For Selim's ear his sweetest song	327	Abydos	1	290
His ear but rang with Hero's song	329	Abydos	2	16
But now too long I've held thine ear	334	Abydos	2	478
The loud Wul-wulleh warn his distant ear	335	Abydos	2	627
His ear with tidings he must quickly meet	340	Corsair	1	136
Without thine ear to listen to my lay	343	Corsair	1	367
Shall soothe or lull--or, should it vex thine ear	344	Corsair	1	438
But sudden sunk; for on his ear the cry	350	Corsair	2	199
To trust their absent echoes in his ear	356	Corsair	3	92
I have a counsel for thy gentler ear	358	Corsair	3	177
When every voice that grated on his ear	358	Corsair	3	214
And now its dashing echo'd on his ear	359	Corsair	3	256
That frantic echo burst the sleeping ear	369	Lara	1	206
And such they were, and meant to meet an ear	369	Lara	1	233
Till louder accents rung on Lara's ear	372	Lara	1	418
Thy heart must answer, though thine ear would shun	372	Lara	1	438
Which it befits Count Lara's ear to know	372	Lara	1	468
Awake their absent echoes in his ear	373	Lara	1	523
For then, ear, eyes, and heart would all awake	374	Lara	1	591
To lend at thy demand a listening ear	375	Lara	2	44
It struck even the besieger's ear	387	Corinth	276
Make music to the lonely ear	396	Parisina	6
Though her ear expects as soft a tale	396	Parisina	22
And Azo's tortured heart and ear	397	Parisina	130
His father's ear; the silent sire	399	Parisina	232
And not an ear but felt as wounded	399	Parisina	320
Was banish'd from each lip and ear	401	Parisina	506
The sweetest song ear ever heard	405	Chillon	254
My ear with uncouth noises rang	412	Mazeppa	575
Hath greater power o'er each true heart and ear	420	Island	2	91
Chains in his eye, and menace in his ear	430	Island	4	62
Replied Orlando, 'So much to your ear	471	Morgante	333
Which pierced a pig precisely in the ear	473	Morgante	498
The merest word that ever fool'd the ear	491	Manfred	3	11
That have cried shame to every ear in Venice	506	Faliero	1	419
To lend a patient ear. Say on. Not thou	506	Faliero	1	488
For your ear only. Prince, I take my leave	581	Sardan	4	195
Worship the word which strikes their ear, and deem	636	Cain	2	10
More to the mind than thunder to the ear	662	Heaven	543
To weary Heaven's ear with thy selfish plaint	667	Heaven	956
To triple Time in the son's ear. I'm cold	701	Werner	3	399
Distinct and keener far upon my ear	715	Werner	5	133
From delicacy to Don Juan's ear	768	Juan	1	1407
Being no Grecian; but he had an ear	793	Juan	2	1202
Meantime Apollo plucks me by the ear	817	Juan	4	55
It has a strange quick jar upon the ear	821	Juan	4	321
The ear becomes more Irish, and less nice	821	Juan	4	328
That broke for nothing on their sleeping ear	862	Juan	6	628
Thine ear, if it should reach--and now rhymes wander	863	Juan	6	739
He scratch'd his ear, the infallible resource	864	Juan	6	799
It seems, has got an ear as well as trumpet	869	Juan	7	120
How sweetly on the sun'd echoes sound	878	Juan	8	37
The ear far more than thunder; for Heaven's flashes	879	Juan	8	47
And shriek for water into a deaf ear	879	Juan	8	85
Upon the ear, and sounds of horror chime	885	Juan	8	462
And yet was what you are: from ear to ear	898	Juan	9	90
To Balaam, and from tongue to ear o'erflows	933	Juan	12	206
That--but my chaster ear will not receive	935	Juan	12	340
And have, or had, an ear that served me prettily	939	Juan	12	600
And then he had an ear for music's sound	960	Juan	14	309
Of deeds and days when they had fill'd the ear	974	Juan	15	365
Came over Juan's ear, which throbb'd, alas	995	Juan	16	957

EARL

To change Earl Osmond's negro to a snake	260	Hints	286
The Earl of--Asterisk, and Lady--Blank	276	Waltz	203
Because the neighbouring Scotch Earl of Giftgabbit	989	Juan	16	604

EARLIER

And with the ills of Eld mine earlier years alloy'd	35	Harold	2	926
Bright are the deeds thine earlier sires display	139	Dorset	66
Fair didst thou shine upon my earlier hours	139	Ossian-A	36
But that was in the earlier ages	233	Nihil	12
There lurk his earlier lays; but soon, hot-press'd	266	Hints	727
'In earlier days, and calmer hours	322	Giaour	1218
In happier mood and earlier time	386	Corinth	187
Six summers, in my earlier age	408	Mazeppa	130
My sister Zillah sings an earlier hymn	630	Cain	1	183
Before the human orison the earlier	662	Heaven	556
Till they were exiled from their earlier bowers	749	Juan	1	140
Who in the earlier ages raised a bustle	752	Juan	1	323
A little earlier than the waning moon	955	Juan	13	884
Which charm most people in their earlier day	974	Juan	15	419

EARLIEST

Oh, known the earliest, and esteem'd the most	19	Harold	1	936
The scenes our earliest dreams have dwelt upon	33	Harold	2	833

EARLIEST

Even in its earliest nurture; what subdued	43	Harold	3	481
Of moody texture from their earliest day	60	Harold	4	301
Haunted by holy Love--the earliest oracle	73	Harold	4	1062
Must fall the earliest prey	167	Dead		38
An only infant's earliest governess	208	Sketch		12
The earliest--even the only paths for me	212	Augusta-C		92
Their leaves, the earliest of the year	218	Bloom		4
From simple childhood's earliest hour	328	Abydos	1	421
Blooming as Aden in its earliest hour	333	Abydos	2	409
And, with to-morrow's earliest dawn	386	Corinth		231
Those best and earliest lyres of harmony	424	Island	2	421
Thou sole pure seraph of my earliest love	456	Dante	1	20
Thou earliest minister of the Almighty	493	Manfred	3	182
And then the daughter of my earliest friend	513	Faliero	2	330
Yon earliest, and the brightest, which so quivers	562	Sardan	2	64
Old hunter of the earliest brutes! and ye	578	Sardan	4	28
So far--let's in. The earliest are most welcome	616	Foscari	4	97
Their earliest fault in fable, and attribute	631	Cain	1	233
And earliest embraces of earth's parents	643	Cain	2	476
Whate'er it now be); and Rome's earliest cement	731	Deformed	1	651
Of old the angels of her earliest sex	741	Deformed	2	414
The lisp of children, and their earliest words	762	Juan	1	984
This was Don Juan's earliest scrape; but whether	771	Juan	1	1585
Like Titus' youth, and Caesar's earliest acts	814	Juan	3	827
Lay at her heart, whose earliest beat still true	824	Juan	4	494
Don Juan now saw Albion's earliest beauties	916	Juan	10	545
That poets were so from their earliest date	950	Juan	13	589
The sea-coal fires the 'earliest of the year	950	Juan	13	614
The earliest knowledge from the tree so knowing	965	Juan	14	619
Earliest to rise, and last to quit the search	991	Juan	16	684

EARLS

Present, Lords A. B. C.'--Earls, dukes, by name	947	Juan	13	426
To silken rows of gay and garter'd earls	949	Juan	13	538

EARL'S

A surgeon's statement and an earl's harangues	299	Age		64

EARLY

His early youth misspent in maddest whim	8	Harold	1	322
If, kindly cruel, early Hope is crost	24	Harold	2	313
Awoke the jocund birds to early song	43	Harold	3	462
And hands which offer early flowers	43	Harold	3	507
Honour to Marceau! o'er whose early tomb	44	Harold	3	541
Not vainly did the early Persian make	49	Harold	3	851
Where early Love his Psyche's zone unbound	51	Harold	3	972
Watering the heart whose early flowers have died	56	Harold	4	44
By the impatience of my early thought	66	Harold	4	680
Heaven gives its favourites--early death; yet shed	70	Harold	4	915
Are clothed with early blossoms, through the grass	72	Harold	4	1046
Dorset! whose early steps with mine have stray'd	93	Dorset		1
Turn to the few in Ida's early throng	93	Dorset		27
The recollection of our early race	94	Dorset		104
Goes late to bed, yet early rises	95	Granta		32
Allan had early learn'd control	102	Alva		67
'Stand, stragglers! stand! why early thus in arms	109	Nisus		308
All, all was mine,--his early fate suspend	110	Nisus		371
Of early science, future fame the source	122	Recoll		38
Each early boyish friend, or youthful foe	123	Recoll		52
Soon must her early song for ever cease	123	Recoll		97
The dear preceptor of my early days	123	Recoll		108
While thus our souls with early passions swell	124	Recoll		147
And here my name, and many an early friend's	124	Recoll		163
Some old companion of my early race	124	Recoll		194
Made, by a parent's early loss, my own	125	Recoll		224
Oh! in the promise of thy early youth	125	Recoll		247
To soothe a youthful rival's early pride	126	Recoll		337
These young effusions of my early days	127	Recoll		358
In friendship I early was taught to believe	129	Becher-A		26
My early vows were paid	131	L'Amitie		32
And hearts with early rapture swell	133	E. N. Long		32
To thee these early faults I owe	134	Lady-D		5
This cheek now pale from early riot	134	Lady-D		30
Had friends--my early friends are fled	135	I Would		26
Deplored by those in early days allied	138	Harrow-B		33
Adieu, thou Hill! where early joy	145	Adieu		1
Since early affection and love are o'ercast	149	Farewell-A		34
For still in thy bosom are life's early seeds	149	Newstead-B		23
So frail is early friendship's reign	153	Friend-A		10
Away! away! my early dream	155	Happy		33
To think of every early scene	156	Lady-F		43
And why that early love was crost	156	Lady-F		51
Teach me--too early taught by thee	165	Thyrza		53
And early valour, glowing, find	184	Parker		23
When the day's promise heralds early Spring	185	Julian		58
Oh! early in the balance weigh'd	185	Belshaz-A		17
When the glow of early thought declines in feeling's dull decay	185	Music-B		2
From thence if thou an early grave hadst found	206	Love, Death		12
If early habits--those false links, which bind	208	Sketch		43
She was my early friend, and now shall be	212	Augusta-C		87
The early truth, which was thy proper praise	213	Lady Byron		48
May no rude hand disturb their early sleep	247	Bards		425

EARLY

The puny schoolboy and his early lay	251	Bards		727
Launch'd into life, extinct his early fire	260	Hints		243
Like early unrequited Love	336	Abydos	2	669
Since far too early and too well obey'd	349	Corsair	2	163
Betray'd too early, and beguiled too long	365	Corsair	3	663
The pride, but not the fire, of early days	367	Lara	1	69
His early dreams of good outstripp'd the truth	370	Lara	1	323
Blest are the early hearts and gentle hands	371	Lara	1	391
And, 'stead of trousers (ah! too early torn	425	Island	1	480
In these my early strength exulted; or	486	Manfred	2	163
Of early nature, and the vigorous race	493	Manfred	3	175
Upon his early, tried, and trusted friend	510	Faliero	2	82
In early life its foe, but, in his manhood	619	Foscari	4	307
'Twould be destroy'd so early. But why war	641	Cain	2	352
The fruits of the earth, the early beautiful	647	Cain	3	105
A dreary, and an early doom, my brother	654	Cain	3	545
Of early delicacy render more	672	Werner	1	40
Hath changed no atom of his early nature	682	Werner	1	729
You are early, my sweet cousin! Not too early	706	Werner	4	151
The stars receding early to our wish	710	Werner	4	409
Life early, and am what the world has made me	716	Werner	5	223
Their feast of peace was early for the times	721	Werner	5	540
The first-born child of the early sun	742	Deformed	3	8
And the early flowers are flinging	742	Deformed	3	70
For early stomachs, to prove wholesome food	752	Juan	1	338
At least 'twas rather early to begin	767	Juan	1	1332
But he died early; and when he was gone	785	Juan	2	692
And woke her maid so early that she grumbled	791	Juan	2	1101
Or by one's early valet's cursed knock	793	Juan	2	1213
And every day by daybreak--rather early	795	Juan	2	1337
Such kisses as belong to early days	797	Juan	2	1484
The old archer's shafts, perhaps the early grave	817	Juan	4	95
For no one, save in very early youth	854	Juan	6	123
Partake of mine; but by to-morrow early	858	Juan	6	367
In early youth, to turn a lady's maid	860	Juan	6	492
They cannot quench young feelings fresh and early	909	Juan	10	150
Of doors 'gainst duns, and to an early dinner	922	Juan	11	228
Of early life; but this is a new land	932	Juan	12	183
(Such, early traveller! is the truth thou learnest	938	Juan	12	510
They separated at an early hour	955	Juan	13	881
But Juan had been early taught to range	959	Juan	14	253
To early risers after a long chase	960	Juan	14	282
Early in years, and yet more infantine	973	Juan	15	353
Some wondering 'twas so early, some so late	987	Juan	16	484

EARN

To earn mild virtue's vain desire, repose	417	Island	1	114
Black with a double treason, now will earn	537	Faliero	4	646
Thou mightst have earn'd thy bread, as thousands earn it	673	Werner	1	139
I will not pardon you, unless you earn it	707	Werner	4	207
He must his laurels separately earn	880	Juan	8	131
Were hardly rude enough to earn their pay	923	Juan	11	320

EARN'D

And see how dearly earn'd Torquato's fame	60	Harold	4	318
Fame, fame is cheaply earn'd by fleeting breath	106	Nisus		51
And here we earn's the conquest dearly bought	124	Recoll		144
And I have earn'd those tortures well	221	Mariamne		23
Where rustics earn'd, and now may beg, their bread	260	Hints		304
Save hers who earn'd it with the natives' gore	303	Age		349
Was earn'd--yet much too worthless for thy hate	357	Corsair	3	144
Well have I earn'd--nor here alone--the meed	359	Corsair	3	286
He earn'd beneath a Moslem name	387	Corinth		317
To see again, a sight they dearly earn'd	416	Island	1	50
The healthy slumber earn'd by sportive toils	422	Island	2	253
To peace and pleasure, perilously earn'd	435	Island	4	418
Rights cheaply earn'd with blood.--Still, still, for ever	455	Venice-B		148
We!--We!--no matter--you have earn'd the right	519	Faliero	3	66
Thou hast done a worthy deed, and earn'd the price	537	Faliero	4	602
Earn'd by the guilty; this I'll not pronounce ye	566	Sardan	2	280
Thou mightst have earn'd thy bread, as thousands earn it	673	Werner	1	139
I've earn'd them; but might have earn'd more from others	692	Werner	2	579
There was no doubt he earn'd his laureate pension	811	Juan	3	640
And, to say truth, it had been fairly earn'd	923	Juan	11	312
And not a joke he cut but earn'd its praise	991	Juan	16	699

EARNEST

Were added after, to the earnest prayer	417	Island	1	93
In earnest councils--we will not be least so	616	Foscari	4	98
With such an earnest brow, upon thy tablets	626	Foscari	5	368
But Abel's earnest prayer has wrought upon me	632	Cain	1	325
A wife makes or takes love in upright earnest	937	Juan	12	508

EARNESTLY

He look'd upon it earnestly	391	Corinth		663
To trust, save to yourself; most earnestly	529	Faliero	4	118

EARNESTNESS

Her earnestness would ne'er have made an end   794 Juan 2 1284

EARNING

In fact and fairness are his earning, Charles   467 Morgante   104

EARNINGS

From their hard earnings, has inflamed them
  further   507 Faliero 1 501

EARS

Tell not the deed to blushing Europe's ears   21 Harold 2 112
And Evan's, Donald's fame rings in each
  clansman's ears   39 Harold 3 234
Its knell in princely ears till the o'erstung   80 Harold 4 1535
My ears with tingling echoes ring   87 Ad Lesbiam   19
What ne'er was meant for other ears   146 Vain Lady   2
Detect with fingers, in default of ears   262 Hints   436
Adds an ell growth to his egregious ears   266 Hints   736
When I cut ears off, I had cut him down   287 Vision   150
The angels stopp'd their ears and plied their
  pinions   297 Vision   818
And red to pale, as through her ears   326 Abydos 1 223
Dear--as his native song to Exile's ears   333 Abydos 2 406
And unto ears as rugged seem'd a song   338 Corsair 1 46
The clang of tumult vibrate on his ears   345 Corsair 1 522
To other ears that death became thee well   359 Corsair 3 229
Now, creaking in the ears of those who may   454 Venice-B   119
Where late my ears rung with the damned cries   456 Dante 1 7
Through all the music ringing in my ears   528 Faliero 4 11
But walls have ears--nay, more, they have
  tongues; and if   542 Faliero 5 281
Never was word yet rung so in my ears   552 Sardan 1 137
To spare mine ears the truth. My own slight
  guard   572 Sardan 3 83
Sound impious in mine ears. Then leave me!
  Never   647 Cain 3 94
Into my ears this truth--'Thou liv'st for ever   656 Heaven   114
Shaking their dripping ears upon the shore   678 Werner 1 438
And dubious notice of your eyes and ears   730 Deformed 1 583
Together by the ears and hearts! I have not   739 Deformed 2 268
They fear'd no eyes nor ears on that lone beach   798 Juan 2 1505
A melody which made him doubt his ears   805 Juan 3 221
Rang in her sad ears like a mermaid's song   820 Juan 4 271
About his ears, and nathless would not bend   844 Juan 5 826
Or wonder'd at her ears without a ring   856 Juan 6 276
Her cheek turn'd ashes, ears rung, brain whirl'd
  round   865 Juan 6 837
The women with their hair about their ears   876 Juan 7 547
All ears, though long; all ages, though so short   877 Juan 7 626
Like the death-watch, within our ears the ills   879 Juan 8 94
Because it might not solace 'ears polite   890 Juan 8 742
And all lips were applied unto all ears   906 Juan 9 618
And intellect, that neither eyes nor ears   951 Juan 13 676
The scanty but right-well thresh'd ears of truth   953 Juan 13 762
To introduce a bon-mot head and ears   955 Juan 13 868
I have brought this world about my ears, and eke   956 Juan 14 73
There's music in all things, if men had ears   969 Juan 15 39
I sometimes almost think that eyes have ears   977 Juan 15 601
To soothe our ears, lest Italy should fail   986 Juan 16 408
No longer ready ears and short-hand pens   991 Juan 16 708

EARSHOT

This much is sure, that, out of earshot, things   977 Juan 15 602

EARTH
(See also UNDER-EARTH)

Love's image upon earth without his wing   3 To Ianthe   13
Since shamed full oft by later lyres on earth   3 Harold 1 3
But not my mother Earth   5 Harold 1 129
Gaul's locust host, and earth from fellest foemen
  purge   6 Harold 1 215
In hope to merit Heaven by making earth a Hell   7 Harold 1 260
Vain are the pleasaunces on earth supplied   7 Harold 1 286
Here Folly dash'd to earth the victor's plume   8 Harold 1 301
Or call with truth one span of earth their own   11 Harold 1 457
Bound to the earth, he lifts his eye to heaven   20 Harold 2 28
On earth no more, but mingled with the skies   20 Harold 2 33
Commingling slowly with heroic earth   33 Harold 2 806
No earth of thine is lost in vulgar mould   33 Harold 2 829
And gaze complacent on congenial earth   34 Harold 2 867
And be alone on earth, as I am now   35 Harold 2 921
Soul of my thought! with whom I traverse earth   36 Harold 3 51
As their own beams; and earth, and earth-born jars   37 Harold 3 120
And foam in fetters;--but is Earth more free   38 Harold 3 164
The earth is cover'd thick with other clay   39 Harold 3 250
Conqueror and captive of the earth art thou   40 Harold 3 325
For sceptred cynics earth were far too wide a den   41 Harold 3 369
And far beneath the earth and ocean spread   42 Harold 3 402
Earth paved like Heaven; and to seem such to me   43 Harold 3 449
Nor could on earth a spot be found   44 Harold 3 532
Is to the mellow Earth as Autumn to the year   44 Harold 3 571
How Earth may pierce to Heaven, yet leave vain
  man below   45 Harold 3 598

EARTH

And names that must not wither, though the earth   45 Harold 3 636
And love Earth only for its earthly sake   46 Harold 3 672
And what behind it lay, all earth shall view   48 Harold 3 773
All heaven and earth are still--though not in
  sleep   49 Harold 3 833
All heaven and earth are still. From the high
  host   49 Harold 3 836
With Nature's realms of worship, earth and air   49 Harold 3 858
And the big rain comes dancing to the earth   49 Harold 3 874
And living as if earth contain'd no tomb   50 Harold 3 917
The earth to her embrace compels the powers of air   52 Harold 3 1021
The revel of the earth, the masque of Italy   55 Harold 4 27
And blood she bore o'er subject earth and sea   57 Harold 4 121
The beautiful, the brave--the lords of earth and
  sea   59 Harold 4 225
Making the sun like blood, the earth a tomb   60 Harold 4 305
Of earth recoils upon us;--let it go   63 Harold 4 465
Here Machiavelli's earth return'd to whence it
  rose   63 Harold 4 486
Did they not to her breast their filial earth
  intrust   63 Harold 4 504
Boccaccio to his parent earth bequeath'd   63 Harold 4 514
The Earth to them was as a rolling bark   64 Harold 4 568
Made the earth wet and turn'd the unwilling waters
  red   65 Harold 4 585
Alas, for Earth, for never shall we see   67 Harold 4 737
Earth with her haughty shadow, and display'd   67 Harold 4 754
And blood of earth flow on as they have flow'd   68 Harold 4 825
Mantles the earth with darkness, until right   69 Harold 4 834
And their free thoughts be crimes, and earth
  have too much light   69 Harold 4 837
On infant Washington? Has Earth no more   69 Harold 4 863
The last of those who o'er the whole earth reign'd   71 Harold 4 994
Or, it might be, a beauty of the earth   72 Harold 4 1032
Oh Love! no habitant of earth thou art   73 Harold 4 1081
Whose root is earth, whose leaves and branches be   74 Harold 4 1130
Unto the things of earth, which Time hath bent   74 Harold 4 1156
Hear me, my mother Earth! behold it, Heaven   75 Harold 4 1208
To build for giants, and for his vain earth   78 Harold 4 1365
And reap from earth, sea, joy almost as dear   81 Harold 4 1583
Man marks the earth with ruin, his control   81 Harold 4 1605
And dashest him again to earth:--there let him lay   82 Harold 4 1620
To mark the spot where earth to earth returns   86 Fragment-A   6
Still dauntless 'midst the wreck of earth he'd
  smile   88 Horace   17
Love and hope upon earth bring no more consolation   92 Caroline-D   19
Some portion of paradise still is on earth   93 First Kiss   23
She fear'd that, too divine for earth   97 To M--   11
'Thrice has the earth revolved her course   104 Alva   209
He said, and dash'd the cup to earth   104 Alva   248
Now o'er the earth a solemn stillness ran   106 Nisus   85
What poor rewards can bless your deeds on earth   107 Nisus   135
Stain'd is the couch and earth with clotting gore   108 Nisus   252
Lowly to earth inclines his plume-clad crest   110 Nisus   377
'Tis surely enough upon earth to be vex'd   117 To Eliza   21
Earth shudders as her caves receive his bones   121 Newstead-A   107
Peruse the record of your days on earth   127 Recoll   403
Earth, ocean, heaven, thy boundless throne   132 Prayer   20
Mix'd with the earth o'er which my footsteps
  moved   138 Harrow-B   30
Which Spring and Nature cull from Earth   139 Anacreon-C   10
Breathes our thoughts from Earth to Heaven   139 Anacreon-C   12
When Earth is darken'd with tempestuous skies   139 Ossian-A   17
The Earth, and all the joys reserved me   144 Becher-B   46
But me she beckons from the earth   146 Adieu   85
And yields thee scarce a name on earth   150 My Son   16
On earth thou wert all but divine   151 Soul-A   5
I died: let earth my bones resign   154 Skull   6
When some proud son of man returns to earth   154 Dog   1
Denied in heaven the soul he held on earth   154 Dog   12
Thou grow'st old--who does not?--but on earth
  what appears   155 Goblet   15
When the box of Pandora was open'd on earth   156 Goblet   25
The poorest, veriest wretch on earth   156 Lady-F   31
To quit another spot on earth   157 Florence   4
On earth thy love was such to me   165 Thyrza   55
Then turn'd from earth its tender beam   166 Away   28
But silent let me sink to earth   166 Euthanasia   9
Too soon return'd to Earth   167 Dead   4
Though Earth received them in her bed   167 Dead   5
Like common earth can rot   167 Dead   16
I'd dash to earth the sweetest bowl   168 Haunts   23
'So now for the earth to take my chance   176 Devil's Dr   25
Then up to earth sprung he   176 Devil's Dr   26
Nor often on earth had he seen such a sight   176 Devil's Dr   38
For men of all might and the monarchs of earth   176 Devil's Dr   50
Who strew'd our earth with hostile bones   180 Ode-A   6
And Earth hath spilt her blood for him   181 Ode-A   82
Of these, the Conquerors of the earth   181 Ode-A   108
That Earth is now as free   181 Ode-A   124
While earth was Gaul's--Gaul thine   181 Ode-A   146
All earth becomes their monument   183 Parker   8
On Earth--but Rage on Ocean's troubled Heart   184 Julian   2

EARTH

He was on Earth--but what was Earth to him	184	Julian		28
And down to Earth he sunk in silent trance	184	Julian		37
And left thee but a mass of earth	185	Belshaz-A		20
Arose and o'ershadow'd the earth with her name	186	Napoleon		2
I made thee the gem and the wonder of earth	186	Napoleon		10
Though Guilt would sweep it from the earth	188	Ode-B		86
Why rise in Heaven to set on Earth	188	On Star		6
Earth rock'd beneath thee to her base	188	On Star		15
Rayless, and pathless, and the icy earth	189	Darkness		4
All earth was but one thought--and that was death	189	Darkness		42
For Earth is but a tomb-stone, did essay	190	Churchill		21
Which Earth and Heaven could not convulse	191	Prometheus-B		43
If the deep barrier be of earth or sea	192	Fragment-C		20
As midnight in her solitude?--O Earth	192	Fragment-C		31
That humbler Harmonist of care on Earth	194	Monody		112
Distance, nor depth of wave, nor space of earth	198	Po		38
Seems proud of the reptile which crawl'd from her earth	203	Avatar		91
Earth is no desert--ev'n to me	210	Augusta-A		44
There was but one beloved face on earth	214	Dream		48
Which is not of the earth; she was become	215	Dream		172
Since then, though heard on earth no more	217	The Harp		16
To soar from earth, and find all fears	217	High World		7
It will not live in other earth	217	Gazelle		18
Earth yawn'd; he stood the centre of a cloud	219	Saul-B		5
Saul saw, and fell to earth, as falls the oak	219	Saul-B		13
All earth can give, or mortal prize	219	Vanity		7
Which all that life or earth displays	219	Vanity		11
All, all in earth, or skies display'd	220	Clay		11
Before Creation peopled earth	220	Clay		17
The wisest of the earth	220	Belshaz-B		22
If the Exile on earth is an Outcast on high	221	False		7
You visit him on earth again	235	Paine		3
Empires have moulder'd from the face of earth	244	Bards		195
Earth, heaven, and Hades echo with the song	259	Hints		204
Whose thistle well betrays the niggard earth	270	Minerva		135
The law of heaven and earth is life for life	272	Minerva		311
Upon earth. Give it way; 'tis an impulse which lifts	283	Blues	2	135
Our spirits from earth; the sublimest of gifts	283	Blues	2	136
'Tis the vision of Heaven upon Earth; 'tis the gas	283	Blues	2	139
Which peopled earth no better, hell as wont	285	Vision		50
He died!--his death made no great stir on earth	286	Vision		65
Its way back into earth, and fire, and air	286	Vision		84
He's dead--and upper earth with him has done	286	Vision		89
On earth, yet ventured in my face to advance	287	Vision		147
In heaven, and upon earth redeem'd his sin	287	Vision		158
Reach'd even our speck of earth, and made a new	288	Vision		213
'Look to our earth, or rather mine; it was	290	Vision		313
'Look to earth, I said, and say again	290	Vision		329
And much of earth and all the watery plain	290	Vision		333
Upon the thrones of earth; but let them quake	290	Vision		376
The faith which makes ye great on earth, implored	291	Vision		378
From our sun to its earth,--as we can tell	291	Vision		435
That you should half of earth and hell produce	292	Vision		499
That look'd as it had been a shade on earth	294	Vision		594
On earth besides; except some grumbling voice	296	Vision		755
Of sullen earth divide each winding sheet	298	Age		20
He wept for worlds to conquer--half the earth	298	Age		35
Whose table earth--whose dice were human bones	299	Age		52
Oh earth! of which he was a noble creature	300	Age		132
To earth, air, ocean, all that felt or feel	301	Age		228
Or drawing from the no less kindled earth	301	Age		247
What is the happiness of earth to them	307	Age		692
That earth has yet to see, or e'er hath seen	308	Age		732
Which gleams, but warms no more its cherish'd earth	311	Giaour		102
Though bent on earth thine evil eye	312	Giaour		196
Unfit for earth, undoom'd for heaven	314	Giaour		436
It fell, and caught one stain of earth	315	Giaour		503
So moved on earth Circassia's daughter	315	Giaour		505
His back to earth, his face to heaven	317	Giaour		668
But first, on earth as Vampire sent	317	Giaour		755
Such looks are not of earth nor heaven	319	Giaour		915
To lift from earth our low desire	321	Giaour		1134
Earth holds no other like to thee	322	Giaour		1184
From earth; why then art thou awake	323	Giaour		1305
Where the tints of the earth, and the hues of the sky	323	Abydos	1	11
And made earth, main, and heaven our own	324	Abydos	1	70
And paints the lost on Earth revived in Heaven	325	Abydos	1	165
God! am I left alone on earth	330	Abydos	2	166
Survey'd Earth, Ocean, Sun, and Sky	332	Abydos	2	346
Earth--sea alike--our world within our arms	333	Abydos	2	453
'Tis from her lowly virgin earth	336	Abydos	2	715
Without one hope on earth beyond thy love	344	Corsair	1	400
Felt--that for him earth held but her alone	345	Corsair	1	480
Flung o'er that spot of earth the air of hell	349	Corsair	2	156
That shines like snow and falls on earth as mute	353	Corsair	2	405
As if the last he could enjoy on earth	353	Corsair	2	457
Oh! she is all that still to earth can bind	354	Corsair	2	487
By this how many lose not earth--but heaven	355	Corsair	2	552

EARTH

Refreshing earth--reviving all but him	355	Corsair	2	562
From earth with ruthless but with open hand	361	Corsair	3	361
Her all on earth and more than all in heaven	363	Corsair	3	530
Their joy and find this earth enough for woe	365	Corsair	3	633
All was so still, so soft in earth and air	368	Lara	1	167
With more capacity for love than earth	370	Lara	1	321
And Youth forget such hour was past on earth	371	Lara	1	395
For him earth now disclosed no other guide	373	Lara	1	526
To know no brotherhood, and take from earth	374	Lara	1	552
The sun is in the heavens, and life on earth	375	Lara	2	6
Nor earth nor sky will yield a single tear	375	Lara	2	14
If yet he be on earth, expect him here	375	Lara	2	34
His glove on earth, and forth his sabre flew	376	Lara	2	54
Defying earth and confident of heaven	378	Lara	2	217
The war-horse masterless is on the earth	380	Lara	2	396
Held all the light that shone on earth for him	381	Lara	2	431
Roll down like earth to earth upon the plain	382	Lara	2	507
They laid him in the earth, and on his breast	383	Lara	2	540
Over the earth, and through the air	384	Corinth		38
Arise from out the earth which drank	385	Corinth		61
And turn'd to earth without repining	387	Corinth		249
'Tis still a watch-word to the earth	388	Corinth		418
And see worms of the earth, and fowls of the air	389	Corinth		491
But dash that turban to earth, and sign	390	Corinth		577
Not earth, that's past--but heaven or me	391	Corinth		634
Hath she sunk in the earth, or melted in air	391	Corinth		676
He tramples on earth, or tosses on high	392	Corinth		727
Strew'd the earth like broken glass	392	Corinth		732
When he fell to earth again	395	Corinth		1034
Its living things, its earth and sky	396	Parisina		31
But here, upon the earth beneath	398	Parisina		213
And to the earth she fell like stone	400	Parisina		348
Could this be still the earth beneath	400	Parisina		373
To whom the goodly earth and air	402	Chillon		9
Of the pure elements of earth	403	Chillon		57
Even from the cold earth of our cave	404	Chillon		151
The flat and turfless earth above	404	Chillon		160
One on the earth, and one beneath	404	Chillon		219
There were no stars, no earth, no time	405	Chillon		245
When skies are blue and earth is gay	405	Chillon		299
And the whole earth would henceforth be	405	Chillon		322
Than thee, Mazeppa! On the earth	408	Mazeppa		101
In the full view of earth and heaven	410	Mazeppa		315
The earth gave way, the skies roll'd round	412	Mazeppa		539
And fill'd the earth, from his deep throne	413	Mazeppa		651
The earth, whose mine was on its face, unsold	416	Island	1	39
Where all partake the earth without dispute	418	Island	1	213
Where Chimborazo, over air, earth, wave	420	Island	2	77
Done for the earth? We feel them in our shame	423	Island	2	321
The world for ever, earth of light bereft	424	Island	2	363
Lives not in earth, but in his ecstasy	424	Island	2	371
Had left the earth, and but polluted heaven	426	Island	3	4
No further home was theirs, it seem'd, on earth	426	Island	3	13
They had gain'd a central realm of earth again	431	Island	4	119
By those who had lost all hope in earth or heaven	434	Island	4	300
His last rage 'gainst the earth which he forsook	434	Island	4	340
The God who was on earth and is in heaven	437	Tasso		28
And mingle with whate'er I saw on earth	438	Tasso		151
Thou didst annihilate the earth to me	439	Tasso		173
But Spirits may be leagued with them--all Earth	439	Tasso		199
And all is ice and blackness,--and the earth	453	Venice-B		54
But for a term, then pass, and leave the earth	454	Venice-B		96
Flew between earth and the unholy Crescent	454	Venice-B		116
Which, if it waned and dwindled, Earth may thank	454	Venice-B		117
That nought on earth could more my bosom move	456	Dante	1	22
The sense of earth and earthly things come back	457	Dante	1	131
And makes your land impregnable, if earth	460	Dante	2	122
That crowds on my prophetic eye: the earth	460	Dante	3	5
To give thee honour and the earth delight	461	Dante	3	42
Some voices shall be heard, and earth shall listen	461	Dante	3	63
But fly more near the earth; how many a phrase	461	Dante	3	73
And fill the earth with feats of chivalry	462	Dante	3	111
Will look on earth and heaven, and who will deign	462	Dante	3	143
Unlaurell'd upon earth, but far more bless'd	463	Dante	4	6
All beauty upon earth, compell'd to praise	464	Dante	4	82
Is it that they on earth, whose earthly power	464	Dante	4	96
Which shut him from the sole small spot of earth	465	Dante	4	134
Composed of branches, logs of wood, and earth	470	Morgante		306
O'er the whole earth is echoing and rebounding	473	Morgante		464
And burst, while cold on earth lay head and hoof	474	Morgante		542
Or lurking love of something on the earth	479	Manfred	1	27
Ye, who do compass earth about, and dwell	479	Manfred	1	31
If it be so.--Spirits of earth and air	479	Manfred	1	41
Strike deep in the earth	479	Manfred	1	93
Was ruled, ere earth began, by me	480	Manfred	1	111
Earth, ocean, air, night, mountains, winds, thy star	480	Manfred	1	132
O'er earth, the whole, or portion, or a sign	480	Manfred	1	141
I have no choice; there is no form on earth	481	Manfred	1	184
It is not of my search.--My mother Earth	481	Manfred	1	268
Ye were not meant for me--Earth! take these atoms	483	Manfred	1	370
Will it then never--never sink in the earth	484	Manfred	2	22

EARTH

The blush of earth embracing with her heaven	485	Manfred	2	116
Of Earth, whom the abstruser powers permit	485	Manfred	2	123
And gaze on thee a moment. Son of Earth	485	Manfred	2	126
The face of the earth hath madden'd me, and I	485	Manfred	2	133
Nor look'd upon the earth with human eyes	485	Manfred	2	146
And spirits that do compass air and earth	486	Manfred	2	182
Hail to our Master!--Prince of Earth and Air	488	Manfred	2	371
Glory to Arimanes! on the earth	489	Manfred	2	387
Child of the Earth! or dread the worst. I know it	489	Manfred	2	405
'Tis taught already;--many a night on the earth	489	Manfred	2	407
What the whole earth accords, beholding not	489	Manfred	2	414
Have been beyond the dwellers of the earth	489	Manfred	2	429
Of earth and heaven, from which no power, nor being	489	Manfred	2	435
Which return'd to the earth	490	Manfred	2	460
Speak to me! I have wander'd o'er the earth	490	Manfred	2	513
Her words will be fulfill'd. Return to the earth	491	Manfred	2	526
Man. We meet then! Where? On the earth	491	Manfred	2	535
Yet shape themselves some fantasy on earth	492	Manfred	3	102
Of mortals on the earth, who do become	493	Manfred	3	139
Or having been, that I am still on earth	493	Manfred	3	153
Centre of many stars! which mak'st our earth	493	Manfred	3	188
Grovel on earth in indistinct decay	495	Manfred	3	290
Like an infernal god, from out the earth	495	Manfred	3	323
In knowledge of our fathers when the earth	496	Manfred	3	377
But all things swim around me, and the earth	497	Manfred	3	407
In face of earth and heaven; for I have never	513	Faliero	4	325
When what is now a handful shook the earth	519	Faliero	3	21
And sees a hundred beings, now in earth	525	Faliero	3	455
Down to the earth, strew'd with their bleeding fruit	527	Faliero	3	615
What ocean is to earth, spreads its blue depths	529	Faliero	4	72
Thou holdest dear on earth or heaven--by all	530	Faliero	4	171
The earth as being the Christian bulwark 'gainst	538	Faliero	5	11
Alone can profit you on earth or heaven	538	Faliero	5	32
Answering to Heaven for what they did on earth	540	Faliero	5	178
Upon the earth would live were all judged justly	543	Faliero	5	365
His life, while earth yet bore his cruelties	544	Faliero	5	443
And as he rose from earth again, he raised	546	Faliero	5	601
To many a triumph! Thou, my native earth	548	Faliero	5	729
Which I have bled for, and thou foreign earth	548	Faliero	5	730
Sink in the earth, and thirteen hundred years	550	Sardan	1	7
While the great king of all we know of earth	551	Sardan	1	33
If they should sweep me off from earth and empire	557	Sardan	1	445
Why, what is earth or empire of the earth	557	Sardan	1	446
On earth, or should you read of it in heaven	566	Sardan	2	311
That there are worse things betwixt earth and heaven	566	Sardan	2	314
From all the taints of common earth--while I	570	Sardan	2	521
Rocks underneath his throne, and the earth yawns	574	Sardan	3	180
As sweeps the air and deluges the earth	576	Sardan	3	318
Gold: all the gold of earth could ne'er repay	577	Sardan	3	360
You have cause, sire; for on the earth there breathes not	578	Sardan	3	426
And fetters us to earth--at least the phantom	579	Sardan	4	61
From heaven or earth--And rather let me see	580	Sardan	4	129
'Tis lost, all earth will cry out, thank your father	582	Sardan	4	289
The sullen earth. Oh! if thou hast at length	583	Sardan	4	351
Assyria is not all the earth; we'll find	583	Sardan	4	355
How hideous upon earth! where peace and hope	587	Sardan	5	5
In heaven a glorious mockery of the earth	587	Sardan	5	14
To that which keeps all earth from being as fragile	588	Sardan	5	45
As now he reigns in heaven, so once on earth	588	Sardan	5	49
Gallant and glorious spirit! must the earth	589	Sardan	5	123
Anon--what the whole earth shall ne'er forget	591	Sardan	5	285
Purged from the dross of earth and earthly passion	594	Sardan	5	473
Their very record! Then farewell, thou earth	595	Sardan	5	487
And loveliest spot of earth! farewell, Ionia	595	Sardan	5	488
Which persecutes me; but my native earth	597	Foscari	1	142
So does the earth, and sky, the blue of ocean	598	Foscari	1	164
Because all earth, except his native land	600	Foscari	1	290
This ducal cap the diadem of earth	603	Foscari	2	80
There! In the earth? To which I am tending: when	603	Foscari	2	142
On earth. And how then shall we judge each other	607	Foscari	2	367
Who are all earth, and I, who am call'd upon	607	Foscari	2	368
And the sweet freedom of the earth and air	610	Foscari	3	145
On earth to bear. Have I not borne? Too much	611	Foscari	3	202
Of your three goodly brothers, now in earth	616	Foscari	4	113
An atom of their ancestors from earth	619	Foscari	4	277
For his inauguration. Earth and heaven	624	Foscari	5	228
Resemble that you exercise on earth	626	Foscari	5	336
Earth, ocean, air, and fire, and with the day	627	Cain	1	10
Needful: the earth is young, and yields us kindly	628	Cain	1	49
The earth, which is thine outward cov'ring, is	629	Cain	1	117
The earth yield nothing to us without sweat	630	Cain	1	182
In nature being earth also--more in wisdom	630	Cain	1	222
To heaven, and Zillah casts hers to the earth	631	Cain	1	251
What ill? To be resolved into the earth	631	Cain	1	285

I cannot answer. Were I quiet earth	631	Cain	1	287
To till the earth--for I had promised--What	632	Cain	1	321
The myriad myriads--the all-peopled earth	635	Cain	1	519
The unpeopled earth--and the o'erpeopled Hell	635	Cain	1	520
Eternity--and heaven and earth--and that	636	Cain	1	546
Which is not heaven nor earth, but peopled with	636	Cain	1	547
Is yon our earth? Dost thou not recognise	636	Cain	2	27
In number than the dust of thy dull earth	636	Cain	2	46
Art thou not nearer? look back to thine earth	637	Cain	2	118
The earth! where is my earth? Let me look on it	638	Cain	2	145
Shalt soon return to earth and all its dust	638	Cain	2	149
Like them the features of fair earth:--instead	639	Cain	2	189
Thou livest. When? On what thou callest earth	640	Cain	2	268
Yes, from their earth, as thou wilt fade from thine	640	Cain	2	280
The earth, thy task--I'll waft thee there in safety	640	Cain	2	310
I must one day return here from the earth	640	Cain	2	312
To earth again? Their earth is gone for ever	641	Cain	2	325
It is not with the earth, though I must till it	641	Cain	2	330
Of the deep woods of earth, the hugest which	641	Cain	2	341
What is it? There is still some such on earth	642	Cain	2	389
Now let us back to earth! And wherefore didst thou	642	Cain	2	433
Approach the things of earth most beautiful	643	Cain	2	454
Like Adah's face: I turn from earth and heaven	643	Cain	2	473
Lay foaming on the earth, beneath the vain	643	Cain	2	496
Mighty pre-Adamites who walk'd the earth	644	Cain	2	564
Clay has its earth, and other worlds their tenants	644	Cain	2	575
With me, then, to thine earth, and try the rest	646	Cain	2	655
The fruits of the earth, the early beautiful	647	Cain	3	105
Jehovah upon earth! and God in heaven	649	Cain	3	248
Or if the sweet and blooming fruits of earth	650	Cain	3	259
Why so? Thy fruits are scatter'd on the earth	650	Cain	3	281
From earth they came, to earth let them return	650	Cain	3	282
Awake!--why liest thou so on the green earth	651	Cain	3	324
The earth swims round me:--what is this?--'tis wet	651	Cain	3	344
Of death, whom I have brought upon the earth	652	Cain	3	420
Deny thee shelter! earth a home! the dust	653	Cain	3	442
Cursed from the earth, which open'd late her mouth	653	Cain	3	472
Be from this day, and vagabond on earth	653	Cain	3	476
Behold, thou drivest him from the face of earth	653	Cain	3	478
A fugitive and vagabond on earth	653	Cain	3	480
Shall slay me? Where are these on the lone earth	653	Cain	3	483
Blood darkens earth and heaven! what thou now art	654	Cain	3	530
But who hath dug that grave? Oh, earth! Oh, earth	654	Cain	3	542
Of Earth, and love her as he once loved Anah	655	Heaven		30
They have touch'd earth! Samiasa! My Azaziel	657	Heaven		159
The refuse of the earth, could be received	657	Heaven		194
To let the inner spirits of the earth	657	Heaven		202
Upon an earth all evil; for things worse	658	Heaven		251
By all that earth holds holiest, speak! Ha! ha	659	Heaven		322
By the approaching deluge! by the earth	659	Heaven		323
For earth and all her children. Ha! ha! ha	659	Heaven		331
How the earth sleeps! and all that in it is	659	Heaven		335
Earth shall be ocean	660	Heaven		350
Of earth nought left but the unbroken blue	660	Heaven		364
Man, earth, and fire, shall die	660	Heaven		370
And to the expiated Earth	661	Heaven		465
Till earth wax hoary	661	Heaven		474
Howl! howl! oh Earth	661	Heaven		500
God hath proclaim'd the destiny of earth	662	Heaven		538
What have we here? Shapes of both earth and air	662	Heaven		576
Dost thou on earth when thou shouldst be on high	663	Heaven		590
Of our great function is to guard thine earth	663	Heaven		592
But all good angels have forsaken earth	663	Heaven		593
Upon the earth to toil and die; and they	663	Heaven		638
No, not to save all earth, were earth in peril	664	Heaven		659
Shall shake these solid mountains, this firm earth	664	Heaven		716
He who made earth in love had soon to grieve	665	Heaven		728
Has not God made a barrier between earth	665	Heaven		741
When earth must be alone	665	Heaven		777
That earth by angels must be left untrod	666	Heaven		785
Earth! which oft saw	666	Heaven		786
And thou! if earth be thus forbidden	666	Heaven		815
Let us still walk the stars. True, earth must die	666	Heaven		825
Cannot this earth be made, or be destroy'd	666	Heaven		828
Earth groans as if beneath a heavy load	668	Heaven		995
The tempest cometh; heaven and earth unite	668	Heaven		1035
And if thou dost not weep for thy lost earth	669	Heaven		1042
The heavens and earth are mingling--God! oh God	669	Heaven		1060
Farewell, thou earth! ye wretched sons of clay	669	Heaven		1069
Should stir all heaven and earth up to destroy	669	Heaven		1106
If he hath made earth, let it be his shame	670	Heaven		1127
And though the waters be o'er earth out-spread	670	Heaven		1150
Whose every drop bows them down nearer earth	672	Werner	1	27
We'll offer a reward; move heaven and earth	684	Werner	2	64

EARTH

The bare knife in your hand, and earth asleep	690 Werner	2	454
Had swept him and all fears of mine from earth	690 Werner	2	470
Nor the lowest his vicegerents upon earth	692 Werner	2	613
Thou flaming Spirit of the Earth! which, sitting	700 Werner	3	334
'Twixt earth and heaven, like envy between man	700 Werner	3	363
The powers of earth shall never make me.'--So	710 Werner	4	359
Like them? Oh that each drop which falls to earth	722 Deformed	1	38
A burden to the earth, myself, and shame	723 Deformed	1	53
On earth, to which I will restore at once	723 Deformed	1	58
Be, that the man who shook the earth is gone	725 Deformed	1	203
That which he exchanged the earth for. Since so far	725 Deformed	1	239
Was he e'er human only? Let the earth speak	726 Deformed	1	253
From the red earth, like Adam	728 Deformed	1	384
On earth to be found	728 Deformed	1	411
And scarce a better to be found on earth	729 Deformed	1	502
The deep hue of the ocean and the earth	731 Deformed	1	655
And sent forth mighty spirits. The past earth	733 Deformed	1	757
The devil, or the devil's vicar upon earth	739 Deformed	2	251
Rebel in hell--you shall obey on earth	740 Deformed	2	325
On earth you have often only fiends for friends	741 Deformed	2	410
Then the earth looks free from trouble	743 Deformed	3	75
Your humid earth enables you to look	744 Deformed	3	143
Beyond you--and your jealousy's of Earth	744 Deformed	3	148
Of things you know not. Well, to earth again	744 Deformed	3	152
Upon the most unquiet imp on earth	750 Juan	1	196
Let's own--since it can do no good on earth	751 Juan	1	283
He thought about himself, and the whole earth	758 Juan	1	729
In Bacchanal profusion reel to earth	762 Juan	1	986
Had signs or footmarks, but the earth said nought	764 Juan	1	1148
For me on earth, except some years to hide	770 Juan	1	1555
To wean him from the wickedness of earth	775 Juan	2	63
Sooner shall earth resolve itself to sea	776 Juan	2	148
'Sooner shall heaven kiss earth (here he fell sicker	776 Juan	2	153
For which their mouths gaped, like the cracks of earth	784 Juan	2	666
To what part of the earth they had been tost	786 Juan	2	797
He knew not, for the earth was gone for him	788 Juan	2	882
Which then seems as if the whole earth it bounded	797 Juan	2	1459
Each was an angel, and earth paradise	800 Juan	2	1632
Earth! render back from out thy breast	812 Juan	3	727
Ave Maria! o'er the earth and sea	815 Juan	3	903
Sink o'er the earth so beautiful and soft	815 Juan	3	908
Earth, air, stars,--all that springs from the great Whole	815 Juan	3	927
But I'm digressing; what on earth has Nero	816 Juan	3	969
The heavens, and earth, and air, seem'd made for them	818 Juan	4	98
Gush from the earth until the land runs o'er	823 Juan	4	435
Afric is all the sun's, and as her earth	823 Juan	4	441
Terror to earth, and tempest to the air	823 Juan	4	452
She had so much, earth could not claim the whole	824 Juan	4	480
By age in earth: her days and pleasures were	825 Juan	4	565
Will sink where lie the songs and wars of earth	829 Juan	4	831
Instinct of gore and glory earth has known	829 Juan	4	839
And air--earth--water--fire live--and we dead	836 Juan	5	310
Her blood was high, her beauty scarce of earth	845 Juan	5	893
Earth being only made for queens and kings	847 Juan	5	1020
('Twas thus he spake) 'and Empress of the Earth	849 Juan	5	1146
Was also certain that the earth was square	850 Juan	5	1194
Of earth was wrinkled by the sins and tears	853 Juan	6	47
But rather skim the earth; while Dudu's form	857 Juan	6	325
But she was a soft landscape of mild earth	859 Juan	6	417
Chill, and chain'd to cold earth, we lift on high	867 Juan	7	5
Then one vast fire, air, earth, and stream embraced	879 Juan	8	53
He rush'd, while earth and air were sadly shaken	882 Juan	8	263
Alone can save the earth from hell's pollution	884 Juan	8	408
On earth, in Paradise; and when once seen	892 Juan	8	886
The earth, which he became like a fell'd tree	893 Juan	8	926
A mode of proving that the earth turn'd round	907 Juan	10	5
I've no great cause to love that spot of earth	915 Juan	10	521
How eager all the earth is for the blow	915 Juan	10	531
From the enjoyment of the earth and air	916 Juan	10	543
The earth, as scarce the eagle in the broad	916 Juan	10	619
Who butcher'd half the earth, and bullied t'other	917 Juan	10	648
He took to regularly peopling Earth	929 Juan	11	701
The twice two thousand, for whom earth was made	947 Juan	13	386
She made the earth below seem holy ground	948 Juan	13	485
The earth has nothing like a she epistle	954 Juan	13	834
But since beneath it upon earth we are brought	958 Juan	14	204
They are so much intertwisted with the earth	963 Juan	14	466
And set the other half of earth to rights	965 Juan	14	655
Like Archimedes, I leave earth as 'twas	966 Juan	14	672
No friend like to a woman earth discovers	967 Juan	14	743
Their earth is but an echo of the spheres	969 Juan	15	40
Where all the dwellers of the earth must dwell	981 Juan	16	30
Or earth beneath, or heaven, or t'other place	983 Juan	16	178
How Earth could round the solar orbit run	997 Juan	17	59

EARTH-ABSORBING

Or harden'd from some earth-absorbing fire	432 Island	4	151

EARTH-BORN

As their own beams; and earth, and earth-born jars	37 Harold	3	120
That bear the form of earth-born being. Ah!	631 Cain	1	260
A son of Adam! What doth the earth-born here	663 Heaven		588
To save an earth-born being; and behold	665 Heaven		734
I could not deem it earth-born: but be calm	716 Werner	5	181

EARTH-COMMANDING

The ocean-born and earth-commanding city	529 Faliero	4	104

EARTHLESS

He's gone, his soul hath ta'en its earthless flight	497 Manfred	3	412

EARTHLY

Few earthly things found favour in his sight	4 Harold	1	16
And love Earth only for its earthly sake	46 Harold	3	672
With an atoning smile a more than earthly crown	67 Harold	4	747
The purity of heaven to earthly joys	73 Harold	4	1068
Of earthly structures, in his honour piled	78 Harold	4	1383
From whom no earthly power can save	88 Catullus		19
Ah! whilst I tread this earthly sphere	133 Prayer		47
A quiet refuge from each earthly care	161 Athos		20
Since earthly eye but ill can bear	167 Dead		44
For earthly Love to merit thee	168 Haunts		40
I should have deem'd thee doom'd to earthly care	175 Sonnet-A		8
Look on thine earthly victims--and despair	209 Sketch		96
An age shall fleet like earthly year	220 Clay		27
Fit consummation of an earthly race	251 Bards		680
Can heavenly mercy dwell with earthly zeal	262 Hints		374
(Just like those cherubs, earthly ministers	285 Vision		27
An earthly peacock's tail, with heavenly dyes	287 Vision		134
With earthly likenesses, for here the night	288 Vision		222
If it be just: if in his earthly span	289 Vision		301
An earthly trinity! which wears the shape	303 Age		396
Ah! had she but an earthly grave	321 Giaour		1124
That this can be no earthly flower	336 Abydos	2	684
No, 'tis an earthly form with heavenly face	353 Corsair	2	397
Of earthly hope, they loved one from thee riven	359 Corsair	3	239
Night wears apace, my last of earthly rest	361 Corsair	3	369
Less clear, perchance, its earthly trials pass'd	365 Corsair	3	666
The sound of words less earthly than his own	368 Lara	1	140
And well he may--his earthly peace	397 Parisina		89
His earthly, his eternal fate	398 Parisina		193
His heart was wean'd from earthly feeling	401 Parisina		468
I had no earthly hope--but faith	405 Chillon		229
And die they do; for earthly life has nought	420 Island	2	119
My earthly sorrows, and to God's own skies	456 Dante	1	5
The sense of earth and earthly things come back	457 Dante	1	131
Where earthly first, then heavenly glory made	459 Dante	2	59
Is it that they on earth, whose earthly power	464 Dante	4	96
Manfred! To-morrow ends thine earthly ills	490 Manfred	2	521
Their earthly errors, so they be atoned	492 Manfred	3	83
Ay--father! I have had those earthly visions	492 Manfred	3	104
And watchings--her, whom of all earthly things	494 Manfred	3	245
Nor will I hence, while I have earthly breath	496 Manfred	3	361
To breathe my scorn upon ye--earthly strength	496 Manfred	3	362
My life, my honour, all my earthly hopes	507 Faliero	1	523
By earthly power omnipotent; but innocence	566 Sardan	2	303
The steel will reach the earthly. But be calm	570 Sardan	2	571
Had earthly monarch half the power and glory	588 Sardan	5	51
Purged from the dross of earth and earthly passion	594 Sardan	5	473
Which looks like that which lit our earthly night	636 Cain	2	31
Of high intelligence and earthly strength	640 Cain	2	298
In virtues nothing earthly could surpass her	749 Juan	1	135
But an unhallow'd, earthly sound of fiddling	805 Juan	3	220
All earthly goods save tithes) and bade them push on	875 Juan	7	510
An earthly paradise of 'Or Molu	926 Juan	11	528

EARTH-O'ERGAZING

Of earth-o'ergazing mountains, and thus take	49 Harold	3	853

EARTHQUAKE

An earthquake reel'd unheededly away	64 Harold	4	563
The earthquake voice of Victory	180 Ode-A		30
The earthquake came, and rock'd the quivering wall	206 Love, Death		13
What! would they spread their earthquake even o'er cash	306 Age		638
As if an earthquake pass'd	395 Corinth		1024
Until the earthquake tear the naiad's cave	421 Island	2	155
The architrave some earthquake might erect	432 Island	4	148
Which, like the pestilence and earthquake, smite	454 Venice-B		95
The unborn earthquake yet is in the womb	459 Dante	2	41
Where the slumbering earthquake	479 Manfred	1	88
The fretwork of some earthquake--where the clouds	487 Manfred	2	308
An earthquake should announce so great a fall	561 Sardan	2	10
As the earthquake saps the hill	735 Deformed	2	42

EARTHQUAKES
He moveth--earthquakes rend the world asunder — 488 Manfred 2 378
With earthquakes, pestilence, and foreign foes — 545 Faliero 5 492
And then he thought of earthquakes, and of wars — 758 Juan 1 732
Like earthquakes from the hidden fire call'd
'central — 801 Juan 2 1720

EARTHQUAKE'S
An Earthquake's spoil is sepulchred below — 37 Harold 3 146
As if they did rejoice o'er a young earthquake's
birth — 49 Harold 3 877
Whose shock was as an earthquake's, and opprest — 81 Harold 4 1547
The whirlwind's wrath, the earthquake's shock — 385 Corinth 50
Its inner crash is like an earthquake's ruin — 966 Juan 14 680

EARTHS
Suns, moons, and earths, upon their loud-voiced
spheres — 649 Cain 3 182

EARTH'S
And traverse Paynim shores and pass Earth's
central line — 5 Harold 1 99
That only Heaven to which Earth's children may
aspire — 25 Harold 2 351
Mountains above, Earth's, Ocean's plain below — 33 Harold 2 848
Earth's troubled waters for a purer spring — 48 Harold 3 800
And laid him with the earth's preceding clay — 68 Harold 4 769
The edict of Earth's rulers, who are grown — 69 Harold 4 852
In air with Earth's chief structures, though their
frame — 78 Harold 4 1403
For earth's destruction thou dost all despise — 82 Harold 4 1615
When calling the dead, in earth's bosom laid low — 91 Caroline-C 24
May rescue thee from earth's embrace — 154 Skull 19
Earth's chief dictatress, ocean's lovely queen — 255 Bards 1002
Earth's coarsest bread, the garden's homeliest
roots — 339 Corsair 1 71
Earth's dust by immortality refined — 460 Dante 3 21
Earth's mist with their pure pinions not agree — 463 Dante 3 171
And earth's and ocean's caves familiar things — 479 Manfred 1 34
The charms of earth's least mortal daughters grow — 485 Manfred 2 109
Be it to the earth's end, from this abhorr'd — 611 Foscari 3 238
Who? Thy sire's Maker and the earth's. And
heaven's — 629 Cain 1 131
And earliest embraces of earth's parents — 643 Cain 2 476
Earth's fruits be ashes in his mouth--the leaves — 652 Cain 3 428
Of my mind overworn. The earth's grown wicked — 658 Heaven 224
When ocean is earth's grave, and, unopposed — 658 Heaven 239
To snatch the loveliest of earth's daughters from — 659 Heaven 302
Earth's seed shall not expire — 660 Heaven 376
And build thy city o'er the drown'd earth's grave — 660 Heaven 408
The sun will rise upon the earth's last day — 662 Heaven 551
Who seek earth's daughters for their beauty?
Patriarch — 665 Heaven 739
Proclaims earth's last of summer days hath shone — 668 Heaven 1007
Whether they live, or die with all earth's life — 669 Heaven 1090
The earth's perfection of all mental beauty — 725 Deformed 1 221
This earth's animation — 728 Deformed 1 417
Lord of the city which hath been earth's lord — 730 Deformed 1 575
If the earth's princes ask'd no more. Be silent — 734 Deformed 1 830
To rise against earth's tyrants. Never let it — 895 Juan 8 1077
Men are but maggots of some huge Earth's burial — 901 Juan 9 312

EARTH-SHOCK
That deadly earth-shock disappear'd — 396 Corinth 1058

EARTH-STARS
Its earth-stars melted into heaven — 386 Corinth 172

EARTH-WORMS
Impossibilities--Away, ye earth-worms — 682 Werner 1 697

EARTH-WORM'S
Than nurse the earth-worm's slimy brood — 154 Skull 10

EARTHY
Still were you happy in death's earthy slumber — 117 Lachin 29

EAR-TRUMPET
Or the ear-trumpet of my good old aunt — 911 Juan 10 269

EASE
And life that bloated Ease can never hope to
share — 9 Harold 1 350
Strange retribution! now Columbia's ease — 18 Harold 1 915
I will not ease my tortured heart — 90 To M.S.G.-A 25
They might have set their hearts at ease — 96 Granta 91
Where confidence and ease the watch disdain — 105 Nisus 27
Stretch'd at his ease, th' incautious king
reposed — 108 Nisus 239
Linger in ease in Granta's sluggish shade — 112 Examination 50
And fashion's ease, without its art — 163 Malta 42
Among my researches for Ease — 234 Ballat 16
Whether thou sing'st with equal ease, and grief — 246 Bards 333
Oh! blest retreats of infamy and ease — 250 Bards 668

EASE
Scarce wrestles through the night, nor tastes of
ease — 261 Hints 313
The name of poet may be got with ease — 263 Hints 472
But fifty dunces can, with perfect ease — 265 Hints 641
The truth is, each writer now quite at his ease
is — 283 Blues 2 148
In comfort, at their own aerial ease — 294 Vision 588
Who fell like Phaeton, but more at ease — 298 Vision 828
Mist fly at last for ease--to hate — 319 Giaour 944
So let them ease their hearts with prate — 333 Abydos 2 385
The Haram's languid years of listless ease — 333 Abydos 2 414
Not thou, vain lord of wantonness and ease — 338 Corsair 1 11
Before our steeds may graze at ease — 408 Mazeppa 115
May see our coursers graze at ease — 415 Mazeppa 856
Which her bold bow flings off with dashing ease — 418 Island 1 228
Pursued her liquid steps with heart and ease — 431 Island 4 114
Because it slips into my verse with ease — 442 Beppo 168
For thence she could discern the ship with ease — 443 Beppo 198
And could not sleep with ease alone at night — 443 Beppo 228
Because they know the world, and are at ease — 444 Beppo 303
And caring little for the author's ease — 446 Beppo 398
To smooth the verse to suit his sovereign's ease — 461 Dante 3 88
And promised him an office of great ease — 470 Morgante 241
And stretch'd himself at ease in this abode — 470 Morgante 307
At ease. 'Tis nothing, child.--But in the state — 511 Faliero 2 181
Fly, son of Noah, fly! and take thine ease — 670 Heaven 1142
At such an hour too! Yes, curse--it will ease
you — 699 Werner 3 277
Some means of restitution, which would ease — 701 Werner 3 444
Through our friend's armour there, with greater
ease — 726 Deformed 1 307
We'll revel at ease — 732 Deformed 1 718
While seated after dinner at his ease — 748 Juan 1 45
She saw that Juan was not at his ease — 758 Juan 1 771
And made them bale without a moment's ease — 781 Juan 2 478
And there he lived exceedingly at ease — 790 Juan 2 1012
His couch; and, that he might be more at ease — 791 Juan 2 1059
With ease; but where I sought for Ilion's walls — 826 Juan 4 615
Europe and Asia, you being quite at ease — 832 Juan 5 38
So now all things are d--n'd one feels at ease — 855 Juan 6 177
A schooner, or--but it is time to ease — 877 Juan 7 677
Where there were fewer houses and more ease — 886 Juan 8 508
Of bricks, to let the dust in at your ease — 921 Juan 11 165
Wars, revels, loves--do these bring men more ease — 931 Juan 12 85
With more ease too she'd tell a different story — 957 Juan 14 104
Especially when we are ill at ease — 961 Juan 14 378
The art of living in all climes with ease — 969 Juan 15 88
The fair Fitz-Fulke seem'd very much at ease — 993 Juan 16 842

EASED
Eased her at last (although we never meant — 778 Juan 2 254

EASIER
Watch'd--follow'd--he were then an easier prey — 357 Corsair 3 150
Easier to stop Euphrates at its source — 584 Sardan 4 400
Our state as render retribution easier — 596 Foscari 1 47
Easier in such a form, or in your own — 725 Deformed 1 226
Through needles' eyes it easier for the camel is — 828 Juan 4 775
And march away--'twere easier done than said — 837 Juan 5 344
A wavering spirit may be easier wreck'd — 966 Juan 14 677
It was not--but 'tis easier far, alas — 975 Juan 15 431

EASIEST
In requisition, but by no means easiest — 738 Deformed 2 220

EASILY
Men are more easily made than machinery — 225 Ode-D 13
Than a poet of t'other, may easily guess — 279 Blues 1 114
Is frail; how easily the world is lost — 447 Beppo 479
And of all sins most easily besets — 512 Faliero 2 208
Which he should be, as easily as the thing — 551 Sardan 1 20
A throne too easily--does it disappoint thee — 563 Sardan 2 134
I'm satisfied. Right easily, methinks — 692 Werner 2 585
I am not so easily recall'd to do — 724 Deformed 1 132
Young, slender, and pack'd easily, he lay — 767 Juan 1 1323
It may be easily supposed, while this — 778 Juan 2 257
The consequence was easily foreseen — 782 Juan 2 545
They are put on as easily as a hat — 854 Juan 6 108
More easily than answer'd,--that he had tried — 864 Juan 6 795
That they as easily might do the youngster — 923 Juan 11 279
Now I could much more easily sketch a harem — 958 Juan 14 163
(By doing easily, whene'er she chose — 986 Juan 16 394

EAST
From spoils of nations, and the exhaustless East — 55 Harold 4 15
And hence, throughout all Hellas and the East — 266 Hints 675
Some east, some west, some every where but north — 270 Minerva 145
'Look to the East, where Ganges' swarthy race — 271 Minerva 221
Slaves of the east, or helots of the west — 302 Age 273
Of Bairam through the boundless East — 314 Giaour 452
'Tis the clime of the East; 'tis the land of the
Sun — 323 Abydos 1 16
Rose Lara's hand, and pointed to the East — 381 Lara 2 467

EAST

Sublime tobacco! which from east to west	425 Island	2	448
Their matins now draw nigh--the east is kindling	662 Heaven		561
Of arms (in the East all arm)--and various dyes	805 Juan	3	215
Thus in the East they are extremely strict	851 Juan	5	1257
An outline of the customs of the East	859 Juan	6	460
Exacted by the customs of the East	863 Juan	6	730
How the new worldlings of the then new East	901 Juan	9	306
As an East Indian sunrise on the main	904 Juan	9	468
In brief, the little orphan of the East	935 Juan	12	383
Thus the low world, north, south, or west, or east	936 Juan	12	446
On roads, east, south, north, west, there is a run	946 Juan	13	332

EASTERN

Soon will the day those eastern clouds adorn	109 Nisus		283
On eastern clouds thy yellow tresses play	140 Ossian-B		24
Nor seek again an eastern shore	164 Friend-B		42
No eastern vision, no distemper'd dream	242 Bards		24
The gate of heaven; like eastern thresholds is	289 Vision		274
The fleets that sweep before the eastern blast	299 Age		107
These Edens of the eastern wave	310 Giaour		15
That best becomes an Eastern night	312 Giaour		179
The insect-queen of eastern spring	314 Giaour		389
The fairest flowers of eastern land	326 Abydos	1	280
Nor fear the fire that lights an Eastern heart	360 Corsair	3	353
Before the eastern flame	413 Mazeppa		648
The greatest heiress of the Eastern Isles	790 Juan	2	1018
An Eastern anti-jacobin at last	811 Juan	3	627
As is the custom of those Eastern climes	842 Juan	5	710
For Eastern stays are little made to pad	849 Juan	5	1115
Expended all their Eastern phraseology	892 Juan	8	858
Beneath the influence of the eastern star	938 Juan	12	548

EASTWARD

Eastward from Eden will we take our way	654 Cain	3	552

EASY

And marvel men should quit their easy chair	9 Harold	1	347
But trust not this; too easy youth, beware	24 Harold	2	263
Now hate rules a heart which in love's easy chains	99 L Adieu		25
Methinks, an easy path perchance were found	105 Nisus		34
And poised with easy arm his ancient shield	106 Nisus		92
Were it not easy, Sir, and is't not sweet	199 Sonnet-E		9
Smooth be the verse, and easy be the strain	242 Bards		26
Or pour the easy rhyme's harmonious flow	253 Bards		864
If false, 'tis easy to disprove the word	372 Lara	1	452
The last not easy, be it known to you	444 Beppo		243
Oh that I had the art of easy writing	446 Beppo		401
What should be easy reading! could I scale	446 Beppo		402
Beyond my easy nature. 'Tis beyond	552 Sardan	1	108
That easy, far too easy, idle nature	552 Sardan	1	109
Were easy in the isolated bower	563 Sardan	2	130
'Tis easy to astonish or appal	588 Sardan	5	79
Nothing more easy. He partakes it now	613 Foscari	3	308
He hath thrown himself into an easy chair	680 Werner	1	597
Not easy to persuade my consort of	681 Werner	1	661
Away!--I'll make all easy. Idenstein	703 Werner	3	543
Ashes are feeble foes: it is more easy	720 Werner	5	436
I'll lie--it is as easy: then you'll praise me	734 Deformed	1	817
This was an easy matter with a man	749 Juan	1	161
Or else 'twere easy to withdraw her waist	761 Juan	1	917
And fits her loosely--like an easy glove	802 Juan	3	20
(And she had some not easy to withstand	828 Juan	4	758
More easy by the absence of all men	856 Juan	6	290
This feeling 'tis not easy to express	956 Juan	14	93
The reason why is easy to determine	957 Juan	14	116
The paper was right easy to peruse	983 Juan	16	206

EAT

Of his impeded soul would through his bosom eat	37 Harold	3	135
Thou! form'd to eat, and be despised, and die	60 Harold	4	334
For Parsons cannot eat without a Living	142 Soliloquy		26
Still let him eat, although at my expense	143 Soliloquy		54
But thou must eat thy heart away	180 Ode-A		54
And will eat himself to pieces	197 Rogers		72
The dogs to be sure have got nothing to eat	225 Ode-D		10
'What ails thee, Dervise? eat--dost thou suppose	348 Corsair	2	117
And tasteless food, which I have eat alone	437 Tasso		14
To eat their salmon, at the least, with soy	441 Beppo		56
You'll give it me? They say you eat no pork	451 Beppo		733
They eat, and drink, and live, and breed together	521 Faliero	3	156
Eat, drink, and love; the rest's not worth a fillip	555 Sardan	1	299
Because 'ye should not eat the fruits of life	630 Cain	1	201
Did they, too, eat of it, that they must die	641 Cain	2	358
Eat, drink, toil, tremble, laugh, weep, sleep, and die	645 Cain	2	621
The bread we eat? For what must I be grateful	647 Cain	3	113
And eat, and drink, and wive	660 Heaven		402
And eat your thoughts--till they breed snakes within you	743 Deformed	3	108

EAT

To eat the head of his arch-enemy	784 Juan	2	659
They would have eat her, olive-branch and all	786 Juan	2	760
That he was faint, and must not talk, but eat	793 Juan	2	1200
'Eat, drink, and love, what can the rest avail us	800 Juan	2	1655
But could not eat them, being in his turn	888 Juan	8	610

EATEN

Thou shouldst have gotten more, or eaten less	306 Age		633

EATING

And he thought himself of eating	178 Devil's Dr		206
Was kill'd and portion'd out for present eating	783 Juan	2	560
And then they left off eating the dead body	784 Juan	2	656
Who all the time was eating up his mutton	807 Juan	3	368
Of eating, with another act or two	835 Juan	5	250
And eating ices, were o'erheard to say	911 Juan	10	238
But thinks less of good eating than the whisper	977 Juan	15	559

EATS

Which eats into itself and rusts ingloriously	42 Harold	3	396
Or eats from out the palm, or playful lowers	805 Juan	3	254
One system eats another up, and this	955 Juan	14	5
And eats her parents, albeit the digestion	955 Juan	14	10
Who eats fire gratis (since the pay's but small	966 Juan	14	662

EBB

So human feelings ebb and flow	153 Friend-A		18
I feel an ebb in my philosophy	212 Augusta-C		71
A touch of hers, his blood would ebb and flow	214 Dream		59
And watch'd his spirit ebb away	321 Giaour		1086
There shrinks no ebb in that tideless sea	388 Corinth		426
But nature's ebb. Beside him was another	428 Island	3	103
The flow and ebb of each recurring age	453 Venice-B		58
For the expected ebb which cometh not	660 Heaven		358
Needful than to the peasant, when the ebb	672 Werner	1	41
Which knows no ebb to its imperious flow	943 Juan	13	126

EBB'D

Till ebb'd the latest eddy it had raised	383 Lara	2	585
The hot blood ebb'd and flow'd again	398 Parisina		226
Pedrillo, and so gently ebb'd his breath	783 Juan	2	603
So Juan's virtue ebb'd, I know not how	849 Juan	5	1130

EBBING

Which, ebbing, leave a sterile track behind	35 Harold	3	25
And through his side the last drops, ebbing slow	76 Harold	4	1256
His wanderings done, his visions ebbing fast	79 Harold	4	1472
As, when the ebbing flames are low	134 E. N. Long		79
As when the ebbing flames are low	148 A Fan		5
Will shrink, as shrinks the ebbing breath	167 Euthanasia		22
But, like an ebbing wave, it dash'd me back	487 Manfred	2	237
Is ebbing from me, yet I do defy ye	496 Manfred	3	360
I feel it ebbing! Let me see the wound	588 Sardan	5	100

EBBS

And ebbs but to reflow!--Renew thy rainbow, God	68 Harold	4	828
Ocean in sullen murmurs ebbs and flows	139 Ossian-A		15
With ebbs and flows is the rough Ocean tost	140 Ossian-A		13
The tide of triumph ebbs that flow'd too well	350 Corsair	2	238
Avoid it--Virtue ebbs and Wisdom errs	355 Corsair	2	547

EBLIS'

To wander round lost Eblis' throne	317 Giaour		750

EBON

The ebon portal of thy peopled cave	192 Fragment-C		36

EBONY

The tables, most of ebony inlaid	810 Juan	3	546

EBULLITION

Was a mere ebullition of the vice	526 Faliero	3	524

ECCLESIASTES

Ecclesiastes said, 'that all is vanity'	867 Juan	7	41

ECCLESIASTICAL

All kinds of dress, except the ecclesiastical	440 Beppo		21

ECHO
(See also RE-ECHO)

As if the clouds its echo would repeat	38 Harold	3	196
Their children's lips shall echo them, and say	40 Harold	3	312
In worship of an echo; in the crowd	52 Harold	3	1053
Has died into an echo; it is fit	82 Harold	4	1658
To echo, from its rising swell	88 Anacreon-A		3
They echo to the gale alone	102 Alva		28
The ceaseless echo of the rhyming throng	119 Answer-A		20
A thousand songs on tuneful echo float	121 Newstead-A		121
It finds an echo in each youthful breast	127 Recoll		364
Yet let me hush this echo of the past	127 Recoll		371
Thy vaults will echo back my knell	145 Adieu		33
Its echo in my heart	240 Cephalonia		6

ECHO

Though soft the echo, scorn a borrow'd tone	254	Bards	889
Though long the sound, the echo sleeps at last	254	Bards	958
Earth, heaven, and Hades echo with the song	259	Hints	204
Shall sink while there's an echo left to air	301	Age	250
Hears 'the lie' echo for his answer round	304	Age	489
Might wake an Echo like relief	313	Giaour	331
His pistol's echo rang on high	334	Abydos 2	520
'Where is my child?' an Echo answers--'Where	336	Abydos 2	663
And shout his name till echo waxeth weak	365	Corsair 3	683
That frantic echo burst the sleeping ear	369	Lara 1	206
Whose steps of lightness woke no echo there	371	Lara 1	400
And echo answer'd from the hill	387	Corinth	263
With an echo dread and new	392	Corinth	762
Where echo roll'd in thunder still	396	Corinth	1068
An echo of the dungeon stone	403	Chillon	64
With Echo for their chorus; nor the alarm	424	Island 2	422
By way of echo to embarrassment	428	Island 3	130
The startled echo of the ocean bird	430	Island 4	16
And ere the word upon the echo died	434	Island 4	303
The echo's echo, usher of the school	449	Beppo	583
The echo of thy tyrant's voice along	453	Venice-B	22
Waves, and the echo of our groans is driven	460	Dante 3	12
The deep echo roll'd	479	Manfred 1	85
Would echo o'er the Stygian wave which flows	507	Faliero 1	539
'Tis true, these sullen walls should yield no echo	542	Faliero 5	280
Must chime in to the echo of his revel	551	Sardan 1	32
I only echo thee the voice of empires	554	Sardan 1	271
And they will swell the echo with a curse	582	Sardan 4	290
Too loud at present to permit the echo	593	Sardan 5	389
Echo the sound to miserable things	636	Cain 2	8
An answer, not an echo. You may seek	679	Werner 1	529
Of long-lived parents finds a jovial echo	701	Werner 3	398
Did I not echo your own wish? Yes, Ulric	706	Werner 4	166
Without your echo? Pardon me, fair baroness	707	Werner 4	206
Let their hearts have an echo in every voice	742	Deformed 3	6
Let their hearts have an echo from every voice	742	Deformed 3	67
The sort of sound we echo with a tear	793	Juan 2	1206
To sounds which echo further west	812	Juan 3	699
Where echo woke as if from a long slumber	839	Juan 5	506
An echo of a syllable that's wrong	935	Juan 12	341
Some deem it but the distant echo given	949	Juan 13	502
Their earth is but an echo of the spheres	969	Juan 15	40
No sound except the echo of his sigh	983	Juan 16	155

ECHO'D
(See also RE-ECHO'D)

What valley echo'd the response of Jove	27	Harold 2	471
And timely echo'd back the measured oar	32	Harold 2	758
And reason's voice be echo'd back by ours	170	Address-A	65
When echo'd to the heart as from his own	346	Corsair 1	549
When every step that echo'd by the gate	358	Corsair 3	212
And now its dashing echo'd on his ear	359	Corsair 3	256
Acquainted with thy vainly echo'd name	490	Manfred 2	508
Ay, doubtless they have echo'd o'er the arsenal	506	Faliero 1	420
Which never echo'd but to sorrow's sounds	608	Foscari 3	2

ECHOED

Echoed their dim light to the mustering stars	424	Island 2	401
Of the last foe is echoed by his own	889	Juan 8	696
Upon debate: the papers echoed yet	952	Juan 13	717
Are somehow echoed to the pretty dears	977	Juan 15	603

ECHOES

While Afric's echoes thrill'd with Moorish matrons' wail	9	Harold 1	395
Would gladly woo thine Echoes with his string	13	Harold 1	619
In Venice Tasso's echoes are no more	55	Harold 4	19
The hills with Latian echoes; I abhorr'd	66	Harold 4	672
And galleries, where my steps seem echoes strangely loud	76	Harold 4	1278
My ears with tingling echoes ring	87	Ad Lesbiam	19
Which echoes through the neighbouring grove	91	Caroline-B	40
But echoes through her shades in vain	103	Alva	122
A brother's death-groan echoes there	105	Alva	316
Wake the dark echoes of the trembling ground	109	Nisus	326
Your deeds on the echoes of dark Loch na Garr	118	Lachin	32
And bids devotion's hallow'd echoes cease	120	Newstead-A	44
echoes of Morven. Then raise thy fair	131	Calmar	201
And echoes back his Patron's voice again	142	Soliloquy	20
The well-remember'd echoes thrill	166	Away	18
Whose strains, the faithful echoes of her mind	252	Bards	757
Till the floor echoes his emphatic foot	267	Hints	776
Thrills the lone heart like echoes from the dead	269	Minerva	70
And every ball-room echoes with her name	275	Waltz	108
Guildhall grows Gael, and echoes with Erse roar	308	Age	771
The cavern'd echoes wake around	312	Giaour	183
In echoes of the far tophaike	312	Giaour	225
Its echoes on the throbbing ear	316	Giaour	638
Till even the scaffold echoes with their jest	353	Corsair 2	451
His hall scarce echoes with his wonted name	366	Lara 1	33
Awake their absent echoes in his ear	373	Lara 1	523
Or gathering mountain echoes as they glide	420	Island 2	90

ECHOES

Had left the echoes to their melancholy	426	Island 3	6
The echoes only, from the rocks rebound	434	Island 4	293
Which echoes Madness in her babbling moods	438	Tasso	90
My soul would drink those echoes.--Oh, that I were	482	Manfred 1	313
His servant echoes back the awful word	492	Manfred 3	65
Unto the echoes of the nation's voice	552	Sardan 1	142
Never profaned by rebel echoes till	575	Sardan 3	252
Were the sole echoes, save my steed's and mine	815	Juan 3	939
A marble fountain echoes through the glooms	838	Juan 5	436
How sweetly on the ear such echoes sound	878	Juan 8	37
Its shriller echoes--like an infant made	948	Juan 13	459
Backward and forward to the echoes faint	982	Juan 16	139
And dreading the chaste echoes of her shoe	995	Juan 16	944
Nigh and more nigh the awful echoes drew	995	Juan 16	965

ECHOING

And oft-times through the area's echoing door	28	Harold 2	509
The rustling tapestry, and the echoing floor	370	Lara 1	262
O'er the whole earth is echoing and rebounding	473	Morgante	464
Of echoing thunder; and then all was hush'd	780	Juan 2	419

ECHOLESS

Until its voice is echoless	191	Prometheus-B	14

ECHO'S

The echo's echo, usher of the school	449	Beppo	583

ECLAT

Turns a diplomatist of great eclat	308	Age	717
The reason's obvious; if there's an eclat	939	Juan 12	617
The Ladies Scilly, Busey;--Miss Eclat	951	Juan 13	628
With the kind view of saving an eclat	963	Juan 14	473

ECLECTIC

A rake turn'd methodistic, or Eclectic	809	Juan 3	523

ECLECTICS

Or mild Eclectics, when some, worse than Turks	265	Hints	593

ECLIPSE

Which far eclipse each minor Glory's rays	139	Ossian-A	4
Sinks those blue orbs in that long last eclipse	364	Corsair 3	613
Yet through this centuried eclipse of woe	461	Dante 3	62

ECLIPSED

A mighty Spirit is eclipsed--a Power	192	Monody	23

ECLOGUES

To match the youthful eclogues of our Pope	262	Hints	388

ECONOMIC

Two weeds which pose our economic Catos	972	Juan 15	296

ECONOMY

'God save the king!' It is a large economy	286	Vision	97
Will turn upon 'political economy	941	Juan 12	704

ECSTASIES

How many sweet thoughts, what strong ecstasies	476	Francesca	17

ECSTASY

With such devotion to their ecstasy	420	Island 2	117
Lives not in earth, but in his ecstasy	424	Island 2	371
Of nature's child in nature's ecstasy	429	Island 3	200

ECSTATICS

I think that Dante's more abstruse ecstatics	803	Juan 3	87

EDDIED

The little whirl which eddied, and slight foam	431	Island 4	75

EDDIES

With its strange whirls and eddies can compare	852	Juan 6	14

EDDY

In its own eddy boiling and o'erwrought	36	Harold 3	57
Till ebb'd the latest eddy it had raised	383	Lara 2	585

EDDYING

Of eddying storms; yet springs the trunk, and mocks	58	Harold 4	176
Yes, when the eddying tempest sighs	102	Alva	33
down from eddying tempests: he rolls his	129	Calmar	13
While eddying whirl and breaking wave	316	Giaour	626

EDEN

Lo! Cintra's glorious Eden intervenes	7	Harold 1	236
And Eden revives in the first kiss of love	93	First Kiss	24
The Garden of Eden would wither without you	117	To Eliza	40
My father could not keep his place in Eden	628	Cain 1	66
The umbrage of the walls of Eden, chequer'd	631	Cain 1	270
Must be all goodness. Was it so in Eden	633	Cain 1	388

E'EN

E'en now the songs of Solyma begin   262 Hints   379
Seem'd weak and shaftless e'en to mortal glance   269 Minerva   82
E'en factions cease to charm a factious land   272 Minerva   276
E'en for thy presence ceased to pine   332 Abydos   2   351
E'en if he fail'd, he still delay'd his fall   378 Lara   2   241
And vain e'en menace--silent to the last   382 Lara   2   527
Nor words a language, nor e'en men mankind   437 Tasso   85
Of coxcombry's worst coxcombs e'en to the pink   449 Beppo   598
E'en when thou wilt. Is it not so, my friends   523 Faliero   3   349
Which e'en in Paradise destroy'd his parents   628 Cain   1   44
When will your names lend lustre e'en to
     partridges   976 Juan   15   536

E'ER

Of the most living crystal that was e'er   65 Harold   4   587
The rest weak and one bleak precipice, as e'er   430 Island   4   25
Was he e'er human only? Let the earth speak   726 Deformed   1   253
'Was it for this that no Cortejo e'er   765 Juan   1 1177
Having no equals, nothing which had e'er   846 Juan   5   946
Some stress on charms, which seldom are, if e'er   847 Juan   5 1029

EFFACE

But feel the shock renew'd, nor can efface   58 Harold   4   210
Thine image, what new friendship can efface   85 Epitaph   24
It was but abjuring my creed to efface   221 False   3
What time shall strengthen, not efface   312 Giaour   193
By Bonnivard!--May none those marks efface   402 Sonnet-F   13
One day of baffled crime must not efface   543 Faliero   5   358

EFFACED

These scenes must be effaced   145 Adieu   20

EFFACING

(Before Decay's effacing fingers   311 Giaour   72

EFFECT

And try the effect of the first kiss of love   92 First Kiss   12
Yet a partial neglect soon takes an effect   115 Pigot   11
Nor with the effect forget the cause   165 Friend-B   56
The stern effect of Giaffir's hate   331 Abydos   2   223
The heart to show the effect but not the cause   370 Lara   1   284
Searching its cause in its effect; and drew   486 Manfred   2   175
Recoils on me; its good in the effect   495 Manfred   3   309
But for the effect, the deadly deep impression   509 Faliero   2   34
So little to effect. This woman's warfare   562 Sardan   2   82
That I had dipp'd the pen without effect   601 Foscari   2   8
And when shall take effect this wondrous spell   661 Heaven   470
Refractory vassals, who can not effect   682 Werner   1   696
You, baron, I believe; but as the effect   693 Werner   2   628
And for the moment it had some effect   778 Juan   2   306
Is in its cause as its effect so sweet   800 Juan   2 1619
This strong extreme effect (to tire no longer   848 Juan   5 1063
Has quite the contrary effect on vice   851 Juan   5 1256
The true effect, and so we had better not   864 Juan   6   782
Before they reach'd a spot to take effect   870 Juan   7   220
But here the effect fell short of their desire   871 Juan   7   246
The effect on Juan was of course sublime   916 Juan   10   585
To leave them hovering, as the effect is fine   967 Juan   14   773
The cause of this effect, or this defect   980 Juan   16   9
'For this effect defective comes by cause   980 Juan   16   10
But so far the immediate effect   987 Juan   16   457
Surprise has this effect--to make one dumb   995 Juan   16   962
Whate'er the cause, are orphans in effect   997 Juan   17   16

EFFECTED

Could have effected. 'Twas a dreadful sight   601 Foscari   1   364

EFFECTIVE

And make the charm effective. Take it all   724 Deformed   1   155

EFFECTS

Our heads such sad effects produce   154 Skull   22
Upon effects, not causes. Stralenheim   720 Werner   5   455

EFFECT'S

Yet their effect's by no means tragic   148 To Author   11

EFFEMINATE

At once Elysian and effeminate   423 Island   2   313
He must be roused. In his effeminate heart   550 Sardan   1   9
Besides, he hates the effeminate thing that
     governs   563 Sardan   2   95
Nursed in effeminate arts from youth to manhood   575 Sardan   3   222
The effeminate garb?'--thus, after a short pause   841 Juan   5   604
And for the effeminate villeggiatura   951 Juan   13   617

EFFICIENT

Let me consider--of efficient troops   505 Faliero   1   353

EFFORT

Good without effort, great without a foe   80 Harold   4 1542
How vain is the effort delight to prolong   148 Farewell-A   14
And vain was each effort to raise and recall   164 Newstead-C   13

EFFORT

He rose and with a feeble effort shaped   184 Julian   34
Pump'd up with such effort, disgorged with such
     labour   278 Blues   1   50
No matter--yet one effort more   334 Abydos   2   518
'One effort--one--to break the circling host   350 Corsair   2   243
With feeble and convulsive effort swept   380 Lara   2   406
With feeble effort still I tried   413 Mazeppa   635
Ah! to what effort would it not persuade   455 Dante   Ded   14
In the vain effort to repress my wrath   516 Faliero   2   533
The very effort which it cost me to   534 Faliero   4   423
They here! all's lost--yet will I make an effort   536 Faliero   4   548
I cannot reach thee with mine utmost effort   549 Faliero   5   803
With slow and staggering effort he arose   788 Juan   2   865
As with an effort she began to speak   793 Juan   2 1196
Cost her an effort, which is a sad toil   966 Juan   14   682
Or careless; but the effort was not valid   985 Juan   16   279

EFFORTS

Yet, should our feeble efforts nought avail   114 Prologue   33
The feeble efforts of my lengthen'd song   126 Recoll   290
Your efforts on yourselves recoil   142 Critics   98
Thine efforts shortly shall be shown   172 Time-B   38
And, after fruitless efforts, you return   267 Hints   785
That owes its deadliest efforts to despair   343 Corsair   1   328
The first, all efforts vainly strove to wean   383 Lara   2   600
Disdain'd all further efforts, save to close   434 Island   4   306
Our efforts to repair the galleys, have   517 Faliero   2   638
Escapes our highest efforts to be happy   587 Sardan   5   38
The noblest efforts for herself and mate   756 Juan   1   595
Despite of all their efforts and expedients   777 Juan   2   227
Their desperate efforts seem'd all useless grown   778 Juan   2   302
To these kind efforts made a low reply   788 Juan   2   904
(So that their efforts should at length prevail   877 Juan   7   614
Of Quixote, shown how all such efforts fail   942 Juan   13   64
'Twill make, if proved, vast efforts without
     paining   943 Juan   13   144
(Though Parry's efforts look a lucky presage   946 Juan   13   309
Or to coarse efforts very loud and long   991 Juan   16   711

EFFRONTERY

Graced with some merit, and with more effrontery   952 Juan   13   727

EFFULGENCE

Dost thou, O Sun! thy vast effulgence pour   140 Ossian-B   4

EFFUSION

The coldest effusion which springs from my heart   148 Farewell-A   4

EFFUSIONS

I court the effusions that spring from the heart   92 First Kiss   15
The light effusions of a heedless boy   119 Answer-A   40
These young effusions of my early days   127 Recoll   358

EGAD

Egad! she seem'd a wicked-looking craft   426 Island   2   513
Egad! I am afraid. You look as if   674 Werner   1   176
Egad! they found the second time what they   883 Juan   8   329

EGERIA

Egeria, sweet creation of some heart   72 Harold   4 1027
Egeria! thy all heavenly bosom beating   72 Harold   4 1055

EGGS

Or to skim eggs unbroke was light enough   474 Morgante   540
Sitting upon strange eggs. Out, urchin, out   722 Deformed   1   27
For breakfast, of eggs, coffee, bread, and fish   791 Juan   2 1064
But Zoe the meantime some eggs was frying   792 Juan   2 1149
But there were eggs, fruit, coffee, bread, fish,
     honey   792 Juan   2 1159
And Zoe, when the eggs were ready, and   792 Juan   2 1161
Eggs, oysters, too, are amatory food   795 Juan   2 1358

EGO

'Non ego hoc ferrem calida juventa   772 Juan   1 1689

EGOTISM

Universe universal egotism   918 Juan   11   10
Of amatory egotism the Tuism   982 Juan   16   103

EGREGIOUS

Adds an ell growth to his egregious ears   266 Hints   736

EGRESS

Combined marauders, half-way, barr'd egress   29 Harold   2   615

EGRIPO

Was he not bred in Egripo   327 Abydos   1   375

EGYPT

As Egypt chose an onion for a god   272 Minerva   258
Egypt! from whose all dateless tombs arose   300 Age   141
Israel left Egypt, stop the waves in stone   464 Dante   4   62
Which usher'd Israel out of Egypt, till   547 Faliero   5   633

EGYPT
We leave a nobler monument than Egypt   595 Sardan   5 482
To Syria, Egypt, to the Ottoman   607 Foscari   2 380
Of Egypt and her neighbour Araby   612 Foscari   3 294
Morocco, betwixt Egypt and Tangier   858 Juan   6 352

EGYPTIAN
Or hieroglyphics on Egyptian stones   895 Juan   8 1093

EGYPT'S
Though shent with Egypt's plague, unkempt,
  unwash'd, unhurt   7 Harold   1 233
Or the light air of Egypt's graceful queen   70 Harold   4 905
Than Egypt's river:--from that gentle side   77 Harold   4 1349
Imperial mimic of old Egypt's piles   78 Harold   4 1361
And on these waves, for Egypt's queen   159 Gulf   3
Can Egypt's Almas--tantalising group   275 Waltz   127
Why, Egypt's gods were rational to these   303 Age   400
Which point in Egypt's plains to times that have 529 Faliero 4   84
What are the hopes of man? Old Egypt's King   773 Juan   1 1745
In Egypt's rays, to harp at a fix'd hour   949 Juan   13 508

EH
Would this assist your knowledge? How!--What!--
  En   699 Werner   3 302

EHRENBREITSTEIN
Here Ehrenbreitstein, with her shatter'd wall 44 Harold   3 554

EIGHER'S
On Eigher's pinnacle, so rested then   494 Manfred   3 238

EIGHT
Though at first view eight feet may seem in vain 262 Hints   405
Through eight long ages of alternate gore   301 Age   263
A senate which hath stood eight hundred years 544 Faliero   5 447
Of Carmagnuola, eight months ere he died   619 Foscari   4 299
With deadly cozenage, eight long months before-
  hand   619 Foscari   4 301
Eight months of such hypocrisy as is   619 Foscari   4 302
We willingly will lengthen them to eight   623 Foscari   5 188
As sign of our esteem. Not eight hours, signor 623 Foscari 5 189
Nor even eight minutes--There's the ducal ring 623 Foscari 5 190
Twelve years! he was but eight then:--beautiful 672 Werner 1   59
Then there was rum, eight gallons in a puncheon 780 Juan   2 376
At half-past eight o'clock, booms, hencoops,
  spars   780 Juan   2 401
I heard a shot--'twas eight o'clock scarce past 835 Juan   5 261
Where is the world of eight years past? 'Twas
  there   927 Juan   11 595

EIGHT-AND-FORTY
Erneis, Radulphus--eight-and-forty manors   912 Juan   10 282

EIGHTEEN
Eighteen hundred years and ten   384 Corinth   2
Whether his winters be eighteen or eighty   936 Juan   12 399
At eighteen, though below her feet still panted 962 Juan   14 437

EIGHTH
And lo! an eighth appears,--'I'll see no more 448 Beppo   527

EIGHTY
The rottenness of eighty years in gold   286 Vision   80
The blood and sweat of almost eighty years   502 Faliero   1 150
Of eighty men, and has great influence   511 Faliero   2 138
Are seldom long of life. And men of eighty   615 Foscari   4   61
Learnt but in eighty years. Brave Carmagnuola 619 Foscari   4 303
Engaged in the chase, draw off the eighty men 705 Werner   4 105
It stands some eighty versts from the high sea 868 Juan   7   71
Also the eighty 'greatest living poets   925 Juan   11 431
'Where is the world?' cries Young, at eighty--
  'Where   927 Juan   11 593
Whether his winters be eighteen or eighty   936 Juan   12 399

EIGHTY-EIGHT
But since the Gallic era 'eighty-eight   285 Vision   5

EITHER
And, gazing upon either, both required   195 Vittorelli   4
Like garden gods--and not so decent either   752 Juan   1 360
I really don't know what, nor Julia either   757 Juan   1 648
And then decide, without great wrong to either 819 Juan   4 199

EITHER'S
In either's eye, as if 'twere less their will 289 Vision   254

EJECTION
Quit; and though death had threaten'd an ejection 912 Juan   10 338

EKE
Where you, and eke your gentle queen   118 Romance   63
Eke out your acts, I pray, with mortal man   260 Hints   292
Some little scandals eke: but all aghast   451 Beppo   693

EKE
I have brought this world about my ears, and eke 956 Juan   14   73
And eke the wise, as has been often shown   970 Juan   15 132
Like all who give and eke receive it gratis   971 Juan   15 226
Fowls 'a la Conde,' slices eke of salmon   976 Juan   15 513

EKENHEAD
Leander, Mr. Ekenhead, and I did   787 Juan   2 840

EKING
And, as he interrupted not, went eking   794 Juan   2 1285

EL
No! as he speeds, he chants 'Viva el Rey   11 Harold   1 508

ELAPSE
Years must elapse ere I tread you again   118 Lachin   34
Elapse, and others share as dark a doom   517 Faliero   2 611

ELAPSED
But several years elapsed since they had met 443 Beppo   209
Some days and nights elapsed before that he   826 Juan   4 594

ELASTIC
I feel so elastic--'so buoyant--so buoyant   282 Blues   2 131

ELATE
Doing his evil will, nor less elate   42 Harold   3 427
If thou hast ever seen me too elate   74 Harold   4 1175
I will say, while with rapture the thought shall
  elate me   97 Harrow-A   35
With joy elate, by snares beset   132 L'Amitie   78
No more with hope or pride elate   320 Giaour   989
He chose the last, and when elate   332 Abydos   2 284
Said, Juan had not got his usual look elate   984 Juan   16 267

ELATES
The sound elates, the sight his hope destroys 109 Nisus   328

ELBA
From Elba to Lyons and Paris he goes   228 Once   3

ELBOW
(See also OUT-AT-ELBOW)
The Count was at her elbow with her shawl   450 Beppo   677
And thus upon his elbow he arose   793 Juan   2 1193
His head upon his elbow, and he saw   794 Juan   2 1250
But seeing at his elbow a mere lad   832 Juan   5   89
Four blacks were at his elbow in a trice   841 Juan   5 640

ELBOWING
At length with jostling, elbowing, and the aid 295 Vision   673

ELD
Lands that contain the monuments of Eld   19 Harold   1 952
Which envious Eld forbore, and tyrants left to
  stand   21 Harold   2 117
And with the ills of Eld mine earlier years
  alloy'd   35 Harold   2 926

ELDER
The elder first address'd the hoary band   106 Nisus   98
Mnestheus to guard the elder youth bestows   108 Nisus   215
Hath scarce been set; I am thine elder far   484 Manfred   2   50
I do not doubt the elder; but in Bertram   517 Faliero   2 580
The prince of whom he was the elder born   621 Foscari   5   82
If, as my elder, I revered thee not   649 Cain   3 197
And suits thee, as the elder. Now prepare   649 Cain   3 213
My brother, as the elder, offer first   649 Cain   3 220
Young, yet her elder, and of brow less grave 788 Juan   2 915
Was, for the elder and the stouter, first   840 Juan   5 538
But when I've added that the elder Jack Smith 869 Juan   7 154
The elder ladies' wrinkles curl'd much crisper 906 Juan   9 619

ELDERLY
Ah, Manuel! thou art elderly and wise   494 Manfred   3 213
The elderly walk'd through the library   954 Juan   13 809

ELDERS
Rough with his elders, with his equals rash   260 Hints   233
The elders of the council: I remember   527 Faliero   3 588
The instance of the elders of the Council   601 Foscari   1 377

ELDEST
When Angus hail'd his eldest born   102 Alva   38
I was the eldest of the three   403 Chillon   69
The eldest born of Fear, which makes you brave 522 Faliero   3 224
But thou, my eldest born, art silent still   628 Cain   1   26
With Cain's, the eldest born of Adam's, blood 664 Heaven   655
The eldest born of man, the strongest, bravest 664 Heaven   685
The eldest was a true and tameless Tartar   892 Juan   8 881

ELDON
As Eldon on a lunatic commission   979 Juan   15 732

ELDON'S
And he saw the tears in Lord Eldon's eyes   177 Devil's Dr   145

ELECT
Come then, some other mode elect   99 Young Lady   31
Who dreaded to elect me, and have since   605 Foscari   2   243
What, if he will not? We'll elect another   615 Foscari   4   36
The public mind,--so few are the elect   814 Juan   3   854
A thing quite necessary to the elect   987 Juan   16   459

ELECTED
(See also SELF-ELECTED)
Elected, and so will I be deposed   624 Foscari   5   253
In glorious homage with the elected 'seven   665 Heaven   780
As any body on the elected roll   911 Juan   10   275

ELECTION
(See also RE-ELECTIONS)
And 'tis for an election that they bawl   293 Vision   534
I sought not, wish'd not, dream'd not the election   541 Faliero   5   211
The bell! St. Mark's, which tolls for the election   625 Foscari   5   281
Awaits it, each new meeting or election   919 Juan   11   72
Talk o'er themselves the past and next election   989 Juan   16   600

ELECTIONEERER
Lord Henry was a great electioneerer   989 Juan   16   601

ELECTIVE
Against the next elective day   95 Granta   12

ELECTOR
From Brandenburg's elector, for the arrest   680 Werner   1   564
I stand well with the elector; in Bohemia   685 Werner   2   176

ELECTRIC
Striking the electric chain wherewith we are darkly bound   58 Harold   4   207
Is link'd the electric chain of that despair   81 Harold   4   1546
Bear hearts electric--charged with fire from Heaven   193 Monody   90
Which stirr'd with its electric qualities   291 Vision   410
From high, and lighten'd with electric thought   373 Lara   1   537
A cold electric shiver ran   401 Parisina   480
Conveying, as the electric wire   409 Mazeppa   242
The electric blood with which their arteries run   462 Dante   3   162

ELEGANCE
Deceived by its gigantic elegance   78 Harold   4   1398
Thou'lt there descry that elegance   87 Rousseau   14
One falls while following elegance too fast   257 Hints   43
Young men with aught but elegance dispense   264 Hints   541
Shed its Ionian elegance, which show'd   808 Juan   3   442
And elegance was sprinkled o'er his figure   960 Juan   14   306

ELEGANT
To separate the elegant and low   262 Hints   434
Out of 'Elegant Extracts.' Well, now we break up   283 Blues   2   154
Into an elegant extract (much less massy   882 Juan   8   269
Of 'elegant' et coetera, in fresh batches   936 Juan   12   423

ELEGIAC
In spite of all this elegiac stuff   238 Snuff-Box   2

ELEGISE
The bard who soars to elegise an ass   245 Bards   262

ELEGY
Ode, epic, elegy, have at you all   242 Bards   46
Of elegy there was the due infusion   286 Vision   70
Of the near fountain my sole elegy   723 Deformed   1   74
A couplet, or an elegy to claim   880 Juan   8   134

ELEMENT
Nor was the ominous element unjust   61 Harold   4   363
The gulf! and how the giant element   65 Harold   4   627
In every element, unchanged, the same   125 Recoll   263
That element may meet thy smile   181 Ode-A   120
Thou other element! as strong and stern   300 Age   185
Roused by the roar of his own element   359 Corsair   3   253
Was as a native's of the element   431 Island   4   107
And the great element, which is to space   529 Faliero   4   71
I have learn'd to-night the price of the pure element   577 Sardan   3   350
To you in that absorbing element   594 Sardan   5   433
Peculiar element; and things which have   644 Cain   2   577
May every element shun or change to him   652 Cain   3   434
For sorrow is our element   656 Heaven   71
Another element shall be the lord   660 Heaven   361
The wide and warring element   660 Heaven   391
Until one element shall do the work   661 Heaven   436
And view; all floating o'er the element   670 Heaven   1144

ELEMENT
In an as perilous, but opposite, element   685 Werner   2   163
Fire! the only element   729 Deformed   1   465
Can every element our elements mar   836 Juan   5   309

ELEMENTAL
Who calm'st the elemental war   133 Prayer   43
Who calm'st the elemental war   146 Adieu   116
So late escaped the elemental strife   185 Julian   45
Lulls his chafed breast from elemental war   269 Minerva   50
Lulls his chafed breast from elemental war   356 Corsair   3   50
While safe amidst the elemental strife   669 Heaven   1095

ELEMENTS
Thus to the elements he pour'd his last 'Good Night   5 Harold   1   117
When elements to elements conform   46 Harold   3   702
These were the elements, and thine no less   53 Harold   3   1096
These are four minds, which, like the elements   63 Harold   4   487
Ye Elements, in whose ennobling stir   81 Harold   4   1589
Round their white summits though elements war   117 Lachin   6
While elements exhaust their wrath   158 Storm   35
Our elements resolved to things untold   192 Fragment-C   38
In other elements, and on the rocks   211 Augusta-C   18
The war of elements no fears impart   334 Abydos   2   458
And seems to dare the elements to strife   339 Corsair   1   94
When all its elements convulsed, combined   352 Corsair   2   329
On that the feebler elements hath raised   367 Lara   1   124
Of the pure elements of earth   403 Chillon   57
Stopp'd by the elements, like a whaler, or   447 Beppo   483
The elements await but for the word   459 Dante   2   44
Which shall control the elements, whereof   480 Manfred   1   142
We have no forms, beyond the elements   480 Manfred   1   181
A conflict of its elements, and breathe   482 Manfred   1   303
Of purer elements; while the hues of youth   485 Manfred   2   111
Of elements the waters shrunk from me   486 Manfred   2   230
The sceptre of the elements which tear   488 Manfred   2   373
A goodly frame of glorious elements   493 Manfred   3   162
The oft discordant elements which form   536 Faliero   4   539
Ye elements! in which to be resolved   548 Faliero   5   724
And watch the warring elements; but this   570 Sardan   2   544
Not yet resolved to separate elements   587 Sardan   5   8
Though men, and gods, and elements, and omens   590 Sardan   5   206
Might move the elements to pause, and yet   596 Foscari   1   62
Will quickly clear the harbour. O ye elements   616 Foscari   4   122
God! who didst call the elements into   627 Cain   1   9
Destruction and disorder of the elements   640 Cain   2   286
In elements which seem now jarr'd in storms   644 Cain   2   584
With all the elements ere they will yield   647 Cain   3   112
I have seen the elements still'd. My Abel, leave me   649 Cain   3   206
The elements; this bosom, which in vain   658 Heaven   231
Leave to the elements their evil prey   668 Heaven   1014
To which the elements again repair   669 Heaven   1079
With all its elements! Heed not their din   669 Heaven   1084
Than did the elements, is come. This way   678 Werner   1   455
In haste, though even the elements appear   679 Werner   1   501
To wring his soul--as the bleak elements   682 Werner   1   723
Amidst the elements, whilst younger trees   689 Werner   2   382
I've seen you brave the elements, and bear   692 Werner   2   614
When man built less against the elements   696 Werner   3   100
Resolve back to her elements, and take   723 Deformed   1   60
Elements, near me   728 Deformed   1   412
Ever relapsing into its first elements   735 Deformed   1   887
Can every element our elements mar   836 Juan   5   309
That e'er were brew'd from elements or gore   941 Juan   12   700

ELEVATION
A Greek had raised around this elevation   868 Juan   7   77

ELEVEN
He may not be disturb'd until eleven   680 Werner   1   599
At six a charming child, and at eleven   753 Juan   1   386
Who bade on till the hundreds reach'd eleven   831 Juan   4   910
Eleven thousand maidenheads of bone   915 Juan   10   495
And rise at nine in lieu of long eleven   991 Juan   16   692

ELEVENTH
I wish she had: his book's the eleventh commandment   972 Juan   15   298

ELF
What harm? In spite of every critic elf   251 Bards   715
By their own rottenness, light as an elf   298 Vision   836
And as my Muse is a capricious elf   826 Juan   4   590

ELGIN
Let Aberdeen and Elgin still pursue   256 Bards   1027
Know, Alaric and Elgin did the rest   269 Minerva   104
See here what Elgin won, and what he lost   270 Minerva   118
And Eratostratus and Elgin shine   271 Minerva   203

ELGIN'S
For Elgin's fame thus grateful Pallas pleads   270 Minerva   107

ELICIT

The torture to elicit the whole truth   542 Faliero 5 300

ELIGIBLE

So that their plan and prosody are eligible   758 Juan 1 719

ELITE

At once the 'lie' and the 'elite' of crowds   951 Juan 13 634

ELIZA

Eliza, what fools are the Mussulman sect   116 To Eliza 1
Could they see thee, Eliza, they'd own their
  defect   116 To Eliza 3

ELIZABETH

Unlike our own half-chaste Elizabeth   906 Juan 9 642

ELL

Adds an ell growth to his egregious ears   266 Hints 736
But take an ell--and make a great sensation   953 Juan 13 781

ELLE

The seal a sun-flower; 'Elle vous suit partout   771 Juan 1 1582

ELM

The elm I clamber'd for your sake   89 To Emma 28
Thou drooping Elm! beneath whose boughs I lay   138 Harrow-B 9

ELMS

High, through those elms, with hoary branches
  crown'd   123 Recoll 121
Thy grove of elms, thy verdant hill   132 L'Amitie 45

ELOISA'S

When Eloisa's form was lower'd beneath   433 Island 4 224

ELOPEMENT

Saw Juan's last elopement with the devil   771 Juan 1 1624

ELOPEMENTS

Elopements, broken vows and hearts and heads   442 Beppo 128

ELOQUENCE

Wrung overwhelming eloquence, first drew   47 Harold 3 728
Not that our heads much eloquence require   112 Examination 29
The beam of Song, the blaze of Eloquence   193 Monody 28
Ye men of wit and social eloquence   194 Monody 107
While Eloquence--Wit--Poesy--and Mirth   194 Monody 111
With native eloquence he soars along   257 Hints 65
Of eloquence between, which flow'd all free   298 Age 16
In saying eloquence meant 'Action, action   304 Age 501
For Truth denies all eloquence to Woe   365 Corsair 3 645
Their eloquence was little worth   409 Mazeppa 277
Nucleus of England's native eloquence   428 Island 3 126
For then their eloquence grows quite profuse   768 Juan 1 1428
Of eloquence in piety and prose   795 Juan 2 1319
The serious Angles in the eloquence   960 Juan 14 298
Yet leave the gate which eloquence slips through   995 Juan 16 963

ELOQUENT

Along his margin a more eloquent green   65 Harold 4 607
Tully was not so eloquent as thou   71 Harold 4 982
And still the eloquent air breathes--burns with
  Cicero   72 Harold 4 1003
Its eloquent proportions, and unroll   78 Harold 4 1411
Who, for years, were the chiefs in the eloquent
  war   204 Avatar 115
So soft, so calm, yet eloquent   216 She Walks 14
My eloquent Ionian! thou speak'st music   559 Sardan 1 563
Hear those sweet lips grow eloquent in aught   578 Sardan 3 431
Her eyes were eloquent, her words would pose   793 Juan 2 1197
The answer eloquent, where the soul shines   794 Juan 2 1293
Here Raucocanti's eloquent recital   827 Juan 4 713

ELOQUENTLY

Which answers to all doubts so eloquently well   52 Harold 3 1003
And language, eloquently false, evince   461 Dante 3 76

ELSE

To nought else constant, hither deign'd to flee   14 Harold 1 670
To me, though to none else, a not ungrateful
  theme   35 Harold 3 36
From your verses, what else she deserved   116 Strephon 10
Else might inspiring Fancy's magic eye   119 Newstead-A 13
Or else at eve, in radiant glory drest   140 Ossian-B 25
The smile none else might understand   165 Thyrza 30
Should I see nothing else to amuse me to-night   177 Devil's Dr 120
Having nothing else to do (for 'the friends'
  each so near   178 Devil's Dr 209
Or else this heavy heart will burst   218 Soul-B 12
Which else had sounded an immortal lay   253 Bards 834
He quits the scene--or else the scene quits him   260 Hints 252
There's pomp enough, if little else, in plays   262 Hints 442
Thus poetry disgusts, or else delights   265 Hints 634

ELSE

And turns--if nothing else--at least our heads   275 Waltz 156
Or else we'll be kept here an hour at their levy   280 Blues 1 147
And hoarse with having little else to do   285 Vision 10
For hoping no one else may e'er be so   286 Vision 107
Or else the ministry will lose their votes   306 Age 603
Else may we dread the wrath divine   319 Giaour 910
That parts all else, shall doom for ever   327 Abydos 1 325
Else vainly had I pray'd or sought the chance   348 Corsair 2 91
Or else he had not seen another sun   359 Corsair 3 247
Who else than Lara could have cause to fear   377 Lara 2 133
As if all else had pass'd away   396 Parisina 35
Else had his rising heart betray'd   398 Parisina 196
Or else a different lot were mine   411 Mazeppa 486
Who think of something else besides the pen   449 Beppo 604
Or else the people would perhaps have shot him   452 Beppo 774
The victory was Almonte's else; his sight   467 Morgante 102
'If you want armour or aught else, go in   476 Morgante 657
In all things else, let me not be shut out   512 Faliero 2 214
Thank Heaven, you were not--all had else been
  marr'd   516 Faliero 2 534
Else I could answer.--Let us to the meeting   520 Faliero 3 82
Who hears me; else why have I been selected   521 Faliero 3 183
Of massacre which else pollutes it wholly   521 Faliero 3 196
Of deeds that else were silent, save on marble   525 Faliero 3 461
Else I should stab thee on the spot, to save   527 Faliero 3 625
Merit forgiveness; else a doubt like this   543 Faliero 5 346
Have I aught else to undergo save death   545 Faliero 5 547
I've heard thy sister talk of nothing else   552 Sardan 1 139
To be aught save a monarch; else for me   556 Sardan 1 411
And mow'd down like the grass, else all we reap   557 Sardan 1 462
None else shall chain them. You hear him, and me   564 Sardan 2 172
Fool! hence--what else should despotism alarm'd   569 Sardan 2 450
Else you had met. That pang at least is spared
  her   585 Sardan 4 455
Else they make an eternity of moments   593 Sardan 5 403
That these are demons: could it be else that   603 Foscari 2 117
Farewell! Farewell! Is there aught else? No--
  nothing   617 Foscari 4 182
To fall upon you! else they would, as erst   624 Foscari 5 218
Else you dare not deal thus by them or me   624 Foscari 5 258
Else--You have reason. I have spoken much   624 Foscari 5 262
Evil; and what else hath he made? But let him   629 Cain 1 147
Aught else but dust! That is a grovelling wish   631 Cain 1 289
Born with me--but I love nought else. Our
  parents   634 Cain 1 430
What else can joy be, but the spreading joy   634 Cain 1 478
Return! be sure: how else should death be peopled   639 Cain 2 200
With me, their sire and brother! What else is   639 Cain 2 233
Another sacrifice! Give way, or else   650 Cain 3 308
Its native soil:--else--I love God far more   651 Cain 3 315
This is a vision, else I am become   651 Cain 3 342
Or else he walks the wild up to the cavern   658 Heaven 248
Alas! what else is love but sorrow? Even   665 Heaven 727
Else it were yours; but this you know, or should
  know   674 Werner 1 203
The only question is--Who else could have   684 Werner 2 58
Werner, or what else? Call me Werner still   700 Werner 3 343
To nothing that may tempt me! Else--Heaven aid
  me   701 Werner 3 413
Who seems the culprit, and--Who seems? Who else   703 Werner 3 530
None else, though all the full-fed train of
  menials   703 Werner 3 576
Nought else.--But I have not the time to pause   706 Werner 4 125
Indeed I have none else left, since my poor
  father   707 Werner 4 174
None else but I, who see it--feel it--keener   709 Werner 4 326
And makes his every thought subservient; else   710 Werner 4 356
To all else--the Hungarian's face! I grew   714 Werner 5 103
You said, and to none else. At dead of night   717 Werner 5 806
You saw none else? You did not see the--No   718 Werner 5 319
For whom or what else did you ever teach it   719 Werner 5 433
I will. Thou canst? Perhaps. Would you aught
  else   724 Deformed 1 119
Nought else would wittingly wear mine. I'll show
  thee   724 Deformed 1 137
Have seen else on this side of the dim shore   726 Deformed 1 243
Or else I would mourn it   743 Deformed 3 80
If you seek aid from me--or else be silent   743 Deformed 3 107
To--God knows where--for no one else can know   746 Juan Ded 72
Any one else--they were become traditional   751 Juan 1 244
And bit her lips (for else she might have
  scream'd   753 Juan 1 430
Or else 'twere easy to withdraw her waist   761 Juan 1 917
Gasps, and whatever else the owners choose   766 Juan 1 1293
But nothing else, the time of words was o'er   767 Juan 1 1302
Or else the thing had hardly come to pass   774 Juan 2 22
Sea-sickness death: his love was perfect, how
  else   777 Juan 2 182
And fed by spoonfuls, else they always burst   794 Juan 2 1264
Else how the devil is it that fresh features   800 Juan 2 1663
Else they shall feel the weight of this my arm   841 Juan 5 651
But tears must stop like all things else; and
  soon   846 Juan 5 961

ELSE

And yet, like all men else, I must allow	877 Juan	7	637
But else unhurt, she open'd her large eyes	890 Juan	8	759
By rendering desperate those who had else repented	940 Juan	12	640
Besides the most sublime of--Heaven knows what else	941 Juan	12	701
If you have nought else, here's at least satiety	957 Juan	14	109
Or else 'twill cost us all another million	966 Juan	14	664
Days better drawn before, or else assume	971 Juan	15	207

ELSE'S

Your Ida, for I would be yours, none else's	707 Werner	4	173

ELSEWHERE

To-morrow, here or elsewhere, as may best	372 Lara	1	469
Me forth to breathe elsewhere, so reassume	457 Dante	1	80
Sole in Assyria, or with them elsewhere	561 Sardan	1	673
But elsewhere than the palace. Wherefore so	564 Sardan	2	146
Nor elsewhere; where the king is, pleasure sparkles	571 Sardan	3	4
Be ashes here than aught that lives elsewhere	597 Foscari	1	139
Elsewhere. And every where. True; but in freedom	624 Foscari	5	210
Than they could do elsewhere. Hark! nearer still	681 Werner	1	633
If not, I'll try my fortune elsewhere. How	695 Werner	3	3
They come! to seek elsewhere what is before them	697 Werner	3	112
Elsewhere was nothing. She had naught to fear	799 Juan	2	1615
Which still elsewhere may rouse a brighter spring	897 Juan	9	84
Elsewhere preserved: the cloisters still were stable	949 Juan	13	523
And senate: when invited elsewhere, truly	951 Juan	13	667
Which you might elsewhere hope to find in vain	980 Juan	16	20

ELUDE

Ye shall not thus elude me: by a power	479 Manfred	1	42

ELUDED

A lucid lake to his eluded thirst	529 Faliero	4	67

ELVES

To mingling bands of fairy elves	118 Romance		22

ELVIRA'S

From Elvira's gates to those	194 Ballad-A		3

ELYSIAN

With thine Elysian water-drops; the face	72 Harold	4	1037
Fit comrades in Elysian regions move	87 Marsus		4
When heart meets heart again in dreams Elysian	325 Abydos	1	164
At once Elysian and effeminate	423 Island	2	313

ELYSIUM

To him it was Elysium to be there	885 Juan	8	420

ELYSIUM'S

Who to the awe-struck world unlock'd Elysium's gates	7 Harold	1	242
Close shamed Elysium's gates, my shade shall seek for none	27 Harold	2	459

'EM
(See also THEM)

In furious mood he would have tore 'em	96 Granta		84
For his merits, would you know 'em	197 Rogers		75
And then, still further to bewilder 'em	230 Murray-A		5
In case you should not know 'em	233 Ballad-B		12
They have a number, though they ne'er exhibit 'em	449 Beppo		559
No bustling Botherbys have they to show 'em	449 Beppo		575
With goods of various names, but I forgot 'em	452 Beppo		772
As if she deem'd that mystery would ennoble 'em	748 Juan	1	104
And said there was analogy between 'em	748 Juan	1	106
But I must leave the proofs to those who've seen 'em	748 Juan	1	108
And all may think which way their judgments lean 'em	748 Juan	1	110
So good--I wonder Castlereagh don't tax 'em	800 Juan	2	1624
Another time he might have liked to see 'em	826 Juan	4	599
You may do right forbidding them to show 'em	830 Juan	4	855
The females stood, as one by one they pick'd 'em	831 Juan	4	927
And for their other matters, meet and share 'em	864 Juan	6	760
Great deeds are doing--how shall I relate 'em	877 Juan	7	646
As now occur, I thought that I would pen you 'em	895 Juan	8	1084
Yet if perchance remember'd, still disdain you 'em	895 Juan	8	1086
Just now,--but by and by the Truth will show 'em	899 Juan	9	173
I say, will these great relics, when they see 'em	901 Juan	9	319
(With more beside if Juan had not stopp'd 'em	912 Juan	10	326
Of all his feelings--only he forgot 'em	914 Juan	10	432
Than these things; and besides, I wish to spare 'em	958 Juan	14	165

EMACIATED

So here, though faint, emaciated, and stark	787 Juan	2	841

EMANATED

Which emanated then, and dazzles now	60 Harold	4	338

EMANATION

A single emanation from one body	524 Faliero	3	407
Emanation of a thing more glorious still	726 Deformed	1	252

EMASCULATED

Emasculated to the marrow It	746 Juan	Ded	114

EMASCULATION

The soul's emasculation saddens all	461 Dante	3	84

EMBALM

Did not my verse embalm full many an act	458 Dante	1	148
To embalm with his celestial flattery	462 Dante	3	144

EMBALM'D

Thy name is yet embalm'd within my heart	126 Recoll		304

EMBARGO

Oh how I wish than an embargo	225 Embargo		1
Napoleon's edicts no embargo lay	260 Hints		301
Than where two wives are under an embargo	863 Juan	6	720

EMBARGO'D

When Rapp the Harmonist embargo'd marriage	972 Juan	15	273
Found his own legs embargo'd from mere walking	997 Juan	17	60

EMBARGO'S

Our embargo's off at last	156 Hodgson		2

EMBARK

The rising morn will view the chiefs embark	347 Corsair	2	37
Embark their wealth and seek a safer strand	357 Corsair	3	152
Nor ever did more love and joy embark	435 Island	4	399
We will embark anon. Fair nymphs, who deign	551 Sardan	1	54
And now to serve for safety, and embark	591 Sardan	5	261
Oh let this child embark	669 Heaven		1097
Her son to Cadiz only to embark	775 Juan	2	58

EMBARK'D
(See also RE-EMBARK'D)

'They are--nay more, embark'd; the latest boat	346 Corsair	1	557
Embark'd, the sail unfurl'd, the light breeze blew	362 Corsair	3	452
Embark'd their guests and launch'd their light canoes	429 Island	3	222
He then embark'd with risk of life and limb	452 Beppo		762
To have ponder'd this before,--ere you embark'd	520 Faliero	3	103
Bear her to where her children are embark'd	584 Sardan	4	421
The queen's embark'd. And well? say that much. Yes	586 Sardan	4	534
Juan embark'd--the ship got under way	775 Juan	2	81
Embark'd himself and them, and off they went thence	836 Juan	5	315
Of the troops were embark'd, the siege to raise	872 Juan	7	306
Here he embark'd, and with a flowing sail	915 Juan	10	505

EMBARKING

Not long ago the senators embarking	509 Faliero	2	4

EMBARKS

Bid to his dukedom. When embarks the son	615 Foscari	4	14

EMBARRASS

Whose little nibbling rustle will embarrass	983 Juan	16	159

EMBARRASS'D

And you, Scamp!--I needs must confess I'm embarrass'd	282 Blues	2	121
Jack was embarrass'd,--never hero more	428 Island	3	131
Embarrass'd at first starting with a novice	756 Juan	1	592
Was much embarrass'd, never having met	847 Juan	5	970
To which embarrass'd people have recourse	864 Juan	6	800
Embarrass'd somewhat both with fire and water	959 Juan	14	240
Nor seem embarrass'd--quite the contrary	993 Juan	16	794

EMBARRASSMENT

By way of echo to embarrassment	428 Island	3	130
So much embarrassment to me just now	700 Werner	3	319
And much embarrassment in either eye	755 Juan	1	556
Baba, with some embarrassment, replied	864 Juan	6	793

EMBASSIES

Have made and marr'd peace oft in embassies	506 Faliero	1	460

EMBASSY

Returning from my Roman embassy	506 Faliero	1	475
From his first fight to his last embassy	510 Faliero	2	115
My Genoese embassy: I saved the life	524 Faliero	3	425

EMBASSY'S

'And'--quoth Satan--'this Embassy's worthy my sight	177 Devil's Dr		119

419

EDEN

But we, thy children, ignorant of Eden	633 Cain	1	397
Ask of your sire, the exile fresh from Eden	635 Cain	1	479
The leaves along the limpid streams of Eden	637 Cain	2	104
Round our regretted and unenter'd Eden	639 Cain	2	252
Adam, could e'er have been in Eden, as	640 Cain	2	275
The cherub-guarded walls of Eden, with	641 Cain	2	344
Which drove your race from Eden--war with all things	641 Cain	2	354
The tree in Eden? Eve, thy mother, best	642 Cain	2	401
Of sorrow--and thou sufferest, are both Eden	642 Cain	2	426
The want of this so much regretted Eden	646 Cain	3	40
Eden and Immortality, resolves	647 Cain	3	73
From Eden, till his children do by him	652 Cain	3	424
The serpent, and my sire still mourn'd for Eden	654 Cain	3	508
Eastward from Eden will we take our way	654 Cain	3	552
An Eden kept afar from sight	656 Heaven		73
Which could not keep in Eden their high place	660 Heaven		342
Her Eden in an endless paradise	661 Heaven		467
Welcome as Eden. It may be they come	663 Heaven		584
Thus was another Eden; they were never	817 Juan	4	74
Where all is Eden, or a wilderness	823 Juan	4	432

EDENS

These Edens of the eastern wave	310 Giaour		15
And Edens in them? It may be. And men	638 Cain	2	170

EDEN'S

When Man, expell'd from Eden's bowers	155 Lady-E		1
As the day closes over Eden's walls	643 Cain	2	471
Of those cast out from Eden's gate	656 Heaven		59
On Eden's streams	656 Heaven		100
Lovely as those which ripen'd Eden's fruit	872 Juan	7	327
She look'd as if she sat by Eden's door	973 Juan	15	359

EDGE
(See also GILT-EDGED, TWO-EDGED)

Could blunt the sabre's edge or clear the cannon's smoke	12 Harold	1	530
And shaped his weapon with an edge severe	51 Harold	3	998
When Brutus made the dagger's edge surpass	67 Harold	4	732
And, blunt myself, give edge to others' steel	263 Hints		486
Shall never blunt its edge on meaner men	265 Hints		600
His teeth were set on edge, he could not blow	297 Vision		824
Let those who shape its edge, beware	319 Giaour		931
Be the edge sharpen'd of my boarding-brand	340 Corsair	1	163
To bare the sabre's edge before a slave	347 Corsair	2	19
Which, once partaken, blunts the sabre's edge	348 Corsair	2	120
Here in thy hold, and with thy falchion's edge	376 Lara	2	52
As it slipp'd through their jaws, when their edge grew dull	389 Corinth		461
But close by the shore, on the edge of the gulf	389 Corinth		473
Since he set its edge anew	400 Parisina		404
Swift-gliding o'er the breaker's whitening edge	422 Island	2	230
And you, ye crags, upon whose extreme edge	482 Manfred	1	274
Nor the false edge of aged appetite	513 Faliero	2	311
Upon the forest's edge, the vehicle	701 Werner	3	433
As o'er the cutter's edge he tried to cross	781 Juan	2	452
Which sets the teeth on edge; and a slight clatter	995 Juan	16	954

EDGES

Save where their brazen-colour'd edges streak	668 Heaven		1009

EDGEWORTH'S

Miss Edgeworth's novels stepping from their covers	749 Juan	1	122

EDICT

The edict of Earth's rulers, who are grown	69 Harold	4	852
Upon some edict; but I have observed	500 Faliero	1	16
This edict. Let him call up into life	619 Foscari	4	273
Would run the edict of the other God	636 Cain	2	6
Of fix'd necessity: against her edict	731 Deformed	1	600

EDICTS

Can tell what edicts sage Lycurgus made	111 Examination		19
Napoleon's edicts no embargo lay	260 Hints		301
The edicts of a power which is not mine	522 Faliero	3	257
Oh, thou wouldst have me doubtless set up edicts	555 Sardan	1	302
The edicts of your orbs, which make Time tremble	561 Sardan	2	7
To edicts of inquisitors of state	607 Foscari	2	383
Their goods and edicts out from pole to pole	915 Juan	10	519
Or starch, as are the edicts statesmen utter	971 Juan	15	212

EDIFICE

Outshining and o'erwhelming edifice	78 Harold	4	1418
When that vast edifice display'd	196 Venice-A		23
An edifice no less sublime than strong	988 Juan	16	517

EDIFYING

A virgin-like and edifying throng	856 Juan	6	235
In a most edifying conversation	994 Juan	16	868

EDINA

And pale Edina shudder'd at the sound	248 Bards		483
For thee Edina culls her evening sweets	249 Bards		532
What then?--Edina starves some lanker son	265 Hints		623

EDINA'S

Edina's brawny sons and brimstone page	256 Bards		1048

EDINBURGH

And that the Edinburgh Review and Quarterly	772 Juan	1	1687

EDITION

Juan was taught from out the best edition	752 Juan	1	345
There's more than one edition, and the readings	770 Juan	1	1509

EDITOR

With the Editor added to make up the three	179 Devil's Dr		245
Till some less rigid editor shall stoop	752 Juan	1	357
I sent it in a letter to the Editor	772 Juan	1	1673

EDUCATE

My politics as yet are all to educate	747 Juan	Ded	133
To educate--ye youth of Europe--you by	848 Juan	5	1046

EDUCATED

And educated as his heir; but then	684 Werner	2	93
Was educated for a monk of all times	732 Deformed	1	668
That sons should not be educated so	753 Juan	1	424

EDUCATION

Or Mrs. Trimmer's books on education	749 Juan	1	123
With persons of no sort of education	749 Juan	1	170
If such an education was the true one	753 Juan	1	379
Perhaps to finish Juan's education	759 Juan	1	806
The great success of Juan's education	775 Juan	2	79
In fact, he had no singing education	827 Juan	4	691
Meantime the education they went through	850 Juan	5	1221
Although their haram education led	875 Juan	7	532
Amongst you, about Leila's education	933 Juan	12	224
To undertake the orphan's education	933 Juan	12	235
Of freedom shall complete their education	940 Juan	12	662
To virtue proper, or good education	945 Juan	13	243
Both lawyers and both men of education	952 Juan	13	731
Their love, their virtue, beauty, education	958 Juan	14	191
For a young gentleman's fit education	962 Juan	14	414
That where their education, harsh or mild	997 Juan	17	13

EDUCATIONS

The best of mothers and of educations	774 Juan	2	5

EDWARD

For the safety of Edward and England they fell	86 Leaving NA		14
When Edward bade his conquering bands advance	111 Examination		15

EDWARD'S

Black Edward's helm, and Becket's bloody stone	916 Juan	10	578

EE
(See also EYE)

But Pride congeal'd the drop within his ee	4 Harold	1	49
'Mid many things unsightly to strange ee	7 Harold	1	228

EELS

Used to it, no doubt, as eels are to be flay'd	832 Juan	5	56

E'EN
(See also EVEN)

And e'en for change of scene would seek the shades below	4 Harold	1	54
Pride might forbid e'en Friendship to complain	19 Harold	1	930
Not e'en a zephyr wanders through the grove	84 Death-B		2
E'en though the numbers did exceed	88 To Ellen		9
Nor e'en your eyes your love bespeak	90 Caroline-B		12
For e'en your lip seems steep'd in snow	90 Caroline-B		17
E'en now a name illustrious is thine own	93 Dorset		9
E'en suns, which systems now control	97 To M--		27
For whom, at last, e'en hostile nations groan	114 Death-A		31
Nor e'en to Pitt the patriot's palm resign	114 Death-A		34
E'en now the gulf appears in view	118 Romance		59
From ruffian fangs escape not e'en the dead	121 Newstead-A		87
Can rank, or e'en a guardian's name, supply	125 Recoll		221
E'en when our lives are on the wane	128 Lady-C		14
When e'en thy smiles begin to pall	135 I Would		44
Not e'en the hope of future fame	146 Adieu		75
Though cold as e'en the dead can be	166 Struggle		47
E'en Pain itself should smile on thee	167 Euthanasia		20
Nor e'en the pawing of the wilder Brute	184 Julian		22
To thee--to thee- e'en in the gasp of death	206 Love, Death		19
E'en then the boldest start from public sneers	242 Bards		33
Still there are follies, e'en for me to chase	242 Bards		41
In mangled prose, nor e'en aspires to rhyme	246 Bards		322
E'en I--least thinking of a thoughtless throng	251 Bards		689
E'en I must raise my voice, e'en I must feel	251 Bards		695
E'en now, what once-loved minstrels may claim	254 Bards		955

EMBATTLED
Or pour his arrows through th' embattled field | 105 Nisus | 4

EMBELLISH
They so embellish, that 'tis quite a bore | 771 Juan | 1 1614

EMBERS
His shivering limbs the embers warm | 89 Anacreon-B | 35
The fires are faint; their embers fail in | 130 Calmar | 105
Extinguish'd with the dying embers | 134 E. N. Long | 86
Extinguish'd with the dying embers | 148 A Fan | 12
The dying embers of an altar-place | 189 Darkness | 58
But no,--their embers soon will burst the mould | 308 Age | 754
The embers of their former fires | 311 Giaour | 117
The dying embers dwindle in the grate | 980 Juan | 15 775

EMBITTER
Will deeply embitter the bowl | 162 Romaic-A | 18

EMBITTER'D
Ah! splendour has raised, but embitter'd, my lot | 136 Highlander | 29

EMBITTERS
Embitters the present, compared with the past | 96 Harrow-A | 2

EMBLAZON'D
(See also WELL-EMBLAZON'D)
Immortal names, emblazon'd on our line | 170 Address-A | 49
And many a bright emblazon'd rhyme | 329 Abydos | 2 74

EMBLEM
Mortality's emblem is given | 97 To M.S.G.-B | 10
His myrtle, an emblem of purest delight | 100 L Adieu | 43
Yet are his tears no emblem of regret | 122 Newstead-A | 145
A fitter emblem of his own | 168 Cornelian-B | 8
From this emblem what variance your motto evinces | 228 Ich Dien | 1
Her emblem sparkles o'er the minaret | 269 Minerva | 40
Emblem of all to whom the land gives birth | 270 Minerva | 136
Be neither name nor emblem spread | 323 Giaour | 1326
Her emblem sparkles o'er the minaret | 356 Corsair | 3 40
The first the emblem (rarely though) of what | 924 Juan | 11 348

EMBLEMS
With emblems well devised by amorous pride | 42 Harold | 3 436
The mingled emblems of his mighty mind | 248 Bards | 489
Are emblems of deeds that are done in their clime | 323 Abydos | 1 2
Emblems and monuments, and prostitute | 464 Dante | 4 86
Or a singultus--emblems of emotion | 968 Juan | 15 10

EMBODIED
Embodied longest. If there be indeed | 579 Sardan | 4 56
Made her a beautiful embodied storm | 848 Juan | 5 1080

EMBODY
Could I embody and unbosom now | 50 Harold | 3 905

EMBOSOM'D
And deep embosom'd in his shady groves | 161 Athos | 10
It stood embosom'd in a happy valley | 948 Juan | 13 441

EMBOSS'D
What silver arms with various art emboss'd | 109 Nisus | 285
A sun emboss'd in gold, whose rays of tissue | 809 Juan | 3 535

EMBRACE
The earth to her embrace compels the powers of air | 52 Harold | 3 1021
The anguish of a last embrace | 89 To Emma | 34
And hope no more thy soft embrace | 90 To M.S.G.-A | 34
If again in the mansion of death I embrace thee | 92 Caroline-D | 23
Then in his warm embrace the boys he press'd | 107 Nisus | 127
And death was heavenly in his friend's embrace | 110 Nisus | 400
May rescue thee from earth's embrace | 154 Skull | 19
To fold thee in a faint embrace | 167 Dead | 60
In one embrace let these arms again enfold him | 205 Hindoo | 14
Pursuing Deities, or in the embrace | 205 Aristom | 9
Of that fair boy his sire shall ne'er embrace | 299 Age | 84
The thought that Conscience must embrace | 313 Giaour | 274
Upon the last embrace of foes | 316 Giaour | 650
She rose, she sprung, she clung to his embrace | 345 Corsair | 1 466
Their arms can scarce forbear a rough embrace | 363 Corsair | 3 501
At once she sought and sunk in his embrace | 363 Corsair | 3 543
But not the form he panted to embrace | 364 Corsair | 3 588
The frequent sigh, the long embrace | 397 Parisina | 53
The frequent sigh, the long embrace | 397 Parisina | 59
And he to that embrace awakes | 397 Parisina | 75
And clasp the mountain in his mind's embrace | 422 Island | 2 283
Raphael, who died in thy embrace, and vies | 445 Beppo | 363
And then Orlando to embrace him flew | 471 Morgante | 361
But my embrace was fatal. Heaven give thee rest | 485 Manfred | 2 87
Of the embrace of angels with a sex | 493 Manfred | 3 177
Come hither, my Bertuccio--one embrace | 535 Faliero | 4 476
Then farewell, Angiolina!--one embrace | 547 Faliero | 5 671
Myrrha, embrace me;--yet once more--once more | 574 Sardan | 3 170

EMBRACE
In sounding. Now, farewell; one last embrace | 594 Sardan | 5 469
Embrace, but not the last; there is one more | 594 Sardan | 5 470
Will never be so white. Embrace me, father | 613 Foscari | 3 359
But first embrace thy son. May his soft spirit | 648 Cain | 3 174
My brother to his cold and still embrace | 652 Cain | 3 375
And I embrace it, as I did my son | 699 Werner | 3 246
My father!--Let me embrace thee! We may be | 699 Werner | 3 272
Embrace me! Yes,--your tone--your look--yes, yes | 702 Werner | 3 471
To embrace him in fight | 742 Deformed | 3 53
There was a depth of feeling to embrace | 987 Juan | 16 431

EMBRACED
Where Rome embraced her heroes? where the steep | 71 Harold | 4 1001
If thus, when to my heart embraced | 91 Caroline-B | 45
Which all embraced--and lighten'd over all | 193 Monody | 35
Than the one which once embraced me | 207 Fare Thee | 19
The women throng'd, embracing and embraced | 435 Island | 4 409
Embraced me, while I shrunk from her, as if | 580 Sardan | 4 156
The music, and the crowd embraced in lieu | 715 Werner | 5 131
And Julia sate with Juan, half embraced | 761 Juan | 1 913
Then one vast fire, air, earth, and stream embraced | 879 Juan | 8 53

EMBRACES
Your last embraces | 200 Stanzas-B | 69
But such a love for you my heart embraces | 475 Morgante | 629
And earliest embraces of earth's parents | 643 Cain | 2 476
Kisses, sweet words, embraces, and all that | 854 Juan | 6 106

EMBRACING
All his toils are repaid when, embracing the maid | 115 The Tear | 23
The women throng'd, embracing and embraced | 435 Island | 4 409
The blush of earth embracing with her heaven | 485 Manfred | 2 116

EMBROIDER'D
(See also GOLD-EMBROIDER'D)
The velvet chair--in his embroider'd night-gown | 683 Werner | 2 34
Embroider'd delicately o'er with blue | 809 Juan | 3 510

EMBROIDERY
Their rival scarfs of mix'd embroidery | 10 Harold | 1 434
Medals, rank, ribands, lace, embroidery, scarlet | 877 Juan | 7 665

EMBRYO
Of embryo actors, to the Drama new | 113 Prologue | 16
Though yet in embryo these perfections shine | 126 Recoll | 293

EMERALD
Making it all one emerald:--how profound | 65 Harold | 4 626
O'er emerald meadows of Kashmeer | 314 Giaour | 390
Near these, with emerald rays beset | 329 Abydos | 2 67
Of desert-loving pine, whose emerald scalp | 459 Dante | 2 64
An emerald aigrette with Haidee's hair in't | 811 Juan | 3 614

EMERALDS
May its verdure like emeralds be | 151 Soul-A | 10

EMERALD'S
While the mild emerald's beam shades down the dies | 930 Juan | 12 63

EMERGE
Don Juan, here permitted to emerge | 826 Juan | 4 625
Our bubbles; as the old burst, new emerge | 980 Juan | 15 790

EMERGENCIES
Show me the law! On great emergencies | 540 Faliero | 5 185

EMERGING
Haply thy sun, emerging, yet may shine | 122 Newstead-A | 153
To hiss and sting through some emerging world | 659 Heaven | 305

EMETIC
But the sea acted as a strong emetic | 776 Juan | 2 168
Three hundred cannon threw up their emetic | 879 Juan | 8 89

EMIGRANT
To her desolate shore--where the emigrant stands | 202 Avatar | 13

EMIGRATION
That half its produce tends to emigration | 972 Juan | 15 294

EMIGRATIONS
Several prepared themselves for emigrations | 911 Juan | 10 237

EMINENCE
(See also PRE-EMINENCE)
Broad eminence I was invested duke | 624 Foscari | 5 242

EMINENT
And all which makes them eminent and bright | 547 Faliero | 5 657
Nor canvass what so 'eminent a hand' meant | 973 Juan | 15 302

EMIR

An Emir by his garb of green	313	Giaour		357

EMIT

Whose fires emit a faint and trembling ray	109	Nisus		276

EMITTING

And some emitting sparks, and some displaying	638	Cain	2	186

EMOTION

Mistake not, sweet sceptic, the cause of emotion	91	Caroline-C		17
But still I perceive an emotion the same	135	Highlander		11
With a full but soft emotion	188	Music-C		15
If their billows excite an emotion	210	Augusta-B		15
Nor feels, forsooth, emotion at his heart	267	Hints		779
This gentle emotion, so seldom our lot	282	Blues	2	134
Perchance from some emotion, doubt, or pride	340	Corsair	1	152
On Lara's glance emotion gathering grew	372	Lara	1	411
Or that of any other strong emotion	804	Juan	3	206
We ponder deeply on each past emotion	816	Juan	4	16
By deep emotion:--you may sometimes trace	866	Juan	6	884
Or a singultus--emblems of emotion	968	Juan	15	10
A theme for Pity or some worse emotion	997	Juan	17	22

EMOTIONS

The fierce emotions of the flowing soul	119	Answer-A		10
That raised emotions both of rage and fear	341	Corsair	1	224
And let such strong emotions stamp your brow	511	Faliero	2	177
I might not yield again to such emotions	534	Faliero	4	397
Extracts emotions beautiful and new	773	Juan	1	1708
He stopp'd.--What singular emotions fill	804	Juan	3	163

EMPEROR

Over the proud Place where an Emperor sued	56	Harold	4	97
An Emperor tramples where an Emperor knelt	57	Harold	4	101
But peace to her, her emperor and diet	274	Waltz		55
Of Charles the Emperor, whom you will find	466	Morgante		28
Know then, oh emperor! that all complain	467	Morgante		110
When Rome's sixth emperor was near his last	492	Manfred	3	88

EMPERORS

Under its emperors, and--changing sex	730	Deformed	1	576
The theatre where emperors and their subjects	731	Deformed	1	619
Emperors are only husbands in wives' eyes	846	Juan	5	917
Arise, when we see emperors fall with oats	900	Juan	9	256

EMPEROR'S

Though an Emperor's taste was displeased with his haste	176	Devil's Dr		57
Oppressive than an emperor's jewell'd purple	682	Werner	1	719

EMPEROUR

For being the last wife of the Emperour	850	Juan	5	1167

EMPHASIS

With emphasis, and also with good sense	960	Juan	14	300

EMPHATIC

Till the floor echoes his emphatic foot	267	Hints		776
And our Sophias are not so emphatic	955	Juan	13	877

EMPHATICALLY

That you repeat the word emphatically	605	Foscari	2	215

EMPIRE

An empire thou couldst crush, command, rebuild	41	Harold	3	338
Fortress of falling empire, honour'd sleeps	64	Harold	4	528
From the first hour of empire in the bud	72	Harold	4	1011
Arch, empire, each thing round thee, and man plods	77	Harold	4	1310
Rose o'er an empire: but beneath thy right	81	Harold	4	1563
An empire for a cell	180	Ode-A		67
Vain froward child of empire! say	181	Ode-A		161
A longer empire o'er the public mind	263	Hints		507
Shall shake your tyrant empire to its base	271	Minerva		222
O'er which from empire she lured Antony	298	Age		30
What though his name a wider empire found	299	Age		93
Survey our empire and behold our home	338	Corsair	1	4
That fearful empire which the human breast	366	Lara	1	15
The empire of the alternate victor's breast	379	Lara	2	275
Glory and Empire! once upon these towers	454	Venice-B		101
Her palace, in whose cradle Empire grew	459	Dante	2	55
Which form the empire of eternity	464	Dante	4	69
Some empire still in his expiring glance	492	Manfred	3	95
Its part with all its empire in this ermine	506	Faliero	1	445
A province for an empire, petty town	548	Faliero	5	751
Of empire ending like a shepherd's tale	550	Sardan	1	8
To have reach'd an empire: to an empire born	550	Sardan	1	15
An empire than thy presence. It may be	552	Sardan	1	104
Who built up this vast empire, and wert made	553	Sardan	1	160
If they should sweep me off from earth and empire	557	Sardan	1	445
Why, what is earth or empire of the earth	557	Sardan	1	446
But what wouldst have? the empire has been founded	559	Sardan	1	596
Taking his last look of Assyria's empire	561	Sardan	2	2

EMPIRE

Ne'er fought more fiercely to win empire, than	576	Sardan	3	313
The empire of eternity. Hence--hence	578	Sardan	4	27
An empire to indulge thee. I must part ye	583	Sardan	4	358
Sweep empire after empire, like this first	594	Sardan	5	444
(A soul by whom you have increased your empire	625	Foscari	5	322
Who made all empires, empire; or recalling	656	Heaven		86
In youth was such as to unmake an empire	673	Werner	1	153
As e'er another prince of the empire. Why	704	Werner	4	8
Not sceptre, an hermaphrodite of empire	730	Deformed	1	577
Have been the circus of an empire. Well	734	Deformed	1	850
'Twere worth one half our empire: his indulgences	739	Deformed	2	276
Of empire and chase	742	Deformed	3	47
Here is the empire of thy perfect bliss	757	Juan	1	699
Which needed not an empire to persuade	847	Juan	5	995
His empire also was without a bound	850	Juan	5	1197
I know its mighty empire now allures	899	Juan	9	181
This is the literary lower empire	926	Juan	11	481

EMPIRES

Still springing o'er thy banks, though Empires near them fall	45	Harold	3	589
Forgets her empires with a just decay	45	Harold	3	637
Of men and empires,--'tis to be forgiven	49	Harold	3	826
Thou wert the throne and grave of empires; still	52	Harold	3	1027
Lone mother of dead empires, and control	66	Harold	4	696
The pyramid of empires pinnacled	71	Harold	4	978
Thy shores are empires, changed in all save thee	82	Harold	4	1630
That will arise, though empires fall	128	Answer-B		16
And swept down empires with its flood	188	On Star		14
Kingdoms and empires in my little day	211	Augusta-C		33
Empires have moulder'd from the face of earth	244	Bards		195
The fall of empires or a yellow leaf	246	Bards		334
Whose game was empires and whose stakes were thrones	299	Age		51
To come, in which all empires shall expire	300	Age		184
Would have depopulated empires, nor	528	Faliero	3	656
To vanquish empires, and refuse their crown	535	Faliero	4	507
Than empires can confer, in quiet honour	540	Faliero	5	156
I only echo thee the voice of empires	554	Sardan	1	271
I cannot go on multiplying empires	559	Sardan	1	597
Of empires, into nothing; but even then	594	Sardan	5	445
Who made all empires, empire; or recalling	656	Heaven		86
Belongs to empires, and has been but borne	730	Deformed	1	538
Then spur away o'er empires and o'er states	759	Juan	1	822
Of empires heave but like some passing waves	980	Juan	15	792

EMPIRE'S

Stop!--for thy tread is on an Empire's dust	37	Harold	3	145
He tasted empire's blessings and its curse	299	Age		96
Look to the annals of thine empire's founders	559	Sardan	1	594

EMPLOY

To me a silent and a sweet employ	127	Recoll		374
And this will form a dear employ	141	Pignus		31
And all my wane of years employ	150	My Son		29
His years need scarce a thought employ	326	Abydos	1	207
Her charms to pontiffs proud, who but employ	464	Dante	4	87
Employ the minutes left in aspirations	547	Faliero	5	651
To employ our means to obtain heaven for the souls	712	Werner	4	488
But she defied all means they could employ	824	Juan	4	471
No less delighted to employ his leisure	881	Juan	8	192
Their natures? or their sovereigns, who employ	890	Juan	8	735

EMPLOY'D

Alike been all employ'd in vain	168	Cornelian-B		4
Must now, every hour of the twelve, be employ'd	280	Blues	2	5
The warrior ere his strength could be employ'd	427	Island	3	50
I have employ'd my penance to record	437	Tasso		31
I am the chief of the arsenal, employ'd	505	Faliero	1	379
Employ'd it for the best. Pronounce in person	565	Sardan	2	189
Though seemingly employ'd like all the rest	587	Sardan	5	33
I am employ'd in such; but you perceive	741	Deformed	2	408
In Juan's case were but employ'd in vain	774	Juan	2	6
Have much employ'd the muse of history's pen	800	Juan	2	1644
Employ'd for, since it is their daily labour	923	Juan	11	322

EMPLOYING

If we should fail, employing bloody means	519	Faliero	3	76
And still more women, spring from not employing	965	Juan	14	623

EMPLOYMENT

I'd pass them in the same employment	144	Becher-B		8
Who could, ye gods! her next employment guess	208	Sketch		11
A fool: his folly shall have such employment	703	Werner	3	559
And this at present was her kind employment	993	Juan	16	848

EMPLOYMENTS

Intrusted by the state with high employments	544	Faliero	5	481

EMPLOYS

Employs a pen less pointed than his awl	252	Bards		766
The unwonted chase each hour employs	314	Giaour		441

EMPLOYS
Has lavish'd all its chief employs upon him   510 Faliero   2   114

EMPOISON'D
Empoison'd all my life before I knew   652 Cain   3   373

EMPOWER
There is resource: empower me with thy signet   555 Sardan   1   334

EMPRESS
(See also EX-EMPRESS)
Oh Stamboul, once the empress of their reign   32 Harold   2   748
And vanquish'd millions hail their empress, Rome   110 Nisus   406
('Twas thus he spake) 'and Empress of the Earth   849 Juan   5   1146
Gulbeyaz was an empress, but had been   855 Juan   6   199
And brought before the empress, who had made   867 Juan   6   941
The armies of the Christian Empress Catherine   875 Juan   7   512
'Glory to God and to the Empress!' (Powers   895 Juan   8   1063
The empress smiled: the reigning favourite
   frown'd   902 Juan   9   362
Besides, the empress sometimes liked a boy   902 Juan   9   375
Then recollecting the whole empress, nor   903 Juan   9   457
Or duchess, princess, empress, 'deigns to prove   905 Juan   9   541
But in such matters Russia's mighty empress   906 Juan   9   615
The favour of the empress was agreeable   910 Juan   10   169
Unto an empress, who preferr'd young men   911 Juan   10   258
The empress was alarm'd, and her physician   912 Juan   10   306

EMPRESSEMENT
But Juan was received with much 'empressement   923 Juan   11   329

EMPRESS'S
All, praised the empress's maternal love   911 Juan   10   256

EMPRIZE
Shrunk from his deeds of chivalrous emprize   25 Harold   2   337

EMPTIED
Vials of wrath but emptied to refill   460 Dante   3   3

EMPTY
(See also LONG-EMPTY)
Have yielded to the stranger: empty halls   57 Harold   4   132
An empty urn within her wither'd hands   66 Harold   4   705
to blue-eyed Mora; let it hang in my empty   131 Calmar   179
In thoughtless throngs and empty noise   134 Lady-D   39
And empty the goblet, and dreary the hearth   164 Newstead-C   12
Than sounding trifles, empty, though refined   263 Hints   508
And find them flown her empty nest   319 Giaour   956
His empty chain above it leant   404 Chillon   162
And seek to honour with an empty urn   465 Dante   4   139
Search empty pockets; also, to arrest   684 Werner   2   70
(Signs of true genius, and of empty pockets   762 Juan   1   1026
As tigers combat with an empty craw   884 Juan   8   389

EMPURPLED
But this empurpled pledge to bear   317 Giaour   720
The very blue of the empurpled night   638 Cain   2   179

EMULATE
Though thus in arms they emulate her sons   13 Harold   1   587
As soars this fane to emulate the last   169 Address-A   27
He was your Master--emulate him here   194 Monody   106
Oh! would thy bards but emulate thy fame   255 Bards   997
To emulate them, and to 'eave behind   530 Faliero   4   173
Ties which bind man to man, to emulate   599 Foscari   1   263
Do we but imitate and emulate   665 Heaven   745

EMULATION
Far distant he goes, with the same emulation   86 Leaving NA   27
Kept the place open for their emulation   913 Juan   10   384
So first there was a generous emulation   933 Juan   12   233

EN
Of all that strut 'en militaire   163 Malta   20
Nor think of poverty, except 'en masque   250 Bards   655

E---N
Oh well done Lord E---n! and better done R---r   225 Ode-D   1

ENABLE
Enough of heaven to enable them to bear   587 Sardan   5   30

ENABLED
Mine hath enabled me to bear her scorn   657 Heaven   171

ENABLES
Your humid earth enables you to look   744 Deformed   3   143
A ready answer, which at once enables   768 Juan   1   1394
Such as enables Man to show his strength   998 Juan   17   91

ENAMOUR
His heart was one of those which most enamour us   444 Beppo   269

ENAMOUR'D
Thus, and enamour'd, were in him the same   47 Harold   3   737
Of an enamour'd Goddess, and the cell   73 Harold   4   1061
Lo! blushing Itch, coy nymph, enamour'd grown   249 Bards   536
There man, enamour'd of distress   310 Giaour   50
Let him who crawls enamour'd of decay   338 Corsair   1   27
And makes the nymphs enamour'd, to the hand   466 Morgante   20
I am almost enamour'd of her, as   741 Deformed   2   413
Patient--but not enamour'd of endurance   998 Juan   17   84

ENCAGE
Which the stern dotard deem'd he could encage   17 Harold   1   804

ENCHAIN'D
More than her fell Pizarros once enchain'd   18 Harold   1   914
Of Lancilot, how love enchain'd him too   477 Francesca   32

ENCHAINS
Enchains the captives of their hate   196 Venice-A   16

ENCHANT
A smile can enchant, or a tear can dissuade   91 Caroline-C   20

ENCHANTED
And life's enchanted cup but sparkles near the
   brim   36 Harold   3   72
The charm of this enchanted ground   44 Harold   3   527
Here didst thou dwell, in this enchanted cover   72 Harold   4   1054
At seventeen, too, the world was still enchanted   962 Juan   14   435

ENCHANTER
That great enchanter, at whose rod's command   902 Juan   9   347

ENCHANTER'S
As from the stroke of the enchanter's wand   55 Harold   4   4
By this old black enchanter's unsought aid   842 Juan   5   664

ENCHANTING
It sings of Love's enchanting dream   92 Lady-A   3

ENCHANTMENT
Enchantment over passion, and from woe   47 Harold   3   727
Because he turn'd a fruit to an enchantment   554 Sardan   1   235

ENCHANTMENTS
Its false and true enchantments--art and nature   529 Faliero   4   63

ENCHANTRESS
Me the enchantress ever flies   132 L'Amitie   86

ENCHANTRESSES
Ye young enchantresses of gay Licoo   419 Island   2   58

ENCHANTS
Enchants you like the Girl of Cadiz   160 Cadiz   24
The gesture which enchants, the eye that speaks   805 Juan   3   260

ENCIRCLE
Clouds there encircle the forms of my fathers   117 Lachin   23

ENCIRCLED
(See also ZONE-ENCIRCLED)
Encircled by insulting rebel powers   120 Newstead-A   58

ENCLOS
Ugly; for instance--Ninon de l'Enclos   844 Juan   5   784

ENCLOSE
And caves their sullen roar enclose   133 E. N. Long   56
The Turkish tyrants now enclose   158 Florence   36
Dispatch the letter which I must enclose   224 J.C.H.   10

ENCLOSED
No common be enclosed without an ode   252 Bards   786
The purest ore enclosed the whitest skin   810 Juan   3   567
The Gothic chamber, where he was enclosed   982 Juan   16   115

ENCOMIAST
'Though I doubt if this drivelling encomiast of
   War   177 Devil's Dr   127

ENCOMPASS
Which encompass Rome, the mother   735 Deformed   2   51

ENCOMPASS'D
Encompass'd with its dark and rolling shroud   438 Tasso   115

ENCORE
His anguish doubling by his own 'encore   261 Hints   310

ENCOUNTER
Nor solely dare encounter hostile rage   31 Harold   2   718
The full encounter of his searching eye   341 Corsair   1   216
They could encounter as a veteran may   379 Lara   2   303

ENCOUNTER
All who encounter me and mine, be sure   524 Faliero 3 397
What thy remoter offspring must encounter   644 Cain 2 522
It may be, may again encounter, why   676 Werner 1 322
How to encounter with this martial scold   864 Juan 6 763
Which best it is to encounter--Ghost, or none   998 Juan 17 105

ENCOUNTERING
At length encountering meets the mutual gaze   372 Lara 1 409
From the point of encountering blades to the hilt   392 Corinth 767

ENCOURAGE
You should rather encourage my passion than
  shock it   280 Blues 1 144
Was not such as to encourage him to shine   977 Juan 15 598

ENCOURAGED
The foster'd feud encouraged to beguile   302 Age 293

ENCOURAGEMENT
Because it left encouragement behind   786 Juan 2 790
With this encouragement, he led the way   843 Juan 5 737

ENCOURAGES
What Nature naturally most encourages   972 Juan 15 278

ENCOURAGING
Upon the same ground, and encouraging   589 Sardan 5 109

ENCROACH
I could say more, but do not choose to encroach   921 Juan 11 181

ENCROACHING
Unanswer'd save by the encroaching swell   662 Heaven 509
By rebel pachas, and encroaching giaours   850 Juan 5 1199

ENCRUST
Of gem and marble, to encrust the bones   64 Harold 4 534

ENCUMBER
My back-shop glut, my shelves encumber   231 Doctor 32
By stealth her husband's temples to encumber   763 Juan 1 1102
Not finding that the additions much encumber   802 Juan 3 24
Here wealth had done its utmost to encumber   839 Juan 5 510
Their clay for the last time their souls encumber   880 Juan 8 141
Nor did she find the quantity encumber   913 Juan 10 382
Variety itself will more encumber   945 Juan 13 237

ENCUMBER'D
(See also PRAISE-ENCUMBER'D)
Rot piecemeal on his own encumber'd shores   272 Minerva 270
The route on to Bohemia, though encumber'd   698 Werner 3 197
But like a hawk encumber'd with his hood   745 Juan Ded 14

ENCUMBERING
Which still recoils from its encumbering clay   463 Dante 4 22

ENCUMBERS
The lust which stings, the splendour which
  encumbers   886 Juan 8 533

ENCYCLOPEDIZE
Which encyclopedize both flesh and fish   976 Juan 15 542

END
Far as the eye discerns, withouten end   9 Harold 1 354
Nor mortal eye the distant end foresees   18 Harold 1 912
We once have loved, though love is at an end   23 Harold 2 200
Mingling, and made by Love, unto one mighty end   51 Harold 3 958
Until it seems prolonging without end   52 Harold 3 1016
My daughter! with thy name thus much shall end   53 Harold 3 1068
Where he had plunged it. Glory without end   60 Harold 4 323
Deep in his throat its end the weapon found   110 Nisus 395
Their lives did not end when they yielded their
  breath   129 Becher-A 19
Thy season o'er, thy days will find their end   139 Ossian-A 26
Thy years shall have an end, and thou no more   140 Ossian-B 31
Here's a rope's end for the dogs   157 Hodgson 52
And shouldst thou seek his end to know   173 Origin 5
I have something for both at the end of their
  race   176 Devil's Dr 24
Were it not that all life must end in one   190 Churchill 24
It may be both--but one day end it must   192 Fragment-C 21
Yet this was not the end I did pursue   212 Augusta-C 101
No matter how, to the desired end   213 Lady Byron 57
The means were worthy, and the end is won   213 Lady Byron 59
To end in madness--both in misery   216 Dream 206
That will at once put an end to mistake   225 Ode-D 8
A sort of end which I should take indeed ill   230 Murray-A 19
To end at once:--that bard for all is fit   264 Hints 543
Being, end, aim, religion--rent, rent, rent   306 Age 631
Woe without name, or hope, or end   313 Giaour 276
The day shall have a stormy end   316 Giaour 664
Yet must thou end thy task, and mark   318 Giaour 771

END
I would remind him of my end   322 Giaour 1224
Since all must end in that wild word, farewell   344 Corsair 1 455
To count the hours that struggle to thine end   358 Corsair 3 227
Where thousand thoughts begin, to end in one   365 Corsair 3 642
But whatsoe'er its end below   401 Parisina 528
The wretch still hopes his woes must end   414 Mazeppa 748
At the same end by pathways not the same   417 Island 1 116
And such a truant boy would end in woe   438 Tasso 160
(Though such was not my ambition's end or aim   456 Dante 1 52
And to the end illuminate my mind   466 Morgante 16
Mix'd, and contending without end or order   493 Manfred 3 166
Is to dare all things for a righteous end   493 Manfred 3 170
Is its own origin of ill and end   496 Manfred 3 391
My object is to make your cause end well   518 Faliero 2 694
And secret plot, although to a good end   519 Faliero 3 77
The noble end must justify them. What   535 Faliero 4 510
The hour may be a hard one, but 'twill end   545 Faliero 5 546
Its everlasting page the end of what   561 Sardan 2 13
Ho! tyrant--I will end this war, Even so   575 Sardan 3 270
Death all than such a being! And the end   580 Sardan 4 130
Unto what end? what purpose? I will grant   581 Sardan 4 217
But at the least, whate'er the past, their end   583 Sardan 4 297
I am not what I should be--let it end   583 Sardan 4 334
Ends as such partings end, in no departure   583 Sardan 4 364
Prolong it--end it. Then let us end both   587 Sardan 4 573
The end I would have chosen, had I saved   589 Sardan 5 125
They work by different means to the same end   603 Foscari 2 89
To one great end, must be maintain'd in vigour   607 Foscari 2 413
Be it to the earth's end, from this abhorr'd   611 Foscari 3 238
No end; and some, which would pretend to have   638 Cain 2 157
And to what end have I beheld these things   645 Cain 2 622
Nothing can err, except to some good end   649 Cain 3 234
When they end, let mine end with them, or thee   673 Werner 1 148
But no, 'it must,' and there's an end. How now   681 Werner 1 609
I would be fain, and there's an end. Perhaps   686 Werner 2 241
He hath not lured you here to end your? or   690 Werner 2 474
Brawls must end here. They shall. You have
  wrong'd me, Ulric   693 Werner 2 633
Descend in rain and end, but spreads itself   700 Werner 3 362
This is so--Nay, but hear me to the end   718 Werner 5 341
With the first cock-crow. Which, if it end with   731 Deformed 1 634
For malice still imputes some private end   755 Juan 1 526
And so is spring about the end of May   759 Juan 1 811
By dole or ink; 'tis sweet to put an end   762 Juan 1 1002
Few mortals know what end they would be at   763 Juan 1 1061
Why, don't you know that it may end in blood   768 Juan 1 1366
What is the end of Fame? 'tis but to fill   773 Juan 1 1737
Her earnestness would ne'er have made an end   794 Juan 2 1284
He hers, until they end in broken gasps   798 Juan 2 1550
But those who have ne'er end with only one   802 Juan 3 32
In poesy, unless perhaps the end   816 Juan 4 2
And such an end! that he who many a day   836 Juan 5 293
We know where things and men must end at best   839 Juan 5 501
Might probably attain both in the end   840 Juan 5 547
A thousand times of him had made an end   844 Juan 5 830
The spirit in the end will have its way   845 Juan 5 880
There was no end unto the things she bought   845 Juan 5 901
Of which the surest sign is in the end   852 Juan 6 7
There was a way to end their strife, although   864 Juan 6 756
But such precipitation may end ill   866 Juan 6 909
Might end in acting as his own 'Jack Ketch   866 Juan 6 925
Yet, in the end, except in Freedom's battles   878 Juan 8 31
But let me put an end unto my theme   894 Juan 8 1009
There was an end of Ismail--hapless town   894 Juan 8 1010
They write, and for what end; but, note or text   901 Juan 9 327
Selfish in its beginning as its end   905 Juan 9 578
To end or to begin with; the next grand   906 Juan 9 602
This is the way physicians mend or end us   912 Juan 10 329
At the great end of travel--which is driving   916 Juan 10 576
Meaneth the west or worst end of a city   924 Juan 11 354
But these are few, and in the end they make   933 Juan 12 201
Peruse! 'Tis always with a moral end   934 Juan 12 306
Of epic Love's beginning, end, and middle   935 Juan 12 360
An end to answer, or a plan to lay   937 Juan 12 462
Thirdly, commence not with the end--or, sinning   950 Juan 13 583
In this sort, end at least with the beginning   950 Juan 13 584
Or make a Werter of him in the end   963 Juan 14 506
Or grave Lord George, with whom perhaps might end   972 Juan 15 260
To bring what was a jest to a serious end   978 Juan 15 630

ENDANGER'D
Endanger'd glory, life itself beset   352 Corsair 2 343

ENDANGERS
An almost twelvemonth's constancy endangers   845 Juan 5 848

ENDEAR'D
By every honest joy of love and life endear'd   34 Harold 2 881
Which only make more mourn'd and more endear'd   61 Harold 4 399
Endear'd to all in childhood's very name   125 Recoll 212
I think of those eyes that endear'd the rude
  scene   136 Highlander 36
Endear'd by days gone by   159 Storm 58

ENDEAR'D
The vision thus endear'd to me   173 Mrs. Lamb   10
While thou--whose softness long endear'd   332 Abydos   2   333
To give thee back to all endear'd below   355 Corsair   2   531
A thing which each endearment more endear'd   818 Juan   4   128

ENDEARING
Is, that such lips, of looks endearing   100 Marion   29
Thus must I cling to some endearing hand   125 Recoll   241
Endearing Waltz!--to thy more melting tune   275 Waltz   109
At once love's most endearing thought resign   277 Waltz   238
So beautiful, unnumber'd, and endearing   635 Cain   1   512

ENDEARMENT
A thing which each endearment more endear'd   818 Juan   4   128

ENDEARMENTS
In vain with endearments we soothe the sad heart   99 L Adieu   5

ENDEARS
Yes, she, whose gen'rous aid her name endears   21 Harold   2   115
Of roused-up millions: all that most endears   38 Harold   3   178
Endears it to my memory ever   113 Cornelian-A   2
Say, if remembrance days like these endears   127 Recoll   391
And more thy buried love endears   168 Dead   71
Our own, surviving Love endears   217 High World   2
Shall sound each tone thy long-loved voice
    endears   333 Abydos   2   407
Because that number rarely much endears   760 Juan   1   854
No doubt we weep for those the heart endears   776 Juan   2   119

ENDEAVOUR
To part would be a vain endeavour   88 To Ellen   11
In spite of every vain endeavour   134 Lady-D   42
To forget our dissension we both should endeavour   137 Delawarr   35
But, ah, in spite of Hope's endeavour   150 Harrow-C   14
And Time's endeavour   199 Stanzas-B   3
I will endeavour. And you, signor? Lady   606 Foscari   2   284
Be firm, my son! I will do my endeavour   614 Foscari   1   403
Endeavour--Oh, my husband! Give it way   621 Foscari   5   70
And will endeavour patiently to obey   664 Heaven   695
We'll have one more endeavour   732 Deformed   1   701
Though all Exchequer chancellors endeavour   993 Juan   16   830

ENDEAVOURING
The expression, and endeavouring to resume   807 Juan   3   349

ENDEAVOURS
Should, after all, our best endeavours fail   114 Prologue   34
'Tis hush'd, and my feeble endeavours are o'er   148 Farewell-A   30
With all his best endeavours, only squall   264 Hints   554
As Love or Hymen your endeavours guide   275 Waltz   105

ENDED
If David, when his toils were ended   96 Granta   81
And--though our dream at last is ended   98 To Lesbia   23
And the hour when thy glories were ended   222 Babylon   15
Begun in folly, ended in disgrace   251 Bards   681
With George the Third's--and ended long before   275 Waltz   134
Its grief seem'd ended, but the sex confess'd   382 Lara   2   517
On him whose life and love thus ended   401 Parisina   482
Thou too art ended--what is left me now   437 Tasso   43
When the first act is ended by a dance   445 Beppo   327
But Caina waits for him our life who ended   476 Francesca   11
But 'tis by this time ended. I perceived   509 Faliero   2   3
Are ended. Yet, I dread thy nature will   584 Sardan   4   393
Your poverty my likeness ended; but   695 Werner   3   15
All comedies are ended by a marriage   802 Juan   3   66
His head, until the ceremony ended   843 Juan   5   760
But ended in his being found out and sack'd   865 Juan   6   830
The London winter's ended in July   946 Juan   13   337
The conference or congress (for it ended   975 Juan   15   481

ENDING
Of empire ending like a shepherd's tale   550 Sardan   1   8
Ending in 'ischskin,' 'ousckin,' 'iffskchy,' 'ouski   869 Juan   7   127
Quicksilver small talk, ending (if you note it   933 Juan   12   207
The English winter--ending in July   946 Juan   13   329
(Especially as the sixth year is ending   993 Juan   16   806

ENDLESS
But slave succeed to slave through years of
    endless toil   31 Harold   2   737
And boil in endless torture; while the sweat   65 Harold   4   618
Dark-heaving;--boundless, endless, and sublime   82 Harold   4   1643
Where endless pleasures virtue's deeds repay   84 Death-B   16
Her only boy, reclined in endless sleep   106 Nisus   74
Which make me wish for endless night   113 Quaker   36
Of him whose meed exists in endless fame   114 Death-A   10
Whence are the beams, O Sun! thy endless blaze   139 Ossian-A   3
And so, with endless truth and hurry   232 Doctor   89
Like a soul's in endless woe   401 Parisina   493
Their days in endless strife, and die alone   458 Dante   1   152
If sire or mother suffer endless thrall   472 Morgante   413

ENDLESS
Endless, and all alike, as sands on the shore   484 Manfred   2   54
Through an aerial universe of endless   637 Cain   2   107
And the infinity of endless ages   645 Cain   2   640
Of endless beings; skirr'd extinguish'd worlds   647 Cain   3   64
Her Eden in an endless paradise   661 Heaven   467
Gone home. To the endless home of unbelievers   711 Werner   4   459
Of endless torments and perpetual motion   746 Juan   Ded   104
But pays off moments in an endless shower   798 Juan   2   1534
The endless soot bestows a tint far deeper   909 Juan   10   115
Would you have endless lightning in the skies   967 Juan   14   750

ENDOR
Of Endor; and the Spartan Monarch drew   487 Manfred   2   276

ENDOW
A being more intense, that we endow   36 Harold   3   47
With knowledge to endow   145 Adieu   4

ENDOW'D
Endow'd with qualities to give happiness   710 Werner   4   372
Which has of old endow'd it; but from you   711 Werner   4   474

ENDOWMENTS
Of wonderful endowments: birth and fortune   717 Werner   5   244

ENDS
Ends:--Some, with hope replenish'd and rebuoy'd   58 Harold   4   192
Clothed in odds and ends of humour   197 Rogers   39
Ends not in dying   199 Stanzas-B   10
(Like patriot speeches) but to paltry ends   257 Hints   22
Another Babel soars--but Britain ends   307 Age   649
The verge where ends the cliff, begins the beach   346 Corsair   1   534
And there unfolds his plan, his means, and ends   346 Corsair   1   586
My life begun and ends the same   399 Parisina   313
But yet where happiest ends in pain   409 Mazeppa   297
Which being finish'd, here the story ends   452 Beppo   790
Or joy that ends in agony or faintness   487 Manfred   2   264
Manfred! To-morrow ends thine earthly ills   490 Manfred   2   521
Ends as such partings end, in no departure   583 Sardan   4   364
These walls are silent of men's ends; they only   609 Foscari   3   71
Ends with his life, and goes not beyond murder   618 Foscari   4   199
The more so in obtaining our own ends   750 Juan   1   236
I doubt, all likeness ends between the pair   769 Juan   1   1488
Here ends this canto.---Need I sing, or say   770 Juan   1   1497
Of us dies with them as each fond hope ends   776 Juan   2   166
Laid with one blast the ship on her beam ends   777 Juan   2   240
The moment after he politely ends   784 Juan   2   660
And having pick'd up several odds and ends   811 Juan   3   658
Which mostly ends in some small breach of both   849 Juan   5   1136
An isle near Ismail, had two ends in view   870 Juan   7   178
And others of themselves and latter ends   874 Juan   7   432
Ends in a rusty casque and dubious bone   916 Juan   10   582
Beginnings are fair faces, ends mere fishes   939 Juan   12   578
Ends. When the body of the book's begun   940 Juan   12   690
And form'd a basis of esteem, which ends   943 Juan   13   119
And hardly heaven--because it never ends   954 Juan   13   835

END'S
So the end's gain'd, what signifies the route   974 Juan   15   408

ENDUED
None that, with kindred consciousness endued   23 Harold   2   231
When Athens' children are with hearts endued   33 Harold   2   794
With all which Demosthenes wanted endued   202 Avatar   39
Eternal, more than other kings, endued   289 Vision   294
But as their nerves may be endued   414 Mazeppa   746

ENDURABLE
Endurable, and temperest the hues   493 Manfred   3   189
Innumerable, more endurable   630 Cain   1   159
What makes my feelings more endurable   644 Cain   2   526

ENDURANCE
Of silent, sharp endurance: he can tell   36 Harold   3   42
In the endurance, and repulse   191 Prometheus-B   41
Prolong'd endurance tames the bold   412 Mazeppa   524
Of such endurance too prolong'd to make   457 Dante   1   95
Most stoical endurance. Without owning   595 Foscari   1   13
In action and endurance than thyself   724 Deformed   1   108
And pass'd for arguments of good endurance   924 Juan   11   412
Patient--but not enamour'd of endurance   998 Juan   17   84

ENDURE
Who can so well the toil of war endure   29 Harold   2   580
Through banks whose beauty would endure for ever   42 Harold   3   444
But this will not endure, nor be endured   48 Harold   3   779
Endure and shrink not, we of nobler clay   58 Harold   4   188
The fire which we endure, it was repaid   79 Harold   4   1460
Ah happy days! too happy to endure   121 Newstead-A   129
But now thy vows no more endure   134 Lady-D   11
What there thy bosom must endure   174 Remember-B   40
And more decreed his glory to endure   183 Address-D   11
Through unborn ages, to endure this blight   190 Churchill   18

ENDURE

We must endure it as a test	198	Duel	53
The soul that must endure it	219	Vanity	24
Its years as moments shall endure	220	Clay	28
The wrongs he made your satellites endure	291	Vision	398
Nor deem'd she, could he long endure	330	Abydos 2	109
To blackest shade, nor will endure a guide	365	Corsair 3	661
Of all that he would do, or could endure	373	Lara 1	503
The few who may endure my lay	385	Corinth	42
For ever in its depth endure	402	Parisina	566
And no Venetian audience could endure a	444	Beppo	247
'And you shall see what weight I can endure	474	Morgante	574
But can endure thy pity. I depart	485	Manfred 2	90
I have so much endured, so much endure	490	Manfred 2	488
Mine have no further outrage to endure	506	Faliero 1	434
In what we have to do and to endure	506	Faliero 1	480
I know it will, and yet I must endure it	544	Faliero 5	471
It is. I can endure it.--And the time	545	Faliero 5	523
Thou may'st endure whate'er thou wilt--the stars	567	Sardan 3	346
Hath nerved me to endure the risk of death	609	Foscari 3	88
That thought would scarcely aid me to endure it	609	Foscari 3	97
I could endure my dungeon, for 'twas Venice	610	Foscari 3	127
In fact but add to), shall endure and do	642	Cain 2	432
Think and endure, and form an inner world	646	Cain 2	668
Endure, and, harder still, bequeath; but since	648	Cain 3	134
Omnipotence, but merely to endure	650	Cain 3	278
Rather than see his mates endure alone	660	Heaven	417
Be it so! but while yet their hours endure	664	Heaven	690
Rather than longer worship dared endure	666	Heaven	833
We have chosen, and will endure	668	Heaven	983
Which colder hearts endure till they are laid	825	Juan 4	564
A town which did a famous siege endure	868	Juan 7	61
Juan replied: 'At least I will endure	891	Juan 8	798
Lord Henry at his table should endure	992	Juan 16	758

ENDURED

But this will not endure, nor be endured	48	Harold 3	779
And full-grown actors are endured once more	249	Bards	565
I have so much endured, so much endure	490	Manfred 2	488
I have endured as much in giving life	599	Foscari 2	242
Its mandate; which thus far I have endured	650	Cain 3	279
Sermons he read, and lectures he endured	752	Juan 1	369
By length I mean duration; theirs endured	798	Juan 2	1489

ENDURES

The bond of affection no longer endures	137	Delawarr	30
The tie which bound the first endures the last	212	Augusta-C	128
A sceptre, and endures the purple robe	454	Venice-B	128
Endures my Love--not meets it. That seems strange	743	Deformed 3	119

ENDURING
(See also ALL-ENDURING)

The enduring produce of immortal Mind	193	Monody	30
Forgetting all thy still enduring claim	300	Age	163
And braved their thirst with as enduring lip	421	Island 2	181
But a continuance of enduring thought	478	Manfred 1	4
Secured, by the short penance of enduring	513	Faliero 2	336
And most enduring:--Shall I blush for him	664	Heaven	686
His Grace was an enduring, married man	963	Juan 14	490

ENEMIES

And they were enemies. They met beside	189	Darkness	57
I thought mine enemies had been but Man	439	Tasso	198
Upon his enemies? Oh! no, no, no	484	Manfred 2	83
Avenging men upon their enemies	488	Manfred 2	362
Heaven bids us to forgive our enemies	512	Faliero 2	260
And please your enemies--a host already	542	Faliero 5	279
Slew fifty thousand of his enemies	555	Sardan 1	307
Unto our enemies. Chief, keep your weapon	565	Sardan 2	218
Inveterate enemies. Now it bears an aspect	593	Sardan 5	366
Your fathers were mine enemies, as bitter	605	Foscari 2	228
Or should be comrades, even though enemies	676	Werner 1	347
Of our dead enemies is worthy those	712	Werner 4	489
Had cost his enemies a long repentance	808	Juan 3	431
Old enemies who have become new friends	908	Juan 10	89

ENEMY
(See also ARCH-ENEMY)

The fault of a friend, bid an enemy live	30	Harold 2	658
Is gall and wormwood to an enemy	41	Harold 3	346
Said, 'Oh that mine enemy, mine enemy had written	179	Devil's Dr	236
The secret enemy whose sleepless eye	193	Monody	69
Yet lowering on his enemy	317	Giaour	670
Seyd is mine enemy, had swept my band	361	Corsair 3	360
An enemy, save in my just defence	484	Manfred 2	86
And the great enemy of man, as subject	545	Faliero 5	493
The aspect of a secret enemy	678	Werner 1	448
I render'd him, I am his enemy	696	Werner 3	81
I have plunged our enemy. You kindled first	720	Werner 5	465
Near enemy; or let me have the long	724	Deformed 1	115
Is for a flying enemy. I gave thee	737	Deformed 2	186
Your ranks more than the enemy. Away	740	Deformed 2	321
Like one who grapples with his enemy	780	Juan 2	415

ENEMY

O'er his worst enemy when at his knees	855	Juan 6	181
But when they saw the enemy retire	871	Juan 7	242
In thinking that their enemy is beat	872	Juan 7	332

ENEMY'S

Our enemy's,--but let not that forbid	44	Harold 3	540
If you regret your enemy's bloodless death	712	Werner 4	505

ENERGETIC

And stoic Franklin's energetic shade	303	Age	386
The worst acts of one energetic master	552	Sardan 1	119
Nought's more sublime than energetic bile	848	Juan 5	1076

ENERGIES

Herself a billow in her energies	421	Island 2	142
Has not all quench'd, and latent energies	550	Sardan 1	11
Then by degrees recall'd his energies	983	Juan 16	196

ENERGISE

To 'energise the object I pursue	274	Waltz	27

ENERGISING

'When energising objects men pursue	170	Address-B	1

ENERGY

By him to whom the energy was given	79	Harold 4	1461
Still in thy patient energy	191	Prometheus-B	40
That deem'd not till they found their energy	357	Corsair 3	96
Hath all the energy which would have made	493	Manfred 3	161
In the last energy of venomous life	521	Faliero 3	150
With words, but deeds. Keep thou awake that energy	557	Sardan 1	429
Their antique energy of mind, all that	610	Foscari 3	152
Their energy like life forms all their fame	824	Juan 4	487

ENERVATING

A most enervating and filthy cheat	637	Cain 2	57

ENFEEBLED

Nor yet enfeebled even his mortal frame	509	Faliero 2	10

ENFER

And his works shall be bound in Morocco d'Enfer	177	Devil's Dr	131

ENFOLD

In one embrace let these arms again enfold him	205	Hindoo	14
I care not; so my arms enfold	323	Giaour	1294

ENFORCE

Not thirty tyrants now enforce the chain	31	Harold 2	706
Such chastisement as will enforce respect	509	Faliero 2	30
Necessity enforce it. I hate all pain	556	Sardan 1	395
I could enforce for my authority	605	Foscari 2	253

ENFORCED

Such as were ne'er before enforced in schools	93	Masters	12
Call'd county meetings, and enforced the laws	266	Hints	672

ENFORCES

Enforces pang on pang, and stifles gasp on gasp	79	Harold 4	1440

ENGAGE

Bleed gladiator-like, and still engage	69	Harold 4	844
And now new thoughts our minds engage	98	To Lesbia	11
Zeal for her honour bade me here engage	255	Bards	993
Because I never heard, nor could engage	442	Beppo	172
But I'll engage, that if seen there but once	686	Werner 2	211
In answering yours. I wish I could engage him	687	Werner 2	258
I will engage for her. So will not I	710	Werner 4	394
We don't much care with whom we may engage	905	Juan 9	547
And happiest they who horses can engage	946	Juan 13	348

ENGAGED

Here once engaged the stranger's view	150	Harrow-C	1
I suppose that to-night you're engaged with some codgers	226	Oh You	11
I'm engaged to the Lady Bluebottle's collation	279	Blues 1	137
Engaged in secret to the Signory	520	Faliero 3	133
Engaged in the chase, draw off the eighty men	705	Werner 4	105
But next, when I'm engaged to sing there--do go	827	Juan 4	704
Suwarrow, though engaged with accents high	875	Juan 7	515
To gentlemen engaged in the assault	880	Juan 8	127

ENGENDER

The fratricide might well engender parricides	653	Cain 3	492

ENGENDER'D
(See also LONG-ENGENDER'D)

And worse than all, the sudden crimes engender'd	453	Venice-B	81
Reptiles engender'd out of the subsiding	640	Cain 2	302
The worst of dreams, the fantasies engender'd	664	Heaven	714
Engender'd monstrous shapes of every crime	888	Juan 8	656

ENGENDERING
Are silently engendering of the day | 548 Faliero | 5 | 742

ENGINE
A further application of yon engine | 539 Faliero | 5 | 71
They--Bade thee stretch me on their horrid engine | 598 Foscari | 1 | 155

ENGINEERING
(Prithee, excuse this engineering slang | 868 Juan | 7 | 86

ENGINEER'S
Whether it was their engineer's stupidity | 870 Juan | 7 | 209

ENGINES
(See also STEAM-ENGINES)
Upon your engines, gorged with pangs already | 538 Faliero | 5 | 47
There's that within my heart shall strain your engines | 542 Faliero | 5 | 305
Our swords when drawn must cross, our engines aim | 676 Werner | 1 | 348
A new-found mammoth; and their cursed engines | 726 Deformed | 1 | 305
With deadlier engines and a speedier blow | 877 Juan | 7 | 635
Of war's most mortal engines, to their foes | 879 Juan | 8 | 59

ENGINE'S
And speaks in thunder through yon engine's roar | 10 Harold | 1 | 410

ENGLAND
England, I joy no child he was of thine | 21 Harold | 2 | 96
For the safety of Edward and England they fell | 86 Leaving NA | | 14
England! thy beauties are tame and domestic | 118 Lachin | | 37
And, England! add their stubborn strength to thine | 182 Address-C | | 10
Him who bade England bow to Normandy | 239 Conquest | | 2
The scourge of England and the boast of France | 244 Bards | | 206
England could boast a judge almost the same | 247 Bards | | 439
Frown not on England; England owns him not | 270 Minerva | | 127
'What George? what Third?' 'The king of England,' said | 287 Vision | | 139
To die for England--why then live?--for rent | 306 Age | | 623
But Heaven preserve Old England from such courses | 444 Beppo | | 295
To England, France, or any other nation | 444 Beppo | | 302
In England 'twould be dung, dust, or a dray | 445 Beppo | | 336
'England! with all thy faults I love thee still | 446 Beppo | | 369
This is the case in England; at least was | 447 Beppo | | 473
Holland, France, England, Germany, or Spain | 774 Juan | 2 | 2
In England a six canto quarto tale | 812 Juan | 3 | 682
In moral England, where the thing's a tax | 856 Juan | 6 | 231
But in old England, when a young bride errs | 938 Juan | 12 | 511
In England ranks quite on a different list | 963 Juan | 14 | 478
Besides, his conduct, since in England, grew more | 969 Juan | 15 | 85

ENGLAND'S
There thou too, Vathek! England's wealthiest son | 7 Harold | 1 | 275
On distant England's name | 158 Storm | | 16
I know that all save England's church have shamm'd | 286 Vision | | 110
His dreams were of Old England's welcome shore | 415 Island | 1 | 19
Nucleus of England's native eloquence | 428 Island | 3 | 126
Let none accuse Old England's hospitality | 947 Juan | 13 | 391

ENGLISH
Who, scarcely skill'd an English line to pen | 111 Examination | | 11
Nor fair her locks, like English lasses | 159 Cadiz | | 6
Our English maids are long to woo | 160 Cadiz | | 17
Yes, happy are they in their cold English graves | 204 Avatar | | 117
For nature then an English audience felt | 243 Bards | | 116
Or Scottish taste decides on English wit | 248 Bards | | 503
To learn, who our first English strollers were | 262 Hints | | 438
An English subject for an English muse | 263 Hints | | 452
What Review? 'Tis the English Journal de Trevoux | 279 Blues | 1 | 126
She liked the English and the Hebrew tongue | 748 Juan | 1 | 105
The English always use to govern d--n | 749 Juan | 1 | 112
Were there not also Russians, English, many | 765 Juan | 1 | 1189
Were in the English newspapers, of course | 770 Juan | 1 | 1504
For we all know that English people are | 794 Juan | 2 | 1241
Much English I cannot pretend to speak | 795 Juan | 2 | 1315
Which make the English climate of our years | 801 Juan | 2 | 1712
He had an English look; that is, was square | 832 Juan | 5 | 81
Are things which make an English evening pass | 838 Juan | 5 | 460
Requires it, that's to say, the English rhyme | 854 Juan | 6 | 138
Who name the French in English, save to show | 870 Juan | 7 | 175
To Russian, Tartar, English, French, Cossacque | 873 Juan | 7 | 362
An English naval officer, who wish'd | 888 Juan | 8 | 639
An English lady ask'd of an Italian | 903 Juan | 9 | 401
Of English, save their shibboleth, 'God damn | 920 Juan | 11 | 90
To think so: for half English as I am | 920 Juan | 11 | 94
Into as furious English), with her best look | 925 Juan | 11 | 415
Cool, and quite English, imperturbable | 942 Juan | 13 | 108
The English winter--ending in July | 946 Juan | 13 | 329
An English autumn, though it hath no vines | 950 Juan | 13 | 601
For ennui is a growth of English root | 954 Juan | 13 | 805
But whether English dukes grew rare of late | 973 Juan | 15 | 332
Which prove plain English truer of the two | 977 Juan | 15 | 574
For Gothic daring shown in English money | 988 Juan | 16 | 520

ENGLISH
Had English influence in the self-same sphere here | 989 Juan | 16 | 605
Is't English? No--'tis only parliamentary | 990 Juan | 16 | 626
As between English beef and Spartan broth | 991 Juan | 16 | 719

ENGLISHMAN
From me a wandering Englishman; I tore | 199 Sonnet-D | | 4
He gloried in the name of Englishman | 990 Juan | 16 | 648

ENGLISHMEN
'Mongst them were several Englishmen of pith | 869 Juan | 7 | 143
Well, like most Englishmen, and loved the races | 944 Juan | 13 | 182

ENGLISHWOMAN
But where an Englishwoman sometimes faints | 451 Beppo | | 707

ENGLISHWOMAN'S
And, above all, an Englishwoman's roves | 922 Juan | 11 | 260

ENGRAVE
Engrave upon the plate, you rose at four | 792 Juan | 2 | 1120

ENGRAVED
Fierce and unfathomable thoughts engraved | 288 Vision | | 190
Whereon engraved the Koorsee text | 329 Abydos | 2 | 70
Flung over these dim words engraved beneath | 545 Faliero | 5 | 499
Engraved in crimson in men's memories | 703 Werner | 3 | 553
It will not be engraved upon my tomb | 714 Werner | 5 | 91

ENGRAVES
Absurdly varying, he at last engraves | 257 Hints | | 47

ENGROSS
And for the fame you would engross below | 745 Juan | Ded | 52

ENGROSS'D
With the substantial company engross'd | 992 Juan | 16 | 764

ENHANCE
War's merit it by no means might enhance | 878 Juan | 8 | 20

ENHANCING
His power enhancing | 200 Stanzas-B | | 41

ENJOIN'D
Slight were the tasks enjoin'd him by his lord | 374 Lara | 1 | 564

ENJOINING
Enjoining silence strict to Zoe, who | 791 Juan | 2 | 1082

ENJOY
For the more that enjoy thee, the more we enjoy | 155 Goblet | | 20
Enjoy the moments as they flee | 173 Quotation | | 30
'Now fare ye well! enjoy your little hour | 272 Minerva | | 259
As if the last he could enjoy on earth | 353 Corsair | 2 | 457
The dangers past that make even man enjoy | 423 Island | 4 | 300
Preserve thine own. At least, I will enjoy it | 559 Sardan | 1 | 598
You came here to enjoy a heartless triumph | 613 Foscari | 3 | 325
Or shadow, madest beings to enjoy them | 627 Cain | 1 | 12
The promised party, to enjoy its sweets | 950 Juan | 13 | 594

ENJOY'D
Since Time hath reft whate'er my soul enjoy'd | 35 Harold | 2 | 925
Enjoy'd, from absence, with enraptured zest | 121 Newstead-A | | 116
A bright renown shall be enjoy'd | 128 Answer-B | | 39
Those scenes to be enjoy'd no more | 137 Clare | | 14
'Tis long since she enjoy'd it: may it be | 601 Foscari | 2 | 12
Enjoy'd them, loved them, and, alas! abused them | 672 Werner | 1 | 78
Enjoy'd the lonely, vigorous, harmless days | 886 Juan | 8 | 487

ENJOYING
Enjoying, with inexorable eye | 302 Age | | 338
Handsome and young, enjoying all the present | 823 Juan | 4 | 404
Your wars eternally, besides enjoying | 880 Juan | 8 | 111
Some hours to make the remnant worth enjoying | 965 Juan | 14 | 624

ENJOYMENT
Existence by enjoyment, and count o'er | 40 Harold | 3 | 305
And yet, I think, with more enjoyment | 144 Becher-B | | 6
Exulting in the enjoyment of the wild | 416 Island | 1 | 44
A bodiless enjoyment--born and dying | 482 Manfred | 1 | 316
Enjoyment! We have cut the way short to it | 571 Sardan | 3 | 14
Things whose enjoyment was to be in blindness | 640 Cain | 2 | 305
It sounds for joy, takes something from enjoyment | 701 Werner | 3 | 392
From the enjoyment of the earth and air | 916 Juan | 10 | 543
And store it up for mischievous enjoyment | 993 Juan | 16 | 847

ENJOYMENTS
Of thine enjoyments a sweet degradation | 637 Cain | 2 | 56

ENJOYMENT'S
Which for an instant clip enjoyment's wings | 908 Juan | 10 | 40

ENJOYS
Enjoys thy person, and inspires thy pen 249 Bards 539

ENKINDLE
'Twere to enkindle the strong tower of our 593 Sardan 5 365

ENLARGED
There is no trait which might not be enlarged 209 Sketch 74
By nature but enlarged by art 330 Abydos 2 101
It hath enlarged my thoughts with a new sense 491 Manfred 3 16
Yes, the enlarged but noble aspect of 580 Sardan 4 133

ENLARGEMENT
Enlargement of existence to partake 796 Juan 2 1378

ENLARGING
Dusky and huge, enlarging on the sight 27 Harold 2 451
While the broken line enlarging 188 Ode-B 67

ENLIGHTEN
Must burn more mildly ere it can enlighten 922 Juan 11 216

ENLIGHTEN'D
The patch'd-up idol of enlighten'd days 38 Harold 3 168
Then pause, and be enlighten'd; there is more 78 Harold 4 1423
There be who say, in these enlighten'd days 253 Bards 849

ENLIGHTENER
The enlightener of nations; and to rise 492 Manfred 3 107

ENLIST
For my part, I'll enlist on neither side 898 Juan 9 125

ENLIVEN'D
Gone was the smile that enliven'd their red 390 Corinth 549

ENLIVENING
Bright through the world enlivening radiance pour 140 Ossian-B 32

ENMITIES
Had stood the test of mortal enmities 43 Harold 3 491

ENNOBLE
As if she deem'd that mystery would ennoble 'em 748 Juan 1 104

ENNOBLED
Like thine ennobled, hardly less divine 107 Nisus 178
By nature vile, ennobled but by name 154 Dog 21

ENNOBLES
Thy name ennobles him who thus commends 125 Recoll 244
Ah, surely affection ennobles the strain 148 Farewell-A 22

ENNOBLING
Ye Elements, in whose ennobling stir 81 Harold 4 1589

ENNUI
After long travel, ennui, love, or slaughter 797 Juan 2 1439
To prove its grand ingredient is ennui 814 Juan 3 872
For ennui is a growth of English root 954 Juan 13 805
This paradise of pleasure and ennui 957 Juan 14 136
The grand antithesis to great ennui 968 Juan 15 11

ENOCH
Must not my daughter love her brother Enoch 633 Cain 1 363
My little Enoch! and his lisping sister 634 Cain 1 435
Our little Enoch sleeps upon yon bed 646 Cain 3 2
And loving him? Soft! he awakes. Sweet Enoch 648 Cain 3 139
So shall our children be. I will bear Enoch 653 Cain 3 456
I hear our little Enoch cry within 654 Cain 3 519
The scroll of Enoch prophesied it long 662 Heaven 541

ENORMOUS
Yet oft the enormous skeleton ye pass 76 Harold 4 1281
Enormous model doom'd the artist's toils 78 Harold 4 1364
Rivets the living links, the enormous asp 79 Harold 4 1439
Of an enormous city did survive 189 Darkness 56
When scaling his enormous crag the wave 426 Island 3 21
From the enormous mountains where it rises 590 Sardan 5 192
And its enormous walls of reeking ruin 595 Sardan 5 481
His grace for your enormous guilt. He was 604 Foscari 2 172
Last night in yon enormous spider's net 609 Foscari 3 105
Enormous liquid plains, and some begirt 638 Cain 2 187
Unfold its gates! Enormous vapours roll 639 Cain 2 198
Of swimming shadows and enormous shapes 639 Cain 2 236
That which it was. And those enormous creatures 641 Cain 2 337
Than an enormous room without a soul 838 Juan 5 447
In mockery to the enormous gate which rose 842 Juan 5 693
And one enormous shout of 'Allah!' rose 879 Juan 8 57
Of this enormous city's spreading span 922 Juan 11 220

ENOUGH
'Enough, enough, my little lad 6 Harold 1 154
'Enough, enough, my yeoman good 6 Harold 1 170

ENOUGH
Enough of Battle's minions! let them play 11 Harold 1 468
Enough, alas, in humble homes remain 16 Harold 1 798
Is't not enough, unhappy thing, to know 20 Harold 2 29
For me 'twere bliss enough to know thy spirit blest 20 Harold 2 81
Yet am I changed; though still enough the same 36 Harold 3 61
They are enough, and if thy tale be true 40 Harold 3 308
More than enough, thou fatal Waterloo 40 Harold 3 310
And meditation chasten'd down, enough 58 Harold 4 165
Enough for my rude boat, where should I steer 70 Harold 4 944
It is enough in sooth that once we bore 80 Harold 4 1493
'Tis not enough, with other sons of power 94 Dorset 43
Full foes enough to-night have breathed their last 109 Nisus 282
'Tis surely enough upon earth to be vex'd 117 To Eliza 21
Enough for Ten; and here I own it 144 Becher-B 4
Thy verse is 'sad' enough, no doubt 147 To Author 1
Not enough to stow Queen Mab in 157 Hodgson 39
And were I vain enough to think 163 Malta 35
It is enough for me to prove 167 Dead 14
It is enough to grieve the heart 181 Ode-A 78
With just enough of learning to misquote 242 Bards 66
But managers for once cried, 'Hold, enough 251 Bards 735
Enough for genius if itself inspire 254 Bards 914
Our men in buckram shall have blows enough 256 Bards 1049
'Tis not enough, ye bards, with all your art 258 Hints 137
There's pomp enough, if little else, in plays 262 Hints 442
And that's enough; then write and print so fast 266 Hints 711
Thy breast--if bare enough--requires no shield 273 Waltz 11
Come near enough--if not to touch--to taint 277 Waltz 243
Quite enough; and, to tell you the truth, my retreat 278 Blues 1 44
Well, time enough yet, when the play's to be play'd 282 Blues 2 84
And yet they had even then enough to do 285 Vision 34
True testimonies are enough: we lose 292 Vision 501
Of him; I've kings enough below, God knows 293 Vision 512
As to speak first? there's choice enough--who shall 293 Vision 518
The angels had of course enough of song 296 Vision 731
When Castlereagh has been up long enough 296 Vision 739
Have wept enough--for what?--to weep again 298 Age 8
Each course enough? or doctors dire dissuaded 305 Age 509
The gout was martyrdom enough for thee 305 Age 527
And ne'er (enough) lamented Castlereagh 305 Age 538
Enough of this--a sight more mournful woos 308 Age 725
Enough--no foreign foe could quell 311 Giaour 133
And if it dares enough, 'twere hard 320 Giaour 1050
Enough that he who comes to woo 326 Abydos 1 205
He found enough to load with heaviest chain 351 Corsair 2 312
It is enough--I breathe--and I can bear 354 Corsair 2 482
From one I never loved enough to hate 354 Corsair 2 514
Leave scarce one thought inert enough to quail 358 Corsair 3 221
It was enough--she died--what reck'd it how 365 Corsair 3 625
Their joy and find this earth enough for woe 365 Corsair 3 633
But long enough to leave him half undone 366 Lara 1 24
Distinct but strange--enough they understand 369 Lara 1 231
A word's enough to raise mankind to kill 378 Lara 2 223
But enough of the past for the future to grieve 389 Corinth 502
It was enough for me to be 409 Mazeppa 259
But yet she listen'd--'tis enough 409 Mazeppa 278
With just enough of life to see 414 Mazeppa 720
Enough to leave my accents free 415 Mazeppa 824
And just enough of water and of bread 416 Island 1 89
This tale; enough that all within that cave 433 Island 4 221
But still enough survived, and mounted still 434 Island 4 315
Enough for seizure, near enough to die 434 Island 4 318
With blasphemies enough to break their jaws 451 Beppo 683
Torture enough without a living tomb 462 Dead 3 148
You know, they can do all--we are not enough 469 Morgante 190
'Is wont to be enough, and you shall see 472 Morgante 418
Or to skim eggs unbroke was light enough 474 Morgante 540
Enough!--I may retire then--say! Retire 487 Manfred 2 257
One were enough; then wonder not that I 493 Manfred 3 151
'Tis strange enough; night after night, for years 494 Manfred 3 202
He will not be judged hardly? 'Twere enough 500 Faliero 1 22
It was reward enough for me to view 506 Faliero 1 466
Matured and strengthen'd. We're enough already 508 Faliero 1 574
And deem you this enough for such foul scorn 509 Faliero 2 48
No. A month's arrest. Is it not enough 512 Faliero 2 224
Enough!--yes, for a drunken galley-slave 512 Faliero 2 225
There seems to me enough in the conviction 512 Faliero 2 230
Enough for Fortune to have granted once 515 Faliero 2 475
As far as I have seen, we are enough 518 Faliero 2 653
And not a thing in robes. We are enough 533 Faliero 4 378
No, not enough to extract an epitaph 547 Faliero 5 682
I leave such things to conquerors; enough 555 Sardan 1 309
Given or received; we have enough within us 556 Sardan 1 396
Enough to overcome all former nature 559 Sardan 1 551
Enough to spare even those who would not spare him 566 Sardan 2 317
One more than mine. It shall have work enough 568 Sardan 2 424
Order my horse out.---There is space enough 573 Sardan 3 105

ENOUGH

But there's enough of that shed; as for wine	577 Sardan	3	349
You know, or ought to know, enough of women	581 Sardan	4	219
In strength enough to venture an attack	586 Sardan	4	554
Enough of heaven to enable them to bear	587 Sardan	5	30
My pangs, without sustaining life enough	589 Sardan	5	129
And your companions; there's enough to load ye	591 Sardan	5	256
I promise. 'Tis enough. Now order here	591 Sardan	5	275
From tyrannous injustice, and enough	611 Foscari	3	203
The dungeon gloom is deep enough without you	612 Foscari	3	264
Because we have waited long enough, and he	616 Foscari	4	63
Lived longer than enough. Hence! in to council	616 Foscari	4	64
That is enough. For them, but not for us	616 Foscari	4	69
But he, who, had he been enough protected	622 Foscari	5	90
Let us return. 'Tis time enough to-morrow	623 Foscari	5	155
Had been enough to charm ye, as before	630 Cain	1	192
Enough?--why should ye differ? We both reign	645 Cain	2	597
Righteous enough to save his children. Would	664 Heaven		648
These were enough to gnaw into our souls	672 Werner	1	47
Friends. You appear to have drunk enough already	674 Werner	1	201
Enough of the Oder to have burst two peasants	675 Werner	1	223
'Tis time enough to ask it when he's able	675 Werner	1	245
But it may be a feign'd one. Like enough	678 Werner	1	427
He has valets now enough: they stood aloof then	678 Werner	1	437
And devilish damp, but fine enough by torchlight	679 Werner	1	514
And that's enough for your right noble blood	679 Werner	1	515
For mettle, he has quite enough: they say	684 Werner	2	104
And circumstance, and proofs; I know enough	691 Werner	2	557
Is the fault mine? Is't not enough that I	692 Werner	2	592
Enough to seize a dozen such? Hence! after him	693 Werner	2	659
His sabre. Take it. No, sir, 'tis enough	716 Werner	5	208
Rich enough to relieve such poverty	718 Werner	5	372
Left graves enough, and woes enough, and fame	725 Deformed	1	205
More than enough to track his memory	725 Deformed	1	206
But I have worn it long enough of late	727 Deformed	1	375
You are brave, and that's enough for me; and quick	733 Deformed	1	809
Why will you vex him? Have we not enough	734 Deformed	1	834
And that's enough. I am thirsty: would I had	738 Deformed	2	218
With just enough of talent, and no more	746 Juan	Ded	94
Are quite enough for me, so they but hold	761 Juan	1	944
A hint, in tender cases, is enough	768 Juan	1	1417
As I, who've cross'd it oft, know well enough	775 Juan	2	84
Was scant enough: in vain the telescope	779 Juan	2	326
But scarce enough to serve them for a luncheon	780 Juan	2	375
And all the rest were thin enough, Heaven knows	784 Juan	2	634
With just enough of life to feel its pain	787 Juan	2	863
Saying, he had gorged enough to make a horse ill	794 Juan	2	1272
Enough.--The faithful and the fairy pair	818 Juan	4	138
Gave light enough to hint their farther way	838 Juan	5	442
But not enough to show the imperial halls	838 Juan	5	443
Was hardly long enough; but Baba found	841 Juan	5	626
Conceived that phrase was quite enough to move	846 Juan	5	928
(Enough, God knows!) would much fall short of this	848 Juan	5	1072
But words are not enough in such a matter	849 Juan	5	1138
Was scarce enough; for he had fifty-nine	853 Juan	6	63
Although her beauty was enough to vex	857 Juan	6	290
'Juanna.'--Well, a pretty name enough	858 Juan	6	346
Your father's son, 'tis quite enough for me	864 Juan	6	744
Science enough, which levels to an ass	867 Juan	7	35
And more might be found out, if I could poke enough	869 Juan	7	118
But fighting thoughtlessly enough to win	880 Juan	8	151
This simile enough for Ajax, Juan	882 Juan	8	231
Over the hills, a fire enough to blind	882 Juan	8	236
The first time thought quite terrible enough	883 Juan	8	330
'Tis strange enough--the rough, tough soldiers, who	893 Juan	8	945
Without me, there are demagogues enough	899 Juan	9	194
Or on, might dread her majesty had not room enough	902 Juan	9	379
For a new flame; a thought to cast of gloom enough	902 Juan	9	381
Her third was feminine enough to annul	904 Juan	9	477
Enough to make a stripling very vain	905 Juan	9	576
And that's enough, for love is vanity	905 Juan	9	577
It is enough that Fortune found him flush	908 Juan	10	38
He was not yet quite old enough to prove	914 Juan	10	420
'Twas strange enough she should retain the impression	914 Juan	10	441
Just now enough; but by and by I'll prattle	918 Juan	10	695
Were hardly rude enough to earn their pay	923 Juan	11	320
Enough to gratify a bee's slight munchings	926 Juan	11	517
And that's enough; succeeded in my youth	931 Juan	12	130
'Twas not her fortune--he has enough without	934 Juan	12	274
Enough to make for port, ere time shall summon	946 Juan	13	316
'Tis not enough to spell, or even to read	950 Juan	13	578
Proud of his learning (just enough to quote	952 Juan	13	723
Ridiculous enough, but also dull	953 Juan	13	754
And quite enough for me to keep in mind	956 Juan	14	67
Of passions, too, I have proved enough to blame	956 Juan	14	68
O Job! you had two friends: one's quite enough	961 Juan	14	377
Whose merit none enough can sing or say	965 Juan	14	650

ENOUGH

Methinks Love's very title says enough	967 Juan	14	751
Perhaps 'twas hardly quite assured enough	970 Juan	15	109
Imagination's quite enough for that	970 Juan	15	123
Strangely enough as yet without miscarriage	972 Juan	15	275
That Juan had enough of maintenance	973 Juan	15	306
In her own mind, and that's enough for woman	973 Juan	15	314
Though ladies' robes seem scant enough for less	975 Juan	15	488
Nor even smiled enough for any vanity	977 Juan	15	620
Slight but select, and just enough to express	978 Juan	15	634
Was weak enough to deem Pope a great poet	987 Juan	16	423
Nor insolent enough to scorn the scorner	989 Juan	16	566
You see here was enough of occupation	989 Juan	16	585

ENOW

Why, what thou'st stole is not enow	227 Thurlow-B		3
Whate'er might Kaled's be, it was enow	374 Lara	1	606
'Ey, ey!' quoth Ben, 'not new, but news enow	426 Island	2	502
Have I not cares enow, and pangs enow	581 Sardan	4	229

ENQUIRE

My business and your own is not to enquire	287 Vision		174
The honey, nor enquire whence 'tis derived	583 Sardan	4	323
Are you of heaven? If I am not, enquire	635 Cain	1	482
No matter; we should ne'er too much enquire	828 Juan	4	761
'At least,' said Juan, 'sure I may enquire	840 Juan	5	588
Let spendthrifts' heirs enquire of yours--who's wiser	931 Juan	12	88

ENQUIRED

Enquired into his state; and when he heard	428 Island	3	151
And not enquired their Maker's breath of me	666 Heaven		802
Enquired, Who was this very new young man	906 Juan	9	626
Fair Adeline enquired, 'If he were ill	984 Juan	16	251

ENQUIRY

Have lately made a sharp Enquiry	144 Becher-B		23
If still more prying such enquiry grew	367 Lara	1	93
Of keen enquiry and of mute amaze	372 Lara	1	410
Came fast enquiry, which unfolded nought	376 Lara	2	105
Enquiry into deeds at distance done	378 Lara	2	239

ENRAGED

But he was most enraged lest such	410 Mazeppa		345

ENRAPTURE

Thy beauty must enrapture all	97 To M--		19

ENRAPTURED

And clasp enraptured all your charms	91 Caroline-B		42
Enjoy'd, from absence, with enraptured zest	121 Newstead-A		116
My soul, enraptured with the past	131 L'Amitie		16
Ossian no longer can enraptured gaze	140 Ossian-B		22
While Gayton bounds before th'enraptured looks	250 Bards		624
Enraptured, thinks to do the same at once	262 Hints		384

ENRICH

The Garlick steams, which half his meals enrich	224 J.C.H.		17
Enrich thee. And live wretched! Think upon	593 Sardan	5	380
I am proud to say, would not enrich the treasury	623 Foscari	5	176
That went before; in these I shall enrich	771 Juan	1	1628
Whose blood the puddle greatly did enrich	887 Juan	8	563

ENRICH'D

Four brothers enrich'd with their blood the bleak field	86 Leaving NA		18
Enrich'd our island's ill-united tongues	257 Hints		86

ENRICHES

Europe's mingling gore enriches	736 Deformed	2	96

ENRICHING

A heritage enriching all who breathe	462 Dante	3	154

ENSANGUINED

Slaked with its ensanguined rain	401 Parisina		459

ENSEMBLE

As suited the ensemble of his toilet	841 Juan	5	631
The 'tout ensemble' of his movements wore a	960 Juan	14	317

ENSHRINED

On Harold's page, Ianthe's here enshrined	3 To Ianthe		39
A fit abode wherein appear enshrined	78 Harold	4	1391
And, gallant Parker! thus enshrined	184 Parker		21

ENSLAVE

Hard is his heart whom charms may not enslave	22 Harold	2	142
Your free-born rights, forbade ye to enslave	271 Minerva		228
The liberty of that I would enslave	733 Deformed	1	778

ENSLAVED

From birth till death enslaved; in word, in deed, unmann'd	31 Harold	2	710

ENSLAVED
The enslavers and the enslaved, their death and
  birth   45 Harold   3   638
He perish'd rather than see Rome enslaved   238 Epigrams   3
But not to govern lands enslaved or free   305 Age   526
Of whom I am the lowest, most enslaved   523 Faliero   3   282
And 'Europe's Liberator'--still enslaved   897 Juan   9   40
His pride, too, felt that she was not enslaved 914 Juan 10   436
While Wellington has but enslaved the Whites 932 Juan   12   159

ENSLAVER
Had stung him from a slave to an enslaver   808 Juan   3   424

ENSLAVERS
The enslavers and the enslaved, their death and
  birth   45 Harold   3   638
Nor the steps of enslavers and chain-kissing
  slaves   204 Avatar   119

ENSLAVING
And by the heart, not hand, enslaving us   199 Sonnet-E   14

ENSNARE
I will disclose--ensnare--betray--destroy   532 Faliero   4   315

ENSUE
But here a sort of scene began to ensue   875 Juan   7   529

ENSUED
So that some disappointment there ensued   895 Juan   8 1042
If in the circumstances which ensued   994 Juan   16   899

ENSUING
As I will tell in the ensuing story   476 Morgante   687
Which put off business to the ensuing session 814 Juan   3   862

ENSURE
Like Lapland witches to ensure a wind   274 Waltz   76
You might obtain a post, which would ensure 685 Werner   2   173
I may ensure the public, and defy   772 Juan   1 1682
Quoth Johnson: 'Neither will I quite ensure 891 Juan   8   796

ENSURED
Thus Giaffir's safety was ensured   332 Abydos   2   292
But how faith is acquired, and then ensured 753 Juan   1   373
But of all verse, what most ensured her praise 987 Juan 16   447

ENSURES
Your worth a lasting love ensures   132 L'Amitie   73
Unless it ensures most infallible Damnation 179 Devil's Dr   214
In that complete perfection which ensures   814 Juan   3   867

ENTAIL
Entail will last him longer than his lands 693 Werner   2   639
If stars and titles could entail long praise 871 Juan   7   291

ENTAIL'D
(See also VICE-ENTAIL'D)
Entail'd on thy less virtuous daughters, grown 549 Faliero 5 778
Have shaving too entail'd upon their chins 958 Juan   14   184

ENTAILING
Entailing, as it were, my sins upon   673 Werner   1   92

ENTANGLE
But here again, why will I thus entangle   979 Juan   15   721

ENTANGLED
With brakes entangled, scarce a path between 109 Nisus   313
Like a good ship entangled among ice   977 Juan   15   615

ENTANGLING
Here entangling   157 Hodgson   28

ENTER
Enter: its grandeur overwhelms thee not   78 Harold   4 1387
I enter thy garden of roses   162 Romaic-A   1
But he heard, as he purposed to enter in there 177 Devil's Dr 135
Be guided who shall enter heaven or fall   297 Vision   804
One chamber where none enter: I would give 494 Manfred   3   209
But though I understand your grief, and enter 502 Faliero 1 173
To enter here till sought for. Though I might 585 Sardan 4 440
And see! they enter. Higher, my good soldiers 593 Sardan 5 357
I know that none who enter there return   599 Foscari   1   256
Requests an audience. Bid her enter. Poor   602 Foscari   2   45
Apart--what's this? Enter! Can I return   639 Cain   2   199
I did not enter Prague alone; and should I 719 Werner   5   390
Could enter into Don Alfonso's head   764 Juan   1 1106
We enter on our nautical existence   775 Juan   2   96
Here I might enter on a chaste description 828 Juan   4   769
On which the Muse has always sought to enter 946 Juan   13   302
Through which the deepen'd glories once could
  enter   948 Juan   13   491

ENTER'D
(See also RE-ENTER'D)
Adieu, thou palace rarely enter'd   163 Malta   3
And thus once enter'd into crooked ways   213 Lady Byron   47
Ne'er to be enter'd more by him or sin   288 Vision   194
But War had enter'd their dark caves   395 Corinth   977
They enter'd and for coffee call'd--it came 451 Beppo   721
Enter'd, he said that he was taught to adore 468 Morgante   165
'Twas well you enter'd by another portal   585 Sardan   4   454
As they have enter'd--many never, but   599 Foscari   1   257
Stir--in my train at least. I enter'd here 624 Foscari   5   273
The gates of death--By what gate have we enter'd 640 Cain 2 319
To be now fully enter'd on) have made   693 Werner   2   680
Past doubt, been enter'd secretly. Excuse me 702 Werner   3   486
Which led to this same night: how he had enter'd 718 Werner 5 329
By the same path I enter'd? Yes; that's safe
  still   721 Werner   5   504
You are well enter'd now. Ay; but my path   730 Deformed 1   569
He enter'd in the house no more his home   807 Juan   3   401
He enter'd in the house--his home no more   808 Juan   3   409
As the black eunuch enter'd with his brace 838 Juan   5   425
Before they enter'd, Baba paused to hint   843 Juan   5   721
Further, old Baba rather briskly enter'd   849 Juan   5 1144
The town was enter'd. Oh eternity   885 Juan   8   473
The town was enter'd: first one column made 887 Juan   8   545

ENTERETH
But whoso entereth within this town   6 Harold   1   225

ENTERING
Entering with every step he took through many a
  scene   36 Harold   3   81
Might entering lead where axe and stake await 358 Corsair 3 213
Entering a separate avenue, and still   524 Faliero   3   372
Now, Don Alfonso entering, but alone   768 Juan   1 1377

ENTERPRISE
Unknown the secret enterprise I brave   107 Nisus   183
A soul for every enterprise   332 Abydos   2   369
With all the thirsting eye of Enterprise   339 Corsair   1   56
Myself this enterprise to-night will share 340 Corsair   1   157
To enterprise like ours: I've seen that man 517 Faliero 2   582
To make the enterprise secure, if 'tis   518 Faliero   2   654
In our great enterprise. Do you repent   520 Faliero   3   104
When once our enterprise is o'er, which must not 521 Faliero 3 179
Now, my lord, to our enterprise; 'tis great 526 Faliero 3   567
These are the men for such an enterprise   533 Faliero   4   365
Why spur me to this enterprise? your own   562 Sardan   60
Unto the savage love of enterprise   685 Werner   2   134
Whom either accident or enterprise   716 Werner   5   234
In such an enterprise to die is rather   733 Deformed 1   783

ENTERPRISING
Our enterprising bards pass nought untried 263 Hints   450

ENTERS
A Guest where old Simony enters   239 Bray   24
He who once enters in a tyrant's hall   461 Dante   3   80

ENTERTAIN
Like to the notions we now entertain   901 Juan   9   301
To entertain, this autumn, a select   947 Juan   13   410

ENTERTAINING
All these are, certes, entertaining facts   813 Juan   3   825

ENTHRAL
The bars survive the captive they enthral   40 Harold   3   286
Though my heart they enthral, I'd abandon them
  all   115 Pigot   23
And the first day which sees the chain enthral 461 Dante 3   82

ENTHRALL
Who would men by man enthrall   187 Ode-B   35
Which tyranny can ne'er enthrall   320 Giaour   1069

ENTHRALL'D
Where Peleus' son? whom Hell in vain enthrall'd 21 Harold 2 120
The grave which enthrall'd thee   490 Manfred   2   477

ENTHRALLS
Too oft remind her who and what enthralls   57 Harold   4   134

ENTHRONED
As sovereigns swathed in purple, and enthroned 592 Sardan 5 325

ENTHUSIASM
There was enthusiasm and much applause   873 Juan   7   370
And rash enthusiasm in good society   945 Juan   13   279

ENTHUSIAST
Rather than thus--But the enthusiast dreams 664 Heaven   713

ENTIRE
Let it at least be simple and entire | 257 Hints | 38
The king who comes has head and all entire | 287 Vision | 170
They furnish'd him, entire, except some stitches | 794 Juan | 2 1279

ENTIRELY
Who love each other so entirely? You | 713 Werner | 5 34
At least entirely--for he had seen too many | 936 Juan | 12 391

ENTITLE
Just to entitle me to make a fuss | 448 Beppo | 542

ENTITY
(See NON-ENTITY)

ENTOMB
Shows that we build when we should but entomb us | 839 Juan | 5 504
Here peals the people's voice, nor can entomb it | 919 Juan | 11 70

ENTOMB'D
Entomb'd the bravest of the brave, Achilles | 826 Juan | 4 603

ENTOMBING
She sunk, with her my joys entombing | 221 Mariamne | 18
From out the wide destruction, which, entombing all | 829 Juan | 4 805

ENTRAIL
So that all mischiefs spring up from this entrail | 801 Juan | 2 1719

ENTRAILS
Yells the mad crowd o'er entrails freshly torn | 15 Harold | 1 691
The thirsty point in Sulmo's entrails lay | 110 Nisus | 351
Of famine fed upon all entrails--men | 189 Darkness | 44
And turn'd the royal entrails to a prison | 305 Age | 505
The hell which in its entrails ever dwells | 463 Dante | 3 193
And rip the hunter's entrails. Ah! I care not | 695 Werner | 3 9
And such things as the entrails and the brains | 783 Juan | 2 614

ENTRANCE
The abruptness of my entrance and my bearing | 542 Faliero | 5 334
Before your entrance in this hall, Zarina | 585 Sardan | 4 451
They shall not balk my entrance. Alas! this | 599 Foscari | 1 258
Is there no other entrance to the chamber | 683 Werner | 2 13
Before the entrance of a cliff-worn cave | 787 Juan | 2 862
Whence is our exit and our entrance,--well I | 903 Juan | 9 435
Which kindle manhood, but can ne'er entrance | 994 Juan | 16 910
A single shade's sufficient to entrance a | 995 Juan | 16 974

ENTRANCING
His long entrancing note | 336 Abydos | 2 693

ENTRATE
Voi che entrate!' The hinge seem'd to speak | 995 Juan | 16 971

ENTRE
Stuck in their loins; or like to an 'entre | 291 Vision | 427
(This should be entre nous, for Julia thought | 757 Juan | 1 671

ENTREAT
The Prince of the Republic, and entreat | 500 Faliero | 1 43
Stop! I command--entreat--implore! Oh, Ulric | 721 Werner | 5 523

ENTREATING
So Juan's spaniel, spite of his entreating | 783 Juan | 2 559
Entreating you to pause before you dash on | 935 Juan | 12 358

ENTREATY
Has been one long entreaty, and a vain one | 598 Foscari | 1 201

ENTREMETS
And 'entremets' to piddle with at hand | 976 Juan | 15 525

ENTRENCHMENT
O'er the entrenchment and the palisade | 880 Juan | 8 119

ENTWINE
For I have been accustom'd to entwine | 64 Harold | 4 545
These locks, which fondly thus entwine | 101 Lady-B | 1
While these a thousand kindred wreaths entwine | 125 Recoll | 237
And rosy wreaths their locks entwine | 139 Anacreon-C | 18
And ivy thy trunk with its mantle entwine | 149 Newstead-B | 4
Where transport and security entwine | 757 Juan | 1 698

ENTWINED
Such is thy name with this my verse entwined | 3 To Ianthe | 37
As the ivy and oak, in the forest entwined | 147 To Anne-B | 9
We are entwined--let death come slow or fast | 212 Augusta-C | 127
None knew, nor how, nor why, but he entwined | 371 Lara | 1 371
To be entwined for ever--but too late | 440 Tasso | 247
Or love.--I won't say more about 'entwined | 757 Juan | 1 710

ENTWINES
The paths, o'er which the far festoon entwines | 950 Juan | 13 603

ENUMERATION
And noble births, nor dread the enumeration | 962 Juan | 14 412

ENVELOPE
Then, Morpheus! envelope my faculties fast | 97 To M.S.G.-B | 5
Envelope a nation | 488 Manfred | 2 345
Envelope mine. You have done well. The greatest | 726 Deformed | 1 284

ENVENOM'D
Envenom'd with irrevocable wrong | 74 Harold | 4 1121
The old man's clench; the long envenom'd chain | 79 Harold | 4 1438
Oh factious viper! whose envenom'd tooth | 114 Death-A | 5
The poisonous heads of whose envenom'd body | 506 Faliero | 1 451

ENVIABLE
Oh, enviable Briareus! with thy hands | 856 Juan | 6 217

ENVIED
Envied, yet how unenviable! what stings | 41 Harold | 3 385
And monarchs gazed and envied in the hour | 56 Harold | 4 98
And lovely form were envied, praised, and eyed | 70 Harold | 4 924
Yet envied every fly the kiss | 89 To Emma | 23
The envied silver cup within his scope | 112 Examination | 28
Death; and envied those who fell | 187 French-A | 14
Till now I had envied thy sons and their shore | 204 Avatar | 121
Their eyes had envied Conrad his repose | 353 Corsair | 2 416
They envied even the faithless fame | 387 Corinth | 316
And envied all he gazed upon | 388 Corinth | 357
As might have envied mine, I offer'd you | 719 Werner | 5 373
By railing at the unknown and envied passion | 935 Juan | 12 354

ENVIES
How he envies the wretch with a soul wrapt in steel | 100 L Adieu | 29
And envies Lais all her Attic beaux | 271 Minerva | 192

ENVIOUS
Provoking envious gibe from each pedestrian churl | 15 Harold | 1 701
Which envious Eld forbore, and tyrants left to stand | 21 Harold | 2 117
Who blames it but the envious fool | 92 Lady-A | 5
Surely some envious demon's force | 99 Young Lady | 5
Are thine; no envious lot shall then be cast | 107 Nisus | 157
Some lurking envious fear intrude | 133 E. N. Long | 14
Chasing the shades of envious night | 142 Critics | 93
While lurking envious foes will smile | 146 Vain Lady | 6
In envious dimness pass'd thy portrait by | 183 Address-D | 48
The envious who but breathe in others' pain | 193 Monody | 72
Mouth which marks the envious scorner | 196 Rogers | 3
That aids his envious treachery | 316 Giaour | 613
That law's chicane or envious kinsmen might | 513 Faliero | 2 338

ENVIOUSLY
Oh! enviously destined Ball | 201 Ode-C | 72

ENVIRON
Ah! what is man? what perils still environ | 806 Juan | 3 281
As will environ a conspicuous man. Some | 927 Juan | 11 581

ENVIRON'D
Which has environ'd thee with snares; but yet | 555 Sardan | 1 333

ENVOY
Have chosen well their envoy. 'Tis their choice | 604 Foscari | 2 193
There many an envoy either dwelt or dwells | 922 Juan | 11 245
The envoy of the secret Russian mission | 947 Juan | 13 416

ENVOYS
Except in shape of envoys, who were sent | 850 Juan | 5 1201

ENVOY'S
One envoy's letters, six composers' airs | 274 Waltz | 73

ENVY
And Boileau, whose rash envy could allow | 60 Harold | 4 340
Envy the innate flash which such a soul could mould | 62 Harold | 4 441
Yet envy not this gaudy state | 85 To E-- | 7
Till envy, with malignant grasp | 85 To D-- | 3
But envy in the other raises | 87 Rousseau | 16
While Envy waved her burning brand | 105 Alva | 287
For friends to envy and for foes to feel | 108 Nisus | 212
Which Envy, wearing Candour's sacred mask | 114 Death-A | 35
Envy dissolved our ties, and not our will | 126 Recoll | 307
I envy now too much to weep | 167 Dead | 33
Whom envy dared not hate | 182 Ode-A | 169
'Tis but envy, when all's done | 197 Rogers | 66
Envy into unutterable praise | 199 Sonnet-E | 6
Of an Irishman's heart, that I envy--thy dead | 204 Avatar | 124
Nor Envy ruffle to retaliate pain | 208 Sketch | 28
Clothe envy in the garb of honest zeal | 247 Bards | 376
That most survivors envy those who fell | 276 Waltz | 170
Need he thou servest envy me my lot | 290 Vision | 316
Do more than niggard envy still denies | 300 Age | 114

ENVY
I envy not his varied joys   321 Giaour   1175
If love or envy made them foes   331 Abydos 2 214
Confess and envy, yet oppose in vain   341 Corsair 1 180
But yet--thou lov'st--and--Oh! I envy those   354 Corsair 2 493
Whom vice and envy made my foes   390 Corinth   594
Which late went down, and envy the lost wreck   430 Island 4 28
No heroes envy them their monument   433 Island 4 268
So that her female friends, with envy broiling   448 Beppo   547
When Venice was an envy, might abate   454 Venice-B   104
To envy every dove his nest and wings   458 Dante 2 168
Curst Gan, with envy bursting, had such need   467 Morgante   85
Scorn'd! what, to be the envy of your sex   585 Sardan 4 461
Had nought to envy him within. Where is he   615 Foscari 4 10
Envy the dead. My lord, if you indeed   624 Foscari 5 235
Was there to envy in the narrow bounds   631 Cain 1 240
The childless cherubs well might envy thee   648 Cain 3 153
Envy the giant patriarchs then no more   660 Heaven   422
'Twixt earth and heaven, like envy between man   700 Werner 3 363
Poor child! Do you pity me? No; I but envy   713 Werner 5 36
To you I envy neither fruit nor boughs   745 Juan Ded 51
The fame you envy and the skill you need   746 Juan Ded 60
And even the good with inward envy groan   748 Juan 1 78
Which make the reader envy his transgressions   753 Juan 1 376
And always envy, though we deem it frantic   818 Juan 4 144
Which hate nor envy e'er could tinge with wrong   886 Juan 8 502
It was not envy--Adeline had none   974 Juan 15 425
No one could envy her deserved prosperity   994 Juan 16 862

ENVYING
Its spark immortal, envying it the light   37 Harold 3 124
Lamenting and yet envying such a doom   44 Harold 3 543

ENVY'S
In which not Envy's self a flaw discovers   749 Juan 1 126

ENWRAPP'D
All were enwrapp'd: the feasted monarchs knew   454 Venice-B   106

EPAMINONDAS
When Thebes Epaminondas rears again   32 Harold 2 793
Epaminondas saved his Thebes, and died   897 Juan 9 58

EPAULETTES
His wings subdued to epaulettes; his quiver   902 Juan 9 354

EPHESIAN
Link'd with the fool that fired the Ephesian dome   271 Minerva   201
I've heard them in the Ephesian ruins howl   899 Juan 9 210

EPHESIANS
My Dian of the Ephesians, Lady Adeline   961 Juan 14 363

EPHESIAN'S
I have beheld the Ephesian's miracle   78 Harold 4 1372

EPIC
The Latian coast where sprung the Epic war   81 Harold 4 1561
He who sublime in epic numbers roll'd   87 Marsus   1
With glowing strings, the epic strain   88 Anacreon-A 13
Who rolls the epic song   132 L'Amitie   82
To roll in Epic, or to rave in Rhyme   142 Soliloquy   8
Ode, epic, elegy, have at you all   242 Bards   46
An epic scarce ten centuries could claim   244 Bards   191
Another epic! Who inflicts again   247 Bards   385
With rhyme by Hoare, and epic blank by Hoyle   255 Bards   966
To themes celestial told in epic song   258 Hints   108
Whose epic mountains never fail in mice   259 Hints   198
No doubt a liquid path to epic fame   417 Island 1 102
And now, my Epic Renegade! what are ye at   745 Juan Ded 5
Most epic poets plunge 'in medias res   747 Juan 1 41
My poem's epic, and is meant to be   771 Juan 1 1593
Me and my epic brethren gone before   771 Juan 1 1610
An epic from Bob Southey every spring   814 Juan 3 868
'Tis being too epic, and I must cut down   816 Juan 3 978
According to the ancient epic laws   851 Juan 5 1267
Make epic poesy so rare and rich   889 Juan 8 720
And epic, if plain truth should prove no bar   896 Juan 8 1101
Of epic Love's beginning, end, and middle   935 Juan 12 360
By that real epic unto all who have thought   942 Juan 13 72
To come between mine epic and its index   964 Juan 14 544
Than I have yet done, in this epic satire   967 Juan 14 790
From any thing, this epic will contain   980 Juan 16 18

EPICAL
My epical pretensions to the laurel   772 Juan 1 1670

EPICENE
The gender still was epicene, at least   859 Juan 6 458

EPICS
While Southey's epics cram the creaking shelves   243 Bards   127
There were Renegade's epics, and Botherby's plays   279 Blues 1 123

EPIC'S
Next rose the martial Homer, Epic's prince   266 Hints   679
So that my name of Epic's no misnomer   771 Juan 1 1600

EPICURE
Mere roast and boil'd no epicure invites   265 Hints   633

EPICUREAN
A mild Epicurean, form'd, at best   305 Age   520

EPICURUS
Thou mak'st philosophers; there's Epicurus   800 Juan 2 1649

EPIDEMIC
Reviews record this epidemic crime   266 Hints   723

EPIGRAM
Were never caught in epigram or witticism   449 Beppo   571
Forth into universal epigram   994 Juan 16 874

EPIGRAMMATIST
The Epigrammatist: while living   239 Martial   3

EPIGRAMS
To all those nauseous epigrams of Martial   752 Juan 1 344
Made epigrams occasionally too   986 Juan 16 419

EPILEPTICAL
Half epileptical and half hysterical   780 Juan 2 399

EPILOGUE
And you promised the epilogue, Inkel. Not quite   282 Blues 2 88

EPILOGUE'S
For a spice of your wit in an epilogue's aid   282 Blues 2 83

EPIRUS'
Epirus' bounds recede and mountains fail   27 Harold 2 478
That look along Epirus' valleys   384 Corinth   27

EPISODE
The bard sighs forth a gentle episode   246 Bards   358
What went before--by way of episode   747 Juan 1 44

EPISODES
New characters; the episodes are three   771 Juan 1 1597

EPISTLE
And never such a treat, as--the epistle of one
    'Vetus   177 Devil's Dr   125
The earth has nothing like a she epistle   954 Juan 13 834

EPISTLE-CRAFT
Then Queen Mary's Epistle-craft   232 Murray-B   40

EPISTOLARY
At this epistolary 'Iron Mask   294 Vision   624

EPITAPH
And be the Spartan's epitaph on me   56 Harold 4 85
My epitaph shall be my name alone   86 Fragment-A   8
Here Harold lies--but where's his Epitaph   161 Substitute   2
An epitaph on every tongue   184 Parker   10
Believe a woman or an epitaph   242 Bards   78
The brass of both his epitaph and tomb   295 Vision   658
And the brief epitaph in danger's day   338 Corsair 1 39
Their life was shame, their epitaph was guilt   433 Island 4 270
And thy grandchildren's love for epitaph   484 Manfred 2 71
No, not enough to extract an epitaph   547 Faliero 5 682
I have read their epitaph, which says they died   596 Foscari 1 34
Their epitaph, attributing their deaths   605 Foscari 2 224
Holds like an epitaph their history   608 Foscari 3 20
His heir's upon his epitaph. Methought   675 Werner 1 247
An epitaph as larceny upon my tomb   696 Werner 3 47

EPITAPHS
Where are the epitaphs our fathers read   829 Juan 4 813

EPITOME
Epitome of what brave chivalry   688 Werner 2 324
Catherine, who was the grand epitome   903 Juan 9 449

EPOCH
The rainbow-like epoch where Freedom could pause   201 Avatar   6
The first will make an epoch with his lyre   462 Dante 3 110
And every moon an epoch of new pleasures   586 Sardan 4 518
Sunrise and sunset form the haunted epoch   587 Sardan 5 21
Of age, if 'tis a day. Which epoch makes   677 Werner 1 377
Without whose epoch my poetic skill   761 Juan 1 963
But since they are, that epoch is a bore   930 Juan 12 12
Epoch, that awkward corner turn'd for days   941 Juan 13 26

EPOCHS
It doth; but actions are our epochs: mine   484 Manfred 2 52

EPOPEE
Some fine examples of the epopee — 814 Juan 3 871

EPROUVEUSE
Named from her mystic office 'l'Eprouveuse — 907 Juan 9 671

EQUAL
A father's sorrows cannot equal mine — 85 Epitaph 20
Equal to Jove that youth must be — 87 Ad Lesbiam 1
With equal ardour seems to burn — 91 Caroline-B 34
With equal ardour fired and warlike joy — 106 Nisus 37
A second shaft with equal force is driven — 110 Nisus 356
Who once could glow with equal fire — 118 Romance 47
As speakers each supports an equal name — 126 Recoll 335
Equal were their swords in battle; but fierce — 129 Calmar 25
His practice is not equal to his years — 143 Soliloquy 60
There are two Souls, whose equal flow — 144 Jessy 29
Our souls were equal, and our lot — 146 Adieu 68
An equal love may see — 163 Parting 6
An equal deed hast done at length — 180 Ode-A 51
But in equal rights and laws — 188 Ode-B 81
Itself--and equal to all woes — 191 Prometheus-B 54
Since thus divided--equal must it be — 192 Fragment-C 19
Or scrawl or scribbler from an equal grave — 242 Bards 54
And rhyme and blank maintain an equal race — 243 Bards 143
Whether thou sing'st with equal ease, and grief — 246 Bards 333
'Heir to my virtues! man of equal mind — 248 Bards 456
Whose pen and pencil yield an equal grace — 253 Bards 860
Be ever hail'd with equal honour here — 270 Minerva 109
I doubt if you'll leave us an equal behind — 282 Blues 2 81
He turn'd as to an equal not too low — 289 Vision 285
About still flows from Fortune's equal urn — 306 Age 611
If won, to equal ills betray'd — 314 Giaour 400
Equal her grief, yet not the same — 326 Abydos 1 259
Of equal rights, which man ne'er knew — 333 Abydos 2 386
Thou ne'er hast seen less equal war — 334 Abydos 2 527
To Greece and Venice equal foes — 385 Corinth 124
Her horn; the equal land without a lord — 416 Island 1 36
Art shall resume and equal even the sway — 463 Dante 4 41
Almost our equal?--Can it be that thou — 496 Manfred 3 367
To make my dowry equal to the rank — 513 Faliero 2 307
Not rash equality but equal rights — 523 Faliero 3 291
Equal to every fortune. Droop not, 'tis — 537 Faliero 4 628
Willing to equal all in social freedom — 579 Sardan 4 81
It galls you:--well, you are his equal, as — 606 Foscari 2 290
The victims are not equal: he has seen — 619 Foscari 4 278
In battle: the rewards are equal. Now — 620 Foscari 4 315
His equal? No;--I have nought in common with him — 632 Cain 1 302
Of space an equal flight, and I will show — 636 Cain 2 23
Fair!--Well, I trust your taste in wine is equal — 677 Werner 1 382
I am your equal. You! Ay, sir; and, for — 691 Werner 2 554
By heart and soul, and make itself the equal — 727 Deformed 1 315
All clay is of equal merit — 729 Deformed 1 457
And saw no equal. Arnold, shouldst thou see — 737 Deformed 2 145
But whether Julia to the task was equal — 757 Juan 1 655
When nights are equal, but not so the days — 832 Juan 5 42
And you an equal courtesy should show — 833 Juan 5 124
His glory might half equal his estate — 871 Juan 7 292
Proved death in battle equal to a pension — 874 Juan 7 464
But still we moderns equal you in blood — 877 Juan 7 640
Which makes all female ages equal--when — 905 Juan 9 546
In birth, in rank, in fortune likewise equal — 943 Juan 13 153
There Rembrandt made his darkness equal light — 950 Juan 13 570

EQUALITY
Not rash equality but equal rights — 523 Faliero 3 291
From my equality with you in birth — 540 Faliero 5 204
Have gorged themselves up to equality — 558 Sardan 1 488

EQUALL'D
Confess'd a love which equall'd mine — 152 Time-A 6
With virtues equall'd by her wit alone — 748 Juan 1 76

EQUALLY
But pardon equally to books or men — 264 Hints 559
Mislead his spirit equally to crime — 371 Lara 1 344
But then, no doubt, it equally as true is — 760 Juan 1 863
Though all deserving equally to turn — 880 Juan 8 133
Why should not Life be equally content — 898 Juan 9 99

EQUALS
Rough with his elders, with his equals rash — 260 Hints 233
We fought to make our equals, not our lords — 519 Faliero 3 35
With kings--my equals. These men sought to be so — 571 Sardan 2 583
With your pure equals. Hence! away! away — 666 Heaven 812
Having no equals, nothing which had e'er — 846 Juan 5 946

EQUANIMITY
Who seem'd the cream of equanimity — 973 Juan 15 323

EQUINOCTIAL
Make my soul pass the equinoctial line — 915 Juan 10 486
For they have pass'd life's equinoctial line — 941 Juan 13 36
Which ne'er can pass the equinoctial line — 945 Juan 13 267

EQUINOX
That horrid equinox, that hateful section — 910 Juan 10 212

EQUIPAGE
Coach, chariot, luggage, baggage, equipage — 946 Juan 13 346

EQUIPMENT
As new artificers for their equipment — 517 Faliero 2 641

EQUIPP'D
Equipp'd for deeds alike on land or deep — 347 Corsair 1 604
Equipp'd for flight, her vassals--Greek and Moor — 362 Corsair 3 439
Next with a virgin zone he was equipp'd — 841 Juan 5 611

EQUITY
You do not then in aught arraign our equity — 541 Faliero 5 271
Forbear! Ha! ha! here's equity! The dogs — 740 Deformed 2 310

EQUIVOCAL
In phrases not equivocal, by you — 691 Werner 2 541

EQUIVOCATION
A vile equivocation; you well know — 692 Werner 2 595

EQUIVOCATIONS
Equivocations, and the thoughts which dwell — 213 Lady Byron 52

ERA
True, the great of her bright and brief era are gone — 201 Avatar 5
But since the Gallic era 'eighty-eight — 285 Vision 5
An era of sweet peace 'midst bloody annals — 586 Sardan 4 512
I know that some would fain postpone this era — 941 Juan 13 33

ERAS
New eras spread their wings, new nations rise — 254 Bards 951

ERA'S
About the day--the era's more obscure — 761 Juan 1 968

ERASE
Whose green, wild margin now no more erase — 72 Harold 4 1040
Had sorrow fix'd what time can ne'er erase — 345 Corsair 1 492

ERASED
Deeply she cut--but not erased — 150 Harrow-C 5

ERATOSTRATUS
And Eratostratus and Elgin shine — 271 Minerva 203

ERE
Crack'd, shiver'd, vanish'd, scarcely gazed on, ere — 927 Juan 11 597

'ERE
(See also THERE)
'Oh Jack! I'm floor'd by that 'ere bloody Frenchman — 920 Juan 11 104

ERECT
Simple, erect, severe, austere, sublime — 77 Harold 4 1306
Still the old man stood erect — 393 Corinth 847
Stern and erect his brow was raised — 398 Parisina 186
The architrave some earthquake might erect — 432 Island 4 148
Breathe save the erect ones? How the lights recede — 638 Cain 2 173
Two beings here erect them unto thee — 650 Cain 3 254
Who shall erect a home — 660 Heaven 374
And thin, produced a plan whereby to erect — 988 Juan 16 510

ERECTED
And snorting, with erected mane — 410 Mazeppa 366
Erected in the Abruzzi to his glory — 466 Morgante 43
Erected by your ancestors, is still — 711 Werner 4 454
Cheops erected the first pyramid — 773 Juan 1 1746
In the new batteries erected there — 870 Juan 7 214
New batteries were erected, and was held — 873 Juan 7 401
Nor use those palisades by dames erected — 963 Juan 14 487

ERECTION
To me appears a stiff yet grand erection — 921 Juan 11 199

ERECTS
Some hand erects a cross of mouldering lath — 7 Harold 1 267
Erects a shrine and idol of its own — 243 Bards 140

EREMITE
More blest the life of godly eremite — 23 Harold 2 235

EREMITE'S
Which seem'd to him more lone than Eremite's sad cell — 4 Harold 1 36

ERIC
Good morrow, worthy Henrick. Eric, is   705 Werner   4   74
You spear'd four with your own hand. True, good
  Eric   705 Werner   4   82

ERIDANUS
Why doth Eridanus but overflow   460 Dante   2   105

ERIN
aid of Erin   130 Calmar   34
where is Cuthullin, the shield of Erin? He   130 Calmar   48
dust of Erin? Let me fall alone. My father   130 Calmar   72
they lie on Erin. The breeze of ocean lifts   131 Calmar   155
Gild over the palace; lo, Erin, thy lord   202 Avatar   55
The miscreant who well might plunge Erin in doubt   203 Avatar   95
Which proclaims that from Erin no reptile can
  spring   203 Avatar   98
Shout, drink, feast, and flatter! Oh! Erin, how
  low   203 Avatar   101
He was what Erin calls, in her sublime   881 Juan   8   177
After the good example of 'Green Erin   923 Juan   11   303
Heart-ballads of Green Erin or Gray Highlands   986 Juan   16   410

ERIN'S
blue waves. Erin's sons fell beneath his   130 Calmar   30
Dabbling its sleek young hands in Erin's gore   746 Juan   Ded   90
Thy clanking chain, and Erin's yet green wounds   747 Juan   Ded   125

ERIZZO
Of Nicolas Erizzo, who slew the late   600 Foscari   1   304
Was slain by Erizzo for private vengeance   600 Foscari   1   308

ERMELLINA
From Ermellina, consort of the Dane   468 Morgante   129

ERMINE
Can stars or ermine, man's maturer toys   127 Recoll   397
Its part with all its empire in this ermine   506 Faliero   1   445
A bull-dog, and a bullfinch, and an ermine   913 Juan   10   393
Judges in very formidable ermine   949 Juan   13   545
There is a sameness in its gems and ermine   957 Juan   14   118

ERNEIS
Erneis, Radulphus--eight-and-forty manors   912 Juan   10   282

EROS
And where these are light Eros finds a feere   5 Harold   1   79
Eros and Anteros, at Gadara   486 Manfred   2   187
Of Eros: but though thou hast play'd us many
  tricks   995 Juan   16   919

ERR
All round us; we but feel our way to err   67 Harold   4   723
Time! the corrector where our judgments err   74 Harold   4 1165
Accord me such a being? Do I err   81 Harold   4 1591
If my memory don't err   235 New Song   23
Better to err with Pope than shine with Pye   243 Bards   102
A hackney'd plot, than choose a new, and err   259 Hints   186
Alas! how could his cabinet thus err   308 Age   721
There ev'n thy soul might err--how oft the heart   333 Abydos   2   438
Too nearly, deadly aim'd to err   335 Abydos   2   575
Do good with Nature, or with Nature err   418 Island   1   222
And what was he who bore it?--I may err   425 Island   2   446
The day may come when she will cease to err   457 Dante   1   73
He never can in any purpose err   472 Morgante   412
'My own free will and act,' and yet you err   527 Faliero   3   635
Nothing can err, except to some good end   649 Cain   3   234
Dost thou not err as we   666 Heaven   818
The wound. You err. My nature is not given   709 Werner   4   329
And, if I err not, not a minute since   714 Werner   5   79
And left no footstep? There you err. His
  substance   725 Deformed   1   204
To beg his pardon when I err a bit   761 Juan   1   960
She was so like a vision; I might err   811 Juan   3   606
A heavy price must all pay who thus err   825 Juan   4   582
So that I do not grossly err in facts   887 Juan   8   587
(If that my memory doth not greatly err   912 Juan   10   283
With this o'erwhelming world, where all must err   914 Juan   10   414
Sometimes a little later. I don't err   946 Juan   13   338
'Tis thus the good will amiably err   970 Juan   15   131
Sometimes, unless my feelings rather err   982 Juan   16   109
Was more Shakspearian, if I do not err   987 Juan   16   428
They err--'tis merely what is call'd mobility   993 Juan   16   820

ERRANT
Where shall we now be errant? Where the world   729 Deformed   1   493

ERR'D
As err'd the sire, so err'd the son   399 Parisina   314
But err'd, for I was fastly bound   412 Mazeppa   541
If I have err'd this time, 'tis on the side   570 Sardan   2   524
I had not err'd, and watch'd him long and nearly   717 Werner   5   263
And plumage (probably it might have err'd   786 Juan   2   747
The fair Sultana err'd from inanition   853 Juan   6   69

ERR'D
Baba thought she would faint, but there he err'd   865 Juan   6   842
They err'd, as aged men will do; but by   923 Juan   11   281
Whose hounds ne'er err'd, nor greyhounds deign'd
  to lurch   991 Juan   16   682

ERREST
Thou errest, Adah!--was not the tree that   633 Cain   1   349

ERRING
O'er erring deeds and thoughts a heavenly hue   47 Harold   3   731
This erring life may fly at last   133 Prayer   64
Yes! for one single erring verse   142 Critics   69
And soon shall its wild erring notes be forgot   149 Farewell-A   33
Such erring trifles lead to serious ills   267 Hints   803
Except an erring sister's shame   314 Giaour   421
Some erring blade or ball should glance   334 Abydos   2   532
An erring spirit from another hurl'd   370 Lara   1   316
And shown their rashness to that erring brood   379 Lara   2   295
The erring arrow launch aside   400 Parisina   362
He died, as erring man should die   401 Parisina   462
The erring spirits who can ne'er return   493 Manfred   3   179
An erring woman finds an opener door   940 Juan   12   630

ERRONEOUS
The book which treats of this erroneous pair   803 Juan   3   94

ERROR
Though every error stamps me for her own   94 Dorset   39
For this wild error which pervades my strain   119 Answer-A   5
Did I my error mourn   132 L'Amitie   62
Half an age's contempt was an error of fame   203 Avatar   67
And if dearly that error hath cost me   210 Augusta-B   37
Reforms each error, and refines the whole   249 Bards   559
To fly from error, not to merit praise   262 Hints   422
And blushes o'er his error, as he eyes   350 Corsair   2   233
And wandering on in error a long space   468 Morgante   149
Where error sits most lightly on that sense   570 Sardan   2   525
More soundly. That's an error, and you'll find
  it   620 Foscari   4   328
The life-tree? He was hinder'd. Deadly error   631 Cain   1   292
Even for our parents' error. What is that   647 Cain   3   75
An error would spoil all. Your lordship seems   679 Werner   1   507
Not now. Your error has redoubled all   698 Werner   3   241
A moment's error in the heat of conquest   740 Deformed   2   334
But with a moral to each error tack'd   831 Juan   5   12
So agitated was she with her error   863 Juan   6   711
For fear of any error, like the late   866 Juan   6   896
The lurking bias, be it truth or error   956 Juan   14   45
He ne'er presumed to make an error clearer   960 Juan   14   295

ERRORS
View ducal errors with indulgent eyes   93 Dorset   15
As all his errors slumber'd in the grave   114 Death-A   16
If errors are forgiven   146 Adieu   104
Of your sweet errors   200 Stanzas-B   74
My errors with defensive paradox   211 Augusta-C   22
But these are better than the gloomy errors   453 Venice-B   32
Their earthly errors, so they be atoned   492 Manfred   3   83
Since aggravated errors on the part   603 Foscari   2   106
To others' share let 'female errors fall   749 Juan   1   127
There lies the thing we love with all its errors   799 Juan   2 1575
To hunt our errors up with a good grace   961 Juan   14   374
Remember, without telling, passion's errors   968 Juan   15   26

ERRS
Avoid it--Virtue ebbs and Wisdom errs   355 Corsair   2   547
If errs my feeble hand, the morning cloud   361 Corsair   3   384
That no stroke errs. And you, ye blue sea-waves   535 Faliero   4   490
But in old England, when a young bride errs   938 Juan   12   511

ERSE
Guildhall grows Gael, and echoes with Erse roar   308 Age   771
Old Erse or Irish, or it may be Punic   881 Juan   8   178

ERSKINES
All are not Erskines who mislead the bar   264 Hints   584

ERST
To fall upon you! else they would, as erst   624 Foscari   5   218
Don Juan shook, as erst he had been shaken   996 Juan   16   985

ERUDITELY
Though you and I, who eruditely know   262 Hints   433

ERUPTIVE
Than the volcano's fierce eruptive crest   463 Dante   3   187

ESAU
Thou sold'st thy birthright, Esau! for a mess   306 Age   632
Like Esau, for my birthright a beef-steak   837 Juan   5   352

ESAU-BRETHREN
Her Esau-brethren that the haughty flag   454 Venice-B   145

DATE DUE

HIGHSMITH 45-220